International Marketing Handbook

International Marketing Handbook

Second Edition

*Detailed Marketing Profiles for 142
Nations, Special Information on Doing
Business with Countries in the Eastern
Bloc and in the Near East and North
Africa, and Fundamental Data for
Developing an Export Marketing Effort
or Importing to the United States*

Volume 2: Indonesia-Trinidad and Tobago

Frank E. Bair
Editor

Gale Research Company
Book Tower
Detroit, Mich. 48226

BIBLIOGRAPHIC NOTE

International Marketing Handbook combines virtually all non-duplicative elements issued from January 1, 1977 to January 1, 1985 of the pamphlet series known as *Overseas Business Reports,* a sub-group in the *Marketing Information Series* (OBR 79-01 through 84-06) published by the U.S. Commerce Department's International Trade Administration (ITA). Also reproduced in whole or in part as sections within this work are the following publications issued by the U.S. Government sources indicated: *A Basic Guide to Exporting,* ITA, November, 1981; *The Export Management Company,* ITA, August, 1981; *Importing into the United States,* Department of Treasury, United States Customs Service, May, 1984; *A Business Guide to the European Common Market,* ITA, April, 1980; *European Trade Fairs: A Guide for Exporters,* ITA; *Growth Markets of the 1980's: Western Europe,* ITA, June 1984; *Sales Promotion Techniques for Marketing in Communist Countries,* ITA, December, 1981; *East-West Trade Financing: an Introductory Guide,* ITA, Bureau of East-West Trade, September, 1976; *A Business Guide to the Near East and North Africa,* ITA, September, 1981; *A Guide to Doing Business in the ASEAN Region,* ITA, October, 1981; *Doing Business with China,* ITA, December 1983; Metric Laws and Practices in International Trade, ITA, February, 1982; *U.S. Trade Performance in 1983 and Outlook,* ITA, June, 1984.

Special government documents research for
this book performed by Margaret Mary Missar

Library of Congress Cataloging in Publication Data

Main entry under title:

International marketing handbook.

    Contents: v. 1. Afghanistan-India—v. 2. Indonesia-Trinidad and Tobago—v. 3. Tunisia-Zimbabwe and area guides and statistics.
    1. Export marketing—Handbooks, manuals, etc.
I. Bair, Frank E.
HF1009.5.I538   1985   658.8′48   85-4333
ISBN 0-8103-2057-6

CONTENTS

VOLUME 1: AFGHANISTAN-INDIA

Marketing Profiles for Countries of the World

VOLUME 2: INDONESIA-TRINIDAD AND TOBAGO

Marketing Profiles for Countries of the World (Continued)

VOLUME 3: TUNISIA-ZIMBABWE
AND AREA GUIDES AND STATISTICS

Marketing Profiles for Countries of the World (Continued)

International Marketing Briefs

MARKETING PROFILES
For Countries
of the World

Marketing in Indonesia

Contents

Report Revised May 1981

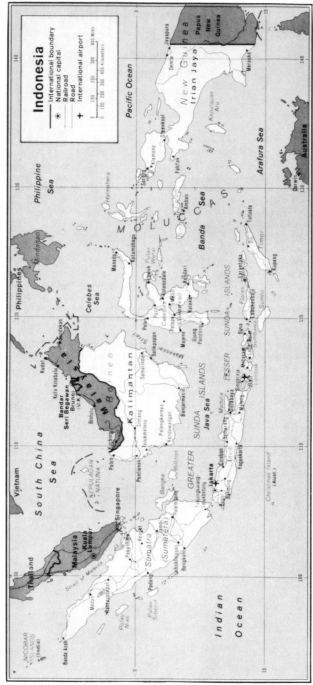

Foreign Trade Outlook

Indonesia's foreign trade outlook is improving substantially as sharp increases in the price of oil, an expected upswing in oil production, and continuing demand for its growing non-oil exports assure considerably higher trade levels in the near and medium term. In the long term, Indonesia is likely to experience a widening resource gap since only modest gains are expected in the output of oil, Indonesia's major export, and increased domestic consumption of oil will reduce oil exports. Thus, it will have to place increased reliance on additional non-oil exports. Continuing high levels of foreign aid will also be required to meet import needs.

However, the improved outlook for the oil industry has alleviated the balance-of-payments constraints anticipated in the Third Five-Year Development Plan(Repelita III), April 1, 1979, to March 31, 1984, and what appeared to be an ambitious development budget now seems well within reach.

Indonesia had a record balance-of-payments surplus of $1.7 billion in 1979/80 (Indonesian fiscal year ending March 31, 1980), and current estimates indicate it was $2.7 billion in 1980/81. Official reserves grew from $4.6 billion at the end of March 1980 to an estimated $7.3 billion at the end of March 1981. Total government debt stood at $15.2 billion as of March 31, 1981. The debt service ratio has declined from 18 percent in 1978 to about 11 percent in 1980.

Indonesia's exports rose from $11.6 billion in 1978 to $15.6 billion in 1979, and imports from $6.7 billion to $7.2 billion, according to Central Bureau of Statistics (CBS) figures (see tables 1 and 2). Since CBS figures omit imports of investment and other goods not subject to duty, actual import levels were appreciably higher and expanded at a more rapid rate in 1980.

A study by the International Bank for Reconstruction and Development(IBRD) in 1979 estimated that the volume of non-oil imports in 1985/86 could well be more than double their volume in 1979/80. Capital goods imports were projected to rise the fastest, by 20 percent annually through 1982 and by 10 percent annually to 1985/86. Intermediate imports were projected to increase by 12.5 percent and consumers goods other than rice by 15 percent annually through 1982 and by 10 percent thereafter.

Foreign aid and direct investment are major factors influencing import growth.

The Inter-Governmental Group for Indonesia (IGGI), made up of 14 donor countries and international lending agencies, has agreed to provide aid valued at about $1.9 billion in 1980/81. About $800 million will come from bilateral donors and $1.1 billion from multilateral institutions (mainly the IBRD and the Asian Development Bank—ADB) and non-IGGI sources. Estimated contributions by major sources are: IBRD, $800 million; ADB, $250 million; Japan, $280 million; Canada, $24 million; the Netherlands, $80 million; France, $65 million; Germany, $68 million; and Australia, $45 million. The United States will provide about $128 million. Development assistance from the United States will be mainly for agricultural development in rural areas, for increasing employment opportunities in rural areas, and improvement of health and education facilities. IGGI also agreed that Indonesia will continue to need significant amounts of external financial and technical assistance for many years to come.

Foreign aid creates trade opportunities for U.S. suppliers through IBRD- and ADB-financed projects and other donor loans for which procurement is not tied to the donor country.

Investment by the private sector, both domestic and foreign, also contributes to import growth. Approved investments under the 1968 Domestic Investment Law totaled Rp. 4,030 billion by the end of 1979 ($6.4 billion at the current exchange rate). Over two-thirds were in industry and had substantial import requirements. Approved investments under the 1967 Foreign Investment Law in fields other than oil totaled $9 billion by the end of 1980, of which many remain to be implemented. Inflows from foreign direct investment amounted to between $200 million and $300 million in 1979/80. Also, considerable imports result from the expenditures of foreign oil companies (mainly U.S.) for exploration and production. These expenditures reached an estimated $1,600 million in 1980.

Indonesia's policy objectives in the export sector are to increase traditional exports by improving their competitiveness, to increase export value by processing, to diversify exports, to improve quality to meet international standards, to develop new commodities, and enlist the participation of businesses from weak economic sectors, and to investigate new markets. To implement the last, Indonesia has formed a Coordination Team for Increased Exports to the Middle East.

In November 1978, Indonesia devalued the rupiah to achieve a rise in export earnings by stimulating production and at the same time increase the competitiveness of Indonesian commodities in international markets.

Indonesia's policy objectives in respect to imports include according high priority to goods needed to develop industry and fulfill other requirements of the development program, and creating import substitution industries, primarily for consumers goods but also for raw materials and other items.

The composition of Indonesia's trade in 1978 and 1979 is shown in tables 1 and 2, based on Central Bureau of Statistics figures, which include oil and gas on a gross basis and omit certain duty-free and other imports.

Timber, Indonesia's second largest export, is expected to continue to contribute substantially to export earnings, while liquefied natural gas, which more than doubled in value (on a gross basis) between 1978 and 1979, will become increasingly important as an export earner.

As indicated in table 2, petroleum is Indonesia's most important import as well as export. Indonesia imports crude oil from Saudi Arabia, saving for export its own low-sulphur crude, which commands a higher price. A significant recent development in Indonesia's import pattern is the virtual elimination of urea fertilizer imports and Indonesia's emergence as a net exporter of fertilizer as a result of increased domestic fertilizer capacity. Imports of cement have declined greatly in the past 5 years and certain types of cement are now being exported.

Japan is Indonesia's major trading partner. Japan supplied 29 percent of Indonesia's imports in 1979 and took 46 percent of its exports. The United States is Indonesia's second trading partner. In 1979, the United States supplied 14 percent of Indonesia's imports (compared with 12 percent in 1978) and purchased 20 percent of its exports.

Table 1.—Principal Indonesian Exports, 1978-79
(in millions of U.S. dollars)

Commodity	1978	1979
Oil and oil products	7,438.5	8,857.9
Liquefied natural gas	546.9	1,292.9
Timber	996.5	1,836.7
Rubber and rubber goods	717.7	940.3
Coffee	491.3	614.5
Tin	281.2	382.0
Fish	180.2	220.7
Palm oil and other vegetable oils	214.0	219.6
Other	776.9	1,225.6
Total exports	11,643.2	15,590.1

SOURCE: Central Bureau of Statistics (CBS).

Note: CBS data exclude investment and other goods not subject to duty and differ considerably from foreign exchange receipts and expenditures compiled by Bank Indonesia that are used as a basis for balance-of-payments statistics.

U.S. Trade with Indonesia

Two-way trade between Indonesia and the United States reached an alltime high of $6.7 billion in 1980, with exports of U.S. domestic merchandise totaling $1,544 million and imports

Table 2.—Principal Indonesian Imports, 1978-79
(in millions of U.S. dollars)

Commodity	1978	1979
Raw Materials	2,664.5	3,328.2
Chemical and pharmaceuticals	153.0	167.5
Fertilizer	57.1	56.0
Newsprint and other paper	122.8	127.3
Cotton	121.0	130.0
Yarns	96.5	122.5
Textile fabrics	64.3	73.1
Cement	28.4	17.2
Concrete iron	87.8	100.4
Iron and steel bars	45.6	82.8
Iron and steel plates	220.0	298.7
Petroleum and petroleum Products	579.7	793.3
Others	1,088.3	1,359.4
Capital Goods	2,829.3	2,691.9
Iron and steel pipes	129.7	102.6
Machines	823.4	914.3
Motors	248.1	258.4
Motor vehicles	654.5	477.0
Others	973.6	939.6
Comsumer Goods	1,196.6	1,182.2
Rice	591.5	596.3
Pharmaceutical preparations	47.8	52.7
Textile fabrics	42.3	72.2
Others	515.0	461.0
Total Imports	6,690.4	7,202.3

SOURCE: Central Bureau of Statistics.

Note: CBS data exclude investment and other goods not subject to duty and differ considerably from foreign exchange receipts and expenditures compiled by Bank Indonesia that are used as a basis for balance-of-payments statistics.

$5,182 million. Continued heavy imports of Indonesian oil by the United States contributed to the $3.6 billion trade deficit. The value and commodity composition of trade are detailed in Table 3.

In 1980, U.S. exports to Indonesia were 58 percent higher than in 1979. Major increases over the 1979 level were for unmilled wheat, chemicals, machinery, aircraft, and various types of manufactured products. Machinery and transportation equipment comprised 36 percent of total exports in 1980, agricultural commodities about one-third, and chemicals 17 percent. Major machinery exports included power generating machinery ($42 million), civil engineer and contractors' equipment ($69 million), agricultural and construction tractors ($10 million), heating and cooling equipment ($14 million), pumps for liquids ($13 million), mechanical handling equipment ($18 million), telecommunications equipment ($10 million), and electronic components ($16 million).

U.S. imports from Indonesia in 1980 were about the same in value as in 1979. Crude petroleum and products comprised 80 percent of the 1980 total. Other major U.S. imports were rubber, coffee, and unwrought tin. In 1979, Indonesia ranked first as a supplier of natural rubber and unground pepper to the United

States. It was the third largest supplier of unwrought tin, the sixth largest supplier of coffee and the ninth largest supplier of crude petroleum.

Indonesia receives the benefits of the U.S. Generalized System of Preferences (GSP). Favorable factors for continued growth of U.S. exports are increased competitiveness of U.S. products resulting from the decline in value of the dollar vis-a-vis other major trading currencies, an increase in U.S. oil exploration and development activities, and Indonesia's implementation of major development projects.

U.S. export levels are highly sensitive to decisions by the Indonesian Government and international financial institutions on major infrastructure projects and to the degree of participation in them by U.S. firms. The American Embassy in Jakarta and the U.S. Department of Commerce are making special efforts to identify pending projects and to alert U.S. suppliers to these opportunities. The Embassy's latest detailed major projects list, revised as of June 1980, lists projects valued at over $22 billion and identifies the funding sources, projected agreement/contract dates, status, and names and addresses of key contacts for each project. Projects are financed by loans from international organizations and donor countries, foreign and domestic investors, Indonesia's own resources, and often a combination of financing groups. Interested firms may obtain the list by requesting it from the ASEAN/South Asia Group, Office of Country Marketing, U.S. Department of Commerce, Washington, D.C. 20230. This list is updated periodically.

Best Prospects for U.S. Exports

Sales prospects are excellent for a wide range of machinery, equipment, and other products. These include construction equipment and building materials; minerals production and processing equipment; power generation, transmission, and distribution equipment; timber production, harvesting, handling and processing equipment; pulp and paper mill equipment; communications equipment; certain types of transportation equipment; agricultural machinery; food processing and packaging equipment; equipment needed for Indonesia's transmigration program; metallurgical and metalworking equipment; and textile machinery. Details on the market for these products are provided below under Sectoral Trends.

Table 3.—U.S. Trade with Indonesia, 1978-80 (f.a.s.)
(in millions of U.S. dollars)

Commodity	1978	1979	1980
U.S. Exports to Indonesia			
Unmilled wheat	71.2	96.9	134.6
Rice	116.9	88.6	66.9
Oilseeds and oleag. fruit	27.2	27.9	57.5
Raw cotton	74.9	81.2	112.4
Chemicals and related products	77.5	136.5	258.9
Medical and pharmaceutical products	8.8	12.6	14.4
Fertilizers and fertilizer material	17.3	6.1	27.0
Synthetic resins; rubber and plastic materials	15.1	45.2	101.0
Machinery	167.6	180.5	262.0
Power generating machinery	39.0	23.5	42.4
Specialized industrial machinery	48.0	66.6	99.4
Telecommunications equipment	7.7	13.8	9.5
Other electrical equipment	15.8	30.7	32.9
Transportation equipment	73.9	226.6	300.2
Road vehicles	13.4	17.5	18.4
Aircraft and associated equipment	46.7	208.3	280.9
Other	140.3	141.7	351.7
Total exports of domestic merchandise	749.5	979.9	1,544.2
Total exports including reexports	751.4	981.5	1,545.1
U.S. Imports from Indonesia			
Fish and preparations	9.5	13.2	17.7
Coffee	178.8	211.1	229.6
Tea and mate	18.2	17.5	20.6
Spices	39.9	35.2	39.3
Natural rubber	337.5	458.1	430.5
Essential oils	10.0	13.4	15.4
Crude petroleum	2,690.3	2,404.5	3,726.1
Petroleum products	151.3	273.2	429.6
Gas, natural and manufactured	29.3	26.6	40.5
Unwrought tin	70.6	79.0	104.4
Electronic components and parts	17.5	33.0	50.8
Other	54.0	55.8	78.0
Total general imports	3,606.9	3,620.6	5,182.5

Sectoral Trends

Development Plans

Indonesia has completed two 5-year development plans, Repelita I and Repelita II. It embarked on the third plan on April 1, 1979. Repelita III has three fundamental objectives: equitable distribution of development gains, economic growth, and maintenance of political and economic stability.

The plan emphasizes the importance of integrated rural development and crop diversification, although increased rice output is also targeted. In the industrial sector, encouragement will be given to industries that create employment opportunities or that fulfill basic domestic needs. Capital intensive industries are expected to rely mainly on private domestic and foreign sources for financing their development. State enterprises in this field will be encouraged to form joint ventures with foreign partners. The plan gives high priority to the expansion of education and health facilities, especially in less developed areas.

Indonesia's economy will experience considerable structural change. The contribution to gross domestic product (GDP) of the major economic sectors by the end of Repelita III, as compared with the first year of the plan, 1979/80, and the average annual sectoral growth objectives are shown below:

Sector	1979/80	1983/84	Average annual growth
Agriculture	31.4	27.2	+ 3.5
Mining	17.9	15.9	+ 4.0
Industry	10.2	12.6	+11.0
Construction	4.9	5.5	+ 9.0
Transportation and communications	4.6	5.4	+10.0
Others	31.0	33.4	+ 8.1
Gross domestic product	100.0%	100.0%	+ 6.5%

Source: Repelita III.

Agriculture's contribution to GDP, which declined from 32.7 percent in 1974/75 to 31.4 percent by the end of Repelita II, is expected to decline further to 27.2 percent by 1983/84. The contribution of manufacturing, on the other hand, rose from 8.3 percent in 1974/75 to 9.3 percent in 1978/79 and is projected to rise to 12.6 percent by the end of Repelita III. The program for the industrial sector envisages an 11 percent annual growth rate in value added. Strategic industries (steel, metal, and chemicals) are expected to grow by 14 percent annually, consumer goods industries (food processing, textiles, household goods, and pharmaceuticals) by 10.7 percent annually, and small and cottage industries by 6-7 percent annually. The mining sector's contribution to GDP, which declined from 22.2 percent to 17.9 percent during Repelita II, is expected to fall to 15.9 percent by the end of Repelita III, due mainly to the slower growth of oil production.

An average annual GDP growth rate of 6.5 percent was initially expected during Repelita III. This compared with the 7.5 percent GDP growth rate targeted for Repelita II and the 6.8 percent actually achieved.

The growth targets were lowered in Repelita III because of the increased emphasis on social considerations in the plan, the declining opportunities for quick-yielding investments, and the increased financial constraints expected at the time the plan was prepared.

In 1979, GDP growth slowed to 4.8 percent, compared with 7.8 percent in 1978, because of a below average performance in rice production due to pest infestation and a poor performance in other sectors, as devaluation created uncertainties in the business climate. However, higher than anticipated oil prices and oil output are expected to raise the overall growth rate in Repelita III to well over 6.5 percent.

Agriculture

Agriculture is the mainstay of Indonesia's economy. Despite the decline in its relative importance to total national output, agriculture's current contribution of 31 percent makes it the largest contributing sector. Including fishing and forestry, agriculture employs about 65 percent of the labor force and accounts for some 90 percent of non-oil and gas exports. During Repelita III, 14 percent of the Government's development expenditures is to be spent on the agriculture sector.

About 12 percent of Indonesia's total land area—nearly 90,000 square miles—is under cultivation. Intensive farming is carried out on some 40,000 square miles in Java, Madura, and Bali. Excessive expansion of cultivated areas has resulted in irregular flooding and soil erosion in parts of Java.

Sumatra and Kalimantan have an additional 77,000 square miles of potentially arable land. The development of this land is a primary goal of the Government's transmigration program.

Within the agricultural sector, the food crop subsector is the most important, accounting for about 60 percent of the value added in agriculture. Apart from rice, the most important crop, the leading food crops are corn, cassava, soybeans, peanuts, sweet potatoes, and sorghum. The main agricultural export products are timber, rubber, palm oil, coconuts, copra, coffee, tea, and tobacco.

Since the growth in food crop production has lagged behind rising demand resulting from population and income growth, Indonesia has had a continuing need for rice imports. Recognizing the constraints on the rapid increase in rice production, the Government changed its agricultural strategy in Repelita III from a goal of self-sufficiency in rice under the first two plans to an increase in the output and consumption of non-rice food crops. Increases in food production are to be realized through intensification programs (i.e., expansion of the supply of essential inputs including disease-resistant, high-yielding varieties; fertilizer and pesticides; and improvement of support services, including extension services and research activities) and the extension of cultivated areas. The core of the latter is water resources development. Repelita III calls for the rehabilitation and improvement of 1,324,000 acres of existing irrigation systems, construction of 1,730,000 acres of new irrigation systems, reclamation of considerable swamp area, and rehabilitation or expansion of canal systems.

Rice.—Rice production rose by 4.5 percent annually during Repelita I, but declined to 2.8

percent annually in Repelita II, considerably short of the plan's target. The increase in rice production is targeted at 4.3 percent annually in Repelita III, compared with a 5 to 7 percent increase in the output of secondary crops.

Rice output reached 17.5 million tons in 1978 and 18 million tons in 1979, 3 percent higher than the record 1978 harvest. Rice imports by BULOG, Indonesia's rice agency, reached an estimated 2.7 million tons in 1979/80 valued at about $800 million. Of this total 2 million tons were commercial imports, valued at $625 million, or 78 percent, and the remainder were aid shipments, including PL 480. BULOG estimates 1980/81 imports at 2.5 million tons.

Sugar.—Indonesia is attempting to rejuvenate this once important industry. Despite considerable success in increasing sugar output, which reached 1,611,000 tons in 1978, Indonesia imported over 430,000 tons of raw sugar, beet, and sugarcane valued at over $180 million in 1978. A rehabilitation program for old sugar processing factories, located mainly in Java, is currently underway. The Government plans to expand sugar output, mainly on dry land, in order to prevent the replacement of rice by sugarcane in the irrigated fields; to modernize sugar processing factories in Java; and to build new factories in other islands. Six new sugar factories are planned during the next few years.

Rubber.—Rubber is Indonesia's second most important non-oil export. Production was 844,000 tons in 1978, of which 269,000 tons were from estates and 575,000 were from smallholders. Almost all production is exported. Exports were valued at $718 million in 1978 and $940 million in 1979.

Coffee.—Coffee became Indonesia's third most important non-oil export because of the rise in world coffee prices in 1977/78; it temporarily surpassed rubber as a contributor to export earnings in 1977. Production in 1978 amounted to 188,000 tons, of which 17,000 tons were produced on estates and the rest by smallholders. Some 80 percent of production is exported.

Fishing.—Fishing activities, both for domestic consumption and export, account for approximately 2 percent of GDP. The most productive fishing grounds are in the Straits of Malacca around the coast of Kalimantan and near the Moluccas. Exports of fisheries products—particularly shrimp and tuna—have become increasingly important and contributed $281 million to export earnings in 1978 and $382 million in 1979. Production in 1978 amounted to 1,655,000 tons, of which 1,255,000 were saltwater and 430,000 tons freshwater fish.

Food processing and packaging industries present a growing market in Indonesia. Market research estimates the import market in 1978 at $35.4 million, of which $18.8 million was food processing equipment, $5.1 million grain milling equipment, $4.3 million food freezing and refrigeration equipment, and $7.2 million food packaging equipment. West Germany had a 19 percent share of the market, Japan 11 percent and the United States 10 percent. The United States has been particularly successful in the supply of food freezing and refrigeration equipment. This market is projected to rise to some $55 million by 1984. Additional information on the food processing and packaging industries and a list of firms in the industry may be obtained from the ASEAN/South Asia Group, U.S. Department of Commerce, Washington, D.C. 20230.

Transmigration

Indonesia has an ambitious transmigration program under which 500,000 families are to be moved from overpopulated Java to 250 settlement areas in Sumatra, Kalimantan, Sulawesi, and Irian Jaya during Repelita III. This represents an eightfold increase in the number of families actually settled during Repelita II. The program involves construction of 26,500 miles of various types of roads, clearance of 1,544,000 acres of land, and construction of 500,000 houses for transmigrants. In addition, transmigrants are to be provided with agricultural inputs such as seeds, pesticides, fertilizers, sprayers, and agricultural extension services. Considerable assistance from international lending agencies is being provided for this program, which will create trade opportunities. The cost of site preparation, community development, and resettlements under the World Bank Transmigration Project II, for instance, was estimated to be $4,250 per family in constant 1979 prices.

Forest Resources

Indonesia has the largest forest resources in Asia and a large share of the world's tropical hardwoods. Over 300,000 acres, or 64 percent of the total land area, are forested. Kalimantan contains 34 percent of the total resources; Sulawesi, the Moluccas, and Irian Jaya 31 percent; and Sumatra 23 percent. The remainder is in Java, Madura, Bali, and Nusa Tenggara.

Indonesia's forest resources have been exploited increasingly in recent years through domestic and foreign investment. Production of logs and sawn timber rose from 18.7 million cubic meters in 1975 to 31.5 million cubic meters in 1979.

Timber exports are Indonesia's principal non-oil export and were valued at $997 million in 1978 and $1,800 million in 1979, or 12 percent of gross export earnings (see table 1).

Government policy aims to exercise greater control and guidance of the timber and wood industry after a decade of rapid and rather unrestrained growth. It aims to ensure reforestation, selective cutting and a sufficient supply of wood products for domestic use, and to promote growth in the number and production capacities of wood-processing industries such as plywood, sliced veneer, chip mills, pulp and paper mills, and furniture making. Development of the latter will add export value by processing and provide additional employment, a priority need.

In order to encourage local processing of timber, the Government increased the number of levies on log exports in 1978, raised the log export tax, and lowered the levy on the exports of processed wood. Also, exports of certain types of logs and timber are banned.

The current policy of the Government is that all concessions operating more than 7 years and all concessions in operation after 1983 must sell 60 percent of log production domestically and must process 40 percent of all log production domestically. To protect domestic supplies, the Government expects to set limits on exports. Teak, ramin, and ebony log exports are currently banned; only 60 percent of meranti logs, 40 percent of other logs, 75 percent of processed ramin, and 25 percent of other processed species are to be exported.

As of early 1980, there were 469 holders of forestry concessions in Indonesia, of which 55 were foreign investment operations (22 Japanese, 3 U.S., and the remainder Philippine, Korean, Malaysian, Singaporean, and other). Total approved domestic and foreign investment in logging and sawmilling was about $2 billion, of which only about 30-35 percent had been realized. Foreign investment applications for new logging, sawmilling and/or rotary veneer ventures have not been accepted for some time (except for Irian Jaya, a special case), and new domestic ventures may be limited.

Indonesia's plywood industry shows great promise. Before 1973, only three or four plywood factories were in operation with a combined production capacity of 30,000 cubic meters per year. The bulk of Indonesia's plywood was imported. Indonesia currently imports less than 3 percent of its plywood and has 18 plywood mills with a total capacity of 735,000 cubic meters.

Actual production in 1978 was 424,000 cubic meters. Ten more factories are planned, boosting total capacity to about 1.3 million cubic meters annually, and it is hoped that they will raise output to as estimated 869,000 cubic meters in 1983.

Indonesia is one of the world's lowest per capita consumers of paper but is heavily dependent on paper imports. Indonesia's domestic consumption reached 440,000 tons of paper in 1979, of which only 180,000 tons were produced domestically. Consumption is expected to reach 675,000 tons by 1983. In order to meet this growing demand, Indonesia has six large-scale pulp and paper mill projects in planning stages as well as several major expansion programs for existing mills. Total cost is to exceed $2 billion, if plans are fully implemented.

There are 28 paper plants in operation in Indonesia—five State-owned integrated plants with total annual capacity of 83,000 tons and 23 nonintegrated private industries with a total annual capacity of 202,000 tons. An integrated plant produces both pulp and paper, while a nonintegrated plant purchases pulp and produces only paper. The plants produce mostly printing and writing grades of paper but also some cigarette paper, tissue, and some light boards. In 1979, Indonesia for the first time exported 12,500 tons of newsprint valued at $9 million.

In 1978, the total Indonesian market for timber harvesting, handling, processing, and production equipment was estimated at $14.3 million and is expected to grow at 7 percent annually, reaching $21.7 million in 1984. Timber harvesting and handling equipment imports, which approximated $4.8 million in 1978, may reach $7.8 million in 1984. Wood production and processing equipment imports may increase from $9.5 million in 1978 to $13.9 million in 1984. Japan, Taiwan, and the United States were major suppliers in 1978. The United States had a 24 percent share of timber harvesting and handling equipment, but only a 2 percent share of the wood production and processing equipment.

In 1978, the market for pulp and paper production equipment and pulp and paper mill equipment amounted to an estimated $9.4 million and is projected to grow to $14.8 million in 1984. The United States had only a 2 percent share of pulp and paper production equipment in 1978 and a negligible share of the pulp and paper mill machinery market. This may change, however, with the implementation of new major projects.

Additional information on the timbering and wood-processing industries of Indonesia is contained in DIB #80-07-027 and on the pulp and paper industry in DIB #80-07-028 (see Sources of Information below).

Minerals

Indonesia's minerals sector is a major contributor to GDP and plays a dominant role in economic growth. It is the most important source of foreign exchange earnings and government revenue and the principal source of energy. Indonesia is endowed with a wide variety of mineral resources, including oil, natural gas, tin, copper, nickel, coal, bauxite, gold, and silver, of which oil is by far the most important. State companies are heavily involved in minerals production. These are Pertamina for oil and gas, P.T. Tambang Timah for tin, P.T. Tambang Batubara for coal, and P.T. Aneka Tambang for all other minerals.

Petroleum.—Indonesia has proven oil reserves of 10-15 billion barrels or 2 percent of the world's total. New exploration is accelerating rapidly, providing hope that additional reserves may be discovered in the future. With production of 1.639 million in 1978 and 1.593 million bbl/d in 1979, Indonesia ranks 14th among world oil producers and 7th among OPEC countries.

Following a 12 percent increase in oil production in 1977 to an average rate of 1.69 million bbl/d, the highest level ever achieved, production declined by 3 percent annually in 1978 and 1979. The declines are believed to have resulted mainly from the slowdown in exploration and drilling activity that occurred between 1975 and 1977 following the renegotiation of the terms of contracts for foreign oil company operations in Indonesia and the advent of certain tax rulings by the U.S. Internal Revenue Service. A secondary recovery program underway in the large Minas field and the renewal of exploration and drilling activity will probably result in a gradual increase in production for the next several years. Most new discoveries are being made offshore in relatively small fields and an intensified drilling program is necessary if new finds are to keep pace with production depletion. Repelita III estimates a production level of 1.83 million bbl/d by 1984.

Of the 1,539,000 barrels per day produced in 1979, 85,000 bbl/d were produced by the State oil company, Pertamina, 764,000 bbl/d by foreign companies under contracts of work, and 744,000 bbl/d by foreign companies with production-sharing agreements.

U.S. companies predominate among foreign oil companies in Indonesia. One U.S. firm, Caltex, produced 46 percent of total oil produced in 1978. Well over 80 percent of total output is currently exported. However, Indonesia imports crude oil for domestic consumption. In 1978, Japan took 44 percent of Indonesia's oil exports and the United States, 35 percent.

Although Indonesia's domestic energy consumption is very low, it has been increasing by more than 13 percent annually since 1969. Unless alternative sources are found, Indonesia's entire oil production could be needed to supply the domestic market by sometime in the 1990's. Presently, 90 percent of domestic energy consumption is satisfied by oil, 8 percent by gas, and only 2 percent by other energy sources.

To save oil for export, the Government's medium- and long-term energy policy aims at development of non-oil energy sources including coal, hydropower, geothermal, solar, and nuclear energy.

On a gross basis, Indonesia's oil exports were valued at $8,858 million in 1979 (see table 1) and comprised 57 percent of total export earnings. Oil also accounts for more than 50 percent of government revenue.

All refining and distribution of petroleum products are carried out by the State oil company, Pertamina, except for one 4,000 bbl/d refinery owned by Lemigas, the petroleum research and training institute. Pertamina owns and operates eight refineries throughout the country. Design capacity of Pertamina's refineries is 522,000 bbl/d; but, because of age, their economic capacity is around 400,000 bbl/d. An increase in refining capacity is planned.

Liquefied Natural Gas (LNG).—Production of natural gas has increased rapidly in recent years because of the completion of the Badak LNG facility in East Kalimantan (operated by the U.S. firm, Huffco) and the Arun facility in North Sumatra (operated by the U.S. firm, Mobil). Total output rose by 50 percent in 1978 to 820 billion standard cubic feet (stdft^3) and is expected to have increased to about 1,000 billion stdft^3 in 1979, or about 175 million barrels of oil equivalent. Despite the construction of these facilities, utilization of natural gas remains limited, and substantial amounts of gas have to be flared in oilfield operations.

Exports of LNG rose from $547 million in 1978 to $1,293 million in 1979, when LNG exports comprised 8 percent of total export earnings (see table 1). Although LNG production is exported exclusively to Japan, an agreement to supply large quantities of LNG to the West Coast of the United States was concluded in 1978. However, the siting of the receiving facilities has yet to clear the U.S. approvals procedures. LNG is used domestically for various urea and cement plants and for the direct reduction units in the Krakatau steel plant. LNG may eventually become Indonesia's most important hydrocarbon resource, both in terms of export earnings and as feedstock for domestic industry.

New major hydrocarbon-based investment projects, which are now at various stages of planning, include the expansion of both the Badak and Arun LNG plants (at a cost of $800 million and $1 billion, respectively), a hydrocracking complex at Dumai (at a cost of $800 million), a refinery on Batam Island ($700-$800 million), an expansion of the Balikpapan refinery ($700-$900 million), an olefin petrochemicals complex in Arun ($1.5-$2 billion), an aromatics petrochemicals complex in Pladju ($450 million), a methanol plant on Bunyu Island ($200 million) off the coast of East Kalimantan, and a carbon black plant.

Tin.—Indonesia is one of the major tin producers in the world and has reserves estimated at from 700,000 to 1 million tons of concentrates. Exports were valued at $382 million in 1979 and were 36 percent higher than in 1978, mainly because of price increases.

Production of tin ore concentrate was 29,436 tons in 1979, compared with 27,437 tons in 1978. By continuing exploration and development activities, rehabilitating aging facilities, and adding new dredges, Indonesia plans to reach a production capcity of 35,000 tons annually by 1984.

P.T. Tambang Timah is the largest producer and sole processor of tin in Indonesia and contributes over 90 percent of total output. Three foreign companies—P.T. Koba Tin, P.T. Broken Hill Proprietary, and P.T. Riau Mining (formery Billiton Exploratie Maatschappij Indonesia)—are also active. Indonesia's tin industry has now been closed to additional foreign investment.

Tin is one of the oldest mined mineral commodities in Indonesia. It occurs in that part of the world's largest "tin belt" which is located in the archipelago: the tin islands of Bangka, Belitung, Singkep, some smaller islands of the Riau-Lingga Group and nearby seas, and the Bangkinang area on mainland Sumatra. New offshore tin reserves have been identified on the tin islands during the past few years. One tin project currently underway is an offshore mining venture near the island of Pulau Tujuh to be undertaken by one of the foreign companies under a contract of work agreement. The mine will cost an estimated $49 million and have an average annual production of 2,250 tons of 70 percent tin concentrate. In 1979, P.T. Tambang Timah ordered a new $25 million dredge with an annual production capacity of 1,100 tons, which will be built on Batam Island. It is likely to come into use within 2 years.

Copper.—Copper deposits occur in Irian Jaya, Sumatra, Kalimantan, Java, and Sulawesi. The only copper producer and exporter is Freeport Indonesia (in which Freeport Minerals of the United States has a controlling interest), which mines the Ertsberg copper deposit in Irian Jaya. In addition to its open-pit mine—that began producing in 1973, Freeport is developing an adjacent underground mine which has an estimated 45 million tons of ore. This mine will cost an estimated $100 million and will have an eventual capacity of 9,500 tons per day. The open-pit mine, which produced 188,769 tons of copper concentrate in 1979, compared with 180,932 tons in 1978, will be mined at least until 1983-84. Copper exports in 1978 were valued at $81.9 million.

In 1978, an Indonesian firm signed a third-generation contract of work with P.T. Copperindo Utama of Taiwan, with reference to 6,178 acres (2,500 ha) of concession area in West Java. In addition, representatives of Indonesia and France signed a cooperation agreement on February 5, 1979, for a geological survey that will map and identify mineral deposits, principally copper, in northwest Kalimantan.

Nickel.—Indonesia has one of the world's largest reserves of nickel, estimated at 824 million tons of nickel bearing laterites and nickel silicates.

Originally P.T. Aneka Tambang was the sole producer of nickel ore. However, P.T. International Nickel Indonesia, a subsidiary of the Canadian-based INCO Ltd., signed a contract of work in 1968, and after years of preparation is now producing. Both operate in southeast Sulawesi: Aneka Tambang at Pomalaa and INCO in the area of Soroako, where its nickel matte plant is located.

Production of nickel ore by P.T. Aneka Tambang totaled 1,265,450 tons in 1978, of which 864,369 tons were exported, a figure slightly higher than the previous year. Since 1976, Aneka Tambang has operated a ferro-nickel plant at Pomalaa, which produced 19,734 tons of ingot in 1978, of which 19,455 tons were exported. INCO produced 1,194,715 tons of wet ore in 1978. INCO began production of nickel-matte in 1977. Production was 5,729 tons in 1978, but full capacity following second-stage expansion is due to be 45,000 tons per year. Indonesia's exports of nickel ore and concentrates in 1978 were valued at $21.4 million. Output of nickel ore and concentrate amounted to 1,551,872 tons in 1979.

Exploration activities and plans for a ferro-nickel plant at Gebe Island have been abandoned by P.T. Indeco due to the prevailing low world price of nickel. Exploration on the island has since been resumed by P.T. Aneka Tambang. Another major nickel project, located on Gag Island, west of Irian Jaya, is under review.

Bauxite.—Indonesia's largest reserves of bauxite are on Bintan Island near Singapore. Mining output by the sole producer, P.T. Aneka Tambang, reached an alltime high of 1,301,416 tons in 1977 and declined to 1,007,764 tons in 1978 and 1,057,905 tons in 1979. Exports totaled 983,324 tons in 1978, of which 98 percent went to Japan. The Government has decided to drop its plans to build a 600,000 ton per year alumina refinery on Bintan Island. However, it is considering other schemes to develop the reserves at lower cost. These include the possibility of transporting below export grade bauxite from Bintan Island to a proposed alumina smelter at Kuala Tanjung, Sumatra, near the Asahan aluminum project. The possibility of exploiting higher grade bauxite deposits in West Kalimantan is also being considered.

Coal.—Indonesia's coal reserves have been estimated by its Mineral Technology Development Center at 525 million tons, not including billions of tons of low-quality coal. Deposits are primarily in Kalimantan, Sumatra, and at a few locations on Java. Modernization and expansion of the coal industry is an important part of the country's development plan and a key factor in its energy planning.

A State company, P.N. Tambang Batubara, operates a deep mine at Ombilin in West Sumatra and an open-pit mine at Bukit Asam in South Sumatra. Production was 264,180 tons in 1978 and 278,589 tons in 1979. Some coal was exported in 1978 to Taiwan and Singapore.

The Government plans to increase coal production at the Bukit Asam mine from the 177,000 tons produced in 1978 to 2.5-3 million tons by 1984/85. The coal will be transported to Suralaya, West Java, to fuel a power plant with initial capacity of 750 MW, and ultimate capacity of 2,500 MW by 1993. The construction contract was awarded to a Canadian consortium. Preliminary estimates place required investment at over $1 billion, of which approximately $350 million will be required for upgrading the mine and constructing the transportation system. The Export Development Corporation of Canada and the World Bank are expected to provide financial support.

To further develop coal resources, P.N. Batubara in 1978 gave approval in principle to six international companies to explore and develop eventually eight blocks in East and South Kalimantan on the basis of a production-sharing arrangement.

Manufacturing

Indonesia's manufacturing sector is in an early stage of development. However, its structure is changing rapidly, and it is becoming a significant source of export earnings. Manufacturing accounts for about 12 percent of GDP and less than 10 percent of total employment in recent years. It has been one of the most rapidly growing economic sectors. Value added by manufacturing rose by 11.3 percent annually in Repelita II and is expected to maintain this growth rate in Repelita III.

Private enterprises producing mainly consumers goods dominate the manufacturing sector. However, the rapid expansion of the sector has been largely attributable to increases in the output of "strategic industries," such as cement, fertilizer, and basic metal products produced mainly by State-owned companies, either independently or in joint ventures with foreign firms.

Foreign investment has played a major role in developing manufacturing industries. Between 1967 and August 1979, projects valued at $4,558 million were approved, of which about half have been implemented. Of the total approved projects, basic metals accounted for 25.3 percent, textiles 25 percent and nonmetallic minerals 12 percent. Investment in basic metals includes the Asahan aluminum project, which comprises approximately two-thirds of total approved investment in this sector.

The production of selected manufacturing industries from 1976/77 to 1978/79 is shown in table 4.

Cement.—Indonesia's cement industry has grown so rapidly that the country became a new exporter of cement during 1979/80. In 1969, there were only three State-owned plants, with a combined production capacity of 400,000 tons per year. By the end of 1979/80 Indonesia had seven major cement plants in operation with a total capacity of 6.85 million tons. With this new capacity coming into operation, cement production increased from 2.9 million tons in 1977/78 to 3.6 million tons in 1978/79, resulting in a decrease in imports from 600,000 tons in 1977 to 300,000 tons in 1978.

Five expansions ranging from 0.5 to 1 million tons are scheduled for completion by 1984/85, as well as five new plants in Sumatra, Java, Sulawesi, and Timor, so that the capacity of the cement industry by the mid-1980's could reach about 14 million tons. Of this, more than 1 million tons should be available for export.

Fertilizer.—Plentiful supplies of natural gas as feedstock and the successful completion of various fertilizer projects have made Indonesia self-sufficient in both urea and triple superphosphate fertilizer. Production of urea fertilizer increased from 406,000 tons in 1976/77 to 1,434,000 tons in 1978/79, or by over 250 percent. In addition to meeting the domestic demand for fertilizer, which increased by 6 percent in 1978/79, Indonesia exported 262,000 tons of urea in 1978/79 valued at $37 million.

There are three State-owned chemical fertilizer plants in operation—P.T. Pupuk Sridjaja, P.T. Petrokimia Gresik, and P.T. Pupuk Kujang, with annual production capacity of about 2.8 million tons—2,200,000 tons of urea, 150,000 tons of ammonium sulphate, 330,000 tons of TSP, 80,000 tons of DAP, and 50,000 tons of NPK. Two additional urea fertilizer plants are under construction in East Kalimantan and Aceh. The Aceh fertilizer plant is a project sponsored by ASEAN to meet regional requirements. The total annual production capacity of each plant will be 570,000 tons of urea.

Metal and Machinery.—A substantial diversification of metal products fabricated in Indonesia is taking place. The automotive industry, initially limited to the assembly of imported parts, now produces such items as radiators, transmission systems, clutches, speedometers, steering assemblies and many other smaller components. Foundry facilities are being expanded and shipbuilding capacity is being increased.

Barata Metalworks and Engineering in the Surabaya area is Indonesia's largest steel casting and metalworking company. Barata makes sugar mill and other agricultural equipment and a variety of industrial equipment, including water pumps, pressure vessels, boilers, pistons, road rollers, gears, and heavy pipe. Boma-Bisma-Indra (BBI), also in the Surabaya area, makes agricultural equipment and assembles diesel engines under license from Deutz of West Germany, making some of the parts.

A large-scale aluminum smelter project (Asahan) under construction in North Sumatra is an important development in the metals sector. This is scheduled to start aluminum production in 1982 at a level of 75,000 tons a year and to reach full capacity of 225,000 tons by 1984. Most of the aluminum produced will be exported to Japan, but Indonesia may purchase up to 30 percent of the project's production for the domestic market.

Steel.—Indonesia has a number of small-scale steel manufacturing companies. At the end of 1977, there were some 74 plants producing reinforced bars, wire, rods, and pipe. However, the major development of the steel industry is the establishment in 1970 of the State-owned company, P.T. Krakatau Steel, which was given two mandates: to complete the former Cilegon steel project, which has been started with Russian aid in 1962; and to develop a national steel industry.

The first of these objectives was achieved by mid-1977 with the completion of a bar and section mill. Cilegon is the first integrated steel plant in Indonesia and is also the first steel complex in Southeast Asia to combine direct reduction of iron ore with electric furnace steelmaking.

P.T. Krakatau Steel's master plan for the achievement of the second objective envisages the gradual construction over the next 10 years of a steel plant with an annual capacity of 2.2 million tons of steel. Construction of infrastructure will also be required. Total cost of the project is nearly $2 billion.

Table 4.—Production of Selected Manufacturing Industries 1976/77-1978/79*

Products	Units	1976/77	1978/79	1978/79**
Cement	thousand tons	1,979	2,879	3,640
Fertilizer				
Urea	thousand tons	406	990	1,434
Ammonium sulphate	thousand tons	105	93	116
Paper	thousand tons	54	84	1,400
Fabrics	million meters	1,247	1,333	1,400
Textile yarn	thousand bales	623	678	900
Reinforcing				
steel bars	thousand tons	296	240	300
Galvanized iron				
sheets	thousand tons	156	185	185
Automobiles (assembled)	thousand units	75	84	99
Motorcycles (assembled)	thousand units	268	272	320
Automobile tires	thousand units	1,883	2,339	2,641
Motorcycle tires	thousand units	1,520	2,429	2,499
Television sets assembled	thousand units	213	482	611
Radio sets (assembled)	thousand units	1,100	1,000	1,128
Radio cassette recorder (assembled)	thousand units	325	548	488
Car batteries	thousand units	480	575	800
Dry-cell batteries	thousand units	420	443	420
Light bulbs	million units	26	25	29
Coconut oil	thousand tons	276	276	319
Other cooking oil	thousand units	33	31	38
Salt	thousand tons	560	786	165
Cigarettes				
Clove	million units	37,900	40,900	45,200
Regular	million units	22,637	23,100	24,200

SOURCE: Indonesian Department of Industry.
*Indonesian fiscal year ending March 31, 1979.
**Preliminary.

There is a substantial market in Indonesia for the sale of metallurgical and metalworking equipment used in the above industries and other sectors of the economy. Market research estimates that the total market for all kinds of metallurgical and metal working equipment in 1978 was $80.4 million, of which metallurgical and primary metals production equipment was $20.2 million; machine tools and equipment for metal products production, $48.1 million; welding equipment, $11.2 million; and control and measuring instruments for metallurgy, metalworking, and machining, $1 million. The United States had only a 6.5 percent share of the market overall but had a 10 percent share of the market for welding equipment and a 12.2 percent share for control and measuring instruments and metallurgy, metalworking equipment. The overall market is estimated to rise to $127.2 million in 1984.

Electronics.—The Indonesian Government places high priority on the development of an electronics industry and is seeking foreign investment. The possibilities offered by the industry for large-scale employment generation are particularly attractive.

The output of electronic products has grown rapidly during the last 10 years. Two U.S. firms, Fairchild and National Semiconductor, already have plants that export integrated circuits. Indonesia exported electronic parts during 1979 valued at more than $70 million. The United States imported integrated circuits from Indonesia valued at $33 million in 1979.

Textiles.—Indonesia produced 1,400 million meters of textile fabrics in 1978/79 and 900,000 bales of textile yarn, increasing output 5 percent and 32.7 percent, respectively, over the preceding year. The Government hopes to increase textile output significantly. The production target for the end of Repelita III is 2.5 billion meters, or a per capita production of 16 meters of textiles. Since consumption levels are estimated at 14 meters per capita, some 280 million meters of textiles and ready-made clothing will be available for export.

The textile industry has been a major area for domestic and foreign investment. Between 1967 and August 1979, approved domestic investment projects in textiles were valued at $791 million and foreign investment projects, primarily Japanese, at $1,141 million.

Since Indonesia has virtually reached self-sufficiency in fabrics, more attention will be placed on raw material producing projects and the garment manufacturing sector. Indonesia currently supplies much of its internal market for modern garments and in 1978 exported clothing valued at $15 million.

Emphasis will be given to the development of the upstream sectors of the industry, such as synthetic fiber making and spinning as Indonesia's textile industry is still highly dependent on imported raw materials. Domestic sources supply less than 50 percent of the total amount of fiber required for the manufacture of textiles in Indonesia. Indonesia is already able to meet its need for polyester fiber but has to import all synthetic raw material. In the future, domestic fiber makers will be able to draw their supplies of synthetic raw material from the aromatic chemical plant now under construction. Expansions are expected in manufacturing capacities of other types of synthetic fiber, such as nylon and acrylic.

Virtually all machinery and 99 percent of the spare parts needed by the industry must be imported. Market research estimates the market for textile and apparel manufacturing equipment at $98.6 million in 1978, of which $34 million was spinning mill equipment, $32.7 million was textile and fabric production equipment, $23 million was textile and fabric finishing equipment, and $8.9 million was apparel and other textile products manufacturing equipment. Imports are estimated to increase to $175 million by 1984. The United States was a minor supplier in 1978, supplying only 2 percent of total imports.

Additional details on the textile industry are available in a report by the American Embassy, Industrial Outlook Report: Textiles, listed in Sources of Economic and Commercial Information below, and in market research available from the ASEAN/South Asia Group, U.S. Department of Commerce, Washington, D.C. 20230.

Transportation

Marine transport services link the islands and form the major trunk system in Indonesia. Roads and railways provide the secondary system. The internal transport network is most developed on Java; the northern and southern parts of Sumatra, Madura, and Bali; and is relatively undeveloped in Kalimantan, Sulawesi, and Irian Jaya. There are railways in Java, Madura, and Sumatra used for the transport of freight and passengers. In the islands without railways and with less developed highways, rivers serve as the main means of transportation. Air transport is still limited but is increasing rapidly.

Because of the high priority accorded the transport sector in Repelita I and II, there was marked improvement in overall transport services. However, a wide gap persists between the capacity and requirements. Repelita III continues to give high priority to transport. Of the development budget for communications and tourism, which totals $5.4 billion, 49 percent has been allocated for road and rail transport, 15 percent for marine transport, and nearly 14 percent for air transport. However, while the current plan maintains the emphasis of the preceding programs on low-cost, quick-return improvement schemes, Repelita III places greater emphasis on improving communications in rural areas and on maintenance of existing systems.

Market research estimates the market for transportation equipment at $861 million in 1978, of which $627 million was for road transport equipment, $62 million for rail transport equipment; $86 million for marine transport equipment; and $86 million for air transport equipment. This is projected to increase by 50 percent to $1,297 million by 1983. In 1978, the United States had market shares of 4.3 percent for road transport equipment, 17.1 percent for railways equipment, 4.8 percent for marine equipment, and 62 percent for air transport equipment.

Road Transport.—Indonesia's road system beyond the village level had a total length of 76,253 miles in 1978, of which 6,943 miles were national highways, 16,747 miles were provincial, and 52,563 miles were district roads. About 43 percent of the total was paved. The road system is most developed in Java, which had 32 percent of the total road system in 1978 but comprises only 7 percent of the country's total land area. Sumatra's roads also accounted for about 32 percent of the total; Sulawesi's 16 percent; and Kalimantan's 8 percent. Village roads constitute an additional road network of about 120,000 miles. Also, agricultural estates, oil companies, and other installations have constructed and maintained their own road systems.

The network of usable roads is inadequate, particularly outside Java, and road conditions, though improved on many arterial links, remain poor over much of the remaining system. The Government considers unstable more than 90 percent of the roads in Indonesia, including those in Java, and special methods are required in order to maintain passable conditions. The World Bank has extended five loans for highway, projects to improve and extend the highway systems.

The systems need further expansion to accommodate the demand for road transport, which is growing rapidly. Highway transport during the second 5-year plan increased by more than 10 percent annually and the total number of motor vehicles increased at about 16 percent per year. From 1973 to 1977, the number of buses increased by 11.5 percent annually, trucks by 16.8 percent, passenger cars by 11.1 percent, and motorcycles by 24.4 percent.

The number of registered motor vehicles throughout the archipelago in 1978 was passenger cars, 532,299; buses, 58,365; trucks, 331,658; and motorcycles, 1,960,237. However, the number of vehicles actually in use was less. In 1972, only about two-thirds of the registered vehicles were on the road. While updated data are not available, there are indications that the proportion in operation has risen in recent years because of the substantial additions to the fleet.

Repelita III allocates $2.6 billion for road transport or nearly half of the total budget for communications and tourism. In line with overall transport strategy, greater emphasis will be placed on maintenance and support works and on the rural road system. During Repelita III, 24,600 miles of rural roads will be rehabilitated and 47,500 meters of bridges in the rural area will be rebuilt, along with the implementation of the provincial and national road improvement program covering more than 6,000 miles of road and 96,000 meters of bridges. In addition, nearly 600 miles of new roads will be built, and 600 miles of urban roads will be upgraded. In addition to these activities, the road rehabilitation and maintenance programs will be continued. Plans are being prepared for added road safety and measuring equipment, including the completion of 40 weighing bridges, 9 load meters, 35 light meters, and 89,905 traffic lights.

Motor vehicle industries in Indonesia produce a limited number of motor vehicle components but mainly assemble passenger cars, trucks, and motorcycles imported in knocked down condition. Indonesia had hoped to create a commercial vehicle industry by 1984 in which all components were manufactured locally, but problems in the industry prevent adherence to the initial time schedule.

In 1978, Indonesia imported road transport equipment valued at $627.3 million, of which automobiles were valued at $102.1 million, buses at $26.3 million, trucks at $371.4 million, other road vehicles at $80.6 million, and automotive parts and accessories at $46.9 million. The United States had a market share of only 4.3 percent overall, but a 6.9 percent share of other (i.e., special purpose) motor vehicles and a 20.7 percent share of parts and accessories. The market for road transport equipment is estimated to increase to $857 million by 1983.

Rail Transport.—The Indonesian State Railways (PJKA)—a government agency with its own management—is the largest railway system in Southeast Asia. It has a total track mileage of approximately 4,100 miles, of which 3,000 miles are in Java. Because of the inadequate highway system, the railway is used extensively for freight transportation and passenger services.

A weakened financial situation in recent years has curtailed freight traffic by railroad as tariff increases necessary to offset large wage costs made the railroad systems less competitive than other alternative distribution modes. The State-owned railway lines are fully subsidized in order to provide transportation for low-income sectors of the society. Service in Java is designed to provide first-, second-, and third-class passenger transportation during medium and long journeys, while still providing mass transit in large cities and suburbs.

Great strides were made during Repelita II in the railroad area of the development plan. Railway lines increased by 1,287 miles and railway bridges by 1,417 miles. Machinery acquisitions included the addition of 673 locomotives, 14,145 freight cars, 1,448 passenger cars, 2 electric railways, and 10 diesel railways. A reservoir of replacement equipment included 130 freight cars, 39 diesel locomotives, and 124 passenger cars.

Repelita III emphasizes the need for better maintenance of rolling stock and the operation of larger and more reliable trains. Increases in services for the transportation of bulk goods, such as cement, fertilizer, oil, and basic commodities, are planned. Industrial considerations earmark the W. Sumatra railway system for priority service to the Indarung cement factory and the Ombilin coal mine. S. Sumatra railway lines will service third-class passengers on long-distance travel, while also transporting freight from mining, industrial, and forestry industries.

In 1979, the railroads carried 27.4 million passengers and 5,295 million tons of freight. By 1983, these are to increase to 36 million and 7,855 million tons, respectively.

In addition to the replacement of over 400,000 miles of railway lines, Repelita III targets include the rehabilitation of 106 and acquisition of 39 locomotives, the rehabilitation of 131 and purchase of 55 passenger cars, and replacement of 3,900 and addition of 1,250 freight cars.

Imports of railway transport equipment amounted to $61.8 million in 1978, of which locomotives, mainly from the United States, were valued at $19.1 million; self-propelled railway cars, mainly from Japan, were $11.2 million; and railway passenger cars, mainly from Yugoslavia, were $28.4 million. Imports declined in 1979, reflecting completion of procurement under the Repelita II program, and are estimated at about $38 million in 1981 and $52 million in 1983, assuming implementation of the South Sumatra

coal project.

Sea Transport.—Indonesia has an extensive port system of about 300 registered ports. Of these, 16 can accommodate oceangoing ships and about 100 can accommodate interisland shipping vessels. Tanjung Priok, serving the Jakarta area, is by far the largest port for general cargo, although the port of Dumai in Sumatra, where the large Caltex oil fields are located, handled the largest volume of exports in 1978. Other major seaports in Indonesia are Tanjung Perak, the port for Surabaya; Cirebon and Cilacap in Java; Belawan, Pangkalan Susu, and Palembang in Sumatra; Banjarmasin and Pontianak in Kalimantan; Ujung Pandang and Bitung in Sulawesi, Ambon in the Moluccas; and Sorong in Irian Jaya.

Of the 147.2 million tons of cargo handled at Indonesian ports in 1977, exports comprised 65 percent; imports, 9 percent; and interisland trade, 26 percent.

Indonesia's shipping fleet is neither large nor modern and carries only a small portion of the country's total cargo trade.

In 1977/78 Indonesia's shipping fleet had a capacity of 955,000 dead weight tons (dwt), and carried about 11.1 million tons of cargo, exclusive of the large volume of cargo handled by special cargo vessels such as log carriers, oil tankers, and other bulk cargo vessels and by merchant sailing ships. The fleet consisted of an oceangoing shipping line of 54 ships, which operates from Indonesia to Japan, Europe, the United States, and Canada; an interisland fleet known as the Regular Liner Service; a coastal shipping fleet; and a so-called pioneer shipping service to help farmers on more isolated islands in their trade. Capacity and cargo handled by the respective services in 1977/78 are shown below:

	DWT	Tons of cargo handled
Oceangoing fleet	490,310	5,580,000
Interisland fleet	310,570	3,635,000
Coastal shipping	141,000	1,832,000
Pioneer Lines	12,872	67,000

In addition, the capacity of a "people's shipping armada," comprised mainly of sailing ships, was 42,900 dwt in 1977/78, and the cargo handled amounted to 968,000 tons.

As of December 31, 1978, the interisland fleet had 322 carriers with a total capacity of approximately 312,000 dwt and the coastal fleet had 1,448 carriers with a total capacity of approximately 187,000 dwt.

During Repelita II, Indonesia increased shipping capacity and improved productivity in cargo handling and continues to have these as priority objectives in Repelita III.

Repelita II also brought improvements in the development of harbor facilities. At the end of the plan, wharves totaled 35,083 meters; warehouses, 678,383 square meters; and cargo yards and clearance space, 770,000 square meters. They were equipped with 351 forklifts, 95 mobile cranes, and various other harbor equipment that permitted servicing of 24.6 million tons of cargo annually. A smoother flow of goods has resulted from increased educational facilities, which have boosted labor productivity in some harbors to 16-18 tons per crew per hour. Harbor productivity has reached approximately 600-700 dwt per year.

Repelita III calls for expansion of "National Fleets," rehabilitation and development of ports, and improvement of port efficiency to meet projected growth needs of 5 percent annually in foreign shipping and 10 percent annually in domestic shipping. It calls for additions of 275,290 dwt to the oceangoing fleet, additions of 6,000 dwt and replacements of 100,300 dwt for the interisland fleet, additions of 45,000 dwt and replacements of 17,500 dwt for coastal shipping, and additions and replacements in the sailing ship fleet of 36,000 dwt. In addition, the log transport fleet is to increase by 104,000 dwt.

The plan also calls for the addition of 6,670 meters of wharves, 83,160 square meters of warehousing space, and 60,304 square meters of cargo yard space. Additional equipment planned includes 164 forklifts and 35 mobile cranes, as well as dredging equipment and new dock facilities.

Containerization is developing in Indonesia. Tanjung Priok, Jakarta's largest port, has a container terminal and two 5-ton capacity cranes, each capable of handling 20 containers an hour. Container traffic has risen by an average of 45 percent annually at the port in the last 4 years reaching 35,345 units in 1978 and 45,875 units in 1979, of which 18,345 units and 23,303 units in the respective years were incoming cargo. Container facilities are now being built at Belawan in North Sumatra, Tanjung Perak in Surabaya, Palembang in South Sumatra, and Pangkai Pinang in the Riau Archipelago to enable them to handle feeder vessels.

Of total imports of marine transport equipment valued at $85.7 million in 1978, ships and boats comprised $49.9 million; marine engines, $30.8 million; and marine transport lifting and loading equipment, $5 million. While the overall market share for the United States was only 4.8 percent, the United States was the second largest exporter of marine engines, with 12.1 percent of the total. The total market for marine transport equipment is projected to rise to $163.4 million in 1983.

Major projects being implemented over the next 5 years include the expansion and modernization of port facilities at Belawan at a cost of $100 million, funded by the Indonesian Government, the Asian Development Bank and West Germany; and the expansion of port facilities at Semarang, Central Java, at a cost of $63 million. Also, Tanjung Priok is being modernized and expanded at a cost of $80 million, $32 million of which is being funded by a World Bank loan.

U.S. flag carriers provide liner services to Indonesia from Gulf and West Coast ports. From Gulf ports, Lykes Bros. Steamship Co. Inc., Lykes Center, 300 Poydras Street, New Orleans, Louisiana 70130, provides breakbulk service and American President Lines, 1509 Cotton Exchange Building, Dallas, Texas 75201, provides Mini-Landbridge Container Service.

From West Coast ports, two U.S. flag carrier services are available. American President Lines Ltd., (APL), 1950 Franklin Street, Oakland, California 94012, provides 14-day frequency containership vessels and dry and refrigerated cargo by relay from Portland (via overland service), Seattle, Los Angeles, and Oakland/San Francisco for discharge in Jakarta. The transit time is 23 days. APL also provides service twice a month from California/Columbia River-Puget Sound areas to discharge ports in Indonesia on inducement. The Lykes Lines, 320 California Street, San Francisco, California 94104, has biweekly service from Portland, Seattle, Long Beach, and San Francisco for discharge in Jakarta. The transit time is 25 days. Vessels provide container, breakbulk, limited reefer container service, and deeptanks for bulk liquid cargo.

Air Transport.—Indonesia's flag-carrying airline, P.T. Garuda Indonesian Airways (Garuda), is the largest air carrier. With the acquisition of the government-owned Merpati Nusantara Airlines by Garuda in 1978, the entire government-owned airlines system for both domestic and international traffic is now under one management. Six private scheduled airlines and additional private operators serve domestic routes or operate charter services. However, these have only a very small share of domestic air traffic and almost none of the international.

Garuda currently has scheduled services to 33 cities and towns throughout Indonesia and international routes to the Netherlands, Australia, Singapore, Malaysia, the Middle East, Hong Kong, and Japan. Merpati Nusantara has mainly domestic routes and served 132 cities and towns in 1978.

Indonesia's air transport services have grown rapidly to keep pace with the country's economic development. Between 1973 and 1978, the distance traveled by domestic aircraft nearly doubled to 66 million craft/km. and the passengers carried grew from 1.6 million to 3.98 million.

Operations by national airlines on international routes have been fairly limited. Between 1973 and 1978, the number of passengers traveling national airlines on international routes rose from 97,000 to 270,000, while cargo transport rose from 3,125 tons to 4,257 tons.

In Repelita III, the annual increase in demand for domestic passenger and cargo air transportation services is projected to be about 18 percent and 25 percent, respectively. To meet this demand, more than 25 airports throughout the country will be improved and expanded. More service must be provided to remote areas of Indonesia. The number of airplanes serving domestic as well as international flights will also be increased.

As of September 30, 1979, Garuda's fleet consisted of 6 DC-10's, 25 DC-9's, 28 F-28's, and 2 DC-8's. Merpati Nusantara operates 38 aircraft. In 1979, Garuda ordered four new Boeing 747 aircraft and six new Airbus A300 aircraft. The 747 aircraft were delivered during 1980 and will be used for Garuda's European and Middle Eastern services, and for its projected service to the United States via the Pacific. Four Airbus A300 aircraft will be delivered in late 1981 and two in early 1982 and will be used on Garuda's most heavily traveled domestic routes and on regional routes.

There were 59 registered airports in 1978. Jakarta's Halim Perdanakusuma International Airport and the Ngurah Rai Airport in Bali are Indonesia's two main international airports. Both accept Boeing 747's and DC-10's. There are about 12 other major airports—three in Java, three in Sumatra, two in Sulawesi, and one each in Kalimantan, East Timor, Maluku, and Irian Jaya—which accept DC-9's and smaller aircraft. Preparatory work has begun on the site for Jakarta's new airport at Cengkareng, about 20 miles northwest of Jakarta. It will replace Halim. The new airport will be built in two stages at an estimated cost of $300 million. The first stage, to be ready by 1982, will be designed to handle Jakarta's air traffic through 1987.

Indonesia's imports of air transport equipment were valued at $86.5 million in 1978, of which aircraft comprised $45.5 million; aircraft engines and components, $17 million; and radio navigation aid apparatus, $24 million. The United States was the principal supplier with market shares of 94 percent for aircraft, 23.4 percent for aircraft engines and components, and 28.4 percent for radio navigation aid apparatus, or an overall market share of 62 percent. The market is estimated at $224 million in 1983.

Indonesia continued to be a significant market for U.S. exports in 1979. U.S. exports to Indonesia of aircraft amounted to $192 million in 1979 and exports of aircraft parts amounted to $16.3 million.

Additional details on Indonesia's transportation sector are available in market research available from the ASEAN/South Asia Group, Office of Country Marketing, U.S. Department of Commerce, Washington, D.C. 20230.

Communications

Indonesia's communications capability has improved substantially in recent years. For international communications, Indonesia established its first satellite earth station in 1969. Major communications projects recently scheduled include expansion of the domestic satellite program, a telex and telegram projects, and a project for telephone exchanges. The aggregate foreign exchange cost of these latter projects is about $780 million (the financing for most of this has already been arranged) and the domestic costs are equivalent to $386 million. The most dramatic addition to Indonesia's communications capabilities was the inauguration in August 1976 of its Domestic Satellite System, consisting of two satellites, Palapa A1 and A2. The system operates with 50 earth stations, 10 of which were added in Repelita II, and links Jakarta with 26 provincial capitals and 14 other major points. The satellite system enables Indonesia to achieve rapid expansion of telephone and broadcast facilities and gives it the capacity of extending multiple channels of television and radio broadcasts to all of its provinces.

Palapa A1 serves domestic communications (telephones, teleprinters, and data and television broadcast), and Palapa A2 serves international needs. The system is leased to neighboring countries, particularly to the other four members of the Association of Southeast Asian Nations (ASEAN). During 1982/83, the second-generation satellites, Palapa B1 and B2, will be launched to replace the existing satellites, which will end their service-life in 1983/84. During Repelita III, 37 more small earth stations will be built, including some to meet requirements for inner-city communications.

Aside from the satellite system, transmission facilities in Indonesia include open-wire carrier, high-frequency (hf), very-high frequency (vhf), and radio and microwave systems.

Indonesia's microwave network was expanded by nearly 800,000 miles in Repelita II and will be expanded further in Repelita III. Direct communication facilities between Jakarta and Ujung Pandang were established on June 16, 1978, when the East Indonesia microwave network began operation. The East Indonesia network joins other established microwave networks already working in Indonesia. The Java-Bali microwave network connects Jakarta, Bandung, Semarang, Jogjakarta, and Surabaya in Java with Denpasar on Bali. The Trans-Sumatra microwave network operates between Telukbetung in Southern Sumatra and Jakarta. Since microwave systems are limited by a line-of-sight requirement between transmitters and receivers, other transmission methods are used to span the long distances between Indonesia's islands. These methods include high-frequency radio and a very-high altitude troposcatter system, which links Surabaya on Java with Banjarmasin on Kalimantan and serves other parts of Kalimantan through two local microwave networks.

During Repelita II, the average number of telephones in service increased from 1.9 to 3.7 per 1,000 population and the long-distance, direct-dial service rose from 126,000 lines to 423,000 lines. The telephone service network is concentrated in the vicinity of Jakarta, which has over 13 telephones in service per 1,000 population. Repelita III calls for the installation of 232,000 new long-distance lines, 65,000 in Jakarta and 166,500 in other cities and localities.

Telex capabilities are being expanded through 7,730 new installations made in Repelita II and 3,910 additional planned in Repelita III to meet increased demand forecast at 25 percent annually. As of 1977, Indonesia had telex services to 57 cities, including all provincial capitals and telex communications with 130 countries.

Various State-owned enterprises provide communications services. PERUM Telekomunikasi (Perumtel) provides the telephone and telegraph services (with the exception of the satellites themselves, the transmission facilities in Indonesia are operated by both private and government companies); Radio Republik Indonesia (RRI) has radio broadcast facilities; Television Republik Indonesia (TVRI) is responsible for television communications; and PERUM Pos dan Giro provides postal services.

Indonesia plans to develop radio and television communications since both media are seen to have great educational, cultural, and social impact. As of 1976, there were about 6 million radio receivers serving an audience of at least 60 million people in Indonesia. RRI had 45 stations throughout the country that comprised the national system. Each of these was linked to one of three regional networks centered in Medan, Sumatra, Jogjakarta in Central Java, and Udjung Pandang in Sulawesi. In addition, 169 privately owned radio stations were registered as of 1976, including stations owned by universities and religious and missionary organizations.

Facilities of RRI and the area served increased considerably during the remaining years of Repelita II and are expected to continue to grow. Radio transmission will expand into FM relay and the quality of programs will be improved.

TVRI is the only television network in Indonesia. There are now an estimated 370,000 television receivers operating throughout Indonesia, of which 247,000 are in Jakarta.

TVRI currently consists of 70 transmitting stations and 11 relay stations reaching 92,000 square miles. Telecasts from Jakarta are received in all provincial capitals including Dili in East Timor. Existing broadcasting stations in Jakarta, Medan, Palembang, Jogjakarta, Balikpapan, and Ujang Pandang received additional telecast facilities in Repelita II, and two additional stations opened in Surabaya and Denpasar at the end of that period. In Repelita III, telecast programs are to run on two channels, and other improvements will be made.

An expanded postal service is planned to meet anticipated increases in demand of 9 percent annually. The construction of 750 post offices at district levels are scheduled to supply transmigration and isolated areas with postal service; 11 large post offices and 4 regional post office bureaus are also planned for provincial areas. Special express posts, air parcel posts, postal receipts, and stamp publication are to be increased.

Power

The Indonesian electric company, Perusahaan Umum Listrik Negara (PLN), is responsible for the generation, transmission, and distribution of electricity in Indonesia. PLN is a State-owned but autonomously operated statutory authority.

Until the early seventies, PLN's expansion was restricted by foreign exchange shortages, and a crash program was undertaken that resulted in the installation of gas turbines. PLN suffered major breakdowns in generating plant, and turbines were seen as the only means of providing generating plant quickly. At the end of 1978/79,

PLN's total capacity was 2,209 MW, of which gas turbines comprised 34 percent; steam, 25 percent; hydro, 21 percent; and diesel, 20 percent. The imbalance in plant will be corrected with the commissioning of 1,000 MW of steam capacity by 1982.

About 70 percent of PLN's total installed capacity in 1978/79 was in Java; also, Java accounted for 80 percent of PLN's total electricity sales in that year, amounting to 4,287 million kWh. In addition to internally generated power, PLN purchases power from other sources, including the 125 MW Jatiluhur hydroelectric station, which is part of a multi-purpose authority.

Since demand for electricity has exceeded the power supply capacity of PLN for a considerable time, privately owned generating capacity has increased steadily. The aggregate installed capacity of captive plants was 1,700 MW at the end of 1978/79. Annual growth in captive plants has fallen to about 5 percent in recent years, compared with about 15 percent in the mid-1979's. Since PLN will be unable to meet the country's power requirements in the near future, however, captive power plants will continue to be installed. PLN's energy sales are projected to grow at 21 percent annually, compared to captive plant growth at 5 percent annually, based on current trends. If this trend continues, the captive generating capacity will constitute only 25 percent of the country's total capacity by 1986/87.

PLN operates about 3,800 km of transmission lines at 70 and 150 kV and 40,000 km of distribution lines, the bulk of which are in Java. About 2,000 km of 150 kV transmission, under construction, are scheduled for completion by 1982. Java will have a fully interconnected grid at 150 kV by 1981 and a 500 kV system is also proposed. Demand in the other islands is not yet sufficient to justify islandwide grids, and some time must elapse before such grids are feasible.

Per capita consumption of electricity in Indonesia is still very small, at about 45 kWh in 1977/78. Overall, only about 6 percent of the households have access to electricity. The degree of electrification varies by regions. It is highest in Java where about 10 percent of the households are connected. PLN estimates that in 1978 about 45 percent of total power sales was to residential users and the remaining 55 percent to industrial and commercial users. Use of electricity is generally limited to urban and a few rural areas.

During Repelita III, new power plants are expected to be built and the generating capacity of existing plants is to be expanded. The planned increase in generating capacity is 2,729 MW, of which 65 percent will be derived from steam, 17.5 percent from diesel, 10.8 percent from hydroelectric, and 6.7 percent from other sources. Currently, some 85 percent of the generating capacity of PLN relies on oil as its power source. During Repelita III, PLN will concentrate on hydropower, coal- and natural gas-fired capacity. One of the major projects planned for startup during this period is the coal-fired power plant at Suralaya, West Java.

The Suralaya power plant will ultimately have an installed capacity of 3,100 MW, consisting of four generating sets of 400 MW and three sets of 500 MW, using coal as fuel. The first stage of the project, consisting of two 400 MW dual-fired (coal and oil), thermal-generating sets and other facilities, has already begun. The total cost of plant and equipment for Stage 1 is estimated at $468 million (including costs of price escalation), of which foreign exchange costs will be about $296 million. The cost of transmission lines and equipment is estimated at $300 million.

The hydropower station under construction at Asahan, North Sumatra, will have a peak capacity of 603 MW when completed in 1984. Capacity not used by the adjacent aluminum smelter will be supplied to the surrounding area. Also during Repelita III, a rural electrification program is planned to supply electricity to 200,000 homes in Java, Sumatra, Sulawesi, and Lombok. This program will receive loan and grant assistance from the United States, Canada, and the Asian Development bank. A trial geothermal plant was dedicated in 1978 at Kamojang, West Java. PLN plans to build a 30 MW geothermal plant near the trial plant by 1982, at an estimated cost of $42.3 million.

Indonesia's market for power generation, transmission, and distribution equipment was estimated at $135.7 million in 1978, of which imports supplied $123.7 million. The United States had a 12 percent market share. Power generation imports were valued $93.4 million and transmission and distribution equipment imports were valued at $30.3 million. The market declined from $172.1 million in 1976, because of a slowdown in the development of captive power due to reduced economic activity, but is expected to expand to $184 million by 1981 and possibly to $245 million by 1984, with the completion of large-scale thermal and hydropower plants. More than 90 percent of the market will continue to be supplied by imports. In 1978, the United States had a market share of 10.5 percent for power generating equipment and 14.5 percent for power distribution and transmission equipment.

Construction

The construction industry is a large and rapidly growing industry, particularly important for the generation of new employment opportunities. In Repelita III, the construction sector is expected to grow at an average annual rate of 9 percent annually, compared with the 6.5 percent growth rate targeted for the economy as a whole and to contribute 5.5 percent to gross domestic product (GDP) by 1983/84, compared with 4.9 percent in 1979/80. Growth may well exceed this target by a substantial margin.

In late 1976 through 1978, the growth rate of the construction industry slowed for a variety of reasons, including depressed economic conditions in Indonesia's major trading partners, reduced investment interest, and a slowing of major project activity. In 1979, following devaluation, both domestic and foreign investment levels continued to be depressed due both to monetary policy and unclear objectives in the investment promotion and approving mechanisms. However, with Indonesia's rapidly rising foreign exchange earnings, the continuing high level of foreign aid, new investment interest, and increased government expenditures, the growth rate of the construction industry is expected to quicken. The development budget in Repelita III calls for expenditures of $35 billion—2.4 times their level in Repelita II.

Expansion plans in the fields of agriculture, transport, manufacturing, and other sectors, discussed below, will require new irrigation projects, roads, bridges, ports, airfields, office buildings, manufacturing facilities, and power plants. New schools and health facilities are required to meet social objectives and hotels to promote tourism.

Together with fresh water supplies and environmentally healthy conditions, adequate housing is another objective of Repelita III. The plan projects that population growth alone would require construction of 3 million additional houses. While the provision of housing is considered the responsibility of the communities, a State enterprise, Perumnas, will build 150,000 low-cost houses through the Housing Mortgage Bank. About 500,000 houses also will be needed for the Government's transmigration program. The projected cost for transmigrant housing is $244 million, of which the foreign exchange cost is about $158 million.

While many foreign construction and engineering firms have established offices in Indonesia and do considerable business, Indonesia is trying to increase the role of national private companies in the construction industry and is giving preferential treatment to *pribumi* (native Indonesian) enterprises.

The market for construction equipment and building products was valued at $1 billion in 1977 and was expected to increase to about $1.5 billion by 1981 if economic conditions continued to improve and the planned major construction projects were implemented. The import market in 1977 totaled $526 million, $150 million for construction equipment and $376 million for building products.

Indonesia is increasing local production of building products, including cement, reinforcing bars, roofing tiles, pipe, finished lumber and plywood, steel shapes and frames, and wire and cables. On the other hand, except for road rollers for which domestic production supplies about one-third of the market, nearly all construction equipment must be imported.

In 1977, the United States supplied the largest share of Indonesia's imports of construction equipment. It supplied 39 percent of the imports of road tractors for hauling and construction and dumpers valued at $31 million; 31 percent of bulldozers, off-road tractors, log skidders, crawler tractors for construction valued at $54 million; and 25 percent of excavators, levelers, loaders for construction valued at $5 million. The U.S. market share was strong also for lifting and loading equipment and other construction equipment. For building products, the United States ws particularly competitive in supplying air-conditioning equipment, plumbing, heating pipe and fittings, steel structures and fabricated parts for houses and buildings, and builders hardware.

Government Role in the Economy

The Indonesian Government and government-owned enterprises are directly involved in a wide range of economic activities. Their active participation in manufacturing, trade, estate agriculture, and other sectors of the economy largely stems from the Government's nationalization of Dutch-owned businesses following the breaking off of diplomatic relations with the Netherlands in 1958 as a result of the conflict over the sovereignty of Irian Jaya. Diplomatic relations between the two countries were resumed in 1962. The Government's involvement in the mining and petroleum sectors is based primarily on the constitutional provisions that all natural resources belong to the State and that the State should control essential minerals activities. In other economic areas, the Government has undertaken to support development in sectors affecting the public welfare or in areas not of interest to private capital. Through State agencies, the Government owns and operates the railroads, the highway network, seaport and airport facilities, the public telecommunications system, and most of the electric power facilities. Air transport is predominantly government operated.

State-owned manufacturing enterprises include plants producing cement, fertilizer, textiles, paper, tires, cigarettes, glass, small aircraft, telephone equipment, and steel products.

In the trading sector, there are four State companies (P.T. Dharma Niaga, P.T. Kerta Niaga Ltd., P.T. Pantja Niaga, and P.T. Tjipta Niaga) that operate like privately owned commercial houses and compete with private enterprise.

State companies operate large rubber, palm oil, tea, cinchona, and other argicultural estates. Most teak is produced by a government agency.

State mining enterprises currently produce nearly all of the country's tin, coal, bauxite, nickel, iron, and other minerals. The State oil company, Pertamina, has a monopoly over all aspects of oil and natural gas production and controls all exploration, development, and production and refining of oil and gas in Indonesia.

The Government has interests in industrial estates and warehousing operations. It also participates in Indonesia's financial sector through government-owned banks and other financial institutions. In the insurance industry, it participates in one credit insurance institution, one casualty insurance company, one life insurance company, one reinsurance company, and four other insurance companies.

While the Government operates in a wide variety of fields, it encourages development of the private sector through various tax and other incentives designed to attract domestic and foreign investment.

Before 1969, State companies could be identified through the use of the prefix P.N. (Perusahaan Negara—State enterprise) before the company name. Unless special circumstances applied, PN's were wholly owned by the Government and operated under a government department.

In accordance with Decree No. 1 of 1969, however, State enterprises are gradually being consolidated and reorganized into three basic categories: (1) departmental agencies, with their capital to be determined annually through the State budget (these are of a public service nature and are designated Perusahaan Jawatan, or PERJAN); (2) public companies, established as entities separate from the departments, with their capital separate from the State budget (these are of a public service nature also operating as businesses and are designated Perusahaan Umum, or PERUM—examples are Perum Telekomunikasi in telecommunications and Perum Listrik Negara in electric power); and (3) public corporations with limited liabilility, or P.T.'s Public corporations are subject to the same rules and regulations as private corporations. They are designated as Perusahaan Perseroan, or PERSERO, but actually bear the same prefix as the private limited liability corporations or P.T.'s (Perseroan Terbatas). However, all or part of the shares of a public corporation must be owned by the Government (National or Provincial), while the remaining shares may be sold to private parties. The Government has been encouraging, and, in some cases, requiring State enterprises to become P.T.'s. The policy intent is to make them into profitable enterprises so that their shares can eventually be sold to private (including foreign) investors, thus reducing public sector involvement.

As of 1979, there were reported to be 113 government-owned limited liability companies subject to the same commercial codes, taxes, and other laws applicable to private enterprise.

Distribution and Sales Channels

Import Channels

The Indonesian Government has reserved for Indonesian companies the fields of importing and exporting and the wholesale and retail distribution of imported or locally produced goods in the domestic market. An Indonesian company is defined as one having 51 percent or more Indonesian ownership and a board of directors consisting mostly of Indonesian nationals.

An exception to this regulation is made for foreign investors engaged in production or manufacturing, whereby they may import raw materials for their own use and also export their own products. However, foreign investors are not permitted to undertake the distribution of their products in the local market. An investor frequently arranges to have a separate trading company owned by its local partner handle distribution.

Domestic investors in production and manufacturing and some government agencies may also be permitted to import for their own use.

Trade Representative Office.—Foreign companies may open and maintain a local representative office subject to permission of the

Indonesian Department of Trade and Cooperatives. The representative may be an Indonesian national or company or a foreign national, but only one representative office per firm is permitted. Foreign trade representatives are not permitted to engage in direct sales but may engage in sales promotion or provide market research and technical advice. Many foreign firms and trading companies have opened trade representative offices in Indonesia and some of these have expatriate representatives on their staffs. In many instances, representative offices of foreign companies have established close connections with Indonesian national importers so that the two companies can operate virtually as one, with the Indonesian company acting as importer-distributor for overseas principals and the foreign company promoting the products and, where necessary because of the technical or specialized nature of particular products, providing technical assistance.

Appointment of an agent.—The services of an aggressive, active agent have always been the most effective means of expanding sales in Indonesia.

Until recently Indonesian regulations did not require the appointment of an agent except when importing fertilizer and specified types of heavy equipment. Since December 1970, the import of certain types of equipment, including road rollers, hoisting and lifting apparatus, tractors and cement-mixing machines, have had to be handled by a national franchise holder or sole agent. Sole agency relationships have also been required for motorcycles, cars, and trucks. At the end of 1980, to spur the development of indigenous business, particularly the "economically weak group," the Government began requiring the State oil company and other government agencies to deal through Indonesian agents when purchasing imported goods and services. Also, the Government began putting pressure on agents to deal directly with foreign manufacturers rather than third-country middleagents. While the full implications of the new practices are still unclear, a foreign firm selling to government agencies would do well to appoint an Indonesian firm as its agent.

Indonesian importers traditionally have not specialized in particular product lines. While it is generally advisable to set up agency arrangements with firms that handle a complementary range of products, this is not essential since substantial sales can often be made by Indonesian firms active in quite different commodity fields. An increasing number of firms identifying themselves as suppliers of "technical goods" concentrate on general industrial machinery and equipment. Such firms often have engineers on their staffs and are prepared to provide engineering assistance and aftersales technical support.

The main difference between a representative office and an agent is that an agent can perform all trade activities and is allowed to have several offices throughout Indonesia. When an agent is appointed, expatriate personnel stationed in Indonesia under representative office status can be assigned to the agent and become employees of the agent for the purpose of satisfying Indonesian law.

In many cases, a separate agreement is signed between the expatriate personnel and the foreign employer for the purpose of regulating the relationship of the expatriate and company outside Indonesia. The tax liability of the foreign firm is limited to the income tax of the expatriates assigned to the representative office, and any other taxes are assessed to and borne by the agent.

Since a commission agent or agent-distributor arrangement may not be satisfactory for the marketing of certain types of products in Indonesia, several forms of association with Indonesian companies have been developed to comply with government policy on trade and distribution that permit the foreign firm to establish a permanent presence in Indonesia.

Cooperation Under Management Agreement.—This form is a step toward a more active role of the foreign company in Indonesia. The forms of management agreement can be classified as follows: (1) Technical Assistance Agreement, (2) Management Agreement, and (3) Management Agreement coupled with a Financial Agreement. In the Technical Assistance Agreement, the foreign party's function is limited to pure technical assistance in the Indonesian company. In the Management Agreement, the foreign firm's role is to manage the company or a division thereof. In the Management Agreement coupled with a Financial Agreement, the foreign company also finances the Indonesian operation either under the name of the Indonesian company or the division thereof. The remuneration of the foreign company can be in one of the following forms: (1) fixed fee, (2) commission, or (3) profit sharing. Whatever basis is used for the remuneration, it must be formulated clearly in the agreement, and it must be applicable under the present Indonesian laws. To protect the foreign company's interest properly, a bona fide and comprehensive agreement must be drawn between the parties concerned.

Distribution Practices

The major islands of Indonesia constitute distinct marketing areas. Each market has ethnic and sociocultural differences with varying degrees of economic development. The Indonesian language is generally understood throughout the country, although there are several hundred dialects.

Java is by far the principal market and the most important distribution point for imports. The country's industries as well as people are concentrated there. Together with Bali and Madura, Java; has about 65 percent of Indonesia's 147 million people. Over three-fourths of Indonesia's imports entered through Javanese ports in 1979. The port for Jakarta in western Java was the major port of entry.

As the capital of Indonesia and the largest urban area, Jakarta is the largest single market. It has a population of some 6 million. It is the site for the largest commercial houses, banks, import and export firms, shipping and transportation facilities, and the Government's administrative machinery for foreign trade. Foreign banks may have branches only in Jakarta and most foreign investors also have offices there. Jakarta's harbor at Tanjung Priok handles about half of the country's incoming foreign cargoes. Surabaya, in east Java, with a population of nearly 3 million, is Indonesia's second largest city and its port, Tanjung Perak, handled 12 percent of total imports in 1979. Other urban centers are Bandung and Cirebon in west/central Java and Malang, Jogjakarta, and Semarang in east/central Java.

Sumatra, with nearly 20 percent of the total population, may be divided roughly into three marketing areas: the north, with Medan the principal urban center, which can be covered from Penang and Singapore as well as Jakarta (Belawan, Indonesia's third largest port, which handled 7 percent of Indonesia's imports in 1979, is near Medan); the southeast, with Palembang the principal center; and the west, with the main urban center of Padang. Both Palembang and Padang have good communications with Singapore as well as Jakarta. Imports through Sumatran ports amounted to about 15 percent of the country's total in 1979.

Sulawesi, with 7 percent of the population, may be divided roughly into the north, with the main center of Menado; and the south, with the main center and principal port of Ujung Padang (formerly known as Makassar). Sulawesi's imports from foreign countries comprised some 3 percent of total imports in 1979. Menado, on the northern tip, has good communications with

Singapore, Hong Kong, and the Philippines, as well as Jakarta and Surabaya. Ujung Pandang has communications with Jakarta, Surabaya and Singapore but is anxious to develop other direct outside contacts.

Kalimantan is a vast land area, but it has only 5 percent of the population and accounted for only about 5 percent of total imports in 1979. Principal urban areas are Banjarmasin, Pontianak, and Balikpapan. For trading purposes, all communications are either through Java or Singapore.

West Irian is the most primitive island of Indonesia and is sparsely populated. Its capital and principal city is Jayapura. Because of extensive foreign investment, communications have been developed between Jayapura and foreign countries but communications with the rest of Indonesia are limited.

Generally it is advisable for foreign firms to appoint distributors in several centers in Indonesia, preferably one company with branches in the different centers. Some Jakarta-based companies may give adequate distribution to the whole of Java and a few may also cover North Sumatra. However, in order to do this, the company has to have active branch offices in areas outside of west Java. It is virtually impossible to service a market adequately by periodic visits from Jakarta.

Servicing of products and adequate stocks of spare parts are extremely important adjuncts of marketing. In many cases, the Indonesian firm's personnel must be given training in servicing equipment.

Government Procurement

Procurement by government agencies and enterprises may be financed by funds appropriated through the Central Government or Regional Government budgets, or through funds derived from their own operations. They also may be financed through funds made available by donor governments or international agencies for specific projects or essential agricultural commodities.

Procurement procedures are not standardized. They vary with the department or agency involved. Also each lending country (including the United States) or international agency has its own regulations for assuring the proper use of the funds which must be met in the procurement process.

Indonesia has not signed the MTN Government Procurement Code.

State enterprises organized as a perjan- or perum-type enterprise (see Government Role in

the Economy, above) receive funds from the Central Government budget, but not State enterprises that have been converted to limited liability companies (P.T.'s). The latter have full responsibility for funds at their disposal.

Indonesia has no Central Government purchasing agency. Each ministry, department, or project receiving budget funds is responsible for its own buying after its budget has been approved by the Finance Ministry. Each such entity can set up its own specifications and select brands of products. However, the Finance Ministry exercises certain controls by requiring approval of proposed purchases with regard to the amount spent at any given time in order to adjust overall government spending to the general profile it desires to maintain.

Most overseas items are procured through a public tender issued by Jakarta. A limited bid tender may be sought if the purchase is urgent or requires special design or handling. For very urgent purchases a previous supplier may be utilized.

Prequalification requirements may be set for firms wishing to bid. Bids in response to tenders are evaluated on the basis of price and payment terms; quality; delivery time; port of delivery; and firm's reliability, experience, and ability to meet technical specifications. For major items, additional considerations are aftersales service and having a representative in Indonesia. Purchases are made on the basis of a purchase contract. Unless credit is involved, payment usually requires about 2 months.

Two regulations enacted in 1980 will have a far-reaching effect on government procurement practices. Kepres 10, of January 1980, establishes a procurement guiding team that must review all government contracts of over Rp. 500 million ($800,000). Major objectives are to ensure that the price is fair, that there is a maximum of local content, and that the contract complies with government efforts to promote domestic production. Kepres 14A, of April 1980, regulates the expenditure and management of State budget funds and establishes a preferential system for all government procurement, including that of State-owned enterprises. The decree emphasizes that priority must be given to purchase of domestic goods and services.

Kepres 14A also provides for preferential treatment of local contractors in bidding on government contracts of up to Rp. 200 million ($320,000). For contracts of up to Rp. 20 million ($32,000), no tenders are required but the contract must be given to a local contractor from an economically weak group. For contracts valued at between Rp. 20 million and Rp. 50 million ($32,000-$80,000), the contract must be given to a local contractor from an economically weak group, but tenders are required. For contracts valued at between Rp. 50 and Rp. 100 million

($80,000-$160,000), tenders are required. Although the contract must still go to a local contractor, all groups are eligible. However, economically weak groups have a 10 percent margin of preference. Contracts of Rp. 100 million to Rp. 200 million ($160,000-$320,000) must go to local contractors, but there is no margin of preference. For contracts of over Rp. 200 million ($320,000), both local and foreign contractors may compete for government tenders.

The International Development Association (IDA) and, in later years, the International Bank for Reconstruction and Development (IBRD) have been major sources of financing for government projects. Between 1969 and April 30, 1980, IDA extended loans valued at $901 million, of which $372 million were undisbursed; and the IBRD extended loans valued at $2,638 million, of which $1,846 million were undisbursed. In addition, the International Finance Corporation had outstanding commitments valued at $26 million on April 30, 1980, as a result of loans or equity investment in Indonesian projects.

The Asian Development Bank (ADB), which started operations in Indonesia in 1967, had extended 60 loans valued at $947 million as of April 30, 1980, of which loans of $785 million were from its ordinary capital resources and loans of $162 million were from its Special Funds resources. Technical assistance valued at $10 million was also provided. Disbursements under ADB loans from both ordinary capital and Special Funds resources amounted to $199 million as of April 30, 1980.

The loans from the international financial institutions have been responsive to the Indonesian Government's development priorities and have covered virtually all major sectors. Emphasis has been given to agriculture, including irrigation and the development of agricultural estates; electric power production, transmission, and distribution; transportation and communications, especially port and highway projects; expansion of fertilizer production; transmigration projects; and urban development.

Key contacts for the international lending agencies may be reached through: World Bank Group, 1818 H St., N.W., Washington, D.C. 20433; World Bank Resident Staff in Indonesia, Arthaloka Building, 8th Floor, Jl. Jenderal Sudirman 2, (P.O. Box 324 JKT), Jakarta, Indonesia; Asian Development Bank, 2330 Roxas Boulevard (P.O. Box 789), Manila, Philippines. Information on the status of projects funded by international organizations is included in the monthly operational summaries and other announcements published by the information offices of the World Bank Group and ADB.

Project information can be obtained in the United States at the Export Information Reference Room, Room 1326, U.S. Department of Commerce, Washington, D.C. 20230, as well as through the U.S. Department of Commerce District Offices. Notification of tenders and bid announcements can be obtained through the Department's Overseas Trade Opportunities Program. In Indonesia, tender announcements are published in leading news media.

The United States has provided extensive financial assistance to Indonesia through the P.L. 480 program and through program and project loans from the U.S. Agency for International Development (USAID). As a result of Congressional action, the thrust of USAID programs was shifted in 1974 from capital development and infrastructure projects to programs having broad social impact. Since then, loans and grants have focused on rural development, transmigration, agricultural education, health care and medical services, family planning, irrigation, sanitation, and water supply.

In U.S. FY 1981, U.S. assistance is likely to total $128 million, of which $67 million will be development assistance and $61 million will be P.L. 480 Title I and Title II assistance. Development assistance will be mainly for agricultural development in rural areas, for increasing employment opportunities in rural areas, for improving health and education facilities, and for assistance with renewable energy and environmental problems. Key contacts for these programs include the Program Office, USAID, American Embassy, Jakarta, Indonesia, and the Agency for International Development, U.S. Department of State, Washington, D.C. 20523.

The Export-Import Bank of the United States (Eximbank) has also made extensive loans to the Indonesian Government and its agencies for projects and equipment. Total Eximbank exposure for long-term loans and financial guarantees was $600 million as of February 29, 1980, approximately the level of exposure for the past 3 years. Most of Eximbank's exposure is accounted for by aircraft, a wide variety of transportation and communications projects, and several mining and oil transactions. Additional information on Eximbank programs can be obtained from the Export-Import Bank of the United States, 811 Vermont Avenue, N.W., Washington, D.C. 20571.

Advertising and Research

The most effective route to end-user sales in Indonesia is personalized sales calls, reinforced by prompt and efficient technical support. Direct mailing of product literature and use of various advertising media and research organizations are important adjuncts to the direct sales effort.

Advertising Media

Newspaper advertising, particularly in Jakarta and West Java where purchasing power is concentrated, is recommended for introducing new products. Numerous newspapers reach a significant portion of the business community. Daily Jakarta newspapers with an estimated circulation of 75,000 or more include "Kompas" and "Sinar Harapan,"—both have large advertisement sections—and "Merdeka." Others are "Berita Buana" and "Suara Karya." English language newspapers include "The Indonesia Times" and "The Indonesian Observer." In 1980, the Government placed restrictions on the amount of space that newspapers could devote to advertising in order to promote the use of government-owned papers. As a result, competition for space in the major independent newspapers, "Kompas" and "Sinar Harapan," has increased substantially.

Various magazines and periodicals also have large circulations within management groups. An excellent advertising medium is the Standard Trade Directory of Indonesia, an official publication of the Indonesian Chamber of Commerce and Industry. The 1980/81 edition contains advertisements in black and white and color by nearly 300 firms. Requests may be made to the publisher at Jl. Hayam Wuruk 4 SX, P.O. Box 4556, Jakarta. There are also specialized trade publications designed for readers in specific business sectors.

Government-owned television and radio networks are effective advertising media. The most concentrated single media force is television. Television Republic Indonesia (TVRI), the only television network in Indonesia, reaches potential customers through nearly 400,000 television sets, of which well over half are in Jakarta. Opportunities for using television for advertising may be more limited, however, since the Government is restricting the use of advertising on television in 1981. Radio networks include the government-owned Radio Republic Indonesia and many private "ham" radio stations throughout Indonesia that handle advertising. Additional media are direct mail advertising—often a low-cost, effective medium if mailing lists are properly prepared, movie films, cinema slides, and posters and signboards for bus exteriors, bus stop shelters, and bridges. It is recomended that these types of publicity be arranged through a local advertising agent. Names can be obtained from the Indonesian

Advertising Agency Association, Jl. Letjen. Suprapto Gedung FORTUNE, Jakarta. Suggestions on reliable advertising firms may be obtained also from the American Embassy in Jakarta.

Further information on advertising media is contained in The 1980/81 Asian Press and Media Directory, Syne Media Enterprises Ltd., 1301 World Trade Centre, Causeway Bay, Hong Kong.

Market Research and Trade Organizations

While a growing number of Indonesian organizations engage in market research, it is sometimes difficult to find the level of competence required by Western firms. Branches of American banks in Jakarta (see section on Banking and Credit, below) will often make market surveys for their customers, and several leading U.S. consulting firms now have affiliates in Jakarta.

Indonesian consulting firms in Jakarta have formed the Association of Indonesian Consultants (IKINDO), whose members perform a wide range of research and consulting services. The address of the Association is Jl. Gondangdia Lama 23, Jakarta.

P.T. Data Consult, Inc. (P.O. Box 108/JNG, Jakarta) publishes a newsletter twice a month entitled "Indonesian Commercial Newsletter" which contains a commodity survey in each issue and other market information. Other consulting and research firms in Jakarta include:

>   Price Waterhouse and Company
>   Jl. Gondangdia Lama 10-12

>   P.T. SGV-Utomo
>   Jl. Let Jend. S. Parman Kav. 56

>   Indonesia Research & Development Co.
>   Jl. Gedung Kasenian 5

>   P.T. Indoconsult
>   98 Jalan K. H. Wahid Hasyim

>   P.T. Spectrum Research
>   Jl. Melawi VII/2
>   Kebayoran Baru.

Advice on these firms and others that can undertake market surveys may be obtained from the Commercial Section, American Embassy, Jakarta.

Market research in Indonesia is difficult because detailed statistics on production and consumption are often not available in published sources. External trade statistics are fairly detailed, and additional data may be obtained for a fee from the Central Bureau of Statistics (Biro Pusat Statisik—CBS), Dr. Sutomo No. 8, P.O. Box 3, Jakarta. Unrecorded trade may distort import values and trends. Also CBS figures understate import values since they exclude duty-free imports (including imports for investment, which are usually duty-free) and certain other transactions.

The major trade association in Indonesia is the Indonesian Chamber of Commerce and Industry (KADIN) whose membership includes representatives from private industry, as well as cooperatives, utilities, public corporations, and State-owned enterprises throughout Indonesia.

In addition to associations of a general nature, there are numerous enterprises with homogeneous interests in trade, industry, transportation, or other sectors of the economy that have organized specialized or professional associations. The Standard Trade Directory for Indonesia for 1979 lists 112 associations covering a wide range of economic activities.

Associations of importers and exporters, most of which are organized on a commodity basis, are organized in turn in the Importers Association of Indonesia (GINSI) and the Indonesian Association of Exporters (GPEI), both of which have head offices in Jakarta. The Jakarta addresses of the above associations are shown below:

>   Indonesian Chamber of Commerce and
>   Industry (KADIN)
>   Jalan Merdeka Timur II

>   Importers Association of Indonesia (GINSI)
>   Jalan Majapahit 1

>   Indonesian Association of Exporters (GPEI)
>   Jalan Kramat Rava Nos. 4 and 6

The Indonesian Government has established within the Department of Trade a National Agency for Export Development to promote exports of less well-known products such as handicrafts (e.g., jewelry, batik, handwoven fabric, and woodcarvings), agricultural and cottage industry products, and new manufactured products. The Agency, which is located on the Sixth Floor of the Sarinah Building, Jl. M. H. Thamrin 11, Jakarta, will assist foreign buyers and importers in establishing contacts with Indonesian companies.

The American Chamber of Commerce in Indonesia, known as AMCHAM, is affiliated with the Asian-Pacific Council of American Chambers of Commerce (APCAC). Its membership of 255, as of January 1980, consists of leading U.S. firms with offices in Indonesia and additional associate, individual, and social members. The Chamber has prepared a number of useful guides to doing business in Indonesia; assists the Embassy in preparing its commercial newsletter, the Jakarta Business Bulletin; and is prepared to help U.S. firms in assessing business opportunities. The Chamber's address is AMCHAM, Indonesia, Seventh Floor, Oil Center Building, Jl. M. H. Thamrin 55, Jakarta.

The American Indonesian Chamber of Commerce Inc., 120 Wall Street, Suite 1021, New York, New York 10005, is the only chamber in the United States that represents the interests of U.S. firms concerned with trade and investment in Indonesia. The Chamber publishes detailed information bulletins and is a major source of information and assistance.

Banking and Credit

Banking

Indonesia's banking system consists of Bank Indonesia (the central bank), State and private (including foreign) commercial banks, development banks, and other financial institutions such as savings banks, development finance companies, and investment banking institutions.

State Commercial Banks.—Commercial banking is dominated by five State banks owned by the Government, which account for 80-90 percent of total outstanding bank credit. Each of the banks is permitted to conduct foreign exchange transactions, and each channels credit to one particular economic sector in accordance with government priorities. State commercial banks, by area of specialization, are Bank Rakyat Indonesia—agriculture, fisheries, cooperatives, and rural development; Bank Ekspor Impor Indonesia—production, and processing and marketing of export products; Bank Negara Indonesia—industry and infrastructure; Bank Bumi Daya—State agriculture and forestry; and Bank Dagang Negara—mining.

Private Banks.—There are 78 private Indonesian banks of which 9 are authorized to deal in foreign exchange. All have relatively small capital and resource bases, including technical expertise.

The number of private banks has decreased from 129 as of March 31, 1971. Since many of them are weak, the government has been providing incentives to encourage them to merge in an attempt to improve their efficiency and strengthen their working capital. The private nonforeign exchange banks are, for the most part, small local banks that use few modern banking techniques and restrict their lending to their immediate localities.

Foreign Banks.—There are 10 branches of foreign banks in Jakarta including 4 U.S. banks: American Express International Banking Corporation, Bank of America, The Chase Manhattan Bank, and Citibank. There is also a joint-venture commercial bank with Japanese capital. No additional foreign banks are being permitted to establish branches. However, foreign banks have established 48 representatives offices. U.S. banks with representative offices include: Bankers Trust New York, Chemical Bank, Continental Illinois Bank of Chicago, Manufacturers Hanover Trust, Marine Midland Bank, Morgan Guaranty Trust Company of New York, United California Bank, and Wells Fargo Bank. The operations of foreign banks are limited to Jakarta except when they establish joint ventures with national banks.

The role a foreign bank is expected to play in Indonesian banking is to facilitate foreign direct investment, capital inflows, and the adoption of modern banking practices in Indonesia. Foreign banks have been expanding their operations rapidly, gaining a comparable share in total loans outstanding to that of private national banks.

Development Banks.—There are 29 development banks or finance companies in Indonesia, primarily involved in granting medium- and long-term credit. The largest development bank is the Development Bank of Indonesia (BAPINDO). Established in 1960, BAPINDO was reorganized in 1970 with assistance from the World Bank Group, with a view to making it the predominant source of medium- and long-term finance for industry. It has received additional World Bank aid. Although most of BAPINDO's credits are for no more than 5 years, it is the only bank authorized to grant loans up to 15 years. It may also make equity investments. All industries are eligible for loans, but priority is given to those considered important for achieving the objectives of the current 5-year plan.

Two other development finance companies that extend medium-term loans and make equity investments are the Indonesian Development Finance Company (IDFC), a joint venture between the Government and the Netherlands Finance Company for Developing Countries in which the Dutch Government has a majority interest, and P.T. Private Development Finance Company of Indonesia (PDFCI), a largely privately owned development bank, which also has received assistance from the World Bank Group. In addition to BAPINDO, IDFC, and PDFCI, there are 26 regional development banks with 123 branch offices providing finance for relatively small projects in industry, agriculture, fishing, trade, and services.

Investment Banking Institutions.—In 1973, the Government authorized the establishment of nonbank financial institutions to stimulate the development of the money and capital market in Indonesia. Except for one, a consortium of Indonesian banks and enterprises, each of these is a consortium of at least three foreign trading and merchant banks (each from a different country) and one Indonesian bank. Operating as investment banks, the financial institutions are not permitted to compete with the commercial banks. However, they provide a wide array of financial services, including investment consultancy and portfolio management, and also engage in money market activities. They may serve as the *pribumi* partner in a foreign investment contract to meet the joint-venture requirement. Also these institutions will act as intermediaries in coordinating and underwriting the issue of securities by companies wishing to list their stocks in the new capital or securities market.

There are nine nonbank financial institutions. Seven of these have a U.S. bank as a participant. Those with an American partner are Asia & Euro-American Capital Corp. Ltd., Goldman, Sachs & Co.; Financial Corporation of Indonesia (P.T. Finconesia), Manufacturers Hanover Trust; Indonesian Investments International (P.T. Indovest), The First National Bank of Chicago; P.T. Inter-Pacific Financial Corporation, Continental Illinois National Bank & Trust Company of Chicago; Merchant Investment Corporation (P.T. Merincorp), Morgan Guaranty International; Multinational Finance Corporation (P.T. Multicor), Chemical Bank; and P.T. Mutual International Finance Corporation, Crocker National Bank.

The Government also has established a specialized institution, P.T. Bahana, as a venture capital and finance company providing medium- and long-term loans, equity finance, and technical assistance to financially weak enterprises.

Capital Market.—While there is no capital market in operation in Indonesia, the Government has taken steps to encourage its development through the establishment of the Securities and Exchange Commission (BAPEPAM) in 1976. BAPEPAM has authority to prepare regulations and supervise the activities of the stock exchange as well as to define offering and trading procedures. In 1976, the Government also created an investment fund, P.T. Dana Reska, which plans to buy shares from companies and convert them into share certificates of relatively small denominations

(Rp. 10,000 or $16) to enable small investors to participate in the stock market. The Government also grants certain tax allowances to companies willing to go public and to individuals who invest in securities traded in the stock exchange.

Credit

Interest rates offered by the State commercial banks are set by Bank Indonesia. However, foreign banks and private nonbank financial intermediaries are not subject to the interest ceilings imposed by Bank Indonesia when using their own resources. Private financial institutions are able to provide financing facilities to borrowers who are not *pribumi* and, therefore, ineligible for the services of the State banks.

Short-Term Credit.—Short-term credit is available from commercial banks (State, private, or foreign) for up to one year. Generally, short-term loans can be rolled over but, with some exceptions, the loans must be repaid when the term is up.

State banks have more favorable lending rates for the production, distribution, and export and import of goods in priority economic areas. As of mid-1980, the rates ranged from 9 to 21 percent, with lower rates applying to priority categories such as food grain distribution and agricultural credit. Lending rates of commercial banks generally ranged from 12 to 36 percent in 1980.

Some Indonesian firms have access to credit in Singapore and Hong Kong through established business or personal relationships. Those who must rely on domestic credit are seriously disadvantaged, especially when importing from non-Asian sources. U.S. suppliers can overcome some of this disadvantage by (1) supplying the Indonesian market from regional depots or bonded warehouses; (2) assisting Indonesian customers to draw on credit facilities through U.S. banks in Singapore, Hong Kong, or elsewhere at rates lower than in Indonesia; or (3) providing direct credit facilities based on credit evaluations from U.S. banks in Indonesia.

Medium- and Long-Term Credit.—Term credit is available from most banks, although foreign banks must obtain Bank Indonesia's approval to make loans with more than 1-year maturity. As indicated under Development Banks, above, BAPINDO is by far the most important source of medium- and long-term credit and provides finance for projects of all sizes in both the public and private sectors. Other major sources of credit are the development banks, IDFC and PDFCI, and the finance company, P.T. Bahana.

The Government has been trying to assist indigenous, or *pribumi* firms, by making credit available at preferential rates. A chief source of term credit for indigenous enterprises is the Kredit Investasi Besar (KIB or "INVESTASI") program initiated by the Government in 1969, through which State banks were authorized to extend 3-5 year credits (with a grace period) for approved projects.

Financing for Small-Scale Businesses.—In addition to the INVESTASI program, the Indonesian Government and Bank Indonesia established P.T. Asransi Kredit Indonesia (P.T. ASKRINDO) to encourage term lending by State banks to small- and medium-sized indigenous entrepreneurs by guaranteeing their loans for up to 75 percent of the total risk. Further assistance to small-scale and economically weak indigenous enterprises was initiated in December 1973 through the Kredit Investasi Kecil (KIK), which finances fixed assets; and Kredit Modal Kirja Penamaman (KMKP) which finances working capital. Both schemes are administered by the State banks (including BAPINDO) and selected regional development banks, with Bank Indonesia refinancing 75-80 percent of the loan amounts disbursed. The annual interest rates for borrowers of KIK and KMKP resources were 10.5 percent and 12 percent, respectively, as of mid-1980.

In 1979, several measures were introduced to broaden the KIK and KMKP schemes. The maximum amount of credit was raised, the size of collateral reduced, and eligibility for the credits was extended to all indigenous enterprises with total assets up to $160,000 if they operate in the construction and industrial sectors and up to $64,000 in other sectors. In addition to these changes, a new special medium-term credit scheme became effective in September 1979, that will provide further credit on concessionary terms to strengthen the expansion of indigenous enterprises.

Trade Regulations

Exchange Rate Systems and Controls

The currency of Indonesia is the Indonesian rupiah. Since November 16, 1978, when the rupiah was devalued by nearly 34 percent, the exchange rate has been stable at about Rp. 625 per U.S. dollar. The central bank uses a basket of currencies of Indonesia's main trading partners to help determine the middle exchange rate, and buying and selling rates are set daily at within 1 percent either side of the middle rate. There are no taxes or subsidies on purchases or sales of foreign exchange.

There are two types of foreign exchange, Devisa Kredit and Devisa Umum. Devisa Kredit (DK), or credit exchange, is a special type of exchange used for imports and related services financed by foreign commodity assistance programs. Devisa Umum (DU), or general exchange, supplied mainly by Indonesia's export earnings, is used for all other trade and invisible transactions. The same rate applies to both DK and DU exchange.

Sabang, an island at the northern tip of Sumatra, is outside the Indonesian exchange and trade control system,[1] but the Indonesian rupiah is legal tender there.

Indonesia has virtually no foreign exchange controls. Payments for the proceeds from invisibles are not restricted or subject to control. Proceeds from invisibles need not be surrendered.

There are no limitations on the remittance to Indonesia of capital in the form of foreign exchange or in commodities. Both residents and nonresidents may hold foreign currency deposits with foreign exchange banks.

Additional information on Indonesia's exchange rate system is available in the Annual Report on Exchange Arrangements and Exchange Restrictions, 1980, International Monetary Fund, Washington, D.C. 20006.

Import Regulations

Indonesia's present import system is basically a free system in which market forces are permitted to determine import priorities. No import licenses are required. There are a few nontariff trade barriers, including a prior import deposit system and a ban on certain imports to protect domestic industry and to encourage local assembly operations. Indonesia has been making substantial reductions in duty rates for raw materials and semifinished goods used in domestic production, but duties are still high on goods less essential for economic development and basic consumer needs and goods competitive with locally produced items.

Indonesia bans imports from Angola and South Africa.

The import of most secondhand goods is banned. However, effective September 5, 1979, certain types of used machinery and accessories may be imported by State trading companies and producer/importers if the product is not made or assembled locally and does not affect Indonesia's standardization program.

---

[1] With the exception that the prohibition on imports of certain automobiles is applicable.

The importing of cloves, rice, wheat and wheat flour, fertilizer, and refined sugar is restricted to specific approved importers.

Imports of certain commodities for the national iron stock are reserved for State enterprises; they include cement, newsprint, certain types of paper and automobile tires, asphalt, cotton weaving yarn, sheet iron, raw materials for maritime industries, pharmaceutical raw materials, and certain other items.

Indonesian has no antidumping legislation.

Import Tariff Structure.—In early 1981, the import tariff structure was changed from the Brussels Tariff Nomenclature (BTN) adopted on January 31, 1973, to the Customs' Cooperation Council Nomenclature (CCCN). This involved only minimal numerical and descriptive changes and the rates were not affected. While Indonesia has eliminated a large number of surcharges and other levies, the system is still complicated and includes surcharges and exemptions.

Import duties are mainly ad valorem, with basic rates ranging from 0 to 100 percent. They are imposed on *check prices* (indicative prices) determined by several ministries on the recommendation of a Check Price Team. These prices are set to reflect c.i.f. prices and are changed when prices abroad differ by more than 10 percent from the check prices for the preceding 3 months. Sales taxes of 2½, 5, 10, and 20 percent may also be levied (see internal taxes below). Items that are exempt from import duties are also exempt from sales taxes. Specific import duties and specific sales taxes are levied on some items, primarily certain foods, textiles, and other consumers goods.

Concurrently with the devaluation of the rupiah in November 1978, Indonesia reduced by 50 percent the import duty and sales tax on nearly 1,000 items, mainly raw materials and complementary goods used in domestic production. Also a total exemption from import duties and sales tax was granted on imports of raw materials and certain other goods used for the manufacture of export products. In September 1979, duties were again reduced on a large number of raw materials and semifinished goods.

Tariff reductions have been made, also, for nearly 1,000 items imported from other ASEAN countries (i.e., Malaysia, the Philippines, Singapore, and Thailand) under the ASEAN Preferential Trading Arrangements. Additional reductions for this area are anticipated. While the mechanism has not yet been developed satisfactorily, Indonesia has introduced a new system under which the customs duties paid for goods processed and subsequently exported will be rebated in order to encourage exports.

Indonesia is a signatory to the General Agreement on Tariffs and Trade (GATT). In 1976, Indonesia obtained permission to withdraw and renegotiate under GATT Article XXVIII its entire GATT schedule of concessions (Schedule XXI Indonesia). In June 1980, the United States and Indonesia completed a bilateral settlement of the Article XXVIII action. However, as of January 1981, Indonesia had not yet completed bilateral negotiations with the European Community and Japan under Article XXVIII and had not submitted its new schedule of concessions to the GATT.

The most recent series of Multilateral Trade Negotiations (MTN) held under the auspices of GATT—the Tokyo Round—was concluded in 1979. Indonesia bound duty rates on 32 product items as a result of bilateral negotiations between Indonesia and the United States during the MTN.

Indonesian regulations governing investment under the Foreign Investment Law of 1967 and the Domestic Investment Law of 1968 authorize various exemptions from duties as investment incentives. Also, under certain conditions, the payment of import duties may be deferred for a period of several months for essential imports.

Imports are grouped into two lists, mainly for tariff purposes, with the highest duties applying to the least essential items.

List 1 consists of four groups:

Group A—Most essential items (rice, cereal flour, cotton, certain iron and steel products, certain organic chemicals and pharmaceuticals, fertilizers, certain agricultural and industrial machinery and equipment, and some raw materials);

Group B—Essential items (these include raw materials and spare parts for industry);

Group C—Less essential items (these include some locally produced goods that require import protection); and

Group D—Luxuries, some consumer goods, and some goods produced locally.

List 2 is a list of over 30 prohibited items. These include built-up sedans and station wagons; components for the assembly of luxury automobiles; built-up commercial vehicles and motorcycles; certain types of aircraft; radio and television sets in built-up or semiknocked-down condition; built-up air conditioners, refrigerators, and electric sewing machines; sarongs; galvanized iron sheets; iron roofing sheets; mosquito sticks; matches; monosodium glutamate; mattresses; certain types of cotton yarn and specified types of textiles; and certain types of automobile tires, batteries, printed matter, office supplies, animal traps, bottles, and lamps and bulbs.

As noted above, State enterprise are permitted to import some of these items for the national iron stock.

Internal Taxes.—Import sales taxes ranging from $2\frac{1}{2}$ percent to 20 percent are levied on a wide variety of goods. Sales taxes have been reduced, however, and fewer items are now taxed at the higher rates. Items that are exempted from import duties are also exempted from sales taxes.

The sales tax is levied on the sum of the c.i.f. rupiah cost of the import; all customs levies (including the basic duty, exemption, or surcharge), and a 5 percent importer markup. The tax must be paid at the time the goods are cleared through customs.

In accordance with Indonesian regulations regarding prepayment of income and corporation taxes, the importer must also pay the Government a certain percentage of c. & f. import value as a tax prepayment.

Information regarding Indonesia's duties applicable to specific products may be obtained free of charge from the Country Marketing Manager for ASEAN/South Asia, Office of Country Marketing, U.S. Department of Commerce, Washington, D.C. 20230; or from any Department of Commerce District Office. Inquiries should contain a complete product description, including CCCN, SITC, or U.S. Schedule E Export Commodity numbers, if known.

Import Procedures.—There is a registry of authorized importers. Since October 31, 1968, only Indonesian nationals may obtain an importer's license, but certain established foreign firms have been permitted to retain their licenses and new foreign investors can obtain an importer's license restricted to the import of materials required for their own projects. Firms engaged primarily in exporting or industrial production may also register as importers. Since December 1970, the import of specified types of heavy equipment must be handled by a national franchise holder or sole agent. Approved importers are assigned an Import Identification Number (API), which remains in effect indefinitely unless it is suspended or revoked for cause.

Sight bankers' letters of credit are required for most private sector imports with the exception of

(1) parcel imports and goods brought in by travelers of a value not exceeding $100, (2) imports specifically authorized by the Ministry of Trade and Cooperatives or by the Investment Coordinating Board in the case of goods constituting part of a foreign investment, (3) imports through the Government's bonded warehouses, and (4) those specific cases in which usance letters of credit and aftersight letters of credit (180 days deferred payment) may be allowed.[2] The central bank has been requiring importers to make an advance deposit of at least 40 percent of the letter of credit value when they submit applications for letters of credit to authorized banks, and to settle the balance upon receipt of the documents, upon arrival of the goods, or within 75 days of the opening of the letter. However, effective May 27, 1980, the amount of the deposit was left to the discretion of the individual foreign exchange bank for certain agricultural imports and certain raw materials, spare parts, and capital goods.

Shipping Documents.—Documents required on shipments to Indonesia include the commercial invoice, the bill of lading (waybill for air cargo), the marine insurance certificate when the insurance is purchased abroad, and certain sanitary or other special certificates in some instances. No consular documents are required for shipments from the United States. Certificates of origin are required only in the case of certain drugs and narcotics.

When an import company applies for a letter of credit, its bank assigns an import reference number that identifies the bank and branch, the document itself, and the year. The control number should be shown on all related financial, shipping, and customs documents.

Commercial Invoice.—The original manufacturers' (suppliers') invoices, plus one copy, must be supplied. No special invoice form is prescribed for shipments to Indonesia. Such forms may be printed on the firm's letterhead and sent under separate cover to the consignee. For all freight shipments, the following information should be shown on the commercial invoice: name and address of shipper, place and date of shipment, name and address of consignee, number and kind of packages, contents and weight of each package, identifying package markings, and the import reference number described above.

---

[2] On March 2, 1978, the Government issued a list of 199 items that could be imported using irrevocable usance letters of credit, which provide credit of up to 180 days, and subsequently enlarged this list. Goods eligible are mostly spare parts and intermediate material needed for further processing in Indonesia.

Bill of Lading.—There are no special requirements affecting the preparation of bills of lading, except that the bills must show separately the amount paid for freight.

Marking and Labeling Requirements.—Indonesian regulations do not require special markings. The marking requirements of the country of origin are acceptable. However, as noted above, the import reference number assigned by the importer's bank when applying for a letter of credit should be part of the outer container markings to facilitate identification. The country of origin may be inserted as well as other marks desired by the supplier to help insure safe delivery at the foreign destination.

The possibility of long storage at dock warehouses in the tropical climate, rough treatment by dock workers, and considerable pilferage at ports should be taken into consideration in packing for this market. Articles affected by excessive heat and humidity should be treated and packed with oil-lined paper so as to prevent deterioration. Nothing should appear on the outer case that will advertise the contents. Cardboard cartons are usually not adequate, and importers are often willing to pay a higher price for strapped wooden cases. Reusable containers (including wooden cases) are of special value in this market. In the case of some consumer goods, for instance, the final buyer prefers a reusable container to plastic wrappings for subsequent food storage or use as a domestic utensil.

There are no special requirements regarding labeling of merchandise. Attractive labels in English are quite acceptable.

Indonesia officially uses the metric system of weights and measures, based on a 1949 law. Discussions on revising the 1949 law began in early 1981. However, there are no requirements for imports to be invoiced, specified, measured, or marked in metric units. Many products from nonmetric countries are imported in nonmetric units. Within Indonesia, they tend to be remarked and sold in metric units. However, some products are sold without conversion.

Senate Concurrent Resolution 40, adopted July 30, 1953, invites U.S. exporters to inscribe, insofar as practicable, on the external shipping containers in indelible print of a suitable size: "United States of America."

Samples and Advertising Matter.— Commercial samples and advertising matter of low- or noncommercial value may be imported into Indonesia (by freight, parcel post, or as part of commercial travelers' baggage) free of duty and without import permits. Samples should be prepared in such manner as to clearly preclude their being of regular commercial use. There is no weight stipulation to determine whether or not a sample is a commercial import.

For commercially valuable samples that will be reexported, actual deposit of guaranty funds with customs is not required. However, a bank guaranty at the shipper's end is required in an amount equal to the sum of all normal costs of importing, plus the full applicable import duty. Payment will not be required if the goods are reexported within the time limit fixed by customs, usually 6 months. In special cases, the time limit for reexport can be extended to 2 or even 3 years.

Bonded Warehousing and Export Processing Zones.—The Indonesian Government plans to expand bonded warehouses and export processing zones in Indonesia to facilitate trade and stimulate manufacturing processing activities. P.T. Bonded Warehouses Indonesia (BWI), a State enterprise, was set up in 1973 to manage bonded warehouse activities. P.T. BWI has 8,000 square meters of covered warehouse space and 12,500 square meters of open storage space at Nusantara Harbor within the boundary of Tanjung Priok (port of Jakarta). It also has 12,500 square meters each of both covered and open storage space at Jakarta Kota, in the capital city. Additional facilities are under construction at Cakung, near Jakarta.

Goods can be shipped to BWI on consignment to be released upon instruction of the supplier. No letter of credit is required. No import duties need be paid. The goods remain the property of the supplier and can be shipped back to any destination outside Indonesia as long as they have not physically entered the Indonesian customs territory.

Importers using BWI do not have to make an advance deposit in order to purchase foreign exchange and open a letter of credit until they wish to take delivery, thus avoiding the higher financing costs involved in purchasing directly from distant suppliers. Only licensed importers may use the bonded warehouse area.

In addition, an export processing zone is being developed adjacent to the warehouses at Nusantara Harbor. This is designed for light manufacturing industries that are labor intensive and export oriented such as electronic semiconductors, garments, food processing, and cold storage industries. Investors intending to establish manufacturing/assembling facilities within this zone must obtain approval from the Capital Investment Coordinating Board (BKPM) through the bonded warehouse administrator.

Limited processing activities can be carried out in the zone, and certain goods can be exported from it. These include goods originating from outside the Indonesian customs area that enter the bonded warehouse for storage and reexport and those produced in the zone that originate either from within or outside of the Indonesian customs area.

In addition to the Jakarta region, the Government plans to build bonded warehouses on Tarakan Island off the northeast coast of Kalimantan; on Batam Island, just south of Singapore; and in Cilacap on the south coast of Central Java. At Surabaya, where bonded warehouses are nearing completion, a duty-free industrial zone is also being planned.

The Government hopes to turn Batam Island, 12 miles south of Singapore, into an industrial area, taking advantage of its proximity to Singapore to attract industries requiring relatively large amounts of land and/or low-cost labor and to attract tourists to the area's extensive beaches. Batam has been designated a free trade zone, although no bonded warehouses have yet been established.

A master plan, drawn up in 1972 by Pacific Bechtel in cooperation with the Indonesian State oil company and Nissho-Iwai, a Japanese firm, envisaged the creation of an area free of many of the bureaucratic problems plaguing the rest of Indonesia. Industrial sectors that are to be given priority include oil-related industries; manufacturing, including value-adding enterprises (i.e., assembling, packaging, and labeling); agro-based industries, including cattle raising and timber processing; and shipbuilding and repair facilities.

So far development has been slow. As of early 1979, 38 companies, including 10 international concerns, had operations on Batam. Several U.S. firms are engaged in manufacturing oilfield-related equipment. Batam's future as an export-processing or -transshipment zone depends on whether significant investment can be attracted to the area. Inadequate infrastructure is currently an impediment. Investors interested in establishing industrial ventures on the island can apply directly to the Batam Authority, which is authorized to appraise and process proposals on behalf of the Investment Coordination Board (BPKM). BPKM, however, has final approval.

Export Regulations

In general, all commodities may be exported freely by registered private firms and by State trading firms subject to registration for the purpose of controlling the surrender of the export proceeds.

All exports to Angola, the People's Republic of China, Israel, and South Africa are prohibited, as are exports to all countries of gold ore and pure gold and certain other commodities. Exports of certain domestically produced commodities are controlled by means of quotas in order to maintain supplies to meet domestic demand, and prior authorization is required for the export of some other commodities.

Certain export transactions may be settled under irrevocable usance letters of credit, which grant credits of up to 180 days. Otherwise, all exporters except the petroleum companies and licensed "border-crossing" traders involved in trade with Malaysia and the Philippines must require their buyers to open a bank letter of credit covering the value of the goods to be exported. These must be sight letters of credit opened by banks abroad in a foreign currency, unless the exporter concerned has deposited foreign currency with a foreign exchange bank in Indonesia sufficient to cover the expected export proceeds. The foreign currency must be approved by the central bank.

Exports are usually "outright exports." Exports on a consignment basis or forward sales basis require a permit from the central bank.

For the principal export commodities other than petroleum, the sales price must not be lower than indicative prices (*check prices*) determined periodically by the Minister of Trade.

Indonesian regulations require the export proceeds, to the full amount of the actual f.o.b. price, be surrendered to Bank Indonesia through the foreign exchange banks except for petroleum, the exports of certain mining companies, and goods exported by licensed border-crossing traders.

Exports of copra cake, sawn timber, hides, rubber, coffee, palm kernels, palm oil, pepper, and a few other commodities are subject to a 5 percent tax, and the major mineral products and unsawn timber to a 10 percent tax.

If an export tax is applicable, the foreign exchange bank deducts it before it reimburses the exporter. It also deducts the withholding tax (MPO) due as advance payment on income or corporation tax. After deduction of these required payments, the exporter is reimbursed in rupiah for the f.o.b. value of the export at the prevailing rate on the foreign exchange Bourse.

Investment in Indonesia

Foreign Investment Climate

The Indonesian Government welcomes foreign investment and technology to assist in the development of its extensive resources and achievement of its economic potential. It grants tax and other incentives to encourage foreign investment. It also expects foreign investors to respond to its own objectives in the investment field. Thus, its legislation restricts foreign investment in certain fields, requires Indonesian co-ownership, and sets up requirements for the development of Indonesian work force. It also limits the validity period of an investment contract but provides opportunity for its extension, if certain standards are met. The Foreign Investment Law of January 10, 1967 (Law No. 1 of 1967), as amended by Law No. 11 of 1970 in respect to tax holidays and other tax concessions, established a sufficiently favorable investment climate that foreign firms had some $9 billion in approved foreign investment contracts other than oil and banking by the end of 1980.

Investors in Indonesia have had to cope with a number of difficulties of doing business. These include the lack of an up-to-date commercial code, port congestion, slow, and bureaucratic customs procedures, unofficial administrative or other payments sought by some public officials, problems in acquiring the use of land, and competing demands for taxes at different levels of government. In addition, new regulations were issued in 1974 that created uncertainties in the investment climate.

Responding to the demands of ethnic Indonesians (*pribumi*) for increased participation in the benefits from development, the Government issued a series of policy directives designed to increase considerably the domestic share of foreign investment projects. Among them were acceleration of the process leading to Indonesian control of foreign enterprises, mandatory reductions in the numbers of expatriate personnel allowed, the introduction of fines for expatriates holding positions in certain sectors the Government felt could be filled by locals, renewed emphasis on training of Indonesians, and removal or limitation of certain investment incentives. These new regulations, the financial crisis in 1975 caused by mismanagement by the State oil company—Pertamina, the Government's renegotiation of the foreign oil contracts in 1976, and a growing reputation for capricious tax assessment led many foreigners to conclude that Indonesia was not an attractive investment site.

The Indonesian Government has since taken numerous steps to improve the investment climate. These include reorganization of procedures for processing applications, reduction in corporation taxes, the use of consulting firms for advice and preparation of publications, and the issuance of an investment priority list that enables investors to learn from published data what the Government considers the most important investment projects. The latest list entitled "List of Priority Scales for Fields of Foreign Investment for the Year 1980" (also known as the DSP list) was released in February 1980.

In 1979, Indonesia began a new service within the BKPM known as the Partner Bank System (PBS) to assist overseas companies in identifying prospective joint-venture partners. PBS is compiling a data bank of references by broad activity, products, sales, and other financial and economic information.

Also, new government regulations in 1980 opened the way for wholly owned foreign investments under certain conditions and provide new incentives in respect to land use to encourage foreign investment in agricultural plantations (Presidential Decree No. 23 of 1980). Most importantly, the considerable additions to capital made by existing investors attest to the ability of firms to work successfully in Indonesia and to the profitability of foreign investment there.

Reports on the investment climate, available from the ASEAN/South Asia Group, Office of Country Marketing, International Trade Administration, U.S. Department of Commerce, Washington, D.C. 20230, include: "Indonesia's Investment Climate," September 1980, prepared by the American Embassy in Jakarta; a "Country Paper," prepared by the Investment Committee of AMCHAM, the American business group in Indonesia, October 1979; and the Indonesian Government's DSP list for 1980.

Value of Foreign Investment

Indonesia has attracted foreign investment capital valued at many billions of dollars. While the Indonesian Government does not publish figures on the total value of foreign investment, the United States is believed to be the largest investor because of heavy investment in oil. In the last 6 years alone (1975-80), expenditures by foreign firms for oil and gas exploration and development are estimated at $7 billion (excluding spending associated with the development of field and processing facilities for the Arun and Badak LNG projects). U.S. companies accounted for possibly 90 percent of these expenditures. In fields other than oil and gas, foreign investment projects valued at $3.4 billion were implemented between 1967 and March 1979, somewhat less than half of the total approved projects.

Between 1967—when the Foreign Investment Law was enacted—and the end of 1979, the Government approved 780 projects valued at $8,193 million in fields other than oil and banking. These figures exclude projects known to be cancelled or transferred to domestic investment but include the additional capitalization of existing projects. Major investors by nationality were Japanese firms with contracts valued at $3,173 million; Hong Kong, $819 million; U.S., $706 million; Philippines, $311 million (predominantly in one forestry contract, mainly with U.S. capital); Dutch, $233 million; and Australian, $224 million. By economic sector, major approved investments were in manufacturing, valued at $5,500 million (mainly in textiles, base metals, chemicals, and rubber products); mining and quarrying, $1,327 million; forestry, $556 million; and financial, real estate, and business services, $238 million.

Annual approvals of foreign investment contracts reached peaks of $1.1 billion in 1974 and $1.7 billion in 1975 but plunged to $455 million in 1976 and have remained at a disappointingly low level. In 1979 (excluding the Japanese-sponsored ASEAN fertilizer project in Aceh, Sumatra), new foreign investment project approvals amounted to only $100 million. On the other hand, many U.S. and other firms already established in Indonesia have found operations highly profitable and have added to their investment stake. In 1980, U.S. firms agreed to invest an additional $70 million in existing operations and $46 million in new non-oil projects.

U.S. Investment.—According to U.S. Department of Commerce figures, the U.S. direct investment position of the United States in Indonesia at yearend 1979 was $1,005 million. Of this, $697 million was in petroleum and $95 million in manufacturing. Since these are based on book value, they probably understate the value of current investment.

Legislation Concerning Investment

Investment Institutions and Procedures.— The Capital Investment Coordinating Board (BKPM), located at Jl. Jenderal Gatot Subroto No. 6, Jakarta, is the overall authority for both foreign and domestic investment. Exceptions are in minerals and forestry where special regulations apply and the appropriate departments (the Department of Mines and the Department of Agriculture, respectively) should be contacted. In addition to approval by the BKPM, each foreign investment project must have written presidential approval.

In October 1977, BKPM was reorganized into a "One-Stop Investment Center" in order to streamline procedures and reduce the time required to grant approval of an investment application. The first step for a prospective investor is an appointment with BKPM to discuss investment opportunities and facilities. Subsequently, the potential investor submits a Model 1 application form. After review and evaluation by BKPM, a preliminary approval will be issued to the applicant if the application is found satisfactory. The next step is to prepare a Model 2 form with the additional information required. If found satisfactory, BKPM will recommend the project for the President's approval. Together with the President's approval, other permits and investment incentives granted to the applicant will be issued. The process through Presidential approval takes 6 months or more. Preliminary approval can be obtained within 3 months.

A foreign investor must form a limited liability company with one or more Indonesian companies or persons to be allowed to invest in Indonesia. Limited liability companies (Perseroan Terbatas) are known as P.T. companies (see Forms of Business Organization below). U.S. firms familiar with doing business in Indonesia advise that the selection of an Indonesian partner should be made with extreme care and that there should be complete understanding between the foreign and local partners as to the basic legal and financial commitments the parties are undertaking. Reaching a fair agreement, understood by all, is more important than executing legal documents that may not be worth much if understanding is lacking.

A foreign investment project must be executed under the terms and in the time period approved by the Government. Unauthorized changes and delays are cause for cancellation and penalties, or at the very least, protracted and expensive negotiation.

Investment Assurances and Incentives.— The Foreign Investment Law grants investors the right to transfer profits, loan obligations, depreciation and capital (but for the latter, while tax concessions are being given). It also provides assurances against nationalization and gives various tax and other incentives.

New enterprises investing in priority areas may be granted a tax holiday of 2 to 6 years. In addition to the basic 2-year tax holiday, further 1-year holidays may be granted for investments meeting each of the following criteria; earning or saving foreign exchange of $250,000 annually during the first 3 years of production; investment exceeding $15 million or investment in a high risk area; location of the project outside Java; or meeting other priority government objectives. Investment in a plantation may also be granted a special 6-year tax holiday.

An investment allowance is granted in priority investments not receiving a tax holiday and also possibly for an expansion project where at least 80 percent of production has been realized and expansion is necessary to achieve a minimum economic size. The investment allowance is 20 percent of the amount invested in fixed capital over a 4-year period at 5 percent annually. The law provides the right to offset losses against profits and to use accelerated depreciation methods.

In addition, certain exemptions are provided from dividend tax and capital stamp duty.

Relief from import duty and sales taxes may be granted on items required for investment, and foreign employees of companies operating under the Foreign Investment Law receive certain duty-free imports.

Priority Foreign Investment Areas.—In the 1980 DSP list, priority is given generally to agriculture, certain types of transportation, machine tools, certain types of agricultural and construction machinery and equipment, pulp and paper products, and basic chemicals and synthetic fibers. The list indicates three degrees of priority. Fields with the highest priority include pulp and paper; basic chemicals (olefines, aromatics, and methanol); basic metals; iron and steel industries; diesel engines, internal combustion engines, and water turbines using locally produced components; and machinery and equipment for the mining industry. Fields with the next highest priority include plywood and veneer; garment manufacture; preservation of meat, primarily for export; fruit and vegetable canning; rubber goods for technical and medical use; ceramic and porcelain goods and building materials; safety glass; portland cement; nonmetallic mineral products; office machines; and scientific and measuring equipment. Since priority areas will change, investors should consult the DSP list in effect at the time they are considering an investment.

Areas Closed to Foreign Investors.—The 1967 investment law prohibited any investment in industries vital to national defense (e.g., munitions manufacture) and full control in fields vital to the public welfare (e.g., harbors, electric power, telecommunications, aviation, and shipping). Subsequent decrees or decisions prohibited new investment in areas the Government felt were sufficiently developed or it wished to reserve for Indonesians.

The 1980 DSP list does not designate areas closed to foreign investors. Of 526 industries open to domestic and foreign investment, 340 areas are listed as open to foreign investment as joint ventures. Of these, 70 must be in cooperation with a partner from the "weak economic group" (i.e., indigenous Indonesian rather than Chinese). However, the Government states that areas not on the list may be fields not yet identified for promotion during Repelita III, as well as fields actually closed. Also not on the list, but possibly permitted, are investments that produce entirely for export. These may be eligible for a tax holiday. The project would have to be located outside the customs zone (i.e., in a bonded warehouse, private entrepôt, or export processing zone).

Import, export, and local wholesale and retail distribution, including services related to trade or distribution, are generally reserved to national companies.

Requirements for Indonesian Participation.—Except in special cases detailed below, all foreign investors must enter into a joint-venture arrangement. Investors are advised to check with the BKPM and review the DSP list in effect at the time of the proposed investment since the priority sectors will carry new incentives to encourage a healthy balance between foreign and Indonesian businesspeople. To increase the capabilities of the latter for a more active and stronger participation, the Government stipulates that at the start of a joint venture Indonesians should own at least 20 percent of the share capital and that within 10 years they should own at least 51 percent. The foreign investor may have either a private or a State-owned company as its Indonesian partner or a combination of the two.

When Indonesia released its 1980 DSP list on February 15, 1980, the Government announced a possible exception to the Indonesian participation requirement. It stated that in specific cases, particularly fields of investment where the total production is exported, where domestic marketing would be impossible, and which create large employment opportunities, straight investment may be considered.

Sufficient time has not elapsed to test the Government's ability to enforce the local participation requirement of 51 percent within the 10-year period. However, prospective investors would be unwise to plan on an extension of this deadline or a modification of the overall objective.

Requirements for Indonesian Work Force.—Although foreign investors are assured full authority to determine their own management personnel, they are required to meet other staffing needs with Indonesian nationals and to institute training programs to meet Indonesian employment targets. Training programs are to be stepped up. Employment in a number of sectors—including mining, oil, gas, and textiles—has been classified in four categories: (1) jobs that are closed to foreigners, (2) jobs that foreigners may hold until qualified Indonesians are available, (3) jobs for which Indonesians must be trained by a specified date, and (4) all other jobs that will remain open to foreigners. A specific decree of April 4, 1974, sets forth a schedule for phasing out of foreign personnel in the forestry sector in which there are the largest number of expatriates, and, in January 1975, a schedule was set up for the oil and gas sector. Companies retaining foreign personnel beyond the specified time frame in job categories designated for Indonesians must pay $100 per month per expatriate employee. This will be used for training Indonesians.

In the last quarter of 1978, the Ministry of Manpower and Transmigration issued decrees regarding "implementation of elimination of foreign labor in the industrial section." Like the earlier decrees for the forestry and oil and gas sectors, these set forth timetables for the phasing out of foreign personnel in each industrial subsector and set a penalty of $100 per month for each expatriate not replaced in the specified time period.

Validity Period of the Investment Contract.—This may not exceed 30 years in the initial contract but may be extended once if certain standards are met.

Special Regulations for Minerals and Forestry.—While the basic investment legislation, Law No. 1 of 1967, applies to all investment areas, the exploitation of mineral and forest resources is subject to special regulations.

Prior to 1966, foreign companies participated in petroleum and natural gas exploration and development in Indonesia as contractors for the State under contract of work agreements. Three contracts are still operative: P.T. Caltex Pacific Indonesia (Caltex); Calasiatic & Topco (C & T), an affiliate of Caltex; and P.T. Stanvac Indonesia (Stanvac). The contract of work agreements with Caltex and Stanvac expire in 1983, and the agreements with C & T expire in 1993.

In 1966, the Government introduced a new type of contractual agreement with foreign oil producers known as a production sharing contract. The duration of the production sharing contracts is 30 years although they expire after an unsuccessful exploration period of 10 years. Under the production sharing agreement, the contractor is required to finance all exploration, development, and production relating to oil and gas resources within a specified area, but the State oil company, Pertamina, is responsible for management of the operations. Also, in contrast to the contract of work agreements, equipment and other property owned by contractors under production sharing contracts and brought into Indonesia become the property of Pertamina at the point of landing.

The contractor is entitled to be compensated for his operating costs, including his capital investment, in the form of crude oil production. The balance of oil production (*shared oil*) is divided between the Government and the contractor at a predetermined sharing ratio.

Since 1978, the agreements in effect provide for the Government to receive 65.91 percent of the shared oil and for the contractor to receive the remaining 34.09 percent. The 34.09 percent share received by the foreign contractor is fully taxable under Indonesian tax law at the normal corporate income tax rate and a further 20 percent dividend tax is applicable to the income remaining after corporate income taxation. On a net basis, the contractor's after-tax income is thus equivalent to 15 percent of the market value of the shared oil. In 1978, the way in which Indonesian corporate income and dividend taxes are paid by contractors operating under production sharing agreements was changed so as to allow U.S.-based contractors to continue to obtain U.S. tax credits for these Indonesian taxes. A U.S. Internal Revenue Service ruling that disallowed foreign tax credit for the share of oil production retained by the Indonesian Government under the earlier production sharing agreements necessitated this change.

In 1977, Pertamina introduced a modified form of production sharing agreement to cover areas where some exploration work had been undertaken either by Pertamina or by a foreign contractor whose contract had expired or been voluntarily terminated. Such agreements are known as joint-operations arrangements and are aimed at reducing Pertamina's own exploration costs while opening up lower risk acreage (mainly onshore) to foreign contractors.

Exploitation of minerals other than oil is governed by Law No. 11 of 1967, which permits foreign companies to explore and develop minerals on the basis of a *contract of work (Kontrak Karya)* with the Government. Application for a contract of work must be made to the Minister of Mines, R/I., 18 Merdeka Selatan, Jakarta. The contract stipulates work stages (for a possible total of 41 years, including 30 years of operation). No tax holidays are granted for corporation tax, but there is a considerable reduction of tax rates for the first 10 years, described under taxation below.

An exception to the contract-of-work principle applies in coal mining where a production sharing contract similar to the pattern of cooperation in the petroleum industry has been signed.

Under a contract-of-work agreement, the foreign mining company usually establishes an operating company incorporated in Indonesia that has full responsibility for production and assumes all related economic risks. Profits are shared between the State enterprise and the foreign contractor.

Because of delays in a government decision on the ground rules for so-called third-generation, non-oil mining contracts, only two new contracts were signed between 1972 and September 1978. However, by the end of 1979, 11 contract-of-work agreements had been signed requiring foreign capital investment totaling about $1.3 billion.

The technical provisions of the new form of contract differ little from the earlier types of contracts, but there are a number of significant changes in the financial provisions. A single tax rate applies to all non-oil minerals. The amount of regional tax is clearly established, exempting the contractor from any further liability. Provision is made for additional taxation in the event that the average rate of return for any 3 consecutive years exceeds a prescribed rate of return of 15 percent. Companies are also guaranteed a fair value for any equity that they may transfer into Indonesian hands in the years following the startup of production.

Investment in forestry is governed by Law No. 5 of 1967. Investment in logging even as a joint venture is now prohibited, but foreign firms may serve as operating contractors for domestic logging companies and may invest in wood processing industries.

Meeting the *Pribumi* Requirement.— Foreign investors have been exploring various means of satisfying the Indonesian Government's requirement of 51 percent *pribumi* ownership while protecting their vital interests in the investment. Partnership arrangements have drawbacks that limit their use as the dominant solution. A stock market of sufficient size is not developing rapidly enough to serve as a generator of equity funding or be of sufficient breadth and depth to provide a fair value of shares. In major projects and special sectors such as mining and forestry, the main means of Indonesianizing are likely to be government share purchases and joint ventures with State enterprises.

For the great majority of medium and small investors, the most practical means of compliance is the use of trusteeship arrangements. Under these, investors designate local nonbank financial institutions to hold shares in trust for future sale to *pribumi*. Indonesian regulations require that the holding of shares by nonbank financial institutions may not exceed 20 percent of the capitalization and the time period may not exceed 5years.

The Private Investment Corporation of Asia (PICA), the respected internationally owned investment bank, is one of several service organizations that can help prospective investors evaluate opportunities in Indonesia, and get the project underway, particularly for manufacturing operations. The Indonesian affiliate of PICA is P.T. Indo-Mas-Utama, Skyline Building, Jalan M.H. Thamrin 9, P.O. Box 429, Jakarta, Indonesia.

Industrial Property Protection[3]

Although Indonesia is a member of the "Paris Union" International Convention for the Protection of Industrial Property (London Revision of 1934), it has only a trademark law. There are no patent, utility model, or design laws. Under the trademark law, U.S. nationals are entitled to the same protection in that country as Indonesia extends to its own citizens. U.S. nationals are also entitled to certain special benefits. For instance, they may apply for a trademark in Indonesia within 6 months after applying for a trademark registration in a member country and claim on the Indonesian application the filing date of the first filed application *(right of priority)*.

Patents.— In the absence of patent legislation, the Indonesian Department of Justice issued a Decree on August 28, 1953, under which an inventor or his/her assignee may file for the record an application for an Indonesian patent, pending adoption of a patent law. Such provisional applications will not be acted upon nor will they be published or made available for public inspection prior to enactment of a patent law. A patent application filed under this Decree will create for the applicant, once a law is passed, a priority claim under the Paris Union Convention over applications submitted at a later date.

Trademarks.— Trademark registrations are granted under the Trade Name and Trade Marks Act (No. 21 of 1961) for 10 years from date of registration and may be extended for like

---

[3]Prepared by the Foreign Business Practices Division, Office of International Finance and Services, International Trade Administration, U.S. Department of Commerce.

periods. The first user of a mark is entitled to the registration for the class of goods for which the mark has been used. In absence of proof of the contrary, the first applicant for registration is considered as having been the first to make use of the mark, provided he/she uses the mark within 6 months after the registration for the goods covered thereby. There is no prior home registration requirement for U.S. nationals seeking to register a trademark in Indonesia. Interested U.S. applicants must file through a resident agent or attorney in Indonesia. Applications are examined and, if found acceptable, registration is granted. A registration grants exclusive right to use of the mark on the designated commodities. There is no provision for opposition before the Trade Marks Office under Indonesian law. However, once a mark is registered, a party who believes the registration violates his/her rights may file a petition to cancel the registration with the District Court of Jakarta. Such a petition must be filed within 9 months of publication of the registration.

Administration of the country's industrial property laws and regulations is vested in the Directorate of Patents and Trademarks, Department of Justice, Jalan Veteran III/8A, Jakarta, I/4.

Copyrights.—The Copyright Law in force in Indonesia is the Netherlands Copyright Act of 1912. Copyright protection for an author's work is granted for his/her life and 50 years after his/her death. The Netherlands is a member of the Universal Copyright Convention to which the United States and about 60 other countries also adhere. Under its provisions, the U.S. author of a work who first publishes and copyrights it in the United States or any other member country has automatic protection for that work in the other member countries by showing thereon his/her name, year of first publication, and the symbol "c" in a circle.

The Netherlands is also a member of the "Berne Union" Convention for the Protection of Literary and Artistic Works. Although the United States is not a member of this convention, U.S. authors may secure its automatic protection benefits in all member countries for a work by publishing that work in a member country simultaneously with its first publication in the United States.

Further information on Indonesian industrial property and copyright protection may be obtained from the Foreign Business Practices Division, Office of International Finance, Investment and Services, International Trade Administration, U.S. Department of Commerce, Washington, D.C. 20230. That Division, however, is not in a position to provide detailed information on fees or other specific step-by-step procedures to be followed in seeking rights under pertinent laws. Competent legal counsel should be consulted for that purpose.

U.S.-Indonesian Commercial Agreements

Indonesia has no Treaty of Friendship, Commerce, and Navigation (FCN) with the United States. However, it has an Investment Guaranty Agreement, which enables the United States to offer insurance to new investors to minimize risks of currency inconvertibility, expropriation, war, revolution, or insurrection, and to assist with investment finance, primarily through guaranties of private loan or equity investments. This U.S. program is administered by the Overseas Private Investment Corporation (OPIC), Washington, D.C. 20527, a public-private joint venture. OPIC also provides pre-investment assistance, is authorized to make direct loans of dollars or local foreign currencies in certain cases, and provides other investor services. Information on this program may be obtained directly from OPIC.

The United States and Indonesia are discussing a tax treaty to prevent double taxation and to facilitate trade and investment between the two countries. Despite periodic talks since 1971, agreement has not yet been reached.

Forms of Business Organizations

The following legal forms of business organization in Indonesia are the most common:

1. The limited liability company (*Perseroan Terbatas*, or P.T.), for most foreign investors, this type of organization is the only relevant form;

2. The full partnership (*Firma*), in which all partners are personally liable for all obligations of the enterprise;

3. The limited partnership (*Perseroan Komanditer*), in which one or more are silent partners responsible for obligations only up to the amounts of their capital participation, while those designated as managing partners are personally liable for all of the firm's obligations;

4. The cooperative (common among farmers and other small entrepreneurs);

5. The sole proprietorship or individual enterprise (*Perusahan Perseorangan*), in which the owner is personally liable for all obligations of the firm he/she owns; and

6. The branch of a foreign business firm.

Organization of Foreign Firms.—The Foreign Investment Law provides that an enterprise operated wholly or for the most part in

Indonesia as a separate business unit must be a legal entity organized under Indonesian law and have its domicile in Indonesia. As this article was subsequently elucidated, the entity must be organized as a limited liability company (P.T.), unless a firm is operating a branch, as foreign banks are permitted to do, or unless special circumstances permit some other arrangement.

Establishing a Limited Liability Company.—The legal characteristics of the P.T. are specified in Articles 36-56 of the Indonesian Commercial Code. A limited liability company may be formed by foreigners alone or by foreigners jointly with Indonesian nationals. A minimum of two persons is required.

The services of an Indonesian Notary Public are required to organize a P.T. The deed must be in the Indonesian language and must use a name for the P.T. that the Ministry will approve (containing the term *"Perseroan Terbatas"* or its abbreviation). In addition, it must state its capitalization in rupiahs (although the capitalization in another currency, in parentheses, may be given as well). The capital structure must be shown in the initial Deed of Establishment, and certain percentages of the authorized capital must have been subscribed and paid in by the time the Deed is approved.

The limited liability of shareholders is recognized. Shares may be in bearer or in registered form, but in practice all shares held by foreign investors are required to be in registered form. Both common and preferred shares are permitted.

Taxation

The principal taxes of importance to the foreign investor are the company or corporate tax; the personal income tax; the interest, dividend, or royalty tax; and the sales tax. Special corporate taxes apply in the minerals field. There are also property taxes, stamp taxes, a personal net wealth tax, excise taxes, motor vehicle or road taxes assessed by local governments, and a variety of other taxes. Investors producing for export may be subject to an export tax.

Corporate Taxes.—The Company Tax Law of 1925, most recently amended on April 1, 1979, provides for a 20 percent tax on profits up to Rp. 25 million, 30 percent on the next Rp. 50 million (i.e., between Rp. 25 million and Rp. 75 million), and 45 percent on profits of over Rp. 75 million. Companies that present financial statements audited by public accountants (as most U.S. firms do) will be taxed at the following rates: 20 percent on taxable profits up to Rp. 100 million; 30 percent on the next Rp. 250 million (i.e., profits

of between Rp. 100 million and Rp. 350 million), and 45 percent on profits of more than Rp. 350 million. Companies that issue shares on the stock exchange may apply different, reduced rates of corporation tax.

All types of partnerships and corporate bodies are subject to the company tax. Following a U.S. Internal Revenue Service ruling that the payments under production sharing contracts did not qualify as income taxes for purposes of U.S. foreign tax credit (previously the corporate tax paid by oil companies derived from the profit split between the Government and the foreign oil company under production sharing contracts), the production sharing arrangements were changed so that the oil producing companies are now directly assessed to corporation tax. The tax is now considered creditable for U.S. tax purposes. Companies producing minerals other than oil are subject to special corporation taxes of 35 percent of taxable profits for the first 10 years of production and up to 45 percent thereafter (according to regulation No. 21 of August 23, 1976, "Taxation and other Levies Against Non-Oil and Natural Gas Mining Operations"). No holidays from corporate tax are granted mining companies under the Foreign Investment Law.

Personal Income Taxes.—Both residents and nonresidents of Indonesia are subject to personal income tax. Foreign individuals who work in Indonesia for a year, regardless of their intentions to reside in Indonesia, are considered taxable residents. Those working for 3 months but less than a year are considered taxable nonresidents. Residents are taxed on all of their worldwide income, defined as the difference between gross income and deductions permitted by law. Dividends received from firms domiciled outside Indonesia are exempt. The expatriate is eligible for a tax credit against taxes paid to a foreign government, at the rates at which the same income would have been taxed if earned and taxed in Indonesia.

Personal income tax rates are applied progressively to 19 income brackets. The lowest rate of 5 percent applies to residual taxable income of less than R. 240,000, as of 1980, and the highest rate of 50 percent to income of Rp. 18 million (about $28,800) or more. This means that foreign personnel are generally paying a rate of 50 percent on a large portion of their income. There are also personal and family tax deductions.

As of 1980, for expatriates earning not less than $12,000 annually, the following deductions apply: a standard deduction of 5 percent of gross income with a maximum of Rp. 180,000 ($288); a deduction for the taxpayer of 10 percent of gross income with a maximum of Rp. 750,000 ($1,200), a deduction for a legal wife of 5 percent of gross income to a maximum of Rp. 437,500 ($700), and a deduction of 5 percent of gross income for up to three children and 7 percent of gross income for over three children, each to a maximum of Rp. 750,000 ($1,200). A deduction is also allowed for pension fund contributions. In addition to personal income taxes, a special tax is levied annually on foreigners—currently Rp. 7,500 for adults and Rp. 3,750 for children. A 0.5 percent wealth tax is payable on net wealth exceeding 15 million ($24,000).

Interest, Dividend, and Royalty Tax.—A withholding tax of 20 percent is levied on payments of interest, dividends, or royalties. If the recipient is a resident, the withholding is considered an advance payment of the corporation or income tax of the recipient. If the recipient is a nonresident, the tax is considered a final tax. In 1973, the withholding tax rate applicable to interest on foreign-based loans was reduced to 10 percent.

Sales taxes and export taxes are described under Trade Regulations, above.

Because tax evasion is so common, tax officials often doubt the accuracy of tax returns and financial statements submitted to them and make their own assessment, sometimes on an arbitrary basis. This can result in a long and frustrating negotiation for a foreign company. Some companies attempt to negotiate in advance with tax officials an acceptable tax base.

Two special withholding tax systems known as the MPS and MPO systems also apply to corporate and personal income taxes. The MPS system is a self-assessment scheme under which companies and individuals make monthly prepayments of taxes due. Under the MPO system, companies or individuals may be appointed tax collectors for other companies or individuals with whom they do business. For example, a manufacturer selling to a wholesaler may invoice an extra percent of the value of the transaction (usually 2 percent) that it forwards to the taxation authorities as an advance payment of the wholesaler's liability.

Industrial Estates

To assist the investor, the Government has opened a number of industrial estates in Indonesia and is planning additional facilities. These offer many advantages in providing easy access to land, infrastructure, and support facilities such as water, electricity, sewage disposal, and telephones.

In the Jakarta area, the major facility is the Pulogadung industrial estate, a $50 million joint venture between the Central Government and the municipal administration. The estate is located in the eastern part of the city about 15 km from Tanjung Priok harbor and 9 km from the Halim international airport. Of some 1,000 acres of raw land earmarked for acquisition, about 80 percent had been acquired as of mid-1979, and 294 acres of developed land had been sold to 99 firms expected to employ around 19,000 people when operating at full capacity. No industries are prohibited in the estate although most firms are in the light-to-medium industrial fields and manufacture products such as glass, textiles, aluminum, chemicals, food products, and beverages. Industrial sites are available to local and foreign investors in plots ranging from 5,000 to 7,000 square meters.

Ten other districts in the outlying areas of Jakarta have been earmarked by the Jakarta municipality for new industrial estates, but planning is only in the initial stage.

A $30 million industrial estate is under development at Rungkut in Surabaya, East Java, with the assistance of loans and technical aid from West Germany. This 500-acre estate, designed to accommodate some 140 enterprises, is conveniently located—only 5 km from the Juanda Airport and 10 km from the port of Tanjung Perak. As of March 1979, about half of the area had been sold to 80 companies, of which 29 were in production commercially or on a trial basis. Foreign firms included Union Carbide (United States), Mitsui (Japan), Kusum Products (India/West Germany), and Dewana (Singapore). The director of the estate states that small- and medium-sized industries suitable for the immediate market of 25 million people in East Java are food processing, beverages, leather, wood, paper and printing, chemicals, glass, metal products, car components, machinery, and electrical products industries.

An industrial estate some 500 acres in area has been developed at Cilacap, Central Java, with the assistance of the Australian Government. This development has been stimulated by the construction of important industrial facilities in Cilacap, including an oil refinery, a cement plant, a frozen sea food processing facility, and a fertilizer bagging and distribution facility. As of early 1979, some 250 acres were available for use. The project cost is estimated at $14 million.

A 500-600 acre industrial estate is underway for Ujungpandang, South Sulawesi, to accommodate 150 plants and absorb 30,000 workers. Japan will provide 28 percent of the financing. The first stage of this three-stage project is to be completed by 1982 and the last by 1990. Some firms have already located there.

Priority will be given to food and beverage industries, textiles, electrical devices, machinery, wood products, equipment industries, and food preservation industries.

A feasibility study has been completed for an industrial estate in Medan, and the site of the first zone (nearly 200 acres) has been acquired. Industrial estates are also planned for Semarang, Central Java, and Samarinda, and East Kalimantan.

Development plans for Batam Island, in the Indonesian Riau Archipelago just south of Singapore, include facilities for industrial estates. Additional details are provided in the discussion of warehousing and export processing zones below.

Labor

The Indonesian labor force is primarily young, unskilled, and minimally educated but highly trainable. Consisting of about 56 million people in 1979, the labor force is projected to reach 90 million workers by the year 2000. Historically, the availability of the labor force has fluctuated with the seasonal changes of the country. Highly productive and labor intensive wet paddy rice cultivation alters the availability of the labor force by about 20 percent. In the rainy season workers are needed to prepare fields, plant, transplant, and harvest. Later, in the dry season, work slacks off and many farmers supplement their incomes by obtaining construction or agricultural jobs with private firms.

The largest segment of Indonesia's population works in the agricultural, forestry, and fishing sector. Detailed results of the last census (1980) have not yet been released. However, the 1976 intercensal survey indicated that 35 million people were in jobs related to agriculture, forestry, and fishing. About 14 million of these people were unpaid farm workers, 6 million were landless agricultural workers, and up to 6 million were fishermen with very meager incomes. About 4 million workers were in manufacturing. Some 6 million worked in the trade segment of the economy; these people included hotel and restaurant workers but also self-employed vendors, scavengers, and food hawkers. About 5 million people worked in community, social, and personal services.

There is a wide divergence in wages earned by the masses of workers in the traditional economy and those who have entered the modern industrial sector. In a labor surplus country, the economic law of supply and demand keeps most wages low. However, employees with skills needed in the modern sector receive substantially higher wages. Also, both skilled and unskilled workers in the modern sector reap higher benefits and better wages than traditional farm workers.

The Government so far has not adopted a minimum wage law for the country. However, it has established recommended minimum wages in different geographic areas that are paid to government laborers and are expected to be followed by private industry employers. The minimum wages are arrived at by utilizing a formula that takes into account the local prevailing wages. Since the minimum wages rely on government persuasion rather than law for enforcement, they are often ignored.

In January-June 1980, average minimum and maximum monthly salaries, by industry, were as follows: plantation, $28 to $306; mining, $107 to $911; manufacturing, $64 to $661; construction, $41 to $594; electricity, $34 to $370; trade and banking, $66 to $658; communications, $81 to $365; and services, $52 to $515. Minimum and maximum monthly salaries paid by the American Embassy in Jakarta as of June 1980 (these were for skilled employees required to speak English) ranged from $136 to $190 for a file clerk and $216 to $312 for a driver to $877 to $1,329 for an electrical engineer. Professional level managers in private sector companies received salaries about 25 to 50 percent or more above the highest Embassy salary for local employees. Most workers in the modern industrial sector in Indonesia also received benefits to supplement their cash income, which often equaled the value of their monetary salary.

The low income levels prevailing in Indonesia are evidenced by the high amount of per capita income spent on food. An International Labor Organization study based on 1976 data indicates that about 75 percent of per capita expenditures in Indonesia are used for food. For the Philippines, Thailand, and Malaysia per capita expenditures for food are in the 50 to 60 percent range. In developed countries the percentage spent on food is as low as 20 percent.

It is Indonesian policy for government, employers, and labor to work together smoothly to achieve an even distribution of economic as well as social and national development. Labor law—including regulations covering the right to unions, policies for collective bargaining and strikes, termination of employees, workday arrangements, and safety and child labor— illustrate the societal aspirations to provide harmonious working relationships between workers and employers.

President Suharto, in his 1973 State Address, urged that each enterprise unionize. Government reorganization of the labor movement and increased trade union membership was spurred by the development of the FBSI (All Indonesian Labor Federation) whose purpose is to unite existing labor organizations as well as to create new organizations.

By June 1980, the FBSI was composed of 21 industrial unions and 9,635 local unions; it claimed 2.7 million members. However, the labor union movement suffers from weaknesses in communications, administration, finances, and organizing and training capabilities. The AFL-CIO sponsored Asian American Free Labor Institute and the West German Friedrich Ebert Foundation have given indirect financial support in supplying equipment, buildings, training programs, seed capital, loans, and scholarships for study abroad.

The official government body delegated the responsibility for most labor functions is the Department of Manpower and Transmigration. Although functioning with a low budget, a small staff, and an insufficiently trained personnel group, the efficiency and importance of the department is growing as teams of ILO (International Labor Organization) experts aid in organization, labor laws and regulations, and employment.

Considerable progress has been made in negotiating collective bargaining agreements. Early in 1976, only 40 of the 50,000 medium-to-large business ventures in Indonesia had collective bargaining agreements with their workers. In an effort to promote collective agreements, the Department of Manpower and Transmigration decreed that companies that had no collective bargaining agreement and that employed more than 50 workers had to prepare regulations explaining conditions of employment including wages, hours, holidays, allowances, and promotion systems. As of June 1980, there were 1,197 collective bargaining agreements registered with the Government. Other enterprises that have not negotiated agreements will be forced to meet the regulation if it is strictly enforced.

The problem of unemployment plays a key role in the concentrated effort of government, employers, and laborers to reach the common goal of national development. Laborers and employers alike realize the need for cooperation; as a result, strikes are rare in Indonesia and require official government approval. Appropriate measures to a legal strike include sanctioning by a Regional Labor Court and by the National Labor Court, both of which are segments of the tripartite organizations of representatives of management, government, and labor. A strike may not be initiated while a court is seeking solution through arbitration or conciliation. It is also illegal for government workers or workers in vital industries to strike. Although spontaneous, unsanctioned strikes have occurred, most of these have been small and shortlived; local law enforcement authorities quickly restored order.

Termination of an undesirable working arrangement between worker and employer is very difficult. In an effort to avoid this problem, a 3-month trial period has been adopted for both the employer and the prospective worker. Termination during this period is a simpler procedure than termination after the 3 months. If, however, dismissal is deemed appropriate after this trial period, the company must obtain approval of each dismissal from an appropriate government authority. High unemployment rates lead government authorities to discourage termination before another replacement position is obtained.

A three-point, mandatory, social insurance plan became effective in January of 1978. The plan includes workers' accident and life insurance programs and a savings plan. The workers' savings plan is payable in the event of total disability or when the employee reaches 55 years of age. Limited financial means in both the private and public sector have posed problems to the implementation of this plan; but, as it stands, the accident insurance is absorbed completely by the employer; in addition, 0.5 percent of the employee's wage is contributed by the employer to cover the life insurance portion of the program. The savings plan is made up of a combination of a contribution of 1.5 percent of the employee's wage by the corporation plus a contribution of 1 percent of the employee's wages paid by the employee. Large multinationals operating in Indonesia have had pension plans, accident insurance, and house purchasing assistance programs in operation before the government plan was put into effect.

National legislation provides for a 7-hour workday, a 40-hour workweek with a 30-minute break after every 4 hours of continuous work. Overtime pay must be 1-1/2 times the basic wage, while work on Sundays and holidays must pay double the usual wage. There are provisions for a rest day each week as well as special regulations regarding employment of women.

An annual labor report, prepared by the American Labor Attache in Jakarta, provides additional information. It is available from the ASEAN/South Asia Group, Office of Country Marketing, International Trade Administration, U.S. Department of Commerce, Washington, D.C. 20230.

Entrance and Residence Information

Visas

A visa is required for a visit to Indonesia of any duration. Visas may be obtained from the Visa Section of the Embassy of Indonesia, 2020 Massachusetts Avenue, N.W., Washington, D.C. 20036; the Consulate General at 5 East 68th Street, New York, New York 10021; the Consulate at 351 California Street, San Francisco, California 94104; and the Consulate at 3540 Wilshire Boulevard, Los Angeles, California 90010.

Businesspeople traveling to Indonesia are required to have a visitor's visa (for business purposes). A visitor's visa for 30 days or less costs $5.50 per passport. For over 30 days up to 3 months, the cost is $22; this includes a landing fee of $16.50. A letter in duplicate from the firm the businessperson represents, stating the purpose of the visit and guaranteeing sufficient funds, is required. Visa forms in two copies must be filled out and two photographs provided. The Indonesian Embassy and Consulates will mail the required forms upon request. The Directorate General of Immigration, Jl. Cikini Raya 93, Jakarta, may grant an extension of the visitor's visa.

A tourist visa is issued for 30 days and a cost of $3. It may be extended for a period of only 15 days. Two forms and two passport photographs are required. The tourist must also provide proof of his/her intention and financial ability to depart from Indonesia, either through a round trip ticket or a letter from a travel agency, airlines, or steamship company confirming the purchase of tickets.

Passports to be submitted with the visitor's and tourist visa application forms must be valid for at least 6 months from the time the visa application is submitted. Visas obtained by mail must be accompanied by a money order covering all fees and $3.50 per passport for postage. The Indonesian Government no longer requires proof of any vaccinations to enter the country.

Persons to be employed in Indonesia may obtain a semipermanent visa for a stay of 3 months to 1 year. While forms may be obtained in the United States, issuance of the visa requires the approval of the Indonesian Department of Immigration. In addition to a valid passport, an application form in triplicate and three photographs, requirements include: a police certificate of good conduct; a biographical sketch; a statement by employer of the nature of work; a copy of employment contract; and copies of degrees, marriage, and birth certificates.

Fees per passport include chantery fee, $2.60; immigration fee, $4; landing fee, $16.50; and mailing fee, $3.50.

Even though a person holds an Indonesian visa, permission to land or enter Indonesia remains at the sole discretion of the Immigration Officer in Indonesia. Also, the visa will not be valid if entry into Indonesia does not take place within the period specified on the visa.

It is advisable for businesspeople visiting Indonesia to register with the American Embassy to facilitate contact in case of an emergency and to acquire a replacement for their passports in the event they are lost or stolen. When traveling in the provinces, all foreigners are expected to report to police officials within 24 hours of their arrival. It is wise to carry your passport and Indonesian Immigration Document (if your stay is long enough to require the latter).

Currency

The Indonesian currency is the rupiah and the current exchange rate of Rp. 625 per U.S. dollar is used for all trade and invisible transactions. There are no restrictions on the import or conversion of foreign currency or travelers checks when entering the country or on reconversion upon departure. However the import or export of Indonesian currency exceeding Rp. 2,500 is prohibited. A money changer is available at the Jakarta international airport. Currency may be exchanged also at any of the foreign exchange banks, including the branches of U.S. and other foreign banks in Jakarta and at many hotels.

Travelers' checks can be cashed at most hotels and banks, including all the branches of U.S. banks in Jakarta. Most of these banks are open between 8 a.m. and 3:30 p.m. Monday through Friday and 8 a.m. to 12:30 p.m. on Saturday.

Customs Bureau Regulations

Customs allows on entry a maximum of two liters of alcoholic beverages; 200 cigarettes, 50 cigars, or 100 grams of tobacco; and a reasonable amount of perfume per adult. Cars, photographic equipment, typewriters, and radios are admitted provided they are taken out on departure. They must be declared to customs.

Airport Tax

An airport tax of Rp. 1,600 ($2.56) is levied by the airport authority for travelers on international routes and Rp. 1,000 ($1.60) for those on domestic routes.

Hotels

There are numerous hotels in Jakarta that provide good accommodations at international standards. Leading ones include the Borobudur Intercontinental, the Hotel Indonesia Sheraton, the Hyatt Aryaduta Jakarta, the Indonesia Sheraton, the Jakarta Hilton International, the Hotel Sari Pacific (non-U.S./Pan Pacific), and the Mandarin (non-U.S. Mandarin International). As of early 1981, rates ran from $35 to $70 per day for a single room, plus 11 percent government tax and 10 service charge. Business discounts of 10 to 20 percent are often given. Except Hotel Sari Pacific, which accepts American Express and Diners Club, all of the above-listed hotels accept all major credit cards. These hotels provide business facilities, including secretarial, translation, and telex services. All offer small function rooms in addition to restaurants and lounges. There are a number of small hotels and guest houses that offer comfortable accommodations at more moderate rates.

Languages

The national language is Indonesian (or Bahasa Indonesia, a form of Malay). Since Indonesia became independent in 1945, Indonesian has been used increasingly throughout the archipelago. It is not only the *linqua franca* between ethnic subgroups, but it is the language of all written communication, education, government, and business. While it is understood in all but the most remote villages, local languages are still important in many areas.

English is the most widely spoken foreign language and is taught in the schools. It also is used in business circles and in most business communications.

Length of Stay

Doing business in Indonesia is more difficult and time-consuming than in the developed countries because of telephone problems, heavy traffic during business hours, and the difficulty of making appointments more than a day in advance. Since it is hard to keep more than three or four appointments during a workday, the length of visit should comprise a number of days, even for an initial survey of the market. Business activities should be started no later than 7:30 a.m.

Health

The general level of community sanitation and public health awareness is low throughout Indonesia. Local hazards include typhoid, hepatitis, cholera, amoebiasis, enteric parasites, tuberculosis, and common infections. Malaria is endemic in much of Indonesia except metropolitan Jakarta. When traveling outside Jakarta, malaria suppressives should be taken. Cholera, typhoid, paratyphoid and tetanus vaccinations are strongly recommended for persons remaining in Indonesia for an extended period. Medication for stomach or intestinal ailments may well be included in a traveling kit.

Except for the large hotels in Bali, tap water is considered unsafe to drink.

Food

The Indonesian staple food is rice, steamed, boiled, or fried. Some accompanying dishes can be pepper hot—big red peppers or small ones; so it is advisable to ask first before ordering. Many restaurants, however, specialize in European, Japanese, and Chinese cuisine. A variety of beverages are available everywhere including very good Indonesian beer. Since tap water is generally unsafe, hot or bottled beverages are recommended. Pork is forbidden for the Moslem population and beef for the Balinese Hindus, but both are available at many restaurants and markets. Fruits may be eaten with comparative safety if carefully peeled. In public places, cold cuts, lettuce, and foods with mayonaise should be avoided.

Clothing

Dress is normally casual in Indonesia and light clothing is advisable due to the hot, humid weather. A jacket and tie are required only for formal occasions or official calls. For travel to mountain areas, a light sweater or coat is recommended.

Manners

Indonesians are very polite people. Handshaking is customary both for men and women on introduction and greeting, and smiling is a national characteristic. The use of the left hand to give or receive is taboo; also crooking one's finger to call someone is considered impolite.

Holidays

Some holidays in Indonesia are on a fixed date while others vary with the lunar calendar. In 1981, Indonesian businesses and government offices are closed on the following holidays: January 1, New Year's Day; January 18,

Mohammad's Birthday; April 17, Good Friday; May 28, Ascension of Christ; May 31, Ascension of Mohammad; August 1, Idul Fitri; August 17, Indonesia's Independence Day; October 8, Idul Adha; October 29, Moslem New Year; December 25, Christmas Day. The American Embassy and Consulates will be open on Good Friday and Ascension Day, but they will be closed on the other holidays as well as on U.S. national holidays. In addition to the holidays listed, business visitors should be aware of the Islamic lunar month of fasting, Ramadan (28 days), when Indonesian Government offices and many business establishments work a shorter business day, generally 8 a.m. to 12 noon. The month of Ramadan is concluded by the holiday of Idul Fitri, which in 1981 falls on August 1. The American Embassy can provide information on the date of movable holidays in subsequent years.

Work Permits

Foreigners employed in Indonesia are required to have work permits from the Ministry of Manpower, Transmigration, and Cooperatives. They may be employed only in occupations that cannot be filled by Indonesian nationals. Information required on the application form includes a description of the occupation to be filled and programs underway or planned by the employer to train Indonesians for the job. Arrangements can be made for a reduction in the work permit fee for employers applying concurrently for a number of permits for employees needed for a given project.

Sources of Economic and Commercial Information

Government Representation

Indonesia is represented in the United States by its Embassy at 2020 Massachusetts Avenue, N.W., Washington, D.C. 20036; by a Consulate General at 5 East 68th Street, New York, New York 10021, where the Commercial Attache is located; by a Consulate at 351 California Street, San Francisco, California 94104; and by a Consulate at 3540 Wilshire Boulevard, Suite 320, Los Angeles, California 90010. Bank Indonesia, the central bank, has an office at 91 Liberty Street, New York, New York 10006. Also, an office of the State commercial bank, Bank Export Import, is located at 100 Wall Street, New York, New York 10005. Pertamina, the State-owned oil company, is represented by George C. Benson (Colonel, U.S.A. Ret.), Suite 829, 1800 K Street, N.W., Washington, D.C.

20006. The company also has an office at 2020 Century Park East Boulevard, Suite 1100, Los Angeles, California 90067.

The United States maintains an Embassy in Jakarta at Jalan Medan Merdeka Selatan No. 5 (tel. 340001-9; telex 44218 AMEMB JKT). It also has Consulates in Surabaya, Jalan Raya Dr. Sudomo No. 33 (tel. 69287/8; telex 31334, AMCON SB) and in Medan, Jalan Imam Bondjoi No. 13 (tel. 322200). U.S. Foreign Service and Foreign Commercial Service Officers in the Economic and Commercial Sections are available to assist American businesspeople visiting Indonesia. A booklet, *Key Officers of Foreign Service Posts*, is published three times annually by the U.S. Department of State. Copies may be purchased for $1.50 each or $4.50 per year on a subscription basis from the U.S. Government Printing Office, Washington, D.C. 20402.

Publications

Indonesian Publications

Business News P.T. Business News, Member of SPS, 70 Abdul Muis, Jakarta Pusat, Indonesia (Biweekly).

Doing Business in Indonesia, 1978. P.T. SGV-Utomo, Jl. Let Jend. S. Parman Kav 56, Jakarta, Indonesia.

Focus on Indonesia, Information Division, Embassy of the Republic of Indonesia, 2020 Massachusetts Avenue, N.W., Washington, D.C. 20036 (Monthly).

Indonesia: A Guide for Investors, The Investment Coordination Board (BKPM), Jalan Gatot Subroto No. 6, Jakarta, Indonesia, April 1980.[4]

Indonesia Development News, National Development Information Office, Republic of Indonesia, Wisata International Building, 8th Floor, Jl. M.H. Thamrin, Jakarta, Indonesia.[4]

Indonesia: Economic Update 1980, National Development Information Office, Wisata International Building, 8th Floor, Jl. M.H. Thamrin, Jakarta, Indonesia.[4]

Indonesia Fact File, June 1978, National Development Information Office, Republic of Indonesia, Wisata International Building, 8th Floor, Jl. M.H. Thamrin, Jakarta, Indonesia.

Indonesia News and Views, Information Divi-

---

[4]Also available from Hill and Knowlton, Inc., 633 Third Avenue, New York, New York 10017.

sion, Embassy of Indonesia, 2020 Massachusetts Avenue, N.W., Washington, D.C. 20036 (Biweekly).

Indonesian Commercial Newsletter, P.T. Data Consult Inc., P.O. Box 108/JNG, Jakarta, Indonesia (Bimonthly).

Jakarta City Business Directory, 1979, CV Pacific Book Co., Jalan Gunung Sahari No. 64, Jakarta, Indonesia.

Kompass, Indonesia, 1980-81. P.T. Gramedia, Bagian Penerbitan, Jl. Palmerah Selatan 22, Lantai 4, Jakarta Pusat.

List of Priority Scales for Fields of Foreign Investment for the Year 1980, Investment Coordinating Board, Jalan Jenderal Gatot Subroto No. 6, Jakarta, Indonesia (55 pp).

Monthly Statistical Bulletin (Indicator Ekonomi), Central Statistical Bureau (Biro Pusat Statistik), Jarkarta, Indonesia.

Standard Trade Directory of Indonesia, 1980/81. Official Publication of the Indonesian Chamber of Commerce and Industry, Jl. Hayam Wuruk 4 SX, P.O. Box 4556, Jakarta.

Statistical Pocketbook of Indonesia, 1978/79, Central Statistical Bureau (Biro Pusat Statistik), Jakarta, Indonesia.

The Third Five-Year Development Plan, Repelita III, the Republic of Indonesia, 1978/79-1983/84, Economic Division, Embassy of the Republic of Indonesia, 2020 Massachusetts Avenue, N.W., Washington, D.C. 20036 (63 pp.).

Department of Commerce Publications

Business Firms, Indonesia, April 1979, $3.00.

Foreign Economic Trends and Their Implications for the United States—Indonesia (semiannual).

Indonesia: A Survey of U.S. Business Opportunities (Country Market Sectoral Survey), May 1977.

Market Profiles for Asia and Oceania, OBR 80-40, December 1980.

World Trade Outlook for the Far East and South Asia, OBR 80-31, September 1980.

Foreign Market Reports[5]

1981

DIB #81-01-001—Industrial Outlook Report—Petroleum, $8.

DIB #81-01-002—Indonesia's Investment Climate, $5.

DIB #81-01-037—Economic Development in W. Kalimantan Province, $5.

DIB #81-03-015—Small Holder Sugar Program in E. Java, $5.

DIB #81-03-016—Annual Labor Report, $6.50.

DIB #81-03-018—Belawan Port Expansion Project, $5.

1980

DIB #80-02-002—Indonesia: Five-Year Plan Project Proposals for 1979/1980, The Telecommunications Sector, $5.

DIB #80-02-004—Indonesia: Five-Year Plan Project Proposals for 1979/1980, the Industry Sector, $5.

DIB #80-02-005 Indonesia: Five-Year Plan Project Proposals for 1979/1980, Radio, Television, Film and Printing, $5.

DIB #80-02-006—Indonesia: Five-Year Plan Project Proposals for 1979/1980, the Electric Power Generation Sector, $6.

DIB #80-02-007—Indonesia: Five-Year Plan Project Proposals for 1979/1980, the Mining Sector, $5.

DIB #80-02-008—Indonesia: Five-Year Plan Project Proposals for 1979/1980, Health and Rural Water Supply, $5.

DIB #80-02-010—Indonesia: Five-Year Plan Project Proposals for 1979/1980, the Transportation Sector, $8.

DIB #80-03-020—Trade Outlook Article for Indonesia, Commercial Attache, American Embassy, Jakarta, $5.

DIB #80-04-002—Food Processing and Packaging Opportunities in Indonesia, $5.

[5]Available from National Technical, Technical Information Services, U.S. Department of Commerce, Springfield, Virginia 22161 (these reports include reports prepared or transmitted by the American Embassy in Jakarta and reports based on market research done in Indonesia).

INDONESIA

DIB #80-05-004—Indonesia's Fishing Industry, $5.

DIB #80-06-021—Indonesia's Investment Climate, as of April 1979, $5.

DIB #80-06-022—Best Prospects for U.S. Exports for FY 1982, $5.

DIB #80-07-027—The Timbering and Wood-Processing Industries of Indonesia, $7.

DIB #80-07-028—The Pulp and Paper Industry of Indonesia, $5.

DIB #80-07-029—American Chamber of Commerce in Indonesia: Country Paper on Indonesia, $6.

DIB #80-11-006—Summary List of Indonesian Major Projects, as of July 1, 1980, $5.

DIB #80-11-007—Industrial Outlook Report: Textile, $5.

1979

DIB #79-02-021—Presidential Non-Fuels Mineral Policy Review, $4.

DIB #79-05-020—Industrial Outlook Report: Textiles, $4.

DIB #79-09-001—Analysis of Indonesian Exports, $4.

DIB #79-09-002—Prospects and Problems in Motor Vehicle and Components Industries, 1979, $4.

DIB #79-09-004—Indonesia: Five-Year Plan Project Proposals for 1979/1980, the Urban Development Sector, $4.

DIB #79-09-006—Indonesia's Petroleum Sector, $4.

DIB #79-09-008—Industrial Outlook Report: Minerals, $4.

DIB #79-09-017—Indonesia: Five-Year Plan Project Proposals for 1979/1980, the Irrigation Sector, $5.25.

DIB #79-09-021—Export and Production of Chinchona Bark and Quinine, Calendar Year 1978, $4.

DIB #79-09-022—Minerals Questionnaire 1978, $4.

DIB #79-09-069—Foreign Trade in Bauxite and Alumina, Indonesia, $4.

DIB #79-09-135—Indonesia: Five-Year Plan Project Proposals for 1979/1980, Rural Cooperatives Development Projects, $4.

DIB #79-012-002—Aircraft Industry, Indonesia, $4.

1978

DIB #78-03-022—Commercial Reporting, Best Prospects for 1980, $4.

DIB #78-03-505—Market Survey for Special Communications Equipment in Indonesia, $10.

DIB #78-03-513—Market Survey for Scientific and Industrial Instruments in Indonesia, $10.

DIB #78-08-009—Mining, Petroleum & Natural Gas, Market Review, $5.25.

DIB #78-10-502—Market Survey for Pumps, Valves and Compressors, Indonesia, $10.

DIB #78-11-005—Annual Labor Report, $4.

DIB #78-12-013—Batam Island: Current Status and Development Prospects, $4.

DIB #78-12-017—Construction and Public Works: Market Review, $4.50.

Other Publications

Annual Report on Exchange Arrangements and Exchange Restrictions, 1980, International Monetary Fund, Washington, D.C. 20006.

Background Notes, Indonesia, June 1978, U.S. Department of State. Superintendent of Documents, U.S. Government Printing Office, Washington, D.C. 20402.

Country Labor Profile—Indonesia, 1979, Bureau of International Labor Affairs, U.S. Department of Labor, Washington, D.C. 20210.

Directory of U.S. Firms and Organizations In Indonesia, 1980, Economic/Commercial Section, American Embassy, Medan Merdeka Selatan 5, Jakarta.

Doing Business in Indonesia, February 1978, Price Waterhouse & Co., 1251 Avenue of the Americas, New York, New York 10020.

Handbook on Marketing in Indonesia, 1979, mprc (asia) sdn. berhad, 132B, Jalan Kasah, Damansara Heights, Kuala Lumpur 23-10, Malaysia.

Indonesia, Ernst & Whinney International Series, January 1980.

Investing, Licensing & Trading Conditions Abroad, Indonesia, Business International, 575 Third Avenue, New York, New York 10017. August 1980.

Jakarta Business Bulletin, Jakarta Supplement in TRADE USA, American Embassy, Manila, the Philippines.

Outlook Indonesia, American Indonesian Chamber of Commerce, Suite 1021, 120 Wall Street, New York, New York 10005.

The Republic of Indonesia, February 1981, Kuhn Loeb Lehman Brothers International, Lazard Freres et Cie., S.G. Warburg & Co., Ltd., One William Street, New York, New York, 10004 (92 pp.).

Market Profile— INDONESIA

Economic Overview

The world recession, the oil glut and OPEC production cutbacks have forced the Indonesian Government to reevaluate its goals for economic growth. Gross domestic product in 1981 was $86 billion, which represents a real growth of 8 percent. Per capita income was $480.

Major Developments

Various development projects are at different stages of planning in Indonesia, including the 500 MW Cirata hydroelectric project in West Java, 39 diesel power plants of 5 and 6 MW at 12 different sites, an aromatics complex at Plaju in South Sumatra, an ammonia/urea complex in Kalimantan, a $1 billion joint venture to build an olefins plant in Northern Sumatra, 2 large fossil fuel power generation complexes on Java, 18 new sugar mill plants and refurbishing of 27 existing mills, the Cilacap integrated kraft paper plant in Central Java, the $700 million Sesayap pulp mill project, and construction of low cost prefabricated and modular housing.

Foreign Trade

Best U.S. Sales Prospects. — Agricultural products, chemicals, machinery and transport equipment, machine tools, energy systems, medical equipment, telecommunications equipment, and engineering and construction services.
Major Suppliers (1981). — Japan (32 percent), United States (13 percent), and Singapore (17 percent).
Principal Exports. — Petroleum, timber, rubber, LNG, coffee, tin, fish, spices and palm products.
Major Markets (1981). — Japan (46 percent), United States (20 percent), and Singapore (13 percent).

Finance

Currency. — As of October 1982, US$1=676 rupiahs.
Domestic Credit. — Banking system consists of central bank (Bank of Indonesia); state, private and foreign banks; development banks and other financial institutions. Both domestic and international credit ratings are strong.
National Budget. — Estimated FY 1981-82 national budget $22.2 billion, of which $12 billion for routine expenditures and $10.2 for development expenditures. Domestic revenues $19.6 billion, external development receipts $2.6 billion.
Balance of Payments. — Official foreign exchange reserves are $6.7 billion, plus $3.5 billion in reserves in commercial banks on which the current Government of Indonesia (GOI) can call: Balance of payments (current account) registered an estimated deficit of $1.5 billion for FY 1981-82, compared with a slight surplus of $887 million in FY 1980-81. The decline is attributed to large declines in non-oil export earnings, particularly in coffee, rubber, timber, and palm oil.

Foreign Investment

The GOI views foreign investment as a vehicle for strengthening domestic technological and management capabilities. The United States is the largest foreign investor in the large oil and gas sector. During the past 6 years, U.S. oil companies accounted for 90 percent of $7 billion spent for oil and gas exploration and development in Indonesia. The largest foreign investor in Indonesia's non-oil sector is Japan, followed by Hong Kong, the Netherlands, and India. The value of approved applications in this sector increased 34 percent in 1981 from $614 million in 1980 ($99 million or 16.2 percent by U.S. firms); and the largest share of foreign capital went to chemicals ($328 million), metal industry ($143 million), and the forestry sector ($140 million).

Basic Economic Facilities

Transportation. — Marine transport services link the islands and form major trunk system. Roads and railways provide secondary system. Indonesia has an extensive port system of about 300 registered ports, a modest shipping fleet, and an Indonesian flag-carrying airline, the largest air carrier in a rapidly expanding air transport system.
Communications. — Telecommunications facilities have improved substantially through domestic satellite system. Current communications projects include expansion of a satellite program, telex and telegram projects, and a project for telephone exchanges. Radio, television, postal, and express delivery services are all being expanded.
Power. — Power capacity estimated at 3,909 megawatts (public 2,209 megawatts, industrial and private 1,700 megawatts). Hydroelectric, diesel, nuclear, and fossil fuel projects underway.

Natural Resources

Land. — Indonesia's seven major island groups span 3,000 miles of equatorial South East Asia (782, 700 square miles).
Minerals. — Indonesia has considerable resources in oil and gas, tin, rubber, copper, timber, palm oil, and coffee. These resources, especially oil and gas, and the country's position between the Indian and Pacific Oceans, make our relations with Indonesia of strategic and economic significance.
Forestry. — Timber is a major export. More than 60 percent of land is forested.

Population

Size. — Indonesia has a population of 155 million (1981), of which over 60 percent is on Java. Annual growth reduced to 2 percent through family planning program.
Labor Force. — 56 million (1979), of whom about 2 percent unemployed and 35-40 percent underemployed.
Education. — Adult literacy rate about 62 percent; primary school enrollment 86 percent.
Language. — Bahasa Indonesia, official. English second language, used in business circles.

Import-Export Trade*
(millions of U.S. dollars)

	1979	1980	1981
Total Imports (c.i.f.)	7,202.3	10,834.4	13,267.0
Imports from the U.S.	1,027.8	1,409.2	1,794.3
Manufactured goods	465.4	581.4	393.1
Agricultural goods	142.3	192.1	167.2
Other	420.1	635.7	123.4
Total Exports (f.o.b.)	15,590.1	21,908.9	22,260.3
Exports to the U.S.	3,170.2	4,303.3	4,083.1
Petroleum	2,540.2	3,570.1	3,517.2
Agricultural goods	569.1	667.2	451.2
Other	60.9	66.0	114.7

*Based on Indonesian data.

Principal Imports from the U.S. in 1981*
(millions of U.S. dollars)

	Value	Percent of Total
Grains	130.3	10
Cotton yarns, fibers	92.1	7
Elevators, wenches	89.7	7
Oil-bearing vegetable materials	86.7	7
Synthetic resins	75.8	6
Fertilizers	55.2	4
Aircraft and space craft	53.4	4
Motor vehicles	52.1	4
Milled grains	49.2	4
Boilers, engines	44.8	4
Total	1,260.5	

*Based on U.S. data.

Market Profile—IRAN

In mid-1979 Iran's economy was still suffering the aftereffects of the revolutionary turmoil which ushered in the Islamic Republic during February 1979. Due to the civil disturbances and change in government, hard statistical information on the Iranian economy is not available. Where possible in this Market Profile, levels of change are given; however, these statistics should be used with caution as all are estimates.

Foreign Trade

Imports (non-military).—$11–$12 billion, 1978–79 (year ending March 20); $14.6 billion, 1977–78. Major suppliers (1977–78): West Germany, 19 percent; United States, 16 percent; Japan, 15 percent; United Kingdom and Italy, 6 percent each. Major imports (1977–78): industrial and agricultural machinery, automotive equipment, industrial raw materials, electrical apparatus, precision instruments, agricultural commodities.

Exports.—$18.4 billion, 1977–78; $20.1 billion, 1976–77. Could reach $21 billion in 1979–80. Oil accounts for more than 95 percent of export value. Other exports: handwoven carpets, cotton, knit goods, hides and skins, lead and zinc ore, currants, pistachio nuts, buses, detergents, aluminum, shoes, caviar. Natural gas piped to U.S.S.R.

Trade Policy.—Import regulations reflect Islamic prohibitions and an autarkic philosophy. For example, vehicle imports are prohibited. Most exporters desire a confirmed letter of credit, and most Iranian banks ask for 100 percent prior deposit. Iranian exporters must agree in advance to sell foreign exchange proceeds to the banking system.

Trade Prospects.—Sales of necessities, including food, pharmaceuticals, paper products and spares, have the most potential. Some government contracts with foreign firms have been canceled, a few have been reconfirmed and a good number remain in suspense. In cases where renegotiation has occurred, downward modifications have occurred in the scale of the project, unit labor costs and expatriate participation.

Foreign Investment

End of 1977 the book value of U.S. private direct investment (excluding oil industry) was about $217 million. Investment prospects remain uncertain.

Finance

Currency.—The Central Bank has a two-tier exchange rate. Officially sanctioned exchanged needs sold at US$1=Iranian Rials 70.60 and other exchange purchases at US$1=IRIs 79.00.

Domestic Credit.—The banking system was reasonably operational in June 1979. The health of the banks was uneven prior to the June 7 nationalization. The foreign exchange market was particularly chaotic, with Central Bank regulations changed almost completely on May 5 and revised often since then. Continuing postponement of domestic and private debt repayment to banks is expected. U.S. banks, with direct outstandings of about $3 billion in early 1979 are slowly reducing exposure. The issue of compensation to private shareholders has not been determined, but the Government has espoused the compensation principle.

Reserves.—Official foreign exchange, mid–June 1979, was a little more than $10 billion.

Economy

Gross National Product.—1978–79 estimate, $70 billion; down 8 percent from previous fiscal year. Per capita GNP $1,988, down 10 percent.

Petroleum.—Iran was world's fourth largest producer after United States, USSR, and Saudi Arabia. Production in June 1979 averaging 4 million barrels/day, almost 40 percent below the level of last year.

Agriculture.—Negative growth in 1978–79. Somewhat favorable prospects for wheat production (5.4 million metric tons); negative prospects for soya, dairy, meat, rice and other production. Major crops: wheat, barley, rice, sugar, beets and cane, cotton, tobacco, nuts, dates.

Industries and Mines.—Food and pharmaceutical industries operating near normal. Most industries operating at about 40 percent of capacity. Major industries: petrochemicals and fertilizers, textiles, foodstuffs, glass, cement, steel, aluminum, motor vehicles, vehicles, tractors, tires, appliances, detergents, tobacco, matches, pharmaceuticals, footwear, paper, plastic products. Lead, zinc, chromite being mined.

Budget.—1978–79 budget (proposed): expenditures $31.8 billion, of which $11.3 billion is for capital expenditures and the balance for current and miscellaneous activities. Stresses agriculture, rural development, housing.

Basic Economic Facilities

Infrastructure including water, electricity, telecommunications and post, are essentially sound.

Transportation.—Iran's transport system comprises more than 5,000 kilometers of railways, almost 19,000 kilometers of paved road and 14 major airports. Before the revolution, Iranian seaports handled about 12 million tons of cargo per year.

Communications.—Radio and TV broadcasting in major cities.

Power.—Electricity consumption is growing at 21 percent a year, and should reach 24 billion kWh by 1980. Natural gas will be an important energy source for industrial and household use in Tehran, Isfahan, Tabriz, Shiraz, and other cities.

Natural Resources

Area of Iran is 628,000 sqaure miles, much of it desert and mountain. Abundant rainfall only along Caspian Sea. Good fisheries potential in Caspian and Persian Gulf. In addition to vast reserves of oil (60–80 billion bbls.) and gas (400 trillion cu. ft. or more), Iran has significant deposits of coal, copper, iron, lead, zinc, chromite, gold, and manganese.

Population

35.1 million (1978 estimate), largely concentrated in north and west. Growth rate 2.6 percent Tehran's population is more than 4.5 million. More than half of the people live in rural areas where illiteracy is widespread. There is heavy migration to the cities. The official language is Farsi (Persian); the main foreign language is English. Shiite sect of Islam professed by 90 percent of population; another 8 percent are Sunnite Moslems; males make up 85 percent of labor force. Unemployment is high.

CAUTION: Major governmental shifts have occurred in this country since this report was made, and some of the above information may no longer apply. A direct inquiry to the International Trade Administration of the U.S. Department of Commerce is advised for those requiring the most current data available. The Administration is headquartered in Washington D.C., and maintains field offices in principal cities of the U.S.

BOUNDARY REPRESENTATION IS
NOT NECESSARILY AUTHORITATIVE

Iran

— International boundary
⊙ National capital
‑‑‑ Railroad
‑‑‑ Road
✚ International airport

0   50   100   150 Miles

0   50   100 150 Kilometers

Market Profile—IRAQ

Foreign Trade

Imports.—$5.5 billion, 1979; $4.2 billion, 1978. Major suppliers are Japan, 17.6 percent; West Germany, 12.6 percent; United States, 4.9 percent. Soviet Union most important trading partner if military sales are included. Principal imports: construction equipment, machinery, motor vehicles, agricultural commodities.

Exports.—$16 billion 1979; $11 billion 1978. Crude oil accounts for 99 percent of total exports, with about 60 percent going to industrial countries. Major customers 1979: France, 16.1 percent; Italy, 13.8 percent; Brazil, 9.3 percent; Japan, 8.6 percent; United States, 3.2 percent.

Trade Policy.—90 percent of imports purchased by state organizations; licenses and exchange permits required for private sector imports. Use of agents restricted, and contracts with private sector agents must be registered with the Government.

Trade Prospects.—Agricultural products and equipment; building supplies and equipment; health care equipment; communications equipment; plastics, rubber and chemical equipment; production process control instrumentation; computers and business equipment; metal-working equipment; food processing and packaging equipment.

Foreign Investment

Foreign equity investment not desired. Technology transfers acquired through service contracts, turnkey contracts, and licensing agreements.

Finance

Currency.—Iraqi dinar (ID) divided into 1,000 fils; 1 ID=$3.38; $1=ID.295. Inflation 18–20 percent annually.

Domestic Credit and Investment.—All banks nationalized; all commercial transactions handled by Rafidain Bank. Other banks: Central Bank, Cooperative Agricultural Bank, Industrial Bank.

National Budget.—$48 billion 1980; estimated $28.5 billion 1979; In 1980 budget, $12.5 billion covers revenue and expenditures for Government, almost $18 billion to development projects, and almost $18 billion for public sector organizations.

Balance of Payments.—Surplus on current account, due chiefly to oil income. Foreign exchange reserves estimated at $8.5 billion (1980).

Development Plan.—Actual expenditures over 1976–80 Five-Year Development Plan period estimated at $30 billion. Assigns priority to agricultural development, housing and social services, and infrastructure. Plan has not met expected goals because of infrastructure bottlenecks and manpower shortages. The plan for 1981–85 will have same emphasis.

Economy

Goal to have modern, independent socialist economy based on oil, industry, and agriculture. Success has been mixed due to problems in assets, planning, and implementation. Long-term outlook is good because of conservative approach to development and plentiful reserves of cash and natural resources. Within 20 years, Iraq may develop into one of the region's major economic powers.

GDP.—Estimated $30 billion 1979; $23 billion 1978. Third largest oil producer in Middle East. Economy largely socialist except for private sector activity in agriculture, construction, light industry, and tourism.

Agriculture.—Potentially self-sufficient in basic foodstuffs but still large net importer of food. About 30 million acres cultivable with about 7 million acres cultivated in any year. Approximately half the cultivated land irrigated but percentage increasing. Major crops: wheat, barley, rice, cotton. World's largest date producer. Major projects underway in irrigation and land reclamation; plans eventually to be a food exporter.

Industry.—Most industry based on exploitation of local materials and import substitution; 75 percent government owned. Industrial development keyed to petroleum sector. Major industries include petroleum refining, textiles, food processing, cement, petrochemicals, paper, glass, vehicle assembly, iron and steel, and various light manufacturing. Large projects in petrochemicals, metalworking.

Basic Economic Facilities

Transportation.—1,462 miles of railroad, all government owned. Major ports: Basra, Umm Qasr, Khor Al-Zubair and Al-Fao. Rapid expansion of port, road, and rail systems underway.

Communications.—Telephone system generally satisfactory but limited to major cities. Introducing electronic telephone exchanges. All communications media owned or controlled by Government.

Natural Resources

Land.—170,000 square miles. Large desert areas, particularly in west of country, broad fertile valley between Tigris and Euphrates rivers, mountains in Northeast; marshes in south coastal area.

Climate.—In lowlands; dry, very hot summers and relatively cool, humid winters, little rainfall. Northeast mountains cooler, with sufficient rainfall for some crops.

Minerals.—Proven petroleum reserves 35 billion barrels, but estimates run as high as 100 billion barrels, crude oil production averaged 3 million barrels per day in 1979. Sulfur and phosphates also produced. Has deposits of iron, chromite, copper, lead, limestone, gypsum, salt and dolomite.

Population

Size.—1980 estimate, over 13 million, almost two-thirds urban, almost half below age 14. Growth rate 3.3 percent. Baghdad, the capital, has about 3 million people. Other large cities are Mosul, Basra, Kirkuk.

Education.—Free. Ordinarily compulsory for all children 6–12 years. Literacy estimated at 45 percent. Enrollment in universities, technical institutes, and vocational training increasing rapidly since early 1960s.

Labor.—Estimated labor force 3.2 million; 53 percent in agriculture, 15–20 percent in industry. Manpower shortage must be filled with imported labor. Attempting to develop the female labor force.

Almost 75% of Iraq's population live in the flat, alluvial plain stretching from north of Baghdad past Basra to the Persian Gulf. The Tigris and Euphrates Rivers, which irrigate the area, carry about 70 million cubic meters of silt annually to the delta. The legendary locale of the Garden of Eden, the region also contains the ruins of Ur, Babylon, and other ancient cities.

The mountains in the northeast are an extension of the Alpine system that runs southeast through the Balkans, the Taurus Mountains of southern Turkey, northern Iraq, and Iran, and into Afganistan, finally ending in the Himalayas.

1246

Marketing in Ireland

Contents

Report Revised May 1978

Economic Trends

Ireland's economic climate today is almost the reverse of that of a year ago. In terms of economic performance, Ireland has climbed dramatically from the bottom rungs of the European Community tables to the top of the growth charts. GNP, which grew by 3.5 percent in real terms in 1976, was at 5.2 percent in 1977, led by a healthy increase in industrial production and a sharp rise in manufactured exports. Inflation, at 18 percent in 1976, was reduced to 10 percent in 1977. Unemployment, at 11 percent in 1976, remains a tough problem, but has been reduced to 10 percent. Anticipating a GNP growth rate of 7 percent in 1978, the present Irish Government, which came to power last June, aims at stimulating the private sector through tax cuts and tax concessions to raise output and manufacturing investment. Although the Government had hoped to hold wage expansion in 1978 to 5 percent in this year's national wage agreement, the present outlook is closer to 8 percent. Labor stability remains a concern, as strikes in the public sector are presently running at five times the rate in the private sector—leading the Government to recognize that much of its optimistic program will depend on reaching agreement with the unions.

Foreign Trade and Export Opportunities

U.S.-Irish Trade

U.S. exports to Ireland in 1976 amounted to $339 million, while imports from Ireland totaled $219 million, leaving a trade surplus in the U.S. favor of $120 million. In January-July 1977, U.S. exports to Ireland rose to $299 million while imports during the same period reached $136 million, leaving the United States with a trade surplus for the 7-month period of $161 million. The U.S. share of total Irish imports rose from 8.3 percent in 1976 to 10 percent in January-July 1977. U.S. exports to Ireland consisted mainly of nonelectric and electrical machinery and goods, unmilled corn, oilseed cake, meal and residues, and textile yarn and fabrics. U.S. imports from Ireland were mostly frozen beef, medicinal and pharmaceutical products, sugar preparations, tobacco products, clothing, alcoholic beverages, glassware, machinery and electronic equipment.

Export Opportunities for U.S. Products

The expanding growth of the Irish economy has stimulated a significant rise in Irish imports in all categories: finished consumer goods, producer's capital goods, and raw and partly processed goods. The general manager of Dublin's largest department store believes there is a good market for American consumer products in Ireland, especially sporting goods. Other American-made consumer products that would seem likely to find a good market in Ireland include made-up garments and other textile products, washing machines and other electro-mechanical household appliances, pleasure boats, phonograph records and hand tools.

On the industrial side, newly established firms will be importing capital equipment, especially machinery of all types, and raw materials, notably chemicals. In the longer range, the

---

HOW TO OBTAIN BACKGROUND INFORMATION ABOUT THESE COUNTRIES

For those who wish *general* data about a country—data which goes beyond marketing and commerce—the editors recommend *Countries of the World and Their Leaders*, published as an annually updated yearbook by Gale Research Company, Detroit, Michigan 48226. Containing 4- to 20-page entries on 168 countries, the volume also provides several hundred pages of supplementary world data. Each report provides some historical insight as well as a look at contemporary trends of lifestyle in the country. Reports also discuss a country's educational system, its press, ethnic groupings and religious practices.

NEW TO EXPORT?

Many basic questions about export and overseas marketing are answered by material which appears at the end of the country-by-country market studies. Three of the information packages appearing there for the benefit of the new exporter are:

* **Basic guide to export marketing.**
* **East-west trade financing.**
* **Metric laws and practices in international trade.**

Check the table of contents for page numbers of these and other special reports.

State-owned surface transportation monopoly Coras Iompair Eireann (CIE) is giving serious consideration to electrification of Irish railways. All its diesel locomotives were purchased from an American company. CIE has also started preliminary studies on a possible Dublic subway system. The state-sponsored fertilizer company, Nitrogen Eireann Teoranta, has announced plans to build a $50 million plant for processing ammonia from natural gas or naphtha in the Cork harbor area. Increased prices for Moroccan phosphates may provide U.S. phosphate producers with an opportunity to sell in Ireland. In the energy field, the Government appears ready to proceed with construction of a nuclear generation plant. Irish Oil Co., Ltd., has announced plans to construct a $180 million oil refinery and terminal near Bantry, County Cork. Recent international loans received or under consideration for Ireland should also provide U.S. export opportunities. The World Bank has approved a $25 million loan for livestock development as part of a $56 million government project. The funds are being channeled through the Irish Agricultural Credit Corporation and will be spent on such items as pasture improvement, water facilities, fencing, buildings and silos, and purchases of stock. Significant imports of construction and farm equipment should be involved. The Irish Government is requesting an additional World Bank loan of $25 million for educational facilities and $15 million for the State-sponsored Industrial Credit Company, which assists industrial expansion and reequipment. The European Investment Bank reportedly will channel a significant portion of a $50 million investment into Ireland's inadequate and outmoded telephone system, to develop and augment automatic exchanges, improve the in-

terurban network, and construct automatic telephone booths. Most existing Irish telephone equipment has been supplied by a Swedish firm, but U.S. manufacturers might be able to sell if their equipment is compatible and price is competitive.

Trade Regulations

Ireland became a member of the enlarged European Economic Community (EEC) effective January 1, 1973. This followed the approval of membership by nationwide referendum in May 1972. The enlarged EEC includes the six original EEC members (i.e., Belgium, France, Germany, Italy, Luxembourg, Netherlands), plus Denmark, the United Kingdom and Ireland.

Tariff Structure

Ireland, under the terms of accession, currently applies the EEC's Common External Tariff (CXT) on imported goods and the Common Agricultural Policy (CAP) on selected agricultural commodities and products. The CAP is a protectionist device designed to elevate world prices to the level prevailing in the EEC.

Trade between Ireland and the other member states of the EEC is duty free. Similarly, Ire-

Table 1.—Principal Irish Imports From The United States in 1976

Thousands of Irish pounds[1]

Horses, etc.	312
Wheat & Meslin, Unmilled	3,434
Maize, Unmilled	13,762
Oats, Unmilled	41
Cereals, Unmilled, NES	2,292
Fruit & Vegetables	2,536
Oilseed Cake, Meal & Residues	13,785
Unmanufactured Tobacco	6,049
Textile Fibres & Waste	567
Sulphur	1
Fixed Vegetable Oils & Fats	291
Chemical Elements & Compounds	4,082
Dyeing, Tanning, Coloring Mats	1,206
Medicinal & Pharmaceutical Products	1,727
Essential Oils & Resinoids	597
Potassic Fertilizers, Unmixed	321
Plastic Materials, Etc.	4,158
Chemical Mats. & Products, NES	1,765
Leather, Leather Manufactures & Dressed Furskins	1,337
Rubber Manufactures, NES	1,517
Wood & Cork Manufactures	1,078
Kraft Paper & Paperboard	3,428
Machine-Made Paper & Boards, NES	1,337
Textile Yarn, Fabrics, Etc.	9,329
Nonmetallic Mineral Manufs.	1,040
Iron & Steel	939
Nonferrous Metals	806
Manufactures of Metal, NES	2,929
Machinery (Nonelectric)	56,674
Electric Machinery, Goods, Etc.	21,472
Transport Equipment	7,596
Professional, Scientific, Etc. Goods, Watches & Clocks	5,879
Misc. Manufactured Articles	6,907
Shannon Imports	9,101
Total	199,023

[1] One Irish pounds in 1976 equaled approximately $1.82.

land, together with the other EEC members, under the term of free trade agreements, accords duty-free treatment to virtually all products imported from the former European Free Trade Association countries (Finland, Austria, Norway, Portugal, Iceland, Sweden and Switzerland) but subjects specified agricultural products to the CAP.

Ireland extends preferential duty rates under EEC agreements to imports from Greece, Turkey, Cyprus, Malta, Spain, Algeria, Morocco, Tunisia, Egypt, Israel, Jordon, Lebanon, Syria and several Caribbean and Pacific countries. Under the provisions of the Generalized System of Preferences (GSP), over 100 developing countries receive tariff preferences from Ireland.

Import Regulations

Ireland exercises import licensing controls on a relatively minor number of items.

The Irish importer applies for licenses at the Ministry of Industry and Commerce if the goods are industrial, and at the Ministry of Agriculture and Fisheries for agricultural products. Licenses are valid for varying lengths of time, ranging anywhere from 3 months to a year. Extensions of the time limits are usually easily obtained on application to the issuing agency.

Tires and tubes for bicycles and tricycles imported from the United States are subject to import licensing requirements. In addition, private cars, buses for the carriage of not more than 16 persons (including the driver), commercial vehicles, industrial roadgoing tractors, and bodies and chassis for these vehicles, require licenses if imported by nonregistered persons.

Agricultural items subject to the approval of import licenses issued by the Ministry of Agriculture and Fisheries include: egg albumin, raw apples, broiler chickens and turkeys (live or dead) and parts, butter, cereals and cereal products, wheat, wheat flour, wheatmeal, certain wheat commodities, maize, oats, hay, straw, certain animal feeding stuffs, raw or processed cheese, eggs, egg yolks, certain fish, specified fruit, fruit juice and fruit pulp, bacon and other meats, dried or powdered milk, raw onions, certain seeds, sugar, raw tomatoes, and tobacco seeds and plants.

Entry.—Before removal from the place of importation is permitted, the customs authorities require that necessary formalities be fulfilled. Entry must be accomplished by the importer or the importer's agent within specified time limits with the presentation to the customs official of prescribed documentation, including a declaration of value and the supplier's commercial invoice, either the original or copies certified as true by supplier.

The importer or agent at the time of entry has several options. These include importation for home consumption, transit shipment, storage in bonded warehouses, or use in the free zone at Shannon Airport.

Warehousing.—Imported goods liable to duty may be deposited in bonded warehouses approved for the purpose at certain ports or places. They may remain there until cleared for home consumption on payment of duty, removed under bond to other ports or warehouses, removed for use as ships' stores, or reexported. These warehouses are the property of companies or private individuals who are responsible to the merchant for the goods and to the state for duty. Partial withdrawal of goods from bonded warehouses is permitted upon payment of duty. Goods liable to ad valorem duty may not be manufactured in bonded warehouses but they may be repacked for exportation.

Certain operations are allowed in bonded warehouses under official supervision. Spirits and wines may be vatted, blended, or racked as often as required by the proprietor. Spirits and foreign wines may be bottled in warehouses for exportation or for ships' stores, and spirits that are not inadmissible may be bottled for home consumption. Dry goods (such as coffee, cocoa, sugar, and tea) that are liable to specific duties may be repacked in bonded warehouses. Further operations, such as bulking, sorting, and blending, also are allowed.

Facilities for the importation and warehousing of tobacco are afforded at Dublin, Cork, Dundalk, and Limerick. Drying, garbling, and butting warehouses are allowed. Unmanufactured tobacco may be manufactured into cavendish or negrohead in a warehouse approved for the purpose, and facilities are granted for cutting, packing, etc., for ships' stores, or for home consumption as well as the making of cigars or cigarettes for exportation or for ships' stores.

Goods may be deposited in general bonded warehouses without payment of duty and subsequently reexported under conditions similar to those governing transit shipments through the country. Goods also may be imported for further manufacture without actual payment of duty on such conditions as will ensure the payment of duty in the event of failure to reexport.

Free Trading Areas.—The customs free airport at Shannon is Ireland's only free port. The airport is excluded from the scope of all laws, with a few exceptions, relating to the importation or exportation of goods between the free airport and foreign countries. Among the restrictions which remain in force are those relating to public health, animal and plant diseases, currency, dangerous drugs, and used clothing.

Goods stored in the free zone are exempt from examination. Processing, sorting, grading, or repacking may take place within its boundaries, and buildings required may be erected by interested persons or concerns, or leased from the state. There are no customs free seaports in Ireland.

Refund of Duty.—Refunds will be made in certain cases. These include such instances as when the buyer returns to the seller, with the seller's consent, goods that were entered and found to be damaged in transit or not in accordance with the contract of sale and when overpayment is made because of incorrect tariff classification or valuation.

Drawback.—Total repayment is made of all duties and taxes paid on imported goods from non-EEC countries that are reexported in the same condition or after having undergone repair, processing or manufacture.

Samples and Advertising Matter

The Republic of Ireland and the United States, among others, are contracting parties to the Internal Convention to Facilitate the Importation of Commercial Samples and Advertising Matter. Based on the provisions of that Convention, commercial samples of negligible value under certain conditions are admitted duty and tax free. Other types of commercial samples can be entered temporarily by individuals who post a bond or cash deposit (cancelled or refunded on reexportation) with the customs authorities to cover the payment of the customs charges or who obtain waivers of duty from the Department of Industry and Commerce and taxes from the Revenue Commissioners. Customs charges are levied at the same rate as on commercial shipments when commercial samples are not reexported.

The United States and other countries, including Ireland, are contracting parties to other conventions that help facilitate the temporary importation of commercial samples and goods. These conventions are entitled "Customs Convention Regarding the E.C.S. (Echantillons Commerciaux-Commercial Samples) Carnet for the Temporary Admission of Commercial Samples" and "Customs Convention on the A.T.A. (Admission Temporaire — Temporary Admission) Carnet for the Temporary Admission of Goods."

Carnets are obtainable for most goods from authorized chambers of commerce in participating countries. However, in the United States, only the A.T.A. carnet is being issued, since it can perform the same function as the E.C.S. carnet. U.S. firms desiring the A.T.A. carnet should secure an application from the United States Council of the International Chamber of Commerce, 1212 Avenue of the Americas, New York, New York 10038 (telephone 212-354-4480). The minimum fee charged is $50 per carnet for merchandise valued up to $499.99. The maximum is $150 for merchandise over $20,000 in value.

Trade catalogs are exempt from import duty. Price lists and trade notices, according to the provisions of the International Convention to Facilitate the Importation of Commercial Samples and Advertising Material, are admitted duty and tax free into Ireland under specified conditions. The catalogs must concern transport or commercial services or goods offered for sale or hire by a person established in the United States or other contracting countries. Each consignment imported into Ireland may consist of not more than one copy of any one document, and not exceed 1 kilogram in gross weight.

Internal Taxes

On imports, the value added tax is levied on the c.i.f. duty-paid value. For the rates, see the section on "taxation."

Advance Rulings on Classifications

Advisory rulings as to the customs classification of particular goods will be supplied in advance of shipment upon application to the Revenue Commissioners in Dublin. This may be done either by the exporter or his agent in Ireland or by the intended importer. A full description of the goods, and where practicable, samples or illustrations should be forwarded with the application. Final or definite rulings as to the amount of duty payable on any goods will not be given in advance of the actual arrival of the shipment.

Fines and Penalties

The extent to which violators of the Irish customs laws may be punished depends on the nature of the infraction. For concealment of goods or falsification of documents to avoid payment of import duty, the consequences may be stiff fines and forefeiture of the goods. In more serious offenses, violations of criminal law may be involved. Convictions may result in the imposition of much more severe penalties than those under the customs law.

Shipping Documents

Consular certification of shipping documents is not required. For ocean freight, air freight, and parcel post shipments, a minimum of two commercial invoices must be sent to the Irish importer. Ordinary kinds are acceptable. They need not be certified by local chambers of commerce or associations. These documents should contain all the necessary details, including country of origin and terms of shipment (f.o.b., c.i.f., etc.), to enable customs to properly assess import duties and applicable additional taxes. In addition, the supplier must certify on all invoices that they are original or true copies and whether or not all charges to the port of entry, such as freight costs, packing and insurance are reflected in the invoices. In the case of textile consignments, the invoices should indicate such particularity as use, proportionate composition, width, number of square yards, net weight, and whether woven, knitted, or of other construction, or made of discontinuous or continuous manmade fiber.

On shipments from the United States of madeira wine, raw and scoured wool, and certain textile yarns, made-up articles and piece goods, two certificates of origin on Irish official forms must be completed and certified by local chambers of commerce or associations. They usually require one additional copy for their records.

Special documentary requirements are specified in various Irish sanitary and plant quarantine regulations. In such instances, the necessary documents should be obtained from the U.S. Department of Agriculture or other Government agencies.

Marking and Labeling Requirements

No general requirement that imports be marked with country of origin notice is specified in the Merchandise Marks Act, 1887, as amended. Imported goods that do not bear or have applied to them any infringing names or marks whatsoever either on the goods directly or on the coverings, wrappers, labels, etc., are not required to bear an indication of origin.

Senate Concurrent Resolution 40, adopted July 30, 1953, invites U.S. exporters to inscribe, insofar as practicable, on the external shipping containers in indelible print of a suitable size: "United States of America." Although such marking is not compulsory under our laws, U.S. shippers are urged to cooperate in thus publicizing American-made goods.

Considered as an infraction of law is any false or misleading description, statement or other indication, direct or indirect, regarding such matters as weight, number, quantity, composition, method and place of manufacture, trademark, patent and copyright, as well as the use of any figure, word, or mark to indicate the preceding.

Certain new furniture and component parts, made wholly or mainly of wood, must be permanently marked with an indication of the country of origin in both the Irish and English languages. Also requiring country of origin marking in Irish and English are ceramics, tableware, and certain other ceramic articles used for domestic or toilet purposes, vitreous enameled ware, plumbers brassfounding and compression couplings, men's and boy's outer garments, electric kettles, aluminum holloware, hosiery, carpets, footwear, knitted and crocheted clothing, jewelry and lead acid batteries.

Exchange Controls

Exchange controls are under the jurisdiction of the Irish Central Bank, which delegates much of its authority to commercial banks. The Central Bank's prior permission must be obtained for ordering goods originating outside the Sterling Area that are to be delivered later than 9 months after the order date or are not to be consumed in Ireland.

Special approval is required for payments exceeding L2,000 to non-Sterling Area members. Importers are required to support with appropriate documents their requests for the allocation of foreign exchange or permission to credit Irish currency or sterling abroad. For permissiole imports, the Irish exchange authorities usually approve reasonable requests automatically.

Export Controls

Ireland has maintained a system of quantitative controls on exports since the beginning of World War II. The export control system is intended to prevent the exportation of items in short supply, to stop reexportation of goods that have been paid for in dollars, and to control the exportation of strategic goods.

Under the export control regulations, certain items in short supply are prohibited exportation to any destination except under licenses issued by the proper Government authorities. Certain other items in short supply or of a strategic nature are prohibited exportation to any destination other than the United Kingdom, except under license.

Applications for licenses must be made by the exporter in writing to the authority charged with the control of the particular export, viz., the Minister for Industry and Commerce for industrial items, the Minister for Agriculture and Fisheries for agricultural products, etc. Each application is considered on its own merits in relation to the ministerial policy in force at the time.

Distribution and Sales Channels

Marketing Areas

The population of Ireland is primarily rural, over half of the population lives on isolated farms or in villages having a population of 1,500 or less. The per capita income in 1976 was estimated at $2,444. This somewhat understates the purchasing power of the more economically significant sections of the country, however, which may be compared roughly to that of Great Britain outside the London area.

The primary marketing segments of the Irish Republic consist of the Dublin, Cork and Limerick metropolitan areas. These three cities and environs account for approximately one-third of Ireland's population. Spaced from 60 to 160 miles apart, Dublin, Cork, and Limerick form a triangle touching three sides of the southern part of the Republic. This includes some of Ireland's most fertile agricultural area. Dublin is at the apex of this triangle, and serving as a natural funnel through which goods flow into it and the rest of Ireland. With a population in excess of 735,000 people greater Dublin is the political, industrial, shipping, and commercial center.

The port of Dublin handles more tonnage than any other in the Republic and contributes importantly to the city's preeminence. Most of Ireland's large purchasing organizations—its wholesalers, retail buying co-ops and department stores—have their headquarters here. In addition, it is the most important manufacturing center. Automobile assembly plants, textile factories, distillers, brewers, food processing, electronic and light manufacturing firms are all located here. For most products, Dublin is the logical starting place in any marketing program aimed at the Irish market.

The second most important business center is Cork (population 217,000, including County Cork). It is a major port and serves as a gateway to southern Ireland through which a great quantity of merchandise for other centers flows. Automobile assembly, shipbuilding, steel making, pertoleum refining, rubber and plastic goods, textiles, distilling, chemical and food processing are among the many industries in the Cork area. Ford, Dunlop, Pfizer, Gulf Oil and Parke Davis are among the plants located near Cork.

The third most important business and commercial center is Limerick (population 82,000 including Limerick County). The city is built on the Shannon River, some 60 miles from the Atlantic and 18 miles above the Shannon estuary. The modern port of Limerick can handle ships up to 10,000 tons deadweight. Food processing, tanning, milling, and furniture manufacturing are Limerick's principal industries. Perhaps even more important, the city lies only 15 miles from the Shannon Free Port and Industrial Estate, which is fast becoming Ireland's most important single export-producing center. Situated near both a sea port and the most important air terminal (Shannon), as well as lying astride the meeting place of roads and railways that link the south and west provinces, Limerick is a natural distributing center for the Irish hinterlands.

Other important market areas include Waterford, a shipping center on the south coast between Dublin and Cork and the home of Waterford glass (population 43,000, including Waterford County) ; Galway, an important tourist center in the west (population 148,000 including Galway County) ; and Dundalk in County Louth, some 50 miles north of Dublin (population 69,000 for the county, which also includes Drogheda between Dublin and Dundalk).

Distribution Methods

A wide range of marketing methods is available in Ireland to American exporters. For American firms that do not establish subsidiaries or branch offices, the most common method of selling is through an agent or distributor. The Embassy in Dublin has in its files the names of more than 1,000 such agents, all representing American firms (and, in most cases, Irish and European firms as well), all interested in expanding their lines and doing more business.

The normal practice of American firms selling in Ireland is to appoint an exclusive agent or representative to cover the entire country. Where local inventories are not maintained, as is the usual practice with commission agents, the marketing area can conveniently be expanded to cover the six counties of northern Ireland as well (population, over 1.4 million), thus susbtantially increasing the market potential. As indicated, Irish agents often represent several different product lines. Occasionally this may lead to conflict of interest, and American exporters should avoid commissioning agents who handle directly competing lines.

The intimate nature of Irish society and the very personalized relationships that characterize Irish business dealings make it desirable for American exporters to develop close personal contacts with Irish agents. Manufacturers seeking an agent should plan to visit Ireland. This will not only provide them with first-hand information but will enable them to judge and choose more wisely from among prospective agents. Finally, it will enable them to build the personal rapport so essential to successful business relationships in Ireland.

Exporters of consumer goods and other items that require maintenance of locally held stocks generally sell through established wholesalers. There are 2,495 wholesale outlets in the Republic of Ireland covering a wide range of products. If demand justifies the carrying of local stocks, an American exporter should find little difficulty in finding a suitable wholesaler. For certain types of products, Aemrican manufacturers may find it advantageous to sell directly to department stores—especially where they also function as wholesalers to smaller outlets in rural areas and consumer cooperatives.

Wholesale and Retail Channels

According to the latest census, there were 33,850 retail and 2,495 wholesale outlets in the Irish Republic. The various classes and number of these establishments are listed below. Examination of this list indicates that the Irish distribution system, especially at the retail level, still consists of large numbers of small, frequently family, units. Of some 9,642 grocery stores in Ireland, for example, only about 50 could be classified as supermarkets, of which there are perhaps six chains. Even among chain supermarkets, volume tends to be small by American standards. Nevertheless, 10 years prior there were 40,900 retail outlets, which clearly demonstrates that the transformation of Ireland's distributive system into larger, more economically viable units is well underway.

Table 2.—Irish Retail and Wholesale Outlets

Retail Outlets

Type of Outlet	Number
FOOD, DRINK, TOBACCO	
Grocery (including supermarkets)	9,642
Grocery with bars	2,346
Public Bars	6,395
Wines and Spirits (not bars)	61
Fresh meat	1,693
Bread and other confectionery	433
Dairy products	72
Fish and poultry	115
Fruit and vegetables	320
Country general shop	87
Tobacco, sweets, and newspapers	2,581
CLOTHING AND FOOTWEAR	
Footwear	454
Men's and boys' wear	480
Ladies', girls' and infants' wear	807
General drapery	1,220
VEHICLES	
Cycle shop	202
Gas station	965
Repair and service garage	800
Vehicle sales	504
ALL OTHER NONFOOD	
Chemist	1,093
Hardware	766
Electrical goods	662
Electrical goods shop with repairs	97
Furniture and carpets	395
General stores (nonfood)	39
Department stores	17
Variety stores	32
Leather, sports and fancy goods	368
Books and stationery	198
Jewelry	319
Solid fuel	187
All other nonfood	500
Total	33,850

Wholesale Outlets

Grocery	218
Tea, sugar, coffee	13
Fruit and vegetables	79
Eggs and poultry	30
Other food	143
Wines and spirits	93
Clothing, textiles and footwear	117
Wool, skins and leather	29
Builders' materials	247
Hardware and electrical goods	98
Chemists' wares, photographic and optical goods	47
Motor vehicles, nonagricultural machinery and accessories	102
Agricultural machinery (including tractors)	116
Petroleum products	104
Grain, forage and fertilizers	583
Paper, stationery, books, etc.	52
All other Nonfood	424
Total	2,495

One of the predictable consequences of this transformation has been that surviving retailers, particularly in the grocery trades, increasingly have tended to cluster around and depend upon grocers associations. There are primarily three—SPAR, VG and Mace—all Irish organizations of their larger European counterparts. In addition, a large number of small cash-and-carry wholesale distributors cater to the very small family grocery stores. A result of the highly fractured structure of the Irish distributive system has been to add another link to its chain. Many goods move in the first instance from a foreign manufacturer to an Irish agent or importer, then to a wholesaler and finally to a retailer.

The markup system ranges widely, from as low as 5 percent to as high as 50 percent. In the hardware trade the rates vary according to product from 15 percent to 20 percent; novelty goods range from 33 percent to 50 percent, all based on wholesale prices. The markup in the grocery trade also varies but, on an average, yields a gross profit of 12 percent on retail sales. In the clothing and jewelry trades the markup is 50 percent. The average markup on wholesale prices is reported to be about 12½ percent. Table 2 shows a breakdown of wholesale and retail outlets in Ireland.

Government Procurement

There is no central government purchasing agency in Ireland. Most government departments have their own contracting sections. The volume of their individual purchases tends to be small except for departments listed below:

Department of Defense, Parkgate, Dublin 8
Office of Public Works, 51 St. Stephen's Green, Dublin 2 (responsible for all government property).
Department of Health, Custom House, Dublin 1.
Department of Posts and Telegraphs, Hawkins House, Hawkins Street, Dublin 2.
Aer Lingue/Irish International Airlines, Dublin Airport, Dublin.
Aer Rianta, Dublin Airport, Dublin.
Waterford Corporation, City Hall, Waterford.
Limerick Corporation, City Hall, Limerick.
Galway Corporation, City Hall, Galway.
Electricity Supply Board, 27 Lower Fitzwilliam Street, Dublin 2.
Coras Iompair Eireann, Heuston Station, Dublin.

Dublin Corporation, City Hall, Dublin.
Cork Corporation, City Hall, Cork.

Government-sponsored bodies also purchase independently, as do municipal authorities. Purchases are generally made on the basis of tenders. It is not necessary to appoint an Irish agent in order to sell to the Government.

The principal Government and State-sponsored agencies purchasing abroad are the Department of Posts and Telegraphs, the Electricity Supply Board, Aer Lingus/Irish International Airlines, Coras Iompair Eirann (transport monopoly), and Aer Rianta (airport management). The Irish Department of Defense (about 8,000 troops) operates on a small budget and purchases very little abroad. Irish policy is to buy Irish-made goods whenever possible.

There are two types of procurement procedures that apply in Ireland. Under the selective tender, bids are invited from both Irish and foreign sources specifically known to be interested and which would be able to supply the item. The second method of procurement is by public tender. This procedure requires that the invitations to tender be advertised and is generally done to ensure competition.

Ireland has only a few standards of its own. The result is that British standards are usually adhered to, sometimes to the disadvantage of American suppliers. Foreign exporters interested in selling in Ireland may register with the contracts section of Government departments and State-sponsored organizations. The Embassy in Dublin is registered with the more important of these agencies, however, and regularly advertises significant requests for bids in the trade opportunities section of the official Department of Commerce biweekly magazine, *Commerce America*. The ability of the seller to provide or arrange credit for large sales is frequently a consideration.

Transportation and Utilities

Selling in Ireland is facilitated by good transportation facilities between the United States and the Republic. Several shipping lines, including the American flag United States Line, maintain regular freight service. Direct air service is also available between the United States and Ireland. Pan American Airways, Trans World Airlines, and Seaboard World Airlines are some of the direct service carriers. Transportation services within Ireland are very good.

Railroads.—The State-owned railroad system provides efficient freight service between all major cities and towns. Ireland in recent years has greatly improved and expanded its rolling stock, with almost a complete changeover to diesel-powered transportation. As mentioned earlier, consideration is being given to electrification of railways.

Domestic Airlines.—Ireland has three international airports located at Shannon, Dublin, and Cork. Aer Lingus and Aerlinte Eirann, Ireland's major airlines, are Government-owned. Aerliste Eirann operates domestic air services, and cross-channel services to and from the continent of Europe. Aerlinte Eirann, Irish International Airlines, which trades under the name Aer Lingus, operates transatlantic services between Dublin, New York, Boston, Chicago, and Montreal. TWA, Pan American and Seaboard World provide service through Shannon.

Highways.—Road freight is a rapidly growing form of goods movement. The most important road carriers are Coras Iompair Eireann (the Transport Company of Ireland or C.I.E.O., the County Donegal Railways Joint Committee, and the Lough Swilly Railroad Company. In addition to these carriers there are over 950 licensed haulers in Ireland. However, only about 116 licensees are authorized to operate through the whole of Ireland. Names of trucking firms may be obtained from the Licensed Road Transport Association, 58 Durrin Street, Carlow, and the Road Transport Organization, 34 Upper O'Connell St. Dubin 1.

Ports.—Ireland has two major ports, Dublin and Cobh, that serve mainly transatlantic lines. There are also less elaborate port facilities at Cork, Waterford, Limerick, Galway, Drogheda, Dundalk and Sligo.

The Shannon Industrial Estate, a free port area at Shannon Airport, provides the unique combination of a 500-acre customs-free industrial zone and direct access to air transport. Raw materials and partly or completely manufactured products may be imported into the Industrial Estate in any quantity free of duty.

Warehousing.—Adequate warehousing facilities are generally available in major Irish cities. Bonded warehouses are operated at Dublin, Cork, Limerick, Waterford, and Galway. The Dublin Port and Docks Board maintains the largest warehousing organization in the country. Almost all the tea and tobacco consumed in Ireland, and a large proportion of the wines and spirits are warehoused by the Board. In addition to the main service of storage, this department provides additional services including sorting, weighing, blending, gauging, racking, bottling; packing, etc., and has a modern motor transport fleet for collection and delivery of goods warehoused. It is the only warehouse in Ireland maintained by a port authority.

Advertising and Research

A full range of advertising media is available in Ireland, all of it available to American exporters.

Radio and Television Advertising.—Radio and television broadcasting in Ireland are the monopoly of Radio-Telefis Eireann, a State-owned corporation. Telefis Eireann operates from 4 p.m. to 11:30 p.m. each day on one channel; Radio Eireann broadcasts from 7:30 a.m. to 11:30 p.m. on one channel as well. In addition, Irish cable television sets can receive British programs broadcast from Wales and numerous British and continental radio stations. Ninety-two percent of Irish homes have radio sets and 66 percent have television, with radio and television audiences at peak times estimated to be 51 percent and 70 percent respectively of the total population.

Radio and Telefis Eireann have a code of standards with which all advertisers must comply. Advertising film must be approved before showing. No advertising of hard spirits is accepted (only wines and beers can be advertised). Detailed rates may be obtained from Radio-Telefis Eireann, Advertising Sales Division, Donnybrook, Dublin 4. Nonpeak advertising, however, must be contracted approximately 6 months in advance.

Newspaper and Magazine Advertising.—Ireland has approximately 60 newspapers, of which four are daily morning papers and three are daily evening papers. Of these, the Irish Independent (Dublin, morning) has the largest circulation, followed by the Evening Press (Dublin) and the Evening Herald (Dublin). The Irish Times has the smallest circulation in Dublin, nevertheless it reaches an important segment of the public concerned with business and finance. The only daily papers published outside Dublin are the morning Cork Examiner and the Evening Echo (also Cork). However, only the Dublin dailies can be regarded as having national distribution. There are approximately 150 periodicals and trade magazines published in Ireland.

Motion Picture Advertising.—Spot films from 15 to 30 seconds in length shown between feature movies are a popular form of advertising in Ireland. Frequently, cinema advertising of this sort tends to be coordinated with parallel television and/or radio advertising. There are more than 160 cinemas in Ireland, all of which accept spot advertising.

Billboard and Poster Advertising.—Billboard advertising is not very common. Posters tend to be limited to advertising political, theatrical, artistic, sporting and similar events involving mass participation including exhibits and trade shows.

Direct Mail Advertising.—Only one major firm engaged in direct mail advertising covers the entire Irish Republic. This firm has lists of the more important industrial, agricultural, professional, educational, and consumer groups. The post office does not accept unaddressed mailouts, and advertising material, as such, does not benefit from special postal rates.

Advertising Agencies.—Ireland has approximately 54 advertising agencies. The larger ones provide a full range of advertising services. Twenty-nine of the principal agencies belong to the Institute of Advertising Practitioners, which is closely associated with the American Association of Advertising Agencies (AAAA). The Institute of Advertising Practitioners prepares a "Code of Advertising Standards for Ireland," to which all Irish advertising agencies are expected to adhere. This code is similar to the Code of Advertising Practices (CAP) used in Britain. Copies may be obtained by writing to the Institute of Advertising Practitioners in Ireland, 35 Upper Fitzwilliam Street, Dublin 2.

Advertising Techniques.—Coupons, sampling, merchandising novelties, premiums, and prizes are all used as promotional techniques. However, laws covering gaming and lotteries as well as restrictive trade practices are strictly enforced by the National Government. Firms advertising and selling their goods in Ireland should inform themselves of the provisions of these laws and adjust their practices accordingly. There is also censorship of publications and films containing "unwholesome" material in the sense of its being "indecent" or "obscene."

Market Research.—There are at least three firms engaged in market research in Ireland, all with headquarters in Dublin. These firms provide the usual range of services, including store audits, consumer market surveys, product tests, advertising media research, attitude and motivation research, etc. One of these market research companies, S.C. Nielsen Ltd., is a subsidiary of an American firm of the same name. The other two companies, Irish Marketing Surveys Ltd. and the Market Research Bureau, are strictly domestic organizations but both have done work for American companies. In addition, the American Embassy in Dublin provides the Department of Commerce with periodic data on the Irish economy as well as with commercial and market information. These data are made available to U.S. companies through the Bureau of Export Development, Department of Commerce, Washington, D.C., 20230, as well as the Department's 43 District Offices.

Trade Organizations.—In addition to market research firms, a number of Irish trade associations can provide extensive information and assistance to American exporters selling goods within certain product categories. Following are the more important Irish trade organizations:

Association of Chambers of Commerce in Ireland
7 Clare Street
Dublin 2

Confederation of Irish Industry
Confederation House
Kildare Street
Dublin 2

National Federation of Drapers and Allied Traders Ltd.
127 Lower Baggot Street
Dublin 2

Pharmaceutical Chemical & Allied Industries Association
13 Fitzwilliam Square
Dublin 2

Irish Wholesale Footwear Association
½ S. Leinster Street, Dublin 2

Wholesale Fruit Importers and Distributors' Association
16 Henry Street, Dublin 1

Retail Grocery, Dairy and Allied Traders' Association
24 Earlsfort Terrace
Dublin 2

Harware & Allied Traders' Association of Ireland
21 Camden Row
Dublin 8

National Association of Irish Steel Merchants,
Eire
90 St. Stephen's Green
Dublin 2

National Federation Retail Newsagents
63 Middle Abbey Street
Dublin 1

Trade Fairs.—Trade fairs provide an important media for introducing new products. Besides serving to help locate distributors for a product, Irish trade fairs attract wide public attendance and can frequently be used effectively to gauge consumer acceptance of a new product.

The most important of the Irish trade fairs is the Spring Show and Industries Fair. It covers almost any product one might wish to display, attracts wide attendance, and is held annually in May at the Royal Dublin Society in Dublin. In addition, a number of more specialized trade fairs are held annually that are confined to specific product categories. These are listed below:

Spring Show and Industries Fair (yearly in May) R.D.S. Balsbridge, Dublin (largest industrial fair).

Irish Export Fashion Fair (yearly) Intercontinental Hotel, Dublin.

Irish Printing and Publishing Exhibition (yearly) R.D.S. Dublin.

Business Equipment Exhibition (yearly) Mansion House, Dublin.

Irish Furniture and Furnishing Exhibition (yearly) R.D.S. Dublin.

Hotel and Catering Exhibition (yearly) Mansion House, and R.D.S. Dublin.

ETEX (Education and Training Exhibition and Conference) (yearly) R.D.S. Dublin.

Irish International Food and Drink Fair (held every 2 years) R.D.S. Dublin.

Further information on these fairs may be obtained from Board Failte Eireann, Baggot St. Bridge, Dublin 2.

Credit

There are two main banking groups in Ireland, Bank of Ireland Group (500 offices including New York and Chicago) and Allied Irish Banks Ltd. (400 offices—representatives in New York and Chicago), as well as the Northern Bank Ltd., the Ulster Bank Ltd., and five North American banks (Citibank, Bank of America, Chase & Bank of Ireland International Ltd., First National Bank of Chicago, and the Bank of Nova Scotia).

Of these, only the Irish banks provide consumer financing, usually through associated companies specifically set up for this purpose. In addition there are approximately 50 firms in Ireland operating as consumer finance companies, referred to locally as industrial bankers, hire purchase companies, or finance houses, including three with U.S. connections—Irish Intercontinental Bank Ltd. (Marine Midland Bank, N.Y.), Trinity Bank Ltd. (Philadelphia National Bank), Royal Trust Co. (Ireland) Ltd. (Royal Trust Corp., Miami).

Regulations

The Irish Government strictly regulates terms for consumer financing, using this right as one of the monetary tools to control the economy. Normal credit at trade and consumer levels is 30 days, occasionally extending to as much as 60 days. The practice of taking a small percent discount for cash on the invoice price is fast dying in Ireland. At the retail level most outlets except grocery stores offer their customers credit, usually 30 days. Charge accounts and credit cards are common; department stores and banks also have begun to issue credit cards.

Quotations and Terms of Payment

Irish importers prefer quotations on a c.i.f. Irish post basis. Without specific information on shipping costs, particularly when goods must travel overland in the United States, Irish importers find it difficult to assess properly the competitiveness and/or profitability of an American product as compared with a European-made product, especially since most European goods are quoted on a c.i.f. basis. American quotations, invariably in dollars, are completely acceptable in Ireland. The usual practice of American firms selling in Ireland is to require cash against documents on the first sale or two. Thereafter, after establishing his credit, the Irish importer will expect to pay by 30, 60 or even 90-day letter of credit, with perhaps a discount for payment within 50 days.

Investment in Ireland

Irish Government Policy on Foreign Investment

In general, Ireland presents a favorable investment climate. Its constitution and its governmental institutions are of a type familiar to U.S. business, and the country has a tradition of free enterprise.

The Irish Government acknowledges the contribution that productive private investment, both domestic and foreign, can make toward economic and social progress, and is actively promoting direct American and other foreign investment in manufacturing subsidiaries in Ireland. In the Government's two development programs, primary emphasis has been placed on productive investment, preferably in the private sector and in industries capable of meeting competition in the export markets. The Industrial Development Act of 1958 relaxed the previous restrictions on foreign investment in export industries.

The Irish Government currently offers some positive forms of assistance to prospective American investors. The Grants Board makes non-repayable loans available for new industries, covering up to two-thirds of the cost of fixed assets and gives generous allowances for training workers. The Industrial Credit Company Ltd. offers facilities to industrialists requiring capital for the establishment of new industries or for the expansion or modernization of existing industries. The Irish Export Board provides a variety of services for exporters and importers.

The Government also offers various tax incentives. New manufacturing companies established in Ireland are not required to pay Irish income tax or corporation profits tax for 10 consecutive years on profits arising from exports of goods manufactured in Ireland. There are also generous allowances made for depreciation, scientific research, staff training, and patent rights.

The Industrial Development Authority (IDA) was set up by the Government to foster the development and expansion of Ireland's industries. The IDA advises on economic conditions in Ireland, market and export prospects, and other points of interest are easily obtainable for the American business community. The IDA's U.S. representative is located at 405 Park Avenue, New York, New York, 10022. The

Shannon Industrial Estate provides the unique combination of a 300-acre customs-free industrial zone and direct access to air transport. Raw materials and partly or completely manufactured products may be imported into the Industrial Estate, in any quantity, free of duty. Also provided are factories for rent, grants for machinery and training, and housing. All profits arising from export business are exempted from Irish income tax and corporation tax until 1990, and profits may be freely repatriated to the investing country.

U.S. Investment In Ireland

A survey conducted by the United States Chamber of Commerce in the summer of 1974 estimated that American direct industrial investment in Ireland stood at $420 million, about double the previous recorded total of $200 million. An annual turnover of about $540 million was estimated to produce $42.5 million in remittances to the United States in the form of royalties, profits, engineering fees, licenses, salaries, and other forms of payments. There are presently more than 200 U.S. manufacturing firms in Ireland producing motor vehicles, paperboard, petroleum products, electronic components, engineering tools, ball bearings and textiles. Total U.S. investment in Irish industry is now being valued at $897 million. U.S. investment is looked upon by the Irish Government to provide the lion's share of new investment capital in the coming years.

Nearly two-thirds of the production of American firms in Ireland is exported, well over half to the other members of the European Economic Community, and accounts for 25 percent of total Irish exports. Total employment in U.S. manufacturing subsidiaries is estimated at 33,-000, about 8.5 percent of the Irish manufacturing industry work force. Some 75 percent of the firms were established after 1959; the firms organized before 1959 are smaller and produce mainly for the Irish market.

These statistics underscore the favorable climate that exists in Ireland for U.S. investment. Attractions include (1) a springboard for sales (eventually duty free) to the other countries of the European Economic Community; (2) the relatively low Irish wage scales that, although rising rapidly, are still less than those in most of the Community; and (3) Irish inducements to investment, including grants and tax exemption on export profits. The emphasis in the Industrial Development Authority's grant scheme is on job creation in the less developed and depressed areas of western Ireland. Investment in Ireland benefits from the Community's regional fund because the entire island has been designated as one of the less developed areas in the Community.

Forms of Business Organization

There are three ways in which a foreign corporation can carry on business in the Republic:

1. Through a sales agent, without establishing a place of business in the Republic;

2. Establishing a branch office with its own place of business;

3. Setting up a subsidiary company registered under the Companies Act of 1963.

Businesses may be proprietorships (or "sole traders"), partnerships or business companies. The word Corporation has a special meaning in Ireland. It usually denotes certain types of municipal authorities. Under the Companies Act of 1963, there are three types of incorporated companies: a company limited by shares, a company limited by guarantee and an unlimited company. Only the first is of interest here.

Company Limited by Shares.—This is defined as "a company having the liability of its members limited by the memorandum (charter) to the amount, if any, unpaid on the shares respectively held by them." A company may thus issue shares before they are fully paid up. Where shares are fully paid up before they are issued, the shareholders have no liability for the debts of the company. Creditors can only look to the assets of the company.

Private and Public Companies.—Private companies legislation restricts the right to transfer shares, limits the number of members to 50, and prohibits any invitation to the public to subscribe for any shares or debentures of the company. Thus, shares of a private company may not be dealt with on a stock exchange. Private companies need not file financial statements with the Registrar of Companies. Incorporation of a private company is performed by a solicitor who prepares a memorandum of association, articles of association, a statement of nominal capital and a declaration of compliance with the Act. Notice of location of the company as well as the particulars of directors and secretaries must be lodged with the Registrar of Companies within 14 days of incorporation.

Public companies require the submission of further documents stating the objects of the company, its name, and the amount of share capital. There is no minimal capital requirement. When stamp duties and other fees are paid, the Registrar of Companies will issue a certificate of incorporation. Every company must have at least two directors. Aliens may be directors.

Republic Branch of a Foreign Company.— Foreign companies, organized under the law of a country other than the Irish Republic, may carry on business in the Republic either with or without having a place of business in the Republic. A place of business must be of more than a fleeting character. If it has merely an independent sales representative or an agent who is an independent contractor and not an employee, it does not come within the provision of the Companies Act. Foreign companies that establish a place of business must deliver to the Registrar of Companies certified copies of its articles of incorporation and by-laws, a list of directors, names and addresses of one or more persons in the Republic authorized to accept on behalf of the company "service of process" and other legal notices, and the address of the company's principal place of business in the Republic. The foreign company must also file annual statements with the Registrar.

Taxation

The Irish tax system is similar to that in the United Kingdom. Revenue is derived primarily from income taxes on individuals and companies, from turnover and wholesale (now being replaced by the value-added tax), customs and excise duties, stamp duties, capital gains tax, and motor vehicle duties. The tax year runs from April 6 to April 5 of the following year.

While Irish residents are liable to tax on all their income, nonresidents are taxed only on that part of their income arising in Ireland. Individuals residing in Ireland and working for a foreign company without becoming residents are subject to taxation on a remittance basis only. To avoid double taxation, Ireland has concluded a number of treaties with other countries to avoid double taxation. Such treaties are in effect with the United States and the United Kingdom.

Individual income tax is chargeable at the rate of 20 percent for the first £500 of taxable income, 25 percent for every £ of the next £1,000, 35 percent for every £ of the next

£3,000, 45 percent for every £ of the next £1,500, 50 percent for every £ of the next £1,000 and 60 percent for every £ of the remainder of taxable income. Wage earners and salaried employees have their tax deducted at the source by the employer. Others pay directly to the Revenue Commissioners by January 1 of the year of assessment and on July 1 of the following year.

Corporation tax is charged on all the profits, wherever arising, of companies resident in the state and on the profits arising in the state of nonresident companies insofar as those profits are attributable to an Irish branch or agency. Profits include capital gains, and these gains are charged to corporation tax in effect at the capital gains tax rate of 26 percent. Corporation tax was chargeable for the financial year 1977 at the rate of 45 percent on companies with profits exceeding £10,000. For smaller companies the rate of tax was 35 percent. Companies with profits of between £10,000 and £15,000 may qualify for a special rate of 25 percent if they are manufacturing companies achieving certain targets of increased employment and output as compared with 1976.

Local taxes on real property, called "rates," are charged to individuals and corporations on land and buildings. Rates are levied by the local authorities and, in practice, currently work out at between 0.3 percent and 1.5 percent of the current capital cost of land and buildings, excluding the cost of machinery and plant.

The value-added tax, enacted in July 1972, replaced the former sales tax system that included retail turnover tax and wholesale tax. The value-added tax is paid on delivery of goods, rendition of services, and on goods imported. Aside from certain exemptions, the value-added tax is assessed at four rate levels, 10, 20, 35, and 40 percent, with the largest category of transactions subject to the 10 percent rate.

Excise duties are levied on hydrocarbon oils, beer, spirits, wines, tobacco, matches and tires.

Labor

The Irish labor force, according to April 1976 estimates, amounts to 1,143,000 persons, of whom 243,000 are employed in agriculture, forestry, and fishing, 304,000 in industry and construction, and 488,000 in other sectors. Labor affairs in Ireland are essentially the responsibility of the Department of Labor, which implements legislation relating to the safety, health and welfare of the country's labor force.

The Irish Congress of Trade Unions (ICTU) is the central authority of the Irish labor movement, with a total membership in excess of 600,000. The ICTU functions primarily as a coordinator of Ireland's 82 different unions, each of which represents a particular trade or profession. At the employer level, the ICTU is paralleled by a national organization representing industry and trade, the Federated Union of Employers. The FUE can provide information and advice to foreign individuals or companies moving to Ireland. The FUE also represents employers in negotiations with the Government or the ICTU.

Conditions of employment are regulated by the Conditions of Employment Act of 1936. The maximum standard working week is 48 hours for persons over 18 years of age and 40 hours for "young" persons between 14 and 18. Women may not be employed in industrial undertakings between the hours of 10 p.m. and 8 a.m. Overtime is limited to 2 hours per day or 12 hours per week. For shift work, a special license must be obtained from the Ministry of Labor. Nonnational management personnel and other key workers have no difficulty in obtaining required work permits, which are renewable every 12 months for 5 years and thereafter indefinitely, as long as the worker remains at the same job.

Guidance for Business Travelers

Entrance Requirements.—Every U.S. citizen entering the Republic of Ireland must have a valid American passport. An American citizen entering Ireland for permanent residence must register with the police (Aliens Office) as soon as possible after entering the country. Anyone not an Irish citizen must have a work permit before being permitted to accept employment. Such permits, which must be applied for by the prospective employer and obtained from the Department of Labor, are usually granted only for specialized work.

Foreign Exchange Regulations.—There are no restrictions on the importation of currency into Ireland. U.S. travelers entering Ireland may bring with them both Irish pounds and foreign currency in unlimited amounts and may take out any foreign currency which they brought into the country. Not more than $60 worth of Sterling Area notes (including Irish currency) and $600 worth of other foreign currency (in addition to what was brought in), may be taken out of the country. There is no restriction on the amount of Irish or other currency that may be taken to the United Kingdom.

Customs Regulations.—The bona fide personal effects of passengers arriving in Ireland are admitted free of duty. These articles include clothing and other wearing apparel, articles of personal adornment, toilet articles, and other personal effects. They may be imported without limit as to quantity or value in personal baggage provided they are necessary and appropriate for the use of the traveler while staying in Ireland and not intended for other purposes or for sale. Handtools and portable professional effects are also allowed duty-free entry. U.S. travelers are permitted to import in personally accompanied baggage, without the payment of duty, the following quantities or values of dutiable goods for their own personal use: Tobacco, 1,000 cigarettes, or 200 cigars, or 2½ lbs. of other manufactured tobacco or any combination of these up to a total weight not exceeding 2½ lbs; wines and spirits, potable spirits, including liqueurs and cordials, 1 quart; wine, ⅓ gallon; and perfume, 1 pint. Although customs does not specify the amount of cameras and film that may be imported duty free, in ordinary practice one or two cameras for personal use and an amount of film sufficient for the traveler's stay are permitted free entry.

Hotel Accommodations.—In view of large numbers of visitors going to Ireland, travelers are advised to make their hotel reservations fairly well in advance in order to assure the type of accommodations they desire.

Clothing.—There is no need for great variations in wardrobe to fit the seasons since the Irish climate is free of extremes. Woolen clothing has been found to be most appropriate owing to the predominantly cool weather. Sturdy, weatherproof raincoats and footwear are essential because of the frequent, light rain.

Health Conditions.—Community sanitation services (e.g., water supply, garbage collection, sewage disposal) are generally adequate. Medical services are generally excellent, and there are several well-equipped hospitals in Dublin and other leading cities.

Communications.—Telephone and telegraph systems are Government-owned and operated by the Department of Posts and Telegraphs. International cables are privately owned by foreign firms. A flat rate is charged for inland telegrams regardless of distance. Government-owned and operated telegraph cables connect Dublin with London and Liverpool. Cable and Wireless, Commercial Cable, and Western Union transmit cables to points outside the British Isles. In figuring the arrival time of a cable message in Ireland, add 6 hours to Eastern standard time. During the spring and summer, Ireland is on daylight saving time.

Business Etiquette.—The most important characteristics of Irish business etiquette are punctuality and courtesy. Delivery terms as well as appointment schedules are expected to be maintained. Titles, when known, should be used in business correspondence.

For expeditious handling of correspondence, air mail should be used at all times. It is advisable to address mail to the firm rather than to individuals.

Commercial Language.—Two languages are spoken in Ireland—Irish and English. Irish is the first official language and English the second. While English is normally used in business contracts and is the language of correspondence, some expressions and words have different meanings from those accepted in the United States; for clarity of meaning it is well to define unfamiliar terms. Prompt acknowledgement of communications addressed to U.S. concerns by Irish firms is always appreciated.

Specifications may be according to U.S. or English measurement standards. The Government of Ireland, however, will change over from these present standards to the metric system in the near future.

Business Hours.—Banking hours are generally 9:30 a.m. to 12:30 p.m. and from 1:30 to 3 p.m. Banks are usually open until 5 p.m. on Fridays.

Offices are open from 9:30 a.m. until 5 p.m. while stores are open from 9:30 a.m. to 5:30 p.m. Because of vacations in July and August, most Irish business executives are not available during these months except by advance appointment.

Holidays.—The following holidays are observed by Irish banks and businesses, except where indicated otherwise: New Year's Day (banks only); St. Patrick's Day (March 17); Good Friday; Easter Monday; First Monday in June (bank holiday); First Monday in August (bank holiday); Christmas (December 25); and St. Stephen's Day (December 28).

Government Representation

Ireland is represented in the United States by an Ambassador and four Consuls General. The Embassy of Ireland is located at 2234 Massachusetts Avenue, Washington, D.C., 20008. The four Irish Consulates General are located at 33 East 50th Street, New York, New York, 10022, at 200 Berkely Street, Boston, Massachusetts, 02116, at 400 North Michigan Avenue, Chicago, Illinois, 60611, and at 681 Market Street, San Francisco, California, 94105. The Irish Industrial Development Authority maintains offices at 200 Park Avenue, New York, New York, 10017 at 515 South Flower St., Los Angeles, Calif., 90071, at Suite 2065, 1100 Milam Bldg., Houston, Texas, 77002 at 1 East Wacker Drive, Chicago, Illinois, 60601, and at Lansdowne House, Dublin 4.

The United States maintains diplomatic representation through its Embassy in Dublin, 42 Elgin Road, Ballsbridge, telephone Dublin 64061/9. Foreign Service Officers in the Economic/Commercial Section of the Embassy are available to brief and assist American business visitors.

Market Profile—IRELAND

Foreign Trade

Imports — Total $7,524 million in 1978; $5,904 million in 1977. From U.S. $633 million in 1978; U.S. share: 8.4 percent. Other major suppliers: U.K. 49.4 percent, West Germany 7.1 percent. Principal imports: machinery and electrical goods, vehicles and parts, chemicals, textiles, petroleum, cereals and other foodstuffs, live animals. Imports from U.S.: Office machines, computer equipment, machinery, feedstuffs and organic chemicals.

Exports. — Total $6,007 million in 1978; $4,810 million in 1977. To U.S. $383 million in 1978; U.S. share: 6.4 percent. Other major markets: U.K. 47.2 percent, West Germany 8.4 percent. Principal exports: live animals, food and food preparations, textiles, machinery and transport equipment and clothing. Exports to U.S.: Electrical equipment and components medicinal and pharmaceutical products, textiles, medical, surgical and veterinary apparatus, glassware, footwear.

Trade Policy. — On January 1, 1973, Ireland became a member of the European Community. Tariffs between Ireland and the other members of the European Community were completely eliminated on July 1, 1977. On that date Ireland also adopted the EEC's common external tariff toward third countries, including the U.S. Member of GATT, OECD and IMF.

Trade Prospects. — Ireland's program of encouraging expansion and modernization of industry offers numerous opportunities for U.S. exporters of machinery and industrial equipment.

Foreign Investment

Investment Prospects. — Foreign investment in Irish industry actively encouraged by the Irish Government. U.S. investment estimated at around $900 million. More than 200 U.S. manufacturing firms in Ireland producing motor vehicles, paperboard, petroleum products, electronic components, engineering tools, ball bearings and textiles. Double taxation treaty with the U.S.

Finance

Currency. — Irish pound = $2.03 in 1978. Pound allowed to float since June, 1972.

Domestic Credit and Investment. — Developed capital market. Modern banking system, bond and stock issues may be floated on any Irish stock exchange.

National Budget. — Current budget expenditure during fiscal year 1977–78 is expected to amount to $4.9 billion. Capital budget expenditures expected to be $1,075 million.

Balance of Payments. — Estimated $335 million current account deficit in 1978.

Economy

GNP, at current prices, $12.8 billion in 1978, a 17 percent rise over 1977. GNP per capita, about $3,867. Agriculture of major importance, but its share of national income is decreasing, while industry's share is expanding.

Agriculture

Agriculture. — Approximately two-thirds of agricultural land is in pasture, which supports large livestock industry. Main crops: wheat, potatoes, sugar beets, barley and oats.

Industry. — Generally on a relatively small scale. Principal industries: Processing of agricultural products into food, drink, and tobacco; clothing; textiles; paper products and printed matter; wood manufactures; metals and engineering and vehicle assembly.

Tourism. — A major industry, actively promoted by Irish Tourist Board, a Government agency. Tourism earned estimated $568 million in 1978.

Development Program. — Regional Industrial Plans (1976-1980) of Irish Industrial Development Authority calls for greater dispersal of economic activity throughout Ireland and creation of 50,000 new industrial jobs. Wide range of regional incentives offered.

Basic Economic Facilities

Transportation. — Railroad route mileage, 1,334. Program of modernization under way. Freight traffic, 3.5 million tons in 1977. Extensive road system; 9,894 miles of main-roads, 42,173 miles of country roads. Motor vehicles (private cars) in 1978, 104,411. Shipping: Irish Shipping Ltd. (Government owned) is largest shipping line. 14 ships, 171,000 deadweight tons. Major ports: Dublin, Cork, Waterford.

Communications. — Telephone, telegraph, radio and television State-controlled. Radios, est. 210,000; television sets 399,000.

Power. — Electric utility industry is Government-controlled. Power generated in 1976: 8,498 million kwh, an increase of 900 million over 1975.

Natural Resources

Land. — Approximately 27,136 square miles. Hilly and sometimes mountainous coastal regions, bordering low-lying, rolling plains.

Climate. — Mild and free of extremes. Generally high humidity and rainy.

Minerals. — Gypsum, limestone, slate, clay, and peat. Deposits of iron, lead, copper, zinc, and silver.

Forestry. — Government program of afforestation.

Fishing. — Relatively small industry. Value of catch over $22.9 million 1978.

Population

Size. — 3,314,000 (1978). Population increasing slowly.

Languages. — English and Gaelic. English is predominant.

Education. — Extensive public school system. Large number of private schools. Several excellent universities.

Labor. — Labor force estimated at 1.1 million: Agriculture, forestry and fishing, 252,000; industry and construction, 328,000.

Marketing in Israel

Contents

Report Revised July 1980

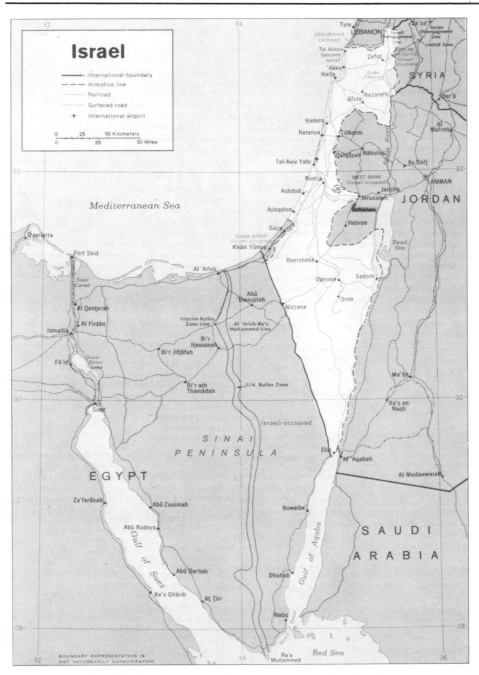

Israel

International boundary
Armistice line
Railroad
Surfaced road
+ International airport

0   25   50 Kilometers
0   25   50 Miles

Note: Dashed lines represent armistice lines. Borders are not necessarily authoritative.

Foreign Trade Outlook

Israel's economy has been characterized throughout the State's history by rapid growth and by dependence on foreign trade. Between 1948 and 1973, Israel's gross national product (GNP) increased an average of 10 percent per year in real terms, a growth rate among the highest in the world. However, due to unusually slow growth in 1976 and 1977, the average real growth rate from 1974 to 1978 was only 3.2 percent. By 1978, the economy came out of the earlier slump and grew 5.2 percent (real) to a total GNP of $12.8 billion or a per capita income of $3,470. In 1979 GNP and per capita income totaled $16.4 billion and $4,332 respectively.

Limited in natural resources, Israel has always had to rely heavily on imports to supply its large defense needs (costing about one-third of the country's GNP) and to provide for the demands of immigrant absorption. In the past, Israel was able to finance the excess of imports over exports by means of loans and gifts from abroad. The current account deficit, however, took on new dimensions following the 1973 war and in 1979 was running at a level of $4.3 billion.

Israel's foreign debt, which had been increasing at rates in excess of 20 percent annually since 1973, slowed to 15.5 percent in 1977. This debt, which reached $12.9 billion in 1978, is quite large in absolute terms and is unusually high for a country of Israel's size. Over 60 percent of the debt is owed to the U.S. Government (39 percent) or to Israel bond holders (21 percent), most of whom are American citizens. The foreign debt increased to $15 billion in 1979 and is expected to reach $17 billion in 1980 as deterioration in the current account of the balance of payments will cause the Government to borrow abroad to finance the excess of imports over exports. Much of this borrowing will be for medium or long terms, and the U.S. Government and Israel bond purchasers will continue to be a major source of financing. The American Government will lend Israel an average of about $800 million in military and economic support loans in 1979 and 1980 plus the special $2.2 billion loan to finance the Israeli withdrawal from the Sinai which will take place in 1980–81.

In October 1977, the Government of Israel announced its New Economic Policy (NEP) which represented a radical departure from the socialist-oriented economic policies of previous administrations. The measures were aimed at reducing the level of government involvement in the economy and moving the country toward greater economic independence. Achieving this independence required tackling the country's

---

HOW TO OBTAIN BACKGROUND INFORMATION ABOUT THESE COUNTRIES

Keeping this book within reasonable size limits has made it necessary to focus on material *directly* concerned with marketing and commerce, and set aside materials only indirectly related. The editors relize, however, that *general* data about a country are also vital to a company's preparations to enter a foreign market, and make a very definite recommendation as to how such expanded information needs can be served.

For those who wish *general* data about a country—data which goes beyond marketing and commerce—the editors recommend *Countries of the World and Their Leaders,* published as an annually updated yearbook by Gale Research Company, Detroit, Michigan 48226. Containing 4- to 20-page entries on 168 countries, the volume also provides several hundred pages of supplementary world data. Each country entry is prepared by the U.S. Department of State to provide a general briefing on the geography, people, culture, and political situation of the particular country. Each report provides some historical insight as well as a look at contemporary trends of lifestyle in the country. Reports also discuss a country's educational system, its press, ethnic groupings and religious practices.

Countries of the World and Their Leaders provides a fresh listing of cabinet ministers of each nation. In addition it lists health conditions the traveling businessman will wish to prepare for and includes information on passport procedures, customs and duties, and world climate conditions.

balance of payments problem. Toward that end the Israeli pound was allowed to float, most controls on foreign exchange transactions were eliminated, and certain import duties, surcharges, and taxes were reduced or removed. Since these measures were designed to develop Israel's export-oriented and import substitution industries, American firms that supply these industries benefited from the new policies.

Israel, over the past several years, recorded substantial export growth of 24 percent in 1976, 28 percent in 1977, 25 percent in 1978 and 16 percent in 1979. The rise during 1979 is impressive since the value of diamond shipments (Israel's largest export) decreased and many of the country's markets were experiencing slow economic growth. In fact, the value of Israel's non-

Table 1.—U.S. Exports to Israel 1978, 1979
(in thousands of dollars)

	1978	1979
Total	1,841,322	1,782,878
Food and live animals	189,874	197,913
Meat preparations	3,554	6,930
Wheat	63,379	86,058
Corn, unmilled	40,294	29,833
Cereals, not elsewhere specified unmilled	64,509	62,011
Beverages and Tobacco	7,952	9,046
Tobacco and tobacco manufactures	7,551	7,827
Crude materials, inedible except fuel	112,889	125,543
Oilseeds and oleaginous fruit	98,882	99,939
Mineral fuels, lubricants etc.	2,323	2,466
Petroleum and products	2,270	2,355
Animal and vegetables oils, fats, waxes	4,792	6,569
Vegetable oils and fats, fixed	4,712	6,497
Chemicals and related products	50,487	80,533
Organic chemicals	12,285	29,259
Explosives and pyrotechnic products	5,688	9,528
Synthetic resins; rubber and plastic materials	8,306	16,392
Manufactured goods by chief material	113,983	172,668
Paper and paperboard	13,454	25,130
Yarn, fabric and articles, textile	22,479	40,512
Diamonds, unset	17,841	21,381
Iron and steel	11,223	14,725
Nonferrous metals	11,143	14,626
Structures, and parts, iron, steel, aluminum, zinc	3,580	17,609
Machinery and transport equipment	516,124	820,281
Steam and vapor generators boilers and parts	6,859	30,226
Internal combustion piston engines and parts	25,726	41,007
Internal combustion engines, not elsewhere specified and parts	30,802	20,601
Rotating electric plant and parts	11,609	13,869
Agriculture and dairy machinery	6,861	10,331
Tractors, agriculture and construction	6,927	23,494
Civil engineering and contractors' equipment	9,708	26,857
Textile and leather working machinery and parts	5,935	6,412
Mineral crushing, sorting, mixing etc.	822	4,273
Special industrial machinery not elsewhere specified	16,241	6,172
Metalworking machinery tools, parts and accessories	5,153	15,036
Heating and cooling equipment and parts.	10,306	12,427
Pumps for liquids	6,155	5,562
Pumps not elsewhere specified, compressing, filtering equipment etc.	11,067	10,551
Mechanical handling equipment	21,367	38,626
ADP and auxiliary equipment	16,569	27,969
Office machine and ADP parts	11,432	18,660
Telecommunication equipment, TV, radio equipment and parts	40,802	43,760
Electric current carrying wiring devices and parts	43,363	44,066
Electronic components and parts	13,398	17,865
Electric machinery and apparatus not elsewhere specified	22,424	31,595
Passenger motor vehicles	11,928	23,217
Trucks and special purpose motor vehicles	14,843	53,788
Motor vehicles and tractor parts	29,766	53,250
Airplanes	47,949	93,536
Aircraft parts	517	82,385
Miscellaneous Manufactured Articles	83,783	87,575
Optical Instruments and apparatus	5,628	9,928
Measuring, checking instruments	48,266	40,320
Photographic apparatus and equipment.	2,894	2,779
Photographic chemical, film, paper and photos	4,046	6,431
Commodities, transactions, not classified elsewhere	21,862	22,100
Special category	737,253	25,183

Source: U.S. Department of Commerce, Bureau of the Census, U.S. Foreign Trade, Exports, World Area by Commodity Grouping, Annual 1978, 1979, FT 455.

Table 2.—U.S. Imports from Israel 1978, 1979
(in thousands of dollars)

	1978	1979
Total	719,397	749,061
Food and live animals	15,655	17,130
Dairy products and birds' eggs	2,226	1,782
Vegetables and fruits	9,909	8,883
Beverages	1,691	2,584
Crude materials, inedible except fuel	13,295	11,799
Fertilizers, crude and mineral except coal	7,905	4,346
Animal and vegetable materials not elsewhere specified	4,580	6,503
Oils and fats, animal and vegetable	1	17
Chemicals and related products	40,591	47,110
Organic chemicals and related products	10,272	8,934
Inorganic chemicals	1,194	4,262
Medical and pharamaceutical products	1,151	1,682
Fertilizer and fertilizer materials	18,403	21,428
Synthetic resins, rubber and plastic materials	2,416	4,838
Manufactured goods by chief material	449,548	398,214
Tires and tubes for tires	15,363	16,074
Diamonds, except industrial not set or strung	389,901	327,704
Nonferrous metals	5,962	9,085
Tools for hand or machine use	7,059	9,228
Machinery and transport equipment	79,044	134,536
Power generating machinery and equipment	6,681	7,278
Agriculture and dairy machinery and parts	1,708	2,608
Textile and leather working machinery	817	1,985
Metalworking machinery	2,836	5,398
Pumps not elsewhere specified, compressors fans, etc.	1,368	1,168
Non-electric machinery and mechanical apparatus not elsewhere specified	1,289	1,898
Non-electric parts not elsewhere specified for machinery	4,133	4,268
Office and ADP machinery	7,014	8,982
Telecommunication and sound reproduction equipment	5,081	13,315
Electronic equipment, current carrying, resistors etc.	4,505	6,508
Electro-medical and radiological apparatus	2,947	3,172
Road vehicles	5,757	7,914
Airplanes	27,380	57,736
Airplane parts	1,183	4,664
Miscellaneous Manufactured Articles	95,393	116,127
Furniture and parts	2,902	3,535
Wearing apparel and accessories and articles made of fur	30,785	21,506
Professional, scientific and control instruments not elsewhere specified	5,429	8,692
Jewelry and related articles	35,832	62,807
Articles not provided for elsewhere	24,182	21,564

Source: U.S. Department of Commerce, Bureau of the Census, U.S. Foreign Trade, Imports, World Area by Commodity Grouping, Annual 1978, 1979, FT 155.

Table 3.—*Principal Imports into Israel from the United States and from the World-1978*
(in millions of dollars)

	Imports from the World	Imports from the U.S.
Total..	5,871	1,125
Wheat and meslin.........................	78	78
Maize	43	43
Millet, sorgum, dura and the like...........	73	73
Soya beans................................	105	105
Bitum minerals raw and petroleum-oils.....	763	—
Insecticides..............................	19	6
Polyamides...............................	16	—
Polyethylene.............................	13	2
Ilomba, mahogany etc, rough wood.........	19	—
Pine and other conifer wood, sawn	35	—
Kraft paper, paperboard	24	11
Synthetic fibres, yarn, not for retail	22	10
Unworked diamonds	1,246	82
Worked industry diamonds	14	3
Other worked diamonds	77	10
Precious, semiprecious stones not elsewhere specified	20	—
Gold, unwrought..........................	53	—
Bars and rods, other not elsewhere specified	35	—
Iron, steel sheets plates....................	103	—
Aircraft engines	18	9
Closed, semiclosed compressors	12	1
Refrigerators and refrigeration equipment .	10	3
Machinery for cleaning, filling, packing etc., not elsewhere specified	12	2
Earth excavation, extraction, machinery, etc...	23	18
Washing machines and parts	12	—
Machine tools for working metal not elsewhere specified	16	2
Automatic statistical machinery............	58	21
Mechanical appliance producing plastic, rubber...................................	16	3
Taps, locks, valves for popes not elsewhere specified	15	6
Radiotelegraph telephone transmission, reception apparatus.....................	10	7
Transmission and reception apparatus, other	16	—
Valves, tubes, other photocells.............	29	21
Tractors for earth work agriculture	28	8
Buses....................................	16	—
Passenger cars...........................	119	8
Chassis	25	9
Parts and accessories for motor vehicles, not elsewhere specified	20	4
Planes, etc...............................	45	45
Parts of planes etc.	71	47
Ships and other vessels	29	—
Medical instruments and appliances	18	8
Electronic measuring, comparing apparatus, not elsewhere specified	12	6
Other....................................	2,483	474

Source: Government of Irael, Central Bureau of Statistics, 1978

diamond industrial exports expanded by more than 28 percent; the fourth consecutive year of growth over 24 percent.

The growth in Israel's export sector has been helped by the GSP and EC agreements. On January 1, 1976, Israel became eligible for the United States generalized system of preferences (GSP). Countries qualifying for GSP may export some 2,700 products to the United States duty-free. Israel agreed to reduce tariffs on over 130 U.S.-made items.

In 1975, Israel entered into an agreement with the European Community (EC) which reduced Israeli customs duties on industrial products

from the EC and which gave Israeli-manufactured goods duty-free access to the EC effective July 1977. This has resulted in increased competition for American firms exporting to Israel.

The United States is Israel's single best customer. American imports from Israel increased slightly from $719 million in 1978 to $749 million in 1979. More than half of U.S. purchases from Israel consist of raw diamonds, imports of which declined from $390 million in 1978 to $328 million in 1979. This decline was offset by American imports of Israeli-manufactured goods and machinery and transport equipment.

The United States is Israel's leading supplier. Despite increasing competition, especially from the European Community, our share of the market increased from 18.9 percent in 1978 to 20.2 percent in 1979. During 1979, American sales declined slightly to $1.8 billion from $1.9 billion in 1978. This decrease was due to a reduction in Israeli purchases of American military goods. U.S. sales of civilian products over this period actually increased to $1.5 billion from $1.1 billion in 1978, a rise of 37 percent. With the demise of the Iran market during 1979, Israel was our second largest Near East customer behind Saudi Arabia. Principal U.S. exports to Israel include agricultural products, chemicals, power generating machinery, telecommunications equipment, mechanical handling equipment, electric apparatus, electronic components, road motor vehicles, aircraft, scientific and control instruments and military goods.

Especially with the fall in the value of the dollar, U.S. goods are more competitively priced in relation to our major competitors, such as the United Kingdom and West Germany. In addition to being price conscious, the Israeli buyer looks for high product reliability and productivity as well as spare parts availability. Therefore, U.S. exporters may benefit from having a reliable Israeli representative to provide after-sales service and spare parts.

Economic Trends

Israel's Central Bureau of Statistics estimates the real growth in the country's gross national product (GNP) at 4.9 percent during 1979, somewhat less than the 5.2 percent real growth in 1978. During the period of low growth following the 1973 war, the Israeli Government instituted several measures to encourage a shift of resources into the export sector so that when growth resumed it would not have to be cut short by a deterioration in the balance of payments. A measure of the success of the policy is the increase in the share of resources devoted to exports from 27 percent in 1978 compared to only 19 percent in 1974. During the same period, investment and government spending dropped in real terms.

In 1978, there was a halt in the reduction in domestic investment, and government spending was up significantly, particularly on defense imports which grew an estimated real 48.8 percent. The trend of increased private consumption continued in 1979 based on real wage gains over the past 3 years. In the first 6 months of 1979, retail sales of consumer durables posted a 28.5 percent increase over the corresponding period in 1978.

The disturbing rise in prices also continued as the inflation rate reached 111 percent during 1979. The high inflation rate is largely due to government budgetary deficits, the rapid depreciation of the Israeli pound in recent years, and reductions in government subsidies for domestic consumption. Inflation has become a political problem for the Government in spite of the real growth and steady rise in Israel's standard of living. Domestic demand is strong and should be further accelerated by military spending on redeployment of Israeli defense forces from the Sinai to the Negev. The official state budget deficit, excluding military expenditures, will grow in real terms by almost 7.5 percent over the next 3 years due largely to the rising cost of fuel and Israel's departure from the Sinai oil fields.

In November 1979, the Israeli Government instituted far-reaching measures to cool off the state's economy. The steps were intended to slow inflation and narrow the gap in the balance of payments. The new measures included complete cancellation of subsidies on cooking oil, margarine, milk and milk products; and reduced subsidies on frozen poultry, bread, and public transport. An import deposit scheme of 10 percent was established effective immediately. The interest-free deposit will be released after 6 months. Government development loans to industry were fully linked to the cost of living index or to the dollar; index-linked loans are charged a 6.0–7.5 percent interest rate. Banks have become more selective in issuing credits. Export credits continue to be available at below market interest rates of 26 percent in Israel pounds and 9 percent in dollars. The interest rate in pounds will be linked to 40 percent of the local free market interest rate, and the dollar rate will rise if Eurodollar rates increase. The development budget in FY 1980 was restrained.

No new public construction projects were to be started, but projects underway would be continued at the same levels. A hiring freeze was instituted in the civil service. Absolutely no new employees would be hired by the central government or local authorities. If attrition did not reduce the number of public service workers, the Government would consult with the Histradrut (labor organization) over measures to force dismissals or early retirements. Utility rates were increased significantly with telephone rates hiked 52 percent and electricity rates up almost 37 percent. To ease the effect on the poor segments of the society, welfare recipients received an 8 percent rise in benefits, and child allowances were boosted 4–5.5 percent. Further, the Government negotiated a special cost of living allowance with the Histradrut that was paid in January 1980.

In March 1980 the Government introduced a change in the name and value of the country's currency. The Israel lirot (pound) was replaced by the biblical shekel, with currency denominations reduced to 10 percent, e.g., one shekel is equivalent to 10 Israel lirot (pounds).

Industry Trends

The following key sectors of the Israeli economy provide the most productive opportunities for greater U.S. private sector involvement.

Building Industry

Important factors affecting the building industry include bureaucratic delays, low productivity, a shortage of skilled labor and the high cost of capital and building materials. While the ultimate effect of Israeli trade with Egypt is unpredictable, it is expected to give Israeli architects and engineers access to a market with 40 million people.

The building industry is strongly influenced by the Government of Israel, especially the Housing and Construction Ministry and the State Lands Administration. Housing is still the hottest domestic political issue, due to acute shortages and skyrocketing rents. New housing construction is all that is permitted under the ban on non-essential construction. Master urban plans, especially in Jerusalem, are being reexamined and upgrading of 29 development towns is being planned. Therefore, the demand for prefab buildings, wall coverings, window and door frames and sanitary and plumbing fixtures offer an attractive opportunity for U.S. firms.

The relocation of defense and civilian installations from the Sinai will create a large demand for earthmoving, construction and transportation equipment, as well as building materials. The estimated cost for the two military bases being constructed under the United States Army Corps of Engineers direction is more than $1 billion. A third base will be built by Israel at a cost of $600 million. Inquiries on these projects should be addressed to the U.S. Army Corps of Engineers, North Atlantic Division, 90 Church Street, New York, New York 10007.

Chemical Industry

Israel has a highly developed chemical industry primarily based on processing domestic and imported crude oil and potash, bromine, magnesia, and phosphates mined in the Dead Sea region. Production of chemicals and chemical products accounts for 28 percent of Israel's industrial production and 30 percent of exports. The value of chemical exports rose from $336 million in 1975 to $439 million in 1978 and an estimated $610 million in 1979.

The value of Israel's chemical production was over $1 billion in 1976 and included fertilizers, insecticides, pesticides, pharmaceuticals, medicines, petrochemicals, nitrates, perfumes, paints, detergents, soaps, cosmetics, flame retardants, glues, food additives and Hanukkah candles. About 150 foreign firms, including several of the largest American conglomerates, have manufacturing facilities in Israel; many were established to penetrate the European Community. U.S. technology has played a major role in the development of most areas of Israel's chemical industry through licensing and joint venture agreements and through engineering of highly sophisticated refining and processing facilities.

During 1977, almost 500 industrial research and development (R&D) projects were approved by the Ministry of Industry, Trade and Tourism, of which 214 were in the chemical industry. In 1978, R&D allocations to the chemical industry rose 30 percent and the number of projects increased 10 percent; during 1979, a 25 percent and 12 percent growth was projected in grants and the number of projects respectively. Almost one-third of the foreign chemical firms operating in Israel are involved in R&D.

Major expansion plans for this industry offer especially good opportunities for U.S.-Israel cooperation. Israel Chemicals Ltd. (ICL), the government-controlled holding company of most of Israel's large chemical firms, has planned a five-year expansion program (1978–82) which would require a total investment of over $260 million. The plan calls for plants to produce titanium dioxide, magnesium oxide, and potassium sulphate, and for additional phosphoric fertilizer production capacity. ICL is interested in involving U.S. firms in joint ventures and licensing agreements for access to markets and new technology rather than direct equity investment. ICL also expects to purchase a substantial portion of its equipment for the new facilities from foreign firms.

Electronics Industry

The electronics industry is one of the key sectors in the Israeli economy. It plays a prominent role in the nation's defense industries and the rapidly expanding export industries. Currently, the United States dominates the field, although additional promotional efforts are required to increase our share of this growing market in the face of rising competition.

The electronics industry is the fastest growing industrial sector in Israel. Output (estimated at $321 million in 1978) increased during 1969–75 by 14 percent per year, representing the highest growth among all industries. Exports during the same period increased by 35 percent annually, again the highest for all industrial sectors. Employment in this field grew from 14,000 in 1969 to 25,000 in 1975, while fixed capital grew by 21 percent per year to a total of $250 million in 1975. Past growth patterns are expected to continue at least until 1985. Real output is expected to grow by 9.8 percent per year in net terms. Specifically, output of the electronics sector is expected to increase (in constant 1975 dollars) from $321 million in 1975 to $1.175 billion in 1985.

A large part of electronic equipment is destined for Israel's defense sector. Fortunately, Israeli defense standards are generally the same as U.S. standards, giving U.S. exporters an advantage in further developing this market.

Solar Energy

Israeli development and use of solar energy devices will be of continuing technical and commercial interest to the United States. Israel's need for alternate energy sources is perhaps more pressing than that of any developed nation. As a result, the Government, despite limited funds, has a broad and innovative energy research and development program.

Israel does not provide a market for "low technology" solar devices made in the United

States. However, the Israelis would be customers for proven U.S. solar devices which they cannot manufacture or which can be manufactured in Israel under license or joint venture arrangements.

The U.S.-Israel Binational Science Foundation assists Israeli research in solar energy, producing useful results in such areas as solar concentrators and aerogenerators. An advantage to the United States is that the research is done in cooperation with American scientists. The Binational Industrial Research and Development (BIRD) Foundation is also expected to be advantageous to the United States in bringing new solar devices to the market, again with full collaboration between U.S. and Israeli firms.

Food Processing Industry

Israel's food processing and packaging industry is one of the country's primary industrial sectors accounting for 20 percent of total industrial output. In 1977, intermediate and finished products amounted to $1.5 billion with real annual growth fluctuating around 6.9 percent.

Israel is one of the leading exporters of both fresh and processed foods, and in 1977 food exports accounted for 12 percent of the country's total industrial exports or about $188 million. By 1980, the Government plans to increase its exports to $350 million. Most of Israel's exports go directly to the European Community where its products are given duty-free entry.

As Israel seeks to upgrade plant facilities to meet growing demand for processed food, U.S. manufacturers of food processing and packaging machinery will find expanded market opportunities for their products. Food processing firms will also find attractive investment incentives. The Israeli market for food processing and packaging equipment is estimated to have reached $40 million in 1976. U.S. exports, on the other hand, only totaled about $8 million, an estimated import share of 20 percent. However, the outlook for U.S. exports and investment opportunities is extremely bright, and best prospects for U.S. firms are mainly in such areas as meat, poultry, eggs, vegetable and dairy processing.

Textile Industry

The textile industry is very important to Israel. There are 827 clothing plants in Israel with 35,000 employees, and 413 textile plants with 25,000 employees. The textile and clothing industry is the third largest industrial sector of the economy (excluding diamonds). Textile output accounts for 11.2 percent of the total value of

industrial output, and 14 percent of non-diamond industrial exports. Textile investments reportedly account for 12.6 percent of the stock of total investments.

No new textile plants are planned for the near future, but investment for expansion and technology infusion are planned in all branches. New machinery will be required, although local manufacturers are better acquainted with European products. Nevertheless, in an interview during 1978, the Director of the Textile Division of Israel's Manufacturers Association felt that, due to the fall in the value of the dollar, American manufacturers could compete successfully with Europeans. The Director further stressed that while many U.S. machines are not as multifunctional as our competitor's equipment, American quality equals or surpasses European models, so cost becomes the key factor.

Electric Power

The government-owned Israeli Electric Corporation (IEC) is continuing to plan for major expansion of power generating and transmission facilities throughout Israel. IEC projects a yearly increase of 8-9 percent in electricity consumption.

One major project which is now being planned is a dual coal and/or oil fired thermal plant, 2X500 MW, to be built in the south, perhaps near the existing Ashdod Power Plant, with start-up planned for 1985-86 for both units. The Hadera coal/oil power plant now under construction between Tel Aviv and Haifa will have its first unit in operation in 1983, followed by one additional unit each year. A decision has been made to proceed with a hydroelectric power station on the Jordan River, north of the Sea of Galilee. This will be a small plant of 120 MW, and completion is expected during 1984-85. In addition, erection of a power station in Eilat at some time in the future is being considered.

Detailed design work on a super grid high voltage (400 kv) transmission system will be carried out during the next 2 years. The new grid will be needed during the 1986-87 period. Additional projects to enable transmission of energy from the Hadera Power Station to the central region, which will require energy supplies from the north by 1982, are being studied.

Although 60-79 percent of existing generating facilities in Israel are U.S. manufactured, there was intensive competition from European firms on the Southern Power Plant with a West German company winning the turbine contract. Germany, the United Kingdom, and Switzerland are the chief U.S. competitors for large engines. Favorable financing is considered an important factor in purchasing decisions.

The Israeli demand for medium and small generators and other electric power equipment totals $30 million per year. Standby generators are required by law for all buildings of eight or more floors. Local generator production is limited to small generators which are assembled from imported alternators and motors. Because domestic production is growing steadily, demand is growing for components and parts.

Alternatives to oil fuel are being developed and emphasized for long-term projects. As the use of nuclear power poses several problems, conversion to coal has progressed substantially during the past 3 years. Solar energy utilization also offers a practical alternative and is being explored.

Other Prospects

In addition to the industrial growth sectors cited above, other attractive markets, including the following, exist for American manufacturers.

Israeli exports of metalworking products and other products requiring the use of metalworking equipment are expected to grow from $174 million in 1975 to over $1 million by 1985. Total industrial production of metalworking products (both for the domestic market and for export) will grow from $1 billion in 1975 to $2.3 billion in 1985 (constant 1975 prices). Total production of other products requiring the use of metalworking machinery will increase from $500 million in 1975 to $1.3 billion in 1985. In addition, the heavy machinery investments which were made in 1968–69 (mostly from German reparation payments) will have to be replaced by the early 1980s. This provides an opportunity for U.S. manufacturerers to displace old equipment made in other countries and thus increase their share of the market.

Domestic production is insigificant; the main competition comes from Europe, especially in the conventional equipment field. Spain is becoming increasingly competitive in the small-to-medium size machines for N/C purposes. A new competitor, Japan, is offering sophisticated equipment, such as machine centers, at competitive prices and with attractive financing packages.

Israeli purchasers are interested in productivity, reliability, and accuracy in metalworking equipment, with price a secondary consideration. Nevertheless, American prices should be more competitive due to exchange rate developments.

Since Israel generally faces a shortage of manpower and a desire to expand exports and the defense sector, data processing technology will continue to be in strong demand. Increased adoption of computer technology in defense-related agencies, manufacturing enterprises, commercial banks, government agencies, insurance companies, medical groups, and educational institutions has already been noted. Current trends also indicate that small-size companies, realizing the need for efficient operating procedures, are buying terminals or subscribing to service bureaus. Furthermore, acquisition of data communications and terminal equipment will be in demand in an effort to upgrade present systems. The trend will be particularly significant in export-oriented industries as a result of duty-free access to the European Community for Israeli manufactured products.

Practically all small, medium, and large computer systems in Israel are of U.S. origin. American products will continue to dominate these product lines as they are regarded by the Israelis to be superior to the products of other suppliers. However, subsequent U.S. services and software support is regarded as only adequate.

Locally produced minicomputers, dominated by Elbit Computers, Ltd., should contribute as much as 30 percent of the market by 1981. Elta Electronics, the second largest local firm, manufactures peripheral equipment such as paper tape readers, high speed readers, modern and intelligent terminals. Third-country competition from West Germany, the United Kingdom, and France will continue, mainly in small business computers.

Local Israeli production of engines and mechanical power equipment is insignificant and limited to small engines. While overall the United States has an impressive share of the market, in some fields, such as large marine and diesel engines, the share is small. Engines and power equipment imports will continue to grow in the years ahead. Expansion of the construction industry (where the trend is toward multi-story buildings), the chemical and petrochemical industries, and oil drilling and refining, among others will require all types of diesel and gas fueled power equipment for auxiliary electrical generating applications.

The Israel Shipyards Ltd., which manufactures commercial and military ships and repairs

Israeli and foreign vessels, is a major importer of electric power equipment. Looking into the future, the government-owned company has ambitious plans for the construction of ships of 200,000–300,000 dead weight tons requiring purchase of large diesel and steam engines, gas turbines, heat exchangers and parts.

Since most Israeli medical care is nationalized, the principal blueprint for future development is the National Economic Plan for 1980. According to the plan, the annual net growth in sales of medical equipment from 1976 to 1980 is expected to be approximately 5 percent, with clinical laboratory equipment increasing slightly faster.

Investment in the medical sector at both public and private facilities is scheduled to grow at an average annual rate of 5 percent from 1976 to 1980, although growth will not be smooth. American manufacturers currently supply about 35 percent of all imported medical equipment; the U.S. share should remain roughly the same through 1980.

Concerted private and public efforts to expand Israel's major process industries should yield a $25 million market for industrial process controls in 1982, an 11 percent average annual increase over the 1978 level of $16.2 million. American industrialists have been Israel's leading suppliers of control instruments for more than 15 years. Their position should remain unchallenged in the high quality, advanced devices needed by the country's technology conscious, capital intensive manufacturing sectors.

Research and Development

Israel's total expenditures on research and development (R&D), including defense spending, in 1978–79 was almost $340 million with the Government contributing almost 63 percent. These expenditures account for about 2.3 percent of GNP, probably among the highest ratio in the world.

Learning in general and scientific research in particular are viewed by Israelis as a part of their cultural heritage as well as a vital element in the drive to establish a modern, productive, and disease-free state capable not only of sustaining its own scientific needs but of sharing in the scientific development of the world community. Even before independence was achieved in 1948, three of Israel's most prominent scientific institutions were well established—Technion Institute, Hebrew University, and the Weizman Institute. In addition, the Mandatory Government established laboratories and a central body for coordinating scientific and industrial research so that, in contrast to most other newly independent states, Israel entered nationhood with a number of important elements of scientific and technological infrastructure already in place.

On the basis of available statistics, the Government's science and technology planners have some reason to be satisfied with what has been achieved since 1969, for there has been not only an increase in R&D but a prounounced shift towards R&D activity in the applied research field relative to basic sciences research activity. There also has been a significant increase in R&D funding on the part of the manufacturing and agricultural sector and an increase in the number of trained engineers relative to the number of researchers trained in the natural sciences.

Data shows clearly the transformation in the relative proportions of basic and applied research between 1966–67 and 1978–79. In the case of civilian R&D (defense R&D data is not available prior to 1976), the ratio between basic research (63 percent) and applied research (37 percent) was almost completely reversed. Considering the entire national effort in 1978–79, including defense R&D, 76 percent was devoted to applied technological research, a ratio comparable to that in a developed country.

As might be expected, the shift to applied R&D was accompanied by an impressive increase of R&D activity and funding on the part of the manufacturing and agricultural sector. While institutions of higher learning continue to be the principal center of R&D performance, the manufacturing and agricultural sector is a close second, having increased its activity from 11 percent in 1966–67 to 43 percent of the civilian R&D effort in 1978–79. At the same time, this sector replaced the educational institutions as the second largest investor of civilian R&D funds, quadrupling its share in 1966–67. This appears to have been due largely to a decline in the income received by the universities from abroad and the obligation of elements of the manufacturing and agricultural sector to invest R&D funds to supplement those provided to them by the various chief scientists in the ministries.

Israel's large number of professional research workers increased 34 percent, from 9,400 in 1974 to an estimated 12,600 by the end of 1979. Of these, the majority are still trained in the natural sciences, medicine and agriculture.

To the extent that R&D policy reflects the goal of helping to reduce the unfavorable gap between Israel's imports and exports, government allocation of R&D's resources appears to have had some success. Although statistics are somewhat imprecise, those available indicate that government R&D spending in recent years has been targeted chiefly at agricultural products (consistently almost half the total spent by government research institutes) and certain industrial sectors, chiefly electrical and electronic equipment, chemical and oil products, and machinery in that order. Agricultural products for some time have ranked as an export commodity second only to polished diamonds and have tripled in value from 1967 to 1977. Informed sources state that, while the private sector has probably overtaken the contributions of the Government in the field of crop improvement, there is no question but that without the initial work of the Agricultural Research Organizations Israeli agricultural exports would not have achieved such success.

Israel participates in a large number of international and bilateral scientific activities. Its cooperative arrangements with the United States, however, are unique in that they include three separate binational foundations, jointly funded and administered, having as their purpose the promotion of R&D projects of mutual interest.

The U.S.-Israel Binational Science Foundation (BSF), established in 1972 with an endowment of $60 million, funds joint basic and applied research projects in the life sciences, natural sciences, medicine, agriculture, energy, and social sciences. Thus far over 600 projects have been approved for funding. Joint industrial R&D projects (non-defense related) are funded by the Binational Industrial Research and Development Foundation (BIRD), which started up in 1977, also endowed with the equivalent of $60 million. This organization is of particular interest to the Israeli Government because of its potential for increasing Israeli industrial exports.

The Binational Agricultural Research and Development Foundation (BARD), established in 1977, funds cooperative projects submitted by U.S. and Israeli laboratories from the interest gained on its initial endowment of $80 million. Fifty such projects have been approved to date.

Industrial Property Protection*

Israel is a member of the "Paris Union" International Convention for the Protection of Indus-

*Prepared by Foreign Business Practice Division, Office of International Finance, Investment, and Services, International Trade Administration.

trial Property (patents, trademarks, commercial names, and industrial designs) to which the United States and about 85 other countries adhere. American businessmen and inventors are therefore entitled to receive national treatment in Israel (i.e., treatment equal to that accorded Israeli citizens) under that country's laws regarding the protection of patents, trademarks, and other industrial property rights. American nationals are also entitled to certain other benefits, such as the protection of their patents against arbitrary forfeiture for nonworking and one-year "right of priority" for filing their patent applications (i.e., 1 year, after first filing a patent application in the United States, in which to file a corresponding application in Israel and receive for the latter the benefit of the first U.S. application filing date). The "right of priority" period for trademark applications is 6 months.

Israel is also a member of the Universal Copyright Convention to which the United States and about 60 other countries adhere. Works of American authors first copyrighted in the United States are thereby entitled to automatic protection in Israel. To obtain such protection in Israel, the author need only show on such work his name, year of first publication, and the symbol "c" in a circle. Israel is also a member of the Berne Copyright Convention, to which about 60 countries, but not the United States, belong. U.S. authors may, however, obtain protection in Berne Union countries by publishing a work in a Union country simultaneously with its first publication and copyright in the United States.

Patents

The basic law for the protection of patents in Israel is the Patents Law, 5727-1967, effective April 1, 1968. Patents are granted for a period of 20 years from the effective filing date of the application. Inventions must be novel (i.e., not published or used anywhere in the world) in order to be patentable. Applications are examined and, if satisfactory, are published for opposition for 3 months. If a patentee does not work his patent to satisfy local needs, it can be subjected to compulsory licensing. Such licensing cannot be ordered, however, before the end of 3 years after the patent grant or 4 years after application filing date, whichever is later.

Trademark

Trademarks are protected under the Trademarks Ordinance of 1938, as amended (reissued in Hebrew version in 5732-1972). For registration purposes, the "Nice International Classification" system (34 classes of goods and eight classes of services) is used. Trademark registrations are valid for several years from the effective filing date of the application and renewable for 14-year periods. Applications are examined; if found satisfactory, they are published for opposition for 3 months. A party who is the first user of the mark and who desires recognized exclusive use by virtue of its registration may apply for and receive a registration and exclusive ownership of the mark. Proprietary rights are conferred by first use or by application, whichever is earlier.

After 5 years, a registered mark becomes incontestable on grounds of prior use or ownership. Non-use of a registered mark for 2 consecutive years can result in its cancellation.

Copyrights

Protection of copyright in Israel is governed by the United Kingdom Copyright Act of 1911, as applied to Palestine in 1924, maintained in force in Israel, and amended up to 1971. The term of copyright protection is for the author's life plus 70 years after his death, for any literary, dramatic, or musical work. This includes the exclusive right to produce and reproduce the work, or a translation of it, to publish such work or translation, to perform it in public, and to authorize others to do the aforementioned.

New or original industrial designs may be registered for protection for 5 years from application filing date and renewed for two periods of 5 years each.

Communications pertaining to patent, trademark, and other industrial property rights matters should be addressed to the Commissioner of Patents, Designs, and Trademarks, Ministry of Justice, Jaffa Road 19, P.O. Box 767, Jerusalem. On copyright matters, communications should be addressed to the Administrative Director in Charge of Copyrights, Ministry of Justice, at the same address.

Further information on the general provisions of Israel's patent, trademark, industrial design, and copyright laws may be obtained from the U.S. Department of Commerce, Foreign Business Practices Division, Office of International Finance, Investment, and Services, International Trade Administration. That Division, however, is not in a position to provide detailed information on fees or other specific step-by-step procedures to be followed in seeking protection

under these laws. Competent legal counsel should be consulted for this purpose.

Transportation and Utilities

Transportation

Israel's merchant fleet, including Israeli ships under foreign flag, numbered 105 in 1978, with a total deadweight of 4.6 million tons. The largest companies are Zim Navigation, El Yam, and Maritime Fruit Carriers.

All Mediterranean traffic—passenger and cargo—is handled through the deepwater ports of Haifa and Ashdod. Haifa Port, which services more than half of Israel's total port turnover, handled 5,447 thousands tons of freight (3,950 thousand tons unloading; 1,497 thousand tons loading) in 1978. The port has over 4,100 meters of wharves in the main port and Kishon Harbor. About 60,000 square meters of closed storage space and 80,000 square meters of open storage space is available in the main harbor. In the Kishon area, 60,000 square meters and 125,000 square meters of closed and open storage space respectively is available. The Kishon area also has cold storage, container, and roll-on/roll-off facilities. The Port of Haifa's passenger terminal, which has been under construction for the past 25 years, was put into regular use in 1979. The port expansion project, costing $40 million, is scheduled to be completed by 1983. The Israel Ports Authority, however, hopes it can be completed by October 1981, well ahead of schedule.

Ashdod Port, accounting for more than one-third of total port turnover, primarily loads and unloads consumer goods. The port handled 4,389 thousand tons in 1978, of which 1,399 thousand tons were imports and 2,990 thousand tons were exports. The port has four piers including a bulk pier and a container pier and three berths for roll-on/roll-off traffic. Ashdod has 500,000 square meters of storage area plus cold storage warehouses.

A third port, Eilat, on the Gulf of Aqaba, has 528 meters of wharves, 200 meters of quays of 6 meter depth, 55,000 square meters of storage area (both open and closed) and cold storage facilities. The port can handle container traffic. Eilat handled 1,027 thousands tons of freight in 1978, of which 314 thousand tons were imports and 713 thousand tons were exports.

Passenger traffic at all three ports totaled 264,332 in 1978; 131,732 arrivals and 132,600 departures.

Two U.S. shipping lines offer regular service to Israel. Farrell Lines serves the Atlantic coast and Lykes Steamship Company operates primarily from the Gulf of Mexico. The New York to Haifa voyage normally requires 2-3 weeks.

Ben Gurion Airport, the only international airport in Israel, is located 15 miles from Tel Aviv. El Al, Israel's national airline, maintains regular service to major European cities, several points in Africa, and New York. Foreign air carriers, including Trans World Airlines, also service Ben Gurion Airport. International air freight and passengers handled in 1977 totaled 107,468 tons and 2.41 million passengers respectively. Domestic air service is provided by a purely internal airline, ARKIA. Regularly scheduled service connects Ben Gurion Airport with Eilat, Mahanaim, Masada and Jerusalem. Charter and nonscheduled services are offered to other parts of the country.

Highways are an important part of the country's internal transport network. The major population centers are connected by good roads; in 1978 Israel had some 11,891 kilometers of road. Trucks and buses provide the most common means of inland transport because of the relatively undeveloped rail system and short distances involved.

Israel's railroad, owned and operated by the Ministry of Transport, is a fairly small system with total trackage of approximately 516 kilometers in 1977. The major passenger and freight lines connect Haifa, Tel Aviv, and Jerusalem.

The Ministry of Transport is still hoping to complete the Eilat railroad project which would link the Red Sea and the Mediterranean. At present, railway connections extend from Ashdod Port to Har-Zin in the Negev, site of the new phosphate mine. Complex reconstruction engineering work was underway in late 1979 for the 24 kilometer section between Har-Zin and Ein Hatzeva. To complete the railway track in the south, 174 kilometers of main line southward to Eilat and an additional 35 kilometers northward to Sdom on the Dead Sea have to be constructed. Eventual completion of the project, which appears economically feasible and which would provide low cost transport for mineral exports through the ports of Ashdod and Eilat, is dependent upon financing.

Power

Electric power is supplied by the government owned Israel Electric Corporation. Electricity generation in 1978-79 (ending March 31, 1979) totaled 11.6 billion kilowatt hours; sales reached 10.4 billion kilowatt hours. Almost 35 percent of electricity sales were purchased by industrial users. The number of electricity consumers on March 3, 1979 was 1.2 million, some 40,000 more than a year earlier. Residential and commercial electric current is 220 volts alternating current, 50 cycles.

Fuel

The following is a list of the main types of fuel used in Israel and the prevailing retail prices including tax, duty and value added tax (VAT) as of December 19, 1979:

Motor Gasoline 83 Octane	$0.71/Liter
Motor Gasoline 94 Octane	$0.75/Liter
Diesel Fuel	$0.29/Liter
Household Kerosene	$0.32/Liter
Gas for Cooking	$9.19/Container of 12 KG
Heavy Fuel Oil (Mazut) for Industry	$160.53/Metric Ton (excl VAT)
Heavy Fuel Oil (Mazut) for Electricity	$151.69/Metric Ton (excl VAT)

Distribution and Sales Channels

Representation

Most U.S. firms exporting to Israel have found it convenient to appoint a local representative. In some cases, particularly for heavy industrial equipment, the representative is a commission agent who conducts a limited promotional campaign and calls on potential buyers but who does not import on his own account. In other instances, especially in the light industrial and consumer goods fields, a distributor will be appointed. The distributor usually imports on his own account, carries stocks sufficient to satisfy immediate demand or to use for demonstration, maintains his own sales organization and supplies spare parts and servicing facilities. In any case, the dependability of after-sales service is a very important sales inducement.

An Israeli law, effective March 20, 1977, regulates all commissions paid to agents of suppliers of military goods. Agents selling equipment to the Israeli defense agencies must now receive prior approval from the Ministry of Defense before receiving any commission. If receipt of a commission is permitted, the Defense Ministry also regulates the amount of the fee.

Contract Procedures

The relatively advanced economic base in Israel means that development efforts are focused on maintaining and upgrading the basic infrastructure and on expanding the capacity and technology level of the sophisticated and diversified industrial base. Despite a highly skilled work force, particularly in the civil engineering and construction industries, the Israelis often seek specialized skills in the world market. Rather than issuing a general tender notice, they generally invite one or more companies with the needed capability to negotiate a contract. The contract is usually for a specific portion of the project. Proposals are seldom requested from consortia or from a turnkey contract.

Though the private industrial sector plays a growing role in the economy, most of the large projects are undertaken by the Government and by organizations which are required to follow the Government's tender regulations. The Israeli customer's willingness to allow some flexibility in the application of the regulations depends on such things as the size of the contract and the number of firms capable of providing the requested service.

The Government encourages the maximum use of local resources on projects in Israel. Preference is always given to the bid which has a low price and proposes the use of a high proportion of Israeli materials and equipment. The local supply may be contracted separately or included in the overall contract. The client will pay for locally produced goods at the price which is current at the time of purchase. All contracts require that 25 percent of the value of the contract be offset by the purchase of Israeli-made goods. The 25 percent is calculated after deducting the local supply included in the contract.

A review of the applicable rules and regulations can be obtained from the U.S. Department of Commerce publication, "An Introduction to Contract Procedures in the Near East and North Africa," February 1978, available from the Superintendent of Documents, Government Printing Office, Washington, D.C. 20402.

Central Government and Municipal Purchasing

Government agencies either purchase through commercial importers or buy directly from foreign suppliers. Tenders are seldom issued, as central government agencies usually "shop around," weighing the merits of quality and price. In the United States, these agencies make many of their purchases through the Government of Israel Supply Mission at Empire State Building, 350 Fifth Avenue, New York, New

York 10001. Defense-related equipment is purchased through a second Government of Israel Supply Mission (Ministry of Defense), 850 Third Avenue, New York, New York 10016. The Histradrut, Israel's General Federation of Labor and the largest employer, makes purchases in the United States through Solcoor, Inc., 415 Madison Avenue, New York, New York 10017.

Tenders frequently are issued by the various municipal governments, but they seldom allow sufficient time or give enough details to allow foreign suppliers to submit bids. The terms of most tenders are usually known in advance by the business community, including representatives of foreign firms. These representatives are also able, through their personal contacts, to apply sales effort where they will be most effective.

Retailing Methods

Israel has over 2,200 retail outlets that employ four or more persons. The shops are predominantly privately owned, specializing in a limited number of items. About 540 of these are food retailers (including supermarkets, small groceries, and cooperatives). The stores, together with many fruit and vegetable stands, are located throughout commercial and residential areas. Dry goods, clothing, hardware, and gift shops can be found in every settlement of any size. Israel's 48 department stores have not yet gained the importance that these outlets have in other countries. However, the one commercial supermarket chain and the cooperative supermarket chain are gaining in popularity.

Time-payment buying has not yet reached the proportions that it has in the United States. Most retail credits do not exceed 12 months and a substantial down payment as well as some form of collateral or consignors are required.

Prices of nearly all goods are high as consumer demand, whetted by the constantly rising standard of living, often exceeds the available supply. In an attempt to control inflation, the Government has imposed a series of price controls over the past several years.

Licensing

Israeli Government controls are not a major problem in establishing licensing agreements in Israel. Israeli businessmen usually prefer to negotiate agreements for an initial 5 years which are automatically renewable for another 5 years. They also prefer agreements where the licensor takes equity with the licensee.

The transfer of fees and royalties is not limited. The normal royalty is 4–5 percent of turnover although higher rates apply for luxury items, authors' fees, and specialized machinery.

A withholding tax of 25 percent on royalties and fees is withheld at the source. Royalties and fee payments are deductible by the licensee in calculating his income tax.

Distribution Practices

About 27 percent of Israel's population (3.8 million in 1979) is concentrated in the metropolitan area of Tel Aviv and Jaffa, which is the center of most of the country's commercial and financial activity. Haifa, the second largest community, accounts for 15 percent of the population, and is the site of most heavy industry, such as oil refining and chemical processing.

The kibbutzim (collective settlements) and moshavin (cooperative settlements) are beginning to seek licensing and know-how agreements in fields that do not require extensive capital.

Almost all goods, especially those that are imported, are distributed through Tel Aviv or Haifa. Only a few firms maintain branches, showrooms, or service facilities in other communities.

Wholesale and Retail Channels

Most marketing of agricultural and dairy products is carried out by cooperatives, which retail the items in their own stores or act as wholesalers to independent merchants. Wholesale firms have not developed as they have in the United States, and in many cases, such as in textile goods and furniture, no wholesale channel exists. Few imported goods, especially consumer-oriented items, pass through wholesalers. Most importers prefer to act as the exclusive representative of their foreign suppliers and maintain their own distribution network.

Advertising and Research

Advertising

Advertising is a relatively new but rapidly growing industry. Although there are over 100 advertising agencies in Israel, many are operated by one or two people in a one-room office. Fewer than 20 provide the comprehensive service available to business in the United States. Agencies are generally paid by media-granted commissions, but a growing number of clients pay retaining fees.

Israel enjoys a high literacy rate (over 90 percent), and the people are avid readers. The mass immigration has resulted in 24 daily newspapers published in 11 different languages. Because of this diversification, graphics design has been emphasized and display advertisements predominate. There are weekend supplements and trade publications covering shipping, medicine, industry, and economics.

Radio and television broadcasting is controlled by the Israel Broadcasting Authority (IBA), the government owned and operated network. Five radio programs are broadcast on 25 wave lengths. The main program is noncommercial, but the others with a more popular content permit advertising. Audience measurement proves radio to be a very effective advertising medium for consumer products, as radio provides the easiest way to reach all segments of the population without placing multiple advertisements. The business office address is Regie Israel Ltd., 224 Ben Yehuda Street, Tel Aviv. Three English language news broadcasts may be heard on radio each day. An English language station broadcasts from outside Israel's territorial waters.

Regular daily television broadcasts, in Hebrew and Arabic, began in November 1969. There are 355,000 licensed television sets in the country. Most of the imported programs are translated into Hebrew and Arabic. Israeli television broadcasts in black and white only. Local television does not accept advertising and does not broadcast in English.

The movie theater is the predominent source of entertainment. Some 240 theaters are in operation throughout the country, featuring domestic and foreign films in their original languages. Generally, only one feature is shown, preceded by a newsreel, advertising film clips and slides. Theater advertisements, many of which are extremely well done, are usually limited to consumer products.

Israel has a well-developed printing industry which regularly turns out multicolor advertisements that are posted throughout the country, especially on wooden fences surrounding new construction. There are some roadside billboards and the use of neon signs is growing. Most outdoor advertising uses both Hebrew and English. Direct mail and leaflet advertising have been introduced with some success.

Market Research and Trade Organizations

Market research is handled by a few competent private firms and the larger advertising agencies. The Ministry of Trade, Industry, and

Tourism has its own Marketing Research Institute located in Tel Aviv. This Institute will conduct research at the request of companies at nominal costs. The Institute's library is probably the most complete in Israel in this field.

There is an active American-Israel Chamber of Commerce and Industry at 500 Fifth Avenue, New York, New York 10035, and Israel-U.S. Joint Business Council (secretariat in the U.S.-Chamber of Commerce, 1615 H Street, N.W., Washington, D.C. 20062), and an Israel-America Chamber of Commerce and Industry in Israel at 35 Shaul Hamelech Boulevard, P.O. Box 33174, Tel Aviv. In addition, there are many businessman's clubs and organizations, such as the Chamber of Commerce of Tel Aviv-Jaffa, 84 Hahashmonaim Street, P.O. Box 20027, Tel Aviv; the Haifa Chamber of Commerce and Industry, 53 Haatzmauth Road, P.O. Box 33176, Haifa; the Jerusalem Chamber of Commerce, 10 Hillel Street, P.O. Box 183, Jerusalem; the Manufacturers' Association of Israel, 29 Hamered Street, P.O. Box 297, Tel Aviv; and the Israel Hotel Association, 18 Idelson Street, P.O. Box 26278, Tel Aviv.

Credit

Local Capital Participation

Specialized institutions, owned by the Government or jointly by the Government and the commercial banks, are the principal sources of medium and long-term credit in Israel. Known generally as mortgage, cooperative, and industrial banks, they cater to the investment needs of housing, agriculture, and industry. Of the 20 mortgage banks, the largest is the Tefahot Israel Mortgage Bank, which recently was purchased by the United Mizrahi Bank. Mortgage banks finance housing and civic amenities while the development banks finance long term development projects. For the most part, the development banks are organized to service a specific sector of the economy. The largest is the Industrial Development Bank of Israel (IDB), which was founded in 1959 by the Government, the "big three" banks, the national labor federation, and the manufacturers association. IDB is the principal source of medium-and-long term industrial financing. The Bank of Agriculture is the single largest institution lending to the agricultural sector. Eight credit cooperatives engage in banking services (with the exception of foreign exchange transfers). Other types of financial institutions are the social insurance funds and insurance companies which invest mainly in government bonds and development banks.

Commercial banks also make available funds for some types of industrial development undertakings, though usually on shorter terms than the mortgage and development banks. Commercial banking activity is dominated by the three largest: Bank Leumi L'Israel B.M., Bank Hapoalim B.M., and the Israel Discount Bank, Ltd. These banks also participate in the ownership and management of some of the 17 smaller Israeli banks. The "big three" have extensive branch networks throughout Israel.

Foreign banks once played a substantial role in Israel, but they have declined in importance as the local banks have grown. Only one Israeli bank is foreign controlled, and no foreign bank has a branch in Israel.

The Tel Aviv Stock Exchange (T.A.S.E.) is the only organized stock exchange in Israel. After a slump, the T.A.S.E. is once again becoming an important means of raising capital. Issues of shares to the general public must comply with regulations promulgated under the Securities Law. The regulations deal with the content of financial statements and prospectuses to assure that the public obtains full and accurate information. The Office of the Commissioner of Financing and the Capital Market reviews a proposed issue from the viewpoint of whether it will be beneficial for the economy.

U.S. Economic Assistance

Since FY 1972, the United States Agency for International Development (AID) has provided loans and grants to Israel to finance non-defense commodity imports and to meet the country's need for cash. From modest economic assistance of $50 million in FY 1972, the program has grown to $785 million annually in FY 1978, 1979, and 1980. In addition to the FY 1979 economic assistance package, the United States provided Israel with $800 million in grants for relocation of air bases from the Sinai to the Negev as part of the post Egypt-Israel peace aid package.

Beginning in FY 1979, U.S. Economic Assistance to Israel shifted to a cash transfer from the previous Commodity Import Program. The Government of Israel has provided written assurances that this shift would not adversely impact the aggregate level of Israel's civilian imports from the United States or access to the Israeli market by American firms. As a result, the level of assistance provides significant financing for a wide variety of American products.

In addition to economic assistance, Israel receives military assitance of about $1 billion, in both grants and loans, from the United States.

Trade Regulations

Tariff Structure

Israel has a single-column import tariff based on the Brussels nomenclature classification. Ad valorem rates predominate, although specific and compound rates are also used. Ad valorem duties are imposed at rates ranging from 3 to 150 percent, and are based on c.i.f. value for air freight via Ben Gurion airport and c.i.f. value plus 2.5 percent of c.i.f. value for sea shipments. Most basic food commodities, raw materials, and machinery for agricultural or industrial purposes are exempt from customs duties. Highest rates are applied to nonessential foodstuffs, luxury consumer items, and manufactured goods of a type produced in Israel.

In May 1975, Israel and the European Community (EC) entered into an agreement which phased out all tariffs on Israeli industrial exports to the EC on July 1, 1977. Israel will phase out tariffs on EC industrial exports, to reach zero by 1989.

Goods of U.S.-origin are guaranteed most-favored-nation treatment under a Treaty of Friendship, Commerce, and Navigation between the United States and Israel in force since 1954. Israel is also a member of the General Agreement on Tariffs and Trade (GATT).

Information regarding Israeli duties applicable to specific products may be obtained free of charge from the Commerce Action Group for the Near East, Office of Country Marketing, U.S. Department of Commerce, Washington, D.C. 20230; or from any Department of Commerce District Office. Inquiries should contain a complete product description, including BTN, SITC, or U.S. Schedule B Export commodity number, if known.

Duties, Surcharges and Taxes

Specific import duties are assessed on the net weight, unless otherwise specified; ad valorem duties are assessed on a cost, insurance, and freight (c.i.f.) basis. The c.i.f. value is the cost of the goods in the country of origin on the day of clearance plus all costs incident to delivery at the port of entry in Israel. If an unreasonable disparity exists between the c.i.f. value, as invoiced, and the current market c.i.f. value of similar goods at the time of importation, the lat-ter value is taken as the basis for levying cutoms. Duties are payable in Israeli currency.

A schedule of purchase taxes is applicable to certain items imported into or produced in Israel. Included in the list of taxable items are building materials, household furnishings, utensils and appliances and luxury goods. Purchase taxes under the New Economic Policy, introduced in October 1977, were lowered and exemptions were made for most raw materials for industry. The tax is levied on the wholesale price, i.e., landed cost plus wholesaler's uplift (used to adjust import cost before imposition of purchase tax).

Other possible charges include a 2 percent port charge on the c.i.f. value and a stevedoring tariff assessed according to the size of the containers.

On July 1, 1976, a Value Added Tax (VAT) came into effect on most goods and services sold in Israel, including all imports. The VAT of 12 percent on imported goods is based on their landed cost plus import duty.

Import Deposit

Effective November 20, 1979, the Government of Israel imposed a 10 percent import deposit scheme. The deposit based on the c.i.f. value is to be paid on all goods on which customs duty is due. The deposit earns no interest and will be returned to the importer after 6 months.

Samples and Advertising Matter

Israeli regulations concerning trade samples and advertising matter are based on international standards and conventions. Trade samples of negligible value in quantities necessary for soliciting orders and not for distribution to the general public are exempt from duty and do not require a license. Trade samples accompanied by an ECS (Echantillon Carnet Samples) may be carried or sent into Israel without an import license, import entries, or securities. An ECS may also be used by engineers, doctors, technicians, or others who wish to take along instruments or other equipment. Arrange for an ECS in advance of travel abroad through the United States Council of the International Chamber of Comerce, Carnet Bureau, 1212 Avenue of the Americas, New York, New York 10036, (212) 354-4480 or 100 California Street, Suite 1100, San Francisco, California 94111, (415) 956-3356.

Trade samples neither of neglible value nor imported under the Enchantillon Carnet Samples regulation may be introduced into Israel without a license by submission of securities.

Advance Rulings on Classification

It is possible to obtain an advance ruling on a customs classification if all pertinent data regarding the goods are supplied and found sufficient. Application for the ruling should be made to the Directorate of Customs, Tel Aviv, Israel.

Fines and Penalties

The penalty provided by law for misinformation on any document, refusal to present documents, or evasion of payment of duty is imprisonment for 2 years and/or a fine of 500 Israeli pounds. The penalty for importation of prohibited goods is 6 months imprisonment and/or a fine of 100 Israeli pounds. As of March 1977, goods entering Israel without proper customs invoices identifying the country of origin must pay an import deposit of 10 percent, refundable only after presentation of a corrected invoice.

In January 1977, Israel passed an antidumping law to protect local manufacturers from unfair competition by foreign suppliers.

Entry and Reexport

Goods landed in Israel are placed in public warehouses or any other place of security approved by the Collector of Cutoms. Port storage fees are charged after 8 days (16 days for cargo in transit or transshipment). Many public bonded warehouses offer facilities for cold and chemical storage. Grain silos and licensed private bonded warehouses are also available

Goods in transit are accepted provided prior declaration on the proper forms is made to the collector of customs at the place of entry. Goods in transit must be reexported within 90 days of their receipt.

Free port zones have been established in Haifa and Eilat.

Marking, Labeling, and Packaging Requirements

All imports into Israel must contain a label indicating the name of the producer, the contents and the weight in metric units. In most instances English may be used, but some items require Hebrew labeling or dual foreign language/Hebrew labeling. Food products to be sold in Israel must be packaged in specific net weight metric units according to the "Standard Weights of Food Products Order," December 1975. Specific information is available from the Director of the Department of Weights and Measures, Ministry of Commerce and Industry, P.O. Box 299, Jerusalem.

Specific label regulations apply to some consumer goods, paper products, handbags, phonographic records, fertilizers, insecticides, chemicals, pharmaceuticals, some food products, seeds, wine, whiskey, beer, and other alcoholic beverages. In addition, special packing material regulations apply to fruit, plants, and meat. Outside and inside containers of dangerous articles such as poisons, insecticides, drugs, inflammable goods, ammunition, explosives, reptiles, insects, bacteria, and radioactive materials should be clearly marked.

If goods bear any marking that is found on examination to constitute a false "trade description," they are liable to detention or seizure.

No marks may be applied (such as the words "Patented," "Registered Design," and "Trade Mark Registered," used alone) that suggests that the patent, design, or trademark has been registered in Israel, if such is not the case.

Imported goods of foreign manufacture bearing the name or trademark of a manufacturer, dealer, or trader in Israel must also indicate the name of the country in which the goods were made or produced.

Although there are no specific requirements as to the marking of outside packing cases, it is customary to use marks and numbers for purposes of identification of the goods upon arrival, thereby assuring their early clearance through customs.

Strong and durable packing is recommended to withstand rough handling of cargo on landing from ships. Secure packing is essential to discourage pilferage.

Senate Concurrent Resolution 40, adopted July 30, 1953, invites U.S. exporters to inscribe, insofar as practicable, on the external shipping containers in indelible print of a suitable size: "United States of America."

Shipping Documents

The documents required for shipments to Israel by ocean or air transport include commercial invoices, and bills of lading (or air waybills). Any other documents relating to the dispatch of goods, their value or charges incurred in transit, such as policies of insurance, may also be needed. A packing list is needed only if a shipment contains more than two packages or when the invoice does not specifiy in detail the contents of each package. Whenever goods are palletized or containerized (full containers door to door or pier to door), a separate packing list should be issued for each pallet/container. In addition, special certificates from the country of origin authorities are required for shipments of live animals, bees, plants, liquors and whiskey, frozen meat, hides and animal parts. Food products may require a Kosher certificate regarding the contents of the commodity. The certificate must be issued by an orthodox Rabbi and be forwarded to the Rabbinate in Jerusalem, or as otherwise instructed. U.S. requirements include a shipper's export declaration.

The following clause must appear on bills of lading for Israel: "This vessel is not to call at or enter the territorial waters of any Yemeni, Jordanian, Saudi Arabian, Iraqi, Lebanese, Syrian, Sudanese, Libyan or other Arab (except Egypt) port prior to unloading in Israel unless the ship is in distress or subject to force majeure. Transshipment is permitted."

Information concerning postal regulations for mailing letter packages, small packets and parcel post shipments to Israel can be obtained from the U.S. Postal Service, North Capitol Street and Massachusetts Avenue, Washington, D.C. 20013; phone (202) 523-2375 or any U.S. Post Office.

Import Licensing

The majority of Israel's imports are free from licensing and administrative or quantitative restrictions. Most products, including textiles, pharmaceuticals, foodstuffs, electrical equipment, and automobiles, which remain on the "Restrictive List" require licenses in order to protect the public's health and safety. A few items cannot be imported.

Israel does not discriminate as to source of supply; however, exceptions may be made for goods available through surplus disposal programs, goods covered by specific tied loan agreements, and imports under bilateral agreements. Imports from Rhodesia are prohibited.

There is no requirement for registration of importers. Previously those wishing to engage in foreign trade had to register at the Ministry of Industry and Trade.

Investment in Israel

Foreign Investment

Since its founding, the Government of Israel has sought in its policy and practice, to encourage foreign investment. Several hundred foreign companies, including 23 which are among the largest 250 U.S. companies on Fortune Magazine's list, have set up manufacturing and/or exporting subsidiaries in Israel. The Labor Government, in power from independence until May 1977, directed investment through the Investment Authority and regulated it through the 1948 Law for the Encouragement of Capital Investments in Israel. The present Likud Government, inaugurated in May 1977, continues to encourage foreign investment within its overall policy of emphasizing private initiative. Specifically, the Likud Government has floated the Israeli pound, liberalized foreign currency regulations and announced plans to divest itself of many of its business operations.

The Government maintains a substantial measure of influence over foreign investment through its power to screen all investments seeking government incentives. The Government determines eligibility for incentives under geographic or industrial criteria. Geographic preference depends on the distance from the central economic zone around Tel Aviv. Industrial criteria favors industries which are export oriented, science based or replace imports. The Government particularly encourages metalworking and electronics investments which produce for export. The policy also favors basic industries, recycling plants, and energy saving or environmental protecting industries. Capital intensive investment is preferred, due to the chronic labor shortage.

The acquisition of real property in Israel by residents of foreign countries is subject to the approval of the Director of Land Registry or that of the Controller of Foreign Exchange. Their decision is based on the amount or method of transfer of the consideration paid or received. In practice, normally no obstacles are raised. Subsurface mineral resources remain the property of the Government, which is authorized to license exploration and exploitation rights for specified periods in specified areas.

Although the Government's policy is to maintain stable terms and conditions of benefits to foreign investment, changes may be deemed necessary from time to time. It is, therefore, advisable to check at an early stage of planning with the Israel Government Investment Authority; 350 Fifth Avenue, New York, New York 10001, phone: (212) 560-0610. The Investment Authority has branch offices at 174 North Michigan Avenue, Chicago, Illinois 60601, phone: (312) 651-5700, and 905 Peachtree Street, N.E., Suite 656, Atlanta, Georgia 30308, phone: (404) 875-6947.

Law for the Encouragement of Capital Investment

Investment is governed by the Law for the Encouragement of Capital Investments of 1959, as amended, which provides a broad range of financial concessions for both local and foreign investors. For the purpose of administering the law, Israel is divided into three geographic areas, with the concessions higher for investment in outlying areas. The concessions include tax reductions, which allow an optional 50 percent depreciation on equipment, long-term loans at subsidized rates of interest, cash grants, and other benefits deemed appropriate to specific investments (see appendix).

The Government encourages development of projects which will result in exports or which will provide import substitution. It also encourages development of science-based industries by providing designated projects with direct financial benefits, research support, and aid in establishing industrial parks.

Under the Law for the Encouragement of Capital Investment, investment projects are designated as belonging to one of the following categories, each one carrying specific incentives and benefits. They are: Approved Enterprise, Approved Investment, Approved Specialist, Approved Loan, and Approved Property. Application for "approved" status is made to the Investment Center in Jerusalem.

Industrial investments which have "approved" status are eligible for government loans through the Industrial Development Bank of Israel (IDBI) or another industrial finance bank. These medium-and-long term loans at subsidized rates are not automatically approved.

Whatever the designated status of an investment project, negotiations between the investor and the Israeli Government will determine what proportion of an investment will be put up by the owner, what portion will be granted by the Government, and what amount will be loaned, under the guidelines of Israeli investment law.

Business Organization

The principal business entities in Israel are the sole proprietorship, general and limited partnerships, cooperative society, societies based on Ottoman law, a branch of a foreign corporation, and three types of companies. The type of company limited by shares and the branch of a foreign company are the entities commonly used by foreign investors.

The individual proprietorship is the most common form of organization in the retail-wholesale trade, but is rare in industry. The cooperative society is important in Israel and used in agricultural activities, marketing, bus and truck transportation, provident funds, and other areas. Ottoman associations are formed under the Turkish Ottoman Association Law of 1909, which is still valid. Only nonprofit bodies such as religious, fraternal, charitable, or political organizations can form Ottoman associations.

The Israeli law of partnership differs from the English law in that a duly registered partnership is a legal person and can sue and be sued in the name of the firm. A partnership formed abroad can carry on business in Israel after having registered with the Registrar of Partnerships.

The Companies Ordinance, as amended, regulates the formation and conduct of companies in Israel. The basic law, the Companies Ordinance of 1929, is modeled on the English law as it stood prior to enactment of the English Companies Act of 1948. It provides for the formation of an unlimited company, a company limited by guaranty, a limited share company, and a company with share capital.

Aids for Exporters

Potential investors seeking to establish exporting projects in Israel can find a number of public and government institutions as well as professional groups to help them deal with specific areas of overseas marketing.

In Israel, firms seeking to enter the export market can avail themselves of these services to learn more about the regulations and characteristics peculiar to overseas markets. For instance, the Ministries of Industry, Trade, and Tourism; Foreign Affairs, Finance and Agriculture conduct ongoing programs covering intergovernmental trade negotiations, determination of export development policies and incentives to encourage export development. Activities of these organizations are coordinated by the Foreign Trade Devision of the Ministry of Industry, Trade, and Tourism through its Documentation and Market Research Center.

The Ministry of Industry, Trade, and Tourism, in cooperation with the Ministries of Foreign Affairs; Finance; and Agriculture maintain a network of economic and commercial representatives in 38 countries throughout the world. This network has broadened and grown, keeping pace with the development of Israeli exports. Today, Israel maintains trade representations in every country which constitutes a singificant market for its exports and in those where export potential exists.

Factors Affecting Investment

As a result of a trade agreement signed with the European Community (EC) in May 1975, most Israeli industrial products enjoy duty-free access to all the Common Market countries. Israel will abolish import duties on manufactured goods from the EC by 1989. Another attraction for foreign investors is the designation of Israel by the United States as a beneficiary of GSP, the Generalized System of Preferences (January 1, 1976). This program permits some 98 developing countries to export about 2,800 products to the United States duty free. Israel also has treaties providing varying degrees of reduction of tariff barriers with Australia, Austria, Canada, Finland, Japan, New Zealand, Norway, Switzerland and Sweden. The Government of Israel hopes that small and medium size American firms will establish operations in Israel to supply the EC, the United States, and other regional markets along with the local market.

At the May 1975 meeting of the U.S.-Israel Joint Committee for Investment and Trade, the governments of the two countries agreed to initiate a treaty to avoid double taxation. The treaty has been presented for ratification according to each nation's constitutional process. Currently the treaty is before the U.S. Senate.

A Treaty of Friendship, Commerce, and Navigation between Israel and the United States has been in effect since 1954. It guarantees the protection and security of American citizens and their property in Israel and prohibits expropriation except for public purposes, in which event prompt and equitable compensation is mandatory. The Treaty further provides for nondiscriminatory treatment of American citizens and firms engaged in business activity for profit, but reserves the right of the Israeli Government to limit the extent to which aliens, including U.S. citizens, may conduct business in the fields of communications, air or water transport, banking, or exploitation of land or other natural resources, with the provision that any such limitation be imposed on a most-favored-nation basis in all events.

The United States has an Investment Guaranty Agreement with Israel under which U.S. investors can secure insurance against inconvertability, expropriation, war, revolution, and insurrection as well as investment guarantees for project financing. This program is administered by the Overseas Private Investment Corporation (OPIC). Additional information on this program may be obtained from the Overseas Private Investment Corporation, Washington, D.C. 20527.

The U.S.-Israel Joint Committee for Investment and Trade, established in 1974, sponsored a U.S.-Israel Joint Business Council to enhance the participation of U.S. business in industrial projects in Israel. The Council identifies projects for U.S. private sector investments and joint ventures, arranges business symposia and visits, and disseminates information on business opportunities in both countries. The local U.S.-Israel Chamber of Commerce and Industry is also active in the promotion of trade and industry.

Taxation

Corporate Tax

The corporate tax consists of two elements, the company tax and the income tax. The corporate tax must be paid by every company within Israel. The company tax is 40 percent of taxable income, and retained earnings (net of the company tax) are subject to a 35 percent income tax. Resident companies are taxed on Israeli-source income only. (Note: These are generalizations and may not apply to all cases. Foreign investors should obtain expert tax advice about specific situations.)

Certain enterprises which received "Approved Enterprise Status" after July 30, 1978, pay company tax only at the rate of 30 percent and are exempt from income tax for 5 years. Earnings distributed as dividends are taxed at a reduced rate. Companies with foreign equity of more than 25 percent or, under certain circumstnaces with foreign ownership of 49 percent or more, are entitled to certain rebates with respect to devaluation of the Israeli pound.

Capital Gains Tax

Capital gains from the sale of any asset are subject to a capital gains tax, except movable assets held by an individual for his personal use or that of his dependents, real property used for residential purposes and not for profit, securities traded on the Tel Aviv Stock Exchange, and government bonds.

The standard capital gains tax is 25–50 percent applicable to the sale of assets on which depreciation is allowable. On the sale of non depreciable assets, the capital gains tax is reduced by 5 percent for every year the asset was held by the seller, up to a maximum reduction of 80 percent. Assets held for 18 or more years are exempt.

Personal Income Tax

Income tax is levied on the gross income a taxpayer derives from his vocation, employment, trade, profession, business, dividends, interest, pensions, rents or royalties. (Employment income includes most employee fringe benefits such as car allowances, telephone maintenance.) Income tax rates, which are steeply progressive, are generally much higher than in the United States, ranging from 25 percent to 60 percent. Individuals are allowed tax credit points based on family status. Tax brackets and credits are linked to the cost of living index.

A foreign resident who is recognized as an "approved specialist" pays income tax on his salary in Israel at a flat rate of 25 percent. A foreign resident who receives a salary for working in Israel for a foreign employer is exempt from income tax if his income does not exceed 50,000 Israeli pounds and if he resides in Israel for less than 90 days.

Property Tax

Immovable assets, inventories, and equipment are subject to an annual levy under the Property Tax and Compensation Fund Law of 1961. The tax, 0.6 percent on houses, 2.5 percent on land and 0.8 percent on inventory and equipment, is calculated as a percentage of the value of the property.

A land betterment tax is levied on the profit realized at the time of sale of real property.

Value added Tax

The Value Added Tax (VAT) was introduced into Israel on July 1, 1976. It is a uniform tax applied to all goods and services at each level of production or distribution. The basic VAT rate of 12 percent is imposed on most commercial transactions. There is also a 6 percent rate on financial institutions, 3 percent on nonprofit institutions, and an exemption granted on certain items (e.g., fresh fruits and vegetables, exports, international transportation, and imports for new immigrants). The VAT applies to all imports, the amount based on the landed cost of an item plus the customs tariff.

Local Taxes

Municipalities and local and regional councils levy several taxes and rates. The main ones are:

Business Tax.—An annual business tax on every enterprise based on net worth, annual sales volume, number of employees, etc. A company is subject to this tax in each municipality in which it has a place of business.

Rates.—General rates, a form of real estate tax, and water rates are paid by tenants or occupiers rather than owners.

Indirect Taxes

The Government imposes numerous indirect taxes, which take the form of taxes on expenditures, taxes on business transfers, and various license fees, as distinct from the direct taxes on income and property covered in the preceding paragraphs.

In addition to tariff duties, mentioned earlier, there are purchase taxes levied on goods for local consumption, whether imported or locally manufactured, fuel taxes on kerosene and gasoline, an entertainment tax, and excise duties on alcoholic beverages, tobacco, and other goods produced locally for domestic consumption.

A revenue stamp tax is imposed on documents such as contracts, mortgages, debt certificates, powers of attorney, and insurance policies; license fees are charged annually for private automobiles, trucks, taxicabs, driving licenses, television sets, radios, and for licenses required in certain trades.

Employment

Labor Force

Israel's total population was 3.8 million at the end of 1979. The labor force of about 1.2 million has a high percentage of technically and academically trained people. The literacy rate is over 90 percent.

In recent years, as the demand for manpower has risen sharply in response to Israel's rapid industrialization and security needs, the unemployment rate has been very low—averaging fewer than 1,000 and concentrated largely among unskilled workers. Some slackening in the employment rate is expected in 1980 as the Government undertakes policies to reduce inflation.

The Israeli industrial worker in 1976 produced less than half as much as a U.S. worker, but wages (including fringe benefits) were less than one-third that of the United States. Wage costs per unit of output, therefore, are believed to be lower than in most industrial countries. Highly trained research personnel are abundant, so research and development operations may benefit from being located in Israel.

Payments and Benefits

Wage and working conditions are regulated by collective agreements, negotiated in most cases by the Histadrut, the principal labor organization, and the Israel Manufacturers' Association, representing management. The Government, where it is an employer, acts as the principal negotiator on the management side, and takes a strong interest in all other negotiations because of a desire for coordinated economic policies.

The basic wage is supplemented by a cost of living (COL) allowance calculated on the basis of the Consumer Price Index, a family allowance, and a seniority allowance. In addition, fringe benefits may cost the employer 26 percent to over 50 percent of wages.

The Hours of Work and Rest Law, 1951, sets the maximum regular working hours at 47 per week. A trend has started toward the 42–45 hour week but only a few companies are at this level. A minimum break of 45 minutes must be allowed. The weekly day of rest falls on Saturday. Ten paid holidays a year are common.

Labor Organization

The General Federation of Labor in Israel, better known as the Histradrut, is a highly developed trade union structure. Its adult membership numbers more than 1.3 million, including housewives. Employees join the Histradrut and are then assigned to one of the over 41 trade unions in the various trades. The Histradrut exercises local jurisdictional control through a network of some 70 local labor councils located in the cities and towns throughout the country.

In addition, the Histradrut controls large enterprises, such as Koor and Bank Hapoalim, that employ one-fourth of the labor force and account for one-fourth of the national product. The Histradrut is also the prime mover in the cooperative movement in Israel, and is active in cultural and educational endeavors as well. It also controls the National Sick Fund, whose membership accounts for more than 70 percent of the Israeli population.

Guidance for U.S. Traders Abroad

Business Customs

Hebrew and Arabic are the official languages of Israel, but English is a common second language. English is used widely in the business community and predominates in specialized fields such as electronics. All correspondence and documentation in foreign trade may be conducted in English.

Business establishments are generally open from 8 a.m. until 1 p.m. and from 4 p.m. to 7 p.m. Some are open 8 a.m. to 7 p.m. Banks are generally open from 8:30 a.m. to 12:30 p.m. and from 4 to 5:30 p.m., Sunday through Thursday. On Wednesdays and Fridays and days preceeding holidays, they are open 8:30 a.m. to 12:30 p.m. Israeli Government offices are generally open to visitors between 9 a.m. and 1 p.m., Sunday through Friday. Working hours usually extend before and after those hours, and if the matter is urgent, most departments will be accommodating to visitors. Most offices and stores close somewhat earlier on Friday and on the day preceding official holidays. On Saturdays (Sabbath), businesses are closed all day. Sundays are ordinary work days. The U.S. Embassy in Tel Aviv is open 8 a.m. until 4:30 p.m., Monday through Friday.

The following are Israeli holidays in 1980. All are based on the Jewish calendar, and therefore, do not fall on the same dates each year. Certain official holidays when banks and schools are usually closed, are marked with an asterisk:

March 2—Purim (in Jerusalem, Purim is celebrated on March 5).
April 1—Passover (1st day)
April 7—Passover (last day)
(Between the first and last day of Passover, some businesses and institutions close half days. A few factories take annual leave; others remain open).
April 21—Independence Day
May 21 –Pentecost
July 22—Tish'ah Be'Av (Communication of the Destruction of the Temple)
September 11—Rosh Hashana (New Year—1st day)
September 12—Rosh Hashana (New Year—2nd day)
September 20—Yom Kippur
September 25—Succoth (Tabernacles)
October 2—Simhat Tora (last day of Succoth)
(Between the first and last day of Succoth, some businesses and institutions close half days. A

few factories take annual leave, others remain open).

Business customs in Israel do not vary markedly from those of Western Europe or the United States and there is no "business etiquette" as such. Business in Israel does tend to be conducted in a somewhat informal atmosphere, and generally Israelis will not hesitate to express an opinion and will welcome frank, open discussion. Most Israelis are well informed on international business developments and are aware of competitive factors.

Credit cards are accepted by some hotels, restaurants, and airlines. The most widely used credit cards are American Express, Diners' Club and Eurocard. Travelers checks are accepted in hotels, restaurants, and by airlines, except El Al. The most widely used travelers' checks are American Express, Thomas Cook, First National City Bank, Bank of America, and Barclays Bank. Travelers' checks may be cashed easily. Bills can be paid in dollars and by check. Sometimes personal checks are not accepted.

There is no maximum amount of foreign currency that can be carried into Israel, nor is there a minimum amount that must be spent each day.

Miscellaneous

The months of April through mid-October, the peak of the tourist season in Israel, are also the hottest months of the year. Taxis are available in most areas; the prices are metered and fixed by the Government. Facilities in the newer hotels are on a par with those in other countries. Telephones are available in hotels and offices but may be difficult to locate elsewhere. Public telephones require special tokens available from post offices and certain stores.

The United States is represented by an Embassy at 71 Hayarkon Street in Tel Aviv (APO New York 09672), phone: 654338, telex: 33376. U.S. Foreign Commercial Service Officers in the Embassy are available to assist American business travelers visiting Israel.

Sources of Economic and Commercial Information

Israel maintains the following offices in the United States:

Embassy of Israel
1621 22nd Street, N.W.
Washington, D.C. 20008
Phone: (202) 483-4100

Israel Consulates General:
Atlanta, Boston, Chicago, Houston, Los Angeles, New York City, Philadelphia and San Francisco

Investment Authority and Branches
Empire State Building
350 Fifth Avenue
New York, New York 10001
Phone: (212) 560-0610

174 North Michigan Avenue
Chicago, Illinois 60601
Phone: (312) 332-2160

6380 Wilshire Boulevard
Suite 1700
Los Angeles, California 90048
Phone: (213) 651-5700

805 Peachtree Street, N.E.
Suite 656
Atlanta, Georgia 30308
Phone: (404) 875-6947

Israel Trade Center
Empire State Building
350 Fifth Avenue
New York, New York 10001
Phone: (212) 560-0660

Israel Supply Mission
Empire State Building
350 Fifth Avenue
New York, New York 10001
Phone: (212) 560-0680

The American-Israel Chamber of Commerce and Industry, Inc., is headquartered at 500 Fifth Avenue, New York, New York 10036; telephone (212) 354-6510. Chapters are located in several cities throughout the United States. The Israel-America Chamber of Commerce and Industry is located in Tel Aviv at 35 Shaul Hamelech Boulevard; P.O. Box 33174; telephone 252341/2; telex 32139 BETAM IL.

A private sector Israel-U.S. Joint Business Council was established in 1975 to complement government-to-government efforts to increase bilateral trade. Independent in matters of policy, the Council is under the administrative aegis of the Chamber of Commerce of the United States, 1615 H Street, N.W., Washington, D.C. 20062, telephone (202) 659-6115.

Publications

Government of Israel

Information about ordering is available from the Government of Israel's Consulates General,

Investment Authority, or Trade Center.

Facts About Israel; Division of Information, Ministry of Foreign Affairs, Jerusalem;

Statistical Abstract of Israel; Central Bureau of Statistics, Sivan Press Ltd., Jerusalem;

Israel Directory of Products and Services Available in the United States; Government of Israel Trade Center and the American-Israel Chamber of Commerce and Industry, Inc., New York, New York; 1976

Israel Publication Catalog; Consulate General of Israel, 800 Second Avenue, New York, New York 10017;

Israel Export Directory; Official Guide to the Ministry of Commerce and Industry, published by Israel Publications Corporation, Ltd., Tel Aviv, P.O. Box 11587;

The Advantages of Investing in Israel (Industry); Government of Israel Investment Authority, October, 1978.

United States Government

Foreign Economic Trends and Their Implications for the United States, Israel, FET 79-062, U.S. Department of Commerce (annual)

Country Marketing Survey: Medical Equipment, Israel, CMS 79-002, U.S. Department of Commerce

Country Market Survey: Industrial Process Controls, Israel, CMS 79-204, U.S. Department of Commerce

Country Market Survey: Electronic Components, Israel, CMS 79-013, U.S. Department of Commerce

A Business Guide to the Near East and North Africa, U.S. Department of Commerce

Market Profiles for the Near East and North Africa, OBR 79-36, U.S. Department of Commerce

Near East/North African Business Costs, OBR 79-19, U.S. Department of Commerce

Other Publications

Economic Horizons: Yearbook and Trade Directory, American-Israel Chamber of Commerce and Industry, Inc.

APPENDIX—Summary of Investment Incentives
Approved Enterprise

QUALIFICATIONS REQUIREMENTS:

Creation or expansion of an enterprise owned by a company incorporated in Israel or registered as a foreign company. Ownership can be fully foreign or any combination of Israeli and foreign investors. Venture should have a reasonable capability of earning foreign currency.

REQUIREMENTS FOR APPROVAL:	*ZONE A*	*ZONE B*	*ZONE C*
Financial Structure paid up capital as percent of fixed assets	30	40	50
investors's financing as percent of entire investment including working capital	30	35	40

INCENTIVES FOR INVESTMENT:	*ZONE A*	*ZONE B*	*ZONE C*
1. Cash Grants Percent of investment in fixed assets	30	15	5
Additional grant for infrastructure costs varies according to circumstances			
For costs of industrial R&D projects in Israel (approved by Government)	50	50	50
2. Development Loans (10 years, given by commercial banks)			
Loan as percent of fixed assets	40	40	40
Interest rate	6	6.5	7.5

3. Export Support
Funds to finance working capital for exports available in Israeli and foreign currency at low interest rates; terms depending on industry branch type of materials financed.

TAX CONCESSIONS:

1. Depreciation
Investment (equity plus loans) in industrial machinery and equipment can be fully depreciated in 2 years (at rate of 50 percent per year).

2. Tax Rates
Three periods of taxation:

a. Before investment paid back by net profits: Total depreciation over 2 years is tax deductible expense, making income tax-free as long as investment in machinery and equipment has not yet been paid back by profits. (Only exception is when profits exceed 50 percent return on investment in first or second year of operation.)

b. Next 5 years:

Corporate tax: 40 percent

Withholding on distributed dividends: 15 percent (no further income tax is payable by stockholder in Israel). Under a new U.S.-Israeli tax treaty (subject to U.S. Senate ratification), U.S. corporate recipients may be subject to a lower effective withholding rate.

Taxation when profits reinvested in approved project or expansion: limited to 40 percent corporate tax. No additional tax due if profits reinvested. Project eligible for additional grants and loans and for new depreciation allowance for new machinery and equipment.

c. Thereafter:

Regular tax rates applied. However, under the proposed tax treaty, a U.S. corporation will enjoy the same siutation mentioned in (b) above.

3. Property Taxes: Building: exempt from two-thirds of property tax during initial five-year period. Equipment, spare parts, finished goods: exempt from one-sixth of tax for 5 years.

4. Import Levies, Custom Duties and Purchase Tax: Imported equipment and machinery for industrial plants are exempt from duty and purchase tax.

Market Profile—ISRAEL

Foreign Trade

Imports.—$7.5 billion in 1979; $5.8 million in 1978. Major suppliers in 1979: United States, 20.1 percent; United Kingdom, 9.2 percent; West Germany, 10.2 percent; Switzerland, 9.4 percent. Major imports were rough diamonds, raw materials, fuel, machinery and transport equipment.

Exports.—$4.6 billion in 1979; $3.9 billion in 1978. Major customers in 1979: United States, 16.5 percent; West Germany, 9.2 percent; United Kingdom, 8.7 percent; France and Hong Kong, 5.4 percent each.

Trade Policy.—In October 1977, the Israeli pound was allowed to "float"; most controls on foreign exchange transactions were eliminated; and certain import duties, surcharges and taxes were either reduced or removed. These measures were designed to contribute to the development of export-oriented and import-substitution industries. A Cooperation Agreement was reached with the European Community (EC) in 1975. This provided for the mutual and gradual reduction of tariffs on industrial goods, with the goal of eliminating entirely EC duties on Israel's exports by July 1977 and Israel's duties on EC exports by 1989. A 1976 agreement with the United States established Israel's eligibility for the Generalized System of Preferences (GSP), which aids sales from developing countries by abolishing U.S. tariffs on 2,700 items. Israel reciprocated by decreasing its duties on 130 U.S. products.

Trade Prospects.—Best sales opportunities in the fields of electronic components, electronics industry production and test equipment, metal-working, computers and peripherals, electrical power, and engines and mechanical power.

Foreign Investment

Several hundred foreign companies, including 23 that are among the largest 250 U.S. firms on Fortune Magazine's list, have manufacturing/exporting subsidiaries in Israel.

Investment Prospects.—Government encourages investment through 1948 Law for the Encouragement of Capital Investments. Israeli Government Investment Authority has offices throughout U.S.

Economy

Israel's economy is characterized by heavy dependence on foreign trade, a high level of industrialization, and rapid growth averaging 10 percent per year in real terms throughout most of the State's existence. A slowdown in economic activity began in 1974, but recent indicators point to an upward trend. Real GNP grew by 4.9 percent in 1979. The most impressive growth has occurred in the export sector. Israeli exports rose by 28 percent in 1977, 25 percent in 1978, and 16 percent in 1979.

Agriculture.—Agricultural production grew by 3.5 percent in 1978. Major products are citrus fruits, vegetables, meat and poultry.

Industries.—Industrial production grew by an estimated 4.9 percent in 1979. Most of the expansion has occurred in the science-based industries such as electronics, chemicals, and metallurgy.

Tourism.—This fast-growing industry is Israel's major net earner of foreign exchange. In 1978 more than 1 million tourists arrived. Tourism between the United States and Israel should increase as a result of the civil aviation agreement between the two countries.

Finance

Currency.—As of May 1980 the exchange rate stood at 4.47 shekels = US$1. In March 1980 the Government replaced the pound with the Israeli shekel with currency denominations reduced to 10 percent, e.g., 1 shekel equals 10 Israeli pounds.

Domestic Credit and Investment.—Long-term credit from government or private sources is offered by some 20 mortgage and development banks. Short-term credit is available throughout the country and abroad.

Balance of Payments.—In recent years, Israel's foreign exchange reserves have grown remarkably, increasing from $1.18 billion in 1975 to $3.1 billion in 1978–9. Israel has successfully reduced its current account deficit from $4.06 billion in 1975 to $3.40 billion in 1978. Israel's foreign debt reached $12.9 billion in 1978, $15 billion in 1979 and a projected $17 billion in 1980.

Basic Economic Facilities

Transportation.—Infrastructure includes 11,891 kilometers of road in 1978. Tel Aviv, Haifa, and Jerusalem are joined by 562 miles of railway. A major rail line is being extended to Eilat. The chief ports are Haifa and Ashdod on the Mediterranean and Eilat on the Gulf of Aqaba. Ben-Gurion Airport near Tel Aviv serves most major international airlines including TWA. ARKIA local airline connects Israel's principal cities.

Communication.—About 210 post offices and branches. Maintains international links via radio telegraph, underwater cable and telex.

Natural Resources

Land and Climate.—About 8,000 square miles (not including areas occupied since hostilities of 1967), 55 percent arable. Inland hill country drier and cooler than coast.

Population

Size—3.8 million in 1979 (not including areas occupied since 1967 hostilities).

Language.—Hebrew and Arabic are official languages. English widely used for business.

Ethnic Groups.—Jewish (85 percent), Arab (15 percent). Religions: Judaism, Islam, Christianity, Druze.

Education.—87.6 percent literacy; Enrollment of 1.2 million in education system in 1978/79.

Marketing in Italy

Contents

Report Revised April 1981

Foreign Trade Outlook

Italy's export-oriented economy dictates the need for the pursuit of liberal foreign trade policies. Italy belongs to the Organization for Economic Cooperation and Development (OECD), the International Monetary Fund (IMF), and the U.N. Economic Commission for Europe, and is a signatory to the General Agreement on Tariffs and Trade (GATT). Italy's external tariffs, and elements of its trade and domestic policy are directed by its membership in the European Community (EC).

Italy has relatively few domestic natural resources and must depend on a heavy volume of imports in these key areas: raw materials, consumer goods, capital equipment, and petroleum. Like many other countries, a significant portion of Italy's inflation problem is due to the high cost of imported petroleum. This has caused the Italian Government's increased exploitation of coal as a substitute for petroleum. A recent study, for example, suggests doubling Italy's use of coal, and at the 1980 meeting of the EC, the nine members endorsed increased European coal production and consumption. For the United States, this increased emphasis on coal should provide excellent sales opportunities for sales of coal equipment, coal storage and environmental protection systems, energy conversion systems, and coal itself.

The United States ranks third in total Italian trade behind the Federal Republic of Germany, and France. Eastern European trade accounts for no more than 4 percent of Italy's foreign trade, and approximately one-half of that is accounted for by the Soviet Union. Other major trading partners are the Benelux countries and the United Kingdom.

America's traditional strength in high technology equipment markets is expected to continue in 1981. Computers and peripherals are likely to do well as Italy's small- and medium-sized companies continue to emphasize investment in labor and energy saving equipment. Special opportunities exist for minicomputers and multiple-function calculators.

Other excellent export opportunities are the following: process control instruments and equipment, avionics/airport equipment, electronic components, electronic production and test equipment, pollution control equipment, and graphic arts machinery. Another notable area in which U.S. companies may increase their market share is security equipment. An increasingly security-conscious Italy will continue to seek protection systems in both the public and private sectors.

Economic Trends

Italy's strong economic performance in 1979 surprised even the most optimistic forecasters. Real gross domestic product (GDP) posted a 5 percent annual growth and a $5.2 billion current account surplus was registered. The Italian lira appreciated against most currencies and was counted among one of the strongest currencies in the European Community (EC).

In 1980, growth based on internal consumption and investment continued, with a 3.5 to 4 percent real annual GDP advance, again one of the highest growth rates for any industrialized nation. This continuing expansion in the face of other industrialized nation's minimal to zero

---

**HOW TO OBTAIN
BACKGROUND INFORMATION
ABOUT THESE COUNTRIES**

For those who wish *general* data about a country—data which goes beyond marketing and commerce—the editors recommend *Countries of the World and Their Leaders*, published as an annually updated yearbook by Gale Research Company, Detroit, Michigan 48226. Containing 4- to 20-page entries on 168 countries, the volume also provides several hundred pages of supplementary world data. Each report provides some historical insight as well as a look at contemporary trends of lifestyle in the country. Reports also discuss a country's educational system, its press, ethnic groupings and religious practices.

Table 1.—Italian Foreign Trade By Major Trading Partner, 1977-79
(millions of U.S. dollars)

	Imports (c.i.f.)			Exports (f.o.b.)		
	1977	1978	1979	1977	1978	1979
West Germany	7,980	9,541	11,102	8,369	10,376	11,333
France	6,615	8,007	9,094	6,438	7,776	8,872
United States	3,284	3,718	5,277	3,005	3,886	4,662
Netherlands	1,975	2,306	2,707	1,702	2,234	2,746
Belgium-Luxembourg	1,590	1,836	2,303	1,603	1,875	2,046
United Kingdom	1,755	2,195	2,613	2,381	3,302	3,915
Eastern Europe	2,615	2,865	3,239	2,303	2,360	2.205
Total World	47,571	54,921	77,798	45,052	54,521	72,111

Note: Exchange rates used: 1977: US$1=882 lira; 1978: US$1=849 lira; 1979: US$1=831 lira.

Source: ISTAT (Italian Central Institute of Statistics)

Table 2.—U.S. Exports to Italy, by Major Commodity Groups 1977-79
(millions of U.S. dollars)

	1977	1978	1979
Food and live animals	405.3	550.9	460.3
Cereals	277.8	362.8	258.4
Animal feed	96.1	150.8	155.3
Tobacco	72.2	84.0	78.5
Crude materials, inedible except fuels	563.3	654.4	1,024.6
Oilseeds and oleaginous fruit	241.3	266.7	285.7
Wood, lumber and cork	59.8	65.8	151.1
Pulp and waste paper	90.8	81.0	117.6
Minerals, fuels, lubricants, etc.	263.5	211.1	338.7
Coal, coke, briquets	213.5	166.0	260.6
Petroleum	50.0	45.1	78.0
Oils and fats, animal and vegetable			
Chemicals	231.5	343.2	479.1
Chemical elements and compounds	70.0	102.9	113.5
Medicinals and pharmaceuticals	50.0	60.2	74.7
Manufactured goods by chief material	242.9	269.0	487.6
Leather	7.4	6.9	17.9
Paper and paper board	29.0	33.5	45.8
Iron and steel	31.2	34.3	70.1
Nonferrous metals	33.8	46.8	73.0
Textiles, fabrics	87.6	89.6	188.4
Machinery and transport equipment	686.6	808.7	1,043.5
Office machines and ADP equipment	124.4	157.0	209.4
Electrical	218.2	140.0	183.4
Transport equipment	92.1	128.9	174.8
Aircraft	74.5	126.1	162.0
Manufactured articles, miscellaneous	153.1	252.6	308.3
Items not classified by kind	14.8	20.2	30.8
Total	2,644.7	3,201.2	4,260.3

Source: U.S. Department of Commerce, Bureau of the Census, FT 455.

Table 3.—U.S. Imports from Italy by Major Commodity Group, 1977-79
(millions of U.S. dollars)

	1977	1978	1979
Food and live animals	58.3	70.1	63.9
Dairy products and eggs	26.2	27.6	24.8
Fruits and vegetables	19.7	15.8	16.4
Beverages and tobacco	135.1	219.4	254.8
Wine	109.3	182.5	216.3
Tobacco	8.2	12.3	11.1
Crude materials, inedible, except fuels	19.2	20.7	21.1
Minerals, fuels and lubricants	304.1	237.9	412.6
Petroleum and petroleum products	292.1	220.9	407.9
Oils and fats, animal and vegetable	14.5	19.6	22.9
Chemicals	206.5	205.9	196.7
Chemical elements and compounds	129.2	117.3	93.4
Medicinal and pharmaceutical products	37.8	39.6	48.9
Manufactured goods by chief materials	556.6	773.3	734.1
Rubber	69.6	58.7	77.2
Textile	121.2	203.5	191.2
Nonmetallic Mineral	94.2	125.9	158.7
Iron and steel	171.0	227.8	133.2
Machinery and transport equipment	704.2	1,004.2	1,189.1
Nonelectric machinery	351.9	203.1	215.8
Transport equipment	295.1	440.3	546.5
Motor vehicles and parts	265.8	409.3	506.0
Miscellaneous manufactures	989.1	1,497.4	1,971.3
Clothing	153.5	187.4	185.5
Footwear	367.5	569.0	801.6
Items not classified	49.2	53.3	51.6
Total	3,036.8	4,101.8	4,918.1

Source: U.S. Department of Commerce, Bureau of the Census, FT 455.

its traditional export market shares and moderate the excessive flow of imports prevalent in 1980. The lira is predicted to be devalued minimally to make imports more expensive and therefore less attractive to Italian consumers and also help to make Italian export goods more price competitive in Italy's traditional export markets.

In general, the Italian economy has been a strong, growing economy with excellent potential for U.S. exports. All trends indicate that Italy will remain one of the prime export market areas of the United States.

Trade Regulations

Import Tariff System

Italy, together with France, Germany, Belgium, Luxembourg, the Netherlands, Denmark, Ireland, and the United Kingdom, are members of the European Community. Greece became the 10th member of the EC on January 1, 1981. The EC is composed of the European Coal and Steel Community (ECSC), the European Atomic Energy Community (Euratom), and the European Economic Community (EEC), popularly known as the Common Market. Unlike the ECSC and Euratom, which are limited to specific fields, the EEC was established for the purpose of creating a free mass market among the member countries. The EEC provides for a common external tariff, a common agricultural

growth is causing some problems. The combined effect of high cost petroleum imports and a reduced ability to export relatively expensive Italian products has caused Italy to run large trade deficits. Inflation is another major problem and is basically traced to the unabated growth of Italy's domestic economy. Inflation grew at an estimated 21 percent annual rate in 1980.

For 1981, the Italian economy is expected to finally slow down in a manner which will permit it to be somewhat in accord with the other industrialized nations. It should be a year of moderation with a 1.5 to 2 percent real GDP growth and an inflation rate at 15 to 17 percent. In this way, Italy is expected to once again regain policy, a joint transportation policy, and the free movement of goods, labor, and capital.

Specific duties are levied on a small number of items. These involve a fixed charge per unit of imported goods; e.g., per hectoliter or 100 kilograms. Where goods are dutiable according to weight, the term "gross weight" is taken to mean the weight of the goods including that of the packaging, and "net weight," the weight of the goods alone, stripped of all inner and outer packaging. In some cases, a fixed tare is used to arrive at a net dutiable weight.

Customs charges are payable in the currency of the country into which the goods are imported. Traders may obtain currency quotations through their banks.

The metric system of weights and measures is used in customs transactions: 1 metric ton equals 1,000 kilograms; 1 kilogram equals 2.2046 pounds; 1 meter equals 39.37 inches; and 1 liquid liter equals 1.0567 quarts.

Customs Surcharges.—Italy does not levy customs surcharges as such, but nearly all imports are subject to a value-added tax (IVA) and some products to excise taxes.

Common External Tariff (CXT) duty rates are applied to all dutiable products imported from non-EEC countries except those governed by the Common Agricultural Policy (CAP) of the Community. The Cap is a single consistent policy on prices, protection levels, and marketing arrangements applying to the entire Community. Import duties on agricultural goods covered by the CAP have been replaced by a system of variable levies, the purpose of which is to equalize the prices of imported commodities with those of commodities produced in the Community. Trade among the nine EEC member states is duty free.

Information regarding Italian import duties applicable to specific products may be obtained free of charge from: International Trade Administration, Office of Country Marketing, Southern Europe Division, U.S. Department of Commerce, Washington, D.C. 20230, telephone (202) 377-3462, or from any Department of Commerce District Office. Inquiries should contain a complete product description, including CCCN (BTN), SITC, or U.S. Schedule B Export Commodity numbers, if known. The EEC employs the Customs Cooperation Council Nomenclature (CCCN), also known as the Brussels Tariff Nomenclature (BTN).

Third-country duty rates listed in the Community's CXT are in two columns, autonomous and conventional. The latter are lower rates and are applied to imports of items from more than 80 General Agreements on Tariffs and Trade (GATT) member states, including the United States, and to countries that have concluded agreements with the EEC incorporating the most-favored-nation (MFN) clause. The EEC countries grant MFN treatment to all countries. The higher autonomous rates are applied only where no conventional rates are listed. Duty rates are not excessive. Most raw materials enter duty free or at low rates of duty, while rates on most manufactured goods fall within a range of 5 to 17 percent; some food products have higher rates.

The EEC members extend preferential tariff treatment under EEC agreements to imports from members of the African, Caribbean and Pacific Convention of Lome, Turkey, Morocco, Tunisia, Algeria, Spain, Israel, Malta, Lebanon, Cyprus, Egypt, Jordan, Syria, and their overseas countries and territories. The EEC also grants tariff preferences to more than 100 developing countries and about 40 overseas territories under the EEC's Generalized System of Preferences. Imports of nearly all semimanufactured and manufactured goods considered to originate in these countries and territories enter the Community duty free. Annual duty-free quotas are established for those products considered "sensitive." Certain processed agricultural products enter duty free or at reduced rates.

Free trade agreements have been concluded between the EEC and the European Free Trade Association (EFTA), which includes Finland, Austria, Norway, Portugal, Iceland, Sweden, and Switzerland. Under the terms of these agreements, the EEC exempted most industrial products and certain processed agricultural products from import duties on July 1, 1977. Specified sensitive products are subject to longer transitional periods of reduction to zero tariff rates, while numerous agricultural commodities are dutiable at the CXT duty rates.

Multilateral Trade Negotiations

The most recent series of Multilateral Trade Negotiations (MTN) held under the General Agreement on Tariffs and Trade (GATT)—the Tokyo Round—was concluded in 1979. These comprehensive and far reaching negotiations, in which the United States and its trading partners played major roles, have resulted in agreements which should liberalize world trade over the next decade.

Of particular interest to U.S. exporters to the EEC are the six agreements which establish new rules, or "codes," on government procurement, product standards, import licensing procedures, subsidies, trade in civil aircraft, and customs valuation, and the protocol which lowers tariffs on industrial and other products in general.

The codes will increase the opportunities for foreign suppliers to sell to government entities; discourages the manipulation of product standards which discriminate against imported products; simplify and harmonize import licensing procedures; provide recourse when facing subsidized competition in foreign markets; reduce government influence on civil aircraft purchase decisions and eliminate tariffs on civil aircraft and their principal components; and replace a number of different systems of customs valuation with a uniform system. The tariff protocol will reduce the EECs average tariff level on industrial product imports from the United States by approximately 35 percent.

The agreements on product standards, subsidies and countervailing measures, import licensing procedures, trade in civil aircraft, and tariffs came into force on January 1, 1980. The codes on government procurement and customs valuation because effective internationally on January 1, 1981, although the customs valuation code was implemented by the United States and the EEC on July 1, 1980.

Tariffs on civil aircraft and their principal components were completely eliminated by the EEC on January 1, 1980. On the other hand, EEC tariff reductions on other industrial products will, with a few exceptions, be spread in equal installments over a period of 8 years. The first cut was made on January 1, 1980; the seven additional cuts are scheduled for each January 1 from 1981 to 1987 (for certain chemicals and plastics the first cut was not made until July 1, 1980). For textiles and steel, six equal cuts are scheduled for each January 1 from 1982 to 1987.

Basis of duty assessment.—Virtually all import duties listed are on an ad valorem basis; that is, percent charges levied on the dutiable value of the imported goods. As of July 1, 1980, Italy agreed to enact the Tokyo Round Trade Agreement on Customs Valuation.

The primary method of valuation is the transaction value. Under this method, the dutiable value is based on the price actually paid or payable for the goods with a limited number of adjustments for things such as selling commissions, packing costs, and certain costs for materials and services used in producing the goods that were borne by the buyer but not reflected in the price paid or payable for the goods. It is anticipated that the transaction value will be used in all but a limited number of cases. One situation in which the transaction value would not be used is where there is a sale between related parties and this relationship affects the price. It should be noted that the existence of a relationship alone is not a sufficient reason to reject the transaction value of a sale between related parties. The Agreement provides a number of important safeguards to assure that transaction value between related parties are not arbitrarily rejected.

If the value cannot be determined by using the transaction value method, it is necessary to proceed through the alternative methods of valuation in a prescribed sequence. The first alternative method is based on the transaction value of identical goods sold for export to the same country of importation. If no value can be established under this provision, then the transaction value of similar goods sold for export to the same country of importation would be the basis for valuation.

If a value cannot be determined under the above methods, then the Agreement provides for the application of a deductive value method, and if that is unsuccessful, a computed value method. However, at the importer's request, the order of application of these two methods will be reversed.

Under the deductive value method, the customs value is calculated by taking the price of the first sale after importation of either the imported good or of identical or similar goods and deducting from it certain costs and charges that are incurred after importation. This method will normally be used only when the imported product is not further manufactured after importation. However, if the importer so requests, this method will be applied to goods processed after importation with due allowances for value added in processing.

Under the computed value method, the customs value is based on the sum of material and manufacturing costs, profits, and general expenses for the goods being valued. If all the above methods turn out to be inapplicable, then the customs officials can use other methods provided that they are reasonable and consistent with the principles of the Agreement and Article VII of the GATT. The Agreement lists a number of existing arbitrary practices that are explictly cited as unreasonable.

Currency

The basic currency unit in Italy is the lira which floats in relation to the dollar. Current exchange rates may be found in major newspapers or may be obtained through banks. The average value of the lira for 1980 was US$1 = lira 815. This represents an appreciation over 1979 when the exchange rate was US$1 = lira 831. Thus the Italian currency has strengthened within the

European Monetary System (EMS).

Italy has been following a tightened monetary policy. From 1978 to 1979, the monetary supply increase was reduced 3.2 percent. In addition, interest rates rose consistently in 1979 along with the yield on Italian Treasury bonds.

With a likely deterioration of the balance of payments in Italy, there may be some depreciation of the lira against the stronger EMS currencies.

Taxes

While Italy imposes no customs surcharges, a value-added tax (IVA) has replaced turnover on all transfers of goods since 1973. Under the IVA system the seller adds the appropriate tax at each stage of the manufacturing distribution chain. The tax is always quoted separately on the invoice. In practice, he periodically deducts all tax paid on his total sales and remits the balance to (or claims a credit from) the Government. This process repeats itself until the product is sold to the final consumer who bears the full burden of the tax. Capital equipment, in effect, is exempt from the tax as the purchasing firm can deduct in full IVA paid on the equipment from its IVA tax liability to the Government.

The IVA is levied on the duty-paid value of imported goods at the same rates that apply to domestic products. Exports are exempt from IVA.

The IVA tax rates range from 1 to 35 percent, with the basic rate being 15 percent for the majority of products.

Shipping Documents

Documents required include the usual shipper's commercial invoice and the bill of lading or air waybill, none of which requires consular legalization. It is good practice to provide a certificate of origin, available through most state chambers of commerce. However, if substantive proof of origin is provided through other accompanying documents as well as through characteristic trademarks, then a certificate of origin is not normally necessary.

Import Licensing

With the exception of a small group of hard core items, largely agricultural, practically all goods originating in the United States and most other free-world countries may be imported without import licenses and free of quantitative restrictions. There are, however, monitoring import measures applying to imports of certain sensitive products. The most important of these measures is the automatic import license for textiles. This license is granted to Italian importers when they provide the requisite forms.

Marking and Labeling

There is no general requirement that imports be marked as to country of origin. Under Italian legislation, the origin of imported merchandise is established through documentation accompanying the shipments arriving in Italy and not through marking of products or their containers. Certain specified commodities, however, must be marked or labeled to show composition, and name and location of manufacturer, in accordance with various laws and regulations.

The following articles are subject to the special marking or labeling regulations: lime, cement and similar binding agents; pianos, automatic pianos, harmoniums and similar instruments; clinical thermometers; ethical medicines; packaged foods; distilled spirits; beer; wine; vinegar; and feedstuffs.

－－－

Senate Concurrent Resolution 40, adopted July 30, 1953, invites U.S. exporters to inscribe, insofar as practicable, on the external shipping containers in indelible print of a suitable size: "United States of America." Although such marking is not compulsory under our laws, U.S. shippers are urged to cooperate in thus publicizing American-made goods.

Temporary Imports

Material may temporarily be imported into Italy without the payment of duties and tax if such material is to be used in the production or manufacture of a product that is to be exported. The importer gives security in the form of a guarantee from an acceptable bank or insurance company in the amount of applicable duties and taxes. Upon exportation of the finished product, the guarantee is released.

Temporary admission of goods intended for reexport in the same condition is permissible free of import duties and taxes upon approval of an application at the Customs Administration.

Samples without commercial value are admitted free of duty and taxes. Samples with commercial value are also admitted duty and tax free, provided that the following conditions are complied with:

(a) The samples are accompanied by a representative of the foreign firm who possesses a statement, notarized by an Italian consulate, identifying him as a commercial traveler and attesting to the intention that the samples are being imported into Italy for the purpose of being shown or demonstrated and that they are to be reexported in due course.

(b) A certificate of origin from a recognized chamber of commerce is submitted.

(c) Applicable import duties and taxes are deposited at the customs house of entry, later to be refunded at time of reexportation.

(d) A list (in duplicate) with a full description of each sample including weight and value is submitted. It is helpful to have such a list in Italian.

U.S. traders should consider a more simplified procedure in the form of a "carnet" for the temporary importation of samples without posting guarantees. Carnets are issued in the United States by the U.S. Council of the International Chamber of Commerce, 1212 Avenue of the Americas, New York, N.Y. 10036, telephone (212) 354-4480. Applications for carnets may be obtained from the U.S. Council or U.S. Department of Commerce District offices.

In practice, samples carried by businesspersons into Italy that are not covered by a carnet valued in excess of lira 1 million (or about $1,175) are practically impossible to clear through Italian customs. It might be advisable for businesspersons carrying samples valued at over lire 1 million and not covered by the ATA Carnet to employ the services of a local freight forwarder.

Free Trade Zones and Warehousing

There are two free trade zones ("punti franchi") located at Trieste and Venice. Goods of foreign origin may be brought into the free trade zones without the payment of customs duties and remain free of all such duties while held in the zones or if subsequently transshipped or reexported. They may be freely negotiated, manipulated, and processed industrially. Operations authorized include loading, unloading, mixing, warehousing, and cargo handling. Retail sale is prohibited. There are no free ports in Italy.

Italy also has more than 800 general warehouses that are similar to the bonded warehouses of the United States; more limited facilities are available in free depots ("depositi franchi") located in 10 port cities.

There are no limitations as to the type or origin of merchandise that can be stored in free trade zones, bonded or customs warehouses. The time limit for such storage is 5 years. Merchandise deteriorated while in storage can be destroyed without payment of duty.

Technical Standards and Requirements

There are numerous mandatory and voluntary standards in existence that define products, processes, or procedures and embrace many fields. The texts of these standards may be obtained directly from UNI, Ente Nazionale Italiano di Unificazione, Piazza Diaz 2, 20123 Milan (i.e., the Italian National Bureau of Standards) or through the American National Standards Institute, 1430 Broadway, New York, N.Y. 10018, telephone (212) 354-3300.

Distribution and Sales Channels

American businesspersons seeking to increase their sales have a ready market waiting for them. They will find that selling in Italy offers new challenges, but that it presents no really difficult problems. Over 6,000 American companies are actively represented in Italy, with approximately 800 of that number having subsidiaries there.

U.S. businesspersons may find some commercial practices different from those in the United States, but many will look very familiar. The system of retail and wholesale distribution, for instance, still centers on small family-operated stores, although the supermarket-type operation has rapidly gained in importance and there are a number of substantial department store operations.

Major Marketing Areas

Italy is almost evenly divided into an industrial northern half and a southern half where economic and market conditions are very different. The northern area with its heavy concentration of large commercial, financial, and industrial enterprises is a ready market for all kinds of capital and consumer goods, and accounts for about 70 percent of total Italian imports. Incomes are almost twice what they are in the south, and the standard of living resembles that of France and Germany. The area's vast industrial complex offers a steady demand for new, more advanced machinery and equipment.

Italy is known for its many large urban centers. Rome, Milan, and Naples all have populations of over a million people, but the market areas of these and other large cities extend much beyond their boundary lines and reach a population well above that of the cities themselves. Each of the major cities forms the nucleus of a particular province that in most cases is densely populated. Thus Lombardy province, where Milan is located, has a population of over 8.5 million. Piemonte, where Turin is situated, has over 4.5 million population. There are about 15 million people in the relatively small area of the Milan-Turin-Genoa industrial triangle. Lazio, where Rome is located, has a population of 5 million and Naples within Campania, has a population of 5 million. These two latter adjoining areas together make up a compact market of close to 10 million people.

In the north, the country's leading commercial-industrial center, is Milan. This city has throbbed with economic activity for centuries and has become the center of Italy's business activities. It serves as headquarters for most of the large industrial firms in Italy. Many firms, including those importing foreign products, usually direct their sales efforts in Italy from Milan. Milan is also the seat of many of Italy's leading industry and trade associations. These include Aschimici, the national association of the chemical industry; Assogomma, the association of rubber products manufacturers; and Assolombarda, the regional industrial association of Lombardy. Also included are the Associazione Cotoniera Italiana (cotton textiles); Associazione dell' Industria Laniera (wood textiles); Assider (iron and steel); Anima (mechanical equipment); and Anie (electrical equipment). The American Chamber of Commerce in Italy has its headquarters in Milan.

The population of Milan is over 1.8 million, and is supplemented by thousands of commuters who come in from nearby towns each day. The greater Milan area accounts for 7.2 percent of the Italian population and includes about 1 million industrial workers, more than 14 percent of all industrial workers in Italy. It is this preponderance of well-trained, well-paid factory workers that sets the pattern for tastes, consumer preferences and demand of the area. Turin is another important commercial-industrial city in the north, and as Italy's automobile capital, it is also one of the country's best markets. Fiat and Lancia cars as well as many subsidiary products of the motor and metalworking industries are manufactured in Turin. The Regions of Piedmonte and Lombardy, of which Turin and Milan are the capitals, together account for 30 percent of Italy's gross national product. They are the richest and most sought after markets in

Italy, and as to be expected, the competition is intense.

Genoa, Italy's major port, is also an important northern commercial and industrial center. The area bounded by these three northern cities, Milan, Turin, and Genoa, is often referred to as the industrial triangle, and it is roughly within this area that the highest standard of living prevails.

Further south, the capital city of Rome, in addition to serving as the location of much government procurement, contains the headquarters of many State-controlled enterprises, the oil industry and the airlines. The State enterprises include transportation services, the national electric company and many major industrial operations. Rome, Italy's largest city, is also an important market sector and serves as a distribution hub for other parts of central and southern Italy.

Naples, a large port city serving Rome and the south, is an industrial city whose importance is continuously increasing under government development programs. Aeritalia, the State-owned aerospace company and Alfa (Romeo) Sud are creating thousands of jobs and satellite industries in the Naples of area.

The area surrounding the cities of Bari-Brindisi and Taranto also has been stimulated by considerable government assistance and private investments.

Marketing Channels

The marketing of foreign products in Italy is accomplished through a variety of channels, depending on the nature of the commodities, the sales territory to be covered, the type of end-user to be serviced, and the sales promotional activities required. Brokers, commission merchants, indent houses, and independent representatives are used extensively for the sale of raw materials, semifinished products, and capital goods to the larger manfacturing organizations. However, well-established distributors are the channels normally employed to reach the smaller industrial firms as well as the large number of wholesalers and retailers engaged in the marketing of consumer goods.

Agency.—Agency contracts (contratto di agenzia) are governed by the Civil Code and by a number of other legislative decrees. An Italian agent for a foreign firm is generally regarded as being authorized to act for the firm. Depending on the contract, the principal may be subject to termination compensation payments and to income taxes and other levies on sales effected through the agent.

Distributorship.—Under this arrangement the local distributor acts in his own name, takes title of the merchandise and assumes all the risks, as well as the obligations to pay all taxes involved in sales to Italian buyers. These agreements are subject only to stipulations made in the contracts themselves. There are no laws or regulations currently in effect in Italy providing for advance notice of termination, termination compensation, or social security payments in connection with these agreements.

Frequently, a domestic distributorship agreement provides for exclusive sales rights. There is nothing in the Italian law preventing exclusive arrangements in all or part of Italy. However, if these agreements provides for exclusive sales rights in all or part of the European Economic Community, they should be examined carefully, and with the assistance of a competent international lawyer, in light of the antitrust provisions of the Common Market Treaty.

Agent/Distributor.—In some instances a firm may act as a commission agent of an American company for some products or for some sales of relatively high value and as a stocking distributor for other products or for relatively low value sales.

Direct Buying.—Direct buying of imported goods occurs frequently in Italy. Certain raw materials and some industrial machinery and equipment having limited markets are purchased by the end-users directly from the foreign manufacturers or suppliers. Voluntary associations of food retailers and food wholesalers make substantial purchases directly from the domestic or foreign manufacturers. The department and chain stores in operation in Italy have purchasing agents abroad (including the United States) through which they place their orders.

Wholesale outlets.—Wholesale establishments are numerous in Italy, but most of these are small firms employing one or two people. Their scope is limited as they sell only to small retailers who are not in a position to buy directly from manufacturers. The larger retail outlets customarily purchase from local wholesalers only those items that they sell in small quantities.

Many of the larger wholesalers in Italy are familiar with foreign trade practices and procedures. They have extended their operations beyond the localities in which they are established to better facilitate distribution of goods on a countrywide basis.

There are 128,854 wholesale establishments in Italy of which 57 percent are in the north, 18 percent in central, and 25 percent in southern Italy. Nonfood wholesalers total 71,002 of all wholesaler establishments in Italy.

Retail Outlets.—Retail trade is still dominated largely by small individual outlets run by the owner with the help of his family or with one or two paid assistants. Small firms are expanding, however, and are adopting new merchandising techniques. Modern retail outlets, however, such as department and self-service stores, have been increasing rapidly, particularly in the cities. The number of stores handling food products exceeds those handling other lines. The proportion of nonfood retailers generally diminishes as one moves from northern to southern Italy. Sales vary considerably according to type of retail establishment. Volume is limited by the consumer's traditional practice of making small purchases as needed on a day-to-day basis. This is especially true in foodstuffs.

According to the Ministry of Industry, there are 411,321 food retail outlets, and 461,412 retailers of nonfood goods in Italy. Not included in that number are 210,098 "coffee" bars, ice cream parlors, cafeterias, restaurants and hotels, and some 250,000 itinerant or door-to-door sales representatives, who sell foodstuffs, housewares, and textile goods.

Department stores (*grandimagazzini*) and supermarkets have gained wide public acceptance in the last few years, but these large establishments only account for 7-8 percent of total Italian retail sales. There are 711 department stores and 1,223 supermarkets in Italy. Issuance of licenses for more department stores and markets has been limited by the need to maintain incomes of small retailers. Nevertheless, the expansion of chain and department stores is resulting in more and more centralized buying by head offices.

Furthermore, the advent of large retail organizations has influenced the streamlining of other distribution outlets. Groups of wholesalers and retailers have formed associations, primarily in the foods sector, to take advantage of bulk purchases for their members. Over 200 mail-order firms operate in Italy. Not more than a few do substantial business; however, current annual mail-order business, estimated at about $250 million (about 1.3 percent of total nonfood retail sales), is a noticeable recent development that shows promise of good growth. Goods sold through the mail-order system consist mainly of wearing apparel and household furnishings. Other types of mail-order goods include books, phonograph and tape recorders, radios, watches, jewelry, optical goods, cameras, musical instruments, electric handtools, plants, flowers, seeds, and bulbs.

Franchising.—The franchising system is not widely known in Italy. Although efforts are being made to expand franchising operations, it is generally agreed that the parent company would need to make substantial investment in company-owned outlets to attract potential franchises and to educate the consuming public.

Franchisors should bear in mind that a business license is necessary for each outlet. These may be difficult to obtain, particularly if the franchise will be competing against small, independent, local companies.

Leasing.—It has become a common commercial practice in Italy to lease, rather than sell, certain types of machinery, especially electronic data processing equipment. The leasing of foreign machines is usually arranged with the Italian clients through the branch offices in Italy of the foreign manufacturers. Commercial importation, application for import licenses, payment of duties, and related customs formalities are required to be made by an entity established in Italy; i.e., either the Italian branch of the foreign manufacturer or directly by the Italian lessee. Whether the lessee, in dealing with firms outside of Italy, is willing to assume the responsibility and inconvenience of handling importation depends on the attractiveness and leasing cost of the equipment compared to that available from U.S. or other entities established in Italy.

Distribution by U.S. Firms.—The successful American company in Italy enjoys this status because its product is marketed with the same diligence employed in the U.S. market. Whether it establishes a manufacturing/sales operation, or sales branch, appoints a commission agent, a stocking distributor, or a combination agent/distributor, a U.S. firm must follow sound marketing practices to sell successfully in the Italian market.

Foreign competition encourages the cliche that U.S. deliveries are poor because of distance and that service on U.S. equipment is undependable. In actual practice, it has been found that the successful American company: (1) offers deliveries as good as or better than foreign competition, (2) makes arrangements so that aftersales service is available in the market, (3) provides for the local stocking of service parts for which a requirement can be anticipated, and (4) gives priority to air shipments of any parts required that are not available in stock.

An American company that is entering the market is well advised to ensure that the arrangements it is considering are adequate to market its product properly and have the growth potential to achieve the sales volume that its product justifies.

The appointment of a resident representative is extremely important. For promotion of business and knowledge of the market, there is no effective alternative to a resident representative who is part of the local business scene and available to his customers. The representative may or may not be a U.S. citizen, but high commercial value is placed on his presence. This is particularly important when the product is technically complex and may be expected to require follow-up servicing or modification. The resident representative, because he is familiar with his product, is in a position to answer questions and solve problems. Such personalized service is frequently demanded by the customers, creates goodwill, and often stimulates repeat sales.

Having selected a strong distributor or agent, the American company normally cooperates with its representative in promoting the sales of its products in the Italian market. This may be done through a cooperative advertising program based upon matching funds up to a certain percentage of sales. The American company also usually assists in the training of key service and sales personnel.

A number of larger U.S. firms maintain their own sales organizations in Italy. Still others sell through specialized importers or appoint sales agents who often are manufacturers' brokers. A large, well-established Italian firm with an efficient nationwide sales organization is likely to insist on an exclusive arrangement.

About 6,000 U.S. firms are represented in the Italian market through agents, branches, subsidiaries, or licensees. Of these, nearly 800 have a substantial direct capital investment in the form of stock, as the sole owner or partner in an enterprise. Generally the sales territory of these firms takes in the whole of Italy, but in many cases it also covers the whole European Community. Sometimes the territory includes the Mediterranean basin.

Installment Sales

Selling on the installment plan was first introduced in Italy in the field of capital goods, and it has played an important role in the industrial development of the country. The payment term usually granted in sales of manufacturing equipment ranges from 180 days to 5 years, with the buyer making an initial cash payment and then settling the balance in monthly, quarterly or semiannual installments. Sales contracts on installment credit for machinery usually provide for a lien against the merchandise on behalf of the seller. As a general rule, the lien is established in favor of a bank which, in turn, makes the funds available to pay the seller.

This kind of credit is extended in the great majority of cases by domestic or foreign (including U.S.) firms already established in Italy or elsewhere in the EC. Installment sales by firms outside the EC are rare. Such sales hold little appeal because an authorization from the Ministry of Foreign Trade is required, the exchange risk (or insurance thereon) must be borne by the buyer, and the buyer must pay a tax on the interest charged by the seller.

Exchange control requirements for installment sales are as follows:

Import Value	Type of Exchange Control
Less than lira 1,000,000	None
Lira 1,000,000-2,000,000	Form required to be filled out by importer
Over lira 2,000,000	Form required to be filled out by authorized bank

Where settlement takes place more than 360 days after importation, the importer must choose an authorized bank as bank of domicile, through which to carry out all payments operations.

Deferred payments for imports are permitted without authorization if 90 percent of the import bill is paid within 360 days of receipt of the goods. In such a case, the remaining 10 percent may be paid over 24 months following receipt of goods.

Advance payments for imports require special approval when they take place more than 120 days before importation. If such payments exceed 2 million lire they must be made in foreign currency borrowed from authorized banks. When prepayments exceed 10 million lire, a 5 percent advance deposits is required.

Installment sales credits are extended, in the majority of cases, by domestic or foreign firms operating in Italy. However, in these instances the buyer bears the foreign exchange risk. Italian firms also make financing arrangements with the Export-Import Bank of the United States. Financing through the Eximbank carries no exchange risk.

Installment sales also are very common in Italy in the field of durable consumer goods. They account for 35-50 percent of all domestic sales of television sets, refrigerators, and washing machines. The Bank of Italy estimates that 35 percent of the automobiles sold in Italy are financed.

The financing of installment credit in connection with sales of consumer goods is accomplished by the local banks through the discounting of bills of exchange submitted by manufacturers or distributors established in Italy. The bills of exchange commonly known as "carta rateale" (installment paper) are signed by the buyers of the goods.

Government Procurement

The Italian Government and its agencies do not ordinarily make purchases abroad except when domestic suppliers cannot adequately meet the needs of government procurement offices. The term "domestic suppliers" does not exclude local subsidiaries, branches and agents of U.S. firms, and importers and distributors of merchandise imported from the United States. It is strongly suggested that U.S. firms utilize the service of Italian agents and distributors of U.S. products rather than attempt to offer their products directly to Italian governmental agencies.

To be eligible for a government contract, a firm must establish its financial and technical eligility by presenting its appropriate qualifications to the agency with which it wishes to do business. The required documents include the firm's legal structure, organization, manufacturing capacity, ownership, employment, financial status, business experience, and work accomplished in the past.

Each Italian agency maintain its own list of eligible contractors and suppliers, and a firm must establish its eligibility directly with each agency with which it wants to contract.

Each of the Italian Government agencies makes its own purchases except for office equipment and supplies. Such items are centrally procured by the Government's central purchasing office, the Provveditorato Generale dell Stato, an agency operating within the Ministry of the Treasury. Items usually purchased by the central office include office furniture, typewriters, calculating machines, stationery, forms, heating fuel, custodial uniforms, and air conditioners.

Procurement for projects developed within the framework of the North Atlantic Treaty Organization (NATO) is open to international competitive bidding. U.S. firms not already certified to participate in NATO bidding should send a resume of their qualifications to the Trade Opportunities Staff, Export Development, U.S. Department of Commerce, Washington, D.C. 20230.

Procurement in the United States of items needed by Italian defense organizations is made through the Italian Embassy in Washington.

Request for clearance of Americans visiting government agencies or Italian firms for defense technology purposes should be submitted to the Italian Security Authority at least 30 days before the proposed date to visit to ensure its proper clearance. The request must include: (a) full name, position, address, date and place of birth of visitor(s); (b) visitor's employing firm and address; (c) visitor's passport number and issue date; (d) visitor's security clearance level, date and by whom issued; (e) date and detailed purpose of visit; (f) highest level of security classification of discussion if any; (g) name and address of firm or government office to be visited and individual(s) to be contacted. The above information is to be furnished to the Commercial Section of the U.S. Embassy in Rome, which will coordinate the request for clearance with the appropriate Italian authority.

Alitalia, the State-owned civil airline, negotiates purchases of equipment and supplies in the United States through its offices at 666 Fifth Avenue, New York, N.Y. 10019.

The Italian State Railway, which controls virtually the entire Italian railway system, customarily procures items not available in Italy directly from foreign producers.

In addition to the Central Government agencies, there are 20 regional governments, 95 provincial administrations, over 8,000 communal authorities and about 30 State universities actively procuring a large variety of goods and services.

The Italian Government owns, through several holding companies, all or part of the stock of hundreds of firms representing a large segment of industry. These firms, organized and operated as private enterprises, are free to buy from domestic or foreign sources whatever equipment and supplies they need for their operations. The general tendency among these firms, as well as among the majority of other large Italian industrial concerns is to make every effort to eliminate what they consider to be the unnecessary costs of intermediaries. Consequently they establish relations with Italian or foreign manufacturers who are in the best position to supply their needs. (See also "Government's Role in Industry.")

At present, Italy is preparing new legislation on government procurement to implement the EEC directive permitting U.S. and European firms to participate in government tenders of certain specified Italian ministries. U.S. firms will be eligible to participate in government tenders as a result of the last GATT agreement.

Multilateral Trade Negotiations Affecting Government Procurement.—The Italian Government, by its membership in the EEC, has signed and will implement the new government procurement codes under the Multilateral Trade Negotiations (MTN). The codes provide for the following:

1. Signatory countries will not discriminate in their government purchases against goods produced abroad when such purchases exceed $200,000.

2. The agreement does not apply to services except those incidental to the purchase of goods.

3. The United States has exempted its minority and small businesses from the Agreement. As a result of the code, signatories must:
   a. Openly publish invitations to bid.
   b. Supply all documentation necessary to bid.
   c. Apply the same purchasing criteria to foreign and domestic firms.

4. Generally provide full information and explanation at every stage of the procurement process. Compliance with MTN regulations has been ensured by the formation of adjudication boards to which complaints of violations may be brought. The signatories have agreed to meet with 3 years to include services and other products under the government procurement agreement not presently covered.

Transportation and Utilities

Transportation

The railroad system is principally operated by the Italian State Railways (FS), a government agency. A small section of the system is operated by private companies on concession. The total length of the railroad network is 12,500 miles, half of it electrified. National as well as international connections are adequate.

The highway/road system is approximately 197,000 miles, including over 3,000 miles of superhighways (autostrade). The network connects the major industrial centers and offers access to Northern Europe. Extension trucking services are mainly operated by private companies under government concession.

Alitalia, a State-owned company, is Italy's principal airline providing both international and domestic service. Additional domestic service is provided by A.T.I., which is wholly owned subsidiary of Alitalia, Itavia, and Alisarda airlines. Charter service is offered by S.A.M. also an Alitalia subsidiary, which air-taxi service is available from Unijet Italia in Rome and Agena in Milan.

Italy has an extensive airport network consisting of 19 international, 17 domestic and 59 general aviation airports.

Italy has six major ports—Genoa, Livorno, Naples, Palermo, Trieste and Venice. In addition, there are 35 smaller ports mostly used for coastal commerce.

Fuel and Power Sources

Italy produces virtually all of the electrical energy it needs. However, it is strongly dependent on imports for its crude oil and coal. Production of electrical power totaled 179 billion kWh in 1979, of which 70.6 percent was thermoelectric, 26.6 percent hydroelectric, 1.4 percent nuclear and 1.4 percent geothermal.

Natural gas is produced domestically but over half of the demand is met by imports.

Because of the high cost of imported oil, Italy's energy plan calls for some expanded use of nuclear energy and for diversification of all energy sources, particularly coal. Presently there are four nuclear power stations. The new plan calls for the construction of eight 1,000 megawatt nuclear power plants to be completed by 1987.

Advertising and Research

Marketing Aids

Advertising Media.—In the last 10 years, advertising in Italy has grown in volume, importance, and sophistication. A relatively new industry, it is nevertheless making itself felt as a strong social, economic, and commercial force in the country. There is a growing awareness of the value of market studies, and use of technical, economic, and social as well as business data in planning promotions to reach the largest market as effectively as possible.

This growth in advertising has been accompanied by a proliferation of advertising agencies and an expansion of services offered. Along with Italian-owned agencies, there are joint ventures with other European or U.S. firms, as well as several American firms with large subsidiaries in Italy. While some agencies specialize in specific services and media, a large number of full service agencies deal with all advertising media and have market research facilities.

An estimated $700 million annually was spent on advertising in 1979 with the following percentage dollar breakdown by media: Magazines, 33.5 percent; radio and television,

22.2 percent; newspapers, 34.5 percent; movie strips, 3 percent; posters, etc., 6.8 percent.

Newspapers and Periodicals.—The main means of product advertising in Italy is through the daily newspapers. Newspapers in all sections of the country work closely with advertising firms, both Italian and foreign. However, since the newspapers themselves do not maintain advertising departments, advertising firms must place their ads with special agencies commissioned by the papers to receive advertising for them.

Of about 90 daily newspapers in Italy, only a dozen or so are read throughout the country, and while some 230 Italian and foreign periodicals are on sale in Italy, only about 20 have a large circulation.

Television.—Italy is served by three television networks operated by Radiotelevisione Italiana (RAI), a government-regulated company in which the State owns a majority interest. The three networks carry commercials in programs presented a few times each evening. In addition, over 100 private television stations were licensed in recent years for local broadcasting. In 1979, there were about 19 million licensed television receivers of which over 3 million were color TV. It is estimated that the television transmission comes into 80 percent of the households of the country.

Radio.—There are three radio stations owned and operated by RAI. These are on the air for a total of more than 340 hours weekly, and commercial time is available. In addition to the three networks there are many local radio stations.

Motion Picture Theaters.—Wide use of slides and film clips is made for advertising purposes. There are some 10,000 motion pictures theaters and many regularly show advertising films. The rates for advertising vary according to the showing time and class of the theater. Advertising is shown during every intermission. This medium may, therefore, be used to reach a wide market, cutting across economic strata.

Posters and Billboards.—Poster advertising is handled by a number of specialized companies, as is electric sign advertising, which is subject to special regulations. Poster advertisement on walls, along streets, in street cars, buses, and other means of transportation are used to reach the consumer market. Both posters and billboards are subject to the approval of provincial authorities and to payment of a tax on poster advertising.

Show Windows and Flyers.—Show window advertising is extensively used in Italy. Displays are usually attractively done and show prices of the items for sale.

Advertising flyers are in general use and street banners are used also for special occasions. Loudspeakers are used for advertising at sporting events.

Direct advertising, through the distribution of gifts, samples, and price reduction coupons, is frequently used to reach the Italian consumer, particularly the lower economic strata.

For such consumer goods as soap, soft drinks, and groceries it is not unusual to enclose in the package a free gift or gift certificate, a discount, or a chance in an advertising lottery. Samples appear to be especially effective in southern Italy.

Consumers are also quite receptive to advertising catalogs, which are frequently passed along from person to person. Distinctive and imaginatively designed letterheads and trademarks are quite important in publicizing a company.

Market Research and Trade Organizations

Market research is closely related to advertising, and a number of firms specialize in this work. There are over 100 market research agencies operating in Italy, of which 9 are the subsidiaries of well-known U.S. companies. Large Italian companies, including the leading manufacturers of consumer goods, conduct market research either through their own specialized departments or by employing market research agencies.

Most of the many different manufacturers' associations are members of the General Federation of Italian Industry (Confindustria), Via dell'Astronomia 30, Rome. This association publishes much material of possible interest to U.S. businesspersons, including an annual review of the Italian economy, and a bulletin in English several times a year.

There are chambers of commerce in all major Italian cities, and some, particularly those in large industrial centers such as Milan, publish economic reviews of their particular regions. A monthly review of the Italian economy is published by the Union of Italian Chambers of Commerce (Unione Italiana Delle Commercio, Industria E Agricoltura), via Piazza Sallustio 21, Rome. The American Chamber of Commerce in Italy, Agnello 12, Milan, publishes a monthly review in English containing information on current business developments.

Several of the leading banks, such as the Banco di Roma, and the Banca Nazionale Del Lavoro, publish economic reviews. There are also a number of periodicals specializing in commercial and financial matters that provide marketing information.

Reports on Italian industry are prepared by US. Foreign Service posts in Italy and are made available to U.S. firms by the Publications Sales Branch, Room 1617, U.S. Department of Commerce, Washington, D.C. 20230.

Credit

Sources of Credit

Italy has a well-developed banking and credit system. Banks are subject to close government supervision since the granting of credit and the administration of savings are considered functions of "national interest." The establishment of a new bank or the opening of a branch of an existing bank must be authorized by the Bank of Italy, the central bank of Italy.

The Italian banking system consists of two sectors: a commercial banking sector (banks that primarily accept demand and short-term deposits and make loans of a short-term nature) and a second sector made up of 70 "special credit institutes" that make medium- and long-term loans.

Short-term financing for foreign and domestic firms is available from the commercial banking sector, including branch offices of many U.S. banks. (See section on Credit Facilities.)

The special institutes generally specialize in particular types of investment finance; e.g., agriculture, industry, real estate, housing, and credit. Principal institutes for medium- and long-term industrial credit are the Instituto Mobiliare Italiano (IMI), Banca di Credito Finanziario (Mediobanca), and Ente Finanziario Interbancario (EFIMBANCA).

U.S. firms desiring to finance a major portion of their investment outside the United States may find capital available in the Eurodollar market. Loans granted by European branches of U.S. banks are exempt from payment of the interest equalization tax. Several major U.S. banks have branches in Italy, principally in Rome and Milan.

There are 10 stock exchanges in operation in Italy, the most important one being in Milan.

Credit Facilities

There are banking offices located in all important cities and towns throughout the country, with nearly 1,200 banks and 10,000 branches performing commercial services. Among the most important are the Banca Nazionale de Lavoro, Banca Commerciale

Italiana, Credito Italiano, Banco di Roma, Banco di Napoli and Monte dei Paschi di Siena. These banks are a principal source of credit information.

Several U.S. banks perform banking services through branches, subsidiaries, or representatives. The Chase Manhattan Bank has offices in Milan and Rome, the Morgan Bank, Chemical Bank, the first National City Bank of New York and the First National Bank of Chicago have commercial banking facilities in Milan and Rome; the American Express Bank in Milan, Venice, Florence, Rome, and Naples; and the Morgan Guaranty Trust Co. in Milan. The Bank of America operates through its subsidiary, Banca d'America d'Italia. The Continental Illinois National Bank and Trust Co., the Marine Midland Bank, and the Manufacturers Hanover Trust Co. have offices in Rome while the Chemical Bank of New York hs an office in Milan.

Most of the commercial banks correspond with U.S. banks, thus enabling the foreign departments of many American banks to give service throughout Italy.

Foreign Exchange Policy

Italy has no restrictions on the amount or type of foreign exchange instruments, including currency and checks, which may be imported. However, the amount of Italian banknotes permitted to be introduced into, or reexported from the country cannot exceed lire 100,000 approximately $117). The amount of foreign exchange instruments that may be exported by nonresidents leaving Italy must not exceed that registered on entry or legitimately acquired in Italy.

Italian foreign exchange regulations are issued by the Italian Exchange Office (Ufficio Italiano dei Cambi (U.I.C.)), Via Quattro Fontane 123, 00184 Rome, under instructions of the Ministry of Foreign Trade. Foreign exchange instruments may be sold or acquired from the Bank of Italy or any of the banks authorized by the Bank or Italy. In practice, all commercial banks in operation are authorized to engage in foreign exchange transactions.

Dollar banknotes, travelers checks, and, in some cases, personal checks, may be exchanged at banks, exchange offices, and authorized tourist offices and hotels.

Quotations and Terms of Payments

While f.o.b. price quotations for certain commodities are readily understood by the larger Italian business firms experienced in dealing with U.S. suppliers, c.i.f. terms are the usual basis for quotations. Experience indicates that use of f.o.b. terms in dealings with the average Italian businessperson can, in some cases, lead to misunderstandings and perhaps even the loss of an order because of miscalculation of what the final landed cost of the import from the United States will be.

The customary terms of sale in Italy are either cash or net. Sales made on cash terms call for payment before delivery, on delivery or shortly after delivery—usually within 10 days from the date of delivery. A 2-to-5 percent discount is allowed on the amount of the invoice. Net terms call for payment of the full amount of the transaction at the end of the specified period—1, 2, 3, or 4-months—from the date of the invoice. The length of the period depends on the commodity involved and the credit standing of the purchaser. A period of up to 2 years is often allowed for payment of capital goods, store equipment, trucks, and similar equipment. Western European suppliers are known to apply terms of sale comparable to those customarily offered in domestic Italian business.

Reports from Italian sources indicate that some American suppliers have been too rigid in their payment terms and have lost business to other suppliers because of it. While these U.S. manufacturers requested payment upon receipt of the goods, successful bidders were offering terms allowing settlement of the account from 60 to 120 days following receipt of the order. In the cases of machinery, store fixtures, and similar equipment, even more liberal terms have been offered.

The use of irrevocable letters of credit in Italian purchases from the United States has declined appreciably in recent years. Although such instruments are still required by American exporters, especially when the Italian customer's credit reputation is not well known, the growing reluctance of Italian businesses to provide letters of credit has forced American exporters to utilize either other avenues for assuring payment or lose to other suppliers in the highly competitive Italian market. The Italian businessperson is understandably hesitant to pay the relatively high fees for a letter of credit when other means are open to his supplier or to himself. U.S. exporters have shown growing confidence in the creditworthiness of Italian buyers and also have put to greater use the export credit insurance and guarantee programs available to them through the Foreign Credit Insurance Association.

There are no collection agencies in Italy. If a case proves troublesome, the debt can be collected only through the courts, and such legal process is usually long and expensive. A list of attorneys is available from the U.S. Department of Commerce, Washington, D.C. 20230.

Information on particular Italian firms is available from the U.S. Department of Commerce through its World Traders Data Reports service. Italian and American banks also provide credit information service. Credit information is available as well from such private agencies as Foreign Credit Interchange Bureau, 475 Park Avenue South, New York, N.Y., 10016; and from Dun and Bradstreet, Inc., 99 Church Street, New York, N.Y. 10007.

Just as the terms of any sales offer should be presented in a clear and detailed manner, shipments should conform to the contract and to any samples which may have been sent to the Italian importer. Special attention should be given to the prompt observance of agreed delivery schedules as, prompt delivery may be a decisive and possibly an overriding consideration of the importer in placing additional orders especially during times of business prosperity.

Investment in Italy

Policy

Italy's general policy toward foreign investment in Italy has been consistently favorable, motivated by the belief that foreign investment contributes to economic growth, employment, and the level of technology. In 1979, total foreign investment in Italy was over $7 billion.

Foreign investment in Italy is in principle governed by Law No. 43 of February 7, 1956, and subsequent implementing regulations. Law 43 guarantees repatriation of foreign capital originally invested in new "productive" enterprises in Italy and unlimited remittance of profits therefrom. ("Productive" investments may be defined as those adding to Italy's stock of physical capital.) Foreign direct investment transactions and transfers are also covered by Italian exchange control procedures. Although both capital and earnings are free of restrictions, strict enforcement of exchange controls may cause some delays in effecting certain international transfers of funds.

In general, Italy does not limit the extent of foreign ownership in an Italian corporation or other business entity. The Italian Government's stance on foreign investment is national treatment; that is, nondiscriminatory either in favor or against foreign investment, as compared with domestic investment. There are some restrictions, however, on medium- and long-term indebtedness in lira of foreign-owned firms that wish to be eligible for the transfer guarantees under Law 43.

Legislation has been in effect in Italy since 1950 that provides for incentives designed to stimulate economic development in southern Italy. These incentives consist mainly of tax exemptions, grants, soft loans, and temporary exemption from the share of payments into the pension fund required to be made by employers. They are extended uniformly, without discrimination, to both domestic and foreign investors. Similar, but somewhat less generous incentives are available for domestic and foreign investments in depressed areas in central and northern Italy.

Multinational firms, which are generally capital intensive, have benefited fully from these incentive programs. Law No. 183 for the economic development of southern Italy of May 2, 1976, has amended the regulations on loans and grants, however, in such a manner as to favor the small- and medium-sized, labor-intensive enterprises. The tax incentives and the exemption from pension-fund payments continue to be granted uniformly to both labor-intensive and capital-intensive firms.

In addition, foreign ownership or management is subject to limitations in certain cases. These include, among other:

(1) Vessels under the Italian flag are required to be owned by a corporation established in Italy in which the controlling interest and management are Italian.

(2) Aircraft cannot be registered in Italy unless they are wholly owned by Italian nationals or by an Italian corporation in which foreign interest does not exceed 40 percent. The same restrictions apply to airlines.

(3) Participation in competitive bidding or construction projects by the Ministry of Public Works is limited to qualified contractors operating in EEC countries. In the case of bids by corporations, the directors are required to be Italian citizens. Italian residence is acceptable in lieu of citizenship for individuals who are nationals of states granting reciprocal treatment to Italian citizens.

(4) The local representative of a foreign life insurance company must be an Italian citizen residing in Italy.

Several fields of activity controlled by the State

are excluded entirely from both Italian and foreign private participation. These include the manufacture and sale of tobacco, tobacco products and matches; and the operation of railroads and the telephone system.

U.S. Investment in Italy

The United States has been the leading foreign investor in Italy for over a decade. Approximately 6,000 U.S. firms have subsidiaries, distributors, or licensees there. Some 40 percent of U.S. investments are estimated to be wholly U.S. owned.

At the end of 1979, the book value of direct investments by American companies in Italy was nearly $3.0 billion. More than half of all U.S. direct investments in Italy are in manufacturing areas (58.6 percent) and in the petroleum and petrochemical sectors (25.4 percent). The majority of U.S. investment is in the Milan-Turin-Genoa area of northern Italy; the remainder is in and around Rome.

There is no longer in Italy a general requirement that all new industrial plants must be authorized by the Ministry of Industry and Commerce. However, major industrial investments are required to be submitted to CIPE (Interministerial Committee for Economic Planning) to verify that the proposed investments conform to the objectives set forth in the economic plan. Job creation and overall economic development by avoiding the over-concentration of industry in northern and central Italy are the primary objectives of the economic plan. Specifically, investments subject to verification are those with a capitalization of more than 5 billion lire (about $8 million) or any investment project in excess of lire 7 billion or ($11.2 million).

Licenses are required for numerous activities including the manufacture of pharmaceutical chemicals and patent medicines, infant foods and meat preparations, explosives, firearms and ammunition, radio and TV sets, and electronic tubes.

Insurance companies cannot operate in Italy without special authorization from the Ministry of Industry and Commerce.

Trading firms wishing to import or export goods subject to licensing procedures must be registered with the Ministry of Foreign Trade.

Any organization dealing in retailing or wholesaling, including mail-order and vending machine sales, must obtain a license from the national and/or local authorities.

Government's Role in Industry

The Italian Government plays an important role in the nation's economy, with State agencies holding controlling interests in a large number of financial, commercial, and industrial enterprises. In Italy, as in other European countries, State participation in key economic sectors is very extensive, particularly in communications and transportation, where telephone, railroads, the national airline Alitalia, and large shipping companies are operated by government holding companies. Most of the production and distribution of electric power is nationalized and, in addition, the Italian Government is also directly and significantly involved in a number of industrial sectors where it competes with private enterprises.

State participation in the industrial sector varies from direct management in the case of the salt and tobacco monopolies to indirect management through State holding companies or joint ventures in which the Government controls the majority of shares. State activities spread over a wide range of industrial branches from engineering, mining, metallurgy, ship-building, automobiles, chemicals, paper mills, printing and publishing, and hotels to the largest banks. Probably about one-third of Italian industrial output comes from State-owned firms. The State is, therefore, an important employer and customer, and its influence is felt in both the domestic and foreign trade sectors.

Most of the government-controlled enterprises are affiliates of four giant holding companies: IRI (Industrial Reconstruction Institute), EFIM (Manufacturing and Financial Holding Agency), and ENI (National Hydrocarbons Agency), which come under the supervision of the Ministry of State Holdings, and of ENEL (Electric Power Agency) under the Ministry of Industry.

Requirements for Business Operation

A foreign citizen wishing to establish temporary or permanent residence in Italy to administer a business or to manage a corporation should obtain a visa for this purpose from the Italian consulate having jurisdiction in the individual's place of residence.

All persons or entities engaging in business in Italy in any capacity must be registered with the local Chamber of Commerce, Industry and Agriculture, a quasi-government office, operating essentially as a field office of the Ministry of Industry and Commerce. To register with this office, an agent for a foreign company must produce a power of attorney duly notarized by an Italian consular or diplomatic official in the country of the principal.

Forms of Business Organization

A foreign businessperson setting up an enterprise in Italy may choose from several types of organizations that are specified in the Italian Civil Code Book V, Title V.

Individual or Sole Proprietorship.—An individual proprietorship established for the production or exchange of goods and services is responsible for its operation to the extent of the proprietor's business assets and his personal property.

Simple Partnership (*Societá Semplice*).—A partnership is a group of two or more persons conducting trade jointly. The simple partnership can be established without any particular formalities. The partnership is set up either through the joint operation of a business or by contract. Each member of the firm is liable for any business debts, unless otherwise specified and publicized, to the full extent of his personal assets. Each partner's share of profits and losses is proportional to his contribution of capital.

General or Unlimited Partnership *(Societá in Nome Colletivo-S.n.c.)*—In an unlimited partnership, all partners are jointly and severally liable without limitation for partnership obligations. An unlimited partnership may not issue bonds. The partnership contract must contain the data specified in Article 2295 of the Civil Code and be filed in the Register of Enterprises at the local court. Any of the partners may be appointed to serve as directors.

Limited Partnership (*Societa' in Accomandita Semplice-S.a.s.*).—Liability in a limited partnershhip is joint, several, and unlimited for the general partners ("*accomandatari*"). Limited partners ("*accomandanti*") are liable only to the extent of their original capital investment. A limited partnership may not issue bonds. Subscribed capital cannot be represented by shares. The articles of partnership, as outlined in Article 2295 of the Civil Code, must specify who are the general and limited partners. The partnership contract is filed with the Register of Enterprises of the local court. Only general partners may participate in the management.

Limited Partnership with Shares (*Societá in Accomandita per Azioni-S.a.p.A*).—A limited partnership with shares has the same structure as a limited partnership, except that holdings of the partners are represented by shares. Companies limited by shares may issue bonds,

within the limits as provided for the joint stock companies in the limited partnership, liability is joint, several, and unlimited for general partners, while limited partners are liable to the extent of the original capital invested. The general partners are by law the directors. The company must be registered in the Register of Enterprises. Many of the regulations governing corporations are applicable to this form of business.

Limited-Liability Company (*Societá a Responsibilita Limitata-S.r.l*).—Owners in a limited liability company are not personally liable for company obligations beyond their subscription quotas. Unlike a corporation, quotas in a limited liability company are not represented by shares of stock. Such a company cannot issue bonds. A limited liability company must have a minimum capital of lire 20 million and does not require a board of auditors unless the capital is over lire 100 million. The company must draw up a contract according to Article 2475, Civil Code, and file it with the Register of Enterprises.

Cooperative (*Societa' Cooperative*).—Cooperatives and mutual insurance or assurance companies (enti mutalistici Art. 2512) may be established to carry out such activities as production, marketing, banking, and insurance. Cooperatives are subject to various restrictions and to governmental supervision. Each partner may not hold more than $400 in shares. The board of directors must approve assigning of shares and admission of new members.

Joint Venture (*Associazione in Partecipazione*). —A joint venture involves the participation by a supplier of capital in the profits of the business. The operator manages the business and is solely responsible for the obligations he assumes toward third parties. The person furnishing capital is responsible for any loss in direct proportion to his share in the net profit, limited to the amount of his original investment.

Corporation (*Societá per Azioni-S.p.A*).—The Italian corporation is similar in form to the corporation in the United States and is usually the most suitable form for large enterprises. Participation quotas are represented by shares of stock. Personal liability is limited to the amount of shares owned. The corporation is a legal person, an entity separate from its shareholders, and is liable for its obligations only to the extent of its assets.

A corporation must have at least two shareholders. A minimum of lire 200 million is required for incorporation, 30 percent of which must be deposited with the Banca d'Italia in a noninterest bearing account until organization formalities are completed. The entire capital stock of the company must be subscribed. If the original stock exceeds lire 2 billion, the Ministry of Treasury must give special authorization.

The article of incorporation (*atto costitutivo*) and the bylaws must be drawn up before a notary public according to specifications in the Civil Code, Art. 2328. The company is incorporated when the articles of incorporation have been approved by the court and the registry tax is paid. Copies of documents concerning the life of the corporation must be filed with the local chamber of commerce.

Employment

Labor protection and social security are provided for in a number of Italian laws, including the Constitution. The principal government agency responsible for implementing these laws in the Ministry of Labor and Social Security, through the Labor Exchanges and the Labor Inspectorates. As the labor practices in Italy are somewhat complex, American companies seeking to invest in Italy should make a careful study of management labor relations to avoid the possibility of serious and costly difficulties in their proposed Italian operations.

Labor Force

The labor force was 22.6 million in 1979 out of the total population of 57 million. About 38 percent of all workers were employed in industry 48.3 percent in services, government, and other servicers, and 13.3 percent in agriculture. The 1979 average unemployment rate was 7.6 percent.

Job placement is a public function and is carried out by public agencies operating under the Ministry of Labor and Social Security. According to law, every person wishing to be employed must register with the Ministry of Labor Employment Office ("Ufficio del Collocament") in his locality. Private employment agencies are prohibited, except in special cases.

Workers may be hired directly or through the Employment Office. Direct employment is permitted; however, only in certain cases, including persons required for executive positions, workers to be employed in plants having less than four workers, or persons employed through public competitive examinations.

An employer seeking to hire workers with specified skills must submit a written request to the Employment Office in his district. The employer has the right to refuse to employ workers referred to him by the Employment Office who have been previously dismissed from other jobs for legitimate reasons and he may dismiss workers who prove to be unsatisfactory. According to Italian law, apprentices must be hired through the Employment Offices, but in certain cases they may be employed directly.

No person under 15 years of age may be employed unless an exemption is obtained from the Ministry of Labor. The employment of women and minors is subject to various restrictions depending on the type of labor involved. There are also requirements concerning the employment of blind, deaf, and disabled workers.

Dismissal of workers.—Dismissal in Italy is governed by labor-management agreements and by law. Both protect workers' interests through a series of provisions: advance notice, compulsory union-management consultations, monetary compensation, and possible reemployment rights, in cases of labor force reductions due to poor business conditions.

Employment of Aliens.—A foreign citizen living in Italy and seeking permission to work in Italy must apply to the "Ufficio Stranieri" (Foreigners' Office) of the Questura (Police Headquarters) having jurisdiction in the place in which he resides. Requests for work permits must be accompanied by written documentation from the prospective employer. The Ministry of the Interior (Direzione General di Pubblica Sicurezza) makes the final decision after consultation with the Ministry of Labor and Social Security.

For foreign citizens living outside of Italy, requests for an Italian work permit, together with documentation from the prospective employer, should be submitted to the nearest Italian consultate. The consulate will in turn transmit the application to the Italian Ministry of Foreign Affairs, which will make a decision after consultation with the Ministry of the Interior and the Ministry of Labor and Social Security.

The principal criteria for obtaining permission to work in Italy are: (a) the foreign applicant must have found a specific job, (b) the prospective employer must have requested permission to employ him; and (c) the employer must be able to justify the employment of a foreigner rather than an Italian on the grounds that no Italian can be located who has the specialized talents required for the job in question.

Persons expecting to remain in Italy for more than 6 months for investment purposes must obtain a visa granted for a period of 6 months to 3 years, depending on the references given and the character of the enterprise. Upon arrival in Italy, the applicant must go to the local police headquarters to obtain a Permit of Stay, which usually corresponds to the validity of the visa and classifies the applicant a resident for the purpose of engaging in business. The permit is easily extended, and U.S. citizens are allowed to remain in Italy as long as they are successfully engaged in their activity.

Foreign workers in Italy enjoy the same social legislation rights as Italian nationals. In cases of unemployment, however, the Italian employment law does not provide for the registration of foreign workers with the Employment Offices. Foreign workers are eligible to receive social security benefits provided for Italian nationals (including old age, disability, family allowances, health and accident insurance). Pensions to workers permanently disabled in occupational accidents or through occupational diseases, as well as disability and old age pensions, are paid to foreign workers wherever they reside.

Taxation

A new comprehensive income tax system entered into force on January 1, 1974. This system is designed to bring about a more equitable tax collection system than was previously utilized. The following information briefly describes new regulations applicable to taxes of principal interest to U.S. businesspersons: the personal income tax, the tax on legal entities, and the local tax on income.

The personal income tax (IRPEF) affects net income accruing from wages and salaries, dividends, interest, and income from professional services. Nonresidents are taxable only with respect to income produced in Italy. A person who resides in Italy for more than 6 months is considered a "resident" for tax purposes. A "resident" in Italy is required to pay IRPEF also on income produced abroad. However, a tax credit is granted on taxes paid in the foreign country in which the income is produced, if a country (such as the United States) grants reciprocity. The rates of IRPEF range from 10 percent on income up to 3 million lire (or $3,500) per year and progressively rises to 25 percent in income of 7.5 to 8 million lire ($8,775-$9,360), 40 percent in incomes of 35 to 40 million lire ($41,000-$46,800), 50 percent on income between 100 and 125 million lire ($117,000-$146,250), with a top bracket of 72 percent on income over 500 million lire (over $585,000).

The tax on legal entities (IRPEG) applies to corporate entities, companies, and, in general, any association of persons. Also subject to this tax are foreign legal entities but only with respect to income produced in Italy. Italian legal entities are required to pay IRPEG on income produced abroad. A tax credit for taxes on such income is allowable. IRPEG is levied on a flat rate of 25 percent of net aggregate income. The rate of this tax is reduced to 7.5 percent in the cases of private holding companies and financial entities. For holding companies and financial entities whose capital is more than 50 percent directly or indirectly owned by the Italian Government, the tax rate is 6.25 percent.

The local tax on income (ILOR), collected for local government utilization, affects income of persons and legal entities but is not applicable to income derived from wages, salaries, pensions, equities, and professional activities.

Industrial Property Protection

Italy is a member of the "Paris Union" International Convention for the Protection of Industrial Property (Patents and Trademarks) to which the United States and about 85 other countries adhere. Thus, U.S. nationals are entitled to the same treatment in acquiring and maintaining patent and trademark protection in Italy as that country extends to its own nationals. A U.S. national is also entitled to a period of 12 months (rights of priority), after first filing a patent application in the United States, within which to file a corresponding application in Italy and receive in the latter area the benefit of his or her first U.S. filing date. The "priority right" filing period for trademarks is 6 months.

Italy is a member of the Berne Copyright Union and also adheres to the Universal Copyright Convention to which the United States and 50 other countries are signatories. A U.S. author can thereby obtain copyright protection in Italy for his work first copyrighted in the United States merely by placing on his work, his name, date of first publication, and the symbol "c" in a circle. Italian authors have the same rights in this country for their works first copyrighted in Italy.

Patent and trademark applications and inquiries should be addressed to:

Ministero dell'Industria e Commercio
Ufficio Centrale Bervetti per Invenzioni
Modelli e Marchi
Via Molise, 19
00187 Rome, Italy

Applications and inquiries concerning copyrights should be addressed to:

Presidenza del Consiglio dei Ministri
Ufficio del Proprietá Letteraria, Artistics e
Scientificia
Via Boncompagni, 15
00187 Rome, Italy

Patents and Licensing.—The principal laws
governing patent protection are Royal Decrees
No. 3731 of October 30, 1859, No. 1127 of June 29,
1939, Law No. 633 of April 22, 1941, and
Presidential Decree No. 338 of June 19, 1979.
Decree 338 amends the former Italian legislation
and implements the European Patent
Convention. To be patentable, an invention must
be novel; i.e., it cannot have been available to the
public anywhere and anyhow before the date of
the filing or of the priority claimed.

Patents are granted for 15 years from the
effective filing date of application. They are
assignable and transferable. A patent can be
subject to compulsory licensing if not worked
within 3 years from date of grant or 4 years from
the filing date of application, whichever is later.

Licensing and technical assistance agreements
with foreign firms are encouraged by the Government and can be entered into without
Government approval. The foreign exchange
necessary to effect payment abroad (including
the United States) of *bona fide* royalties and/or
technical assistance fees can be obtained simply
upon application to the Italian Exchange Office
through a bank. Applicants are required to
produce the original contract with the foreign
concern and to submit a certified copy of such a
contract. A certificate confirming the validity of
the patent should also be submitted in the event
that the contract provides for the use of patents.

Annual taxes must be paid throughout the
period an Italian patent is in force. These taxes
are progressive and range from 1,000 lire for the
first year to 35,000 lire for the 15th year.

Trademarks.—The principal trademark
registration laws are Royal Decree No. 929 of
June 21, 1942, and Presidential Decree No. 795 of
May 8, 1948. Some types of terms are not
registrable as trademarks, such as those deemed
to be generic, those containing false indications of
quality or origin of goods, and those similar to
terms already registered by others in Italy or for
which applications are pending. For some goods,
geographic names may not be used in
trademarks nor can the portraits of persons be
registered without their consent. Surnames,
other than those of the applicant for registration,
cannot be registered if they reflect unfavorably
upon the persons who have the right to use the
names.

Trademark applications are examined for
acceptability of their format and consistency
with the above criteria. If an application is in
order, the mark will be registered. There is no
opportunity for opposition. First applicant is
entitled to registration. However, any other
person who claims to be the first user of the mark
in Italy can have the prior registration cancelled,
provided he can prove his claim. No prior use
claim can be rendered after the registered mark
is 5 years old.

Trademarks are registered for 20 years from
the effective application filing date and are
renewable for similar periods. Failure to use a
mark within 3 years after its registration can
result in cancellation. Trademarks may be
assigned provided such action involves no
deceptive trade practice.

Trademark products are classified under 42
groups (1-34 for products, 35-42 for services);
applications must indicate the appropriate classification. At present, trademark application
fees are lire 1,500. The registration fee for a
trademark classification under one category of
products is 5,000 lire. Additional fee of 3,000 lire
is charged for each new category if the
trademark is classified under more than one
category of products.

Copyrights.—Copyrights are protected by
Law No. 633 of April 22, 1941, and Decree Law
No. 82 of August 23, 1946. Executive recognition
in the form of copyright protection to the author
is accorded intellectual creations pertaining to
science, literature, music, decorative arts,
architecture, the theatre, and motion pictures.
Copyright protection for an author's work exists
for the life of the author, plus 50 years after his or
her death. In the case of motion pictures,
protection is limited to 30 years from the date of
the first public screening. Anonymous works are
protected for 50 years after publication.

Further information on step-by-step
procedures regarding patent, trademark, and
copyright protection in Italy should be obtained
from competent legal counsel. Additional
information on laws and regulations is available
from the Foreign Business Practices Division,
Office of International Finance, Investment, and
services, U.S. Department of Commerce, Washington, D.C. 20230. List of attorneys practicing in
the patent, trademark, and copyright fields in
Italy are available from the Export Information Division, International Trade Administration, Washington, D.C. 20230.

Guidance for Business Travelers

By and large, what is considered good business
practice in this country also applies when doing

business in Italy. Businesspeople there also appreciate prompt replies to their inquiries, and they expect all correspondence to be acknowledged.

In the North, promotional literature and correspondence is short and factual. In the South, where customs are different, Italians place much more value on personal contacts than on correspondence.

Commercial Language.—Italian is the official language and is spoken in all parts of Italy, although minorities in the Alto Adige and Aosta regions speak German and French, respectively. Correspondence with Italian firms, especially if the letter is the first ever sent, should be in Italian. If a reply comes in English then the subsequent correspondence with the Italian firm can be in English. The use of Italian is not only regarded as a courtesy, but assures prompt attention, and prevents inaccuracies which might arise in translation. Most large commercial firms, however, are able to correspond in English and French in addition to Italian.

The importance of having trade literature, catalogues, and instructions for the use of servicing of products printed in Italian cannot be overemphasized. The agent representative in Italy who has such material is in a far better competitive position than the one who can only show prospective customers trade literature in the English language.

Business Hours.—The usual Italian business hours are from 8 or 9 a.m. to noon or 1 p.m. and from 3 to 6 or 7 p.m. Working hours for the various Ministries of the Government are normally from 8 a.m. to 2 p.m. without intermission. Bank hours are from 8:30 a.m. to 1:30 p.m.; they are closed on Saturdays.

Holidays.—Italian holidays to take into account when planning a business itinerary include the following: January 1, New Year's Day; Easter Monday; April 25, Liberation Day; May 1, Italian Labor Day; August 15, Feast of the Assumption; November 1, Feast of all Saints; December 7, Feast of St. Ambrogio (Milan only); December 8, Immaculate Conception; December 25, Christmas; December 26, Feast of St. Stephen.

August is a poor month for conducting business in Italy, since most business firms are closed for vacations.

System of Weights and Measures.—The metric system of weights and measures is used in Italy. The metric system should be used in every quotation where measurement or weight is involved.

Electric Current.—Electrical power supplies are generally 220 volts, 50 cycles, single-phase and 380 volts, 50 cycles, three-phase. Also, usually available are 127 volts, 50 cycles, three-phase. Electricity at 60 cycles is ordinarily not available.

Sources of Economic and Commercial Information

Rome: American Embassy
Via Veneto 119/A
00187-Rome; or APO New York 09794
Tel. (06) 46 74
Telex: 613425 or 610450

American Consulate General, Genoa
Banca d'America e d'Italia Bldg.
Piazza Portello 6, Box G; or APO New York 09794
Tel. (010) 282-741 thru 5

American Consulate General, Milan
Piazza Repubblica 32
20124 Milano; or APO New York 09689
Tel. (02) 652-841 thru 5

Commercial Section
Via Gattamelata 5
20124 Milano
Tel. (02) 498-2241/2/3

U.S. International Marketing Center
Via Gattamelata 5
20124 Milano
Tel. (02) 469-6451
Telex 330-208

Consulate General, Naples
Piazza della Republica
80122 Naples; or Box 18, FPO New York 09521
Tel. (081) 660-966

Consulate General, Palermo
Via Baccarini 1, 90143, or
APO New York 09794 (c/o American Embassy Rome-P)
Tel. 291532-35

Consulate, Florence
Lungarmo Amerigo Vespucci 38; or
APO New York 09019
Tel. (055) 298-276

The United States also maintains a Consulate in Trieste; however, that office performs no commercial functions.

Italian Government Representation

Italy maintains a commercial office of the Italian Embassy located at 1601 Fuller Street, N.W., Washington, D.C. 20009, phone: (202) 328-5500.

Offices of the Italian Trade Commissioners are located in the following cities:

San Francisco—595 Market Street, Suite 2150, San Francisco, California 94105, phone: (415) 398-1574/5

New York—World Trade Center, New York City, New York 10048, phone: (212) 432-9250.

Los Angeles—1801 Avenue of the Stars, Los Angeles, California, 90067, phone: (213) 879-0950.

Chicago—401 North Michigan Avenue, Equitable Building, Chicago, Illinois, 60611, phone: (312) 787-3772.

Houston—3050 South Post Oak Road, Route 1090, Houston, Texas, 77056, phone: (713) 626-5531.

English Language Publications

OECD Economic Survey of Italy. Published annually by the Organization for Economic Cooperation and Development; Publications Office located at: 1750 Pennsylvania Avenue, N.W., Suite 1207, Washington, D.C. 20006.

Italy: Economic Trends. U.S. Department of Commerce (Published semiannually).

Italy: Background Notes, August 1977, U.S. Department of State.

Italy: An Economic Profile. Published annually by the Italian Embassy. Commercial Office, Washington, D.C.

Bank of Italy Annual Reports.

Italian American Business Directory. Published annually by the American Chamber of Commerce in Italy, Via Agnello 12, 20121 Milan, Italy. Price: $25.

The Gulling Report, Italy. Published monthly subscription price: $85 from the Galling Report on Italy, Via dei Tre Orologi 6, 00197 Rome, Italy.

Italian Trends. A monthly letter from the Banca Nazionale del Lavoro, Via Veneto 119, Rome, Italy.

Review of the Economic Conditions in Italy. Published bimonthly by Banco di Rome, Casella Postale 2442, 00100 Rome, Italy.

Economic News From Italy. Published weekly by Elite Publishing Corporation, 11-03 46th Avenue, Long Island City, New York 11101.

Information Service of the European Communities. Available in the United States from the European Community Information Service, 2100 M Street, N.W., Washington, D.C. 20037.

Banca Nazionale del Lavoro, Quarterly Review. Published by the said bank located at Via Vitorio Veneto 119, Rome, Italy.

Kompass. A 2-volume directory of information on Italian firms published by Etas-Kompass, Via Mantegna 6, 20154 Milan, Italy.

Italian Language Publications

Annuario Statistico Italiano. Published annually by Istituto Centrale di Statistics, Rome, Italy.

Bolletino Mensile di Statistic. Published monthly by Instituto Centrale di Statistics, Rome, Italy.

Statistica Mensile del Commercio Con L-Estero. Published monthly by Instituto Centrale di Statistics, Rome, Italy (Foreign trade statistics).

Mondo Economico. Published weekly Mondo Economico Via die Mercanti 2, 20121 Milan, Italy.

Notiziario Istat. Statistical bulletin published monthly by the Instituto Centrale di Statistica, Rome, Italy.

Indicatori Mensili. Monthly bulletin of statistical indicators published by the Instituto Centrale di Statistica.

Successo Magazine. Published monthly by Casa Editrice Successo S.p.A.-Via Manzoni 44, 20121 Milan, Italy.

Market Profile—ITALY

Foreign Trade

Imports.—$77.7 billion in 1979, and $54.9 billion in 1978. U.S. share: 6.8 percent in 1979, and 6.8 percent in 1978. Chief imports from world: crude oil, machinery, iron and steel. Main imports from U.S.: machinery feeds and grains, chemicals, coal, aircraft and parts, paper and paper pulp.

Exports.—$72.1 billion in 1979, and $54.5 billion in 1978. U.S. share: 6.5 percent in 1979, and 7.1 percent in 1978. Chief exports to world: industrial machinery, office machines, motor vehicles, footwear, textiles, agricultural products. Chief exports to U.S.: shoes, apparel, office machines, automobiles, beverages.

Trade Policy.—Liberal, except for agricultural imports which are subject to Common Agricultural Policy of the European Community. Italy is a member of EEC, IMF, OECD, and GATT.

Trade Prospects.—Italian imports increased by 24 percent in 1979, in 1980 they are expected to increase approximately 40 percent over 1979 figures. Imports from the U.S. are moving ahead at a steady pace. Best sales prospects in Italy are for: computers, peripherals, calculators, process control instruments and equipment, avionics/airport equipment, electronic components, pollution control equipment, and security and protection systems.

Foreign Investment

Total foreign investment in Italy is estimated at about $8 billion. U.S. direct investment is estimated at $3.5 billion accounting for nearly 44 percent of all foreign direct investment in the country. U.S. investment is primarily concentrated in heavy industry and chemical sectors. Italy generally encourages foreign investment and has legislation which assures transfer of profits and repatriation of capital. Special legislation is also in effect providing incentives designed to stimulate investment for economic development in southern Italy.

Finance

Currency.—Currency unit is the lira which is traded on a floating exchange rate basis. Average 1979 rate: U.S. $1=831 lire.

Domestic Credit.—Banks and company earnings are major sources of financing. Istituto Mobiliave Italiana (I.M.I.) grants long-terms loans to industry. Stock markets also function.

Balance of Payments.—Balance of payments 1979: total surplus $2.195 billion (current account $1.124 billion), capital account $745 million, errors and omissions $327 million. Balance of trade 1979: total deficit $8,696 billion.

Economy

Gross Domestic Product.—GDP was up 21 percent from $262 billion in 1978 to $323 billion in 1979 in market prices.

Agriculture.—Decreasing in importance, inefficient in the south; employed 14 percent of labor force and accounted for 6 percent of exports in 1979. Agricultural imports accounted for 10 percent of Italy's total import figure. The U.S. accounted for $540 million of Italy's 1979 agricultural imports. Main crops: wheat, corn, sugar beets, grapes, citrus fruits, olives, fruits.

Basic Economic Facilities

Transportation.—Road network very well developed, railway system adequate. Ports adequate but need expansion and modernization. Domestic and international air service available.

Communications.—Domestic and international communications service adequate.

Power.—Expansion program, to include nuclear-powered generating plant, in progress.

Natural Resources

Land.—117,000 square miles, generally mountainous except for Po Valley and some coastal areas.

Climate.—Generally temperate. Temperatures average from 49 degrees F to 65 degrees F.

Minerals.—Limited. Principal materials: mercury, pyrites, potash salts, sulphur. Major imports: Coal, iron ore, copper.

Population

Size.—60 million; yearly increase about 300,000. Rome (capital), 3 million; Milan 1.8 million; Naples, 1.2 million; Turin 1.2 million.

Language.—Italian. Linguistic minorities form less than 5 percent of population. English should be used in correspondence with large firms only.

Education.—Compulsory from ages 6 to 14. Illiteracy about 5 percent.

Labor.—21.7 million in labor force; 7.6 million (35 percent) in industry; 3.1 million (15.7 percent) in agriculture; 9.4 million (43 percent) in tertiary activities. Average unemployment rate in 1979 7.7 percent. Skilled labor available but scarce.

Marketing in Ivory Coast

Contents

Report Revised May 1979

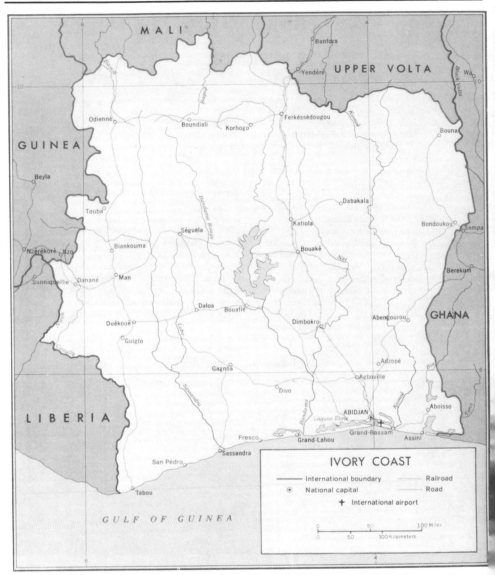

Note: Abidjan is approximately 5,000 miles (8,000 km.) from Washington, D.C.

The Ivorian Market

Political stability, a liberal investment code and nonrestrictive payments policy, a progressive attitude toward private initiative and foreign investment, and an impressive record of growth have contributed to the creation of an attractive business climate in Ivory Coast. Endowed with a climate and soils favorable to tropical agricultural production and boasting one of the continent's richest economies, Ivory Coast has often been hailed as Black Africa's model "success story." It has repeatedly stressed its eagerness to obtain Western skills and capital for State and joint venture operations designed to promote national prosperity.

Many trade and investment opportunities for American suppliers and investors are provided in Ivory Coast's ambitious 1976-80 Five-Year Development Plan. The Plan reserves an important place for foreign and domestic private investment. Important construction projects include ports, highways, airports, mines, tourist facilities, agricultural and forestry projects, urban development, and industrial plants. While the relationship with France remains strong in Ivory Coast, the Government in recent years has demonstrated an increasing interest in diversifying sources of supply and investment. A growing number of American firms are exploring the Ivorian market. Already there are more than

Table 1.—*Public Sector Budgetary Expenditures for Five-Year Development Plan*

(in billions of 1975 CFAF)

	Government	State enterprises	Total	Percent
Economic Activity	196.6	203.7	400.3	39.2
Agriculture	75.4	140.7	216.1	21.2
Livestock Breeding	20.0	6.1	26.1	2.5
Fisheries	5.7	10.7	16.4	1.6
Forests	15.0	1.2	16.2	1.6
Industry	72.5	42.0	114.5	11.2
Handicrafts	3.0	—	3.0	0.3
Commerce	2.9	3.0	5.9	0.6
Tourism	2.1	—	2.1	0.2
Development Infrastructure	164.2	217.8	382.0	37.5
Scientific Research	5.5	—	5.5	0.5
Energy	9.3	140.7	150.0	14.7
Transport & Telecommunications	149.4	77.8	227.2	22.3
Social & Cultural Development	123.2	10.0	133.2	13.1
Population	—	—	—	—
Health	20.6	—	20.6	2.0
National Solidarity	2.6	—	2.6	0.3
Housing & Welfare	78.0	10.0	88.0	8.6
Culture	3.0	—	3.0	0.3
Information	19.0	—	19.0	1.9
Human Development	54.5	—	54.5	5.3
Education	48.3	—	48.3	4.7
Employment	2.2	—	2.2	0.2
Ivorianization	4.0	—	4.0	0.4
Regional Development	30.0	—	30.0	2.9
Administration	20.0	—	20.0	2.0
TOTAL	588.5	431.5	1,010.0	100.0

Table 2.—*Ivory Coast: Direction of Trade From Selected Countries of Origin, 1973-77*

(in percent of total)

	1973	1974	1975	1976	1977
Total exports (millions of U.S. $)	820.0	1,235.0	1,188.0	1,706.5	2,300.8
France	25.8	26.1	27.1	25.5	26.8
Other franc area	10.8	11.8	16.4	10.4	10.1
EEC (except France)	37.1	40.1	30.5	35.8	31.1
United States	11.1	7.1	10.2	10.5	12.0
Japan	2.3	1.0	1.6	2.6	3.0
Other	12.9	13.9	14.2	15.2	17.0
Total imports (millions of U.S. $)	541.0	773.0	1,012.0	1,354.8	1,867.8
France	44.3	38.8	39.3	38.4	42.3
Other franc area	5.0	4.4	6.3	4.9	3.3
EEC (except France)	19.8	19.5	19.7	20.7	21.9
United States	8.9	6.8	7.1	7.4	7.9
Japan	2.8	3.5	4.0	5.1	5.8
Other	19.2	27.0	23.6	23.5	18.8

Source: Ministere de l'Economie et des Finances, Direction de la Statistique et des Etudes Economiques, *Bulletin Mensuel de Statistique*

300 U.S. firms selling there, and total U.S. investment passed the $160 million mark during 1978. A flourishing Ivorian economy, fueled by increasing revenues from sales of coffee, cocoa, timber and other agricultural products, should offer excellent sales opportunities throughout 1979.

Foreign Trade Outlook

Led by increased demand for American transport vehicles, construction and mining machinery, kraft paper, refrigeration and cooling machinery, chemicals and foodstuffs, U.S. exports to Ivory Coast should exceed $100 million in 1979. This year U.S. imports of Ivorian coffee, cocoa and other tropical products are expected to grow by nearly $100 million and approach $500 million. As is true for most African markets, an unfavorable bilateral trade imbalance presently exists for the United States.

Ivory Coast has consistently registered a healthy trade surplus in recent years. During the 4-year period 1974-77, positive trade balances of $223 million, $57 million, $351 million, and $433 million were recorded. Healthy trade surpluses are projected for both 1978 and 1979.

The principal obstacles to increasing U.S. sales are now the lack of independent agents and distributors (most are owned by or tied to European suppliers), the necessity of doing business in French (a point that should not be overlooked), and the need to overcome traditional trading patterns. Buyers in Ivory Coast respect the technical superiority and price competitiveness of American products but must be reassured that U.S. suppliers will meet delivery dates and that they will provide servicing and spare parts. Major trade opportunities for U.S. exporters over the next few years are expected to be in telecommunications equipment, energy systems, industrial refrigeration, food processing machinery, agribusiness enterprises, cereal products, agricultural and industrial chemicals, consumer goods, earthmoving equipment, business systems, building supplies and equipment, textile machinery, commercial aircraft, and motor passenger and transport vehicles.

U.S. Department of Commerce trade promotion events in Ivory Coast through September 1980 will include an Energy Systems Technical Trade Mission in June 1979, a Construction Firms and Equipment Trade Mission in October 1979 and an Industrial and Agricultural Chemicals Trade Mission in November 1979. U.S. firms interested in obtaining more information or participating should write or phone (202-377-4927) the Country Marketing Manager, African Area, Office of Country Marketing, Industry and Trade Administration, U.S. Department of Commerce, Washington, D.C. 20230.

Development Planning

Ivory Coast's 1976-80 Development Plan was finally enacted in January 1977. While main-

Table 3. — Key Economic Indicators, 1975-77

Indicator		1975	1976	1977	Percent Change 1976-77
GDP at current prices	U.S. $ Million	3,628	4,830	6,639	37.4
GDP price deflator	1973 = 100	135.5	160.3	204.4	27.5
GDP real growth	percent	7.0	12.5	7.8	
GDP per capita	U.S. $	540	690	910	31.8
Money supply	U.S. $ Million	782.2	1,130.9	1,613.5	42.7
Foreign exchange	U.S. $ Million	37.4	87.0	245.7	182.4
Gross fixed capital formation	U.S. $ Million	809	1,044	1,718	64.5
General operating budget	U.S. $ Million	551	668	862	29.0
Capital development budget	U.S. $ Million	308	398	950	138.7
Official external debt, disbursed	U.S. $ Million	935	1,225	1,870	53.0
Debt service payments	U.S. $ Million	128.7	216.5	310	43.0
Debt service ratio	Percent	9.3	10.7	12.4	
B/P on current account	U.S. $ Million	−358	−236	−335	42.1
B/P on capital account	U.S. $ Million	192	318	565	77.8
Exports f.o.b.	U.S. $ Million	1,107.0	1,706.5	2,300.8	34.8
Imports c.i.f	U.S. $ Million	1,049.6	1,354.8	1,867.8	37.9
Trade Balance f.o.b./c.i.f	U.S. $ Million	57.4	351.7	433.0	23.1
Coffee production	thousands of tons	196	270	308	13.9
Cocoa production	thousands of tons	242	227	233	2.5
Oil palm production	thousands of tons	967	974	905	−7.1
Sugar production	thousands of tons	4.7	21.6	31.5	45.8
Cotton production	thousands of tons	60.9	66.0	76.4	15.8
Pineapple production	thousands of tons	240	268	286	6.9
Bananas production	thousands of tons	192	147	132	−10.3
Electricity production	gWh	962	1,114	1,242	11.5
Consumer price index, European	1970 = 100	155.3	175.0	198.8	13.6
Consumer price index, African	1970 = 100	145.1	161.3	207.1	28.4

Source: U.S. Embassy, Abidjan

taining traditional Ivory Coast economic policy goals of agricultural expansion and diversification, the 4500-page Plan also envisions massive new expenditures in the areas of public works, export-oriented industrialization, and social development. Seven broad objectives are specified: (1) Modernization of agriculture and rural life in general; (2) establishment of a diversified, export-oriented industrial sector; (3) acceleration of Ivorianization; (4) governmental reform; (5) accelerated development of the less-prosperous regions of the country; (6) reform of the educational system, and (7) evolution toward a synthesis of the varied cultural heritage of the Ivorian people. The Ivorians hope to maintain an 8.7 percent average of real economic growth over the Plan period, raising the gross domestic product (GDP) from 813 billion CFA francs ($3.8 billion) in 1975 to more than 1,100 billion francs ($5.1 billion) in 1980 (in constant 1975 francs). In 1976 and 1977, the GDP actually grew at a real growth rate of 12.5 percent and 7.8 percent, respectively, with 1978 and 1979 also expected to be very good years.

Ivory Coast envisioned total investment during the 5-year Plan period of 1,591 billion CFA francs (constant 1975 prices) to realize its de-velopment objectives-a figure likely to be far exceeded, based on investments through 1977. That would mean maintaining a rate of investment of about 31 percent of GDP over the Plan period. Of the projected investment totals, public investment (government and parastatal enterprises) were to account for 1,020 billion CFA francs, and private investment (private enterprises and households) were to provide the remaining 571 billion CFA francs.

Under the Plan, the Ivorians expected to borrow 579 billion CFA francs from external sources, resulting in a net inflow of 298 billion CFA francs after debt service payments of 281 billion CFA francs over the 5-year period. Based on their export projections, the Government expected to be able to hold its external debt service to exports ratio to no more than 13 percent through 1980. Due to a rapid increase in borrowing, the debt service ratio already stood at 12.4 percent in 1977. Since then the Government has cut back considerably on its borrowing from domestic and foreign sources. It now appears that the Ivory Coast probably will be able to avoid an untenable debt position in the years ahead.

Table 4.—Ivory Coast: Planned and Realized Public Investment, 1971–80

(In millions of CFA francs)

| | Planned investment for 1971–75[1] | Realized investment 1971–75 | | Planned investment for 1976–80[3] | Realized investment 1976 | Revised estimates of investment in 1977 | Planned investment under the Program-Law | | |
		In 1970[2] prices	In current prices				1978	1979	1980
Agriculture and natural resources	86,200	80,323	107,961	292,500	55,033	100,041	155,914	132,680	102,193
Industry and mining	17,000	7,942	11,723	117,500	3,214	8,141	8,028	17,000	22,143
Energy	33,000	40,900	53,798	149,300	22,915	38,521	51,564	55,400	31,727
Transport and communication	54,480	68,989	99,225	227,200	51,106	78,443	99,128	115,011	73,090
Transport	45,590	60,862	88,196	189,700	47,432	70,461	82,737	98,139	67,906
Communication	8,890	8,127	11,029	37,500	3,674	7,982	16,391	16,872	5,185
Urban development and housing	33,790	38,603	55,698	100,300	17,898	53,595	58,459	50,061	32,310
Finance, commerce, and tourism	—	9,917	12,933	8,000	3,655	13,883	7,916	3,297	895
Social services	38,070	29,340	41,809	99,700	17,208	42,569	64,833	64,225	52,442
Education	18,290	19,520	29,966	48,300	12,579	30,347	49,609	39,648	32,220
Health	9,390	3,673	4,193	20,600	3,437	7,427	12,271	13,821	9,509
Other	10,390	6,147	7,680	30,800	1,192	4,795	2,953	10,756	10,713
Other services	11,370	21,420	30,448	20,000	9,760	16,454	24,743	17,604	6,896
General administration	6,790	12,449	16,871	20,000	5,506	2,712	4,458	1,029	816
Defense and security	4,580	8,971	13,577	—	4,254	13,742	20,285	16,575	6,080
Research	3,090	1,742	2,213	5,500	1,185	3,243	2,173	1,837	1,500
TOTAL	277,000	299,176	415,838	1,020,000	181,974	354,890	472,758	457,953	323,196

Source: Ministere de l'Economie, des Finances et du Plan, *Loi programme des investissements publics.*

[1] In 1970 prices.
[2] Adjusted using the World Economic Outlook (WEO) import price deflator as most investment relates to imports. However, the WEO import price deflator, which is based on the composition of total exports of Ivory Coast's partner countries rather than that of their actual exports to Ivory Coast alone, understates Ivorian imports of manufactured goods, machinery, and equipment.
[3] In 1975 prices.

Agriculture

Agriculture is the main economic activity in Ivory Coast. Together with forestry, animal husbandry, and fishing, it provides a livelihood for the bulk of the active population and has accounted for a quarter of GDP at current prices in recent years and for some three–quarters of total export earnings. Furthermore, agricultural commodities form the basis of the country's principal processing and manufacturing industries. Table 5 shows Ivory Coast's agricultural production for 1975 and projections for 1980 and 1985.

Agricultural policies are the responsibility of four ministries, represented at the regional level by directors. Implementation of agricultural policies is generally entrusted to autonomous or semiautonomous agencies, so-called Societes de Developpement, which are within the purview of the four ministries. These agencies are involved in the development of specific sectors and commodities, usually in association with the research institute concerned with that commodity. In addition, two regional public agencies have been set up to promote the overall economic development of certain parts of the country: the Bandama Valley Authority (AVB) and the Southwest Regional Development Authority (ARSO). In addition, a decree was issued in October 1977 that, among other things, divided the country into three main regions, with one large Societe de Developpement Rural (SDR) in charge of overall agricultural development in each region.

Leading public sector agricultural corporations (all with headquarters in Abidjan) include:
Caisse de Stabilisation et de Soutien des Prix des Produits Agricoles

Societe d'Assistance Technique pour la Modernisation Agricole de Cote d'Ivoire (SATMACI)

Societe pour le Developpement et l'Exploitation du Palmier a Huile (SODEPALM)

Compagnie Ivoirienne pour le Developpement des Textiles (CIDT)

Societe des Caoutchoucs de Cote d'Ivoire (SOCATCI)

Societe pour le Developpement des Fruits et Legumes (SODEFEL)

Societe pour le Developpement de la Motorisation de l'Agriculture (MOTORAGRI)

Since independence in 1960, agricultural policy has been geared mainly to alleviating the vulnerability of the Ivorian economy, which was based on three main export commodities (coffee, cocoa, and timber), through the introduction and expansion of new cash crops, the development of processing capabilities for the three traditional as well as other newer commodities, and the development of food crops to cater to domestic needs and reduce imports of foodstuffs. A key element of this policy has been the setting of producer prices at remunerative levels so as to encourage production and increase rural incomes. In addition, an efficient stabilization fund

Table 5.—Agricultural Production for 1975 with Projections for 1980 and 1985

	1975 Quantity[1]	1975 Value[2]	1980 Quantity[1]	1980 Value[2]	1985 Quantity[1]	1985 Value[2]
Industrial and Export Production						
Coffee (green)	270,000	40,500	330,000	49,500	360,000	54,000
Cocoa (beans)	230,000	40,250	335,000	58,625	480,000	84,000
Oil palm (kernels)	959,000	7,205	1,262,000	9,605	1,700,000	13,180
Coprah	18,000	900	61,000	3,050	145,000	7,250
Rubber (latex)	17,000	1,820	21,000	2,250	47,000	5,030
Fresh pineapple (exports)	70,000	2,625	150,000	5,250	230,000	8,050
Canned pineapple	155,000	1,200	215,000	1,720	270,000	2,160
Banana (exports)	160,000	3,200	200,000	4,000	220,000	4,600
Sugar Cane	115,000	290	1,500,000	3,750	5,500,000	13,750
Cotton (unginned)	65,000	4,485	105,000	7,245	195,000	13,455
Soybeans	—	—	10,000	650	100,000	6,500
Production for Domestic Consumption						
Rice (paddy)	450,000	29,250	800,000	52,925	1,030,000	66,950
Corn	255,000	6,630	360,000	9,360	560,000	14,560
Other cereals	47,000	2,350	51,000	2,550	56,000	2,800
Yams	1,880,000	37,600	2,170,000	43,400	2,550,000	51,000
Manioc	650,000	11,700	750,000	13,530	890,000	16,020
Plantain	780,000	7,800	900,000	9,000	1,060,000	10,600
Vegetables	26,000	780	69,000	2,340	159,000	6,000

[1]in metric tons
[2]in millions CFAF

has for many years shielded producers from fluctuations in world commodity prices.

During the decade of the Eighties, if present forecasts are realized, Ivory Coast will be the world's principal cocoa producer, the second or third largest producer of coffee, and the second or third principal producer of palm oil. In addition, Ivory Coast will be processing domestically about 50 percent of its cocoa production, or at least 200,000 metric tons annually, and will be a major supplier of fruits and vegetables. Under the Loi–Programme covering 1979 agricultural investment, 140 billion CFA francs ($600 million) are to be spent for development purposes. This compares with 105 billion francs for the 5-year period 1970-74. The sugar industry is to receive the bulk of public funding: 85 billion francs. Other agricultural sectors slated to receive allocations include: Palm oil (3.5 billion francs), coconut (1.7 billion francs) rubber (6.9 billion francs), coffee (12.6 billion francs), and cocoa (27.1 billion CFA francs). In addition, sizable investments are expected to expand Ivory Coast's cotton production. Among these various sectors , there are several opportunities for U.S. capital investment, American construction companies, management consultants, and U.S. suppliers of machinery and equipment. The construction of sugar mills alone is expected to call for millions of dollars in machinery purchases.

The United States is a well-established supplier of agricultural machinery to Ivory Coast. Several American companies have strong representation there. The continuing expansion of Ivorian agriculture—in traditional crops as well as in sugar, cotton, corn, rice, soybeans and tropical produce—will increase sales opportunities in 1979 and beyond for capital equipment. To date U.S. exports have been mainly heavy duty tractors and harvesting equipment. There is only limited local production of simple agricultural tools. American companies should be able to compete effectively in the market for machinery with high technological complexity.

Within the food processing and packaging equipment field, the United States enjoys a 15 percent share overall and a 30 percent share of the market for commercial refrigeration equipment. Projects underway or envisaged that will require food processing equipment include fisheries, sugar refining, cocoa and coffee processing. Machinery for processing agricultural products and tropical fruits and commercial refrigeration equipment will continue to have major sales opportunities in Ivory Coast.

Table 6.—Major U.S. Exports to Ivory Coast, 1974–77

(in U.S. dollars)

Commodity	1974	1975	1976	1977
Rice, milled	484,902	629,805	1,244,020	11,862,427
Cereals, unmilled	23,114	—	—	461,864
Tobacco, unmanufactured	661,576	19,976	224,492	267,917
Cigarettes	112,221	167,344	374,734	619,851
Waste materials from textile fab	4,261,115	5,208,439	2,323,985	823,541
Lubricating oils & greases	624,305	252,535	606,540	542,249
Organic chemicals	786,939	1,188,192	1,358,330	2,043,273
Fertilizers	90,920	376,277	989,552	1,170,903
Insecticides, fungicides	—	838,834	633,084	455,782
Artificial waxes, prep. additives	313,831	285,486	748,541	613,277
Rubber tires & tubes	66,586	177,262	363,330	414,723
Kraft paper & paperboard	6,787,588	5,276,090	4,373,962	4,003,475
Iron & steel tubes & pipes	1,475,692	261,343	166,452	301,092
Aluminum & aluminum alloys	113,186	109,592	1,156,341	284,101
Finished struc. parts and structures	550,349	142,953	435,655	302,347
Power generating machinery	596,665	452,905	1,167,567	3,691,894
Tractors, except road & industrial	3,067,670	6,695,117	7,846,117	12,109,788
Agri. mach. & appr. nec & pts.	—	122,206	139,051	906,029
Office machines & pts.	131,140	126,069	134,831	442,959
Textile machinery	333,160	1,007,892	353,065	868,048
Food processing machinery	1,221,035	392,421	787,968	1,858,689
Construction & mining machinery	3,473,369	10,414,947	10,619,628	10,079,987
Heating & cooling machinery	2,623,872	3,126,583	3,339,455	4,633,462
Pumps, centrifuges	262,586	569,716	1,053,992	1,281,065
Mechanical handling mach. and parts	3,692,314	1,909,760	3,085,398	3,442,531
Machinery & mechanical appl.	950,237	366,905	250,557	509,603
Parts & acces. for machinery	—	182,823	159,007	517,747
Electric power machinery	165,329	784,856	950,325	2,444,686
Telecommunications equipment	244,352	712,861	322,052	1,891,544
Electric household equip. and appl.	81,411	165,474	273,733	215,159
Batteries and parts	272,366	346,805	302,025	827,568
Passenger cars and trucks	1,605,097	2,770,361	4,649,707	2,726,297
Motor vehicle & trac. pts.	904,099	606,321	1,801,030	3,913,509
Aircraft-heavier than air	5,233,764	23,623,488	196,147	3,069,088
Aircraft, pts. & acces.	438,422	590,549	429,023	378,320
Ships and boats, (civilian)	40,837	266,054	3,327,620	442,905
Measuring, control inst.	134,248	212,694	533,481	326,664
Phonograph records & other sound media	144,283	121,419	178,773	123,506
Other	7,057,250	7,707,986	6,525,684	7,023,445
TOTAL	49,025,830	78,300,230	63,425,354	88,091,315

Source: U.S. Department of Commerce

Fisheries and Livestock

Fish is an important source of protein in the Ivorian diet, supplying about three-fourths of all animal protein consumed. Fish consumption has increased from 95,000 tons in 1970 to approximately 210,000 tons in 1978. The local catch at present supplies about 30% of needs. Consumption requirements officially are projected to reach 350,000 tons by 1985, of which imports are to supply 125,000 tons. In reality import needs are likely to exceed that total, or else consumption will be artificially restrained due to high prices.

Industrial fishing has had mixed success over the past decade, with production being unable to break out of the 40–60,000–ton annual range. The Ivorian fleet at the end of 1976 consisted of 23 companies, of which 20 had only one or two vessels, comprising 51 boats, including 21 sardine seiners, 19 deep-sea trawlers, 6 tuna seiners and 6 shrimpers. Meanwhile in 1976 about

240 foreign fishing boats visited the port of Abidjan.

The competitiveness of the Ivorian fisheries industry will depend upon the conpanies' ability to purchase vessels capable of traveling the long distances to the major fishing grounds and refrigerating their catch during the return voyage, as well as the companies' ability to process the catch for sale. In addition, the Government of Ivory Coast will have to negotiate reciprocal fishing rights with other African nations—agreements that could necessitate payment of substantial fees since Ivory Coast's own coastline is relatively poor in fish resources. So far only one accord has been reached—with Senegal in January 1977. At last report several other bilateral agreements were being discussed.

The Ivorian five-year plan calls for investments in the fishing industry of 17.6 billion CFAF—16.4 billion CFAF from public sources and 1.2 billion private (Table 7). Eighty percent

of the total, 14.1 billion CFAF, will be spent expanding Ivory Coast's deep-water fleet and port processing facilities.

Meat consumption in Ivory Coast is increasing rapidly, paralleling the rise in per capita income. Consumption is projected to rise from 10.4 kg. per year per person in 1975 to 27.3 kg in 1990. To date tropical diseases (notably trypanosomiasis), together with the lack of experience of most Ivorians with livestock breeding, have kept domestic production quite low. In the past, Ivory Coast imported much of its meat from the Sahel. Now with world meat prices escalating and Sahelian production still suffering from the effects of the drought, Ivory Coast must become more self-sufficient in meat production over the long run (Table 8).

The projected total investment in the livestock sector for the 1976–80 Plan period is 38.2 billion francs, more than half of which will be allocated to development of large-scale, industrialized production. A major effort is being made to expand cattle, sheep, and goat raising by: (1) Developing more productive, disease-resistant cross-breeds and expanding herds, with imports of female breeding animals playing a large role (2) expanding industrial-scale production, making use of both agro-industrial products (molasses, cottonseed cake and oil, palm oil, and soybean cake and oil), and improved pasturage for feeding purposes; and (3) encouraging improved methods among traditional producers. Nevertheless, through 1985 the Government of Ivory Coast expects to import more than half of the country's requirements of beef, lamb and goat meat. Ivory Coast already produces 98 percent of its own pork.

Plans are under way to expand substantially both consumption and production of poultry over the next decade. Special emphasis is being placed on expanding and modernizing productive capacity, including henhouses and incubators (most chicks are currently imported from Eur-

Table 7.—Investment in the Fishing Sector 1976-80

(CFAF millions)

	State	State Enterprises	Private	Total
Industrial Fishing	3,000	9,910	1,190	14,100
Creation of a modern, deep-water fleet	1,280	6,800	420	8,500
Tuna fleet expansion	450	2,100	450	3,000
Coastal fleet expansion	50	350	100	500
Abidjan fish port development	400			400
San Pedro fish port development	600			600
Port refrigeration facilities	220	660	220	1,100
Coastal Village Fishing	330	800		1,130
Lagoon Village Fishing	225			225
Coastal and Lagoon Fishing Research & Development	125			125
River and Lake Fishing	1,050			1,050
Fish Breeding	1,000			1,000
TOTAL	5,730	10,710	1,190	17,630

Table 8.–Livestock Breeding

(thousands of metric tons)

	1975 Consumption	1975 Production	Percent	1980 Consumption	1980 Production	Percent	1985 Consumption	1985 Production	Percent	1990 Consumption	1990 Production	Percent
Beef	30	6.9	23	50	13.5	27	60	27	45	83	58	70
Sheep/Goats	13.5	5.5	40	20	9	45	40	19	47	75	60	80
Pork	5.1	5	98	10	10	100	20	20	200	35	35	100
Poultry/Eggs	20.7	18.2	88	40	38	95	75	75	100	170	170	100
Milk (fresh equivalent)	79	3.5	5	100	9	9	125	30	24	155	115	75
Other (game, etc.)	16	16	100	14	14	100	12	12	100	10	10	100
TOTAL	164.3	55.1	34	234	93.5	40	332	183	55	528	448	85

ope), feed-grain production, and slaughter and processing facilities.

Forestry

Traditionally, timber has been one of Ivory Coast's richest natural resources. For many years the nation has been Africa's largest exporter of wood; however, this resource is being depleted very rapidly. Forest reserves have been reduced by approximately 50 percent in 20 years; at the current rate of production, the 19 most desirable species will be exhausted by 1988. Whether the 80 other species of lumber, which have been largely unaffected, will be commercially exploitable remains to be determined.

The 5-year Plan outlines an integrated, long-term program for assuring the preservation of Ivory Coast's forest reserves. Overall the Plan envisions an investment of 16.2 billion CFA francs in the forestry sector during 1976-80 to be borne entirely by the government and state enterprises, with no private participation. Of this amount, 11.8 billion CFA francs are to be spent on a reforestation program, with the remaining 4.4 billion CFA francs devoted to the essentially administrative tasks of surveying forests and protecting them against illegal destruction, encouraging improved harvesting and marketing efforts. The International Bank for Reconstruction and Development (IBRD) has indicated an interest in a $40 million project likely to begin in 1979, involving the creation of 20,000 hectares of industrial wood plantations.

In 1977, total exports of wood brought in 87 billion CFA francs, 11 percent more than the 1976 figure.

There are approximately 75 companies involved in the wood industry in one form or another. Of these there are 12 major companies that were responsible in 1974 for 68 percent of all sawn lumber, 100 percent of all plywood production and 100 percent of particle board. The remaining companies are generally logging operations and are almost exclusively European-owned and operate by negotiating with Ivorians who hold the rights to exploit timber within delineated sections. They primarily export logs to Europe. As such they have limited equipment needs, consisting of a few felling saws and a bulldozer. Transport is hired, and logs are exported as they are cut.

The 12 wood processing operations account for approximately 13 percent of Ivory Coast's industrial exports and provide about a quarter of all

employment in modern industry. These firms offer the best sales opportunities to American suppliers, even though all have strong ties with European manufacturers. The most important companies include: Compagnie des Scieries Africaines (S.C.A.F.), the Societe Industrielle Ivorienne des Bois (S.I.B.O.I.S.), Compagnie Industrielle du Bois (C.I.B.), the Groupe Lalanne, Societe d'Exploration des Produits de la Cote d'Ivoire (S.E.P.C.), Ateliers de Kahankro, Scieries du Bandama and Societe Industrielle et Forestiere de Cote d'Ivoire.

Based on existing sources of supply, competition for U.S. suppliers of wood-processing equipment can be expected from Angelo-Cremona of Italy, Muller of Switzerland, Brenta-Antwerp and Dankert of Belgium, Torvedge and Hildebrand of West Germany, and Valette-Garrault and William Gillet of France. Useful trade association contact points include the Syndicat des Producteurs Forestiers de la Cote d'Ivoire (B.P. 318, Abidjan) and the Syndicat des Exportateurs et des Industriels en Bois (B.P. 1979, Abidjan). Addresses of the above firms and other timber companies in Ivory Coast can be obtained by contacting the African Area, Office of Country Marketing, Industry and Trade Administration, U.S. Department of Commerce, Washington, D.C. 20230.

The major industrial project in the Plan involving the timber sector is the approximately $400 million San Pedro pulp-paper mill. The Government of Ivory Coast plans to take 100 percent of the equity, with a new parastatal enterprise to be established to undertake the scheme. Financing arrangements have delayed project commencement. It had been hoped to begin engineering studies by year-end 1977, actual construction by year-end 1978, and production by 1980-82. If and when the project begins, it offers a good possibility for a turnkey contract as well as exports of U.S. machinery.

Mining

The mining sector is of little importance to Ivory Coast. Its share of the gross domestic product (GDP) declined from 1 percent in 1960 to 0.3 percent in 1974. Manganese production, which amounted to 180,000 tons in 1965, was discontinued in 1970, and diamond production, which reached the record level of 334,000 carats in 1972, declined to 278,000 carats in 1974, 209,000 carats in 1975 and 60,100 carats in 1976. Ivory Coast's chief diamond producer, the Waston company, discontinued its operations in June of 1977.

Ivory Coast believes it has the potential to be an important mining country with regard to oil, iron, nickel and gold. While not yet producing crude petroleum, Ivorians are encouraged by the discovery made by the ESSO Shell PETROCI Consortium of a commercial petroleum offshore deposit 40 km southeast of Abidjan. Production is scheduled to begin in early 1980 at an annual level of 400,000 metric tons, or about 25 percent of the country's current import requirements—which amounted to $154 million in 1976. The deposit is expected to produce for 10 to 11 years.

Other petroleum companies also are carrying out exploration efforts. A permit has been granted for oil exploration in 19,000 square meters off the Ivorian coast to a consortium made up of four companies—one of which is European—AGIP (Italian Petroleum Enterprise), two are American—Phillips, which will supervises the work, and SEDCO; and one Ivorian—PETROCI, the national oil company. Test drilling began in September 1976. Traces of oil and natural gas have been found to date. In the oil processing industry a refinery at Abidjan (Societe Ivoirienne de Raffinage) refines imported crude for consumption in Ivory Coast. Capacity has been enlarged to about 2 million tons of crude per year. Production in 1975 totaled 1.49 million metric tons. In October 1975 PETROCI, took over the government interest in the petroleum sector. It has begun exploratory onshore drilling in the Jacqueville area west of Abidjan.

The principal industrial mining investment during the current Plan period involves exploitation of the Mount Klahoyo iron ore deposits. Investigations of the iron deposits carried out between 1966 and 1972 by Societe pour le Developpement Minier de la Cote d'Ivoire (SODEMI) and a U.S. company, Pickands Mather of Cleveland, indicated that the deposits, located west of the town of Bangolo near the Liberian border, contained ore reserves equivalent to 200 million metric tons of pellets. Drilling, followed by metallurgical testing, revealed that the crude ore contains 36 percent iron and very few impurities except for 37.4 percent silica. Reserves at Mount Klahoyo are now estimated at 350 million tons, enough for 30 years mining at 12 million tons of pellets a year. Spin-off projects from the mining operation and pelletizing plant were to include a slurry pipeline to the port of San Pedro and power supply through the construction of a dam at Soubre. However, at last report the original British, French, Dutch, Japanese and Ivorian consortium participants had decided to shelve the $2.25 billion project indefinitely

due to the current depressed condition of the market for iron pellets. Inquiries concerning all aspects of the Mount Klahoyo development project can be addressed to : Mr. Augustin Douoguih, Office of the Financial Counselor, Ivory Coast Development Office, 521 Fifth Avenue, Suite 1604–06, New York, New York 10017, (212-661-9700).

For several years SODEMI (Ivory Coast Mining Development Company) has been investigating the possibility of exploiting known nickel deposits and gold-bearing placers. The contents of a nickel field in the region of Biankouma, north of Man, has been estimated at 5.6 million tons at 2 percent nickel content. A second nickel field has been discovered at Saabela. Falconbridge of Canada has expressed interest in the Biankouma deposit.

SODEMI's 1977 report also confirms the existence of a copper-molybdenum anomaly at Dyenguele and the discovery of seven zones of strong radioactivity in the north near Kebi and Serihio. With regard to gold a consortium composed of SODEMI (60 percent), French public and private interests and the British firm, Lonrho, has been formed to develop the Ity goldfield, southwest of Man. Production is expected to begin at the end of 1979 at the rate of 10 to 15 tons of gold per year according to the Ivorian Ministry of Mines.

Energy

Ivory Coast's situation with regard to energy is characterized by: (1) Rapidly increasing production; (2) heavy reliance upon petroleum products, both for direct consumption, and for production of electricity; (3) consequent heavy dependence on imports. Taking into account the anticipated new large industrial projects (iron ore, paper pulp), Ivorian electricity consumption is projected to increase from 962 million KWH in 1975 to 3 billion KWh in 1980, and to 5 billion KWh in 1985.

Ivory Coast seeks to assure itself of energy supplies sufficient to sustain its ongoing economic development program at the lowest possible cost. Table 9 gives the Ivory Coast's production of electricity from 1970 to 1977 with projections for 1978–80. The 1976–80 development Plan calls for a massive energy development program over the coming 15 years, based heavily on hydraulic as opposed to thermal generation. Ongoing and possible projects include: (1) Completion by 1979 of the Taabo dam on the Bandama River

Table 9.—Ivory Coast: Production of Electricity, 1970-80

	Interconnected network Hydro-production (GWh)	Percent of total	Thermal[1] Production (GWh)	Unconnected Power Plants Thermal Production (GWh)	Total Production (GWh)
1970..........	260	49	178	97	535
1971..........	139	24	360	89	588
1972..........	226	33	398	68	692
1973..........	168	21	556	72	796
1974..........	277	32	520	58	855
1975..........	383	39	524	55	962
1976..........	358	32	700	57	1,115
1977[2]..........	270	22	917	63	1,250
		Projections			
1978..........	270	19	1,049	76	1,395
1979..........	620	31	1,265	88	1,973
1980..........	1,760	62	1,069	8	2,837

Source: Energie Electrique de Cote d'Ivoire (EECI)

[1]Includes thermal production of unconnected power plants not shown separately
[2]Provisional

downstream from the Kossou dam; (2) completion by 1980 of the Buyo dam on the Sassandra River; (3) evaluation studies of possible dam sites on the Cavally (in cooperation with Liberia) and Comoe Rivers.

Ivory Coast depends on imports for all elements of its energy production and transmission system. Additional attention by U.S. suppliers to this market can reap incremental sales. U.S. sellers must be prepared to do business in the French language. European suppliers have the advantage of long-established trading and technical assistance ties (Electicite de France for example has provided much engineering counsel to E.E.C.I.). American firms can counter with early reaction to planned major projects, strong local representation, and frequent visits by sales personnel. American companies interested in Ivorian power projects should contact: M. Lambert Konan, Directeur General, E.E.C.I., B.P. 1345, Abidjan, Tel. 32-23-45.

Manufacturing

The $850 million manufacturing sector has been one of the most dynamic elements of the Ivorian economy. Its share in GDP rose from 4 percent in 1967 to 12 percent in 1976. In current prices, the value added by manufacturing rose tenfold during the decade 1960-70 and more than doubled between 1970 and 1976, reflecting in part the establishment of new industrial plants. The volume of production rose 11 percent in both 1975 and 1976.

In the early years industrial policy in Ivory Coast was geared mainly to import substitution. This policy proved successful, but the scope for further industrialization along this pattern appears limited. Accordingly, the Government's policy is to concentrate increasingly on encouraging the establishment of export-oriented industries based largely on locally available agricultural raw materials. The objective is to increase the share of manufactured exports from 30 percent of total exports in 1975 to about 45-50 percent in 1980. The achievement of this objective will require both the expansion of existing industries and the establishment of new industrial units, particularly in the following areas: Coffee and cocoa processing, fruit canning, cotton spinning and weaving, edible oil refining, sugar production and refining, paper pulp production, and tire manufacturing.

The Government hopes the manufacturing sector/GDP ratio will be 30 percent by 1980. The current Development Plan foresees an annual industrial growth rate of 12 percent through 1985. Industrial exports are projected to grow 15 percent annually. Between 1976-80 total investments in manufacturing enterprises have been set at 120 billion ($600 million) CFA francs (1975 prices) and at 160 billion CFA francs ($800 million) between 1981–85. The share of Ivorian capital investments in industrial enterprises reached nearly 37 percent of the total in January 1976 (24.6 percent from the State and 12 percent from the private sector). In September 1976 the Ivorian Government had some ownership participation in 221 firms (50 of which were wholly State-owned) out of 486 industrial enterprises. Capital from 26 other countries provided the remainder. French investors were easily the most important source (39.3 percent in 1976; American investment in manufacturing enterprises that year stood at 2.71 billion CFA francs (4.21 percent of the total).

The prospects for the textile industry in particular look promising. Ivory Coast is now the second largest producer in Africa, with three-quarters of its production sold overseas. Turnover totaled 44.5 billion CFA francs among 36 enterprises between October 1975 and September 1976. Plant capacity reportedly doubled during 1976. Development efforts, which will involve large-scale machinery, includes a plant to produce 10,000 metric tons of polyester annually by 1980, expanding to 14,000 metric tons by 1985. The Ivorians also are planning to augment their facilities for cotton-spinning, weaving, bleaching, dyeing, printing, and garment-making. Production expansion is projected as follows:

	1975	1980	1985
Thread (cotton and polyester)	10,000 m.t.	38,500 m.t.	47,500 m.t.
Cloth	11,000 m.t.	32,000 m.t.	41,000 m.t.
Garments (for export)	—	8,000 m.t.	18,000 m.t.

1329

There is no production of textile and garment-making machinery in Ivory Coast. U.S. suppliers face keen competition from European and Japanese competitors, but stand a good chance of gaining an increased share of a growing market. U.S. firms may wish to participate in the biennial SITHA textile exhibition, which brings together buyers and sellers from African and European countries. For more detailed information, interested firms should contact M. Adrien Kouadio, Centre Ivorien du Commerce Exterieur, B.P. V68, Abidjan.

Transportation

Ivory Coast is placing major emphasis on the construction of an adequate transportation network. Government authorities are stressing the establishment of comprehensive road and rail systems, as well as the expansion of existing port facilities. Since 1970 major developments within the transport sector have included opening the new port of San Pedro in May 1971, the extension of facilities at the port of Abidjan, a vast increase in the national road system, modernization of several links of the Abidjan-Ouagadougou railway line, and a rapid expansion of the Ivorian railway line. The transport system consists of 43,000 km of roads, about 640 km of railroads, two major seaports, about 400 km of navigable lagoons, two international airports, and 14 airfields served by regularly scheduled domestic flights.

A very important recent development has been the significant growth of the Ivorian shipping company, the Societe Ivoirienne de Transport Maritime (SITRAM). Ivory Coast plans to triple its shipping fleet with a view to carrying 20 percent of total two-way cargo in Ivorian bottoms by 1980. Eight new general cargo ships were recently purchased, and SITRAM plans to purchase 12 specialized ships over the next few years.

There are considerable sales opportunities for U.S. contractors and suppliers with regard to Ivory Coast's major projects in roadbuilding. At the end of 1976, the road network included 43,000 km of roadway, of which 2,200 km were paved and 17,000 km were earth roads. A continuous major effort is being made to upgrade Ivory Coast's road system. At the beginning of 1978, bids let totaled 120 billion CFA francs, including construction projects. Roads totaling 1,115 km were to be upgraded and paved between 1978 and 1980, representing an investment of 72 billion CFA francs. In addition, a number of urban road work sites are being constructed or planned, at a cost or 43 billion CFA francs, and the third Abidjan bridge has been underwritten for 9 billion CFA francs.

Urban transport has been reorganized in recent years. The public mass transportation service is run by the Abidjan Transportation Company (SOTRA), which carried more than 135 million passengers in 1976. SOTRA's pool contained 418 units, including three hundred sixty-seven 100-seat buses and thirty 25-seat express jitneys, in 1976. By 1980, it will have about 1,000 units, including some 800 large buses and about 100 express jitneys. SOTRA's 1976–77 investment program, indicative of future requirements, called for the purchase of 227 large buses, the purchase of 100 market supply cars and taxi baggage vehicles, the purchase of 30 express jitneys and eight 30-seat touring buses (including six with air-conditioning); and the construction of various servicing facilities. An urban public transportation service using boats on the lagoon was put in operation by SOTRA in 1978, involving over the 1977–80 period an investment of 2.5 billion francs for 45 boats and 3 docks.

The Abidjan-Niger Railway Administration (RAN) operates 1,173 km of railroad, including 628 km on Ivory Coast territory. In 1976 its commercial traffic totaled 3.2 million passengers, or 1.04 billion passenger-kilometers, and 865,700 tons of goods. RAN has embarked on a vast modernization program to increase its transport capacity, productivity, speed, comfort and safety. Proposed investments in the 1976–80 Development Program amount to 42 billion francs. The development budget for 1977 came to 9.9 billion CFA francs, up 53 percent from 1976; and covered, among other things, infrastructure and construction projects, the purchase of self-propelling cars, traction equipment, and financial charges. Plan purchasing requirements for the system included 31 locomotives, 37 locotractors, 94 autorail cars, 649 closed freight cars and 63 flatcars. Other projects involve the building of sorting yards and workshops at four different sites.

Inquiries concerning railway projects in Ivory Coast can be made to: (1) M. Lansine Konate, Directeur General, Regie Abidjan-Niger, P.O. Box 1394, Abidjan, Tel. 32-02-45, Telex 564 FERDIA: (2) M. Kouadio Wilson, Charge de Mission, Ministere des Travaux Publics et des Transports, P.O. Box V6, Abidjan, Tel: 32-08-88, Telex 2108.

There are two deep-water ports, one at Abidjan and the other at San Pedro in the southwest.

Commercial traffic in 1977 at Abidjan Port totaled 7,863,333 metric tons, up 2.3 percent from 1976, and reached 1,358,510 metric tons at San Pedro, up 10.9 percent from the previous year. Imports accounted for 4,729,093 and 40,786 tons of the totals, respectively. Facilities at Abidjan Port consist of 19 general cargo and 4 specialized berths, with additional facilities for handling bananas, timber, ore, fish, oil and river traffic.

Development plans for Abidjan include a proposed port expansion on the Locodjo Peninsula, including: 3 container piers; 12 piers for general merchandise; a duty-free zone of 90 hectares; an industrial zone of 200 hectares adjacent to the port facilities; and a mineral port to handle the expected flow of manganese from the Tambao project in Upper Volta. Spin-off construction projects include a new access channel to the mineral port, a sugar port, a cereals port, a new fishing port, a new access road to the port area, railway line extensions to connect the port area with the existing Abidjan-Ouagadougou line. Specific types of equipment that will be needed include containers, stockpiling equipment for containers, tugboats, motorized launches, trolleys, mooring buoys and electric lines. All construction contracts are expected to be awarded through bids at some future date. Interested companies, according to project authorities, would do well to include financing packages in their proposals. Interested companies can address themselves to: M. Antonen Ibo, Directeur General, Port of Abidjan, B.P. 1360, Abidjan.

Air transportation continues to develop very rapidly. At the Port Bouet-Abidjan International Airport, traffic rose from 228,537 to 546,727 passengers and from 13,821 to 16,800 tons of goods between 1970 and 1976. Domestic traffic handled by the national company Air-Ivoire, which links Abidjan to 11 cities in the interior, rose 185 percent between 1970 and 1975. Air Ivoire's traffic in 1976 totaled 69,826 passengers and 408 tons of freight and mail. Some 89 aircraft were registered in 1976. In addition, 33 other aircraft (including one helicopter) registered in France had been granted flying rights and were legally resident in Ivory Coast by 1977. Various major airport construction, including an upgrading to international standards of the airport at Bouake, and improvement projects were being considered in late 1978.

U.S. firms should be able to benefit from the local preponderance of U.S.-built aircraft, the local prestige of U.S. airlines, and an increased appreciation of U.S. equipment among the African management of ASECNA, the multi-government owned corporation with headquarters in Dakar, Senegal, responsible for Ivorian airport maintenance and development.

Inquiries concerning ASECNA's operations and plans can be addressed to: M. Paul Malekou, Directeur General, B.P. 3144, Dakar, Tel. 359-49-40, Telex 680. ASECNA's mailing address in Abidjan is: B.P. 1365.

Communications

The national telecommunications investment program for 1976-78 totaled 19.4 billion CFA francs (about $97 million). Among the projects embarked upon were the reconstruction and expansion of the telephone network of greater Abidjan; the refitting, extension and automatization of about 50 exchanges in the interior; the construction of large capacity microwave links; the expansion of the telex switching center at Abidjan; and the laying of a submarine cable from Abidjan to Dakar, Senegal. Substantial capital purchases also are anticipated for the upgrading and expansion of Ivory Coast's TV and FM broadcasting network. Finally, Ivory Coast may be a good market for point-to-point and mobile VHF and HF communicatons gear.

U.S. supplies (other than the French subsidiary of ITT) have not fared well in the Ivory Coast market for common carrier telecommunications equipment because of the entrenched position of European manufacturers and the close and continuing relationship between the Ivorian OPT and INTELCI and their French counterparts, the PTT and France Cables et Radio. In recent years representatives of numerous U.S. manufacturers of telephone and telex equipment have sought to enter this market. Prospects are good, as the Ivorian communications network appears ready for an infusion of new technology. Some major U.S. firms have begun to give the Ivorian market serious attention. In the telephone/telex market, they are finding genuine interest but have much groundwork to prepare if they are to be accepted as serious business contenders. U.S. suppliers of such items as multiplexers and concentrators, which confronted no foreign competition, found their products accepted immediately.

One major source of resentment among end-users of radio communications and broadcasting equipment has been the difficulty experienced in obtaining spare parts from U.S. suppliers, both in terms of responsiveness to inquiries and of a refusal to correspond in French. As few spare parts or substitutes were available locally, this is a major factor in the sale of equipment.

Ivory Coast has little production of telecommunication equipment. Societe Ivoirienne de Cables (SICABLE) was established in 1975 by TREFIMETAUX, a Pechiney (France) subsidiary; SONAFI, IVOIRAL and SIDELAF. The firm manufactures low tension electrical transmission and telecommunications cable.

Cie. Generale de Constructions Telephoniques (CGCT), an ITT subsidiary, enjoys the greatest market share for the central switching equipment, including virtually the entire Abidjan network. Ericcson of Sweden is a major supplier of telephone switchgear and PBX equipment. Thomson-CSF (transmitters, antennas), SODE-TEG (construction, buildings, maintenance), Schlumberger-I.S. (LF and HF equipment studios) also are active in Ivory Coast.

Only telephone equipment that has been type-accepted by the PTT may be connected to the telephone system. Furthermore, the firm selling and installing the equipment must itself be an approved service organization. A manufacturer or its representative applies for type-acceptance (agrement des appareils) by submitting schematic diagrams and descriptive literature, including technical details of operations in French, to: M. Robert Banti, Sous-Directeur des Installations des Postes de l'Etat, Poste 13, 2e Etage, Direction Generale de PTT, Abidjan. The PTT desires that manufacturers have a designated representative in Ivory Coast.

A firm handling installation becomes approved by submitting a list of its personnel and their qualifications to the same office. In general, only installations with more than three extensions or with PBX or key systems may be serviced by such private firms. PTT-installed equipment is now obtained by bulk purchases, normally on a sealed bid basis. Because of limited lead times, it is not practical for a U.S. firm to bid without operating through a local agent or dealer. The larger agents such as Peyrissac and CFAO do not have autonomy in the selection of product lines. Such firms have offices throughout Francophone Africa, and their Paris headquarters centralize purchasing decisions.

The full 1976–80 Third Five-Year Plan for communications envisages the following major programs: (1) 65,000 telephone subscribers nationwide, including 48,000 in Abidjan with the addition of 22,000 new lines to existing exchanges in 1979–80, (2) a fully automated system by 1980, (3) major new international links, (4) new multiplex aerial and microwave lines, (5)

$110 million invested in switchgear, transmission equipment, electric generators, vehicles and tools; (6) a new earth satellite station to communicate through the Indian Ocean network.

In the radio and television field, there is no market for citizens band (11 meters) equipment in Ivory Coast, as operation of such equipment is banned. There is an important market for commercial and government point-to-point radio. In 1976 there were 154 licensed operators of commercial HF and VHF stations, 58 marine stations, and 12 aeromobile stations. The OPT operates a marine operator position, and the Port of Abidjan maintains a station for contact with incoming vessels. The petroleum refinery, and numerous other major enterprises, including hotels, forestry companies and agribusiness enterprises, maintain private radio communications networks.

As regards radio and TV broadcasting, the Ministry of Information has a project to extend FM radio and TV (for educational TV—a top priority in Ivory Coast) coverage to the entire nation. All radios sold in Ivory Coast are to be required to have FM reception capability. AM transmission is to be discontinued when the project is complete—perhaps by 1986. The entire project may cost as much as $50 million.

While the Ministry of Information claims familiarity with U.S. broadcast equipment, technical advisors there cite several obstacals to increased sales of U.S. equipment: (1) Nonresponsiveness of U.S. firms to correspondence; (2) difficulty in spare parts, particularly when it is necessary to deal through a French intermediary; (3) absence of local agents for U.S. goods; (4) the tendency of European technical advisors and European-trained technicians to look first to Europe as a source of supply.

Useful contact points in Ivory Coast for U.S. communications firms and sellers of communications and information network equipment are:

(1) Direction Generale des Telecommunications (domestic)
    M. Yapi Bancouli, Director
    Poste 13, 2e Etage, Grande Poste
    Abidjan
    Tel: 32-46-67

(2) Telecommunications Internationale de la Cote d'Ivoire (INTELCI)
    M. Thierry du Roizel, Direction of International Telecommunications
    B.P. 1838
    Abidjan
    Tel: 22-58-03, Telex; 790

(3) Radiodiffusion Television Ivoirienne (RTI)
Director for Radio Broadcasting
B.P. V191, Abidjan
Tel: 32-41-52

(4) Radiodiffusion Television Ivoirienne
M. Frederic Kouami, Director of Television
Broadcasting
B.P. 8883, Abidjan
Tel: 34-92-06, Ext. 202

Tourism

During the past decade, Ivory Coast has made substantial expenditures in its tourism industry, notably for the construction of a chain of first-class SIETHO (Societe Ivoirienne de'Equipments Touristiques et Hoteliers) hotels in a large number of major cities. During 1970–74, public investment in the tourism sector totaled 7.1 billion CFA francs, more than 75 percent of which went to developing the Assinie and Assounde beach resorts and expanding Abidjan's Hotel Ivoire. The Novotel in Abidjan (288 rooms, four stars) opened in December 1978 (cost-2.7 billion CFA francs). The first stage of the Sebroko complex, on the heights of Banco Bay, will be ready this year (cost $3.3 billion). The expansion of the President Hotel in Yamoussoukro is in progress. Hilton and Sheraton are considering building hotels in Abidjan; various other facilities are planned, including major resort hotels east of Abidjan.

The tourism flow (122,200 in 1976) should increase with the development efforts underway. In 1976 tourism made a contribution of 14.4 billion CFA francs (up 2.5 billion from 1975), 65 percent of which was due to hotel receipts.

Total investment in tourism during 1976–80 is projected at 26.1 billion CFA francs. However, the Government hopes to take a lower profile in this effort than in previous periods, restricting its investment to 2.1 billion francs and leaving the field open for private enterprises to make up the remaining 24 billion francs. Henceforth, the Government efforts will focus in the support area; the provision of services to major tourist centers, personnel training, tourist information services, and selected financing, rather than in hotel construction itself. Development of the southeastern resort area stretching from Assinie to Grand Bassam will continue to receive a large proportion of available funds in recognition that Europeans are the primary potential source of tourist revenue and that Ivory Coast's beaches remain its principal attraction to them.

Development Assistance

Development assistance from both bilateral and multilateral sources has been significant since independence and totaled $904 million between 1973–76; in 1976 aid amounted to $385 million. World Bank and International Development Administration loans amounting to $396.2 million had been approved by July 1978. The European Development Fund and European Investment Bank also have made sizable loans. The United Nations Development Program (UNDP) has been disbursing technical assistance in recent years at an annual rate of nearly $4 million. About $19 million has been earmarked for 1977–81 for disbursal through the U.N. family of specialized agencies.

Bilateral aid has come primarily from France. Other important donors have been West Germany, other Western European countries, Canada, Nationalist China, and Japan. Ivory Coast to date is the only country in Francophone Africa that has not benefited from Arab bilateral development assistance. The African Development Bank, to whose African Development Fund the United States is making allocations, has its headquarters in Abidjan (B.P. 1387; telex AFDEV Abidjan 717) and has financed projects throughout sub-Saharan Africa.

The United States provided or earmarked $60.8 million in economic assistance through September 1977 under its bilateral aid program. It also provided assistance through USAID's West African Regional Program. Eximbank exposure amounted to $157 million by the end of June 1978. OPIC has been actively involved in Ivory Coast with its programs. The United States has had a Peace Corps program for more than a decade and currently provides Ivory Coast with a group of about 85 volunteers.

Trade Regulations

General Information

Trade Policy.—Ivory Coast is a member of the six-nation Economic Community of West Africa (CEAO), which replaced the West African Customs Union (UDEAO) on January 1, 1974. The other CEAO members are Mali, Mauritania, Niger, Senegal, and Upper Volta. The CEAO treaty provides for a common external customs tariff (CXT) and for the harmonization of member states' customs regulations regarding external trading partners. In actual practice the various members have tended to impose their own tariff schedule. For many years the Ivory

Coast's tariff structure placed higher duties on goods originating outside the French franc zone and the European Economic Community (EEC). Imports from the EEC countries entered the country duty free as a result of the Yaounde Convention of Association signed in 1968 between the EEC member countries and 18 African and Malagasy states. On July 21, 1975, Ivory Coast abolished the "reverse preferences" for imports from the Common Market, thus equalizing the duties applied to imports from the United States and making American products more competitive.

Ivory Coast is a member of the four-country Conseil de l'Entente (Council of the Entente), which also includes Benin, Niger and Upper Volta. It aims to increase regional economic cooperation. The Ivory Coast also belongs to the 15-country Economic Community of West African States (ECOWAS) established by treaty signed May 27, 1975. ECOWAS is working toward elimination of trade barriers among its membership, and, in addition, hopes to achieve harmonization of overall commercial policy, including investment projects planned in member countries.

In connection with payment for imports, foreign exchange controls do not apply to France or any country whose bank of issue is linked with the French treasury by an Operations Account. All other countries, such as the United States, are subject to exchange controls, generally through the delegation of authority to commercial banks for transfer of funds. Controls are not considered restrictive: the banks ordinarily transfer foreign exchange promptly upon presentation of satisfactory documentary evidence that the proposed transaction is legitimate and the imported goods have arrived in Ivory Coast.

Currency.—Ivory Coast is a member of the West African Monetary Union (UMOA), together with Benin, Niger, Senegal, Togo, and Upper Volta. The countries share a common currency, the CFA franc, which is issued by a common central bank, the Banque Centrale des Etats de l'Ouest (BCEAO). The convertibility of the CFA franc into French francs is guaranteed through a monetary cooperation agreement with France. The exchange rate is officially maintained at 50 CFA franc per French franc. In the first quarter of 1979 the rate of exchange approximated 230 CFA francs = US$1.

Technical Standards.—The metric system is the official standard of weights and measures. The standard electric current used in Ivory Coast is 50 cycles 220/380 volts (wye system), but there are variations from that norm.

Language.—French is the official language and is generally understood throughout the country. All correspondence as a general rule should be written in French. Shipping documentation should also be prepared in French to expedite customs formalities.

Duties and Taxes on Imports

Tariff Structure.—Ivory Coast has two basic customs charges: (1) A fiscal duty levy (droit fiscal), which generally is between 5 and 20 percent but can go as high as 55 percent; and (2) a customs duty levy (droit de douane), which generally is between 5 and 15 percent, but can reach 40 percent for items that are locally produced. Goods from all developed counties are now admitted on a nondiscriminatory basis. Additional import taxes include: a levy of 0.6 percent in favor of the Centre Ivorien du Commerce Exterieur and the Conseil Ivorien des Chargeurs; a tax on value added ranging from 10 to 33.5 percent (usually 22 percent); and excise taxes on tobacco and alcohol.

Most of the duties are ad valorem rates assessed on the "normal price" wholesale market value of the goods in the country of origin, plus all costs and expenses incurred up to the time of their arrival in an Ivorian port. For the few imported goods chargeable with duty by weight (i.e. specific), the duty is levied on the net weight unless otherwise specified in the tariff. Import duties and all other taxes on ad valorem goods are based on c.i.f. (cost, insurance, freight) values.

Ivory Coast uses the Brussels Tariff Nomenclature (BTN) for classifying products. Advance rulings on customs classification can be supplied on written request to the Chef du Bureau des Douanes (Chief of Customs Office) in the locality where entry is to be made. A prescribed form must be submitted in quadruplicate to the Customs Office.

Information regarding Ivorian duties applicable to specific products may be obtained free of charge from the African Area, BED/OIM, Industry and Trade Administration, U.S. Department of Commerce, Washington, D.C. 20230, or any Commerce District Office. Inquiries should contain complete product description, including BTN, SITC, or U.S. Schedule B Export Commodity Numbers if known.

Other Trade Regulations

Imports from foreign countries, such as the United States, are subject to licensing according to an annual import program that establishes for each country a quota for bilateral commercial agreements and a global quota that can be applied to any of the countries. Import licenses are required for goods subject to quotas, while import certificates are needed for goods that are "decontrolled," which means they are not subject to the quota system. Two import certificate forms are used for "decontrolled" products: c.1.1 (where payment is made by letter of credit) and c.1.2 (where payment is made by cash against documents). Raw materials, spare parts for machinery, and semifinished goods largely make-up the "decontrolled" products list.

Import licenses and certificates are issued by the Subdirectorate for Licenses and Foreign Trade Regulations in the Directorate of Economic Affairs and External Economic Relations of the Ministry of Economy and Finance. Import licenses are valid for 6 months from date of delivery of the license and are normally easy to obtain. Licenses may be extended for 6 months: one time for consumer goods and three times for capital goods. License expiration is calculated from the loading date. Extension requests should be accompanied by the so-called "Import" copy of the license and supported by a letter from the supplier stating the reasons why the goods could not be shipped within the stipulated period.

All import transactions relating to foreign countries must be domiciled with an authorized bank when their value exceeds 500,000 CFA francs; transactions of lower value must be domiciled if a financial transaction is to be undertaken before customs clearance. The import licenses or import attestations enable importers to purchase the necessary exchange, but not earlier than 1 month before shipment before a documentary credit is opened or 8 days before the payment is due if the commodities have already been imported.

Since July 1, 1975, Ivory Coast has authorized the Societe Generale de Surveillance, S.A. (SGS) of Geneva, Switzerland, or its agents to perform a qualitative, quantitative, and price comparison inspection of all imports. Clarifications of the original decree require that all goods valued at 100,000 CFA francs f.o.b. or more must be accompanied by a "Declaration of Intent to Import" when shipped to Ivory Coast. Goods valued at 500,000 CFA francs f.o.b. or greater are subject to full inspection by SGS or its agent and cannot enter Ivory Coast without an inspection certificate, a notice of refusal to grant a certificate, or an exemption from the Ivorian Government. Sellers must notify SGS or its agent of the intent to ship goods, they must make the goods available to the agent for inspection, and they must bear all costs of the inspection prior to shipment. In most cases the inspection will be visual and the price comparison will be cursory.

Certain goods imported into Ivory Coast are exempted from inspection prior to shipment. Such items include medicine, food products, jewelry, publications, personal effects and gifts, and petroleum products. Exempted from qualitative inspection are cosmetics, dyes, paints, chemical products, insecticides, wines in bulk packaging, and spirits. The representative of SGS in the United States is the Superintendence Company, Inc., with offices at 17 Battery Place North, New York, N.Y. 10004 (212-052-6300), and other major ports. Exporters should send their inspection requests to the New York office, which will refer them to the appropriate regional office for the inspection to be carried out.

Shipping Documents. — Import documentation is not excessive nor is it applied in a discriminatory fashion. Customs formalities and procedures are enforced uniformly. Documents required by Ivorian customs officials on shipments from the United States include the commercial invoice (two copies in French, or with a French translation), a certificate of origin (two copies) and a bill of lading (or air waybill). No consular certification is required. In addition, the exporter must furnish his importer with a pro forma invoice in French or with a French translation, which must be attached to the importer's application for a license. Heavy fines are imposed for even minor irregularities in the above documents.

Marking, Labeling and Packaging. — All cartons, cases, crates and packages containing American-produced merchandise must bear marking identifying the United States as the country of origin (i.e., "Made in U.S.A.") before it will be allowed to enter Ivory Coast. Marking should be placed on each box, case, or package, just below the brand name. Lettering should be legible and at least 3 mm in height. Marks of origin in either English or French also are required on the labels of products exported to Ivory Coast. Labels should also indicate the date of production.

Other than for hazardous materials, which should be packaged in a standardized manner, there are no specific regulations on packaging.

However, goods shipped to Ivory Coast should be security padded to withstand tropical heat, moisture, pests, rough handling and pilferage. Importers recommend that American shippers avoid thin cardboard or plywood containers since they are easily broken into and readily damaged if exposed to weather. Many goods entering Ivory Coast by sea must be transshipped by truck a considerable distance. To ensure safe arrival at their destination, all packages should be of sturdy construction, properly supported (preferably on the inside), and banded on the outside with steel strapping.

Senate Concurrent Resolution 40, adopted July 30, 1973, invites U.S. exporters to inscribe, insofar as practicable, on the external shipping container in indelible print of a suitable size: United States of America. Although such marking is not compulsory under law, U.S. shippers are urged to cooperate in this publicizing of American-made goods.

Entry and Warehousing of Goods. — All goods are allowed to remain warehoused without customs entry in Ivory Coast for up to 1 month. Goods entered for transshipment, if removed within the alloted time, are not subject to customs duty, although they are liable for accrued storage and handling charges. All other goods, if not retrieved within 30 days from the customs area, are sold at public auction by the customs authorities after 4 months. Goods placed in a commercial bonded warehouse can remain undeclared for up to 18 months, with the possibility of two additional legal delays of 6 months each. Afterwards the goods may be sold at public auction. Various freight forwarding companies in Ivory Coast operate bonded warehouses.

Air Shipment. — Shipments by air cargo to Ivory Coast require the same documentation as those arriving by ocean freight and are subject to regulations applicable to shipments by vessel. In addition, copies of the air waybill are required for such shipments, as well as other required documents. For shipments by air cargo the shipping documents should either accompany the goods or be attached to the consignment notes and air mailed separately. At present seven international airlines, including Pan American, offer scheduled air cargo services from the United States to Abidjan.

Transits. — Ivory Coast maintains a transit zone facility at Abidjan for goods destined to Mali, Niger, or Upper Volta. These facilities allow duty-free storage within the transit area.

Merchandise in transit must be bonded. The bonding usually takes the form of a guarantee by a bank, freight forwarder, or major importing firm that the goods will, at a later date, either be transshipped or entered through Ivory Coast customs.

Samples and Advertising Materials. — Samples that are of no commercial value or that have been rendered unusable by mutilation or otherwise damaged may be entered free of duty. Such goods must, however, be marked "aucune valeur commerciale" (i.e., "no commercial value"); otherwise they will be subject to full duty.

Advertising materials are dutiable when imported in quantity. Single catalogs or small packets of brochures are normally allowed free entry if marked "imprime" ("printed matter") and sent by parcel post. Ivory Coast also admits duty-free, under the cover of carnets, commercial samples, advertising material and professional equipment.

Embargoes and Special Requirements. — Embargoes have been placed on various types of products. Items whose general importation have been restricted or prohibited include live animals, arms or munitions, distilling equipment, obscene publications or films, saccharin, narcotics, explosives, and living plants or seeds. Exemptions may be granted in certain instances by the appropriate government agency. The importation of used clothing was prohibited in 1975. In addition, all pesticides must be registered prior to their sale, distribution, or use in Ivory Coast. Biscuits, any kind of rice, and textile imports falling within tariff chapters 50 to 63 of the Ivorian Customs Code require prior issue of a visa from the Direction du Commerce Exterieur. Pro forma invoices, which must be included with import license applications, must show the number of cubic meters and global and unit weight in addition to other information. The importation of alcoholic beverages with an alcohol content exceeding 20 percent is also subject to special regulation, including registration with the Direction du Commerce Exterieur.

Selling in Ivory Coast

Distribution Systems

Distribution Centers. — The estimated population of Ivory Coast in mid-1978 was 7.6 million persons, with an annual growth rate of 3.5 percent (including net immigration). About 20 percent of the population originates from outside the country. The largest cities in Ivory Coast are Abidjan (population 900,000)—which is the capital and financial center of the country, and Bouake (population of 200,000) which is located in the center. Roughly 25 percent of the population lives in urban centers. The projected rate of growth of urbanization to 1980 is 8 percent a year. Other cities with populations exceeding 50,000 include Adzope, Agboville, Daloa, Divo, Gagnoa, Korhogo and Man.

The Ivorian distribution system is both traditional and modern. In the modern sector distribution is handled for the most part by large trading companies that cover all aspects of selling from importing to retailing and servicing. Among the larger firms involved are: C.A.E.I., CFA, DACIVO, Hamelle Afrique, Metco Ivorie, PEYRISSAC, Socaci, SCOA, and SOGIEXCI. More than 200 American companies are represented by local firms. Several of the import houses, especially those dealing in consumer goods, have set up stores and supermarkets that retail groceries, liquors, household goods, hardware, and clothing. Several chain stores (PAC, Chaine Avion) have branches in every major town.

Forms of Representation.—The specific type of representation that a U.S. firm might establish in Ivory Coast should conform to the marketing requirements of the product to be sold. The principal means are employing the services of an agent, utilizing a distributorship or dealer, and establishing a direct sales branch or subsidiary.

Agents are used exclusively for the distribution of a wide range of both durable and nondurable consumer goods and for some industrial raw materials. This form of representation may be particularly appropriate for highly competitive products appealing to a specialized market.

In appointing an exclusive representative in Ivory Coast, the U.S. exporter is legally entitled to certain exemptions from U.S. antitrust laws. The Webb-Pomerene Act allows a limited exemption from antitrust laws for direct exports by allowing exporters to agree on prices, sales terms, territorial division, and other activities in export trade that would be prohibited in U.S. domestic commerce. More information on the Webb-Pomerene Act is available from the Foreign Business Practices Division, Office of International Finance and Investment, Industry and Trade Administration, U.S. Department of Commerce, Washington, D.C. 20230.

Consumer goods requiring maintenance of stocks and industrial equipment and building materials are often exported to Ivory Coast through local distributors. The prospective distributor should be willing to carry a sufficient parts supply and maintain adequate facilities and personnel to perform all normal servicing operations. An efficient servicing capability is a virtual prerequisite for selling machinery in tropical Africa. American companies are urged to monitor closely the performance of their dealers.

Another method of representation for an American firm selling in Ivory Coast is to establish a branch office or sales subsidiary. This method is particularly appropriate where a large continuing market exists for a product where regular maintenance service or frequent contacts with the Government are required.

Credit

Apart from the Banque Centrale des Etats de l'Afrique de l'Ouest (BCEAO), the banking system in Ivory Coast consists of 13 commercial banks and 5 specialized public credit institutions, the most important being the Caisse Autonome d'Amortissement (CAA), which manages the Government's debt. Other financial intermediaries that perform some banking operations include the Treasury, the Post Office, and the National Savings Bank.

Citibank, N.A. and Chase Manhattan have branches in Abidjan, and Chemical Bank has a representative office there. Other U.S. banks with major interests in Ivory Coast include Bank of America, Bankers Trust Company, and Morgan Guaranty. The U.S. accounting firms of Arthur Andersen, Price Waterhouse, Deloitte, Haskins and Sells, and Coopers and Lybrand have regional offices in Abidjan. The Washington, D.C. law firm of Duncan, Allen & Mitchell also has an office there.

To assist U.S. exporters in formulating sound credit policies applicable to local markets, credit information on individual Ivorian firms is available from the World Traders Data Report (Export Information Service, Industry and Trade Administration U.S. Department of Commerce.) Some of the principal U.S. sources include the Foreign Credit Interchange Bureau, National Association of Credit Management, 229 Fourth Ave., New York, N.Y. 10003; American Foreign Credit Underwriters Corp., 253 Broadway, New Yor, N.Y. 10007; and Dun and Bradstreet, Inc., 99 Church St., New York, N.Y. 10007.

Government Procurement

Procurement of goods and services by the Ivory Coast Government comes under the supervision of the Ministry of Finance, which in most cases is in a position to control the purchases of other ministries. Ordinarily, ministries order from local importing houses or from those foreign sources with which they are most familiar, which often means French suppliers. There is a growing interest in American sources of supply. Occasionally international calls-or-bids are issued, particularly for large-scale projects. Requests for bids are published in local newspapers and in various trade and government publications such as the *Daily Bulletin of the Chamber of Commerce*. All invitations for bids are advertised in the *Journal des Marches*.

The American Embassy in Abidjan watches all announcements of bids and promptly reports them to the Department of Commerce, where they are made available to the American business community through the Trade Opportunities Program (TOP). Frequently short lead times make it impossible for foreign firms to bid except through a local agent. The Government relies heavily on French technical advisors and consultants, and bid specifications are often based on those used in France, although IBRD (International Bank of Reconstruction and Development) and African Development Bank-financed projects have more broadly drawn specifications and have enjoyed good participation by U.S. firms. Bids may be handled by one of several methods depending on the work, type of service, and goods required. The principal method is competitive bidding.

American firms which are interested in supplying equipment, materials or services to the Ivorian Government or to a semipublic corporation will require reliable, persistent representation. Besides attractive pricing, major selling points are prompt delivery, availability of spare parts, and, if required, an effective local servicing capability.

Market Research and Trade Organizations

The main firm in Ivory Coast for market research is the Institut Ivorian d'Opinion Publique, whose address is B.P. 21,044, Abidjan. This firm is a subsidiary of the Paris-based affiliate of the U.S. Gallup Institute. Local support for market research projects may also be obtained through the Chamber of Commerce, B.P. 1399; the Chamber of Industry, B.P. 1758; and the Chamber of Agriculture, B.P. 1291, all of Abidjan. American and Ivorian researchers and business visitors are encouraged to use the U.S. Embassy's commercial library in Abidjan.

The Government of Ivory Coast publishes economic data that can provide valuable assistance

to the U.S. exporter in formulating a marketing plan. The best available statistical sources are the *Statistiques du Commerce Exterieur*, and other statistical publications issued by the Direction de la Statistique, Ministere de l'Economie et des Finances, B.P. 222, in Abidjan and by various Ivorian banks. Other useful sources of commercial information include the respective *Bulletin Mensuel* (Monthly Bulletins) of the Chambers of Commerce, Industry and Agriculture. A most valuable aid in marketing is the *Annuaire National de la Republique de Cote D'Ivoire* (National Year Book) printed every year by Chastrusse et Cie., Rue Andre-Devaud; 19105 Brive, France. *La Cote d'Ivoire en Chiffres* is a statistical yearbook published by the Ministry of Planning. Ediafric, 57 Avenue d'Iena, 75116 Paris publishes *Societes et Fournisseurs d'Afrique Noir*, a comprehensive directory of public and private companies.

Marketing Aids

Advertising Media.—Advertising is available in Ivory Coast in almost any medium: newspapers and magazines, television, by short films in movie houses, over the radio network, via local exhibitions and displays and through direct mail. To be fully effective the advice of local specialists should be sought before embarking on a publicity campaign.

Printed Materials.—There are two French language newspapers, published in Ivory Coast, a daily and a weekly. *Fraternite Matin*, the daily, has a circulation of more than 35,000. *Fraternite Hebdomadaire* (circulation of 15,000) is the official newspaper of the country's sole political party, the PDCI. Advertising in these papers is inexpensive. Several magazines enjoy a wide circulation, including *Bingo, Paris Match, Jeune Afrique*, as well as the European editions of *Time* and *Newsweek*. *Le Monde*, the influential French daily, is read widely. Many Ivorian business people also read some of the African business publications that carry advertising. These periodicals include *Afrique Industrie Infrastructures, Le Manager, Marches Tropicaux et Mediterraneens, Moniteur Africain du Commerce et de l'Industrie, Bulletin de l'Afrique Noire, African Development, and West Africa*. French trade journals are read widely within their respective industries.

Investment in Ivory Coast

Investment Climate

Foreign investment in Ivory Coast had a book value of about $500 million in 1977. Ameri can investment amounted to approximately $160 million, primarily in the services sector. As in many cases loans and accounts payable far exceed the cash investment. More than 100 U.S. firms are operating wholly owned subsidiaries or branches or are partners with other firms and the Government in manufacturing, tourism, banking, insurance, mining and petroleum marketing services. These firms, include Exxon, Bank of America, Bankers Trust Company, Citibank, Chase International Investment Corporation, Lazard Freres and Company, IBM Corporation, American International Assurance Company, AFIA Worldwide Insurance, Union Carbide, and Riegel Textile Corporation. Additional American capital expenditures are under way that will increase substantially the total U.S. investment.

Government Policy on Foreign Investment

The Government encourages private foreign investment in projects that contribute to the country's economic development. For nearly two decades it has had one of the most liberal investment codes in Africa. Law No. 59-134 of September 3, 1959, lays down the conditions governing private investment by defining what constitutes a "priority enterprise" and by specifying the requirements with which an undertaking must comply to be approved as such. The Law also provides for important tax exemption and relief measures that will benefit all priority enterprises without distinction, and, in regard to some enterprises, the long-term taxation scheme that is designed to ensure fixed taxation for a period not exceeding 25 years. Establishment agreements between the Ivory Coast Government and the firms concerned, specifically provided for by the law, lay down the terms and conditions of the establishment and activities of enterprises using the long-term scheme.

The following categories of enterprises in the Ivory Coast are eligible for priority status: (1) Real estate; (2) industrial crops and related processing industries—oilseeds, rubber, sugar cane, etc.; (3) industrial preparation or processing by mechanical or chemical means of local vegetable and animal products—coffee, cocoa, timber, cotton, etc.; (4) manufacturing and assemblying goods and articles for large-scale consumption—textiles, building materials, fertilizers, pharmaceuticals, etc.; (5) extractive industries—mining, enriching or processing of mineral and related handling and transport industries, oil prospecting; (6) power production; and (7) tourism (by Law No. 73-368 of July 26, 1973).

If priority status is sought, the investor must submit a proposal to the Ministry of Planning. The Bureau du Developpement Industriel (Industrial Development Office) within the Ministry will provide counseling services and pinpoint government interests. Formal government approval for priority status is granted by decrees passed by the Council of Ministers and published in the *Journal Officiel* (official gazette). More detailed information concerning specific benefits offered investors under the investment code, as well as copies of the 1959 law itself, can be obtained from the African Area, Office of Country Marketing, Industry and Trade Administration, U.S. Department of Commerce, Washington, D.C. 20230.

Although Ivory Coast has no specific legislation limiting the degree of foreign participation in investment enterprises, the Government vigorously encourages joint venture projects with Ivorian nationals. Prior authorization of the Office des Changes, Ministry of Economic and Financial Affairs, is mandatory for all direct foreign investment in Ivory Coast involving transactions outside the franc zone.

International Agreement.—Ivory Coast is a signatory of the Convention of the Settlement of Investment Disputes between States and Nationals of other States, which has also been ratified by the United States. Ivory Coast and the United States also have concluded an Investment Guarantee Agreement. This agreement makes available the investment services of the U.S. Overseas Private Investment Corporation (OPIC) to U.S. investors approved by the Government of Ivory Coast.

Industrial Property and Copyright Protection

Patents and Trademarks.—Ivory Coast is a member of the Office Africain et Malgache de la Propriete Industrielle (OAMPI). This organization establishes a common system for obtaining and maintaining protection for patents, trademarks and industrial designs among its member states (Central African Empire, Benin, Gabon, Ivory Coast, Niger, Rwanda, Senegal, Togo, Upper Volta, Mauritania). Inquiries and applications should be directed to OAMPI, B.P. 887, Yaounde, Cameroon.

Ivory Coast is a member of the "Paris Union International Industry Property Convention" (patents and trademarks). U.S. nationals are thus entitled to national (i.e. equal) treatment under that country's laws in maintaining their patent and trademark rights. They also are entitled to certain special advantages such as 1 year preservation of patent filing rights after first filing in the United States (6 months for trademarks) and protection against arbitrary cancellation of patents and trademarks for non-use. Invention and design patents as well as trademarks are valid for 20 years.

Copyright.—The Ivory Coast is not a party to any copyright convention to which the United States adheres. But it is a member of the Berne Copyright Convention. American authors may receive automatic copyright protection in Ivory Coast for a work if it is published in one of the 55 other countries adhering to the Berne Convention at the same time it is first published in the United States. Further general information on industrial property and copyright protection may be obtained from the Foreign Business Practices Division, International Economic Policy and Research, Industry and Trade Administration, U.S. Department of Commerce, Washington, D.C., 20230. Information related to step-by-step procedures on fees, documents, and related matters, however, should be secured by consulting legal counsel.

Business Organizations

Types of Organizations.—Foreign investors engaging in commercial activity may operate under one of two forms in Ivory Coast: (a) A branch, which is not considered a separate legal entity, or (b) an Ivorian company by either participating in an existing firm or establishing a new one. The forms of business organization sanctioned in Ivorian law are the sole proprietorship (commerce par les interesses); the partnership (societe en nom collectif); the limited liability joint stock company (societe a responsabilite limitee) and the corporation (societe anonyme).

Ivorian requirements for organizing a business enterprise closely follow French legal practice. Information related to procedures for setting up a business should be secured from experienced legal counsel (a list of local attorneys in Ivory Coast can be obtained from the American Embassy in Abidjan or the U.S. Department of Commerce in Washington, D.C.). For further information concerning Ivorian formalities and regulations concerning enterprises to be established in the country, contact the Bureau de Developpement Industriel of the Ministry of Planning, B.P. 4196, Abidjan.

Taxation

I. Taxes on Income and Profits

A. *Companies, partnerships and individual enterprises.*—This is an annual tax levied on the net profits realized from activities (including real estate) carried on in Ivory Coast. The basic rate is 25 percent on individual enterprises and 40 percent for companies. There is also a 10 percent contribution to the Fonds National d'Investissement (FNI). Low-cost housing companies are exempted. Authorized deductions include property taxes and losses incurred during the 3 previous years.

B. *Individuals*

1. Tax on noncommercial profits.—An annual tax levied on earnings from the exercise of independent professional activity. The basic rate is 25 percent plus a 10 percent contribution to the Fonds National d'Investissements (FNI). Authorized deductions include property taxes and losses incurred during the 3 previous years.

2. Tax on salaries and wages.—An annual tax levied on earnings from employment, pensions, and annuities of residents, withheld at source. A basic rate of 1.5 percent applies, plus a progressive component ranging from 1.5 percent (for monthly salaries between 30,000 to 100,000 CFA francs) to 10 percent (for monthly salaries of more than 150,000 CFA francs). Certain exemptions and deductions are allowed.

3. General income tax.—An annual tax levied on total net income of residents. Foreigners are taxed on Ivory Coast income. A graduated split system is in effect with a progressive rate of 0–60 percent applied. Total tax is obtained by multiplying the tax on each split by the number of splits. Retirement fund contributions (up to 6 percent) and specified expenses (up to 15 percent) are deductible. A family situation is taken into account through a system of income splits, up to five.

C. *Other.*—Tax on income from movable capital.—A withholding tax on dividends introduced in 1974. The standard rate is 12 percent. The tax is deductible from the general income tax payable.

II. Social Security Contributions

A. *Retirement.*—The employer is as

sessed at a rate of 1.8 percent of the employee's salary.

B. *Family allowances.* — The employer pays at a rate of 5.5 percent. There is a ceiling of 840,000 francs annual salary.

C. *Worker's Compensation.* — The employer pays at a rate of between 2 and 5 percent.

III   **Employer's Payroll Taxes.** — An annual tax payable by employers on total wages and salaries paid in cash or in kind. The assessed rate is 12 percent for Ivorian employers and 17 percent for private non-Ivorian employers.

IV.   **Taxes on Property**

A. *Tax on developed property.* — This tax is levied on the rental value of buildings constructed of nontraditional materials. A rate of 10 percent is imposed. Standard deductions are 80 percent for housing and 50 percent for other buildings.

B. *Sewerage assessment.* — The rate is 5 percent.

C. *Tax on undeveloped property.* — This charge is levied on the assessed market value of vacant urban land. A rate of 4–6 applies, depending upon the number of years since purchase.

D. Mortmain tax. An annual tax on property held in mortmain by corporations and associations. Fifty percent of the equivalent property tax is levied. Real estate companies are exempted.

E. Tax on insufficiently used land. Levied on the excess of the market value above three times the normal rental value. It is not applied if conditions beyond the control of the owner prohibit construction.

V.   **Taxes on Goods and Services**

A. *Turnover and value-added taxes*

1. Domestic value-added tax. — A tax based on turnover after deduction of purchases. It is levied at the production stage. Exports, many basic commodities, most primary sector activities, and low-cost housing construction are exempted. There are three rates (1) Normal — 22 percent, (2) reduced — 10 percent, and (3) increased — 33 percent.

2. Value-added tax on imports. — This is levied on the c.i.f. value of imports plus all import duties. Fertilizer, newspapers, cereals are exempted. Rates are the same as for the domestic value-added tax.

3. Tax on services. — This is levied on all services, notably restaurants and insurance commissions. Rates are the same as for the domestic value-added tax.

B. *Taxes on use of goods and property* (Business license tax.). — An annual tax levied on any person or company engaged in trade, industry, or profession not expressly exempted. There is a temporary exemption for new enterprises. A fixed levy is imposed depending upon the type of business, plus a proportional levy of 10 percent on the rental value of the premises. There is also at present a surcharge of 10 percent.

C. *Export duties.* — Levied on most agricultural products, minerals, diamonds, and gold on the basis of standard values. Rates are ad valorem, generally 0–30 percent. Reductions are made on exports by priority enterprises.

Avoidance of Duplicate Taxes. — The United States and Ivory Coast have not concluded a tax treaty with one another. Under U.S. law, however, American companies operating in Ivory Coast may claim a credit against U.S. taxes for such taxes paid to Ivory Coast.

Employment

Labor Force. — There has been no comprehensive census of the economically active population. The vast majority of the working population is engaged on a nonsalaried basis, primarily in farming. The number of permanent wage earners in the private sector in 1977 has been estimated at 350,000 to 370,000 (or roughly 10 percent of the labor force). About 50,000 persons are employed by the Ivorian Government. Employment in the so-called modern sector rose by 22 percent in 1976.

Labor for modern enterprises is usually available; but the workers possess few technical skills and must be trained on the job. Lack of highly skilled laborers has resulted in the employment of about 15,000 non-African (mostly French) workers in advanced technological jobs and administrative and managerial positions).

Unemployment remains a relatively minor problem in Ivory Coast compared with other African countries, although in urban centers, particularly Abidjan, the number of unemployed persons has increased in recent years, and young educated people with inappropriate qualifications and lack of experience have some difficulty getting jobs.

Payments and Benefits.—Ivory Coast has a system of guaranteed minimum wage rates consisting of the Salaire Minimum Agricole Garanti (SMAG) for agricultural workers and the Salaire Minimum Interprofessional Garanti (SMIG). The SMIG minimum wage is presently 920 CFA francs per 8-hour day, and the SMAG is about to be raised retroactively from the present 240 CFA francs per 8-hour day.

Actual wages in many sectors are governed by collective agreements (conventions collectives), which are negotiated by a committee of employers' and workers' representatives. Relationships between employers and employees are covered by the Labor Code (Law No. 64–290 of August 1, 1964, as amended). The Union General des Travailleurs de Cote d'Ivoire (UGTCI) represents all organized workers in the country.

Ivorianization Policy

The Commission d'Ivorisation (AICI) was created in 1973 with the stated political goals of Ivorianizing capital and senior officer positions in the public service and the promotion of Ivorian enterprise. The Government has fixed 1980 as its target for Ivorianization, although the extent to which its objectives will be achieved is unclear. In enterprises with priority status under the 1959 Investment Code, which are required to employ and train a prescribed number of locals, the Ivorians' employment share rose from 66 percent in 1974 to 80 percent in 1976.

Ivorianization also is promoted through the Manpower Office in the Ministry of Labor and Ivorianization of Employment. The Office must be informed of any vacancies, which it attempts to fill with Ivorian candidates; if no suitable Ivorian is found, the employer may take any candidate of his choice.

In addition, firms doing business in Ivory Coast are required to file reports with AICI indicating the number of Ivorians, non-Ivorian Africans, and other expatriates employed. Work permits may be canceled for those expatriates whose positions are not reported to the AICI as

required. Information on current regulations is obtainable from the Secretariat General of the Association Interprofessionnelle des Employeurs de C.I., B.P. 1340, Abidjan.

Guidance for Business Travelers

Correspondence and Communications

French is the language of business, government and social exchange. To conduct business effectively in Ivory Coast a working knowledge of French is a necessity. Commercial correspondence is ordinarliy conducted by means of airmail letters, which arrive from the United States twice a week. Transit time usually is between 1 and 2 weeks. International airmail letters from the United States to Abidjan cost $0.31 for a letter weighing one-half ounce; airform letters cost $0.22. Post Office box numbers (B.P.) rather than street numbers should be used in addresses.

Cables are frequently used to supplement airmail communication. For telegrams, the full rate per word from all places in the United States is $0.34, subject to a seven word minimum. Communications in the other direction, i.e. from the Ivory Coast to the United States, are considerably more expensive.

Local telephone service is available in Abidjan and all provincial centers. International calls to the United States may be made 24 hours a day and cost 30 CFA francs (about 13¢) for each 1.49 seconds on direct-dialed calls to the continental United States. Telex facilities can be found in Abidjan, Bouake, and other commercial centers. Most major businesses have their own telex numbers. The larger international hotels will send and receive cable/telex messages.

All business pertaining to mail, telegrams and telephones is transacted at the offices of the P&T (Posts et Telecommunications). The following is a list of Post Offices in the Abidjan area: Place de la Republique; Abidjan Plateau; Treichville; Adjame; Cocody; 220 Logements; Port Bouet; Airport; Kaemassi. Stamps may be purchased also at bookstores, hotel desks, and at the kiosk near City Hall on the Plateau.

Entrance Requirements

American travelers must have a valid U.S. passport and visa when entering Ivory Coast, which does not grant airport visas. Visas may be applied for in person or by mail. If by mail, postage for passport return by certified or other mail should be included. In Washington, D.C., applications should be made at the Ivorian Embassy, 2424 Massachusetts Av., N.W., 20008; in New York, apply at the Ivory Coast Visa Office, Suite 1404, 521 Fifth Av., 10017; and in Los Angeles visas can be obtained from the Ivory Coast Consulate, Suite 1402, 9000 Sunset Boulevard, 90069.

Visas are usually issued in 2 to 3 days and are valid for up to 3 months. There is no charge, but four photos are required and four copies of the visa application must be completed and submitted in French. For a business trip the applicant should submit a letter from the company indicating position held, destination, purpose of travel, proposed length of stay, and stating that expenses will be borne by the company. An international health certificate showing vaccination against smallpox, yellow fever, and cholera should accompany the application. Business travelers who reside outside Ivory Coast and whose activities necessitate their frequent presence in the country may obtain entry and reentry visas from the Service du Documentation in Abidjan.

Exchange Controls

There are no limitations on the importation of dollars, travelers checks, or other instruments of payments, but travelers may be asked to declare this amount at the time of entry. Nonresident travelers may take out foreign bank notes up to the amount declared on entry and a maximum of 25,000 CFA francs. Currency can be exchanged at the Abidjan airport exchange office or at leading banks downtown at a slightly less favorable rate. French francs are freely interchangeable without commission at a rate of 50 CFA francs to one French franc. Banks are open Monday through Friday from 7:30 a.m. to 11:30 a.m. and 2:30 p.m. to 4 p.m.

Business Hours.—Business hours for firms and government offices are 8 a.m. to noon and 3 to 6 p.m. Monday through Friday and 8 a.m. to 12 noon on Saturdays. U.S. Embassy hours are 8 a.m. to noon and 2 to 5:30 p.m., Monday through Friday.

Holidays.—Official holidays observed in Ivory Coast include January 1 (New Year's), April 16 (Easter Monday)* May 1 (Labor Day), May 24 (Ascension)*, June 4 (Pentecost)*, August 15 (Assumption), August 22-23 (Id-el-Fitri)*, October 31 (Tabashi)*, November 1 (All

*Variable Christian or Moslem Holiday-dates given are for 1979.

Saints), December 7 (Independence Day), December 25 (Christmas).

General Information About Abidjan

Abidjan is composed of various areas: A business district centered on the Plateau; a residential area, Cocody, where the Hotel Ivoire is located; and several African townships, the most important of which are Treichville and Adjame. Much of the city is attractive. Travelers are reminded that English-speakers are relatively scarce in Abidjan, and they cannot count on English to explain directions, give orders, and so forth.

Climate.—The Ivory Coast climate is tropical, with two distinct seasons. The rainy season lasts from May to October and is characterized by cloudy, hot and humid weather interspersed with frequent showers ranging in intensity upward to monsoon force. The dry season, November to April, is very sunny, slightly warmer, and less humid. Sea breezes, especially in the evening, frequently alleviate the heat and humidity. Mid-June to early September is generally a bad time to visit Ivory Coast because key government and business officials are often on leave.

Local Time.—Ivory Coast is on Greenwich Mean Time (GMT). This is 4 hours ahead of Eastern Standard Time.

Taking Pictures.—It is recommended that you obtain the permission of persons you wish to photograph. Many Africans, particularly orthodox Moslems, have a strong dislike of being photographed, although some are pleased by the attention. *DO NOT* photograph people against their will. *DO NOT* take photographs in the National Museum.

Car Rentals.—Cars can be rented from: (1) Hertz (Renault), at the Hotel Ivoire, Hotel des Relais, Hotel du Parc, and Airport; (2) Europcars (Renault) at Air Service Ivoirien, Hotel Tiama, and Airport; (3) Locauto (Fiat), at Station AGIP—Autoroute; and (4) Transivoirauto (Datsun) at 15 Boulevard de Gabon.

Taxis.—City taxis (red) are reasonable, numerous and available on the main streets and boulevards in most sections of the city day or night. All are metered, minimum charge is 80 CEA francs, and rates are doubled (legally) between midnight and 5 a.m. The average charge between the Hotel Ivoire and the Plateau is about 700 francs. On the Plateau taxis usually may be found in front of the Hotel du Parc or the

Hotel Tiama as well as in the Nour-al-Hyat and Score supermarket areas.

Tipping.—As a general rule, 10 percent of the price is recommended. Taxi drivers appreciate but do not expect tips. As a general rule, baggage porters are tipped.

Prices.—All persons should be aware of high prices charged in Abidjan restaurants, gift shops and bars. Inflation has hit the Ivory Coast with full force, therefore the prices quoted below are only approximate and will quickly become dated.

Hotels.—All of the following hotels are air conditioned:

1. Hotel Ivoire (Intercontinental)
   B.P. 8001, Tel: 34-94-81, Telex 550

   The most deluxe hotel in Ivory Coast, featuring 750 rooms, 7 restaurants and bars, a night club, an 800-seat cinema, casino, swimming pool, bowling alley, shopping arcade, and 2,000 seat convention hall. Room prices per day range from 15,000 to 18,000 CFA francs.

2. Hotel Le Tiama (UTH)
   B.P. 4643, Tel. 32-08-22, Telex 494

   A 150-room international class hotel in central Abidjan. Contains restaurant, bar, and conference rooms. Room prices per day range from 11,300 to 13,800 CFA francs.

3. Hotel du Parc (UTH)
   B.P. 1775, Tel. 22-23-86, Telex 619 UTAPAR

   A comfortable 80-room hotel in downtown Abidjan. Good French restaurant. Room prices per day range from 10,300 to 12,600 CFA francs.

4. Grand Hotel
   V.P. 1785, Tel. 32-64-38

   A relatively inexpensive hotel in the downtown Plateau district with 100 rooms. Room prices per day range from 6,500 to 7,500 CFA francs.

5. Forum Hotel du Golf
   B.P. 8018, Tel. 34-84-32, Telex 2368

   A new tourist-oriented hotel with 300 rooms located on the outskirts of Abidjan. Features several restaurants, swimming pool, tennis, golf, and nautical sports. Room prices per day range from 10,000 to 13,000 CFA francs.

Restaurants.—Abidjan's restaurants are many and varied, with offerings of many international specialties and excellent fish in addition to the predominately French cuisine. Luncheon is usually served between 12:30 and 2 p.m. and

dinner from 8 p.m. onward. A few cafes and snack bars are open 24 hours a day.

1. Chez Valentin, Avenue Reine Pokou (Avenue 16) in Treichville serves excellent French food. A small, popular place where it is best to call ahead for a table. Telephone 32-47-16. Expensive.

2. Hotel du Parc, on the Plateau. Call 22-23-86 for a reservation. The hotel's sidewalk cafe (drinks only) is a popular place from which to watch passersby. The indoor restaurant serves excellent French food and is air conditioned. Moderate to expensive.

3. La Petite Auberge, rue des Pecheurs, Zone 3, behind the Treichville Hospital. First class with tasteful decor. Open evenings only. Telephone 35-66-00. Very expensive.

4. La Santa Maria, a floating restaurant on the lagoon, offers a pleasant view, a cool breeze and superb cuisine. The service is impeccable and very friendly. Located on Boulevard de Marseille, just before Sorrento. Telephone 35-54-66. Moderate to expensive.

5. Chez Babouya, Rue 7, Avenue 7, across from the Information Hall, Treichville. A cushion-strewn intimate setting in the heart of Treichville offering Mauritanian and North African specialties. Best for larger groups. By reservation only. Moderately priced.

6. L'Aquarium, Boulevard Pelieu, on the Plateau. Informal dining around on the loveliest public pools in Abidjan. A splendid view of the lagoon from the terrace, where drinks are served.

7. Le Manguier, Grill Room, Hotel Tiama, small and comfortable. Features wood fire grilling. Good but limited menu. Moderate prices. Telephone 32-08-22.

8. Brasserie Abidjanaise, Boulevard de la Republique, near Avenue Terrasson de Fougeres. The most moderately priced, air conditioned restaurant on the Plateau, serving good food in a quiet setting. Telephone 22-67-51.

9. Dragon, Chinese restaurant located around the corner from the Pyramide building. Favorite of the local Chinese community. Service is often very poor. Moderately priced. Telephone 32-34-15.

10. La Pizza di Sorrento, Boulevard de Marseille, Km 6. First class pizza served under open cabanas. Selection of other regional Italian foods also on the menu. Reservations are necessary on weekends. Expensive. Telephone 35-57-75.

11. Les Pecheurs, near the fishing port. A very attractive restaurant serving excellent seafood. Moderate to high. Telephone 35-42-35.

12. Les Tourelles, on the road to Grand-Bassam just past Port Bouet, has a saltwater pool which faces the ocean. Restaurant not particularly noteworthy, but a pleasant place to spend an afternoon. A ye-ye band plays after 5 p.m. on Sundays. Inexpensive.

13. Toit d'Abidjan, at the Hotel Ivoire 4,000 CFA minimum per person without drinks. Open from 7 p.m. to 11 p.m. daily except Sundays. Elegant, fine view of city lights.

Churches. —

Catholic:

Saint Paul Cathedral (Plateau): Sunday Mass at 7:30, 9:30 and 11 a.m. Telephone 30-20-38.

Saint-Jean (Cocody): Sunday Mass at 7:30 and 10 a.m. and 7 p.m. Telephone 34-92-60.

Notere-Dame du Perpetuel Secours (Treichville): Father Florian speaks English. Sunday Mass at 6, 7:30 (choir) and 9 a.m. and 6:45 p.m. Telephone 35-64-54.

Saint Michel (Adjame): Sunday Mass at 6:30, 8: (with drums and African Choir), and 9:30 a.m. and 7 p.m.

Protestant

Eglise Protestante Methodist (Plateau): Service every Sunday at 9:30 a.m. English service third Sunday of each month at 11 a.m. Telephone 32-11-93.

First Baptist Church (Marcoury): Every Sunday at 10:45 a.m. A Nigerian service with excellent choir and drum accompaniment.

Health Precautions and Medical Information

Water and ice in the Hotel Ivoire are safe for consumption, as the Ivoire has its own purification plant. Water and ice served in other establishments should be avoided. Travelers should drink only bottled water, which is available in most restaurants. (Evian, Vittel and Volvic are popular brands). Beer and bottled soft drinks also are considered safe.

Travelers should avoid eating salads and uncooked vegetables. Meat (no matter what kind) should be well done. Fish (if fresh, of course) is safe. Milk and milk products (cheeses, ice cream, butter, cream) of unknown origin should be avoided. Milk from sealed cartons or bottles is considered safe, as are imported cheeses, butter, cream, and ice cream. Most of the items served in restaurants are imported, but if there is any doubt, do not eat them.

The inner lagoons of Abidjan are badly polluted, and travelers ar advised not to swim nor water ski in them. While the salt waters at the ocean beaches near Abidjan are unpolluted, it is extremely dangerous for even the most expert swimmers to swim in thses waters due to the strong surf and treacherous undertow. The pool at the Hotel Ivoire is filtered, cleaned regularly, and is supposed to be safe. The salt water pools at the beaches are usually safe.

Hospitals and Clinics

Treichville Hospital
Telephone 35-56-03
CHU Cocody (University Hospital).
Telephone 31-24-45
Clinique de Plateau (Obstetrical Clinic).
Telephone 22-20-29

Principal Pharmacies*

Pharmacie Moderne (Plateau)
Telephone 22-21-31
Pharmacie Centrale (Plateau)
Telephone 32-19-64
Pharmacie du Commerce (Plateau)
Telephone 32-12-12
Pharmacie de Cocody (Cocody)
Telephone 34-94-95

Diplomatic Representatives

Government of the Ivory Coast

Embassy of the Republic of Ivory Coast
2424 Massachusetts Avenue, N.W.
Washington, D.C. 20008
Tel: 202-483-2400
Ambassador, Timothee N'Guetta Ahoua
Mission of the Republic of Ivory Coast
46 East 74th Street
New York, New York
Tel: 212-988-3930
Consulate of the Republic of Ivory Coast
9000 Sunset Boulevard, Suite 1402
Los Angeles, California 90060
Honorary Consulate of the Republic of Ivory Coast
26555 Evergreen Road
Suite 1602
Southfield, Michigan 94104
Tel: 313-355-0300

---

*Since most of the pharmaceutical products available in Ivory Coast are French, you will have to see a doctor and show him your U.S. prescription so that he can prescribe the French equivalent. The U.S. Embassy publication *Drum Beat*, published every week, lists doctors and pharmacies on duty during the weekend.

Honorary Consulate of the Republic of Ivory
Coast
3151 Southwest Fairmont Boulevard
Portland, Oregon
Tel: 503-226-3201

Honorary Consulate General of the Republic of
Ivory Coast
44 Montgomery Street
San Francisco, California 94104
Tel: 415-981-6330

Government of the United States

American Embassy
5 Rue Jesse Owens
P.O. Box 1712
Abidjan, Ivory Coast
Tel. 32-09-79
Telex: 660
Cables: AmEmbassy Abidjan
Ambassador: Monteagle Stearns

Government Offices

The offices listed below are located in Abidjan.

Presidency
B.P. 1354

State Ministry for Public Health and Population,
B.P. V4
Tel: 32-08-88

Ministry of Justice,
B.P. V107,
Tel: 32-43-37

Ministry of Foreign Affairs,
B.P. V109
Tel: 32-08-88

Ministry of Armed Forces and Civic Service,
B.P. V11
Tel: 32-02-88

Ministry of Economy, Finance and Plan
B.P. 125-IMM. SCIAM
Tel: 32-05-66

Ministry of Construction and Urbanization
B.P. V153
Tel: 32-08-88

Ministry of Agriculture,
B.P. V 82
Tel: 32-08-33

Ministry of Scientific Research,
B.P. V 151
Tel: 32-06-88

Ministry of Technical and Vocational Training,
B.P. V 141
Tel: 32-06-88

Ministry of National Education,
B.P. V 120
Tel: 32-68-88

Ministry of Trade,
B.P. V 143
Tel: 32-56-26

Ministry of Public Works and Transports,
B.P. V6
Tel: 32-08-88

Ministry of Animal Production,
B.P. V 185
Tel: 32-29-63

Ministry of Labor,
B.P. V 119
Tel: 32-08-88

Ministry of Information,
B.P. V 138
Tel: 32-06-88

Ministry of Mines,
B.P. V 50
Tel: 32-50-03

Ministry of Water and Forests,
B.P. V 94
Tel: 32-08-33

Ministry of Elementary Education and T. V.
Education,
B.P. V 40
Tel: 32-43-53

Ministry of Cultural Affairs,
B.P. V 39
Tel: 32-20-77

Ministry of National Security,
B.P. V 121
Tel: 32-23-00

Ministry of Posts and Telecommunications,
B.P. 20.927
Tel: 32-46-52

Ministry of the Marine,
B.P. V 67
Tel: 32-08-88

Ministry of Tourism,
B.P. V 184
Tel: 32-53-50

Ivorian Governmental Parastatal
Organizations

The organizations listed below are located in
Abidjan

Centre D'Exploitation Industrielle Du Betail
B.P. V 185
Tel: 32-29-63

Centre Ivoirien De Gestion Des Enterprises
(CIGE)
B.P. 7322
Tel: 35-34-84

Centre National Des Bureaux De Fret (CNFB)
B.P. V 116
Tel: 37-44-05

Ste Pour Le Developpement Et L'Exploitation Du Palmier A Huile (Groupe Sodepalm)
B.P. 2049
Tel: 32-00-79
Telex: 347-708

Ste. Pour Le Developpement Minier De La Cote-D'Ivoire (SODEMI)
B.P. 2816
Tel: 31-17-65
Telex: 552

Ste. Pour Le Developpement De La Motorisation De L'Agriculture (MOTORAGRI)
B.P. 20.835
Tel: 37-46-17

Ste. Pour Le Developpement Des Plantations De Canne A Sucre, L'Industrialisation Et La Commercialisation Du Sucre (SODESUCRE)
B.P. 2164
Tel: 32-37-71
Telex: 451

Ste. Pour Le Developpement Des Plantations Forestieres (SODEFOR)
B.P. 20.860
Tel: 31-24-25

Ste. Pour Le Developpement Des Productions Animales (SODEPRA)
B.P. 1249

Ste. Pour Le Developpement De La Production Des Fruits Et Legumes (SODEFEL)
B.P. 20.122
Telex: 2100

Ste. Pour Le Developpement De La Rivera Africaine (SDRA)
B.P. 4136

Ste. Pour Le Developpement De La Riziculture
B.P. 2766

Energie Electrique De La Cote-D'Ivoire (EECI)
B.P. 1345
Telex: 738

Ste. D'Equipment De Terrains Urbains (SETU)
B.P. 21.181

Ste. De Gestion Financiere De L'Habitat (SOGEFIHA)
B.P. 9278
Telex: 534

Institut Pour La Technologie Et L'Industrialisation Des Produits Agricoles Tropicaux (ITIPAT)
B.P. 8881

Ste. Ivoirienne De Cinema
B.P. 304
Telex: 344

Ste. Ivoirienne De Construction Et De Gestion Immobiliere (SICOGI)
B.P. 1856

Ste. Nationale De Conditionnement (SONACO)
B.P. 119
Telex: 2288

Telecommunications Internationales De La Cote D'Ivoire
B.P. 1838
Telex: 790

International Organizations

The organizations listed below are in Abidjan unless otherwise stated.

African Development Bank (B.A.D.),
B.P. 1387,
Tel: 22-56-61
Telex: 498 and 717

European Development Fund (EEC),
B.P. 1821,
Tel: 22-69-20
Telex: FEDKOKS 729

International Labor Organization,
B.P. 75
Bingerville
Tel: 30-30-08

United Nations Development Program,
B.P. 1747
Tel: 32-10-49

United Nations Industrial Development Organization (UNIDO),
B.P. 1747
Tel: 22-63-95

UNICEF, B.P. 4443
Tel: 32-31-31
Telex: 340 UNICEF ABIDJAN

World Health Organization
B.P. 2494
Tel: 32-26-60

World Bank (IBRD),
B.P. 1850
Tel: 32-24-01
Telex: 533

Trade Associations and Business Organizations

The organizations listed below are in Abidjan.

Chambre D'Agriculture De La Cote D'Ivoire
B.P. 1291
Tel: 32-16-11

Chambre De Commerce De Cote D'Ivoire,
B.P. 1399
Tel: 32-46-79

Interpretation Services

Artaud, Joane
19 Ruye des Palmiers
B.P. 11636
Tel: 35-64-41

Bouquier, Pierre,
B.P. 1387
Tel: 31-18-01

Interstar,
B.P. 1318
Tel: 35-57-10

R.L. School, Imm. le General,
B.P. 8437
Tel: 22-73-47

SIPRESTAS
36 Bd. de la Republique
B.P. 2597
Tel: 32-39-41

Sosoo, Leonard,
B.P. 8435
Tel: 34-91-64

Sources of Economic and Commercial Information

Ivorian Government Information Services

Direction des Etudes de Developpement
Ministry of Planning
B.P. 649
Abidjan

Direction Centrale des Marches
Ministry of Economy and Finance
B.P. 20.346
Abidjan

Ivory Coast Development Office
Office of the Financial Counselor
Suite 1604–06
521 Fifth Avenue
New York, New York 10017
Tel: 212-661-9700

Ivory Coast Stabilization Fund
Office of the Commercial Counselor
Suite 2507
1 World Trade Center
New York, New York 10038
Tel: 212-466-0180

Information about investing in Ivory Coast

Economic Counselor
American Embassy
5 Rue Jesse Owens
B.P. 1712
Abidjan, Ivory Coast
Tel: 23-25-81, Ext. 347
Telex: 660

American Businessmen's Club
c/o Duncan, Allen and Mitchell
Imm. SMGL, Av. Barthe
B.P. 20484
Abidjan, Ivory Coast
Tel. 32-67-66
Telex: 2435

Autorite pour l'Amenagement de la Vallee du Bandama (AVB)
Av. Lamblin
B.P. 20.887
Abidjan
Tel. 32-33-34
Telex: 518

Autorite pour l'Amenagement de la Region du Sud-Ouest (ARSO)
Bd. de l'Ouest
B.P. 21.058
Abidjan
Tel: 32-50-78

Chambre d'Industie de Cote d'Ivoire
11 Avenue Lamblin
B.P. 1758
B.P. 1758
Abidjan
Tel: 22-55-04

Bureau de Developpement Industriel (BDI)
Residence Diana
B.P. 4196
Abidjan
Tel: 32-42-86
Telex: 793

Information about marketing in Ivory Coast

Commercial Attache
American Embassy
5 Rue Jesse Owens
B.P. 1712
Abidjan, Ivory Coast
Tel: 32-25-81, Ex. 348
Telex: 660

Chambre de Commerce de la Cote d'Ivoire
6 Avenue Barthe
B.P. 1399
Abidjan, Ivory Coast
Tel: 32-46-79

Syndicat des Commercants, Importateurs et Exportateurs de la C.I.
B.P. 20.882
Abidjan, Ivory Coast
Tel: 22-24-83

Information about Ivorian Products

Centre Ivoirien du Commerce Exterieur (CICU)
Immeuble de la CSSPPA
7th Floor
B.P. V68

Abidjan, Ivory Coast
Tel. 32-08-33
Telex. 460
Chambre d'Agriculture de la Cote d'Ivoire
Av. Lamblin
B.P. 1291
Abidjan, Ivory Coast
Tel: 32-16-11

Information about accounting, business and taxes—U.S. accounting firms

Arthur Andersen & Co.
AMCI, B.P. 20.262
Abidjan, Ivory Coast
Tel. 32-42-97, 32-56-72
Telex. 2107

Coopers & Lybrand
La Pyramide, 3eme etage
B.P. 1361
Abidjan, Ivory Coast
Tel. 32-22-76
Telex: 3304 COLYBCI

Deloitt Haskins & Sells
Alpha 2000, 18eme etage
B.P. V245
Abidjan, Ivory Coast
Tel. 33-15-62; 34-94-56

Pannell Kerr Forster
Res. Nogues, 13eme etage
B.P. 4618
Abidjan, Ivory Coast
Tel. 32-40-70

Price Waterhouse & Co.
Imm. Alpha 200
B.P. 20,011
Abidjan, Ivory Coast
Tel. 32-51-21
Telex. 2250

Information about Ivorian laws and lawyers*

List of English-speaking lawyers in Ivory Coast, distributed by Consular and Commercial Sections
American Embassy
Abidjan, Ivory Coast
Association du Barreau, c/o M. Assi Camille ADAM
B.P. 698
Abidjan, Ivory Coast
Tel. 37-47-99

---

*All Government of Ivory Coast laws and decrees cited in the text of this Report are available through the Department of Commerce District Offices or the African Area, Office of Country Marketing, Industry and Trade Administration, Department of Commerce, Washington, D.C. 20230.

Duncan Allen and Mitchell
B.P. 20484
Abidjan, Ivory Coast
Te. 32-67-66
Telex. 2435

Information about insurance—U.S. insurance companies

AFIA, St. Paul Fire and Marine Insurance Co.
Imm. SMGL
2nd Floor
11 Ave. Barthe
B.P. 20,457
Abidjan, Ivory Coast
Tel. 32-47-11
Telex. 2440

American International Assurance Co.
Nour Al Hayat
10th Floor
B.P. 8873
Abidjan, Ivory Coast
Tel. 22-66-31, 22-31-91
Telex. 2391

American Life Insurance Co.
Imm. Nour Al Hayat
10eme etage, Av. Chardy
B.P. 8873
Abidjan, Ivory Coast
Tel. 32-30-91

U.S. airlines and steamship lines

Pan American World Airways
Room M-26, Hotel Ivoire
B.P. 8392
Abidjan, Ivory Coast
Tel. 34-91-32
Telex: 780

Delta Lines
c/o Ste. TRANSAFRIC
Zone des Entrepots Portuaires
B.P. 21,172
Abidjan, Ivory Coast
Tel. 32-31-80
Telex: 3670

Farrell Lines
c/o UMARCO
Rond-Point du Nouveau Port
B.P. 1559
Abidjan, Ivory Coast
Tel. 22-24-61
Telex. UMARCO 309

U.S. Banks

Bank of America, NTSA
c/o Banque Internationale pour le Commerce et l'Industrie en Cote d'Ivoire (BICICI)

Av. Franchet d'Esperey
B.P. 1298
Abidjan, Ivory Coast
Tel. 32-03-79
Telex. 651
Citibank, N.A.
Imm. AMCI
B.P. 20,788
Abidjan, Ivory Coast
Tel. 32-46-10
Telex: 2121
Chase Manhattan Overseas Corp.
B.P. 20408
Abidjan, Ivory Coast
Tel. 32-68-17
Telex: 2435
Chemical Bank
Imm. Alpha 2000, 15eme etage
B.P. 1872
Abidjan, Ivory Coast
Tel. 32-73-50
Fidelity Bank
Alpha 2000
B.P. V245
Abidjan, Ivory Coast

Ivorian Banks

Bank of Credit and Commerce International (Overseas) Ltd.
B.P. 1279
Abidjan, Ivory Coast
Banque Internationale pour l'Afrique Occidentale (BIAO)
10 Av. Barthe
B.P. 1274
Abidjan, Ivory Coast
Tel. 22-27-71/6
Telex: 641
Banque International pour le Commerce et l'Industrie en Cote d'Ivoire (BICICI)
16 Ave. Franchet d'Esperey
B.P. 1298
Abidjan, Ivory Coast
Tel. 32-93-79, 32-08-79
Banque Real De Cote d'Ivoire
22 Blvd. Clouzel

B.P. 4411
Abidjan, Ivory Coast
Tel: 32-27-82
Ste. Generale de Banques En Cote d'Ivoire (SGBCI)
5 Av. Barthe
B.P. 1355
Abidjan, Ivory Coast
Tel. 32-03-33
Telex: 776 and 437
Ste. Ivoirienne de Banque (SIB)
16 Av. Barthe
B.P. 1300
Abidjan, Ivory Coast
Tel. 32-00-00
Telex: 751 and 406

Ivorian National Development Banks

Banque Ivoirienne De Developpement Industriel (BIDI)
B.P. 4470
Abidjan, Ivory Coast
Tel. 32-01-11
Telex: 484
Banque Nationale Pour Le Developpement Agricole (BNDA)
B.P. 2508
Abidjan, Ivory Coast
Tel. 22-52-37
Telex. 2298
Banque Nationale Pour L'Epargne Et Le Credit (BNEC)
B.P. 9256
Abidjan, Ivory Coast
Tle. 32-20-31
Telex. 2285
Le Credit de la Cote d'Ivoire (CCI)
B.P. 1720
Abidjan, Ivory Coast
Tel. 32-19-13
Ste. Nationale de Financement (SONAFI)
B.P. 1591
Abidjan, Ivory Coast
Tel. 32-05-45
Telex: 508

Market Profile— IVORY COAST

Foreign Trade

Imports.—$2,404 million in 1981; $2,093 million in 1982. Major 1981 suppliers: France, 33 percent; United States, 7 percent; Venezuela, 5.7 percent and Japan, 5.1 percent. Principal imports: rice and wheat, capital equipment, semifinished metals, transportation and construction equipment, paper products, textiles, crude petroleum, and chemicals. Imports from United States: aircraft, tractors, small ships, mechanical handling equipment, and construction equipment (total $95.6 million in 1982).

Exports.—$2,536 million in 1981; $2,441 million in 1982. Major markets in 1980: France, 21.7 percent; Netherlands, 15.1 percent; United States, 8.4 percent; and Italy, 10.2 percent. Principal exports: coffee, lumber, cocoa, pineapples, and bananas. Exports to United States: coffee, cocoa, and lumber (total $303 million in 1982).

Trade Policy.—Grants preference to members of West African Customs Union; member of the Conseil de l'Entente and Economic Community of West African States. Seeks to diversity trade and investment. Has ended trade preference for imports from European Economic Community.

Trade Prospects.—U.S. exports decreased significantly during 1982 to $96 million level. Textile machinery, agricultural machinery, roadbuilding equipment and materials, food processing, transport vehicles, and energy systems equipment are best opportunities.

Foreign Investment

Substantial foreign investment, mainly French; U.S. investments totaled approximatly $160 million in 1981; petroleum exploration, refining and distribution, banks, manufacturing, and service industries. Close to 100 U.S. firms maintain offices in Abidjan.

Investment Prospects.—Government seeks foreign investments; liberal investment code. Investment opportunities in agribusiness, tourism, and light industry.

Finance

Currency.—Communate Financiere Africaine (C.F.A.) franc (399 CFA=US$1); floating with French franc, issued by seven-nation Central Bank of West African States.

Domestic Credit and Investment.—Commercial and industrial credit available. Discount rate of 12.5 percent applied in 1982.

National Budget.—1982 administrative budget $1.3 billion; development budget set at ca. $900 million. Major emphasis on education, public works, health, and agricultural development.

Balance of Payments.—Negative trade balance of $1.16 billion in 1982 up sharply from $470 million in 1979. Disbursed foreign debt is estimated at approximately $6 billion in 1982.

Foreign Aid.—United States assists through loans and guarantees of Eximbank, and OPIC programs. Development assistance also granted by international organizations, including African Development Bank/Fund with headquarters in Abidjan.

Economy

A major world exporter of coffee, cocoa, and tropical wood.

Increasing industrialization and agricultural diversification sought. Due to world recession, tourism sector contracting from a high of 200,000 visitors in 1978, 150,000 in 1980.

GDP.—Real annual GDP growth rate of 7 percent in the 1970's followed by virtual stagnation in 1981 and 1982.

Agriculture.—Traditionally strong in coffee, cocoa, and timber. Diversification into palm oil, bananas, pineapples, cotton, sugar, and rubber.

Industry.—705 firms manufacturing as of 1980. Industrial sector turnover of $2.75 billion in 1979. Number of workers in industry put at 67,443 in mid-1979. Cumulative capital investment placed at $2.5 billion.

Commerce.—Cost of living rising about 10-15 percent per annum. Government promotes greater Ivorian participation in business. Stock exchange in Abidjan. Private sector significant by African standards.

Development Plan.—New Five-Year Plan published in 1981 and revised substantially in 1982.

Basic Economic Facilities

Transportation.—Transport system generally adequate, relying heavily on extensive road network linking all parts of country. Future emphasis on maintenance and improvement of feeder road network. Railroad runs 500 miles through Ivory Coast linking the port of Abidjan with Ouagadougou, Upper Volta.

Communications.—Adequate telephone service from Abidjan to interior cities and overseas. National radio and television networks.

Power.—Soubre dam construction expected to begin in 1984.

Natural Resources

Land.—125,000 square miles; slightly larger than New Mexico.

Climate.—Tropical. Temperature stays between 70 and 90 degrees fahrenheit with humidity averaging 84 percent. Two rainy seasons, March-July and September-November.

Minerals.—Iron ore reserves of 350 million tons may be developed during 1980's. Some diamonds are exported. Other mineral potential in nickel, gold, and oil. Petroleum discovered late in 1977 and production began in 1980. A second more significant, field which was discovered in 1980, began production in mid-1982. Total oil production is estimated at 30,000 barrel per day in 1982, the self-sufficiency level.

Forestry.—The leading African exporter of tropical logs and lumber. Several expansion projects underway. Depletion of prime species currently depressing tropical hardwoods exports.

Population

Size.—8.8 million in 1982; rate of growth 3.5 percent; urbanization 40 percent. Capital city, Abidjan, 1.2 million; interior commercial center, Bouake, 250,000.

Language.—French is official and commercial language. Knowledge of English is limited.

Education.—Primary school enrollment, 46 percent.

Labor.—375,000 wage earners; 40 percent in agriculture.

Marketing in Japan

Contents

Report Revised June 1980

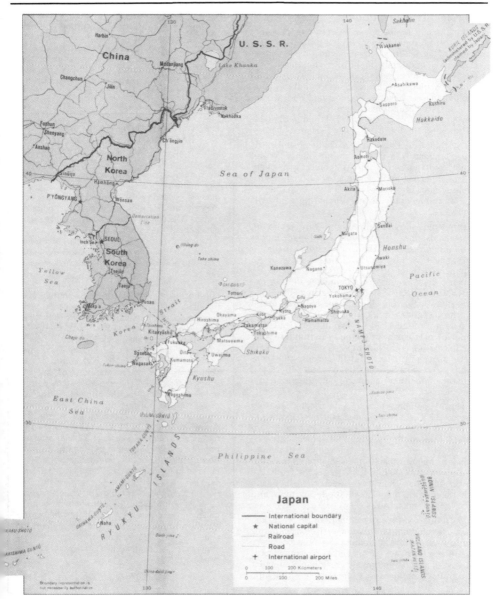

Japan

International boundary
★ National capital
Railroad
Road
+ International airport

0   100   200 Kilometers
0   100   200 Miles

Foreign Trade Outlook

Japan, our largest overseas trading partner, offers outstanding opportunities for U.S. exports of agricultural commodities, basic industrial raw materials including chemicals and forestry products, advanced technology products and high quality consumer merchandise. Thus the Japanese market remains sound and attractive despite recent emergence from a severe recession, threat of a new round of double digit inflation, and the unsolved energy crisis.

Our bilateral trade deficit challenges American manufacturers to increase productivity and American traders to compete more aggressively in the Japanese market. Japan must also insure greater market access for U.S. goods and services by reducing tariffs and elminating non-tariff barriers.

Important activities directed toward achieving these goals since 1978 include: The Japan Import Promotion Mission to the United States in March 1978; the U.S. Export Development Missions to Japan in October 1978; the efforts of the U.S.-Japan Trade Facilitation Committee (TFC); the USDOC-JETRO[1] Seminar Program; Boatique America—a floating department store mounted on the Japanese exhibition ship Shin Sakura Maru; and four trade missions of Boatique America participants designed to stimulate long term trading relationships. These programs were especially successful in encouraging continuing relations between buyers and sellers and greater understanding among both Japanese and Americans.

The 91 members of the Japan Import Mission visited 17 U.S. cities and 2,000 businesses between March 2-18, 1978. The resulting sales contracts totaled $1.94 billion of which approximately $646 million were achieved as a direct result of the Mission. Japanese buyers concentrated on purchasing U.S. products from the power industry, machinery sector, fashion and leisure goods, processed foods, wines, and spirits, and housewares.

In October 1978, 137 members of the U.S. Export Development Missions visited the major marketing centers of Japan. The Missions were organized into seven specialized groups: Advanced scientific equipment; original equipment automotive components; food processing and

[1] U.S. Department of Commerce—Japan External Trade Organization

packaging equipment; general industrial machinery; modern management equipment; investment in America; and a spokespersons team. The primary goals were achieved with American sellers realizing that Japan provides a highly profitable market, and Japanese buyers realizing that U.S. companies are committed to a permanent presence in the local market.

HOW TO OBTAIN BACKGROUND INFORMATION ABOUT THESE COUNTRIES

Keeping this book within reasonable size limits has made it necessary to focus on material *directly* concerned with marketing and commerce, and set aside materials only indirectly related. The editors relize, however, that *general* data about a country are also vital to a company's preparations to enter a foreign market, and make a very definite recommendation as to how such expanded information needs can be served.

For those who wish *general* data about a country—data which goes beyond marketing and commerce—the editors recommend *Countries of the World and Their Leaders*, published as an annually updated yearbook by Gale Research Company, Detroit, Michigan 48226. Containing 4- to 20-page entries on 168 countries, the volume also provides several hundred pages of supplementary world data. Each country entry is prepared by the U.S. Department of State to provide a general briefing on the geography, people, culture, and political situation of the particular country. Each report provides some historical insight as well as a look at contemporary trends of lifestyle in the country. Reports also discuss a country's educational system, its press, ethnic groupings and religious practices.

Countries of the World and Their Leaders provides a fresh listing of cabinet ministers of each nation. In addition it lists health conditions the traveling businessman will wish to prepare for and includes information on passport procedures, customs and duties, and world climate conditions.

The TFC was established in September 1977 by the Secretary of Commerce and Japan's Minister of International Trade and Industry (MITI). It is meeting regularly to encourage increased Japanese imports of American manufactures and commodities. A principal function of the TFC is to help U.S. exporters resolve problems involving Japanese Government import restrictive regulations or actions which impede the free flow of U.S. goods to Japan. Through January 1, 1980 the Department of Commerce received 89 cases for its review, 21 of which have been forwarded to the TFC. Fifteen of these have been favorably resolved.

During 1977–1979 joint-USDOC/JETRO Seminars were held in 35 American cities. This program focused on "How To Do Business In Japan" and included presentations by Japanese government and business officials, American businesspersons with experience in the Japanese marketplace, and the Commerce Department's own country experts. Over 2,000 businesspersons have attended these seminars.

Boatique America offered U.S. products directly to consumers on a tour of 13 major Japanese ports from October 12 to December 9, 1979. Over 140 American manufacturers presented 10,000 different items with a total retail value of $13 million. Major product categories included apparel and accessories, housewares and home furnishings, sporting and recreation products and American beef. Average per capita sales amounted to $16 for 475,000 visitors.

Trade Opportunities

While market conditions for high technology and quality consumer goods generally remain good, a sophisticated market such as Japan requires careful study before making any substantial commitments. Computers and peripheral equipment, electronic components and other equipment used in the electronic field, analytical and control instruments, laser and laser systems, food processing and packaging, and biomedical equipment, are among the most saleable items.

Goods with lesser sales opportunities include such products as metal working equipment, materials handling equipment, building systems and materials, automotive products, industrial process control instrumentation and business equipment.

Japan continues to buy a wide range of agricultural products and the United States remains an important and dependable supplier. In 1978, U.S. agricultural shipments to Japan were valued at $4.4 billion, representing an increase of 15 percent over the previous year. For the first 9 months of 1979, by contrast, exports of these commodities totaled $3.7 billion for a gain of 20 percent over the same period of 1978. Japan's principal imports in 1977 and 1978 are shown in table 1. U.S. exports to Japan, which benefited earlier from the strong Japanese demand, favorable exchange realignments, rising affluence, and growing shortages of industrial and consumer products, competed in an economy substantially recovered in 1979.

Over the first 9 months of 1979, Japan's imports (c.i.f.) from the United States accounted for an estimated 19 percent of Japan's total imports and were valued at $14.8 billion. Japan's expanded import efforts have been successful, even with Japan's rising crude oil costs which still account for almost 30 percent of the total import bill. For example, during January-September 1979, Japan's imports (c.i.f.) of oil increased 25 percent over the same period in 1978, and cost $21.6 billion compared with an overall import increase of 33 percent while Japan's imports from the United States rose an impressive 36.7 percent to equal the $14.8 billion previously mentioned.[2]

Industry Trends

Gross National Product

Japan's Gross National Product (GNP) registered a real growth of 5.5 percent in FY78 (April 1, 1978–March 31, 1979) with a first quarter advance of 1 percent, a second quarter growth of 0.9 percent, a third quarter increase of 1.8 percent and a fourth quarter gain of 1.8 percent. Due mainly to the phenomenal expansion of exports the growth rate was 5.9 percent in FY76 and 5.6 percent in FY77. Significantly, growth in FY78 did not derive primarily from exports but rather from the expansion of domestic demand which increased about 8.1 percent. Important factors contributing to this growth were a 5.5 percent increase in individual expenditures which usually account for more than 50 percent of growth in GNP; and 11.7 percent advance in industrial capital expenditures and a 5.8 percent expansion in government expenditures. These positive developments were offset by a 2.1 percent decline in exports and a 14 percent rise in imports, the net effect of which constituted a probable 2 percent reduction in GNP.

The Japanese Government recently reaffirmed its projection of a real growth rate of 6.3 percent

---

[2] Change is in aggregates denominated in yen not dollars.

Table 1.—Japan's Principal Imports 1977 and 1978 *

(in millions of U.S. dollars)

	1977 From World	1977 From U.S.	1977 U.S. Share	1978 From World	1978 From U.S.	1978 U.S. Share
Beef	136	21	16	220	47	21
Pork	330	73	22	407	100	25
Wheat	744	431	58	831	481	58
Corn (Maize)	1,070	883	83	1,231	993	81
Grain Sorghums	585	279	48	574	265	46
Sugar	721	—	insig	588	—	insig
Soybeans	1,099	1,042	95	1,134	1,096	97
Cattle Hides and Skins	292	229	78	368	282	77
Wool	550	—	—	556	—	insig
Cotton, Raw	1,148	354	31	1,061	372	35
Iron Ore	2,223	—	—	2,004	—	—
Iron and Steel Scrap	136	81	60	334	266	80
Nonferrous Metal Ores	571	46	8	477	61	13
Copper Ore	891	3	insig	945	5	insig
Bauxite	97	—	insig	96	—	insig
Zinc Ores and Concentrates	188	1	insig	125	—	—
Rubber, Natural	227	—	—	344	—	—
Logs and Lumber (Selected List)	3,816	1,250	33	4,117	1,362	33
Coal, Coking	3,177	947	30	2,764	550	20
Oil, Crude	22,579	—	—	22,909	—	—
Petroleum Products	1,423	13	insig	1,544	20	insig
Fuel Oil	1,782	—	insig	1,505	15	insig
Liquified Petroleum Gas	1	—	—	21	—	—
Chemicals	1,434	563	39	1,814	721	40
Machinery and Equipment	3,256	1,630	50	3,808	1,935	51
Aircraft	140	138	99	307	300	98
Aircraft Engines	89	78	88	63	58	92
Automobiles, Passenger	287	100	35	990	413	42
Computers	17	4	23	16	4	22
Computer Parts	137	76	56	138	85	62
Pumps & Centrifuges	51	29	56	67	36	53
Metalworking Machinery	86	21	25	121	42	34
Telecommunications Equipment	16	8	52	18	9	51
Electrical Measuring & Controlling Instruments	205	147	72	264	193	73
Scientific and Optical Instruments	288	129	45	365	172	47
Paper Products	183	82	45	246	110	45
Iron and Steel Products	474	132	28	835	345	41
Total of Above	50,449	8,790		53,207	10,338	
Total Imports	71,122	12,480		79,655	14,803	

*Source: Japan Exports and Imports, Ministry of Finance, Published by the Japan Tariff Association. IMF Exchange Rates 1977, Y269=US$1.00; Y210=US$1.00.

of FY79. Japan's real growth in the first quarter of FY79 was 2.3 percent (6.1 percent annual). Industrial production is expected to advance 7 percent. While wholesale prices are projected to rise almost 10 percent, the inflation rate for consumer goods will be held under 5 percent. Unemployment should remain at about 2 percent. The trade balance will approach equilibrium with a current account deficit of approximately $5 billion at the close of the third quarter of FY79. Exports and imports will total $105–$110 billion respectively for FY79 compared with an original government projection of $103.5 billion for exports and $94 billion for imports. These economic conditions are reflected against a background of rising inflation, unresolved energy problems, a weakening of growth prospects abroad, and mounting concern over the government's deficit financing.

Investment and Growth

The projected growth of industrial capital investment by large Japanese corporations for FY1979 is estimated at $41 billion for a 13 percent increase over FY 1978. Investments by manufacturing firms are expected to advance approximately 20 percent which is the first year-over-year gain in 5 years. Investments in the non-manufacturing sector are expected to grow about 10 percent which represents the fourth consecutive year to year gain.

Specific industries anticipating substantial investment increases over FY78 include the automobile industry up 35.3 percent, textiles, up 28.2 percent, chemicals and steel up 12.4 percent. However, electric power firms will only advance 7.1 percent which is a sharp decline from the 32.2 percent growth in FY78.

This expansion of private sector investment for FY79 is a persuasive indicator of strong economic recovery in Japan, particularly when compared with equipment investment growth rates in recent years. For instance, investment in all industries declined by 8.2 percent in 1975, rose

2.3 percent in 1976, increased 3.5 percent in 1977 but only advanced 0.8 percent in 1978. Several conditions encourage industry to expand investment in plant and equipment. Many manufacturers recognize the need to replace obsolescent equipment and to streamline operations with the introduction of new labor-saving equipment. Further a general sense pervades industry that now is the time to develop new product lines, new technology, and new areas of business. This expansion of domestic demand is displacing exports and public works spending as the primary source of sustained economic growth. However, the threat of a continuing energy crisis and a return to double digit inflation generate uncertainty which may contribute to a decline in investment. Nevertheless, Japan's major industrial managers project the expansion of plant and equipment investment to range between increases of 8.5 to 10 percent on an annual basis for the next several years.

One of Japan's major concerns is the threat of a new round of double digit inflation. The wholesale price index rose 5 percent in 1976 over 1975, but only 1.9 percent in 1977 over 1976, and actually declined 2.5 percent in 1978 from 1977. However in the first 10 months of 1979 the wholesale price index averaged 5.6 percent higher than the annual index for 1977. The consumer price index has advanced steadily since 1973. For the January–October 1979 period the consumer price index averaged 4 percent over the index for all of 1978.

Government Expenditures and Controls

The Government approved a budget of $194.4 billion (Y219=US$1.00) for FY80 (April 1980–March 1981). This expenditure represents a 10.3 percent increase over FY79 but remains the lowest annual expansion in over 20 years. The shift toward austerity originally signaled in the FY79 budget will continue in FY80.

The new budget maintains a sharp contrast with the FY78 budget which was 20.3 percent over FY77 and specifically designed to reflate the economy through spending on large public works projects intended to stimulate industrial activity and expand domestic demand.

The trend toward austerity derives from diminishing revenues and concern with an increasingly proximate threat of double digit inflation. Over the last decade financing government expenditures through national bond issues has risen from 4.2 percent to almost 40 percent in FY79. The total debt, including national bonds, local government bonds, and other debt guarantees outstanding is currently about 30 percent of Japan's gross national product.

The Government is committed to a radical reduction in dependence on deficit financing. Tax revisions have been designed to raise an additional $1.6 billion during FY80. Tax, stamp, and miscellaneous revenues are expected to rise over 21 percent from FY79 budget estimates. An attempt to increase revenues through imposition of a general consumption tax failed because of political and popular opposition. With this newly proposed tax eliminated as a viable option to deficit financing, the Government plans to issue $4.6 billion less in national bonds in FY80 and to reduce the ratio of bonds to budget to 33.5 percent from the current level of 39.6 percent with consequent reductions in domestic welfare programs. By 1983, if this plan succeeds, government bond issues will be used exclusively to support public works projects with no bonds funding current expenses.

The Fiscal Loan Investment Program (FLIP) for FY80 totals $83 billion and represents an 8 precent advance over FY79. Allocations under the FY80 general account operating budget in billions of U.S. dollars include social security at $37.5, 19.3 percent of the budget, up 7.7 percent over FY79; education $20.7, 10.6 percent, up 5.2 percent; servicing the national debt $24.2, 12.5 percent, up 30.2 percent; pensions and other payments $7.5, 3.9 percent, up 9.3 percent; local finance $33.7, 17.3 percent, up 23.3 percent; national defense $10.2, 5.2 percent, up 6.5 percent; public works $30.4, 15.6 percent, up 1.7 percent; economic cooperation $1.7, 0.9 percent, up 17.5 percent; other $26.9, 13.8 percent, up 5.4 percent; reserves $1.6, 0.8 percent, no change from prior fiscal year.

The Japan Tobacco and Salt Public Corporation controls the importation and sale of tobacco and salt. Other State-traded commodities are industrial alcohol, dairy products, and grains. The importation, distribution, and sale of rice, wheat, barley, and various dairy products are administered by the Food Agency of the Ministry of Agriculture and Forestry. While the importation of these products is administered by the public corporations, the actual import transactions are delegated to specified trading companies and, to the extent government-traded commodities are of prime importance to the well-being of the nation, control is maintained through issuance of import allocation certificates and licenses.

Economic Planning

The Japanese Government publishes both short-and long-term plans for industrial development, social welfare, labor relations, and related major sectors. Japanese Government planning, however, bears little resemblance to government planning by most other nations. Plans, as announced, represent the consensus of not only government but also of the private sector concerned and academia. The latter two sectors carry considerable weight in policy determination. Thus, plans as such are not forced onto the private sector whether investments, imports, industry trends and direction, or similar major decisions. The private sector has full knowledge through its considerable input to any government planning. In the Japanese connotation, planning or plans represent goals which the government would like to see achieved. It is not dictated fiat but a goal toward which the government and private industry will strive.

To achieve its goal, especially to keep inflation under control and to aid imports from developing nations, Japan grants preferential duties to most imports from these nations. Additionally, this action helps to maintain their bilateral balance of trade with Japan within more manageable limits.

For the intermediate term, Japan's Economic Planning Agency has designed a new Seven Year Plan (1979–1985) to restructure and redirect the Japanese economy. The plan concentrates on correcting the imbalance among various sectors of the economy, restructuring the industrial organization, and improving the quality of life in Japan by creating a welfare society, If implemented, the plan will generate steady growth at a reduced rate through the continued expansion of domestic demand and the curtailment of production for export markets. There will be a correspondent shift from an economy based primarily on heavy industry to one based on more high technology, knowledge, service and information industries. The success of the program will finally depend on the Government's ability to control inflation, the availability of funds, and the resolution of Japan's energy needs. The formulation of this plan indicates fundamental attitudinal changes and a continuing commitment to realize full economic recovery with a smooth transition to a new economic and social order.

Economic planners from the government, private, and academic sectors have formed a consensus in identifying the major problems which confront Japan through the intermediate term.

Agreement focused on the necessity to correct imbalances among various sectors of the economy, to reduce petroleum dependance, and to improve the quality of life in Japan. The following specific goals have been established to resolve these problems by 1985:

Projected annual real growth averaging 5.7 percent over the next seven years (FY79–FY85) would be maintained by expanding domestic demand rather than basic reliance on expanded exports.

The unemployment rate will be reduced to less than 1.7 percent.

Consumer prices will be stabilized at the current 5 percent level.

Trade and current account balances will be restored to equilibrium and maintained.

Official development assistance is projected to increase 100 percent over FY77 within 3 years.

Fiscal reform will be achieved by reducing bond issues and increasing tax rates. The Government suspended plans to establish a 5 percent general consumption tax due to the universal negative public reaction.

Conservation and development of alternate sources of energy remain concerns of the highest priority.

Stable sources of supply for food and raw materials will be secured with a correspondent movement toward greater self-sufficiency in foodstuffs.

Efforts to increase environmental protection and improvement will be strengthened.

Larger government and private sector allocations will be made to support expanded research and development programs.

Finally, investment in social overhead capital projects will be accelerated to improve the quality of life in Japan.

Success in achieving this program depends fundamentally on the expansion of domestic demand. The prospects for Japan attaining these goals appear highly probable if external conditions remain relatively stable.

Research Promotion

Japan's total research and development (R&D) expenditure for Japan FY77 rose 9.9 percent (3.6 percent in real terms) from FY76 to $12.6 billion. The ratio of this amount to national income was 2.1 percent which compares unfavorably with 2.5 percent for the United States and 2.6 for West Germany. The Prime Minister's Council for Science and Technology has repeatedly called on the Government to take necessary measures for raising Japan's R & D spending/national income ration to 2.5 percent and eventually to 3 percent.

For all industries basic research accounted for 5 percent of R & D allocations, applied research 20 percent, and development 75 percent. In comparison with FY76, expenditures for information processing remained constant, space activities declined by 13 percent, and environmental protection was down 24 percent.

Outlays for marine science and engineering increased 5 percent, petroleum and coal products advanced 50 percent, precision machinery grew 32 percent, rubber products were up 30 percent and publishing and printing also gained 30 percent.

The growth rate for researchers, research assistants, and technicians had declined since FY75. As of April, 1978, the number of researchers totaled 273,102, an increase of only 0.4 percent over the previous year. The total number of persons engaged in scientific research is estimated to be approximately half that of the United States.

Private industry accounted for 65.2 percent of the nation's total R & D expenditure for FY77, with universities and research institutes accounting for 19.5 percent and 15.3 percent respectively. While private industry's share of the total R & D expenditure for Japan has always been high, its spending has grown at a low rate since 1974. Further, private industry has tended to spend much less on basic and applied research and correspondingly more on development. The share of corporate R & D expenditure for basic and applied research declined from 38.6 percent in 1967 to 30.8 percent in 1972 to 23.9 percent in 1977.

The Japanese Government set aside about $1.4 billion for the promotion of science and technology, exclusive of university research, in its general account budget for FY 1979. This sum represents an increase of about 13 percent over the allocation for FY78.

Wholesaling

Wholesale trade, which was valued at $1,484.5 billion in 1978, increased by 12 percent over the previous year compared with an increase of about 9 percent between 1976 and 1977. In 1978,

sales of food and beverages rose nearly 8 percent to $116.3 billion while sales of apparel and accessories increased by almost 15 percent for a total value of $57.1 billion. Building materials showed a rise from $57.9 billion to $80.9 billion, machinery and equipment by over 14 percent to $280.9 billion, and chemicals by almost 10 percent for a value of $48.7 billion.

Retailing

Retail sales of $276 billion grew 11 percent in 1978, compared with a 9 percent increase in 1977. During 1978, the sale of fabrics and accessories increased by $4.1 billion to a value of $30.3 billion, while sales of food and beverages remained constant. General merchandise registered a gain of 12 percent between 1978 and 1977, with sales value at $49.1 billion.

Distribution and Sales Channels

Although a variety of importing methods exists side by side in Japan, overshadowing all others is the pervasive influence of the Japanese trading company. Direct sales contacts between Japanese end-users and foreign producers are not common. Most prefer to deal through intermediaries.

In many cases, the average small Japanese manufacturer has neither the financial resources, the technical competence to import products, nor the ability to communicate in a foreign language. The help he needs is available through the nearly 6,000 "trading firms." These firms run the gamut from large, diversified, multifunction organizations often closely linked to large manufacturing companies and banks to small, specialized importers that operate in narrow commodity areas.

Trading firms may be divided into three groups: (1) general trading companies, (2) specialized trading companies, and (3) maker or retailer "captive" trading companies. The general trading companies, including the 10 to 14 largest trading firms, each handle between 7,000 to 10,000 different items and provide a wide variety of services ranging from all phases of importing to financing, warehousing, transporting, wholesaling, and servicing.

Japan's general trading firms are represented abroad in almost all the world's major cities. Reliance on a general trading company may often by warranted, but in some instances there may be a disadvantage. The decision to tie up with a general trading company should be based on a careful investigation of the Japanese distribution channel for the product involved.

If the product is other than a bulk commodity or raw material, then a smaller, more specialized trading company may offer the best prospect for a successful sales effort in Japan. It limits itself to a narrow range of products and handles most phases of the product's journey through customs to the end-user. Sophisticated industrial items such as electronic instruments are often handled by specialized trading companies.

Maker or "captive" trading companies import, export, and sell for particular manufacturing companies. They are of use to those firms primarily interested in exporting to the parent manufacturing company and in certain instances may be the only route open to that company.

An alternative possibility is the establishment in Japan of a facility to import, warehouse, market, and service one's own product. The Japanese Government permits the establishment of wholly foreign-owned subsidiaries for this purpose, provided that the products involved are not petroleum, leather and leather products, or primary products.

Distribution Practices of U.S. Firms

The Japanese distribution system is complicated and very fragmented. Up to this point, many American exporters have been content to leave the importation and distribution of their products to trading companies. Where industrial products of considerable sophistication are involved, the trading company is likely to be one of the smaller, specialized trading firms having the technical competence to install and service the product as well as sell it through its developed distribution network. Occasionally, rather than using a trading company for distribution, an American firm may appoint a Japanese manufacturer of complementary equipment as its agent to take advantage of the natural compatibility of the American firm's products with the Japanese firm's own lines and to use the Japanese firm's distribution network.

Because of their unfamiliarity with the Japanese market and the language, most Americans have not attempted to undertake direct sales operations without the assistance of an independent Japanese representative. However, direct sales operations at the wholesale level— and at the retail level when permitted by the government—through subsidiaries or branches may be quite feasible, assuming the U.S. seller is able to hire competent Japanese to assist in making the sales presentation.

Distribution Channels

Distribution channels in Japan vary considerably from industry to industry and from product to product. Historically, the most common wholesaling setup in Japan consisted of three or more layers.

Urban retail stores in the traditional setting tended to be either very small neighborhood outlets handling a limited line of goods or large department stores. The neighborhood store, usually a family operation of very small physical dimensions and sales volume, serviced a limited clientele. Typically, these stores tended to specialize in one, or at most a few, product lines and were clustered on shopping streets near residential areas.

There are today approximately 1.4 million retail outlets in Japan—one retail store for every 80 persons. Nearly 90 percent of these stores have fewer than four employees and one half have a floor space of less than 200 square feet. The largest retailers, those having 100 employees or more (1.3 percent of the total), account for 21 percent of total retail sales. It is easily seen that the vast majority of the small stores are marginal.

Recently, Japan has experienced a new phenomenon, the growth of self-service or superstores patterned after the American-style supermarket but, on an average, much smaller. Self-service stores now number over 10,600 outlets. The biggest chain of superstores, Daiei and Seiyu, have over 100 stores and pose a significant challenge to the dominant position in retail sales long held by department stores. At present, self-service stores account for about 10 percent of total retail sales in Japan as compared to the department stores' 14 percent. The superstores have followed the formula of centralized buying, self-service, and limited selections of goods and have been able to undersell the small retailers and department stores by from 10 percent to 20 percent on most items. The use of tertiary wholesalers has been almost totally eliminated by superstores and the role of secondary wholesalers has been reduced. The self-service stores now buy certain products, such as clothing and household appliances, directly from manufacturers.

Self-service stores have in some instances purchased directly from foreign suppliers. However, the trading companies are strongly entrenched in the import sector and have begun to expand beyond wholesaling to retailing through tie-up with self-service store chains.

Superstores and the large trading companies, initially at odds because of the superstores' fear of domination by the trading firms, seem now to have reached an accommodation. The superstores realize that to achieve their ambitious expansion objectives they need capital for expansion, deferred payments for merchandise, and overseas sources of inexpensive goods. The 10 largest trading companies supply roughly 10–12 percent of the trade credit outstanding to suppliers and purchasers in Japan. The trading companies are, in effect, banking intermediaries and serve as borrowers of record, thereby decreasing the lending risk for the banks.

Department stores in Japan are similar to those found in Western countries and have an important place in retailing in Japan's major cities. The average big city department store carries approximately 500,000 items, all in very small supply, and makes 80 to 90 percent of its purchases from as many as 1,500 wholesalers, many of which supply goods on consignment and must accept return of those items that do not sell. Even in the multistore operations, centralized buying is the exception rather than the rule. Some stores, however, are now establishing central purchasing offices to rationalize buying for all stores, including both parents and affiliates.

It is readily apparent to Japanese and foreigners alike that a less cumbersome wholesale and retail system would eliminate great numbers of medium- and small-sized wholesalers and increase the size of retail operations. Clearly discernible trends indicate this is happening. The numbers of wholesalers involved in the distribution chains of many commodities are decreasing and the triple-layered wholesale system is tending to decrease in importance.

Wholesalers to larger retailers have found it necessary to expand through growth or merger and to modernize their operations by introducing labor-saving equipment. They also are helping to organize their small retailer customers into larger units, which are called "voluntary chains," for the purpose of joint purchasing. Such trends will in the long run increase the efficiency of the wholesale system

It should be noted, however, that the neighborhood retail store is exhibiting unusual staying power in resisting these trends toward consolidation. Several factors account for this tenacity: (1) the strongly ingrained Japanese habit of shopping in the immediate neighborhood; (2) the heavy traffic which discourages automobile trips out of the neighborhood; (3) the high price of land which prevents the spread of self-service or department stores to urban sites; (4) the advantage of Japanese income tax laws which permit the small shop owner to deduct his family member's salaries as business expenses; (5) the necessity of most homeowners to shop daily for their perishables because of the small-size refrigerators in use in Japan; and (6) the assessment of land taxes based on actual use, not potential value.

Mention also should be made of the distribution of imported processed food. These imports are relatively small, but are expected to increase in the future. However, sales will be limited if distribution is made through specialty and department stores as in the past. Foreign food processors and their agents have often opted for ease of distribution through department stores and supermarkets and have missed the mass market serviced by the neighborhood stores.

In some industrial areas, Japan has a number of small end-users of capital goods who function as subcontractors for larger manufacturers. Such small- and medium-sized firms (firms employing from 1 to 299 persons) account for 99.4 percent of the number of enterprises involved in light and heavy industry, employ 70 percent of the persons involved in manufacturing and produce 50 percent of total output in the light and heavy industrial sectors. Thus, it is clear that Japan's industry is far from monolithic and that the problem of distribution is not simply one of selling to the largest firms and ignoring the small outlying factories. To sell to this type of end-user, it is often necessary to follow a multilayered wholesale distribution system similar in many respects to those in the consumer goods field.

Each exporter must investigate his own market and should attempt to find out (1) where his product or similar products are sold and in what quantities; (2) whether his product is sold through neighborhood stores, self-service stores, or department stores and in what proportion for each type of outlet; (3) which wholesalers have access to the largest portion of the retail sector and what methods other producers use in motivating these wholesalers; and (4) whether the product is suitable for the Japanese taste, and the extent to which it should be modified.

In most cases, the American exporter should attempt to obtain a degree of control over distribution. This might be accomplished through supplying a large portion of the sales items in a particular type of store. Perhaps groups of companies operating together could accomplish this through sales made directly to an exclusive retail outlet. If this approach is impossible or inappropriate, the exporter might tie up with a major trading company, wholesaler, or retail chain in order to take advantage of the prestige and influence of these established firms. At a minimum, an exporter should maintain close personal contact with his agent, trading company, or wholesaler, through frequent visits to Japan. Leaving an agent to his own devises is not practical. He must have support via promotional materials, training, and other incentives.

For business on a continuing basis, a branch operation can be set up which, for legal purposes, will be treated as any Japanese company.

Establishing an office brings with it the problems of management, office rents, staffing, housing, expense account, and the recruiting and training of a sales force. While very expensive, it may pay off if the market warrants and cannot be reached effectively through an established channel.

The social aspects of doing business apply equally to relationships with an agent or distributor. An advantage of frequent trips to Japan is that the American exporter's presence is tangible evidence of his interest in the Japanese agent's efforts. A foreign company's conduct is carefully watched in Japan. An insensitive handling of an agent, such as an abrupt dismassal may be considered "bad form" and seriously damage the foreign company's reputation. This is not to say changes in representation cannot be made, but only that such changes are delicate matters and care must be exercised so that all parties fully understand the reasons compelling the change.

Licensing

Many American businessmen seeking to develop trade, licensing, and other investment activities in Japan are vitally concerned about the protection available there for patents, trademarks, designs, and other industrial property rights. Protection of copyrights in that country is also important to their business interests. Failure to secure protection for such rights under pertinent Japanese laws, and under convention procedures, can result in the loss of marketing and licensing opportunities. This section provides general information on protection available in the country for such rights, including Japanese activity relative to licensing transactions.

Technological assistance contracts concerning the transfer of patents, trademarks, and other industrial property rights as well as other similar technological rights or the actual use of such rights whose duration or term of payment of compensation exceeds 1 year (called A-class technological assistance contracts) including such contracts where no compensation is to be paid, are subject to validation under the Law Concerning Foreign Investment. All other contracts (called B-class technological assistance contracts) are subject to licensing under the Foreign Exchange and Foreign Trade Control Law.

Since June 1, 1968, technological assistance contracts have become, in principle, subject only to validation by the Bank of Japan, except in certain instances. Two of these instances are the processing of new technological assistance contracts and the screening process carried out by the Fair Trade Commission (FTC).

The validation by the Bank of Japan automatically becomes effective 1 month after the application is made, provided the concerned ministers have not issued instructions to subject the matter in question to individual examination on the grounds that the proposed contract is liable to be greatly detrimental to the national economy.

However, contracts for the induction of technology without compensation and with a contract duration of 1 year or less, and with compensation to be received in yen by resident foreign investors are not subject to any restrictions. Effective April 1, 1974, the induction of technology without compensation by branch offices in Japan of foreign corporations or Japanese corporations whose management is controlled by nonresidents, are subject to licensing, even if the duration of the contract is 1 year or less. When validation or a license has been obtained, compensation in foreign currency may be remitted abroad in accordance with the conditions attached to the validation or license.

In addition to these regulations, technological assistance contracts are subject to screening by the FTC. The FTC is authorized to act if the contract may be interpreted to constitute unreasonable restraint of trade or unfair business practice.

Japan's accelerated use of foreign technology is also reflected in its payments figures over the past 15 years. Japanese payments or royalties and related management fees for foreign technology, which totaled $62 million to the United States in 1961, rose to $306 million in 1971, to $485 million in 1976 and $744 million in 1978.

Complete information concerning Japanese patents, trademarks and licensing is available in OBR 73-04, February 1973, *Patents, Trademarks, and Licensing in Japan.* Additional information may be found in *Foreign Business Practices, Materials On The Practical Aspects Of Exporting, International Licensing And Investing,* available from the Superintendent of Documents, U.S. Government Printing Office, Washington, D.C. 20402.

Franchising

A Ministry of International Trade and Industry (MITI) and Smaller Enterprise Agency franchise white paper shows approximately 15,000 franchise stores with total sales of nearly $350 million. Of these stores, about half are restaurants, while foodstuffs and beverage retail outlets accounted for slightly more than one-fourth, apparel 7 percent, and service stores 7 percent. In sales, however, foodstuffs and beverage stores accounted for the largest portion, contributing nearly 30 percent of the total.

Franchisers and franchises are linked generally by contract fees, guarantee fees, management guidance, and commodity supplies. The partnership pattern in Japan, however, is somewhat different from that in the United States where the franchise system was devised. The average contract fee in Japan was roughly $1,250, guarantee fee $2,500, royalty 1.75-2 percent of sales, and about 1 percent for advertising expenses.

Most Japanese franchise firms require either contract money or royalty. This presents a sharp contrast to the U.S. pattern, which specifies almost without exception a substantial amount in contract fees and royalties. The Japanese place heavy emphasis on the use of franchise names and the supply of goods. Since the franchise system is still young in Japan, the guidance of parent companies is essential. In a leading franchise chain system, for example, 10 percent of new members have either seen their partnership contracts cancelled or have gone bankrupt. As a consequence of such disasters, the Fair Trade Commission has restricted, within the framework of the anti-monopoly law, exaggerated solicitation by franchise organizers. Additionally, the Smaller Enterprise Agency in the Smaller Retail Store Promotion Bill, has requested the franchisers to make public the contents of franchise contracts and information on system management. The franchise industry itself has worked on a code of practice in an attempt to carry out voluntary restraints.

The most promising sector in the nation's franchise system appears to be fast foods backed by foreign capital. The increased opportunities of dining out and longer hours for pleasure seeking among the Japanese are creating new markets for fast food restaurants and do-it-yourself kit stores. Competition, however, is growing in the foods and restaurant sectors with the advance of newcomers.

Japanese Government Procurement

There are three methods of Japanese Government procurement: (1) public notice, (2) selective tender, and (3) private or free contract.

Public Notice.—The public notice procedure regulations require that under normal circumstances public announcements (newspapers, notice board, etc.) of the procurement project be made at least 10 days prior to the closing of bids. Included in such announcements are: Objects for which tenders are sought; qualifications necessary for bidders; place from which to obtain bid specifications; time and place where bids will be opened; and matters concerning financial guarantees. However, only firms deemed qualified and appearing on so-called "eligible" lists drawn up by the government agencies concerned may submit bids. The criteria for determining eligibility are largely left to the individual government agency. Moreover, government contract officers are authorized to award the contract to the next lowest bidder where the lowest bid is considered "extremely inappropriate."

Selective Tender.—Where the government agencies determine (a) that "a rather limited number of firms is interested" or (b) that public tender is "disadvantageous depending on the nature or objective of the contract," the selective tender procedure must be used. This procedure may be applied in lieu of the public notice procedure when the value of goods to be procured is limited. Under this procedure, invitations to bid are sent to selected suppliers (more than 10 "if possible") drawn from "eligibles" lists similar to those under the public notice procedure. Agencies are authorized, however, to dispense with the preparation of such lists.

Private Contracts.—Private contracts, which are directly negotiated with selected suppliers or a single supplier at the discretion of the purchasing entity, must be used "(a) when the nature and objective of the contract do not allow competition; (b) urgency is required in procurement; and (c) it is deemed that disadvantage is caused by competition." In addition, private contracts may be resorted to in a host of cases such as those where the scheduled costs of various goods or services to be procured do not exceed specific amounts, e.g., 1.5 million yen (about $6,000) for "work or manufacture."

Transportation and Utilities

Excellent air and water transportation services link Japan and the United States. There are frequent sailings of cargo vessels and departures of scheduled air freight services from U.S. ports and major cities to points in Japan. For rates, exact schedules of sailings, and related information, freight forwarders or local offices of steamship companies and airlines should be contacted. Currently, a nonstop Yokohama-San Francisco trip takes between 12–13 days while nonstop to New York takes approximately 29 days.

Seaports and Inland Waterways

Japan's more than 600 harbors provide facilities for trade, fishing, and shelter. Most of the 26 major ports are located on Honshu, the largest island. The most important are Yokohama and Nagoya, on the Pacific side, and Kobe and Osaka, in southern Honshu on the Bay of Osaka. Other important shipping centers include Tokyo, Yokkaichi, and Shimizu on Honshu; Otaru, Muroran, and Hakodate on Hokkaido; and Kagoshima, Nagasaki, and Hakata on Kyushu.

Inland waterways, although numerous, are relatively unimportant in the transportation system of Japan. Most streams are largely unnavigable; however, some lowland rivers are used by small boats to carry products locally. Small boat traffic is extensive on river tributaries and canals in the vicinity of some large cities, especially Osaka.

Railroads

The core of Japan's land transportation system is the Japan National Railways (JNR), the largest land transportation enterprise in the country. In addition to its railroad activities, it operates ferries, buses, coal mines, power plants, and other activities. Total trackage in Japan is about 31,000 miles. In 1970, a law was passed providing for the construction of an ultra high speed 5,400-mile railroad network linking the principal cities in Japan. The program is scheduled to be completed by 1985 at a cost of $31.4 billion. The new network is to consist of an artery railway line connecting Sapporo in the north to Fukuoka in the south and having branch lines.

Highways

Japan's present road system totals about 648,481 miles, of which 243,212 miles are paved. The rugged topography of Japan makes both highway and railway construction expensive. A construction program currently underway will complete a nationwide network of expressways totaling 4,712 miles by 1985 at a cost of $14.5 billion.

The number of registered motor vehicles grew more than three times between 1969 and 1978. Of the 34.1 million vehicles registered in 1978, 21.2 million were passenger cars, and 12.8 million consisted of trucks, buses and special purpose vehicles. In addition, there were 10 million registered motorcycles.

Air Transportation

The main airports used by international services are Tokyo International Airport (Narita), and Osaka International Airport. The former is among the world's busiest. A new Kansai International Airport to handle the increased air traffic to the Osaka area is in the planning stage. Other important airports are located at Fukuoka, Nagoya, Kagoshima, and Chitose (near Sapporo).

Fuel and Power

Japan is nearly totally dependent upon overseas sources for its major energy source—crude oil—with only about 1 percent of its requirements being produced locally. Any action taken by the Organization of Petroleum Exporting Countries (OPEC) and other suppliers, therefore, has direct multiple effects on Japan and its economy. The petroleum emergency of 1973–74 indicated the extent to which the Japanese economy depends on imported crude. A comparison of the first 10 months of 1974 with the same period of 1978 shows this vividly. During the former period, Japan imported about 224 million kiloliters at a total cost of $15.4 billion. Over the same period of 1978, however, 214 million kiloliters cost Japan $19.1 billion. Even with conservation measures reducing total oil import volume by 10 million kiloliters for this period, the cost of imported crude oil has increased over $3.5 billion.

Electric power is available throughout Japan but at costs significantly higher than for similar use in the United States. Further, because of the continually increasing demand for power, which tripled over the past decade, the possibility exists for a future shortage of capacity.

The nine major suppliers of electric power in Japan generated 476 billion kWh in fiscal year 1975 and 448 billion kWh in 1976 compared with 490 billion kWh in 1978.

Because of the high cost of fuel, the growing inaccessibility of suitable land and space, and rising wages, continued cost inflation is expected. Recognizing these conditions both the public and private sectors are making a concerted effort to conserve energy, to rationalize the power generation industry, and to promote technological development. To achieve these goals the Ministry of International Trade and Industry (MITI) is currently preparing a long-term program to reduce dependence on imported oil and organize resources to develop alternate sources of energy. If approved and successfully implemented MITI's plan will reduce the oil share of the power generation fuel market from an estimated 35 percent in fiscal 1985 to approximately 20 percent in fiscal 1995. Atomic power will expand from 16.5 percent in fiscal 1985 to 27 percent in fiscal 1995. The LPG portion will grow to 16 percent and coal will increase from 5.5 percent to 12 percent.

Telephone and telegraph services, which are public corporations, blanket the country but with available telephone lines still considerably less than demand. For nonbusiness use, therefore, there may be a considerable wait before installation.

Advertising and Research

Advertising Agencies

There are several basic differences in the roles that Japanese advertising agencies play compared with advertising in most other nations. Originally, the function of Japanese advertising agencies was to finance certain media, initially newspapers, later radio and television, by purchasing space in advance, then selling it to companies interested in advertising time or space. In sharp contrast to the practice in the United States, this initial function of advertising agencies in Japan led to companies specialized by media in handling accounts for a variety of companies, including competitors. For this reason, Japanese companies rely on advertising agencies primarily to secure the necessary time or space and secondly, where needed, the necessary talent to produce advertising copy.

Despite the differences in the role of Japanese advertising agencies, they rank high internationally in total sales volume. Japan's largest advertising agency is the world's largest in total volume of advertising with 1978 billings of $2.1 billion, while two others produced billings of $719 million and $414 million respectively. The agencies can be extremely useful to overseas firms, particularly if their roles and services are supplemented by internal planning for "in channel" promotion. (Promotional methods which motivate both wholesalers and retailers including setting appropriate and competitive rebates and supplying certain services to wholesalers and retailers, are called "in channel" promotion, as distinct from advertising and promotion aimed primarily at the end-consumer).

Advertising Media

Japan is ideally suited for the use of mass media advertising. Its 114 million inhabitants, tightly concentrated in an area smaller than the state of California, are highly literate and homogeneous. Both the quality and quantity of advertising, a relatively new phenomenon in Japan, have grown enormously in recent years. There are now about 4,000 advertising agencies servicing the country through newspapers, television, magazines, radio, and outdoor advertising. In 1978, total advertising expenditures amounted to about $9 billion, with television accounting for about 37 percent; newspapers, 33 percent; outdoor advertising, 15 percent; magazines, 5 percent; direct mail, 5 percent; and radio, 5 percent.

Advertising rates vary throughout the country depending upon access to the main consumer markets. In general, rates in Tokyo are higher than elsewhere. In 1978, the average unit rate (1 column by 1 centimeter) for the Tokyo editions of such national newspapers as the Asahi Shimbun, Mainichi Shimbun, and the Yomiuri Shimbun were the most expensive with cost ranging between $130 and $230. Rates are lower for smaller papers in the outlying areas and even for limited circulation papers such as the English-language dailies in Tokyo. Television and radio rates in Tokyo also are the highest in Japan, varying between $780 and $2,600 for a 15-second television spot, depending upon the time of day or evening. Magazine rates vary significantly depending on reader audience and circulation.

The expense of advertising is often discouraging to an American business executive; however, it should be understood that famous American brands known "worldwide" are often unknown in Japan and without effective advertising are likely to remain that way. If a foreign mass consumption product with domestic competition is to be distributed through a long and complex distribution channel, a promotional boost through a concerted advertising campaign will be essential to establish the product's image.

Market Research and Trade Organizations

Market research is essential for an effective selling program in Japan. There are many specialized market research firms, independent organizations with their own field personnel, that perform public opinion research, consumer and retail surveys, advertising research, television audience measurement, product and package testing, and motivational research. Advertising agencies may also have independent research facilities to assist their clients.

U.S. exporters interested in conducting their own market research in Japan should be able to develop a considerable amount of useful information from the numerous and readily available Japanese Government statistical and economic publications. These sources provide detailed data on foreign trade, population, consumption patterns, personal income, employment and wages, industrial output, and changes in industrial sectors and various other economic, financial, and fiscal information.

Of great potential help to American exporters is the Japan External Trade Organization's (JETRO) series of publications on marketing and business information which are expressly tailored for new-to market firms. Inquiries may be addressed to the Japan Trade Center offices in Chicago, New York, Los Angeles, San Francisco, and Houston. Additional material describing various Japanese manufacturing and service sectors may be obtained from Japanese trade associations.

Potential exporters should also be aware of reports on Japanese industries prepared by the U.S. Foreign Service posts in Japan. A 1978 U.S. Department of Commerce publication of special interest to businessmen and women dealing with Japan is *U.S. Export Opportunities to Japan*, which surveys growth and marketing potential for U.S. sales to Japan in 14 industry sectors.

The book is available from the Superintendent of Documents, Government Printing Office, Washington, D.C. 20402. The names and addresses of Japanese trade associations, chambers of commerce, banks and individual firms may

also be obtained from the U.S. Department of Commerce.

Credit

Banks and Other Financial Institutions

In Japan, a very large portion of the external funding of private corporations comes from bank borrowings followed by sale of securities and finally by bond issues.

The role played by private financing institutions is very high. In private financing, there are more than 7,400 organizations including city banks and agricultural cooperatives. In addition to banks, private financing includes insurance and securities companies. The banks are tops in their important role as financiers. The bank law classifies banks as (1) ordinary banks, (2) trust and banking companies and (3) specialized foreign exchange banks, long-term credit banks, and mutual loan and savings banks. Excluding the mutual loan and savings banks, the other types are called national banks of which the ordinary banks have the most deposits, accounting for about half of the total amount of such deposits.

Commercial banking is well developed in Japan. These banks include the so-called city banks with headquarters in the prefectures. The operations of some of these local banks, however, are as large as city banks. In terms of total assets the leading city banks include Fuji, Mitsubishi, Sumitomo, Sanwa, and Mitsui, with the 12 leading city banks maintaining over 1,800 branches, including those established overseas. Commercial banking activities are not restricted by prefectures. Consequently, the large city banks have branches in virtually every major Japanese city.

Foreign banks, including U.S. banks, operate through branches and are engaged in foreign exchange transactions, loan activities, and have deposit facilities. As of October 1977, 58 foreign banks operated 80 branches while 83 foreign banks maintained resident offices in Japan. Twenty-two U.S. banks had 34 branches in Japan while 12 other American banks maintained representative offices in Japan. U.S. branch banks represent about 66 percent of the total assets of the foreign banks in Japan.

Unlike American firms, Japanese companies usually borrow on the basis of 60–180 day promissory notes. These notes, however, are often rolled over for a number of years. While the maintenance of a compensating balance is a frequent requirement, since the borrowings are technically short term, they are treated as current liability on the balance sheet.

The firm's borrowing capacity frequently depends on the company's contacts, past relationship, credit standing, and influence with bank officials. From the bank's standpoint, factors determining loans include the influence it exerts on the firm's liquidity and receptiveness of the firm to the bank's advice on company operations. Because of these factors, foreign companies often find local financing more difficult to obtain than do similar Japanese companies. By contrast, in joint ventures with a Japanese partner representing a large firm, the Japanese partner frequently can influence bank officials to grant loans to the joint venture.

Another common method of lending and borrowing money in Japan is the use of the overdraft account. If the bank judges a firm to be credit worthy, the firm will be allowed to open such an account with the limit decided by the bank. Interest is charged on the use of funds represented by the overdraft.

Some loans are unsecured but for most the usual types of collateral are required with banks frequently insisting that the parent company guarantee a loan authorized for its subsidiary. Foreign banks often assist nationals of their home countries in securing loans from Japanese banks.

One feature of commercial banks worth noting is that their funds are derived primarily from deposits—both demand and savings. Thus, the saving habit of the Japanese forms a major element in providing funds to enterprises.

Among the long-term credit banks specializing in supplying loans are the Industrial Bank of Japan, Long Term Credit Bank, and the Hypothec Bank of Japan. The two governmental banks are the Japan Development Bank and Export-Import Bank of Japan.

Until recently, the securities of foreign enterprises were not sold on the open market in Japan. Pacement of securities with private banks by companies specializing in handling securities was, however, not uncommon. Currently, several foreign companies are listed on the Tokyo Stock Exchange and the door is open for other firms provided the requirements for the exchange are met. It should be noted that the banks in Japan are excluded from stock market activities. They may, however, hold up to 10 percent of the stock of a private firm, but underwriting and handling stock are performed exclusively by security companies. While private placement of company bonds through security companies is a further possibility for raising funds, the bond market in Japan is not yet sufficiently developed to make this a satisfactory method of raising funds. The main purchasers of bonds are banks and other financial institutions, rather than individuals.

Foreign Exchange Controls

The basic law providing for the control of foreign exchange and trade transactions is the Foreign Exchange and Foreign Trade Control Law of 1949. Accordingly, foreign exchange and foreign trade transactions have been controlled by the ordinances and regulations issued under this law.

The Law concerning Foreign Investment, affecting the inflow of foreign capital, was instituted on May 10, 1950, as a special law taking precedence over the Foreign Exchange and Foreign Trade Control Law for the purpose of facilitating the induction of "sound" foreign capital. The law is international in character, for it was formulated by reference to the Agreement of the International Monetary Fund and to the principles and systems of control existing in other countries.

Foreign exchange control administration is conducted by the Ministry of Finance, Ministry of International Trade and Industry, or the Bank of Japan and authorized foreign exchange banks entrusted by the ministries to exercise controls, in accordance with the Foreign Exchange and Foreign Trade Control Law.

The Ministry of Finance is charged with the administration of policy matters concerning international finance and foreign exchange. It designates currencies to be used for the settlement of external transactions and establishes the method of settlement, administers authorized foreign exchange banks, and money changers, controls invisible trade transactions, determines foreign exchange rates, administers and operates foreign currency funds, and controls the inflow of foreign capital and investments and outflow of funds abroad. The Ministry of International Trade and Industry controls foreign trade and exercises foreign exchange control over invisible trade transactions incidental to the export and import of goods.

Under the direction of the Ministry of Finance, the Bank of Japan operates the Ministry of Finance accounts held in U.S. dollars and pounds sterling, administers the operation of the Foreign Exchange Fund Special Account, and conducts exchange equalization operations. In addition, the Bank is entrusted by the Minister of Finance or the Minister of International Trade and Industry with tasks such as the granting of permission of invisible trade transactions coming within its competence, post examination of these transactions, collection of reports, and compilation of statistics.

In view of Japan's heavy dependence on foreign trade, there was a growing recognition that an influential foreign exchange bank of extensive capacity be established to streamline foreign trade finance and control. Under these circumstances, the Foreign Exchange Bank Law was enacted on April 10, 1954 and the Bank of Tokyo, the successor to the Yokohama Specie Bank, was licensed under the Law on August 2 of the same year to function as the sole specialized foreign exchange bank. Banks authorized under the Foreign Exchange and Trade Control Law are together referred to as the "authorized foreign exchange banks."

While conducting ordinary exchange transactions such as the purchase and sale of foreign exchange, the authorized foreign exchange banks are also empowered to administer various businesses relating to foreign exchange control. On December 11, 1979 the Diet approved new legislation radically liberalizing Japanese foreign exchange controls. For details see section on Exchange Regulation.

U.S. Financial Institutions in Japan

Commercial

Bank of America
Tokyo Kaijo Bldg.
1-2-1 Marunouchi
Chiyoda-ku 100, Tokyo

Citibank, N.A. (FNCB)
Shin Otemachi Bldg.
2-2-1 Otemachi
Chiyoda-ku 100, Tokyo

Chase Manhattan Bank
AIU Bldg.
1-1-3 Marunouchi
Chiyoda-ku 100, Tokyo

Continental I.N.
Bank & Trust
Mitsui Seimei Bldg.
1-2-3 Otemachi
Chiyoda-ku 100, Tokyo

American Express
International Banking Corp.
Toranomon Mitsui Bldg.
3-8-1 Kasumigaseki
Chiyoda-ku 100, Tokyo

Morgan Guaranty Trust Co.
Shin Yurakucho Bldg.
1-21-1 Yurakucho
Chiyoda-ku 100, Tokyo

Manufacturers Hanover Trust Co.
Asahi Tokai Bldg.
2-6-1 Otemachi
Chiyoda-ku 100, Tokyo

Wells Fargo Bank, N.A.
Fuji Bldg.
3-2-3 Marunouchi
Chiyoda-ku 100, Tokyo

Security Pacific National Bank
Yurakucho Bldg.
1-10-1 Yurakucho
Chiyoda-ku 100, Tokyo

Chemical Bank
Mitsubishi Shoji Bldg. Bekkan
2-3-1 Marunouchi
Chiyoda-ku 100, Tokyo

United California Bank
Shin Yurakucho Bldg.
1-12-1 Yurakucho
Chiyoda-ku 100, Tokyo

First National Bank of Chicago
Time Life Bldg.
2-3-6 Otemachi
Chiyoda-ku 100-91, Tokyo

Bankers Trust Co.
Otemachi Bldg.
1-6-1 Otemachi
Chiyoda-ku 100, Tokyo

Irving Trust Co.
Tokyo Shoko Kaigisho Bldg.
3-2-2 Marunouchi
Chiyoda-ku 100, Tokyo

National Bank of Detroit
Togin Bldg.
1-4-2 Marunouchi
Chiyoda-ku 100, Tokyo

Rainer National Bank
Fuji Bldg.
3-2-3 Marunouchi
Chiyoda-ku 100, Tokyo

Mellon Bank N.A.
Shin Yurakucho Bldg.
1-12-1 Yurakucho
Chiyoda-ku 100, Tokyo

Marine Midland Bank
Kokusai Bldg.
3-1-1 Marunouchi
Chiyoda-ku 100, Tokyo

The Bank of California N.A.
Palace Bldg.
1-1-1 Marunouchi
Chiyoda-ku 100, Tokyo

Seattle-First National Bank
Kokusai Bldg.
3-1-1 Marunouchi
Chiyoda-ku 100, Tokyo

Crocker National Bank
AIU Bldg.
1-1-3 Marunouchi
Chiyoda-ku 100, Tokyo

Representatives

First National Bank of Dallas
Fuji Bldg.
2-3 Marunouchi 3-chome
Chiyoda-ku, Tokyo

Allied Bank International
Asahi Tokai Bldg.
6-1 Otemachi 2-chome
Chiyoda-ku, Tokyo

Republic National Bank of Dallas
Yurakucho Bldg.
10-1 Yurakucho 1-chome
Chiyoda-ku, Tokyo

Texas Commerce Bank N.A.
Palace Bldg.
1-1 Marunouchi 1-chome
Chiyoda-ku, Tokyo

Union Bank
Shin Tokyo Bldg.
3-1 Marunouchi, 3-chome
Chiyoda-ku, Tokyo

First Union National Bank of North Carolina
Shin Yurakucho Bldg.
12-1 Yurakucho 1-chome
Chiyoda-ku, Tokyo

First City National Bank of Houston
Shin Tokyo Bldg.
3-1 Marunouchi 3-chome
Chiyoda-ku, Tokyo

The Fidelity Bank
AIU Bldg.
1-3 Marunouchi 1-chome
Chiyoda-ku, Tokyo

First Pennsylvania Bank N.A.
Yurakucho Bldg.
10-1 Yurakucho 1-chome
Chiyoda-ku, Tokyo

Harris Trust & Savings Bank
Yurakucho Denki Bldg.
7-1 Yurakucho 1-chome
Chiyoda-ku, Tokyo

Pacific National Bank of Washington
Shin Yurakucho Bldg.
12-1 Yurakucho 1-chome
Chiyoda-ku, Tokyo

Republic National Bank of New York
Nihonbashi Tokai Bldg.
7-17 Nihonbashi 1-chome
Chuo-ku, Tokyo

The World Bank
Kokusai Bldg.
1-1 Marunouchi 3-chome
Chiyoda-ku, Tokyo

Trade Regulations

Import Regulations

Commodities on the Ministry of International Trade and Industry's (MITI) list of "Non-Liberalized Items" are subject to the Import Quota System (IQ). To obtain permission to import any item subject to quota, an importer must apply to MITI for an import quota allocation certificate.

Commodities other than those covered by the Import Quota System may now be freely imported. Licenses are no longer required but an importer must "declare" his intention to import a commodity to a foreign exchange bank. The new system uses a simplified version of the former Automatic Approval System (AA) import license application (Form T2010).

For clearance through customs, the importer or his customs broker must submit; (1) for IQ items, an import license, usually valid for 6 months from date of issuance; (2) an import declaration; (3) a commercial invoice; (4) a packing list; (5) a certificate of origin if the goods are entitled to favorable duty treatment; e.g., GATT rates; (6) bill of lading or, if shipped by air, air waybill; and (7) any other document that may be required by the customs office of jurisdiction to determine the value of goods in assessing duties.

The Plant and Animal Quarantine Regulations of the Ministry of Agriculture, Forestry, and Fisheries specify the requirements for the importation of plants and animals into Japan. A commercial invoice and certificate of origin are not required for shipments by mail, but commercial shipments arriving by the postal system are subject to customs examinations and duty payment.

Shipments to Japan of certain plants, seeds, animals, meat, hoofs, horns, skin, poultry, eggs, and other such products must be accompanied by an inspection certificate showing that such shipments are free from infectious materials or diseases. Further information may be obtained from the Plant Quarantine Division or the Animal Health Division, Agricultural Research Service, U.S. Department of Agriculture, Federal Center Building, Hyattsville, Maryland 20782.

Consular documents are not required for shipments to Japan.

Commercial Invoice.—No special form of commercial invoice is prescribed, but two copies on the shipper's letterhead and signed by the shipper must accompany each shipment. The commercial invoice is required by customs for valuation of the goods and must contain the following information: (1) mark, number, name, description, quantity, and value of the goods including freight, insurance, and shipping charges, gross and net weights; (2) place and date of preparing the invoice; (3) destination and consignee; and (4) conditions of the contract relating to the determination of the value of the goods. Neither consular legalization nor certification by a recognized chamber of commerce is required.

Bill of Lading.—Three signed original bills of lading (or air waybill for aircargo) are usually sent through banking channels, and at least two unsigned copies are sent to the consignee. The bill of lading should show the name of the ship; the shipper; the ultimate destination and, if applicable, the intermediate consignee(s); the markings and number of packages; and a description of the goods, including the gross metric weights and measures. However, actual requirements are generally specified in the consignee's letter of credit. Air waybill forms for aircargo are available from international airline companies and freight forwarders.

Certificate of Origin.—There is no general requirement that imports be marked as to country of origin. However, a certificate of origin should accompany merchandise that, by reason of its origin, is entitled to the lower import duty rates negotiated under the GATT. U.S. goods are accorded the benefit of GATT or Temporary

rates.[3] Certificates of origin are ordinarily authenticated by local chambers of commerce or by a Japanese consular or diplomatic official at the place of production, procurement, purchase, or shipment. Authentication by a consular officer is not required, however.

Exceptions to the general rule that a certificate of origin must accompany goods imported from the United States if such goods are to be entitled to the benefits of GATT or Temporary import duty rates are as follows:

• Foodstuffs and beverages, canned, bottled, or in jars (excluding liquors other than bourbon and rye whiskey), pharmaceuticals, chemicals, cosmetics, toilet soap, and photographic developing materials (not developed) in packages for retail sale, if the country of origin can be identified by the printed (not types or mimeographed) label on the package.

• Motion picture film (including motion picture soundtrack film, and limited to developed film).

• Fabrics, the origin of which can be identified through marks woven into the fabric's border.

• Merchandise (including parts and accessories) described in tariff chapters 84 through 93 (machinery, transport equipment, scientific equipment, clocks and watches, musical instruments, television sets, tape recorders, and arms and ammunition) on which the country of origin can be identified by stamped nameplates fastened thereto.

• Fountain pens, ballpoint pens, and mechanical pencils in which the country of origin can be identified by stamped marks.

For merchandise other than the above, nonsubmission of a certificate of origin must have the advance approval of the Ministry of Finance to ensure the application of GATT or Temporary rates of duty. In cases of such approval, other import documentation, such as manufacturer's invoices, bills of lading, insurance documents, contracts, shipping documents, or agreement that would enable customs to identify the country of origin, will be required.

There is no standard certificate of origin form devised for use by Japanese consular offices. Shippers can use either the general form available from commercial printers and stationers or submit a document that shows the following in-

---

[3]Japan's import duties, including GATT rates, are listed in Customs Tariff Schedules of Japan 1979, published by the Japan Tariff Association, 4-7-8 Kojimachi, Chiyoda-ku, Tokyo at a price of Y7,000 excluding passage.

formation: place of origin; marks and/or numbers of the commodities; commodity description; number of packages; quantities of merchandise; value; port of shipment; and destination. In addition, the certificate should include a statement that the commodities enumerated were produced or manufactured in the place of origin shown on the form. Finally, the document must be signed by the applicant and the certifying officer, and the date of certification must be shown. Two copies should accompany the shipment, and one copy is retained by the certifying authority.

Import License.—Import allocation certificates are required only for commercial shipments of import quota items into Japan.

Import Declaration.—The import declaration, which is prepared and filed by the Japanese importer, must show (1) the mark, shipping number, description, quantity, and value of the goods; (2) the place of origin, purchase, and shipment of the goods; (3) the name or registered mark and nationality of the vessel or aircraft by which the goods are carried. Once the import declaration has been accepted by customs, it cannot be altered without special approval of customs.

Import Tariff System

Tariff Structure.—Japan's Customs Tariff is administered by the Ministry of Finance through its Customs Bureau. Japan adheres to the Brussels Tariff Nomenclature (BTN) classifications.

In the recently concluded Tokyo Round[4] of the Multilateral Trade Negotiations (MTN) Japan agreed to reduce duties on 2,600 industrial items and 225 agricultural, forestry and fishery products over the next 8 years. Tariff cuts on GATT-bound duties will decline by a trade weighted average of nearly 50 percent.

Prior reductions on items of particular interest to the United States included automobiles from 6.4 percent to zero, computer mainframes from 13.5 to 10.5 percent, peripheral equipment from 22.5 to 17.5 percent, integrated circuits from 15 to 12 percent, and color film in rolls from 16 to 11 percent. Further phased reductions will establish the duty on computer mainframes at 4.9 percent, peripheral equipment at 6 percent, integrated circuits at 4.2 percent, and color film in rolls at 4 percent as of January 1, 1987.

Additional commitments were received to expand the import quotas on leather and leather products, citrus fruit, and beef and to reduce or

eliminate non-tariff barriers such as custom valuation procedures, government procurement policies and standards approval.

As a contracting party to the GATT, Japan accords most-favored nation tariff treatment to most of its trading partners, including the United States.

Basis of Duty Assessment

Under the Customs Tariff Law, the value for customs assessment is the price of the goods sold in ordinary wholesale quantity and in the ordinary course of trade in the exporting country at the time of exportation, plus freight, insurance, and other incidental costs incurred in connection with the shipment. The dutiable value for air shipments is usually determined on the basis of transportation other than air. Most duties are levied on an ad valorem basis. However, for some commodities, the import duty rate is a specific one based on the number of units imported. For a few commodities, the tariff prescribes both an ad valorem and a specific rate, giving the customs official the option of assessing whichever duty yeilds the higher revenue. Duties are payable in Japanese yen effective at the official exchange rate.[5]

The 1951 Measurement Law of Japan made mandatory the use of the metric system from January 1, 1959. Consequently, imported products to be sold at retail in Japan must show only metric weights and measures, as must the shipping documents.

Information regarding Japanese duties applicable to specific products may be obtained free of charge from the Regional Marketing Manager for Japan, Korea, and Hong Kong Office of Country Marketing, U.S. Department of Commerce, Washington, D.C. 20230; or from any Department of Commerce District Office. Inquiries should contain a complete product description, including BTN, SITC, or U.S. Schedule B Export Commodity numbers, if known.

Internal Taxes

Seventeen groups of commodities, mostly of a luxury or semiluxury type, are subject to indirect commodity taxes. The commodity tax is applicable to both imported and domestic goods and ranges from a high of 30 percent down to 5 percent. The tax base for imported commodities is the recipient's price on receipt from customs (c.i.f. value plus duty). The tax base for most items of domestic manufacture is the manufacturer's sale price, although the tax on jewelry,

---

[4] The "Tokyo Round" is the name given to the Seventh Round of Trade Negotiations conducted in Geneva from 1973 to 1979 under the auspices of the GATT.

[5] As of February 1980, the yen was floating at about 245=$1.

precious metal products, furs, and carpets is levied on the retailer's sale price.

Representative commodity taxes are as follows: Boats, golfing equipment, billiard equipment, and rifles, 30 percent; jewelry with precious and semiprecious stones, precious metal products, and furs, 15 percent; electrical appliances such as refrigerators, washing machines, and air conditioners, 15 and 20 percent; small automobiles, musical instruments, record players, records, cameras and film, 15 percent; and perfume and toiletries, 5 and 10 percent. A taxable minimum value is prescribed for many items subject to the commodity tax.

Internal taxes applicable to other commodities not covered by the commodity tax are the liquor tax, the gasoline tax, the liquefied petroleum gas tax, the sugar excise tax, and the playing cards tax.

Information regarding Japanese internal taxes for specific products may be obtained from the Regional Marketing Manager for Japan, Korea, and Hong Kong, Office of Country Marketing, U.S. Department of Commerce, Washington, D.C. 20230, or from any Department of Commerce District Office.

Marking and Labeling Requirements

The labeling, marking, and packing of commercial shipments to Japan are covered by specific regulations for certain items such as food, pharmaceuticals, and electrical household products. Where discrepancies in marks of origin are shown and detected, the importer, upon notification from customs, must either cancel or correct the indication of origin or return the goods.

The Food Sanitation Law of Japan contains provisions under which standards may be established for packaging, marking, and labeling food products. Detailed requirements for specified foodstuffs are contained in ordinances issued by the Ministry of Health and Welfare; distribution of food products that are not labeled, marked, or packaged in accordance with these ordinances is prohibited.

Requirements for labeling, packing, and marking drugs and cosmetics are governed by the Pharmaceutical Affairs Law and by ordinances of the Ministry of Health and Welfare.

With respect to both pharmaceutical and food products, the content and directions for use must be in the Japanese language. All imported food products, including confectionery and chewing gum, must state in Japanese whether the product contains artificial coloring or preservatives and state the name and address of the importer.

The Electric Appliance Control Law specifies standards for both domestic and imported consumer electrical appliances and commercial electrical apparatus. Marking and labeling requirements for electrical appliances and apparatus are also prescribed by the law to assure conformity to technical standards established by MITI. Many of these appliances require MITI's approval of their safety based on actual laboratory testing before they can be sold in Japan. For example, air conditioners must be uniformly labeled in a prescribed manner to indicate rated capacity in kilocalories and other information concerning performance.

The Measurement Law provides that the conventional Japanese measurements and the yard-pound system are prohibited for all transactions and certifications, except for those specifically exempted under government ordinances.

Bonded Areas

Foreign goods may be transported in bond only between ports of entry, customs airports, bonded areas, customs offices, or places specified by the Director of Customs. In such cases, the director may, if he deems it necessary, require security equivalent to the amount of the customs duty payable. The security will be released upon arrival of the goods in bond at the specified destination within the stated transportation period.

Japan has five kinds of bonded areas: (1) designated bonded areas; (2) bonded shed; (3) bonded warehouse; (4) bonded factory; and (5) bonded exhibit site. The Japanese Customs Bureau is equipped to handle inquiries from American businesspersons concerning bonded facilities in Japan. Such inquiries may be addressed to: Chief, Inspection Section, Customs Bureau, Ministry of Finance, 1 Kasumigaseki 3-chome, Chiyoda-ku, Tokyo, Japan.

Senate Concurrent Resolution 40, adopted July 30, 1953, invites U.S. exporters to inscribe, insofar as practicable, on the external shipping containers in indelible print of a suitable size: "United States of America."

Samples and Advertising Matter

Samples and advertising matter including brochures, photographs, films, and models of no commercial value are exempt from customs duty. Samples having commercial value will be permitted duty-free entry provided they are to be exported from Japan within 1 year from the date of the permission for duty-free import. Should these samples be used for purposes other than advertising or order-taking, or if they are not exported from Japan within the 1-year period, the duty becomes immediately payable. Articles intended for display at trade fairs, competitions, prize shows, or other similar events will be permitted duty-free entry, provided they are to be exported within 1 year of the day of entry.

With approval from the Director of Customs, foreign goods may be taken from a bonded area on a temporary basis for use as samples. As a signatory of the International Convention to Facilitate the Importation of Commercial Samples and Advertising Material, Japan admits valuable samples temporarily duty-free under deposit of bond for the amount of duty.

Technical Requirements

The principal agency for establishing standards in Japan is the Japan Industrial Standards Committee (JIS), an agency of the Ministry of International Trade and Industry (MITI). Many Japanese Industrial Standards have been modified to conform to international or U.S. practices, but in general, it is desirable to conform to JIS standards to assure acceptance of imports. The published standards are available from the Japanese Standards Association 1-24 Akasaka, Minato-ku, Tokyo or the American National Standards Institute, 1430 Broadway, New York, New York, 10018.

Indicating devices must be tested in Japan prior to sale. Responsibility for monitoring compliance with standards rests with the Industrial Technical Institute of MITI. Inspection policy is determined by the Industrial Manufacturers Inspection Institute, an agency of MITI with 10 branches located throughout Japan.

The electrical power characteristics of low voltage lines are 100 volt single-phase and 200 volt three-phase. The frequency is 50 cycles in the Kanto area (Tokyo) and 60 cycles in the rest of the country. High voltage distribution lines are either 3,000 volt or 6,000 volt three-phase with 6,000 volt lines being increasingly installed to replace existing lower voltage lines. There are also 10,000 and 20,000 volt lines fed to larger plants and buildings.

Investment in Japan

Value of U.S. Investment

U.S. investments in Japan remain small, registering a total value of $4.1 billion as of December 31, 1977. The 7.5 percent advance in U.S. investment between 1976-1977 compares unfavorably with the 15 percent increase between 1975-1976. However, a recent MITI survey confirmed that U.S. investors accounted for 54.9 percent, the dominant share, of total foreign investment as of March 31, 1977.

Growth of U.S. investments in Japan is slow because of the limited availability of land, the difficulty of providing potential employees with benefits equivalent to those offered by local companies, and the high cost of establishign an independent presence in Japan which is compounded by shifting exchange rates.

While these U.S. investments in Japan include nearly all industrial activity, the major areas of interest are concentrated in the petroleum, chemical, transportation equipment, nonelectric machinery, and the food industries. Additional investments, however, are found in international trade and retail sales.

Investment Climate

Effective May 1, 1973, the Japanese Government adopted a new policy toward inward foreign investment. The main feature of it is the change from the principle of limiting foreign investments to 50 percent in new companies and less than 25 percent (a maximum of 10 percent per individual foreign investor) in existing companies. The new principle permits up to 100 percent foreign investment in both new and existing companies, with significant exceptions. Exceptions are: (1) where, with regard to investment in an existing company, the proposed investment is a "take-over plotted against the wishes of the company concerned" and (2) where the proposed investment is in (a) agriculture, forestry and fishing (b) mining, (c) petroleum, including refining, and (d) leather and leather products.

The principal law under which the Japanese Government controls the nature and extent of inward foreign investment are the Foreign Exchange and Foreign Trade Control Law (Law No. 228, December 1, 1949) as amended, and the Law Concerning Foreign Investment (Law No. 163, May 10, 1950), as amended.

Forms of Business Organizations

Foreign investment in Japan usually takes one of the following forms: Wholly-owned subsidiary, joint venture, branch office, portfolio investment, or licensing agreement. The following are the types of business organizations open to both Japanese and foreign investors:

Limited Stock Company. *(Kabushiki Kaisha)*—The most popular form of business organization for foreign investors is the limited stock company whose principal characteristics are similar to those of a U.S. corporation. A minimum of seven promoters or incorporators is required to organize a limited stock company and may be juridical entities or natural persons. They need not be Japanese citizens or residents but all must subscribe for at least one share. Many foreign investors find it convenient to use Japanese agents as promoters by issuing powers of attorney to local residents and then transferring the shares to the real party of interest after completion and corporation registration.

The principal costs to be considered in incorporating a stock company as a joint venture with foreign participation are notary fees, the registration tax amounting to 7 percent of capital, and legal fees.

Branch *(Shiten)*—The establishment of a branch in Japan by a foreign enterprise is controlled by Articles 479–485 of the Commercial Code, by the Foreign Exchange Control Law, and by special licensing requirements which apply to certain business areas. A legal representative with full authority to represent the branch must be appointed in all instances where a foreign entity wishes to engage in commercial transactions on a continuing basis. After government approval, the branch must be registered at the local registration office of the Ministry of Justice. The information submitted to this ministry should include the state or country of the parent company's incorporation, information about its capital structure, names and addresses of its directors, address of the Japanese branch office, the purposes of the branch, and stated capital. Providing such data, paying a nominal registration tax, and sending notifications to income and other tax offices complete the registration requirements.

Limited Liability Partnership *(Goshi Kaisha)*—This organization is similar to the unlimited liability partnership except that it includes one or more limited partners whose liability for partnership obligations is limited to the capital contributed as well as partners whose liability is unlimited. The articles of incorporation must specify whether each member's liability is limited or unlimited.

A limited partner's capital contribution must be in cash or property. He cannot participate in the management of the partnership and the trade name must include the words *goshi kaisha*.

Unlimited Liability Partnership *(Gomei Kaisha)*—The partners under this organization have joint and unlimited liability for all partnership obligations. Only natural persons may be partners since the Commercial Code prohibits any entity with limited liability from assuming unlimited liability in another entity. Each partner in a *gomei kaisha* has implied authority to represent the partnership and to perform all acts relating to the partnership business.

Sole Proprietorship.—The Japanese Commercial Code defines a sole proprietor as a person who engages in commercial transactions as a business on his own behalf. The business name of a sole proprietorship may be the surname or full name of the entrepreneur or any other designated trade name. Because of high individual income taxes it is unusual for foreigners to operate a sole proprietorship in Japan.

Industrial Property Rights

The basic Japanese industrial property rights statutes are the Patent Law (No. 121), Trademark Law (No. 127), Utility Model Law (No. 123), and Design Law (No. 125), all enacted April 13, 1959, and effective April 1, 1960, and subsequent amendments.

Applications to register patents, trademarks, utility models, and designs should be addressed to Director-General of the Japanese Patent Office, 1–3–1 Kasumigaseki, Chiyoda-ku, Tokyo. Foreigners must maintain a local agent to prosecute filings and pay fees, including those for maintaining patents in force. Applications and all other documents must be prepared in Japanese.

Trademarks

The first applicant for a trademark is entitled to its registration. Another person widely using a mark before the first application filed for it by someone else may be permitted to continue its use, even after its registration to the applicant (concurrent use).

A separate application is needed for a trademark in each class of goods for which it is intended to be used. There are 34 classes of goods for trademarks.

Trademark applications are examined by the Patent Office as to registrability, distinctiveness, and resemblance to other registered marks. Acceptable marks are published in the Trade Mark Gazette, for opposition for 2 months from date of publication. The provisions for op position and appeal from Patent Office decisions are the same as for patent applications.

Trademark registrations are issued for 10 years from the registration date, renewable for like periods.

A registered mark cannot be contested, after 5 years, on grounds of well-known use by others, or of being confusingly similar to others, or of being identical to a prior registration.

Trademarks not registrable are those which are identical with Japanese national emblems, or emblems of any member country of the "Paris Union" Convention. Also not registrable are names or symbols of government bodies and associations; marks injurious to public order or morals; and marks widely recognized by the public as indicating the goods of another person, or which are liable to cause confusion with the goods of another person, or which may cause deception as to the quality of the goods. Marks identical to existing registration are not registrable.

If an unregistered mark is used on merchandise displays at an exhibition held by the Japanese Government, or at an official international exhibition so designated by the Patent Office, the person who exhibited the trademarked goods has 6 months from the last day of such exhibition in which to apply for a trademark registration in Japan. The application shall be considered to have been filed at the time of first exhibition of the goods.

A registered trademark not used on the designated merchandise within Japan for a period of 3 or more consecutive years may be subject to cancellation unless there is a justifiable reason for not using the mark.

Trademark owners may seek injunctive relief and damages in infringement cases. The infringement of a trademark may also be punishable by imprisonment. Prison sentences may also be imposed on those who are found guilty of obtaining trademark registrations through fraud or perjury. For complete details, see OBR 73-04 *Patents, Trademarks and Licensing in Japan.* Additional information may be found in *Foreign Business Practices; Materials on Practical Aspects of Exporting, International Licensing, and Investing,* available from the Superintendent of Documents, U.S. Government Printing Office, Washington, D.C. 20402.

There are no restrictions on the repatriation of capital or the outward payment of royalties provided the original venture had received prior Japanese Government approval.

Taxation

Tax legislation is drafted by the Tax Bureau of the Ministry of Finance in Japan, and enacted by the Diet (parliament), both for national and local taxes. The national tax is administered by the Tax Administration Agency for the Ministry of Finance and local taxes by the appropriate local authority.

The present Japanese taxes imposed by national and local governments can be classified into four groups: Income, property, consumption, and transfer of goods. Of these, the most significant is income.

Income taxes are assessed by corporate (subdivided into corporation-national, enterprise-local, municipal-local, and prefectural-local) and individual (subdivided into national, municipal-local,[6] and prefectural-local).

Corporate income taxes are payable on self-assessed basis by filing tax returns within 2 months after the end of the corporate fiscal period. They are based on the fiscal period of corporation (not exceeding 12 months) with many domestic corporations having 6 month fiscal periods ending in March and September. Corporations having a 12 month fiscal period are required to make estimated tax payments of 50 percent of the preceding year's taxes due, or alternately, payments based on the actual results of operations during the initial 6 months of the current fiscal year.

All corporations paying taxes are classified either as domestic or foreign corporations. Domestic corporations, i.e. corporations established under the laws of Japan, are subject to tax on their worldwide income, while foreign corporations having branches in Japan are taxed on their Japanese source income. Generally, Japanese source income includes all income arising in Japan or from Japanese sources. This may include income which is not entered in the books of the foreign branch in Japan, for example, royalties paid to a head office abroad by a Japanese domestic corporation, or interest on a loan, usually in foreign currency to a Japanese domestic corporation but which is carried on the books of the head office of a bank in, for example, New York or London.

Foreigners paying national taxes are permitted the following deductions: Basic personal exemption, employment income deduction, wife, other dependents, deduction for old age, deduc-

---

[6]Sometimes also collectively called inhabitants', residents' or ward tax.

tion for widows under 65 with a dependent, and medical expenses in excess of Y100,000 or 5 percent of taxable income, whichever is less.

An individual who is subject to Japanese income tax must declare the following: Income from employment, business, interest, dividends, real estate, and capital gains.

Local government taxes (ward taxes) are assessed on the income declared for national taxes but are payable in the following year. Thus, an individual will pay his ward tax in four equal installments, for example, on June 30, 1972 through January of the following year but the income on which the assessment is based is that of the national tax for 1971 filed on or before March 15, 1972.

Labor Relations

For foreign firms interested in setting up in Japan, one area of prime interest is the availability of qualified labor, especially since labor practices have often been described as uniquely Japanese.

There are three basic points of difference between Japanese labor practices and those elsewhere: (1) Japanese firms practice lifetime employment for permanent employees, that is, the employee in a typical white collar job is hired for life, (2) wages and positions within the company are determined largely by age and length of service, and (3) labor unions in Japan are organized on a company basis, with the typical company union only loosely tied to a national organization.

The foreign investor is faced with adopting the Japanese practices as they are, in a slightly modified form, or adopting a very clear policy of not following these labor practices but providing economic and other incentives to offset the riskier Western-style labor employment system.

While some of the company unions are extremely large and powerful, such as the union of the Japan National Railways, the typical company union represents only a small fraction of the nation's work force. This makes for a very different balance of power between union and management in Japanese firms. Since it is difficult to obtain employment by leaving one company for another, the unions rarely press their demands as to seriously damage the company. Forcing a company into bankruptcy, for example, would put the employees at the mercy of the labor market.

The number of trade unions in Japan at the end of 1978 was estimated at 70,868 with a total membership of over 12,232,000. Membership increases were most notable in the public service, finance, insurance, and real estate sectors.

In total, about 8 million trade unionists are involved directly or indirectly in the spring wage struggle. In spite of this large number, the unions of single companies are the bargaining units.

Wage gains won during the spring of 1979 in the private sector averaged 6 percent or Y9,959. This increase represented an advance of only 0.1 percent over 1978. Further, 1979 was the second consecutive year in which the average settlement fell below Y10,000 and the third lowest settlement in postwar history. However, recognizing that the 1978 increase in the consumer price index was only 3.4 percent, the wage boost for 1979 resulted in a substantial increase in workers' real wages.

Guidance for Business Travelers

Entrance Requirements

In addition to a valid passport, other formalities are required for entry into Japan and as far as Japanese immigration is concerned, there is no deviation from the law.

To obtain a visa, it is necessary to submit three copies of the application form with the necessary letters and two pictures of the applicant to a Japanese Foreign Office in charge of the district where the applicant resides. The type of visa will depend upon the purpose of the trip to Japan. Wives who wish to work in Japan must apply for a special work permit. The commercial entrant visa (4–1–5) is valid for 4 years with a period of stay up to 3 years while the tourist visa (4–1–4) is also valid for 4 years with a period of stay up to 60 days without renewal.

Forms vary according to the desired status or residence but three copies are common requirements. For a commercial visa, there is the additional requirement of three copies of "Affidavit of Support" usually supplied by the resident employer.

Health requirements.—For information concerning inoculations, call upon: (1) the nearest representative of the United States Public Health Service; (2) the Division of Foreign Quarantine, Public Health Service, Department of Health and Human Resources, Washington, D.C. 20025; or (3) the nearest consular representative of Japan in the United States.

Unaccompanied Baggage.—Form C–5002–Declaration of Unaccompanied Baggage pertains to all articles not accompanying the entrant, and must be filled out in duplicate and verified by customs at the time and port of entry for articles arriving in Japan by any other means of transportation. These articles must arrive within 6 months of the entrant's arrival in Japan.

Personal effects.—Personal effects imported must not be sold and must be retained for a period of 2 years.

Pets.—Entrants may bring pets with them to Japan but they should be declared orally upon entrance by owners or, if unaccompanied, on Customs Form C–5002. Japanese regulations regarding their importation, especially in the case of dogs, are quite explicit and rigidly enforced. Proof that dogs have been inoculated against rabies not less than 30 days nor more than 120 days prior to entry into Japan, and a veterinarian's certificate endorsed by an Inspector-in-Charge, U.S. Department of Agriculture, are required.

These inspectors are located in each state except Delaware, which is serviced by the Baltimore Office. In the case of cats, the Japanese Government requires only a certificate of good health signed by a licensed veterinarian. While there is no Federal agency specifically charged with the responsibility for endorsing these certificates, the State Office of the Bureau of Animal Husbandry's Inspector-in-Charge will provide such endorsements as a special service.

Currency

There is no restriction on the amount of money brought into the country. It may be in U.S. currency, letters of credit, travelers' checks, and other instruments drawn in U.S. dollars.

Foreign currency may be exchanged for yen by an authorized bank or money changer such as travel agencies or hotels. Yen may be changed to American currency upon leaving Japan.

U.S. dollar checks can be written in Japan to any Foreign Exchange Bank and cabled for yen at the prevailing rate of exchange; remittances from abroad can be received through the same banks. In addition, foreign residents in Japan may open and maintain a yen bank account. However, it should be noted that payment by check has not been established in Japan to the extent it is in the United States.

Exchange Regulations

The exchange control system is operated by the Ministry of Finance, MITI, and the Bank of Japan as the Government's agent. However, much of the authority for approval of normal payments is delegated to authorized foreign exchange banks.

Before March 31, 1978 payment for goods imported into Japan was generally required within a period of 4 months from the receipt of the shipping documents or customs clearance. In certain cases prepayment or partial payment was allowed on designated items or shipments of specific value. For c.i.f. transactions, the standard method of settlement was payment of at least 90 percent of the total cost within 4 months after customs clearance and the balance within 6 months.

Payments for invisible trade transactions such as transportation and insurance do not require separate application if approval has been granted to import the commodities.

Certain contracts require approval, but when a license for a contract has been granted, any payment arising from the contract may be made freely.

After April 1, 1978 the payment period for imported goods was extended from 4 months to 1 year after customs clearance in the case of capital goods, consumer durables and sales commissions and to 6 months for other types of merchandise. Prepayment is now permitted for imports up to a year in advance of delivery.

However, legislation liberalizing foreign exchange regulations has recently been approved with an effective date set for the fall of 1980. The new law will make capital transactions virtually free of government control except in emergencies. Further, without government approval, Japanese businesses will be able to offer bond issues overseas with a reciprocal privilege for foreign enterprises in Japan. Most significantly for American traders, the legislation will abolish the current system requiring exporters and importers to conform to specified settlement methods except for a few special transactions. The net effect of this change could reduce the need for government approvals from 100,000 to about 600 per year.

The two basic treaties concerning commercial relations with Japan are the Treaty of Friendship, Commerce and Navigation, effective October 30, 1953 and the Convention Between the United States of America and Japan for the

Avoidance of Double Taxation With Respect to Taxes on Income, agreed to on March 8, 1971.

In addition to those financial institutions listed previously (under Credit), the following Japanese banks can assist in foreign exchange transactions. The main office addresses follow:

The Fuji Bank
5-5 Otemachi 1-chome
Chiyoda-ku, Tokyo

The Taiyo-Kobe Bank
56 Naniwa-cho
Ikuta-ku, Kobe

The Bank of Tokyo
Nihonbashi 6-3, 1-chome, Hongoku-cho
Chuo-ku, Tokyo

The Daiwa Bank
21 Bingo-machi 2-chome
Higashi-ku, Osaka

The Industrial Bank of Japan
3-3 Marunouchi 1-chome
Chiyoda-ku, Tokyo

The Mitsubishi Bank
7-1 Marunouchi 2-chome
Chiyoda-ku, Tokyo

The Mitsui Bank
12 Yurakuchol 1-chome
Chiyoda-ku, Tokyo

The Sanwa Bank
10 Fushimi-machi 4-chome
Higashi-ky, Osaka

The Sumitomo Bank
22 Kitahama 5-chome
Higashi-ku, Osaka

The Tokai Bank
21-24 Nishiki 3-chome
Naka-ku, Nagoya

The Yasuda Trust and Banking Co.
2-25 Yaesu 1-chome
Chuo-ku, Tokyo

Also, there are a large number of banks bearing prefectural names which can carry out foreign transactions on behalf of their clients. Generally, these banks act as intermediaries between their clients and the banks listed above and in the section on Credit.

Holidays

Japan will observe the following holidays in 1980:

January 1	New Year's Day
January 15	Adult's Day
February 11	National Foundation Day
March 21	Vernal Equinox Day
April 29	Emperor's Birthday
May 3	Constitution Day
May 5	Children's Day
September 15	Respect for the Aged Day
September 23	Autumnal Equinox Day
October 10	Sports Day
November 3	Culture Day
November 23	Labor Thanksgiving Day

Most Japanese firms and government offices traditionally observe year-end and New Year Holidays from December 29–January 5.

Language

While English is widely used in business, a wide range of language ability is to be found in correspondence, oral and aural comprehension, and skill. Everyday social English may present little problem but the technical or legal areas are best served by capable translators or interpreters. It should not be assumed that most Japanese businesspersons speak or understand English.

Hotels

Excellent western-style hotel accommodations are available in major cities and most smaller cities. Room costs measured by American standards, however, are substantially higher, as well as for food served in these hotels. Costly as accommodations are, especially in Tokyo, businesspersons contemplating a trip to Japan should make early room reservations since space is limited.

Sources of Economic and Commercial Information

U.S. Government Representation

The U.S. Government maintains an embassy in Tokyo at 10-1 Akasaka 1-chome, Minato-ku, (Tel: (03) 583-7141). Consulate General offices are located at:

Sankei Kaikan Building, 9th Fl.
4-9, Umeda 2-chome
Kita-ku, Osaka
Tel: (06) 341-2754

10 Kano-cho 6-chome
Ikuta-ku, Kobe
Tel: (078) 331-6865

No. 2129 Gusukuma
Urasoe City, Okinawa
Tel: (0988) 77-8142

American Consulates are located at:

Kita 1-Jyo Nishi 28-chome
Chuo-ku, Sapporo
Tel: (011) 641-1115

5-26 Ohori 2-chome
Chuo-ku, Fukuoka
Tel: (092) 751-9331

Foreign Service Officers in the Economic/ Commercial sections of these posts are available to brief and assist American business executives visiting Japan. A booklet, *Key Officers of Foreign Service Posts*, is published quarterly by the U.S. Department of State. Copies may be purchased on a subscription basis from the Government Printing Office, Washington, D.C. 20402.

In addition, there is an American Commercial Information Office in the Aichi-ken Sangyo, Boeki Kaikan Nishikan, 4-7 Marunouchi 2-chome, Naka-ku, Nagoya. Tel: (052) 231-7791.

The U.S. Trade Center in Tokyo is operated by the U.S. Department of Commerce with the cooperation of the Foreign Service of the United States. Since its inauguration in April 1963, it has served American manufacturers effectively as a site for introducing their products into Japan and finding respresentatives or expanding sales if they are already established in this important market. The Center is equipped to handle virtually any exhibition situation and is staffed by professionals with many years of experience in the promotion and display of foreign products in Japan.

Millions of dollars in sales attributable to exhibitions at the Trade Center are realized each year by U.S. companies and their representatives. When the Center is not occupied by the Department of Commerce, it is available to American firms or their Japanese representatives for private exhibitions of U.S. products, sales meetings, technical seminars, or other commercial activities.

In November 1978 the U.S. Trade Center, Tokyo relocated offices and exhibition space to the World Import Mart, 7th Fl. 1-3, Higashi Ikebukuro 3-chome, Toshima-ku, Tokyo. Tel (03) 987-2441. The new Trade Center site is part of a comprehensive Japanese import promotion center which provides all the functions necessary for promoting sales to Japan.

In September 1972, the U.S. Department of Commerce opened an exhibition center in Osaka. This facility, called American Merchandise Display Osaka (AMDO), is located on the premises of the American Cosulate General in Osaka. Since its inauguration, AMDO, managed by the commercial staff of the Consulate General, has been successfully used by hundreds of American manufacturers and their representatives to intensify exposure of their products in the large and affluent market of Western Japan.

A small exhibition space is also available in the U.S. Consulate in Fukuoka City to American manufacturers and their representatives who desire to further their penetration of the Kyushu market.

The American Consulate at Sapporo also offers promotional services including space in a new building for U.S. exporters to display their products.

Japanese Government Representation

The Japanese Government maintains an embassy in the United States at 2520 Massachusetts Avenue, N.W., Washington, D.C. 20008. Consulate General offices are located in the following U.S. cities:

280 Park Avenue
New York, New York 10017

625 North Michigan Avenue
Chicago, Illinois 60611

1021 Main Street
Houston, Texas 77002

400 Colony Square Building
1201 Peachtree Street, N.E.
Atlanta, Georgia 30361

Guam International Trade Center Building
Tamuning, Guam 91910

1538 International Trade Mart
No. 2 Canal Street
New Orleans, Louisiana 70130

614 Norton Building
801 Second Avenue
Seattle, Washington 98104

2400 First National Bank Towers
1300 S.W. 5th Avenue
Portland, Oregon 97201

250 East First Street
Los Angeles, California 90012

1742 Nuuanu Avenue
Honolulu, Hawaii 96817

It also maintains a Consulate at 909 West 9th Avenue, Anchorage, Alaska 99501.

Japan Trade Centers are located at:

1221 Avenue of the Americas
New York, New York 10020

555 South Flower Street
Los Angeles, California 90017

1737 Post Street
San Francisco, California 94115

230 North Michigan Avenue
Chicago, Illinois 60601

One Houston Center
Suite 1810
Houston, Texas 77002

An additional source of information is the United States-Japan Trade Council, 1000 Connecticut Avenue N.W., Washington, D.C. 20036.

Japanese Publications

English-language daily newspapers available in Japan include the Japan Times, the Yomiuri, Asahi Evening News, and the Mainichi Daily News. In addition, there is the weekly *Japan Economic Journal* and the monthly *Oriental Economist*. These are reliable economic and business journals and highly useful to executives interested in Japan. The *Japan Quarterly* and the *Journal of Social and Political Ideas in Japan* are useful by providing good assessments of contemporary Japanese thinking in the political and cultural fields.

Other sources on Japanese companies may be found in such English-language publications as the *Japan Company Handbook* (published by the *Oriental Economist*), *Japan Directory* (The Japan Press), *Standard Trade Index* (Japan Chamber of Commerce and Industry), *Foreign Capital Affiliated Enterprises in Japan* (Business Intercommunications), *Japan Chemical Directory* (the Chemical Daily), *Setting Up Enterprises in Japan* (Bank of Tokyo), and others.

In addition, the various Japanese ministries, the Economic Planning Agency, banks, associa-

tion, and other private organizations publish information too numerous to mention. A sampling is presented as an example of the wide variety of information available on a regular basis.

(Ministry of International Trade and Industry)
Industrial Statistics Monthly
Yearbook of Machinery Statistics

(Ministry of Finance)
Japan Exports and Imports
Quarterly Bulletin of Financial Statistics

(Ministry of Labor)
Monthly Labor Statistics and Research Bulletin
Yearbook of Labor Statistics

(Economic Planning Agency)
Japan Economic Indicator
Economic Survey of Japan

(Office of the Prime Minister)
Monthly Statistics of Japan
Japan Statistical Yearbook

(Bank of Japan)
Economic Statistics Monthly
Short-Term Economic Survey of Principal Enterprises in Japan
Economic Statistics Annual

U.S. Department of Commerce Publications

These Overseas Business Reports are available from any Department of Commerce District Office or from the Publications Sales Branch, Room 1617, U.S. Department of Commerce, Washington, D.C. 20230, or from the Superintendent of Documents, U.S. Government Printing Office, Washington, D.C. 20402.

Patents, Trademarks and Licensing in Japan, OBR 73-04 (30 cents)

Market Profiles for Asia and Oceania, OBR 79-14 (80 cents).

Foreign Economic Trends, Japan, FET 79-93 (50 cents).

World Trade Outlook for the Far East and South Asia, OBR 80-10 ($1.25)

Market Profile—JAPAN

Economic Overview

Real Japanese economic growth for both the calendar and fiscal year (April 1, 1983—March 30, 1984) should not exceed 3.0-3.5 percent. This percentage range is barely higher than the actual percentage for 1982, but it does represent the highest expected rate among the OECD countries. Inflation and unemployment should remain steady at about 3 percent and 2.5 percent, respectively. Most of the economic growth will occur in the latter half of the year, assuming accelerated personal consumption expenditures and expanded exports. Business investment—particularly by small and medium-size enterprises—housing, and public expenditures will continue to lag. Weak domestic demand is not likely to boost imports to any degree. Japan's global current account surplus will therefore probably top $15 billion. The yen should continue to strengthen from 1982's average rate of 249 per dollar but the effect on U.S. exports may be delayed until the end of the year.

Major Developments

The U.S. and Japanese Governments in February 1983 accepted the recommendations of the U.S.-Japan Working Group on High Technology Industries with a view to improving the conditions for trade in such key sectors as computers, semiconductors, and telecommunications equipment

The Government of Japan also announced in February 1983 that it will continue its unilateral export restraints on automobile shipments to the United States. The restraint level for the third year (April 1, 1983-March 31, 1984) is set at the same level as in the two previous fiscal years (1.68 million units excepting certain shipments and about 1.8 million without the exceptions).

The Administration is considering proposals to lift the legislative ban on exports of Alaskan crude oil—a step which, it is said, could add $3-$4 billion (perhaps more realistically about $1 billion) in U.S. exports to Japan.

Foreign Trade

Best U.S. Sales Prospects. — Analytical instruments, computer hardware, electronic components, medical equipment, telecommunications equipment, sporting goods and recreation equipment, metalworking machinery, coal and pulp, paper and paperboard, fish, avionics, inorganic chemicals, and construction equipment.

Major Suppliers (1981). — United States (17.7 percent), Indonesia (9.3 percent), EEC (6.0 percent), Australia (5.2 percent), and Canada (3.1 percent).

Principal Japanese Exports. — Motor vehicles; iron and steel; radio and television receivers and tape recorders; scientific, medical, and optical equipment; and motorcycles.

Major Markets (1981). — United States (25.4 percent), EEC (12.4 percent), Korea (3.7 percent), Taiwan (3.6 percent), Hong Kong (3.5 percent), and China (3.4 percent).

Note: Fastest growing U.S. exports in 1982 were petroleum products (up 213 percent to $621 million), mining and oil and gas well-drilling machinery (up 51 percent to $254 million), toys and sporting goods (up 37 percent to $162 million), aircraft engines and parts (up 18 percent to $177 million), metal manufactures (up 15 percent to $174 million), and pharmaceuticals (up 14 percent to $489 million).

U.S. exports to Japan (1982—U.S. data), $20,966 million; U.S. imports from Japan, $37,744 million; merchandise trade balance, -$16,778 million.

Foreign Investment

U.S. value of direct investment, end 1981, was $6.8 billion. Principal fields of U.S. investment are petroleum, trade, nonelectrical machinery, transportation equipment, electric and electronic equipment, and food products. A Treaty of Friendship, Commerce and Navigation and a Convention for the Avoidance of Double Taxation and the Prevention of Fiscal Evasion are in effect between the United States and Japan.

Import-Export Trade*

(millions of U.S. dollars)

	1980	1981	1982
Total Imports, (c.i.f.)	140,528	143,280	131,970
Imports from the U.S.	24,408	25,297	24,162
Raw materials and mineral fuels	93,752	92,598	84,513
Foodstuffs	14,666	15,913	14,604
Manufactures	32,110	34,779	32,853
Total Exports (f.o.b.)	129,807	152,030	138,831
Exports to the U.S.	31,367	38,609	36,341
Industrial Products	125,353	147,636	134,875
Foodstuffs	1,588	1,739	1,401
Other	3,166	2,655	2,555

*Japanese data

Principal Exports from the U.S. in 1932*

(millions of U.S. dollars)

	Value	Percent of Total
Agricultural Commodities	5,547	—
Corn	1,290	6.2
Soybeans	971	4.6
Wheat	564	2.7
Nonagricultural Commodities	15,118	—
Bituminous coal	1,525	7.3
Inorganic and organic chemicals	1,303	6.2
Logs and lumber	1,045	5.0
Aircraft and parts	906	4.3
Office machining and computers	838	4.0
Electrical machinery and parts	618	2.9
Medical equipment and measuring and controlling instruments	549	2.6
Paper-base stocks	488	2.2

*U.S. data

Government policies on direct portfolio investment by nonresidents follow OECD patterns. In principal, 100 percent foreign capital allowed except for four industrial sectors: agriculture, forestry, and fishing; mining (50 percent); petroleum; and leather and leather products.

Economy

Industrialized nation with the world's second largest market economy. Increasing emphasis on high-technology products and services.

GNP. — CY 1981 $1,128 billion, or about a 3 percent real increase over 1980. Per capita GNP $9,560. Average annual real growth 1971-1981 4.8 percent.

Agriculture. — Average farm size about 2.5 acres. Principal crops: rice, wheat, barley, vegetables, fruit, and tea.

Industry. — World's largest producer of motor vehicles, motorcycles, merchant vessels, and consumer electronics; second in computers, electronic components (including semiconductors), household electric appliances, crude steel, zinc; third in refined copper, synthetic rubber, and newsprint.

Commerce. — Average 1981 wholesale price index up 1.4 percent, consumer price index up 4.9 percent. Retail sales for 1981, $318 billion.

Finance

Currency. — Yen (Y); floating. Average exchange rate for 1982: 249 Y=US$1.

Domestic Credit and Investment. — Official discount rate was 5.50 percent in January 1983. Plant and equipment investment has been relatively flat.

National Budget. — FY 1983 (April 1983—March 1984) planned total expenditure of 50,379 billion yen (about $202 billion at 1982 exchange rate) or 1.4 percent higher than FY 1982 budget. No growth in general expenditures; local finance, -20.4 percent; education and science, -0.9 percent; foreign aid, 7.0 percent; defense, 6 percent; energy, 6 percent; national debt service, 4.6 percent; social security, 0.6 percent; and public works, no increase.

Balance of Payments. — Calendar 1982, overall balance $5 billion deficit, current balance $6.9 billion surplus, trade balance $18.2 billion surplus; calendar 1981, overall balance $2.1 billion deficit, current balance $4.8 billion surplus, trade balance $20 billion surplus. Gold and foreign exchange reserves at yearend 1982, $23.3 billion, down $5.1 billion from 1981.

Basic Economic Facilities

Transportation. — Railroads are main domestic carriers. Merchant fleet is world's second largest. Transportation facilities well developed.

Communications. — Government and private radio and television stations reach all areas. Telephone and telegraph systems are operated by public corporation (NTT).

Power. — Electric power available throughout Japan, including active nuclear power facilities; 523 billion kilowatt hours generated in 1981 by public stations.

Natural Resources

Land. — Four main islands, approximately 147,000 square miles (size of Montana). Mountainous, about 16 percent arable.

Climate. — Similar to U.S. East Coast but more humid.

Minerals. — Low-grade bituminous coal, iron pyrites, limestone, and sulfur. Domestic requirements, especially for oil, met through imports.

Forestry. — Heavily forested but about two-thirds of log supply imported.

Fisheries. — World's largest fishing industry in terms of value, variety of fish, and areas of operation. Important food source and export/import item.

Population

In 1981, 117.9 million; 0.7 percent annual increase. Capital: Tokyo, population 11.6 million. Principal cities: Osaka, 2.6 million; Yokohama, 2.8 million; Nagoya, 2.1 million; Kyoto, 1.5 million; Kobe, 1.4 million. About 76 percent urbanized.

Market Profile—JORDAN

Foreign Trade

Imports.—$2 billion in 1979; $1.5 billion in 1978. Major suppliers of non-military goods in 1979: United States, 16.4 percent; West Germany, 10 percent; United Kingdom, 9.2 percent; Italy, 6.3 percent; Japan, 5.8 percent. Principal non-military imports: oil, foodstuffs, machinery, and transportation equipment.

Exports.—$275 million in 1979; $211 million in 1978. Major customers 1979: Saudi Arabia, 22.1 percent; Syria, 17.2 percent; Kuwait, 7 percent; India, 6.2 percent; Iraq, 5.9 percent; United Kingdom, 4.8 percent, United States, 1.4 percent. Principal exports: phosphates, vegetables, and fruits.

Trade Policy.—Free market system. Government holds important equity positions in many larger enterprises.

Trade Prospects.—Tractors; irrigation and agricultural equipment; construction, mining, and materials handling equipment; medical supplies and equipment; building materials and supplies; air conditioning and refrigeration equipment; telecommunications equipment; electric power equipment; consumer durables.

Foreign Investment

Investment strongly encouraged under favorable legislation that provides tax holidays, exemptions from customs duties, and other incentives, including 100 percent foreign ownership of local enterprises. Legislation also provides for repatriation of capital and dividends. Small U.S. investment in banking, insurance, and footwear manufacture. Good potential in light industrial joint ventures as well as consulting. Investment Guarantee Agreement with U.S. Registration of Foreign Companies Law of 1975 provides incentives for firms to locate regional offices in Amman; around 170 have done so, including more than 50 Americans.

Finance

Currency.—Liberal foreign exchange controls. Jordanian dinar (JD) divided in 1,000 fils; 1 JD equals US$3.33. Inflation rate approximately 14 percent in 1979.

Domestic Credit.—Central Bank, 16 commercial banks, including two U.S. Six specialized credit institutions.

National Budget.—$1,769 million for 1980, a real decrease from 1979 when adjusted for inflation.

Foreign Aid.—Economy heavily dependent on foreign assistance, primarily from the United States, Saudi Arabia, and Kuwait.

Balance of Payments.—Perennially large trade deficit ($1,682 million in 1979) financed by foreign aid and remittances from Jordanians working abroad. International reserves $1.5 billion in 1979.

Economy

GNP.—Estimated $2.8 billion in 1979; $2.3 billion in 1978.

Agriculture.—Wheat, barley, and other crops grown on rainfed lands; production fluctuates widely with rainfall. Fruits and vegetables grown on irrigated land. Major crops: wheat, barley, vegetables (particularly tomatoes), citrus, and other fruits. Declined in importance in 1979 because of poor growing conditions.

Industry.—Major industries are phosphates, cement, and oil refining. Small industries include textiles, pharmaceuticals, cigarettes, batteries, steel rods, food processing, soap, insecticides, and ceramics. Industry accounts for 27 percent of the GDP

Tourism.—Number of tourists averages 900,000–1.2 million per year, providing net receipts of more than $100 million. Hotels and other infrastructure being expanded.

Development Plan.—Five-Year Plan (1976–80) set high growth rate of 12 percent and total investment of $2,318 million. Emphasis is on growth of commodity producing sectors, expansion of exports, and reduction of trade gap through development of agriculture and irrigation, minerals-based industry, mining (particularly phosphates), tourism, and related infrastructure. Indications are that the next five-year plan will continue to deal with improvements in infrastructure and industry, but will place more emphasis on social services.

Basic Economic Facilities

Transportation.—Narrow gauge, single-track railway from Syrian border to port of Aqaba. East Bank has 6,782 miles of roads, of which 4,832 are paved. Aqaba, sole port, handled 1.5 million tons of cargo, about 12 percent of which was transit traffic mainly for Iraq and Saudi Arabia. Construction expected to increase capacity to 4.5 million tons per year. Most important exports passing through are phosphates. Major airport at Amman served by international carriers; new Amman airport under construction. Smaller international airfield at Aqaba. Royal Jordanian Airlines (ALIA) serves Middle East, Western Europe, Asia, and United States.

Communications.—Good telephone system with intercity connection and satellite international links. Television and radio stations.

Power.—1979 production 774.1 million kWh.

Natural Resources

Land.—30,000 square miles (including West Bank); 80 percent desert.

Climate.—Arid and semi-arid subtropical. Summers hot and dry. Winters cooler, with rainfall in some areas from November to April. Periodic droughts.

Minerals.—Phosphate production in 1979 2.8 million metric tons. Potash is the other major mineral resource. Copper under development. Some potential in manganese, petroleum, and other minerals.

Population

Size.—Population in early 1980 estimated at over 2.1 million (East Bank). Annual rate of increase 3.4 percent. More than half urban. More than half under 15 years. Figures based on 1979 census.

Language.—Arabic. English widely used in commerce and government.

Education.—Compulsory elementary education. Nearly two-thirds of population literate; about one-third of population enrolled as full-time students.

Labor.—Estimated size of labor force 383,000; about 60 percent in services sector, 20 percent in agriculture, 20 percent in industry, construction and mining, with a shift from agriculture toward industry. The labor force is relatively well educated. A shortage of skilled and semi-skilled workers exists because of the large-scale labor migration to Arab oil producing countries. This has resulted in the import of significant amounts of unskilled foreign labor. About 75,000 foreign workers.

Marketing in Kenya

Contents

Report Revised May 1982

KENYA

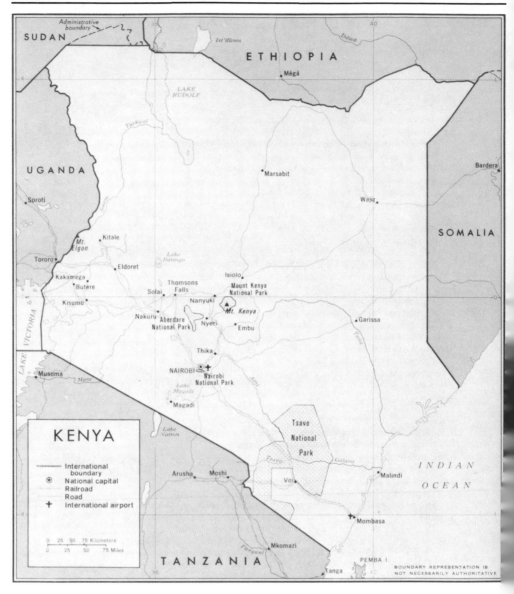

1386

Trade Outlook

Declining export receipts and rampant population growth spell a continuation of foreign exchange shortage and more hard times ahead for the Republic of Kenya.

Once characterized by a rapid growth rate from its earliest days of independence in 1963, Kenya's economic difficulties came to a head in the late 1970's, then boiled over into the 1980's as real growth lost pace with the country's soaring population increase, causing a decline in per capita gross domestic product (GDP). In addition to an annual population growth rate of nearly 4 percent (the world's highest), the principal factors in Kenya's economic stagnation are a high-priced, import-intensive industrial sector, low world prices for coffee and tea, continued bottlenecks in the agricultural sector, and rapidly increasing prices for manufactured imports. In 1981, these factors combined to hold down U.S. sales to Kenya to $150 million, just 6 percent above the 1980 level. With the GDP growth rate expected to run below 3 percent per annum over the next 3 to 5 years, U.S. exports to Kenya may face more serious constraints if the country experiences further deterioration in its terms of trade and continued foreign exchange difficulties.

A resurgence in world prices for exports of coffee and tea would go a long way toward easing some of Kenya's problems. In the meantime, the Kenyan Government has taken steps to implement the provisions of a Standby Agreement from the International Monetary Fund (IMF) designed to tide the country over the upcoming structural adjustment period. The Kenya shilling was devalued by 30 percent against the dollar in 1981, and major revisions were made in Kenya's tariff schedule. Differential duties have replaced the previous quota system for many imports. Kenya is now attempting to emphasize agriculture and agribusiness, as well as improved industrial efficiency and investment in labor and export intensive projects. However, the gravity of current conditions, particularly in the wake of unfavorable international economic trends, leaves little hope for any strong improvements in Kenya's economy for the forseeable future.

Opportunities for U.S. Exports

Notwithstanding the country's dim prospects, Kenya still offers one of the more attractive investment climates in Africa. Private direct investment by U.S. firms is approximately $315 million, comprised of both manufacturing and sales and service facilities. Over 200 U.S. firms have established regional offices in Kenya due to the excellent transportation and communications infrastructure. Concessions and protection offered to private investors will not be as generous as in the past, but foreign investment will continue to be welcomed. As in years past, priority will be given to firms involved in labor-intensive, export-oriented industries that utilize local raw materials and introduce new technology. U.S. suppliers may find opportunities for sales of agricultural chemicals, medical supplies and equipment, aviation equipment, business machines, and computers and peripherals.

Economic Sectors

Kenyans became accustomed to rapid economic growth during the years following independence. Between 1964 and, 1973, real GDP growth averaged 6.6 percent annually. That average dropped to 4 percent between 1973 and 1977. It has remained about 2 percent since 1979 and appears unlikely to exceed 3 percent before 1984, still well below the targeted rate of 5.4 percent established in the country's latest 5-year Development Plan initiated in early 1979. A major result of this has been the decline in real per capita national income as Kenya's population has grown at a staggering 3.96 percent annual rate.

Kenya's rapid population growth means steadily increasing burdens on government services, such as education and health, and on the ability of the economy to absorb the more than 250,000 new job seekers each year. Population growth also places great pressure on agriculture to provide food and employment, sufficient foreign exchange earnings to finance industrial development, and adequate inputs for developing agribusiness. Between 1964 and 1974, agricultural output grew at a real rate of 4.7 percent per annum. The rate was only 2.4 percent between 1974 and 1979, and was less than 1 percent per annum in 1980 and 1981. Shortfalls in maize production resulted in sizable imports in 1980 and 1981, a drain in foreign exchange of over $150 million. Many farmers, as well as expert observers, believe government intervention in pricing and market controls have contributed to production instability, to supply and demand distortion, and to substantial losses by farmers and government marketing bodies. In effect, the urban consumer has been subsidized at the expense of the farmer.

Kenya also must come to grips with an industrial structure that has grown increasingly out of kilter with Kenya's needs. Under the import substitution (or import reduction) strategy of the 1960's and 1970's, manufactured output grew at a rate of about 9 percent per annum in real terms and by 10.5 percent between 1972 and 1978. That growth rate was achieved behind extensive import barriers, primarily quantitative, and overvaluation of the shilling. Price setting, market sharing, and other administrative practices also contributed to development of inward looking, relatively high priced, and capital import-intensive manufacturing. The available Kenyan market is so small that most goods are produced on a less-than-optimal scale, and thus at higher-than-optimal cost. Large firms have tended to encourage redefinition of demand away from traditional, often labor-intensive, indigenous products in favor of packaged, name brand products that may or may not be of better quality. Resources were bid away from other existing or potential sectors such as capital and intermediate goods, agriculture, and export manufacturing. The import component of manufactured output is often 60 percent or more and cost more in foreign exchange than would imports of the finished products that now have been eliminated. Manufactured exports dropped from 23 percent of total exports in 1972 to only 11 percent in 1978.

Persistent balance-of-payments difficulties, coupled with impending shortfalls in government revenues caused by reduced levels of economic activity, has resulted in a major reassessment of the goals of Kenya's 1979–83 Development Plan. Lower than expected revenue growth has necessitated a 12-percent cut in anticipated government expenditures during the 4-year period of the Plan from the original $8.5 billion. However, the reductions have been made more heavily in the development budget (down 17.6 percent) than in recurrent expenditures (4.8 percent). The cut in planned government-financed capital formation is a result of the need to reduce foreign commercial borrowing, which has become much more expensive than originally anticipated. The World Bank estimates that Kenya will require over $5 billion in external resources over the next 5 years, of which about $2.7 billion is expected to be provided by assistance agencies. Thus, $2.3 billion plus will have to come from private sector sources, either in the form of direct investment or commercial loans. There are indications that the next few years may see a dramatic increase in the country's debt service burden, which could dampen private sector enthusiasm for financial involvement.

Real per capita income at constant prices fell by 1.5 percentage points to $251 in 1981. This followed a decline of 1.3 percent in real per capita income in 1980. Current population is estimated at over 16 million.

Agriculture

General

About 90 percent of Kenya's population lives in rural areas and depends primarily upon agriculture, which provides over 25 percent of recorded wage employment. In 1980, the sector contributed about 30 percent of GDP, of which about 16 percent is provided by subsistence agriculture and 14 percent by monetary agriculture. Less than 20 percent of Kenya's land has high or medium agricultural potential. Most of the better land is in the highlands in western Kenya or along the coast. Because of geographic and climatic variations, diverse farm commodities are produced. The principal export products are coffee, tea, sisal, beef, and pyrethrum. The major food products marketed domestically are maize, wheat, sugar, livestock, and dairy products. Maize is the main subsistence crop. Pulses, cassava, millet, and bananas also are grown for subsistence. Before independence, the agricultural market sector was dominated by large-scale holdings generally operated by Europeans. Most of these holdings have been transferred to Africans either intact or subdivided. Considerable efforts have been made to develop smallholder agriculture in the traditional farming areas, especially through encouraging the production of high value export crops, such as coffee, tea and pyrethrum, and through introducing hybrid maize and improved cattle. As a result of these developments, small-scale farms produce about 50 percent of total marketed agricultural production.

Agricultural exports have increased faster than the total value of agricultural product. During 1967–73, the value of agricultural exports increased an average of 11.8 percent per annum, in contrast to the 7.6-percent gain for total agricultural production and the 9.8-percent increase for production in the monetary sector. At the beginning of the period, agricultural exports were valued at 71 percent of total exports compared with about 68 percent at the end of this period. Total exports rose an average of 12.2 percent per annum during the period.

During the period from 1963 until 1973, Kenya was successful in expanding its important agricultural sector by an average real growth rate of over 4 percent annually. A significant part of this growth was attributable to private large-scale farming. Substantial progress also was achieved by smallholders. The latter mainly focused on export cash crops such as tea, coffee, and pyrethrum, which are promoted by single crop statutory boards. More recently, Kenya has recognized the need to give higher priority to the needs of less privileged small farmers in areas largely excluded from the development process. Kenya now aims to both widen the social impact of development and the production base to strengthen the economy suffering from a number of adverse international economic factors. The Kenyan Government has prepared the Integrated Agricultural Development Program to meet these objectives. Increased emphasis is being placed on decentralized planning and projected implementation and its aim to progressively develop comprehensive farm systems rather than the promotion of a single crop or farming activity. In both respects, this program represents a significant change in the approach to smallholder agriculture.

Government direct services to agriculture are delivered through the Ministries of Agriculture, Cooperative Development, Natural Resources and Works, as well as through more than 15 statutory corporations and boards. Apart from the installation and maintenance of roads, water supplies, and other agricultural infrastructure, these services include the provision and regulation of research, extension and staff and farmer training, input and output marketing, credit, price controls for inputs and outputs, and regulation of land title.

Active locations and detailed coverage of each project are to be determined by work plans prepared at least once a year and agreed upon by the Kenyan Government and the World Bank.

Climate.—Equatorial Africa provides two distinct rainy seasons, the long rains (essentially from March through May) and the short rains (September through November). These seasons are separated by the two driest months (January and July).

Soils.—In the higher altitudes, there are deep red, friable loams where the rectification of phosphate deficiency leads to good crop yields. Available soil moisture usually is adequate to help the crop through the two dry seasons at the beginning and mid-year periods. For annual arable cropping, especially of shallow-rooted crops, the soil moisture availability can often be critical. This has been indicated in the occasional years of low cereal yields.

On the plateaus below the higher elevations there is a range of soil types. The more common type has a lateritic horizon often with impeded drainage. A second type, also found at lower elevations, is the "black cotton" soil commonly found in Nyanza, the Kano Plain, and some of the coastal shores of Lake Victoria. These soils become difficult to manage under very wet conditions and generally have low nutrient quality. Available soil moisture is less than the red soils at higher elevations. In general, there are less optimum yield levels at these lower altitudes.

Irrigation

Only 25,000 acres of land in Kenya are irrigated. The irrigable potential of the country is at least 500,000 acres and probably a great deal more. Since its formation in 1966, the National Irrigation Board (NIB) has undertaken six large schemes while the Ministry of Agriculture continues to oversee minor irrigation. NIB's schemes are (1) Mwea, 15,000 acres of Pakistani paddy rice; (2) Ahero, 2,000 acres of paddy rice and sugar cane; (3) Bunyala, 500 acres of paddy rice; (4) Perkerra, 770 acres of onions, chilies, and other horticultural crops; (5) West Kano, 2,000 acres of paddy rice and sugar cane; (6) Hola, 2,100 acres of cotton, maize, and pulses. The gross value of the produce from these schemes is $4 million annually. Approximately 5,000 tenant farmers supply the labor and derive income.

Mwea has already realized its maximum potential, but there is considerable expansion possible in the West Kano scheme for rice and sugar cane in the Kisumu Valley. In 1968, President Kenyatta directed that a 2,000-acre irrigation scheme be undertaken for rice at Kisumu, but the endeavor was troubled by blast disease and hailstones. NIB shifted to a more resistant variety of rice.

The Hola scheme already yields 2,500 pounds of excellent cotton per acre. Since 1969, however, Hola has been a pilot experiment for the development of a more extensive area in which sugar cane as well as cotton appears promising. In 1956, Alexander Gibbs Partners identified the region of the upper Tana River (surrounding Meru and Garissa) as the potential nucleus of an irrigable stretch of 1 million acres. The Dutch financed the research station at Hola and commissioned the Dutch consulting firm ILACO to do a feasibility study for the lower Tana as well. Completed in 1972, the study identified Bura area on the west bank of the Tana River's basin as also irrigable, with a potential of 200,000 acres suitable for cotton, rice, and sugar cane. About 11,000 families eventually will settle as tenants upon invitation. The population of the scheme is expected to reach 100,000. NIB will construct a diversion weir across the Tana River, then construct a main canal of 61 kilometers with secondary and tertiary canals and surface drainage; the motive force will be gravity. Total cost of Dura is projected at $168 million. The World Bank confirmed $46 million; the Netherlands, $15 million; the Commonwealth Development Corporation, between $5 million and $10 million (at 8 percent); the European Community, $12 million; the Federal Republic of Germany, $20 million; and the Government of Kenya, suppliers credits up to $2.3 million.

Irrigation techniques are needed to mine aquifiers, recharge water-bearing strata, catch storm runoffs, or desalinate. Other possible techniques might be flash distillation; electrodialysis, vacuum freezing, reverse osmosis, filtration under pressure, mising volatile hydrocarbons with sea water, solar distillation, windmill pumps, and hydraulic rams.

Livestock

Livestock represents a major national resource for Kenya. The livestock population consists of about 9.5 million cattle (including 500,000 dairy cows) and about 8 million sheep and goats. Half of the cattle is concentrated in densely populated agricultural areas and the other half is widely spread over the sparsely settled rangelands. About 500,000 are found on large-scale commercial ranches; these are the principal source of quality beef production. Over 800,000 head of cattle are slaughtered annually, a total offtake rate of about 9 percent. Only about 285,000 head are marketed through commercial farms and ranches and half from traditional pastoral areas. Domestic per capita beef consumption (about 13 kilograms) is high in comparison with that of other countries in eastern Africa.

The indigenous Zebu, with a total of about 8.8 million head, is the most important type of livestock in Kenya. Two subtypes and a number of intermediate stages also are identifiable. The large East African Zebu that occupies the northern and northeastern range areas totals about 1.6 million head. The small East African Zebu, which is indigenous to the highlands and southern range areas, totals about 5.1 million head. An estimated 2.1 million head are of intermediate size. The major part of Kenya's commercial beef cattle consists of improved Boran and its crosses with exotic breeds; there are about 500,000 such animals in the country. The majority of dairy cattle are owned by smallholders and settlement farmers in Central Province. Dairy cattle are increasing rapidly in the high potential areas of eastern Kenya. The annual increase in the number of dairy cows currently is about 8 percent. A large proportion of the dairy herd is comprised of crossbreds of exotic dairy breeds and the indigenous Zebu.

The major animal disease problems include trypanosomiasis, East Coast and other tickboner fevers, Contagious Bovine Pleuropneumonia, and Foot and Mouth Disease. Rinderpest has been almost eliminated. The standard of veterinary service is good and an active program of disease control is being carried out.

All livestock markets, stock routes, and holding grounds are owned and operated by the Livestock Marketing Division (LMD) of the Ministry of Agriculture. LMD acts as buyer of last resort and is the largest buyer of cattle from Northeast Province. In 1972, LMD purchased about 18 percent of total cattle marketed, and purchases were almost entirely from Northeast Province.

The Kenya Meat Commission

The Kenya Meat Commission (KMC) agency, has a monopoly over exports of meat and meat products. About 50 percent of its total production is exported. Most of the canned beef is exported to the United Kingdom and the chilled and boneless beef recently have been sent to Italy, Spain, and Switzerland. KMC owns and operates two large meat packing plants at Athi River and Mombasa. The processing capacity of these facilities is about 155,000 and 60,000 head, respectively. The Athi River plant is within the disease-free zone and generally is considered to meet export standards.

Forestry

Heavy dependence on wood for fuel and housing are effectively depleting Kenya's forest reserves leading to serious land degradation in certain areas of the country. To reverse conditions, the Forestry Department of the Ministry of Environment and Natural Resources replanted 4,000 hectares of forest in 1980 bringing the total forest plantation area increased to an estimated 146,500 hectares.

Hectares within the Turbo afforestation areas are earmarked to supply timber to the pulp and paper mill at Webuye. The $35.4 million pulp and paper mill at Webuye, which began operations in late 1974, has a log intake of 275,000 cubic meters and produces 45,000 metric tons of paper annually. In addition, three plywood mills, with an output capacity of 3.8 million square meters, are in production. Two other plywood mills are to be built in the Transmara and northeastern Mt. Kenya areas. When all are completed, the five mills are expected to have a combined annual production of 5.4 million square meters. A fiberboard mill at Elburgon, which was completed in 1974, has an output capacity of 700 metric tons of manufactured hardboard for domestic use.

Fisheries

In 1981, the Government of Kenya completed construction on a Kenya shelling (Kshs.) 19 million fish processing plant near Lake Turkana. The plant received funding from the Norwegian Agency for International Development and is capable of processing 6,000 kilos of fish per week. Kenya is a net importer of fish and fishery products.

Manufacturing

Diversification of Industry

Although manufacturing accounts for only 13 percent of GDP, Kenya is industrially the most developed country in East Africa. Manufacturing no longer centers entirely on mining and agricultural processing as it did before independence. The diversification of industry has been rapid under a policy of protection for import substitution industries and a more recent policy of exporting agricultural commodities already processed. In this latter category come the food processing industries—meat processing, sugar refining, fruit canning, dairy products, brewing, instant tea and cashew nuts processing—as well as the manufacture of sisal and hessian goods, cotton spinning and textiles, pyrethrum products, animal feeds, hides and skins, and pump and paper. Kenya also produces cement and cement products, petroleum products, chemical products including soap, paint and pharmaceuticals, and metal products.

Motor Vehicle Assembly

The Kenyan Government, through ICDC, has 51 percent and the General Motors Corporation of the United States 49 percent of the shares of a commercial vehicle assembly plant in Nairobi. The plant assembles Bedford and Isuzu light, medium, and heavy vehicles and Chevy Luv, a pickup truck. The Kenyan Government also has a majority share in the British Leyland plant at Thika, which assembles and exports trucks, buses, Land Rover and Range Rover four-wheel drive vehicles and Volkswagen light commercial vehicles. A plant at Mombasa is operated by Associated Vehicle Assemblers, a London-based consortium of Inch Cape, MacKenzie, and Lonhro. It uses imported Ford, Mercedes, Peugeot, Datsun, and Toyota components. In 1981, the American Motors Corporation (AMC) of the United States announced plans to establish its first Sub-Saharan Africa assembly facility in Kenya. AMC proposes to assemble 4-wheel drive deisel jeeps for distribution throughout Kenya and East Africa.

Mining and Minerals

Mineral exploration in Kenya intensified in the 1970's. Discoveries include exploitable deposits of nickel and chrome ore and a ruby deposit reported to be the world's richest. Lead, silver, and zinc ore in production, in addition to crude minerals (including fertilizer), comprised natron (natural sodium bicarbonate or soda ash), fluorspar, lime, limestone, salt, carbon dioxide, magnetite, and minor quantities of barites, feldspar, magnesite, diatomite, vermiculites, woolastonite, copper, gold, sapphires, garnets, tourmalines, and aquamarines. A deposit of green garnets has been discovered in addition to the red garnets already produced. Deposits of niobium and europium (rare earths used in stainless steel) have been discovered in the coastal area.

A number of other minerals are present in exploitable quantities, and some are actively mined in years when rising demand brings the world market price above the cost of extraction. The lack of cheap energy resources and the distance of deposits from industrial centers or transport has precluded development of several minerals.

Kenya has been attracting considerable interest from numerous oil prospectors, and the World Bank is helping provide assistance in collating and compiling available geographical and geological information, as well as legal aspects of exploration. No commercial finds have been recorded to date, but the oil-bearing formation discovered in southern Sudan might well extend down the Rift Valley into Kenya. Cities Service has drilled several exploratory wells off Kenya's northern coast, but the results thus far have been inconclusive. In value terms, soda ash is still the most important mining operation although the quantity mined has declined slightly in recent years.

Trade Policy and Regulations

Import Duties

For 10 years Kenya, along with Tanzania and Uganda, was a member of the East African Community. Under the Treaty of East African Cooperation (EAC), the three countries maintained a common external tariff, abolished quantitative restrictions on movements of manufactures between themselves, and maintained East African corporations to run their airways, railways, harbors, posts and telecommunications and other services. This cooperation was terminated in 1977. EAC services have now been absorbed into the national civil services of the member countries.

Kenya uses the Brussels Tariff Nomenclature (BTN) system. Under the Customs Tariff Amendment of 1975, which came into force in Kenya on January 1, 1976, tariff preferences to the European Economic Community (EEC) were abolished and the former three-column tariff was reduced to a single column. Ad valorem duties on most items imported range from 12.5 to 75 percent. Ad valorem duties are assessed on the c.i.f. value comprising the original cost of the goods plus freight, insurance, commissions, and all other charges incurred in the making of the sale and delivering the goods to the port of entry. If this information is not available, duties are assessed at the port of entry on the price that the goods would command in the local market.

Specific duties also cover a wide range of rates. The amount of duty depends largely on whether or not the item is considered essential or a luxury or if it is readily available locally. Specific duties, where applicable, are based on the weight, length, area, volume, or number of the imported goods. Where duty is assessed according to weight, the net weight is used. However, if the package does not indicate the net weight of its contents or if no one can furnish the net weight, then the duty is assessed on the gross weight of the package and its contents.

In 1981, the Kenyan Government unveiled a new imports policy linked to a revised tariff schedule in an effort to shift emphasis from import substitution to promotion of industrial exports and the elimination of quantitative restrictions and import licensing. Henceforth, all imported goods will be categorized into three import schedules on the basis of their importance to the Kenyan economy. The three schedules are as follows: Schedule I (most essential, i.e., raw materials, capital goods, spare parts, etc.), Schedule II A (priority goods used in industry or agriculture and petroleum products), and Schedule IIB (nonessential, goods for which domestic equivalents or substitutes exist). Schedule IIB items will receive the foreign exchange remaining after the demand for the importation of more essential goods is satisfied.

For information on the import tariffs applying to specific products, contact the International Trade Administration's Africa Division, U.S. Department of Commerce, Washington, D.C. 20230, or call (202) 377-4564.

Sales Taxes

Most imports are subject to a sales tax of 10 percent of the c.i.f. value plus the import duty. Only medicines and farm inputs are exempted.

Advance payment

Advance payments for imports are allowed only in exceptional circumstances. Exchange for import payments normally is not granted until after customs clearance. This does not apply to imports by the Government or parastatal organizations. In all cases, payment is made 60 days after shipment or railment.

Import Licensing

Beginning in 1971, and modified during each subsequent year, Kenya has imposed import procedures and restrictions to conserve reduced or threatened foreign exchange reserves. Controls that were established in 1974 on capital transfers and local borrowing by foreign-controlled companies continue to be enforced.

Duty Exemptions

Exemptions from import duties normally are allowed for emergency medical equipment, items for personal use, diplomatic and consular goods, and items for the use of the Kenyan Government, charitable organizations, educational, and other similar institutions. Duty refunds often are granted for imported materials to be used for local production. The Minister in charge may also grant refunds of duty where he believes it would be in the public interest to do so or where payment of duty would operate harshly or inequitably. Suspended duties are found on a number of items for which local production is nonexistent or insufficient, but for which expanded production is planned.

Customs Surcharges

No customs surcharges are imposed in Kenya.

Excise Duties

Excise duties are assessed *ad valorem* on beer, sugar, tobacco, and its manufactured products, matches, spirits, soap and soap products, woven fabrics, paints, varnishes, lacquers, enamels, and distempers.

Pre-Inspection

All commodities imported into Kenya are subject to preshipment inspection for quality and quantity as well as for price comparison. The General Superintendence Company, Ltd., a private Swiss firm, conducts the inspection in the country of original shipment of the goods. Suppliers should give General Superintendence at least 7 days notice before indicating the place where the goods can be inspected and the expected time of shipment. Upon satisfactory completion of the inspection and receipt of all required documents, General Superintendence will issue a "Clean Report of Findings." Banks may not make payment against a letter of credit or a bank draft unless a Clean Report of Findings has been issued. The cost of the inspection services will be paid by the Government of Kenya.

The General Superintendence Company, Inc. has offices at 17 Battery Place, North, New York, N.Y., 10004; 1110 S. Highland Avenue, Baltimore, Md. 21224; 325 Chestnut Street, Philadelphia,. Pa. 19106; 203 North Wabash Street, Chicago, Ill. 60601; 4100 Tchoupitoulas Street, New Orleans, La. 70115; 6001 Gulf Freeway, Houston, Tex. 77017; and has agents in all other ports.

Shipping Documents

No prescribed form of invoice or consular document is needed for shipments to Kenya and there are no consular fees. Documents required are the commercial invoice, the bill of lading, and certain sanitary and other certificates. Required documents for goods sent by air are the same as those for goods sent by ship or other forms of transportation.

Shipping documents should be forwarded as soon as possible by air mail separately from the goods to ensure their receipt by the consignee prior to the arrival of the goods at the port of entry of goods into East African ports or clearance will be delayed.

Any alterations made on any required document prior to its acceptance by the various customs authorities must be made in such a manner as to show the error and the alteration in legible form. Each alteration must be initialed and dated by the person making the correction.

The ordinary customs declaration, submitted in duplicate, can be used for import declarations. The following information should be shown on the invoice: The country of origin; quantity of goods; the true market value in the country of origin; all costs of packing, insurance, and freight up to the port of entry; the exact nature of any discounts and/or commissions given by the seller to the buyer; and the import license number.

Shipping marks and numbers on bills of lading, on the goods themselves, and on the invoices, should correspond exactly to ensure prompt clearance by customs. In addition, weight measure on which freight is charged may also be added, if possible.

Although not required by law, a packing list facilitates clearance through customs. If used, the list should contain the following information: Marks and numbers of packages, gross and net weight of each package, and a careful description of each package and its contents. These lists are especially recommended for consignments of miscellaneous goods.

There are no special requirements for the preparation of bills of lading. Only the particulars usually shown on such documents need be inserted. No invoice is normally required for bona fide private parcel post shipment. In the case of "trade goods" (packages other than those addressed to a private individual for his own use) shipped by parcel post which exceed $28 (224 shillings) in c.i.f. value, must be accompanied by the proper customs invoice.

Sanitary and Other Special Certificates

Importation of animals, plants, seeds, and used clothing is subject to quarantine regulations. Except for used clothing, importation is allowed only at designated ports of entry.

Every imported animal must be accommpanied by a certificate, from a qualified veterinary surgeon, that it was free from disease at the time of exportation. Examination by a veterinarian at the port of entry is also required.

Kenya requires a special import permit for plants and seeds issued by the Kenyan Director of Agriculture. This permit is also required for fresh fruits, as well as a certificate signed by an appropriate government official in the exporting country. In addition, such imports are subject to examination by an agricultural officer at the designated port of entry. Plants not covered by this special permit will be destroyed. Seeds not covered by permit will not be destroyed unless they come from the following plants: coffee (except roasted beans), cotton, tobacco, tea, cacao, coconuts, groundnuts, lucerne and clover, rubber, maize, wheat, cloves, peach, barberry, buckthorn, and potatoes.

A certificate of disinfection must be presented to the customs authorities for the import of used clothing intended for sale.

Labeling and Marking Requirements

There are no specific requirements as to the labeling or marking of imported goods, except for condensed milk, paints and varnishes, and vegetable and butter ghee. However, all goods bearing any wording in the English language should indicate the country of origin.

Under customs law, manufactured articles bearing the name, address, or trademark of any manufacturer or dealer or bearing the name of any place in the United Kingdom or any member country of the Commonwealth calculated to impart to them a special character of British manufacture, though not of such manufacture, are prohibited imports. Also banned are any articles marked, without authority of Her Majesty, with the royal arms or monogram, or arms or monogram so closely resembling the same as to be calculated to deceive.

———

Senate Concurrent Resolution 40, adopted July 30, 1953, invites U.S. exporters to inscribe, insofar as practicable, on the external shipping containers in indelible print of a suitable size: "United States of America." Although such marking is not compulsory under our laws, U.S. shippers are urged to cooperate in publicizing American-made goods.

Metric System

Kenya indicated its intention to switch its weights and measures to the metric system in 1968. Gradually varying sectors of the economy and specified municipal areas have been instructed to adopt the metric system exclusively.

In the remaining economic and geographic sectors, the dual English and metric measures continue to be used. Items to be sold by specific weight or measure may be published by the government from time to time. Labeling indicating quantities in denominations other than those specified must be obliterated.

A special ordinance provides that imports of prepackaged paints and allied products must be sold by net metric weight or metric fluid measure. Paints packed in tubes or boxes, commonly sold as artists' or children's paints, are excepted from these regulations.

Imports of pharmaceutical products from the United States may be labeled according to U.S. pharmacopoeia standards.

All goods should be securely packed to withstand excessive tropical heat, moisture, rough handling, and pilferage. East African importers recommended that American shippers avoid use of thin cardboard and plywood containers because such containers are easily broken into and readily damaged if exposed to the weather. To ensure safe arrival at the port of destination all packages should be of sturdy construction, properly supported, preferably on the inside, and banded on the outside with steel strapping.

Special Customs Provisions

Entry, Transit, and Reexport

Kenya operates no free trade zones, free ports, or any other customs privileged facilities. Goods imported are admitted for home consumption, warehousing, transit, and transshipment. Entry must be made within the prescribed time after arrival of the ship in port.

Goods inadmissible at port of entry are removed to a government warehouse after 21 days from the date of commencement of unloading and are sold if still not admitted after 3 months and after advertisement in the appropriate official gazette.

Goods admitted in transit are allowed to pass through Kenya under security bond. They are under customs control until reexported. Goods for transshipment can be transshipped directly from the importing vessel or within 21 days if the appropriate customs officer permits. Goods admitted in transit or for transshipment under bond on which import duties were not paid can be reexported from a bonded warehouse without payment of import duties.

Where goods are reexported and duties were paid at the time of importation, a refund of the amount originally paid can be obtained. A claim for such a refund (or drawback) can be made provided the owner produces such goods for examination, describes the goods on the prescribed form, makes and subscribes to a declaration that such goods have actually been exported and will not be reimported into Kenya and that the owner was and is the person entitled to the drawback, and presents his claim for drawback within 12 months of exportation of the goods.

No drawback is allowed if the value of such goods for home consumption is less than the amount of the drawback that may be allowed, if the import duty thereon was less than 40 shillings ($5), if the exported goods have been destroyed by accident on board aircraft or vessel, or if the goods have been materially damaged at any port or place in the country. Furthermore, no drawback is allowed unless the goods are exported in the original packages in which they were imported or unless contents were unpacked and repacked by authority and under supervision of a customs official.

The duty will be remitted on any goods lost or destroyed by accident on board vessel or aircraft, or in removing or unloading from any customs areas or warehouse before they are delivered out of customs control. Duty also will be refunded on any duty paid in error. No duty refund will be allowed for reexported goods unless the claim is submitted within 12 months of time of exportation.

Warehousing

Goods may be stored in a bonded warehouse for a period of 2 years, after which, if not rewarehoused or cleared by the owner, they may be sold by the Customs Collector.

Goods admitted for domestic consumption that remain in any warehouse more than 14 days may be forfeited to the Government or destroyed as the Commissioner of Customs and Excise may direct. This regulation is rarely implemented. Dutiable goods on first importation may be stored in a bonded warehouse without payment of duty.

Goods deposited in a government warehouse are subject to rent and other charges as may be prescribed. If these charges are not met, the goods may be sold and the proceeds applied to the charges. Goods that have been abandoned to Customs will be destroyed or disposed of at the owner's expense. Duty on such goods may be remitted or refunded on application to the customs officer.

Samples and Advertising Matter

Kenya is a member of the International Convention to facilitate the Importation of Commercial Samples and Advertising. Samples that the Commissioner of Customs and Excise decide are of no commercial value may be admitted free of duty. The duty on samples not so exempted must be paid on entry, and the deposit later refunded, provided the samples are reexported within 6 months of the date of importation. The period of 6 months may not be extended. Imports of samples and advertising matter into Kenya are subject to normal licensing and documentary requirements.

Price list and catalogs are permitted duty-free entry. Showcards and similar printed matter advertising goods grown or produced, or services to be supplied from outside Kenya and imported for advertising purposes only (but not including calendars, diaries, date indicators, desk pads and other advertising stationery) are also admitted free of duty.

Advance Rulings on Classification

Requests for advance rulings on customs classification of merchandise not specifically mentioned in the customs tariff or on a doubtful classification may be submitted in writing (together with a sammple, if practicable, or advertising notes) to the Commissioner of Customs and Excise at any Customs House in Mombasa or Nairobi. However, such advance rulings are not binding on the authorities.

Appeals and Claims

The Commissioner of Customs and Excise, with the consent of the importer, may settle a dispute between the importer and a customs officer. Otherwise, the dispute will be settled in court. There is no appeal against decisions of the Commissioner of Customs and Excise where the accused offender has consented to accept the Commisioner's decision. In cases heard by the courts, penalties and forfeitures inflicted by the courts may be appealed in accordance with the rules of the court.

When any vehicle or goods have been seized by customs authorities as forfeited, the Commissioner may—by written notification—require the claimant to institute suite against him for recovery or may himself cause suit to be instituted in any competent court for the forfeiture of the vehicle or goods. In the former instance, if the claimant does not enter his suit against the Commissioner within 2 months, the goods are automatically forfeited. If the Commissioner fails to notify the claimant within 2 months or fails to institute proceedings himself, ownership of the goods reverts to the claimant.

In any case of dispute as to the amount or rate of duty payable or as to the liability of goods to duty, the duty should be paid in accordance with a prescribed procedure. The owner may sue for the recovery of such duty paid provided he commences the suit within 6 months after the date of payment.

Credit and Finance

Currency

The official currency is the Kenya shilling (KSh.), which is divided into 100 cents. The par value of the shilling is 0.103133 gram of fine gold. A central rate of KSh. 9.66 = 1 Special Drawing Right (SDR) of the International Monetary Fund was established on October 27, 1976. In transactions with authorized banks, the Central Bank of Kenya stands ready to issue Kenya shillings in exchange for U.S. dollars and to supply U.S. dollars in exchange for Kenya shillings at rates posted on the IMF's daily calculation of the U.S. dollar/SDR rate. As of December 31, 1981, approximately KSh. 10.0 was the equivalent of US$1.

Banking

The Kenyan Central Bank performs the functions of issuance and redemption of notes and coins and the administration, regulation, and direction of the currency system and the banking system in accordance with the economic policy of the Government.

Commercial banking in Kenya is relatively well developed and generally is used in financing wholesale and retail trade, manufacturing, export crops, and other major business functions. Commercial banking operations have been subject to increasing degrees of government participation over the last several years.

In mid-1970, the Kenyan Government announced it would take 60 percent participation in the operations of the National and Grindlays Bank. The Kenya Commercial Bank has taken over 78 of the existing 81 branches of Grindlays Bank. The remaining three branches formed another bank, Grindlays Bank International (Kenya), Ltd., in which the Kenyan Government holds 40 percent of the shares and the National and Grindlays Bank, 60 percent. The British-owned Barclays Bank and Standard Bank, Ltd., have branches in Kenya.

Seven American banks have branches or affiliations: The Bank of America, the Chase Manhattan Bank, Citibank, Chemical Bank, the Continental Illinois Bank, Manufacturers Hanover, and the First National Bank of Chicago. Bankers Trust is in the process of opening a representative office.

Other foreign commercial banks operating in Kenya include the Bank of India, Ltd.; the Bank of Baroda, Ltd.; the Algemene Bank Nederland N.V.; Habib Bank (Overseas) Ltd.; The Ottoman Bank; and the Commercial Bank of Africa. Two local Kenyan commercial banks—the Cooperative Bank of Kenya, Ltd., and the National Bank of Kenya—began operations in 1968.

Other financial institutions operating in Kenya include a Post Office Savings Bank, building societies (which provide mortgage loans for residential and commercial buildings), savings and loan companies, hire-purchase firms, and insurance companies. A stock market operates in Nairobi where trading takes place in shares and public securities.

Distribution and Sales Channels

Kenya has a relatively low cost distribution system and price competition in wholesale and retail trade is intense. The local import trade is dominated by several large trading companies affiliated with British and continental European suppliers. Their influence as wholesalers, retailers, and investors is felt at all levels of commerce.

Distribution Centers

The main points of population concentration are Nairobi, the capital (850,000), Mombasa (400,000), Visumu (150,000), Nakuru (130,000), Machakoo and Meru to the East (85,000 and 70,000, respectively), Eldoret (50,000), and Thika in central Kenya (41,000).

Nairobi, the commercial hub of East Africa, is centrally located in both Kenya and East Africa as a whole. It is located at the edge of the prosperous agricultural settlements of the Kenya Highlands, and is the focal point of regional transport and communications. The city is also an industrial center, producing vegetable oils, pyrethrum extract, processed coffee, beer, carbonated beverages, cigarettes, knitwear, shoes, furniture, tires, containers, metal structures, glassware, batteries, plastic products, soaps and detergents, paints, bricks, and a wide variety of consumer and light industrial products for local and regional use, as well as export.

The preeminence of Nairobi as a center for wholesale distribution is evident in each of the several levels of its commercial hinterland. At the lowest level, Nairobi serves as a domestic trading center, supplying local markets. Although much of the region to the south and west is sparsely populated, purchasing power is high in the prosperous farming districts to the north and east—an area of affluent European population and dense African settlement, which has become increasingly significant as cash incomes have risen. A wide range of goods is involved in this provincial trade, and merchants in towns such as Nyeri and Meru may be entirely dependent on suppliers in Nairobi.

Nairobi also serves as a regional wholesale distribution center. Many firms operating throughout the region have their headquarters in Nairobi. Finally, despite its inland location, Nairobi is the center for the major portion of the region's export trade. The city also serves as a retail center for a large part of the surrounding area. The relative affluence of Nairobi's civil servants and business and industrial workers has fostered the development of a relatively sophisticated retail sector in the city and, in a more recent development, the establishment of groups of up to 20 shops in Nairobi's upper-income suburbs, in the shopping center pattern familiar to American retailing.

Nairobi derives a certain commercial advantage from its role as an administrative center, and most of those marketing services normally available in a major distribution center are available there. U.S. exporters should not hesitate to avail themselves of these services in developing sales promotion programs geared to the regional market.

Mombasa is the leading port and major distribution center of Kenya. Some of the larger import/export firms and many smaller ones are based there. Several others have offices have offices and warehouses in the industrial area of the city. Monbasa is equipped to play a regional distributive role. The city is also actively involved in the export trade, and in addition to the numerous private export houses, the Uganda Coffee and Lint Marketing Boards maintain large warehouses there.

Although Mombasa is the chief center for the trade of Kenya's Coast Province, its function in retail and local wholesale trade is small in relation to its size. Its effective area of distribution is considerably reduced by its coastal location. Large sections of its immediate hinterland consist of arid, sparsely populated areas where modern market activity is virtually nonexistent.

Nakuru and Eldoret developed principally as trading centers for the affluent European settlers of Kenya's former White Highlands area. They are distinguished by large-scale commercial units, including the Kenya Farmers Association which distributes agricultural machinery, fertilizers, and supplies.

Kisumu, serving a large area of dense African settlement, is becoming increasingly important as the commercial center of western Kenya. Provincial administrative centers also play a significant role in distribution; the importance of which is generally related to the size, population, and prosperity of the area they serve. Most merchants in these areas are retailers, although several may also sell goods to smaller traders in the more remote areas and buy some local agricultural produce as well.

Below the level of provincial centers, the size and frequency of trading centers will vary with the density of population and the local level of income. Throughout the rural areas, African traders are entering the retail trades in increasing numbers. Groups of African shops are found every few miles along the road, particularly in the area of Kikuyu settlement north of Nairobi.

Distribution Channels

Although Kenya offers the U.S. exporter a wide variety of methods for distributing and selling his product, the specific means chosen must be tailored to fit the individual requirements of the product and its potential market alike. The principal methods used are as follows: Employing the services of an agent of distributor, selling through established wholesalers or dealers, selling directly to cooperatives and other indigenous organizations or establishing a branch or subsidiary.

Many U.S. firms now operate their own offices in Kenya. This method has several advantages for firms with an established market for their product. Most are principally promotional offices with actual sales handled through local representatives.

Agents are often used for the distribution of a wide range of both durable and nondurable consumer goods and for some industrial raw materials. This form of distribution may be particularly appropriate for highly competitive products which lack a large local market. Agents are located in most of the larger cities and those in Nairobi or Mombasa may be able to effectively cover the regional market.

The choice of an agent is particularly important. It can be a deciding factor in the eventual success or failure of the marketing effort. In making this decision, the U.S. exporter is well advised to weigh the relative merits of the larger, well-established import houses against those of smaller, newer firms. Many firms in the first category tend to be overburdened with agencies and frequently find it difficult to allocate sufficient time and personnel resources to the promotional effort required for fewer product lines. Alternatively, smaller agents are ordinarily prepared to devote considerable time and attention to individual product lines but may lack the capital, personal contacts, and physical facilities necessary for a successful sales effort. As agents often represent several different product lines, the U.S. exporter should avoid appointing an agent who currently is handling a directly competitive brand.

The exporter also is advised to give serious consideration to government programs designed to favor African as opposed to noncitizen traders. Recent legislation restricting noncitizen merchants to trade in specified commodities and commercial centers may severely limit the ability of noncitizen agents to provide adequate representation in this market.

Capital goods and equipment are often best handled by stocklist-distributor who buys on his own account and carries a wide range of spares. Distributors also handle other commodities, such as chemicals, pharmaceuticals, and brand name products.

In appointing an exclusive representative in Kenya, the U.S. exporter is legally entitled to certain exemptions from U.S. antitrust laws. The Webb-Pomerene Act allows a limited exemption from antitrust laws for direct exports by allowing exporters to agree on prices, sales terms, territorial divisions, and other activities in export trade that would be prohibited in U.S. domestic commerce. More information on the Webb-Pomerene Act is available from the International Business Practices Division, Office of Service Industries, U.S. Department of Commerce, Washington, D.C. 20230.

U.S. exporters seeking an agent or distributor in Kenya should plan to visit the country since first-hand knowledge of the market is highly desirable before any long-term commitment is made and since such a visit provides an opportunity for a personal appraisal of the relative merits of prospective agents or distributors. For those products requiring servicing, the exporter should ensure that qualified personnel and the necessary parts and components are readily available for the after-sales service. European competitors particularly capitalize on their geographic proximity to the Kenyan market by making spare parts and even service personnel available to local customers on short notice. More than one U.S. firm has lost a valuable order through failure to provide prompt and efficient service for its product.

Consumer goods requiring maintenance of stocks and industrial raw materials are often exported to Kenya through established wholesalers. Further information concerning wholesale and retail distribution in Kenya is presented in the "Commercial Practices" section below.

Many American exporters of agricultural supplies, equipment, and accessory materials have found it most profitable to reach potential customers in the agricultural sector through the local cooperative organizations. Through its own organizational and marketing structure, the cooperative already possesses the distribution channels to reach local farmers who might have little other contact with the market place. In addition, the cooperative can often provide two other commodities in short supply in rural Kenya, credit and service.

Commercial Practices

Wholesale and Retail Channels

Distribution is affected almost entirely through independent wholesalers and retailers although a substantial amount of buying is still done through commission indent agents and manufacturers representatives. Manufacturers of cigarettes, beer, tea, and shoes and distributors of petroleum products have developed their own sales networks. All manufacturees, however, rely heavily on independent wholesalers and retailers for the later stages of the distribution of their products.

Trading companies affiliated with English and other European firms are among the largest and most influential importers, wholesalers, and in some cases retailers in Kenya. They usually are supplied by purchasing agents or confirming houses in the United Kingdom and continental Europe or directly by foreign suppliers.

These latter trading companies may engage in a variety of commercial activities. They may be importers on their own account, supplying capital goods for investment projects in which they hold an interest or for other enterprises that wish to order through them. They may act as wholesalers for a wide variety of consumer goods and capital equipment probably carrying as many as 30 or 40 sole agencies. They may specialize in a single product line, managing their own sales and service outlets.

Retailers.—There is an almost total lack of specialization among retail outlets in Kenya. Practically all shops are general stores stocking a wide range of goods and only in the larger towns are there any specialty shops. There are no extensive chain stores.

The distribution of retail establishments closely parallels the pattern observed in the wholesale trade. Approximately one-third of the establishments are located in the Nairobi area. The majority operate on a small scale; more than half are individual proprietors and the greater portion of the remainder are partnerships; only three are organized as public enterprises or public registered companies.

Wholesalers.—Almost all goods pass through wholesale channels and wholesalers play an important role in the distribution system. Local produce trading and wholesale distribution may be very closely linked, particularly in the more rural districts. Although the major cash crops are now marketed through cooperatives and the various marketing boards, most of the minor cash crops are still handled by traders who are also wholesale distributors.

Nearly one-half of all wholesale establishments are located in the Nairobi area. Other concentrations occur in the Coast, Rift Valley and Central Provinces. The smallest number are located in the sparsely populated North-Eastern Province. The greatest portion of Kenya's wholesalers are private registered companies or partnerships.

Pricing

Kenya has a relatively low-cost distribution system. Wages are low and overhead is kept to a minimum. Advertising is used infrequently; premises are inexpensive, and few customer services are provided. Cost conscious wholesalers typically hold inadequate stocks and very few do any active market development. The single exception appears to be the import trade. As there is an element of monopoly in the agencies held by these firms, they tend to emphasize services, stock, maintenance, and advertising rather than costs.

Price competition in both wholesale and retail distribution is intense. This concentration on price often means that better quality lines are not stocked. Increasing competition in recent years has tended to diffuse distribution activities so that there is no clear cut distinction between importers, wholesalers, and retailers. All except the largest wholesalers do some retailing and the retail sales of subwholesalers may account for more than half their annual turnover.

U.S. products are generally believed to be higher priced than similar commodities available from competing suppliers, and local traders rarely make any systematic price comparisons before ordering from traditional sources in Europe and Japan. Even in those lines where the United States is a higher priced supplier, the willingness of the Kenyan consumer to pay a premium for quality is often frustrated by an arbitrary decision based solely on price. U.S. exporters therefore are advised to emphasize the price and/or quality advantages of their product when seeking local distributors.

Resale price maintenance is almost unknown in Kenya, and there are virtually no conventionally established prices for most commodities. With the exception of foodstuffs, prices at all level of trade are determined by bargaining, and it is therefore difficult to establish a meaningful "normal" markup for any given sector.

The maintenance of a relatively stable price/wage structure has become a major objective of government economic policy. Specified commodities especially susceptible to manipulation and extreme price fluctuations are now being distributed by government trading organizations at fixed prices. Commodities in this latter category include rice, salt, khaki drill, printed khangas, cotton fabrics, charcoal irons, bicycles, flashlights, secondhand clothing, and cinematographic film.

Consumer Financing

Consumer credit is not widely used in Kenya. Local banks may provide credit to firms selling personal and household articles, and some banks offer hire-purchase facilities to selected clients.

Africanization

Africanization of the commercial sector is a major objective of government policy. The Kenya National Trading Corporation (KNTC) has been designated the principal agent of Africanization in the distributive trades. KNTC provides credit facilities and general business training to African traders and maintains exclusive rights to import selected consumer items for distribution through citizen traders. Also designed to favor citizens in the wholesale and retail trades is the Trader Licensing Act, which excludes noncitizen businesspeople from trading in specified commodities and commercial districts outside the largest towns.

Quotations and Terms of Payment

In quoting prices to Kenyan importers, costs should be computed on a c.i.f. basis. In general, clarity of price quotations is vital to successful selling and an effort should be made to quote in terms with which the Kenyan importer is familiar.

Local sources of commercial credit are generally inadequate to finance the growing volume of import transactions. In most instances, liberal credit terms offered by a foreign supplier can outweigh a considerable differential in price. The ability of the U.S. exporter to extend liberal credit terms is therefore an extremely important factor in determining the overall success of the Kenyan marketing effort. Foreign competitors ordinarily grant credits for a period of up to 180 days for consumer goods and 24 months for small machinery and equipment.

Long-term credits for the purchase of more expensive capital equipment have been extended for firms in Italy and Germany for as long as 7 years, with a 5-percent payment at time of order and a 10-percent payment on delivery up to a year later. Some Japanese suppliers may extend similar credits for 10 years. The German, Italian, and Dutch Governments discount paper for their exporters at similarly liberal terms and at low interest rates.

U.S. firms may also lose potential sales by requiring cash payment in advance for Kenyan orders. Local foreign exchange regulations do not permit such cash payments abroad and require importers to prove that goods ordered actually have entered the country. This proof must include an invoice and a customs certification that duty has been paid or that the item has been entered duty free. Moreover, local commercial banks will open letters of credit only on the basis of specific pro-forma invoices.

To assist U.S. exporters in formulating sound credit policies applicable to local markets, credit information on individual Kenyan firms is available through the World Traders Data Reports (WTDRs) service. WTDRs, prepared by the U.S. Commerce Department's U.S. Foreign Commercial Service, are available from the U.S. Department of Commerce for $40. Such information is also available from private agencies.

Government Procurement

The importance of governmental action in the import sector has increased. Government procurement for ordinary supplies as well as materials and equipment requirements of public development programs is a significant factor in the total trade of Kenya. Government action also is evident in programs designed to ensure citizen control of local commerce and the maintenance of a stable price structure in basic commodity markets.

Imports required by Kenya's Ministry of Education, police forces, and the East African Power and Light Corporation (EAP/L) are purchased through the Crown Agents. The Crown Agents, a British quasi-governmental organization, serves as an overseas purchasing agent for 15 African governments. The Crown Agents representative for U.S. suppliers is located at 3100 Massachusetts Avenue, N.W., Washington, D.C. 20008 (202-462-1340, extension 2128).

The Ministry of Works obtains goods and services locally through the Central Tender Board. In Kenya, the orders are placed by the Chief Supplies Officer. The Central Tender Board must approve the selection of contractors utilized by the Chief Supplies Officer for Kenya. The address of the Central Tender Board is P.O. Box 30346, Nairobi, Kenya.

Advertising and Research

Marketing Aids

Several advertising agencies with headquarters in Nairobi offer a full range of sales promotion services throughout East Africa.

Most local distributors of imported merchandise expect their suppliers to provide substantial advertising and promotional support, particularly when introducing a new product or brand name. Good sales ability is the most important element in selling the product. Clear and simple operating instructions, displays of the product in use, sample handouts, and frequent personal visits are all vital tools for the successful sales representative in Kenya.

Advertising Media

A variety of newspapers and magazines, in both English and Swahili, are read by East African consumers. Among the English-language newspapers, Nairobi's *Daily Nation, Sunday Nation,* and *The Standard* report the largest circulation. Venacular favorites include *Taifa Kenya* and *Taifaleo* (Nairobi). Black and white newspaper advertising costs vary from 54 KShs. to 62 KShs. per column inch. Full color ads range from 4,213 KShs. to 4,634 KShs. per column inch. In addition, specialized trade and industry journals also are published by various local industry groups, commodity marketing boards, and government institutions, offering an opportunity to address a population whose interest in a specific area is known.

The Voice of Kenya, offers advertising facilities on both its radio and television services. Radio spot announcement rates vary from 450 KShs. for 15 seconds to 1,500 KShs. for 1 minute. Sponsored-program costs range from 3,000 KShs. for 15 minutes to 7,500 KShs. for a 1-hour show (6 minutes commercial content). Television spot announcement rates range from 500 KShs. for 15 seconds to 1,200 KSHs. for 60 seconds. A 15-minute sponsored program costs 2,400 KShs.; a 1-hour show, with 6 minutes of commercial content, 6,000 KShs. Voice of Kenya advertising inquiries should be addressed to the Commercial Manager, Voice of Kenya, P.O. Box 30456, Nairobi, Kenya.

Another popular form of advertising for consumer articles is the film short; a number of these are run with each showing in local movie houses. To show a 30-second film costs 720 KShs. per week (16 showings) at major theaters. For advertising in more remote areas, East African Touring Circuits, managed by Factual Films, Ltd. of Nairobi, operates 17 mobile theaters, each of which gives 29 shows per month at 464 towns and villages in selected agricultural areas throughout Kenya. Audiences average 2,000 per show, and exhibition charges per circuit per month range from 300 KShs. for a 10-second filmlet to 900 KShs. for a 60 second presentation. Longer films are prorated to the 60-second rate. Factual films also will accept advertising records and arrange for the distribution of leaflets in exhibition areas.

Posters and point-of-sale reminders are an important part of the advertising package in Kenya. Brochures and special advertising materials can be prepared by local printers at standard rates. Billboard advertising is used in some localities but is prohibited in urban areas. Neon signs are rigidly controlled by local authorities. Both billboard advertising and neon signs are permitted in railway stations and are used extensively by local advertisers. Interior and exterior bus advertising is also popular.

The role of packaging is an extremely important sales factor. Eye appeal has proven to be the most effective means of attracting consumer attention, and the supplier who takes into account consumer tastes in color and design and appeals to habits and attitudes—peculiar to the locality—enhances his product's saleability. Popular among low income African consumers is a reusable container—a bottle, jar, or box that may be used for later storage—and may be a determining factor in a competitive situation.

Participation in Kenya's trade fairs also can offer the U.S. exporter an opportunity to develop local interest in his product. Among the best known is Kenya's Nairobi Show, usually held during the last week of September, which offers broad agricultural-through-industrial coverage.

Market Research and Trade Organizations

The major Kenyan advertising agencies will undertake special market research activities for their clients.

A complete selection of economic research and consultant services is available from the Economist Intelligence Unit (EIU), Spencer House, 27 St. Jame's Place, London SW1, England. The Intelligence Unit, which regularly publishes regional economic revies and supplementary studies in developing countries, also will prepare materials for clients on a commission basis according to their specific needs. The EIU maintains a research office in Nairobi at 56 Marlborough Road, P.O. Box 14210.

Kenyan banks will also provide assistance on market research. These services are frequently available in the United States through correspondent arrangements.

Local support for market research projects also may be obtained through the National Chamber of Commerce and Industry, Kenya P.O. Box 47024, Nairobi, Kenya. The Chamber has branches in all major towns and is increasingly effective in its representation of African businesses.

The Kenya Association of Manufacturers, P.O. Box 30225, Nairobi, Kenya, is a representative organization of industrialists who seek to advance the interest of the private sector and to make their experience available to potential investors and traders. The Association also publishes a list of members and their products, which is a useful guide to local industry.

Among the other informative publications dealing with East African commerce in its various aspects, the following are particularly noteworthy. The *East African Trade and Industry* is a monthly journal on developments in the engineering, construction, electricla, textile, furniture, hardware, automobile, and shipping trades in East Africa. It is privately published. In addition, the Kenya Export News is published by the Kenya External Trade Authority and deals primarily with external trade.

Power

General

Electric current in Kenya is 240 volt, 50 cycle, single; 415 volt, 50 cycle, three phase; and higher voltages in certain areas.

Kenya's consumption of all types of electricity increased by 34 percent between 1976 and 1980 with consumption of hydroelectricity rising particularly fast. The share of imported electricity fell from 21 to 20 percent of the total between 1976 and 1980. In 1980, total generating capacity in Kenya amounted to 485 MW of which 65 percent was hydroelectric. It is expected that supplies will most economically be provided by several methods of generation. The Tana River at present supports installed capacity of 295 MW, but it has a total exploitable potential of 540 MW. Coastal regions will almost certainly be supplied by oil-fired stations. Geothermal energy in the Rift Valley and natural gas potential are being explored. Oil prospecting, in North-Eastern Province and offshore, has so far failed to yield positive results.

Water

Adequate supplies of water for both personal and industrial purposes are available. A number of improvements and additions to the existing water supply systems have been completed recently, are underway, or are planned for the near future. The largest and most important project is the renewal of about 16 km of the Mzima transmission pipeline. While this project should remove the most serious pipeline weaknesses, others will remain and interruptions in service will continue to occur, although less frequently. Improvements to increase the capacity of the Marere Springs pipeline to about 15,900 cubic meters per day has been completed with the addition of a booster pumping station on the main line and a development of alternative sources—three boreholes and a small intake and treatment plant on the Pemba River.

Tourism

Tourism has become one of Kenya's most important sources of foreign exchange, its receipts in 1980, at KSh. 82.5 million, accounting for about 7 percent of total exports of goods and services (although its net contribution is, of course, smaller than this).

The future of Kenya's tourism lies in the coastal areas. The opening of the Mombasa jet airport, the proposed development of the Diani Beach complex, the existing hotel facilities on the coast and their proximity to Tsavo and other game parks is expected to move the tourist center away from Nairobi in the coming years.

Another development is the increase in business travel to Kenya. The Kenyatta Conference Centre is a tourist asset bringing thousands of delegates to Nairobi. Thus Nairobi, which already draws the business travelers, also is accommodating conference visitors.

The responsible ministry for tourist information in Kenya is the Ministry of Tourism, P.O. Box 30027, Nairobi, Kenya. The visitors' information bureau has two locations at: Mama Ngina Street, P.O. Box 42278, Nairobi, Kenya (tel: 2 32 85) and Moi Avenue, P.O. Box 95072, Mombasa (tel.: 2 54 28).

Transport and Communications

Transportation

Kenya has 51,368 km of established roads, of which 5,336 km are bitumen surfaced. Buses and coaches operate everywhere, but services are not yet well developed outside the towns. The stock of vehicles at the end of 1975 totaled 199,715, of which 83,676 wre private motor cars, 58,349 utilities and pickups, 20,875 lorries and 4,605 buses and mini-buses. Driving is on the left.

The Kenya Railways Corporation operates some 2,114 km of railway, of which 1,070 km is the main line between Mombasa and the Uganda border. Modern trains, with sleepers and dining cars, run between Mombasa, Nairobi, and Kisumu. Fares are moderate.

The Eastern African National Shipping Line, which was established by Kenya, Tanzania, Uganda, and Zambia in 1969, ceased trading operations in March 1980. Mombasa port serves Uganda, Tanzania (in normal times), Rwanda, Burundi, and Zambia, as well as Kenya. Mombasa, one of the finest natural harbors in the world, has 15 deepwater quays, numerous transit sheds and back-of-port sheds for dry cargo, the Kipevu Oil Terminal capable of accepting tankers up to 65,000 tons, and a lighterage wharf. The rapid growth in traffic at Mombasa has often caused congestion, creating bottlenecks in Kenya's seaborne commerce. Total freight handled at Mombasa in 1980 reached 6 million metric tons. The channel and part facilities are being expanded to accommodate larger vessels.

Air travel and air freight are well developed, with major airports at Mombasa, (Moi International) and Nairobi (Jomo Kenyatta International Airport). In addition, many towns such as Kisumu and Malindi have airports, and there are innumerable "bush" airstrips throughout the country. With the winding up of East African Airline in 1977, Kenya Airways was established and operates on international as well as domestic routes; it achieved 1,018 million passenger-km and 111.6 million kg/km of freight in 1980.

Telecommunications

Responsibility for the former East African Posts and Telecommunications Corporation, which handles local services, and its subsidiary, East African External Telecommunications, which handles communications with the world outside East Africa, hasxo been taken over by the Ministry of Transport and Communications.

Radio and Television.—The Voice of Kenya (VOK), transmitting in English, Swahili, and Hindustani, provides effective coverage of Kenya as well as adjacent sections of Tanzania and Uganda from three medium-wave stations. Parts of the country beyond the coverage provided by the medium-wave system are served by a short-wave relay station at Langata. In Kenya, almost 1.4 million radios reach about 85 percent of the total adult population.

Kenya television—also provided by the Voice of Kenya—serves the Nairobi and Mombasa areas, including the main cities in the Rift Valley and Kisumu. Approximately 40 hours of English, Swahili, and Hindustani are broadcast weekly.

Telephone and Telex Facilities.—Kenya has over 46,000 direct exchange lines and more than 70,000 telephones in use. Telegrams may be phoned in. There also is an all-night service at the Government Post Office. Telex services are available at some hotels and public telex offices. Local telephone calls cost 60 cents, and there are public phone booths at all the large hotels as well as the main post office.

Press

There are two daily newspapers in English (*Daily Nation* and *Standard*) and one in Swahili (*Taifa Leo*). There are three weekly newspapers: *Sunday Nation, Sunday Standard,* and *Coast Week*. Kenya also has two periodicals that are published weekly: *The Weekly Review* and *What's On,* a free weekly guide to current events in Kenya published by the National Group of Newspapers.

Investment

Kenya Policy

Since independence, the Kenyan Government has taken a positive stance toward foreign investment in the country, particularly when there is Kenyan equity participation. It actively encourages private foreign investment in projects that contribute to Kenya's general economic development. Most foreign investment in the country has been in the production of consumer goods. Government policy has been increasingly to encourage diversification into higher technology industries.

Investment Climate

Most American investors find it in their interest to share equity in their operations with local organizations. The most commonly used local organizations are parastatal bodies owned by the Kenyan Government. While these parastatal bodies take equity participation in given enterprises they seldom take a very active role in the day-to-day management of the enterprise. The largest and most commonly utilized parastatal bodies are the Industrial and Commercial Development Corporation (ICDC), Industrial Development Bank (IDB), Kenya Tourist Development Corporation (KTDC), and the Agricultural Development Corporation (ADC).

For further information potential investors should contact the Industrial Survey and Promotion Center of the Ministry of Industry located in Maendeleo House, P.O. Box 30430, Nairobi, Kenya.

It is important that a potential investor be aware that Kenya Government policy has favored local firms over foreign firms for purposes of allocating locally raised capital. Many foreign firms are required to look outside of Kenya for loan capital.

The Kenyan Government provides protection for locally manufactured goods through a system of import controls and duties on competing products. Firms manufacturing locally are also eligible for 20 percent export subsidy for goods made in Kenya and sold outside East Africa. For any investment in plant and machinery located outside of the Nairobi and Mombasa areas, the Government allows firms to write off 120 percent of their investment as depreciation.

Repatriation of Capital

Applications for the introduction of foreign capital for direct investment in Kenya are considered on an individual basis. If the investment is accepted because the project can contribute to Kenya's development, a "Certificate of Approved Status" may be granted. This certificate guaranteees the right to repatriate capital profits after taxes and dividends.

Under the Foreign Investments Protection Act of 1964 as amended in 1976, the Minister of Finance may issue the certificate to foreign nationals who invest foreign assets or reinvest their profits in Kenya if the Minister is satisfied that the investment will be of "economic benefit to the country." This has generally been interpreted to mean that a project will.

(a) lead to either an earning or a saving of foreign exchange;

(b) result in a gain of technical knowledge to the country; or

(c) increase economic wealth and social stability by raising the national income or promoting the diversification of the economy.

Amendments to the Act in 1976 stipulate the investor rather than Kenya must assume the foreign exchange risks of his investment; the Kenyan Government will not guarantee in advance the repatriation of capital gains realized upon liquidation of an investor's assets; guaranteed repatriation of the original investment is a clear right; and the schedule for repatriation of profits (capital gains) must be negotiated.

Depreciation allowances are up to 2.5 percent annually on buildings and 12.5 percent on equipment. Corporation taxes are 45 percent for local firms and 52.5 percent for branches of foreign companies. While the Kenyan Government allows profits to be repatriated annually, it has deferred payments of dividends overseas when a firm has outstanding loans locally. To date, the Kenyan Government has had a flexible attitude toward overseas payments for technology transfer payments and management fees. Potential investors should clarify their position with the Government on this issue prior to entering into any agreement.

Foreign Investment

The main source of foreign private investment in Kenya continues to be the United Kingdom, the former colonial power. During recent years investment interest on the part of companies in Western Europe and Japan has increased significantly.

Reliable figures on total private foreign investment in Kenya are not available. Figures for total industrial capital formation in Kenya during the years following independence indicate a steady increase in the volume of investment.

Foreign nationals who have invested or plan to invest foreign assets in approved industries are protected from loss due to nationalization by guarantees incorporated in the Kenyan Constitution and by the Foreign Investment Protection Act of 1964, as stated above.

The number of American firms with direct representation in Kenya has risen dramatically from 20 in 1962 to over 200 in 1981. The book value of U.S. private direct investment in Kenya is estimated at $315 million. With few exceptions, U.S. investments in Kenya have proven successful but the recent economic difficulties have adversely affected the returns of many of the U.S. firms. Kenyan officials have expressed particular interest in increased investment for American business as they have been favorably impressed by U.S. management capabilities.

U.S. firms manufacture batteries, soap products, and can Kenyan agricultural products for home consumption and export. They manage modern hotels, provide banking and insurance services, provide international transportation, and contribute many other products and services to the economy. Included among American firms with major manufacturing facilities in Kenya are Firestone, Colgate-Palmolive, Crown Cork, Del Monte, Union Carbide, General Motors, CPC International, and Coca-Cola.

Franchising and Licensing

Kenya law does not contain specific provisions for franchising or licensing. The primary consideration in either arrangement is the formalization of a remittance procedure for any fees, royalties, etc., to the franchisor or licensor.

International Agreements

Kenya is a signatory of the Settlement of Investment Disputes Between States and Nationals of Other States, which also has been ratified by the United States. An investment guaranty agreement is in force between the United States and Kenya. The investment service of the U.S. Private Investment Corporation (OPIC) are therefore available for Kenya.

Trade Licenses

A company engaged in wholesale or retail trade must obtain a license after it has acquired a place of business. Noncitizens are precluded from operating in many towns; it is therefore essential to determine in advance whether the location is in what is termed a "general trading area."

Manufacturing firms are not allowed to distribute their local produced merchandise but must sell through African distributors.

Foreign Ownership of Business Entities

There are no restrictions on the right of foreign nationals to acquire and own business entities in Kenya. Most foreign companies investing there are urged to have Kenya participation in the new business. Local financial participation increases Kenyan support and provides the benefits of local knwoledge and experience.

Permission must be obtained at the outset to appoint directors who are not residents of Kenya. Similar permission must be obtained to issue shares to nonresidents.

Ownership of Real Property

Foreign interests are permitted to own or lease land on industrial sites in Kenya, subject to the country's land-tenure laws and regulations. Land in Kenya is held on either a freehold or lease-hold basis, and is available to industry for periods of 99 years. Rentals for industrial sites are established by reference to prevailing market prices in Kenya. One-fifth of the assessed value of the undeveloped land must be paid by the lessee as a lump sum, followed by a yearly payment of 5 percent on the remaining four-fifths; this rental remains constant during the 99-year tenure. The purchaser also is required to pay the development costs for the installation of railway sidings, roads, sewers, etc. Major approved industrial enterprises may be able to negotiate favorable terms for the acquisition of land.

There are normally no onerous covenants contained in the leases other than that which requires the construction of the building of suitable design or stipulated minimum value within 2 or 3 years of the date of the grant.

Investors obtaining industrial plots in Kenya are advised to contact the Ministry of Industry, P.O. Box 30430, Nairobi, Kenya. The Kenyan Government controls the rights to all minerals within the boundaries of its jurisdiction, and prospecting is lawful only under a license granted to qualified persons for a nominal fee. Exploitation of any mineral or petroleum deposits discovered requires payment of royalties to the Government.

Kenya's laws governing the issuance of prospecting licenses are quite liberal; the license must delineate the area covered and specify an obligation to drill and to expend a minimum sum of money. Kenyan Government negotiators have wide leeway to set the specific terms of licenses, although their duration is limited to 10 years. Succession or inheritance of land by noncitizens is protected by the Constitution of Kenya and therefore is not affected by these controls. The President may prohibit any transactions involving agricultural land and may exempt any person or transaction from the provisions of the Act.

Types of Business Organizations

American firms that desire to set up operations in Kenya may incorporate a local subsidiary company or establish a branch of representative office. Trading may be carried on only by a locally incorporated company or branch of the U.S. company. An authorized representative can trade on the company's behalf only as an agent, but may collect orders for the company's products. Firms doing business in Kenya must have a resident bank account.

As mentioned above, Kenya officials have strongly endorsed the joint enterprise type of investment arrangement. In order to regulate establishment of business operations, Kenya has published a Companies Act patterned after the United Kingdom Companies Act of 1948. Companies that may be organized under the terms of this legislation include limited-liability companies, partnerships, individual proprietorships, and companies limited by guarantees.

Limited-Liability Companies.—Limited-liability companies are limited by the number of shares that they may distribute. The liability of each individual shareholder is restricted to the amount, if any, unpaid on the shares that he holds. This is the usual type of corporate business organization in Kenya and may be either public or private.

A public limited-liability company is comparable with the typical U.S. corporation. This type of company must have at least seven shareholders.

Private companies, on the other hand, are usually formed to obtain the advantages of limited liability for family businesses, for small companies similar to partnerships, and for companies subsidiary to other companies. Most overseas firms establishing a branch in Kenya set up private companies. In accordance with their articles of association, such companies must restrict the transfer of shares and prohibit any invitation to the public to subscribe to any shares or debentures. The number of shareholders must be not less than two or more than 50.

Partnership.—The partnership is used for professional enterprises, small trading concerns, and frequently for the business of manufacturers' representatives that handle or distribute imported commodities. A partnership may be constituted between two but not more than 20 persons, either orally or in writing. Each of the partners must contribute either capital or labor for the joint benefit of the partnership and with the object of making a profit. Should these essentials be lacking, no partnership is deemed to exist. The liability of the partners cannot be limited by private agreement, and each partner is jointly and severally liable for all debts contracted by the partnership.

Limited-Liability Companies Established Outside East Africa.—Each company incorporated outside East Africa that establishes a place of business in Kenya must, within 30 days of such establishment, file with the Registrar of the country the following materials: a certified copy of the charter, statutes, or memorandum and articles of the company or other instrument constituting or defining the constitution of the company; a list of the directors and secretaries of the company; a statement of all subsisting changes created by the company; the names and addresses of one or more resident persons authorized to accept on behalf of the company service of process and notice required to be served on the company; and the full address of the registered or principal office of the company.

Industrial Property Protection

Kenya is a member of the "Paris Union" International Convention for the Protection of Industrial Property (patents and trademarks) to which the United States and about 80 other countries adhere. Thus, American businesspeople and investors are entitled to the benefits of this Convention, such as national treatment and "priority right" recognition for their patent and trademark filing dates, in these countries. U.S. firms interested in securing patent and trademark rights in Kenya should consult with competent legal counsel to determine what steps should be takne.

Patents

Kenya has not yet promulgated an independent national patent law and continues to use preindependence procedures in providing patent protection. Only the holder of a valid U.K. patent can obtain patent protection in Kenya. As such, only those patents first registered in the United Kingdom may be registered in Kenya; such applications for registration must take place within 3 years of the date of the original U.K. patent grants on which they are based. A patent registered therein continues for the term of the original U.K. patent.

Trademarks

Trademark applications must be filed in order for the mark to be registered; there are no provisions for automatic protection or recognition of a mark previously registered in the United Kingdom. In Kenya, registrations are valid for 7 years from application date and renewable for 14-year periods. The first person to apply for a mark as its user or intended user is entitled to its registration. Applications are published for opposition for 60 days. Registration is subject to cancellation if the mark is not used with 5 years. The office responsible for receiving trademark applications is the Department of the Registrar General, P.O. Box 30031, Nairobi, Kenya.

Copyrights

Kenya adhered in 1966 to the Universal Copyright Convention to which the United States and about 50 other countries also adhere. As such, U.S. nationals who have a U.S. copyright on their works receive automatic copyright protection in Kenya by inserting on their works their name, date of first publication, and the "c" in a circle (symbol of copyright registration).

Taxation

Corporate and personal income taxes in Kenya are levied according to rules specified in The Income Tax Act 1973, as amended. The amounts of personal allowances and taxation rates are fixed by the Act. The machinery for assessment and collection is operated by the Kenya Income Tax Department.

Corporate Taxes

The corporate tax rate for industrial enterprise is 45 percent of the net profits, excluding dividends received from resident companies. The tax on the income of branches of foreign firms is 52.5 percent. Profits from life insurance business and the mining of certain specified minerals are taxed at a lower rate. New mining companies are afforded partial tax relief by paying only 27.5 percent for 5 years after the company first makes a profit. Although the tax on undistributed income was abolished after 1964, companies that deliberately accumulate profits so that shareholders can avoid taxation or distribute them in nontaxable form, nevertheless can be subjected to further tax under the anti-avoidance provisions of The Income Tax Act. A 15-percent withholding tax on dividends and a 12.5-percent withholding tax on interest has been introduced to be paid by both residents and nonresidents. A withholding tax of 20 percent has been imposed on all payments of management fees and royalties to nonresidents.

Personal Income Tax

Residents and nonresidents alike must pay tax on income accrued in or derived from Kenya. Taxes on chargeable income are usually withheld from employees on a "pay-as-you-earn" system.

Tax Concessions

In addition to expenses wholly and exclusively incurred in the production of income, Kenya tax law specifies various other permissible deductions.

Annual deductions for certain classes of capital expenditure incurred for business purposes are allowed as follows:

(a) Industrial buildings, such as factories (4 percent) and "approved" hotels (6 percent annually on the expenditure incurred).

(b) Plant and machinery: heavy self-propelling vehicles such as tractors—37.5 percent on the written down value; other self-propelling vehicles such as cars—25 percent; all other machinery, including ships—12.5 percent.

(c) Mining: 40 percent of expenditure in the first year and 10 percent in each of the following years.

(d) Farm works: 20 percent of expenditure in the first and each of the 4 following years.

An investment deduction also is given (which is not deducted in calculating written down values for the annual deduction) at the following rates or capital cost of construction:

(a) Ships—40 percent.

(b) New factory buildings and new machinery installed in them—20 percent.

(c) New hotels—20 percent.

Expenditures on clearing and planting land and on scientific research are allowed as incurred.

No balancing deductions on charges are made when a business as a whole is disposed of. Purchasers of assets are entitled to write off the residue of expenditure not allowed to the vendor. A loss in business (calculated after allowing capital deductions as above) is set off against other income of the same year. If a deficit results, the losses may be set off against profits of the preceding year or carried forward indefinitely and set off against profits of succeeding years. The provisions apply to all approved companies, both public and private, that operate in Kenya, whether incorporated in Kenya or overseas.

Guidance for U.S. Business Travelers

Entrance Requirements

A valid U.S. passport and Kenyan visa are required for entry to Kenya. Visas are issued by the Kenyan Embassy, 2249 R Street, N.W., Washington, D.C. 20008, and by the Principal Immigration Officer at Nairobi. Visas may be for either single or multiple entries; a letter of recommendation from the company the traveler represents also is required.

Temporary entry is usually granted for a maximum period of 6 months, with two extensions of 6 months each. Visitors wishing to remain longer, but not wishing to apply for permanent residence, must leave the country and seek readmission.

Visitors are not permitted to accept remunerative employment unless they hold a valid Temporary Employment Pass issued by the Immigration authorities. Such permits are ordinarily granted only if personnel with comparable skill are not locally available and, in most cases, immigration officials will require a Security Bond covering each alien so employed.

Entry requirements for persons wishing to take up residence or to seek long-term employment are more stringent. All persons traveling to Kenya must have been vaccinated against small pox and inoculated against yellow fever and carry with them International Yellow Fever and Smallpox Certificates. Typhoid, tetanus, thyphus, plague, cholera, and diphtheria inoculations are recommended. The regular use of a malaria suppressant is advisable. There are no limitations on the importation of dollars, travelers checks, or other instruments of payment, although travelers must declare this amount at the time of entry. Where there are no restrictions on the use of U.S. dollars,

departing American travelers will not be permitted to export foreign currencies, travelers checks, or letters of credit in excess of the amount declared at entry. The importation and exportation of Kenyan currency is prohibited.

Business travelers entering Kenya are required to complete a passenger's baggage declaration certifying those items of baggage that are liable to duty.

Free entry is permitted of necessary wearing apparel and personal effects that are proved to have been in personal or household use by the traveler and are not for sale, and of instruments and tools for professional use.

With the exception of stipulated personal allowance of alcoholic beverages and tobacco products, all other goods, whether imported for personal use or sale, including goods intended for residents of Kenya, are subject to duty.

Travelers wishing to import any vehicle (including trailers or cycles) or other goods intended for their use, convenience, or comfort, but not for consumption, must deposit at the time and place of importation a sum equal to the duty that would be imposed. Simultaneously, a claim for temporary exemption should be presented in duplicate. The vehicle or goods must then be exported within 6 months or such further period as the Commissioner of Customs and Excise may allow. These conditions also apply to articles imported for exhibition or demonstration and subsequent reexport. If the prescribed conditions are not met, the visitor will be liable for the full duty of the vehicle or goods imported. A guaranty may be made by an authorized organization, however, in which case no deposit is required. The organization thereby assumes the liability for the duty if the vehicle or goods is not reexported within the prescribed period.

Business Etiquette

In general, business customs are similar to but less formal than those in the United Kingdom. Americans stand a good chance for commercial success in the Kenyan market because of favorable dollar-shilling exchange rate, quality durability and reputation of product, and Keyan recognition of direct, ethical business practices of Americans. Kenyans sometimes complain about slow and unreliable deliveries, cumbersome formalities, irregular spare parts or followup services, and generally stiffer credit terms than the major competitors. American firms are urged to confirm current Kenyan requirements and procedures through their bank, the General Superintendence Company (see above under Pre-Inspection).

Although Swahili is the official language of Kenya, English is widely used in business and commerce. Business correspondece, catalogs, and advertising material prepared in English are readily understood by most potential buyers. Business cards are widely used. They are usually imprinted in black and white, although there is no objection to the colored American styles. Academic titles and degrees are most frequently cited by members of the European and Asian expatriate communities. U.S. businesspeople will ordinarily use their firm's name and their title within the organization.

Correspondence and personal calls each play a significant role in the conduct of business in Kenya. Expeditious handling of correspondence is expected and greatly appreciated.

Usual daytime dress is quite informal. Standards of appropriate business attire in the larger towns are comparable to those in most U.S. cities. In the coastal areas, tropical weight clothing is appropriate throughout the year; in the highlands, wool suits may be more comfortable. A raincoat is essential particularly during the April to June and October to November rainy season; a topcoat is rarely worn.

Personal visits are warmly welcomed and generally regarded as the most efficient method of establishing new trade contracts. Punctuality is important to Kenyan businesspeople and the business visitor should make every effort to be on time for appointments. As a general rule, appointments should be made in advance of a business call.

Local telephone service is available in most cities and larger provincial towns, although delays of from 1 to several hours are often experienced on long distance calls within the region. Long-distance telephone service to the United States, which cost approximately $15 for the first 3 minutes, can usually be made with a few minutes delay. International telex service through London provides teleprinter communication between Kenya and some 50 countries in Europe, North America, Asia, and Australia.

Commercial airmail rates to Nairobi are 40 cents for a letter weighing one-half ounce. Airform letters, costing 30 cents, are less expensive. Post office boxes, not street numbers, are used when addressing business firms, and cables are frequently used for speedier business communication. In estimating the time of a cable's arrival, 8 hours should be added to the time of dispatch (Eastern Standard Time).

Living Conditions and Costs

Most business travelers and residents find the Kenyan climate healthy and agreeable. Although the incidence of malaria is negligible in the cities and at altitudes over 5,000 feet, it is advisable to take an antimalarial preparation in the lower regions. Medical facilities in the major cities are generally adequate. British and Dutch equivalents of standard household medicines, including vitamins and pain relievers, can be purchased at local "chemists." Any special medicines should be carried with the traveler.

Kenya has several large hotels in Nairobi (Ambassador, Brunners Hotel, Nairobi Hilton, Hotel Inter-Continental/Nairobi, Embassy, New Avenue, New Stanley) and in Mombasa (Dolphin, Oceanic, New Carlton, Hotel Splendid, Rex, Nyali Beach Hotel, and the Mombasa Beach Hotel). Hotel accommodations in Kenya are often difficult to obtain and reservations should be made well in advance. Hotels in the principal cities are generally comparable to first rate American standards, but accommodations in smaller towns may be less satisfactory.

Suitable long-term housing accommodations are often difficult to obtain, and business travelers planning a lengthy visit should allow 4 to 8 weeks in a hotel until more permanent housing can be located. Boarding houses, which are considerably less expensive, are available, but generally do not provide accommodations of the standard considered satisfactory by Americans.

Eating habits are generally comparable to those prevailing in Western Europe or the United States, and American travelers ordinarily experience no difficulty in adjusting to the local cuisine.

Buses and taxis serve the residential areas of the cities, but the schedules are such that they may not be considered a reliable means of transportation for business purposes. Private cars are available for hire in the main commercial centers, with or without chauffeur. Railway service is available only between the largest cities.

Business Hours

Business establishments and government offices in Kenya are open Monday through Friday from 8:15 a.m. to 12:30 p.m. and from 2 p.m. to 4:30 p.m. Most offices also are open on Saturday from 8:15 a.m. to noon.

Holidays

The official Kenyan holidays are as follows:

New Year's Day	January 1
Good Friday	Varies
Easter Monday	Varies
Labor Day	May 1
Madaraka Day	June 1
Id-ul-Fitr	Varies
Kenyatta Day	October 20
Independence Day	December 12
Christmas Day	December 25
Boxing Day	December 26

General Advice

Visitors to Kenya should show respect for the President and all he symbolizes. They should stop before a Presidential motorcade, stand for the national anthem, and under no circumstances destroy or deface a portrait of the President. The normal spending money of Western visitors amounts to a small fortune for many Kenyans, and foreigners are therefore asked not to spend money ostentatiously.

Since there is virtually no drug addiction in Kenya, the import and unauthorized use of addictive drugs is a particularly serious offense.

Embassy Assistance

U.S. business visitors are encouraged to use the U.S. Embassy in Nairobi and the Kenya Embassy and Consulate-General in the Unied States. The U.S. Embassy in Kenya is located at the corner of Moi and Haile Selassie Avenues, P.O. Box 30137, Nairobi (tel: 334141). There is a U.S. Consulate in Mombasa, located in Palli House, Nyerere Avenue, P.O. Box 88079, Mombasa, (tel.: 315101). Kenya is represented in the United States by an Embassy at 2249 R Street, N.W., Washington, D.C. 20008, (tel.: (202) 387-6101). and by its Mission to the United Nations, 15 East 51st Street, New York, N.Y. 10022, (tel.: (212) 421-4740) and its Consulate at 9100 Wilshire Boulevard, Beverly Hills, Calif. 90212, (tel.: (213) 274-6635).

APPENDIX A—Banks

Algemene Bank Nederland N.V.
Koinnage Street
P.O. Box 30262
Nairobi
Tel.: 21130, 21164

Bank of Baroda
Bank of Baroda Building
Mondlane Street
P.O. Box 33033
Nairobi
Tel.: 27611, 333089

Bank of India
Kenyatta Avenue
P.O. Box 30246
Nairobi
Tel.: 21414

Bank of Tokyo
Silopark House
Mama Ngina street
P.O. Box 30441
Nairobi
Tel.: 20951

Beclays Bank International Ltd.
Local Head Office
P.O. Box 30120
Nairobi
Tel.: 23085

Central Bank of Kenya
Haile Selassie Avenue
P.O. Box 30463
Nairobi
Tel.: 2643

Chase Manhattan Overseas Corporation
P.O. Box 57051
Nairobi
Tel.: 334990

Chemical Bank
P.O. Box 61631
Nairobi
Tel.: 333036

Citibank (Regional Office)
P.O. Box 30490
Nairobi
Tel.: 334286

Citibank (Kenya)
P.O. Box 30711

Nairobi
Tel.: 33524

Commercial Bank of Africa Ltd.
Wabera Street
P.O. Box 30437
Nairobi
Tel.: 28881

Continental Bank
P.O. Box 42938
Nairobi
Tel.: 28698

Co-operative Bank of Kenya Ltd.
Government Road/Haile Selassie Avenue
P.O. Box 48231
Nairobi
Tel.: 25370

First National Bank of Chicago
International House
Mama Ngina Street
P.O. Box 47842
Nairobi
Tel.: 333960/28389

Grindlays Bank International
   (Kenya) Ltd.
Kenyatta Avenue
P.O. Box 30550
Nairobi
Tel.: 335888

Habib Bank (Overseas) Ltd.
Nkrumah Road
P.O. Box 83055
Mombasa
Tel.: 20829

Kenya Commercial Bank Ltd.
Government Road
P.O. Box 30081
Nairobi
Tel.: 336681

Manufacturers Hanover Trust Company
International House
P.O. Box 45433
Nairobi
Tel.: 28181/337088

National Bank of Kenya Ltd.
Development House
Government Road
P.O. Box 72497
Nairobi
Tel.: 29541

Standard Bank Limited
Government Road
P.O. Box 30003
Nairobi
Tel.: 331210

APPENDIX B—Public Sector Entities

General Government Agencies

Kenya Tea Development Authority
National Irrigation Board
University of Nairobi
Egerton College
Kenyatta University College
Kenya National Parks Authority
Museum Trustees of Kenya

Trading Organizations

Kenya Meat Commission
Pyrethrum Marketing Board
Mombasa Pipeline Board
Cotton Lint and Seed Marketing Board
Maize and Product Board
Kenya National Trading Corporation

Financial Institutions

Agricultural Development Corporation
Central Bank of Kenya
Cooperative Bank of Kenya
Industrial Development Bank
National Bank of Kenya
Post Office Savings Bank
Agricultural Finance Corporation
Development Finance Company of Kenya
National Housing Corporation
Industrial and Commercial Development
   Corporation
Kenya Tourist Development Corporation

Cereals and Sugar Finance Corporation
Agricultural Settlement Fund
Kenya National Assurance Company
State Reinsurance Corporation
Kenya Commercial Bank, Ltd.
First Permanent (E.A.), Ltd.
Housing Finance Co. of Kenya, Ltd.
Kenya Industrial Estates, Ltd.

Public Enterprises

Mumias Sugar Company
Mataara Tea Factory Co., Ltd.
Linten Tea Factory Co., Ltd.
Nyankoba Tea Factory Co., Ltd.
Chinga Tea Factory Co., Ltd.
Ragati Tea Company, Ltd.
Kenya Mining Industries, Ltd.
Kenya Mining Company
Kenya Cashew Nuts, Ltd.
Kibos Ginnery, Ltd.
Mwea Cotton Ginnery, Ltd.
Mambale Ginnery
Mea Garments
Wananchi Sawmills, Ltd.
Pulp and Paper Co. of E.A., Ltd.
Kenya Engineering Industries, Ltd.
E.A. Oil Refineries, Ltd.
E.A. Power and Lighting Co., Ltd.
Kenya Wine Agencies, Ltd.
Kenya Poultry Development Co., Ltd.
Panagric Hotels, Ltd.
Kenya Shiping Agency, Ltd.

APPENDIX C—Tables

Table 1.—FOREIGN EXCHANGE RESERVES
K£ '000*

As at end of Month	Central Bank of Kenya**	Commercial Banks		Govern-ment***	Total
		Net Balances with banks outside Kenya	Other		
1976 December	114,332	−2,118	799	799	114,828
1977 December	210,396	−5,790	1,163	1,214	206,983
1978 December	135,202	615	879	1,420	138,116
1979 December	237,587	244	1,409	1,828	241,068
1980—					
January	253,786	510	1,130	1,597	257,023
February	256,026	3,937	1,596	1,461	263,020
March	248,534	6,028	1,241	3,098	258,911
April	252,257	421	1,231	2,597	256,506
May	237,734	6,655	856	2,185	247,430
June	220,309	4,024	885	2,272	227,490
July	196,709	3,475	998	2,269	203,451
August	180,135	3,700	982	2,099	186,916
September	167,996	3,145	1,030	2,406	174,577
October	195,519	6,228	1,244	2,389	205,380
November	190,336	6,370	1,103	2,567	200,376
December	186,092	3,134	1,146	3,097	193,469
1981—					
January	179,975	7,927	1,588	3,028	192,518
February	183,019	8,014	1,507	2,626	195,166
March	185,318	8,091	1,249	4,281	198,939

Source: 1 Kenyan Pound = 20 Kenyan Shillings. Central Bank of Kenya.
**Includes net balances with the Banks of Tanzania and Uganda.
***Includes Securities of the Kenya Post Office Savings Bank.

Table 2.—BALANCE OF TRADE
K£ '000*

Year/Quarter/Month	Imports			Exports			Visible Balance
	Commercial	Government	Total	Domestic	Reexports	Total	
1976	377,330	29,667	406,997	318,658	26,403	345,062	−61,935
1977	495,589	35,857	531,446	480,259	21,560	501,819	−29,627
1978	631,121	30,004	661,125	369,965	25,747	395,712	−265,413
1979	582,700	37,456	620,156	385,534	27,253	412,787	−207,369
1979—							
1st Qr.	121,168	10,524	131,692	84,935	6,159	91,093	−40,599
2nd Qr.	144,928	10,437	155,365	89,272	5,454	94,726	−60,638
3rd Qr.	143,109	9,773	152,882	93,001	5,191	98,191	−54,691
4th Qr.	165,325	14,442	179,767	118,321	10,450	128,771	−50,997
1980—							
1st Qr.	217,533	22,447	239,980	121,695	7,355	129,050	−110,930
2nd Qr.	174,875	12,064	186,939	131,396	8,222	139,618	−47,321
3rd Qr.	231,341	9,557	240,898	92,104	8,289	100,393	−140,505
4th Qr.	166,416	30,193	196,609	140,159	4,560	144,719	−51,890
January	56,654	12,448	69,102	39,230	2,148	41,378	−27,723
February	94,211	5,696	99,907	41,895	2,367	44,262	−55,645
March	65,413	4,304	69,717	40,146	2,841	42,987	−26,730
April	52,994	3,680	56,674	42,657	2,579	45,236	−11,437
May	53,123	5,871	58,994	36,636	2,275	38,911	−20,082
June	62,547	2,466	65,013	38,260	3,313	41,572	−23,441
July	50,149	2,601	52,750	29,319	4,644	33,963	−18,787
August	83,438	2,064	85,503	25,656	1,447	27,103	−58,400
September	43,171	4,846	48,016	31,921	1,948	33,869	−14,148
October	55,680	20,437	76,117	31,634	1,647	33,281	−42,836
November	46,581	3,576	50,157	33,129	1,193	34,322	−15,835
December	49,665	5,824	55,489	43,904	1,656	45,500	−9,929

*1 Kenyan Pound = 20 Kenyan Shillings.
Definitions—
(1) *Imports.*—Goods entered at the time of importation for consumption or for warehousing in Kenya, including, in both cases, goods which are subsequently reexported.
(2) *Reexports.*—All imported goods, other than scrap metals in any form, which are subsequently reexported in the form in which they were imported, to places outside Kenya, or as aircrafts' or ships' stores.
(3) *Domestic Exports.*—Goods grown, produced or manufactured in Kenya exported to places outside Kenya or as aircrafts' or ships' stores. Scrap metal is included.
(4) *Valuation*—Imports.—C.I.F. port or place of importation. Exports and Reexports.—F.O.B. part or place of exportation.
Source: Customs and Excise Department.

Table 3.—Livestock Production*
(In thousands of head)

Year/Quarter/Month	Cattle and Calves	Sheep and Lambs	Goats	Pigs***			
				Baconers	Porkers	Larders**	Total
1976	228.5	12.8	4.6	38.7	3.7	2.3	44.6
1977	158.1	11.2	6.1	40.7	4.0	2.5	47.2
1978	68.0	11.6	10.4	40.7	7.7	2.7	51.0
1979	67.7	10.1	2.0	34.1	8.5	2.7	45.4
1980	55.9	6.2	2.6	28.3	6.2	2.5	36.9
1979—							
2nd Qr.	16.2	2.3	0.7	9.2	2.2	0.5	11.9
3rd Qr.	21.8	3.9	0.9	7.8	2.5	0.8	11.0
4th Qr.	11.7	0.1	0.1	7.3	1.8	0.8	9.8
1980—							
1st Qr.	18.9	2.4	0.5	6.1	1.7	0.7	8.5
2nd Qr.	10.1	1.0	1.1	5.3	1.3	0.7	7.3
3rd Qr.	14.8	1.2	1.0	8.3	1.6	0.5	10.4
4th Qr.	12.1	1.5	—	8.7	1.5	0.6	10.7
January	5.6	1.2	—	2.0	0.5	0.3	2.8
February	6.3	0.8	—	1.5	0.6	0.2	2.3
March	6.9	0.5	0.5	2.5	0.5	0.3	3.4
April	3.3	0.3	—	1.5	0.5	0.2	2.3
May	3.2	0.2	0.2	1.8	0.4	0.2	2.3
June	3.6	0.6	0.9	1.9	0.5	0.2	2.7
July	5.2	0.1	1.0	2.6	0.5	0.2	3.3
August	5.6	0.9	—	2.7	0.5	0.1	3.3
September	4.0	0.2	—	3.0	0.6	0.2	3.8
October	5.4	0.6	—	2.9	0.5	0.2	3.7
November	3.6	0.5	—	2.6	0.5	0.1	3.2
December	3.1	0.4	—	3.1	0.5	0.2	3.8
1981—							
1st. Qr.	13.7	2.4	—	....	....	....	....
January	4.6	0.9	—	....	....	....	....
February	4.0	1.0	—	....	....	....	....
March	.1	0.5	—	....	....	....	....

*Recorded deliveries only.
**After June 1971, the grade was changed to manufactures, which includes valuation.
***From January 1975, slaughters outside Uplands Bacon Factory by licensed butchers are included.
Source: Kenya Meat Commission, Pig Industry Board and Uplands Bacon Factory.

Table 4.—Dairy Production

Year/Quarter/Month	Recorded Milk production	Milk Processed By The KCC						
		Whole milk and cream	Butter and ghee	Cheese	Evaporated milk	Dried whole milk powder	Dried skim-milk powder	Other products
	000 litres	000 litres**	Metric tons	Metric tons	Metric tons	Metric tons	Metric tons	Metric tons
1976	208,658	150,422	3,067	177	2,099	3,009	1,489	2
1977	259,450	157,880	4,342	445	1,321	5,262	3,440	1
1978	269,796	185,557	3,871	253	489	4,236	2,956	—
1979	240,559	212,255	3,134	264	188	1,439	1,218	—
1980	186,885	186,892	2,174	150	44	128	80	270
1979—					—			—
1st Qr.	65,309	48,637	921	55		896	630	
2nd Qr.	66,496	54,626	949	110	188	283	573	
3rd Qr.	60,308	57,755	694	61	—	260	14	—
4th Qr.	48,446	51,237	571	38	—	—	1	—
1980—								
1st Qr.	31,526	34,653	338	26	—	—	1	—
2nd Qr.	44,222	44,196	495	56	44	12	75	83
3rd Qr.	59,334	58,988	781	58	—	74	5	62
4th Qr.	51,803	49,055	559	9	—	43	—	125
January	13,162	13,691	144	13	—	—	—	—
February	9,874	10,849	104	11	—	—	—	—
March	8,490	10,114	91	2	—	—	1	—
April	8,084	8,620	87	7	44	—	—	—
May	15,466	7,110	159	21	—	—	—	—
June	20,672	18,466	249	28	—	12	75	83
July	20,537	20,522	252	18	—	74	5	42
August	19,510	20,326	276	31	—	—	—	20
September	19,287	18,140	253	9	—	—	—	—
October	16,409	16,917	195	1	—	—	—	—
November	18,752	15,337	173	4	—	—	—	61
December	16,642	16,802	191	4	—	43	—	64
1981—								
January	....	18,155	148	12	—	—	—	—
February	....	15,584	73	2	—	—	—	—

*Deliveries of milk and butterfat to the Kenya Co-operative Creameries and other sales licensed by the Kenya Dairy Board
**Whole milk equivalent.
Source: Kenya Co-operative Creameries and Kenya Dairy Board.

Table. 5—Production of Certain Industrial Commodities

Year/Quarter/Month	Soda Ash	Wheat Flour	Biscuits	Sugar	Spirits	Beer	Mineral Waters	Tobacco	Cigarettes
	*000 Metric Tons		Metric Tons	Metric Tons	Litres	*000 Litres		Kg.	Million Sticks
1976	107.3	137.8	1,651	170,546	356,838	165,586	81,193	5,950	3,703
1977	....	148.4	1,653	182,141	420,183	195,160	99,411	5,575	3,944
1978	185.7	246.3	2,485	238,000	437,389	199,110	108,019	4,305	4,493
1979	....	141.2	2,947	295,998	415,694	208,933	118,926	5,320	4,554
1980—									
1st Qr.	56.3	42.4	701	110,674	326,631	52,281	37,475	1,219	1,153
2nd Qr.	53.2	50.0	856	65,886	311,767	54,578	39,425	1,311	1,109
3rd Qr.	55.7	55.0	649	115,004	437,522	58,074	35,043	676	1,139
4th Qr.	51.6	51.4	819	111,752	413,233	56,809	33,791	1,088	1,153
January	18.7	12.3	261	35,878	151,615	15,395	14,065	592	425
February	17.9	13.2	200	36,759	44,272	17,127	12,171	338	367
March	19.7	16.8	239	38,037	130,744	19,759	11,239	298	361
April	17.2	14.4	250	27,607	115,506	18,608	12,205	504	383
May	20.3	17.5	306	13,734	143,057	18,335	10,973	400	382
June	15.7	14.8	300	24,544	149,287	17,635	16,247	402	344
July	17.4	17.8	298	40,716	155,825	19,161	14,359	278	436
August	20.4	17.4	152	38,661	140,949	18,239	11,293	130	348
September	17.9	16.2	198	35,727	140,748	20,674	10,729	268	355
October	19.0	16.9	304	36,687	140,929	20,005	11,576	276	397
November	16.8	17.6	217	38,337	144,462	19,775	11,147	406	378
December	....	16.9	298	36,728	128,023	17,029	11,068	406	378

*Of crude Petroleum.
Source: Oil Refinery—E.A., Magadi Soda Co. Ltd., E.A. Power and Lighting Co. Ltd., Cement Companies. Flour milling Companies, Customs and Excise Department.

KENYA

Table 6.—Electricity Production and Consumption
(Millions of KWh)

	1976	1977	1978	1979	1980
Total available	1,400	1,385	1,599	1,728	1,805
of which:					
generated locally	1,158	1,113	1,382	1,568	1,490
imported	242	272	217	160	325
Total sales	1,152	1,273	1,371	1,479	1,539

Source: Kenyan Economic Survey 1981.

Table 7.—Selected Imports
K£*000*

Year/Quarter/Month	Crude Petroleum	Motor Vehicles and Chassis	Agricultural Machinery and Tractors	Industrial Machinery (including electrical)	Iron and Steel	Fabrics of Cotton	Fabrics of Synthetic Fibers	Paper and Paper Products	Pharmaceutical Products	Fertilizers
1976	93,470	23,620	7,097	69,886	28,172	971	3,301	7,599	6,734	5,225
1977	100,158	40,764	16,598	91,844	32,643	444	3,233	9,031	10,175	9,473
1978	92,338	68,797	18,575	130,180	41,816	436	2,119	10,261	13,187	10,012
1979	120,085	45,122	7,568	113,252	37,631	405	1,883	12,304	11,230	5,344
1979—										
1st Qr.	19,934	10,339	2,317	27,786	8,783	93	490	3,523	2,189	186
2nd Qr.	36,475	11,204	2,226	27,606	8,168	133	527	2,133	2,782	874
3rd Qr.	28,282	10,565	1,780	27,111	8,381	69	460	3,890	2,985	2,251
4th Qr.	35,395	13,014	1,244	30,367	12,302	110	405	3,014	3,274	2,292
1980—										
1st Qr.	70,260	17,089	2,243	41,731	10,755	90	446	3,092	4,389	7,799
2nd Qr.	19,035	16,972	2,288	32,874	15,410	112	792	2,853	3,951	4,403
3rd Qr.	85,355	15,426	2,188	34,772	14,188	122	433	3,173	4,105	1,026
4th Qr.	10,155	18,078	3,446	40,938	10,156	958	579	3,789	3,453	2,605
January	5,746	6,126	634	18,994	4,406	72	80	1,020	1,316	2,395
February	45,923	5,322	995	9,238	3,748	6	238	807	1,652	3,624
March	18,591	5,640	623	13,403	2,611	12	128	1,265	1,421	1,433
April	5,379	4,319	757	9,490	4,535	31	286	1,164	1,267	3,039
May	—	8,201	875	12,642	5,126	58	109	1,153	1,473	525
June	13,656	3,913	652	10,014	5,320	23	396	454	1,156	838
July	—	5,271	388	10,921	5,436	76	150	1,364	1,653	557
August	33,565	5,913	656	12,023	5,643	3	151	1,075	1,273	5
September	—	4,236	1,134	11,126	3,038	43	131	729	1,174	389
October	—	6,391	1,331	12,575	4,391	478	249	1,097	1,528	664
November	—	4,747	1,174	11,952	1,828	19	141	980	930	1,368
December	5,466	4,884	695	13,004	3,067	421	109	1,567	968	574

*1 Kenyan Pound = 20 Kenyan Shillings.
Source: Customs and Excise Department.

Table 8.—Principal Domestic Exports
K£'000*

Year/ Quarter/ Month	Coffee (not roasted)	Sisal (fibre and tow)	Tea	Pyrethrum (extract and flowers)	Meat and Meat Products	Hides and Skins (undressed)	Manufactured Goods*				
							Soda Ash	Wattle Extract	Petroleum Products	Cement	Other
1976	93,348	4,194	31,763	6,887	8,386	8,561	3,033	2,686	57,603	8,070	47,309
1977	204,366	4,114	71,779	6,040	7,597	8,023	2,687	1,832	72,398	8,566	34,910
1978	124,679	4,038	63,187	4,622	2,721	9,825	3,684	1,487	60,216	9,008	34,165
1979	110,573	4,800	62,843	5,765	2,688	13,770	5,577	1,966	68,051	8,347	37,203
1979—											
1st Qr.	25,576	758	15,219	1,223	585	2,908	1,691	196	12,188	2,006	7,235
2nd Qr.	24,519	1,084	17,291	982	601	5,311	1,311	692	11,854	2,081	7,718
3rd Qr.	20,151	1,293	14,884	1,044	625	2,228	1,690	451	24,103	2,180	10,051
4th Qr.	40,328	1,665	15,451	2,309	878	3,323	864	627	19,900	2,081	12,199
1980—											
1st Qr.	31,707	2,293	15,614	2,322	475	4,347	1,270	517	23,210	2,270	14,423
2nd Qr.	38,162	1,895	14,419	1,502	218	1,995	921	318	40,291	2,553	11,238
3rd Qr.	15,888	1,809	12,766	2,511	424	1,337	848	611	25,878	2,677	9,314
4th Qr.	22,372	2,849	15,050	2,739	464	1,868	2,033	660	61,047	2,654	10,483
January	6,993	399	6,073	646	95	1,760	682	235	8,330	710	4,522
February	11,362	1,266	5,460	854	78	1,257	527	73	8,127	663	5,165
March	13,357	639	4,150	822	300	1,247	61	209	6,533	898	4,620
April	13,333	591	4,634	529	70	1,567	371	81	9,876	898	3,792
May	13,596	789	4,641	499	101	886	398	15	5,073	687	3,680
June	11,261	516	5,091	474	45	334	155	222	10,956	968	3,501
July	5,141	521	5,415	417	119	227	43	201	6,561	746	3,993
August	2,606	607	4,178	710	182	1,003	663	125	5,997	939	3,939
September	8,142	681	4,092	1,384	123	522	456	286	7,373	991	3,037
October	9,997	993	4,755	1,328	79	202	896	234	3,243	809	3,188
November	7,682	960	4,819	574	166	372	535	283	7,028	883	4,082
December	5,349	951	5,507	913	217	1,295	602	143	18,611	961	3,212

*Manufactured good include S.I.T.C. Section 5–8 and Petroleum Products.
*1 Kenyan Pound = 20 Kenyan Shillings.
Source: Customs and Excise Department.

Market Profile— KENYA

Foreign Trade

Imports.—$2.1 billion in 1981: $1.7 billion in 1982. Major suppliers. 1981: Saudi Arabia, 21.8 percent: United Kingdom, 17.5 percent: United States. 7.9 percent: and West Germany. 7.8 percent. Principal Imports: crude petroleum, machinery, iron and steel products, and vehicles. Imports from United States: aircraft and parts, telecommunications equipment. fungicides, and pesticides: $95.6 million in 1982.

Exports.—$1.2 billion in 1981: $1.1 billion in 1982. Principal markets. 1979: United Kingdom, 12.8 percent: West Germany. 11.1 percent: Uganda, 10.6 percent: and Singapore, 5.6 percent. Principal exports: coffee, tea, pyrethrum extract. sisal fibers. and wood carvings. Exports to United States: $71.3 million in 1982.

Trade Policy.—Exchange and import authorization required for most imports. Sales tax of 15 to 25 percent on most imports and domestic manufactures.

Trade Prospects.—Import restraints least likely to be applied to industrial raw materials, intermediates, capital goods, and agricultural products.

Foreign Investment

Government encourages private foreign investment in enterprises that utilize local resources for export industries. Priority given to investors willing to transfer technology and export output. Companies with equity held by nonresidents may not remit annual dividends of more than 10 percent of equity and reserves. No formal code. Investment guaranty agreement with United States and Foreign Investment Protection Act of 1964 in force. U.S. direct investment estimated at $315 million in 1982.

Finance

Currency.—Kenya shilling (Ksh). (Ksh 13.3=US$ in Oct. 1983). Money supply: $1.974.6 million in 1981.

Domestic Credit and Investment.—Credit and venture capital available from domestic. foreign, and international lending agencies.

National Budget.—FY (July-June) 1981 expenditures estimated at $7.5 billion.

Balance of Payments.—Overall surplus was $275 million and external public debt $705.6 millon at yearend 1979. Foreign exchange reserves totaled $158.1 million in 1982.

Economy

Mixed economy. A major world exporter of coffee and tea. Tourism is significant foreign exchange earner.

GDP.—In 1981. GDP was $6.5 billion (current prices): per capita GDP $330.6: annual real growth rate 3.1 percent. Rate of inflation. 14 percent.

Foreign Aid.—$200.3 million in grants and loans from United States in fiscal years 1982 and 1983.

Agriculture.—Major products. 1979: coffee, tea, pyrethrum extract, cattle and calves, milk, beer, and maize. Corn, millet, and cassava are main subsistence crops.

Industry.—Major industries include food processing: tobacco curing: automobile assembly: oil refining: and production of textiles, tires, cement, and paper. Industrial Production Index (1976=100) rose 7.1 percent to 139.8 during 1978-79.

Commerce.—Consumer Price Index (1976=100) was 194.3 in 1981, up 15 percent from 1980.

Development Plan.—Plan calls for $11 million expenditures in 1979-83. Emphasis on creation of employment in rural areas and on export industries.

Basic Economic Facilities

Transportation.—30,000 miles of road, 3,200 paved. Mombasa is chief port in eastern Africa. International airports at Nairobi and Mombasa. Rail network of 3,670 miles is major means of freight transport. Freight handled in 1978: 6 million metric tons at Mobassa port: 31,600 metric tons at Nairobi airport: 23,000 metric tons at Mombasa airport. 200,000 vehicles registered.

Communications.—Radio relay links: open wire lines: 144,000 telephones: 2 million radios: 4 AM and 2 FM radio stations. Five television stations in 1979, 82,000 TV's. Four daily papers.

Power.—In 1980, 485,000 kW capacity: 1.5 billion kWh consumption. 65 percent hydro.

Natural Resources

Land.—244,900 square miles: 13 percent agricultural. Low marsh strip along Indian Ocean: large arid northern region and high southern plateau interrupted by rugged volcanic mountains: north-south Great Rift Valley.

Climate.—Wide ranging altitudes contribute to temperature-tropical variations.

Minerals.—Fluorspar production. Small soda ash and salt but no known coal or petroleum deposits. Imported crudes refined for local consumption and reexport.

Population

Size.—17.8 million (1982): 98 percent African: 50 percent under age 18: average annual growth rate, 4 percent. Principal cities: Nairobi, capital, 959,000: Mombasa, 401,000: and Nakurku, 66,006.

Language.—Swahili is official. English widely understood.

Education.—In 1978, literacy 35 percent. Enrollment: primary schools, 2,977,679: secondary school, 240,615: University of Nairobi, 5,942.

Labor.—Employment in monetary sector about 972,300: 5.4 million in labor force.

Health.—1978: 255 hospitals, 201 health centers, 1,101 dispensaries. 1,466 doctors. 130 dentists, and 6,388 nurses. Infant mortality rate 83 per 1,000: life expectancy: 51.3 years for men and 55.2 years for women.

Market Profile— KIRIBATI *

Foreign Trade

Exports.—In 1978, $21.2 million. Copra and phosphates accounted for 99 percent of export earnings.

Imports.—In 1978, $18.4 million worth of food, livestock, machinery, transportation equipment, fuel and petroleum products and manufactured goods.

Trade Policy.—A single-line metricated tariff structure was introduced in 1975, thereby eliminating Commonwealth preference tariffs. Tariff matters are handled by the Division of Customs and Excise within the Ministry of Finance.

Trading Agencies.—The Wholesale Society—a public corporation which uses the Kerr Bros. Pty., Ltd.; and Schutz and Wilder—private, based in Tarawa. Oten Trading Company—private, based in Betio.

Finance

Currency.—Australian currency is used. Sterling coins are accepted but circulate at par with Australian coins. American dollars are used at Canton and accepted elsewhere.

Foreign Aid.—Western (non U.S.) commitments in 1979 totaled $46 million. An aid agreement with Australia will provide $8.1 million during the 3-year period 1980-83.

Banks.—The Bank of New South Wales Ltd.

Economy

GDP.—GDP for 1979 was $36 million, per capita GDP was $630.

Commerce.—A hot, disagreeable climate and the lack of any scenic attractions seem to preclude the hope for a tourist industry on the islands.

Basic Economic Facilities

As of 1976 the Japanese Daiwa Shipping group began operations in the area. Services are fully containerized. Port facilities for large overseas vessels are at Canton Island. Small vessels elsewhere tie up at buoys or in lagoons. Interisland freight is operated by a colonial government fleet. Air Pacific and Air Nauru provide service via Nadi, Fiji, to the Colony at the airport on Tarawa Island twice weekly. There also is a domestic airline, Air Tungory, which operates between various islands within the colony. Most islands have roads running the length of the island. They are adequate for bicycles and other small vehicles which are the chief modes of transportation. Interisland trans-portation is underdeveloped. The islands are surrounded by lagoons, so transportation is either by domestic air service or through the lagoons.

Communications.—The Government provides radio communications to all the islands for 18 hours daily.

Power.—Electricity of 240 volts, 50 cycles is supplied continuously by the Public Works Department of Tarawa; availability is limited.

Natural Resources

Location.—Kiribati, a newly independent government as of July, 1979, is located 500 miles north of Nadi, Fiji.

Climate.—Hot, rainfall varies from 40 to 120 inches per year.

Minerals.—Phosphate, in rock form. However, the supply is becoming exhausted.

Population

Size.—As of 1982, 59,000 inhabitants.

Language.—English is the language of business; many dialects of Micronesian spoken.

Education.—As of 1974, 15,000 students enrolled in over 206 schools.

---

* Formerly Gilbert Islands.

Marketing in Korea (South)

Contents

Report Revised July 1980

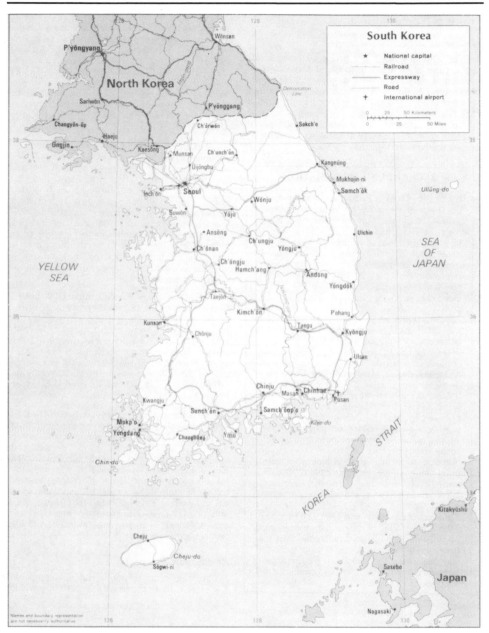

South Korea

* National capital
  Railroad
  Expressway
  Road
+ International airport

1421

Foreign Trade Outlook

Introduction

The Korean market has produced exceptional opportunities in recent years, and the country's record of dynamic growth augurs well for U.S. exporters. Building upon an already diversified industrial base, Korea's planners have targeted the next decade for the country's emergence as a developed economy. To accomplish this objective, Korea will require increasingly sophisticated products and technologies.

BACKGROUND INFORMATION

Keeping this book within reasonable size limits has made it necessary to focus on material *directly* concerned with marketing and commerce, and set aside materials only indirectly related. The editors relize, however, that *general* data about a country are also vital to a company's preparations to enter a foreign market, and make a very definite recommendation as to how such expanded information needs can be served.

For those who wish *general* data about a country—data which goes beyond marketing and commerce—the editors recommend *Countries of the World and Their Leaders*, published as an annually updated yearbook by Gale Research Company, Detroit, Michigan 48226. Containing 4- to 20-page entries on 168 countries, the volume also provides several hundred pages of supplementary world data. Each country entry is prepared by the U.S. Department of State to provide a general briefing on the geography, people, culture, and political situation of the particular country. Each report provides some historical insight as well as a look at contemporary trends of lifestyle in the country. Reports also discuss a country's educational system, its press, ethnic groupings and religious practices.

Countries of the World and Their Leaders provides a fresh listing of cabinet ministers of each nation. In addition it lists health conditions the traveling businessman will wish to prepare for and includes information on passport procedures, customs and duties, and world climate conditions.

As a result of annual growth of real GNP averaging about 10 percent for almost two decades, Korea has entered the 1980's with its international trade totaling over $35 billion. Although export oriented, its economy is drawing increasing strength from domestic growth. The economy nonetheless continues to be sensitive to downturns in the growth of its few major trading partners. Moreover, soaring oil import costs and other sources of inflation have tested Korea's proven ability to continue its rapid growth.

Korea's imports from other parts of the world exceeded $20.3 billion in 1979, an increase of 36 percent over 1978. Except for a small decline in imports of transportation equipment, almost all other categories showed large gains. Imports of grains were up 58 percent and other food items, 51 percent. Other categories registering above average growth were chemicals, mineral products, and nonferrous metals: in part due to significant price increases. In particular, Korea has become a key market for expensive and complex projects in such areas as power generation and telecommunications.

The U.S. share of Korea's import market rose from 20 percent in 1978 to 23 percent in 1979. In contrast, Japan's share dropped from 40 to 33 percent. The previous edition of this report noted that in 1975 Korea was the 15th largest market for U.S. exports. Korea ranked 11th in 1979. Moreover, Korea was the second largest market for U.S. exports in the East Asia region, after Japan. Table 1 shows selected U.S. exports to Korea by major commodities.

The Korean Government is committed to a long-term policy of liberalization of the economy, including the financial structure, imports monopolies, and capital flows. To reach developed country status, and recognizing that Korea's competitive edge will not remain in labor-intensive industries, Korea aggressively has moved into development of heavy and chemical industries. This indicates that there will be substantial new opportunities for U.S. companies to participate in capital-intensive, high-technology projects.

Best Export Prospects

The wide range of industrial development in Korea as well as increased interest in providing

Table 1.—Selected U.S. Exports to Korea by Major
Commodities
(Millions of dollars)

Commodity	1977	1978	1979
Total	2,369	3,160	4,170
Agricultural products			
Wheat	202	215	258
Corn	119	209	319
Rice and barley	51	1	44
Hides and skins except furskins .	94	115	129
Cotton	315	378	398
Animal fats and oils	38	41	58
Nonagricultural products,			
Chemicals	105	169	377
Metalworking machinery	14	46	73
Office machines, computers, and			
parts	32	43	48
Telecommunication equipment...	68	83	71
Electronic components and parts	145	166	196
Other machinery	289	321	596
Road motor vehicles, engines, and			
parts	29	85	107
Commercial aircraft, engines, and			
parts	89	146	186
Logs and lumber	51	84	90
Pulp and waste paper	52	55	114
Iron and steel scrap	98	118	153
Nonferrous metal scrap	33	58	61
Coal	28	41	60
Phosphate fertilizer	36	46	57

medical and social services provides numerous opportunities for U.S. exporters. Although there are many more best prospects, 11 product areas have been identified as having good longer-term prospects. They are: metalworking and finishing machinery; materials handling equipment; power generation, transmission, and distribution equipment; construction and mining equipment; process control instrumentation; communications equipment; scientific and laboratory instrumentation; computers and peripheral equipment; medical equipment; electronics industry production and test equipment and electronic components; and textile and apparel machinery. The Industry Trends section below provides some explanation for the selection of these products; additional analysis of each product category is available in the annual Best Prospects Report prepared by the American Embassy in Seoul, Korea, which can be obtained from the Japan/Korea/Hong Kong Branch, Office of Country Marketing, International Trade Administration, U.S. Department of Commerce, Washington, D.C. 20230.

Industry Trends

GNP Development

The Korean economy has grown rapidly since the early 1960's. During 1962-78, gross national product (GNP) grew at a real average annual rate of 9.5 percent, exceeding the expectations of the First, Second, Third, and Fourth Five-Year Plans. In 1978, GNP reached $47.4 billion in current prices ($28.7 billion in 1975 prices), achieving a real growth rate of 11.6 percent. GNP per capita reached $1,279, compared with $965 in 1977 and $87 in 1962.

Forecasts for economic growth based on the Economic Management Plan (1979-81) are that GNP will grow at an average annual rate of 9.3 percent during 1979-81. GNP is projected to reach $86 billion in 1981 with per capita GNP at $2,210.

Principal Growth Sectors and Economic Priorities

Korea's economic growth has been led by increases in the mining and manufacturing and social overhead capital and other service sectors. From 1962 to 1978, mining and manufacturing grew at an average annual rate of 17.4 percent and social overhead capital grew at 10.2 percent. Agricultural production has lagged behind the industrial sectors, increasing at an average annual rate of only 3.9 percent.

A significant shift in the industrial structure has occurred. The percentage share of mining and manufacturing GNP steadily increased from 11.6 percent in 1962 to 32.9 percent in 1978, while agriculture, forestry, and fisheries declined from 43.5 to 19.1 percent in the same period. Export growth also has contributed greatly to overall economic growth. Commodity exports grew by an average rate of 41.2 percent annually during 1962-78.

The Fourth Five-Year Economic Plan emphasizes economic self-reliance, social development, and the enhancement of technology and productivity. To meet these objectives, the Plan aims at: (1) boosting grain production and improving farm income through promotion of the "Saemaul Movement," a program initiated early in the decade to assist agricultural development; (2) strengthening import substitution through active continuation of heavy and chemical industries development; (3) promoting education, including vocational and technical training and improving the social welfare system; and (4) developing technology and (5) stabilizing prices. During the Plan period, the average sectoral growth of GNP is projected to be 4 percent in agriculture, forestry and fisheries; 12-15 percent in mining and manufacturing; and 6-8 percent in social overhead capital and other services. The ratio of gross investment in GNP is forecast at

28–30 percent. Among the investment ratios, private and government savings are projected at 20–25 percent and 6–8 percent, respectively. With respect to external transactions, visible exports are projected to grow at a 16 percent annual rate, with visible imports scheduled for an annual growth of 12 percent.

Key growth sectors in the economy are those chosen for a special industrial development program announced in January 1979 that would inject $46 billion in government investment funds into facility expansion projects by 1986. Some of the major goals of the development program are discussed below.

Iron and Steel.—Korea's annual production capacity of crude steel in 1978 totaled 7.8 million tons. By 1980 annual production capacity is targeted to reach 20.6 million tons with Korea becoming the 10th largest producer in the world. Korea's only integrated steel plant, the state-controlled Pohang Steel Co. (POSCO), is expanding its production capacity from the current 5.5 million tons to 8.5 million tons (crude steel basis) by 1981, under its fourth-phase expansion project. POSCO's capacity will be further expanded to 9.5 million tons by 1982 and 13.2 million tons by 1986. The Korean Government has selected POSCO to construct a second integrated steel mill by 1982, at a cost of $2 billion, which will have an initial capacity of 3 million tons of crude steel per year. The capacity of "POSCO II" will be expanded in four stages to reach 12 million tons. Through the construction of POSCO II, the Korean Government hopes to help overcome Korea's shortage of crude steel, which is now estimated to reach 7.8 million tons by 1986. Plans for a third integrated steel mill, which would also have an annual capacity of 12 million tons, are now under review by the Government.

Machinery.—Machinery is slated to become Korea's major export industry by 1986 with exports of $10 billion. A total of $1.6 billion will be invested in the machine industry to raise the self-sufficiency ration in machinery to 88 percent by 1981 as part of the Machine Industry Development Program of the Fourth Five-year Economic Development Plan. Machinery production is projected to rise to $5 billion by 1981 compared with $2.1 billion in 1977, with a wide range of heavy machines produced including metalworking machinery, power generation equipment, and construction machinery. The Korean Government has undertaken a comprehensive set of measures to help the local machinery industry meet these goals, including subsidized loans, import protection and other incentives to selected firms. A key element in reaching Development Program goals is significant new private investment in the Changwon Machine Industrial Complex, which has been under development since 1974. Approximately 200 plants are to be located in the Changwon Complex. There are currently 61 plants in operation and 25 others under construction. By 1981 the Changwon Complex is expected to produce more than 40 percent of total Korean machinery output and more than 50 percent of total machinery exports.

Shipbuilding.—Korea expects to become one of the five largest shipbuilders in the world by 1986 with an annual capacity of 6.5 million gross tons. Plans call for prior approval for installation of private shipbuilding facilities so as to effectively promote expansion projects, financial support for the exportation of yachts and marine structurals as well as oceangoing vessels, and an updating of the 1967 Shipbuilding Industrial Development Law. Small shipyards also will be expanded and developed into export industries by means of increased financial assistance from the Government. A shipbuilding industrial development plan designed to meet the 1981 export goal of $1.2 billion calls for domestic shipyards to increase their construction capacity from 2.77 million gross tons in 1977 to 4.25 million gross tons in 1981, and their renovation capacity from 10.7 million metric tons in 1977 to 14.6 million metric tons by 1981. As of May 31, 1979, overseas orders for shipbuilding totaled $194 million, or 39 percent of the year's target of $500 million, for 19 vessels.

Automobiles.—The Korean Government plans to invest $7.1 billion in both domestic and foreign capital by the end of 1986 for the development of three major automobile makers — Hyundai, Saehan, and Kia. The plan envisages expanding the nation's annual automobile production capacity from the current 278,400 units in a move to raise annual automobile exports to $1.4 billion and advance Korea to ninth place among the world's automobile producing nations. The proportion of domestically produced automotive parts used is expected to increase rapidly as the Automotive Parts Manufacturers Development Plan takes effect. The Ministry of Commerce and Industry tentatively has designated 115 firms as potential specialized makers of automobile parts. Designated firms will receive administrative and financial support. Specific automotive parts covered include: bolts and nuts, gaskets, fuel pumps, oil pumps, switches, bulbs, drive shafts, shock absorbers, steering wheels, steering knuckles, springs, horns, thermostats, seat belts, rocker arms, and hub drums. In the first 7 months of 1979, four domestic automobile and automotive parts makers exported a total of $65 million, an increase of 69 percent over the same period in 1978 and 50 percent of 1979's $130 million export goal. Automotive parts accounted for $20 million of the total. Through July 1979 automobiles were exported to 51 countries and automotive parts to 70 nations.

Electronics.—Korea ranked 11th among the world's producers of electronic products in 1978 with a production value of $2.3 billion, up from $56 million in 1968. During the 10-year period, exports of electronic products grew at an average rate of 53 percent and in 1978 accounted for 11 percent of Korea's total exports. According to the "Long-Term Demand Prospects and Plant Construction Plan," prepared by the Korean Fine Instruments Center, $2.6 billion will be invested in the Korean electrical and electronic products industry during the next 9 years. A total of 944 new plants will be built, 230 plants to make home appliances, 209 to make industrial apparatus and 496 to make components. By 1986 Korean production value of electrical and electronic products is expected to reach $12.7 billion. Exports are projected at $7.3 billion with domestic consumption reaching $8.4 billion, of which $3 billion is to be imported. Government development plans envisage the production of 57 new electronics products by 1981. The Government will provide assistance to the manufacturers of nine high-priority items—fabricated silicon waters, fabricated wafers for LEDs, minicomputers and microcomputers, microprocessors, computer peripherals, data transmission equipment, electronic communications switching systems, computer terminals, and software. The 48 projects to be developed by the private sector will be monitored closely. Much of this production will take place in the Gumi Electronics Industrial Complex.

Petrochemicals.—By 1986 Korea has a goal of total annual production capacity of 1.5 million tons, which would raise Korea's petrochemical self-sufficiency ratio to 83 percent and make Korea the world's 10th largest producer of petrochemicals. Various expansion projects are planned for the Ulsan and Yochon Petrochemical Industrial Complexes and plans to build a third petrochemical complex at Yochon by 1984 also have been announced. Broad outlines for the proposed new complex call for the construction of a 350,000 ton-per-year naphtha cracking center, plus nine downstream plants requiring an investment of approximately $1.5 billion in domestic and foreign funds. The Korean Government is reportedly working out a master plan for a fourth petrochemical industrial complex that would start being constructed in the early 1980's. Likely to be sited at Ulsan or Onsan, the fourth complex also will have a naphtha cracking plant with annual capacity of 350,000 tons of ethylene, and downstream plants.

Cement.—Plans call for annual output of cement to rise from 16 million tons in 1978 to 28.6 million tons by 1982 and 40 million tons by 1986, placing Korea sixth among world cement producers. Ssangyong Cement Company will be the largest domestic cement manufacturer with production of 11.6 million tons by 1982, followed by Tong Yang Cement with 6.1 million tons. Tong Yang Cement Co. plans to expand its facilities by adding two kilns, each with a daily capacity of 4,200 tons, that will be financed in part by a $60.4 million loan from the U.S. Export-Import Bank.

Nonferrous Metals.—By 1986 Korea hopes to attain self-sufficiency in refining and production of copper, lead, zinc, and aluminum ingots. Construction of a new nonferrous metal industry complex is underway at Onsan. The Onsan Copper Refinery has commenced operation of its 80,000 ton-a-year refinery, which cost $180 million to build. The plant also will produce 260,000 tons of sulfuric acid, 1,500 kg of gold and 23,500 kg of silver each year. Korea's zinc metal production capacity is to be increased from the present level of 80,000 tons per year to 130,000 tons per year by 1983. The Government is now studying the feasibility of building a 100,000 ton-per-year aluminum refinery to produce the 42,500 tons of aluminum currently being imported as well as exportable surplus.

Textiles.—Korea's textile and apparel industry continues to be its principal foreign exchange earner. Government plans call for continued expansion with Korea becoming the number one world textile exporter by 1986 with $10 billion in exports and 10 percent of the world market share. The Korean textile industry has an ambitious plan to boost Korea's exports of textile products that will require investment of about $1.1 billion by 1981. The Government is directing industry toward import substitution for fibers and yarns and toward improvement of product quality rather than general expansion in the fabric field. In 1979 there was an expansion of synthetic fiber production facilities designed to reach total capacity of 1,387 tons per day with 273.8 tons of nylon yarn, 602 tons of polyester fiber, 345.5 tons of acrylic fiber, 33 tons of polypropylene fiber, 109.2 tons of viscose fiber and 15.5 tons of acetate fiber. To help further expansion, the Ministry of Commerce and Industry has drafted a bill that, if passed, provides for the formation of a fund for textile industry modernization, the replacement of worn-out facilities, and the establishment of integrated textile industry estates. The acquisition of foreign technology and development of new and high-quality products would be fostered.

Government Role in the Economy

Korea has a free market economy based on private ownership of the means of production and distribution. However, the Government does own part or all of approximately 35 companies, which are organized and operated as private companies with independent management. Some of these firms are: Agriculture Development Corporation, Chinhae Chemical Co. Ltd., Korea General Chemical Industry Corp., Korea Electric Co., Korea Fertilizer Co., Ltd., Dai Han Coal Corp., Korea Trade Promotion Corp., Korea Oil Corp., Yong Nam Chemical Co., Ltd., Korea Housing Corp., and Pohang Iron and Steel Co. Ltd. In addition, the Government traditionally has controlled the economy through its overall economic development plans, specific industry expansion plans, price controls, and other special economic measures taken to achieve stabilization and growth.

Distribution and Sales Channels

Major Marketing Areas

Most large Korean firms maintain headquarters in Seoul, the nation's capital and leading industrial center. About one-third of the value added in manufacturing is accounted for by industry in this area. However, a growing number of important firms have head offices in other main cities.

Other key industrial cities are Pusan, Daegu, Inchon, Suwon, Masan, Ulsan, and Pohang. Many of these specialize in certain industries. For example, Daegu, is known for textile manufacturing; Pusan is important in food processing, shipbuilding, plywood, and rubber products; Ulsan is a center for the chemical and petrochemical industry and the site of the impressive new Hyundai shipyard; Seoul is prominent in the wearing apparel field and paper and printing; Masan is the site of a free export zone. Additional industrial areas are under development.

For example, Gumi is the site of the new electronics complex, and a new machinery complex has been established at Changwon. Yochun is the site of the new chemical and petrochemical industry.

Importers, Agents, Distributors

Local representation in the Korean market is crucial for successful penetration. In marketing their products in Korea, U.S. suppliers have a number of alternatives. These include establishment of a branch sales office managed by home office personnel, appointing one of the U.S. trading firms in Korea as their representative, selecting a registered trading firm to act as their agent, or making a registered offer agent their agent in Korea. Frequently, foreign suppliers will appoint several agents to represent the company's different product lines or will pursue a mix of the above alternatives, such as establishing a branch office with responsibility for formulating and executing a general sales campaign in the country and for supervising other agents. Distribution methods vary with the product and with individual situations and must be tailored to fit the particular conditions.

U.S. suppliers seeking representation in the Korean market may obtain help and advice through the Agent Distributor Service (ADS), which is offered for a nominal fee by the U.S. Department of Commerce District Offices. The U.S. Trade Center offers REPFIND services for those firms scheduling a visit to Seoul. These services include temporary free entry to demonstration equipment and samples, identification and contacting of prospects, and hiring for the account of the U.S. firm a qualified interpreter/ secretary. In effect, upon arrival, the visitor will have ready a temporary office and staff in Seoul and can then devote full time to interviewing agency prospects and potential customers. Other sources of assistance are the Korean Traders Association (KTA) (to which all licensed traders belong), the Korea Trading Agents Association (to which all offer agents belong), the Korea Chamber of Commerce and Industry, and the U.S. branch banks in Seoul. The KTA maintains an office in New York City.

Registered Traders.—By law only registered traders are authorized to import goods in their own names. All imported merchandise is handled by registered traders with the exception of goods brought into Korea by end-users under foreign economic assistance programs, goods imported in connection with foreign private investment, raw materials and components imported for processing and then reexported, and Korean Government procurement.

Trader's licenses are issued by the Government on the basis of the applicant's export performance. (Criteria for obtaining a license are discussed in the Trade Regulations Section.) A growing number of manufacturing firms export their products and are registered traders. This enables the manufacturer to import needed raw materials and equipment for his operation without recourse to a middleman. However, not all registered traders conduct a general import business. As of December 31, 1978, 3,148 firms were registered traders with a substantial number of these acting as agents for foreign suppliers. In 1974, the Government established criteria for so-called conglomerate trading companies, and to date 10 Korean firms have qualified.

Appointing a registered trading firm rather than an offer agent as the supplier's agent has an advantage in that such a firm can handle the paper work of importing and can also import for its own account. As registered traders split their business between exports and imports, however, they may not be able to give as much attention to importing as do offer agents. Although large trading firms may be better known, they may not be able to devote as much attention to a single principal as do some of the smaller firms. On the other hand, because of their size, large trading firms may be more influential as a representative and may be more willing to extend credit or to vouch for a prospective client.

Offer Agents. — There are about 1,400 offer agents or commission agents registered with the Ministry of Commerce and Industry. These include 65 branches or liaison offices of foreign firms, of which 19 are U.S. and 21 are Japanese. These agents act as representatives of foreign manufacturers and suppliers and make offers on behalf of their principals. Unless they are also registered traders, however, they are not authorized to import on their own or to hold title to imported merchandise. In many cases, offer agents pay a small fee to registered traders to overcome this limitation.

Foreign Trading Companies. — Nineteen U.S. trading firms in Korea handle a diversified line of products and represent primarily, but not exclusively, U.S. suppliers. Several trading firms are managed by Europeans. Much of Japan's trade with Korea is handled by the Korean branches of 21 Japanese trading firms which include all the giant Japanese trading houses, such as Mitsui, Mitsubishi, C. Itoh, and Nissho-Iwai.

Both Japanese and U.S. trading firms are registered as commission or offer agents.

Selecting a U.S. trading firm in Korea to act as an agent may offer the advantage of having a representative of the firm who is keeping an eye open not only for sales, but for other interests as well. There is also the advantage inherent in a bond of language and a common way of doing business. Like the large Korean trading firms, however, U.S. firms may sometimes handle too many agencies for maximum effectiveness or may not be aggressive in searching out new business, concentrating instead on larger and well-known Korean clients.

Commissions. — Registered traders or agents usually receive a 3 to 8 percent commission. In the few cases in which there is a secondary step in the distribution system, with a wholesaler acting as an intermediary between the end-user and the import agent, the wholesaler earns commissions ranging between 5 and 30 percent. The price the end-user pays for imported machinery is usually about 15 percent higher than the supplier's initial price quotation.

Selling Techniques

To be competitive a U.S. firm must consider other key areas of an effective sales effort once it has obtained a local representative. These key areas are: credit, continued personal contact, delivery, servicing, availability of spare parts, and pricing. Credit is discussed in a separate section. The other factors are outlined below.

Personal Contact. — In selling to manufacturers, personal contact is important not only because of the value placed on personal discussions in the Orient, but also because such discussions serve to bring the end-user in touch with new processes and equipment. Korean businesspeople are open to new ideas and technology, but their knowledge of what is available may be limited. Frequently, Korean firms in the market for equipment to expand and modernize their plants are not aware of what U.S. suppliers can offer, and the contract may go to a Japanese firm by default. Such occurrences reflect, in general, the underrepresentation of U.S. suppliers in Korea and the less-than-adequate dissemination of catalogs and similar information by U.S. suppliers.

In view of the competition offered by Japanese suppliers, who often visit potential and existing customers throughout Korea, U.S. suppliers should consider: (1) making visits to Korea to augment the efforts of the local representative;

(2) holding more demonstrations, seminars, and exhibitions of their products in Korea, utilizing such facilities as the U.S. Trade Center in Seoul; (3) increasing the distribution of technical data and descriptive brochures to potential buyers, teachers and industry associations (the Commercial Library at the U.S. Export Development Center in Seoul displays catalogs of American firms); and (4) improving the follow-up on initial sales leads.

U.S. suppliers should be knowledgeable of developments and technology in the potential customer's industry and should be able to emphasize how purchasing their product will specifically benefit the customer's operations, particularly with respect to cost reduction and quality improvement. Plant visits are a virtual necessity for effective sales presentations. Such visits give the supplier the opportunity to talk to plant engineers and foremen and thereby help pave the way for a favorable procurement decision. Although purchasing decisions are made by the headquarters staff of the company, whose offices are often in downtown Seoul, engineers located at the plant typically will be consulted and their recommendation given strong consideration.

Delivery.—The ability to supply goods in a prompt and timely manner is a positive factor when competing in any market. Delivery schedules take on an added significance in the Korean importer's purchasing decisions because of the Government's requirement for advance import deposits and the prevailing high interest rates. In most instances, Korean importers must deposit foreign exchange certificates, equal to or greater than the value of the goods to be imported, in noninterest bearing accounts when the import license and letter of credit are issued. The importer's capital is thus tied up for the length of time required for the goods to arrive in Korea after the import license is issued. Even if he is able to borrow the money from a local bank to make the advance deposit, his interest payments (prime lending rate rose to 24.5 percent in January of 1980) become extremely costly if delivery is in any way delayed. Under these conditions, fast turnover and prompt delivery become crucial considerations to the buyer. A few sales have been won by the U.S. firm's agreeing to postpone issuance of the letter of credit until after shipment of the goods, thus reducing the carrying costs to the Korean buyer.

Japan, of course, enjoys a significant advantage with respect to delivery time. Shipping transit time from Yokohama to Pusan is 24 hours and from Kobe to Pusan 18 hours, while goods shipped to Korea from the United States take considerably longer. Although little can be done to reduce transit time direct from the United States, the possibility of maintaining stocks of rapid-turnover goods will require more serious consideration in the future, as will all other methods designed to combat Japan's competitive advantage of close proximity. At present, only a few agents for U.S. firms stock equipment in Korea. These are primarily in the instruments, office equipment, and spare parts fields.

In view of the above, U.S. suppliers should make every effort to handle foreign orders on a priority basis to speed up delivery as much as possible. Production schedules should be more flexible, promised delivery dates should be more accurate, and the importer should be made aware that his U.S. supplier is doing everything possible to effect delivery as efficiently as possible.

Servicing.—In the lean years following the Korean conflict, when foreign exchange was exceedingly scarce and imports were kept to a minimum, owners of machinery learned to rely on their own resources or on the many small machine shops to repair machinery. Equipment parts were often replaced by locally tooled spares. This tradition still remains but, with heavy competition among foreign suppliers in the Korean market, servicing has become a more important part of selling.

Japan's proximity to Korea allows Japanese manufacturers to send teams of specialists at little cost to offer skilled advice in installation, maintenance, and repair. Some agents for U.S. firms have qualified maintenance personnel familiar with the equipment being sold, and some emphasis has been given recently to training such personnel in formal programs in the United States. U.S. firms should give consideration to establishing regional servicing facilities which can effectively support equipment sold in Korea.

Private traders and offer agents often have engineers available to install equipment. For specialized installations, however, the best sources of assistance should be the Korea Institute of Science and Technology, the National Industrial Standards Research Institute, the Korea Institute of Machinery and Metals, and other Government laboratories. Importers of equipment normally have close relations with members of the Government laboratories and institutes and are able to call upon their services. Fees are not fixed and are negotiable. For complex installations requiring a great deal of time and specialized technicians, U.S. manufacturers should budget approximately the same amount as that required for similar installations in the United States.

Pricing.—U.S. goods have a reputation among Korean buyers for quality and performance; yet Koreans tend to be very price conscious and often regard the U.S. label as being too expensive. Two important factors help to explain the price consciousness of Korean customers. First, the general shortage of funds has resulted in very high local interest rates, which favor the smallest possible outlay of capital. Second, in an export-oriented economy where finished products must be able to meet keen competition in the world market, many local manufacturers believe that it is essential to buy raw materials and equipment from the cheapest source. Under these conditions, goods from Japan and other countries are frequently considered to be a better buy, even though it is widely recognized that their quality and durability often do not compare with products made in the United States.

U.S. exporters might consider: (1) adapting their products for the Korean market by stripping them down to the basic production unit; (2) taking into account in their price quotations, as their competitors do, the repeat business generated by the demand for spare parts and components and auxiliary equipment; (3) emphasizing and selling the idea that the superior quality of U.S. products ultimately results in lower production costs; and (4) investigating possible warehousing arrangements in Korea that would allow larger shipments and cheaper freight rates for the trans-Pacific voyage.

Wholesale and Retail Channels

The market for most consumer products is concentrated in the major cities. Retail distribution is accomplished through a network of millions of outlets, the majority of which are small one-family stores, stalls in markets, or street vendors. There are several middle-sized department stores in Seoul and Pusan, serving retail customers from the immediate vicinity. In addition there are approximately 1,100 supermarkets throughout the country.

Wholesalers tend to dominate the distribution system and are often in a position to dictate terms of manufacturers. Traditionally, the wholesaler obtains considerably longer credit terms from the manufacturer than he extends to the retailer, sometimes earning substantial interest on the difference.

Local manufacturers require that wholesalers tender an inventory consignment bond or, alternatively, take a lien on the wholesaler's property. Because of the inherently dominating position of the wholesalers, some large manufacturers have set up their own national distribution networks. The chain store and supermarket concept is developing rapidly, with 38 major retail chains and thousands of stores, but most retail trade continues to be conducted by small family establishments.

Franchising

Franchising as practiced in the United States is still unknown in Korea. There are no regulations prohibiting franchise operations; however, franchise operations would be subject to the same laws as those which govern other types of business organizations.

Wholesale and Retail Sales

The Seoul wholesale and retail trade index shows that average wholesale trade grew from 100 in 1975 to 196.8 in 1978 and that retail trade increased to 212.9 during the same period.

Government Procurement

The Office of Supply, Republic of Korea (OSROK), is responsible for supervising the procurement of government agencies and government-owned enterprises in which the Government holds a majority share. Formal public invitations to bid are issued for all procurement, although occasionally OSROK is obligated to purchase under negotiated procurement, as in the case of spare parts for specialized equipment. Purchases are financed either by government-owned foreign exchange (KFX) or by loan and credit funds from foreign aid programs and international financial organizations. The invitation to bid specifies which source of financing is to be used to pay for the goods and services.

In the case of foreign aid funds, procurement is usually limited to the country extending the credit; in the case of KFX funds, on the other hand, bidding is worldwide. In general, the deadline for receiving bids is 40 calendar days after the invitation to bid is used. By law, the award is made to the lowest qualified bidder conforming to the terms and conditions of the bid invitations, taking into account the price, delivery time, quantity, specifications, and financial terms most advantageous to the Government. Bids for a single product valued at $100,000 or more are in two parts, the first consisting of specifications and details of the offer (excluding price) and the second consisting of price alone. Only bidders whose specifications have been accepted are eligible to have their price bids opened during the evaluation by the end-user agency.

Procurement needs for the government agencies are formulated by the ministries and agencies concerned and then screened by the Ministry of Commerce and Industry to see whether those requirements can be met from local sources. If not, the Ministry of Finance allocates the necessary foreign exchange funds. Specifications are normally drawn up by the government agency requesting the goods and services, and these agencies frequently call upon representatives of foreign suppliers for information and assistance. Thus, if the U.S. supplier wishes to participate in Korean Government business, it is helpful to have a local representative. Having a local representative also proves useful in keeping abreast of developments in procurement plans of government agencies and of invitations to bid.

If the bid is made by the supplier's agent in Korea, he must be registered with the Ministry of Commerce and Industry as an agent of the supplier with the authority to make offers on his behalf. If the supplier or manufacturer submits a tender directly to OSROK, the bid must be certified by the Korean Mission or Consulate covering the region in which the supplier is located, or by the local chamber of commerce, as having been made by the manufacturer or supplier making the offer.

Transportation and Utilities

Shipping from the United States

Ocean.—Ocean shipping to Korea from the United States takes a minimum of 21 days from the East Coast to 14 days from the West Coast if the shipment is direct, and longer if routed through other ports. Most imports enter Korea through Pusan, the country's major port, or through Inchon which is the port of Seoul. Other major ports include Gunsan, Mukho, Masan, Pohang, and Mokpo. The Pusan harbor has cargo handling capacity for up to 14 million tons and Inchon 9.2 million tons; both ports are undergoing improvement and expansion projects. Both Pusan and Inchon are serviced by American, Japanese, and other foreign flag lines, including about 520 Korean flag carriers owned by 68 shipping companies that serve the United States and other countries. As of the end of September

1979, there were 523 oceangoing vessels with a combined tonnage of 4,638,000 tons including 105 vessels (1,040,148 tons) secured on a conditional (acquisition of title) bare charter basis. All the oceangoing vessels under the management of the Korean shipping firms, including "other chartered vessels", numbered 546 totaling 4,927,216 tons. Each month, over 1,500 international ships, primarily from Japan and the United States, land at Korea's ports.

Containerized shipping has been increasing rapidly, with an annual growth rate of about 12 percent. A container terminal has been completed in Pusan, and Inchon's container terminal began operations in 1974.

Air Freight.—Korea has three international airports that have facilities for handling jet aircraft: Kimpo Airport for Seoul and Inchon, the Pusan-Kimhae Airport, and the Cheju Island Airport. Kimpo Airport is served by six international airlines that handle cargo: Korean Airlines, Northwest Airlines, Japan Airlines, Cathay Pacific Airlines, Flying Tiger Airlines, and Braniff International. Kimpo airport is implementating expansion plans.

Recent improvements in the nation's highway network and the extensive use of coastal shipping makes it possible for cargo to be forwarded within Korea with little delay. The three largest Korean freight forwarders are Hanjin Transportation, Dong Bang Forwarding Co., and Korea Express Co.

Domestic Transportation Systems

Road.—Road transportation is expanding rapidly. An extensive highway network for shipping materials and products is already in place, and all major cities are connected by hard-surfaced roads. The total road mileage is 45,955 kilometers of which 13,544 are paved. In June 1970, a 428–kilometers four-lane expressway connecting Seoul and Pusan was completed. At the end of 1978, the total expressway length was 1,225 kilometers. Two new two-lane expressways with a combined length of 129 kilometers were inaugurated on October 14, 1975 in the rugged mountain area of Kangwon-do. The roads span the 97 kilometers linking Saemal with Kangnung and the 32 kilometers between Kangnung and Mukho. They are extensions of the first leg of the 104-kilometer Yongdong Expressway stretching to Seoul, which was opened in December 1971.

During the Fourth Five-year Plan, a 128 kilometer expressway from Daegu to Pusan through Masan will be completed. By 1981, it is projected that expressways will connect nearly every district of the country in a "one-day" travel network.

There are about 1,050 privately owned trucking companies serving major cities and urban areas. Of the total, 21 handle route cargo and the remainder local cargo. Road freight rates vary depending upon the kilometric tonnage transported and are US$171 for 411–460 kilometers/4.5 tons and $313 for 411–460 kilometers/12 tons for one way. Discounts of 20 percent are allowed for round trip.

Coastal Shipping.—With the expansion and improvement of ports, intercoastal freight service is of major importance in the transportation network. Although there are 1,300 ports scattered along the coastline, only 14 are suitable for large trans-ocean ships. In 1978, the total volume of marine transportation within the country totaled 17.2 million metric tons; that of marine transportation to and from overseas ports totaled 77.9 million metric tons.

Air.—Domestic air transportation has been steadily expanding to service all major cities and industrial estates. At present, 17 major cities in Korea are connected by daily service with Seoul. In 1978, the number of domestic passengers was 1.5 million and international air passengers 2.7 million. The U.S. Export-Import Bank (U.S. Eximbank) approved a $24 million loan for the expansion of Seoul's Kimpo International Airport in a 5-year project ending in 1979. Korea Airlines introduced Boeing 747 and DC-10 flights between Los Angeles and Seoul. Northwest Orient introduced daily DC-10 flights from Seoul to New York in June 1973, and Japan Airlines implemented 747 service between Tokyo and Seoul in July 1973. Korean Airlines is expanding its route system almost continuously. KAL inaugurated its direct Boeing 747 flight on the Seoul-New York route in 1979; and the opening of the Pusan-Tokyo and Pusan-Abu Dhabi routes is to follow soon.

Rail.—The total share of freight carried by rail has increased in recent years despite increased expressway and harbor construction. Due to subsidization, the freight rate structure is extremely attractive. All major urban areas are connected by railroad. At the end of 1978, the total mileage was 5,788 kilometers. The government-owned and operated Korea National Railway (KNR) maintains a commercial network of 3,153 kilometers.

During the Fourth Five-year Plan, the electrification and double-tracking of certain lines continues, with foreign exchange costs for these

projects amounting to $29 million. The major ports of Pusan and Inchon are connected to Seoul by double tracks.

Utilities

Fuel.—Oil, coal, and wood are the main fuels.

Electricity.—Electricity is available in all industrial areas and towns. Installed capacity was 6.9 megawatts in 1978, and production reached 31.5 billion kilowatt hours. Reserve power capacity is reported to be 7.7 percent. Electricity production is primarily thermal, but one nuclear powered generating plant has been completed and several others are under construction or planned for the near future. Korea's Fourth Five-Year Plan provides for an extensive program of rural electrification, and the Government proposes to complete the rural electrification project by the early 1980's. The Fourth Five-Year Plan calls for an increase in installed capacity to 10.4 megawatts by 1981. The government-owned Korea Electric Company (KECO) controls most electric power generation and all distribution in Korea. Industrial power rates vary in accordance with the consumer, amount used, voltage, and other factors.

Water.—The Fourth Five-Year Plan also continues a comprehensive development scheme for water resources. Projects are currently underway in many major water areas to meet increasing demands and to develop an adequate and suitable industrial water supply. The capacity of water supply systems in Taegu, Kwangju, Masan, Chinhae and Changwon will be expanded during 1980–82 at a total investment of 73.8 billion won ($152.6 million) including $60 million in foreign capital, by a total of 1 million tons daily in these cities. Rates vary depending on industrial areas, with $0.01446 basic rate and $0.4132 excess rate per cubic meter in Seoul.

Communications.—Although they have improved dramatically in recent years, communications facilities remain inadequate. The number of telephone subscribers was 1,916,878 in 1978. Long distance facilities increased to 39,648 circuits in 1978, and overseas telegraph, telephone, and television connections are now handled by communications satellite. In the evening it is possible to reach a party in the United States within 10 minutes. A second earth station for the Indian Ocean satellite system at Kumsan, partially financed with U.S. Eximbank support, was completed in 1977.

The Ministry of Communications operates a 2,900 line telex system. Communications with industrial estates are possible. Telecommunication charges from the United States as of the beginning of 1980 were approximately $2.45 per minute for telephone calls, under $3 per minute for telex and under $.50 per word for telegraph. There are severe delays in obtaining installation of new telex or telephone lines in Korea although in certain cases it is possible to purchase a working line from the previous subscriber.

Advertising and Research

Advertising Media

The basic media for advertising in Korea are, in order of importance, newspapers, radio, television, magazines, and movies.

Newpapers.—As over 90 percent of the Korean population is literate, newspapers are the most commonly used medium for advertising. There are 27 daily newspapers in the country. Of the total, 13 are located in Seoul, including two English language newspapers (Korea Herald and Korea Times) and one Chinese newspaper (Han Hwa Daily News). All of the Seoul newspapers are circulated throughout the nation. The four major newspapers, which have an individual circulation of over a half million, are the Dong-A Ilbo, the Chosun Ilbo, the Han Kook Ilbo, and the Joong Ang Ilbo.

Advertising rates in the larger newspapers vary for a single-column centimeter from a high of 23,000 won to a low of 15,000 won.

Radio.—Radio advertising is the second most common medium, and there were nearly 12.3 million radios as of December 31, 1978. There are four privately owned radio broadcasting stations in Seoul: MBC, CBS, TBC, and DBS. With 19 stations, MBC has the largest network, followed by CBS with four and TBC with two.

Prime time is from 7 to 9 a.m. and noon to 1 p.m. during the day. The prime time rate in Seoul for a 20 second spot is 45,700 won.

Television.—Television is rapidly becoming an important advertising medium. At the end of December 1978, there were 5,135,496 sets, and this number is increasing rapidly.

The prime time is from 8 to 10 p.m. There are two commercial television stations in Seoul, MBC-TV and TBC-TV. MBC has relay stations in Pusan, Daegu, Kwangju, Jeonju, Taejon, Ulsan, Masan, and Cheju', and TBC has a station in Pusan. The prime rate in Seoul ranges from 434,000 to 599,000 won for 20 seconds.

Magazines.—There is a wide range of weekly and monthly magazines, with circulations rang-

ing from an estimated 10,000 to 180,000. Many of the magazines are of interest to women. The rate in the leading magazine for a single page black and white advertisement with an offset picture is 250,000 won.

Film.—All motion picture houses project advertising strip or stills, ranging in length from 30 seconds to 1 or 2 minutes, in both color and black and white. The advertiser may prepare his own material or use the services of an advertising agent.

Market Research Services

The Korea Marketing Association was established in Seoul in 1970 under the administration of the Ministry of Commerce and Industry. It provides information in such related fields as market development planning, marketing of various products, and export marketing. The Center is also a repository for statistical data for use in market research and development. In addition, there are a number of privately owned research firms engaged in contract research work, including Korea Management Development Institute, ASI Market Research Inc. (Korea), Korea Industrial Development Research Institute, International Management Institute of Korea University, and Industrial Management Research Center of Yonsei University.

The American Embassy in Seoul supplies the U.S. Department of Commerce with information on the Korean economy as well as commercial and market information. There are also a limited number of market studies available to U.S. companies through the Office of Export Planning and Evaluation, International Trade Administration, U.S. Department of Commerce, Washington, D.C. 20230.

Advertising Agencies.—Korea has a number of advertising agencies able to assist in placing advertisements in any of the mass communications media. Representative agencies are: Hap dong Advertising Agency, Union Advertising Inc., Korea First Advertising Company, International Marketing Corp., and Pacific Media Korea. All have headquarters in Seoul.

Credit

Availability of Capital

Korean corporations reply primarily on bank to supply operating and capital expansio financing. Banks in Korea are divided into tw broad groups: commercial banks, which offe short-term financing, and specialized banks which offer long-term credits. The 32 foreign branch banks in Korea also extend medium-term loans in local and selected foreign currencies. All foreign loan transactions, whether quaranteed or not, require government authorization. The cost of won funds is high by Western standards, and funds are usually tight. Commercial banks in early 1980 were required to pay 24 percent for 1-year deposits. The previous rate in effect until January 1980 was 18.6 percent. Depending on the fund sources and type of use, interest rates will range up to 25 percent per annum for won loans, with a prime rate of about 24.5 percent.

Term lending, as it is known in the United States, is usually not practiced by the Korean commercial banks. In general, Korean commercial banks grant short-term loans against promissory notes. It is not uncommon for these notes to be renewed on a continuing basis.

Most Korean commercial banks take security in the form of mortgages on land and, less frequently, equipment. As a rough rule, the value of the land and buildings, as determined by the Korea Appraisal Board, must be equal to 125 percent of the loan amount. By the end of 1978, the total amount of won loans and discounts outstanding was 6,609 billion won.

Sources of Financing

Korean Banking System.—Government and semigovernment banking institutions dominate Korea's banking system. The supervisory institution is the Bank of Korea (BOK). Established in 1950 as the central bank of the country, it serves as the bank of issue and as the depository for government funds. The Bank's operations are administered by the Monetary Board, which was also established in 1950, and is presided over by the Minister of Finance. The Board formulates the country's monetary, credit, and exchange policies, and has broad powers over the operations of the Bank and the banking system as a whole, with the exception of the Korea Development Bank, which is specifically exempt from the Board's control.

The Korea Exchange Bank (KEB) was established in 1966. The KEB has assumed most of the foreign exchange functions previously performed by the BOK. In addition to its wholly owned subsidiary, the Korea Exchange Bank of California, it has branch offices in Los Angeles, Chicago, New York, Tokyo, Osaka, Hong Kong, Kowloon, Paris, Singapore, London, and Frankfurt. It also is represented in Toronto, Guam, Sao Paulo, Vienna, Milan, Jakarta, Bangkok, Beirut, Brussels, and Panama City.

The Korea Development Bank (KDB), which is under the jurisdiction of the Ministry of Finance, acts as an intermediary for channeling government funds and foreign loans to industry. The loans extended by the KDB are heavily concentrated in the manufacturing and electric power sectors and are mostly medium or long-term loans for large industries.

The National Agricultural Cooperative Federation (NACF) emphasizes service to the agricultural sector. It extends loans to farmers and provides commercial banking facilities for farmers and urban customers.

The Medium Industry Bank (MIB), the Citizens National Bank (CNB), the Korea Housing Bank (KHB), and the Export-Import Bank of Korea are government-controlled banks designed to meet the needs of certain sectors of the economy. The purpose of the MIB is to finance small and medium-size industries. It is engaged in short-term operational financing and longer-term capital lending. The CNB specializes in extending loans and accepting mutual installment deposits and ordinary deposits. In principle, to avoid competition with commercial banks, it is limited to granting loans only to those persons having a deposit account with the bank. The KHB was established in July 1957 to make home building loans available to middle-income families. Like its U.S. counterpart, the Export-Import Bank, which opened for business in July 1976, provides support for Korean export industries.

There are 15 domestic commercial banks currently in operation, of which 5 operate nationwide. There are 634 branch facilities throughout the country. The five so-called city banks are the Hanil Bank, the Commercial Bank of Korea, the Choheung Bank, the First Bank of Korea, and the Bank of Seoul & Trust Co. With the exception of the Commercial Bank of Korea, the Government is the largest single shareholder in these banks, which provide conventional commercial banking facilities and are authorized to handle international business through correspondent banks.

In 1967, the Korean Government began granting permission to foreign banks to open branches in Korea, and 32 such branches have since been opened in Seoul, of which 12 are American, 5 French, 4 Japanese, 4 British, 2 Canadian and 5 others. In addition, 19 foreign banks, including 8 American and 9 Japanese banks, maintain representative offices in Seoul.

The Korea Development Finance Corporation (KDFC), incorporated in 1967, is a private institution which makes loans in both foreign and local currencies to private manufacturers and assists in the establishment of joint ventures. The KDFC's capital is based on foreign loans and stock subscriptions from the International Finance Corporation, foreign banks, Korean banks and private investors, and the Korean Government. This is Korea's first private institutional source for long-term industrial loans and equity financing.

Korean Stock Market.—The Korean capital market is still relatively thin, and the Korean Government is actively engaged in efforts to further the development of the securities market as one response to this problem. Three hundred and fifty-five firms are presently listed on the exchange.

In the past, bank time deposits offered a much higher return than the cash dividend yield on stock. In addition, bank deposits were safer and mostly tax free. The reduction in time deposit rates that accompanied the August 1972 Decree was to set in motion an adjustment of relative yields that were likely to make investment in stocks more attractive; but rates were raised again as a result of recent price hikes.

Foreign Financing Sources.—In the last decade, Korea has obtained substantial loans and credits from foreign aid programs (primarily the United States and Japan), and from international finance organizations, such as the International Bank for Reconstruction and Development and the Asia Development Bank. As the level of foreign aid programs decreases, there is a rising dependency on commercial loans and credits, such as those extended by export-import banks. The U.S. Export-Import Bank has played an important role in financing U.S. exports in recent years.

List of Banking Institutions

The following is a list of banking institutions in Korea:

The Bank of Korea
110, 3-Ka, Namdaemoon-ro
Choong-Ku, Seoul 100
CPO Box 1448 Seoul

Korea Exchange Bank
10, Kwanchul-dong, Chongro-ku
Seoul 110
CPO Box 2924, Seoul

National Agricultural Cooperative Federation
75, 1-ka, Choongjeong-ro

Seodaemoon-ku, Seoul
CPO Box 1051 Seoul

The Medium Industry Bank
361, 2-a, Ulchi-ro
Choong-ku, Seoul 100
CPO Box 4153 Seoul

The Korea Development Bank
140-1, 2ka, Namdaemoon-ro,
Choong-Ku, Seoul 100
CPO Box 28 Seoul

The Bank of Seoul & Trust Co.
10-1, 2-Ka, Namdaemoon-ro
Choong-Ku, Seoul 100
CPO Box 276 Seoul

The Cho-Heung Bank, Ltd.
14, 1-ka, Namdaemoon-ro
Choong-ku, Seoul 100
CPO Box 2997, Seoul

The Commercial Bank of Korea, Ltd.
111, 2-ka, Namdaemoon-ro
Choong-ku, Seoul 100
CPO Box 126, Seoul

Korea First Bank, Ltd.
43-1, 1-ka, Choongmoo-ro
Choong-ku, Seoul 100
CPO Box 2242 Seoul

The Hanil Bank, Ltd.
118, 2-ka, Namdaemoon-ro
Choong-ku, Seoul 100
CPO Box 1033 Seoul

The Bank of Pusan, Ltd.
8, 1-ka, Shinchang-dong,
Choong-ku, Pusan 600
PO Box 73 Pusan

The Daegu Bank, Ltd.
20-3, Namil-dong
Choong-ku, Taegu 630
PO Box Taegu 122

Gyeong Nam Bank, Ltd.
172 Chang-dong
Masan City 610

The Che-ju Bank, Ltd.
1349, 2 do, 1-dong
Cheju City

The Kangwon Bank Ltd.
72-3, Woonkyo-dong,
Chunchon, Kwangwon-do

The Citizens National Bank
9-1, 2-ka, Namdaemoon-ro
Choong-ku, Seoul 100
PO Box 815, Seoul

Korea Development Finance Corp.
60, 1-ka, Yeoido-dong
Yungdungpo-ku, Seoul 160

The Korea Housing Bank
61-1, 1-ka Taepyung-ro
Choong-ku, Seoul 100

Korean branches of American banks are:

The Chase Manhattan Bank, N.A.
50, 1-ka, Ulchi-ro,
Choong Ku, Seoul 100

Bank of America, NT & SA
250, 2-ka, Taepyungro,
Choong-ku, Seoul 100

Citibank N.A.
28, Sokong-dong,
Choong-ku, Seoul 100

The First National Bank of Chicago
286, Yang-dong
Choong-ku, Seoul 100

American Express Int'l Banking Corp.
286, Yang-dong,
Choong-ku, Seoul 100

Continental Illinois Bank of Chicago
286, Yang-dong,
Choong-ku, Seoul 100

Citibank N.A. (Pusan)
257-5, Buchun-dong,
Pusanjin-ku, Pusan City

Bank of America NT & SA (Pusan)
77-1, Choongang-dong,
Choong-ku, Pusan City

Morgan Guaranty Trust Company of New York
250, 2-ka, Taepyung-ro,
Choong-ku, Seoul 100

Chemical Bank
250, 2-ka, Taepyung-ro,
Choong-ku, Seoul 100

Manufacturers Hanover Trust Company
286, Yang-dong,
Choong-ku, Seoul 100

Bankers Trust Company
91-1, Sokong-dong,
Choong-ku, Seoul 100

In addition, the following U.S. banks have representative offices in Seoul:

The Chase Manhattan Bank, N.A. (Pusan)
5-1, 1-ka, Dongkwang-dong,
Choong-ku, Pusan City

Marine Midland Bank (Seoul)
91-1, Sokang-dong,
Choong-ku, Seoul 100

Security Pacific National Bank (Seoul)
286, Yang-dong
Choong-ku, Seoul 100

United California Bank (Seoul)
10-1, 2-ka, Namademoon-ro,
Choong-ku, Seoul 100

Wells Fargo Bank N.A. (Seoul)
286, Yang-dong
Choong-ku, Seoul 100

Union Bank (Seoul)
286, Yang-dong,
Choong-ku, Seoul 100

The First National Bank of Boston (Seoul)
17-7, 4-ka, Namdaemoon-ro,
Choong-ku, Seoul

Crocker National Bank (Seoul)
250, 2-ka, Taepyung-ro,
Choong-ku, Seoul 100

Importance of Credit in Selling to Korea

The low level of equity capital in many Korean firms, the resultant high debt-equity ratio, and the high interest rates on routine commercial bank loans all make credit a very important factor in selling to Korea. The advance import-deposit system, under which the deposit margin decreases with the length of payment time, accentuates the demand for purchases on credit terms. The general unwillingness of U.S. suppliers to sell on credit, or to accept commercial risk unless guaranteed by a bank in Korea, are in contrast to the selling practices of Japanese and other foreign suppliers. Although a ceiling is placed on the amount that can be imported on a short-term credit basis of up to 180 days, Japanese firms have taken up a much larger portion of this ceiling than have firms in the United States, even though shipping time from Japan is less than that from the United States.

Before extending credit, American suppliers usually prefer to secure a foreign currency guarantee from the Korea Exchange Bank. This process requires that the Korean end-user secure from a commercial bank a guarantee denominated in won, which the commercial bank is formally only willing to grant if it holds a first or second mortgage on the firm's assets (the only sort of collateral that Korean banks will accept), and if the margin between the value of the mortgage and the firm's debts to the bank is substantial. Japanese firms are more willing to accept the local won guarantee and often extend credit on the basis of the firm's general reputation in Korea.

The financing package is a critical factor in selling major equipment to Korean end-users. Korea has been a major recipient of U.S. Export-Import Bank credits, and the demand for these has outstripped the supply. U.S. sellers of industrial machinery and other big-ticket items should be prepared to discuss alternative financing packages with their Korean prospects.

Trade Regulations

Import Tariff Systems

Tariff Structure.—Korea maintains a three-column import tariff schedule comprised of general rates, temporary rates, and GATT rates. There also is a separate set of concessional tariff rates relating to trade negotiations among developing countries (TNDC rates). Very few special temporary rates, GATT rates and TNDC rates are now in effect. The 1967 revision of the Customs Law authorizes the Executive to specify special tariff rates within 50 percentage points of the tariff schedule under certain circumstances.

Two separate special tariff schedules, effective until the end of 1979, were announced, one on February 13, 1979, and the other on May 17, 1979 under this authority, officially designated as the Flexible Tariff Systems. The principal effect of that action was to group under one listing the items benefiting from special reduced rates on the basis of the above-mentioned authority. Wheat, soybeans, beef tallow, cotton, Bunker C oil, raw rubber, cement, rolls for rolling mills of cast iron, ferrous waste and scrap, ferrite magnet, other raw materials for export processing, and construction supplies for heavy

and chemical industry plants make up the 66 items in the current elastic tariff schedule. An additional 43 items, mostly petrochemicals are expected to be added to the existing list soon. The elastic tariff system is designed primarily to ensure effective support for the development of export industries and heavy and chemical industries and to help stabilize the domestic prices of related products.

Most Korean duties are assessed on and ad valorem basis. Specific rates apply to a few items and both ad valorem and specific rates apply on a few others. The dutiable value of imported goods is the normal c.i.f. price at the time of import declaration. Tariffs are payable in won before goods are permitted to clear customs.

Under the 1979 tariff, industrial raw materials and equipment for basic industries not locally produced are subject to ad valorem duty rates ranging from 5 to 20 percent; goods produced by domestic industries receiving import protection are subject to duties ranging from 25 to 60 percent; and rates of duty on nonessential imports range between 80 to 150 percent.

Import duties are not assessed on capital goods and raw materials imported in connection with foreign investment projects. Authorization to import on a duty-free basis those equipment items and supplies designated in the foreign investment application to the Economic Planning Board (EPB) usually accompanies the EPB's approval of a foreign investment project.

In addition, raw materials used in the production of export goods are exempt from duty and certain machinery, materials and parts used in designated industries may enter Korea either duty-free or at reduced rates.

Information regarding Korean import duties applicable to specific products may be obtained free of charge from the Japan/Korea/Hong Kong Branch, Office of Country Marketing, U.S. Department of Commerce, Washington, D.C. 20230 or from any Department of Commerce District Office. Inquiries should contain a complete product description, including BTN, SITC, or U.S. Schedule B Export Commodity numbers.

Customs Surcharges.—No customs surcharges, as such, are currently levied against goods imported. Since 1973, however, a temporary import surcharge law has been in effect. Under the law, the Government may impose import surcharges, up to a uniform rate of 30 percent of the dutiable value of imports, whenever balance-of-payment considerations dictate that import levels be controlled. Implementation of the law requires a Presidential Decree, which has yet to be issued.

Defense Tax.—On July 16, 1975, the Government promulgated the National Defense Tax Law. This law was amended on December 28, 1979, to remain in force until 1985. Taxable items range from commodity imports to luxury consumer goods and services, property, and corporate incomes. The defense tax is assessed at the rate of 2.5 percent of the c.i.f. value of all imports, excluding those imported duty free in accordance with the Foreign Capital Inducement Law and other pertinent laws. The tax applies to imports reported for customs clearance on and after July 16, 1975.

Customs Classification.—The tariff classification is based on the Customs Cooperation Council Nomenclature (CCCN), which is similar to Brussels Tariff Nomenclature (BTN). A ruling regarding the customs classification on items not shown in the tariff schedules or the dutiable status of goods on which there is some question may be obtained in advance of shipment upon written application to the Collector of Customs in Seoul. It is desirable, although not mandatory, that samples be submitted with the application. Should this be impractical or impossible, photographs, specifications, and descriptive literature may be required, and it would be prudent to forward these with the application.

Value Added Tax.—In December, 1976, the Government carried out an overall tax reform on a grand scale, including introduction of a value added tax (VAT) and special excise tax system in the field of indirect taxation. Eighteen tax laws were newly enacted or amended under the reform. The traditional indirect tax system including a cascade-type business tax was replaced by the consumption-type value added tax and the supplementary special excise tax system, mainly to simplify the tax system and its administration. At present, a single flat rate of 10 percent is applicable on all imports of items subject to the value added tax (VAT= 10% of c.i.f. Value + Customs levies).

Nontariff Import Controls

Import Licensing.—An import license, obtainable from the Korea Exchange Bank or from any one of the other Class A foreign exchange banks, is valid for 6 months. A license is required for every transaction and before a letter of credit may be opened in favor of a foreign supplier. Under the system of licensing introduced in July 1967, all commodities may be freely imported (i.e., applications for import licenses will be approved automatically) unless they are included on a negative list, which includes commodities that are either prohibited or restricted. The negative list is revised by the Ministry of Commerce and Industry every 6 months and is published as the Semi-Annual Trade Plan.

Applications for licenses for the import of items currently in the restricted category are approved on a case-by-case basis after screening by the government agencies concerned, or by the manufacturers associations. Included in the restricted categories are such items as selected foods, domestic appliances, certain pumps and boilers, various chemical elements and compounds, varnishes, lacquers and some pigments, essential oils and resinoids, synthetic fibers, metalworking machine tools, and certain types of office equipment. As soon as local producers can match a foreign-made product, the Government's policy is to provide protection to the local industry by restricting the importation of foreign items. However, the Government will not restrict importation of good where local manufacturers cannot meet the precision and quality standards required by the local market.

Quotas are established by the Ministry of Commerce and Industry for a number of restricted items. The importation of quota items is linked in various complex ways to the import performance and the record of producers of domestic raw materials used for exports. This linked quota system is designed to encourage exports and the increased use of domestic raw materials by granting the exclusive right of import of attractive quota items to such exporters and raw materials producers.

All applications for import licenses must be accompanied by firm offers issued by a foreign supplier, in most cases through the supplier's qualified local agent. Such proforma invoices are then checked to see whether the offer prices exceed the maximum import prices set by the Government. Only firms that are registered as foreign traders are eligible to receive import licenses.

Licensing of Traders.—According to Korean trade law, all persons desiring to engage in foreign trade must register with and obtain a license from the Ministry of Commerce and Industry. Exceptions are granted for government procurement, foreign aid-financed goods imported by end-users, and imports entering Korea for processing and reexport or imported in connection with foreign investment projects.

An applicant for a new trading license must have a paid-in-capital of not less than 50 million won and must have met one of the following requirements: (1) received letters of credit totaling $500,000 or more; or (2) signed a consignment processing contract for net foreign exchange earnings of at least $150,000; or (3) manufactured and supplied export goods valued at more than $500,000 through the use of local letters of credit during the 6 months prior to the license application; or (4) received letters of credit totaling $200,000, as well as a recommendation of the Office of Fisheries Administration (only for those licensed and approved under provisions of Articles 8, 11, 12 and 23 of the Marine Products Industry Law).

Even firms already licensed and registered as traders may not import general commodities until exports valued at $1 million have been achieved. A minimum of $1 million export sales must be maintained annually in order to qualify for the renewal of a trade license. As of January 1, 1980, 2,208 firms were registered traders.

In 1975, the Ministry of Commerce and Industry established criteria for the designation of conglomerate trading firms eligible for a series of preferential measures tied to the importation of major raw materials, participation in international tenders, and the like. The revised criteria as in effect on January 1, 1980, are: (1) firm must have gone public; (2) annual export sales corresponding to at least 2 percent of all Korean exports; (3) a product line of at least five major export items (those with annual export records of at least $1 million); (4) at least 20 overseas branches. As of January 1, 1980, the Ministry had designated 10 firms as consolidated trading houses. These are Samsung Company, Dai Woo Industrial Company, International Chemical Company (ICC), Hyundai Corp., Sun Kyong Ltd., Bando Trading Company, Kum Ho & Company, Hyosung Moolsan Company, Ssangyong Trading Company, Korea Trading International, Inc. (established specifically to help small, independent manufacturers market their products abroad).

"Offer agents" must submit their agency agreement to the Ministry of Commerce and Industry for registration. To remain qualified, a registered offer agent must earn a minimum of $50,000 in sales commissions annually.

Early in 1976, the Ministry of Commerce and Industry delegated to the Korea Trading Agents Association the authority to handle applications for the registration of local trading agents. Applications for the registration of foreign trading agents continue to be handled by the Ministry.

As of January 1, 1980, there were 1,508 offer or commission agents registered with the Ministry of Commerce and Industry. They include 65 branches or liaison offices of foreign firms, of which 19 are American, 21 are Japanese, and 10 are Hong Kong based firms. These agents act as representatives of foreign manufacturers and suppliers and make offers on behalf of their principals. Unless they are also registered traders, however, they are not authorized to import on their own. In many cases, offer agents pay a small fee to registered trading firms who import for them.

Import Deposit Requirements. — Korea maintains advance import deposit requirements on most categories of private sector imports. Requirements for imports financed with government-owned foreign exchange (KFX) are met by the deposit of local currencies at the importer's bank when the import letter of credit is opened or, in the case of imports financed by documents against acceptance (D/A) and documents against payments (D/P), either at the time of application for an import license or when the license is approved. (See Exchange Controls section.) For most KFX imports under sight letters of credit, local currencies (cash or certified check issued by banking institutions) equivalent of 110 percent of the f.o.b. value plus 10 percent must be deposited. A 200 percent deposit is required for items categorized as nonessential or luxury goods. The advance deposit rates for goods imported on a D/A and a D/P basis range from 5 to 200 percent depending upon the type of goods being imported.

Imports by the private sector under loan and credit funds from international finance organizations and foreign aid programs are subject to prior cash payments (in won) of part of the import settlement.

Shipping Documents

Documents required for nearly all surface shipments to Korea are a full set of clean, on board, ocean bills of lading, made out to an exchange bank designated by the importer; marine insurance policy or certificate, in duplicate, endorsed in blank for 110 percent of the invoice value (for c.i.f. shipments); signed commercial invoice in quintuplicate; and packing list in duplicate. A certificate of origin in duplicate is required only for shipments of certain selected goods from certain selected countries. Such a certificate must be issued by a Korean Consulate and show the marks, numbers, commodity descriptions, quantities, prices and the country of origin. Exporters should bear in mind that before the importer can open a letter of credit it must possess a notarized pro-forma invoice legalized by a Korean Consulate, unless such pro-forma invoice or firm offer has been issued to the importer by an authorized local agent of the foreign supplier.

To minimize delays in the clearance of livestock imports, it is advisable to obtain certain quarantine certificates issued by appropriate governmental agencies of the exporting country. The same is applicable for dogs, cats, and other pets, except that in those cases a certificate should be issued by the appropriate agency in the last country in which the pet resided. Dogs and cats require current rabies vaccination certificates in addition to health certificates.

An application for a quarantine certificate must be filed with the National Veterinary Quarantine Station upon arrival of the live-stock in Korea. The issuance of such a certificate is required before customs clearance is permitted. Sanitary certificates also are required for shipments of plants and vegetable products.

Certificates of inspection and statements of authority to manufacture, issued by the appropriate authority in the United States, are required for shipments to Korea of pharmaceuticals, medical instruments, sanitary materials, and cosmetics. Such certificates are required for each item in these categories, except such as may be exempted by the Korean Ministry of Health and Social Affairs or where such or similar certificates have been previously submitted.

Marking and Labeling Requirements

All commodities must be labeled and marked to show the country of origin, except where unnecessary according to international practices.

No special packing requirements are in effect for imports into Korea, but care should be taken that items are packed so as to avoid loss through damage, rough handling, pilferage, or deterioration.

Senate Concurrent Resolution 40, adopted July 30, 1953, invites U.S. exporters to inscribe, insofar as practicable, on the external shipping containers in indelible print of a suitable size: "United States of America."

Free Zones and Warehousing

Free Zones. — The Government has designated two free export zones for the bonded processing of imported materials into finished goods for export. The free export zones are specially established industrial areas where foreign invested firms can manufacture, assemble, or process export products using freely imported, tax-free raw materials or semifinished goods. Generous tax incentives are provided for foreign invested firms, and the Government constructs various facilities for sale or lease, including plant sites or factory buildings for the initial occupant industries. The Masan Free Export Zone, established in 1971, is located near Pusan at the southern end of the country. The Iri Free Export Zone opened in March 1975 and is still recruiting foreign occupants. It is located near Gunsan on the western coast of Korea. Information on free export zones may be obtained from the Director, Bureau of Industrial Estates Management, Ministry of Commerce and Industry, 4th Floor, Unified Government Building, 77 Sejong-ro, Chongro-ku, Seoul 110, Korea.

Warehousing. — Adequate bonded storage facilities are available in Korea; all of which are under the direct supervision of the Collector of Customs. Storage of goods in such "bonded storage places" is restricted to 4 months. The maximum storage period in a bonded warehouse is 24 months, although extensions may be granted on request. The Customs Law also provides that privately owned and operated bonded warehouses may be established with the approval of the Collector of Customs. There are currently over 100 licensed commercial bonded warehouses in Korea. In addition, approximately 110 manufacturing enterprises operate as licensed private bonded facilities. With the permission of a Collector of Customs, goods stored in bonded facilities may be repacked, stored, divided and combined, or repaired, provided that the nature and quality of the goods is not changed in so doing.

The above storage periods do not apply to the storage of live animals or plants, perishable merchandise, or other commodities that may cause damage to other merchandise or to the warehouse. The Collector of Customs bears no responsibility for goods while they are stored in customs facilities.

Samples and Advertising Matter

Pursuant to Article 30 of the Korean Customs Law, advertising matter and samples of merchandise are exempt from customs duties, provided that such items are used solely for these purposes. All other samples and advertising matter are subject to payment of normal commercial duties. In general, duty-free entry of advertising matter is left to the discretion of the customs officials at the ports of entry and at post offices.

Technical Standards and Requirements

In Korean foreign trade, metric weights and measures are in common use. However, the domestic system presently used in Korea is a combination of several systems of weights and measures, including metric, pound, yard, and chockkwan (the traditional oriental system of weights and measures, which originated in China). A Weights and Measures Law, promulgated on May 10, 1961, specified that only the metric system of weights and measures was to be used after January 1, 1964. This legislation has not yet been applied to export-import cargoes, however.

Electric current is 60 cycles, 100/200 volts, a.c., single and three phase.

As of 1978, all American appliances functioned on the 100-volt, 60 cycle A.C. current. However, the Government has already begun a program to change over to 220-volt by 1982. Locally made electric appliances will be required to have converters so that they will function on 100 and 220 volts.

The Industrial Standardization Law of September 1961 established the Korean Bureau of Standards and the Council for Industrial Standardization. The Bureau establishes and publishes standards and urges voluntary adherence. Thus far, standards have been published for mechanical, electrical, civil and metallurgical engineering; mining; construction; the textile and chemical industries; foodstuffs; and ceramics. Local firms meeting the standards are allowed to place the mark "KS" on their products, and government organizations are urged to purchase such products. As past and pending standardization legislation is patterned on American models, equipment acceptable in the United States will be acceptable in Korea.

Investment in Korea

U.S. Investment in Korea

U.S. direct investment approvals in Korea from 1962 to December 1978 amounted to $293.9 million in 123 projects, 21.9 percent of total foreign direct investment approvals of $1,008.4 million in 857 projects. Japanese investment was $583.6 million in 665 projects or 57.9 percent of the total. Foreign equity investment approvals culminated in a record high in 1973 of $264.7 million. Approvals were $72.7 million in 1977 and $148.7 million in 1978.

The major fields of foreign investment are chemicals (19.2 percent), tourism and hotels (16.2 percent), electric and electronics (13.0 percent) textiles and garments (9.9 percent) machinery and parts (7.6 percent), petroleum (7 percent), and steel and metals (4.8 percent). Major U.S. investments are in chemicals, electrical machinery and electronics, petroleum, transportation equipment, fertilizers, and electricity. Some of the larger American investors in Korea are Gulf Oil, Union Oil, Caltex, Dow, Skelly, Swift, Control Data, Motorola, General Motors, Fairchild Semiconductor, IBM, Chemtex, and Sperry Rand.

Korean Policy on Investment

Korea welcomes foreign direct investment, particularly from the United States. As its $14 billion heavy and chemical industry development plan requires large inputs of foreign capital (60 percent financing anticipated from foreign sources), there are many opportunities for prospective investors. A special office in the Korean Economic Planning Board assists potential investors in their initial investigations and offers help in carrying out the necessary procedures. Inquiries may be directed to the Bureau of Economic Cooperation, Economic Planning Board, Seoul, Korea. An additional source of assistance is the Korea-U.S. Economic Council located at C.P.O. Box 6754, 10-1, 2-ka Hoehyun-dong, Choong-ku, Seoul, Korea, or its American counterpart, the U.S.-Korea Economic Council at Suite 2-L, 88 Morningside Drive, New York, N.Y. 10027. Korean Government representatives at its Embassy and Consulates in the United States also stand ready to assist. (See Sources of Economic and Commercial Information Section).

Korea's Foreign Capital Inducement Law offers liberal tax and other incentives to foreign investors. Four principles govern Korea's encouragement of foreign equity investment: (1) the contribution that the investment will make to the improvement of the balance of payments, (2) introduction of advanced technology into the economy, (3) establishment of industries providing for increased employment of Korean labor, and (4) utilization of domestic resources.

The Korean Government has recently raised the minimum allowable foreign investment in Korea to a uniform level of $500,000 from the previous $50,000 to $200,000, retroactive to September 8, 1979, with the exception of the $200,000 minimum requirement for investment by a Korean resident overseas. The action has been taken in a move to meet the increasing demand for foreign investment in those industrial areas that require capital-intensive and high-technology industries as the national economy expands with rapid industrialization. The categories of industries in which foreign investment is permitted are classified by the new guidelines as follows:

(1) Large-scale facilities that cannot be built/operated independently by domestic enterprises, and industries for the production of metal, machinery, electric/electronic products;

(2) Export-oriented projects for which overseas markets cannot be effectively explored independently by domestic enterprises;

(3) Projects contributing to the development/utilization of domestic resources;

(4) Chemical industrial and other projects deemed necessary by the Economic Planning Minister.

The principle of restricting foreign equity to 50 percent or less will be maintained, except for: (a) multinational enterprises requiring highly sophisticated technology and management techniques, (b) projects contributing to diversification of investment sources, (c) electronic/machinery industries to be accommodated within the Kumi-Changwon Estates, (d) industries to be accommodated within free export zones.

The Government has issued guidelines favoring investments directed to the development of the country's heavy industry and has also established 17 industry categories, each with different conditions, to govern foreign investment; e.g., minimum capital to be invested, percentage of foreign ownership, permitted production capacity, and export requirements to be met. The Government is currently reviewing once again the conditions of the Foreign Capital Inducement Law and further modifcations to the Law are anticipated.

Forms of Business Organization

In principle, foreigners are permitted to operate in the following types of organizations: joint stock corporation, limited partnership, unlimited partnership, limited company, and branch.

Joint Stock Company.—The joint stock corporation (Chusik Hoesa) is the company structure most commonly utilized by foreign investors. The legal concept and regulations of the joint stock company in Korea are similar to those found in the United States, Japan, and Germany. To establish a joint stock company, Articles of Incorporation must be drawn up and notarized. Seven or more promoters, none of which need be Korean, are required for the incorporation of a joint stock company. After incorporation the number of shareholders may be reduced to one. The minimum par value of a share is W500, and shares may be registered as bearer, common, or preferred. Common shares must carry voting rights.

The application for registration must then be submitted to a District Court. Upon registration and payment of the registration tax (2 percent of capital for Seoul and Pusan and 0.4 percent for other areas), the company acquires the status of a juridical person. At such time it may enter into contracts, acquire rights and obligations, possess intangible property such as patents and copyrights, own real estate, establish commercial credit, and undertake business transactions.

Within 30 days of the commencement of business a company must apply to a district tax office for a business license. The license must then be certified twice yearly by government authorities.

An annual independent audit by a certified public accountant is not required, except for those companies listed on the Korea Stock Exchange; local banks and branches of foreign banks; foreign investment companies remitting dividends overseas; companies remitting royalties overseas, to the extent of the sales on which the royalties are based; and Korean branches remitting gains of over 100 percent of its authorized operating capital or over 50 million won during a specific business year. A number of international auditing firms are represented in Korea.

Branch of a Foreign Corporation.—Licenses issued by the Bank of Korea are required for the establishment of branches (branch offices, branch shops, liaison offices, etc.) by foreign corporations intending to make remittances of gains to their head offices overseas, according to the new rules enforced by the Ministry of Finance on September 15, 1979. Formerly, no such license was required. However, foreign branches requiring no remittance of gains will continue to be required to simply file "reports on establishment" with the Bank of Korea. Other significant points of the new "Regulations Concerning Establishment of Foreign Enterprises' Branches" are as follows:

1. The licenses will have to be renewed every 3 years, unless otherwise-approved in accordance with a pertinent law.

2. Prior to the issuance of such licenses, prior consultation with other government agencies concerned will be held with respect to possible adverse influence on the domestic economy/security.

3. In the case of foreign branches requiring remittance of gains, prior approval of the Bank of Korea will be required for the inducement of over $1 million of operating capital.

4. Money lending, acquisition of securities and other deals not specifically covered under the license will be banned; acquisition of securities deemed necessary for the discharge of functions permitted in accordance with a pertinent law will be allowed, provided approval of the governor of the Bank of Korea is secured.

5. No remittance of gains accrued from businesses not covered by the license will be approved.

6. In a move to ensure effective management of foreign exchange transactions, each branch will be required to designate a single foreign exchange bank through which all foreign exchange transactions will be dealt.

Appointment of an Agent.—Foreign exporters who wish to be represented in Korea but cannot justify an office of their own may appoint an agent to act on their behalf. An individual with special qualifications may be chosen, although the customary practice is to select from among the hundreds of offer agents and registered traders currently operating in Korea.

Acquisition of Stocks.—Foreign acquisition of existing stocks or shares is prohibited under the Foreign Capital Inducement Law. Investment may be made by subscribing to stock or shares of a newly established corporation or by subscribing to a new issue of an existing enterprise. Capital for subscription may be in cash, kind, industrial property rights, technology related to industrial property rights, and rights to the use of such technology.

Licensing Agreements

Licensing and technical assistance agreements provide another alternative means of entry to the Korean market. Korea regulates patent and trademarks for the protection of industrial property rights, provided that such patents and trademarks are registered in Korea.

There are no specific limitations on licensing agreements. Approval of agreements is based on internal and unpublished policy guidelines of the Economic Planning Board. It may be said in general, however, that priority is given to technical and licensing agreements in the export and highly sophisticated machinery industries.

In April, 1979, the Korean Government substantially liberalized restrictions on the inducement of foreign technology under the second phase of its liberal technology inducement plan. Under the second phase: (1) prior approval of the competent ministry will be required only for nuclear energy and defense industries; (2) for other industries, the Minister of Economic Planning Board may approve foreign technology transfer proposals (without having them put through the complicated procedures of review by the ministries concerned), provided that the contract terms fall under the following criteria: a contract (payment of royalty) period of 10 years or less, downpayment of $500,000 or less, running royalties of 10 percent or less of net sales, or a fixed fee of $1 million or less. However, no inducement of foreign technology will be allowed in the following instances: (a) contracts designed simply to allow the use of designs, brands, or trademarks, (b) contracts designed to sell raw materials or components only, (c) contracts containing unfair and restrictive terms on exports, etc., (d) contracts for outdated, low-grade, and declining technology, (e) contracts for specific technology designated by the Minister of Science and Technology for domestic (independent) development, and (f) such other contracts as may be deemed unnecessary by the Minister of the Economic Planning Board.

From 1962 through December 31, 1978, 1,210 technical assistance and licensing agreements had been concluded by Korean enterprises. The United States accounted for 282, and Japan, 717; 29.4 percent of these agreements were related to machinery and parts, 19.1 percent to the electric and electronics industry, 17.3 percent to petroleum refining and chemical engineering, 9.4 percent to the metallurgical industry, and 24.8 percent to other industries (textiles, communications, shipbuilding, power generation, etc.). Total remittances of royalty payments since 1962 have amounted to $256.7 million, with 27.7 percent going to the United States and 45.6 percent to Japan.

Investment Regulations

Application Procedure.—With the exception of investments in the free export zones, all foreign direct investment, technology assistance agreements, and the repayment of loans exceeding 3 years and $200,000 are regulated by the Foreign Capital Inducement Law (1966, amended in 1973) and its Enforcement Decree. An application for approval of a foreign investment must be submitted to the Economic Planning Board (EPB) in quintuplicate, together with necessary supporting documents including the project plan, a certification of nationality, articles of incorporation of a new firm, a proxy authorization, and, when applicable, a joint-venture agreement. It is desirable that the application for authorization be submitted in the Korean language. Joint-venture agreements should be submitted in English. Reliable Korean law firms are available to assist in preparing joint-venture agreements and to provide translation services.

The application should discuss in detail the nature and scope of the proposed foreign investment. All ambiguities should be clarified in the initial planning stages, so as to minimize the risk of problems arising once production has begun. Agreements regarding government concessions and exemptions should be stipulated in writing and affirmed by the highest government officials. Following an initial screening by the Bureau of Economic Cooperation, Economic Planning Board, the application will be forwarded to the competent ministry, depending upon the nature of the proposed investment. The ministries are required by law to submit an opinion to the EPB within 20 days (10 days for a foreign investment of less than $1 million) from the date of the receipt of the application. The investment application will then be forwarded to the Minister of the Economic Planning Board for clearance.

The final clearance comes from the Foreign Capital Inducement Deliberation Committee (FCIDC). The FCIDC reviews the established criteria as well as the comments and recommendations received from the ministries and the Screening Committee. If FCIDC approves the application, the Minister of the Economic Planning Board authorizes the proposed foreign investment project and advises the applicant accordingly. Under special conditions, the Minister may approve an investment application without FCIDC's clearance notifying the FCIDC of the action taken. There are two special conditions: (1) investments up to $1 million and (2) licensing agreements for all industries other than those related to nuclear energy and defense industries, with a contract period of 10 years or less, downpayment of $500,000 or less, and running royalties of 10 percent of net sales or less, or a fixed fee of $1 million or less. The entire review procedure is usually completed within 30 to 40 days.

Should an application be disapproved during the clearance procedure, the applicant may consult with officials in the Bureau of Economic Cooperation of the Economic Planning Board to determine the reasons for the disapproval and, if possible, to make adjustments that will be mutually agreeable.

Profit Remittance.—Remittance of profits is guaranteed by the Government, although approval must be obtained from the Ministry of Finance before remittances may be made.

Ninety days before the end of each fiscal year, firms operating under the Foreign Capital Inducement Law must submit a schedule of projected remittances for the forthcoming year to the Economic Planning Board and the Ministry of Finance. When an application for a remittance is submitted, the Ministry of Finance is authorized to examine the company books if the remittance appears "excessive." In most cases, the determination of eligibility is a simple procedure, and the requested amount of foreign exchange is promptly released.

Foreign firms not covered by the Foreign Capital Inducement Law are allowed to make remittances directly through a foreign exchange bank after obtaining government approval, a procedure that takes from 1 to 3 months.

Capital Remittance.—After 2 years of operation, a firm may repatriate each year up to 20 percent of its invested capital. When a business enterprise is liquidated, the total amount of foreign investment capital may be repatriated.

Reinvestment of Dividends.—In most cases, reinvestment of dividends is allowed as a matter of course. When such reinvestment exceeds the amount of the original investment, however, specific approval must be obtained from the Minister of the Economic Planning Board.

Industrial Property Rights

Patents and Trademarks.—Korea announced its intention to join the "Paris Union" International Industrial Property Convention effective

May 4, 1980, and it implemented a revised Trademark Law on January 1, 1980. In addition, through court decisions, Korea is providing greater protection for well-known foreign trade marks. Patents and trademarks fall under the jurisdiction of the Ministry of Commerce and Industry.

Patents are granted for a 12-year period and are not renewable. Trademarks registered with the Patent Bureau are protected by law for 10 years and may be renewed indefinitely for 10-year periods. Trademarks must be used to remain valid, and those not used within a year of registration may be subject to cancellation.

Through a reciprocal provision of the Treaty of Friendship, Commerce and Navigation between the United States and Korea, U.S. investors may register patents and trademarks directly in Korea. In the absence of a commercial agreement, foreigners must file for patent or trademark registration through a licensed agent. Firms desiring counsel in patent or trademark matters may obtain a list of English-speaking patent attorneys from the Korea Patent Attorney's Association, Room No. 307, Sambo Bldg., 113-1, Banpo-dong, Kangnam-ku, Seoul. The cost of acquiring patent and trademark rights is nominal.

Items construed as vital to national defense or to the public interest are not patentable. Food, beverages, and pharmaceutical products fall within this category, although related processess may qualify for coverage.

Copyrights.—Korea is not a member of the Universal Copyright Convention (UCC), nor has it entered into any other agreement with the United States for mutual protection of copyrights. Under Korea's Copyright Law, only Korean nationals may apply for copyright registration of books and other literary works and enforce such registration against unauthorized users. Although foreign publishers may not apply for copyright protection of their works, the Bureau of Culture of the Ministry of Culture and Information, which administers the Copyright Law, has agreed to a procedure whereby Korean book publishers who have licenses from U.S. publishers to publish in Korea may apply for local copyright protection of the latter's U.S.-copyrighted books. Books copyrighted under these procedures will thereby be entitled to the full protection of the Copyright Law.

Ownership of Land.—Foreign investors may legally own and lease land throughout Korea. In practice, however, the purchase of land has not been allowed unless provided for in the investor's contract under the Foreign Capital Inducement Law. Foreign nationals are subject to the regulations of the Alien Land Law, which requires firms with a foreign interest of 50 percent or more to obtain approval for land ownership from the Ministry of Home Affairs.

Property Guarantee.—All the property of foreign-invested enterprises is guaranteed and protected from requisition or expropriation. The same rights, privileges, and protection enjoyed by Korean nationals are extended to foreign nationals and enterprises, except in cases specifically prescribed by law.

Taxation

Korea offers foreign investors a number of tax exemptions and benefits under its Foreign Capital Inducement Law and other tax laws. Table 2 lists the major tax privileges. The foreign investor, creditor, or supplier of technology has the option to request that taxes not be exempted or reduced.

In addition, the following benefits are provided:

1. Tax Credit on Investment.—In the case of capital invested in shipbuilding, iron making, steel making, lead making, chemical fertilizer, power generation, chemical fibers, major automobile parts, machines, chemical pulp, soda ash, mining, marine and livestock products processing industries, national land development projects, and petrochemical, electronics and heavy and electric power industries, 8 percent of the total amount of investment may be deductible from the amount of income tax or corporation tax.

2. Nonapplication of Five-Fold Rates of Registration Tax.—On the registration of real estate or business offices, branches and factories of corporations in Seoul and Pusan, five-fold rates of tax are applied. Application of the five-fold rate of tax is withheld, in the case of foreign-invested enterprises engaged in manufacturing.

3. Exemption of Real Estate Speculation Control Tax.—In cases where land is invested in kind for the establishment of a foreign-invested enterprise under the Foreign Capital Inducement Law, the income tax and the additional corporation tax on capital gains may be exempted.

4. Deduction of Presumptive Dividend Tax.— For enterprises established under the

Foreign Capital Inducement Law, 50 percent of the amount of presumptive dividends is deductible from the tax.

5. Tax Exemption and Reduction for Disaster.—In cases where an enterprise is deemed unable to pay taxes because of a loss of more than 50 percent of the total amount of its business assets due to an "Act of God" or any other disaster, the corporation tax and business tax on the enterprise may be exempted or reduced according to the ratio of the value of the lost assets.

6. Depreciation Allowances.—In cases where a foreign investor, as defined in the Foreign Capital Inducement Law, takes 40% or more of the stock or shares of a domestic corporation, the computation method of depreciation may be changed with approval from the head of the competent district tax office. An application for change in the computation method must be filed within 30 days of the beginning date of the business year in which it is intended to apply the changed depreciation method.

On fixed assets used in certain designated businesses, additional depreciation is allowed over the ordinary depreciation. Depreciation is normally allowed on the basis of government specifications of the useful life of all fixed assets. The depreciable base of an asset is the original

Table 2.—Major Tax Reductions and Exemptions Applicable to
Foreign Invested Enterprise in Korea

	Taxation Bases	Tax Rates	Tax Reduction or Exemption
Income Tax on Unincorporated Enterprises	Amount of Income or Earnings	6–62%	(1) Exemption for 5 years in proportion to the ratio of stock or shares owned by the foreign investors (2) 50% reduction of the above for following 3 years
Corporation Tax	(1) Income in Each Business year (2) Liquidation Income	(1) Open Corporation 20–35% (2) Closed Corporation 20–40%	(1) Exemption for 5 years in proportion to the ratio of stock or shares owned by the foreign investors (2) 50% reduction of the above for following 3 years
Wages and Salary Income Tax	Salary or Wage of Foreign Employee Working in Foreign Invested Enterprise	6–62%	Exemption for 5 years
Dividend Income Tax	Amount of Dividends Received	5–62%	(1) Exemption for 5 years on foreign investor (2) 50% reduction of the above for following 3 years
Tax on Technology Income	Amount of Income Received from Supplying Technology (Royalty)	6–62%	(1) Exemption for 5 years (2) 50% reduction of the above for following 3 years
Interest Income Tax	Interest or other income accruing from loan contract	5–62%	Full exemption for loans approved
Value Added Tax	Amount of CIF value plus customs duty	10%	Full exemption on imported capital goods
Customs Duty	Ad Valorem Basis (c.i.f. Price) for importation	5–62% by Commodities	Full exemption on capital goods approved
Property Tax	Assessed Value of Land, buildings, Vessels, Mining District, etc.	(1) Land 0.3–5% (2) House & Vessels 0.3–5% (3) Per/ha of Mine Lot W50	(1) Exemption for 5 years in proportion of the ratio of stock or shares owned by the foreign investors (2) 50% reduction of the above for following 3 years
Property Acquisition Tax	Acquisition Price of Real Estate, Motor Vehicles, Land, Buildings, and Ships	2%	(1) Exemption for 5 years (2) 50% reduction of the above for following 3 years

cost less a 10 percent allowance for salvage value.

Corporate tax returns are normally due 60 days after the close of an accounting period. The Ministry of Finance is charged with the ultimate responsibility for fiscal matters, with the enforcement and processing functions of collection handled by the Office of National Tax Administration. Tax audits on foreign investments should be expected each year.

Labor Force

At the end of 1978, Korea's labor force totaled 13.5 million. The agriculture, forestry, and fishing sectors accounted for 38.4 percent of the employed labor force. Other categories were mining and manufacturing, 23.2 percent; and social and overhead capital and other services, 38.4 percent (construction 6 percent and other 32.4 percent).

The labor force is one of Korea's main resources. With a 90 percent literacy rate and an emphasis in the school system on technical education and vocational training, there is a good supply of well trained, skilled workers and competent supervisory personnel. Korean workers are traditionally bright, hard-working, and aggressive.

Payments and Benefits.—Korea has no legal minimum wage system, although the Labor Standards Act authorizes the Director-General of the Office of Labor Affairs to set a minimum wage according to industry. Base wages make up only part of worker's income. Fringe benefits make up 50–60 percent of a wage-earner's salary and, in some cases, may amount to 80 percent of total compensation. In 1978, average monthly earnings for all workers were about $197. Highest average monthly earnings were paid by the petroleum refining industry ($597) and the lowest by the wearing apparel industry ($126).

In addition to an employee's base salary, bonuses of 100 percent or higher of monthly salary are paid several times a year. Many companies provide meals at lunch and commuter services. One month's average salary for every year of employment is given as severance pay by employers employing more than 16 workers.

Working Hours.—The standard work week is 48 hours-8 hours a day for 6 days. Working hours may be extended to 60 hours per week by mutual agreement, a practice that has become common in manufacturing and export industries. Further extension of overtime hours requires prior approval of the Office of Labor Affairs. Anything above the standard work week is considered overtime and is subject to compensation at 150 percent of the standard hourly rate. Minors, ages 13–16, are permitted to work 42 hours a week (7 hours a day). There are 14 legal holidays in Korea. In addition, employees are entitled by law to eight paid holidays a year if they have perfect attendance or if their attendance is 90% perfect.

Social Benefits.—An employer employing more than 16 workers must provide at least one physical examination a year. For an on-the-job injury, industrial accident compensation practice provides that the employer pay medical costs, 60 percent of the employee's ordinary wages during the period of medical treatment, and compensation for physical handicaps. In case of death, 1,000 days of wages and funeral expenses (90 days wages) must be furnished to the employee's family. For firms employing 16 or more workers, industrial accident compensation insurance is mandatory.

Labor Relations

There are three basic laws concerning labor: The Labor Standards Law, the Labor Union Law, and the Labor Dispute Settlement Law. In addition, a temporary special law dealing with foreign-invested enterprises has been appended to the latter law. This special law provides for the establishment of a Foreign-Invested Enterprises Labor Dispute Settlement Committee in the Ministry of Health and Social Affairs. In case of a suspension of operations or the closing of a foreign enterprise, the Korean Government must adjust labor disputes within 20 days. Foreign investors may be given up to 5 years exemption from having to recognize a union.

The labor union movement is still in the developing stage. Under the Labor Union Law, workers are entitled to form and participate in the activities of labor unions, to conduct collective bargaining, and to take collective action in order to maintain and improve working conditions. Use of violence and destructive acts in labor disputes are prohibited, and conciliation, mediation, and compulsory arbitration are the approved means of settlement. At the end of 1978, there were 17 industrial unions, all affiliated with the Federation of Korea Trade Unions (FKTU). The number of companies with a labor union chapter was over 5,000, most of which had concluded collective bargaining agreements. Agreements that have been concluded voluntarily need not necessarily be registered with the Office of Labor Affairs. Foreign investors wishing to enter into a collective bargaining agreement shall submit an application to the Office of Labor Affairs for a decision, which will be made within 30 days.

Investment in Industrial Estates

Korean law permits the building of new plants only in industrial areas. The Government's policy of decentralization, aimed at relieving congestion in Seoul, entirely prohibits new factory construction in the city. There is, however, no problem in selecting industrial estates. The Korean Government is building many industrial estates and is providing the necessary infrastructure facilities in coastal and inland areas. There is particular interest in attracting foreign investment to these areas.

There are 29 industrial estates classified in six groups: 12 local industrial estates, 2 special export industrial estates, 2 private industrial estates, 6 export industrial estates, 5 heavy and chemical industrial estates, and the Iri and Mason Free Export Zones. All offer low land costs, adequate power and water, transportation and support facilities, and special administrative assistance. All of the industrial estates are open to foreign as well as local enterprises.

Some of the more interesting estates to potential foreign investors are the Gumi Electronics Zone, established for the assembly of electronic items and the manufacture of electronic components, materials, and related industrial products; the Iri and Masan Free Export Zones (described in the Trade Regulations Section); the Changwon Industrial Complex designed as an integrated machinery manufacturing base; and the Yochun Petrochemical Industrial Estate designated as a petrochemical products manufacturing base.

Additional information on the industrial estates may be obtained from the Director, Bureau of Industrial Estate Management, Ministry of Commerce & Industry, 4th floor, Unified Government Bldg., 77 Sejong-ro, Chong-ro-Ku, Seoul.

Guidance for Business Travelers

Entrance Requirements

Visitors must have a valid passport, a visa to enter the country, and a quarantine certificate. Visas are granted gratis by any Korean diplomatic or consular post. Three kinds of visas are issued: a tourist visa valid for a stay of 60 days (except in the case of Japanese nationals, for whom a tourist visa is valid for 15 days), a transit visa valid for 15 days, and an entry visa for a stay of more than 60 days. Either of the two latter may be issued if the visit is mainly for business purposes. Visas may be extended for valid reasons, but application must be made prior to expiration of the original visa.

A tourist staying 120 hours or less need not obtain a visa, provided a confirmed air reservation is produced. In such cases, a shore pass is given on arrival, and an extension may be granted upon request. In addition, a visa is not required for transit passengers stopping over for up to 72 hours, provided that a valid passport is produced and for the condition that the traveler comes from an area where there is no Korean diplomatic or consular representative. Persons desiring to remain in Korea over 60 days must obtain a residence permit from the Ministry of Justice.

At present, no vaccination certificate is required under Korea's Quarantine Regulations, unless the visitor has come from an epidemic area. It is recommended that travelers, particularly those traveling to a number of countries, carry with them a current international immunization record.

Pertinent Treaties

A Treaty of Friendship, Commerce and Navigation signed by the United States and Korea in 1956 reciprocally grants to the citizens of one country the right of residence and trade in the territories of the other and confers national rights on them in the commercial field. Each country accords the other unconditional most-favored-nation treatment in commercial matters.

Foreign Exchange Controls

Under Korea's Foreign Exchange Control Law, all foreign exchange transactions are subject to control. The Law is administered by the Ministry of Finance and the Bank of Korea. Exchange certificates are required for all foreign exchange expenditures, except for payment of imports under U.S. Public Law 480, and for payments by the commercial banks in connection with their banking transactions.

All transactions between Korea and other countries must be denominated in one of 48 designated currencies, which include U.S. dollars, Japanese yen, Canadian dollars, Hong Kong dollars, British pounds, German marks, Italian lira, French francs, Swiss francs, Swedish krona, Australian dollars, Danish kroner, Belgian francs, Austrian schillings, Norwegian krones, and Dutch guilders.

With very few exceptions, all foreign exchange proceeds must be surrendered to the Korea Exchange Bank or to one of the designated foreign exchange banks (see below) against payment in won or against delivery of equivalent foreign exchange certificates. The exceptions are largely limited to transportation and insurance companies and to foreign nonresidents.

Foreigners may bring into Korea any amount of authorized foreign currency in any form. They make take out any authorized foreign currency originally brought in and declared to customs. Prior to departure, visitors also may convert won back to foreign exchange, up to the value of US$500, at any authorized foreign exchange bank.

The basic unit of exchange in Korea is the won. The exchange rate floats to the market price, with the Korea Exchange Bank acting as the center. The central bank authorities may regulate the supply and demand of funds in the foreign exchange market so as to stabilize the exchange rate, however, and the won was effectively stabilized at a rate of 485 won to US$1 from December 1974 to January 1980. After a devaluation of 20 percent announced January 12, 1980, the exchange rate was 582 won to US$1.

In addition to the Korea Exchange Bank, 58 banks, including 32 branches of foreign banks, have been authorized to deal in foreign exchange. These banks have been authorized to handle international business through correspondent banks. Previously, only the Bank of Korea and the Korea Exchange Bank had overseas correspondents.

Language, Business Hours, Holidays

Commercial Language.—Although Korean is the language of the country, many Koreans speak and understand English. Many business firms are able to correspond in English. Knowledge of Japanese is also fairly widespread. Catalogs, promotional literature, and instructions are acceptable in English.

Business Hours.—Most offices, government and private, are open from 0900 to 1700 on weekdays, with 1 hour at noon for lunch, and from 0900 to 1300 on Saturday. Banks close at 1600 daily, but are also open until 1300 on Saturday. Service establishments, such as department stores, shops, restaurants, hospitals, and barber shops, may remain open as late as 2200 and on weekends and public holidays. Except for Cheju Island and Chungchongbukdo province, a curfew is in effect from 2400 to 0400.

Holidays.—Public and business offices close on the following statutory holidays: January 1–3, New Year Celebration; March 1, Independence Movement Day; March 10, Korean Labor Day; April 5, Arbor Day; April 8 (lunar), Buddha's Day; May 5, Childrens Day; June 6, Memorial Day; July 17, Constitution Day; August 15, Liberation Day; September 23, Korean Thanksgiving Day; October 1, Armed Forces Day; October 3, National Foundation Day; October 9, Hangul (Korean Alphabet) Day; December 25, Christmas Day. On Labor Day, March 10, most business offices are closed. However, public offices remain open.

Sources of Economic and Commercial Information

General information concerning the Korean market (economic trends, commercial development, production, trade, etc.) may be obtained from the Office of Country Marketing, International Trade Administration, U.S. Department of Commerce, Washington, D.C. 20230.

The United States is represented by an Embassy at 82 Sejong-Ro Chongro-Ku, Seoul. The telephone number is 72-2601 through 72-2619. The U.S. Export Development Office (EDO), is located in the same building and provides exhibition and conference areas for business visitors. Members of the staff of the Commerce and Industry Section of the Embassy are available to brief and assist American businesspeople and to discuss EDO programs designed to assist U.S. exporters. From the United States, mail may be directed to the Commerce and Industry Section or to the U.S. Trade Center through Armed Forces postal facilities. The address is American Embassy Seoul, APO San Francisco 96301.

Korean Government Representation in the U.S.

The Republic of Korea maintains an Embassy in the United States at 2320 Massachusetts Avenue, N.W., Washington, D.C. 20008. It also maintains Consulates General at the following U.S. locations:

500 North Michigan Avenue
Chicago, Illinois 60611

2756 Palihighway
Honolulu, Hawaii 96817

508 World Trade Building
1520 Texas Avenue
Houston, Texas 77002

Suite 1101
Lee Tower Building
5455 Wilshire Boulevard
Los Angeles, Califronia 90036

460 Park Avenue
New York, New York 10022

3500 Clay Street
San Francisco, Califronia 94118

Suite 2301
Harris Tower
233 Peachtree Street
Atlanta, Georgia 30303

Suite 1125
United Airlines Building
2033 6th Avenue
Seattle, Washington 98121

Suite 1405
New World Tower
100 North Biscayne Boulevard
Miami, Florida 33132

In addition, Korean Trade Centers are maintained at:

Hahn Kook (USA), Inc.
460 Park Avenue
New York, New York 10022

111 East Wacker Drive
Chicago Illinois 60601

Suite 660
Two Embarcadero Center
San Francisco, California 94111

Occidental Center
1149 South Hill Street
Los Angeles, California 90015

World Trade Center
Room 155
2050 Stemmons Freeway
Dallas, Texas 75258

1 Biscayne Tower
Suite 1984
Miami, Florida 33131

The Bank of California Center
900 4th Avenue
Seattle, Washington 98164

Suite 2501
Peachtree Center Building
229 Peachtree Street, N.E.
Atlanta, Georgia 30303

300 Town Center
Suite 1040
Southfield, Michigan 48075

ITM Building
Suite 824
2 Canal Street
New Orleans, Louisiana 70130

Watergate Building
Suite 630
600 New Hampshire Avenue, N.W.
Washington, D.C. 20037

All of these trade centers are operated by the Korea Trade Promotion Corporation (KOTRA), a government organization.

Korean banks with representation in the United States are:

Korea Exchange Bank
460 Park Avenue
New York, New York 10022

33 North Dearborn Street
Suite 400
Chicago, Illinois 60602

Korea Exchange Bank Agency
One Wilshire Building
Suite 2510
624 South Grand Avenue
Los Angeles, California 90017

Bank of Korea
40 Wall Street
New York, New York 10005

The Korea Development Bank
250 Park Avenue
Room 905
New York, New York 10017

The nongovernment Korean Trader's Association has a branch at:

Hahn Kook (U.S.A.), Inc.
460 Park Avenue
New York, New York 10022

The Korean Shipping Corporation is located at:

80 Broad Street
New York, New York 10004

Other Korean organizations located in the United States are:

Korean Trader's Association
(a private organization)
Hahn Kook (U.S.A.), Inc.
460 Park Avenue
New York, New York 10022

Korean Shipping Corporation
80 Broad Street
New York, New York 10004

U.S. Korea Economic Council
(a private organization)
88 Morningside Drive
New York, New York 10027

Publications

The following is a list of publications available from private and public sources that treat current economic and commercial matters in Korea and provide information on trade and investment.

Korean Government

Economic Planning Board
4th Five-Year Economic Development Plan
(1977–1981)

Economic Planning Board
Major Statistics of Korean Economy (Annual)

Economic Planning Board
Korea Statistical Yearbook (Annual)

Economic Planning Board
Monthly Statistics of Korea

Economic Planning Board
Report on Mining and Manufacturing Survey
(Annual)

Economic Planning Board
Economic Survey (Annual)

Economic Planning Board
Guide to Investment in Korea (Annual)

Economic Planning Board
(Slides, updated periodically)

Korea Development Institute
Long-Term Prospect for Economic and Social
Development, 1977–1991), 1978

Office of Customs Administration
Statistical Yearbook of Foreign Trade (Annual)

Office of Customs Administration
Monthly Foreign Trade Statistics

Ministry of Communications
Statistical Yearbook of Communications (Annual)

Ministry of Agriculture & Forestry
Yearbook of Agriculture and Forestry

Office of Fisheries Administration
Yearbook of Fisheries Statistics (Annual)

Office of National Tax Administration
Statistical Yearbook of National Tax (Annual)

Banks

Korea Development Bank
Industry in Korea, 1976

Bank of Korea
Economic Statistics Yearbook

Bank of Korea
Quarterly Economic Review

Bank of Korea
Monthly Economic Statistics

Bank of Korea
The Korean Economy, Performance & Prospects

Bank of Korea
Financial System in Korea, 1978

Private

Korea Traders Association
Korean Trade Directory (Annual)

Korea Traders Association
Laws Relating to Foreign Trade, 1977

Korea Traders Association
Terminal Export-Import Notice of the Ministry
of Commerce and Industry
(Semiannual)

Korea Trading Agents Association
Korea Trade Agents Directory (Annual

Korea Chamber of Commerce & Industry
Korean Business Directory (Annual)

The Korea Directory Company
Korea Directory (Annual)

Federation of Korean Industries
Korean Business Review (Monthly)

Korea Trade Promotion Corporation
Korea Business (Montly)

American Chamber of Commerce in Korea
Living in Korea, 1978

Hapdong News Agency
Korea Annual (Annual)

Market Profile—KOREA

Economic Overview

Korea continues its slow recovery from the 1980 recession, with a projected 6.5 percent real GNP growth for 1982. In 1981, real GNP grew 7.1 percent, led by a 23 percent increase in the agricultural sector. The Korean Government (ROKG) is continuing its policy of economic stabilization in 1982 by closely controlling the money supply, narrowing the current account deficit, and focusing on what is considered the primary goal—controlling inflation. The 1983 Korean Economic Management Plan is characterized by its focus on consolidation of price stability gained in 1982 and real growth of 7.5 percent.

Major Developments

Korea's Fifth Five-Year Development Plan contains a number of ambitious development projects, including several nuclear power plants, telecommunications expansion, Pusan subway, expansion of shipbuilding capacity, and sewage treatment facilities. Other transportation, industrial, and environmental projects are in various stages of planning. Korea, a major coal importer, is developing alternative energy resources.

Foreign Trade

Best U.S. Sales Prospects. — Medical instruments and equipment, analytical and scientific instruments, energy conservation systems and equipment, electrical and nonelectrical machinery, industrial controls, construction equipment, telecommunications equipment, coal, chemicals, scrap metals, and logs.

Major Suppliers (1981). — Japan (28 percent) and United States (21 percent).

Principal Exports. — Textile products, metal products, electrical products, and footwear.

Major Markets (1981). — United States (30 percent) and Japan (21 percent).

Finance

Currency. — Korean won valued in June 1982 at 738.4 won = US$1 under floating exchange rate system. Money supply (M2) for yearend 1981, $6,517 million; $5,769 million in 1980.

Domestic Credit. — An economic stimulus package was introduced in July 1982, which included measures to cut back interest rates and corporate taxes, a modest loosening of the money supply, and banking reforms. Prime rate was 10 percent at mid-year 1982, down from 13.5 percent at beginning of 1982.

National Budget. — $13.7 billion for 1982, up 19.1 percent over 1981. Defense 34.4 percent, education 20.8 percent, and economic development 17.6 percent of total 1982 budget.

Balance of Payments. — The current account deficit narrowed from $5.3 billion in 1980 to $4.7 billion in 1981. Korea's external debt service ratio remains under 14 percent. Foreign exchange reserves at end of 1981: $7.1 billion.

Foreign Investment

U.S. direct investment is estimated at $460 million, the second largest book value of foreign investment in Korea. Major U.S. investments are in oil refineries, chemicals, automotive industry, electronic components, and textiles.

Investment Prospects. — On September 25, 1981, Korea liberalized its regulations governing the entry of foreign investment. Korea seeks U.S. investment, with emphasis on technology and capital intensive projects and incentives for export-oriented industries.

Import — Export Trade*
(millions of U.S. dollars)

	1979	1980	1981
Total Imports (c.i.f.)	20,339	22,292	26,131
Imports from the U.S.	4,603	4,890	6,044
Manufactured goods	11,563	9,914	11,671
Agricultural goods	1,654	1,992	2,925
Other	7,122	10,386	11,535
Total Exports (f.o.b.)	15,055	17,505	20,992
Exports to the U.S.	4,374	4,607	5,667
Manufactured goods	13,570	16,151	19,508
Agricultural goods	519	458	431
Other	966	896	1,053

*Korean data.

Principal Imports from U.S. in 1981*
(millions of U.S. dollars)

	Value	Percent of Total
Grains	1,091.5	21.8
Cotton yarns, fibers	489.6	9.8
Aircraft and space craft	396.6	7.9
Boilers, engines	234.3	4.7
Electrical machinery	230.6	4.6
Minerals	162.2	3.2
Papermaking products	129.3	2.6
Oil-bearing vegetable materials	126.2	2.5
Hides and skins	122.1	2.4
Iron and steel	115.5	2.3

*U.S. data.

Basic Economic Facilities

Transportation. — Modern highway network being completed. Domestic and international air service well developed. Significant coastal and foreign shipping.

Communications. — Government and private radio and television stations reach most areas. Major cities serviced by international telegraph and telephone circuits. Telecommunications capabilities are being expanded in preparation for the 1988 Summer Olympics.

Power. — Electricity production 36.4 billion kilowatt hours in 1981. Generating capacity presently meets demand. Active nuclear program underway.

Natural Resources

Land and Climate. — About 38,000 square miles, mostly mountains. Climate similar to northeastern United States.

Minerals. — Meager mineral resources include anthracite coal, tungsten, and some iron ore.

Forestry and Fisheries. — Forest and fisheries resources are depleted.

Population

Size. — Estimated 41.1 million in 1982, with annual growth rate of 1.6 percent. Capital city, Seoul, 8.1 million.

Labor. — Korean labor force estimated at 15.4 million.

Education. — Literacy rate over 90 percent. Compulsory attendance through 6 years.

Language. — Korean, English. English is used widely in business circles and is also taught in Korean high schools.

Marketing in Kuwait

Contents

Report Revised June 1979

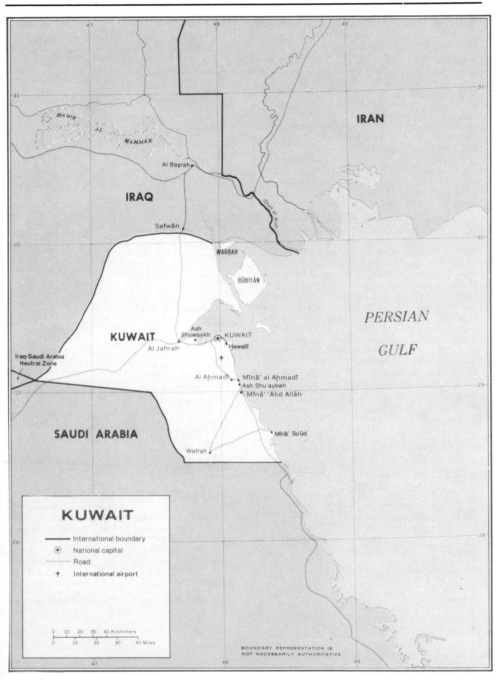

IRAN

MAWR AL HAMMAR

Al Baṣrah

IRAQ

Shaṭṭ al Arab

Safwān

WARBAH

BŪBIYĀN

PERSIAN

KUWAIT

Ash Shuwaykh

KUWAIT

Al Jahrah

Hawallī

Iraq-Saudi Arabia
Neutral Zone

GULF

Al Aḥmadī

Mīnā' al Aḥmadī

Ash Shu'aybah

Mīnā' 'Abd Allāh

SAUDI ARABIA

Mīnā' Su'ūd

Wafrah

KUWAIT

International boundary

National capital

Road

International airport

0 10 20 30 40 Kilometers

0 10 20 30 40 Miles

BOUNDARY REPRESENTATION IS
NOT NECESSARILY AUTHORITATIVE

1453

Foreign Trade Outlook

Introduction

Kuwait, with a relatively small population of 1.1 million, has one of the highest per capital income levels in the world ($15,480 in 1976). Since Kuwait depends on imports for virtually all of its foodstuffs and most of its requirements for raw materials and manufactures, the country is also one of the world's most intensive purchasers of foreign goods. Foreign purchases, which totaled $84 million in 1954 and $886 million in 1972, rose to $3.3 billion in 1976. The 1975 product mix of goods imported into Kuwait was split between agricultural products (17 percent) manufactured goods (18 percent), machinery and transport equipment (46 percent) and other (19 percent).

Since the late 1960s, increasing competition in the Kuwait market has caused the United States to lose its earlier preeminent role when it had 20 percent of the market. By 1976, the United States was the second largest supplier to Kuwait, after Japan, with 13 percent of the market. Nevertheless, U.S. exports, sharing the expansion of the market, totaled $548 million in 1977. Major commodities were food, live animals, and cigarettes ($30 million); motor vehicles ($178 million); heating and cooling equipment ($70 million); construction and mining equipment ($23 million), power generation machinery ($16 million); mechanical handling equipment and electric power machinery ($15 million each); and electric household appliances ($13 million).

Table 1.—Kuwait: Commodity Classification of Imports

(thousands of dollars)

Commodity Group	1972*	1973*	1974*	1975*
Food and live animals	$140,244	$179,900	$236,364	$365,800
Beverages and tobacco	19,796	25,930	32,207	31,222
Crude/materials inedible except fuels	12,026	18,604	29,643	29,056
Mineral fuels and lubricants	7,895	9,753	18,660	14,114
Animal and vegetable oils and fats	3,159	3,597	6,302	8,615
Chemicals	38,717	45,741	65,131	92,526
Manufactured goods	171,200	222,086	385,033	427,000
Machinery and Transport equipment	260,078	362,442	532,720	1,090,931
Miscellaneous manufactured articles	142,339	173,409	234,039	317,438
Unclassified commodities	1,563	11,411	11,758	14,666
TOTAL	$797,018	$1,052,873	$1,551,857	$2,391,368

*The value of the imports is listed in Kuwaiti Dinars in the Abstract. The exchange rate used here is $3.04 for 1 KD in 1972; $3.39 in 1973; $3.41 in 1974; and $3.45 in 1975.

Source: 1976 Annual Statistical Abstract from the Kuwait Ministry of Planning.

Table 2.—U.S. Exports to Kuwait 1975–77

(thousands of dollars)

Commodity	1975	1976	1977
Cereals and Prepations of cereal, flour, etc	$740	$1,555	$2,376
Fruits and vegetables	2,098	3,492	2,935
Other foods and live animals	4,209	6,658	9,669
*Cigarettes	14,501	18,237	15,125
Essential oils, perfume, soaps, etc	2,763	1,847	2,321
Chemical proudcts, n.e.c. including reagents, etc	5,017	1,964	5,407
Rubber tires and tubes for vehicles and planes	2,415	2,404	4,128
Made-up articles of textile materials n.e.c	1,995	2,794	3,216
Carpets and rugs	440	2,652	3,261
Nonmetallic mineral manufactures, n.e.c.	2,434	4,098	5,439
Iron or steel pipes, tubes and fittings	3,508	9,019	5,919
Finished iron and steel structure and parts	2,840	5,230	6,030
Tools for use in hand or in machines	1,842	2,873	3,083
Steam engines, turbines and parts	213	224	4,770
Engine—internal combustion aircraft and parts	4,807	8,138	8,106
Tractors except road and industrial	2,375	3,002	3,590
Office machines and parts	728	856	3,217
Construction and mining mach and pts, n.e.c.	12,123	14,338	23,469
Mineral working and glass working machinery and parts	1,223	2,860	11,694
Heating and cooling machinery and equipment and parts	22,082	43,481	69,991
Pumps, centrifuges, etc, and parts	7,579	14,968	12,924
Mechanical handling machinery, and equipment and parts	12,879	19,041	15,427
Parts and accessories for machinery n.e.c.	2,434	3,289	4,768
Electric power machinery and parts	18,845	38,047	10,199
Electrical apparatus for making etc. electrical circuits	586	1,140	4,452
Telecommunications equipment n.e.c	1,974	14,148	11,196
Electric household equipment appliances and parts	5,650	10,608	13,059
Electical machinery and apparatus, and parts n.e.c.	3,862	4,607	5,639
Passengers cars, trucks etc—all fuel	143,544	128,761	161,422
Motor vehicles and tractor parts and accessories n.e.c.	7,755	13,620	15,993
Aircraft and aircraft parts and accessories	15,756	11,162	6,096
Ships and boats exc military incl special purpose	2,407	1,359	2,038
Furniture	421	786	2,016
Travel goods, handbags, etc.	1,826	4,869	3,108
Clothing ex furs, knit, elastic, fabric articles, etc	3,876	4,244	6,072
Scientific optical etc apparatus	2,477	6,427	7,112
Miscellaneous manufactured articles n.e.c	4,315	5,919	8,500
Special category	4,867	5,717	7,343
Other	30,335	47,083	56,690
Total	$362,175	$471,497	$547,800

SOURCE: U.S. Department of Commerce, Bureau of the Census FT-455

Japan has steadily improved its market position with a sustained and effective competitive effort and in 1976 supplied 21 percent of Kuwait's market. West Germany and the United Kingdom were also important suppliers to Kuwait capturing 10 percent and 8 percent of the market respectively.

Because of the large increases in the posted

Table 3.—Kuwait: Source of Imports 1973-76)

(millions of dollars)

	1973	1974	1975	1976
United States	$147	$219	$430	$480
Japan	186	265	387	689
West Germany	82	173	273	364
United Kingdom	107	127	244	252
France	28	61	79	169
Italy	44	62	108	147
India	27	44	53	129
Australia	28	21	57	74
China	36	47	50	75
Taiwan	27	29	41	72
Hong Kong	17	22	32	57
Korea	10	18	31	52
Netherlands	25	34	50	51
Belgium	17	41	30	42
Spain	7	22	70	35
Switzerland	14	24	29	35
Other	241	347	424	508
Total	$1,043	$1,556	$2,388	$3,231

*Annual data derived from partner countries export reports to the International Monetary Fund.
SOURCE: IMF, Direction of Trade. 1976 information derived from December 1977 report.

price of crude oil in 1973-1974, Kauwait's foreign exchange earnings have risen dramatically to an estimated $8.5 billion in 1977. In addition, the government receives revenues of approximately $1.5 billion on investments and $500 million in service income. In the next year or two when the new LPG plant comes on stream, making use of gas now being flared to produce products based on gas, the government's financial position will be further enhanced. Revenues of this magnitude considerably exceed the country's absorptive capacity—even with the most ambitious of development programs. As a result, the government will have continually rising surplus funds to invest overseas and to maintain and perhaps increase foreign assistance.

Using their expanded financial resources over the past several years, Kuwait has developed a well integrated infrastructure by regional standards. Kuwait also has made remarkable strides in industrial development, especially in the petroleum sector. Despite the progress, Kuwait expects to spend $16.6 billion over the period 1977-81 on further economic development.

Execution of these programs will require importation of capital goods, supplies, and services. The continuing growth in the economy will also result in rising disposable personal income giving an impetus to the demand for consumer goods.

Best Export Prospects

The major opportunities for American companies will be in the export of technology and in design, construction, equipment supply, and

management of the many public works and industrial projects to be undertaken. The Government is presently implementing a number of projects including housing construction ($4 billion), extension of motorways ($1 billion), expansion of electric generation and water desalination capacity ($1.2 billion), LPG plant ($1 billion), hospital construction ($200 million), marina/recreational facilities ($400 million), telecommunications and port expansion ($750 million), and tanker purchase ($300 million). In addition, there are a number of plans under consideration for development of petrochemical and hydrocarbon-based production facilities, as well as other light industry. The hydrocarbon-based

---

HOW TO OBTAIN
BACKGROUND INFORMATION
ABOUT THESE COUNTRIES

Keeping this book within reasonable size limits has made it necessary to focus on material directly concerned with marketing and commerce, and set aside materials only indirectly related. The editors relize, however, that general data about a country are also vital to a company's preparations to enter a foreign market, and make a very definite recommendation as to how such expanded information needs can be served.

For those who wish general data about a country—data which goes beyond marketing and commerce—the editors recommend Countries of the World and Their Leaders, published as an annually updated yearbook by Gale Research Company, Detroit, Michigan 48226. Containing 4- to 20-page entries in 168 countries, the volume also provides several hundred pages of supplementary world data. Each country entry is prepared by the U.S. Department of State to provide a general briefing on the geography, people, culture, and political situation of the particular country. Each report provides some historical insight as well as a look at contemporary trends of lifestyle in the country. Reports also discuss a country's educational system, its press, ethnic groupings and religious practices.

Countries of the World and Their Leaders provides a fresh listing of cabinet ministers of each nation. In addition it lists health conditions the traveling businessman will wish to prepare for and includes information on passport procedures, customs and duties, and world climate conditions.

Table 4.—Kuwait Petroleum Exports

(in million barrels)

	1970	1971	1972	1973	1974	1975	1976
Crude Oil	941.7	1008.9	1070.6[1]	966.0	804.8	652.6	655.6
Kuwait Oil Co.	879.5	946.9	994.8	894.4	736.2	594.1	598.5
Arabian Oil Co.[2]	62.2	62.0	75.6	71.6	68.6	58.5	56.8
Refined products:	154.6	155.0	146.5	148.9	132.7	106.8	147.1
Kuwait Oil Co.[3]	92.8	87.2	76.6	77.5	61.0	38.1	50.9
American Independent Oil Co.	28.6	30.6	29.1	26.8	29.7	26.2	30.8
Kuwait National Petroleum Co.	33.2	37.2	40.8	44.6	42.0	42.5	65.4
TOTAL	1096.3	1163.9	1217.1	1114.9	937.5	759.4	802.7

Source: Ministry of Oil, Government of Kuwait
[1] Including slight exports by the American Independent Oil Co.
[2] Kuwait's share.
[3] Including bunker and liquefied petroleum gas.

projects are the area of greatest uncertainty in projecting future Kuwaiti expenditures, because the government has not reached agreement on the appropriate level of investment.

Other product categories offering opportunities for American business follow.

Computers, Business Equipment and Systems.—Significant growth in U.S. exports of business equipment and systems to Kuwait is forecast for the 1980's. The country's modernization efforts, supported by an expanding business infrastructure, need more of this equipment. Rising labor costs, shortages of skilled workers and professionals in many sectors, and increasing workloads and paper flow are prompting Kuwaiti merchant establishments, as well as governmental agencies, to adopt modern office procedures. Kuwait's continuing role as a regional financial center and a force in the world's financial markets ensures that the number of potential business equipment purchases is both large and growing.

U.S. exports of office equipment and systems to Kuwait totalled $1.2 million in 1976, nearly three times the value of 1975 export sales. The 1977 export figures are estimated at $1.5 million. U.S.-made equipment with good sales potential in Kuwait include: reprographic equipment, both microfilm and microfiche; combination input-output terminals with Arabic c.r.t. or printout capacity, terminal-related accessories; machines used in blueprinting; electronic calculators; electric typewriters; authomated word processing machines, accounting and statistical machines, and parts and components for business equipment.

U.S. export statistics for 1977 show sales of computers and peripheral equipment exceeded $2.5 million, a reflection of the increase in EDP consulting activity and the need to update and replace present facilities. Demand is expected to continue to grow as advanced computer-related equipment is being installed by some government agencies, including those concerned with social security, housing, and public utilities. Concerted market promotion efforts on the part of American firms can realize a sizeable part of the possible $10 million market for EDP hardware, software, and services.

Refrigeration, Chilling and Condensing Equipment.—Reliable, high capacity air conditioning and refrigeration equipment is needed to counteract Kuwait's extreme summertime heat. Of Kuwait's total summertime electrical output, more than 70 percent is needed for air conditioning units. Local firms are extremely interested in acquiring either agency lines or manufacturing licenses and technical assistance in order to compete in the local market.

Since Kuwait imports nearly 100 percent of its food requirements, cold storage facilities on a warehouse and retail level have been developed. Studies are underway to build a 300,000 square meter public cold storage facility—reportedly the first of a series. The continuing growth of Kuwait's nascent food processing and packaging industry will spur on sales in these areas.

In response to Kuwait's development boom in both residential, office, and institutional construction, U.S. export sales in refrigeration, chilling, and condensing equipment increased to almost $70 million in 1977. Housing construction should be tapering off by 1982, when the present projects of the National Housing Authority are due to be finished. The market potential for these product lines should hold rather constant at approximately $50 million during this period. Replacement sales and sales of spare parts will become an increasing component of future sales, however.

Competitive Factors

Competition in Kuwait from traditional sources (Japan, the United Kingdom, West Germany) and increasingly from third world countries (e.g. Korea) is intense, requiring close and continuing cultivation by prospective sellers. The decline in the U.S. market share described above is the result, in part, of the determined effort by these and other suppliers in providing attention to the market, dealer support (technical, advertising, etc.) and after sales service. Business dealings in Kuwait are highly personalized. The company willing to send representatives to Kuwait on a regular basis to meet with its agent and prospective customers has a decided advantage.

Kuwait seeks the best and the latest in technology and equipment for its development program and has the capacity to pay for it. Quality and timely delivery are important factors in procurement decisions and may to some extent offset price differentials. Price is still an important element in such decisions, however, and should be considered carefully by prospective U.S. suppliers in the preparation of bid proposals. Competition for major development projects is intense, but the potential for American companies is excellent because of U.S. technological strength in the more sophisticated industrial fields. U.S. companies also gain from Kuwait's appreciation of the quality of American products and techniques.

Industry Trends

GNP Development

Kuwait has long been one of the more economically prosperous countries in the Near East. Economic expansion was especially marked in 1974 and 1975 following the oil price rise. Kuwait's Gross National Product (GNP) doubled in only 1 year. Since then, the economy has continued to mature at a moderate rate. GDP totaled $12,524 million in FY 1976.[1]

Kuwait's economy is mostly petroleum based. Production of crude oil and natural gas account for approximately 70 percent of GDP, and petroleum refining is the predominant manufacturing industry. Transport, trade, and finance along with services, public administration and defense account for 15 percent and 10 percent

[1] Kuwait's fiscal years 1975 and before ended March 31. FY 1976, a transitional year covering 15 months, ended June 30, 1976. Fiscal years since then end June 30.

respectively of GDP. Industry is presently a relatively small part of the total Kuwaiti economy, and agricultural production is negligible.

Further industrial expansion and diversification to achieve a more balanced economy is a priority objective of the Government of Kuwait. Primary emphasis will, of course, be on power and capital intensive industries to take advantage of Kuwait's cheap energy from gas and its abundant capital. Other economically viable industries capable of producing for either the domestic or export markets are also encouraged. Ownership of these new ventures may be public, private or mixed government/private, and foreign investment is welcomed.

Most industry in Kuwait is located in one of the three major industrial areas—Shuwaikh, Shuaiba, and East Ahnadi. Most of the smaller plants are in the district of Shuwaikh, Kuwait City's western surburb. Heavier industries, including most petroleum-based concerns, are located in Shuaiba, 30 miles south of Kuwait City. The semi-autonomous Shuaiba Area Authority provides integrated infrastructure and facilities for firms relying directly or indirectly on oil or natural gas. The newest zone, East Ahamadi, is near the town and oil harbor of Fahaheel.

Principal Growth Sectors

Crude Oil Production.—Kuwait is a member of the Organization of Petroleum Exporting Countries (OPEC) and the Organization of Arab Petroleum Exporting Countries (OAPEC). Kuwait's production and pricing policies are consistent with the decisions of these groups.

Kuwait is the world's eighth largest producer of crude petroleum. Oil production is carried out by two companies, the Kuwait Oil Company (KOC) and the Arabian Oil Company (AOC). KOC, originally owned by Gulf Oil and British Petroleum, was nationalized in 1975; it produces almost 90 percent of the country's crude oil. AOC, the second largest oil company, operates offshore in the neutral zone divided equally between Kuwait and Saudi Arabia. The Government of Kuwait now owns 60 percent and a Japanese consortium 40 percent of the company.

The Kuwait Ministry of Oil exports the bulk of Kuwait's crude through KOC's facilities. Most is sold in long-term sales agreements directly to foreign governments and to international oil companies. Crude oil production increased steadily until 1972 but has shown a decline since then. The drop reflects the government's desire to limit output to conserve petroleum reserves and the recent reduction in world oil consumption. Production declined in 1977 to about 2 million barrels per day in comparison to 2.15 million barrels per day in 1976.

Petroleum Refining.—Kuwait has three major refineries; the largest at Mina al Ahamadi is run by KOC and is a conventional topping plant with refining capacity at the end of 1976 of 300,000 barrels a day. The KOC also has a refinery at Mina Abdullah which produces 145,000 barrels per day. The third refinery, located in the Shuaiba industrial complex, is owned by the Kuwait National Petroleum Company (KNPC). KNPC, a fully owned government company, markets the refined oil both locally and internationally. Production at the sophisticated Shuaiba facility is 200,000 barrels per day. The majority of the refined oil from all the facilities is exported, since Kuwait's domestic daily requirement is only about 20 thousand barrels.

KNPC industrial facilities, a number of which were completed in 1978, include a 28,000 ton per year lubricating oil blending plant, a sulpher recovery unit and a $110 million hydrocracker unit. In addition, a 250,000 ton per year asphalt (or bitumen) plant is being built for KOC. Several additional refinery projects totaling $1.5 billion are under consideration.

Natural Gas Production.—All of Kuwait's natural gas is presently produced in association with the extraction of crude oil. Known reserves totaled 31.8 billion cubic feet in early 1976, or 1 percent of the world's reserves. The gas is used for reinjection into oil fields, for desalination and distillation of water, and for generation of electric power. In addition, natural gas is used as a raw material in the production of fertilizers and petrochemicals.

Kuwait uses over 70 percent (table 6) of its gas production. In fact, there is growing concern about the amount of gas use, because the supply is dependent upon oil production. With large gas-using projects coming onstream shortly, the country may experience a shortage of natural gas. Also oil production could drop due to economic or political reasons.

Petrochemical Industry.—The petrochemical industry is the most important industrial sector after oil production and refining. The Petrochemical Industries Company (PIC), a wholly owned Government concern, is the main vehicle for production of petrochemicals in Kuwait. Its two fertilizer plants annually produce approximately 1.65 million tons of ammonia. Another PIC company produces chlorine, caustic acid, salt in bulk, table and industrial salt, hydrochloric acid, sodium hydrochloric, and distilled water.

Table 5.—Production of Crude Oil

(in million barrels)

	Kuwait Oil Company (KOC)	American Independent Oil Company (Aminoil)	Arabian Oil Company (AOC)	Total	Total Average Daily Production
1965	791.9	36.5	33.1	861.5	2.36
1966	830.7	29.5	46.5	906.7	2.48
1967	836.7	24.8	50.9	912.4	2.50
1968	886.1	15.3	55.2	956.6	2.61
1969	940.0	12.9	58.8	1,011.7	2.77
1970	998.1	29.9	62.6	1,090.6	2.99
1971	1,067.8	33.3	65.3	1,166.4	3.20
1972	1,097.7	28.9	75.0	1,201.6	3.28
1973	1,004.8	25.8	71.9	1,102.5	3.02
1974	830.7	30.1	68.6	929.4	2.55
1975	671.0	30.3	59.4	760.7	2.08
1976	699.9	30.1	55.8	785.8	2.15

Source: Ministry of Oil, Central Bank of Kuwait, and various oil industry publications.

Table 6.—Production, Use of Natural Gas

(in billion cubic meters)

Year	Gas Produced	Gas Used	Percentage Used to Produced	Used by Companies	Used for Reinjection	Consumed by State public Facilities
1970	570.4	188.0	33.0	90.0	45.3	52.7
1971	643.7	227.5	35.3	94.8	89.5	63.2
1972	647.8	246.8	38.1	95.2	65.9	85.7
1973	581.1	265.1	45.6	101.0	79.0	85.1
1974	466.9	251.4	53.8	94.3	83.2	93.9
1975	382.4	226.0	59.5	79.7	42.2	104.1
1976	395.8	243.8	61.6	89.6	46.7	107.5

Source: Kuwait Ministry of Oil

PIC's potentially most ambitious undertaking is a proposed $300 million aromatics plant, which would make use of naptha produced as a by-product of the oil refineries to produce benzene, ortho-xylene, para-xylene and several other compounds. Despite tentative government approval, the project has experienced numerous delays and is not expected to be tendered until 1980.

Other petrochemical developments include the formation of the Kuwait Melamine Industries Company which intends to produce 150,000 tons per year of melamine. Construction of the plant was expected to begin in 1978. The Government has also approved a $40 million project to build a synthetic rubber plant with a capacity of 42,000 metric tons per year.

Construction materials.—The Kuwait National Industries Company (NIC), owned 51 percent by the government, produces building materials including bricks, cement, asbestos and pretressed concrete. In addition, NIC is a minority shareholder in companies which produce prefabricated buildings, metal pipes and cement.

Expansion of the Kuwait Cement Company's (KCC) facilities was expected to bring total productive capacity to 1 million tons of cement annually by 1978. The company is also studying proposals to produce white cement and manufacture clinker from local raw materials. A significant development for KCC is its entrance in joint venture arrangements with other countries of the Gulf. In Oman, KCC has signed a preliminary agreement with the Sultanate to produce clinker and cement from local raw materials. KCC has also agreed to set up a cement plant in Saudi Arabia with local interests to produce 3 million tons per year.

Other Kuwaiti companies have been formed to produce glass fiber, cement block, plywood, sinks, bathtubs, ceramic tile, sewage pipe, concrete prefabricated building elements, and steel buildings.

Government Role in the Economy

Although Kuwait has a free market economy permitting much scope for private training and industrial activities, the government has a predominant role in almost all aspects of the economy.

Historical factors determined the Government's leading role rather than any dedication to socialist principles. The Government is the channel for the receipt of the large oil export revenues and thus is the primary source of local capital. The Government's functions over the past two decades in investing this income in basic infrastructure development and in redistributing income to private Kuwaiti citizens has been fundamental to the progress of the economy.

As the developer of Kuwait's basic infrastructure, the Government owns and controls directly such important fields as electricity, power, water desalination, communications (including radio and TV), hospitals and other social welfare institutions. To the extent possible, the Government has delegated control of some of these operations to decentralized authorities, controlled by both public and private directors.

The Government also participates directly or indirectly in other commercial and industrial activities, often in participation with private capital partners. Among these important enterprises, are the Kuwait Foreign Trading, Contracting, and Investment Corporation; the Kuwait National Industries Company; the United Fisheries Company of Kuwait and the Kuwait National Petroleum Company.

Another major function of the Government is its extensive social welfare programs including free education, health care and housing subsidies for low income groups. Through the Kuwait Supply Company, the Government implements a price subsidy program for basic food items such as rice, sugar, edible oils and milk. In addition, direct subsidies are provided to producers and importers of cement, dairy products, flour, sand, limestone, iron rods, and live animals.

The Government does not engage in state trading and most import trade is in the hands of private traders who compete through tenders for government contracts, which account for a high portion of the country's total imports. The Government exercises certain price control powers on imported commodities, principally basic foodstuffs and medicinal products.

Government agencies are also responsible for much of the basic scientific and economic research being undertaken in Kuwait.

Social Infrastructure

Education.—The illiteracy rate for children between 10 and 14 is 8.5 percent; the rate for older citizens is 50 percent.

Children of Kuwaiti citizens and of journalists and teachers are legally entitled to free primary and secondary education in Kuwait. However, in practice the State provides free education to all children living in Kuwait. About 40 percent of the 202,000 students enrolled in the state schools in 1975–76 were children of expatriates; more than 50 percent of the university students were expatriates or children of expatriates. At the university level, a number of Kuwaitis, particularly male students, study overseas, usually in the United States or Cairo.

The Government has allocated funds to build 180 primary and secondary schools, a number of which were completed in 1978. Funds are also earmarked for expansion of Kuwait University to accommodate 15,000 students. In general, construction will be done by local contractors, but school supplies and equipment will be imported.

Public Health.—Kuwait introduced free health service in the early 1960's. Although hospital admissions increased from 41,000 in 1964 to over 100,000 in 1976, only the four new hospitals currently under construction have been built since 1963. The present construction is part of a program to provide five hospital beds for every 1,000 people by 1979, which would double the existing hospital bed capacity to 6,000. In addition to the four major city hospitals nearing completion, the Amiri Hospital, a 390 bed hospital to be built by the Ministry of Public Works, a 500 bed military hospital, and new hospitals to concentrate on fever cases, pediatrics, geriatric diseases, and orthopedic medicine, will be built. Other projects under consideration are orthopedic, chest diseases, maternity, geriatric, and psychiatric clinics.

The construction of new facilities will exacerbate the serious shortage of medical staff, resulting in the need to recruit 300 doctors and 2,000 nurses over the next several years. Kuwait is looking toward the United Kingdom, India, South Korea, Egypt, the Sudan and several other nations for recruits.

Recreation Facilities.—The Touristic Enterprises Company (TEC), a wholly owned government organization, and the Ministry of Public Works are undertaking projects to provide the country with recreation facilities. TEC has employed a Korean firm to assist in developing the archeological site on Failaka Island into a tourist resort. The firm will erect chalets and a ferry port on the Island; supermarkets, restaurants, swimming pools, a hotel and an amusement park are also planned. In addition, TEC is planning to build chalets and other facilities near Mina Abdulla on the southern coast and several small amusement parks in other parts of the country. The Ministry of Public Works has several projects under consideration including a thematic amusement park, an aquarium, a zoo and a national theater.

The Government has authorized a number of private local firms to either expand or build new hotel facilities. The Sheraton, Hilton and Messilah Beach hotels plan to add 150–200 rooms each to their present facilities. Hilton Inn, Hyatt, Marriott, Holiday Inn, Intercontinental and Meridien hotel chains plan to build new hotels in Kuwait over the next several years.

Transportation, Utilities and Communications

Shipping from the United States

Two American flag carriers provide regular liner service to Kuwait from U.S. East, Gulf and Pacific Coasts. The American President Lines, 1950 Franklin St., Oakland, California 94612, telephone: (415) 271-8000. provides container service from the West Coast, Gulf Coast and Pacific. Waterman Steamship Corporation, 120 Wall Street, New York, New York 10005, telephone: (202) 747-8550 provides lash barge service from the Gulf and East Coasts. There are regular sailings to Kuwait from the East coast of the United States by Eastcoast-and Gulf-based shipping lines on a monthly basis. There is no conference agreement for this trade route but shippers operate under the "8900 Lines" rate agreement.

The sailing time from East coast ports to Kuwait around the tip of Africa is normally 30 to 40 days. This time is reduced by at least 5–6 days when using the Suez Canal and possibly by even more time for vessels with less stops before Kuwait.

Information on air cargo to Kuwait may be obtained from the New York office of Kuwait's wholly government-owned airline. The address is Kuwait Airways, 30 Rockefeller Plaza, New York, New York 10020.

Port Facilities and Shipping.

Kuwait has four ports capable of handling cargo. Shaweikh, adjacent to Kuwait City, is the largest and most important; the port has 18 wharves with a maximum depth of 33 feet. The other general cargo port, Shuaiba, has five wharves with depths between 22 and 34 feet. It serves as the export facility for the Shuaiba industrial area and as the off-loading area for high priority government construction projects. Mina al-Ahmadi is the crude oil and gas terminal for the Kuwait Oil Company; it has 16 wharves varying in depth between 44 and 58 feet. Completed expansion of the port of Doha has eased the congestion at Shuwaikh by serving Kuwait's fishing fleet and barge traffic.

The port congestion experienced in late 1976 and 1977 has been eased by increased storage fees, expanded work force and mechanized cargo handling, improved management, and streamlined customs procedures. The waiting period for off-loading ships has been reduced to several days at most.

The shipping industry in Kuwait is heavily influenced by Government participation via loans and other forms of financial support. Three major shipping lines, all of which have significant government participation, operate out of Kuwait. The Government owns 49 percent of the Kuwait Oil Tankers Company (KOTC) which operates crude oil tankers. The company has 10 crude tankers in operation with a dryweight capacity of over 2 million tons; additional product and LPG tankers are on order.

The Arab Maritime Petroleum Transport Company (AMPTC), an Arab multinational crude tanker company affiliated with the Organization of Arab Petroleum Exporting Countries, has its headquarters in Kuwait. AMPTC has eight crude tankers in operation with a dryweight capacity exceeding 2 million tons and two LPG ships on order for delivery in 1978-79. The United Arab Shipping Company (UASC) is a joint venture shipping line owned by Iran, Kuwait, Saudi Arabia, Bahrain, Qatar and the United Arab Emirates. The company was expected to have 62 ships in operation by the end of 1978.

The only private shipping firm is the Kuwait Livestock and Transport Company which operates four 18,000 gross ton vessels.

Road Transport

Land movement along the coast is helped by a good highway system, which extends from Saudi Arabia and the Neutral Zone partition line to Mina al-Ahmadi and northwest through Kuwait City. It then proceeds west to Al Jahara and north across the desert into Iraq and the city of Basra. The country's already modern road system is being expanded by an ambitious $1 billion plus motorways program. The U.S. Federal Highway Administration is providing consultative services for this program on a fully reim-

bursable basis. More than 335,000 cars are registered in Kuwait and the number is growing rapidly.

Air Transport

In addition to Kuwait Airways, the national airline, Kuwait is served by Gulf Air, Saudi Arabian Airlines, Iran National Airlines British Airways, Air France, KLM, and Lufthansa German Airlines. Kuwait's International Airport is currently being expanded and will be able to handle 4 million passengers and 30,000 tons of cargo per year when completed in 1979.

Utilities

Demand for both power and water has grown in the past decade, reflecting expansion of Kuwait's industrial and social sectors. Kuwait now ranks third in the world in per-capita energy and water consumption. The demand for power rose 20-25 percent annually in the early 1970's, then slowed to approximately 12-15 percent, and is expected to level out at 7-8 percent by 1980. The government is currently implementing plans to expand electric capacity from 1,718 MW in 1977 to 2,500 MW by 1980.

Ten percent of Kuwait's water supply comes from a brackish water underground reservoir near the Iraqi boarder and is used basically to add "taste" to the distilled water coming out of the tap. Production at the reservoir is being phased down due to depletion and increased salinity. The balance of the country's water supply is dependent upon desalination plants. Since the demand for fresh water is growing at about 20 percent annually, the Ministry of Electricity and Water plans to increase the capacity of its desalination plants to 220 million gallons daily by 1980 compared to estimated capacity in 1978 of 100 million gallons per day.

Communications

Despite good telephone, telex, and cable systems, facilities have not been able to keep abreast of demand. Businesses or residences in a newly developed suburb often wait 2 to 3 years for a telephone due to a shortage of lines and equipment. Therefore, the Ministry of Communications is modernizing and enlarging its telecommunications links.

Kuwait has two earth satellite systems and good direct dial telephone communications to many parts of the Near East, Europe, and the United States. Kuwait may add a third ground station when a satellite employing a new, multi-channel system is launched.

Trade Regulations

Trade Policy

Dependent on imports for most of its foodstuffs, consumer goods, and capital goods, Kuwait maintains a liberal trade policy. Tariff duties are minimal, and very few products are subject to administrative control. Restrictive measures have been implemented only to insure that the profits on foreign trade accrue to Kuwaiti nations.

Kuwait has bilateral trade agreements with several Near East countries but no bilateral payments agreements. It is a party to the Arab League Trade and Payments Agreements, which accord preferential rates to specified products of Arab League member states. Kuwait is also a signatory to the General Agreement on Tariffs and Trade and receives preferential tariff treatment from British Commonwealth countries. There is a general prohibition on relations with South Africa, Rhodesia, and Portugal; Kuwait participates in the Arab League's boycott of Israel.

Import Regulations

Kuwait does not permit the import of alcoholic beverages; pork products or foodstuffs containing pork; industrial and medical oxygen gas; spiral weld pipe of 6 to 48 inches outer diameter; medicines containing cobalt salt; or used trucks and buses which use gasoline and are more than 10 years old. The Kuwait Flour Mills Company is the only firm permitted to import flour and wheat. The Ministry of Public Health must issue a special license before insecticides may be imported and given written consent before ethyl alcohol, or any substance containing any percentage of ethyl alcohol, may be imported into the country.

Otherwise, there are no administrative restrictions or prohibitions on imports. Specific licenses are not required for individual import transactions; however, commercial imports may be affected only by Kuwaiti nationals or firms (i.e., a firm at least 51 percent Kuwaiti owned) licensed by the Ministry of Commerce and Industry to engage in import trade. For the most part, open general import licenses are issued to well established importers who have been operating in a variety of import fields. Others who have confined their operations to a few com-modities are granted licenses to import specific goods. Licenses are normally valid for a period of 1 year but are renewable.

Import Tariff System

Kuwait imposes a flat 4 percent ad valorem duty on the c.i.f. value of most imported goods. Goods transshipped through Kuwait are subject to a 2 percent ad valorem duty. Exempt from customs duty are items imported by government departments and oil companies, a number of imports used by local industries and specified foodstuffs and flour mills and ice machines.

The Government accords "infant industry" treatment to several local products. These products, charged with a duty of 10 percent—15 percent, include biscuits, macaroni, bitumen for insulation, steel furniture, wooden household furniture, certain cast iron products, industrial paints, chemical detergents and shampoo, motor car batteries, pipe joints, aerosal products, steel wool and certain aluminum and plastic products. There are no customs surcharges or other taxes on imports.

All international trade transactions which involve weights and measures must use only the metric system as a unit of standards.

Information regarding Kuwait's duties applicable to specific products may be obtained free of charge from the Commerce Action Group for the Near East, Industry and Trade Administration, U.S. Department of Commerce, Washington, D.C. 20230 or from any Department of Commerce District Office. Inquiries should contain a complete product description.

Shipping Documents

A commercial invoice, certificate of origin, bill of lading, packing list, steamship certificate and insurance certificate must be included with each Kuwait shipment. All the documents must be certified by a stipulated chamber of commerce (see below). An officer of the Kuwait Embassy must legalize the document, such as the letter of credit, unless the Kuwaiti purchaser has specifically included a phrase stating that the certification is unnecessary. The documents should be in duplicate when legalization is not required; otherwise they must be in triplicate.

The exporter may use the ordinary form of commercial invoice. The invoice should include an accurate description of the goods and give the weight (in kilos) for each type of good as well as the quantities and the value. The invoice must show the name of the carrying vessel (if by sea), give the name of the processor or manufacturer (in the case of manufactured goods) and be signed by the exporter or supplier. The certificate of origin must list the country (ies) of the product's origin, the name of the manufacturer or processor and the name of the exporter. There are no special requirements for the bill of lading; however, Kuwaiti authorities emphasize that it must state whether the freight is prepaid or collectable. Two original copies must be given to the shipping companies.

Kuwaiti law requires certification by the U.S.-Arab Chamber of Commerce, New York, for goods manufactured or exported by companies operating in New York State; the Mid-American-Arab Chamber of Commerce, Inc., Chicago, for products exported from the state of Illinois; the American-Arab Chamber of Commerce, Houston, for products exported from Texas, or the U.S. Arab Chamber of Commerce (Pacific), Inc. for California products. Companies exporting from other parts of the country may use any authorized chamber of commerce. (Addresses of the Chambers may be found at the end of this publication.)

Live animals may be imported only with a veterinary certificate. Animal products require a health certificate and, for all meats, a statement that slaughtering has been conducted in conformity with Islamic law. Pork is prohibited, except for non-Muslim consumption. Sanitary certificates are not required for the import of plants and plant products. Pharmaceutical products must be registered in Kuwait in compliance with Ministry of Health regulations.

Documentation requirements for shipments by parcel post are subject to the same customs regulations as imports in general. Parcel post shipments are turned over to the Kuwaiti customs. The exporter must obtain a local delivery order from the Post Office and present it, together with an invoice or customs declaration, if available, to the consignee upon payment of the customs duty.

As a member of the Universal Postal Union, Kuwait accepts and delivers packages of a maximum gross weight of 44 pounds, 42 inches in length or 72 inches in length and girth combined. Group shipments are not permitted. Parcels may be insured up to $200 but may not be registered. Insured packages must be sealed. Parcel post packages must be accompanied by one customs declaration tag (Form 2966–A), giving exact details of the contents and quantity. In addition, a dispatch note (Form 2972), properly filled out,

and an international parcel-post sticker (Form 2922) are required. A U.S. Shippers Export Declaration must be enclosed if the value of the shipment exceeds $250 or an export license is required.

Dutiable articles in letters or packages prepaid at the letter rate of postage may be sent to Kuwait up to a weight limit of 4 pounds (or single books weighing up to 11 pounds) provided there is a green label on the address side. (Form 2976), giving exact details of the contents and indicating that it is subject to customs inspection at destination. The length, breadth and thickness combined should not exceed 36 inches—the greater length being 24 inches. The customs declaration (Form 2976–A) must be enclosed inside the package if the sender does not describe the contents on the outside.

The maximum weight limit on "small packets" to Kuwait is 2 pounds. The dimensions for small packets are the same as for letters and letter packages.

Samples and Advertising

Advertising materials and samples are admitted free of duty if sent in packages which both describe the advertising nature of the contents and identify the sender. Material considered to be in excess of reasonable requirements will be subject to normal customs duty.

Advance Rulings on Classification

Advance rulings on customs classification are unnecessary, since almost all imports into Kuwait are subject to one simple ad valorem duty. The Director of Customs occasionally makes a ruling on whether or not a given shipment is for the account of the Government or oil company or for the account of a private contractor. All such rulings by the Director are considered final.

Fines and Penalties

The usual penalty for importing prohibited goods, refusal to present documents, or evasion of payment of duty is confiscation of the goods in question. Each case, however, is subject to an individual decision by the Director of Customs. In some cases, the consignee is fined while in the more serious cases the goods may be confiscated and the guilty persons turned over to the Kuwait authorities for judicial action.

Marking and Labeling

An Amiri Decree, published in the official

gazette on July 3, 1977, established that all imported packaged and canned foodstuffs must have a printed sticker affixed listing, in Arabic, the contents of the package, its characteristics, the date of manufacture and the date of its expiration. (The expiration date has been eliminated on food products unaffected by climate conditions, such as dry milk and cereals.) The sticker may be placed over the regular label. The Kuwait Municipality will be in charge of enforcement of the decree. Further information may be obtained from the Kuwait Municipality Food Division, P.O. Box 10, Safat, Kuwait.

Containers containing fats and oils should bear the name of the factory or its proprietor, address of the factory or its proprietor, name of the plant from which the fat or oil was extracted, net weight of the contents and degree of goodness. If the oil is mixed, the container should have the words "Mixed Oil" with the name and proportions of oils used.

A high standard of export packing is essential because of the long sea voyage, the high temperatures which are experienced for most of the year, and the likelihood of transshipment.

Import Prohibitions

The Government of Kuwait prohibits imports from South Africa, Rhodesia, and Israel. It participates in the Arab League boycott against Israel and to the secondary boycott against third-country firms found to have certain economic relationships with Israel. Accordingly, it is possible that at some stage of a transaction with Kuwait, a firm will be asked to participate in a restrictive trade practice or boycott.

Pursuant to section 3(5) of the Export Administration Act of 1969 (the Act), as amended by PL 95-52 (The Export Administration Amendments of 1977), it is the policy of the United States (a) to oppose restrictive trade practices or boycotts fostered or imposed by foreign countries against other countries friendly to the United States, and (b) to encourage and, in specified cases, to require United States persons engaged in the export of articles, materials, supplies, or information to refuse to take actions, including furnishing information or entering into or implementing agreements, which have the effect of furthering or supporting such restrictive trade practices or boycotts. Implementing regulations were issued by the Department of Commerce on January 18, 1978 (15 C.F.R., Part 369 et. seq.).

The receipt of any request to participate in a restrictive trade practices or boycott *must be* reported to the Department of Commerce, in accordance with Section 369.6 of the above-cited regulations. The necessary forms, DIB-621, may be obtained from the local district offices of the U.S. Department of Commerce.

The U.S. Government, by furnishing information and assistance to U.S. firms directly involved, has attempted to minimize the adverse impact on U.S. trade of foreign boycotts and other restrictive trade practices. In addition to reporting such requests as noted above, firms confronted with boycott problems may wish to discuss them with the Commerce Action Group for the Near East, U.S. Department of Commerce, Washington, D.C. 20230 (telephone: 202-377-5767).

Distribution and Sales Channels

Major Marketing Areas, Distribution Centers

The city of Kuwait, which is located on the southern shore of Kuwait Bay, is the commercial and marketing center of the country. The suburbs of Salmiyah and Hawalli, as well as the satellite towns, such as Ahmadi and Fahaheel, have also become increasingly important retail and service centers. The government ministries, major trading houses and the banking community are clustered around the old "suq" or bazaar in Kuwait City and constitute the nerve center of the country.

Distribution Practices

Any American firm wishing to sell in Kuwait must adhere to Kuwait Commercial Law (Law No 2/1961) and do so through an agent or distributor. This representative must be a Kuwaiti national or a company with at least 51 percent Kuwaiti ownership. Serious consideration should be given to the selection of a representative; whenever possible, it should be done on the basis of a personal visit to Kuwait.

The practice of appointing exclusive representatives is generally followed in Kuwait. American firms should avoid assigning one regional agent to cover the entire Middle East and should deal directly through a local Kuwaiti establishment. American firms should also take care to see that their agent is not handling competitive lines.

Termination of agency or distributor relationships can be tedious and damaging to a company's reputation. Therefore, a thorough investigation of a potential agent should be conducted before a final agreement is signed.

Nearly all Kuwaiti importers prefer to receive quotations from the United States and most other countries on a cost, insurance and freight or c and f basis, Kuwait. Of the two, merchants tend to choose c and f since it allows them to arrange insurance with a local company. A few merchants who operate their own charter vessels and handle bulk shipments prefer to deal on an f.o.b. basis.

Most Kuwaiti firms still deal on a nonconfirmed irrevocable Letter of Credit basis. Roughly 70–80 percent of all shipments from Europe and about 85 percent of all transactions involving the United States contain this type of payment terms. Sight drafts and usance drafts are used less extensively in orders involving construction materials, clothing items, and foodstuffs. Most payment drafts are made for 60–90 day periods although in more competitive lines, such as consumer electronics, longer periods are extended. In general there has been a recent trend toward more liberal credit terms. The Japanese, for example, occasionally deal on a 180-day payment basis while the French offer lower interest rates for financing purposes. U.S. firms seeking a long-term marketing position in Kuwait should be prepared to extend every possible advantage to their Kuwaiti dealer.

Lower product prices reflecting recent dollar devaluations are one way in which U.S. exporters can compete more effectively on price-elastic goods and services.

Wholesale and Retail Channels

Kuwait is almost totally reliant on imports for the supply of consumer and industrial products. As a result, a well-developed commercial sector presently exists in the country. The leading merchant families were active in Kuwait and the Gulf long before oil was discovered. They have paralyed Kuwait's fabulous oil wealth into dozens of large, modern trading houses, many of them with branches throughout the region. Some of these firms have turnover amounting to hundreds of millions of dollars per year. A few could be termed "mini-conglomerates." Many of them hire Western and Arab personnel fully conversant with the most modern marketing techniques.

Most Kuwaiti firms consist of two main divisions: trading and contracting. The former deals primarily with the stocking and sale of consumer and industrial items on a retail or tender-purchase basis; the latter division is exclusively concerned with bidding on government or oil company tenders for the construction or installation of buildings and facilities. At the present time, a well defined wholesale network does not exist except for foodstuffs and textiles. This reflects the common preference of Kuwaiti merchants to act as exclusive agents and, at the same time, their dislike for dealing through middlemen. A typical major merchant establishment will consist of a downtown retail showroom located along the main shipping street of Kuwait City and an industrial warehouse in Shuwaikh. Branch showrooms are appearing in increasing numbers in Kuwait's expanding suburbs. The number of department stores is rapidly expanding.

Retail pricing of goods and services reflects Kuwait's dependence on outside imports as well as the traditional open market economy. In essence, a mark-up system prevails. On essential items such as foodstuffs, a mark-up factor of 5–20 percent above landed costs is common. Nonessential, fastmoving items are subject to an increase of about 25 to 50 percent while the mark-up on luxury items may range from 75 to 150 percent. Increased competition in the form of new products and/or new firms entering the market is beginning to exert a downward pressure on these mark-up margins, particularly in consumer product lines. In an effort to curb a recent rise in the cost of living, the Government intervened in the market in mid-1972 and fixed prices on a variety of foodstuffs and medicines. Among the food items on the list are cheese, powdered milk, corn oil, tea, rice, and sugar. A list showing the complete schedule of price controls is available at the Ministry of Commerce and Industry, P.O. Box 2944, Kuwait.

Consumer Financing

No formalized system of consumer credit or installation buying has yet been established in Kuwait. However, one of the largest credit houses in the Middle East is housed here. Yusuf Ahmad Alghanim and Sons, the local General Motors agent, sells 70 percent of its 15,000 vehicle volume on credit, and the company itself provides the consumer financing. The company regards its credit operation as so vital a marketing tool that it has established additional credit lines with international lending institutions. The other automobile and construction machinery agencies are beginning to follow Alghamin's lead. Despite these trends, the prevalent rule is "pay as you go."

Franchising and Licensing

U.S. firms should not overlook new techniques

such as licensing in an effort to link up American know-how with Kuwaiti capital to respond to the new technical requirements of established industries. Similarly the outlook for franchising appears very promising. A growing number of private Kuwaiti individuals and firms are exploring investment possibilities in service industries. They have been particularly interested in franchising services sold by U.S. firms working in the fast food field. The same care used in identifying a potential agent should be used in selecting a licensee.

Government Tendering Procedures

Basic tendering regulations are detailed under the Public Tenders Ordinance (Law No. 37/1964). The order established a central ordinance Tenders Committee (CTC) consisting of representatives of the Ministry of Finance, the Ministry of Commerce and Industry, the Ministry of Public Works, the client ministry for which the project has been tendered and six representatives appointed by the Council of Ministers.

The tender regulations apply specifically to the Ministry of Electricity and Water, the Ministry of Communications and the Ministry of Public Works, which is the principal construction supervisor of the Kuwait Government. Other entities such as the Shauiba Area Authority, the National Housing Authority, the Ministry of Defense, the oil sector and the private sector are not subject to the regulations, although they often adhere to them.

Invitations to tender usually are issued by the CTC and published in Kuwait's Official Gazette, Kuwait Al Youm. However, the law permits the limitation of tender issuance to companies listed by the client government agency. The CTC receives and awards tenders for construction and supply contracts. Tenderers must be Kuwaiti citizens or companies or foreign firms represented by a Kuwaiti agent or joint-venture partner. Contractors seeking public works contracts must be prequalified by the CTC to undertake a project of the kind being tendered. The award of the contract must be made to the lowest bidder unless the bid is determined to be unreasonable or the Council of Ministers decides to make the award to a higher bidder at the request of the CTC.

Regulations for bid and performance guarantees apply by law only to the civilian ministries. However, they also are widely used by the Ministry of Defense and National Authority. Kuwait practice normally calls for a 90-day bid bond of up to 2 percent and a 5–10 percent performance bond.

An advance payment of 15 percent of the value of equipment will be made to the contractor against a bank guarantee when he shows a letter of intent to purchase the necessary equipment. An additional 65 percent will be paid when the equipment is imported, and the remainder is paid on completion of the contract.

Further information on Kuwait's contracting procedures can be found in "An Introduction to Contract Procedures in the Near East and North Africa" prepared by the Commerce Department. It can be obtained from the Superintendent of Documents, Government Printing Office, Washington, D.C. at a cost of $2.20. Checks should be made payable to Superintendent of Documents.

Regulations Governing Commercial Activity

All Kuwaiti firms, as well as all non-Kuwaiti business organizations having agents in Kuwait are required to be listed in the Commercial Register which is maintained by the Registrar of the Ministry of Commerce and Industry. Names, dates of the start of operations, addresses of head and branch offices, and business backgrounds of the owners of firms are among the basic items required for registration. By government regulation, a firm wishing to do business in Kuwait must also register with the Kuwait Chamber of Commerce and Industry. No company is allowed to bid on government tenders unless it is registered with the Chamber of Commerce and Industry. Non-Kuwaiti firms are not permitted to submit bids directly to the Ministries, but must do so through a registered Kuwait agent. Consulting firms, however, must deal directly with the Kuwait Planning Board and not through an agent.

A municipality registration must also be obtained if a firm plans to open an office in Kuwait town.

Advertising/Market Research

Advertising is being used more in Kuwait due to the increasing sophistication of Kuwait's consumers and professionalism of local advertising agencies. Listed below are the major types of advertising facilities in Kuwait.

Press.—Newspaper advertising is still the principal publicity medium. The five major Arabic languages dailies have a net circulation of 115,000, the larger of which are the *As-Siyasse* at P.O. Box 2270, Kuwait, Kuwait and the *Al Qabas* of P.O. Box 21800 Shuwaikh, Kuwait. The two English newspapers, the *Daily News* at P.O. Box 695, Shuwaikh, Kuwait and the *Kuwait Times* at P.O. Box 1301, Fahed Al Salem

Street, Kuwait, have a total circulation of approximately 20,000. All newspapers are printed in offset at eight columns to the page. The centimeter columnar rates range from $10 to $12 for the front page with interior pages costing from $3.50 to $5.00.

The eight weekly Arabic language magazines cater to different readerships ranging from political analysis to sports. Their net circulation totals 171,000, the most popular being Al Nahda and Al Taliah. Their respective Kuwait addresses are P.O. Box 695 Safat, Kuwait, and P.O. Box 1082 Safat, Kuwait. The advertising charge for a color spread on the cover ranges from $250 to $1050; charges for black and white advertising on inside pages are $50 to $350 depending on the size of the advertisement and the magazine circulation.

The Kuwait Chamber of Commerce and Industry prints a monthly bulletin, which publishes, free of charge, notices from foreign firms. Interested firms should write to the Secretary of the Kuwait Chamber of Commerce and Industry, Majed Bader Jamal Uddin, P.O. Box 775, Kuwait. Full details about the goods and services involved and the terms offered should be included.

Movie Theaters.—The 10 cinemas in Kuwait had a total attendance of 5.3 million in 1976. They are owned and managed by the government owned National Cinema Company which screens commercials prior to and between the feature firms and main attractions. The rate for 30-second film spots varies from $70 to $140; 60-second spots cost between $125 and $160. Slide advertisements range from $22 to $28 each.

Television.—There are 375,000 television sets in Kuwait but only one channel, which is in color and operated by the Ministry of Information. The channel's broadcast range includes Bahrain, Basra (Iraq), and the Eastern Province of Saudi Arabia. The government was expected to open a second channel in 1978. Advertising rates vary depending on the time and programming, with rates highest at the presentation of popular sport events. They range from as low as $125 for a 10-second spot to as high as $1,130 for a 90-second spot.

Billboard and Poster Advertising.—Billboards and posters are used, on a limited basis, to promote products. New electric billboards, capable of programmed advertisements are being introduced and may prove more successful. The Kuwait Municipality sets the charges for the posters and billboards.

Special Exhibits.—In order to capitalize on consumer interest in new products, several merchants have successfully held single product line exhibitions at one of the local hotels. These are prepared in coordination with the firm's foreign partner who arranges the display of the products or equipment. A license from the Ministry of Commerce and Industry must be obtained by the local agent which often takes a number of months to be issued.

Advertising Agencies.—There are several well-established and well-staffed advertising agencies serving both Kuwait and the Gulf states. A number have affiliates or parent companies in Beirut and Cairo. The largest Kuwait advertising agency, Kawmia, had in 1976 billings of $3 million. Many local companies retain the services of such firms on a full-time basis while a few have formed their own marketing and advertising departments to promote their products and corporate image.

Market Research.—Market research analysis and new product testing have gradually evolved in Kuwait. Several new market consulting and research firms have entered the market, responding to a widespread perception among the business community that better marketing tools are now needed. Leading advertising and marketing companies include: Kaumai, P.O. Box 23915, Safat, Kuwait; Grant Advertising and Association (Group) P.O. Box 36546 Ras, Kuwait; McKann Erickson Advertising, Puli-Graphies, P.O. Box 1035, Safat, Kuwait; Mass Consultants, P.O. Box 2064, Kuwait; and Pan Arab Computer Co., P.O. Box 921, Kuwait. The latter only conducts market surveys.

Business Information Source.—The Kuwait Chamber of Commerce and Industry (P.O. Box 775, Safat, Kuwait) through its monthly bulletin, frequent guest lecturers, and well-stocked library and files provides up-to-date business information and keeps its members abreast of domestic and foreign market developments.

The Kuwaiti Contractors Union (P.O. Box 5712 Kuwait), whose members include nearly all of the country's construction firms, is an excellent source of information on what is happening Kuwait's booming construction market.

Credit

Availability of Credit

There is an abundance of capital in Kuwait. The financial sector consists of a central bank, seven commercial banks, three specialized banks, at least 25 investment companies, 20 insurance companies and a number of foreign exchange dealers and stock brokers.

Banking

The Central Bank of Kuwait was established in 1969 to supervise the banking system, formulate and regulate credit policies, secure the stability of Kuwait's currency and insure free convertibility of the currency into foreign currency. The bank has recently begun to monitor the changes and growth of the financial system, requiring statistical reporting from the banking system and other financial institutions.

The foreign exchange rate is determined by the Central Bank using the performance of a weighted basket of the six major currencies Kuwait uses to carry out its international transactions. The official parity rate is 0.2710 Kuwait dinars to US$1 or KD1 to US$3.69. The dinar is divided into 1000 fils.

The government limits the number of commercial banks in the country and, until recently, allowed only local ownership. The law has recently been amended to permit other Arabs to secure part ownership in a Kuwaiti bank. The seven commercial banks have over 92 branches and include the Burgan Bank which opened its doors in 1977, and the Bank of Kuwait and Bahrain which opened in 1978. The others, the Commercial Bank of Kuwait, the National Bank of Kuwait, the Gulf Bank, the Al-Ahli Bank of Kuwait, and the Bank of Kuwait and the Middle East, have been in existance for some time and are among the largest in the Near East. Four are owned by the private sector and the other two, the Burgan Bank and Bank of Kuwait and the Middle East, are jointly held by the government and the private sector. The Bank of Kuwait and Bahrain is owned by private Bahraini interests and Kuwaiti public and private entities.

A large portion of the total resources of Kuwaiti commercial banks is invested in foreign assets, particularly negotiable deposits and short term certificates of deposit. In Kuwait the principal lending operations of the banks are short term financing of foreign trade (mostly imports) and local business operations. On November 17, 1976, the Commercial Law was amended to allow Commercial Banks, subject to approval by the Ministry of Finance, and institutions to vary their interest rates within a determined range. Central Bank Resolution Number 1 of 1977 with an effective date of February 20, 1977, established a ceiling of 10 percent on loans

of Kuwaiti Dinars; 7 percent for short term credit on trade, manufacturing and construction activities; and 8½ percent for all other short term loans. Minimum interest rates on saving deposits were raised to 4½ percent while rates on time deposits are negotiable subject to a 10 percent ceiling.

Specialized banks include the Industrial Bank of Kuwait (see industrial sector), the Savings and Credit Bank and the Kuwait Real Estate Bank. The principal function of the former is to finance industrial projects and of the latter two banks to finance real-estate activities. The Savings Bank also lends money for industrial and agricultural purposes. All the banks are permitted to participate in foreign investment opportunities.

Stock Market

Thirty-eight firms are listed on the stock exchange, 22 in the private sector and 16 in the joint public/private sector; only 34 trade their stocks. A primitive trading floor was opened in April 1977 but most trading occurs in brokers' offices. U.S. firms planning to go into a joint venture with a local firm will find the stock market of little financial assistance.

Investment Companies

The investment companies in Kuwait operate both as closed corporations and as shareholding firms. Most were established after 1974. The best known and only ones publicly listed on the stock exchange are the Kuwait International Investment Company (KIIC), the Kuwait Investment Company, (KIC) and the Kuwait Foreign Trading, Contracting and Investment Company (KTRCIC). The latter two firms are owned respectively 50 percent and 80 percent by the Kuwait Government. In 1976 the three firms accounted for 92.5 percent of the total assets and 97.3 percent of the total capital and reserves of all investment companies. The Government owns 2 percent of the Kuwait Real Estate Investment Consortium. Eight other firms, including KIIC, KFTCIC, KIC, and the Kuwait Hotels Company, hold equal equity in the company. It was established in 1974 to coordinate real estate investment overseas and is an example of government and private cooperation.

Investment in Kuwait

Government Policy on Investment

Kuwait's vast oil wealth endows it with one o

the highest levels of per capita income in the world. Constantly increasing income from oil has resulted in a far reaching program of social welfare. The Government also actively encourages the investment of more of the country's wealth in new industries within Kuwait in order to broaden the economic base beyond its natural concentration in petroleum and petro-chemicals.

In addition to providing legal incentives to private investment and financing necessary infrastructure facilities, the Government uses joint participation with private capital as an important means of promoting the development of new industrial enterprises. From the private investor's viewpoint, government participation not only provides financial resources but also opens the door to future contracts in the public sector, which is the major consumer of the nation's output of services. The Government, either directly or through its various shareholding entities, is a partner in some of the country's most important industrial enterprises.

Industrial investments are governed by the National Industries Law of 1965 and its 1971 amendment, whereby approved industries may be accorded the protection of increased tariff rates and restrictions on imports of competing products. Several industries are now benefiting from such protection (e.g., certain woodwork, tiles, paints and furniture). Approved industries may also be granted exemption from customs duties on their raw material and equipment imports.

A license issued by the Ministry of Commerce and Industry is required for new processing, manufacturing, blending, assembling, or packing industries. License applications are judged on the basis of the economic feasibility of the venture and its compatibility with Kuwait's social and economic needs. This law stipulates that 25 percent of the employees of each industry must be Kuwaitis, but this requirement may be waived by the Ministry if sufficient numbers of qualified Kuwaiti applicants are not available. It also gives the Government a nominal measure of control over the activity of industries to assure sound labor management and fiscal practices, and minimum standards of quality in the products of the industry.

The Law of Commercial Companies (Law No. 15/1960) prescribes that non-Kuwaitis may not establish a business in Kuwait except in joint participation with Kuwaiti nations or firms. It limits the foreign participation in any business established in Kuwait to 49% of the total capital of the joint business, whether a partnership or

share company. Foreign firms establishing a branch in Kuwait must do so through a Kuwaiti agent. Bank are dealt with under a separate law. Non-Kuwaits may now own real property.

Subject to these limitations, foreign capital is welcomed both because it tends to bring with it needed technical and managerial experience and because it provides access to international markets. Foreign capital is accorded equal treatment with local capital. Kuwait affords the foreign investor the climate of an open market with well-developed financial and investment institutions. In addition, the Government offers opportunities to exporters of the design, engineering, and construction services required by its extensive welfare program which includes housing, schools, hospitals, and other health and municipal facilities.

Forms of Business Organization

The following five different types of company organizations are authorized under Kuwait's Law of Commercial Companies:

1. A General Partnership formed by two or more persons under a particular name to carry on commercial business. Its members are bound jointly and severally for its liabilities, which are covered by the entire assets of each member.

2. A Limited Partnership comprised of two membership groups: active members who manage the company and are bound jointly and severally for its obligations, the liability of each extending to his private assets, and inactive members who simply provide the company with capital, the liability of each being limited to the sum of his investment.

3. A Joint Venture, which is defined as a commercial company, not a legal entity, formed between two or more persons. It is not subject to registration in the Commercial Register. Since it has no legal character, a third party can have no relationship with it except through contract with individual members. If, in a transaction with a third party, the member is not of Kuwaiti nationality, he is required to have a Kuwaiti stand surety for him. A Joint Venture may not issue transferable shares or debentures.

4. A Joint-Stock Company consisting of a number of persons who subscribe to its transferable shares. Individual liability for the company's obligations is limited to the nominal value of the shares for which each person has subscribed. Every joint-stock company incorporated in Kuwait must be Kuwaiti controlled. All of its Directors would normally be Kuwaitis and its registered home office is required to be in Kuwait. However, subject to the provision that Kuwaiti capital be not less than 51 percent of total capital and that an authorization to this effect must be obtained from the Government, a non-Kuwaiti (other than a bank or insurance company) may participate if there is need for foreign capital or foreign technical competence.

5. A Limited Liability Company consisting of a body of persons whose number shall not be less than two (three, if the two are husband and wife) and shall not exceed 30. The liability of each is limited to his share in its capital. Members must be natural persons i.e., not corporate bodies. A limited liability company may not be incorporated nor may money be borrowed on its behalf by public subscription. It is also prohibited from engaging in insurance, banking or investment.

Entry and Repatriation of Capital

The strong foreign exchange position provided by Kuwait's oil wealth permits the operation of a free exchange system without limitations on international payments and transfers. No restrictions are placed on receipts from exports, re-exports, or invisibles, or on the transfer to and from Kuwait of resident or nonresident capital in any currency. When a firm in which non-resident capital is involved is liquidated, permission for capital repatriation can be obtained quickly from the Central Bank. Foreign nationals working in Kuwait experience no difficulty in remitting their basic wages and salaries abroad.

Industrial Property Protection[1]

Kuwait is not party to any treaties or conventions for the protection of patents, trademarks, or copyrights.

Trademarks.—The basic trademark statute is Law No. 2 (1961), with regulations adopted in 1961 and 1962. The first applicant for a mark is entitled to its registration. If the Registrar of Trademarks, upon receipt of the application, decides to refuse, or accept it conditionally, the applicant may appeal therefrom with 30 days to the AL KULLIYA (Commercial Division) Court, which can uphold or refuse the appeal. If the Registrar accepts the mark, it is advertised in three consecutive issues of the Official Gazette. Any interested party may file an application within 30 days of the last advertisement. The Registrar's decision in an opposition proceeding

[1] Prepared by Joseph M. Lightman, Foreign Business Practices Division, Office International Finance and Investment, Bureau of International Economic Policy and Research.

is subject to appeal to the Court within 10 days of the applicant's being notified of the decision. Trademarks are classified into 33 classes of goods, identical to the International Classification System, except marks are not registrable for beer and ale in class 32. Class 33 is deleted and 34 substituted therefore. Separate application is required for each class.

A trademark may be registered for one product or for one unit or group of similar products for 10 years renewable for similar periods. Continuous use of a trademark for 5 years from the date of registration without a contest of its validity makes ownership of the mark incontestable. The owner of a registered trademark may at any time apply for any addition or alteration of his mark which does not materially affect its character. The proprietor of the right of the trademark can guarantee the continuation of protection for new periods if he submits a renewal application during the last year of the initial protection period.

Patents.—The Kuwait Patent Law (Law No. 4/1962) provides for the issuance of a patent for every new invention suitable for industrial use and not used in Kuwait in last 20 years. Kuwaiti nationals, foreigners residing or having business in Kuwait, and foreigners in countries which grant reciprocal rights to Kuwaitis may apply for patent rights. Applications are examined as to form only. The period covered by a patent is 15 years and it may be renewed for another 5 years. Patents for chemical inventions related to food, medical drugs, or pharmaceutical compounds cover an unrenewable period of 10 years. Adverse decisions by the Patent Office may be challenged before a Kuwait court within 30 days from the date of notification. If the application is accepted it is published for 2 months opposition period. Applications for trademarks and patents should be sent to the Industrial Affairs Department, Ministry of Commerce and Industry, P.O. Box 2944, Kuwait, State of Kuwait.

Taxation

There are no personal income taxes levied in Kuwait. This applies alike to citizens and aliens residing in Kuwait.

Kuwait's income tax law, Decree No. 3/1955, as amended, provides for the taxation of incomes of "bodies corporate", wheresoever incorporated, that carry on trade or business in Kuwait. These taxes are fixed on a sliding scale rising from 5 percent to a maximum of 55 percent on taxable income above U.S. $1,050,000.

The law defines a "body corporate" as an association formed and registered under the laws of any country or state and recognized as having a legal existence entirely separate from that of its individual members. Corporations, domestic or foreign, engaging in a partnership in Kuwait are subject to taxes on their share of the parternship profits; individuals engaging in a partnership are exempt from income taxes. The law defines the carrying on of a trade or business to mean "the purchasing and selling of property, goods, or rights thereto, and maintaining a permanent office in Kuwait where the contracts of purchase and sale are executed, the operation of any other manufacturing, industrial, or commercial enterprise in Kuwait; the letting of any property in Kuwait; and the rendering of services in Kuwait."

The law stipulates that a corporation carrying on trade or business in the country either directly or through an agent, is liable to pay the Kuwaiti corporate income tax on its earnings in Kuwait. The Ministry of Finance and Oil has interpreted this, however, to apply only to firms actually registered in Kuwait (not to be confused with registration in the Commercial Register). For purpose of the law, the term "agent" does not include commission agents or distributors representing foreign firms in straight sales transactions.

When enacted in 1955, the law was intended to apply only to foreign corporations (i.e. oil companies), since Kuwaiti law at that time made no provision for the local formation of such entities. All "bodies corporate" subsequently formed in Kuwait under the Law of Commercial Companies of 1961 are normally subject to the income tax law. But in practice, only foreign firms and the foreign share of local firms' profits are taxed.

There is no convention for the avoidance of double taxation between the United States and Kuwait. Under U.S. law, a credit against U.S. taxes is allowable for the taxes paid to foreign countries by U.S. companies operating in them.

Labor

Of Kuwait's total population of about 1.1 million over half are non-Kuwaitis. Foreigners comprise more than 70 percent of the labor force and the majority of those with professional training. In contrast to many Arab countries, Kuwait is employing a growing number of Kuwaiti and expatriate women, particularly in office work and as teachers and nurses.

There is no unemployment in Kuwait; rather the country's major development constraint is the shortage of skilled and unskilled labor. Therefore, contractors on most projects are required to recruit 80 percent of their labor from overseas. The contractor must arrange for housing and other facilities for these employees.

The Government is emphasizing Kuwaitization of employment in the technical and administrative fields in both the public and private sectors. It has aimed at increasing the number of Kuwaiti technicians by: increasing educational and vocational training opportunities; sending missions abroad for training; and encouraging private enterprise—especially the oil companies—to provide more training. The Government, along with the United Nations, has organized an Industrial Training Center at Shuwaikh to train craft instructors, supervisory personnel, and skilled workers.

Without an agricultural sector, and with nonpetroleum industries in their infancy, the Government provides the bulk of jobs sought by Kuwaiti nationals. The Government employs over 150,000 people. This has resulted in great government influence over wage patterns. Most large, private sector employers are obligated to adjust their pay scales to reflect the Government's rates for workers of like or similar skills.

Wages and Benefits

Salaries in the public sector have increased substantially in the past several years, in part to cover the high inflation which the country has recently experienced. Allowances for education, housing and health have also increased to about 30-50 percent of the basic salaries. The Government also subsidizes housing, and food for its employees.

High level western expatriate executives are often paid between 60,000 and $100,000; middle management executives earn between $20,000 and $50,000; technicians, such as computer technicians, $25,000 to $35,000; secretaries (they normally are required to have English fluency) $10,000 to $20,000; skilled workers such as plumbers and electricians $15 to $35 a day, and day laborers $25 daily. Many employers augment the salaries of the lower paid workers with a food allowance and either a housing allowance or company housing.

Labor Legislation

The basic labor law for the private sector,

Law No. 38/1964, covers all private sector employees except domestic servants and workers in small non-mechanical establishments (employing less than five workers). A special law, No. 28/1969, was passed as an amendment to the basic labor law and covers workers engaged in operations pertaining to the search, discovery, production, refining, processing, transporting or shipping of oil or natural gas. It also applies to Kuwaiti workers engaged in construction, erection, maintenance or operation of installations and equipment and all related service work connected with the oil industry. The 1964 law is applicable to oil workers in matters not covered by the 1969 law.

Under the 1964 law, youths below the age of 14 may not be employed; youths from 14 to 16 years of age must obtain permission from the Ministry of Social Affairs and Labor. They may work only 6 hours a day and may not do night or dangerous work. Women may not be employed in night work, with certain exceptions, or in dangerous industries. Pregnant workers are entitled to a maximum of 30 days leave before and 40 days after delivery with full pay. Women and men must get equal pay for equal work. Employers are responsible for eliminating industrial accidents and health hazards in accordance with regulations laid down by the Ministry of Social Affairs and Labor. Provisions of these laws relating to work week, overtime, holidays, leave, compensation for injury, termination benefits, and other matters may be acquiried from the Commerce Action Group for the Near East, Bureau of Export Development, U.S. Department of Commerce, Washington, D.C. 20230.

Labor Relations

The Labor Law of 1964 authorizes the formation of employer and employee organizations to promote their respective interests and legislates procedures for the formation of unions, election of officials, and keeping of records and books. A labor union must have at least 100 members, and only one union is allowed in a single establishment or trade. Non-Kuwaitis may become nonvoting members once they have resided at least 5 years in Kuwait. Other non-Kuwaitis may select a representative to express their views before the union's administrative council. No worker may belong to more than one union. Union participation in political, religious, or ideological matters is officially prohibited, as well as the use of union funds for financial, real estate, or speculative ventures. Unions may receive donations or legacies only after agreement

from the Ministry of Social Affairs and Labor has been received.

Federations may be formed from unions representing single industries or similar industries. In turn, these federations may join in a general labor confederation (only one is allowed), which may become affilated with an international labor federation. In December 1967, the General Federation of Kuwait Workers and Employees (GFKWE) was formed to unite all legally organized and recognized labor unions in Kuwait. Subsequently, it joined the International Confederation of Arab Trade Unions. The General Federation consists of two smaller federations, the Federation of Government Employees and Workers and the Federation of Petroleum Workers. Recently, a federation for workers in the petrochemical industries was also formed. It will become part of the General Confederation.

The basic labor law of 1964 also provides for the following steps in arbitration of labor disputes involving private sector non-oil company employees. First, the employer and employee engage in direct negotiations. If a settlement is reached, the agreement must be registered with the Ministry of Social Affairs and Labor. Second, if a settlement is not reached, one or both of the parties may request the Ministry to settle the dispute. Third, if the Ministry fails to mediate a settlement within 15 days, the dispute is passed to a committee for the arbitration of labor disputes. The committee is composed of representatives from the High Court of Appeal, the Attorney General, and the Minister of Social Affairs and Labor. Its decision is final and binding.

Employment of Aliens

The Government, in various laws, memoranda, and development plans, has encouraged employers to recruit the largest possible number of Kuwaitis, or other Arabs if Kuwaitis are not available. Foreigners are recruited only when qualified Arabs are not availalbe. All non-Kuwaitis seeking employment must obtain prior permission before entering the country and must keep the Passport Department informed of their residence. Each must have a "nonobjection certificate" issued by the Ministry of the Interior, a certificate of good conduct approved by the Ministry of the Interior, and a declaration by an employer that they are, in fact, employed by a specific firm in order to maintain visas and residence permits. Companies will not be permitted to import foreign personnel when qualified technicians are already in the country. A residence permit will be issued only to persons having commercial or industrial activities authorized in accordance with Kuwaiti laws.

Guidance for Business Visitors Abroad

Entrance Requirements

Business representatives wishing to visit Kuwait must have a valid passport and possess a visa. The latter can be obtained from the Kuwait Embassy in Washington or the Kuwait Mission to the U.N. in New York. If the traveler is outside the U.S. and wishes to come to Kuwait, a visa can be obtained at the nearest Kuwaiti Embassy or Consulate. Transit visas are not normally available for business visitors coming directly from the States.

Visitors must have proof of health inoculations. Certificates of Vaccination against smallpox and cholera are required and travellers arriving from infected areas must have a certificate of vaccination against yellow fever.

Certain vaccinations are recommended or required by the United States Government for Americans going abroad. Since these requirements may change with prevailing conditions, anyone contemplating a trip abroad should obtain the latest information from the U.S. Public Health Service, Department of Health, Education, and Welfare, Washington, D.C. 20230 or from any local facility of the service.

For information on regulations covering foreigners working in Kuwait, see the above sub-section Employment of Aliens under the section Investment in Kuwait.

Language, Business Hours, Holidays

Commercial Language.—Arabic is the official language, but English is widely spoken and is generally acceptable in business and government circles. Catalogs and promotional literature in English are acceptable. Use of Arabic by foreign firms in corresponding with Kuwaitis is greatly valued in Kuwait as a mark of consideration, however, and consequently could be of competitive advantage to the foreign firm.

Business Hours.—Friday is the Muslim sabbath, and all government and business offices are closed. Government offices are generally open from 0800 to 1300, Saturday through Thursday. Bank employees usually work from 0900 to 1130 and 1430 to 1800 Saturday through Wednesday. Business and shop office hours vary but generally are between 0730 and 1300 and 1600 to 1930 Saturday to Wednesday and from

0800 to noon on Thursday. Business, bank and government offices have shorter working hours during the one month Ramadan fasting period and often open and close their offices one hour earlier in the summer.

Holidays.—Kuwait uses the Hejira calendar, which is based on a lunar year about 11 days shorter than the Gregorian, or solar year. Religious holidays vary from year to year, therefore, on the Gregorian calendar. The Department of Commerce publishes each year in its bi-weekly publication Business America a complete listing of holidays throughout the world. The listing usually appears in the last issue of the year preceding the year covered. The only fixed holidays in Kuwait are New Years Day and Kuwait National Day (February 25).

October through May or June generally is considered the best period for foreign business visits to Kuwait. The summer months are intensely hot and many local business people are absent from the country during this period.

Sources of Economic and Commercial Information

General information concerning the Kuwait market (economic trends, commercial development, production, trade regulations and tariff rates) may be obtained from the Commerce Action Group for the Near East. U.S. Department of Commerce, Washington, D.C. 20230. Such information may be obtained also from any of the Departments District Offices throughout the United States.

Government Representation

The Kuwait Government maintains an Embassy at 2940 Tilden Street, N.W., Washington, D.C . 20008 (telephone 202-966-0702), and consular office at 801 2nd Avenue, New York, New York 10017, telephone 212-661-1580.

The United States maintains an Embassy at P.O. Box 77, Safat, Kuwait, telephone 424-151-9.

Trade Organizations

U.S. Arab Chamber of Commerce, Inc.
One World Trade Center
Suite 4657
New York, New York 10048
Telephone: 212-432-0655

U.S. Arab Chamber of Commerce, Inc. (Mid-
   Atlantic Chapter)
1819 H Street, N.W., Room 470

Washington, D.C. 20006
Telephone: 202-293-6975

American Arab Chamber of Commerce
World Trade Building
Suite 319
Houston, Texas 77002
Telephone: 713-222-6152

Mid American-Arab Chamber of Commerce, Inc.
136 South LaSalle Street
Suite 2050
Chicago, Illinois 60603
Telephone: 312-782-4654

U.S. Arab Chamber of Commerce (Pacific), Inc.
230 California Street
San Francisco, California 94111
Telephone: 415-397-5663

American Arab Association for Commerce and
Industry, Inc.
342 Madison Avenue
New York, New York 10017
Telephone: 212-986-7229

U.S. Government Publications

U.S. Government.—(Available from the Superintendent of Documents, U.S. Government Printing Office, Washington, D.C. 20402, and the Department of Commerce District Offices.)

A Business Guide to the Near East and North Africa, May 1978, prepared by the Commerce Action Group for the Near East, Department of Commerce.

An Introduction to Contract Procedures in the Near East and North Africa, February 1978, prepared by Cherie Loustaunau, Commerce Action Group for the Near East.

Foreign Economic Trends and Their Implications for the United States—Kuwait, November, 1977 prepared by the American Embassy annual.

Background Notes–Kuwait. December 1977—prepared by the Department of State.

Market Profiles for the Near East and North Africa October 1978, prepared by the Commerce Action Group for the Near East, Overseas Business Report, semi-annual.

Near East/North African Business Costs, (January 1978) prepared by Commerce Action Group for the Near East, Overseas Business Report.

Trade List, Business Firms in Kuwait July 1978. Department of Commerce publication. $3.00.

Market Share Reports, Country Series, Kuwait 1971—5, U.S. Department of Commerce, for sale by the National Technical Information Service, 5285 Port Royal Road, Springfield, Virginia 22161; $4.75.

Market Profile—KUWAIT

Foreign Trade

Imports.—$5.7 billion in 1979; $4.6 billion in 1978. Leading 1979 suppliers: Japan, $966 million; United States, $841 million; United Kingdom, $546 million; France, $478 million. Major imports: machinery, transport equipment, iron and steel, electric appliances, textiles and clothing, food and live animals, tobacco.

Exports.—$17.6 billion in 1979; $10.5 billion in 1978. Major 1979 markets: Japna, $3.9 billion; United Kingdom, $1.4 billion; Italy, $639 million; Korea, $522 million; United States, $86 million. Major export is petroleum; other exports include chemical fertilizers, building materials, metal pipes, and shrimp.

Trade Policy.—Liberal. Most items duty free or charged 4 percent ad valorem. Commercial importing restricted to Kuwait nationals and firms. No exchange controls on imports.

Foreign Investment

Investment welcomed, but limited to 49 percent foreign participation in industrial and commercial concerns. Low cost, long-term loans available for some industrial projects. No personal income taxes and low corporate rates; no restrictions on repatriation of profits.

Finance

Currency.—Kuwait dinar (KD)=$3.75; US$1-.267 KD in June 1980. Divided into 1,000 fils. Money supply March 1980 was $2.5 billion; currency in circulation was $800 million.

Domestic Credit and Investment.—Six commercial banks, three specialized banks, and Central Bank of Kuwait. Foreign participation not generally allowed.

National Budget.—1979–80 (ending June 30) estimated revenue, $11.8 billion (oil revenue 95 percent); expenditures, $6.2 billion; development projects, $2 billion; State reserves, Kuwait Fund for Arab Economic Development, Fund for Future Generations, $3.6 billion. In addition, $1.8 billion income was earned from foreign investment during FY 1978–79. Per capita income $14,900 in 1979.

Balance of Payments.—Current account surplus in 1979 was about $15 billion. Gold and foreign exchange reserves were estimated at $3.3 billion in June 1980. Government foreign assets exceed $25 billion in early 1979.

Economy

Estimated GDP at current prices in 1979 was $24 billion. Annual GDP growth through 1983 should average 5 percent. Inflation rate 10–12 percent in 1978.

Agriculture.—Only 1 percent of land is cultivated, due to absence of natural sources or irrigation.

Minerals.—Has one of world's largest known oil reserves. Production totaled 777 million U.S. barrels in 1978, up 8.2 percent from 1977. Estimated gas reserves are 32.5 trillion cubic feet; 1978 production of 393 billion cubic feet was up 8.3 percent from 1977.

Industry.—Manufacturing investment should continue to increase, but it will be concentrated in the oil sector. Two major refinery expansion/modernization projects are scheduled for completion by 1986. Additional ammonia manufacturing facilities will also be added, but the bigger proposed petrochemical projects more likely will not be contracted for until after 1983. The bulk of heavy manufacturing facilities are in the petroleum field. However, nonpetroleum projects also will be built; for example, a tire factory may be established.

Transportation.—Some $800 to $900 million worth of highway construction is currently underway, and this figure will increase substantially over the next 3 years. Port expansion and possibly the construction of Kuwait's first railroad will add to the activity in this sector.

Utilities.—Very high per capita electricity consumption coupled with a rapidly growing population have made it difficult for the GOK to meet electricity demand. Meanwhile, demand for water also is growing rapidly. Thus, as the giant Doha West electrieity/water desalination facility nears completion, the Government is speeding plans for the next complex to be located at Ras Jalaya. In addition, a network of 19 gas turbines will be built during 1981 to build up capacity quickly.

Communications.—Radio (AM and FM) and TV (color) both government owned. Good domestic and international telephone and cable services. Two satellite ground stations in operation.

Natural Resources

Land.—10,000 square miles of flat, rolling desert.

Climate.—Intensely hot and often humid in summer; milder climate November to April. Average rainfall less than 4 inches annually.

Fisheries.—Plentiful fish supply in territorial waters. Privately owned concern, United Fisheries of Kuwait, has modern fleet and area monopoly on fishing.

Population

Size.—Estimated 1.27 million inhabitants, more than half living in greater Kuwait City. More than 52 percent of population are nationals of other countries, including Egypt, Iran, India, Pakistan, and Iraq.

Language.—Arabic. English is widely spoken.

Education and Health.—Free education to all citizens through high school; 8 years attendance compulsory. Literacy rate above 65 percent. There were 287,120 students in public and private schools during 1976–77; in Kuwait University, 7,528. Free medical services are provided by the government.

Labor.—There are roughly 300,000 people in the labor force; 70 percent are expatriates.

Market Profile—LEBANON

Note: Due to the Lebanese Civil War (1975–76) and the resulting turmoil, only partial information is available on the economy. Damage from the war is estimated at $2–$3 billion; productive capacity may only be two-thirds of the 1974 level. Because security conditions in the country are poor, the U.S. Embassy Staff has been reduced to a minimum, and business visitors are advised to use caution in visits to Lebanon.

Foreign Trade

Imports.—Estimated at $1.7 billion in 1978. Principal imports: automobiles, lumber, pig iron, chemical raw materials, foodstuffs, tobacco, machinery, and consumer appliances. Fifty-four percent of all 1978 imports from Western Europe, United States, and Japan; U.S. imports accounted for 8.3 percent of total. Statistics highly unreliable, and actual imports certainly greater (e.g. gold imports omitted and figures do not reflect extensive smuggling). Partial figures reflect 1979 recovery, with documented imports of $2.2 billion and smuggled imports of perhaps a third again of that figure.

Exports.—Estimated at $650 million in 1978 and $790 million in 1977; probably higher in 1979, perhaps back to 1977 level. Principal exports: construction materials, chemicals, paper, metals and fabrications, cement, machines and appliances, and agricultural products including smuggled hashish. Eighty-two percent of 1978 exports to Arab countries; Saudi Arabia had largest share.

Trade Policy.—Liberal, free enterprise system. Negligible exchange controls. Moderate tariffs; import license required for commodities that are produced domestically.

Foreign Investment

Welcomed under liberal legislation. Tax concessions and other incentives available. Moderate U.S. investment concentrated in oil transport, storage, and refining facilities. Light industry to supply regional market could be an attractive possibility if security conditions allow. National Organization for the Insurance of Investments against losses from war and civil disturbance.

Finance

Currency.—Lebanese pound (LL) divided into 100 piasters; $1=LL3.30; LL1=$.30, Pound remains weak, however, and is expected to deteriorate further. Inflation rate approximately 25 percent in 1979.

Domestic Credit and Investment.—At the beginning of 1979, there were 74 banks operating in Lebanon, and about a dozen new ones either applied for licenses or opened during the year. Also 56 representative offices of foreign banks, 5 specialized medium- and long-term financial establishments, and the Central Bank.

National Budget.—Council of Ministers approved 1980 budget of record $1.4 billion; 1979 budget $1 billion. Government's inability to control interior means a loss of tax revenues.

Balance of Payments.—Estimated 1979 surplus of $200 million, same as 1978, reflecting strength of invisible earnings and emigrant remittances.

Economy

Traditionally private enterprise, with Beirut the principal financial, trading, and commercial center of the Middle East until the outbreak of fighting in 1975.

GNP.—Estimated at $3 billion for 1979. Still below pre-war levels.

Agriculture.—Contributes about 9 percent of GNP. Principal crops: fruits and vegetables. Had good year in 1979.

391,000 hectares cultivable, of which 174,00 are neglected but reclamable, 152,000 cultivated with rainfall, 65,000 cultivated with irrigation.

Industry.—Mostly light industries producing consumer goods. Principal industries: textiles, food processing, consumer goods, metal processing, oil refining, petrochemicals, cement, and fertilizer. Contributed approximately 17 percent of GNP.

Tourism.—Was a major foreign exchange earner, accounting for about 8 percent of GNP in 1974, but tourist infrastructure has suffered heavy damage.

Development Program.—Reconstruction and Development Council established in 1977 to prepare and execute a medium-term development plan for reconstruction of Beirut and other damaged areas. Medium-term development needs can be financed in part by Lebanon's reserves, present commitments from foreign lenders, and foreign aid for telecommunications, water and sewage, highways, vocational training schools, port and electricity development. Additional funding is anticipated from Near East OPEC countries. Price for all of Lebanon's reconstruction has been estimated at $7 billion; figure will have to be revised upward because of inflation.

Basic Economic Facilities

Transportation.—Road traffic predominates; good network with about 5,100 miles, 74 percent paved. About 250 miles of railroad connecting Beirut with Sidon, Tripoli, and Syria. Beirut International Airport, a major regional airport, now operating again. Beirut port handled 4.1 million tons of cargo in 1974, one-quarter of which was transit cargo. Major port facilities have been repaired and are steadily recovering commercial importance; handled 2.6 million tons in 1979.

Communications.—Had excellent telecommunications systems, linked to outside world by three submarine cables, earth station, and microwave cables. System suffered heavy war damage and is being rebuilt on priority basis. System is fair to good internationally, poor within country. Postal system again in service. Telex service good but inconsistent.

Power.—Production in 1974 was 1,975 MkWh. Power largely restored after wartime disruptions. Hydroelectric power production down in 1979 because of dry winter and spring.

Natural Resources

Land.—About 4,100 square miles, about the size of Connecticut. Seventy percent mountainous.

Climate.—Mediterranean; cool, rainy winters, and warm dry summers.

Minerals.—Lacks any significant petroleum, coal, or metal resources.

Population

Size.—Approximately 3 million in 1978; large emigration during civil war, but many Lebanese now returning. Major city Beirut. Urban population about 1 million.

Language.—Arabic official. French and English widely used.

Labor.—Shortages in certain categories because of war-induced emigration. About 20 percent each in agriculture and industry, remainder in services. Skilled labor more abundant north of Beirut, unskilled south. In general, capabilities of labor force highly rated, although availabiliy varies geographically.

Education.—Literacy rate about 85 percent, highest in Arab world. Extensive public and private education system, four universities and five colleges.

Lebanon

- International boundary
- --- Armistice Line, 1949
- --- Province boundary
- ★ National capital
- ⊙ Province capital
- Road
- Railroad

0   5   10   15 Kilometers
0   5   10   15 Miles

SYRIA

Al Hamidiyah
Nahr an Nahr
Tall Kalakh
An Nahr al Kabir
Bahrat Hims
Al Qubayyat
Halba
Al Qubayr
Al Mina'
Nahr al Musa
Tripoli
Al Hirmil
ASH SHAMAL
Al Qa'
Shikka
Amyun
Nahr al Asi
Bsharri
Al Batrun
Duma
Nahr al Jawz
Nahr Ibrahim
Jubayl
AL BIQA
Nahr al Litani
Ba'labakk
Juniyah
Bikfayya
Beirut
BAYRUT
Zahlah
Riyaq
B'abda
JABAL LUBNAN
Shtawrah
Mediterranean Sea
Alayh
Al Qutayfah
Ad Damur
Bayt ad Din
SYRIA
Barja
Jubb Jannin
Nahr Barada
Ad Dimas
Sidon
Nahr al Awwali
Damascus
Duma
Buhayrat al 'Utaybah
Jazzin
Al Qir'awn
Rashayya
Az Zahrani
Nahr al Hasbani
Qatana
An Nabatiyah at Tahta
Nahr al A'waj
Marji'yun
Nahr al Litani
AL JANUB
UNDOF Zone
Tyre
Baniyas
GOLAN HEIGHTS (Israeli occupied)
An Naqurah
Bint Jubayl
Rumaysh
Al Qunaytirah
As Sanamayn
As Surah as Sughra
Jordan River
Qadaf
Nahariyya
ISRAEL
Boundary representation is not necessarily authoritative

1477

Marketing in Liberia

Contents

Report Revised August 1982

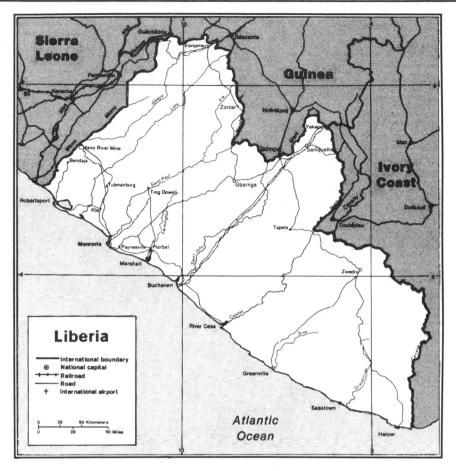

Note: Monrovia is about 6,400 kilometers (4,000 mi.) from Washington, D.C.

The Liberian Economy

Although the Liberian economic situation is continuing to improve from a low point following the coup of 1980, Liberia continues to struggle with low export earnings and financial instability. The Government recognizes that its principal needs are an infusion of private investment capital and a restoration of business confidence.

The United States is traditionally Liberia's leading supplier, although its market share has declined in recent years. From a high of 32 percent in 1975, the U.S. share fell below 24 percent in 1979 and is expected to drop still further. Following the coup of April 12, 1980, which toppled the government of President William Tolbert, several factors combined to depress the level of Liberia's imports from the United States. Political instability led to a decline in business confidence. Consumers cut back on purchases, and the Government reduced expenditures on capital goods in order to pay higher salaries and meet essential foreign obligations. Duty surcharges for nonessential imports, imposed as part of a 2-year IMF (International Monetary Fund) stabilization program, have also helped squeeze generally higher-priced U.S. goods out of the market.

Use of the U.S. dollar as Liberia's currency unit contributed to massive capital flight following the coup. Without effective exchange controls, individuals and firms were free to transfer assets out of the country, causing a contraction of the money supply and a severe financial crisis, especially in government accounts.

Demand for U.S. exports, when it occurs, is mainly generated by major development projects designed and financed by the World Bank and other international lending institutions through the issue of competitive tenders by the Liberian Government. In the longer term, attendant to the restoration of the Liberian economy, demand for consumer items will emerge from a private-enterprise based wholesale and retail trade. There are approximately 1.8 million consumers in Liberia, with an annual population growth rate of 3.3 percent. Imports from the United States in 1980 consisted principally of machinery and transportation equipment, 32.5 percent; food, 28.2 percent; and manufactured materials, 14.4 percent.

Apparent consumption of domestically produced goods and imports declined overall from $722.1 million in 1977 to $719.9 million in 1979 as a greater percentage of production and imports were directed to exports.

The private sector accounted for 59.3 percent of consumption, i.e., commercial, industrial, and consumer, while the public sector accounted for 40.7 percent, but 28.4 percent of private consumption was devoted to revenue for government services.

Development Planning and Assistance

Head of State and Chairman of the People's Redemption Council (PRC) Samuel K. Doe outlined the elements of Liberia's Four-Year Development Plan in a nationwide address on July 17, 1981. The Plan will form from the fiscal year 1981/82 through 1984/85. It is expected that the total amount of $615 million will be invested by the public sector during the life of the plan. This investment will concentrate on such priority sectors as agriculture, forestry, rural development, roads, electricity, industry and commerce, education and training, and health and social welfare.

Between the rice riots of April 1979 and the coup of April 1980, a number of foreign investors left Liberia and sent dollars in large quantities out of the country. The resulting capital shortage was exacerbated by a precipitous fall in world demand for Liberia's chief exports: iron ore, rubber, and timber. In addition, Liberia has had to borrow extensively to pay for its oil imports. During the 1982 fiscal year, the U.S. Government allocated $35 million in Economic Support Funds (ESF) for Liberian Government budgetary support, mostly for oil purchases, and will provide $75 million in various types of assistance in 1982. This represents the largest aid program in West Africa, and one of the largest on the continent. It is also reflective of the close political ties between Liberia and the United States.

In June 1982, Liberia completed a 2-year standby arrangement with IMF, which provided $85 million. The Liberian IMF program has been the most successful one on the continent; with the Government consistently meeting performance criteria. Liberia is also the recipient of an EEC aid package that is worth $32 to $37 million. Approximately three quarters will be in grant form and the rest in long-term loans. This aid derives from the second Lome Convention, which became effective in 1981. Under the first convention, Liberia was allotted $30 million of which only 34 percent had been spent by the end of 1980. The balance is still available for use by Liberia in addition to the new commitments. Liberia could also benefit from EEC regional aid to West Africa, in particular, from a project that will develop the Mano River basin.

Liberia has also been promised a loan of $11 million from West Germany to improve the electricity and sewerage services in Monrovia, as well as water supplies in Robertsport, to rehabilitate the country's ports, and to assist in the revival of a timber company in eastern Liberia. A $5 million loan from the World Bank and a $5 million loan from its soft loan affiliate, the International Development Agency, are being lent to various rural institutions in support of the development of cash crops by small farmers in three southeastern countries. The World Bank is also lending the Ministry of Agriculture some $15 million to expand existing projects in Lofa County and other new projects involving the production of rice, cocoa, and coffee in addition to the development of wells, feeder roads, and agricultural services. A $67 million loan, the major portion of it from the World Bank and a consortium of private American banks, is being used to rehabilitate the National Iron Ore Company mine.

Economic Sectors

Agriculture

Agricultural output totaling $97.8 million in 1980 was comprised of rubber, coffee, cocoa, palm products, and other export crops, with rubber accounting for 63 percent of the total value.

The structure of the agricultural sector is characterized by (a) foreign concessions, (b) Liberian-owned commercial farms, and (c) small traditional farms that comprise more than 90 percent of agricultural holdings in Liberia. Foreign concessions are limited principally to large rubber plantations and timber exploitation. The basic features of these enterprises are highly trained expatriate managerial and technical staff, extensive capital investment, large-scale modern technology, and high levels of efficiency.

The Liberian-owned commercial farms produce rubber primarily, but they have been expanding into poultry, livestock, coffee, cocoa, oil palm, and some rice and vegetables. They employ moderately capital intensive technology and have relatively easy access to capital and other resources, often against the security of their own interests. Most of the ownership is absentee, and management is poor, except in cases where the farm is large enough to support an experienced professional manager. The traditional sector is largely outside the monetized economy. It is located in areas with minimal infrastructure

and is comprised of farms in which fewer than 10 acres are cultivated each year. The sector primarily produces rice, cassava, yams, and other subsistence crops along with some coffee, cocoa, oil palm, and sugar cane that are grown as cash crops.

Land Tenure.—Apart from small holdings, primarily in urban areas that are freeholdings, land in Liberia is owned by the State. Within each tribal area the traditional authorities are responsible for the administration of land and allocate its use to members of the community and others. This practice is common in West Africa and provides tenure in areas where population pressure is light. Land allocated to an individual may not be sold or otherwise disposed.

Coffee and Cocoa.—Liberia is not a major world producer of coffee and cocoa nor is incremental production of coffee forseen to be large enough, in terms of world production, to have a measurable effect upon the supply and price situation. Coffee constituted only 5 percent of Liberia's export earnings in 1979. World prices for cocoa have been dropping, a major disincentive for increased production. Liberia is not a member of the International Cocoa Agreement.

Livestock.—Cattle are scarce because of health (the tsetse fly), and climatic conditions. Most of the rural protein intake comes from small wild animals and fish.

Until 1978, the Netherlands had been a principal supplier of fertilizers to Liberia, running first and then second to West Germany. In the agricultural machinery sector, Japan moved into first place in 1979 with its agricultural tractors.

Forestry

Liberia's timber industry ranks third in export earnings after iron ore and rubber. Earnings from lumber and log exports doubled from $29.3 million in 1977 to $58.5 million in 1979. About half of the country's 45 forestry concessions, which cover 9 million acres, are active. The available 250 tree species are suitable for all types of wood industries, including veneer, plywood, furniture, prefabricated structures, parquet blocks, and pulp and paper processing. The maximum exploitation of all Liberian timber acres on a sustained yield basis is presumed to be about 500,000 cubic meters, with an average of 25 years assumed needed for the major species to grow to size. Before 1975 logs were the principal forest export. However, in a move to increase timber exports, the Government has set minimum local processing requirements. As a result, some concessions plan to expand into veneer, wood paneling, prefabricated housing, and paper manufacture. New investments in a plywood plant and sawmill facilities have taken place. In light of the changed markets conditions, the average stumpage fee is $18 per cubic meter.

The Liberian Government has prescribed model concession arrangements with obligations as follows: Annual cuttings to be limited to sustained yield levels, scientific reforestation of the concession area, and processing in Liberia of progressively larger percentages of its timber harvest.

Fishing

Commercial ocean fishing is a growing activity carried out from Liberian ports. The substantial and steady increase in fish landings is largely due to foreign fishing boats unloading frozen fish for the Mesurado Fishing Company and the Liberian Storage Company. The Mesurado Fishing Company handles over 80 percent of the fish in the Liberian fish market. Over 95 percent of the total fish landed by Mesurado is frozen at sea, the bulk of which is purchased from Soviet and other fishers.

Mesurado operates a shrimp fleet. The catch is processed and exported in frozen form. The industry continues to expand, and the outlook is bright for increased production both for local consumption and export. Fishing and fish processing have already attracted substantial investment, but much remains to be done to develop Liberia's rich fish resources, especially tuna. Liberia also offers excellent potential for fresh fish culture, and it has ample fresh water resources.

Mining and Minerals

Mining is the most important sector in Liberia's economy, a sector dominated by the iron ore industry. However, the continuing slump in the world steel industry has left the demand for iron ore and its price only slightly above 1978 levels. In 1979, iron ore accounted for 54 percent of export earnings as opposed to 71 percent in 1976, the last strong year for the international steel industry. Receipts for iron ore are expected to remain low through at least 1982, but are expected to pick up by the middle of the decade. Serious exploration for uranium and gold is underway.

Iron Ore.—Two major iron ore mining companies, National Iron Ore Company and Bong Mining Company, were on the verge of closing their mines, a result of serious financial difficulties, threatening the jobs of some 25,000 Liberians. The World Bank, together with other lenders, is now lending $67 million to rehabilitate the National Iron Ore Company, and the Liberian Government has offered various subsidies to help the Bong Mining Company, a joint venture with West German and Italian interests. The Liberian Iron and Steel Corporation (LISCO), suspending its operation at the Wologisi Mine after the coup of April 1980 now has had its concession extended for 1 year but is obliged to report regularly to the Liberian Government and to announce when it is starting to commence commercial production. Upon payment of $135,000 by a Japanese group that has an optional contract to buy 51 percent of its shares, LISCO applied for the extension.

An exception to the gloomy outlook for iron ore exports occurred when Nigeria's Delta Steel Company signed an agreement to purchase 4.5 million tons of iron ore from Liberia over a 5-year period. The iron ore will be supplied by LAMCO's mine at Mount Nimba beginning in July 1981 with 550,000 tons, increasing to 600,000 tons in 1982, and to 1 million tons by 1985 as Delta Steel's production rises. The price will vary annually to accord with LAMCO's f.o.b. price in Europe. This will be the first time that Liberia has sold iron ore to Nigeria. The five largest companies engaged in the production of Liberian iron ore are the Bong Mining Company (DELIMCO), Liberian-American-Swedish Minerals Company (LAMCO), Liberian International American Corporation (LIAC), Liberian Iron and Steel Corporation (LISCO), and National Iron Ore Company (NIOC).

Diamonds.—Diamonds are mined in the Lofa River area. Data on total production are unreliable, as there is reported to be considerable smuggling of diamonds from Sierra Leone into Liberia. Diamond export production increased 23 percent between 1977 and 1979 while its value increased 85 percent. In 1981, 336,000 carats, primarily of gem diamonds, valued at $23 million, were produced.

Gold.—Gold is reported to exist in the Lofa River area and the southwestern part of the country. Both U.S. and European companies are likely to continue to explore and to produce gold. Production was valued at over $5 million in 1981.

Petroleum

A French firm has completed an offshore seismic survey for the Liberian Government that was paid for by a $5 million loan from the World

Bank. The Government plans to use the data produced by this project to induce oil companies to invest risk capital in exploration drilling. U.S. firms now have an opportunity both to bid for exploration concession areas and to establish support facilities for any companies that do eventually begin drilling. Seminars were held in Monrovia and Houston in early 1982 to present the results of the survey to interested companies; over 40 oil companies were represented.

Manufacturing

The manufacturing sector contributes about 8 percent of gross domestic product (GDP). Real growth in the sector averaged 21 percent a year during 1973–78. The bulk of the sector's output is sold domestically. Exports of manufactured goods account for a small proportion of output, although exports of processed fish and wood products are growing in importance. The domestic market is small, and industries largely have been limited to import substitution, such as petroleum refining, cement, food and beverages, construction materials, clothing, and furniture. Although many of the major establishments are owned by foreigners, the number of Liberian entrepreneurs is increasing. Most industries are privately owned. Employment in manufacturing numbers 6,500.

Lumber Industries.—Vanply of Liberia began sawmill operations in 1975 and plywood production in 1976. Vanply, a subsidiary of the Skelly Oil Company of Tulsa, Oklahoma, is located in Sinoe County near Greenville. It has 1.6 million acres of timber resources for its operation. The plant fits well into the Liberian Government's program to encourage development of the country's natural resources and expand lumber exports. The plant's major structures include a power plant, sawmill, plywood factory, lumber drying, woodworking buildings, water treatment plant, and warehouses.

Rubber Processing.—The Liberian Rubber Development Unit has just launched the building of a new rubber processing plant in Bong County. This project is being financed by the World Bank and the Commonwealth Development Corporation.

The IDA, the World Bank's soft loan subsidiary, has offered $4 million in credits to help the Government to finance wholly Liberian-owned small and medium-scale enterprises in industries such as woodworking and metalworking, building materials, machine repair and maintenance, tailoring, food processing, and automotive trans-

portation. One million dollars will be allocated to the small-scale segment and $2.4 million to the medium, financing both fixed and working capital. Part of the loan, $6,000, will be spent on technical assistance to the newly created National Investment Commission (NIC).

Utilities

Power.—With an electric power capacity of 327,000 kilowatts in 1977, Liberia produced 980 million kilowatt hours of electricity, or 620 kilowatt hours per capita. About half of the power generated is used by the mining companies. By African standards, consumption per capita is high even after discounting electricity consumed by the concessions. The Liberia Electricity Corporation (LEC) supplies about 40 percent of the power consumed, the remaining 60 percent being supplied by the iron ore mining companies. LEC's installed capacity is 149 megawatts (MW), consisting of 69 MW hydro capacity (46 percent), and 81 MW thermal capacity (54 percent). The mining companies, together with small privately owned installations, have an estimated capacity of 150 MW. The main centers of population and power loads are Monrovia, the capital; Buchanan, an important port; Robertsport; and Bong Mines and Tubmanburg (mining centers).

The Monrovia system is the main source of public power. LEC also operates seven secondary centers in rural areas that generate 5 percent of the country's total output. All non-hydroelectric power is generated from imported petroleum or its derivatives. Half of the power supplied to Monrovia comes from the Mt. Coffee dam, Liberia's only hydroelectric power plant, on the St. Paul River. Other rivers with hydroelectric potential are the Cavalla, the St. John, the Mano, and the Cestos. Two feasibility studies for hydroelectric dam projects are underway. One of the studies being conducted by a U.S. engineering firm involves the construction of two storage dams, two generating dams, and installation of additional generating capacity at Liberia's existing hydroelectric dam. This project would cost approximately $550 million and will have to be financed by such international lending institutions as the World Bank, and African Development Fund, as well as through suppliers' credits. The other study is being conducted by a French firm for the Mano River Union, a developing common market-type organization comprised of Liberia, Sierra Leone, and Guinea. Whichever of the two projects obtain Liberian Government approval and international funding, the result will reduce the devastating effects of Liberia's increasing oil import bill and produce an energy savings of immense proportions.

Telecommunications.—Liberia's telecommunications network consists of telephone, radio, television, and international microwave and satellite systems. A U.S. firm installed and equipped the radio network with transmitter, receivers, towers, antennas, and power supply in the 1960's.

The transmitter site for the international communications network is located in Paynesville. French Cables Company, equipped with two transmittters, provides telephone and telegraph circuits to Paris. Liberia Telecommunications Corporation (LTC) operates five Technical Material Corporation (TMC) 10 kW transmitters, one RCA and one TMC 1 kW transmitter, all of which are used on international circuits. Another transmitter serves ship-to-shore communications. Established international telephone circuits provide telephone links to New York, Rome, Frankfurt, Stockholm, Freetown, and Lagos. In 1976, ITALCABLE, in a joint venture with the Liberian Government, installed and currently operates a nonstandard satellite ground station in Monrovia to tie in with the international satellite communication system. Although capable of television transmission, the station is used for international telephone and telex. The Liberian Government presently is considering upgrading the installation to a standard station. Liberia also is cooperating with neighboring countries in linking up with the Pan African Telecommunications System (PANAFTEL).

There are 8,500 telephones (0.5 per 100 population). The U.S. Government maintains two major communications facilities in Liberia—a Voice of America transmitter and a diplomatic communications facility, as well as a Coast Guard navigation station.

Services

Banks and Insurance.—Banking and insurance are important segments of services offered in Liberia. Besides the Government's central bank, The National Bank of Liberia, there are six commercial banks, two indigenous, three U.S.—namely Chase Manhattan Bank N.A., Citibank (Liberia) and Intrusco (affiliated with International Bank of Washington)—and an Italian, Liberian Trading and Development Bank Ltd. (TRADEVCO), a subsidiary of Mediobanca of Milan.

There are eight insurance companies, five of which have a U.S. affiliation: American International Underwriters, American Life Insurance Co., Insurance Company of Africa, Intrusco, and Lone Star Insurances, Inc. Other companies are Minet James Liberia, Inc., Royal Exchange Assurance (British), and United Security Insurance Agencies, Inc.

Government Services.—The 1980 Coup brought changes to the organizational structure of the Liberian Government. Superimposed over the 17 cabinet ministers is a 22-member Peoples Redemption Council (PRC), including a five-member executive committee, all of them Liberian soldiers of tribal origin who planned and executed the coup against the century-old Americo-Liberian ascendancy. Head of State Doe has promised to return the country to civilian rule on April 12, 1985, the fifth anniversary of the coup. A constitutional commission is drafting a new constitution for the return to democracy. The 17 cabinet agencies in the Liberian Government and noncabinet agencies that offer special services, employ some 29,000 civil servants. The latter includes the National Investment Commission (NIC), an autonomous body that negotiates investment incentive agreements on behalf of the Government; the Liberia Industrial Free Zone Authority in Monrovia, the Liberian Produce Marketing Corporation that exports Liberian produce, provides industrial facilities for processing of agricultural products, and participates in agricultural development programs; and the National Ports Authority.

Radio and Television.—The Liberian Broadcasting Corporation controls all forms of broadcasting.

There are 5 AM and 2 FM radio stations. ELBC, founded in 1960, is a commercial station sponsored by the Liberian Government. In 1977, it took part in a $3.5 million expansion and modernization of its radio and television capability by acquiring new transmitters and other equipment, and the construction of new studios. ELWA, founded in 1954, is a station of the Sudan Interior Mission and broadcasts religious, cultural, and educational broadcasts in English, French, Arabic, and 42 West African languages. ELNR, the LAMCO Information and Broadcasting Service, is located in Nimba and provides Liberian news, political, educational, music, and cultural programs in English; national news and all nationwide broadcasts from ELBC; and local news in English and African languages for LAMCO employees.

There are three television stations in Liberia. ELTV is a commercial station sponsored by the Liberian Government which broadcasts for 6½ hours daily. There were 260,000 radio receivers and 10,000 TV receiver sets in Liberia in 1974. The U.S. Agency for International Development (AID) is working with the Government of Liberia on a $17.5 million rural broadcasting project ($11.7 million from the United States and $5.8 million from Liberia) which will provide seven rural transmitters to broadcast news and information in local languages.

Medical Services.—There are 32 hospitals (2,500 beds) in Liberia, 52 percent government owned, 28 percent owned by concessionaires (investors), 14 percent owned by foreign missions, and 6 percent private. There are 24 health centers and 276 clinics.

Consumers

Of the 1.8 million consumers in Liberia, 38.3 percent are employed at a gainful occupation, either in money or kind, according to the 1979 enumeration. Students, housewives, retired persons, and others who do not seek employment comprised 39 percent, while 23 percent are unemployed.

Based on a 1978 estimate showing the employed population at 417,046, the labor force was comprised, by industry, of agriculture (76 percent), services (16 percent), and industry (9 percent). The table below shows the breakdown by occupational groups.

Agricultural Workers	67.3%	280,476	Unskilled	66.8%
Production Workers	14.2%	59,170	Semiskilled	10.6%
			Skilled	4.1%
Sales Workers	9.5%	39,540		
Clerical Workers	2.5%	10,468		
Service Workers	1.7%	7,255		
Professional Workers (Teaching)	1.6%	6,800		
Professional Workers (Nonteaching)	1.6%	6,728		
Owners of Small Business Establishments	1.0%	4,227		
Professional Workers Decisionmaking Senior level Teaching and nonteaching	0.5%			
Managing-Owners, Managers of Large Enterprises	0.1%	256		

Trade Policy and Regulations

Duties and Taxes on Imports

Liberia has a single-column tariff with no preferential or differential rates. The value for ad valorem duty in Liberia is c.i.f. The net weight of merchandise on which a specific duty is prescribed is the weight of the article without internal packing. Specific duties apply to foodstuffs, beverages, petroleum products, and certain rubber and textile products. Under the Tariff Schedule of the Republic of Liberia, 1974, customs duties fall into the following categories: 75 percent on luxury goods (plus import duty surcharges of up to 25 percent on cosmetics and perfumes, luxury jewelry articles, beer and malt beverages, alcoholic spirits, and cigars and cigarettes). The import duty surcharges of up to 25 percent on all nonessential items were imposed by the Liberian Government on September 1, 1980, in acordance with its 2-year standy agreement with the IMF.

Foreign concessionaires investing in development projects related to iron ore mining, rubber plantations, etc. are exempted from payment of duties and other customs on all imports required for the construction, maintenance, and operation of their projects (see Investment section). The Government's trade policy complements its current program for expanded agricultural production and industrialization. Business in Liberia is entirely free of foreign exchange regulations. To protect domestic industries, the Government has occasionally imposed new or increased import duties on competing imports. Under the Investment Incentive Code, additional tariff protection may be granted to approved projects. In some cases, quantitative restrictions have been imposed. The level of tariff protection usually is not determined until the enterprise is in operation.

Export Duties

Liberia taxes exports of precious metals and stones and ivory ad valorem as follows: Gold, other precious metals and minerals, unrefined, 15 percent; refined, 10 percent; diamonds, other precious stones, rough or uncut, 16 percent; cut and/or polished, 10 percent; ivory manufactured, per pound, 10 percent. There is an export sales tax on rubber of 1, 1.5, or 2 cents per pound depending upon the selling price.

Import Licensing and Controls

Import Licenses as such are not required except for pork, pork products, and matches. Import permits are required for firearms, ammunition and explosives, gold in any form, medicines, narcotics and dangerous drugs, live animals, plants, and used clothing.

All paints are subject to import controls, and all orders for them must be channelled through the Ministry of Commerce, Industry, and Transportation before being ordered overseas. Additionally, orders for imports of toilet tissues, paper napkins, kitchen towels, roofing, galvanized nails, petroleum jelly, rubber footwear, car batteries, wheelbarrows, household candles, crown corks, nails, brooms, and brushes must also be channelled through this agency of the Government. Imports from South Africa and imports of shotgun shells and various items tending toward the subversion of the public's morals and health are prohibited. Meat is imported only by the Liberian Supply Corp., and petroleum and petroleum byproducts by the Liberian Petroleum Refinery Company. Cement is not presently being licensed. Sugar imports are not permitted.

Entry and Transit of Goods

The Free Port of Monrovia is operated in much the same way as free trade zones in U.S. ports. Goods may be delivered for domestic consumption, warehousing, transit, or transshipment.

Entry of goods into the Liberian customs territory must be accomplished within 7 days after the goods are unloaded to avoid assessment of storage charges. Ammunition, dynamite, and other explosives will be confiscated unless they are cleared through the port immediately following offloading.

Transshipment of goods may be made under bond or may be transferred from one ship to another in the free port for transshipment under a permit issued by a collector of customs. No duty is payable on foreign merchandise unloaded for transshipment that does not enter the Liberian customs territory.

Prohibited goods may not be unloaded for any purpose. Foreign goods that have entered the Liberian customs territory may be reexported upon application to a collector of customs, but only 60 percent of the duty paid will be refunded.

Foreign merchandise may be released from the free port area for transit overland to another country upon the written authorization of a Collector of Customs. Similarly, foreign goods may be brought in transit into the free port for reexport from Liberia. While goods in transit are not subject to import or export duties, all handling charges and warehouse costs must be paid before shipment is effected.

Storage and Unclaimed Goods

There are bonded warehouses and other storage facilities inside and outside the free port. Space may be leased from the National Port Authority for storage, assembly, or manufacturing operations, as well as from private warehouse operators for storage and cargo-handling operations.

Charges for storage and handling in the free port are calculated on a cubic tonnage basis and vary according to the type of goods. The storage rates applied to goods being transshipped are lower. Goods unclaimed or abandoned in the free port are subject to auction.

Samples and Advertising Matter

Bona fide samples having no commercial value are admitted duty free, but they must be marked, mutilated, or perforated in such a manner as to prevent their sale. Advertising matter—such as catalogs, brochures, and posters—imported for display purposes only are admitted duty free. The article or its container should be marked "Free Sample" or "Free Specimen." The address side of the package should be marked "Sample of Merchandise." Advertising articles such as ashtrays, cigarette lighters, hats, pens, mechanical pencils, playing cards, and drinking glasses are subject to duty, even though they bear the name of a product or firm.

Shipping Documents

Documents required by Liberian customs authorities on shipments from the United States are the bill of lading, commercial invoice (2 copies minimum), a packing list, insurance documents, and any special certificates that might be required due to the nature of the shipped goods or as may be requested by the importer. Shipping marks and numbers on bills of lading must correspond exactly with those of the invoices and on the goods. No special invoice or consular forms are required.

Marking, Labeling, and Packaging

Merchandise imported into Liberia is not required to show the country of origin. However, the packaging of most consumer goods must be accompanied by a descriptive text in English. Crates must bear clear, distinctive and indelible marks and numbers, and places of destination that agree with the invoice and the ship's manifest. All goods should be securely packed and wrapped in waterproof covers to withstand excessive tropical heat, moisture, rough handling, and pilferage. West African importers recommend that U.S. shippers avoid the use of thin cardboard or plywood containers because they are readily damaged if exposed to the elements. Most goods entering Liberia by sea must be transported by rail or truck for distribution or transshipment. To ensure safe arrival at destination, all packages should be of sturdy construction, properly supported, and banded on the outside with steel strapping. A separate packing list showing packing detail, description of goods, weights, marks, and numbers should be attached to the Liberian commercial invoice as there normally is insufficient space for such detail.

Distribution and Sales Channels

Distribution Centers

The urban centers, the prime markets for imported manufactured goods, are concentrated along the coast, the main roads to the interior, and near the large iron ore and rubber concessions. Although overall population density is relatively low (approximately 30 persons per square mile) the figure is as high as 150 in the cities. Major centers and their estimated populations (as of 1978 census) are Monrovia 240,000 est.; Harbel and Harbel Plantation 60,000; Buchanan 25,000; Yekepa (Nimba) 16,000; Harper and Harper Plantation 14,000; and Greenville 10,000. Other towns generally have fewer than 4,000 inhabitants. The foreign residents are distributed similarly, with 9,000 living in Monrovia.

Although Liberia's per capita income ($481 in 1975) is high by African standards, income and purchasing power are not evenly distributed. They are highly concentrated in the major urban centers. Approximately 10 percent of the population is employed in the monetary economy. Over 70 percent of the total work force is engaged in agriculture, primarily on a subsistence level, and is only marginally attached to the monetary economy. The remainder is employed in the major concessions.

Monrovia's market characteristics and unique positon make it the focal point for firms seeking to enter the Liberian market. Monrovia is the country's largest city, the national capital, chief seaport, chief free port, and commercial manufacturing center. The population of Monrovia represents most of Liberia's purchasing power. It is comprised of a high proportion of the country's wage earners, foreign residents, government leaders, and a large and continuous influx of migrants from the rural areas. Almost all of the major enterprises in Liberia have offices in Monrovia that can serve as initial points of contact with the extractive operations in the interior. In addition, Monrovia is the national wholesale and retail distribution center. Thus, an association with one of the leading importers/wholesalers in Monrovia can lead to wide product distribution throughout Liberia.

Distribution Channels

The major import channel for suppliers wishing to enter the Liberian market is the large or medium-sized, predominantly foreign-owned, trading house. About 30 of the more important of these companies are also represented in other West African countries. An exporter may gain broader market exposure by dealing with one of these firms. The principal trading houses generally handle a wide variety of goods, ranging from food products and radios to automobiles and industrial equipment. In many cases, importers prefer to hold exclusive agency rights for the various noncompeting lines they handle. But it must be noted that the present government has opposed exclusive agency agreements unless they involve servicing and the provision of spare parts.

In the past, the Liberian Government had granted import monopolies to individual traders. However, the largest commercial establishments often are subsidiaries of foreign companies, including a number of U.S. interests. This situation results in a relatively stable line of business for many importers, particularly in such areas as technical equipment where aftersales servicing is an important factor requiring the training of technicians and the stocking of spare parts. Middle Eastern and Asian merchants appear less hesitant to change their sources of supply as they do not have close links with a specific industrial country. With respect to foodstuffs and other nondurable consumer items, price, quality, and other purchase criteria are often more essential in introducing new products. Although the larger import houses have tended to concentrate on wholesale functions, many of them also have retail outlets in Monrovia and branch stores in several other population centers. Increasingly, these companies are specializing in capital equipment and consumer durables, leaving most nondurable consumer items to the small importer-distributor. At present, there are large firms specializing in earthmoving vehicles and related machinery, household appliances, furniture and furnishings, food products, and consumer goods suitable for supermarket sales. A number of small merchants specialize in textile imports and sales.

Sales to the large, foreign-owned mining and rubber concessionaires present an additional import channel. These companies purchase their industrial equipment and supplies as well as consumer goods for their employees, either directly or through subsidiary trading companies that may also serve the general public.

Webb-Pomerene Act

In appointing an exclusive representative in Liberia, the U.S. exporter is legally entitled to certain exemptions from U.S. antitrust laws. The Webb-Pomerene Act allows a limited exemption from U.S. antitrust laws for direct exports by allowing exporters to agree on prices, sales terms, territorial division, and other activities in export trade that would be prohibited in U.S. domestic commerce. More information on the Webb-Pomerence Act is available from the International Business Practices Division, Office of Service Industries, International Trade Administration, U.S. Department of Commerce, Washington, D.C. 20230.

Government Procurement

With certain exceptions noted below, procurement practices of the Government of Liberia are handled on a decentralized basis by the individual departments or agencies. However, purchase requests must be approved by the Bureau of General Supplies before presentation to the Bureau of General Accounting. The General Services Agency (GSA) has responsibility for government procurement. Government procurement of medical and pharmaceutical products is handled either through bids solicited from foreign firms or directly from local suppliers of imported goods. Semiautonomous government agencies, such as public utility corporations, do their own purchasing, either from local wholesalers or directly from overseas suppliers. These public companies usually issue invitations to bid on major purchasing requirements.

Although purchases are made from local wholesalers whenever possible, there are significant direct sales opportunities for U.S. suppliers. The Liberian Government's use, as a general rule, of U.S. specifications gives U.S. manufacturers an advantage in selling to the Government. However, this factor does not eliminate the desirability of some type of representation in Liberia to maintain contact with GSA and other agencies that make buying decisions.

Commercial Practices

Quotations and Terms of Payment

Price quotations are usually requested on a c.i.f. basis in dollars by Liberian importers. In well-established trade relationships with larger firms, some import transactions, including those with U.S. suppliers, are conducted on a 60-to-90-day sight draft basis. Interest is charged at an effective annual rate of 10 to 12 percent. Products from Eastern Europe are imported on a straight sight draft (i.e., no delayed payment). Importers do not pick up sight drafts until arriv-

al of the goods at the port of Monrovia. Most U.S. exporters require irrevocable letters of credit, a procedure that is recommended in new trade relationships with all firms. In certain cases, credits available through the Export-Import Bank of the United States (Eximbank) can make quotations more competitive with those of third country suppliers. Payments by the large, foreign-owned firms are often handled through the parent companies. In nearly every instance, import transactions with Japan, Hong Kong, and Singapore are on the basis of irrevocable letters of credit. Some Japanese products, particularly motor vehicles, are imported on open account (i.e., on consignment).

Pricing and Markup

The cost and time involved in shipping to Liberia has resulted in a situation of high markups on imported goods. Generally, markups are greater on consumer durables than on food and beverages and rise as distances from Monrovia increase. In some cases, low-priced imports may retail at several times their landed cost to counterbalance those product lines that are sold below cost to induce quick turnover. In an effort to hold down prices, the Government has established price controls on a number of the most widely used imported foods. These controls are enforced by the Minister of Commerce, Industry, and Transportation.

Credit

Due to critical foreign exchange shortages, Eximbank and the Foreign Credit Insurance Association offer a limited range of loans and credit insurance for export of U.S. products to Liberia only after verification that the importer has foreign exchange cover for each transaction. Credit was widely used in Liberia with commerce and manufacturing receiving a large proportion of commercial bank credit. Lending arrangements ranged from the usual commercial methods—such as open account, letters of credit, and short-term bank financing—to complex and informal credit relationships based on personal acquaintance among the different levels of trading and their customers outside of the banking system. As most Liberian banks borrow from foreign sources to supplement their loanable resources, interest rates reflect those prevailing in the New York and Eurodollar markets.

To assist U.S. exporters in formulating sound credit policies applicable to local markets, credit information on individual Liberian firms is available through the World Traders Data Reports (WTDRs) service. The WTDRs, which are compiled by the U.S. Foreign Commercial Service, are available from the U.S. Department of Commerce (ITA), World Traders Data Reports, Room 1033, Washington, D.C. 20230, for $40 for each company on which a report is requested. Credit information may also be available from private agencies. Some of the principal U.S. sources include Foreign Credit Interchange Bureau, National Association of Credit Management, 229 Fourth Avenue, New York, New York 10003; American Foreign Credit Underwriters Corp., 253 Broadway, New York, New York 10007; and Dun and Bradstreet, Inc., 99 Church Street, New York, New York 10007.

Credit information also may be available from the following banks located in Monrovia in which U.S. banks have interests: Citibank, N.A.; Chase Manhattan Bank; and International Trust Company of Liberia (International Bank, Washington, D.C.).

Market Research and Trade Organizations

Market research techniques have not been widely developed in Liberia; however, their use is gradually becoming more important. Large trading firms occasionally conduct limited market surveys for specific products, usually in co-operation with their suppliers. Several local advertising agencies conduct market research and consumer services. Liberian banks also will provide assistance in market research, and these services are frequently available in the United States through correspondent arrangements. U.S. banks that have interests in Liberia are listed in Appendix A.

There are several business organizations in Monrovia—including the Liberia Chamber of Commerce, the Junior Chamber of Commerce, and the Monrovia Marketing Association—which may be able to furnish market information and can put suppliers in contact with their members. (See Appendix B for addresses.) The American Businessmen's Association, which was organized in late 1976, works closely with the Economic/Commercial Section of the U.S. Embassy. The Liberian Journal of Commerce and Industry, an official Liberian publication, contains information and data pertaining to the Liberian economy but is issued only sporadically. Other government publications issued from time to time deal with specific topics of economic and commercial interest.

Advertising

While advertising is not as widely utilized in Liberia as in the United States, its use is growing as the money economy expands. Most major advertising media are available in Liberia, and a multimedia approach is generally considered the most effective in gaining acceptance for new products. Advertising campaigns are desirable and are used extensively in introducing certain consumer goods to the market. In the case of the more expensive and technical items, local distributors are often reluctant to carry new products without promotional support from their suppliers. Publicity should be simple and direct, concentrating on the product's benefits or prestige rather than its technical characteristics. Items should not appear to be specifically designed for the African market, as such goods often are regarded as inferior to articles sold in the United States or Europe and do not sell well in Liberia. Acceptance of a product by leaders of the People's Redemption Council (PRC) will often lead to wide acceptance in all areas.

Printed Materials.—Advertising is generally confined to the press in Monrovia, all of which is in English. This includes the *New Liberian*, published by the Ministry of Information, Cultural Affairs, and Tourism, Monday through Friday, the independent *Liberian Observer*, and the weekly *Sunday Express*. Each newspaper has an estimated circulation of 5,000. The Government also publishes mimeographed news sheets in outlying areas, and missionary and other private groups publish small local papers. Leading American and European news magazines are read widely by the expatriate community and by Liberians in government, business, and professional circles. The *International Herald Tribune* also is available at Monrovia's newsstands and at supermarkets and book stores. Pictorial magazines directed toward West Africa, such as *Drum*, *Flamingo*, and the African edition of *Ebony*, are popular as are such publications as *West Africa*, and *African Development* (published in London). Various business directories that carry advertising are published locally from time to time.

Journals in which exporters may wish to place ads include the *Dictionary* and *Who's Who*, published by A&A Enterprises, Inc., P.O. Box 103, Monrovia; and the *Liberian Trade and Industry Handbook*, P.O. Box 1498, Monrovia.

Radio, TV, and Motion Pictures.—The country's radio and television are dependent on advertising revenue. Due to widespread illiteracy in the country, the broadcasting medium is an important means of reaching consumers, especially those living outside Monrovia. There are three classes of radio time, "Premium," "AAA," and "AA"; advertising rates vary accordingly. Inquiries concerning radio or television advertising should be addressed to General Manager, ELBC/ELTV, P.O. Box 594, Monrovia, Liberia. Liberia has 23 movie theaters that accept advertising. Seven theaters in Monrovia have a combined seating capacity of over 6,000, and 17 in the larger towns and major iron ore and rubber concession enclaves have a total capacity of 5,500.

Other Media. —Other types of advertising that should not be overlooked include billboards, posters, transportation displays, and point-of-sale advertisements and demonstrations. Of these, point-of-sale demonstrations, such as food product sampling held in supermarkets, have proved highly effective. Flyers, either distributed by hand or as newspaper inserts, are also used.

Investment

Investment Climate

Liberia is heavily dependent on the export of a few primary commodities for its livelihood, chiefly, iron ore, and rubber. To exploit these resources, the Government of Liberia has maintained an open door policy on foreign investment and freedom of capital transfers. Adverse conditions in world markets for Liberia's exports, rising oil prices, combined with unsettled political conditions following the military coup in April 1980, have resulted in little or no real growth for several years and a substantially reduced level of economic activity.

The new Government has emphasized on several occasions its intention to continue the liberal investment policies of its predecessors and is actively seeking new investment. A number of fiscal incentives, including special benefits to investment in the industrial free zone, established to encourage enclave industries, will be continued. Although a number of economic and political uncertainties still face potential investors in Liberia, continuing progress toward internal security has been evidenced following the initial chaos of the post-coup era, and this has led to optimism that the country's current difficulties can be surmounted.

Since taking office, the military government headed by Head of State Samuel K. Doe has been faced with a serious financial crisis, inherited in part from the previous regime. The crisis was aggravated by capital flight reflecting uncertainty by investors and substantial salary increases granted to the military and civil servants, actions that were accompanied by declining customs revenues related to falls in import levels in the months following the coup. Agreement with IMF on a stabilization program has given the Liberian Government substantial new financial resources and important foreign bilateral assistance, including an enlarged U.S. Agency for International Development (AID) program. Some restoration of confidence within the business community also has permitted economic conditions to stabilize, though at a lower level than existed prior to the coup.

Liberian laws of incorporation are simple and favor foreign investors. Liberia uses the U.S. dollar as its currency, and there are no restrictions on repatriation of profits or capital. Tax holidays and tariff exemption and sometimes tariff protection are granted to new investments under Liberia's Investment Incentive Code in activities considered economically desirable by the Liberian Government. Special "concession" agreements have been negotiated between the Government and important foreign investors, particularly for iron ore mining, rubber production, and timber exploitation, which together account for almost 90 percent of the total value of Liberian exports. The Government's goal is a 50 percent share in the profits of the operation through taxation of equity participation. Although there are no known laws or regulations governing the use of local raw materials and other inputs, such use is obviously encouraged and might well figure in negotiations between the Liberian Government and a potential investor seeking incentives and privileges.

Legislation

U.S.-Liberian relations are formalized in the Treaty of Friendship, Commerce, and Navigation of 1938. The United States and Liberia also concluded an Investment Guarantee Agreement that makes available the programs of the U.S. Overseas Private Investment Corporation (OPIC). OPIC extends its full range of services to Liberia and has about $46 million in active maximum coverage insurance. Liberia is a signatory to the Convention on the Settlement of Investment Disputes Between the States and Nationals of Other States.

The main instrument of Liberia's open door policy is the Investment Incentive Code, which was introduced in 1966 and essentially amended in 1973. In the case of new industries, the code provides for exemption from customs duties, tax levies, and other charges for the following: (a) approved imports of construction machinery, equipment, and materials necessary for the provision of facilities for the enterprise; and (b) raw, semiprocessed, or processed materials required in the manufacture of articles by the approved investment project for a period of 5 years from the first importation.

Under the revised code, the total cumulative new income exempted from taxation is generally limited to a maximum of 150 percent of the total capital investment at the time production is begun. Capital investment includes the cost of land, buildings, and equipment, as well as unamortized intangible exploration and development costs.

Other benefits include provisions for certain technical assistance, the possibility of Liberian Government loans or equity participation, and leasing arrangements of government-owned land in industrial parks within the city of Monrovia. Benefits and incentives are negotiable with the Government of Liberia, and they are granted upon application to the Ministry of Commerce, Industry, and Transportation after review and approval of an interagency concession board.

Private foreign investment has figured prominently in the economic development of Liberia. The large rubber plantations are owned by foreign companies. Many commercial and nearly all banking operations are financed and managed by foreigners—Lebanese, Americans, Swedes, Germans, Italians, Dutch, Israelis, and others. The four iron ore mining ventures are primarily owned and operated by U.S. and European interests with some equity held by the Government of Liberia and individual Liberians (the arrangements vary from company to company). The U.S. Department of Commerce estimated the U.S. direct investment position in Liberia at $278 million at yearend 1980, the second largest figure in black Africa.

Industrial Free Zone

The international industrial free trade zone contains 71 plots of 1 acre each (total area including all facilities with provision for expansion is approximately 110 acres). The Liberian Government is presently seeking financing for the $32 million zone. Factories thought to be best suited for the area are those producing pharmaceuticals, agricultural machinery, pumps and valves, office machinery, photographic and other scientific equipment, electrical equipment, and motor vehicles and aircraft equipment assembly. Interested firms may contact the Minister of Commerce, Industry, and Transportation,

Monrovia, Liberia or the Managing Director, Liberia Industrial Free Zone Authority, PMB 9047, Monrovia, Liberia.

Industrial Property Protection

Liberia is not a member of the International Convention for the Protection of Industrial Property. However, the U.S.-Liberia Friendship, Commerce, and Navigation Treaty guarantees in part the rights of property ownership and lease protection under the law; noninterference in professional, scientific, religious, philanthropic, manufacturing, and commercial activities subject to local laws; and equal status with Liberians in regard to taxation, judicial proceedings, and protection.

Copyrights

Liberia is a signatory of the Universal Copyright Convention. Application for copyright of a literary, scientific, or artistic work must be made to the Liberian Ministry of Foreign Affairs. The author of a work copyrighted in Liberia has exclusive lifetime rights and his heirs have exclusive rights for 20 years after his death to reproduce, sell, or authorize reproductions, and to forbid the sale in Liberia of reproductions made abroad without permission.

Further general information on industrial property and copyright protection can be obtained from the International Business Practices Division, Office of Service Industries, International Trade Administration, U.S. Department of Commerce, Washington, D.C. 20230. However, information related to step-by-step procedures on fees, documents, etc., should be obtained from legal counsel.

Patents

Patents are obtained by making a written application to the Bureau of Archives, Patents, Copyright, and Trademarks in the Ministry of Foreign Affairs. Any alien receiving a patent must put it into active operation within 3 years from the date of issuance or abandon it to the public. Invention patents are valid for 20 years after grant to the applicant, and his heirs, administrators, executors, or assignees. Prior public knowledge, publication, or use in Liberia is prejudicial. There are no specific exclusions from patentability, no novelty examination, and no opposition provision.

Trademarks

Applications for trademarks must be made to

the Ministry of Foreign Affairs. Trademark protection is granted for 15 years and may be renewed upon application for a second 15-year period. A proprietor of a trademark may rectify or alter it upon filing notice in the Ministry of Foreign Affairs within 3 months from the date of registration. Rectification or alteration that materially alters the original design is considered an original trademark. A trademark may be assigned or transmitted. Use of a trademark without the express consent of the proprietor is a civil offense. Infringement action is not possible if based on an unregistered mark. First applicant is entitled to registration, but he or she must prove that the mark is not in use by anyone else. There are examination procedures but no opposition provisions. The mark must be used within 2 years of registration date; otherwise it is cancellable. It is also cancellable if the owner neglects legal action against infringer or adopts a new similar mark.

Business Organization

The types of business organization most common in Liberia are similar to those in the United States. These are corporations, individual proprietorships, and partnerships. The Liberian Corporation Law and other business laws fail to provide specifically for the establishment of branch offices. Most foreign firms, however, will find it advantageous to organize as a corporation in Liberia, as domestic corporations that are more than 50 percent owned by foreign interests enjoy a number of important corporate and tax advantages.

Sole proprietorships, with the exception of those with assets of under $500, are required to pay a flat fee of $100 a year. Regardless of size, corporations pay annual fees of $200.

Foreign enterprises in Liberia include individual proprietorships in trading and services, joint ventures, major industrial and agricultural projects under government concessions grants; and architectural, engineering, and construction operations working under Government and private contract. A high percentage of firms, particularly those in trading, are wholly owned by foreign companies or nationals. U.S. business interests in Liberia are engaged largely in mining, industrial, and agricultural ventures; marketing and distribution; banking; insurance; shipping; construction contracting; and engineering and architectural services.

Taxation

Corporate Taxes

Liberia assesses a progressive tax on the net income of every domestic corporation, incorporated association, joint stock company, and insurance company as well as on the income of those firms existing under foreign law and doing business in Liberia. No statutory deductions from gross income are allowed, but corporations may claim ordinary deductions of necessary business expenses, uninsured business losses, other taxes paid, reasonable amortization and depreciation allowances and charitable contributions not to exceed 15 percent of net income. Net income is taxed according to the following table:

Net Income		Percentage Tax Rate
$ .01 to	$ 5,000.00	5
5,000.01 to	10,000.00	10
10,000.01 to	20,000.00	15
20,000.01 to	50,000.00	20
50,000.01 to	75,000.00	25
75,000.01 to	100,000.00	30
100,000.01 to	500,000.00	35
500,000.01 to 1,000,000.00		40
Over $1,000,000.00		45

Personal Income Tax

Net income of both individuals and partnerships is subject to a progressive tax ranging from 2 to 35 percent. Both are allowed a statutory deduction of $1,500 from gross income, as well as certain ordinary deductions similar to those allowed under U.S. income tax laws. Liberian law provides that every employer be responsible for the withholding of income tax from the wages, salaries, or other compensation of employees and for the payment of such taxes to the Bureau of Internal Revenue, Department of the Treasury. Net income is then taxed according to the following rates:

Net Income		Percentage Tax Rate
$ 0.01–$	1,500	2
1,500.01–	4,000	4
4,000.01–	6,000	6
6,000.01–	8,000	8
8,000.01–	10,000	10
10,000.01–	20,000	15
20,000.01–	50,000	20
50,000.01–	75,000	25
75,000.01–	100,000	30
Over 100,000		35

Ordinary deductions for individuals include payments of interest on indebtedness and of other taxes, all losses not covered by insurance, and contributions to charitable or philanthropic organizations.

Other Taxes

Other taxes include the following: import and export duties (see above under Trade Regulations); a real estate tax of 0.5 to 1 percent of the assessed value of buildings; a realty lease tax of 10 percent of the annual rental; a stumpage tax on lumber; an export tax on diamonds; various revenue stamps for a variety of documents, business, and professional licensing fees; and various excise taxes and registration fees on vehicles and tonnage fees for vessel registration.

The United States does not have a bilateral tax treaty with Liberia. Under U.S. law, however, U.S. companies operating in Liberia may claim a credit against U.S. taxes due for the taxes paid to Liberia. In addition to the ordinary business deductions, Liberia provides important exemptions for domestic corporations in which aliens or nonresidents of Liberia hold majority voting rights. Such corporations are exempted from tax on income derived from sources outside the Republic of Liberia—unless from the sale of goods grown, produced, or manufactured in whole or in part within the Republic; business transactions, including insurance, in foreign commerce not involving Liberian products; income from the sale of any property, real or personal, tangible or intangible, which is not physically within the Republic of Liberia or which is held in custody in Liberia by a domestic bank or trust company; earnings from the operation of Liberian-documented vessels not engaged for the operation of Liberian coastal trade (applies both to alien-owned domestic and to foreign corporations); and interest received on tax-exempt obligations of the Republic of Liberia.

All income tax returns must be filed with the Collector of Internal Revenue not later than April 1 of the year following the end of the tax year of December 31. Alien-owned Liberian firms earning all their income from sources outside of Liberia are not required to file income tax returns.

Iron Ore Profit Sharing

The Liberian Government shares in the profits-in-lieu-of-income tax receipts of the four iron ore mining companies. The oldest of these companies now shares its profits with the Government on a 50-50 basis. The single exception applies to Bethlehem Steel's one-quarter share.

Employment

The total Liberian labor force is estimated to be 510,000. Within the monetary economy the labor force numbers about 160,000, and approximately one-half is employed in agriculture, mainly in rubber plantations. The Government is also a significant employer. While productivity varies with the type of work performed, it tends to be low among industrial and clerical workers. Unskilled laborers and drivers maintain a higher productivity level. It has been calculated that productivity of all workers is about 40 percent of that of workers in the United States. In the private sector, aliens dominate the managerial, administrative, and most skilled positions (95 percent). Liberians are expected to become more numerous in such positions.

Payments and Benefits

Laws exist establishing maximum hours of work, paid vacations, worker's compensation, medical care, retirement, restrictions on the employment of aliens, and control of labor unions. The normal work week is five 8-hour days. The minimum wage is established at 15 cents an hour for industrial workers and 12.5 cents an hour for agricultural workers.

Fringe benefits vary greatly with the industry and the employer. Industrial workers sometimes receive transportation and lunch money. Plantation workers receive a full range of benefits—including housing, medical care, subsidized food, and sometimes scholarships for their children. Fringe benefits range from zero to 33 percent of a worker's wages.

Labor Organization

The bulk of Liberia's economically active population is outside the wage-earning sector; there is some degree of labor organization among wage-earning workers including commercial, clerical, mining, transportation, petroleum, distribution, mechanics, dock workers, seamen, and domestic workers. Labor unions were first approved in 1949, although the first collective bargaining agreement was not concluded until 1963. Liberia has occasionally been criticized by the ILO for practices at variance with conventions of the International Labor Organization, such as a prohibition against trade union organizing of agricultural workers (which was lifted in 1980) and civil servants. Following the April 1980 coup, the ruling People's Redemption Council banned strikes, although it allowed other forms of labor activity to continue. The Liberian Government is currently working on a comprehensive revision of the country's labor code, which is expected to streamline the current labor laws and the adjudication of labor disputes.

Prior to the April 1980 coup, unions generally associated themselves with influential members of the Americo-Liberian elite and did not challenge the government. Since then, more indigenous labor leaders have emerged, but the Liberian labor movement remains weak by Western standards.

Liberia has one national labor federation, the Liberian Federation of Trade Unions (LFLU), which includes eight member unions and approximately 2,000 dues-paying members. There are several significant unions not affiliated with LFLU, such as the National Agricultural and Allied Workers of Liberia (NAAWUL), which represents the 17,000 workers of the Firestone Rubber plantation, and LAMCO Mine Workers Union.

Liberian labor law prohibits the employment of foreign labor, except in administrative, supervisory, or technical capacities unless there is a shortage of qualified Liberians capable of supplying the needs of the employer. If the employer can find no qualified Liberian on lists maintained by the Liberian Government, he so certifies to the Minister of Labor, Youth, and Sports, who may then issue a special work permit for the foreigner to engage in the work designated. The employer must obtain this permit before attempting to obtain a visa for a worker to be imported. Likewise, a foreign employee must have a work permit in hand before applying for a residence permit. Prospective foreign investors in Liberia should be aware that the trend is toward "Liberianization" in all employee categories, including management.

No foreign employee may be paid at a wage rate different from that paid Liberian citizens in similar work, except that some allowance is made for differentials to compensate for an alien's overseas employment status.

Guidance for Business Travelers Abroad

Communications

Business correspondence is normally conducted by airmail which arrives four times weekly from the United States. International airmail letters from the United States to Monrovia cost 40 cents for a letter weighing ½ ounce; 40 cents for each additional half ounce up to 2 ounces; and form letters cost 30 cents. The normal weight limit of 4 pounds applies to letters and letter packages.

Telephone service is limited. The regular rate for a long distance call to the United States is $12 for the first 3 minutes and $3.40 a minute thereafter Monday through Saturday. Special Sunday rates to the United States are $9 for the first 3 minutes and $2.60 a minute thereafter. Rates to Europe are less expensive. Telephone company credit cards are honored for calls to the United States. Collect calls are accepted to the United States.

Telegraphic rates to the United States are 25 cents a word for a straight message and $2.25 per 22 words and 12½ cents for each extra word for a night letter.

Currency

The U.S. dollar is the basic monetary unit in Liberia. U.S. coin and bills in denominations up to $20 are legal tender. The Liberian Treasury issues 1, 2, 5, 10, 25, and 50 cent, $1, and $5 coins. There are no exchange controls.

Technical Standards

Liberia's system of weights and measures is the same as that currently in use in the United States. The former President of Liberia had recommended the adoption of the metric system of weights and measures.

Language

English is the official and commercial language.

Entrance Requirements

All persons entering Liberia must have a valid passport and a Liberian visa. Visas can be obtained from the Liberian Embassy, 5201 16th Street, N.W., Washington, D.C. 20011, or consular posts in Chicago, Detroit, Houston, Los Angeles, New Orleans, New York City, Philadelphia, and Port Arthur, Texas. Requirements needed to obtain a Liberian visa in the United States are as follows: possession of a valid U.S. passport; two completed application for visa forms and two passport-size photographs (one attached to each copy), and vaccination certificates for smallpox, cholera, and yellow fever. Any person or persons being sponsored by a company or organization should present a letter assuming financial responsibility for the proposed visit, either a round-trip ticket, or if in transit, visa to country of ultimate destination must be presented. For those seeking a resident visa, a police certificate of good conduct from the applicant's last place of residency and a Liberian Ministry of Foreign Affairs authorization for Resident Visa.

Visas are $2 for a visitor's visa and $20 for a resident visa. Cash or money orders are acceptable in payment of visa fees. Personal checks will not be accepted. Visitors visas are usually issued 48 hours after submission of applications and requirements with passports. Resident visas are required to be obtained from the Ministry of Foreign Affairs. All persons departing Liberia, other than those remaining at Robertsfield and leaving within 48 hours, must have an exit permit issued by the Immigration Office. An airport tax of $10 is levied on all departing passengers.

Holidays

The following are commercial holidays in Liberia:

January 1	New Year's Day
February 11	Armed Forces Day
Second Wednesday in March	Decoration Day
March 15	J.J. Roberts Birthday
Friday Preceding Easter Sunday	Day of Fasting and Prayer
April 12	Redemption Day
May 14	National Unification Day
July 26	Independence Day
August 25	Flag Day
First Thursday in November	Thanksgiving Day
November 29	The Late President Tubman's Birthday
December 25	Christmas Day

Business Hours

The business hours of most stores and firms are generally 8 a.m. to noon and 2 p.m. to 6 p.m., Monday through Friday. On Saturday, most firms and stores are open from 8 a.m. to noon. Many small shops and supermarkets stay open later. Government offices are open from 8 a.m. to 4 p.m., with varying times taken for lunch. Government offices and nearly all business establishments are closed on Sundays and holidays. Office hours at the American Embassy are 7:30 a.m. to 4:30 p.m., with lunchtime from noon to 1 p.m., Monday through Friday. The U.S. Embassy is closed on weekends and on American and Liberian holidays.

Diplomatic Representation

Embassy of Liberia
5201 16th Street, N.W.
Washington, D.C. 20011
Tel: 202-723-0437

Consulate General of Liberia

820 Second Avenue
New York, New York 10017
Tel: 212-687-1033

American Embassy
United Nations Drive
Monrovia, Liberia
Tel: 22991, 22992

Correspondence may be sent through the U.S. mail using the following address:

American Embassy
APO New York 09155

Commercial Banks in Liberia

Citibank, NA
Corner of Ashmun and Randall Street, or
P.O. Box 280
Monrovia
Tel: 21300
U.S. affiliate: CITICORP

Chase Manhattan Bank, N.A.
Ashmun and Randall Streets, or
P.O. Box 181
Monrovia
Tel: 21500, 21103

International Trust Company of Liberia (INTRUSCO)
80 Broad Street, or
P.O. Box 292
Monrovia
Tel: 21600
U.S. affiliate: International Bank of Washington, D.C.

Liberian Trading and Development Company (TRADEVCO)
57 Ashmun Street, or
P.O. Box 293
Monrovia
Tel: 21800, 21302

Sources of Economic and Commercial Information

Business Information

Liberian Chamber of Commerce
P.O. Box 92
Monrovia

Junior Chamber of Commerce
Monrovia

Monrovia Retailers Association
Monrovia

Government Information

Liberia Industrial Free Zone Authority

PMB 9047
Monrovia, Liberia

Ministry of Commerce, Industry, and
Transportation
88 Ashmun Street
P.O. Box 9014
Monrovia, Liberia

Ministry of Planning and Economic Affairs
P.O. Box 1096
49 Broad Street
Monrovia, Liberia

Ministry of Agriculture
Tuban Boulevard, Sinkor
P.O. Box 9010
Monrovia, Liberia

Ministry of Lands and Mines
144 Tubman Boulevard, Capitol Hill
P.O. Box 9039
Monrovia, Liberia

Ministry of Public Works

100 Lynch Street
P.O. Box 9011
Monrovia, Liberia

Ministry of Information, Cultural Affairs,
and Tourism
150 Tubman Boulevard, Capitol Hill
P.O. Box 9021
Monrovia, Liberia

Liberian Bank for Development and
Investment
P.O. Box 547, or
Tubman Boulevard
Monrovia, Liberia

National Bank of Liberia
P.O. Box 2048, or
Broad Street
Monrovia, Liberia

Liberia Electricity Corporation
P.O. Box 165
Monrovia, Liberia

Appendix

Selected Import Markets

Agricultural Industry Markets

Fertilizers

Total Import Market Size:
Average Annual (1975–79): $3.3 million; 1979: $4.1 million
Average Annual U.S. Share (1975–79): 7.1 percent
Leading Suppliers 1979: Germany, 25.9 percent; United States, 15.1 percent; Belgium Luxembourg, 1.8 percent

Pesticides, Fungicides, Disinfectants

Total Import Market Size:

Average Annual (1975–79): $7,000; 1979: $1.4 million
Average Annual U.S. Share (1975–79): 23.1 percent
Leading Suppliers 1979: United Kingdom, 49.7 percent; United States, 25.9 percent; Netherlands 9.2 percent

Agricultural Machinery

Total Import Market Size:

Average Annual (1975–79): $6.2 million; 1979: $6.5 million
Average Annual U.S. Share (1975–79): 55.3 percent
Leading Suppliers 1979: Japan, 47.3 percent; United States, 31.1 percent; United Kingdom, 10.9 percent

Forestry Industry Markets

Hand Tools for Agriculture and Forestry

Total Import Market Size:

Average Annual (1975–79): $731,600; 1979: $552,000
Average Annual U.S. Share (1975–79): 7.0 percent
Leading Suppliers: United Kingdom, 71.7 percent; United States, 11.5 percent; Germany, 8.3 percent

Machine Tools for Working Wood

(Includes sawmill machines and equipment; veneer, plywood, and cratemaking machines; and machines for working wood)

Total Import Market Size:
Average Annual (1975–79): $930,000; 1979: $655,000
Average Annual U.S. Share (1975–79): 17.6 percent
Leading Suppliers 1979: Germany, 36.3 percent; Italy, 21.7 percent; Belgium-Luxembourg 14.5 percent; United Kingdom, 10.7 percent; United States, 9.2 percent; France, 7 percent

Papermill and Pulpmill Machinery

Total Import Market Size:

Average Annual (1975–78): $136,800; 1978: $450,000
Average Annual U.S. Share (1975–78): 14.3 percent
Leading Suppliers 1978: Italy, 98.4 percent; United States, 1.3 percent; United Kingdom, 0.2 percent

Fishing Industry Markets

Present organization of trade data obscures the identification of Liberian import markets for ships/boats (fishing vessels) and fish processing equipment. Imports of ships are concealed in data that provide the value of ships that are registered as Liberian flag of convenience vessels, and fish processing equipment is included under the general heading of food processing machinery and equipment.

Mining and Mineral Industry Markets

Imports of mining, mineral processing, and materials handling equipment in West Africa are principally arranged by the mining concessionaires in their respective home countries rather than at the mine head as prevails in Southern Africa, but these types of machinery and equipment, nevertheless, form a large portion of U.S. exports to Liberia.

Excavating Levelling Machinery

Total Import Market Size:

Average Annual (1975–79): $14.7 million; 1979: $12.7 million
Average Annual U.S. Share (1975–79): 38.2 percent
Leading Suppliers 1979: United States, 60.2 percent; Germany, 17.8 percent; United

Kingdom 7.0 percent; Belgium Luxembourg, 5.3 percent; Japan 4.7 percent

Mineral Crushing, Sorting, Washing, Etc. Machinery and Parts

Total Import Market Size:

Average Annual (1975–79): $6.7 million; 1979: $3.7 million
Average Annual U.S. Share (1975–79): 22.6 percent
Leading Suppliers 1979: United Kingdom, 30.8 percent; Germany, 28.7 percent; United States, 21.9 percent; Italy 13.4 percent

Lifting, Loading, and Conveying Machines and Equipment

Total Import Market Size:

Average Annual (1975–79): $5 million; 1979: $4.5 million
Average Annual U.S. Share (1975–79): 38.2 percent
Leading Suppliers 1979: United States, 37.2 percent; Germany 33.7 percent; United Kingdom, 13.8 percent; France, 3.6 percent; Sweden, 2.5 percent

Trucks, Truck Chassis, and Truck Tractors

Total Import Market Size:

Average Annual (1975–79): $12.5 million; 1979: $13.1 million
Average Annual U.S. Share (1975–79): 27.9 percent
Leading Suppliers 1979: Japan, 38.4 percent; United States, 30.6 percent; Germany, 11.2 percent; France, 10.3 percent

Electric Utility Industry Markets

Demand in this market sector is expressed principally through the advertisements of competitive tenders.

Electric Power Machinery

Total Import Market Size:

Average Annual (1975–79): $5.8 million; 1979: $9.6 million
Average Annual U.S. Share (1975–79): 31.1 percent
Leading Suppliers 1979: Sweden, 37.3 percent; United Kingdom, 32.4 percent; United States, 17.5 percent; Germany, 4.9 percent.

Switchgear

Total Import Market Size:

Average Annual (1975–79): $3.9 million; 1979: $4.7 million
Average Annual U.S. Share (1975–79): 17.4 percent
Leading Suppliers 1979: Sweden, 44.2 percent; United States, 24.2 percent; Germany, 14.8 percent

Insulated Wire, Cable (shared by telecommunications industry)

Total Import Market Size:

Average Annual (1975–79): $2.1 million; 1979: $2.3 million
Average Annual U.S. Share (1975–79): 18 percent
Leading Suppliers 1979: Sweden, 38.4 percent; Germany, 25 percent; United States, 20 percent; United Kingdom, 10.9 percent

Electric Insulating Equipment

Total Import Market Size:

Average Annual (1975–79): $187,200; 1979: $179,000
Average Annual U.S. Share (1975–79): 63.5 percent
Leading Suppliers 1979: United States, 64.3 percent; Sweden, 29.1 percent; United Kingdom, 6.1 percent; Japan, 1 percent

Telecommunications Industry Markets

Telephone and Telegraph Equipment and Parts

Total Import Market Size:

Average Annual (1975–79): $2.2 million; 1979: $4.7 million
Average Annual U.S. Share (1975–79): 8.4 percent
Leading Suppliers 1979: Belgium, 37.7 percent; Germany, 21.5 percent; Sweden, 10.1 percent; Italy, 3.7 percent; United States, 1.5 percent; United Kingdom, 0.6 percent

Telecommunications Equipment, not elsewhere classified

This category embraces the whole continuum of radio and television communications equipment from transmitters and radio frequency amplifiers, single sideband high frequency transceivers, mobile and microwave signal equipment through commercial radio and TV broadcasting equipment, to electronic navigational, and search and detection apparatus, including radar.

Total Import Market Size:

Average Annual (1975–79): $2.8 million; 1979: $3.1 million

Average Annual U.S. Share (1975–79): 48.7 percent

Leading Suppliers 1979: United States, 40.1 percent; Germany, 30.9 percent; United Kingdom, 3.2 percent

Service Industry Markets (Banks and Insurance; Government)

Typewriters and Checkwriters

Total Import Market Size:

Average Annual (1975–79): $310,400; 1979: $327,000

Average Annual U.S. Share (1975–79): 4.4 percent

Leading Suppliers 1979: Germany, 70.3 percent; Italy, 10.1 percent; Netherlands, 7.6 percent; Sweden, 6.1 percent; United States, 3.0 percent; Japan, 2.1 percent

Calculating, and Accounting Machines, Electronic Computers, and Computer Peripheral Equipment

Total Import Market Size:

Average Annual (1975–79): $515,400; 1979: $407,000

Average Annual U.S. Share (1975–79): 15.8 percent

Leading Suppliers 1979: Germany, 25.6 percent; Japan, 21.6 percent; United States, 16 percent; United Kingdom, 11.8 percent

Duplicating and Addressing Machines

Total Import Market Size:

Average Annual (1975–79): $109,400; 1979: $163,000

Average Annual U.S. Share (1975–79): 29.9 percent

Leading Suppliers 1979: Germany, 54 percent; United Kingdom, 30.1 percent; United States, 5.9 percent; Sweden, 4.3 percent

Office Machine Parts, NEC

Total Import Market Size:

Average Annual (1975–79): $231,000; 1979: $238,000

Average Annual U.S. Share (1975–79): 15.8 percent

Leading Suppliers 1979: United States, 22.9 percent; United Kingdom, 16.8 percent; Italy, 16.4 percent; France 16 percent

Health Industries Markets

Medical and Pharmaceutical Products

Total Import Market Size:

Average Annual (1975–79): $4.9 million; 1979: $6.1 million

Average Annual U.S. Share (1975–79): 8.1 percent

Leading Suppliers 1979: United Kingdom, 44.7 percent; Germany, 18.5 percent; United States, 5.3 percent; France, 4.9 percent

Electro-Medical Equipment

Total Import Market Size:

Average Annual (1975–79): $45,000; 1979: $116,000

Average Annual U.S. Share (1975–79): 42.8 percent

Leading Suppliers 1979: Sweden, 41.4 percent; United States, 29 percent; United Kingdom, 10.3 percent

Medical, Dental, Surgical, Ophthalmic, and Veterinary Instruments and Apparatus

Total Import Market Size:

Average Annual (1975–79): $384,600; 1979: $473,000

Average Annual U.S. Share (1975–79): 36.4 percent

Leading Suppliers 1979: United States, 32.5 percent; Germany, 31.5 percent; United Kingdom, 26.2 percent

Mechanical Physical Therapy Appliances, Psychological Testing Apparatus, and Respiratory Equipment

Total Import Market Size:

Average Annual (1975–79): $41,200; 1979: $87,000

Average Annual U.S. Share (1975–79): 51.7 percent

Leading Suppliers 1979: United States, 71.5 percent; Germany, 17.2 percent; United Kingdom, 3.4 percent

Retail Industry Markets (Consumer Goods)

Perfumery, Cosmetics, Dentifrices, and Other Toilet Preparations

Total Import Market Size:

Average Annual (1975–79): $1.3 million; 1979: $1.3 million

Average Annual U.S. Share (1975–79): 39.6 percent

Leading Suppliers 1979: United States, 51.3 percent; France, 26.6 percent; Germany, 17.4 percent; and Italy, 2.7 percent

Domestic Mechanical Food-Processing Appliances

Total Import Market Size:

Average Annual (1975–79): $26,400; 1979: $73,000

Average Annual U.S. Share (1975–79): 25.3 percent

Leading Suppliers 1979: United Kingdom, 84.9 percent; Sweden, 9.6 percent; and United States, 6.4 percent

Domestic Water Heaters

Total Import Market Size:

Average Annual (1975–79): $18,600; 1979: $52,000

Average Annual U.S. Share (1975–79): 72.2 percent

Leading Suppliers 1979: United States, 100 percent

Domestic Electric Refrigerators

Total Import Market Size:

Average Annual (1975–79): $915,200; 1979: $1.3 million

Average Annual U.S. Share (1975–79): 57.8 percent

Leading Suppliers 1979: United States, 71.7 percent; Germany, 13.2 percent; Netherlands, 2.9 percent; United Kingdom, 2.9 percent

Electro-Mechanical Appliances

(Electric blenders, vacuum cleaners, floor waxing, and polishing machines, etc.)

Total Import Market Size:

Average Annual (1975–79): $212,600; 1979: $208,000

Average Annual U.S. Share (1975–79): 25.5 percent

Leading Suppliers 1979: United States, 44.1 percent; Japan, 29.3 percent; United Kingdom, 13 percent; Germany, 2.9 percent; Sweden, 2.9 percent

Electric Household-Type Cooking Equipment and Thermic Appliances

Total Import Market Size:

Average Annual (1975–79): $439,200; 1979: $481,000

Average Annual U.S. Share (1975–79): 44.4 percent

Leading Suppliers 1979: United States, 52.4 percent; Italy, 19.5 percent; Sweden, 9.8 percent; Germany, 9.4 percent

Radio Broadcast Receivers

Total Import Market Size:

Average Annual (1975–79): $1.7 million; 1979: $831,000

Average Annual U.S. Share (1975–79): 8.6 percent

Leading Suppliers 1979: Japan, 92.7 percent; Germany, 4.2 percent; United States, 1.5 percent; France 0.5 percent

Television Receivers

Total Import Market Size:

Average Annual (1975–79): $274,000; 1979: $304,000

Average Annual U.S. Share (1975–79): 16 percent

Leading Suppliers 1979: United States, 36.1 percent; Japan, 34.5 percent; Germany, 15.1 percent; United Kingdom, 11.7 percent

Clothing (Excluding Fur Products)

Total Import Market Size:

Average Annual (1975–79): $3.6 million; 1979: $3.9 million

Average Annual U.S. Share (1975–79): 33.3 percent

Leading Suppliers 1979: United States, 54.7 percent; Japan, 15.9 percent; France, 9.6 percent, United Kingdom, 8.1 percent; Italy, 5.9 percent

Footwear

Total Import Market Size:

Average Annual (1975–79): $1.1 million; 1979: $2.1 million

Average Annual U.S. Share (1975–79): 22.5 percent

Leading Suppliers 1979: Italy, 46.8 percent; United States, 23 percent; Netherlands, 11.9 percent; Germany, 8.5 percent; United Kingdom, 4.4 percent

Air-Conditioning Machinery and Equipment

Though more of a commercial than a consumer/retail market in Liberia at the present time, it is included here for lack of suitable economic market sector designation.

Total Import Market Size:

Average Annual (1975–79): $1.4 million; 1979: $1.8 million

Average Annual U.S. Share (1975–79): 82.6 percent

Leading Suppliers 1979: United States, 65.5 percent; United Kingdom, 18.6 percent; Japan, 8.8 percent

Market Profile— LIBERIA

Foreign Trade

Imports.—$477.4 million in 1981; $533.9 million in 1980. Major suppliers, 1981: United States, 29.7 percent; Saudi Arabia, 19.1 percent; Germany, 10.2 percent. Chief imports: crude petroleum, food, machinery, transportation equipment (excluding ships), and petroleum products. From United States, 1982 ($112.1 million): rice, 24.4 percent; chassis parts, 8.2 percent; mechanical shovels, nspf, 8.2 percent; aircraft, 7.7 percent; textile fabrics, nspf, 4.2 percent.

Exports.—$529.2 million in 1981; $600.4 million in 1980. Major markets, 1981: Germany, 25 percent; United States, 23.3 percent; Italy, 13.3 percent. Chief exports: iron ore, 61.5 percent; rubber, 16.4 percent; logs, 6.1 percent; diamonds, 4.4 percent; and coffee, 3.7 percent. To United States, 1982 ($91.2 million): iron ore, 47.2 percent; natural rubber, 36 percent; precious and semiprecious stones, 5.2 percent; coffee, 4.5 percent; shellfish (excluding clams), 1.8 percent.

Trade Policy.—Moderate, nondiscriminatory tariff. Most goods admitted by open license. No foreign exchange or quota controls. Signatory Lome Convention. Member of ECOWAS, Mano River Customs Union with Sierra Leone and Guinea.

Trade Prospects.—Established product acceptance makes U.S. goods attractive. Best prospects: mining equipment, timber processing equipment, motor vehicles, building construction materials, air-conditioning equipment, agricultural machinery and implements, water pumps, and agricultural chemicals. Major African export market (1981): Guinea, 48 percent; major African supplier (1981): Ivory Coast, 21.6 percent.

Foreign Investment

United States is major source with about $350 million, mainly in iron ore and rubber. Investment Guaranty Agreement with United States. Liberia Industrial Free Zone (LIFZA) in Monrovia.

Investment Prospects.—Investment Code of 1973 provides attractive incentives. Investment opportunities in light manufacturing, mining, timber, and agro-industries.

Finance

Currency.—Liberia uses the U.S. dollar and Liberian dollar. Liberian dollar par value with U.S. dollar.

Domestic Credit and Investment.—Loans available from nine commercial banks. Credit also available from Liberian Bank for Development and Investment. Money supply 307.5 million in Dec. 1981.

National Budget.—1981/82 budget revenue of $223 million; recurrent expenditure of $241 million; deficit of $18 million; $57.1 million for development.

Foreign Aid.—U.S. and International Monetary Fund leading sources of capital and technical assistance. U.S. economic assistance FY 1982, $74.9 millon; development assistance, $12 milion (28 percent); economic support funds, $35 million (46.7 percent); PL 480, $15.3 million (20.4 percent); foreign military sales (military aid program) $12 million (16 percent); IMET, $594,000 (0.8 percent).

Balance of Payments.—In general, Liberia traditionally runs a substantial deficit on nongoods items in the current account. Given the absence of new investments, the private capital account has also been negative, and despite substantial receipts of official capital, the overall balance of payments has been negative.

Economy

Based on production and export of iron ore and rubber by largely foreign-owned firms, plus subsistence agriculture. GDP (current rices) 1981. $715 million; GDP per capita $384.4

Agriculture.—(35 percent of GDP.) Primarily of subsistence nature; coffee, palm oil, rubber, lumber, and logs are major exports. Food crops include rice, cassava, yams, and vegetables.

Industry.—6 percent of GDP. Chief products: processed rubber, petroleum products, foods, beverages, iron pellets, explosives, and wood products, cement, and consumer products.

Commerce.—Trading and distribution mainly in hands of Lebanese and Indian expatriates.

Mining.—44 percent of GDP, world's 10th largest iron ore exporter. Two pelletizing plants. Growing importance of diamonds. Largely unexploited resources of barite, kyanite, gold, and others.

Development.—The first socio-economic development plan (1981-85) contemplates a public sector expenditure of $615 million.

Basic Economic Facilities

Transportation.—Road network of 5,300 miles (500 miles paved), 310 rail miles mainly used by mining firms, four ports. Third largest merchant fleet in world due to liberal laws permitting flage-of-convenience ship registry. Two major airports; 23,000 vehicles.

Communications.—7,700 telephones (0.5 per 100 people); seven radio stations (two AM, four FM); one TV station, one Atlantic Ocean satellite station.

Power.—In 1982, 460,000 kW capacity; 2-3 billion kWh produced; 1,140 kWh per capita.

Natural Resources

Land.—43,000 square miles, slightly smaller than Pennsylvania; generally rolling terrain; mountain ranges (to 4,500 ft) in north.

Climate.—Tropical and humid, rainy season from April to November, balance of year dry.

Forestry.—40 percent of country is forested; industry growing but still underdeveloped. Plywood factory in operation.

Fisheries.—Annual landings of fish and shrimp around 13,484 metric tons; half is exported. Processing industry expanding. Coastal waters supply local market. Interior fishponds are source of fish.

Population

Size.—2.1 million (1983); annual growth 3.2 percent.

Language.—English official and commercial language.

Education.—Literacy rate 18 percent; compulsory education 11 years. Attendance primary schools 40 percent, secondary 16 percent.

Labor.—Labor force slightly in excess of 510,000, of which 160,000 in monetary economy. Agriculture, 70.5 percent; services, 10 percent; industry and commerce, 4.5 percent; other, 14.2 percent.

Market Profile—LIBYAN ARAB REPUBLIC

Foreign Trade

Imports.—$7,898 million (1979), $4,603 million (1978). Major suppliers (1979): Italy (27 percent), West Germany (16 percent), France (8 percent), Japan (8 percent), United Kingdom (8 percent). Major imports: Foodstuffs, oil drilling equipment and machinery, motor vehicles, power generating equipment, clothing. From United States (1979, $468.1 million): Soybeans, cigarettes, construction and mining machinery, pumps, aircraft, telecommunications equipment.

Exports.—$15,236 million (1979), $9,503 million (1978). Major markets (1979): United States (33 percent), West Germany (18 percent), Italy (18 percent), France (4 percent). To United States (1979, $5,256.0 million): Crude oil, petroleum products, gas.

Trade Prospects.—Libyan Government is spending large sums on agriculture, industry, social development, and infrastructure. Sole buyers are government agencies and semi-autonomous corporations. Best U.S. sales prospects: Agricultural equipment, pumps, transport and communications equipment, building materials, health care and educational materials, construction machinery, electric power equipment, filtration and purification equipment, and technical services.

Foreign Investment

U.S. investment in the hydrocarbon sector totals an estimated $750 million. Libya has nationalized 51 percent or more of virtually all foreign oil company operations.

Finance

Currency.—Libyan dinar=US$3.38 since 1973. Money supply: $4.4 billion (December 1978). Money in circulation: $2.7 billion (1978 est.).

Domestic Credit and Investment.—Nationalized commercial banks finance foreign trade and provide loans for construction, business, and consumption. Two government banks provide interest-free loans to farmers and builders.

Balance of Payments.—End of 1978, balance-of-payments deficit of $300 million. Foreign exchange reserves $4.9 billion (December 1978).

Economy

Petroleum provides more than 85 percent of government revenues. Government seeking to diversify economy through development of agriculture and industry.

GNP.—$18 billion in 1978 (est.); $17.5 billion in 1977. GNP distribution: oil (56 percent), construction (11 percent), public services (6 percent), transportation and communications (6 percent), wholesale and retail trade (6 percent).

Agriculture.—Principal crops include barley, wheat, peanuts, olives, vegetables, dates, and grapes. In 1976-80 Development Plan $5 billion allocated to agriculture, with emphasis on large-scale projects. Production expected to increase as subterranean water supplies are tapped for irrigation.

Industry.—Libyan Government seeking to expand and diversify industrial base with emphasis on building materials, food processing, and mechanical-electrical industries. During 1976-80 Plan, $4.1 billion allocated to this sector (including mining).

Development Plan.—Latest Development Plan (1976-80) calls for investments exceeding $31.3 billion, with priority on non-oil sectors. Bulk of these resources allocated to agriculture and industry, followed by housing, transport, communications, and education.

Minerals.—Oil production in 1979 averaged 2.2 million barrels per day. Petroleum reserves are estimated at 25 billion barrels. Other minerals include iron, uranium, phosphates, and gypsum.

Basic Economic Facilities

Transportation.—Jet airports at Tripoli, Benghazi and Sebha. No functioning railway system, but 1,270 kilometers of railroad are planned. Modernizing underway of Tripoli, Benghazi Derna, Misuratah, Zuara and Tobruk ports. More than 1,200 miles of oil pipelines link oilfields with five oil ports.

Communications.—International telephone, telegraph and telex service is available. Facilities being rapidly expanded; plan allocated $950 million to improvement of communications system.

Power.—Present service inadequate to meet expanding requirements. Major upgrading of facilities underway.

Natural Resources

Land.—Area is 679,358 square miles, 90 percent of which is desert. Narrow coastal plains adjoin mountainous plateaus.

Climate.—Mediterranean along most of the north coast; subtropical or tropical desert in southern and central regions.

Population

Size.—2.76 million (est. for 1978), 3.6 percent growth rate. Approximately 95 percent in northern coastal fringe. Tripoli (281,000 and Benghazi (131,000) are largest cities.

Language.—Arabic is official language; legislation requires that all signs and legal documents be in Arabic. English and Italian are understood.

Education.—Literacy rate estimated at 36 percent. 1976-80 Plan allocated $1.8 billion to education.

Labor.—1978 labor force estimated at 773,000 persons; mostly male. Distribution: 20 percent, agriculture; 20 percent, services; 22 percent, construction; 8 percent, transport and communications; 5 percent, manufacturing.

Housing.—Government subsidies and credits encourage construction. National goal is a proper home for each family by 1984.

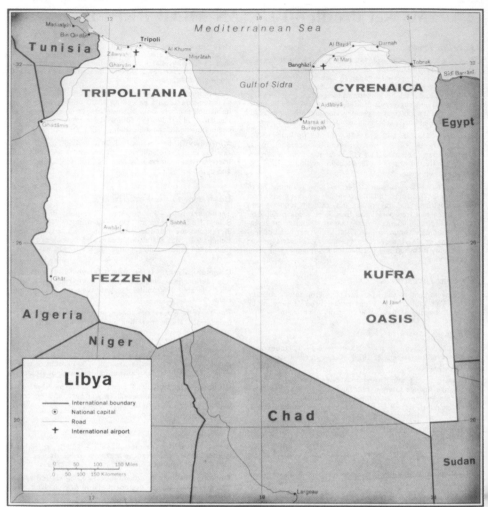

518192 9-76

Market Profile— MADAGASCAR

Foreign Trade

Imports.—$492 million in 1981; $522 million in 1982. Major suppliers: France, 27 percent; Saudi Arabia, 14 percent; and United States, 10.1 percent. Major imports: rice, vegetable oils, crude petroleum, transport machinery, and electrical appliances. Imports from United States: $23.9 million (1982): animal oils, fats, aircraft and parts, agriculture and construction equipment, and mining machinery.

Exports.—$386 million in 1981; $433 million in 1982. Major markets: France, 18 percent; and United States, 20 percent. Major exports: coffee, meat, fish, petroleum products, sugar, cloves, vanilla, and raffia. Exports to United States: $69 million (1981): coffee, vanilla, cloves, and other spices.

Trade Policy.—Madagascar is an associate member of the EEC. Tariff preferences for goods from EEC countries were abolished on Jan. 1, 1976. Import quotas allocated to importers based on taxes paid and previous import levels. All imports, regardless of source, are subject to quotas and must be licensed except for industrial raw materials, spare parts, and pharmaceuticals which receive automatic licenses not subject to quotas. All import licenses to Malagasy importers by the Ministry of Economy and Commerce are subject to prior payment authorization by the Central Bank of Madagascar.

Trade Prospects.—Best sales opportunities are in construction and mining equipment, agricultural and livestock equipment, food processing machinery, and textile and metalworking machinery. Also, specialized equipment and machinery not available elsewhere.

Foreign Investment

Small, mostly French. Some U.S. investment in petroleum exploration. United States has investment guaranty agreement with Madagascar. All future foreign investors will be required to be minority shareholders with local partners, usually government or state-owned companies.

Investment Prospects.—New private investment in Madagascar very limited. Incentives in the Investment Code promulgated in 1973 have been inadequate to attract much interest. Best prospects in mining and fertilizer production.

Finance

Currency.—Malagasy franc (FMG) 423.47 FMG=US$1 Oct. 1983. Money and near-money supply $645.7 million as of 1979 (est.).

Domestic Credit and Investment.—Four commercial banks supply short-term loans. All commercial banks and insurance companies were nationalized in June 1975. Domestic credit: about $110 million in 1982.

National Budget.—Expenditures for 1982 estimated at $565 million; $348 million in revenues.

Foreign Aid.—$237.7 million in development assistance, 1980. France provides the bulk of foreign assistance; European Development Fund, the United States, and West Germany also give assistance.

Balance of Payments.—Estimated overall balance-of-payments deficit of $73 million in 1982.

Economy

Predominantly agriculture; GNP estimated at $2.3 billion in 1980. Government controls 70 percent of the national economy (13 percent in 1975).

Agriculture.—Production of sugar (115.6 million metric tons), coffee (69.4 million metric tons), and cotton (934 million metric tons). Other crops include vanilla, cloves, tobacco and rice.

Industry.—Major industries include extraction of chromite and graphite; agricultural processing, light consumer goods, industries cement plant, auto assembly plant, paper mill, and oil refinery.

Commerce.—State trading company (SONACO) established in 1973 and aims to control over half of country's foreign trade.

Basic Economic Facilities

Transportation.—Two unconnected public railroad systems total 549 miles of 1-meter track. Of 17,000 miles of roads, about 2,800 miles are paved. Major seaport is Tamatava. Antananarivo and Majunga airport accommodate long-distance jets; Air Madagascar is national carrier.

Communications.—Domestic and international telephones and telegraph service via cable and satellite earth station. 37,100 telephones; 11 AM radio stations; 4 TV stations.

Power.—The island is not electrified outside urban centers. Production estimated at 465 million KWh in 1977. Extensive hydroelectric potential.

Natural Resources

Land.—Island's total area is 226,656 square miles. Mountainous plateau rises sharply in east and descends gradually in terraces to west. 58 percent pastureland, 21 percent forested, and 5 percent cultivated.

Climate.—Warm and rainy in eastern coastal strip, moderate in central highlands, and hot and dry on south-western coast.

Minerals.—Graphite, mica, chromite, and uranothorianite mined and exported. Vast unexploited petroleum reserves in tar and deposit.

Forestry.—Forests covering 10-20 percent of the land are important source of building materials and fuel. Raffia is exported.

Fisheries.—Limited development of saltwater fishing. Freshwater fishing is important for domestic market. 1978, 51,380 metric tons catch.

Population

Size.—Estimated at 8.90 million in 1982, 38 percent rural; annual growth rate 2.4 percent. Principal cities: Antananarivo, the capital, 321,000; Tamatave, 49,400.

Language.—Official languages: Malagasy and French.

Education.—Literacy rate 45 percent of population 10 and over.

Labor.—90 percent engaged in subsistence agriculture. Organized labor: 4 percent of labor force.

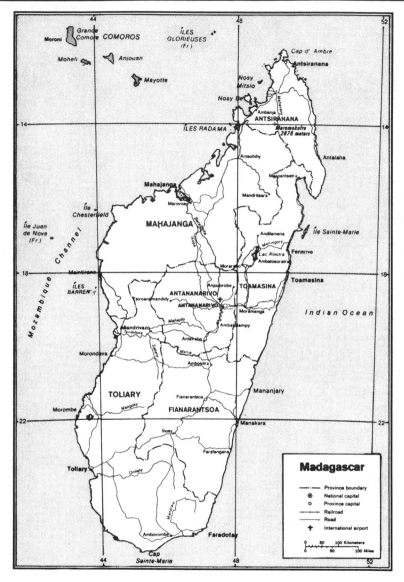

Market Profile— MALAWI

Foreign Trade

Imports.—$348 million in 1981: $291 million in 1982. Major suppliers in 1981: South Africa. United Kingdom. West Germany. Zimbabwe. Japan. and United States. Imports from United States. $5 million in 1981. $3.0 million in 1982.

Exports.—$277 million in 1981: $232 million in 1982. Major markets in 1981: Australia. United Kingdom. and United States. Exports to United States: $61.6 million in 1981. $30.7 million in 1982.

Trade Policy.—No restrictive import licensing or exchange controls on most U.S. goods. Signatory of 1979 Lime II Convention. Trade agreement with South Africa in force.

Trade Prospects.—Best U.S. export prospects for agro-industry. food processing and construction equipment. motor vehicles. chemicals. and textiles. U.S.-produced chemicals. plastics and rubber. wood. paper and base metal articles. precision instruments. office machinery. railway equipment. agricultural machinery and tools.

Foreign Investment

The book value of total foreign investment in Malawi is $350-$500 million. and is primarily British ($250 million) and South African ($100-$200 million). U.S. direct foreign investment is over $20 million. U.S.-Malawi Investment Guaranty Agreement in effect since 1967: double taxation agreement also in effect.

Investment Prospects.—Foreign investment strongly encouraged. Basic corporate tax rate is 45 percent of net profit. Investment opportunities exist for participation in fertilizer. cement. and glass works plans: telephone exchange systems: agriculture and food processing industries.

Finance

Currency.—Malawi Kwacha 1.14 Mk=US$1. Oct. 1983 pegged to Special Drawing Rights. Money supply was $114.88 million in April 1982. Foreign reserves: $27.92 million in August 1982.

Domestic Credit and Investment.—Commercial banking by Commercial Bank of Malawi and National Bank of Malawi: Industrial Development Bank of Malawi (Indebank) makes long-term loans and may take equity interest in new enterprise.

National Budget.—For 1981. government revenues were $239.66 million. and government spending was budgeted at $402.88 million.

Foreign Aid.—Official development aid commitments $143.3 million in 1980. Major donors are the World Bank. United Kingdom. South Africa. West Germany. the United States. and Denmark.

Balance of Payments.—Total change in reserves $26.7 million in 1980.

Economy

Almost 90 percent of population derives its livelihood from agriculture. 1980 GDP (at current prices) was $1.191.1 million.

Agriculture.—Agriculture accounts for 43 percent of GDP and 50 percent of paid employment. As Malawi is now virtually self-sufficient in food production. greater emphasis is being placed on increasing and diversifying agricultural exports. Sugar. peanuts. and rice have been targeted as crops with additional export potential.

Industry.—Agri-based industries appear to offer the best prospects. The country is handicapped. however. by a small internal market: difficulty in exporting to its neighbors due to their financial problems and difficulty in exporting to the world's major markets due to high transportation costs.

Commerce.—Government encourages Malawian participation in wholesale and retail trade.

Development Plan.—A Five-Year Development Plan embarked upon for fiscal year 1981/82. total nearly $1 billion. Sectors receiving the largest percentage of development money will be transport and communication. 35 percent: agriculture. 30 percent: education. health. and welfare. 19 percent: and construction and urban deveopment. 10 percent.

Basic Economic Facilities

Transportation.—2.000 miles of paved roads. 754 km of 1.067 meter gauge. Two rail links to Mozambican ports of Beira and Nacala. Malawi Railways Ltd. has 5-year development program. Principal airport at Blantyre; limited service at Kamuzu International Airport. Lilongue.

Communications.—Facilities exist for international communications. Fair system of open-wire lines. radio-rely links. and radio communications stations. Main urban centers connected by telephone: Blantyre. Zomba. and Muzuzu: 28.800 phones (0.5 per 100 people). Six AM and four FM radios. no TV stations. One Indian Ocean satellite station.

Power.—310 million kWh of electricity produced in 1978: 60 kWh per capita: 124.000 kW capacity 1980.

Natural Resources

Land.—36.700 square miles of which one-fifth is lake water. Main geographical feature is the Great Rift Valley which bisects Malawi from end to end: high plateau rises in the west.

Climate.—Hot and humid in lowlands: more moderate in western plateau.

Minerals.—Production limited to quarrying constructional stone and limestone. Known deposits of uranium. bauxite. and coal.

Forestry.—Large reserves. mostly hardwood.

Fisheries.—Fish important in diet. Annual catch estimated at 14.000 tons.

Population

Size.—6.4 million (1982). Annual growth rate 2.9 percent. Principal cities: Blantyre. 170.000: Zomba. 20.000: Lilongwe (the capital). 70.000.

Language.—English is official. Local language is Chichewa.

Education.—Adult literacy: 25 percent of population.

Labor.—Total employment was 369.000 persons in 1979. Monthly average earnings $46.28.

MALAWI

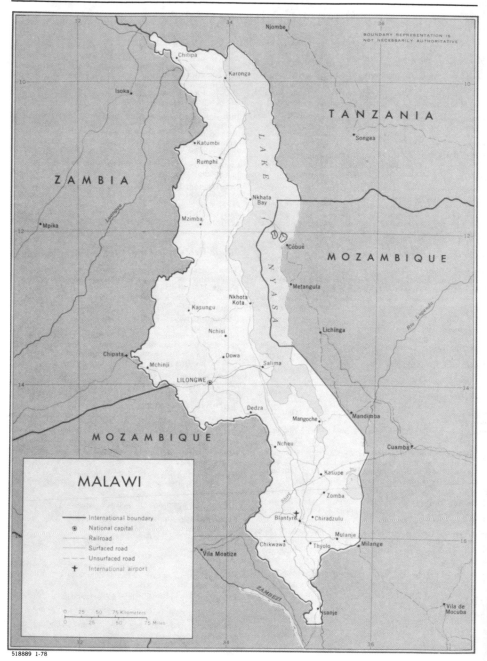

Note: Lake Nyasa is now called Lake Malawi.

1508

Marketing in Malaysia

Contents

Report Revised March 1981

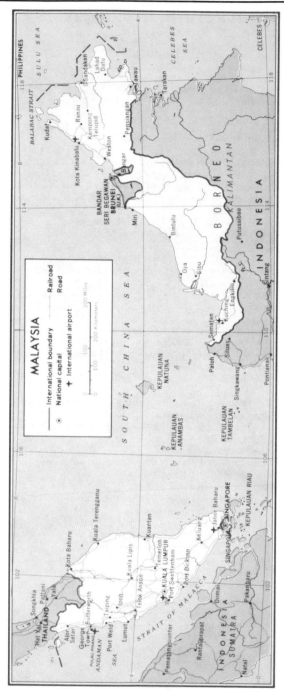

Foreign Trade Outlook

The Malaysian economy has shown impressive growth in recent years, with both industrial and agricultural sectors growing steadily in keeping with the goals of the Third Malaysia Plan (1976-80). Manufacturing, petroleum products, and electronics assembly are stimulating real growth, 8.3 percent in 1979 and an estimated 8 percent for 1980. Foreign trade is flourishing.

Economic performance is reflected in the 1979 gross national product (GNP) of US$10,724 million in constant prices, as compared with US$9,900 million in 1978. Exports constituted nearly 57 percent and imports 40 percent of this GNP. Gross exports increased 40.5 percent to US$11,071 million, with rubber the mainstay of the export commodities list. Gross imports rose 24.6 percent to US$7,860.8 million in 1979.

The expanded exports, along with high prices for Malaysia's primary products, resulted in a trade surplus of US$3,210.2 million in 1979, an increase of 104.6 percent over 1978. While exports were expected to grow at a slower rate in 1980, the Ministry of Finance forecast surpluses in the current and capital accounts, and a final balance-of-payments surplus of US$800 million.

The U.S. share of Malaysia's imports has grown both in relative and in absolute terms. The United States reached a 15.2 percent market share in 1979, as compared with 13.9 percent in 1978. Japan is expected to remain Malaysia's foremost trading partner, with a 23.3 percent share of Malaysia's import market, but the United States has now moved to second place, ahead of Singapore. In dollar value, Malaysia imported US$1,196.3 million of U.S. goods in 1979, an increase of 36.4 percent over 1978.

As the Government of Malaysia continues to encourage foreign investment and rapid development of the industrial sector through creation, expansion, and modernization of productive facilities, prospects for U.S. sales remain bright in the 1980's.

The United States has already invested over US$1 billion in Malaysia, primarily in the petroleum industry, although U.S. investment in electronics and banking is also significant.

Best Prospects

Particular areas of sales interest to U.S. firms are telecommunications, power generation, building and construction equipment, pollution control equipment, and timber processing

*Foreign exchange rate December 1, 1980: M$2.18=US$1.

Table 1.—Malaysia: Gross Imports by Economic Functions

(US $ millions)

Item	1975	1976	1977	1978
Consumption Goods	716.2	875.4	1,011.7	1,333.8
Food	256.1	304.5	362.0	485.3
Beverages and Tobacco	35.4	67.7	65.0	79.0
Consumer durables	108.3	117.6	166.2	237.1
Other	316.4	385.6	418.5	532.4
Investment Goods	1,140.9	1,263.0	1,439.1	1,803.1
Machinery	395.6	335.2	405.5	568.7
Transport equipment	104.1	186.9	166.6	171.4
Metal products	229.0	265.2	325.8	465.4
Other	412.2	475.7	541.2	597.6
Intermediate Goods	1,551.5	1,669.4	2,057.4	2,696.0
For manufacturing	839.9	891.6	1,092.9	1,627.4
For construction	70.8	110.2	121.9	130.0
For agriculture	137.4	146.7	186.9	208.1
Crude petroleum	276.9	274.2	349.0	401.1
Other	226.5	246.7	306.7	329.4
Imports for Re-export	168.6	144.0	123.5	135.2
Tin ore	110.3	46.0	56.9	96.6
Crude natural rubber	16.7	24.4	31.7	38.4
Crude petroleum	41.6	73.6	34.9	—
TOTAL	3,577.2	3,951.8	4,631.7	5,968.1

Source: Malaysian Department of Statistics

Table 2.—Malaysia: Trade by Commodity with the World and the United States, 1978

(US$ millions)

Commodity	Imports		Exports	
	World	U.S.	World	U.S.
Food and Live Animals	855.4	31.9	383.1	16.6
Beverages and Tobacco	80.3	35.7	7.0	—
Crude Materials, Inedible, Fuels	311.9	28.7	2,747.6	211.2
Mineral Fuels, Lubricants and Related Materials	634.9	3.2	1,011.7	288.1
Animals and Vegetables	11.2	0.2	909.2	90.8
Chemicals and Products of Chemical Industries	530.3	99.0	44.6	4.3
Manufactured Goods	977.5	67.8	1,218.0	336.9
Machinery and Transport Equipment	2,135.5	468.2	786.0	380.8
Miscellaneous Manu-factured Articles	312.6	68.7	214.1	37.2
Transactions and Com-modities, nes	61.5	18.1	59.6	8.4
TOTAL	5,911.1	821.5	7,380.9	1,374.3

Source: Bank Negara Malaysia

equipment. In addition, the main contract to engineer, procure and construct the Bintulu Liquefied Natural Gas Plant in Sarawak, the largest project in Malaysia's history, was awarded to a joint venture of JGC Corporation of Japan and the Pullman Kellogg Division of Pullman Incorporated of the United States. This project will provide a number of export opportunities for U.S. firms. Also, Petronas (Malaysia's national oil corporation) has appointed Stone & Webster Engineering Corporation of New York as the project technical consultant to advise Petronas on technical matters related to the implementation of the ASEAN Second Area Project, as well as to assist

Petronas in the supervision of construction work on the project. Other major projects underway or to be undertaken include: the refinery in Trengganu (25,000-30,000 barrels per day); the fourth Malaysian refinery (150,000 barrels per day); the Port Kelang Thermal Power Station; the Penang Bridge project; a new port on Pulau Lumut, Selangor; the National Electricity Board's Paka combined cycle project; the Pahang Port, expansion—phase III; and the Kota Bharu Airport expansion.

Industry Trends

Malaysia's strong economic growth and economic stability reflect the strategy for rapid expansion and diversification laid out by the Third Malaysia Plan—1976-80. Investment is the mainstay of this plan; however, investment by the private sector during the early years of the Third Plan fell short of the Government's goals, probably due to a worldwide investment lag and uneasiness concerning the Industrial Coordination Act (ICA). Consequently, the slack has been taken up by increased government spending and investment. For 1980, the final year of the plan, the budget called for an increase of as much as 39 percent in overall spending by the Federal Government and an increase of up to 100 percent in spending for development projects alone. Public investment in 1979 increased about 22 percent to US$1,113 million.

When the Industrial Coordination Act, which many view as a tool to aid the economically disadvantaged Malays, was introduced in 1975, the general opinion was that private investment (primarily by Chinese Malaysians) would decline. During the first years of the ICA, this prediction held true, but in recent years this investment has recovered and even exceeded planning targets. This performance indicates the strength of the economy and the opportunity that exists. The Government is aware of the problems and is constantly monitoring the impact of its policies upon the private sector. Investors on the other hand apparently have accepted these policies, albeit with some complaint.

In 1979, industrial production grew by an estimated 9 percent, absorbing much of the increasing labor force; in 1980 industrial production was expected to decline somewhat. Unemployment was reduced to an estimated 6.1 percent in 1979, with inflation reported at 5 percent. Unemployment was estimated at about 6 percent for 1980; with inflation estimated at about 7 percent. The inflation rate is believed actually to be somewhat higher since the consumer price index is heavily weighted by goods with prices that are controlled and therefore not subject to the inflationary pressures of an otherwise expansionary policy. The money supply grew an estimated 17.9 percent over 1978 to US$3.9 million, and gold and foreign exchange reserves increased about 9.3 percent to approximately US$3.6 million.

Growth in manufacturing led the way in the expanding 1979 economy. Manufacturing, which now constitutes 20 percent of gross domestic product (GDP), increased its share of the nation's exports and also provided domestic goods as substitutes for imports. Electronics, with its output increase of 10 percent in 1979, is a front-runner attracting significant U.S. investment, with plans for expansion underway. The processing of petroleum products is also increasing and attracting new investment. In 1980, petroleum was expected to replace rubber at the head of Malaysia's exports.

The agricultural, forestry, and fisheries sector played a dominant role in the economy, contributing 25 percent of real GDP in 1979. Production in this sector in real terms increased by 5.6 percent to M$5,787 million in 1979, compared with a growth rate of only 1 percent in 1978. Malaysia's three main crops—rubber, palm oil, and rice—all registered significant gains in 1979.

Rubber production for 1979 totaled 1.65 million tons, an increase of 3 percent, and is expected to increase 1.5 percent in 1980. Rubber exports increased 3.5 percent by volume and contributed about 19 percent of total export earnings in 1979. Malaysian Government officials forecast that rubber prices will increase further with growing demand and decreased competition from the petroleum-based synthetic industry. The Government has decreased the export duty on rubber to encourage greater planting of rubber trees for the future growth of the industry. Malaysia and the United States are members of the newly negotiated International Natural Rubber Agreement designed to stabilize world prices in natural rubber.

Output of crude palm oil rose by approximately 17 percent to reach over 2 million tons in 1979. Total exports of crude palm oil are estimated to have declined 6 percent over 1978, due mainly to an increase in domestic consumption. Exports of crude palm oil in 1980 are estimated to increase by about 11 percent to 600,000 tons.

Rice production for 1979 is estimated to have increased 34 percent over the 1978 drought year. Current production levels of padi meet about 85 percent of domestic needs.

The Government of Malaysia is encouraging a higher level of domestic processing of timber and also seeking to conserve forest resources. With restrictions imposed on the export of logs, particularly in Sabah, total exports of sawlogs from Malaysia were estimated to decrease by 3.7 percent to about 16 million cubic meters. Exports of sawn timber in 1979, however, were estimated to rise by 4.7 percent to 2.9 million cubic meters, with Peninsular Malaysia accounting for 95 percent of the total.

Malaysia is the world's largest producer of tin (32 percent of world supply). Despite high prices for tin in 1979, production increased only 2.2 percent, as increased operating fuel costs resulted in foreclosure of marginal tin mines. The Government decreased the tin export duty in an effort to stimulate the mining by gravel pump operators with marginal profitability levels. Both the United States and Malaysia are members of the Fifth International Tin Agreement designed to stabilize the world market prices of tin.

In 1979, prices for Malaysia's primary commodity exports were very favorable. Overall, the prices of these major export commodities may decline slightly, after the rapid rise in 1979.

Government of Malaysia Plans

Malaysia is successful in meeting its 5-year goals. In the Second Malaysia Plan (1971-75), growth rates exceeded projections, and investment projects devoted primarily to rural and agricultural development (23 percent) reached their targets. The Third Malaysian Plan (1976-80) is meeting with comparable success in the key areas of GNP growth and expansion of the industrial and agricultural bases. The Federal Land Development Authority in 1979 expended over US$100 million to develop 45,850 hectares of land involving 21 schemes for the planting of rubber, palm oil, cocoa, coffee, and sugar cane. The elimination of poverty is somewhat below projected levels. Public spending on development and infrastructure were further accelerating in 1980, the final year of the Third Malaysia Plan. Details on the Fourth Malaysia Plan are not yet available, but the Government of Malaysia is expected to place considerable emphasis on the development of resource-based heavy industry.

Malaysia will establish a Heavy Industries Corporation to stimulate the development of resource-based heavy industries in the country, as part of its industrial strategy for the 1980's. The Government decided to proceed in the development of heavy industries that are, by

nature, capital intensive with long payback periods. The Government would like to promote the development of an integrated steel complex, an aluminum smelter, and other basic projects as part of the corporation's functions—in joint venture with foreign firms if necessary.

Table 3.—Malaysia: Development Expenditure
of the Federal Government, 1975-1979

(US$ millions)

	1975	1976	1977	1978	1979
General Administration...	51.4	44.0	62.7	86.7	86.4
Economic Services	836.9	874.4	1,389.8	1,684.5	1,816.9
Agriculture	281.9	237.1	339.9	458.0	441.2
Transport and Communication	294.0	366.9	562.3	633.9	773.9
Trade, Industry, and Mining..............	144.2	100.3	271.6	397.8	291.3
Feasibility Studies	3.3	1.3	4.1	7.0	6.7
Other (inc. utilities).....	113.5	168.8	211.9	187.8	303.8
Social Services	186.4	192.6	305.4	360.3	472.9
Education...............	89.7	120.6	172.6	182.6	219.4
Health	31.4	23.7	41.5	44.2	52.2
Other	65.3	48.3	91.3	133.5	201.3
Security	122.2	129.8	306.9	275.7	224.4
Defense	90.8	78.7	219.8	161.2	153.2
Internal...............	31.4	51.1	87.1	114.5	71.2
TOTAL	1,196.9	1,240.8	2,064.8	2,407.2	2,600.6

Note: Figures for 1979 are estimates.
Source: Malaysia Ministry of Finance.

Trade Policy

U.S.-Malaysian trade is affected by certain trade policies of the respective governments, agreements negotiated in international forums, and Malaysia's membership in the Association of South East Asian Nations (ASEAN). The following are of most interest to U.S. traders and investors:

U.S. Generalized System of Preferences (GSP)

Title V of the Trade Act of 1975 authorized the President of the United States to grant generalized tariff preference to imports from developing nations for a period of 10 years. Other major industrialized countries had previously adopted this program of assistance to developing countries, which aims to decrease their need for outside financial help by building up their export opportunities. The scheme permits voluntary, general and nonreciprocal tariff preferences for imports of certain products from the developing countries. In 1979, $184 million worth of Malaysian exports was covered by GSP. Approximately $55 million worth of imports actually entered duty free under the program, while $63 million worth was statutorily excluded for reasons of competitive need. The remaining $66 million was not granted duty-free treatment for administrative reasons, i.e., failure to meet the value-added criteria or failure to include a certificate of origin with shipments. Major Malaysian products eligible for GSP are: cocoa butter, unsweetened cocoa, seamless gloves of rubber, electric sound or visual signaling apparatus, hardwood lumber, wood handles for brooms and mops, chairs other than folding, solid-state radio receivers, and movements and other parts of music boxes.

U.S.-Malaysia Textile Agreement

The United States and Malaysia have negotiated a new 4-year restraint agreement covering all cotton, wool, and synthetic textile and apparel exports to the United States. The new agreement will be effective January 1, 1981, through December 31, 1984.

International Natural Rubber Agreement

Both Malaysia and the United States are members of the newly negotiated International Natural Rubber Agreement (INRA), which is designed to stabilize world prices in natural rubber. The headquarters for the organization will be in Kuala Lumpur.

International Tin Agreement

The United States and Malaysia are members of the Fifth International Tin Agreement, which is designed to stabilize world market prices in tin through mid-1981. The agreement is being renegotiated.

Multilateral Trade Negotiations

During the Multilateral Trade Negotiations (MTN), the United States gave tariff concessions to Malaysia on 11 product categories. Malaysia was the principal supplier in 1976 of seven of these products: palm kernel oil, palm oil, wood dowels, tin wire, electric luminescent lamps, and watch movements. Malaysia was the substantial supplier of compressed wood tool handles, broom and mop handles, and natural rubber. The United States also reduced tariffs on an additional 16 products of export interest to Malaysia, conditioned upon adequate reciprocity from other suppliers. Total U.S. tariff concessions to Malaysia covered trade equaling $153.7 million in 1976.

In return, Malaysia conceded tariff reductions or bindings to the United States on 27 product categories, with a total 1976 trade value of $33.2 million. Industrial products composed 97 percent of these concessions. Most significant were natural juices and other food preparations, peptones and other protein substances, insecticides, kraft paper, refrigerator and air conditioner compressors and parts, refrigerators, typewriters, other machinery parts, and motor vehicle parts.

As of this writing, the Malaysians have not signed any of the MTN codes on nontariff measures that inhibit trade, including subsidies, government procurement, customs valuation, licensing, and standards.

Association of South East Asian Nations

Malaysia is a member of the Association of South East Asian Nations (ASEAN), along with Indonesia, Philippines, Singapore, and Thailand. The Association was formed in 1967 to facilitate economic, social, and cultural development and the promotion of peace and stability. Among other things, the members have negotiated tariff preferences within ASEAN, and they will continue to negotiate such preferences; members also accord preferential treatment on government purchases and in financing, and they are developing industrial complementation schemes.

In the past, the ASEAN tariff preferences were narrow and did not include products figuring prominently in U.S.-Malaysian trade. ASEAN has now begun to increase the depth of cuts. The margin of preference on government contracts does not appear to have hindered U.S. contractors to date. The first complementation scheme, one for cooperation in the automotive industry, has just recently been approved by the ASEAN economic ministers. U.S. exporters and investors should be aware of the Association in trading with or investing in Malaysia, particularly over the long term.

Sales and Distribution Channels

Trading Companies

The marketing of imported goods in Malaysia is, in most part, conducted by trading companies that operate sales outlets in the principal cities. They regard Peninsular Malaysia and Sabah and Sarawak as a composite market to be cultivated by branches and traveling salespersons. Although some of these firms are headquartered in Singapore with branches in Malaysia, many have head offices in Kuala Lumpur, the capital of Malaysia.

The entire range of importing services is available in Malaysia. The larger houses provide the full gamut of marketing services. They import for their own account; maintain inventories of goods and spare parts; provide maintenance services; sell or process indent orders for delivery to customers, including end-users; and sell to wholesalers and retailers. A few of the small- and medium-sized companies offer the same services but most operate as indent merchants, placing and handling import orders for the account of others.

A few large, foreign-owned and -managed trading companies are responsible for moving as much as one-half of the import trade of Malaysia. Included among the major trading companies are over a dozen large and successful British trading houses. Most began their trading activities supplying the requirements of the numerous plantations and tin mines started by British investors in the early days of the former colonial relationship. Many of these firms perform as managers or custodians of British firms that have large investments in Malaysian rubber and palm oil operations.

Among the major trading companies are several firms owned and managed by other foreign nationals that operate mostly as branches. These include several branches of U.S.-owned firms. Although their parent firms have considerable assets and a large international sales volume, their marketing role in Malaysia is secondary to that of the large British companies. A typical major trading company may represent several hundred foreign suppliers and be involved in the marketing of several thousand individual product items. It may sell to factories and other producing enterprises, to government agencies owning and operating public facilities, to construction and building companies, and to wholesale and retail outlets.

A large number of small- and medium-sized, locally owned and managed trading firms and a smaller number of locally owned major firms now account for about one-half of Malaysia's foreign trade. Such firms are usually owned by Chinese Malaysians and to a lesser extent by Indian Malaysians. Participation in foreign trade by native Malaysians is small, but it is being encouraged by government authorities who are making progress.

Many of these small- and medium-sized firms are well diversified in the range of products they handle; however, some prefer a specialization such as electrical equipment; medical and scientific instruments and equipment; and motor vehicles, parts, and supplies. These firms also take orders from customers, sell to end-users, and engage in wholesale and retail trade. Mainly, such firms are located in the

Peninsular Malaysia cities of Ipoh, Penang, and Malacca and in the East Malaysian cities of Kuching and Kota Kinabalu. Their import activities are for the benefit of local customers or end-users in these cities and the adjacent markets. For example, Ipoh, in the heart of the tin mining region and close to the rice bowl sections of West Malaysia, is served by trading firms specializing in tin mining and rice farming equipment and supplies, as well as by branches of the large trading complexes having countrywide marketing facilities.

There are other variations in the distribution pattern. A large department store may operate as an importer/retailer and also import through indent orders placed with trading companies representing foreign suppliers whose merchandise the store requires. Retail dealers specializing in food and other shelf goods follow the same pattern. There are instances of local sales branches maintained by foreign manufacturers who staff them with local management and technical personnel, though maintaining home office management and supervision in residence or by frequent visits as the case requires, and who provide full sales and service facilities. U.S. firms are included in this category.

The greater portion of the foreign goods moving into and out of Sabah and Sarawak is handled by trading firms headquartered in Singapore and Peninsular Malaysia. The area is served through branch sales outlets or by salespersons who make frequent visits to small local dealers and distributors, or end-users. Only a small amount of international trade is conducted directly between foreign suppliers and strictly local East Malaysian importers and distributors. However, branch sales offices of Malaysian and Singaporean trading firms are often given autonomy in arranging import transactions with foreign suppliers who have agency contracts with parent firms or on a single transaction basis.

Wholesale and Retail Facilities

Wholesale and retail facilities range from the most modern warehouses and department stores to small owner-shops. Modern, western-style retail outlets are increasing in popularity as are U.S. merchandising methods.

Wholesalers usually grant credit to those retailers who agree to stock their products. Generally, the trading companies handle the wholesaling and to some degree the retailing functions. They maintain large warehouse complexes in connection with their trading activities; the retail market is supplied from these facilities.

Direct Procurement

There is direct infrastructure equipment procurement by government agencies for power, water, irrigation, and transport development. These purchases are arranged with foreign suppliers in response to international tendering. However, direct transactions are waning as it becomes clearer to foreign suppliers that dealing through a competent local agent or distributor greatly enhances their chances of making sales to government agencies.

Selecting an Agent

Trading companies serving foreign suppliers in these markets are generally capable of effective sales techniques; however, foreign suppliers often face the problem of inadequate agency selling performance. A contributing factor is the overcommitment by local distributors, particularly the larger firms, in representation of foreign suppliers. The result is that they give appropriate attention only to some of the more salable products they handle and ignore those that require more effort to sell. Foreign suppliers, including many American exporters, have learned to cope with this situation by making a careful search for more flexible agents, often found among the less committed trading firms, and by providing their own market promotion and development. The agent should be a local—not a third-country—agent. A visit to Malaysia by a company executive to select an agent and to learn firsthand the subleties of the culture, government policies, and the market is a wise investment of company resources, particularly in light of increasing competition from other countries.

Despite the problems in finding a suitable marketing outlet, foreign suppliers are making successful representation arrangements and selling their products. This success is based largely on a genuine interest in exporting, an awareness of the market situation, careful selection and training of agents, active support in a sales campaign, and appropriate monitoring of distributor performance. The implementation by a supplier of a marketing program should be a continuing process in which there is room for restructuring of an agency arrangement and sales campaign.

Agent Support

While followup attention to the distributor and his performance by the U.S. supplier is a key factor in the success of the agency arrangement, an important and probably more difficult requirement is to make the distributor feel he is a member of the supplier's firm. All of the support elements are needed in such a relationship. Probably the most vital element is technical and training support. Effective marketing of hard goods in these countries through a local distributor demands full assistance from the U.S. supplier in all phases of selling, particularly in identification of requirements, installation, operation and maintenance of facilities and equipment, and sales training and use of equipment. To give this supplier role proper meaning, frequent contact between the U.S. supplier and the local distributor is essential.

Selling the Market

Import and distributing firms that have advanced to the role of "selling the market," have often had the benefit of advice and help from foreign suppliers who understand and apply this concept. The conversion from a habit of order filling to a role of finding buyers has been and continues to be a gradual process, and success is found in proportion to the competitive spirit and market development interest shown by the supplier. Thus, a foreign supplier who has found a likely distributor or agent in these markets should anticipate working with the agent to advance selling techniques in pursuing an effective market development program.

Training

Foreign trading firms have gradually substituted locals for foreign sales staffs and have trained them in selling methods and product know-how. Also, supervisory and management positions in these firms are being increasingly filled by promotion from within. Sales techniques by the foreign trading firms have spilled over into local trading firms as sales personnel have transferred to better job opportunities.

Foreign trading firms have frequently supplemented on-the-job sales training with training abroad in the headquarters of the foreign suppliers that they represent. This training, generally financed by suppliers, includes product orientation and application by exposure of trainees to the manufacturing processes in plants of suppliers. In addition, local talent for selling positions in foreign-owned and local establishments is increasingly drawn from college graduates who have received degrees in business administration and other specialties from universities in Malaysia, the United

Kingdom, Canada, Australia, or the United States.

Sales training of local sales staffs is also provided by company representatives of foreign suppliers who are stationed in Malaysia or make frequent visits to the area from company headquarters or from regional marketing offices. This training is available to sales personnel of local as well as foreign trading firms.

Product expertise, vital in the sale of machinery and equipment, is not widely available among the sales staffs of local distributors. While this situation is being corrected by increased education and training, foreign suppliers of machinery and equipment frequently augment the product know-how and engineering skills of their agent with an office in the region. The company officials at such an office, particularly in the case of important requirements for factory equipment in the private sector or government procurement of infrastructure equipment, are able to provide the essential product application knowledge that helps swing sales to their company.

Services

Value added in the services sector, which comprises 46 percent of real GDP, was estimated to expand by about 7 percent in real terms in 1979 to about US$4,800 million, following the increased demand for services from the agricultural and manufacturing sectors. Wholesale and retail trade, which accounted for about 13 percent of real GDP, rose further by 7 percent in 1979 in line with the overall expansion in demand in the economy. The other services sectors—including transport, storage, and communications—and producers of government services rose by 8 percent and 7.6 percent, respectively, thus helping to sustain economic output in 1979. Reflecting mainly the slower increase in bank lending, the finance, insurance, real estate, and business services sector rose moderately by 5 percent, compared with 10 percent in 1978.

Transportation

The development of transportation facilities has received a large share of the Government's attention. In both the Second and Third Malaysia Plans, approximately 17 percent of investment by the Government was devoted to transportation infrastructure. The highway program, aimed at consolidating and improving existing facilities, is a major undertaking. Expansion and modernization of port facilities, which handle 90 percent of the total volume of international trade in Peninsular Malaysia, is scheduled or underway. Eleven airport projects were initiated or continued in the Third Malaysia Plan, catering to both domestic and international transportation. Malaysia now possesses some of the most modern facilities in the region. Finally, the government-owned railway system, converted to diesel powered locomotives, plays an important role despite the expansion of other modes of transportation.

Highway Transport

The highway network generally serves all the settled areas in Malaysia, connecting principal commercial centers and reaching into the newly settled land development areas opened up by the Federal Land Development Authority. Roadways were modernized to accommodate the expected 12.5 percent increase in traffic during the Third Malaysia Plan. This growth, which is occurring along the major traffic corridors on the west coast, as well as in specific sections of the east, results from the rapid rate of land development and urbanization.

The present highway network includes links of commercial and strategic importance between the settled western areas of Peninsular Malaysia and its less populated east coast. One is in the south between Batu Pahat and Mersing. Another link is in the south-central region connecting the west coast with Kuantan on the east coast. The north-south link serves the economically important west coast area and provides good access to Singapore in the south and Penang and Thailand in the north. A northern east-west highway is being completed between Butterworth and Kota Bahru.

To ease traffic congestion in Kuala Lumpur, a public transport system and road maintenance, as well as a new bridge connecting Penang with the mainland throughways, are receiving attention.

A sum of M$1,277.7 million was allocated under the Third Malaysia Plan to implement road programs in Peninsular Malaysia. Projects that commenced the expansion of the Federal road network include the East-West Highway connecting the northern states with the more developed areas on the west coast, the Kuantan-Segamat Road, the Kuala Lumpur-Karak Road, the Jerangau-Jabor Road, and the Kuala Lumpur-Petaling Jaya Highway.

About 400 miles of development and feeder roads are being constructed in the three regional development areas of Johor Tenggara, Pahang, Tenggara, and Trengganu Tengah in order to support agriculture, land development, and urbanization programs. The sum of M$198.5 million has been allocated to these projects, some of which have also received loans from the Asian Development Bank. A total of M$205.9 million, including a grant of M$107 million by the Federal Government, has been devoted to State and rural road development, which forms an important part of the overall integrated rural development program for raising the productivity and incomes of these areas by providing greater access to marketing and distribution outlets.

The road systems in Sabah and Sarawak are being developed, and expansion is considered vital by planners for development of exploitable virgin areas. In the Third Malaysia Plan, M$250 million each was allocated for the Sarawak and Sabah regions.

Rail Transport

The government-owned Malayan Railway Company operates a relatively modern and efficient railway system in Peninsular Malaysia; there is also a small network in Sabah but none in Sarawak. The rail network in Peninsular Malaysia continues to fill a vital need in the nation's transportation system despite the faster growing role of the road carriers.

In Peninsular Malaysia, the main line extends from Singapore, connected with Malaysia by a causeway, and runs through the key commercial centers, including Johore City, Kuala Lumpur, Ipoh, and Prai (adjacent to Penang), and on to Bangkok in Thailand. Important branch lines connect with Port Kelang, Port Dickson, Telok Anson, and Port Weld, and there is a link between Prai and Butterworth. There is also a 327-mile line along the east coast to the Thai border. Rail service between principal commercial centers and Singapore is frequent and efficient.

The Government of Malaysia included M$200 million in the Third Malaysia Plan for extension and improvement of the railway network, with a view to strengthening the role of the Railway in the national transportation system. Improvements in training programs for Malayan Railway personnel are also being made.

Ocean Transport

Transport time from the East Coast of the United States to Malaysia is 40 to 50 days, depending on the number of ports of call, or can be as little as 30 days if freight is forwarded by rail to U.S. West Coast ports for shipment. From western U.S. ports to Malaysia requires 22 to 35 days, compared with about 20 days from Europe and 10 days from Japan. Shipping lines serving U.S.-Malaysia routes regularly include American President Lines, Maersk Line, Knutsen Line, Sea Train Lines, Inc., Lykes Bros. Steamship Co., United States Lines, Sea-Land Service, EAC Lines, Hapag-Lloyd, Neptune Orient Line, Barber Steamship Lines, Inc., and SCINDIA Steamship Navigation Co. Ltd.

Ocean shipping is vital to Malaysia, due to its heavy dependence on foreign trade and separation by water of the Peninsular from the East Malaysian States. Most of Peninsular Malaysia's foreign trade moves via Port Kelang—27 miles from Kuala Lumpur and the facilities in Penang, which include berths on the mainland in Butterworth. The commissioning of the new ports at Johore Bahru and Kuantan, in 1977 and 1978, respectively, is adding to the handling capacity of Peninsular Malaysian ports. The capacity of the major Peninsular ports is expected to double from 6.8 million tons in 1975 to 11.4 million tons in 1980. These major areas are supplemented by numerous minor ports.

Improvement in existing facilities is highlighted by the significant expansion in the Penang and Kelang ports. An allocation of M$121 million was made under the Third Malaysia Plan for the Penang facility. The port of Penang will be increasingly important in serving the north Malaysia region.

It is anticipated that under the Fourth Malaysia Plan (1981-85) a new port will be built on Pulau Lumut, just off Port Kelang. The port, projected to cost more than US$1 million, will serve Kuala Lumpur.

Port facilities in East Malaysia have also been expanded and modernized. The Sabah Ports Authority administers seven ports, but the bulk of the State's trade is confined to three—Kota Kinabalu, Sandakan, and Tawau. Kota Kinabalu's and Sandakan's port facilities were commissioned in 1977, while the Tawau port expansion is being undertaken in 1978-82. Sarawak's main ports are Miri, Sibu, and Kuching, which were greatly expanded in 1975. Construction of a port in Bintulu is now underway, at an estimated cost of US$128.6 million.

Malaysian ocean shipping is performed exclusively by the Malaysian International Shipping Corporation (MISC), a national line that began operations in early 1970. It is a joint venture company between the public and the private sectors. Frequent ocean freight service by international conference and nonconference lines is available between Malaysian ports and the rest of the world by many foreign shipping lines. Given the distance involved, delivery schedules should be coordinated with the shipping lines to avoid delays and complications.

Air Transport

The Malaysian Government attaches considerable importance to the accommodation of international air flights and to expansion of domestic aviation. Total expenditure for civil aviation projects under the Third Malaysia Plan was estimated at M$211 million, underscoring its importance in the region's development. Peninsular Malaysia has two international airports: one in Subang near Kuala Lumpur and the other in Penang. The Subang airport, completed in 1965, is among the most modern in the region and can handle jumbo jets. The airport in Penang has been expanded and modernized to handle international flights by aircraft of the Boeing 707 class. Recent construction included a new terminal building, control tower, and safety features. Under the Third Malaysia Plan, development of the Kota Kinabalu Airport in Sabah into an international airport was accomplished in order to accommodate the expected 5.5 percent yearly increase in traffic.

Airports for domestic flights in Peninsular Malaysia are located in Kota Bharu, Kuala Trengganu, Kuantan, Alor Star, Ipoh and Malacca. Planned expansion of these airports was completed under the Third Malaysia Plan or is underway. (Kota Bharu will be further developed into an international airport beginning in 1982.)

The Government of Malaysia regards the development of air transport facilities in Sabah and Sarawak as vital for an integrated domestic air transport system. In Sarawak, the present airport network inclues the Bintulu, Sibu, Miri, and Kuching facilities. Expansions of the latter two have been undertaken, as they are considered essential in view of the rapid agricultural and industrial development within the region. In addition, construction of the Limbang Airport was initiated in 1978. Sandakan and Tawau Airports in Sabah are undergoing renovation.

Foreign suppliers are finding it feasible and competitive to ship a widening range of goods to the Malaysian market via air freight. The advent of the jumbo jet with its more efficient handling of freight has helped the U.S. exporter overcome the time-distance delivery problem, although adding to the costs of the product.

Regional Warehousing

U.S. exporters of a variety of products may also be able to overcome the time-distance delivery problem by developing facilities for warehousing and regional marketing and distribution in a single commercial center. Malaysia, as well as several other Southeast Asian countries, is suitable for this operation.

A basic element in a regional marketing operation is the storage of selected products in warehouses for future delivery to customers in markets located a reasonable distance from the distribution point. Requirements for this operation are adequate port facilities, including warehouses; inland transportation and lighterage; frequent shipping connections with market areas in the region; capable trading establishments; and banking services. Malaysia has an abundance of the necessary facilities and is being used increasingly by foreign suppliers as a regional distribution and marketing center. Port areas have considerable public warehouse space, and new warehouses are being added steadily. Also, many of the trading firms maintain warehouses convenient to port areas.

Regional warehousing and distribution operations have been discussed here in the context of improving U.S. exporters' competitiveness by enabling earlier deliveries of goods ordered in Malaysia and other market areas in Asia. These kinds of operations may also result in increased sales by U.S. exporters to customers in those Asian countries requiring advance import deposits.

Communications Facilities

Malaysia's government-owned telecommunications system is modern and efficient. All the principal cities and towns are linked by telephone, and calls may be placed immediately to most points by direct dialing. Overseas radiotelephone service between Malaysia and most foreign countries is available via Singapore. Telephone and telegraphic connections can be made through the Southeast Asia Commonwealth Communications System (SEACOM) to the Commonwealth global system. Thus, there is direct dialing between Kuala Lumpur and the United Kingdom, the United States, Canada, Australia, and Japan. The SEACOM system also reaches Kota Kinabalu in Sabah and Brunei. A troposcatter station in Sarawak provides high-quality telephone channels and permits automatic or semiautomatic dialing into the Peninsular Malaysian subscriber trunk dialing system. Telex service, a quick means of international communication for commercial use, is also available to subscribers.

An effective telegraph system serves all the principal cities in Malaysia, and local and overseas telegrams are accepted at main telegraph offices, post offices, and hotels and by private phone. Overseas telegrams from Malaysia are sent by the Malaysian Telecommunication Department using radioteletype facilities. Telegrams to Hong Kong and Kota Kinabalu are transmitted directly from Kuala Lumpur via the SEACOM cable. To all other countries, they are transmitted by the Singapore Telecommunications Department via submarine telegraphic cable or short-wave radio.

Malaysia entered the space link age by opening a Satellite Communications Earth Station in Kuantan in 1970. This facility links Malaysia to the Indian Ocean INTELSAT III Satellite to Tokyo and provides a high-quality overseas service for telephone, telegraph, and telex circuits.

The government-owned domestic radio communication system reaches a wide audience in Malaysia. Radio transmission takes place in the languages common in the area: Malay, various Chinese dialects, Tamil, and English. Commercial advertising is accepted.

Malaysia maintains an efficient postal service with two mail deliveries daily in the larger commercial centers. Airmail service between Malaysian points and the outside world, including the United States, is considered excellent.

Utilities

The major supplier of electric power in Peninsular Malaysia is the government-owned National Electricity Board (NEB), with an installed capacity in 1979 of 1,778 megawatts (MW) and with a demand at just over 1,200 MW. Of this, the percentage composition was 55 percent thermal, 34 percent hydro, 6 percent gas turbine, and 6 percent diesel. A substantial number of the diesels serve the rural areas and are not connected to the national grid network. In addition to the principal system, Penang is supplied separately by a municipally owned facility, and smaller privately owned thermal plants operate in several regions. In the State of Perak, private hydroelectric facilities operate. NEB's generating capacity was to be increased to 2,137 MW during 1980. To meet demand, growing at a high annual rate of 12 to 13 percent, and to further the expansion and development of the national grid system, the NEB plans to carry out a comprehensive construction program that is to be completed by 1985. Included in the program are the Bersia and Kenering hydroelectric projects, expected to be commissioned in 1982-83, as well as a large, multipurpose hydroscheme in Trengganu, to be commissioned in 1984-85. Funding for power projects under the Third Malaysia Plan was increased to US$1,216.1 million from the original allocation of US$718 million. Increases in generating power in 1975-78 were 28.3 percent per annum, illustrating the attention given to this area.

NEB installations and major private facilities are on alternating current at 50 cycles, 3-phase. Commercial and domestic suppliers are uniform at 400-415 volts single-phase and 230-240 volts single-phase and 230-240 volts 3-phase. Major consumption by industrial and commercial users is in the ratio of about 70 to 30, but growth in commercial use has been outdistancing the rise in industrial use. The rates charged by the National Electricity Board are considered moderate. The charges vary according to location and purpose, as well as the number of units consumed.

In Sabah, electricity is supplied by the State-owned Sabah Electricity Board (SEB). Similarly, in Sarawak, the Sarawak Electricity Supply Corporation (SESC) meets the needs of the region. The principal load centers in Sarawak are located at Kuching, Sibu, Miri, and Bintulu and are currently served by diesel generation. Demand in this region depends on the realization of major industrial projects in Bintulu—an aluminum smelting project, an iron fabrication plant, and the LNG plant. The Batang Ai hydroelectric facility is expected to accommodate demand in the Kuching region beginning in 1985.

Water supply is under the jurisdiction of the various state governments—except for Malacca and Penang City—which have their own authorities. Rates are moderate and vary from state to state and according to the purpose for which the water is used.

Advertising and Research

Advertising

Advertising as a sales tool is widely used in Malaysia. There are several advertising and public relations firms that will assist the U.S. exporter or his/her agent in media presentations. U.S. firms (or local companies with American equity participation) in advertising and public relations located in Malaysia include: Ted Bates (Malaysia) Sdn. Bhd., Burson-Marsteller (Malaysia) Sdn. Bhd., Eric White Associates

(Malaysia) Sdn. Bhd., SSC & B Lintas Sdn. Bhd., McCann-Erickson (Malaysia) Sdn. Bhd. (Interpublic Group in New York), and PTM Thompson Advertising Sdn. Bhd.

The most effective media advertising is done in the daily newspaper. These publications have a wide circulation and reach readers in the major local languages. While Malay is the national language, most of the business community can be reached in the English language press. The principal English language newspapers are the New Straits Times and The Sunday Times. Other publications include the Malay Mail, The Asian Wall Street Journal, and Business Times.

Advertising in American publications also reaches the Malaysian market. U.S. consumer and trade journals have a wide circulation—often reaching a worldwide readership, particularly among the more affluent business and professional customers, many of whom are headquartered in Malaysia.

Radio and television are being used increasingly by distributors to advertise consumer goods. Rising family incomes make these media very popular methods of advertising. The majority of the population listens daily to Malaysian radio broadcasts. Television operates over two channels offering a full range of programming. Both radio and television offer commercial "spots."

In addition, all types of advertising familiar to the exporter are available in Malaysia. The type of promotion will depend upon the product and the target market. Flyers, billboards, store displays, television, radio, and newspapers are all used as successful marketing techniques.

In Malaysia, the Advertising Standards Authority was established in 1974. The agency administers and updates the Code of Advertising Practices (1972), which sets guidelines for "legal, decent, honest and truthful" advertising. Recent revisions in the code ban all television liquor advertisements, place time restrictions on advertising of some products, restrict cigarette advertising, and ban advertisements in general that feature scantily dressed women, Malaysians who look like foreign celebrities, and children.

Market Research

Market research, as it is known in the developed economies, is being recognized as an essential and effective marketing tool. It is being utilized with increasing frequency in Malaysia with very satisfactory results. Several firms, including Asian ones, have been established to supply this service and have developed an acceptable competence in professional market research. These firms are constantly expanding their activities to meet the growing demand for their expertise. Market research firms based in Singapore and Hong Kong also take on commissions in Malaysia.

Although professional market investigation services are available, many local trading firms conduct market inquiries on a rule-of-thumb basis. While the results are often good, they vary according to the competence of the firms and the staffs responsible for market planning and development. Foreign suppliers having agency contacts with local firms are able, in many cases, to obtain very useful market analyses and market development guidance from these agents. Business organizations, both government and private, may also be helpful as sources of market information.

There are several chambers of commerce organized on an ethnic basis. They have good membership support and are loosely tied into a single united chamber in an effort to achieve a consolidated approach when representing the viewpoint of private enterprise in its relations with the Government. The largest chambers have been organized by Malaysian businesspersons of Chinese origin and are located in Kuala Lumpur, Ipoh, and Penang. Membership includes a large number of importers and exporters.

Banking and Credit

Malaysia has a well-developed, sophisticated banking system that provides an important source of capital for commercial and industrial development. The Central Bank (Bank Negara Malaysia) was established in 1959 to promote monetary stability and the development of a sound financial structure and to influence the credit situation to the advantage of the country. Bank Negara Malaysia is charged with the responsibility of formulating and implementing the country's monetary and banking policies within the framework of the overall national economic policy. Specifically, it is empowered to issue currency, to keep the external reserves safeguarding the value of the currency, to act as banker and financial adviser to the Government, and to act as a banker's bank. Bank Negara provides banking facilities to commercial banks, finance companies licensed as borrowing companies, merchant banks, discount houses, and a few other financial institutions.

Malaysia's numerous commercial banks and commercial branch banks are all members of the Association of Banks aimed at promoting sound banking practices. Commercial banks are centered mainly in Kuala Lumpur and other urban areas. American banks represented in Malaysia include Chase Manhattan, Citibank, Bank of America, Seattle First National Bank, and Manufacturers Hanover Trust Company. The commercial banks are free to determine and quote exchange rates for all currencies to their customers; they are also permitted to deal forward in all currencies. There are no taxes or subsidies on purchases or sales of foreign exchange.

Finance companies licensed as borrowing companies constitute the second most important source, next to commercial banks, of private sector lending in Malaysia. These finance companies, numbering over 30, finance hire purchases; commercial, industrial, and residential construction; leasing transactions; factoring; and a variety of other purposes, including bridging finance and refinancing.

Merchant banking is a fairly new development in Malaysia, the oldest bank being only 10 years old. Effective January 1, 1979 merchant banks were brought under the scope of the Banking Act of 1973, to ensure that they undertake their functions effectively, conform with the objectives of national policy, and operate on sound management principles. However, the 12 merchant banks operating in Malaysia were exempted from certain provisions of the Banking Act, in recognition of the specialized nature of their operations and activities which complement the activities of commercial banks and finance companies.

Medium- and long-term development finance is provided by the Malaysian Industrial Development Finance Berhad (MIDF). Originally a private financial institution, MIDF was reorganized in 1963 with the participation of the Malaysian Government and the World Bank. Shareholders include the Malaysian Government, commercial banks, insurance companies, and industrialists. Its advances have been mostly in the form of long- and medium-term loans to local and foreign investors. Other facilities offered by MIDF include underwriting of capital issues; advisory service for industry; and equity, preference share, or debenture participation. As of September 1980, financing was offered by MIDF at 8½ to 9½ percent interest rates. (See also "Exchange Control Regulations" section.)

Trade Regulations

Foreign Trade Regime

The Government of Malaysia seeks to promote economic integration and development of the country and simultaneously to keep trade controls to a minimum. To effect this policy, the Federal Government has taken steps to form a Common Customs Area throughout the country. Almost all goods are exempt from tariffs when moved within Malaysia. External duties are low or nonexistent on most raw materials and capital goods and are moderate on most manufactured goods unless there is local production. Nontariff import controls are not extensive but include license and quota restrictions to protect locally produced goods, antidumping regulations, customs and health protective measures.

Tariff Structure

Effective January 1, 1978, a new Customs tariff based on the Customs Cooperation Council Nomenclature (CCCN) came into force. Applying to all of Malaysia—which includes Peninsular Malaysia, Sabah, and Sarawak, it sets out, inter alia, the common Malaysian tariff to be levied on imports into Customs areas of Malaysia. With the exception of certain items, mainly petroleum products and live animals, both locally made and foreign-made goods moving between the three areas are free of internal import duties.

Ad valorem rates range from zero to 75 percent, although only a few items are dutiable at over 25 percent. The average import Customs duty rate is approximately 15 percent, relatively low among the countries in Southeast Asia. Most capital machinery may be imported duty free.

The Government is empowered to raise tariff rates on a number of items, both manufactured and agricultural; however, enforcement thereof has been suspended until a more opportune time when domestic production of such items is adequate for Malaysia's needs. One purpose of this measure is to encourage investors to produce locally those goods on which duties will be increased in due course.

Information regarding Malaysian duties applicable to specific products may be obtained free of charge from the Regional Marketing Manager, ASEAN/South Asia Branch, Office of Country Marketing, U.S. Department of Commerce, or through the Commerce District Offices. Inquiries should contain a complete product description, including BTN, SITC, or U.S. Schedule E Export Commodity numbers, if known.

Basis of Duty Assessment

All Customs areas base ad valorem duty on the c.i.f. value of the product. Specific duties are levied on only a few items. Containers and packing materials are excluded from duty assessment when specific duties are levied on a weight basis. The standard measures for length and weight throughout Malaysia are undergoing a transition to the metric system. The Metric Weights and Measures Bill of 1971 asserts that both metric and imperial systems may be legally used until January 1, 1982, when complete conversion to metric will be enacted. However, as of January 1, 1978, the Customs tariff was metricated. From that date forward, all import, export, and excise duties as well as regulations pertaining to the imposition of duties can only be based on metric units.

In Malaysia duties are stated and paid in Malaysian currency at the time the goods are cleared through Customs. Conversion of foreign values is effected at the market rate for foreign currencies. There is a 5 percent surtax imposed on the c.i.f. value of most imports and a 5 percent sales tax on the c.i.f. value plus Customs duty and surtax. However, machinery for new or expanded industrial facilities may be exempted from the 5 percent surtax, and raw materials imported for industrial purpose may also be taxed at a reduced rate.

Special Customs Provisions

In 1971, the Malaysian Parliament passed the Free Trade Zone Act. Once an area has been declared a free trade zone, goods of any description, not specifically prohibited by law, may be brought into the specific area without payment of customs duty. However, goods in a free trade zone may only be removed for export or for transfer to another free trade zone area in Malaysia. Goods brought into a free trade zone may be broken, repacked, assembled, distributed, mixed, or reassembled for export or transfer to another free trade zone.

Samples of no commercial value may be admitted free of duty into Malaysia; other samples are subject to prevailing duties. Dutiable samples may be brought in by commercial travelers upon deposit of duty. The deposit is refunded if the samples are exported within 3 months or within such further time as the authorities may grant. Samples imported into Malaysia by parcel post, whether for free distribution or for sale, are subject to prevailing import duties. Provisions for reexportation of parcel post samples are similar to those which apply to reexports. No restrictions are imposed on the reexportation of duty-free goods. Printed advertising matter imported into Malaysia is subject to an import duty of 55 Malaysian cents per kilo, plus the normal 5 percent surtax and 5 percent sales tax.

Advance Rulings on Classification

When an importer is in doubt as to the classification of goods, a sample and description of goods may be sent to an appropriate Customs officer. Any ruling that the Customs officer may make is purely advisory and not binding. However, the Customs officer may elect to send a sample of the goods to the Comptroller of Customs for a ruling on the classification of the article. Such a ruling is considered binding.

Shipping Documents

Documents required by Customs authorities for air and surface shipments entering Malaysia include the commercial invoice, the bill of lading for surface shipments, an air waybill for air freight, a certificate of origin, and the import declaration. Special documents are also required for the importation of certain plant materials, birds, and animals. Consular documents are not required.

Commercial Invoice.—Special commercial invoice forms are not required. Invoices may be printed on an importer's letterhead, but they must be signed by a responsible person of the firm and must show the proper description, quantity or weight, c.i.f. value, and country of origin of goods. Three copies of the commercial invoice are forwarded under separate cover to the consignee. The original copy of the invoice must be submitted to the Customs authorities.

Bills of Lading.—The bill of lading covering shipments to Penang should show the name of the shipper, consignee, and steamer; the exporter's mark and number of packages; and a description of goods. For other ports, the bill of lading should show the name of the shipper and the consignee and a description of the goods, including measurements and weights.

Certificate of Origin.—A certificate of origin is required for banking purposes when dollar exchange is supplied by the local control authorities. There is no special form for the certificate, which is usually issued in letter form by the Ministry of Commerce and Industry.

Import Declaration.—Importers are required to present an import declaration for all imports.

Marking and Labeling Requirements

Labels are required for imports of food, drugs, and liquors, and the labels must specify the country of origin. Prepacked foods must be labeled to show, in English, the appropriate designation of the food content, printed in capital letters at least 1/8 inch in height; whether foods are compounded, mixed, or blended; the minimum quantity stated in weight or measure (intoxicating liquors, soft drinks, and condensed or dried milk are exempt from this provision if prepackaged in a container for retail sales); the name and address of the manufacturer or seller; and the country of origin.

A description of the contents of the package may be added to the label, provided the additional language is not contrary to, or a modification of, any statement (in English) on the label. Pictorial illustrations must not be misleading as to the true nature or origin of the food.

Food that must adhere to standards must be labeled to conform to these standards and be free from added foreign substances. Packages of food described as "enriched," "fortified," "vitaminized," or in any other way which implies that the article contains added vitamins or minerals, must show the quantities of vitamins or minerals added per pound, ounce, or fluid ounce.

Special labels are required for certain foods, including invalid's food, margarine, coffee mixtures, vinegar, milk, milk products, and diabetic food.

Drugs and medicines must be labeled to indicate the amount of active constituents or ingredients. Cosmetics and toilet preparations containing lead or its components are prohibited. Where applicable, drugs, medicines, and cosmetics are subject to the provisions of the Malayan Poisons and Dangerous Drugs Ordinances.

Although not prescribed by law, it is advisable to inscribe marks on the outside of packing cases to correspond with the marks shown on the bill of lading and to indicate the port of discharge. Further information should be obtained from importers or agents in Malaysia since many requirements are not published.

Senate Concurrent Resolution 40, adopted July 30, 1953, invites U.S. exporters to inscribe, insofar as practicable, on the external shipping containers in indelible print of a suitable size: "United States of America."

Import Licensing

Most goods may enter under an Open General License, but some are admissible only under a specific validated license which is issued by the Comptroller of Customs. Some imports are totally prohibited by orders issued under the Customs Ordinance of 1952. This Ordinance is the enabling law authorizing the issuance of various Customs orders.

The Open General License is simply an authorization by the Government to import or export specified goods without recourse to a specific validated license for each transaction. A validated license is issued upon application and authorizes a firm to import or export a particular article. Products may require an individual license for surveillance purposes.

Trade controls are exercised over certain goods through legislation other than the Customs Ordinance of 1952, and licneses issued under the Customs Ordinance are issued without prejudice to the provisions of such legislation. For example, there is special legislation covering food and drugs, the field of veterinary controls, security, and exchange controls.

The Comptroller of Customs, who administers trade controls, has authorized officers of the Trade Division, Ministry of Commerce and Industry, located in Kuala Lumpur and Penang, to issue necessary import and export licenses.

Validated licenses are required to import several types of products, including primate animals; arms and ammunition; brandy and whiskey, unless certified as stored in wood for at least 3 years; diamonds; and certain food products, among others.

Imports of motor vehicles are subject to specific licensing with quantitiative restriction. Certain other imports are subject to quantitative restrictions as a temporary measure to protect local industries; these restrictions are reviewed from time to time.

A number of meats or meat products for human consumption imported into Malaysia require the certification of a competent government veterinary officer of the country of origin and are also subject to approval for import by an authorized State Veterinary Officer serving in the area into which imported.

An import license and a health certificate are also required on all imports of live plant and planting material.

The importation of some goods is absolutely prohibited. These goods include indecent or obscene articles or prints and articles bearing the imprint or reproduction of any currency note, bank note, or coin that is current or has ever been issued in any country. There is also a prohibition on the import into Malaysia of goods from the Republic of South Africa and Israel.

Certain goods are exempted from import and export licensing under the Customs Ordinance. These are goods imported (or exported) by government procurement bodies, approved personal baggage, and bunkering and stores requirements for ships and aircraft.

Export Controls

The Federal Malaysian Government is

empowered to legislate with respect to exports from any of the Malaysian areas. Individual export licenses are required to authorize some exports and reexports. Exports of rubber from Peninsular Malaysia require a certificate from the Malaysian Rubber Exchange and Licensing Board. Exports of steel bars, formic acid, wheat flour, rice bran, and sugar were subject to specific licenses at mid-year 1980, and licenses for these and a few additional items (e.g., fertilizers and pig iron), may be denied. Exports of the following were also subject to licensing: all textiles, some confectionery items, tiles, fish meal, "dollar area goods," all commodities used in barter trade, and other goods as specified in the second schedule of the Customs (Prohibition of Exports) Order, 1978, of the 1967 Customs Act.

The export of certain strategic materials and products is controlled to assure adequate domestic supply; steel, scrap metal, cement, bricks, timber, and petroleum products were subject to quantitative restrictions at mid-year 1980.

The export of strategic goods to Communist countries is controlled in the interest of national security by requiring a validated license for the export of all strategic materials to all destinations. In addition, Malaysia has adopted an import certification/delivery verification procedure by which diversion of strategic materials to the Communist Bloc may be prohibited.

All exports to South Africa and Israel are prohibited.

Export Taxes

In the 1980 Government of Malaysia budget speech, a number of export tax changes were announced. The tax structure is now based on a "cost-plus" approach, with the cost of production of a particular commodity to be taken into account and appropriate duties to be imposed only at prices above the prevailing cost of production. Also, the maximum marginal rates will be limited to 50 percent for all commodities. Producers in Sabah and Sarawak will continue to pay only 70 percent of the assessed tax.

The duty revision has decreased the tax burden on rubber in order to encourage greater planting of rubber trees for the future growth of the industry. The tin export duty was also decreased in an effort to stimulate the mining of tin by gravel pump operators with marginal profitability levels. Although all tin mines benefit from the decreased duty, larger concerns also became subject to an increase in the tin profits tax levied on corporate incomes above specified minimum levels.

Limitations on Business Activities of Foreigners

Exchange Control Regulations

Exchange control regulations were liberalized in June 1979. The following are the exchange control regulations of most interest to U.S. traders and investors:

Remittances.—If the amount to be remitted abroad is below M$5,000, no permission is required and no exchange control form needs to be completed. For amounts of M$5,000 up to M$2 million, exchange control forms must be completed and approval is given by the commercial banks. For amounts greater than M$2 million, exchange control forms must be completed and approval of the Controller of Foreign Exchange must be obtained.

Exports.—For exports valued at M$5,000 f.o.b. and above, exchange control forms must be completed. These forms must be approved by a commercial bank (acting on behalf of the Controller of Foreign Exchange) before submission to the Customs authorities.

Payments for exports must be made in a specified currency or in Malaysian dollars obtained from the sale of a specified currency to a bank in Malaysia, according to the timing of payment stated in the sales contract, which should not be later than 6 months from the date of exportation.

Investment.—Foreign direct and portfolio investments by Malaysian residents are freely allowed subject to the completion of an exchange control form for amounts of M$5,000 and above. For amounts up to M$2 million permission is given by commercial banks, and for amounts greater than M$2 million, the permission of the Controller of Foreign Exchange is required.

Nonresidents are allowed to make portfolio and direct investment in Malaysia without prior exchange control permission. Repatriation of capital and remittance os profits are freely permitted subject to the completion of exchange control forms for amounts of M$5,000 or more.

A company in Malaysia controlled by nonresidents is permitted to borrow amounts up to M$5,000 from Malaysian commercial banks; exchange control permission from the Controller of Foreign Exchange is required for loans beyond this amount. Such approval will be given based on the genuine need of the nonresident controlled company. To ensure that nonresident controlled companies regard their investments in Malaysia as long-term propositions, they are required to bring in some funds of their own to finance their projects. The Exchange Control also requires that nonresident controlled companies obtain 50 percent of their domestic borrowings from locally incorporated banks, unless the required funds are not available from these banks.

Malaysian dollar (ringgit) bank accounts of residents of other countries are ordinarily designated as "external accounts." Deposits are freely permitted subject only to the completion of exchange control forms on amounts above M$5,000; the proceeds from the sale of any foreign currency may be credited to external accounts. There are no restrictions on withdrawals.

Land and Real Estate

In Peninsular Malaysia all dealings in land other than land for mining are governed by the National Land Code of 1965. The code established uniform land laws for all of the individual States of Peninsular Malaysia, which continue to exercise the responsibility for controlling land ownership. The code also provides for the methods by which land may be made security for debts.

Land and real estate dealings in East Malaysia are governed by the Sabah and Sarawak Land Codes. With certain specific exceptions, there is no basic restriction on land ownership in Malaysia. Land may be acquired by persons or companies domiciled outside Malaysia provided they conform in all respects to existing land laws. Title to land is derived either from a grant by the Crown or from rights granted as the result of duly recognized and registered clearing and cultivation. Most land is held by long-term lease ranging from 33 to 99 years, subject to the payment of fixed annual rental. The present policy of the state governments is to transfer land by lease rather than by perpetual grant. All states have the power to acquire any land that may be needed for a public purpose, but a fair and reasonable compensation must be paid. Title under the various land codes conveys surface rights only, with state governments retaining all rights to minerals below the surface.

Foreign Investment

U.S. Investment

U.S. Investment in Malaysia totaled over US$1 billion at yearend 1979. While the majority of this investment is in the petroleum industry, there are also significant U.S. investments in the electronics industry (assembly) and the banking sector. The future for U.S. investment is positive, given the abundance of natural resources, able labor force, numerous government investment incentives, and the political stability of the country.

Malaysian Government Policy on Investment

The basic attitude of the Malaysian Government towards foreign investment revolves around two policy objectives. First, the desire to restructure the economy, providing a more equitable distribution of employment and equity holdings for bumiputra (Malay and other indigenous people) as established in the New Economic Policy (NEP). Secondly, Malaysia's interest in diversifying its exports through development of the manufacturing sector plays an important role in encouraging foreign investment. Joint ventures are the official form for such projects.

The importance of foreign investment in government policies is reflected in the presence of the Malaysian Industrial Development Authority (MIDA), which was established in 1967 and initially called the Federal Industrial Development Authority. Its goal is not only to attract new industry but also to expand existing industry and to disperse industry throughout the country. The actual functions of the Authority include economic feasibility and pre-investment studies of specific products and industries, the promotion of local investment, recommendations on policies on industrial site development, the evaluation of applications for pioneer status and other investment incentives and generalized aid to investors. In promoting and coordinating joint ventures, the MIDA has established the Registry of Potential Investors and Entrepreneurs. The registry provides names of potential investors and attempts to bridge the gap between investors who have the capital but lack technical know-how and those with relevant knowledge who require additional capital.

The principal law relating to investment and the NEP is the Industrial Coordination Act (ICA), which took effect in May 1977 (amended 1979). The law requires that all manufacturing firms above a minimum size obtain a license from the Minister of Trade and Industry. The license contains a number of technical conditions pertaining to production, pollution control, etc.; however, its main thrust is towards fulfillment of the goals of the NEP. It states the conditions related to the holdings allowed in the case of foreign firms; it also stipulates an effort must be made toward achieving the goal of about 50 percent bumiputra participation at all levels of the firm including middle management by 1990. The ICA increases the amount of government control over firms, but as promised, it has displayed considerable flexibility in enforcing it. Most Americans have had little difficulty obtaining licenses. This flexibility should continue because of the Government's desire to increase investment, especially in manufacturing.

The achievement of a 30 percent bumiputra share of equity holding by 1990 is of great concern to the Government of Malaysia. From this concern, stems the heavy yet flexible emphasis on its NEP goal, while also encouraging export oriented investment in manufacturing. The guidelines are as follows:

Projects for the Domestic Market.—If the technology involved is available in Malaysia, and especially if similar projects already exist there, such projects should be 100 percent Malaysian owned. Where the technology is *not* available, up to 30 percent foreign ownership may be allowed.

Export-Oriented Projects Based on Imported Components and Parts.—Where a new investment project plans on exporting between 80 and 100 percent of its product and basically utilizes imported component parts, the Ministry of Trade and Industry will generally allow majority foreign ownership. The extent of foreign ownership will usually be negotiated within the range of 51 to 70 percent, depending on the nature of the project. In exceptional cases, where 100 percent export-oriented projects can make a case for 100 percent foreign ownership, the Minister of Trade and Industry may approve such ownership.

Export-Oriented Industries Utilizing Nondepleting Domestic Raw Materials.—The investment policy in manufacturing industries using nondepleting domestic raw materials (rubber, palm oil, tapioca, etc.) is flexible. Manufactured products of timber are also included in this category. Depending on the type of project, its location, the nature of the product, the level of technology, and the number of similar projects already established in Malaysia, foreign ownership of from 30 to 55 percent may be allowed.

Export-Oriented Industries Utilizing Depleting Domestic Raw Materials.—Resources (tin and other minerals).—In this category, foreign companies will generally only be allowed to have 30 percent equity participation. In some cases, foreign companies may *initially* be allowed to hold between 35 to 45 percent on the condition that this be reduced within a stipulated and agreed upon period.

Despite the Government's flexibility in issuing licenses, Malaysia's goal *is* to reduce foreign participation to 30 percent by 1990. This trend is in evidence in recent years as total foreign ownership has been declining throughout the seventies, from 63.3 percent in 1970 to a projected 43.6 percent in 1980.

Regardless of the uncertainties raised by these policy measures, the Government of Malaysia offers eight major forms of investment incentives, indicative of its active investment recruiting. Companies that produce goods not already manufactured on a commercial scale suitable to the economic requirements of Malaysia may qualify for Pioneer Status Incentives, which exempt them from income tax, development tax, and excess profits tax for 2 to a maximum of 10 years. Firms not enjoying pioneer status may be eligible for another type of tax incentive, such as Investment Tax Credit (which allows part of the investment cost to be deducted and is attractive in projects with high investment levels and a long gestation period before profits); Labor Utilization Relief (for labor intensive industries); export incentives (which include export allowances, accelerated depreciation allowance, deduction for promotional expenses overseas, and the export refinancing facility); Increased Capital Allowance; hotel incentives; locational incentives; or special incentives for approved agricultural industries.

Other benefits are import duty relief for necessary components and tariff protection for infant industries. The Government also exercises preferential purchasing of locally manufactured goods. State governments have established economic development corporations directed toward helping investors find suitable sites and facilities in specially created free trade zones. They offer special incentives to attract the industries they desire, complementing government efforts to ensure balanced regional growth.

An additional incentive for American investors is the availability of Overseas Private Investment Corporation (OPIC) insurance and finance programs in Malaysia. OPIC programs, or the programs of its predecessor agency, have been operating in Malaysia since 1959.

On balance, the investment climate in Malaysia remains attractive. The racial friction, infrastructure problems, limitations on expatriates, and bureaucratic problems can be overcome if cultural sensitivity, careful advance planning, and development of good relations are practiced. The substantial positive factors of abundant natural resources, an honest and stable government, a strong economy, relatively low wages, productive workers, weak unions, flexible rules, and numerous tax incentives make

Malaysia a site with high potential for prospective investors.

Requirements for Business Organization

The basic instrument of law governing business enterprises in Malaysia is the Companies Act of 1965. This ordinance, which is based on English law, sets the guidelines for incorporation and details the manner in which the enterprise may borrow funds. The act provides for the formation of any profit-seeking enterprise by foreign nationals that conforms to the laws, public policy, and morals of Malaysia.

All companies that wish to operate in Malaysia must register with the Registrar of Companies under the Ministry of Trade and Industry. Within the Ministry of Trade and Industry, the Malaysian Industrial Development Authority (MIDA), known as the "one-stop agency for investment," handles all applications for the establishment of businesses in Malaysia. This agency has the primary responsibility for promoting and coordinating all industrial development. Its functions include evaluating applications, conducting economic feasibility studies of proposed industries, coordinating information for business, governmental oversight of progress and problems of industrialization, and recommending policy regarding the country's industrial development.

Other institutions of interest to potential investors are the Malaysian Industrial Development Finance Berhad (MIDF), which is a public corporation providing ancillary or complementary financial, technical, and managerial assistance; the Foreign Investment Committee (FIC), which formulates policy guidelines on foreign investment and coordinates and regulates all asset acquisitions, mergers, and takeovers; and the Petroleum National Berhad, which regulates all petroleum ventures (exploration through manufacturing).

Four types of business may be set up in Malaysia: (1) public companies, (2) private companies, (3) sole proprietorships and partnerships, and (4) branches of foreign companies.

Three types of public companies may be incorporated: (1) a company limited by shares, (2) a company limited by guaranty, and (3) an unlimited company. In a company limited by shares (analogous to that under U.S. law), the liability of members is limited to the amount paid on shares. In a company limited by currency, the liability of members is limited to a specific amount undertaken by the member. An unlimited company has no limit on the liability of the members and resembles a general partnership in this respect.

Private companies, as distinguished from public companies, may be limited or unlimited. A private company: (1) restricts the right to transfer its shares, (2) limits its membership to not more than 50 (not including employees), and (3) prohibits public subscription to its shares.

All companies must pay registration fees based on the amount of authorized capital. The fees range from a minimum of M$300 to a maximum of M$35,000. The following documents must be filed with the Registrar of Companies at the time of registration: (1) memorandum of association, (2) articles of association, (3) statutory declaration of compliance with the Companies Act of 1965, (4) list of directors, with a certificate of identity, (5) statutory declaration by the appointed director that he/she is not an undischarged bankrupt nor has he/she been convicted of fraud or other offenses connected with setting up a company, and (6) address of company's registered office.

In addition, the secretary and a minimum of two directors must have their principal or only place of residence in Malaysia; company auditors must be approved by the Malaysian Government; and companies must hold a general meeting within 18 months of incorporation followed by one per year thereafter.

Both sole proprietorships and partnerships must be registered with the Registrar of Business, with additional requirements spelled out by the Registration of Business (Amendment) Act of 1967. The registration fee is M$50 with an annual renewal cost of M$25. Partnerships permitted are: unlimited, where all partners (at least 2 but not more than 20) are jointly liable without limit; or limited, where at least one partner must have unlimited liability. The Registrar must be furnished with a statement covering such particulars as the business name; general nature of the business; address; and names of partners, officers, or directors.

A company incorporated outside but doing business in Malaysia must deposit with the Registrar of Business, within 1 month of local establishment: (1) a certified copy of the charter, bylaws, memoranda and articles of the company, or other instrument(s) delineating the constitution of the company; (2) list of directors; and (3) the names and addresses of one or more persons resident in Malaysia who are authorized to act legally and responsibly in its behalf. Each foreign company is required to submit annually to the Registrar a balance sheet containing the same particulars of operation as are required of companies formed locally under the Companies Act.

Registration of Trademarks and Patents

Registration of trademarks and patents is carried out under the provision of the Trade Marks Ordinance and the United Kingdom Patents Ordinance, respectively. There are presently separate items of legislation for Peninsular Malaysia, Sabah, and Sarawak, which, however, will eventually be consolidated.

Applications for registration of trademarks are made on prescribed forms available free from the pertinent Registrar. Foreign applicants are required to submit their application through locally resident agents and to provide a local address for service. Registration of the mark is effective for 7 years and renewable for periods of 14 years each.

There are 34 classes based on the International Classification of Goods. One application must be submitted for each trademark in each class.

Under the provisions of the United Kingdom Patents Ordinance, patents that have previously been registered in the United Kingdom may be registered in Malaysia within 3 years from the date of the patent. Applications for registration with the local registry have to be accompanied by a Certificate of Registration issued by the Patent Office in the United Kingdom and a certified copy of the specifications relating to the invention. Foreign applicants have to appoint local agents as powers of attorney to prosecute the applications on their behalf, and the power of attorney must be executed on a prescribed form. The life of a patent is 16 years.

Contracts

The Contract Ordinance of 1950 codifies the laws of contract. Except for minor differences, its provisions follow the principles of contract law as practiced in the English courts.

All contracts with the Government of Malaysia include a malpractice clause to the effect that should the private company be found guilty by a Malaysian court of anything illegal under Malaysian law, it would be subject to an unlimited penalty. However, the U.S. Embassy in Kuala Lumpur states that it knows of no government contracts that have been terminated as a result of this clause. Malaysia's judiciary has a reputation for ability, honesty, and independence.

Taxation

Income Tax.—Individual income tax is applicable to all resident individuals in Malaysia. Income is defined to include gains or profits from any trade, business, profession, or vocation arising anywhere in the world; all earnings from employment, direct or in the form of food, clothing, and housing; net annual value of land and improvements used by the owner on a rent-free basis; dividends, interest, and discounts; most pensions and annuities; rents, royalties, and earnings from property; wife's income; and other gains or profits of an income nature. Income tax is imposed on chargeable income, i.e., gross income, less allowable deductions; capital allowances, including unabsorbed, carried-forward allowances (on income from business only); business losses; and personal allowance (in the case of resident individuals only).

Residents of Malaysia are taxed according to a progressive rate schedule. A person allowance of M$5,000 is tax deductible from the income of resident taxpayers; additional deductions are allowed for a wife (M$2,000) and for children educated abroad. Life insurance premiums and certain contributions to retirement funds are also deductible as personal allowances.

Nonresidents of Malaysia are not eligible for any personal allowances and are ordinarily taxed at a flat levy of 40 percent. In most cases, nonresidents are not subject to tax on income from employment in Malaysia if the period of employment is less than 60 days in any 1 year.

The profit of a business carried on by nonresidents who operate partly inside and partly outside Malaysia is considered derived in Malaysia to the extent to which the profit is not directly attributable to operations outside Malaysia and Singapore. Nonresidents operating transportation facilities are liable for the full profit deemed to accrue in Malaysia from the transport of passengers, mail, and goods.

A company is taxed on its chargeable income at the rate of 40 percent. An exemption of 5 percentage points from the 40 percent tax rate is being given for assessment years 1980-82 to any company having paid-up capital or net assets of not less than M$1 million, which conforms to the NEP equity restructuring requirement. (Pioneer companies and those qualifying for other tax incentives are not entitled to this incentive.) Income earned from petroleum operations is taxable under a special Petroleum Act. In all companies, the manager or principal officer in the area is answerable for all matters regarding the assessment and payment of tax.

Deductions at prescribed rates are provided for qualifying capital expenditures incurred in connection with business operations, and, depending upon the nature of the particular business, they may take the following forms: (1) plant, machinery and equipment, etc.; (2)

industrial building, used as factory, dock, wharf, warehouse, etc.; (3) plantation/forest expenditure clearing of land, planting of approved crops, construction on roads and quarters, etc.; and (4) prospecting and development expenses on the acquisition of mining rights. Similar deductions are allowed for sole proprietorship and partnerships.

An accelerated depreciation allowance has been granted to all industries for assessment years 1979-83. A reinvestment allowance of 25 percent of capital expenditure on plant, machinery, and industrial buildings has been given to manufacturing and processing industries undertaking expansion approved by the Ministry of Trade and Industry for assessment years 1980-83.

The Investment Incentives Act provides for certain specific income tax relief incentives for companies and persons with approved pioneer status, as mentioned above; it also provides for relief from the Development Tax and Excess Profits Tax cited below.

Excess Profits Tax.—For a resident company, the Excess Profits Tax is 5 percent of chargeable income exceeding 25 percent of its shareholders' funds or M$200,000, whichever is the greater. For branches of nonresident companies, the tax is 5 percent of chargeable income exceeding M$200,000. For an individual, the Excess Profits Tax is imposed on chargeable income exceeding M$75,000. However, income from tin mining operations, timber extraction, pioneer companies (during a specific qualifying period), and petroleum companies is excluded from the scope of this tax. While tin mining and timber operations are exempt from this tax, they are levied respectively with a Tin Profit Tax and a Timber Profit Tax on proceeds from their operations. These taxes are additional to income and development taxes. Petroleum income is taxed under the Petroleum Act of 1967.

Development Tax.—A Development Tax is payable at the rate of 5 percent on net income from business or rents above M$3,000. For partnerships, the levy is 5 percent on income above M$2,000.

Real Property Gains Tax.—Gains arising from the disposal of property are subject to the Real Property Gains Tax. The rate of tax is on a diminishing scale in accordance with the length of the holding period.

Stamp Tax.—A Stamp Tax is imposed on a wide range of documents. The rate of tax varies, depending on the type of document and the amount of money involved. Firms transacting business in Malaysia should check carefully which, if any, of their business forms are subject to the Stamp Tax.

Sales Tax.—A 5 percent Sales Tax is levied on the sale of goods manufactured and sold or otherwise disposed of—with certain exceptions—and on imported goods for domestic consumption. The tax may be rebated if the goods are subsequently exported.

Labor Market and Organization

The Government of Malaysia gives priority to the basic education of its population and to specific training to meet the growing need for skilled labor. The literacy rate more than doubled between 1960 and 1975 and continues to rise; it is now over 60 percent in Peninsular Malaysia and approximately 25 percent in East Malaysia. The total labor force is nearly 5 million; unemployment is 6.1 percent.

Primary schooling in Peninsular Malaysia is both compulsory and free between ages 6 and 15. Greater efforts are being made by the Government to increase educational opportunities for the low income groups, especially in the rural areas. Numerous secondary vocational and technical schools have been established, as well as training courses and programs to increase labor skills.

Within the Government, the Ministry of Labor and Manpower assists in the formulation of labor policy and its implementation. Its major functions include protecting and promoting the welfare of workers, promoting good employer/employee relations and sound industrial relations, equipping unemployed persons with basic industrial skills and raising the skill level of the labor force, and making maximum use of the nation's manpower and generating employment.

The Trade Unions Ordinance of 1959 requires registration of trade unions and provides for their supervision and specific rights and privileges. The Employment Ordinance of 1955 governs employer/employee contracts of service.

Additional information on labor may be found in *Country Labor Profile for Malaysia, 1980*, published by the Bureau of International Labor Affairs, U.S. Department of Labor, available from the Superintendent of Documents, U.S. Government Printing Office, Washington, D.C. 20402.

Employment Permits for Expatriate Staff

It is government policy to encourage foreign companies investing in Malaysia to employ as many Malaysian personnel as possible, and the entry of expatriate staff is, therefore, subject to restrictions.

If the Government believes that the investing company operates an adequate training program to prepare Malaysians for the higher posts in the company, it will allow the investing company to bring in such technical experts and executive personnel as are considered necessary for the proper functioning of the company. Most of these foreign experts and executives are expected to be replaced as soon as local employees have been adequately trained, but each company is allowed to retain a number of "key posts" that can be filled by expatriate personnel indefinitely. The number of key posts that can be retained in expatriate hands and the speed of Malaysianization required is not laid down, but each case is considered by the Government on its merits. These regulations apply to expatriates of every nationality, including citizens of Singapore.

All foreigners who intend to become employed in Malaysia must obtain a work permit in accord with the Immigratioin Ordinance of 1959 and the Immigration Act of 1963.

Guidance for Business Travelers

Entrance Requirements

Passports are required for all visitors to Malaysia, but visas are not required for purposes of business, tourism, in transit, or social visits for a period of stay of less than 3 months. Those desiring clearance for stays of longer duration or those seeking employment, education, or research should consult the Embassy of Malaysia in Washington, D.C. Visitors staying for more than 1 year are required to obtain a national registration card. Each person entering Malaysia must have an International Certificate of Vaccination against smallpox that certifies vaccination against this disease not more than 3 years before the date of entry. A certificate of inoculation against cholera issued not less than 6 days or more than 6 months before entry is also required. It is also advisable to have shots for typhus and typhoid. Further, gamma globulin for hepatitis is recommended for travelers; malaria tablets are recommended for those visiting other than the urban areas. Health conditions and facilities for medical care are good. Water is safe to drink, except in some of the more remote rural areas and small towns.

Many goods entering Malaysia are not subject to import tariffs. Used portable goods in the possession of visitors are normally exempt from import duty; however, Customs may require registration of articles such as expensive cameras and watches. Such personal items may not be sold within a 3-month stay. In general, household and personal effects may be brought into Malaysia duty free.

Pertinent Treaties

Malaysia has no treaty of friendship, commerce, and navigation with the United States. Malaysia has no bilateral payments agreements. All payments for current transactions are to be made in convertible currencies. Malaysia has an Investment Guarantee Agreement with the United States under which U.S. investments in Malaysia may be insured against loss from expropriation, inconvertibility, war, resolution, and insurrection, as well as some commercial risks. The United States does not now have a double taxation agreement with Malaysia. Generally, there is no restriction on repatriation of capital, profits, or dividends provided approval of the Government has been obtained. This approval is freely granted.

Currency

The Malaysian currency is the Malaysian dollar, or ringgit. The external value of the Malaysian dollar is determined on the basis of its relationship to a weighted basket of currencies of Malaysia's major trading partners, including the United States.

There is no limitation on the amount of U.S. currency or travelers checks and letters of credit brought into the country; the restriction on the export of currency notes of other countries was lifted in 1979. A maximum of M$10,000 per person may be brought in. Visitors are allowed to depart with all of the U.S. currency they brought with them provided this amount was declared by the visitor and formally noted by the Customs authorities at the time of arrival. They may have a maximum of M$5,000 in their possession when departing the country. No limitations are imposed on the import by travelers of currency notes of other countries.

The exchange rate of the Malaysian dollar, or ringgit, in terms of the U.S. dollar, the intervention currency, is determined in the foreign exchange market, and the Central Bank of Malaysia intervenes in order to promote relative stability in the value of the ringgit in relation to the basket of currencies. Rates for all other currencies are determined on the basis of the ringgit-U.S. dollar rate and U.S. dollar rates for those currencies in markets abroad.

Climate

The temperature and humidity readings are in

the high ranges, and the average annual rainfall is about 100 inches. There are no appreciable seasonal variations in temperature, and the difference between daytime and nighttime temperature runs about 15 to 20 degrees throughout the year. The humidity rises at night, but it is considerably dissipated during the almost consistently sunny days. Rainfall is generally of short duration, a few minutes or so, followed by clearing skies. Rainfall is more frequent between April and October; in the early months of the year, drought conditions exist, sometimes reaching a degree of severity that threatens the water supply of some metropolitan areas.

Exceptions to these climatic conditions are noted both in the less populated east coast area of Peninsular Malaysia, subject to monsoonal rains during the April to October period, and in the highlands, where the resort areas are located, which have an average annual rainfall of up to 200 inches. The climate in Sabah and Sarawak is tropical and influenced by monsoons. Daytime temperature in the settled areas of Sarawak averages 85 degrees, with high humidity, and the average annual rainfall is from 120 to 160 inches. In Sabah, daytime temperature in the coastal areas ranges from 74 to 88 degrees, and at night the temperature is about 72 degrees. Rainfall ranges from 60 to 160 inches.

Facilities

Malaysian cities have good hotel facilities, giving the traveler a wide choice of comfortable accommodations. These include the new, modern, luxurious hotels and the older establishments, many of them having fine international reputations. Advance reservations are advised for the traveler seeking lodging in the modern and better known facilities. Conference rooms and secretarial services are available at most first-class hotels.

The cities are well and inexpensively served by taxi cabs. Passenger cars can be rented in the principal cities by visitors with international drivers' permits. The taxis and rental cars are usually the small-sized vehicles common to these areas; they are equipped with right-hand drive, since traffic moves on the left side of the roadway.

Language

The population of Malaysia is a racial melange. Malaysian, Chinese, Indian, Eurasian, and others make up the total population. The mix of languages and dialects rivals the racial mix. Bahasa Malaysia is the official language. English is understood and spoken in most business circles. In addition, Tamil, Hindi, Mandarin, and several southern Chinese dialects are spoken.

Business Hours

Most business establishments have office hours from 8:30 or 9:00 a.m. to 1:00 p.m., and from 2:30 to 4:30 or 5:00 p.m. on Mondays through Fridays. Most offices are open on Saturday from 9:00 a.m. to 1:00 p.m. Most government offices observe similar hours through the week and on Saturday morning.

On the other hand, in the States of Kedah, Kelantan, Trengganu, and Johor the weekend is observed on Thursday and Friday.

The U.S. Embassy in Kuala Lumpur is open Monday through Friday, 7:45 a.m. to 4:30 p.m.

Holidays

The Malaysian Ministry of Information in Kuala Lumpur announced the following national public holidays for 1981: January 1 (New Year's Day); January 18 (Prophet Muhammad's Birthday); February 5 and 6 (Chinese New Year); May 1 (Malaysia Labor Day); May 18 (Wesak Day), June 3 (Birthday of His Majesty the Yang di-Pertuan Agong); August 1 and 2—subject to change (Hari Raya Puasa); August 31 (Malaysia National Day); October 8—subject to change (Hari Raya Haji); October 26 (Deepavali); October 29 (First Day of Muharam); December 25 (Christmas Day).

Please note that when a holiday falls on a Sunday the following Monday is then a public holiday.

Sources of Economic and Commercial Information

Government Representation

The United States is represented by an Embassy in Malaysia. The address is A.I.A. Building, Jalan Ampang, P.O. Box 35. Telephone: 26321.

Foreign Service Officers in the Economic and Commercial Sections of the Embassy are available to brief and assist American business-persons visiting Malaysia.

The Malaysian Government representation in the United States is an Embassy in Washington, D.C., Trade Center offices and Malaysian Industrial Development Authority (MIDA) offices in New York and San Francisco, and the Permanent Mission of Malaysia to the United Nations. The Embassy is located at 2401 Massachusetts Avenue, N.W., Washington, D.C. 20008. The telephone is (202) 328-2700. The New York Trade Center office and the New York MIDA (investment) office are at 600 Third Avenue, 3rd Floor, New York, New York 10016. Both offices are expected to move by the end of April 1981 to 630 Third Avenue, 11th Floor, New York, New York 10016. The San Francisco Trade Center office and the San Francisco MIDA office are located on the 36th Floor, Transamerican Pyramid Building, 600 Montgomery Street, San Francisco, California 94111. The Mission is on the 30th Floor, 666 Third Avenue, New York, New York 10017.

U.S. Government Publications

The U.S. Government has a broad range of export-oriented publications. These include: Overseas Business Reports, which examine individual countries in terms of marketing factors and trade regulations; the Foreign Economic Trends series, which covers over 100 country economies and their potential for U.S. exports; foreign market reports monthly indexes, Commerce research studies, Foreign Service-prepared economic-commercial reports; and a wide variety of marketing intelligence from around the world. Global Market Surveys and Country Market Surveys, summarizing Commerce's market research findings, provide a detailed marketing picture for specific high export potential products in individual overseas markets. The flow of foreign market data is further augmented by the international commerce section of the biweekly magazine *Business America*, The Background Notes series, prepared by the Department of State, gives profiles of individual foreign countries and the addresses and phone numbers of the American Embassies and Consulates and the key officers assigned to them. In addition to being available on an individual basis, many publications can be obtained by subscription. The following are of particular interest on Malaysia:

Foreign Economic Trends and Their Implications for the United States—Malaysia, March 1981 prepared by the U.S. Foreign Service, U.S. Department of Commerce, FET 81-027. Publication Sales Branch, U.S. Department of Commerce, Room 1617, Washington, D.C. 20230.

Background Notes—Malaysia, December 1979, U.S. Department of State, Washington, D.C. 20520.

Country Labor Profile for Malaysia, published by the Bureau of International Labor Affairs, U.S. Department of Labor, available from the Superintendent of Documents, U.S. Government Printing Office, Washington, D.C. 20402.

U.S. Firms and Representatives in Malaysia '80, published by and available from Gray & Associates Sdn. Bhd., Kuala Lumpur, Malaysia (in cooperation with the Embassy of the United States, Kuala Lumpur).

Malaysian Government Publications

Information Malaysia 1976-77, incorporating Malaysia Year Book, Berita Publishing, Sdn. Bhd., Kuala Lumpur, Malaysia, 1975.

Third Malaysia Plan, 1976-1980, Government Printer, Kuala Lumpur, 1976.

Annual and Monthly Statistical Bulletins, West Malaysia, Department of Statistics, Kuala Lumpur, Malaysia.

Malaysian Industrial Development Authority Publications, P.O. Box 618, Kuala Lumpur.

Bank Negara, Malaysia Annual and Quarterly Reports, Central Bank of Malaysia, Kuala Lumpur.

Peninsular Malaysia Annual Statistics of External Trade, Department of Statistics, Kuala Lumpur, Malaysia.

Statistics of External Trade-Sarawak Department of Statistics, Kuching, Sarawak, Malaysia.

Statistics of External Trade-Sabah, Department of Statistics, Kota Kinabalu, Malaysia.

Other Publications

The New Straits Times Directory of Malaysia, 1977/78. Berita Publishing Sdn. Bhd. 31, Jalan Riong, Kuala Lumpur, Malaysia.

Trade Index of Malaysia, July 1980. Printrade Corporation (Malaysia) Sdn. Bhd. 47B & 47C, Jalan Ipoh, Kuala Lumpur 02-12, Malaysia.

International des Douanes—Malaysia, No. 12, 4th ed., International Customs Tariffs Bureau, 1980.

Market Profile—Malaysia

Economic Overview

The world recession has slashed foreign demand for Malaysian exports and has resulted in slower economic growth. Despite the lack of encouraging news relating to the international economy so important to Malaysia's growth, the country maintains its attractiveness as a trade and investment partner. On the negative side, real growth during 1982 may drop as low as 3.5 percent, and the country will experience what for it is a most uncharacteristic situation, with its trade account moving sharply into deficit. On the positive side, inflation has abated considerably, and despite substantial foreign borrowing, the debt-service ratio should not top 4.6 percent this year. The United States is a leading source of foreign investment in Malaysia, with total investment of about $2 billion, and supplies 14.5 percent of imports.

Major Developments

The weak foreign trade picture mirrored a weakening in the Government's financial position. In May 1982, Prime Minister Mahathir announced that the Government would abandon its policy of countercyclical spending and tighten its belt in response to continuing slackness in the world economy. Although this means that some development projects will be postponed or cancelled, for most companies interested in competing for large projects the main impact will be a need to concentrate on price competitiveness.

Foreign Trade

Best U.S. Sales Prospects. — Transportation equipment, telecommunication equipment, petroleum production and refinery equipment, power generation and distribution equipment, building and construction supplies and equipment, timber processing equipment, pulp and paper equipment, medical equipment, computers, pumps, valves, and compressors.
Major Suppliers (1975. — Japan (23.3 percent), United States (15 percent), EEC (17.5 percent).
Principal Exports. — Petroleum and petroleum products, electrical and electronic goods, rubber, sawn logs and timber, palm oil, and tin.
Major Markets (1979). — Japan (22 percent), United States (19 percent), EEC (18 percent), and Singapore (17 percent).

Finance

Currency. — The value of the Malaysian dollar, or ringgit, is determined on the basis of its relationship to a weighted basket of currency of Malaysia's major trading partners. Currently US$1 = M$2.3.
Domestic Credit. — Malaysia has a well-developed, sophisticated banking system that provides an important source of capital for commercial and industrial development. In 1981, the commercial prime rate ranged from 8.5 to 9.5 percent.
National Budget. — Reflecting an uncertain economic picture for 1983, the Government has proposed a "no-frills" budget for the year. Allocations are over $100 million less than estimated expenditures for 1982 and represent a substantial decline in real terms across-the-board.
Balance of Payments. — At the end of 1981, foreign reserves stood at US$4.37 billion.

Foreign Investment

The United States is a leading source of foreign investment in Malaysia, along with Japan, Singapore, the United Kingdom, the Netherlands, and Hong Kong. U.S. investment in Malaysia was estimated at $2 billion at mid-year 1982. This was concentrated in petroleum production and distribution, manufacturing (including 19 plants assembling electronic components), banking, trading companies, and insurance.

Import/Export Trade*
(millions of U.S. dollars)

	1979	1980	1981
Total Imports (c.i.f.)	7,461	10,413	12,447
Imports from the U.S.	1,115	1,572	1,804
Total Exports (f.o.b.)	10,530	12,476	12,390
Exports to the U.S.	1,819	2,048	1,790

*Malaysian data.

Principal Imports from the U.S. In 1981*
(millions of U.S. dollars)

	Value	Percent of Total
Electrical machinery	726.9	50
Aircraft and space craft	100.5	7
Elevators, winches	51.3	4
Boilers, engines	48.8	3
General machinery	47.1	3
Tobacco	45.2	3
Motor vehicles	28.5	2
Oil-bearing vegetable materials	25.1	2
Synthetic resins	23.4	2
Electrical machinery	21.8	1

*U.S. data.

Investment Prospects. — Malaysia maintains a liberal investment code, with easy profit repatriation, accelerated depreciation, and possible tariff protection. Additional incentives for new foreign investment that contribute to national development are available. OPIC insurance also is available to qualified U.S. investors.

Basic Economic Facilities

Transportation. — Peninsular Malaysia is relatively well linked by sea, air, rail, and road. Key cities in Sabah and Sarawak accessible by sea and air.
Communications. — Telephone, telegraph, and postal facilities, including overseas, well developed. Satellite earth station operational. Radio and television in common use.
Power. — Electricity capacity in Peninsular Malaysia (1979), 1,778 megawatts. Further expansion underway.

Natural Resources

Land. — Combined total about 128,000 square miles. Much of land area is primary forest containing a variety of flowering plants and immense but diminishing timber reserves. Production important to economy.
Climate. — Tropical. Average year-round maximum and minimum daily temperatures are 32°C (90°F) and 24°C (75°F). Annual rainfall ranges from 60 to 200 inches.
Minerals. — Tin, copper, petroleum, natural gas, bauxite, manganese, and iron ore.

Population

Size and Composition. — 13.3 million (1979), annual growth about 2.7 percent. Percentage Malay (50), Chinese (36), and Indian (10).
Religion. — Muslim, Hindu, Buddhist, and Christian.
Language. — Malay replaced English as sole official language September 1967. English used in government and business circles. Chinese also used.
Labor Force. — Labor force (1979) nearly 5 million, about 42 percent agriculture, about 32 percent industry and commerce, about 12 percent services, about 14 percent government; unemployment 6.1 percent.
Education. — Literacy rates about 25 percent in East Malaysia and over 60 percent in Peninsular Malaysia. Facilities include national university and technical colleges.

Market Profile—MALI

Foreign Trade

Imports.—$365 million in 1981; $330 million in 1982. Major suppliers in 1981 by percentages: France, 32.5; Ivory Coast, 23.9; People's Republic of China, 13.3; Senegal, 8.3 percent. Major imports from United States: old clothing and other textiles, textile and leather working machinery and parts, wire products (not insulated electric) special textile fabrics and related products, parts of road vehicles and tractors, and rice. Imports from United States in 1982: $7.6 million.

Exports.—$155 million in 1981; $146 million in 1982. Major markets in 1981 by percentages: Belgium, 21.7; People's Republic of China, 19.2; France, 14.2; and Ivory Coast, 8.3. Major exports to United States: artworks, collectors pieces, antiques, wood, shaped or simply worked, and wood manufacturers. Exports to United States in 1982 $1.1 million.

Trade Policy.—Associate member of European Economic Community (EEC). One of six countries forming the West African Customs Union; imports from these countries exempt from customs duties. Not a member of GATT. Member of Economic Community of West African States.

Trade Prospects.—Foodstuffs, household appliances, office equipment, and capital goods for agriculture and infrastructure development.

Foreign Investment

Traditionally small, predominantly French. Minimal American presence limited to banking interest, distribution of petroleum products, and mineral exploration. Investment Guaranty Agreement with United States since 1964. Government invites foreign private capital and management to join in venture. Investment Code of 1971 offers 5-year profits tax holiday and 10-year exemption from import duties and taxes. U.S. investment in petroleum, $2 million.

Investment Prospects.—Meat packing, other agribusiness, and transportation of meat products. Long term: mining, fertilizer production.

Finance

Currency.—Malian franc (798.8 MF=US$ in Oct. 1983), issue controlled by Central Bank, freely convertible with backing French Treasury. Money and near-money supply: $339.7 million in July 1980.

Domestic Credit and Investment.—System includes Banque Centrale du Mali (BCM), Development Bank of Mali (BDM), two commercial banks, Societe de Credit Agricole et d' Equipment Rural (SCAER), and a postal checking system.

National Budget.—Estimated at $188.2 million in 1979. Deficit of $1.7 million. Over 60 percent of total expenditures for government employment.

Foreign Aid.—Mainly from France, EEC, United States, and UNDP.

Balance of Payments.—Characterized by persistent deficits; $10 million in 1980, balance-of-trade deficit: 125 million.

Economy

Adverse climate severly hinders economy. Subsistence agri-culture; hopes pinned on livestock, increased basic manufacturing and mineral potentials.

GNP.—$1.2 billion in 1980 (estimated); (at current prices) $163 per capita; agriculture and livestock account for 50 percent of GNP.

Agriculture.—Traditional small-scale farms product sorghum, millet, rice, and corn for food; peanuts and cotton for export. Cotton is major export earner.

Industry.—11 percent of GDP in 1979. Main activity is in food processing, textiles, leather, cement, and electric power; some oil exploration by U.S. affiliates. Existing plants being expanded.

Commerce.—Six state enterprises predominate representing 30 percent of total business and 60 percent of business by modern firms. One company, COMIEX, has a monopoly over all internal and external trade.

Development Plan.—5-year plan (1981-85) shifts emphasis from state-owned companies to mixed enterprises.

Basic Economic Facilities

Transportation.—State-operated. 9,755 miles of roads; 10.6 percent paved. 400 miles of railroad being increased with IBRD loans. 37 usable airfields. 1,128 miles of inland waterways, 25,000 vehicles.

Communications.—State-owned and operated; domestic system poor and provides only minimal service. Open-wire and radio communication used for long distance telecommunications. Two AM radio stations; one Atlantic and one Indian Ocean satellite station. 11,000 telephones.

Power.—State-controlled. Hydroelectric potential on Niger River. 46 MW capacity in 1980 (mostly thermal). 45 MW capacity dam completed in 1982.

Natural Resources

Landlocked, 465,000 square miles, almost twice as big as Texas, half is desert or semidesert. Average elevation less than 1,000 feet above sea level.

Climate.—Hot; average annual rainfall ranges from arid in the northwest to 40 inches in the extreme southwest, mainly July through October.

Minerals.—Salt and gold extracted on limited basis. Traces of bauxite, petroleum, uranium, iron ore, copper, manganese, and phosphates have been found. Mining and petroleum codes revised in 1969 to encourage more systematic prospecting.

Fisheries.—Important to people living along Niger River; surplus smoked, salted, or dried and exported.

Population

Size.—1980, 6.9 million; growth rate 2.7 percent; 11 percent urban. Principal cities: Bamako, the capital, 200,000 people; and Sayes, Mopti, and Segou, about 30,000 each.

Education.—15 percent schoolage children in school; 235,000 students. Literacy under 5 percent.

Languages. French (official) and Bambara.

Labor.—90 percent of population engaged in agriculture and livestock raising. 150,000 wage earners.

MALI

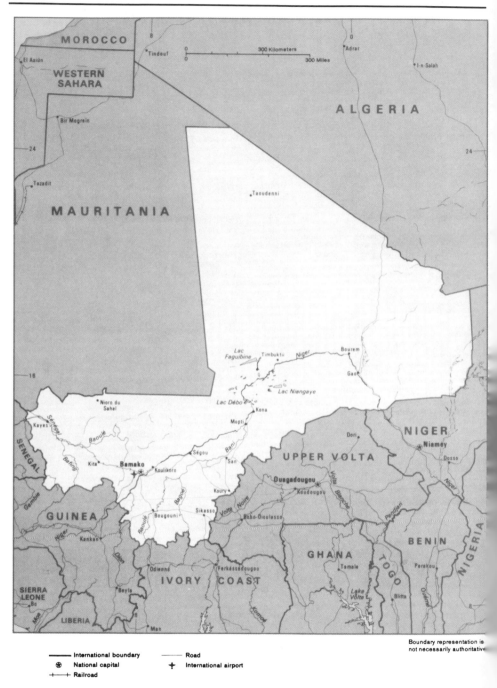

Market Profile— MAURITANIA

Foreign Trade

Imports.—$408 million in 1981: $445 million in 1982. Major suppliers. 1981: France. Spain. Netherlands. Senegal. United States. Principal imports: foodstuffs, other consumer goods, petroleum products, vehicles, electrical equipment, and building materials. From United States, 1982 ($26.9 million): mechanical shovels, NSPF, 39.8 percent; railway locomotives, 27.7 percent; automobile trucks, 3.6 percent; wheat, 2.8 percent; dried milk and cream, 2.5 percent.

Exports.—$331 million in 1981; $256.5 million in 1982. Major markets 1981: Spain. France, Japan, and United States, 12th. To United States, 1982 ($467,000): wearing apparel (women's, girls, infants) other textile materials, 24.2 percent; shellfish (excl. clams), 15.8 percent; postage stamps, 4.3 percent; models and construction kits, 1.1 percent.

Trade Policy.—Associate member of the European Economic Community as Signatory of Lome Convention. Member of ECOWAS. Import licenses required for all products. All import licenses, import certificates, and advance payments for imports require exchange control approval by the Central Bank.

Trade Prospects.—Products having best potential are: fishing and fish processing equipment, agricultural equipment, and mining equipment. Principal African export market (1982): Congo (Brazzaville). Principal African Supplier (1982): Senegal.

Foreign Investment

The 1979 investment code provides for tax exonerations for periods up to 12 years on exports, raw material imports, and reinvested profits. The sector offering best investment opportunities is the fishing and fish processing industry.

Finance

Currency.—Ouguiya (53.95 Oujuiyas=US$1 in Oct. 1983). Currency issued by Mauritanian Central Bank. Money supply: $135.2 million the first quarter 1982.

Domestic Credit and Investment.—Central Bank, five commercial banks, and one foreign bank (French). Four of the commercial banks controlled by the Government.

National Budget.—In 1980, $204 million expenditures; $140.4 million revenues.

Foreign Aid.—Chief donors are Arab countries, France, and IDA. U.S. economic assistance 1982, $9.7 million: development assistance, $6.3 million (64.8 percent); PL 480, $3.4 million (35 percent); IMET, $25,000 (0.3 percent).

Economy

Industry.—Several poorly designed capital intensive projects including: sugar processing, petreleum refinery, steel mill.

GDP.—Projected $720.7 million in 1982: $453 per capita. 2.4 percent growth.

Agriculture.—Livestock raising important (23 percent GDP). Mauritania is a member of Organization pour la Mise en Valeur de Fleuve Senegal (OMVS), along with Senegal River Basin, permitting irrigation of 494,000 acres in Mauritania. Under 1 percent of land under cultivation. Development of Gorgol Noir River in south central section will increase arable land by another 17,971 acres.

Commerce.—State trading company SONIMEX controls imports of essential foodstuffs. Private companies also active in this sector.

Basic Economic Facilities

Transportation.—4,685 miles of road (839 paved.) 404 miles private railroad. Two major seaports and airports at Nouakchott and Nouadhibou. 500,000-ton capacity port to be finished at Nouakchott in 1984.

Communications.—Poor system of cable and open-wire lines; minor radio relay links and radio communication stations. 5,200 telephones (0.2 per 100 people). Two AM radio stations.

Power.—88,000 kW capacity (1982); 150 million kWh produced (1982). 95 kWh per capita.

Natural Resources

Land.—419,229 square miles. Flat desert and savannah except for low central ridge.

Climate.—Hot. Very little rainfall, particularly in the north.

Minerals.—High-grade iron ore and gypsum exported. Research licenses have been issued for nickel, chrome, cobalt, gold, phosphate, manganese, uranium, and petroleum. High-grade copper reserve.

Fisheries.—Resources among the richest of the world. Local estimated catch, 12,000 metric tons (1980). Commercial fishing exports, 135,000 metric tons in 1981.

Population

Size.—1.6 million (July 1983); 2-percent growth rate; 21 percent urban. 30 percent Moors. 30 percent black. 40 percent mixed.

Language.—French is commercial language. Arabic widely used.

Education—Literacy rate 17 percent. Primary enrollment is 24 percent; secondary school, 4 percent.

Labor.—45,000 wage earners estimated in 1980.

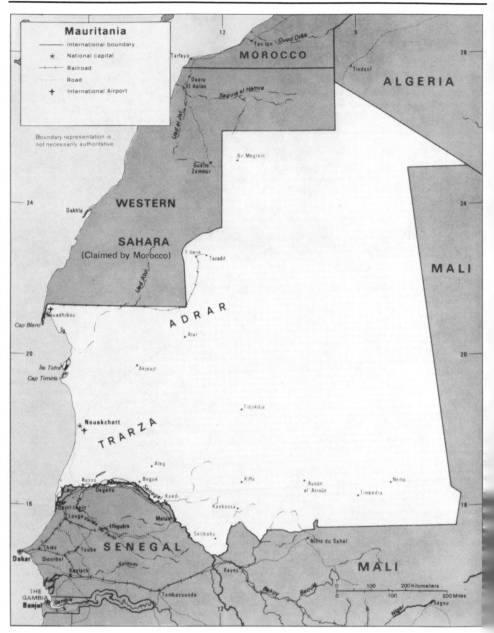

1538

Market Profile— MAURITIUS

Foreign Trade

Imports.—$554.28 million in 1981; $463 million in 1982. Major suppliers, 1981: Bahrain, 12.7 percent; West Germany, 10.7 percent; United Kingdom, 10 percent; South Africa, 9.7 percent. Major products: electrical machinery and apparatus, fixed vegetable oils (soft—crude or refined), rice, animal oils and fats, inorganic chemicals. Imports from United States in 1981 $18.2 million, in 1982 $15 million.

Exports.—$323 million in 1981; $365 million in 1982. Major markets in 1981: United Kingdom, 40.9 percent; France, 23.5 percent; Germany 7 percent; and United States, 7 percent. Major Products: sugar, syrups, molasses and honey, fish, fresh (chilled or frozen), ferrites and electrical machinery and equipment, eyeglasses, eyeglass frames and parts, electric components and parts.

Trade Policy.—No restrictive licensing or exchange controls on most U.S. goods. Associate member of EEC. Signatory to 1979 Lome Convention.

Trade Prospects.—Best for import from United States of manufactured goods, light industrial machinery, automotive vehicles and parts, chemicals.

Foreign Investment

Foreign investment, which accounts for most investment in Mauritius, is largely by French (sugar plantation) and British interests. Modest U.S. participation in joint venture fertilizer plant underway. U.S.-Mauritian Investment Guaranty Agreement in effect.

Investment Prospects.—Government actively encouraging foreign investment. Opportunities offered for establishment of tourism facilities, paper and paper products plant, and fish cannery; others exist for processing of rice, peanuts, copra, and for flour milling. Export processing zones provide facilities at concessionary rates, exemption of import duties on capital goods and raw materials, and 10-20 year tax holiday for export industries.

Finance

Currency.—Mauritian rupee (11.32=US$1 in Oct. 1982). Mauritius is a member of the Sterling Area. No restrictions on transfers of profits and dividends. Capital transfers subject to 35.7 stamp tax. Money and quasi-money supply was $257.5 million in May 1982.

Domestic Credit and Investment.—Expanding bank services offered by five commercial banks. Development Bank of Mauritian finances medium- and long-term loans; can provide equity investment for agricultural and industrial projects.

National Budget.—1982 estimated receipts about $249 million, total expenditures about $400 million.

Balance of Payments.—Financial position varies directly with returns from sugar crop. Gross reserves of Central Bank estimated at about $41 million in 1982.

Basic Economic Facilities

Transportation.— Excellent road system totaling 1,786 km,

of which 91 percent is paved. No railroad. Main harbor at Port Louis. Major international air carriers provide frequent direct connections between Plaisacs Airport and Paris, London, Rome, Frankfurt, Nairobi, and other major cities.

Communications.—Domestic telephone service (36,400 telephones, 4 per 100 people) and telegraph service with Reunion, Madagascar, Seychelles, Zanzibar, and west of Africa. One AM radio station, and four TV stations, one Indian Ocean Satellite Station.

Electric Power.—Plant capacity 180,000 kW, 370 million kWh produced in 1980.

Economy

Essentially agricultural, centered on large sugar plantations. GDP was $102 million in 1980, about $130 million in 1982.

Agriculture.—Forty percent of land for sugar cultivation. Other commercial products: sugar, sugar products, tea. Main subsistence crops: potatoes, peanuts, corn, manioc. Rice, the staple food, is imported.

Industry.—Small but expanding base. 23 sugar processing plants. Also processing facilities for tea, tobacco, fibers, matches, alcoholic beverages, shoes, bricks. Plants include dehydrating plant for fruits and vegetables, wig factory, diamond cutting plant, woven/knitted goods factory. Fertilizer plant under construction. Electronic components manufactured and assembled. IBRD financing industrial estate.

Commerce.—Most retail trade dominated by Sino-Mauritian sector of population. Consumer Price Index (1975=100) in 1982 was 248.6

Development Plan.—Ten-Year Plan (1971-81) called for capital expenditures of $99 million. Port Louis—Curepipe road; sewage systems, low-cost housing, a hydroelectric plant and thermal station; deep water quay. IBRD loan of $7.2 million for tea development.

Natural Resources

Land.—Pear-shaped island of 720 square miles in Indian Ocean, 38 miles long and 29 miles wide. Situated some 500 miles east of Madagascar; low-lying coast rises to plateau in center; characterized by many rivers. Dependencies include Rodrigues Island and small islands up to 580 miles north.

Climate.—Tropical. Cyclones can occur December-April.

Minerals—No known mineral deposits; only quarrying.

Fisheries.—Good prospects for development. Excellent deep sea sport fishing

Population

Size.—930,000 (July 1982). Over 40 percent under age 15; density 1,171 persons per square mile; average increase 1.1 percent in 1982.

Language.—English is official; French and a Creole patois are widely spoken.

Education.—Literacy, 61 percent over 21; 90 percent of school age.

Labor.—Labor force 335,000, 30 percent agriculture, 6 percent industry, 24 percent government services, 14 percent unemployed, underemployed or self-employed.

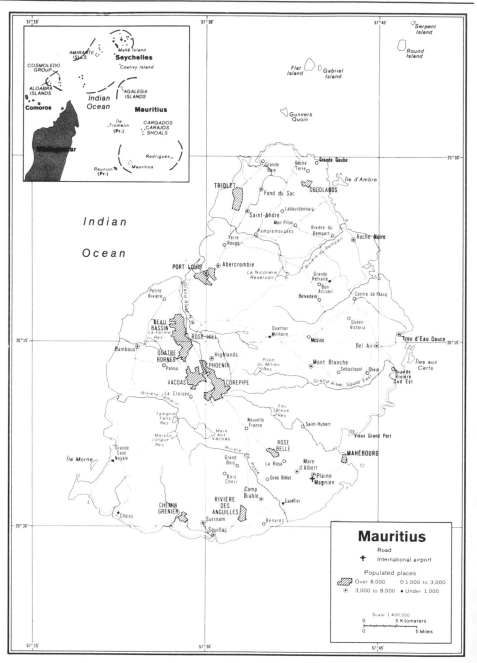

Marketing in Mexico

Contents

Report Revised May 1981

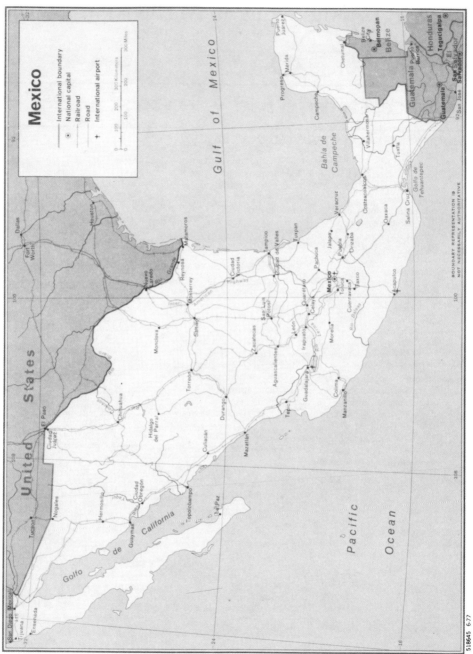

Mexico

- —— International boundary
- ⊙ National capital
- —+— Railroad
- — Road
- + International airport

0 100 200 300 Kilometers

0 100 200 300 Miles

51864S 6-77

Foreign Trade Outlook

Mexico, with a fast-growing population—now about 68 million, a politically and economically stable government, a broad agricultural base, increasingly important oil production, and a rapidly expanding industrial plant, offers an important and growing market for U.S. exports. Between 1977 and 1980, U.S. exports to Mexico have almost tripled, growing to the $15 billion level in 1980.

Table 1.—Mexican Imports and Exports by Country and Region 1979-80

(in thousands of dollars)

	1979	Percent	1980	Percent
IMPORTS				
North America	7.724.993	64.5	12.507.317	67.3
United States	7.540.179	62.9	12.154.577	65.4
Canada	184.814	1.5	352.740	1.8
South America	539.931	4.5	674.505	3.6
Argentina	117.378	1.0	109.614	0.5
Brazil	273.422	2.3	419.030	2.2
Chile	37.191	0.3	38.144	0.2
Venezuela	40.085	0.3	28.197	0.1
Others	71.855	0.6	79.520	0.4
Central America and Caribbean	119.290	1.0	244.290	1.3
Netherlands Antilles	35.392	0.3	12.190	—
Guatemala	9.969	—	25.876	0.1
Nicaragua	975	—	186	—
Cuba	3.868	—	120.100	0.6
Panama	22.142	0.2	21.399	0.1
Others	46.944	0.4	25.378	0.1
Europe	2.604.618	21.7	3.467.285	18.6
Fed. Rep. Germany	778.951	6.5	971.954	5.2
Spain	210.318	1.7	423.804	2.3
France	500.239	4.2	516.325	2.7
United Kingdom	251.187	2.2	405.042	2.1
Italy	221.112	2.1	305.169	1.6
Switzerland	153.392	1.3	186.516	1.0
Sweden	115.138	0.9	152.676	0.8
Netherlands	82.227	0.7	98.435	0.5
Others	292.054	2.4	407.364	2.1
Other Countries	953.284	7.9	1.333.979	7.2
Japan	726.573	6.0	988.811	5.3
Peoples Rep. of China	41.300	0.4	66.074	2.4
Australia	30.309	0.3	32.688	0.3
Singapore	36.103	0.3	35.186	0.2
Morocco	21.274	0.2	1.269	—
Others	141.126	1.2	554.780	2.9
TOTAL	11.985	100.0	18.572	100.0
EXPORTS				
North America	6.254.910	71.1	9.629.378	62.9
United States	6.180.328	70.3	9.466.875	61.8
Canada	74.582	0.8	162.504	1.1
South America	415.849	4.7	608.105	4.0
Argentina	38.443	0.4	44.301	0.3
Brazil	149.789	1.7	348.808	2.3
Chile	37.732	0.4	27.152	0.2
Venezuela	95.199	1.1	61.772	0.4
Others	94.686	1.1	126.072	0.8
Central America and Caribbean	276.648	3.1	997.756	6.5
Netherlands Antilles	16.137	0.2	459.305	3.0
Guatemala	52.843	0.6	59.201	0.4
Nicaragua	3.939	—	43.286	0.3
Cuba	7.422	0.1	26.757	0.2
Panama	20.058	0.2	21.948	0.1
Others	176.249	2.0	387.259	2.5
Europe	1.097.697	12.5	2.217.718	14.5
Fed. Rep. Germany	213.078	2.4	255.954	1.7
Spain	457.512	5.2	1.061.911	6.9
France	71.686	0.8	271.851	1.8
United Kingdom	45.101	0.5	72.354	0.5
Italy	56.415	0.6	210.405	1.4
Switzerland	27.281	0.3	23.106	0.2
Sweden	16.862	0.2	19.211	0.1
Netherlands	46.206	0.5	100.943	0.7
Others	163.556	1.9	201.983	1.3
Other Countries	750.229	8.5	1.277.589	8.3
Japan	248.150	2.8	563.166	3.7
Peoples Rep. of China	114.344	1.3	93.415	0.6
Australia	5.695	—	8.268	—
Singapore	1.459	—	1.446	—
Morocco	38	—	249	—
Others	383.453	4.1	1.187.979	7.8
TOTAL	8.798.245	100.0	15.307.480	100.0

Figures are preliminary and do not include insurance and freight.
Source: *Indicadores Economicos*, January, 1981, Bank of Mexico, Mexico City.

During that same time, U.S. imports from Mexico grew more than 2½ times, to $12.5 billion. As a result, Mexico is now the third largest U.S. trading partner for both imports and exports, rising from fifth 2 years ago. The United States is Mexico's leading supplier and principal customer. In 1980, 65.4 percent of all Mexico's purchases abroad came from the United States and 61.8 percent of all Mexican exports went to this country, and indications are that similar market shares continued through 1980.

U.S. exporters have a number of advantages in competing in the Mexican market. Mexico's geographical proximity permits fast delivery, lower transportation costs, and easily accessible servicing and technical assistance. U.S. products have a reputation for quality; many are long established in the market and are well liked. Much of Mexico's production that goes to the United States market must meet U.S. standards and therefore incorporates components or uses processes for which this country is the source. Other foreign suppliers are now actively competing for a larger share of Mexico's international purchases through the traditional marketing strategies of lower prices and favorable credit terms and delivery dates. In a few cases they are benefiting also from bilateral commercial agreements providing for favorable treatment in specific instances.

Mexico's expanding industry is increasing the types of goods produced, both in consumer durables and in intermediate equipment and materials such as chemicals and petrochemicals. The country will require increasing quantities of capital equipment and raw materials and components to maintain its growing industrial base and to keep pace with the Government's wide-ranging development projects.

Table 2.—United States Exports of Principal Commodities to Mexico in 1979 and 1980
(in thousands of dollars)

	1980	1979
Food and live animals	1,908,555	755,847
Dairy products and eggs	78,447	27,680
Cereals and preparations, flour, etc.	1,207,980	492,612
Vegetables and fruits	256,034	35,468
Sugar, sugar preps, honey	145,504	66,262
Animal feeds, excl. cereals	100,032	56,442
Beverages and tobacco	2,630	3,992
Crude materials—inedible except fuels	1,078,685	652,491
Hides and skins—undressed	69,860	102,124
Oilseeds—oleaginous fruit	506,091	124,696
Wood, lumber, and cork	57,990	33,632
Pulp and waste paper	185,570	107,357
Raw textile fibers and waste	30,804	26,224
Fertilizers, crude, and minerals, excl. coal	64,017	54,750
Metalliferous ores and metal scrap, NSPF	218,010	154,849
Mineral fuels, lubricants, etc.	340,863	220,107

Coal and lignite	33,697	29,690
Compositions used for fuel and coal coke	15,693	15,704
Petroleum products—refined	109,141	73,651
Residual petrol prods and related	40,826	30,114
Gas—natural and mfrd.	141,499	70,945
Animal vegetable oils, fats and waxes	90,273	39,062
Animal oils and fats	50,495	37,184
Chemicals and related products	1,441,454	1,053,019
Specified hydrocarbons and derivates	199,071	158,401
Organic chemicals and products NSPF	392,548	326,945
Inorganic chemicals and products NSPF	198,296	135,155
Medicinals and pharmaceutical products	58,887	35,549
Fertilizers and materials	78,815	33,773
Synthetic resins, rubber, and plastic materials	315,867	212,842
Manufactured goods by chief material	2,063,395	1,209,484
Tires and inner tubes	93,117	42,069
Paper and paperboard	181,782	98,465
Paper, pulp, and paperboard articles	79,697	62,763
Textile yarn and thread	19,017	14,749
Manmade fabrics, woven	23,987	14,868
Special textile fabrics and related products	66,649	44,370
Cement, clay, and refractory construction materials	43,972	32,565
Glass	38,462	26,184
Iron and steel primary forms	112,613	18,981
Iron and steel bars, rods, angles, etc.	110,538	48,879
Iron and steel plates and sheets	243,140	84,665
Iron and steel tubes, pipes and fittings	173,468	178,164
Copper and alloys	39,943	29,977
Aluminum wrought and unwrought alloys	147,558	92,530
Structures and parts, iron, steel, aluminum, and zinc	145,283	59,508
Tools for use in hand or machines	53,948	40,542
Machinery and transportation equipment	6,563,454	4,659,430
Internal combustion piston engines and parts	314,444	242,622
Internal combustion engines, NSPF and parts	198,285	164,603
Rotating electrical plant and parts	104,706	64,463
Power generating machinery and parts	50,710	31,196
Agricultural and dairy equipment	166,971	88,779
Tractors, agricultural and construction	209,897	187,411
Civil engineer and contractor equipment	352,886	308,935
Textile and leather machinery	83,200	66,221
Specialized industrial machinery	241,916	163,245
Metalworking machinery, tools, parts and acc.	168,735	88,475
Metalworking machinery, NSPF and parts	39,568	29,245
Pumps, compressors and parts	258,291	189,169
Mechanical handling equipment	213,821	125,676
ADP	107,810	71,420
Parts for office machines and ADP equipment	153,112	94,703
Office machines	25,758	23,283
Telecommunications sound repro. eq.	374,360	247,484
Electrical equipment, NSPF	926,313	192,551
Passenger motor vehicles, excl. pub. soc.	31,329	22,080
Trucks and special purpose motor vehicles	114,462	84,067
Parts for road vehicles and tractors	1,128,296	25,265
Motor buses and truck tractors	27,923	771,544
Motorcycles, adult bikes, wheel chairs	7,445	3,295
Railway vehicles and accessories	150,880	106,510
Aircraft and accessories	402,646	220,804
Ships, boats, floating structures	88,277	5,257
Miscellaneous manufactured articles	856,575	632,895
Heating, plumbing, and light fixtures	19,902	12,464
Furniture and parts	42,083	19,386
Apparel articles and accessories	172,572	127,832
Professional, scientific, and control instruments	226,891	188,551
Photo equipment	108,221	72,880
Miscellaneous manufactures	267,134	204,463
TOTAL	14,884,767	9,666,803

Source: U.S. Exports Annual 1979 FT 455; Exports of Domestic Merchandise EM 450/455, November 1980. U.S. Department of Commerce, Bureau of Census, Washington, D.C.

Despite the attractiveness and size of the Mexican market, it is a good market for only selected goods. Policies protecting domestic producers limit imports of consumer goods to such items as bulk shipments of grain, dry milk, and pharmaceuticals. The Mexican market is primarily a producers goods market, with about 80 percent of total imports composed of heavy industrial equipment, automotive parts for assembly, construction machinery, tractors and heavy agricultural equipment, locomotive and railway equipment, scientific apparatus, iron and steel items and scrap, chemicals, and a wide variety of raw and semiprocessed material for further industrial processing.

Industry Trends

Gross Domestic Product Development

Mexico has enjoyed uninterrupted economic growth for almost 30 years.

In current prices, GDP reached $166 billion in 1980, with a per capita GDP of $1,827. This was an apparent real per capita increase of 4.5 percent.

The economic growth rate in 1980 of 7.4 percent marked the third consecutive year of growth over 7 percent and it is hoped that this will be the new "normal" growth rate instead of the post World War II average of 6 percent.

New public sector investment for the year was reported at $22 billion, equivalent to 12.1 percent of GDP and a record high. New private fixed investment of $25 billion was also a record, up 14.9 percent over 1979. Together, these were the most significant elements in the stimulation of growth of aggregate demand. The pressures of demand confronting a relatively inelastic domestic productive capacity, caused a significant increase in both production and imports as well as an increase in the rate of inflation which reached 26.3 percent, on an average annual basis as measured by the National Consumer Price Index and 29.8 percent on a December to December basis. Principal factors cited by Mexico's Central Bank for the strong rate of real growth in 1980 included very good showings by the petroleum, petrochemical and construction industries which increased activity 17.5, 12.0 and 12.8 percent, respectively, in real terms. Agriculture recorded a better than expected 7 percent rise.

Mexico's foreign exchange reserves rose $1.15 billion in 1980, due to a marked increase in net inflow to the capital account to a total of $8.5 billion. This was enough to offset an increase in the current account deficit which totalled $6.5 billion, up from $4.8 billion in 1979. The trade deficit was $3.2 billion in 1980, accounting for less than half, rather than the usual 70 percent of the current account deficit.

Payments for financial services, up $1.5 billion in 1980 over the year before to $4.8 billion, and a small drop in border transactions and tourism revenue were the other principal contributors to the negative current account.

Net income from gold and silver exports rose to $843 million in 1980, up 73 percent over the year before due to favorable prices on the volatile international market for these commodities. Value added by the "in-bond" industries was $773 million, a significant 21 percent increase in view of the recession in the United States where the products are marketed.

Private sector financial services payments jumped to $1.4 billion, a 91.5 percent increase, attributed to higher international interest rates. The comparable public sector payment was up 37 percent to $3.9 billion. Together, financial

Table 3.—Mexican Imports and Exports by Commodity 1979-1980

(in thousands of dollars)

Imports	1979	1980
Chemical products	1,104.3	1,485.0
Automotive assembly material	786.1	949.1
Corn	101.6	588.9
Steel laminates	236.5	564.5
Sugar	—	562.0
Basic petrochemicals	339.6	535.1
Paper, newsprint, cellulose	264.6	481.9
Steel tubing	439.4	474.3
Metalworking machinery, equip.	214.2	408.9
Automotive spare parts	237.4	394.3
Automotive vehicles	360.7	392.4
Farm tractors, combines, implements	310.6	367.1
Textile industry machinery, parts	254.4	337.2
Soil conditioning machinery, parts	275.8	327.1
R.R. locomotives, equipment, parts	168.2	313.2
Grain sorghum	160.1	308.2
Petroleum derivates	251.3	291.8
Electrical installations equip. parts, pieces	178.0	258.4
TOTAL	11,985.6	18,572.2

Exports	1979	1980
Crude oil	3,764.6	9,429.6
Natural gas	—	448.9
Petroleum derivates (¹)	96.4	427.3
Automotive vehicles, parts, components	383.1	415.4
Coffee	574.9	415.2
Chemical products (¹)	335.8	389.8
Frozen shrimp	358.9	382.4
Cotton	309.7	320.9
Metallic minerals	131.6	252.2
Non-metallic minerals	185.5	250.7
Electrical, electronic equipment, accessories	104.5	244.2
Industrial machinery and equip.	184.5	242.1
Tomatoes	206.9	185.4
Fresh vegetables	153.9	172.4
Textiles and wearing apparel	173.6	161.1
Basic petrochemicals	113.2	116.7
Fresh fruits	86.7	108.6
Canned or processed fruits, juices, vegetables, etc.	84.2	87.5
TOTAL	8,798.2	15,307.5

¹Excludes exports of basic petrochemical products.

Source: Bank of Mexico, Mexico City.

services accounted for 73.3 percent of the net current account deficit in 1980, a 5 percent rise over 1979.

Mexico's public sector borrowed $7.7 billion of long term capital abroad in 1980, a significant drop from the 1979 figure of $10.4 billion; amortizations were down from $7.2 billion to $3.7 billion for the same years. Private sector borrowing doubled to $2.1 billion and foreign direct investment inflows during 1980 brought in $963 million, up 40 percent over the 1979 figures of $665 million.

The Bank of Mexico's gross primary international reserves reached a record $4 billion, an increase of $915 million over the prior year, Secondary international reserves increased to $3.2 billion which was $576 million over the 1979 level and also a record.

Role of Government

Mexico is a market economy with a very large involvement in business and industry by government corporations which manufacture, service, and sell many items that are the preserve of the private sector in the United States. Government corporations may be wholly owned or in conjunction with private capital, both Mexican and foreign. There are approximately 550 government entities, known locally as "parastatals," ranging from the multibillion dollar Petroleos Mexicanos oil monopoly to agricultural growers cooperatives with nominal assets.

Under the law, activity in the fields of petroleum, basic petrochemicals, nuclear energy and radioactive substances, designated mining activities, electricity, railroads, telegraph and wireless communicaiton is reserved to the Government.

No bilateral foreign assistance is currently being received by Mexico. Active and diversified programs are in effect by the Interamerican Development Bank and the World Bank. Although emphasis is on infrastructure modernization and expansion, there are programs to finance industrial exports and provide funds to expand manufacturing enterprise.

Research and Development

The Mexican private sector makes a modest contribution to scientific and technical research in Mexico. It is estimated to be about 4 percent of the total, to which should be added another 6 percent contributed by subsidiaries of international enterprises.

The remaining 90 percent is undertaken by Mexico Government organizations, with the National Council of Science and Technology (CONACYT) taking the lead role in financial support of research. CONACYT prepared the National Program for Science and Technology 1978-82 which seeks to strengthen the Mexican position in scientific matters through setting research priorities and specific goals during that period. In order to stimulate research and development activity, a program of tax incentives which provides up to 15 percent tax credit to research institutions was promulgated in late 1980.

Table 4.—Balance of Payments
(figures in millions of dollars[1])

	1979	1980
I. Current Account	-4,856.4	-6,596.6
Income	16,131.5	24,819.5
Merchandise exports	8,798.2	15,307.5
In-bond processing services	637.6	773.4
Nonmonetary gold and silver	488.0	843.6
Transportation	335.0	449.9
Tourism	1,443.3	1,670.1
Transactions	2,919.2	3,660.6
Investment income	589.2	939.8
Other services	664.5	864.6
Transfers	256.4	310.0
Expenditures	20,987.9	31,416.1
Merchandise imports, f.o.b.	11,985.6	18,572.2
Freight and insurance	610.0	944.8
Nonmonetary gold	151.8	61.8
Transportation	529.5	768.9
Tourism	713.6	1,010.8
Border transactions	2,241.2	3,056.4
Investment related expenditures:	3,902.5	5,778.1
Profits remitted by enterprises with foreign ownership	284.0	422.3
Interest on Public sector loans	2,888.4	3,957.6
Other Services	730.2	1,398.2
Transfers	821.3	1,181.3
II. Capital Account (net)	32.5	41.8
Long-Term Capital (net)	4,332.3	8,541.3
Public Sector (net)	4,186.9	6,182.4
Loans and bond placements	3,146.7	4,058.5
Amortization of loans and bonds	10,415.0	7,771.1
Loans made abroad (net)	-7,285.9	-3,723.4
Private Sector (net)	17.6	10.8
Direct foreign investment	1,040.2	2,123.8
Purchase of foreign firms	665.0	963.0
Foreign debt (net)	-39.6	-9.5
Firms with foreign equity (net)	473.8	1,287.4
Other firms (net)	186.5	1,096.3
Transactions with stocks (net)	287.2	191.0
Short-Term Capital (net)	-59.0	-117.0
Liabilities	145.4	2,358.9
Public sector (net)	1,906.1	4,421.7
Private sector (net)	205.5	67.8
Assets (net)	1,700.7	4,354.0
III. Special Drawing Rights	-1,760.7	-2,062.8
IV. Errors and Omissions	70.0	73.5
V. Change in Bank of Mexico reserves	873.0	-867.3
(sum of I, II, III, IV)[2]	418.9	1,150.9

Source: *Indicadores Economicos*, Bank of Mexico, January 1981.
[1]Preliminary figures.
[2]Reserves figured according to International Monetary Fund criteria plus silver. Gold holdings are valued at $42.22 per ounce.

Standards

The Mexican Bureau of Standards (Direccion General de Normas, DGN) publishes standards for the country. These are available to firms in the United States through the American National Standards Institute, 1430 Broadway, New York, N.Y. 10018.

Mexico uses the metric system and equipment going to that country should have metric markings. There is widespread use of U.S. equipment and consequently, in a number of instances, the Mexican practice is identical with that in this country.

Distribution and Sales Channels

The Mexican market for imported products can be divided three ways: the free zones and perimeters, the in-bond industries, and the Mexican market as such.

The Free Perimeter Market

The border regions of Mexico have historically looked abroad for a large part of their requirements. Recognition of this trading pattern has resulted in a special set of rules which apply only to these regions and allow the importation of a number of items which cannot be sold in the rest of the country.

Strips 20 kilometers wide along the borders of the United States and Guatemala are known as free perimeters. Free zones cover the peninsula of Baja California and the State of Quintana Roo on the Yucatan peninsula.

As the central economy of Mexico is considered to be able to supply the demand for a particular product, the previous exemption is lifted and special treatment ceases for that product. The aim is to eventually completely integrate the economy of these areas with that of the rest of the republic. Until that happens, however, a number of special opportunities exist. Under the program of "articulos gancho" for promotional items, Mexican retailers in border towns are allowed to sell consumer goods such as apparel and personal items rather than have their sales go to merchants across the border. Generally, U.S. wholesalers in the border city immediately next to the Mexican city service these accounts. The border cities are the only areas of Mexico where U.S. made automobiles may be sold and then only to local residents in very small quantities of specified models, four years old, and identical to those made in Mexico.

The In-Bond Industries

Since 1965, Mexico has had legislation (article 321 of the Customs Code) permitting the assembly in-bond of foreign-made components that are then reexported and sold abroad. The companies are known as "maquiladoras" from the Spanish term for the portion of flour, retained by the miller in payment for grinding the wheat. These regulations make it possible for U.S. manufacturers to set up operations under Tariff Schedules of the United States 806.30 and 807.00.

While initially called "border industries," since 1972 there has been no geographical restriction on the site within the country, and Mexican planners have encouraged location in the interior of Mexico where labor is plentiful and wages are more favorable than along the northern border. Nevertheless, in-bond plants are still 90 percent concentrated in border cities.

The major restriction on in-bond industry manufactures is that they may not be sold in Mexico unless physically reexported from the country and entered with payment of import duty and compliance with all other formalities. In-bond plants normally purchase from their domestic suppliers in the United States.

The Mexican Market

The rest of the Mexican market presents more problems and more opportunities to the potential exporter. The Government has a conscious policy of encouraging the growth of local industry and protecting nascent industries. To effect this policy, many items are not permitted to be imported, and duty rates, in general, are high. Import liberalization is now proceeding, however, and fewer items are restricted with some further liberalization expected.

The largest segment of the Mexican market centers around Mexico City—the country's political, economic, and cultural capital. The population of the metropolitan area is about 18 million which represents more than 20 percent of the total urban population. It has 35 percent of the industry, 40 percent of the purchasing power, and 35 percent of the motor vehicle registration.

Mexico City is the financial center and the hub of the railway, airline, highway, and communications systems of the country. It is connected by expressway with Toluca, Queretaro, Puebla, Acapulco and Pachuca. Mexico City is also a major tourist center of Mexico, with its parks, boulevards, fine hotels and restaurants, and nearby archeological sites and museums.

There are several other important business and commercial centers. The most important are described below.

Guadalajara, with a population of about 2.5 million, is the second largest city in Mexico. It is the most important financial and commercial center in the central-western part of Mexico. Guadalajara accounts for 6 to 7 percent of Mexico's purchasing power and about the same percentage range of the country's motor vehicle registration and TV and radio ownership. There are an estimated 19,500 retired Americans living in the Guadalajara area.

Monterrey, with a population of 2.1 million, is Mexico's third largest city. However, it is the second most important industrial center. In Monterrey are located Mexico's second and third largest steel producers, a large glass manufacturing complex, one-fifth of Mexico's textile and clothing industry, a major brewery, a large and growing chemical industry, and a well-developed paper and cardboard industry. Also produced are cement, refractory bricks, tile and construction bricks, processed foods, and a wide range of manufactures, ranging from television sets to bus and truck bodies.

Monterrey dominates northern Mexico in commerce and banking. Regional trading centers outside of Monterrey are Saltillo, Torreon, Durango, and San Luis Potosi. Monterrey has made a strong effort to expand tourism and has been quite successful in attracting fall and winter conventions.

Communications by rail, highway, and air between Monterrey, the United States, and Mexico City are good. The city has the advantage in both commerce and tourism of lying astride the principal north-south routes from the United States to Mexico City. The variety and level of sophistication of Monterrey's industry, together with its proximity to the United States, offers U.S. exporters an attractive market for modern machinery and equipment, industrial raw materials, and technology.

Importers, Agents, and Distributors

The main import channels are importing distributors, sales agents, direct importers, branch houses or subsidiaries of foreign suppliers, and the Government.

Importing distributors are playing a decreasing role for many products because of the high proportion of stock in capital goods to total imports and the tendency to import direct whenever possible. Importing distributors tend to purchase simpler and cheaper lines for their own account and to act as sales agents for other larger more expensive and more specialized items for direct delivery to the user.

A common method of selling is through sales agents who solicit business on behalf of their principals. This method is well suited for sales of capital goods direct to end-users. The preference in Mexico for purchasing direct from the foreign manufacturer whenever possible is encouraged by the Government which sometimes grants import permits as well as import duty reductions only to the end-user. Aftersales service, however, is an important competitive advantage in this market. The "sell it, order it, install it, and forget it," approach of some local sales agents does not help to promote long-range sales of American products. If a U.S. firm cannot economically justify its own distribution network in Mexico, a local agent or distributor should be required to maintain a properly trained service person or staff and a reasonable selection of spare parts where required or have very quick access to U.S. parts and service sources. Alternatively, the supplier should be prepared to give quick service from the United States. This is made difficult by restrictions on and requirements for prior approval for the import of service parts and equipment. In many instances, it would profit the U.S. firm to subsidize its agent or distributor's service program and spare parts stock.

Entering the Mexican Market

The Mexican market must be viewed realistically. Many foreign products are not importable. The first step for U.S. exporters not familiar with Mexico is to ascertain if their products can be imported. If a product is found to be importable, it should be examined in terms of its sales potential in the market. The exporter should also determine where his major markets are in Mexico. If his choice for a representative in Mexico City is not strongly represented in other potential sales areas, especially along the border, he should consider other agent or subagents for those areas.

Although a neighbor to the United States and accustomed to buying American in preference to other foreign articles, Mexico is no mere extension of the U.S. market. Purchasing power is smaller and income groupings are different. Market statistics by products are not available, and sellers must frequently make special surveys to obtain information needed for a sales program.

Because of recent and projected increased foreign earnings, Mexico is one of the more rapidly expanding markets in Latin America. It is being cultivated by the industrialized countries, Latin American Integration Association members, and virtually all trading nations. As a result, Mexico has become a highly competitive market and is likely to become even more so.

Personal contact is very important in selling in Mexico. The development of a close working relationship between the Mexican sales representatives and the U.S. exporter will contribute a great deal to the success of the mutual effort. If the sales agents have good support from their suppliers they will usually try to do a good job.

Government Procurement Practices

Government imports represent over 40 percent of the country's purchases from abroad.

In keeping with its import substitution policy, government entities purchase domestic products whenever possible. Foreign purchases are made when similar items are not available from Mexican sources in required quality, quantity, delivery date, when international lending requires it, or when a price differential is exceeded. As of year-end 1980, local products were preferred if their price was lower than the landed duty-paid cost of the import, plus 15 percent.

Purchasing committees for each entity are made up of representatives from that organization plus representatives from other Secretariats, such as Commerce, concerned with the bidding procedure. Purchasing committees prepare standards for purchase and leasing of goods, supervise and schedule their execution, make sure commitments are carried out according to law, and transmit to the responsible, supervisory-mixed consultative commission their requirements for imported capital goods.

A "mixed consultative commission" is made up for each government entity and composed of representatives of that entity; four other government secretariats; and representatives from the National Confederation of Industrial Chambers, the National Chamber of the Transformation (manufacturing) Industry, and other chambers as thought necessary.

The mixed consultative commissions are involved only in purchases of raw materials, merchandise, or goods from foreign countries and, as noted, include private sector representatives who are in a position to provide definite information about availability of the goods in question from local sources. Recommendations of a mixed commission are not binding upon the purchasing committee and appeals are possible from mixed commission decisions.

Bidding is not required when an organization is buying for resale in government stores, when three separate suppliers are not available, when

products are part of general supply contracts negotiated by the Federal Government, when standardization or the technical characteristics of replacement equipment dictate a particular brand, or in the event of an emergency.

Suppliers may offer a fixed price which remains unchanged until delivery or one subject to monthly change, either on a fixed or variable basis. The rate of increase of a fixed escalating price may not exeed the monthly inflation index of the Mexican Central Bank in the case of local suppliers or of the central bank of the nation of the foreign supplier. A variable rate of increase must take into consideration the costs of direct labor, raw materials, parts, and subcontracting.

Sellers to any Mexican Government entity must register with Licenciado Abel Rasgado, Jefe de la Unidad de Analysis y Registro de Proveedores del Gobierno Federal, Secretaria de Comercio, Alvaro Obregón No. 121-1er Piso, Mexico 7, D.F. Mexico. Forms for registration are available directly from the organization named or from: Regional Market Manager, Mexico/Central America, OCM/ITA, U.S. Department of Commerce, Washington, D.C. 20230. Initial registration is accepted during the first three-quarters of the year with the last quarter reserved for annual re-registration. Fee for initial registration is 1,000 pesos (about US$45), and re-registration costs 500 pesos (about US$23). Payment is made to Secretaria de Hacienda y Crédito Público.

The registration process is often taken care of by the local representative of the foreign company, who is usually designated as the exclusive representative of the firm for government sales of a particular product line. Registration forms are in Spanish, and data must be supplied in that language.

In addition to registration with the Secretariat of Commerce, firms must register with the individual purchasing office of the government organization.

Four agencies account for over half of the Government's imports: the Mexican Petroleum Company (Petroleos Mexicanas, PEMEX); the Mexican National Railways (Nacionales de Mexico, N de M); the Federal Electricity Commission (CFE); and the National Popular Supply Company (CONASUPO), which buys basic foodstuffs such as wheat, corn, and powdered milk. Other agencies that import on a significant scale are: Productora Importadora de Papel, S.A. de C.V. (newsprint); Altos Hornos de Mexico, S.A. (steel manufacturing equipment); Secretariat of Human Resources and Public Works (construction equipment); Secretariat of Agriculture and Hydraulic Resources (construction, farming, and livestock equipment); Secretariat of Communications and Transportation (communication and transport equipment); Secretariat of National Defense (military equipment); Fertilizantes Mexicanos, S.A. (chemicals, materials and equipment to produce fertilizers); Department of the Federal District (roadbuilding and repair equipment); and Diesel Nacional, S.A. (motor vehicle components).

Channels of Distribution

Mexico has about 562,000 commercial establishments that employ about 1,880,000 persons. Of this number, 29 percent are in the Federal District (Mexico City) and 9 percent in the State of Mexico (suburbs of Mexico City). Jalisco, the state in which Guadalajara is located, has 8 percent.

Larger businesses have characteristics influenced by the marketing techniques of the United States, and, in recent years, several modern techniques have become common in Mexico. These include self-service for non-edibles, suburban shopping centers, and automated checkout in discount stores. Techniques such as sales stimulation by price leader merchandising and easier credit access are now also common. The growth of bank credit cards in the last few years has made credit available in just about every type of store or outlet.

Small establishments predominate numerically. The average number of employees per business outside Mexico City is two, while those in the city average only about three. These proprietorships continue their marketing in the traditional way.

The wholesale and retail channels for the distribution of commodities in Mexico are similar to those in the United States, but they differ in certain important characteristics. For example, Mexico has no nationwide chain of supermarkets or drug stores, although the larger cities have modern supermarket chains. There has been accelerated growth in the number of supermarkets and other chain stores in the last few years. Central Mexico has four major supermarket chains, and it is estimated that they account for about 25 percent of total food sales in the urban areas of Mexico City, Puebla, Toluca, and Cuernavaca. Of the total 900 self-service stores nationwide, 215 are in Mexico City; of the total 8,700 drug stores, 2,500 are in Mexico City. Although the public markets located in all Mexican cities and villages tend to specialize in fresh fruits and vegetables, they also sell a large variety of goods ranging from clothes to cosmetics.

Department stores have seen increasing competition from the smaller specialized outlets that are growing at a very fast pace. The department stores have responded by opening new outlets and by creating boutiques and specialized sections within their stores.

Franchising

Franchising opportunities in Mexico have been best in the fast food restaurants, hotels and motels, and rental services for automobiles and trucks. However, a saturation point may have been reached for the time being in some of these fields, given the limited number of people in income brackets able to afford such services, and the fact that the Government does not assign a high priority to such investments. Other franchise operations offer limited potential. Import restrictions may pose special problems to those franchise companies that require their franchisers to install specialized equipment that may not be importable.

Leasing

The first leasing company in Mexico was established in 1960. Operations have expanded rapidly since then. Leasing offers two important advantages. It can conserve working capital for corporate purposes and reduce taxes by charging leasing fees to operating costs. As in the United States, the client frequently may choose at a later date to convert the rental contract into a sale.

The market is dominated by five firms, all of which are controlled by Mexican banks, several with minority capital participation by U.S. banks. These firms offer lease financing on anything from a single machine to a complete plant. The client submits his or her requirements to the leasing company, which does not attempt to offer planning assistance in the setting up or expansion of plants. There are several smaller firms, mostly specializing in a particular field such as construction equipment or transportation units. All leasing companies require a license from the Finance Secretariat and operate under its general supervision.

Leasing across the border is attempted very rarely and is feasible only in extremely limited circumstances. To bring in equipment belonging to a U.S. leasing company, a temporary import permit would have to be obtained and a bond posted for the amount of the calculated duties, plus 10 percent. Such permits are for a limited time only, and the cost is considerable. Mexican

Customs authorities have taken the position that temporary import permits for leasing equipment will not ordinarily be given. However, they have made exceptions when very specialized projects have required large and expensive equipment that was not available in Mexico and had so little demand that purchase was not feasible.

Across-the-border leasing is feasible and practiced in the so-called maquiladoras or in-bond processing industry. Across-the-border leasing is possible whether the lessee is the company operating in Mexico or the U.S. parent. Machinery and equipment imported temporarily for use in the in-bond processing industry without paying import duties requires that a bond be posted against it.

Licensing

The 1973 law for the Control of Transfer of Rights of Technology and the Use and Exploitation of Patents and Trademarks requires that all contracts or other documents for the transfer of such rights, technical assistance, and related transactions be registered with the Secretariat of Patrimony and Industrial Development. The stated purpose of the law is to regulate the transfer of technology to Mexican companies, enabling them to obtain the maximum benefit at a minimum cost, reducing the outflow of foreign exchange.

The Government considers that charges for the use of foreign patents or technical assistance should not exceed 3 percent of sales, although in special cases with specific government approval higher charges have been acceptable.

A few types of agreement are exempted from the registration requirement, including those providing for (1) visits of technicians to install or repair machinery, (2) assistance in repairs and maintenance arising under a contract that has already been registered, and (3) the operation of in-bond processing companies that reexport their products.

Transportation, Communication, and Utilities

Mexico has a well-developed transportation system although increasingly it is unable to meet the needs of the rapidly expanding economy and growing population. There are 25,100 kilometers (km) of railroad track that connect at several border points with U.S. railroads. There is an all-weather road network of 60,000 km that links with the road systems of the United States and Central America. Two Mexican shipping companies and a number of foreign carriers provide service for international seaborne commerce. It has been estimated that two-thirds of Mexico's imports are carried by truck and rail, however, and that the greater part of the country's internal distribution is by truck.

Railways

Modernization of Mexico's railways is a major priority, with annual expenditures on rolling stock in the several hundred million dollar range. Total spending on modernization through 1982 is expected to be over $2 billion. Track is U.S. standard gauge, and diesel locomotives are used exclusively. The principal railroad is the government-owned Ferrocarriles Nacionales de Mexico with 8,745 miles of track and 2,100 locomotives. A program is underway to consolidate all Mexico's railroads into one system to centralize direction and maximize economies of scale.

Highways

The most important highways, like the principal railways, run mainly north and south and converge in Mexico City from the northern border points of Matamoros, Nuevo Laredo, Piedras Negras, Ciudad Juarez, and Nogales; and from the southern border points of Tapachula and Cuauhtemoc. Transverse highways extend from Matamoros (opposite Brownsville, Texas) to the Pacific port of Acapulco on the west coast; and from Coatzacoalcos on the Gulf Coast across the Isthmus of Tehuantepec to Salina Cruz on the Pacific Coast.

Now that the Government has completed the expansion of the highway system, it is placing more emphasis on constructing secondary and feeder roads.

In passenger traffic, auto transport occupies first place by a wide margin, moving about 70 percent of all passengers using public facilities and about 60 percent of all freight.

The operation of commercial truck and bus service is restricted to Mexican individuals and to Mexican companies with an exclusion of foreigners clause who are granted route concessions by the Secretariat of Communications and Transportation. Despite government regulations setting forth trucking tariffs, it is estimated that nearly half of the country's commercial trucking is carried out by firms and individuals at freely negotiated rates determined by market forces.

In 1980, estimates indicate that over 1 million trucks, 70,000 buses, and 7 million automobiles operated on Mexican highways.

Air Service

There are more than 50 commercial air lines operating in Mexico, of which approximately 33 provide scheduled international service. Mexico has 28 international airports, 19 major domestic airports, and about 435 smaller airfields. Mexico City is the center of the airways system that extends to 60 Mexican cities and towns, to a number of the larger cities in the United States and Canada, to other Latin American countries, and to Europe. Aeromexico and Compania Mexicana de Aviacion are the Mexican interational airlines.

Shipping

The merchant marine has about 98 seagoing ships in operation. The largest shipping line is Transportacion Maritima Mexicana, S.A. (TMM). Its affiliate, Transportes Maritimos Anahuac, S.A., operates a tanker fleet. Overall, the total deadweight tonnage is about 1,075,688; oceangoing vessels account for most of the tonnage.

The Government operates the facilities of the principal sea ports. Mexico has two principal shipyards, Astilleros Unidos de Veracruz on the Gulf Coast, and Astilleros de Mazatlan on the Pacific Coast, both government-owned.

In 1979, 36.4 million metric tons of cargo were loaded at Mexican ports and 58.9 million metric tons were unloaded, including coastwise shipping. Details of U.S. flag services to Mexico are available from the Division of Commercial Cargo, Office of Market Development, Maritime Administration, U.S. Department of Commerce.

Communications

The postal service is operated by the Government. It makes extensive use of air transportation and has developed a network of 7,000 offices and postal routes extending a total distance of 350,000 kilometers. Approximately 1.5 billion pieces of mail are handled annually.

Mexico's telecommunications services are regulated by the General Directorate of Telecommunications of the Secretariat of Communications and Transportation. National and international telegraphic service is operated by the government-owned Telegrafos Nacionales de Mexico. The Government also owns and operates the international radio-telegraph and radio-telephone facilities, and in remote areas operates some telephone offices in conjunction with the telegraph system. In 1979, the national network included 3,000 telegraph and 4,283 telephone offices; and some 223,161 kilometers of line over which 46 million telegrams were transmitted.

Utilities

Mexico's needs for energy double every 6 years, and the country suffers a chronic power shortage. After unprecedented brownouts during summer 1980, expansion plans were further accelerated. The Federal Electricity Commission (CFE), wholly government-owned, produces and distributes 95 percent of electricity. The stated policy of the Government is to develop the electrical power system through the use of resources other than petroleum which is presently by far the leading energy source.

A major coal-fired plant near the large coal field at Rio Escondido in northern Mexico and the Laguna Verde nuclear power plant near Veracruz are the principal alternative fuel projects currently under construction.

Water and sewerage systems in Mexico are overloaded due to the rapid urban growth, but there are continuing construction programs, some with international financial backing and supply of equipment.

Petroleum

Mexico's oil monopoly, Petroleos Mexicanos (PEMEX), is the world's oldest government-owned integrated oil company. It has a refining capacity of 1.476 million barrels of crude per day, placing it 11th in the world in this regard. Production of crude oil as of yearend 1980 is to be limited to 2.5 million barrels per day (bbl/d), with a 10 percent additional capacity to cover contingencies. Of this amount, it is proposed to export 1.5 million bbl/d.

Mexico's proven reserves of petroleum and natural gas equivalents are listed at 67 billion barrels, with additional probable reserves of 45 billion barrels and total possible reserves, including the two figures given, of 250 billion barrels.

Mexico's policy is to restrict petroleum production to a level that the economy can absorb without inflation. Exports are to be diversified as much as possible, with no single buyer to receive more than half of total exports.

Natural gas associated with liquid petroleum production is piped to the United States through a 48-inch line which connects in Texas to the U.S. distribution system.

Advertising and Market Research

Principal advertising media in Mexico are television, radio, and newspapers, accounting for 47, 11, and 11 percent, respectively, of billings. There are about 150 advertising agencies in Mexico, about half of which are located in Mexico

City and include well-known U.S. firms.

The most serious problem is fragmentation. For example, Mexico City alone has 22 daily newspapers, of which 14 have a circulation of over 10,000 copies. Newspapers are local in coverage; only a small percentage of circulation is outside the city of publication. Most cities have two or three daily papers. Magazines have similar fragmentation problems in that circulation of each of 31 exceeds 100,000 copies nationwide.

Mexican television, however, presents a different picture. In urban areas with populations of more than 100,000, television penetration is usually 70 percent or higher, and it is 83 percent in Mexico City. In Mexico City there are six TV channels—five commercial, and one educational. Guadalajara and Monterrey each have four, and most other cities over 50,000 inhabitants have at least one channel.

There are 550 radio stations with penetration of 80 percent or more of Mexican homes. In most of the large urban areas, penetration is over 90 percent of all homes.

Movie theaters are an excellent medium for advertising in Mexico. The average attendance is 2.2 times weekly, and the audience cuts across all socioeconomic levels as admission prices are low. Advertising consists of 20- to 60-second commercials inserted in the local firm program.

Billboard advertising is relatively common in large cities. However, legal restrictions limit the use of them on highways, so they are not as prevalent as in the United States.

With the growing importance of the Mexican market and its industrial complex, market research is becoming more common and a growing number of firms are entering the field. In addition to market research firms, the service also is offered by advertising agencies, management consultant firms and the like. Government agencies, as well as private corporations, contract for research. Some 30 firms, several with international reputations, are doing indepth market research at the present time. Their services include market analysis, sales analysis and forecasting, and distribution analysis.

Detailed information on advertising media in Mexico is compiled by Medios Publicitarios Mexicanos, A.C., Av. Mexico No. 99, Mexico 11, D.F. This firm, which is affiliated with the Standard Rate and Data Service, Skokie, Illinois, furnishes circulation and rates for radio and television stations and for newspapers and magazines.

Credit

Credit for private sector companies has been tight over the past several years as Mexico's public sector financial needs have generally taken priority. As a result, credit requirements, particularly those of companies with significant foreign ownership, are often met from foreign sources and denominated in foreign currency. There are no restrictions on such borrowing, nor are there any foreign exchange controls.

Mexico has a highly developed banking system. Several banks have nationwide branch networks and offer a complete range of banking services. Mexico's General Law on Credit Institutions and Auxiliary Organizations was amended recently to permit a single institution to include commercial, investment, and mortgage banking. Such institutions are called "multibancos," and the largest are Bancomer, Banamex, Comermex, and Serfin.

Effective interest rates on bank credit denominated in pesos runs higher than rates in the United States. Mexican banks make loans in dollars, funded either domestically or externally. U.S., Canadian, European, and Japanese banks supply substantial foreign currency denominated credits to U.S. firms operating in Mexico. In mid-1979, the Mexican loan portfolio of U.S. banks amounted to $11 billion.

Banks from other industrialized countries probably had a portfolio of at least half this amount. More than 200 foreign banks are actively engaged in making loans to various entities in Mexico. About 100 of these are represented in Mexico. The only U.S. bank with a branch in Mexico is Citibank, and its activities are relatively limited.

In addition to the private Mexican banks, there are several government-owned financial institutions and trust funds that lend directly or indirectly to the private sector. The largest and most important of these is Nacional Financiera, which lends mostly to industry. Other such institutions include Banrural, largely for agricultural credit; Banobras, for lending associated with public work projects; Banco Nacional de Comercio Exterior, which finances foreign trade. The Banco de Mexico (the Bank of Mexico) is the country's central bank. The Government has a number of trust funds (fideicomisos) that makes funds available for a variety of specific purposes, usually at below-market rates. These trust funds are operated through the national credit institutions or private credit institutions. They are not usually available to foreign-owned companies on the grounds that such companies enjoy access to foreign sources of credit. Among these trust funds are FOGAIN (loans to purchase capital equipment for small- and medium-sized industry), FOMEX (export promotion loans), FONATUR (tourism development), FIDEIN (industrial parts), FONEP (preinvestment studies), and FIRA (agricultural projects).

The bulk of industrial credit comes from the banking system. However, there are efforts to strengthen the capital market in Mexico. Bond issues are becoming increasingly popular for the larger and better known Mexican firms. The large Mexican banks have brokerage firms.

The Mexico City Stock Exchange is the country's exchange, with over 500 companies listed; branches operate in Monterrey and Guadalajara. The shares of foreign companies cannot be traded on the exchange without specific authorization by the Ministry of Finance. No foreign companies are presently listed although the shares of Mexican subsidiaries of foreign companies are traded. Many foreign-owned firms incorporated in Mexico have used the stock exchange to "Mexicanize" in recent years; this option is limited to firms established in Mexico for at least 2 years.

The Export-Import Bank of the United States has authorized more than $1.4 billion in credits to Mexican Government agencies and private firms for the purchase of U.S. goods. It also supports U.S. sales to small- and medium-sized Mexican firms by offering financial assistance under its Relending Facility Program.

The following companies in Mexico City offer credit information services:

Compania Jarbic, S.A., San Juan de Letran 13-505

Dun & Bradstreet, S.A., Av. Hidalgo 5-7 Piso

Etica Comercial, A.C., Londres 25-305

Intercambio Mosert, S.A. de C.V., Arquimedes 98

Retail Credit Co. Mexico, Napoles 36-7 Piso

Trade Regulations

Trade Policy

Mexico's trade policy has long emphasized import substitution as a means to develop domestic manufacturing industries. Proteciton has been accomplished mainly through a system of import licenses or permits that are required for a wide range of products and which are generally not granted if "acceptable substitutes" are manufactured locally. Manufactured imports primarily are products required for industrial growth, such as industrial production and processing equipment, spare parts, components, instrumentation, and advanced, high-technology items such as computers. This policy has stimulated the growth of a sizable domestic manufacturing sector that, although generally inefficient, supplies many of the country's needs, particularly in consumer products.

The current administration is placing considerable emphasis on the development of export markets for Mexican manufactured goods in order to prevent the country from becoming dependent on raw materials exports as a source of foreign exchange. Some preliminary steps have thus been taken to increase the international competitiveness of domestic industry through a gradual liberalization of the import regime.

Until the 1975 imposition of a permit requirement on 100 percent of the import tariff, about 40 percent of import tariff items were under permit control and about 60 percent by value of Mexico's imports came in under an approved import permit. Since 1977, the Government has removed the import permit requirement from a large number of items, generally substituting higher tariffs, some of which have increased up to 80 percent ad valorem, although most increases have been considerably lower. The intent of the import permit removals is to require local manufacturers over time to meet world market standards through lessening the degree of protection they receive from foreign competition by adjustment of the tariff rates. The intent has never been to open the market to foreign competition.

As of May 1981, the permit requirement remains on some 2,000 items, about 25 percent of total tariff classifications. Phase II of the import permit liberalization process is now scheduled to remove the import permit requirement from all but 700 items by yearend 1982, but the degree of opposition from manufacturers associations and opposition political groups is now intense and it is expected that remaining liberalizations will be slow in coming.

In October 1980, some 70 consumer items on which import permit requirements had been removed had them reimposed. Spokespersons cited "luxury" consumption of these items as undesirable for policy reasons. Additional reimpositions on approximately 300 items took place in March, April, and May 1981.

Import Permits

When an item requires an import permit, the purchaser in Mexico must submit to the

Secretariat of Commerce a request form, a pro forma invoice from the foreign supplier and, if the item warrants it, a technical description of the item in question. The request is considered by one of 13 committees that specialize in a particular portion of the tariff or by a special committee that considers all requests for permits from government entities. Requests are acted upon within 2 weeks or within 72 hours if in an emergency. The fee for a permit is a fraction of the invoice value of the goods, and an approved permit is valid for 6 months from date of issue and will be accepted for a shipment varying 10 percent from the approved value and quantity.

Committees rely on industry associations for advice as to local availability of an item that could perform the function of the import, as well as information on cost and delivery date of the Mexican equivalent.

Another reason for denial of a permit request is if an item has been determined to be a luxury item that is undesirable as an import for policy reasons.

Permits are issued based on the end use of the item. Often an end-user will be able to obtain a permit when the agent or distributor for the product cannot. It is also normal for a business starting up to obtain blanket import permits for the items necessary for production over a period of up to several years. State-owned companies such as PEMEX and the Federal Electricity Commission are often able to obtain more liberal rulings than other applicants.

Import permits for shipments of needed spare parts not valued over 10,000 pesos (U.S.$440) may be obtained through industry chambers and associations. Exceptions are parts for the automotive and textile industries, pumps, and motors.

Informal opinions as to whether an import permit would be granted on a particular item are given by the Secretariat of Commerce in Mexico City upon inquiry in person. A U.S. business wishing to find out the importability status of its products may send a request to the Director, U.S. Trade Center, Liverpool 31, Mexico 6 D.F. Mexico, with product literature and a check for $15 per item to the United States Trade Center to cover the cost of translation if literature is not in Spanish. Opinions are unofficial and are not binding. There is a limit of five items per request.

Tariff Structure

The Mexican tariff generally follows the Brussels Tariff Nomenclature. The Tariff Act published in 1974 eliminated specific duties and established a General Ad Valorem Duty to be levied at varying rates based on the "official price" or the purchase price, whichever is higher. In July 1979, a new law of customs valuation went into effect eliminating the official price on most items. Initially, 860 products remained on the official price list and several hundred more have since been added. For other items, Customs calculates duties based on the "standard value" of the product and will accept the invoice as evidence, usually combined with a Declaration of Value form submitted under oath.

Industrial machinery needed for development purposes generally has a 20 percent duty. Equipment for which there is less urgent need is levied at rates from 20 to 60 percent. Luxury items, including most importable consumer products, encounter duties from 60 to 100 percent. (These levies do not appear to be a serious barrier to sales of a wide range of items, however, due to the high prestige value of owning foreign goods.) Some products are imported free of duty, including certain essential raw materials, agricultural products, chemicals, tractor engines and parts, airplane tires, and books, catalogs, and publications in languages other than Spanish. Lower rates or duty-free treatment apply to a variety of items entering the free zones and free perimeters.

Mexico is the only major trading nation that is not a member of General Agreement on Tariffs and Trade (GATT). It rejected accession in March 1980, after a national opinion-sounding process, on the basis that GATT membership would impose too many restrictions on Mexico's trade policy, which is designed to promote industrial development.

Mexico applies its tariff rate in a nondiscriminatory manner with the exception of fellow Latin America Integration Association (LAIA formerly LAFTA) members (Argentina, Bolivia, Brazil, Colombia, Chile, Ecuador, Paraguay, Peru, Uruguay, and Venezuela), which receive reductions or exclusions from tariffs as well as import permit requirements on specific items, particularly in the chemical and electrical sectors.

Information regarding Mexican duties applicable to specific products may be obtained free of charge from the Office of Country Marketing, International Trade Administration, U.S. Department of Commerce, Washington, D.C. 20230. Inquiries should contain a complete product description, including BTN, SITC, or U.S. Schedule B Export Commodity number, if known.

Other Taxes on Imports

Surcharges of 2 percent ad valorem, earmarked for an export promotion fund, and 3 percent of the base duty, earmarked for port improvement are collected on virtually all imports except for basic foodstuffs. A 10 percent surcharge applies to mail shipments.

Since 1980, Mexico has collected a value-added tax (VAT or IVA in Spanish) of 10 percent on all imports in the same manner as on sales of the same products manufactured domestically. The rate drops to 6 percent in the free perimeter areas, and no VAT is collected on a number of items intended for basic consumption and lower income groups.

A luxury tax, known as Intercambio Compensado, is collected on items considered to be luxuries or nonessentials. The rate varies from 1 ½ to 12 percent ad valorem.

Advance Rulings on Customs Classifications

The Mexican Customs Service will furnish, upon request, information concerning the customs classification applicable to specified merchandise.

This service is usually rendered to a U.S. company through a customs broker in Mexico by the Departmento Pericial Calificador, Direccion General de Aduanas, Mexico, D.F. To obtain an advance opinion, the application should be accompanied by a sample of the product, preferably in its customary container, together with descriptive pamphlets, labels, etc. Where the nature of the item precludes submission of a sample, it may be substituted for by photographs or drawings accompanied by pamphlets, catalogs, specifications, descriptions of the component materials, and other data designed to describe fully the nature and use of the article. It is mandatory for the import or customs broker to make appropriate arrangements with the customs authorities before forwarding samples and related data. Opinions are advisory and not binding.

Marking and Labeling Requirements

Marking.—To be fully protected, goods having their trademarks registered in Mexico should bear the words "marca registrada," the trademark, and the location of the factory, including the name of the country of manufacture (for example, New Haven, Connecticut, U.S.A.). If the product is too small to accommodate these data, they may be shown on the label. Such markings are particularly advisable on wearing apparel and on leather goods. The use of the metric system is obligatory, but labeling in both systems is permitted.

Labeling of Goods.—There are labeling regulations applicable on the following products:

silver, silver- and nickel-plated articles, articles of wearing apparel, and leather goods in general, as well as packaged foodstuffs and beverages, pharmaceutical products, veterinary preparations, prepared feeds, fertilizers, and insecticides. The regulations vary from product to product and are too detailed to be included in this report. It is suggested that the importer or customs broker obtain the requirements directly from the Mexican Government agency concerned with the applicable products.

Senate Concurrent Resolution 40, adopted July 30, 1953, invites U.S. exporters to inscribe, insofar as practicable, on the external shipping containers in indelible print of a suitable size: "United States of America."

Customs Warehousing

Goods entering Mexico are deposited in a Customs warehouse and may be entered for consumption upon the presentation of the required documents and the payment of duties and other charges. Storage charges begin after 15 days from the time the shipment is unloaded. Goods that are not claimed within 90 days after unloading are considered legally abandoned (tacit abandonment) and become the property of the Customs administration.

Goods stored in Customs warehouses may be reexported without payment of duty, provided the goods are not prohibited in Mexican trade, have entered the country legally, and are still under customs custody, and provided the applicable duties have not been paid and tacit abandonment has not occurred. Products requiring import licenses normally require a special permit for reexportation. However, once goods have cleared the Mexican Customs, they are considered as having been nationalized. If subsequently reexported, no refund of import duties will be made and the shipment, moreover, will be subject to applicable Mexican export duties and regulations. Most exports, however, are free of duty and of restrictions.

Veracruz and Tampico are the only ports of entry that have bonded warehouses. With the exception of these ports, merchandise intended for storage in bond must be transported to Mexico City, where the merchandise may be placed in an authorized bonded warehouse for a maximum period of 1 year, renewable for another year, without paying import duties.

Shipping Documents

The documents needed for surface shipments to Mexico are the commercial invoice, bill of lading, packing list, shipper's export declaration, as well as the insurance policy, if available. These documents are prepared by the exporter. The insurance policy is prepared upon request of the exporter. The Mexican import clearance documents that are required usually are supplied by the Mexican customs broker at the port of entry. Documents may be in Spanish or in English with a Spanish translation.

Commercial Invoice.—This document, normally prepared in six copies, is required for all land or maritime shipments, of merchandise valued at more than 1,000 pesos.

Commercial invoices covering land and maritime shipments valued at 1,000 pesos or less are required in triplicate. Mail shipments valued at more than 1,000 pesos must be accompanied by commercial invoices in original and three copies, signed by the exporter. An additioinal copy should be sent directly to the consignee. For air shipments, three copies of the invoice, signed by the exporter, should be furnished the carrier, regardless of the content and value of the package, and these invoices must accompany the shipment. Some carriers require one or more additional copies. Heavy fines are imposed on shipments arriving without properly executed invoices. The seller must certify by signature on all copies that "the value and other details on the invoice are true and correct." These requirements are being enforced even more stringently under the customs valuation system that came into effect in 1979 and eliminated most official prices.

Bill of Lading.—This document is required only on maritime shipments, but freight forwarders usually request it on rail shipments as well. The bill of lading shows the marks, quantity and the kind of packages, and the gross weight of goods in units of the metric system. Most merchandise shipped to Mexico by rail is sent on local bills of lading in care of the customs broker or forwarding agent in the border city. "To order" bills of lading are acceptable. Freight collect shipments are generally recognized.

Packing List.—This document should be furnished in triplicate (additional copies are sometimes required), to the customs broker or forwarding agent at the border for use in preparing the necessary customs document and in any repacking of the goods. The packing list should show the gross, legal, and net weights and indicate whether box, crate, carton, or keg (if this information is not given in the commercial invoice); the total number of packages; and the gross, net, and legal weights of the entire shipment.

Air Waybills.—On air shipments the required number of copies of the air waybill (used instead of the bill of lading) varies according to the type of shipment and the carrier. However, when the package is delivered to the carrier, the shipper should furnish a full description of the goods giving their value (data on the commercial invoice are usually sufficient) and sign the air waybill.

Other Documents.—Sanitary certificates, in quadruplicate, must accompany other documents when shipping live animals, certain animal products, seeds, and plants and plant products. They are issued at the place of origin by the veterinary inspector of the U.S. Department of Agriculture, by the local authorities of the State concerned, or by an accredited veterinarian. The original must be legalized by the nearest Mexican consulate.

Samples without commercial value are admitted free of duty into Mexico. Samples considered usable or salable are subject to import duty at the rates applicable to ordinary commercial shipments. However, with the prior approval of the Director General of Customs, such samples may be rendered unusable prior to clearance and thereby qualify for duty-free entry.

Convention and Exhibit Materials

Mexico permits temporary duty-free entry of convention and exhibition materials. Requests for exemption must be addressed to the Director de Convenciones, Consejo Nacional de Turismo, Mariano Escobedo No. 726, Mexico 5, D.F., telephone (905) 531-0949, giving details of the convention and samples of the materials the convention wants to import. At least 2 months lead time is needed, preferably more. As it is not uncommon for convention materials to be impounded by Customs on technicalities, it is safest to work through a reliable customs broker.

The U.S. Trade Center (USTC) in Mexico City has been granted special in-bond status for the purpose of commercial exhibitions. Part or all of this facility may be rented, subject to USTC schedules and policies, at reasonable rates by U.S. firms who wish to stage private exhibitions or seminars with a minimum of customs problems. For further information, contact Director, Office of Export Promotion, International Trade Administration, U.S. Department of Commerce, Washington, D.C. 20230.

Advertising Matter

Catalogs in a language other than Spanish do not require an import license and may be imported free of duty and value added tax.

Free Zones and Perimeters

Mexico's Free Zones were established in order to encourage development of these once remote and underpopulated regions. Free zones currently exist in the States of Baja California, Norte, and Sur, the northwest corner of Sonora, and the State of Quintana Roo on the Yucatan Peninsula. A preimeter zone 20 kilometers wide parallels the U.S. border and includes the border cities. Certain items may be shipped to these zones at reduced duties or free of duty. A number of consumer products that are excluded from the rest of the country may be exported to these zones (including consumer electronic goods and some motor vehicles). Goods sold to the special zones may not be transferred to the rest of the country without payment of duties (checkpoints exist at the boundaries of the zones).

Since the list of products eligible for duty free or license exempt entry into free zones and perimeters is subject to change without notice, and because special treatment for an import is withdrawn when it is determined that a Mexican produced one is available to take its place, exporters should check the status of their shipments beforehand. The special zones are administered by the Secretaria de Hacienda y Credito Publico (Secretariat of the Treasury and Public Credit), which has offices in the major border towns. Customs brokers in the border towns will also be familiar with the latest regulations.

Investment in Mexico

Foreign Investment

Direct U.S. investment at yearend 1979 was estimated by the U.S. Department of Commerce at $4.57 billion, of which $3.42 billion was in manufacturing divided as follows in millions of dollars: Chemicals and related, 915; machinery, 640, food products, 281; transportation equipment, 510; primary and fabricated metals, 288; and other, 775. Investment in other sectors in millions of dollars: Trade, 696; finance and insurance, 136; mining, 113, and petroleum, 81.

Total accumulated foreign investment in Mexico at yearend 1979 is estimated by the Mexican Foreign Investment Commission at $8.4 billion, with a U.S. share of 70 percent; Germany, 6 percent; Japan, 5 percent; United Kingdom, 4.5 percent; and Switzerland, 4.5 percent. Foreign investment is about 4 percent of total private investment in Mexico. As of 1978, there were 4,854 companies with foreign participation.

Investment Policy and Legislation

Mexico regards foreign investment as a privilege that will be granted to applicants who meet criteria established to maximize the benefits to the nation of that investment.

The 1973 Law to Promote Mexican Investment and to Regulate Foreign Investment codifies administrative practices and previous legislation on the subject. The law establishes the principle that foreign investment will be permitted only on a minority basis in association with Mexican investment.

A National Commission on Foreign Investment was created to administer the Foreign Investment Law and manage the newly created National Registry of Foreign Investments. All foreign individuals and corporations with equity investments in Mexico and Mexican companies with any foreign ownership must register with the National Registry of Foreign Investment. The Foreign Investment Commission is empowered to approve or disapprove contracts governing the transfer of technology; e.g., royalties, patents, trademarks, and know-how.

The law stipulates that new foreign equity investments will not exceed 49 percent of a firm's total equity. Expansion, relocation, and new products by existing firms are treated as new investment. Although exceptions to the 49 percent rule may be granted by the Commission, it rarely does so. A regulation of the Foreign Investment Commission permits 100 percent foreign ownership of the so-called "in-bond" industries; i.e., those firms that assemble components for export under sections 806.30 and 807 of the U.S. Tariff Code.

Foreign investment in certain industries is restricted to less than 40 percent, or prohibited altogether. In companies mining national mineral reserves (excluding those reserved for the public sector), foreign ownership is limited to 34 percent, and it is limited to 40 percent in companies engaged in the manufacture of automotive parts and secondary petrochemical products. The entire petroleum industry, including basic petrochemicals, is reserved to the government-owned monopoly, Petroleos Mexicanos. In addition, there are prohibitions on foreign ownership of real property in zones along the country's borders and seacoasts and requirements of Mexican ownership of enterprises engaged in banking, news dissemination, transportation within Mexico, land settlement, and exploitation of forest and marine products.

The Foreign Investment Commission uses 16 criteria to screen applications by potential foreign investors. Among these are whether the proposed investment will be complementary rather than competitive with Mexican investment; the technology brought into Mexico; the impact on exports, imports, and employment; the extent to which it is financed from abroad; the country from which the investment is made; the extent of the foreign investor's interest in Mexico, and the investor's connection with foreign centers of economic decision, and its location.

Another important law affecting foreign investors, promulgated in 1973, is the Law on the Registration of the Transfer of Technology and the Use and Exploitation of Patents and Trademarks. This law makes the registration of all contracts involving the transfer of technology, including patents, compulsory. The Registry of the Transfer of Technology, under the Ministry of National Properties and Industry, can declare contracts null and void under a variety of circumstances, including excess cost, local availability of the technology in question and attempts to use such contracts to control management of Mexican firms. A rule of thumb used by the Registry limits contracts to 3 percent of sales for a nonrenewable 10 year period although exceptions are possible.

As noted in the Industrial Property Protection section below, Mexico's Law on Inventions and Trademarks is more restrictive than most national laws in defining the rights granted by a patent and in defining the products that can be patented. For example, chemicals, pharmaceuticals, pesticides, herbicides, and several other commonly patentable products cannot obtain patent protection in Mexico. The validity of patents has been shortened to 10 years, and if a patent is not exploited within 3 years, the Government can assign the right to exploit it to someone else. A certificate of invention can be obtained in place of a patent. It conveys the same rights as a patent with the exception of exclusive exploitation. The section on trademarks has been troubling to foreign firms because it requires that all products produced in Mexico carry a distinctive Mexican trademark, equally linked if necessary, with the foreign or international mark. The Government has shown some flexibility in implementing this law and the Mexican trademark provisions.

Copies of the Patent and Trademark Law, the Law for the Promotion of Mexican Investment and Regulation of Foreign Investment, and the Law on the Registration of the Transfer of Technology and the Use and Exploitation of Patents and Trademarks are available from the Marketing Manager, Mexico/Central America, OCM/ITA, U.S. Department of Commerce, Washington, D.C. 20230.

The United States and Mexico have never signed an investment guaranty agreement nor an agreement to prevent double taxation.

In-Bond Industry Investment

Mexico legislated provisions in 1965 to allow investors to establish plants to produce finished goods from imported components that are then reexported for sale. In addition to blanket authorization for 100 percent foreign ownership, in-bond plants (known as "maquiladoras") operate under a variety of other exemptions which include among others the use of U.S. trucks to haul material to the plant from the border and duty-free entry of expendable items.

In-bond plants were initially limited to the immediate border area but, since 1972, can be located anywhere in Mexico. Nevertheless, over 90 percent of the approximately 619 plants are still located in border cities.

Products of maquiladora plants receive the same treatment in the Mexican market as do wholly foreign made products.

Fiscal Incentives

The 1979 National Industrial Development Plan (NIDP) restructured previous investment incentives in an effort to provide a coordinated program to encourage new industry. Priority development zones established by the NIDP set up five geographical categories with highest preference (IA) given to the industrial port areas of Lazaro Cardenas, Michoacan on the Pacific coast and Tampico, Tamaulipas and Coatzacoalcos, Veracruz on the Gulf of Mexico. Salina Cruze, Oaxaca, originally designated an industrial port, was withdrawn from special development status in 1980. Ninety municipalities in 20 states have second place status (IB), and new industry there will receive virtually all possible incentives. No encouragement is given to growth in new industry in the Mexico City and State of Mexico region (IIIA), and new industry in Guadalajara and Monterrey is also discouraged.

Priority industries established by a 1979 executive order have been estimated to provide 60 percent of the present gross value of industrial production and are split into two categories with the highest including agro-industry and a number of capital goods manufacturing categories. A special program exists for small business.

Tax credits take the form of certificates known as CEPROFI's (Certificados de Promocion Fiscal) which are valid for payment of most

Federal taxes and are not regarded as income for tax calculation purposes.

Benefits as a rule are available only to Mexican-owned companies, although some benefits may be given to firms with minority foreign capital.

Benefits include:

• A 5 percent tax credit on purchases of approved Mexican-made new machinery and equipment.

• A new employment tax credit of up to 20 percent of the minimum wage for each new job.

• Tax exemption on profits from sale of real assets in region IIIA, if reinvested in an approved relocation.

• Up to 30 percent subsidy of fuel costs in Zones IA and IB.

In addition, capital goods manufacturers may benefit from up to 100 percent reduction of import duties on raw materials and up to 75 percent reduction of the duties on machinery and equipment not made in Mexico, accelerated depreciation, and reduction of up to 75 percent of the net Federal gross receipts tax on priority capital goods.

Foreign Exchange

Mexico has no exchange control; therefore, foreign investors are permitted freedom in foreign exchange operations. Capital, profits, and dividends may be readily transferred to and from Mexico. The rates at which foreign exchange may be bought and sold are governed by those quoted by Mexico's central bank the Banco de Mexico, S.A.

The Mexican monetary unit is the peso, which is approximately equivalent to US$0.04. On September 1, 1976, the peso was allowed to float on the market after 22 years at the fixed rate of 12.50 pesos to US$1. The peso was valued at approximately 23.50 pesos to US$1 in early 1981, with little depreciation over the past 3 years. Earlier the rate had fluctuated between 20 and 28.50 pesos to US$1.

Forms of Business Organization

The General Law of Mercantile Companies provides for counterparts of the forms of business organization known to American law and also provides corporations to be formed with variable capital.

In Mexico, there is also provision for a form of operation in which the participant's liability is limited to the amount of his or her contribution to the enterprise's capital, the Sociedad Anonima de Responsabilidad Limitada.

The most common type of corporate organization is the Sociedad Anonima. The Sociedad Anonima is a corporation consisting of a minimum of five stockholders. The permission of the Ministry of Foreign Relations is required for establishing a corporation with foreign participation.

The application for permission must state the objective or purpose of the corporation; e.g., to manufacture, purchase, and sell goods. The application must also state that every foreign stockholder will agree: (1) to be considered a Mexican insofar as shares of stock or other interests in the corporation are concerned; and (2) not to invoke the protection of his or her government under penalty, should he or she fail to keep his or her agreement, of forfeiting such shares or interest to the Mexican nation. This clause must also be inserted in the corporate charter and in titles or certificates representing the stock of Mexican corporations.

This clause, known as the Calvo Clause, is founded on the principle that no foreigner shall have greater rights in Mexico than the country's own citizens. It does not in any way affect the U.S. or other foreign citizenship of an individual.

Taxation

Mexican taxes applying to investments generally are moderate. Mexican tax laws and regulations are comprehensive and are amended frequently; therefore, only a brief summary of the tax structure can be given here. Business enterprises, whether sole proprietorships, partnerships, or corporations, are subject to a global income tax. This means all income of business enterprises must be included in their annual tax return except dividends received from Mexican corporations, CEPROFI's, and earnings of funded pension plans approved by the Income Tax Department.

The principal taxes payable by commercial and industrial enterprises operating in Mexico and in certain cases by foreign companies as well as by individuals are: import and export duties, taxes on income, mercantile revenue tax (gross receipts tax), value-added tax, local taxes on proceeds of capital and real property, and payroll taxes, principally social security.

The corporate income tax is a graduated tax with income up to 2,000 pesos being entirely exempt. Income between 2,000.01 and 3,500.00 pesos is assessed at the rate of 5 percent, and income between 3,500.01 and 5,000.00 pesos is assessed at 75 pesos, plus 6 percent on the excess over 3,500.00 up to 5,000.00.

When taxable income exceeds 500,000 pesos, the entire income is taxed at 42 percent, except that if the total taxable income is between 500,000 and 1,500,000 pesos, an amount equivalent to 6.65 percent of the difference between 1,500,000 pesos and the taxable income will be deducted from the tax calculated at the rate of 42 percent.

With the exception of any expenditures deemed to be ordinary, necessary, and in proportion to the size of the business, only those deductions specifically authorized by law are allowable. Capital expenditures are not deductible.

Gross income earned in Mexico by nondomiciled corporations or individuals is taxed at the flat rate of 21 percent or the graduated corporate rate, at the election of the taxpayer. Tax on this type of income must be withheld by those who make such payments. It includes: technical service fees, interest on loans of foreign banks, royalties of all types, occasional commission income, advertising and publicity for use within Mexico, and rental of equipment.

The Secretariat of Finance and Public Credit maintains a register of foreign credit institutions that are entitled to be taxed on their interest income from Mexican sources at the flat rate of 15 percent. The specific requirements for registration are contained in regulations issued by the Secretariat. Interest paid to official lending institutions of foreign countries is also subject to a withholding tax of 15 percent. A 21 percent rate applies to interest paid to foreign suppliers on sales of machinery and equipment included in the fixed assets of a purchaser resident in Mexico, when the latter is engaged in activities that merit encouragement in the opinion of the Secretariat of Finance and Public Credit. Interest on loans made by nonresident foreign companies, which are considered by the Secretariat of Finance and Public Credit to be in the general interest, is also taxed at a same rate. The interest income of foreign companies that have not qualified for this special treatment is subject to a flat rate of 42 percent.

A value-added tax (VAT, or IVA in Spanish) went into effect in 1980, replacing a turnover tax and a number of specialized levies. Mexico's IVA follows the European model by adopting a 'consumption" system in which tax paid on all purchases including capital assets, is deductible from the VAT due on sales during the same period. The base rate is 10 percent with a 6 percent rate applying in the free zones and the northern free perimeter. Exempt from VAT are professional services, many government transactions, agricultural products, and necessities for low-income consumers. The tax is collected on imports and rebated on exports.

The straight-line method of depreciation and amortization, at fixed annual rates, is required. Annual depreciation rates range from 3 to 35 percent.

The Secretariat of Finance and Public Credit is authorized to grant accelerated depreciation rates as economic development incentives, but these may be granted only to a general type of activity or in a specified geographic area, not to individual firms. Depreciation may be commenced in the fiscal year in which the assets are placed in use or in the following year, at the election of the taxpayer.

Other taxes include production taxes, Federal excise taxes, and certain State and local taxes.

Industrial Property Protection*

Mexico is a member of the "Paris Union" International Convention for the Protection of Industrial Property (patents and trademarks) to which the United States and 90 other countries belong. It entitles American businesspersons and inventors to receive national treatment in Mexico; i.e., treatment equal to that accorded Mexican citizens, under its laws regarding the protection of patents and trademarks. U.S. nationals also are entitled to certain other benefits such as having 1 year after filing a patent application in the United States in which to file a corresponding application in Mexico and receive for the latter application the benefit of the first U.S. filing date (right of priority). The "priority" period for trademark applications is 6 months.

Applications or inquiries pertaining to patents and trademarks should be addressed to the Director General of Industrial Property, Secretariat of Commerce, Hermosillo 26, Mexico D.F., Mexico.

Mexico is also a member of the Universal Copyright Convention to which the United States and about 60 other countries belong. It is also a member of the Buenos Aires Copyright Convention adhered to by the United States and about 17 other countries. Works of American authors first copyrighted in the United States are entitled to automatic protection in Mexico under these conventions. To obtain copyright protection in Mexico, the author need only show on such works his or her name, year of first publication

---

*Prepared by Foreign Business Practices Division, Office of International Finance, Investment and Services, International Trade Administration.

and the symbol "c" in a circle. Mexico is likewise a member of the "Berne Union" Copyright Convention. Although the United States is not a member of this Convention, U.S. authors may obtain protection in Berne Union countries by publishing a work in a Union country at the time it is first published and copyrighted in the United States (simultaneous publication).

The new Mexican Law on Inventions and Trademarks was enacted December 30, 1975. Implementing regulations were published October 14, 1976 and February 20, 1981. There is also the Law on the Registration of the Transfer of Technology and the Use and Exploitation of Patents and Trademarks of December 28, 1972, under which all agreements for the licensing of patents, trademarks, and technology must be approved by government authorities and recorded in the National Registry for the Transfer of Technology.

Patents.—Patents are registered for a term of 10 years from the date of grant. A patent must be worked within 3 years from such date or 4 years from filing date, otherwise it is subject to compulsory licensing. Importation is not considered to fulfill the working requirements. If a party acquires a compulsory license under a patent, he or she must initiate the working within 2 years of the license grant. If, after 3 years from issue of a patent, more than 1 year elapses without the patent being worked or compulsory licenses issued, the patent shall lapse.

A patented product must bear the patent number; otherwise, the other may be unable to take legal action against possible infringers.

The Government may issue, at any time, "public utility licenses" for exploitation of certain patents on grounds of public health, national defense, or other decisions deemed to affect the public interest.

The law enables owners of inventions for chemicals and pharmaceuticals, nuclear energy, and antipollution equipment not patentable under the law to apply for and obtain a special form of recognition for their inventions, known as "Certificates of Invention." The certificates are issued for 10 years and are subject to licensing upon request by interested parties. Licensees must pay royalties to the owner for the invention's use. The owner also may personally exploit the invention but he or she has no exclusive rights to its exploitation.

Trademarks.—The law provides for protection of product and service marks. The first person to apply for a mark is entitled to its registration and exclusive use. Marks not registerable are those that are generic or in common use for the products or services, or are not otherwise distinctive of the products; that constitute official government emblems or insignia; that reproduce coins or bank notes; that consist of geographic origin names; that are identical to marks already registered; or that are contrary to good morals and public order.

Use of a registered mark cannot be denied to someone who used the mark for the same product or service more than 1 year before the registration. The prior user has 1 year after the registration to himself or herself as the excusive owner. Trademarks that have lapsed because of nonrenewal or nonuse may be reapplied for by any person within 1 year of the lapsed date.

Applications are examined for novelty and, if any similar registrations exist or questions arise for the examiners, the applicant is notified and given 15 to 45 days to modify or substitute the application. Otherwise, the registration will be denied. The trademark classification system is comprised of 50 classes, somewhat similar to the old U.S. classification system.

Trademarks are registered for 5 years from application filing date and are renewable indefinitely for 5 year periods. A registered mark must be used within 3 years of registration. If not used to the Government's satisfaction, the mark is considered cancelled. Registration notice must appear on the mark; otherwise, it is not enforceable against infringers.

The Government may, in the public interest, require the registration and use of trademarks on any product or service. It may also prohibit use of trademarks, whether or not registered, on particular products. Marking under a generic name may be ordered for specific products within an industrial sector. Persons selling foreign-made goods bearing foreign registered marks not registered in Mexico, must indicate clearly the place of registration on the product, or for the service.

Every trademark of foreign origin or owned by a foreigner, used on articles made in Mexico, must be used jointly with a mark originally registered in Mexico; both marks to be displayed in an equally visible manner. All contracts for licensing and use of foreign-owned marks on locally produced goods must contain this co-use requirement. Otherwise, such contracts will be denied government approval and registration with the National Registry for the Transfer of Technology. The Mexican Government has delayed the entry of this provision into force several times; the latest delay expires December 31, 1981. Further extensions should not be expected, although they are possible.

The owner of a mark registered in Mexico may authorize other parties to use the mark and record the "authorized user" contracts with the General Bureau of Inventions and Trademarks, and with the National Registry for legal recognition and enforcement.

The law also specifies procedures under which cancellation of registered marks may be sought by parties who believe that such marks have been improperly registered by reason of similarity to prior registration, prior use by others, false indications of origin, or application by a local agent without prior permission of the foreign owner. A mark may also be cancelled when the Government determines that the owner has improperly priced or represented the quality of the product or service covered by the mark, to the public detriment.

Copyrights.—The Federal Copyright Law of December 28, 1956, was amended by Law of November 4, 1963. The term of copyright protection is for the author's life plus 30 years after death for literary, dramatic, musical, and artistic works. Copyright includes the sole right to produce and reproduce the work or a translation of it, to publish such work or translation, to perform it in public, and to authorize others to do the aforementioned. The Law is administered by the Copyright Directorate of the Secretariat of Education.

Further information on the general provisions of Mexico's patent, trademark, and copyright laws may be obtained from the Foreign Business Practices Division, Office of International Finance and Investment, International Trade Administration, U.S. Department of Commerce, Washington, D.C. 20230. That Division, however, is not in a position to provide detailed information on fees or other specific step-by-step procedures to be followed in seeking protection under these laws. Competent legal counsel should be consulted for this purpose.

Labor

The 1979 economically active population was estimated at 17.9 million, with 7.5 million in agriculture, forestry, and fishing and 3.2 million in manufacturing. Employment for the country's rapidly growing population is a major government concern and the national industrial development plan emphasizes job creation and decentralization of industry with a view to deconcentration of the population from the central plateau region.

Mexico's unemployment is not excessive, but underemployment is a serious problem. President Lopez Portillo announced in late 1980 that economic growth had for the first time in recent years allowed the creation of more jobs than new entrants into the labor force. The National Employment Plan seeks to give employment to 2.2 million from 1980 to 1982 or to create jobs at an annual rate of 4.2 percent in order to lower unemployment to a level of 5.5 percent. One indirect indicator of job growth has been the growth of industrial workers covered by the social security system which was up 10.2 percent in 1979, and 9.6 percent in the first 8 months of 1980.

The Mexican labor force is characterized by an excess of unskilled workers and a shortage of trained workers. The labor in short supply ranges from semiskilled factory laborers to craftworkers, line supervisors, technicians, and managers. This shortage of skilled labor is one of the most serious problems facing Mexican industry.

Trained workers are concentrated largely in and around Mexico City and in other industrial cities such as Monterrey, Guadalajara, and Puebla.

Wages and Salaries.—Minimum wages are set annually by tripartite minimum wage boards composed of workers, employers, and government representatives. In practice, minimum wages fall far short of satisfying the normal needs of a worker's family; hence, wages are often higher than the minimum. This is particularly true in newer industries and in more modern plants. Wages are also generally higher in foreign-owned plants, partly because they are among the most modern and highly unionized. Similarly, wages in government-operated industries are higher than the average.

Labor Organization

About 4 million Mexican workers are organized, representing about 38 percent of the nonagricultural labor force. In the industrial sector, more than 90 percent of production workers in establishments of over 25 employees are organized. The most highly unionized sectors of the economy are the Federal Government, the mining and petroleum industries, the transportation and communications industries, and the major manufacturing industries. The development of a strong Mexican trade union movement has been facilitated by close relations with the Government and the dominant political party, the Institutional Revolutionary Party (Partido Revolucionario Institucional—PRI). Unions have succeeded generally in establishing the union shop, and most of the larger industries operate under a closed-shop system.

Guidance for Business Travelers Abroad

Entrance Requirements

An alien wishing to enter Mexico for business purposes must obtain an entry permit. This is issued by the Secretariat of Interior.

Nonimmigrant.—A nonimmigrant alien may enter on a Visitor's Card for a period of 6 months (renewable once) for lawful and temporary business purposes. If trip purposes are scientific, technical, artistic, or athletic, the card is renewable twice. U.S. nationals specifically denominated as qualified nonimmigrants include traveling salespeople; officials of agricultural, industrial, commercial, and mining or other institutions who enter to negotiate business contracts or confer with associates; and persons wishing to promote or conclude business transactions.

Businesspeople may enter Mexico under the special category "Counselor" to attend meetings of a firm's administrative council or to provide consultation or perform certain company transactions on a temporary basis. Admission under this category is for 6 months, nonrenewable, but with permission for multiple entries during the period, none for more than 20 days each.

Immigrant.—An alien who wishes to enter Mexico for business purposes other than those entitling him to nonimmigrant status can gain entry only if he satisfies the requirements for one of the following classificaitons of an immigrant visa.

Investors in Business.—An alien can obtain the immigration status of "inversionista" or investor, if he or she guarantees to assume an active role in any livestock, agricultural, industrial, or export business in which he or she will invest a minimum of 600,000 pesos, if the business is established in the Federal District or the industrial zones adjoining the Federal District, or of 200,000 pesos, if the investment is made elsewhere in Mexico.

Investors in Securities.—An alien can obtain immigrant status if he or she agrees:

1. That he or she will invest capital in (a) Federal Government certificates, securities, or bonds; and (b) securities or stocks issued or guaranteed by national credit institutions or issued by decentralized or State-participating institutions. In each case, the stock referred to in (b) must be for financing basic activities for Mexico's economic development.

2. That the capital he or she invests in those securities will be sufficient to produce the minimum amount of income required for "rentista" (see below).

Recipients of Fixed Income.—An alien rentista or recipient of fixed income can gain immigration status upon submissioin of proof that he or she will receive regular income from abroad (from pensions, savings, bank accounts, or other income sources) equal to $300 monthly, plus $80 per month for each relative or dependent over 15 years of age whom he or she agrees to support in Mexico.

Professionals.—In the few instances where alien professionals are permitted to practice in Mexico, immigrant status is accorded.

Persons Assuming Positions of Trust.—An alien who is to assume an administrative position or other position of responsibility and trust in a company or institution in Mexico can obtain immigrant status when the employing company, institution, or individual requests it. The company or institution must show, however, that it has been operating in the country at least 2 years (except in the case of an industry considered essential), that it is legally established, and that its paid-up capital is not less than the minimum required for investors.

Technicians and Specialized Workers.—An alien technician or specialist who renders services that, in the Ministry's judgment, cannot be rendered by a Mexican resident can attain immigrant status when a company, institution, or individual operating in Mexico requests it and justifies the permanent need for the technician or specialist.

The technician or specialist is obligated to instruct at least three Mexicans in his or her specialty, except where the Ministry may require otherwise. Within 60 days of the time the foreign technician or specialist has assumed his or her position, the person requesting his or her entry must submit to the Ministry the names of the Mexicans who are to be instructed.

Language

Spanish, the official language, is spoken by most of the inhabitants, although about 1 million people speak only Indian dialects. Many Mexicans speak or understand English, especially in the larger cities and along the U.S.-Mexican border. Many firms are accustomed to carrying out business correspondence in English, but this ability should not be taken for granted. Catalogs and technical literature should be provided in careful translations. In the case of visits to Mexican Government offices, U.S. businesspeople who do not speak Spanish should be accompanied by an interpreter. If the visiting businessperson has already established relations with a Mexican firm, the services of a bilingual employee of the latter can often by obtained. If not, there are a number of persons in Mexico City offering this service.

Holidays

January 1 (New Year's Day), February 5 (Anniversary of Mexican Constitution), March 20 (Juarez' Birthday), April (Holy Thursday and Good Friday), May 1 (Labor Day), May 5 (Anniversary of the Battle of Puebla), September 1 (President's Annual State of the Union Address), September 16 (Anniversary of Proclamation of Mexican Independence), October 12 (Columbus Day), November 2 (All Souls), November 20 (Revolution Day), December 25 (Christmas).

U.S. holidays are not included in the schedule; they should be considered when appointments are made with U.S. Commercial Officers abroad.

Mexican Government employees are given vacations of a week to 10 days in May and approximately 2 weeks in December. While most offices leave a few employees on duty during these periods, it is almost impossible to transact any business.

Business Hours

Business offices in Mexico City are usually open from 9 a.m. to 6 p.m. Most still close for lunch, but it is increasingly common to stagger lunch hours to stay open throughout the day. Some firms have adopted the custom of remaining closed all day Saturday, although this is most common among Mexican affiliates of U.S. companies. Retail establishments customarily open at 10 a.m. and close at 7 p.m., without closing for lunch. Banks open at 9 a.m. and close to the public at 1 p.m. Government offices customarily open at 8:30 a.m. and close to the public at 2:30 p.m. for the rest of the day.

Time

Central Standard Time prevails throughout Mexico except in lower California where Pacific Standard Time is used, and in Sonora, Sinaloa, and Nayarit where Mountain Standard Time is used.

Electrical Current

Mexico has 115 volt, 60 cycle alternating current. Three-phase and single-phase 230 volt current is available.

Sources of Economic Information

Information about the Mexican market and tariffs and trade regulations may be obtained from the Office of Country Marketing, International Trade Administration, U.S. Department of Commerce, Washington, D.C. 20230, or from the Department's District Offices.

Mexican Government Representation

The Mexican Institute for Foreign Trade, an export promotion organization, has the following offices in the United States:

CHICAGO
Instituto Mexicano de Comercio Exterior
875 North Michigan Avenue, Suite 3737
Chicago, Illinois 60611
Telex: 266 70 06
Telex: 255 5172 COMLCONMEX CGO

DALLAS
Instituto Mexicano de Comercio Exterior
120 World Trade Center
2050 Stemmons Freeway
Dallas, Texas 75258
P.O. Box 58258
Tels: 742 8554 and 742 8374
Telex: 730537 IMCE DAL

LOS ANGELES
Instituto Mexicano de Comercio Exterior
The Equitable Building
3435 Wilshire Boulevard, Suite 2416
Los Angeles, California 90010
Tels: 388 2201
Telex: 67 4463 IMCE LSA

NEW YORK
Instituto Mexicano de Comercio Exterior
115 East 57th Street
Galleria Building, 4th Floor
New York, New York 10022
Tels: 371 3823
Telex: 12 7504 IMCEMEXICO NYK

The Mexican Government maintains an Embassy at 2829 16th Street, N.W., Washington, D.C. 20009.

The Trade and Fiscal Office of the Embassy is located at Suite 505, 1101 15th Street, N.W., Washington, D.C. 20005. Tel. (202) 785-3214.

Mexican consulates are located in many cities throughout the Untied States.

U.S. Representation in Mexico

The U.S. Foreign Commercial Service is represented at the United States Embassy,

Avenida de la Reforma 305, Mexico 5, D.F., tel: (905) 553-3333, Telex number 1775685, and an Export Development Office (formerly U.S. Trade Center) Liverpool 31, Mexico 6, D.F., Mexico, tel: (905) 591-0155. Telex number 1773471, answer back, USTCME.

Consulates in Mexico are:

American Consulate General
924 Av. Lopez Mateos
Ciudad Juarez, Chihuahua
Tel: 34048
Telex: 033-840

American Consulate General
Progreso 175
Guadalajara, Jalisco
Tel: 25029098; 25027-00
Telex: 068-2-860

American Consulate
Av. Primera 232
(Between Azucenas and Azaleas)
Matamoros, Tamaulipas
Tel: 252-50
Telex: 035-827

American Consulate
6 Circunvalacion No. 6
(At Venustiano Carranza)
Mazatlan, Sinaloa
Tel: 1-29-05
Telex: 066-883

American Consulate
Paseo Montejo 453
Merida, Yucatan
Tel: 7-70-78
Telex: 75885 AMCONME

American Consulate General
Av. Constitucion 411 Poniente
Monterrey, Nuevo Leon
Tel: 43-06-50
Telex: 038853

American Consulate
Avenida Allende 3330
Colonia Jardin
Nuevo Laredo, Tamps
Tel: 4-05-12, 4-06-18
Telex: 036-849

American Consulate General
Tapachula 96
Tijuana, Baja California
Tel: 386-1001

Foreign Service Officers are available to brief and assist American businesspeople visiting Mexico.

Business Organizations

Many trade and industry chambers and associations operate in Mexico. Some are confined to a single industry or product and others extend across industry and product lines. All except the smallest firms are required by law to belong to a chamber for their particular kind of business.

Chambers vary widely in the scope and efficiency of their services to members and in the efforts made to publicize among them the trade offers received from abroad. Some of the more active chambers publish directories listing the products of individual members. The larger chambers issue bulletins and magazines and in some cases answer specific questions from foreign inquirers.

The American Chamber of Commerce of Mexico, affiliated with Chamber of Commerce of the United States, located at Lucerna No. 78 in Mexico City, includes among its members Mexican firms doing business with the United States as well as U.S. firms in Mexico. It publishes a number of titles on a variety of business topics.

The United States-Mexico Chamber of Commerce which includes corporate members from both the United States and Mexico is interested in furthering trade between the countries. It has offices at 1800 K Street, N.W., Suite 410, Washington, D.C. 20006, and at Balderas 144-107, Mexico 1 D.F., Mexico.

The Mexico Chamber of Commerce of the United States, Inc., is located at 5 World Trade Center, Suite 6343, New York, New York 10048.

The principal Mexican business organizations in Mexico include the following (all located in Mexico City):

Confedration of National Chambers of
Commerce (Confederacion de Camaras
Nacionales de Comercio-Concanaco)
Balderas 144-2o. piso

Confederation of National Chambers of
Industry (Confederacion de Camaras In-
dustriales de Los Estados Unidos
Mexicanos-Concamin)
M.Ma. Contreras 133-8o. piso

National Chamber of Manufacturers (Camara
Nacional de la Industria de Trans
formacion)
Av. San Antonio 256, Piso 4

Importers and Exporters Association
Asociacion Nacional de Importadores y
Exportadores de la Republica Mexicana-
ANIERM)
Monterrey 130

Mexico City Chamber of Commerce
(Camara Nacional de Comercio de la
Ciudad de Mexico)
Paseo de la Reforma 42-1 er. 2o y 3 er. pisos

National Construction Industry Chamber
(Camara Nacional de la Industria de la Con-
struction)
Colima 254

National Electronics Industry Chamber
(Camara Nacional de la Industria Elec-
tronica y de Communicaciones Electricas)
Guanajuato 65

National Communications and Transportation Chamber (Camara Nacional de Transportes y Comunicaciones)
Turin 45 ler piso

National Paper Industries Chamber
(Camara Nacional de las Indutrias de Papel)
Lafayette 138

National Chamber of Graphic Arts (Camara
Nacional de la Industria de Artes Graficas)
Ave Rio Churubusco 428 4o piso

Radio and Television Industry Chamber
(Camara Nacional de la Industria de Radio
y Television)
Paseo da la Reforma 445 9o. piso

Textile Industry National Chamber
(Camara Nacional de la Industria Textil)
Rio Rhin 27-2o. 3er piso

National Advertising Association (Asociacion
Nacional de la Publicidad)
Jalapa 147

Mexican Automotive Industry Association
(Asociacion Mexicana de la Industria
Automotriz)
Ensendada 90 Piso 1

Iron and Steel Industry Chamber (Camara
Nacional de la Industria del Hierro y
del Acero)
Amores 338

National Association of Manufacturers of
Automotive Products (Asociacion Nacional
de Fabricantes de Productos Automotrices)
Paseo de la Reforma 369, Edif. 8-402

Chemical Industry National Association
(Ascociacion Nacional de la Industria
Quimica)
V. Suarez 13

Paint and Ink Manufacturers National
Association (Asociacion Nacional de
Fabricantes de Pinturas y Tintas)
Manzanas 44 Piso 1

National Plastic Industry Association
(Asociacion Nacional de Industrias del
Plastico)
Sullivan 199-402

Bibliography

For sale by the Superintendent of Documents,
U.S. Government Printing Office, Washington,
D.C. 20402.

Order No.		
OBR 79-13	*Investing in Mexico,* OBR 79-13,	$.80
FET 81-018	*Foreign Economic Trends and their Implications for the United States—Mexico*	$.50
		$.50
	Background Notes— Mexico, April 1981, Department of State Publication 7865	$.50
	Area Handbook on Mexico, Department of Army Publication 550-79	$7.45

The following reports are available for $10
each from the National Technical Information
Service (NTIS), U.S. Department of Commerce,
Springfield, Virginia 22161, Tel: (703) 487-4600.
Rush service guarantees same day special
delivery certified mailing for an additional $10.
The rush service fee if publication is picked up is
$6. Telephone (703) 487-4700. Purchaser's
deposit account will be billed or several charge
accounts are accepted.

The market surveys (The Mexican Market
for. . . .) listed below are based on research
supplied by private Mexican market research
firms under contract to ITA or by commercial
officers at the American Embassy or the U S.
Export Development Center in Mexico City.

Order No.

DIB 78-10-504	*Motor Vehicle Maintenance Equipment*, 68p.
DIB 80-02-508	*Dictation and Word Processing Equipment*, 72p.
DIB 78-10-006	*Pemex Petrochemical Projects*, 5p.
DIB 79-05-507	*Computers & Related Equipment*, 105p.
DIB 78-03-514	*Product Machinery, Test Instruments & Special Materials for Electric Components*, 104p.
DIB 79-11-005	*Electronic Components*, 15p.
DIB 79-10-002	*Fishing Industry*, 12p.
DIB 80-07-017	*Fishery Developments*, 46p.
DIB 80-08-506	*Commercial Fishing Equipment*, 162p.
DIB 80-08-505	*Food Processing & Packaging Equipment*, 166p.
DIB 78-06-502	*Forestry & Sawmill Machinery*, 35p.
DIB 80-03-505	*Graphic Industries Equipment*, 149p.
DIB 80-02-507	*Industrial Process Controls*, 85p.
DIB 80-07-508	*Laboratory Instruments*, 41p.
DIB 78-08-502	*Machine Tools & Related Equipment*, 220p.
DIB 78-03-508	*Industrial Instruments*, 79p.
DIB 78-06-501	*Ceramics & Glass Manufacturing Equipment*, 58p.
DIB 78-12-500	*General Industrial Products*, 201p.
DIB 79-06-500	*Heavy Construction & Mining Equipment*, 148p.
DIB 80-04-504	*Plastics & Rubber Products Equipment*, 67p.
DIB 80-04-003	*Air & Water Purification & Pollution Control Eq.*, 15p.
DIB 78-03-512	*Communications Equipment*, 114p.
DIB 80-08-504	*Communications Equipment*, 123p.
DIB 78-11-508	*Furniture Manufacture and Woodworking Eq.*, 71p.
DIB 80-09-008	*Woodworking Equipment*, 10p.

Country Market Surveys summarizing the detailed studies are available as listed below for 50 cents each from Publications Distribution, Room 1617, U.S. Department of Commerce, Washington, D.C. 20230.

CMS 79-004	*Medical Equipment in Mexico*, February 1979
CMS 79-011	*Electronic Components in Mexico*, March 1979
CMS 79-920	*Textiles in Mexico*, December 1979
CMS 80-005	*Graphic Industries Equipment*, September 1980
CMS 80-210	*Industrial Process Controls*, September 1980

Also available from NTIS are Industrial Outlook Reports:

DIB 81-03-088	*Iron & Steel Industry—Mexico*, Nov. 5, 1980.
DIB 81-03-091	*Power Equipment—Mexico*, Nov. 24, 1980.
DIB 81-03-104	*Minerals—Mexico*, May 31, 1979

Other titles available at NTIS include:

DIB 81-03-100	*Law to Promote Mexican Investment and to Regulate Foreign Investment*, March 9, 1973.
DIB 81-03-103	*Law on the Registration of the Transfer of Technology and the Use and Exploitation of Patents and Trademarks*, January 11, 1973.
DIB 81-03-102	*Commercial Reporting—Best Prospects FY 1982, Mexico*, September 24, 1979.
DIB 81-03-101	*Living Conditions in Mexico*, March 1980.
DIB 81-03-099	*Directory of Business Services*, January 1979.

Tax and Accounting

Business Study—Mexico, Touche Ross International, 1633 Broadway, New York, N.Y. 10019 —Dec. 1979. Free

Doing Business in Mexico, Price Waterhouse and Company, 1251 Avenue of the Americas, New York, N.Y. 10020. Free upon written request.

Mexico, Ernst & Ernst International, series 1979, Free from E & E offices in major cities.

Taxation in Mexico, International Tax and Business Service, Deloite Haskings & Sells, 1114 Avenue of the Americas, New York, N.Y. 10036. Free.

Company Formation in Mexico, Alexander C. Hoagland Jr., Lloyds Bank International, Ltd. London, England, 1980.

Doing Business in Mexico (2 volumes) Edited by S. Theodore and Anne E. Reiner; Matthew Bender, 235 E. 45th Street, New York, N.Y. 10017, $150.

Listings of American Companies

American Firms, Subsidiaries & Affiliates in Mexico, Uniworld Business Publications, Inc.,

Suite 805, 50 E. 42nd Street, New York, N.Y. 10017. $9 plus 75 cents postage.

In Bond Industry

Mexico In Bond Industry 1980, Instituto Mexicano de Comercio Exterior, Alfonso Reyes No. 30, Mexico 11, D.F.—a "how to do it-" manual. Free.

Annual Reports on the Economy

Analysis 80, The Mexican Economy, Publicaciones Ejecutivas de Mexico S.A., Homero 136, Mexico 5, D.F. Annual, available in March. Obtainable from firms in Mexico who advertise in it.

Mexican Markets in Action, Editorial Marynka, S.A. Sinaloa 9-503. Annual $45.

Tips for the Newly Assigned to Mexico

Update: Mexico, Moran, Stahl & Boyer, Inc., 355 Lexington Avenue, New York, N.Y. 10017, December 1979.

Business Developments

Business Latin America, Business International Corporation, One Dag Hammarskjold Plaza, New York, N.Y. 10017. Weekly.

Business Trends, Publicaciones Ejecutivas de Mexico, S.A. Homero 136, Mexico, 5 D.F. foreign subscription $200.00, single copy $8.00 Weekly.

Comercio Exterior de Mexico, Banco Nacional de Comercio Exterior, Av. Chapultepec 230, 2 piso, Mexico 7 D.F. monthly.

The American Chamber of Commerce of Mexico A.C., Lucerna No. 78 Mexico 6 D.F., includes among its members Mexican firms doing business with the United States as well as U.S. firms in Mexico. Its publications are available through the mail with a $4 charge to cover postage and handling.

Business Mexico (1978) Articles on 40 key areas of business interest by recognized authorities. $45.

Directory of Members of the American Chamber of Commerce of Mexico (annual). $42.

Energy Mexico. Details on Mexico's power sources with statistical tables. 1980. $35.

Agribusiness Manual. Listing of products and services offered in the agribusiness sector. 1980. Price to be announced.

Directory of American Companies Operating in Mexico. Name and addresses of U.S. companies and product category. Biannual. 1980. Edition $90.00.

Survey of Salaries and Benefits in Mexico—Executive Level. Analysis of 30 top executive position salary and fringe benefit levels. Annual $180.

Survey of Salaries and Benefits in Mexico—Salaried Employee Level. Detailed coverage for 60 job categories. Annual $180.

Summary Tables of Mexican Labor Negotiations. Results of labor contract negotiations in real and percentage terms. Biannual $100.

Family Expenditure Survey, Mexico City. Budget for goods and services including price averages and ranges for food, rent, transportation, education, etc. Biannual $115.

Industrial Location in Mexico. Details on each of Mexico's States to help in relocating in less developed zones of the country. Includes decentralization and regional development incentives. 1980. $60.

Noticias. Specialized monthly, includes new trade opportunities in Spanish only.

Mexican-American Review. The Chamber's official monthly. Subscription $20, $2.00 for single copy.

Quarterly Economic Report Analyzes timely issues. $18.

The Organization of American States, 17th and Constitution Avenue, N.W., Washington, D.C. 20006 publishes *Statements of the Laws of Mexico in Matters Affecting Business*, cost $10. Other titles cover aspects of Mexico's history and culture.

1569

Market Profile—MEXICO

Foreign Trade

Imports.—1980, $18.5 billion; 1979, $12.1 billion; U.S. share, 1980 65.4 percent. Major suppliers: Japan, 5.3 percent; West Germany, 5.2 percent; France, 2.2 percent; Brazil and the United Kingdom, 2.4 percent each. Major imports: industrial machinery, organic chemicals, iron and steel products, automotive parts, and electrical machinery.

Exports.—1980, $15.3 billion; 1979, $8.9 billion; U.S. share, 1980, 61.8 percent; Spain, 6.9 percent; Japan, 3.6 percent; and Netherlands Antilles 3.6 percent. Major exports: crude oil, coffee, chemicals, cotton, machinery, transport equipment, and shrimp.

Trade Policy.—Protection of local industry through tariff and import permit restrictions on competing products. Export promotion, rationalization, and diversification of industrial base now has priority over import substitution. Mexico is not a member of GATT. As a member of LAIA, Mexico grants concessions to other members.

Trade Prospects.—Equipment for the petroleum, construction, mining, communications, electrical power, agricultural and metal working sectors are current best prospects. Consumer goods imports discouraged.

Foreign Investment

Direct U.S. investment at end of 1979 estimated at $4.57 billion, of which $3.42 billion was in manufacturing and divided as follows (in million): chemicals and related, $915; machinery, $649; food products, $281; transportation equipment, $510; primary and fabricated metals, $288; and other, $775. Investment in other sectors (in millions): trade, $696; finance and insurance, $136; and mining and petroleum, $113. Book value of foreign investment in Mexico as of the end of 1979 is estimated at $6.8 billion, with the United States having about 69.8 percent; Germany, 6 percent; Japan, 5 percent; United Kingdom, 4.5 percent; Switzerland, 4.5 percent. In 1978, there were 4,854 companies with foreign equity.

Investment Policy.—Foreign investment, welcome in most fields when it provides significant new employment and new technology, increases exports, substitutes for imports, or aids regional development. Majority Mexican ownership requred for new investment except for rare exceptions.

Finance

Currency.—The peso has no fixed exchange rate. Over the past 3 years it has held steady between 22 and 23 pesos to US$1. In December 1980, it was traded at 23.25 to US$1. No exchange control. Currency in circulation including checking accounts was 345.9 billion pesos in December 1979.

Domestic Credit and Investment Fund Sources.—The Bank of Mexico sets policy and regulates the commercial banking system. New foreign deposit banks are not permitted.

National Budget.—For 1980, the Federal budget totaled $73 billion, evenly divided between decentralized agencies, government corporations, and the executive branch secretariats. The budget deficit in 1978 was $2.7 billion.

Balance of Payments.—The current account for 1980 was in deficit by $6.5 billion compared to a deficit of $4.2 billion in 1979. The deficits were offset by capital inflows, largely loans, with 1980 recording a surplus of $8.5 billion compared to $222 million in 1978. The Bank of Mexico's foreign exchange reserves as of December 1980 were $4 billion.

Foreign Aid.—At year end 1980, World Bank loans authorized total $4.8 billion of which $681 million has been repaid. Interamerican Development Bank loans as of the end of 1980 totalled $2.7 billion with $406 million repaid.

Economy

Economic Growth.—Mexico has had uninterrupted economic growth since 1934. Growth in the postwar years averaged about 6 percent in real terms.

GDP.—In 1980, the economy grew at the rate of 7.4 percent in real terms with GDP reaching $166 billion in 1980 in current prices.

Agriculture.—Mexico produces a wide range of temperate and tropical products, but has to import increasing amounts of basic foodstuffs.

Industry.—Growing in almost every field, with manufacturing accounting for 23.8 percent of GDP in 1978.

Commerce.—Accounted for 29.3 percent of GDP in 1978. Distribution patterns are changing with increasing trend toward shopping centers and discount stores in large cities.

Basic Economic Facilities

Transportation.—The nation's highways, ports, and railways are inadequate to serve the needs of a rapidly growing population and economy. They are the targets of increasing government investment. The airlines provide good national coverage.

Communications.—National and international telegraph and telephone service is government-operated.

Power.—Public service is government-owned. Installed capacity at the end of 1978 was 13,700 megawatts and power generated during 1978 was 55,203 million kWh, about 69 percent hydrocarbon based. Mexico has chronic power shortages, but the Government is making heavy investments to increase capacity.

Natural Resources

Land.—761,000 square miles, approximately a quarter as large as the United States; about 15 percent is arable.

Climate.—Temperature ranges with altitude from cool (53-63°F) to hot (77-94°F). Mexico City cool at night, warm during day. Generally insufficient rainfall except in coastal areas.

Minerals.—1978 production in thousands of metric tons: iron ore 3,492; sulphur 1,762; lead 170; copper 6; zinc 240; silver, in tons, 1,567. Petroleum production reached 1.8 million barrels per day at the end of 1979.

Marketing in Morocco

Contents

Report Revised December 1979

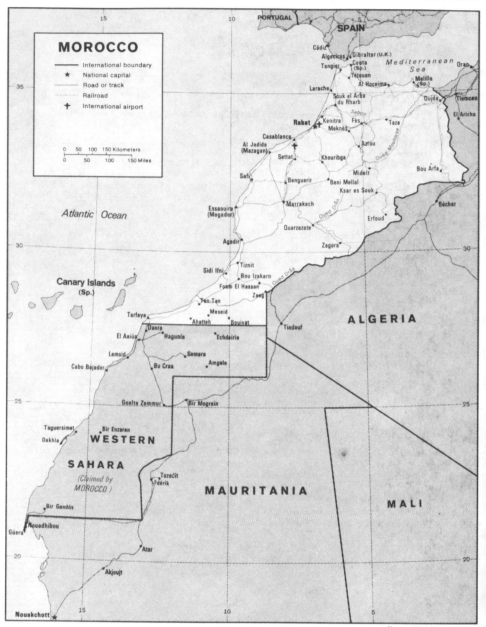

Foreign Trade Outlook

Introduction

For American exporters, Morocco offers a $3 billion market for a variety of capital and consumer goods. In 1978, Morocco's gross domestic product reached $11 billion ($742 per capita) and imports from the United States exceeded $400 million. Given the country's immense reserves of phosphate rock (about 65 percent of the world's total) and its potential for greatly increased agricultural output, the long-term outlook for the Moroccan economy is favorable.

Morocco operates a mixed economic system with both the public and private sectors playing important roles. Certain activities, such as phosphate production and utilities, are state controlled. Private enterprise in the commercial and industrial sector is encouraged, except where the resources of the state are required to initiate and develop capital-intensive projects considered essential to the economy.

The key factors affecting Morocco's economic development are workers' remittances, exports of phosphate rock, agricultural production, tourism, and light manufacturing. The country's Fifth Five-Year Development Plan (1968–72) concentrated on agricultural and irrigation projects. Over the period, the economy achieved an average annual rate of growth in gross domestic product of 5.6 percent in real terms. During the Sixth Development Plan (1973–77), emphasis shifted to industrial expansion and the Government became an increasingly important source of fixed capital investment. The economy grew at an overall rate of 6.8 percent in real terms, somewhat below the targeted 7.5 percent.

Various factors, including a softening of the world demand for phosphates, the country's major earner of foreign exchange, poor harvests and hostilities in the Western Sahara, led to a serious economic downturn in 1977 which is expected to continue through 1980. As a consequence, the 1978–82 Development Plan was replaced by an interim plan which envisages more moderate growth rates over a 3-year period (1978–80) of transition and consolidation.

Direction of Trade

The European Economic Community (EEC) as a whole is Morocco's main trading partner, France being the leading country (as shown on table 3). The EEC's dominant share of imports and exports, which has not changed perceptibly in recent years, is explained by EEC tariff concessions on most major Moroccan exports and by geographic and historic links with France. Aside from EEC countries, major Moroccan trading partners include the United States, Spain and

---

**HOW TO OBTAIN
BACKGROUND INFORMATION
ABOUT THESE COUNTRIES**

Keeping this book within reasonable size limits has made it necessary to focus on material *directly* concerned with marketing and commerce, and set aside materials only indirectly related. The editors relize, however, that *general* data about a country are also vital to a company's preparations to enter a foreign market, and make a very definite recommendation as to how such expanded information needs can be served.

For those who wish *general* data about a country—data which goes beyond marketing and commerce—the editors recommend *Countries of the World and Their Leaders*, published as an annually updated yearbook by Gale Research Company, Detroit, Michigan 48226. Containing 4- to 20-page entries on 168 countries, the volume also provides several hundred pages of supplementary world data. Each country entry is prepared by the U.S. Department of State to provide a general briefing on the geography, people, culture, and political situation of the particular country. Each report provides some historical insight as well as a look at contemporary trends of lifestyle in the country. Reports also discuss a country's educational system, its press, ethnic groupings and religious practices.

Countries of the World and Their Leaders provides a fresh listing of cabinet ministers of each nation. In addition it lists health conditions the traveling businessman will wish to prepare for and includes information on passport procedures, customs and duties, and world climate conditions.

MOROCCO

Table 1.—Market Shares by Country
(Percentage of Total)

Country Sources of Moroccan Imports	1974	1975	1976	1977
France	27.5	30.2	29.2	27.3
West Germany	10.2	7.9	8.1	6.7
Benelux	5.4	5.9	4.5	5.8
Italy	4.2	3.9	5.6	7.0
United Kingdom	2.7	3.3	4.1	3.5
Other EC	0.8	0.6	0.5	0.7
EC Subtotal	50.8	51.8	52.0	51.0
United States	9.0	7.6	8.6	6.3
Spain	4.1	4.4	6.3	8.6
Iraq	3.1	5.4	5.1	4.9
U.S.S.R.	3.0	2.9	2.6	2.6
Others	30.0	27.9	25.4	26.6
Total	100.0	100.0	100.0	100.0
Markets for Moroccan Exports				
France	22.9	21.7	23.7	24.7
West Germany	7.3	6.5	9.6	10.5
Benelux	9.1	10.3	9.9	9.3
Italy	7.4	7.5	7.3	6.1
United Kingdom	6.0	6.7	5.8	4.3
Other EC	2.0	1.4	0.9	1.1
EC Subtotal	54.7	54.1	57.2	56.0
United States	1.1	0.7	1.1	2.0
Spain	5.5	5.3	5.4	7.5
Poland	5.1	7.0	4.7	2.0
U.S.S.R.	1.8	3.0	4.3	3.9
Others	31.8	29.9	27.3	28.6
Totals	100.0	100.0	100.0	100.0

Source: *Statistiques des Echanges Extérieurs du Maroc*—1974-77

Table 2.—Major Moroccan Imports 1975-77
(In thousands of U.S. dollars)

Commodity	1975	1976	1977
Foodstuffs, beverages, tobacco	619,947	440,523	462,703
Bread wheat	229,404	161,145	139,724
Sugar	232,156	135,412	121,423
Tea	24,970	20,496	102,757
Fuels and lubricants	267,818	289,281	397,315
Crude oil	214,386	234,259	295,382
Gas oil and fuel oil	20,364	20,513	49,677
Other hydrocarbons	12,271	14,852	26,651
Raw materials of animal or vegetable origin	212,989	192,905	276,264
Raw vegetable oil	97,790	49,234	82,084
Rough and sawn lumber	41,813	54,634	79,948
Raw materials of mineral origin	24,999	192,039	276,264
Synthetic textile fibers	11,142	15,618	17,189
Semimanufactures	479,235	525,319	705,396
Chemical products	68,454	58,717	78,946
Fertilizers, natural and chemical	41,776	20,541	19,228
Cement	9,065	25,852	48,248
Plastic materials	39,973	44,370	55,662
Paper and carbons	23,898	30,740	13,247
Synthetic textile fiber thread	33,246	40,161	43,264
Iron bars	69,301	86,054	109,322
Iron and steel sheets	41,917	48,136	66,025
Agricultural equipment	34,041	24,470	41,403
Agricultural tractors	18,667	13,298	21,121
Industrial equipment	722,884	740,210	1,141,609
Machine tools	65,003	81,004	110,115
Piston motors	33,509	38,562	23,074
Pumps and compressors	18,626	18,030	25,532
Food processing machinery	12,410	23,259	12,836
Crushing, conveying machinery	21,322	25,563	59,934
Textile machinery	23,839	34,913	26,621
Railway rolling stock	20,207	31,095	33,801
Mining equipment	17,767	24,878	59,382
Ships	46,230	74,214	21,145
Consumer goods	267,631	294,479	321,467
Medicines	16,488	18,443	26,131
Finished paper and paper products	14,158	13,890	19,178
Plastic articles	6,008	6,463	9,047
Household goods	7,767	9,405	13,798
Stoves and heaters	3,667	5,118	6,035
Radios and TV receivers	16,488	23,767	29,332
Automobiles	65,603	63,459	70,653
Automobile parts	44,416	49,780	16,112
Bicycles and motorcycles	14,032	12,111	15,773
Totals	2,484,096	2,565,118	3,427,544

Sources: Ministére des Finances, Office des Changes: *Statistiques du Commerce Extérieur; Statistiques des Echanges Extérieurs du Maroc.*

[1] One U.S. dollar = Moroccan dirham 4.18 in 1975, 4.48 in 1976, and 4.32 in 1977.

the Soviet Union. Iraq is the country's major supplier of crude oil. Poland is an important market for phosphate rock.

U.S. exports to Morocco have grown dramatically in recent years, rising from $199 million in 1975 to $406 million in 1978. Wheat and wheat flour are the main U.S. exports, followed by soybean oil, cigarettes, raw cotton, animal fats and oils, aircraft, construction and mining machinery, and trucks. Although the United States is Morocco's second largest supplier after France, Moroccan exports to the United States traditionally have been quite limited. Major U.S. purchases from Morocco include vegetables, phosphate rock, manganese ore, molasses, cotton fabrics, carpets, footwear, and leather goods and wool products.

Best Prospects for U.S. Exports

In July 1978 the Moroccan Government, faced with an increasing shortage of foreign exchange and heavy debt obligations, adopted a program of austerity that entailed lower development spending and restrictions on many imports, either through prohibitions or licensing. Despite these measures, development activities in the priority sectors—agriculture, mining,

tourism—are generating a demand for the types of equipment listed below.

Agricultural Equipment.—Agriculture has traditionally been Morocco's most important economic sector, employing about 60 percent of the labor force. About 34 percent of Morocco's agricultural land—held by 3 percent of the farming population—is utilized in large-scale operations. These modernized agribusiness operations produce over 85 percent of the commercial agricultural production, including almost all citrus products, fresh vegetables, wine, and other export crops. With programs seeking to overcome seasonal demand fluctuations and facilitate

Table 3.—*Major Moroccan Exports 1975-77*
(In thousands of U.S. dollars)[1]

Commodity	1975	1976	1977
Foodstuffs, Beverages, Tobacco	348,046	401,552	393,967
Tomatoes	41,257	28,343	26,503
Citrus fruit	97,135	132,373	142,179
Canned fish	40,939	52,584	52,902
Fuel and Lubricants	13,694	17,490	21,170
Raw Materials of Animal or vegetable Origin	57,898	62,222	52,350
Raw and refined olive oil	22,430	14,667	14,774
Wood pulp	11,550	14,469	10,541
Raw Materials of Mineral Origin	880,955	553,942	582,026
Calcium phosphates	819,876	488,568	487,665
Lead ore	15,575	14,599	35,797
Manganese ore	8,724	9,020	12,276
Semimanufactures	60,254	66,261	130,172
Natural and chemical fertilizers	25,239	16,335	25,159
Phosphoric acid		14,826	51,672
Industrial Equipment	10,586	4,572	6,967
Consumer Goods	144,263	148,004	166,904
Carpets and rugs	34,397	36,866	48,271
Clothing	23,796	35,482	43,480
Fabrics of synthetic and artifical fibers	3,916	3,755	3,988
Articles of leather and travel goods	7,461	8,529	8,307
Totals	1,490,802	1,244,187	1,353,569

[1] One U.S. dollar = Moroccan dirham 4.18 in 1975, 4.48 in 1976, and 4.32 in 1977.
Source: Ministére des Finances, Office des Changes *Statistiques du Commerce Extérieur, Statistiques des Echanges Extérieurs du Maroc.*

Table 4.—*Moroccan Trade with the United States, 1976-77*
(In thousands of U.S. dollars)

Commodity	1976	1977
U.S. Exports to Morocco		
Wheat, unmilled	79,739	33,557
Wheat flour	6,373	6,844
Malt	2,988	1,273
Cigarettes	3,851	6,511
Soybeans	3,932	9,407
Raw cotton	1,549	3,706
Animal fats and oils	3,511	4,216
Peanut oil	2,522	410
Soybean oil	2,687	8,167
Tractors	2,940	2,533
Construction and Mining Machinery	10,299	31,655
Heating and Cooling Machinery	492	5,300
Pumps, centrifuges	1,115	4,407
Machine handling machinery and equipment	2,173	6,968
Electric power machinery and parts	801	2,177
Telecommunications equipment	7,578	4,371
Passenger cars	5,331	6,499
Passenger car parts	7,883	5,361
Aircraft	45,018	25,909
Aircraft parts	7,507	9,213
Railway locomotives	2,147	
Special category	46,151	159,178
Totals	296,431	371,303
U.S. Imports from Morocco		
Vegetables, fresh, dried, preserved	1,193	2,554
Spices	746	726
Phosphates	616	4,215
Crude mineral substances	3,106	2,351
Manganese ores and concentrates	1,545	2,351
Lead	861	561
Travel goods, handbags, personal goods	1,853	1,803
Clothing	1,083	629
Carpets	389	514
Totals	16,471	21,840

Source: Bureau of the Census, U.S. Department of Commerce.

export diversification, the government is stressing development of food storage and packaging, deep freezing and growth of vegetables under cover.

U.S. firms able to provide technical and managerial expertise in these areas should find attractive opportunities. Items of interest to U.S. manufacturers in the agricultural field are sugar machinery, dairies, tractors, harvesting combine machinery, and packaging machinery and raw materials for packaging.

Moroccan imports of agricultural equipment totaled $37 million in 1978, with U.S. exports in that field at $1 million. The major competition for U.S. exporters in this area comes from France, Italy, Spain, and West Germany.

Irrigation Equipment.—Despite the application of modern agricultural technology to help cultivate the most promising export products, Moroccan agriculture remains dependent on the often extreme variations in rainfall. As a consequence, irrigation is a high priority of the Moroccan Government. By the end of this century, the Government projects that one million hectares will be irrigated.

A number of dams have been completed and others are planned or under construction. There also is strong demand for irrigation systems to distribute the water. U.S. firms marketing sprinkler systems, especially mobile ones, will find promising opportunities in Morocco.

U.S. firms that produce water desalination systems and equipment should find Moroccan Government interest keen. Desalination projects for some coastal cities in the southern provinces of Morocco and the former Spanish Sahara are either underway or projected by the Ministry of Water Supply (Office National de l'Eau Potable) in Rabat. A small water desalination plant has been built at Boujdour, and two mobile water treatment facilities are operating at El Ayoun and Smara.

Moroccan imports of irrigation equipment in 1978 totaled $27 million, while U.S. sales were $2.3 million or 8.5 percent of that market. Other major suppliers of irrigation equipment were France, Great Britain, Italy, and West Germany.

Mining Equipment.—Morocco's economic planners have based their economic development strategy primarily on rapid industrialization, a major element of which is the exploitation and in-country processing of its potentially vast mineral wealth. In terms of current production, export revenues, estimated reserves and projected utilization, phosphates are Morocco's most important mineral resource. With 65 percent of the world's proven deposits of phosphate rock, Morocco is the world's largest exporter of phosphates and presently the third largest producer, after the United States and the Soviet Union. Over the long term, Morocco's economic planners hope to stimulate economic development as a consequence of achieving a predominant role in the international phosphate market.

Production of other mineral resources, including coal, iron ore, lead, zinc, cobalt and copper will require continuing imports of capital equipment. American products are well received in heavy mining equipment, and the U.S. reputation for durability and quality has proven more important than price. Although the U.S. market share is already substantial, favorable opportunities exist for U.S. firms in this key sector. Small and medium-sized processing equipment, such as trucks, drilling machines, conveyor belts, are of special interest to Moroccan firms, but in this area the United States faces price competition from European and Japanese suppliers.

Total Moroccan imports of mining equipment grew from $24.9 million in 1976 to $60 million in 1978, an increase of 141 percent. U.S. sales of mining equipment reached $17 million in 1978, totaling 28 percent of the market. Other major suppliers of such equipment are France and West Germany.

Aviation and Avionics Equipment.—Due to an unexpectedly strong demand for its services, Royal Air Maroc has dramatically increased its fleet of aircraft. In April 1979, the fleet included three Boeing 707s, seven Boeing 727s, three Boeing 737s and one Boeing 747.

In addition to its international activities, the Government of Morocco is increasing and improving air transport facilities to upgrade its inland transport systems. Its 10 international airports are being equipped with up-to-date equipment, and numerous smaller airports used exclusively for internal flights will be equipped with navigational equipment.

In this field, U.S. manufacturers are in an excellent position, owing to the technical qualities of their products, despite price competition from other nations producing aircraft, avionics, and parts. Moroccan imports in this category totaled $53 million in 1978. U.S. sales of aviation and avionics equipment in 1978 were $49.9 million or 94 percent of the Moroccan market. Other suppliers in this area include Great Britain, West Germany, and France.

Railway Equipment.—The Government of Morocco continues to increase and modernize its fleet of railway cars, locomotives, lines, trucks, and other products in this area, offering possibilities for sales by U.S. firms. The Budd Company of Troy, Michigan, recently received a contract for six self-propelled diesel cars. Projected large industrial projects such as the long-term development of the Meskala phosphate deposit, Jorf Lasfar petrochemical complex, and Nador steel complex are expected to greatly increase the need for railroad equipment and an expansion of lines. In addition, an engineering study is in progress for a proposed railway link between Marrakech and El Ayoun. A U.S. firm, Parsons-Brinkerhoff-Centec, in cooperation with other foreign firms, is conducting this study.

The United States exported $70,000 of railway equipment to Morocco in 1978, or 0.8 percent of the total market. Other major suppliers are France, Belgium, and West Germany.

Industry Trends

GDP Movement

The Moroccan economy grew at a rapid rate during 1974–77, averaging 6.8 percent annually. This growth was largely the result of a sharp and sustained increase in public investment, which led to an average annual growth rate of 9.6 percent in the industrial sector. The most rapid expansion was experienced in construction and public works, which averaged 27.7 percent annually. Movement in the agricultural sector in 1974–77 averaged a declined 0.9 percent annually and was characterized by marked fluctuations in output. The services sector grew at an average annual rate of 6.6 percent while government services, largely due to annual increases in personnel, grew 12.2 percent.

The disparity between the sectoral growth rates led to major changes in the structure of the Moroccan economy during 1974–77. The share of agriculture in the GDP, which in 1974 amounted to 24.9 percent, declined to 17.5 percent in 1977. This development was accompanied by the rising importance of the industrial sector which, due entirely to rapid growth in construction and public works, increased from 26.7 percent of GDP in 1974 to 30.4 percent in 1977. The share of the services sector increased only marginally to 37.7 percent in 1977. The marked expansion of government services, however, led to an increase in the public sector's share of GDP from 12.1 percent to 14.4 percent.

Development Planning

Given the country's mixed economy, Moroccan development plans have largely been efforts to coordinate government and private investments into a single national program for economic development.

The Sixth Development Plan, covering the 1973–77 period, emphasized industrial expansion, employment maximization, and redistribution of wealth. New programs included redistribution of land, increased spending on social services and low-cost housing, and programs for the poor in underdeveloped rural areas. In late 1974 and in 1975, a five-fold increase in phosphate revenues led the Government to revise the initial target for public and semipublic investments upward from $2.8 billion to $5.9 billion. New development allocations were focused on industry, agriculture, and defense. However, due to a lack of growth in the agricultural sector as well as stagnation in the world phosphate market, the economy grew at an overall annual rate of 6.8 percent in real terms—somewhat short of the targeted 7.5 percent.

In mid-1978, the Seventh Five-Year Development Plan (covering 1978–82) was replaced by a more modest, transitional 3-year program designed to conserve foreign exchange. Investment allocations during the 1978–80 Plan (not published in its entirety) are to be directed toward export-generating and import-substituting industries, with greater stress placed on the expansion of labor-intensive industries.

Total investment during 1978–80 will reportedly amount to $9.4 billion, with $1.7 billion allocated to housing, $1.5 billion for industry, and $1.5 billion for rural development. Large capital projects likely to receive high priorities include an additional phosphate rock production site at Sidi Hajjaj, a new phosphate acid plant at Safi, an extension of the oil refinery at Mohammedia, infrastructure for a integrated chemical complex and industrial port to be built at Jorf Lasfar,

continued expansion of Atlantic ports, and additional irrigated land development.

Growth Sectors

Agriculture

Agriculture has traditionally been Morocco's most important economic sector, employing 60 percent of the labor force. Agriculture supplies one-third of domestic food requirements and about 40 percent of the country's total merchandise exports. Although the most important goal in this area is to achieve and maintain agricultural self-sufficiency, the sector has become increasingly export-oriented as well. The Office de Commercialisation et d'Exportation (OCE), at 45 Avenue de l'Armée Royale in Casablanca, holds export monopolies for fruits, vegetables, wine, olive oil, cotton, and canned fish. It is responsible for coordinating and directing export promotion by seeking new markets and encouraging development of export-oriented agricultural products.

The country's agricultural sector is one of contrasts: on the one side, there exists a system of modern agriculture inherited from the Europeans with an emphasis on cash and export crops; on the other, there exists a traditional, small-scale subsistence agriculture involving the bulk of the farm population. Despite attempts to distribute the land, large farms of 20 hectares or more which accounted for 34 percent of all agricultural land in 1977 were held by only 3 percent of the farmers. These modernized agribusiness operations contribute 25 percent of all crops by value and over 85 percent of commercial agricultural production.

Cereals are planted on about 80 percent of the arable land. The main cereal crops—barley, hard wheat, and corn—provide the stable diet of the country. Small quantities of sorghum, millet, and oats also are raised, and in recent years sufficient rice has been grown in irrigated areas to meet the small local demand. The largest percentage of cereal production is consumed by the farm family itself or is sold in local markets. There are more than 8,000 small flour mills in the countryside grinding grain for local use.

Wheat is generally planted north of the Atlas mountain ranges where the annual rainfall is more than 10 inches annually. Major wheat growing areas include the Fez, Meknes, and Chaouida, as well as the Rharb and Tadla plains.

In 1978 Moroccan grain production totaled 4.7 million tons; bread and durum wheat production, at 1.9 million tons, was marginally above the 1970–77 average. Morocco is traditionally Africa's largest producer of wheat.

Other important crops are citrus, pulses, grapes, vegetables, sugar beets, cotton, oilseeds, and nuts. Citrus fruits have been cultivated for centuries in Morocco, but only since the 1920s have these been raised commercially for export. By the late 1970s, the citrus industry provided employment for about 50,000 Moroccans and has become the country's largest single export earner after top-ranking phosphate rock. To increase the production of citrus, old citrus orchards are now being replanted under a new government program. Also, a project to improve the varieties of citrus fruit through grafting is yielding encouraging results.

Despite success in raising citrus production in recent years, exports of citrus products have run into marketing difficulties in Europe. On January 1, 1979, Morocco lost its preferential access to the French market it had enjoyed for its citrus exports under the 1976 Association Agreement with the European Economic community (EEC). Morocco also faces keen competition from other Mediterranean suppliers, which will grow with the future enlargement of the EEC to include citrus-producing Spain and Greece. Attempts by the Moroccan Government to divert their citrus exports away from Western Europe have met with some success. In early 1978, a 10-year contract was signed with the Soviet Union for annual citrus deliveries of 190,000 tons.

Truck gardening is carried out close to the large cities, particularly near Casablanca. About 8,000 commercial vegetable farms with intensive use of irrigated land produce high yields and provide employment for thousands of persons. Some of the vegetables, especially tomatoes and potatoes, are raised as early vegetables for export to Western Europe, where they have a 2- or 3-week harvest edge on production in southern Spain, France, and Italy. Morocco produces about 1 percent of all the vegetables in the world and accounts for 10 percent of world vegetable exports.

Prominent among the difficulties facing agricultural growth in Morocco is a lack of water and the year-to-year unpredictability of rainfall. To increase production of high-yielding export and food crops, the area under irrigation has been greatly expanded in recent years. By 1977, about 480,000 hectares, or approximately 10 percent of the total cultivated land area, had been brought under cultivation. A national goal has recently been set to bring one million hectares under irrigation by the end of the century. To help achieve this target, nine dams will be completed and four new ones begun under the 1978–80 interm development plan. The plan also provides for an additional 46,000 hectares that will be irrigated with sprinklers, of which 21,210 hectares will be installed in 1979 and 24,869 in 1980.

Livestock raising, which is estimated to account for about one-third of total agricultural production by value, is primarily carried out on crop stubble after harvests or on marginal pastureland. Future development of the livestock sector in Morocco is limited largely by inadequate feed supplies and insufficient water. Little feed for livestock is raised or stored and, in years of very low rainfall, the livestock population is subject to abrupt losses. Sheep and goats are the main sources of meat and milk. Cattle are raised more for their dairy produce than meat. A number of measures are being taken to improve dairy herds, since less than half of milk consumption in Morocco is met by domestic production.

Energy

Morocco consumes more energy than it produces, and the deficit continues to grow. By 1979 almost 80 percent of the country's energy needs were imported, mostly in the form of crude oil. Oil imports are refined in Morocco, where the annual refining capacity is about 5 million tons. This capacity will rise to almost 8 million tons when expansion of the country's largest refinery in Mohammedia is completed in early 1980.

The balance of energy produced in Morocco is derived from domestic coal, gas, and hydroelectricity. About 85 percent of the coal mined in Morocco is used to fuel thermal electric plants. The coal-fired thermal unit in El-Jerida, constructed with financial and technical assistance from the Soviet Union, produces about 34 percent of the electrical power used in Morocco. Several new hydroelectric facilities are under construction, including installations at the Oued Makhzan dam on the Loukko River near Larache and at the Idriss I dam near Fes. A long-range program through 1990 includes the building of 20 new hydroelectric facilities on tributaries of the Sabou, the Oum Er Rbia, and other rivers.

The Office National de l'Electricite (ONE) provides more than 90 percent of the total electrical energy generated. About 48 percent of this total is consumed by industry, with the phosphate monopoly being the largest single user. Morocco's high-tension power grid, built before independence from the French, is being continually extended, integrated, and upgraded. By 1977 all major cities, 70 percent of the country's small towns, and 11 percent of the rural areas were electrified. In 1980 ONE will begin an $85 million, 4-year project to extend electrical service to about 220 village centers in 17 rural provinces. This project will be the first stage of a 15-year village electrification program aimed at providing electricity from the national grid to 1,800 villages.

Electric current in Morocco is 115/200 volts.

Mining

Although mining activities contribute a relatively small share to GNP, their share of export earnings is very large—ranging between 30 percent and 50 percent annually. Phosphate rock is the most important mineral, accounting for 90 percent of all Moroccan mining activity by value. Morocco's known phosphate deposits are estimated at 57 billion tons. An additional 9 billion tons of phosphate rock is estimated to exist in the portion of the former Spanish Sahara administered by Morocco.

Phosphate deposits were nationalized in 1920, and the Office Chérifien des Phosphates—(OCP) was created with a monopoly for the mining, processing, and exporting of phosphates. The OCP, located at 305 Avenue Mohamed V, Rabat/T(elex: 31013), is the largest company in the country and a major employer. From a labor force of more than 13,000 in 1973, OCP employees numbered 21,000 by 1977 as numerous facilities were expanded. Most phosphates are still exported in rock form, but OCP aims at greatly increasing its capacity to produce phosphate intermediaries, such as phosphoric acid, so that eventually more than one-third of phosphate rock production will be processed in Morocco. OCP thus operates a growing number of subsidiaries, including chemical plants, fertilizer plants, and seaports.

Phosphates are extracted at several locations in Morocco, including the areas of Khouribga, Youssoufia, and Ben Guerir. In addition, at Ben Guerir, a new mine is being opened to produce 2 million tons of rock annually by 1981, with this figure gradually rising to 10 million tons. More long-term projects include mines at Sidi Hajjaj

and Meskala, both with an eventual annual capacity of 10 million tons. The Meskala mine is to be built with financial and technical assistance from the Soviet Union within the framework of a comprehensive cooperation agreement signed in early 1978. The agreement, under which Moroccan phosphates will be exported to the U.S.S.R. for 30 years, represents a major breakthrough in OCP's efforts to diversify export markets. In a similar vein, OCP exported its first shipment of phosphate rock to the United States in 1977.

Moroccan output of phosphate rock reached 19.7 million tons in 1974 but then declined steadily for 2 years as world demand fell. Production rose to 16.4 million tons in 1977 and then, thanks to increased world demand, climbed 28 percent to almost 21 million tons in 1978. The largest customers for Moroccan phosphates in 1977 were Poland, the United Kingdom, France, and Italy.

In their drive to increase the country's processing capabilities, the Moroccans are pushing ahead with plans to put the Maroc-Phosphore II plant being built at Safi into production by 1982. The plant will have an output capacity of 495,000 tons of phosphoric acid annually. Eurodollar financing secured for this project has totaled $438 million to date.

The Maroc-Phosphore III project, at Jorf Lasfar, is planned to begin production after 1985. This complex, requiring external financing of $1 billion, will also have a capacity of 495,000 tons of phosphoric acid per year and will produce important quantities of DAP, ammonia, and urea. In another area, OCP's fertilizer subsidiary FERTIMA plans to build eight new mixing and bagging plants for fertilizers needed domestically. Capacity of these plants will total 700,000 tons per year, with a stocking capacity of 200,000 tons.

Besides phosphates, Morocco has a number of other important mineral reserves. The Bureau de Recherches et de Participation Minieres (BRPM), 27 Avenue Moulay Hassan, Rabat (Telex: 31066), is a government agency engaged in mineral exploration and development (excluding phosphates) and is a major shareholder in most private mining enterprises in Morocco. New foreign private investment in mining is generally made via a joint venture with BRPM. Usual terms provide that BRPM obtain the permits and supply all previous geological and mineralogical studies while the foreign partner carries out the in-depth study of mineral deposits. Exploitation, if any, is usually on a 50-50 basis.

Morocco's second most important mineral export is lead. Production amounted to 146,000 tons of concentrate in 1977, earning more than $37 million in export revenues. At a time when older lead mines are nearing exhaustion, new reserves have recently been found at Bou Azzer, Bou Shour, and Zeida. A notable increase in the world price for lead has spurred plans for the construction of two new lead foundries. One of these, to be built at Meknes, is expected to produce 75,000 tons of metal annually and will create an estimated 300 jobs.

Other minerals include iron ore, which is mined at Ait Amar and Nixan. Production, 375,000 tons in 1973, rose to more than 433,000 tons in 1977 in response to plans for development of a major steel complex at Nador. Morocco has no known deposits of coking coal, but it does have large reserves of anthracite coal near Jerada in the northeast. The coal has a high sulfur content and is used as a fuel for thermal electrical plants. Production of manganese ore amounted to 114,000 tons in 1978, 35 percent of which is treated in the Sidi Marouf factory.

Zinc is mined at Boukber, Touissit, Aouli, and Mikbladen. Due to declining reserves, the output of zinc has fallen from 101,000 tons in 1959 to 22,000 tons in 1977. Cobalt is produced at Bou Azzar and copper at Blida; production in 1977 was 8,000 tons and 14,000 tons, respectively. In a consortium with the Moroccan Government, two Japanese firms and one French company plan to build a factory to process copper extracted from the Blida deposits. Annual production is expected to reach 255,000 tons, half of which will be exported to Japan.

Domestic production of oil and natural gas meets only about 4 percent of local requirements, and production has been declining since the early 1960's. This decline is caused not only by depletion of the country's few oil fields but partially by pumping and storage problems. Despite continuous exploration since 1950, no sizable oil or gas deposits have yet been found. Virtually the entire offshore Atlantic Coast, which has been considered geologically the most potentially productive area, is under exploration by foreign oil firms, in some cases under partnership arrangements with the BRPM.

Morocco possesses important deposits of oil shale at Timahdit and Tarfaya which have received extensive study over the past few years by both Soviet geologists and American private contractors. There are plans to produce 3 million tons of oil annually from these deposits, but the project is still in its early stages.

Although Morocco must import almost all of its crude oil, it has the facilities to refine most petroleum products. Two State-owned refineries, one at Sidi Kacem and the other at Mohammedia, are increasing their refining capacity to a total of about 8 million tons annually by the end of 1979, thus making Morocco self-sufficient in all specialized refined petroleum products and providing a sizable saving in foreign exchange. In 1974, all foreign-owned petroleum-marketing companies that operated service stations were nationalized and a newly created state petroleum products company took a 50 percent interest in all firms engaged in the domestic distribution of petroleum products.

Manufacturing

Manufacturing's contribution to GDP has remained about 12 percent for the past several years. Between 1973-77, output of the manufacturing sector increased at an average annual rate of 7 percent. The most important manufacturing subsectors include foodstuffs and beverages, metal transformation, textiles, chemicals, and construction materials. Many of these subsectors depend heavily on imported raw materials and semimanufactures.

Employment in modern manufacturing in 1977 was estimated at 746,000 full time workers. Development of this sector since independence had been encouraged by public investments in large government-approved or organized industries including chemicals, fertilizers, pharmaceuticals, textiles, metal working and machinery, construction materials, sugar, petroleum, vehicle assembly, and paper and paper products.

As with agriculture, manufacturing is divided into modern and traditional areas comprising a few large-scale production units and many small-scale operations. Small-scale industry, defined by the Government as enterprises employing between 10 and 50 persons and each having assets under $1,250,000, accounted for about three-fourths of total industrial employment and 40 percent of production by value in 1975.

The existing manufacturing infrastructure consists of:

Food Processing. — Food processing is a major industry and includes sugar refining, vegetable and fruit canning, and production of juices, vegetable oils, wine, and tobacco products. Flour mills meet all domestic needs, but much wheat is imported. A large number of factories process fruits and vegetables, with most of them using unexportable fresh fruits and vegetables that have not met export standards. The oil seed industry, composed of a consortium of private and State-owned refineries, has the sole right to import oilseeds and unrefined vegetable oil. The consortium, Moroccan Cooperative for Edible Oils (Cooperative Marocaine des Huileries Alimentaires—COMAHA), also has the responsibility of stabilizing the domestic price of vegetable oils. The production, importation, distribution, and sale of all tobacco products is a monopoly of the State-owned Tobacco Authority.

As a result of continued growth, a number of new plants for food processing are planned. A feasibility study has been completed for a plant at Berkane, near Oujda, for the production of vegetable preserves, and studies are in progress for a tomato concentrate and dried vegetable plant at Khemis Zemmamra, near El-Jadida. Discussions are also taking place with potential foreign partners on a dried fruit and vegetable plant at Souk El-Sebt, in Beni Mellal.

Fishing.—The Atlantic coastal waters abound in sardines, tuna, mackerel, and anchovies. The commercial fishing industry, the most important in Africa, has grown appreciably since its inauguration in the early 1920s and, including the more than 150 small fish canneries, provides employment for about 20,000 persons. Despite the large domestic fishing industry only small amounts of fish are consumed locally. Most of the annual catch is exported. Morocco has become a major world fish exporter, particularly of canned sardines, fish meal, and fish oil. The ports of Agadir and Safi are centers of the fishing industry, although many of the canneries are in Casablanca.

To modernize the fleet, consisting mostly of short-range, nonrefrigerated vessels, the Office National des Pêches (ONP) is seeking joint ventures using refrigerated, long-distance fishing vessels and on-shore cold storage plants. ONP has entered into several joint ventures, including those with Spanish, Japanese and French fishing companies.

Textiles.—About one-fourth of Morocco's industrial work force is employed in textile mills. In 1978 there were over 800 textile factories with 58,000 employees, and the country was almost entirely self-sufficient in clothing and textile needs. The textile industry is concentrated in Casablanca and Tangier (over 80 percent of the plants are located in those two cities). The industry has become highly modernized with new equipment installed in most plants, although about 20 percent of production still comes from small producers and artisans. The 30 largest textile firms produce more than half of total production. There is very little government participation in the textile industry; almost all plants are privately owned.

Leather.—The leather industry includes a labor-intensive, traditional sector producing a variety of handicrafts. In 1978 there were 30 shoe-making establishments with a production capacity of 8 million pairs annually. Moroccan earnings from exports of leather shoes climbed dramatically from $3.4 million in 1973 to $11.1 million in 1977.

Forestry.—Forestry is run by the State, which owns most of Morocco's 8 million hectares of forest. These contain cork, the most important commercial forest product, and lesser woods (mostly eucalyptus) which yield plywood, veneer, and paneling. Factories manufacture paper, cardboard, cartons, sacks for cement and fertilizer, and miscellaneous paper products.

Chemicals.—The Moroccan Government is committed to a long-term expansion of domestic processing of the country's mineral wealth. Thus, while phosphate derivatives such as phosphoric acid, superphosphates, and fertilizers are already produced locally, a great expansion of local processing is projected for the 1980s and 1990s.

The existing production units in Morocco, near Safi, have a capacity of 858,000 tons of phosphate acid and are equipped to produce small quantities of other phosphatic intermediate or final products.

The Office Chérifien des Phosphates (OCP), a State-owned company, plans to more than double annual production capacity at Safi by the mid-1980s. In the long term, the OCP plans to build additional units near the port of Jorf Lasfar to produce phosphoric acid, mono and diammonium phosphates, and triple superphosphate.

Plastics.—The Moroccan plastics industry expanded significantly through 1977, encompassing 200 businesses which employed 15,000 people. Articles fabricated include irrigation equipment, housewares, packaging materials, shoes, and records. Sales of this industry reached $335 million in 1977 but declined to $267 million in 1978.

Metalworking and Machinery.—Metalworking plants fabricate a wide range of iron, aluminum, steel and galvanized products, metal cans, containers, and agricultural equipment.

Morocco makes most of its electric cables and wire, and about half of its steel wire, gauze, cables, tubes and nails, aluminum and lead pipes. Machinery products include locally assembled automobiles, trucks, motorcycles, bicycles, agricultural machinery, railroad equipment, heaters, motors, pumps and compressors, industrial office equipment, and some electric machinery.

Construction materials. — The output of Morocco's cement plants totaled 2.6 million tons in 1977, a 26 percent increase over 1975. During the same period, due to a rapidly rising demand caused by a boom in construction, consumption rose 62 percent to 3.6 million tons. Moroccan cement plants are located at Agadir, Tangier, Meknes, Casablanca, and Tetouan. In February 1979, a new cement plant opened near Oujda which will produce 1.4 million tons of cement annually.

Morocco also produces tiles, bricks, refractory products, cement pipe, and asbestos-cement products. Related glass and glassware factories produce pots, bottles, jars, and lamps. In addition, prefabricated cement items have been manufactured in Morocco since 1976.

Tourism

Morocco developed rapidly as a tourist center during the 1970s. Tourism is responsible for about 200,000 jobs and is an important source of foreign exchange. Its development also has had indirect beneficial effects on other sectors of the economy such as construction, handicrafts and services. More than 1.5 million tourists visited the country in 1977, an increase of 24 percent over 1976. Receipts of $390 million were generated and the pace increased in 1978. Most of the tourists were French, Spanish, English, and American.

Development of the tourist industry is one of the priorities of the Development Plan. Government programs have concentrated on development of infrastructure, promotion and professional training. As a result, Morocco boasts 57,000 beds in classified hotels as well as 12,000 in vacation camps. There are 22 five star hotels, 68 four-star hotels and 119 three-star hotels. Most hotels are booked from March to October and during the holiday seasons.

The Government of Morocco is actively seeking investment in the tourist sector and offers many incentives to encourage it. These include the possibility of 100 percent foreign ownership, tax exemptions of up to 10 years depending on the location of the investment, and the availability of long-term, low-interest financing through the Credit Immobilier et Hôtelier (CIH). Sources of funds for the CIH include the World Bank, the Kuwait International Investment Company, and Citicorp of the United States.

Infrastructure

Developments in Morocco's infrastructure include:

Ports. — The Moroccan Government continues to emphasize the expansion and development of the country's ports. Construction of the port of Nador is nearly completed. This will be of considerable importance to the northern part of the country. Construction has begun on Jorf Lasfar, a new port on the Atlantic to the south of El Jadida, which will include a major chemical complex and phosphate exporting facilities. The ports of Casablanca and Mohammedia are being expanded under a $200 million program. Other ports slated for major improvements during the next few years include Agadir, Tan Tan, Tarfaya, and El-Ayoun.

Roads and Highways. — Many roads are projected for expansion to outlying areas, including paved roads linking urban centers of the former Spanish Sahara with each other and with the north. Work is continuing on the Casablanca Rabat expressway, and a new beltway around Casablanca is being completed.

Railroads. — Ongoing expansion is planned. In 1978, a Moroccan firm with U.S. participation undertook a detailed engineering study of a projected new railroad to the south, linking Marrakech with Agadir and El Ayoun. New projects also include a railroad spur linking Nador with the existing Fez-Oujda railroad, and the double tracking of the railroad between Casablanca and Rabat.

Power Plants and Dams. — New power generation plants are under construction at Mohammedia and Kenitra. In addition to the hydroelectric projects already started, the Moroccan Government anticipates starting work in the near future on the Mjara Dam in the north. A considerable amount of power will be produced when the diversion of the Sebou River into the Idriss I Dam near Fez is completed. Also, work is being completed on the El Massire Dam on the Oum ErRhiba River.

Housing. — The Moroccan Government is giving high priority to the social sector, with heavy investment in low-cost housing and other social services. There is an estimated shortage of some 600,000 housing units, and the present construction target is about 40,000 units per year.

With the assistance of the World Bank, a pilot housing project of 12,000 units is to be undertaken in Rabat.

Education.—Emphasis is being placed on augmentation of the country's educational infrastructure. Several thousand classrooms for primary and secondary schools were completed in 1978, and major expansion of Morocco's university facilities is continuing. An estimated $225 million will be invested in the educational sector during 1978–80.

Distribution and Sales Channels

Domestic Trade

Traditional trading has long been dominated by Moroccan entrepreneurs. An estimated 1,000 small town souks, or weekly markets, have schooled Moroccans in the intricacies of a market economy in which bargaining has assumed an important and characteristic business formality. The traditional trading sector, however vibrant and important to an understanding of Moroccan society and character, is not fully addressed in this report. The reader should, however, keep in mind its importance in the life and buying styles of the average Moroccan consumer who lives outside the modern sector. Self-sufficient farmers and villagers (62 percent of the population) consume little foreign merchandise. It is estimated that only 6 percent of Morocco's 17.5 million people participate in the European-influenced, affluent society and can be considered modern consumers.

Regulation of Distribution and Sales Channels

The role of the private sector in Morocco has been strengthened as a result of the "Moroccanization" decrees issued in 1973, as its composition shifted from foreign to Moroccan control. (Moroccanization is discussed in a subsequent section). State enterprises and government agencies have preferred to order from local manufacturers and from local agents of foreign suppliers whenever possible.

The Government has, however, insisted on its right to monopolize domestic and export marketing of certain agricultural products which ensure basic consumer needs or which earn foreign exchange surpluses. Thus, most fruits, vegetables, canned fish, wine, raw cotton, and cotton byproducts are marketed domestically and overseas by the Office de Commercialisation et d'Exportation (OCE). Exports of handicrafts and fresh and frozen fish are subject to OCE's administrative control. Other State marketing monopolies are: OCIC (Office Chérifien Inter-professionnel des Céréales): wheat and barley; ONTS (Office National du Thé et du Sucre): tea, sugar beets, and cane sugar; COMHA (Cooperative Marocaine des Huileries Alimentaires): edible oils; Régie des Tabacs: tobacco and tobacco products; and the Société National des Produits Pétroliers: distribution of petroleum products.

Other State enterprises include the Office Chérifien des Phosphates, which controls phosphate production and exploration, SAMIR, which imports most crude petroleum, and the Office National des Pêches, which has entered into joint ventures with foreign firms.

Since 1957, the Government has exercised controls on the prices of certain basic foodstuffs and other consumer necessities, and on electricity, gas, farm machinery, and transport. Several decrees since 1971 including "Arrête" No. 3–334–71 of February 4, 1972, have set up administrative machinery for expanded price controls on virtually all foodstuffs, construction materials, clothing, fuel, agricultural inputs, and commercial services, although the decrees and controls have not been fully implemented. Prices of controlled goods are regulated at the distributor, wholesale and retail levels, with a temporary maximum permissible 7 percent profit on sales. Government approval is required for price increases in such businesses.

"Moroccanization"

"Moroccanization" defines a government-decreed program to turn over to actual (rather than nominal) Moroccan control specified commercial businesses and light industries which the Government finds to have been too closely controlled by foreign firms and individuals. Depending on the activity of the business, the Moroccanization law specified under a decree issued March 2, 1973 requires that Moroccan citizens or Moroccanized companies hold at least 50 percent of the share capital and constitute a majority on the board of directors, or that all partners and capital be Moroccan.

Under the law, companies involved in commercial, banking, insurance, and service activities were required to Moroccanize. Although not required to do so, some companies involved in manufacturing activities, the so-called tertiary sector, have voluntarily Moroccanized by taking on Moroccan partners. Except for exporting enterprises and companies in the tourist industry, new companies formed in Morocco, although not necessarily subject to this law, may find that by Moroccanizing they can take advantage of increased investment incentives.

Wholesale and Retail Channels

Most of the wholesale and retail commercial enterprises in Morocco are family-run businesses which perform a variety of commercial roles, depending upon the commodity and buyer concerned.

Most foreign-made goods are imported at Casablanca by companies with headquarters and warehouses there that distribute either directly to the public through branches in other towns or to other wholesalers, semiwholesalers, or retailers. Mark-ups may range from 25–35 percent although current price control tends to keep them lower. Goods may also be imported by commission agents who deliver the goods directly to semiwholesale and retail warehouses. The agent's mark-up represents only a 3 to 5 percent commission.

Locally manufactured products are ordinarily distributed by the manufacturer directly through the firm's own transportation service to wholesalers, semiwholesalers, or retailers. This system, motivated by strong price competition, eliminates certain middlemen and helps maintain competitive pricing. Manufacturers' mark-ups range between 20 and 30 percent depending on the product; those of distributors from 10 to 15 percent.

In choosing agents or distributors, U.S. manufacturers can take advantage of the Agent/Distributor Service (ADS) of the Department of Commerce. For a small fee, the U.S. Embassy in Rabat or Consulate General in Casablanca will locate up to three Moroccan firms which appear to meet the needs of the requesting company and which have expressed an interest in a business relationship. For details, consult the nearest Department of Commerce District Office.

U.S. exporters seeking an agent or distributor are encouraged to visit Morocco in person before making any long-term commitment with prospective agents or distributors. The importance of ensuring the availability of qualified personnel and necessary spare parts and components for after-sales service cannot be overstressed. European competitors particularly capitalize on their geographic proximity and historical/cultural ties to Morocco by making spare parts and even service personnel available to local customers on short notice. More than one American firm has lost a valuable Moroccan order through failure to provide prompt and efficient service.

Licensing and Franchising

Franchising in Morocco is regulated by the Exchange Office of the Finance Ministry. Franchise firms pay royalties for the use of the franchisor's trademark and process by filing requests periodically with the Exchange Office. Royalties are renewable annually and do not exceed 1 or 2 percent according to Exchange Office regulations. Products and services under license in Morocco include vehicle rental, assembly of vehicles, and manufacture of consumer goods such as soft drinks, perfumes, cosmetics and shampoos, textiles, and clothing.

Activities offering additional franchising opportunities in Morocco include hotels/motels, automotive product services, campgrounds, business aids and services, recreation/entertainment/travel, and fast food restaurants.

Addresses of Moroccan Government Buying and Merchandising Offices

BRPM (Bureau de Recherches et de Participations Minières)
27 Avenue Urbain-Blanc
(Chana Moulay Hassan), Rabat

Ministère des Travaux Publics et des Communications
Quartier Administratif, Rabat-Chella

OCE (Office de Commercialisation et d'Exportation)
45, Avenue de l'Armée
Royale, Rabat

OCP (Office National des Phosphates),
305, Avenue Mohamed V. Rabat

ONCF (Office National des Chemins de Fer du Maroc)
19, Avenue Allal ben Abdallah, Rabat

ONCL (Office National des Céréales et Légumineuses,
ex-OCIC), 25, Avenue Urbaine
Blanc, Rabat

ONE (Office National de l'Electricité), B.P. 498,
65 rue Aspirant laFuente, Casablanca

ONEP (Office National de l'Eau Pôtable), 6 bis,
rue Patrice Lumumba, Rabat

ONP (Office National des *Pêches), 13-15, rue Chevalier Bayard, Casablanca*

ONTS (Office National du Thé et du Sucre), km
10, Route de Rabat, Ain Sebaa, B.P. 618, Casablanca

Regie des Tabacs, Blvd. Idriss I, Casablanca

SOGETA (Société de Gestion des Terres Agricoles), Rabat

Government Procurement Practices

Morocco has no central government purchasing office. Instead, government bureaus and ministries publish invitations to bid on goods and services. All types of awards can be granted by open or limited competitive bidding per conditions noted in Decree No. 2–65–116 of May 19, 1965, as amended. Open bidding invites anyone to submit a bid; in limited competitive bidding only preselected suppliers are invited to submit bids on the basis of technical or other considerations.

Notices of government invitations to bid are relayed to the Department of Commerce by the American Embassy in Rabat and Consulate General in Casablanca. This information is disseminated to subscribers to the Trade Opportunity Program (TOP), and/or published in the bi-weekly Business America magazine or in Commerce Business Daily. The Commerce Action Group for the Near East, Bureau of Export Development, U.S. Department of Commerce, Washington, D.C. 20230, also contacts directly potential U.S. exporters on major projects.

In practice, most government purchasing is supplied from private, local importing houses. Local representation by one of these firms is therefore recommended. Among other services, local representatives can obtain advance information and tender documents on potential government purchases and on big-ticket projects, and can arrange for extensions of bid deadlines or orders for supplies not open to competitive bidding.

Moroccan bid specifications are frequently based on those used in France. The Government also relies to some extent on French technical advisors and consultants in drawing up specifications and reviewing bids, a practice which may work to the disadvantage of U.S. firms.

Payment by the Government may take 6 months or more after delivery of the goods. Under such conditions, the more generous terms of credit offered by the foreign supplier could tip the balance in the mind of the local importer.

To obtain consideration as a potential supplier and to expedite receipt of tenders and other information, U.S. firms should send their names and addresses, catalogs, price lists and company resumes in French to appropriate buying officials of the government offices to which they wish to sell.

Further information useful for firms tendering and negotiating contracts in Morocco can be found in *An Introduction to Contract Proce-dures in the Near East and North Africa*, Bureau of Export Development, U.S. Department of Commerce, Washington, D.C. 20230.

Advertising and Research

Advertising Agencies

A number of advertising agencies provide the services an American seller would expect. Among the larger firms, Cie. Cherifienne d'Editions et de Publicité, 71 Rue Allal Ben Abdallah, Casablanca, is associated with an international group of advertising companies which includes an American firm among its members.

Most local distributors of imported merchandise expect their suppliers to provide substantial advertising and promotional support, particularly when introducing a new product or brand name. Good salesmanship is itself the most important element in selling the product, and clear and simple French-language operating instructions, displays of the product in use, sample handouts and frequent personal visits are vital for successful sales in Morocco.

Advertising Media

Newspaper advertising is the most commonly used medium reaching the mass audience, and Morocco offers a variety of journals, in French, Arabic and Spanish, including nine major daily publications with a total circulation of 200,000. Of these, the French-language papers have the largest readership.

Ad placement rates range from $0.75 to $0.25 per column millimeter. The Casablanca edition charges higher than the Rabat or regional editions. Full-page rates range from $1,600 to $1,400.

The leading daily papers, published in Casablanca in French, include Le Matin, Maroc Soir, and Maghreb Information, L'Opinion, and Courier Economique. La Vie Economique is a business/economic weekly.

In addition, specialized trade and industry journals are published by several local industry groups.

Street posters are an important advertising medium in Morocco. Special wooden panels for posters of 105 by 75 centimeters are provided in all major cities. Printing charges range from $0.75 to $2.25 each, depending on the number of colors and the quantity ordered. Space rentals normally run from $2.50 to $3.50 a month for each location.

Commercial time is also available on the government-owned television service in 10 to 15 second "spots," aired two or three times daily. Costs are about $1,000 per minute. The film, which must produced abroad, is provided by the advertiser. Advertisers may also choose a still picture viewed for 6 seconds for $7.

Advertising is prohibited on the government-owned radio.

Local cinemas include commercial messages at their showings, charging from $0.25 to $2.75 per meter weekly, depending on the size and type of establishment. As in the case of television, the film must be furnished by the advertiser and be produced abroad.

In addition to the foregoing commercial techniques, some companies employ sound trucks to advertise their products, particularly in areas not well covered by other media.

Suppliers who appeal to consumer tastes, habits and attitudes will attract Moroccan buyers. Packaging for eye appeal is effective in Morocoo.

Participation in one of Morocco's trade fairs can also offer the U.S. exporter an opportunity to develop local interest in his product. The largest is the biannual Casablanca International Fair, at which an estimated one million persons visited the U.S. pavilion in 1977. Other fairs are held in Marrakech, Fez, Mekness, and Kenitra.

Market Research and Trade Organizations

There are a few firms in Morocco which engage in market research. Advertising agencies, law offices, and consultants also undertake research assignments for clients.

Local Moroccan trade organizations such as the Chambers of Commerce and Industry located in major cities also may assist U.S. exporters by providing market information or arranging business appointments. Chambers have been established in Casablanca, Rabat, Fez, Meknes, Marrakech, Tangier, Tetouan, Kenitra, Safi, Oujda, El Jadida, Esaouira, Taza, Larache, and Nador. In addition, the American Chamber of Commerce in Morocco, located in Casablanca, can provide the U.S. business traveler with an on-the-spot appraisal of local business conditions.

The Statistical Division of the Secretariat of State for the Plan in the Prime Minister's Office is primarily responsible for collection of statistical data relevant to economic and business conditions in Morocco, although other agencies, including the Exchange Office in the Ministry of Finance, share this task.

Among the publications which can provide valuable assistance to the U.S. exporter in developing his marketing groundwork are the Bulletin Mensuel: Statistiques, the Statistiques des Echanges Extérieur du Maroc, The Bulletin Mensuel d'Informations and the Statistiques du Commerce Extérieur.

In addition, numerous other government bureaus and State agencies, such as the Office de Commercialisation et d'Exportation, the Banque nationale pour le Dévélopment Economique, and the Banque du Maroc, publish statistical reports and economic surveys of interest to the U.S. exporter.

Transportation, Communications and Utilities

Shipping to and from the U.S.

Morocco has good air and sea links with the United States and Europe. Trans World Airways provides service to Casablanca from New York and Chicago via Lisbon. Royal Air Maroc provides direct service to New York from Casablanca and Tangier. Other international carriers include Air France, Alitalia, Iberia, Sabena, and Swissair.

Casablanca is served by more than 100 foreign and U.S. maritime companies including, among U.S. firms, American Export Isbrandtsen Line, Prudential Line; Yugoslav Line, Medlakes Services, Orient Mid-East Line, and Waterman Line. Tangier is served by Yugoslav Line and Medlakes Services. Shipping times to Casablanca from New York average 8 days; from Baltimore, 10 days; from New Orleans, 12 days.

Two U.S. flag carriers, Lykes Brothers of New Orleans and Farrell Lines of New York City, serve Casablanca on a scheduled basis and other Moroccan ports on inducement. Lykes serves Casablanca weekly with both breakbulk and container service. Farrell serves Casablanca with conventional breakbulk service; deeptank space is usually available.

For information on American flag capacities worldwide, contact: Division of Commercial Cargo, Office of Market Development, Maritime Administration, U.S. Department of Commerce, Washington, D.C. 20230, tel.: 202-377-4180.

Domestic Transportation System

Morocco has six major ports on the Atlantic: Casablanca, one of the largest deepwater ports in Africa, handles 63 percent of all Moroccan freight; Tangier is a free port; Safi is the point of export for phosphates; Mohammedia specializes in petroleum imports; and Kenitra and Agadir handle citrus and fish. A total of 25.2 million tons of goods was handled in Moroccan ports in 1976, a 12 percent rise over 1975. There are currently plans to build two new major harbor complexes—one at Jorf Lasfar (for phosphate exports), the other at Nador (on the Mediterranean).

The government-run railway is operated by the Office National des Chemins de Fer (ONCFM). It serves all large industrial cities and phosphate mining centers from Marrakech to Tangier and from Safi to Oujda, where it joins the Algerian system. Track totals 1,778 kilometers, including 730 kilometers of electrified service; the rest of the tracks are diesel. Rail freight costs range from $0.22 to $0.67 per ton/kilometer. In 1976 more than 20 million tons of freight carried by rail.

Morocco's paved highway system is one of the best in Africa and totals over 26,000 kilometers. In 1976 there were some 348,000 passenger cars and 146,000 commercial vehicles in use and almost 6.8 million tons of freight were carried by road transport. Major projects underway include the construction of an expressway from Casablanca to Rabat as well as an urban expressway within Casablanca.

The railway and highway systems together provide a relatively efficient means of internal distribution. Intercity, common carrier road freight is allocated exclusively by the government's Office National de Transport. ONT also establishes trucking tariffs and levies road taxes. Road haulage costs $0.028 per ton/kilometer, weighted average.

Several Moroccan airfields serve international flights. They are Casablanca, Rabat, Tangier, Marrakech, Fez, Agadir, and Oujda. There are 10 smaller commercial fields as well as about 50 landing strips for light aircraft. The number of passengers handled rose from 728,000 in 1968 to 1.8 million in 1976.

International service is provided by Royal Air Maroc (RAM), which is owned by the Moroccan Government. RAM flies Boeings and Caravelles to 13 foreign countries from several Moroccan cities; direct flights are provided from Casablanca and Tangier to New York. Its volume of business in 1977 was $155 million, up 41 percent over 1976. As of April 1979, the RAM fleet included three Boeing 707s, seven Boeing 727s, three Boeing 737s and one Boeing 747. Domestic air service is provided by Royal Air Inter (RAI), a subsidiary of RAM.

Communications

Business correspondence is normally conducted by air mail. Transit time for air mail from the United States averages between 4 and 6 days. Surface mail takes 4 to 6 weeks; parcel post is slow and handling is unreliable. Cables and telex supplement air mail communication. In estimating the time of arrival of a radio or cable message in Morocco, 5 hours should be added to Eastern Standard Time of dispatch.

Morocco has a modern telephone system which serves most parts of the country. At the end of 1977, telephones in use were estimated at 230,000. Internationally, direct automatic dialing has been instituted in telephone calls with several European countries. Semiautomatic service is in effect with the United States. Delays are brief and line quality is good. The person-to-person rate for a 3 minute Morocco-U.S. call is $12; $3 for each additional minute.

Television is broadcast in color and black and white and in both Arabic and French; no English language programs are broadcast. Local radio stations, owned by the Government, broadcast English language programs 3 hours daily.

Utilities

Production and distribution of electricity in Morocco are State-controlled through the Office National d'Electricité (ONE), which produces 90 percent of Morocco's electricity. Annual production was 2.8 billion kwh in 1975, with 35 percent of all electric power coming from the country's extensive hydroelectric system. Additional dams are under construction, but the share of power produced by hydroelectric plants has declined sharply as the thermal complex at Jerrada, powered by coal, has been connected into the national power grid. Built with substantial financial and technical assistance from the Soviets, the Jerrada complex produces about 34 percent of all the electric power used by Morocco.

Credit

Morocco has a well developed monetary system, consisting of a central bank (Banque du Maroc), 16 private commercial banks (most of which have foreign capital participation), and a number of specialized public and semipublic financial institutions that provide commercial credits and normal banking services. In accord-

1587

ance with Moroccanization requirements, foreign-owned banks, insurance and credit agencies became at least 50 percent Moroccan-owned and majority Moroccan-directed on May 31, 1975.

The Banque du Maroc issues currency, rediscounts bills, extends credit to commercial banks, and acts as banker to the Government, to other banks, credit institutions, and certain state enterprises. It does not lend directly to the private sector.

In controlling the overall credit volume extended by commercial banks, the Banque du Maroc relies on a combination of rediscount ceilings, minimum reserves and a requirement that commercial banks hold a specified percentage of their demand and time deposits in Treasury bonds.

Currency issued by the central bank is backed by gold or convertible currency to the amount of at least one ninth of total currency in circulation.

In addition to the private commercial banks (listed at the end of this section), the specialized public financial institutions are important sources of credit for equity participation in Moroccanized joint ventures.

The development bank, Banque Nationale pour le Développement Economique (BNDE). Place des Alaouites, B.P. 407, Rabat, provides medium- and long-term financing for development projects and takes equity in joint ventures. During the last few years, BNDE has played an active role in financing private manufacturing, trade and tourism. Loans carry an interest rate of 10 percent; this can be lowered to 7 percent through government subsidies to the borrower.

Foreign trade financing is the specialty of the semipublic Banque Marocaine de Commerce Exterieur, 241 Blvd. Mohammed V, B.P. 425 Casablanca. BMCE operates a Cooperative Financing Facility with the U.S. Export-Import Bank.

Crédit Immobilier et Hôtelier (CIH), 159 Ave. Hassan II, Casablanca, is the primary source of medium- and long-term credits for housing and hotels. As spelled out by the August 1973 investment code, CIH offers financing at 4.5 percent with a 20-year maturity for hotel ventures, and interest-free advance equal to 50 percent of the value of the new investment, which is repayable over a 10-year period (including 5 years' grace). Companies and individuals domiciled in Morocco may apply for housing loans bearing 10 percent interest.

The Caisse Nationale du Credit Agricole (CNCA), Place Duclos, Rabat, is the principal source of agricultural credit. The CNCA provides loans to farmers for new equipment and supplies and for development of crops and animal husbandry. CNCA charges 7 to 8.5 percent on most loans; 6 to 8.5 percent for stock and crop financing, respectively.

The Caisse de Depôt et de Gestion, 1 rue Patrice Lumumba, B.P. 408, Rabat, extends medium- and long-term loans and participates with equity capital in public and private investments, including Moroccanized joint ventures. A small percentage of the Caisse's resources is invested in housing and hotel construction.

The Caisse Centrale de Garantie guarantees repayment of Moroccan Government loans extended to private and public enterprises. Its resources, derived from commissions from the guarantee, are applied in the fields of energy, mining, transportation, agriculture and housing.

The Caisse Marocaine des Marchés supplies short-term credit for public and private business transactions. Its main function is to finance government contracts (marchés publics) and other contracts of public interest.

The Banque Centrale Populaire (BCP) is designed to encourage handicraft and cottage industries through credits to small Moroccan businesses and artisans. It also receives for deposit transfers from Moroccan workers overseas.

Another source of financing for preinvestment studies and Government participation in joint ventures is the Office de Developpement Industriel, established in 1973 to replace the former BEPI in planning and promoting industrial development.

Private savings are mobilized by the 16 private commercial banks and by the BCP, which together maintain 291 permanent offices throughout the country. In addition, the Post Office accepts demand deposits through the Postal Checking System and administers the National Savings Fund (Caisse Nationale d'Epargne).

Other members of the financial system include some 35 insurance companies, two equipment leasing firms, several consumer credit institutions, a national investment fund, and the Casablanca Stock Exchange.

The Casablanca Stock Exchange (Bourse des Valeurs), in existence since 1967 under the authority of the Ministry of Finance, lists stocks and shares in about 135 private and public Moroccan-based companies as well as 30 foreign securities.

The Société Nationale d'Investissement, (SNI), 6 Rue Omar Saloui, Casablanca, and three affiliates function as national investment funds. SNI, formed in 1966, mobilizes private savings for investments, particularly through equity participation in Moroccanized joint ventures.

Consumer Financing

Consumer credit is not widely used in Morocco other than for automobile purchases. Several companies which offer such financing give terms up to 24 months (sometimes longer), generally at 10 percent interest. Some retail outlets may offer 6-month to 1-year credit terms on purchases of durable household goods, but most retail consumer purchases are self-financed. Firms which do offer financing normally charge customers only the bank discount rate, since retailers discount the customer's note at their bank.

Local banks may provide credit to selected clients but usually only for sizable transactions. BCP and CNCA loans to artisans, small businesses and farmers do not normally finance consumer-type purchasers. Commercial bank loans, even if available, generally include interest rates sufficiently high to exclude all but the most affluent borrowers.

Import Financing

Most Moroccan importers, relatively short of working capital, rely heavily on sight drafts and overdrafts to finance trading activities. Since local importers can usually anticipate a sales return in excess to the 6 to 8 percent interest generally charged on overdrafts, proceeds from the sale of imported goods often are reinvested rather than used to reduce outstanding balances.

An estimated 60 percent of Moroccan imports are paid for by sight drafts due upon receipt of documents by the importer at the port of destination. This is particularly the case for goods available from suppliers' stock and which require no special modification for the Moroccan market.

Another 15 percent of Moroccan imports, principally those which must in some way be modified or adapted to Moroccan requirements, are covered by 30-, 60- or 90-day notes, or are carried on open account.

More specialized industrial or capital goods are commonly financed by irrevocable confirmed letters of credit opened at the time the order is placed with the foreign supplier. Because the largest share of American commercial sales to Morocco falls within this latter category, the importance of attractive competitive credit terms should be self evident.

In most cases, the total amount outstanding on import orders must be paid in full prior to the import license's expiration date, commonly 6 months after issuance. Sales providing for payment beyond this date must have prior written approval for the Exchange Office, though such approval is generally granted readily.

Credit extended by third country competitors, such as firms in Italy or West Germany, have included terms as soft as 7 years with 5 percent payment with the order, 10 percent upon delivery. Japanese suppliers have been known to offer 10-year terms. Also, some European governments discount paper for their exporters at equally liberal terms and at low interest rates.

Terms offered by American exporters often do not match those available from competing suppliers. This is especially true because many American firms require irrevocable letters of credit whose terms very often are too rigorous even for the most sympathetic Moroccan importing house. When U.S. suppliers and Moroccan buyers become acquainted, it is to the advantage of both to ensure that credit terms be mutually advantageous and as liberal as possible.

In this connection, Foreign Credit Insurance Association (FCIA) insurance offers clear advantages to U.S. exporters of goods and services, particularly in its protection of foreign receivables against nonpayment due to unforeseen occurrences. For information on FCIA, contact its Office of Ombudsman, Ninth Floor, One World Trade Center, New York, N.Y. 10048, tele: 212-432-6300.

U.S. Export-Import Bank (Eximbank) assistance is also available to U.S. suppliers in the form of loans and guarantees for the export of goods and services. Eximbank has also made available to the Banque Marocaine du Commerce Extérieur a line of credit (Cooperative Financing Facility) which enables the Moroccan bank, in turn, to loan to Moroccan buyers of U.S. goods and services.

Financial and credit information about Moroccan firms can be obtained by U.S. suppliers from their banks in the United States, or from private agencies such as the Foreign Credit Interchange Bureau, National Association of Credit Management, 229 Fourth Ave., New York, N.Y. 10003; American Foreign Credit Underwriters Corp., 253 Broadway, New York, N.Y. 10007; or Dun and Bradstreet, Inc., 99 Church St., New York, N.Y. 10007.

Private Commercial Banks in Morocco

Algemene Bank Nederland (Maroc) S.A.
Place du 16 Novembre, Casablanca

Arab Bank Limited
Casablanca and Rabat

Banco Expanol en Marruecos, S.A.M.
Blvd. Mohammed V, Casablanca

Bank of America
73 Ave. del L'Armée Royal, Casablanca

Banque Americano Franco-Suisse pour le Maroc
(U.S. interest: Continental Bank of Illinois)
26 Ave. Des Forces Armées Royales,
B.P. 972, Casablanca

Banque Commerciale du Maroc S.A.
1 rue Idriss Lahrizi, Casablanca

Banque Marocaine pour le Commerce et L'Industrie
26 Place Mohammed V. (B.P. 573) Casablanca

British Bank of the Middle East (Morocco)
80 ave. Lalla Yacout, (B.P. 880), Casablanca

Compagnie Marocaine de Crédit et de Banque S.A.
1 ave. Hassan II, Casablanca

Crédit du Maroc S.A.
B.P. 579, 48-58 blvd. Mohammed V., Casablanca

First National City Bank (Maghreb)
52 Ave. Hassan II, Casablanca

Société Marocaine de Dépôt et Crédit, Casablanca
(formed in April 1974 by merger of Banque de Paris et de Pays-Bas and Worms et Cie).

Union Bancaria Hispano Marroqui
69 rue de Prince Moulay Abdullah, Casablanca

Bank-Uni Casablanca

Société Générale Marocaine de Banque, Casablanca

Union Marocaine de Banque, Casablanca

Trade Regulations

Import Procedures

The Moroccan Import Program, revised annually, is a three-part list of goods subject to licensing, goods on open license (about 75 percent of all Moroccan imports) and prohibited imports.

Imports subject to licensing require an Import Certificate (Certificat d'Importation) from the Ministry of Commerce countersigned by the Office des Changes (Exchange Office). Requests for Import Certificates must bear the stamp of the government-approved Moroccan bank that has been designated by the importer to handle his international banking transactions. The commercial bank pays for imports by purchasing necessary foreign exchange from the Bank of Morocco and transferring it to the foreign supplier's bank.

Approved Import Certificates are used to clear goods through customs and to arrange for their payment. Normally Import Certificates are valid for 6 months but may be extended by the Office des Changes for 1 month or less or by the Ministry of Commerce for longer periods if necessary.

Automatically renewable Import Certificates may be obtained by industrial importers of semifinished goods which are needed on a recurring basis. Importers must file copies of *pro forma* invoices in duplicate with all applications for Import Certificates.

Imports of goods on open general license generally do not require countersignature by the Office des Changes. They do, however, require the formalities of an Import Commitment (engagement d'importation). Those persons or firms which are inscribed in the Commercial Register and which have been trading in the goods in question for at least 1 year are permitted to submit Import Commitments to authorized banks, which then effect the required exchange transactions. Countersignature by the Office des Changes is required only if the country of origin of the goods differs from the country of shipment or if the goods are purchased on a c.i.f. (rather than c. & f. or f.o.b.) basis.

Import Commitments are valid for 6 months and may be extended up to 3 months by the Office des Changes upon application by the importer.

Special Customs Provisions

Goods arriving in Morocco, if not declared for consumption, may take advantage of a number of special customs provisions that provide for bonded, duty-free, temporary import, reexport or storage.

Merchandise placed under one of these duty-suspended categories ("regimes suspensifs") must be secured by payment of a deposit ("acquit de caution"). This deposit will be returned to the depositor when the goods are removed from their special customs category.

The special customs provisions include the following (bonded warehousing and the Tangier Free Trade Zone are described elsewhere);

Temporary Entry (admission temporaire).—This permits duty-free entry of goods for further processing followed by reexportation. Goods that may be imported under this regime must be specifically authorized by decree of the Finance Ministry. The Customs office may authorize other goods on an individual basis. The time limit for temporary entry is 6 months, with the possibility of one 6-month extension.

Temporary entry is permitted through the following points of entry: Casablanca, Mohammedia, Rabat, Kenitra, Tangier, Tetouan, Oujda, Fez, Meknes, El Jadida, Safi and Agadir.

Temporary Importation (importation temporaire).—This permits duty-free entry of goods which will be reexported in their identical condition after use, such as personal possessions and other goods identified by the Finance Ministry. Duration of the temporary importation privilege varies according to the goods involved. Goods must be reexported after expiration of the time-limit, unless permission for storage or further use is first obtained from the Customs office.

The following goods, among others, qualify for temporary importation: foreign-owned material to be used in industry or for a project within a specified time period; rented films; packing and containers, including empty bags, boxes, and tubes of wood, plastic or metal; containers filled with candies or bottled gas; barrels; wire for packaging; packing materials of wood or paper; samples and models; exhibit materials, testing materials; objects and animals belonging to professionals which are tools of the profession; negatives; commercial vehicles for international use; animals used in sporting competitions; other goods permitted under international laws accepted by Morocco.

Temporary export for foreign processing (trafic de perfectionnement a l'exportation).—This permits provisional duty-free exportation of goods to be processed in another country and returned to Morocco. Upon return of the processed goods, these will be subject to normal import duties and taxes for the foreign value-added position only.

Most of the goods allowed under temporary importation may also be temporarily exported under this category.

Temporary exportation (exportation temporaire).—This allows the transfer abroad of goods to be used abroad for a specified time, such as personal possessions of Moroccans who temporarily take up foreign residence. The goods must be returned in their original condition and within an agreed-upon time limit, and will be admitted duty free.

Goods in Transit.—This permits the movement of goods under bond from one customs area to another or from one warehouse to another within Morocco, free of duties and taxes. At the point of destination, the goods so transferred may qualify for any of the special customs provisions or for regular importation.

Drawback.—A drawback is a partial refund of duty and taxes paid in the case of certain goods which are imported for use in the manufacture of local products. Drawback is granted at the time of exportation of the finished local product, e.g., on containers for sardines and edible oils. However, if an item is imported and declared for consumption, drawbacks will not be paid even if the goods are later reexported.

The list of goods which qualify for drawback privileges and the amount of drawback is determined by Customs. The list is subject to revision upon request of a manufacturer.

Tariff Structure

Morocco has adopted the Brussels Tariff Nomenclature (BTN) and maintains a two-column tariff system in which the second column gives the effective rate of import duty. The first column indicates only how high the tariff could be raised without prior notification.

Customs duties apply equally to imports from all countries. Duties on nonessential consumer goods, luxury products or commodities competing with local manufacturers range from 30 percent to 400 percent *ad valorem*. Producer goods, fuels, raw materials, and essential imports are generally subject to lower tariffs ranging between 5 percent and 25 percent *ad valorem*.

Exemption from customs duties on machinery and equipment may be granted to certain enterprises under special regulations designed to encourage investment. This exemption applies only to the customs duties themselves and not to other taxes mentioned below.

Customs Classification

The customs authorities will not give a binding ruling on customs classification in advance. However, an informal advisory opinion may be obtained upon written request to the Directeur des Douanes, Direction Générale des Douanes, Blvd. Rachidi, Casablanca.

Tariff Preferences

Morocco applies tariffs equally to all supplying countries. It is linked to the European Economic Community (EEC) through a limited association agreement. On April 27, 1976, Morocco signed a trade and cooperation agreement with the EEC to replace that of 1969. Of unlimited duration, the agreement provides free access to the EEC markets for all Moroccan industrial products and privileged access for the agricultural products of major importance to Morocco. In addition, the 1976 agreement also abolished Moroccan tariff preferences for EEC products.

Customs Surcharges

Special Import Tax.—Ten percent *ad valorem* c.i.f. value on all dutiable goods; Stamp Tax: 2 percent of duty plus Special Import Tax, on all dutiable goods; Control and Stamping Tax: 5 percent *ad valorem* c.i.f. on imported rugs; Special Tax and Fee on tobacco imported by private persons; Warrant and Assay Fees on platinum, gold, and silver; Plant Inspection Fee on imported vegetables, fruit, and plants; Veterinary Inspection Fee on imported animals and meat.

Basis of Duty Assessment

Virtually all import duties are assessed on an *ad valorem* basis, which includes the wholesale value of the goods in the country of origin and all costs up to their arrival to Morocco. The dutiable value is determined by the customs office on the basis of both the importer's declaration and the wholesale value of similar goods in the local market.

Customs duties are payable in cash at the office where clearances take place, unless payment is warranted by a deposit of funds. Payment must be in local currency.

Import Documentation

Commercial Invoice.—No special invoice form is necessary, nor is a consular visa or consular certification required. Invoice prices must be quoted f.o.b. or c.i.f. (AID- or PL480-financed goods may be quoted c.i.f.). The commercial invoice should fully describe the goods in both English and French. Certification as to country of origin of the goods is required. Invoices should bear the signature of the responsible officer of the supplying firm and include the name of the bank and the account number to which payment is to be made. Payments are made through bank-to-bank transfers as provided by Moroccan exchange control regulations.

Pro forma invoices must be provided in most cases. The invoice, which should be on company letterhead, is required for both import licenses and foreign exchange transfers.

Bill of Lading/Air Waybill.—"To order" bills are acceptable. The bill of lading/airwaybill should show gross weight in pounds, volume measurement in feet and inches, identification marks, import license number, value of goods, cost of freight, and name and address of consignee.

Bills of lading by American shipping companies are acceptable. To ensure prompt identification and clearance by customs, shipping marks and numbers on the bill of lading/waybill, containers, and commercial invoice should correspond.

Sanitary and Other Special Certificates.—Shipments of potatoes, tomatoes, and eggplant must be accompanied by a phytosanitary certificate stating that the produce is free from all parasites and that it was packed and shipped under sanitary conditions. Chamber of Commerce certification of seeds is required. A number of other vegetables and some animal products not requiring phytosanitary certificates are subject to sanitary inspection upon arrival. Prior consultation with the importer is therefore recommended in all shipments of animal and vegetable products.

Marking and Labeling.—No special regulations apply to the marking of outer containers for shipments to Morocco. However, an indication on outer containers of the net weight in kilograms, together with other identification markings, will assist in locating goods on arrival and speed their clearance through customs.

Free Zones.—A commercial Free Zone was created at the port of Tangier in 1961. Merchandise entering or leaving the Free Zone is exempt from Customs, fiscal, and exchange controls. Duties must be paid, however, if goods are subsequently transferred into Moroccan customs territory.

Only "commercial" as opposed to "industrial" processing of goods is allowed in the Commercial Free Zone. Permissible operations include sorting, mixing, sampling, screening, repacking, and preserving. Ship chandlering and, subject to cer tain conditions, the sale of goods to foreign tourists also are authorized.

Financial and brokerage transactions are also permitted in the Zone. Within the Zone Moroccan currency is considered foreign exchange. There are no taxes on operations or profits in the Zone. Merchandise may be stored in the Free Zone for up to two years. Operators may use storage platforms and warehouses of the Free Zone management or lease areas and construct their own facilities. Address: Zone Franche, Tangier, Morocco.

A Tangier Industrial Free Zone, also authorized in 1961, has not significantly developed.

Warehousing

There are three kinds of warehousing (entrepôt de douane): Public communal, private communal, and private industrial. Any of these are termed "special" warehouses if the goods stored therein require special installations, e.g. oil storage tanks.

Public communal warehouses are bonded by the Finance Ministry, guarded by customs agents and managed by a city or chamber of commerce.

Private communal warehouses are authorized by the Finance Ministry but are owned and operated by private firms or individuals, such as freight forwarders.

Private individual warehouses, authorized by the Customs Office, may be set up by individual businesses for their exclusive use.

Goods may be stored for 2 years (plus two extensions of 6 months each) in public warehouses and for 1 year (plus two 6-month extensions) in private communal warehouses. At the end of this period, the goods must either be exported, imported with payment of normal duties, or transferred to one of the special temporary-entry categories described elsewhere in this report.

The following operations are permitted in public warehouses: unpacking, rebottling, reassembly or disassembly of packages and all other operations necessary to conserve or commercially prepare the goods in question. Goods stored for exportation may be mixed with other foreign or domestic origin goods as required.

Goods can be stored for 1 year (plus two 6-month extensions) in private, individual warehouses. The owner is responsible for building the warehouse and housing customs agents. After verification of the goods to be warehoused, the business may bottle, mark, imprint its trademark, or seal the goods as it sees fit. However, further processing of the goods while in private individual warehousing is forbidden.

If goods are abandoned, they will be sold by the Government. If merchandise is spoiled or found unfit for consumption, the importer is required to have it destroyed. If he refuses, the Government will do so at the importer's expense.

Samples and Advertising Matter

Samples may be admitted free of duty on posting a deposit or bond which is refunded if the sample is reexported within a year.

Advertising matter which has no commercial value is admitted duty free. Items such as ash trays, knives, key rings or other items customarily traded in commerce which have a utility value are subject to usual duties. Small noncommercial parcels may be subject to a standard duty of 10% *ad valorem* or be admitted duty free under conditions stipulated by the Minister of Finance.

Morocco does not adhere to the ATA Carnet Customs Convention for the temporary admission of goods. It also does not adhere to the customs Convention on the temporary admission of pedagogic material.

Technical Standards and Requirements

The metric system is standard in Morocco.

Electric power in Morocco is 50 cycle, one and three phase, with nominal voltage in the largest cities at about 115 or 200 volts.

Investment

Value of U.S. Investment

American investment in Morocco is relatively small—$33 million. Some 56 U.S. firms have direct investments or maintain branch offices in a number of sectors: cattle ranching, agribusiness, industries such as tires, chewing gum, pharmaceuticals, detergents, telephone equipment, sewing machines and food processing equipment, and a variety of services including banking, insurance and oil exploration. Morocco is also the site of regional/area sales offices for several American firms.

The American Chamber of Commerce in Morocco, created in 1966, is the only such organization in Africa affiliated with the Chamber of Commerce in the United States. Its address is 53, Rue Allah Ben Abdallah, Casablanca; telephone: 27-49-68; telex 21947.

Moroccan Policy on Foreign Investment

The Moroccan Government has traditionally welcomed private foreign direct investments in most sectors, reserving to itself only sectors considered vital, such as air and rail transport and phosphates. At the same time, the Government has encouraged a voluntary effort on the foreign investor's part to provide opportunities for Moroccans to share in business equity and management.

Since 1973, Morocco has enacted a series of laws (known as investment codes) that provide incentives for investment. These laws are designed to foster a liberal, profit-oriented economy offering many opportunities for profitable business ventures to investors. The investment codes cover six major areas: industrial manufacturing, tourism, maritime, handicrafts, mining, and all export industries. The codes provide their incentives through exemption from duties and taxes, loans with liberalized terms, and guarantees of transfer of capital and dividends. Long-term loans are available at reduced rates to investors mainly through two banking groups, the National Bank for Economic Development (B.N.D.E.) and the Credit Immobilier et Hotelier (C.I.H.)

The investment incentives summarized below apply to the six sectors mentioned above:

Exemption from import duties on new equipment and materials and on used machinery when authorized by the Ministry of Industry, except when such goods can be supplied locally at less than 20 percent extra cost. Full exemption from production taxes on purchases or leasing of domestic or imported equipment.

Complete exemption from production profits tax during the first 10 years of operation for firms that locate in Tangiers, Tetouan, Taza, Al Hoceima, Oujda, Nador, Ksar, Es Souk, Ouarzazate, Tarfaya and the District of Essaouira. A 50 percent reduction of the profit tax (usually levied at a rate of 48 percent after some deductions) during the first 10-year period for investments in other areas. This is with the exception of Casablanca, where an accelerated depreciation of twice the normal rate may be used for tax purposes.

Reduction of registration tax from 1.5 percent of capital invested to 0.5 percent. Five-year exemption from the annual license tax.

Guaranteed repatriation from the annual license tax of capital, investment by the foreign company.

Guaranteed transfer of dividends out of the country.

Export industries receive a 10-year exemption from profit tax on profits gained from export business no matter where they are located. In addition, 3 percent of total export turnover may be transferred overseas to run offices, conduct foreign market studies or to pay for advertising.

The national development bank, the B.N.D.E., grants loans up to 60 percent of the total capital investment for authorized industrial development projects. As further incentive to industrial investments, the Government intervenes to reduce prevailing interest rates by 2 percent. Similarly, the C.I.H. finances long-range tourism-related projects at a favorable interest rate of 6 percent.

For all investments exceeding $6.5 million, further privileges may be granted through special agreements negotiated with the Moroccan Government.

There also are additional incentives in tourism, fishing, and mining. For tourism investments, aside from normal financing available from the C.I.H., which can amount to up to 55 percent of the total investment, 15 percent may be borrowed interest-free for 10 years with a 5-year grace period for repayment. Additionally, there is a 100 percent 10-year exemption on profit taxes for development in El Judida, Setlat, Beni Mellal and Safi. In other areas, the exemption is 50 percent. In the fishing and shipping sector, the Government will subsidize up to 15 percent of the purchase of commercial vessels less than 5 years old. The subsidy may also apply to onboard or onshore related equipment. There is also an additional selection grant of 15 percent of the cost for certain types of vessels—including refrigerated fishing boats, bulk carriers, ferrics and oil tankers over 2,000 tons. For mining ventures in which the investment is over $110,000 or creates more than 50 jobs, the Government will contribute up to one-half of the project-related infrastructure costs.

An investment advisory service (Service d'Accueil des Investissements) has been set up within the Economic Council of the Prime Minister (Direction des Affaires Economiques aupres de Premier Ministre) and should be consulted for details. Its address is: 23 bis, ave, Moulay El Hassan, Rabat, Morocco. Tel: 348.37.

Further information on Moroccan investment regulations is available from the Commerce Action Group for the Near East, Bureau of Export Development, U.S. Department of Commerce, Washington, D.C. 20230.

Treaties

The 1836 Treaty of Peace and Amity between Morocco and the United States is still in force providing certain basic guarantees, including most-favored-nation trading rights.

An Investment Guaranty Agreement between the United States and Morocco, signed March 31, 1961, covers risks of war, convertibility and expropriation and applies to all American investments approved by the Moroccan Government.

A treaty to avoid double taxation of income was signed by the United States and Morocco on August 1, 1977. It still awaits approval, however, by the U.S. Senate.

Types of Business Organization

The organization of industrial and commercial activities is governed by the Commercial Code of August 12, 1913, as amended. Based on the French legal system, the code recognizes four basic types of company, in addition to sole proprietorship (commerce prive or enterprise individuel). The Commercial Code freely permits the constitution, extension or merger of firms. The only formalities required to form a company consist of entering the statutes with the secretariat of the Court of First Instance and in the Commercial Register kept by the Court.

As in the United States, a person may create or purchase a business without incorporating. The owner of such a business (sole proprietorship) has responsibility for all operations and transactions, and in case of debts, personal goods and chattels as well as business assets may be attached.

The four main types of companies are: partnership (societe en nom collectif), limited partnership (societe en commandite) and two forms of joint-stock companies: limited-liability company (societe a responsibilite limitee, SARL) and corporation (societe anonyme, S.A.). The characteristics of these forms of business organization are similar to those of their American counterparts.

Patent, Trademark, and Copyright Protection*

There is not as yet a unified patent and trademark law for the Kingdom of Morocco;

separate laws exist for former French Morocco and for the former Tangier Zone. As indicated below, it is necessary to file separate applications for each of these areas. The situation regarding the former Spanish Zone and the Western Sahara is unclear.

The Kingdom of Morocco is a member of the Paris Union International Convention for the Protection of Industrial Property, to which the United States and 85 other countries adhere. Under this Convention, American business executives and investors are entitled to receive patent and trademark protection equal to that accorded Moroccan citizens. In addition, American nationals are entitled to a "right of priority" after first filing an application in the United States. A period of 1 year for patents and 6 months for trademarks is allowed in which to file a corresponding application in Morocco and receive for the latter the benefit of the first U.S. application filing date.

The Nice Trademark Classification System (34 product and 8 service classes) is used in Morocco.

Morocco is a member of the Universal Copyright Convention to which the United States adheres. As such, U.S. authors receive automatic protection for their works first copyrighted in the United States (must show name, year, date and "C" in circle). Morocco also is a member of the Berne Union Copyright Convention. Although the United States is not a member of this convention, U.S. authors may obtain copyright protection in Berne Union Countries, including Morocco, by simultaneous publication of a work in the United States and a Union country.

Patents.—Patent applications in the former French zone of Morocco should be filed with the Office Marocain de la Propriete Industrielle, Casablanca. Patents for use in this region are granted for 20 years commencing with the effective filing date of the application. A patentee who is a national of a Paris Union country must work his patent within 3 years from date of grant; for others, the time limit is 3 years from filing of application.

In the former Tangier Zone, patent applications should be filed with the Bureau de la Propriete Industrielle, Tangier. Regular patents are granted for 20 years from application filing date. Patents of importation are granted for an exclusive right to manufacture locally, but not to prevent importation of similar foreign articles, for

*Prepared by Foreign Business Practices Division, Office of International Finance and Investment, Bureau of International Economic Policy and Research, U.S. Department of Commerce.

10 years from the application date. Applications are examined for conformity to formal requirements and patents are granted upon acceptance of application. Patents must be worked within 3 years from the date of the grant and for a minimum of 3 consecutive years.

In the former Spanish Zone, patent registrations applied for in Spain prior to April 7, 1956 are reportedly valid for their original terms. No provisions exist for accepting new applications and it is not yet clear whether registrations in the other Zones are applicable here.

Trademarks.—Trademarks in Morocco are valid for 20 years from the date of registration and in the former Tangier Zone from application filing date and are renewable for like periods. Applications for the registration of trademarks should be filed with the Office Marocain de la Propriete Industrielle in Tangier, as appropriate. The prior user of a mark is entitled to its registration but the registration of a mark by another becomes exclusive unless the prior user takes steps to provide this right. In the former Tangier Zone, trademark applications are published for opposition for 2 months; this is not true in the former French Zone.

The situation regarding protection of trademarks in the former Spanish Zone suffers from the same ambiguity surrounding the protection of patents in that region.

Copyrights.—Morocco's copyright law was enacted effective October 7, 1970. Literary and artistic works are extended copyright protection for the author's life plus 50 years after death.

Further information on the patent, trademark, and copyright laws of Morocco may be obtained from the Foreign Business Practices Division, Office of International Finance and Investment, Bureau of International Economic Policy and Research, U.S. Department of Commerce. For more specific information and advice on step-by-step procedures in Morocco for obtaining such protection, the services of specialized legal counsel should be secured.

Entry and Repatriation of Capital

Exchange controls are administered by the Exchange Office (Office des Changes), 12 Charii Amr Ibn Al Aas, b.P. 71, Rabat, an agency under the Ministry of Finance. The Office has delegated the execution of certain exchange control measures to authorized banks ("approved intermediaries"). Most foreign transactions, including import and investment capital, transfer of investment income, repatriation of salaries, changes in the makeup of investments in Morocco, and import/export licensing, are subject to Exchange Office regulations and procedures.

American or other foreign investment in Morocco can be undertaken without prior permission from the Exchange Office but the eventual repatriation of such investments may be difficult. Retransfer abroad of capital invested by foreigners in Morocco is guaranteed by the Moroccan Government if a retransfer guarantee is obtained when the investment is made. To obtain this retransfer guarantee, the investor must finance his investment by exchanging convertible currency through the Bank of Morocco either directly from abroad or by withdrawing funds from a "foreign convertible account," which contains convertible dirhams maintained in a Moroccan bank.

The retransfer guarantee is an irrevocable undertaking by the Exchange Office to authorize, whenever requested, the full or partial transfer of the value of an investment into the currency or type of account from which it was originally financed. Notable types of investment which are not eligible to receive transfer guarantees are those financed by contributions in kind. Money from blocked accounts which is reinvested can be transferred after 5 years pursuant to investment code guidelines.

All investment income earned by nonresidents in Morocco may be transferred abroad by the investor regardless of whether the invested capital itself is retransferrable. Investment income for this purpose includes interest payments, dividens, mortgage interest, operating profits, rents and similar earnings from capital. Appropriate taxes must be paid.

Some 20% of the salary of a foreign salaried employee who is single or whose family resides with him in Morocco and 50 percent in the case of an employee whose family resides abroad may be repatriated upon authorization by the Exchange Office after certification of the amount of the salary by the Ministry of Labor. The same percentage applies for professional workers up to a DH 12,000 ($2,675) annual maximum. A certificate of residence for a family residing abroad must be submitted in support of the 50 percent remittance request. Authorizations normally must be renewed every 6 months.

Foreigners engaged in agricultural, industrial or commercial activities or in skilled crafts may transfer abroad a similar percentage of their income subject to a monthly limit of DH 300 ($67).

Nonresident travelers to Morocco are not required to declare the amount of foreign exchange brought into the country. All foreign exchange must, however, be exchanged at authorized banks. Import or export of Moroccan currency over DH 10 (2.25) is prohibited.

Residents (defined as persons residing in Morocco more than 6 months or having their principal activity in Morocco or companies established in Morocco) must cede all incoming transfers of foreign exchange to the Bank of Morocco. Residents of foreign nationality have the right to hold assets outside the country.

Nonresident Accounts

Various forms of nonresident accounts are maintained by Moroccan banks but two are of special interest to U.S. executives: Foreign Accounts in Convertible Dirhams and Capital Accounts.

Foreign Accounts in Convertible Dirhams may be credited freely with authorized payments due to nonresidents (except payments for imports, for which other regulations apply) and with dirhams obtained from the sale of convertible currencies to the Bank of Morocco. This account may be debited freely for payments in Morocco and for purchases of convertible currencies from the Bank of Morocco.

Capital Accounts are credited with funds that cannot be transferred abroad. Capital Account funds may generally be used to purchase Moroccan securities or shares of Moroccan companies listed on the Casablanca stock exchange; to buy government or state enterprise bonds; and may be debited for limited personal expenses (up to DH 100, or $22.50, per day) and costs of upkeep, taxes and insurance on real estate located in Morocco. Interest and dividends from government bonds are freely transferrable abroad. All other operations through Capital Accounts require individual approval.

Labor Force

Morocco's working population reached 4.49 million in 1977, equivalent to 27 percent of the population. Of the total labor force, 83 percent are gainfully employed in Morocco, while the remainder are either occupied in the public work relief program, have emigrated to Europe, or are unemployed. The Government's work relief program (Promotion Nationale) employed 70,000 workers or 1 percent of the labor force in 1977. Emigration, mainly to Western Europe, amounted to 130,000 workers or 3 percent of the labor force.

Agriculture provides jobs for 51 percent of the total working population, followed by manufac-turing (11 percent), services (8.8 percent), commerce (7.8 percent), construction and public works (7 percent), transport and communications (3 percent), and energy and mining (1 percent each).

Moroccan labor is generally well organized in the major cities and is particularly strong in the transport, mining, petroleum, administrative, and hotel sectors, as well as among post workers. Organized labor has been dominated by the *Union Marocaine du Travail* (U.M.T.) for the past 20 years. Membership figures are unavailable, but total strength probably does not exceed 100,000.

Labor Legislation

Moroccan labor legislation is well developed and provides for a maximum 48-hour week, (10-hour day), and a comprehensive social security system including old age pension, sickness, accident, invalid, death, and survivor benefits. All apprentices and salaried or wage earning personnel in industry, commerce, or professions are covered. Agricultural workers are covered by a minimum wage.

Establishment of a new industrial or commercial enterprise must be declared to the provincial Labor Inspectorate, which is responsible for overseeing the application of labor laws and mediating labor disputes.

All employees are obliged to affiliate with the National Social Security Fund (Caisse National de Securite Sociale, CNSS) and should mention their affiliation number on company letterheads and other documents.

Manpower must be recruited, initially through the local Labor Exchange in the area where a new enterprise will be located. If candidates sponsored by the Exchange are unsuitable to the employer, the latter may recruit the employees and inform the Exchange of those chosen within one week.

Work contracts between employer and employees, whether written or verbal, are governed by two decrees dated August 12, 1913, and October 23, 1948, which together describe minimum reciprocal rights and duties of employee and employer. An employer may make more favorable arrangements by securing an agreement with the Ministry of Labor. Wages must be paid at least twice a month, salaries at least monthly. Overtime pay must be at least 25 percent additional (50 percent between 10 p.m. and 5 a.m.). These rates are doubled for work during normal days off. Work contracts of non-

Moroccan employees must be approved by the Ministry of Labor.

In 1977 the minimum wage stood at 35 cents an hour for industrial workers and $1.80 per day for agricultural workers. Wages actually paid to workers are generally higher than the minimum.

Although annual bonuses are not required by law, most employers pay employees a *gratification de fin d'annee* in the form of an additional month's salary at the end of the calendar year. In addition, wage earners are also due a *prime d'anciennete* of 5 percent if they have worked for 2 years in the same establishment and 10 percent after 5 years in the same firm or under the same employer. Social welfare contributions from employers generally add about 30 percent to a worker's wages. Benefits (as a percentage of total salary) include: paid leave: 8.4 percent (18 days per year plus three paid holidays: March 3, May 1, and November 18).

Contribution to CNSS: with (1) 5 percent for general social security up to DH 500 ($112.50) maximum (an additional 2.5 percent is withheld from pay-checks by the employer) and (2) 8 percent for family allowances; medical coverage (only for firms employing more than 50 persons or using products liable to cause occupational diseases): 1.5 percent; workmen's compensation (accidents, sick leave): 10 percent.

Taxation

Morocco's tax system is based on taxes on income and profits, on property and on production and consumption. There are also license and stamp taxes, a Government bond, and an investment reserve requirement. Customs duties and surcharges and social security contributions are discussed in other sections of this report.

Taxes on income and profits include:

1. The business profits tax *(Impôt sur les Benefices Professionels)* is levied on commercial, industrial and professional profits of firms and individuals, Rental income is generally not subject to this tax. For firms, the tax is 40 percent for income under DH 500,000, 44 percent for income between DH 500,000 and DH 2 million, and 48 percent for higher income. For individuals, the tax rate is progressive, ranging from 5 percent (on income under Dh 3,000) to 48 percent (over DH 2 million).

2. Dividends tax *Impôt sur les Revenues):* Dividends paid to Moroccan residents are subject to a progressive tax similar to the business profits tax.

3. Tax on wages and salaries *(Prelevement sur les Traitments et Salaries)*: for residents, the tax is levied on income for all countries; for non-residents, on Moroccan income only. The progressive rate ranges from 6 percent (minimum DH 3,000 income) to 36 percent (over DH 60,000). An additional complementary tax *(Contribution Complementaire)* is applied on total net income exceeding DH 24,000 per year, whether or not this income is already subject to the business profits tax. The rate for the complementary tax is progressive, ranging from 3 percent to 45 percent (the latter on taxable income exceeding DH 75,000).

4. Agricultural tax *(Impôt agricole)*: levied on the productive capacity of farms, fruit trees, or the livestock headcount. The rate ranges from 8 percent to 20 percent of income.

Taxes on property include an urban tax, based on the rental value of urban buildings; a municipal tax, applied in some cities in addition to urban tax; and taxes on the transfer of property.

Taxes on production, transactions and consumption are as follows:

1. Product and services tax *(Taxe sur les Produits et les Services)*:

These are levied on most imported and domestically produced goods and services. The product tax, like a value-added tax, is applied to the productive value added to the good, not counting value already taxed at a previous stage. Certain goods, including exports, are excluded from this tax. The product tax is 15 percent on most goods; it is 20 percent on large cars, gems, and spirits; lower on certain foodstuffs (9 percent to 12 percent), pharmaceuticals, raw materials, radio-TV materials (8 percent), and utilities and petroleum products (6.38 percent). The services tax is generally 7.5 percent but varies according to the service from 4 percent to 9 percent.

2. Consumption tax: levied on specified goods such as spirits, petroleum products, explosives, sugar, tea, spices, chocolate, matches, tires and mineral waters.

Other taxes include the license tax (impôt des patents), levied on all industrial and commercial enterprises and on professional services according to the rental value of the premises, number of employees, and characteristics of the business; there are also registration, notarial, and stamp taxes.

Government Bond Program.—Wage and salary earners who earn over DH 6,000 yearly net are required to purchase non-negotiable government bonds as a form of forced savings. Subscriptions are deducted by employers in the following percentage: 0.5 percent of annual income between DH 6,000 and DH 12,000; 1 percent between DH 12,000 and DH 24,000; 1.5 percent for higher amounts.

Investment Reserve.—Firms whose taxable business profits are greater than DH 50,000 must each year set aside an investment reserve consisting of a fixed percentage of profits. The reserve is carried over from year to year for the life of the firm. A specified percentage of the reserve must be set aside to purchase 10-year equipment bonds at 5 percent interest. The balance remains with the assets of the firm and can be used to cover losses or increase capitalization. It cannot be distributed with other profits until the eventual merger or dissolution of the firm.

Guidance for Business Travelers

Entry Requirements

U.S. citizens must possess a valid U.S. passport but a visa is not required for a stay of 90 days or less. Smallpox and cholera vaccinations are required, and it is recommended that travelers to Morocco be immunized for typhoid, typhus and cholera.

Persons proposing to establish residence must possess a work contract delivered by the employer and approved and certified by the Ministry of Labor and Social Affairs. Work contracts will be approved for foreigners only if qualified Moroccans cannot be found for the position. Applications to renew these contracts or to change employment will be considered on the same basis as original applications for entry. Within two weeks of arrival, foreigners who intend to apply for resident status must register for a "Carte d'Etranger" at Casablanca.

Customs regulations permit duty-free entry of clothing, personal effects, and household items intended for personal use, subject to specified limits on the amount of film, tobacco, and the like. Travelers wishing to import a vehicle must present the registration papers issued in the country of origin.

This initial dispensation expires at the end of six months at which time the vehicle becomes subject to the usual import formalities. With the exception of stipulated personal allowances for alcoholic beverages and tobacco products, all other goods, whether imported for personal use of sale, are subject to duty.

Languages

French is the commercial and working language of Morocco. Arabic is the official language. Berber dialects are spoken by one-third of the population. Spanish is also understood in northern areas. Business correspondence, including bids on tenders, always should be in French. English is rarely understood.

Business Hours

Government offices are open most of the year, from 8:30 a.m. until noon and 2:30 to 6 p.m., Monday through Thursdays, 8:30 until 11 a.m., and 4 to 6 p.m. on Fridays, and 8:30 to noon on Saturdays. In July and August they are open 8 a.m. to noon, and 4 p.m. to 7 p.m. Business shop hours vary but generally are 8:30 a.m. to noon, and 3 to 7 p.m. Monday through Friday, and 8:30 a.m. to 1 p.m. on Saturday.

In summer some offices work from 8 a.m. 1 p.m., Monday through Saturday.

The U.S. Embassy is open 8:30 a.m. to 12:30 p.m. and 2 to 6 p.m. Monday through Friday, with summer variations. Some suggested hours to meet executives are early morning and early afternoon for private business; late morning and late afternoon for government officials.

Hotels

Rabat.—Tour Hassan; Rabat Hilton; Cellah.

Casablanca.—El Mansour; Marhaba; Hotel Casablanca.

Tangier.—Rif Hotel; Grand Hotel; Intercontinental Hotel; Villa de France.

Transportation

TWA and Royal Air Maroc provide service to Casablanca from the United States. There are air connections with most major European cities as well as with Algiers and Tunis. Taxis and cars are plentiful in major cities. There are good paved roads and the rail system is well-developed. Telex, telegraph, and telephone service is available to Europe and the United States.

Holidays

Official holidays and others on which government offices and business establishments are likely to be closed in 1980 are:

New Year's Day	January 1
*Moulid al Nabi	January 28 or 29
Throne Day	March 3
Labor Day	May 1
Youm Eddahab	August 14
*Aid al Fitr	August 12 or 13
*Aid al Adha	October 21 or 22
Anniversary of the Green March	November 6
Independence Day	November 18
*Fatih Moharram	November 10

Holidays marked with asterisks are based on the lunar calendar and change every year. Christians and Jews may also celebrate their respective holidays: Easter Monday, Ascension Day, Whit Monday, Assumption Day, All Saints Day, Christmas, Passover, Rosh Hashana, and Yom Kippur. During the month of Ramadan most business and Government activities are considerably curtailed.

Sources of Economic and Commercial Information

Government Representation

American Embassy
1 Ave de Marrakech
Rabat, Morocco
Phone: 30361, 30362
Telex 31005

American Consulate General
No. 8 Blvd. Moulay Youssef
B.P. 675
Casablanca, Morocco
Phone: 60521/23, 60562
No telex

American Consulate General
Chemim des Amoureux
Tangier, Morocco
Phone: 35904
No telex

Embassy of Morocco
1601 21st St., N.W.
Washington, D.C. 20009
Phone: (202) 462-7979/82

Consulate General
(includes Moroccan National
  Tourist Office)
597 Fifth Ave.
New York, N.Y. 10017
Phone: (212) 421-5771

Commerce Action Group for the Near East
Bureau of Export Development
U.S. Department of Commerce
Washington, D.C. 20230
Phone: (202) 377-5737

Moroccan Government Publications

Statistiques du Commerce Extérieur, Office des Changes, Ministère des Finances. Annual; in French.

Statistiques des Echanges Extérieure du Maroc, Office des Changes, Ministère des Finances. Monthly; in French.

Bulletin Mensuel d'Information, Office de Commercialisation et d' Exportation (OCP). Monthly; in French.

Revue Bimensuelle d'Informations, Banque Marocaine du Commerce Extérieur. Bi-monthly; in both French and English.

La Situation Economique de Maroc, Direction de la Statisque, Secrétariat d'Etat au Plan et au Dévéloppement Régional. Annual; in French.

Bulletin Mensuel, Direction de la Statistique, Secrétariat d'Etat au Plan et au Développement Régional. Annual; in French.

Le Maroc en Chiffres. Direction de la Statique and Banque Marocaine de Commerce Extérieur. Annual; in French.

Activité du Secteur Pétrolier, 1976, Direction de l'Energie, Ministère du Commerce, de l'Industrie, des Mines et de la Marine Marchande. In French.

U.S. Government Publications

Morocco, A Country Study, 1978, printed by American University, Washington, D.C. and available from Government Printing Office, Washington, D.C. 20402. Publication number DA Pam 550–49.

Background Notes: Morocco, published October, 1978, by U.S. Department of State, Washington, D.C. Publication number 7954.

Other Sources

Middle East Economic Digest (weekly). published by MEED, 84–86 Chancery Lane, London WC 2A 1DL, United Kingdom.

The Middle East and North Africa, Annual, published by Europa Publications Ltd., 18 Bedford Square, London, United Kingdom.

Appendix

Selected Moroccan Government Ministries and Agencies

Ministry of Industry and Commerce
Quartier des Ministères
Rabat-Chellah
Tel.: 65951

Ministry of Energy and Resources
Quartier des Ministères
Rabat-Chellah
Tel.: 65951

Ministry of Agriculture
Quartier des Ministères
Rabat-Chellah
Tel.: 61535

Ministry of Finance
Quartier des Ministères
Rabat-Chellah
Tel.: 67171

Ministry of Tourism
Quartier des Ministères
Rabat-Chellah
Tel.: 61701

Bureau de Recherches et de Participations
Minières (BRPM)
27, Charia Moulat Hassan
P.O. Box 99
Rabat
Tel.: 63035

Office Cherifien des Phosphates (OCP)
305, avenue Mohammed V
Rabat
Tel.: 60277

Office de Développement Industriel (ODI)
8, rue Ghandi
Rabat
Tel.: 32181

Office National de Commercialisation et
d'Exportation (OCE)
45, avenue des F.A.R.
Casablanca
Tel.: 224103

Office National des Pêches (ONP)
13-15, rue Chevalier Bayard
Casablanca
Tel.: 240551

Secretariat of State for Economic Affairs in the
Prime Minister's Office
Quartier des Ministéres
Rabat-Chellah
Tel.: 65630

Service d'Accueil des Investisseurs
23, avenue Moulay Hassan
Rabat
Tel.: 64710

Crédit Immobilier et Hôtelier (CIH)
159, avenue Hassan II
Casablanca
Tel.: 222959
Telex: 22839

Direction de la Marine Marchande et des
Pêches Maritimes
Avenue El Hansali
Casablanca
Tel.: 261733

Direction Générale des Douanes et Impôts
Indirects
Place des Nations Unies
Casablanca
Tel.: 262301

Market Profile—MOROCCO

Foreign Trade

Imports.—$3.7 billion in 1979; $3.1 billion in 1978. Major suppliers (1979): France, (32 percent), Spain (10 percent); United States (6 percent), West Germany (6 percent), Italy (6 percent). Principal imports: crude petroleum, wheat, iron and steel products, crude vegetable oils, chemicals. From the United States (1979, $271.3 million): grain, aircraft, automobile parts, trucks, cotton, machinery, scientific instruments.

Exports.—$1.9 billion in 1979; $1.6 billion in 1978. Major markets (1979): France (28 percent), West Germany (10 percent), Spain (7 percent), Italy (5 percent), Netherlands (5 percent). Principal exports: phosphates, citrus fruit, canned fish, rugs, lead. To the United States (1979, $39.3 million): phosphates, vegetables, manganese ore, crude mineral substances, travel goods.

Trade Policy.—Nondiscriminatory tariff. Partial association agreement with European Economic Community (EEC) gives EEC reserved subquotas (which in practice have no discriminatory effect) for commodities subject to global quotas and licensing.

Trade Prospects.—Excellent prospects for goods needed to meet development goals. European competition tough, but Eximbank credits facilitate U.S. suppliers. U.S. firms must emphasize after-sales service, financing, and competitive prices.

Foreign Investment

Government encourages foreign investment in selected targets (mining, tourism, export industries) governed by 1973 investment codes. Moroccanization decrees issued in 1973 require that specified businesses be 50 percent Moroccan-owned and a majority of board directors and board chairmen be Moroccan. Existing foreign investment, primarily French, includes 56 U.S. firms. There is an Investment Guaranty Agreement with the United States.

Finance

Currency.—Moroccan dirham 3.8=US$1 as of April, 1980. One dirham=100 centimes. Money supply $6,208 million in March 1980.

Domestic Credit.—Available from 16 private commercial banks and several semi-public financial institutions.

National Budget.—1979 expenditures $5,733 million. 1980 planned expenditures $6,200 million. Primary emphasis is on the social sector, especially education and housing.

Balance of Payments.—Current account deficit in 1979 $1,205. Foreign exchange reserves $288 million (May 1980).

Development Plan. Emphasis of "interim" Three Year Development Plan (1978–80) is on export-oriented industry, agricultural and fish processing, and mining. Education, public health and low-cost housing will receive increased attention.

Economy

Basically agricultural with growing manufacturing, tourism and mining sectors. Real GDP $8 billion in 1979 (per capita $805). Distribution: commerce (22 percent), manufacturing (17 percent), government (14 percent), agriculture (13 percent), building and public works (6 percent), transport and communications (5 percent), mining (3 percent), other services (15 percent).

Agriculture.—Leading products include grains, citrus, vegetables, wine grapes, wool. Efforts to increase and diversify agricultural production for export. Major investment in irrigation and flood control.

Industry.—Industrial production increasing moderately, led by food and mineral processing, metalworking, and textiles.

Mining.—Phosphate production 20,061,000 metric tons in 1979. Other minerals include iron ore, coal, manganese, lead, flourite, cobalt and copper.

Tourism.—Tourist arrivals rose 2.9 percent in 1978 to 1.5 million, generating receipts of $413 million. The Government, in cooperation with private capital, is undertaking substantial expansion of tourist facilities.

Basic Economic Facilities

Transportation.—26,000 kilometers of paved roads; 1,778 kilometer railway network services mining, industry, and major cities. International airports located at Casablanca, Rabat, Fes, Tangier, Oujda, Marrakech and Agadir. Casablanca is the principal port; others include Safi (phophates), Kenitra, Mohammedia, Agadir, and Essauoira.

Communications.—State-owned and operated; 230,000 telephones; 95,000 radios; 183,000 TV sets.

Power.—Electric power generated 1979: 4,371.6 million kWh. Grid covers entire country.

Natural Resources

Land.—171,800 square miles. Rif and Atlas mountain ranges separate agricultural zones from Sahara.

Climate.—Mediterranean: mild winters and warm, dry summers. Desert climate south and east of Atlas Mts.

Forestry.—12 percent of total land area, State-owned. Exports include cork, dwarf palm fiber, wood pulp.

Fisheries.—Important and growing industry. 1979 catch: 280,000 tons. Sardines, mackerel and tuna are principal exports.

Population

Size.—19.1 million (1978). Annual growth 2.9 percent. (35 percent urban). Cities: Rabat, the capital (385,000); Casablanca, commercial center (2 million); Marrakesh (333,000); Fez (322,000).

Language.—Arabic is the official language, and Berber is common in remote communities. French is used in business and government.

Education.—Literacy: 23.5 percent of school age and above; 42 percent primary school enrollment.

Labor.—Total labor force 4.5 million (1977); of these 51 percent in agriculture, 20 percent in industry, 29 percent in services.

Market Profile— MOZAMBIQUE

Foreign Trade

Imports.—$819 million in 1981; $792 million in 1982. Major suppliers in 1981: France, 11.4 percent; Brazil, 10.3 percent; Saudi Arabia, 9.3 percent; United Kingdom, 7.8 percent; and Bangladash 7 percent. Imports from United States in 1981 $35 million, in 1982 $26.5 million. Principal imports were petroleum, food and dranspont goods.

Exports.—$382 million in 1981; $303 million in 1982. Major markets in 1981: United States, 71.5 percent; Venezuela, 11.8 percent; Kenya, 10.3 percent; and Singapore 9 percent. Exports to United States in 1981: $83.1 million, $50.9 million in 1982. Principal exports cashews and sugar.

Trade Policy.—Lack of unified legal system for trade disputes, foreign exchange shortage, and "red tape" impede personal sales contacts.

Trade Prospects.—Transactions should be on basis of irrevocable letter of credit or other assured method of payment. Opportunities continue for sales of capital goods, grains, fertilizers, chemicals, and pharmaceuticals.

Foreign Investment

Government has recently accelerated its efforts to attract foreign investment. Decree-law 18/17 of April 1977, guarantees investors the rights of profit repatriation and protection from nationalization, and outlines the terms of foreign participation. Petroleum Activity Law of October 1981 clarifies government policy toward foreign investment in petroleum and natural gas development. Natural resources development (mining, energy, agriculture, fishing) seems to offer the most promise for investors at the present time. Investment opportunities also exist on fisheries, forestry management and development, and hydroelectric power generation. U.S. investments $2 million in 1982.

Finance

Currency.—Mozambique metical (40.92 MM=US$1 in Oct. 1983). Cumulative money supply in 1977 was $822 million.

National Budget.—Estimated budget of $1 billion in 1981. Deficit of $75 million on recurrent expenditures of $523 million. Investment budget of $661 million, said to be balanced. Total external debt: approximately $454 million.

Foreign Aid.—$184.2 million, 1980. Largely East Bloc; United States has PL-480 food program.

Balance of Payments.—Overall deficit of $187.6 million for 1981. Gold and foreign exchange reserves, which were $231.8 million in 1977, are believed to have fallen substantially. Foreign exchange remittances of workers outside Mozambique important to economy. External debt said to be $454 million, 1980.

Economy

Based primarily on subsistence agriculture. Industry and mining play minor roles. GNP estimated at $1.8 billion in 1981, per capita GNP, $140.

Agriculture.—Main cash crops: sugar, coconuts, copra, cashew nuts, timber, tea, sisal, cotton, tobacco.

Industry.—Mainly food processing, tobacco, and textile manufacturing, vegetable oil refining, assembly of transistor radios.

Mining.—Some copper, bauxite, beryl, bismuth, iron ore, columbo-tantalite, and gold, extensive effort underway to inventory mineral resources. Large coal deposits, production 319,608 metric tons 1979. Offshore and onshore petroleum exploration underway.

Development.—The 1978-79 Development Budget called for $104 million in capital investment in highways, $70 million in ports and railways, and $68 million for water projects. Other priority sectors for development funds are construction of public buildings, mining, housing, air and marine transport and fisheries.

Basic Economic Facilities

Transportation.—3,436 km of railway and 26,498 km of roads (17 percent). Major airports and seaports at Beira and Maputo and seaport at Nacala. Local LAM airline provides domestic and regional service. Seaports and rail lines also serve Zambia, Malawi, South Africa, Swaziland and Zimbabwe.

Communications.—Fair system of troposcatter open-wire lines, and radio communications. Telephones: 52,200 or 0.5 per 100 people; 10 AM and, two FM radio stations. No TV stations. One Atlantic Ocean satellite station.

Power.—2.1 billion kW electric power capacity; production of 11.3 billion kWh in 1981; 1,000 kWh per capita. Cabora Bassa Dam, completed in 1977, is the largest power facility in Africa. Ultimate capacity 18 million kWh. Massingir Dam being constructed primarily for irrigation.

Natural Resources

Land.—303,769 square miles, divided into coastal low-lands, middle and high plateaus, and mountains.

Climate.—Varies from tropical to subtropical except in a few upland districts.

Forestry.—Large reserves. Main products: timber, fuel wood, mangrove bark.

Fisheries.—Fishing industry produces primarily for domestic consumption. Shellfish and canned fish exported.

Population

Size.—12.7 million 1982 (est.). Major cities: Maputo, the capital, 500,000; Beira, 115,000; Nampula, 31,000. Majority is rural.

Language.—Portugese is official.

Education.—Literacy rate estimated at 15 percent. Higher education institutions include the University of Maputo and teacher colleges in Maputo and Beira.

Tourism.—Tourism is not encouraged.

Labor.—Labor force includes 900,000 Africans (mostly unskilled), of whom 300,000 work outside the country, 44,000 Europeans and Asians. 90 percent of population engaged in family/subsistence agriculture.

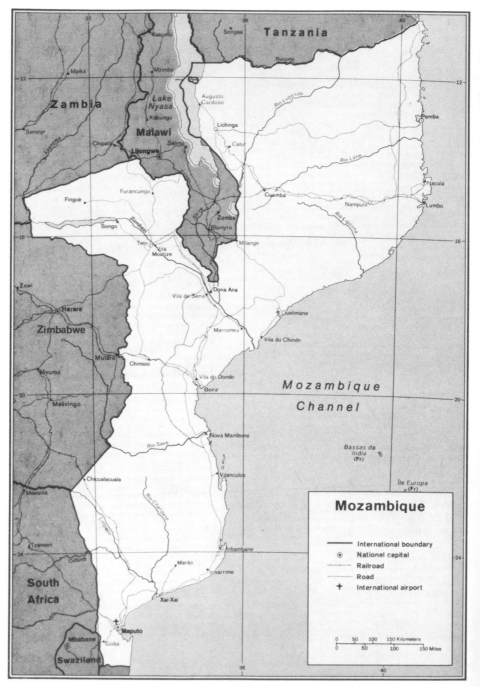

Mozambique

- International boundary
- ⊛ National capital
- Railroad
- Road
- ✚ International airport

Market Profile— NAMIBIA

Foreign Trade

Because South Africa administers Namibia (originally under a League of Nations mandate and since 1966 illegally on a de facto basis), its foreign trade statistics are included in South Africa's foreign trade statistics. According to U.S. trade statistics, U.S. imports from Namibia totaled $26.3 million, and U.S. exports totaled $7.4 million for yearend 1981.

Foreign Investment

Since May 1970 the U.S. Government has officially discouraged American investment in Namibia. The United States Government has announced that investment rights acquired through the South African Government following the termination of the mandate in 1966 will not be protected against the claims of a future lawful government in the territory. Export-Import Bank guarantees and other facilities are not available for trade with Namibia. The United States maintains no permanent diplomatic or consular representation in Namibia.

Finance

Currency.—South African Rand. R0.89=US$1 in Oct. 1983. Inflation rate of 15 percent in 1981.

Domestic Credit and Investment.—Fully integrated into the Rand Monetary System; most of the principal South African banks operate branches in the main town.

National Budget.—1983/84 budget $952 million. Revenues $897 millon; borrowings of $179 million.

Foreign Aid.—South Africa is only donor. Provided $2 billion during 1974-83.

Balance of Payments.—Balance-of-trade deficit of $41 million (1981).

Economy

GDP.—GDP decline 1.6 percent 1982; $896 GNP per capita (1980).

Agriculture.—Livestock raising predominates. Several subsistence crops are grown (millet, sorghum, corn, and wheat), but most food must be imported. Together with fishing provides 10 percent of GDP.

Manufacturing and Mining.—Consists of meat packaging, fish processing, copper, lead, diamond and uranium mining, and dairy products. Provides over 35 percent of GDP.

Basic Economic Facilities

Transportation.—Railways total 600 km; 54,500 km of highways, 7 percent paved; 2 major ports; 17 airports with hard surface runways; 1 with runway over 4,500 m; three with runways over 2,500 m.

Communications.—Good urban and fair rural service. Microwave relay connects major towns while wires extend to other population centers. There are 5.2 telephones per 100 people; 10 FM stations; 1 TV station. FM Radio services broadcast in English, Afrikaans, and German. Shortwave broadcasts in Ovambo, Herero, Damara, and Kavango.

Power.—400 MW capacity (1982); 1.3 billion kWh produced (1980); 1251 kWh per capita.

Natural Resources

Minerals.—Diamonds (1.6 million carats in 1980), uranium (5,000 tons of oxide in 1980), copper (38,000 tons in 1980), and lead (37,000 tons in 1980).

Fishing.—Up 14 percent to 247,800 metric tons (1981).

Land.—823,620 km²; mostly desert except for interior plateau and area along northern border.

Climate.—West coast is damp, cool, and rainless; inland climate is dry. All rain falls in summer months. Daytime summer temperature is high, nightime is cool. Winters are cool.

Population

Size.—1 million in 1981: Blacks (85.6 percent), White (7.5 percent), Mixed race (6.9 percent). Principal towns are Windhoek (capital), Andangwa, Tsumeb, and Luderitz. Growth rate 3 percent; 15 percent urban.

Language.—Official are Afrikaans and English; German also used.

Education.—Literacy high for white population, 28 percent for nonwhite; 1980 literacy rate for urban population, 15 percent.

Labor.—In 1981, there were 500,000, of which 12 1/2 percent are unemployed; 60 percent in agriculture, 6 percent in mining, and 19 percent in industry and commerce.

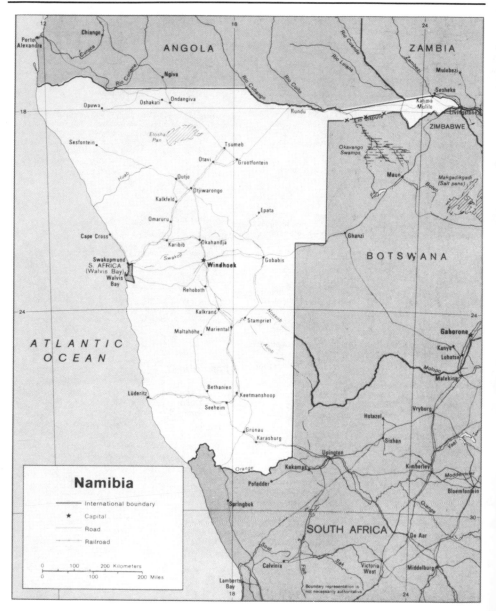

Market Profile—NAURU

Foreign Trade

Exports.—Exports in 1977 totaled $50.4 million, consisting primarily of phosphate.

Imports.—Imports were $32 million in 1977, with major imports of machinery, transportation equipment, foodstuffs, and meats.

Trade Policy.—The latest available tariff laws specify import duties on cigarettes and beverages, with low, nominal rates. All goods imported for government use are duty free.

Best Trade Prospects.—Machinery, transportation equipment, and foodstuffs.

Trading Associations.—Nauru Pacific Shipping Company, and British Phosphate Commission, which charters ships.

Finance

Currency.—Australian currency.

Banks.—The Bank of Nauru.

Economy

GNP.—In 1977, $155.4 million, with per capita income $21,400.

Industry.—Because phosphate deposits cover 80 percent of the island, the mining of phosphate has made Nauru the richest island in the Pacific. At the current production rate of 2 million tons annually, deposits will be depleted in approximately 25 years. However, mining operations will remain quite extensive for the next several decades because there are still phosphate pockets at levels below the present 24 meter mining limit that have not been tapped.

Commerce.—The Government is systematically making investments in Australian real estate to pay for the Nauruan welfare state once the phosphate revenues have ceased.

Basic Economic Facilities

Transportation.—Nauru has its own airline, Air Nauru, and an international airport. Air Nauru operates services from Nauru to Japan, Taipei, Hong Kong, the Philippines, Guam and Micronesia, the Solomon Islands, Western Samoa, New Caledonia, and Australia. The Nauru Pacific Line operates vessels servicing the island and also offers regular commercial cargo services to other users. Passenger and cargo handling is by barge, there are no harbors or wharves. Vessels are usually tied to deep-sea moorings, and cargo transportation is carried on from there. There is an excellent road system around the island linking all villages. There also is a railway line in connection with phosphate recovery.

Communications.—In 1975, Nauru began operations with a worldwide telephone communication system. Telex is also available. There also is a modern internal telephone system on Nauru.

Power.—The Nauru Public Service supplies all the electricity which is 240 volts, 50-cycle AC.

Natural Resources

Location.—Nauru is located 1,250 miles northwest of Nadi, Fiji.

Climate.—Climate is hot, the amount of annual rainfall varies. The wet cycle is from November to February.

Minerals.—Phosphate covers 80 percent of the island.

Forestry. — No resources of any commercial value.

Population

Size.—As of 1982, 9,000 inhabitants.

Language.—English is the language of business.

Education.—Education is free and compulsory for children between the ages of 6 and 16.

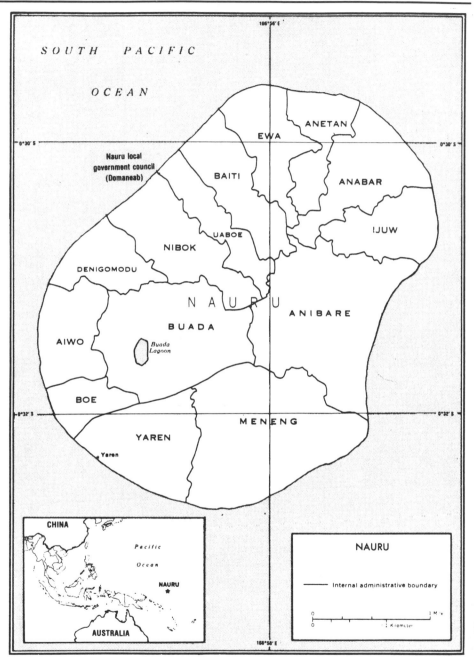

Marketing in The Netherlands

Contents

Report Revised March 1982

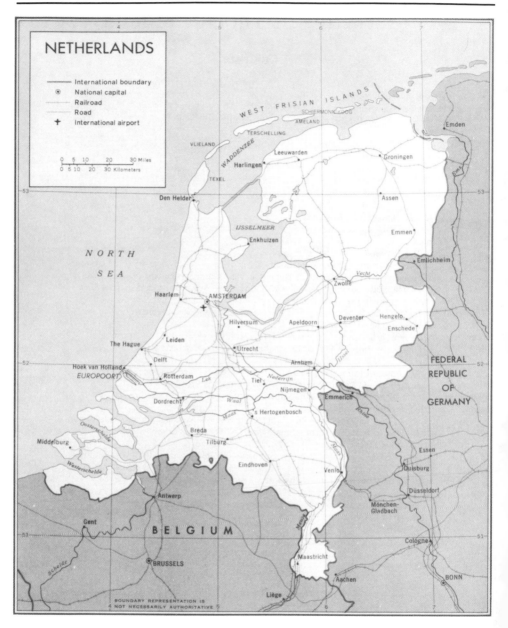

NETHERLANDS

——— International boundary
⊙ National capital
········· Railroad
——— Road
✈ International airport

0 5 10 20 30 Miles
0 5 10 20 30 Kilometers

WEST FRISIAN ISLANDS
SCHIERMONNIKOOG
AMELAND
TERSCHELLING
VLIELAND
WADDENZEE
Leeuwarden
Harlingen
TEXEL
Den Helder
Emden
Groningen
Assen

IJSSELMEER
Enkhuizen
Emmen
Emlichheim

NORTH
SEA
Vecht
Zwolle
Haarlem
AMSTERDAM
Hilversum
Apeldoorn
Deventer
Hengelo
Enschede
The Hague
Leiden
Utrecht
Delft
Arnhem
IJssel
FEDERAL
REPUBLIC
OF
GERMANY
Hoek van Holland
EUROPOORT
Rotterdam
Lek
Tiel
Nederrijn
Nijmegen
Emmerich
Dordrecht
Waal
's Hertogenbosch
Maas
Rhine
Oosterschelde
Breda
Tilburg
Middelburg
Westerschelde
Eindhoven
Venlo
Essen
Duisburg
Düsseldorf
Antwerp
Mönchen-Gladbach
Gent
BELGIUM
Cologne
Scheide
BRUSSELS
Maastricht
Aachen
BONN
Liège

BOUNDARY REPRESENTATION IS
NOT NECESSARILY AUTHORITATIVE

The Netherlands Economy

The Dutch economy is based on private enterprise. The Government has little direct ownership or participation, but it is heavily involved in the economy, with more than 60 percent of the gross national product (GNP) involved in its operations and social programs (including transfer payments). Government at all levels makes its presence felt through numerous regulations and permit requirements pertaining to almost every aspect of economic activity.

With the exception of large supplies of natural gas ashore and beneath its sector of the North Sea, the country has no significant natural resources. It has relied instead on its excellent location at the hub of Europe's transportation network and has based its development heavily on trade and services as well as industry, construction, engineering, agriculture, and fishing.

Services, which account for more than 42 percent of the natural income, are primarily in transport and financial areas, such as banking and insurance. Industrial activity provides about 33 percent of the national income and is dominated by the metalworking, chemical, and food-processing industries. Construction amounts to over 7 percent of the national income. Agriculture and fishing, although visible and traditional Dutch activities, account for only 5 percent of the national income.

Foreign trade influences the Dutch economy, with exports accounting for over 40 percent of GNP. The Netherlands has found a liberal commercial policy advantageous and participates as a charter member in the European Economic Community (Common Market), the Benelux Economic Union, and the European Monetary System (EMS). It is a firm supporter of the General Agreement on Tariffs and Trade (GATT) and a subscriber to the successful conclusion of the multilateral trade negotiations in establishing freer and expanded world trade.

The vast Slochteren gasfield in Groningen Province, which came into production in 1959, is the largest producing natural gasfield in the world. The Netherlands also has available large gas deposits in the North Sea's Continental Shelf. At present, total proven natural gas reserves (mainland and North Sea) amount to 1.8 trillion cubic meters. The reserves of other Dutch gasfields, including the Dutch North Sea sector, total about 34 percent of those of Slochteren. Current gas production is running annually at about 100 billion cubic meters, half of which is exported to EC member countries.

Dutch economic growth in the last several years has been limited by the world's general economic slowdown, with growth in 1979 about 2 percent and less than 1 percent in 1980 and 1981. Inflation, brought down from relatively high levels in the mid-1970's to about 4–5 percent in 1978–79, was up again in 1980 to 6.5 percent, with 1981 projections at the same level. The Netherlands' usual balance-of-payments current account surplus changed to a deficit from 1978 to 1980. This has been caused partly by the decision to conserve natural gas and to export less. Another factor has been the general economic malaise affecting the Netherlands major export markets since 1980.

The United States has found the Netherlands an attractive market. U.S. exports to the Netherlands totaled $8.6 billion in 1981, which gave the United States a bilateral trade surplus of $6.3 billion. The United States remains the largest source of foreign private investment in the Netherlands. Direct investments totaled $7.9 billion in book value at the end of 1980. The Dutch were also in first place in foreign investment in the United States, as their total rose to $16 billion in book value at yearend 1980.

The Netherlands Market-Trade Outlook

The Netherlands is the third largest European market for U.S. exports and the sixth largest in the world. Following 20-percent increases in 1978 and 1979, U.S. exports to the Netherlands jumped 25.3 percent in 1980 to an all-time record level of $8.7 billion, taking a 14.6-percent share of the Dutch import market. More impressive, our trade balance with this small country was in surplus by over $6.6 billion. In 1981, U.S. exports were down 1 percent to $8.6 billion. With Dutch industrial output, investment, and consumption falling, we cannot expect a repetition soon of the strong advances made by U.S. exports to the Netherlands in the recent past. The decline in Dutch imports in 1981 due to reduced domestic demand was amplified, in the case of imports from the United States, by the sharp appreciation of the dollar. If

---

FOREIGN BUSINESS INFORMATION

For information on foreign economic trends, commercial development, production, trade regulations, and tariff rates, contact the Central European Division, Office of the European Community, International Trade Administraion, U.S. Department of Commerce, Washington, D.C. 20230. This information is also available from any of the Department of Commerce district offices located throughout the United States.

NETHERLANDS

Table 1.—Key Economic Indicators, as of October 1, 1981

Income, production, and employment	1980	1981		1982 (E)	Pct. Change*
GNP at current prices ($ mil.)	132,920	138,520	(E)	149,240	plus 7.7
GNP at 1980 prices ($mil.)	132,920	131,220	(E)	132,787	plus 0.8
Per capita GNP, current prices ($)	9,355	9,749	(E)	10,504	plus 7.7
Per capita GNP, 1980 prices ($)	9,355	9,270	(E)	9,346	plus 0.8
Plant & equipment investment ($ mil.)	15,000	14,900	(E)	15,800	plus 6.8
Indices: 1975=100					
Industrial production	112	106	(AUG)	—	minus 1.9
Avg. Labor productivity	127	132	(QI)	—	minus 1.5
Avg. Industrial wage (1972=100)	204	210	(AUG)	—	plus 2.4
Disposable personal income, at current prices ($)	71,452	74,608	(E)	—	plus 4.4
Per capita income, current prices ($)	8,470	8,854	(E)	—	—
Disposable income per capita, at current prices ($)	5,076	5,150	(E)	—	—
Employment (000's) (end of year)	4,785	4,714	(E)	4,678	minus 0.8
Average unemployment rate (%)	5.8	9.1	(E)	10.81	—
Housing starts (units)	105,672	66,764	(JAN-JUL)	—	plus 15.4
Money and prices					
Money supply (M1) ($mil) (end of period)	26,234	27,796	(JUN)	—	plus 1.7
Money supply (M2) ($mil) (end of period)	42,687	47,092	(JUN)	—	plus 6.6
Public debt domestic (end of yr) ($mil)	31,236	34,567	(APR)	—	plus 26.2
Public debt external (end of yr) ($mil)	0	0		—	—
Central Bank discount rate (end of yr)	8.0	9.0	(AUG)	—	—
Domestic credit outstanding (end of yr)	47,454	49,023	(JUN)	—	plus 8.2
Indices: ($ mil)					
Retail sales (value): 1980	100	100	(E)	—	unchanged
Avg. wholesale prices: 1970=100 (excl. VAT)	128.4	141.3	JUL	—	plus 9.3
Avg. consumer prices: 1975=100	133.8	143.2	(E)	152.5 (E)	plus 6.5
Balance of payments and trade					
Gold and foreign exchange reserves (end of yr))$ mil.)	13,938	13,931	(AUG)	—	plus 7.4
Balance-of-payments current account (transactions) ($ bil.)	-1.9	1.0	(E)	40.0 (E)	—
Balance of merchandise ($ bil.)	-3.1	-0.4	(E)	+2.8 (E)	—
Total exports F.O.B. ($bil.) Dutch stats.	59.4	70.0	(E)	82.4 (E)	plus 17.8
Total imports C.I.F. ($bil.) Dutch stats.	62.5	70.4	(E)	79.6 (E)	plus 13.1
U.S. imports from Netherlands C.I.F. ($bil)**	2.04	1.16	(JAN-JUN)	—	plus 20.8
U.S. exports to Netherlands FOB ($ bil.)** (incl. reexports)	8.67	4.2	(JAN-JUN)	—	minus 7.0

Main imports from the United States (in thousand metric tons (TMT) and millions of U.S. dollars ($ mil.) Jan-Jun 1981: oilseeds, 1,638 TMT/$ 509 mil.; corn. 566 TMT/$ 91 mil.; animal feed except grains, 1,748 TMT/$ 341 mil.; chemicals, $433 mil.; aircraft and parts, $96 mil.; measure and control equipment, $80 mil.; automatic data processing equipment, $104 mi.; nonferrous ores, 11 TMT/$ 100 mil.; coal, 1917 TMT/$ 132 mil.

Percentage changes compare full year results or estimates, when available; otherwise comparable periods.
**U.S. Department of Commerce Statistics.
Note: The value of the guilder through October 1981 averaged about US$1=Dfl 2.50. For the most meaningful comparison with earlier years, 1979 and 1980 guilder figures also have been converted at that rate. Those who want to convert at actual rates should use US$1=Dfl. 1.99 for 1979 and 1.97 for 1980.
Sources: Central Bureau of Statistics (CBS), Netherlands Central Bank, Central Planning Bureau (CPB), U.S. Department of Commerce, IMF International Financial Statistics

this is not reversed, it will be hard for the United States to maintain its present share of the Dutch market. The U.S. Foreign Commercial Services (FCS) in the Netherlands recently canvassed leading Dutch importers of U.S. goods and ascertained that, while low-technology U.S. products are being hurt by price increases stemming from the appreciation of the dollar (coming on top of the price effects of a higher inflation rate in the United States than in the Netherlands and our main competitor, West Germany), technologically advanced and high-quality U.S. goods should continue to sell well. U.S. industry, however, will have to exert greater efforts to maintain the market position it achieved when the U.S. dollar was weak.

Looking at U.S export preformance from January through July 1981, the big losers were oil seeds (−20.3 percent), metal ores and scrap (−27.3 percent), nonferrous metals (−57.1 percent), and transport equipment (−20.5 percent). Modest declines were shown in the following categories: Metalworking machinery (−22.5 percent), nonpassenger vehicles (−35.5 percent), apparel (−35.9 percent), telecommunication and reproduction equipment (−15.4 percent), parts for nonpiston engines (−11.8 percent), complete computer systems (−9.3 percent), and computer CPUs (−59 percent). (Note: Big losers and gainers refer to categories that involved export values of more than $110 million in the 7-month period. Modest declines and gains refer to categories that involved export values of less than $60 million in that period.)

The big gainers were grains and cereal products (+12 percent), fertilizers (+31.1 percent), bituminous coal (+82.2 percent), office machines and ADP equipment (+11.6 percent), and airplane parts (+13.8 percent). Modest gains were shown in the following categories: paper (+25.6 percent), furniture (+19.4 percent), footwear (+16.2 percent), plywood (+134 percent), aircraft engines and parts (+105.4 percent), construction and mining machinery parts (+37.5 percent), parts for pumps (+39.6 percent), typewriters and word processors (+55.4 percent), electromedical equipment (+12.6 percent),

X-ray equipment (+33.4 percent), and photographic film and paper (+17.6 percent). The export losses and gains in some of these categories may indicate periodic shifts in trade volumes.

U.S. commercial opportunities are not rosy, but neither are they uniformly gray. The dollar-guilder exchange rate will be important, but the major determinant of the performance of U.S. exports will be the expansion of Dutch investment, production, and consumption. Only a gradual improvement can be hoped for in 1982 and modest growth, even in the best of circumstances, through 1985. Even so, the Netherlands is one of our best customers, and our exports will remain substantial. In some product areas—such as agricultural goods, office machines, computer equipment, specialized industrial machinery, and scientific, and process control systems—the opportunities for major gains are promising. Consider the fact that the Netherlands' economy has been in the doldrums for a number of years and, since 1977, has had less than 1-percent growth in GNP and foreign trade. Yet during this same period for reasons cited above, U.S. exports to this country have been bounding ahead at more than a 20-percent rate of increase in 1978 and 1979 and over 25 percent in 1980.

Dutch consumers are well known for their conservative tastes and thriftiness. They are quality and price conscious, expect delivery dates to be honored, and demand courteous, competent service. Also, the Dutch are wary of high-pressure merchandising efforts. Although the average Dutch citizen's disposable income is below that of the average American, the Dutch citizen is interested in many of the same items as the average American, but less emphasis is placed on luxury goods. American products are often considered to be more practical, to show more ingenuity in construction, and to be of better quality than many goods of Dutch domestic or other foreign origin.

The United States has traditionally been the third-ranking supplier to the Netherlands, following the Federal Republic of Germany and Belgium/Luxembourg. The commodity composition of Dutch imports from the United States has remained fairly stable in recent years, with manufactured goods accounting for about 50 percent of the total. The principal product groups imported from the United States are shown in table 2.

Macroeconomic Outlook-Industry Trends

The economic situation in the Netherlands in 1980 was sluggish, with real GNP growing by only 1 percent, unemployment rising to over 5 percent, and stagnant levels of international trade. The primary cause of this poor performance was declining domestic demand combined with depressed economic conditons in the Netherlands' major trade partners. Actual GNP in 1980 was $160.5 billion at the average 1980 exchange rate of US$1=Dfl. (Dutch guilder (florin)) 2.50.

Economic conditions in 1981 continued to deteriorate, and real GNP for the year is now expected to have declined by about 1 percent. During 1981-84, however, real GNP growth is expected to average about 0.5 to 1 percent per year. The projected GNP in 1984 will only be about $132 billion in real terms (i.e., constant 1980 prices) at the forecasted average 1984 exchange rate of US$1=Dfl. 2.50.

Sectoral growth during 1980-84 is expected to continue the same general trend as shown in the past, with relatively higher growth for the service sectors than for industry or agriculture. Overall output in the service sector—including finance, commerce, house ownership, medical services, and some quasi-official services—is expected to rise at an average rate of 2 percent per year. The slowest growing sector will be construction, where output in 1980-84 is projected to rise by only 0.1 percent per year. Agriculture and fishery production will rise by about 1.7 percent annually while output in the industrial sector (mining, manufacturing, and public utilities) will rise by about 1.5 percent per year.

Within the broad economic categories mentioned above, certain sectors will show more potential for growth as a result of gradual restructuring of the Netherlands' economy. In the energy field, the prospects for further continued rises in energy prices will necessitate the ongoing restructuring of energy-intensive industries to more efficient forms of production. In addition, fuel sources for electric power generation will be reoriented so that by 1985 some 20 percent of the Netherlands' electricity will be from coal-fired plants, as compared with 11 percent in 1980. The increasing use of coal by Dutch public utilities and private firms, together with large increases in coal use in other areas of Northern Europe, will require major expansions in the coal terminals and transshipment facilities in Rotterdam and Amsterdam. The planned reduction in Dutch output of natural gas will further reinforce this conversion to coal.

Higher energy prices also will have a negative impact on the chemical industry, which will face increasing competition in petroleum based bulk products from the oil producing nations. The

Table 2.—Principal Netherlands Imports from the United States, 1978–80

Sched-ule E Code	commodity	1978	1979	1980
		All methods, value (dollars)		
00	Animals—live	1 320 063	986 454	1 341 192
01	Meat preparations	37 491 903	43 844 942	48 431 018
02	Dairy products and birds' eggs	850 126	1 250 983	1 919 124
03	Fish (including shellfish) and preparations	20 772 276	26 740 857	29 521 805
04	Cereals and preparations of cereal, flour, etc	411 338 028	390 053 450	394 832 004
05	Vegetables and fruits	62 401 436	69 960 480	105 827 455
06	Sugar, sugar preparations, and honey	3 850 180	2 727 665	2 551 727
07	Coffee, cocoa, tea, spices, and manufactures	1 745 554	2 667 704	789 931
08	Animal feedings-stuff, excluding unmealed cereal	371 078 960	559 587 201	1 008 049 530
09	Miscellaneous food preparations	9 681 280	4 990 282	5 272 451
11	Beverages	1 018 358	2 117 422	2 304 314
12	Tobacco and tobacco manufactures	80 907 652	83 810 165	125 143 375
21	Hides, skins, and furskins—undressed	4 567 381	10 590 284	2 860 390
22	Oilseeds and oleaginous fruit	1 269 844 188	1 310 613 385	1 624 383 656
23	Crude rubber, including synthetic and reclaimed	14 427 715	29 054 445	28 799 591
24	Wood, lumber and cork	36 605 883	40 072 078	34 843 389
25	Pulp and waste paper	39 438 285	47 575 064	62 873 062
26	Raw textile fibers and their waste	13 973 297	15 880 870	16 459 977
27	Fertilizers, crude and minerals, excluding coal	57 063 045	115 994 424	140 891 710
28	Metalliferous ores and metal scrap	174 019 070	247 356 435	302 597 736
29	Animal and vegetable material, NSPF, crude	14 301 979	18 921 208	24 302 056
32	Coal, Coke, and briquettes	61 378 230	121 869 547	225 447 725
33	Petroleum and petroleum products	80 082 783	115 616 897	137 289 943
34	Gas—Natural and manufactured	52 756	3 502 095	597 587
41	Animal oils and fats	58 554 110	54 435 699	61 388 376
42	Vegetable oils and fats—fixed	20 567 241	26 938 412	40 729 442
44	Animal and vegetable oils and fats, NSPF, hydrogenized	376 667	915 098	2 498 944
51	Organic chemicals	390 710 003	563 523 789	636 714 872
52	Inorganic chemicals	83 025 380	117 252 562	109 376 445
53	Dyeing, tanning, and coloring materials	9 807 996	11 423 359	12 855 570
54	Medicinal and pharmaceutical products	59 894 347	32 914 859	54 476 579
55	Essential Oils, perfumery, soaps, etc	14 295 726	17 582 593	19 278 032
56	Fertilizers and fertilizer material, NSPF	2 143 620	6 264 787	845 724
57	Explosives and pyrotechnic products	39 207	1 102 228	1 142 762
58	Synthetic resins; rubber and plastic materials	120 786 678	171 477 025	201 899 598
59	Chemical materials and products, NSPF	72 241 198	92 356 377	122 869 908
61	Leather and leather manufactures, NSPF and DRSD, furskin	3 127 183	6 230 565	7 509 795
62	Tires and tubes for tires	2 547 059	3 752 540	3 786 670
63	Cork and wood manufactures, excluding furniture	6 194 631	11 149 701	10 274 830
64	Paper, paperboard and manufactures	51 142 764	48 907 308	58 613 585
65	Yarn, fabric, and articles, textile	26 855 569	39 157 226	47 489 530
66	Nonmetallic mineral manufactures, NSPF	28 875 264	19 057 902	31 558 177
67	Iron and steel	13 751 009	15 902 875	28 067 666
68	Nonferrous metals	104 003 439	183 530 484	364 039 533
69	Manufactures of metal, NSPF	60 430 881	71 224 221	78 506 646
71	Power generating machinery and equipment	120 108 139	153 748 387	167 931 595
72	Specialized industrial machinery	103 645 063	131 631 371	163 900 092
73	Metalworking machinery	21 324 538	22 488 876	28 303 603
74	Industrial machinery, NSPF; and machine parts, NSPF	134 076 947	152 409 137	178 733 607
75	Office machines and automatic data processing equipment	211 576 619	281 725 174	384 981 645
76	Telecommunications and sound reproduction equipment	48 952 202	72 259 410	61 587 694
77	Electrical equipment, nspf, and electrical parts, nspf	181 182 480	213 307 310	243 283 953
78	Road vehicles (including air-cushion) and parts	81 912 851	93 606 779	65 270 816
79	Transport equipment, NSPF	269 695 263	312 875 569	366 849 446
81	Heat, plumbing, and light fixtures, NSPF	4 725 004	6 279 447	10 393 266
82	Furniture and parts thereof	6 368 483	5 107 771	7 869 815
83	Travel goods, handbags, etc	1 127 252	1 067 413	507 759
84	Apparel articles and accessories	7 647 000	18 918 646	27 078 173
85	Footwear, new	812 095	956 083	1 533 215
87	Professional scientific and control instruments NSPF	123 919 584	150 531 991	190 466 063
88	Photographic equipment, optional goods, and timing apparatus	114 932 530	136 220 517	141 589 999
89	Miscellaneous manufactured articles, NSPF	90 789 932	130 492 212	147 271 546
93	Special transactions not classed by kind	13 851 717	31 589 805	34 166 873
94	Live animals, NSPF (zoo animals etc)	295 836	222 116	226 578
95	Military arms, ammunitions, vehicles, etc	47 497	16 085	17 838
96	Metal coins, not yet legal tender	153 731	69 071	32 259
97	Nonmonetary gold, except ores, etc	75 839 462	125 304 601	66 665 691
99	General merchandise, under $251, estimated	15 420 654	22 317 782	29 393 735

Source: FTT 455, 1978, 1979, 1980.

rate of investments in the chemical industrial will be down slightly in coming years and can be expected to be concentrated in facilities to produce downstream, high-quality derivatives rather than bulk products.

The reasons for this rather pessimistic outlook are the continuing problems of high labor costs, declining productivity, low profit levels and insufficient investment. The generally recognized cause of these problems is the rapid growth in the past

Table 3.—The Evolution of the Dutch Economy, 1970–81

Year	Budget Deficit/ NNI (%)	Current Account/ NNI (%)	Real Product Growth (GNP) (%)	Unemployment (%)	Share of Labor Costs in Value Added (%)
1970	3.8	−1.6	6.4	1.4	83.5
1971	3.8	−0.4	4.2	1.7	85.8
1972	2.0	3.2	3.6	2.8	85.1
1973	1.5	4.4	6.1	2.9	85.0
1974	2.9	3.4	3.6	3.5	87.8
1975	5.3	2.7	−1.9	4.9	93.9
1976	5.1	3.5	5.6	5.3	90.6
1977	4.0	0.9	2.4	5.2	91.2
1978	4.4	−1.0	2.1	5.2	91.5
1979	5.5	−1.5	2.3	5.3	93.0
1980[1]	6.0	−1.6	1.0	5.9	95.0
1982[2]	5–5.5	−0.3	0.5	6.9	97.5

Sources: Central Planning Bureau, Central Bureau of Statistics, and De Nederlandsche Bank.
[1] Estimates
[2] Projections

two decades of the public sector claim on the net national income (NNI). The government share of NNI was 41 percent in 1962 but had grown to 66 percent by 1980. Most of this increase has resulted from a wide range of social security and welfare programs. While attractive in themselves, these programs have in aggregate raised labor costs, reduced work incentives, and limited corporate profitability.

Rising unemployment in recent years has aggravated the problem and has contributed to even larger government deficits which, through the crowding-out phenomena, has further inhibited investment in production facilities. Real gross investment by enterprises was down by 6 percent in 1980 and was expected to drop another 9 percent in 1981. These trends (low investment levels, slow growth, rising unemployment, etc.) are not expected to improve in the immediate future, but there may be some improvement over the medium term. The Netherlands' inflation rate is relatively low (6.5 percent in 1981), and labor unions have agreed on the need to restrain wage costs.

These two factors, plus the recent depreciation of all European currencies, will tend to increase Dutch export competitiveness over time. A further source of optimism is the possibility of strong economic growth in the United States in 1982–84 as forecast in the Administration's economic recovery program. Such growth could serve as a major stimulus to European exports to the United States and could lead to a growth surge in the Netherlands. The depreciated value of the guilder would serve to reinforce this export-led growth surge. If such a surge does occur, GNP growth in the latter part of the 1980–84 period could be somewhat higher than the 1- to 2- percent range suggested above.

Best Prospects

The following product areas are believed to hold the greatest potential for increased U.S. export sales through 1984. The first five—computers, software, oil and gas equipment, laboratory and other instruments, and coal—are expected to offer significant long-range potential; i.e., beyond 1984. In addition to the product categories detailed below, excellent opportunities also exist for safety and security equipment; hand and power tools; air-conditioning, refrigeration, and heating equipment; hotel and restaurant equipment; and printing and graphic arts equipment.

Computers and Peripheral Equipment.—The Netherlands offers an important and rapidly growing market for computers and peripheral equipment. Imports account for about 90 percent of the market. U.S. manufacturers are the leading suppliers. In spite of the current depressed economic situation, strong growth is forecast for the next few years. Best prospects for U.S. sales include the following: Minicomputers; microcomputers, including personal computers; terminals, particularly graphics terminals and banking terminals; advanced input/output equipment; hard discs and floppy discs; and data and communication equipment.

Computer Software.— The Dutch market for computer software products and services is rapidly expanding. A market growth of 15 percent annually in real terms is forecast for the next few years. Best prospects for U.S. sales include, in general, all types of software products that do not require major conversion for use in the Dutch market. Specific products needed include: Application packages, particularly production and process control, scientific packages and cad/cam software; systems software; and microcomputers software.

Oil and Gas Production Equipment.—Oil and gas production from the North Sea is currently running at record levels. More than 300 drillings are planned for the coming years. Approximately 30 platforms will be needed, of which some will be leased from contractors. Annual investment in capital goods will run at over $350 million in the early eighties. U.S. suppliers based in the Netherlands and the United States benefit from a $1.2 billion opportunity involving compressor stations, turbines, generators, and glycol dehydrating units for natural gas and telemetery equipment. Best sales prospects in this sector include the following: drill bits, core heads, head speed stabilizers, blowout prevent-ers, bushings, churn drills, elevators, spiders, hooks and connectors, float collars, float shoes, kelly joints, pitmans, rotary tables, slips, stabilizer mandrels, swivel sockets, geophysical surveying equipment, mucking pumps, and compressors and valves.

Laboratory, Scientific, and Engineering Equipment. —The Netherlands offers a dynamic market for laboratory, scientific, and engineering instruments. Trade sources expect an annual increase of 12 percent in the laboratory instruments sector. Government expenditures on R&D is predicted to rise to $2.457 billion in 1985. Specific product categories offering best prospects for U.S. sales include the following: Spectrometers, spectrophotometers and instrumental analyzers, electron microscopes, materials testing instruments (for metals), laboratory cryogenic instruments and controls, and environmental controls.

Coal. —In the year 2000, coal is expected to furnish some 20 percent of the Netherlands' total energy needs. Coal imports for electricity generation are expected to rise from the present 2.6 million tons to 26 million tons by the turn of the century. Substantial expansion of coal use is to be based on secure supplies through long-term contracts. The Dutch Government is promoting participation in overseas coal production in order to contribute to the security of supply. The most salable product is steam coal with a sulphur content lower than 1.5 percent.

Apparel. —The Dutch apparel market, estimated at $3 billion in 1980, depends heavily on imports. Imports were $2.7 billion in 1980. The United States had a share of $38 million, an increase of 80 percent over 1979. Sportswear and leisure wear are still believed to offer the best prospects for U.S. apparel sales in the Netherlands.

Process Central Instrumentation. —After an impressive 20-percent growth in Dutch imports of U.S. process control instrumentation from 1978 to 1979, imports of this equipment from the United States jumped another 37 percent in 1980 to $130.5 million. The demand for laborsaving and energy-saving process control instrumentation is expected to continue strong over the next 4 years. The most salable products are the following: Top-quality sensing instruments, computerized display terminals offering a number of control features, high-density/high frequency multiplexing equipment, sophisticated and specialized data acquisition systems, and more highly developed microprocessor-based systems.

Automobile Parts and Accessories. —Demand for automobile parts and accessories is good, particularly if suitable for European-size cars. A considerable revival in car sales is expected again after 1982 due to a surge in demand for new and economy cars. Parts in particular demand are maintenance-free batteries, adjustable shock-absorbers, exhaust systems, asbestos-free brake linings, energy-saving lubricants and additives, LPG installations, radial tires, and sun roofs. Growth of garage equipment sales in the coming years should rise from $160 million this year to $234 million in 1984. Interest is mainly in equipment that can be used universally on large and small vehicles and tools that are compatible with metric standards. Particular interest is in hand and pocket testers, optical electronic diesel testers, computer test equipment, electronic wheel balancing and alignment equipment, body repair equipment, and specialized tools.

Medical and Health Care Equipment. —The Netherlands market for medical and health care equipment, which has steadily increased over the last 5 years, will experience less growth in the early 1980's. The demand for health care products will remain steady. Products with the best sales opportunities for U.S. manufacturers will exist in the following areas: Central cardiographic monitoring stations, cardio pacemakers and catheters, ultrasonic scanners for obstetrics and cardiology, X-ray systems for population screening, prosthetic and orthopedic apparatus, patient monitoring systems, sophisticated medical, surgical laser instruments, nuclear magnetic resonance equipment, automated cell counters, blood/gas analyzers, enzyme analysis and microbiological test kits, and ultrasonic therapy units.

Electronic Components. —The Netherlands is a major trader in electronic components, as well as an important end-user and producer. The market is expected to grow during the next few years, as a result of the many new technologies and rapidly increasing number of applications of semiconductor components. Recently, the Government announced measures to stimulate and support wider application of microelectronics by small- to medium-sized manufacturers. Major end-user sectors are communications equipment, business equipment, aviation and avionics equipment, measuring and test equipment, and consumer electronics. Best prospects for U.S. exports to the Netherlands are state-of-the-art semiconductors—particularly mass produced digital ICs, professional tubes, capacitors, and connectors.

Multilateral Trade Negotiations

The most recent series of Multilateral Trade Negotiations (MTN) held under the General Agreement on Tariffs and Trade (GATT)—The Tokyo Round—was concluded in 1979. These comprehensive and far-reaching negotiations, in which the United States and its trading partners played major roles, have resulted in agreements that should liberalize world trade over the next decade.

Of particular interest to U.S. exporters to the European Economic Community (EEC) are the six agreements that establish new rules, or codes, on government procurement, production standards, importing licensing procedures, subsidies, trade in civil aircraft and customs valuation, and the protocol that lowers tariffs on industrial and other products in general.

The codes will increase the opportunities for foreign suppliers to sell to government entities, discourage the manipulation of product standards that discriminate against imported products, simplify and harmonize import licensing procedures, provide recourse when facing subsidized competition in foreign markets, reduce government influence on civil aircraft purchase decisions and eliminate tariffs on civil aircraft and their principal components, and replace a number of different systems of customs valuation with a uniform system. The tariff protocol will reduce the EEC's average tariff level on industrial product imports from the United States by approximately 35 percent.

The agreements on product standards, subsidies and countervailing measures, import licensing procedures, trade in civil aircraft, and tariffs came into force on January 1, 1980. The codes on government procurement and customs valuation were scheduled to take effect internationally on January 1, 1981, although the customs valuation code was implemented by the United States and the EEC on July 1, 1980. Tariffs on civil aircraft and their principal components were completely eliminated by the EEC on January 1, 1980. On the other hand, EEC tariff reductions on other industrial products will, with a few exceptions, be spread in equal installments over a period of 8 years. The first cut was made on January 1, 1980; the seven additional cuts are scheduled for each January 1 from 1981 to 1987 (for certain chemicals and plastics the first cut was not made until July 1, 1980). For textiles and steel, six equal cuts are scheduled for each January 1 from 1982 to 1987. Specific details on the Government Procurement Code, the Tariff Protocol, and the Technical Standards code can be found on pages 12, 18, and 24, respectively.

Distribution and Sales Channels

The Netherlands is one of the most densely populated countries in the world, with about 413 persons per square kilometer. The Dutch market is compact, homogeneous, and easily serviced. Distances are short: from Groningen, the most northernly major city to Maastricht, at the southern tip of the country, the distance is about 200 miles by road; the west-east distance from Rotterdam to Enschede, near the German border, is about 120 miles. Transportation is excellent by road, rail and water. Shipments within the Netherlands can usually reach their destination overnight. Given the small area of the country and the excellent transport means available, nationwide distribution of any product is handled with ease.

Import Channels

The Netherlands has a variety of highly developed import channels with experienced import-

Table 4.—Netherlands: Main Economic Aggregates, 1960–80

	GDP volume growth	GDP volume growth per occupied person	Unemployed in labor force	Rise in consumer prices	Compensation per employee	Current account balance of payments	General government balance	Savings ratio of households[1]	Money supply growth M2[2]
	%[3]	%	%	%[2]	% GDP	% GDP	%	%	
1960–72	5,0	4,0	1,0	4,9	11,0	0,4	0,6		9,3
1973	5,7	5,7	2,4	9,3	15,1	4,0	1,7	20,6	21,9
1974	3,5	3,5	3,0	10,1	15,8	3,2	0,9	20,3	20,0
1975	−1,3	−0,4	4,2	10,7	13,3	2,5	−2,2	16,6	5,7
1976	5,3	5,5	4,6	8,8	10,9	3,2	−1,8	17,3	22,7
1977	2,4	2,2	4,5	6,0	8,1	0,8	−1,1	15,5	3,6
1978	2,5	2,0	4,5	4,4	7,1	−0,9	−2,3	15,3	4,2
1979	2,2	1,3	4,5	4,6	5,9	−1,4	−3,0	13,8	7,3
1980	1,1	1,2	5,1	6,9	5,5	−1,4	2,3	12,0	5,5

[1] Private sector.
[2] End of year.
[3] Percent change over previous period, annual rate.

ers, agents, and distributors well-versed in foreign trade techniques.

A fairly large percentage of imported commodities sold in the Netherlands is handled by importers who purchase for their own accounts and distribute throughout the country. Because of the size, excellent accessibility, competitive nature and makeup of the Dutch market, importers often insist on an exclusive distributorship of imported products. This often yields the best results. Wholesalers constitute an important segment of importers doing business in this manner. They are the primary sources of import supplies for the small- and medium-size retail outlets, which often find it impossible to buy directly from manufacturers requiring large orders.

Closely resembling the importing wholesaler are purchasing associations, formed by independent small- and medium-size retailers. These associations combine orders and operate their own warehouses, thus performing the function of importing wholesalers.

There are also many commission agents and brokerage houses in the Netherlands. These firms handle a large percentage of raw material imports, such as grains, lumber, wool, metal ores, and tropical products, as well as some industrial equipment and consumer goods.

With the considerable rise in living standards of the population in recent years, there has been a rapid growth of sales through chain stores, department stores, and supermarkets. Hence, direct selling to large retail organizations is becoming increasingly important. While large Dutch retail organizations usually insist upon having exclusive lines, an approach to more than one organization may be successful in selling consumer goods.

The approach used for selling some raw materials, as well as capital goods for which there are a limited number of potential buyers or users, is direct selling. However, U.S. manufacturers selling capital equipment (even if only to a handful of customers) should appoint a local agent capable of providing aftersales service.

Cooperatives and some chain and department stores have established central purchasing offices in the Netherlands to provide for their import needs. The larger Dutch department and chain stores have buying agents in New York City. These agents assist in placing orders and in arranging for shipments. Since these agents are often represent stores located in a number of countries, they have the bargaining advantage of strong purchasing power. These agents offer American exporters an opportunity to sell simultaneously and directly to stores in several countries.

The Netherlands has also become the European base of operation for a substantial number of U.S. firms. These subsidiaries act as sales agents, assemblers, or manufacturers of the firm's products. In many instances, the subsidiary is a combination of all three. Such firms import for warehousing against future sales in the Netherlands and other parts of Europe, for servicing products of the parent company, for assembly and sale, or for manufacturing.

Agent/Distributor Arrangements

Usually, the entire country can be covered by one agent. Unless it is specifically agreed upon to the contrary, such an agreement is considered exclusive if it offers the agent a designated area and a specified line of customers. The choice of a good agent is paramount for successful selling. While at present there is no specific agency law in the Netherlands, some rules are included in the commercial and civil codes that protect the interests of the representative. Consequently, such agreements should always be in writing and care should be taken in selecting an agent. Professional legal advice also is recommended before finalizing an agency agreement.

The principal agent relations that are governed by the commercial and civil codes follow: In the absence of termination provisions in the agreement, the law provides a minimum term for serving notice of termination of 4 months. Parties may agree upon other terms, provided the period agreed upon is not less than 1 month. A definite term agreement terminates on the agreed expiration date. If parties continue to operate under the agreement after that date, the agreement is deemed extended for a further identical period but not for more than 1 year, with the result that notice of termination of definite term agreements should be given.

Rotterdam Revises List Of Practicing Attorneys

The U.S. Consulate General in Rotterdam has revised its list of attorneys practicing in the Rotterdam Consular District. The list is current as of December 29, 1980, and covers the four southern provinces of the Netherlands: South Holland, Zeeland, North Brabant, and Limburg. Rotterdam and The Hague are the principal cities in the district.

For a copy of this list, contact Robert McLaughlin, Office of European Community, International Trade Administration, U.S. Department of Commerce, Washington, D.C., 20230; tel. 202-377-3371.

Termination of an agreement without adequate notice makes a principal liable for compensation, leaving the agent the choice to claim the amount of the commissions that would have accrued during the termination period or the amount of the actual damages suffered. Exceptionally, and only for just and urgent causes, an agreement may be terminated without notice, provided the other party is immediately advised of such cause or causes. In cases like these, the party concerned may also request the court to terminate the agreement.

At the expiration of the agreement, by whatever means, an agent who has increased the value of the business of the principal by additional customers is in principle entitled to an adequate remuneration. The amount of this remuneration shall not exceed the average of the commissions in 1 year. Claims are subject to an expiration term of 1 year. No specific rules exist concerning distributorships.

Distribution Practices of U.S. Firms

Distribution methods of U.S. firms selling in the Dutch market vary with the product. Generally, American exporters find it best to sell their products through a distributor carrying stocks while staple commodities, capital, and some industrial equipment are sold through a commission agent or brokerage house.

There are a number of channels through which suitable agents and distributors may be located, including the agent/distributor service and other programs of the U.S. Department of Commerce, American and Dutch banks, Dutch trade associations and through visiting Dutch trade exhibitions—particularly those in which the U.S. Government participates.

Many U.S. companies have established sales offices in the Netherlands. To obtain optimum market penetration in the Netherlands, as well as through Western Europe, many American manufacturers insist upon taking on direct responsibility for developing their overseas distribution network—training their sales force, participating in trade shows, handling sales promotion, and controlling inventories in local warehouse facilities.

Some American firms have formed sales companies in association with Dutch partners or have made arrangements whereby Dutch manufacturers supplement their own product line by adding the articles of the U.S. exporters. Such relationships are often coupled with licensing agreements or other reciprocal arrangements.

American firms also use the services of U.S.-based export management companies (EMC's), which specialize in exporting and handle the products of several different companies.

Experienced U.S. food exporters have found that the best approach to the Dutch food market is through the buying organizations of the cooperatives and independent retailers who dominate the field. Limited space in most retail stores makes it difficult for the U.S. exporter to establish competing lines in the small independent retail outlets.

Since Dutch wholesalers and retailers generally do a considerably smaller volume of business than their American counterparts, the Dutch importer usually purchases in smaller lots from the U.S. supplier than is the custom in the United States.

Wholesale and Retail Channels

Although wholesale trade traditionally has been marked by large numbers of small units, the number of wholesale firms has been declining in recent years. A major structural change is evident. A growing number of purchasing organizations, cooperatives, department stores, and chains are ordering directly from manufacturers and foreign suppliers, bypassing the wholesaler to avoid wholesale markups. Wholesalers have begun to branch out, taking on agencies and distributorships for foreign firms and carrying stocks of their principals' goods. Many Dutch wholesalers are familiar with international operations and have their own connections abroad. Therefore, a Dutch enterprise can cover other European countries simultaneously.

Retail trade has also been undergoing a structural change. The number of retail establishments has been decreasing steadily, falling from 188,041 in 1968 to 157,916 in 1979. (However, the total volume of retail business has continued to grow.) This general decline in number has been led by small grocery and food stores due to the trend toward chain and self-service stores and supermarkets. The rising affluence of the Dutch consumer, however, has been reflected in an increase in the number of establishments servicing the luxury trade, e.g., florists, jewelers, photographic suppliers, and glass, china, and luxury goods outlets. Table 5 gives the number of various retail outlets for 1977, 1978, and 1979.

A retailer's annual sales quota is normally predetermined in consultation with either the retailer's wholesaler or manufacturer if the retailer buys direct; and the retailer usually finds it difficult, if not impossible, to obtain extra orders if demand should exceed expectations. On the other hand, an unsold portion of a sales quota may not ordinarily be returned to the wholesaler, and the retailer must dispose of it.

Chain and Department Stores. —Chain store retailing has expanded steadily in recent years. There are now over 150 organizations operating chain stores selling chiefly food, clothing, photographic supplies, books, medicines, cosmetics, furniture, and household goods.

Department stores, which may be members of chains or independent, buy directly from producers and foreign suppliers if possible. Otherwise they buy from agents.

American goods sold in Dutch department stores fall mainly in the textile, clothing, household article, and foodstuff categories. Aside from the sales opportunities that they afford the U.S. exporter, Dutch department stores play a prominent role in developing popular tastes and in setting the pace for smaller retail units. Hence, exposure in department stores can play a valuable role in gaining consumer acceptance for new products or styles.

The major chain stores in the Netherlands are as follows:

- C & A, with 55 branches plus some boutiques

- De Bijenkorf, with 6 branches and 120 Hema stores and some boutiques

- Vroom and Dreesman, with 60 stores and 400–500 small shops (and growing rapidly)

- Peek and Cloppenburg, with 27 stores

- A-Hejn with, 678 food stores

- Hij Heerenmoden, with 70 stores

- Brons Textiles, with 155 stores

Food Stores and Supermarkets. —The most striking change in Dutch retailing in recent years has been in the field of food distribution. The small, family owned food store has been giving way to self-service outlets, supermarkets and grocery chains. Voluntary chains include 75 percent of all retail grocery outlets. The total number of grocery outlets dropped from 23,793 in 1961 to 15,462 in 1972, and now there are about 12,000. Self-service shops accounted for much of this decline.

The self-service grocery outlets experienced a period of growth in the sixties, increasing from 2,210 stores to 6,869 during the decade, but since dropped to about 5,000.

Most striking has been the rapid rise of the supermarket. The number of supermarkets rose from 42 in 1961 to a current total of more than 3,000. The Dutch consumer is showing a marked preference for one-stop shopping.

Cooperatives. —The consumer cooperative is declining in importance in the Netherlands. In 1969, there were 44 cooperatives with 453,720 members serviced by 761 shops. By 1971, there were only 31 cooperatives with 350,833 members serviced by 519 shops, In 1973, a large number of takeovers and liquidations took place. After this drastic reorganization, there are only six cooperatives with an estimated 125,000 members serviced by 111 shops.

Mail-order and Discount Houses. —Mail-order houses are widely accepted in the Netherlands and appear to be becoming more popular, especially if deferred payment plans are provided. There are six general-goods mail-order companies. The others are smaller and more specialized in such products as textiles, house furnishings, books, etc. Only one of the major mail-order companies operates a retail store.

Franchising

Franchising has grown significantly in the Netherlands in the past few years, although it is not as common as in the United States. There are over 160 franchisors in the Netherlands, some of which are American. The Dutch Government considers franchising a necessary means of restructuring medium- and small-sized business enterprises. Franchising accounted for 15 percent of all retail sales in 1980, and expectations for the 1980's appear to be good for American franchisors.

The rapid rise of operating costs of independent firms, the management expertise and other

Table 5.—Number of Establishments in Distributive Retail Trade on January 1st

	1970	1975	1978	1979	1980
Foodstuff, beverages and tobacco					
Alcoholic and nonalcoholic beverages	3,720	3,784	3,498	3,434	3,341
Bread and pastry	9,630	7,135	6,196	6,019	5,926
Fish	2,295	1,962	1,985	1,982	2,000
Groceries	17,778	13,718	12,022	11,744	11,538
Ice-cream	1,889	1,734	1,933	2,042	2,182
Meat and meat products	8,410	7,380	7,031	6,986	6,928
Milk and dairy produce	9,821	7,783	6,529	6,310	6,244
Pastry and confectionery	3,354	3,141	2,971	2,917	2,866
Potatoes, vegetables and fruit	10,410	8,204	7,048	6,889	6,780
Poultry	791	745	790	797	816
Tobacco goods	8,822	6,409	5,320	5,087	4,895
Other consumer goods					
Accessories for cars and motor cycles	324	1,913	2,148	2,160	2,324
Animals, animal requirements, feedingstuffs and angle-sport articles	1,235	1,633	1,860	1,952	2,034
Antiques	1,213	1,946	2,607	2,797	2,888
Bicycles and powered bicycles	7,027	5,612	4,975	4,807	4,722
Books	1,055	1,481	1,784	1,935	2,160
Books/stationery	1,269	1,022	825	771	707
Cleaning materials and petroleum	879	593	413	385	377
Clocks and watches	1,416	1,252	1,161	1,150	1,146
Domestic articles	5,059	4,356	3,892	3,815	3,709
Drugs	3,893	3,539	3,243	3,154	3,079
Electrical articles	4,707	4,463	4,355	4,342	4,373
Flowers and plants	7,083	7,301	7,687	7,812	8,099
Fuels	5,014	2,732	2,108	1,983	1,925
Furniture	4,525	4,617	4,720	4,751	4,789
Glassware, china, luxury goods, etc.	1,921	2,326	2,835	3,120	-3,344
Gold and silverware	1,140	1,216	1,315	1,381	1,428
Heating and cooking apparatus	2,102	1,760	1,482	1,452	1,439
Ironware and tools	3,965	3,296	3,141	3,139	3,158
Leatherware and travelgoods	968	777	756	790	810
Medical instruments and bandages	249	222	210	206	211
Motor cycles	607	456	182	223	248
Musical instruments	748	657	692	719	737
Office furniture and machines	395	411	406	439	458
Optical articles	761	892	1,057	1,100	1,136
Paints and window glass	3,416	3,337	3,165	3,145	3,125
Perfumery and cosmetics	404	447	526	599	632
Photographic articles	1,542	1,569	1,650	1,675	1,698
Pictures and frames	340	352	399	445	520
Radio and television	2,486	2,408	2,462	2,491	2,495
Sanitary ware	1,871	2,404	2,413	2,482	2,484
Second-hand and irregular goods	1,266	1,469	2,178	2,399	2,680
Sewing machines	606	545	533	539	538
Shoes	4,857	4,307	4,090	4,053	4,079
Sportware	656	868	1,295	1,463	1,625
Stamps	271	260	340	366	413
Stationery	959	827	801	806	814
Textiles	20,749	19,119	20,221	20,815	21,084
Toys	378	448	537	578	598
Wallpaper	1,241	1,086	985	957	932
Wood and woodware	1,406	1,808	2,081	2,222	2,339
Miscellaneous[1]	1,492	2,285	3,632	4,294	4,694
Total	178,414	160,037	156,476	157,919	159,567

[1] Including trade in baby carriages and market and street trade in other articles.
Source; Central Registration Office Retail Trade/Handicraft Trade (Central Registratiekantoorr Detaihandel-Ambacht).

assistance provided by the franchisors, as well as the demand for improved services, offer good opportunities for franchise operations. The number of registered small firms that are operating on a franchise basis rose from 8,119 in 1977 to 8,480 in 1980. This rise is expected to further increase as many large purchasing associations and independent affiliates are expected to concentrate their activities. Consequently, a growth of 30 to 35 percent in total retail sales is not unrealistic, according to industry sources.

The best opportunities for American franchisors lie in the following areas: Handicraft shops, fast food restaurants, home repairs and interior decorating, hotels and motels, drycleaning, lawn and garden care, recreation and sporting equipment, computer services, automotive maintenance systems and diagnostic centers, and clothing.

While the capabilities of U.S. franchisors are well regarded, local experts warn foreign franchisors to approach the potential market cautiously and to conduct an extensive market survey before setting up a "pilot" store. Failure to grasp local customs could lead to the downfall of a potentially viable franchise.

Additional information, including legal background and regulations affecting franchising operations, is available from the "Stiching Franchise Voorlichting"—The Foundation for Franchising Information, Amersfoortsestraat 73, Ooesterberg, The Netherlands. The functions and goals of this organization are similar to those of the International Franchise Association in the United States. Most commercial banks also have their own franchise experts.

Government Procurement

The compliance of the Netherlands with the provisions of the Government Procurement Agreement began on January 1, 1981. Listed below are the Netherlands Government purchasing entities and their specific areas of buying responsibility.

• The Netherlands Government Purchasing Office, P.O. Box 10200, 6000 GE Zwolle: Furniture; office supplies, office machines and graphic equipment; textiles and uniforms; food; fuel; household supplies; music instruments; and leather; laboratory and scientific instruments; hospital supplies, electromedical and health care equipment for 58 academic and special hospitals, and chemicals, medicines, and photographic equipment; commercial kitchen catering equipment; and light aircraft and ground avionics on special request of ministry of transportation

• PTT Services, P.O. Box 20901, The Hague: Post office equipment *only*: automatic handling, sorting, and delivering equipment; postage stamp vending equipment; and printing telephone directories

• State Printing and Publishing Office, P.O. Box 20014, 2500 EA The Hague. Printing Dutch government publications and books

• Directorate for Ijsselmeer Polders, P.O. Box 600, 8200 AP Leystad: Construction, engineering, and architectural work involving the Ijsselmeer polders

Dutch Government purchasing entities issue tender summaries in Dutch and English. All other tender documents are in Dutch. Bids should be made in Dutch. Even though English is widely understood in the Netherlands, the Dutch entities may refuse bids in English. However, bids on highly technical projects such as aircraft or electronics are, reportedly, acceptable in English if the specifications are issued in English. Documentation for each specific tender will provide information on the language(s) in which bids must be made.

Dutch entities provide gratis copies of tender notices, summaries, and documents. Tender notices are published in Dutch in the *Official Gazette, The Nederlandse Staatscourant*. Tender notices covered by the Procurement Agreement also are published in the *Official Journal* of the EC in English. The minimum deadline time for tenders is 30 days, but 40 days appears to be average. Tender summaries are usually only a few pages long.

The Netherlands Government Purchasing Office generally uses the open tendering system. Its practice, however, is to contact suppliers directly when a special project for which there is only a limited number of qualified firms is concerned. Selective tendering is usually done by entities that tender construction contracts; *e.g.*, the Directorates of Water Control and for Ijsselmeer Polders. Construction contracts are not covered by the Procurement Agreement.

It is not mandatory that U.S. firms have a local agent to bid on government tenders. As a practical matter, however, having an agent would likely have a positive influence on a bid, especially when installation of equipment, servicing, and spare parts are involved. U.S. firms with no local representation or servicing facilities should consider either subcontracting some of the work in the Netherlands or arranging to service directly from the United States. For high-technology equipment, these might be the only ways to win a contract.

The Government Purchasing Office annually prepares its own buyers manual (*Handleiding*), which consists of firms—mainly in the Netherlands—that have successfully bid for contracts for common articles. For more sophisticated purchases that cannot be made through the *Handleiding*, bids are requested locally. In its dealings with foreign sources of supply, the Netherlands Government Purchasing Office only occasionally buys directly from the manufacturers abroad. The usual practice is to make purchases through the local representatives of foreign companies to facilitate settlement of possible difficulties. Firms submitting bids on public works must have a Netherlands' domicile. In practice, this means a domestic engineering office, although this is not specifically required by Dutch law.

All U.S. firms interested in participating in future Dutch tendering, especially those not represented in the Netherlands, are advised to confirm that interest in writing with the Netherlands Government Purchasing Office. The letter should briefly explain the firms products and services and request that the firm be included in the annual buyer's guide, a guide used when Dutch entities wish to order goods. A descriptive company catalog also should be included giving export prices. The letter should explain how servicing will be handled.

There are no practices, requirements, or policies employed by the Netherlands that would have a negative impact on the ability of U.S. firms to bid. U.S. firms are advised to be exact on pricing, using c.i.f. (cost, insurance, and freight), metric standards, and electric current in 220 volts, 50 cycles. American firms should also be aware of the need to meet Dutch and EC standards as specified in the technical specifications of the tender. If these standards are missing from the tender, firms should check with the issuing Dutch entity in time to be able to bid.

Regarding projects of the North Atlantic Treaty Organization (NATO), foreign firms have the same bidding rights as domestic ones, provided they are qualified and have been acknowledged as such by their respective governments. Firms interested in bidding on NATO projects should obtain a copy of the pamphlet "Doing Business with NATO" from the International Trade Administration, Major Projects Division, Office of Export Marketing, U.S. Department of Commerce, Washington, D.C. 20230. This brochure outlines the action necessary for a firm to take to be placed on the list of eligible bidders, and it provides the address of the Netherlands Government agency connected with NATO projects.

Transportation and Utilities

Transportation

With its key position on the North Sea at the mouths of the Rhine, the Meuse, and the Scheldt, the Netherlands has traditionally been a center for trade, transport, and transshipment. It has efficient, modern ports that are constantly being expanded and improved as well as an excellent inland transport system and good connections with neighboring countries. Bulk and cargo shipments from the United States can be delivered readily from the Netherlands' ports to the principal industrial areas in the Ruhr, Belgium, and northern France.

U.S. flagship lines servicing Dutch ports from U.S. Gulf ports include Lykes Brothers Steamship Company, Inc., Sea-Land Services Inc., Waterman Steamship Company, and United States Lines; from U.S. Atlantic ports, United States Lines, Sea-Land Services Inc., and Farrell Lines Inc.; from U.S. Pacific ports, Sea-Land Services Inc., Farrell Lines Inc., and United States Lines. Lykes Brothers Steamship Company, Inc., also offers mini-landbridge service from these Pacific ports. Shipping time to Dutch ports averages 15 days from the Great Lakes, 8 days from the Atlantic Coast, 11 days from the Gulf Coast, and 21 days from the West Coast.

Rotterdam handles more cargo than any other port in the world. In 1981, Rotterdam handled 253 million metric tons (mmt) of freight. Europort, the extension of the port of Rotterdam, continues to expand and is now accessible to 300,000 deadweight ton tankers. Container ship traffic at Rotterdam has been increasing markedly. In 1981, 21 mmt of containerized cargo passed through the port. Coal shipments grew by 21 percent in 1981 over 1980 and totaled 14 mmt, up from 11.4 mmt. The address of the Rotterdam Port Authority is as follows: Habenbedriji Der Gemeente Rotterdam, P.O. Box 3002 AP Rotterdam, Telephone 010–896911, Telex 23077 Eurot NL.

There is an extensive inland waterways system consisting of over 3,500 miles of navigable rivers and canals. Rhine transport—linking the Netherlands with industrial centers of Germany, France, and Switzeralnd—handles 130 million tons of goods. The Netherlands inland fleet actually used for transport includes over 650 tankers with carrying capacity of approximately 600,000 tons and over 8,000 barges with a carrying capacity of 4.5 million tons.

The Netherlands has an excellent system of

railroads, which includes frequent service on approximately 3,000 kilometers of track. Fifty-eight percent of the system is electrified.

Approximately 85,000 kilometers of good-to-excellent surfaced roads provide ready access to all markets. The fully developed transportation infrastructure is further evidenced by Dutch trucking companies, which are responsible for moving 40 percent of the goods shipped in Europe. The Netherlands is a right-hand-drive country, with one automobile to every three inhabitants.

The main international airport in the Netherlands is Schiphol, just southwest of Amsterdam. Schiphol is a large and modern airport that provides efficient passenger and cargo handling facilities. Rotterdam also has an international airport and smaller regional airports that provide facilities for short distance international air traffic within Europe. The official Dutch airline is KLM-Royal Dutch Airlines.

Utilities

Coal and Fuel Oil.—Since the last coal mine in the Netherlands was closed in 1974, the country has been dependent exclusively on imports for its supplies of coal. With about 8 mmt of coal imported in 1980, the Netherlands is presently a relatively small user of this fuel. Annually, about 2.5 mmt of coal are used by three electric power plants 3.2 mmt by industry, and the remaining 2.3 mmt is reexported.

Currently, 6.6 percent of the needs for electric energy are supplied by coal, 6.6 by nuclear energy, 7.2 percent by oil, and 79.4 percent by natural gas. The oil is imported mainly from the Middle East and Nigeria, and the natural gas is supplied by large gasfields within the Netherlands. Since the Dutch Government wants to be less dependent on oil imports and plans to conserve its natural gas for the future, the rise of coal and coal gasification will become increasingly important in the Netherlands' energy picture. By the turn of the century, coal is expected to furnish about 20 percent of the Netherlands' total energy needs. Coal imports, therefore, are expected to increase from today's 1.5 million tons to 26 million tons by the year 2000.

Because the Dutch Government wishes to guarantee its supplies of coal by diversifying its sources of supply as much as possible, incremental sales of U.S. coal to the Netherlands can best be realized by offering long-term contracts. It would also be useful to invite Dutch officials of the Ministry of Economic Affairs and/or leading Dutch coal trading companies to the United States to interest them in buying larger amounts of steam coal for electric power generation. It is now the policy of the Dutch Government that, in principle, natural gas and oil will no longer be used for newly constructed electric utilities. Coal prices in the Netherlands are regulated by the European Coal and Steel Community.

The principal coal trade association in that country is Nederlandse Organisatie van Olie-en Kolenhandelaren "NOVOK,"'s-Gravendij Kwal 103, 3021 EH Rotterdam.

Natural Gas.—Accounting for 55 percent of the Netherlands total primary energy supply, natural gas reserves remain plentiful for current-and near-term domestic demand. However, as indicated by the 79-billion-cubic-meter drop in proven reserves in 1979, a gap will develop in the 1980's unless new sources are secured.

Although the Netherlands has long been one of the largest exporters of natural gas in the world and the EC's largest supplier, emphasis now is placed on conserving existing supplies and on increasing imports.

Nuclear Power.—Due to the high population density and consequent limited possibilities for power stations and waste storage sights, nuclear energy is a controversial subject. At present, only two plants, a pressurized water reactor in Borssele and an experimental reactor in Dodewaard, are in operation. Politically sensitive decisions on the construction of additional nuclear power plants have been postponed for some time.

Electric Power.—Voltage rates vary according to geographic location, cost of production, quantity consumed, maximum power required, and periods of utilization. The SEP, short for N.V. Samenwerkende Electriciteits Productiebedrijven, is the umbrella organization of 13 provincial power distribution companies in the Netherlands. These companies all have different electricity rates. Production capacity in the Netherlands has been increased recently by approximately 6,800 megawatts to 18,000 megawatts. This expansion does not include plans for new nuclear power stations.

Advertising and Market Research

Advertising is widespread and its technique well developed in the Netherlands. Advertising is done through a wide variety of media, including the press, radio and TV, billboard posters the cinema, direct-mail advertising, trade fairs and even banner-towing by airplanes.

Press advertising is regulated by the Code and Rules of Dutch Press Advertising. TV and radio advertising is supervised by an Advertising Council. Medical and medicinal advertising must be approved by a special medical board.

Advertising Agencies

There are over 185 recognized agencies in the Netherlands that plan advertising, write copy, and insert advertisements. As most American advertising must be adapted to Netherlands customs and conditions, American exporters should confer with local agents about selecting a Dutch advertising agency for their publicity needs. Brand names, general themes, and part of the illustrations used in the United States may be applicable to the Dutch market, but layout, copy, and overall effect of the advertisement may often have to be changed to conform to Dutch advertising practices and to appeal to the attitudes and tastes of the Dutch public.

Most leading advertising agencies in Holland have reciprocal arrangements with U.S. agencies. Some are wholly owned subsidiaries of American companies. Services of advertising agencies are covered by a commission of 15 percent of media billings. Charges for artwork, production costs, and special services such as market research are made in addition to the regular fees for advertising services.

English copy presents no translation problem. All copy, except highly technical material, is translated as part of the normal service. If a technical translator is required, costs are charged to the advertiser.

Advertising Media

Newspapers and Periodicals. —Expenditures for newspaper and periodical advertising still exceed those for any other media. Daily newspapers in the Netherlands have a total daily circulation of 4.5 million. There are no Sunday newspapers.

Most newspapers are small, regional papers—only 10 are national. There also are newspaper chains, which facilitate the placing of advertisements. The provincial papers have considerable influence and should not be overlooked as a medium for advertising consumer goods.

Trade, professional, and opinion journals are important media, with wide circulation and alert readership. Women's magazines are also an important vehicle for advertising. Directories and yearbooks are also used.

Direct-Mail Advertising. —Direct-mail advertising in the form of letters, folders, circulars, newsletters, catalogs, and calendars is widespread.

Outdoor Advertising. —Outdoor advertising in the form of posters, electric signs, streetcar and bus advertisements is widely used. Outdoor poster sizes are standardized. Billboards are available in railroad stations throughout the country, but they are not allowed on trains. Billboards and posters are generally prohibited on highways.

Radio and Television. —Until recently, advertising on radio and television was prohibited. In the last 10 years, however, advertising has been permitted on both of these communications means. Such advertising is strictly limited both in terms of length of commercials and the subject that can be advertised. Practically every home has a TV set, and about 90 percent of the population watches television.

Cinema. —Advertising by film shorts in motion picture theaters is common, but attendance has been steadily declining in the past decade due to the popularity of television.

Trade Fairs. —Another excellent form of publicity is participation in trade fairs and exhibitions. (Table 6 lists major specialized fairs that take place in Amsterdam.) The Netherlands has several each year, including the large general spring and fall international industries' fairs at the Jaarbeurs exhibition site in Utrecht, and other large (some international) trade exhibitions either at the Jaarbeurs or at the RAI exhibition buildings in Amsterdam. Smaller, regional, technical and specialized exhibitions also are held throughout the year covering consumer goods, technical items, and industrial products. Many exhibitions are open only to executives and professional personnel associated with the commodity sectors concerned, but some allow the general public. While some expressly limit participation, the majority are open to American and other foreign exhibitors. Most specialized trade fairs are annual or biennial and are particularly useful for introducing a new product to the Dutch market or for finding an agent or representative.

Market Research

Market research, as known in the United States, is relatively new to the Netherlands. Although basic economic data utilized in market studies are readily available, some market indicators (such as production and sales data for many industries) are not published.

Market research services are provided in the Netherlands by a number of specialized firms and many advertising agencies. The names of Dutch advertising agencies, market research organizations, and management and public relations counseling firms—including U.S. subsidiaries in the Netherlands specializing in these activities—may be found in appropriate publications including the *International Directory of Market Research Houses and Services*, by the American Marketing Association, 420 Lexington Avenue, New York, New York 10017 (phone: 212–687–3280); and *Bradford's Directory of Marketing Research Agencies and Management Consultants in the United States and the World*, P.O. Box 276, Department N, Fairfax, Virginia 22030 (phone: 703–560–7484).

In addition, the U.S. Department of Commerce commissions market research in selected commodity and geographic areas in connection with its export promotion programs. These reports, which are listed in the Department's *Monthly Index to Foreign Market Reports*, may be obtained through any of the Department's district offices.

Foreign trade information may also be obtained from the larger Dutch banks, industry associations, Dun and Bradstreet, the Netherlands Chamber of Commerce in the United States (which maintains offices both in the Hague and New York City), and the Netherlands Economic Information Service of the Ministry of Economic Affairs (151 Bezuidenhoutseweg, The Hague).

Credit

Terms of Payment.—Sales terms generally follow normal worldwide credit terms, varying with the commodity and the credit standing of the purchaser. As a rule, the Netherlands business community *does not like letters of credit. In most cases, sight or time drafts are used as the means of payment.* U.S. suppliers may often find it necessary to offer their best payment terms in order to land sales contracts in the highly competitive Dutch market.

Prices should be quoted on a c.i.f. port of entry basis. Quotations should preferably be made in terms of guilders, although it is generally satisfactory to make them in dollars.

Credit Facilities.—There are approximately 71 commercial banks—including the branches, subsidiaries, and affiliates of foreign banks—in the Netherlands. By far the greatest part of credit needed by Dutch importers can be provided by the commercial banks in the Netherlands. The five major banks, including The Netherlands Bank (the country's central bank), are Algemene Bank Netherlands N.V., Centrale Rabobank N.V., Amsterdam-Rotterdam Bank N.V., and Nederlandse Credietbank N.V.

Many American banks—including Bank of America, Continental Illinois National Bank and Trust Company of Chicago, Citibank, First National Bank of Chicago and Crocker Bank—have banking presence in the major Dutch cities and also have correspondent relationships with Dutch banks. The foreign departments of many

Table 6.—Major Specialized Fairs in Amsterdam

EXHIBITION/FAIR	PRODUCT	HELD	ORGANIZER a/o AUTHORITY	U.S CONTACT
HISWA	Boat Show	annual	R.A.I. Gebouw B.V., 8 Europaplein, Amsterdam	The Netherlands Chamber of Commerce in the United States One Rockefeller Plaza New York, New York 10020 (212) 265–6460
PETROTECH	Oil and natural gas	biennal	see above	see above
AQUATECH	Water: treatment, storage, transport	biennial	see above	see above
FIAREX	Industrial electronics	biennial	see above	see above
HORECAVA	Hotel, restaurant, institutional Equipment	annual	see above	see above

U.S. banks are well equipped to give service and advice in matters concerning credit documentation, foreign exchange, finance, and the general investment climate of the country.

Credit to business generally takes the two traditional forms of discount credits and loans. Terms follow normal international practice. Credit information on Dutch firms is available from the World Traders Data Report Service, produced by the U.S. Foreign Commercial Service and the U.S. Department of Commerce and obtainable through Department of Commerce District Offices. Additional information may be obtained from merchantile credit agencies.

Trade Regulations

The Netherlands, together with Belgium and Luxembourg, is a partner in the Benelux Economic Union, which provides for the removal of all obstacles to the free movement of labor and capital in the Benelux countries and for harmonization of economic policies to bring about final economic consolidation of the member countries. Goods of origin in any one Benelux country can be imported duty free into another.

Together with its Benelux partners and France, the Federal Republic of Germany, Italy, Denmark, Ireland, and the United Kingdom, the Netherlands is a member of the European Communities (EC). Greece became the 10th member of the EC on January 1, 1981, following ratification by the parliaments of the current EC members and Greece. The EC consists of the European Coal and Steel Community (ECSC), and the European Atomic Energy Community (EURATOM), the European Economic Community (EEC)—popularly known as the Common Market.

The EEC was established in 1958, at the same time as EURATOM, for the purpose of creating a free mass market among the member countries. The EEC treaty provides for a Common External Tariff (CXT), a Common Agricultural Policy (CAP), a joint transportation policy, and the free movement of goods, labor, and capital.

The customs union of the nine member countries of the EEC was achieved on July 1, 1977, with the establishment of the CXT and the dismantling of internal import duties.

Tariff Structure

The tariff structure of the CXT consists of an autonomous and a conventional column of duty rates, the former being applicable if no conven-

tional (lower) rate is shown. The EEC accords most-favored-nation treatment (conventional rates) to all countries. The rates of duty applied are not excessive. On most raw materials, duty rates are free or low. The import duties on most manufactured goods range between 5 and 17 percent, with some food products bearing higher rates.

Nonagricultural imports have been almost completely liberalized; i.e., they are admitted without quantitative restrictions, and items still restricted or subject to licensing are for the most part liberally treated.

The establishment of the CAP means that imports of certain major commodities are regulated by policies developed by the EEC as a whole rather than by the Netherlands. The usual method for controlling the level of imports into the EEC from third countries is to subject certain commodities (e.g., cereals, eggs, and poultry) to a system of variable levies, which results in raising and maintaining the threshold or minimum prices of these commodities slightly above their EEC equivalents. The internal market of the EEC is supported at an intervention price slightly below the threshold price, at which surpluses are bought through its agricultural fund.

The Netherlands grants preferential duty rates to various countries with which the EEC has concluded trade and association agreements. In addition, the Netherlands extends such treatment to over 100 less developed countries.

After the entry of the United Kingdom and Denmark into the EEC in 1973, the remaining EFTA countries—namely Austria, Finland, Iceland, Norway, Portugal, Sweden, and Switzerland—concluded agreements with the EEC. The provisions of these agreements included a schedule of the mutual abolition of import duties. With a few exceptions, no import duties have been levied on industrial products since July 1, 1977, provided these products have been in free circulation and have originated in the EFTA countries.

Tariff Reductions

The most recent series of Multilateral Trade Negotiations (MTN) held from 1973–79 under the General Agreement on Tariffs and Trade (GATT)—the Tokyo Round—resulted in substantial reductions in tariff duties. The tariff concessions agreed upon in the MTN will generally be phased in at 1-year intervals over a 7-year period, with the first cuts implemented on January 1, 1980.

Tariff Reductions Between the United States and the EEC. —The tariff negotiations resulted in reductions in duties covering about $126 billion or 90 percent of industrial trade (1976 imports) among the major developed countries. The average tariff on total industrial imports (dutiable plus duty free, excluding petroleum) will decline for the United States from 6.1 percent to 4.2 percent (32 percent cut) and for the EEC from 6.3 percent to 4.6 percent (27 percent cut). The bilateral tariff reductions made by the EEC countries in terms of industrial products exported to them by the United States is even more substantial. The EEC reduction is from 7.2 percent to 4.7 percent (34 percent cut).

Significant gains were made by the United States on certain chemical items, certain kraft paper items, printing machinery, automated metalworking machine tools, electrical machinery, scientific and controlling instruments, and photographic equipment. For example, in the photographic equipment sector, the EEC reduction will be from an average tariff of 11.2 percent vis-a-vis products from the United States to an average rate of 6.5 percent (42 percent cut). Closely related to the tariff negotiations, the EEC also expanded its duty-free tariff quota on plywood from 400,000 cubit meters to 600,000 cubic meters. In return, the United States improved its offered reductions on leather gloves, some textile items, watch and bicycle parts, and on future products in the chemical sector.

International Status of the MTN Tariff Reductions. —The MTN tariff reductions are formally contained in two legal instruments: (1) the Geneva (1979) Protocol to the General Agreement on Tariffs and Trade and (2) a supplementary protocol to the Geneva (1979) Protocol. These documents, signed by 32 countries and the EEC thus far (see appendix), constitute legal bindings under the GATT of the tariff concessions made in the course of the Tokyo Round. Individual tariffs "bound" in the protocols can be changed in the future but may only be raised at a price. "Bound" tariffs are subject to exacting procedures in the GATT, which are designed to maintain a balance of concessions among the signatories. Accordingly, any future raising of a "bound" tariff must—with some limited exceptions—be offset by an equivalent lowering of a tariff on other trade items.

Additional Information. —The following publications contain details concerning the U.S. implementation of the tariff agreements and are available from the Superintendent of Documents, U.S. Government Printing Office, Washington, D.C. 20402 (Telephone: (202) 783-3238).

- December 13, 1979, Federal Register, Book II, Part IV, Proclamation 4707 (President's proclamation on U.S. tariff concessions, staging details, and other matters)
- 1980 edition of the Tariff Schedules of the United States (TSUS) (USITC Publication 1011)
- Trade Agreements Act of 1979

Foreign tariff concessions are available for viewing in Room 3029-A, U.S. Department of Commerce, 14th Street and Constitution Avenue, N.W., Washington, D.C. 20230 (Telephone: (202) 377-3268).

Basis of Duty Assessment

Virtually all CXT (Dutch) duties are levied on an ad valorem basis. Briefly stated, such value is the normal price of goods at the time of importation, negotiated under open market conditions between the Dutch buyer and foreign seller. That price includes freight, insurance, commission, and all other costs, charges, and expenses incidental to the sale and delivery of the goods to the buyer at the port or place of importation with the exception of additional taxes.

Customs Valuation/Import Licensing/ Antidumping. —As of July 1, 1980, the legislation for implementing the customs valuation (Agreement on Customs Valuation) developed in the MTN was effective in the Netherlands. The legislation is controlled jointly by offices within the Ministries of Economic Affairs and Finance. The controlling officer of customs value forms is the Inspector of Customs and Excise Taxes at the port of entry. The Ministry of Finance, under whose jurisdiction these inspectors fall, is the executing body for this legislation.

All import goods exceeding Dfl. 4,500 (approximately US$1,850) require a declaration of particulars relating to customs values submitted on a special form (D.V.I.) which replaces the previous Benelux 80 Form.

The primary method of valuation is the *transaction value.* Under this method, the dutiable value is based on the price actually paid or payable for the goods, with a limited number of adjustments for things such as selling commissions, packing costs, and certain costs for materials and services used in producing the goods that were borne by the buyer but not reflected in the price paid or payable for the goods. It is anticipated that the transaction value will be used in all but a limited number of cases. One situation in which the transaction value would not be used is where there is a sale between related parties and this relationship affects the price. It should be noted that the existence of a relationship alone is not a sufficient reason to reject the transaction value of a sale between related parties. The Agreement on Customs Valuation provides a number of important safeguards to assure that transaction values between related parties are not arbitrarily rejected.

If the transaction value cannot be determined because the consignment has no buyer and if the importer faces delay in the final determination of the value, then alternative value methods are introduced and the importer can clear the goods from customs by providing a guarantee in the form of a deposit. However, 95 percent of the customs are determined by the transaction value method.

The first alternative method is based on the *transaction value of identical goods* sold for export to the same country of importation. If no value can be established under this provision, then the *transaction value of similar goods sold* for export to the same country of importation would be the basis for valuation.

If a value cannot be determined under the above methods, then the Agreement on Customs Valuation provides for the application of a *deductive value method*, and if that is unsuccessful, a *computed value method*. However, at the importer's request, the order of application of these two methods will be reversed.

Under the *deductive value method*, the customs value is calculated by taking the price of the first sale after importation of either the imported good or of identical or similar goods and deducting from it certain costs and charges that are incurred after importation. This method will normally be used only when the imported product is not further manufactured after importation. However, if the importer so requests, this method will be applied to goods processed after importation with due allowance for value added in processing.

Under the *computed value method*, the customs value is absed on the sum of material and manufacturing costs, profits, and general expenses for the goods being valued.

If all the above methods turn out to be inapplicable, then the customs officials can use other methods provided that they are reasonable and consistent with the principles of the Agreement and of Article VII of the GATT. The Agreement lists a number of existing arbitrary practices that are explicitly cited as unreasonable.

There are relatively few specific duties in the Dutch tariff. Such duties are based on net or gross weight, length, volume, or on the number of units imported. The metric system of weights and measures is used in customs transactions: 1 metric ton equals 1,000 kilograms; 1 kilogram equals 2.2046 pounds; 1 meter equals 39.37 inches; and 1 liquid liter equals 1.057 liquid quarts.

Duties are payable in Dutch currency (florin or guilder, divisible into 100 cents); the conversion into foreign currencies, including the U.S. dollar, is made at the rate of exchange prevailing on the foreign exchange market.

Information regarding the Netherlands' duties and taxes applicable to specific products may be obtained free of charge from the Policy Division, Office of the European Community, International Trade Administration, U.S. Department of Commerce, Washington, D.C. 20230. Inquiries should include a complete product description and Brussels Tariff Nomenclature (BTN) number of the new Customs Cooperation Council Nomenclature (CCCN) number.

Customs Surcharges. —There are no customs surcharges in the Netherlands. However, practically all imported goods are subject to a value added turnover tax, an indirect tax on consumption ultimately paid by the consumer. Some items are subject to additional excise taxes. These levies are explained more fully in the section entitled "Indirect Taxes."

Special Customs Provisions

Entry. —The law requires that shortly after a ship berths at an official port of entry, a general (unspecified) declaration must be submitted by the captain to the customs authorities before unloading can begin. However, under certain circumstances, the customs authorities may permit unloading before the submission of the declaration. If the goods appear on the transportation entry (the "VOLGLIJST") of the general declaration, the importer or agent is required to determine within specified time limitations their disposition. There are several possibilities available to the importer or agent. These include importation for home consumption, storage in bonded warehouses or customs sheds, transit shipment, transportation to another place for delivery or reexportation.

Temporary Importation. —The Netherlands provides for a procedure of temporary exemption from duty and taxes on goods reexported in exactly the same state within a specified time, provided a security in the form of a cash deposit, bond, or other means is posted with the customs authorities. Upon reexportation, the security is returned. A security may not be required in instances when containers holding merchandise are certain to be reexported. The following are typical examples of categories of temporary importation: means of transportation for goods and passengers; goods for display at exhibitions, fairs, and similar events; goods admitted for inspection and testing; and samples and advertising matter.

Transit.—International customs transit procedures are in effect in the EEC. The United States and the EEC, including the Netherlands, are contracting parties to the customs convention, entitled "International Transport of Goods under Cover of TIR Carnets." Under the provisions of this convention, shipments can be transported in road vehicles within the Netherlands or across the frontiers of other contracting parties, without intermediate reloading, to the ultimate destination in another contracting party where import duties and taxes become payable. The convention provides for the acceptance of the TIR carnet as a security for import duties and taxes on the goods covered. The carnet is obtainable for a fee from the U.S. Council of the International Chamber of Commerce Inc., 1212 Avenue of the Americas, New York, New York 10036. Telephone (212) 354-4480.

An alternative transit procedure similar to the TIR carnet is compulsory when the crossing of two or more frontiers is involved. It requires the certification of a declaration to accompany the goods at the customs office of the place of departure, as well as the posting at the customs office of the place of departure of a security to cover the cost of duties and taxes levied at the country of destination. At each frontier crossing, the certified declaration is submitted to the customs officials, where one copy of the declaration is receipted and returned to the customs office at the place of departure. This procedure, which requires the execution of only one set of transit documents, helps expedite the movement of the goods by reducing the amount of paper work en route.

The EEC's transit procedure for shipping goods by rail is simple. Among the various rail authorities of Western Europe, a common system of accounting for and apportioning railway revenue based on specific railway consignment notes exists. The members of the EEC use these forms and procedures for customs control purposes without interfering with their original intentions. The rail authority accepting goods for

shipment assumes responsibility for delivery of the goods to their destination. Consequently, the shipper is not required to provide a security to cover any customs charges.

Processing.—Customs favored processing is of two types: (1) inwards processing—used within the customs territory of the Netherlands; and (2) outwards processing—practiced outside the EEC customs territory. Prior authorization is required and is granted only to individuals and companies resident in the EEC. The authorization sets forth requirements to be met in allowed processing operations; for example, time limits and surveillance procedures.

(1) Inwards Processing.—Merchandise imported for processing (including assembly, repair, overhaul, finishing, and mounting), following which a certain portion of the processed goods are to be reexported out of the EEC, is eligible for customs favored treatment. The reexported goods may be partly or totally in the processed state. Import duty and tax are charged only on those goods sold in the EEC. Security may be required as described under the section on Temporary Importation.

Use of the inwards processing procedure is granted where it contributes to the creation of favorable conditions for the exportation of processed goods without encroaching upon essential interests of domestic (Community) producers. These conditions would be met in the following cases:

(a) The importation of goods needed to execute a work contract done to order for a person domiciled in a third country;

(b) goods that are not available within the Community;

(c) goods the use of which is necessary to comply with provisions relating to the protection of industrial and commercial property rights;

(d) goods required because those items available within the Community do not meet specifications.

The reexported processed goods can be derived from materials other than those admitted for customs favored processing if: (1) these materials are judged to be of the same type and quality with identical technical characteristics and (2) no identity requirement is present. Authorization for processing may be transferred to a qualified third party. Goods under the inwards processing regime are eligible for deposit in a customs warehouse or for clearance to the transit regime or another customs regime with a view to their subsequent reexportation.

(2) Outwards Processing.—Under this procedure, goods in free circulation may be shipped out of the Dutch customs territory for processing outside the EEC customs territory. The duty charged on the reimported processed product is reduced to reflect the Dutch materials that went into its manufacture. The processed goods must be reimported within 1 year to the original exporter's account. No import duty is charged on imported goods returned to the manufacturer for repair done without charge under a guarantee or to correct previously undetected manufacturing flaws. Goods exported from one member country for processing abroad can be reimported into any other member country subject to reduced duty charges.

Storage of Goods Under Customs Control

The Netherlands customs' legislation, which is harmonized with the European Communities' directives on the matter, provides for two kinds of storage with respect to goods that are under customs control:

(1) Customs storage (pending submission of a declaration for import, for placing in a bonded warehouse, or for transit) and

(2) Storage in a bonded warehouse (pending receipt of instructions as to further destination of the goods, without duty being payable).

Customs Storage.—Here a distinction is made between short-term storage in a warehouse and longer term storage in a warehouse.

Short-term storage may take place without a detailed declaration, by making use of the customs documents with which the goods were delivered. Its main purpose is to make the means of conveyance available as quickly as possible for a subsequent consignment. The duration of such storage is limited to a period not exceeding a few months.

Longer term storage, which can take place only after short-term storage, may take place after submission of a declaration by the keeper of the building or site and may not exceed a period of 5 years.

Storage in a Bonded Warehouse.—There are three kinds of bonded warehouse: public, private, and fictitious.

Public bonded warehouses are bonded warehouses that are sealed or guarded by the Customs and are intended for use as storage space by anybody. With this type of official supervision, stocks need not be checked, and the keeper does not have to pay duty on any goods lost during storage. These warehouses, unlike other bonded warehouses, can be established only at a limited number of places, namely in Amsterdam, Delfzijl, Dordrecht, the Rotterdam port area, Schiphol, and Flushing. The storage is unlimited.

Private bonded warehouses are bonded warehouses that are sealed by the Customs and intended for storage by the warehouse keeper. With this type of official supervision, stocks are not checked, except for alcoholic substances, beer and tobacco products, which are checked against a storage and release account kept by the customs authorities. Provided the requirements of customs supervision are met, establishment can be permitted anywhere in the country. The storage period is unlimited.

Fictitious bonded warehouses are warehouses for the storage of certain easily identifiable goods. These warehouses are not officially sealed or guarded and are intended for storage by the warehouse keeper. As these warehouses are not officially sealed, stocks are checked against a storage and release account kept by the customs authorities. Moreover, the warehouse keeper must give security for any duty that may be payable. Provided the requirements of customs supervision are met, establishment can be permitted anywhere in the country. The storage period is limited to 5 years.

For a number of years, Netherlands customs legislation also has made provision for bonded warehouses in which the aforementioned checking of stocks is replaced partly or altogether by checking against the keeper's business and financial accounts, which in such cases must satisfy certain requirements. At the same time, customs documents are no longer required for release for certain permitted destinations. Since identification of the goods no longer plays a decisive role with this modern type of checking, any kind of goods can be stored in such a bonded warehouse.

Manipulations During Storage Under Customs Control.—During customs and bonded warehouse storage, goods may undergo certain (so-called normal) manipulations to ensure their being kept in good condition or to improve their presentation or marketability. Manipulations other than the aforementioned may take palce outside the storage establishments only in accordance with the rules in force for "active veredelingsverkeer" (temporary admission for inwards processing), whereby the goods are

In 1981, the average warehouse charges in Rotterdam were as follows:
(1) Warehouse costs, $4 per ton per month
(2) Documentation charge, $17.50 per transaction
(3) Unloading at storage site, $12.50 per ton
(4) Movement from warehouse to truck, $12.50 per ton
The charges for cargo handling are per metric ton and are based on the condition that the goods are harmless, not voluminous, and not loaded on pallets.
The average rent of office space at prime location in Rotterdam amounts to $110 per year per square meter excluding service and heating charges and taxes.

imported temporarily on certain conditions. This temporary admission for inwards processing, which is not normally subject to physical official supervision, can take place anywhere in the Netherlands; there is no need for the customs authorities to approve the establishment where manipulation takes place.

Refund of Duty

Duties and taxes are refundable under certain conditions. They may be refundable if it's determined after a protest that they are excessive. They also may be refunded if, while under customs supervision, the goods are destroyed by force majeure or accident. Other legal grounds also exist for claiming refunds. As a condition precedent, goods almost invariably must be unused and returned to the seller or destroyed in the presence of the customs authorities. Claims must be submitted by the payer or designee in a written application to the customs office of collection. Included among the legal grounds for claiming refunds are the following: Goods not in conformity to contract or damaged in transit, goods unordered, faulty merchandise, and goods found to be unusable for the purposes intended.

Duty-Free Material

The United States and the Netherlands are parties to an agreement entitled "Importation of Educational, Scientific, and Cultural Materials." This agreement provides for the dutyfree importation of specified books, publications and documents, works of art, collectors' pieces, visual and auditory materials, and articles for the blind. In addition, scientific instruments and apparatus may enter duty free under the Florence Agreement, subject to the approval of the Dutch Government on the grounds that such items are not manufactured in the country and are consigned to approved public and private educational and scientific institutions. EEC regulations, effective January 1, 1976, broadened the area of manufacture to include any EEC member country.

Samples and Advertising Matter

Under the terms of the International Convention to Facilitate the Importation of Commercial Samples and Advertising Matter, to which the Netherlands and the United States are parties, samples of negligible value are exempt from import duties and taxes. Other samples, which are representative of particular categories of goods, also are admitted on a temporary exemption basis on conditions that they are imported solely for soliciting orders and are not sold or put to normal use except for purposes of demonstration. The posting of a bond or deposit to cover the amount of customs charges is required. Samples of commercial value, which are not reexported within 1 year from the date of importation, are subject to the same customs regulation charges as ordinary commercial shipments.

Outside of the Convention's provisions, trade advertising material is dutiable at 9 percent ad valorem plus a turnover tax of 18 percent.

As a result of the U.S. accession to the Customs Convention on the ATA Carnet for the Temporary Admission of Goods, procedures for the importation of samples have been simplified considerably. The Convention provides for the acceptance by the contracting parties, including the United States and the Netherlands, of an ATA carnet instead of a security for import duties and taxes and customs documents. This instrument, valid for 1 year, is obtainable from the U.S. Council of the International Chamber of Commerce, located at 1212 Avenue of the Americas, New York, New York 10036, telephone (212) 354-4480. Applications for carnets are available from the U.S. Council or U.S. Department of Commerce district offices. The price of a carnet varies from $50 to $150, depending on the valuation of the merchandise being covered.

Advance Rulings on Classification

Tentative or advisory rulings on the customs classification of particular goods will be supplied on request by the Dutch customs authorities. It is desirable to submit samples, but this is not always necessary. To obtain advance rulings in writing, send applications to the Ministry of Finance, Director of Customs, 's-Gravenhage, Korte Voorhout 7, The Hague, Netherlands.

Internal Taxes

As required by EEC rules designed to unify the tax structure within the EEC, the Netherlands in 1969 changed its turnover tax from a cascade-type system to the Tax on Value Added (TVA). On imports, the tax is assessed on the cost-insurance-freight (c.i.f.) duty-paid value plus excise taxes, if applicable.

Most items are taxed at 18 percent while such goods as foodstuffs, books, farm products, artificial limbs, hearing aids, certain medicines and works of art are subject to a 4 percent tax rate. Seagoing vessels (except pleasure craft) and aircraft intended for use principally for public transportation on international routes are exempt from the turnover tax. A special consumption tax of 17.5 percent (or 16 percent if the catalog price is below Dfl. 10,000) is also applied on passenger cars. The rates assessed are the same on domestic and imported items; however, exports are exempt from the TVA.

The TVA paid by a firm on capital equipment purchased domestically or abroad is fully deductible from the total amount owed to the Dutch Government due to the firm's collection of the TVA on the sale of its product.

Excise taxes are levied on soft drinks, wine, beer, spirits, substances containing methyl, propyl, or isoproply alcohol, sugar, products containing sugar, tobacco products, and petroleum products. Identical rates are assessed on both imported and domestic goods.

Shipping Documents

The shipper must transmit to the consignee two signed copies of the commercial invoice. Neither consular legalization nor chamber of commerce certification is necessary.

Although no special form or phraseology is prescribed for the commercial invoice, it is advisable to include the following: Date and place of shipment; name (firm's name) and address of the seller and buyer; method of shipment; number, kind, and markings of the packages and their numerical order; exact description of goods—customarily a commercial description according to kind, quality, quantity, grade, weight (gross and net, preferably in metric units), etc., with special emphasis on factors increasing or decreasing their value; agreed price of the goods—unit cost, total cost f.o.b. factory plus shipping, insurance and other charges (see earlier discussion on valuation); delivery and payment terms; and the signature of a responsible official of the shipper's firm.

Bills of lading should bear the name of the party to be notified. The consignee needs the original bill of lading to take possession of the goods.

A certificate of origin is not usually required by customs regulations. However, if requested by a Dutch importer or needed to comply with a stipulation in a letter of credit, it must be certified by a recognized U.S. chamber of commerce.

The regulations concerning health certificate and plant quarantine requirements are complex and are frequently amended. In the United States, the Dutch agencies mentioned under "Sources of Economic and Commercial Information" should be contacted. The Animal and Plant Health Inspection Service, U.S. Department of Agriculture, located in the Federal Center Building, Hyattsville, Maryland 20782, not only inspects and certifies through numerous local offices but also can furnish information to U.S. exporters. In the Netherlands, information on health certification and on plant quarantine requirements may be obtained from the Plantenziektekundige Dienst, Geertjesweg 15, Wageningen.

Marking and Labeling Requirements

An existing law (Commodity Act) empowers the appropriate authorities to issue regulations on the required marking, labeling, packing, and composition of individual commodities. Such regulations, which vary considerably and are issued and amended frequently, apply to many individual commodities, mainly foodstuffs.

No regulation has been promulgated requiring that imports in general indicate foreign origin, but false indications of origin are prohibited. However, specific regulations are applicable to certain items such as eggs, flavors, gravies and soups, powdered milk, and honey. Complete and detailed information may be obtained from the Keuringsdienst voor Waren (Food Inspection Service), Prinsegracht 50, The Hague.

Under the provisions of EEC regulation 158/66, the country of origin is required on the packing of various fruits and vegetables. In addition, the quality class (EEC grade) and variety of the fruit or vegetable must be mentioned on the packing. U.S. exporters desiring assistance in this regard should contact the Foreign Agricultural Service, U.S. Department of Agriculture, Washington, D.C. 20250.

Hallmarking of gold and silver articles with small tolerances allowable for error is required before they can be offered for sale in the

Netherlands. The hallmarking may be done by a Netherlands hallmarking office after importation. On gold articles, karat marking is permissible.

Nontariff Import Controls

Import Licensing. —Only 64-digit BTN industrial product categories, broken down to up to 7-digit subcateogries, are subject to import licensing requirements in the Netherlands. These are mainly coal and coke products (BTN tariffs 27.01 and 27.04), selected textile mill, apparel and textile products (in the 51 through 62 BTN tariff groups), certain base metal products (in the 73 and 79 BTN tariff groups), electronic calculators (BTN tariff 84.52), and a range of small arms and ammunition (in the 93 BTN tariff group). The vast majority of manufactured goods are free of import registration and licenses.

Practically none of the imports requiring licenses are subject to quantitative limitations; if they are, licenses are normally issued immediately and automatically. Licenses are valid for 6 months for overseas countries, including the United States; importation must occur within that period. Extensions as well as renewal of unused licenses may be authorized at the discretion of the Dutch licensing authorities.

The Central Import and Export Agency (CDIU) administers the licensing system. In the case of agricultural and fishery items, however, the Minister of Agriculture and Fisheries has delegated this authority to 13 Commodity Boards, which are quasi-governmental bodies supervising the marketing of such items.

Exchange Controls. —Payments for imports may be made freely in any foreign currency. Residents, including importers, may freely grant credit on imports of goods and accept suppliers' credits with maturities customary in the trade. However, they must obtain prior approval from the Netherlands Bank to accept suppliers' credits in excess of traditional maturities. Such approval is rarely authorized.

Exchange controls are administered by the Netherlands Bank on behalf of various ministries.

Technical Standards and Requirements

The Nederlands Normalisati Instituut (NNI) coordinates all work and research relating to standardization in the Netherlands. The NNI works closely with professional, industrial, and governmental organizations that perform much of the technical work, including testing. NNI prepares new and revised standards, subjects them to public inquiry, and finally submits them to the appropriate Ministry for approval. Specific inquiries about standards in the Netherlands should be directed to the: Nederlands Normalisatie Instituut, (Netherlands Standards Institute), Polakweg 5, Rijswijk (Z.H.)

The Netherlands also applies standards that result from the EEC program for harmonizing industrial standards. Over 100 EEC directives have been approved to date.

Another source of information with regard to standards include the American National Standards Institute, 1430 Broadway, New York, New York 10018; tel: (212) 354-3300.

The European Electrical Standards Committe (CENEL) is a private organization that administers an agreement on harmonized standards and testing for electronic components to which several European countries, including the Netherlands, adhere. The system sets technical specifications for components and provides that a certification of quality, issued by an authorized institution in any member country, be recognized in the other participating nations with no additional testing required.

Electrical current in the Netherlands is distributed at an alternating current of 50 cycles. Alternating nominal voltage is normally distributed either through a three-phase wye (star) or through a delta (triangle), four-wire secondary distribution system. In the wye or star distribution system, a nominal voltage example is 220/380, which is typical of most cities in the Netherlands. One and three are the conventional phases that are available in the Netherlands. The number of wires used most often are two, three, and four; the frequency stability is stable enough for electric clocks. The standard plug B (round pin attachment plug) is used, but the use of adapters is prohibited in the Netherlands.

Electric Current Abroad, a publication of the U.S. Department of Commerce, provides information on electric current for a number of Dutch cities. Copies may be obtained from the Superintendent of Documents, U.S. Government Printing Office, Washington D.C. 20402, or from any Department of Commerce district office.

Investment in the Netherlands

The Netherlands' adherence to a liberal commercial policy is exemplified by its participation as a charter member of the Common Market and the Benelux Economic Union. Ideally situated at the mouth of Europe's busiest internal waterways system and boasting the world's largest port (Rotterdam), the Netherlands has become one of the most active trading nations on the Eurasian continent. The Netherlands' economic well-being is largely dependent upon the climate for world trade. U.S. direct investment in the Netherlands increased by 25 percent in 1980. The cumulative amount of U.S. investment in 1980 was $7.9 billion, with manufacturing in first place and the petroleum industry next in order of importance.

The Dutch Government has never played a strong regulatory role in the economy. However, it has determined that the national interest occasionally requires some degree of government participation in industry. Examples of this participation are found in coal, mining, salt, transportation and communications, steel, arms and munitions works, and natural gas industries.

Foreign Ownership

There are no specific provisions in the Netherlands' commercial code that deal with the status of foreign enterprises located in the Netherlands. Their status is exactly the same as enterprises entirely owned by Dutch citizens. There are no provisions that establish a required ratio of foreign to Dutch capital in a company; an enterprise may be wholly foreign owned. No differentiation is made between Dutch and foreign companies in so far as either public or private issue of shares is concerned.

There are no legal provisions requiring the appointment of Dutch nationals to the board of directors, to the management, or to the staff of a company. Board meetings may be held at any place the company chooses, but meetings of shareholders must be held in the Netherlands.

Commercial Treaty with the United States

A Treaty of Friendship, Commerce, and Navigation between the United States and the Netherlands sets forth the signatories' mutual rights and privileges. Basically, each country agrees to accord the citizens of the other's country equal treatment with respect to the conduct of commercial, industrial, and financial activities.

Investment Incentives

The Dutch Government provides a wide range of incentives to stimulate the economy and to encourage investors to move out of the traditional industrial areas, such as the "Randstad," into the western and central part of the Netherlands. There are three basic instruments of investment facilitation: The Investment Account Law (WET Investerings Rekening—WIR), the Selective Investment Law (Selective Investerings regeling—SIR), and the Investment Premium Law (Investerings Premie Regeling—IPR). In addition, there is a wide array of other incentives, which include special loans and participation, training subsidies and fiscal incentives.

In 1978, the Investment Account Act (WIR) was established to encourage investment in fixed or capital assets. Under this act, the Government provides free tax bonuses that are offset against tax assessment. Moreover, any firm whose tax liability is too small to absorb such a bonus may be given a tax-free cash payment instead. Thus, firms at any stage of their life cycle and at any part of the profitmaking spectrum can benefit from these incentives. The investment bonuses consist of a basic subsidy, which ranges from 10 to 18 percent and may be increased by one or more of four types of supplement: The small scale grant, the large projects grant, the regionalization grant, and the special region grant. In order to maintain eligibility for these grants, the firm's assets must be situated in the Netherlands and the minimum investment must be Dfl. 2,200 (approximately $1,000) in any calendar year. Bonuses are not given for land investments. Improvements to existing assets do not qualify for bonuses unless they are depreciated at rates not higher than 12.5 percent for buildings or 15 percent for plants.

In order to help alleviate the congestion in the Randstad and other populated areas, the Dutch Government imposes a levy, the SIR, which reduces WIR bonuses in those areas already heavily industrialized. The SIR law is applied exclusively to investment in new buildings or for important alterations or fixed equipment in the so-called SIR area. This underdeveloped region is located in the Provinces of Zuid Holland, Utrecht, the southern part of Noord Holland, and the western part of Gelderland. Under the SIR, there is a system of levies plus a compulsory notification system. The levy is 13 percent for new buildings and 8 percent for fixed equipment in open air. The amount of $125,000 for buildings and $250,000 for fixed equipment are exempted from the levy.

IPR investment premiums are granted to new industries settling in the target areas of the Northern Netherlands (NOM), South Limburg (the LIOF), parts of Overijssel (the OOM), the Gelderland, and Noord Brabant. Moreover, IRI premiums are granted to new establishments tagged as "dynamic service enterprises of more than regional importance." These investments are eligible for a premium of 15 to 25 percent of capital expenditures on fixed assets. These include the cost of land and acquisition of buildings and machinery. As a rule, the maximum premium is $2 million. The principal conditions for the application of the IPR are (1) the capital expenditure on fixed assets should be at least $100,000, (2) at least 35 percent of the capital expenditure on fixed assets should be financed by the entrepreneur, and (3) after the project has been realized and after the premium has been granted, the shareholders' equity must be a proportion of the net investment acceptable to the Dutch Ministry of Economic Affairs.

The Dutch Government has established an industrial commission to attract new investments in a coordinated manner. It has a full-time staff of 25 people in offices located in New York and Tokyo while officials in The Hague are responsible for European regions. The Government also has launched a full-scale 5-year industrial development plan with a $14.5 billion budget. This aid is available to both Dutch and foreign-owned companies. Over $11 billion will be spent to stimulate investment nationally and in the regions. A further $2.25 billion will be spent on solving the problems of ailing industries while $1 billion will help companies develop new technologies and applications for their products. By introducing this policy, the Government is veering away from its former practice of subsidizing weak industries and will now focus on a more selective, sectoral policy of assisting innovative, high-technology firms having the best potential for export. The primary point of contact for prospective U.S. investors seeking further information on investment in the Netherlands is the Industrial Commissioner of the Netherlands in the United States, One Rockefeller Plaza, New York, New York, 10020 telephone (212) 246-1434.

To qualify for any of the investment incentives, certain conditions have to be met. In all cases, premiums are only granted to entrepreneurs who are subject to Dutch taxation. To obtain the most favorable tax advantages, the establishment or relocation will have to be made in a priority-designated area. Under the WIR and IPR programs, certain minimum capital expenditures are set as a principal condition.

Business Organizations

The Netherlands Commercial Code recognizes the following major types of business organizations: (1) Proprietorship (Eenmanszaak), (2) general partnership (Vennootschap onder firma), (3) limited partnership (Commanditaire Vennootschap), (4) civil partnership (Maatschap), (5) limited partnership with shares (Commanditaire Vennootschap op Aandelen), (6) cooperative (Cooperatie), (7) corporation (Naamloze Vennootschap or N.V.), and (8) private company (Besloten Vennootschap met beperkte aansprakelijkheid or B.V.).

Newly formed companies of any type must comply with certain administrative and commercial regulations. All business organizations are required by law to keep books and prepare yearly balance sheets. Records of business organizations must be preserved for at least 10 years. Besides the formalities discussed below in connection with corporations, new companies must register with the Office of Direct Taxation, the Office of Indirect Taxation, and the Social Security offices. In addition, business organizations as well as individuals who are in business for themselves are required to register in the Commercial Trade Register kept by the appropriate chamber of commerce.

The most frequent types of business organization are the private firm or partnership for smaller enterprises and the public corporation (N.V.) or private corporation (B.V.) for larger enterprises. Sizable firms in which foreign capital is to be invested will usually find the N.V. or B.V. best adapted to their use.

Public Corporations.—There are four steps to be taken in the establishment of a public corporation: (1) Execution before a notary of the articles of incorporation by at least two of the company's founders, (2) submission of the notarized articles to the Netherlands' Minister of Justice for declaration that the articles comply with the legal requirements, (3) publication of the articles and ministerial declaration in the *Official Gazette* (Nederlandse Staatscourant), and (4) registration of the newly established company in the Commercial Register of the appropriate chamber of commerce. When these steps have been taken and at least 20 percent of the subscribed capital has been paid in, the corporation is considered "established" and has the full rights and obligations of a legal entity.

The articles of incorporation must be in Dutch and must be executed before, and registered by, a notary. They must give the name and the location of the principal administrative office and the purpose of the company. The amount of company capital, the number and nominal value of the shares, and the number of shares owned by each of the founders must also be indicated. The first board of directors, if there is to be one, is named in the articles; later appointments to the board are made by the general meeting of the stockholders.

The articles of incorporation must mention any special agreements entered into on behalf of the company being set up and out of which arise rights and obligations for the company, whenever the latter, after establishment, either expressly or tacitly confirms them. Such agreements may relate to the acceptance of shares whereby special obligations are assumed by the company; the acquisition of shares on a basis different from that whereby participation in the company is made available to the general public; assurances of any profit to a founder of the company or to a third party connected with the establishment; and the paying-in on shares in a manner other than payment in legal Netherlands currency. After a company has been established, the management only can enter into such agreements if it has been given explicit authority in the articles of incorporation.

The name of the corporation must begin or end with the words "Naamloze Vennootschap" written in full or abbreviated to "N.V." The name should either be in Dutch or in another language with some additional name such as "Nederland," "Holland," or the place of establishment of the company.

A business name previously in legal use by another company or differing only slightly may not be used if confusion might result because of close proximity and/or similarities of the two businesses.

The principal administrative office of a Dutch company or foreign subsidiary must be in the Netherlands if it is to have Netherlands' nationality. Transfer abroad of the principal administrative office deprives the company of Dutch nationality. The question of where the activities of the company are actually carried on is of no relevance in establishing nationality if the company's principal administrative office is in the Netherlands.

The N.V., whether it be domestically or foreign owned, may raise capital by public issue or by private placing of shares in the Netherlands. Official listing of shares on the Amsterdam Stock Exchange may be applied for if the share capital amounts to not less than Dfl. 500,000. Quotations and dividends are expressed as a percentage of the nominal value of one share. Netherlands law does not recognize shares without nominal value.

Shares may be expressed in terms of equal or varying values and may be subdivided into fractional shares. The number of votes of each stockholder is determined by a formula based on the value of shares owned.

Share certificates are drawn up in name or to the bearer. The latter type of share must generally be fully paid up. Stockholders are liable only for the par value of their shares and may not be obligated without their consent beyond full payment of their shares.

The typical N.V. has three separate and distinct authorities; namely, the stockholders, the board of directors, and the managing board. Regulations among these three bodies are governed by the articles of incorporation, subject to the relevant provisions of the Commerical Code.

The supreme authority of the corporation is vested in the general meeting of shareholders, at which each shareholder has voting rights proportionate to the stock held.

The board of directors is charged by the general meeting of shareholders with supervision of the management. Directors may not receive remuneration unless the articles of incorporation contain provisions for it.

The managing board is entrusted with managing the affairs of the company, administering its property, and representing the corporation before the courts and other authorities. Each member of the managing board has the right to represent and obligate the company unless the articles of incorporation prescribe otherwise.

Private Corporation. —The B.V. or private company is a relatively new form of enterprise introduced in June 1971, which is organized similarly to the N.V. but has a more closed character as shown by differences in the legal provisions concerning the shares and the absence of an obligation to publish its annual accounts. A directive of the Council of the European Communities has obliged all limited liability companies to publish their financial data without regard to their size or purpose. The B.V. was introduced to provide an appropriate alternative to smaller companies.

The shares of a B.V. must be registered. A shareholder may transfer shares only to a very limited category of relatives without the prior approval of one of the company organs designed for that purpose or without first offering them to co-shareholders. Most important, the private company, B.V., is under no obligation to publish its financial reports as must a public company (N.V.). Exceptions to this rule are a B.V. in the insurance or banking business, that has issued bearer bonds or certificates thereof, and that has its shares or debentures listed on the stock exchange. However, a subsidiary B.V. in one of these three classes may be exempted from the need to file financial reports if the parent company has filed a consolidated financial statement that incorporates the accounts of the subsidiary.

An independent annual audit is required of those private companies that has an issued capital of not less than Dfl. 500,000 or have aggregate assets of not less than Dfl. 8 million, have more than 100 employees, carry on banking or insurance business, or have bearer debentures or certificates thereof in circulation.

Proprietorship (Eenmanszaak). —An individual may operate a business as a sole proprietorship, in which case that individual has sole responsibility for the business and all of the assets, both business and personal, is subject to attachment for his/her business debts.

General Partnership (Vennootschap onder Firma). —The general partnership is an association of individuals to operate a business under a common name. The partners are the owners and managers of the firm and are jointly and severally liable for obligations of the firm with regard to third parties. Transfer of an interest in a partnership must be approved by the other parties. If partners retire, they remain responsible for liabilities incurred before their retirement. A written partnership agreement is required by law; the rights and duties of the respective partners among themselves must be clearly defined therein.

Limited Partnership (Commanditaire Vennootschap). —A limited partnership has two kinds of partners: one or more general partners who are unconditionally liable for all the firm's activities and one or more limited partners who are not active in the management of the firm and whose liability is limited to their capital contribution. A limited partner's name may not appear in the firm's name unless he/she was previously a general partner.

Civil Partnership (Maatschap). —This special type of partnership, formed under and governed by civil law rather than commercial law, is usually used only in the professions and is a relatively unimportant type of business organization in the general commercial field. Because of the peculiarly personal nature of a civil partnership, special provisions cover the rights and duties of the partners.

Limited Partnership with Shares (Commandi- *taire Vennootschap op Aandelen).* — This type of busines organization is similar to the limited partnership, except that the interests of the limited partners are represented by transferable shares.

Cooperative (Cooperatie). —The cooperative is a special type of legal entity formed to represent the collective interests of its members, such as buying or selling, rather than primarily an establishment to make profits for investors. The extent of the liability of the members must be clearly defined and must be identified in the firm's name, which must also specify that the firm is a cooperative.

For further information concerning the establishment of a business in the Netherlands, contact the Ministry of Economic Affairs, Foreign Investment Commission, Bezuidenhoutseweg 30, 2594 AV, The Hague, tel. (070) 81 41 11.

Industrial Property Protection

Patents. —Persons not domiciled in the Netherlands are required to submit patent applications through a Dutch patent attorney. Patents are granted by the Octrooiraad (Patent Council), Patentlaan 2, Rijswijk (Z.H.), The Netherlands.

The Netherlands is a member of the "Paris Union" International Convention for the Protection of Industrial Property (Patents and Trademarks) to which the United States and about 80 other countries adhere. U.S. businesspersons and investors are thereby entitled to the same treatment in protecting patent and trademark rights in the Netherlands as that country extends to its own nationals. Under the Convention, a U.S. national is entitled to a period of 12-months' right of priority after first filing a patent application in the United States or any other Convention country. The priority right filing period for Benelux trademarks is 6 months.

Once granted, patents are valid for 20 years from the date of issue. Applicants have 7 years to request novelty examination; if not requested, the appliction lapses. Compulsory licensing is possible after 3 years if a patent is not used adequately.

Transfer of expense through licensing agreements is common place in the Netherlands. Technical and financial considerations often underlie the motive for licensing. Furthermore, there is a demand in the Netherlands for the acquisition of licenses, since many medium-size and small companies do not have the means to carry out research. A few companies in the

Netherlands are specialized in the negotiation of licensing terms and joint venture agreements and in preparing the texts of the agreements reached, paying special attention to patent and trademark interests, Common Market interests, Common Market antitrust regulations, and other legal aspects. The Netherlands does not require government approval of licensing agreements. There are also no restrictions on foreign exchange operations that would limit the availability of dollars for the payment of royalties. Taxation of royalties is covered by the statement: "Royalties paid to a resident or corporation of one of the contracting States shall be exempt from tax by the other contracting State" (Article IX, paragraph (27)). Royalties paid to the American licensor by a Dutch company are exempt from taxation; this is not the case if the investor forms a permanent establishment in the Netherlands. The exemption may also be lost if the royalty fees appear excessive to the Dutch tax authorities.

Trademarks. —The Uniform Benelux Law on Trademarks governs the registration and protection of trademarks in the Netherlands, Belgium, and Luxemburg. Under this law, it is no longer possible to register a trademark for only a part of the Benelux territory. Applications for trademark registration may be filed at the Benelux Merkenbureau (Trademark Office), Bankastraat 149/151, The Hague, or at one of the international offices. Trademarks are protected for 10 years from the date of filing of the application for registration. Registrations can be renewed for periods of 10 years. The right to a trademark expires automatically if not used within the Benelux during the first 3 years counted from the filing date, or during any uninterrupted period of 5 years. International registrations under the Madrid Agreement are effective in the Benelux.

Copyrights. —The law of the Netherlands accords copyright protection to literary, scientific, or artistic works including all writings, dramas, lectures, choreography, musical works, works of graphic arts, motion pictures, and applied industrial art. Copyright in the Netherlands generally subsists for a term of life of the author plus 50 years. However, the term of protection for works authored by public institutions, associations, foundations, and partnerships, as well as posthumously published works, is 50 years from the time the work was first made public. The Netherlands is a member of both the Berne Copyright Union and the Universal Copyright Convention, to which the United States is also a party.

Taxation

The burden of taxes and social security contributions in the Netherlands is one of the highest among Organization for Economic Cooperation (OECD) countries. In 1980, these two accounted for 53.5 percent of Dutch GNP (compared with 43.2 percent in Belgium, 39.6 percent in France, and 32.3 percent in the United States). However, income taxes are only imposed by the State. Provinces and municipalities are not authorized to impose tax on income and may only impose other taxes to a limited extent.

Corporation Income Tax, Basis and Rates

The corporation income tax (Vennootschapsbelasting) is levied on the net profits of resident corporations (i.e., firms incorporated under Netherlands laws) and of nonresident or foreign corporations. The profits of the latter are taxable only if they are earned within the Netherlands and are attributed to a permanent establishment situated in the Netherlands.

Dividends are taxed as income received by the shareholder. No account is taken of the corporation tax already levied. An exception to the rule is made if the shareholder is a limited liability company holding interest of more than 5 percent. In such cases, the corporation need not pay corporation tax on dividends received. The corporate tax rates applicable to the various levels of corporate income are 45 percent on taxable profits of Dfl. 40,000 or less; 45 percent plus 15 percent of the excess over Dfl. 40,000 on profits of Dfl. 40,000 to Dfl. 50,000; and 48 percent on profits of over Dfl. 50,000.

Depreciation Allowances

Deductions for depreciation are allowed for buildings, plant, machinery, equipment, goodwill and other intangible property, but not for land. However, land and a building erected on it may be regarded as one asset for depreciation purposes, thus increasing both the basis for depreciation and the salvage value.

Deferral of a depreciation expense is not permitted in any year, even a loss year. The depreciable basis of an asset is its cost less its estimated salvage value. The depreciation method used is generally left up to the taxpayer, e.g., depreciation of a given percentage of the purchase or production cost (straight-line method), depreciation of a given percentage of the book value (declining balance method), or depreciation according to intensity of use. Additional depreciation is allowed if the value of capital assets has deteriorated considerably owning to extraordinary circumstances (e.g., a fire). The method of depreciation elected may not be changed without justification.

Investment Allowances

Depreciable assets (except for dwelling houses, securities, and land not used for industrial building purposes) are eligible for an investment allowance, the amount of which is chargeable against taxable income without reducing the depreciable basis of the asset. Since the investment allowance is used as an instrument to control the national economy, the rules change frequently, but never retroactively. Land, including industrial sites on which plants are located, is exempt from the investment allowance.

Inventory Valuation

All methods of inventory valuation that conform to generally accepted accounting principles are allowable in determining taxable income applied. Among the acceptable methods of determining cost are first-in, first-out (fifo); last-in, first-out (lifo); the average cost; and the base-stock methods.

Carry-Forward Provisions and Operating Costs

Net losses incurred by a corporation during the first 6 years of its existence may be carried over indefinitely. Subsequent profits must offset losses incurred within the 6-month period prior to application of normal losses. Operating losses may be carried back 1 year and forward 6 years. An exception to the rule takes place between the years 1974 and 1978 when losses may be carried back 2 years as well as forward 6 years.

Personal Income Tax

A resident of the Netherlands is subject to individual income tax. (Inkomstenbelasting) on his/her total worldwide income. There are certain allowances for compulsory expenses (old age insurance, etc.). Nonresidents are subject to the income tax only with respect to income from certain sources within the country. Non-Dutch employees of foreign companies transferred to the Netherlands can request, and are usually granted, a predetermined deduction of a flat 35 percent of their total taxable income from Dutch sources during the first 5 years of their stay in the Netherlands. This includes any extra allowances the employee receives as compensation for working abroad. The major factors that determine a person's residency for tax purposes include length of stay, intentions regarding the length and nature of the visit, and similar considerations. Residence abroad does not necessarily preclude the possibility of a place of residence in the Netherlands.

Under the United States-Netherlands Double Taxation Agreement, a resident of the United States shall be exempt from Dutch taxation on compensation for labor or personal services performed within the Netherlands if temporarily present within the Netherlands for a period or periods not exceeding 183 days during the taxable year and if compensation is received for labor or personal services performed as an employee of, or under contract with, a resident of the United States or an American corporation, provided it is not deducted as such in computing the profits of a permanent establishment in the Netherlands.

The income that a person derives from all sources, such as wages, dividends, etc., is included in taxable income. Wage and salary earners are subject to a withholding tax or wage tax (Loonbelasting). This tax is levied as an advance payment on the income tax. At the time of the final assessment, the amount of wage tax withheld is deducted, and if this amount exceeds the tax due, a refund is made. The tax is imposed on a sliding scale. Married persons may not file a joint return for income from wages. A working wife is to report her wage income independently from that of her husband's. It is currently taxed at a separate, and more progressive, rate to allow time to adjust the tax system to this change. Married persons may file a joint return for a husband's wage income plus the nonwage income of both husband and wife. Individuals do not pay tax on capital gains, except the gains from shares in family-owned companies.

The rates of income tax in the Netherlands are set forth in schedules and are levied according to the appropriate tax brackets. In 1980, the rates varied from 20 percent on the first Dfl. 7,568 to 72 percent on incomes exceeding Dfl. 175,126.

Other Direct Taxes and Fees

A number of other taxes and fees are applied. Among those of importance to foreign investors is the dividend tax (Dividendbelasting), which is imposed on the dividends of shares, profit-sharing notes, and profit-sharing debenture bonds issued by corporations resident in the Netherlands.

The rate of the dividend tax for Dutch tax-liable citizens is 25 percent of the gross proceeds, and it is withheld form the distributed profits by the distributing company. Dividend tax paid is credited against income tax or company tax, if the dividend itself is included in the taxable income or in the profits. If neither of these taxes is due, the dividend tax is only repaid in certain cases. The same rate applies to foreigners who are tax liable, unless a lower rating is provided by a treaty for prevention of double taxation.

A wealth tax (Vermogenvelasting) is payable on most assets owned by an individual. Resident individuals are distinct from nonresident individuals for tax purposes. Resident individuals are assessed on their entire net property. Wherever situated after an exemption of Dfl. 90,000 for capital invested in business. Nonresident individuals are taxed for specific items of their net property located in the Netherlands, such as real estate mortgages and fixed assets of an industrial nature; generally, however, nonresidents are not entitled to the aforementioned deductions. Residents are liable for taxation on all their property, wherever it is located.

Where total liability to income tax and wealth tax exceeds 80 percent of taxable income, a refund of the excess is granted.

In addition to the above taxes, there are several other minor taxes levied in the Netherlands. Transfer taxes are imposed on a number of transactions; e.g., the acquisition of real estate, premiums paid to insurance companies or their authorized agents, the issuance of stock, and the purchase and sales of securities. A transfer tax is levied on property passing either by gift or inheritance. An automobile tax is imposed on the owners of most motor vehicles on an annual basis. There are also certain minor taxes levied by the municipal authorities.

Tax Treaty with the United States. —U.S. citizens, residents, and corporations are eligible for the benefits accorded under a convention for the avoidance of double taxation between the United States and the Netherlands.

In general, U.S. citizens, residents, and corporations are subject to Dutch taxes on income from certain sources in the Netherlands. The United States allows as a credit against its tax the appropriate amount of taxes paid to the Netherlands. Income from real property is taxable in the country in which the property is located.

Dividends paid by a corporation of the Netherlands to a U.S. resident or corporation are taxed at the maximum rates specified in the U.S.-

Netherlands tax agreement rather than at the 25-percent, dividend-tax rate mentioned above. These rates are as follows: (1) At a rate not exceeding 15 percent of the gross amount actually distributed or (2) at a rate not exceeding 5 percent of the gross amount actually distributed if during the part of the paying corporation's taxable year that precedes the day of payment of the dividend and the whole of the prior taxable year (if any), the recipient is a corporation owning at least 25 percent of the voting stock of the paying corporation, either alone or in combination with another corporation of the United States, provided each recipient corporation owns at least 10 percent of such voting stock. The rule cited in point (2), above, does not apply if more than 25 percent of the gross income of the paying corporation for such prior taxable year (if any) consisted of interest and dividends (other than interest derived in the conduct of a banking, insurance, or financing business and dividends or interest received from subsidiary corporations, 50 percent or more of the voting stock of which was owned by the paying corporation at the time such dividends or interest were received). The foregoing provisions do not apply if the recipient of the dividends has a permanent establishment in the Netherlands and the shares with respect to which the dividends are paid are effectively connected with such permanent establishment.

Another provision of the U.S.-Netherlands tax agreement calls for distinguishing between operating profits and investment income earned by a permanent establishment owned by a U.S. firm. The former will continue to be taxed at current Netherlands profits tax rates, while the latter will be subject to special arrangements provided for in the convention. This means that interest and royalty payments to the U.S.-owned company will be exempt from Dutch taxes, except for those categories of income that are effectively connected to the operation of the firm.

A third feature permits a U.S. firm to send an employee to the Netherlands for business experience and pay him up to Dfl. 18,000 (approximately $9100) before the employee is subject to Dutch income tax. This provision is applicable, however, only in cases where the U.S. company has less than a 50-percent interest in the Dutch firm. A resident's total income, including the income of a foreign national, is subject to Dutch individual income tax. Under certain circumstances, deductions are permitted under the double taxation agreement with the U.S. Internal Revenue Service.

Refund of VAT To
Foreign Entrepreneurs

As of January 1, 1981, the Dutch Turnover Tax Act has been brought into line with the EEC eighth directive. The changes all refer to the refund of VAT to foreign entrepreneurs.

Although this was already included in Dutch law, the following adjustments were made:

(1) The form was changed.

(2) The period to which a request for a refund relates must be at least 3 months and at most 1 year; the period can be shorter than 3 months if it represents the remaining part of a calendar year.

(3) The period during which the request must be made must be within 6 months after the end of the calendar year in which the right to a refund arose.

(4) The minimum amount for a request that refers to a calendar year or the remaining part of a calendar year must be at least Dfl. 70. A request for any other period, must be at least Dfl. 550.

(5) The foreign entrepreneur is no longer required to choose a domicile in The Netherlands.

(6) The original invoices must be sent together with the form to the tax inspectorate.

Indirect Taxes

Turnover Tax (Valued Added Tax). —This tax is levied in accordance with the value added system (TVA). All deliveries of goods and services, including retail sales and imports, are subject to this tax. For tax rates, see "Internal Taxes," page 1633. The tax is levied on the sales price charged by the entrepreneur. The entrepreneur, however, does not pay the entire amount of the tax, but deducts from it the amount already charged by the previous links in the consumption chain for services, raw materials, components, and so on. Thus, at each step, the tax is levied on the value added. The general rate is 18 percent, with a lower rate of 4 percent applying to such necessities of life as foods, medicines, and transportation. Exported goods are exempt.

Excise Taxes. —These are levied on soft drinks, wine, beer, spirits, tobacco, sugar, and petroleum products. See "Internal Taxes," page 1633, for additional information.

Employment

Labor Force and Unemployment

The labor force in the Netherlands consists of 4.3 million people or 30 percent of the total population. The services industry employs the largest part of the labor force, 45 percent, followed by the manufacturing industry, with 30 percent. Women comprise only 28 percent of the labor force. This percentage grows slowly and is still low in comparison with other European countries. More than half of the working population, for both sexes, is in the 20-to-40 age group.

For many years the unemployment rate remained relatively stable at 2 percent of the work force or 100,000 people. However, this situation changed drastically in 1974 following the oil crisis. Within 3 years, the number of unemployed doubled to about 200,000 or more than 4 percent of the total work force. By late 1981, unemployment, reflecting the economic slowdown in the Dutch economy, had risen to 474,000 or about 8 percent of the total labor force. The figure is expected to average 475,000 or 11 percent for full year 1982. Dutch labor force statistics, it should be noted, exclude self-employed and professional people and therefore tend to understate the real number of jobless.

Wages and Hours

The usual workweek is 5 days, and average working hours range from 40 to 42.5. The Labor Act (Arbeidswet) regulates such matters as maximum working hours (48 weekly), rest periods, weekly half-days and full days of rest, overtime for male workers, and working hours and overtime for women and young people. Overtime is strictly forbidden by law for people under 18. In most industries, overtime pay equals at least 25 percent for the first 2 hours and 50 percent for all other hours, except Sundays and holidays, which require at least 100 percent of the basic hourly wage.

Wages in most industries are set by collective bargaining agreements (CAO's), which may apply to entire industries or to single plants. CAO's are usually negotiated for a year at a time, although sometimes longer, and they are negotiated between the employers' organizations and the trade unions. Subject to government restrictions, collective agreements generally provide for wage increases based on rises in the cost of living. Discrimination in matters of pay between men and women doing equal work is illegal. There is a statutory minimum wage fixed at Dfl. 1,925.30 per month for employees between 23 and 65 years of age. This amount decreases per year by an additional 10 percent to the age of 19.

The law provides for a bonus of 7 percent of wages to be paid at annual vacation time, but in practice this bonus varies between 7 percent and 8 percent in accordance with CAO provisions. Employers frequently pay what is called 13-month bonus as extra compensation, which is usually given at Christmas time. Employees over 18 are entitled to a vacation or annual holiday of 3 working weeks, and those under 18 to 4 working weeks. These are minimum entitlements, which employers often exceed by about a week. Employees receive overtime for the following legal holidays: New Year's Day, Easter Monday, Queen's Birthday (April 30), Ascension Day, Whit Monday, Christmas Day and the day after, and sometimes for Good Friday and Liberation Day (May 5, once in 5 years). Leave without pay is permitted for legally specified periods of time on such occasions as the birth, marriage, and death of close relatives, examination for military service, and voting in elections.

The hiring of employees in the Netherlands involves employment contracts, which can be concluded in writing or by verbal agreement. These contracts cannot contain provisions that are less demanding than those required by law or by any applicable labor agreement. The usual employment contract may be for an unlimited term, although no employee can specifically bind himself/herself for more than 5 years. A trial period for a maximum of 2 months can form part of the contract. Within this period, both partners can discontinue the contract at any time with no obligations. Employment may be terminated at any time by mutual agreement between employee and employer. In the absence of mutual agreement, the approval of the director of the regional labor office is required. By law, the term of regular notice need not be longer than 13 weeks for the employer and 6 weeks for the employee. Employment cannot be terminated by the employer during illness of the employee, unless the illness has lasted for at least 2 years.

The Unemployment Insurance Act insures the unemployed person (below the age of 65) against the financial consequences of involuntary unemployment. This benefit amounts to 80 percent of the daily wage to a maximum of $112.60. This insurance is valid for a maximum of 26 weeks per benefit year. After this period, the Unemployment Provisions Act comes into force for 2 years and provides for 75 percent of daily wages.

Nonwage Labor Costs

The social security system in the Netherlands is extensive, complex, and compulsory. The system covers the costs of illness and ensures a minimum income for those unable to earn their living as a result of illness, serious injury, unemployment, or retirement. Both employers and employees contribute to various social insurance funds. The premiums paid by the employees are deducted from their wages by the employer. Together with his/her own contributions, the employer pays these amounts periodically to the Industrial Insurance Board. Each year, the amount of premiums to be paid is fixed, with the change normally following the trend of wages. The amount of contribution as of January 1, 1979, is 27 percent of the insurable wage for the employer and 24 percent for the employee.

The Ministry of Social Affairs may require all groups employed in any sector of industry to participate in an industrial pension fund. Contributions to such a fund, which must provide for old age, widows', and orphans' benefits, are made equally by employers and employees. Private pension schemes are supervised by the Government under the Pension and Savings Fund Act. Broadly, the act requires an employer to insure his/her scheme with an appropriate insurance company, to join an industry-wide scheme, or to set up a company fund.

In addition to the compulsory social charges, there are a number of other employee benefits furnished voluntarily by the employer or agreed upon in collective labor agreements. These may include such fringe benefits as paid holidays, vacation allowances, Christmas bonuses, cafeterias, recreational facilities, company magazines, and saving plans.

Labor Relations with Management

The Netherlands has a very good record with regard to few days lost by strikes. Strikes have not been the primary means of achieving union aims, and labor-management disputes have been settled by negotiation. Unofficial or wildcat strikes have been largely unknown, and in general, the unions have so far had few problems in controlling their members.

Three union groups coexist in the Netherlands and comprise about 39 percent of the total labor force. The Protestant unions are affiliated to the Federation of Christian National Workers Unions (CNV); the Roman Catholic unions, to the Federation of Netherlands Catholic Trade Unions (NKV); and the nondenominational unions, to the Netherlands Federation of Trade Unions (NVV). Additionally, there are Federations for middle and higher level employees organized in the Council for Medium and Higher Employees. In 1976, the NVV and NKV set up a joint organization (FNV), which represents 60 percent of organized workers.

Most unions are organized on an industry-wide basis. Union membership is not compulsory—except in the printing and allied industry, where, in accordance with its collective agreement, only union members may be employed. Although the unions may represent only a minority of the workers, the collective agreements that they and the employers' organizations conclude are usually imposed on the entire industry by the Minister of Social Affairs. Representatives of all the union groups participate in collective bargaining and other negotiation.

Employers are associated with two organizations, the nondenominational Union of Netherlands Enterprises (VNO) and the Federation of Catholic and Protestant Employers' Unions (NCW). These two groups cooperate closely. In addition, two organizations cater to medium- and small-scale businesses; and three, to agriculture.

In 1945, the central organizations of employers and employees set up the Foundation of Labor as a body for joint consultation and, if possible, negotiations at a national level in the areas of labor agreements. This foundation has contributed considerably toward a good relationship between employers and employees.

The Social and Economic Council (SER) also has had a positive influence on industrial relations. It consists of 45 membres, of whom 15 are elected by the trade unions, 15 are elected by the employers' organizations, and 15 are independent experts appointed by the Government. The Government is required by law to seek the advice of the Council on major social and economic matters.

To foster good labor relations and employee participation, every enterprise having 100 or more employees must establish a Works Council. Its members are employees chosen by their coworkers. The number varies from 7 to 25 depending on the size of the company. The law states that the employer must seek the advice of the Works Council regarding important decisions such as takeover, closure, change of location, important reorganizations, and changes in working conditions.

Employment of Foreign Workers

Citizens of most countries, including the United States, do not need visas to enter the Netherlands, a valid passport being sufficient. A national of an EEC or EFTA (European Free Trade Association) country (except Portugal) or of the United States who wishes to stay in the Netherlands for 3 or more months must apply for a residence permit to the local Netherlands municipal police within 8 days of arrival. A national of any other country must obtain an authorization for provisional stay at the Netherlands embassy or consulate in his/her country of origin.

A foreign national from any country outside the EEC wishing to take up paid employment, even in a managerial position, must obtain a work permit from a regional labor office before he/she is allowed to work in the Netherlands. This permit is usually valid for 1 year and can be extended.

Guidance for Business Travelers Abroad

There is a solid potential for U.S. goods in the Dutch market. However, this is a highly competitive market, and the U.S. exporter must keep certain factors in mind to achieve maximum success. The U.S. exporter should establish close liaison with distributors and customers to exchange information and ideas. Customary business courtesy, especially replying promptly to requests for price quotations and to letters placing orders, is a primary prerequisite for success in the Netherlands market. Exporters should be aware that ocean shipping requires stronger, more weatherproof packing than that used for domestic freight.

A vigorous and sustained promotion is often needed to launch products in the Netherlands because of conservative buying habits. In many cases, the Dutch consumer is not prepared to accept rapid changes in styles, colors, and materials of consumer goods. A good educational selling campaign can help considerably in overcoming this resistance to change. Advertising, if done carefully and in good tase, can be very effective.

Since the market is very competitive, the Dutch importer is in a position to request, and obtain, strict adherence to terms of sale. It follows that meeting delivery schedules is of prime importance. It is much better to quote a later delivery date that can be guaranteed than an earlier one that is not completely certain.

The terms of payment are generally from 30 to 90 days after delivery, although this varies considerably. Letters of credit are disliked by some Dutch business people. Drafts are occasionally used as a means of payment, the periods varying extensively.

Since Dutch wholesalers and retailers generally do a lower volume of business than their U.S. counterparts, the Dutch importer usually purchases smaller lots of goods than is the custom in the United States.

Close control should be maintained with Netherlands distributors. In most instances, mail and telegraphic and telephone communications are sufficient, but the understanding developed through periodic personal visits is the best way to keep distributors appraised of new developments and to avoid the complacency that sometimes evolves after a period of time.

Further, U.S. exporters should plan stockpiling in Europe to supply and to service customers speedily, support distributors' sales efforts by sharing advertising costs, be aware of and provide competitive credit terms, quote prices c.i.f. rather than f.ob., and adapt electrical equipment to the local 220 volt, 50 cycle alternating current.

English can be used in business correspondence, however, not all Dutch know this language. Therefore, the use of Dutch is essential in advertising, labeling, and instructions for assembling and using machines and appliances. If literature in Dutch cannot be provided, an English version is preferable to one in any other language.

Entrance Requirements.

Every traveler must have a valid passport. No visa is required of U.S. citizens visiting the Netherlands (see "Employment of Foreign Workers," page 1644, for further details). The Netherlands has no vaccination or inoculation requirements.

Business Etiquette

Initial dealings with Dutch businesspeople usually leave a correct impression of great courtesy and earnestness. Most do not use first names until a firm friendship has been formed. Friendships are highly valued, however, and once an American executive has gained his/her partner's confidence, he/she usually can count upon the partner's full cooperation.

Hotel Accommodations

Hotel rooms are difficult to find during the tourist season (May–September), and reservations should be made well in advance.

Clothing

Because of the damp and chilly climate, men wear winter-weight suits most of the year. American summer-weight suits will find only occasional use in the Netherlands. Women also wear suits during most of the year. Woolen dresses, sweaters, blouses, and skirts should also be included in a wardrobe for the Netherlands. Rainwear is imperative, as there is frequent participation during most of the year.

Health

Medical services are generally excellent and compare favorably with those in the United States. Large, well-equipped hospitals are located in Amsterdam, The Hague, and Rotterdam. Diagnostic clinics and laboratory facilities are very good. All common medical supplies are readily obtained, and special supplies are normally available on short notice.

Commercial Languages

The official language of the Netherlands is Dutch, but English, French, and German are commonly known by Dutch businesspeople. An American firm can usually expect to receive replies to its inquiries in English.

Business Hours

A 40–45 hour, 5-day workweek is typical for offices and factories, which are usually closed on weekends. Banking hours are 9 a.m. to 3 p.m., Monday through Friday. Shops are open daily from 9 a.m. to 6 p.m. Stores are required by law to close one morning or afternoon a week. Many large stores are closed Monday mornings. In some of the larger cities, the stores are open one evening a week.

Holidays

The following commercial holidays are observed in the Netherlands: New Year's Day (January 1); Good Friday (varies—March/April), Easter Monday (varies—March/April), the Queen's Birthday (April 30), Ascension Day (varies—May), Whit Monday (varies—May/June), St. Nicholas Eve (December 5), Christmas Day (December 25), and Second Day of Christmas (December 26). The entire building industry is usually on vacation for 3 weeks in July/August.

Weights and Measures

The metric system of weights and measures is used throughout the Netherlands

Communications and Local Transportation

The telephone system is very modern. Virtually the entire network is based on the automatic dial system.

Good public transportation is available in the major cities and fares are reasonable. Taxicabs are plentiful, day and night. Bicycles, scooters, and motorbikes are widely used.

To operate a car in the Netherlands, a valid U.S. driver's license is sufficient. Upon first arrival, driving in town may be a little disconcerting because of the many cyclists who often make quite unexpected turns or who must be passed at very close range. Right-hand traffic has the right-of-way, except at intersections of roads or streets marked as preferential fast traffic roads.

Domestic Payment

In the Netherlands, payments are usually made in cash through a transfer from the payer's account maintained with a bank or with the postal clearing service to the account of the payee (transfer system) or by "payment checks" or "Eurochecks." The checks are guaranteed by banks up to $50.00 and to $150,000 respectively, per check. Payments by ordinary checks not guaranteed for payment by a bank are less customary. A convertible guilder account may be maintained in a Dutch bank by any nonresident of the Netherlands. Without special license, deposits may be made to such an account by the holder of the account or any other nonresident. A convertible guilder account may be debited without license for any transfer anywhere in the world, but in a few special cases, payments to a Dutch resident require a license.

A convertible guilder account may be found useful during the initial stages of a new venture for collecting dividends, for paying travel and other expenses, and for keeping funds in an easily transferable form. Both a foreign-managed international distribution center in the Netherlands and a foreign supplier wishing to free Dutch customers from all foreign exchange formalities can take advantage of a convertible guilder account.

Sources of Economic and Commerical Information

U.S. Government Sources

General information concerning the market (economic trends, commercial developments, production and trade statistics, etc.), tariffs and trade regulations, and U.S. trade promotion efforts in the Netherlands may be obtained from the Netherlands Country Specialist, Central Europe Division, Office of the European Community, International Trade Administration, Washington, D.C. 20230 (phone (202) 377-3371), or from any of the Department of Commerce District Offices.

Information on exporting U.S. agricultural products to the Netherlands may be obtained by writing the Foreign Agricultural Service, U.S. Department of Agriculture, Washington, D.C. 20205.

In the Netherlands, the United States maintains an Embassy in The Hague at 102 Lange Voorhout (telephone: 070-624911) and Consulate Generals in Amsterdam at Museumplein 19 (telephone 020-790321) and in Rotterdam at Vlasmarkt 1 (telephone 010-117560). U.S. Foreign Service Officers in each Economic/Commercial Section are available to assist American business travelers. To keep U.S. business travelers informed of key Foreign Service appointments, the U.S. Department of State publishes trimesterly a booklet entitled *Key Officers of Foreign Service Posts: A Guide for Business Representatives*. Copies may be purchased for $2.25 each, or $5 per year on a subscription basis from the Superintendent of Documents, U.S. Government Printing Office, Washington, D.C. 20402.

Dutch Government Representation

The Netherlands maintains its Embassy at 4200 Linnean Avenue, N.W., Washington, D.C. 20008 (phone: 202-244-5300), and Consulate Generals at the following addresses: Rockefeller Plaza, New York, New York 10020 (phone: 212-246-1429); 2 Illinois Center, Suite 1900, 233 North Michigan Avenue, Chicago, Illinois 60601 (phone: (312-856-0110); 712 International Building, 601 California Street, San Francisco, California 94108 (phone: 415-981-6454); Central Plaza, 3460 Wilshire Boulevard, Room 509, Los Angeles, California 90010 (phone: 213-380-3440); and Suite 610, Post Oak Bank Building, 220 South Post Oak Road, Houston, Texas 77056 (phone: 713-622-8000). These offices should be contacted only regarding the importing of Dutch goods into the United States and Dutch consular matters.

The Industrial Commission of the Netherlands to the United States offers information on investment incentives. It is located at One Rockefeller Plaza, New York, New York 10020; telephone 212-246-1434.

The Dutch Government Tourist Office, an official tourist information agency, is located at 576 Fifth Avenue, New York, New York 10036; telephone 212-245-5320.

Other Information Sources

• The Netherlands Chamber of Commerce in the United States, Inc., One Rockefeller Plaza, New York, New York 10020; phone:

212-265-6460; for Midwester and Pacific Coast States: Wrigley Building, 410 North Michigan Avenue, Chicago, Illinois 60611, phone: 312-943-1580.

- American Chamber of Commerce in the Netherlands, Carnegieplein 5, The Hague; phone: (070) 659808

- Amsterdam Chamber of Commerce and Industry, Department for Commercial Information, Koningin Wilhelminaplein 13, Amsterdam; phone: (020) 172882

- Rotterdam Chamber of Commerce and Industry, Department for Commercial Information, Coolsingel 58, Rotterdam; phone (010) 117450

- The Netherlands Chamber of Commerce for America/Netherlands, Center for Trade Promotion, phone (070) Kettingstraat 2, 2501 CA, The Hague

- Chamber of Commerce of the United States, 1615 H Street, N.W., Washington, D.C. 20006

European Community Information Service, 2100 M Street, N.W., Washington, D.C. 20037; phone (202) 862-9500; maintains a variety of publications on EEC-related economic and social issues.

OECD Publications Center, 1750 Pennsylvania Avenue, N.W., Washington, D.C. 20006; offers economic information prepared by the Organization for Economic Cooperation and Development on its member countries. Publications on sale include annual economic surveys with forecasts, trade statistics, and economic indicators.

Commercial and economic trends and technical developments also are given coverage in specialized trade journals and publications of trade associations and banks.

Market Profile—NETHERLANDS

Foreign Trade

Imports.—In 1979, $52.3 billion: in 1980, $59.4 billion. From United States: $6.9 billion in 1979; $8.7 billion in 1980. Major suppliers: West Germany, United States, France, United Kingdom, Italy. Major imports: Machinery and transportation equipment, mineral fuels, lubricants. From the United States: Agricultural products, aircraft and parts, measuring and controlling equipment, ADP equipment, nonferrous ores.

Exports.—In 1979, $51 billion; in 1980, $58.3 billion. To United States: $1.85 billion in 1979, $2.04 billion in 1980. U.S. share: 3 percent. Major markets: West Germany, France, United Kingdom, Italy. Major exports: Semifinished goods, chemicals, manufactured goods, petroleum products. To United States in 1980: aircraft and parts, alcoholic beverages, organic chemicals (hydrocarbons), nonelectric engines and motors.

Trade Policy.—Liberal, except for agricultural prodcts subject to EEC Common Agricultural Policy. Member of the Benelux Economic Union, EEC, OECD, GATT, and IMF.

Trade Prospects.—Export prospects for the United States good despite modest economic growth projections. High-technology items and coal will experience strongest growth.

Foreign Investment

Largest investors are United States, United Kingdom, Belgium, West Germany. Total book value of U.S. direct investment in the Netherlands end of 1980, $7.9 billion. Direct investments have been concentrated mainly in manufacturing, primary and fabricated metals, and petroleum. Dutch investment in United States, end of 1981: $16.2 billion. U.S.-Netherlands treaties: Convention for Avoidance of Double Taxation; Treaty of Friendship, Commerce and Navigation.

Investment Prospects.—The Netherlands welcomes foreign, particularly U.S., investment. Incentives for locating outside of highly industrial western region.

Finance

Currency.—Basic unit, guilder (Dfl.) of 100 cents. Floating exchange rate, guilder value averaged $1 = 2.50 Dfl. in 1981.

Domestic Credit and Investment.—Commercial banks grant short- and medium-term loans. Long-term capital is available from insurance companies and investment banks. Securities may be listed on the Amsterdam Stock Exchange. Central Bank discount rate, 9 percent, August 1981.

National budget.—The 1982 forecast budget calls for total outlays of Dfl. 152 billion and revenues of Dfl. 133 billion. Planned deficit amounts to Dfl. 18 billion.

Balance of Payments.—Surplus on current account in 1981, $1 billion. Official gold and foreign exchange reserves in August 1981, $14 billion.

Economy

GNP.—For 1980, $133 billion at current prices; 1981 estimated GNP at current prices, $139 billion.

Industry.—Most important sector, producing a wide variety of capital and consumer goods. Major industries: Metalworking, petroleum refining, chemicals and petrochemicals, food processing, electronics, textiles. The volume of output declined by 2 percent in 1981.

Commerce.—Government measures have been relatively successful in combating inflation. Retail distribution changing from small establishments to larger units.

Agriculture.—Many small, well-managed farms, intensive cultivation—mainly dairy, livestock, fruits and vegetables.

Basic Economic Facilities

Transportation.—Extensive modern railway network with excellent domestic and international connections. Good road system, with most centers connected by limited access highways. One car to every 3.5 inhabitants. The principal port, Rotterdam, is one of the largest ports in the world in tonnage handled. It provides excellent connections with Germany, France, and Switzerland via the Rhine and other inland waterways. The second port, Amsterdam, has the main international airport, Schiphol.

Communications.—Government-owned postal, telegraph, and fully automated telephone services. Radio and TV broadcasting facilities are government-owned and leased to private broadcasting companies. Limited advertising permitted.

Power.—Net exporter of energy. Virtually all premises connected to national electricity and gas grids. Utilities owned by municipalities and provinces. Current is 220 volt, 50 cycles.

Natural Resources

Land Area.—16,464 square miles. Almost totally flat.

Climate.—Temperature: maritime. Mild, wet winters; cool summers.

Minerals.—Considerable reserves of natural gas.

Population

Size.—14.2 million (1980). Negligible positive growth rate; 870 inhabitants per square mile. Principal cities: Rotterdam, Amsterdam, The Hague (seat of government), Utrecht.

Language.—Official language is Dutch. English is widely used in business. French and German also widely understood.

Education.—Compulsory attendance, ages 6–15.

Labor.—Total labor force in 1980, 4.3 million; highly skilled. Services, 45 percent; manufacturing, 30 percent. Unemployment rate as of December 1981, 11 percent. Average industrial wage index (1972=100): 1979=196.

Market Profile—NETHERLANDS ANTILLES

Foreign Trade

Imports.—1975 (Curacao and Aruba) $2,591 million (U.S. share 2.7 percent nonpetroleum imports). Major imports: crude petroleum, chemicals, industrial machinery, electrical machinery and equipment, iron and steel, clothing.

Exports.—1975 (Curacao and Aruba) $2,621 million; Major exports: petroleum products, chemicals, electrical machinery and apparatus.

Trade Policy.—Due to association with the European Economic Community, Netherlands Antilles grants reverse traiff preferences on some EEC imports. Many goods are subject to duties of 4.5 percent, but some imports bear rates ranging from 20 percent to 55 percent to protect local industries. St. Eustatius, St. Maarten, and Saba are free ports. Licensing system in force since 1971.

Trade Prospects.—Best prospects continue to be consumer goods and transport equipment, principally trucks and boats, as well as pumps, heating and cooling machinery and equipment, and construction machinery. Others are oil storage tanks, aluminum plant equipment and phosphate mining machinery. In the consumer goods field, specific trade prospects appear to be textiles, stylish clothes, caluculators, new foods, and car accessories.

Foreign Investment.—Foreign capital welcomed, but is licensed so that projects can best serve the country. New industries, if oriented mostly toward overseas markets, can acquire non-resident status, and non-resident accounts in foreign currencies can be opened free of exchange controls. Total U.S. investment estimated at $450 million, mostly in oil refining; $6 million in solt mining; $40 million in manufacturing. Total foreign invesment estimated at $900 million.

Finance

Currency.—The Netherlands Antilles Guilder or florin, (NA Fl.) equals US$0.56, or 1.79 NA Fl. equal US$1. In addition to a Central Bank, the islands have ten commercial banks in operation, three of which have branches on more than one island.

Economy

G.N.P.—Estimated at $209 million in 1973.

Industry.—Petroleum refining and storage is the leading industry, employing some 5,000 people. Among industrial enterprises are a chemical plant, a large electronic equipment factory, and a drydock, mainly for ship repairing, which handles ships of up to 120,000-ton capacity. There are a number of small firms producing for the local market.

Tourism.—In 1975, the number of tourist arrivals increased by 10 percent to total 311,000. Principal tourism activities centered in Curacco, Aruba, and St. Maarten, with Aruba showing considerable growth, while Curacao experienced a decrease.

Basic Economic Facilities

Transportation.—A good network of roads exists. Air transport service to Curacao is provided by international carriers. Modern and well-maintained harbor and docking facilities help commerce and tourism; Curacao is expanding its harbor facilities to take care of VLCCs.

Communications.—These islands have direct radio-telephone connections with each other and with the United States, Western Europe, and most Latin American countries. TV stations operate on Curacao and Aruba and ten radio stations operate on six islands.

Power.—Except in Aruba, which obtains its electric power from the Government-owned Water and Energy Works, eletricity is generated by privately-owned thermal stations of English and American manufacture (diesel).

Natural Resources

Land.—Combined area, 383 square miles, comprising the three major A.B.C. islands, with two satellites (Klien Curacao and Klein Bonaire), three smaller islands, St. Eustatius, St. Maarten, and Saba.

Climate.—Trade winds bring mild tropical weather to these islands. October to March is the rainy season. Rainfall is of short duration, with greater precipitation on the three smaller islands. Average temperature is 81.6 degrees.

Minerals.—Mining is limited to phosphate and the extraction of solar salt.

Population

Size.—Totaled 240,000 in 1975, a slight increase over 1974. Nearly 152,000 in Curaco, 62,000 in Aruba, 8,000 in Bonaire and 10,000 in St. Maarten.

Language.—Dutch is the official language, but English is spoken in the smaller islands.

Education.—Government spends nearly 30 percent of its budget on education, which is not compulsory. However, there is virtually no illiteracy among the younger people and very little in the older age group.

Labor.—Work force of 67,000 people in 1973. Services and manufacturing employed 44 percent. Some 6,000 laborers work in the oil refineries.

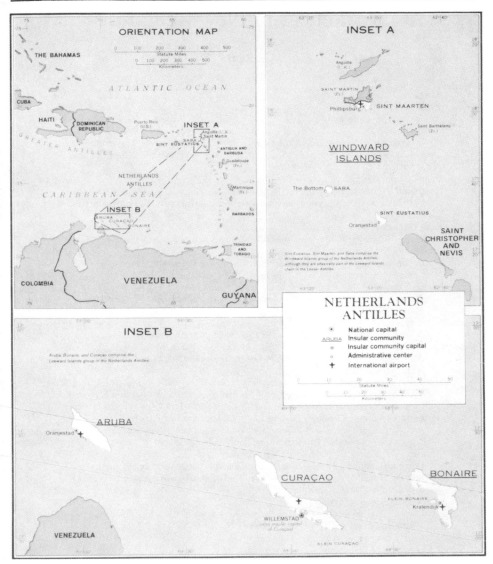

ORIENTATION MAP

THE BAHAMAS

ATLANTIC OCEAN

CUBA

HAITI
DOMINICAN
REPUBLIC

Puerto Rico
(U.S.)

INSET A

GREATER ANTILLES

SINT EUSTATIUS

Anguilla (U.K.)
Saint Martin

ANTIGUA AND
BARBUDA

Guadeloupe
(Fr.)

NETHERLANDS
ANTILLES

Martinique
(Fr.)

CARIBBEAN SEA

INSET B

ARUBA
CURAÇAO
BONAIRE

BARBADOS

TRINIDAD
AND
TOBAGO

COLOMBIA

VENEZUELA

GUYANA

INSET A

Anguilla
(U.K.)

SAINT MARTIN
(Fr.)

Phillipsburg   SINT MAARTEN

Saint Barthélemy
(Fr.)

WINDWARD
ISLANDS

The Bottom   SABA

SINT EUSTATIUS

Oranjestad

SAINT
CHRISTOPHER
AND
NEVIS

Sint Eustatius, Sint Maarten, and Saba comprise the
Windward Islands group of the Netherlands Antilles,
although they are physically part of the Leeward Islands
chain in the Lesser Antilles.

NETHERLANDS
ANTILLES

⊙   National capital
ARUBA   Insular community
⊛   Insular community capital
○   Administrative center
✚   International airport

Statute Miles

Kilometers

INSET B

Aruba, Bonaire, and Curaçao comprise the
Leeward Islands group of the Netherlands Antilles.

ARUBA

Oranjestad

BONAIRE

CURAÇAO

KLEIN BONAIRE

Kralendijk

WILLEMSTAD
(also insular capital
of Curaçao)

KLEIN CURAÇAO

VENEZUELA

Marketing in New Zealand

Contents

Report Revised October 1981

Foreign Trade Outlook

Foreign trade is vital to the overall health of New Zealand's economy. Currently, the country's annual export earnings on goods and services are running at a level equal to approximately 25 percent of its gross domestic product (GDP). Agricultural and forest industries products account for about 70 percent of foreign exchange earnings. Prior to entry into the European Economic Community (EEC), the United Kingdom provided New Zealand with a stable export market for up to 40 percent of total export sales. Sales to the United Kingdom were predominantly agricultural and pastoral products. Loss of such a large share of New Zealand's market forced that country not only to seek new markets for its agricultural products but to promote actively the growth of its industrial sector in an effort to broaden the range of products having export potential.

Current trade patterns—*i.e.*, projected export sales figures for 1980—show that the United States is New Zealand's principal export market with 14.4 percent sales, followed by the United Kingdom, 14.2 percent; Japan, 12.6 percent; and Australia, 12.6 percent. New Zealand's terms of trade have deteriorated steadily since the oil squeeze of 1973 by the oil-producing exporting countries (OPEC). The principal cause is the worldwide drop in prices for goods from the primary sector against steadily rising prices for machinery and raw materials for industry and agriculture. New Zealand's major suppliers during 1980 were Australia, 19 percent; the United Kingdom, 14.4 percent; the United States, 13.5 percent; and Japan, 12.6 percent.

Table 1 lists New Zealand's principal imports from the world for 1977, 1978, and 1979.

Table 1.—Value of Principal Imports from the World
(NZ$1,000)

Commodity	1977	1978	1979
Food and live animals	148,763	152,302	155,364
Beverages and tobacco	28,629	29,547	31,283
Crude materials, inedible, except fuels	122,816	119,538	184,510
Mineral fuels, lubricants, and related materials	468,970	466,257	502,228
Animal and vegetable oils and fats	13,707	14,925	16,900
Chemicals	423,861	417,492	453,451
Manufactured goods classified chiefly by material	723,143	618,327	785,468
Machinery and transport equipment	1,091,036	952,747	1,155,206
Miscellaneous manufactured articles	203,498	215,493	264,093
Commodities and transactions not classified according to kind	19,934	31,529	25,638
Total Merchandise Imports	**3,537,982**	**3,018,158**	**3,574,139**

Note: Annual average conversion rates: 1977, NZ$1=US$0.97; 1978, NZ$1=US$1.04; 1979, NZ$1=US$1.02; 1980, NZ$1=US$0.97.

Source: Department of Statistics, Wellington.

Outlook for U.S. Exports

The largest share of U.S. exports consists of machinery, equipment, and materials necessary for New Zealand's efforts to expand both agricultural and industrial production and processing (table 2). There are strong indications that total imports will increase by 16 to 20 percent annually in terms of current prices over the next 2 to 3 years. U.S. exports should be able to profit from such a growing market. Exporters may expect to see significant expansion in the forest products industry, food processing industry, various energy-related fields using natural gas and coal, and the fishing industry. Planned projects that should provide major sales opportunities for goods and services over the next 5 to 7 years include expansion of an oil refinery, methanol plants, a synthetic gasoline plant, an ammonia/urea plant, expansion of a steel mill, aluminum smelters, a silicon-carbide plant, pulp and paper mills, and a cement plant.

Industry Trends

Economic Progress

New Zealand must import all crude and many refined petroleum products. There are, however, substantial supplies of natural gas and coal available, which when added to hydroelectric and thermal power supplies favor the country with a wealth of energy resources. Inflation is high,

---

**HOW TO OBTAIN
BACKGROUND INFORMATION
ABOUT THESE COUNTRIES**

For those who wish *general* data about a country—data which goes beyond marketing and commerce—the editors recommend *Countries of the World and Their Leaders*, published as an annually updated yearbook by Gale Research Company, Detroit, Michigan 48226. Containing 4- to 20-page entries on 168 countries, the volume also provides several hundred pages of supplementary world data. Each report provides some historical insight as well as a look at contemporary trends of lifestyle in the country. Reports also discuss a country's educational system, its press, ethnic groupings and religious practices.

Table 2.—Principal U.S. Exports to New Zealand
(f.a.s. US$1,000)

Commodity	1978	1979	1980
Fruit	1,695	1,592	1,452
Tobacco, unmanufactured	6,653	7,897	8,030
Rubber, synthetic	1,595	3,395	2,576
Wood, simply worked	1,178	1,978	943
Lubricating oil and grease	1,898	1,948	2,907
Organic chemicals	13,304	21,561	21,246
Inorganic chemicals	7,460	8,515	9,739
Electrical, medical, and radiological apparatus	3,113	2,698	3,490
Synthetic resins, rubber and plastic	22,536	41,590	32,052
Paper and paperboard	3,592	4,671	4,382
Fertilizer	10,869	18,662	23,502
Aluminum and alloys	944	860	753
Aircraft parts	38,351	39,339	38,294
Aircraft	4,225	6,853	6,900
Motor vehicle and tractor parts	6,980	15,471	16,952
Agricultural and dairy machinery	2,745	5,221	7,396
Tractors (agricultural and construction)	2,346	2,568	6,125
Office machinery	1,955	1,730	2,981
Civil engineers and contractors equipment	7,480	6,512	7,102
Pumps	5,145	7,628	9,459
Mechanical handling equipment	3,680	5,612	6,409
Printing and bookbinding machinery	3,188	5,294	5,107
Measuring, controlling instruments	12,874	13,714	18,885
Printed books and pamphlets	4,225	6,853	6,900
Total U.S. Exports to New Zealand	402,838	526,672	591,841

Source: U.S. Department of Commerce, Bureau of the Census.

running at a rate of 14 to 16 percent, but the rate of registered unemployed has been held to 3 percent or less and projections for the next year indicate it should not worsen appreciably.

Sparked by a number of planned, energy-intensive major projects and anticipated growth in forest products, food processing, and fishing industries, the New Zealand economy may be expected to move out of its present recessionary position and into a satisfactory level of annual growth by the end of 1982 or beginning of 1983.

It should also be noted that significant improvement in the economies of the United States, Japan, and the EEC countries undoubtedly would be reflected promptly in an improved New Zealand economy.

Gross Domestic Product

New Zealand's economy is going through a low-growth period. According to the New Zealand Institute of Economic Research (NZIER—an independent, nonprofit society under the direction of a board of trustees representing academic, business, and government), the country may experience a zero real growth rate during 1981. NZIER predicts a definite upturn in the economy beginning early in 1982.

Estimated GDP statistics, at current price levels, and projected by NZIER are as follows: March 1980, NZ$20.6 billion; March 1981, NZ$23.8 billion; and March 1982, NZ$27.9 billion. A deflator factor of 13 to 14 percent for the March 1981 year would account for a real

growth rate of zero to 1 percent, while an estimated 15 percent deflator for the March 1982 year would still allow for an estimated real GDP growth of up to 2.5 percent.

Industrial Sector

Even though most New Zealand industry is privately owned and managed, private enterprise is subject to a high degree of gvernmental direction. The Government is dominant in the fields of transportation, communication, and electric utilities. Government enterprise competes with private enterprise in such sectors as coal mining, banking, tourism, and insurance.

New Zealand industry is characterized by a predominance of relativley small-scale establishments. In 1975-76, 51 percent of all factories employed 10 or fewer persons; 88 percent employed fewer than 50; and only 2.2 percent employed more than 200. However, statistics indicate a trend during the past decade toward large manufacturing units. Large-scale industrial expansion has been particularly noted in the forest-based and metal-processing industries. For example, the establishment of the basic steel and aluminum industries has significantly widened the range of metal products able to be manufactured in New Zealand.

During recent years, industrial development has progressed at a fairly healthy rate. From FY 1966 to FY 1978, manufacturing output increased significantly faster than agriculture, the average annual rate being 4.8 percent and 1 percent, respectively, in terms of real GDP. During the same period, overall real GDP increased at an average annual rate of 2.95 percent.

While New Zealand continues to be heavily dependent on its agricultural and forest products for export earnings (approximately 69 percent for the years ending June 1979 and June 1980), the Government is particularly eager to assist the industrial sector in improving its export earnings range of products offered overseas buyers.

The most important types of manufacturing, in terms both of value added and employment, are food processing, metal products, paper and paper products, chemical products, transport equipment, wood products, electrical machinery, and textiles. Table 3 presents statistics for New Zealand manufacturing during the Fiscal Year 1976-77 (the New Zealand Fiscal Year runs from April 1 through March 31).

Government's Role in Industry

The Government is actively supporting a

Table 3.—New Zealand Manufacturing, FY 1976-77

Industry Group	No. of Factories	Persons Engaged	Salary. Wages (NZ$ mil.)	Turnover* (NZ$ mil.)
Food	1,084	66,979	393.7	2,367.0
Beverages	117	4,712	27.3	186.1
Tobacco	6	1,330	7.9	63.5
Textiles	408	19,566	100.0	439.9
Clothing, footwear	868	27,108	114.5	335.5
Leather	142	3,418	15.6	82.0
Wood products	875	16,957	102.7	463.6
Furniture	477	7,298	38.6	143.7
Paper and paper products	104	10,436	81.4	594.6
Printing and publishing	570	18,077	108.2	318.6
Rubber products	83	4,602	31.6	131.3
Chemical products	296	12,837	82.5	573.0
Petroleum, coal products	31	741	42.6	68.0
Plastic products	198	6,222	34.8	151.1
Nonmetallic mineral products	496	11,270	72.1	355.8
Basic metal industries	115	6,702	50.2	356.5
Metal products	1,253	24,327	145.8	707.5
Machinery (except electrical)	858	14,378	83.0	385.9
Electrical machinery	299	17,502	102.7	458.0
Transport equipment	421	20,059	126.9	569.3
Professional and scientific equipment	43	1,107	5.4	21.5
Miscellaneous products	275	4,430	21.7	81.6
Total	**9,019**	**306,177**	**1,801.7**	**8,987.2**

*Turnover: The total of all sales and other income except interest, dividends, royalties, patent fees, and insurance claims received, plus the value of capital work done by own employees.

Source: Department of Statistics, Wellington.

number of measures to develop infrastructure in support of industrial development. Its goal is to broaden the base of production and to add to the variety of goods produced for export. Agriculture will continue to form the foundation for the country's economy, but it is the manufacturing sector that has the greatest potential for growth. The Development Finance Corporation (DFC) is a government development bank established to assist with the establishment of new industries and the expansion of existing viable industries. DFC is governed by a board of directors consisting of two government and six private sector representatives. DFC's principal contribution to development is in the financing of plant and equipment for promising industrial projects.

Regional Economic Development

A program of financial incentives designed to stimulate development in areas having below-average growth rates has been in existence since 1973. Presently, there are 11 geographic areas, each with its own Regional Development Council that reports to the New Zealand Cabinet Minister of Regional Development. Main incentives provided under the program are loans on very favorable terms to firms processing renewable resources or introducing technology that is new to the region and "establishment grants," which assist with the cost of feasibility studies or the

initial cost of establishing a plant or other business.

Promotion of Research and Development

The Government's Department of Scientific and Industrial Research (DSIR) is responsible for implementing research and development in the fields of manufacturing, agricultural production and processing, energy, natural environment, transport, and building and construction. DSIR's scientific expertise and services are available to industry and government departments, as required. During the year ending March 31, 1979, DSIR had a staff of over 2,000 and an operating budget of NZ$47 million, of which NZ$5.3 million was allocated to research institutions or associations in the form of grants. There are a number of industry research associations jointly funded by industry and government. Industries involved in such activities include building, coal mining, dairy, fertilizer, heavy engineering, textiles, leather and shoe, logging, meat, concrete, ceramics, and wool. Additional information on its activities and interests may be obtained from the Department of Scientific and Industrial Research, Private Bag, Wellington, New Zealand.

Trade Regulations

Import Tariff System

Duties on goods imported into New Zealand are calculated usually as a percentage of the value of the goods (ad valorem rate). In some cases, they are calculated on the basis of a charge on a specified unit of weight, volume, or other measurement ("specific" rate) and occasionally on the basis of a combination of ad valorem and specific rates. Ad valorem duty is assessed on the "current domestic value" of the goods; i.e., the fair market value of the goods when sold for cash for home consumption in the principal markets of the country from which they are exported. On July 1, 1978, New Zealand introduced a new customs tariff based on the Customs Cooperation Nomenclature (formerly the Brussels Tariff Nomenclature). In the New Zealand Tariff, rates of duty are shown in two columns titled "Preferential Tariff," listing lower rates for Australia, Canada, Malaysia, and developing countries; and "Normal Tariff," applicable to imports from all other countries. British preferential rates were terminated in June 1977.

Generally, goods not manufactured in New Zealand, especially materials and machinery required by local manufacturers and farmers, are subject to moderate rates. Under the Generalized System of Preferences (GSP) introduced on July 1, 1976, New Zealand extends special low rates of duty to approximately 160 developing countries.

The New Zealand-Australia Free Trade Agreement (NAFTA), in effect since 1966, provides for periodic reductions of duties on goods covered in the Agreement, and for negotiations to expand the coverage of goods involved in two-way trade between the two countries. Items listed cover about 65 percent of imports from Australia including forest products, petroleum products, meat and dairy products, metals, chemicals, and some machinery.

New Zealand is a Contracting Party to the General Agreement on Tariff and Trade (GATT), and has granted concessions on imports in a number of negotiations under the Agreement.

Information regarding New Zealand rates of duty applicable to specific products may be obtained free of charge from the Regional Marketing Manager for ASEAN/Australasia, Office of Country Marketing, International Trade Administration, U.S. Department of Commerce, Washington, D.C. 20230, or from any Department of Commerce District Office. Inquiries should contain a complete product description, including the Customs Cooperation Nomenclature (CCN) or Standard International Trade Classification (SITC) commodity classification, if known.

Information regarding tariff classifications and rates of duty given by these offices should be regarded as an opinion only, based on the information supplied by the inquirer. The furnishing of authoritative advice on these matters is the sole prerogative of the Collector of Customs at the port of importation, who may require a sample of the goods before a tariff classification and duty rate can be given.

SAMPLES AND ADVERTISING MATTER.— New Zealand admits samples of negligible value free of duty. Small shipments of trade catalogs and price lists printed outside New Zealand and advertising products produced abroad are admitted duty free if they bear the name and address of the foreign manufacturer and are not designed to advertise the sale of those products by any company, firm, or person with a business established in New Zealand. Temporary, duty-free admission of advertising films is also permitted, provided that the films relate to the products or equipment offered for sale and meet other specified conditions. No import licenses are required for samples and advertising materials supplied free of charge and not exceeding NZ$100 (c.i.f.) or for goods up to a value of NZ$20 imported by mail for the importer's use and not for business or sale.

Samples of commercial value may be imported temporarily under bond or deposit of the amount of the duty to which they are liable. Such samples are subject to the same customs regulations and duties in New Zealand as are ordinary commercial shipments of the commodities represented. They are also accorded the same import licensing treatment as commercial shipments of such goods. Trade catalogs, price lists, posters, circulars, handbills, programs, calendars, play bills, and fashion plates other than those listed above are dutiable.

There is no provision for the prepayment of such duties in the United States. However, an overseas firm sending printed advertising parcel or letter post to New Zealand and desiring to ensure prompt delivery may, prior to the actual shipment of the material, advise the Secretary of the General Post Office at Wellington of the number, weight, and value of each posting and forward a specimen. It should also arrange for the payment by its New Zealand agent of the duty involved; or enclose an international postal money order made out to the Director-General, General Post Office, Wellington, to cover the estimated amount of duty (including sales tax, if applicable) or the entire lot; or lodge an amount with the Director-General, General Post Office, Wellington, New Zealand, to meet the claims as they arise. When this procedure is followed, each packet should bear the notation, "Duty remitted to the G.P.O., Wellington," whether remittance is made direct or through an agent of the exporter.

ADVANCE RULINGS ON CUSTOMS CLASSIFICATION.—The Customs Department at Wellington will give an advance ruling on goods that are intended to be shipped, provided a sufficient description of the goods is furnished (and, if requested, samples submitted) for it to determine the correct customs classification. Such decisions are regarded as binding, but no responsibility for changes that may subsequently be made in the tariff rates is assumed by the customs authorities. Application for an advance ruling may be signed by the shipper in the United States, by the importer in New Zealand, or by any other interested person. Inquiries should be addressed to the New Zealand Customs Department, Private Bag, Wellington, New Zealand.

Shipping Documents

The New Zealand Customs Department requires that each original bill of lading or air waybill for imported goods be accompanied by an Invoice and Combined Certificate of Value and Origin for Exports to New Zealand (New

Zealand Government Form 55). Only one copy of this form is required although the importer may request additional copies. Printed forms of the invoice and certificate of value may be purchased at commercial stationery stores located in major port cities, and exporters may consult the nearest District Office of the U.S. Department of Commerce for advice on the most convenient source of supply. No consular visa or notarial service is required for the invoice and certificate of value.

The Government has established a requirement that exporters' declarations must include a statement to the effect that any wooden or plywood packing cases, crates, wooden containers or cargo pallets destined for New Zealand have been inspected before shipment and found free from bark and visible signs of insect and fungal attack. This declaration must accompany all bills of lading and other shipping documents.

Items such as fruits, plants, seeds, and the like must be accompanied by certificates from the competent authorities in the country of origin to the effect that the items have been examined and have been found to be free of disease. These certificates should be forwarded to the consignee in New Zealand.

Marking and Labeling

New Zealand prohibits the importation of all goods bearing false trademarks or those calculated to deceive. It also prohibits the entry of any goods of foreign manufacture that bear the name or trademark of a New Zealand manufacturer or trader, the name of a place in New Zealand, or words that would be likely to associate the goods with New Zealand unless the names or words are accompanied by a definite indication of the country of origin.

There is no general requirement that the country of origin be indicated on all imported goods. If any goods are marked with the country of origin, such markings must be true, accurate, and not misleading. The country of origin must, however, be shown on footwear, clothing items, and dry-cell batteries.

The Merchandising Marks Act 1954, as amended, is designed to ensure that goods are not incorrectly marked or advertised as to their nature, quality, or the place where they are manufactured or produced. Very detailed regulations are in effect regarding the labels that must be attached to various prepared, blended, compounded, mixed, or imitation foodstuffs. Paints and colors containing lead, electrical appliances and equipment, footwear, drugs, toilet preparations, and food products must also be specially labeled. Wool products, defined as any product containing 50 percent or more by weight of wool, must be marked to show in English the trade description of the main fabric in the product and the percentage by the weight of the wool in the product. Regulations also provide that all packaged goods bear an indication of the net weight of the contents and specify how such weights are to be indicated for each commodity.

With the exception of movie film and dangerous goods, there are no regulations governing the marking of outside packing cases. However, according to good shipping practice, packages should show the consignee's mark, including post mark, and they should be numbered unless the shipment is such that the contents of the package can readily be identified without numbers. It is also advantageous to show net and gross weight on the outside packing cases.

Movie film must be marked on the outer package as "FILMS" in black letters not less than 2 inches high and with the name of the owner, distinguishing mark, or number. There are detailed regulations covering the marking of dangerous goods.

Senate Concurrent Resolution 40, adopted July 30, 1953, invites U.S. exporters to inscribe, insofar as practicable, on the external shipping containers in indelible print of a suitable size: United States of America. Although such marking is not compulsory under our laws, U.S. shippers are urged to cooperate in thus publicizing American-made goods.

Free Zones, Customs Entrance, Warehousing, and Reexportation

There is neither a free zone nor a free port in New Zealand.

Goods may be entered for home consumption, for warehousing, for removal within New Zealand, or for reexport. The appropriate customs entry forms are completed by the importer or his/her agent from information contained in the invoice, and they are submitted to customs officials along with the import license and all shipping documents except the bill of lading. When entered for consumption, duties must be paid at once. There are adequate provisions permitting an importer having insufficient evidence on invoices or no invoices to enter goods on a sight entry, to be completed later, when full particulars for making a complete entry can be supplied by the importer. In such cases, a deposit adequate to cover the duty must be made.

Within 21 working days after the arrival of any goods at any port, entry shall be made of the goods at that port. If they are not entered within that time, the customs collector may have them removed to a warehouse and, if not claimed and entered within 3 months after warehousing, duties become due and payable. The goods may be sold by the collector if the duties are not paid on demand. Entry of only a portion of the contents of a package is not permitted unless the goods are placed in a bonded warehouse.

There are wharves, approved by the customs for the discharge of overseas cargoes, and licensed and manufacturing warehouses. Licensed warehouses are of two kinds—those for the warehousing of dutiable goods in general and those for the storing of any particular class or classes of dutiable goods, subject to restriction imposed by the Minister of Customs.

Manufacturing warehouses are those licensed for the purpose of utilizing products in the manufacture of perfumery and other articles in which spirit is a necessary ingredient or in the manufacture of any other goods, such as tobacco, which may be permitted by regulations to be prepared in a manufacturing warehouse. Goods entered for internal consumption from manufacturing warehouses are subject to duty at the rates prescribed in the "Table of Excise Duties," if applicable.

Importers may be permitted to sort, bottle, pack, or repack goods in any licensed warehouse. Warehoused goods may be taken temporarily from the warehouse for use as commercial travelers' samples; for inspection, trial, exhibition, or demonstration; or for other temporary purposes. Special regulations govern the warehousing of dangerous goods.

Uncleared goods may be left in transit sheds temporarily (normally 1 night) free of charge, the period differing in various ports; after that time, storage is charged. For uncleared goods stored in warehouses, there is no period of free storage. When warehouse dues are in arrears for a period of 6 months, the merchandise may be sold upon request of the licensee. Goods warehoused for 3 years must at the end of that period be entered for consumption and duties paid, be entered for reexportation, or be rewarehoused.

Special permission of the collector must be obtained for rewarehousing, and, if permission is granted, the process is the same as if the goods were entered for the first time, with reexamination at the expense of the importer. The duties must then be paid on any goods found deficient at the time of reexamination. Goods removed from a warehouse may be remeasured, reweighed, regauged, and so forth. If goods become damaged or deteriorate while under customs control, they may be revalued, and duty is payable on the value then determined.

Imported goods, including those removed from a warehouse, may be transshipped or reexported upon completion of the appropriate entry and under the security of a bond. Customarily, such entries are passed by custom agents under the security of their general bond.

Import Licensing

New Zealand has been controlling imports through a licensing system since December 1938. Import licensing is not a serious obstacle to import of most manufactured goods of major interest to the United States. About one-fourth of total imports (by value) are subject to licensing requirements. Various types of licensing categories and different quotas have been established, but similar goods receive the same licensing treatment regardless of overseas source.

Licenses are currently issued on the following basis: Most licenses (called "basic" licenses) are issued to importers according to a percentage allocation, which varies by commodity groupings, based either on the amount of their previous period's licenses or on the amount of actual goods imported during the previous period; other applications for licenses are considered individually.

In general, where allocations are based on the licenses issued for a previous period, basic licenses are automatically issued. Where the allocation is based on actual imports, specific applications for basic licensees are required.

In some cases, basic licenses for small amounts are issued for certain approved classes of goods, the import of which is normally restricted. The object is to ensure that some selection of imported goods be kept before the public and to enable local manufacturers to keep abreast of foreign trends in production and style.

The Government has a system of export incentives to encourage the export of goods manufactured in New Zealand. The plan provides for the issuance of additional import licenses to manufacturers for raw materials and components used in manufacture for export.

While the onus for obtaining an import license is on the New Zealand importer, foreign suppliers should satisfy themselves that licenses have been obtained (if required for their category of goods). Goods imported without a license, where required, are subject to forfeiture, and the importer is liable to penalties provided under the law.

Internal Taxes

Most goods, both imported and domestic, are subject to a sales tax. The tax is nondiscriminatory and payable only once, at the point where the goods pass to the retailers. The most common rate of sales tax is 20 percent. Other specific rates are as follows: Television sets, radios, and tape recorders, 30 percent; jewelry and ornaments, 40 percent; machinery and aircraft, 10 percent; motor vehicles are subject to a tax that increases from 30 to 60 percent as the engine capacity increases. Food, clothing, and footwear are generally exempt from sales tax. On imported goods, the tax is assessed on the dutiable value of the merchandise plus duty.

Excise taxes are levied on gasoline and other motor spirits, tobacco, sugar, beer, wines, and distilled spirits.

During the New Zealand fiscal year ending March 1980, various indirect taxes accounted for the following shares of the Government's total tax receipts of NZ$7.2 billion: Customs, 4.9 percent; sales tax, 11.2 percent; fuel tax, 2 percent; highway tax, 2.5 percent. (For purposes of comparison, income tax, as a direct tax, provided 75.5 percent of total taxes.)

Trade Customs

Technical Standards and Requirements

The Standards Association of New Zealand has responsibility for industrial standardization on a national basis. The organization issues not only New Zealand standards regarding materials and products but also standard codes of practice. Standards may relate to such aspects of industrial practical as terminology, dimensions, specifications of performance and quality of products, test methods, and safety or design codes. In general, these standards are adopted voluntarily due to their intrinsic merit, but in those cases in which safety of life or property are involved, their adoption may be compulsory through statutory reference. Although compliance with these standards is obligatory only under certain circumstances, as stated above, many customers prefer items that meet these specifications. Thus, compliance with such standards may be an important factor in sales promotion. Copies of New Zealand standards may be obtained from The American National Standards Institute, 1430 Broadway, New York, New York 10018, or from the Director, Standards Association of New Zealand, Private Bag, Wellington, New Zealand.

Weights and Measures

The metric system for weights and measures is now in use. Conversion to metrics was completed by the beginning of 1977.

Electrical Current

Electric circuits generally carry 230 volts, single phase, or 400 volts, triple phase, at a frequency of 50 cycles per second.

Distribution and Sales Channels

Import Channels

The principal import channels are sales agents, importer-distributors, direct importer-users, and combinations thereof. Sales agents are the common medium for selling a variety of products, including producer's materials bought according to specifications and consumer goods for distribution to large wholesalers and retailers. The preference for buying direct from manufacturers is well established in New Zealand. A number of sales agents with a broad range of products have special departments and technical personnel to sell products requiring specialized knowledge.

Agents or importer-distributors (distributors who import and stock certain lines and take orders for direct shipment of others) are a common channel for the distribution of products involving technical knowledge, service, repairs and parts, and other more involved services for the manufacturer. Typical products handled are metalworking machinery and equipment; agricultural and electrical machinery; transportation, medical, and scientific equipment; measuring and testing instruments; and certain kinds of consumer durables. Importer-distributors are also frequently used to sell certain kinds of chemical products, textiles, foodstuffs, and other consumer goods where stocking is an important factor. A number of large retailers also buy through purchasing offices in the United States and other countries.

Numerous subsidiaries of foreign manufacturers import direct from parent companies and distribute products to round out or supplement their domestic production. Importing and distributing by a New Zealand branch or subsidiary is common when the volume is substantial and the foreign parent company wishes to retain control over distribution.

A number of well-established companies with nationwide networks of offices perform, in addition to trading activities, a broad range of other functions including transportation, packaging, manufacturing, and distribution at both the wholesale and retail levels. These firms are usually excellent representatives for new products seeking market penetration, although they usually import products to complement existing lines.

Wholesale and Retail Channels

With the growth of the New Zealand economy, there has come some blurring of the traditional pattern of the channels of distribution. In the past, wholesalers provided the link between manufacturers and retailers. Large department and chain stores, dealing direct with manufacturers or having factories of their own, and associations of retailers buying in bulk, together account for a significant volume of goods. In addition, some manufacturers have established organizations for the purpose of selling direct to retailers, while smaller manufacturers often sell to retailers located in the area adjacent to their factories. On their part, wholesalers now sometimes extend the scope of their activity into the field of manufacturing and retailing.

As of April 1978, more than 220,000 members of the labor force worked in wholesale and retail trade.

WHOLESALE TRADE.—The 1978 Census of Distribution lists 6,183 establishments. At that time, wholesalers employed more than 77,385 people, earning approximately NZ$526 million, and had an aggregate income of approximately NZ$9.8 billion. Wholesale trade was shown as being heavily concentrated in the Auckland and Wellington urban areas, which between them accounted for 49 percent of all wholesale stores (65 percent of the total volume of business).

RETAIL TRADE.—The 1978 Census of Distribution lists 27,878 retail stores, having a total of 142,849 employees who earned NZ$550 million and doing a total business of NZ$6.5 billion for that year. Retail shops were broken down into several major categories, including the following: Unprocessed primary products, 705; food, beverages, and tobacco, 8,752; textiles, clothing, and footwear, 4,787; paint, wallpaper, and hardware, 914; household appliances, furniture and floor coverings, 2,455; paper products, 1,240; chemical products and petroleum, 2,537; motor vehicles and other transport equipment, 2,584; gift, handcraft, and souvenir, 722; watch and clock dealers and jewelers, 574; department stores, 421; general stores, 421; and sports goods dealers, 340. As in the case of wholesale outlets, retail stores are heavily concentrated in the Auckland and Wellington areas. Approximately 60 percent of the country's retail trade outlets are located in the two urban areas. Retail trade income for the year ending April 1978 reached NZ$6.5 billion.

There is a trend in retailing toward the growth of self-service stores, supermarkets, and shopping centers. To a certain extent, this has been accompanied by the disappearance of the smaller retail outlets, particularly in the small neighborhood grocery field. With relatively few exceptions, there is no weekend shopping as stores (except for small delicatessens or neighborhood milk bar/food stores close on Saturdays and Sundays.

Marketing methods are becoming increasingly organized and competitive. An increasing range of locally produced goods and imported foods, consumer durables, and clothing reflect the growing sophistication of the New Zealand market.

The 1978 Census listed a total of 6,563 service establishments, employing 24,473 and having an income of about NZ$441 million for the 1978 census year. Service shops include laundries and cleaning, 2,518; repair services, 3,522; beauty shops, 1,108; and photographic studios, 789.

The New Zealand Consumer Price Index (CPI), based on the December Quarter of 1977 equals 1,000. The CPI for the year ending December 1980 reached 1,490.

Consumer Financing

Installment credit buying, which in New Zealand includes "hire-purchase" agreements, budget accounts, and credit sales agreements, has increased greatly during recent years and is used in many lines of business. Arrangements for deferred payments are usually made for the purchase of automobiles, machinery, household appliances, and furniture. Retail outlets have "lay-by" systems for customers who want a store to hold merchandise until full payment is completed. Retailers or finance companies provide the financing.

As of December 1980, NZ$646 million was the amount owing under "hire purchase." The percentage of payments overdue was 2.5.

Commercial Practices

QUOTATIONS AND TERMS OF PAYMENT.— Quotations should be c.i.f. New Zealand port, whenever possible. In addition, an f.o.b. U.S. port price, including inland freight to the nearest port of export, should be provided for customs purposes. Estimates of U.S. inland freight charges are not readily obtainable in New Zealand, and an exfactory price makes calculating landed cost difficult.

Quotations may be made in either New Zealand or U.S. dollars. Exporters making quotations in New Zealand dollars should consult their bank for the prevailing rate of exchange.

To determine the most suitable payment terms for its needs, a business firm must also take into account the type of products involved. The foreign departments of most major U.S. banks are well equipped to give service and advice in matters of foreign trading, particularly terms of credit.

Credit Information

Credit data on individual New Zealand firms are available through World Traders Data Reports, which are compiled by U.S. Commercial Officers stationed overseas and are available from the U.S. Department of Commerce. Information is also available from private agencies. Principal U.S. credit reporting agencies include the Foreign Credit Interchange Bureau, National Association of Credit Management, 475 Park Avenue South, New York, New York 10016, and Dun and Bradstreet, Inc., 99 Church Street, New York, New York 10007. American companies may also obtain credit information by requesting their own U.S. bank to obtain a "bank opinion" from its New Zealand correspondent bank located nearest the company in question.

Export Credit Facilities

The major banks in the principal U.S. seaports and industrial centers maintain large, experienced foreign departments. These banks account for the bulk of export financing in the United States. Through their correspondent relationships with banks in New Zealand and other foreign countries, they provide a direct channel to overseas customers. Other sources of export credit include factoring houses, export management companies, financing firms and confirming houses. The Export-Import Bank of the United States (Eximbank) is also a source of credit, particularly for very large overseas projects that warrant credit maturities of 5 years or longer. The Foreign Credit Insurance Association (FCIA) provides coverage against commercial credit risks. Another instrument for U.S. export financing is the Private Export Funding Corporation (PEFCO), owned by 62 investors, mostly commercial banks. PEFCO finances only the export of goods and services of U.S. manufacture and origin, and its loans generally have maturities in the medium-term area.

Transportation and Utilities

Transport Services Between
New Zealand and the United States

In regard to shipping, New Zealand port facilities are being improved, and emphasis is placed on keeping abreast of developments in handling containerized cargo and cargo from roll-on/roll-off and LASH vessels. Most of the overseas cargo, which amounted to more than 36 million metric tons in 1976 is handled by the major ports of Auckland, Wellington, Lyttleton, Bluff, Timaru, Taranaki, Whangarei, and Napier.

Shipping service between New Zealand and the U.S. east coast is provided by the U.S. flag carrier Farrell Lines Inc. (four container vessels, Columbus Line (five vessels), and Pace Line (five vessels). Service from the west coast is provided by the U.S. flag carrier Farrell Lines Inc. (three container/"Lash" vessels), Columbus Line (four vessels), and Star Line (two vessels). Transit times run between 15 and 25 days.

The geographical distances from New Zealand to the United States, Europe, South America, and Asia have led to a growth in the use of international air transportation for both passengers and air cargo.

The United States is represented by Pan American World Airways, which operates weekly several 747 and 747SP passenger and air cargo services, including a weekly nonstop flight between Auckland and Los Angeles, and by Continental Airways, which operates three flights weekly to New Zealand. Additional service is provided by Air New Zealand, the country's government-owned airline, and UTA French Airlines. Airports in both Auckland and Christchurch are capable of handling the largest international commercial jets.

Transportation System

RAILWAYS.—New Zealand has an extensive government-owned railway network operated by the Railways Department of the Central Government. The Ministry of Works carries out most new construction projects on behalf of the Railways Department.

The total distance of railway track open for traffic on March 31, 1975, was 4,797 kilometers, of which 2,555 were in the North Island and 1,981 in the South Island. Total amount of freight carried during 1979 was 11,722 metric tons.

Increasing attention is given to improving the movement of goods by pallet, containers, and other new methods of bulk transport employing new loading techniques and equipment. Rolling stock and locomotives in use as of March 31, 1979, totaled 312 main-line diesel-electric locomotives, 193 diesel shunting locomotives, 14 electric locomotives, and 28,597 goods and livestock wagons (wagons have a capacity of 493 million kilograms). The rail lines of the North and South Islands are connected by a ferry service operated by the Railway Department across the Cook Strait.

HIGHWAYS.—Commercial road transportation is used mainly for short hauls (under 100 miles) of freight to areas not served by railways. This involves feeder service and transporting agricultural goods from the farm to the market or processing plant. Although public transportation is supplied by the local authorities in most of the major cities, use of these facilities has been declining in recent years because of the preference for private transportation.

On March 31, 1978, New Zealand had more than 96,525 kilometers of roads and streets, of which approximately 48 percent were paved. Administration of the country's road and highway system is exercised by municipalities in the case of city streets, county councils for county roads, and the National Roads Board for State highways.

There were slightly more than 22 million motor vehicles licensed as of June 30, 1980, including 1.3 million cars; 261,891 trucks; and 387,000 trailers and caravans (RV's).

SHIPPING.—Ocean shipping, including both coastal and overseas, is very important to the New Zealand economy because of the country's dependence on international trade. During 1979, 3,438 overseas vessels called at the country's 19 ports with inward and outward cargo each equal to 18.3 million metric tons.

Both east and west coasts of the United States are served by vessels of the container-carrying type. Service is frequent and reliable. Farrel Lines of New York is the principal American carrier. The country has substantial container-handling facilities in both the North and South Island ports, primarily in Auckland and Wellington in the north and Lyttleton in the south.

Although there are good facilities available to handle ship passenger traffic in both Auckland and Wellington, the flow of shipboard passenger traffic has slowed to a trickle during recent years and is now confined to a relatively small number of transit tourists aboard cruise ships.

Although New Zealand has a vast network of inland waterways, most of them are not suitable for navigation. There are no regular passenger or cargo services on any of the rivers. The only inland-water shipping is the service on Lake Wakatipu. Passengers and cargo, mostly livestock, are carried from Queenstown to other points on the lakeshore.

AIRWAYS.—Air travel is very important to New Zealand, both internationally and domestically. In some areas of the South Island, the mountainous topography makes travel between isolated domestic locations extremely difficult and time consuming by other means.

New Zealand ranks among the leading nations in the world in use of air transportation per head of population. A most important use of aircraft in agriculture has emerged in the country. The topography of the pasture land has made aerial topdressing, seed sowing, and the spraying of pesticides and weedicides economical. More than 50 percent of fertilizer is spread by airplanes.

On matters concerning air safety, ground facilities, and services, civil aviation in New Zealand is the responsibility of the Civil Aviation Division of the Ministry of Transport.

International air service is provided by Air New Zealand Ltd., the government-owned airline, Pan American World Airways, UTA French Airlines, Singapore Airlines, Polynesian Airlines, Air Pacific, Qantas, British Airways, and Continental Airlines. Scheduled international airlines transported 1,415,000 passengers and 51,575 metric tons of freight and mail during 1979. Domestic air travel, apart from small tourist sightseeing and charter services, also is handled by Air New Zealand and its subsidiary air freight company, Safe Air Ltd. Air New Zealand provides regularly scheduled service to 23 cities and towns throughout the two islands. Utilizing a fleet of Boeing 737's and Fokker Friendships, it transported 2,388,718 passengers during 1979.

Power and Fuel

New Zealand is endowed with natural resources that can be economically developed to generate electric power. Lakes provide natural reservoirs for hydroelectric projects, while melting snow and rain constantly replenish waters used in generating electricity. Geothermal steam, generated by volcanic activity, provides another source for power. Natural gas, in substantial quantities, has been found on North Island, and its use as a major energy source includes the generation of electricity, premium household fuel, and industrial applications. A major gas field off the west coast of the North Island was discovered in 1969 and is being actively developed. Although an aggressive search for petroleum has been carried out by experienced overseas exploration companies for a number of years, it has so far been unsuccessful. Coal exists in significant quantities, but extraction and transportation costs have limited its use during the past years. The Government and private mining companies are reexamining the economics of coal use in the face of current high prices for crude and refined petroleum products, all of which New Zealand must import.

ELECTRICITY.—In the year ended March 1979, the generation of electricity reached 21,693 million kilowatt hours (kWh): 16,209 million kWh from hydroelectric sources and 5,483 kWh from thermal plants. This represents almost a 20-percent increase over 1974. Government projections indicate that between 28,000 and 34,200 million kWh will be required by 1994. Annual per capita consumption is currently at 6,932 kWh.

The New Zealand Electricity Department, a government agency that produces about 97 percent of all electricity retailed in the country, had made a total capital outlay of about NZ$3 billion by 1979.

Electric power is distributed through a network of government electric power boards and county councils. (As of March 31, 1979, there were 37 boards, 22 municipal supply authorities, and 2 county councils active in distribution.) More than 99 percent of New Zealand's population has electricity in the home. Electric circuits generally carry 230 volts, alternating current at a frequency of 50 cycles. Retail rates are low by world standards and usually provide for reduced rates for large industrial and commercial customers.

The Government will grant special reduced rates or water rights for the generation of electricity to approved new industries. This applies to industries in which the cost of power is an important part of the total cost of production and when the industry cannot operate competitively unless electric power is available at special low rates. Such concessions will be granted only to industries that are in the national interest and that require a large and continuous supply of electricity.

GAS.—Total gas production reached 48,146.7 terajoules in 1979. Of this amount, 1,011.4 terajoules was manufactured gas from coal-gas plants owned either by private companies or municipalities. In addition to the production of gas, these plants supply coke, tar, and a variety of minor byproducts.

Advertising and Market Research

Advertising Media

The largest share of advertising in New Zealand is handled by the eight daily newspapers in the four major metropolitan areas and by the four Sunday newspapers. These papers are followed by television, newspapers from smaller cities and provincial towns, magazines, radio, motion pictures, and outdoor media.

Circulation of the eight major newspapers is approximately 694,000; an additional 30 papers are published in provincial towns, plus 110 general interest nondailies. Also, there are four national newspapers issued weekly, as well as women's magazines, sports publications, and an increasing number of periodicals concerning technological fields, business, finance, farming, hobbies, and entertainment.

Total advertising revenue of newspapers, magazines, journals and periodicals was NZ$80.9 million in the year ending June 1977. Figures for other media are not available.

Currently, three independent public corporations control most radio and all television transmission under the control of the Broadcasting Council of New Zealand.

Radio New Zealand provides programming for 56 medium-wave stations and 2 short-wave stations. Two television channels had telecast to 889,000 sets at the end of 1979. Programs reached 94 percent of New Zealand homes. Service is based on the 625-line system. Private commercial radio transmission consists of 10 licensed stations.

Market Research and Trade Organizations

MARKET RESEARCH.—Market research is a growing service industry in New Zealand. A substantial number of advertising and market research firms have developed expertise and experience in covering the consumer goods market. These firms, and others more recently undertaking research, are expanding activities to cover the industrial and investment market. Some 22 firms are currently listed as being active in the market research field, including several with U.S. affiliations.

The following trade associations can be useful in establishing contact with an appropriate market research firm: The Association of New Zealand Advertisers, P.O. Box 3846, Wellington, New Zealand; and the Accredited Advertising Agencies Association, P.O. Box 643, Wellington, New Zealand. Additionally, the reports and findings of New Zealand's leading economic organizations and banks frequently provide valuable source material for market studies.

TRADE ORGANIZATIONS.—There is a New Zealand trade association for almost every form of agricultural, commercial, and industrial endeavor.

New Zealand trade organizations conduct market research on behalf of their members and prepare a variety of their other reference material. They sometimes make information available to nonmembers, but they may choose to do so only within the framework of a reciprocal exchange of data.

The New Zealand Chamber of Commerce, P.O. Box 1071, Wellington, New Zealand, is the national coordinating body for the activities of more than 50 chambers of commerce located throughout New Zealand. These chambers provide services similar in every respect to those provided by regional and municipal chambers in the United States.

The American Chamber of Commerce in New Zealand (AMCHAM) has its head office in Wellington (P.O. Box 3408, Wellington, New Zealand) and branch offices in Auckland and Christchurch. AMCHAM maintains close active contact with the U.S. Chamber of Commerce and effectively represents over 200 members, including companies and firms engaged in almost every phase of manufacturing, commerce, transportation, and banking and investment finance.

Trade Fairs

New Zealand trade fairs offer an opportunity for introducing firms and products new to the New Zealand market. These fairs also serve as meeting places for producers to check on competitive lines, for licensors to negotiate arrangements, and for technicians to exchange ideas and catch up on recent developments in their fields.

Although Auckland and Wellington are the principal sites for the international trade fairs held alternate years in New Zealand, Christchurch and smaller centers host a number of specialized fairs. The trend in New Zealand is toward the specialized vertical fair and away from the so-called universal or horizontal, multi-industry fair.

Space is limited and often rented by perennial exhibitors. Newcomers wishing to participate must, therefore, apply early. New Zealand customs regulations permit foreign products to enter duty free for display at scheduled fairs and exhibitions.

Participants can achieve best results by supplying the fair's management and the press with the necessary promotional and pictorial material about 10 weeks before opening day. Since fair catalogs are used as standard reference documents long after the gates close, special care should be given to the preparation of the firm's entry and advertising in the catalog. An ample supply of catalogs, price lists, and other promotional literature should be on hand for distribution throughout the exhibit.

In addition to New Zealand's major international trade fair, the venue for which alternates between Wellington and Auckland, the following regularly scheduled exhibitions may be of interest to American companies: the New Zealand Building Field Days (building and construction equipment), the New Zealand Agricultural Field Days (agricultural equipment and materials), and the New Zealand Transport Field Days (all types of transportation equipment). The Field Days are all organized by the New Zealand National Field Days Society Inc., Private Bag, Hamilton, New Zealand. Additional information on these and other exhibitions may be obtained from the American Chamber of Commerce in New Zealand or from the New Zealand Department of Trade and Industry, Private Bag, Wellington, New Zealand.

Credit

*Banking System and Other
Financial Institutions*

The banking system of New Zealand is comprised of the Reserve Bank of New Zealand (the central bank), 5 nationwide trading banks (i.e., commercial), and 14 trustee savings banks. In addition, finance companies, insurance companies, building societies, and 10 merchant banks are engaged in the capital investment business. Finally, stock exchanges are located in five cities and engage in the trading of domestic and certain foreign securities. The State-operated Bank of New Zealand, which accounts for the largest share of business transacted by the five trading banks mentioned above, is the only trading bank with headquarters in New Zealand. The remaining four trading banks are the Australia and New Zealand Bank (London), the National Bank of New Zealand (London), the Bank of New South Wales (Sydney), and the Commercial Bank of Australia (Melbourne). The trading banks undertake the customary business of receiving deposits, handling checks, granting advances (overdrafts), and buying and selling foreign exchange. These banks also discount bills, but this is not a highly developed practice in New Zealand. These banks, which operate primarily in the short- and medium-term credit sectors, maintain the usual liaison with banks in the major financial countries of the world.

The interest rate charged by the trading banks on overdrafts is subject to control by the Government. This interest rate varies from less than 6 percent to over 20 percent. The weighted average for the half-year ending September 1980 was 13.2 percent (compared with 8.59 percent in September 1977). Interest is paid by the trading banks for fixed deposits. It is the policy of the Reserve Bank to ensure that trading bank loans are confined mainly to advances of working capital to their customers—for stocks, work in progress, and wages. It is also expected that the amount of overdraft shall ot be excessive in relation to the capital of the enterprise. The trading banks require collateral and follow the customary safeguards in determining credit-worthiness.

In 1971, the Government permitted overseas companies to participate in establishing merchant (investment) banks. Since then, the number of such banks has increased to 10. These banks offer a wide variety of services to industrial clients, manage investment portfolios, and deal in commercial bills. They also underwrite new company share issues, advise on and finance mergers and takeovers, and lend to companies requiring funds for expansion purposes. Several U.S. banks are participants in New Zealand merchant banks.

The short-term money market in New Zealand is a comparatively recent innovation, having only achieved significance and official standing (by being granted access to "last resort" loans from the Reserve Bank) in September 1961. There are at present several recognized dealers comprising the market. By regulation, the dealers may only accept deposits or "buy back" transactions of NZ$20,000 or more from any customer. This ensures that the market complements rather than competes with other facilities, notably savings banks, interest-bearing tax prepayment and short-term deposits with trading banks.

The total average monthly balance of official short-term money in the market during 1979 was NZ$320 million. The interest rates on total deposits held (percent per annum) averaged 10.48 percent during 1979.

Availability of Capital

The main sources of capital for new development in New Zealand are undistributed profits, the share market, merchant banks, insurance companies, savings banks, finance companies (including hire-purchase companies), private sources, and the investment by overseas companies in New Zealand branches and subsidiaries and joint venture companies.

An additional source of capital for industry was provided by the Government when it established the Development Finance Corporation (DFC) in 1965. DFC holds the right to borrow substantial sums with full government assistance. The Corporation is fully controlled by the Government and is funded by secured debenture stock subscribed by the New Zealand public, overseas loans, and government investment. Its purpose is to fund small or medium-sized manufacturing ventures, especially where there is export potential, to aid New Zealand's growing industrial base by filling a gap in providing medium- to long-term industrial finance. The Corporation's Act requires it to "evaluate each proposal having regard to the economic worth of the industry concerned, its usefulness to the New Zealand economy, the extent to which it will be owned or effectively controlled by persons domiciled in New Zealand, and the prospects of it becoming profitable within a reasonable time."

For further information on DFC assistance available for development purposes, see "Industry Trends" on page 1655.

Availability of U.S. Funds

Prospective exporters interested in doing business in New Zealand should be aware of the facilities available from the U.S. Export-Import Bank for financing, guaranteeing, and insuring payment for U.S. goods and services. Long- and medium-term loans are available for capital goods for projects and industries that assist the economic development of New Zealand.

Investment in New Zealand

Value of U.S. Investment

Foreign direct investment has played a significant role in the development of New Zealand. Although the Government does not publish figures covering total value of direct investment (noting that book values bear little relationship to what investments would realize on sale), it does make available statistics on the total investment changes during recent years. Drawing on this source, it is possible to determine that the inflow of direct investment during FY 1970/71 through FY 1979 averaged NZ$173.3 million. Those areas of industry that historically have attracted the greatest amount of interest from foreign investors include meat and dairy products, chemical and mineral products, metal fabricating and transport equipment, wholesale and retail trade, banking, insurance, and ownership of property.

Although the United Kingdom is the principal source of overseas direct investment, U.S. investments have become increasingly significant during recent years. The U.S. direct investment position at the end of 1979 was US$530 million. Annual average income on direct investment in

New Zealand was 26 percent during 1976-79. The major U.S. investments are in the following sectors: Motor vehicle assembly, oil refining, tire production, chemicals, and food processing. A Double Taxation Convention is in effect between the United States and New Zealand. Although a number of U.S. companies have subsidiary branches in New Zealand, many American companies operate through local agents while others are associated in joint ventures. Many New Zealand firms manufacture products under license with royalties payable to U.S. companies.

Investment Climate

The New Zealand economy has been characterized by an expanding industrial base in recent years, complementing its highly efficient agricultural sector. The gross national product (GNP)—in current prices—has increased by an average of almost 11.5 percent during 1973-78, and gross domestic capital formation as a percentage of GNP has averaged almost 25 percent over that period. Nevertheless, business and Government recognize that foreign investment has an important part to play as a supplement to domestic capital in continuing New Zealand's economic expansion.

Amid the changes in the pattern of capital investment, private enterprise has found, and will continue to find, avenues for profitable investment in many types of industry and trade. During the 1980's, considerable capital will be required to develop mineral resources, heavy industry, and tourism, in addition to such traditional sectors as forestry, food processing, manufacturing, agriculture, and wholesale and retail trade, all of which have attracted the greater portion of capital investment during the last 20 years.

Especially welcome is foreign capital that brings with it technical knowledge, skill, and modern methods that will assist New Zealand's development. Foreign capital is also welcome for its contribution toward receipts of foreign exchange.

The New Zealand Government plays a strong role in economic development; however, New Zealand has no all-inclusive economic plan. The volume and pattern of production and consumption reflect, for the most part, the decisions of the private sector.

In the financial system, there is a degree of State ownership of financial institutions, including insurance, mortgage lending, small savings, and banking. These institutions, nevertheless, enjoy virtually complete freedom from political control.

The Government contributes substantially to the provision of transportation, communications, and electricity. Postal, telegraph, telephone, and railway service are provided by the Government. A government corporation operates both the international and the domestic air service; the Government also has equity participation in the iron and steel mill near Auckland and in Tasman Pulp and Paper, the country's largest producer of forest products.

Government Policy on Foreign Investment

The New Zealand Government clearly recognizes the need to encourage an inflow of foreign investment on a selective basis to assist in its basic economic goal of achieving the highest possible standard of living for the people of New Zealand. The Government particularly encourages investment proposals that introduce new or improved technology, make substantial sums of capital available for the development of local resources, or assist in obtaining increased access to overseas markets for New Zealand exports.

To ensure that investment proposals satisfy New Zealand's major objectives of developing the country's natural and human resources in its best interests (while preserving the social and physical environment) and maximizing the benefit available from the inflow of capital and technology to promote a satisfactory rate of economic growth, the Government adopted legislation in the form of the Overseas Investment Act 1973. The Act established an Overseas Investment Commission, administered through the Reserve Bank of New Zealand, which considers investment proposals in accordance with government policy and pertinent regulations governing the transfer of money into and out of the country. The Commission also advises the Government and generally supervises all aspects of foreign investment.

All foreign investment in New Zealand, whether direct or in the form of licensing or royalty agreements, requires the prior approval of the Government. Any proposal by an overseas person or entity to take over control of 25 percent, or more, of the capital stock in a New Zealand company also requires prior approval by the Government.

The main regulations relating to overseas investment in New Zealand are The Exchange Control Regulations 1978, the Overseas Investment Act 1973, the Overseas Investment Regulations 1974, and the Commerce Act 1975. These acts and regulations consolidate and supersede all previous legislation on the subject of direct investment, portfolio investment, and company takeovers. The Commerce Act 1975 established a Commerce Commission—which has jurisdiction over certain aspects of trade practices, monopolies, oligopolies, mergers, and takeovers. Accordingly, both the Overseas Investment Commission and the Commerce Commission may be involved in examining investment plans of foreign companies.

In 1974, the Government introduced new regulations that relate to companies predominantly or wholly overseas owned or controlled. (A non-resident company is defined as one in which foreign interests have a holding of at least 25 percent.) In assessing the amount that such a company can borrow in New Zealand, the degree of local equity in a company will be a determining factor. In general, foreign companies will need to raise the largest portion of their capital and borrowing overseas, thus leaving the local money market largely to New Zealand companies. The 1974 legislation strengthened existing regulations on foreign takeovers and increased the power of the Government to prohibit those foreign takeovers that it considers contrary to public interest.

Foreign investment in activities affecting national security—i.e., communications, transportation, and defense production—are closely controlled. As noted above, investment in the information media field is also restricted. Two other areas in which foreign investment is not encouraged are fishing and farming—unless new technology is introduced.

U.S. companies or individuals seriously considering investment in New Zealand, either direct investment or portfolio investment that will result in the acquisition of 25 percent of company shares (25 percent or more of the company's voting power) or assets the value of which exceed NZ$500,000, should obtain detailed information from The Director, Investment Unit, Department of Trade and Industry, Private Bag, Wellington, New Zealand.

Foreign Ownership of Real Property

ACQUISITION OF LAND.—The acquiring of certain kinds of land in New Zealand, either by foreign citizens or companies controlled by foreign citizens, requires government approval in accordance with the Land Settlement Promotion and Land Acquisition Act 1952. This legislation restricts the absentee ownership of New Zealand land by overseas interests; it pertains principally to acquisition of rural lands and off-shore islands. The Act does not relate to land zoned for residential or commercial use.

Inquiries concerning land acquisition should be directed to the Lands and Survey Department, Head Office, Private Bag, Wellington, New Zealand.

Foreign Ownership of Business Entities

The New Zealand Government prefers local participation in the ownership and control of New Zealand subsidiaries of foreign concerns, but there are no fixed rules requiring any minimum proportion of equity capital to be held by New Zealanders. While local participation in overseas investments is not mandatory, partnership involving overseas and New Zealand capital can substantially benefit the foreign investor in terms of goodwill and familiarity with local conditions and customs. The Government would also like to see New Zealand influence in the policies of expanding and profitable concerns to ensure that a significant part of the rewards of growth accrue to New Zealand. The participation of New Zealand residents in overseas investments also will make it easier for the overseas company to obtain local capital. The extent of local borrowing approved by the Government will generally reflect the degree of New Zealand equity participation. Access to the local capital market is adjusted according to the country's current internal and external liquidity.

The borrowing or raising of funds in new Zealand by a company that is not incorporated in New Zealand or by a company incorporated in New Zealand but of which 25 percent or more of the voting capital is foreign controlled must be approved by the Overseas Investment Commission. Current guidelines for "overseas persons" wishing to borrow in New Zealand include the following: No restrictions on amounts up to NZ$300,000, no restriction on companies predominantly New Zealand owned and controlled, and companies 50 percent or more overseas owned or controlled may borrow 15 percent of total turnover in previous financial year plus an additional 20 percent on export sales. Companies exactly 50-50 New Zealand-overseas owned may increase local borrowing limits by NZ$3 for every NZ$1 raised overseas.

Two areas in which foreign investment is not encouraged are fishing and farming unless new technology is introduced. However, in practice, all proposals are considered on their merits.

Forms of Business Organization

INDIVIDUAL PROPRIETOR.—As in the United States, an individual may, subject to various formalities and authorizations that apply to specific types of activities, establish a business without incorporating. The owner has the sole responsibility for the operation in which he/she engages, and, in settlement of debts, not only business assets but also personal goods and property may be attached.

PARTNERSHIP.—The types of partnerships and the general principles relating to the rights and liabilities of partners are similar to those applying under English or American law. A special partnership, which is similar to limited partnership of English law, may be formed for the transaction of business other than banking and insurance. Such a partnership must be registered and consists of general partners and special partners, the latter contributing to the capital specific sums in money beyond which they are not generally responsible for any debt of the partnership.

COMPANY.—The New Zealand Companies Act 1955, as amended, is closely in line with similar legislation in the United Kingdom. No company, association, or partnership consisting of more than 25 persons may be formed for the purpose of carrying on any business that has for its object the acquisition of gain unless legally registered as a company.

A company may be limited by shares, limited by guaranty, or unlimited. The great majority of incorporated industrial and commercial enterprises are established as limited (by share) liability companies, which may be either public or private in organization. The shareholders of limited liability companies are liable to creditors in the case of winding up only to the extent of the amount, if any, unpaid on their shares. There are no restrictions as to nationality of directors or shareholders.

A company may not use a name that is identical with that resembling the name of a company already carrying on business in New Zealand. In addition, such words as "Royal," "Imperial," "National," "Anzac," and "Standard" may not be used except with the consent of the Governor-General in Council. The Registrar of Companies may refuse to register a company by a name containing a trademark or a word so nearly resembling an existing trademark as to be calculated to deceive or to cause confusion.

A company limited by shares or by guaranty must have the word "Limited" as the last word of its name.

Private companies are formed to obtain the advantages of limited liability for family businesses, for small companies closely akin to partnerships, and for companies that are subsidiaries of other companies. In addition, this form of business organization need not observe all the requirements of the Companies Act, examples being the rules in connection with forming a

company, the passing of resolutions, and audit. If it is desired to impose restrictions on the transfer of shares and if the capital required by the undertaking can be raised without the necessity of offering shares to the public, incorporation as a private company is the more convenient form, particularly in the establishment of a New Zealand subsidiary by an American corporation. A private company must have a minimum of 2 members and may not have more than 25 members.

PUBLIC COMPANY.—The term "public company" is normally used to describe a limited company other than a private company. The public form of organization is used when it is deemed advisable or necessary to raise capital by offering shares to the general public. Any seven or more persons may incorporate a public company.

REGISTRATION AND LICENSE FEES.—Permission must be obtained from the Overseas Investment Commission and registration must be granted by the Registrar of Companies before any overseas company may commence business in New Zealand. To obtain registration, companies must disclose details of the following: Country of incorporation and whether limited liability applies wherever the company exhibits its name, certificate of incorporation or the equivalent, certified copy of the company constitution or charter, list of directors and the company secretary, and name of a New Zealand resident (either a company or an individual) authorized to act as the overseas company's agent for the purpose of accepting notices served on the company.

All overseas companies must register in the Wellington office of the Registrar of Companies. Further information, including the cost of registration and reregistration fees, is available from the Registrar of Companies, Department of Justice, Private Bag 1, Government Buildings, Wellington, New Zealand.

Organization of Foreign Firms

Part XII of the Companies Act 1955 provides for companies that are incorporated outside New Zealand and are carrying on business in New Zealand. Such companies must, within 1 month from the establishment of a place of business, deliver to the Registrar of Companies a certified copy of the charter, statutes, or other instruments defining the constitution of the company; a list of the directors; names and addresses of one or more persons resident in New Zealand and authorized to accept on behalf of the company service of process and other notices; and a verified copy of the certificate of incorporation. These companies are required to keep in New Zealand accounts relating to their New Zealand business and to register a balance sheet and profit and loss account once in a calendar year.

Both assets and liabilities are required by the Act to be classified in the balance sheet. The most important groups of assets are fixed assets, current assets, investments, preliminary expenses, and goodwill, patents, and trademarks. On the liabilities side a distinction must be made between fixed liabilities, current liabilities, bank loans and overdrafts, share capital, premium on shares, capital reserves, revenue reserves, and provision for dividends. In the profit and loss account, special mention must be made of investment income (interest from government and local body stock, dividends, and other investments), expenditure on debenture interest, depreciation, taxes, dividends, and directors' and auditors' fees.

Every overseas company must exhibit in every place where it carries on business in New Zealand and on all letterheads, invoices, and bill heads the name of the company, the country in which it is incorporated, and the fact that the liability of the company is limited.

EVIDENCE OF INCORPORATION.—A certificate of incorporation is deemed conclusive evidence that the company has been duly incorporated. This applies if the certificate is given under the hand of any officer who may be authorized to grant such a certificate by law of any country outside New Zealand providing that the company purports to be incorporated and that the certificate is duly verified by declaration made by one of the directors, the manager of the company before a notary public, a Commonwealth representative, or other person authorized to take the declaration.

Repatriation of Capital and Foreign Remittances

Repatriation of overseas capital and capital gains is normally permitted, provided that the original funds have come to New Zealand through the banking system or in some other equivalent approved form and that the formal approval of the Reserve Bank of New Zealand is obtained. It is also the policy of the New Zealand Government to allow the remittance of profits, interest, and dividends earned by overseas investors. This policy applies to loan investment as well as to direct and portfolio investments. However, application must be made under the exchange control regulations, and these require Reserve Bank approval for almost all overseas remittances.

Both in the case of remittances and the repatriation of capital, the approval of the Reserve Bank is, in fact, only a technical requirement and will be automatic once an auditor's certificate or the required proof of the remittance of the investment funds through the banking system has been produced.

Licensing and Royalty Agreements

Any proposed royalty agreements, together with particulars of the article to be produced, its use, demand, and the like, must first be submitted to the Reserve Bank for approval.

The Reserve Bank treats royalty payments to foreign firms in a uniform manner, regardless of whether the recipient is a parent company of a New Zealand subsidiary, a substantial joint venture partner, or an independent licensor.

The question frequently arises as to what a U.S. principal can consider as valid evidence that a proposed licensing or royalty agreement between the U.S. firm and its New Zealand counterpart has been approved. Although the Reserve Bank provides no standard approval form, U.S. firms can request their New Zealand counterparts to provide a copy of the Reserve Bank letter that reflects either approval or the rejection of the proposed agreement. This also applies to technical services to be provided by U.S. firms. U.S. principals should be satisfied that approval has been granted before finalizing any agreements or incurring any expenses related to such agreements.

Industrial Property Protection

PATENTS AND DESIGNS.—The Patents Act 1953 and the Designs Act 1953 represent the basic New Zealand legislation governing these forms of industrial property protection. During FY 1979, 3,221 applications were received; 1,138 originated in New Zealand, 700 in the United States, 390 in the United Kingdom, 247 in Australia, 158 in Switzerland, and the balance of 618 from 33 countries.

Patents are obtainable for "any manner of new manufacture," a phrase to which a wide interpretation is given.

Those who wish to protect an invention by a patent should arrange for a search of Patent Office records to determine what has been done in the same field. If the invention appears capable of being registered as a patent, an application may be filed at the Patent Office, accompanied by either a provisional or a complete specification describing the invention. The documents must meet formal requirements, and the fee must accompany the application.

An application for a patent not filed subject to the "priority right" provision of the "Paris Union" International Convention may be made in either of two ways: (1) the applicant may apply in the first instance with a provisioinal specification and may file a complete specification at any later date within 12 months or with application for extension of time within 15 months; or (2) the applicant may file complete specification at the time of making application.

Under the "Paris Union" International Convention for the Protection of Industrial Property, to which New Zealand is a party, or under pertinent bilateral arrangements with certain countries, a person (or his/her personal representative or assignee) who has filed an application for a patent in a Convention Country has the right, within 12 months from the date of the first application in a Convention Country, to claim priority—i.e., the filing date of first application—for a subsequent application in respect of the same invention in any other Convention Country. An application in New Zealand for a patent for an invention in respect of which protection has been applied for in a Convention Country must be accompanied by a complete specification, together with copies of the papers filed abroad, simultaneously or within 3 months.

The specifications are examined for formalities and for novelty of the invention by examiners; the invention must be novel in New Zealand only at the date of priority. If the application passes the examination stage, it is accepted and publicized in the *Patent Office Journal.* Thereafter the application is open for a period to opposition by any interested person. If the opposition stage has passed successfully, the patent is granted for a 16-year term.

A New Zealand patent is a limited monopoly granted by the Crown to make, use, exercise, and vend an invention and its products throughout a 16-year period, with the proviso that it may be terminated in certain circumstances. Those who infringe the patent are liable for damages and other penalties.

The Patent Office is forbidden by law to make searches for members of the public (except trademark searches), but will assist inquirers to use the system of classifying and recording patents. No search fees are charged. The Office has a complete record of all patents granted in New Zealand. There is also a comprehensive library of specifications from overseas countries.

Those not familiar with the practice of the Patent Office are advised to employ a patent attorney for searches and all work relating to patents. The Patent Office will supply a list of attorneys on request.

The import into New Zealand of articles that are subject to patent rights granted in New Zealand is subject to infringement action.

Inventions are either subject to patent rights or in the public domain. If subject to patent rights, they may be used only under license, normally obtained from the patentee. The Patents Act 1953 gives protection against the abuse of patent rights, and compulsory licenses and other remedies are available.

Designs may be registered to obtain protection for the shape, configuration, pattern, or ornament applied to articles by an industrial process or means.

The law in relation to the marking of registered designs and the system for searching is much the same as for patents. To register a design, an application must be made, supplemented by drawings or photographs of the design. The application is examined and a search for novelty is made, but this is, of necessity, limited to designs previously registered. The term of registration is for 5 years, which may be extended to 15. The registration of the design may be canceled if found to be invalid for any reason.

TRADEMARKS.—The Trade Marks Act 1953 provides the registration, in respect to particular goods or classes of goods, of a distinctive mark, stamp, device, brand, or name. The Commissioner of Trade Marks may refuse to accept any application with representations of Royal or official coats of arms or some other items.

Registration may be permanent subject to payment of renewal fees. It is necessary in registration to have used or to propose to use the mark, and a trademark may be expunged from the register on the grounds of non-use. It is possible to register trademarks only in relation to goods, not services. The only protection given the name of a service is under common law, where a case may be laid complaining that another person is passing off as the complainant.

The registration of trademarks is not essential for protection, but those who use marks without registering them must rely for their protection on common law rights and remedies. Definite statutory rights are given to registered proprietors. Because the value of a well-known trademark may be high, its registration is desirable.

Of the 4,155 applications for trademarks during FY 1979, 1,788 originated in New Zealand, 890 in the United States, 384 in Great Britain, 278 in Austria, and the remaining 815 were distributed among 37 other countries.

COPYRIGHT.—Copyright in New Zealand in literary, dramatic, musical, and artistic works and in cinema films extends to all countries that are parties to the Universal Copyright Convention and to all countries that are parties to the International Convention for the Protection of Literary and Artistic Works (Berne Copyright Union). New Zealand is a party to both conventions.

Labor Relations

LABOR FORCE.—New Zealand follows a policy of full employment. Over the last 30 years, the annual rate of unemployment has been low by U.S. standards; i.e., out of a labor force of approximately 1.3 million, the number of registered unemployed was about 50,000 in December 1980 (3.8 percent). The distribution of the labor force (in thousands as of October 1976) was as follows: agriculture, hunting, forestry, and fishing, 144.1; mining and quarrying, 4.4; manufacturing, 289.2; construction, 90.6; wholesale and retail trade, 190.1; transport, storage, and communications, 110.7; finance, insurance, and real estate, 77.3; service industries (public and private), 269.1.

The annual rate of growth of the labor force has been slow during recent years, averaging about 1.6 percent during 1972-76. According to recent projections by the New Zealand Department of Statistics, the labor force could reach approximately 1.8 million by 2001.

Although the productivity of the New Zealand agricultural worker is high by world standards, productivity in manufacturing and other major industries is not high by those standards. The small size of the domestic market partially accounts for this, as a 3.1 million person market makes it difficult for industry to achieve any significant economies of scale.

There are no requirements concerning the nationality of the staff, although qualified New Zealanders would expect to fill most available positions. There have been a few cases where New Zealand unions have opposed foreign companies employing aliens to work on public projects.

OVERSEAS STAFF.—At times fear has been expressed that appointment of foreigners by the parent organization to senior positions in the New Zealand unit may deny New Zealanders the opportunity to develop their talents and use their initiative. A study by a member of the Reserve Bank's Economic Department, produced little evidence to suggest that this was true. Only one-third of the respondents had managing directors (or the equivalent) sent from overseas associates. In few cases was this procedure adhered to

dogmatically, and in most instances, it was a reflection of the shortage of appropriate New Zealand personnel. This was endorsed by the fact that the figure was only slightly lower for companies with local equity participation, as compared with wholly foreign-owned enterprises.

Considerably less than 1 percent of all employees in the sample had been sent out from foreign associates, and again, in almost all cases, the absence of sufficient skilled labor in New Zealand was offered as the reason. This was particularly noticeable with firms setting up new industries. Many of these employees were permanent immigrants.

PAYMENTS AND BENEFITS.—Wages are paid at either an hourly rate or by the week. The standard week for most workers is 5 days totaling 40 work hours. Some clerical workers have a 35 hour week. Many workers receive a substantial amount for overtime. In general, there is no limit on the amount of overtime that adult males may work, except for underground miners.

Wage rates are determined by collective bargaining or by conciliation or arbitration with government participation. The minimum weekly wage rate is presently NZ$77.07 for both men and women. The Equal Pay Act 1972 provided for the gradual phasing in of equal pay for equal work at a rate that achieved parity between male and female workers on April 1, 1977. The legal minimum is established for about one-half of the New Zealand work force through the framework of the Industrial Relations Act 1973. However, in actual practice many employees are paid at "ruling rates" considerably higher than award rates established through bargaining or as a result of government conciliation. There are also regional differences in wages paid workers performing similar jobs. In February 1980, the countryside average weekly wage for adult workers was NZ$180.44.

Employees, including farm workers, are provided an annual holiday of 3 weeks on full pay. There are 11 public holidays per annum. Labor legislation also provides for compensation for job-connected injuries or death; comprehensive factory, shop, and office regulations to ensure the worker's safety, health, and welfare; and a system of conciliation and/or arbitration for disputes of rights or personal grievance.

Other benefits to labor include social security payments, youth housing, and recreational facilities. Many industries have their own training program, apprenticeships, and other vocational schooling.

LABOR ORGANIZATION AND RELATIONS WITH MANAGEMENT.—Although membership is voluntary, a very large proportion of wage and salary earners are union members. Most unions are registered under the provisions of the New Zealand Government's Industrial Relations Act 1973 and accordingly agree to avail themselves of the system of mediation, conciliation, and arbitration machinery available under the Act. There were 289 registered unions at the beginning of 1979 while a few important unregistered unions and professional associations remain outside the system (mainly unions of central and local government employees and workers in the pulp and paper industries). Certain provisions of the Industrial Relations Act are designed to deter the proliferation of unions and to simplify the amalgamation of unions. Most unions are occupational or craft-based, and industry agreements frequently require the cooperation of numerous unions. Registered unions range in size from more than 40,00 down to a legislated minimum of 10. Approximately 487,000 workers, 38 percent of the work force, belonged to unions at the beginning of 1979.

Although union membership is voluntary, according to a "qualified preference" clause in most union-management agreements, non-union workers may be hired only if no competent union member wants the position. The effect is to make membership in a union practically compulsory. This clause is generally an automatic part of an award or agreement (contract) unless specified to the contrary.

Most government workers are union members, although membership is voluntary. Separate tribunals and commissions set the wages and work standards for all Central Government employees.

Unions are normally required to admit everyone, except persons "of generally bad character."

Most major employers in New Zealand belong to management organizations known as Unions of Employers. By registering under the provisions of the Industrial Relations Act 1973, the employers secure all the rights of a union and can exercise them with only minor differences, in the same manner as a union of workers.

A considerable amount of collective bargaining occurs in New Zealand, both privately and within the system of mediation and conciliation. Labor-management negotiations usually begin with talks between employers and union representatives. If a registered union does not reach agreement with management, either the union or management may submit its case to the Industrial Mediation Service, the Industrial Conciliation Service, or both. If parties are unable to reach a settlement under mediation and conciliation proceedings, the dispute is referred to the Industrial Commission for arbitration. The Commission is comprised of five members, two of whom are appointed on recommendation of the central organizations of the union and the employer. The remaining three members of the Commission are appointed by the Government, which carefully screens them to ensure impartiality.

EMPLOYMENT OF ALIENS.—U.S. nationals are generally permitted to be employed in New Zealand on the same basis as New Zealand citizens. All persons other than New Zealand citizens must obtain permits to enter the country. U.S. citizens are reminded that in most cases a guarantee of employment is one of the conditions of entry into the country as a long-term resident.

Information regarding visa requirements and employment of aliens may be obtained from the Embassy of New Zealand or its consulates-general, which are listed in this report under the heading of "Government Representation."

Taxation

Reviews of the New Zealand tax structure were conducted during the late 1960's. Although the income tax still serves as the cornerstone of the country's tax system, there has been an increasing proportion of indirect taxes, the most important of which are the Sales Tax, Customs Duty, National Roads Fund Tax, Beer Tax, and Stamp Duties.

Fundamental provisions governing the Income Tax are contained in the Income Tax Act 1976, Land Tax Act 1976, and amendments. With certain exceptions, income tax is levied on all income, which includes receipts from such sources as labor or effort, investment in property, business, dividends, interest, royalties, estates and trusts, and pensions. The value of such benefits as free meals or board received by employees is taxable.

The collection of income taxes, levied by the country's Central Government, is the responsibility of the New Zealand Inland Revenue Department. Because the country has no federal system, there are no provincial or State income taxes. As a result, the services that such taxes would usually finance are generally provided in New Zealand by the Central Government. For the year ending March 31, 1979, the Department collected from individuals and companies income tax exceeding NZ$3.6 billion, which amounted to 73 percent of the country's total tax revenue.

Copies of New Zealand's tax legislation may be obtained from the Government Printing Office, Publications Branch, Private Bag, Wellington, New Zealand. Inquiries concerning New

Zealand Income, Land, Estate, and Gift Taxes, as well as Stamp Duties, may be addressed to The Commissioner of Inland Revenue, Head Office, Inland Revenue Department, Private Bag, Wellington, New Zealand.

A brief summary of several forms of New Zealand taxation that are of particular interest to U.S. firms and private persons follows.

Domestic Company Taxes

INCOME TAX.—For domestically owned companies, the income tax is a flat rate of 45 percent. Special tax provisions are available for mining companies, petroleum exploration companies, insurance companies, corporations, overseas shipping companies, and forestry companies.

EXCESS RETENTION TAX.—Privately controlled New Zealand investment companies are liable for this tax if they do not pay a dividend equal to at least 40 percent of its tax-paid profits. The tax does not apply to overseas companies trading in New Zealand through a branch of a wholly owned and subsidiary company.

Nonresident Company Taxes

For foreign-owned companies, the flat rate of tax is 50 percent on taxable income. There are rebates against this tax for nonresident life insurance companies receiving income from development assets in New Zealand and nonresident companies paying dividends to shareholders resident in New Zealand. In addition, income received from interest, dividends, royalties, and "know-how" is subject to a withholding tax of 15 percent, which is a final tax in many cases.

Personal Income Tax

For wage and salary earners, income tax is deducted at the source on the pay-as-you-earn (PAYE) system. Self-employed persons pay their taxes in installments during the March 31 fiscal year. Income tax rates in 1980 applying to representative levels of income include the following: to NZ$4,900, 14.5 percent; NZ$1,501 to NZ$16,000, 48 percent; and over NZ$22,000, 60 percent.

Nonresidents are liable for tax on their New Zealand income, unless the income is exempt under the general law or a double taxation agreement. A visitor to New Zealand who is liable for income tax in his/her own country and who resides in New Zealand for not more than 92 days a year performing personal or professional services for an overseas employer is exempt from income tax in New Zealand. (These provisions do not apply to entertainers, who are liable for tax ‚ on income earned.) In general, the same condi-

tions apply to visitors from countries with which New Zealand has a double taxation agreement, provided that the visitor and his/her employer reside in the same country. In this case, however, the visitor is exempt from income tax if he/she remains in New Zealand for 183 days or less in the income year.

Interest, Royalties, and Dividends

Interest and royalties derived in New Zealand by nonresidents are subject to a withholding tax of 15 percent of the gross amount payable. With the exception of cultural royalties and interest payments where the borrower and lender are not associated persons, the withholding tax is a minimum tax. The nonresident is liable to later assessment if the rate of income tax payable on the income received is greater than 15 percent. Interest paid to an overseas pension fund exempt from tax in its own country is also exempt from New Zealand tax. Dividends paid to nonresidents are subject to a withholding tax of 15 percent, deducted at the time of payment. This tax is final, and the payments are not subsequently included in any annual assessment.

CAPITAL GAINS TAX.—New Zealand has no capital gains tax.

Sales Tax

The Sales Tax Act 1974 provides legislation for the collection and payment of sales tax. Administered by the Customs Department, the tax is chargeable on all goods (which are not specifically exempted from this tax), either at the time of importation or sale. The tax is payable on the sale's value of the goods at the prescribed rate. The basic rate of sales tax is 20 percent but other rates currently applying are 10, 30, 37½, 40, 50, and 60 percent. The higher rates apply to motor vehicles, which are taxed according to engine capacity at rates varying from 60 percent for the largest models down to 30 percent for cars with engines of smaller capacity. Tax on machinery is 10 percent. Additional major commodity groups subject to sales tax are motor vehicle parts; confectionery; cosmetics and perfumes; jewelry and watches; radios, record players, sound recordings, and television sets; wines and spirits (except beer, which is subject to a separate tax); typewriters and accounting machines; and printed stationery.

The tax is not a turnover tax but is payable only once, usually at the point where the goods pass to the retailer. Taxable goods imported by other than a licensed wholesaler are taxed prior to their removal from customs control, either at the time of importation or when the goods are taken from a bonded warehouse.

Land Tax

The Valuer-General is charged with the duty of examining property and estimating the value of the land, the value of buildings or other improvements, and the capital value of the property. Improvement on land is defined as any work done on or for the benefit of the land by any owner or occupier resulting in its increased value, except for such work as draining, reclamation, grading, leveling, removal of rocks and vegetation, and the arresting or elimination of erosion. Capital value is the sum of the land value plus the value of improvements.

Land tax is levied on the total value of the land (i.e., capital improvements are not included) after making the following deductions; NZ$157,000 if the land value does not exceed NZ$175,000 or NZ$175,000 diminished at the rate of NZ$1 by which the land value exceeds NZ$175,000 with the result that no deduction remains when the land value amounts to NZ$350,000 or more.

The tax rate, based on the value of the land after allowing the deduction, is as follows: For a land value not exceeding NZ$20,000, the rate is 0.2 cents for each dollar; if the value exceeds NZ$20,000 but does not exceed NZ$30,000, 0.4 cents for each dollar; if the value exceeds NZ$30,000 but does not exceed NZ$40,000, 0.6 cents for each dollar; finally, if the value exceeds NZ$40,000, 0.7 cents for each dollar. Land used for agricultural activities is exempt from the Land Tax.

Depreciation

Ordinary depreciation on assets used in production of assessable income is deductible from gross income at various rates approved by the Commissioner of Inland Revenue. Recent examples of the ordinary depreciation allowances include 1 to 2½ percent a year on the cost price of buildings. The rate of depreciation on plant and machinery is generally 10 percent on the diminishing value, while the rates for motor vehicles and office equipment, furniture, and fittings are 20 percent.

Tax Concessions

A wide range of incentive provisions is contained in the Income Tax Act 1976.

New Zealand's dependence on international trade and export earnings has resulted in particular emphasis being given to tax incentives for export-oriented businesses.

Concessions are available for expenditures related to developing export markets. Qualifying expenditures might include the expenses of overseas travel, advertising, publicity, free samples, market research, packaging, and production of new lines.

Increased export sales qualify for another type of tax concession. Under this plan, 25 percent of the increase in export sales is exempt from tax. A qualifying increase is the differential between the actual export sales in the income year and the average export sales made in a base period of the first 3 of the immediately preceding 7 years. As each income year elapses, the base period moves forward 1 year so as to leave a 4-year gap between the end of the base period and the beginning of the income year with which the comparison is to be made. New Zealand's traditional exports of meat, wool, dairy products, newsprint, and minerals do not qualify.

The tourist promotion expenditure concession is similar in scope to the export market development concession. An additional deduction of 67.5 percent from assessable income can be claimed for qualifying expenditures to attract tourists. Qualifying expenditures include advertising overseas, tourist market research overseas, the costs of bringing travel agents to New Zealand, and the cost of overseas sales missions by individual businesses.

The taxable incomes of companies mining specified minerals and of petroleum exploration and mining companies are determined solely on the basis of dividends they declare.

Investment allowances, in addition to the first year depreciation allowance, may be allowed with respect to new manufacturing plant and machinery used for various purposes. An allowance of up to 20 percent of the cost price of new manufacturing plant and machinery is allowable where that plant or machinery will contribute substantially to export production and has been installed by businesses that have achieved a significant export performance in goods qualifying for the increased export taxation incentive (mentioned earlier) or by businesses planning substantial increases in production for export.

There is also a regional investment allowance of up to 20 percent for high priority regions on new manufacturing plant and machinery and new road transport equipment purchased by licensed goods service operators (trucking companies, moving companies, etc.).

The regional investment allowance is in addition to the export investment allowance so that a maximum investment allowance of 40 percent is available in the case of new plant and machinery which is to be used for export production or to be used in plants located in areas designated as having a high priority for planned industrial development.

Expenditure for new farm plant and machinery qualifies for an investment allowance of 40 percent. The same rate of allowance is available for new road transport vehicles used wholly or principally to service the farming industry and new fishing boats and new fish farming plant and machinery other than onshore processing facilities.

Double Taxation Convention

A convention is in effect between New Zealand and the United States for the avoidance of double taxation and prevention of fiscal evasion with respect to taxes on income.

A U.S. enterprise is not subject to New Zealand tax on its industrial or commercial profits unless it is engaged in trade or business in New Zealand through a permanent establishment in New Zealand. If it is so engaged, New Zealand tax may be imposed on its entire income derived from sources within New Zealand.

The term "industrial or commercial profits" includes manufacturing, mercantile, mining, financial, and farming profits, but it does not include income in the form of dividends, interest, rents, or royalties; insurance premiums; management charges; or remuneration for personal services.

The term "permanent establishment" means a branch management, factory, mine, farm, or other fixed place of business, but it does not include an agency unless the agent has and habitually exercises a general authority to negotiate and conclude contracts on behalf of the enterprise or regularly fills orders on the agency's behalf from a stock of goods or merchandise. An enterprise is not deemed to have a permanent establishment in New Zealand merely because it carries on business in New Zealand through a bona fide broker or general commission agent acting in the ordinary course of his/her business.

Profits derived by a citizen of the United States who is not resident in New Zealand, from operating ships or aircraft are exempt from New Zealand tax.

Rental of motion picture films derived from New Zealand sources by a U.S. resident who is not engaged in trade or business through a permanent establishment in New Zealand is exempt from New Zealand tax. However, it is provided that the foregoing exemption shall not be construed to affect the New Zealand film hire tax or the income tax imposed by New Zealand on incomes that are taxable under New Zealand law

and are derived by any person from the business of renting motion picture films.

An individual who is a resident of the United States is exempt from New Zealand tax on remuneration received for personal and professional services performed in New Zealand in any year if he/she is present in New Zealand for a period or periods not exceeding 183 days during that year and if the services are performed on behalf of a U.S. resident. A teacher who is normally a U.S. resident and who receives remuneration for teaching during a period of temporary residence not exceeding 2 years at an educational institution in New Zealand is exempt from New Zealand tax on such remuneration, provided it is taxed in the United States. A student or a business or trade apprentice who is normally resident in the United States and who is receiving full-time education or training in New Zealand is exempt from New Zealand tax on payments made to him by persons in the United States for the purpose of his/her maintenance, education, or training.

Reciprocal provision is made for granting credit for income tax paid in the other country. U.S. taxpayers who are also subject to tax in New Zealand should consider the provisions in the U.S. Internal Revenue Code; namely, section 901 (formerly 131 which is cited in the Convention). Sections 164, 902 through 905, and 911 may also be of interest to such taxpayers.

Guidance for Business Travelers

Entrance Requirements

A U.S. citizen is required to have in his/her possession a valid U.S. passport to enter New Zealand. For stays of 30 days or less, no visa is required. For longer stays, the New Zealand Embassy should be contracted for information pertaining to visas and alien registration. A valid passport is also required for departure from New Zealand.

Customs Procedures

The following are among the used personal effects that a visitor may bring into New Zealand free of duty: Wearing apparel; personal articles, including jewelry, toilet requisites, and the like; personal sporting requisites; two cameras of a noncommercial kind; a pair of binoculars; one radio; one portable phonograph, tape recorder, or both; and one portable television set. Visitors may also import duty free small amounts of cigarettes or cigars, as well as 1 quart of spirits where, in accordance with its collective agreement, only union members may be employed. Although the unions may represent only a minority of the workers, the collective agreements that they and the employers' organizations conclude are usually imposed on the entire industry by the Minister of Social Affairs. Representatives of all the union groups participate in collective bargaining and other negotiation.

Employers are associated with two organizations, the nondenominational Union of Netherlands Enterprises (VNO) and the Federation of Catholic and Protestant Employers' Unions (NCW). These two groups cooperate closely. In addition, two organizations cater to medium- and small-scale businesses; and three, to agriculture.

In 1945, the central organizations of employers and employees set up the Foundation of Labor as a body for joint consultation and, if possible, negotiations at a national level in the areas of labor agreements. This foundation has contributed considerably toward a good relationship between employers and employees.

The Social and Economic Council (SER) also has had a positive influence on industrial relations. It consists of 45 members, of whom 15 are elected by the trade unions, 15 are elected by the employers' organizations, and 15 are independent experts appointed by the Government. The Government is required by law to seek the advice of the Council on major social and economic matters.

To foster good labor relations and employee participation, every enterprise having 100 or more employees must establish a Works Council. Its members are employees chosen by their coworkers. The number varies from 7 to 25 depending on the size of the company. The law states that the employer must seek the advice of the Works Council regarding important decisions such as takeover, closure, change of location, important reorganizations, and changes in working conditions.

Employment of Foreign Workers

Citizens of most countries, including the United States, do not need visas to enter the Netherlands, a valid passport being sufficient. A national of an EEC or EFTA (European Free Trade Association) country (except Portugal) or of the United States who wishes to stay in the Netherlands for 3 or more months must apply for a residence permit to the local Netherlands municipal police within 8 days of arrival. A national of any other country must obtain an authorization for provisional stay at the Netherlands embassy or consulate in his/her country of origin.

A foreign national from any country outside the EEC wishing to take up paid employment, even in a managerial position, must obtain a work permit from a regional labor office before he/she is allowed to work in the Netherlands. This permit is usually valid for 1 year and can be extended.

Guidance for Business Travelers Abroad

There is a solid potential for U.S. goods in the Dutch market. However, this is a highly competitive market, and the U.S. exporter must keep certain factors in mind to achieve maximum success. The U.S. exporter should establish close liaison with distributors and customers to exchange information and ideas. Customary business courtesy, especially replying promptly to requests for price quotations and to letters placing orders, is a primary prerequisite for success in the Netherlands market. Exporters should be aware that ocean shipping requires stronger, more weatherproof packing than that used for domestic freight.

A vigorous and sustained promotion is often needed to launch products in the Netherlands because of conservative buying habits. In many cases, the Dutch consumer is not prepared to accept rapid changes in styles, colors, and materials of consumer goods. A good educational selling campaign can help considerably in overcoming this resistance to change. Advertising, if done carefully and in good tase, can be very effective.

Since the market is very competitive, the Dutch importer is in a position to request, and obtain, strict adherence to terms of sale. It follows that meeting delivery schedules is of prime importance. It is much better to quote a later delivery date that can be guaranteed than an earlier one that is not completely certain.

The terms of payment are generally from 30 to 90 days after delivery, although this varies considerably. Letters of credit are disliked by some Dutch business people. Drafts are occasionally used as a means of payment, the periods varying extensively.

Since Dutch wholesalers and retailers generally do a lower volume of business than their U.S. counterparts, the Dutch importer usually purchases smaller lots of goods than is the custom in the United States.

usually given at Christmas time. Employees over 18 are entitled to a vacation or annual holiday of 3 working weeks, and those under 18 to 4 working weeks. These are minimum entitlements, which employers often exceed by about a week. Employees receive overtime for the following legal holidays: New Year's Day, Easter Monday, Queen's Birthday (April 30), Ascension Day, Whit Monday, Christmas Day and the day after, and sometimes for Good Friday and Liberation Day (May 5, once in 5 years). Leave without pay is permitted for legally specified periods of time on such occasions as the birth, marriage, and death of close relatives, examination for military service, and voting in elections.

The hiring of employees in the Netherlands involves employment contracts, which can be concluded in writing or by verbal agreement. These contracts cannot contain provisions that are less demanding than those required by law or by any applicable labor agreement. The usual employment contract may be for an unlimited term, although no employee can specifically bind himself/herself for more than 5 years. A trial period for a maximum of 2 months can form part of the contract. Within this period, both partners can discontinue the contract at any time with no obligations. Employment may be terminated at any time by mutual agreement between employee and employer. In the absence of mutual agreement, the approval of the director of the regional labor office is required. By law, the term of regular notice need not be longer than 13 weeks for the employer and 6 weeks for the employee. Employment cannot be terminated by the employer during illness of the employee, unless the illness has lasted for at least 2 years.

The Unemployment Insurance Act insures the unemployed person (below the age of 65) against the financial consequences of involuntary unemployment. This benefit amounts to 80 percent of the daily wage to a maximum of $112.60. This insurance is valid for a maximum of 26 weeks per benefit year. After this period, the Unemployment Provisions Act comes into force for 2 years and provides for 75 percent of daily wages.

Nonwage Labor Costs

The social security system in the Netherlands is extensive, complex, and compulsory. The system covers the costs of illness and ensures a minimum income for those unable to earn their living as a result of illness, serious injury, unemployment, or retirement. Both employers and employees contribute to various social insurance funds. The premiums paid by the employ-ees are deducted from their wages by the employer. Together with his/her own contributions, the employer pays these amounts periodically to the Industrial Insurance Board. Each year, the amount of premiums to be paid is fixed, with the change normally following the trend of wages. The amount of contribution as of January 1, 1979, is 27 percent of the insurable wage for the employer and 24 percent for the employee.

The Ministry of Social Affairs may require all groups employed in any sector of industry to participate in an industrial pension fund. Contributions to such a fund, which must provide for old age, widows', and orphans' benefits, are made equally by employers and employees. Private pension schemes are supervised by the Government under the Pension and Savings Fund Act. Broadly, the act requires an employer to insure his/her scheme with an appropriate insurance company, to join an industry-wide scheme, or to set up a company fund.

In addition to the compulsory social charges, there are a number of other employee benefits furnished voluntarily by the employer or agreed upon in collective labor agreements. These may include such fringe benefits as paid holidays, vacation allowances, Christmas bonuses, cafeterias, recreational facilities, company magazines, and saving plans.

Labor Relations with Management

The Netherlands has a very good record with regard to few days lost by strikes. Strikes have not been the primary means of achieving union aims, and labor-management disputes have been settled by negotiation. Unofficial or wildcat strikes have been largely unknown, and in general, the unions have so far had few problems in controlling their members.

Three union groups coexist in the Netherlands and comprise about 39 percent of the total labor force. The Protestant unions are affiliated to the Federation of Christian National Workers Unions (CNV); the Roman Catholic unions, to the Federation of Netherlands Catholic Trade Unions (NKV); and the nondenominational unions, to the Netherlands Federation of Trade Unions (NVV). Additionally, there are Federations for middle and higher level employees organized in the Council for Medium and Higher Employees. In 1976, the NVV and NKV set up a joint organization (FNV), which represents 60 percent of organized workers.

Most unions are organized on an industry-wide basis. Union membership is not compulsory—except in the printing and allied industry, and 1 quart of wine. In addition, there are concessions that are subject to certain conditions by which items not classified as personal effects may enter the country duty free. Further information is available from any New Zealand consular office or customs representative. For information concerning the admission of samples land advertising material, see "Import Tariff Systems," page 1656.

Foreign Exchange Regulations

Travelers may enter New Zealand with any amount of New Zealand bank notes. However, travelers from New Zealand are permitted to take abroad only up to NZ$1000 per month (to a maximum of $4000 annually).

Accommodations and Services

HOTELS.—Information concerning many accommodations available in New Zealand is presented in the "New Zealand Accommodation Guide," published by the New Zealand Tourist and Publicity Department, available from the New Zealand Government Tourist Office, Suite 530, 630 Fifth Avenue, New York, New York 10020.

TELEPHONE AND TELEX SERVICES.—More than 1.7 million telephones are currently in service in the country. Telephone calls can be placed to most foreign countries. A telex service permits direct telex calls to be made overseas. Phototelegraph services are available.

Holidays

New Zealand's business holidays are as follows (included are three anniversary days* that could affect visiting U.S. business travelers):

January 1—(New Year's Day)
January 25—(Wellington Anniversary Day)
February 1—(Auckland Anniversary Day)
April 9—(Good Friday)
April 12—(Easter Monday)
April 25—(Anzac Day)
June 7—(Queen's Birthday)
October 25—(Labor Day)
December 16—(Canterbury/Christchurch Anniversary Day)
December 25—(Christmas Day)
December 26—(Boxing Day)

Sources of Economic and Commercial Information

Government Representation

The United States Embassy is located at 29

Fitzherbert Terrace, (P.O. Box 1190), Wellington, New Zealand. There is a U.S. Consulate General located at Fifth Floor, Old Northern Building Society Building, Queen and Wellesley Street (P.O. Box 7140 Wellesley St. Post Office), Auckland, New Zealand.

The Embassy of New Zealand is located at 37 Observatory Circle, N.W., Washington, D.C. 20008. The New Zealand Government maintains consulates general at the following addresses: Suite 530, 630 Fifth Avenue, New York, New York 10020; 153 Kearney Street, San Francisco, California 94108;k and 510 West Sixth Street, Los Angeles, California 90014.

Trade Commissioners are also located at the New Zealand consulates general in New York, San Francisco, and Los Angeles. New Zealand Commercial and Trade Officers are prepared to discuss proposals for U.S. investment in New Zealand and can answer many points that may occur to potential U.S. investors.

In addition to the office listed above, a trade correspondent is located at 2270 Kalakau Avenue, Waikiki, Honolulu, Hawaii 96815.

Bibliography

NEW ZEALAND GOVERNMENT PUBLICATIONS.—The following publications are available from the Government Printer, Private Bag, Wellington, New Zealand:

Economic Review (annual). Treasury Department.

New Zealand Official Yearbook (annual). Department of Statistics.

External Trade of New Zealand (annual). Department of Statistics.

Facts About New Zealand. Tourist and Publicity Department.

Investment in New Zealand (annual). Department of Trade and Industry.

Monthly Abstract of Statistics. Department of Statistics.

New Zealand Official Yearbook (annual). Department of Statistics.

New Zealand Pocket Digest of Statistics (annual). Department of Statistics.

New Zealand Taxes and Duties. Inland Revenue Department of New Zealand.

---

*Dates of some holidays vary from year to year. Anniversary days are observed only in the Province of that anniversary.

Reserve Bank of New Zealand Bulletin (monthly). Reserve Bank of New Zealand.

UNITED STATES GOVERNMENT PUBLICATIONS.—The U.S. Department of Commerce has published, in addition to *Marketing in New Zealand*, the following special reports on New Zealand that are available from any Department of Commerce District Office or from the Publications Branch, Room 1617, U.S. Department of Commerce, Washington, D.C. 20230:

Foreign Economic Trends. New Zealand (biannual).

Market Profiles for Asia and Oceania

World Trade Outlook for Far East and South Asia (biannual).

OTHER PUBLICATIONS.—

ANZ Quarterly Survey.

Businessman's Guide to New Zealand. Australia and New Zealand Banking Group, Wellington.

Life and Business in New Zealand. Bank of New Zealand, Wellington.

Economic Review (quarterly). The Commercial Bank of Australia Ltd., Wellington.

New Zealand Business Who's Who. FEP Productions Ltd., P.O. Box 2798, Welington.

Market Profile—NEW ZEALAND

Economic Overview

The short-term outlook for New Zealand is not particularly bright. The most basic of New Zealand's industries, agriculture, has been hit by escalating costs and drought; manufacturers are expecting a decline in demand; consumer and investor confidence is weakening and more labor unrest is probable. Inflation is expected to remain high, and the slowdown in real growth has unhappy implications for employment. For the somewhat longer term, however, New Zealand's economic situation seems more promising. As major energy projects are completed, world demand for New Zealand's food, forest, and other primary based products should also pick up. Given good economic management and a reasonable international economic environment, New Zealand should do better than many countries in the years ahead.

Major Developments

The New Zealand Government has moved to implement its "think big" development strategy, which calls for economic development through a series of major projects. Among these are construction of the world's first natural gas-to-gasoline plant using a catalytic process developed by Mobil Oil Company and the natural gas from New Zealand's extensive Maui gasfield. In addition to several natural gas-based resource projects, the Government has approved an expansion of New Zealand's only oil refinery at Marsden point near Whangerei. And the long-projected expansion of New Zealand Steel's Glenbrook plant, which produces steel from New Zealand's iron sand deposits has been approved and is currently undergoing preliminary engineering studies.

Foreign Trade

Best U.S. Sales Prospects. — Computers and accessories, equipment for industries based on natural gas, on forest products, and on food processing.

Major Suppliers (1981). — Australia (14 percent), Japan (13 percent), United Kingdom (13 percent), and United States (13.5 percent).

Principal Exports. — Meat, dairy products, wool, and forest products.

Major Markets (1981). — Australia (19 percent), United States (18 percent), Japan (15 percent), and United Kingdom (10 percent).

Finance

Currency. — New Zealand dollar worth US$.72 in Dec. 1982.

Domestic Credit. — Banking systems and stock exchanges are well established. Commercial bank prime rate averaged 12.75 percent in 1981.

National Budget. — Public account expenditures and public debt totaled $11.6 billion in year ending March 1981.

Balance of Payments. — Official overseas reserves were $695 million in March 1981. Balance-of-payments (current account) deficit was estimated at $770 million that month.

Foreign Investment

Bilateral economic aid commitments (1970-79), $400 million.

Basic Economic Facilities

Transportation. — More than 58,000 miles of road and over 3,000 miles of railroad track provide good internal transportation service. All major cities and towns linked by air services, 1.32 million licensed automobiles in June 1980, 19 deepwater ports.

Import — Export Trade*
(millions of U.S. dollars)

	1979	1980	1981
Total Imports (c.i.f.)	3,917	5,017	5,090
Imports from U.S.	499	630	833
Manufactured goods	2,249	2,672	2,676
Agricultural goods	190	239	220
Other	1,206	1,753	1,824
Total Exports (f.o.b.)	4,148	4,997	5,125
Exports to the U.S.	645	700	673
Manufactured goods	763	930	990
Agricultural goods	1,902	2,205	2,437
Other	1,483	1,862	1,698

*New Zealand data.

Principal Imports from the U.S. in 1981*
(millions of U.S. dollars)

	Value	Percent of Total
Computers	39.8	56.5
Instrumentation	26.9	43
Medical instruments	7.0	41
Printing and graphic arts equipment	9.1	50
Food processing machinery	2.4	25
Pulp and paper machinery	5.2	24

*U.S. data.

Communications. — 1,321 post offices, 569 telephones per 1,000 population, sophisticated overseas network including cable, satellite and radio connections. There are 59 medium wave and two short wave radio stations and more than 885,000 television receivers.

Power. — Distribution systems are well developed. Electricity reaches 99.5 percent of the population at 230 volts, 50 cycles, a.c.

Natural Resources

Land. — 104,000 square miles, principally two elongated islands extending 1,000 miles. A land of infinite variety, much of which is mountainous.

Climate. Most of the country is in the temperate zone.

Minerals. — Iron sands from the base of a growing iron and steel industry. Substantial quantities of offshore natural gas are being exploited and provide a base for a variety of industries, including petrochemical, synfuels, and LPG.

Forestry. — Presently accounts for 8 percent of total export earnings, but there are substantial resources.

Fisheries. — Presently contributes only 3 percent of export earnings, but the industry has great potential.

Population

Size.—3.20 million (as of Dec. 1981), an increase 0.010 percent from the previous year. Population is highly urbanized.

Major cities: Wellington (capital), 100,00; Auckland, 200,000; Christchurch, 200,00; and Dunedin, 100,000.

Education. — Free and compulsory for all children between the ages of 6 and 15 years. Free university education available based on scholastic achievement in secondary school.

Labor Force. — 1.3 million in April 1981, 34.2 percent female. About 3.8 percent registered unemployed in Dec. 1980.

Religion. — Protestant 63 percent, Catholic 16 percent, Hebrew 0.1 percent, Hindu 0.2 percent, Buddhist 0.1 percent, other 1.1 percent at time of last count (1976).

Language. — English.

Market Profile—NICARAGUA

Foreign Trade

Imports.—(C.I.F.) 1976, $525 million; 1975, $516.9 million. U.S. market share 1976, 31 percent. Major imports: petroleum, fertilizers, chemical, pharmaceuticals, agro-industrial supplies.

Exports.—(F.O.B.) 1976, $526 million; 1975, $375.9 million. U.S. market share 1976, 30.2 percent. Major exports: cotton, coffee, sugar, meat, seafood.

Trade Policy.—Member of Central American Common Market (CACM). Intra-CACM duties eliminated on almost all goods, but some controls and restrictions continue. Common external CACM tariff in effect for 95 percent of production categories. Preferential interchange and free trade egreement with Panama on certain specific items.

Trade Prospects.—Excellent opportunities for U.S. exporters exist despite increased competitiveness in pricing and financing from Europe and Japan. Best prospects include equipment for agriculture, health care, communications, hotels and restaurants and energy systems.

Foreign Investment

Figures for U.S. investment in Nicaragua are unavailable. Estimated at approximately $160 million in 1976. Nicaragua actively promotes foreign investment. Investment Guaranty Agreement with U.S. covers inconvertibility, expropriation, war and extended risk.

Finance

Currency.—7 Cordobas equal US$1.

Domestic Credit and Investment.—Liquidity is high in Nicaragua due to a 40 percent increase in export earnings during 1976. Deposits in commercial banks and savings and loan associations have increased at a faster rate than loans outstanding. Most Nicaraguans seem shy about investing or spending this new-found liquidity and seem content to allow it to remain in the bank for the time being.

National Budget.—1976, $317.5 million.

Foreign Aid.—AID, the several international lending agencies and the Central American Bank for Economic Integration are major sources of external financing.

Balance of Payments.—Estimates for 1976 indicate $29 million surplus in Nicaraguan balance of payments position and net foreign reserves at $45.3 million. Nicaragua's 1977 balance of payments surplus is projected at $25 million.

Economy

GDP.—Estimated at $2.1 billion in current prices for 1977; per capita GDP in 1976 was $825. GDP 1976 growth rate in real terms, 7 percent.

Agriculture.—The heart of the Nicaraguan economy; accounted for 25 percent of GDP in 1976. 70 percent of land could be used for some form of agriculture but only 30 percent is utilized. Government is planning to invest heavily in this sector. Principal agricultural products: cotton, sugar, meat, coffee, shellfish.

Manufacturing.—Generated about 21 percent of GDP in 1976. Depends to a large extent on agricultural inputs. Investment in manufacturing sector grew by 60 percent in 1976. Most important manufacturing activities: food and beverage processing, chemical and petroleum products, textiles and clothing, metal products.

Basic Economic Facilities

Transportation.—8,965 miles of roads in 1975, of which 1,530 miles were paved and 2,830 miles all-weather. Well served by shipping and air lines. Domestic bus and rail service not well developed; trucking services adequate.

Communications.—Local and international telephone and telegraph service is available in Managua and a few other urban areas.

Power.—Present capacity is approximately 295MW, 195MW from fossil fuel plants and 100MW from hydroelectric.

Natural Resources

Land.—Area 57,000 sq. miles (about the size of Iowa). Ample virgin land, with abundant water. Coastal plain and hills along Pacific; low mountains through center; wide flat coastal plain along Caribbean. Two very large lakes in southwest.

Climate.—Lower elevations tropical, average 84°F with little fluctuation; mountains somewhat cooler. Rainy season May to November, but amount varies: 60-65 inches annually on Pacific coast, 150-plus inches on Caribbean coast.

Minerals.—Gold, silver, and copper have been significant exports in the past though they have diminished in importance. Deposits of gypsum, lead and zinc now being mined. Petroleum exploration under way.

Forestry.—Almost 60 percent of nation forested; 10 percent marketable pine, rest tropical hardwoods.

Population

Size.—2.2 million (1975 est.), about 50 percent urban, with growth rate of 3.6 percent (1975). Low density (38.5/sq. mile), but half of the population is concentrated near Pacific around the capital, Managua, in 7 percent of area.

Language.—Spanish. Most leading businessmen and high government officials speak some English.

Education.—Primary education free but, in practice, not compulsory. Enrollment in 1975: 389,020 in primary schools (about 80 percent of school-age population), and 82,722 at secondary level (about 25 percent of school-age population). Two government and one private university-level institutions had a combined enrollment of 12,000 in 1975.

Labor.—About 50 percent in agriculture, 10 percent in manufacturing, 32 percent in services. Serious urban underemployment and seasonal unemployment in rural areas. Shortage of educated, skilled labor.

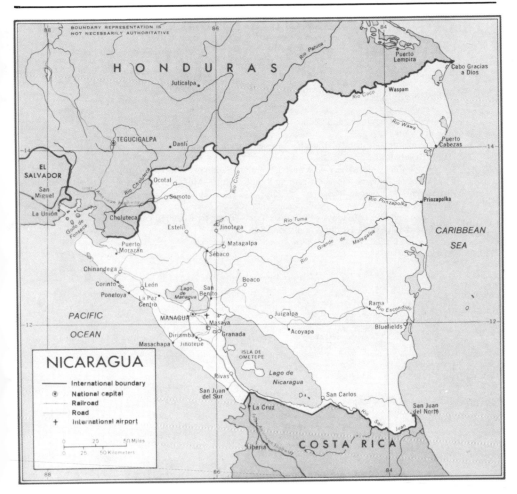

Marketing in Niger

Contents

Report Revised July 1981

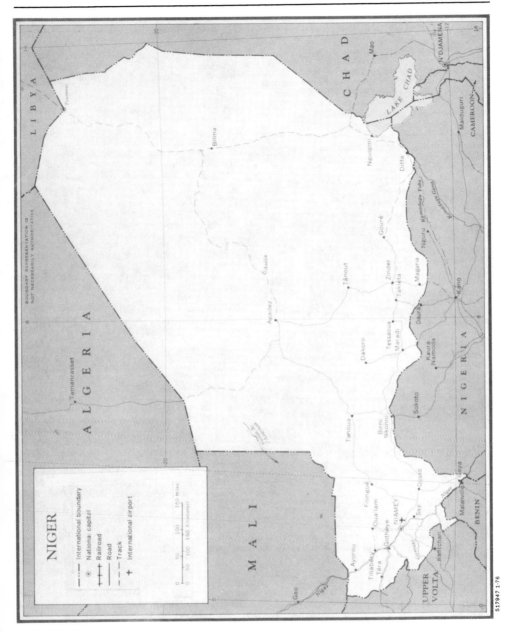

1683

Market Overview

Traditionally an agrarian economy, Niger experienced rapid growth during 1979-80 due largely to excellent harvests and the doubling of its uranium production. As world uranium prices soared, the mineral became the engine of the country's economic growth.

Faced with a decline in uranium prices, Niger's economy and balance of payments will suffer at least a temporary downturn. However, a revival of world uranium prices should renew interest in Niger's ample reserves, which should result in continued commercial opportunities for certain American goods.

Once avoided by many American manufacturers who preferred the more accessible English-speaking markets of coastal Africa, Niger is attracting the attention of a number of U.S. producers and investors who view it as a progressive and stable nation and regard France's dominant trade position there as a result of historical and cultural factors rather than competitive commercial development. Niger, an integral part of French West Africa until 1958, has served as an exclusive market for French products for over three decades. Today, through increased knowledge of the high performance of U.S. goods and services, Niger should gradually shift from its traditional source of imports to make way for more tested American products and a more competitive marketplace in the future.

Best prospects for U.S. exports to Niger are aircaft, mining, and construction equipment; airconditioning equipment; road equipment; irrigation equipment; heavy-duty vehicles; and prefabricated housing.

Profile Niger: Geography and People

The Republic of Niger covers an area of 1,268,500 square km (490,000 mi.²) and is larger than the States of Texas and California combined. Landlocked, it is bordered by seven states: Algeria and Libya to the north, Chad to the east, Nigeria and Benin to the south, Upper Volta to the southwest, and Mali to the west. Niamey, the capitol of Niger, is located in the southwest on the Niger River.

Four-fifths of Niger is arid desert. The remainder is savanna suitable mainly for livestock and limited agriculture. The Niger River flows for 480 km (300 mi.) along the southwest border, permitting the cultivation of rice and truck produce.

Rainfall, which comes in June through September, ranges from 10-82 cm (4-32 in). The climate is hot, dry, and dusty, especially in April and May.

Niger is predominantly a country of small villages with a population totaling 5 million. Because the north is largely mountainous or desert, 90 percent of the population is concentrated in a narrow band along the southern border. The population is divided roughly along tribal lines: the Hausa, whose homelands extend into northern Nigeria, predominate in the eastern portion of Niger and comprise 50 percent of the population; Djerma-Songhai, 23 percent; Fulani (Peul), 15 percent; and Tuareg and Toubou, 12 percent. Although French is the official language, Hausa and Djerma are widely spoken. The predominant religion in Niger is Islam.

The Economy

Since 1974, the Nigerien economy, through sound fiscal policies, has experienced a period of rapid growth averaging between 8 and 10 percent. In 1979, the growth rate surged to 15 percent as a second uranium mine neared capacity production. Uranium is the backbone of Niger's economy, providing 75 percent of Niger's total foreign trade receipts in 1980 and $122 million in government earnings. But maintaining high growth in the near future will be difficult. Niger's uranium sales price was not increased in 1980, breaking a 6-year trend, and will be lower in 1981 to a level nearer the world market price. Consequently, Niger will find itself with falling export revenues in addition to declining foreign investment as the development of several new mines is postponed.

Foreign assistance attracted by the Government's dedication to development totaled over $190 million in 1979 and will probably increase further in the near future. This increase will mitigate the effects of declining export earnings and reduced private capital inflows on Niger's balance of payments, but the deficit registered in 1979 ($2.4 million) will probably worsen in the immediate future.

Inflation remains a persistent problem in Niger. In 1979, the GDP deflator rose to 15 percent, from 12 percent the year before, while "European" and "African" consumer price indexes rose by 18 percent and 11 percent, respectively. The principal cause of Niger's inflation is the rise in the price of imports, particularly petroleum and capital goods. (For additional information on key economic indicators see tables section.)

Although the decline in uranium prices threatens to weaken the short-term outlook for

Niger's economy, there remain many opportunities for sales of American products and technology. Construction of several large projects not directly connected to the uranium sector will probably begin during 1981. In addition, the long lead time associated with mine development assures that the first sign of a recovery in uranium prices will renew interest in Niger's substantial reserves.

Other serious threats to Niger's economy are external. Relations with Libya deteriorated when Libyan troops moved into Chad. The Government of Niger is deeply concerned about Libyan designs on its territory and meddling in its internal affairs. Niger's fears about further Libyan expansionism are tempered by continued close ties to France and amicable relations with its other neighbors. There is no significant domestic opposition to the Government in Niger.

Agriculture

Current government policy gives top priority to improving grain production to meet domestic consumption needs and to upgrading the animal herds, which provide the livelihood of Niger's substantial nomadic population. Production in 1980 of the principal food crops of millet and sorghum totaled 1,749,150 metric tons (MT) according to government estimates. This represents a surplus of 120,000 MT over the grain requirements of Niger's population. Other sources agree that very favorable weather conditions and modest pest losses have contributed to a bumper crop, probably the biggest since independence. Even so, a substantial quantity of rice will need to be imported to satisfy urban demand.

Niger's livestock sector was the hardest hit by the Sahel drought. Between 1972 and 1974, the cattle herds dropped by 35 percent, a loss of nearly 2.2 million head; in some areas losses were total. The Government's livestock reconstitution program, begun in 1974, consisted of a ban on the export of fertile adult animals as well as herd improvement measures financed largely by the international community. It was officially terminated in early 1980. At that time, the Government announced that the goals of the program had been realized. However, research and experimentation in the livestock sector continue unabated.

Growth of Niger's main cash crops, peanuts and cotton, has been neglected in recent years. Government policy and private demand for food grains have undermined farmer interest in cultivation of peanuts and cotton. Crop losses due to destruction by rodents and insect-borne disease reinforce this downward trend. Exports of both of these crops have been halted for several years as deliveries of peanuts to the oil mills have fallen from 145,000 MT in 1972 to under 9,000 MT in 1979, and raw cotton production in 1980 fell below 6,000 MT, less than one-third of installed ginning capacity. Although the Government is hoping higher prices and reconstituted private grain reserves will revive farmer interest in these traditional cash crops, there is no sign of a turnabout yet. Production of cowpeas or niebe, a highprotein legume mainly exported to Nigeria, increased dramatically after the drought. However, as production has grown, it has become more difficult to market the whole crop in Nigeria. Production in 1980 dropped to 245,000 MT from the high of 300,000 MT recorded the previous year.

Minerals

Niger's uranium production increased dramatically in 1979 and 1980. Begun in 1971 in the remote Air region, it reached 4,000 MT in 1980, compared with a total of 2,000 MT in 1978. The difference is attributable to the attainment of capacity production, 2,200 MT, by Niger's second mine, Akouta. Operated by the consortium COMINAK, incorporating Nigerien, French, Japanese, and Spanish partners, it opened in 1978. Niger's first mine, Arlit, which is operated by SOMAIR, recently remodeled its mill and increased capacity to 2,300 MT. However, production in 1980 did not exceed the previous year's total of 1,800 MT.

Niger's estimated uranium reserves exceed 160,000 MT and to date have attracted exploration efforts by 16 foreign companies from 9 different countries. In 1979, there were three different groups planning to begin mine construction almost immediately. Included among these were the SMTT group for which operating permits and financing had already been arranged, and a Nigerien-French-American (CONOCO) consortium, which planned to exploit the huge Immouraren reserves. However, as a result of the recent and severe decline in world uranium prices, all three of these projects have been postponed. In the case of SMTT, the length of the delay is not known and may depend to some extent on the Nigerien Government's posted price for 1981 uranium sales. For both the others, the foreign partners probably will not reconsider their plans until world uranium prices recover. The Nigerien Government holds equity participation in all present uranium mining concessions through its National Minerals Office (ORAREM); however, this is not required by law.

The search continues for petroleum deposits in Niger's eastern (Lake Chad) and northern (Djado) regions. To date, no finds have been made, but recent strikes in neighboring Chad offer some promise. Other minerals found in Niger are coal, tin, phosphate, copper, and iron ore. Phosphate deposits in southwest Niger are being evaluated for possible commercial value. The copper and iron ore reserves are probably not commercially exploitable at this time.

Industry

Niger's small industrial sector contributed less than 5 percent to the gross domestic product in 1979. The Government is directly involved as a partner in Niger's 27 parastatal companies and is determined to maintain its presence in the modern sector. The parastatals include most of Niger's largest industrial concerns: e.g., the national electricity utility (NEGELEC), the cement plant (SNC), and the chemical plant (SPCN), as well as a number of agro-industries—the national peanut company (SONARA), tanneries (SNCP), rice processing plants (RINI), and the textile company (SONITEX). Growth of the industrial sector is limited by a lack of domestic raw materials and a small internal market.

The construction sector continues to boom. Even the postponement of new mine construction will not seriously depress the industry as there are several other large projects ready to begin; among these is the Islamic University at Say, to be financed by Arab loans. Construction of the Kandadji Dam has become the highest priority of Niger's Government, and work could begin as early as 1983. Office and residential construction is brisk, and Niamey's first international class hotel is nearing completion.

Development Plans

In March 1980, the Government published Niger's first Five-Year Plan, covering 1979-83. As expected, the basic development strategy outlined in the Plan emphasizes the modernization of the rural sector and the attainment of self-sufficiency in food production. The industrial and energy sectors are also targeted for large investment, and the important role of private enterprise and foreign investors in reaching these goals is recognized.

Niger's Central Government budget was $336.4 million in 1980, an increase of approximately 20.7 percent over 1979 and 42.8 percent over 1978. In keeping with the direction of the Government's development plans, roughly 40 percent ($134.6 million) of the 1980 total was allocated for use through the nation's National Investment Fund (FNI). Priorities of FNI are rural development, improving social and physical infrastructure, and development of the country's human resources through increased education and health services.

A coal mine-electricity generating plant being built by the Societe Nigerien de Charbon (SONICHAR) is nearing completion. Coal is already being mined and stockpiled in anticipation of production of the first electricity in April 1981. The principal beneficiaries will be the two uranium mnes and the city of Agadez. A second construction phase doubling installed capacity to 32 MW will follow directly on the first. Production from the first phase alone will reduce Niger's petroleum imports by approximately 25 percent. The total cost of the project exceeds $125 million.

The Second Maradi Rural Development Project, an extension of the ongoing Maradi Rural Development Project, will be implemented over a 5-year period from July 1980 to June 1985. Financed by France, the World Bank, Niger, and the United States, the project seeks to increase agricultural production and extend irrigation to improve farm incomes. Total cost of the project is estimated at $47.5 million.

Feasibility studies have been completed on the Kandadji Dam Project on the Niger River. Construction is not to begin until 1983 and is expected to take 4 years. The construction cost of the dam and hydroelectric facilities is estimated at $370 million. For information write: Haut Commissioner, Autorite du Barrage du Kandadji, Niamey, Niger, West Africa.

Niger Economic Indicators

(All values in U.S. millions of dollars and represent period average unless otherwise indicated.)

	1979	1978	1977
Production and Government Expenditures			
GDP at Current Price	2,802.5	1,523.2	564.5
Population (millions).................	5.3	5.23	5.1
Per Capita GDP, Current Prices	393.9	295.8	110.6
Central Government Budget	278.8	192.3	141.6
Money and Prices			
Money Supply (M2)....................	314.5	240.2	156.1
Interest Rates			
Central Bank (BCEAO).............	5.5-8%	5.5-8%	5.5-8%
Commercial Banks	6.5-13%	6.5-13%	6.5-13%
Consumer Price Indices: (1964=100) ...			
Low Income......................	331.6	306.1	278.1
High Income	256.3	218.5	197.5
Balance of Payments and Trade			
Net Foreign Reserves.................	117.5	112.9	88.2
External Debt.......................	547.0	394.0	158.9
Balance of Payments	-2.3	7.9	—
Balance of Trade	-61.0	-101.0	-78.2

Note: Exchange Rates: (1979) US$=212.72 fCFA, (1978) US$=225.64 fCFA, (1977) US$=242.33 fCFA.

Source: Foreign Economic Trends—Niger, prepared by the American Embassy in Niamey.

Trade Regulations

Trade Policy

Niger is an associate state of the European Economic Community (EEC) and a member of the following organizations:

Council of the Entente—coordinates member countries' economic and commercial policies. Council tries to eliminate trade barriers among members. Other member states include: Benin, Ivory Coast, Togo, and Upper Volta.

Economic Community of West African States (ECOWAS)—represents the largest (and potentially the most important) single economic grouping in Africa. Other member nations are Benin, Gambia, Ghana, Republic of Guinea, Guinea-Bissau, Ivory Coast, Liberia, Mali, Mauritania, Togo, Nigeria, Senegal, Sierra Leone, Upper Volta, and Cape Verde. The Community's objectives are cooperation in industry, transport, telecommunications, energy, agriculture, natural resources, commerce, monetary and financial matters, and social and cultural functions.

West African Economic Community—organization seeks to better coordinate and develop policies among member states with regards to transport and communications, agricultural and industrial products, energy and external trade. Members include Ivory Coast, Mali, Mauritania, Senegal, and Upper Volta.

Lome Convention—Niger is also an adherent to the Lome II Convention. This 5-year, trade-and-aid treaty between the EEC and 54 African, Caribbean, and Pacific (ACP) nations was negotiated in 1979. The accord, which replaces previous agreements (e.g., Lome I, the Yaounde Convention, and the Arusha Agreement), does not require that member countries extend preferential tariff treatment to EEC nations. It includes provisions to compensate countries dependent on raw material and farm exports for price and production level fluctuations.

Currency

The currency of Niger is the African Financial Community (Communite Financiere Africaine) franc or CFA franc. The CFA franc is officially maintained at the rate of 50 CFA francs per French franc (255.27 CFA francs=$1, April 1981). All duties and taxes are payable in local currency and conversion of foreign currencies into CFA francs is guaranteed by the Bank of France at the official rate.

Technical Standards

The metric system of weights and measures is used in Niger. Electric current is A.C., 50 cycles, 220/380 volts, 1, 3 phases, and 2, 3, 4 wires.

Import Controls

Imports are divided into two groups: those requiring an import license and liberalized imports which may be brought in without quantitative restrictions on the basis of an import certificate made out by the importer. When import licenses are required, they are valid for 6 months from issuance date and may be extended for 3 months on the basis of reliable proof from the supplier that such an extension is necessary. Goods should be shipped before expiration of the license. A 5 percent tolerance in licensed valued of goods (maximum 25,000 CFA francs) may be permitted if specified circumstances appear.

Imports of soap, cement, and certain printed cotton fabrics are prohibited, irrespective of origin, unless a special authorization is issued by the Ministry of Economic Affairs, Commerce, and Industry. The import from any source of rice, wheat flour, butane gas, many types of fabric, certain footwear, and certain plastic goods requires prior authorization, irrespective of whether an import license or import certificate is also required.

The Societe Nationale de Commerce et de Production du Niger (COPRO-NIGER), Boite Postale 615, Niamey, has a monopoly over the importation of various consumer goods—including dried or concentrated milk, tomato puree, matches, tomatoes, green tea, wheat, wheat flour, certain cane and beet sugar and malt extractions for infant foods, cigarettes, crude salt in sacks, certain textiles, cotton blankets, and jute-bags (new or used). Imports from South Africa are prohibited.

The import license or import certificate entitles importers to purchase the necessary exchange, provided that the authorized bank is satisfied that the import transaction is genuine and in accordance with the import title. Import certificates require the visa of the External Finance Bureau when the goods have to be paid for before they are imported. All import transactions with foreign countries must be domiciled with an authorized bank when valued at more than 25,000 CFA francs, c.i.f. Nigerien border.

Duties and Taxes on Imports

Customs duties are levied on an ad valorem c.i.f. basis, which includes the purchase price, transport charges, export duties, price of packaging not dutiable separately, insurance, commissions, freight, and other expenses incurred in shipping the goods to the port of entry. Dutiable value, however, does not include charges for transportation within the country (e.g., from the dock to the warehouse).

In addition to customs duties, Niger levies the following taxes on imported goods:

Statistical Tax.—This tax is levied at a rate of 2.5 percent of the c.i.f. value or of the "fixed market value" (valeur mercuriale), if any, for all imported goods, (unless specifically exempted therefrom).

Standard or Transaction Tax.—This tax is assessed at 26 percent of the c.i.f. value plus fiscal duty, customs duty, and statistical tax paid on most imported goods. For a list of specified commodities comprising, in the main, various medications (including some veterinary medicines), raw materials for industry, machinery, industrial equipment, and vehicles the rate is 12 percent. Some basic food products such as cereal grains, sugar, fresh milk, and salt, butter, as well as certain types of cigarettes and insecticides, are exempted from the payment of this tax.

Consumption Tax.—This tax is assessed at varying rates on ship biscuits (hardtack), tobacco products, peanut oil, alcoholic beverages, and cotton fabric. In most cases, the tax is levied on a specific basis; estimated ad valorem equivalents range between 1 percent and 10 percent of the duty-paid value. The tax is applicable to domestically produced items, as well as to imports.

Information regarding the duties applicable to specific products entering Niger may be obtained free of charge from the Asia/Africa Division, Office of Country Marketing, International Trade Administration, U.S. Department of Commerce, Washington, D.C. 20230; or from any Department of Commerce District Office. Inquiries should contain complete product description, including CCCN, SITC, or U.S. Schedule E Export Commodity numbers, if known.

Special Customs Requirements

Commercial Invoice.—No special form is required. The invoice should contain the names of exporter and consignee, number and types of packages, marks and numbers on packages, net and gross weights, the c.i.f. value; terms of sale, and an accurate description of the merchandise. To meet the requirements in relation to the price and distribution regulations, the importer must have the following information: Ex-factory price, f.o.b. price, and cost of shipping and insurance.

Bills of Lading.—No special regulations exist for bills of lading, but marks of identification and name and address of consignee should be clearly indicated. To ensure prompt clearance by Customs, the shipping marks, the number on bills of lading, and the number on invoices should correspond exactly with those on the goods.

Packaging List.—Although not legally required, a packing list is recommended.

U.S. Shipper's Export Declaration.—This form is necessary if the value of the shipment is more than $250 or where a validated export license is required. The $250 exemption applies to foods under each Schedule E number in a single shipment from one exporter to one importer.

Certificate of Origin.—A certificate of origin is required. In cases of doubt as to the origin of goods, Nigerien Customs officers may request in addition to a certificate of origin whatever other documents they consider necessary to ascertain the true origin of the goods. A combined invoice and certificate of origin may be used instead of separate forms for the commercial invoice and certificate of origin. Printed forms of this document are available from commercial stationers, but typewritten copies are usually acceptable if they follow the form exactly.

Samples and Advertising.—In general, samples that have no commercial value or that have been made unusable by mutilation may enter free of duty. However, such goods must be marked "No Commercial Value (Aucune Valeur Commerciale)." Single catalogs or small packets of brochures marked "Imprimes" are allowed entry free of duty.

Marking of Goods.—All goods should be marked with country of origin. For the United States, "Made in U.S.A." should be satisfactory. All merchandise that originates in one country and transits another country before entering Niger should have markings identifying the true country of origin.

Marking of Packages.—There are no regulations for marking packages. According to sound shipping practice, these packages should bear the consignee's mark including port mark and be numbered unless the shipment is such that the contents of the packages can be readily identified without numbers.

Labeling/Packing of Hazardous and/or Restricted Materials.—Many, if not most, United Nations members have adopted the UN recommendations for the labeling and packing of hazardous materials in a standardized manner and style. Exporters to Niger should ascertain from their importers in that nation whether or not Niger is currently adhering to these requirements, and if so, how they should conform in order that the goods in question will be importable. In addition, shippers must take into consideration any special Nigerien requirements in this regard. If goods are shipped by air, International Air Transport Association regulations regarding packing, labeling, and documentation must be met (the international airline chosen can assist in explaining the latest measures). For goods shipped by boat, the latest International Maritime Consultative Organization requirements usually have to be met. Subscribers exporting from the United States or whose goods will transit the United States must meet strict U.S. regulations, irrespective of the mode of transport used. (Some are additional to international requirements; others are based on such requirements.)

Modes of Shipment

Air Cargo.—The carrier's Air waybill, commercial invoice in duplicate, and U.S. Shipper's Export Declaration are required.

The following carriers operate to Niamey:

Air Afrique
683 Fifth Avenue
New York
(Regular service from New York via Dakar to Niamey).

UTA French Airlines
9841 Airport Boulevard
Suite 1000
Los Angeles
(Regular service from New York, Boston, Washington, D.C., Chicago, Philadelphia, Houston, and Los Angeles, via Paris, to Niamey).

Air Niger
P.O. Box 865
Niamey
(national air service)

Shipping Information.—Since Niger is a landlocked nation, all of its trade moves through ports of neighboring countries, chiefly through the port of Cotonou, Benin. Inland transportation is either by road or a combination of rail from Cotonou to Parakou and then 580 km by road to Niamey.

Investment

The investment code in effect since March 1974, provides for two major grace periods of tax relief and tariff protection (if necessary) allocated according to levels of investment in selected fields: energy production, mineral exploration and mining, textiles, agriculture, fertilizers, consumer goods, forestry, husbandry, fishing, and hotels. While foreign investors have concentrated investments in the mining sector, the code seeks to encourage and attract private investment and participation, foreign and local, throughout the economy. Government participation in commercial ventures is common in Niger, but it is not required by law. Principal investment disincentives are red tape, the shortage of local capital, the unavailability of suitable labor, and the limited local market.

Niger's principal banks are B.I.A.O., Banque de Developement de la Republique du Niger and Banque Centrale des Eats de l'Afrique de l'Quest, and Citibank.

Travel Notes

Legal and Bank Holidays

The following days are observed as legal and bank holidays in Niger: Jan. 1; April 15, April 16, Easter Monday; May 1, Labor Day; Aug. 3, Independence Day; Dec. 18, Proclamation of the Republic; Dec. 25. In addition, there are Muslim religious days (in particular, Id Al-adha, Maulid al-nabi, and Id al-fitr) whose dates cannot be determined accurately far in advance as they are based on the lunar calendar. Banking hours are 8 a.m. to 11:30 a.m. and 4 p.m. to 5 p.m., Monday through Friday. Banks are closed on Saturdays.

Business Hours

Office hours in Niger are from 7:30 a.m. to 12:30 p.m., and 4-6 p.m. Monday through Friday and 7:30 a.m. to 12:30 p.m. on Saturdays.

Passport Requirements

Applications for visas should be made either to the Nigerien Embassy in Washington, D.C. or to the Permanent Mission to the United Nations in New York. For addresses of these offices see the section on Niger's representatives in the United States.

Transit Visa.—The following information is needed for a Transit Visa: A valid passport, two applicaiton forms fully completed and signed, two recent photographs, and international vaccination certificates (yellow fever and cholera).

Tourist Visa.—The following information is needed for a Tourist Visa: Same items as needed for a Transit Visa plus a letter from the travel agent stating that a round trip ticket has been purchased or a letter from the bank stating that the traveler has at least $500 in savings account (this applies to travelers who are going by road).

The fees for the visas are as follows: 1 to 7 days, $2.10; 8 to 30 days, $4.20; and 30 to 90 days, $8.30. For a stay of over 3 months, prior arrangements must be made by applicant with the Ministry of Foreign Affairs in Niamey.

Communications

Niamey has reasonably good telephone and telegraph facilities. However, long distance calls from the United States may take several hours to complete and the quality of reception can be uncertain (improvements are underway). A 3 minute call from the eastern United States to Naimey costs about $16. The time difference between Eastern Standard time and Niamey is 6 hours. International airmail letters to or from the U.S. east coast take from 6 to 10 days and cost 40^c per half ounce from the United States to Niamey, and about 55^c from Niamey to the United States, for each half ounce. International parcel post can be used for packages and magazines, but service is unreliable.

Health

Immunization is suggested for yellow fever, tetanus, typhoid, typhus, and polio. Although Niamey has a filtering plant, water is unsafe to drink and should be filtered and boiled or treated with purification pills before use. Outside Niamey, use extreme caution in drinking water.

Transportation

Travel within Niger and to neighboring countries is by air and road. Scheduled air service is available to Niger's important towns (Tahous, Maradi, Zinder, and Agadez) and to capitals of neighboring countries (Cotonou, Abidjan, Ouagadougou, Bamako, Lagos, and Dakar). Major airlines operating in Niger are UTA and Air Afrique.

Of the three major roads leading from Niamey one is paved for the first 100 km (60 mi.), another is paved for 960 km (580 mi.), and the third is not paved. Other roads in Niger are paved for short distances.

The only adequate public transportation in Niamey is the taxi, which is inexpensive and generally obtainable in business areas or near the markets.

The following are principal hotels in Niger: Niamey: Grand Hotel du Niger, Hotel Rivoli, Hotel Terminus, Hotel Le Sahel, Hotel Tenare, and Hotel Gaweye; Maradi: Djan Gorzo Hotel; and Zinder: Damagaram Hotel.

Information Contacts

Nigerien Representation in the United States

Niger is represented in the United States by an Embassy at 2204 R Street, N.W., Washington, D.C. 20008 (Telephone: (202) 483-4224) and by a Mission to the United Nations at 417 East 50th Street, New York, New York 10022 (Telephone (212) 421-3260, 9 a.m. to 5 p.m., closed Saturdays). There is also an Honorary Consulate at 417 East 50th Street, New York, New York 10022.

United States Representation in Niger

The United States is represented in Niger by the American Embassy at Niamey (Address: Boite Postale 201 Telephone: 72-26-61/62/63/64 and 72-26-70).

Additional Sources of Information

Chamber of Commerce,
Agriculture and Industry
B.P. 209
Niamey

Caisse de Stabilisation
des Prix des Produits du Niger
P.O. Box 480
Niamey

COPRO-NIGER (state trading company)
B.P. 615
Niamey

Office National du Tourisme
P.O. Box 612
Niamey

Market Profile—NIGER

Foreign Trade

Imports.—$547 million in 1981; $480 million in 1982. Major suppliers in 1981 by percentage: France, 47.6; West Germany, 11.1; Ivory Coast, 5.2; and United States 3. Major imports from U.S. in 1982: civil engineer and contractors equipment, trucks and special-purpose motor vehicles, telecommunications equipment, rice, mechanical handling equipment, tobacco. Total from United States $10.3 million.

Exports.—$336.5 million in 1981; $306.6 million in 1982. Major markets in 1982 by percentage: France, 73.4; Germany, 5.6; United Kingdom, 3.9; Algeria, .9. Major exports to United States in 1982: manufactured articles, collectors artwork pieces and antiques. Total to United States $0.7 million.

Trade Policy.—Associate member of European Economic Community. Member of Economic Community of West African States, and one of five members of the Conseil de l'Entente. Member of West African Economic Community and adherent to Lome Convention.

Trade Prospects.—Capital goods and engineering services as needed in support of development projects.

Foreign Investment

Primarily French, significant Canadian and Libyan interest. Investment guarantee agreement with United States in force. Growing American interest in banking and minerals. Liberal investment code in 1974.

Investment Prospects.—Energy production, mineral exploration, textiles, agriculture, fertilizers, consumer goods, forestry, livestock, fishing, and hotels.

Finance

Currency.—CFA franc (399 CFA francs=US$1, Oct. 1983), issued by Central Bank of West African States which serves six member nations of the West African Monetary Union. France guarantees unlimited convertibility of CFA francs into French franc. Money and near-money supply $358 million as of 1981.

Domestic Credit and Investment.—Central Bank, one commercial bank, three development banks, a credit institution, postal checking system, and a French public institution, Caisse Centrale de Cooperation Economique. Deposits of the price stabilization board ease Niger's banking system.

National Budget.—The Central Government Budget for 1981 was estimated at $293.1 million.

Foreign Aid.—Foreign aid totaled $240 million in 1981, principally French, including technical assistance, development projects, and budget subsidy. World Bank, U.N., EEC, West Germany, and Canada are other significant contributors.

Balance of Trade.—A deficit of $231 million in 1981. Foreign reserves were $92.2 million in 1981. External debt $550.2 million.

Economy

Agricultural and pastoral. Geographically remote, arid climate, poor soil. Continued 4-percent net growth rate will depend on mineral exploitation and regional cooperation.

GDP.—$2.2 billion in 1981; $403.9 per capita.

Agriculture

Agriculture.-Contributes 60 percent of GDP. Principally subsistence. Millet, cowpeas, and sorghum are main food crops. Government is moving increasingly to irrigated agriculture with emphasis on rice production. Peanuts, cotton, and cowpeas are major foreign exchange earners.

Industry.—Accounted for 10 percent of GDP in 1981; electricity production, metalworking, chemicals, cement production, food processing, tanneries, and textile plant.

Commerce.—Virtual government monopoly. Contributes about 20 percent to GDP.

Mining.—Uranium: Niger's known uranium reserves rank fifth in world. Extensive phosphate deposits are being evaluated.

Development Plan.—The Government Five-Year Development Plan, 1979-83, emphasizes greater agricultural productivity, an improved rural infrastructure, and development of the country's human resources through increased education and easier access to health services.

Basic Economic Facilities

Transportation.—Niger River is least expensive trade route. New international air terminal at Niamey; 62 usable airfields. Approximately 26,001 motor vehicles estimated in 1980. 4,711 miles of road (23 percent paved, 37 percent gravel). No railroad, but planning underway to construct one by mid-1980's.

Communications.—Improvements planned in telecommunications system with African Development Bank loan. Government radio and TV broadcasting facilities. Approximately 8,000 telephones in country. 10 AM radio station and 1 TV station; 1 Atlantic Ocean satellite station.

Power.—70 million kWh produced in 1977, with 20,000 kW capacity, 10 kWh per capita.

Natural Resources

Land.—490,000 square miles, approximately the size of Texas, Oklahoma, and New Mexico combined. Landlocked plateau; mainly savanna to the south, desert to the north, mountainous center, about 3 percent cultivated.

Climate.—Hot and dry, particularly in north. Extreme differences between day and night temperatures. June to September precipitation.

Forests. Over 10 percent of total area, almost all in the southwest.

Population

Size.—5.4 million in 1980, annual growth rate 2.8 percent; less than 5 percent urban. Principal city and capital, Niamey, 100,000, Zinder, 25,000, Mardi, 20,000.

Language.—French.

Education.—Literacy rate, 6 percent. 14 percent of school-age population attend school. College d'Enseignment Superieur, only university, opened in October 1972.

Labor.—90 percent in agriculture. Approximately 26,000 wage earners.

Marketing in Nigeria

Contents

Report Revised April 1983

Trade Outlook

Despite recent declines in its oil income, Nigeria remains the richest country in Black Africa, with substantial petroleum reserves and large, unexploited deposits of natural gas. It continues to offer significant business opportunities to American firms with a strong commitment to the market over the long term. The priorities given in the annual budget messages offer the best market guide. In general, Nigeria is seeking import substitution and industries in areas where it has raw materials.

Relying on oil exports for over 90 percent of its foreign exchange earnings and 80 percent of government revenues, Nigeria needs high oil sales to sustain its economic growth. During 1982, Nigeria's balance-of-trade position deteriorated as oil production declined about 8 percent following a 30 percent drop in 1981. It is estimated that Nigeria's current-account deficit amounted to $5 billion in 1982. Because Nigeria had already drawn down its foreign reserves, this deficit was financed by slow payment of short-term obligations. These pressures forced Nigeria to lower its oil prices in the face of severe competition from North Sea crude.

Steep oil price increases early in 1980 and a relatively strong level of production yielded record export earnings in 1980 of over $26 billion. This high level of income not only fueled a 62 percent increase in imports, to $15.8 billion, but supported a doubling of external reserves to $10.7 billion. During 1981, Nigeria's balance of trade deteriorated significantly; oil income was $17 billion, but imports continued to climb, to $24 billion ($18 billion for merchandise imports and $6 billion for services). Exports amounted to $17 billion and imports $19 billion during 1982.

The oil crisis brought about a reversal of the slight liberalization in foreign exchange and import measures evidenced in 1980. In April 1982, the Government imposed a series of fiscal, monetary, exchange, and antismuggling measures designed to cut Nigeria's imports by a third. The list of prohibited imports and licensable imports was extended. On January 1, 1983, the Government imposed additional controls designed to hold imports to $11 billion annually. Practically all imports goods now require import licenses.

Fourth National Development Plan

Although Nigeria's President has acknowledged that the country's Fourth National Development Plan will have to be restructured in terms of timing and funding, the Plan, announced in January 1981, still provides a general guide to Nigeria's economic priorities. The basic goals of the Fourth Plan are to develop Nigeria's physical and social infrastructure, and agricultural and industrial bases so that the country will be less dependent upon the fluctuations of the world oil market. Over 7,900 projects were listed in the Plan, with estimated investments totaling $125-150 billion during 1981-85. Priority sectors are agriculture, industry, and housing. High priority also was given to construction of the new Federal capital at Abuja.

The 1983 Federal Budget, announced in November 1982, is an austere budget predicated on an oil production level of about 1 million barrels per day (bpd). Budget expenditures total $4.9 billion, while capital expenditures, estimated at $10.4 billion, are 10 percent less than the 1982 levels. A significant increase is projected for foreign borrowing, which is estimated to reach over $4.5 billion for the year. Areas scheduled to receive capital expenditures cuts are housing (63 percent), health (28 percent), and education (24 percent). Funds for industrialization, primarily iron and steel projects, and construction of the Federal capital at Abuja, which will receive 2.5 percent of the budget, were increased.

Trade with the United States

In 1981, the value of U.S. exports totaled $1.5 billion, a 32 percent increase over 1980 and a 141 percent increase over the $632 million worth of exports in 1979. In spite of this increase, the U.S. market share remains at less than 9 percent, with major competition coming from the United Kingdom (19 percent), West Germany (12 percent), and Japan (10 percent). In 1982, U.S. exports totaled $1.3 billion, down 13 percent from the 1981 level. Nigerian imports dropped sharply in 1982 as a result of new import control measures.

While Nigeria is the second largest supplier of crude oil to the United States, behind Saudi Arabia, the United States has consistently maintained a negative balance of trade with Nigeria. In 1982, U.S imports from Nigeria totaled $2 billion, 99 percent of which was oil.

Although it is faced with the need to adjust to declining demand and prices for oil, Nigeria remains a viable long-term market. It offers excellent opportunities for firms willing to meet the challenge. The following areas offer the best prospects for U.S exports to Nigeria: agriculture/agribusiness services supplies, and equipment; engineering services building equipment and supplies; industrial machinery, particularly for agribusiness and food processing; petrochemicals; metallurgy; telecommunications equipment and services; office equipment and supplies; and consultancy contracts.

U.S. Export Promotions

Several events have improved the climate in Nigeria for American busines.

In January 1982, Secretary of Commerce Baldrige and Secretary of Agriculture Block led a high-level trade and investment mission of 25 senior U.S. executives to Nigeria. The mission uncovered substantial opportunities in such sectors as agriculture commodities, agribusiness, construction, communications, and mining. The two Secretaries, along with the Chairman of the Export-Import Bank and the President of the Overseas Private Investment Corporation, met a spectrum of government leaders at the highest levels to discuss further areas of cooperation.

The Commerce Department's exhibition at the Kaduna International Trade Fair in February 1982 was the first U.S. commercial exhibition in northern Nigeria and the first anywhere in Nigeria in several years. The 60 American companies promoted a variety of products. Those enjoying the greatest interest were involved in agricultural development (grain storage, farm equipment, solar energy, and water resources), agricultural commodities, office equipment, and consumer goods (housewares, prepared foods, and cosmetics).

The U.S. Chamber of Commerce and the Nigerian Association of Chambers of Commerce, Industry, Mining, and Agriculture have signed an agreement to form the U.S. Nigerian Business Council, which will exchange information and will act to improve commercial relations and to remove impediments to increased economic cooperation between the United States and Nigeria.

The Government's Role in the Economy

The Federal Government's Structure

On October 1, 1979, after 13 years of military rule, a new constitution for the Federal Republic of Nigeria entered into force. The basic structure of the constitution resembles that of the United States, providing for a government with separate and independent executive, legislative, and judicial branches.

The executive branch consists of a president and vice president, elected every 4 years. The president nominates the cabinet and the ministers of the executive branch departments and also serves as commander-in-chief of the armed forces. The constitution provides for a governor of each state who has roughly parallel executive powers.

The National Assembly is a bicameral legislative body all of whose members are elected every 4 years.

The Senate consists of five members from each of the 19 states, and the House of Representatives consists of 449 members apportioned among the states by population. Each of the 19 states has its own unicameral House of Assembly.

Political Parties

There are currently six political parties registered with the Nigerian Federal Electoral Commission (FEDECO): the ruling National Party of Nigeria (NPN), headed by President Shagari, who was inaugurated in October 1979; the Unity Party of Nigeria (UPN), the Nigerian Peoples Party (NPP), the Peoples Redemption Party (PRP), the Great Nigeria Peoples Party (GNPP), and the Nigeria Advance Party (NAP). The constitution provides that additional parties can be formed, but they must prove that they have a national character. They cannot be based solely on tribal or regional consideration.

The Federal Government's Authority

The Federal Government plays the dominant role in Nigeria's economic progress. It is the largest employer of salaried Nigerians—employing 15 percent of the work force. It controls the purse strings of the national budget—an estimated $15.3 billion in FY 1983—and revenues from oil—an estimated $10 billion for 1983. It apportions funds to the states, coordinates and encourages growth of each state in the national interest, and establishes national development planning priorities. It maintains operational authority over parastatal corporations.

The Federal Government is the principal importer and exporter. It grants subsidies or makes loans and attempts to control inflation in the interest of balanced real growth. It makes commercial and economic policy and implements decisions with respect to diversification, indigenization, foreign interests, increased trade, and investment.

State Governments' Authority

While Nigeria is a federation of 19 states and the new constitution outlines a system of government in which the states have a certain amount of autonomy, the states receive most of their revenue from the Federal Government according to a formula based on population and other factors. A new allocation system, devised in 1981, allocates roughly 55 percent of revenues to the Federal Government, 35 percent to the states, and 10 percent to local governments.

Although they have relatively few resources for generating revenue within their borders, the states may individually determine policy on matters such as education, health care, and local industrial development.

Growth Trends

Gross Domestic Product

Gross domestic product (GDP) real growth averaged approximately 8 percent during the 1970's. In 1973-74, when revenues from the oil boom first enabled the Nigerian Government to embark upon a massive effort to accelerate economic development, through 1978-79, the fastest growing sectors were transportation, construction, solid minerals, manufacturing, and government services. The crude oil sector, estimated at 45 percent of GDP in 1973-74, grew at only 3.4 percent from 1973-74 to 1978-79, due to the up and downs of the world oil market.

The Fourth Plan, based on 1977-78 constant prices, predicts that GDP at factor costs will grow from an estimated 36.1 billion naira ($54.9 billion) in 1980 to about 51.1 billion naira ($77.7 billion) in 1985. This represents an annual growth rate of 7.2 percent over the 5 year period. The fastest growing sectors are expected to be manufacturing, utilities, and communications (15 percent each); transport and government services (12 percent each); wholesale and retail trade and other services (10 percent each); and housing (8 percent). According to the Plan, agriculture is expected to grow at an annual rate of 4 percent, construction at 5 percent, and mining and quarrying, 2 percent. In line with the objective of diversifying the economy,. the mining sector (including oil) is expected to decline from 23.5 percent of GDP in 1980 to 18.3 percent in 1985. Manufacturing is expected to rise from 7.4 to 10.5 percent. The public sector is expected to account for 86 percent of capital investment spending.

In current prices, there was a 12.7 percent increase in GDP from 44.9 billion naira ($68.2 billion) in 1979 to 50.6 billion naira ($76.9 billion) in 1980. This is largely attributed to the increase in the price and production of oil during that period. This growth slowed considerably in 1981 to an estimated 6.7 percent.

Nigeria, with a population of 80-100 million, is one of the world's 10 most populous nations. Estimated per capita income is about $750, with the majority of wealth in the hands of a very few. Approximately 75 percent of the population consists of subsistence level farmers.

Agriculture, once the mainstay of the Nigerian economy, now takes a back seat to petroleum. Oil now accounts for about 23.5 percent of GDP, more than 90 percent of exports, and 80 percent of Federal Government revenues. As a result, Nigeria has developed many of the characteristics of a dual economy, dominated by the oil sector in all measures of relative importance save employment.

Natural Resources

Petroleum. — Nigeria is among the 10 largest crude petroleum producing nations in the world. Proven recoverable reserves are estimated at 16.7 billion barrels, sufficient to sustain production levels of 2-2.5 million bdp well into the 1990's. Production, which averaged 2.06 million bpd in 1980, is currently under 1.3 million bdp. Approximately 90 percent of Nigeria's crude is exported, nearly 50 percent to the United States. In 1982, Nigeria supplied about 18 percent of the crude petroleum imported by the United States.

Over 3,000 exploratory and development wells have been drilled in Nigeria. Most of the oil is pumped presently from some 148 fields, mostly onshore fields in the Niger Delta area in the southeastern part of the country. Exploration also is being carried out in the Anambra and Lake Chad basin areas.

There are 12 main companies exploring for or extracting petroleum in Nigeria. The major one is Shell, which accounts for over 50 percent of total production. Gulf is a distant second followed by Mobil. Others include AGIP/Phillips, ELF, Texaco, Pan-Ocean, and Ashland. The Federal Government, through the Nigerian National Petroleum Corp. (NNPC), is the largest shareholder (60 percent) in all production operations.

Nigeria has three operating petroleum refineries: one at Alesa-Eleme near Port Harcourt with a 60,000 bdp capacity; one at Warri with a 100,000 bdp capacity; and one at Kaduna, which came into operation in 1980, also with a 100,000 bdp capacity. According to the Fourth Plan, there are plans to build a fourth refinery with a 200,000 bdp capacity at Warri and to raise the production capacities at Warri and Kaduna to 120,000 bdp each. Nigeria is a net importer of refined oil.

Domestic consumption of petroleum is still relatively low at about 225,000 bdp. Demand is estimated to be growing at 20 percent per year and could represent as much as 50 percent of production by 1990.

A network of pipelines and storage depots to distribute petroleum products throughout the country was planned during the Third Plan period (1975-80). Some of these pipelines and depots have been completed while others are still under construction. During the present Plan period, emphasis will shift to consolidtion of the pipeline network and construction of more depots.

Natural Gas.—Natural gas, produced mostly in association with crude oil, is being flared at a rate of 2 billion cubic feet per day. However, most of Nigeria's gas production is lost through flaring; less than 1 percent of production is being recovered and used domestically (mostly in power generation). The Government has sought to address this problem by requiring each producing company to develop specific proposals to eliminate flaring by January 1, 1984.

Nigeria's primary hope for exploiting its gas reserves, estimated at 75 trillion cubic feet, had been the Bonny Liquified Natural Gas (LNG) project, which would have exported close to 2 billion cubic feet per day in liquid form. Because of increasing costs and continued delays, the shareholders in the Bonny company (60 percent of which was owned by the NNPC) decided in early 1982 to liquidate the Bonny project. The Government of Nigeria has, however, reiterated its commitment to the development of an LNG project. The completion date of such a facility is now not likely before the late 1980's.

Minerals.—In addition to oil, Nigeria has deposits of other important minerals including tin, lime, coal, iron ore, lead, zinc, columbite and tantalite. However, some of these resources have not been adequately explored, and the income from them is insignificant.

Following World War II, Nigeria had been the fifth largest producer of tin in the world, but the deposits, located near Jos, have gradually been depleted and now remain only at difficult-to-reach depths. The Government, in patnership with a private company, is developing an underground mine at Ririwari in Kano State that is forecast to yield an estimated 1,000 tons of tin concentrate per year. The Government intends to hold this mine in readiness for future exploitation. Limestone is mined to supply cement factories. However, the supply of limestone still falls short of domestic demand.

The main emphasis in Nigerian mining is on iron ore and coal for the new steel plants at Ajaokuta and Warri. Nigeria has proven coal reserves of 639 million metric tons. Annual production for 1980-81 was only 114,875 metric tons. To increase production, the Nigeria Coal Corporation is re-equipping and rehabilitating the Enugu Coal Mine in Anambra State, which is expected to have a capacity of 2.5 million metric tons per year by 1985. Improvements are also being made at the Okaba, Onyeama, and Okpara mines. Investigation of the coking coal seams at Lafia/Oki is continuing with a view to exploiting sufficient quantities for the Ajaokuta blast furnace. The Associated Ores Mining Company is developing an iron ore mine at Itakpe, which is to provide 7.28 million metric tons per year for the complexes at Ajaokuta and Warri.

Agriculture

Nigeria has an area of 98.3 million hectares with 71.2 million hectares of arable land, of which only 34 million are under cultivation. Agricultural production is labor intensive. The sector employs 75 percent of the labor force, 95 percent on small farms of 2 hectares or less. Once the backbone of the economy, agriculture now contributes less than 23 percent to GDP and is growing at a rate of 1-2 percent in real terms—significantly less than the population.

Nigeria's main cash crops are cocoa, sugar, cotton, tobacco, and oil palm. Major staples include cassava, cocoyams, sweet potatoes, guinea corn, and millet. Some maize and wheat also are grown, and rice production has increased recently in response to government incentives. Livestock production is limited to beef and sheep in northern areas, and poultry throughout the country. Dairy farming is still virtually nonexistent.

Drought in the northern farm belt, increased incidence of disease and pests, the exodus of rural labor, a general lack of incentives to farmers, and low government-instituted price ceilings have combined to depress agricultural production. Except for cocoa, the major traditional bulk exports are no longer exported.

As recently as the early 1970's, Nigeria had been a net exporter of agricultural commodities. Now it is a net importer of foodstuffs. Provisional estimates indicate that Nigeria's total imports of agricultural commodities reached $2.25 billion in 1982.

Although agricultural production is low, Nigeria has the conditions necessary for vigorous agricultural development of many crops for internal consumption as well as for export. According to the International Institute for Tropical Agriculture, the low crop production and yields are due to inferior crop varieties; inadequate distribution and use of fertilizers; limited use of pesticides and fungicides; insufficient farmer credit, research, and extension services; inaccessible markets; and unattractive prices.

The Federal Government is committed to agricultural development and has made it the first priority of the Fourth National Development Plan. Over 1,200 projects and an original budget of $13 billion are identified in the agriculture section of the Plan. The Plan incorporates the stategies of the Green Revolution Program, announced in 1980, which sets forth a strategic plan for achieving agricultural self-sufficiency in the 1980's.

There are three major aspects of the Nigerian Green Revolution Program. The first, and most successful to date, is the World Bank-type projects which work with the small farmer to improve crop production potential through the provision of proper input and extension services. These programs are operated mainly through the World Bank and its rural integrated development schemes. The second aspect is the program of the 11 River Basin Development Authorities, which operate under the Ministry of Water Resources. These Authorities are attempting to revitalize Nigerian agriculture through large-scale, government-run irrigation projects. A tremendous amount of money has been spent in construction of major dams and irrigation schemes. The third aspect is an effort to promote and establish private joint ventures in all sectors of Nigerian agriculture. The U.S.-Nigerian Joint Agricultural Consultative Committee, which was established in 1980 to facilitate and expedite U.S. private investment in Nigerian agriculture, has been a leader in promoting this effort.

Of the nearly $2 billion in loans which Nigeria has received from the World Bank, roughly 43 percent of it goes to agricultural development. Presently, 21 projects are underway; 3 near completion. Most of the loans are for the development of cash crops such as cocoa and palm oil and for the Accelerated Development Area Program-Agricultural/Rural Development Projects. The U.S. Food and Agriculture Organization also is involved heavily in Nigerian agricultural projects.

The 1981-82 cocoa crop came to 180,000 metric tons. Due to the additional output from some 6,000 hectares newly planted under various World Bank programs, the outlook for the future is some-what improved. Of two planned processing plants, each with a 30,000 ton capacity, one began operation in 1982. These plants should triple the output of the Nigerian cocoa processing sector.

Production increases in the tobacco sector have been the most successful agricultural development efforts by far in the past few years. Production in 1981 was about 13,000 tons, a level which when coupled with a large increase in smuggled tobacco products has created a surplus of domestic tobacco.

Production of raw sugar during the 1982 crop year increased by 8,000 tons to 32,000 tons. The entire production increase is attributed to the new Savannah Sugar Plantation in Gongola State, which finally began limited production.

Cotton production in 1982 increased even though farmers continued to move into the production of food crops. Outturn of cotton lint was in the 28,000 ton range, far short of the amount needed by the domestic textile industry.

The oilseeds sector showed little change, and there was no reported commercial production of groundnuts. The major development in the oilseeds sector is the continued steady growth of vegetable oil imports.

Estimated grain production increased by some-what over 2 percent (150,000 tons) in 1982, mainly of continued expansion in the rice sector. Estimated rice production increased 10 percent to 1.4 million metric tons, primarily because of increased pressure from the Federal Government on the River Basin Development Authorities to bring increased acreage under rice production. Early season crops of corn and millet did reasonably well, and both showed marginal production increases. However, the late season crops (sorghum and in some areas rice) were adversely affected when the rains ended early.

Estimated production of root crops (cassava, sweet potatoes, and cocoyams) decreased as severe insect infestation problems hurt cassava output. Estimated production of other food crops such as pulses, bananas, and soybeans appears to be virtually unchanged from earlier years.

The poultry subgroup of the livestock sector continued to expand in 1982; however, no real change took place in beef, dairy, sheep, and goats production.

As far as the United States was concerned, the most significant factor about the Nigerian agricultural scene in 1981 was the continued expansion of Nigeria as a major market for U.S. agricultural exports. Sales of U.S. food stuffs to Nigeria in 1981 increased to an estimated $550 million, a 50 percent increase over the 1980 level and a 150 percent increase over 1979. U.S. sales in 1982 were $468 million.

Nigeria is still heavily dependent upon imports to meet some 90 percent of its agricultural equipment needs. Imports of tractors and other agricultural machinery totaled about $69 million in 1980 and about $96 million in 1981. It is unlikely that imports will account for less than 80 percent of agricultural machinery and equipment sales before 1986.

Construction

The construction industry has been dominated by infrastructure development—particularly roadbuilding, which at times has consumed up to 30 percent of annual capital expenditures. While the Government of Nigeria intends to continue the development of basic infrastructure, it is placing increasing importance on building construction.

With a rapidly growing population that is becoming increasingly urbanized, providing adequate housing is a major consideration for the Nigerian Government. To tackle this problem, the Federal Ministry of Housing and Environment was to construct 2,000 houses annually in each of the 19 states at a cost of $1.5 billion. The Plan also budgeted $2.4

billion to a joint Federal and State urban development project. Other housing projects are under various government rural development projects. The Federal Ministry of Industries predicts that Nigeria will need to build 750,000 housing units a year over the next 50 years to meet its needs.

The Plan allocates $3 billion to construct buildings for the secondary and college-level education system. This does not include expenditures for primary education, for which preliminary estimates are that over 150,000 classrooms will be built during the next 5 years.

The biggest construction project currently active in Nigeria is the development of the new Federal capital at Abuja. The project, the largest public works project in Africa, is estimated to cost about $17 billion. Under the Fourth Plan, $3.8 billion was allocated to Abuja for 1981-85. The Government originally expected that by 1983 the population of the new city would reach 150,000 and by the year 2000 it would reach 1.5 million. Although much of the government staff housing has been completed, building is behind schedule. However, even with the current loss of oil revenues, Abuja remains a priority project.

Most construction machinery and building materials and supplies need to be imported, although the Government has made some progress in increasing local production of certain materials, in particular bricks and cement. British, German, Italian, French, and Japanese firms who have established themselves in Nigeria actively compete on most of the major construction projects. (See Government Procurement)

Manufacturing

Apart from agriculture, the Government sees manufacturing as offering the greatest prospects for rapid development and transformation of the economy and places high priority on developing this sector during the Fourth Development Plan period. During the Plan period, the manufacturing sector is expected to grow at 15 percent a year. A total of $15.2 billion was allocated originally to the public sector program in this area. Approximately $9.7 billion is to support Federal Government participation in already identified areas such as the iron and steel industry, and the production of nitrogenous fertilizers. Approximately $1.2 billion is for the Nigerian Industrial Development Bank and the Nigerian Bank for Commerce and Industry to help make more financing available to private sector enterprises. The remaining funds are being allocated to State and local governments, some of which have substantial industrial programs.

Although the Government will continue to guide the manufaturing sector, it is encouraging private investors to take an active role in developing this sector. Encouragement is being offered to both large and small manufacturers through increased availability of financing, additional investment incentives, and the development of industrial estates. Industries that the Government has placed high priority on developing include agro-based and food processing; building materials; including such products as bricks, lime, and slag; automobile assembly; chemicals and petrochemicals; and metallurgy. Particular emphasis is being placed on increasing local content requirements. To encourage this, incentives are being offered to firms willing to integrate backwards to produce their own components or components for other industries.

Agro-based Industries. —Substantial investments have been made in food and beverage processing; however, output still fails to meet domestic demand. The beer and soft drink industries have developed rapidly. Investments also have been made in mills for grains and sugar, oil production, and some canning industries. The Government is directly involved in some other agro-based industries including two integrated dairy products and several pulp and paper projects.

Building Materials. —Another priority area is the local production of building materials. During the Third Plan period (1975-80), cement, lime, and plaster products were expanded to reduce dependence on imports. Factories at Nkalagu, Ukpilla, Calabar, and Lagos were expanded, and new factories were constructed at Asaka and Shagamu. With the exception of Nkalagu, the Federal or State Governments have an equity position in the plants. These plants still only account for about two-thirds of consumption. During the Fourth Plan period, the Federal Government plans to reduce its own involvement in this area and encourage the private sector and State governments to advance activity. Most other building materials and supplies have to be imported; therefore, the Government also is encouraging investment in these industries.

Automobile Assembly Industry. —Nigeria has two assembly facilities for passenger cars. Volkswagon, located in Lagos, produces approximately 140 cars per day. Peugeot, located in Kaduna, assembles about 75,000 cars per year and controls 64 percent of the market. Peugeot also assembles pickup trucks in Lagos. There are five major assembly facilities for commercial vehicles: Bedford in Lagos, British Leyland in Ibadan, Mercedes Benz in Enugu, Fiat in Kano, and Steyr/Ford in Bauchi. Together, they produce about 13,300 trucks and tractors (Fiat and Steyr) per year. Under the agreement each automotive assembly plant has with the Nigerian Government, the local content is eventually to reach 100 percent. Under these terms, the companies are to obtain 30 percent of their components from local sources by the end of the 3rd year of operation, 50 percent by the 5th year, 75 percent by the 8th year, and 100 percent by the 12th year. However, none of the firms is close to being able to fulfill its agreement. Production of local inputs includes tires and tubes, batteries, paints, plastic materials, mufflers/exhaust pipes, seals radiators, seat frames, and windshield glass.

Chemicals and Petrochemicals. —A major area of priority is the development of chemicals and petrochemicals. The Nigerian National Petroleum Corporation has implemented a plan for petrochemicals production, which is in its early stages. The first phase, on which construction has begun as adjuncts to the refineries at Warri and Kaduna, consists of plants for polypropylene, carbon black, detergents, benzene, and solvents. The second phase is to be an ethylene complex near Port Harcourt, consisting of the following units: VCM, PCV, caustic soda chlorine, low density polyethylene, high density polyethylene, ethylene oxide, and ethylene glycol. This phase is scheduled for completion by 1986. A third phase, which will not be underway until the mid-1980's, will be centered on aromatics, and aimed at plastic fibers, wood processing, resins, polyurethane foam and explosives.

A key project for the Government is the development of a nitrogenous fertilizer plant, for which a contract has already been signed with a U.S. technical partner. The overall cost of the project is expected to be about $623 million, excluding the cost of infrastructure development. The plant is expected to produce 1,000 metric tons of ammonia, 1,500 metric tons of urea, and 1,000 metric tons of NPK per year.

Metallurgical Industries. —The development of a steel industry has been given top priority by the Government. Under the auspices of the Ministry of Steel Development, Nigeria is attempting to meet demand of about 3.5 million metric tons of steel per year through the construction of a blast furnace complex at Ajaokuta (Ajaokuta Steel Company) and a steel reduction mill at Warri (Delta Steel Company). The completely integrated steel complex at Ajaokuta, which is being financed by the USSR, will be capable of carrying out the entire process from receiving ore to producing rolled structural sections. The ultimate production goal of 5.2 million tons of steel per year is envisaged for 1995. completion of a rolling mill using imported ingots may be completed in 1983.

Construction of the Warri (Aladja) direct reduction mill, financed by Germany and Austria, began in 1978. The Warri mill, which started operations in 1982, will eventually have a yearly capacity of 1 million tons of crude steel. In addition, rolling mills at Oshogbo, Jos, and Katsina, with an initial capacity of 210,000 tons of rolled products per year, are designed to produce rods and bars from billet to be supplied from Warri. Due to transportation problems, Katsina is being redesigned into a full ministeel complex based on scrap metal.

Trade Policy

Nigeria is a member of the General Agreement on Tariffs and Trade (GATT) and maintains a nondiscriminatory import tariff. It is also a signatory to the Lome Convention, which provides duty-free entry into the European Economic community (EEC) for certain categories of goods. Nigeria is one of the founding members of the Economic Community of West African States (ECOWAS), formed in May 1975, which seeks to facilitate trade between the 16 member nations and to promote joint development efforts. Although actual implementation of a customs union is still several years away, the treaty calls for eventual reduction or elimination of import duties among the member states.

Nigeria is a member of the British Commonwealth, the United Nations and a number of its subsidiary organizations, the World Bank, and the African Development Bank. It is a party to a number of international commodity arrangements including the following: International Cocoa Organization, International Coffee Organization, International Rubber Organization, International Cotton Advisory Committee, International Institute for Cotton, the West African Groundnuts Council, the International Tin Council, and the Organization of Petroleum Exporting Countries (OPEC).

Treaties and agreements in force between the United States and Nigeria relating to consular matters, aviation, mutual security, economic and technical cooperation, extradition, property, taxation, and trademarks were concluded originally between the United States and the United Kingdom and were continued by Nigeria upon independence in 1960. The agreement on investment guarantees was concluded in 1969 and renewed in 1975. The U.S.-Nigeria Tax Treaty expired in 1979 and is being renegotiated. Through ongoing bilateral economic discussions, the two nations have sought to continually resolve differences and to find new ways to cooperate in the areas of trade and investment.

The Nigerian Ministries of Commerce, Industries, and National Planning have responsibility for trade policy. Organizations such as the Nigerian Association of Chambers of Commerce, Industry, Mining and Agriculture and the Manufacturers' Association also influence trade policy. The Ministry of Finance, supplemented by the Central Bank of Nigeria, has responsibility for foreign exchange matters. The enforcement of importation and exportation regulations and customs, including customs and excise duties, are administered by the Board of Customs and Excise.

Trade Regulations

Current trade policy and changes in regulations and tariffs and licensing requirements are contained in the annual budget and its supplements, which are published in the *Federal Republic of Nigeria Official Gazette.* These annual changes have usually appeared each year in the March or April edition. The most recent of these, the Finance Act of 1981, which contains the 1980 budget provisions, appeared in March 1981.

In addition to these budget changes, customs and excise, as well as foreign exchange, requirements are subject to frequent changes, often with little or no prior notice. Import prohibitions have been issued by the Nigerian Government to help relieve port congestion, encourage local production, conserve foreign exchange, and curb inflation. The most recent example of this occurred in March-April 1982, when the Government acted to control Nigeria's deteriorating foreign exchange position. (See Trade Outlook.) The specific monetary, fiscal, and foreign exchange measures which President Shagari outlined on April 20, 1982, went into effect immediately, and are included, where appropriate, in the following sections.

Import Prohibition and Licensing

The Import Prohibition Order of 1980 (Finance Act of 1981) specifies goods which are absolutely prohibited in Schedule 1, defines countries (South Africa and Namibia) from which the importation of all goods is absolutely prohibited in Schedule 2, and lists items subject to import under certain conditions and which require specific import licenses in Schedule 3.

Schedule 1 prohibits, among other things, the importation of various weapons; blank invoices; matches; second-hand clothing; most spirits; beer; cigarettes; live poultry (excluding day-old chicks); vegetables, roots, and tubers; wood in the rough; eggs (except those imported by recognized hatcheries); pastry and biscuits; nuts; fruits; potatoes; tomatoes (fresh or chilled); sugar confectionary; most textiles and madeup articles of textiles; towels; most articles of domestic glassware and most other articles of glass; most domestic articles and ware of plastic;

enamelware and galvanized buckets; fresh milk; flavored or colored beet sugar; macaroni and spaghetti; most footwear; carpets; most furniture; jewelry; clothing; household candles; pearls, precious and semiprecious stones; Christmas cards, greeting cards and calendars, almanacs and diaries; toothpicks; rice in containers of less than 50 kilograms; toothpaste; specified bicycle tires and tubes; and components of the above goods imported, unassembled or disassembled.

Schedule 3 contains two parts. Part I lists goods prohibited unless imported under certain conditions specified on an item-by-item basis. Part II, which changes continually, specified those goods which may be imported for trade only under specific import licenses.

On January 1, 1983, the list of items requiring an import license was extended to cover virtually all goods. U.S. exporters should contact the nearest U.S. Department of Commerce District Office for the latest provisions.

Goods not specifically mentioned in Schedules 1, 2, or 3 or in subsequent modifications to the Finance Act's Import Prohibition Order, or those imported for the Nigerian Army, Navy, or Air Force, bona fide commercial travelers' samples or patterns, personal effects, and Nigerian returned goods may be imported under open general license.

Shippers should familiarize themselves with the import requirements for their goods and make sure that importers in Nigeria have obtained the proper license, when required, from the Internal Trade Office, Federal Ministry of Commerce. Applicants for special licenses must provide a tax clearance certificate for the past 3 years (this also is required of imported goods under open general license—see Taxes), detailed information about their company and the product to be imported, and must pay a processing fee. The application is then reviewed and approved or disapproved by the Import Licensing Review Committee. Special licenses are usually valid for the calendar year in which they are issued, although the Ministry of Commerce can revoke or modify the license at any time. When goods are shipped in contravention of licensing regulations or after a license has expired they are liable to forfeit.

Tariffs

The Nigerian Customs and Excise Tariff uses the Brussels Tariff Nomenclature (BTN). A single-column, nonpreferential import tariff schedule applies equally to all countries. Duties are either specific or ad valorem depending on the commodity. Duties are computed on the c & f value, and all imported goods must be insured by an indigenous insurance company. All import duties are payable on entry in Nigerian currency. Goods classified as nonessential or luxury items are subject to duties of 100 percent or more. Many items essential for economic development or imported by and for government use are admitted duty free.

Tariff rates, by African standards, are moderate; they favor imports of capital goods for industrial development yet tend to protect infant industries and attempt to provide an incentive to produce goods locally through high tariffs on some capital and essential consumer items. All goods entering Nigeria via Nigerian air or seaports are assessed a 5 percent port development surcharge, based on the duty payable, to aid in the development of Nigerian ports.

Import duties on raw materials necessary for local industries are generally a maximum of 10 percent ad valorem. Excise duties, imposed on most manufactured goods, are generally about 5 percent. Import duties on building materials not produced locally also are low.

A special duty may be imposed on imported goods if, in the opinion of the Government, such goods are being dumped or are being unfairly subsidized by a foreign government so as to materially injure the Nigerian market or threaten potential or established industry.

Duties previously paid may be remitted, refunded, or drawn back on abandoned, reexported, damaged, or destroyed goods, provided proper claim is made before the goods have left customs custody. Permission for reexportation must be obtained from the Board of Customs and Excise. A destruction certificate must be obtained from a customs officer to obtain a refund of duties paid on goods destroyed.

If goods mainifested for Nigeria are landed elsewhere, duties paid on them in Nigeria will be refunded only upon presentaiton of a customs certificate attesting to their landing in the other country.

Overpaid duties may be refunded upon application to Customs within 12 months of importation.

Under the Customs (Drawback) Regulations, full or partial rebate may be made if materials are imported for use in the local manufacture of goods which are then exported. The same regulations apply on materials which are purchased by and for the use of organizations or persons entitled to duty-free importation of such goods, such as with duty concessions under the "Approved User Scheme." Nigerian regulations do not, however, provide for duty suspensions, drawbacks, or rebates for temporary importation of goods except when exported by temporary residents and removed at the end of such residence, not exceeding 6 months.

Bona fide samples or patterns of no commercial value, to be used for the purpose of soliciting orders, are usually admitted duty free, at the discretion of customs officials. Nigeria is a signatory to the United Nations International Convention to Facilitate the Importation of Commercial Samples and Advertising Material. Samples of value may be imported duty free under bond. The bond, in the amount of duty leviable on such goods, is cancelled and any deposit is refunded when the samples are reexported. The Board of Customs and Excise is authorized to permit the temporary importation, without payment of duty, of motion picture films intended for advertising, educational, and scientific purposes or for exhibition at international fairs, trade shows, or similar events. Catalogs and similar printed matter imported solely for advertising purposes and other advertising matter of no commercial value, other than for the solicitation of orders, are permitted duty-free entry. The Board of Customs and Excise will accept properly documented requests for advance rulings on customs classifications of merchandise, but such rulings are only advisory.

Intent to defraud customs and similar offenses are punishable by forfeiture of the goods, a fine, prison term, or all three. Persons wishing to contest seizure of any article must file their appeal with the Board of Customs and Excise within 1 month. In addition, recent measures state that foreigners and foreign firms who are known to engage in fraudulent practices and foreign exchange malpractices will be blacklisted. Foreigners with proven cases of fraudulent practices will be deported.

Export Controls

Most agricultural products are under export controls. Under the Export Prohibition Order of 1980 (Finance Act of 1981) the following products are prohibited from export: beans, cassava tuber, groundnut oil, maize, palm oil, rice, timber (excluding ebony), milk, sugar, flour, and all imported food items. Most other agricultural items, goods manufactured outside of Nigeria, goods made wholly or partly of imported compounds, and minerals including petroleum require specific export licenses. A single tariff schedule exists for specific Nigerian exports. Unless specifically listed or under the Export Prohibition Order goods to be exported are exempt from payment of export duties. Most export duties are levied on a specific basis, as opposed to ad valorem.

There are special arrangements for taxes, royalties, duties, and other government revenue from crude oil and oil products produced and exported.

Further information or specific questions regarding Nigerian trade regulations and practices may be obtained from: the Office of African Affairs/ITA, U.S. Department of Commerce, Washington, D.C. 20230 (202-377-4388). Requests for Nigerian duties should contain a complete product description, including BTN, SIC, SITC, or U.S. Schedule B Export Commodity Number for a more accurate response.

Exchange Control

All overseas payments for goods, investment capital, profits, dividends, interest, royalties, and fees are subject to stringent foreign exchange controls. To avoid excessive and unnecessary delays and problems in the repatriation of funds from Nigeria, a thorough understanding of exchange regulations and procedures is necessary.

The Exchange Control Act of 1962, as amended, vests overall authority for exchange control with the Minister of Finance. Under the Nigerian Exchange Control (Anti-Sabotage) Decree No. 57 of 1977, anyone violating exchange controls will be subject to official sanction.

The Ministry of Finance administers some controls itself and delegates others to the Central Bank of Nigeria. According to the terms of the Exchange Control (Payments for Imports) Order Amendment 1975, the Governor of the Central Bank of Nigeria and authorized dealers (mostly commercial and merchant banks) shall release foreign exchange "in accordance with the supplier credit terms arrnged by the importer with approval of the Federal Ministry of Finance . . ." or the Bank.

The Ministry of Finance directly administers controls for the following activities: repatriation of capital and profits and dividend to any country outside Nigeria; raising of external loans, including repayments of such loans; granting of "Approved Status" to nonresident investments in Nigeria; payment for copyrights, patents, and royalties; any dealings in foreign securities, including those dealt in on the Nigerian Stock Exchange; miscellaneous payments, purchase of ships and aircrafts; purchases of Nigerian Embassies; Ministry of Defense expenditures; official tours; medical tours (public); and requests for resident, nonresident, and external accounts.

The Central Bank administers controls for football pools and any betting arrangements; compensation deals; payment for imports; education, students, etc.; commissions and brokerages; fees for airline, shipping, and fishing charters; insurance (trade and nontrade); business travel; private leave and medical tours; educational tours; home remittance, bonus gratuity, monthly remittance by salaried foreign nationals in arrears for more than 3 months, final remittance, and leave payments in excess of

more than 3 months; pension funds; cash gifts; miscellaneous payments; official tours; request for resident, nonresident, and external accounts; and pilgrimage services.

Prior Approval and Preshipment Inspection Requirements

Prior approval for all payments in Nigerian currency on any foreign currency/securities to or for the credit of any nonresident of Nigeria is required by the Exchange Control Act of 1962. Nigerian residents or companies resident in Nigeria must receive this approval before letters of credit or other banking instruments for overseas payments can be issued. The following application forms are used for exchange control purposes: Form M, application to purchase foreign currency for imports only; Form MFMF, application to purchase foreign currency/ open letters of credit (for the public sector only); and Form A, application to purchase foreign currency not for imports (ie., income, dividends, royalties, fees, etc.). These forms are obtainable from the Central Bank, its branches, and local banks.

Form M (submitted in sextuplicate) should be accompanied by a tax clearance certificate and for copies of the seller's pro forma invoice showing the price split between f.o.b. (free-on-board) and freight, with all ancillary charges such s commissions and interest charges shown separately. Where appropriate, a copy of a special import license, proof of "Approval Status," and other company information also are required. Where both the sale of goods and service are involved, as with turnkey projects, both Forms M and A are required. To avoid inspection approval and payment problems, care should be taken to make application for each component (ie., goods versus services) on the appropriate form.

Commercial and merchant banks are authorized to approve applications for Form M up to a maximum of 5,000 naira. Authorized dealers must file applications exceeding this amount with the Central Bank's approval. Form M is now valid for only 6 months.

Prior approval is closely linked to another foreign exchange requirement, the preshipment inspection. Since January 1, 1979, a Swiss company, Societe Generale de Surveillance (SGS) has been employed by the Nigerian Government to conduct preshipment inspections of most goods destined for Nigeria and to certify such goods as to quantity, quality and price. Goods valued at 5,000 naira or less are exempted from preshipment inspection.

Application for the preshipment inspection is made by the importer on Form M. Upon receipt of the Inspection Order copy of Form M, SGS contacts the seller to arrange an inspection date. To be safe, shippers should contact SGS themselves when anticipating shipment to Nigeria.

Upon completion of inspection SGS will issue a Clean Report of Finds if the inspection is satisfactory or a Non-Negotiable Report of Findings if discrepancies are revealed. Authorized dealers cannot effect payment against a letter of credit, bills for collection, or any other form of payment unless the documents presented for payment include a Clean Report of Findings by SGS.

For further information on preshipment inspection shippers should address inquiries to: SGS Control Services, Inc.; 17 Battery Place North, New York, N.Y. 10004 (212-482-8700).

Advanced Deposits on Imports

Effective April 21, 1982, the Central Bank imposed compulsory advanced deposits against the c & f value of imports as follows:

Items	Percentage deposits relative to the c & f value of imports
Raw materials	10
Spare parts	15
Food (except rice)	50
Medicaments	50
Building materials	50
Capital goods	50
Books	50
Motor vehicles and trucks	200
Motor cars	250
Other goods	250

In the case of imports under letters of credit, banks are directed to obtain the required percentage advance deposits for the particular imports from the importer before opening the letter of credit. In the case of imports under usance bills of less than 6 months' maturity from the date of shipment of goods to Nigeria and for bills for collection and payments on accounts of less than 6 months duration from the date of shipment of goods to Nigeria, importers are required to make advance deposits for imports not later than 10 days before the vessel carrying the goods arrives at any Nigerian port. All such deposits are held interest free by the Central Bank. This advance deposit requirement is waived where credit facilities of over 6 months are obtained.

Payment for Imports

Payments for imports can be approved by commercial banks if the shipping documents are presented or in accordance with such credit terms as may be arranged between importer and exporter. Payment in advance of shipment requires the ap-

proval of the Central Bank, except where prepayment is made against a letter of credit, in which case an inspection certificate for quality and value must be presented. Payments for imports of plant and machinery valued at 100,000 naira or over must be approved by the Central Bank or Ministry of Finance. The payment schedule may be arranged as follows: up to 15 percent payable against documents or signing of contract, up to 20 percent payable on delivery of goods or completion of construction, balance of about 65 percent payable according to a schedule agreed upon by importer and supplier based on the normal credit terms for the types of goods imported.

Exporters should be aware that delays in payment, often 4 to 6 months, are common. Excessive delays can usually be avoided by careful documentation and compliance with regulations. Applications for payment should be supported by the following: copy of letter of credit or bill history, original copy of approved Form M, copy of pro forma invoice, attested invoice (Form C16 includes combined certificate of origin and value), nonnegotiable bill of lading, customs bill of entry (evidence of receipt of goods), copy of certificate of insurance, SGS clean report of findings (where value of the goods exceeds 5,000 naira), tax clearance certificate, certified copy of import license where appropriate, and copy of certificate of registration of order where applicable (for goods valued at 100,000 naira or more sold on credit).

If letters of credit call for payment in foreign currencies, it is suggested that they include the following clause: "In accordance with the requirements of Nigeria Exchange Control Regulations, drafts drawn within terms and conditions of this credit will only be paid after the related goods have been landed in Nigeria and currency cover is provided by the Central Bank of Nigeria." When suppliers charge interest on payments for imports into Nigeria from the date on the bill of lading until the release of Nigerian foreign exchange and/or overdue charges, the draft covering the respective shipment should bear a clause explaining such rates, within the legal maximum, for prior approval of the bank.

Exporters are cautioned against shipping to a customer when they are not certain of the buyer's credit rating. Disreputable importers have been reported to have drawn fraudulent letters of credit and to have perpetrated other sorts of fraud. Exporters should be particularly wary of orders accompanied by bank drafts and other requests which are in obvious violation of Nigerian customs and excise and/or exchange control regulations. Credit checks on Nigerian firms should be requested from the Nigerian Embassy (Commercial Section); commercial banks with international departments; or the nearest Department of Commerce District Office, which can provide World Traders Data Reports (WTDRs) prepared by the U.S. Embassy in Lagos.

Exporters can check with the World Traders Data Reports Division, Office of Trade Information Services (OTIS/ITA, U.S. Department of Commerce, Washington, D.C. 20230; 202-377-2988) to see if a report is available on the particular firm. A "List of Nigerian Firms of Questionable or Unknown Reliability" is available for $12 through the Commerce Department's Publications Distribution Center, Room 1617 (202-377-5994). Exporters should bear in mind, however, that this list is by no means all-inclusive and should be used only as a guide.

An additional source for credit information is the Dun and Bradstreet agent in Lagos: Taibeth and Associates Group Ltd.; 5th Floor, 9 Nnamdi Azikwe Street; P.O. Box 6240; Lagos, Nigeria (Telex: 22294 TABETA NG).

Trade complaints should be referred to the Nigerian Embassy or the U.S. Embassy in Lagos via the nearest Department of Commerce District Office. Cases of fraud are beyond the jurisdiction of the U.S. Government, and exporters should be aware that once a fraud has been perpetrated it is virtually impossible to trace. For assistance, victims of criminal fraud should write to: Assistant Commissioner of Police; Interpol, Force CID; Alagbon Close, Ikoyi; Lagos, Nigeria.

Exporters are strongly recommended to insist upon confirmed, irrevocable letters of credit.

Value of Imported Goods

The value of imported goods is defined in the Second Schedule to the Customs and Excise Management Act, No. 55 of 1958, as amended. In computing the statutory value of imported goods, deductions normally allowable include trade discounts, quantity discounts, quality discounts, cash discounts, export discounts, nonassembly discounts, and bank commissions. Not alowable as deductions from statutory value of imported goods are sample discounts, pattern discounts, special consideration discounts (such as claims for breakage), currency discounts, contingency discounts, unspecified discounts, those discounts not freely available, freight, rebates, and buying commissions.

Shipping Documents

The minimum documents which the exporter must provide for commercial shipments to Nigeria irrespective of value or mode of transport, are as follows: the proforma invoice; commercial invoice (a special form—Form C16—must be used which also incorporates a certificate of value and a certificte of origin); bill of lading or air waybill; packing list, if not incorporated in the invoice; and depending on the nature of the goods being shipped or as requested by the importer/bank/letter of credit clause, various special certifictes (e.g., veterinary, sanitary, free sale, etc.) which are usually issued by the appropriate government agency in the country of origin. In addition, a U.S. Shippers Export Declaration will be required by the United States if the value of the shipment is over $500 or a validated U.S. export license is necessary. To effect entry, the importer must fill out the appropriate entry form and a Certificate of Value form based on the information furnished in the documents by the exporter. The importer also must be in possession of the following documents: import licenses (where applicable); other special import permits or certificates (where applicable) for items such as arms and ammunition, vaccines, certain chemicals, alcohol, etc.; tax clearance certificate; registration certificate (where applicable); and certificate of insurance. All imports must be covered by a Form M and by a Clean Report of Findings, unless specifically exempted from SGS preshipment inspection. Depending on circumstances, the Nigerian Customs may request various other documents from the importer.

Form C16.—Goods may be entered into Nigeria only on a special commercial invoice (Form C16) which has an "Invoice and Declaration of Value for Shipments to Nigeria" on the front and a "Certificate of Value" and "Certificate of Origin" on the back. This form is available from commercial printers such as: Unz and Co., P.O. Box 308, Jersey City, N.J. 07307 (201-795-5400); and Wolcott's, 241 South Spring St., Los Angeles, Calif. 90012 (213-624-4943)

Generally, four to six copies (at a minimum) of this invoice are required. Additional copies may be required by the importer. The invoice should be filled out strictly in accordance with detailed instructions. Experience has shown that a maximum of six adequately described tariff items may be accommodated in the space provided on one form. Continuation sheets are not permitted. Invoices covering piece goods consisting of mixed materials must show the percentage of such materials.

Among the more important details to be contained on the invoice is a clear indication of whether the exporter is the manufacturer, supplier, or in any way connected with the importer of goods. Total f.o.b. and c.i.f. prices of the goods showing component costs, i.e. unit price, packing, freight, insurance, commissions, as may be permitted under current exchange regulations, and other charges, must be clearly indicated. The invoice must be signed by the manufacturer, supplier, or exporter, and witness, or attested to by a U.S. chamber of commerce which has been approved for the purpose by the Nigerian Federal Ministry of Finance (Chambers of commerce in most large U.S. cities are approved.) Consular legalization or authentication of the attesting signature, is then required. Consular legalization is obtainable normally in 1 business day from the Nigerian Embassy in Washington, D.C. or from the Nigerian Consulate in New York City for $3.87 per signature.

Company stamps and facsimile signatures are unacceptable on the original invoice. Photographed copies are permitted as duplicates only. Supporting documents to the original invoice may be photographed copies. A separate packing list showing packing detail, description of goods, weights, marks, and numbers should be attached to the Nigerian commercial invoice form since there normally is insufficient space for such detail.

Bill of Lading or Air Waybill. — No special bill of lading or air waybill form is required. Separate bills of lading or air waybills must be prepared for each port or interior destination. Shippers should make certain that bills of lading are correct in every detail and that trade names are qualified by sufficient description of such goods. Descriptions, shipping marks, and numbers on the ship's manifest, bill of lading, packing list and invoice must all match with those on the actual goods.

To speed port clearances, avoid heavy storage fees, assist the importer in entering the goods, and initiate payment action, it is urged that bills of lading or air waybills contain a "Notify Address" at the port of entry of the goods, especially in Lagos or Apapa. For shipments by air, it is advisable to forward documents direct to whomever is expediting entry.

On government purchases, exporters should forward all shipping documents by air mail direct to the Government Coastal Agent, Coastal Agency, 3 Creek Road, Apapa, Nigeria, immediately after ship departure so that the documents will arrive before the goods.

Application for foreign exchange to pay for imported goods must be accompanied by the exchange control copy of the customs bill of entry, properly stamped with date of clearance, and a copy of the bill of lading or air waybill. It is advised that U.S. shippers provide at least one extra copy of the bill of lading to facilitate this procedure since, normally, applications for foreign exchange submitted to the Central Bank by the importer's commercial bank require at least 30 days for processing.

Special Requirements

Under the Food and Drugs Decree of 1974, which

became effective in 1976, stringent controls were placed on the sale and manufacture of food, drugs, cosmetics, and items such as pesticides. The Decree requires that all imports of such goods be accompanied by a certificate from the manufacturer to the effect that the good was manufactured in accordance with any existing standard or code of practice pertaining to such product or, where such standard or code of practice does not exist for the particular product, in accordance with international standards laid down; and a certificate issued by or on behalf of the government of the country where it was manufactured to the effect that its sale in that country would not constitute a contravention of the law of that country. Goods not accompanied by this type of certificate may experience delays on arrival or may even be refused entry into the country.

The U.S. Food and Drug Administration (FDA) *does not* issue a Certificate of Free Sale for articles of export. However, a factual statement of the status of a specific article subject to FDA jurisdiction may be provided on request. What is acceptable is subject to the demands of the Nigerian authorities at the time of shipment. In some cases, this statement will suffice. In other cases, only the statement and signature of a senior officer of the manufacturing company may be required. At other times, an attestation and legalization, such as is required for the commercial invoice, may be required.

All pharmaceuticals must be registered in Nigeria. Application for registration must be accompanied by detailed product information. Inspection officers have the right to take samples for purposes of examination and analysis of any food, drug, or cosmetic imported for use in Nigeria. Samples, data sheets, and the method of analysis of any new drug or cosmetic must be sent to the Nigerian Food and Drug Administration 3 months before the product arrives in Nigeria. The Certificate of Analysis, along with the Certificates of Manufacture and Free Sale, will be required in addition to the usual export documents.

Certain animal products, plants, seeds, and soils may not be imported into Nigeria without sanitary certificates from exporters. (In the United States, these are usually issued by the U.S. Department of Agriculture.) In addition, special Nigerian import permits or licenses are required for many of these items.

Entry and Storage of Goods

Goods imported into Nigeria may be entered for consumption or for warehousing, transit, or transshipment. Entry of goods must be accomplished within 3 days after landing, if storage charges are to be avoided. Preentry is permitted and is advisable to prevent costly warehousing charges. Preentry is required in the case of hazardous goods of any kind.

Goods properly entered for transshipment or transit are exempt from duty. Goods entered for warehousing are not subject to duty until removed and reentered for consumption. Goods entered in transit are deposited under bond in transit sheds, a government warehouse, or other secure place under customs control until transshipment. They may remain so up to 7 days free of charge. However, any handling or other warehousing charges must be paid before transshipment.

Goods may be examined and samples taken with customs officials' permission without payment of duty. However, duty is payable on the full quantity or value entered, and no duty allowance is made for samples which customs official may require for examination or analysis.

Goods dutiable on an ad valorem basis may not be withdrawn from storage piecemeal; the entire shipment must be withdrawn at once. Any part of the shipment of goods, dutiable according to other than ad valorem standards, however, may be removed from storage provided duty is paid on the portion removed and entered for consumption.

Under Customs supervision, warehoused goods may be packed, repacked, sorted, separated, or otherwise rearranged as may be necessary for their preservation or for sale or shipment. Goods may be transferred to other warehouses or removed temporarily under bond if Customs officials approve.

Goods not worth the duty assessed on them may be destroyed without payment of duty, if the Board of Customs and Excise approves. Bulky or dangerous goods are likely to incur extra storage charges if stored under government supervision and control.

Goods in transit or pending transshipment must be rewarehoused or reexported or entered for consumption within 2 years or be subject to government disposal or sale.

A bill of sight may be presented by the importer to allow examination of goods in the company of Customs officials in the event of inadequate documentary evidence of shipment interfering with perfect entry.

There are no free ports or zones in Nigeria.

During the late 1970's, port congestion, particularly in Lagos, resulted in delays of more than 60 days for the entry of merchandise. Although port capacity has increased and the situation has improved, port congestion still becomes a problem from time to time. Exporters should, therefore, take precautions and ascertain through shipping agents that their goods are properly scheduled for unloading by the Nigerian Ports Authority. Exporters will generally have to bear the cost of any demmurage charges.

Unclaimed Goods

Generally, unclaimed goods are transferred to a govenment warehouse a month after discharge. Goods which have remained in a government warehouse for one month may then be advertised for sale in the *Federal Republic of Nigeria Official Gazette.* One month after the appearance of this advertisement, unclaimed goods will be sold and proceeds used to pay for duties, storage, handling, auctioning, and other charges due. The remainder, if any, is paid to the owner of the goods if they apply within 4 years of sale; otherwise the surplus is payable to the account of the Federal Government. Goods so sold must be removed by the purchaser within 14 days, or the goods are subject to resale by the Government.

It has been common practice among less ethical importers to purposely leave goods unclaimed so as to pick them up for less than invoiced value at auction. Once again, it is important for exporters to know their importer's performance record.

Labeling, Marking, and Packing

Nigeria adopted the metric system in 1973. Since January 1, 1979, under the provisions of the Weights and Measures Decree 1974, all items entering the country must be labeled in metric terms exclusively. All products with dual (metric and nonmetric) markings will be confiscated or refused entry.

The Merchandise Marks Ordinance forbids importation of goods labeled in such a way as to infringe on trademark rights of other manufacturers. Goods bearing trade and other marks which are false or misleading also are prohibited, especially use of the Royal Arms of Great Britain or facsimiles.

All packages and goods imported into Nigeria should be marked according to shipping practice, in the absence of specific Nigerian regulations. Containerized imports must have identifying marks and numbers clearly and indelibly displayed on the container, and they must agree with the ship's manifest. When the container holds more than one consignment of goods or a consignment consists of goods of a different description, such details also must be shown on the ship's manifest.

Packages or containers of sales samples should be marked "Free Sample" or "Free Specimen" and the address side of the container must be marked "Sample of Merchandise."

Special marking regulations cover a limited group of articles, coinciding in most cases with those imports requiring licensing, certificates or permits.

including, for example: flour, gunpowder, nails, rice, salt, some soaps, yarns, wools, crochet cotton, blueing, candles, and sugar.

Parcels should be securely packed and wrapped in waterproof covers to guard against the elements, pilferage, and rough handling. Goods packed in straw may be refused entry due to limitations on material, such as straw originating from small cereals.

Distribution and Sales Channels

Distribution Centers

Approximately one-quarter of Nigeria's 80-100 million people live in urban centers of 20,000 or more. At least 24 cities have populations exceeding 100,000. There are three areas of high density: the ever-widening Lagos-Ibadan commercial and manufacturing area to the southwest, the Port Harcourt oil-producing area to the southeast, and Kano and Laduna area in the northern agricultural belt.

Lagos is the Federal Capital, chief seaport, largest commercial and manufacturing center, and largest city with about 4.5 million residents. Traditional concentration of industry in Lagos has attracted more people than can be accommodated or employed. While the new Federal Capital being build should alleviate the problem of overpopulation, Lagos, the entrepot for Nigeria and adjacent or landlocked counties, will remain the headquarters for most foreign and major domestic business and government procurement authorities for some time to come.

Ibadan, with a population of several million people, is the largest traditional African city. It is in the heart of the cocoa producing region and serves as the most important distribution center in the western portion of the country.

Port Harcourt is a fast-growing city with more than 500,000 people. It is the second-ranking port in the country and serves a large native population in the southeast as well as foreigners drawn by crude oil exploration and refining.

Kano with about 1 million people and Kaduna with about 500,000 are important market and distribution centers for neighboring countries and the north, where agriculture and associated processing industry is receiving special emphasis.

Sales Channels

Based upon managerial and financial strength, distributors in Nigeria may be divided roughly into three categories: large trading conglomerates; Nigerian, Lebanese, and Indian firms; and petty traders.

There are approximately 20 large trading conglomerates with European equity and management. These companies are the recommended distributors for products requiring technical servicing, an adequate supply of spare parts, and a large financial commitment. While many of these firms already have full product lines, they will drop or add a line to maintain a market share through specialization. Several of these companies, which also have department stores, offer the only nationwide distribution network. Decisions about new product lines are reached jointly between the Nigerian company and the European headquarters.

The next level of distribution—Nigerian, Lebanese, and Indian firms—tends to serve only one region. However, these distributors are frequently more dynamic than the large trading companies. They have a tendency to move in and out of product lines at will. Such distributors, while requiring continuing marketing and technical assistance, represent the best choice for many products of intermediate technical complexity and financial banking.

The third category of distributors, the numerous petty traders, generally market less complex consumer goods and tools. Many of these traders are inadequately financed, lack managerial skills, and cover only a small marketing area. They move in and out of product lines continuously and are often forced out of business. Such firms should be considered for only one or two transactions and then only on the basis of confirmed, irrevocable letters of credit.

Neglect of the distributor is a major cause of failure in the Nigerian market. It is essential to visit the distributor to develop personal relations, to demonstrate a commitment to the market, and to learn the conditions in the market.

It is not necessary to sign an exclusive marketing agreement for the whole country with a distributor, although the distributor may ask for exclusive rights in his region. It is permissable to drop a distributor.

Most of the large construction companies, petroleum service firms, and banks avoid the high costs and long delays of the Nigerian distribution system by buying equipment directly from or through their European or American headquarters. Products embodying high technology are almost always ordered in this manner. Local distributors are used only for service and for emergency requirements that can be met out of stock.

Government Procurement

Historically, the Nigerian Government has used consultants, such as the British Crown Agents, to procure its goods and services. A similar system has been incorporated into the ministries, which hire consultants to work as Nigerian Government employees and solicit services or equipment from firms through one of three methods of tendering. The consultants are warned against any nationalistic bias in selecting companies to perform a specific task. Ministries not only have this type of consultant but also have architects and architectural firms attached to them which draw up plans, recommend contractors, supervise jobs, and issue completion certificates at various stages of the contract.

Procurement Methods.—The Nigerian Government uses three methods for procuring goods and services: open competition, negotiated contract, and selective tender.

Open competition is used for standardized, generally available goods and services or World Bank projects.

The negotiated contract is used for specialized goods and services. It is opened to a select number of firms that are known to the tendering body through its past experience with them. Under the negotiated contract, the tendering body simply explains what it needs done, and the final cost and conditions are negotiated.

The selective tender has become the dominant form of government procurement at both the Federal and State level, particularly for major projects. It requires that a registration or prequalification statement be filed with the tendering ministry or agency.

The prequalification statement should contain the following information: name and address of main office; authorized capital; main business activities; name and address of parent company, if any; names and addresses of associated/subsidiary companies, if any; issued and paidup capital; projects in Nigeria already completed and/or being implemented and date of commencement of each project; projects undertaken within 3 years to date outside Nigeria already completed and/or being implemented; pretax profits (losses) for past 3 years (i.e. annual reports); financial stability; directors; bankers; and any other information relevant to the company's ability to perform.

It is particularly important to highlight overseas experience in the prequalification statement—(in descending order of preferability—in Nigeria, Africa, Third World, anywhere).

If a firm's various divisions offer different product/services, each division will have to prequalify independently.

Until a firm has prequalified, it will not be considered. Once it has prequalified for a project with a given government entity, it is usually considered qualified for all future projects of the same general type for that entity. However, maintaining contact is essential, as there is no central registry and prequalification procedures can be very informal.

Invitations to bid for a specific project are sent to firms having already prequalified. This constitutes the so-called long list. (On rare occasions, firms that have not prequalified are placed on the long list.) Companies on the long list may be asked to submit further qualifications tailored to the specific project. It is important to provide such elements as the ability to provide financing or comprehensive training programs.

From the list of companies responding to the invitation to bid is drawn the short list, those five or six companies who are actually sent the tender documents. Sometimes a short list is established without a long list. Under Nigerian law it is illegal to change an established short list.

In addition to prequalifying, firms must continue to demonstrate their interest in working in Nigeria. This demonstration should consist of having a local agent and visits by home office officials.

Incorporation Requirements.—In almost all cases to qualify to bid on public work contracts, construction firms must be incorporated in Nigeria with a Nigerian partner holding 60 percent equity. The Nigerian Indigenization Decree does exempt foreign firms bidding on their first contract from having to establish a company in Nigeria. However, this exemption has become increasingly difficult to obtain, and only about one-fourth of the applications for exemption are being approved. This same rule applies to subcontractors.

To be able to take advantage of opportunities as they arise, firms are advised to establish a local company early on. Reliable partners can be found for small joint ventures. These partners will be able to assist in winning the first vital contract. Local bank funds can be used for expansion, reducing the need to import more foreign capital, and initial expenses can be deducted from Nigerian taxes.

Registration Requirements.—In addition to submitting prequalification statements to the appropriate government entities and complying with incorporation requirements, contractors interested in large construction projects also must register with the Federal Work Registration Board, Federal Ministry of Works. Registration requirements are dependent upon the size and nature of the project and are aimed at ensuring that firms are financially and technically capable of undertaking projects. A registration fee is required.

A company's eligibility to bid is based upon qualifications described in the registration form. For example, if the project requires a road builder, only those firms registered as road builders will be invited. If the job requires a mechanical electrical firm as well as a building/civil engineering firm, only firms registered for both will be invited.

Contractors intersted in registering in the mechanical/electrical category should produce evidence of a valid license issued by the Nigerian Electric Power Authority (NEPA). Contractors interested in providing consultant services should apply to the appropriate ministry, Permanent Secretary, Planning Section. Those who intend to employ expatriates must apply to the Ministry of Internal Affairs for an expatriate quota.

Publicizing of Tenders.—Although tenders are publicized in the *Federal Republic of Nigeria Official Gazette* and newspapers, the tenders themselves usually must be purchased from the issuing body. While it is not encouraged, appeals may be made to extend bid deadlines. If granted, this extension would affect all potential bidders. Selection of bidders is made usually in a closed meeting.

State Tendering Practices. —Tendering practices vary somewhat among the states, although many now use selective tendering for major projects. As with Federal contracts, a firm must be registered to bid on the construction tender. In fact, some states require registration of structural engineers, architects, surveyors, and electrical/mechanical contractors as well. Some states require registration with the State Registration Board (usually located in the Ministry of Works or the Ministry of Finance and Economic Planning). Others require only Federal registration. Some require both. When firms register with the state government, they are classified according to their capacity. The firm's classification defines the magnitude of the projects it may bid upon.

Franchising and Licensing

Franchising is relatively unknown in Nigeria, but it is starting to grow. Hertz and Avis Rent A-Car, the only known franchisers operating in Nigeria, essentially cater to overseas visitors to pay for services under U.S. and European credit card arrangements. New interest in fast food and vehicle diagnostic and repair servicing is apparent, but the absence of a legal or regulatory framework governing fees, royalties, payments, and protection of parties to an agreement remains the basic impediment. Some forms of licensing arrangements, such as use of a hotel name backed by a management contract, are more acceptable, but competent legal guidance is advisable since most of these innovative business forms must accommodate indigenization.

Credit and Monetary Policy

Formal Credit System

The formal credit system in Nigeria includes the Central Bank under the auspices of the Ministry of Finance, 20 commercial banks, 7 merchant banks, 3 development banks, the Federal Mortgage Bank, the Federal Savings Bank, several finance corporations and insurance companies, and 3 stock exchanges.

In 1980, the commercial banks maintained 650 branches and had combined assets of close to $24 billion. Under the Government's "Nigerianization" policy, all banks must be at least 60 percent Nigerian owned. Of the 20 commercial banks, 11 are indigenous and 9 are affiliates of foreign financial entities. Commercial banks are involved in a full range of commercial banking services such as collections, letters of credit, foreign exchange, transfers, local currency loans, etc.

Most of the merchant banks are affiliated with U.S. banks, and all but one are majority owned by the Nigerian Government. In 1980, combined assets of merchant banks totaled $900 million. Merchant banks offer many of the same services as commercial banks do, but they cannot take personal deposits or do banking related to personal or retail business. Their main functions include wholesale banking, leasing, medium-term lending, syndications, underwritings, and equity investments.

Commercial banks are required to put 8 percent of loans and advances in the agriculture sector, 2 percent in mining, 36 percent in manufacturing, and 13 percent in construction. The credit allocation for export financing has been reduced from 5 to 3 percent.

For merchant banks the "preferred sectors"—including agriculture (5 percent), mining (3 percent), manufacturing (41 percent), and construction (20 percent)—must account for not less than 79 percent of total bank lending, merchant banks must observe longer maturity periods for their loans than commercial banks. A minimum of 40 percent of total loans and advances must be of a medium- and long-term nature with maturity of not less than 3 years. A maximum of 20 percent of loans and advances can be of a short-term nature with a maturity of less than 12 months. A maximum of 15 percent of total assets can be in the equipment leasing business.

All banks must maintain a minimum credit allocation of 80 percent to indigenous borrowers, a certain percentage of which must go to small-scale enterprises. Under a new 1982 guideline, banks are required to lend not less than 30 percent of deposits collected in rural branches to customers in rural areas. The minimum specified liquidity ratio is 25 percent, and the ratio of cash to demand deposits is 5 percent for banks with deposit liabilities of 300 million naira or more and 4 percent for banks with deposits of 100-300 million naira. As of April 20, 1982, the leading minimum commercial lending rate is set at 10.5 percent. There is a lower rate of 8 percent for agricultural production and low-cost housing.

The three development banks—the Nigerian Agricultural and Cooperative Bank, the Nigerian Bank for Commerce and Industry (NBCI), and the Nigerian Industrial Development Bank (NIDB)—the Federal Mortgage Bank, and the Federal Savings Bank are federally controlled. NBCI and NIDB have similar structures and objectives, both providing term financing to industry. NBCI also lends to services and is involved in commercial lending.

The Nigerian Stock Exchange, founded in 1961, has branches in Lagos, Kaduna, and Port Harcourt. The exchange is becoming increasingly active. In 1980, it provided a market for the shares of 155 companies.

The increasing demand for services from the private sector, ever-changing government regulations, and the Government's policy of bringing banking services closer to the people through an extensive rural branch banking program have placed tremendous pressure on the Nigerian banking system. Inefficiency and administrative and bureaucratic delays are common as the banks are unable to find enough qualified personnel to deal with the increasing load of paperwork. The commercial banks, in particular, are under constant pressure from the business community to improve their services.

Monetary Policy

Lending to the private community has expanded rapidly since the early 1970's and in the process, the guidelines for Nigerian commercial and merchant banks have become among the most rigorous in the world. In 1976, limits on the growth of bank lending and credit allocation requirements were introduced to promote the flow of credit to what were termed "directly productive sectors," particularly agriculture and manufacturing. To carry out such policies, there are strict aggregate, sectoral, and maturity targets for loan portfolios with rather severe financial penalties if they are not adhered to.

Monetary policy is usually set forth once a year at budget time in the form of a monetary policy circular issued by the Central Bank. For 1982, monetary and credit policy measures were designed to impove Nigeria's balance of payments, restrain inflation, and mobilize domestic savings. Under current regulations, most banks are restricted to a 30 percent expansion of credit over the previous year. Small banks, those with loan advances not exceeding 100 million naira as of December 31, 1980, may expand their credit up to 40 percent, or up to 70 percent of their total deposit liabilities, whichever is higher. Loans for agriculture, residential building construction, purchasing motor cars, and for the purchase of shares by Nigerians under the Indigenization Scheme are not counted against a bank's lending.

Consumer Credit

For consumer items on the mass market, credit is casually arranged and based on the personal relationships of the parties involved. Thus, the wholesaler, agent, or distributor extends credit to the traders and the traders to the end-user in an interlocking pattern. Family sharing plays an important role in the intricate mass distribution complex. For capital goods imports, supplier credits tend to be highly competitive and are frequently necessary.

Financing Nigerian Imports

Letters of credit play an important part in financing Nigerian imports. Irrevocable, confirmed letters of credit are recommended to collect payments for U.S. exports to Nigeria. As a general rule, only after a trading relationship has matured should a U.S. supplier begin to consider use of other credit terms.

Foreign nationals must be protected against the action of fraudulent Nigerian companies and individuals who have presented themselves as authorized dealers in foreign exchange, purporting to have powers to engage in banking activities and particularly to issue letters of credit. The names of duly authorized Nigerian banks officially licensed and recognized as authorized dealers with powers to undertake banking business are listed below (Foreign bank affiliations are noted parenthetically):

Commercial Banks

African Continental Bank Ltd.
Allied Bank (Nigeria) Ltd.
Arab Bank Ltd.
Bank of the North Ltd.
Bank of India (Nigeria) Ltd.
Co-operative Bank Ltd.
Co-operative Bank of Eastern Nigeria Ltd.
First Bank of Nigeria Ltd. (Standard Bank, U.K.)
International Bank for West Africa Ltd.
Kaduna State Cooperative Bank Ltd.
Kano State Cooperative Bank
Mercantile Bank Ltd.
National Bank of Nigeria Ltd.*
New Nigeria Bank Ltd.
Nigerian Bank for Commerce and Industry
Pan African Bank Ltd.
Savanah Bank of Nigeria Ltd. (Bank of America)

Societe Generale Bank Nigeria Ltd.
United Bank for Africa Ltd. (BNP)[1]
Union Bank (Barclays)
Wema Bank Ltd.

Merchant Banks

Chase International Merchant Bank ltd. (Chase Manhattan Bank)
ICON Ltd. (Merchant Bankers) (Morgan Guaranty Trust Co. of N.Y.)
International Merchant Bank Ltd.
(The First National Bank of Chicago)
NAL Merchant Bankers (Continental Illinois National Bank)
Nigerian American Merchant Bank Ltd. (The First National Bank of Boston)
Nigerian Merchant Bank Ltd.

Transportation, Communications, and Power

Ports and Shipping

Sea Ports. — Nigeria's principal general cargo ports are Lagos (Apapa and Tin Can Island), Port Harcourt, Warri, and Calabar. (Bonny and Burutu are the main petroleum ports.) These ports serve a market of up to 100 million people, including transit cargo for countries such as Niger and Chad. In 1980, general cargo passing through the four main complexes totaled an estimated 18 million metric tons. The Nigerian Ports Authority (NPA), which has operated and administered the general cargo ports of Nigeria since 1955, is responsible for the administration and operation of the country's port facilities.

The Lagos complex, with about 50 berths, handles about 75 percent of Nigeria's general cargo traffic. In 1980, Lagos alone handled about 10 million metric tons. Facilities are well developed for handling container traffic, but facilities for bulk unloading and for liquids are still poor.

The $198 million Federal ocean terminal under construction at Onne in River State is expected to be completed this year. The complex is intended to relieve traffic congestion at Apapa and Port Harcourt, to service east and northeast Nigeria, and to cater to the needs of the Ajaokuta steel project. Onne, a deepwater port, eventually will have a 1 mile dock with six berths. There will be facilities for both container and bulk cargo handling.

The Government has instituted a variety of measures to help alleviate port congestion, and, in general, long delays are no longer encountered at the Lagos port complex as they were during the late 1970's when ships had to queue up to unload. However, dockworkers' strikes do cause temporary delays from time to time. In addition, the Government has recently closed most of the country's estimated 200 private jetties in an effort to control smuggling. This measure has brought about some delays. Theft and pilferage as well as open piracy are common problems, particularly at Lagos.

There are no free port facilities in Nigeria.

Inland Waterways. — Nigeria's 5,331 miles of navigable inland waterways, using principally the Niger and Benue Rivers and their tributaries, constitute an extensive waterway system. The Government emphasizes the need for the year-round navigability of the Niger River not only for normal river traffic, but also to meet the needs of the Ajaokuta steel mill. During the Fourth Plan period, funds are being allocated to the Department of Inland Water Ways to facilitate dredging, river training, and the construction of inland river ports.

Shipping. — Nigeria also is interested in expanding its shipping capacity. The Nigerian National Shipping Lines, formed in 1958, has been wholly owned by the Government since 1961. At present, Nigerian carriers have only about a 12 percent share of the country's maritime traffic. The Government has instituted a new shipping policy with the objective of encouraging the development and maintenance of Nigeria's merchant marine capacity, and increasing Nigeria's share of earnings derived from external trade and shipping. The adoption of the UNCTAD 40-40-20 cargo sharing formula is the cornerstone of the new policy. As this policy is implemented, Nigerian national carriers will have carrying rights of at least 40 percent of the freight in revenue and volume of the total trade to and from Nigeria. Recognized national carriers will have carrying rights of 40 percent, and all third flag carriers will have the remaining 20 percent. The policy also calls for the formation of new national carriers which may be 40 percent foreign owned. Two U.S. flag carriers, Farrell Lines and Delta Lines, serve Lagos on a scheduled basis as members of the American West African Freight Conference. Shipping times from U.S. ports to Nigeria range from 9 to 50 days depending upon intermediate stops and delays.

Air Service

There are two federally owned organizations that dominate civil aviation in Nigeria. These are the Nigerian Airport Authority (NAA), responsible for the operation of some 14 airfields around the coun-

---

[1] The United Bank for Africa Ltd. and the National Bank of Nigeria Ltd. have recently opened representative offices in New York City.

try, and Nigeria Airways, which operates a full internal and international route network. Nigeria Airways has a fleet of about 25 aircraft including 6 medium/long haul jets. To improve its domestic, African, and international services, Nigerian Airways is planning to expand the fleet. Several medium haul jets are already on order. There are also several aviation charter firms in Nigeria, and many private interests, notably the oil companies, operate their own aircraft.

Airport development received substantial attention during the Third Plan period (1975-80) when 14 airports were simultaneously under construction in Lagos, Kano, Ilorin, Kaduna, Sokoto, Maiduguri, Enugu, Port Harcourt, Calabar, Hos, Ibadan, Benin, Makurdi, and Abuja (still under construction). The Government is trying to emphasize proper upkeep and maintenance for security and safety reasons.

International travel has been eased by the completion of the modern Murtala Muhammad International Airport in Lagos. There are also international flights to Kano and Port Harcourt. Pan Am and Nigeria Airways are the only airlines that fly directly from the United States to Nigeria. Each has two direct flights a week between New York and Lagos. Daily flights are available from Europe.

Land Transportation System

Roads. — Roads are the dominant mode of transportation in Nigeria, accounting for about 80 percent of the movement of goods and services in the country. The road network is quite well developed by African standards.

The country's road network is over 60,000 miles, of which more than 11,000 are paved. The 19,000 miles of the network under Federal administration, called Trunk A roads, consist of those linking the major population centers, those serving the seaports and airports, and those leading to the border with neighboring countries. The roads serving the secondary towns are designated Trunk B roads and are the responsibility of the state governments. Local roads (Trunk C) and city streets are the responsibility of local government councils.

During the Third Plan period, the Government placed a high priority on linking the major ports and the state capitals. Developments included the 68-mile Lagos-Ibadan toll expressway, a circumferential highway around Lagos, and completion of the Carter Bridge which links Lagos with the mainland. Roads linking the Federal Capital Territory at Abuja to Kaduna and Lagos have recently been improved, although much remains to be done in this regard. During the Fourth Plan period, the Government has pared down its projects for additional highway construction and is focusing instead on rehabilitation and maintenance of existing roads.

In 1980, the total number of registered cars, trucks, and buses in Nigeria stood at an estimated 500,000. The annual growth rate for passenger vehicle registrations is about 10 percent. Facilities for vehicle servicing and maintenance still are developed poorly.

The road transport industry is characterized by diffusion of ownership and small firm size. The reasons for this situation include free market entry (no common carrier regulation), small capital requirements, lack of specialization in the transport market, and high-risk/high-profit situations.

Larger, more specialized firms—often working on long-term contracts and moving products such as petroleum, refrigerated goods, steel, and construction equipment requiring special vehicles—have begun to appear in Nigeria. Foreign entrepreneurs, often long-term residents of Nigeria, controlled most of the larger cargo and passenger transport companies in the past. Since the Enterprises Promotion Decree of 1972, the transport of goods (except petroleum) and passengers by road has been reserved exclusively for Nigerian citizens.

In the near absence of any regulations concerning routes or rates, vans and trucks may ply wherever their business takes them, carrying whatever goods or passengers are available at freely negotiated rates. In practice, there is some natural specialization with regard to local or long-distance markets, particular types of commodities, routes, and clients. In addition, many private bus lines will operate only within a given state or region.

Railroad. — Nigeria's 2,200 mile, 42-inch (1067 mm) guage system is owned by the Nigerian Railway Corporation (NRC), a semiautonomous statutory corporation of the Ministry of Transport. It is the only authorized railroad operator in Nigeria. The basic rail systems run north-south from Kano to Lagos and from Maiduguri to Port Harcourt. It was completed in 1929.

In the past, rail service was generally slow and inefficient, and the NRC had been running at a loss for over 10 years since the late 1960's. In 1978, the Nigerian Government negotiated a 15 million naira ($23 million) contract with the Indian state-owned firm, Rail India Technical and Economic Services (RITES). The contract called for RITES to improve and manage the rail system for a 3-year period ending in mid-1982 and to train local people to run it themselves when the contract was over.

RITES improved the management and maintenance of the system and has rehabilitated much of the track and original diesel locomotive fleet of 219. Over 500 Nigerian staff are receiving on-the-job training, and another 100 have gone to India for specialist training. Confidence in the system is returning among the general public and Nigeria's business community. Passenger journeys increased from less than half a million per month in 1979 to 1.2 million by 1980. Daily freight loads have increased by almost 500 percent, rising from 65 wagons a day in 1979 to 312 wgons in 1980. Freight wagons are usually available when and where they are needed. In 1980, freight traffic accounted for almost half the railway's earnings.

During the Fourth Plan period, emphasis is on augmenting the existing fleet of 216 locomotives, 650 passengers coaches, and 7,000 wagons by acquiring locomotive and rolling stock, improving telecommunications, and repairing bridges. A major standard guage rail line is planned between Port Harcourt and Ajaokuta to facilitate the transportation for the iron and steel project at Ajaokuta. This system will eventually cover the entire country.

Communications

Business correspondence is normally conducted by air mail, which arrives from the United States daily. Transit time averages between 7 and 14 days. Surface mail takes 6 weeks to 3 months; parcel post is slow and handling is unreliable. It is suggested that for important letters, documents, and packages, a courier be used. DHL International, Ltd., which has offices in most major cities in the United States, has service to Lagos. For service within Nigeria, International Messenger of Nigeria, Ltd. (INML) enjoys a good reputation. IMNL is located at 17 Laide Tomori Street, Afrijet House, P.O. Box 634, Ikeja, Lagos (phone: 933948).

Cables and telex supplement airmail communication. Lagos is 6 hours ahead of Eastern Standard Time. Local telephone service is available in most cities and larger towns although service is generally slow and not always satisfactory. Intercity phone capacity is rare. Telephone service between the United States and Nigeria is more reliable than local service.

The Department of Posts and Telecommunications (P&T), Ministry of Communications, has responsibility for communication within Nigeria. According to its statistics for March 1981, there were 100,000 exchange lines connected, serving some 173,000 telephone instruments (0.2 per 100 population). The highest density of telephones is in the Lagos area where there are some 40,000 telephones, an estimated 1 telephone per 100 people. There is believed to be considerable suppressed demand for service particularly in and around state capitals. There were 1,875 telex lines installed by March 1981 with a waiting list of 2,898 and remaining capacity of 1,000 lines within

the system. Again the majority of telex lines are in the Lagos area and considerable suppressed demand exists elsewhere. Telex is referred to as the General Telex (Gentex) System.

Nigeria External Communications Ltd. (NET) operates Nigeria's external communication systems, linking the country to the international telecommunications network primarily through its two INTELSAT antenna and the West African submarine cable. It serves 5,000 subscribers nationwide, of which 4,000 are in the Lagos area. These are normally connected to the NET system by P&T lines.

Power

Electric current in Nigeria is 230 volt, 50 cycle, single phase AC and 415 volt, 50 cycle, three phase AC, with higher voltages in certain cases. Most principal cities and towns are electrified. The government-owned National Electric Power Authority (NEPA) has responsibility for production and sales throughout Nigeria. A grid-connected plant supplies over 95 percent of energy sales. In terms of energy sale in megawatts, residential end-users consume about 32 percent, the industrial sector consumes 41 percent, and the commercial sector consumes 23 percent. Roughly 1.3 percent is sold to Niger.

Plant capacity in 1981 is estimated at 1,760 megawatts. By 1985, the Government plans to have a total installed generating capacity of about 4,600 megawatts, which would be sufficient to meet an estimated loan of 3,460 megawatts and provide a reserve margin of 1,140 megawatts to ensure uninterrupted supply of power at all times. Approximately 50 percent of the electric power in Nigeria is presently generated by hydro plants. By 1985, it is expected that 75 percent will by hydrogenerated. As the new plants thereafter will stress thermal generation, the ratio by 1990 is expected to be 60 percent hydro and 40 percent thermal.

Demand for electrical power is expected to grow 25 percent a year during the Fourth Plan period as distribution is extended to the rural areas. Emphasis also is being placed on reinforcing and improving service to urban and commercial centers already supplied. Estimated demand in 1981 was 9,987,780 megawatt hours.

Industrialization of the country is hampered by unreliable power supplies. The Nigerian Manufacturers Association estimates that on the average, 60 production hours per month are lost by each manufacturing entity in Nigeria. Power surges and low voltages are frequent, outages routine.

Marketing Aids

Advertising Aids

Advertising is becoming more and more important in Nigeria, although it is still not as widely used as in the United States. Advertising campaigns should be specifically created for the Nigerian market with the needs, desires, and lifestyle of the Nigerian consumer in mind. Care should be taken to account for language, ethnic, and religious differences.

Nigeria has one of the most highly developed media systems in developing Africa, and coverage is available through the press, billboards, radio, and television. Most of these services are concentrated in urban areas, although radio coverage is becoming more widespread. Advertising directed at the mass consumer should be largely oral and visual because of widespread illiteracy. Information is still spread by word of mouth, particularly in rural areas, in marketplaces and by itinerant traders.

Brand consciousness and brand loyalty, particularly to established British trademarks, are still very important factors among the urban African population, but Nigerian consumers are extremely quality conscious and appreciate "Made in U.S.A." goods.

Printed Material

There are 14 major daily newspapers, approximately 20 weekly newspapers (including Sunday editions of the dailies), and about 25 magazines published in Nigeria. All of the dailies are printed in English as are most of the weeklies and periodicals. There are six vernacular weeklies, three in Lagos and two in Ibadan in Yoruba, and one in Kaduna in Hausa. Total circulation of the newspapers is between 1.5 and 1.8 million.

Sixty percent of the Daily Times Group, the major publishing house in the nation, is owned by the Federal Government. The *Daily Times*, based in Lagos but distributed over most of Nigeria, is the largest daily with a circulation of about 400,000. The *Sunday Times*, the largest weekly, sells over 400,000 copies each week. The weekly *Business Times*, with a circulation of about 35,000, is the most important for the business reader.

The *New Nigerian*—a Kaduna-based, 100 percent Federal Government-owned daily—has a printing plant in Lagos. A number of state government-owned papers also have national standing: the *Nigerian Observer* of Benin, the *Daily Sketch* of Ibadan, and the *Daily Star* of Enugu. The most prominent independently owned newspapers are the *Tribune* of Ibadan, the *Punch* (Lagos), and the *National Concord* (Lagos). The latter (founded in 1980) claims the second largest circulation in the nation (120,000 daily and 140,000 Sunday).

Among the more popular periodicals in Nigeria are *Drum*, a pictorial publication designed for African readers (circulation 172,000), *Headlines*, (circulation 205,000), *Spear* (circulation 150,000), and *Women's World* (circulation 31,000). The number of specialized trade magazines is limited. However, firms should consider advertising in some of the technical and specialized magazines, such as *West African Technical Review*, which are published in Europe for the West African market. Advertising in these newspapers and magazines is expensive but worthwhile.

Billboards and poster art are inexpensive and a widely used means of advertizing, particularly effective in the cities and when affixed to vehicles.

Radio and Television

Radio broadcasting is the most reliable way of reaching the Nigerian people. The Federal Radio Corporation of Nigeria (FRC) is solely responsible for broadcasting to all parts of Nigeria from its main base in Lagos and through its zonal stations in Enugu, Ibadan, and Kaduna. All FRC programs are transmitted in English, concentrating on Nigerian domestic news. The Voice of Nigeria (the FRC external service) broadcasts to other African countries, Europe, and the Middle East in English, French, Hausa, and Arabic. None of the zonal stations is allowed to carry commercial advertisements.

Each of the 19 states has an autonomous radio station, broadasting in local languages as well as English. Since the broadcasting system was reorganized in 1978, state stations can no longer broadcast on short wave and are confined to broadcasting only in their areas. These state-owned stations accept network news and policy guidance from FRC Lagos. They do accept commercial advertising.

There are an estimated 18 to 20 million radios in Nigeria, the majority of them in urban areas. Most Nigerians have access to medium-wave broadcasts. Ownership of short-wave receivers is estimated at approximately 5 million

Television is a rapidly expanding medium, but its audience is still mainly limited to the urban elite. The Nigerian Television Authority (NTA) oversees all TV broadcasting in Nigeria. NTA produces the nightly network news which must be carried by all stations. For transmission purposes, the country is divided into six zones with three or four production centers in each. Nineteen TV stations (one in each state) plus the NTA flagship station provide regular broadcasting to the Nigerian people. There are over 2.5 million licensed TV sets in use with an estimated audience of close to 22 million. NTA accepts advertising.

Many of the state governments also are interested in developing their own TV broadcasting facilities. At present, only Lagos and Anambra states have operational services. Both NTA and FRC have expansion programs planned, including new production centers at Abuja.

In addition to radio and television advertising, firms should consider advertising at movie theaters. Motion pictures are very popular in Nigeria, and although there are still only about 100 cinemas in the country, they do accept commercial advertising and can provide additional coverage for certain cities and towns.

Packaging

Packaging techniques are very important to successful selling in Nigeria. Container designs should be as attractive and eye-catching as possible and geared towards the Nigerian consumer. Once an item has been introduced to the market, packaging changes should be subtly introduced so as not to sacrifice customer familiarity with a specific product's identity and brand loyalty. The competitive position of consumer goods often can be improved by enclosing them in containers, such as bottles or boxes which can be reused by the purchaser.

Market Research and Trade Organizations

Prepared market research is not readily available. In most cases, firms wishing in-depth sectoral and product information will need to contract out for a study or undertake one themselves. Even then, companies will find that statistical information is generally inadequate. Statistics, when they are available, tend to be out of date and of questionable accuracy. As a consequence, marketing decisions tend to be made more subjectively in Nigeria than in many other markets and may entail more risk of trial and error.

The Association of Advertising Practitioners of Nigeria has about 30 to 40 members, although over a half of the business is handled by four or five top firms. Some of these ad agencies will undertake market research for their clients. Some banks and accounting firms also can provide assistance in market research.

There are several business organizations in Nigeria which may be able to furnish market information. These include the Nigerian Association of Chambers of Commerce, Industry, Mines, and Agriculture (131 Broad St., P.O. Box 109, Lagos), The Lagos Chamber of Commerce and Industry (131 Broad St., P.O. Box 109, Lagos), and the Manufac-

turers' Association of Nigeria (30 Marina St., P.O. Box 3835, Lagos). Various Nigerian Government ministries also may be able to provide market information for their areas of responsibility.

For information on trade shows and exhibitions being staged in Nigeria, contact the Lagos International Trade Ground, Badagary Expressway, Lagos. In the United States, information may be obtained from the Nigerian-American Chamber of Commerce, Inc. (122 East 42nd St., Room, 1700, New York, N.Y. 10168) and from the African-American Institute (833 U.N. Plaza, New York, N.Y. 10017). To organizations which frequently sponsor exhibits in Nigeria are IC Publications (122 East 42nd St., New York, N.Y. 10017) and Glahe International Inc. (1700 K St., N.W., Washington, D.C. 20006).

The Office of Africa, within the International Trade Administration of the U.S. Department of Commerce, (202-377-4388) can provide information on market research available from the U.S. Government and recommend other sources for market research and information on trade events. This office also can provide information on upcoming U.S. Government-sponsored trade promotion events in Nigeria.

Investment in Nigeria

At yearend 1981, the United States direct investment position in Nigeria was $218 million. This figure is an estimate of the book value of U.S. direct investors' equity in, plus loans outstanding to, their Nigerian affiliates. It does not describe the value of U.S. corporate assets of plant and equipment expenditures in Nigeria.

Investment Climate

The Government of Nigeria supports and encourages foreign investment, both in cash and in kind by way of equipment, technical expertise, and services as a means of increasing the supply of investment capital to the economy and of encouraging technology transfer to Nigeria. It offers incentives to both foreign and domestic investors to strengthen those sectors of the economy which the Government believes contribute most toward economic development. At the same time, the Government strictly regulates the establishment and operations of foreign investment through laws and decrees it has adopted over the years since Nigeria gained its independence from Great Britain in 1960. The two main laws affecting foreign investment, the Companies Decree of 1968 and the Nigerian Enterprises Promotion Decree of 1977, ensure that all foreign investment is government approved and has indigenous equity participation. The Government's primary interest in regulating foreign investment to this extent is merely another facet of its interest in regulating and guiding the economy to self-sustained and indigenously controlled development. Aside from the continued execution of these existing laws, the Government plans to scrutinize increasingly the extent to which firms owned in part by foreigners use locally produced inputs and train their Nigerian employees..

Indigenization or Nigerianization should not be misconstrued to mean nationalization of industry by the Nigerian Government. It is not the Government's intention to participate in the private sector except in such strategic economic sectors as petroleum, iron and steel, communications, utilities, and in some cases, banking. Under its policies, the Government will take an equity position in a going venture only to make it comply with the Nigerian Enterprises Promotion Decree if private capital in unavailable or Nigerians are unwilling to invest.

Investing and operating in Nigeria is not easy. It is generally acknowledged that the most successful foreign companies are those that have had prior experience in other developing countries. In addition to the legal restrictions on the amount of foreign equity involvement, other obstacles face the potential foreign investor. Limitations on repatriations of earnings, expatriate quotas, conflicting priorities among ministries, constant issuance of decrees (some of which have been retroactive) changing investment terms, proliferation of government red tape and slowness of paper processing, corruption, and lack of adequate infrastructure can make investing in Nigeria a frustrating process. In many cases, because of these difficulties and high startup costs, investors do not realize a return on their investment for several years. In addition, because of import controls, there is a serious lack of consumer items and other amenities to which many foreigners are accustomed. This factor, the high cost of living, and the high incidence of serious crime make life more difficult for expatriate staff living in Nigeria.

Nevertheless, the wealth and dynamism of the country and its population provide an attractive area of expansion for those willing and able to withstand the rigors. Joint ventures in agricultural production and processing, mining, the construction industry, the manufacture of building materials and supplies, and the manufacture of basic and intermediate chemicals, offer some of the best investment opportunities in Nigeria.

All firms investigating the possibility of investing in Nigeria should visit the Nigerian Investment Information and Promotion Center (9th Floor, the Federal Ministry of Industries, New Federal Secretariat, Ikoyi, Lagos). This office can provide advice and information on investment opportunities in the various states, prospective joint-venture partners, reputable suppliers of machinery and raw materials, the status and availability of State and Federal Government incentives, sources of financing, investment laws and regulations, and the latest procedures for establishing a business in Nigeria. In addition, the Ministry of Industries has opened a Nigerian Investment Promotion Center in the United States which provides similar assistance. The Center is located at 100 East 42nd St., New York, N.Y. 10017; telephone (212) 883-1980.

Business Organizations

Aside from government-owned concerns and statutory corporations, the principal forms of business organization in Nigeria are incorporated companies, partnerships, and sole proprietorships.

Partnerships. — Partnerships are governed by the English Partnership Act of 1890, unless the agreement provides otherwise. In a partnership, there may be no less than 2 and no more than 20 partners, although they may be of any nationality and may be a corporate body. In general, the partners are jointly liable for the debts and obligations of the firm. In addition, each partner is personally liable to the extent that debts of the partnership have not been discharged from the firm's assets.

Incorporated Companies. — The Companies Decree of 1968 provides for incorporation, regulation, and operation of companies. Subject to certain exceptions, Part X of the Decree provides that no company may carry on business in Nigeria unless it is incorporated as a separate entity in Nigeria. Incorporated companies may be unlimited, limited by guarantee, or limited by share, with the last named the most commonly adopted by foreign investors in Nigeria. The liability of each member of a limited by shares company is limited to the amount, if any, unpaid on the shares held by that member. Once a member has paid for those shares, there is no further liability. There is no maximum or minimum amount of share capital, and shares may be pegged at any value.

A limited-by-share company may be incorporated either as a public or as a private company, although in practice there is little difference between the two. Public companies are normally formed to enable the investing public to share in the profits of an enterprise without taking any part in the management. Such companies usually have no limitation on the maximum number of members (but must have a minimum of seven). Their Articles of Association provide for transfer of shares and for subscription from the public. A public company is not necessarily quoted on the Nigerian Stock Exchange. A private company must have at least 2, but no more than 50 members. It may restrict the right to transfer its shares and prohibit any invitation to the public to subscribe for its shares or debentures.

Foreign Companies Exempt from Incorporation. — The Companies (Special Provision) Decree of 1973 empowers the Government to exempt certain specified categories of foreign companies from complying with Part X of the companies Decree. Only the following categories of foreign companies are eligible for exemption: nonprofit corporations, companies invited by or with the approval of the Federal Government to execute specified projects, companies executing specific loan projects on behalf of donor countries or international organizations, foreign government-owned companies engaged solely in export promotion activities, and engineering consultants and technical experts engaged in specialized projects under contracts with any of the state governments or any of their agencies or with any person where such contracts have been approved by the Federal Government.

The granting of Part X exemption status is becoming increasingly rare. Only about one-quarter of the applications for exemption are now being approved, and entities previously enjoying this status are generally unable to obtain renewal once the initial period expires. In addition, the ability to perform as a local entity has become an important factor in the awarding of government contracts to construction firms and consultants of all types.

Nigerian Enterprises Promotion Decree

Under the Nigerian Enterprises Promotion (Indigenization) Decree of 1977, the minimum level of Nigerian equity participation in any business enterprise is 40 percent. The Indigenization Decree, first enacted in 1972 and modified in 1977, established three schedules of enterprises and minimum percentages of Nigerian financial participation under each schedule. In Schedule 1 are enterprises reserved exclusively for Nigerians. Operations of firms in this schedule are relatively noncapital intensive or do not involve high levels of technological input. Schedule 2 enterprises are those whose ownership must be at least 60 percent Nigerian. These firms generally use more capital-intensive production processes or more sophisticated technology than firms in Schedule 1. In Schedule 3 are enterprises which must be at least 40 percent owned by Nigerians. Firms in this category typically use high inputs of both capital and technology. Appendix A contains a list of business categories, by schedule, under the Nigerian Enterprises Promotion Decree.

The Nigerian Enterprises Promotion Board (NEPB), established to monitor compliance with the provisions of the Decree, is responsible for issuing a certificate of compliance to those companies that have met all the requirements of the act. The Board issues detailed guidelines to companies and conducts post-compliance inspections before final certification is given. To receive a certification of compliance, companies must submit the following documents to NEPB:

(1) Evidence of acquisition of shares

(2) Evidence of payment of purchase consideration

(3) List of board of directors. At least two of the Nigerian directors must be an executive for a Schedule 2 enterprise, and at least one must be a director for a Schedule 3 enterprise. (In addition, the Board has adopted a policy requiring that the composition, by nationality, of a company's board of directors reflects the proportional ownership of the company.)

(4) Copies of business permit and expatriate quota authorizations

(5) Memorandum and articles of association

(6) List of appointed indigenous distributors (for manufacturers) and lists of suppliers (for commercial or trading companies) and their addresses (Manufacturers are not allowed to appoint only one distributor.)

(7) Evidence of compliance with the mandatory workers' participation in equity (equal to 10 percent of the foreign investor's interest) with at least 50 percent of the mandatory proportion having been sold to non-marginal employees

(8) Copy of company's tax clearance certificate

The Investment Process

Establishing a foreign investment in Nigeria has four major steps: (1) application to establish a business and (if necessary) to employ expatriates, (2) incorporation and registration of the company, (3) notification of intention to incur capital expenditures, and (4) application for "approved status" to obtain approval for the repatriation of capital and income. In addition, any application for particular concessions or incentives schemes should be made at the time a company is established. Investors should ensure that required approvals are granted by the appropriate ministries for all the above before commencing business in Nigeria. Approvals will be required from the Ministries of Finance, Industries, Commerce, and Internal Affairs. In some cases, the involvement of other ministries will be required.

During the investment process, the assistance of the Nigerian partner is important to monitor the decision process and to obtain necesary assistance from contacts in smoothing out any bottlenecks which may be encountered. In addition, investors should obtain professional advice and assistance from lawyers and accountants at an early stage in the process. In general, the process of officially establishing a company in Nigeria will require from 6 to 12 months, if not longer, to complete.

Permission to Establish a Business and Employ Expatriates. — The Ministry of Internal Affairs grants permission to establish a business in Nigeria. Form T1, obtainable from the Ministry, is a combined application for permission to establish a business and to employ expatriates in Nigeria (expatriate quota). Without the approval of Form T1, a foreigner may not be employed in Nigeria. Expatriate quotas usually entail a negotiating process as the Government is committed to involving the Nigerian population in the economy as soon and as much as possible. Thus, the Government tends to limit the number of expatriates employed. In 1980, the Government announced its intention to tie new approvals for expatriate quotas to the firm's plans for training of Nigerian staff. The Government also has warned firms directly that it will monitor these plans. Quotas are normally granted for a 3 year period and may be extended upon request. If necessary, due to future expansion of the business, an increase in the size of a company's quota will be considered. Application for any additional expatriates should be made on Form T2. When approval is granted, the Ministry will issue a business permit and authorization for an expatriate quota.

Incorporation and Registration of Companies. — The documents which must be drawn up and filed with the Registrar of companies, Ministry of Commerce include the following: memorandum of association, articles of association, statement of nominal capital (Form C.O.2. for companies limited by share), declaration of compliance with the Companies Decree of 1968 (Form C.O.1.), notice of location of the registered office of the company (Form C.O.6.), and particulars on the directors and secretary (Form C.O.7.). The statutory application forms are available from bookstores. The memorandum and articles of association must be printed. A stamp duty, assessed at scaled rates, is payable on the authorized share capital, along with filing and registration fees.

The memorandum of association must contain the objectives of the company; the company's name with the word "limited" as the last word (the name must not conflict with that of any other company and must have the prior approval of the Ministry of Commerce); the amount of nominal share capital, the number of shares into which it is to be divided, and the nominal or par value of each; and the location of the registered office of the company. It must be signed by subscribers to the original issue of shares and witnessed. If an undertaking is a sole proprietorship, a partnership, or for professional practices, the application for the registration of the business name is required on Form 1 or Form 2; both are obtainable from the Registrar.

If upon examination, all the documents are in order, Registry officials will issue a certificate of incorporation. After being issued a certificate of incorporation, construction companies must then apply for classification through the Ministry of Works (see "Government Procurement").

Notification of Intention to Incur Capital Expenditures. — Whenever initial or additional expenditures of 20,000 naira or more are made, a notification of intention to incur capital expenditure must be filed with the Industrial Inspectorate Division of the Ministry of Industries. The information on Form 1, which is obtainable from the Inspectorate, establishes the value of plant equipment and machinery contributed to the enterprise from abroad. This step is important, as the certificate of value of the investment must be submitted for obtaining final approved status.

Application for Approved Status. — To repatriate earnings and capital from Nigeria foreign investors must obtain approved status from the Ministry of Finance. The approval should not be confused with the "approved user's status" granted under one of the investment incentive schemes. Although not a guarantee of foreign exchange availability, approved status grants permission to the concern to apply for repatriation of earnings and capital and carries with it the implication that the Ministry will give sympathetic consideration to such applications.

Application for approved status is generally a two-step process. before capital is brought into the country, approved status, in principle must be obtained by submitting a letter of application, based on a Ministry of Finance questionnaire, to the Exchange Control Division of the Ministry of Finance. In the application it is necessary to describe fully the proposed project, its initial and future objectives, and the proposed capital structure of the company, with distinctions between loans, debentures, and preferred and ordinary shares, benefits to the Nigerian economy such as increased exports or decreased imports, creation of new industry or introduction of new technology, or increased employment should be included. Authorities also will consider the ratio of share capital to loan capital to current account balances and bank borrowings of the proposed Nigerian company, in granting approved status. This letter should be supported by copies of the memorandum and articles of association, the business permit, and the certificate of compliance issued by the Nigerian Enterprises Promotion Board.

Approved status, in principle, is valid for 12 months, but can be extended. Final approved status is granted once the capital has been imported into

Nigeria. Documentary evidence including the Central Bank's certificate of capital importation of cash or the original customs bill of entry for the machinery equipment and the valuation of the machinery from the Industrial Inspectorate Division of the Ministry of Industries.

Remittance of Profits and Dividends

Annual remittances of profits and dividends can be made subject to any ceilings imposed by law and subject to approval from the Ministry of Finance. Application should be made on a Form A (see Trade Policy), accompanied by a current tax clearance certificate, proof of approved status, and any other supporting documents as may be required.

The Government restricts annual dividend declarations to 60 percent of net profits after taxes. Royalty payments are limited to 1 percent of sales, except for books and records where the fee is negotiable. Overseas payments for management and technical fees are limited to 2 percent of pre-tax profits.[2] Where consultants are not resident in Nigeria, up to 30 percent of consultants' fees may be remitted abroad to cover offshore costs. A higher percentage can be negotiated in special cases. All dividends, royalties, and fees are subject to withholding tax.

Foreigners employed in Nigeria are allowed to remit up to 50 percent of their net after tax income on a monthly basis. When leaving Nigeria, such employees may remit their surplus naira earnings provided that the authorities are satisfied that the amount to be repatriated is "reasonable" in terms of the individuals personal living expenses while in Nigeria.

National Office of Industrial Property Act

The Ministry of Finance must approve the terms and conditions of all licensing and other agreement which involve the transfer of technology to Nigeria. This includes such things as trademarks, patents, designs, technical and managerial expertise, and the supply of machinery and plant. This function is to be transferred to a new National Office of Industrial Property. Under the National Office of Industrial Property Act of 1979, all agreements involving the transfer of technology must be specifically approved and registered before foreign exchange approval will be authorized.

---

[2] However, the Government has stated that in the future such agreements will only be approved for local entities that are not well established. A Nigerian firm that has been in business for several years may not be allowed to enter into a management or technical service contract.

There is detailed legislation for the protection of registered patents, designs, trademarks, and copyrights. Most of the legislation was inherited from the United Kingdom. Patents granted in Nigeria are valid for a 20-year period starting with the date of application. The application can be made by the inventor or an assignee. Trademarks are registered initially for 7 years and may be extended thereafter every 14 years provided the application for the extension is made within 3 months of the registration expiration date. Nigeria is a signatory to the International Convention for the Protection of Industrial Property.

Price Controls

Price controls were introduced in 1977. The federally appointed Price Control Board, with the assistance of state Price Control Committees, enforces a system of price controls on various commodities ranging from locally manufactured goods to major imported items including food. The Board advises the Government on general policies and guidelines pertaining to prices, productivity, and personal incomes. Guidelines are issued annually, and once approved by the Government, they have the force of law. Violators are subject to fines or imprisonment.

The Corrupt Practices Decree

The Nigerian Corrupt Practices Decree of 1975, designed to suppress corrupt practices in both the public and private sectors, provides stiff penalties for any person found guilty of bribery and corruption but exempts bona fide customary gifts.

Residence Permits

Any foreigner entering the country for purposes of employment must obtain a residence permit, which may take some time to obtain. Inquiries about residence and work permits, expatriate quotas, and multiple-entry visas should be addressed to the Nigerian Embassy or its consulates or to the Chief Federal Immigration Officer, Immigration Department, Federal Ministry of Internal Affairs, Lagos.

Investment Incentives

The Government offers special incentives to industrial enterprises where such incentives are considered necessary to the overall economic interest of Nigeria.

Pioneer Status. — The "Industrial Development (Income Tax Relief) Act of 1958," as amended by Decree No. 22 of 1971, grants "pioneer" firms relief from income tax for the first 3 years of operations; the relief period can be extended for 2 years upon approval by the Ministry of Industries. In considering an extension application, the Ministry will examine the progress and efficiency of the company, the amount of local raw materials used, the training of Nigerian personnel undertaken, the relative importance of the industry in the economy, and such other relevant matters as may be required.

Capital expenditures made during the tax relief period may be deducted from taxable profits arising after the tax relief period. The minimum capital expenditure required to qualify is 150,000 naira for foreign-controlled firms and 50,000 naira for indigenous-controlled firms.

Firms applying for pioneer status must be engaged in activities classified as pioneer by the Ministry of Industries and must be public, limited-by-share companies. Applications are evaluated on the basis of the firm's potential for producing at a satisfactorily large scale, the prospects for favorable further development of the industry, and the import-substitution potential of the investment.

The granting of pioneer status is subject to the recipient's observance of the following conditions:

(1) The company shall not engage during the tax relief period in any enterprise except the industry for which the pioneer status is granted.

(2) The company shall start to operate within 1 year of the date estimated by the company in its application.

Pioneer industries are generally industries where there is an insufficient supply of the goods and services provided by that industry. However, companies that want to engage in an industry not classified as pioneer may still apply for pioneer status. Appendix B contains the 38 industry categories presently enjoying pioneer status.

Approve User Scheme. —The approved user scheme allows qualifying firms total or partial exemption from import duty on materials brought into Nigeria for use in manufacturing, processing, or the provision of services. To qualify, applicants must show either that an exemption is needed to enable them to charge prices low enough to complete with imports or that the duties on the imported finished article are lower than the sum of duties on raw mterials needed to make the product. Under the terms of the approved user program, import duty relief is intended to be temporary in nature and limited to the time needed to establish a new industry or to allow an existing company to expand to an economically visible scale. Therefore, the Approved User Certificte is valid for a maximum of 3 years and is not valid for relief on imported materials which are available locally. Application for this status is channeled through the Ministry of Industries which advises the Ministry of Finance on whether or not to approve the application.

Repayment of Import Duty. —The Customs (Drawback) Regulations of 1959, with amendments, provide that importers may claim repayment of import duty in full if materials imported were for use of local manufacture of exported goods.

Protection Against Dumping. —The Customs Duties (Dumped and Subsidized Goods) Act of 1958 protects Nigerian manufacturers against goods dumped at low prices in Nigeria or against the import of goods at prices subsidized by a foreign government.

Industrial Estate. —As an added effort to encourage industrial development, the State and Federal Governments have established throughout the federation a number of industrial estates which provide roads, power, water, and supporting services and complementary activities to new companies.

Nigerian tax laws allow quick depreciation of capital assets with corresponding accumulation of liquid reserve—a feature intended as an additional incentive to industrial investment. Developers of housing estates are entitled to higher capital allowances: 30 percent during the first year and 10 percent thereafter. To qualify, such housing estates must contain at least 50 units.

Investment Incentives for Agricultural Sector. —Capital expenditures on plant and equipment used in agricultural production receive a special 10 percent investment allowance in addition to the normal capital allowance. Farming establishments may carry forward loses for an indefinite period of time as opposed to the normal 4 years. Agricultural implements and irrigation equipment can be imported duty free by companies with approved user status. Fish and shrimp caught and landed by Nigerian-flag vessels are imported without duty.

Industrial Free Zones. —The Govenment plans to create industrial free zones for eport industries, although incentives for firms producing in such zones have not yet been announced.

Taxes

There are three basic direct taxes in Nigeria: income tax, capital gains tax, and the petroleum profits tax. The tax year ends December 31.

There is no double taxation agreement in effect between Nigeria and the United States. In April 1979, Nigeria withdrew from the U.S.-U.K. Tax Treaty to which it had acceded in 1959. Negotiations have been underway for some time to institute a new bilaterial tax treaty.

NIGERIA

All companies operating in Nigeria are subject to tax. These taxes are administered by the Federal Board of Inland Revenue, Federal Ministry of Finance, according to laws enacted in the Income Tax Management Act of 1961, the Company Tax Act of 1979, the Capital Gains Tax Act of 1967, the Petroleum Profits Tax Act of 1959, and numerous subsequent amending acts. Generally speaking, all gains of a revenue nature which accrue in, are derived from, are brought into, or are received in Nigeria are regarded as taxable income of companies established in Nigeria.

The current rate of company income tax is 45 percent. Companies entitled to pioneer status (see Investment) are exempt from income tax during the pioneer period. Companies engaged in building or construction projects are assessed on 2½ percent of turnover or the normal adjusted accounts profits, whichever is the higher.

All expenses which are "wholly, exclusively, necessarily and reasonably" incurred in the production of profits are allowable as tax deductions. Generally all taxes, duties and fees are deductible. Taxes on income or profits levied in Nigeria, however, are not deductible. Foreign income taxes are deductible, unless they qualify for credit.

Credit for foreign income tax, against Nigerian tax, is granted to reduce or eliminate double taxation.

In lieu of depreciation, capital allowances are granted for prescribed assets. These allowances consist of initial allowances based on cost and annual allowances computed on the written-down value of the qualifying capital expenditure. They have the effect of accelerating the writeoff of capital assets. For example, the initial (first-year) allowance for agricultural plantations is 25 percent. Since the 15 percent annual allowance also is granted the first year, 40 percent of the value of the new agriculture plant can be written off the first year. Expenditures for the acquisition of land, goodwil, trademarks, patents and other intangible assets do not qualify for capital allowances.

The rate of withholding tax on dividends is currently 12½ percent. Interest, royalties, management fees, and consultancy fees ar subject to a withholding tax at 45 percent of the gross amount less applicable expenses. Firms providing technical and consulting services or involved in construction projects which have both onshore and offshore elements will find that the tax consequences will vary depending on the nature of each contract and the specific circumstances involved.

Foreign employees are liable for Nigerian personal income tax on business profits; salaries, wages, or other employment compensations; dividends;

interest; pensions; annuities; and rents. The only exception is for employees of non-Nigerian entities who work in Nigeria for less than 183 days a year and who are liable for personal income tax in another country. Collection of personal income tax is under the jurisdiction of the states. The rates, which are uniform throughout the country and are eased by various exemptions and deductions, are as follows:

Taxable (naira) income	Percentage	Cumulative Income	Tax
0-2,000	10	2,000	200
2,001-4,000	15	4,000	500
4,001-6,000	20	6,000	900
6,0001-8,000	25	8,000	1,400
8,001-10,000	30	10,000	2,000
10,001-15,000	40	15,000	4,000
15,001-20,000	45	20,000	6,250
20,001-30,000	55	30,000	11,750
Over 30,000	70		

There is a 20 percent capital gains tax arising from disposal of assets. The tax affects all companies, including pioneer companies, individuals, and noncorporate bodies. The capital gain is determined by deducting from the sum received the cost of the acquisition to the person or entity realizing the chargeable gain plus expenditures incurred, improvements, or expenses incidental to the realization of the asset. There are exemptions to the tax for certain charitable institutions and for the disposal of certain assets including Nigerian Govenment securities, private road vehicles, land compulsorily acquired, and tangible, movable property sold for less than 1,000 naira. A capital loss arising from the disposal of one asset cannot be set off against a gain from the disposal of another asset.

Companies engaged in petroleum operations, including the extraction and transportation of petroleum oil and natural gas, are subject to a petroleum profits tax of 85 percent. Income generated by nonpetroleum-related operations of the company are subject to normal company tax rules.

An investment tax credit of 5 percent can be taken for onshore production, and an investment tax credit of from 10 to 20 percent is permitted for offshore production, dependent upon depth of drilling.

A tax clearance certificate certifying that all taxes due for the three immediately preceding fiscal years have been settled in full is a prerequisite for practically all official transactions, for both companies and individuals. This certificate is demanded.

- From private companies applying for government loans
- On the first registration of motor vehicles
- On application for a gun license
- On application for foreign exchange control permission to remit funds
- On application for a certificate of occupancy
- On tendering for government contracts
- On application by a trader for a trading license
- On application for approval of building plans
- On application for property transfer documents
- From electoral candidates
- From applicants for import/export licenses
- From applicants for state land
- From applicants for buying agents' licenses
- From applicants for pools or other gaming licenses
- From applicants for distributorship
- From applicants for Approved Users' Certificates
- From candidates for appointment as chairperson or members of public corporations and other institutions

Tax clearance certificates are issued to companies upon application to the Federal Board of Inland Revenue and to individuals upon application to the Internal Revenue Division of each state. These certificates are valid for 1 year.

Inquiries on taxation may be directed to the Federal Board of Inland Revenue, Lagos. Some of the best sources of information, not only on taxation, but on investment and contractual matters in general, are the branch offices of major accounting firms.

Labor

The Nigerian labor force is believed to number about 33 million. Approximately 75 percent of this work force is employed in the rural agricultural sector; 15 percent in government; and 10 percent in industry, commerce, and services. Statistics on unemployment and underemployment are not available. Among skilled workers, unemployment is rare, but underemployment of unskilled workers and agricultural workers is prevalent. Productivity tends to be low, primarily because of shortages of managerial and technical personnel and skilled laborers.

Legislation

The Federal Ministry of Employment, Labor, and Productivity has overall responsibility for labor matters. In general, Nigeria closely follows English jurisprudence in labor matters. The major piece of Nigerian legislation is the Labor Act of 1974. This act, among other things, places certain limits on the general freedom of employers and employees to enter into binding employment contracts and restrictions on child labor.

With few exceptions, there are no standard employment contracts. Although contracts need not be in writing, it is usually wise to do so for major employment contracts. Rules governing the termination of employment contracts form an important part of Nigerian labor laws and regulations. Employees have legal recourse for wrongful dismissal.

There is also legislation which deals with the health, safety, and welfare of workers in certain industries. Details of employment such as working hours, paid holidays, sick pay, and other benefits are generally left to bargaining between employers and employees. There is a stipulated minimum wage of 125 naira (approximately $186).[3]

The Nigerian Labor Movement

The Trade Union Decree of 1978 obliges companies to recognize legal trade unions and to deduct trade union dues directly from employees' salaries. Between one and two million workers are members of trade unions.

The Nigerian labor movement—which was rationalized by the former military government into 42 trade unions under a single national labor federation, the Nigerian Labor Congress (NLC)—became increasingly restive during the first 2 years of civilian rule as it pressed for increases in the national minimum wage, restoration of car loans for government workers, and other fringe benefits. In response, the Government has approved substantial increases in the minimum wage and other benefits but has also indicated that it will support legislation which could dilute the influence of NLC by making union affiliation with NLC optional.

Shortly after coming to power, the administration of President Shagari increased the national monthly minimum wage from 69 to 100 naira. However, NLC continued to press its demands for a 300 naira minimum wage, an amount deemed by the Government and even many trade unionists to be unrealistic and inflationary. NLC pressure culminated in a 2-day general strike in May 1981, which, although not supported by all 42 unions, ultimately led to National Assembly approval of 125 naira monthly minimum wage which was signed into law on

---

[3]One naira equals US $1.45 at current exchange rates.

September 3, 1981. Although it covers both public and private sector employees, the bill does exempt seasonal workers and firms with fewer than 50 employees. Representing more than a 100 percent wage increase over an 18-month period, the new minimum wage has created problems for some marginal, labor intensive companies, such as the textile industry which, already faced with problems created by competition from illegal imports, may be forced to retrench as a result of the higher labor costs.

Over and above the minimum wage, civil servants also are paid a minimum 25 naira per month housing and transport allowance, a fringe benefit which most private employers also provide. Firms which do not have their own retirement plans are required to make modest monthly contributions to the National Provident Fund for their employees, and employers with more than 500 workers also are required to provide housing near the place of work.

During 1980 and 1981, there was a series of industrial actions by workers in both the public and private sectors involving teachers, university professors, doctors, nurses, civil servants, dock workers, petroleum workers, and employees of the Central Bank. According to Nigerian Government figures, the nation lost 2 million work days as a result of industrial strikes between January 1, 1981 and February 23, 1982, in disputes involving 366,323 workers. Given the lack of union strike funds, the majority of strikes were of short duration. They were often resolved in favor of the workers. Strikes by State and Federal Government employees resolved primarily around issues related to wage demands and alleged government nonimplementation of the minimum wage or car loans for government workers. Month-long strikes during 1981 by university professors and doctors focused on demands for improved conditions of service in government institutions and hospitals.

In March 1982, a 6-day strike by employees of the National Electric Power Authority (NEPA), who were demanding payment of an end-of-year bonus and greater autonomy for the parastatal organizations, caused massive disruption of power and water distribution throughout the country and generated proposals in the National Assembly to prohibit workers in essential services from participating in labor unions. In March 1982, the National Economic Council rejected a demand for a 300 naira per year across-the-board wage increase for civil service employees.

Because of revenue shortages created in part by reduced petroleum production in 1981, several state governments experienced problems funding both the minimum wage and other fringe benefits; this situation remains unchanged. Worker actions to force implementation of wage and benefit agreements can be anticipated. Thus far, the Government has been reluctant to take strong action against the unions, even in certain cases where strikes have taken place in contravention of existing legal procedures for dispute resolution.

Guidance for U.S. Business Travelers

Entrance Requirements

All individuals entering Nigeria must possess a valid passport and a Nigerian Government visa, which costs $2.55 in the United States. To obtain a visa, visitors must submit to the Nigerian Embassy in Washington, D.C. or to the consulates in Atlanta, New York, or San Francisco, a properly completed Nigerian visa application with a valid U.S passport, one visa photograph, and an International Health Certificte showing a current inoculation against yellow fever. (This inoculation must have been administered at least 14 days before the traveler arrives in Nigeria or entrance may be refused.) In addition, travelers must submit a copy of their round-trip air ticket or other proof of passage to and from Nigeria and a letter from their company explaining the purpose of the visit. In some cases, a copy of a letter of invitation from the appropriate entity in Nigeria also may be requested. Visa applications should be submitted well in advance (at least 4 weeks) of departure for Nigeria. Visas are not issued upon arrival in Nigeria, and persons arriving without a valid Nigerian visa will be refused entry.

Nigerian consulates and embassies are supposed to issue 1-year multiple-entry visas to serious business representatives, but compliance is sporadic. To procure a multiple-entry visa, applicants should submit detailed letters of explanation from their companies and a letter of invitation from the appropriate Nigerian Government agency or private company stating why multiple entry will be required to the Director of Immigration, Federal Ministry of Internal Affairs. The Ministry will telex its approval to the issuing embassy or consulate in the United States. Exact requirements may vary from case to case.

Travelers should be aware that the Nigerian Embassy and consulates in the United States will not issue visas to applicants with South African visas or customs stamps in their passports. This policy also has been applied to Israel from time to time. It is recommended that applicants who are also traveling to these countries either obtain a second passport or request that these countries issue their visas on detachable forms.

Living Conditions and Costs

Although the climate is tropical throughout Nigeria, considerable variations exist between the south and the north. Temperatures range from 79°F to 90°F in the south and from 65°F to 100°F in the north. High humidity prevails throughout the year in the south and in May-October in the north. There are two rainy seasons in the south, March-July and September-November, and one in the north, April-October. The dry season in the north is usually made dusty by Saharan winds called "harmattan." Rainfall varies from 150 inches a year on the coast to 25 inches or less in the extreme north.

A number of infectious diseases are prevalent in Nigeria. The foreign visitor should avoid unboiled water, ice, peeled fruits, and raw vegetables. Regular use of malaria suppressants is strongly recommended. Vaccinations for typhoid, tetanus, and gamma gobulin for hepatitis are also highly recommended. Visitors should consult with their physician, visa agency, or their local health department about the current inoculations required and recommended prior to a visit to Nigeria.

Adequate medical facilities are not readily available in Nigeria. Many common American household medicines are available locally, but any special medicines should be carried with the traveler.

There are several large hotels in the Lagos area and some comfortable hotels in major towns throughout Nigeria. The three major hotels in Lagos are the Eko Holiday Inn, the Federal Palace, and the Ikoyi. Others include the Mainland, Bristol, Airport, and Durbar. It is advisable to make reservations well in advance, particularly for Lagos hotels, which generally require up to 6 weeks' notice. Visitors without reservations will find it very difficult to find accommodations. It is important to note that most hotels require payment in advance and will only guarantee or confirm a reservation if an advance deposit has been made for the entire length of the stay. Visitors who fail to arrive forfeit their deposit.

The price of an air-conditioned single room with bath at one of the major hotels in Lagos is about $90 per day plus a $30 per day deposit for food, of which the unused portion is refundable upon demand. The deposit on such a room is about $120 per day. Upon arrival, travelers may find themselves accommodated in double rooms costing about $100 per day, or in a single room at the double room rate. Visitors should also be prepared to find that the air-conditioning does not work due to frequent power shortages.

In Lagos, there are some air-conditioned restaurants serving Arab, Indian, Chinese, and European dishes. Meals are expensive—$40 to $60 per day.

There are several night clubs, one or two of which include a cabaret, and a few casinos; all are expensive by U.S. standards.

Taxi service is available in Lagos and most other urban areas; however, it is frequently expensive and unreliable due to traffic. Fares should be negotiated in advance, particularly from the airport. (From the airport to Ikeja to Victoria Island, the fare should be under $20.) Cars with drivers can be rented for about $100 per day. U.S. business visitors to Nigeria should figure on about $200 per day for expenses. Visitors to Lagos are advised that the incidence of armed robbery is fairly high, so that travel in and around the cities should be limited after sunset and before dawn.

Lagos airport is often congested, and the traveler can expect long delays entering and leaving the city. Domestic airline schedules are unreliable—flights may be cancelled on a moment's notice. Reservations made may not be honored as overbooking by the airline is common. Travelers should plan on arriving at the airport at least 1 hour before the flight.

Business appointments generally have to be made by personal calls or sending notes by hand, as the telephone and postal systems are unreliable and slow. Visitors should write to their contacts well before their departure from the United States informing them of the departure date, itinerary, and hotels to be used. The international telex is fairly reliable and should be used if possible. Cable traffic is also generally reliable; cables should carry a Private Mail Bag (PMB) or Post Office Box (P.O. Box) as well as a street address. Important documents or correspondence is best sent by courier (see "Communications").

Marketing Tips

Steps to Achieving Profitable Operations.—All foreign business representatives face the same situations—endless negotiations, considerable prepayment for services anticipated and administrative delays—in dealing with Nigerian customers. Americans, however, stand a good chance for commercial success in Nigeria. Common language, quality, durability, and reputation of U.S. products are to their advantage. Many American firms already have tailored their presence in Nigeria to suit the market. They make the most of sales potential by appointing local agents or distributors, selling through established wholesalers and dealers, or direct investment.

Three proven steps have become evident in achieving profitable operations in this difficult market. First, build a company, product or service profile that can withstand scrutiny. Direct product or service literature (with ample pictures and indication of satisfied overseas customers) to key agent candidates, buyers, end users or government authorities. Do your homework on the market before you sign or ship. Expeditious handling of correspondence is expected and greatly appreciated. Second, visit the market. Do not expect to arrive and sign invoices or contracts and leave the next day. Lagos is a difficult city in which to communicate because of inoperative telephones and serious traffic jams (go-slows), which often result in long delays and an inability to meet tightly drawn schedules. Third, start small; practice moderation at first. From the moment you hint at an interest in Nigeria you will be inundated with contacts, facilitators, promoters, consultants, etc. [4] Complete the first sale, contract, or job well and let successive sales build your acceptance in Nigeria's market.

Business visitors should be well dressed. Casual dress in many cases connotes a casual attitude, especially to European-trained Nigerians. Titles should be used, especially the honorific titles of traditional leaders. Company representatives should be flexible in business dealings and be able to make decisions on contractual matters without lengthy referral to their home offices. In Nigeria, business of any consequence is consummated face to face. No worthwhile transactions can be completed either impersonally or quickly. Follow-up visits are common. As a developing nation determined to upgrade its standing of living and committed to integrate fully its peoples into the economic mainstream, Nigeria prefers those proposals which include measures to train its people and are in concert with its long-range development goals.

Language.—English is the official language of Nigeria, although for many Nigerians it is a second language. Business travelers will find that most government officials and business people speak English well. However, travelers should not use American slang and idioms.

Business Hours.—Business establishments and government offices are generally open from 7:30 a.m. to 4 p.m., Monday through Friday. Lunch is generally taken from about 1 to 2 p.m. Many government offices and businesses hold staff meetings on Monday and Friday mornings, sometimes making it difficult to see people at these times. In the Muslim north, all establishments close at 1 p.m. on Friday.

Holidays.—The official Nigerian public holidays are as follows.

Holidays falling on Saturdays are likely to be observed on the preceding Friday, while those falling on Sunday are likely to be observed on the following Monday. While the Muslim holidays of Eid-El-Fitri and Eid-El-Kabir are usually ei brated for 2 consecutive workdays, their celebration dates, as well as the celebration date of Eid-El-Maulud, vary according to the actual sighting of the crescent of the new moon. Confirmation of the dates is normally issued by the Ministry of Intenal Affairs approximately 2 weeks prior to the holidays.

New Year's Day	January 1
Eid-El-Maulud	variable
Good Friday	variable
Easter Monday	variable
Eid-El-Fitri	variable
Eid-El-Kabir	variable
National Day	October 1
Christmas Day	December 25
Boxing Day	December 26

Currency.—Nigeria decimalized its currency in 1973. This currency, the naira, is divided into 100 kobos. (One naira equals about US $1.45.)

Travelers must declare all currency upon entering and leaving Nigeria. Foreign exchange controls regulations allow travelers into and out of Nigeria to import or export up to 50 naira in Nigerian currency. There is no restriction on the amount of foreign currency that can be brought into the country.

Since credit cards are not widely accepted in Nigeria, travelers are advised to use travelers' checks

Embassy Assistance

U.S. business visitors are encouraged to use the commercial staff at the U.S. Foreign Service posts in Nigeria and the Nigerian Embassy and consulates in the United States for guidance on doing business in the Nigerian market. The Embassy in Nigeria is at 2 Eleke Crescent, Victoria Island, P.O. Box 554, Lagos; (phone: 610097); telex: 21670 USEMLA NG. There is a U.S. Consulate at Kaduna, in northern Nigeria, located at 5 Ahmadu Bello Way, P.O. Box 170, Kaduna (phone: 062-213276).

Nigerian Embassy in the United States is located at 2201 M Street, N.W. Washington, D.C. 20037, phone: 202-822-1500. (The commercial and consular sections are located at the Nigerian Embassy Annex, 2215 M Street.) There are three Nigerian consulates in the United States: 575 Lexington Avenue, New York, NY, 10022 (phone: 212-935-6100); 225 Peachtree Street, N.E., Suite 1000, Atlanta, GA 30302, (phone: 404-577-4800); and at 360 Post Street, Suite 502, San Francisco, CA, 94108, (phone: 415-433-6500).

[4] American firms are urged to check current Nigerian requirements, procedures, terms, and credentials with their bank, export company, international commercial information facility, or their nearest Department of Commerce District Office.

Appendix A
Business categories under the Nigerian Enterprises Promotion Decree

Schedule 1.—Enterprises Exclusively Reserved for Nigerians

1. Advertising and public relations business
2. All aspects of pool betting business and lotteries
3. Assembly of radios, radiograms, record changers, television sets, tape recorders, and other electric domestic appliances not combined with manufacture of components
4. Blending and bottling of alcoholic drinks
5. Blocks and ordinary tile manufacture for building and construction works
6. Bread and cake making
7. Candle manufacture
8. Casinos and gaming centers
9. Cinemas and other places of entertainment
10. Commercial transportation (wet and dry cargo and fuel)
11. Commission agents
12. Departmental stores and supermarkets having an annual turnover of less than 2 million naira.
13. Distribution agencies excluding motor vehicles, machinery, and equipment and spare parts
14. Electrical repair shops other than repair shops associated with distribution of electrical goods
15. Estate agency
16. Film distribution (including cinema films)
17. Hairdressing
18. Ice-cream making when not associated with the manufacture of other dairy products
19. Indenting and confirming
20. Laundry and dry-cleaning
21. Manufacturers' representatives
22. Manufacture of suitcases, briefcases, handbags, purses, wallets, portfolios and shopping bags
23. Municipal bus and taxi services
24. Newspaper publishing and printing
25. Office cleaning
26. Passenger bus services of any kind
27. Poultry farming
28. Printing of stationery (when not associated with printing of books)
29. Protective agencies
30. Radio and television broadcasting
31. Retail trade (except by or within departmental stores and supermarkets
32. Singlet manufacture
33. Stevedoring and shorehandling
34. Tire retreading
35. Travel agencies
36. Wholesale distribution of local manufactures and other locally produced goods

Schedule 2—Enterprises in Which Nigerians Must Have 60 Percent Equity Participation

1. Banking (commercial, merchant, and development banking)
2. Basic iron and steel manufacture
3. Beer brewing
4. Boat building
5. Bottling of soft drinks
6. Business services (other than machinery and equipment rental and leasing) such as business management, consulting services, and fashion designing
7. Clearing and forwarding agencies
8. Canning and preserving of fruits and vegetables
9. Coastal and inland wateways shipping
10. Construction industry
11. Departmental stores and supermarkets having annual turnover of not less than 2 million naira
12. Distribution agencies for machines and technical equipment
13. Distribution and servicing of motor vehicles, tractors, and spare parts thereof or similar objects
14. Fish and shrimp trawling and processing
15. Establishments specializing in the repair of watches, clocks, and jewelry, including imitation jewelry for the general public
16. Garment manufacture
17. Grain mill products including rice milling
18. Industrial cleaning
19. Insecticides, pesticides, and fungicides
20. Internal air transport (scheduled and charter services)
21. Insurance (all classes)
22. Lighterage
23. Manufacture of bicycles
24. Manufacture of biscuits and similar dry bakery products
25. Manufacture of cosmetics and perfumery
26. Manufacture of cocoa, chocolate, and sugar confectionery
27. Manufacture of dairy products, butter, cheese, milk, and other milk products
28. Manufacture of food products like yeast, starch, baking powder, coffee roasting; processing of tea leaves into black tea
29. Manufacture of furniture and interior decoration. Manufacture of metal fixtures for household, office, and public building
30. Manufacture of jewelry and related articles including imitation jewelry
31. Manufacture of leather footwear
32. Manufacture of matches
33. Manufacture of paints, varnishes, or other similar articles
34. Manufacture of plastic products such as plastic dinnerware, tableware, kitchenware, plastic mats, plastic machinery parts, bottles, tubes, and cabinets
35. Manufacture of rubber products, rubber footwear, industrial and mechanical rubber specialties such as gloves, mats, sponges, and foam
36. Manufacture of tires and tubes for bicycles, motorcycles, and motor vehicles
37. Manufacture of soap and detergents
38. Manufacture of wire, nails, washers, bolts, nuts, rivets, and other similar articles
39. Other manufacturing industries such as nonrubber and nonplastic toys, pens, pencils, umbrellas, canes, buttons, brooms and brushes, lamp-shades, tobacco pipes, and cigarette holders
40. Mining and quarrying
41. Oil milling, cotton ginning, and crushing industries
42. Paper conversion industries
43. Printing of books
44. Production of sawn timber, plywood, veneers and other wood conversion industries
45. Petrochemical feedstock industries
46. Publishing of books, periodicals, and such like
47. Pulp and paper mills
48. Restaurants, cafes, and other eating and drinking places
49. Salt refinery and packaging
50. Screen printing on cloth, dyeing
51. Inland and coastal shipping
52. Slaughtering, storage associated with industrial processing and distribution of meat
53. Tanneries and leather finishing
54. Tin smithing and processing
55. Wholesale distribution of imported goods
56. Photographic studios, including commercial and aerial photography

Schedule 3—Enterprises in Which Nigerians Must Have 40 Percent Nigerian Equity Participation

1. Distilling, rectifying, and blending of spirits such as ethyl alcohol, whisky, brandy, gin, and the like
2. Fertilizer production
3. Tobacco manufacture
4. Manufacture of basic industrial chemicals (organic and inorganic)
5. Manufacture of synthetic resins, plastic materials, and man-made fibres except glass
6. Manufacture of drugs and medicines
7. Manufacture of pottery, china, and earthenware
8. Manufacture of glass and glass products
9. Manufacture of burnt bricks and structural clay products
10. Manufacture of miscellaneous nonmetallic mineral products such as concrete, gypsum, and plastering products (including ready-mixed concrete) mineral wook, abrasive; asbestos products; graphite products
11. Manufacture of primary nonferrous metal products such as ingots, bars and billets; sheets, strips, cirales, cecrous rods, tubes, pipes and wire rods; casting and extrusions
12. Manufacture of (fabricated metal) cutlery, hand tools, and general hardware
13. Manufacture of structural metal products, components of bridges, tanks, metal doors and screens, and window frames
14. Manufacture of miscellaneous fabricated metal products, except machinery and equipment, such as safes and vaults; steel springs furnaces; stoves; and the like
15. Manufacture of engines and turbines
16. Manufacture of agricultural machinery and equipment
17. Manufacture of metal and wood working machinery
18. Manufacture of special machinery and equipment, such as textile and food machinery, paper industry machinery, oil refining machinery and equipment, and the like
19. Manufacture of office, computing, and accounting machinery
20. Manufacture of other machinery and equipment except electrical equipment, pumps, air and gas compressors; blowers, air-conditioning and ventilating machinery; refrigerators; and the like
21. Manufacture of electrical industrial machinery and apparatus
22. Manufacture of radio, television, and communication equipment and apparatus
23. Manufacture of electrical appliances and housewares
24. Manufacture of electrical apparatus and supplies not elsewhere classified, such as insulated wires and cables, batteries, electric lamps and tubes, fixtures and lamp switches, sockets, switches, insulators, and the like
25. Shipbuilding and repairing (excluding boat building)
26. Manufacture of railway equipment
27. manufacture of motor vehicles and motorcyles
28. Manufacture of aircraft
29. Manufacture of professional and scientific and measuring and controlling equipment, such as laboratory and scientific instruments, surgical medical and dental equipment, instruments and supplies, and orthopaedic and prosthetic appliances
30. Manufacture of photographic and optical goods
31. Manufacture of watches and clocks
32. Manufacture of cement
33. Manufacture of metal containers
34. Plantation agriculture for tree crops, grains, and other cash crops
35. Plantation sugar and processing
36. Ocean transport/shipping
37. Oil servicing companies
38. Storage and warehousing—the operation of storage facilities and warehouses (including bonded and refrigerated warehouses) for hire by the general public
39. Textile manufacturing industries
40. Hotels, rooming houses, camps, and lodging places
41. Data processing tabulating services (on a fee or contract basis)
42. Production of cinema and television films (or motion picture production)
43. Machinery and equipment rental and leasing
44. All other enterprises not included in Schedule 1 or 2 not being public sector enterprises

Appendix B

Industries Enjoying Pioneer Status

1. Cultivation and processing of food-crops, vegetables, and fruits
2. Manufacture of cocoa products
3. Processing of oilseeds
4. Integrated dairy production
5. Cattle and other livestock ranching
6. Bone crushing
7. Fishing (a) Deepsea trawling and processing
   (b) Coastal fishing and shrimping
   (c) Inland lake fishing and processing
8. Manufacture of salt
9. Mining of lead zinc ores by underground mining methods
10. Manufacture of iron and steel from iron ore
11. Smelting and refining of nonferrous base metals and the manufacture of their alloys
12. Mining and processing of barytes and associated minerals
13. Manufacture of oil-well drilling materials containing a predominant proportion of Nigerian raw materials
14. Manufacture of cement
15. Manufacture of glass and glassware
16. Manufacture of lime from local limestone
17. Quarrying and processing of marble
18. Manufacture of ceramic products
19. Manufacture of basic and intermediate industrial chemicals from predominantly Nigerian raw mateials
20. Manufacture of pharmaceuticals
21. Manufacture of surgical dressings
22. Manufacture of starch from plantation crop
23. Manufacture of yeast, alcohol, and related products
24. Manufacture of animal feedstuff
25. Manufacture of paper-pulp, paper, and paperboard
26. Manufacture of articles of paper-pulp, paper, and paperboard
27. Manufacture of leather
28. Manufacture of textile fabrics and man-made fibers
29. Manufacture of products made wholly or mainly of metal
30. Manufacture of machinery involving the local manufacture of a substantial proportion of components thereof
31. Manufacture of goods made wholly or partly of rubber
32. Manufacture of nets from local raw materials
33. Processing of local wheat and flour milling
34. Oil palm plantation and processing
35. Rubber plantation and processing
36. Gum arabic plantation and processing
37. Integrated wood projects
38. Manufacture of fertilizers

Market Profile—NIGERIA

Foreign Trade

Imports.—$14 billion in 1982; $19 billion in 1981. Major suppliers, 1981: United Kingdom, 18 percent; West Germany, 13 percent; Japan, 12 percent; France, 10 percent; United States, 9 percent. Chief imports: machinery and transport equipment, manufactured goods, construction and mining machinery, pumps, iron and steel, transport equipment, agricultural machinery, and chemicals. Imports from United States: $1.3 billion in 1982.

Exports.—$15 billion in 1982; $18.4 billion in 1981. Major markets, 1982: United States (45 percent), West Germany, Netherlands, France, and Italy. Chief exports: crude petroleum, cocoa, tin, palm nuts, and oil, rubber, hides and skins, and leather products. Exports to United States: crude oil and cocoa. Exports to United States: $7.0 billion in 1982.

Trade Policy.—Nonpreferential, nondiscriminatory; preshipment inspection required. Favors establishment of domestic manufacturing over imported products. Import controls include outright bans, licensing, high tariffs. Import deposit scheme imposed in April 1982.

Trade Prospects.—Communications equipment and systems, building and construction supplies and equipment, health care items, energy systems, oil-field process plant equipment, agricultural machinery, business equipment, material handling equipment, motor vehicle maintenance equipment, and food processing and packaging equipment.

Foreign Investment.

Over $2 billion, about $400 million from United States, primarily in crude oil exploration and production.

Investment Prospects.—Government welcomes foreign investment. Nigerian participation required in all types of enterprises, and government participation and control required in certain "strategic" industries. Tax and import concessions subject to negotiation. Investment guarantee agreement with United States in effect since March 1975.

Finance

Currency.—Niara (N). (1N=US$1.34, in Oct. 1983). Money supply: $10.2 billion (1982). Current overall inflation rate 20 percent in 1982.

Domestic Credit and Investment.—Twenty-one merchant, commercial, or cooperative banks; four government banking institutions. Lagos stock exchange and local credit institutions expanding operations as result of oil income.

National Budget.—FY 1983 planned Federal budget of approximately $15.3 billion.

Foreign Aid.—IBRD is the largest source; United Kingdom, France, Japan, West Germany, Netherlands, United States, and Canada are other significant technical assistance sources.

Balance of Payments—Had a $5 billion balance-of-payments deficit in 1982. Foreign exchange reserve totaled $1.5 billion in January 1983.

Economy

Based on subsistence agriculture, but oil provides most of disposable income. Growing manufacturing sector.

GDP.—$75 billion in FY 1982; about $730 per capita; real annual growth rate about 3.7 percent.

Agriculture.—Food production is not adequate to supply domestic demand. Normally world's largest exporter of palm products, second in cocoa; large rubber and cotton producer.

Minerals.—Crude oil production was 1.3 million barrels per day in 1982. Oil accounts for 94 percent of total export earnings. Tin, coal, marble, and limestone are mined. Steel works began in 1982.

Industry.—Traditionally textile oriented. Oil revenues have fostered growth in construction, food processing, oil-related, and import substitute manufacturing.

Commerce.—The Nigerian Enterprises Promotion Decree of January 1977 requires a minimum of 40 percent participation by Nigerians in all business enterprises.

Development Plan.—The Fourth Development Plan, 1981/85, stresses agriculture, industry, education and housing, but has been modified until revenue picks up.

Basic Economic Facilities

Transportation.—Present 64,000-mile road network (29,000 paved) accommodates over 600,000 registered vehicles; railways carry 1.3 million tons of freight and provide passenger services for approximately 6 million people per year over its 2,700 miles of track; international airports in Lagos, Kano, Port Harcourt, and internal airfields at 19 state capitals and other cities. Port Harcourt, Lagos, often congested.

Communications.—International telegraph, radio, television, telephone and telex facilities are government-operated. 17 newspapers; 154,000 telephones operated.

Power.—Demand for power will require about $75 million annually to sustain the required 350 percent growth over the next decade. Present capacity estimated at 2,200 MW, mostly from petroleum. Frequent black outs.

Natural Resources

Land.—356,700 square miles; a little larger than Texas and Utah combined. Mangrove swamps, tropical rainforest in south, central plateau, northern savanna.

Climate.—Tropical in south, northern areas hot and dry. Wet season May to October.

Forestry.—12 percent of land in forest reserves.

Fisheries.—Commercial fishing: shrimp for export.

Population

Size.—About 85-95 million; 20-25 percent urban. Principal cities: Lagos, 3 million; Ibadan, 1.6 million; Kano, 1 million; and Kaduna, 500,000. Estimated non-African population 50,000.

Language.—Official and business language is English.

Education.—Literacy 30 percent. Universal Primary Education introduced at a cost of $5 billion between 1975 and 1980.

Labor Force.—About 33 million, of which 53 percent in agriculture, forestry, and fishing.

Marketing in Norway

Contents

Report Revised December 1979

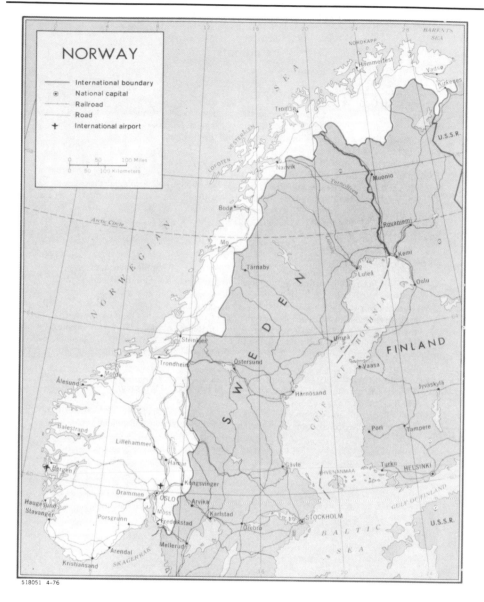

518051 4-76

Note: Oslo is 3,200 miles (5,150 km.) from Washington, D.C.

Foreign Trade Outlook

Introduction

Norway is an excellent market for U.S. products. Its sound and growing economy offers U.S. exporters opportunities to sell a wide range of goods and services. The people of Norway enjoy one of the highest standards of living in the world.

Norwegian industry is modern and technologically advanced. Norway is a receptive market for industrial equipment and supplies, quality consumer products, and agricultural commodities. The availability of foreign exchange, low tariff rates, few trade restrictions, and a well organized commercial system make business in Norway easy and profitable.

The economy of Norway was based for a long time on the country's traditional industries of fishing, shipping, forest products and metals. During the 1970s, the exploration and development of Norway's oil and gas resources changed the balance and relative position of these industries and altered the outlook of Norway's economy.

Norway is a maritime and trading nation. Its economy is based heavily on foreign trade. In addition to its imports and exports, Norway's fleet of merchant ships carries a sizable portion of the world's international trade. Revenue from the shipping industry is a major source of foreign exchange for Norway and important to its economy.

The Norwegian market is much larger in volume and value than would be expected for a country with 4.5 million inhabitants.

Norway's imports from the world in 1978 totaled $11.4 billion (table 1) a decrease of 11.6 percent from 1977. Imports from the United States were $775 million in 1978. The United States held a 6.8 percent share of the import market. The United States ranks as Norway's fourth largest supplier, following Sweden, West Germany, and the United Kingdom.

Current Economic Situation

The Norwegian economy is in readjustment. It slowed somewhat in 1978 as the GNP rose by about 3.1 percent compared with 4.3 percent in 1977. The weakest sectors continued to be the shipbuilding and pulp and paper industries while metal smelting improved. Manufacturing production, which declined in 1977, remained relatively unchanged in 1978. The year-end figure on unemployment doubled to more than 30,000 but was still less than 2 percent of total work force.

Inflation in 1978 was an estimated 8.5 percent while consumer demand remained at 1977 levels. At latest prices the GNP was equivalent to $39.7 billion (at the average 1978 exchange rate of NKr. 5.30/US$), or to about $9,920 on a per-capital basis.

While imports declined 11.4 percent in 1978 to an estimated $11.4 billion, exports rose 16 percent to about $9.9 billion.

The balance of payments deficit is estimated to have been reduced by more than one half to $2.4

HOW TO OBTAIN BACKGROUND INFORMATION ABOUT THESE COUNTRIES

For those who wish *general* data about a country—data which goes beyond marketing and commerce—the editors recommend *Countries of the World and Their Leaders*, published as an annually updated yearbook by Gale Research Company, Detroit, Michigan 48226. Containing 4- to 20 page entries on 168 countries, the volume also provides several hundred pages of supplementary world data. Each country entry is prepared by the U.S. Department of State to provide a general briefing on the geography, people, culture, and polical situation of that particular country. Each report provides some historical insight as well as a look at contemporary trends of lifestyle in the country. Reports also discuss a country's educational system, its press, ethnic groupings and religious practices.

Table 1. —Norway: Imports from World and from Unites States, 1978

(millions of U.S. dollars)

	From World	From U.S.	U.S. Share Percent
Food, total	742.3	75.7	10.2
Meat	42.2	.5	1.2
Fish	26.8	1.0	3.7
Cereals	111.1	38.0	34.2
Vegetables and fruit	187.9	32.1	17.1
Beverages	33.7	3.8	11.3
Tobacco	38.9	11.0	28.3
Industrial raw materials	825.4	90.7	11.0
Oil seeds	77.3	71.6	92.6
Wood	135.0	4.5	3.3
Crude fertilizers	82.7	6.5	7.9
Metal ores and scrap	372.7	3.9	1.0
Mineral fuels and lubricants	1,354.5	61.9	4.6
Animal and vegetable oils and fats	27.7	2.6	9.4
Chemicals	756.8	43.3	5.7
Organic	101.4	9.0	8.9
Inorganic	68.4	4.1	6.0
Dyes	56.1	2.3	4.1
Pharmaceutical	107.6	3.7	3.4
Plastics	220.8	9.9	4.5
Basic manufactures	2,126.1	53.0	2.5
Rubber products	108.1	4.1	3.8
Paper and paper products	181.5	5.6	3.1
textile yarn, fabrics and products	367.7	9.5	2.6
Nonmetal mineral manufacture	180.1	3.9	2.2
Iron and steel	474.7	6.0	1.3
Machinery and transport equipment	3,856.4	342.4	8.9
Power generating equipment	212.9	30.7	14.4
Specialized industry equipment	582.2	72.7	12.5
Metalworking machinery	73.4	3.1	4.2
General industrial machinery	565.2	45.9	8.1
Office machines and computers	186.1	59.2	31.8
Communications and recording equipment	279.8	24.4	8.7
Electrical machinery and appliances	533.6	47.2	8.8
Miscellaneous manufactured articles	1,569.7	84.6	5.4
Apparel and accessories	492.1	6.3	1.1
Scientific and control instruments	150.7	30.6	20.3
Photographic, optical, and time devices	132.3	22.5	17.0
TOTAL	11,422.3	775.3	6.8

Note: Import values are c.i.f. Norwegian Kroner values have been converted to U.S. dollars values at an average 1978 rate US$1=5.2423 NKr

Source: Central Bureau of Statistics, Manedsstatistikk over Uternrikshandeln (Monthly Bulletin of External Trade). December 1978 totals may differ from detail due to rounding.

billion. At the end of the third quarter, total net foreign exchange reserves were $2.5 billion, 19 percent above the corresponding figure for 1977.

Norway's exports of raw and refined petroleum and products in 1978 (Jan.-Nov.) increased 23 percent to 17.2 million metric tons (MT) valued at $1.8 billion while imports declined 13 percent to 9.1 million MT valued at $1 billion.

Best Export Prospects

While Norway is a small country, its market potential is greater than might be suspected at first glance. For one thing it is among the world's wealthiest countries in terms of per capita gross national product. Furthermore, there are several fields that offer market potential out of proportion to the size of the population. Among them are the offshore oil industry, the maritime industry, and the metals working industry.

The oil industry warrants particular attention. Oil field development continues to be a major market for U.S. products and services. Work is nearing completion on the Statfjord A platform and is in progress on the Valhall/Hod Field. Maintenance and upgrading of facilities continue at Frigg and Ekofisk. Construction contracts have been awarded for the multibillion dollar Statfjord B. project. Any commercial finds in newly licensed North Sea blocks are sure to lead to further projects. Two sites north of the 62nd parallel could be opened to exploratory drilling in 1980—the first probing in an area many times the size of Norway's continental shelf, which is under development.

Partnerships between American and Norwegian companies in oil field services are proving advantageous to both sides. The American companies have the experience and technology, but benefit from the Norwegian marine expertise and understanding of local conditions. They also get a foot in the door when it comes to Norwegian Government policy, which hopes for its industry to provide at least 60 percent of offshore goods and services. Licensing Norwegian firms to manufacture from American designs is another possibility for U.S. manufacturers.

The Norwegian market also offers opportunities in a number of product categories.

It is expected that there will be a continuation of strong demand for high technology products for industry. Norwegian industry needs such products to diversify and to minimize the high cost of labor. Some of the most promising exports to Norway are described here.

Process Control Instrumentation.—The demand for process control instrumentation in Norway is expected to grow. Local production is limited and most demands are met by imports from U.S. and European suppliers. total imports in 1977 totaled $20 million. Projected growth indicates an import market of $26 million by 1981. U.S. equipment has a good hold in this market, supplying more than 60 percent, of which 25-30 percent is manufactured in the U.S.

Major foreign suppliers of these products are the United States, West Germany, and the

NEW TO EXPORT?

Many basic questions about export and overseas marketing are answered by material which appears at the end of the country-by-country market studies. Three of the information packages appearing there for the benefit of the new exporter are:

- **Basic guide to export marketing.**
- **East-west trade financing**
- **Metric laws and practices in international trade.**

Check the table of contents for page numbers of these and other special reports.

United Kingdom. Domestic production of process control instrumentation is limited—less than 9 percent of total consumption. Local production is not expected to expand. The United States will probably continue as a major supplier to this market. Exports of U.S. manufactured process control equipment to Norway increased 25 percent from 1976 to 1977.

Major competitors to U.S. manufacturers are West Germany suppliers, especially in the fields of nonelectric instruments and control valves.

Norwegian processing industries are characterized by high costs and slow growth. The processing industries have a great interest in modernization and cost reduction projects. This will entail a greater use of process control instruments. The largest and most sophisticated end-user in Norway, the chemical industry, is expected to enjoy a steady growth during the 1980s.

An area of special interest to suppliers of process controls is an anticipated expansion of the relatively new petrochemical industry when offshore oil and gas activities move into new exploration areas off northern Norway.

Laboratory, Scientific and Engineering Instruments.—The market for laboratory, scientific and engineering instruments is expected to expand rapidly. The market increased from $81 million in 1975 to $127 million in 1977. There has been substantial growth in imports of laboratory and scientific instruments. U.S. exports of these products to Norway almost doubled from 1976 to 1977, particularly in scientific instruments, which accounted for 15 percent of total consumption. The US market share for scientific instruments is estimated at 30 percent, while the import share for instruments in general is above 17 percent.

Although West Germany still dominates this import market, there is evidence of increased interest in U.S. equipment, particularly research instruments. U.S. sales of these items gained considerably during the past 2 or 3 years. Domestic production of instruments is limited and chiefly concentrated in fields of flow instruments (echo-sounders) and instruments for checking electrical quantities.

Of late, there has been an increase in research and development budgets within industry as well as on the federal and local government level. Among the sectors of concentration are offshore and onshore oil and gas activities, stringent anti-pollution measures and controls, and alteration of the Norwegian shipbuilding industry, which is seeking new production alternatives. Among the factors which stimulate the higher degree of research and development is Norway's high labor costs.

Among the items for which there is an active interest are physical properties testing equipment, computers for scientific applications, hospital laboratory instruments, sampling and analyzing instruments for pollution control applications, and electro-optical instruments.

Communications Equipment.—The Norwegian market for communications equipment will continue to grow. U.S. deliveries increased some 120 percent from 1976 to 1977, after a relatively slow investment rate in Norway during 1976. Plans for modernization and construction of new communications systems indicate excellent opportunities for U.S. suppliers. The market for communications equipment in Norway was estimated at $220 million in 1978, in which telecommunication systems/equipment represented some $120 million. The market size is expected to increase to almost $350 million by 1981. These figures, however, do not incorporate TV/Radio broadcast equipment, audio-video and alarm-signaling equipment.

There is a high degree of interest in Norway in U.S. technological developments in communications systems and equipment. Recent contracts for earth satellite station equipment and automation system for public telephones were won by U.S. suppliers in competition with Japanese and European companies. U.S. suppliers have established a good hold in some segments of this market, but strong competition is expected from domestic and European suppliers.

Future plans of the Norwegian Telecommunication Administration include an additional earth station for satellite communication, a continuous conversion from analog to digital telecommunication system, and an inter-Scandinavian and domestic data transmission network system.

Investments also will be made to modernize and replace ground aviation equipment, administered by the telecommunication authorities.

The feasibility of an interScandinavian satellite TV system, is being debated. Plans also are being developed to expand the present satellite communication system to include more offshore oil/gas rigs and platforms in the North Sea. These plans, however, will be the concern of the oil companies operating there. Expansion of the North Sea oil drilling activities is also expected to boost sales of other communications equipment, such as tropospheric scatters and microwave line of sight.

Metalworking Equipment. — In the past several years, the U.S. share of the market for this equipment has increased substantially. The United States is supplying some 10 percent of the metalworking equipment imported into Norway.

The traditional suppliers, West Germany, Sweden, United Kingdom, and Switzerland, are still strong in this market. But depreciation of the U.S. dollar, new technologies and product developments combined with good quality and realiability of U.S.-manufactured equipment, are important factors to Norwegian end-users.

The growth of the oil and gas industry will present Norwegian industry with a number of future opportunities requiring modern and high-technology equipment. High labor costs is a special reason for the continuing search for advanced technology. Plans for industrial development in the metals industry, and, in particular, incentives to improve and increase the level of processing within the Norwegian aluminium industry, will stimulate demand for metalworking equipment.

Electronic Components and Production Equipment. — The Norwegian electronics industry is expected to achieve a considerable growth rate during the next few years, especially in the communications and data processing fields. Expansion of the electronics industry consequently will result in more imports of advanced components, since domestic production is limited. The U.S. share of the import market is growing steadily. The total 1978 import market for components is estimated at $121 million. Projections indicate a 1981 market of nearly $250 million.

There is no domestic Norwegian production of electron tubes, limited production of semiconductors and intergrated circuits, but considerable production of passive components. The United States has a lead in marketing advanced electronic components but competition from European suppliers is expected to become stronger in the years ahead. This will call for greater promotional efforts from U.S. companies and emphasis on new technology if the United States is to maintain or strengthen its present share of the market.

Norway is attempting to stimulate the growth of its electronics industry. The Norwegians, through industrial assistance programs, hope to expand the production of electronic equipment to make electronics a more important sector in Norway's future industrial development and reduce its reliance on its traditional industries. Future expansion of the electronic industry will present opportunities for U.S. exporters of electronic components and electronic production and test equipment.

Many of the major U.S. trade publications in the electronics field are read by Norwegian electronics professionals. U.S. companies receiving inquiries from Norway should be alert to potential sales in Norway and respond promptly to such inquiries.

Building Equipment, and Supplies. — U.S. exports of building equipment and fixtures to Norway have grown rapidly in the last few years. Total U.S. sales of these products to the Norwegian market total almost $7 million. Prospects for expanding their sales are good. The Norwegian construction industry is affected by high labor cost. U.S. advances construction techniques have stimulated Norwegian interest in labor-saving building supplies, new building methods and materials.

Most of Norway's requirements for building materials and equipment are supplied by domestic production but a sizable volume of these products is imported, mostly from Sweden and West Germany. Although the U.S. share of the market is not large, it is significant to warrant attention and promotion by U.S. suppliers.

Among the product categories in which the United States appears to have good sales potential are refrigeration systems and equipment, plastic materials, plumbing and hardware equipment, and prefabricated building technology. A significant interest also has been noted in solar energy systems and equipment.

Other Products With Sales Potential. — In addition to those industries and products, already mentioned, the Norwegian market appears to offer good prospects for expanded U.S. exports in a number of other product categories. Among these are food processing and packaging equipment, computers and peripherals, aviation and avionics equipment, medical equipment, graphic arts equipment, and pumps, valves, and compressors.

Industry Trends

Industrial Development

For a long time Norway relied on a few traditional industries to support a sound, stable, relatively prosperous economy. These cornerstores included the shipping, fishing, forest products, and the metals industries. Norway has only a very small percentage of its land suitable for farming. Only about 3 percent of Norway's land area is cultivated. The country is favored, however, with an abundance of energy resources. Inexpensive hydroelectric power spurred industrial development, particularly in the metals and in other industries needing low-cost power.

Norway grew into a modern, industrialized country based on mining, manufacturing and transportation. In recent years, several events have changed the relative importance of the traditional industries and will have an impact on future industrial development in Norway. Among these events were the discoveries of oil and gas in commercial quantities, the extension of the 200-mile economic coastal zone, and the Norwegian people's decision to remain out of the European Economic Community.

Norwegian industry, which in the past had been evolving along predictable lines, is now has expected to make some dramatic changes with significant expansion in oil-based industries, petrochemicals, plastics, and electronics.

The traditional industries, however, will continue to be important sectors in the country's economy.

Forest Products Industry. — The forest products industry accounts for about 10 percent of Norway's exports. It is greatly affected by world demand for pulp and paper, which in turn depends on the economies in the industrialized countries. Norwegian exports of these products have been doing well lately but Norway must remain price competitive to keep it market position. If U.S. industrial growth slows down with a consequent decline in American demand for pulp and paper, then the relatively high cost Norwegian producers will be hard pressed to defend their position against U.S. exporters.

Efforts to hold down prices through improved technology and modernization will generate opportunities to sell equipment to the pulp and paper industry.

The largest Norwegian company in this field is Aktieselskapet Borregaard. Starting in the forest products field, this firm has diversified into chemicals, petrochemicals, and textiles.

Shipbuilding Industry. — The Norwegian shipbuilding industry is one of the largest in Europe and one of the most technologically advanced. One major company, the Aker Group, builds large tankers. Another firm, Moss-Rosenber, is noted for the country's merchant fleet. A large number of ships is exported.

The shipbuilding industry in Norway, as well as in much of the rest of the world, is in a slump due to overcapacity and a decline in demand. At the moment some Norwegian shipyards have no backlog of orders and are facing curtailment of activity and substantial reductions in employment. The shipyards provide employment for 34,000 people. It is expected that it will be several years before there is a rebound in the shipbuilding industry. In the interim, Norway is attempting to restructure the industry and reduce its overcapacity.

Electrochemical Industry. — The electrochemical industry began with the production of nitrogen and nitrogenous fertilizers. One of Norway's largest firms, the State owned Norsk Hydro, had its beginnings in this field. It is now the largest exporter of nitrogen products in Europe.

Electrometallurgical Industry. — The electrometallurgical industry is one of Norway's important industrial fields. Norway is one of the world's leading aluminum producers. Ardal og Sunndal Verk and Norsk Hydro are two of the country's aluminum processing companies.

Norway's ferro-alloy, nickel, and zinc industries — all are based on abundant and economical hydroelectric power. The firm, Elken-Spigerverki A/S, operates the largest ferro-silicon smelter in Europe as well as an aluminum smelter.

Electronics Industry. — Norway's electronics industry, though small, is highly sophisticated and can be expected to expand during the next few years. It produces telecommunications equipment, televisions, tape recorders, and other electronic apparatus.

Other Industries. — Other significant industries in Norway include mining (chiefly iron ore pyrites), metal fabrication, fishing and fish processing, and food processing. Table 2 shows number of establishments, number of employees, and sales values of production for major Norwegian industries in 1976.

Research and Development. — One factor that gives a solid foundation to Norway's industrial growth and diversity is its commitment to research and development. R&D expenditures have increased during the past few years. Research institutes, business enterprises, and the universities cooperate closely. It is estimated that expenditures on research and development exceed 1 percent of GNP.

Norway has three main research councils: Norges Almenvitenskapelige Forskningsrad (NAVF, The Norwegian Research Council for Science and the Humanities); Norges Teknish-Naturvitenskapelige Forskningsrad (NTNF), the Norwegian Research Council for Scientific and Industrial Research); and Norges Landbruksvetenskapelige Forskningsrad (NLVF) The Norwegian Agricultural Research Council.

NTNF and NLVF include representatives of government research institutions and business and industry, while NAVF comprises members from Government research institutions and business.

The three councils (as well as a coordinating body representing all three) perform all no research work and have no scientific functions. Their activity is organizational, consultative and financial in nature. They plan an active part in developing and coordinating Norwegian research, giving advice and making recommendations to government departments and research institutions. They also promote closer contact between research institutions and industry. Their activities in these fields have a significance in shaping Norwegian research policy far beyond the direct application of the financial means at their disposal.

Government Role in the Economy

Norway has a free-market economy based on private ownership of the means of production and distribution. Approximately 94 percent of the total value of mining and manufacturing for example, is contributed by the private sector.

The number of government-owned enterprises is only a small share of the total of Norwegian enterprises, but these play a significant role in the economy. These enterprises are mostly public utilities, special monopolies, e.g., railroads, grain, broadcasting and other activities which for reasons of public policy are operated for the public benefit.

The Norwegian Government's participation in industry stems from special needs of the country, such as employment and other social needs; from providing capital for enterprises where the requirements are too large or risky for domestic interest; from the takeover of shares of companies previously owned by German interests as part of World War II reparations; and from participation in enterprises jointly financed with private organizations.

The degree of government participation in the major State-owned enterprises ranges from 50 to 100 percent. Of the total gross investment in Norwegian industry, 12.5 percent is government owned.

Some large industrial firms partially or fully state owned are Statoil, petroleum; Norsk Hydro, aluminum, fertilizers, petrochemicals, power; Sydvaranger, iron mining; Norsk Jernverk, steel; Norsk Olje, petroleum products distribution; and Ardal og Sunndal Verk, aluminum.

The Norwegian Government is also a major shareholder along with the Danish and Swedish

Table 2.—Norway's Major Industries in 1976

Industry	No. of Establishments	No. of Employees	Gross Value of Production (million dollars)
Total manufacturing	13763	379,811	20,052
Food Processing	2761	50,179	3,669
Beverage and tobacco	78	6,139	470
Textiles	481	12,439	390
Wearing apparel except shoes	469	9,603	214
Wood products except furniture	1765	24,735	1,187
Wood furniture and furnishing	655	10,508	365
Pulp, paper and paperboard	209	19,976	1,292
Graphic arts and printing	1481	33,248	908
Chemical raw materials	64	8,695	645
Chemical products	191	7,920	442
Oil refining	7	697	978
Petroleum products	49	1,601	135
Rubber products	89	2,768	80
Plastic products	322	8,140	314
Cement, concrete, etc.	613	12,748	603
Iron and steel	62	16,416	902
Nonferrous metals	82	12,385	1,069
Metal products	1542	27,650	964
Machinery	973	31,459	2,027
Electrical apparatus and equipment	382	23,393	924
Transport equipment	981	51,198	2,236
Professional and scientific instruments, photo and optical goods	51	1,116	37

Note: Norwegian kroner values are converted to U.S. dollar values at an average rate of exchange for 1976 (One US $=5.4545 N kr.)

Source: Central Bureau of Statistics, Industristatistikk 1976 (industrial Statistics 1976, table #11), Olso.

Governments, in Scandinavian Airlines System (SAS).

Norwegian industrial companies, in which the Government has a share of the ownership, are operated and managed on the same basis as joint stock companies that are privately owned.

In addition to limited ownership of manufacturing and mining facilities as described above, the Norwegian Government plays a major role in overall economic and industrial planning. Planning is being done for the exploitation of Norway's oil and gas resources. Norway sees a new industrial future in petrochemical production. The Government also has become involved in plans for the restructing and modernizing of such basic industries as shipbuilding and forest products. In these fields the Government is concerned with maintaining employment and international competitiveness.

The Government also places emphasis on regional industrial development, i.e., the encouragement of industry to locate facilities in less-developed, economically disadvantaged regions of the country. Information on this program is available from the Regional Development Fund (Distriktenes Utbyggingfond) Mollergaten 1/3 Oslo 1, Norway.

In industrial planning, as in other matters, the Government works closely with private industry and labor. In Norway arriving at a consensus and taking a rational approach with cooperation and understanding is an important element in government and private enterprise transactions.

Transportation and Utilities

Transportation

Ocean shipping from the eastern seaboard of the United States to Norway is rapid and convenient. Four U.S. shipping lines offer services to Norway, three of which have weekly sailings from Atlantic Coast ports and the fourth offering service from the major Gulf ports to Norway. The Atlantic Coast carriers are Farrell Lines, Inc.; Sea Land Services, Inc.; and United States Lines, Inc. Lykes Bros. Steamship Co., Inc. provides Gulf Coast services.

Farrell Lines Inc. provides container service to Oslo via Bremerhaven from the ports of New York, Norfolk, and Baltimore with feeder service from Savannah, Philadelphia and Boston. Transit time from the last U.S. port to Norway is 10 days. For additional information call (212) 482-8916 or write Farrell Lines, Inc., one

Whitehall St., New York, New York 10004. Sea-Land Service, Inc., has weekly container ship sailings from New York, Boston, Baltimore, Charleston, Portsmouth, Savanah, Wilmington, NC and Philadelphia. Cargo for Norway is transhipped at Bremerhaven. Transit time from the last U.S. port to Norway is 10 days. For further information call (201) 494-7400 or write Sea-Land Service, Inc., Edison, New Jersey 08817. United States Lines, Inc. provides weekly containerized service sailing from the ports of New York, Philadelphia, Baltimore, Norfolk, Charleston, Jacksonville, and Savannah. Cargo is transhipped to Norway via Rotterdam. United also offers refrigerated, open top and flat bed equipment on request. Transit time to Oslo is 12 days. Further information may be had from (201) 272-9600 by writing to United States Lines, Inc., 27 Commerce Drive Cranford N.J. 07016. Lykes Bros. provides service from the major Gulf ports of New Orleans and Galveston transhipped to Norway through Bremerhaven. Contact (504) 523-6611 for additional information or write Lykes Bros. Steamship Co., Inc., Lykes Center, 300 Poydras Street, New Orleans, Louisiana 70130.

Norway's principal seaports are Oslo, the main port of entry for the southeastern area; Bergen and Stavanger, providing access to the west-central and southwestern areas respectively; Kristiansand, serving the extreme southern region; and Trondheim and Tromso in the north.

Shipping to Norway by air freight or air express is facilitated by frequent regularly scheduled air passenger and freight service. Oslo is served by two airports-Fornebu, about 10 minutes from the city center, and Gardemoen, about 36 miles from the city. Two other major airports handle international traffic—Sola airfield at Stavanger and Flesland airfield near Bergen.

Railroad services are available to most of the principal cities and between Oslo and Stockholm, Sweden, and Oslo and Copenhagen, Denmark, via southwestern Sweden. Oslo is the key rail center of the country. Railroad construction and maintenance is difficult because of Norway's climate and rugged terrain. No service is provided to many west coast points because of the deep fjords; Narvik can be reached by rail only through Sweden.

Highway trucking services, although not yet developed to an extent comparable with that found in the more populous European countries, has developed steadily over the past few years. The best system of highways radiates from Oslo, linking that city with Kristiansand, Bergen, Stavanger, and Sweden.

Utilities

Electricity, generated mainly by hydroelectric plants, is abundant and relatively inexpensive. Norwegian production of electricity was 81.1 billion kilowatt hours in 1978. Norway has the world's highest per capita consumption of electricity.

Telephone and telex services in Norway are operated by the State telegraph service (Televerket).

Distribution and Sales Channels

Major Marketing Areas

Selling in Norway is simplified by the fact that the population is concentrated within a few relatively dense areas. About half of the inhabitants live in Eastern Norway, a relatively small area centered in the political and business capital, Oslo. Another quarter of the population resides in the southwestern coastal area that includes Bergen and Stavanger.

During this century Norway has been transformed from a rural to an urban economy. The share of inhabitants living in urban areas increased from only 35 percent in 1900 to about two-thirds of the population today. Especially rapid has been the growth of suburban areas outside the central cities.

These are four major commercial-industrial centers. Each of these forms the core of a larger marketing and distribution area. They are: (1) the Oslo metropolitan area, (2) the Bergen area; (3) the Trondheim area, and (4) the Stavanger area.

Oslo, capital and commercial heart of Norway, has a population of 460,000 (including adjoining suburbs). Oslo serves a wider area traditionally called Ostlandet (Eastern Norway) whose population is about 2 million. Oslo includes head offices of most major firms and industrial associations, banks and financial institutions. Its industry is diversified, including shipping, shipbuilding, machinery manufacturing, steel, food processing, textiles. Radiating from Oslo, particularly to the south along the Oslofjord, are numerous smaller centers such as Sarpsborg (forest products), Drammen, Skien, Porsgrunn. Largest of these centers are the Sarpsborg-Fredrikstad area (90,000), Drammen (51,000), and Skien-Porsgrunn area (91,000). The Eastern

Norway commercial area, focussed on Oslo, contains half of Norway's population, 60 percent of its economic activity, and about half of the commercially usable agricultural and forest land. Most of the country's wood-processing industries such as paper, pulp, and board) are located in this area.

Bergen, with a population of 212,000 including suburbs, is the second largest commercial center. The greater Bergen area is important from a marketing standpoint because of its industrial and commercial growth. Norsk Hydro, one of the country's largest firms, has built a huge refining-petrochemicals complex at nearby Mongstad. Bergen long has been a major shipping and commercial center. It serves much of the area traditionally known as Vestlandet (Western Norway). Because waterfalls abound in this region, it is the site of several large electrometallurgical and electrochemical plants which use hydroelectric power.

Trondheim is Norway's third largest commercial center. The city proper has a population of 135,000. It serves a larger marketing area in central Norway, called Trondelag, whose population is about 366,000. This important marketing area includes large metal and mining facilities and is noteworthy for its agriculture and fishing.

Stavanger (population 88,000), located about 100 miles south of Bergen, is Norway's fourth major commercial center and Norway's "oil capital", a base for oil drilling and exploration operations in the North Sea. Stavanger, like Bergen, is in the Vestlandet (Western Norway) administrative region.

A survey of Norwegian marketing areas also should include reference to Sorlandet, an area at Norway's southern tip. It principal city is Kristiansand (population 61,000). Sorlandet (Southern Norway) is of growing importance for tourism; it also includes several metal plants and shipping ports.

At Norway's opposite extreme is Nord-Norge (Northern Norway). Despite its relatively large land area (most of it north of the Arctic circle), it includes only 12 percent of the population. It is the site of several impressive manufacturing plants, including Norway's largest iron and steel works at Mo i Rana and one of the largest aluminum plants at Mosjoen.

Harstad (21,363), selected by the Government to be the center of offshore oil field supply operations for northern Norway, will grow as oil field activity increases and as a neighboring Coast Guard station is developed. Other important towns are Tromso (45,000), Mo i Rana (26,000) and Bodo (37,000). Narvik (19,000) is a significant iron ore port.

Importers, Agents, Distributors

Norway offers the American exporter a wide range of methods of distributing and selling a product. This section will consider the most generally used of these methods.

Selling Through an Agent or Distributor. — Exporters of capital goods, industrial raw materials, and related commodities usually employ Norwegian commission agents. Normally one exclusive agent is appointed with offices in Oslo to cover the entire Norwegian market. Such representatives often work through subagents in Bergen, Trondheim, and Stavanger as well as other principal centers. The Norwegian Federation of Purchasing Agents is headquartered in Oslo.

Norwegians strongly favor dealing with agents in Norway rather than being served from other Scandinavian or European locations. This is particularly so in high technology products. The concern is not as great if a Swedish or other European agent has an active subagent in Norway, but it bothers Norwegians when a small company located outside Norway, without adequate sales or service facilities, gets exclusive Scandinavian distributor rights and then proceeds to ignore their market.

Norwegian agents often represent several different foreign firms and carry a number of different product lines. In selecting an agent, the exporter should avoid commissioning one who handles directly competing products.

In Norway, it is important that an agency contract be terminated prior to entering into negotiations with another potential agent. If the contract between the principal and the agent has not been satisfactorily terminated, other agents will generally decline any offer of representation. When a principal plans to change agents, he should bear in mind that compensation may be demanded for goodwill that the agent has built up — a sum representing as much as his average annual commission over the previous 5 years. Although goodwill compensation is not yet written into law in Norway, it is already an established practice.

In view of the customary practice of appointing exclusive representatives in Norway, U.S. exporters should know that they are legally entitled to certain exemptions from U.S. antitrust laws. The Webb-Pomerene Act allows a limited exemption from antitrust laws for direct exports by allowing exporters to agree on prices, sales terms, territorial divisions, and other activities in export trade which are forbidden in U.S. domestic trade. More information on the Webb-Pomerene Act is available through the Foreign Business Practices Division of the Office of International Finance and Investment, U.S. Department of Commerce, Washington, D.C. 20230.

Manufacturers seeking an agent in Norway should also plan to visit the country. It is the best way of making a first-hand appraisal of the relative merits of prospective agents. Besides acquainting the exporter directly with the market, it also gives him an opportunity to discuss policy and sales campaigns with the agent.

Close contact between the American principal and the Norwegian distributor is very desirable and should be developed early. Certain products and equipment entail servicing to maintain them during their useful life. The exporters should make provision for such servicing by qualified personnel in Norway or a neighboring Scandinavian country.

Selling Through Established Wholesaler. — Consumer goods, components, hardward products, and industrial raw materials are often imported through these channels (see section below on "Wholesale and Retail Channels").

Selling Directly to Retail Organizations. — American exporters of consumer goods may find it advantageous to sell directly to department stores, consumer cooperatives, voluntary chains, and other retail outlets. A few of the larger Norwegian retailers have purchasing agents in the United States.

Establishing a Sales Subsidiary in Norway. — This method of reaching the Norwegian market has become increasingly significant; a number of U.S. firms now operate their own sales offices.

Commercial Practices

Norwegian importers generally prefer sales quotations on a c.i.f. port of destination basis. Quotations and invoices are usually in terms of the currency and country of origin.

In view of the competitive nature of the Norwegian market, exporters seeking a foothold have had to grant increasingly favorable credit terms. In recent years there has been a trend toward more liberal financing, as opposed to payment by letters of credit or cash. Letters of credit are customarily used mainly for handling certain staple commodities and transit shipments. Knowledge of the market competition and of the customer are generally the prime considerations in deciding whether to use sight drafts, time drafts, or open accounts.

General terms of sale are payment within 30 to 90 days after delivery, varying with the commodity and credit standing of the purchaser.

Wholesale and Retail Channels

Because of rising labor costs and continued concentration of the Norwegian population in cities and towns, there is a strong trend in both wholesaling and retailing toward concentration into larger and fewer units.

Small and medium-sized retail merchants usually purchase imports through wholesaler-importers. Large retail merchants (including department stores) often prefer to purchase imports directly from the foreign manufacturer.

Wholesale Channels.—Total turnover in the Norwegian wholesale trade reached $20 billion in 1976, while the number of wholesale establishments exceeded 9,000. Wholesale sectors with the largest turnover and number of establishments are: food and beverages, machinery and equipment, building materials, raw materials, automobiles and accessories, and fuels and lubricants. Many of the largest wholesalers are highly organized through the Association of Norwegian Wholesale Merchant and Importers based in Oslo.

Retail Channels.—Links between wholesalers and retailers are highly developed in Norway, with substantial reliance on central buying organizations, especially in consumer goods. This simplifies the task of locating a Norwegian distributor.

Turnover in the Norwegian retail trade was 12 billion in 1976 while the number of establishments was over 33,000.

The food trade is dominated by four wholesaler groups, each covering roughly one fourth of the total turnover in that sector: 1) Joh. Johannson — family-controlled importer/distributor organization—with local wholesale outlets in most or Norway (address: Postboks 130—Sentrum, Oslo 1,); 2) KOFF—a retailer-owned import organization, (address: Ruselokkveien 14, Oslo 1); 3) Loken Group (address: Hans Loken & Co. A/S, N Griegsgate 30, 1500 Moss); and 4) NKL—(Norges Kooperative Landsforening), the central organization for Norway's consumer cooperative consisting of

approximately 700 local association (address: Revierstredet 2, Oslo 1). NKL is the second largest trading company in Norway, with an annual sales turnover exceeding $200 million.

The S–Kjeden retail stores, operated by the cooperatives, include approximately 2,000 outlets. Groceries account for half of their total turnover. The consumer cooperatives also sell hardware, wearing apparel, household appliances, etc. About 20 percent of Norway's grocery retail turnover and 11 percent of total retail turnover are in the hands of consumer cooperatives.

Vivo is a large voluntary food chain, with almost 300 retail outlets and seven wholesale distributors. Large private chains also include the Irma stores (which originated in Denmark) and the Bonus stores in Oslo.

The hardware trade is also characterized by a close linkage between wholesalers and retailers. Eight major hardware wholesale firms are represented by the purchasing organization Nordjern A/L. In the same field, approximately 100 hardware retailers have formed a wholesale organization, Jernia Norsk A/S.

In the electrical equipment field, 40 Norwegian retailers have established a voluntary chain called Sesam/Serviceringen. The El–Kjop and Elgros Group of firms are major purchasing organizations in the electrical equipment field.

Paints and a similar products also are sold through highly organized distribution channels. Seventy-two retailers beong to the Samkolor group. Samkolor in turn belongs to the all-Nordic purchasing agency, Norcolor, which includes retailers in Denmark, Sweden and Finland. Farveringen, a group of about 13 wholesalers, is another paint distributor.

In the textiles and wearing apparel field there are several voluntary chains: Samtex, a voluntary chain of about 46 retailers, sells men's wear; Nortextil, a voluntary chain of some 35–40 members, retails women's wear and home furnishings. A rapidly growing chain of shoe stores, Falkinger, now has about 150 sales outlets and 50% of the shoe market.

Future Distribution Trends.—A Norwegian study indicates that the rapid growth of modern merchandising facilities and techniques will continue, with emphasis on more self-service stores, supermarkets, and department stores.[1] The

[1] The study is "Norsk Detaljhandel fram til 1980" by Dr. John Arndt of the Norwegian School of Economic and Business Administration, Bergen.

growth of these more efficient units will probably bring a substantial decline in the number of retail shops. In some product groups, voluntary buying chains can be an effective counter to the competition of larger enterprises (e.g. hardware, textiles, shoes, paints, sporting goods, electrical goods). The growth of branch stores and department store chains will probably continue.

Competition in price, assortment, and service may be expected to continue increasing. Various combinations of these competitive techniques are found in self-service stores (which number about 4,000,), discount houses (accounting for some 25–30 percent of consumables turnover in Bergen, where they have been most prominent), supermarkets, and department stores.

Wholesale and Retail Sales

Norway's 9,000 wholesale establishments had a turnover of nearly $20 billion in 1976. Of total wholesale turnover, 50 percent was transacted in the Oslo area, 7 percent in Bergen, and 8 percent in the south western county (Rogaland), which includes Stavanger. In terms of commodities, wholesale turnover was distributed as follows: food, beverages, tobacco, 26 percent; raw materials, 25 percent; machinery and equipment; 16 percent; hardwood and construction materials (12 percent); other (21 percent).

Norway's 33,000 retail establishments in 1976 had a turnover of $12 billion, including the value added tax and other sales taxes. Of total retail turnover, 27 percent was transacted in the Oslo area, 10 percent in Bergen and surrounding areas, and 10 percent in Rogaland (which includes Stavanger). In terms of commodities, retail turnover was distributed as follows: food, beverages, tobacco, 36 percent; motor vehicle, parts and accessories, 20 percent; wearing apparel and textile goods, 11 percent; furniture, 8 percent; other 25 percent.

Licensing and Franchising

Licensing.—Licensing has become a rather general practice, and both American and other foreign firms have licensed the manufacture of a considerable variety of products in Norway. Each licensing arrangement must be approved by the Bank of Norway in order for the Norwegian licensee to remit royalty payments. Americans entering into licensing arrangements in Norway should make certain that this requirement has been properly carried out.

Approval of licensing arrangements by the Norwegian authorities is determined on the merits of each individual case. The dollar-saving,

and the dollar-earning prospects offered by the particular arrangement are given particular attention by the licensing authorities.

Franchising.—While franchising is not yet a widespread practice in Norway, the outlook is good for future development. There are no discriminatory laws or regulations aimed at franchising. Particularly attractive opportunities for franchising exist in automotive products and services, fast food restaurants, motels, laundry and dry cleaning services, educational services, and nonfood retailing.

It is recommended that any U.S. company considering franchising in Norway conduct a qualified legal study to ensure full validity and enforcement of its franchise agreements. To use an American form of franchise agreements without adjustments to Norwegian laws and practices could be detrimental to the franchisor's business.

Government Procurement

Government procurement in Norway is decentralized with the various agencies controlling their own purchases. The procedures for procurement of commodities at the national government level are regulated by legislative enactment (Forskrifter for bortsettelse av leveranser og arbeider for statens regning, Royal Norwegian Ministry of Industry, Oslo, 1968). These rules and regulations are, with a few exceptions, nondiscriminatory, making no distinction between domestic and foreign suppliers or contractors. Procurement at the national government level is, as a general rule, made on the basis of competitive bidding. Invitations to bid are made either by public advertisements (Norsk Lysningsblad and newspapers), or by circular letters to known suppliers or contractors. The underlying rule is that strict business principles should form the basic criteria for a government institution or agency in the awarding of contracts. In addition to price, importance is thus attached to quality, delivery time, ability to meet required standards and specifications, and the general reputation of the bidder.

An exception to Norway's generally nondiscriminatory procurement policies has been made in the field of offshore oil equipment. Concession agreements for oil exploration and drilling contain a clause requiring the procurement of equipment from Norwegian sources whenever feasible, given similar price, quality, and delivery. This applies to concessions held by private as well as State-owned companies.

Also the procurement regulations do not apply to the State monopolies (the State Grain Corporation, the Wine Monopoly, the State Fish Tackle and Gear Monopoly, and the State Medical Depot), or to the government-owned corporations which manufacture goods under the same conditions as privately owned enterprises. These monopolies and corporations follow established commercial practices in their procurement.

There is no general legislative enactment regulating local governments' (counties', cities' and rural municipalities') procurement of commodities and services.

Advertising and Research

Advertising Media. — All major types of advertising media are available in Norway with the important exception of radio and television. Expenditures on advertising (except point of sale advertising) amounted to Nkr 780 million in 1970 or 0.87 percent of GNP. While on a per capita basis, advertising expenditures are less than in Sweden, nevertheless they are respectable for a country the size of Norway.

Publications — newspapers, magazines, and trade and professional journals — account for the lion's share of advertising expenditures, almost 75 percent, direct mail accounts for 16 percent. Other media include cinema advertising, outdoor posters and billboards, transit cards, and point-of-sale advertising.

Neither radio nor television carries commercial advertising in Norway. Broadcasting is carried out by a State-controlled corporation, and is financed through payment of annual license fees by set owners.

Advertising in Norway is self-policed by means of an "advertising agreement" concluded between associations representing the three interests concerned: the media; the advertiser, and the advertising agency. With few exceptions, all advertising agencies in Norway are members of the Association of Authorized Advertising Agencies (Autoriserte Reklamebyråers Forening—ARF). Advertisers are represented by the Norwegian Advertisers Association (Norske Anmonsørers Forening—NAF). Publications, the most important advertising media, are organized in the Norske Avisers Landsforbund (Federation of Norwegian Newspapers) and Norsk Ukepresse (Norwegian Weekly Press).

Publication. — Norway has an extremely high rate of newspaper readership. In 1977 there were 72 dailies with a total circulation of about 1.6 million. Circulation figures are audited by the newspaper publishers' association. Extensive demographic information concerning readership is available. Distinctions are drawn between the 4 major metropolitan areas and other, so-called trade districts, numbering about 100. The 3 leading metropolitan newspapers (Aftenposten—morning edition, Dagbladet, and Verdens Gang—both afternoons papers) had a combined national weekday circulation of 500,000.

Advertising space rates in Norwegian newspapers are relatively low. A full page, black-and-white advertisement in the largest circulation daily costs between 32,000 and 38,000 kroner, depending on location. Rates for weekend editions and color pages are higher. Copy in English is acceptable.

Magazines also enjoy wide circulation in Norway and are a prime medium for advertising of consumer goods. The most widely read magazines are consumer-family journals, the largest of which are 3 weeklies: Hjemmet, circulation 365,000 in 1978; Norsk Ukeblad, circulation 314,000 in 1978; Allers, circulation 248,000 in 1977; and A-Magasinet (a weekly supplement to aftenposter), circulation 257,000 in 1977.

Billboard and Poster Advertising. — Expenditure on billboard and poster advertising, including transit cards, amounted to Nkr. 11.7 million in 1978. Poster advertising is found almost exclusively in large towns. Highway billboard advertising is strictly regulated by law and is mostly local in character, (e.g., advertisements for nearby inns, etc. Display cards are found both inside and outside public transport vehicles.

Direct Mail Advertising. — Although direct mail advertising is widespread in Norway, it is an expensive medium in view of high postal rates. There are a number of advertising firms that specialize in direct mail in Norway and that offer mailing lists by target audience category.

Other Forms of Advertising. — Cinema advertising is used extensively in Norway and is considered an effective medium for the promotion of consumer goods. Advertising shorts, which are screened before the feature film begins, usually run for approximately 60 seconds. Point-of-sale advertising is also important, and considerable emphasis is placed by merchants on attractive window and store dislays.

Trade Fairs. — Only in recent years has a conscious effort been made to give Norwegian trade fairs an international character, and with the important exception of the biennial shipping fair—Nor-Shipping—more foreign firms' participation in Norwegian trade fairs is through their local agents.

Market Research.—In preparing a preliminary survey of the Norwegian market for any product, the exporter may wish to make use of the excellent Norwegian statistical publications.

Market research is well developed in Norway. The techniques used in the United States are generally available. Market research is for the most part undertaken by advertising agencies and marketing consultant firms. Opinion and customer attitude surveys are available, as are retail audits. While most trade associations follow developments within their sector, their findings are often made available only to their members.

The American Embassy in Oslo supplies the U.S. Department of Commerce with information on the Norwegian economy as well as commercial and market information. There are also a limited number of short market studies available to U.S. companies through the U.S. Department of Commerce, Washington, D.C. 20230, as well as the Department's District Offices.

Credit

Availability of Capital

Major sources of loan capital in Norway are commercial banks, savings banks, state banks, insurance companies and loan associations. In recent years the state banks have expanded more rapidly than private banking, a trend which some Bank of Norway and other government officials see a need to reverse. Other specialized credit institutions also play a significant role in providing credit. Relatively insignificant amounts of credit are obtained through the stock and bond markets.

Sources of Financing

The Central Bank.—Norges Bank is a joint stock company in which the Government took over all shares in 1949. Norges Bank, which has 20 branches throughout Norway, handles the usual central bank functions such as regulating foreign exchange transactions, conducting open market operations, establishing the central discount rate. It is the sole bank of currency issue. In conjunction with the Ministry of Finance, Norges Bank formulates national monetary and credit policy.

Commercial Banks.—there are 27 commercial banks, of which the largest have branches throughout Norway. Total loans made to the public by commercial banks at the end of December 1978 totaled 43.3 billion kroner. The largest banks transact a large share of the banking business and predominate in international transactions. These are:

Den Norsk Creditbank
Kitgegaten 21
Olso, Norway

Chiristania Bank of Kreditkasse
Stortorvet 7
Olso, Norway

Bergens Privatbank
P.O. Box 826
5001 Bergen, Norway

There are no branches of foreign banks in Norway; however, the First National City Bank of New York and Manufacturers Hanover Trust Company have opened representative offices in Oslo. Although not engaged in banking operations, a representative office maintains and develops contacts, responds to inquiries, and cooperates with Norwegian banks in banking transactions.

Norwegian commercial banks provide most short- and medium-term loans to business and industry. The most common types of credit are overdraft facilities, loans based on promissory notes, and discounting of bills of exchanges and hire purchase contracts. To a lesser extent the commercial banks grant building loans and long-term loans.

Savings Banks.—From 500 units in 1970, the number of savings banks in Norway has reduced through mergers to about 370 today. Customers loans and long-term mortgage loans have traditionally been granted by savings banks. These also finance agriculture to a considerable extent. Recent legislative ammendents have brought their operations more closely into line with those of commercial banks. Savings banks' total loan commitment to the public in December 1978 stood at 33.7 billion kroner.

State Banks.—Norway has eight state-owned banks which concentrate on medium-and-long-term investment loans. These banks supplement the private capital market, especially in areas such as the financing of industry, regional development and housing. Loans outstanding from state banks in December 1978 amounted to 67.1 billion kroner, of which 30.6 billion in kroner were attributable to the State Housing Bank.

The Norwegian Bank for Industry, which is 51 percent state-owned, grants mortgage loans to industry. Another specialized credit is Strukturfinans, establishing jointly by the State and private credit institutions. Its aim is to provide assistance to Norwegian companies which are restructuring their operations to achieve greater efficiency. It normally grants medium-term (1-12 year) loans, which may be use for plant rationalization, expansion, product development, etc. These two institutions merged in January 1978.

The Regional Development Fund provides loans and grants to promote development in less developed regions of the country.

Other banks owned and controlled by the Government are the Postal Giro, which provides basic money transfer facilities through Post Office outlets and the Post Office Savings Bank. When deemed appropriate by the Government, these banks supplement private lending for trade and industry.

Insurance companies/Pension Funds. — Insurance companies provide long-term, first mortgage loans to the business community and to private parties. Life insurance companies and pension funds are more restricted in the administration of their funds, most of which are placed in long-term mortgage loans. Non-life insurance companies are not as restricted and may place their funds at higher levels of risk. Loans outstanding from insurance companies in June 1978 totaled 15.8 billion kroner, of which 14.6 billion kroner to the private and municipal sectors, and 1.2 billion kroner to the central government and to financial institutions.

Loans Associations. — These institutions were established to grant credit to certain sectors of industry such as shipbuilding, export and real estate. They fund themselves through issuing bearer bonds. Authorities establish a lending quota each year. Loans totaling 21.3 billion kroner were on record in September 1978, of which 7.3 billion kroner were made by the Real Estate Loan Association and 8.1 billion kroner by the Ship Mortgage Association.

Private Finance Companies. — Certain other types of companies also operate in the capital market. Some specialize in factoring and leasing. Their share of the market is fairly small with 4.2 billion kroner of loans outstanding in September 1978.

Norges Hypotekforening for Naeringslivet, established in 1972, grants long term, first mortgage loans to Norwegian industry.

Eksportfinans, an institution established by the commercial banks, grants medium-term credits to trade and industry, especially for the financing of Norwegian exports.

Stock and Bond Market. — The Norwegian stock market is small and does not function as a major source of capital. The ratio of share capital to GNP in 1976 was 5 percent for Norway, compared with ratios of 14 percent for Sweden, 28 percent for the United Kingdom and 54 percent in the United States. New issues on the Oslo Stock Exchange in 1977 totaled 329 million kroner while turnover for the year was 194 million kroner. Domestic bond issues are strictly regulated by the Ministry of Finance and a license is required. Larger manufacturing enterprises, power companies and municipalities float both domestic as well as international issues for their financing requirements.

Trade Regulations

Norway is heavily dependent on foreign trade and the earnings of its merchant fleet to maintain a high standard of living for its people. Its trade policy is aimed at expanding its foreign trade and shipping services.

There are few restrictions on imports and Norwegian duty rate are relatively low.

Norway takes an active role in international organizations engaged in promoting the freer movement of trade. It participates in the General Agreement on Tariffs and Trade (GATT), is a member of the Organization for Economic Cooperation and Development (OECD), and has membership in the International Monetary Fund and the International Bank for Reconstruction and Development (World Bank). Norway took an active part in the formation of the European Free Trade Association (EFTA). As a participant in the programs of these international organizations, Norway has liberalized its import trade as rapidly as its balance-of-payment position permitted. Relatively few commodities remain subject to control.

Tariff Structure

Norway's tariff is a single-column tariff using the Brussels tariff nomenclature (BTN) for commodity classification. The BTN, which is also referred to as the Customs Cooperation council Nomemclature (CCN), is an international system for classifying goods for customs purposes. It also is used by Norway for statistical reporting.

Norwegian Import duties apply to all countries receiving most-favored-nation treatment, including the United States. Tariffs on most machinery are in the 5 to 10 percent range. Those on most semimanufactures and raw materials are quite low. Rates on wearing apparel and other finished textile articles are relatively high, often falling within the 15 to 30 percent range. Certain items, mainly machinery, of a type not produced in Norway, may be admitted duty free provided this is authorized by the Norwegian Customs Department. That Department may also authorize raw materials and auxiliary products for industry to be imported duty free or at a lower rate than that provided in the tariff, if circumstances warrant.

Norway was an active participant in the Tokyo Round of the GATT multilaterial trade negotiations concluded in 1979, and agreed to make substantial duty concessions. The reductions are to be staged over an 8-year period begining January 1, 1980.

Preferential Trade Agreements With EFTA and EEC. — As a member of the European Free Trade Association (EFTA), Norway began a gradual elimination of its duties on practically all industrial products originating in other EFTA nations on July 1, 1960. The final reduction to duty-free entry was made on December 31, 1966. At that time EFTA consisted of Austria, Denmark, Finland, Norway, Portugal, Sweden, Switzerland, and the United Kingdom. Iceland became a member in 1970. Then on January 1, 1973, Denmark and the United Kingdom withdrew from EFTA to become members of the European Economic Community (EEC).

Norway, along with other EFTA countries that did not join the EEC, entered into an industrial free trade agreement with the Community. The agreement provided that Norway and the EEC eliminate in stages over a 4-year period their duties on trade in most industrial goods. Reductions of 20 percent were carried out on July 1, 1973; January 1, 1974; 1975 and 1976. The final reduction of 20 percent was made on July 1, 1977 so that there is virtually free trade in industrial goods between Norway, the other members of EFTA, and the nine member nations in the EEC.

Basic of Duty Assessment. — Most duties are levied on an ad valorem (a percentage of the c.i.f. value of goods). The dutible value is described in Norwegian customs regulations as the normal price plus certain other costs. The normal price is the price the goods would command when offered for sale in the open market by an independent seller to an independent buyer on the day of customs clearance. The "other costs," added to the normal price, include cost of packing, shipping, insurance.

Information regarding Norwegian duties applicable to specific products may be obtained free from any U.S. Department of Commerce District office or from the Norway Country Specialist, Office of Country Marketing, Bureau of Export Development, U.S. Department of Commerce, Washington, D.C. 20230. The Country Specialist also can provide information about Norwegian duty rate concessions resulting from the GATT negotiations.

Inquiries should contain a complete product description, including BTN, SITC, or U.S. Schedule B Export Commodity numbers, if known.

Customs Surcharges and Taxes. — Norway has no customs surcharges although some port and traffic charges are levied at the point of entry into the customs territory of Norway. Virtually all imports are subject to the Norwegian value-added tax, capital equipment to the investment goods tax, and certain goods to excise taxes. These taxes apply equally to imports and to goods produced in Norway. Further information is presented in the section of this report, "Taxation."

Advance Rulings on Classification. — Prior to signing a long-term contract or sending a shipment of considerable value, it may be prudent for the Norwegian importer or U.S. exporter to obtain an official ruling on customs treatment. Requests for advance information regarding the customs classification of products may be addressed directly to the Finansog Tolldepartmentet, Akersgaten 42, Oslo, Norway. The application should describe the product in full detail. Samples, catalogs, photographs, or other descriptive literature should be submitted whenever possible. The application should be signed by the manufacturer, or by the exporter or his representative in Norway.

While the customs authorities will not in all cases give a binding decision, the decision will usually be considered binding if the goods are found to correspond exactly to the sample or the description.

Import Restrictions. — Industrial goods originating in the United States are not subject to import restriction by Norway. Agricultural commodities are in some instances subject to global quotas; these quotas apply to all countries.

Control of certain commodities is exercised by State monopolies in Norway. The State Grain Corporation has a sole right to import grain and grain products. The Wine Monopoly has the exclusive right to import alcoholic beverages. The Norwegian Medical Depot has the exclusive right to import pharmaceutical products.

Sanitary certificates.—Shipments of pickled meat require a health certificate issued by a veterinary and signed by a Norwegian consul in the country of origin of the goods.

The following commodities may be imported only by special permission of the Ministry of Agriculture, and in some instances sanitary certificates of origin may be required: live animals; meat other than tinned or pickled; milk products; seeds of red and white clover, timothy, and alsike; disinfected hair and bristles; salted guts and bladders, living plants with roots; fresh vegetables and edible roots; certain animal products.

Marking and Labeling Requirements

In general, labels or other markings should indicate accurately the nature and contents of the package and should not be misleading. Goods so marked as to cause misunderstanding of their true origin are not permitted entry for the retail market. While the responsibility for compliance with national regulations falls on the Norwegian importer, U.S. exporters should follow carefully any marking and labeling instructions from the importer. Failure to do so may cause problems in clearing customs and loss of subsequent sales. If the merchandise is to be repackaged by the importer, he may wish to apply the proper marking, labeling, and display of price at that time. It is desirable to consult with your importer on this matter.

Most articles of precious metals require hallmarking before clearance is permitted.

Shipping documents

The documents required by Norway from the exporter on ocean or air shipments include a commercial invoice (with a certificate of value, signed by the consignee, and a verification of freight, insurance, and other costs for goods liable to ad valorem duty), a bill of lading, and sanitary or health certificates in certain instances.

All shipping documents may be made out in the English language. The use of the metric system of weights and measures, though preferable, is not compulsory.

Consular invoices and regular certificates of origin are not required.

Commercial Invoice.—No special form of commercial invoice is required. Invoices should be forwarded in at least two copies; the original stays with the bill of lading and the duplicate is sent direct to the importer. The invoice must include a description of the goods and their value; the number of cases, parcels, or containers; and the number or mark affixed to the cases, parcels, or containers. Invoices covering machinery, apparatus, tools, or parts therefore must specify net and gross weights.

If the entire shipment covered by the invoice consists of only one type of merchandise, the total net and gross weights should be indicated. If the shipment is made up of different types of merchandise, the net and gross weights of each type must be indicated; this data may be given on a separate sheet attached to the invoice.

Bill of Lading.—The usual ocean bill of lading (or air waybill for air shipments) suffices for shipments to Norway. The bill of lading must be prepared in accordance with the invoice. The date of the bill of lading and the invoices must be identical. "To order" bills of lading are accepted.

Numerous articles must be marked to show origin. Among these are yeast, potatoes, butter and oleomargarine, meat extract, seeds, plywood, cast-iron articles, batteries, razor blades, veneer, rubber goods (including rubber footwear), various textile fabrics, cordage, glassware, paints, paint brushes, and matches. Leather footwear must be marked to show quality as well as origin. Except in the case of footwear and a few other articles, marking can be done after arrival in Norway. There are no special regulations for marking outside cases or packages shipped to Norway except that packages upon arrival must be marked to correspond with the bill of lading and the invoice, and gross weight must be marked on single packages exceeding 1 metric ton in weight.

Labeling of pharmaceuticals is strictly regulated.

Customs-Privileged Facilities

Norway has no free ports or free trade zones.

Customs-privileged facilities in Norway are limited to three categories: (a) customs warehouses, (b) bonded warehouses, and (c) entrepots or transit zones. According to customs legislation (the Customs Law of June 10, 1966, chapters VII and VIII) customs privileges mainly cover storage of commodities. The customs authorities are entitled to permit repacking, but no further processing of customs-privileged imports. Customs-privileged facilities are under the supervision of Tolldirektoratet, (the Customs Directorate), Schweigaardsgate 15, Oslo—an agency under the Ministry of Finance. Tollvesenet is the executive arm of Tolldirektoratet.

Customs Warehouses.—Customs warehouses are owned and operated by Tollvesenet or by forwarding firms, shipping companies, or the Norwegian State Railways. Such facilities only allow short-term storage of imported goods. Foreign firms or nationals can put imported goods into customs warehouses, but such goods can only be removed for domestic distribution by Norwegian nationals or by firms registered in Norway.

Bonded Warehouses.—There are only three bonded warehouses in Norway for public use:

Oslo Havnelager A/S, Langkaia, Oslo Bergen Havnelagers Frilager A/S, Dokkeskjaerkaien, Bergen
Kristiansands Frilager, Odderøykaien, Kristiansand S.

In addition some shipping lines and private importers operate private bonded warehouses for storage of their own imports. Bonded warehouses and entrepots or transit zones can only be used for goods imported by firms registered in Norway.

Entrepots or Transit Zones.—The establishment of entrepots or transit zones is dependent on permits granted by Tolldirektoratet. Such facilities so far established in Norway are owned and operated by oil companies or private companies otherwise engaged in the North Sea oil exploration and exploitation. Only commodities subject to customs duty can be stored in entrepots today. The Tolldirektoratet, however, is considering extending entreport storage permits to duty-free commodities to avoid having to collect the 20% value added tax which must be refunded when the goods are removed (exported) from the entrepot or transit zone.

Samples, Carnets

Norway is a member of the "International Convention to Facilitate the Importation of Commercial Samples and Advertising Matter." Samples may be imported into Norway free of customs charges if they are of little or no commercial value, or if they have been made unfit for use. If they do not meet these requirements the samples are subject to customs duty.

However, samples intended exclusively for the obtaining of orders in Norway may be temporarily exempted from payment of duty providing a bond is posted upon entry of the samples into Norway. When the merchandise is reexported the bond is cancelled. Such samples, as well as pattern books and pattern cards, that may be carried by a commercial traveler must be declared at the first customhouse on arrival in the country.

Samples may also be imported temporarily by using the ATA Carnet. The ATA Carnet is a simplified customs document by which commercial samples or professional equipment may be sent or taken into Norway and any of the other 34 foreign countries participating in this arrangement. The ATA Carnet is a guarantee to the Customs authorities that duties and taxes will be paid if the goods are not taken out of the country. The carnet permits making customs arrangements in advance in the United States and is especially useful when visiting several countries, since the same document may be used and remains valid for a 12-month period.

In the United States ATA Carnets are issued for a fee by the U.S. Council of the International Chamber of Commerce, 1212 Avenue of the Americas, New York, N.Y. 10036, (212) 354-4480. Application forms may be obtained from your local U.S. Department of Commerce district Office.

Technical Standards and Requirements

Since Norway uses the metric system, equipment for sale by Norway should be adapted to it whenever possible.

For information on Norway's metric regulations and usage contact Norge Standiseringsforbund Haakon VII, gate 2, Oslo 1, Noway.

Electric current is 50 cycle, 220 volts A.C., single and three phase.

Electrical equipment sold in Norway must be approved by the Norwegian Electrical Control Board (Norges Elektriske Materiellkontrol) or

NEMKO, at Gustadalleen 30, Blindern, Oslo 3, Norway.

Information about Norwegian industrial standards may be obtained free from the Standards Information Service of the National Bureau of Standards, (301) 921-2587. This reference service can determine if there is a standard for a specific product, provide a reference number and the name of a private U.S. organization from which to obtain the standard.

Since the diversity of foreign standards, regulations, inspection procedures, and certification requirements constitute a considerable barrier to increasing U.S. exports, U.S. firms may want to take advantage of the Technical Help to Exporters program provided by the National Technical Information Service of the U.S. Department of Commerce. This service can provide foreign standards and regulations that a product must meet in a specific or regional market overseas. Customized work projects may also be undertaken to meet your needs in the standards area on a cost reimbursable basis. For additional information contact: National Technical Information Service, Technical Help to Exporters, U.S. Department of Commerce, Springfield, Va. 22161, (703) 557-4732.

Investment in Norway

U.S. Investment in Norway

U.S. direct investment in Norway totaled $1.63 billion at the end of 1977. Of this total, 73 percent was in petroleum, 21 percent in manufacturing, and 6 percent in other sectors (chiefly commerce).

About 100 U.S. firms have direct investments in Norway. Most of these are in sales subsidiaries. Within certain fields (petroleum, alloys, telephone and electronic equipment, ice cream products, medical supplies, and a few others), U.S. firms have manufacturing subsidiaries. By far the most vigorous field for U.S. direct investment at this time is offshore oil operations. U.S. subsidiaries in this field include Phillips Petroleum, Amoco, Esso, Gulf, Union Oil, Texaco, Mobil, Tenneco, Conoco, Superior Oil, Areo Amerada, Texas Eastern, and Getty.

Norwegian Policy on Investment

Officially, Norway accepts direct foreign investment, and foreigners are offered national treatment with a few minor exceptions. Public attitudes toward foreign investment are by and large positive.

As a general rule licenses or concessions must be obtained for all kinds of productive and manufacturing activity. Trade and merchandising, however, are in practice free from restriction.

Legislative impediments to foreign direct investment are contained in a number of concession laws which, for the most part, govern the conditions under which foreigners are permitted to own or develop natural resources, including real estate. (Largely, these regulations also apply to nationals). Interpretation of regulations by government authorities tends to inhibit foreign investment in such fields as banking and insurance. Also, foreign takeover or Norwegian companies is normally not permitted, and foreign investment in "new" enterprises is subject to approval. In practice, however, since all transfers of capital into Norway require foreign exchange licenses, the authorities have complete control over foreign investment, and all investment applications are handled on a case-by case basis.

Applications for investment in new enterprises are carefully screened. Preference is given industry which is new to Norway and capital intensive, incorporating a high level of technology. In view of the government's concern with unemployment, especially attractive would be investment which would absorb labor from declining industries (e.g. textiles, apparel, leather, shipbuilding and wood processing).

Once investment permission is granted, the right of physical establishment is controlled by the authorities in accordance with national social and demographic policies. Investment incentives are granted on a nondiscriminatory basis to both Norwegian and foreign firms locating in less developed areas of Norway. In effect, these areas comprise a large portion of the country.

Direct and indirect taxes are levied on a nondiscriminatory basis, and both foreign and Norwegian firms are bound to adhere to legislation regulating the conduct of business, labor relations, social welfare and the like. With respect to offshore oil and natural gas activity, special legislation and regulations have been adopted governing the conditions under which Norwegian and foreign firms can obtain exploratory and production concessions. All oil companies operating in Norway must agree to procure Norwegian equipment and services whenever these are competitive in all respects.

Norwegian policy toward foreign indirect (portfolio) investment has been highly restrictive in the past, but the Government's attitude toward purchase of shares in Norwegian companies has been liberalized to some extent. The more liberal approach to foreign portfolio investment, which may be viewed as an experiment, does not imply any change in Norway's highly restrictive policy toward foreign takeovers of Norwegian companies.

Requirements for Establishing a Trading Enterprise

A number of licenses must be obtained before establishing a new trading or manufacturing enterprise in Norway. These licenses are listed below (and are described in greater detail in later sections):

(1) A concession or new establishment license;
(2) Trading license (Handelsbrev);
(3) Capital import license from the Bank of Norway.

Registration is required both with the fiscal authorities and with the Register of Companies in the municipality where the company's head office is to be located.

Forms of Representation

Agent.—Foreign firms are permitted to engage Norwegian firms as agents to carry out most types of temporary business in Norway without formal establishment. There are no special requirements or registration formalities for agency agreements. However, the sale of commodities and the provision of services in Norway require registration and a trading license.

Subsidiary/Branch.—The setting up of either a subsidiary or a branch is the frequent choice for a permanent business establishment in Norway. A branch with a separate board of directors requires registration. The board must be authorized to make commitments on behalf of the company similar to the board of a Norwegian limited liability company.

Frequently used forms of business in Norway are described in some detail below. Of these, the corporation and the branch of a foreign corporation are those forms chosen most often by foreign investors.

Forms of Business Organizations

Corporation (Aksjeselskap).—The corporation, or joint stock company, is regulated by Norwegian law, the special act of June 4, 1976. Participants are personally liable for the company's obligations up to the face value of shares held.

The minimum share capital is 50,000 Kroner and may be owned by one or more shareholders. Foreigners are permitted to own 100 percent of the share capital. At least half must be paid in by the time of registration; the other half may be paid in up to one year after the signing of the memorandum of association.

At least one board member is required for corporations having share capital up to 1,000,000 kroner. Otherwise the minimum number is three. At least half of the board members, as well as the managing director, must reside in Norway and have resided there for the last two years; this requirement may be dropped at the discretion of the Ministry of Commerce.

Since January 1, 1973, all corporations having over 200 employees must establish a corporate assembly (bedrifts-forsamling), an institution intended to give employees a greater voice in management. It must have at least 12 members, one third of them chosen by and among the firm's employees, the remaining two thirds by the general stockholders meeting: The corporate assembly elects the company's board of directors and is be the firm's highest authority in matters pertaining to significant investment or to rationalization or other changes having a significant effect on the work force.

Corporations must register at the Commercial Registry, in the office of the local justice, within 6 months after signing the memorandum of understanding. At the time of registration there is a stamp duty of 1 percent of authorized shared capital. Application for registration of a company must include specified data. The abbreviation is A/S or A.S.

Branch of A Foreign Corporation (Filial av utenlandsk aksjesel-skap).—A corporation validly established in its home country is permitted to carry out activities in Norway through an independent branch. The branch, similar to the Norweigian corporation, must have its own board of directors, which can make binding decisions for the organization.

Before commencing operation in Norway, the board is required to provide the commercial registrar in the municipality where the branch is to be located with information concerning the nature of the business, its capitalization, board of directors and auditors. Until properly registered, the boards of directors of the branch and the foreign corporation are jointly liable for the liabilities of the branch. Following registration, the foreign corporation is fully liable for the liabilities of the branch. All business documents of the branch must clearly indicate, as part of the letterhead, that it is a branch of a foreign corporation with limited liability.

General Partnership (*Kompaniskap*).—Each member of the general partnership is liable for its debt to the full extent of his personal assets. This form of partnership is a separate legal entity and can sue and be sued. General partnerships are of two types: trading partnerships which carry out trading activities and require a trading license, and civil partnerships which carry out activities not requiring a trading license. The relationship between the partners (e.g. how to share profits and losses) should be stated in the partnership agreement. The application for registration must include the names of all the partners. All partners who are entitled to sign for the firm must be holders of a trading license. The name of the partnership must contain the name of at least one of the partners, and, if only one name is used, it must be followed by "and company," indicating that it is a partnership.

Limited Partnership (*Kommanditselskap*).—A limited partnership is composed of one or more (general) partners fully responsible for the partnership's liabilities, and one or more (limited) partners who are responsible for its liabilities only up to an agreed amount—"the share", which is usually paid in full or in part at the time of formation of the partnership. The limited partnership may be a commercial or a civil partnership. There is no special law regarding limited partnerships; therefore, the partnership agreement is the governing document.

The limitation of liability is the main reson for using a limited partnership. As in the case of the general partnership, the partners (not the partnership) are subject to taxation. Moreover, partners may limit their liability to a certain amount. Often the general partner is a limited liability company owned by the limited partners.

The name of the limited partnership must include the name of at least one of the general partners together with a supplement indicating a partnership but not the limited liability. The trade license and registration requirements are the same as for the general partnership.

Individual Enterprise (*Selvstendig Firma*).—An individual enterprise is owned and operated by one person, the owner being liable with all his business and personal assets for debts. Application for registration must include (1) name of the enterprise (2) name and address of owner, (3) description of the nature of the company, and (4) name of the municipality in which the company is located. The owner must have a trading license if the nature of the business requires it. The name of the company shall contain the family name of the owner and must not include anything to indicate that it is a partnership or corporation.

Entry and Repatriation of Capital

There are no formal criteria regarding the requirements to be fulfilled by a private foreign investor to obtain approval of his investment project. However, the Concession Law of December 14, 1917, is the usual basis for the admission to Norway of foreign private enterprises, particularly industrial enterprises of any size. An authorization by the Norwegian exchange control authorities is required in all instances for the entry of private foreign investment. When investment requiring a concession agreement is being considered by the Ministry of Industry, that Ministry consults with the exchange control authorities.

A prospective investor should apply by letter, with a description of the proposed investment plan, to the Norwegian Ministry of Industry, which is responsible also for clearing with interested local municipal authorities certain other aspects of the investment proposal.

It is not always clear in what cases the Concession Law applies; but, negotiations will ordinarily be necessary for an enterprise of any size. Sometimes relatively unimportant rights for utilization of real property under the Concession Law thus become the starting point of negotiations. Not only real estate but also such subjects as dividends and taxes are often covered in the final agreement with the Government. If building is involved, a building license must be obtained. However, the Ministry of Industry consults on the requirements with the Housing Directorate in the Ministry of Municipalities and Labor in this respect, and a building license is ordinarily given if a concession agreement is granted.

Transfer of Dividends and Profits.—There are no limitations on the transfer of dividends occurring from foreign investment approved by the Bank of Norway. Similarly, contractual amortization of loans and interest on debentures and mortgages are freely transferable.

Transfer of Royalties.—Norwegian exchange regulations allow the free transfer of royalties derived from approved projects.

Transfer of Earnings.—United States nationals who are employed in Norway may transfer home salaries, fees, wages and other earnings after the deduction of living expenses, taxes and social insurance. When leaving Norway to return home they may arrange for the transfer of any capital assets they may own.

Foreign Ownership of Business Entities

There are no general prohibitions against foreign ownership of business entities. However, the participation of foreigners in the following fields is restricted: ownership of commercial banks, other financial institutions, Norwegian ships and Norwegian aircraft; and operation of domestic airlines.

A foreign corporation may register and conduct a business in Norway by means of a branch corporation under a separate board of directors. New local corporations, with their own boards of directors, may also be set up by foreigners. There are no limitations on the amount of foreign ownership of either branch or new corporations. In order to rent or own real estate, however, a foreign corporation, or a Norwegian company with foreign participants, must become a party to a concession agreement with the Norwegian Government in all cases involving an industrial establishment. Any foreigner or foreign corporation must have a concession to own real estate.

The amount of foreign ownership is, in practice, relevant to the negotiations of not only a concession agreement regarding real property but other agreements with the Government regarding matters such as dividends and taxes. Obtaining an agreement with the Government is not precluded even if more than 50 percent of the share capital of the corporation is foreign owned. A number of foreign corporations are doing business in Norway today on this basis.

With respect to real estate, a 1974 law tightened existing legislation on ownership and transfer of real estate. The object of the law is to regulate the transfer of real estate and to allow governments (national and local) to obtain title to real estate when this is deemed to be in the best interest of society from the points of view of (1) agriculture, horticulture, and forestry; (2) the need for building and construction sites; and (3) general environmental protection and recreational purposes. According to the law, real estate, regardless of size, can in principle only be sold if the purchaser has obtained a concession or permit from the Ministry of Agriculture; there are a few stipulated exemptions but they do not apply to corporations purchasing real estate.

In view of the complexity of Norway's concession laws, any company considering direct investment in Norway is advised to seek qualified legal counsel.

Mandatory Requirements.—There are a few mandatory requirements spelled out by the Concession Law. Some of the conditions required by the Norwegian Government in granting concessions are:

The corporation's seat must be in Norway.

A majority of the board of directors must be Norwegian citizens.

A certain part of the capital stock must be in the hands of Norwegians.

Norwegian capital must have equal opportunity to share in any extension of a corporation's share capital.

Fringe benefits must be granted to employees, including, if in isolated areas, adequate housing, commissary facilities, and schools.

Any damage to roads, quays, or other public property must be repaired.

A certain production fee must be paid to the State.

The property may not be sold or transferred without permission.

Preference must be given to Norwegian labor and materials.

It may be said, generally, that a decision on individual concession application is made only after an appraisal of the advantages and disadvantages involved in admitting foreign capital for the enterprise in competition with existing or planned Norwegian industries. In addition, the specific requirements of the prospective foreign investor are taken into account. These requirements include items such as (1) foreign exchange —for example, for import of machinery, raw material, license fees, (2) building material, (3) domestic scarcity of raw materials, and (4) manpower that might be employed for other purposes with greater advantage.

Industrial Property Protection[2]

Norway is a member of the "Paris Union" In-

---

[2]Prepared by the Foreign Business Practices Division, Office of International Finance and Investment.

1753

ternational Convention for the Protection of Industrial Property (patents, trademarks, commercial names, and industrial designs) to which the United States and about 85 other countries adhere. American businesspeople and inventors are thus entitled to receive national treatment in Norway (treatment equal to that accorded Norwegian citizens), under laws regarding the protection of patents and trademarks. American nationals are also entitled to certain other benefits, such as the protection of patents against arbitrary forfeiture for nonworking and a 1-year "right of priority" for filing patent applications (1 year after first filing of patent application in the United States in which to file a corresponding application in Norway and receive in the latter the benefit of the first U.S. application filing date.) The right-of-priority period for trademark applications is 6 months.

Norway is also a member of the Universal Copyright Convention to which the United States and about 60 other countries adhere. Works of American authors first copyrighted in the United States are thus entitled to automatic protection in Norway. The author need only show on such works, his name, year of first publication, and the symbol "c" in a circle to obtain copyright protection.

Norway is also a member of the "Berne Union" Copyright Convention. Although the United States is not a member of this Convention, U.S. authors may obtain protection in Berne Union countries by publishing a work in a Union Country at the same time it is first published in the United States (simultaneous publication).

Applications or inquiries pertaining to industrial property rights should be addressed to Norwegian Patent Office, (Styret for det Industrielle Rettsvern,) Middlthunsgate 156, Oslo. 3

Patents. — The Patents Act of 1967 became effective January 1, 1968. Patents are granted for 17 years from the effective filing date. Applications are examined by novelty and, if acceptable, published for opposition for 3 months. If no opposition is filed, or it is successfully overcome, the application is allowed and a patent granted. If a patentee does not work his patent within 3 years from date of grant (or 4 years from application), a compulsory license may be ordered.

Trademarks. — Trademarks are protected under the Trade Marks Act of March 3, 1961, effective October 1, 1961. Norway has adopted the Nice International Classification System for registration purposes (34 product and 8 service classes). Trademark registrations are valid for 10 years from the date of registration and are renewable for like periods. The first applicant for a mark is entitled to receive a registration and exclusive ownership. If another party, however, can prove he was the first user, he may have the mark canceled and reregistered to himself. After 5 years, a registration becomes incontestable on grounds of prior use. Applications are examined and, if acceptable, published for opposition for 2 months. Not registrable as trademarks are marks incapable of distinguishing applicant's goods from others, marks consisting solely of statements regarding nature, quality and quantity of goods, marks connoting a matter taken as a firm's name, marks contrary to law or public order, marks likely to be deceptive, marks consisting of official seals and emblems, marks similar to those already in use by others, if applicant was aware of such use. Use of a mark is not compulsory.

Copyrights. — Protection of copyrights in Norway is governed by Law of May 12, 1961, as amended on December 20, 1974. The term of copyright protection of a work is for the author's life plus 50 years after death. It includes all literary, dramatic, musical, and artistic works. Copyright includes the sole right to produce and reproduce the work or a translation of it; to publish such work or translation; to perform it in public; and to authorize others to do so.

Further information on the general features of Norway's laws on patent, trademark, and copyright protection may be obtained from the U.S. Commerce Department's Foreign Business Practices Division, Office of International Finance and Investment, International Economic Policy and Research. That Division, however, cannot provide detailed information on fees or other specific step-by-step procedures in seeking protection under the laws. Specialized legal counsel should be consulted.

Taxation

Corporate Taxes. — The national corporate income tax is 27.8 percent of net taxable profit. In addition, corporations are subject to two other direct taxes; (1) the local (municipal) corporate income tax, which is 22 percent; (2) the "contribution to the tax equalization fund" which is 1 percent. Total direct taxes on corporations thus equal 50.8 percent. However, dividends paid by Norwegian corporations are deductible from the national corporate income tax assessment but not from the other direct taxes. The total income taxes payable by the company on distributed profits are thus reduced to 23 percent (representing the local income tax, and the tax equalization fund contribution). In other words, Norway has a "split rate," which provides for a 23 percent on distributed profits compared with a 50.8 percent tax on retained profits.

Deductions are in general allowed for all expenses incurred in the course of the income year for the purpose of earning, securing or maintaining the company's income. Companies are, moreover, subject to a capital tax of 0.7 percent of the company's net capital value exceeding 10,000 or more.

Depreciation Allowance.—Norwegian depreciation regulations permit ordinary and accelerated depreciation. Under the ordinary depreciation allowance regulation, such items as commercial buildings, office and shop equipment, machinery, most types of ships, and motor vehicles are depreciable. The rates are based on the useful life of the asset, and the straight line method of depreciation should be used. The tax authorities have established rates for most types of assets. For example, the rates for most types of machinery vary between 5 and 15 percent, for buildings between 1 and 3 percent, and for motor vehicles between 10 and 25 percent. The rates are reviewed by the tax authorities each year and are subject to change. Accelerated depreciation consists of additional, initial and advance depreciation.

In addition to the ordinary depreciation allowance, a taxpayer may request an additional depreciation allowance. This is in the form of an additional allowance available for productive assets other than motor vehicles and commercial buildings. Under the rules governing the additional depreciation allowance, a taxpayer may write off an asset the first year it is used and for 4 succeeding years at a rate of 50 percent of the normal annual allowance subject to a maximum of 5 percent of the cost in any one year. The maximum to be claimed as additional depreciation is 15 percent of the cost of the asset.

Initial depreciation may be claimed for buildings and plants used for the production or storage of goods, or for the construction and repair of aircraft, ships, etc., and for movable drilling rigs. This initial allowance may be claimed in addition to the ordinary depreciation allowance described above. The intital depreciation allowance is limited to 25 percent of the cost in excess of 500,000 kroner. It may not exceed 50 percent of the assessed income in any one year. Special exemptions are granted under this rule for aircraft and ships, but the maximum allowed is 25 percent of the cost of the asset.

Investment in northern Norway may, in addition to ordinary, additional and initial depreciation, also be subject to advance depreciation. This allowance is available on the whole appreciation cost, not just on the excess over 500,000 kroner. The maximum deduction through advance depreciation is 50 percent of cost.

The cumulative depreciation of an asset cannot exceed cost reduced by the value of any grants or subsidies received from the state, municipality, or other public body.

Individual Taxes.—Norwegian residents are subject to personal income taxes at both the national and local (municipal) levels. The tax burden on middle and upper income brackets is heavy because of the progressive character of the national personal income tax. Capital taxes are levied, at both the national and municipal levels, as well as social security premiums in support of the National Insurance Scheme and the National Health Scheme.

Petroleum Revenue Tax.—Pursuant to National Act No. 35 of June 13, 1975, a special tax is levied on income from the exploitation and pipeline transportation of petroleum. This act extends Norwegian tax jurisdiction generally to all activities on the Norewegian continental shelf.

Value Added Tax.—By far the most important indirect tax in Norway is the value added tax (VAT), levied at the rate of 20 percent on both domestic and imported goods. Exports from Norway are not subject to the VAT.

The VAT is levied at each sale transaction along the production and distribution chain. But as the name of the tax implies, it is only the value added at each phase of production or distribution that is taxed. In effect, each taxpayer pays the difference between the tax on his own sales and the tax included on his purchases from other producers or distributors.

On imported goods, the value added tax is payable to Norwegian Customs Authorities at the time of entry in much the same way as customs duties. The VAT is levied on the c.i.f., duty-paid value of the imported product. The effective rate is 20 percent.

The Norwegian VAT applies to almost all goods and services. There are a few specific exemptions from the VAT, however, including exports from Norway to foreign countries; goods and services for use in the North Sea area in connection with exploration and exploitation of offshore oil/natural gas resources; goods and services for use by foreign ships and aircraft; regularly published newspapers; sale and rental of real property.

All capital equipment enjoys practical exemption from the VAT (this is partially compensated for, however, by the Investment Goods Tax, explained below). When capital equipment is imported into Norway, the importer must pay the 20 percent VAT. However, VAT paid at time of purchase of capital equipment can be deducted from the buyer's VAT remittances to the Government on those sales. Thus, in effect, the VAT does not apply to capital equipment.

Investment Goods Tax.—In order to conpensate for the fact that capital goods are exempt from the VAT, Norway levies a 13 percent investment goods tax (5 percent for enterprises engaged in manufacturing and mining tax on all purchases of capital equipment.) The investment goods tax is levied in all cases in which the buyer obtains the practical exemption for VAT described in the preceding paragraph.

Other Indirect Taxes.—The Norwegian Government levies excise taxes on several items, including alcoholic beverages, tobacco, chocolate, confectionery, cosmetics, electric power, mineral oil, gasoline, motor vehicles. Certain documents are subject to the stamp tax.

Guidance for Business Travelers

Entrance Requirements

Foreigners entering Norway must have a valid passport. (Citizens of Denmark, Finland and Sweden are exempted from this requirement.) U.S. citizens do not need to obtain a visa to enter Norway.

Foreigners wishing to remain in Norway longer than 3 months are required to obtain a residence permit from local police.

Norway has no vaccination requirements.

A visitor to Norway is permitted to bring in, free of duty and taxes, clothing and other items of personal use, including cameras, jewelry, toilet articles, and the like.

Foreign Exchange Regulations

Foreign exchange is provided readily for all imports except for a relatively small number of commodities still subject to import license requirements and those of Rhodesian origin. It is sufficient for the importer to show the bank an original invoice stamped by the customs authority at the time of clearance, for the bank to arrange the transfer of foreign exchange to the seller. Payment is also provided for goods subject to import license when the proper license is presented to a foreign exchange bank.

Foreign exchange transactions are governed by Law 10 of July 14, 1950. Under this law, only Norges Bank (Central Bank of Norway) and banks authorized by the Ministry of Commerce may carry on transactions in foreign exchange. Approval must be obtained from the Ministry of Commerce of Norges Bank to raise loans and credits abroad, grant loans or credits abroad, issue or receive guarantees or surety for financial obligations abroad, or engage in security transactions abroad.

Approval given by the Ministry of Commerce or Norges Bank for foreign exchange transactions is valid for 3 months from time of approval unless otherwise specified.

Languages, Business Hours, Holidays

Many Norwegian business executives, especially import and export, dealers are fluent in English, the preferred commercial language. The business visitor will discover, however, that as one travels from Oslo, Bergen, and Stavanger, one finds fewer English-speaking businesspeople.

Norwegian business executives often travel in the United States and in Europe. Moreover, they generally read English-language trade and technical magazines and books. Americans will quickly note that Norwegians are often well informed about U.S. trade and business practices.

Business Hours.—Business hours throughout Norway are generally from 9 a.m. to 4 p.m. The time in Norway is 6 hours ahead of Eastern Standard Time and 5 hours ahead of Eastern Daylight Saving Time.

Holidays.—Commercial holidays are: New Year's Day, Holy Thursday, Good Friday, Easter Monday, Labor Day (May 1), Norwegian Constitution Day (May 17), Whit Monday, Christmas Day, and the day following Christmas. At Easter time many businesses close at noon on the Wednesday prior to Easter and remain closed until Tuesday morning following Easter.

July and August are the traditional vacation months in Norway. Serious business visitors would be advised to avoid traveling to Norway during this period as they could find Norwegian executives unavailable, unless they have made prior arrangements. In particular, the last three weeks in July is the most popular time. Many Norwegian firms close during these weeks.

Sources of Economic and Commercial Information

General information concerning the Norwegian market (economic trends, commercial development, production, trade, etc.) may be obtained from the Germany/Nordic Section, Office of Country Marketing, Bureau of Export Development, U.S. Department of Commerce, Washington, D.C. 20230, or from any of the Department's District Offices.

Government Representation

The Norwegian Embassy in the United States is located at 3401 Massachusetts Ave., N.W., Washington, D.C. 20007.

Consulates General are located at:

360 N. Michigan Ave.
Chicago, Ill. 60601

4543 Post Oak Place Dr.
Houston, Texas 77027

360 South Figueroa St.
Los Angeles, CA 90071

800 Foshay Tower
Minneapolis, MN 55402

17 Battery Pl.
New York, NY 10004

One Embarcadero Center
San Francisco, CA 94111

In addition the following offices in the U.S. are concerned with Norwegian interests:

Norwegian-American Chamber of Commerce
800 Third Ave.
New York, NY 10022
Tel.:(202) 421-9210

Norwegian Information Service
825 Third Ave.
New York, NY 10022
Tel.: (202) 421-7333

Export Council of Norway
800 Third Ave.
New York, N.Y. 1002
Tel.: (202) 421-9210

Norwegian National Tourist Office
75 Rockefeller Plaza
New York, N.Y. 10019
Tel.: (202) 582-2802

The United States is represented in Norway by an Embassy located at Drammensveien 18, Oslo, Norway; telephone 56-68-80. Telex 18470.

Foreign Service Officers in the Economic/Commercial Section are available to brief and assist American business visitors in Norway. In October 1979 the Counselor for Economic and Commercial Affairs, was John A. Boyle and the Commercial Attache, F. Brenne Bachmann.

Tax Treaty With the United States. — A revised Convention for the Avoidance of Double Taxation Between the United States and Norway came into force on November 29, 1972. It applies to national income taxes in the United States and Norway and to local income taxes in Norway. Its benefits apply both to individuals and to corporations in the two countries. The key, for Norwegian taxation purposes, is whether an American enterprise operates in Norway through a "permanent establishment" (Article 4), defined as "a fixed place of business through which a resident of one of the Contracting States engages in industrial or commercial activity." If so, then all "industrial and commercial profits" made in Norway are taxable by the Norwegian Government (and exempt from taxation by the United States). The identical rule applies, of course, to Norwegian-operated permanent establishments in the United States.

Tax treatment of royalties is spelled out in Article 10 of the Convention, as follows: "Royalties derived from sources within one of the Contracting States by a resident of the other Contracting State shall be exempt from tax by the first mentioned Contracting State." However, the Convention stipulates that this rule does not apply "if the recipient of the royalty, being a resident of one of the Contracting States, has in the other Contracting State a permanent establishment and the property or rights giving rise to the royalty are effectively connected with such permanent establishment."

Tax treatment of interest on bonds, etc. is dealt with in Article 9 of the convention, as follows: "Interest derived from sources within one of the Contracting States by a resident of the other Contracting State shall be exempt from tax by the first-mentioned contracting State." However, this rule does not apply if "the recipient of the interest, being a resident of one of the Contracting States, has a permanent establishment in the other Contracting State and the indebtedness giving rise to the interest is effectively connected with such permanent establishment." Tax treatment of dividends is treated in Article 8 of the Convention.

Norwegian Trade Organizations

Specific industries, trades, and professions are almost invariably grouped into associations. In turn, these associations are often represented in larger trade federations which have more general purposes. The most important, from the standpoint of export and import trade, as well as domestic business activity, are listed below.

1. The Federation of Norwegian Industries (Norges Industriforbund), located at Drammensveien 40, Oslo. Membership consists of the major trade associations, local industry associations, and individual Norwegian firms. The Federation plays an active role in the formulation of Norwegian industrial, business, and trade legislation, as well as foreign economic policy. Professional staff members follow industrial trends in Norway and foreign countries. The Federation publishes a biweekly magazine, Norges Industri (Norway's Industry).

2. The Federation of Norwegian Wholesale Merchants and Importers Norges Grossistforbund), located at Drammensveien 30, Oslo. The Federation represents 28 branch associations (e.g., automotive accessories, hardware, textiles) whose member-firms act as importers, wholesalers, distributors for all kinds of goods. Many member firms are active in the import trade.

3. The Export Council of Norway (Norges Exportrad), located at Drammensveien 40. The Export Council is charged with the development of Norwegian exports and the coordination and promotion of various measures for increasing the sale of Norwegian goods in foreign markets. It also acts as a consultative organ for the Government in matters of trade and exports. The Council maintains 15 overseas offices and permanent trade centers in London, Stockholm, and Hamburg. The Export Council publishes an English-language journal, Norway Exports. Its New York office is at 800 Third Ave., New York, N.Y. 10022 (Tel. 212-421-9210).

4. The Norwegian American Chamber of Commerce, is incorporated in the U.S. with headquarters at 800 Third Ave., New York, N.Y. 10022, and Norwegian headquarters at Drammensveien 40, Oslo 2, Norway. U.S. branch offices are located at:

36 N. Nichigan Ave.
Chicago, IL. 60601

800 Foshay Tower
Minneapolis, MN 55402

17 Briar Hollow Lane
Houston, Texas 77027

350 South Cigueroa St.
Los, Angeles, CA 90071

2727 Ranier Bank Tower
Seattle, WA 98101

One Embarcadero Center
San Francisco, CA 94111

5. The Association of Machinery Wholesalers (Maskingrossistenes Forening), Drammensveien 30, Oslo. The Association has membership of about 130, covering the entire country in distribution. It circulates offers concerning distributorships or agencies among its members.

6. The Import and Export Agents Association, Drammensveien 30, Oslo. This association is the largest division of the Norwegian Federation of Agents, with Oslo being the main Norwegian trade center. Jointly with the Norwegian Federation of Agents the Association issued a monthly, "Agentur," in which proposals from foreign firms seeking agents in Norway are published. The association also assists, free of charge in establishing business relations between principals and potential agents.

Other Norwegian agencies and organizations are:

The Royal Norwegian Ministry of Finance
(Finans- og Tolldepartmentet)
Akersgaten 42
Oslo 1
Tel.: (02) 11 90 90

The Royal Norwegian Ministry of Industry
(Industri- og Handverksdepartementet)
Akersgaten 42
Oslo 1
Tel.: (02) 11 90 90

The Royal Norwegian Ministry of Petroleum and Energy
(Olje- og Energidepartementet)
Tolbugaten 31
Oslo 1
Tel.: (02) 41 91 50)

The Royal Norwegian Ministry of Public Labour and Municipality Affairs
(Kommunal- og Arbeidsdepartementet)
Pilestredet 33
Oslo 1
Tel.: (02) 20 22 70

The Royal Norwegian Ministry of Foreign Affairs
(Utenriksdepartementet)
7. Juni plass 1
Oslo 1
Tel.: (02) 20 41 70

The Royal Norwegian Ministry of Commerce and Shipping
(Handelsdepartementet)
Fr. Nansens plass 4
Oslo 1
Tel.: (02) 20 51 10

The Regional Development Fund
(Dsitriktenes Utbyggingsfond)
Mollergaten 1/2
Oslo 1
Tel.: (02) 20 63 10

Directorate of Labor
(Arbeidsdirektoratet)
Halbergsplass 7
Oslo 1
Tel.: (02) 11 10 70

The Royal Norwegian Ministry of Defense
Defense Procurement Division
Storgaten 33
Oslo 1

The Norwegian Employeer's Confederation
(Norsk Arbidsgiverforening)
Kristian Augustsgate 23
Oslo 1
Tel.: (02) 20 25 50

The Norwegian Federation of Trade Unions
(Landsorganisasjonen i Norge)
Youngs gate 11
Oslo 1
Tel.: (02) 20 67 70

The Bank of Norway
(Norges Bank)
Foreign Exchange Department
Ovre Slottsgate 2
Oslo 1
Tel.: (02) 41 01 50

Publications

Norwegian Government

Bank of Norway Annual Report. Oslo: Bank of Norway. Available in English; describes economic and financial trends.

Economic Bulletin. Oslo: Bank of Norway. Published quarterly in English.

Industristatistikk (annual production statistics). Central Bureau of Statistics, Oslo.

Manedstatistikk over Utenrikshadeln (monthly foreign trade statistics). Oslo: Central Bureau of Statistics.

News of Norway. Washington: Norwegian Embassy Information Service, 4301 Massachusetts Avenue, N.W., Washington, D.C. 20007. Weekly news bulletin, often contains useful information about eocnomic and commercial developments.

Statistisk Arbok (statistical yearbook). Oslo: Central Bureau of Statistics.

Statistisk Mandeshefte (monthly bulletin of statistics). Oslo: Central Bureau of Statistics.

Economic Trends. An appraisal of tendencies in the Norwegian and foreign economies. Central Bureau of Statistics.

Quarterly Bulletin of Private and Public Banks. This publication contains data from the monthly, quarterly and annual statistics of the banks. Central Bureau of Statistics

Guide to Norwegian Statistics. A survey of Norwegian official statistics, systematically arranged by subject. Central Bureau of Statistics.

In addition to the quarterly, monthly and weekly bulletins, the Central Bureau of Statistics issues about 100 publications annually.

A comprehensive survey of official statistical publications released by the Bureau or other institutions, is listed in the publication Catalog of Norwegian Statistics and other Publications published by the Central Bureau of Statistics 1828-1976 (NOS A 957).

Others

Arntzen and Bugge, Doing Business in Norway. Oslo: Den Norsk Credibank, Kirkegaten 21, Oslo 1. Detailed account of Norwegian business legislation in English.

Economic Surveys of the OECD: Norway. Paris: Organization for Economic Cooperation and Development. This and other annual country surveys may be obtained from: OECD Publications Center, Suite 1207, 1750 Pennsylvania Ave., N.W., Washington, D.C. 20006

Financial Review. Oslo: The Economic Research Institute of the Commercial Banks of Norway. Published quarterly in English. The Norwegian Bankers Association, Post Box 1989 Vika Oslo 1, Norway.

Norway—A Brief Business Guide. Bergen Bank Torwalmenning 2 N-5001 Bergen, Norway. A report in English on the Norwegian economy and how to establish a business in Norway.

Nordisk Handels Kalender. Copenhagen: Scan-Report A/C. Comprehensive directory for industry of firms in Norway and other Nordic countries.

Norway Exports. Oslo: Export Council of Norway. Periodical in English with information on industrial developments.

Norwegian American Commerce. New York: Norwegian American Chamber of Commerce, 800 Third Ave., New York, N.Y. 10022, quarterly.

The Scandinavian Market. Zurich: Nor-Finanz-Bank. Survey in English of Norwegian and other Nordic markets. Available from Den Norsk Creditbank, Kirkegaten 21, Oslo 1.

Setting Up in Norway, Oslo: Andersens Bank A/S. Useful, brief account in English of Norwegian company law, taxation, exchange regulations, and other aspects related to establishing a business in Norway.

Norway—Economic Trends and Their Implications for the U.S. Prepared semi-annually by the American Embassy, Oslo, and issued by the U.S. Department of Commerce.

Norway—Background Notes. Information on the geography, people, history, government and economy. Prepared and issued by the U.S. Department of State.

Marketing in Oman

Contents

Report Revised August 1981

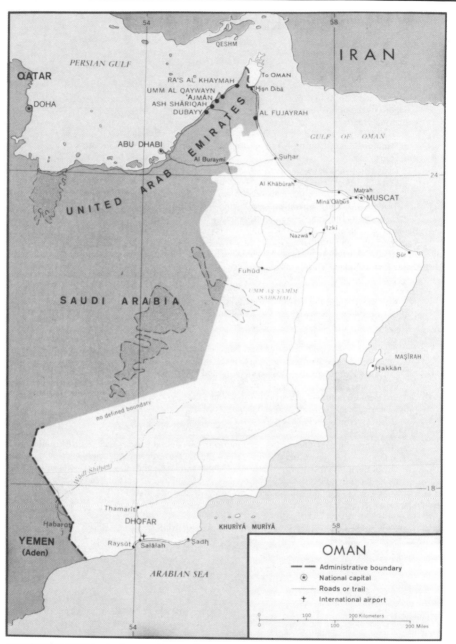

Note: **Oman's northwestern borders are undemarcated.**

Foreign Trade Outlook

The Sultanate of Oman is by international standards a minor oil producer. Nevertheless, oil and gas revenues account for the major portion of its earnings. Recognizing that the country's oil reserves (estimated at 2.4 billion barrels) will almost certainly be depleted by the end of the century, the Government began in the 1970's to develop Oman's economic infrastructure. Before the reign of the current sultan, Qaboos bin Said, Oman was one of the backwaters of the Arab world, a country without schools, health facilities, or even effective control of its own hinterland, living by fishing and subsistence agriculture.

Oil revenues provided the means to introduce change. In addition to putting down a guerrilla war in the province of Dhofar, Sultan Qaboos welcomed back qualified Omani expatriates and undertook a rapid development program. Although this program has slowed down since 1976, its thrust remains to develop the oil sector to insure a continuing income while providing basic social services to the population. This healthier, better trained and educated population will then be used to help diversify Oman's economy so that the country has something to fall back on when the oil runs out. As yet, little has been done toward diversifying the economy, but Oman has development potential in agriculture, fishing, copper mining, and some light industry.

Oman recognizes the need for foreign capital, technology, management, and marketing expertise. It hopes to attract these as part of its economic development program. Consequently, Oman's investment laws are designed to encourage capital investment. Joint ventures are welcomed as the preferred form of business investment. The legal requirements for Omani participation in business and trade preclude the establishment in the country of most foreign wholly owned enterprises.

Firms contemplating entering the Omani market should familiarize themselves with local social and business customs, tax laws, and agency and import regulations. There is no substitute for a good personal relationship with an Omani representative because Omani practices favor ties of kinship, friendship, and business partnership. Many Omani business people are also civil servants. Moreover, government regulations maximize the business benefits to foreigners who have Omani agents or partners.

Oman does not have the most sophisticated business community in the area, but it has rapidly learned a great deal from the lessons of the 1970's. More Omani projects are now opened to competitive bidding, and such outside agencies as the World Bank and the U.S. Agency for International Development as well as development funds of other Arab States are asked to help evaluate tenders. Moreover, having begun its development program much later than its neighbors, Oman is able to learn from their mistakes. In short, Omani business people and government officials are not easy marks, and they are alert to attempts to do business in other than good faith.

Presently, there are disincentives to investment. One of these is the small size of the market. Accompanying this is a shortage of a skilled labor force, limited availability of raw materials, and a dearth of infrastructure facilities in some parts of the country. Just as important is the solidly entrenched position of the United Kingdom. This harkens back to Great Britain's traditional, but now abandoned, position as protector of the Gulf States. While its official military presence is gone, its commercial dominance remains. This is the case not only because so many years of close association with the British brought a preference for their goods but also because many decisionmakers or advisors in both the Government and the private sector are either British-educated or British nationals. Other competition comes from the United Arab Emirates (mainly reexports) and Japan, both of which have larger shares of the Omani market than the United States.

In August 1980, the United States and Oman formed a joint economic commission. In addition to overseeing the distribution of $90 million in U.S. economic aid during 1981-82, the

---

HOW TO OBTAIN
BACKGROUND INFORMATION

For those who wish *general* data about a country—data which goes beyond marketing and commerce—the editors recommend *Countries of the World and Their Leaders,* published as an annually updated yearbook by Gale Research Company, Detroit, Michigan 48226. Containing 4- to 20-page entries on 168 countries, the volume also provides several hundred pages of supplementary world data. Each country entry is prepared by the U.S. Department of State to provide a general briefing on the geography, people, culture, and political situation of that particular country. Each report provides some historical insight as well as a look at contemporary trends of lifestyle in the country. Reports also discuss a country's educational system, its press, ethnic groupings and religious practices.

Table 1.—OMAN—DATA SUMMARY
(1979 data unless otherwise indicated)

Geographic data (estimates)

Population: 865,000
Expatriate population: 140,000
Population growth rate: 3%
Literacy rate: 20%
Population under 15 years old: 45%
Life expectancy: 47 years

National Income Accounts

Gross domestic product: $3.4 billion
GDP per capita: $3900
GDP growth rate: 31% (nominal, reflection oil price rise)
Composition of GDP

Agriculture and fishing	2%
Petroleum	61%
Construction	8%
Manufacturing	1%
Transport and Telecommunications	3%
Electricity and water	1%
Internal trade	7%
Banking	1%
Ownership of dwellings	2%
Public administration and defense	11%
Other services	1%
	100%

Composition of Labor Force

Agriculture	48%
Petroleum	2%
Services	50%

Composition of Civil Imports

Food and beverages	13%
Fuels and lubricants	7%
Industrial and building supplies	20%
Automobiles	10%
Other transport equipment	12%
Capital goods, n.e.s.	18%
Consumer goods, n.e.s.	13%
	100%

Origin of Imports 100%

Western Europe	42%
Federal Republic of Germany	(6.5%)
United Kingdom	(17%)
Middle East	18%
United Arab Emerates	(15%)
Asia	27%
Japan	(15%)
Australia	2%
United States	9%

Exchange Rate: 1 Omani Rial (RO) = US$2.92
(Pegged to U.S. dollar)

Inflation Rate: 10% (Est.)

Money Supply Growth Rate: 8%

External Debt: $478 million

Exchange Reserves: ($720 million as of 4/80)

Balance of Payments ($ millions)

Trade balance	852
Exports	2240
(petroleum)	(2159)
Imports, c.i.f.	1428
Services balances	-492
Profit remittance	-135
Worker remittance	-281
Other	-76
Official loan and grants	168
Grants	179
Net loans	11
Net oil sector	
Capital flow	25
Errors and omissions	57
OVERALL BALANCE	325

Fiscal Data ($ millions)

Revenues	2180
Oil revenues	1839
Customs	20
Public utilities	31
Foreign grants	180
Other	110
Expenditures	1885
National defense	779
Recurrent	556
Capital	223
Civil	851
Recurrent	475
Development	376
Government's share of oil operations	255
Operating	69
Development	185

commission's activities will focus on developing the infrastructure necessary to support expanded industrial development. The hope is that as more U.S. money flows into Oman as a result of economic and military agreements, Omanis may become eager to purchase more U.S. goods and services.

In November 1980, Sultan Qaboos announced a new 5-year plan for 1981-85. Still mainly concerned with infrastructure development, the plan ensures a variety of opportunities for U.S. suppliers. For the duration of the plan, the Omani Government will emphasize development in telecommunications, oil and gas, electricity and water, agriculture and fisheries, minerals, roads and ports, light industry, housing, and vocational training.

Economic Trends

GDP

In 1979, the last year for which statistics are

relatively complete, Oman's gross domestic product (GDP) was $3.4 billion. By far the largest component of this was the petroleum sector, which contributed 61 percent. The contributions of other sectors are indicated in table 1.

Oman's GDP is highly sensitive to changes in the price of oil. Inflation is running at a rate of about 10 percent per year. Almost all of this is attributable to import price changes.

Government Budget

The Government of Oman was greatly aided by the more-than-doubling price of Oman's crude oil export during 1979. The 1979 budget anticipated a deficit of $315 million; however, the price rise permitted the repayment of $199 million worth of long-term debts as well as a budgetary surplus of $202 million. Although Oman officials still refer to the Sultanate as the poor man of the Gulf and foreign businesspeople encounter repeated protestations of how poor they are compared with the Saudis, Oman is in the enviable position not

Table 2.—Key Economic Indicators

(All values in millions of dollars unless otherwise indicated)

	1977	1978	% Change	1979
Income and Production				
GNP at current prices	2124.9	2227.4	+4.8	
Government investment ...	671.3	555.1	-17.3	
Private investment	236.2	265.4	+12.4	
Crude oil production				
(000 bbl/d)	340.0	314.2	-7.6	295.1
Private sector expatriate				
labor (000)	96.7	102.2	+5.7	e106.0
Money and Prices				
Money supply	330.8	344.9	+4.3	363.8
Quasi-money	258.1	314.2	+21.8	346.0
Commercial bank assets ..	937.8	950.1	+1.3	1193.3
Imported food price index				
(1972 = 100)	164.4	187.5	+14.1	e204.2
Government Finance				
Government revenues	1790.8	1486.3	-17.0	p2161.4
Government expenditures .	1560.2	1635.2	+4.8	p1747.9
Budget surplus or deficit .	+209.4	-166.7	-179.6	p+201.9
External public debt				
services	81.3	135.0	+66.1	
Balance of Payments				
Value of oil exports (f.o.b.)	1594.0	1523.7	-4.4	p2177.4
Non-oil exports (f.o.b.)	39.4	88.2	+123.9	p126.1
% of Oil exports to U.S. ...	15.4	15.8	+2.6	13.1
Imports (c.i.f.)	1147.3	1279.8	+11.5	p1399.0
Recorded Imports from				
U.S.*	63.0	60.3	-4.3	e125.9
Balance of trade..........	+486.2	+332.0	-31.7	p+964.6
Balance on current				
account ....+35.6	-89.4	-351.1	p+408.5	
Official loans and transfers	358.6	-3.5	-101.0	p+133.7
Overall balance	+221.3	-97.8	-144.2	p+328.2
Gross official reserves	438.6	418.1	-4.7	609.7
Net foreign assets	313.6	215.8	-31.2	544.3

*Does not include U.S. goods reexported from United Arab Emirates; based on Omani figures.

e = estimated; p = provisional.

only of being solvent but of having far greater financial resources at its disposal than ever before. The 1980 budget projected total revenues of $3.5 billion ($3.2 billion of which are oil revenues) and a surplus of $432 million transferred directly to the General State Reserve Fund. When final figures are available, they are expected to show that revenues doubled, taking into account further rises in oil prices, increased production, and a probable shortfall in civil development expenditures. Since at least 1978, the Government has been unable to spend the full amount it has budgeted for civil capital expenditures and development, largely because of a shortage of technically trained personnel. It simply has not been possible to translate general development plans into programs ready for implementation.

Ordinarily, Oman has devoted between 30 and 40 percent of its total expenditures to defense and national security. This includes outlays for the Royal Oman Police and related internal security functions.

About $1.7 billion was earmarked for civil programs in 1980. One-third of this was managed by the Ministry of Communications, which is responsible for developing the telecommunications sector, roads, ports, and airports. The other principal spenders are the Ministries of Petroleum and Minerals, Electricity and Water,

Agriculture and Fisheries, Land Affairs and Municipalities, and Education.

The budget for the second 5-year plan (1981-85) projects expenditures of $21.5 billion. Defense expenditures account for $8.7 billion of this, while $4.1 billion has been allocated to civil development projects and $2.3 billion for the Government's share of the capital and operating expenses of Petroleum Development Oman. The ministries that received the lion's share of the 1980 budget, along with the Ministry of Labor and Social Affairs will manage the bulk of development funds under the 5-year plan budget.

Development Planning

The Omanis are pleased with the results of their 1976-80 5-year plan. This concentrated on roads, ports, water supply, electricity, low-cost housing, education, and health. In large measure, planning for 1981-1985 is a logical extention of the earlier plan. Where the first plan succeeded in bringing education to 85 percent of the population, the second foresees improved education facilities as well as the construction of

Table 3.—U.S.-Oman Trade

($ million)

Year	U.S. Exports to Oman*	U.S. Imports from Oman
1973	9.1	13.1
1974	36.5	24.3
1975	74.7	58.4
1976	57.1	222.6
1977	56.9	424.3
1978	65.1	354.0
1979	87.9	316.7
1980	94.9	344.3

*Actual U.S. exports may be higher than indicated. Because of high shipping costs from the United States for small shipments and the inadequate storage facilities available in Oman, an unknown quantity of U.S. goods were transshipped to Oman by wholesale dealers in the United Arab Emirates.

Source: U.S. Department of Commerce, Bureau of the Census/FT 990.

Table 4.—U.S. Exports to Oman by Major Products Category 1979

($ million)

Food and live animals 1.8
Beverages and tobacco 17.0
Crude materials (inedible) 1.2
Chemicals 3.4
Manufactured goods 5.5
Paper products..35
Floor coverings...50
Mineral manufactures 24
Manufacturers of metal..2.4
Iron and steel 1.2
Machinery and transport equipment 51.3
Engines 1.5
Electrical parts and generation equipment 5.2
Tractors 1.8
Contractor equipment 14.8
Specialized machinery 3.4
Heating and cooling equipment 2.8
Pumps 5.8
Mechanical handling equipment..1.1
Nonelectric parts 1.8
Telecommunications equipment 3.9
Passenger vehicles 2.9
Trucks and special purpose vehicles 2.5
Road vehicle parts 1.1
Miscellaneous manufacturing equipment 4.1
Unclassified items 2.1

OMAN

Table 5.—Imports by Broad Economic Category 1975-80
(RO million)*

Broad Economic Category	1980 1st quarter	1979					1978	1977	1976	1975
		Total	4th quarter	3rd quarter	2nd quarter	1st quarter				
Food and beverages	19.4	56.7	14.0	12.6	13.8	16.3	45.1	42.3	33.8	29.2
Industrial supplies nes	33.0	86.2	26.4	19.8	21.0	19.0	73.3	65.2	57.5	62.8
Fuels and lubricants	8.5	28.4	7.0	6.5	6.9	8.0	27.6	20.4	16.6	9.1
Capital goods	16.7	69.3	15.2	21.5	17.6	15.0	27.6	52.3	16.6	51.4
Transport equipment	30.1	94.9	28.5	26.3	23.7	15.0	45.8	52.3	45.9	51.4
Consumer goods	16.9	61.6	15.0	13.7	19.3	16.4	75.8	58.8	45.7	34.4
Goods, n.e.s. and n.e.c.	1.2	33.3	13.1	15.8	2.1	13.6	52.0	53.2	41.8	31.9
TOTAL	125.8	430.5	119.2	116.2	104.4	2.3	7.6	9.9	9.3	45.5
						90.6	327.2	302.1	250.5	264.3

*Exchange rates: 1980: US$1 = RO 0.345; 1979: US$1 = RO 0.3456; 1975-78: US$1 = RO 0.3454.
Notes: nes: not elsewhere specified   nec: not elsewhere classified
Sources: Directorate General of National Statistics, Oman, and *Middle East Economic Digest*.

a university. More important, Oman is hoping to use some of its better trained and educated citizens in jobs that previously would have required South Asians or British expatriates.

During the first plan, the Omanis became impressed with the value of natural gas. This can be attributed to their relatively modest oil reserves and the fact that Oman must import refined petroleum products. Consequently, the new plan envisions using gas for Oman's own development while exporting crude oil. Going hand in hand with this is the projected construction of a pipeline grid for the nationwide distribution of gas.

The areas of greatest expenditure will be communications, social services, and defense. The Development Council has elected not to concentrate on industries based on processing imported raw materials. A continuing effort, unfulfilled under the 1976-80 plan, will be the attempt to turn such sectors of the economy as mining, agriculture, and fisheries into income earners so that the country's revenues are not so overwhelmingly dependent on oil.

Petroleum and Gas

During 1980, Oman's oil production averaged 283,000 barrels per day. The Government set a production ceiling of 330,000 barrels per day, a level it expects to maintain for the next several years. The country has an estimated 2.4 billion barrels in recoverable reserves. Petroleum exports account for more than 60 percent of its GDP and more than 90 percent of government revenue. Known oil fields have an expected life of 25 years, and progress in locating new oil has been ahead of schedule. As yet, Oman has no refinery.

The major producing company is Petroleum Development Oman (PDO), 60 percent government owned but operated by a Royal Dutch/Shell management staff. Since November 1980, the Elf-Sumitomo-Wintershall consortium also has been producing 12,000 barrels per day from the Sahmah field in

the group's Butabol concession. Discovered Omani oils have API gravities ranging from 19 degrees to 48 degrees, and they can produce an acceptable blend without having to be combined with oil from elsewhere. Omani planners see oil as a product primarily for export, although this may change when a 50,000-barrel-per-day refinery is completed in 1982 or 1983.

While there are only two oil producers in Oman, they by no means represent the whole story. Shell (34 percent), Campagnie Francaise de Petroles (4 percent), and Partex (2 percent) are minority owners of PDO. Elf-Aquitaine, BP (with AGIP and Deminex), Sumitomo, Wintershall AG, Gulf, Quintana, Occidental, Cluff, Hispanol, and Amoco, either individually or in combination, also have concessions either within the country or offshore. Oman's generous concessions have avoided the rancor that frequently arises between governments and oil companies. Largely for social and political reasons, the Government has placed a priority on having trained Omanis replace foreigners.

Given the importance of oil revenues, it should come as no surprise that PDO—and the oil sector as a whole—exerts considerable influence in domestic affairs. PDO will manage the Government's $100 million, 50,000-barrel-per-day refinery, and it is building an oil town at Rima to complement already existing towns at Fahud and Marmul. The total cost of construction at Rima will be about $12 billion. Although the oil sector employs only 2 percent of the indigenous labor force, its earnings provide jobs for the 30-50 percent of that labor force engaged in the services sector. Moreover, oil exports have brought in plentiful foreign exchange, allowing a flood of imports. The combination of increased imports and urban migration encouraged by oil revenues has further depressed the traditional agricultural and fishing sectors.

Nonassociated natural gas reserves are estimated to be 4 to 5 trillion standard cubic feet down to abandonment pressure, enough to last 80 years at the unpressurized pipeline delivery capacity of 140 million standard cubic feet per day. This is more than enough gas to start a gas industry even after filling Oman's own needs, but government planners have for now ruled this out. Conservation of gas resources for domestic use is the byword: it is hoped that by 1983 gas will no longer be wasted by flaring. Gas now fuels the Ghubra power and desalination plant, and a 120-mile pipeline to Sohar is being constructed to provide gas in the copper mining and smelting operation to begin there by 1982.

In 1979, a natural gas liquids (NGL) plant was commissioned at Yibal. This will produce from associated gas about 3,500 barrels per day of gasoline liquids. These are in turn used to improve the quality of crude. Smaller plants are also in operation at Fahud, Lekhwair, and Saih Rawl.

Mining

Oman will become the first country on the Arabian Peninsula to make a major commitment to export natural resources other than gas or oil. It has deposits of chromite, coal, manganese, limestone, marble, asbestos, phosphates, zinc, and nickel of undetermined exploitability, but its major effort is the mining of copper. A $150 million copper ore smelting project at Sohar is expected to export the metal by 1982. Plans are to produce 20,000 tons of copper ore annually. At this rate, known deposits will last about 12 years, but there is reason to believe other deposits exist elsewhere in the country. Financing to the extent of $100 million has come from the Saudi Fund for Development.

As costs increased, the Omani Government took over the operation from foreign partners. Using foreign consultants and contractors, the Government is developing the area around the project, a site with limited agricultural potential. In addition to a power plant, a smelter, crushing plant, laboratory, housing, and jetty are being constructed. The Government's approval suggests a long-term commitment to the project, which fits in well with its stated goal of economic diversification. The final product will be blister blocks of 99 percent or higher purity. The Government is also studying the feasibility of an electrolytic refinery and the production of copper rods, wire and cable, extrusions, and copper water pipes.

Manufacturing

A major subsector of Oman's small manufacturing sector is the production of pipes. It is protected by a 20-percent tariff against imported pipe. Production is expected to increase under the 1981-1985 5-year plan. The larger of Oman's two pipe plants, located in the Rusail industrial area, produces asbestos cement pipe. The smaller, in Ghubrah, makes plastic pipe.

The other major area of manufacture is cement. The Government has awarded contracts for the construction of two cement plants. The Rusail plant, near Muscat, will be operated by the government owned Oman Cement Company. The contract for the construction of this 624,000-ton-per-year plant, valued at $146 million, was awarded to Krupp-Polysius AG of West Germany. It will be completed in 1983. The $58 million Raysut plant, near Salalah, will be built by West Germany's Babcock Krauss-Maffei Industrienlangen. When it is completed in 1983, it will produce 210,000 tons per year.

The Government also owns 60 percent of Oman Flour Mills, which was producing three types of flour at full capacity by mid-1980. This operation has been so successful that the Government was able to reduce its percentage of ownership by selling shares to the public. It has scheduled an expansion program to produce animal feed.

An industrial zone is being constructed at Rusail, near Muscat. Work is already underway to provide roads, water and sewage pipes, power, drainage, and communications. The total cost of the zone will be just under $60 million. The Government hopes that by March 1982, 28 buildings will have been constructed and more than 3,000 jobs will have been created. Rusail Industrial Zone presently contains the Amiantit Asbestos Cement Pipe Plant and the National Gas Company gas bottling facility. In addition to the new cement plant, a 200 MW, gas turbine, electric power plant and a detergent factory also will be built in Rusail.

The second 5-year plan places increased emphasis on encouraging private Omani interests, sometimes in joint ventures with foreigners, to develop light industries based on indigenous raw materials. The Government may be expected to modify its free-trade philosophy to provide tariff protection for nascent industries.

Agriculture and Fishing

Agriculture is the prime source of income for the majority of Oman's population even though it and fishing combined account for only 3 percent of GDP. Rural to urban migration, conservatively estimated at 5,000 persons per year (mainly young males), continues to deplete the agricultural work force. Several other constraints also contribute to the sluggishness of agricultural production. Foremost is the scarcity of rainfall; virtually all agriculture in the country requires irrigation. Much of the farming is done at sites remote from the primary domestic markets. In addition, there is widespread reliance on traditional techniques. About 95 percent (36,000 hectares) of the land under cultivation is located along the Batinah coast in the north. Land suitable for cultivation could be increased by 250 percent if underground water reserves were exploited and if rural migration to urban centers, especially to the capital area, were stopped.

Oman's major crop is dates, which are a major item in the diet of the rural population. Other important agricultural produce includes limes, bananas (which are protected against imports by a 25-percent tariff), mangoes, melons, onions, and coconuts. Production of all other goods is far from adequate.

The focus of distribution for agricultural produce is the market at Matrah. This is not a wholesale market in the generally accepted sense, but an area set aside for some retailers and importers/wholesalers. Locally produced fruits and vegetables are delivered directly by farmers to Matrah or to retailers in smaller markets. Agricultural produce also is marketed in the outdoor market at Ruwi.

Two types of wholesalers distribute imports. Those at Matrah deal mostly in local produce and goods imported from Dubai. Produce from Dubai is delivered daily, so the wholesalers have no need for cold storage facilities. They sell to the low-income population through small retailers. The other type combines importing, wholesaling, and retailing. They import produce from Jordan, Lebanon, Turkey, India, Australia, and Western Europe and sell either through their own outlets or to other supermarkets, hotels, or the Government. Most of their customers are in the higher income sector of the population.

Following its practice in some other sectors, the Government has invested its own money in agricultural joint ventures with foreign companies in hope of divesting some of its shares to private Omani citizens once the project is operating successfully. It joined with a Swiss company to start a dairy farm at Sohar and a pilot farm at Salalah. In addition to serving as models for integrated irrigated farming and providing a source of technical expertise, these farms are already producing for the local markets. Furthermore, with outside help the Government is establishing an agricultural training center and is already operating agricultural research facilities. The Ministry of Agriculture has announced plans for a $1.5 million banana ripening and packaging plant with an annual capacity of 10-15,000 tons.

Oman's long coastline on the Gulf and the Arabian Sea provides a productive fishing ground. Its catch is estimated at 40,000 tons per year, but experts believe this could be increased tenfold without overexploitation. The Government's intention is to develop this industry in such a way that small fishers will still be able to participate and reap the benefits from it.

The Government's principal agent in fisheries development is the Oman National Fisheries Company (ONFC), which is owned by the Government (20 percent), traditional fishers (20 percent), and private Omani investors (60 percent). With $3 million capital, ONFC plans as one of its earliest projects to construct and operate a 20-ton-per-day cannery, processing, and fishmeal complex near Salalah. This plant presently is only in the planning stage. Koreans also operate a concession that trains Omanis and turns over 30 percent of its catch to the Government.

Health and Education

The Government has decided not to encourage private health care companies. As a result, it has made a considerable effort to bring health care facilities to the country's interior. Oman now has 14 hospitals, 11 health centers, 4 small-scale maternity clinics, and 60 dispensaries. For out of the way communities, the Government has established mobile medical teams and one integrated rural health service that handles 25 villages.

As in other areas, the Government wants to increase the number of Omanis in the health service. To this end, it operates health training centers at home and sends some of its citizens abroad for advanced training. It already runs a 3-year nursing course and plans to start paramedical training. A malaria control training center soon will be turning out 40 trainees annually.

The Sultanate is proud of having stayed mostly free of cholera since 1970. There are national committees for mass vaccination, tuberculosis control, and trachoma.

During the 1970's, the Government took education and training to the countryside. During the 1980's, the effort will be to upgrade educational facilities and provide a university for those who were educated in the last decade. It is estimated that 85 percent of the population have received some education or training. The Ministry of Education runs 375 schools for 100,000 children from ages 6 to 18, and it hopes to reach 20,000 more children in remote areas within the next 5 years. There is also the nucleus of a secondary and further education program, with 12

Table 6.—Gross Domestic Product (GDP) by Industry,* at Market Prices
(RO million)

	1979	1978	1977	1976	1975	1974	1973	1972	1971	1970
Agriculture and fishing	32.0	27.1	24.0	21.4	20.2	17.4	16.7	17.0	16.8	16.6
Mining (oil)	721.0	498.4	534.8	530.4	486.8	389.0	94.5	76.4	73.9	71.6
Construction	90.7	85.3	84.2	83.0	70.8	58.0	24.0	22.6	20.4	10.6
Public administration and defense	125.9	105.9	83.4	71.0	53.0	46.4	13.1	11.0	4.1	2.3
Others	202.9	176.1	153.7	121.2	93.4	57.7	21.1	13.8	9.9	5.7
Total GDP (at market prices)	1172.5	892.8	880.1	827.0	724.2	568.5	169.4	140.8	125.1	106.8
Minus indirect taxes	-8.1	-4.6	-4.6	-4.5	-2.5	-2.8	-2.0	-1.6	-1.1	-1.1
Gross domestic product* (at factor costs)	1164.4	888.2	875.5	822.5	721.7	565.7	167.4	139.2	124.0	105.7

*Estimates relating to 1970-74 are World Bank estimates. From 1975, the estimates are made by the Development Council, Oman. Hence, the two series are not strictly comparable.
Note: Exchange rates: 1979: US$1=RO 0.3456; 1978: US$1=RO 0.3454; 1977: US$1=RO 0.3454; 1976: US$1=RO 0.3454; 1975: US$1=RO 0.3454; 1974: US$1=RO 0.3454; 1973: US$1=RO 0.3486; 1972: US$1=RO 0.386; 1971: US$1=RO 0.41; 1970: US$1=RO 0.42.
Sources: Directorate General of National Statistics, Oman, and *Middle East Economic Digest.*

Table 7.—Oman: Capital Expenditure of Ministries and Government Authorities in the Second 5-Year Plan (1981-85)
(RO million*)

	1981	1982	1983	1984	1985	Total
Diwan of Protocol	8.0	8.0	8.0	8.0	8.0	40.0
Governorate of the Capital	0.6	0.6	0.6	0.6	0.6	3.0
Ministry of Royal Diwan Affairs	0.5	0.5	0.5	0.5	0.5	2.5
Ministry of Foreign Affairs	3.0	3.0	3.0	3.0	3.0	15.0
Ministry of Health	5.0	5.0	7.0	8.0	10.0	35.0
Ministry of Education	5.0	7.0	8.0	10.0	10.0	40.0
Ministry of Interior	1.0	1.5	1.5	1.5	1.5	7.0
Ministry of Communications	54.0	48.0	48.0	45.0	45.0	240.0
Ministry of Social Affairs and Labour	6.0	8.0	8.0	9.0	9.0	40.0
Ministry of Petroleum and Minerals	19.0	19.0	19.0	14.0	14.0	85.0
Ministry of Awqaf and Islamic Affairs	0.5	1.0	1.0	1.0	1.0	4.5
Ministry of Information and Youth Affairs	5.0	5.0	5.0	5.0	5.0	25.0
Ministry of Commerce and Industry	20.0	18.0	12.0	10.0	10.0	70.0
Ministry of Agriculture and Fisheries	15.0	18.0	20.0	22.0	25.0	100.0
Ministry of Justice	0.6	0.6	0.6	0.6	0.6	3.0
Ministry of National Heritage and Culture	3.0	3.0	3.0	3.0	3.0	15.0
Ministry of Land Affairs and Municipalities	4.0	5.0	6.0	7.0	8.0	30.0
Ministry of Post, Telegraphs and Telephones	10.0	10.0	9.0	13.0	8.0	50.0
Ministry of Electricity and Water	23.0	27.0	32.0	32.0	31.0	145.0
Ministry of Public Works	0.5	0.5	0.5	0.5	0.5	2.5
Ministry of State for Dhofar	3.0	3.0	3.0	3.0	3.0	15.0
Office of Deputy Prime Minister for Legal Affairs	0.3	0.3	0.3	0.3	0.3	1.5
Musandam Development Committee	0.5	0.5	0.5	0.5	0.5	2.5
Other government authorities**	27.5	32.5	43.5	59.5	77.5	240.5
Total	215.0	225.0	240.0	257.0	275.0	1,212.0

**Including Development Council allocation, financing of Development Bank and Housing Bank and support for private sector.
*US$1=RO 0.3457.
Source: *Middle East Economic Digest,* London.

secondary schools to date and advanced studies in Islam, teacher training, and agriculture. In addition, the Ministry expects to set up schools for commercial studies.

Advanced education is for the most part provided at universities in Europe and other Arab countries, although a high school for technical training is planned for the capital area. Technical on-the-job training is also provided at various project sites, and often training programs are offered as adjuncts to larger projects. Presently, fewer than 900 Omani students are at universities abroad; 230 of these are in the United States.

Table 8.—Oil Production and Export
(million barrels)

	Production	Exports
1967 (August-December)	20.9	21.0
1968	87.9	88.1
1969	119.7	119.2
1970	121.3	121.4
1971	107.4	106.3
1972	102.8	103.2
1973	107.0	106.3
1974	105.8	105.9
1975	124.6	124.8
1976	133.7	134.3
1977	124.1	122.0
1978		
1st quarter	29.2	28.1
2nd quarter	28.4	29.8
3rd quarter	28.6	27.6
4th quarter	28.5	30.4
1979		
1st quarter	27.2	27.2
2nd quarter	27.6	27.3
3rd quarter	26.6	26.0
4th quarter	26.3	27.1
1980		
1st quarter	25.4	24.5
2nd quarter	25.6	24.8
3rd quarter	25.5	26.9
4th quarter	26.8	25.6
Total 1980	103.3	101.8

Sources: Department of Petroleum and Minerals and Petroleum Development Oman, Directorate General National Statistics, Development Council, and *Middle East Economic Digest.*

Selling In Oman

Distribution and Sales Channels

Commerce in Oman has a long history of free enterprise. Although most of the population was engaged in subsistence pastoralism or agriculture, trading was an important economic activity. Situated on the Indian Ocean littoral, Omanis, and Arabs in general, were leaders of the flourishing trade in that area before the Portuguese wrested this trade from them in the 16th century. According to tradition, Sindbad the Sailor of the *Arabian Nights* was based in Sohar, and the exotic adventures attributed to him were evocative of the also exotic, if more mundane, experiences of his real life counterparts.

Trade remains so ingrained that little distinction is made between economic activities and public duties. Often officials who themselves or whose close relatives hold public office are also engaged in the private sector, and use their public influence to their own private advantage. This is not regarded as a conflict of interest in Omani terms, although it may potentially create

Table 9.—Destination of Oil Exports
(million barrels)

Destination	1980	1979	1978	1977	1976	1975	1974	1973	1972	1971	1970	1969	1968	1967
Japan	51.5	68.6	65.8	62.7	58.2	46.8	37.5	38.1	43.7	35.9	36.5	31.9	27.0	9.0
Malaysia	–	–	–	–	–	–	–	–	–	14.9	21.6	17.3	23.6	1.6
Singapore	11.1	–	–	–	1.4	7.4	0.9	6.6	8.6	5.2	2.5	0.8	–	–
France	1.0	0.5	2.1	4.7	8.6	8.6	12.7	18.4	15.4	10.7	11.4	10.2	5.2	1.3
Netherlands	11.0	7.6	7.2	11.1	19.6	25.6	1.9	9.2	4.8	12.2	10.8	26.0	6.8	0.8
Italy	–	–	3.1	1.3	1.2	0.6	8.6	–	–	–	–	0.6	1.2	–
West Germany	8.4	0.5	2.8	1.3	1.6	0.7	0.6	–	–	–	0.8	–	–	–
United Kingdom	1.5	6.0	0.8	1.3	1.7	8.3	5.7	3.4	3.7	5.7	5.9	9.2	9.7	2.0
Sweden	–	–	1.0	4.1	–	–	3.4	7.3	7.7	8.7	14.5	11.5	9.7	3.9
Norway	2.9	5.2	7.6	3.8	0.6	1.5	3.2	5.4	10.7	9.4	11.2	5.0	2.3	–
Denmark	–	–	–	–	–	–	1.0	0.5	3.4	3.0	6.2	6.7	2.6	2.4
South Africa	–	–	–	–	–	–	–	0.3	–	0.6	–	–	–	–
United States	3.1	14.2	17.5	18.8	21.2	7.2	3.1	2.0	3.0	–	–	–	–	–
Canada	–	–	–	–	8.0	4.8	12.4	10.5	2.2	–	–	–	–	–
Taiwan	3.0	–	–	–	–	–	0.4	1.6	–	–	–	–	–	–
Pacific Islands	–	–	–	11.1	10.4	13.3	3.9	2.0	–	–	–	–	–	–
Brazil	–	1.3	–	–	–	–	4.9	1.0	–	–	–	–	–	–
Belgium	–	–	–	–	–	–	3.4	–	–	–	–	–	–	–
Portugal	3.0	–	–	1.2	–	–	1.3	–	–	–	–	–	–	–
Switzerland	–	–	–	–	–	–	0.8	–	–	–	–	–	–	–
Sri Lanka	–	–	–	–	–	–	0.2	–	–	–	–	–	–	–
Others	7.3	4.0	7.7	0.6	1.8	·	–	–	–	–	–	–	–	–
Total	101.8	107.9	115.6	122.0	134.3	124.8	105.9	106.3	103.2	106.3	121.4	119.2	88.1	21.0

Sources: Petroleum Development Oman, *Central Bank Quarterly Bulletin*, and *Middle East Economic Digest*.

difficulties for U.S. firms who must consider the U.S. Foreign Corrupt Practices Act.

Specialization in trade is not commonly found in the Omani private sector. The "typical Arab trading firm" combines the functions of importer, wholesaler, exclusive distributor, retailer, and so on. The larger trading firms often have interests in such other activities as construction, manufacturing, and shipping.

There are a number of common problems that hamper U.S.-Omni commercial relations and that discourage Omani businessmen from seeking U.S. products. Examples of such complaints by Omanis include failure to provide proper shipping documents, improper labeling, delays (sometimes of up to 6 months) in delivery, shipping to Dubai or Saudi Arabia instead of directly to Muscat, and failure to respond to telexes and letters.

Legal System

The Omani legal system in theory rests on the decisions of Muslim religious courts, which use the precepts of the Quran and the body of law known as the Shari'a as the basis for their decisions. Each case is considered by a board of three judges, often without reference to recent precedents. In actual fact, the Quranic legal system has been considerably modified, as criminal jurisdiction is now divided between the criminal code administered by police magistrates and the Quranic law administered by Qadis, or judges of the religious courts. Decisions can be appealed to a court of review, and from there can be appealed to the Sultan. It is possible, however, for legal contracts to be written to provide for external arbitration. Omani officials have on occasion expressed a readiness to abide by decisions of such bodies as the World Court. In addition, the Omani business community has a Committee for the Settlement of Commercial Disputes, described below.

The Omani commercial legal system is still evolving. Businesspeople, therefore, should not be surprised if they are unable to obtain definitive answers about regulatory matters or if actual practice does not match legal theory.

The most important pieces of legislation for the foreign businessperson are the Banking Law of 1974, which created the Central Bank of Oman and regulates banking business in the Sultanate (including banking transactions and commercial paper); the Commercial Companies Law (CCL) of 1974; the Commercial Register Law (CRL) of 1974; the Foreign Business and Investments Law (FBIL) of 1973; and the Commercial Agencies Law (CAL) of 1977.

FBIL stipulates Omani participation in companies operating in Oman. For most companies, the Omani share of capitalization and profits should not be less than 35 percent. For companies engaged in public utilities, real estate, or the registration of aircraft, the Omani share must be 51 percent; and for press and information activities, 66 percent. Special agreements with the Government or a decree from the Sultan can exempt a company from these provisions. No commercial company with any direct or indirect foreign ownership interest may own land in Oman. An automatic exemption from Oman's partnership requirements is available to any person or firm having a government contract. Service professionals such as lawyers, architects, and consultants are not subject to the law, nor are international transportation companies, offshore banks, and companies participating in projects that the Ministry of Commerce has designated as development projects.

FBIL sets a minimum of Omani Rial (RO) 150,000 on the paid-in capital of any investment in which a foreigner has an interest. This minimum may be reduced to RO 30,000 on the recommendation of the Committee on the Investment of Foreign Capital, which consists of representatives of the Ministry of Commerce and Industry, the Ministry of Agriculture and Fisheries, the Ministry of Petroleum and Minerals, the Directorate General of Finance, the Development Council, and the Chamber of Commerce. The Committee considers whether the project is of benefit to economic development and fixes the amount of Omani participation.

CAL requires representatives or distributors of foreign firms to be Omani citizens, or, if a company, to have at least 51 percent Omani ownership. Under CAL, all imports into the Sultanate must be made through an authorized agent. Manufacturers are required to reimburse their agents for all expenses incurred by them for all commitments made in carrying out the terms of the agreement. Repair facilities and spare parts are required where appropriate. Certain contracting companies may be exempted from CAL and allowed to import such items for their own use as heavy equipment, but special permission will have to be obtained. The law entitles authorized agents who find the companies they represent dealing with other agents to file claims for normal commissions and seek enforcement of their rights from the Ministry of Commerce and Industry.

Commercial agency agreements, along with any subsequent amendments, must be in writing and approved by the Omani Chamber of Commerce. If executed outsde Oman, they must be approved by an Omani Chamber of Commerce or consulate or, in its absence, by a consulate of any member of the Arab League. The agreement must then be filed and registered with the Ministry of Commerce and Industry. Registration is valid for 2 years but is renewable for additional 2-year periods.

Resolution of Commercial Disputes

Oman has created a special organ to hear cases of commercial disputes, the Committee for the Settlement of Commercial Disputes. This body consists of the Under Secretary of the Ministry of Commerce and Industry, the President of the Oman Chamber of Commerce and Industry, and five prominent Omani businessmen. Decisions of the Committee are guided by its perceptions of equity and fairness and customary business practice in Oman. They are final and unappealable and may be enforced through the local police authorities. Legal representation in disputes before the Committee is possible. More details are provided in the section on Bidding and Awarding of Contracts.

Agents

All foreign firms selling goods in Oman are required to appoint an Omani company or individual as an agent. Only holders of import licenses can bring goods into the country for local sale, and these licenses are issued only to Omani citizens or to companies in which Omanis own 51 percent. Agencies, whether firms or individuals, must be listed in the Commercial Register, be members of the Chamber of Commerce, and have their principal place of business in Oman. Firms working directly for the Omani Government do not need a local agent. In actual practice, the Ministry of Commerce is not likely to approve the formation of a company with foreign equity if it intends to act in an agency capacity. It makes no distinction between an agent and a distributor of goods. Provisions of CAL are discussed under "Legal System," above.

In addition to the legal requirement, there also are sound practical reasons for using an agent, and the selection of effective representation is extremely important. On one level, agents in Oman provide such important services as arranging for entry visas, hotel reservations, and making appointments with government officials. An attempt to make these arrangements directly can require expenditure of an inordinate amount of time and effort by a foreign firm. A good local representative should also have important contacts in government decisionmaking circles. These will enable him to collect valuable information on approaching tenders and allow him an opportunity to acquaint key government officials with the product or service provided by the foreign firm.

To be effective, an agent must have good local contacts and a good business reputation. In addition, the agent must be willing to market product lines aggressively. Most large merchant establishments in Oman hold literally scores of sales agencies for products ranging from sewing needles to heavy construction equipment, often for several competing product lines. In such situations, the distributor obviously will not give equal attention to all agencies but instead will actively market only those products that offer the greatest sales potential and the highest profit margin. The larger Omani trading firms combine the functions of importer, wholesaler, exclusive distributor, and retailer, along with their involvement in such areas as construction or shipping.

Omani firms will usually stipulate that an agency agreement provide the right of exclusive distributorship. If the exclusive distributor is also a major retailer, very often the product will appear only in that one retail outlet.

Profit margins imposed by Omani distributors often are quite high. For representing international companies that win tenders to major projects, most agents charge from 1 to 10 percent, the larger the project the lower the rate.

Personal contact is an essential prerequisite for a successful marketing effort in Oman. Representatives of foreign firms should visit Oman prior to selecting an agent and follow up with regular trips thereafter. Omanis like to see the home office representatives of the firms with which they deal, and the display of interest symbolized by frequent visits can make the difference between making and losing major sales.

U.S. businesspeople have reported that Omani importing agents have balked at accepting risks or responsibilities that the American might assume would devolve on him/her according to Western standards of business. U.S. businesspeople may find it advantageous to take upon themselves the responsibility for such things as financing. Omanis have been known to expect U.S. businesspeople to supply them with goods at no cost to themselves and with no firm assurance of sales or other commitment of activity on their part. They prefer to be commissioned agents rather than stocking distributors, at least until a firm market for any good is established. A constant feature of business is that Omani businessmen will take great pains to make clear that they lack the economic and financial resources of their Saudi neighbors.

The U.S. Department of Commerce and the U.S. Embassy in Muscat can assist in identifying potential agents or distributors through Commerce's Agent/Distributor Service. Local chambers of commerce and commercial banks also can help.

Bidding and Awarding of Contracts

Though the complete informality that traditionally has characterized business transactions in Oman is falling prey to increasing regulation, Omanis attach a high degree of importance to personal relationships. Therefore, business is conducted almost entirely with companies that have a local presence. Frequent visits by the foreign firm's home representatives are virtually a prerequisite for market penetration even after local representation is established. Furthermore, opportunities for consultants, architects, engineers, or contractors are not always published; information on upcoming projects can best be obtained by a competent local representative.

The Oman Government undertakes all the major infrastructure projects and is a joint-venture partner in the large industrial projects. Oman's active private sector is composed primarily of traders or merchants who spend much of their time representing foreign companies seeking government contracts. The Ministries of Defense, Communications, Electricity and Water, Petroleum and Minerals, and Agriculture and Fisheries are the biggest users of consultants and engineers.

The Ministry of Communications, with its project consultants, has the primary responsibility for the evaluation of bids and selection of contractors for civil construction and highways. The Ministry of Electricity and Water does the same for electric power and desalting projects. The Ministry of Petroleum and Minerals has a similar role in contracts for natural gas and oil pipelines, refineries, mining activities, and other projects related to natural resources. The Ministry of Commerce and Industry is primarily involved in nonpetroleum-related industrial projects, while agricultural and fisheries projects are the responsibility of the Ministry of Agriculture and Fisheries.

The Government does not generally award turnkey contracts. The design/engineering and construction contracts are awarded separately. Contracts for the design/engineering phase of small projects are awarded on a negotiated basis to Oman-based firms. On the large projects, the executing or client agency generally will invite a few firms to submit proposals. Normally, other firms who become aware of the project may submit prequalification information and ask to be included on the list of those presenting proposals.

In contrast to the negotiated contracts of the mid-1970s, the Government of Oman now prefers competitive bidding in the award of major contracts.

Government ministries regularly submit proposed projects to the Development Council. This body must grant approval before the Finance Council may release funds for implementation.

The Government established a Tender Board, comprising officials from various government agencies, to make information on projects available to foreign contractors. Only firms with a local presence or ones registered with the Board are invited to submit a bid. There is no formal prequalification process. In order actually to submit a bid, contractors must have not only a local sponsor or Omani partner but must also be registered with the Tender Board and the Ministry of Commerce and Industry. Bidders must put up a bid bond of 5 percent of the tender price in the form of a temporary bank guaranty. Ministry of Defense projects are not handled by the Tender Board. On some contracts the involved government agency will invite a small number of firms to submit bids. The Development Council then hires consultants to evaluate the bids. The contract will not necessarily be awarded to the lowest bidder: the Tender Board is allowed to reject the lowest bidder on the grounds of financial responsibility, past history, available equipment, or other reasons. Additional negotiations ordinarily follow the selection of the winner and precede the signing of the contract. From preliminary selection through the awarding of the contract and final signing usually takes about 60 days.

Within 15 days of notification of the award, the contractor must submit a performance bond for 10 percent of the award in the form of a bank guaranty. It is difficult to have the required amount of either the bid bond or the performance bond reduced. No exception is made for firms that have already performed successfully in Oman.

Force majeure clauses are defined in the tender conditions and include unforeseen circumstances such as wars and natural disasters. Labor disputes and delays due to port congestion are not considered force majeure, but in practice, they do not occur in Oman.

Contracts and commitments exceeding RO 250,000 require the signature of the competent minister or other authorized individual and the approval of both the Deputy Chairman of the Financial Affairs Council and the Director of the Office of Financial Affairs. Contracts between RO 50,000 and 250,000 must be signed both by the Secretary of the Procurement Department and the competent minister or a legally appointed representative. Contracts under RO 50,000 must be signed only by the competent minister or a legally appointed representative.

Omani law requires that private business controversies be submitted to the Committee for the Settlement of Commercial Disputes. The Committee is composed of the Chairman of the Chamber of Commerce, three officials in the Ministry of Commerce, and five local merchants. It seeks a settlement that is mutually agreeable to the parties concerned. Its decisions are binding and cannot be appealed. It is not clear whether disputes to which an Oman Government entity is a party must be submitted to the Committee. It is unlikely that the Government would be obliged to do so, but it could undoubtedly turn commercial disputes over to the Committee if it wished. Most controversies between the Government and foreign firms are handled by direct negotiation. Provisions for international arbitration, usually under the auspices of the International Chamber of Commerce, are routinely written into most contracts. However, few, if any, disputes have to be referred to international arbitration.

Advance payments of 10 to 20 percent of the value of the contract can be obtained. However, the Omanis prefer contractors who can finance the project themselves or can line up commercial bank financing.

Arabic is the official language in Oman, but English is used in government and commercial circles and is generally acceptable for bids and contracts. The metric system of weights and measures is used.

Price

There are no government regulations for pricing contracts. Contracts with a negotiated fixed price, contracts with escalation clauses, and cost-plus-fee contracts are used. For most large projects, prices are fixed during the negotiations after the contract has been awarded and before it is signed.

The Government does not guarantee the prices of commodities. Generally, there are no provisions made for escalation of the contract price for demurrage charges nor for escalation in the price of parts.

Equipment and Materials

A customs duty of 2 percent of the c.i.f. value of the goods is applied to most imports. However, a waiver may be negotiated for machinery, equipment, and materials for government projects. Used machinery and equipment need not be reexported. There are no bonded areas.

Oman does not produce the commodities needed for construction projects, so there are no requirements to use local supplies. However, contracts often stipulate that goods be purchased through local importers rather than directly from the overseas manufacturers.

Price Controls

Various essential goods are subject to price control administered by the Omani Department of Commerce. Exporters are advised to check with that office either directly or through its agents, as the list of items and their prices change frequently.

Terms of Payment

Payment is typically by letter of credit.

Japanese sellers, and some European firms, are well known for their willingness to offer attractive time draft terms, extending for as much as 2 or 3 years. U.S. firms generally have been unable to offer more than 180-day terms.

The Export-Import Bank of the United States, 811 Vermont Avenue, N.W., Washington, D.C. 20571, telex 89-461, phone 202-382-8400, and the Foreign Credit Insurance Association, (FCIA), One World Trade Center, Ninth Floor, New York, N.Y. 10048, phone 212-432-6311, can help U.S. exporters cover the risk involved in lengthening their credit terms. A similar private organization is the Private Export Funding Corporation (PEFCO), 280 Park Avenue, New York, NY 10017.

Real Property

Foreign companies or individuals may not acquire property for personal or investment purposes in Oman without the permission of the Ministry of Land Affairs. Corporate bodies can obtain permission to lease land on a long-term basis, ordinarily 49 years. On the average, after 15 years the property and buildings become the property of the local partner, although their use is guaranteed to the company for the period of the lease.

Only Omanis may hold clear individual title to land. Foreigners are now being permitted to buy freehold leases on houses at the new town of Madinat Qaboos. Local law remains unclear regarding rights of transfer in case of sale to a third party.

Patents, Trademarks, and Copyrights

There is no formal copyright, patent, or trademark protection legislation in Oman. Such rights can be advertised in the local and regional press, and cases of infringement may be decided by the Ministry of Commerce and Industry.

Packaging

The use of Islamic religious symbols or sayings on packages should be avoided. Bold tones seem to be favored over soft ones, and red, green, black, and white are preferred colors. Elsewhere in the Arabian Peninsula, such colors as pink, violet, and yellow have a negative impact. Photographs or illustrations of pigs or wrappings simulating pigskin should be avoided. Because Oman is taking part in the anti-Israel boycott, allusions or references to Israel in packaging or promotional material may have an adverse effect. In some adjacent countries, reusable bottles or tins have appeal.

All goods consigned to Oman should be packed to withstand rough handling, extreme heat, and high humidity and to afford protection against pilferage. Ideally, boxes should be waterproofed inside and out, and double strapped with metal bands. Simple crating of merchandise does not give sufficient protection from weather or the possibility of careless stevedoring.

For food items, dates of manufacture and expiry (i.e., the life of the product) must appear on the outside of packages or boxes as well as on individual items. These dates need not appear on crates or containers used for shipping.

Marketing

Most marketing is subject to the abilities and discretion of the local agent, who will order only what he feels he can sell. The most decisive factors in determining whether or not a product is purchased may be its international reputation or word-of-mouth recommendation.

English and Arabic language newspapers accept advertising. The rate for the English newspapers is $700 per page. For mass market consumer goods, billboards and filmed cinema advertisements may be more effective, considering the high rate of illiteracy. Neither television nor radio accepts advertising.

The U.S. Army Corps of Engineers

The U.S. Army Corps of Engineers has begun to act as a consultant to the Omani Government in contracting design and construction work on certain military and development projects. On behalf of Oman, the Corps can contract with architectural and engineering firms, usually American, to draw up and design specifications for these projects. After approval by the Omani Government, the Corps can issue tenders for international bid for construction and supply.

U.S. firms must prequalify with the Corps at this address:

U.S. Army Corps of Engineers
Middle East Division (Rear)
P.O. Box 2250
Winchester, Virginia 22601
Telephone: 703-677-2295, ext. 2179
Telex: 89584

Construction firms must submit Form 3627, "Prequalification Statement for Prime Construction Contractors," to the above address, attention: MERPS-C, telephone extension 2179. Architect-engineering firms must submit Standard Forms 254 and 255 to the above Winchester, VA, address, attention: MEDED-MC, telephone extension 2206. Suppliers of other equipment and services must file Form SF 129, "Bidder's Mailing List Application," to the above address, attention: MERPS, telephone extension 2155. It also is recommended that suppliers obtain current lists of architect-engineers and contractors undertaking Corps-sponsored projects and supply them with information on products of interest.

Solicitations for architect-engineering services, certain supplies, and other services are advertised only in "Commerce Business Daily," which may be ordered from the Superintendent of Documents, U.S. Government Printing Office, Washington, D.C. 20402 ($105 per annual subscription). Construction and major supply and service projects are advertised in "Commerce Business Daily"; "International Construction Week," published by Engineering News-Record, McGraw-Hill Publications Co., P.O. Box 950, New York, N.Y. 10020; "Middle East Economic Digest," available from 21 John Street, London WC1N 2BP, England; and "Middle East Trade Letter," available from Airport Office Center, P.O. Box 3444, Charlotte, N.C. 28203.

U.S. firms that bid on Corps projects will be subject to Omani regulations. The Corps accepts surety bonds in lieu of bank guarantees to cover bid and performance bonds on Omani projects.

Currently, the Corps is engaged in the design and construction of military facilities in Oman. The program, potentially valued at $200 million to $250 milllion, is to improve existing facilities for use by the U.S. Air Force at Seeb, Thumrait, Al Khasab, and Masirah Island. U.S. firms must by law be used almost exclusively in these projects, and any supplies shipped to Oman for use in them must go by U.S. flag carrier.

The Corps address in Oman is as follows:

U.S. Army Corps of Engineers
P.O. Box 6096
Ruwi
Sultanate of Oman
Telephone: 601382, 601386
Telex: 3034 CEOMAN MB

The U.S.-Oman Joint Commission

The U.S.-Oman Joint Commission for Economic and Technological Cooperation was established in 1980 to channel funds from U.S. Government agencies, private business, and financial and educational institutions to Oman to assist its development. Once this government-to-government program gets underway, the Omani and U.S. commissioners will evaluate and initiate development projects using U.S. funding and expertise. To date, Joint Commission projects include the construction of a water catchment in the capital area, still in the consultancy stage; and primary health care projects, still being discussed with the Omani Government.

Correspondence to the Joint Commission in Oman should be addressed to:

U.S.-Oman Joint Commission
U.S. Representative
P.O. Box 6001
Ruwi, Muscat
Sultanate of Oman
Telephone: 702438, 701357

In Fiscal Year 1981, the Commission will receive $5 million in grants; in Fiscal Years 1982 and 1983, it will receive $5 million in grants and $10 million in soft loans. The figures for 1982 and 1983 are still subject to congressional approval. Beginning in Fiscal Year 1982, the Omani Government will provide matching grants of $10 million each year.

Banking, Credit, and Sources of Capital

Twenty commercial banks operate in Oman, many with branches in Salalah and the northern interior. Citibank of New York is the only U.S. commercial bank in the Sultanate, but other U.S. banks have equity participation or management contracts with local banks. There are no controls on the free entry or exit of capital, and commercial banks make liberal use of foreign borrowings to finance the working capital of local firms.

Because of the great expansion of credit and banking in Oman in the early 1970s, the Government established a Central Bank in 1975 with full powers to manage the economy, supervise commercial banks, and regulate credit. This institution has largely supplanted British financial institutions in managing government finances, having imposed loan restrictions, interest rate ceilings, and reserve requirements on the commercial banks. The Central Bank is recognized as one of Oman's best run institutions.

During 1980, the Central Bank issued regulations dealing with reserves and assets of banks operating in the Sultanate and established guidelines for banks to follow when assessing their reserves. Commercial banks are required to keep up-to-date information on each customer so that the Central Bank auditors can assess their accounts. There has been a general tightening of banking documentation both to comply with changing laws and regulations and to meet with increasingly demanding standards of Central Bank audits.

Oman also has set up the Oman Development Bank and the Oman Housing Bank. The former is owned 40 percent by the Government, 20 percent by private Omanis, and 40 percent by foreign institutions, firms, or organizations. Its main aim is to serve as the principal vehicle for promoting Omani private enterprise, while at the same time creating a channel between the local and international monetary and capital markets. It also is considered an important means of providing studies and financial advice to members of the private sector who are interested in initiating new projects. The Oman Housing Bank was capitalized at RO 10 million, with 51 percent held by the Government, 39 percent by the Kuwaiti Ministry of Finance, and 10 percent by the British Bank of the Middle East. It makes loans for private homes for Omanis. Neither bank will be involved in traditional commercial banking. They will handle the medium- and long-term requirements of private enterprise in Oman for projects in industry, mining, and oil. The Government also has authorized the establishment of a new Agriculture and Fisheries Development Bank to open in the fall of 1981 with a capitalization of $55 million.

The Central Bank was concerned that a lack of credit would dampen economic development. To avoid this, it issued in February 1980 regulations covering the purchase, discount, and rediscount of commercial paper. Previously, and traditionally, credit was generated by overdraft, and bankers had to meet liquidity requirements through dollar swaps. In part as a result of these policies, credit was expanding by late 1980 at an annual rate of 27 percent.

There is no stock exchange or long-term capital market in Oman.

New banks incorporated in Oman are now required to have 51-percent Omani shareholding.

Two international financial institutions headquartered in Saudi Arabia are sources of finance in other countries:

Islamic Development Bank, P.O. Box 5925, Jidda, phone 33994, 33995, telex 401137 BISLAMI SJ. Established in 1975, the Islamic Development Bank consists of 33 Muslim countries with an authorized capital of $2.4 billion. It provides loans, guarantees, foreign trade financing, leasing, and equity investment to the most needy in its member countries.

Arab Petroleum Investment Corporation, P.O. Box 448, Dhahran Airport, phone 43883, 43411, 44663, telex 671009 PETMARK SJ, Attention APIC. Established in 1976, with authorized capital of $1.1 billion, the Arab Petroleum Investment Corporation provides financing for the petroleum and related industries with an emphasis on joint ventures in Arab countries.

Oman also obtains financing from the following institutions: the Kuwait Fund for Arab Economic Development (KFAED), the Abu Dhabi Fund for Arab Economic Development (ADFAED), and the Arab Fund for Economic and Social Development (AFESD).

Transportation and Utilities

Roads

In the late 1970s, Oman had over 1,300 km of paved roads. These included roads from the capital to the border with the United Arab Emirates (UAE), and to Nizwa, Ibra, Rustaq, and other towns in the mountains. A route linking the capital with Quriyat is expected to be extended along the coast to Sur, and the major towns in the northern part of the country are now linked by road. Road construction is also underway in the Musandam Peninsula, separated from the rest of Oman by the UAE. When completed, this road will be linked to the rest of Oman by joining with existing paved highways in the UAE. A north-south highway stretching 800 km from Nizwa to Thumrait is scheduled for completion in early 1982.

In 1979, there were 36,783 commercial vehicles and 32,104 private vehicles registered in Oman. Basic bus service is provided from Matrah to Sohar, Nizwa, and other points in the interior.

There are no plans for mass transportation in Muscat or Salalah or for a transportation system that would run throughout the country. However, bus service does run from Matrah to Sohar, Nizwa, and other destinations, and cars and trucks may be rented. Taxis are available in cities.

Ports

Oman's ports are managed by the Port Services Corporation, 60 percent of which is owned by the Government. The major cargo port is Mina Qaboos, near Matrah in the capital area. Oman's next most important port is at Raysut, near Salalah. Smaller ports or jetty facilities are being planned for Sur, Sohar, and Khasab. The country's only oil terminal is at Minal al Fahal. From here oil can be loaded into supertankers offshore.

With a 2-million-ton capacity, Mina Qaboos is generally far less congested than other ports in the Persian Gulf. It has 12 berths and is able to accommodate vessels with maximum drafts of 45 feet. The port also has a grain silo with a 50,000-ton capacity. Maximum waiting time for offloading ships is 3 days. Mina Qaboos has container-handling capability and, in 1980, was acquiring cranes to speed container handling.

Raysut harbor has six berths that can handle freighters of more than 35,000 tons. It averages 220,000 tons of cargo annually and is being expanded to a 1-million-ton capacity.

Although Oman does not yet receive direct service from U.S. shipping lines, Hansa, Concordia, Nedlloyd, and Maersk, among other lines, provide scheduled steamship service from the eastern and southern United States. The Omani Government does not plan to enter the shipping industry.

Airports and Airlines

Seeb Airport, 20 miles (36 km) from Muscat, is the only international airport in Oman. Served by more than a dozen carriers, it has become a stopover point for British Airways and UTA flights to the Far East. Together, the carriers provide service to about a dozen countries. The Seeb runway has been improved to permit large aircraft to use it year round without reducing their loads. No U.S. airlines fly into Oman on a scheduled basis. Flights to Seeb are available from Dhahran, Kuwait, Bahrain, Qatar, Abu Dhabi, Karachi, and Salalah.

An airport of international standards has been completed at Salalah, but it receives no international flights. It is served by daily flights from Muscat—the capital, but permission to fly to Salalah must be obtained beforehand from the office of the Governor of the Capital. Both the Seeb and Salalah airports are maintained by Pan American.

Electrical Power

Electric power and water are under the Ministry of Water and Electricity. Prior to the Ministry's formation in 1978, the capital area was plagued by power shortages. This situation was eased by the construction in that year of the Ghubrah power and desalination plant. Further capacity was installed in 1979, and the Government plans to increase its capacity from 260 to 460 MW in the early 1980s. The govern-

ment is taking steps to provide electricity throughout Oman during the 1980s to include three 30-MW generating plants, one near Nizwa and two on the Batinah coast. Twenty-six power stations recently completed in rural Oman will be operated by the newly formed National Electric Company, sponsored by the Government but privately owned.

Water

Oman possesses greater water resources than other countries in the Arabian Peninsula. Ground water from rainfall in the mountainous interior is transported by a system of canals to towns and villages. Tenders have been invited for construction of water supply systems for Sur, Sohar, and Buraimi, and water systems for other towns in the interior are planned. Desalination supplies more than 80 percent of the water to Muscat. Most of this (6 million gallons per day) comes from the Ghubrah desalination plant. This plant is being doubled in size. Water production and consumption throughout the country, but especially in Muscat, are increasing rapidly.

Communications

The Omani telephone system comprised over 11,000 lines in the late 1970s, and 7,000 more lines were being added in the capital area. It is operated by the General Telecommunications Organization (GTO). Despite this expansion, Oman in 1979 still had one of the lowest ratios of telephones to population of any country in the Middle East, with only about one telephone per

Table 10.—Electricity, Energy

	1979	1978	1977	1976	1975	1974	1973	1972	1971	1970
Government			**Installed capacity***							
Power House.										
Riyam and Ghubrah (megawatts) ..	264.5	139.4	116.2	66.2	37.4	37.4	17.1	12.2	3.0	3.0
Salalah (megawatts)	41.0	24.0	22.0	17.5	15.3	6.6	2.3	1.8	0.9	0.1
Petroleum Development (Oman)										
Mina al-Fahal (megawatts) ..	10.8	10.8	7.1	8.4	7.6	7.6	7.6	7.6	7.6	7.6
Fahud (megawatts)	34.0	25.2	25.2	24.0	25.8	22.8	22.8	22.8	22.8	22.8
Government			**Gross Production****							
Power House Riyam and Ghubrah	497.7	376.7	329.2	214.2	121.9	72.6	38.9	22.2	12.0	8.0
Salalah.......	86.4	84.4	79.5	51.7	32.5	18.5	8.0	3.4	1.0	—
Petroleum Development (Oman)										
Mina al-Fahal	29.4	30.6	29.2	28.9	28.1	27.5	26.7	25.9	24.6	20.3
Fahud	109.9	100.7	105.7	102.1	104.0	102.2	98.9	78.5	73.3	76.6

*In megawatts.
**Units generated—millions of kilowatt hours.
Sources: Directorate General of National Statistics, Oman, and the *Middle East Economic Digest.*

100 population. Service is available in the capital and Salalah. Substantial expansion is expected during the next few years. Although improving, telephone service remains unreliable. Waiting time for a telephone is 1 year, and the installation cost is about $300. A call to the United States costs $5.50 per minute. Direct dial is now possible with many other countries.

International telex facilities have recently been increased, and satellite communications are being improved. Waiting time for a telex is also 1 year, and installation costs about $300. The cost of a telex to the United States is $5.50 per minute. There is a monthly service charge of about $120.

International mail services Oman, but delays are sometimes encountered. Omani businessmen prefer the use of telex to the mails.

Oman is nine time zones ahead of the eastern United States.

Trade Regulations

Trade Policy

The trade policy of Oman is liberal. Oman participates in the Arab League's economic boycott of Israel, but normal trade regulations between the United States and Oman have generally not been affected. Certain goods cannot be imported for reasons of health, morality, or security. Import licenses are not required, and there are no limitations on obtaining exchange for payments abroad typically by letter of credit.

Oman has no exchange controls. The Omani Riyal (RO) is pegged to the U.S. dollar at an official rate of 1 RO equals US$2.92.

Customs Provisions

The Customs Department is a branch of the Royal Oman Police. The rate of customs duties applicable is generally 2 percent of the c.i.f. value of imports for most items, although liquor has a 75-percent duty. The Ministry of Commerce has discretionary authority to raise tariffs up to 25 percent to protect local industry. Thus far, only imports competing with domestically produced asbestos cement pipe, plastic pipe, ice cream, bananas, and emulsion paints are subject to protective tariffs. Moreover, as additional domestic industries emerge, extension of tariff protection to them is likely. In addition to the tariff, a 2-percent municipal tax is imposed on most items. Samples are generally duty free if they cannot be sold.

Contractors are sometimes allowed to import duty-free items used for government projects.

Duty is payable on items that the customs authorities consider are not part of a visitor's essentials for traveling.

The Government announced that, effective January 1, 1981, the duty on imported tobacco products would be 30 percent. Additional measures affecting the import of tobacco are discussed under Import Controls.

Import Controls

Magazines like *Playboy* are considered pornographic and are confiscated. It is possible to get a permit from the police for firearms and alcohol—two items usually prohibited—although the duty on the latter is 75 percent. Goods of Israeli origin are prohibited, and there are special regulations governing cigarettes and items intended for reexport.

No plants or plant products or their filling or packaging materials are allowed to enter the Sultanate without the approval of the agricultural quarantine authorities of the Ministry of Agriculture and Fisheries. These authorities must be given assurances that the plants in question are free of agricultural pests prior to shipment from the exporting country. If the percentage of damage of agricultural shipments exceeds a percentage permitted by law, the entire shipment may be returned or destroyed without compensation. Special permission must be obtained for the import of agricultural soil and organic manure. Cereals, seeds, and seedlings must be accompanied by an agricultural health certificate issued by the government in the country of export. The Minister of Agriculture and Fisheries has the discretion to prohibit the entry even of undiseased plants or plant products.

No animals may enter Oman without specific permission of the Ministry of Agriculture and Fisheries. To obtain such permission, a medical certificate from the country of export is necessary, stating that the animals have been examined and are free from disease, along with reports testifying that they have had no contact with diseased animals. Prior written permission must be obtained from the Directorate-General of the Ministry of Agriculture and Fisheries for the importation of sheep and goats.

The Omani Ministry of Commerce and Industry announced that, as of January 1, 1981, the import of cigarettes containing more than 20 mg of tar or 1 mg of nicotine would be banned. Cigarettes with lower levels of tar and nicotine must have the levels printed on each package. All imported tobacco products must bear the warning: "Smoking is a major cause of cancer, lung disease, and diseases of the heart and arteries."

Nontariff Controls

Oman subscribes to the Arab economic boycott against Israel, but the free-trade sympathies of Omani businessmen and government officials have made them generally more accommodating to U.S. business than their counterparts in many other Arab countries. In general, the Omanis are eager to establish business relations with new companies.

Oman follows the lead of the Central Boycott Office in Damascus. Boycott administration is in the purview of the Royal Oman Police.

It is the policy of the U.S. Government to oppose restrictive trade practices or boycotts fostered or imposed by foreign countries against other countries friendly to the United States. The Export Administration Act of 1979 (Public Law 96-72) and the U.S. Department of Commerce's implementing regulations (Export Administration Regulations, 15 C.F.R. Part 369) prohibit certain forms of compliance with foreign boycotts including furnishing information or entering into or implementing agreements. Violators of the U.S. antiboycott law are subject to severe penalties, including fines, imprisonment, and revocation of export license privileges. U.S. exporters are required by law to report to the U.S. Department of Commerce any request for action in support of such restrictive trade practices or boycotts in accordance with Section 369.6 of the Export Administration Regulations. Reporting forms (ITA-621P or ITA-6051P) may be obtained from the Office of Antiboycott Compliance, International Trade Administration, U.S. Department of Commerce, Washington, D.C. 20230.

U.S. exporters should also familiarize themselves with antiboycott provisions of the Tax Reform Act of 1976, administered by the U.S. Treasury Department. Violation of Treasury antiboycott regulations risks tax penalties rather than criminal prosecution. These tax penalties can extend to business operations in nonboycotting countries.

The U.S. Department of Commerce seeks to minimize the adverse impact on U.S. trade of foreign boycotts and other restrictive trade practices by furnishing information and assistance to U.S. firms directly affected. In addition to reporting such requests, firms confronted with boycott problems may wish to discuss them with the Commerce Action Group for the Near East.

Shipping Documents

Certificates of Origin.—To be issued by the manufacturer or exporting company, this certificate must state that the goods were wholly and exclusively produced in the United States, and that the certificate is true and correct. If the goods are not entirely of U.S. origin, the certificate must show the itemized percentages of foreign components, and country of origin of each itemized percentage. The U.S. Department of Commerce's position is that the following statement is acceptable as a positive statement of origin:

"The undersigned, _____ , does hereby declare on behalf of the above-named supplier/manufacturer, that certain parts or components of the goods described in the attached certificate of origin are the products of such country or countries, other than the country named therein as specifically indicated hereunder:

"Country of origin and percentages of value of parts or components relative to total shipment: _____ ."
(notarized)

The certificate must also give the complete name and address of the manufacturer, as well as other information commonly found on such documents or required by the importer under terms of a letter of credit.

Commercial Invoices.—These documents ordinarily require an accurate description of the goods, with weights, quantities and values, in addition to whatever information is required by the importer, or by a letter of credit, or is commonly provided for particular goods. The complete name and address of the manufacturer must be given. The same information about origins of the product and its components provided in the certificate of origin is also usually given. The shipment must contain a signed statement that the invoice is true and correct.

Special Documents.—See Customs Provisions for requirements for shipping plants or animals.

Packaging Lists.—These are not required but may help in the clearance of goods.

Insurance and Steamship Certificates.—These are unnecessary except as required by the importer or by a letter of credit.

Bills of Lading.—This should agree with the invoice and show gross weight, volume, measurement, marks and name/address of the consignee. Marks and numbers should agree with those on the invoice and containers. Generally, freight charges should be prepaid.

U.S. Shipper's Export Declaration.—This is necessary if the value of the shipment exceeds $250 or where a validated export license is required.

Certification and Legalization.—The certificate of origin and the commercial invoice have to be certified by a recognized chamber of commerce and then legalized by an Omani consular official. Oman recognizes the U.S.-Arab Chamber of Commerce, One World Trade Center, Suite 4657, New York, N.Y. 10048, 212-432-0655; the Mid American-Arab Chamber of Commerce, Inc., 135 La Salle Street, Suite 2050, Chicago, Ill. 60603, 312-782-4654; the American-Arab Chamber of Commerce, 319 World Trade Building, Houston, Tex. 77002, 713-222-6152; and the U.S.-Arab Chamber of Commerce (Pacific), 433 California Street, Suite 920, San Francisco, Calif. 94104, 415-397-5663. Each of these chambers will require an additional copy of any document it certifies, just as the Omani Embassy or an Omani consulate will require a file copy of any document it legalizes. Thus, the minimum number of copies of any document that is both certified and legalized is three. It may in certain circumstances be desirable to have more than three copies: This is a matter on which the Omani importer can best advise shippers. The legalization fee for each copy of a certificate of origin or commercial invoice is currently $7.50.

If legalization is to be done by the Omani Embassy in Washington, D.C., the shipper should first send the document to one of the approved chambers, along with checks to cover the necessary fees and a stamped envelope addressed to the Omani Embassy. The chamber will then forward the certified documents to the Embassy. If legalization is to be done by Oman's consulate in New York, the documents (already certified) should be mailed directly to the consulate, along with a check and a self-addressed, stamped envelope for their return. These documents should not be presented in person.

If Omani officials require U.S. Department of State authentication, the documents should be presented to the Authentications Office, Room 2813, U.S. Department of State, Washington, D.C. 20520, telephone 202-632-0406.

Marking Requirements.—There are no regulations governing the marking of packages or goods other than food products (see *Packaging* section of Selling in Oman). For your own protection, packages should bear the consignee's mark, including the port mark, and be numbered unless identifiable by other means. If the shipment includes hazardous or restricted material, shippers should ask the advice of the Omani importer regarding labeling requirements. U.S. exporters must meet U.S. requirements, as well as International Air Transport Association requirements if the goods are shipped by air.

Senate Concurrent Resolution 4, adopted July 30, 1953, invites U.S. exporters to inscribe, insofar as practicable, on their external shipping containers in indelible print of a suitable size "United States of America."

Investment in Oman

Attitude Toward Foreign Investment

The Government generally encourages direct foreign investment, although at least 35-percent Omani participation is required. The Government prefers joint ventures to full government ownership of natural resources and other industries. Particular encouragement is given to foreign firms that produce commodities that reduce imports or will develop such priority sectors as petroleum, agriculture, fishing, and minerals.

Total direct foreign investment in Oman was estimated at about $200 million in the mid-1970s, but there are no official statistics. While about half of that represented the assets of the private shareholders of Petroleum Development Oman, an increasing amount of public and private funds from Kuwait and the UAE is being invested there. Total U.S. investment in Oman was established at $5 million.

The Government set up the Foreign Capital Investment Committee in 1972 to control foreign private investment. Foreign investors must get specific approval to establish a business or invest in an Omani business. Approved economic development projects are eligible for tax credits.

Forms of Companies

The Companies Law permits the five forms of companies discussed below. Each may own property except the joint venture.

Joint Ventures.—These are usually formed for specific purposes or jobs. They are not required to be in the Commercial Register because, under law, they have no legal personality of their own. They are the preferred approach to doing business in Oman, and the Government offers incentives to promote them. Although the term ordinarily refers to a business partnership between a government, individual, or company and a foreign partner, it is legally defined as a commercial company formed between two persons, natural or legal. Third parties are not affected unless they have entered into a contractual relationship with one or both participants.

Limited-Liability Companies (Sharikat Dhat Masuliyya Mahduda).—These are the most commonly used type of company. It must have a fixed capital of not less than RO 10,000 divided into shares held by not less than 2 or more than 30 natural or legal persons. The company name must include the words "with limited liability" or its abbreviation. Each shareholder is responsible for the nominal value of his own shares.

Joint-Stock Companies (Sharika Mussahama).—These are commercial companies with a fixed capital of RO 25,000 divided into shares held by at least three natural or legal persons. The company's name must include the words "Omani joint stock company" or its abbreviation, and may also include reference to limited liability. The company must have at least a three-member board of directors.

General Partnerships (Sharikat Tadhamun).—These may be formed by two or more persons bound jointly and severally for all liabilities. These liabilities in turn are covered by the entire property of each member. The name of the company consists of the names of one or more of the partners and the words "and company." Negotiable certificates of ownership may not be issued.

Limited Partnerships (Sharika Tawsiyya Bassita).—These consist of active partners who manage the company and are liable for its obligations. Inactive partners provide capital investment and are each liable only for the sum of individual investment.

There are also laws detailing requirements regarding directors, management, meetings, ownership and transfer of shares, legal reserves, distribution of dividends, and liquidation procedures for each of the above.

In addition, audits are required for all joint-stock companies and for limited-liability companies that meet any of the following conditions:

(1) The company has more than 10 shareholders.

(2) Its capital is greater than RO 50,000.

(3) Its articles of association require the appointment of an auditor, or it is requested by holders of shares representing not less than 20 percent of the company's capital.

Audits may also be legally required of other forms of companies.

Establishing a Business

The Foreign Business and Investment Law (FBIL) is the legislation covering the requirements for establishing a business. Under this law, foreign firms wishing to operate in Oman must be represented by an Omani company. Such branch operations as banks may be exceptions to this law, but these must be registered none the less.

To register, a company must file the FBIL application in Arabic, the company's articles of association, and the application for registration in the Commercial Registry. For the last, the following information is required:

(1) Name and legal structure of the company.

(2) The company's objectives.

(3) Principal place of business and address of all branches and agencies.

(4) Name, nationality, date and place of birth of each shareholder except in the case of joint-stock companies, where the information is required only about its directors.

(5) Name, nationality, date and place of birth of the company's authorized signer and a description of the extent of his/her power to do so.

(6) The company's capital including the value of capital contributed in kind or in services.

(7) The company's dates of formation and termination (if any).

(8) Date and authorization number issued by the Government for non-Omani shareholders.

Any changes in the original registration document must be reported to the Commercial Registry. The Registry is located in Muscat with a regional office in Salalah. Additionally, all firms must be members of the Chamber of Commerce and Industry.

Once the application for the formation of a company is submitted to the Ministry of Commerce, it is reviewed by the Committee on the Investment of Foreign Capital, which makes a recommendation to the Ministry. Obtaining a favorable recommendation rests on several factors, including the utility of the project to the country and whether or not the company meets minimum capitalization requirements (RO 150,000 for foreign firms) and minimum requirements for equity participation by Omani nationals (35 percent). At its discretion, the Ministry of Commerce may additionally require a 1-year, on-demand bank guaranty from a local bank for the equivalent amount of equity capital.

Engineers and Architects

All architects and consulting engineers operating in Oman are required to register with the Tenders Board and the Minister of Commerce and Industry.

Flag of Convenience

An Omani maritime law of April 1975 provides an Omani registry for both foreign-owned and local ships. The Oman Maritime Administration has an office at One State Street Plaza, New York, N.Y. 10004 (Telephone: 212-269-9110).

Insurance Programs

In 1976, the Governments of Oman and the United States signed an agreement authorizing U.S. Overseas Private Investment Corporation and Export-Import Bank of the United States guarantees and financing for U.S. ventures in Oman.

The U.S. Overseas Private Investment Corporation (OPIC), 1129 20th Street, N.W., Washington, D.C. 20527, phone 202-632-9646, provides political risk insurance for bid and performance bonds and advance guarantees that may be required.

The Export-Import Bank of the United States, (Eximbank), 811 Vermont Avenue N.W., Washington, D.C. 20571, phone 202-566-8096, and the Foreign Credit Insurance Association, One World Trade Center, Ninth Floor, New York, N.Y. 10048, phone 212-432-6300, offers a wide range of credit insurance and guarantees for exports. Eximbank also offers a U.S. Contractors Guarantee Program, which insures U.S. contractors against the risks of inconvertibility, confiscation, war, and failure by the client to honor an arbitration award or comply with an agreed dispute-settling mechanism.

Labor Situation

Oman, like other Gulf countries, has a population too small to carry out its economic development plans unaided. European (mainly British) managers and South Asian laborers and clerical staff comprise almost half the non-agricultural work force. The Omani Labor Department estimates that over 85,000 expatriates are employed in Oman, a large portion of whom are from India and Pakistan. Expatriates are especially prominent in the construction, petroleum, finance, and transportation industries, although government policy requires that whenever possible Omanis be hired before expatriates.

To overcome the shortage of talented local labor, the Government has made a major effort to upgrade the education of younger Omanis and to insure their placement in positions of responsibility. It pays for a number of students to receive higher education in the United States and Europe, and by 1980, it had opened five, and planned several additional, vocational training institutes in Oman. Moreover, firms employing more than 50 persons are required to provide formal training programs for Omanis or to pay a training levy. While the rapid expansion of the educational system may be expected in the long run to increase the availability of skilled Omani workers, it had by 1980 delayed their entry into the work force.

The law governing labor relations is the Omani Labor Law of 1973. It gives equal protection to Omani and foreign workers, as well as to males and females. It applies to any business, public sector organization, or institution that hires employees, with the exception of the army, police, national and municipal employees (covered by a separate Civil Service Law), domestic workers, casual workers, students employed temporarily, and firms with fewer than five employees.

Employers must have a written contract with their workers. The contract must specify duties, wages, and such other provisions of employment as duration of the contract and the notice period required for termination. Where the contract is less advantageous on specific items to the employee than the Labor Law, the latter will apply. One copy of the contract must be given to the worker; another retained by the employer. When the worker is Omani, the contract must be in Arabic.

Workers may not enter into a contract for more than 2 years, although contracts may be indefinitely renewed while a worker continues to work for the same employer. The contract expires if the worker is absent for illness for 10 weeks in 1 year or when the worker reaches age 60.

Any initial probationary period must be defined in the contract, and no worker may be hired on a probationary status more than once by the same employer. A successfully completed probationary period counts toward the period of normal employment.

Employers are required to post conspicuously work instructions and disciplinary measures to be taken in the event of infringements. A worker cannot be accused of an offense more than 15 days after its discovery or punished after other specified time limits. An employee may not be fined more than 5 days' wages nor suspended for more than 5 days in a single month, regardless of the number of offenses he/she commits. An exception is that workers accused of a crime at work may be suspended for up to 2 months while an investigation is conducted.

The Labor Law specifies causes for which a worker may be dismissed without notice, recompense, or severance pay. The worker in turn may appeal his/her dismissal to the Labor Office, which has the authority to disallow the dismissal and reinstate the worker with all privileges due him/her under the Labor Law or his/her contract.

Firms are generous in paying fringe benefits to local employees. Most firms pay a housing and utilities allowance of up to 50 percent of basic salary. The labor regulations provide for a maximum workweek of 48 hours (36 during Ramadan), paid vacation of 14 days per year, and severance pay of 14 days for each year of the first 3 years of service and 30 days for each additional year. After completing 3 months of consecutive service, the employee is entitled to 10 weeks compensated sick leave over 1 calendar year upon presentation of a valid medical certificate from an employer-approved doctor. Women may have up to 6 weeks unpaid maternity leave, although after a year of service this may be compensated as sick leave. The Ministry of Health settles disputes related to sick leave. Additionally, workers are entitled to the following special paid leaves:

(1) 3 days for marriage (once during period of service).

(2) 3 days for the death of an immediate relative and 1 or 2 days for the death of a more distant relative. For these leaves the worker must present a death certificate.

(3) 15 days for pilgramage to Mecca (once during the period of service).

(4) 130 days to a working wife on the death of her husband.

In addition, employers are required to bear the cost of hospital care, outpatient treatment, and medication for employees, regardless of whether the illness or injury is work related. Transportation, meals, drinking water, and other accommodations must be supplied for workers at a site some distance from their homes, and medical and first aid personnel must be at any site where 100 or more employees work.

Children under 13 cannot be employed, and juveniles between ages 13 and 16 cannot be employed between 6 p.m. and 6 a.m., at strenuous or hazardous work, or on feast days or holidays. Women also cannot be employed at night, at hard labor, or at work damaging to their health and morals. The agricultural sector is exempt from these restrictions, but it may be governed by other regulations.

The Ministry of Labor and Social Affairs is responsible for labor conditions and for ensuring adequate pay, housing, and health facilities. The Government tries to set some guidelines for private sector wages and to keep wages from rising much beyond the general rate of inflation. It controls the importation of foreign workers by requiring labor permits. Ordinarily, it will reject a request to import an employee if a qualified citizen is available. The Ministry maintains a register of job seekers that is matched against job requirements. Expatriate workers may not change jobs unless they have served in their current job at least 1 year.

There is no organized labor in Oman. Strikes, lockouts, and slowdowns are forbidden, and labor unions are nonexistent. The Government requires companies that employ 50 or more workers to set up worker committees as a mechanism for communicating information about wages and working conditions. While the Ministry of Social Affairs and Labor adjudicates disputes between all workers and employers, its main concern is to assist Omani employees. There has been a tendency to give Omani workers the benefit of the doubt in labor disputes with expatriate employers.

Labor offices have been set up throughout the country to enforce the provisions of the Labor Law.

Taxation

Income Tax

There is no personal income tax in Oman, nor is there an estate or gift tax, a capital gains tax, a tax on interest or dividends, or a sales or transaction tax. The only tax is on profits from trade or business. This is imposed on every "body corporate" that carries on trade or business in the Sultanate during any portion of the tax year through a permanent establishment in Oman, regardless of where the firm is incorporated. This includes corporations that act as agents for others or that conduct business either directly or through an agent, provided such an agent is a corporation. When a corporation conducts its trade or business in Oman through the agency of a second corporation, the taxable income of the second corporation is restricted to payments received from the first corporation through its agency activities.

There is no tax on profits below RO 20,000. According to Royal Decree 65 of 1977, the tax rate is a flat 15 percent for companies with 51 percent or greater Omani ownership. If Omani participation is between the minimum 35 percent and 51 percent, the tax rate is set at 20 percent.

Types of business that produce taxable income include the sale and purchase of goods; the operation of any manufacturing, industrial, or commercial enterprise in the Sultanate; the leasing of any property located in Oman; and the rendering of services in Oman.

The tax year is from January 1 through

December 31, unless the Director of Income Tax has given the taxpayer authorization to follow a different annual accounting period. Both the accrual method and the cash receipts and disbursements method of commercial accounting are considered as fairly reflecting income. Taxable income may be computed in a foreign currency only by special agreement with the Sultan.

The Omani tax law allows the following deductions:

(1) The costs of goods sold or services rendered in connection with doing business in Oman.

(2) Expenses that accrue or are paid in the tax year in connection with such business.

(3) A "reasonable amount" for depreciation, obsolescence, exhaustion, or amortization of physical and intangible assets. The latter includes any expenditure, wherever incurred, before or after the commencement of carrying on trade or business (other than on physical assets). An agreement with the Sultan may establish what constitutes the "reasonable amount."

(4) Losses sustained in carrying out trade or business that are not compensated by insurance or other means. The amount of loss is the excess of the depreciated value over any proceeds realized. If proceeds are greater than the depreciated value, this difference is taxable income.

(5) The amount of any net operating loss in any earlier tax year that has not previously been allowed as a deduction.

(6) Any payments made to the Sultan, other than oil royalties. These may include payments to make up the Sultan's share of profits.

Other Taxes

There is a 5-percent municipal tax in Muscat. Moreover, a 5-percent payroll tax is required for firms with more than 50 employees. Because this tax is used to finance vocational training, it is waived for firms that have their own training program.

A small service charge is sometimes imposed by hotels and restaurants.

Tax Holiday

To stimulate foreign capital investment, the Government allows a tax holiday of up to 5 years for firms investing in such priority sectors of the economy as industry, agriculture, fishing, as well as to companies that have a paid-up capital of more than RO 100,000 and are involved in developmental projects. The same tax advantage

was extended to wholly owned Omani companies that began operations before June 11, 1980. Under current law, this tax holiday may be taken advantage of through July 1, 1985. Consulting firms are subject to a local income tax if the firm does private business in Oman through a branch or a subsidiary. Consulting firms working directly for the Government of Oman are exempt from paying the local income tax.

Tax Administration

Every taxpayer with taxable income greater than RO 20,000 is required to file with the Director of Income Tax a provisional tax declaration for the tax year. This is due on or before the last day of the third month following the end of that tax year. The tax is payable in four equal installments, due on the last day of the 3rd, 6th, 9th, and 12th month following the end of the tax year.

In addition, by the last day of the ninth month, the taxpayer must file a final tax declaration. The final payment is adjusted on the basis of this declaration.

A taxpayer who fails to file a declaration or to pay the tax due may be fined 1 percent of the tax every 30 days while the failure continues. The penalty is not assessed when the Director of Income Tax determines that the failure is for reasonable cause. Fines, prison sentences or both may be assessed if books and records are knowingly falsified.

Disputes over taxation are referred to the Sultanate's courts unless submitted to arbitration by agreement between the taxpayer and the Director of Income Tax.

Guidance for Business Travelers

Entrance Requirements

All persons entering Oman must be sponsored by a person or institution resident in the country. The sponsor applies for the entry on the applicant's behalf, and a reason for the trip must be given. Because the Government does not encourage tourism, using it as a reason would very likely cause rejection of the application. There have been instances when visitors arriving without advance permission have been denied entry and departed on the next plane.

There are three ways that the sponsor in Oman may obtain permission on behalf of an applicant:

(1) The sponsor may get a "no objection certificate" (NOC). This is the usual procedure. Most NOCs are obtained from the Immigration Department of the Royal Oman

Police, but if the applicant has a diplomatic or official passport, the sponsor goes to the Foreign Ministry. To get an NOC, the sponsor needs to know at least the applicant's name, date and place of birth, passport type and number, and passport date and place of issue. Once obtained, the NOC document may be mailed to the applicant for carrying and presenting on arrival, or it may be held by the sponsor to pass to the applicant at Seeb International Airport. Sponsors who hold airport passes can simply meet the traveler as he/she gets off the plane; others must use an office at the airport that, for a fee, takes NOCs and transmits them to arriving passengers. Sometimes the Immigration Department will stamp on the NOC that it must be seen by an Omani Embassy before the traveler boards the plane for Oman, a requirement that precludes holding the NOC in Oman. This requirement is only sporadically enforced and seems to be used more with Arab and subcontinent nationals than with Americans and Europeans. The validity period of an NOC is nowhere stated, but in practice, it seems to be about 3 months from its date of issue. An NOC issued by the Foreign Ministry, however, states a validity period that usually depends on the travel plans mentioned in the application, which must therefore be known by the sponsor in addition to the applicant's birth and passport data.

Businesspersons without specific local commercial sponsorship may apply for an NOC by letter to the Oman Chamber of Commerce, P.O. Box 4400, Muscat. If the Chamber of Commerce is satisfied of the applicant's serious intent, it will sponsor an NOC. When seeking sponsorship, potential travelers should keep in mind that the Omani Government regards sponsorship as a connection with the applicant and an endorsement of the applicant's bona fides.

(2) To obtain a visa, as opposed to an NOC, an applicant must present the following documentation:

(a) An invitation from his/her Omani sponsor. A letter will suffice.

(b) A letter from his/her firm, identifying his relationship with it and explaining the purpose of travel.

(c) A letter from any local U.S. chamber of commerce with which his/her firm is registered. This letter should certify the bona fide membership of the firm represented and the good reputation of the visa applicant.

(d) Two application forms and two passport-size photographs.

The visa costs $9, is valid for 3 months, and permits a stay of up to 1 week. The Embassy generally requires 3 days to issue a visa, although it may require more time if it has to consult with authorities in Oman.

(3) A rare procedure is for the sponsor to persuade an Omani Government agency, through the Foreign Ministry, to instruct an Omani Embassy abroad to issue a visa. The applicant can then present himself/herself at the Embassy and get the visa stamped in his/her passport.

There are some variations and restrictions on the above procedures. These are as follows:

(1) There is a restriction barring from entry single adult females who are not diplomatic or official passport holders. The dimensions of this policy are as yet unclear. Apparently, entry will be permitted if a valid, specific reason other than visiting relatives or friends is given.

(2) If entry is by road rather than through Seeb International Airport, the applicant must have not only an NOC or visa (a separate one for every non-Omani traveler in the vehicle) but a road permit as well. This, like an NOC, is obtained by the sponsor in Oman. One road permit may cover all non-Omani passengers traveling together, but each must be named. As a rule, the permit must specify which entry and exit points are to be used and must list the license plate number, the make, and the color of the vehicle. Frequently it is possible for the sponsor to get a road permit valid for any entry and exit point. It is also possible, although less common, to waive the vehicle designations. The period of validity of a road permit is specified on the document and may vary depending on the applicant's stated travel plans.

(3) Generally only single-entry NOC's, visas, and road permits are granted. Exceptions are possible in the case of visas and, less often, road permits, but a strong case for multiple entry must be made. A single-entry NOC is surrendered on arrival when the traveler's passport is stamped. A single-entry road permit applies to one entry and one exit and should not be relinquished to the border official on entry.

(4) Transit passengers at Seeb International Airport do not need visas or NOCs, but such travelers should be aware that, in principle, a minimum transit time of 2 hours and a maximum of 6 hours are allowed. Exception to this rule may be possible, but only if a good reason is given.

The traveler must always have a reserved-seat ticket and all documentation for his/her onward travel. With rare exceptions, he/she must wait in the transit lounge. The airport immigration authorities will usually hold his/her passport during the transit period.

(5) Travel to Dhofar is a special case. People going there must travel through Muscat because of airline schedules: Flights directly to Salalah may occur in the future, but at present all traffic to Salalah must go through Muscat. It is possible to ticket travel from outside Oman to Salalah, merely transiting Muscat, but this may be unwise unless the traveler has Omani Government sponsorship and his/her NOC or visa specifies that it will be honored at Salalah Airport. The safer course is to terminate the flight at Muscat and count on spending 2 or 3 days there arranging onward permission and a plane reservation to Salalah.

Oman's health and customs rules are about normal for the region. Only if the Government perceives a special problem is one likely to be given exceptional scrutiny.

A current cholera shot is required if one has entered or transited an infected area within 5 days prior to entering Oman. Six months is the validity period recognized for a cholera vaccination. Transit passengers not leaving Seeb Airport and children under 1 year of age are exempted.

In practice, inoculation records are rarely checked either at Seeb Airport or at border posts, though travelers should be prepared. During past cholera scares, the airport health authorities not only checked all shot records, but required every incoming passenger to swallow four Tetracycline pills whether or not their cholera vaccination was current.

Business Hours and Holidays

Hours of business are as follows:

Government: 7:30 a.m. to 2 p.m., Saturday to Wednesday and 7:30 a.m. to 1 p.m. Thursday.

Banks: 8 a.m. to 12 p.m., Saturday to Wednesday and 8 a.m. to 11:30 Thursday.

Merchants: 8 a.m. to 1 p.m. and 4 p.m. to 7 p.m. Saturday to Thursday.

American Embassy: 7:30 a.m. to 3:30 p.m. Saturday to Wednesday (commercial office: 7 a.m. to 3 p.m. Saturday to Wednesday).

The weekly day off is Friday. Saturday and Sunday are normal working days.

Visits should be scheduled with the following list of Omani holidays in mind:

Hejra New Year (Muslim New Year)*
Maulid an Nabi (Birth of the Prophet)*
Lailat al Miraj (Ascension of the Prophet)*
Eid al Fitr (feast of the breaking of the fast, end of Ramadan)*
National Days (November 18-19)
Eid al Adha (Feast of the Sacrifice)*

The U.S. Department of Commerce District Office nearest you keeps a listing of the approximate dates of these holidays.

In addition to the dozen or so public holidays, officials and businesspersons are sometimes difficult to find during the Muslim fasting month of Ramadan (also determined by the lunar calendar) and during the hot summer months. Appointments for these times would best be arranged well in advance.

Language

The official language of Oman is Arabic, although it is also possible to find speakers of English, Farsi, Urdu, and Indian dialects. English is the business language. Though not all business or government officials speak English, they will usually have someone available to interpret. Regardless of the use of English in commerce, the law may require business documents, such as those to register a company, to be filed in Arabic.

Most people likely to be encountered by the visitor to the capital area (with the exception of taxi drivers) will probably have at least a small working English vocabulary. The English language papers *Times of Oman* and *Akhbar Oman* are among a growing number of newspapers and magazines published in the country. International news magazines are available about 1 week later than the same issue would appear in the United States. The most important Arabic publications are the newspaper *Oman* and the magazine *Al Akidah*.

Radio and television broadcasts are operated by the Government. Although most of the broadcasting is in Arabic, there are a few hours of English-language broadcast daily. The British Broadcasting Corporation also broadcast in English to Muscat.

Living Conditions and Costs

Oman's climate is one of the hottest in the world, with temperatures ranging from 95 degrees to 120 degrees F. from April to September, and humidity reaching 80 percent.

*Dates are determined by the Muslim lunar calendar.

Light clothing, preferably cotton, is mandatory in the summer. From late October to March, the climate is milder, with temperatures ranging from 60 degrees to 90 degrees F. Medium-weight clothing is suitable for these months. Business dress is tie and short sleeved shirt in the summer and a regular shirt in the cooler months. Evening entertainment frequently requires a business suit. Local clothing is expensive and limited in alternatives. There is occasional rainfall during the winter. Many U.S. businesspeople regard Oman with its scenic beaches and relaxed social atmosphere, as more pleasant than other States on the Arabian peninsula.

Accommodations are not as limited as they once were, but visitors should still make arrangements in advance. Many business visitors to Muscat stay at the Al Falaj Hotel and the Ruwi Hotel because they are close to the commercial center. The Gulf and Inter-Continental Hotels offer a deluxe standard of accommodation and more extensive restaurant and recreational facilities. In 1981, single-room hotel rates ranged between $69 to $91 per night. (See box on next page.) Most hotels and restaurants accept major credit cards. Travelers checks are not commonly accepted in restaurants, but they can be used in hotels or for airline payment.

After a period of decline, rents are again rising. Two-bedroom flats rent for $580 to $870 per month. Detached homes ("vilas") rent for $870 to $2,900 monthly. Rent for a three-bedroom house averages $2,000 per month. Ordinarily payment for 2 years is required in advance. Tenants are responsible for maintenance, furnishings, and appliances.

Diseases causing the greatest problems in Oman are malaria, trachoma, tuberculosis, and gastrointestinal virus infection. Visitors generally drink bottled or boiled water. The government has undertaken a program to expand and upgrade health facilities, the objective being to insure that no one is more than 2-hours travel time from a health center. In 1980, coverage was reasonably good in terms of facilities, but there remained a need to upgrade the quality and kind of health care available through these units. Serious illness may require evacuation to Europe. There has been a substantial expansion in the number of doctors, nurses, and other trained specialists. About 90 percent of the doctors and nurses are non-Omani. More than 600 hospital beds are available in the capital area, more than 1,000 throughout the rest of the country.

Teachers are being recruited from the United Kingdom. This is part of an effort to upgrade both the facilities and quality of instruction at the English-speaking elementary school.

The electric supply is 220/240 volts, 50 cycle. It is not stable enough for electric clocks. Receptacles accept a round pin attachment plug and square pin attachment plug. Both plugs and adapters are readily available in the capital area. Electricity costs about 6 cents per kWh.

Most social life revolves around sports and home entertainment. Some of the larger hotels offer swimming pools and other recreational facilities, and several large companies have athletic facilities for their employees. Oman television offers some English programming, and a few cinemas regularly show English language films.

Western foods and beverages, including alcohol, are available but expensive. Restaurants used by businesspeople charge about $6 for breakfast, $9 for lunch, and $12 for dinner. These prices include a service charge.

Wages and Salaries

Annual salaries for high level executives range from $25,000 to $40,000. Middle management salaries are between $15,000 and $21,000. Technicians receive about $12,000, and secretaries fluent in English get about $10,000. Skilled workers are paid between $300 and $450 per month; unskilled workers between $150 and $250 per month. Only unskilled workers are available locally. Holiday or overtime work receives 125 percent of base pay or compensatory time off.

Office Rentals

The monthly cost of renting an office is about $3 per square foot. There does not seem to be a problem with the availability of rental space. Landlords ordinarily do not provide furnishings.

Getting Around

Japanese, U.S., and European automobiles are available, but servicing and repairs are very expensive. Comprehensive insurance is recommended. Omani drivers' licenses are required, and can be obtained for RO 5 with the presentation of a valid foreign license. Women may drive.

Taxis, generally the most convenient means of transportation for foreigners, are available for travel between the airport, the hotels, and the capital-area communities of Muscat, Mutrah, and Ruwi. There are no taxi meters, and the following fare schedule was in force in May 1980 (RO 1 = $2.92):

Hotels

Name	Rooms and Rates	
Al-Falaj Hotel P.O. Box 5031, Muscat Telephone: 702311 A. C. Papayannis, Managing Director Telex: 3229 MB Hotel Located in Ruwi	150 Rooms Single: Double: Suites:	 RO 18-22 RO 28-30 RO 60-70
Gulf Hotel P.O. Box 4455, Ruwi Telephone: 600100 Michael E. T. McFayden, General Manager Telex: 3416 GULFOTEL MB Located in Qurum	115 Rooms Single: Double: Junior Suite: Senior Suite: Presidential Suite:	 RO 25 RO 31 RO 55 RO 75 RO 95
Mina Hotel P.O. Box 3504, Ruwi Telephone: 734226 Sukesh Hoogon, Manager Telex: 3350 CORNICHE MB Located in Mutrah	31 Rooms Single: Double:	 RO 14 RO 18.200
Muscat Inter-Continental Hotel P.O. Box 1398, Mutrah Telephone: 600500 Georgio Bagnasco, General Manager Telex: 3491 IHCMCT MB Located in Qurum	308 Rooms Single: Double: Standard Suite: Royal Suite: Service charge included	 RO 31 RO 37 RO 70 RO 175
Mutrah Hotel P.O. Box 4525, Ruwi Telephone: 734401 T. A. John, Manager Telex: 3226 MUTROTEL MB Located in Mutrah	37 Rooms Single: Double: Continental breakfast included	 RO 12-15 RO 14-20
Ruwi Hotel P.O.Box 5195, Ruwi Telephone: 704244 James Lennox, Manager Telex: 3456 RUWIOTEL MB Located in Ruwi	88 Rooms Single: Double: Suite:	 RO 23 RO 32 RO 50
Salalah Holiday Inn P.O. Box 8870, Salalah Telephone: 461777 Hermann Frommrich, Manager Telex: 7638 HOLISAL MB Located in Salalah	 Single: Double: Suite:	 RO 23 RO 27.50 RO 55

A 10-percent service charge and 5-percent municipal tax are extra. 1 RO=US$2.92.

Airport to Gulf/Inter-Continental
Hotels .... RO 5.000
Gulf/Inter-Continental Hotels to
Muscat 4.000
Falaj/Ruwi Hotels (Ruwi) to Matrah ...750
Falaj/Ruwi Hotels to Muscat 1.350
Muscat to Matrah 600

Taxi service within Muscat, Matrah, or Ruwi can be difficult to find. Vehicles with drivers can be rented from hotels or through local businessmen for rates of $30 to $50 per day. Few drivers speak English. Not all streets are named.

Cars and trucks are generally available for rent. Daily rental for a medium-sized car is about $45; daily rental for a truck, approximately $90.

Business Customs

As in the rest of the Middle East, business

transactions are characterized by the importance attached to personal relationships and local presence. Personal visits to Oman are virtually a prerequisite for market penetration by foreign companies even after local representation is established. It is generally necessary to make more than one visit to establish all necessary contacts. Although some firms can conclude sales through the Department of Commerce's Trade Opportunities Program without ever visiting Oman, these are the exceptions. Above all it should be remembered that unwritten customs and ways of doing business are more significant than commercial regulations, and doing business "by the book" may not be effective.

A typical visit to the office of an Omani businessman will involve some of the following elements. Appointments will not be made until after the foreign businessperson arrives in Oman. After arriving at an office, he/she may wait for about 15 minutes and may even discover that others have appointments at the same time or have arrived without one. A 9 a.m. appointment tends to mean a morning appointment.

When the visitor finally gets into the office, which may be a government office since many Omani businessmen are also civil servants, the phone will invariably interrupt the conversation every few minutes. A closed door insures no privacy as other visitors or employees may enter without knocking and exchange several minutes of conversation with the host. Coffee or tea will probably be offered, unless the Muslim fasting month of Ramadan is in progress. It is important to realize that the host is not necessarily indicating a lack of interest; the style of business is simply unstructured.

Visiting businesspersons should also remember that politeness is valued. One almost never receives a blunt statement of no interest in his/her product or service, even if such is the case. This pattern may differ at the many companies having a European top-level manager or perhaps an Indian middle-level staff.

Hands are shaken in greeting, and it is customary to look someone straight in the eye when talking to him. Allowing the soles of one's shoes to be seen by others creates a bad impression, and may be regarded as offensive; if you cross your legs while sitting, keep your feet pointed toward the floor.

Devout Omani Muslims pray five times daily. The first prayer during business hours is at about 12:45 p.m. You should be sensitive to businessmen who may wish to break off further discussion at this point, leaving visitors while they retire to a prayer room.

Air Carriers

Alia (Royal Jordanian Airlines), Pakistan International Airlines, and Trans Mediterranean Airlines (an all-cargo line)—all with offices in New York—have regular service from New York to Muscat. They stop first in Amman, Karachi, and Beirut, respectively.

British Airways, UTA, Air India, and Saudia also have New York offices and provide service to Muscat, as do Gulf Air and Kuwait Airways. From Muscat, British Airways and Gulf Air offer nonstop service to London, and UTA has direct flights to Paris. Travelers should obtain the most current information from airline offices or travel agents.

Shipping Lines

The following lines provide ocean cargo service to Muscat from Atlantic ports: Central Gulf Lines, Concordia Line, Gulf Ocean Lines, Hansa Lines, Nedlloyd Lines, P & O Strath Services, Sea-Land, and Seatrain.

The following provide service to Muscat from Gulf of Mexico ports: Concordia Line, Gulf Ocean Lines, P & O Strath Services, Sea-Land Service, Inc., and Seatrain Lines.

The following provide service to Muscat from northwest and Pacific ports: Sea-Land Service, Inc., Seatrain Lines, Inc., and Showa Line.

Publications

U.S. Government

(Available from the Superintendent of Documents, U.S. Government Printing Office, Washington, D.C. 20402)

Area Handbook for the Persian Gulf States, U.S. Government Printing Office, Washington, D.C., 1977.

Foreign Economic Trends and Their Implications for the United States—Oman (annual).

Background Notes—Oman.

Private

British Bank of the Middle East, *Business Profile Series: Sultanate of Oman*, Doha, Hong Kong, and London.

Useful Addresses

U.S. Government

Commerce Action Group for the Near East
U.S. Department of Commerce
Room 3200
Washington, D.C. 20230
Telephone: (202) 377-5767

U.S. Army Corps of Engineers
Middle East Division
P.O. Box 2250
Winchester, Va. 22601
Telephone, Public Affairs Office: (202) 554-7960,
ext. 2460

Oman office:
P.O. Box 6096
Ruwi
Sultanate of Oman
Telephone: 601382, 601386
Telex: 3034 CEOMAN MB

Regional Trade Development Office (for Near East)
c/o U.S. Embassy
91 Vasilissis Sophias Blvd.
Athens, Greece
Telephone: 712951, 718401
Telex: 21-5548

U.S. Oman Joint Commission for Economic and Tech-
nological Cooperation
P.O. Box 6001
Ruwi, Muscat
Sultanate of Oman
Telephone: 703000, 701357

Omani Representation in the United States

Embassy of the Sultanate of Oman
2342 Massachusetts Avenue, N.W.
Washington, D.C. 20008
Telephone: (202) 387-1980

Combined Consulate and Permanent Mission to the
United Nations
605 Third Avenue, Room 3304
New York, N.Y. 10016
Telephone: (212) 682-0447

U.S. Representation in Oman

U.S. Embassy
P.O. Box 966
Muscat, Oman
Telephone: 745231
No Telex
Hours: 7:30 a.m. to 3:30 p.m., Saturday through
Wednesday

U.S. Embassy Economic-Commercial Office
Ruwi, Across from the Abdul Redha Sultan Mosque
Telephone: 703287
Hours: 7 a.m. to 3 p.m., Saturday through Wednesday

U.S. Chambers of Commerce

American-Arab Association for Commerce and Industry,
Inc.
342 Madison Avenue
New York, N.Y. 10017
Phone: (212) 986-7229

U.S.-Arab Chamber of Commerce, Inc.
One World Trade Center, Suite 4657
New York, N.Y. 10048
Phone: (212) 432-0655

American-Arab Chamber of Commerce, Inc.
World Trade Building, Suite 319
Houston, Tex. 77002
Phone: (713) 222-6152

U.S.-Arab Chamber of Commerce (Pacific), Inc.
433 California Street, Suite 920
San Francisco, Calif. 94104
Phone: (415) 397-5663

Mid-American-Arab Chamber of Commerce, Inc.
135 South La Salle Street, Suite 2050
Chicago, Ill. 60603
Phone: (312) 782-4654

Omani Government Agencies

Ministry of Agriculture and Fisheries
P.O. Box 467, Muscat
Telephone: 702066
Telex: 3503 MB
Location: Ruwi
H. E. Abdul Hafidh Salim Rajab, Minister
H. E. Hassan Abdulla al-Morazza, Under Secretary
Mohammed Redha Hassan, Director General of
Agriculture
Abdulla Ali Bakhateri, Director General of Fisheries

Ministry of Awqaf and Islamic Affairs
P.O. Box 767, Muscat
Telephone: 702233
Location: Ruwi
H. E. Sheikh Waleed Bin Zahir al-Hinai, Minister
H. E. Sheikh Abdulla Bin Salim al-Zeidi, Under Secretary

Governate of the Capital
P.O. Box 875, Muscat
Telephone: 722516
Telex: 3201 GCM MB
Location: Muscat
H. H. Sayyid Thuwaini Bin Shihab, Governor
H. H. Sayyid Salim Bin Ali Al-Saeed, Deputy Governor

Oman Chamber of Commerce and Industry
P.O. Box 4400, Ruwi
Telephone: 702259
Telex: 3389 AL-GURFA MB
Location: Ruwi
Sheik Ahmed Mohamed Bin Omeir, President
Suhail Bahwan, Vice-President

Ministry of Commerce and Industry
P.O. Box 550, Muscat
Telephone: 745301
Telex: 3351 WIZARIH MB
Location: Muscat
H. E. Mohammed al-Zubair, Minister
H. E. Ali Daoud, Under Secretary
Suleiman Barakat al-Lamki, Director General of Industry
Mohammed Mirza, Director General of Commerce
Mohammed Abdul Rahman Faqir, Director General of
Economic Affairs

Ministry of Communications
P.O. Box 684, Muscat
Telephone: 702233
Telex: 3390 MWASALAT MB
Location: Ruwi
H. E. Sayyid Salim Bin Nasser Al-Busaidi, Minister
H. E. Salim Ahmed Khalfan, Under Secretary for Roads
and Ports

Directorate General of Civil Aviation
P.O. Box 204, Muscat
Telephone: 619310
Location: Seeb Airport
Eng. Mohammed Rajab al-Baomar, Director General

Directorate General of Roads
(Same address as Ministry of Communications)
Tariq Mohammed Al-Mandhari, Director General

Port Services Corporation
P.O. Box 133, Muscat
Telephone: 772191
Location: Mina Qaboos in Mutrah
Awad Salim al-Shanfari, General Manager

Ministry of Defense
P.O. Box 246, Muscat
Telephone: 701109
Telex: 3228 DEFENCE MB
Location: Ruwi at Bait al-Falaj
H.H. Sayyid Fahar Bin Taimur, Deputy Prime Minister
for National Security and Defense
H.E. Col. Salim Abdulla al-Ghazali, Under Secretary
W. J. (Pat) Hurley, Chief, Support Services (Military
Procurement)

Ministry of Defense Purchasing Agent
Charles Kendall & Partners, Ltd.
7 Albert Court
Prince Consort Road
London SW2, England

Development Council
P.O. Box 881, Muscat
Telephone: 745558
Location: Muscat
Dr. Sharif Lotfy, Secretary General

Ministry of Diwan Affairs
P.O. Box 246, Muscat
Telephone: 722841
Location: Muscat
H.E. Sayyid Hamad Bin Hamoud, Minister

Ministry of Education
P.O. Box 3, Muscat
Telephone: 702233
Location: Ruwi
H.E. Yahya Mahfudh al-Mandhari, Minister
H.E. Sheikh Amer Ali Omeir, Under Secretary

Ministry of Electricity and Water
P.O. Box 4491, Ruwi
Telephone: 702233
Telex: 3358 DIRELEC MB
Location: Ruwi
H.E. Sheikh Hamoud Bin Abdulla al-Harthy, Minister
H.E. Saif Salim al-Ma'mari, Under Secretary

Directorate General of Finance
P.O. Box 506, Muscat
Telephone: 745240
Telex: 3333 MALIYA MB
Location: Muscat
H.E. Mohammed Redha Musa, Under Secretary

Ministry of Foreign Affairs
P.O. Box 252, Muscat
Telephone: 701211
Telex: 3337 MFA MB
Location: Muscat
H.E. Qais Abd al-Munim al-Zawawi, Minister of State
H.E. Yusuf Abdulla al-Alawi, Under Secretary

Ministry of Health
P.O. Box 393, Muscat
Telephone: 600177
Telex: 3465 SIHA MB
Location: Ghubra
H.E. Dr. Mubarak al-Khaduri, Minister
H.E. Dr. Salim Hamdan, Under Secretary

Ministry of Information and Youth Affairs
P.O. Box 600, Muscat
Telephone: 600022
Telex: 3454 INFORM MB
Location: Qurum
H.E. Abdul Aziz Rowas, Minister
Salim Said al-Siyabi, Director General for Radio and
Television
Hamad Yahya al-Kindi, Director of Technical Affairs

Ministry of the Interior
P.O. Box 3127, Ruwi
Telephone: 702877
Location: Ruwi
H.E. Sheikh Badr Bin Saud Bin Harib, Minister
H.E. Abdulla Bin Ali al-Qutubi, Under Secretary

Ministry of Justice
P.O. Box 3354, Ruwi
Telephone: 702233
Location: Ruwi
H.E. Sayyid Hilal Bin Hamad al-Sammar, Minister
H.E. Sheikh Hilal Bin Sultan Bin Said al-Hosni, Under
Secretary

Ministry of Land Affairs and Municipalities
P.O. Box 173, Muscat
Telephone: 701655
Location: Ruwi
H.E. Ahmed Abdullah al-Ghazali, Minister
H.E. Sheikh Suleiman Bin Hamad al-Harthy, Under
Secretary (Munic.)
H.E. Ahmed Mohammed Nabhani, Under Secretary
(Land Affairs)

Musandam Development Committee
P.O. Box 5286, Ruwi
Telephone: 704599
Telex: 3103 MDCMT MB
Location: Ruwi
H.E. Sheikh Hamoud Bin Abdullah al-Harthy, Chairman

Ministry of National Heritage and Culture
P.O. Box 668, Muscat
Telephone: 602555
Location: Ghubra
H.H. Sayyid Faisal Bin Ali al-Said, Minister

Ministry of Petroleum and Minerals
P.O. Box 551, Muscat
Telephone: 702066
Telex: 3280 PLANDE MB
H.E. Said Ahmad al-Shanfari, Minister
H.E. Salim Mohammed Abdullah Shaaban, Under
Secretary
Ali Thabit al-Battashi, Director of Economic and Legal
Affairs
Khalifa Mubarak al-Hinai, Director of Technical Affairs
Mohammed Hussein Kassim, Director of Minerals

Royal Oman Police
P.O. Box 2, Muscat
Telephone: 600099
Telex: 3377 COMPOL MB
Location: Qurum
Col. Felix d'Silva, Inspector General of Police and Customs
Supt. Bakheet Said al-Shanfari, Director General of
Customs
Abdul Aziz Hussain, Principal Immigration Officer

Ministry of Posts, Telegraphs, and Telephones
P.O. Box 3338, Ruwi
Telephone: 702888
Telex: 3225 MB
Location: Ruwi
H.E. Karim Ahmed al-Harami, Minister

General Telecommunications Organization (GTO)
P.O. Box 3789, Ruwi
Telephone: 701844
Telex: 3400 OMANTEL MB
Nur Mohammed Nur, General Manager

Ministry of Public Works
P.O. Box 215, Muscat
Telephone: 704280
Telex: 3359 ASHGHAL MB
Location: Ruwi
H.E. Dr. Assim al-Jamali, Minister
H.E. Sheikh Musallim Bin Mohammed al-Amri, Under
Secretary

Ministry of Social Affairs and Labor
P.O. Box 560, Muscat
Telephone: 702233
Location: Ruwi
H.E. Halfan Bin Nasser al-Woheibi, Minister
H.E. Maqbool Hameed, Under Secretary

Oman Tender Board
P.O. Box 787, Muscat
Telephone: 722222
Telex: 3201 GCM MB
Location: Muscat
H.H. Sayyid Thuwaini Bin Shihab, Chairman
H.E. Dr. Assim al-Jamali, Deputy Chairman

Public Authority for Water Resources
P.O. Box 5255, Ruwi
Telephone: 704188
Telex: 3629 MB
Location: Ruwi
H.E. Engineer Abdul Hafidh Salim Rajab, Chairman
Dr. Robert Dale, Secretary

Government Financial Institutions

Central Bank of Oman
P.O. Box 4161, Ruwi
Telephone: 702222
Telex: 3288 MARKAZI MB
Location: Ruwi
Dr. Abdul Wahab Khayata, Deputy Chairman and
President

Oman Development Bank
P.O. Box 309, Muscat
Telephone: 745021
Telex: 3179 ODB MB
Location: Muscat
Bechir Ben Uthman, General Manager

Oman Housing Bank
P.O. Box 5555, Ruwi
Telephone: 704050
Telex: None
Location: Ruwi
Mahmoud Abu Teen, General Manager

Oil Companies

BP Petroleum Development Ltd.
P.O. Box 3703, Ruwi
Phone: 702500
Mike Roberts, Manager
Location: Ruwi

ELF Aquitaine Oman
P.O. Box 3352, Ruwi
Phone: 702264
Phillippe Thiebierge, Managing Director
Telex: MB 3314 ELF Oman
Location: Ruwi

Gulf Oman Petroleum Ltd.
P.O. Box 5271, Ruwi
Phone: 701079/702067
Kenneth Attrell, Manager
Telex: MB 3488 Gulf
Location: Ruwi

Petroleum Development Oman, LLC
P.O. Box 81, Muscat
Phone: 607505
Hans Brinkhorst, Managing Director
Telex: MB 3212 Petro
Location: Mina al-Fahal

Sales of Refined Products

BP Arabian Agencies, Ltd.
P.O. Box 9092, Mina al-Fahal
Phone: 600801/600645
David Glov , Area Manager
Telex: MB 3419 BEEPEE

Shell Markets (Middle East) Ltd.
P.O. Box 9038, Mina al-Fahal
Phone: 601743
Jim McGrory, Manager
Telex: MB 3257
Location: Mina al-Fahal

Commercial Banks

Arab Bank Ltd.
P.O. Box 991, Muscat
Abdul Kader Askalan, Manager
Telephone: 722831/2/3
Telex: 3285 Arabnk MB

Bank Melli Iran
P.O. Box 410, Muscat
Mohsen Pirzadeh, Manager
Telephone: 722646
Telex: 3295 MB

Bank of Credit & Commerce International
P.O. Box 4442, Ruwi
Mohammed Ashraf Khan, Manager
Telephone: 701892
Telex: 3317 BCCI MB

Bank of Oman, Bahrain & Kuwait
P.O. Box 4708, Ruwi
Charles Lewelyn, General Manager
Telephone: 701528/722966
Telex: 3290 BOBK MB

Banque de Paris et des Pays Bas
P.O. Box 425, Muscat
D. Fahmy, Manager
Telephone: 722740/722391
Telex: 3360 PARISBAS MB

Chartered Bank Ltd.
P.O. Box 5353 Ruwi
K. Waynforth, Manager
Telephone: 703999/703574
Telex: 3217 CHARBANK MB

Commercial Bank of Oman Ltd.
P.O. Box 4696, Muscat
Sajid Ali Abbasi, General Manager
Telephone: 773327/734021
Telex: 3392 COMBANK MB

Habib Bank A.G. Zurich
P.O. Box 7338, Ruwi
Wazir Mumtaz Ahmed, General Manager
Telephone: 772686/734314
Telex: 3331 SWISSHABIB MB

al-Bank al-Ahli al-Oman, SAO
P.O. Box 3134, Ruwi
D. J. Fletcher, General Manager
Telephone: 701044
Telex: 3450 BK AHLI MB

Bank of Baroda
P.O. Box 7231, Mutrah
J. T. Ahuja, Manager
Telephone: 734556
Telex: 3470 Baroda MB

Bank of Oman & The Gulf
P.O. Box 4175, Ruwi
Desmond R. Burnie, Manager
Telephone: 702584/703443
Telex: 3403 BNKHALIF MB

Bank Saderat Iran
P.O. Box 4269, Ruwi
Masood Ahmed, Manager
Telephone: 773474/5
Telex: 3191 MB

British Bank of the Middle East
P.O. Box 234, Muscat
F. X. Paul, Manager
Telephone: 722253/722442
Telex: 3213 BBME MB

Citibank N.A.
P.O. Box 918, Muscat
Bill Serumgard, Manager
Telephone: 722508
Telex: 3444 CITIBANK MB

Grindlay's Bank Ltd.
P.O. Box 3550, Ruwi
Ian G. McIntosh, General Manager
Telephone: 702848/702023
Telex: 3393 GRINDLY MB

Habib Bank, Ltd.
P.O. Box 7326, Mutrah
Sarfaz H. Abidi, Manager
Telephone: 772155/722839
Telex: 3283 HABIBBANK MB

National Bank of Abu Dhabi
P.O. Box 5293, Ruwi
Ali Abdel Sadiq, General Manager
Telephone: 772842
Telex: 3452 ALMASHRAF MB

Oman Arab-African Bank
P.O. Box 4216, Ruwi
Anthony R. Kelly, General Manager
Telephone: 703614
Telex: 3364 MD

National Bank of Oman
P.O. Box 3751, Ruwi
S. Mohammed Shafi, General Manager
Telephone: 734411
Telex: 3434 NATBANK MB

Union Bank of Oman
P.O. Box 4565, Ruwi
R. S. Frank, General Manager
Telephone: 703091
Telex: 3434 ETIHAD MB

Major Omani Trading Companies

Muscat

Abdulla & Hussain Hamza al-Asfoor
P.O. Box 4812, Ruwi
Phone: 702075/704079
Telex: 3326 ALASFOOR MB

Location: Ruwi (Wadi Kabir)
Ali Hamza and Monem al-Asfoor, Directors
Business: furnishings, household appliances, general
  traders

Abdul Aziz & Bros.
P.O. Box 5, Muscat
Phone: 772371
Telex: 3373 MB
Location: Mutrah (Corniche)
Abdul Rehim Jaffer, Manager
Business: household appliances, pharmaceuticals, general
  traders

Assarain Enterprise
P.O. Box 4475, Ruwi
Phone: 773295/6/7
Telex: 3293 Assarain MB
Location: Mutrah
K. A. Jilla, Manager
business: household appliances, furnishings, travel agents,
  department store, building materials, construction, gen-
  eral traders

Bahwan, Suhail & Saud
P.O. Box 169, Muscat
Phone: 734201
Telex: 3274 Bahwan MB
Location: Mutrah
Suhail & Saud Bahwan, Directors
Alex Borges, Project Manager
Business: auto sales, construction, household appliances,
  communications, electronics, travel agents, super-
  markets, general traders

Bhacker Haji Abdul Latif Fazul
P.O. Box 4068, Ruwi
Phone: 734651
Telex: 3320 Bhacker MB
Location: Mutrah
Ahmed Ali Abdul Latif, Manager
Business: shipping agents, insurance.

Darwish, Mohsin Haider
P.O. Box 3880, Ruwi
Phone: 703777
Telex: 3230 Lugaina MB
Location: Ruwi
Mohsin Haider Darwish, Proprietor
Business: auto sales, gas plant, construction, department
  stores, electronics, general traders

Al-Darwish Enterprises
P.O. Box 704, Muscat
Phone: 734624
Telex 3357 Muwaffaq MB
Location: Mutrah (Riyam)
Hussain Haiden Darwish, Proprietor
Business: travel agent, shipping, furniture, general traders

General Electric & Trading Co.
P.O. Box 7006, Mutrah
Phone: 703208
Telex: 3332 GENETCO MB
Location: Ruwi
Sadiq Hassan Ali, Director
Business: household appliances, electronics, photo equip-
  ment, general traders (and foodstuffs through Fairtrade
  Ltd., P.O. Box 1436, Mutrah)

GETCO Group of Companies
P.O. Box 84, Muscat
Phone: 702133
Telex: 3278 MB
Location: Ruwi
Kamal Daud, Partner
Business: auto sales, construction, building materials, gen-
  eral traders

Al-Harthy Corporation
P.O. Box 4248, Ruwi
Phone: 702456
Telex: 3417 Harthcor MB
Location: Ruwi
Sheik Zaher Al-Harthy, Proprietor
Business: auto sales, construction, general traders

Al-Hashar & Company
P.O. Box 1028, Mutrah
Phone: 702646/702555
Telex: 3245 MB
Location: Ruwi
Saeed Nasser al-Hashar, Director
Business: auto sales, household appliances, office equipment, electronics, general traders

Khimji Ramdas
P.O. Box 19, Muscat
Phone: 745601
Telex: 3289 Broker MB
Location: Muscat
Anil Matradas, General Manager
Business: auto sales, construction, department stores, building materials, household appliances, foodstuffs, general traders

Lashko Group of Companies
P.O. Box 118, Muscat
Phone: 703733
Telex: 3286 Lashko MB
Location: Ruwi
Nasser Abdulla Lashko, Director
Business: building materials, construction, travel agents, gas factory, general traders

Mazoun Establishment
P.O. Box 415
Phone: 601417, 601804
Telex: 3336 Mazoun MB
Location: Wattiyah
Sheikh Yaqub al-Harthy, Proprietor
Business: household appliances, office equipment, generators, general traders

Moosa Abdul Rahman Hassan
P.O. Box 4, Muscat
Phone: 701486/701566
Telex: 3222 MB
Location: Ruwi
Abdulla Moosa, Director
Business: auto sales, service station, furniture, pumps, general traders

Al-Moosa Establishment
P.O. Box 287, Muscat
Phone: 702722
Telex: 3269 MB
Location: Darseit
Mohammed Moosa Ali, Manager
Business: household appliances, electronics, general traders

Muscat Overseas Co.
P.O. Box 3488, Ruwi
Phone: 703844
Telex: 3323 MOAC MB
Location: Ruwi
Taher Jamali, Director
Business: auto sales, communications, pumps, agricultural equipment, general traders

Mustafa & Jawad Trading Company
P.O. Box 4918, Ruwi
Phone: 772168/734646
Telex: 3291 MB
Location: Mutrah
Mustafa A. R. Sultan, Manager
Business: department stores, household appliances, travel agents, general traders

Ahmed Mohammed Bin Ameir Estab.
P.O. Box 5157, Ruwi
Phone: 701495/701870
Telex: 3205 MB
Location: Ruwi
Ahmed Mohammed Ameir, Proprietor
Business: construction, agricultural equipment, household appliances, building materials, general traders, poultry farm

Oman Holdings International, LLC
P.O. Box 889, Muscat
Phone: 702666
Telex: 3398 AMMAR MB
Location: Ruwi
Rodger Drystale, Manager
Business: auto sales, travel agents, communications, insurance, household products, pharmaceuticals, general traders

Omar Zawawi Establishment (OMZEST)
P.O. Box 879, Muscat
Phone: 722239/40/41
Telex: 3542 OMZEST MB
Location: Muscat
Charles A. Stewart, Coordinator
Business: general traders, construction

Oman International Corporation
P.O. Box 4769, Ruwi
Phone: 734211/12
Telex: 3312 MB
Location: Mutrah
Mohamed Amin Al-Min, General Manager
Business: household appliances, insurance, general traders

Oman Trading, Industrial, and Engineering Company
P.O. Box 5063, Ruwi
Phone: 701331
Telex: 3841 MB
Location: Ruwi
A. Longinos, Manager
Business: commission-agents for construction, communications, furniture, general traders

Qais Omani Establishment
P.O. Box 656, Muscat
Phone: 734267/734939
Telex: 3300 MB
Location: Mutrah
Noel Hugh McGrath, General Manager
Business: general traders, general commission agents

SABCO Enterprises
P.O. Box 4086, Ruwi
Phone: 701483
Telex: 3456 Ruwihotel MB
Location: Ruwi
Hassan al-Misbah, Manager
Business: general traders

Bin Salim Enterprise
P.O. Box 808, Muscat
Phone: 701382/772202
Telex: 3430 Binsalim MB
Location: Mutrah
Sheikh Aflah H. S. al-Rawahy, Director
Business: construction, household appliances, generators, drilling equipment, general traders

Shanfari Trading company
P.O. Box 783, Muscat
Phone: 702560/703846
Telex: 3321 MB
Location: Ruwi
Peter F. Bailey, Manager
Business: construction, household appliances, general traders

SICO, The Industrial and Trading Company
P.O. Box 508, Muscat
Phone: 701976/702566
Telex: 3415 SICO MB
Location: Ruwi
Juman Ashour Rajab, Director
Business: general traders

Suleiman Ibrahim Najwani & Co.
P.O. Box 6, Muscat
Phone: 734136
Telex: 3320 MB
Location: Matrah
Ahmed Haji Salman, Director
Business: household appliances, foodstuffs, furnishings,
    general traders

al-Taher Enterprises
P.O. Box 3378, Ruwi
Phone: 734602
Telex: 3408 alTaher MB
Location: Mutrah
Sheikh Saud al-Khalili, Proprietor
Business: construction, general traders

Technical & Commercial Development Company
    (TECODEV)
P.O. Box 520, Muscat
Phone: 734602
Telex: 3383 MB
Location: Mutrah
Dr. Hamed Riyami, Proprietor
Business: household appliances, medical supplies, general
    traders

United Enterprises Co., LLC
P.O. Box 3588, Ruwi
Phone: 701471/701472
Telex: 3457 MB
Location: Ruwi
Mohammed A. Jamali, Director
Business: building materials, service stations, construc-
    tion, general traders

W. J. Towell & Co., LLC
P.O. Box 7061, Mutrah
Phone: 772131/5
Telex: 3214 MB
Location: Mutrah
Kamal A. R. Sultan, Director
Anwar Sultan, Mgr.
Business: automobiles, hardware stores, shipping agents,
    construction, consumer items, rice, general traders

Waleed Associates
P.O. Box 437, Muscat
Phone: 745101/105
Telex: 3270 MB
Location: Muscat
Commander John Howe, Manager
Business: general commission agent, medical supplies,
    communications, consumer items, general traders

Yahya Enterprises
P.O. Box 286, Muscat
Phone: 702615
Telex: 3239 Nassib MB
Location: Ruwi
Yahya Mohammed Nassib, Proprietor
Business: construction, general traders, communications

al-Yousef International Enterprises
P.O. Box 200, Muscat
Phone: 734969
Telex: 3247 MB
Location: Mutrah
G. R. Evans, Manager
Business: general commission agent, communications,
    general traders

Zawawi Trading Company
P.O. Box 58, Muscat
Phone: 600102
Telex: 3232 Zawawi MB
Location: Qurum
Michael H. Akeroyd, General Manager
Business: automobiles, construction machinery, agricul-
    tural equipment, electrical equipment, communications,
    pharmaceuticals, general traders

Zubair Enterprises
P.O. Box 127, Muscat
Phone: 722821/3
Telex: 3258 Mustarad MB
Location: Muscat
Dr. Charles Sawaya, General Manager
Business: automobiles, furnishings, electrical and elec-
    tronic equipment, insurance, travel agents, construc-
    tion, oilfield supplies, general traders

Salalah

Cement Marketing Company, LLC
P.O. Box 8196, Salalah
Phone: 461824
Telex: 7670 MB
Ali Mohammed Akeel, Partner
Business: tile factory, building materials, general traders

Hamdan Group of Companies
P.O. Box 8190, Salalah
Phone: 461984
Telex: 3478 MB
Abdul Rehman M. A. Gadallah, Manager
Business: transportation, building materials, general
    traders

Nasr Arabian Company
P.O. Box 8122, Salalah
Phone: 460820/460660
Telex: 7660 MB
Saeed Abdulla al-Bahar, Director
Business: road building, construction

Oman Building & Contracting Co.
P.O. Box 8212, Salalah
Phone: 461430/461779
Telex: 7634 Marhoon MB
Ahmed Salim Saeed al-Marhoon
Business: building contractors, general traders

Omani Import & Export Company
P.O. Box 8713, Salalah
Phone: 461923
Bakheet Ali Shanfari, Proprietor
Business: drilling equipment, building materials, general
    traders

Shanfari & Partners
P.O. Box 8026, Salalah
Phone: 461805/461351
Telex: 7617 MB
Abdul Aziz Saba, Director
Business: foodstuffs, consumer products, construction,
    general traders

General Trading Companies with
Foreign Partnership

Fanal Trading Company
P.O. Box 4979, Ruwi
Phone: 734724/734735
Telex: 3116 MB
Location: Mutrah
Safat Malik, Manager
Business: building materials, chemicals, cement, general
    traders

Ramniklal B. Kothary
P.O. Box 66, Muscat
Phone: 703863
Telex: 3169 MB
Location: Ruwi
Harshand Mody, Manager
Business: department stores, foodstuffs

Mutawa Trading Company
P.O. Box 1017, Mutrah
Phone: 701841
Telex: 3287 Etertrade MB
Location: Ruwi
Suhail Sharabati, Manager
Business: building materials, Swedish Trade Center

Oasis Trading and Equipment
P.O. Box 1002, Mutrah
Phone: 602272
Telex: 3329 MB
Location: Azibah
A. L. Knox, Branch Manager
Business: construction machinery, automobiles

Oman Catering Company
P.O. Box 654, Muscat
Phone: 701429
Telex: None
Location: Ruwi
Rafic Shammas, Manager
Business: foodstuffs, catering services, liquor

Oman United Agencies
P.O. Box 3985, Ruwi
Phone: 701291/702362/704129
Telex: 3215 MB
Location: Ruwi
Richard Tatham, Managing Director
Business: shipping, travel agents, marine contractors, insurance, liquor, general traders

al-Sadoon & Musaad al-Saleh
P.O. Box 5204, Ruwi
Phone: 704808
Telex: 3439 FAWZI MB
Location: Ruwi
Ibrahim Zawawi, Manager
Business: building, road construction machinery, real estate

Al-Seeb Technical Establishment (SARCO)
P.O. Box 3966, Ruwi
Phone: 734893
Telex: 3399 GENEVCO MB
Location: Mutrah
Mohammed Abu Shaeria, Manager
Business: central air-conditioning, construction machinery, general traders

Sharikat Fanniya Omaniya
P.O. Box 4949, Ruwi
Phone: 704400
Telex: 3227 Fanniya MB
Location: Ruwi
John Stubbs, Manager
Business: foodstuffs, office equipment, household appliances, furnishings, liquor

Yusuf Bin Ahmed Kanoo & Company
P.O. Box 7310, Mutrah
Phone: 772253/4
Telex: 3352 Kanoo MB
Location: Mutrah
Alan Cottingham, Manager
Business: shipping, travel, general traders

Omani Joint-Stock Companies

Amiantit Oman
P.O. Box 4807, Ruwi
Phone: 620604
Telex: 3304 MB
Location: Rusail
Business: asbestos-cement pipes

Construction Materials Industries
P.O. Box 4791, Ruwi
Phone: 704603
Telex: 3199 MB
Location: Ruwi
Hamzi K. Moghrabi, Managing Director
Business: lime bricks

Oman Cement Company, S.A.O.
P.O. Box 3560, Ruwi
Phone: 701377/701512
Telex: 3112 MB
Location: Ruwi; plant to be located in Rusail
Engr. Suleiman Barakat Lamki, Deputy Chairman
Business: cement

Oman Flour Mills Company, Ltd.
P.O. Box 3566, Ruwi
Phone: 701154
Telex: 3422 OFM MB
Location: Mutrah
Mohammed al-Battashi, Marketing Manager
Business: flour and feed products

Oman Mining Company
P.O. Box 758, Muscat
Phone: 603501
Telex: 3492 HUMUS MB
Location: Wattayah
Jack Wali, Managing Director
Business: mining

Oman National Dairy Company
P.O. Box 3610, Ruwi
Phone: 603425
Telex: 3456 MB
Location: Ghubrah
Kristen Jorgensen, Manager
business: dairy products

Oman National Electric Company
P.O. Box 4393, Ruwi
Phone: 701633
Telex: 3528 MB
Location: Ruwi
R. R. Harper, Manager
Business: electricity management

Oman National Insurance Company
P.O. Box 5254, Ruwi
Phone: 702677/701522
Telex: 3290 OBK MB
Location: Ruwi
J. A. McRobbie, Manager
Business: insurance

Oman Sun Farms, S.A.O.
P.O. Box 3604, Ruwi
Phone: 701886
Telex: 3476 OSFARM MB
Location: Ruwi
Mehboob Rasuh, General Manager
Business: livestock, vegetables production

Sadolin Paints (Oman) Ltd.
P.O. Box 3531, Ruwi
Phone: 602780
Telex: 3484 MB
Location: Khuwair
A. K. Ayya, General Manager
Business: paints

al-Sharika al-Ahliya Letamween
P.O. Box 3236 Ruwi
Phone: 602540
Telex: 3608 MB
Location: Ghubrah
Farouk Hussein Sharfi, Manager
Business: foodstuffs

Shipping Agents

Ambola Contracting and Trading Company
P.O. Box 3158, Ruwi
Phone: 704367
Telex: 3355 MB
Location: Ruwi
Agent for: Hellenic

Bhacker Haji Abdul Latif Fazul
P.O. Box 4086, Ruwi
Phone: 734651
Telex: 3220 MB
Location: Mutrah
Agent for: Hansa, Nedlloyd, United Arab Shipping Co.,
  Shipping Corporation of India, Watersteamship Cor-
  poration

al-Fayha Shipping Agencies
P.O. Box 1395, Mutrah
Phone: 772325
Telex: 3329 MB
Location: Mutrah

Gulf Agency Company (Oman)
P.O. Box 3740, Ruwi
Phone: 734888
Telex: 3284 MB
Location: Mutrah
Agent for: Scanmel, North American Van Lines, Scindia,
  Vyk Line, Tokyo Shipping, Futiwara, Sinchiao Ship-
  ping

Kassar Transport (NALCO)
P.O. Box 3028, Seeb Airport
Phone: 610211
Telex: 3306 MB
Location: Seeb Airport
Agent for: Sea Land Inc

M. A. al-Konji Shipping Department
P.O. Box 3899, Ruwi
Phone: 734497
Telex: 3271 MB
Location: Mutrah
Agent for: Central Gulf Lash

Muscat Maritime Agency
P.O. Box 1420, Mutrah
Phone: 773111
Telex: 3277 MB
Location: Mutrah
Agent for: Gulf Shipping Line

Mutrah Shipping Agency
P.O. Box 4984, Ruwi
Phone: 734984
Telex: 3309 MB
Location: Mutrah
Agent for: MTO, Citiola Oceanic

Oman United Agencies Ltd.
P.O. Box 3985, Ruwi
Phone: 701299
Telex: 3215 MB
Location: Ruwi
Agent for: P&O, Jugolinija, APCL, Showa, Mearks, Mitsui
  OSK

Suwaidi Shipping Agency
P.O. Box 263, Muscat
Phone: 600315
Telex: 3338 Suwaidi MB
Location: Ruwi
Agent for: Coastal Line

W. J Towell & Company LLC Shipping Division
P.O. Box 7061, Mutrah
Phone: 773266
Telex: 3214 MB
Location: Mutrah
Agent for: Saudi Concordia, Mercanidia Lines

Transport Services Oman
P.O. Box 268, Muscat
Phone: 702461
Telex: 3301 MB
Location: Mutrah
Activity: Clearing and forwarding services

Yousuf Bin Ahmed Kanoo & Company
P.O. Box 7310, Mutrah
Phone: 772253
Telex: 3352 MB
Location: Mutrah
Agent for: Blue Star Line, Vanpac International, Hough
  Ugland Auto Liner, Nosac, Cunard Brock Bank, Com-
  panhia de Paulista

Market Profile—OMAN

Foreign Trade

Imports.—Almost $1.4 billion in 1979; estimated $1.3 billion in 1978. Major suppliers (1979 provisional): United Kingdom, 17 percent; Japan, 15 percent; United Arab Emirates, 15 percent; United States, 9 percent. Principal imports: transportation equipment (including passenger cars), industrial and building supplies, capital goods, foods and beverages, and consumer goods.

Exports.—$2.3 billion in 1979; estimated $1.6 billion in 1978. Petroleum constitutes bulk of exports. Non-oil exports are dates and limes. U.S. has 14 percent share of Omani exports.

Trade Policy.—Liberal, with no exchange controls and few limits imposed on trade. Import licenses are not required, but all firms selling products in Oman, except those working directly for the Oman Government, are required to appoint an Omani individual or company as an agent.

Trade Prospects.—Foodstuffs; air conditioners; telephone equipment; passenger and heavy vehicles; navigation and communications equipment; data processing equipment.

Foreign Investment

Foreign investment encouraged. Minimum 35 percent Omani participation required except in banking, professional offices, and government contracts. Five year tax holiday for firms in agriculture, fishing, and industrial development. Majority of U.S. firms are involved in petroleum and minerals. Investment Guarantee Agreement with U.S. signed in 1976.

Finance

Currency.—One Omani rial (R.O.) equals US$2.895. US$1 = R.O. .345. Domestic Credit: 20 commercial banks (the government established maximum), mostly foreign owned. Two U.S. banks have operations in Oman. Central Bank began operations in 1973. Establishment of the State General Reserve Fund in January 1980.

Balance of Payments.—Surplus of $328 million in 1979. Negative balance of $98 million in 1978. Surplus should increase further in 1980. Exchange reserves $720 million in April 1980.

Economy

GNP.—$2.2 billion in 1978; $2.1 billion in 1977.

Agriculture.—36,000 hectares (about .12 percent of Oman's 300,000 square kilometers) under cultivation. Employs about half the country's total work force, but produces only about 3 percent of GNP. Nearly half total cultivated area is date palms, intercropped with alfalfa. Limes and onions are of importance, followed by fruits, wheat, tobacco. Domestic production supplies only about 60 percent of Oman's food requirements. Fishing is an important but underexploited activity carried out, like agriculture, on a subsistence basis.

Industry.—A light industrial zone has been established. Flour mill; copper processing; plans are being prepared for a small refinery, a steel rolling mill, and a cement plant. Implementation of the last two is uncertain.

Tourism.—Government policies discourage tourism despite good potential and presence of excellent international grade hotels.

Development Program.—1976–80 Five Year Plan emphasizes diversification of economy toward income-generating projects in agriculture, minerals, and light industry. Results have been mixed. 1981–85 Five Year Plan will also emphasize diversification of production and promotion of private sector investment.

Basic Economic Facilities

Transportation.—1,760 km of paved roads; 13,497 km of graded earth roads. No railroads. New airport near Muscat served by international carriers.

Communications.—Telephone and telegraph facilities with international links in capital area and Salalah. TV and radio stations.

Power.—Available in capital area, Salalah, and some rural towns. Production in 1978: 612.9 million kWh.

Natural Resources

Land.—Between 82,000 and 100,000 sq. miles, depending on where unresolved borders are fixed; 1,200 mile coastline. Coastal plain; interior is mountainous, with large desert areas.

Climate.—Arid and very hot. Humid along the coast, dry in the interior.

Minerals.—Petroleum output declined to an average of 295,000 barrels per day in 1979. Production is expected to increase to about 350,000 barrels per day by the end of 1980 and stay at that rate at least through 1984.

Population

Size.—No census has been taken. Estimated 865,000 with about 140,000 expatriates mainly from India and Pakistan. Oman Government officially uses a figure of 1.5 million for planning purposes. More than 40,000 in capital area. Estimated annual growth rate of 3 percent. Life expectancy about 47 years. Estimated 45 percent of population under 15 years.

Language.—Arabic. Baluchi spoken along coast. Indian dialects in capital areas. English used in government and business circles.

Education.—Estimated 20 percent literacy rate. Schools built since 1970; first secondary school opened 1973. 85 percent of schools located outside capital area. Government also operates teacher training institutes, vocational training centers, literacy centers, and adult education centers.

Labor.—Shortage of skilled and unskilled labor. Large numbers of expatriate workers. Distribution of labor force: agriculture, 48 percent; petroleum, 2 percent; services, 50 percent.

Market Profile—PACIFIC ISLANDS TRUST TERRITORY

Foreign Trade

Exports.—Exports for 1980 were $13.67 million, consisting of fish, copra, handicrafts, and fruit.

Imports.—Imports for 1978 were $38.85 million, consisting of foodstuffs, petroleum products, building materials, timber, and textiles.

Trade Policy.—An ad valorem tax of 3 percent is levied on most imported products. However, some specific items are subject to higher rates. There is an export duty levied on the major export items.

Best Trade Prospects.—Foodstuffs, petroleum products, and building materials.

Trading Associations.—Ponape Federation of Co-Op Association, Truk Trading Company, Yap Shipping Co-Operation Association, and EMI Enterprises.

Finance

Currency.—U.S. Currency is used.

Banks. — Bank of Hawaii, Bank of Guam, California Trust Bank, and Micronesian Development Bank.

Aid.—U.S. appropriations and grants cover the majority of aid programs.

Foreign Investment.—Foreign investment is encouraged by the Government as long as domestic employment increases and domestic economic development improves.

Economy

GNP.—The computed figure for 1979 was $107 million, with a per capita income of $810.

Industry.—The industrial sector is very small, but production is adequate to supply the basic needs of the islanders.

Commerce.—The Government plans to develop tourism into a major industry. The number of visitors has increased from 19,000 in 1975 to some 26,000 in 1979. The construction of facilities has kept pace with the growing demand for accommodations.

Development Plans.—The Government is pursuing the development of existing industries, such as tourism, fishing, rice, and general agriculture.

Basic Economic Facilities

Transportation.—Micronesian Interocean, Inc provides shipping from the United States to eight islands where there are commercial docks. From there, smaller vessels provide inter-island service. The shipping industry is well developed and efficient. A total of seven shipping lines provided service to the islands as of 1976. Continental/Air Micronesia, Japan Airlines and Air Pacific International are the three international airlines with scheduled stops. The Trust Territory is well served on interisland routes by Air Micronesia, Aloha Airlines, and United Micronesian Development Association. The roadway system is small. Most main thoroughfares are paved; the smaller roads are generally dirt with coral-finished surfaces.

Communications.—Through the hookup at Guam the Radio corporation of America provides worldwide connections.

Power.—There is an adequate supply of diesel-generated electricity in all districts. The voltage is 110 volts.

Natural Resources

Location.—The Pacific Island Trust Territory, a possession of the United States with three island districts, is located to the north, south, and west of Guam.

Climate.—Tropical and pleasant. The western section of the territory is subject to typhoons, which occur almost annually.

Minerals.—No minerals are available for commercial exploitation.

Forestry.—There is not a sufficient amount of quality timber for commercial use.

Fisheries.—A valuable and growing industry.

Population

Size.—As of 1980, 134,000 inhabitants.

Language.—English is the business language. Many dialects of Micronesian spoken.

Education.—Education is free and compulsory for children between the ages of 6 and 16.

Marketing in Pakistan

Contents

Report Revised January 1982

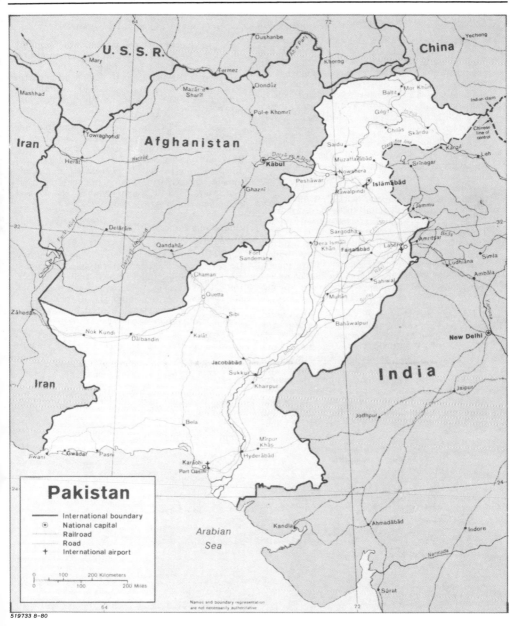

Pakistan

— International boundary
⊙ National capital
  Railroad
  Road
✦ International airport

0   100   200 Kilometers
0   100   200 Miles

Names and boundary representation
are not necessarily authoritative

519733 8-80

Foreign Trade Outlook

Pakistan continues to be an expanding market for U.S. exports. Pakistan's total imports for Fiscal Year (PFY) 1980 (July 1979–June 1980) amounted to $4.8 billion, 29 percent higher than the previous year. Spurred by an expanding economy and a newly liberalized import policy, Pakistan's imports for PFY 1981 (July 1980–June 1981) approached $5.5 billion in initial reports.

Despite the rapid growth of imports, Pakistan's balance of payments situation—and thus its ability to pay for imports—has continued to improve. The country's foreign exchange earnings from exports were $3 billion in PFY 1981, up 26 percent as compared with PFY 1979. The continued growth in remittances received from Pakistanis working abroad has also been helpful. These remittances were expected to reach $2.1 billion in PFY 1981. In addition, the International Monetary Fund provided a $1.7 billion loan to Pakistan in 1980, and the Government was able to reschedule a large portion of its international debt payments falling due during 1981.

Foreign assistance plays a major role in financing Pakistan's imports. Pakistan averages over $1 billion a year in foreign assistance, although for PFY 1979 this figure rose to $1.7 billion. The Pakistan Consortium, consisting of 12 industrialized countries, the World Bank, and the Asian Development Bank, supply the majority of this assistance. For PFY 1981, the Consortium pledged $954 million, of which the World Bank, the Asian Development Bank, Japan, and the United Kingdom were the largest contribu-

tors. The United States, which is a member, contributed $50 million in PFY 1981.

Of growing importance is assistance from oil producing Near East Arab States. As of March 1981, they have contributed a total of $1.5 billion to Pakistan. Beyond loans to pay for oil imports, Saudi Arabia and Kuwait have supplied Pakistan with almost $400 million for specific development projects.

Japan was Pakistan's largest trading partner for PFY 1980. Total two-way trade amounted to $673 million. The United States was second with $648 million. Together, the United States and Japan accounted for 22 percent of Pakistan's imports and exports. Other major trading partners were Kuwait, Saudi Arabia, the United Kingdom, and West Germany.

Pakistan's Imports from the United States

The United States accounts for approximately 15 percent of Pakistan's total imports. After reaching a record high of $591 million in PFY 1981, U.S. exports to Pakistan have started to fall. The primary reason for this drop was a decline in wheat shipments, caused by Pakistan's growing self-sufficiency in wheat.

Nevertheless, as Pakistan's total import bill grows, opportunities, especially for U.S. manu-

Table 1.—Pakistan Imports by Major Commodities

(in millions of dollars)

	PFY 1980	PFY 1979
Total	4,740	3,676
Crude petroleum and petroleum products	1,079	530
Machinery	747	601
Transport equipment	596	250
Iron and steel	282	210
Fertilizers	274	284
Edible oils	230	268
Synthetic and artificial silk yarn	156	115
Wheat	105	354
Tea	96	101
Medicinal preparations	76	61
Chemicals (excluding fertilizers and medicines)	69	195
Paper and paper products	60	48
Synthetic fibers	49	52
Milk and milk food	40	28
Tires and tubes	31	23
Others	850	556

Pakistan Fiscal Year (PFY): July 1 to June 30.
Source: Central Statistical Office, Government of Pakistan.

Table 2.—Pakistan Principal Imports from the United States

(in millions of dollars)

	PFY 1980	PFY 1979
Wheat unmilled	39.6	282.8
Soybean oil	51.6	67.7
Animal tallow	27.0	29.6
Fertilizers	19.6	23.6
Sheets iron and steel	29.3	14.9
Tinned plates eletrolytic	5.9	4.9
Synthetic textile yarns/fibers	4.2	5.5
Used apparel/clothing	9.8	7.0
Insecticides/pesticides	2.6	3.1
Tobacco, raw	1.5	1.2
Medicinal and pharmaceutical products	6.4	5.4
Chemical products	5.0	4.0
Electrical machinery and parts	7.2	6.3
Air-conditioning and refrigeration equipment	6.2	4.3
Parts and accessories of machinery	8.0	7.5
Pumps and parts	2.5	2.1
Telecommunication equipment	3.8	0.5
Railway locomotives and parts	9.0	4.2
Road transport equipment and parts	11.0	9.0
Aircraft	67.2	—
Petroleum and gas drilling machinery	2.7	2.7
Oil refinery machinery and parts	5.2	—
Earthmoving, mining, and construction machinery parts	13.2	12.0
Machinery and mechanical appliances	6.7	0.9
Scientific instruments and parts	3.0	2.8
Totals	527.20	584.92

Pakistan Fiscal Year (PFY): July 1 to June 30.
Source: Central Statistical Office, Government of Pakistan.

factured items, are also growing. Best prospects for U.S. exporters to Pakistan are: chemicals, pharmaceuticals, fertilizers, synthetic fibers and yarns, edible oils, animal tallow, and iron and steel products including scrap, as well as power generation, telecommunications, port, and construction equipment.

Details on the market for these products are provided below under Growth Sectors.

Industry Trends

Government Policy

Since 1977, the administration of President Mohammed Zia-ul-Haq has consistently sought to allay the private sector's concerns about nationalization and to encourage both foreign and domestic investment. The business community has responded favorably to this policy by increasing its rate of investment in agriculture, transportation, real estate, and services. In PFY 1980, new projects sanctioned by the Government investment banks and the Investment Promotion Bureau rose by 60 percent over 1979 to a record $663 million. More than half of these investment proposals were put forward by business firms from the Persian Gulf area.

Industrial Performance

Production in the industrial sector for PFY 1981 rose by 9.2 percent over PFY 1980. This growth was a major contributor to the growth in the gross domestic product (GDP), which rose 6 percent in real terms for the third consecutive year. Major gains in the industrial field were sugar refining (up 47 percent over 1979), fertilizer (up 31 percent), jute goods (up 19 percent), and vegetable oil (up 12 percent). The performance of Pakistan's two largest industrial sectors, cotton yarn and cotton cloth, were mixed. Cotton yarn rose 2 percent while cotton cloth fell 10 percent.

Development Plan

Pakistan's current Five-Year Plan, announced in July 1978, involves a total outlay of some $4 billion in the industrial sector for the period PFY 1979 through PFY 1983, of which $2.1 billion is for the public sector and $1.9 billion for the private sector. A major portion of the investment outlay, both public and private, is for expansion of cement; fertilizer; edible oil; iron and steel manufacturing; production of agricultural machinery and parts; production of automobile, tractor, and truck parts; manufacture of heavy electrical machinery; modernization of the cotton industry and other industries that either save or earn foreign exchange.

However, actual investment in projects during the first 2 years of the Plan has been disappointingly low. Consequently, the fifth Plan is being reviewed by the Government and may be replaced by a new Three-Year Plan during 1982. Regardless of any changes, Government priorities show a consistent pattern favoring investment in the energy, water, transportation, and communication fields.

Large major projects that have been started and require ongoing imports or are in the advanced stage of planning include: a $1.12 billion Lakhra coal mine and thermal power plant, a $1.01 billion hydroelectric power extension at Tarbela dam, a $568 million Port Qasim construction project near Karachi, and a $404 million integrated mineral exploitation project in Baluchistan province. U.S. businesses interested in learning more about these and other major projects in Pakistan should contact the Major Projects Division, Office of Export Marketing Assistance, U.S. Department of Commerce, Washington, D.C. 20230.

Growth Sectors

Based on current Government of Pakistan economic planning objectives, the following sectors are priority areas and will provide excellent opportunities for U.S. business firms:

Agriculture and Agro-Related Industries. —Agriculture's share of the GNP is about 30 percent. Farm production has grown by 4 to 5 percent in the last 2 years, and increasing agricultural production remains a top economic priority. Major crops are wheat, rice, sugarcane, and cotton. Raw cotton and rice supplied over $1 billion in export earnings for Pakistan in 1980. Opportunities for U.S. exporters derive mainly from services and supplies needed to support Pakistan's agricultural growth. Especially attractive are Pakistan's programs to improve food grain storage and irrigation facilities.

Pakistan encourages agriculture-based industries, especially the upgrading of rice milling facilities. Plans for the next 5 years call for adding two to four rice milling plants at a total estimated cost of $5 million. The Government also plans to expand sugar producing capacity from 900,000 tons per year to about 1.5 million tons in the next few years. Despite the Government's interest in using the maximum amount of locally manufactured sugar-producing equipment, substantial imports will be required. Export opportunities exist for U.S. boilers, centrifuges, regulatory instruments, complete with mill houses (including shredders and revolving knives), turbines, and generators.

Chemicals.—Agriculture is also the basis for Pakistan's rapidly growing consumption of chemicals and allied products. In PFY 1978 imports under this category amounted to $334 million; this increased by 119 percent to $735 million in PFY 1981. Imports consist of both organic and inorganic industrial chemicals, fertilizers, insecticides, and plant equipment. Pakistan's imports of chemicals and related equipment constitute approximately 15 percent of total imports. Pakistan's fifth Five-Year Plan allocated $103 million in foreign exchange for investment in plant and equipment for the expanding chemical industry, but the failure to invest in this sector during the early part of the plan and inflation have pushed this figure up dramatically. Trade sources in Pakistan now estimate procurement in the next 3 years may be worth more than $600 million. At the same time, plant expansion is not expected to keep up with growing demand, meaning that Pakistan will also remain a good market for direct chemical exports from the United States.

Electric Power.—Pakistan's power generation and transmission industry is under the responsibility of the Water and Power Development Authority (WAPDA). Present installed capacity is 3,535 MW, of which 1,566 MW is hydro, 1,684 MW is thermal, and 100 MW is nuclear. By 1984, 2,655 MW of capacity have to be added to the system at a cost of approximately $769 million. Imports over the next 2 years are estimated at about $387 million. The U.S. share of the market has been about 6 percent. With more commitments for economic assistance available from the untied sources such as the Asian Development Bank and OPEC countries, the U.S. share should increase between 10 and 12 percent in the next 3 years. Growing interest is being shown in the development of nontraditional sources of energy, including solar. Implementation of these projects will depend on availability of international financing. Pakistan has several firms engaged in manufacturing a limited range of power generating equipment. Export opportunities exist for turbines, transformers, capacitors, electric motors, generators, switch-gears, high voltage transmission cables, and other allied equipment.

Telecommunications.—Pakistan's telecommunication network consists of 345,000 phones located in 49 cities. This system is linked to 17 countries through a satellite communications system. There are 178 overseas channels via satellite, of which 162 are speech circuits and 16 are for telegraph. The principal end users are the Pakistan Telephone and Telegraph Department and the Ministry of Defense.

Pakistan has approximately 1.55 million radios and 700,000 television sets. The Pakistan Broadcasting Corporation (PBC) has 33 short-wave and medium-wave transmitters, with a total radiating power of 3.171 kilowatts. Short-wave broadcasts reach 100 percent of the population; and medium-wave, 88 percent. The Pakistan Television Corporation covers 74 percent of the population.

Pakistan places a high priority on expanding its communication network, both civilian and military. Total imports of industrial and public service telecommunication equipment should exceed $300 million during the next 2 years. In the past, U.S. restrictions on supplying defense communications to the Pakistan military have limited the U.S. share of the telecommunications market. It is expected, however, that with increased U.S. military assistance to Pakistan, the U.S. share of the market will grow from about 10 percent to between 15 and 20 percent.

Cement—Until recently, the cement industry was exclusively under and controlled by the State Cement Corporation. This corporation plans to add a 1,000-tons-per-day cement plant at the Darwza cement project, and a 2,000-tons-per-day plant at the D.G. Khan cement project. The total foreign exchange cost will be $120 million. In addition, the private sector has now been permitted to establish three to four plants of 1,000-tons-per-day capacity at an estimated cost of $140 million. Despite these expected increases in production, the need for cement is growing very rapidly. Pakistan is likely to import approximately $200 million worth of cement in the next 2 years.

Construction Equipment.—Pakistan will import construction equipment worth approximately $250 million in the next 2 years. These imports are needed for development of roads, irrigation projects, and mineral development and for construction of large civil works and urban and rural development projects. The U.S. share of the market has ranged from 8 to 31 percent. Since a major part of the equipment is for the public sector, the equipment purchases will depend heavily on foreign assistance. The U.S. share of the market will be very sensitive to how much of this assistance is funded from untied sources.

Textiles.—Pakistan produces cotton, woolen,

and synthetic yarns and fabrics. It also produces jute goods and has developed a capacity for manufacturing synthetic fibers, including rayon acetate, nylon, and polyester fiber. However, cotton textiles is the premier industry of the country. The installed capacity of this industry at the end of June 1980 was 3.7 million spindles and 26,162 looms. In PFY 1980, the spinning mills produced 362.9 million kilograms of yarn while cloth production was 342.3 million square meters. Export earnings from this production was $445.6 million. Pakistan also produces a wide variety of cotton products including hosiery, knitted garments, and apparel. A large part of the installed equipment in the textile mills is over 20 years old and needs replacing. Development plans call for modernizing existing plants and possibly establishing new plants. Pakistan is expected to import textile machinery and equipment, including accessories worth more than $304 million between 1982 and 1984.

Pharmaceuticals. —While domestic use of pharmaceuticals is still very low by international standards, 172 firms, using primarily imported ingredients, manufacture medicine in Pakistan. Considerable scope exists for increasing U.S. exports of pharmaceutical preparations, both in finished form and in bulk for reprocessing and packaging by local industry. Total imports during 1980 amounted to approximately $65 million and are growing 10 percent annually. There are also good opportunities for expanding manufacturing. The fifth Five-Year Plan allocated $50 million for expansion of the industry. The pharmaceutical industry is exempt from all duties and taxes; e.g., import duty, central excise duty, and sales tax.

Oil and Gas Development. —To reduce the heavy reliance on oil imports, which cost Pakistan close to $2 billion in PFY 1980, the Government has given highest priority to exploration and development of Pakistan's oil and natural gas resources. During 1981 11 oil companies engaged in petroleum exploration, 8 of which were U.S. companies. The exploration and development activities have accelerated, and development plans call for the drilling of 30 oil wells per year as opposed to an average of only 3 in past years. Between 1982 and 1984, Pakistan plans to import $156 million worth of oil and gas exploration, production, and refining equipment. The U.S. share of the market is approximately 40 percent and could go up to 45 percent during the next 3 years.

Industrial Process Control, Material Testing and Quality Control Equipment. —The Govern-

ment of Pakistan is keen to develop the industrial infrastructure of the country to achieve lesser reliance on imports in particular sectors such as fertilizers, oil refining, cement, and sugar. Moreover, it is placing emphasis on promoting production of quality goods for export and domestic consumption. For this purpose, the Pakistan Standards Institution requires its certification marking on 51 items meant for export and on 9 articles meant for domestic consumption. Consequently, an increasing number of industrial units are adding quality control instruments to their production facilities. In addition, more industrial units based on process control operations, such as cement, fertilizer, chemicals, and food processing are under installation or being planned which should accelerate demand for the product category. The total market for all items in this category is estimated to be about $110 million between PFY 1982 and 1984.

Railroad Equipment—Pakistan's annual average import of railroad equipment during PFY 1982–84 is estimated at $60 million. The Government-owned Pakistan Railways, with its headquarters at Lahore, has elaborate plans for expansion, modernization, and replacement. Net growth rate of imports is estimated at 5 percent annually above inflation. Major items to be procured include sophisticated and special purpose machine tools for modernization of railways workshops and equipment production units, signaling and telecommunications equipment, expansion and replacement of rolling stock, diesel and electric locomotives, and track materials, as well as equipment and materials for local production/assembly of freight and passenger cars.

To assist U.S. business firms in responding to these prospects, the U.S. Foreign Commercial Service in Pakistan has prepared market research in the following areas: Food processing and packaging; American books and periodicals; sugar processing and refining; cement plant equipment; mining, earthmoving, and construction; hotel supplies; American agricultural machinery; textile machinery; metalworking and finishing; oil exploration and production; railroad equipment; telecommunications; engineering, management and marketing, auditing, and accountancy consultant firms in Pakistan; computers and related equipment; and American material testing, quality control, industrial process control, and measuring instruments. These research reports may be obtained from the National Technical Information Service, U.S. Department of Commerce, Springfield, Virginia 22161, or from the Pakistan Country Desk Officer, U.S.

Department of Commerce, Washington, D.C. 20230.

The U.S. Department of Commerce also assists U.S. business firms by sponsoring commercial promotions (trade missions or catalog exhibitions) in Pakistan. These events are planned for 1982 and 1983: construction equipment catalog exhibitions, industrial process controls catalog exhibition, and mining and excavation trade mission. Interested firms should contact: Special Promotions Division, Office of Export Promotion, U.S. Department of Commerce, Washington, D.C. 20230.

Distribution and Sales Channels

Since the primary channel for selling U.S. merchandise in Pakistan is through a resident agent, U.S. firms should appoint imaginative, active, and technically trained local agents. A local agent may be authorized for industrial consumers, to bid on Government tenders, or to place orders to book indent orders for his/her own account. U.S. firms will often find that agents handle competitive lines.

Major Marketing Areas

Pakistan estimates its population at 84 million, with an annual growth rate of almost 3 percent. Urban dwellers represent over 26 percent. The principal cities are Karachi, Lahore, Hyderabad, Faisalabad, Multan, Rawalpindi, Islamabad, and Peshawar. The largest city in Pakistan, Karachi, is the center of trade, finance, and industry and is also the only port. Lahore, in northeastern Pakistan, is an increasingly important distribution center. Islamabad, the capital, is located in the northern part of the country and is not a major marketing center.

Wholesale and Retail Channels

Retailers located in populous areas usually purchase or obtain on credit supplies sufficient to last them for a week. Representatives of firms in more rural areas generally travel to the large cities, such as Karachi, to inspect the goods and to place orders sufficient to last a month or more.

While a number of retail stores carry general merchandise, only a few carry a wide enough range to be considered small department stores. The typical retail shop sells a single commodity; e.g., tires, cooking utensils, textiles, or jewelry. It is frequently located in a bazaar area near a number of other shops carrying similar goods

and is likely to be small and crowded. In recent years the concept of the department store has gained some ground, especially in big cities like Karachi, but such stores are relatively very small. A retailer's markup on imported merchandise is between 30 percent and 40 percent over his/her cost. The markup on locally produced goods is about 25 percent. About one-fifth of the wholesalers in Karachi sell on a consignment basis. Less than one-third of the wholesalers allow discounts to their customers. Granting of 15 to 30 day credit by wholesalers is common. The financial resources of retailers are generally limited; retailers usually sell only for cash. Consumer credit is still an insignificant portion of total commercial credit.

Government Procurement Procedures

The Pakistan Government, including the large autonomous organizations and numerous Government-controlled corporations, is the country's largest importer. Import requirements are handled through bids. Orders are generally placed with the lowest bidder. The Director General, Department of Supplies in Karachi, processes import requirements of a number of Central Government Departments and issues the invitations to bid. In addition, a number of other Government agencies, autonomous organizations, and public sector corporations import their requirements directly through tenders, which are publicly announced and/or issued to registered suppliers. Some of the major Government agencies that purchase their requirements directly include: Ministry of Defense through the Directorates of Procurement for Army, Navy, and Air Force; Department of Telegraph and Telephone; Pakistan International Airlines; Pakistan Railways; Karachi Shipyard and Engineering Works; Pakistan Atomic Energy Commission; Water and Power Development Authority; Pakistan Broadcasting Corporation; Pakistan Television Corporation; Oil and Gas Development Corporation; Pakistan Steel Mills Corporation Ltd.; and other corporations controlled by the Government. The Provincial Governments of Punjab, Sind, and North West Frontier and Baluchistan Province purchase equipment through their respective Directorates of Industry located in the provincial headquarters of Lahore, Karachi, Peshawar and Quetta, respectively.

Agent Registration

Local agents intending to participate in Government bids must register in accordance with the rules of the respective purchasing agency.

These agencies usually require Pakistani firms representing foreign manufacturers or suppliers to submit documentary proof of their agency agreements, attested to by the Embassy of the foreign firm. In some instances, the Government procurement office may require a local agent to prove he/she has an exclusive representation in Pakistan. Bank references of the foreign supplier may also be required. A deposit of earnest money is usually required with the submission of bid documents.

Transportation

Owned by the Central Government, the Pakistan Railway has 7,764 miles of tracks, of which more than 90 percent is broad gauge. In recent years, trucks have become increasingly successful competitors of rail transport. Pakistan's road network includes 30,000 miles of road, of which 10,000 miles is concrete or asphalt surfaced. Large proportions of the roads are in poor condition and not suitable for modern motor traffic.

The total size of the automotive market in Pakistan is approximately 40,000 to 45,000 vehicles a year, with a growth rate of 10 percent a year. Mini-commercial vehicles and tractors are top sellers. The market for imports, however, is very restrictive because Pakistan has committed itself to a firm policy for progressive domestic manufacturing of selected, standard makes of motor vehicles, including tractors. The import of assembled passenger vehicles is banned, and the domestic content of all vehicles made in Pakistan is expected to climb to 80 percent by 1985. Some opportunities do exist for joint ventures, for both auto and tractor assembly plants, as well as parts manufacturing. Interested U.S. firms should contact the General Manager, Pakistan Automobile Corporation, Sixth Floor, NSC Building, Moulvi Tamizuddin Khan Road, Karachi.

International airports are located at Karachi, Lahore, Rawalpindi, and Peshawar. The country is linked to other parts of the world by 28 different airlines. Pan American is the sole U.S. carrier to Pakistan, with two flights weekly originating in New York. Pakistan's one airline, Pakistan International Airline (PIA), has connecting domestic flights to 20 cities and towns. PIA also serves as Pakistan's flag carrier for international flights.

The shipping conference servicing U.S. companies exporting to Pakistan is the West Coast of India/Pakistan/USA/Conference located at 19th Rector Street, New York, New York 10006. Shipping time from the east coast of the United States to Karachi is between 15 and 20 days. American President Lines and Waterman Steamship Corporation maintain regular service from the United States to Pakistan. For further information pertaining to American flag service capabilities worldwide contact: Division of Commercial Cargo, Office of Market Development, Maritime Administration, U.S. Department of Transportation, Washington, D.C. 20590.

The size of Pakistan's only sea port at Karachi is being expanded from 24 to 28 berths. Construction is to be completed by 1984. Important improvements also include the mechanization of the cargo handling system, procurement of 19 mobile road cranes, and containerization equipment. Construction also is underway on a new port with eight berths near Karachi. This construction at Port Qasim is scheduled for completion by 1985. Contacts are: Chairman, Karachi Port Trust, Port Trust House, Karachi, and Chairman, Port Qasim Authority, Pipri, Karachi.

Advertising and Research

There are over a dozen major advertising agencies. Advertising agency commissions are usually 15 percent of the ad cost. Additional information concerning advertising agencies in Pakistan can be obtained from the Pakistan Advertising Association, 232 Hotel Metropole, Abdullah Haroon Road, Karachi.

While the daily press has a generally small circulation, and in some cases reproduction and illustration standards are not high, newspaper advertising is the most widely used method of advertising. Other media used include radio, television, billboards, trade journals and periodicals, and slides and commercial film shorts in movie theaters.

The principal English-language daily newspapers are Dawn, Pakistan Times, Business Recorder, the Muslim and Morning News. These dailies have an average sale ranging from 50,000 to 200,000 copies per day. The principal English-language weekly economic magazine is the Pakistan Economic Weekly.

Pakistan had approximately 700,000 television sets as of 1980. This figure is growing by 50,000 sets per year. Television reaches 62 percent of the population, and programming in English and Urdu totals 45 hours per week. The number of radios in Pakistan is estimated to be 1.5 million.

Medium-wave and short-wave broadcasts reach 100 percent of the population. The Government-owned headquarters for radio and television are located in Rawalpindi.

A few firms in the Karachi area have the capability to undertake market research.

Banking and Credit

Banking System

Pakistan's banking system consists of the State Bank of Pakistan, five nationalized banks, foreign banks, and development institutions. The State Bank of Pakistan, acting as the country's Central Bank, exercises control over the central reserve system, in which all banks must participate.

The Government fixes interest rates to encourage small farmers and Pakistan exporters. Subsistence farmers, for example, are granted interest-free loans. While exporters of machinery can obtain 2 percent loans, other exporters can obtain 3 percent loans. Eleven percent loans are given to investors in agriculture, other industries and hotels. The Central Bank discount rate in August 1981 was 10 percent. Commercial loans not eligible for discounts average 14 percent. The interest rate for savings deposits at commercial banks ranges between 7.5 and 8.5 percent.

The Central Bank sets monetary policy by controlling the amount of credit available under each of these interest rate categories. Although credit is expected to remain tight in each category over the next 2 to 3 years, businesses are expected to receive funds for projects given high priority by the Government. (see Industry Trends for sectors most likely to receive high priority.)

Pakistan's five nationalized banks are the National Bank of Pakistan, Habib Bank, United Bank, Muslim Commercial Bank, and Allied Bank. To cater to the requirements of the country, the banks have an extensive, nationwide network, with several having branches abroad. The National Bank is the leading commercial bank and the most active in the agricultural sector. The Muslim Commercial Bank and the Allied Bank are especially active in importing and exporting.

In 1981, the five nationalized banks initiated "interest-free" banking accounts. The new "profit-and-loss sharing" (PLS) accounts pay dividends based on the bank's profit and loss balance in lieu of fixed interest. The purpose of eliminating interest payments is Pakistan's determination to conform more closely to Islamic law, which prohibits interest but does allow a variety of other ways for lenders to earn a return on their investment. None of the foreign banks has opened PlS accounts. Foreign bankers expect no adverse reaction from this policy providing the Government takes no further steps in this area.

Fifteen foreign banks have branches in Pakistan. Four are U.S.: American Express, Bank of America, Chase Manhattan, and Citibank. Citibank also has a share in British-owned Grindlays Bank, which has branches in Pakistan. A number of Pakistan banks act as representatives of other U.S. banks, including Morgan Guaranty Trust, Irving Trust, Chase Manhattan, and Continental Illinois.

In addition to commercial banks, Pakistan has a large number of other sources for financing industrial and developmental projects. For U.S. business, the two most important sources are the Pakistan Industrial Credit and Investment Corporation (PICIC) and the Industrial Development Bank of Pakistan (IDBP), which is 51 percent government-owned. PICIC is primarily a source for foreign exchange loans for new and existing large industrial projects. As of December 1979, total loans and guarantees amounted to over $570 million, 95 percent of which were in foreign exchange. Major foreign exchange suppliers are the World Bank and various sources from the United States. PICIC loans normally range from $750,000 to $20 million. IDBP provides financing ranging from $500,000 to $20 million for medium- and small-scale industries in the private sector. Total loans have amounted to $260 million, of which 75 percent were in foreign exchange.

Credit

Short-term Credit. —The primary sources of short-term loans are commercial banks, both Pakistani and foreign. Foreign banks, including U.S. banks, can make loans up to $470,000 or 10 percent of their total capital, depending on which is greater.

Medium- and Long-term Credit. —The World Bank Group, through its two lending agencies, the International Development Association (IDA) and the International Bank for Reconstruction and Development (IBRD) has been a major source of credit for Pakistan Government projects. Through July 31, 1981, IDA has extended $864.6 million in low-interest loans to

Pakistan and the IBRD another $316.1 million at commercial market rates. In addition, Asian Development Bank (ADB) loans total $1.2 billion and technical assistance $4.1 million up to March 30, 1981.

The assistance of both banks has been in response to the Government of Pakistan's development priorities and has covered virtually all major sectors of the economy. For the future, they will continue to be major sources of funds for Pakistani development projects.

Information on the status of projects funded by international organizations is included in the monthly operational summaries and other announcements published by the information offices of the World Bank Group and ADB. Key contacts may be made through: World Bank Group, 1818 H Street, N.W., Washington, D.C. 20433; and Asian Development Bank, 2330 Roxas Boulevard (P.O. Box 789), Manila, Philippines.

Project information also can be obtained in the United States at the Export Information Reference Room, Room 1326, U.S. Department of Commerce, Washington, D.C. 20230, as well as through the U.S. Department of Commerce district offices. Notification of tenders and bid announcements can be obtained through the Department's Trade Opportunities Program.

U.S. assistance to Pakistan has until recently been limited to food programs because of U.S. laws restricting assistance to countries believed to be engaged in nuclear weapons research outside the scope of international safeguards. In September 1981, however, the U.S. lifted the restrictions on assistance to Pakistan and authorized a 5-year, $3.2 billion military and economic assistance program. While approximately half of this amount will be in direct military sales, the economic assistance portion is expected to generate opportunities for agricultural imports, especially phosphate fertilizer, irrigation equipment, and farm machinery. Significant opportunities also exist for energy development projects. Key contacts for this program are the Agency for International Development, 320 21st Street, N.W., Washington, D.C. 20523; and the U.S. Department of State, 2201 C Street, N.W., Washington, D.C. 20520.

The Export-Import Bank of the United States (Eximbank) long-term loans and financial guarantees to Pakistan amounted to $72.8 million as of mid-1981. Most of this was accounted for by the sale of aircraft to Pakistan's single airline, Pakistan International Airways (PIA). Additional information on Eximbank programs

can be obtained from the Export-Import Bank of the United States, 811 Vermont Avenue, N.W., Washington, D.C. 20571.

In 1980, the two stock exchanges in Pakistan, Karachi and Lahore, listed 309 securities. The Securities and Exchange Authority of Pakistan (SEAP), is in Karachi and regulates both exchanges. For foreign corporations, the exchanges provide a vehicle for offering equity shares in joint ventures to Pakistani citizens. Such offerings can increase the percentage of Pakistani ownership in joint ventures, a policy favored by the Government.

Trade Regulations

Import Policy

During 1980 and 1981, Pakistan liberalized its import policy for the private sector. This liberalization is expected to increase Pakistan's imports from $4.7 billion in 1980 to $6.3 billion by 1982. Government officials maintain the new policy will improve Pakistan's industrial efficiency, make the country's exports more competitive, and dampen inflation.

The International Monetary Fund (IMF) was instrumental in convincing Pakistan of the need for liberalization. The IMF granted Pakistan a $1.6 billion loan to assist in offsetting the expected increase in trade deficits.

Basic to the new liberalized policy is the expansion of Pakistan's official "Free" and "Tied" Lists of Imports to the private sector. The Free List has three parts: (1) goods that may be imported by all registered importers; (2) goods that can only be imported by public sector agencies/corporations/companies; and (3) goods that can only be imported by industrial users. The Free List consists of items importable either from worldwide sources against Pakistan's own foreign exchange or under aid credits and barter. The Tied List is comprised of items importable under barter or aid credit only. The Government prohibits the import of goods to the private sector that are not on either of these two lists. In addition, the Government uses a combination of restrictions and quotas on Free List items to limit imports into Pakistan to protect foreign exchange reserves.

The new policy has expanded the List of Permissible Imports in three ways. First, it increased the number of items on the Free List that can be imported by the private sector. Second, it expanded the total number of items on the Free List. Third, it moved items from the

Tied List to the Free List so that they could be imported on a cash basis. The items affected are raw materials—such as aluminum, copper zinc, and lead—some industrial chemicals, agricultural equipment, and various types of light machinery.

Besides an expansion of permissible imports, the new policy removed quotas on established importers and lifted its ban on the expansion of the number of importing firms. Also the Government no longer requires its prior approval for the import of new machinery up to $1 million on a cash basis for new projects with investments up to $2 million. Finally, the new policy abolished import ceilings for 10 consumer products—including ballpoint pens, dry cell batteries, and glucose—and it raised the ceiling on 28 others by 15 percent.

Pakistan announces changes to the Free and Tied Lists, as well as changes in restrictions or quotas on July 1, the beginning of each fiscal year. Further information on Pakistan's import policy can be obtained from the Pakistan Country Specialist, Office of Country Marketing, U.S. Department of Commerce, Washington, D.C. 20230.

Tariff Classification and Structures

Pakistan is a signatory to the General Agreement on Tariffs and Trade (GATT). In 1979, negotiations sponsored by GATT—often called the Tokyo Round—resulted in six major international proposals on nontariff measures. As of mid-1981, Pakistan has signed one, the Agreement on Subsidies and Countervailing Measures. This prescribes permissible limits on government subsidies to its industries.

Tariff Structure.—Pakistan uses a single column, Customs Cooperation Council Nomenclature (CCCN)—formerly called Brussels Tariff Nomenclature (BTN)—to classify and describe items. Ad valorem duties predominate. Most rates vary from free to 125 percent. Information regarding Pakistan duties applicable to specific products may be obtained from the Pakistan Desk, U.S. Department of Commerce, Washington, D.C. 20230, or from any Commerce Department district office. Inquiries should contain a complete product description, including CCCN or U.S. Schedule B Export Commodity numbers, if known.

Basis of Duty Assessment.—Pakistan customs authorities normally accept the invoice price as the dutiable value unless they doubt its reasonableness or authenticity. Where the invoice price is not available or acceptable, the dutiable value is the c.i.f. (cost, insurance and freight) value. Authorities assume this value includes the right to use any foreign patent, trademark, or design in respect to imported goods. The net weight is most commonly used to assess goods subject to specific duties.

Advance Rulings on Classification.— Importers or exporters may obtain advance rulings on the probable tariff classification of goods by submitting to the Collector of Customs, Karachi, a full description of the goods, accompanied (if practicable) by a sample. But custom authorities may revise their rulings on actual importation of goods.

Fines and Penalties.—If an exporter or importer attempts to import prohibited goods in Pakistan or if authorities find goods differing widely from the description in the bill of entry, the goods may be confiscated and the offender fined.

Authorities will confiscate goods warehoused illegally or in violation of warehousing regulations. Goods found in a warehouse in excess of those registered therein are subject to a fine of five times the ordinary duty on the excess products.

Pakistan has no special antidumping legislation.

Additional Charges.—The Government collects a 10 percent surcharge on all imports excepting those that are duty free or are specially exempted (petroleum products, tea, machinery, tractors, and used clothing). The 10 percent surcharge is on the cost and freight value of the imported product.

When foreign exchange reserves are low, Pakistan uses an additional "development tariff" to dampen the flow of imports. It applies to consumer goods imported during first 6 months of the year and ranges from 10 to 15 percent.

The Government levies a single point sales tax—10 to 30 percent in most cases—on a wide range of goods produced in, or imported into Pakistan. Items considered essential to the lower income groups are taxed at a reduced rate, usually 7.5 to 15 percent. Authorities tax raw materials and semimanufactures imported by a licensed manufacturer when the firm sells the finished products. They grant exemptions for capital goods, many food stuffs, cotton goods, goods manufactured in Pakistan for export, and certain other items.

Exporters and importers pay duties and other

charges in Pakistan rupees. Effective January 8, 1982, Pakistan un-linked its rupee from the U.S. dollar and floated the rupee on the basis of an undisclosed basket of foreign currencies. The rupee parity rate is now determined daily by the State Bank of Pakistan. As of late January 1982, the rate was Rs. 10.5 per U.S. dollar. By mid 1982 the rupee is expected to stabilize at about Rs. 11.00 to U.S. $1.00.

Metric System.—Pakistan uses the metric system as its standard for imports. Public sector agencies, the country's major importers, use metric measurements and specifications in tender documents. These agencies may ignore quotations not providing metric equivalents.

Entry and Reexport.—Pakistan has no free port facilities, but regulations permit similar privileges while goods are warehoused. Goods must be landed within the period specified on the bill of lading or within 15 working days after entry of the vessel in port. Once the goods have been entered and the duties assessed, the importer must clear them for consumption (by paying the duties and other assessed charges) or warehouse them. Ample public and bonded warehouse facilities, most of which are owned by the port trust organizations, exist for the storage of goods.

Export Processing Zone.—Work on an Export Processing Zone is underway at Karachi. U.S. and other foreign firms with 100 percent or less investment, all in foreign exchange, will be encouraged to establish processing facilities exclusively for export. Liberal incentives have been provided, including exemptions from customs duty, excise duty, sales tax, and other local taxes. Application of local labor laws may also be exempted and will not be subject to Pakistan's import/export or exchange control regulations. For approval, investors should apply to the Chief Executive of the Export Processing Zone Authority, Karachi, which, without involvement of any other authority, will process and permit investment within the Export Processing Zone.

Other Import Regulations

Shipping Documents.—Authorities require a commercial invoice and a bill of lading (or air waybill). Exporters should forward documents separately if shipment is by sea but should include them with air shipments. Certificates of origin are not legally required but may be requested by the consignee or his/her bank. When a certificate of origin is not requested, a statement as to the country of origin should appear on the invoice. Consular invoices are not required.

Custom authorities require special certificates for imports of plants and plant products.

Markings and Labeling Requirements.—Pakistan strictly enforces requirements for country of origin markings as distinct from certificates of origin on imported goods. Penalties range from detention or confiscation of the goods to imposition of fines.

Authorities assume any article bearing English words to be of British origin, unless otherwise marked. Every article, label, or wrapper bearing any English words must also bear an adequate, indelible indication of the country of origin. If more than one language is used on the article, the mark of origin should be repeated in all languages. Goods or packages entirely unmarked require no mark of origin. Special regulations apply for marking of textile piece goods, dyes, chemicals, and pharmaceuticals.

_____

Senate Concurrent Resolution 40, adopted July 30, 1953, invites U.S. exporters to inscribe insofar as practicable, on the external shipping containers in indelible print of a suitable size: "United States of America."

Import Licensing.—The Government issues licenses to the following: (1) any Pakistani national who has a registration certificate under the Registration of Importers and Exporters Order (1952); (2) all commercial importers and industrial consumers already registered under the above order; (3) importers without import registration who apply for an import license for an amount not exceeding $200 at a time; and (4) actual users without import registration provided the specified items are for their personal use only and do not exceed $200 in value.

Import licenses generally are valid for 6 months from the date of issue. Licenses for parts and accessories of machinery and mill work are valid for 12 months. In cases where the item must be specifically fabricated and the lead time is over 12 months, the license may be issued for a period of 24 months. For Tied List items, authorities validate licenses for 6 months and require a letter of credit to be opened within 45 days through banks designated by the State Bank of Pakistan.

Samples and Advertising Matter.—Pakistan collects no duty on printed advertising matter. Authorities admit samples duty free if they are only representative parts of a complete shipment or unsuitable for sale. The duties applicable to commercial shipments apply on samples having a commercial value. In the case of dutiable samples, seven-eigths of the duty paid may be refunded if samples are registered with customs at the time of arrival, are reexported within 2 years, and are identifiable by the customs collector when the refund is claimed.

Even for imports involving no remittance of foreign exchange Pakistan requires import permits. Authorities waive this requirement, however, in the case of: (1) written publicity materials in the form of brochures, posters, pamphlets, calendars, and technical literature supplied free of charge; and (2) bona fide samples within a specified limit, provided the importer and indentor is registered or has obtained exemption from registration.

Second-Hand Machinery and Tractors. — Under guidelines issued by the Department of Investigation Promotion Bureau, the Government of Pakistan permits the import of rebuilt machinery and secondhand tractors against externally held foreign exchange. Such machinery may be financed out of the earnings of Pakistani nationals working abroad or by foreign investors in Pakistan. In addition, the Bureau may approve the import of secondhand and reconditioned machinery by industrial consumers and construction firms.

Exchange Controls

To control the outflow of foreign exchange, the Government limits imports by using Free and Tied Lists (see Import Policy section), and only Government-approved commercial banks can handle private foreign exchange transactions. All foreign exchange must be bought and sold at rates set by the State Bank of Pakistan. The State Bank also raises or lowers margin requirements against import letters of credit. During 1981, most goods required a 25 to 30 percent margin, while many industrial raw materials required none. Sufficient supplies of foreign exchange, made available under the 1980 loan from the IMF, should preclude the need of the State Bank from drastically changing margin requirements over the next 2 years.

Transactions with U.S. exporters are generally conducted through confirmed, irrevocable letters of credit. The letter of credit must specify that the shipment must be made on or before the expiration date of the import license. To collect the credit, the U.S. exporters must present an on-board bill of lading and a signed commercial invoice.

Export Policy

Pakistan strongly encourages exports. It exempts from import duty most machinery used to establish new textile manufacturing units and to improve all other types of existing manufacturing units. Also exempt are most raw materials used by export industries. Many tax incentives are available to exporters. In addition, the Government provides compensatory rebates on the export of cotton yarn, textiles, and a number of other domestic manufactured products.

Pay As You Earn (PAYE) Scheme. —PAYE provides guaranteed but deferred payment for capital goods and equipment used in 55 export-oriented industries. The plan allows advance payment in foreign exchange for 15 percent of the cost and freight value of the equipment. Further, businesses may remit foreign exchange earnings attributed to the operation of the equipment, plus royalties and various incidental expenses. If this allotment does not meet the debt service liability, the State Bank will authorize a shortfall subject to a penalty of 27 percent.

Details about this scheme and other export incentives may be obtained by writing to the Export Information and Advisory Center, Export Promotion Bureau, Shareef Place, Outram Road, Karachi (Cable address: EXPROM).

Investment in Pakistan

General Policy

Under President Zia, the Government's announced policy is to encourage foreign investment, reversing a nationalization trend that prevailed during the mid-1970's. This reversal stems from the importance the country now places on foreign private investment for accelerating industrial development. Especially encouraged are foreign investments in industrial sectors requiring sophisticated technology or large amounts of capital and in export-oriented and import-substitution industries.

Steps taken to improve the investment climate include a law passed in 1979 to strengthen foreign investment protection against uncompensated nationalization. A few previously nationalized industrial units have been returned to their former owners. The Government now encourages private investment in some industrial sectors previously reserved for the public sector such as cement, edible oils, chemicals, fertilizers, tractors, heavy duty engineering, automobiles, and basic metals.

Despite these efforts, political uncertainties and lingering problems with the bureaucracy have caused investment to remain at a level far below the Government's expectations. Private investors especially complain about delays in obtaining Government approval, price controls that severely depress profit margins, and overzealous interpretation of tax laws. Occasional restrictions on imports of raw materials occur due to lack of foreign exchange.

Amount of Foreign Investment

The value of U.S. private direct foreign investment in Pakistan at the end of 1978 was $145 million. Major U.S. investments are in fertilizer projects undertaken by American Cyanamid, Hercules, and Exxon Chemical in response to the needs of Pakistan's large agricultural sector. More recently, U.S. petroleum companies have been investing in oil exploration.

Details of total foreign investment in Pakistan are not officially published, but, according to the State Bank of Pakistan's annual balance of payments figures, direct foreign investment between 1971 and 1979 totaled $270 million. Based on estimates from this same data, U.S. investment accounts for the largest share, followed by the United Kingdom. The pattern is changing, however, as Middle East oil countries increased their direct investment in Pakistan.

Treaties and Agreements

To facilitate commercial relationships, the United States has signed a Treaty of Friendship and Commerce and an Investment and Guaranty Agreement with Pakistan. The Treaty of Friendship and Commerce provides a comprehensive, legal framework within which enterprises and nationals of either country can make investments, carry on business within the territories of the other, and settle disputes. It also contains provisions assuring basic personal freedoms and protection of persons and property and grants most-favored-nation status to nationals, corporations, and trade goods of each country.

Under the Investment and Guaranty Agreement, the United States can offer insurance to new investors to minimize risks of currency inconvertibility, expropriation, war, revolution, or insurrection. This agreement also provides for assistance with investment finance, primarily through guarantees of private loan or equity investments. It is administered by the Overseas

Private Investment Corporation (OPIC), which also provides investment counsel, makes direct loans of dollars or local foreign currencies, and provides other investor services. Further information may be obtained from the Overseas Private Investment Corporation, 1129 20th Street, N.W., Washington, D.C. 20527.

Joint Ventures

No law exists limiting the level of foreign equity participation in Pakistan. While the normal practice is to limit foreign ownership to the value of imported equipment, technology and expertise, this constraint can be removed in areas where foreign technology or expertise is especially needed. Pakistan is also interested in establishing joint ventures in areas of priority interest even though they may be reversed for the public sector.

In actual practice, foreign companies have found it advantageous to limit themselves to joint venture shareholding of up to 49 percent. Furthermore, most new investors find advantage in a strong local partner who is effective in dealing with the Pakistani Government and private parties.

Licensing

The Department of Investment Promotion and Supplies appproves foreign licensing agreements. Approval is usually granted within 3–9 months. Technical fees to cover research and use of patents and trademarks are generally easier to negotiate than know-how royalties. The Government encourages local procurement and discourages arrangements to purchase parts or materials from the licensor. Companies may enter into technical assistance and know-how agreements.

Organized Private Support of Foreign Investment

The Overseas Investor Chamber of Commerce and Industry (see Sources of Economic and Commercial Information for address) is the principal private organization that serves the interest of foreign investors, more than 90 percent of whom are members. The Chamber is often consulted by the Government in matters relating to foreign investment.

There is no American Chamber of Commerce and Industry and it is not clear whether existing law would permit the formation of such a body.

Investment Approval Procedure

All foreign firms and individuals intending to start a business, enter into a partnership, or change existing agreements in Pakistan must first obtain written permission from the Investment Promotion Bureau (IPB), Karachi. Investors must also receive approval in the following four areas.

Screening.—All applications to establish new units or expand existing ones involving foreign investments must be made to the Department of Investment Promotion and Supplies (Investment Promotion Wing), Karachi. Application forms can be obtained on request from the Department free of charge.

Registration.—A business in Pakistan may be organized as a sole proprietorship, a partnership, or an incorporated or unincorporated association. Foreign investors establishing enterprises in Pakistan usually form corporations or "companies" as corporate enterprises are called in Pakistan.

Government regulations require that companies register their memorandum and articles of association with the Registrar of Joint-Stock Companies. Partnerships may register under the Partnership Act with the Registrar of Firms, although this is not required. Unregistered firms, however, are unable to enforce claims against third parties, and any partner of such a firm is unable to enforce his/her claims against either third parties or against fellow partners.

Issuance of Capital.—No company or industrial undertaking may issue capital or invest in shares of securities without the consent of the Controller of Capital Issues, Ministry of Finance, Government of Pakistan, Islamabad. No firm can raise a loan against the assets of a company or industrial undertaking unless authorized by the Controller. General instructions to be followed can be obtained from the Controller.

Import License.—A foreign investor in possession of permission to invest in Pakistan is required to make application to the Director General of Investment Promotion Bureau, Industries Division, Ministry of Industry, Government of Pakistan, Karachi, for import license for any plants or machinery required for the investment. In past years, some firms, both domestic and foreign have experienced difficulties in securing sufficient import licenses for raw materials, components, and spare parts needed to keep their factories in full production.

Agreements between the Government and for-eign investors engaged in packaging or assembly operations sometimes specify that the investor must progressively increase the use of Pakistani raw materials and parts. Prospective U.S. investors in projects that will require imported materials are urged to review carefully all agreements, which define the types and amounts of raw materials and spares the investor or his or her firm will be allowed to import.

Pakistan's investment procedures—from the submission of the proposal to the receiving of import licenses—often take months and even longer to complete. Even though the Investment Promotion Board will assist in completing these procedures, the Government recognizes the need for reducing the investment approval time and has stated its intention to "streamline and simplify" its current procedures.

Foreign Ownership of Real Property

Foreigners may freely own land and buildings, subject only to regulations applicable to everybody. Mineral concessions, except for petroleum and minerals of interest to the Pakistan Atomic Energy Commission, are the responsibility of the Minerals Department of Provincial Governments in Karachi, Lahore, Peshawar, and Quetta. The Pakistan Mineral Development Corporation handles the exploitation of minerals in the public sector; petroleum concessions, petroleum pricing, and other related functions are the responsibility of the Ministry of Fuel, Power and Natural Resources; and all other petroleum and natural gas functions pertain to the Oil and Gas Development Corporation. The Resources Development Corporation has been established to exploit Baluchistan Province copper deposits.

The basic act governing the development of Pakistan's mineral resources is the Regulation of Mines and Oil-Field and Mineral Development (Federal Control) Act, 1948, amended and supplemented by the Mining Concessions Rules, 1960, and the Petroleum Production Rules, 1949. The Regulation of Mines Act of 1948 empowers the Central Government to enact legislation and issue rules on granting exploration licenses, prospecting licenses, and mining concessions; refining minerals; and fixing prices and controlling production, storage, and the distribution of minerals and mineral oils.

The Mining Concession Rules of 1960 regulate the granting of prospecting licenses and mining leases for most minerals other than petroleum and natural gas.

The Petroleum Production Rules of 1949 regulate the issuance of certificates of approval for exploration and prospecting licenses and mining leases for petroleum and natural gas concessions.

Industrial Property Protection

Pakistan has laws for the protection of patents, trademarks, and copyrights. Although Pakistan is not a member of the Paris Convention for the Protection of Industrial Property (principally patents and trademarks), it has joined the World Intellectual Property Organization (WIP), effective January 6, 1977. Pakistan accords U.S. citizens national treatment in patent and trademark matters. It is a member of the Universal Copyright convention and the Berne Copyright Union.

Patents.—Patent applications should be addressed to the Patent Office, 30-A Maqbool Chambers, Shaheed-e-Millat, Karachi. Patent applications are subject to a novelty examination. On acceptance, the application is published for opposition. The opposition period is 4 months. Patents are granted for 16 years and may, in unusual cases, be extended an additional 5 to 10 years. Pakistani law permits the licensing of patents. Patents are subject to compulsory licensing within 3 years if not worked or if inadequately worked in Pakistan.

Trademarks and Brand Names.—Applications for the registration of trademarks should be addressed to the Trademarks Registry, 67 Islamabad, Karachi. The right to a trademark registration belongs to the first user of the mark. A registration is valid for an initial period of 6 years and may be renewed for 15-year periods thereafter.

Copyright.—An author who owns a copyright in the United States or any country that is a member of the Universal Copyright Convention automatically receives copyright protection in Pakistan. Pakistani copyrights are valid for the life of the author and for 50 years after his or her death. According to the Copyright (Amendment) Ordinance of 1972, the Central Government has been given power to reprint, translate, adapt, and publish any works for the purposes of teaching, studying, or researching in educational institutions. Additional information on laws and regulations regarding the protection of patents, trademarks, and copyrights in Pakistan may be obtained from the Foreign Business Practices Division, Office of International Services, U.S. Department of Commerce, Washington, D.C. 20230.

Repatriation of Capital and Remittance of Profits

Investors may repatriate foreign capital from Government-approved industries established after September 1, 1954, at any time up to the amount of the original investment. Investors may treat profits reinvested in approved projects and appreciated capital investment as investment for repatriation purposes. To determine the investment value of goods and services, Pakistan uses the rupee value recorded in company books. Repatriation rights do not extend to the purchase of shares on the stock exchange unless the purchase is an integral part of an approved investment project. A prospective investor may wish to obtain a guaranty of capital repatriation from the Investment Protection Bureau, Karachi, at the time of application for approval of the investment. The guaranty is communicated to the applicant along with the approval of the investment.

Taxation

Personal Taxes.—Personal income tax rates range from 15 to 60 percent depending on the level of income. The Government imposes a surcharge equivalent to 10 percent of stated income tax on individuals with taxable income over $5,000. All individuals earning an income in Pakistan must pay income tax, and no provision exists for deductions for dependents.

Pakistan defines taxable income as employment income, business and professional income, interest, rents, royalties and technical assistance fees, and income arising from property. Not included is income from agriculture or capital gains. Dividend income from public corporations is taxed only above the first $1,500.

Corporate Taxes.—Private companies pay an income tax at a rate of 30 percent on taxable income plus a Super Tax of 25 percent for a total of 55 percent. The Super Tax on banking companies is 35 percent; it ranges from zero to 30 percent on registered partnerships, depending on income. On top of these taxes, companies pay a 10 percent surcharge on collectable taxes.

Taxable income for companies and partnerships include business and professional income; income from interest, rents, royalties; and technical assistance fees; but not agricultural income or capital gains. Income is taxed after deduction of exempt income, casualty losses, and deductible expenses. Deductible expenses include: Salaries, rents, bad debts, repairs, insurance premiums, and interest on business and depreciation allowance loans for the purpose of the business. Dividends received by a private company are not included in taxable income but are subject to a 30 percent Super Tax.

The Central Government's 1974 moratorium on the taxation of capital gains is still in effect. Provincial governments, however, tax income resulting from the sale of immobile property (such as buildings), while both provincial and city governments collect some property taxes.

To make income distribution more egalitarian as required by Islamic Law, the Government imposed a wealth tax (called Zakat) in 1980. It applies to all Muslim and majority Pakistan-owned companies at a rate of 2.5 percent on assets. To avoid undue loss of investment confidence, the government can be expected to make further moves with extreme caution.

Tax Incentives. —A variety of tax incentives exist. These incentives include: a 55 percent return on all taxes generated by export income, a 5-year tax holiday on industrial undertakings in Baluchistan Province and other specified underdeveloped regions, tax credits ranging from 15 to 30 of the cost of machinery that will improve productivity, and a major increase in depreciation allowances for firms employing a double and triple shift. Pakistan uses these incentives to encourage the establishment of industries in underdeveloped regions, to modernize the textile and other export industries, and to promote export substitution industries.

Double Tax Protection. —A double taxation convention between the United States and Pakistan has been in effect since 1959.

Employment

Labor Force

Population is currently estimated at 84 million. According to 1981 preliminary census estimates, the self-supporting civilian labor force is 24 million, with 55 percent engaged in agriculture and 12 percent in manufacturing. Pakistan continues to have a shortage of administrative, managerial, professional, and technical skills.

Labor productivity is low because of the shortage of skills, a high rate of absenteeism, dietary deficiencies, and generally poor living and working conditions. In spite of the prevalence of unemployment and underemployment in Pakistan, labor shortages occur as a result of labor exodus to the relatively large and lucrative Middle East market.

Labor Costs

In the larger towns, unskilled workers earn approximately $2.50 per day; semiskilled workers $4; and skilled workers $10. Although basic labor rates are low, overall labor costs are not as low as might first appear because of the low output and absenteeism, mentioned above as well as liberal leave benefits. Other expenses include cost-of-living allowances or bonus payments plus housing, medical, retirement, and other benefits. Representatives of the textile industry estimate that an unskilled worker's legislated minimum wage of $14 per month actually costs employers three times as much because of these fringe benefits and allowances. In addition, foreign enterprises are expected to pay higher wages and provide superior benefits to their employees. Rarely are employees of foreign enterprises paid less than $100 per month including fringe benefits.

Labor Policy

Besides the financial benefits, Palistani labor laws provide that:

1. Workers will be given participation in management.

2. Each shop or department in a large industrial unit should have a shop steward who will represent the workers' interest and point of view in the management of that shop and will act as a link between the workers and management.

3. Every establishment employing 50 or more persons is to have a Works Council consisting of representatives of employers and employees. The Works Council promotes measures for securing and preserving good relations and particularly promotes settlement of differences through bilaterial negotiations.

Labor Organization and Relations

Estimates place membership of the country's large unions at about 1 million. Most trade unions are formed by the workers in a single factory. Industrial, craft, or nationwide unions in the same trade or industry are virtually nonexistent.

Since the imposition of strict martial law in 1977, the Government has banned strikes and lockouts. Although this ban has created apparent industrial peace, there are undercurrents of dissatisfaction because of a relatively slow increase in wages in the last 2 years.

Employers have especially complained about the difficulty in discharging an employee. To discuss this and other labor relations issues, the Government formed a Tripartite Labor Conference representing the Government, workers, and employers, but thus far the Conference has been unable to find a way that is acceptable to both labor and management.

Employment of Foreign Nationals

Foreigners must submit applications for employment to the Investment Promotion Bureau in Karachi on a prescribed form. The Government expects that expatriates will only be employed as necessary to take care of specialized jobs for which Pakistanis of suitable qualifications and experience are not yet available. Foreign companies must undertake a progressive increase in the percentage of Pakistanis in management positions. The Government requires annual reports showing both progress toward this goal and future plans, but a foreign-owned firm may permanently maintain a foreigner as its chief executive.

Foreigners employed in Pakistan are permitted to make monthly remittances to their home country out of their savings to cover family maintenance, insurance premiums, educational expenses of children, legal charges, mortgage payments, loans, interest, etc. Such remittances are allowed up to 50 percent of net income subject to a maximum of $500 per month or its equivalent. Authorized banks allow remittances for family maintenance, subject to presentation of the permission letter for employment in Pakistan issued by the Investment Promotion Bureau.

Upon leaving Pakistan and presenting documentary evidence, foreigners are permitted to request transfer of their savings overseas by the State Bank of Pakistan.

Guidance for Business Travelers

Entrance Requirements

Pakistan requires no visas for U.S. citizens passing through Pakistan in 15 days or less or visiting Pakistan for less than 30 days. Single journey visas are issued for a stay of 3 months. Unusual circumstances may change visa requirements. Visitors are advised to check with the Pakistan Embassy in Washington or the Consulate General in New York. (See addresses in Sources of Economic and Commercial Information.)

Smallpox and cholera inoculations are required. Typhus, typhoid, and yellow fever immunizations are recommended. Americans going to this area should check the nearest office of the U.S. Public Health Service for information on any unusual occurrences that might necessitate additional protection.

Exchange Controls

Visitors entering or leaving Pakistan are limited to 100 rupees, but no restriction exists on foreign currency.

Travelers may exchange currency only at banks and hotels authorized by the State Bank of Pakistan. Reconversion facilities for unspent rupees is limited to Rs. 150 per person. Travelers need prior State Bank approval for transactions exceeding this amount.

Business Customs

Although business is conducted on a somewhat more leisurely pace than American visitors may be accustomed to, a "down to business" attitude is also characertistic. Pakistani businesspeople have a definite pro-Western bias, and Americans are welcomed in Pakistan as friends.

Urdu is the national language, but English is widely accepted in Government and business throughout Pakistan.

Calls on Pakistani Government officials and commercial establishments are best scheduled for morning and early afternoon. Central Government offices are open from 7:30 a.m. to 2:30 p.m., Saturday through Thursday. Offices are closed on Friday. The U.S. Embassy and Consulates are open from 8 a.m. to 4:30 p.m., Sunday through Thursday.

Clothing

Local taste and tailoring in men's clothing are similar to that in the United States. During the long, hot summer, entertainment is usually casual and either short sleeved or sport (bush) shirts are worn.

Women's dress is similar to that in the United States but more modest. In the office and within the Western community, anything acceptable in the United States is appropriate. On the street, however, and in the bazaars or rural areas, women are advised not to wear short skirts, low-necked or sleeveless dresses, or tight or revealing shorts or pants.

Health Standards

Sanitation throughout Pakistan is a constant problem. The public water supply is unsafe everywhere. Drinking water must be boiled; sewage systems are antiquated or inadequate; refuse collection is erratic; and refrigeration and sanitary packaging of foodstuffs in public markets are rare.

Hotels

International hotels with good accommodations are located in all major cities in Pakistan. They include: the Intercontinental, Metropole, and Mehran in Karachi; the Holiday Inn and Islamabad Hotel in Islamabad and the Intercontinental and Hilton Lahore International in Lahore.

Tourist Information

Tourist Information Centers are located at: Karachi, Shafi Chambers, Hotel Intercontinental, and the International Arrival Lounge, Karachi Airport; Islamabad, Islamabad Hotel; Lahore, 5, Transport House.

Holidays

The following national, religious, and public holidays were scheduled for observance by the Central Government and most commercial establishments during calendar year 1982: January 8—Eid-I-Milad-Un-Nabi; March 23—Pakistan Day; May 1—May Day; July 1—Bank Holiday; July 24 and 25—Eid-Ul-Fitr; August 14—Independence Day; September 6—Defense of Pakistan Day; September 11—Death Anniversary of Quaid-i-Azam; September 29 and 30, and October 1—Eid-Ul-Azha; October 27 and 28—Ninth and Tenth of Muharram; December 25—Birthday of Quaid-i-Azam and Christmas; December 28—Eid-i-Milan-un-Nabi; December 31—Bank Holiday.

Bank holidays, July 1 and December 31, are for banks only. The seven religious holidays are subject to visual sighting of the moon and thus could vary from the dates noted above.

Sources of Economic and Commercial Information

Numerous chambers of commerce and industry and industrial and trade associations are lo-cated in Pakistan's major cities. All are affiliated with the Federation of Pakistan Chambers of Commerce and Industry, located at St-28 Sharah-e-Firdousi, Block 5, Kehkeshan, Main Clifton, Karachi. Although there is no American Chamber of Commerce, many U.S. firms operating in Pakistan are members of the Overseas Investors Chamber of Commerce and Industry located at the Karachi Chamber of Commerce Building, Talpur Road, Karachi. Other trade organizations in Pakistan are the Lahore Chamber of Commerce and Industry, 11 Race Course Road, P.O. Box 597, Lahore; and the Karachi Chamber of Commerce and Industry, Aiwan-e-Tijarat Road, Karachi.

In the United States, the U.S.-Pakistan Economic Council promotes trade with and the investment in Pakistan. The Council is a private, nonprofit association of U.S. and Pakistani business firms. It publishes a bimonthly newsletter, holds monthly information meetings in New York, and sponsors periodic commercial missions to Pakistan. The address is: U.S.-Pakistan Economic Council, Inc., Professional Building, 55 Lake Avenue, St. James, New York 11780 (tel. 212/662-861).

Government Representation

Government of Pakistan representation in the United States includes Pakistan Embassy, 2315 Massachusetts Avenue, N.W., Washington, D.C. 20008; and Pakistan Consulate General, 12 E. 65th Street, New York, New York 10021.

The United States Embassy is in Islamabad at the AID/UN Building, P.O. Box 1048 (tel. 24071; telex 82-05-864). Consulate addresses are: Karachi, 8 Abdullah Haroon Road (tel. 515081; telex 82-02-611); Lahore, 50 Zafar Ali Road, Gulberg 5 (tel. 870221); Peshawar, 11 Hospital Road (tel. 73405). The U.S. Department of Commerce Foreign Commercial Officer for Pakistan is located in Karachi. U.S. Department of State Economic/Commercial Officers are located in Islamabad and Lahore. These officers assist American businesspeople visiting Pakistan.

Publications

Budget 1981–82 in Brief, Finance Division, Islamabad. (Yearly)

Foreign Trade, Statistics Division, Government of Pakistan, 1 S.M.C.H. Society, Post Box No. 7766, Karachi-3. (Monthly)

Industrial Investment Schedule for Fifth Five-Year Plan, 1978 to 1983. Ministry of Industries and Investment Promotion Bureau, Islamabad.

Pakistan Economic Survey, 1980–1981, Government of Pakistan, Finance Division, Economic Advisors Wing, Islamabad. (Yearly)

Pakistan's Key Economic Indicators. Statistics Division, Government of Pakistan, 1 S.M.C.H. Society, Post Box No. 7766, Karachi-3. (Monthly)

Statistical Bulletin, Statistics Division, Government of Pakistan, 1 S.M.C.H. Society, Post Box No. 7766, Karachi-3. (Monthly)

Other Pakistani Publications

Federation of Pakistan Chamber of Commerce and Industry, *Directory of Exporters*, 1981, Reprographic Offset Press, Karachi.

U.S. Department of Commerce Publications:

Foreign Economic Trends and Their Implications for The United States (FET)—Pakistan (annual)

Market Profiles for Asia and Oceania, OBR 80-14, December 1980.

Other Publications:

Exporters Encylopedia: Pakistan, 1981. Dun and Bradstreet, International Ltd., 99 Church Street, New York, New York 10007.

International Trade Reporter, 1981, *Pakistan,* The Bureau of National Affairs, 1231 25th Street, N.W., Washington, D.C. 20037.

Investing, Licensing & Trading Conditions Abroad, Pakistan, 1981, Business International Corporation, 575 Third Avenue, New York, New York 10017.

Market Profile—PAKISTAN

Foreign Trade

Imports.—$5,486.3 million, PFY 1980–81; $4,864, PFY 1979–80. Major suppliers: Japan (11.6 percent), United States (11.1 percent), Kuwait (10.1 percent), Saudi Arabia (6.9 percent), and United Kingdom (6.1 percent). Principal imports: Petroleum and petroleum products, machinery, transport equipment, iron and steel, and fertilizer.

Exports.—$2,598 million, PFY 1980–81; $2,341, PFY 1979–80. Major export markets: Hong Kong (7.9 percent), Japan (7.7. percent), China (6.2 percent), West Germany (6.1 percent), and Saudi Arabia (5.4 percent).

Trade Policy.—Licenses required for all imports. Permissible imports are itemized under two lists: Free— importable from worldwide sources, and Tied—importabl e exclusively from specific countries under credit, loan, or barter arrangements. Import of certain items is limited to public sector agencies.

Trade Prospects.—The best prospects for U.S. exporters to Pakistan are in the areas of chemicals, fertilizers, telecommunications equipment, port equipment, power generation and distribution equipment, steel scrap, edible oils, drilling and oilfield equipment, textile machinery, food processing equipment, and hotel industry equipment.

Foreign Investment

Direct foreign investment between 1971 and 1979 is estimated to total $270 million. The value of U.S. private direct investment was $100 million at the end of 1978.

Investment Prospects.—The Government welcomes foreign investment in certain areas. An investment schedule published by the Government lists investment opportunities. Major stress is on sugar refining. textiles, fertilizers, petrochemicals, cement, mineral development, and agricultural machinery.

Finance

Currency.—Pakistan rupee. Exchange rate: Rs 9.84 = US$1 (October 1980).

Domestic Credit and Investment.—Limited short- and long-term credit availability. Ceilings are placed on local borrowing by foreign-controlled firms, based on level of equity.

National Budget. Expenditures for PFY 1980–81 are estimated at $5.82 billion.

Foreign Aid.—Major sources of assistance are the World Bank, Consortium countries, and oil exporting countries. Assistance averages over $1 billion annually.

Balance of Payments.—In FY 1980–81, Pakistan's trade deficit was slightly more than $2.5 billion, but overseas remittances make up most of this deficit.

Economy

GNP.—GNP in current prices is estimated at $27.8 billion in PFY 1980–81 ($23.3 billion in 1979–80).

Agriculture.—About 43 percent of total cultivated acreage was assigned to wheat, 15 percent to cotton, 12 percent to rice.

Industry.—Cotton textile production is the largest industry, employing well over half the industrial labor force. Other important sectors are cement, fertilizers, sugar, industrial chemicals, and petroleum refining.

Commerce.—PFY 1980–81 wholesale price index up 20.2 percent; consumer price index up 15 percent.

Development Plan.—The fifth Five-Year Development Plan, covering the period 1978–79 to 1982–83, calls for investments of about $4 billion.

Tourism.—Almost 300,000 tourist arrivals in 1978. Tourism receipts totaled $83 million in 1978.

Basic Economic Facilities

Transportation.—The Government-owned railway consists of 5,475 route miles. The road network totals about 31,000 miles, of which about 16,000 are paved. Karachi is the major seaport, with an annual handling capacity of 10 million tons of cargo. The national airline provides services to major cities, to important tourist attractions, and to more than 20 countries.

Communications.—Telegraph and telephone facilities are Government-operated and provide links to major cities and towns in Pakistan and internationally. There are five television stations.

Power.—Total generating capacity was 3,535 MW in 1981. Supply of electricity is still considerably short.

Natural Resources

Land.—310,000 square miles. The land is relatively arid except for the fertile Indus river valley. Mountainous terrain is found in the northwest and west.

Climate.—Temperatures vary from 40 degrees F in winter to 120 degrees F in summer. Average annual rainfall is low.

Minerals.—Except for large natural gas reserves, an oil field, and Baluchistan copper deposits for which development is planned, known mineral resources are minimal.

Forestry.—Forest areas represent about 10 percent of the land area; however, much consists of unproductive scrub.

Fisheries.—Production estimated at 263,000 tons in PFY 1980–81. Export earnings from fisheries was $56.6 million in PFY 1979–80. Shellfish account for 84 percent of fish exports.

Population

Size.—About 84 million; 26 percent urban. Density more than 200 per square mile. Cities with population of more than 250,000 are: Karachi, Lahore, Hyderabad, Lyallpur, Multan, Rawalpindi, Peshawar, Quetta, and Sialkot.

Ethnic Division.—Punjabi, Sindhi, Pushtun (Pathan), Baluchi.

Religion.—97 percent Muslim.

Doing Business with Panama

Contents

Report Revised July 1984

Introduction

Panama is the country bridging Central and South America. Factors contributing to Panama's unique position in Latin America include: the Panama Canal, use of the U.S. dollar as the medium of exchange, the presence of over 125 foreign banks with total assets in excess of $49 billion, and the operations of the Colón Free Zone, the largest free trade area in the Western Hemisphere. Panama, including the Colón Free Zone, is now the largest export market for the United States in the Caribbean and Central American region, and U.S. investment in Panama is one of the highest in the entire Latin American area. These elements act together to offer U.S. companies attractive commercial opportunities in Panama. This report is designed to inform U.S. firms of the many export and investment opportunities in Panama and to provide basic information on doing business there.

Foreign Trade Outlook

Panama's market is dual in nature. One distinct market is made up of Panama's imports for domestic consumption; the other is the Colón Free Zone, where goods are imported, warehoused and then re-exported to third countries in the Caribbean and in Central and South America. (For more information on the Colón Free Zone, see page 1839 below). In 1982, imports into the Colón Free Zone alone exceeded $1.7 billion, while imports into the rest of Panama amounted to approximately $1.4 billion. The combined Panamanian and Colón Free Zone 1982 imports of $3.1 billion make this market the region's largest.

This high import level in relation to size (2.0 million population and $4.2 billion GDP in 1982) can be attributed principally to relatively high per capita income levels for the area and to a dependence on imports as a result of a narrow industrial base and an inefficient agricultural sector.

U.S. exports to the Panamanian market over the last 5 years have roughly followed Panama's overall economic growth. Beginning in the late 1970's and continuing through the first part of 1981, Panama grew at an accelerated rate, and U.S. exports to Panama grew proportionately. According to U.S. Department of Commerce data, U.S. exports to Panama (including the Colón Free Zone) grew from $364.2 million in 1974 to $832.5 million in 1981, before falling to $825.2 million in 1983.

Presented in table 1 are Panama's leading import market categories. Drawn from Panamanian statistics, they represent 72 percent of all imports into Panama and 42 percent of all imports into the Colón Free Trade Zone. For comparative purposes the tables below show the percentage of the import market held by a given country in a particular product category. To arrive at absolute dollar figures from the percentages, multiply them by the total dollar value presented in the last column.

Best Export Prospects

The products and services discussed in this section offer significant opportunities to U.S. exporters due to their importance in the Panamanian economy, their growth prospects and/or U.S. competitive advantage. The mix reflects the dual character of Panama's market, with the Colón Free Zone importing a larger quantity of goods for eventual reexport than the country imports for its own consumption. The list should be considered indicative and not all-inclusive; market conditions, especially those in a small developing country, can change rapidly, making specific market forecasts difficult.

Engineering, Architectural and Consulting Services.— As a developing country, Panama is in the process of expanding and upgrading its infrastructure. Roads, bridges, ports, utilities, schools, and airports are being constructed or improved. To assist in the feasibility studies for these projects, as well as their design and supervision of construction, foreign firms are being employed. While there is no hard data on the size and composition of the market for these services in Panama, it is estimated that the public and private sectors spent over $15 million in 1981 on consulting services, with U.S. companies receiving a majority of the contracts. U.S. consulting engineering and architectural firms must register with the Government's Pre-Investment Fund before they may participate in Government projects. For more information about registration, U.S. firms may wish to contact the Technical and Operations Secretary, Pre-Investment Fund, Ministry of Planning and Economic Policy, P.O. Box 2694, Panama 3. Panama (telephone: 69-5435).

*Materials Handling Machinery.—*Although the $7.1 million market in Panama in 1982 for this product line was not a major one, it is anticipated that moderate growth will occur within the next five years. The expected increase is based on the expansion plans of the Colón Free Zone (see page 1839) and on the plans to develop light industrial parks throughout the country, particularly in areas that recently reverted to Panama as a consequence of the Canal treaties, and on plans for major improvements in the Cristóbal and Balboa ports.

The most promising product lines include computerized warehouse locators, multi-line conveyors, stacking systems, lift trucks and general packing equipment and supplies.

*Automotive Parts and Accessories.—*Panamanian imports of automotive parts and accessories have increased steadily for several years. Notwithstanding a declining U.S. share of the automotive import market in Panama, the volume of U.S.-made automotive parts and accessories exported to Panama has increased. This trend is the result of the preference of Panamanian owners of Japanese, European and Korean cars for U.S.-made replacements parts and automotive accessories which are more easily obtainable than those made by the original manufacturer. Delays in shipments, recurrent price increases, and problems occasioned by shifts of foreign currency values make it more difficult for local parts dealers to maintain adequate stocks of non-U.S. parts to serve a growing market.

Table 1—Imports to Panama by Type and Origin, 1981-82

(in percent of total)

Industry and Subgroup	U.S.		Japan		Colón Free Zone		W. Germany		Mexico		Various Countries (identified)		Other Countries		Total (in thousands of dollars)	
	1981	1982	1981	1982	1981	1982	1981	1982	1981	1982	1981	1982	1981	1982	1981	1982
Const. Equip.															39,668	36,375
Wheel Tractors	44.0	53.0	4.3	10.0	9.0	—	7.2	7.0	—	—			35.0	30.0	6,022	5,853
Tracklaying Tractors	79.0	86.0	4.4	4.0	—	—	—	—	—	—			16.6	10.0	23,046	17,439
Mech. Shovels	80.0	14.0	—	—	—	52.3	—	—	—	—			20.0	33.7	46	172
Oth. Cons. Mchy.	60.0	78.0	13.0	4.0	11.2	14.0	—	—	—	—			15.8	4.0	5,076	4,586
Mixers	35.0	32.0	27.2	34.3	—	—	—	—	—	—			37.8	33.7	789	1,922
Oth. Parts & Acc. Equip	69.0	69.0	—	—	—	—	5.0	10.0	—	—			26.0	21.0	4,689	6,403
Auto. Parts & Service Equip.															20,821	22,446
Tires & Wheels	27.0	32.0	25.2	—	12.0	7.4	—	—	—	—	S. Korea 20.0	13.0	15.8	47.6	11,625	12,608
Motors	31.0	49.0	4.0	2.3	—	—	—	—	—	—			65.0	48.7	821	810
Oth. Trans. pts.	82.0	92.0	14.0	3.0	—	1.4	—	—	—	—			4.0	3.6	755	1,173
Telecommunication Equipment															17,408	18,749
Radio Transmitter	44.0	90.0	—	—	—	—	—	—	—	—	Canada 53.0		3.0	10.0	120	58
Radio Station Equipment	94.0	80.0	—	—	3.0	—	—	—	—	—			3.0	20.0	67	25
TV Transmitter	48.0	28.0	—	—	52.0	28.0	—	—	—	—			—	44.0	409	683
TV Studio Eg.	19.0	21.0	59.0	48.0	17.2	30.0	—	—	—	—			4.8	1.0	1,089	1,151
Radio/TV Comm. Equipment	57.0	60.0	5.0	—	30.0	32.0	—	—	—	—			8.0	8.0	1,882	1,876
Oth. telegraphic Apparatus	87.0	76.0	—	12.0	6.0	8.0	—	—	—	—			5.9	4.0	4,962	4,285
Receivers	42.0	34.0	1.8	14.0	3.3	6.2	—	—	—	—	Sweden 49.3	45.0	3.6	0.8	8,879	10,671
Agricultural Equipment															12,136	13,442
Tractors/Agric	66.0	64.0	3.0	28.2	21.4	—	—	—	—	—			9.6	7.8	523	609
Planting/cultivation equip	63.0	51.0	—	—	—	—	—	—	—	—			37.0	49.0	917	1,065
Harvesting mchy	53.0	52.0	—	—	—	—	—	6.0	—	—			47.0	42.0	4,283	4,288
Oth. Equip.	84.0	82.0	—	6.0	—	—	—	—	—	—			16.0	12.0	391	1,627
Tractors parts	44.0	53.0	4.3	10.4	9.0	—	7.2	7.0	—	—	Brazil 22.1	24.0	13.5	5.6	6,022	5,853
Trucks, Buses and Other Vehicles															81,145	83,751
Automobiles	18.0	20.0	59.0	65.0	4.2	—	4.0	5.0	—		—		14.8	10.0	39,944	48,424
4 WD Vehicles	28.0	25.0	58.0	72.0	5.3	—	—	—	—	—			8.7	3.0	3,374	4,936
Buses	56.0	38.0	37.0	53.0	—	—	—	—	—	—			7.0	9.0	9,800	7,817
Trucks	52.0	42.0	29.0	39.0	3.3	—	—	—	—	—			15.7	19.0	18,441	15,381
Ambulances	100.0	98.0	—	1.4	—	—	—	—	—	—			—	0.6	138	412
Funeral cars	100.0	100.0	—	—	—	—	—	—	—	—		—			58	19
Trash Trucks	63.0	89.0	7.2	—	—	—	—	—	—	—		—	29.8	11.0	1,498	651
Oth. Vehicles	44.0	13.0	52.4	84.3	2.0	—	—	—	—	—			1.6	2.7	7,322	6,042
Bodies (Buses)	86.0	54.0	—	—	—	—	—	—	—	—			14.0	46.0	124	11
Bodies without Motors	91.0	41.0	—	38.0	—	—	—	—	—	—			9.0	21.0	446	58
Hotel & Rest. Equipment															5,734	6,235
Water coolers	70.0	77.7	—	—	—	8.0	—	—	—	—			30.0	15.0	2,461	2,456
Acc. & parts	88.0	83.0	—	8.0	5.0	6.3	—	—	—	—			7.0	2.7	3,246	3,769
Dishwashers	15.0	30.0	—	—	—	70.0					Canada 85.0		—	—	27	10
Security and Safety Equip.															1,210	1,258
Sec. glasses	43.0	22.0	12.0	18.0	—	—	—	—	—	—	Colombia 18.2		26.8	60.0	208	266
Fire extinguishers	80.0	66.0	—	—	—	—	—	—	—	—			20.0	34.0	407	467
Fire alarms	84.0	88.0	—	—	3.0	7.0	—	—	—	—			13.0	5.0	132	84

Table 1—Imports to Panama
by Type and Origin, 1981-82—Continued

(in percent of total)

Industry and Subgroup	U.S. 1981	U.S. 1982	Japan 1981	Japan 1982	Colón Free Zone 1981	Colón Free Zone 1982	W. Germany 1981	W. Germany 1982	Mexico 1981	Mexico 1982	Various Countries (identified) 1981	Various Countries (identified) 1982	Other Countries 1981	Other Countries 1982	Total (in thousands of dollars) 1981	Total (in thousands of dollars) 1982
Security and Safety Equip. (Cont'd)																
Oth. sound or visual signl'g	83.0	74.0	—	—	4.0	7.0	—	—	—	—			13.0	15.0	463	441
Agric. Chemicals															31,105	28,483
Acids	66.0	72.0	—	—	—	—	9.2	7.3	—	—			24.8	20.7	140	191
Fertilizers	41.0	51.0	—	—	—	—	30.0	26.3	—	—	C.Rica 28.0		1.0	22.7	15,593	10,068
Insecticides & Pesticides	48.0	53.0	—	—	—	—	8.0	6.3	—	—	C.Rica 19.0 Guat. 8.9	6.8 14.2	16.1	19.7	15,372	18,224
Household Appliances															16,143	22,242
Table serving	1.0	1.0	—	5.0	17.0	75.0	—	—	—	—	C.China 47.0		35.0	19.0	2,636	1,426
Table serving and other dom. equip	36.0	47.0	—	—	12.0	20.2	—	—	—	—	C.Rica 24.0	9.1	28.0	23.7	789	868
Elec. iron	30.0	14.0	—	—	64.0	76.0	—	—	—	—			6.0	10.0	344	355
Toasters	41.0	43.0	—	—	46.2	53.1	—	—	—	—			12.8	3.9	919	799
Radios	17.0	1.0	—	—	79.0	92.3	—	2.2	—	—			4.0	4.5	232	354
Tape recorders & Stereo sets	3.0	1.0	—		96.1	99 0	—	—	—	—			0.9	—	5,010	5,644
TV Sets	2.0	—	—	—	96.4	96.4	—	—	—	—			1.6	4.0	4,092	4,743
Dryers and curling irons	45.0	49.0	—	—	17.0	24.0	—	—	—	—			38.0	27.0	355	374
Spare parts (TV and Stereos)	64.0	83.0	—	—	15.0	12.3	—	—	—	—			21.0	4.7	432	617
Oth. Household appl (vacuums)	53.0	46.0	—	—	39.0	47.0	—	—	—	—			8.0	7.0	1,197	1,306
Stereo sets	55.0	10.0	—	—	45.0	44.0	—	—	—	—			—	46.0	73	644
Acc. & parts	46.0	52.0	8.0	3.0	45.0	44.0	—	—	—	—			1.0	1.0	114	112
Oth. tape rec.	2.0	4.0	1.0		97.0	96 0	—	—	—	—			—	—	1,866	1,647
Domestic items	56.0	—	—	—	9.1	—	—	—	—	—			34.0	—	078	—
Dom. items plas.	76.0		—	—	—	—	—	—	—	—			24.0	—	63	—
Mat. Handling															8,699	7,265
Forklifts, Elevators	22.0	5.0	55.1	11.0	—	—	—	—	—	—	Brazil 9.2 Italy 5.3	31.0 23.0	8.4	30.0	2,130	1,488
Conveyor belts	81.0	72.0	—	—	2.0	2.2	—	—	—	—			19.9	25.8	5,338	4,626
Loading & unloading machinery	62.0	46.0	30.3	35	3.5	17.2	—	—	—	—			4.2	1 8	1,231	1,524
Elevator for Liquids	—	18.9	—	—	—	—	—	—	—	—			—	—	—	22
Air Conditioning and Ref. Equipment															11,910	12,050
Air conditioner	57.0	49.0	—	1.4	34.0	49.3	—	—	—	—			9.0	1.7	5,728	5,216
Ref. Equip. for Industrial use	73.0	77.0	—	—	8.3	8.0	—	—	—	—			18.7	15.0	2,456	2,456
Ice makers and ice cream mch	90.0	94.0	—	—	10.0	5.2	—	—	—	—			—	0.8	480	609
Spare parts	88.0	83.0	—	8.0	4.8	6.3	—	—	—	—			7.2	10.7	3,256	3,769
Airplanes & Parts															845	2,116
Airplanes	100.0	—	—	—	—	—	—	—	—	—	Brazil	100.0		—	187	1,572
Spare parts	99.0	74.0	—	—	—	—	—	—	—	—	Brazil	15.8	1.0	10.2	658	544
Pharmaceutical Preparations															36,309	38,715
Vitamins	9.0	6.0	—	—	—	—	—	—	—	—	Honduras 47.1	62.1 16.0	43.9 9.8	31.9 20.9	284 519	383 809
Plasma & Vaccine Virus (H.use)	61.0	57.0	—	—	13.2	—	—	—	16.0	6.1	Switzerland —					

Table 1—Imports to Panama
by Type and Origin, 1981-82—Continued

(in percent of total)

Industry and Subgroup	U.S. 1981	U.S. 1982	Japan 1981	Japan 1982	Colón Free Zone 1981	Colón Free Zone 1982	W. Germany 1981	W. Germany 1982	Mexico 1981	Mexico 1982	Various Countries (identified) 1981	Various Countries (identified) 1982	Other Countries 1981	Other Countries 1982	Total (in thousands of dollars) 1981	Total (in thousands of dollars) 1982
Preparations (Cont'd)																
Antibiotics (Not prepared)	11.0	—	—	—	—	—	—	—	—	—	Switzerland 21.0 Italy 44.0		24.0	—	139	391
Salts & derivates ..	4.0	9.0	—	—	84.0	62.0	5.	9.6	—	—			6.4	19.4	426	93
Glucose & salts	3.0	—	—	—	—	—	—	—	—	—			—	—	3	—
Orthopedic pro.	17.0	12.0	—	—	44.0	45.0	—	—	21.0	15.0			18.0	28.0	901	1,057
Inject. medic.	59.0	48.0	—	—	30.4	25.4	—	—	—	6.1			10.6	20.5	2,315	3,040
Oral medic.	6.0	5.0	—	—	28.2	38.3	—	—	8.2	8.5	Guatemala 22.0 C.Rica 12.0	19.0	23.6	29.2	18,261	18,525
Hidracids	—	—	—	—	—	—	—	—	67.0	71.0	El Sal. 18.0	17.0	15.0	12.0	6	7
Other drugs (vet.use)	14.0	15.0	—	—	—	—	—	—	—	8.9	C.Rica 31.0 Guatemala 33.0	32.3 27.0	22.0	25.7	2,157	2,023
Inj. antibiotics	9.0	4.0	—	—	75.0	78.0	—	—	—	—			16.0	18.0	2,283	2,290
Oral via antibiotics.	1.0	—	—	—	36.0	28.0	—	—	20.4	14.0	Guatemala 25.1	14.0	17.5	44.0	2,209	2,309
External use antibiotics	4.0	2.0	—	—	45.0	54.3	—	—	16.4	19.2	Guatemala 28.0	14.1	6.6	10.4	789	712
541-09-15	1.0	1.0	—	—	81.0	51.0	—	—	4.2	—			13.8	48.0	166	303
Non specified drugs.	17.0	24.0	—	—	48.4	34.0	2.4	—	—	—			32.2	42	1,367	2,129
Pumps, Valves & Compressors															8,956	11,830
Pumps	70.0	62.0	4.3	4.6	—	—	—	6.1	—	—			25.7	27.3	5,515	6,289
Valves	87.0	80.0	—	—	—	1.8	—	—	—	—			13.0	18.2	1,667	3,769
Compressors	88.0	67.0	—	—	—	—	1.0	8.3	—	—			11.0	24.7	1,774	1,772
Construction Equipment															6,226	5,918
Wheel Tractors Tracklaying	1.0	1.0	83.2	55.0	—	—	13.2	38.2	—	—			2.6	5.8	5,124	3,331
Tractors	55.0	49.0	45.0	32.1	—	—	—	—	—	—				18.9	915	809
Mixers	9.0	81.0	—	3.5	—	—	—	—	62.0	—			29.0	15.5	187	1,778
Elect. Power Gen. and Dist. Equip.															1,084	890
Generators	60.0	66.0	23.2	8.9	—	—	1.4	6.7	6.8	—			8.6	18.4	897	656
Elect. Conduits	9.0	23.0	—	—	—	—	—	—	62.0	35.0			29.0	42.0	187	234
Const. Material and Equipment															6,663	5,048
Paints & Enamel ..	34.0	32.0	—	—	—	—	—	—	—	—	Denmark 54.2	45.0	11.8	23.0	1,482	1,406
Steel Doors	79.0	97.0	—	—	—	—	—	—	—	—			21.0	3.0	290	108
Buil. Wires and Cables	10.0	4.0	—	—	—	—	—	14.0			Mexico 89.0 Brazil	21.3	1.0	60.7	464	192
Nails	3.0	20.0	—	—	—	11.0	—	—	—	—	Switzerland 48.0 Spain	15.0	49.0	54.0	1,375	164
Lavatories (Non Metal)	95.0	51.0	—	—	5.0	14.0	—	—	—	—			—	35.0	57	132
Lavatories (Metal) .	85.0	84.0	—	—	—	9.5	—	—	—	—			15.0	6.5	97	199
Lamps, shades & Oth. glass acc	12.0	24.0	3.7	—	21.6	12.3	—	—	51.0	44.0			11.7	19.7	2,928	2,847
Agriculture Equipment															7,346	4,833
Agric. Equip	70.0	30.0	5.9	32.4	—	—	—	—	—	—			24.1	37.6	1,428	1,289

Table 1—Imports to Panama
by Type and Origin, 1981-82—Continued

(in percent of total)

Industry and Subgroup	U.S.		Japan		Colón Free Zone		W. Germany		Mexico		Various Countries (identified)		Other Countries		Total (in thousands of dollars)	
	1981	1982	1981	1982	1981	1982	1981	1982	1981	1982	1981	1982	1981	1982	1981	1982
Agriculture Equip. (Cont'd)																
Planting & Cultivating Equipment	14.0	15.0	—	—	—	—	53.0	82.1	—	—			33.0	2.9	794	213
Tractors and parts	—	1.3	85.0	55.0	—	—	15.0	38.2	—	—			—	5.5	5,124	3,331
Buses, Trucks and Other Vehicles															19,129	28,189
Automobiles	3.0	2.0	15.0	21.0	—	—	—	—	—	—	USSR 57.0 W. Germany 19.2	45.2 27.4	5.8	4.4	10,953	17,656
Buses, Trucks & Ambulances	39.0	7.0	6.3	5.5	—	—	—	—	—	—	USSR Brazil 54.3	77.0	0.4	10.5	392	2,028
Bodies (Buses)	5.0	20.0	36.2	33.3	—	—	—	—	—	—	USSR 26.0	30.0	32.8	17.7	7,784	8,515
Food Processing Packing Equipment															6,515	7,067
Refrigeration Equipment	63.0	57.0	21.2	23.2	—	—	—	—	—	—			15.8	19.8	3,891	5,289
Meat processor	72.0	81.0	—	3.5	—	—	—	—	—	—			28.0	15.5	2,624	1,778
Automotive Parts and Serv. Equip															3,104	3,280
Tires & Wheels	70.0	30.0	5.9	32.4	—	4.8	—	—	—	—			24.1	32.8	1,429	1,289
Motors	55.0	81.0	—	7.1	—	—	—	—	—	—			45.0	11.9	1,675	1,991
Office Equipment															37,615	33,518
Typewriters (electric)	4.0	6.0	68.0	70.0	9.8	4.8	—	—	—	—			18.2	19.2	12,821	12,023
Calculators	11.0	9.0	85.0	82.0	—	—	—	—	—	—			4.0	8.0	24,794	21,491
Telecomm Equipment															9,551	8,467
Radio Transmitters	12.0	8.0	57.0	55.0	8.4	6.2	—	—	7.2	10.7			15.4	20.1	6,952	5,901
Receivers	21.0	21.0	25.0	47.1	45.0	17.0	—	—	—	—			9.0	14.9	2,599	2,566
Medical Equipment															40,510	34,766
X-Ray	9.0	1.0	50.0	79.0	41.0	12.4	—	—	—	—			—	7.6	206	971
Medical Furn.	63.0	57.0	—	—	18.2	32.0	—	—	—	—			18.8	11.0	1,339	1,926
Artifical Lung	44.0	29.0	46.0	64.0	—	—	—	—	—	—			10.0	7.0	6,928	5,433
X-Ray Films	74.0	74.0	—	—	—	—	8.9	—	—	—			17.1	36.0	23,211	21,364
Others	12.0	13.0	50.0	28.4	13.0	11.0	—	—	15.0	17.0			10.0	30.6	8,826	5,072
Security and Safety Equipment															2,918	2,034
Sec. glasses	100.0	—	—	—	—	—	—	—	—	—	Italy		100.0	—	59	7
Fire extinguishers	72.0	81.0	—	3.5	—	—	—	—	—	—			28.0	15.5	2,624	1,778
Fire alarms	71.0	55.0	3.8	21.2	19.1	9.6	—	—	—	4.8			6.1	9.4	235	249
Agriculture Chemicals															3,718	3,509
Acids	100.0	100.0	—	—	—	—	—	—	—	—			—	—	60	47
Fertilizers	100.0	100.0	—	—	—	—	—	—	—	—			—	—	1	17
Insecticides & Pesticides	2.0	3.0	1.3	—	—	—	7.1	5.4	—	—	Colombia 49.0 Switzerland 40.0	29.3 52.2	0.6	10.1	3,657	3,445
Household Appliances															451,645	246,709
Table serving	4.0	2.0	21.0	24.0	13.0	23.0	—	—	19.0	4.2	Spain 19.3	22.3	23.7	24.5	6,152	4,333

Table 1—Imports to Panama by Type and Origin, 1981-82—Continued

(in percent of total)

Industry and Subgroup	U.S. 1981	U.S. 1982	Japan 1981	Japan 1982	Colón Free Zone 1981	Colón Free Zone 1982	W. Germany 1981	W. Germany 1982	Mexico 1981	Mexico 1982	Various Countries (identified) 1981	Various Countries (identified) 1982	Other Countries 1981	Other Countries 1982	Total (in thousands of dollars) 1981	Total (in thousands of dollars) 1982
Household Appliances (Cont'd)																
Table serving & other domestic items	17.0	5.0	—	15.0	27.0	30.0	—	—	12.2	13.0	S.Korea 24.4	22.0	19.4	15.0	1,172	856
Elect. items	34.0	28.0	16.1	22.1	49.0	8.6	—	—	—	—			0.9	41.3	6,633	7,403
Radios	12.0	8.0	57.0	55.0	8.4	6.2	—	—	7.2	10.7			15.4	20.1	376,953	195,901
Oth. household appliances	35.0	29.0	41.0	43.0	9.2	10.2	—	—	8.3	8.4			6.5	9.4	25,941	18,804
Stereo Sets	3.0	1.0	89.0	80.0	—	—	—	—	2.0	10.4			6.0	8.6	33,505	18,631
Domestic Items	21.0	15.0	15.4	23.0	6.4	20.4	—	—	40.4	36.0			16.8	5.6	1,289	781
Mat. Handling Equipment															3,959	3,246
Forklift and elevators	55.0	49.0	26.0	32.1	—	—	—	—	—	—			19.0	18.9	714	809
Loading and unloading mach	8.0	10.0	81.4	89.0	—	—	—	—	—	—			10.6	1.0	421	659
Liquid elevator	72.0	81.0	2.9	3.5	—	—	—	—	—	—			25.1	15.5	2,624	1,778
Air Conditioning and Ref. Equipment															3,891	5,289
Air conditioner	63.0	57.0	21.2	23.3	—	—	—	—	—	—			15.8	19.7	3,891	5,289
Pharmaceutical Preparations															113,681	96,314
Vitamins	—	—	—	—	—	—	48.2	—	—	—	W. Germany 50.0		1.8		56	7
Plasma & vaccine virus	35.0	81.0	—	—	43.0	—	—	—	—	—	Mexico 22.0	10.3	—	8.7	82	154
Antibiotics (not prepared)	33.0	33.0	25.0	23.2	—	—	16.3	13.2	—	—			25.7	30.6	15,867	12,267
Alcaloids, salts & other derivat.	—	—	—	—	—	—	84.3	96.0	—	—	W. Germany 7.5	2.7	8.2	1.3	160	72
Glucose and their salts	13.0	10.0	—	—	—	—	9.5	6.8	—	—	Switzerland 25.2 / W. Germany 14.2	29.0 / 16.0	38.1	38.2	97,516	83,814
Pumps, Valves and Compressors															3,878	2,634
Pumps	76.0	82.0	12.0	8.7	—	—	—	—	—	—			12.0	9.3	185	641
Valves	76.0	81.0	2.8	—	—	—	—	—	—	—			21.2	19.0	1,069	215
Compressors	72.0	81.0	2.9	3.5	—	—	—	—	—	—			25.1	15.5	2,624	1,778

It is expected that the current $25 million automotive parts and accessories market will continue to grow at a high rate as total car imports expand to meet the demand of an increasingly affluent population and local banks continue to provide accessible financing to new car buyers. Particular emphasis should be given to this market by U.S. manufacturers of parts for non-U.S. vehicles. U.S. firms should also consider working through the Colón Free Zone. Imports of automotive parts by Free Zone companies in 1980 amounted to about $7 million, with U.S. goods accounting for less than 10 percent of the total.

Franchising Services.—Panama has proved itself highly receptive to U.S. franchising. The market potential for both specific and general franchising opportunities is high, since Panama maintains no control on royalty payments or transfers. Recreation, entertainment services, automotive, as well as hotel and motel franchising operators will find a fertile market as Panama becomes more of a metropolis and its population demands upgraded services and facilities.

Security and Safety Equipment.—Development of Panama's banking center and a widening range of service industries has created new and growing demand for security and safety equipment. The National Guard and National Investigation Department have increased their personnel to guard Panama's suburban centers on a 24-hour basis. The numerous bank buildings and other multi-story buildings have a need for private security forces equipped with the latest equipment to provide effective and professional protection.

Fisheries and Aquaculture.—Commercial fishing and aquaculture are important and growing sectors of the Panamanian economy. Of 25 agroindustrial business ventures approved for loans by the National Finance Corporation (Cofina) in 1981, twelve involved fishing or aquaculture. Examples included a tuna processing plant, a red snapper fishing and processing operation, and five shrimp farming enterprises.

Shrimping is the most important branch of the fishing industry. In 1981 Panama exported about $55 million of shrimp to the United States. Shrimp farming is a rapidly increasing activity. Although the largest shrimp farming producer (Agromarina, S.A.) is a subsidiary of Ralston Purina, eight Panamanian firms have entered the field. Pipe, pump systems and related equipment should be in demand for private shrimp farms and a projected Government shrimp larvae hatchery.

A number of Panamanian fish species are underexploited, notably red snapper, croaker, shark and black skipjack. An American seafood company has recently established an affiliate in Panama to ship red snapper to the United States. The firm plans to construct a processing plant at the Vacamonte fishing port to produce snapper fillets for export. The Government of Panama is actively pursuing investment from U.S. sources in seafood processing plants and other fishing/maritime related enterprises, and has expressed willingness to take the requirements of U.S. firms into consideration in the design of an expanded Vacamonte port and on-shore facilities.

The Panamanian fishing fleet consists of 279 shrimpers, 40 boats serving the fishmeal and oil industry, and 5 tuna boats. Although the Panamanian tuna fleet is minuscule, there is a large service industry supplying the needs of foreign tuna fleets (nets, fuel, cold storage facilities, helicopter spotting for tuna, etc.).

Due to climatic and environmental conditions, there is rapid deterioration of fishing craft and equipment. A shrimp boat, for instance, usually must be withdrawn from normal use after 5 years of regular service. Although no new shrimp boats may be constructed (in order to prevent overfishing), existing boats may be repaired. There is a steady demand for marine hardware such as winches, chains, navigation equipment, pumps, generators and diesel engines.

Building Products.—According to local industry dealers and distributors, the market for building products is now expected to grow less rapidly because the construction of high rise condominiums and commercial buildings has peaked. By the same token, the construction of major, publicly financed, projects are already completed or near completion. However, the Government has stated an intention to commit funds for the construction of more than 10,000 housing units for 1984, and beyond. In response to official incentives, the private sector will start the construction of new apartment buildings for rental purposes, thus alleviating a pressing shortage of this type of living quarters.

Panama's Bureau of Statistics show this industry's imports to have increased from 1981 to 1982 by 27 percent, while U.S. exports only increased 12 percent for the same period. Still, the United States held a predominant 56 percent share of the $49.9 million import market.

Panama has had a shortage of one and two-bedroom apartments since 1973, when the Government froze all leases below $300 per month. This effectively halted the construction of buildings for rental purposes in Panama. If the private sector responds to the stimulus by the Government and the pent-up middle class demand for housing, construction should begin to take place in mid-1984. At that time most of the active construction companies will have completed their present contracts.

Once the new construction begins there will be a good market potential for U.S.-made building material and fixtures, since this type of construction will demand some quality products. Opportunities for the transfer of U.S. technology may also arise as large construction companies look for ways to erect high rise buildings more efficiently. Government-financed housing projects, on the other hand, do not represent a major opportunity to higher-priced U.S. building products since housing contracts are awarded on a lowest price per unit basis.

The distribution of building materials and hardware supplies serving the construction industry is done through retail outlets such as hardware stores. According to trade sources the traditional hardware store building cycle is from January to September, and most dealers use supplier credits of from 60 to 90 days. Most of the established concerns work with export companies or jobbers, and only few work directly with manufacturers. Almost all local hardware stores use the port of

Miami for consolidation of shipments. Third country suppliers, especially those in Spain, Taiwan and Brazil, have been aggressive in opening new markets in the last 3 years through Government-sponored exhibitions, discount pricing, attractive financing packages and by selecting aggressive agents.

Food Processing.—Most of Panama's basic food processing production is consumed locally, although some large plants export to Central America and the United States. The food processing industry represents about half of Panama's total manufacturing output.

Traditionally, the market for food processing equipment has been growing at about 8 percent annually. U.S exports in 1982 increased by 14 percent to U.S. $12 million, a 67 percent market share. Panamanian industrialists continue to show a strong preference for competitively-priced U.S. equipment because of the service and parts supply offered by the local representatives of U.S. manufacturers.

Panama imports more than $130 million worth of food (mostly sold through large supermarket chains) and exports no more than $5 million (excluding sugar and seafood). The Ministry of Agriculture is interested in further developing Panama's weak agricultural sector and is presently promoting the creation of small to medium-size ventures for the processing of some tropical fruits and vegetables. In the fishing industry the Government is actively promoting the creation of new processing facilities. Several commercially exploited fish have been found to have a ready market in the U.S. and Europe, e.g., the frozen red-snapper fillets mentioned above. The Ministry is also going ahead with the construction of a centrally located produce market to better distribute some of Panama's most commonly consumed produce. All of these policies should increase the local demand for food processing equipment.

It is expected that within 5 years some privately-owned processing ventures will be exporting to the U.S. market taking advantage of the recently approved Caribbean Basin Initiative. Nevertheless, some local sources maintain that investors will not engage in intensive agriculture or processing if the Government does not lift some price controls, provide better marketing facilities, and make concessionary financing available to them.

Several proposed projects currently offer sales potential, including a rice by-products processing plant and a meat packing plant in the province of Chiriquí, a vegetable packing facility, a palm-oil processing plant and, in Vacamonte, a tuna canning facility.

Medical Instruments, Equipment and Supplies.—Panama's imports of medical equipment and supplies increased by 18 percent in the last 4 years, as both the Government and the private sector expanded health services with more and better-equipped hospitals and clinics. Yet, there's a serious need for far more services and hospitals.

The U.S. suppliers account for half of a total import market of about $7 million. U.S. market share may be harder to maintain as the total market increases by an average of 18 percent annually and as more third country suppliers promote and sell their products in this expanding market.

The Government sector is presently reviewing its health programs and facilities with a view to upgrade and expand services. A Health Master Plan sponsored by the Pan American Health Organization is expected to detail equipment and service needs for the entire country. The Plan is to be completed during in 1984. Suppliers may wish to include their offerings in a reference catalog the Ministry of Health is preparing as a companion to the Master Plan.

Through its social security system, the Government now provides health services to almost half of the working population. In the future the Ministry of Health would like to see health services extended to Panama's most remote areas, where availability is currently limited.

Private hospital facilities increasingly offer the most advanced health equipment and medical services. The goal is to render services not only to Panama's growing population, but to attract patients from close-by countries as well. Private clinics have also expanded tremendously in the last 5 years, as doctors have grouped together to provide almost all medical services, in a central location and at lower cost.

The demand for U.S. health products and equipment should continue to be strong, since local buyers are well attuned to U.S. product technology. Nevertheless, U.S. products face strong marketing competition from Japanese and other third country suppliers who actively promote their products with better financing terms and more in-house training. The total market for medical equipment will offer important opportunities to technologically advanced companies with good products and a strong local marketing and service network.

Office Equipment.—The sale of business and office equipment, including computers, has become more price competitive during the last 3 years as Panamanian and reexport markets have shrunk. Third country suppliers of business equipment e.g., Canon, Brother, Olympia and Facit, have set up distribution centers in Panama City and no longer handle the Panama City market merely as an extension of reexport activities centered in the Colón Free Zone. Both Japan and Korea are expected to begin shipping typewriters and other office equipment into the Panamanian market directly. Also, faced with intense competition and a shrinking local market, IBM has decided not to serve the market through its own selling channels but rather through exclusive subdistributors. This is an entirely new concept for IBM of Panama, and it is through this mechanism that IBM is competing head-to-head with third country suppliers. These decisions reflect a change in the market, a market that has become more sophisticated. Not only is competition more intense but the product mix is also changing. The electric typewriter and the expensive photocopying machines are no longer the most valuable office equipment assets; the word processor and the computer have become more important.

To date, most word processors and large computers have been bought by Panama's more important banks.

But as Panama's sophisticated banking system slowly induces expansion in the financial service industry generally, there will be increased demand for all products in the business and office field. Also, Panama's medium to large manufacturing companies, advertising agencies, legal firms, CPA firms, and insurance companies are making more efficient use of computers and electronic office equipment to speed to day-to-day transactions so as to provide better service. They represent the future customers in this market.

During 1982, sales of business and office equipment dropped by 12 percent compared to 1981. U.S. exports of these goods to Panama decreased by 8 percent during the same period, although they kept a 47 percent share of the total U.S. $12 million market.

Power Generation and Distribution Equipment.—Since the early 70's Panama's State-owned power company, IRHE, has followed a policy of substituting alternative energy sources for those based on petroleum, which it must import IRHE is now carrying out an extensive program to supply electricity with hydroelectric plants, and once the La Fortuna 300 megawatt plant comes on line virtually all of Panama's electric power needs will be met from hydroelectric sources.

The World Bank has loaned $32.1 million to partially finance a distribution project that will permit Panama to expand its electrical network to serve 62 percent of the country's population. The project has a total cost of $64 million and is estimated to be completed about mid-1986. The project will incorporate about 50,000 new subscribers and improve services in zones already covered by the electrical network.

According to IRHE's planning department, development of the Changuinola hydroelectric plant has been postponed until 1989, due to budgetary constraints. Nevertheless, IRHE hopes to negotiate another loan to obtain $37 million in financing for the VII Distribution Project. This project calls for the installation of lines and the replacement of some substations in the interior of Panama.

U.S. manufacturers generally maintain close contact with IRHE planning and bidding departments. U.S. suppliers often travel to Panama and most retain active and well informed agents who seek out information on IRHE bid proposals well ahead of formal proposal announcements.

The 1983 import requirements for this industry sector doubled from the previous year to U.S. $41 million reflecting large transformer and generator purchases for the La Fortuna Dam project. U.S. imports over the same period increased by half and accounted for more than half of the total market.

With regard to prices, U.S. suppliers enjoy a favorable competitive position in most subgroups of this category. Import statistics for 1982 show that U.S. suppliers held a dominant share in generators, switchgears and switches, while Sweden held the lead in transformers. If IRHE follows plans to expand and upgrade equipment, U.S. firms should be able to increase their exports to Panama in coming years. However, U.S. suppliers have not been successful recently in competing against third

country suppliers on IRHE's hydro plants. This reflects poor U.S. financing schemes and noncompetitive supplier credit.

Domestic Economic Trends

Following 4 years of high growth fueled by an expansionary Government fiscal policy, Panama is now facing a period of budgetary austerity and diminished commercial activity in its service-oriented economy. While real GDP growth averaged 5 percent each year from 1978 and 1981 and was only 0.2 percent in 1983, most sectors of the economy contracted. In 1984 it is expected to be zero or slightly negative. The Government of Panama is faced with the need to decrease unemployment which is how in the 15-20 percent range, improve the balance of trade, and reduce its fiscal deficit and foreign debt.

Over the next few years real growth should increase from 1 percent to 3 percent annually depending on the economic condition of Panama's traditional trading partners in Latin America and Panama's ability to take advantage of export opportunities to the U.S. through the Caribbean Basin Initiative.

Overview

Panama's service sector accounts for 70 percent of the country's Gross Domestic Product (GDP) and employs half of the total work force. Of special significance in this sector are the Colón Free Zone, the Panama Canal, the banking industry, and the new Trans-isthmus oil pipeline, all mainstays of the Panamanian economy.

Manufacturing, construction, and agriculture contribute roughly 10 percent each to the GDP. In contrast to the service sector, these activities serve a small domestic market and have limited export potential

The Colón Free Zone serves as a trade center between Asia and Europe and the countries of Latin America. From 1977 to 1980 its services grew at a rate of 20 percent per year. But by 1982 its value had sharply contracted as its Latin American trading partners experienced severe economic and financial problems.

The Panama Canal contributes about 11 percent to the GDP. With the completion of the Trans-isthmus pipeline to transfer Alaskan crude oil and slower world commerce generally, transits slowed in 1983 from their 1982 record level.

Banking and financial services contribute 6 percent to total GDP. Over 125 banks have located in Panama to take advantage of its relaxed banking laws and minimal financial flow restrictions. Combined assets of all banks exceeded $49 billion in 1982. Lending in Panama is competitive with regard to rates but the decline in economic activity in 1983 reduced the demand for loans.

Manufacturing.—Manufacturing contributes 10 percent of the GDP and employs about 10 percent of the labor force. It is presently constrained by the small domestic market and weak Latin American foreign markets.

1831

Food processing, beverages and tobacco account for one half of this sector. Their growth is erratic, spending on the weather and world prices.

Petroleum products have been Panama's leading export ($174 million in 1982) but have been decreasing in value as world prices drop. Clothing the textiles comprise 10 percent of manufactures but no growth is seen as they have been excluded from the CBI and no healthy foreign markets exist.

Previously the Government industrial policy emphasized import substitution, guaranteeing market protection to new industries. Now export oriented industries are also receiving preferential treatment such as tax exemptions. Though investment has fallen off recently the Government hopes the CBI will provide the necessary markets for expansion. Best prospects seem to be light industry assembly, chemicals and plastic products.

Construction.—For the last several years growth in construction has been one of the principal forces behind Panama's economic development. In 1982 construction alone contributed 9 percent to the GDP, a 17 percent increase over 1981. In this growth the building of La Fortuna Dam, laying a trans-isthmic pipeline, and the private construction of luxury housing and commercial offices figured largely. In 1983 there was a sharp contraction of construction volume compared to 1982, when growth slackened as the market for high-rise apartments and commercial offices became saturated and major public projects were completed.

Major public-financed projects are not foreseen in the near future as Panama tightly restricts its capital expenditures in line with agreements with the IMF and World Bank. Exceptions to this policy are:

(1) Guaranteeing the financing of lower-middle income housing ($25 million).
(2) Paving of the Divisa-Chitre-Las Tablas highway ($32 million).
(3) Various programs for improving rural roads and reconditioning city streets financed with Inter American Development Bank and World Bank loans.

As the Government will no longer be able to stimulate this sector to the same extent as in the past, it plans to provide the necessary laws and incentives for the private sector to increase its participation.

Agriculture.—Panama's agricultural sector has traditionally been weak due in part to price controls which dampened interest in investing in modern technology and equipment. Only in the last 2 years have relaxed price controls helped stimulate growth in this sector.

In 1982 agriculture accounted for 10 percent of the GDP and employed over one quarter of the active labor force. Agriculture also provided over half of domestic merchandise exports, primarily bananas, sugar, rice and coffee. Though price supports have helped in some areas, drought and low world commodity prices hurt the dollar value of exports in 1983.

Livestock growth has been less stable as a result of export quotas and poor processing facilities. The Government believes there is potential though, and is discussing a $25 million dollar project with the World Bank to develop the industry. Also, by yearend 1983 the Government removed export quotas on beef.

Fishing and aquaculture are also important. Shrimp is now the second largest export commodity, with 1982 shipments of $53 million. Shrimp farming, though small, is also being developed with a $22 million dollar loan from the Inter-American Development Bank. Marlin, red snapper and tuna are other currently underexploited commercial fishing possibilities.

Other Economic Considerations

Balance of Trade.—Panama continues to follow a downward trend in its foreign trade balance. Typically, imports have become more expensive as export prices increase more slowly or even decrease. Main commodity exports are petroleum products, shrimp, bananas, sugar and coffee. In 1983 exports were valued at $304 million, while in 1981 they had been $353 million. In 1982 shrimp exports remained strong, increasing 24 percent from $42.7 million to $52.9 million. At the same time sugar dropped 55 percent from $52.6 million to $23.77 million. To increase exports Panama must necessarily explore new markets and develop new products while Latin American markets recover.

Prices.—Panama's open economy links its domestic inflation rate closely to world and U.S. trends. In 1982 inflation dropped from 7.3 to 4.2 percent (consumer prices) and from 10 to 8.3 percent (wholesale prices). Government price controls on some basic goods tend to hold down the price level.

Price controls, meant to assure low prices for basic food-stuffs, have had undesirable consequences on industrial and agricultural production. Due to the administrative inflexibility of price controls producers often find themselves with insufficient incentives to supply the market at the prescribed prices given their costs of production.

Unemployment.—Unemployment continues to be a growing problem in Panama. With a predicted 2.5 to 4 percent real growth rate over the next few years Panama will be short approximately 10,000 new jobs each year. Unemployment, now 15-20 percent could reach 25 percent.

To confront the problem of a rapidly growing labor force, the Government of Panama will promote labor intensive projects and industries.

Panama and the Caribbean Basin Initiative

Panama has been designated as a Caribbean Basin Initiative (CBI) beneficiary country.

The intent of the CBI is to improve the economic conditions of countries in the Caribbean Basin including Panama by stimulating productive private enterprise activities which will offer employment to the area's un- and under-employed. The key feature of the CBI is the duty-free access to the U.S. market until 1995 of goods produced in "beneficiary" countries. At least 35 percent of the value of the goods must be comprised of labor and materials from the beneficiary countries. Goods excluded from the program, include textiles and apparel, leather goods, canned tuna, petroleum and petroleum products.

The CBI principally addresses the industrial and agricultural communities of the "beneficiary" countries offering duty free-entry of their products into the U.S. market. U.S. business, however, can also participate in CBI-related activities. In Panama, U.S. investors can participate through wholly-owned enterprises or as joint-venture partners in export-related facilities. U.S. companies may also look to CBI activities as export market possibilities for processing and packaging equipment. On the import side, U.S. companies can fill a gap in the marketing knowledge existing among CBI-country exporters.

To assist CBI participants in evaluating Panama's potential the following information reviews Panama's general investment attractions; highlights Government assistance from the U.S. and Panama; examines critical issues; reports on the opinions of doing business in Panama expressed by Panamanian and foreign businessmen; and suggests some strategies for investment.

General Investment Attractions

What has made Panama an international banking and commercial center, even before the advent of the CBI, are three macro-economic conditions that will continue to distinguish Panama among CBI beneficiary countries. They are:

Use of U.S. Currency.—The dollar is a freely circulating medium of exchange in Panama. The country does not issue paper bills, U.S. bills are used instead. Because of the dollar's role in the local economy there is no exchange risk regarding Panamanian transactions with U.S. parties. Further, capital and income flows are unrestricted.

Geographic Location.—Panama is at an international maritime and airline crossroads. Domestic transportation facilities are excellent and complement the country's international traffic.

Stable Government.—Panama's history is characterized by peace with its neighbors and social stability domestically.

Government Assistance—U.S.

Promoting the CBI.—The U.S. Government, through the Departments of Commerce and Agriculture, offers to facilitate information between U.S. investors and beneficiary country prospects. The Caribbean Basin Business Information Center (CBIC) at the Department of Commerce in Washington, D.C., US&FCS, acts as a point of contact in the exchange of information related to the Caribbean Basin Initiative. The CBIC's telephone number is 202-377-2527. Much additional information on Panama of interest to investors is available from the Panama Desk of the Caribbean Basin Division, OMCB/WH/IEP, H3016 U.S. Department of Commerce, Washington, D.C. 20230. The Department of Commerce has nearly 50 offices throughout the U.S. that can assist in providing market information, import/export contacts, and investment contacts. Other agencies like the Overseas Private Investment Corporation (OPIC) and the Agency for International Development (AID) will work in conjunction with the Department of Commerce.

Government Assistance—Panama, Legal Provisions

Panama incorporated legal provisions for promoting industrial production sometime before the passage of the CBI. With its passage these established incentives are worth reviewing.

Contract with the Nation.—Under this contract an investor enters into an agreement with the Panamanian Government to realize a project within a period of time specified in the contract. In return the Government exempts the investor from all import duties on imported machinery, raw materials, production equipment, and spare parts. Also, profits from exports are exempted as are income taxes reinvested in fixed assets.

Should a plant locate in a district designated for development, a so-called Contract with the Nation allows for full exemption from income taxes during the first 5 years and partial exemption during the next 3 years.

Investments in production facilities aimed partly at the local market enjoy an additional advantage: they may negotiate for protection of their infant industries in the form of high tariffs or import quotas. There is a concommitant requirement, however, that products meet standards of quantity, quality and price.

Light Industry Assembly Program.—This export-promotion program, commonly referred to as the "Maquila" program provides for a total exemption from income, capital gains, and export taxes All inputs into production are also exempt from duties. Production must be totally aimed at export markets.

Certificates of Tributary Payment (CAT).—These certificates are meant to benefit the exporters of non-traditional products which are manufactured wholly or partially in Panama. A certificate's value equals 20 per cent of the value added to exported goods, and can be applied to the payment of national taxes and import duties.

Bilateral Treaties.—Panama and the United States signed a Bilateral Investment Treaty in October, 1982, which will take effect once it is formally ratified by the U.S. Senate. Panama has since concluded bilateral investment treaties with France, Great Britain, Switzerland and West Germany.

Government Assistance—Panama, Institutional Assistance

Investment Council of Panama.—The CNI (Spanish acronym) seeks to attract investments in export-oriented facilities. Labor-intensive operations which have little need for local financing get CNI's prioity when it renders assistance. The multi-lingual CNI staff assists the investor in identifying potential projects given Panama's economic conditions. The staff also provides the investor with a "one-step" clearinghouse for official documents, saving the investor the time of visiting any number of ministries for official project clearance. Investors can also be directed to qualified professionals for legal counsel, the hiring and training of Panamanian labor, and financing advice. The Council's address is as follows:

Consejo Nacional de Inversión
Edificio Banco Nacional de Panamá
Torre A (8° piso)
Panamá, Rep. de Panamá
Telephone: 64-7211
Telex: 3499 INVEST PG

National Finance Corporation.—Cofina (Spanish acronym) is an autonomous Government agency which provides financing for projects deemed to be in the national interest such as agri-business, tourism, and export promotion. Cofina also engages in studies to determine the feasibility of projects which may be in the national interest. The agency will consider joint-ventures with outside investors if the project meets the criterion of serving a national economic objective.

At present Cofina's available funds are much reduced from previous levels as the agency seeks to put itself on a more business-like basis. A current reorganization proposal suggests that Government participation in the agency be reduced to 40 percent in a corporation where 60 percent will be privately held, half by Panamanians, and half by international entities.

Industrial Zones.—Panama has a wide variety of completed and nearly completed industrial zones located around the country. Industrial parks with paved roads and utility services are in place in Colón, Chitre and David. These parks have ample supplies of fresh water, telephone and telex installations, illuminated streets and reliable electricity.

Colón Free Zone.—This commercial and industrial zone is of great importance to Panama and the CBL, it receives a separate and detailed treatment on page 1839 of this report.

Financial Center.—Though the center is comprised of private international banks its financial activities were institutionalized by Panamanian Government law and this may be viewed as an indirect form of Government assistance to the private sector. Some 125 banks from over 30 countries are located in Panama. In 1983, bank assets totaled $49.0 billion. Like Switzerland, Panama is one of few countries that offers complete banking secrecy. Though primarily aimed at off-shore transactions, the availability of international banking services so close at hand certainly facilitates the financial service requirements of international ventures in Panama.

Critical Issues

Industrial Policy.—As noted in the general economic overview of this report, industry and agriculture are minor contributors to Panama's GDP. The principal economic fact about Panama is that its market is small and does not lend itself to the minimum capacity for production that the smallest available equipment can deliver. Almost all Panamanian industry runs at a fraction of its capacity.

To support new industry the Government has adopted protective measures using the import-substitution argument as a justification. Quotas (now being gradually phased out) and high tariffs are directed at those imports that directly compete with domestic production. In fact, an investor can be guaranteed protection (Contract with the Nation) even before the first unit of production rolls off the line. Import substitution had its greatest success in the 1960's, especially in consumables like food, beverages and clothing. In the 1970's the Government sought to promote exports as an added market for Panamanian industry. Laws such as the Contract with the Nation, the CAT, and the Maquila were passed in support of the export effort.

Though export incentives have been in place for some years now—since the mid-70's—the hoped for stimulation of export-led growth has not taken place. The incentives themselves tended to be vague and sometimes self-defeating. For instance, tax exemptions on machinery and raw material inputs tended to encourage importation of raw materials and the use of capital intensive machinery, shutting out labor-intensive Panamanian inputs. Given this tendency to favor capital equipment, the Panamanian industrialists engaged production facilities that were of too large a scale for the local market. To be profitable the industrialist had to find a large export market. However, tariff walls in neighboring countries (except for Panama's small Central American neighbors) combined with a poor knowledge of the U.S. market, largely compelled Panamanian industrialists to sell at home, at high prices.

Labor Code.—Panama's labor code is one of the most comprehensive in Latin America but it leaves considerable room for interpretation by Government officials, often in the favor of the laborer. For example, after 2 years of work it is very difficult to dismiss a worker, even if incompetent, because such dismissals can be reviewed by the legal system at the discharged laborer's request. The process can be lengthy and costly to the employer. Also, there is no system for rewarding a worker for exceptional performance. Any bonus or cash award becomes a permanent increase in salary, a definite discouragement to recognizing discrete individual achievements.

Price Controls.—The Price Regulation Board, consisting of representatives of several ministries, is responsible for preserving the purchasing power of low-income consumers and for assuring the constant provision of essential goods and services. The Board realizes its objectives by administering controls on prices of essential goods and services, of medicines, and of products produced by firms who have entered into Contracts with the Nation.

Price controls have had undesirable side effects on certain industries. When the prices for raw materials are too high, relative to world prices, they tend to make export products using those materials uncompetitive. Also, when input prices are raised by the Board but no corresponding price increase is granted to the producer of the manufactured good, then the producer's profit margin become discouragingly thin. Appeals to the Board for price increases for a product often encounter long administrative delays.

Price controls, of course, apply to products sold domestically. Those industries which are able to find markets overseas, (assuming their capacity utilization is sufficient to realize economies that translate into competitive prices) are unaffected by domestic price controls. Textiles are an example.

Business' Views on Doing Business in Panama

Panamanian Business' View.—Interviews with Panamanian entrepreneurs, conducted by the Foreign Commercial Service and two independent firms, have tended to confirm the contradictions between incentive laws and price controls. They have also confirmed that the labor code is a disincentive to investment. However, Panamanian businesses also admit that their analysis is based on sales to the Panamanian market.

To fully exploit Government incentives and to circumvent price controls on some items, Panamanians recognize the need to export. However, they see very strong competition from elsewhere due to either lesser production costs using similar equipment (neighboring Central American countries) or higher productivity due to better equipment (some Oriental countries and the U.S.).

The Panamanian industrialist has little alternative in his future plans. Given Panama's small market, an industrialist must diversify or export to grow, even though exporting means entering an extremely competitive world economy. Recent restrictive financial and economic policies among many of Panama's trading partners, however, have put a damper on those few markets where some Panamanian exports were beginning to be competitive.

Panamanian businesspeople also reported that investment plans were difficult since no national industrial policy exists. For example, calls for regional agri-industrial development are not complemented with incentives to agricultural production. Only recently has the Government addressed this plaint by lifting price ceilings on a number of agricultural goods and by allowing the unrestricted exportation of beef. The Government still directs by improvisation, say Panamanian businessmen, and not in accordance with a well-defined, comprehensive plan.

Shipping is also a sore point. Ironically enough for the maritime crossroads of the world, shipping is at higher rates for Panama than for other countries in the area, due to the conference rate structure. Many goods originating in distant points (like the Orient) can be shipped to the U.S. cheaper than from Panama to the U.S. To compound matters further, docking fees are relatively high.

Foreign Business' View.—A study, available to the FCS, queried foreign businesses in Panama about the desirability of investing in Panama. Concerned about financial security, foreign businessmen found the use of the U.S. dollar as a common unit of currency a most attractive feature. For U.S. businesses it meant no foreign exchange risk and an inflationary risk equal to that in the U.S. Political stability was regarded as average to above average by nearly all those interviewed. Panama's proximity to Central American troublespots obscures the country's long tradition of political tranquility and social harmony.

Foreign businessmen are aware of the Government's general encouragement of private investment but only a minority are acquainted with the CAT or the Maquila program. They are, however, very aware of Panama's excellent infrastructure both physical (transportation, communication) and human (a high level of bi-lingualism). There is some desire that technical skills among the work force be improved, however.

Like their Panamanian counterparts, foreign businessmen keyed on the labor code and the price control system as disincentives to investment.

Finally, for a foreign resident, Panama is a very pleasant place to work offering amenities far exceeding its size.

Suggested CBI Investment Strategies

Panama is a country with a very long commercial tradition whose people, like potential U.S. investors, are well-versed in modern business practices. The fact that English is widely spoken makes the communication between the Panamanian and the American businessman even more effective. The information conveyed in these pages makes clear that Panama has its positive and negative aspects as a site for investment like any other nation, and in its mature business culture, these may be fully discussed. Information for making sound investment decisions abounds in Panama and is accessible to the potential investor, a considerable investment attraction in itself.

A preliminary review of economic and business conditions suggests that an investor could do well in Panama if he introduces a labor-intensive, export-oriented product. He should have a good sense of existing foreign markets for his product and regard Panama as an attractive production site because of its various investment incentives and its communication, transportation, financial and social features. In manufacturing, these considerations point to light-assembly manufacturing, preferably low volume products with high profit margins. In agriculture, nontraditional fruits and vegetables which could be processed and packaged in Panama would be feasibile investments.

Specific Strategies.—The National Investment Council of Panama is currently engaged in a research project which will specifically identify those industrial and agricultural products that are likeliest to be profitable investments in Panama. Preliminary results suggest the following industrial investment prospects: Telephone and telegraph apparatus, assembly (labor intensive components) (SIC—3661); Toys (SIC 3944); Electrical test equipment assembly (labor intensive components) (SIC 3825); Sporting goods (SIC 3949); Pharmaceutical manufacturing with U.S. origin inputs for South American markets (SIC 7834); Off-shore data (SIC

7372-7374); Electrical automotive industry, assembly (SIC 2694);

Some preliminary agricultural prospects are: Honeydew melons, yucca, green peppers, tomatoes, carrots, mushrooms, tamarinds, tobacco, fresh flowers.

Among fish and shellfish are: red snapper, anchovies, sardines, crab meat.

A higher return on the total agri-business investment would result if appropriate processing and packaging of the above agricultural and fish products were carried out in Panama.

Lastly, there is considerable unused capacity in Panama's industrial sector which could benefit from an association with U.S. firms whose market knowledge would help to place increased production runs of Panamanian goods in the U.S. market. Some such industries are packing cartons, construction materials and specialty metals.

Trade Policy and Regulations

While not a member of the Central American Common Market, Panama has bilateral trade agreements with each of the Central American countries. These agreements provide for duty-free trade in certain specified articles. Of Panama's total 1980 imports of $1.3 billion, $42 million was imported duty-free under these agreements. About half of this duty-free trade had its origins in Costa Rica. Because of a serious trade imbalance with Costa Rica caused by the falling value of the Costa Rican colon vis-a-vis the U.S. dollar (Panama's circulating medium of exchange) and serious foreign exchange shortages in Costa Rica (in September 1981), the Panamanian Government instituted an import license requirement on Costa Rican products covered by the bilateral trade agreement and later took other measures to reduce the increasingly unfavorable trade balance with Costa Rica.

Tariff Structure

Panama has devised its own tariff nomenclature which is based on the Standard International Trade Classification (SITC) system for the first 5 digits and on the standard tariff nomenclature used by the Central American countries for the last 2 digits. In general, the duties range from zero for agricultural machinery to 30 percent ad valorem for a variety of manufactured products. Although there are exceptions, import duties are relatively light as Panama attempts to promote itself as the commercial crossroads of the world. Many luxury goods enter at negligible duty rates. Duties on most manufactured items are in the 5-20 percent range. Certain manufactured goods that compete with local production are subject to higher tariff rates, and some items are protected by import quotas. The Government of Panama is planning to eliminate most quota arrangements and replace them with relatively high tariffs, which would make goods available only to those consumers willing to pay the higher prices. Of course, goods imported into the Colón Free Zone are not assessed import tariffs.

Customs Surcharges

In addition to the import tariffs, all imports into Panama, including those from the Colón Free Zone, are assessed a surcharge of 7.5 percent on the f.o.b. value except for foodstuffs, which pay 3.5 percent and medicines and pharmaceutical products which are taxed at a 2.5 percent rate. A 5 percent transfer or value added (I.T.B.M.) tax is also levied on the c.i.f. value plus import duty and surcharge of imports, excluding foodstuffs and medicines.

Basis of Duty Assessment

Panama has a single-column tariff schedule, with imports subject to either a specific or an ad valorem duty. Unless otherwise provided, the specific duty is assessed on the weight or measure of the commodity and is expressed in Balboas per kilogram, liter, or other unit. For duty purposes the weight may be calculated on the net, legal, or gross weight, as indicated in the tariff. Net weight means the intrinsic weight of the merchandise without any wrapping or container. The legal weight includes the weight of the goods plus that of an immediate container or wrapper. The gross weight includes the weight of the merchandise plus that of all containers and wrappers, interior and exterior. Most of Panama's specific duties are levied upon the gross weight.

Ad valorem duties are levied on the f.o.b. value, port of export. Duties are assessed and paid in either Balboas or dollars.

Exemptions for New Investment

The Government of Panama provides fiscal benefits, through contracts, to national or foreign enterprises which wish to avail themselves of the existing industrial incentive legislation. New producers may negotiate protection in the form of high tariffs or of quotas to protect their infant industries. They may also obtain exemptions from the payment of import duties on raw materials, component parts, and capital goods for the new investment.

Non-tariff Barriers

Other than quotas, Panama has few, if any, non-tariff barriers directed at physical imports. The Government does impose some health and safety requirements on certain foodstuffs and pharmaceuticals. These requirements are often imposed on national as well as foreign products and are not designed as a protection for local production.

Service sector professionals can expect some barriers due to procedural requirements. Foreign engineers and architects may practice their profession in Panama only after they have been certified by the Panamanian Technical Board of Engineers and Architects. Certifications are granted when certain documentation is provided by the foreign professional. The documentation basically establishes that: the foreign applicant has bona fide credentials; Panamanians enjoy the same professional privileges in the country to which the foreign applicant belongs and, a reasonable effort has been made to employ local professional talent without success.

Foreign architects or engineers are granted authorization by the technical board to work in Panama for periods not to exceed 12 months. The 12 month authorizations of the technical board may be renewed. If the period for which a foreign professional is hired, including extensions, exceeds 12 months, the contracting agency is obliged to hire a Panamanian professional so that he may receive on-the-job training with the foreign professional.

Import Quotas, Licensing and Other Controls

Import quotas had been imposed on approximately 250 kinds of goods. Among the products affected were various food products, certain textiles, edible oils and fats, clothing, footwear, luggage, lumber, toilet preparations, soaps and detergents, filing cabinets, certain industrial goods, certain paper products and various other articles produced in Panama. These quotas are gradually being replaced by higher import duties.

Import licenses are required on a substantial list of products, such as salt, tomatoes and their by-products, flour, meats, eggs, chickens, milk and milk products, beverages, canned or preserved goods, fresh and dried fruits and vegetables, textiles, clothing and footwear, soaps, washing powders and detergents, cotton plush, pharmaceuticals, drugs and cosmetics, wire screening and substitutes, steel rods and bars, and products which compete with locally made goods. Licenses are obtained by the importer upon application to the Office of Price Regulation in the Ministry of Finance. However, in some special cases, the Ministry of Agricultural Development and the Ministry of Commerce and Industries also grant import licenses.

All imported foods and beverages which are packaged or bottled must be approved by and registered with the Ministry of Public Health before their sale is allowed. Under these regulations, the Ministry's approval depends upon a laboratory analysis of each product by the University of Panama. The original registration of foodstuffs is valid for 10 years. A list of ingredients must accompany the application for registry of the product. Spot checks are made by the laboratory to ensure that no unauthorized changes take place in the composition of the products. Spanish language labels giving the names of the products and instructions for use are required, although this requirement apparently is flexibly enforced.

Pharmaceuticals, drugs, cosmetics and other similar products are also subject to regulations. Before importation is allowed, the following types of products must be approved by and registered with the Ministry of Public Health:

(1) Chemical products with scientific names for therapeutic use and corresponding to a determined chemical formula, indicating composition and structures.

(2) Pharmacological products, drugs and base preparations corresponding to the nomenclature found in the official pharmacopoeia and distributed under these names.

(3) Biological products such as serums and vaccines, organotherapeutic products or substances prepared with organs or glands extracted from healthy animals, or chemical substances of other origin but with similar physiological action.

(4) Vitamin products, and extracts or preparations that contain vitamins as the principal components.

(5) Cosmetics, contraceptives of whatever nature, and in general, all internal and external applications that regularly are purchased in pharmacies and which are used for the health of the individual or the group.

The registration of the above products is accomplished by the same procedure as outlined under food regulations except that the list of ingredients must include more details on composition. Laboratories outside Panama must submit a document certified by a Panamanian consul affirming that the laboratory is authorized to produce (and presumably sell) pharmaceutical products where it is located. Pharmaceutical products not accompanied by this certified document will be denied entry.

Import Procedures and Requirements

Entry

Merchandise imported into Panama by freight must be cleared through customs by a customs broker licensed by the Government of Panama. Exceptions are made for goods which are imported duty-free, consigned to national and municipal governments, imported by foreign diplomats, for sale to authorities of the Canal Area, sold to vessels transiting the Canal, or intended for reexportation. For the customs clearance of merchandise, the customs broker must submit a customs declaration covering the goods, accompanied by a legalized consular invoice and a bill of lading, as well as legal proof that the importer has paid his Panamanian income taxes.

If for any reason the consular invoice and bill of lading cannot be presented within 24 hours after the shipment has arrived, clearance of the goods will be permitted by posting a bond equal to double the amount of import duties. The bond is cancelled if the prescribed documents are presented in due form within a period of 90 days, extendable in justified cases for an additional 90 days.

Warehousing and Transit

Merchandise and effects not removed from the custom houses within 24 hours after the duties have been paid will be subject to storage fees which must be settled before the goods can be withdrawn. When such charges have accrued up to the value of the goods, the merchandise will be subject to sale at auction.

All goods arriving at the cities of Panama and Colón to be reshipped to vessels other than those in which they arrived must be deposited in special warehouses designated by the Government. In special cases merchandise stored in these warehouses may be authorized for sale or consumption within Panama upon payment of double the amount of all the charges involved. Merchandise may be declared for warehousing if desired. If the importer has no bonded repository of his own, merchandise may be deposited in a Government warehouse for 6 months. Goods remaining in Government warehouses for more than 12 months without being reexported or without payment of warehouse fees will be considered as having been abandoned. Storage charges are 50 cents per case per day after the first 24 hours for up to 30 days: thereafter, the charge is 75 cents per case per day. The Government of Panama maintains bonded warehouses in Panama City and Colón.

Samples.—Samples having commercial value will be examined and evaluated by the customs authorities and admitted provisionally, if accompanied by a bond or cash deposit covering the amount of the import duties to guarantee that they will be reexported within the 6 months from the day of importation. If the samples are not reexported within that period of time, the amount of bond or deposit will be applied to the duty which is owed on them.

Samples having no commercial value are admitted duty-free. Articles of common use will not be considered as samples without commercial value unless they arrive in unusable form or are made unusable after their arrival. Jewelry, tobacco in various forms, alcoholic beverages, pencils, pens, blotters, rulers, pen knives, matches, ashtrays and other similar articles will not be admitted free of duty as samples without commercial value. Shoes for the left foot only will be considered without commercial value.

Samples of medicinal products and of other similar substances must be in containers of less than one ounce if they are in liquid form and in containers of less than one-quarter ounce if they are creams, pomades, pastes, or preparations in solid or semisolid form. If samples arrive in large containers they will be dutiable even though marked as free samples or as samples for doctors.

Advertising Matter

Trade catalogues, circulars, prospectuses and instruction pamphlets of foreign firms and tourist literature for other countries may be admitted duty-free. Similar printed material promoting Panamanian manufactured goods and Panamanian tourism is dutiable at a rate of one Balboa per gross kilogram unless available in sufficient quantity within the country, in which case the import duty will be six balboas per gross kilogram. It is suggested that shipments of advertising matter be clearly marked as such.

Temporary Duty-Free Importation

Goods brought to Panama for exhibition purposes may be imported duty-free for a temporary period upon deposit of double the applicable duties as a guarantee the goods will be reexported. Goods must be bonded while in the Republic, and import duties are only paid if the merchandise is sold. Exhibitors who move goods through the Colón Free Zone will benfit from the added convenience of being able to ship their goods from the Free Zone for exhibit in the Atlapa Convention Center with a minimum level of inconvenience.

Labeling and Marking Requirements

All packaged, bottled or canned goods sold in Panama, whether produced locally or imported, must bear labels containing the following information in Spanish: name or commercial designation and ingredients (if the articles are other than eggs, meat, etc.) specifying the class or type of mixture not known under specific names, net weight or volume of contents and the country of origin. Imported beer and carbonated beverages must have the word "Panama" printed or stamped in visible characters on the labels and caps. Special labeling requirements are also in effect for imported cigarettes and tobacco, wines, certain foodstuffs, patent medicines, and pharmaceutical specialties.

All goods arriving in Panama, consigned to residents of the Republic, but intended to be reexported immediately must be marked "PANAMA IN TRANSIT" on the boxes or outside containers. All accompanying documents should indicate that goods are "In Transit" merchandise. Packages may be marked with either brush or stencil. Weights are not required to be indicated, but it is preferable to show them.

Shipping Documents and Fees

A consular invoice, commercial invoice and bill of lading are the basic documents required for freight shipments to Panama, regardless of value. No consular documents are required on shipments by parcel post or air cargo or on shipments to the Colón Free Zone. Shipping documents must be presented to a Panamanian Consulate for legalization within 8 working days after the issuance date of the ocean bill of lading. To avoid fines, the issuance date should be the sailing date of the vessel rather than the date the bill is presented to the steamship company.

Consular Invoice

Consular Invoices on prescribed official forms sold by Panamanian Consulates are required on all freight shipments to Panama. They must be prepared in Spanish, in triplicate, and presented for legalization to the same Consulate where they were purchased. Two copies will be retained by the Consulate. The consular invoices may be written either in ink or on a typewriter, but must be free from erasures or corrections. The heading of the consular invoice should be filled out by the shipper to show the port of shipment, the name of the consignee, the port of entry, and the final destination.

On the back of the invoice is a statement to be signed under oath to the effect that the invoice is accurate in all respects and includes no goods the importation of which is prohibited. In the columns for descriptive information there should be indicated the numbering used on the packages, number of packages, capacity in liters (if applicable), net and gross weights, description of the merchandise, including its total value and the value per unit (f.o.b. value port of shipment). If other expenses are shown (ocean freight, insurance, etc.), they should be shown separately and not included in the f.o.b. value of the goods.

Bill of Lading

The bill of lading must be presented to the Panamanian Consulate in triplicate, after having been signed by the steamship company. The original will be certified by the Consulate, which will retain two nonnegotiable copies. "To order" bills of lading are accepted provided the shipper is a responsible party and has a responsible agent at the port of entry. The name of the person to be notified must be given. This document must, of course, show the freight charges.

Commercial Invoices

The commercial invoice, in quadruplicate, may be prepared in either English or Spanish and should contain the following: name and address of the person or firm selling the goods, and the purchaser or consignee; the kind, quality and description of the goods, classified separately according to their value, partial prices and total price invoiced. The value to be shown is f.o.b. port of shipment. If ocean freight and insurance are shown, they must be separated from the f.o.b. value.

Merchandise may not be declared under generic names, such as "hardware" or "tools", but must be listed in accordance with the tariff nomenclature, such as "nails", "saws", "hammers", "handles" and "clamps."

Gross and net weights in kilograms must be given if the goods are assessed on a weight basis; otherwise in meters, liters, or other units as appropriate. In addition, the unit value of each item must be shown.

Each copy of the commercial invoice must contain a sworn statement to the effect that the information contained is true and correct and that the selling price is as stated without deduction of any kind. If a commission or discount is granted, the amount must be shown. The sworn statement must be in Spanish and read as follows:

"Conste bajo la gravedad del juramento, con la firma puesta al pie de esta declaracion, que todos y cada uno de los datos expresados en esta factura, son exactos y verdaderos y que la suma total declarada es la misma en que se han vendido las mercaderias." (I swear under oath and under the hand of the declarant that the information set forth here is true and correct and the sale is effected for the sum total as declared without deductions of any kind.)

A fine of 5 percent of the total value of the invoice is levied for failure to include this declaration.

Other Documents

Import License.—On shipments of meat, eggs, milk and milk products and by-products, live animals and tanned leather, the import licenses issued by the Panamanian Department of Animal Health in the Ministry of Agricultural Development must be presented to the Consulate together with other documents.

Phytosanitary Certificate

This certificate is required on all shipments of meat and meat products, and it may be obtained from the U.S. Department of Agriculture. It is legalized free of charge by the Panamanian Consulate and returned to the shipper.

Certificate of Free Sale

Certain merchandise must be accompanied by a certificate to the effect that the sale of the merchandise in question is permitted in the country of origin. This document is prepared by a local chamber of commerce or similar body, notarized and legalized by the nearest Panamanian Consulate.

Consular Fees

Fees for consular services are as follows, but are subject to change:

Consular invoice forms, per set—$3.00; Legalization of commercial invoice for shipments to Panama—$10.00; Legalization of the commercial invoice for shipment of the Free Zone of Colon—$5.00; Legalization of letters of correction (a set of one original and 4 copies)—$5.00; Legalization of an additional copy of the consular invoice or the bill of lading—$0.50; Legalization of County Clerk's signature—$5.00; For the immediate return of documents ("rush tickets")—$3.00; Legalization of sanitary certificate—Free.

Documents legalized on Sunday or on a Panamanian holiday are subject to double the usual fee. A fee of 5 percent ad valorem is collected as part of the consular fee on goods consigned to Government-bonded warehouses. This fee, which is not refundable, may be credited to the payment of import duties when the merchandise is subsequently cleared by Panamanian customs.

Special Zones

There are two special zones in Panama in which imports are treated differently by the Government of Panama. These zones are the Colón Free Zone and the Panama Canal Area. U.S. firms interested in the Panamanian market should be aware of the special nature of these two markets.

Colón Free Zone

Established by law in 1948 and made operational in 1953, the Colón Free Zone (CFZ) is now the oldest and largest free trade zone in the Western Hemisphere. With over $3.5 billion in trade (imports and exports) in 1982, the CFZ is second only to Hong Kong among the free trade zones of the world. Currently, some 465 companies representing about 1,000 foreign firms, operate in the CFZ. Approximately 11,200 employees work in the CFZ.

In the 1970-1980 period, the CFZ experienced a remarkable average annual growth rate of about 24 percent. The year 1980 was an especially good one, with the value of total imports and exports increasing nearly 35 percent. The rate of growth fell to 8.8 percent in 1981 and was negative in 1982, about 7 percent drop in value, because of the depressed economies of many Central and South American countries. Turnover was off 50 percent or more during the last months of 1982 and the first half of 1983. The longer term outlook for the CFZ, however, promises a rebound as neighboring countries recover and the CBI takes effect.

Modes of Operation.—Companies may use the CFZ for warehousing, exhibition, packing and unpacking, manufacturing, bottling, mounting, assembling, refining, purifying, mixing, converting, and manipulation of all types of goods, products, raw materials, containers and other articles.

Most CFZ activity is related to reexportation. Beverages and tobacco, electronic and home electrical applicances, pharmaceutical, medical and laboratory supplies, photographic equipment, tools, perfumes and cosmetics, watches and jewelry, textiles and apparel and footwear comprise the greatest volume of goods reexported from the Free Zone. Products from Japan, Taiwan, Korea and Hong Kong account for the bulk of the CFZ imports; the United States' share is approximately 15 percent of total CFZ imports.

Goods which enter, are stored or leave the CFZ destined for foreign ports are free of tax, charges, and all other fees. There are no licenses or permits to be bought from any municipal or governmental agency. Profits from CFZ reexports are taxed at preferential rates.

All land within the CFZ complex, which includes the original 94 acres in Colón, the 87 acres recently opened in France Field and a new industrial park area now being developed, is owned by the CFZ Administration, an agency of the Panamanian Government. Virtually all land in the original CFZ area and in France Field has been leased. U.S. firms interested in establishing themselves in the CFZ, rather than being represented by a local firm already there, may purchase a lease contract from a Free Zone leaseholder for prices ranging from $500 to $1,000 per square meter or may rent space for rates in the $15 to $35 per square meter per month range. In either case, the CFZ Administration levies a $0.30 per square meter monthly fee.

Benefits of a Free Zone Operation.—U.S. firms which are new to the Latin American markets should view the CFZ as a one-stop way to reach the entire region. By having goods represented by a CFZ firm with contacts and salesmen throughout the region, a firm can achieve Latin American coverage by just shipping to the Free Zone. The shortened pipeline also enables reduced shipment time to customers particularly during peak production periods. Moreover, the particular invoice and

documentation requirements for the many countries in the region are done by the Free Zone representative, relieving the U.S. firm of that administrative burden.

The advantages, privileges and facilities afforded by the CFZ to its users can be summarized in the following points:

(1) Outstanding geographic location providing the possibility of stategic distribution to points all over the world.

(2) The traditional cooperation of the Panamanian authorities with foreign investors.

(3) Facilities for the assembly of different items, manufacturing and processing of industrial products at low cost.

(4) Availability of experienced or easily trained workers, many with English language skills.

(5) Facilities for the exhibition of articles intended for sale.

(6) Facilities for bulk storage and for repacking and reexport in small quantities.

(7) Quick invoicing and collection of accounts.

(8) Complete absence of import licenses.

(9) Possibilities of quick delivery to customers in nearby countries in cases of emergency.

(10) Greater speed in the movement of stocks, with the resultant better use of credit lines.

(11) Daily express air freight service to major cities around the world.

(12) Frequent ocean shipping services to leading ports worldwide.

(13) Reasonable rates for air freight and express.

(14) Fast and efficient handling of orders received, at a lower cost than in the United States.

(15) The Panamanian balboa is in effect the United States dollar.

(16) Excellent international banking facilities, with moderate service rates.

(17) No tax of any kind on the export of capital or the payment of dividends abroad.

(18) Preferential income tax rate.

(19) Import and reexport of goods free of taxes, charges, and any other type of feee.

(20) Public warehousing service to receive, repack, and dispatch goods, according to orders, without it being necessary for the user to install himself materially in the Free Zone.

U.S. firms interested in finding a representative in the CFZ should contact the nearest U.S. Department of Commerce District Office and request the Agent/Distributor Service.

Expansion of the Free Zone.—Since its founding, the CFZ has been limited to a 94-acre area in the city of Colón. Until the entry into force of the Panama Canal Treaty in 1979, neither Colón nor its Free Zone, enveloped as they were by the territory of the Canal Zone, was able to expand. With the treaty-mandated reversion of much of the surrounding land to Panamanian use, vast amounts of new acreage has become available for the Zone's expansion, necessary to accommodate the more than 200 new firms which have expressed interest in initiating CFZ operations.

In 1980, the World Bank and a consortium of banks led by the Industrial Bank of Japan agreed to grant the GOP a financing package totaling $105 million for the expansion of the CFZ and for improvements in the Port of Cristobal and in the city of Colón itself. At the heart of the 4-year program, called the Colón Urban Development Project, is the proposed doubling of the CFZ and the creation of an industrial park to eventually cover 350 acres. Already 30 new warehouses have been built in the new commercial area and others are now under construction. Among the companies reportedly moving into this expansion area are: National Cash Register, SKF of Sweden, NTN of Japan, and Samsung of Korea. About 90 acres are currently being prepared for the new industrial park. Companies wishing more information about the Colón Free Zone should contact the CFZ Promotion Director, P.O. Box 1118, Colón, Republic of Panama (telex: 328-9287; telephone: 45-1033).

Documents on Shipments to Colón Free Zone.—Freight shipments consigned to established commercial interests in the CFZ must be accompanied by a bill of lading and a commercial invoice. No consular invoice is required, but the commercial invoice requires consular legalization. It should be presented to a Panamanian Consulate in duplicate, the original having been notarized, along with the original bill of lading which must first be signed by the steamship company. The commercial invoice must contain the sworn declaration mentioned on page 34 above. The Consulate will return the documents to the shipper. The invoice must clearly show the destination of the goods as "ZONA LIBRE DE COLÓN."

The Canal Area

On October 1, 1979 two treaties entered into force which superceded all previous understandings between Panama and the United States concerning the Panama Canal. One treaty insures the neutrality of the Canal; the second governs the operations and defense of the Canal and provides for Panamanian territorial jurisdiction over the former Canal Zone. The latter treaty, known as the Panama Canal Treaty, expires on December 31, 1999 at which time Panama will assume full responsibility for Canal operations and maintenance. During the term of the Panama Canal Treaty, the Panama Canal Commission, a U.S. Government agency which replaced the Panama Canal Company, will operate and maintain the Canal. Five Americans and four Panamanians constitute the Commission Board. Until 1990, the Canal Administrator will be an American, and the Deputy Administrator will be a Panamanian. Beginning in 1990, the Canal Administrator will be a Panamanian and the Deputy Administrator will be an American.

The Canal Area, or former Canal Zone, has long been the single most important factor affecting the Panamanian economy. Some 12,000 Panamanians are employed in the Canal Area and an estimated $450 million is contributed annually to the Panamanian economy in the form of wages and purchases of goods and services. The Panama Canal Treaty has increased the importance of the Canal Area to the Panamanian economy. Under the Treaty, more than 1,000 square kilometers have been transferred to Panamanian use, or about 64 percent of the former Canal Zone. Panama's earnings from the Canal have also risen, not only because of an increase in the annual cash payments before the Treaty (about $80 million as compared with $2.3 million before the Treaty), but also because of the development of lands and facilities which have reverted to Panamanian use, such as major port facilities and the trans-isthmian railroad.

One of the most important end-users of U.S. goods and services in Panama is the Panama Canal Commission. For fiscal year 1982, the Commission operated with a budget of $425 million, of which almost $20 million was designated for capital projects and equipment acquisitions. Of particular importance for U.S. firms interested in selling to the Commission is the Storehouse Division of the Commission's General Services Bureau. The Storehouse Division's Inventory Management Bureau is responsible for repeated purchases of over 40,000 different items from soap to lock gears. The Purchasing and Contracts Branch of the Storehouse Division is responsible for the procurement of big-ticket items such as tug boats and towing locomotives. U S firms interested in making contact with this unit of the Commission may wish to communicate with Mr. E. How, Chief, Purchasing and Contracts Branch, Storehouse Division, Panama Canal Commission, APO Miami 34011. (telephone 52-3216).

Goods imported by the Panama Canal Commission and by U.S. government agencies in the Canal Area are exempt from Panamanian import duties and other charges. Panamanian goods purchased by the Commission or by other U.S. Government agencies in the Canal Area are considered Panamanian exports: nonPanamanian goods are considered Panamanian reexports and in both cases the commerce is registered in Panamanian trade statistics.

For further information on the operations of the Panama Canal, interested persons may wish to contact the Office of the Secretary, Panama Canal Commission, 425 Thirteenth St. N.W. Washington, D.C. 20004 (Telephone 202-724-0104).

Distribution and Promotion Channels

Most foreign goods are handled in Panama by local agents or distributors. Panama has a rather detailed law governing relations between companies and their agents, representatives or distributors. The law is Cabinet Decree/344 of October 1969, as amended by Executive Decree No. 9 of February 7, 1970. An informal translation of the major provisions of the law follows. Readers are cautioned, however, that this information should not be used in lieu of competent legal advice in matters pertaining to obligations under the law. Representatives here include agents and/or distributors.

The preamble states that merchants and corporations who act as representatives, agents and/or distributors of domestic and foreign firms must be indemnified when the contracts under which they perform these functions are unilaterally nullified without just cause.

Article 1 defines an authorized representatives as one who has legally registered a written document to that effect before competent authority. The agreement may be exclusive or on any other legal basis. Article 2 states that if he can prove that he has effectively served as the representative, he shall be considered to be the legal representative.

Article 3 requires that representation agreements be registered with the Department of Commerce of the Ministry of Commerce and Industries. The registration fee is B/500, to be paid in fiscal stamps.

Article 5 sets forth the schedule according to which representatives must be indemnified if the firm, without just cause, cancels, modifies or does not renew the contract. The basic indemnity is a multiple of the equivalent of the average gross annual earnings (*utilidades brutas anuales*) of the representative over a stated period. For agreements in force up to 5 years, the indemnity is the average gross annual earnings over the whole period. For agreements in force 5-to-10 years, the indemnity is twice the annual gross earnings during the last 5 years. For agreements in force 10-to-15 years, the indemnity is three times gross annual earnings over the last 5 years. For agreements in force 15-to-20 years, the multiple is 4 times gross annual earnings over the last 5 years. Over 20 years, the indemnity is 5 times annual gross earnings during the last 5 years.

Article 5 also requires that the firm shall buy back the representative's stock of its products and pay any expenses accrued while the stock was in his warehouse.

Article 6 explains what constitutes just cause for cancellation, modification or refusal to renew a representative's contract. These conditions are: lack of compliance with the contract; fraud or abuse of confidence; ineptitude or negligence; sustained decrease in sales attributable to the representative except when caused by the imposition of import quotas; disclosure of confidential information; any action attributable to the representative detrimental to the good conduct of the business for which the agreement was set up.

Article 7 states that the Ministry of Commerce and Industries shall rule on conflicts under the law. This ruling may be appealed to the Executive Branch within 5 days of notification of the ruling. Article 8 states the types of evidence admissible for an appeal.

Article 9 states that unless the case is proven prior to the cancellation, modification, or refusal to renew, such action will be assumed to be unjustified. The plaintiff may obtain a suspension of the agreement while the case is being argued by posting a bond for the amount of the indemnity to which the defendant would be entitled. Once the deposit is made, the plaintiff can enter an agreement with a third party for representation. If the plaintiff loses the case, he pays the cost of the suit in addition to the indemnity.

Article 10 states that the failure to comply with the law will result in a suspension of imports into the country of the products of the company violating the law.

Article 11 states that the protection granted by this law cannot be renounced except with the approval of the Ministry of Commerce and Industries. Conflicts under the law can be compromised or arbitrated by third parties, however, when confirmed by the Ministry.

Atlapa Convention Center

U.S. firms considering market entry in Panama and in other countries in the area may wish to consider participation in one of the several trade shows being planned in 1984-85 at the Atlapa Convention Center. Inaugurated in June of 1980, the Center is considered by experts to be the most modern exhibition and conference center in Latin America.

The Atlapa Center, which takes its name from the Atlantic and Pacific Oceans, has a main exhibit hall of 32,000 square feet, two theaters (one seating 3,000), a modern communications/translation system, and other first-class facilities. The Center is declared a customs-bonded site for all exhibit materials; all customs duties on display materials are waived.

Panama's central location in Latin America, its good airline connections (26 international air carriers serve Panama) the availability of first-class hotels (a new 400-room hotel opened in mid 1982 adjacent to the Atlapa Convention Center), and the country's political stability will help to draw visitors to the Center's trade shows from all over Latin America. For additional information about Atlapa, you may wish to contact Atlapa Convention Center Promotion Office, Box R, Panama 9A., R.P. Tel. 26-4202.

Guidance for Business Travelers Abroad

Entrance requirements for U.S. Citizens

U.S. citizens can enter Panama with a Tourist Card issued by transportation companies. The Card is valid for 30 days and may be extended for two more 30-day periods. Business executives employed by branches of U.S. firms in Panama should apply for a Special Temporary Visitor's Visa. The U.S. firm must certify that the applicant is an executive and that his salary comes from a non-Panamanian source, that his salary is in excess of a certain amount (subject to change), that he will be employed in a section of the firm dealing with operations with another country and that he will be repatriated upon the completion of his work.

U.S. citizens wanting to invest in a Panamanian enterprise should apply for an Investor's Visa. A minimum of $40,000 must be invested and $600 must be deposited in advance, $500 with the Ministry of Government and Justice and $100 with the National Treasury. Further details on entry requirements are obtainable from Panamanian consulates throughout the United States.

National Holidays

There is no official business conducted on national holidays and government offices are closed. The following days are considered national holidays:

- January 1—New Year's Day
- January 9—Mourning Day
  Carnival Tuesday; Good Friday
- May 1—Labor Day
- October 11—Anniversary of Revolution
- November 3—Day of Independence
  from Colombia
- November 4—Flag Day
- November 10—First Call for Independence
  from Spain
- November 28—Independence from Spain
- December 8—Mother's Day (Feast of the
  Immaculate Conception)
- December 25—Christmas

Language

Spanish is the official language, but English is widely understood in the major cities, particularly in business and official circles. English is the mother tongue of the West Indian community (14 percent of the total population).

Communications

Telephone service in Panama City is good. Long-distance service is available to all parts of the country. Telephone calls from Panama to the former Canal Zone are considered long distance and the cost may vary from $0.08 to $0.30 for 3 minutes, depending on location. Facilities are excellent for telephone calls to the United States and to other parts of the world via satellite. Rates vary depending on the U.S. time zone or the overseas country involved. For station-to-station calls to the United States, weekday rates are $7 for the first 3 minutes and $2 for each additional minute. Night, Saturday and Sunday rates vary from $4.30 for the first 3 minutes and $1.10 for each additional minute.

Certain areas of Panama have direct long-distance dialing capability to the United States and to other overseas countries. Panama is expanding its direct dial capability to all sections of Panama City. Cable facilities are excellent and offer worldwide service.

Currency and Weights and Measures

The official currency of Panama is the Balboa (symbol B/.) which is on par with the U.S. dollar. The Balboa exists only in coin form of the same denomination and size as U.S. coins. The official paper currency of Panama is the U.S. bill.

Both the U.S. system of weights and measures and the metric system are used in Panama. Speed limits are posted in miles per hour in some places, kilometers per hour in other places and some signs have both miles and kilometers per hour limits given.

Sources of Economic and Commercial Information

U.S. Government Representation in Panama

The United States is represented in the Republic of Panama by an Embassy in Panama City located at Avenida Balboa at 38th Street, Panama City. The telephone number in Panama City is 27-1777. U.S. Foreign Commercial Service Officers and U.S. Foreign Service Officers in the Commercial and Economic Sections of the Embassy are available to assist American businessmen visiting Panama. A booklet, *Key Officers of Foreign Service Post*, which provides names of current officers at U.S. Embassies, is published quarterly by the U.S. Department of State. Copies may be purchased for 70 cents each, or $2.00 per year on a subscription basis from the Government Printing Office, Washington, D.C. 20402.

Government of Panama Representation in the United States

The Government of Panama maintains an Embassy in Washington, D.C. at 2862 McGill Terrace, 20008, telephone (202) 483-1407. Consulates are located in New York City at 1270 Avenue of the Americas, 10020, telephone (212) 246-3773, as well as in Baltimore, Houston, Miami, New Orleans, Philadelphia, Los Angeles and San Francisco. Consult local telephone directories for addresses and telephone numbers. There is also a Panama Government Trade and Investment Center located at Suite 208, 2355 Salzedo St., Coral Gables, Florida 33134. Telephone 305-446-3343.

Chambers of Commerce

American Chamber of Commerce and Industries
Aptdo. 168
Estafeta Balboa
Panama, Rep. of Panama
Calle Richardo Arias—Edif. America
Tel. 69-3525, 69-3881

Camara de Comercio, Industrias y Agricultura de Panama
(Chamber of Commerce, Industry and Agriculture of Panama)
Aptdo. 74
Panama 1, Rep. of Panama
Avenida Cuba y Ecuador 33A-18
Tel. 25-1158, 25-0833

Camara de Comercio de Colón
Aptdo. 5076
Colón, Rep. of Panama
Aptdo. 322
Ave. Amador Guerrero
Colón, R.P.
Tel. 47-8181, 47-8323

Camara de Comercio de David
Aptdo. 225
David, Prov. de Chiriqui
Panama
Tel. 75-4851

Other Panamanian Trade Associations

Camara Panamena de la Construccion
(Panamanian Chamber of Construction)
Calle Aquilino de la Guardia
Aptdo. 6793
Panama 5, R.P.
Tel. 64-2255, 64-2466

Asociacion de Ganaderos
(Cattlemen's Association)
Edificio Vallarino, Piso 2
Calle 32 y Ave. Justo Arosemena
Aptdo. 6494
Panama 5, R.P.
Tel. 25-1236, 25-1337

Sindicato de Industriales de Panama (SIP)
(Panamanian Industrialists Union)
Ave. Ricardo J. Alfaro (Tumba Muerto)
Aptdo. 952
Panama 1, Rep. of Panama
Tel. 67-4665, 67-4666

Asociacion Panamena de Ejecutivos de Empresa
(APEDE)
(Panamanian Association of Business Executives)
Calle 42 y Avenida Balboa
Aptdo. 1331
Panama 1, Rep. of Panama
Tel. 25-3720, 25-0757

Asociacion Bancaria de Panama
(Banking Association of Panama)
Edificio Banco Union
Piso No. 15
Aptdo. 4554
Panama 5, Rep. of Panama
Tel. 69-7044, 69-7252

Asociacion de Usurarios de la Zona Libre
(Association of Free Zone users)
Aptdo. 3118
Zona Libre de Colón
Tel. 41-4992, 41-4244

Consejo Nacional de la Empresa Privada (CONEP)
(National Council of Private Enterprises)
Calle 52 y Aquilino de la Guardia
(in front of Ejecutivo Hotel)
Aptdo. 1276
Panama 1, Rep. of Panama
Tel. 69-5105, 69-5196

Publications

Descriptive Background on Panama

—*Panama—A Country Study.* Area Handbook Series No. 550-46. U.S. Government Printing Office.

—*Foreign Economic Trends and their Implications For the United States; Panama*; (Dept. of Commerce, 1983). A brief, macro-level report on recent economic trends. Excellent primer.

—*Investment Climate Statement for Panama*, U.S. Embassy (July 1982). Embassy-prepared background information of interest to potential investors, available from USDOC.

Statistics on Panama

—*Memoria, Ministerio de Comercio e Industrias,* Republica de Panama (1982), Spanish only, Ministry of Commerce and Industry Annual Report. Very complete summaries of government activities in various sectors of the economy.

—*Economic Financial and Social Information Concerning the Republic of Panama*, Banco Nacional de Panama (1982). This report stresses banking information—chartered banks, deposits, loan activity, etc. There are some good tables and charts on the performance of certain economic sectors.

—*Panama en Cifras*, Anos 1976-1980, Contraloria General de la Republica. Spanish only (Nov. 1981). An annual compendium of official government statistics.

—*Market Share Reports, Panama*, U.S. Department of Commerce (1978-80). A statistical analysis of exports to Panama by product and country of origin (14 industrialized countries).

Guides for Doing Business in Panama

—*Panama*, Ernst, Whitney, International Series (July 1981). Very quick review stressing financial and tax aspects.

—*Taxation in Panama*, Deloitte, Haskins and Sells International Tax and Business Service (March 1981). Specific information on tax issues. Very thorough.

—*Doing Business in Panama*, Price, Waterhouse Information Guide (July 1980). A handbook for businessmen. Slightly dated in illustrative data but quite current with respect to laws governing business. Designed for quick reading.

—*Panama: A Business Profile*, Arosemena, Noriega y Castro Investigacion y Desarrollo, S.A. (1980). More specific citation and application of laws and regulations.

—*Panama*, Business International Corp., Investing, Licensing, Trading Conditions Abroad (June 1980). A good, brief look at investment, licensing and trading though examples are somewhat dated.

Legal Foundation for Doing Business in Panama

—All publications below, except for *Brief Corporative Analysis of Panamanian Corporation Laws* and *Statement of the Laws of Panama in Matters Affecting Business*, are the actual texts of laws of particular interest to exporters and investors. They are often cited by other publications listed in this report.

—*Brief Comparative Analysis of Panamanian Corporation Laws*, Fabrega, Lopez y Pedreschi (1981).

—*Light Assembly Industry in Panama*, Republic of Panama (1979).

—*Measures with Regard to Reinsurance Operations in Panama*, (Reglamentacion de las Operaciones de Reaseguros en Panama), English and Spanish texts, Republica de Panama (1977).

—*Compilacion de Leyes del Comercio y la Industria*, in Spanish with English Guide to Sections, (January 1978).

—*Statement of the Laws of Panama in Matters Affecting Business*, Organization of American States (1974). An English language presentation of Panamanian business laws. The most complete source book of its kind.

—*Regulations for Representation, Agency and/or Distributorship of Products or Services of Manufacturers of Domestic or Foreign Firms in the Republic of Panama* (1969).

Doing Business in the Free Trade Zone

—*Zona Libre de Colon*, (quadrilingual) Republica de Panama. A pictorial presentation of the FTZ. An instructive text is included.

—*Memoria 1982-1983, Zona Libre de Colon*, (Annual Report—only in Spanish).

Doing Business in the Panama Canal Area

—*Panama Canal Handbook*, 1982-1983, Boyd Steamship Corporation (1983). Up-to-date description of Canal operations.

—*How to Conduct Business in the Panama Canal Area*, Contracting offices of the Department of Defense (July 1982). A guide to Armed Forces purchasing.

—*Panama Canal Commission*, Canal Commission tenders are published in the Commerce Business Daily, U.S. Department of Commerce. The procedures for submitting bids are found in the Federal Procurement Regulations as the PCC remains a U.S. Government Agency).

Caribbean Basin Initiative, Panama

—*Panama Country Team Plan for Implementing the Caribbean Basin Initiative*, Combined Foreign Service Agencies Report (July 16, 1982). Excellent link of CBI

proposals to actual and prospective socio-economic conitions in Panama. Prepared by the U.S. Embassy.

—*Country Development Strategy Statement, FY 1984: Panama*, Agency for International Development (January, 1982). Annual recapitulation of socio-economic events in Panama's recent past.

Other Publications

—*Report to the Government of Panama on the Betterment of Working Conditions and Environment*, (Spanish only—Informe al Gobierno de Panama sobre el Mejoramiento de las Condiciones y del Medio de Trabajo) International Labor Organization (1982). A recently completed study on actual working conditions in Panama which will form the documentary basis for policy-making conferences among Panama's business, labor, and government leaders.

—*A Qualitative and Quantitative Analysis of Panama's Investment Assets and Liabilities as Perceived by Foreign Executives*, American Chamber of Commerce in Panama (August 1983). Self-explanatory. Methodologically-sound, a well-documented survey.

—*Estudio Motivacional Sobre la Empresa Privada y su Proyeccion en la Comunidad*, (Spanish only) American Chamber of Commerce and Industry of Panama (August 1982). A survey of Panamanian attitudes towards private enterprise and its effect on the community.

—*Estudio de Opinion Publica Sobre Imagen y Actitudes hacia las Empresas Norteamericanas en la Republica de Panama*, (Spanish only) American Chamber of Commerce and Industry of Panama (June 1981). A study of public opinion regarding U.S. companies in Panama.

—*Directorio Comercial Industrial de Panama* (Spanish only but easily decipherable (1980-1981)

- *Informe Anual de la Junta Directiva, Asociacion Bancaria de Panama*, (Spanish only). Annual report including complete Panama banking directory.

Business Profile—Panama

Foreign Trade (in U.S. Dollars)

Imports.—1983: Total, 1,245.0 million; U.S. Share, 393.0 million. 1980: total, 1,288.9 million; U.S. share, 424.2 million. Major items in Panama's imports from the United States include industrial machinery, transportation equipment, telecommunications equipment, paper and paperboard products.

Exports.—1983: total, 303.5 million; U.S. share, 163.9 million. 1980: total, 352.4; U.S. share 172.3 million. Major exports include shrimp, sugar and bananas.

Trade Policy.—Some import restrictions exist in an effort to promote and protect new domestic industries, but overall trade policy is liberal. Preferential trade agreements exist with other Central American countries.

Trade Outlook.—U.S. will continue to be Panama's major trading partner. Promising products for export include building materials, fertilizers, and business equipment. Panama is expected to increase non-traditional exports to the U.S. market under the CBI.

Foreign Investment

Panama encourages foreign investment, offering generous incentives to investors. CBI beneficiary status further enhances Panama's investment climate. Panama reports a total of $338.7 million of foreign investment for 1980. Total cumulative U.S. investment as of yearend 1981 was $3.78 billion, about half of which concentrated on the services sector, primarily finance and insurance.

Finance

Currency.—The *balboa*, of 100 *centesimos*, is the official unit of exchange. However, the U.S. dollar is the sole paper currency in circulation.

Public Sector Finances.—Panama's public sector deficit fell to −$246 million in 1983, but the external debt rose to $3.45 billion.

Foreign Aid.—Local development projects continue to benefit from AID, IDB and World Bank lending, despite a shortage of local counterpart funds. A Structural Adjustment Loan was signed recently with the IMF, and Panama has pledged to remain within IMF guidelines on public sector deficits and borrowing.

Balance of Payments.—Large deficits on trade account have been largely offset by income from the Panama Canal, the trans-Panama oil pipeline and capital flows from abroad.

Economy

GDP.—Estimated 1983 GDP at current prices, $4,400 million: 1981's growth rate of 4.2 percent increased to 5.5 percent in 1982, but fell to 0.2 percent in 1983.

Agriculture.—Less than 25 percent of land area farmed. Fertile soil and wet climate provide conditions for cultivation of tropical fruits and vegetables. Development of agriculture (including food processing) a top priority of Panamanian Government.

Industry.—Main industries include food processing, textiles, clothing, shoes, cement, pharmaceuticals, and furniture. No heavy industry.

Basic Economic Facilities

Transportation.—In 1980 there was a total of 8,612 miles of roads of all types of surfaces. Panama is served by a variety of shipping lines and airlines.

Communications.—In 1980 there were 172,000 phones in Panama. The country is well served by radio, telephone and international radio telegraph systems.

Power.—1980 installed capacity 519,140 k.w. Current is 110 volt, 3 phase, a.c., 60 cycle for lighting, and 220-volt for power.

Natural Resources

Land.—Area 28,575 square miles, not including 10-mile wide Canal Zone that bisects the country. Largely mountainous and hilly.

Climate.—Temperature in mountains: at lower levels tropical. Year-round temperature variation between 70 degrees and 90 degrees F. Rain on Caribbean coast averages over 100 inches per year: about 63 inches on the Pacific coast. Mean relative humidity is 80 percent.

Minerals.—Many minerals, but known deposits either low grade or of undetermined value. Explorations being conducted: major copper and molybdeum deposits uncovered.

Forestry.—Tropical rain forests in Caribbean side and deciduous forests on Pacific are part of extensive forest resources. About 75 sawmills and three plywood manufacturing plants in operations.

Population

Size.—As of 1981, 1.986 million, of which 56 percent urban and concentrated in low-land areas adjacent to Canal. As overall growth rate of about 3 percent.

Language.—Spanish is official, but English widely used.

Education.—Enrollment (1980) 338,674 primary and 172,422 intermediate level. Primary education free and compulsory, but dropout rate high. Illiteracy about 14 percent. Two universities with a total of 40,000 students in 1980.

Labor.—Economically active population 1979, 580,000. 29.5 percent in agriculture and related activities, 27.5 percent in services, 10.0 percent in manufacturing. Unemployment estimates: Panamanian government—12 percent: private—15-20 percent.

Market Profile— PAPUA NEW GUINEA

Foreign Trade

Exports.—Exports for FY 1979 were $960 million, and the major products exported were coffee, cocoa, copra, ores, and wood.

Imports.—Total imports for FY 1980 were $1.025 billion, consisting primarily of meat, rice, petroleum, metals, machinery, and transportation equipment.

Trade Policy.—Imports subject to duties at rates of up to 50 percent ad valorem, but many items exempt (i.e. food, agricultural inputs, construction materials, chemicals, etc.) Average rate of duty on total merchandise imports less than 10 percent. (An additional import levy of 2.5 percent was imposed.)

Best Trade Prospects.—Forestry and refrigeration equipment, transportation equipment, and consumer goods.

Trading Association.—Burns Philp and Company, Ltd.; Steamship Trading Company, Ltd.; and W.R. Carpenter (P.O. Box 704, Port Moresby).

Finance

Currency.—The Kina. Exchange rate: 1 Kina = US$1.18 (1982).

Banks.—The major development banks are Reserve bank of Australia, and Papua New Guinea Development Bank. The major trading banks are: Commonwealth Bank, Bank of South Wales, Australia and New Zealand Banking Group, and National Bank of Australia.

Foreign Aid.—An aid agreement with Australia provided $1,158 million during the 5-year period, 1976-81. Additional agreements already concluded will provide a total of about $45.5 million worth of aid from the European Economic Community, the Asian Development Bank, and the World Bank. Most aid will be utilized to expand industrial and agricultural output, to improve transportation facilities, for hydroelectric power, and for education.

Foreign Investment.—Papua New Guinea would like to attract investors. However, the Government closely controls the allocation of resources and the taxation policies to ensure reasonable benefits for its citizens. Investment in forestry and timber, fishing, and agriculture-related industries, as well as large scale mineral development, is welcome.

Economy

GNP.—The final figure for FY 1979 was $2.05 billion.

Industry.—The Government is concentrating on developing this area of the economy. Development projects are generally aimed for improvement in light industries such as the processing of agricultural products and the production of import substitutes.

Agriculture.—Agricultural industries are the largest market for labor. Principal products are copra, coffee, cocoa, rubber, timber, tea, palm oil, and cattle. The Government is interested in developing sugar, spice, and rice production.

Development Plans.—The investments are designed to develop the country's industries and transporation system. The Government has obtained loans to help initiate the development projects.

Basic Economic Facilities

Transportation.—The Farrell Lines offers direct shipment from the United States to Lae, one of two major ports. Domestic shipping companies run regularly from Lae to Port Moresby, the other major port. There are direct flights to Papua-New Guinea by Air Niugini, Qantas, and Air Pacific. An intricate system of air routes connects the small airports throughout the island.

Communications.—Overseas Telecommunications operates coastal radio stations at Port Moresby, Lae, and Rabaul. Madang is a terminal for the SEACOM coaxial cable. The internal radio system and postal telegraph system is large and efficient.

Power.—Electricity consumption per capita per year is 352 kWh.

Natural Resources

Location.—Papua New Guinea is located 200 miles north of Australia. It is an independent nation, and an American Embassy located in Port Moresby represents the United States.

Climate.—Tropical and moist, with no definite dry season.

Minerals.—Reserves of gold, silver, and copper. As of 1976, there were large proven reserves of copper, which the copper industry is now attempting to develop.

Population

Size.—As of 1982, 3.1 million.

Language.—English is the business language. Dialects of Melanesian and Papuan also spoken. There are approximately 700-800 spoken languages.

Education.—The educational system is in the process of development. In 1976, a 5-year education plan was adopted, providing for 6 years primary and 4-6 years of secondary education.

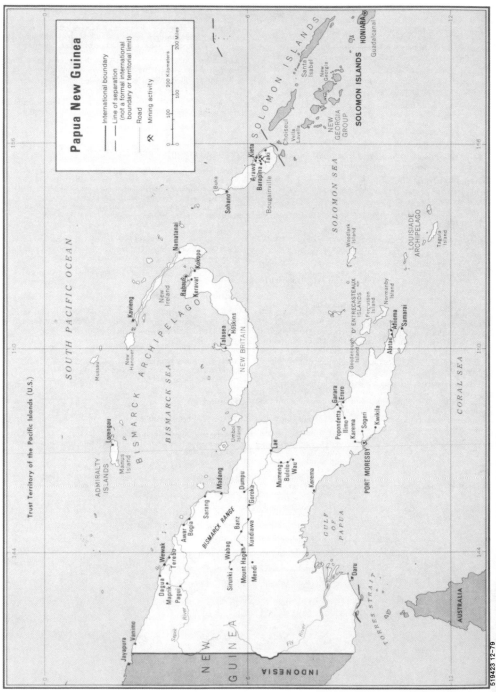

Papua New Guinea

International boundary

Line of separation
(not a formal international
boundary or territorial limit)

Road

Mining activity

0   100   200 Kilometers
0   100   200 Miles

SOLOMON ISLANDS

HONIARA

Guadalcanal

SOLOMON ISLANDS

Choiseul
Santa
Isabel
New
Georgia
NEW
GEORGIA
GROUP

Vella
Lavella

Arawa
Kieta
Barapina Taki
Buka
Bougainville

Sohano

SOLOMON SEA

Namatanai

Kakopo
Rabaul
Keravat

Kavieng

New
Ireland

New
Hanover

BISMARCK   ARCHIPELAGO

Talasea
Hoskins

NEW BRITAIN

Woodlark
Island

D'ENTRECASTEAUX
ISLANDS

Fergusson
Island

Goodenough
Island

Normanby
Island

LOUISIADE
ARCHIPELAGO

Tagula
Island

Ahioma
Samarai

Alotau

SOUTH   PACIFIC   OCEAN

Mussau

BISMARCK   SEA

Lugengau

Manus
Island

ADMIRALTY
ISLANDS

Umbol
Island

Garara
Eroro
Popondetta
Ilimo
Karema
Kwikila
Sogeri

PORT MORESBY

Lae

Mumeng
Bulolo
Wau
Kerema

Madang
Dumpu
Goroka

Sarang

BISMARCK RANGE

Banz
Kundiawa

GULF
OF
PAPUA

Trust Territory of the Pacific Islands (U.S.)

Awar
Bogia

Wewak
Terebu

Dagua
Maprik
Pagui

Sirunki
Wabag
Mount Hagen
Mendi

Sepik   River

Javapura
Vanimo

NEW

GUINEA

INDONESIA

Daru

TORRES   STRAIT

Fly   River

CORAL   SEA

AUSTRALIA

1848

51942.3 12–79

Marketing in Paraguay

Contents

Report Revised September 1980

PARAGUAY

— International boundary

⊙ National capital

— Railroad

— Road

✛ International airport

| 0 | 50 | 100 Kilometers |
| 0 | 50 | 100 Miles |

1850

Introduction

Paraguay has undergone a rapid economic transformation in recent years. This country, with its 2.97 million people and total land area of 154,047 square miles, since 1977 has experienced an average annual growth rate of 10 percent, one of the highest in Latin America.

Historically, the development of landlocked Paraguay had been restricted by political turbulence, remoteness from foreign markets, scattered population, and a weak transport network. Not until the 1970's has the economic potential of the country come to be fully realized. Growth has been stimulated by the development of two of Paraguay's most important physical resources—vast land areas and the huge hydroelectric potential of the Parana River. Work on the Itaipu dam has expanded the construction sector and generated the demand for various industrial products. This, along with the expansion of the agricultural sector, has resulted in accelerated growth, expanding employment, and a rise in per capita income. Other improvements in the standard of living have accompanied the economic boom. For example, the literacy rate has increased and the infant mortality rate has declined. A continued high rate of GNP growth will call for increased government expenditures for education, health, and rural development programs.

The economic policies of the Government, which came to power in 1954, favor private initiative and a free market. Public investment, limited to basic infrastructure and services not provided by the private sector, will increase with GNP growth. Planning policies are aimed at expanding agro-industrial exports through the creation of a favorable climate for private investors.

Three hydroelectric projects underway in the Parana River region have attracted large infusions of investment capital and income. For this reason, the Central Bank was able to increase its foreign reserves and assets to a record level of $612.9 million at the end of 1979 in spite of a $126.6 million trade deficit. Although the Government has maintained cautious fiscal policies, this huge inflow of capital contributed to the inflation rate, which rose from 10.6 percent in 1978 to 28.2 percent in 1979.

The current account deficit has caused the Government to direct development policies towards the transformation of the country's raw materials, production for export, and import substitution. Because of agricultural growth and favorable international prospects for cotton and soybeans, exports are projected to grow at 13 percent a year during 1980–83. GDP growth should maintain a 10 percent annual growth rate in real terms during this period.

In later years, however, the economy is expected to enter into a period of transition during the time between reduced construction activity on the hydroelectric projects in the early eighties and substantial exports of electricity in the late eighties, which will stabilize the balance of payments. During this term increased borrowing may be required to maintain both public and private investment as well as growth.

With the completion of the three hydroelectric plants, Paraguay will become one of the world's major energy producers. This energy, whether used domestically or exported, will be a major factor in government plans to improve and expand transportation, communications, education, and health services. These developments will serve to expand the Paraguayan import market for U.S. manufactured goods and provide greater opportunities for U.S. investment.

Foreign Trade Outlook

As Paraguay's economy continues to grow, the demand for imported goods will increase, especially demand for those that are essential to government plans for continued development of infrastructure, as well as the agricultural and agro-industrial sectors of the economy. Most elements of Paraguay's population are sharing in the exceptional GDP growth. Higher wages and full employment have stimulated the demand for consumer goods. During 1979–83, imports are projected to grow at a rate of 9 percent per annum. An encouraging factor is Paraguay's record level of foreign exchange reserves at approximately $613 million in 1979.

The outlook for foreign investment is highly favorable in Paraguay's laissez-faire and increasingly prosperous economy. The current account deficit of the balance of payments has forced the Government to actively encourage investment that will help to stimulate export-oriented production. Few restrictions are imposed on types of industries that fit into developmental plans. Looking towards the future, opportunities for investment will increase if economic growth continues as expected and as the country begins to benefit from the exploitation of its hydropower.

Implications for the United States

The U.S. share of Paraguay's import market has declined in the past decade as neighboring Argentina and Brazil have capitalized on their location to acquire a larger share of the market. However, U.S. products, helped by dollar devaluation, are doing well in Paraguay's current boom and are expected to do better in the future. The United States exported about $128.2 million worth of goods to Paraguay in 1979, up from $89.7 million one year before, an increase of 42 percent.

Further hydroelectric power development should provide an excellent market for sales of U.S. manufactured construction equipment and electro-mechanical equipment for generation, transmission, and distribution of electric power. Increased attention to the improvement and expansion of agricultural production will lead to greater demand for earthmoving equipment and agricultural machinery and equipment for processing agricultural products. The Government is also promoting construction of cement, fertilizer, and paper plants, as well as steel and aluminum mills.

The information supplied in this report is not intended to serve in lieu of legal counsel. Such advice may be obtained from attorneys in the United States who specialize in foreign law. A list of attorneys in Paraguay may be obtained from the Office of Country Marketing. Bureau of Export Development, U.S. Department of Commerce, Washington, D.C. 20230, or from Department of Commerce District Offices located in 47 cities around the United States.

Best prospects include, but are not limited to:

- construction and earthmoving equipment
- land clearing and logging equipment
- medium and heavy-duty trucks and transportation equipment
- farm machinery equipment
- poultry and dairy equipment
- cotton ginning equipment
- vegetable oil plants and equipment
- cement, fertilizer and paper plants and equipment
- micro-computing hardware and software
- electric motors and equipment
- telecommunications equipment
- woodworking and metalworking equipment
- medical and health care equipment
- central home air-conditioning
- all types of consumer goods

Industry Trends

The Government's development strategy aims at sustaining the growth momentum of agriculture and agro-industry, giving high priority to land settlement and the provision of transport infrastructure to facilitate the flow of goods to domestic and foreign markets.

In 1979, Paraguay's agricultural sector made up 39 percent of the GDP and employed 46 percent of the labor force. Agricultural goods accounted for 95 percent of export earnings and reached a value of $290 million in 1979. There exists a large margin for increased agricultural production since only 20 percent of the arable farm land is now being utilized and more intensive use of the land already being farmed could be undertaken. Commercial agriculture is centered in the area around Asuncion and in the departments of Itapua and Alto Parana. Elsewhere farming activity is predominantly of the subsistence type. The Government of Paraguay is promoting the extension and development of land use through colonization—resettlement programs. Agricultural export growth of 13 percent per annum during 1973–77, resulted primarily from increases in the export of soybeans and cotton. Other principal exports included soybean byproducts, tobacco, vegetable-oils, and lumber. The demand for these products is expected to continue to grow in international markets as well as in Paraguay's domestic market.

The industrial sector is heavily dependent on agriculture since two-thirds of the sector's value-added production is derived from processing agricultural products. Consumer goods, in general, account for more than 80 percent of manufactured goods of which only 3.6 percent are capital intensive goods. Small firms predominate, many of which are concentrated around Asuncion, the main consumer market. Development of the industrial sector will depend on improvement in the availability of raw materials and continued growth and diversification of agricultural production. Essential to industrial growth is the availability of long-term financing as well as the maintenance of a favorable investment climate for private investors.

Paraguay has to import virtually 100 percent of its petroleum requirements. The country has no known reserves of any important mineral, although an American company is currently doing extensive exploration in Eastern Paraguay with a special view toward radioactive materials. Exploitation of the country's main physical resource, hydropower, is proceeding under treaties with Brazil and Argentina that set up two binational authorities for the construction and operation of three hydroelectric plants.

The $9 billion Itaipu project, being built with Brazil on the Parana River, is scheduled to come on line in 1983. When it is completed it will be the world's largest hydroelectric facility, with an annual production capacity of approximately 80 billion kWh per year. Financing has been provided by Brazil's state-run electric power holding company, Brazilian financial institutions, and international lenders. Both countries will be entitled to one-half of the power generated, with Brazil having the option to buy Paraguay's surplus energy. According to the terms of the Itaipu treaty, Paraguay must decide 2 years before the installation of the first turbine in 1983, the amount of energy that the country will use

out of its 50 percent share of the total for the next 20 years.

The two other dams, Yacyreta and Corpus, are being built with Argentina. Yacyreta, downstream from Itaipu, is slated to start energy production in 1986. Construction of housing and other related infrastructure is already underway. Argentina will provide most of the financing with the remainder being supplied by international sources. Corpus, still in the planning stages, will be located between Itaipu and Yacyreta on the Parana River.

These hydroelectric projects are crucial to the development of Paraguay's economy. Their importance lies in the creation of construction and other related jobs, the income they will generate with the sale of electricity to neighboring countries (see table 6 in statistical information section), and their vast potential for energy intensive industrial development. Higher economic growth rates have already resulted from massive investment inflows into the energy sector. Other benefits of the projects will include the improvement of navigation conditions and flood control, the extension of commercial fishing, and the development of recreation areas.

With these dams operating at full capacity, Paraguay will have available, at a relatively low cost, about 65 billion kWh per year, 300 times the present national consumption. The Government intends to use as much of this energy as possible for industrial development. The range of potential industries will be determined by many factors: the price the industries would be required to pay for the energy, the country's lack of known mineral resources, its disadvantageous geographic position vis-a-vis potential markets, and the small size of the economy, which limits economic linkages. In any case, much of Paraguay's vast amounts of energy is certain to be exported. The expectation of energy sales to Brazil provides a favorable outlook for the balance of payments for Paraguay in the years to come.

Marketing Areas

Paraguay's population, estimated at 2.97 million, is small in relation to its land resources. Population density is only 7.3 persons per square kilometer. The country is divided by the Paraguay River into two widely disparate regions. Eastern Paraguay lies in the temperate zone. Receiving ample rainfall, the area consists of gently rolling countryside with tropical forests and fertile grasslands. The Chaco, west of the Paraguay River, comprises almost 60 percent of the country's land area but contains only 5 percent of the population. Its unfavorable climate has caused economic development to be limited to extensive ranching. The little cultivation that has been done in the area is associated with the Mennonite Colonies.

Urbanization has occurred gradually in Paraguay, with only 37 percent of the population living in the urban-areas, namely Asuncion and less than a dozen other towns. There has been a tendency toward decentralization from around Asuncion to the area around Ciudad Presidente Stroessner and Encarnacion where economic activity is expanding rapidly. Development of the eastern and southern parts of the country has been accelerated with the construction of roads and official colonization programs. Yet Asuncion remains the center of Paraguay's political, economic, and cultural life. Most commercial activity takes place in Asuncion; two-thirds of all cargo enters, leaves, or enters and leaves through its port.

The literacy rate is 80 percent in Paraguay. However, about 85 percent of the population 15 years or older has not studied beyond the primary level. Access to education facilities and the quality of such facilities in Paraguay need to be improved to meet the increasing demand for skilled labor. Per capita income has increased significantly in the past few years, along with employment, although the standard of living among the bulk of those living in rural areas remains low, owing in part to limited access to social services. Since there are no strong unions except in the banking sector, labor-management relations are peaceful and strikes are a rarity. Paraguay places no restrictions on the employment of Americans; however, all foreigners must have an official work permit before they can be employed in the country.

Sales Methods

Foreign manufacturers enjoying sustained sales of their products imported into Paraguay typically utilize the services of an agent or distributor. Other manufacturers rely on their subsidiary manufacturing facilities or branch sales offices in neighboring countries such as Argentina and Brazil to achieve sales.

Regardless of the sales methods employed, the most successful foreign manufacturers institute and maintain a substantial market presence in the area. This is accomplished by a variety of techniques.

Trained Sales and Service Personnel.—This is crucial with technologically advanced equipment. Successful foreign manufacturers provide training programs for their personnel or the employees of their sales agents or distributors. Frequently, review training is also provided so that both sales and service employees are familiar with the manufacturer's latest technology. Some American manufacturers have found it necessary or beneficial to bring selected personnel to the United States for on-site training and orientation at their principal plant.

Technical Training and Use Seminars.— Manufacturers often offer free training and use-instruction seminars to prospective buyers in Latin America. This gives the manufacturer an opportunity to instruct in the proper use of the equipment and to exhibit and demonstate it as well. Some American manufacturers bring prospective buyers to the United States to provide a first-hand view of the manufacturing facility and a more direct familiarization with the entire line of equipment and machinery.

Appropriate and Effective Sales Brochure and Materials.—Sales materials in Spanish that provide detailed information on a manufacturer's equipment line and that can be supplied to numerous prospective buyers are an effective means of introducing the equipment. These must be followed up, however, with frequent visits to prospective buyers to further outline the features and advantages of the equipment or products. Weights and measures should be expressed in metric terms.

Regional Supply, Servicing, and Repair Facilities.—Some manufacturers have achieved sales through their ability to provide repair services, assistance with difficult operational problems, and rapid delivery of spare parts through regional repair and supply facilities.

U.S. manufacturers will find that the major factors affecting a decision to buy their products are:

- Quality
- Price
- Delivery time
- After-sale servicing
- Compatibility with installed systems

The order of importance of these factors will vary, of course, depending upon the product and the industry. U.S.-manufactured products are generally regarded as high in quality and competitive in price in Paraguay, but they are frequently rated low on what is regarded as the single most important factor in the decision to buy—financing. American manufacturers offering flexible, innovative, and competitive credit terms will overcome their most difficult hurdle in achieving sales in Paraguay.

Business Approach

Paraguay is racially homogeneous, with 95 percent of the population a mixture of Spanish and Indian descent. Although the Indian tongue, Guarani, is generally spoken, Spanish is the language of government, business, and the usual medium of communication among the more educated.

Americans should be aware of the accepted manner of doing business in Paraguay. Business dress and appearance, as well as one's general approach to business relations, should be conservative. A prior appointment for a business call is usually necessary and considered a customary courtesy. Typically, business is discussed after social amenities. Personal visits and efforts to establish personal contacts are appreciated in Paraguay, as are business cards in Spanish. Patience must be exercised. Entertaining is common and much business is conducted over lunch. The local herbal tea or expresso-type coffee can be expected with many afternoon business appointments.

The best months for business travel in Paraguay are April through September. Businesspeople typically take vacations in January and February during the southern hemisphere's summer season. It is best to avoid business travel in Paraguay during the 2 weeks before and after Christmas and during the week before Ash Wednesday (Carnival) and Easter. Visas are not required for a stay of less than 4 months. A U.S. passport and smallpox vaccination are necessary.

Paraguay enjoys a temperate climate throughout the year. The summer is long (October through March) and hot, with a mean temperature of 84°F. During winter (June through August) the temperature usually does not fall below 30°F.

National holidays include: January 1 (New Year's), Feburary 3 (St. Blas, Patron of Paraguay), March 1 (Heroes Day), April 3 (Holy Thursday), April 4 (Good Friday), May 1 (Labor Day), May 14 and 15 (Independence Day), June 5 (Corpus Christi), June 12 (Chaco Armistice), August 15 (founding of the City of Asuncion), August 25 (Constitution Day), September 29 (Victory of Boqueron), October 12 (Day of the Race), November 1 (All Saints' Day), December 8 (Virgin of Caacupe), December 25 (Christmas Day), and December 31. In addition, there are a number of local patriotic or religious holidays, especially feasts of patron saints, which may be observed by part or all of the community in various cities or provinces.

Government offices are open from 7:00 a.m. to 12:00 p.m. throughout the year. Banking hours vary but are usually from 7:00 to 11:00 a.m. All banks and government offices are closed on weekends and holidays. In general, commercial business hours are 7:00 a.m. to 12:00 p.m. and 3:00 to 6:00 p.m.

Principal hotels in major cities include: Asuncion—Hotel Chaco, Hotel Parana, Hotel Guarani, Hotel ITA Enramada, Gran Hotel del Paraguay, Hotel HUSA; Concepcion—Central, Frances; Encarnacion—Gran Hotel International, Central, Suizo.

Transportation and Utilities

The role of the transportation sector is crucial to government plans to expand agricultural capacity and production, as well as promoting industrialization in all regions. The sector has recently been receiving the largest share of public investment and a basic transportation system now exists. However, the high rate of economic growth that is expected will depend on its continued improvement and expansion.

Rivers and Ports

Paraguay's most important transportation system is the inland waterway, which connects Paraguay's inland ports with the Atlantic Ocean. It begins with the Paraguay River, which runs north-south across the country, and the Parana River, which serves as a border with Brazil and Argentina and continues past the Argentine ports of Rosario and Buenos Aires. Together with the Rio de La Plata, the inland waterway constitutes a 3,170 km system of transport that handles over 60 percent of the international traffic in the area.

Asuncion is by far the largest port. It serves Paraguay's most important productive areas and is the only port with modern berthing facilities and cargo-handling equipment. The facilities are limited, however, and the transit areas are highly congested. In an effort to relieve the congestion, there are plans to expand the port and construct bulk cargo-handling facilities 25 km south of Asuncion at Villeta, rerouting most of the port's bulk cargo.

There are smaller ports at Villeta, Concepcion, Valle Mi, Bahia Negra, Encarnacion, and Puerto Presidente Stroessner, all of which are inadequate. With the completion of the Itaipu, Yacyreta, and Corpus hydroelectric projects, water levels on the Parana River should increase from Encarnacion to Saltos del Guaira. This will open the Parana River to oceangoing vessels, increasing the importance of both Encarnacion and Puerto Presidente Stroessner as inland ports.

The Flota Mercante del Estado (Flomeres) is a semi-autonomous government shipping agency with a total carrying capacity of about 20,000 tons. Its representative in New York is Constellation Navigation, Inc. (Telephone: (212) 791-8450). Ships leave once a month. Holland-Pan American Lines also give regular service to Paraguay, leaving New York every 3 weeks. Transit time is 30 days, although customs and other freight clearance procedures can increase shipping time by an additional 10–14 days. Free port arrangements are available in Paranagua, Brazil; Antofogasta, Chile; and more recently in Rosario, Argentina.

Air

Air transit time is usually 16 hours. Braniff International has two flights a week from Miami, Washington, D.C., and New York. Other airlines flying to Paraguay are Varig (via Sao Paulo and Rio de Janeiro), Iberia (via Madrid), and Lineas Aereas Paraguayas (three direct flights a week from Miami also via Buenos Aires, Montevideo, Santiago, Sao Paulo, Rio de Janeiro, and Santa Cruz). National airlines are Transporte Aereo Militar (TAM) and Lineas Aereas de Transporte Nacional (LATN). Domestic air traffic is small but important as it often constitutes the only means of transport among various sections of the country, especially during bad weather conditions. There are two all-weather international airports, one at Asuncion and another under construction at Mariscal Estigarribia, halfway between Asuncion and Santa Cruz, Bolivia. There is a third restricted all-weather airport, under the control of the Itaipu Binational Authority, north of Puerto Presidente Stroessner. There is also a concrete strip at the cement plant at Valle Mi, a partially completed concrete strip at the textile center of Pilar, and a compacted clay and gravel strip at Concepcion.

Of the 400 registered landing fields throughout the country, most are not really airports, but dirt or grass strips that are susceptible to closure due to rains and flooding.

Railways

The state-owned railway Ferrocarril Presidente Carlos Antonio Lopez (FCPAL), is directly responsible to the Ministry of Public Works and Communications. The neglected condition of both the rolling stock and the 441 km of track has made railway service inefficient, unattractive, and uneconomical. Service has declined enough over the years that the majority of freight and passengers now move by truck or bus.

While there has been a great deal of discussion concerning the modernization of the existing line between Asuncion and Encarnacion, the cost of modernization and existing traffic patterns make this highly unlikely. More likely is the construction of a second line between Asuncion and Saltos del Guaira on the Brazilian border to handle the increasing volume of agricultural exports.

Highways

Paraguay's highway network totals about 8,500 km. Approximately 8 percent is unpaved and susceptible to closure, due to rains and flooding, for up to 100 days per annum. Much of the government investment in infrastructure has been directed towards expanding and improving the highway system. Main and feeder systems are being expanded to meet rapidly increasing demands of agricultural development by linking agricultural production areas to river, railway, and highway transport systems.

The area best served by roads is the southeast portion of the country, east of the Paraguay River, where the major economic activity of the country is concentrated. The principal all-weather paved highways are Highway 1, between Asuncion and Encarnacion; Highway 2, between Asuncion and Coronel Oviedo; Highway 7, between Coronel Oviedo and Puerto Presidente Stroessner; and Highway 6 between Encarnacion and Pirapo.

Construction is currently underway to extend Highway 6 as far as Puerto Presidente Stroessner. This will complete a long envisioned transportation triangle between Paraguay's three most important cities—Asuncion, Encarnacion, and Puerto Presidente Stroessner. It will also serve to further integrate the hydroelectric projects of Itaipu and Yacyreta into the national economy. A far more reaching effect will be the redirection of agricultural exports from Highway 1, the port of Asuncion, and the port of Buenos Aires to Highway 6, Puerto Presidente Stroessner, and the Brazilian port of Paranagua.

The only other all-weather highway is Highway 9, linking Asuncion with Kilometer 300 in the Chaco region. Construction is underway between Kilometer 300 and Mariscal Estigarribia, the site of the new all-weather international airport, also under construction.

Current plans are to extend the highway as far as General Eugenio A. Garay on the Bolivian border, linking Paraguay to the Bolivian market. The Remanso bridge, just north of Asuncion on Highway 9, is Paraguay's only bridge across the

Paraguay River and the link between Highway 9 and the highways of Eastern Paraguay.

Plans for the future include the construction of Highway 5, between Concepcion and Pedro Juan Caballero on the Brazilian border, a second bridge across the Paraguay River at Concepcion, and the construction of a highway between Concepcion and Pozo Colorado in the Chaco region.

In the past 10 years, there has been a shift away from river transportation to Buenos Aires toward highway transportation to Paranagua. This trend will continue as construction is completed on Highways 5 and 6 and on the narrow gauge railway linking Asuncion and the Brazilian rail network.

Domestic trucking, which is growing rapidly, is highly competitive, loosely regulated, and handled by small local firms or individuals. Adding to an already competitive situation is extensive illegal competition from Brazilian trucking firms. Bus transport also is highly competitive but more closely regulated. Road travel is the most common mode of transportation for domestic freight and passenger travel. More than half of the traffic on the road system consists of trucks and buses.

Electric Power

Alternating 50 cycle electric current is available for normal household use at 380 volts between 3 phases and 220 volts between any phase and neutral. Normal household outlets are 220 volts.

For industrial use, commercial power is 23,000 volts between 3 phases.

Communications

Recent research places the press as the most important medium of mass communication in the country, followed by radio and television. Research also indicates that radio is the most penetrating form of communication with greater reach into the Paraguayan interior.

Newspaper readership has grown as a result of technical improvements in printing and distribution and a definite, if uneven, easing of government censorship.

Asuncion currently has five daily newspapers, all of which cover the local news and depend upon international wire and syndicated column services. Daily circulation for the above newspapers is as follows: *ABC Color*—75,000; *Ultima Hora*—27,000; *Hoy*—22,000; *LaTribuna*—7,000; *Patria* (the official Colorado Party paper)—5,000. In addition there are weekly newspapers: *El Pueblo* (the official Febrerista party paper and *Sendero* (published by the Catholic Church). There are no newspapers published in the interior.

The broadcast power of the nation's 42 radio stations ranges from 5 to 50 kilowatts. In Asuncion there is one government-owned and eight privately owned AM stations and seven privately owned FM stations. The government-owned station is unique in that it broadcasts 50 percent of its programs in shortwave. In the interior, there are 20 privately owned AM stations and 6 privately owned FM stations. There are an estimated 650,000 radio units in daily use, with a weekly audience of approximately 2 million.

In Asuncion there is one privately owned television station, Channel 9, which has been operating since 1969. Authorization has been granted for a second privately owned station, Channel 13, which is expected to begin broadcasting in September 1980. Outside of Asuncion, there is one privately owned station in Encarnacion, Channel 7, which began broadcasting in 1976.

All broadcasting is currently in black and white. The Government of Paraguay has recently authorized the PAL-N color system, and Channel 9 has already begun experimental color transmissions.

Along the borders with Argentina and Brazil, reception of neighboring broadcasts are received more easily. As a result, the eastern and southern sections of the country are more influenced by broadcasts from Paraguay's neighbors.

In Asuncion, only three commercial magazines publish with any regularity: *Aqui*, with a weekly circulation of 20,000; *Nande*, with a biweekly circulation of 5,000; and *Comercio*, with a monthly circulation of 2,000. Other commercial and professional concerns publish monthly or quarterly journals, but their appearance is irregular. There are no periodicals published outside of Asuncion.

Telecommunications.—Telephones are serviced by Antelco, the national telephone company. Service is good, although installation can take up to 6 months and cost as much as $1,000.

Communications outside the most important towns are conducted by shortwave radio. As a consequence, there is an active ham radio organization throughout the country.

The quality of international telephone and telecommunications is considered good. In part this is due to the recent installation of a satellite communications center in Arequa, 30 km east of Asuncion.

The Financial System

The Central Bank of Paraguay is an autonomous agency of the State, which determines the nation's monetary, credit, and exhange policies in coordination with the Government's development policies. The bank regulates available credit by establishing interest rates and reserve levels as well as controlling the issuance of currency.

Exchange transactions take place on a dual exchange market. Transactions in the official exchange market, Mercado Libre Bancario, must be carried out through the Central Bank or at authorized commercial banks at the rate of 126 guarani per U.S.$1. Imports and exports, current invisibles, registered private capital transactions, profit remittances and governmental transactions must all be conducted on the official exchange market. All other transactions can be conducted in the fluctuating free market (Mercado Libre Fluctuante) through licensed exchange houses. As of June 1980, the exchange rates were 136 guarani per US$1 buying and 134 guarani per US$1 selling. All purchases and sales of exchange by banks are subject to a tax of 1½ percent, except transactions with foreign embassies, diplomats, and meat packing plants, and transactions relating to investments in Paraguay that are covered by legislation (see Foreign Investment section). Banks also charge a commission of 2 percent on sales of all foreign exchange.

Payments between Paraguay and Argentina, Bolivia, Chile, Colombia, Mexico, Peru, and Uruguay must be made through accounts of the Central Bank of Paraguay and other central banks concerned maintain with each other, within the framework of the LAFTA multilateral clearing system.* Payments through this

system are made promptly. Those on the official exchange market may be delayed from time to time as a result of weekly releases of foreign exchange to the private commercial banks by the Central Bank.

The principal banks in Paraguay are: Citibank, Bank of America, First National Bank of Boston, Chase Manhattan Bank, Deutsche Bank, Banco Holandes Unido, Banco Exterior de Espana, Banco do Brazil, Banco de la Nacion Argentina, Banco Union, and Banco de Asuncion.

Trade Regulations

Most imports into Paraguay are unrestricted; the importer need only obtain a permit for foreign exchange purposes. Narcotics, arms, and ammunition imports, however, require a special import license from the Ministry of the Interior. The imports of a few commodities are prohibited, including sugar, rice, flour, and certain other agricultural products. Requests to import certain yard and textile goods, dry cell batteries, and certain wire and wire products are considered on a case-by-case basis.

Imports of most commodities are subject to an advance deposit of 100 percent of the f.o.b. value of the import, which is retained for 120 days, or for only 90 days for nonexempt commodities imported through the free zone. Advance deposits are not required for public sector imports, petroleum and petroleum derivatives, certain machinery and agricultural equipment, wheat, newsprint, imports from neighboring countries, and imports listed in Investment Decree No. 550/75 and Law No. 216/70. The Central Bank also has authority to grant exemptions on a case-by-case basis.

Ad valorem duties are levied on the c.i.f. value, which the Paraguayan customs authorities calculate as 120 percent of f.o.b. value. Decree No. 34535 (October 1977) placed an ad valorem duty of 25 percent on imports of specific electrical appliances. Decree No. 40940 (July 1978) placed a common duty rate of 12 percent on imports of raw materials and semiprocessed industrial goods.

Other charges on imports are as follows: a consular fee of 5 percent, an import clearance fee of 1 percent, and a customs surcharge of 1½ percent. Additional surcharges are applied on some products. For example, imports of construction materials are subject to an additional customs surcharge of 1 percent, the proceeds of which go to the Institute of Housing and Urbanization.

*Members of the Latin America Free Trade Association (LAFTA) are Argentina, Bolivia, Brazil, Chile, Colombia, Ecuador, Mexico, Paraguay, Peru, Uruguay, and Venezuela. The objectives of LAFTA, as stated in the preamble of the Treaty of Montevideo, include "efforts to establish, gradually and progressively a Latin American Common Market and, hence, to continue collaborating with the Latin American governments as a whole in the work already initiated for the propose and . . . to pool their efforts to achieve the progressive complementarity and integration of their national economies on the basis of an effective reciprocity of benefits . . ."

Fuel derived from petroleum is subject to a surcharge of 15 percent. A surcharge of ½ to 1 percent is levied for the benefit of the Small Farmers Credit Agency (CAH) on all imports except those of wheat and flour, crude petroleum and its derivatives, and pharmaceuticals. There also is an additional surcharge of 5 percent on imports, from all sources, of telephone and telegraphic equipment, television receivers, radios, record players, and their parts and accessories.

These surcharges are collected by the banks at the time of delivery of the documents for customs clearance or when the import payment is made, whichever is earlier. Commodities exempt from advance deposit requirements also are exempt from surcharges. Imports of investment goods and raw materials for export industries may receive exemptions on a case-by-case basis.

A tariff surcharge is levied on certain imports by virtue of Law No. 1334/67, which implemented Decree No. 451 of March 31, 1967 and Decree No. 10 of August 29, 1968. On goods that are not exempt, surcharges range from 12 to 24 percent and are levied on the c.i.f. value. Exempt from this complementary import duty are public sector and diplomatic imports, raw materials and equipment for the production of goods that are subject to internal consumption taxes, imports under Investment Decree 550/75 and Law No. 216/70, and all imported goods taxed under the Internal Consumption Tax Law. Most imports ae subject to a sales tax ranging from 5 to 10 percent, which is higher than the sales tax levied on locally produced goods.

Even though there are no quantitative restrictions, customs duties and surcharges can seriously affect the marketability of some imports into Paraguay. The amount of duties and surcharges applied to each item depends on the product itself—whether it is considered an essential import, a nonessential import, or luxury item. If a similar product is produced locally, duties will be high to protect the national producer.

The origin of the import is also important as products from LAFTA member countries are allowed into Paraguay without the application of surcharges and often with lower tariffs. In return, Paraguay, as a less developed country within LAFTA, is accorded special concessions to stimulate its exports to the more developed LAFTA countries. These concessions take the form of lists of nonextensive tariff concessions bilaterally granted by a more developed LAFTA member.

Inquiries on Paraguay—including tariff and nontariff barriers, the market, and recent developments in the country—should be directed to the Paraguay Desk, Room 4039, International Trade Administration U.S. Department of Commerce, Washington, D.C. 20230. Telephone: (202) 377-4170.

Import Procedures

The customary shipping documents are required for exporting to Paraguay for all goods valued at $100 or more f.o.b. The consular invoice must have four copies prepared in Spanish. All shipping expenses, except ocean freight, must be shown on the consular invoice as one item under the heading "gastos de despacho." The commercial invoice, requiring five copies in Spanish, must have the shipping expenses itemized. The bill of lading requires three originals and one copy, which should be marked as to the country of origin. Goods not going directly to Asuncion should include labels indicating the route used, for example: "Buenos Aires en Transito para Paraguay," or "Montevideo, en Transito para Paraguay." Shipments can be addressed to any individual resident or organization, but retaining a legitimate business representative or distributor is advisable. Specific information is required for all shipments, including the full name and address of the exporter, means of shipment and date and place where the documents were legalized. It is essential that accurate data be given for weights, dimensions, and bulk of the shipment as well as its quantity and value. The composition of such items as fabrics, chemicals, and other liquids must be clearly stated.

For goods under $100 f.o.b., no consular invoice or certificate of origin is necessary. Two copies of the commercial invoice should accompany the shipment. Consular legalization is not required.

Consular Fees

Certain consular fees are paid in Paraguay by the importer. The following are paid to the Consulates of Paraguay in dollars:

Transfer of assignment of trademark ...20.00
Extension and revalidation of
    trademark 20.00
Medicinal certificate giving ingre-
    dients of drugs, etc 20.00
Sanitary certificate 10.00
Special power of attorney 10.00

General power of attorney 20.00
Consular Invoice blanks per set of
four sold only at Consulate 8.00
Registration fee 10.00
Additional copies of commercial in-
voice, when requested .... 2.50 each
Extra copy of Consular invoice at
same time set of four is
presented .... 5.00 each
Extra copy of bill of lading .... 2.50 each
Letter of correction 20.00
Extra copy of certificate of origin .... 2.50 each

Shipping documents are received from 10:00
a.m. to 2:00 p.m. and returned 2 days later.
Consular documents, together with the bills of
lading, must be presented to the consulate for
legalization no later than 2 working days after
the sailing of the vessel.

Special Documents

Sanitary documents are required, in Spanish,
for all live animals, seeds, and grains. The certificate must be signed and notarized by a
County Clerk of the Secretary of the State of
origin. After legalization by the Paraguayan
Consulate, it is returned.

Shipments of drugs and pharmaceuticals require proper identification and a complete list of
ingredients (in Spanish). These shipments also
must be approved by the Consulate and authorities from the country of origin.

Marking of Goods

Individual items need not be marked as to
country of origin. Empty containers must indicate on the labels the importer's or manufacturer's name, registration number, and an
adequate description of the items they will contain. Capacity and weight also should be indicated.

Samples

Samples that have no commercial value are
admitted duty free. Those that have commercial
value are subject to appropriate tariffs as determined by the Brussels Tariff Nomenclature
(BTN) classification. Advertising material also is
subject to duties.

Foreign Investment

The Government of Paraguay is firmly in favor
of private enterprise and welcomes foreign investment. U.S. investment in Paraguay is estimated at $120 million. Total private foreign in-

vestment as of January 1980 is probably over
$1,200 million, with Argentina and Brazil the
largest single participants. Most U.S. investment has been in land development, but areas of
continued and potential investment include
agro-industry and hotels.

Law 550, promulgated in 1976, promotes new
investments by granting special benefits for
projects that will increase the production of
goods and services (for export and import substitution) as well as stimulate the development
of certain geographic regions of the country.
Special benefits include: complete or partial
exemption from duties on machinery and capital
equipment imports, exemption from certain
complementary customs and exchange charges,
and reduction of corporate income taxes. All applications for benefits under Law 550 should be
submitted to the Ministry of Industry and Commerce.

Investments are classified into two
categories—necessary and advantageous, with
necessary investments receiving greater tax
benefits. Necessary investments are defined as
those that have priority in the economic development of the country and that will produce
or process raw materials as well as create exports. Advantageous investments are defined as
those that will contribute to the substitution of
imports and to a greater utilization of natural resources.

Remittance of payments on foreign investments for profits, dividends, interests, and
royalties may be sent abroad through banks authorized to operate on foreign exchange. All remittances are subject to a 10 percent tax. Repatriation of invested capital can be made only after
3 years and will be in annual quotas, not to exceed 30 percent of the incorporated capital.
Under Law Number 367 (January 1973) foreign
corporations and individuals domiciled in
Paraguay are now subject to a 30 percent tax on
fees, commissions, interest, royalties, rents, and
similar incomes. There is no personal income tax
in Paraguay.

Local participation in investment projects is
not required, although such a relationship is
useful, particularly with engineering firms when
bidding on government contracts. The Government does not promote or care to participate as a
partner in joint ventures. There is no antitrust
legislation or regulations affecting acquisitions
or mergers. There have been no cases of expropriation in Paraguay nor are there any outstanding investment disputes. No major changes on

investment legislation are expected in the near future.

Sources of Economic and Commercial Information

The address of the U.S. Embassy in Paraguay is: 1776 Mariscal Lopez Avenue, Asuncion, Paraguay. Telephone: 201–041.

A booklet, *Key Officers of Foreign Service Posts: Guide for Business Representatives*, is published quarterly by the U.S. Department of State. Copies may be purchased for $1.50 each or $4.50 per year on a subscription basis from U.S. Government Printing Office, Washington, D.C. 20402.

Information may also be obtained from the Paraguay Desk, Room 4039, International Trade Administration, U.S. Department of Commerce, Washington, D.C. 20230. Telephone: (202) 377-4170.

The Embassy of Paraguay is located at 2400 Massachusetts Ave., N.W., Washington, D.C. 20008 (Telephone 202-283 6960). A Consulate General of Paraguay is located at One World Trade Center, New York, New York 10048 (212-432-0733). Office hours for receiving documents are 10 a.m. to 2 p.m., Monday through Friday. Documents will be returned 2 days later during business hours.

Other Consulates of Paraguay are located in Albuquerque, Boston, Chicago, Denver, Miami, New Orleans, Los Angeles, and San Francisco.

The following may be useful sources of information on marketing in Paraguay:

Government of Ministries and Agencies

Ministerio de Industria y Comercio
(Ministry of Industry and Commerce)
Avenida Espana 477
Asuncion, Paraguay

Ministerio de Obras Publicas y
Comunicaciones
(Ministry of Public Works and
Communications)
Oliva y Alberdi
Asuncion, Paraguay
Telephone: 44-411/4

Administracion Nacional de Electricidad
(ANDE)
(National Administration of Electricity)
Padre Cardozo 560 y Avenida Espana
Asuncion, Paraguay
Telephone: 22-713/6

Ministerio de Agricultura y Gamoderia
(Ministry of Agriculture and Livestock)
Presidente Franco 472
Asuncion, Paraguay

Key Trade Associations

FEPRINCO-Federacion de la Produccion
Industria y Comercio
Calle Palma 751
Asuncion, Paraguay
Telephone: 46638

Main group of trade associations of businesspeople, ranchers, farmers, industrialists, etc. Publishes newsletter and accepts, without charge, brief notices from foreign firms.

UIP–Union Industrial Paraguaya
Calle Cerro Cora 1038
Asuncion, Paraguay
Telephone: 27758

Industrialists trade association. Circulates information, without charge, from foreign firms among its members.

Central de Importadores
Calle Montevideo 671
Asuncion, Paraguay
Telephone: 41295

Importers and foreign manufacturers' agents trade association. Publishes newsletters and accepts, without charge, brief notices from foreign firms.

Camara y Bolsa de Comercio
Calle Estrella 550
Asuncion, Paraguay
Telephone: 93321

Only chamber of commerce in Paraguay. Publishes newsletter and accepts, without charge, brief notices from foreign firms.

CEPEX-Centro de Promocion de las
Exportaciones
Avenida Espana 374
P.O. Box 1774
Asuncion, Paraguay
Telephone: 24880

Government agency for promotion of Paraguayan exports. Reports export opportunities, prepares business reports, and contracts market research.

Companies Specializing in Selling Lands to Foreign Investors

Peter Siemens
Calle Azara Esquina Antequera
Casilla Posta 1428
Asuncion, Paraguay
Telephone: 45042, 94166

Consultants for Investment in Paraguay-CIP

Casilla Postal 730
Calle 15 de Agosto 120
Asuncion, Paraguay
Telephone: 44426

Mersan
Casilla Postal 693
Calle Yegros 837
Asuncion, Paraguay
Telephone: 49052

Guido Masi
Calle 25 de Mayo 1315
Asuncion, Paraguay
Telephone: 24612, 23538

Inmobiliaria Chaco
Calle Yegros 620
Asuncion, Paraguay
Telephone: 92774

Espirtu Santo Agro Industrial del Paraguay
Calle 14 de Maya No. 970
Asuncion, Paraguay
Telephone: 48701, 90315

Luis Enrique y Javier Zavala
Grupo Administrativo Rural y Asociados-GAR
Casilla Postal 2111
Calle Presidente Franco 573
Asuncion, Paraguay
Telephone: 46227, 49309, 99750

Table 1.—PARAGUAY: GNP at Current and Constant Prices
(Millions of U.S. dollars)

Year	GNP at Current Prices	% Change Over Previous Year	GNP at Constant Prices[1]	% Change Over Previous Year
1970	594.6	—	700.7	—
1971	664.6	+11.8	731.4	+4.4
1972	769.0	+15.7	769.0	+5.1
1973	995.5	+29.5	829.4	+7.8
1974	1,333.5	+34.0	898.0	+8.3
1975	1,511.4	+13.3	943.2	+5.0
1976	1,699.0	+12.4	1,014.1	+7.5
1977	2,092.1	+23.1	1,133.8	+11.8
1978	2,560.0	+22.4	1,250.5	+10.3
1979	3,455.8	N.A.	N.A.	N.A.

[1] At 1972 Prices
Source: Central Bank

Table 2.—PARAGUAY: GNP, Percentage Breakdown by Principal Sectors at Constant Prices [1]

	1970	1975	1976	1977	1978
Agriculture	17.8	18.2	17.9	18.1	17.5
Livestock	13.9	12.2	11.9	11.1	10.4
Forestry	4.2	4.2	3.9	3.8	3.9
Fishing	0.1	0.1	0.1	0.1	0.1
Mining	0.1	0.2	0.3	0.4	0.4
Industry	15.7	15.1	14.9	15.7	15.4
Construction	2.4	3.4	3.8	4.4	5.3
Electricity	0.8	1.4	1.7	1.7	1.8
Sanitation Services	0.2	0.3	0.3	0.3	0.3
Transportation and Communication	3.8	4.6	4.5	4.4	4.5
Commerce	23.0	23.1	23.6	23.7	24.2
Government	5.1	4.0	4.0	3.8	3.7
Housing	2.8	2.6	2.6	2.5	2.5
Other Services	10.1	10.6	10.5	10.0	10.0
Total	100.0	100.0	100.0	100.0	100.0

[1] At 1972 Prices
Source. Central Bank

Table 3.—PARAGUAY: GNP by Principal Sectors at Current Prices
(In Million of U.S. dollars)

	1975	1976	1977	1978
Agriculture	299.4	357.5	470.7	502.0
Livestock	189.1	169.2	172.8	239.2
Forestry	67.8	58.7	68.2	76.4
Fishing	1.3	1.7	2.0	3.3
Mining	2.9	4.2	5.4	6.3
Industry	236.2	271.6	356.9	431.9
Construction	56.8	71.7	83.8	122.8
Electricity	18.3	25.4	31.4	40.4
Sanitation Services	3.5	4.2	5.2	7.1
Transportation and Communication	60.3	69.1	81.5	103.1
Commerce	346.1	408.7	524.0	666.6
Government	51.5	60.5	81.6	100.9
Housing	39.9	44.2	48.2	59.5
Other Services	138.3	152.3	160.4	200.5
Total	1,511.4	1,699.0	2,092.1	2,560.0

Source: Central Bank

Table 4.—PARAGUAY: Per Capita GNP at Current and Constant Prices
(In U.S. dollars)

Year	Per Capita Current Prices	% Change Over Previous Year	Per Capita GNP Constant Prices[1]	% Change Over Previous Year
1970	258	—	305	—
1971	281	+8.9	309	+1.3
1972	316	+12.5	316	+2.3
1973	398	+25.9	332	+5.1
1974	518	+30.1	349	+5.1
1975	571	+10.2	356	+2.0
1976	624	+9.3	372	+4.5
1977	746	+19.6	404	+8.6
1978	886	+18.8	433	+7.2
1979	930	—	—	—

[1] At 1972 prices
Source: Central Bank

1863

Table 5.—PARAGUAY—Sources and Uses of Resources, 1970–77 as percent of Real GDP (1972–100)

	As Percent of Real GDP (1972—100)							Percent Change (%)			
	1970	1971	1972	1973	1974	1975	1976	1977	1970–75	1972–77	1976–77
GDP at market prices	100.0	100.0	100.0	100.0	100.0	100.0	100.0	100.0	6.1	8.1	11.8
Terms of trade adjustment	—	0.5	—	3.5	3.6	2.7	5.4	7.7	—	—	—
Gross domestic income	100.0	100.5	100.0	103.5	103.6	102.7	105.4	107.7	6.7	9.7	14.3
Resource gap	1.1	2.6	0.1	−0.8	1.7	4.9	6.5	6.4	—	—	—
Imports, goods and nfs	15.2	16.1	13.9	15.9	17.5	18.8	22.7	25.3	10.8	22.0	24.8
Exports, goods and nfs	14.0	13.1	13.8	13.2	12.2	11.2	10.8	11.3	1.4	3.8	16.3
Exports (capacity to import)	14.0	13.5	13.8	16.7	15.8	13.9	16.2	18.9	5.9	15.2	30.8
Available resources	101.1	103.1	100.1	102.7	105.3	107.6	111.9	114.1	7.5	10.9	14.0
Consumption	86.9	88.4	85.0	82.4	84.6	83.4	83.8	83.3	5.3	7.6	11.1
Private	78.1	80.0	77.0	75.5	78.2	76.0	76.8	76.8	5.5	8.0	11.8
Public	8.8	8.4	8.0	6.9	6.4	7.4	7.0	6.5	2.7	3.7	3.7
Investment	14.2	14.7	15.1	20.3	20.7	24.2	28.0	30.8	18.0	24.0	22.8
Fixed Capital formation	13.2	13.6	13.7	17.5	18.0	20.5	24.8	28.5	16.2	25.0	28.2
Private	(9.8)	(9.9)	(9.2)	13.5)	(14.4)	(15.2)	(17.9)	(22.0)	(15.7)	(29.0)	(37.6)
Public	(3.4)	(3.7)	(4.5)	(4.0)	(3.6)	(5.3)	(6.9)	(6.5)	(16.1)	(16.4)	(4.3)
Changes in inventories	1.0	1.1	1.4	2.8	2.7	3.7	3.2	2.3	38.0	20.0	−19.6
Gross domestic savings	13.1	12.1	15.0	21.1	19.0	19.3	21.5	24.4	14.7	19.1	26.6
Factor service income	−1.6	−1.5	−1.5	−1.1	−1.0	−0.9	−1.2	−0.9	—	—	—
Net transfers	0.8	1.2	0.8	0.6	0.3	1.0	0.3	0.1	—	—	—
Gross national savings	12.4	11.7	14.3	20.6	18.4	19.4	20.7	23.5	16.1	19.2	27.0
Gross national product	98.4	98.5	98.5	98.9	99.0	99.1	98.8	99.1	6.3	8.2	12.1

Source: Central Bank

Table 6.—Projection of Revenue to Paraguay from Itaipu and Yacyreta

	1984	1985	1986	1987	1988	1989
ITAIPU						
Gross generation (GWh)	10,000	20,000	40,000	60,000	70,000	80,000
ANDE usage (GWh)	800	1,100	1,400	1,600	1,800	2,000
Ceded to Brazil by ANDE (GWh)	4,200	8,900	18,600	28,400	33,20	38,000
Compensation to ANDE at US $300/GWh (US $ millions)	1.26	2.67	5.58	8.52	9.96	11.40
Compensation for management and supervision						
at US $50/GWh (US $ millions)	0.25	0.50	1.00	1.50	1.75	2.00
Royalty US $650/GWh but not less than						
US $9 million (US $ millions)	9.00	9.00	13.00	19.50	22.75	26.00
Total Revenue from Itaipu (US $ millions)	10.5	12.17	19.58	29.52	34.46	39.40
YACYRETA						
Gross generation (GWh)		2,500	5,000	15,000	20,000	26,000
Ceded to Argentina by ANDE (GWh)		1,250	2,500	7,500	10,000	13,000
Compensation to ANDE at US $2998/GWh						
but not less than US $9 million (US $ millions)						
(plus monetary readjustments)[1]		14.63	15.15	39.19	54.06	72.73
Compensation for management and supervision at						
US $166/GWh (US $ millions) (plus monetary						
readjustments)*		0.32	0.67	2.09	3.60	4.01
Total Revenue from Yacyreta						
(US $ millions)		14.95	16.17	41.28	57.60	76.74
Grand Total revenue to Paraguay from						
Itaipu and Yacyreta (US $ millions)	10.5	27.12	35.75	70.80	92.06	116.14

[1] Note: The readjustment is made on the basis of half of the World Bank Projected Index of International Inflation which probably will understate the actual readjustment of the treaty.

Source: Mission Projections.

Market Profile—PARAGUAY

Foreign Trade*

Imports.—(f.o.b.) 1979, $431.7 million; 1978, $317.7 million; U.S. share: 1979, $49.8 million (15.3 percent); U.S. share 1978, $34.75 million (11 percent). Major imports 1979: Cigarettes, machinery and motors, textiles and manufactures, vehicles and transportation equipment, chemical and pharmaceutical products, agricultural machinery.

Exports.—(f.o.b.) 1979, $305.17 million; 1978, $257 million; U.S. share: 1979, $17.63 million (5.8 percent); U.S. share 1978, $22.2 million (8.6 percent). Major exports: Soybeans, cotton, tobacco, sugar, frozen meats, lumber and other wood products.

Trade Policy.—Few value or volume restrictions on goods for resale. Tariff barriers prótect infant industries located in the country. Some LAIA (Latin American Integration Association) members receive special tariff concessions.

Trade Prospects.—further hydroelectric power development should provide an excellent market for continued sales of U.S. equipment. Many other opportunities will develop as income from energy exports is invested. Opportunities are good for the following products: Agricultural equipment; construction and earthmoving equipment; medium and heavy-duty trucks and transportation equipment; cement, fertilizer, and paper plants and equipment; telecommunications equipment; medical and health care equipment.

Foreign Investment

Total foreign investment is over $1,200 million (as of January 1980). Total U.S. investment is estimated at $120 million.

Investment Prospects.—The Government of Paraguay welcomes foreign investment. Special benefits are granted for those projects that will increase the production of goods and services (for export and import substitution) as well as stimulate the development of certain geographic regions of the country.

Finance

Currency.—Guarani. Fixed rate: 126 Guaranis per dollar. Flexible rate: 136 Guaranis per dollar. (June 1980).

Domestic Credit and Investment.—Interest rates are on the rise because of the Central Bank's tight money policies. Credit is below the inflation rate.

Balance of Payments.—1980 (projected), +$160 million; 1979, +$160 million; 1978, +168 million.

National Budget.—1980 budget $424.6 million as compared with $331.7 million in 1979, an increase of 28 percent.

Economy

GNP.—At current prices: 1980 (projection), $4,386 million; 1979, $3,348 million; 1978, $2,573 million. At constant 1972 prices: 1980 (projection), $1,523 million; 1979, $1,372 million; 1978, $1,247 million; Real GNP growth in 1979 was 10 percent. Agriculture, 39.1 percent; industry, 20 percent; services, 40.5 percent; unallocated, 0.4 percent.

Agriculture.—Chief products are: Cotton, soya, sugar, coffee, wheat, cattle, basic foodstuffs. Agricultural goods accounted for approximately 80 percent of export earnings at a value of $290 million and employed 46 percent of the labor force in 1979.

Industry.—Composed mostly of agroindustries, wood products, cement, refined oil products, hydroelectric power, and some consumer goods. Employed 14 percent of the labor force in 1979.

Tourism.—In 1978 accounted for 14.5 percent of the f.o.b. value of exports with total earnings of $46 million for the year.

Basic Economic Facilities

Transportation.—Being landlocked, maritime communications are indirect. Outlets to Atlantic by way of the Parana and Paraguay Rivers. Railways link Asuncion and other areas of the country with Argentine ports. International airlines offer passenger and cargo service. Main road plan connects with Argentine and Brazilian road systems.

Communications.—Long-distance telephone service is available almost worldwide. Telegram service not always reliable.

Power.—Actively engaged in Itaipu, Yacyreta, and Corpus hydroelectric projects. Paraguay will become a major energy exporter during the next decade. Estimated 1978 production 670 million kWh.

Natural Resources

Land.—157,047 square miles.

Climate.—Semitropical.

Minerals.—There is virtually no mineral production except for small amounts of kaolin, clay, and gravel.

Forestry.—Large tracts of virgin timberland in eastern sections of country.

Population

Size.—2.97 million with an annual growth rate of 2.6 percent. Population density is 7.3 persons/km².

Labor.—Estimated employment 1,038,000 in 1978, unemployment rate 3.9 percent in 1978.

Language.—Spanish and Guarani.

Education.—Literacy rate of 80 percent; however, about 85 percent of the population 15 years or older has not studied beyond the primary level.

---

*In analyzing Paraguayan trade figures, one must bear in mind the large amount of unrecorded trade, both import and exports, that goes on in this small country. However, in dealing with the official figures we make the assumption that trends in figures as reported reasonably reflect trends in the country's overall trade.

Marketing in Peru

Contents

Report Revised June 1984

PERU

International boundary
National capital
Railroad
Road
International airport

100   200 Miles
100   200 Kilometers

ECUADOR

Guayaquil

Cuenca

Tumbes
Santa Rosa
Loja

Talara
La Tina
Sullana
Piura
Huancabamba
San Ignacio
Nazareth

Chiclayo
Cajamarca
Pacasmayo
Cartavio
Trujillo
Salaverry
Galgada
Tayabamba
Chimbote
Huallanca
Huarás

Paramonga
Huacho
Ancón
Callao   LIMA
San Vicente de Cañete

PACIFIC
OCEAN

Chachapoyas
Moyobamba
Santiago de Chuco
Mollebamba
Juanjui

Yurimaguas

Contamana

Pucallpa

Huánuco
Pozuzo
Goyllarisquizga
Cerro de Pasco
La Oroya
Yauyos
Huancayo
Huancavelica
Ayacucho
Piaco
Ica
Nazca

Luisiana
Huadquiña
Abancay
Cusco

Iquitos

COLOMBIA

BRAZIL

Rio Napo

Rio Putumayo

Amazon

Rio Marañón

Rio Yavari

Rio Ucayali

Rio Jurad

BRAZIL

Rio Madre de Dios

Puerto Maldonado

Ayaviri

Juliaca
Puno

LAGO
TITICACA

Arequipa
Desaguadero
LA PAZ
Guaqui

BOLIVIA

Matarani
Mollendo
Moquegua
Toquepala

Ilo
Tacna

Arica   CHILE

Boundary representation is not necessarily authoritative

1867

Foreign Trade Outlook

Largely because of the international recession and debt burdens, trade slowed perceptibly in 1983 after several years of accelerated growth. Peruvian imports at about $3.8 billion in 1982 dropped slightly from 1981 levels, after rising sharply from $1.7 billion in 1978 (when the military government imposed severe restrictions on all imports.) Lower import levels continued in 1983—at $2.7 billion—and are likely to remain low well into 1984 before any rebound may be expected. A resumption of import growth will depend on a sustained economic recovery by Peru's principal industrialized trading partners, improvement in international commodity prices and demand, and sufficient credit available from abroad to alleviate pressures on the balance of payments. It will also depend on the extent of the current economic contraction brought on by a combination of factors: the world recession, IMF-mandated austerity measures to bring income and expenditures into better balance, and disruptions and losses caused by the unusual weather associated with the El Nino current. The gross domestic product (GDP) is estimated to have declined by 11-13 percent by 1983.

Despite lower import levels, Peru's market has several interesting characteristics. The United States is the single largest source of imports. It is estimated that up to 39 percent of all products entering Peru originate in the United States. American technology is respected and desired for its high quality. Peru is also a market that is very accessible to U.S. suppliers, since transportation links are shorter from the United States than from our industrialized competitors and costs correspondingly lower. The main Peruvian market is concentrated in the Lima/Callao area, so contacts are simpler. There are relatively few import restrictions. In the face of increasing protectionism worldwide, the Peruvian Government has maintained an open market philosophy, although there were increasing domestic pressures to limit imports in early 1984.

To sell successfully in this market, U.S. suppliers must pay particular attention to price, financing, and service to meet strong competition. The constant devaluations of the Peruvian currency—the sol—with respect to the U.S. dollar make U.S. goods somewhat less price competitive. In a market characterized by high debt/equity ratios and expensive credit, price considerations become as important as quality.

Financing has become the single greatest impediment to increased trade flows. Costs of unguaranteed trade credits are at historically-high real levels. U.S. companies otherwise face competition from countries which often offer government-to-government lines of credit at very favorable terms. The U.S. Export-Import Bank usually is active in Peru. Its exposure increased 50 percent in 1982 to about $300 million. However, suppliers must recognize the need to be flexible and creative in their requirements for payments from customers and representatives. New-to-market companies may find that many distributors are reluctant to make large initial purchases because of the costs of financing inventories; interest on bank loans in soles run about 100 percent annually. Even well-established distribution companies seek to reduce their operating costs by cutting back on their stocks. Although some U.S. companies have asked about barter possibilities, barter has not been a significant factor in promoting trade in recent years.

The quality of support services offered is perhaps more important now than ever. As companies try to keep their capital equipment working longer, facilities for maintenance, repair and rapid parts service become more critical. One foreign competitor in the mining equipment field leaves spare parts on consignment with its best customers. An alternative approach suppliers might consider is placing supplies of spare parts in bonded warehouses in Peru at their own expense to serve the local market.

With respect to major economic development projects, U.S. suppliers of goods and services face formidable challenges in the coming years. In line with current austerity measures, the government is substantially reducing its investments. This means some projects will be cancelled while others are postponed or implemented slowly. However, Peru is and will continue to seek international financial assistance in developing the basic infrastructure that must be put in place to support sustained industrial and agricultural growth. There is a strong need for improved roads and highway networks, seaports, airports, irrigation, water and sewerage facilities, and electric power. Sorely needed improvement will continue to be sought for the social sector, i.e. in housing, education and health. The 1981-85 development plan calls for expenditures in foreign currencies of about $5 billion for these development projects. In addition, the mining and petroleum sectors, which are vitally important to Peru's economy—accounting for close to 70 percent of exports and a large portion of the Government revenues—will continue to be significant importers. Imported consumer goods continue to be popular, although subject to relatively high duties and charges.

The United States exports a wide range of products to Peru. Principal items are given in Table I while the main categories comprising total Peruvian imports are presented in Table II.

TABLE I—*Leading Items in U.S. Domestic Exports to Peru, 1979-1983*
(In thousands of dollars; f.a.s. value)

Description	1979	1980	1981	1982	1983
Wheat	68,744	117,030	164,427	155,089	126,448
Mining machinery and equipment					
Mechanical shovels[1]					
nspf[2]	136,938	138,891	143,076	123,093	97,654
Corn, seed for planting purposes	14,961	73,895	48,959	51,028	57,074
Rice, not parboiled	23,089	36,101	41,054	16,300	43,299
Soybean oil	17,446	20,577	28,481	18,153	39,318
Aircraft	30,972	6,305	9,053	13,523	34,470
Crude petroleum	—	1	—	5	23,887
Chemical mixtures and preparations	24,320	27,713	27,901	27,631	18,980
Aircraft, parts	5,918	7,470	6,629	11,055	11,430
Nitriles and their derivatives	6,862	8,465	11,655	15,690	9,056
Parts of piston-type engines	8,031	12,902	10,775	8,464	8,596
Polyethylene resins	8,308	17,213	9,700	9,604	8,170
Non-piston-type engines	52	777	3,345	1,116	8,086
Digital computers	5,125	8,586	11,644	14,409	7,996
Tractors, wheel-type parts	10,835	19,444	12,823	9,350	7,496
Parts of comp-ignition engines	6,644	8,060	11,281	11,877	7,342
Chassis, parts	12,407	28,113	31,186	14,717	6,966
Oils	1,342	2,574	6,298	9,286	6,984
Passenger cars	4,309	19,015	44,176	14,537	6,366
General merchandise less than $500	6,497	9,489	13,494	8,340	6,024
Menhaden oil	—	5,232	2,056	—	5,924
Generators	5,239	15,521	10,549	19,522	5,796
Wheat, milled, for human consumption	3,943	3,245	4,173	4,316	5,311
Parts of office machinery, other	1,526	3,349	5,556	4,835	5,263
Dried milk and cream	398	438	1,502	897	5,166
Pumps for liquids	10,824	13,409	19,016	13,131	5,032
Radiotelegraphics, other	1,556	3,136	4,006	10,279	4,989
Motor fuel, including gasoline	—	—	5	5	4,927
Piston-type engines	2,145	2,900	4,991	6,770	4,726
Antibiotics, antineoplastic ag	2,111	5,564	4,366	5,120	4,667
Sorting machinery	3,977	6,066	13,008	4,890	4,162
Sodium tripoly phosphate	1,051	1,775	1,580	2,882	4,137
Natural gas, methane, ethane	63	43	30	718	3,942
Automobile trucks	3,913	8,968	22,241	11,535	3,508
Chemical wood pulp	1,288	2,033	1,892	5,766	3,324
Mobile cranes	4,582	6,520	8,691	5,775	3,233
Other machinery parts	569	2,234	10,400	9,819	3,221
Navigational instruments	617	1,030	2,734	2,711	3,197
Mechanical shovels[1]	—	15,108	10,945	5,702	3,184
Re-exports	1,334	1,962	1,937	2,505	3,179
Pipe, seamless, not alloyed	5,389	5,377	4,080	8,827	3,166
Edible preparations	2,447	3,091	5,217	3,480	3,082
Corn, milled, for human consumption	1,764	1,608	2,489	2,006	3,013
Total, all U.S. items exported to Peru (millions of dollars)	719.5	1,171.5	1,485.5	1,116.9	899.5

[1] Coal cutters, excavators, scrapers, bulldozers, and other excavating, levelling, boring, and extracting machinery.
[2] Not specially provided for.
Source: Compiled from official statistics of the U.S. Department of Commerce.

TABLE II—*PERU: PRINCIPAL IMPORT CATEGORIES, f.o.b., 1976-1982*
(In millions of U.S. dollars

	1976	1977	1978	1979	1980	1981	1982
Minerals, petroleum products	298.9	318.8	67.3	41.3	53.1	61.7	42.6
Machinery, parts	400.9	276.2	276.2	313.9	521.5	705.9	564.1
Motor Vehicles, tractors, parts	133.8	148.5	72.9	83.9	206.3	429.8	341.4
Cereals (mostly wheat)	145.8	130.8	99.9	203.3	294.9	269.7	230.3
Iron and Steel and articles thereof	114.1	92.6	81.2	72.5	104.1	294.7	220.3
Electrical machinery equipment and parts	103.3	75.5	74.0	89.9	162.7	246.1	216.1
Organic chemicals	94.1	69.8	65.9	82.6	122.7	117.9	104.2
Total Peruvian Imports	2,100	2,164	1,600	2,090	3,062	3,803	3,787

Source: Ministry of Economy, Finance and Commerce, Lima, Peru.

Best Export Prospects

Oil and Gas Field Machinery and Equipment

Petroleum is one of the key sectors in the Peruvian economy. Daily production in 1982 averaged 195,100 barrels per day (bpd). About one-third of production is exported, generating $715 million in export income in 1982. Production and exports both declined in 1983, due to disruptions in production associated with the "El Nino" weather phenomenon, to an estimated 172,000 bpd and $555 million, respectively.

The government continues to seek expansion of the petroleum sector. In December 1980, a new petroleum law was issued providing tax credits of 40 percent of net income for foreign as well as foreign/Peruvian oil companies operating north of latitude 7 degrees south (the northern part of Peru) and 50 percent for those south of latitude 7 degrees south (the southern part of Peru).

The tax incentives began to pay off in 1981 with the signing of three operating contracts. The continual expansion of activities by Petroperu, Occidental and Belco, supplemented by the exploration and drilling of the relative newcomers—Hamilton Brothers, and Royal Dutch Shell, among others—should help support a higher level of imports of oil and gas field equipment through 1985.

Imports of oil and gas field equipment from the United States declined in 1980 by 7.5 percent, then jumped by 19.5 percent in 1981 in response to the new drilling activity created by the petroleum law. Less rapid but very respectable growth of 10-15 percent is projected in the next two to three years. The U.S. share of the market measured against 19 major supplier countries averaged 86.6 percent through the decade of the seventies. While U.S. suppliers dominate this market, some inroads may occur via competition from Brazil and Argentina. Peru is not expected to become a significant producer of oil and gas field equipment in the immediate future.

There are opportunities in oil and gas exploration, development, gathering and distribution equipment. Best U.S. prospects are for rotary drilling bits, core bits and reamers, oil and gas drilling and boring machines, oil well and field pumps, geophysical and mineral prospecting instruments, oil well tubing and casing pipe.

Trucks and Trailers

Import demand for trucks and trailers was strong in the 1979-1981 period. The number of units imported grew by 65 percent in the period 1980-81 and in the same period the value of U.S. exports shot up by 108 percent. Figures for exports of the units from 19 countries show a surge of 129 percent in the period 1979-1980.

In 1983, the market for trucks slowed considerably. However, there are underlying needs in the economy for basic transportation which will support the market, though smaller sales are expected. When economic recovery occurs, specific items with strong sales prospects include certain types of gas fuel trucks, platform and van-type trailers.

Automotive Parts and Accessories

There are approximately 500 automobile parts importers in Peru, the vast majority of which are small or medium-sized. At the retail level, sales were off in 1982 by 15-25 percent due to the poor economy. Trade sources indicated that the market was somewhat congested in 1982. There were approximately 120,000 American vehicles registered in Peru is 1982. Imports of American cars with engines having a 2,000 cc displacement or more have been subject to a selective 40 percent tax since the beginning of 1982. Thus, many American cars are not price competitive and the expected record growth of the market for U.S. automotive parts has not materialized. However, given the size of the market and the respectable growth achieved to date, this product category still offers some good sales prospects.

Best U.S. sales prospects are for tires, brake fluids, ignition equipment, sealed beam headlights, lubricating equipment, batteries, transmissions, shock absorbers, brakes and spark plugs.

Electrical Energy and Irrigation Equipment

Peru has one of the lowest rates of per capita power usage in Latin America. Some 64 percent of the population did not have access to power at the end of 1981.

The generation and supply of electric power is a key component in the government's plan to encourage investment in industry, to develop rural sections of the country and to create new employment opportunities. To meet the challenge of generating electricity throughout the country, a major development program is underway which includes the construction of eight hydroelectric plants, four thermal plants and six transmission lines. If fully implemented, the electric development program will nearly double Peru's generating capacity by 1992. Approximately 18 percent of Peru's new fixed investment in the 1981-1985 period is to be made in this sector.

Electroperu, the government-owned electric company, will be the organization responsible for most of these projects. Electroperu produces approximately 64 percent of Peru's electrical energy output.

Peru has a total of 3.7 million hectares of crop land of which about one-third are irrigated. The government is implementing a series of irrigation projects with the assistance of the Inter-American Development Bank and the World Bank.

Although Peru produces some of the basic products required for these development programs, import requirements will continue to be high due to the large size of the proposed plans. Best U.S. prospects include power transfer valves and parts, reciprocating pumps, hydraulic fluid power pumps, centrifugal pumps, rotary pumps, portable air compressors and parts of air and gas compressors.

Computers and Peripherals

Despite of the world recession, which became evident in 1981, not more than two small categories of products within this group showed declines in Peru's imports from the United States in that year. The law of labor stability in Peru makes it very difficult for firms to reduce their labor forces in bad times, and many companies use computers for routine processing work in place of people. A new banking regulation will permit the entry into local retail banking of new foreign bank branches for the first time in 15 years. These new firms will bring in computers, and the existing Peruvian banks will be forced to follow suit. Thus, the market is set for an expansion, the size and timing of which will be influenced by general business conditions.

There is presently a shortage of adequately-trained technicians capable of repairing computers. New U.S. firms entering this market should carefully analyze the service capabilities of any prospective agent/distributor. In the next few years this shortage of technicians should ease as graduates of local technical schools enter the job market.

The market for computers in Peru is relatively underdeveloped but growing. Small to medium size computers are the types presently most in demand, and this trend will continue. One of the most important applications for computers is in inventory control as firms strive to lower the financial burdens of excessive inventories. Companies with large amounts of paperwork, such as banks, insurance companies, and finance companies, will also be buyers.

U.S. firms presently dominate the Peruvian computer market, and the main competition is from U.S. -owned or -licensed firms operating from third countries such as Brazil and Argentina.

Telecommunications Equipment

Peru has all the requirements to support a growing market for telecommunications equipment for the foreseeable future. Its existing communications infrastructure is one of the least developed in South America. Peru needs good communication links because of its mountainous terrain and the government's desire to stimulate growth outside the big cities. The government also favors the free exchange of ideas, which has stimulated the growth of the broadcast industry.

Around 30 earth satellite stations are programmed for the next 5-10 years, several new TV and radio stations are in the planning stages, and the expansion of the telephone network is underway. Since the country produces little telecommunications equipment, most of its needs have to be met through imports.

Best U.S. sales prospects are for telephone switching and switchboard equipment, teleprinting and teletypewriting machines, transceivers, TV cameras, and other TV apparatus and depth sounding apparatus and their parts.

Economic Trends

Declining demand and prices for Peru's exports together with a reluctance on the part of international credit sources to extend further credit to Latin American countries in the wake of the Mexican debt crisis significantly reduced the volume of financial resources available to Peru in 1982 and 1983. In June 1982, The Government of Peru (GOP) and the International Monetary Fund (IMF) entered into an arrangement allowing Peru to draw nearly $1 billion over the 1982-84 period, subject to Peru's meeting certain conditions. Essentially, these conditions call for limits on: (1) public sector foreign borrowing for maturities of one to ten years; (2) net annual international reserves losses; (3) domestic borrowing by the non-financial public agencies; and (4) net domestic assets of the monetary authorities.

In line with these conditions, the government is grappling with fiscal deficit problems: It sought to reduce the deficit from 8-9 percent of GDP in 1981 and 1982 to 4.1 percent in 1983. However, natural disasters—floods, landslides and drought—in 1983 exacerbated Peru's economic difficulties by adversely affecting agriculture, oil output and transportation, making the government's goals that much more difficult to achieve. Thus, the goal was not achieved; in fact, the deficit in 1983 was around 10 percent. A new agreement was worked out with the IMF at the beginning of 1984 which calls for substantial cuts in government investment expenditures (down from 10 percent of GDP in 1982 to 7 percent in 1983 and to about 6 percent in 1984), reductions in government subsidies, more efficient tax collections, and continuation of the 10 percent ad valorem import tariff surcharge.

Weather-related damages to the economy in 1983 were estimated at upwards of $1 billion. This led to increased inflationary pressures and a rise in the consumer price index of 125 percent. This rise was due not only to the disrupted food supply caused by natural disasters, but also to the freeing of controlled prices and to substantial, real devaluations of the sol with respect to the U.S. dollar.

Overall, 1983 was a year of severe contraction. In 1982, the GDP grew by only 0.7 percent, with per capita GDP declining by 1.9 percent. Preliminary estimates indicate that GDP fell by 11-12 percent in 1983 as austerity measures and natural disasters took their toll; per capita GDP declined by about 14 percent.

With respect to Peru's international trade, demand and prices for Peru's traditional mineral, agriculture and fisheries exports continued the decline that began in 1980, although there were signs that the decline was bottoming out in mid-1983. A decline of about 20 percent in exports and an increase in imports of 24 percent in the 1980-82 period, together with net interest payments abroad, led to substantial current account deficits of $1.7 billion and $1.6 billion in 1981 and 1982, respectively. The deficits—combined with scarce new borrowing opportunities and the need for large capital inflows—forced the Government to a rescheduling/refinancing of the public sector's foreign debt in 1983 and to seek additional funds. Continued balance of payment difficulties in 1984 will require yet another rescheduling/refinancing arrangement for Peru's public sector debt.

Like many other Latin American countries, Peru has found it necessary to seek assistance in meeting its international obligations. Peru's external debt was about $12.3 billion at the end of 1983, with a debt service equal to about $12.3 billion at the end of 1983, with a debt service equal to about 63 percent of exports (without effects of refinancing included). To alleviate immediate international debt burdens, Peru agreed in June 1983 with major foreign bank creditors to stretch out over eight years with three years grace more than $320 million in public sector medium-term debt amortizations maturing over a 12 month period, while obtaining $450 million in new money. Peru also arranged the rescheduling of some $2 billion in short-term trade and working capital credits. Under an extended funding facility (EFF) agreement with the IMF, Peru has commitments to receive about $1 billion over the 1982-1985 period, subject to implementation of belt-tightening economic policies; in early 1984, a more limited agreement was being considered to replace the failed EFF. Additionally in 1983, Peru's rescheduled repayment terms of over 8 years official debt to foreign government and official lending agencies, including guaranteed credits to suppliers and banks, through The Paris Club arrangement.

Since 1980, the present Peruvian Government has sought to rebuild a market economy upon the statist base it inherited from the preceding 12 years of military rule. This has been difficult during a period of international recession. However, significant steps have been taken to liberalize the economy under policies aimed at ensuring greater economic efficiency. Specifically, this has meant trade liberalization, free access to foreign exchange and maintenance of a realistic exchange rate, decontrol of prices, raising interest rates more in line with inflation, the abolition of government monopolies—though not Government participation—in the marketing of certain agricultural and mining products, partial removal of subsidies in publicly-controlled prices (with total removal the objective), opening the economy to foreign investors with particular emphasis on new legislation designed to stimulate investment in mining and petroleum, initiatives by the Government to sell state-owned firms outright or shares to the private sector, and, in general, creation of a climate favorable to private business activities with a view to bringing about higher living standards. These initiatives will need both short-term resources and worldwide economic recovery before they can be realized.

Trade Regulations

Trade Policy

The Peruvian Government believes that opening up the economy to more imports will improve the efficiency of domestic industry through increased competition, provide lower cost inputs for needed industrial recovery, and help reduce inflationary pressures. The import liberalization program, begun in 1979 and accelerated by the Belaunde Administration in 1980, has eliminated many restrictions, such as import licensing and other "invisible" barriers to trade. In addition, tariffs have been lowered and simplified, although a surcharge and other fees and charges are levied on imports.

Import Tariffs and Taxes

Maximum import duties have been lowered from 150 to 60 percent, with the unweighted average duty now at about 41 percent. Capital goods and intermediate products and materials are dutiable at relatively low levels, e.g., from 10-25 percent, while consumer and luxury imports are subject to the maximum rate of 60 percent. Duties are imposed on the c.i.f. value of imported merchandise.

Surcharge—A 10 percent surcharge was imposed on the c.i.f. value of all imports beginning in March 1983. This probably will not be eliminated during 1984.

Additional Surcharge—A one percent surcharge is levied on the c.i.f. value of most imports. The proceeds are used to promote Peru's non-traditional exports.

Ocean Freight Tax—A tax of 10 percent is levied on freight charges for a large number of import transactions. The proceeds are used to help support Peru's merchant marine. Some agricultural and medical products are exempt.

Sales Tax—A 18 percent valued-added tax is imposed on nearly all products. The tax is applied to the c.i.f. value, plus the duty and all other taxes and fees, including the selective consumption tax (see below).

Selective Consumption Tax—This is a tax on goods considered luxuries, e.g. video games, jewelry, cigarettes, etc. The tax rates are mostly between 10 and 40 percent, with some rates in excess of 60 percent for cigarettes, gasoline and liquor. The tax is levied on the value of the import transaction after duties and other charges have been applied, but before the sales tax, freight tax and administrative charges.

Consular and Customs Broker Fees—Consular fees are collected at Customs. Fees range from $8.00 to $400.00 depending on the value of the shipment. For each set of the Bill of Lading, there is a $40.00 fee. If a certificate or origin is required, the fee is $10.00. In addition, customs broker fees are normally required.

An example of the duties and charges applicable to a color television set imported from the United States is given in Table 3.

TABLE 3—Calculation of Tariffs and Other Charges: Importation of a Color TV.

	CCCN Number 85.15.04.11 (%)	(U.S. Dollars)
FOB value		350.00
Freight		100.00
Insurance		15.00
Total CIF		465.00
Tariff on CIF value	60	279.00
Surtax on CIF value	10	46.50
FOPEX on CIF value	1	4.65
Consular and Bill of Lading Fees on CIF value	1.5	6.97
Sub-Total		802.12
Selective Tax on Sub-total	10	80.21
Sub-Total		882.33
Sales Tax on Sub-total	18	158.19
Sub-Total		1,041.5
Freight Tax	By air	—
Administrative Cost (approximately) of Sub-total	5	52.06
Sub-Total		1,093.21
Total Cost		1,093.21

Duty Exemptions

In the past, the government granted duty exemptions on a variety of goods usually when these were destined to support a specific goal or program of the government. Starting in 1984 all items but books are subject to a minimum one percent tariff, and liberation from other taxes and fees have been severely restricted.

In addition, the following goods which were previously exempt from duty will now pay the minimum tariff: agricultural machinery and equipment; machinery and equipment for gold mining; aircraft, components and parts imported by national companies (80 percent owned by Peruvian citizens), but only with the approval of the appropriate ministry.

Trade Agreements

Peru is a signatory of the Agreement of Cartagena, informally known as the Andean Pact or the Andean Common Market (ANCOM); other signatories include Bolivia, Colombia, Ecuador and Venezuela. Preferential duty rates apply to most imports from other members of ANCOM, and there is a program for automatic annual import duty reductions. By the end of 1983, import duties on products subject to automatic reduction were to be completely eliminated when traded among Peru, Venezuela, and Colombia. Imports into these countries from Bolivia and Ecuador are already exempted from import duties with certain exceptions. However, due to the difficult trade situation of these countries in 1983, barriers to trade were generally raised rather than lowered. The NACOM nations hope to establish a common external tariff (CXT) applicable to imports from outside countries, but this appears unlikely in the near term

due to the growth of protectionist measures within the region. Moreover, there has been no agreement on CXT levels. In the cases of CXT rates assigned for production under joint country programs to develop the metalworking, automotive, and petrochemical sectors, the rates only exist on paper.

The United States signed a bilateral trade agreement with Peru in 1980 within the framework of the Multilateral Trade Negotiations (MTN). In accordance with the agreement Peru agreed to reduce and bind its tariffs at 30 percent on certain plastic materials and at 20 and 35 percent for "chemical wood pulp, other" and automatic door closers, respectively. Peru also agreed to bind its tariffs on a small number of items under a U.S.-Andean Pact Agreement in December 1979.

Peru is a member of the Latin American Integration Association, (LAIA), the successor to the Latin American Free Trade Association (LAFTA). In addition to the Andean members, Argentina, Brazil, Chile, Mexico, Paraguay and Uruguay are members of LAIA. Peru is also a member of the General Agreement on Tariffs and Trade (GATT), the principal international trade policy instrument used for the governing of world trade.

Information regarding Peruvian duties, taxes, and import controls applicable to specific products may be obtained free of charge from the Office of South America, International Trade Administration, U.S. Department of Commerce, Washington, D.C., 20230, Telephone (202) 377-4303. Written inquiries should contain a complete product description, including CCCN (BTN), SITC or U.S. Schedule E Export Commodity number, if known.

Free Ports and Zones

Iquitos, a city located in the Amazon Basin in Peru has been declared a free port. In addition, certain legal provisions—basically the Peru-Colombia frontier agreement—give a portion of the Amazon Basin region a status analogous to that of a free zone, permitting duty-free imports for regional consumption and dispatch to other parts of the country if some value has been added in the area.

Used Goods

Current regulations governing the issuance of import licenses establish that goods to be imported should all be new, except in specific cases which require prior governmental authorization for permitted entry. Used goods are liable for the payment of duties at the same rates as those applicable to new goods. The Customs authorities will use the declared prices in determining value provided that these prices correspond to the condition of the used goods. Prices of used goods may not be lower than 50 percent of the price of similar new goods.

Samples and Advertising Matter

Samples of no obvious commercial value are admitted into Peru free of duty. Samples regarded as salable and, therefore, having commercial value are to be declared as ordinary commercial shipments; they are subject to the duties regularly applying to imports of similar commodities. If, upon inspection of dutiable samples, such samples are mutilated to make them unsalable, they are admitted duty-free. The declaration of dutiable samples as "without value" is penalized by a fine.

Samples of all kinds, with the exception of fine jewelry, may be imported temporarily duty-free into Peru for a maximum period of 6-months, upon application to the Peruvian customs authorities. Samples of articles normally sold by length may not exceed 30 cm. Items never considered "samples" are chemical products, drugs, toilet articles, and liqueurs, whether or not in miniature bottles. These are assessed full duties.

Advertising matter—including catalogs and sales promotional material—is subject to duty. It is recommended that advertising materials not contain any representations of the Peruvian map.

Advance Rulings on Customs Classifications

Advance rulings may be obtained from the Administrator of Customs at the Peruvian port of entry. An application for a ruling can be submitted directly, or, preferably, by a customs broker or local attorney. Appeals of a classification ruling must be presented within 3 days after notification to the Customs Board (Comision Consultiva de Aranceles de Aduana). Decisions by the Customs Board apply for all subsequent imports of identical goods.

Import Licensing

On September 12, 1980, the Peruvian Government, under Supreme Decree number 211-80-EF, eliminated the requirement of an import license for most goods. Goods which still require an import license are those required for defense and national security, petroleum and by-products, fertilizers, and agricultural products which appear on the restricted list. Another set of about 120 items are importable but subject to prior approval ("observacion") from the appropriate ministry. They include items subject to public sector monopoly, where applicable, or deemed in need of protection or detrimental to public welfare. Even though almost all goods are currently without licensing requirements, importers of goods in Peru must be listed in the Register of Importers. Imports valued at up to U.S. $2,000 a year are free from licensing or registration requirements.

Imports from ANCOM countries, do not require an import license and need only be registered with the Direccion de Comercio Exterior (Bureau of Foreign Trade), as well as imports of raw materials and intermediate goods for the production of non-traditional exports. However, all of these imports are subject to the presentation of the corresponding Origin Certificates.

Import Monopolies

The Government of Peru has been relaxing controls on exports and imports of basic products and raw materials which are made through its purchasing agencies and monopolies. The marketing of fishmeal and fish oil is controlled by PESCA-PERU, while fish, crusta-

ceans and mollusks for human consumption are controlled by EPSEP. Imports and exports of crude petroleum and petroleum derivatives are controlled by PETRO-PERU, metallic and non-metallic minerals by MINERO-PERU, steel and related products by SIDER-PERU, and tobacco and cigarettes by ENATA. ENCI controls the importation of products such as cattle, meat, milk products, fruits and vegetables, coffee, rice, corn, soybeans, oil for human consumption, cottonseed and cotton fiber, phosphoric rock, fertilizers, and television sets for the jungle areas.

Exchange Controls

The currency of Peru is the Peruvian Sol. The exchange rate for the sol is established by the Central Reserve Bank and is adjusted daily in relation to inflation and to a group of seven currencies (of which the U.S. dollar is the most important). In 1983, the exchange rate of the sol depreciated about 130 percent against the U.S. dollar, the result of regular minidevaluations. The policy of regular devaluations to maintain parity is expected to continue for the foreseeable future.

The sol is freely convertible, there is no extra-legal market, and purchases of dollars are possible in banks or exchange houses. There are, however, different rates of exchange depending on the application of the funds. The official rate is used by the government in many transactions to which it is a party. The buying and selling rate for certificates of deposit denominated in U.S. dollars are the most commonly used rates for commercial transactions and, therefore, for most import transactions. The exchange house rate varies according to supply and demand factors but is primarily of interest only to tourists.

The government has indicated that it intends to create a new currency unit that will be the equivalent to 1000 of the old soles (sol de oro). The actual currency will not be replaced completely until later this decade. The move is required—according to government sources—to facilitate accounting procedures, which have been ponderous due to inflation.

Banks and nonbank financial institutions may open foreign exchange demand and time deposit accounts for residents and nonresidents. In addition, banks may issue certificates of deposit denominated in foreign currencies, including the U.S. dollar. Funds deposited in these accounts or used to purchase bank certificates must not be derived from exports. Foreign currency certificates of deposit must be for amount of not less than $1,000 and have maturity of not longer than 360 days. They are freely negotiable both in Peru and abroad and may be used by the holder for making all permitted payments and transfers, including import payments. With respect to imports, most products may be imported, and foreign exchange is made available for payment thereof, as long as the importer is registered in the National Register of Importers.

Remittances overseas of capital and net profits require approval. For those derived from foreign direct investment, the approval of CONITE is required, while for most other transfer the appropriate agency is the Central Reserve Bank. Loan amortization repayments of the private sector are authorized by the Central Reserve Bank and those of the public sector by the General Directorate of Public Credit in the Ministry of Economy, Finance and Commerce.

Shipping Regulations

Peruvian regulations require that Peruvian vessels carry imports of goods that have been liberated from import duties as well as Peruvian Government cargos. However, the U.S. lines serving Peru—Delta Steamship Lines, Inc., Lykes Brothers Steamship Company, and Carribbean Container Transport—have entered into associate arrangements with the Compania Peruana de Vapores (the Peruvian Steamship Company) whereby these companies may continue to participate in all cargos to Peru, whether or not liberated (see Transportation and Utilities for futher information).

Freight Insurance

Maritime insurance on imports must be secured from Peruvian insurance companies, in accordance with Decree-Law No. 20019 of May 15, 1973. Public sector entities must insure freight on imports through the Peruvian Government organization, Compania de Seguros Popular y Porvenir in accordance with Decree Law 21088 of January 28, 1975. (The law provides that the Banco de la Nacion will sell the foreign exchange necessary for premiums when local companies' policies are insured in foreign currencies.)

Shipping Documents

Regardless of value or mode of transport, commercial shipments must be covered by the following documents: bill of lading, commercial invoice, and certificate of origin (when requested). A packing list is not required but is recommended in order to facilitate clearance of goods. Special certificates also may be necessary depending on the nature of the goods shipped.

Bill of Lading.—The original and two copies of the bill of lading are required. It may be prepared either in Spanish or in English with a Spanish translation. The bill of lading must show gross weights in pounds and kilograms or measurements in metric units and must give freight charges.

Commercial Invoice—Three copies of the commercial invoice are required and must be prepared in Spanish (each English word must have a Spanish translation typed underneath it). The following data are required:

(a) Name and address of shipper
(b) Invoice number and place and date issued
(c) Order number and date
(d) Number and date of letter of credit, if applicable
(e) Name and address of importer
(f) Number of packages, quantity and type of packages and gross weight of packages
(g) Detailed description of merchandise, including serial number and value of each item
(h) Orgin of merchandise

(i) Unit value of merchandise
(j) Total f.a.s., f.o.b. or c.i.f. values
(k) Discounts, if any, explained
(l) Declaration and tariff numbers

If errors are made on the commercial invoice, a letter of correction can be submitted to the customs administration explaining the errors up to the time of presentation of the import manifest. In the letter of correction, the importer must show the name of the carrier and merchandise, the arrival date, the bill of lading number, and the quantity, types and weights of the packages listed so that the shipment can be identified.

Certificates of Origin—Generally, the certificate of origin is necessary only when requested by the importer or the intervening bank. Certificates should be certified by a Chamber of Commerce in the exporting country. The importer should notify the exporter whether legalization by a Peruvian Consular official is required.

Special Documentation

Sanitary and Purity Certificates—Some farm and fish products in all their forms and types—e.g., plants, seeds, cuttings, fresh fruits, preserved vegetables and fish (i.e., bottled, canned, dried, etc.) and live farm animals—require import permits issued by the Peruvian Ministry of Agriculture.

For more information on documentation relating to animals and plants, and their products, write to: Animal and Plant Health Inspection Service (APHIS), U.S. Department of Agriculture, Hyattsville, MD 20782.

Alcoholic beverages must be registered with the Peruvian Ministry of Agriculture in accordance with detailed regulations. Such beverages require registration and a certificate of analysis issued by a competent authority in the country of origin. Whiskey shipments, regardless of origin, require an age certificate.

Only pharmaceuticals, drugs, and veterinary medicines that are registered with the Peruvian Ministry of Public Health may be imported and sold in Peru. All shipping documents should show the product's registration number. Patent medicines, in addition, must always be covered by a separate set of commercial invoices that show any discounts granted; the metric weight, size, and volume; the technical or commercial name; the kind and capacity of the container; and the quality of the product. Also, imports of toilet preparations, cosmetics and perfumery are subject to prior analysis, approval and registration by the Ministry of Public Health.

A special import permit is required for the importation of any fish products and of firearms, ammunition, or explosives.

Quality Certification

According to Chapter III of the General Industry Law (Ley General de Industrias) imported merchandise is subject to quality standards. All imported goods must be equal or superior to already existing domestic products. Quality standards are set by ITINTEC (Instituto de Investigacion Tecnologica Industrial y de Normas Tecnicas), and all imports goods are subject to ITINTEC's approval. Information on some 200 ITINTEC standards is available through the National Center for Standards and Certification Information, B166, Technology Building, National Bureau of Standards, Washington, D.C. 20234; tel. (301) 921-2587.

Air Cargo.—Requirements for shipping documentation, with the exception of the presentation of an airwaybill instead of a bill of lading, are the same as for maritime shipments.

For air cargo in transit, four copies of a "Manifest of Air Cargo in Transit" in Spanish or with a Spanish translation must be presented, along with other documents, by the airline to the Peruvian customs authorities. Data on this manifest must include airline, flight number, date of arrival, country of origin, airway-bill number, number of packages, description of goods, weight, name and address of consignee, and place of final destination. This last item should be in Spanish and not in code.

Parcel post—Parcel post shipments must be supported by a commercial invoice written in Spanish. For clearance purposes, the commercial invoice must be presented to the Customs Administration, together with the importer's declaration, in the same manner as ocean freight shipments. All parcel post shipments not withdrawn within 60 days after the date of the post office's notification will be returned to place of origin in accordance with the Universal Postal Union Agreement.

Labeling, Marking, and Packing

Picture labels should be avoided. Special labeling requirements apply on the importation and sale of medicinal preparations, pharmaceutical specialties, and processed milk.

Packages may be marked with either stencil or brush and should show gross weight in kilograms on each package. Weight, serial numbers, and other markings must agree with those indicated on the shipping documents.

All foreign industrial products must clearly bear the inscriptions listed below prior to being marketed in Peru.

(a) Brand name (consumer products)
(b) Country of origin
(c) Date of expiration (for food products, medicinal products for human and veterinary consumption, photographic materials and others subject to expiry terms)

If it is not possible to make the above inscriptions because of the product's physical characteristics, inscriptions must be made on labels, decalcomania, containers or other similar means. In the case of imported wearing apparel, shoes, electric appliances, automotive parts, liquors and soft drinks, the name and tax identity card number of the importer must be added as well. Furthermore, wholesalers and retailers of imported products that divide them into fractions or parts, repack or reprocess them locally must maintain identifying inscriptions on such products. Advertising must indicate the product's brand name and country of origin.

Foreign manufactured products not meeting the above requirements are considered illegal for entry purposes and are subject to public auction.

Entry and Warehousing

Imported merchandise must be declared either for consumption or for warehousing within 30 days of its arrival; if not, it will be stored temporarily. All imported goods must be cleared from customs with 60 days of arrival in Peruvian ports.

Goods shall be considered abandoned and subject to public auction if no request for clearance is presented to the Customs Administration within 3 months of discharge at the port of destination for goods arriving by sea or waterways and 2 months for goods arriving by air or land.

Import duties and other customs charges must be paid within a period of 5 days from the date of arrival of the customs bill at the Cashier's Office. If the goods are not withdrawn within this time limit, a 2 percent surcharge per month, or fraction of a month, is applied on the import duties. However, in 1983 a law was passed allowing payment of duties over a period of 10 months on approval of the importer's petition.

Merchandise may be deposited in special customs warehouses at the request of the consignee for a longer storage period. Such "merchandise in deposit" must be cleared or reembarked within 6 months of the date of deposit or it will be considered abandoned. Dangerous cargo in customs yards must be cleared with 48 hours of its arrival at any port. If not withdrawn within this time limit, significant surcharges are applied.

Merchandise entered for warehousing is subject to the same fines and penalties as are applicable to goods declared for immediate clearance. Any fines or penalties imposed must be paid before the goods will be permitted to be warehoused. Warehousing of foodstuffs and other goods subject to deterioration is limited to 90 days. In special circumstances, an additional 90 days may be allowed.

Iquitos, a city located in the Amazon Basin in Eastern Peru, has recently been declared a free port. There also are entry ports at Matarani and Mollendo for shipments in transit to Bolivia.

Imported machinery, equipment and parts, which at the time of clearance from customs or after installation is found to be defective, may be returned abroad temporarily without presentation of customs bond.

Confiscated merchandise cannot be reshipped and will be sold at public auction.

Temporary Imports

In order to guarantee the exportation of goods imported into Peru on a temporary admission basis, the beneficiaries are required to present to the Customs Administration a bond for the full amount of import duties.

Supreme Resolution No. 126-81-EFC/11 of November 1981 allows temporary duty-free entry of both accompanied and unaccompanied baggage for tourists and for persons who visit the country for cultural, technical, scientific, sports, business and other reasons for a period less than one year. Items of baggage subject to this privilege are articles of personal clothing, cosmetics, medicines, articles of personal adornment, books, magazines and documents, a portable musical instrument, portable typewriter, non-professional camera equipment, a portable radio or recorder, six phonograph records or cassettes, a portable calculator, a portable hair dryer, toys personal sports equipment, 20 packs of cigarettes, other articles up to a value of $300 for gifts, and necessary suitcases and other baggage.

In addition, the regulation permits the entry of personal goods and household objects which correspond to the traveler's profession, job or occupation. Visitors who fall into these categories should bring a detailed list of the goods they wish to import temporarily in duplicate in both Spanish and English. On arrival, customs will stamp one copy which will be rechecked upon departure. No monetary deposits on these imports are required.

Distribution and Sales Channels

Import Channels

There are four principal types of commercial import channels in this market: (1) import houses, (2) commission or sales agent, (3) branches and subsidiaries of foreign manufacturers, and (4) direct importation by the end-users.

Leading import houses import on their own account, although they often agree to represent foreign concerns on a commission basis as well. These firms often have a network of branches, sub-distributors, and an extensive sales force to canvass retailers, wholesalers, and consumers. This method offers the foreign exporter a certain degree of financial security since the import house assumes the risk involved and offers the use of well established and experienced distributors.

A more common type of representation is the commission of indent sales agent who takes orders on a direct shipment basis. Frequently, the most effective type of representation in this field is the agent who specializes in a small group of similar but non-competitive lines. The advantage of this arrangement is that as a specialist he will have intimate knowledge of the product (particularly important in the case of technical equipment) and that he may cater to a number of established customers.

The establishment of a local subsidiary provides the greatest guarantee that the foreign manufacturer will obtain efficient and aggressive promotion of his product and permits him to retain control over the product. This method, however, involves a considerable investment and can only be justified on the basis of sales volume or of the need for very efficent servicing facilities or inventories. It also involves adjustment to the restrictions applicable to foreign investors contained in Decision 24 and amendments (the Andean Foreign Investment Code—see below).

Direct purchases by the consumer also are an important channel. The large mining and industrial enterprises, railways, commercial airlines, public utilities, large retailers such as supermarkets, and government agencies frequently import their own equipment directly. The Peruvian Government, through various official entities, has in recent years become an increasingly important purchaser of foreign goods. (For additional information see Government Procurement.) They may occasionally send buyers abroad, correspond directly with foreign suppliers, or may buy through a purchasing agent abroad. Many large American mining, industrial, and commercial companies in Peru make their overseas purchases through their home offices in the United States.

Considerable care should be exercised in selecting representation. It is not only important to select the type of distribution system most suitable for the needs of the exporting firm and its product, but it is equally important to appoint a representative with experience, character, aggressiveness, and financial solvency. Some manufacturers and exporters are known to seek only the largest and best-known import houses, but in many cases large concerns represent too many lines to push effectively the sales of a particular product. Experience has shown that giving the representation to a smaller firm—probably less well-known but alert, responsible, and anxious to succeed—can sometimes result in better coverage.

The U.S. supplier should make periodic visits to assist the distributor or agent. This provides an opportunity for both to assess the market jointly and permits personal contact with representatives and customers which is a very important aspect of doing business in Peru.

Wholesale and Retail Merchandising—Merchandising occupies the time and efforts of hundreds of thousands of Peruvians. In general, the distribution of products in Peru is made through one or more types of distribution organizations but the lines of division are not clear, with wholesalers also operating as retailers, retailers as wholesalers and producers selling directly both to wholesalers and retailers. Large producers of such products as plastics, televisions, radios, refrigerators, and stoves often have their own retail outlets in the larger cities. This type of distribution is suitable only for large volume operations and so far only accounts for a small percentage of the total products distributed.

Large and Small Wholesalers.—The initial distribution of nearly everything sold in Peru takes place through some sort of wholesaler. Importers and distributors who buy for their own account use wholesalers to move their products to retailers and "ambulantes" (street vendors). Many wholesalers import directly and then distribute through retail outlets. Sales agents for foreign firms sell, in large part, to wholesalers. Wholesalers may be described either as large (those who distribute more than one line of goods), or small (those who handle only line). It is estimated that there are approximately 75,000 commercial establishments in Peru of which some 30,000 are classified as wholesalers. Most of the small wholesalers have only one or two employees (in addition to the owner) and often sell consumer goods only to Peru's omnipresent street vendors. The large wholesalers distribute to industrial buyers and deal in capital goods as well as consumer items.

Retailers.—A number of chain-type retail stores have developed in Peru in recent years, led by Sears Roebuck & Co. Others, such as Oechsle, Monterrey and SCALA S.A., are giving Sears vigorous competition. There are also large supermarket chains in Lima—"Todos," "Galax," and "Monterrey". Most of the retail stores in Peru, however, are small in size with only a few employees and little volume. They are indispensable for the distribution of products with limited sales such as those produced in workshops ("talleres") and by small, family-type factories. To reach these stores and gain good distribution of their products, U.S. exporters must find agents and representatives with the right connections who can move their goods through the wholesalers into the small retail stores.

Government Procurement

Peruvian government ministries and agencies usually do their own procurement. Each ministry and agency, under the general supervision of the Ministry of Economy, Finance and Commerce, receives funds through the Federal budget to carry out its programs and each decides how best to spend the funds allocated. In the case of a major project, the following approvals must be obtained before a project requiring foreign financing can go to bid: (1) Project approval from the pertinent ministry (after initiation at the operating company level); (2) Certification from the National Planning Institute that the project is in accordance with national priorities; (3) Approval from the Office of Public Credit for the use of foreign credit; (4) Approval of the Council of Ministers.

Peruvian legislation on government purchasing requires that public tenders be issued for all purchases over 2 million soles unless the Government grants a special dispensation to purchase directly. These tenders, published regularly in the official gazette of Peru, "El Peruano," are open to foreign firms. Furthermore, for all purchases made with funds supplied by the Inter-American Development Bank and the World Bank, bid tender are sent to the U.S. Embassy in Lima and other countries that support the two financial organizations, for submission to firms abroad. Public bids need not be issued for purchases of less than 2 million soles, although it is customary for ministries and agencies to obtain three bids from reliable suppliers before awarding contracts.

American firms desiring to provide goods and services to the Peruvian Government must have, according to Peruvian law, a local address or associate in order to qualify to bid. Bidders are normally required to make a deposit with their bid of not less than 6 percent of the total amount of their bid. The deposit is refundable if the bid is unsuccessful. Peruvian laws governing purchasing also require that domestic products be given preference over similar foreign products provided the domestic products meet quality and quantity requirements.

Most important government bid requests follow the "two envelope" system after prequalification and short listing of potential bidders. The prequalification process establishes the bona-fides of the bidder (financial information, record of previous work, proof of ability to supply the products or services desired, etc.). Envelope No. 1 contains the economic or technical proposal, and Envelope No. 2 contains the financial proposal. Dates are established by the government for the submission of both envelopes and all bids are opened publicly in the presence of interested bidders and of a notary who records the offers and any formal observations made.

The Peruvian Government is a major buyer of Peru's requirements of machinery and equipment through such entities as CENTROMIN and MINERO-PERU (mining, PETRO-PERU (petroleum and petroleum products), ELECTRO-PERU (electricity), ENTEL-PERU (telecommunications), ENAFER (railroads), SIDER-PERU (iron and steel products), ENAPU-PERU (port equipment and supplies) and ENCI (basically food products), or government ministries such as the Ministries of Agriculture; Mines and Energy; Transport and Communications; Industry, Tourism, and Integration; and Economy, Finance and Commerce.

The names and addresses of the more important government agencies active in procurement are given below: All are located in or just outside Lima.

CORPAC (Corporacion Peruana de Aeropuertos y Aviacion Comercial) Casilla 680, Callao; Aeropuerto Internacional Jorge Chavez, Callao, (Peruvian Airport and Commercial Aviation Corporation)

ELECTRO-PERU (Empresa del Electricidad del Peru) 144 Avenida Paseo de la Republica, Lima (Electric power)

ENAFER-PERU (Empresa Nacional de Ferrocarriles del Peru) Casilla 1379, Lima 100; Jiron Ancash 207, Lima 1 (National Railroad Enterprise of Peru)

ENAPU-PERU (Empresa Nacional de Puertos) Casilla 260, Callao; Terminal Maritimo del Callao, Callao (National Ports Enterprise)

ENCI-PERU (Empresa Nacional de Comercializacion e Insumos) Casilla 1834, Lima 100; Avenida Bernardo Monteagudo 210, Lima 17 (National Enterprise for the Marketing of Basic Food Products)

ENRAD-PERU (Empresa Nacional de Radiodifusion del Peru) Avenida Jose Galvez 1040, Lima 14 (National Radio of Peru)

ENTEL-PERU S.A. (Empresa Nacional de Telecomunicaciones del Peru) Las Begonias 475, Lima 27 (National Telecommunications Enterprise of Peru)

ENTUR-PERU (Empresa Nacional de Turismo S.A.) Casilla 4475, Lima 100; Jiron Junin 455, Lima 1 (National Tourism Enterprise)

EPSEP (Empresa Publica de Servicios Pesqueros) Casilla 11119, Santa Beatriz, Lima 1; Avenida Javier Prado Este 2465 Lima 30 (Public Enterprise of Fishery Services)

HIERRO-PERU (Empresa Mineral de Hierro del Peru) Apartado 1229, Lima 100; Avenida Paseo de la Republica 3587 Lima 12 (Iron Producer)

ITINTEC (Instituto de Investigacion Tecnologica Industrial y de Normas Tecnicas) Casilla 145, Lima 100; Jiron Morelli Cuadra. 2; Urbanizacion San Borja, Lima 34 (Research Institute for Industrial Technology and Technical Standards)

Autoridad Autonoma de MAJES Avenida Larco 383 — Piso 4, Lima 18 (Large Irrigation and Power Project)

Proyecto Especial de Irrigation Chira-Piura (Ministerio de Agricultura y Alimentacion) Avenida Republica de Chile 350; Lima 1 (Special Irrigation Project)

Proyecto Especial de Irrigacion Tinajones (Ministerio de Agricultura y Alimentacion) Larrabure y Unanue 299, Piso 7, Santa Beatriz Lima 1 (Large Irrigation Project)

Agency Agreements

In Peru, there are no special protective laws which regulate the termination of agency agreements. Rather, principal/agent agreements are covered by the Peruvian Civil Commercial Code.

Under the code, the principal may terminate an agency agreement at any time. There are no laws providing for special compensation in the event of an agency agreement termination. However, in the event of a disputed contract termination, Peruvian commercial law provides the party which feel injured by the termination the right to file suit for compensation. Therefore, it is highly recommended that U.S. firms include causes and methods for termination of an agency agreement in the legal contract to preempt any possible future contract disputes.

Transportation and Utilities

Ocean Shipping

U.S. maritime trade routes to Peru comprise three shipping systems. The first extends from the U.S. Atlantic ports through the Panama Canal to the West Coast of South America; the second connects the U.S. Pacific ports with the West Coast of South America; and the third connects the U.S. Gulf ports with Peru via the Panama Canal. Three U.S. shipping lines serve Peru. These are Delta Steamship Lines, Inc. from the east and west coasts, Lykes Brothers Steamship Co., Inc. from the Gulf ports, and Coordinated Caribbean Transport (CCT) from the east coast.

Delta calls on the port of Callao every 2 weeks, sailing from Philadelphia, Charleston and Miami. Additional ports in Peru are on an inducement basis. The transit time from Charleston to Callao is 14 days, and the line offers breakbulk, container, reefer, and liquid bulk service. For additional information call (212) 432-4700, or write: Delta Steamship Lines, Inc., One World Trade Center, New York, N.Y. 10048. From the west coast, Delta has service (containers, breakbulk refrigeration) between Seattle/Tacoma, Portland, San Francisco, Los Angeles, and Callao (and Matarani on inducement). The transit time is 20 days from the last U.S. port to Callao. The line has 13 voyages from the west coast per year. For further information call (415) 777-2800, or write: Delta Steamship Lines, Inc., One Market Plaza, Steuart St. Tower, Suite 2700, San Francisco, CA 94106.

Lykes Brothers Steamship Co., Inc., provides regular monthly service from U.S. Coast ports to Callao, Matarani, and Ilo, and also calls, on inducement, at the ports of Talara, Paita, Salaverry, and Pimentel. Transit time from the last U.S. Gulf port to the first Peruvian port is 12 to 15 days. For further information call (504) 523-6611, or write Lykes Brothers Steamship Co., Inc., 300 Poydras Street, New Orleans, La. 70130.

CCT operates a container roll on roll off service between Miami and Paita in northern Peru. The frequency is every 15 days.

For further information pertaining to U.S. flag service capabilities worldwide contact Mr. Carime P. Gerace, International Trade Specialist, Division of Commercial Cargo, Office of Market Development, Maritime Administration, U.S. Department of Transportation, Washington, D.C. 20590; Telephone (202) 426-6211.

Ports

Peru has an extended seaboard on the Pacific Ocean of 1,400 miles with 29 ports. The principal port is Callao, which has berths for 17 vessels, 11 roofed warehouses, and a variety of cargo-handling equipment, including for containers. Lift capacity is 150 tons.

Other important ports are Paita, Talara, Salaverry, and Chimbote (the leading fishing port) in northern Peru, and Matarani, Pisco, Ilo, and San Nicolas (the principal iron ore shipport port) in southern Peru.

Peru also has two important river ports in the Amazon Basin—Iquitos and Pucallpa. Other important river ports include Yurimaguas and Puerto Maldonado, and there are three lake ports on Lake Titicaca, the highest lake in the world—Desaguadero, Puno, and Yunguyo.

Storage

Storage facilities in Peruvian ports are generally insufficient, and there is a significant shortage of roofed warehousing. Even though in recent special police forces have been charged with vigilance and control of activities in all ports of the littoral, pilferage continues to be a considerable problem. Therefore, it is recommended that U.S. shippers and exporters use special and safe export packing, such as weatherproof and pilferproof containers.

Highways and Roads

Peru has a moderately developed road transportation system. It has two primary highways: the Pan American Highway, running along the West Coast from the northern to the southern border, and the Central Highway, extending east from Lima over a 1,600 meter pass to La Oroya and beyond.

There are also a number of penetration roads leading into the jungle area and the incomplete Marginal Highway running along the eastern border. The present approximate mileage of public roads, including asphalted, improved and unimproved, is 56,654 kilometers. By 1985 the government plans to have completed an additional 8,000 kilometers.

Railroads

Peru has approximately 2,192 kilometers of railroads. There is no integrated railroad system, most rail lines having been built to provide service between the coast the mining centers of the Sierra. ENAFER, a government enterprise, provides passenger and freight services on the most important railroads. The scenic Central Railway connects Lima with the central highlands and is the world's highest standard gauge railway, crossing the main range of the Andes at over 15,000 feet. The more extensive Southern Railway connects the Pacific port of Mollendo with Arequipa, Juliaca, Cusco and Puno. From the latter point, there is irregular steamer service across Lake Titicaca to the Bolivian port of Guaqui, which is connected by rail to La Paz.

Energy

Petroleum is the dominant element in Peru's energy system. Oil provides about 70 percent of the country's commercial energy needs and 66 percent of total energy requirements. The country's total crude reserves at the end of 1982 were estimated at 775 million barrels or 11 years supply at current production levels. Estimates of undiscovered reserves range from two to twenty billion barrels. Crude oil production amounted to about 195,061 barrels per day in 1982. The total number of wells drilled for exploration, development and secondary recovery was 353 in 1982, 129 in 1983 and is expected to be 216 in 1984. Petroleum products were Peru's principal export in 1981, at 19 percent of total value of exports. However, the country could become a net importer by 1986. The only producers are Occidental Petroleum, Belco Petroleum and the state oil company, PETRO-PERU.

Electric power is produced primarily by the state-owned entity ELECTRO-PERU, its major subsidiary, Electrolima, and by smaller regional utilites. Total electrical output amounted to 9,959 GWH in 1982. About 60 percent of electricity is produced from hydro sources; the remainder from thermal sources. The cost of electricity for the industrial sector presently varies between $0.03 and $0.08 per kilowatt hour.

Peru's abundance of rivers provides enormous potential for the development of hydroelectric power. While the present generating capabity is 3,253 megawatts (MW), the country's hydroelectric potential is estimated to be approximately 60,000 MW. Current electric consumption on a per capita basis is only 590 KW/hour compared to an average of 1,100 KW/hour for Latin America. This low consumption rate is partially a result of the difficulty in providing electricity across the country's rough terrain and distances in order to serve small population centers. The Peruvian Government, with assistance from international financial agencies such as the World Bank, is undertaking a large number of hydro power projects to meet the needs of consumers, which are estimated to be increasing at an annual rate of 7-8 percent in this decade.

Electric Current Characteristics

The industrial power for older factories is 2300v and for the larger and more modern factories 10,000v AC, 60 cycles. Domestic use is generally 220v AC, 60 cycles, but in the regions of Arequipa and Iquitos the current is 220v AC, 50 cycles and 110v AC respectively. Plugs are 2 pins, both round and flat, and lamp fittings are the screw type.

Advertising

The development of Peruvian advertising has progressed rapidly in recent years. The Lima area is by far the principal advertising center having nearly one-third of the total population. Literacy is approximately 78.4 percent. There are 52 advertising agencies operating in Peru, of which J. Walter Thompson Peruana, McCann Erickson Corp. and Forum, an associate of Ogilvy & Mather, are the leading firms. An agency's commission is usually 15 percent of the gross cost of advertisements. The principal media for advertising is television, followed by radio and press. Other media include motion picture theaters, signs, fairs, billboards, and direct mail.

Television.—There are six operating TV stations in the country and an estimated 750,000 TV sets. The average viewing audience in Lima is five persons per set. Stations broadcast on the average of 14 hours daily. Program listings are a mixture U.S. network shows, Latin soap operas and feature films, with limited local production consisting of news, game shows, and debates.

Television has been one of Peru's fastest growing industries. In the future, broadcasting expenditures are predicted to reach $4 million, some of which will finance the development of three additional TV stations, now in the planning stage, and color TV modernizing equipment.

The commercial rate for a 60-second, prime time TV spot ranges from $205 to $1,025. As many as 10 spots are usually grouped together European-style.

Radio.—There are an estimated 3.5 million radio receivers in Peru and 229 radio stations, including Radio Nacional and its three branches owned by the Government.

Publications.—Publications in Lima include a variety of newspapers and magazines of every type and political persuasion. Publications of particular interest to business persons include the daily newspapers, El Comercio, La Prensa and La Cronica, the weekly magazines. Caretas and Oiga and the monthly magazines The Andean Report and Peru Economico. El Peruano, the daily official gazette, contains laws, decrees, and regulations, as well as news concerning Government actions and programs.

Laws Governing Content.—The laws require that advertisements be aimed at promoting the development of local production, that they avoid "the use of alienating motivations and patterns of consumption, and that they contain true and verifiable information."

Credit

Terms and Quotations

The government is fighting inflation by keeping a tight rein on credit, a policy that is expected to continue indefinitely. Since domestic credit is very tight, it is important that attention be given by the supplier to providing sufficiently flexible credit terms. This may be the key factor in successful selling in this market. Importers may request credit of up to 180 days in some cases.

Imports to Peru are commonly financed by letters of credit. Althouh the cost of these instruments varies, a price of 5 to 6 percent of the amount is not uncommon when all fees and charges are considered. In addition, a cash deposit or other security is also frequently requested by the opening bank.

Foreign suppliers are no longer required to provide credits for specific periods of time. The elimination of this requirement even affects major capital goods transactions of over $1 million. However, in the case of loans for capital goods for public sector entities, the terms sought normally are for a period greater than 10 years with a grace period of 30 months. There may be some flexibility in these rules depending on the urgency of the purchase and the tenor of competing offers.

The maximum rate of interest paid on government debt cannot exceed the rate currently authorized by Peruvian law, which is usually the average rate granted for similar loans. The law is flexible, in that adjustments can be made by decree. These regulations now apply to virtually all public sector purchases, involving foreign indebtedness.

Business Financing

Credit to foreign enterprise in Peru is regulated by the Andean Common Market rules. Only short-term financing (for periods of less than one year) is obtainable and in amounts not exceeding invested capital plus reserves. There are some specific exceptions including loans for promotion of exports of manufactured goods, loans to firms that have signed a transformation contract with the state, and special loans from the government.

The Peruvian banking system consists of a Central Bank (Banco Central de Reserva), five state-owned development banks, (Agricultural, Industrial, Mining, Housing and Central Mortgage), and four state-owned commercial banks: Banco de la Nacion, Banco Popular, Banco Continental, and Surmebanc-International. There are also several privately-owned commercial banks and a group of small regional banks set up in the early 1970's. All of the commercial banks provide normal banking services, *e.g.*, they accept deposits for both checking and savings accounts and lend only at short and medium term. The State development banks also accept deposits from the public and provide loans at longer maturities and lower interest rates than the commercial banks. The State-owned Banco de la Nacion acts as a commercial bank with a very special role: it acts as the sole agent of the government in a wide selection of transactions; it is by far the single largest bank in the system, due to its unique role.

Consumer Financing

Consumer financing through the banking system in Peru is relatively scarce and quite expensive. Nevertheless, most major personal purchases such as cars, TV sets, motorcycles, bicycles, and even clothing are financed through some form of installment buying. The costs for such financing are high, since nonpayment incidence is high, and the commercial banks and "financieras" (finance houses) that provide credit seek to protect themselves.

Commercial banks do not ordinarily furnish personal consumer loans, but the credit card system is coming into wider use and the well known international credit cards are honored in better hotels, airlines, restaurants, and similar tourist facilities. Personal consumer credit is granted for the most part by the seller and this is another reason for its scarcity and expense. For most people, it is still necessary to save for a purchase before it can be made.

Other important sources of consumer credit are consumer cooperatives, mutual funds, professional credit unions, military commissaries, and saving cooperatives. In addition, two department stores have introduced the revolving credit system to finance consumer purchases.

Multilateral Development Banks

Multilateral development banks such as the World Bank group (International Bank for Reconstruction and Development, International Development Association, and International Finance Corporation) and the Inter-American Development Bank provide both conventional and concessionary financing for projects to promote the economic development of member countries. In most cases, procurement is based on international competitive bidding open to suppliers and contractors from member countries. Peru and the United States are both members of these organizations.

PERU

Export-Import Bank

In addition to U.S. commercial banks, the Export-Import Bank of the United States (EXIMBANK) is an important source of export financing. The buyer credit or project financing program provides direct loans with fixed interest rates and long terms (normally 5-10 years) and financial guarantees of private loans for large projects. The supplier credit program offers medium-term (181 days to 5 years) commercial bank guarantees. Short- and medium-term export credit insurance is available through the Foreign Credit Insurance Association. Other Eximbank programs include agricultural export programs, contractors' guarantees, leasing, and feasibility studies.

For more information, consult your commercial bank or write directly to:

Export-Import Bank of the United States
811 Vermont Avenue, N.W.
Washington, D.C. 20571
Tel. 202/566-2117
Telex 89-461

For information on export credit insurance, contact:

Foreign Credit Insurance Association (FCIA)
One World Trade Center, 9th Floor
New York, New York 10048
Tel. 212/306-5000

Other offices FCIA are located in Atlanta, Chicago, Cleveland, Detroit, Houston, Los Angeles, Milwaukee, San Francisco and Washington, D.C.

Investment

The following information is not intended to be a complete review of the many factors affecting foreign investment in Peru. Prospective investors are strongly advised to obtain legal counsel within Peru which specializes in assistance to foreign businesses.

U.S. Investment

The United States accounts for the majority of all foreign direct investment into Peru. U.S. direct investment in Peru amounted to $2,236 million at the end of 1982. Most foreign direct investment in Peru is concentrated in petroleum and mining, and to a lesser extent in manufacturing, commerce, service, and finance.

Investment Climate

Since the late 1970's, the government has been much more receptive to foreign direct investment. The new Peruvian Constitution of 1979 demonstrates the country's positive attitude towards foreign investors through its provisions for equality of treatment under the law for foreigners and Peruvians; the inviolability of private property; recognition of rights of authorship, patents, trademarks and technology; and prohibition of retroactive law.

Peru enacted a new Industrial Law (Law No. 23407) in 1982 aimed at stimulating domestic and foreign investment. The legislation reestablishes those areas where the state will invest but eliminates provisions reserving certain sectors for state enterprises. The new Law provides that the state will refrain from unfair competition, monopolies, and restrictions on both the production and sale of local or imported goods. This stipulation addresses the acknowledged need to eliminate the vestiges of the statist economic policy introduced in the 1970s, under which the government was responsible for much of the country's commerce and production. The new Industrial Law also offers a series of important tax incentives (see taxation).

Authorization of Investments

Investors are required to obtain authorization from Peruvian Government agencies before undertaking investments. The Comision Nacional de Inversiones y Tecnologias Extranjeras—CONITE (National Commission for Foreign Investment and Technology), located at 500 Avenida Abancay, Lima, Peru, is the coordinating agency responsible for approving foreign investment plans. There also are a number of complementary offices whose approval is required for establishing foreign entities in Peru. For industrial investments and transfers of trademarks, licenses, patents, etc., approval is required from the Direccion General de Industrias (Bureau of General Industries), the Instituto de Industrias (Bureau of General Industries), the Instituto de Investigacion Tecnologica Industrial y de Normas Tecnicas—ITINTEC (Research Institute for Industrial Technology and Technical Standards), and the Ministerio de Economia, Finanzas y Comercio (Ministry of Economy, Finance and Commerce).

The following criteria are used by the Peruvian authorities in determining whether to authorize an investment: employment generation in Peru; contribution to development of the country's outlying regions; increased production; promotion and diversification of exports; import substitution; and development of the Andean integration process. In practice, all legitimate investments are welcomed.

Andean Foreign Investment Code

Peru is a signatory of the Treaty of Cartagena and subscribes to Decision 24 of that agreement (often referred to as the Andean Foreign Investment Code—AFIC). The AFIC is structured to protect the Andean market from foreign domination and to assure that the member countries are not drawn into outbidding one another in attracting foreign capital and technology.

Decision 24 states that companies which wish to take advantage of the Andean Common Market must be at least 51 percent owned by national investors. Foreign enterprises (those with more than 49 percent foreign ownership), which agree to become at least 51 percent owned by national investors over a 15-year period, may also benefit from these incentives. However, the Peruvian government has interpreted the Decision so that foreign-owned enterprises not taking advantage of the special tariff concessions of the Andean Pact do not have to be 51 percent national. Thus, it is possible for a U.S. investor to own 100 percent of the equity in a company established in Peru.

CONITE's policy is to authorize investments in all areas which are not expressly prohibited by law. In processing these authorizations, CONITE must adhere to a strict schedule in order to be responsive to potential investors. CONITE has also interpreted Decision 24 to allow dividend remittances, after taxes, equal up to 20 percent of a firm's registered foreign capital. However, this rule was liberalized in 1983 to allow foreign firms to repatriate profits beyond 20 percent when certain performance criteria are met.

All companies are permitted to borrow from sources abroad provided such borrowings are registered with the Central Reserve Bank of Peru. Both foreign and domestic companies can also borrow from domestic financial institutions; however, foreign companies may only borrow at terms of up to one year in the Peruvian market. Local long-term financing is reserved for majority or wholly national companies. Remittances abroad of profits, dividends, royalties, capital and interest can be made directly through the banking system. Foreign investors formerly had to convert incoming capital into local currency at the official rate, in order to have the right to repatriate such capital using the same rate, but new rules introduced in 1983 permit a company to keep capital denominated in foreign currencies if it wants to.

CONITE further clarified Decision 24 by establishing that only companies wishing to take advantage of the intra-Andean trade benefits are required to transform into mixed companies (51 percent locally-owned). If a company opts for these benefits, it must meet a schedule requiring conversion to a mixed corporation within 15 years. The conversion may be carried out by direct sale of existing stock or by issuing new stock sold to local investors. For new enterprises, at least 15 percent of the equity must be held by local investors at the start of production, at least 30 percent when one-third of the agreed upon term has elapsed, and at least 45 percent after two-thirds of the term has passed. If the company fails to comply with the conversion contract, it loses the advantage of intra-Andean tariff benefits. Corporations may remain as much as 70 percent foreign-owned and still be entitled to the tariff benefits, if the state has a minimum of 30 percent participation and has veto power on crucial decisions affecting operations.

Peru also enacted Decision 169 which regulates the creation of Andean multinational enterprises. These enterprises must have investors from at least two Andean countries accounting for more than 80 percent of the total capital with the remainder of the capital from foreign sources. The primary objective of this legislation is to promote the flow of intra-Andean investment and technology. In order to accomplish this goal, Decision 169 offers a number of benefits for Andean multinational companies. These include simplified incorporation procedures, automatic branch registration, full access to local credit, intra-Andean tariff benefits, full remittance

of profit (both for national and foreign investors) and avoidance of double taxation within the region.

Taxation

The following tax information is of a general nature concerning taxes that may be payable by corporations and individuals. It is highly recommended that expert assistance be obtained from companies in Peru specializing in taxation matters.

Corporate Taxes

The principal tax affecting corporations is the income tax. However, there are various other taxes that may be applicable.

Corporate income tax rates are progressive and have recently been modified to allow for inflation adjustment. The basis for calculation is now the income tax unit ("UIT"). The value of this unit is determined annually; for 1984 it is 2,200,000 soles ($880 at the exchange rate of 2,500 soles per U.S. dollar). Rates are set forth below for 1984.

Tax units	Soles ('000)	Tax Rate (%)
First 150	330,000	30
150-1499	2,970,000	40
1500-2999	3,300,000	50
Over		55

Branches of foreign corporations are subject to the same taxes as foreign corporate subsidiaries but must also pay a 32 percent complementary tax on after tax income whether or not profits are remitted.

Mining companies also pay the corporate tax plus a territorial rights tax at the rate of 0.1 percent a tax unit per hectare per year; 1 percent of profits to the Institute of Geology and Metallurgy; sales and export levies and social security and housing payroll taxes. The value of mining rights may be depreciated over a period corresponding to the probable life of the mine. Reinvested profits may be taken as a full tax credit for 3 successive years. There are no excess profits taxes.

Patrimony tax for 1984 is as follows: up to nine income tax units 1.5 percent; from ten to 29 units, 1.8 percent; over 29 units, 2.5 percent. A variety of other taxes such as income tax and cash dividends constitute tax credits before calculating this tax. Mining companies are exempt from this tax. Capital gains are normally taxed as ordinary income. Labor community taxes totalling 25 percent of pretax income must be paid under certain circumstances: (see Industrial Community). Fixed assets may be revalued periodically by indices determined by the government. Such revaluations may result in a tax, if so, it is deductible for corporate income tax purposes.

---

[1]The tax is reduced in the case of corporations to 32 percent when, any foreign tax credit nonwithstanding, the recipient would otherwise be subject to a home-country tax of 32 percent.

Dividends paid to non-resident corporations and persons are generally subject to a withholding tax of 40 and 32 percent, respectively.[1] Royalties paid to non-residents for trademarks, patents and licenses are taxed at 55 percent.

Taxable income is defined as gross receipts minus the cost of goods sold and necessary expenses. Dividends received are excluded from personal income. Payments abroad are a deductible expense if the recipient pays taxes (usually withheld by the payer). Compensation to directors is deductible up to a total of 6 percent of taxable earnings. Also deductible are equity of companies operating in high-priority sectors, e.g., tourism, mining, and hiring. Certain industries located in jungle and frontier areas receive special exemptions.

Depreciation rates must be negotiated with the Superintendency of Taxation. Some typical rates per annum are: buildings, 3 percent; industrial machinery 5-10 percent; agricultural machinery 5-30 percent; furniture and fixtures 5-15 percent and for automobiles and trucks 20-30 percent.

Personal Taxes

Persons become domiciled for tax purposes after residing in Peru for 2 consecutive years. Nondomiciled persons can request to be treated as domiciled after 6 months of residence in Peru. Domiciled taxpayers must declare their worldwide income. Income tax paid abroad is allowed as a tax credit against Peruvian income tax.

Some examples of allowable deductions include one tax unit for the taxpayer spouse, each child and each additional dependent; mortgage interest payments, charitable contributions, social security and pension contributions, life insurance premiums, real estate and certain other taxes and medical expenses.

Tax Rates—After May 1984, the tax rates are 12 percent and 15 percent on monthly salary tax units of 1.0-1.5 and over 1.5, respectively. A tax unit equals 2.2 million soles in 1984 ($880 at the exchange rate of 2500 soles per U.S. dollar). Earnings from professional activities such as consulting is taxed at a flat 10 percent rate.

Value–Added Tax

A value-added tax ("VAT") is also levied on the sale of goods and services in Peru including imports, but not exports. The single rate of 18 percent applies to sales prices at each stage of production, acquisition, and distribution. The VAT on imports is levied on the c.i.f. value plus customs duties and other charges.

Employer Taxes

All employers and employees are required to contribute to a national social security system that includes the national health and maternity system as well as the national pension system. The employer contributes approximately 10 percent of the salary of the employee and the employee approximately 5 percent to this system. There is also a payroll tax of 2.5 percent paid by the employer.

Tax Incentives

Tax incentives have been created to stimulate investment and reinvestment in various sectors of the economy. Credit and tax benefits are also granted for investments made in the less developed regions of the country. Exports of non-traditional goods may obtain significant tax reimbursements ("Certex") for taxes paid locally.

The certex rebate system for exports is to remain in force until 1992, with the value of certexes to be determined by new criteria, including indirect taxes paid, use of local inputs, level of value added and competitiveness in export markets.

Labor

The Peruvian labor force approximates 6 million (December 1981 estimate). In 1983 Peru suffered from a 8.8 percent level of unemployment; only an estimated 37.3 percent of the total population was adequately employed. Furthermore, of the economically-active Peruvians, roughly half are underemployed or earn less than Peru's very low minimum wage (about $2.80 a day).

Labor Organizations

The information concerning the number of trade unions and federations and their registered membership is often unreliable. This is due to frequent changes in the size of unions and shifts in union affiliation due to internal political changes. It is estimated that 11 percent of the economically-active population, or 33 percent of wage and salary earners, are members of unions and about 8 percent of the economically active population, or 24 percent of wage and salary earners, are covered by collective bargaining agreements.

The Confederacion General de Trabajadores del Peru (General Confederation of Peruvian Workers), the Communist led labor federation, controls a majority of the labor unions (claiming between 45-60 percent of all organized labor). The labor confederation of the moderately left APRA party represents approximately 20 percent of the active Peruvian work force.

The rights of private sector workers to organize, bargain collectively, and strike are guaranteed by law and generally observed in practice. Those industries considered the most highly unionized include banking, utilities, construction, transportation, ports, petroleum, metals, textiles, sugar, mining, and maritime.

Workers in the public sector also are organized. The most highly organized include: teachers, social security workers, health and sanitation personnel, and employees of the Ministries of Agriculture and Economy.

Strikes.—The number of strikes, workers involved, and hours lost decreased between 1982 and 1983. The number of strikes in 1982 decreased from 809 to 506 in 1983. Over the same period, the number of man hours lost decreased from 22,525,975 to 19,916,176. The major factor contributing to the decrease in strikes probably was the country's poor economic situation, which made workers somewhat reluctant to risk their jobs, even though national legislation gives workers with more than 3 years seniority a high degree of job protection.

Wages

In recent years, the level of real wages and salaries has declined. In February 1983, real wages were only 67.3 percent of their 1973 levels while real salaries were only 60.8 percent of 1973 levels.

In February 1983, the average wage was 304,014 soles monthly, the average daily salary was 5,937 soles per day and the minimum wage 4,500 soles (1,008 soles = US$1.00 on February 16, 1983). The transport, communication, and finance sectors registered the highest wages and salaries while commerce and services registered slightly lower.

Most businesses have established a 40-hour workweek. In general, after 260 days of continuous service, workers are entitled to 30 paid vacation days a year. Overtime rates range from 25 to 100 percent of basic wages. There are no restrictions on the number of hours that may be worked overtime. Social security contributions, remuneration tax, vacation and holiday pay, and bonuses amount to about 56.5 percent of an employer's basic manual workers' payroll costs. Upon termination of employment, workers are entitled to compensation based on number of years of service in some cases equalling as much as a month's salary for each year.

Peruvian pension benefits are available to men at age 60 and to women at age 55. The minimum pension for eligible workers is 72,000 soles a month; the maximum is 432,000 soles.

Industrial Community

The new Industrial Law has modified the basis for labor participation in profits within the industrial sector. Under the new law, labor can either continue to participate under the previous system, or choose a new profit share alternative. Under the previous system, 10 percent of pre-tax income is distributed to labor in cash, 1.5 percent is set aside for administrative cost of the labor community, and 13.5 percent is issued in the form of non-voting stock. Employees also have the right to elect up to one-third of the company's board of directors. Under the alternative system, labor is entitled to 17 percent of pre-tax income and elects up to 20 percent of the company's board of directors; companies that increase their capital by public subscription must offer a first option of no less than 10 percent of such common share subscriptions to labor. If the second alternative is chosen, shares held by labor as of the date of effectiveness of this law have to be redeemed in a maximum term of 10 years, with a minimum of 10 percent of the shares per year.

Employment of Foreigners

Employment of foreigners is sharply restricted. Decree Law 22452 of 1979, is aimed at protecting the rights of Peruvian workers to fill job vacancies. To employ a foreign national, an employer must demonstrate the need for such an individual and must prove that no suitable candidate is available locally. This requirement, however, does not apply to technicians or highly specialized foreign personnel or to those on international business with the Peruvian Government. The law requires that:

Employers must have a minimum of 90 percent Peruvian national employees;

Peruvian nationals must be trained to succeed foreign workers;

Contracts with foreign nationals must be approved by a special Peruvian Government committee prior to issuance of the corresponding visa, and no one may work on a tourist visa;

No foreign national will be permitted to work in Peru more than 6 years.

The following are not considered foreign personnel: foreigners who are individual investors or who have resided in Peru for more than one year and have renounced the right to repatriate capital; foreigners with Peruvian spouses or children, transportation personnel, personnel covered by bilateral or multilateral agreements, among others.

Guidance for Business Travelers

Requirements for U.S. Citizens

U.S. citizens may enter Peru on a tourist basis for 90 days with a valid passport. No visas are required, but such travelers must have fully-paid onward or return tickets out of Peru. In addition, travelers must either have in cash or in some negotiable document a minimum of eight dollars for each day of stay up to the 90-day maximum. A business visa is also available for $50.00 but it is not recommended for travelers who come on short inspection visits. Persons traveling on a business visa must fill out a report on income earned in Peru and pay taxes before leaving. Travelers entering Peru on business matters must have a valid passport.

A special travel permit is available for business travel by foreigners resident in Peru. Permit holders are allowed to leave the country and return as often as they like within a 6-month period, although absence from the country may not exceed 30 days on each trip. The permits may be renewed only for a further period of 6 months.

Smallpox vaccination is not required in order to enter Peru, but yellow fever and anti-malarial medication are recommended for jungle travel. Gamma globulin is recommended against hepatitis.

An airport tax of $10 is applied to all business persons or tourists leaving the country.

Further information may be obtained at one of the Peruvian Consular Offices located in the United States (see Peruvian Government Representation in the United States).

Trade Customs

Business customs if Peru are similar to those in the United States and Western Europe. Many Peruvian business persons have visited both the United States and Europe and are familiar with how business is done in the more industrialized countries. This means that they expect to be taken seriously by the foreign exporter. Generally, they will give more serious attention to the promotion of a foreign firm's products when they receive occasional personal visits from representatives of the foreign firm and when correspondence and other communications are given expeditious and courteous handling. In other words, they respond well to being treated just as any U.S. company would expect to be treated.

Business travelers wishing to introduce new products should allow sufficient time for their dealings with Peruvian business persons. Decisions are not likely to be made on the spot and a certain degree of patience on the part of the traveler is required.

As their efforts prove successful, distributors and agents expect to be invited to the foreign supplier's installations in order to familiarize themselves with production techniques and home office personnel. In other words, they wish to be made an integral part of the supplier's overall business effort, and those exporters operating in this way may be rewarded. The Japanese, for example, are pursuing this technique with great diligence and their success in the Peruvian market has been remarkable.

Punctuality is becoming more important to Peruvian business persons and government purchasing officers. Also, it is recommended that appointments be made in advance of a business call.

Language

Spanish and Quechua are the official languages in Peru, but Spanish is the language of business. Many business persons in Peru have a command of the English language, but naturally they prefer to use their native tongue. U.S. business firms should present their quotations, catalogs, illustrations, price lists, and other trade information material in Spanish, if possible. Bilingual business persons should speak Spanish when contacting their Peruvian counterparts with a view to generating friendly feelings and confidence. If unable to speak Spanish, the use of English colloquial expressions or phrases should be avoided.

Legal and Bank Holidays

January 1 (New Year's), Holy Thursday, Good Friday, Countryman's Day, The Feast day of Saints Peter and Paul, July 28-29 (Independence Days), August 30 (Saint Rose of Lima), October 8 (Battle of Angamos), November 1 (All Saints Day), November 12 (Immaculate Conception), December 25 (Christmas). Actual dates vary for some of these holidays, so travelers should check the holiday schedule when planning their trip.

Office Hours

The year's working time is divided into summer office hours (January through March) and winter hours (April through December). The workday of 8 hours generally begins at the following times each morning:

	Summer	Winter
Private company offices	7:45 to 8:15 a.m.	8:00 to 9:00 a.m.
Government offices	7:45 to 8:00 a.m.	8:00 to 9:00 a.m.
Factories	6:00 to 8:00 a.m.	6:00 to 8:00 a.m.
Department and Retail		
Stores sales personnel	9:15 to 10:00 a.m.	9:15 to 10:00 a.m.
Administrative personnel	8:00 a.m.	8:00 a.m.

In the summer, ministries and some public entities work limited hours per day (7:45 a.m. to 1 p.m.); however, top executives are often willing to accept appointments outside of regular hours. Bankings hours are generally 8:30 a.m. to 11:30 a.m. in the summer and 8:45 a.m. to 12:45 p.m. in the winter, with most banks closed on Saturdays. Some banks have more extended service hours.

Health

Community sanitation conditions are not a serious problem. Lima has a number of good restaurants; however, outside Lima it is best to take reasonable precautions. Although the water in Lima is treated, all drinking water should be boiled or otherwise treated. Risk of malaria exists in Peru outside of Lima and vicinity and the coastal area south of Lima. At high altitudes in the Andes, the schedule of activities should allow time for adjusting to the altitude.

Telecommunications and Transportation

The telecommunications system in Peru is adequate for most requirements, and it is undergoing constant growth. In 1980 there were 456,156 telephones with a density of 2.7 per 100 population. Local service is sometimes erratic and long-distance calls, both national and international, frequently require long waits. However, the new capacity will be in operation in 1984, and some of these problems are expected to be eased.

Telecommunications facilities are principally owned by Peruvian government companies. Corporacion Peruana de Telefonos is responsible for the Lima area, and Entel Peru is responsible for other areas of the country as well as international service.

The total road network in 1980 was approximately 58,685 kilometers, of which 11 percent was paved, 21 percent was gravel and the balance unimproved. About 60 percent of all inland freight and 90 percent of all passengers are carried over roads. There was a total of 570,245 motor vehicles registered in Peru in 1982. A number of bus companies provide regularly-scheduled service to the cities of the coast and major cities in the mountains.

Two major publically-owned railroads, the Central railroad and the Southern railroad, cross the Western chain of the Andes in the center and the south, respectively, and tranverse parts of the Sierra longitudinally.

Lima is served by several international airlines, and regular commercial flights interconnect Peru's cities.

There are 29 maritime ports; the principal port is Callao (the port of Lima).

Taxis are available in Lima and in practically all cities. Rental car service is available in Lima, but U.S. drivers should note that the traffic of Peru is much more freewheeling than in the United States.

Hotels

There are several well-equipped hotels centrally located in Lima, including one of the Sheraton chain. The state tourist agency, ENTUR-PERU, provides relatively good accommodations in Peru's other major cities.

Currency

The official currency unit of Peru is the sol, which is freely convertible. Travelers checks, dollars and/or other currency can be exchanged for Peruvian currency at most of the larger hotels, private and government commercial banks, and authorized exchange brokers. The exchange rate for the sol is established by the Central Reserve Bank in relation to the U.S. dollar. In the coming years, the sol will be replaced by a new currency that will essentially eliminate three zeros to the left of the decimal point; therefore, one thousand soles of today will be worth one unit of the yet-to-be named new currency.

Sources of Economic and Commercial Information

U.S. Foreign Service Posts in Peru

The United States is represented in Peru by an Embassy located at Avenida Inca Garcilaso de la Vega y España No. 1400, Lima (P.O. Box 1995) and a Consular Agency at Piura: Walter Carlson, Avenida Los Cocos 334, Urbanizacion Grau, Piura, telephone number 32-8460, 32-4683, 32-5211. The telephone number of the Embassy is 28-6000/28-6200 or, if dialing directly from U.S., 011-51—14-286-000, Telex: 25028 PEUSCOMATT. Personnel of the U.S. Foreign Commercial Service and Economic Officers are available to assist U.S. business persons visiting Peru.

A booklet, Key Officers at Foreign Service Posts, is published quarterly by the U.S. Department of State. Copies may be purchased for $1.50 each from the Superintendent of Documents, Government Printing Office, Washington, D.C. 20402.

Peruvian Government Representation in the United States

The Embassy of Peru in the United States is located at:

1700 Massachusetts Avenue, N.W.
Tel: 202-833-9860
Washington, D.C. 20036

Consulates General are located in the following cities:

Los Angeles, CA 20013
1212 Wilshire Boulevard, 2nd. Floor
Tel: 213-975-1152 or 975-1154

San Francisco, CA 94102
870 Market Street, Suite 485
Tel: 415-362-7136 or 362-7137

Chicago, IL 60603
8 South Michigan Avenue, Suite 2003
Tel: 312-782-1599

New York, NY 10020
10 Rockefeller Plaza, Suite 729
Tel: 212-644-2850

Houston, TX 77002
1520 Texas Avenue
World Trade Building, Suite 326
Tel: 713-781-5297

Washington, D.C. 20036
1700 Massachusetts Avenue, N.W.
Tel: 202-833-9896

Honorary Consulates are located in Tuscon, Arizona; San Francisco, California; Denver, Colorado; Honolulu, Hawaii; New Orleans, Louisiana; Boston, Massachusetts; Minneapolis, Minnesota; St. Louis, Missouri; Tulsa, Oklahoma; Portland, Oregon; Santurce, Puerto Rico; Dallas and Fort Worth, Texas; Salt Lake City, Utah; and Seattle, Washington.

A commercial office was opened in New York City in 1983 at 747 Third Avenue. Tel: 212-688-9110.

The following Peruvian enterprises also maintain offices in the United States:

MINERO-PERU (Peruvian State Mining and Mineral Merchandising Corporation)
600 Third Avenue
New York, NY 10016
Tel: 212-972-0910

PETRO-PERU (Peruvian State Petroleum Corporation)
6065 Hillcroft Avenue, Suite 608
Houston, TX 77036
Tel: 713-777-8251

ENCI (National Enterprise for the Marketing of Basic Products)
527 Madison Avenue, Room 1603
New York, NY 10022
Tel: 212-838-9453

Peruvian-American Association, Inc.
50 West 34th Street
6th. Floor, Suite C-2
New York, NY 10004
Tel: 212-564-3855

Chambers of Commerce and Trade Associations

Chamber of Commerce of the United States in Peru:

Richardo Palma 836
Lima 18

Federacion Nacional de Camaras de Comercio del Peru
(National Federation of Peruvian Chambers of Commerce)
Gregorio Escobedo 398
Lima 11

Camara de Comercio de Lima
(Lima Chamber of Commerce)
Gregorio Escobedo 398
Lima 11

(Engineering)
Colegio de Ingenieros del Peru
Avenida Arequipa 4947
Lima 18

(Exporters)
Asociacion de Exportadores (ADEX)
Av. Salaverry 1910
Lima 11

(Industrial Management)
Instituto Peruano de Administracion de Empresas (IPAE)
Avenida La Marina Cuadra 16
Lima 32

(Industry Promotion)
Asociacion Promocional de Industrias
132 Pasaje Tello
Lima

(Industrial Relations)
Asociacion de Relaciones Industriales
Avenida Mariategui 548
Lima 11

(Economists)
Colegio de Economistas
Avenida Central 671
Lima 27

(Lawyers)
Federacion de Colegios de Abogados del Peru
Tarma 119
Lima

(Marketing)
Centro Nacional de Productividad
Pablo Bermudez 214, piso 10
Apartado 5442
Lima

(Merchants)
Confederacion Nacional de Comerciantes
Apartado 2528
Avenida Abancay 210—Piso 3
Lima

Industry Associations

(Automobiles)
Camara Automotriz del Peru
Raimondi 297
Lima 13

(Construction)
Camara Peruana de la Construccion
571 Avenida Paseo de la Republica
Lima 1

(Fishing)
Sociedad Nacional de Pesqueria
Avenida Inca Garcilaso de la Vega 911
Lima 1

(Manufacturing)
Sociedad Nacional de Industrias
Los Laureles 365
Lima 27

(Mining Engineers)
Instituto de Ingenieros de Minas del Peru
Las Camelias 555—Piso 2
Lima 27

(Pharmaceutical Laboratories)
Asociacion Nacional de Laboratorios Farmaceuticos
Calle 41 No. 975
Urbanizacion Corpac
Lima 27

(Rice Millers)
Asociacion Peruana de Molineros de Arroz
Avenida Antonio Miro Quesada 113
Lima 1

Bibliography

U.S. Department of Commerce

This is a list of selected current reports on commercial and economic conditions in Peru available from the various offices of the U.S. Department of Commerce. Some of these reports were prepared within the Office of South America (OSA), while others were submitted by the U.S. Foreign Commercial Service. These reports make up only a part of the information resources at the disposal of OSA's Andean Division. In addition, there are a number of valuable reference works and periodicals, the most important of which are listed in the Bibliography section below. However, the best way to obtain guidance on using the Division's total information resources is to contact the Country Specialist, Room 3314, U.S. Department of Commerce, Washington, D.C. 20230. (Tel: (202) 377-4303).

The following publications are available from the Publications Distribution Branch, Room 1617, U.S. Department of Commerce, Washington, D.C. 20230 (Tel. (202) 377-5494).

World Trade Outlook for Latin America—Semiannual, price $1.50

Andean Common Market: Current Trends—February, price $1.00 (OBR 78-06).

Foreign Economic Trends-Peru—price $1.75; appears semiannually under different FET numbers.

Foreign Business Practices Materials on Practical Aspects of Exporting, International Licensing and

Investment (worldwide by country) May 1981, price $5.50.

The following publications are for sale by the Superintendent of Documents, U.S. Government Printing Office, Washington, D.C. 20402:

U.S. Exports/World Areas by Schedule E. Commodity Groupings Report FT 455, Annual 1982, $15.00.

U.S. Exports, Schedule E, Commodity by Country Report FT 410, December 1982, $9.50.

Selected U.S. Foreign Service Reporting on Peru

The following reports are available from the National Technical Information Services (NTIS), 5285 Port Road, Springfield, Virginia 22161; (703) 487-4650. Consult NTIS for prices.

Country	Research date/or Subject	ITA/DIB No.
Peru	Agriculture Equipment	ITA 81-12-028
Peru	Construction Machinery and Materials Handling Equipment	ITA 81-09-048
Peru	Food Processing and Packing Machinery	ITA-82-04-018
Peru	Non-rubber Footwear	ITA 82-06-001
Peru	Printing and Graphic Arts Equipment and Machinery	ITA 81-09-049
Peru	Printing and Graphic Arts Equipment	ITA 81-12-009
Peru	Annual Labor Report	ITA 81-10-030
Peru	Metalworking Machinery and Equipment	DIB-80-05-010
Peru	Annual Minerals Report	ITA 82-09-011
Peru	Annual Petroleum Report	ITA-82-09-007

Information on Peru is included in the following Annual Worldwide Industry Review (AWIR), a multi-country review of a particular U.S. Industry's export prospects. For further information and prices, consult the Office of Trade Information Services (OTIS), U.S. Department of Commerce, P.O. Box 14207, Washington, D.C. 20014, (202) 377-2432.

Title/Industry	Order No.
Agricultural Machinery and Equipment	AWIR/AGM/1XX/84
Computers and Peripheral Equipment	AWIR/CPE/1XX/84
Food Processing and Packaging Equipment	AWIR/FPP/1XX/84
Medical Equipment	AWIR/MED/1XX/84
Security and Safety Equipment	AWIR/SSE/1XX/84

U.S. Department of State

Background Notes, Peru, March 1980, price $1.25. Available from Superintendent of Documents, U.S. Government Printing Office, Washington, D.C. 20402.

Government of Peru (in Spanish)

Boletin del Banco Central de Reserva del Peru, (Spanish), Banco Central de Reserva del Peru (monthly)

Other Sources

Area Handbook for Peru, Superintendent of Documents, U.S. Government Printing Office, Washington, D.C. 20402, 1981.

Directorio Industrial de Peru 1982, (Spanish) published by Sociedad de Industrias, Lima.

Guia Verde Industrial y Comercial 1979, (Spanish) published by Sirob Ediciones, Lima.

Economic and Social Progress in Latin America, Inter-American Development Bank, (Annual Reports), Washington, D.C.

Peruvian-American Digest, Weekly Newsletter, published by Peruvian-American Association Inc., 50 West 34 Street, 6th Floor, Suite C-2, New York, NY 10001.

Industria Peruana. (Spanish), monthly magazine of Sociedad Nacional de Industrias, Los Laureles 365, Lima 27.

Comercio y Produccion, (Spanish), monthly publication of La Camara de Comercio de Lima.

Anuarium de la Construccion (Spanish), annual publication of Camara Peruana de la Construccion, Lima.

Report on the Economic Situation of Peru, Banco Continental Lima, quarterly.

A Statement of the Laws of Peru in Matters Affecting Business General Secretariat, Organization of American States Washington, D.C. 1973.

Pesca (Spanish), bimonthly, Apartado Postal 877, Lima 100.

The Andean Report, monthly. The Editor, Apartado 2489, Lima 100.

Business Peru, bimonthly, the American Chamber of Commerce, Lima, Peru.

American Firms, Subsidiaries & Affiliates in Peru, 1979, available from the World Trade Academy Press, Inc. New York.

Report from Bank of America's man-on-the-spot in Peru, Bank of America, monthly.

Exporters Encyclopedia, World Marketing Guide, Dun and Bradstreet International, Ltd., 99 Church St., New York, NY 10007.

International Trade Reporter, the Bureau of National Affairs, Inc., 1231 25th Street, N.W., Washington, D.C. 20037.

Operating in Latin America's Integrating Markets: ANCOM, CACM, CARICOM, LAFTA, Business International Corporation, New York, NY, January 1977.

Grupo Andino, (Spanish) Junta del Acuerdo de Cartagena, Lima, Peru, monthly; English edition available from Communications Unit, Junta del Acuerdo de Cartagena, Casilla 3237, Lima 100.

El Informativo ALALC (Spanish), Conferacion de Camaras de Comercio de Grupo Andino, edited and printed by Camara de Comercio de Santiago, Santiago de Chile, weekly.

PERU

Market Profile

Foreign Trade

Imports.—1983, $2.7 billion; 1982, $3.8 billion; 1981, $3.8 billion. Market shares in percent 1982; United States, 36%; E.E.C., 14.3, Argentina/Brazil, 11.5; and Japan, 12.4%. Principal imports: machinery and mechanical appliances and parts, iron and steel products, motor vehicles and tractors, organic chemicals, and cereals (wheat, rice).

Exports.—1983, $3.0 billion; 1982, $3.2 billion; 1981, $3.2 billion. Market shares in percent 1982: United States, 38.0%; E.E.C., 16.2%; Japan, 14.4%; and Columbia/Panama/Brazil, 8.6%. Principal exports: petroleum, copper, silver, lead, zinc, iron, gold, fishmeal, sugar, coffee, cotton, textiles, chemicals, paper products.

Trade Policy.—The government is attempting to open the economy up to foreign competition by lowering some trade barriers. Peru is a member of GATT, the Andean Common Market, and the Latin American Integration Association.

Trade Prospects.—The United States should maintain a strong position in the market. Best export prospects: oil and gas field machinery and equipment; irrigation and electrical energy equipment, automotive parts and accessories, computers and peripherals, telecommunications and transportation equipment.

Finance

National Budget.—Central Government budget in 1983 was $4.4 billion. Public sector deficit reached over 10 percent of GDP in 1983, overwhelmingly financed by foreign borrowing. Government expenditures as percent of total: current goods and services, 50 percent; investment, 12 percent; debt service, 39 percent. Public sector external long-term debt (over one year maturity), $9.3 billion, as of December 31, 1983.

Balance of Payments.—Trade Balance, 1983:+$300 million, 1982:−$557 million, 1981:−$553 million; Current Account, 1983:−$882 million, 1982:−$1.6 billion, 1981:−$1.7 billion; Net Basic Balance, 1983:+$362 million, 1982:−$383 million, 1981:−$1,011 million; change in International Reserves at end of year, 1983:−$50 million, 1982:+$124 million, 1981:−$504 million.

Economy

Gross Domestic Product.—1983, $16.2 billion; 1982, $19.8 billion; 1981, $20.1 billion; 1980, $16.8 billion. Sectoral contribution to GDP, 1982: manufacturing, 23%; agriculture, 13%; mining and petroleum, 9%; construction, 6%; fishing, 1%; government, 8%; and other, 40%.

Agriculture.—Coffee, sugar, cotton, and wool are important crops. Corn, sorghum, wheat, barley, potatoes, and rice are subsistence crops.

Industry.—Fishmeal production; textiles; mining of metals; metal refining; food and beverages; paper, tire, and rubber manufactures; shoes, cement, glass, and basic steel production; electrical appliances; automotive vehicle assembly; shipbuilding, petroleum.

Basic Economic Facilities

Transportation.—Fairly well-developed rail, highway, shipping and air transport facilities; total highway network 56,654 km of which 6,030 is paved; railroad track network 2,192 km; Callao is the major port. Domestic airports in all major cities; and international airport in Lima.

Telecommunications.—Fairly adequate for most requirements; new nationwide radio-relay system; one Atlantic ocean satellite station, 7 domestic antennas; 487,000 telephones (2.8 per 100 people); 212 AM, 17 FM, 73 Television transmitters.

Energy.—Sources (in percent): oil (51.6), firewood and dung (22.5), hydro (15.6), natural gas (8.1), coal and other (2.2). Electric power is 60 percent hydro- and 40 percent thermally-generated. Total energy consumption: about 13 million tons of oil equivalent.

Natural Resources

Land.—496,222 square miles, consisting of coastal belt, Andean highlands and Amazon jungle.

Climate.—Coastal areas: mild and sunny except in winter when foggy and chilly, little precipitation; highlands: warm at midday, chilly to frigid at night, some precipitation; eastern lowlands: hot and humid.

Minerals.—Most important are petroleum, copper, silver, zinc, lead, and iron ore. Also bismuth, cadmium, tin, gold, antimony, tungsten, selenium, and telurium, and nonmetallic minerals such as coal and barite.

Forestry.—Undeveloped land, largely inaccessible hardwoods in eastern jungle region.

Fisheries.—In 1982, Peru's marine fishing catch increased to 3.5 million metric tons, up from 1981's level of 2.7 million metric tons. In 1982, 17 percent of marine fishing catch was for direct human consumption; the remainder for industrial processing (mostly fishmeal and oil).

Population

Size.—Estimate at 19.1 million (July, 1983); 2.6 percent annual growth rate (1982). About 4.9 million located in Lima (1980 estimate). Over 42 percent of the population under 15 years of age.

Distribution.—Urban population: 65 percent (1982); urban growth rate during 1970-80: 4.3 percent per year.

Language.—Spanish and Quechua. Aymara also used in Southern Highlands.

Labor.—Approximately 6 million in work force (1981, estimate); 65.4% were adequately employed in 1982, leaving over a third of the work force either underemployed or unemployed; employed labor force distribution, as follows in percent (1982): agriculture, 35.3; services, 26.0; commerce, 14.5; industry, 14.2; transportation, 4.5; construction, 3.7; mining, 1.8; and financial sector, 1.0.

Education.—Adult literacy rate: 80 percent.

Public Health.—Infant mortality rate of 80 per 1000

live births. Average life expectancy of 58.0 years. 2,000 medical facilities and 30,000 hospital beds.

Ethnic Groups.—Indian, 45 percent; Mestizo, 37 percent; Caucasian, 15 percent; Blacks, Asians, and other, 3 percent.

Marketing in the Philippines

Contents

Report Revised May 1983

PHILIPPINES

* National capital
  Railroad
  Road
+ International airport

SOUTH

CHINA

SEA

LUZON STRAIT

BATAN
ISLANDS

BABUYAN
ISLANDS

Laoag   Aparri
Vigan   Tuguegarao

Ilagan

San
Fernando   Bayombong
Bolinao   Baguio

Dagupan   San Jose
Tarlac   Cabanatuan
Iba   San
Olongapo   Fernando   Quezon   LUZON
Manila   Santa Cruz
Lucena
Batangas
Calapan

MINDORO
Mansalay

MASBATE

Roxas
PANAY   Daanbantayan
Iloilo   Bacolod
CEBU
NEGROS   Cebu   Maasin
Cauayan   BOHOL
Bayawan   Tagbilaran

Puerto Princesa

PALAWAN

SULU SEA

BALABAC STRAIT

Kudat

Kota Kinabalu
(Jesselton)   Sandakan

MALAYSIA

INDONESIA   Tawau

PHILIPPINE

SEA

CATANDUANES
ISLAND

Legazpi

Sorsogon

Matnog   Catarman   SAMAR

Catbalogan

Tacloban

LEYTE
GULF   LEYTE

Surigao

Butuan

BOHOL
SEA

Sindangan   Ozamiz   Cagayan de
Oro

MINDANAO

Cotabato   Davao

Zamboanga   Basilan   MORO   Digos
BASILAN   GULF
ISLAND

Jolo

SULU   ARCHIPELAGO

MINDANAO   SEA

PULAU
MIANGAS
(Indonesia)

PULAU KARAKELONG
(Indonesia)

1893

Foreign Trade Outlook

Imports

The Philippine market remains one of the easiest foreign markets for Americans to enter. Among Filipinos, American products are well known and enjoy a reputation for quality.

In 1981, the United States had the largest share of the $8 billion Philippine market, 22.5 percent, compared with 18.8 percent for Japan. Retaining that lead, however, will require many U.S. companies to be flexible, particularly on supplier credits.

High oil prices have set the scene for the Philippine import market in the next few years. During the past decade, substantial oil imports moved Saudi Arabia into the number three position. In 1981, 13.1 percent of Philippine imports came from Saudi Arabia.

To reduce oil imports, the Philippines has begun an energy diversification program. As a result of this program, American companies will have many opportunities to provide equipment and services during the 1980's.

The program contains very ambitious plans for developing domestic coal deposits. In order to realize these plans, a tremendous amount of investment will have to be made for exploration, mining, handling, and finally transporting coal to end-users. Other energy areas encompassed by the program include geothermal, solar, biomass, and small scale hydroelectric power.

A $4 billion program of major industrial projects is also underway in the Philippines to develop several basic industries. The strength of the U.S. position in the market will be affected substantially by the nationality of companies investing in those projects and the competitiveness of companies bidding on the supply of equipment for the projects.

Balance of Trade

For the last 2 years, the Philippine trade deficit increased at a slower rate. In 1981 and 1982, it increased roughly 14.5 percent each year compared with 26 percent in 1980. The deficit for 1982 was estimated at $2.5 billion.

Traditional exports fared very poorly in 1982. Figures from early in that year indicated the value of coconut oil exports dropped 22 percent compared with already depressed levels in 1981. Sugar was down 68 percent, and lumber exports decreased by 46 percent. On the brighter side, nontraditional exports of semiconductors and clothing showed spectacular growth in 1982.

Table 1—1981-82 Major U.S. Exports to Philippines[1]
(in millions of U.S. dollars)

	1981	1982
Machinery and Transport Equipment		
Industrial machinery (specialized and not elsewhere specified	205.8	180.6
Pow. generating machinery equipment	56.8	112.6
Metalworking machinery	13.0	10.3
Office machines and ADP equipment	22.0	22.2
Telecommunication and sound reproduction equipment	35.2	35.6
Road vehicles and parts	51.2	42.6
Aircraft	62.5	20.9
Professional, scientific and control instruments	26.5	27.0
Electronic components and parts thereof	388.6	446.5
Food and live animals		
Cereals	201.8	198.3
Other food items	39.6	68.3
Manufactured goods by chief material		
Yarn fabric and articles textiles	34.3	21.4
Paper, paperboard and manufactures	33.5	39.3
Iron and steel	17.0	16.7
Chemicals		
Organic	43.8	42.2
Inorganic	30.3	19.0
Synthetic resins and plastic materials	45.4	54.4
Other		
Cellulosic fiber	15.4	18.9
Cotton	22.7	17.9
Tobacco (unmanufactured)	31.4	49.9
Total (all exports)	1,774.0	1,845.5

[1]The figures in this table may differ from Government of Philippines figures used elsewhere in this report.
Source: U.S. Bureau of the Census.

Assistance for U.S. Investors

On February 25, 1983, the U.S. and Philippine Governments signed an agreement at the Commerce Department to facilitate U.S. investment in the Philippines. It encourages additional U.S. investment through an exchange of information and by promotional activities such as investment missions and seminars. The agreement emphasizes investment facilitation in electronics and agribusiness because past investments in those sectors have benefited both countries. A number of U.S. electronics and agribusiness firms currently are operating in the Philippines. Firms interested in participation in the investment missions and seminar should contact the Philippines Country Specialist (Rm. 2310), International Trade Administration, U.S. Department of Commerce, Washington, D.C. 20230.

Table 2.—Trade Partners, 1980-81
(f.o.b. value in million U.S. dollars)

	1980	% Share	1981	% Share
United States	3,374.1	24.9	3,644.0	26.2
Japan	3,064.5	22.7	2,783.0	20.0
EEC	1,808.3	13.4	1,780.5	12.8
Middle East Countries	1,747.0	12.9	1,816.5	13.0
Socialist and Communist Countries	500.6	3.7	460.0	3.3
Escap Countries (excluding Japan, Iran, USSR, PRC, Netherlands, France, U.K. and U.S.)	2,122.4	15.7	2,365.9	17.1
Other Countries	897.8	6.7	1,058.1	7.6
TOTAL (All Countries)	13,514.7	100	13,908.0	100

Source: National Census & Statistics Office.

Best Export Prospects

Food Processing and Packaging Equipment.— The rapid expansion of population along with a gradual increase in income will result in a higher demand for processed foods. The encouragement of nontraditional exports, of which processed foods is an important component, also will improve the market for food processing and packaging machinery. Because the Philippines has substantial advantages in food production, the Government is strongly encouraging foreign investment in agribusiness and food processing and packaging.

Good opportunities exist for U.S. exporters because expansion programs are planned in sectors which use predominantly U.S. equipment. In fact, the United States is expected to overtake West Germany as the leading supplier for this reason.

In 1981, the United States was the number two supplier of the food processing equipment market, with a 25 percent share. It was the leading supplier of food packaging equipment, with a 27 percent share. Total imports of food processing equipment were valued at $42 million, and total imports for food packaging equipment were valued at $3 million. The following product groups should be popularly accepted if promoted:

- Meat and poultry processing equipment
- Fish processing equipment
- Dairy products equipment
- Fruit and vegetable processing equipment

Table 3.—Ten Principal Philippine Imports, 1980-81
(f.o.b. value in milion U.S. dollars)

	1980	U.S. Share 1980 (%)	1981	U.S. Share 1981 (%)	Increase (Decrease) (%)
Mineral fuels, lubricants, and related materials	2,248.4	0.5	2,605.0	0.6	15.9
Machinery Other than electric	1,015.1	34.9	959.4	32.4	(5.4)
Materials and accesories for the manufacture of electrical equipment	548.9	65.4	631.2	62.7	14.9
Transport equipment	533.4	26.8	491.0	15.6	(7.9)
Base Metals	501.3	5.7	393.6	5.5	(21.4)
Electrical machinery	312.1	33.0	393.1	26.0	25.9
Chemical elements and compounds	267.0	24.7	310.4	25.0	16.2
Cereals and cereal preparations	214.3	79.9	233.0	80.0	8.7
Explosives and miscellaneous chemical materials and products	197.0	39.2	213.8	33.5	8.5
Manufactures of metal	132.8	33.1	140.1	28.2	5.5
Others	1,756.6	24.2	1,829.4	52.2	4.1
Total Imports	7,726.9	23.1	8,200.0	22.5	6.1
Total Ten Principal Imports	5,970.3	—	6,370.6	—	6.7

Source: National Census & Statistics Office.

- Beverage equipment
- Refrigeration, cold storage, and chilling equipment
- Packaging machinery (especially can closers/sealers and fillers)

Alternative Energy Generation Equipment.—To decrease their dependence on imported sources of energy, notably oil, the Philippine Government has embarked on a program to develop domestic sources. This emphasis on the accelerated utilization of alternative energy sources includes direct and indirect solar, biomass, wind, hot springs, coal, mini-hydro, and waste heat projects. Philippine energy officials predict that by 1986 only 37 to 45 percent of its oil requirements will come from foreign sources, an impressive reduction from 92 percent in 1980. To date excellent progress has been made toward that goal.

To achieve these objectives, along with continuing its electrification plans, investment of $7.6 billion is planned between 1981 and 1987. This presents substantial business opportunities to firms in the fields of energy resource exploration, energy generation, transmission and distribution equipment, along with non-conventional energy sectors. It is in this area that some of the best opportunities for sales of U.S. equipment exist. Several U.S. companies are already participating in geothermal development, and others have made major sales of coal handling equipment.

Computers and Peripheral Equipment.—The Philippines relies solely on imports for computers and peripherals and has no plans for significant domestic production. The market for such equipment has been growing steadily since 1977; 1980 imports more than doubled from the previous year. The size of the market is expected to grow from $22.4 million in 1980 to $79.3 million in 1986, reflecting an annual growth rate of 23 percent.

From 1978 to 1980, imports of computers and peripheral equipment totaled $49.5 million. Total imports for this equipment grew at an average annual rate of 34 percent, from $12.4 million to $22.4 million. U.S. firms accounted for 65 percent of these imports during this period. They held 60.4 percent of the market for minicomputers; 39 percent of the market for small, medium, and large computer systems; 91.3 percent of the market for peripherals; and 85.7 percent of the market for data communication equipment.

U.S. producers of such equipment are favored because of their product reliability, serviceability, speed and capacity; but they are also, in most cases, more expensive. However, U.S. producers have established a good foothold and a large brand following, and these factors will be beneficial for further sales.

The high rate of growth in the market is due to a realization of smaller local firms that computerization increases both their efficiency and productivity. End-users for such equipment are in the sectors of manufacturing, banking, finance, and wholesaling. The following product groups are popular:

- Small business computers (minicomputers, microcomputers, and small computers)
- Medium- and large- scale computers
- Computer peripherals—disk and magnetic tape drives, terminals, disk key, diskette key and tape key data entry devices, and high speed printers
- Data communications equipment, particularly controllers, modems, multiplexers, and concentrators

Security and Safety Equipment.—The total Philippine market for security, safety, and plant maintenance equipment was estamated at $66.8 million in 1980, growing by 28 percent over the 1979 level of $56.6 million. The market is expected to continue its vigorous growth during the 1981-85 period at an average annual rate of 13 percent.

Imports will continue to comprise the bulk of this market. Total imports amounted to $63.1 million in 1980 (94 percent of market), up 17.1 percent over 1979. The United States is the major source of this equipment, with a market share of 43 percent ($27.4 million) in 1980. A U.S. security and safety equipment trade mission in 1980 was received with overwhelming enthusiasm and interest from both the Philippine Government and local industry.

Increased demand for American made products will continue, and U.S. suppliers are expected to maintain more than a 40 percent market share through 1985. The record of durability, quality, advanced technology, and efficient after-sales service will maintain the high demand for U.S. products.

In 1980, Japan sold $12.9 million worth of equipment, down slightly from 1979. Due to very low prices, the value of China imports has risen from $1.8 million in 1979 to $7.4 million in 1980. The following product groups are much in demand:

- Premises protection devices—alarms (fire, smoke intrusion detection) equipment, power packs, and systems components
- External security devices—closures (automatic) equipment screens/grills, and alarm signaling systems
- Internal security—cameras, fasteners, and dummy CCTV

- Commodity protection—containers, locks, safes, and systems
- Sound and visual reproduction—CCTV cameras, detectors, equipment, and systems
- Fire control and abatement—extinguishers, pumps, and systems

Textile Machinery.—The Philippine Government and the textile industry have embarked on an industrywide modernization and rehabilitation program designed to increase the efficiency and competitive position of local manufacturers. Although the progress has been slow, the modernization program should provide an increasing market for textile machinery. The purchase of such equipment should continue over the next 3 years as the program goes into full swing.

Thirty-one Philippine textile firms have qualified with the Board of Investments (BOI) for the program. The program will cost about $450 million, of which the World Bank has provided $157.4 million and the balance will come from the textile firms with assistance by the BOI and the Development Bank of the Philippines (DBP). Sixteen foreign suppliers, including one group of U.S. firms have prequalified with the BOI for the bidding on $100 million worth of equipment to be imported.

Scientific and Industrial Analytical Equipment.—An explosive expansion of imports occurred in the latter half of the 1970's in which sales soared from $8.1 million in 1975 to $45.2 million in 1980. Strong growth in the Philippine market for laboratory instruments is anticipated through 1985 at a 15 percent annual rate. Though Japanese competition exists, U.S. firms are expected to retain the lead for the foreseeable future. Local scientists, many trained in the U.S., consider U.S. equipment the best in technology, design quality, reliability, and breadth of products lines.

Research and development expenditures in the Philippines are growing at 7 percent annually and are projected to top $156 million by 1983. This is due primarily to the country's attempt to revitalize industry and promote energy self-sufficiency. Government laboratories, food products manufacturers, textiles manufacturers, chemical manufacturers, and pharmaceuticals manufacturers are the primary end-users of such equipment. The prospects for sales in these industries are good.

In 1979, the U.S. share of the market for scientific and industrial analytical equipment climbed to a hefty 48 percent, and trade sources predict that the U.S. market share should remain at about 42 percent to 1983. U.S. suppliers can achieve greater penetration by improving service and maintenance facilities, providing adequate technical training to local agents, maintaining an adequate inventory of spare parts, and establishing regional service/maintenance facilities to increase aftersales service. The following product groups should be popularly accepted if promoted.

- Chromatographs
- Spectrophotometers
- Analyzers
- pH meters
- Refractometers
- Microscopes
- Laboratory balances
- Centrifuges/ultra centrifuges
- Electrodes

Economy

GNP Growth

Most analysts agree that in the long term the Philippine economy has many of the elements for strong economic growth. These elements include an energetic, low wage workforce and highly competent technocratic leadership.

Currently, the Philippines' economic performance remains somewhat depressed compared with high growth in the late 1970's. The world recession, depressed commodity earnings, domestic financial difficulties, and a decline in the activity in the private sector were major factors in 1982.

In real terms, the 1981 GNP (gross national product) growth rate was 3.8 percent while the 1980 rate stood at 4.4 percent. The 1982 estimate was 2 percent. GNP for 1981 was $38.7 billion and the estimate for 1982 is $44 billion.

The real rate of GNP growth has fallen from 6.8 percent in 1978 to 5.4 percent in 1980 and 3.8 percent in 1981 and is estimated to be 2 percent for 1982. This decline comes about from lessened demand and lower world prices for Philippine commodities as a result of the world recession. Per capita GNP has risen from $460 in 1977 to $801.4 in 1981.

Real income growth during 1979-81 has been small due to high inflation rates. The Consumer Price Index in 1981 was 11.8 percent and moderated in 1982 to 10.5 percent. The Philippines, with its low cost, efficient labor force and abundant natural resources has very strong long-term prospects.

The new Five-Year Development Plan (1983-87) predicts an average annual real rate of GNP growth of 6.5 percent. The plan includes an estimated real rate of growth of 7.9 percent for manufacturing; 7.3 percent for construction; 6.6 percent for mining and agriculture, fishery, and forestry; 8.9 percent for electricity, gas, and water; 5.8 percent for transportation, communication, and storage; 6.5 percent for commerce; and 5.6 percent for other services.

Principal Growth Sectors

The industrial sector, which accounts for 37 percent of the gross domestic product (GDP), continued to show the strongest growth in 1981 with a rate of 6.7 percent compared with 6.1 percent in 1980. Manufacturing increased 6.6 percent over 1980, mining and quarrying 7.6 percent, construction 6.7 percent, and utilities 6.7 percent.

In 1981, the largest sector was agriculture, fisheries, and forestry with 25.6 percent of the GDP. Manufacturing held 24.9 percent and commerce 20.5 percent.

The new Five-Year Development Plan (1983-87) aims to establish more competitive industries and to upgrade the capability and competitiveness of the existing ones. To fulfill these goals, various strategies have been implemented including the following:

1. commencement of construction of several of the 11 major industrial projects

2. rationalization and restructuring of existing key industry sectors

3. focus upon export promotion

4. accelerated dispersal of industries

5. government and private sector cooperation in industrial policy formulation and implementation

6. encouragement of foreign investments in selected areas.

Industry.—Industrial output is expected by the Philippine Government to grow 5.6 percent in 1983 and 8.6 percent in 1987. Increased activity in the basic industrial, infrastructure, and export-oriented industries is expected to propel annual manufacturing growth to 7.9 percent during 1983-87, with electrical and electronic equipment and components, garments and furniture as setting the pace.

Until recent years, the Philippines' industrial strategy has focused on meeting the needs of the domestic consumer market. As a result of protection from foreign competition, inefficient industries have evolved. To provide an incentive for the

Philippine Government to reduce duties on consumer goods, the World Bank is providing a series of annual "structural adjustment" loans. Under this agreement with the World Bank, duties will be reduced to a maximum of 50 percent.

Agriculture.—The agriculture, fishery, and forestry sector—which makes up 25.4 percent of GNP—had a 4.3 percent growth rate in 1981 compared with 4.9 percent in 1980. This was primarily due to international economic developments and bad weather during the growth seasons. The slackening in world prices of sugar and coconut oil and demand for these commodities caused a severe decline in Philippine foreign exchange earnings.

Policy objectives for agricultural development include the stepping up of production to meet domestic and export demand and import substitution. This should present opportunities for U.S. firms as the Philippines strive to attract appropriate technology to extend the downstream processing of the country's agricultural products.

Special incentives are offered to foreign investors in several agribusiness sectors, particularly agriculture and truck farming. An investment mission for U.S. agribusiness firms is planned for the spring of 1984. Interested firms should contact the Commerce Philippines Specialist on (202) 377-3875.

Fisheries will expand their production capacity as new vessels begin operating and as integrated area developmental activities continue. Intensification of fishing in existing areas and promotion of new activities, such as fresh water fish ponds, fish pens, and sea farming are planned.

Sugar is a traditional export crop for the Philippines. In the 1980-81 crop year, centrifugal sugar production totaled 2.4 million metric tons (mt). Exports amounted to 1.5 million mt that year. All exports are sold by the National Sugar Trading Corporation (NASUTRA), the Philippines' state trading arm for sugar, on long-term contracts.

In 1981, coconut production, another traditional foreign exchange earner, totaled 3.1 million mt. Of the coconut oil production, 1 million mt were exported; 198,565 mt were consumed locally; 633,110 tons of copra cake and meal, and 87,634 tons of dessicated coconut were exported.

In an effort to reduce petroleum imports, a coco-diesel program was implemented in the fall of 1982, using coconut oil in a 5/95 percent mixture with diesel. Although the program had difficulties initially, experiments using a 30/70 mixture in buses have proven successful.

In 1984, a coco-chemical plant to produce coco fatty alcohol for use in soaps and detergents is expected to be completed. It will be a joint venture between United Coconut Mills (UNICOM) and Lurgi of Germany.

Paper and Pulp.—Since its beginning in 1941, the Philippine pulp and paper industry has come a long way. The existing four pulp mills and five integrated pulp and paper mills in the country have a combined annual rated capacity of 300 thousand metric tons (MT), of which 87 percent was wood pulp and 13 percent other fibers, largely bagasse and abaca.

In 1980, there was an estimated 5 percent increase in domestic production and a 17 percent decrease in imports of all wood pulp paper grades compared to 1979. Total imports of wood pulp in 1980 were 55 thousand mt and imports for 1981 continue to show a decline in imports. This trend will probably be reversed in 1982 due to a loss of the Bataan Pulp and Paper Mills which burned down in December 1981.

The United States has an 11 percent share of Philippine pulp imports. Imports originating from the United States were 56 percent bleached sulphate and 19 percent sulphite, all paper grades.

Among the Philippine planned major projects is the expansion of the PICOP Paper Mill which remains under active consideration by the National Development Company. The project will be staggered in two phases. The first will be small with a larger stage coming into being when enough wood is available.

Forests.—Forests in the Philippines have been overcut in recent years causing severe erosion in certain areas. The Philippine Government has instituted a number of measures to reforest denuded areas, protect "vanishing" species, and increase the domestic value added portion of wood products exports. At the same time, it has strengthened regulations governing logging operations to protect forested areas. However, illegal cutting remains a serious problem.

Textiles and Garments.—The textile industry has experienced considerable difficulties in recent years. Domestic demand has been falling since 1978, and there is reportedly strong competition from significant quantities of smuggled goods. In addition, increased labor problems and a financial crisis have worsened the industry's situation just as the Government completed plans for a major rehabilitation and modernization program. The World Bank has agreed to provide a loan of $157 million of the total $450 million needed for the first phase program. Phase one is supposed to be completed by 1985. The major objectives of the program are as follow:

1. To modernize existing facilities.

2. To upgrade product quality to international standards.

3. To increase plant size to an economically viable size.

4. To increase labor productivity.

5. To encourage specialization in the industry.

Plans call for domestic manufacturers to supply an increasing share of the requirements of garment exporters which normally use imported fabrics.

The garment industry is an important one in the Philippines. There are reportedly over 1,000 garment manufacturers in the country, employing 450,000-500,000 workers. Garment exports have grown dramatically in recent years, rising from $500 milion in 1980 to $685 million in 1981, an increase of 37 percent. Further increases in exports depend mainly on economic conditions in the major export markets (United States 49 percent and EEC 27 percent), the terms of a bilateral textile trade agreements negotiated in 1982, and increasing costs of production.

Construction.—The construction sector grew at a 6.7 percent rate in 1981 after a slow year in 1980. Industry sources and the new Five-Year Plan predict a real annual growth rate of this sector to be 7 to 9 percent for 1983-87. This growth will depend largely on the availability of suitable financing schemes for the construction industry and the realization of numerous government projects.

Several construction projects have been planned in the Philippines and are at various stages of development. These include the five-year housing program, the construction of a steel mill, a copper smelter, a fertilizer plant and various plants, and the expansion of the cement industry and the PICOP paper mill. These should provide U.S. firms with markets for construction equipment and building materials.

Minerals and Oil Production.—The Philippines possesses vast amounts of mineral wealth which has only just begun to be tapped. In 1981, mineral production totaled more than $1.5 billion and should increase in the years to come as mineral prices rise from current low levels.

The most valuable metalic minerals now being mined include gold, silver, copper, and nickel. The Philippines also produces nonmetallic minerals including cement and coal.

Mineral production value showed a decline in 1981 from 1980 of 2.3 percent. This was primarily due to declining world demand, low market prices and rising costs of production. The value of copper production showed a decline of 12.7 percent. A decline in the value of gold and silver by

9.6 percent negated a 17.5 percent and 3.6 percent, respectively, increase in quantity produced.

In 1981, in terms of value, copper concentrates accounted for 32 percent, fine gold 22 percent, and cement 18 percent of total mineral production. Nickel metal followed with a 9 percent share.

Oil deposits are also a possible resource for the Philippines where there are 12 sedimentary basins. An active oil exploration program has been underway since the 1970's and should continue but at a moderate pace for some time. Producing fields are located offshore near the island of Palawan. On-shore exploration is being conducted by the Philippine National Oil Company (PNOC) on the island of Mindoro and Northern and Central Luzon.

Total domestic production was 3.8 million barrels in 1980 and 2.5 million in 1981. In 1982, the Cadlao and Matinloc fields came on stream, but they are considered marginal in their production.

Export Processing Zones.—There are three export processing zones (EPZ) operating in the Philippines. Located on the Bataan peninsula at the mouth of Manila Bay, the Bataan EPZ with light and medium industries, is the largest operation. Some progress has been made in solving the problems of adequate power supply, higher labor costs and inadequate shipping arrangements. Mactan EPZ, located near the city of Cebu, is operational with several light industries including electronics and watch assembly. Among the priority concerns of the Export Processing Zone Authority are to assure firms in the Mactan EPZ of reliable power and water supply. A third EPZ is located in Baguio. It contains mainly electronics and garment manufacturers. Plans call for a fourth EPZ, to be located in Cavite, to house some heavy industries including a petrochemical complex and a coco-chemical complex. The Government has plans for establishing EPZ's in a number of other areas, including Davao, Zamboanga, and Bacolod. The pace of development will depend on the resources available and the demand by investors in exporting industries.

The Export Processing Zone Authority offers incentives that parallel investment incentives available to investors under the Board of Investments program (See Investment section for details.)

Service Sector.—The service sector comprised 38 percent of GDP in 1981, with transport, communication, and storage accounting for 5.2 percent; commerce, 20.5 percent; and services, 12.3 percent. In 1981, growth for the sector was 3 percent. The Government's campaign to further develop Manila as a tourist and convention center is expected to stimulate growth.

Role of Government

State enterprises in the Philippines can be divided into two categories. One category is made up of enterprises which the Government operates by conscious investment decisions and which are now considered by it to constitute a normal part of government activity in the supply of goods and services in the community. These include the National Power Corporation, Philippine National Oil Company, and others. There are 91 such entities. The other category consists of companies in which the Government, most often through the Development Bank of the Philippines (DBP) or the Philippine National Bank (PNB), has acquired an equity position as DPB and PNB loans were converted to equity following the financial crisis of 1981. There are over 120 such companies in this category. Examples of such companies include the Construction Development Corporation of the Philippines (CDCP) and Galleon Shipping Company. Many companies would have gone into receivership without support. The Government has stated its policy to divest itself of these companies whenever it is feasible.

Distribution and Sales Channels

Major Marketing Areas

National Center.—Despite periodically renewed programs for decentralizing commercial/industry activities in the Philippines, the country's national center is still Manila. With a metropolitan population of more than 5 million people, it is the principal port and chief financial, commercial and industrial center. Manila provides the whole country with a variety of specialized central services. It also serves as an interregional center for all the northern provinces and a major center for a large immediate hinterland. It is the country's nerve center of industrial activity, transportation and communications, trade, educational and developmental services, governmental, and various administrative and social services. Approximately 85 percent of Philippine foreign trade passes through the port of Manila; 90 percent of imports enter this port to be distributed to the other principal cities via trucks and interisland vessels.

About 90 percent of all Philippine industries are located in the greater Manila area in three major locations. The first, an area of heavy industries, is situated along the banks of the Pasig River, which flows through the city and the port area into Manila Bay. Cargo discharged from vessels in the Bay is often loaded on barges and lighters for transport via the Pasig to the industrial area

The second industrial district—containing medium-sized plants—is located about 15 miles outside of Manila at Antipolo, in the Marikina Valley. Supplies and raw materials are generally carried from the port area by truck.

The third major industrial area is located in Makati, one of the newer and most prosperous of the Manila suburbs. In addition to small manufacturing plants, a considerable number of distribution centers, trading firms, and banks are located here. Makati is also a shopping area of the higher income group of residents.

Outside Manila, a large private industrial estate, Laguna Estates, is being developed at Canlubaung, at the end of the South Super Highway. The estate is within an hour's drive south from Manila.

Interregional Centers.—In addition to Manila, the other major interregional centers are Cebu, Iloilo, Davao, and Zamboanga.

Cebu City, the second largest city in the Philippines, is the prime trading center in the southern part of the archipelago. It has an advantage over Manila in domestic trade by water since its hinterland is accessible by boat. Its trade by land, however, is quite limited.

Iloilo shares with Cebu the servicing of the country's central area. In recent years, it has been meeting increasing competition from Bacolod City, which is located almost directly across a narrow strait in Negros, Occidental Province. The sugar trade of Negros, which formerly was channeled through Iloilo, is being shipped more and more directly to offshore ships on the Negros coast. The construction of excellent highways replacing the older water transport has aided greatly in the rise of Bacolod City as the direct center of the rich sugar area.

Davao enjoys a trade monopoly in Southern Mindanao, due mainly to the presence of land and water connections with its nearby provinces.

Zamboanga functions partly as an interregional center. Transportation to the hinterland is almost entirely by water since there are only a few roads along the penisula.

Major and Secondary Centers.—Furnishing the archipelago with basic economic, political, and social services are about 40 major and 35 secondary centers situated throughout the Philippines. These are more or less similar to retail outlets and relatively small, ranging in population from about 15 to 60,000. Their importance lies in the fact that they render essential urban services to their respective territories. Most of these centers are on the coasts and a number of them are fair ports.

Minor Centers.—Minor trade centers total about 150. In the areas served by the minor centers, there are about 17,000 barrios (villages). Among the few rudimentary central services available to the barrio, the schools stand out as the most important and widespread function.

Importers, Agents, Distributors

The establishment of reliable trade contracts that can provide continuous product development in the Philippines is perhaps the most important single decision to be made by prospective U.S. exporters. Business relationships are highly personalized and require continuous cultivation.

Nationwide marketing, as contrasted with selling in Manila, still remains limited by an inadequate distribution system for most products. Also, for many product lines, limited demand outside the Manila area often does not warrant the establishment of a nationwide distribution system. Buyers from throughout the islands visit Manila periodically. In many instances, a sales agent in Manila, with branches, travelers, or representatives regularly covering the interregional centers, can provide adequate coverage of the country. The product or product line itself helps decide what type of representation is needed.

Private companies with extensive retailing outlets generally set up franchise dealerships, a highly effective marketing technique. Certain firms also extend consumer credit to help finance purchases. However, credit is seldom extended for large amounts. As a result, installment purchasing is not yet highly developed. Retailers generally depend on a high markup and low turnover and limit their extention of credit to an open account for established customers.

A high percentage of import orders are handled by large trading companies with trained staffs. For the most part, such companies serve as indentors, placing orders with foreign suppliers only after cutomers' orders have been received. Trading houses also often serve as distributors.

In addition to the trading houses, which handle the bulk of Philippine imports from the United States, there are a large number of smaller importer-distributor firms that also act as indentors. These smaller firms represent the traditional trading economy that has been closely associated with the Chinese community. They generally handle a more limited range of products and have more limited promotional activities and market coverage than the trading houses. Lower commission fees of these smaller firms enable them to compete with the large trading houses. They have been particularly effective in offering representation that covers the small quality market—department stores and the established larger wholesale or retail outlets in the urban areas—and the traditional market of petty traders and small sari-sari stores (small retail outlets).

In certain product lines, foreign suppliers do not have agency relationships. Instead, they sell directly to industrial end-users. Larger Philippine companies that are able to station a buyer abroad are moving away from placing orders with local agents.

A large trading house may represent as many as 600 foreign firms. Maintenance of inventories for so many lines is difficult. This large-scale representation of firms and products also limits the degree to which the trading house can promote aggressively the sale of any one product line. The trading house emphasizes customer relations rather than specific product selling to assure a steady flow of orders. Trading firms, however, are in a better position to promote sales through advertising than are smaller importer-distributor firms. Generally, they have more widespread distribution facilities in major Philippine cities. The smaller firms work with less operating capital and find difficulty in advertising extensively.

A number of larger manufacturers, mining concerns, and agricultural cooperatives buy raw materials, fertilizer and other agricultural chemicals, and machinery and equipment directly from foreign suppliers. For the most part, they write to these foreign suppliers directly, relying heavily on catalogs and literature for product selection. Sometimes, buyers are sent aborad, and foreign firms in turn send sales representatives to the Philippines.

However, there is a real need for good distributorship systems and adequate support from American principals. Distributors can provide negotiation, representation and back-up services not available through direct sales methods. Most importantly, they can maintain the personal contact which is critical to doing business in the Philippines.

Certain enfranchised Philippine distributors representing U.S. machinery manufacturers have recently had difficulties as a result of their principals' selling to "jobbers," or intermediaries making spot sales in the Philippines. These sales have been at lower prices resulting in the distributors being undercut. As a result, these distributors are becoming skeptical about the value of developing U.S. lines.

Commercial Practices

The irrevocable letter of credit (L/C remains the most common method of payment. All imports valued at more than $1,000 must be effected through L/Cs (to be opened on or before the date of actual shipment). Exceptions to this policy follow.

1. Importations on Document against acceptance D/A) basis and open account (O/A) arrangement (by prequalified firms of their raw material requirements falling under the "EP" category).

2. No-dollar imports covered by Central Bank Circular No. 849 dated February 15, 1982.

3. Importations valued at less than $1,000 which may be paid for through remittance of foreign exchange upon submission of original shipping documents.

Even if the importation is valued at less than $1,000 the L/C requirement shall still apply where it is shown that there is more than one importation of the same commodity from the sale supplier, the aggregate value of the importations exceed $1,000 and the importations were shipped on the same date on the same vessel or were mailed on the same or successive dates.

The uniform minimum rate on margin deposits for import L/Cs is 35 percent. On July 1, 1983, it will be reduced to 25 percent.

Wholesale and Retail Trading

Only 100 percent Filipino-owned firms may engage directly or indirectly in retail business. The Philippine Retail Trade Nationalization Law (1964) established this requirement, which did not apply to U.S. firms until July 3, 1974 when the Laurel-Langley Trade Agreement expired.

The legal status of wholesale trading is not clear from a literal reading of the law and subsequent cases. However, for exporters to the Philippines, the key factor is that manufacturers or processors selling to industrial or commercial consumers are exempted from the Retail Trade Nationalization Law.

Franchising and Licensing

Transfer of Technology.—Technology transfer arrangements have to be filed with and approved by the Technology Transfer Board (TTB), an agency of the Ministry of Industry, Trade and Investment, to have legal efffect and enable royalties to be remitted to the licensor. The agreement has a maximum term of 5 years and may be renewed. The royalty base is either related to net sales[1] or local value added,[2] and is usually 2 to 3 percent. An additional 2 percent, based on net foreign exchange earnings, is generally granted where the licensed products are exported by the licensee. Because the rates of return for a technology leasing agreements are considered low, some foreign business consultants advise their clients to go into a joint venture manufacturing arrangement with a local partner rather than license technology to a domestic producer.

Moreover, TTB does not allow new agreements involving the use of foreign trademark without accompanying technology or economic benefits accruing to the Philippines.

Government Procurement

The Philippine Government itself is a large direct importer, usually through competitive bidding, of many essential products including roadbuilding and maintenance equipment, cement, machinery and equipment for the various government projects. Government pruchase decisions are generally made in Manila.

Government agencies pattern their regulations and procedures after those of the Bureau of Supply Coordination of the U.S. Government's General Services Administration. The major government purchasers are the National Electrification Administration, National Power Corporation, National Irrigation Administration, National Housing Authority, National Computer Center, and the Philippine National Oil Company.

Philippine Government procurement regulations permit a foreign company to bid on government procurement only if it maintains a registered branch office or a registered resident agent in the Philippines. The first step in obtaining government business is to be placed on the Bidder's Mailing List of the agency with which the applicant wishes to do business. This is done by sworn application accompanied by certified copies of the company's Application for the Certificate of Registration issued by the Philippine Bureau of Commerce, articles of incorporation, a receipted franchise tax bill, an up-to-date financial statement, and other attachments as required. Application forms of the various procurement agencies are substantially the same in most respects. As mentioned in the section "Limitation on Business Activities," bidding preferences are accorded to Philippine firms whose lowest bids do not exceed lowest foreign bids by more than 15 percent.

Currently, the governments of the United States and the Philippines are negotiating on conditions for Philippine accession to the Government Procurement Code under the General Agreement on Tariffs and Trade. If agreement is reached, discrimination against imports by both governments' procurement organizations will be reduced. For example, bidding preferences by agencies covered by the code will be eliminated.

Transportation, Utilities, and Living Conditions

Shipping

Because of its insular character, the Philippines is heavily dependent on marine transport. Hundreds of shipping routes service both freight and passenger movements among the islands. Also, the Philippines depends heavily on ocean shipping in international trade.

The Philippines has 473 ports, 81 of which are national and the remainder, municipal. Less than half of the national ports are open to international shipping. Manila is the most important of these, handling more than 60 percent of the country's imports and almost a fifth of the exports. Next to it is Cebu in the Visayas. Both handle domestic and overseas shipping.

There are 12 ports and 30 subports[3] of entry throughout the Philippines. In addition to Manila and Cebu, the other designated principal ports are the Manila International Airport, Davao, Iloilo, San Fernando, Batangas, Legaspi, Cagayan de Ore, Surgiao, Tacloban, and Zamboanga.

Depending upon the vessel and its itinerary, shipping time from San Francisco to Manila (6,000 nautical miles) normally can range from 18 to 25 days. Very often, schedules of cargo ships arrange for calls to Manila on the homeward leg of a cruise. From New York (11,400 nautical miles), the average time can vary from 18 to 32 days and from Gulf ports, from 22 to 34 days. The following is a list of carriers and the specific details of their service to the Philippines.

---

[1] Net sales is the invoice value based on actual sale less (a) trade, quantity or cash, discounts and brokers or agents' commission; (b) return credits and allowances; (c) any tax, excise or any government charges; and (d) freight, insurance and packaging expense.

[2] Local value added is defined as net sales (as defined above) less the landed cost of imported raw materials and components.

[3] Subports can process import/export documents, enforce customs rules and regulations, accept and release importations and exercise such other powers that principal ports of entry may exercise under existing customs rules and regulations.

U.S. Carriers
U.S. East Coast/Philippines

Ocean Carrier	American President Lines Ltd. 61 Broadway New York, N.Y. 10006 (212) 480-0600	Sea-Land Service. Inc. P.O. Box 800 Isilin, N.J. 08830 (201) 632-2000	Waterman Steamship Corp. 120 Wall Street New York, N.Y. 10005 (212) 747-8550
Contact	Mr. Joel Greenberg Regional Sales Mgr.	Mr. Albert Pierce	Mr. James Devine Sr. Vice President
Frequency of Service	Weekly	Weekly	Monthly
Transit Time	31 days	32-39 days	18-21 days
Type of Service	Container (mini-landbridge)	Container (mini-landbridge)	Break Bulk Lash Barge
Ports of Exit	Boston, New York Philadelphia, Baltimore Norfolk, Charleston Savannah, Jacksonville, Miami	Boston, New York Philadelphia, Baltimore Portsmouth, Charleston, Savannah, Jacksonville, Miami	New York, Philadelphia Baltimore, Norfolk, Savannah
Ports of Call	Manila Cebu Legaspi	Manila Cebu Legaspi	Manila Davao Cebu

U.S. Gulf Coast/Philippines

Ocean Carrier	American President Lines Ltd. Canal Place One New Orleans, LA 70130 (504) 525-1126	Lykes Bros. Steamship Co. Inc. Lykes Center 300 Poydras Street (504) 523-6611	Waterman Steamship Corp. 708 Richards Bldg. New Orleans, LA 70112 (504) 586-0500
Contact	Ms. Lynn Wochomurka Export Coordinator	Mr. R.V. Whittaker Traffic Mgr.	Mr. Angelo Spinato Traffic Mgr.
Frequency of Service	Weekly	Monthly	Monthly
Transit Time	22 days	35 days	35-37 days
Type of Service	Container Break Bulk (mini-landbridge)	Container Break Bulk	Break Bulk Lash Barge
Ports of Exit	New Orleans, Baton Rouge, Mobile, Lake Charles Houston, Galveston Beaumont, Corpus Christi, Brownsville, Freeport, Dallas	New Orleans[2] Mobile Galveston	New Orleans[2] Houston
Ports of Call	Manila Cebu Legaspi Mariveles	Manila[2]	Manila[2]

U.S. West Coast/Philippines

Ocean Carrier	American President Lines Ltd. 1395 Middle Harbor Road Oakland, CA 94607 (415) 271-8273	Sea-Land Service, Inc. 1425 Maritime Street Oakland, CA 94607 (415) 271-1278	Lykes Bros. Steamship Co., Inc. 320 California Street San Francisco, CA 94104 (415) 433-7400
Contact	Mr. Peter Feldbrugge Sales Manager	Mr. John W. Sullivan Sales Manager	Mr. Gerard D. Doyle Director of Sales
Frequency of Service	Weekly	Twice Weekly	Every 18 days

Transit Time	18-24 days	24-28 days	23 days
Type of Service	Container	Container	Container Break-Bulk Roll-on/Roll-off
Ports of Exit	Seattle, Tacoma Los Angeles, San Pedro Oakland, San Francisco	Seattle Long Beach Oakland	Long Beach San Francisco
Ports of Call	Manila Cebu Legaspi/Mariveles	Manila Cebu Legaspi	Manila[1]

[1]Less than container loads accepted at New Orleans, Houston, and Dallas.
[2]Other ports by inducement.

Air Freight

Air freight and air express shipments are becoming more economical for some imported merchandise. Manila is roughly 18 hours from the West Coast of the United States by jet plane. The Philippines is accessible by air to practically any part of the world. Pan American World Airways and Northwest Orient Airlines have frequent scheduled flights to and from the United States. Other airlines serving the Philippines are Flying Tiger Line, Philippine Airlines, Air France, Air Micronesia, China Air Lines, Korean Airlines, Japan Airlines, Thai International Airways, Cathay Pacific Airways, British Airways, Canadian Pacific Airlines, EgyptAir, Garuda Indonesian Airways, KLM Royal Dutch Airlines, Kuwait Airways, Lufthansa German Airlines, Malaysian Airline System, Pakistan International Airlines, Qantas Airways, Sabena Belgian World Airlines, Saudi Arabian Airlines, Scandinavian Airlines System, Singapore Airlines, and Varig Brazilian Airlines.

The Philippines has 86 operational airports of which 2 are regular international airports (Manila and Mactan, Cebu). Out of the 86, 40 airports are being used for scheduled air carriers while the other 46 are general aviation airports.

Railroads

Because of fragmentation of land areas and the high investment needed to build railroads, they are not a dominant mode of transportation. The Philippine National Railways has a network of 643 miles of main lines and about 625 miles of branch lines and siding. Railroads carrying freight and passengers are limited to the islands of Luzon and Panay. A light rail system (LRT), which will serve metro Manila, is under construction.

Water Supply

Water supply in Manila and the surrounding provinces is potable, except during the dry season and after heavy rains. Safe water supplies exist to a lesser extent in the more rural areas. The Government has put priority on investment in water treatment facilities to improve the situation.

Communications

Communication facilities are operated by government and private organizations. Local telephone and telegraph service is only fair but is improving under the Philippine Telecommunication Development Plan. Long-distance service is available to areas outside Manila and to most other countries.

Surface and airmail facilities are provided and include postal money order service and registered and special delivery mails. Airmail letters between the Philippines and the United States are usually delivered between 7 and 10 days. However, courier service is recommended for transmittal of important documents. Companies which offer courier service are DHL (Philippines) Services Corp., Apollo Deliveries, Inc., and World Courier Philippines, Inc. Within Manila, it is best to send local mail by messenger/delivery service.

Housing

Housing facilities are generally available. Most foreign business people live in villages (subdivisions), apartments and compounds throughout Manila. Condominium buildings in the area offer individual dwelling units for sale or lease. A condominium dwelling may come either furnished or unfurnished. Electric power is supplied in

Manila on a 110/220 volt 60 cycle AC basis. Kitchen ranges are powered by either electricity or bottled gas. *Living in the Philippines*, published by the American Chamber of Commerce, contains much valuable information for families moving to Mainla. (see Bibliography)

Clothing

Summer clothing that is normally worn in the temperate zones is suitable for the Philippines. Western-style informal apparel is available throughout the country. Shirt and tie is ordinary business attire. Suits are worn mostly by middle and top management, as well as the traditional "barong" shirt. Clothing for both sexes is usually custom made. There is a large number of tailoring and dress shops that charge reasonable prices. Excellent shoes are manufactured locally, but exceptionally large sizes may have to be specially ordered. Dry cleaning facilities are available. Cosmetics items are sold widely. Beauty and barber shops abound.

Food

A wide variety of fresh and canned food is available locally. Fresh food is sold at supermarkets, smaller grocery stores, and public market stalls. There should be no difficulty in maintaining a diet familiar to the Westerner.

There are fine restaurants in Manila offering varied choices of excellent international cuisine. Bottled beverages, including those carrying American trademarks, are plentiful. Local beer is of the first quality; there is also an assortment of locally made liqueurs. Domestically manufactured cigars and cigarettes present a wide selection. Imported liqueurs and cigarettes are also available.

Health

Manila has modern and adequate medical facilities in all areas. Medical fees are reasonable and pharmaceuticals of all types are easily procured. A-lower level of sanitation exists in the Philippines than in the United States requiring precautions with food and drinking water.

Advertising and Research

Advertising Media

The Philippines is a brand-conscious market. Advertising plays a significant part in promoting the sale of most goods, particularly nondurable consumer types and those selling at low-unit cost.

Although the local advertising business is by no means new, its largest and most rapid expansion has been since World War II. Most advertising agencies (of which there are currently more than 40) have patterned their organizations after American advertising agencies with account executive and media specialist staffing arrangements. Although most advertising expenditures are channeled through local agencies, several American concerns have found it advantageous to establish "house" agencies.

In print, radio, television, outdoor, cinema, direct mail, and point of purchase, all indications point toward a continued increasing trend in budget and activity. In recent years, an estimated overall national breakdown of total media expenditures indicates approximately 45 percent going to television, 20 percent each to radio and the press, and the remaining 15 percent to a combination of all other forms.

Television and Radio

The availability of inexpensive mass-produced transistorized radio receivers and the growth of radio stations throughout the country have made radio the unrivaled medium of communications in the Philippines. It is the cheapest way to reach the rural population. Almost two-thirds of all families own one or more radios. More than 200 stations are in operation, 60 of which are located in the greater Manila area. Four of the Manila stations operate nationwide networks; the rest are small unaffiliated stations.

Some of the largest radio stations have branched out into television transmission. Three television stations currently operate in Manila, all of which have network-affiliated stations in other major cities primarily rebroadcasting taped programs. While television has grown rapidly in the last decade, it is concentrated mostly in Manila and other urban centers. Almost half of Manila's families own a television set, as against the national average of about 5 percent. The high cost of television sets and the absence of television stations in many parts of the country still make television viewing a remote possibility in the rural areas.

Cinema

Theater-screen advertising has increased rapidly in popularity among advertisers. It is an especially popular medium for launching products that appeal to the under 25 age group (e.g., soft drinks and cosmetics). Yearly cinema attendance runs at least 180 million at the 300-400 cinema theatres throughout the country.

Press

Six national daily newspapers, all published in Manila, provide domestic and international news, as well as an expanding standard medium for advertising.

The primary business daily is *Business Day*, which serves as the Phillippine equivalent to the *Wall Street Journal*. The telex number for *Business Day* advertising is 742-2011.

Other widely read newspapers are the Manila Daily Express, Bulletin Today, and the Times Journal. In point of circulation, Philippine magazines have outpaced daily newspapers. There are at least 20 leading magazines that are used consistently by local advertisers. These magazines are published weekly, either as independent publications or as weekend supplements to the daily newspapers. There are some 15 trade and professional journals with growing monthly circulations. Most are published in English. There is a journal for almost every trade or profession; including commerce, industry, engineering, marketing, insurance, architecture, agriculture, medicine.

Market Research

Several companies in the Manila area offer a range of services covering product and consumer research, trade surveys, advertising and media research, panel services, motivational research, and public opinion studies. Four of the most capable companies are as follow:

SGV & Co.
SGV Development Center
P.O. Box 7658 MIA Airmail Exchange, M.M.
105 De La Rosa,
Makati Metro Manila
Telex: 45096 PH

International Research Associates
161 Roxas Blvd. Ext.
Parangue, Metro Manila

Feedback Inc.
Suite 114 Limketkai Bldg.
Ortigas Ave., Greenhills
San Juan, Metro Manila

Asia Research Organization Inc.
ABC Building
P.O. Box 3361 MLA; 1379 MCC
Pasong Tamo
Makati, Metro Manila

Credit

Stock Exchanges

The Philippines has three stock exchanges: the Manila Stock Exchange established in 1927, the Makati Stock Exchange established in 1965, and the Metropolitan Stock Exchange which began operations in 1974. However, the Government eventually may implement its plan of merging three operating stock exchanges in order to rationalize the stock market. Two options are being considered in pursuing the planned merger: through voluntary agreement of the member-brokers of the exchanges or through the setting up of a new exchange, which will be the only exchange allowed to operate.

With the promulgation of Presidential Decree 167, securities approved for listing by the Securities and Exchange Commission are automatically listed in all stock exchanges. In January 1980, there were 194 stocks listed on the three stock exchanges. In 1981, total value of stock transactions dropped to 1.3 billion pesos compared with 4.6 billion pesos in 1980. Total volume of stocks traded in 1981 was 52 million shares, down 48 percent compared with the 1980 figure.

Banking System

The banking system is made up of commercial banks, investment banks, rural banks, and savings banks. There are 24 Offshore Banking Units (OBU's) engaged primarily in refinancing activities and several Foreign Currency Deposit Units (FCDU's). Both the Government and the private sector are involved in banking, the former specializing in long-term agricultural, industrial, and commercial loans; the latter in short-term financing.

Control and supervision over all banks and credit institutions is exercised by the Central Bank (established 1949) which is also administrator of monetary policy. The Central Bank is charged with the duty of maintaining the monetary and banking stability of the country, preserving the international value of the peso, and promoting a rising level of production, employment, and real income. It is also the depository of all other banks and the source of loanable or additional capital funds through the system of rediscounting. It represents the Government in all negotiations and transactions with international financial institutions.

Commercial banks dominate the Philippines banking picture. As of March 5, 1982, there were 34 commercial banks with total assets of 171 billion pesos. Four of them are branches of foreign banks (Bank of America and the Citibank of the United States, Chartered Bank of the United Kingdom and Hong Kong, and Shanghai Banking Corporation of Hong Kong). The most important Philippine commercial banks are the government-owned Philippine National Bank (PNB), Bank of the Philippine Islands, Allied Banking Corporation, and Metropolitan Bank and Trust Company.

Another important source of funds is the Development Bank of the Philippines. Its major function is promoting high priority agriculture and industry by providing technical know-how and financing through medium- and long-term credit facilities at reasonable rates. It also promoted private development banks, supplies public works loans to the Government, and provides real estate financing.

In November 1976, The Central Bank issued guidelines for the establishment of OBU's and FCDU's. OBU's may accept foreign currency deposits from external or nonresident sources. These offshore funds may be loaned out freely, without being subject to Central Bank regulations or restrictions, to nonresident users or to other OBU's. Also, subject to appropriate Central Bank regulation or restrictions, these offshore funds may likewise be loaned to Philippine residents, as well as to commercial banks and local branches of foreign banks authorized to receive money under the Foreign Currency Deposit Act. Foreign Currency Deposit Units (FCDU's may accept foreign currency funds not otherwise required to be surrendered to the commercial banking system, from both resident and nonresident sources.

There are approximately 971 operational rural banks designed to promote and expand the rural economy through the extension of credit facilities to small merchants, rural industries, and cooperatives. Savings and mortgage banks service the requirements of smaller depositors. Credit is most often channeled into the encouragement of livestock breeding, the purchase of fertilizer, machinery, and other productive goods; and the improvement of real estate in cities and municipalities.

Finance companies abound in the country. Commercial finance companies, factoring companies or factors, sales finance companies and commercial paper houses handle short-term financing requirements. The long-term capital finance companies include investment banks or security houses, investment companies or investment trusts, brokerage firms, trust companies, insurance companies, and savings and loan associations or building and loan associations.

Trends in Bank Regulation

"Universal banking" was instituted in 1980 through revised banking laws which eliminated the distinctions between different categories of banks and allow any financial institution to offer all types of financial services if it can meet Central Bank requirements. Minimum capitalization of 500 million pesos is required for "unibank" status. A significant effect has been that the large commercial banks are now able to engage in investment banking and long-term lending.

Recovery from the collapse of the Philippine money market in early 1981 is nearly complete now. The collapse resulted from the departure of a Filipino industrialist who left behind $80 million in unsecured debt. A rescue effort by the Central Bank has been accompanied by long-term reforms which are strengthening the banking system. As part of these reforms, interest rates on all commercial loans have been freed to adjust to market requirements. New financial instruments, such as certificates of deposits, have been introduced and the Government is actively promoting development of a secondary market for commercial paper and government notes.

Trade Regulations

Philippine trade policy is aimed at diversifying the country's markets and sources of supply, broadening its export base, and protecting local industry. The Philippines has sought both to retain its position in the U.S. market and to diversify export trade to lessen its current dependence on U.S. and Japanese markets, which take more than 50 percent of total Philippine exports.

A wide range of goods that are being or could be locally produced or that are otherwise considered unessential are subject on importation to high protective tariffs and internal taxes, as well as to stringent controls on the method of payments. Imports of some items are banned through the use of exchange controls. In January 1981, 1,300 items were removed from the list of banned products in response to World Bank recommendations that import restrictions be reduced. In mid-February 1982, additional trade liberalization moves were announced. These include removal of Central Bank approval for foreign currency to import some 610 items which were originally in the list of banned items and liberalization of the importation of caustic soda, basic iron and steel products, and gasoline and kerosene engines for trucks and tractors.

The United States-Philippine Trade Agreement expired on July 3, 1974. Although it had constituted a bilateral framework for U.S. Commercial relations with the Philippines since the country became independent in 1946, the absence of a treaty has not affected the business climate, nor prevented bilateral accords such as the agreement on trade concessions signed on October 30, 1979, in conjunction with Philippines accession to the General Agreement on Tariffs and Trade.

Tariff Structure

Executive Order No. 609 of August 1, 1980, modified the Philippine tariff schedule. The minimum tariff rate in general is now 10 percent for producer goods not available locally and 5 percent for "certain critical raw matrials" needed by the local food and steel manufacturing industries.

Imported materials that can be obtained locally are assessed at 10 to 25 percent, while semiprocessed goods used in domestic production have a 20 to 30 percent duty. Finished goods have a maximum tariff rate of from 20 to 50 percent. The former ceiling rate of 100 percent will be brought down to 50 percent by 1984, without exception.

Duties are levied on the "home consumption value" (HCV is selling price by manufacturer to a domestic customer; it must be the same value as shown on the invoice) plus 10 percent. Effective January 1983, all duties and taxes must be paid by the applicant when a letter of credit is opened.

Firms registered with the Board of Investments under Presidential Decree 1789 (Omnibus Investment Code) as export producers and those registered with the Export Processing Zone Authority enjoy full exemption from taxes and duties on imported raw materials, supplies, and capital equipment.

Under the ASEAN Preferential Tariff Agreement, 17,000 products from ASEAN countries are given preferential tariff rates (generally 20 percent less than the most-favored-nation rate) in trade between Indonesia, Malaysia, Philippines, Singapore, and Thailand.

Information regarding Philippine duties applicable to specific products may be obtained free of charge from the Philippines Country Specialist, Room 2310 U.S. Department of Commerce, Washington, D.C. 20230; or through any Department of Commerce district office. Inquiries should contain a complete product description, including BTN, or SITC numbers, if known.

Other Tariffs

Effective January 1983, an additional 3 percent *ad valorem* duty is applied to nearly all imports except those products entering bonded warehouses.

Internal Taxes

Most imported products, as well as most locally produced goods, are subject to either a specific tax, a percentage sales tax, or a compensating tax.

Specific Taxes.—Specific taxes represent a set amount assessed per unit of weight or quantity. Payment of this tax, if applicable, is due before release from customs custody if the article is imported. These taxes are levied only on alcoholic beverages, tobacco products, matches, firecrackers, mineral fuels, cinematographic films, playing cards, and saccharine.

Sales and Compensating Taxes.—Advance sales tax is collected both on imports of goods which are intended for resale in the same form and on imports of raw materials to be used in the manufacture of articles for sale. The tax is payable prior to withdrawal of the goods from customs custody. It is computed on the basis of home consumption value or price (excluding internal excise taxes there of) plus 10 percent of such HCV or price including postage, commission, customs duty, and all similar charges, except freight and insurance plus the corresponding markup of 25, 50 or 100 percent of the total landed cost on ordinary, semiluxury and luxury goods, respectively. The advance sales tax rates are 10 percent for ordinary goods, 5 percent for certain procured local products, 25 percent for semiluxury goods, and 50 percent for luxury goods (except automobiles, which are subject to higher sales tax rates)

Compensating tax (or use tax as it is known in other countries) for sales to end-users is charged at the same rate as advance sales tax but without the corresponding markup.

Advance Rulings on Customs Classification

When an article cannot be identified in the Philippine Tariff and Customs Code, information regarding applicable duty rates and taxes may be requested from the Philippine Tariff Commission 5th Floor, Philippine Heart Center for Asia Diliman, Quezon City, P.O. Box 2479, Manila.

When possible, a sample should be enclosed with a request. When this is impractical, a complete description of the article plus photographs may be required to assist the custom appraiser. The article becomes dutiable under the heading indicated by the Commission at the rate in effect at the time of importation.

MTN Codes

The most recent round of the Multilateral Trade Negotiation, the Tokyo Round, under the General Agreement on Tariffs and Trade (GATT) was concluded in 1979. A major accomplishment was an agreement on nontariff barriers to trade which took the form of several codes which required further negotiations.

The Philippines has signed both the Standards and the Licensing Codes. It is expected that agreements will soon be reached on other codes including the Government Procurement Code, the Subsidies Code, and the Customs Valuation Code.

Because the Philippines is a developing nation, it will be accorded certain special privileges under the codes. The long-term effect, however, will be to further open the Philippine economy to imports.

Shipping Documents

Executive Order No. 736 dated September 26, 1981, abolished the authentication requirement on commercial invoices. The requirement for a consular invoice was eliminated previously. Executive Order 736 also provides that all importations covered by a formal entry with an invoice value of 5,000 pesos and above shall be subject to a fixed import processing fee of 250 pesos. This fee shall be paid by the importer/consignee to the authorized agent bank.

Marking and Labeling Requirements

With certain exceptions, every imported or locally manufactured product must be labeled to indicate brand, trademark, or trade name; country of manufacture; physical or chemical composition; net weight and measure if applicable; and address of manufacturer or repacker.

The country of origin lettering must be permanent enough to appear on the article at least until it reaches the ultimate purchaser. The lettering, which may be abbreviated, should either be in Filipino, English, or Spanish. The designation "Made in U.S.A.," for example, is generally acceptable for indicating the United States as the country of origin. If the article cannot be marked prior to shipment without injury or prohibitive expense, is a crude substance, or was produced more than 20 years prior to importation, it is exempt from the marking requirement. However, the container must indicate the country of origin. Any article (or its container) that does not bear a proper mark of origin at the time of importation is subject to a marking duty of 5 percent ad valorem.

All packages and cases, except those of bulk shipments or shipments of more than 500 barrels or cases, must be numbered consecutively in each separate shipment.

Mislabeling, misrepresentation, or misbranding may subject the entire shipment to seizure and disposal. Exporters violating these regulations are subject to fines, prison sentences, or both.

Licensing and Exchange Controls

The Philippine Government has a generally unrestricted import policy although imports of certain commodities are prohibited on the grounds of health, national welfare, and security. The importation of certain commodities is subject to prior approval by appropriate government agencies/committees responsible for implementing the import substitution/industry rationalization program for the Government. (a list of these commodities is available from the Commerce Department's Philippines Specialist).

Merchandise import regulations of the Central Bank may be classified according to the degree of restriction involved into the three categories discussed below.

Prohibited Imports.—Those originating from the Union of South Africa; built-up trucks in the light commercial vehicle category up to 2,000 kgs. or 4,000 lbs.; garlic, onions, potatoes, cabbages, and coffee in any form; used tires; explosives, firearms, weapons of war; printed material advocating the overthrow of the government and forcible resistance to any law; pornographic materials; narcotics, drugs, and materials producing unlawful abortion; gambling paraphernalia; misbranded or adulterated article of food and drugs; precious metals and alloys of precious metals with no indication of fineness or quality.

Imports subject to prior approval on a case-by-case basis. Commodities falling under Unclassified Consumer (UC), Non-Essential Consumer (NEC), Semi-Unclassified Consumer (SUC) categories in the Philippine Standard Commodity Classification Manual; specific textile items; magazines, reviews, and journals, synthetic fibers and yarns; container and packaging requirements by manufacturers/producers or perfumery cosmetics and other toilet preparations; newsprints; Chinese medicinal herbs; meat of bovine cattle and beef veal; mackerel; sardines, synthetic fibers and yarns; tires, those originating from socialist and communist countries except Yugoslavia; refined petroleum products; electonic products; gamefowls for breeding; basic urn; steel products, specific electronic products; parts covered by the Electronics Local Content Program; cellophane hydrogen peroxide, vinyl asbestos, asbestos-vinyl tiles; soybeans; feedgrains and other feed substitutes.

In February 15, 1982, the Central Bank issued Circular No. 850 delisting about 610 items belonging to the NEC and UC list and authorized banks to sell foreign exchange to cover their importation. About 75 percent of the 610 items are in the categories of textile and garments, food and beverages, electrical and electronics appliances. However, although banks are now authorized to sell without limit the required foreign exchange to cover the importation of the listed items, imported items will still be subject to tariff rates of at least 50 percent.

No-Dollar Imports.—Another class of imports are those effected on a "no-dollar" basis requiring no direct foreign exchange remittance from the Philippines, which generally require prior Central Bank approval. Evaluation on such matters are made on a case-by-case basis in accordance with specified guidelines promulgated by the Monetary Board and Mangement.

Samples and Advertising Matter

Samples that are unsalable or of no appreciable commercial value, models not adapted for practical use, and samples of medicine properly marked "physicians" samples, not for sale," are permitted entry without duty. Samples of commercial value, except those that are not readily identifiable (precious and semiprecious stones, for example), also may be imported without duty, provided the value of any single importation does not exceed $1,500. However, the importer must post bond equal to two times the ascertained duties, taxes, and other charges with the Collector of Customs and export the samples within 6 months of their entry. When a single shipment of samples is valued at more than $1,500, the importer may select any portion of the shipment not exceeding $1,500 in value for entry as stated above; the remainder may be entered in bond or entered for consmption by paying the applicable import duties and taxes. Printed material, including pictures and photographs containing printed material—such as lithographs, posters, signs, catalogs, price lists, pamphlets, booklets, and folders for advertising foreign products and foreign business—may be imported without payment of duties. Accompanying documents should indicate that the articles are samples or advertising matter and not for sale.

Samples and printed materials for advertising Philippine products and Philippine business houses, firms, offices, associations, corporations, trades, or professions are subject to payment of duties. Calendars of all kinds are also subject to duty.

Weights and Measures

In 1978, the Philippine Interim Assembly passed Cabinet bill no. 14 which calls for conversion to a modern metric system by 1983.

The Product Standards Agency of the Ministry of Trade and Industry is responsible for conversion. It has issued regulations which require products to be sold in wholenumber metric sizes and labeled accordingly. The mailing address of the agency is P.O. Box 2363, Makati Commercial Center, Makati, Metro Manila, Philippines.

Investment in the Philippines

U.S. Investment

U.S. investment in the Philippines is mostly direct investment. The book value of U.S. direct investment in the Philippines in 1981 was $1.3 billion, up from $644 million in 1972. Current asset value is well over $2 billion.

Until 1970, U.S. firms accounted for 80 percent of all foreign investment. From February 1970 to December 1981, of the $1.6 billion of Central Bank (CB) approved investment, the United States accounted for 54 percent compared with Japan's 15 percent. Japanese investment, as of March 1982, totaled $687 million or 20 percent of all foreign investment in the Philippines.

While the value of U.S. investment has risen, the trend in percentage of U.S. share of total foreign investment has been downward in recent years. Of those investments approved by the Board of Investments (BOI), the U.S. share was 25 percent of the 1981 total of $252 million, compared with 44 percent of $15 million in 1970. (BOI and CB approvals are separate.)

Trend in Investment Levels

Data from CB and BOI on levels of new foreign investment in 1981 indicate that foreign investments registered under the BOI supervised incentive laws increased by 27.9 percent from 1980 figures. Total Central Bank-approved foreign investment in 1981 amounted to $273 million, compared with $221 million in 1980.

Philippine Policy on Investment

If a foreign enterprise qualifies to do business in the Philippines, it may obtain comprehensive tax and other benefits provided it is qualified to register with BOI under the Omnibus Investments Code (Presidential Decree 1789) as amended in April 1983. This Code consolidates all those laws which were enacted previously to encourage both local and foreign entrepreneurs to invest in preferred areas of economic activity as determined by BOI and enumerated in the Investment Priorities List.

Generally, only citizens of the Philippines or domestic corporations, 60 percent of the capital stock of which is owned and controlled by citizens of the Philippines and at least 60 percent of the members of the board of directors are citizens of the Philippines, are qualified to avail themselves of the incentives under the Investment Code. However, the nationality requirement is waived if the applicant will export 70 percent of its total production or will engage in a pioneer enterprise.

A pioneer enterprise is one that manufactures goods that have not been heretofore produced in the Philippines on a commercial scale; or employs a formula, process, or production scheme which has not yet been tried in the Philippines; or engages in agricultural activities or services, especially food processing, which contributes to the national goal of self-sufficiency, or produces nonconventional fuels or manufactures equipment which utilizes nonconventional sources of energy. In all the foregoing instances, the final product or process should involve substantial use of domestic raw materials, whenever available.

Although BOI waives the nationality requirement with respect to an applicant which exports 70 percent of its total production or engages in a pioneer project, the applicant is required to attain the status of a Philippine national (i.e., for corporations, at least 60 percent must be owned and controlled by Philippine citizens) within 30 years from date of registration or such longer period as determined by BOI. However, registered enterprises exporting 100 percent of its production need not comply with this divestment requirement.

Foreign investors are guaranteed repatriation of investments, remittance of profits, freedom from expropriation and requisition of investment, protection of patents and their proprietary rights and, under certain circumstances, exemption from capital gains tax.

On April 28, 1983, President Marcos signed the Investment Incentive Policy Act of 1983, which changes the Omnibus Investment Code incentives system. Under the new system, the total number of fiscal incentives will be reduced from 20 to 8 (see table 4). Of these eight incentives, two are major new incentives; the other six incentives are available under the current system, but will be substantially modified. The first major new incentive is available to all registered enterprises, whether producing for the domestic or export market. This incentive takes the form of a tax credit based on value added and is available to new investments during the first 5 years of commercial production. It is performance oriented. It replaces the large number of incentives which are available to domestic producers under the current system, many of which provide considerable inducement to capital-intensive investments.

The other major incentive is specific to export production. In addition to the above-mentioned tax credit and the already existing provisions designed to give exporters access to capital equipment, raw materials, and intermediate inputs at free trade prices, exporters will receive a tax credit based on the net local content of export production for the first 10 years of commercial operations. This measure is designed to provide compensation for the discrimination against exports arising from the tariff and trade regime. While this incentive is not expected to fully compensate for the anti-export bias of the protection system, it will provide significant encouragement to new export production.

Under the new system, only one tax incentive related to investment in capital equipment will be retained in form, but change considerably in substance and scope. The complete exemption from taxes and duties on imported capital equipment and the corresponding tax credit on locally purchased capital equipment will continue to be available to export producers to put them on a free-trade basis. However, for domestic producers, this incentive will be in effect a deferred payment of taxes and duties; their amount will be deducted from future tax credits on value added. Also, only 50 percent of these taxes and duties will be deferrable.

An enterprise registered under the Omnibus Investments Code may establish its factory within an Export Processing Zone and thus qualify for the incentives available to zone enterprises in addition to the incentives it enjoys under the Investment Code.

Historically, manufacturing investment has been concentrated in the Manila area. To encourage the dispersal of industry into non-urban areas and at the same time generate employment in relatively underdeveloped regions in the Philippines, the Government has prohibited the establishment of factories within a 50 kilometer radius from Manila.

Table 4.—Summary of the New BOI Fiscal Incentives

Incentive	Rate and eligibility				Conditions
	Domestic producer		Export producer[a]		
	Pioneer	Non-pioneer	Pioneer	Non-pioneer	
1. Tax credit on net value earned.[b]	10%	5%	10%	5%	Available only for new or expanded capacity. Tax credit earned for the first 5 years of commercial production.
2. Tax credit on net local content of export production.[c]	10%	10%	10%	10%	Tax credit earned during 10 years of operation, for last 5 years on increment of local content. Incentive also available to indirect exporters. For existing export producers[d] tax credit payable on increment of local content only.
3. Tax credit for taxes and duties paid on raw materials, supplies used in export production................	Yes	Yes	Yes	Yes	Available for an indifinite period to all export producers.
4. Exemption from export taxes and fees	Yes	Yes	Yes	Yes	As for incentive (3).
5. Exemption from taxes and duties on imported capital equipment.	100% (deferred payment)	50% (deferred payment)	100%	100%	
6. Tax credit for locally purchased capital equipment (equal to value of taxes and duties which would waived for imported equipment).	100% (deferred payment)	50% (deferred payment)	100%	100%	
7. Net operating loss carry-over.	Yes	Yes	Yes	Yes	Losses incurred in any of the first 10 years of operations may be carried over as a deduction from taxable income for a maximum period of 6 years following the period in which the loss was incurred.
8. Tax credit for withholding tax on interest on foreign loans.	Yes	No	Yes	No	Available for loans taken during the first five years of registration or operation.

[a] Producers exporting at least 50% of output from new or expanded capacity.

[b] Net value earned is calculated as value of sales minus purchases of raw materials, supplies, utilities and some specifically excluded commodities.

[c] Net local content of export production is calculated as value of export sales minus imported raw materials and supplies, depreciation of capital equipment, and some specifically excluded commodities.

[d] Registered enterprises already engaged at the time of registration in the production, manufacturer or processing of export products.

Another government action (Presidential Decree No. 1851) recently liberalized existing laws on foreign investment. Under the new decree, special investors' resident visas will be conferred to aliens willing to invest at least $200,000 in business in the Philippines, provided they can prove that they have remitted such amount in "acceptable foreign currency in the Philippines." Furthermore, Presidential Decree No. 1851 provides that as a holder of the special investors resi-

dent visas, an alien shall be entitled to "reside in the Philippines while his investment subsists."

Additional Sources on Investment

The most current publication containing details on Philippine Investment Laws is *Doing Business in the Philippines 1982*, publishd by SGV & Co. and is available from its office at Suite 250, 1819

H Street, Washington, D.C.; telephone: (202) 659-5722.

The Philippine Government's *Investment Priorities Plan*, the *Investment Incentive Policy Act of 1983*, and the current *Investment Climate Report*, prepared by the U.S. Embassy in Manila, are available from the Philippines desk, U.S. Department of Commerce; telephone (202) 377-3875.

Export Processing Zones

The Philippine Government embarked on the Export Processing Zone project in 1972, and since then, the concept has assumed a more important role in national development. These zones are designed to promote the processing of goods for export, thereby earning foreign exchange, generating employment, and broadening the industrial base.

There are at present five such zones. The program is to develop a total of 15 zones in various parts of the country. Development of these zones follows the requirements of a modern industrial area, where aside from the basic utilities, the amenities of community life also are provided.

The industry mix in the zones gives significant weight to labor-intensive operations. As a matter of policy, however, all categories of manufacturing activity are evaluated on their overall contribution to the attainment of zone objectives. A large number of companies now operate in the zones, and they represent investments from the United States, United Kingdom, Australia, Canada, Austria, Germany, France, Japan, Italy, Korea, Malaysia, Taiwan, Norway, Singapore, Indonesia, and Hong Kong. U.S. companies now located in the zones include Texas Instruments, Timex, Ford Motor Co. and many others.

The organization mandated to develop and manage the zones is the Export Processing Zone Authority (EPZA), created in 1972 as a government corporation. Capitalized by the Government, the Authority exercises financial and operational autonomy in the conduct of its affairs. The organization and operation of the Authority are designed to provide maximum service to zone companies.

For more details on what the zones offer contact EPZA at 4th floor, Legazpi Towers III, Roxas Boulevard, Metro Manila, Philippines, cable address: "Bataanzone" Manila, telex: 40723 EPZA/PM, tel. 507-507; 507-588.

Forms of Business Organization

The Philippines permits various types of business organizations under rules comparable with those in the United States. The most important business forms are sole proprietorships, partnerships, and corporations. Other less common business forms include joint stock companies, joint accounts, business trusts, and cooperatives.

In general, citizenship is not a requirement for establishment of a business except in specified undertakings. Foreign individuals and firms may conduct business in the Philippines through the appointment of agents or resident representatives, opening of branches, or formation of wholly or partially owned domestic corporations.

The Securities and Exchange Commission (SEC) administers the corporation law, which sets out the documentary and other requirements for registering a corporation. The corporation acquires a legal personality distinct from that of its shareholders when the SEC issues its certificate of incorporation. The liability of shareholders in a corporation is limited to their subscription.

Like a corporation, a partnership also has a separate legal personality, although all partnerships must have at least one partner with unlimited liability. In the ordinary partnerships, all partners are personally liable for the contracts of the partnership once its assets have been exhausted. In a limited partnership, only one partner need have unlimited personal liability. A partnership with more than 3,000 pesos in capital must register with SEC. Except for professional firms that are not allowed to incorporate, most business ventures of any size adopt the corporate form of organization.

Regulatory Agencies

The SEC is the government agency with general regulatory power over business enterprises. Its main role is to issue certificates of incorporation to domestic corporations and licenses to foreign corporations, and to register securities for public sale. It also is responsible for the enforcement of the corporation laws and related laws.

The National Economic and Development Authority (NEDA) was created according to the provision of the new constitution calling for the creation of a central planning and implementing authority for social and economic development. NEDA is empowered to act as a regulatory body and to recommend to the National Assembly continuing, coordinated, and fully integrated social and economic plans and programs. NEDA is charged with oversight for the development plan.

NEDA also supervises the Oil Industry Commission, The Price Control Council, and the Wage Commission. The Oil Industry Commission regulates the petroleum industry, which is considered vital to the national interest. The Wage Commission establishes reasonable levels of wages. The Price Control Council fixes prices of essential consumer commodities.

Most business entities are supervised by specific government agencies. The Central Bank of the Philippines exercises fairly close control over the activities of the nation's banks, including issuance of letters of credit to importers and regulates financial institutions. Insurance companies are supervised by the Office of the Insurance Commissioner. All domestic and foreign corporations that enjoy benefits under the Investment Incentives Act and the Export Incentives Act are subject to some supervision by the Board of Investments.

Aside from approving service contracts, the Petroleum Board overseas the management and operation of contractors who enter into service contracts with the Government pursuant to the Oil Exploration and Development Act of 1972.

The Industry Section of the Ministry of Trade and Industry (MTI) is the primary policymaking body as well as the planning, programming, coordinating, and administrative entity of the Government in the development, expansion, and diversification of industry. The Trade Section is charged with the task of developing, expansion, and diversification of industry. The Trade Section is charged with the task of developing, promoting, and expanding domestic and international trade.

The Technology Transfer Board (TTB) under (MTI) formulates policies, including a system of priorities which would promote an integrated approach to the developmental and regulatory roles of the Government in the field of technology transfer. All technology transfer arrangements are required to be registered with TTB.

The Product Standards Agency (PSA) under MTI was created to issue rules and implement regulations to carry out the metrication program of the Government.

The Ministry of Labor and Employment (MOLE) is the executive arm of the Government charged with implementation of labor policies and the enforcement of labor laws. Specifically, MOLE is charged with the promotion of industrial peace based on justice, protection of workers, and employment promotion and manpower development.

The Government, through EPZA, encourages and promotes foreign commerce as a means of making the Philippines a center of international trade. It was envisioned that through the establishment of export processing zones, the country's export trade and foreign position would be strengthened.

The National Pollution Control Commission (NPCC or PCC) was established to determine if pollution exists in any waters and/or atmosphere of the Philippines. The Commission issues permits for the installation or operation of sewage works and disposal systems of industrial firms.

The Philippine Patent Office (PPO) regulates the issuance of patents, register trademarks, trade names, and service marks. The Philippines is a member of the Paris Union for the Protection of Industrial Property.

Industrial Property and Copyright Protection

The Republic of the Philippines is a member of the "Paris Union" International Convention for the Protection of Industrial Property (patents and trademarks), to which the United States and about 80 other countries adhere. American nationals are therefore entitled to receive the same treatment under Philippine laws regarding the protection of patents, trademarks, and other industrial property rights as that country extends to its own citizens (national treatment). American nationals also are entitled to certain other benefits such as the protection of their patents against arbitrary forfeiture for nonworking and a year "right of priority" for their patent applications (i.e., 1 year after first filing a patent application in the United States in which to file a corresponding application in the Philippines and receive for the latter the benefits of the first U.S. application filing date). The "priority right" period for trademark application is 6 months.

The Philippine Republic also is a member of the "Berne Union" Copyright Convention. Although the United States is not a member of this Convention, U.S. authors may obtain automatic copyright protection for a work in Berne Union countries by publishing that work in a Union country at the time it is first published and copyrighted in the United States (simultaneous publication).

Patents for inventions are granted for 17 years from the date of grant. Inventions must be novel (i.e., not patented, used or published in the Philippines or abroad more than 1 year before the application) to be patented. Applications are examined for novelty; there is no prior publication or opposition period. The owner of a patent must work it within 3 years after its registration. A patent may be subject to compulsory license, if it is not properly worked for 3 years after its registration date.

Patent and trade name infringement inquiries should be directed to: Attorney Cesar C. San Diego, Acting Director, Philippine Patent Office, P.O. Box 296, Manila. His office is located at the 5th floor, Midland Buendia Bldg., 403 Buendia

Avenue Extension, Makati, Metro Manila. His telephone number is 8184145.

Licensing.—Technology transfer arrangements have to be filed with and approved by the Technology Transfer Board, an agency of MTI, to have legal effect and enable royalties to be remitted to the licensor. The agreement has a maximum term of 5 years and may be renewed. The royalty base is either related to net sales or local value added, and is usually 2 to 3 percent. An additional 2 percent based on net foreign exchange earnings is generally granted where the licensed products are exported by the licensee.

Trademarks.—Trademark registrations are valid for 20 years from the registration date and are renewable indefinitely for similar periods. The first user of a trademark is entitled to its proprietary rights. Registration confers prima facie evidence of legal ownership. Trademark applications are examined and, if satisfactory, published for a 30-day opposition period. A registered trademark must be used within its 5th, 10th, or 15th anniversary, otherwise it may be cancelled during these periods. Goods bearing counterfeiting marks may be seized by the customs authorities.

To prevent registration by unauthorized parties, U.S. firms should register their names and marks in the Philippines. Registration will also provide a stronger foundation for possible legal action against infringers.

The Philippines has a trademark classification system consisting of 52 classes of goods. Items not registered as trademarks are official state emblems, or the Red Cross emblem, or marks likely to be confused with one already registered and used in that country. Descriptive marks and surnames cannot be registered.

Copyrights.—Applications for copyrights are filed with the Philippines National Library. Infringement actions may be filed by proprietors; damages and injunction action, as well as criminal penalties, may be sought by the aggrieved party. Copyrights are granted for the life of the author plus 50 years after his death.

U.S. nationals may apply directly for copyright protection of their works in the Philippines under that countries copyright statute (Decree No. 49). But, the extent to which copyrights protection may be available for U.S. works under the law is rather uncertain. Since 1973, the Philippine National Library (PNL) has been authorized to grant to local publishers reprint rights to copyright scientific, cultural and educational works without permission of the copyright owner, domestic of foreign, if the PNL determines that the price level of such works is too high to make them readily accessible to the public. The copyright owner is entitled to collect a royalty on each copy sold by the reprinter, of 2 percent of the foreign list price of works published abroad, or 7 percent of local list price of works published in the Philippines.

Further information on the general provisions of the Philippines patent, trademark, and copyright laws may be obtained from the International Business Practices Division, Rm 1130, Office of Service Industries International Trade Administration, U.S. Department of Commerce.

Limitations on Business Activities of Foreigners

While foreign investment in the Philippines generally is encouraged, there are specific regulatory limitations in certain areas as to the scope of foreign business activity and participation. Hence, only Filipino citizens or corporations at least 60 percent Filipino owned may own land, develop natural resources, or operate public utilities. However, foreign oil exploration companies may enter into service agreements with local petroleum concessionaries with the prior approval of the Department of Industries or the Government, subject to the approval of the Petroleum Board. Other types of businesses require varying Filipino equity; finance companies require at least 60 percent Filipino ownership; commercial and private development banks require 70 percent; rural banks must be 100 percent Filipino owned.

Preference is given to Filipino citizens in the awarding of government contracts. Filipino and 75 percent Filipino-owned corporations are preferable to foreign bidders for the construction or repair of public works if their lowest bid does not exceed the lowest foreign bid by more than 15 percent. Government supply contracts must be awarded only to Filipino citizens or 60 percent Filipino-owned corporations or to citizens or corporations of countries that grant similar rights to Filipinos. Again domestic (i.e., Filipino or 75 percent Filipino-owned) bidders must be given supply contracts where the lowest foreign bid including customs duty, is over 2,000 pesos (roughly US$300) and the domestic bid does not exceed it by more than 15 percent. No foreign bid is allowed for construction or repair of buildings and structures for national defense.

Because of its vital importance to the national welfare and security, the interisland shipping industry also is reserved only to 75 percent Filipino-owned firms. While, under certain conditions, aliens may engage in the culture, production, milling, and processing of rice and corn, only 100 percent Filipino-owned firms may retail such cereals.

Similarly, the Retail Trade Nationalization Act prohibits aliens or companies not wholly owned by Philippine citizens from engaging directly or indirectly in retail trade. Individuals already involved in retail trade at the time the act was passed are allowed to continue until death or voluntary retirement from business. Also an exception is made for manufacturers or processors selling to industrial or commercial consumers who will use the goods to render service to the general public.

The Philippines Securities and Commission (SEC), in compliance with the provisions of the new Philippine corporation code has made it mandatory for all foreign corporations wanting to do business in the Philippines to submit a "Certificate of Reciprocity" in applying for a local license. The certification should be made under oath by authorized officials of the home state or country of origin of the corporation to the effect that the laws of such state or country permit reciprocal rights to Filipino corporations to do business there.

The Office of the Secretary of State in the state in the United States where the firm is incorporated generally provides these certificates to U.S. firms.

There are also certain restrictions which apply to foreign consultants operating in the Philippines. To provide consulting services, it is necessary for a foreign firm to have a Philippine partner.

Construction projects are generally reserved for Filipino firms except for those financed by multilateral lending institutions or awarded by the Philippine Government through international bidding. Also, their may be requirements to use local subcontractors, labor, and construction materials.

Taxation

Local corporations and resident foreign corporations are taxed at the rate of 25 percent of their annual net taxable income up to 100,000 pesos (approximately $10,989) and 35 percent of the annual net taxable income above that level. In addition, a 10 percent corporate development tax based on the entire net taxable income is charged if the corporation is "closely held." (See tax information sources in bibliography for definition.)

A nonresident corporation (i.e., one not engaged in trade or business in the Philippine) is subject to a flat rate of 35 percent on its gross income from Philippine sources. Individual citizens and resident aliens are taxed at graduated rates ranging from 1 percent to 35 percent on compensation income and 5 percent to 60 percent on business income. Nonresident alien individuals engaged in trade or business in the Philippines are taxed at the same rate on income from Philippine sources. Nonresident alien individuals who are not engaged in trade or business in the Philippines are subject to a flat rate of 30 percent on only their gross income derived from Philippine sources. A nonresident alien is deemed engaged in trade or business if he is in the Philippines for more than 180 days in any calendar year.

A flat 35 percent tax is charged on all profits remitted by consultants to their home-country.

An income treaty between the United States and the Philippines became effective on October 16, 1982. It adopts the usual foreign tax credit procedure as the basic method to avoid double taxation.

Labor Force

The Philippine population in 1981 was 49.7 million. Of this total, 17.5 million are in the workforce. With 600,000 new entrants each year, the average annual growth rate of the workforce is roughly 3.4 percent.

There is a surplus of unskilled and professional manpower in the Philippines. Furthermore, labor is literate and quick to acquire technical and mechanical skills. However, because of the relatively rapid buildup of industry, trained personnel are in short supply, and on-the-job training is normally required. The National Colleges Entrance Examination aims to channel a greater percent of high school graduates to technical courses thus meeting the need to fill blue collar jobs in the expanding industrial base of the economy.

Labor productivity, which is still low when compared with that in industrialized countries, is partially offset by much lower wage rates. Vocational and technical training schools, with Philippine Government, U.S. and United Nations aid, are raising standards and increasing the output of qualified personnel.

As in most other countries, the Philippines has a number of laws designed to ensure decent working and living conditions for laborers. Eight hours per day or 48 hours per week is the maximum period an employee may be required to work at a regular rate of pay. Additional hours of work must be paid at 125 percent the regular rate. This law is applicable to all workers except managerial employees, outside sales personnel, domestic help, those in the personal service of another, and workers who are members of their employer's family. Employers are required to furnish free emergency medical and dental supplies and treatment on a scale graduated according to the number of employees.

Effective March 22, 1981, the current legal effective daily minimum wages (legal minimum wage plus mandatory cost-of-living allowance plus daily portion of mandatory 13th month pay) range from 37.63 pesos ($4.14) for large establishments in Metro Manila to a low of 18.53 ($2.04) for agricultural workers employed by small firms. Minimum wages vary according to nonagricultural and agricultural firms, whether located in Metro Manila or outside Metro Manila, and capitalization of entrprise. The Department of Labor, however, may require higher wages than those in certain industries to maintain the employee's health and well-being. Most foreign companies in the Philippines pay wages substantially above the legal minimum. Workers on piecework basis are guaranteed wages not below the applicable minimum wage rates. The minimum wage law does not apply to farm tenants, domestic servants and persons working at home in needlework or in any cottage industry registered under the National Cottage Industry Act.

The right of labor to strike is guaranteed by the Industrial Peace Act. Until recently however, Presidential Decree No. 823, which was enacted in November, 1975, prohibited the staging of strikes and picketing in vital industries. A new law, known as National Assembly Bill 130, removed the ban on strikes in a long list of industries which had embraced virtually the entire economy.

The law provides for the right to strike or lockout in the private sector, except over issues involving inter-union or intra-union disputes. Thirty-day notice of strike or lockout must be filed in cases of collective bargaining impasses, and 15 days in case of an alleged unfair labor practice. The decision to strike must be approved by two-thirds of the members.

In granting the right to strike the new law removed the prior clearance employers had to obtain from Ministry of Labor and Employment before they could terminate an employee. Employers, however, must introduce due process procedures under which workers may appeal unfair dismissals. A provision of the Peaceful Picketing Law permits companies to freely take into and out of the company premises company products.

Several thousand Filipino workers are currently working abroad, many of them on construction projects. Firms interested in hiring Filipinos should contact the Filipino Overseas Employee Administration, 1130 Perez St., Paco, Manila.

Guidance for Business Travelers

Entrance Requirements

Foreign nationals desiring to enter the Philippines for business purposes can come under one of four nonimmigrant classifications:

1. They may enter as temporary visitors. A temporary visitor must have a round trip or through ticket. With this, they can get visas abroad at a Philippine embassy or consulate, or upon their arrival in the country by immigration authorities. In the latter case, the allowable period is 59 days. This may be extended for another 6-month period and then another 4-month period for a total duration of 1 year. The entry of "restricted aliens" requires the approval of the Philippine Commission on Immigration and Deportation.

2. The Government immigration policy allows the entry of foreign business people as special nonimmigrants. Foreign capitalists and stockbrokers investing in the Philippines are permitted to remain in the country under a semipermanent nonimmigrant status. In effect, the immigration policy allows an extension of the liberalized 72-hour no visa period of stay applicable to foreign investors coming into the country. A principal feature of this policy is the waiver of the requirements of finger-printing and deposit of cash bonds. Foreign businesspeople seeking this special privilege, however, must show satisfactory proof of their intention to make a substantial investment in the Philippines. Substantial investment should mean capital investment of not less than $100,000.

Foreign personnel of multinational companies that will establish their regional or area headquarters in the Philippines also are accorded this same entry privilege under certain conditions. Along with their dependents (their spouses and unmarried children under 21 years of age), foreign personnel of such headquarters may come into the country as nonimmigrants and shall be issued special multiple entry visas valid for 1 year and renewable.

3. Foreign businesspeople may be admitted under the prearranged employment status. Foreign technicians, however, are admitted on this basis only if they possess skills not available in the Philippines. Prearranged employment status en-

titles the visitor to stay for a period of 1 year. The stay may be renewed annually with the Commission on Immigration and Deportation. Foreign nationals to be employed by an enterprise inside the Bataan Export Processing Zone are allowed to reside in the Philippines for a period of 5 years on a nonimmigrant status.

4. Foreign businesspeople may be admitted into the Philippines under the provisions of an economic treaty. Thus, they are to carry on substantial trade principally between the Philippines and the foreign state of which they are nationals or to devlop and supervise the operations of an enterprise in which they have substantially invested. Under this treaty-trader or treaty investor classification, foreigners may stay for a period of 1 year, which again may be renewed annually.

Dependents of foreign businesspeople coming in as treaty-traders or investors, prearranged employees or special nonimmigrants also may enter the country. Multiple entry visas may be granted, but clearance must be obtained prior to each departure. (The electronics industry has been granted special treatment through issuance of multiple entry visas to foreign employees.)

The reentry of a single-entry visa holder necesitates the issuance prior to departure of a special reentry permit, which is valid for 6 months.

Every foreign national (unless otherwise exempted) entering the Philippines for a stay exceeding 59 days is required to pay a tax of 25 pesos at the time of entry. He also is required to register with the Commission on Immigration and Deportation. Upon payment of a 50 pesos fee, he is issued an Alien Certificate of Registration (ACR). Furthermore, he must report yearly to the Commission or, if residing outside Manila, to the office of the city or municipal treasurer to review his ACR and pay an annual fee of 10 pesos. The Commission must be notified of any change of address or status.

Foreign businesspeople entering as treaty-traders, treaty-investors, prearranged employees or as special nonimmigrants are generally required, along with their dependents, to undergo extensive medical examinations before departure for the Philippines. In addition, the usual vaccination record must be shown at the time of entry.

Foreign Exchange Regulations

The official monetary unit of the Philippines is the peso (100 centavos). Since February, 1970, the Central Bank has enforced the floating exchange rate system. In 1982, the exchange rate was 8.54 pesos to US$1. In 1983 it is expected to average about 9.44 pesos to US$1.

Foreign exchange receipts from exports and invisible sources may be converted freely into Philippine pesos at the market rate prevailing daily in the foreign exchange market. All foreign exchange must be sold to authorized agent banks within 3 business days after they are received. Likewise, all foreign exchange payments may be negotiated at the free market rate. Authorized agent banks may sell foreign exchange for imports and invisible disbursements. However, all importations valued at $100 or more must be covered by letters of credit. Exception is made for prequalified producers and importers under documents against acceptance (D/A) and open account arrangements (O/A).

In March 1973, the Central Bank issued rules and regulations (CB Circular 365) setting out the following guidelines for registration and repatriation of foreign investments:

1. Investments in export-oriented industries certified by the Central Bank may be repatriated in full or in annual installments to the extent of the applicant's share in net foreign exchange earnings of the firm for the preceding year.

2. Investments in BOI-registered enterprises engaged in the production of import-substitute and/or export items not covered by (1) above may be repatriated in three equal annual installments or to the extent of the total net foreign exchange earnings, whichever is less, starting 1 year after liquidation of investment.

3. Investments in BOI-registered enterprises not engaged in the production of import substitute items and in industries that did not use domestic credit resources may be repatriated in four equal annual installments starting 1 year after liquidation of investment.

4. Investments in all other industries may be repatriated according to the following schedules.

$250,000 or less	Five equal annual installments after liquidation of the investments
Over $250,000 to $500,000	Seven equal annual installments after liquidation of the investments
Over $500,000	Nine equal annual installments after liquidation of the investments

Between the sale of investments and actual repatriation, the proceeds of cash sales may be invested by the foreign investor in foreign currency deposits, government securities, and shares of stocks in BOI-registered or CB-certified export oriented industries, subject to the prior approval of any registration with the Central Bank. Earnings from these investments are net of taxes, fully remittable.

CB Circular 365 also prescribed the following rules for remittances of profits and dividends:

1. Remittances of profits and dividends accruing to non-residents out of net profits realized beginning January 1, 1973 and thereafter shall, net of taxes, be allowed in full at the prevailing exchange rate.

2. Remittances of retained profits and dividends which were earlier held because of a 25 percent limitation on nonresidents' equity participation shall be allowed, with prior Central Bank clearance, provided that such remittances will not be financed by domestic borrowings. These remittances may be staggered by the Central Bank over a period of 2 years, depending on the amounts involved.

3. Capital gains, profits, and dividends, net of taxes, if any realized by foreign investments made in Central Bank-approved Philippine securities listed in the local stock exchanges shall be paid in full at the prevailing rate of exchange.

Payment of royalty on or rentals of patents, trademarks, and copyrights may be allowed up to 50 percent thereof, provided that the gross roydoes not exceed 5 percent of the wholesale price of the commodity locally manufactured under the royalty contract. Remittance of royalties on reprints of textbooks approved by the Department of Education and of highly technical and scientific books may be allowed up to 15 percent of the wholesale price of such provided that the payment shall not exceed 50 percent of the royalties incurred during the year for which the remittance is made. However, if the reprinting contract confers the right to export reprinted books, the royalties may be paid in full provided that it does not exceed the net export proceeds.

Payment of the producer's share of earnings on motion picture films and rentals on television films imported without foreign exchange payments may be allowed up to 50 percent of the producer's share of the earnings or rentals.

Commercial Language

There are three official languages in the Philippines: English, Spanish, and Pilipino. However, English is widely spoken and is the major language used in the Philippine school system, as well as the usual language of commercial correspondence. In an attempt to develop a common language other than English, the Philippine Government has supported the creation of Pilipino, based on Tagalog, as a national language, and requires it to be taught in the schools.

Relatively few Filipinos any longer speak or use Spanish.

Business Hours/Holidays

Office hours for business firms and the Philippine Government normally are from 8 a.m. to 5 p.m., with 1 to 2 hours for lunch. It is best to attempt to accomplish business objectives in the morning or late afternoon. Many business deals are completed informally during meals or entertainment.

Offices are generally closed on Saturdays and Sundays and on the following public holidays: January 1, New Year's Day; Easter Holidays, which include Holy Thursday and Good Friday; May 1, Labor Day; June 12, Independence Day; July 4, Philippine-American Day; November 30, National Heroes' Day; December 25, Christmas; December 30, Rizal Day. In addition, special holidays such as General Election Day may be called by the President of the Republic.

Weather

The climate of the Philippines is generally tropical, with warm days, cool nights, and balmy sea breezes. January and February are usually considered the most pleasant months; they are warm, but not hot, with usually clear, bright skies. March, April, and May become warmer. June brings the end of the hot season and start of the rainy one, which last until into November. December, leading into the "best" months again, also is known for its moderate weather.

Sources of Economic and Commercial Information

U.S. Government Representation

American business visitors should contact the U.S. Foreign Commercial Service (FCS). FCS maintains an office in Makati, the heart of the Philippine business and financial center. The address is Second Floor, 395 Buendia Avenue Extension, Makati, Metro Manila, Phone 818-5482, Telex 7227366.

Visitors also might wish to contact the U.S. Embassy in Manila at 1201 Roxas Blvd., Phone 59-80-11. A consulate also is located in Cebu, Phone 31-51. Officers at the FCS Office, the Embassy, and the Consulate are available to brief and assist American business visitors.

Other U.S. agencies represented in the Philippines that are concerned with economic/commercial activities are the Agency for International Development (AID), Peace Corps, Department of Agriculture, Federal Aviation Agency, Maritime Administration, and the Treasury Department's Internal Revenue Service. U.S.I.A. has an active establishment in the Philippines.

Philippine Government Representation

The Philippine Government maintains an Embassy at 1617 Massachusetts Avenue, N.W., Washington D.C. 20036 open 9 to 12 a.m. and 2 to 5 p.m. Monday-Friday. It also maintains Commercial Attaches at its consular offices in New York City (15 East 66th St.); San Francisco (World Trade Center, Ferry Building); Los Angeles (448 South Hill St.); Seattle (1721 Smith Tower Building); New Orleans (International Trade Mart, 124 Camp St.); Chicago (Suite 1914, 201 North Wells St.); and Honolulu (2433 Pali Highway).

The recently established Philippine-U.S. Business Development Council plays a supportive role for the objectives of the Commercial Attaches. The headquarters of the Council is located at the Philippine Embassy in Washington D.C. There is also an office in the Philippines at 1201 J.P. Laurel St., San Miguel, Metro Manila. The Council plans to open offices in several U.S. cities.

Chambers of Commerce

The American Chamber of Commerce (ANCHAM) of the Philippines, with headquarters in the Corinthian Plaza Building, Paseo de Roxas Makati, Metro Manila is the principal private organization representing U.S. business interests in the Philippines. The Chamber was organized in 1920 and plays an active representational role. AMCHAM's Telex number is 45181 (Amcham PH) and its telephone number is 865-115.

In the United States, the Philippine American Chamber of Commerce—at 565 Fifth Avenue, New York, N.Y. 10017, telephone: (212) 972-9326—and the Philippine Association 501 Madison Avenue, New York, N.Y. 10022 are actively interested in Philipine economic and commercial matters and publish weekly news bulletins covering important Philipine political, economic, and commercial developments.

The leading private organization representing Philipine trade interests in the Philipines is the Philippine Chamber of Commerce and Industry (PCCI). Its address is CCP Building, Magallanes Dr., Intramuros.

Asian Development Bank

American business visitors to Manila who are interested in bidding on Asian Development Bank (ADB) projects should plan to visit the Office of U.S. Executive Director, 2330 Roxas Blvd., Pasay City (telephone 831-7251). The Executive Director's office can arrange meetings with ADB staff members and provide a general briefing on how to bid on ADB projects. Also, information kits on ADB procedures are available upon request (Telex 23103 ADB).

Philippine Government Publications

Annual Report, Central Bank of the Philippines.

Statistical Bulletin, Central Bank of the Philippines.

Philippine Financial Statistics, Central Bank of the Philippines.

Central Bank News Digest, Central Bank of the Philippines.

Foreign Trade Statistics of the Philippines," Bureau of the Census and Statistics.

The Philippine Economic Atlas, National Economic Council.

Bataan Export Processing Zone, Export Processing Zone Authority.

Questions and Answers on Foreign Investment in the Philippines, Board of Investments, P.O. Box 676, Makati, Metro-Manila.

Primer on the Establishment of Regional Headquarters in the Philippines, Bureau of Foreign Trade, Ministry of Industry and Trade Filcap ital Bldg., Ayala Ave., Makati, Metro Manila.

Other Philippine Publications

Doing Business in the Philipines; the SGV Group, Manila: or the SGV Washington Office on (202) 659-5722.

1,000 Largest Corporations, Business Day, Manila.

Bulletin Today (newspaper), Manila.

Fookien Times Yearbook, Fookien Times Co., Inc., Manila.

Weekly Economic Review, Philippine Association, Manila.

The Weekly Bulletin, Philippine American Chamber of Commerce", New York, N.Y.

The Journal of the American Chamber of Commerce of the Philippines, Manila.

Living in the Philippines, American Chamber of Commerce, Manila.

Industrial Philippines, Philippine Chamber of Industries, Manila.

Business Day (newspaper), Manila No. 72, Quezon City, Metro Manila.

U.S. *Private Publications*

Doing Business in the Philippine, Price-Waterhouse Inc.

Exporter's Encyclopedia, Dun and Bradstreet Inc.

Investing, Licensing and Trading Conditions Abroad, Business Internatonal Corp.

Taxation in the Philippines, Deloitte, Haskins and Sells, 1114 Avenue of the Americas, New York, N.Y. 10036.

Key Philippine Government Agencies

Ministry of Agriculture
MA Building
Diliman, Quezon City, Philippines
Tel. 99-87-41 to 54

Fertilizer and Pesticide Authority
6th Floor, Raha Solayman Bldg.
Benavidez St., Makati
Metro Manila, Philippines
Tel. 89-96-20

Philippine Coconut Authority
Don Mariano Marcos Avenue
Diliman, Quezon City, Philippines
Tel. 99-45-01

National Food Administration
(Previously National Grain Authority)
Matimyas Bldg.
E. Rodriguez Avenue
Quezon City, Philippines
Tel. 61-35-07

Ministry of Education and Culture
MEC Building
Arroceros St., Manila, Philippines
Tel. 40-47-44; 40-29-49

Educational Development Projects
Implementating Task Force (EDPITAF)
5th Floor, Marvin Plaza
2153 Pasong Tamo, Makati
Metro Manila, Philippines
Tel. 86-39-71 to 75

Ministry of Energy
7901 Petrophil Buildg.
Makati Avenue, Makati
Metro Manila, Philippines
Tel. 85-90-61 to 65

National Power Corporation (NPC)
Anda Circle Cor. Bonifacio Drive
Port Area, Manila, Philippines
Tel. 48-20-11; 47-21-41; 40-44-71

Philippine National Oil Company (PNOC)
7901 Petrophil Bldg.
Makati Avenue, Makati, Metro Manila
Philippines
Tel. 85-90-61

National Electrification Administration (NEA)
Capitol Building
Quezon Avenue, Quezon City
Philippines
Tel. 99-87-81 to 85

Bureau of Customs
Port Area, Manila
Tel. 48-41-61; 48-13-23; 47-17-07

Ministry of Health
San Lazaro Hospital Compound
Rizal Avenue, Manila, Philippines
Tel. 26-68-77; 21-80-16

Food and Drug Administration (FDA)
San Lazaro Hospital Compound
Rizal Avenue, Manila, Philippines
Tel. 21-25-44; 20-51-71

Ministry of Human Settlements &
Environmental Management
TRC Building
Buendia Avenue Extension
Makati, Metro Manila, Philippines
Tel. 85-98-11 to 26; 85-87-31 to 33

National Pollution Control Commission
772 Pedro Gil St. Cor. Taft Aven.
Ermita, Manila
Tel. 50-30-41

Technology Resource Center (TRC)
TRC Building
Buendia Ave. Ext., Makati
Metro Manila, Philippines
Tel. 85-87-31

Ministry of Industry
Industry & Investment Bldg.
385 Buendia Ave. Ext., Makati
Metro Manila, Philippines
Tel. 81-81-831

Board of Investments
Industry & Investment Bldg.
385 Buendia Ave. Ext., Makati
Metro Manila, Philippines
Tel. 81-81-831

Export Processing Zone Authority
4th Floor, Legaspi Tower 300
Vito Cruz Cor. Roxas Blvd.
Manila, Philippines
Tel. 57-40-21

Ministry of Labor
MOL Bldg.
Gen. Luna Cor. Muralla St.
Intramuros, Manila
Tel. 48-48-52; 47-02-64; 49-47-22

Ministry of National Defense
Camp Aguinaldo, Quezon City, Philippines
Tel. 78-69-11; 78-29-61; 78-29-71

Armed Forces of the Philippines
Deputy Chief of Staff for Logistics
General Headquarters
Camp Aguinaldo, Quezon City, Philippines

National Economic & Development Authority
(NEDA)
Padre Faura St.
Ermita, Manila, Philippines
Tel. 50-39-71

National Development Company (NDC)
2nd Floor, National Steel Corp. Bldg.
377 Buendia Ave. Ext., Makati
Metro Manila, Philippines
Tel. 85-27-58

Ministry of Natural Resources
Visayas Avenue, Diliman, Quezon City, Philipines
Tel. 97-66-26

Ministry of Public Highways
2nd St., Port Area, Manila, Philippines
Tel. 40-83-71

Ministry of Public Works
MPW Bldg.
Bonifacio Drive, Port Area
Manila, Philippines
Tel. 47-57-38; 40-13-08

National Irrigation Administration (NIA)
NIA Building
National Government Center
Quezon City, Philippines
Tel. 96-10-21; 96-45-10

Philippine Ports Authority (PPA)
South Harbor
Manila, Philippines
Tel. 47-34-41

Ministry of Industry and Trade
Yupangco Building
Buendia Ave. Ext.
Makati, Metro Manila, Philippines
Tel. 89-38-09; 89-46-42

Philippine Patent Office
Quezon City Development Bank Bldg.
Quezon Avenue, Quezon City, Philippines
Tel. 99-41-78

Ministry of Transportation & Communication
PhiliComCen Bldg.
Ortigas Ave., Pasig, Metro Manila, Philippines
Tel. 79-55-77

Central Bank of the Philippines (CB)
A. Mabini St. Cor. Vito Cruz St.
Manila, Philippines
Tel. 50-70-51

Securities & Exchange Commission (SEC)
7th Floor, SEC Building
EDSA, Greenhills, Mandaluyong
Metro Manila, Philippines
Tel. 79-84-92; 70-68-93

Metropolitan Waterworks & Sewerage System
(MWSS)
176 Arroceros St.
MWSS Building
Manila, Philippines
Tel. 49-23-77; 40-78-87

Market Profile—PHILIPPINES

Economic Overview

The demand for U.S. products increased 5 percent in 1982 despite a general slowdown in the Philippine economy. The Philippine Government is developing alternative energy resources and revitalizing basic industries in order to reduce dependence on imported oil. The Philippines experienced a trade deficit of $2.6 billion in 1982, with inflation of about 10 percent. These trends are expected to continue through 1983.

Major Developments

Major projects include a copper smelter, an integrated steel mill, a phosphatic fertilizer complex, a diesel engine manufacturing plant, the development of heavy metalworking industries, conversion to coal in mining and cement sectors, coconut industry downstream processing, manufacture of alcogas and a pulp and paper mill. Principal goals of the Philipine Development Plan (1983-87) are to sustain economic growth, distribute equitably the fruits of development, and achieve total human development.

Foreign Trade

Best U.S. Sales Prospects. — Textile machinery; security and safety equipment; computers and peripherals; energy conservation and generation equipment; metal working equipment; food processing and packaging equipment; construction equipment; instrumentation for medical, scientific, and laboratory purposes; chemicals; and cereals.
Major Suppliers (1981). — United States (22 percent) and Japan (22 percent).
Principal Exports. — Electronic components, sugar, coconut oil, copper concentrates, logs, lumber, copra, clothing, cement, and textiles.
Major Markets. — United States (30.8 percent) Japan (23.9 percent).

Finance

Currency. — Peso depreciated gradually from 7.59 to 8.2 (almost 8 percent) during 1981, expected to continue through rest of 1982. Rate as of December 1982, 9 Pesos=US$1.
Domestic Credit. — Prime rate about 16 percent. External debt reached an estimated $16 billion at the end of 1982.
National Budget. — $6.4 billion in 1983. Projected 1983 deficit is 2.3 percent of GNP.
Balance of Payments. — International reserves totaled $2.5 billion at the end of 1982.
  The 1982 current account deficit was $2.8 billion and the 1983 figure is forecast to be slightly less. The 1982 balance-of-payments deficit was $900 million.

Foreign Investment

The Philippine Government (GOP) is in the process of establishing a new investment incentive program in the light of an IBRD-sponsored industrial restructuring program. The new incentives, which will encompass many aspects of investment and development, will be administered in a manner more simplified and consistent with proposed projects. U.S. direct investment exceeded $1.3 billion (book value) in Dec. 1981.

Basic Economic Facilities

Transportation. — Inadequate land transport facilities include about 750 miles of railroads, mainly in Luzon, and 40,000 miles of roads, largely unpaved. Coastal shipping provides interisland service; domestic airlines serve major cities. Regular international air and sea services.

Import—Export Trades*
(millions of U.S. dollars)

	1979	1980	1981
Total Imports (c.i.f.)	6.142	7,726	7,946
Imports from the U.S.	1.400	1,785	1,744
Manufactured goods	999	1.253	1,744
Agricultural goods	1.392	2.235	N/A
Other	3.751	4.258	N/A
Total Exports (f.o.b.)	4.601	5.788	5,722
Exports to the U.S.	1.372	1.576	1,907
Manufactured goods	N/A	N/A	N/A
Agricultural goods	N/A	N/A	N/A
Other	N/A	N/A	N/A

*Philippine data.

Principal Imports from the U.S. in 1981*
(millions of dollars)

	Value	Percent of Total
Electrical machinery	388.5	22.2
Grains	187.7	10.7
Boilers, engines	65.1	3.7
Aircraft and space craft	62.5	3.5
Motor vehicles	57.2	3.2
General machinery	42.9	2.4
Elevators, winches	41.4	2.3
Synthetic resins	40.3	2.3
Fertilizers	39.4	2.2
Boilers, engines (other)	45.9	2.0

*U.S. data.

Communications. — Telephone service extends to all principal islands. Radio network serves entire Philippines. Television stations in major population centers; participation in international satellite network.
Power. — Electric power production in the Philippines is barely adequate to meet the nation's development needs, but should improve under the 5-year energy plan. Electric power is supplied in Manila on a 110/220 volt 60 cycle AC basis.

Natural Resources

Land. — 7,100 islands comprising 115,707 square miles. Climate, tropical with generally abundant rainfall. Agriculture 29 percent of GDP in 1980.
Minerals. — Coper, nickel, iron, petroleum, and smaller deposits of gold, silver, coal, and others.
Forestry. — Hardwood forests being rapidly depleted.
Fisheries. — Account for 5 percent of GNP. Domestic fishing industry has remained undeveloped; GOP will modernize fishing, storage, processing, and marketing facilities.

Population

Size. — 49.4 million in 1981. Annual growth rate 2.5 percent, mostly Malay or Chinese. 83 percent Catholic.
Labor Force. — Estimated 17.5 million, 1981. Agriculture 47, percent industry and commerce 20 percent, services 13.5 percent.
Education. — Literacy rate about 88 percent; 95 percent attendance for compulsory 6 years elementary school.
Language. — English, Spanish, and Pilipino. English is widely used and is the language of commercial correspondence.

Marketing In and Trading With Poland

Contents

Report Revised September 1978

Introduction

U.S. commercial relations with Poland have expanded vigorously in the 1970's. Bilateral trade has grown from $168 million in 1970 to a high of $940 million in 1976. The range of products traded has become more diversified and American companies have won contracts for a number of major turnkey projects. Several ventures for cooperation in production and sales of machinery also have developed successfully in the last several years. The number of American companies trading regularly with Poland has grown substantially and 20 have developed business warranting the establishment of company offices in Warsaw.

U.S.-Polish trade developed gradually, but steadily, throughout the 1960's following the extension of nondiscriminatory tariff treatment (Most-Favored-Nation status) to Poland in 1960. Developments in the early 1970's, especially the general improvement in East-West relations and the new directions taken by the Polish economy, created a favorable climate for bilateral efforts to diminish obstacles and facilitate trade. The visits of three American Presidents to Poland (Nixon—1972; Ford—1975; Carter—1977) and that of Polish First Party Secretary Gierek to the United States (1974), as well as the numerous meetings of other high-level government officials stimulated important initiatives in bilateral commercial relations.

The creation of the Joint American-Polish Trade Commission in 1972 was followed rapidly by the extension of Export-Import Bank credits to Poland, creation of the U.S. Trade Development Center in Warsaw, negotiation of improved business facilities for the firms of both countries including the establishment of company offices, and exchanges of letters concerning arbitration of commercial disputes and port access. The Joint Statement on Economic, Industrial, and Technical Cooperation and the Joint Statement on Agricultural Cooperation, as well as the agreements for the joint funding of research and for cooperation in coal research, environmental protection, health, and housing signed during the October 1974 visit of First Secretary Gierek to the United States

set new goals and commitments for trade expansion and economic cooperation. A firm foundation for commercial relations has been laid through agreements for textile trade, bilateral airworthiness certification, fisheries, avoidance of double taxation, and civil aviation. Bilateral discussions continue, through the Joint Trade Commission, concerning ways to facilitate industrial cooperation, greater availability of commercial information, participation by small- and medium-sized firms in U.S.-Polish trade, and business operating conditions.

Contacts between industrial decision-makers of the two countries have been encouraged through the formation of the Polish-U.S. Economic Council. The Council, which is under the aegis of the Chamber of Commerce of the United States and the Polish Chamber of Foreign Trade, brings together annually more than 50 senior executives of each country for a discussion of business trends and practical ways in which U.S.-Polish trade can expand.

BACKGROUND INFORMATION ABOUT THESE COUNTRIES

For those who wish *general* data about a country—data which goes beyond marketing and commerce—the editors recommend *Countries of the World and Their Leaders,* published as an annually updated yearbook by Gale Research Company, Detroit, Michigan 48226. Containing 4- to 20-page entries on 168 countries, the volume also provides several hundred pages of supplementary world data. Each report provides some historical insight as well as a look at contemporary trends of lifestyle in the country. Reports also discuss a country's educational system, its press, ethnic groupings and religious practices.

These developments have created a favorable climate for trade and economic cooperation. This publication is designed as a basic guide for U.S. companies interested in trading and investing in Poland.

Market Scope

The Economy

In both area (312,354 km²) and population (35 million), Poland is the largest country in Eastern Europe and seventh largest in Europe. Its 1977 Gross National Product (GNP) of $95 billion ranked eighth in Europe and second after the Soviet Union within CMEA. On a per capita basis, however, which was $2,743, this placed Poland behind Czechoslovakia and the German Democratic Republic (GDR) and on a par with Spain and Greece. Of the 17.2 million labor force, 26 percent are employed in industry and 38 percent in agriculture.

Organization.—Poland's economy is centrally planned and controlled, with the state-owned sector dominating the economy. All the great industrial and construction enterprises, transportation and communication, domestic trade, foreign commerce, and banking are directly controlled and administered by the Government. In 1977, it produced more than 75 percent of the national income. The cooperative sector operates some industrial, handicraft, construction, service and agricultural enterprises. The State closely directs and supervises the cooperatives. The private sector predominates in agriculture and operates in a very limited degree in artisan, service, and construction activities. This sector is indirectly controlled through regulation, taxation, and pricing.

Central planning is exercised through 5-year and annual plans which determine the rate of growth, the level and direction of investment, sectoral priorities, and social benefits. For basic raw materials and industrial consumables, such as coal, steel, copper, and grains, the plan specifies production, export, and import targets in physical units as well as in the value terms that are used for all sectors and branches of the economy. Targets also are set for employment, productivity, investment, wages, real income, consumption, and national income.

These plans are prepared by the Planning Commission of the Council of Ministers on the basis of past performance, current needs, and available resources. Their execution is assigned to the ministries that oversee production units: the ministries for the Chemical Industry, Food Industry and Purchase, Forestry and Timber Industry, Heavy and Agricultural Machine Industry, Light Industry, Machine Engineering Industry, Metallurgy, Mining, Power and Atomic Energy.

The main job of assigning goals and directives to individual enterprises and allocating funds within particular branches of industry rests with the industrial associations. Each of the approximately 175 associations are groups of enterprises engaged in similar lines of production, e.g. textile machinery, mining machinery, optical and medical equipment, inorganic chemicals, etc. Most industrial associations also include a research and design institute and sometimes also a foreign trade organization.

"Large economic organizations" (abbreviated in Polish as "WOG") have been created in the

Table 1.—Growth of the Polish Economy

(Annual growth rates in percent)

	Average 1971-75	Plan Average 1976-80	Actual 1976	Actual 1977	Plan 1978
Net Material Product	10.0	7.1	7.5	5.6	5.4
Industrial Output	10.3	8.3	10.7	8.6	6.3
Agricultural Output	3.7	3.3	−0.7	0.8	6.0
Capital Investment	21.5	7.4	5.8	2.5	n.a.
Average Real Wages	7.0	3.0	3.8	2.3	1.8
Total Exports	10.7	11.8	7.5	11.3	10.3
Total Imports	15.3	4.7	10.8	5.4	3.9

Source: Central Statistical Office of Poland.

Table 2.—Profile of Polish Industry

(Percent of total industry in 1977)

	Gross Output	Employment	Fixed Capital*	Share of Investments*	Exports	Imports
Electric	2.4	2.1	11.8	8.1	16.4	11.0
Fuels	5.9	8.8	13.1	10.7		
Ferrous Metallurgy	6.1	3.9	7.4	13.1	6.0	13.2
Non-ferrous Metallurgy	3.7	1.5	3.3	5.2		
Machinery	33.3	33.4	23.1	24.6	46.2	41.3
Chemicals	9.6	6.7	11.3	11.4	8.6	11.4
Construction materials	3.7	6.1	6.5	6.2		
Wood processing, paper	5.2	5.9	4.2	4.8	2.3	2.2
Textiles, clothing, leather	12.3	17.2	7.1	5.3	9.0	4.5
Food Processing	15.0	10.8	11.1	9.0	6.7	5.5
Other	2.8	3.6	1.1	1.6		

* 1976.

1970's on an experimental basis as part of an effort to stimulate managerial initiative and move to more sophisticated and less direct command of the economy. Managers of the WOGs— which may be an industrial association, combine, or multi-plant enterprise — exercise greater control over plant organization, wages, employment, and investment from their own funds or credits than do other units. Their performance is judged on the basis of added production (value added) and profit.

While the majority of major investment projects, and certainly all the important ones, are covered by the plan, the concept of an "open plan" and "self-financing investment" has been experimented with in recent years. Under this principle, investments which are desirable but couldn't be included in the plan can be undertaken if the foreign credit needed for imported capital equipment can be repaid within a given period of time through export earnings generated by the new production. In some cases, the self-financing scheme also has had to cover local costs out of foreign credits. During 1971– 75, investment projects carried out under the self-financing basis accounted for just under 5 percent of total investment outlays. There are indications that the self-repaying principle has been extended recently to some planned investments requiring hard currency imports in order to control the growth of hard currency debt. These have been approved on the condition that there be no net outflow of hard currency in any year of the investment project.

Resources.—Poland is one of the world's leading producers of coal and is continuing large investments in developing new and modernizing old mines. Development of its copper ore fields promises to give Poland world rank in this resource also. Other important mineral resources include zinc, lead, and salt. Poland, in turn, depends heavily on imports of crude oil, iron ore, aluminum oxide, phosphates, apatite, and potash.

Industry.—Machine building ranks first within Poland's diversified industrial sector, accounting for 33 percent of total industrial output in 1977. Its wide variety of products includes railroad locomotives and cars, ships, automotive equipment, generators, electronic equipment, mining machinery, construction equipment, and machine tools. In spite of the heavy investments, rapid growth, and increasing export capability in this industry, Poland

continues to depend heavily on imports of machinery. Output of the chemical industry has increased with heavy investment in the 1970's, and in 1977 accounted for 9.6 percent of total industrial output. Recent emphasis has been on increased production of nitrogen and phosphorous fertilizers, and on the development of a large-scale petrochemical industry to provide the basis for increased output of plastics, synthetic fibers, and synthetic rubber.

Poland's iron and steel industry is the 10th largest in the world and its copper industry is slated to become a leading world producer. Both have been receiving substantial investments and infusion of foreign technology in the 1970's. Investment and output in Poland's traditional industries such as food processing and textiles have picked up in the 1970's and these industries are important earners of hard currency.

Poland has rapidly developed a major fishing capability and currently produces one-fifth of the world's fishing vessels. Its own fishing fleet of 342,300 gross registered tons netted 668,500 tons of fish in coastal and deep sea fishing in 1977. Seeking to adapt to new worldwide fishing conditions, Poland's fishing industry has shown interest in assisting third world countries in development of their own industry and also in joint ventures elsewhere.

Agriculture.—Poland is distinguished among the Communist economies by the continuation of private farming which in 1977 accounted for 78 percent of total agricultural production. Although Poland is a world-ranking producer of rye, potatoes, oats, sugar beets, and milk, farm output is not large enough to meet the rapidly growing domestic demand for food. In recent years Poland has had to rely on imports of grain to meet its planned growth in livestock production and human consumption. Although food products, especially meat, provide a substantial proportion of Poland's hard currency earnings, Poland has become a net food importer in the last several years.

Development.—Poland's economy has grown dynamically during the 1970's. Under the two-pronged economic development strategy launched in 1971, both the industrial and consumer sectors have received sizeable investments and registered rapid growth. The average growth rate of GNP, as calculated by Western experts, was 7.4 percent annually during 1971–75, and industrial production grew at an annual rate of more than 10 percent. Investment grew by more than 20 percent annually and the share of Gross Domestic Product (GDP) devoted to investment rose to a high of 35 percent in 1975. Real wages increased by 40 percent during that 5-year period.

The rapid expansion of the early 1970's was accompanied by higher-than-planned growth of investments, imports, and wages which placed a strain on the resources of the economy. Demand exceeded supply for both industrial and consumer goods, and overburdened the transport and power infrastructure. Inclement weather and poor harvests in 1974 and 1975 lowered agricultural production, turned around the livestock expansion effort, and forced large imports of grain. World inflation of raw material prices and slower demand for Polish exports induced by the recession in the West resulted in growing trade deficits and hard currency debt. Late in 1976, a "new economic maneuver" was launched with revision of the key points of the 1976–80 economic plan.

On the investment front, slower growth and redirection were ordered until the end of the decade. Investment's share in the national income has been pared back from a third of the Gross Domestic Product in 1975 to a quarter in 1977 and 1978. At the same time, funds are being redirected from the construction of new facilities to the modernization of existing plant and completion of projects already begun. Greater resources also have been allocated to industries producing for the home market and for export, while investment in capital goods production is being carefully controlled. The agricultural, food processing, and housing construction sectors are to receive 42 percent of all the capital outlays during the 1976-80 period. Greater central control of wage funds has been instituted and real wages are to grow by an annual average of 3.4 percent during the entire plan period. Under the new economic policies, the services sector is expected to double during 1976-80, and consumer goods availability is to increase faster than income.

Foreign Trade Policy

Foreign trade has played an important role in the rapid modernization pursued in Poland in the 1970's. Complete industrial installations, discrete production lines, and selected technologies were imported for all the major industrial sectors, especially the metallurgical, automotive, chemical, electronics, and engineering industries. Selected consumer-oriented industries such as textiles and food processing also benefited from foreign equipment. Imports of raw materials, semimanufactures, and components to supply these new installations also rose sharply. Purchases of feed grains and other agricultural products also rose in order to support rapid growth of livestock and improve consumption patterns. Thus, Poland's total trade grew from $8 billion in 1971 to $27.2 billion in 1977. Average annual growth of imports during 1971-75 was 15.3 percent and export growth was 10.7 percent.

The fastest growing sector in foreign trade has been the electro-engineering industry. By 1977, this sector provided 46 percent of Poland's exports and absorbed 42 percent of its imports. In the 1976-80 period, electro-engineering exports are slated to increase by 98 percent, considerably more than exports in general, and its imports should be up by some 28 percent.

The import-oriented modernization strategy has been carried out by a conscious recourse to trade deficits and foreign credits. Repayment of loans is to come from the increased production and exports made possible by the imported plant and equipment. As a consequence, the export-generating potential of imports receives particular consideration in purchasing decisions.

Under this policy, Poland's trade with the industrialized West, including the United States, has grown even more rapidly than its trade in general. Trade turnover with these countries increased from $2.25 billion in 1971 to $10.1 billion in 1976. However, this trade development was imbalanced, with imports growing twice as fast as exports. Imports from the West grew particularly rapidly, increasing from $1.1 billion to $6.7 billion between 1971 and 1976. Poland imported almost $10 billion in machinery and equipment alone from the West between 1970 and 1976. Polish exports to the West did not grow apace, increasing from $1.1 billion in 1971 to only $3.4 billion in 1976. Trade deficits of $2-3 billion were thus incurred in each of the last 4 years, resulting in a total hard currency debt, according to most estimates, of $13 billion at the end of 1977.

Along with the growth in trade, there has been an increasing emphasis on long-term industrial cooperation projects by which Polish industry is linked with Western firms in production and marketing of manufactured goods. The importance which has been attached to cooperation arrangements epitomizes the commitment of contemporary Poland to a continuing and increasing involvement in international trade and commerce with the West.

Current Trends.—While the thrust of this trade-led development policy remains intact, immediate plans call for slower import growth and rapid expansion of exports. The revised 1976-80 plan sets imports to grow only 26 percent over the period, but slates exports to expand by 75 percent. An even sharper contrast is planned for trade with the industrialized West.

In 1977, overall Polish imports grew 5.5 percent and exports 11.4 percent, but in trade with the industrialized West, imports declined 4.5 percent at the same time that exports increased by 9.9 percent. For 1978, the annual plan calls for foreign trade to show a 9.9 percent increase in total exports, while imports move up by 4.2 percent. The trend of 1977 has accelerated during the first 6 months of 1978, as Poland's exports to the West increased 10 percent over the same period of the preceding year, while imports declined by 10 percent.

Imports can be expected to be sluggish through the end of the decade as the Polish economy strives to achieve a balance in its hard currency trade. Administrative procedures for the allocation of hard currency, even for priority imports, and for the issuance of import licenses to Polish buyers are being tightened. The ability to import has been tied closely to exports. Individual ministries, and to some extent individual industrial associations and foreign trade enterprises, now operate under annual trade balances which require that a planned ratio of exports to imports be maintained. Failure to achieve export targets can result in decreased import capability. Thus, suppliers can expect to be under pressure for more liberal credit terms, longer deferred payments, more countertrade, and cooperation arrangements which minimize expenditures of hard currency.

Prospects for U.S. Exports

U.S. exports to Poland in 1977 totaled $437 million, of which manufactured goods comprised $118 million. Both figures were down from peaks of $621 million (1976) and $181 million (1975), respectively, reflecting Polish reductions in investment and imports of capital equipment.

Although total U.S. exports to Poland, other than agricultural products, are not expected to increase substantially over the next 2 years, specific sales opportunities should continue for suppliers to priority sectors, such as agricultural equipment and chemicals, food processing and packaging, and production of building materials and furniture. Equipment for mining and metallurgy, feedstocks for successful export-oriented industries, and equipment for the wood, pulp, and paper industries also will be in demand. Equipment and processes for improving production efficiency, particularly through conservation of energy and materials, should enjoy sales chances. Export opportunities can be expected to open up after 1980 as deferred projects and modernization plans are picked up again.

Table 3. Poland's Foreign Trade By Area

(in millions of Dollars)

	1973	1974	1975	1976	1977
Total Exports	6,432	8,321	10,289	11,024	12,274
To Communist countries	3,903	4,638	6,116	6,582	8,100
To Non-communist developed countries ..	2,063	2,865	3,059	3,420	4,400
To Less developed countries	466	818	1,064	1,022	1,050
Total Imports	7,862	10,489	12,545	13,853	15,400
From Communist countries	4,062	4,659	5,749	6,478	8,300
From Non-communist developed countries ..	3,431	5,233	6,096	6,738	6,300
From Less developed countries	369	597	700	637	800

Source: *Rocznik Statystyczny Handlu Zagranicznego.*

Table 4.—U.S.-Polish Trade

(in millions of Dollars)

	1974	1975	1976	1977
U.S. Exports	394.6	580.1	621.1	436.5
Manufactured goods (SITC nos. 5-8)	131.7	180.5	127.8	114.3
Agricultural goods	253.3	367.7	481.3	293.0
Other	9.6	31.8	12.0	29.2
U.S. Imports	265.9	243.1	318.8	329.0
Manufactured goods (SITC nos. 5-8)	168.3	113.4	153.4	172.1
Agricultural commodities	88.4	120.0	144.7	126.6
Other	9.2	9.7	20.7	30.3

Source: U.S. Department of Commerce.

Table 5.—Major U.S. Exports To and Imports From Poland in 1977

(in millions of dollars)

	value	% of total
Exports		
Corn, wheat, grains, sorghums	198.8	46
Soybean oil, cake, meal	41.3	9
Phosphate hard rock and land pebbles ...	21.2	5
Rolling mills, presses machines and equipment for metals industry	14.7	3
Cattle hides, sheep/lamb skins	13.6	3
Tracklaying tractors	12.9	3
Tobacco and cigarettes	11.0	3
Glass working machines	9.6	2
Apparatus for treating materials with changing temperature	8.5	2
Food production and processing equipment	3.5	1
Imports		
Canned hams and other pork products	107.7	33
Clothing	35.8	11
Steel plates and flat bars	18.8	6
Machinery and machine tools	16.2	5
Wire, iron and steel nails, screws, bolts ...	15.1	5
Leather footwear	13.6	4
Various woven fabrics	12.1	4
Frozen cod, whiting, pollock, turbot and other fish	11.1	3
Gasoline	9.9	3
Organic chemicals	9.0	3
Bituminous and lignite coal	7.9	2

Source: U.S. Department of Commerce.

Considerable interest exists in Poland in the development of industrial cooperation ventures with U.S. firms. These ventures involve ongoing exchange of technology, co-production, and joint marketing efforts between the Polish and U.S. firms. A dozen such U.S.-Polish ventures already are in existence covering such products as earthmoving and heavy construction equipment, sewing machines, and light aircraft. Negotiations for some 18 new industrial cooperation projects between U.S. and Polish firms are currently being conducted. Lists of additional areas for cooperation of interest to Polish firms are periodically submitted through the Joint American-Polish Trade Commission.

Foreign Trade Structure

A number of different types of economic organizations are involved in foreign trade in Poland, and in the process of conducting a transaction, American firms will deal with at least one and possibly several. Although the foreign trade organizations (FTOs) are the main point of contact for foreign traders, access to other Polish organizations is relatively easy.

Ministry of Foreign Trade and Maritime Economy

Foreign trade is a state monopoly administered by the Ministry of Foreign Trade and Maritime Economy. The Ministry formulates the country's foreign trade policy and coordinates the work of all institutions engaged in foreign trade. It also oversees maritime matters such as shipping, seaports, maritime services sea fishing, and maritime administration. The Ministry of Foreign Trade's responsibilities include:

—Drafting the annual and long-term foreign trade plans;

—Allocating foreign exchange resources and setting the import, export, and foreign trade balance targets for its own sub-units and for other ministries having units authorized to engage in foreign trade;

—Defining customs and foreign trade credit policies;

—Issuing export and import licenses;

—Establishing principles governing foreign trade prices and supervising their implementation;

—Negotiating and concluding trade and cooperation agreements with foreign countries;

—Directing, supervising, and coordinating commercial representatives and enterprises abroad;

—Authorizing foreign firms to establish commercial and technical offices in Poland;

—Conducting joint commissions with foreign countries.

The Ministry is directed by the Minister of Foreign Trade and Maritime Economy, who is assisted by a number of deputy ministers. The Ministry is organized into departments which have operational, functional, or geographic responsibility. Depending on the nature and size of the commercial transactions, American companies may need to have contact with the following departments: Trade Policy Department III (Industrialized Western Countries) which includes officials responsible for U.S.-Polish trade; Department of Machinery Trade and Cooperation (industrial cooperation agreements); and Department of Management (concerning company offices in Poland). Each Department is headed by a director.

The address is:

Ministry of Foreign Trade and Maritime Economy
ul. Wiejska 10
00-489 Warszawa, Poland
Telephone: 21-03

Other Ministries and Commissions

Ministries and commissions other than the Ministry of Foreign Trade also are involved in foreign trade decisions.

The Planning Commission of the Council of Ministers establishes general guidelines for the development of the economy as a whole and its particular sectors, and the general direction of foreign trade development. Its authorization is required for purchase of major capital investment projects from abroad. Given the need for tight control on new investments and on imports from the West, at least through 1980, the Planning Commission has assumed an even greater role in determining which projects will take place, and on what terms.

The Ministry of Finance directs the allocation of financial resources. Since January, 1977, the Government has attempted to assure that new industrial projects will not result in a net outflow of hard currency in any year over the life of the project. This approach has increased the importance of the Ministry of Finance in the negotiation of large projects.

The individual economic ministries, such as those for the engineering or light industries, set the guidelines for investment, export and import targets, and operating principles for the industrial associations, large economic organizations (WOGs), and foreign trade organizations under their jurisdiction. Most of these ministries have a department for economic cooperation with foreign countries which coordinates trade and industrial cooperation with foreign companies. In the case of major projects, the department of investment and appropriate vice ministers may be involved in foreign commercial decisions.

Foreign Trade Organizations

Only Foreign Trade Organizations (FTOs) are authorized to negotiate and sign contracts with foreign firms. Their role is that of intermediary between foreign suppliers or buyers and Polish firms, negotiating according to the instructions and guidelines of the responsible ministry and industrial association. The FTO itself is responsible for evaluating a proposal's commercial features—price, buyback, guarantees, etc. The technical evaluation of a product or proposal usually is performed by the end-user, generally through the industrial association's research and design office.

There is normally little choice of the FTO with which a company will deal, as the FTOs specialize in given lines of goods and services. As a rule, the FTOs seek competitive bids on sales offers, and in the case of major contracts are required to receive at least three bids.

The FTOs operate within the framework of the overall foreign trade plan. Since January 1, 1976, the FTOs operate under plans which focus on the particular FTO's balance, in value terms, between imports and exports, and their ability to import is related to their export achievements. This increases the importance which FTOs attach to offset purchases by their suppliers.

There are 49 enterprises and offices entitled to engage in foreign trade in Poland, of which 18 are directly subordinated to the Ministry of Foreign Trade and Maritime Economy. The remaining enterprises are supervised by industrial ministries, cooperatives, or large economic organizations (WOGs). There are also specialized enterprises rendering services in advertising, organization of trade exhibits, transport, forwarding, cargo inspection, inspection, and tourism. The Foreign Trade Organizations are listed in Appendix A.

Banks

Three banks are authorized to deal in foreign exchange.

The Bank Handlowy w Warszawie (The Foreign Trade Bank) is most directly involved in foreign trade activities. It supervises, handles, and finances the banking operations of Polish foreign trade organizations. Handlowy negotiates financing for most imports of industrial equipment. Polish FTOs sometimes make a purchase contract contingent on Handlowy's securing "competitive financing" from the United

States. Handlowly usually negotiates directly with U.S. banks, including the Export-Import Bank, in this regard. Handlowy's general functions include the financing and crediting of the operating and investment activities of the foreign trade organizations; the settlement of accounts in foreign trade turnover and foreign trade services; and the granting of foreign exchange credits to units of the socialized sector. The Bank also is authorized to grant and receive foreign credit to secure loans and accept warrants in foreign trade, and to carry out foreign currency operations. The address is:

Bank Handlowy w Warszawie, S.A.
ul. Traugutta 7
00-950 Warsaw
Telephone: 26-92-11 to 15
Telex: 814811

The Narodowy Bank Polski (National Bank of Poland) is the bank of issue and the central credit, savings, clearing, and foreign exchange bank. It regulates the circulation of currency, participates in drafting economic plans, fixes foreign exchange rates, supervises foreign currency transactions of other banks and institutions, and extends credits to Polish enterprises.

Bank Polska Kasa Opieki, S.A. (Bank PKO, Ltd.) renders foreign exchange services to the population. It carries interest-bearing foreign currency accounts for Polish citizens as well as foreigners; purchases foreign exchange checks and settles accounts with foreign countries for old-age and disability pensions, inheritances, gifts, and other transfers in favor of Polish citizens. The Bank PKO, Ltd. also accepts payments in convertible currencies for commodities being sold within the framework of the so-called "internal exports."

Decisionmaking Process

Purchasing of turnkey plants, machinery, and equipment, and other imported products are all subject to the same basic procedures. The industrial association, its research and design office, its parent ministry, the foreign trade enterprise, as well as the Planning Commission, the Ministries of Finance and Foreign Trade, and the Bank Handlowy are involved in the process.

The factory where a machine or new production line is to be installed is, by American definition, the "end-user." Under the Polish system, the factory belongs to an "investor," i.e., an

Association (Zjednoczenie) which is an amalgamated grouping of all factories in a given line of production. Each such Association has its own managing director, director of investments, technical director, and its own design office. Each Association is subordinate to a ministry from which it receives its hard currency investment "limits" for a given year. The limits are generally determined by relative priorities established by the current national Five-Year Plan and, in turn, assigned by the minister and his advisers to development and modernization projects within their ministry.

The initial technical requirements for investment projects are written in the design office (Biuro Projektow) of the Association, and this can be a good point for stimulating demand for a U.S. company's products. The proposals of the design office are then forwarded through the investment and technical directors of the Association to the ministry and eventually to the foreign trade enterprise. Upon completion of the negotiations, which can be long and complex, a director from the responsible foreign trade enterprise signs the contract for the Polish side. Large contracts also may be countersigned by a representative of the investor, who vouches for its technical aspects.

By regulation, the foreign trade enterprise must have at least three bids on a major contract. The proposals are evaluated for their technical, commercial and financial provisions. Poland's sole commercial bank, the Bank Handlowy, is almost always involved in the negotiations, seeking the best possible credit terms. The foreign trade enterprise is responsible for securing commercial aspects of important contracts, which may include buy-back arrangements as well as the customary warranty services, guarantees, and arbitration clauses.

Before a major contract is signed, it is reviewed by the responsible ministry and the Ministry of Foreign Trade, which may have commercial policy reasons for favoring one source of supply over another. The Planning Commission and Bank Handlowy also will look at it from the perspective of financing, hard currency obligations, and investment priorities. Throughout the negotiating process it is, therefore, useful to keep in touch from time to time with the ministries, commission, and bank, as well as the investors, design offices, and foreign trade enterprise.

Information and Assistance

Up-to-date information on business opportunities in Poland and assistance in establishing contacts with Polish firms is available from a number of sources in both the United States and Poland. These include the publications and consulting services of both commercial firms specializing in East-West trade and agencies of U.S. and Polish Governments.

Department of Commerce Services

The U.S. Department of Commerce offers a variety of services to U.S. firms interested in developing trade with Poland. Commerce District Offices located in 43 cities can provide publications, basic assistance, and information about the Department's programs.

The Bureau of East-West Trade in Washington offers assistance in numerous areas, including economic information, marketing advice, business counseling, and promotional events. Companies wishing to avail themselves of these services should contact the Poland Desk Officer, Eastern European Affairs Division (202–377–2645) or the Trade Development Assistance Division (202–377–5500). The mailing address for these divisions is Industry and Trade Administration, U.S. Department of Commerce, Washington, D.C. 20230.

Information on the Polish market and advice on doing business in Poland is carried in the Department's regular and occasional publications. A *Foreign Economic Trends* report on Poland appears annually, and current trade information is carried in the semiannual *East-West Trade Update: A Commercial Fact Sheet for U.S. Business*. Current developments are reported in the biweekly magazine *Business America*. Copies on an individual or subscription basis are available from the Superintendent of Documents, U.S. Government Printing Office, Washington, D.C. 20402 or from any U.S. Department of Commerce District Office.

U.S. firms also can subscribe to the Department of Commerce Trade Opportunities Program. It will automatically bring to their attention trade opportunities in their particular product line in Poland or any other specified country. The Trade Opportunities Program is available on a pre-paid subscription basis. To subscribe, write to the Office of Export Development, Room 2323, Industry and Trade Administration, U.S. Department of Commerce, Washington, D.C. 20230.

Export distributors and managers, trade associations, banks, and others who desire a comprehensive listing of all trade opportunities appearing under the Trade Opportunity Program (TOP), can subscribe to the TOP bulletin by writing to the above address. The weekly bulletin is a compilation of all trade opportunities appearing under the TOP and includes all information contained in the individually distributed trade opportunities.

Warsaw Trade Development Center

The U.S. Trade Development Center in Warsaw assists American companies in establishing contacts with Polish Foreign Trade Organizations, end-users, and government agencies. It offers the visiting American counseling on market conditions and business opportunities in Poland and will assist in identifying and arranging meetings with key purchasing officials for specific products. The Center also has facilities for small conferences and business seminars, along with logistic support for such events. Companies can use the Center's facilities for mounting single company exhibitions and catalog displays. Other facilities include reproduction and telex equipment which can be used by American business representatives at their expense; a commercial reference library on U.S. trade and industry; assistance in arranging for translators, interpreters, and secretarial services. The address is:

U.S. Trade Development Center
Mr. William Schrage, Director
Ulica Wiejska 20
00-490 Warsaw, Poland
tel: 21–45–15/16
telex: 867/813934

Polish Commercial Offices

Polish commercial representatives stationed at the Polish Embassy in Washington, the Commercial Counselor's offices in New York and Chicago, and the Delegation of the Polish Chamber of Foreign Trade in San Francisco are actively involved in promoting trade between Poland and the United States. They do not themselves take part in business negotiations or sign contracts. However, they are important sources of information about trade opportunities and can facilitate contacts with Polish trading organizations. The addresses are:

Commercial Attache
Embassy of Poland
2640–16th St., N.W.
Washington, D.C. 20009
(202) 387–5484

Office of the Polish Commercial Counselor
One Dag Hammerskjold Plaza, 14th Floor
New York, N.Y. 10017
(212) 486–3150

Polish Commercial Consulate
333 East Ontario St., Suite 39068
Chicago, Ill. 60611
(312) 642–4102

Delegate of the Polish Chamber of
Foreign Trade
40 Montgomery St., Suite 2070
San Francisco, Calif. 94104
(415) 956–2266

Chamber of Foreign Trade

The Polish Chamber of Foreign Trade (Polska Izba Handlu Zagranicznego) is Poland's chamber of commerce for international economic relations and trade promotion. Its members include FTOs, industrial associations, individual enterprises producing for export, banks, service enterprises, the insurance company, and transport and forwarding organizations.

The Chamber provides special services for Polish institutions, such as market research abroad, information on customs and maritime procedures, issuance of certificates of origin authorizing invoices and other documents, organization of Polish participation in foreign trade fairs and exhibits, and organization of international trade fairs in Poland. The Chamber also maintains a Court of Arbitration for disputes with foreign firms over commercial activity, transportation, or insurance.

The Chamber also can provide assistance to foreign firms such as arranging contacts with Polish organizations and providing information on trade practices in Poland. The Foreign Relations Department of the Chamber is staffed by specialists directly responsible for relations with the United States. Recently the Chamber established a special unit to help small- and medium-sized foreign firms do business in Poland.

Together with the U.S. Chamber of Commerce, the Polish Chamber of Foreign Trade co-sponsors the Polish-U.S. Economic Council, which was created in October 1974 to provide a channel for direct communication between U.S. business interests and Polish commercial decision-makers.

The Chamber issues a number of publications which are available in English, including *Information for Businessmen Trading with Poland* (biennial), *Polish Foreign Trade* (monthly), *Polish Economic Survey* (biweekly), *Polish Technical Review* (bimonthly), and *Polish Maritime News* (monthly), *Food From Poland* (quarterly), *Polish Fair Magazine*, and several other industrial branch publications.

The address is:

Polish Chamber of Foreign Trade
Trebacka 4
00–950 Warszawa
Tel: 26–02–21
Telex: 814361 pihz pl

Marketing Techniques

Companies new to the Polish market will want to concentrate their efforts on making their company name, product, and services known to potential buyers. This section outlines the principal techniques for marketing in Poland.

Market Research

American companies accustomed to extensive market research prior to entering a new market will need to adapt their techniques and expectations to the Polish system of central planning and FTO monopoly of foreign trade. Some indication of market potential can be gained by looking at the priority assigned to particular sectors in 5-year and annual economic plans and at production, import, and export statistics. Country affairs officers at the Department of Commerce often can assist in obtaining such information. In many instances, however, sufficient market information is not readily available and can be developed only through making contacts and marketing efforts.

Initiating Contact

Since Polish FTOs specialize along product lines, identifying potential purchasers is fairly simple. The organizations listed in the "Information and Assistance" section can assist in determining which of the FTOs listed in Appendix I are appropriate contacts for a given company. The major hurdle, however, is gaining recognition for one's company and product or services by the FTOs and the end users who purchase through them.

Initial contact generally has to be made by the American seller. If an item is of high import priority, the U.S. Trade Development Center in Warsaw may receive an inquiry about American suppliers. Similarly, if a company's product or service is unique and has wide repute, a request for specifications and price quotation may be received from the Polish purchaser. In most cases, however, it is the seller who must initiate contact.

An American company's first contact in Poland is normally the FTO responsible for importing the type of product the company is selling. The company should provide the FTO with information on its product lines and capabilities, and on particular items it wishes to trade. Brochures should contain complete specifications in metric terms if possible, delivery dates, and other information emphasizing the advantages of a firm's products vis-a-vis major competitors. Samples may be sent if feasible.

Although such information can be transmitted by correspondence, most firms doing business in Poland have found that pursuit of market opportunities requires one if not several visits to Poland by company representatives. Such a visit would follow some indication of sale potential and permits the American to become acquainted with the different organizations involved in the decision-making process. Appointments with the FTO should be requested in advance, either directly or through the assistance of the Polish commercial offices in the United States or the U.S. Trade Development Center in Warsaw. This insures that officials competent to deal with a firm are present during the visit. Receipt of an invitation from the FTO will facilitate obtaining a business visa.

Once contact is established, the FTOs can assist U.S. firms in contacting other organizations such as the industrial association, research and design institute, and ministerial departments if appropriate. New-to-market firms should coordinate contacts with end-users through the FTO. Access to end-users is relatively easy in Poland, and after the initial contact, American companies have found it possible to have continuing contacts with Polish end-users without repeatedly going through the concerned FTO.

Visits to end-users may not provide immediate sales; however, development of contacts throughout an industry should prove worthwhile in time, as new import plans are generated. Initial technical requirements for investment projects are drafted in the research and design offices of the end-users' industrial associations. Awareness by the specialists in these offices of particular products and processes increases the likelihood that these will be eligible for consideration when purchases within these requirements are made. In addition, a trader may gain valuable business information through such meetings with end-users.

In general, a new-to-market company will find that contacts with several parts of the Polish trade network are essential to successful market development.

Sales Promotion

Other ways of promoting sales and bringing products to the attention of Polish purchasing officials include exhibiting at trade fairs and specialized exhibitions, participating in trade missions and technical sales seminars, and mounting company-sponsored displays.

Poznan Fair and Exhibits.—The Poznan International Technical Fair is one of the major trade shows in Eastern Europe. Held annually in June at the fairgrounds in Poznan, it features both industrial and consumer goods displayed in national pavilions. The Poznan Fair is attended by Polish trade officials and end-users from all parts of the country, as well as by purchasers from other CEMA countries, and affords an excellent opportunity to display U.S. products.

The U.S. exhibition, sponsored by the Department of Commerce and housed in the American pavilion, provides American exhibitors with extensive services in mounting of displays, attracting potential purchasers, and arranging meetings or representational functions. The Fair's "America Day," presided over by a designated representative of the President of the United States, has traditionally attracted high Polish Government officials to view the U.S. displays and meet with exhibitors. The U.S. pavilion recently has been air-conditioned and shortly will be expanded to accommodate the growing number of American firms which find exhibiting at Poznan a useful promotion technique. Exhibitors are charged on the basis of the space and services for which they contract. Since demand exceeds available space, companies should initiate inquiries at least 8 months in advance of the particular fair at which they wish to exhibit in the U.S. pavilion. The U.S. Trade Development Center in Warsaw is responsible for recruiting participants, and information or applications for space can be obtained by contacting:

U.S. Trade Development Center
ul. Wiejska 12
Warszawa, Poland

Most American companies prefer to exhibit in the U.S. pavilion for the easy identification and services it offers them. Companies unable to secure space in the U.S. pavilion or requiring more space than it has available can rent space in the various pavilions maintained by the Poznan Fair authorities. Inquiries and applications should be addressed to:

International Poznan Fair
ul. Glogowska 14
60–374 Poznan
Telex: 041–5210
Cable: Targ Poznan

In addition to the Fair, a number of specialized exhibitions are held in Poland each year in October and April. Events which have been scheduled repeatedly during the fall include: Chemia—chemistry; Fotokinotechnika–photography and cinematography; Poligrafia—printing equipment; and Taropak—storage, packing and handling equipment. Industries highlighted in the spring have included: Salmed—medical and laboratory equipment and pharmaceuticals; Secura—industrial safety devices; Intermasz—equipment for the textile, leather, clothing, and footwear industries; Interbiuro—office and data processing equipment. Companies inter-

ested in exploring possible participation in these specialized exhibitions should contact the Poznan Fair authorities at the address given above. Since the U.S. Department of Commerce occasionally sponsors a show at these events, U.S. companies can also check the Department's trade promotion schedule.

Trade Missions and Sales Seminars.—The U.S. Department of Commerce has a continuing trade promotion program employing a variety of techniques. The Technical Sales Seminar, concentrating on technical presentations in a specific industry category, has proven to be a particularly effective promotion technique and the Department sponsors five or six such seminars in Poland each year. Information about the schedule of events and participation opportunities can be obtained from the Trade Promotion Division, Room 4821, Industry and Trade Administration, U.S. Department of Commerce, Washington, D.C. 20230, (202) 377–4161.

Single Company Displays.—Individual companies often find it advantageous to stage their own display or seminar, especially to feature a particular product line with good sales potential. The U.S. Trade Development Center offers facilities and logistical support for displays requiring a limited amount of space. Use of the facility should be arranged directly with the Center's Director.

There are also several Polish agencies which can arrange private exhibitions for foreign companies on a contract basis. These include the AGPOL Advertising Agency, Sienkiewicza 12, 00–950 Warszawa; and the National Technical Organization (NOT), Czackiego 3/5, 00–950 Warszawa.

Advertising.—General advertising is considerably less important in Poland than in most Western markets. The technical journals directed toward specific industrial specialties probably offer the best media for most suppliers of industrial goods. Advertisements in these and all other Polish media must be placed by foreign firms through the AGPOL Advertising Foreign Trade Agency, Sienkiewicza 12, 00–950 Warszawa, telex: 81–35–67.

Since the aim of any publicity effort in Poland is to reach the specialists in the design offices and end-user enterprises who draft specifications for imported materials and equipment, companies may want to look into using the information collecting and disseminating network of the following two agencies:

The Center of Information on Firms (OIF-Osrodek Informacji Firmowej, ul. Pankiewicza 3, Warszawa) distributes to all Polish enterprises technical materials which may be of interest to their specialists. Description of company products and services sent to OIF should be in a form which can be easily sent on to those enterprises.

The National Technical Organization (NOT-Naczelna Organizacja Techniczna, ul. Czackiego 3/5, Warszawa) is an umbrella organization for a large number of professional, scientific, and technical societies. Its functions include disseminating information to the more than 200 regional information centers in the various industrial branches and to the more than 2,000 departments for scientific-technical information at the factory level which provide enterprise managements with information on which purchasing decisions are based.

The commercial bulletin *Wiadomosci Handlowe U.S.A.*, put out in Polish by the U.S. Trade Development Center in Warsaw, is distributed to a selected group of several thousand Polish commercial and technical specialists. It carries a section with information on new products and technology and on cooperation and licensing opportunities which may be of interest in Poland. Items to be featured are selected from those submitted by U.S. companies through the *New Product Information Service* (NPIS), sponsored by the Office of International Marketing, Industry and Trade Administration, U.S. Department of Commerce, Washington, D.C. 20230.

Commercial Representation

Examination of the various methods of commercial representation is advisable during the initial stages of market development. Such factors as cost, market potential, technical product complexities, the desired frequency of contact and a firm's individual needs should determine the form of representation. Forms of commercial representation and their characteristics are:

Visits by Parent Company or Subsidiary Offi-cials.—Company officials have the important advantage of in-depth knowledge of the product line and may also be able to speed up the negotiating process by making on-the-spot decisions without reference to higher management. Polish FTOs often prefer to deal directly with the U.S. supplier, because decisions can be made faster and the cost of an intermediary, such as an agent, is eliminated. Companies with Western European subsidiaries should ensure that any sales they make directly from the U.S. to Poland are priced to include a contribution to overhead for the subsidiary office, especially if it is a sales or service office only, since that office may be requested by the purchaser to perform the necessary guarantee work.

Because of the expense and time involved in travel to Poland, visits by U.S. home office personnel may be less frequent than those of European competitors. Companies which depend on occasional visits may have difficulty in finding adequate facilities, communications, and secretarial services. Partly in response to this last factor, the U.S. Trade Development Center in Warsaw provides visiting American business representatives with copying and telex facilities. Center personnel also will assist in locating competent secretaries and translators, arranging business appointments and other services. Any direct costs, such as telex charges, must be reimbursed to the Center.

Visits by Western Agents or Consultants.—Intermediary agents, often based in Western Europe, can be helpful to a U.S. company in the early stages of market penetration, because of their established contacts with the FTO, research institute, end-user, and ministerial personnel and their knowledge of the Polish purchasing system. Agents generally operate on a retainer and commission basis and perform a wide range of marketing services at the supplier's discretion. These can comprise merely an initial introduction to FTO contacts or all necessary functions up to contract negotiation and signature.

Agents represent a number of clients and may not be able to give the individual attention to each sale that company officials would, and they usually lack the product familiarity of home office personnel. As previously mentioned, FTOs sometimes try to avoid dealing with intermediaries in order to eliminate the added expenses of the agent's commission as part of the purchase price. The Trade Development Assistance Division of the U.S. Department of Commerce's Bureau of East-West Trade can provide American firms with names of agents interested in representing U.S. companies in Eastern Europe. In addition, the U.S. East-West Trade Development Support Office in Vienna can help U.S. firms to locate agents.

Polish Commercial Agents.—American companies with a need for continuous representation in Poland but which do not want the expense of opening their own office, can employ one of the 11 Polish commercial agencies authorized by the Government to represent foreign firms in trading with local entities. These agencies, whose addresses are listed in Appendix B, are Dynamo, Ltd., Eximpol Ltd., Maciej Czarnecki and Company, Mundial Ltd., Polcomex S. A., Poliglob S. A., Polimar S. A., Timex S. A., Transactor S. A., Transpol S. A., and Unitex Ltd. Each is headquartered in Warsaw; several have branches in important industrial centers such as Lodz and Katowice.

In Poland each representational agency usually handles the entire range of products offered for sale by a company, rather than specializing in particular categories. Generally, agents do not represent competing manufacturers simultaneously.

Depending on the anticipated volume of sales, a commercial agency may assign one or more of its employees to represent a Western client on an exclusive basis. A large firm with diversified products may have several agency employees working full or part-time on its behalf. An average size agency has a staff of approximately 50, some of whom are former FTO employees or specialists in particular industries. Agents generally do not take on new clients if market prospects for their products appear poor.

The duties of a commercial agent vary according to company needs. In general, a commercial agent's duties involve information and research, servicing, and commercial activities. The agent conveys market information to the seller and price and product details to FTO and plant technicians. Agents can speed up the exchange of views during contract negotiations if not actually conduct them; however, contract signature is usually handled by company personnel. Promotional activities may include as-

sistance in preparation and placement of advertisements suitable to the Polish market; organizing receptions, seminars, and exhibitions at trade fairs; and planning visits of company personnel to Poland and of Polish officials to the United States for inspection tours and technical training. Agents may maintain stocks of parts on consignment, perform after-sales servicing, arrange for training of Polish technicians, handle translations and facilitate entry of goods into Poland.

For a company comparatively new to the market, a local Polish-speaking commercial agent with lifelong acquaintance with Polish methods of doing business offers certain advantages over other forms of foreign representation. A good agent will ensure that correspondence is handled expeditiously, and will be familiar with bureaucratic procedures which often frustrate foreigners. The agent's contacts among decision-makers throughout the Polish trade network are vital to a marketing effort. A good agent can sometimes provide early information about Polish purchasing plans and projects. Employment of an agent can substantially reduce the amount of time U.S. personnel need to spend in Poland.

On the other hand, Polish agents in a sense represent the Ministry of Foreign Trade and have divided loyalties. Therefore, U.S. firms should be cautious in the information they reveal to their agents, particularly pertaining to negotiating tactics and points on which they are willing to make concessions. Also, some firms have found that agency fees make their products uncompetitive. American companies should also be sure that the person chosen to represent them is familiar with the type of products to be promoted and has useful contacts in that industry. Although the U.S. company may not be allowed to actually choose the exclusive agent, it can interview prospects and make its preferences known to the manager of the representational agency.

Company experiences with Polish agents have been mixed. Some large European firms with lengthy histories of trade with Poland reportedly have developed satisfactory business relationships with various Polish agencies. On the other hand, a number of Western firms have become dissatisfied with this type of representation. The most prominent complaint concerns problems in motivating the agent. Local personnel employed by the agencies generally represent several foreign firms and are paid a salary which is unrelated to the sales volume the agent generates. Hence some agents may not pursue business opportunities as diligently as may be expected. An exclusive agent, on the other hand, may devote more time to the company's marketing effort, but the company must be willing to pay a retainer fee, a commission on sales, plus travel expenses.

Agents also may move or be transferred from one firm to a competing firm, taking with them company knowledge, confidential information, and experience. A strong contractual commitment with the agency, as described below, may effectively bond the agent and company for the duration of a project or contract.

Companies are warned to employ only those agents who are officially provided by the state representative agencies and authorized to represent Western companies in Poland. The employment of Polish citizens who are not agents but who offer expertise as consultants for a fee is illegal and may impair the company's ability to operate effectively in Poland.

An agreement signed with a commercial agent should specify exactly what services the U.S. firm expects to receive, the duration of the arrangement, and payment terms. A contract may cover a variety of services, or a specific event, such as a trade fair. The length of the agreement may vary from a 1-year trial period in order to gauge market receptivity (with renewal options), to several years if more time is required to develop a market. American companies should be sure the contract reflects the length of time they anticipate needing an agent, specifies under what conditions the company may terminate the agreement, change to another agency, or be entitled to a new agent if the original agency employee is unsatisfactory.

Polish agencies operate on a commission basis plus a monthly retainer fee. Monthly costs include a minimum $500 retainer, along with agent's travel expenses including an automobile and commission. The agent's salary and advertising may be extra or included in these fees. Commissions range from 2–10 percent of product value and depend on sales volume, cost of each item, and anticipated amount of time spent promoting sales. As sales rise, commissions are usually reduced, and the retainer may be waived. Payment is made in dollars to the agency, which then pays the exclusive representative. An agreement should specify whether sales made without the benefit of agency assistance will result in a commission.

Corporate Offices in Poland.—Companies which are doing a substantial amount of business with Poland on a continuing basis may find it advantageous to establish an accredited representation office in Warsaw or other principal center of activity. Of the various possible forms of commercial representation, the company office offers the most exclusive, continuous, and responsive servicing of a company's interests. Against its advantages must be balanced the high cost of operating an office in Poland. In deciding whether to grant a license to a foreign company office, Polish authorities consider the volume of a firm's trade with Poland and the nature of any cooperative arrangements it may have with Polish industry. Company officials considering opening an office in Poland will want to look at these factors too.

The establishment and operation of representation offices is governed by Decree No. 63 of the Council of Ministers of February 6, 1976, which gives the Minister of Foreign Trade and Maritime Economy jurisdiction over the granting of licenses for commercial activities in foreign trade. In fields such as transportation, tourism, or cultural services, licenses are granted by the appropriate Minister in consultation with the Minister of Foreign Trade.

Company representation offices may be of three types:

Commercial Branch Office.—The commercial branch office is authorized to conduct the full-range of a company's activities in Poland, including sales promotion, contract signing, maintenance of a consignment warehouse, and servicing. It is subject to taxation as regulated by the order of the Minister of Finance of May 23, 1977.

Technical Information Office. — Publicity, product information, scientific research, and auxiliary or preparatory services can be carried out by a technical information office. It is not authorized, however, to conduct the commercial activities of a branch office.

Supervisory Office.—Normally such an office is established only by companies constructing turnkey projects or involved in industrial cooperation requiring on-the-spot supervision. The office may be provided for in the project contract and usually lasts only for the duration of construction and start-up. It cannot perform commercial or technical information services.

The application for a license to open a representation office must be made in writing and include: (1) an abstract from a commercial register with data on the foreign firm, (2) a declaration by the management of the company's intention to establish representation in Poland, and (3) a declaration stating that the firm's representative will observe Polish laws. These three documents must be submitted along with Polish translations and notarization by a Polish Diplomatic Mission or Consular Office at or near the parent company's home office. An application for opening a supervisory office should include a statement from the appropriate Polish Foreign Trade Organization indicating that such an office would be beneficial to the execution of an existing contract. However, this statement is not required if the supervisory office is established on the basis of a contract concluded between a Polish Foreign Trade Organization and the foreign firm.

Once a license is granted, the representation office must follow certain requirements: (1) maintain its bookkeeping and accounts in the Polish language and in Polish currency; (2) make timely payments of taxes and fees; and (3) maintain an account at the Bank Handlowy, S.A., in Warsaw, and settle all accounts and payments in accordance with Polish currency regulations.

Licenses are issued for a specified period of time, usually 2 years. Applications for extension must be made in writing no later than 3 months before the expiration of the existing license. The license is void if the representation office is not opened within 3 months after the license's date of issue. A fee must be paid at the time a license is issued or extended.

The representation office may employ Polish nationals who have been granted employment permits by local Polish authorities. These special permits must be renewed annually. While the government authorities usually have ap-proved renewals routinely, some Western firms feel constrained by this requirement, especially when considering long-term training for their local employees. Foreign nationals also can be employed by the representation office provided that the Polish authorities issue them a permit to exercise their profession in Poland.

Rents for suitable office space and housing for non-Polish personnel are on par with or exceed those in major Western capitals. The exact rent for an office or apartment is determined on the basis of floor space, location, and quality of facilities.

Commercial offices, but not technical and supervisory offices, are subject to income tax (tax on profits). Western offices do not pay a turnover tax, but the company's turnover in Poland is the basis for determining the tax on profits. The company's taxable profit is determined on the basis of all the company's transactions in Poland, regardless of where the contract was concluded or the role of the representation office in concluding the contract. The taxable profit is established on the basis of either the company's accounting books or the following percentages of total turnover: 5 percent of total contract value for sale of commodities and equipment; 10 percent of turnover for construction and assembly work; 60 percent of turnover resulting from commissions. The Western staff of all the representation offices is subject to personal income taxes. The tax rate is progressive, but for foreign companies with commercial offices the tax on net profits and on personal income is limited to 50 percent of the taxable income. Establishment of tax liability is complicated and firms are advised to obtain competent legal advice.

Copies of the relevant regulations and further information about establishing and operating an office in Poland can be obtained from the Commerce Department in Washington or the U.S. Trade Development Center in Warsaw.

Negotiating the Transaction

This section highlights points to be kept in mind in early negotiations, especially by firms new to the market. While successful negotiation of major contracts may be lengthy and arduous, sales of individual machines, instruments, and other items can be made with far less difficulty often with only a purchase order.

The Negotiation Process [1]

The process leading to a signed contract is essentially the same whether an American company is negotiating a major project in Poland, for which several bids are required, or a small sale for which there is little competition. Only written contracts are valid in Poland; therefore, Polish negotiators place heavy emphasis on extensive, often exhaustive, discussions of contract details. As a result, negotiating sessions are usually both time-consuming and costly. Numerous persons are brought into the discussions at various points. Representatives of the FTO, the Bank Handlowy (Commercial Bank), the end-user plant, research institutes, the Ministries of Trade and Finance, and other concerned ministries must be satisfied before a contract is signed. The vice president of the FTO or the head of the pertinent FTO department usually conducts the negotiations, which may take place both in Poland and the United States.

Unless the FTO is under pressure to complete the deal within a specified time period, a company usually engages in protracted talks and numerous visits to Poland. This is especially true when the trading partners are dealing with each other for the first time or have had minimal prior contact. The Poles are cautious about accepting new methods and suppliers. After confidence is established, negotiations on subsequent projects are likely to be less protracted. U.S. companies often have had to overcome Polish preferences for contracts with European sources with whom they have developed traditional working relationships.

A U.S. company's chances of concluding a contract are better if negotiators have the authority to deal with their Polish counterparts on an equal basis. A personal working relationship developed with the Poles can facilitate negotiations. For this reason, firms often have found it useful to have the same company representatives participate in each session.

Negotiations with each of the most promising bidders who have submitted preliminary

[1] Prepared by David Bowie, Trade Development Assistance Division, Office of East-West Trade Development.

proposals to the FTO are divided into two distinct phases—the technical and the commercial. During the former, project specifications are reviewed extensively to determine what best fulfills Polish requirements. At this stage, American firms have frequently had to provide substantially more information (in the form of drawings, blueprints, descriptions, samples, and visual aids) than is normally the case in Western transactions. If the U.S. product is new in Poland or higher priced than that of competing bidders, the U.S. firm will have to spend the time and effort needed to demonstrate the product's advantage and justify the added cost of technology. It is sometimes useful to arrange to have the Polish engineers and negotiators visit the U.S. firm's plant either in the United States or Western Europe.

Because of the exhaustive format of the technical negotiations, a U.S. firm's negotiating team should include qualified specialists who are thoroughly familiar with the product, in order to avoid loss of time while technical questions are referred to the home office. The Polish side generally consists of well-informed technical personnel, including plant managers, product engineers, and research institute staff.

After technical agreement is reached, Polish officials hold discussions with other bidders and appraise bids. Commercial talks, which lead to final selection of one bidder, may in fact be conducted with several firms at the same time to obtain the best terms available. These sessions focus on the project's financial aspects, including price, financing, penalty payments, and a myriad of other subjects such as delivery schedules, arbitration, and training of personnel. Additional Polish officials, usually from the Bank Handlowy, Ministry of Finance, and central planning offices, are brought into the talks.

Countertrade

Polish companies are increasingly turning to countertrade as a tool for expanding exports and reducing hard currency outlays. The term "countertrade" is generally used to describe arrangements under which the U.S. seller agrees to accept full or partial payment in manufactured goods or commodities supplied by the Polish buyer. In addition to the recent growth in the number of transactions involving countertrade, Polish demands for offsetting purchases are increasing as a percentage of the

Western export contract value. Present indications point to expansion of this practice.

In Poland, countertrade involves primarily two types of transactions. In a *counterpurchase transaction* the U.S. seller agrees to purchase Polish goods equivalent to a given percentage of the value of the sale. Normally two separate contracts are involved, one for the sale of the American goods and another for the purchase of Polish goods. Usually the Polish FTO will urge the U.S. seller to buy products handled by that particular FTO, or even a particular FTO division with which the seller is dealing. Counterpurchases from other FTOs are possible but difficult to arrange. Concurrence of the Ministry of Foreign Trade is necessary and usually must involve the services of the DAL or Torimex FTOs. Companies buying and selling in various sectors of the economy should seek Ministry of Foreign Trade approval for all purchases by the entire company to be applied toward fulfillment of its countertrade obligations.

Since readily sellable items are usually difficult to obtain under counterpurchase arrangements, the American company may find it difficult to locate sufficient quantities of marketable Polish merchandise to fulfill its countertrade commitments. Recently, some U.S. companies have concluded that payment of penalty fees for non-fulfillment of counterpurchase commitments may constitute a given cost of doing business that may be difficult to avoid. If using a trading company to dispose of its countertrade purchases, the American company also should take into account the likely commission and discount costs.

In selling technology, plant, or equipment, the American vendor may be asked to take payment in products produced by the equipment. Such *compensation* arrangements are usually much larger in value and take place over a longer period of time than counterpurchase transactions.

For further information on countertrade, U.S. exporters are referred to the publication *East-West Countertrade Practice: An Introductory Guide for Business*, U.S. Department of Commerce, August 1978, available from the Department or from the U.S. Government Printing Office, Washington, D.C. 20402.

Pricing

A company's pricing strategy can range from very simple to very complex depending upon the business proposal under consideration. The simplest case is when a company is selling an off-the-shelf item that has a standard price f.o.b. The most complicated cases occur when product, technology, licenses, technical assistance, and financing all are being included in one contract.

In the more complicated cases the buyer will try to get the seller to quote a firm price as soon as possible in the negotiations. The seller should delay quoting a final price as long as possible and preferably only after all other terms and conditions have been set. Since this is not always possible, the seller, when quoting his price, should explicitly define exactly what is included in his price and what is not. This will preclude unforeseen costs such as living expenses for Polish technicians sent to the United States for preshipment inspections, additional expenses for seller's technicians during technical assistance periods, and many other items. During the pricing negotiations the Polish side will aim to get the maximum price reduction possible. Remember that these are professional negotiators whose job is to get reduced prices. If a firm price is agreed to early in the negotiations the seller may find the buyer trying to add additional items or services into this price, thus gaining an effective price reduction. Thus the importance of not quoting an early price and of explicitly defining what the price covers.

The seller should have sufficient flexibility built into the price to allow for lowering it during negotiations. However, if at all possible, the seller should try to gain a concession from the buyer for this price reduction. The seller also should not quote a price so high that it has no credibility in order to be able to give dramatic price reductions. The buyer will have a reasonable idea of what a fair price should be, and may in fact be negotiating with others at the same time and thus have comparative pricing information.

Also very important is that the seller should specify the time period for which the price remains valid to guard against increased costs, in the event that a long time lapse occurs between the final price quote and contract signing.

The pricing of technology or manufacturing licenses presents special problems. Poland and other Eastern European countries prefer not to pay royalties on production but would rather pay a lump sum, sometimes payable over a period of years. In this case the seller must make sure to negotiate a fair return in any such payment scheme. In addition, the seller may also try to negotiate periodic payments over the life of the contract as recovery of research and development costs for technology improvements attached to the product or process being sold.

Other factors that the seller must consider in quoting a price are inflation forecasts over the contract period, interest rate differentials that may occur as the result of using certain financing methods, and the increased costs of marketing in Poland. This last factor is especially important because it is more expensive to carry out a marketing campaign in Eastern Europe than it would be in Western Europe.

In no case should a company agree to a price that will not provide the minimum return on investment that the company requires. Firms cannot buy into the market hoping to make up any initial losses in future contracts. Each contract must be considered separately.

During the negotiations, some firms have found it advisable to provide their own interpreters, particularly if they are company officials, as those supplied by the Poles are often not fully qualified to translate technical details. The Polish negotiators should be informed immediately of an interpreter's presence. Other U.S. companies have not needed interpreters as their counterparts spoke English.

A flexible approach with well-considered alternatives in case of impasse is invaluable during the arduous negotiating sessions. U.S. firms have sometimes found that difficult points left temporarily unresolved can be taken up successfully in later negotiations. It is also advisable to note what items have been agreed to each day to preclude attempts to reopen the same questions at subsequent sessions, although this may be unavoidable as representatives of different Polish agencies join the talks.

Standard Contract Provisions [2]

As mentioned above, contract negotiations in Poland are divided into two phases, the technical and the commercial. During the technical discussions, there may be little attention to commercial issues. Contract terms, other than price, often are not discussed until the technical phase has been successfully concluded. It is at that point that commercial negotiations with the actual Polish contractual party, the FTO, begin in earnest.

When commercial negotiations with a U.S. firm begin, the Polish FTO will usually offer one of its form contracts and urge its adoption. Most FTOs have several form contracts, each suitable for a different type of transaction. Those forms which are used for transactions involving technology transfer, such as licensing agreements and turnkey contracts, tend to be more complex and detailed than those designed for simple equipment purchases. The main body of a form contract outlines the basic commercial terms of the transaction. Often there are extensive appendices covering matters such as the technical specifications for the equipment and technology being purchased, the installation and commissioning of the equipment, and the training of buyer's personnel.

Form contracts vary in certain respects from FTO to FTO. However, the forms share many common elements, since they are in large measure based on the COMECON General Conditions. (The COMECON General Conditions are a codification of commercial law which carry the force of law in trade among the members of COMECON[3], the international trade organization that includes the USSR and most of Eastern Europe.)

Polish FTOs often are adamant about incorporating form contract provisions, and while changes and concessions are possible, the final product will generally resembel the form contract in at least its basic structure. The following discussion treats some, but by no means all, of the provisions found in FTO form contracts that typically cause problems during commercial negotiations.

---

[2] Prepared by Daniel D. Stein, Trade Development Assistance Division, Office of East-West Trade Development.

[3] COMECON (Council for Mutual Economic Assistance) includes Bulgaria, Cuba, Czechoslovakia, German Democratic Republic, Hungary, Mongolia, Poland, Romania, and the U.S.S.R.

Financing, Price, and Terms of Payment.— Largely because of hard currency shortages, U.S.-Polish trade financing continues to present problems. Given the shortage of convertible currency and increasing Polish indebtedness, only a limited number of transactions can be handled on a cash or short-term credit basis. In these cases, traditional payment methods such as irrevocable letters of credit and cash against documents are normally used. Some U.S. companies even have agreed to extend unsecured short-term credits. In many instances, however, the Polish trading partner will insist upon medium or long-term financing, or some form of countertrade. Recently, U.S. and other foreign suppliers of industrial commodities, such as chemicals, steel, and textile fibers, have had to obtain 2-to-3 year credits to maintain their market share.

Penalties for Late Delivery.— The Communist countries are "performance-oriented" in their approach to contracts, in contrast to Westerners, who are more often considered "breach-oriented." Virtually all contracts for Polish purchase of equipment or technology include penalty clauses for late or incomplete delivery of goods and technical documentation, as well as the rigorous performance or output guarantees discussed below.

Given the nature of the planning system in centrally-run economies, it is not surprising that penalties rather than damages are the standard remedy for late delivery. In these countries each component of the economic plan, including foreign trade, is designed as part of an organically complete system. A breakdown or bottleneck at any single point has repercussions for the whole economy. Thus, the stiff penalty clause in the contract is primarily meant to assure prompt delivery rather than to provide an accurate measure of damages.

A typical clause found in Polish form contracts provides that delays in delivery of equipment, spare parts, and technical documentation are to be penalized at the rate of .5 percent of the value of the equipment overdue for every week, up to a maximum stated percentage of the value of the delayed goods. Generally, there is a provision that if the delay exceeds a certain time period, usually somewhere between 4-6 months, the buyer may cancel the contract without compensation to the seller. Penalty clauses may be particularly troublesome for turnkey contracts. Delays by Polish construction teams and the need to adapt the Polish company to new technology can cause postponements for which the foreign partner may be blamed.

Guarantees.— U.S.-Polish contracts generally include a detailed and comprehensive clause spelling out all of the seller's guarantee obligations. These usually include boilerplate provisions such as guarantees that the equipment being delivered has been manufactured using high quality materials and workmanship, that it conforms to the terms and conditions of the contract, and that it represents the most advanced technical level for such equipment available in the seller's country at the time of the sale.

The seller is uniformly obligated to guarantee normal operations of the equipment for a specified period of time—typically 12 months from the date the equipment is put into operation, but not more than 18 months from the date of delivery. The latter limitation is of utmost importance to a U.S. seller since Polish buyers often fall far behind schedule in putting new equipment into operation. If the guarantee period were to run only from the date the equipment is put into operation, the seller's guarantee obligations might not begin to run until 2 or 3 years after delivery. Even worse, the seller would not be entitled to the 5 or 10 percent of the contract price that is often retained by the buyer during the guarantee period as a type of performance bond.

Polish purchasers often require stricter performance and output guarantees in licensing agreements and turnkey contracts than in other types of contracts. The seller is typically requested to guarantee that the equipment and/or technology being supplied will enable the purchaser to manufacture a specified quantity of goods of an agreed quality. Such a guarantee is risky for a U.S. seller since it may have little control over the installation and operation of the equipment and technology it supplies. Thus the seller should attempt to substitute alternative language which may serve to limit the scope of its obligations.

Polish purchasers of both equipment and technology usually require the seller to guarantee that it possesses the rights to all relevant patents and inventions for the materials supplied; that the purchaser may employ such equipment and technology in the manner called for in the contract without violating the rights of third parties; and that the seller will indemnify the purchaser against patent infringement claims. The most typical provision calls for the seller or licensor to defend against any suit or settle any claims by a third party whose rights have been infringed by the purchaser's use of the equipment or technology furnished under the contract. Often the seller's maximum liability under such an indemnification clause is limited to a specified dollar amount.

Quality Control and Inspection.—Technical specifications and provisions for technical documentation are characteristically an important part of a supply contract, often filling dozens of pages of small print. The Polish party will expect such contractual provisions to be followed to the letter, and will be certain to raise the issue if it believes that technical specifications or quality guarantees are not being met.

In order to assure compliance with specifications and guarantees, the Polish FTO will generally insist on inspection before shipment of any equipment it is purchasing. Specific contract provisions are generally included to permit factory inspections at the seller's or its subcontractor's plant, and to deal with issues such as who will pay buyer's inspection costs. Similar provisions are necessary when the buyer's personnel are to be trained by the seller in the use of the equipment, either at the seller's plant or at the installation site. Final inspection and approval by the buyer usually take place after the goods have arrived at their destination, or in the case of equipment, when it has been installed and put into operation.

Shipping Terms and Insurance.—The majority of contracts for sales of U.S. equipment to Poland call for f.a.s. or f.o.b. port-of-shipment terms, under which the buyer assumes the risk of loss at the time the goods are brought alongside or loaded on board the ship. Polish sales to the United States are usually made on a c.i.f. basis. These arrangements allow the Polish FTOs to arrange insurance coverage with Warta, the Polish state insurance agency.

Force Majeure.—A force majeure clause is an integral part of every U.S.-Polish contract. The effect of such a clause is to release a party from responsibility for non-fulfillment of its contractual obligations if its failure to perform is caused by certain circumstances. A U.S. seller would want to include among such circumstances natural disasters, wars, strikes, unavailability of raw materials, and other unforeseen and unavoidable circumstances. The contract normally provides for notification of the event by the affected party within a specified time period.

Arbitration.—Almost universally, the Communist countries prefer arbitration to court litigation of commercial disputes. For many years, Polish FTOs insisted upon arbitration before the Court of Arbitration of the Polish Chamber of Commerce. However, in a November 1972, exchange of letters, the United States and Poland agreed to "encourage" arbitration in a third country. U.S. companies have recently found Polish FTOs quite willing to agree to arbitration in "neutral" countries such as Switzerland and Sweden, and in a few cases, the Poles have even agreed to arbitration in New York under the auspices of the American Arbitration Association.

Industrial Property Protection [4]

The Patent Office of Polish People's Republic, which administers the law on patents, inventors' certificates, designs, and trademarks, is located at 188/192 Aleja Niepodleglosci, Warsaw, 68. Foreigners are represented before the Patent Office by the Patent Attorney Office (PATPOL) with the Polish Chamber of Foreign Trade, P.O. Box 168, 2 Slawki Street, Warsaw, 00950.

Poland is a member of the Paris Union International Convention for the Protection of Industrial Property, having adhered to the Stockholm Revision (1967) on March 24, 1975. U.S. nationals are thereby entitled to receive the same treatment under a country's patent and trademark laws as that country extends to its own citizens (national treatment). U.S. nationals are also entitled to a "right of priority" for patent and trademark applications. Under this procedure, a U.S. inventor has 1 year after first filing a patent application in the United States in which to file a corresponding patent application or an inventor's certificate in Poland and receive on the latter the date of the

---

[4] Prepared by: Joseph M. Lightman, Foreign Business Practices Division, Office of International Finance and Investment.

first filed U.S. application. The priority period is 6 months for trademarks.

Poland is also a member of the Universal Copyright Convention (UCC) to which the United States and about 60 other countries belong. Under the UCC, works of American authors first published and copyrighted in the United States are entitled to automatic copyright protection in Poland. To obtain such UCC protection, the U.S. author need only show on such works his name, year of first publication, and the symbol "C" in a circle .

Poland is also a member of the Berne Convention for the Protection of Literary and Artistic Works. Although the United States is not a member of this convention, a U.S. author can receive automatic protection for his work in the 60 member countries by publishing it in any member country simultaneously with its first publication in the United States. A reciprocal copyright protection arrangement has been in effect between the U.S. and Poland since February 14, 1927.

Patents.—The applicable legislation is the Law on Inventive Activity, No. 272 of October 19, 1972, effective January 1, 1973. Under this law, U.S. nationals can apply for and receive patent registrations for their inventions. A patent vests in the owner the exclusive right to use the invention and to enforce it against infringers. The law provides for issuing regular patents valid for 15 years from application filing date, and for provisional patents, valid for 5 years from such date. Regular patents are granted after a complete examination and provisional patents are granted after a limited examination. An applicant for a provisional patent may, within 4 years from the filing date, apply for a regular patent with payment of the fee for a complete examination. The law also provides for patents of addition, i.e., valid for the unexpired term of the original patent, and for grants or certificates on utility models for five-year periods.

The law further provides for issuance of inventors' certificates, similar to the system in the USSR. Such certificates are granted for an unlimited term and are awarded by the State to a party, upon application, for inventions considered useful to the State. They entitle the inventor to certain payments by the State based on its use of the invention. The State assumes complete ownership of the invention upon grant of an inventor's certificate.

Patent applications are examined for novelty, and in order for an invention to be patentable, it must not have been used or exhibited prior to the filing. The only exception is that if an invention was disclosed at an exhibition and the application was filed within 6 months of such disclosure, the novelty will not be prejudiced. Pharmaceutical products are not patentable, but processes for making such products can be patented. Oppositions to patent applications may be filed within 6 months of their publication in the Patent Office Journal. Until the application is published, the specifications are not available for public scrutiny.

A patent must be worked by the registrant or his licensee within 4 years of filing or 3 years from date of grant, whichever is later. The Patent Office may order a compulsory license under a patent if it deems such action necessary in the interest of the economy. Also, the Government may expropriate a patent for the State's use and fix the indemnity to be paid to the owner.

The law provides for criminal penalties on patent infringers or those who lay false claims to proprietary rights to inventions.

Trademarks.—Legislation on trademarks is embodied in the Act of March 28, 1963. Under the law, the first applicant for registration of a mark is entitled to its registration and exclusive use. A person who can later prove themselves to be a prior user of a mark registered to someone else, can apply for its cancellation and registration in their name. A registered trademark is enforceable against unauthorized use by others.

Trademark applications are examined. If the Patent Office considers a mark unregistrable, it so notifies the applicant, and if the applicant does not respond within a given time period, the application will be considered abandoned. The following marks are not registrable: marks which are not distinctive, cause confusion as to origin, represent official names and insignia, infringe names of others, or are contrary to law or public morals.

Marks are registered for 10 years from application filing date and are renewable for 10-year periods. There are 34 product classes for registration purposes, corresponding to the Nice Classification System.

The Council of Ministers may require registration of trademarks to be used in connection with certain specified products. Otherwise, there is no compulsory use of a mark for products to be sold in Poland. A mark may be licensed but the license agreement must be recorded to be enforceable. Infringement suits based on a trademark registration are subject to a filing limitation of three years after each illegally committed act.

Copyrights.—Under Poland's Copyright Statute (Law No. 234, July 10, 1952), the period of copyright protection for the work of an author continues for the duration of his life and 20 years after his death. Copyright on photographic works expires 10 years after first publication. Copyright protection is available for writings, musical works, fine art, and cinematographic art, as well as photographs.

Further information on the general provisions of Poland's patent, trademark and copyright laws may be obtained from the Foreign Business Practices Division, Office of International Finance and Investment, U.S. Department of Commerce. The Division, however, is not in a position to provide detailed nformaton on fees or other specific step-by-step procedures to be followed in seeking protection under these laws. Competent legal counsel should be consulted for this purpose.

Licensing.—Polservice is the Polish agency charged with buying and selling licenses abroad. It represents other State trading organizations and can be contacted in the United States through the Polish Trade Office, 500 Fifth Avenue, New York City, or the Commercial counselor of the Embassy of Poland, Washington, D.C.

Experience indicates that firms interested in licensing activities with Polish enterprises should also make contact with the ultimate end-user enterprise, if possible, as well as with Polservice. It is also desirable, when seeking licensing arrangements, to contact the Polish Ministry involved in the particular industry. In any licensing negotiations that may take place with other State enterprises, Polservice may be signatory to the final contract.

Once a potential licensee is identified, mutual interests established, and negotiations undertaken, the process may move forward very slowly. The Polish authorities may insist on exploring every provision in minute detail before including it in a contract in order to arrive at as precise an agreement as possible. Once the matter is concluded, however, State enterprises involved are usually very careful about observing the terms. Also, if such enterprises establish good contractual relations with a particular foreign firm, they may tend to accelerate future dealings with that firm.

U.S. companies interested in licensing arrangements with Polish enterprises should secure the services of an experienced attorney or consultant for assistance in drafting the contract and negotiating its provisions on such matters as the type of technical property rights to be licensed, protection of trade secrets, training of technicians, flow of new improvements, duration of contract, marketing territory, compensation, arbitration, termination, and cancellation.

Financing

Payment/Collection Mechanism.—Since the Polish zloty is not convertible, U.S. firms trading with Poland generally require payment in U.S. dollars or some other agreed-upon hard currency or blend of currencies. Arrangements for payments in U.S.-Polish trade use many of the same instruments applied in other international trade.

Short-term transactions (up to 1 year) are usually dealt with through normal commercial banking channels. For the U.S. trader inexperienced in exporting to Poland, the irrevocable letter of credit offers the most secure payment instrument. Currently, however, cash-against-documents has become the most frequently used method of payment by Polish FTOs. When used, Polish letters of credit are usually irrevocable and payable on sight (cash) rather than deferred (credit).

For medium- and long-term deals, Polish officials have emphasized that bank-to-bank credit arrangements are preferred to supplier credits. In addition to consulting with his banker, the American trader inexperienced in doing business in Poland, prior to entering into a contract, may find it useful to refer to *East-West Trade Financing: An Introductory Guide,* published by the U.S. Department of Commerce. It is available for $2.20 from the Superintendent of Documents, U.S. Government Printing Office, Washington, D.C. 20402.

Eximbank Credits.—The Export-Import Bank of the United States (Eximbank) provides financing in support of U.S. exports of goods and services to Poland through several programs. Direct loans supplement private financing sources and are made to the Bank Handlowy (Polish Foreign Trade Bank) for a portion of the U.S. contract value, with commercial banks providing the remainder of the financing. Eximbank is prepared to provide a preliminary commitment (P.C.) outlining the amount, terms, and conditions of the financial assistance it would extend in a particular transaction, which assists the exporters in concluding negotiation of the financial terms of a contract. Eximbank also may extend its financial guarantee assuring the repayment of credits provided by private lender to Poland for the purchase of U.S. goods and services. Guarantees can be extended regardless of whether direct Eximbank financing is used.

Under the Cooperative Financing Facility (CFF), Eximbank extends medium-term (1 to 5 years) lines of credit in dollars directly to the Bank Handlowy, which uses the funds for dollar credits to Polish buyers of U.S. goods and services. The U.S. supplier whose export sale to Poland is financed under CFF is paid immediately in cash by a cooperating institution, often the U.S. exporter's own commercial bank. The Polish buyer, acting either on their own initiative or at the suggestion of the U.S. supplier, normally initiates the request for financing assitance by applying to the Bank Handlowy. While the direct loan program is designed for relatively large contracts (usually more than $5 million), the CFF is well adapted to facilitating numerous sales of smaller dollar value.

A counseling service is provided by Eximbank for exporters, banks, and financial institutions seeking information on financing for U.S. exports. For further information concerning Eximbank's programs and customary terms contact: Export-Import Bank of the United States, 811 Vermont Avenue, N.W., Washington, D.C. 20571.

CCC Credits.—Financing assistance for sales of agricultural products to Poland can be obtained, as available, under the Commodity Credit Export Sales Program administered by the U.S. Department of Agriculture. Availability of credits depends on the domestic commodity supply situation and requests by Polish importers and U.S. exporters.

The commodities eligible under the program vary depending on available export supplies. Therefore, exporters seeking CCC credit financing should obtain a listing of currently eligible commodities.

The U.S. exporter initiates action by submitting an application for export financing. Following issuance of financing approval, the U.S. exporter has 90 days to register a firm sale on a deferred payment basis. Upon shipment of the commodities and submission of required documents, the exporter is paid in cash by CCC. Detailed information on the program can be obtained from the Export Programs Division, Commodity Credit Corporation, U.S. Department of Agriculture, Washington, D.C. 20250, 202-447-7791.

Foreign Investment and Joint Ventures

Foreign investment in Poland is governed by Decree 123 of the Council of Ministers of May 14, 1976, "On the Granting of Licenses to Foreign Legal and Physical Persons for Conducting Certain Kinds of Economic Activities." While foreign investment in Poland was fairly substantial before the Second World War, all of it was liquidated during the war and in the immediately following period of nationalization. With this decree, foreign investment in Poland again becomes possible.

The decree sets out in general the procedures and conditions for investing in Poland, but the whole area of foreign investment must be considered as subject to evolution and case-by-case negotiation. Because of the decree's recent enactment, the subjects omitted from its purview, and the lack of practical experience with such investments, initial investors can expect to face a long and difficult negotiation process.

Several aspects of the law should be noted by the potential investor. For instance, the Polish decree clearly permits wholly-foreign-owned businesses, but is silent on the question of joint ventures between foreign and Polish firms. In this it differs markedly from the Romanian and

Hungarian laws. According to Polish officials, joint ventures are not excluded, but for the time being will be considered only if they would generate significant levels of exports, and must be negotiated on a case-by-case basis. Financial aspects of joint ventures, however, are covered by Order 110 of the Minister of Finance.

The decree, furthermore, specifies artisan, retail catering, hotel, gastronomic, and other service enterprises as open to foreign investment. These are the areas of the Polish economy in which the private sector already plays a limited role and is receiving increasing state encouragement. Industrial and extractive operations are not mentioned in the foreign investment decree, but like the question of joint ventures they may be open to negotiation and future evolution.

The foreign investor, according to the decree, can be an individual, a company, or an association. Polish ethnic associations in foreign countries and individuals of Polish background taking up residence in Poland receive special mention as potential investors, even though investment rights are not limited to these.

The key provisions of Decree 123 governing the establishment and operation of foreign investments are outlined below.

Application Procedures.—Permission for investment is obtained through a license issued by the provincial (voivodship) government in the location where the enterprise is to be established. Investment by companies or associations also requires the approval of the Ministry of Foreign Trade and Maritime Economy. Application for a license can be made through either a proxy or a Polish diplomatic mission. Investors residing outside Poland must delegate a proxy, either an individual or the FTO Polimar, who is a permanent resident of Poland. The application for a license must be accompanied by an estimate of the total investment and an undertaking to meet all investment costs in convertible currency. Up to 30 percent of the estimated investment must be deposited in convertible currency with the Bank PKO before the license is granted, unless other arrangements are authorized.

Operating Conditions.—The license for a foreign investment is valid for up to 10 years and is renewable, but the period of validity cannot exceed the life of the lease for any facili-

ties which are occupied. The number of employees which may be hired is stipulated by the licensing authority. In the case of investors residing abroad, activities of the enterprise must be conducted by a proxy with permanent residence in Poland. A license to do business in Poland does not ensure the investor of access to raw materials and other factors of production. The enterpreneur must negotiate access to these local resources.

Financial aspects of investing in Poland are regulated by Order 109 of the Minister of Finance of May 26, 1976, which is outlined below.

Currency Accounts.—Foreign investment in Poland is done by opening a convertible currency account at the Bank PKO, S.A. These funds can be used for purchases of goods and real estate under the internal export scheme, for imports ordered through Polish foreign trade organizations, for the services of Polish enterprises entitled to receive payment in foreign currency, and when converted to zlotys, for paying Polish nationals. A zloty account also should be opened by the foreign investor for the deposit of receipts received from the sale of goods and services, payment of expenses incurred by the enterprise, and for the owner's personal expenditures.

Repatriation of Profits.—The financial regulations do not directly cover repatriation of profits, but through regulations providing for converting funds in local currency accounts from zlotys to convertible currencies. Under this provision, up to 50 percent of the net income of the enterprise, but not in excess of 9 percent of the hard currency investment, can be converted annually to hard currency. In effect, the maximum return which can be repatriated is 9 percent annually. This 9 percent maximum does not apply where at least 50 percent of the turnover of an enterprise is accounted for by hard-currency exports. There is a 10-year limitation on the right to convert local currency to foreign exchange.

Repatriation of Capital and Capital Gains.—If an enterprise is sold to an alien for foreign currency, the seller can transfer abroad the sum obtained from the sale, less the tax on the sale. If the sale is to a Polish national holding foreign currency, the seller can transfer abroad the amount invested plus 50 percent of the net income obtained from the sale of the enterprise.

In both cases, the income from the sale is subject to a capital gains tax.

Financial provisions for mixed-capital joint ventures are covered separately in Order 110 of the Minister of Finance of May 26, 1976. This regulation deals with the establishment, operation, and dissolution of enterprises having both Polish and foreign capital.

Tax Provisions.—Taxation is regulated by the Order of the Minister of Finance dated May 23, 1977. The foreign investor is liable for three types of tax charges in Poland: (1) license fees, which vary according to the type of activity; (2) turnover tax, which is levied as a percentage of the gross receipts—the percentage varies according to the nature of the business; and (3) income tax, modified by provisions of treaties for the avoidance of double taxation concluded between Poland and certain countries such as the United States.

Copies of the foreign investment decree, financial orders, and explanatory information can be obtained from the U.S. Department of Commerce.

Polish Investment Abroad.—American companies also may find opportunities for establishing a joint venture with a Polish company in either the United States or a third country. Over the last several years, an increasing number of companies have been established by Polish FTOs in the West, including the United States. While many of these are wholly Polish-owned, many also draw upon foreign capital. The foreign partner usually contributes a minority share.

Almost all of the existing ventures are either trading companies engaged in exports and imports or service firms related to foreign trade such as freight forwarding or shipping. The total capital involved in each of these normally is not large. However, several production ventures have been formed recently. Polish interest in joint ventures abroad is likely to increase along with the growing importance of foreign trade in the Polish economy and the concomitant concern with access to raw materials and markets.

As in the case of industrial cooperation, an investment venture has the greatest likelihood of success where the partners are well ac-

quainted through an established trading relationship. Establishment of a Polish-U.S. joint venture in the United States is accomplished through incorporation under State laws and the potential American investor should follow all the accepted legal and business practices common to the establishment of any company.

U.S. Regulations

Johnson Act.—The Johnson Debt Default Act of 1934, as amended (18 U.S.C. Section 955) prohibits private extension of credits and other private financial transactions with a foreign government in default on paying its obligations to the United States. The Act applies to all private U.S. individuals, partnerships, corporations, or associations. Because of its failure to repay certain indebtedness to the United States, Poland is currently affected by the Johnson Act. However, the Attorney General's interpretation of the Johnson Act provisions, issued on May 9, 1967, clarified the application of the Act. In an advisory opinion, the Attorney General stated that the Johnson Act does not prohibit export financing and credit arrangements if the terms of such transactions are based on *bona fide* business considerations and do not involve a public distribution of securities. Export credits, therefore, are allowed for Poland as long as they are comparable with those commonly given for export of the same commodities to other countries.

Export Controls.—Exports to Poland and other Communist countries are permitted subject to the provisions of the Export Administration Act of 1969, as amended. Under this Act, wide categories of goods may be exported under exemption from the individual licensing requirement; other exports to Poland and the Communist countries of Eastern Europe require validated export licenses. The export licenses are issued by the Office of Export Administration, U.S. Department of Commerce, Washington, D.C. 20230, upon receipt of export license applications from U.S. companies. The objective of the licensing procedure is to prevent the export of goods and technology which would be detrimental to the national security of the United States. Restrictions to Poland have been less severe than for export to other Eastern European countries (except Romania). For answers to basic questions on export licensing requirements, U.S. exporters should consult the Export Administration Regulations and supplementary Export Administration Bulletins. U.S. firms also are encouraged to contact the Office of Export Administration, U.S. Department of Commerce, Washington, D.C. 20230, on possible or pending transactions. While no official determination on licensing can be made before formal application is filed, the Office of Export Administration can often informally give a good idea of the prospects.

Shipping.—Ships from Communist countries enter U.S. ports under certain restrictions. Polish merchant and passenger vessels must submit an entry request 4 working days in advance of a planned entry. Polish fishing vessels calling on the ports of Baltimore, Philadelphia, New York, Boston, Seattle, San Francisco, and Portland must submit a notice of entry 4 days in advance. A request for entry must be submitted 14 days before entry into all other ports by Polish fishing vessels. The appropriate request or notice is directed to the U.S. Coast Guard. Also, Polish crew list visas must be obtained 7 days in advance of the scheduled arrival of a Polish vessel at its first U.S. port.

U.S. Flag Vessels.—Public Resolution 17 provides that where loans or credits are made or guaranteed by an instrumentality of the U.S. Government to foster exports of agricultural or other products, such cargo shall be carried exclusively in vessels of the United States. However, in special circumstances, a waiver can be granted by the Maritime Administration providing tor shipment of up to 50 percent of such cargo in vessels of the purchasing country. This resolution applies to credits of the Export-Import Bank which usually include a requirement that shipments be made in U.S.-flag vessels except to the extent a waiver of that requirement may be granted by the Maritime Administration.

Guidance for Business Travelers

Correspondence.—Correspondence to Polish organizations should be addressed, if at all possible, to the appropriate division or position (e.g., Import Department, Technical Manager). Responses to Polish inquiries should bear the reference identification number appearing on the incoming correspondence. Receipt of unsolicited offers or product descriptions is usually not acknowledged by Polish FTOs. Understaffing and shortage of English-speaking personnel in the FTOs often cause delays in answering communications. In particularly urgent cases, the U.S. Trade Development Center may be able to assist in ascertaining whether the U.S. company's communication was received and facilitate the receipt of a response.

Visiting Poland.—In conducting business in Poland, Americans should try to make personal visits. Such visits help to establish contacts, get specific answers, and speed up the processing of transactons. These visits, however, must be well programmed and appointments arranged in advance for maximum effectiveness. The U.S. Department of Commerce, U.S. Trade Development Center, and the Polish commercial offices described above can assist in arrangements.

Visas.—Americans visiting Poland on business must have a valid U.S. passport and a Polish visa. Visas are of two types:

Regular. Valid for a definite period to time up to 90 days for either a single or double entry.

Transit. Valid for up to 48 hours, requires applicant to be in possession of the visa of the country of final destination.

If the visitor has an official invitation from an FTO, enterprise, or ministry, the visa can be issued within 1 day. Persons applying for a visa without an official invitation may wait from 10 days to 1 month before the visa is issued. A large number of visa applications is received by Polish consulates during the tourist season from April through October. It is advisable that the visa application for a visit during that period be submitted 2 to 3 months prior to the desired departure date. To expedite the issuance of a visa, a business traveler can apply for a support letter to the Polish commercial offices located in New York and Chicago. Additional visa information and applications can be obtained from the folowing Polish consulates:

Polish Consulate General, 233 Madison Avenue, New York, *New York* 10016: Residents of Delaware, Connecticut, Maine, Massachusetts, New Hampshire, New Jersey, New York, Ohio, Pennsylvania, Rhode Island, and Vermont.

Polish Consulate General, 1530 North Lake Shore Drive, Chicago, Illinois 60610: residents of Alaska, Arizona, Arkansas, California, Colorado, Hawaii, Idaho, Illinois, Indiana, Iowa, Kansas, Louisiana, Michigan, Minnesota, Missouri, Montana, Nebraska, Nevada, New Mexico, North Dakota, Oklahoma, Oregon, South Dakota, Texas, Utah, Washington, Wisconsin, and Wyoming.

Consular Division of the Polish Embassy, 2224 Wyoming Avenue, N.W., Washington, D.C. 20008: residents of other States.

Customs and Currency Regulations.—There are no limitations on the amount of foreign currency a visitor may bring into Poland. Personal items and gifts can be brought into the country free of duty. A customs and currency declaration of all foreign currency, checks, and gifts brought into Poland must be completed at the time of entry. Visitors are required to exchange a minimum of $12 per person per day for expenses for each day of their stay. This regulation does not apply to U.S. business representatives visiting Poland at the invitation of ministries, FTOs, or enterprises which will pay for their expenses while in Poland. However, a copy of the invitational letter must be presented to customs officials at the point of entry. On leaving Poland, only the amount of money declared on arrival less all expenses incurred in Poland can be taken out of the country. Any attempt to take out more foreign currency than was listed in the declaration is punishable by law and the currency is subject to confiscation. Foreign currency brought into Poland from abroad may be exchanged for Polish zlotys at ORBIS (Polish Travel Office), exchange counters at the border stations, hotels, ORBIS branch counters at the border stations, ORBIS branch offices, or branch offices of the Polish National Bank located in all major Polish towns. Any exchange of currency through unauthorized individuals (black market) violates Polish exchange regulations and may have legal consequences.

Import and export of Polish currency is prohibited. Polish currency not spent in the country must be deposited with the customs office at the border upon departing Poland.

A traveler may take out of Poland duty free up to 1,000 zlotys worth of Polish goods. All items purchased in Poland for foreign currency in stores designated for that purpose are duty free.

Further information on customs and currency regulations can be obtained from the Polish consulates mentioned above.

Office Hours and Holidays.—Offices and FTOs in Poland are open Monday through Friday from 0800 to 1500 hours. Ministries are open from 0900 to 1500 hours. FTOs and other offices are open most Saturdays from 0800 to 1300 hours. Poland has begun introducing "free Saturdays," and business visitors planing to schedule appointments on Saturdays should check in advance. Public holidays observed are: January 1 (New Year), Easter Monday, May 1 (Labor Day), May 9 (Victory Day), Corpus Christi, July 22 (National Day), November 1 (All Saints Day), and December 25–26 (Christmas).

Hotels.—Hotel accommodations are on the whole adequate. Warsaw has several luxury hotels and at least one first class modern hotel is located in each major Polish city. Hotels run by ORBIS are usually the best. They can be identified by the word ORBIS included with their name. Due to a chronic shortage of hotel accommodations, advance reservations are strongly recommended. For hotel reservations contact the Polish National Tourist Offices at 500 Fifth Ave., New York, N.Y. 10036 or at 333 North Michigan Ave., Chicago, Ill. 60601.

Car Rental.—Cars can be rented on either a drive-it-yourself or chauffered basis through Obris-Avis and advance reservations are recommended.

Railroads.—The Polish railroad network is adequate and all major cities are connected by electric rail. In general, no reservations are required for rail travel. However, during the tourist season it is advisable that reservations be made for longer trips. First class tickets should be bought in all seasons. Trains are frequently crowded and passengers should arrive at the railroad station at least 30 minutes before departure to secure a seat.

Air.—All major Polish cities are connected by several daily flights run by the Polish airline LOT. Most of the airplanes are the fairly comfortable twin-engined Soviet Ilyushins. Reservations are a must and should be made at least a week in advance of the planned travel date. For additional information on internal air travel in Poland, contact LOT Polish Airlines, 21 East 51 St., New York, N.Y. 10022.

Bibliography

Polish Statistical Publications

Concise Statistical Yearbook of Poland, annual in English.

Rocznik Statystyczny (Statistical Yearbook), annual, in Polish.

Rocznik Statystyczny Handlu Zagranicznego (Statistical Yearbook of Foreign Trade), annual, in Polish.

Biuletyn Statystyczny (Statistical Bulletin), monthly, in Polish.

Polish statistical publications are available from: Glowny Urzad Statystyczny, al. Niepodleglosci 208, 00-925 Warsaw, Poland.

Polish Business and Economic Publications

Polish Foreign Trade, an illustrated monthly devoted to trade policy and basic information on foreign trade.

Polish Fair Magazine, an illustrated quarterly providing information on the International Trade Fairs at Poznan.

Polish Economic Survey, a bi-monthly on current information on the Polish economy and foreign trade.

Polish Economic Review, a bi-weekly publication containing economic information intended for the foreign press, government, industrial, commercial and educational institutions.

Polish Technical Review, a monthly published by the Central Technical Organization "NOT" providing information on recent Polish technological developments.

Polish Maritime News, a monthly published by the Maritime Branch in Gdynia of the Polish Chamber of Foreign Trade which is devoted to maritime matters.

Food From Poland, a quarterly of information and advertisements for the Polish food, agriculture, fishing, and forest industries.

Polish Engineering Offers, a monthly on Polish engineering capabilities.

Information for Businessmen Trading with Poland, Warsaw, 1977. Published bi-annually by the Polish Chamber of Foreign Trade, ul. Trebacka 4, Warsaw, Poland.

Information about and subscriptions to Polish publications should be addressed to: Ars-Polona-Ruch, Krakowskie Przedmiescie 7, P.O. Box 1001, 00-068, Warsaw, Poland.

U.S. Department of Commerce Publications

East-West Trade Update: A Commercial Fact Sheet For U.S. Business, OBR 78-23, July 1978. Revised semi-annually.

Foreign Economic Trends and Their Implications for the United States—Poland, FET 78-075, June 1978. Revised annually.

World Trade Outlook for Eastern Europe, Union of Soviet Socialist Republics and People's Republic of China, OBR 78-38, 1978. Revised semi-annually.

U.S. Trade Status With Communist Countries, monthly.

Selected Trade and Economic Data of the Centrally Planned Economies, December 1977. Revised annually.

East-West Trade Financing: An Introductory Guide. September 1976.

East-West Countertrade Practices: An Introductory Guide For Business. August 1978.

The Helsinki Final Act: A Guide for the U.S. Business Community. April 1977.

Export Administration Report, Semi-Annual Report on U.S. Export Controls to the President and the Congress.

Other U.S. Publications

Background Notes: Poland, U.S. Department of State. Revised annually.

East-West Foreign Trade Board Report. U.S. Department of the Treasury. Quarterly.

East European Economies Post Helsinki. A compendium of papers submitted to the Joint Economic Committee of the Congress of the United States, August 1977.

U.S. Government Publications can be ordered from the U.S. Government Printing Office, Superintendent of Documents, Washington, D.C. 20402.

Appendix A—Foreign Trade Organizations

AGROMET—MOTOIMPORT
ul. Przemyslowa 26
P. O. Box 990
00-950 Warsaw
Phone: 28-50-71
Telex: 813511 or 813665 moto pl.
Cable: MOTORIM WARSZAWA

Supervising Agency: Ministry of Heavy and Agricultural Machines Industry.

Import–Export: Tractors and other agricultural machinery, equipment, tools, and spare parts.

AGROS
ul. Zuriawia 32/34
P. O. Box P-41
00-950 Warsaw
Phone: 21-64-21 to 29
Telex: 814391 or 812694 agros wa.
Cable: AGROS WARSZAWA

Supervising Agency: Ministry of Foreign Trade and Shipping.

Import–Export: Alcoholic beverages, sugar products, tobacco, fruit and vegetable preserves, mushrooms, citrus fruits, dried fruit, coffee, tea, spices, pharmaceutical raw materials.

ANIMEX
ul. Pulawska 14
02-512 Warsaw
Phone: 49-48-51
Telex: 814491 ax pl.
Cable: ANIMEX WARSZAWA

Supervising Agency: Ministry of Foreign Trade and Shipping.

Import–Export: Meat and meat products, poultry, feathers and down, live animals, dairy products, frozen and canned game.

ARS POLONA-RUCH
Krakowskie Przedmiescie 7
P. O. Box 1001
00-068 Warsaw
Phone: 26-12-01
Telex: 813498
Cable: ARSPOLONA WARSZAWA

Supervising Agency: Workers' Publishing Cooperative "Prasa–Ksiazka–Ruch" responsible to the Ministry of Communications.

Import–Export: Books, periodicals, printing services, articles made of silver and precious stones, stamps, coins. Organizes yearly International Book Fair in Warsaw.

BALTONA
ul. Pulaskiego 6
P. O. Box 365
81-963 Gdynia
Phone: 21-60-36
Telex: 054361 balt pl
Cable: BALTONA GDYNIA

Supervising Agency: The Ministry of Foreign Trade and Shipping.

Responsible for:
—sales of goods in free zones outside Poland,
—shipchandlers and suppliers to diplomatic and consular corps in Poland and abroad,
—sales of provisions and personal articles at international fairs in Poland,
—sales of domestic and imported goods against foreign currency for tourists on border passages, ferry landing places, ships, and on board aircraft of LOT, the Polish Airlines.

BEFAMA
ul. Powstancow Slaskich 6
43-300 Bielsko Biala
Phone: 23-061
Telex: 035333 or 035290 bfmw pl.

Supervising Agency: Ministry of the Machine Industry

Export: Textile machinery, apparatus and equipment.

BUMIS
Al. Ujazdowskie 41
P. O. Box 58
00-950 Warsaw
Phone: 28-81-81
Telex: 812773 bomis
Cable: BUMIS WARSZAWA

Supervising Agency: Office of Management of Supplies

Export: Surpluses of machinery and raw materials.

BUDIMEX
ul. Zurawia 3/5
00-503 Warsaw
Phone: 29-23-97
Telex: 813473 chzb pl.
Cable: BUDIMEX WARSZAWA

Supervising Agency: Ministry of Building and Building Materials Industry

Export: Engineering, assembly and installation of complete plants and industrial buildings; renovation and preservation of historic architecture.

BUMAR
ul. Marchlewskiego 11
P. O. Box 85
00-828 Warsaw

Phone: 20-46-61 Bmar pl.
Cable: BUMAREX WARSZAWA

Supervising Agency: Ministry of the Machine Industry

Import–Export: Construction, mining and transportation machinery and equipment; vertical and horizontal transportation equipment including materials handling facilities; cement and brickmaking machinery.

H. CEGIELSKI
ul. Dzierzynskiego 223/229
P. O. Box 41
60-965 Poznan
Phone: 32-12-31
Telex: 0415343 pl.
Cable: HACEGIELSKI POZNAN

Supervising Agency: Ministry of Heavy and Agricultural Machines Industry

Import–Export: Ship engines and auxiliary equipment, complete ship engine plants, stationary engines and engines for diesel locomotives.

CENTROMOR
ul. Okopowa 7
P. O. Box 384
80-819 Gdansk
Phone: 31-22-71
Telex: 051376 or 051161 cemor gd.

Supervising Agency: Ministry of Heavy and Agricultural Machines Industry

Import–Export: Merchant ships, fishing vessels, LPG & LNG tankers, container ships, scientific–research and other vessels, marine equipment; consultations and designs for the construction of ships and shipyards.

CENTROZAP
ul. Ligonia 7
P. O. Box 825
40-036 Katowice
Phone: 51-34-01 to 09
Telex: 0312416 to 0312418 or 0312287 czap pl.
Cable: CENTROZAP KATOWICE

Supervising Agency: Ministry of Foreign Trade and Shipping

Import–Export: Foundries and equipment for metallurgical plants; specialists in mining and drilling machines and equipment except coal-mining and oil-drilling industries; complete plant for iron, steel and nonferrous metal works.

CIECH
ul. Jasna 12
P. O. Box 271
00-950 Warsaw
Phone: 26-90-01 to 09 or 26-90-31 to 35

Telex: 814561 cie pl.
Cable: CIECH WARSZAWA

Supervising Agency: Ministry of Chemical Industry

Import–Export: Pharmaceuticals, dyestuffs, pesticides, photochemicals, inorganic chemicals, fertilizers, plastics, glues, cosmetics, sulphur, salt, rubber and rubber products, oil, oil and coke derivatives, paints, licenses and know-how.

Specialized Divisions:

Ciech-Polfa

Import–Export: Drug products

Ciech-Organika
ul. Stawki 2
00-193 Warsaw
Phone: 30-91-11
Telex: 822356

Import–Export: Inorganic chemicals, dyestuffs

Ciech-Nitroplast

Import–Export: Plastics and Fertilizers

Ciech-Pollena
ul. Stawki 2
00-193 Warsaw
Phone: 39-91-11
Telex: 822356

Import–Export: Cosmetics

Ciech-Stomil
ul. Jaracza 78
90-243 Lodz
Phone: 819-63
Telex: 886258

Import–Export: Rubber and rubber products

Ciech-Petrolimpex
ul. Jasna 10
00-013 Warsaw
Phone: 26-71-01
Telex: 814691

Import–Export: Oil

Ciech-Technochem
ul. Stawki 2
00-193 Warsaw
Phone: 39-91-11
Telex: 822351

Export–Import: Licenses and know-how

COOPEXIM
ul. Zurawia 4
P. O. Box 257
00-950 Warsaw
Phone: 21-64-11

Telex: 814211 cox pl.
Cable: COPEX WARSZAWA

Supervising Agency: Central Union of Work Cooperatives

Import–Export: Ready-made clothes, bed covers, textiles, toys, Christmas tree ornaments, wickerwork, folk arts and crafts; leather and non-leather fancy goods; brushes.

Specialized Divisions:

Elksportu Konfekcji i Tkanin
ul. Mysia 3
00-496 Warsaw
Phone: 21-64-11

Export: Ready-made clothes and textiles

Artykulow Wikliniarskich
ul. Hibnera 5
00-018 Warsaw
Phone: 26-64-42

Import–Export: Wickerware

Wyrobow Ludowych i Artystycznych
ul. Rutkowskiego 8
00-020 Warsaw
Phone: 26-60-31

Import–Export: Folk arts and crafts

DAL
ul. Swietokrzyska 12
00-044
Phone: 20-03-11
Telex: 814831 dal pl.
Cable: DALOS WARSZAWA

Supervising Agency: Ministry of Foreign Trade and Shipping.

Responsibility: Arranges compensation deals, industrial cooperation, participation in mixed companies, re-export, export-import brokerage through commercial agencies in foreign countries.

DESA
Al. Jerozolimskie 2
00-374 Warsaw
Phone: 27-87-75
Telex: 812372 bhzd pl
Cable: BEHAZETDESA WARSZAWA

Supervising Agency: Ministry of Culture and Arts

Import–Export: Contemporary art, artistic glass and pottery, jewelry, replicas of antique furniture, coins, medals, posters.

ELEKTRIM
ul. Czackiego 15–17
P. O. Box 638

00-950 Warsaw
Phone: 26-62-71 to 79
Telex: 814351 hzem pl
Cable: ELEKTRIM WARSZAWA

Supervising Agency: Ministry of Foreign Trade and Shipping.

Import–Export: Electrical power plants and equipment, transmission lines, cables, wire communication equipment, lighting fixtures; electronics equipment.

ELWRO
ul. Ostrowskiego 32
53-238 Wroclaw
Phone: 69-031
Telex: 034518 eluro pl

Supervising Agency: Associated with FTO Metronex, attached to the Ministry of Machine Industry.

Import–Export: Computers, electronic calculators, peripheral equipment, software, assemblies and subassemblies.

ENERGOPOL
Al. Jerozolimskie 53
P. O. Box 367
00-950 Warsaw
Phone: 29-80-81
Telex: 813663 or 812487
Cable: ENERGOPOL WARSZAWA

Supervising Agency: General Management of Hydroenergy Constructions and Pipelines, Ministry of Building and Building Materials Industry

Export: Construction of water energy facilities, pipeline construction for natural gas and oil with associated plants; services in designing, know-how and construction of pipelines.

FILM POLSKI
ul. Mazowiecka 6/8
P.O. Box 161
00-950 Warsaw
Phone: 26-04-41
Telex: 813640
Cable: IMEXFILM WARSZAWA

Supervising Agency: Ministry of Culture and Arts.

Import–Export: films of all kinds. Provides services to foreign producers making films in Poland and arranges for studios, technical equipment and personnel including directors, cameramen, actors and actresses, etc.

HORTEX-POLCOOP
ul. Warecka 11a
P.O. Box 199
00-950 Warsaw
Phone: 26-52-81
Telex: 814451 hor pl
Cable: HORTPOL WARSZAWA

Supervising Agency: Central Union of Agricultural Cooperatives "Samopomoc Chlopska"

Import–Export: fruit, vegetables, fresh and frozen preserves, honey, potatoes, ready-made dishes, fodder, fertilizers, fresh flowers, bilateral exchange of consumer goods.

IMPEXMETAL
ul. Lucka 7/9
P.O. Box 62
00-958 Warsaw
Phone: 20-70-51
Telex: 814371
Cable: IMPEXMETAL WARSZAWA

Import–Export: all non-ferrous metals, semi-finished products, ball and roller bearings.

Supervising Agency: Ministry of Foreign Trade and Shipping

INTRACO
ul. Stawki 2
P.O. Box 812
00-950 Warsaw
Phone: 39-91-11
Telex: 812341 Traco pl

Supervising Agency: Ministry of Foreign Trade and Shipping. Rents office space and housing for foreigners in Poland: buildings administration and maintenance services; investments in Poland and abroad.

KOLMEX
ul. Mokotowska 49
P.O. Box 236
00-950 Warsaw
Phone: 28-44-41
Telex: 813270 kolx pl
Cable: KOLMEX WARSZAWA

Supervising Agency: Ministry of Heavy and Agricultural Machines Industry

Import–Export: Electric and diesel locomotives, rolling stock, electric trains, freight and special cars, machines and equipment for construction and maintenance of tracks.

KOPEX
ul. Grabowa 1
P.O. Box 245
40-952 Katowice
Phone: 58-00-45 to 48
Telex: 0315237 kopx pl
Cable: KOPEX KATOWICE

Branch Office:
ul. Krucza 36
00-921 Warsaw
Phone: 28-02-41
Telex: 813581

Supervising Agency: Ministry of Mining.

Import–Export: Complete plant equipment and services for coal mining and coal processing industries; oil rigs and equipment. Complete natural-ore enrichment plants; training of specialists and technical advisory services.

LABIMEX
ul. Stawki 2
P.O. Box 261
00-950 Warsaw
Phone: 39-91-11
Telex: 814230 lbmex pl
Cable: LABIMEX WARSZAWA

Supervising Agency: Ministry of Foreign Trade and Shipping.

Import–Export: scientific research apparatus, measuring and control equipment, laboratory equipment and glassware, microwave equipment, complete laboratories, know-how.

LOCUM
ul. Marchlewskiego 13
Phone: 20-03-51
Telex: 812399 zsm pl
Cable: LOCUM WARSZAWA

Supervising Agency: Central Union of Housing Cooperatives.

Sales of housing for convertible currencies.

METALEXPORT
ul. Mokotowska 49
P.O. Box 442
00-950 Warsaw
Phone: 29-92-41 or 28-22-91
Telex: 184241 mex pl
Cable: METALEX WARSZAWA

Supervising Agency: Ministry of Machine Industry.

Import–Export: Complete plants for metal working machine-tool industry, metal working machines, parts and equipment.

METRONEX
Al. Jerozolimskie 44
P.O. Box 198
00-950 Warsaw
Phone: 26-20-11 or 26-22-21
Telex: 814471 metronex wa
Cable: METRONEX WARSZAWA

Supervising Agency: Ministry of Machine Industry.

Import–Export: equipment for industrial automatic control process; electric and electronic measuring and testing equipment, computers (computer equipment and peripherals), apparatus and installations for nuclear engineering; all office equipment.

MINEX
Krakowskie Przedmiescie 79
P.O. Box P1002
00-950 Warsaw
Phone: 26-64-31
Telex: 814401 min pl
Cable: MINEX WARSZAWA

Supervising Agency: Ministry of Foreign Trade and Shipping.

Import–Export: building materials, products of the glass and ceramic industry, lead crystal articles, porcelain, mineral raw materials, cement, asbestos and asbestos products, insulating materials, silicon products, refractories.

NAVIMOR
ul. Matejki 6
P.O. Box 249
80-952 Gdansk
Phone: 47-09-13
Telex: 051453 navi pl
Cable: NAVIMOR GDANSK

Supervising Agency: Ministry of Foreign Trade and Shipping.

Import–Export: floating docks, fishing boats, cargo and passenger vessels for inland and coastal waters, yachts, sport and pleasure craft; ship repairs and modernization, ship equipment including engines for small vessels, refrigeration and fish processing equipment, rafts, life boats, etc.

Complete plant: inland ports, shipyards and their elements, coastal and inland fishing bases, shipyard equipment.

PAGED
Plac Trzech Krzyzy 18
P.O. Box 991
00-950 Warsaw
Phone: 29-52-41
Telex: 814221 pgd pl
Cable: HAZAPAGED WARSZAWA

Supervising Agency: Ministry of Forestry and Wood Industry.

Import–Export: timber, plywood, all wood products, cardboard, cellulose, paper and paper products; furniture.

PEWEX
ul. Stawki 2
P.O. Box 240
00-950 Warsaw
Phone: 39-91-11
Telex: 815404
Cable: PEWEX WARSZAWA

Supervising Agency: Ministry of Internal Trade Services.

Sale of goods for convertible currencies in special shops and kiosks in Poland.

PEZETEL
ul. Przemyslowa 26
P.O. Box 371
00-950 Warsaw
Phone: 28-50-71
Telex: 813430 pzl pl
Cable: PEZETEL WARSZAWA

Supervising Agency: Ministry of the Machine Industry.

Import–Export: aircraft, helicopters, gliders, air navigation equipment, jet engines, agricultural air services, motorcycles, golf carts, internal combustion piston engines.

POLEXPO
ul. Lopuszanska 38
P.O. Box 46
02-363 Warsaw
Phone: 46-04-01 to 09
Telex: 813633
Cable: POLEXPO WARSZAWA

Supervising Agency: Ministry of Foreign Trade and Shipping.

Organization, designing and arrangement of exhibitions in Poland and abroad; construction of layouts, models, and stands including interiors and exhibits.

POLIMEX-CEKOP
ul. Czackiego 7/9
P.O. Box 815
00-950 Warsaw
Phone: 26-80-01
Telex: 814271 poli pl
Cable: POLIMEX-CEKOP WARSZAWA

Supervising Agency: Ministry of Foreign Trade and Shipping.

Import–Export: machines, equipment and complete plants for food processing and sugar industry, building materials, glass, chemicals, wood and paper industries; installation of water treatment facilities, pumping stations, compressors and refrigeration equipment.

POL MOT
ul. Stalingradzka 23
P.O. Box 16
00-963 Warsaw
Phone: 11-00-01
Telex: 813901 or 813621 pompo pl
Cable: POLMOT WARSZAWA

Supervising Agency: Ministry of the Machine Industry.

Import–Export: passenger cars, trucks, buses, spare parts, car accessories, subassemblies.

POLSERVICE
ul. Szpitalna 5
P.O. Box 335
00-950 Warsaw

Phone: 27-80-61 to 67
Telex: 813539 upol pl
Cable: POLSERVICE WARSZAWA

Supervising Agency: Ministry of Foreign Trade and Shipping.

Import-Export: scientific, technical and economic co-operation; patents, licenses, know-how, technical services, technical documentation, consultation and assistance on technical and economic problems; skilled Polish engineers and technicians available for service abroad. Other technical services for: metallurgy, machine building industry, mining, shipbuilding, power and chemical industries, animal breeding, food engineering.

POLTEL
ul. J.P. Woronicza 17
P.O. Box P-35
00-950 Warsaw
Phone: 43-81-91
Telex: 812511 rtv pl
Cable: POLTEL WARSZAWA

Supervising Agency: State Committee for Radio and Television.

Import-Export: TV film, services, coproduction.

POLSKIE WYDAWNICTWO MUZYCZNE
ul. Krakowskie Przedmiescie 7
P.O. Box 26
00-950 Warsaw
Phone: 26-12-01
Telex: 813498 ap pl
Cable: PEWUEMBEHAZET

Supervising Agency: Ministry of Culture and Arts.

Import Export: musical scores, records, tapes.

POLSKI ZWIAZEK MOTOROWY
ul. Marszalkowska 124
P.O. Box 237
00-950 Warsaw

Supervising Agency: Committee for Sports and Tourism.

Sells spare parts to passenger cars of Western makes for convertible currencies.

RAFAMET
ul. Staszica 1
47-420 Kuznica Raciborska
Phone: 21
Telex: 036489 or 036405 rafam
Cable: RAFAMET KUZNIA RACIBORSKA

Supervising Agency: Ministry of Machine Industry.

Import-Export: special lathes for machining wheel sets for rolling stock; universal turning and boring mills.

ROLIMPEX
Al. Jerozolimskie 44
P.O. Box 364
00-950 Warsaw
Phone: 26-20-11 or 26-24-11
Telex: 814341 rolx pl
Cable: ROLIMPEX WARSZAWA

Supervising Agency: Ministry of Machine Industry.

Import-Export: grains, seeds, spices, sugar, fats, fodder, brewery raw materials, medicinal plants and cooking herbs, reproduction of seeds.

RYBEX
ul. Odrowaza 1
P.O. Box 60
70-965 Szczecin
Phone: 22-08-11 to 19
Telex: 0422326 ab rx pl
Cable: RYBEX SZCZECIN

Supervising Agency: Ministry of Foreign Trade and Shipping.

Import-Export: fish, processed fish, fish products, crab-fish.

SKORIMPEX
ul. 22 Lipca 74
P.O. Box 133
90-950 Lodz
Phone: 250-50
Telex: 886255
Cable: SKORIMPEX LODZ

Supervising Agency: Ministry of Light Industry.

Import-Export: skins and hides, leather and fur garments, leather and textile shoes, calfskin, pigskin, horse-hides, other leather and fur articles; tannings and extracts and semi-finished products for the leather industry; wooden sole footwear.

STALEXPORT
ul. Plebiscytowa 36
P.O. Box 401
40-922 Katowice
Phone: 51-22-11 to 19
Telex: 0312361 or 0312484 stex pl
Cable: STALEX KATOWICE
Branch Office:
ul. Krolewska 27
00-060 Warsaw

Supervisory Agency: Ministry of Foreign Trade and Shipping.

Import-Export: rolled steel products, quality steel products, scrap iron, ferro alloys; ores: iron, chrome, maganese, other metals.

TEXTILIMPEX
ul. Trangutta 25
P.O. Box 320
90-950 Lodz

Phone: 286-20 or 251-80
Telex: 886470 to 79
Cable: TEXTILIMPEX LODZ

Supervising Agency: Ministry of Light Industry.

Import-Export: Textiles, clothing, knitwares, hosiery, carpets, rugs, curtains, raw materials; design of textile mills.

TORIMEX
ul. Nowogrodzka 35/41
P.O. Box 394
00-950 Warsaw
Phone: 29-60-11
Telex: 813611
Cable: TORIMEX WARSZAWA

Supervising Agency: Ministry of Internal Trade and Services.

Import-Export: consumer goods, bilateral exchange between Polish and foreign department stores; supplies Polish specialized stores.

UNITECH
ul. Ratuszowa 11
03-450 Warsaw
Phone: 19-22-85
Telex: 813299 pl
Cable: UNITECH WARSZAWA

Supervising Agency: Ministry of the Machine Industry.

Service of electronic equipment, telephone and teletype service.

UNITRA
Al. Jerozolimskie 44
P.O. Box 66 Pl
00-950 Warsaw
Phone: 26-20-11 to 19 ; 26-22-21 to 29
Telex: 813827
Cable: ELUNI PL

Supervising Agency: Ministry of the Machine Industry.

Import-Export: electronic consumer goods: radios, TV sets, tape-recorders, etc., professional radio and TV equipment, automotive and marine electronic equipment; incandescent and fluorescent lamps.

UNIVERSAL
Al. Jerozolimskie 44
P.O. Box 370
00-950 Warsaw
Phone: 26-20-11 to 19 or 26-22-21 to 29

Telex: 814431 univ. pl
Cable: UNIVER WARSZAWA

Supervising Agency: Ministry of Foreign Trade and Shipping.

Import-Export: consumer household appliances, sewing machines, sporting, hunting and camping equipment, various household plastic and metal articles, bicycles, baby carriages, musical instruments; miscellaneous wire and metal products.

VARIMEX
ul. Wilcza 50/52
P.O. Box 263
00-950 Warsaw
Phone: 28-80-41 or 28-84-81
Telex 814311 pl
Cable: VARIMEX WARSZAWA

Supervising Agency: Ministry of Foreign Trade and Shipping.

Import-Export: medical apparatus, optical and photographic equiment; textile, shoe, tanning and clothing machinery; water and sanitary installations, printing machinery, equipment for restaurants, commercial and industrial scales, xerographic and typographic equipment, metal building fittings.

WEGLOKOKS
ul. Armii Czerwonej 119
40-156 Katowice
Phone: 58-24-31 to 39
Telex: 0312384 to 6 weks pl
Cable: WEGLOKOKS KATOWICE

Supervising Agency: Ministry of Foreign Trade and Shipping.

Import-Export: coal, coking coal, coke, electric power, water, gas.

ZJEDNOCZENIE GOSPODARKI TURYSTYCZNEJ
ul. Bracka 16
P.O. Box 195
00-950 Warsaw
Phone: 26-02-71
Telex: 814761 orb pl
Cable: GOSTUR WARSZAWA

Supervising Agency: Office for Import of Investments of the Union of Tourist Economy attached to the Committee for Sports and Tourism.

Import: Turnkey hotel facilities.

Compiled by Richard Lesczynski

Appendix B—Commercial Agents

MACIEJ CZARNECKI
ul. Marszalkowska 87
P.O. Box 215
00-950 Warsaw
Phone: 28-02-96 or 21-26-61
Telex: 813278 czar pl
Cable: CZAR WARSZAWA

DYNAMO
ul. Olszewska 8
P.O. Box 30
00-957 Warsaw
Phone: 49-31-51
Telex: 813428 dywa pl
Cable: DYNAMO WARSZAWA

EXIMPOL
ul. Stawki 2
P.O. Box 810
00-950 Warsaw
Phone: 39-91-11
Telex: 814640 exim pl
Cable: EXIMPOL WARSZAWA

MUNDIAL
Ul. Czerniakowski 58
P.O. Box P-6
00-950 Warsaw
Phone: 39-57-54
Telex: 813689 pl
Cable: MUNDIAL WARSZAWA

POLCOMEX
ul. Marszalkowska 140
P.O. Box 478
00-950 Warsaw
Phone: 28-84-41
Telex: 813452 pl
Cable: POLCOMEX WARSZAWA

POLIGLOB
ul. Stawki 2
P.O. Box 40
00-950 Warsaw
Phone: 39-91-11

Telex: 813557 glob pl
Cable: POLIGLOB WARSZAWA

POLIMAR
ul. Stawki 2
P.O. Box 151
00-193 Warsaw
Phone: 39-68-45
Telex: 814895 poli pl
Cable: POLIMAR WARSZAWA

TIMEX
ul. Stawki 2
P.O. Box 268
00-950 Warsaw
Phone: 39-91-11
Telex: 813678 tim wa
Cable: TIMWA WARSZAWA

TRANSACTOR
ul. Stawki 2
P.O. Box 276
00-950 Warsaw
Phone: 39-91-11
Telex: 813288 trwa pl
Cable: TRANSACTOR WARSZAWA

TRANSPOL
ul. Stawki 2
P.O. Box 280
00-950 Warsaw
Phone: 39-91-11
Telex: 813844
Cable: TRANSPOL WARSZAWA

UNITEX
ul. Stawki 2
P.O. Box 404
00-950 Warsaw
Phone: 39-91-11 or 39-93-11
Telex: 813751 utx pl
Cable: UNITEX WARSZAWA

UNITRONEX
ul. Stawki 2
00-950 Warsaw
Phone: 39-62-18 or 39-91-11 ext. 259
Telex: 812488

Marketing in Portugal

Contents

Report Revised May 1980

PORTUGAL

——— International boundary
⊛ National capital
········· Railroad
——— Road
✛ International airport

0   25   50   75 Miles
0   25   50   75 Kilometers

517921-12-75

Foreign Trade Outlook

The bulk of Portugal's foreign trade involves its partners in the European Free Trade Association (EFTA)[1] and member nations of the European Economic Community (EEC).[2] Since the 1974 Revolution, there have been substantial shifts in the volume, product composition, and geographic distribution of Portugueese trade. The trade deficit, already increasing rapidly since the end of the 1960's, widened considerably due to a number of external and internal factors: the political, social, and economic unrest following the April 25, 1974 Revolution; the sharp deterioration in the terms of trade due to the rise in oil prices and the contraction of traditional export markets; and the loss of Portugal's African territories. As a partial response to these developments, the Portuguese Government resorted to increased import restrictions and devaluation of the escudo.

During 1978 and 1979, there was substantial progress in reducing Portugal's growing payments deficits. In large part this was the result of a resurgence of emigrant worker remittances, tourist receipts, and exports. Portugal consequently has reduced some of its import restrictions.

Portugal's trade policy has also been influenced by its membership in the Organization for Economic Cooperation and Development (OECD), the General Agreement on Tariffs and Trade (GATT), and the International Monetary Fund (IMF). Portugal also has opened membership negotiations with the EEC or Common Market.

Trade with the World

Historically, Portugal has imported more than it has exported, creating trade deficits in its balance-of-payments ledgers. Statistics measuring a 6-year period demonstrate this growth, with Portuguese exports totaling $1.7 billion in 1973 and increasing by 39 percent by 1978 to $2.5 billion. Portuguese imports jumped by 80 percent over the same period from $2.8 billion in 1974 to $5.2 billion in 1978. Realignments of ex-

change rates and inflationary conditions account for much of this expansion.

The distribution of trade as shown in table 1 indicates that the two European economic blocs, the EEC and EFTA, dominate Portuguese trade patterns. Portugal's principal suppliers in 1978 were West Germany, the United States, the United Kingdom, France and Italy. Principal customers for Portuguese products were the United Kingdom, West Germany, France, the United States, Italy and Sweden. The share of the countries in the former escudo area (Angola, Mozambique), which represented privileged markets, had dwindled to less than 7 percent in 1978.

HOW TO OBTAIN BACKGROUND INFORMATION ABOUT THESE COUNTRIES

For those who wish *general* data about a country—data which goes beyond marketing and commerce—the editors recommend *Countries of the World and Their Leaders,* published as an annually updated yearbook by Gale Research Company, Detroit, Michigan 48226. Containing 4- to 20-page entries on 168 countries, the volume also provides several hundred pages of supplementary world data. Each country entry is prepared by the U.S. Department of State to provide a general briefing on the geography, people, culture, and political situation of the particular country. Each report provides some historical insight as well as a look at contemporary trends of lifestyle in the country. Reports also discuss a country's educational system, its press, ethnic groupings and religious practices.

Countries of the World and Their Leaders provides a fresh listing of cabinet ministers of each nation. In addition it lists health conditions the traveling businessman will wish to prepare for and includes information on passport procedures, customs and duties, and world climate conditions.

---

[1] Members of EFTA are: Austria, Iceland, Norway, Portugal, Sweden, Switzerland, and Finland (associate member).
[2] Members of the EEC are: Belgium, Denmark, France, Ireland, Italy, Luxembourg, the Netherlands, the United Kingdom, and West Germany.

Trade with the United States

U.S. exports to Portugal rose to a record $691 million in 1979, a sharp increase over $525 million in 1978. At the same time, imports from Portugal reached $243 million in 1979, up from $179 million in 1978. The United States has traditionally had a surplus in its trade with Portugal, one which reached an all time high of $448 million in 1979. As of 1978, the United States was Portugal's second major supplier (12 percent of total imports) and third best customer (7 percent of total exports). Traditionally, over half of U.S. exports to Portugal have consisted of agricultural exports, particularly corn, soybeans, wheat, and rice. U.S. industrial exports include iron and steel products, medicines, electrical machinery, and transportation equipment. Major U.S. imports from Portugal include wine, fish products, cork and cork products, canned vegetables, and sisal goods.

The composition of U.S.-Portuguese trade in 1978 and 1979 is shown in table 3.

Best Export Prospects

The demand for imported goods and services in the Portuguese market is varied and changing, but the following categories deserve special note.

Construction, Mining and Materials Handling Equipment. — This field offers promising opportunities for U.S. exports, both for individual products and potentially for the awarding of large project contracts. The government has announced a program for the construction of 100,000 new homes over the next few years. Other projects are underway or contemplated for petrochemical refineries, schools, public transportation, health clinics, highways, bridges, irrigation, water and sewage systems and mining. U.S. exporters have particularly good markets in prefabricated and modular housing, water and sewage systems, power generating facilities, highway construction and railway upgrading, and expansion of the automobile and automotive parts industries.

Metalworking Machinery and Finishing Equipment. — Projects for expansion and modernization of existing metalworking plants will increase demand for metrically calibrated advanced machine tools, foundry equipment and welding machinery. As certain large investment programs which have been delayed over the past few years are implemented, demand for fabricated metal forms, fittings and structures can be expected to rise rapidly. These projects include

railroad modernization, expansion of the automobile assembly industry, subway expansion and steel.

Food Processing, Packaging and Bottling Equipment. — Major objectives in this sector include satisfying increasingly sophisticated tastes of domestic consumers and tourists as well as strengthening the export competitiveness of the canned fish, tomato paste, vegetable, olive and orange juice industries. Agricultural assistance programs have been developed to encourage the establishment of farmers' cooperatives to improve production and processing capacity. Problems of seasonal supply variations and distribution bottlenecks are to be solved through a national slaughter-house network. The private sector is expected to be stimulated for new investments in swine production, sausage and meat processing, fruit and vegetable canneries and modernized fish processing.

Agricultural and Refrigeration Equipment. — Modernization of the agricultural sector has long been a high priority element in government economic planning. Food imports are a major contributor to the country's sizeable trade deficit. Improved technology and equipment will be needed to deal with the problems of small scale farming and antiquated production methods. Modernization will entail an improved

Table 1.—*Distribution of Portugal's Trade by Geographic Areas in 1978*
(in millions of U.S. dollars with percent of total in parentheses)

	Imports		Exports	
Total	5,170	(100%)	2,440	(100%)
Total OECD	3,987	(77%)	1,985	(81%)
Europe	3,151	(61%)	1,744	(71%)
EEC	2,368	(46%)	1,354	(55%)
West Germany	718	(14%)	318	(13%)
United Kingdom	520	(10%)	441	(18%)
France	465	(9%)	217	(9%)
Italy	282	(5%)	139	(6%)
Netherlands	181	(4%)	99	(4%)
Belgium-Luxembourg	164	(3%)	78	(3%)
EFTA	458	(9%)	323	(13%)
Switzerland	218	(4%)	92	(4%)
Sweden	123	(2%)	111	(4%)
Norway	48	(1%)	65	(3%)
Other countries of OECD total	325	(7%)	281	(11%)
Spain	282	(5%)	53	(2%)
Eastern Europe & U.S.S.R.	137	(3%)	79	(3%)
Africa	127	(2%)	174	(7%)
Angola	13	—	99	(4%)
Mozambique	20	—	34	(2%)
Latin America	167	(3%)	89	(4%)
Brazil	66	(1%)	25	(1%)
United States	613	(12%)	170	(7%)
Far East	251	(5%)	53	(2%)
Japan	168	(3%)	28	(1%)
Middle East	597	(12%)	31	(1%)
Iraq	257	(5%)	3	—
Saudi Arabia	155	(3%)	3	—
Iran	149	(3%)	3	—

Source: OECD Foreign Trade Statistics, Series A.

Table 2.—*Portuguese Trade with the World by Principal Categories, 1977-78*
(in millions of U.S. dollars)

Categories	Portuguese Imports 1977	1978
Food & live animals	714	646
Wheat	52	94
Corn	141	194
Animal feedstuffs	73	75
Sugar	65	55
Beverages & tobacco	19	32
Crude materials, inedible, except fuels	651	554
Oilseeds	131	132
Cotton	189	155
Mineral fuels, lubricants, etc.	737	819
Crude oil	610	649
Oils & fats, animal & vegetable	23	26
Chemicals	561	627
Medicinal & pharmaceutical preparations	101	124
Organic chemicals	176	148
Manufactured goods by chief value	789	829
Textile yarn	57	67
Iron or steel ingots	48	60
Iron or steel plates	97	90
Iron or steel bars	57	53
Aluminum	52	54
Machinery & transport equipment	1,301	1,423
Textile & leather machinery	39	72
Heating & cooling equipment	41	70
Motor vehicles	373	223
Motor vehicle parts	64	81
Internal combustion engines	46	50
Tractors	59	48
Misc. manufactured articles, n.e.c.	166	181
Items not classified by kind	2	5
Total	4,964	5,142

	Portuguese Exports 1977	1978
Food & live animals	169	186
Vegetables, preserved or prepared	60	54
Fish & fish preparations	67	84
Beverages & tobacco	135	164
Alcoholic beverages	134	163
Crude materials, inedible, except fuels	242	241
Wood, simply worked	57	60
Pulp & waste paper	94	73
Mineral fuels, lubricants, etc.	34	42
Oils & fats, animal & vegetable	11	13
Chemicals	103	129
Manufactured goods by chief value	667	836
Cork manufactures	121	137
Paper & paperboard	33	34
Textile yarn & fabrics	311	401
Pearls, precious & semiprecious stones	34	44
Machinery & transport equipment	299	328
Telecommunications equipment	54	71
Electrical machinery	41	71
Ships	52	22
Misc. manufactured articles, n.e.c.	320	439
Apparel & clothing	223	303
Footwear	48	63
Items not classified by kind	34	48
Total	2,013	2,426

Source: OECD Foreign Trade Statistics, Series B

distribution and warehousing system of which a cold storage network is a critical element.

Health Care Industries Instrumentation and Equipment.—As part of its overall program of improved social services, the government has stressed the importance of providing expanded health facilities and services to all sectors of the population, especially rural areas. In addition to remodeling and improving existing facilities, the government is studying the construction of 17 new health care centers throughout the country and a school of nursing in the Azores.

Hotel and Restaurant Equipment.—Tourism, long a major offset to Portugal's traditional trade deficit, has rebounded sharply in recent years. Official estimates project a 50 percent increase in visitors or 6 million tourists by 1985, particularly in the Algarve. Sales opportunities appear particularly strong for air conditioning systems and possibly elevators.

Table 3.—*U.S. Trade with Portugal by Value of Principal Categories, 1978-79*
(in millions of U.S. dollars)

	U.S. Exports 1978	1979
Food & live animals	263.4	355.1
Wheat	69.5	89.1
Corn	141.0	206.9
Beverages & tobacco	1.9	2.7
Crude materials, inedible, except fuel	111.1	146.0
Oilseeds, oil nuts	88.4	102.4
Raw cotton	13.4	12.0
Mineral fuels, lubricants, etc.	17.3	18.8
Coal	16.3	17.8
Oils & fats, animal & vegetable	2.8	5.6
Chemicals	13.7	20.6
Medicinal & pharmaceutical products	5.8	7.5
Synthetic resins & plastic materials	1.8	8.2
Manufactured goods by chief value	6.8	11.2
Machinery & transport equipment	63.9	109.9
Aircraft & spacecraft & parts	10.7	43.8
Office machines & ADP equipment	17.3	18.3
Electronic components	4.2	1.5
Telecommunications equipment	4.2	5.5
Misc. manufactured articles, nec	10.5	12.8
Items not classified by kind	10.4	2.8
Special category	3.3	—
Total	525.1	691.3

	U.S. Imports 1978	1979
Food & live animals	16.9	18.3
Vegetables & fruit	5.6	7.0
Fish & fish preparations	7.8	9.7
Beverages & tobacco	30.2	34.6
Wine	29.7	33.8
Mineral fuels, lubricants, etc.	—	30.4
Crude materials, inedible, except fuel	7.0	7.0
Oils & fats, animal & vegetable	.8	.8
Chemicals	5.9	7.7
Medicinal & pharmaceutical preparations	2.8	4.9
Manufactured goods by chief value	56.9	69.7
Cork manufactures	14.2	13.9
Yarn & fabric, textile	17.0	18.8
Iron & steel	8.6	12.5
Machinery and transport equipment	26.9	30.4
Office machines	2.0	2.4
Telecommunications equipment	—	.1
Misc. manufactured articles, nec	29.5	38.7
Jewelry	2.9	5.3
Wearing apparel	13.9	13.2
Items not classified by kind	5.1	5.8
Total	180.1	243.5

Source: U.S. Bureau of the Census, Department of Commerce, FT 455 and FT 155, 1978 and 1979.

Textile Machinery and Equipment. — The textile and wearing apparel industry is one of the most important segments of the Portuguese economy and constitutes a leading source of foreign exchange. Due to increased labor costs and low productivity, introduction of modern technology and more sophisticated machinery will be indispensable for the textile sector to maintain its position. The textile industry employs over 17,000 workers and provides about 30 percent of Portugal's total exports.

Distribution and Sales Channels

Distribution Centers

The Portuguese population is mainly concentrated on the coast where the largest urban centers of Lisbon, in the south, and Oporto, in the north, are located. These two cities and their zones of influence comprise the industrial and commercial centers of Portugal. Portuguese industry, including manufacturing, construction and energy production, contributed 44 percent of GDP in 1977 and employed about one-third of the labor force.

Major industries located in the Lisbon industrial area include oil refining, chemicals, cement, iron and steel, electronics, food products, beverages, shipyards and machinery. Oporto's major industries are textiles, rubber, footwear, fish canning and preserving, wine, machinery and oil refining. Petrochemical complexes are being constructed in the Sines area.

Other centers of commercial or industrial importance in Portugal are: Setubal, an industrial and fishing center specializing in fish canning, cork, automobile assembly, metallurgy, woodpulp and cement; Coimbra, the university center of Portugal with food products, textiles, beer and chemical industries located there; Braga, an ideal location for activities requiring large and quickly adaptable labor, e.g., assembly plants for radio sets, clothing, textiles, cutlery and furniture; Aveiro, an area manufacturing wood products, footwear, engines and also a dairy farming region; and Faro, a tourism area in the Algarve.

Sales Channels

As elsewhere, the key to successful selling is an astute assessment of market requirements and the ability to satisfy these demands by providing the right products taking into consideration price, timing and location.

Portugal is a relatively small market where most foreign firms limit themselves to one representative for the entire country. Different types of products produced by the same company sometimes are represented by different firms, but most local firms want exclusive rights to market. Imports are normally made by importers, distributors or sales agents who also operate as wholesalers and retailers. Industrial equipment and raw materials are frequently imported by large industrial firms and end users. Most product lines are handled by relatively few firms, i.e. 10 or 20, but usually no more than one or two. Experienced service capability and spare parts availability varies widely.

Most U.S. — made goods can be easily imported, but drugs and pharmaceutical products are imported only by firms registered with the Regulating Commission for Chemical and Pharmaceutical Products, 43-3 Calçada do Carmo, 1200 Lisbon.

Business activities and operations are generally concentrated in Lisbon and Oporto. However, most importers and wholesalers have branch offices in the principal towns or sales agent networks covering the entire country. The islands of Madeira and the Azores are generally covered by firms with headquarters in Lisbon.

Consultation with the American Embassy Commercial Section for guidance regarding distributor capabilities is recommended. Those firms that wish to visit Portugal to interview potential distributors can count on the full cooperation of the Embassy in Lisbon and Consulate in Oporto.

Mail-Order Selling

The Portuguese lack confidence in products marketed door-to-door or sold by mail. Also the large number of small retail shops handicaps such sales techniques. Mail-order and door-to-door sales are growing, however, despite a recent law that forbids selling by mail unless products are duly ordered.

Leasing

Equipment leasing services are virtually nonexistent except for some types of construction and roadbuilding machinery. Leasing of heavy equipment such as materials handling machinery is starting to be used by large industrial firms.

Installment Sales

Installment selling is used in the marketing of motor vehicles, radio and television sets, household appliances and foreign travel. For certain commodities and services, there are regulations on the minimum initial cash payment and time period over which installments may extend. There is legislation which establishes limits on installment sales. For example, the minimum downpayment for automobiles costing less than $7,000 is 25 percent with the balance repaid over 2½ years; for automobiles costing more than $7,000 but less than $9,000, the downpayment is 40 percent with the balance repaid over 2 years; for automobiles costing more than $9,000, installment sales are not allowed.

Franchising

There are no local laws prohibiting franchising. As is the case with any capital outflow, approval by the Bank of Portugal is required. The following sectors are considered promising for franchise development: fast-food restaurants; educational products; audio-visual systems; and the construction of prefabricated materials for office buildings, plant sites, schools and military establishments.

Government Procurement

U.S. firms desiring to expand their exports of goods or services to Portugal through participation in government tenders can accomplish this most effectively through association with a reliable and active Portuguese firm or the establishment of a local branch or subsidiary. Association with a registered Portuguese company is essential in bidding on public works projects as the requisite licenses are normally not granted to foreign firms and Portuguese engineers must supervise or participate in the supervision of the project. U.S. contractors should insure themselves that their local agents possess the necessary licenses and maintain contact with the government's Development Planning Commission.

The general system of calls for bids is issued by the Ministry of Public Works, which is responsible for all major construction and engineering projects in Portugal. Government tenders are published in the *Diario da Republica* and in one or two national daily newspapers. Tenders for public works also are published in the local newspaper of the region where the project is to be constructed.

Except for the licensing of public work projects, there are no restrictions against direct bidding by foreign firms, but such bids have less chance of success because preference is given to Portuguese firms and their products, if of comparable quality. Bids submitted by foreign firms represented locally are welcome.

Each U.S. bidder, or the bidder's agent, normally must submit a statement, notarized at the Embassy in Lisbon or the Consulate in Oporto, stating compliance with the general conditions of the tender and with Portuguese courts of law, without claim to any privileges based on nationality. Bids must be submitted in the Portuguese language, in prescribed official format, on the day specified in the announcement. Time limits for submission of bids may range from 10 days to 5 or 6 months, depending on the total bid value and the complexity of the specifications. The bidder, or the bidder's representative, must be present when bids are opened.

The right to cancel the tender, to make partial bid awards, and to accept a bid other than the lowest is reserved by the Government.

Industrial Property Protection

Patents and Trademarks. — Portugal is a member of the International Union for the Protection of Industrial Property and a party to the Madrid Agreements on international registration of trademarks and on the prevention of the use of false origins.

A patent is defined as a certificate granted by the State that gives an exclusive right to employ or use an invention in industry, and to introduce into commerce or offer for sale, articles produced in accordance with the specifications of the protected property. There are two essential requirements that must be fulfilled before issuance of a patent. The applicant must have a property right on the device or technique to be patented and the novelty of the invention must be shown.

An affidavit is submitted by the applicant to the Industrial Property Bureau of the Ministry of Economic Coordination by a local agent of the foreign firm, with detailed specifications in Portuguese, in duplicate, plus drawings. Application for a patent is limited to five products in one class. A notice is then published in the Industrial Property Bulletin describing the device. After a 90-day wait, during which objections to the granting of the patent can be received, the patent rights are granted. The life of the patent is 15 years, which may not be renewed.

A trademark is understood to mean any sign of physical medium which is used to identify a product and serves to distinguish it from similar products in commerce and industry. Trademarks on all products may be registered in Portugal by foreign and domestic firms. Under Portuguese law, registration is the same as ownership of a trademark with registration accepted by one firm, or jointly by two or more. Exporters wishing to qualify for government assistance must have their trademarks registered in the countries of destination and Portugal.

U.S. applicants interested in registering trademarks in Portugal are required to submit a certificate of U.S. registration. Generally, the U.S. Patent Office Seal is acceptable evidence of registration. The certificate must be submitted within 90 days from the date of publication of the application in the Industrial Property Bulletin. Extensions of the time limit may be granted.

Trademarks are registered for a 10-year period and are indefinitely renewable. To remain in effect, a trademark must be used within 3 years. Slogans are to be written in Portuguese, except for goods to be exported. Protection for industrial designs and models is for a 5-year period, renewable indefinitely.

The payment of taxes and fees is required to keep a patent or trademark in force. Payments may be made through an official agent of the industrial property or some other third person resident in Portugal having power of attorney from the patent or trademark owners.

Trade Fair Schedule

Portugal annually hosts a number of national and international fairs. Occasionally, the U.S. Department of Commerce participates in Portuguese fairs or sponsors promotional events, e.g. trade missions, seminar missions or industrial catalog shows. Additional information concerning Portuguese fairs and trade promotion activities may be obtained from the nearest Commerce Department District Office or the Office of Country Marketing, International Trade Administration, U.S. Department of Commerce, Washington, D.C. 20230. The 1980 trade fair schedule for Portugal is shown below by city and month:

Aveiro
July—AGROVOUGA (Agricultural and cattle breeding). Annual

Braga
April—AGRO (Agricultural fair). Annual
June—Motor (Motors, automobiles). Annual
July—MOVELNOR (Wood furniture). Annual

Coimbra
June—CIC (Commercial and industrial fair). Annual

Lisbon
January—FILGRAFICA/FILEME (Graphic industry, office furniture). Annual
March—FILMODA (Textiles, fashion). Annual
March—NAUTICAMP. (Camping, sports). Annual
May—International Fair. Annual
June—JUVENTUS (Children and youth activities). Annual
November—INTERCASA (Furniture). Annual
December—FILDECOR/FILOTEL (Decoration, household appliances, hotel equipment). Annual

Oporto
February—PORTEX (Textiles, apparel). Annual
April—FIMAP (Woodworking machinery). Annual
May—EXPOMOVEL (Furniture, decoration). Annual SEQUIATO (Automobile industry equipment). Annual
October— International Metalworking Fair, Annual.

Santarem
June—Agricultural Fair. Annual

Tomar
October—Agricultural Fair. Annual

Vale de Cambra
June—LACTI (Dairy, agricultural, commercial and industrial). Annual

Viseu
August—St. Mathews Show (Handicrafts). Annual

Trade Regulations

Import Tariff System

The customs tariff for metropolitan Portugal (European Portugal, Madeira and the Azores) uses the Customs Cooperation Council Nomenclature (CCCN), which was formerly the Brussels Tariff Nomenclature, and comprises a maximum and a minimum rate schedule. The maximum tariff is, in principle, applicable to goods originating in countries that have not signed commercial treaties with Portugal granting them special benefits. The minimum tariff is applied to goods from all countries entitled to the benefits of the most-favored-nation treatment (i.e., members of the General Agreement on Tariffs and Trade—GATT—and countries with which Portugal has signed trade agreements), including the United States and most other countries.

As a rule, duties are fairly low on raw materials and on manufactured products not produced by domestic industry. Many raw materials are temporarily exempt from import duties and certain capital equipment used in specified industrial sectors also is exempt from duty when not produced in Portugal.

As a result of concessions, granted by Portugal in the GATT tariff negotiations of 1960–61 and 1964–67, a limited number of products enter at reduced minimum rates when imported from GATT countries, including the United States.

Information regarding Portugal's duties applicable to specific products may be obtained free of charge from the Office of Country Marketing/International Trade Administration, U.S. Department of Commerce, Washington, D.C. 20230, telephone 202-377-4508; or from any Department of Commerce District Office. Inquiries should contain a complete description, including BTN, SITC, or U.S. Schedule B Export Commodity numbers, if known.

Trade with EEC and EFTA.—Almost all nonagricultural imports from EEC and EFTA countries enter duty free or at 20 percent of the minimum rates. According to a decision taken by EFTA in 1979 and by the EEC in 1972, all such import duty rates were to be eliminated in stages at the latest by January 1, 1980. However, in March 1979, Portugal was authorized by its EFTA partners, and in December 1979, by the EEC countries (through a complementary protocol to the 1972 Portugal-EEC trade agreement) to levy up to 20 percent of the duty rates on certain industrial products. The duty rates are to be eliminated in stages by the end of 1984.

Imports from Denmark and the United Kingdom, members of EFTA until 1973, continue to be accorded preferential tariff treatment largely as before.

Portugal has started membership negotiations with the EEC with entry expected sometime in 1983. An extensive transitional period of tariff adjustment, particularly for sensitive product categories, may be expected.

Portugal-Spain Trade.—Portugal, together with its six EFTA partners, signed a multilateral trade agreement with Spain in 1979 which contains special provisions aimed at eliminating trade barriers between Spain and Portugal. Free trade is to be achieved in two consecutive phases, commencing with the treaty's entry into force sometime in early 1980.

Special Import Charge.—In addition to the import duty, there is a special import charge of 10 percent for most products and a 60 percent rate for luxury goods such as wines, tobacco, alcoholic beverages, prepared foods, furniture, cameras, watches, perfumes and cosmetics.

Basis of Duty Assessment.—Most Portuguese duties are specific duties and are levied on the dutiable basis indicated in the tariff. This basis may be gross, legal net, or actual net weight. The metric system of weights and measures is used in customs transactions.

For ad valorem duties the value of an import is taken to be its normal price, i.e., the sale price in the open market between a buyer and seller independent of each other. This normal price is based on the following assumptions: (1) that the goods are treated as having been delivered to the buyer at the place of entry into Portugal; (2) that the seller includes in the price of the goods all costs, freight charges, insurance, and expenses incidental to the sale and delivery of the goods to that place, and (3) that the buyer will bear any duties and taxes payable in Portugal.

The normal price also presupposes that price is the sole consideration, and that the price is not influenced by any commercial, financial, or other relationship between the buyer and seller other than that relationship created by the sale of the goods in question.

For customs purposes the invoice price may be taken as the value of an import, provided the calculation thereof fulfills the conditions required in the determination of the normal price, and no doubt exists as to the accuracy of the details supplied.

The foregoing does not apply to medicinal products, which are dutiable on the sales price to the public.

All duties are payable in current Portuguese escudos. It is suggested that banks or the financial page of major newspapers be consulted for the current value.

Import Licensing

Portuguese importers must have an import license (also called a bulletin of import registration) for nearly all shipments into Portugal, including Madeira and the Azores. However, most products have been liberalized, which means that licenses for these products are granted automatically. Imports of liberalized products valued at less than 5,000 escudos do not require an import license.

Generally, each application for an import license for nonliberalized products is considered on its own merits by the Directorate-General of Commerce based on the relative needs of the national economy. General criteria include the availability of similar products of domestic origin, more favorable prices or terms available from other foreign sources, and trade and payment agreement commitments.

Licenses are valid for 90 days for clearance of goods from Customs and cannot be extended beyond that time. Once the deadline has passed, a new license must be obtained. For payment purposes, validity of the license is 120 days and can be extended up to one year, following the clearance of the goods through Customs. The U.S. exporter should be certain that the Portuguese importer has a license which will be valid when the shipment arrives.

Import licenses for shipments valued up to 5 million escudos are issued by the Foreign Trade Division of the Directorate General of Commerce or by duly authorized agencies. The latter include: the Public Enterprise for Cereal Supplies-EPAC, 26 Ave. Almirante Gago Coutinho, 1000 Lisbon; the National Bureau of Livestock Products, 20 Rua Castilho, 1200 Lisbon; and the Regulatory Commission for Chemical and Pharmaceutical Products, 43-3 Calcada do Carmo, 1200 Lisbon.

Licenses for shipments exceeding the value of 5 million escudos are issued by the Foreign Trade Control Commission of the Ministry of Finance.

In certain cases, special Bulletins of Import Registration or Global Bulletins may be issued with a one year validity. Global Bulletins are designed to facilitate automatic issuance of import licenses for each fraction of the shipment, but they do not replace the regular import license which has to be secured for each shipment or portion of a Global Bulletin.

Imports of passenger motor vehicles and a number of other products, including household appliances, domestic sewing machines, radio and television sets, tape recorders, firearms, are subject to quotas.

Exchange Controls. — Controls over foreign exchange transactions are exercised by the Ministry of Finance through the Bank of Portugal and the various local banks. The same document that serves as an import license serves as a foreign exchange permit. The issuance of the import license guarantees the availability of the necessary foreign exchange. The importer must declare that the foreign exchange is to be used solely for the payment of the respective imports. If the goods are not imported, the importer must sell the foreign exchange back to the bank from which the importer purchased it.

For transactions valued less than 5,000 escudos, for which an import license is not required, the importer must present a pertinent commercial document in order to obtain the necessary foreign exchange.

Internal Taxes. — The most important tax affecting imports is the Transactions Tax or "Imposto de Transaccoes." The basic rate of the tax is 15 percent although a number of basic items and food products are exempt. The tax may range up to 75 percent on luxury items such as private aircraft, jewelry, watches, sporting equipment, tobacco, perfumes, alcoholic beverages and cameras. If the importer is also a registered wholesaler or manufacturer, the tax is charged on the wholesale value of the imported item. If the importer is not a registered wholesaler or producer, the tax is levied at the time of clearance on the total value of the imported item, including freight, insurance and duty.

Shipping Documents

To entitle Portuguese importers to the minimum rates of the Portuguese tariff, the following documents are required for ocean or air cargo shipments to Portugal (including Madeira and the Azores): a bill of lading or an airwaybill accompanied by a commercial invoice stating the origin and certified by a chamber of commerce (or, in the absence of such a chamber of commerce, by the Customs or Port authorities) and, in certain instances, by a certificate of origin.

Bills of Lading and Airwaybills. — Bills of lading and airwaybills require no consular legalization. However, these documents should, if possible, state the origin. "To order" bills of lading are acceptable if they bear the shipper's endorsement. Two copies in Portuguese or English are required.

Commercial Invoices. — When a commercial invoice is presented without proper certification, the bill of lading or airwaybill will suffice provided these documents state the origin.

In the cases involving commodities that have undergone industrial transformation not representing full process of manufacture in the country of origin or which have passed through free ports or zones, the respective commercial invoice shall bear notation issued under the terms of the preliminary instructions of the Portuguese import tariff by the Portuguese Consulate having jurisdiction in that area.

Certificate of Origin. — Certificates of origin are not required on direct shipments (ocean, air, or parcel post) or for goods transshipped via a third country on a through bill of lading or airwaybill in which the origin is stated. Importers in Portugal, however, sometimes request certificates of origin.

To qualify for the minimum rates of the Portuguese tariff, certificates of origin must be furnished for shipments not covered by a commercial invoice, a through bill of lading or airwaybill stating the origin. Certificate-of-origin forms are obtainable from Portuguese consulates. The certificates must be visaed by the Portuguese consul, upon presentation of satisfactory evidence of origin, either at the port of original shipment or the port of transshipment.

Articles imported from countries enjoying the minimum rates, and made of parts originating in more than one country, will be subject to such favorable rates if it is proven by a consular certificate that the value of the material from the country in question, increased by the cost of labor, represents at least one half the value of the articles.

Foreign goods arriving in Portuguese ports from free zones or free ports must be accompanied by a certificate or origin visaed by a Portuguese consul in the free area.

Indirect shipments (those not covered by a through bill of lading, an airwaybill, or a certified commercial invoice in which the origin is stated) require a certificate or origin.

Postage affixed to packages sent by parcel post is sufficient proof of their origin.

Special Customs Provisions

Entry and Reexport. — There is no fixed period during which goods must be declared after arrival, whether for consumption, transit, temporary admission, warehousing, or reexportation. If goods arrive before their related documents, they are stored ex officio by the Port Authority, the expense of storage varying with the merchandise

Declarations for clearance ("Declarações de despacho") must be presented on regular printed forms and must contain the usual information accompanied by documentation required under Customs regulations. Declaration of certain easily classified articles must be made in accordance with official customs classification nomenclature.

The importer may examine the goods to find out their exact descriptions for the declaration.

Free Zones and Ports. — There are, properly speaking, no free trade zones, free ports, or transit zone facilities in Portugal. However, existing customs-privileged facilities described below permit the accomplishment of most commercial and industrial operations traditionally carried out in free trade zones and similar facilities.

Warehousing. — Several types of warehouses and related facilities exist under current Portuguese customs legislation where goods subject to import duties and taxes may be stored without the payment of these charges until their clearance through customs or reexportation. Depending on the nature of the warehouse, goods stored therein may be subject either to direct customs control (no modification of the packing or the goods is permitted) or to customs supervision (alteration of the goods or their packing may take place). Current legislation permits the operation of any industry in warehousing facilities under customs supervision.

Among the warehouses directly controlled and operated by customs are transit warehouses for the temporary storage of goods imported into the country prior to reshipment to other destinations. Associations, corporations, companies and other businesses can, with government authorization, establish transit warehouses by the prior posting of bond. Imported goods expressly marked "in transit" may be stored up to 2 months. Transshipment warehouses, similar to those described above, can be established on vessels and are permanently policed by customs guards.

The warehousing facilities described below are merely supervised by the customs. They differ basically from those described above in that the law permits any industry to operate within them.

Bonded warehouses ("entrepostos"), which are maintained for the storage of goods intended for later consumption in Portugal or for exportation, are currently in operation in the Lisbon area. These are enclosed and policed areas providing open and covered storage space where goods of foreign origin may be stored duty free for 2 years. Operations such as assembling, storing, sampling, mixing, blending, sorting, repacking, and manipulating of goods are permitted; however, no buildings are available under lease for these operations. Exhibiting and manufacturing are not permitted within the warehouses. Entry is denied to explosives, dangerous commodities and easily-perishable goods.

Free or bonded zones ("depositos francos") are established within fenced areas where certain industries can set up assembly or manufacturing operations utilizing materials of domestic and foreign origin to produce goods for export. Any products sold locally must be imported, i.e. clear customs. The Government must approve applications to establish free zones, and it stipulates conditions under which they are to be set up and operated, in particular relating to the use of domestic raw materials and products. Electrical, electronic and automotive production facilities are located in the most important free zones in operation.

Free zones ("zonas francas") also may be fenced areas at seaports or neighboring localities that are equipped for loading and unloading goods, for supplying fuels and foodstuffs to vessels or for warehousing commodities that are to be transformed and later reexported.

Goods deposited in any of these warehouses that exceed the warehousing period, or are abandoned, are ordinarily transferred to a customs auction warehouse and sold, with the proceeds used to pay the charges due.

Goods stored in all these warehouses are subject to the duties and customs regime in force on the date payment is made, and not to those in force when the goods entered the warehouse.

Duty Refund.—Duties are not refunded once goods have been cleared through customs, but excess payments to customs can be claimed within a period of 2 years from the date of payment. The Minister of Finance, however, may authorize the reimbursement of duties collected on imports of merchandise, namely machinery, which—having been entered into consumption in execution of a firm sales contract—have to be returned abroad or destroyed under customs supervision upon authorization expressly given by the General Administration of Customs because such merchandise was found defective or for some other reason does not comply with the terms of the contract.

Temporary Admission.—Goods imported under the temporary duty-free admission regime must be reexported, as a rule, within 6 months. An extension may be granted, but if it is refused the goods must be reexported within 20 days from the date the notice of refusal is received by Customs. A clearance deposit or guaranty is required on a good admitted under the temporary free-admission regime, which is returned or canceled when the reexportation is completed.

Drawback.—The drawback system in Portugal may be applied in two different manners: (1) After the export of a commodity there is reimbursement, of any duties paid on raw materials, parts or components imported for the purpose of manufacturing the commodity; or (2) exemption of import duties on raw materials, parts of components upon their entry into Portugal on the condition that the said duties shall be paid if the goods manufactured with the raw materials, parts of components are not exported within 2 years from the date of importation. Requests for drawback treatment are to be made to the Ministry of Industry and Technology.

Samples and Advertising Matter

As a member of the Convention to Facilitate the Importation of Samples and Advertising Matter, Portugal grants duty-free entry to properly labeled samples (except samples of tobacco and matches) when the reduced duty on each sample does not exceed 2 escudos or when the duty on a set of samples does not exceed 50 escudos. Samples for which the duty is greater than these amounts are admitted under deposit of duty or bond, which is returned or canceled as is appropriate, if the samples are reexported with 6 months. This period is extendable.

Samples are subject to the same documentation requirements that apply to ordinary commercial shipments when the duty on one sample exceeds 2 escudos or the duty on a set of samples exceeds 50 escudos.

Catalogs, pricelists, and trade notices enter duty free provided that: the name of the manufacturer or sellers is readily apparent; each shipment consists of not more than one document; or, if it consists of more than one document, does not exceed 1 kilogram gross weight.

All the other shipments of advertising matter are dutiable.

Carnets.—As a result of various customs conventions, to which both Portugal and the United States are parties, simplified procedures in the form of the "carnet" are available for the importation of commercial samples, advertising materials including film, and medical or other professional equipment into Portugal for a limited time. The carnet is a customs document that eliminates extensive customs procedures for temporary imports; with the carnet such goods may be imported without the payment of duty and tax, or the provision of additional security.

Professional equipment includes equipment for the press or for radio or television broadcasting; cinematographic equipment; engineering, topographical, surgical, electrical, archeological, and entertainment equipment. Commercial samples generally refer to those imported solely for demonstration purposes in the solicitation of orders from abroad. Items not included in the carnet system are items already sold or offered for sale, unmounted gems, and handmade one-of-a-kind articles such as carpets, certain pieces of furniture, paintings and sculpture.

Carnets are issued for a fee in the United States by the U.S. Council of the International Chamber of Commerce, Inc., 1212 Avenue of the Americas, New York, New York 10036, telephone (212) 354-4480. Applications for carnets are available from the U.S. Council or from U.S. Department of Commerce District Offices. Carnets are valid 1 year from the date of issuance.

Advance Rulings on Classification

Advance binding rulings on tariff classifications may be obtained upon presentation to the customhouse at Oporto or Lisbon of seven samples of the article in question, duly packed, labeled and signed by the petitioners, with a petition declaring the commercial or industrial name of the product, the raw materials that enter into its composition, its applications or uses, value, the place from which it will be shipped to Portugal, and the place where it is manufactured or originates. In the case of machines, apparatus, or other articles for which it is not possible to present samples, a set of drawings, models, or photographs, accompanied by a detailed description of the quantity and kind of the component parts and the purpose for which the machine or apparatus is intended, may be substituted.

When a change of classification results by virtue of a legislative measure, or by a ruling of the "Tribunal Técnico Aduaneiro" (Technical Customs Tribunal) and this classification change affects an advance ruling, the advance ruling will remain in force with respect to merchandise already in Portugal or already enroute before the date on which the change is made, unless 1 year has elapsed since the date the advance ruling was announced.

Prior consultations on the classification of products of indefinite composition, or those which cannot readily be identified, are not permitted. Analyses are made at the expense of the interested party.

Antidumping Provisions

If the practice of dumping results or is likely to result in serious losses to Portuguese producers, or results or is likely to result in a considerable delay in the installation of a new line of production in Portugal, the importation of the commodity in question may become subject to a special duty called "antidumping duty," which shall amount to no more than the margin of dumping.

Similarly, if the concession of foreign government subsidies results or is likely to result in the above-mentioned injuries, the commodity in question may become subject to a special duty called "compensatory duty," which shall amount to no more than the amount of the subsidy which was granted.

Portuguese producers can request their Government to investigate cases in which they feel they are being injured because of dumping or subsidies.

Marking and Labeling Requirements

Imported goods need not be marked with an indication of origin unless they bear the mark of a Portuguese house. False indication of origin is prohibited.

There are no special regulations for the labeling of general merchandise. However, some products require markings before they may be sold in Portugal. These are pharmaceutical products, tobacco, food pastes, fertilizers, wines, brandy, and foodstuffs containing preservatives or artificial colorings. Jewelry and other articles of gold, silver or platinum must be assayed and hallmarked in Portugal by the assayer's offices in Lisbon or Oporto; the regulations as to the content of such articles are stringent. The importation of these articles is limited to those firms or persons registered in the assayer's offices.

There are no special requirements for marking the outside of cases for shipment to Portugal. If weights are shown on packages, they should be in kilograms.

Cases or bales bearing the same mark, united or bound together to form one package containing various goods, or even containing one kind of goods, must be accompanied by a declaration stating the number and total weight of the cases or bales so united.

Portugal's Export Controls

Exports exceeding 5,000 escudos require an export license, also known as a "Bulletin of Export Registration—BRE", which is valid for 90 days for customs purposes and 120 days for payments purposes. Export bulletins are issued freely with few exceptions. The primary purpose of this procedure is to enforce comformity to currency and surrender regulations.

Personal baggage and exports of merchandise the value of which does not exceed 5,000 escudos do not require a bulletin.

Exporters are required to sell to an authorized bank, within the period stipulated in the export bulletin, the total amount of the export proceeds, in the foreign currency indicated in the bulletin. The maximum period for repatriation of export proceeds is fixed at 4 months. The Bank of Portugal may authorize the deduction of commission expenses abroad, and freight, insurance or other charges, from the total amount of the export proceeds subject to surrender.

Portugal has no export duties.

Transportation and Communications

Transportation

All Portuguese railway lines are operated by Companhia dos Caminhos de Ferro Portugues, a nationalized company since 1975. The Portuguese government is planning a major program to upgrade its railway and subway services. Plans call for the extension and upgrading of the 3,566 kilometer rail grid, including narrow and wide gauge, and replacement or renovation of most rolling stock.

The 12-kilometer Lisbon metro, operated by the public enterpise Metropolitano de Lisboa, is also receiving extensive budgetary allocations for the renovation of rolling stock. Plans for 1980 call for a 2-kilometer expansion of the metro network. Both projects are expected to result in significant opportunities for imports of U.S. rolling stock and accessory equipment.

The Portuguese road network is 18,731 kilometers long, about 57 percent of which is rated first class, the balance being second and third class gravel roads. The road network is concentrated along the western coastal plain, particularly the long corridor between the cities of Lisbon and Oporto in which most of the country's economic activity is located. At the end of 1977, there were 1,376,888 commercial and passenger automobiles, 90,382 motorcycles, 81,813 tractors and 77,070 trailers.

The international movement of goods and services into and from Portugal is overwhelm-ingly by sea. The port of Lisbon, Portugal's largest, is of international importance due to its location and reexport trade. Lisbon and the two other major ports of Leixoes and Setubal are fully equipped and have adequate warehousing facilities.

The large shipping lines and two of the three principal shipyards were nationalized in 1974. Regular freight and passenger service is provided to the Azores and Madeira, Europe, Brazil and North America. Among the American companies providing service to Portuguese ports include American Export Lines, Atlantica, Dar Containerline and East Coast Overseas Corp.

Due to Lisbon's geographical position, Portela Airport is a major European air terminal and transit point for some 18 airlines, including Trans World Airlines. A new airport for Lisbon is under consideration with the first stage, pending government approval, scheduled for completion in 1985. Other airports in Portugal are Pedras Rubras serving Oporto, Faro in the Algarve region, Santa Catarina in Funchal and Santa Maria in the Azores. An expansion project for Santa Catarina is scheduled to start during 1980.

Portuguese domestic and international airlines are well developed. The government-owned line, Transportes Aereos Portugueses, renamed Air Portugal in 1979, operates flights within the country, between Lisbon and most major cities and also serves larger European cities and several in the United States, South America and Africa. As of January 1980, the Air Portugal fleet consisted of 2 Boeing 747s, 12 Boeing 707s and 8 Boeing 727s. Two Boeing 727s are on order. The fleet for regional flights consists of 1 BE 90 (King-Air), 2 BE 58 (Baron) and 1 Twin-Otter. Another Twin-Otter is on order.

Communications

Portugal is an important international gateway for cable and radio connections. Circuits are operated from Lisbon to most major foreign cities by the Companhia Portuguesa Radio Marconi. Domestic telegraph services are operated by the public enterprise Correios Telecomunicacoes de Portugal/Telefones Lisboa e Porto (Post and Telecommunications Co.) which also operates the telephone system for the entire country.

Television is government owned and broadcasts on one UHF and one VHF channel with separate programming, using nine subsidiary transmitters throughout Portugal. There are an estimated 2 million licensed television sets with an estimated potential audience of 4 million. Programming is varied, ranging from news and children's programs to American features, shown in English with Portuguese subtitles. There are two nation wide radio networks operating on medium wave and FM.

Advertising and Market Research

Portugal offers a reasonably priced market in which to advertise. The primary advertising media are newspapers, magazines, radio, television, outdoor posters, billboards and the cinema; newspapers and commercial television are the most popular. There are about 50 advertising agencies. Six firms specialize in television, 20 in radio commercials and two in direct mailings. Market research services are performed by about 20 firms, but not more than two or three offer complete services. There are several agencies with foreign capital participation.

The press consists of numerous newspapers, with a combined total readership of over a million people. Newspapers circulated in Lisbon and Oporto are the most influential; the following are the most important newspapers: Expresso, Tempo, Diario de Noticias, O Commercio do Oporto, Primeiro de Janeiro, Jornal de Noticias, O Dia, Correio da Manha, Diario Popular, Tarde.

Over 300 periodicals are published in Portugal. A number of periodicals are devoted to consumer areas, particularly women's and general news. Trade and technical publications are not very effective, although fields of interest such as engineering, motor vehicles, agriculture and the metal industry are well represented by good publications.

Credit

The amount of invested capital available locally, while not abundant, has been traditionally sufficient for meeting modest economic expansion. With the nationalization of all banks in 1975, credit policies have been greatly reoriented. Credit to most individuals and private companies, even to smaller and medium-sized firms, has been limited. Companies with foreign capital have access to short- and medium-term capital although access to the latter is subject to special rules. Long-term loans can be obtained only through the National Development Bank or the Caixa Geral de Depositos, Credito e Previdencia. Generally these banks provide only for investment in undertakings of interest to the country's economic development.

Since May 1978, the lending rate charged by credit institutions has ranged from 18.25 percent for 90-day loans to 22.25 percent for loans exceeding 5 years.

Currency

The basic unit of currency in Portugal is the escudo. It is divided into 100 equal parts called "centavos." The symbol for the escudo is $ and is placed between the escudo and the centavo in written amounts. Thus 2.5 escudos is written as 2$50. There are eight coins in the following denominations: 10, 20, and 50 centavos; 1, 2.5, 5, 10 and 25 escudos. Notes are for 20, 50, 100, 500 and 1,000 escudos. A 1,000 escudos is called a "conto."

As is the case with many other major foreign currencies, the escudo is presently floating. Once a day, the Bank of Portugal fixes buying and selling rates and the rates for currencies used for payments under bilateral agreements or arrangements.

Sources of Credit

Following the 1974 Revolution there was a substantial reorganizaton of the credit system and the overall banking structure. With the nationalization of all commercial banks and insurance companies in 1975, most financial institutions were brought under government ownership. All banking operations and all import/export operations involving private capital are supervised by the Bank of Portugal to reinforce government control of the banking system.

Three institutions perform credit functions and all other acts in conjunction with the functions of a bank in Portugal.

Bank of Portugal.—In addition to its responsibilities in the control of the money supply, the Bank of Portugal or Banco de Portugal has the usual regulatory powers over credit institutions and establishes maximum interest rates as well as reserve requirements. It offers rediscount facilities to credit institutions and uses a system of preferential rates to orient credit toward priority sectors. The Bank of Portugal is the sole institution entitled to manage the country's foreign currency resources. Commercial banks and special credit institutions are required to buy from and sell to the Bank of Portugal all foreign currencies that they buy and sell.

Commercial Banks.—The principal activities of commercial banks are to grant short- and medium-term credit with an emphasis on short-term credit, to meet the other needs of business.

In 1975 all Portuguese commercial banks were nationalized although the banks have been able to retain an appreciable degree of financial and administrative autonomy. The largest commercial banks in Portugal are: Banco Espirito Santo e Comercial de Lisboa, Banco Pinto Sotto Mayor, Banco Portugues do Atlantico, Banco Nacional Ultramarino, Banco Totta & Acores, Banco Borges & Irmao, Uniao de Bancos Portuguesas, and Banco Fonsecas & Burnay. Three foreign banks maintain branches in Portugal: the Bank of London and South America, Banco do Brasil and the Credit Lyonnais (through the Credit Franco Portugais). Citibank, Manufacturers Hanover Trust and other foreign banks have representative offices.

Special Credit Establishments.—The National Development Bank or Banco de Fomento Nacional was created in 1959 to stimulate the economic and social development of the country. It makes medium- and long-term loans, mainly to industry, transport and public utilities. The bulk of the credit granted has been absorbed by industrial concerns with a heavy concentration in the manufacturing industries. In practice, credit terms do not exceed 10 years.

Other special credit institutions are the 19 savings banks, Credito Predial Portugues, and the Sociedade Financiera Portuguesa. Special funds also exist for tourism, agriculture, the merchant marine and fishing. Interest rates charged by these special credit institutions may not exceed the interest rate limits for commercial banks.

Personal credit facilities for the purchase of consumer goods are still relatively undeveloped.

Stock Exchanges

Portugal's two stock exchanges, located in Lisbon and Oporto, were closed following the 1974 Revolution. The Lisbon exchange reopened in 1977 although limits have been imposed on security trading. All securities traded on the exchange must be registered with the Chamber of Stockholders (Camara dos Correctores). Shares and bonds of corporatons must be approved by the Chamber as being legally issued and adequately guaranteed. The Portuguese stock exchange, as a source of investment capital, has never been fully developed. Although foreign securities are not traded on the stock exchange, limited transactions are made outside of it.

Investment in Portugal

Direct Investment

The Portuguese government wishes to encourage the establishment of new, technologically advanced industries and the expansion and reorganization of existing operations to enhance export capacity and reduce import requirements. To achieve this goal, the government is seeking to attract foreign investment and technology, both in the form of direct investment as well as joint ventures in association with Portuguese firms.

Based on the 1977 Foreign Investment Code, foreign investment is subject to authorization and registration with the Foreign Investment Institute. Direct investment is permitted in all sectors, except those reserved for the public domain, e.g. defense industries, public utilities, banking and insurance activities. The Code contains relatively liberal profit remittance regulations and allows foreign firms access to all tax incentives available to national companies. Additional incentives can be negotiated under a contractual regime.

Authorization will not be granted in those cases where investment is for mere acquisition or absorption by foreigners of already established companies unless it results in programs of technological improvement, increased productivity or significant financial reorganization considered to be in the interest of the national economy and which may generate the creation of new jobs.

An important attraction for investment in Portugal is the tariff preferences or free entry accorded Portuguese exports to the European Free Trade Association (EFTA), the European Community and Spain. Other import attractions include the availability of skilled and unskilled labor, moderate wage costs and government financial and fiscal incentives.

Investment Incentives.—Foreign investments deemed to be of special interest because of their magnitude or long-term benefits can ob-

Table 4.—Direct Foreign Investment in Portugal

(in millions of U.S. dollars)

By countries of origin	1976	1977	1978 (est.)
EEC countries	38	21	31
EFTA countries	10	17	18
United States	10	16	7
Japan	1	1	0
Canada	—	1	2
Other	2	1	4
Total	61	57	62

Source: Bank of Portugal

tain special fiscal and/or other incentives. Such benefits, given on a contractual basis include: priority of dividend and profit transfers; priority access to domestic medium- and long-term credit at favorable interest rates; guarantees for foreign credits to import capital goods; State assistance in providing infrastructure for the project; and special fiscal benefits, e.g. reduced tax rates, exemption from or reduction of customs duties.

The Code also guarantees that the Bank of Portugal will authorize the purchase of foreign exchange for remittance of dividends, profits and proceeds from the sale or liquidation of foreign investments. The timing for exchange availability, however, depends on the state of Portugal's foreign exchange reserves and its balance of payments.

The following criteria will be used to evaluate the proposed investment under the Code: number of new jobs created; contribution to the balance of payments; value added through national production; contribution to industrial reconversion projects; maximization of regional development; introduction of advanced technology; training of Portuguese workers; and minimizing industrial pollution. Foreign investors seeking additional incentives under the contractual regime must meet the following specific performance requirements: create at least 250 permanent jobs; generate a net export surplus; guarantee that transfers of profit and technology payments will not exceed the amount of its total imported capital for a specified period of years, depending on the nature of the project; and use the company's own capital to finance at least 50 percent of the fixed capital investment.

Technology transfer contracts must be authorized by the Foreign Investment Institute, They may not contain clauses that restrict the structure and volume of production, restrain markets to which the technology importer has access, or allow the technology seller to fix prices for the final product.

Foreign investment is concentrated in automobile assembly plants, electronics, cosmetics, metal products, electrical machinery, pharmaceuticals, paint, property development, and tourism, woodpulp, textiles and clothing, and petrochemicals.

Forms of Business Organization

Foreign companies and foreign nationals may, in principle, engage in all sectors with the following exceptions: public services, monetary and financial institutions, insurance, advertising and other nationalized sectors. Legally constituted companies abroad may establish themselves in several forms of organization or as branches subject to the Portuguese Commercial Code, compliance with the registration and publication of the companies; constitution and designation of powers of attorney in their representatives. Foreign companies and foreign nationals may also freely associate in existing Portuguese companies by acquiring shares, quotas and in other forms of participation. In these cases, the Portuguese party is entitled to the option right in case of transfer or liquidation of the foreign share under the same conditions as the would-be foreign purchaser.

The types of commercial organization recognized in Portugal are individual proprietorships, partnerships, corporations, limited liability companies and branches.

Individual Proprietorship.—This form of business organization is chosen by small business owners and professional individuals. For tax reasons, the individual proprietorship is preferable to the general partnership. Individual proprietors are required to register with the Tax Division of the Ministry of Finance, and if dealing with certain products, also with the appropriate government board or institute. Individuals normally use their own name as their business name and the nature of their business may be included in the trade name.

Partnerships.—There are three forms recognized in Portugal. The general partnership (sociedade collectiva) is where each partner is jointly and individually liable for the debts of the firm to the extent of all of the partner's assets. Each partner has equal voting rights with the firm's name ending in "e companhia." This form of unlimited liability is not frequently used.

The limited partnership (sociedade em comandita simples) and the limited partnership with shares (sociedade em comandita por accoes) are also infrequently used. The former is composed of one or more general partners, with unlimited liability, but shareholders take the place of the special partners. All shares of the limited partnership must be registered. Both types of "sociedade" must submit a notarized deed stating the amount of capital, object of the business, names of the partners and the extent of liability and participation of the partners. The firm must be registered with the Tax Divison of the Ministery of Finance, and its trade name, to be protected, must also be registered. Depending on the nature of the product or products in which the firm deals, it may be necessary also to register with the relevant government agency.

The two organizational forms of particular interest to foreigners wishing to establish a business are the following:

Corporations.—The "sociedade anonima de responsabilidade limitada" (SARL) is equivalent to the U.S. corporation or the British public limited company. There must be at least 10 founders with no limitation as to nationality or residence. Capital must be fully subscribed with 10 percent paid in before the start of the business. This sum must be deposited with the Caixa Geral de Depositos but remains at the dispoal of the board of directors.

All corporations are required to put into a special legal reserve at least 5 percent of their annual profits until reserves equal 20 percent of the incorporated capital. This 20 percent reserve can be used only to absorb losses. A corporation may be given a fixed life but it is usually created for an unlimited period of time.

Limited Liability Companies.—The "sociedade por quota" has features of both a partnership and a corporation. It is a convenient form of organization for small and medium-sized firms with a small number of members and not requiring publically subscribed capital. The liability of a participant is limited to the amount of the individual's contribution, except that the participants are jointly liable for the payment of any unpaid capital contributions due by other members.

A limited liability company must have a minimum of two shareholders with at least 50,000 escudos in capital, each partner's share being 5,000 escudos or more. It need not disclose financial information to the public, and transfers of part of its capital may be made only subject to management's approval. This organizational form is most widely used by both domestic companies and subsidiaries of foreign firms.

Branch.—This is the simplest form for a nonresident wishing to operate a business through a permanent establishment in Portugal. Such an enterprise could range from a sales office to a highly developed business, but a branch must comply with Portuguese laws regarding the establishment and operation of businesses.

A foreign corporation or partnership organizing a branch must register with the Commercial Registry. This registration must indicate the nature and extent of the powers of the representatives. Failure to record the nature and extent of the powers of the representatives renders them personally and jointly liable for acts performed in the name of the corporation. A foreign corporation with a branch or branches in Portugal must also register its foreign articles of incorporation in Portugal together with a certificate from a Portuguese Consulate stating that the corporation is a legal entity in its parent country.

Foreign Ownership of Real Property

The Portuguese Government does not impose restrictions on the ownership of property by foreigners.

Repatriation of invested capital and income is permitted provided that the capital importation has been authorized by and registered with the Bank of Portugal. Under no circumstances should a prospective buyer make payment on a property unless the buyer does so with funds imported under a regular authorization. Transfers of funds out of the country also must be registered with the Bank.

Deeds must be registered with the Real Estate Registry Office in the area in which the property is situated, otherwise the title will not be valid against third parties. Rental income of rural property is normally subject to an annual tax of 10 percent; if the property is not duly cultivated, the tax rates increase substantially. Urban property rental income is subject to different taxes according to the amount of the income and the location of the property. Prospective buyers should acquaint themselves with Portuguese ways and manners of doing business. Etimates of the time necessary to complete construction and other arrangements are sometimes overly optimistic.

It is strongly recommended that all usual precautions in connection with real estate purchases elsewhere be observed, including a personal inspection of the property, investigation of the seller, and good legal advice.

Repatriation of Capital

The transfer of funds is governed by the 1977 Foreign Investment Code. The code guarantees that the Bank of Portugal will freely authorize the purchase of foreign exchange for remittance of dividends, profits and proceeds from the sale or liquidation of foreign investments. The annual transfer of dividends and profits can, however, be delayed because of foreign exchange and balance of payments problems, but not for more than 1 year. When the Council of Ministers decides that transfers, due to their amounts, might cause serious financial disturbances, it can set up a plan for partial transfer yearly over a period of 5 years.

Royalties.—There is no limit on the percentage of royalties or fees, but transfers are subject to prior authorization by the Bank of Portugal. Transfers must be made through an authorized bank in accordance with a regulation that requires information as to the identity of the principals involved and the nature of the transaction.

Royalties are normally based on the gross value of sales but a minimum level of sales is often agreed upon as a floor for computation purposes. The range of royalties depends upon the type of technical know-how and the quantities sold. Examples of royalty payment include the following: 6–8 percent for pharmaceuticals; 4–5 percent for diesel engines; 6–8 percent for machine tools; and 5–7 percent for electrical goods.

Nationalization.—Nationalization and expropriation are permitted by the Portuguese Constitution in cases of public interest and upon payment of a just indemnity. In October 1977, the government published the text of a compensation law for properties nationalized after the 1974 Revolution. Implementing regulations for compensation are virtually completed. The Foreign Investment Code offers the possibility of recourse to international arbitration for those foreign firms whose assets have been expropriated or nationalized.

Taxation

Under the 1976 Constitution, the Assembly of the Republic has the exclusive right to impose taxes and to alter any revenue system in force. District and municipal authorities also have been delegated certain powers in the imposition of taxes. Much of the Portuguese revenue system is in the process of being revised.

The tax year is the same as the calendar year. This is a legal requirement and the official books of companies must also be kept on a calendar year basis.

Industrial Tax

This is the basic tax on business income, which is also subject to the Commerce and Industry and the Complementary taxes referred to below. Resident corporations are subject to tax on their worldwide income; nonresident corporations with a permanent establishment in Portugal are subject to tax on Portuguese source income only. Taxable income is based on book profits from fi-nancial statements prepared according to sound accounting principles and adjusted to comply with tax rules.

The income from private investments of persons with business activities is not subject to this tax nor are capital gains since these are taxed separately.

Tax Incentives.—Various laws provide for reduction or exemption from the Industrial Tax. The most important are: (1) businesses set up to operate hotels or similar establishments considered beneficial to the tourist industry, and (2) companies operating in economically underprivileged regions as well as those setting up industries for development of local resources. These incentives are generally granted for up to 10 years, depending on the size and nature of the investments involved, upon application submitted before the investments are initiated.

Tax Rate.—The industrial tax rate on income under 1 million escudos is 18.9 percent. Income above 1 million but not over 5 million escudos is subject to a 22.7 percent rate; income in excess of 5 million escudos is subject to a 25.2 percent rate. These rates are then increased by the Commerce and Industry and Complementary taxes, resulting in an effective corporate tax burden of between 21 percent and 44 percent (approximately 50 percent in 1978).

Commerce and Industry Tax

This tax is levied by municipal authories on all individuals or companies subject to the Industrial Tax. The rate of tax, as fixed by municipal authorities, may not exceed 10.8 percent of the amount of tax paid or payable to the national government in the previous year. Exceptions to this rate are the cities of Lisbon and Oporto, where the maximum rate is 48.6 percent, and in those areas where indirect taxes are not levied. Taxpayers carrying on activities in more than one municipality pay the highest rate of the applicable taxes.

Complementary Tax

This is essentially an overlapping income tax on individuals and companies. For companies, the tax is levied on the undistributed net income before taxes reduced by the applicable industrial tax and surcharges, at a graduated rate of from 6 to 12 percent. For individuals, the tax is levied on total income from all sources reduced by the applicable income taxes and surcharges and by certain minor allowances, at a graduated rate of from 4 to 80 percent.

Tax on Real Property Income

A property or real estate tax is levied on the income, either real or presumed, arising from immovable property. The tax is divided into two sections, rural and urban property taxes.

Rural properties are defined as those that are used, or can be used, for agriculture, forestry or cattle raising. Urban buildings are considered to be those used for any other purpose or those that cannot be used for agriculture. The rate for urban houses ranges from 16 to 50 percent depending on income received, for rural houses 14 or 36 percent.

Exemptions from the rural and urban property taxes include the following: income from certain farming properties, income deriving from urban buildings when used rent free in activities subject to the industrial tax, recipients of income arising from properties used as hotels or similar establishments for a 10-year period starting in the first year of operation.

Capital Tax

The capital tax is levied on interest, dividend and royalty income and on other actual or presumed income arising from capital investments. The general rate is 34 percent, but reduced rates are applied to certain types of income: 18 percent for interest on deposit accounts, patents, licenses for production, commercial trademarks, etc.; 21 percent for profit distributions to members of companies and for amounts received through profit-sharing.

Professional Tax

Compensation received for services performed in Portugal, including benefits in kind and bonuses, as well as royalties on copyright in intellectual works, etc. are taxable.

The rates are applied to total annual income, and vary between 1 percent for income below 100,000 escudos and 22 percent for annual income over 900,000 escudos.

The following are exempt from the professional tax: medical assistance, pensions and disability allowances of the taxpayer and family allowances received from the social security agency. The following persons are exempt from the professional tax: public workers, members of the diplomatic and consular corps, and taxpayers whose annual taxable income does not exceed 60,000 escudos.

Capital Gains Tax

This tax is levied on certain realized capital gains, which are not subject to the Industrial Tax. The following are the principal types of transactions subject to the tax: sales by businesses of fixed assets, rights and patents; sales of leases on offices; issue of a stock dividend into share capital to the existing members; sales of land in urban areas when such land is intended for construction purposes.

In general, the taxable income is the difference between the selling price of the asset and the cost of the acquisition adjusted for depreciation and inflation. The rate of tax is 23 percent on transactions in land for construction, 6 percent on the receipt of stock dividends, and 12 percent in all other cases.

Other taxes

Sales Tax. — A turnover or sales tax is imposed at a single stage on the sale of goods by a producer or wholesaler to a retailer. Goods imported for resale are also subject to this tax. The tax is levied at the rate of 15 percent except for nonessential or luxury items which are subject to rates of 30–75 percent. Services, exports, fuel, foodstuffs, pharmaceuticals, books and various consumer durables are usually exempt.

Stamp Tax. — Certain documents, books, acts and products are subject to this tax at varying rates.

Inheritance and Gifts Tax. — The gratuitous transfer of movable and immovable property located in Portugal is taxable. The tax falls on those whom the property is transferred to, irrespective of their place of residence. The tax base is progressively higher as the value of the property increases and the relationship of the heir to the donor is less direct. The rate varies from 4 to 75 percent. Transmission of public debt securities, shares and bonds is subject to separate provisions.

Double Taxation Treaty

Residents of treaty countries are generally exempt from Portuguese tax on income from personal services rendered in Portugal, provided that they work temporarily in Portugal for not more than 183 days in a calendar year. In addition, the employer must be resident in the treaty country, and a permanent establishment in Portugal must not bear the compensation.

Unearned income relief differs among the various treaties. Income from real estate is generally taxable only in the country where the real estate is situated. Other types of unearned income are subject to reduced rates. Portugal has double taxation agreements with Austria, Belgium, Brazil, Denmark, Finland, France, Norway, Spain, Switzerland and the United Kingdom.

Labor Relations

Labor Force and Emigration

The labor force of Portugal in 1980 is estimated at approximately 3.6 million workers divided more or less equally among agriculture, manufacturing, commerce and services. With increasing industrialization and vocational and technical training by the government and private industry, there has been in recent years a shift from a heavy predominance of unskilled manual workers towards a greater number of skilled workers.

Unemployment reached an estimated 13 percent in 1979 owing in great part to the arrival over the previous four years of over 600,000 refugees from Portugal's former colonies, demobilization of the armed forces and a sharp decline in worker emigration connected with the economic difficulties being experienced by most West European countries. During the sixties and early seventies, over 100,000 workers yearly left Portugal in search of higher paying jobs in the more industrialized countries, especially France and West Germany. Emigration in 1978 totaled only an estimated 18,651 workers.

Labor Organization and Wages

The Ministry of Labor is responsible for the administration, implementation and execution of labor legislation in Portugal. Due to major labor unrest following the 1974 Revolution, the Government has come to play an increasingly active role in collective bargaining, wage regulation and the setting of working conditions. Labor laws and regulations apply equally to multinational and domestic corporations.

Among the major official goals of the government since 1974 has been the reduction of wage inequalities and the more even distribution of income. Therefore, most labor legislation dealing with wages, worker participation, strikes and dismissals has been substantially revised. Industrial wages and fringe benefits have been sharply increased.

In October 1979, the government raised the monthly minimum wage level for rural workers to 6,100 escudos, for urban workers to 7,500 es-

cudos and for domestic servants to 4,700 escudos. The national maximum salary is set at 60,000 escudos per month. Under the Foreign Investment Code, the salaries of foreign citizens working in Portugal are not subject to the maximum national salary limits unless the foreign citizen intends to live in Portugal for more than 5 years. Overall wages differ considerably among industries and regions and even vary from enterprise to enterprise in certain fields.

Compulsory work benefits include employer's contribution to social insurance (sickness, disability and old-age benefits) totaling 19 percent of basic wages, an unemployment fund of 3 percent and paid holidays plus a holiday bonus. Common fringe benefits include a 13th month salary bonus given at Christmas and often a 14th month salary bonus given in July. Employees pay a 7.5 percent contribution for social insurance, a 3 percent unemployment tax and a professional tax.

More specific information concerning labor matters may be obtained from the Ministry of Labor (Ministerio de Trabalho) located at Praca do Londres, 2, 1000 Lisbon.

Work Permit. — Foreigners wishing to take up residence or employment in Portugal must obtain a residence permit, normally issued for the calendar year. Persons applying for residence must prove adequate support for themselves and their family. Where an individual is taking up employment in Portugal, a statement of responsibility from the employer constitutes proof of support. Once a work permit has been issued, there is little difficulty in obtaining a residence permit. Those wishing to stay and work for shorter periods of time must obtain a special visa that is renewable every 60 days. A person not wishing to work in Portugal normally does not need the entry visa renewed every 60 days. Work permits are applied for by the employer and issued for each calendar year—though it may be for a shorter period in cases of temporary employment by foreign residents.

According to Decree 97-77 of March 1977, firms may only employ, even if unpaid, foreigners if their staff, when consisting of more than five workers, is at least 90 percent Portuguese. A suitable contract and all required legal dispositions must be completed and approved by the Ministry of Labor prior to the foreigner's employment. Temporary employment of under 60 days in certain fields need not be fully authorized.

Foreign citizens may not engage in certain professions or occupations. The professions of law and medicine are subject to special restrictions. In general, engineering may be practiced only by Portuguese nationals although there are certain exceptions. Foreign engineers qualifying for exceptions must have their credentials approved by the Portuguese Engineers Association.

Personal and household goods owned at least 1 year prior to the date of importation by foreign national taking up residence in Portugal may enter free of duty. A notarized declaration attesting to the 1-year period of ownership and a list of the goods must be certified by the Portuguese Consulate in the country of former residency. The importation of motor vehicles is subject to stricter controls, and only cars owned for several years will escape import duties.

Vacations.—Most employers provide any employee who has worked more than 90 days in 1 year a specified vacation. Annual vacation time after 1 year of service normally is 30 days. In addition to pay during the vacation period, most employees receive a bonus equivalent to the normal pay for the statutory minimum vacation period.

Guidance for Business Visitors Abroad

Entrance Requirements.—Except for French, Spanish, German, and Swiss citizens whose national identity cards suffice, all foreigners wishing to enter Portugal are required to carry a passport.

Visas are not required of Americans entering Portugal as tourists, on business, or for health reasons as long as their stay does not exceed 60 days. This period may be extended for 30 days if an application is submitted to the Servicios de Estrangeiros at least 7 days before the expiration of the initial period.

For Americans entering Portugal with the intention of setting up residence, a visa is required. Application for a resident's visa should be made at a Portuguese Consulate accompanied by a valid passport and statements on the applicant's financial means and reasons for desiring to reside in Portugal. Residence visas must be revalidated in January of each year. Further information on residency requirements can be obtained from the Servicos de Estrangeiros.

Foreign travelers are free to carry foreign banknotes, traveler's checks, and letters of credit and may leave with the same currency.

Visitors, however, must complete on arrival a form listing currencies in their possession should their value exceed 20,000 escudos to be authorized to take out the said amount. Visitors can depart with Portuguese banknotes up to the value of only 5,000 escudos unless special arrangements are made.

Business Hours.—Normal business hours are from 9 a.m. to 1 p.m. and 3 p.m. to 7 p.m., Monday through Friday. Some firms are closed on Saturday. Banking hours are 9 a.m. to 12:00 noon and 2 p.m. to 3:30 p.m. from Monday through Friday.

Time Zone.—Portuguese Standard Time is 1 hour ahead of Greenwich Mean Time, and 6 hours ahead of U.S. Eastern Standard Time.

Mail Service.—There is daily airmail service to the United States. Transit time is 2–4 days. Surface mail takes about 3 weeks.

Holidays.—Public holidays vary in number according to the locality. Local patron saints' days for each city have been omitted in this listing. Portuguese national holidays are:

New Year's Day, January 1
Carnival Tuesday, date varies
Good Friday, date varies
Revolution Day, April 25
Labor Day, May 1
Corpus Christi, date varies
Portugal Day, June 10
St. Antonio Day, June 13 (Lisbon)
Assumption, August 15
Day of the Republic, October 5
All Saint's Day, November 1
Independence Day, December 1
Conception, December 8
Christmas, December 25

System of Weights and Measures.—The metric system has been adopted in Portugal and should be used where measurement or weight is involved.

Electric Current.—AC 50 cycle, one or three phase, and nominal voltage is 127/220 and 220/380; most outlets for ordinary current are European (tubular prong) type and require an adapter. Transformers also may be needed.

Commercial Language.—Portuguese is the official language of the country, but French and English also are used in business matters.

Interpreters.—Interpreters are generally available for hire on an hourly or daily basis in Portugal's major cities. Names of reputable interpreter services can be obtained from the American Embassy and Consulate in Portugal.

Sources of Economic and Commercial Information

Portuguese Government Agencies

Ministerio do Trabalho
(Ministry of Labor)
Praca de Londres, 2
1000 Lisbon

Secretaria de Estado de Emigracao
(Secretariat of State for Emigration)
Largo do Rilvas
1300 Lisbon

Secretaria do Estado das Financas
(Secretariat of State for Finance)
Rua da Alfandega
1100 Lisbon

Subsecretaria do Estado do Tesouro
(Subsecretariat of State for Treasury)
Av. Infante D. Henrique
1200 Lisbon

Secretaria de Estado de Agricultura
(Secretariat of State for Agriculture)
Praca do Comercio
1100 Lisbon

Secretaria de Estado do Comercio Externo
(Secretariat of State for Foreign Trade)
Av. da Republica, 79
1000 Lisbon

Secretaria de Estado das Pescas
(Secretariat of State for Fishing)
Praca do Comercio
1100 Lisbon

Dirrecao Geral dos Combustiveis
(Directorate General of Fuels)
Av. da Republica, 45-6-D
1000 Lisbon

Direccao Geral das Alfandegas
(Directorate General of Customs)
Rua da Alfandega
1100 Lisbon

Inspeccao Geral dos Produtos Agricolas e Industrias
(Inspectorate General of Agricultural and Industrial Products)
Av. De Berna, 1
1000 Lisbon

Junta de Energia Nuclear
(Nuclear Energy Board)
Rua de S. Pedro de Alcantara, 70
1200 Lisbon

Inspeccao de Creditos
(Inspectorate of Credits)

Bank of Portugal
Av. da Republica
1000 Lisbon

Inspeccao de Seguros
(Inspectorate of Insurance)
Ministry of Finance
Av. Infante D. Henrique
1200 Lisbon

Direccao Geral das Minas e Servicos Geologicos
(Directorate General of Mines and Geological Services)
Rua Antonio Enes, 7
1000 Lisbon

Instituto do Investimento Estrangeiro
(Foreign Investment Institute)
Av. da Liberdade, 258-5
1200 Lisbon

Secretaria do Estado das Obras Publicas
(Secretaria of State for Public Works)
Praca do Comercio
1100 Lisbon

Secretaria do Estado dos Transportes e Comunicacoes
(Secretariat of State for Transport and Communications)
Praca do Comercio
1100 Lisbon

Secretaria do Estado da Habitacao e Urbanismo
(Secretariat of State for Housing and Urban Affairs)
Av. Columbo Bordalo Pinheiro, 5
1000 Lisbon

Secretaria de Estado da Marinha Mercante
(Secretariat of State for Merchant Marine)
Rua da Prata, 8-3
1100 Lisbon

Direccao Geral de Aeronautica Civil
(Directorate General for Civil Aeronautics)
Av. da Liberdade, 193
1200 Lisbon

Direccao Geral dos Portos
(Directorate General of Ports)
Rua da Prata, 8-3
1100 Lisbon

Aeroporto e Navegacao Aerea
Av. Sidonio Pais, 8-5
1000 Lisbon

Gabinete da Area de Sines
(Sines Area Project Office)
Rua Artilharia 1, 33
1200 Lisbon

Instituto Nacional de Estatistica
(Portuguese National Institute of Statistics)
Av. Antonio Jose de Almeida
1000 Lisbon

Junta Nacional de Investigao Cientifica
e Tecnologica
(National Scientific and Technological Research
Board)
Rua de D. Carlos, I, 126
1200 Lisbon

Registo da Propriedade Literaria, Cientifica e
Artistica
(Copyrights)
Camp Grande, 83
1700 Lisbon

Secretaria de Estado da Industria e Energia
(Secretariat of State for Industry and Energy)
Rua Horta da Seca, 15
1200 Lisbon

Portuguese Representation in the U.S.

Embassy of Portugal
2125 Kalorama Road, N.W.
Washington, D.C. 20008

Office of the Commercial Counselor
2310 Tracy Place, N.W.
Washington, D.C. 20008

Portuguese Trade Office
548 Fifth Avenue
New York, N.Y. 10036

Portuguese Trade Office
One Park Plaza
3250 Wilshire Blvd.
Los Angeles, Calif. 90010

Portuguese consulates are located in major
U.S. cities.

U.S. Representation in Portugal

American Embassy
Avenida Duque de Loule, 39
1098 Lisbon Codex

American Consulate
Apartado 88
Rua Julio Dinis, 826-30
4000 Oporto

American Consulate
Avenida D. Henrique
Ponta Delgada, Sao Miguel
9502 Azores

U.S. Foreign Commercial Service Officers are
available to brief and assist American firms and
individuals visiting Portugal and the Azores.

Other Organizations

Portugal-U.S. Chamber of Commerce, Inc.
5 West 45th St.
New York, N.Y. 10036

American Chamber of Commerce in Portugal
Rua D. Estefania, 115-5
Lisbon 1

Associacao Industrial Portugues
(Portuguese Industrial Association)
Praca das Industrias
Lisbon 3

Publications

The following publications are useful sources
of economic and commercial information:

Area Handbook for Portugal
Superintendent of Documents
U.S. Government Printing Office
Washington, D.C. 20402

Anuario Geral de Portugal
Anuario Comercial de Portugal
(Portuguese language—Yearbook of Portugal/
Commercial Yearbook of Portugal)
Empresa Publica dos Jornais Noticias e Capital
Rua Rodrigues Faria, 103
Lisbon-3

Export Directory of Portugal
(English/Portuguese)
Interpropo, Lda.
Pr. Jose Fontana, 16-A
Lisbon

*The Economic Transformation of Spain and
Portugal*
Eric N. Baklanoff
Praeger Publishers
New York, N.Y.

Estatisticas Industrias
(Industrial Statistics)
Anuario Estatistico
(Statistical Yearbook)
Estatisticas do Comercio Externo
(Foreign Trade Statistics)
Instituto Nacional de Estatistica
Lisbon

OECD Economic Surveys—Portugal
OECD Publications Center
1750 Penna. Ave., N.W.
Washington, D.C. 20006

Foreign Investment Code
(Offcial English translation)
Secretaria de Estado da Comunicacao Social
Direccao Geral da Divulgacao
Lisbon

International Customs Journal—Portugal
International Customs Tariff Bureau
Rue d l'Association, 38
B-1000 Brussels, Belgium

Guia Professional de Portugal
(Portuguese Professional Guide)
Edicoes J. Corte-Real, Lda.
Rua Rodrigo da Fonseca, 60
Lisbon

Background Notes: Portugal
U.S. Department of State
Washington, D.C.
July 1979

Foreign Economic Trends: Portugal
U.S. Department of Commerce
Washington, D.C.
November 1979

Business Report
Portugal-U.S. Chamber of Commerce
New York, N.Y.

Market Profile—PORTUGAL

Foreign Trade

Imports.—In 1978, $4,748 million ($2,027 million in 1977). Principal products imported: Nonelectrical machinery and appliances, petroleum products, sugar, wheat, corn, chemicals, transport equipment, and metal manufactures. U.S. is leading supplier with 11.8 percent of total. Other major suppliers: West Germany, U.K., France, Spain. Imports from U.S., $552 million in 1978 ($457 million in 1977). Principal products from the U.S.: Corn, soybeans, wheat, cereals, rice, coal, iron or steel hoop, cotton, medicines, and oilseeds.

Exports.—In 1978, $2,433 million ($2,027 million in 1977). Principal exports: Clothing, fabric, pulp, cork manufactures, canned vegetables, wines, and fish products. U.S. is a leading customer with 6.9 percent of total. Other major customers: U.K., West Germany, France, Italy. Exports to U.S., $170 million in 1978, ($136 million in 1977). Main exports to U.S.: Wine, fish products, cork products, canned vegetables, sisal goods, and pig iron.

Trade Policy.—Trade agreement with EEC, creating free trade area. Portugal has formally applied for EEC membership. Import surcharge of 10 or 60 percent and quotas imposed on a wide range of products. Member of EFTA, GATT, OECD and IMF.

Trade Prospects.—Despite political situation and economic difficulties, strong export sales opportunities exist for the following U.S. products: Construction, mining, and materials handling equipment, metalworking machinery and finishing equipment, food processing, packaging and bottling equipment, agricultural and refrigeration equipment, health care industries instrumentation and equipment, hotel and restaurant equipment and textile machinery and equipment.

Foreign Investment

Lack of domestic capital and technology ensures continued foreign investment opportunities. Liberal foreign investment code adopted in 1977. Total U.S. investment in Portugal at the end of 1979 estimated at $200–$250 million.

Finance

Currency.—Escudo, floating, approx, 48.75 escudos = $1 on March 12, 1980. Money supply, December 1978, 726.6 billion escudos.

Domestic Credit and Investment.—Bank lending for short- and medium-term loans extremely tight. All Portuguese-owned banks and insurance companies have been nationalized. Interest rates varies between 18.25 and 22.25 percent.

National Budget.—Expenditures in 1979 estimated at 273 billion escudos with revenue planned at 190 billion escudos; priority given to public works, housing, urbanization, construction, and public debt financing.

Balance of Payments.—Deficit amounted to an estimated $776 million in 1978 versus $1.5 billion deficit in 1977. Increased tourism and emigrant workers' remittances.

Economy

Political and social unrest coupled with low investment levels have severely disrupted economy. GDP estimated to have grown by 2.5 percent in 1979. Per capita GDP in 1978, $1,922, although highly inflated due to currency fluctuations. Economy turning more to industrialization, although agriculture, forestry and fishing remain important and economy not self-sustaining.

Agriculture.—About 28 percent of labor force employed in agriculture, which contributed some 18 percent of GDP in 1976. Government expropriation of local private holdings and concomitant worker occupations ceased. Some farms being returned to original owners. Production handicapped by climate, eroded soil, lack of machinery and investment. Chief products: Grains, fruits, vegetables, wines and cork.

Industry.—Generally on a small scale. Contributed 44 percent of GNP in 1977. Principal industries: Textiles, clothing, petroleum derivatives, electronics, shipyard, and electrical equipment. Industrial activity has fallen sharply.

Natural Resources

Land.—Continental Portugal, 34,139 square miles. Mountainous in north, flat in south.

Minerals.—Wolfram, cassiterite, sulfur ore, copper pyrites, titanium and iron ore. Imports: phosphates, coal.

Forestry.—World's leading cork producer and important producer of naval stores.

Fishing.—In 1977 total landed catch 253,057 metric tons

Population

Size.—Continental Portugal, Azores and Madeira: 9.8 million. Influx of Portuguese from former African territories and slowdown in worker emigration.

Principal Cities.—Lisbon (capital), 1.8 million; Oporto, 1.5 million.

Language.—Portuguese; French and English also customary in international commerce.

Labor.—Labor force, 3.7 million; wages lowest in Western Europe. Substantial unemployment (13 percent in 1979).

Marketing in Qatar

Contents

Report revised August 1981

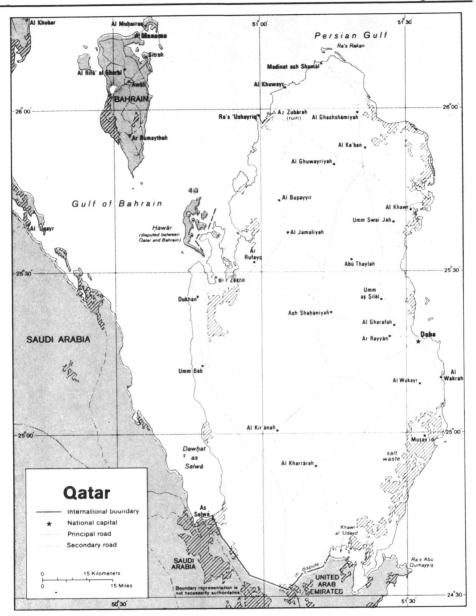

Qatar

——— International boundary
★ National capital
——— Principal road
——— Secondary road

0   15 Kilometers
0   15 Miles

1991

Introduction

A traditional Islamic monarchy, Qatar is located on a barren, sand-covered peninsula extending about 100 miles north from the eastern Saudi Arabian mainland. Prior to the first shipment of oil in 1949, there were no modern settlements in the country. Nomadic Bedouin tribes roamed the interior, while other Qataris, living along the coast, were engaged in fishing and pearling. Doha, the capital, was a small trading center but did not have the entrepot business and importance of such Gulf ports as Manama, Dubai, and Kuwait City.

Since the arrival of oil wealth, an almost constant stream of merchants and immigrant workers, attracted by the prospects of relatively high wages and lucrative contracts, have swollen the country's estimated population from 20,000 in 1949 to approximately 250,000 today. Foreign workers now account for over 80 percent of the total labor force with some, primarily British and Egyptian in origin, playing an important role in the Qatari government and business communities.

Despite these changes, and the steady expansion of the country's infrastructure, Qatar remains a relatively modest market. American exporters would do well to concentrate on those areas of the economy slated for future expansion.

Foreign Trade Outlook

Overview

Qatar, with significant revenues from oil exports and a reltively small population of 250,000, has among the highest per capita income levels in the world (estimated at $26,000 in 1980). Since Qatar depends on imports for a large part of its foodstuffs and most of its requirements for raw materials and manufactures, the country has become an important market for U.S. exporters. Foreign purchases, which totaled $80 million in 1969 and $194 million in 1973, rose to $1.5 billion in 1980. The 1978 product mix of goods imported into Qatar was split between agricultural products (12 percent), manufactured goods (19 percent), machinery and transport equipment (59 percent), and other items (10 percent).

The American share of Qatar's imports has remained close to the same general level during the past few years. In 1980, the United States ranked as third largest supplier to Qatar, after Japan and the United Kingdom, with 11.3 percent of the market. Major U.S. exports in 1980 were food, live animals, and cigarettes ($15.8

million); trucks ($11.6 million); construction and mining equipment ($11.3 million); passenger motor vehicles ($11.2 million); heating and cooling equipment ($8.0 million); mechanical handling equipment ($2.8 million); and iron and steel scrap ($3.3 million).

American firms face stiff competition in Qatar, especially from U.K., West German, and Japanese companies. The United Kingdom has a long history of close commercial ties with Qatar, and the Qataris have a strong sense of loyalty toward established trading partners. The Japanese, with a sustained and effective competitive effort, have done very well in winning major contracts and in maintaining, since 1976, their position as first supplier. West German firms are also known for their aggressiveness and competitive prices. In 1980, Japan supplied 18.3 percent of the Qatari market, with the United Kingdom and West Germany capturing 17.7 percent and 6.1 percent, respectively.

Qatar is a small but economically important country. Because of the large increase in the posted price of crude oil, the country's foreign exchange earnings have risen dramatically, reaching an estimated $5 billion in 1980. Future development goals are based on upcoming exploitation of the Northwest Dome, a nonassoci-

Table 1.—U.S. Exports to Qatar
(thousands of U.S. dollars)

Commodity	1979	1980
Cereals and preparations of cereal, flour, etc.	439	2,666
Fruits and vegetables	555	725
Miscellaneous food preparations	804	926
Cigarettes	12,641	10,634
Chemical mixtures and preparations	1,051	1,501
Iron or steel waste or scrap	15,117	3,348
Floor coverings	1,752	3,335
Made-up articles of textile materials, n.e.c.	358	261
Cosmetic goods	678	1,184
Iron or steel pipes, tubes and fittings	1,450	113
Finished iron and steel structures and parts	303	1,232
Paper and paper products	1,253	1,152
Power generation machinery and equipment	2,430	2,664
Construction and mining machinery	8,171	11,277
Hearing and cooling equipment and parts	5,744	7,973
Pumps, centrifuges,and parts	3,990	3,246
Mechanical handling machinery	1,640	2,890
Parts and accessories for nonelectric machinery, n.e.c.	1,114	763
Telecommunication equipment and parts	6,090	3,356
Household refrigerators and freezers	826	1,169
Radio transceivers and transmitters	4,531	754
Parts of TV, radio and sound reproduction equipment	1,203	1,719
Passenger motor vehicles	11,897	11,193
Trucks	6,475	11,563
Special purpose motor vehicles	1,457	967
Aircraft	23,705	1,415
Nonmilitary ships and boats	1,387	839
Furniture	639	699
Apparel articles and accessories	418	813
Scientific and control instrumentation	1,948	2,456
Miscellaneous manufactured articles, n.e.c.	1,112	1,342
Special category	100	664
Other	14,288	28,299
Total	135,566	123,138

Source: U.S. Department of Commerce, Bureau of the Census, FT-455.

Table 2.—Qatar: Sources of Imports (1973-80)
(millions of U.S. dollars)

	1973	1974	1975	1976	1977	1978	1979	1980[1]
United States	19.9	27.7	51.3	65.1	117.2	118.9	152.1	164.5
Japan	21.6	48.4	61.7	235.7	327.1	233.8	264.4	265.9
West Germany	10.5	16.7	38.4	63.6	87.0	219.6	96.1	89.0
United Kingdom	53.4	37.9	87.1	138.2	231.4	186.0	220.6	257.1
France	9.6	7.1	14.4	36.3	70.1	86.1	175.1	78.4
Italy	3.8	7.9	12.1	32.2	34.3	55.0	66.5	—
Netherlands	4.2	8.3	13.4	24.3	42.3	48.6	34.5	—
Austria	1.3	3.1	2.6	4.5	8.5	4.4	28.1	—
India	5.0	8.0	11.4	13.8	27.0	25.5	24.2	—
United Arab Emirates	4.5	7.0	12.7	39.7	56.8	15.3	22.4	—
Other	60.6	98.8	104.7	165.5	224.4	190.7	341.2	—
Total	194.4	270.9	409.8	818.9	1,226.1	1,183.9	1,425.2	1,450.8

[1]1980 information derived from unpublished sources.
Source: IMF, Direction of Trade.

ated offshore gas field that could prove to be the world's largest. The Government of Qatar plans to utilize this resource for export and the development of a diversified economy.

As the channel for the receipt of oil export revenues, the Government is by far the largest purchaser of goods and services in Qatar. Functioning as developer of Qatar's basic infrastructure, the Government owns and controls directly such important fields as electricity, power, water desalination, communications (including radio and TV), hospitals, and other social welfare institutions. The private sector is active, but a large part of the activity of many Qatari firms results from representation of foreign companies seeking government contracts.

American firms must keep in mind that business transactions are characterized by the high degree of importance attached to personal relationships. Personal visits to Qatar are virtually a prerequisite for market penetration by foreign companies even after local representation is established. Competition is heavy, and it is generally necessary to make more than one visit in order to establish and develop key contacts.

Best Export Prospects

The major opportunities for American companies will be in the export of technology and in design, construction, equipment supply, and management of the various public works and

Table 3.—Qatar Exports of Crude Oil, 1972-79
(in thousands of barrels)

Year	Onshore	Offshore	Total
1972	88,739	87,572	176,611
1973	91,257	116,895	208,152
1974	80,798	105,898	186,696
1975	62,404	94,201	156,606
1976	85,916	92,180	178,097
1977	70,206	83,336	153,597
1978	83,506	91,286	174,793
1979	80,715	100,226	180,901

Source: Qatar General Petroleum Corporation, Government of Qatar.

industrial projects to be undertaken in Qatar. The Government is presently undertaking a number of projects including the construction of electric generation facilities ($1.5 billion), hospital construction ($227 million), expansion of water desalination capacity ($425 million), development of sewage facilities in Doha ($160 million), and expansion of motorways ($175 million). In addition, there are a number of plans under consideration for development of new petrochemical and hydrocarbon-based production facilities, as well as other light industries. The most significant project under consideration is the development of the Northwest Dome offshore gas field. This project, involving at least $4 billion in expenditures, will be of special interest to U.S. firms with expertise in that area.

Although limited by the relatively small Qatari population, there is a promising market for consumer durables and transportation vehicles. These include house furniture, passenger, motor cars, and household appliances.

Industry Trends

GDP Development

Petroleum has furnished Qatar with the resources to become one of the more economically prosperous countries in the Near East. The country's development into a modern State began in 1949, when the first cargo of crude was exported, and continued at a gradual rate into the early 1970's. In 1974, oil revenues jumped to almost $2 billion—a 500-percent increase over 1973 earnings. This influx of wealth continues with Qatar's income from oil reaching $5.8 billion in 1980.

The Qatari Government does not publish data on national income or gross domestic product, making the performance of the non-oil sector of the economy difficult to assess. Growth has been rapid throughout the economy, however,

1993

reflecting the Government's efforts to broaden the base of the economy by developing a modern infrastructure. Developments have been concentrated in the areas of power generation, water desalination, and road and port facilities. Emphasis is also on capital-intensive industries to take advantage of Qatar's cheap energy from gas and its abundant capital reserves. Other economically viable industries capable of producing for either domestic or export markets are also encouraged. Ownership of these new ventures may be public, private, or mixed public and private. Foreign investment is encouraged.

Industry in Qatar is centered at Umm Said, about 30 miles south of Doha. Gas is piped in from the Dukhan field on the west coast and raw materials are imported through the Umm Said port, which is being expanded. The complex, which will have a population of approximately 25,000 by 1985, includes plants for the manufacture of NGL, cement, fertilizer, petrochemicals and steel, as well as facilities for oil refining.

Government Budget

There is no formal development planning in Qatar. Instead, future economic goals are outlined in the Government's annual budget for major projects, also known as the development budget.

Total allocations for the 1981 development budget increased by 20 percent over the 1980 level of $2.5 billion. Major spending areas are $819 million for industry and agriculture, $475 million for water and sewage development, $268 million for housing and public construction, $221 million for transportation and communications, and $187 million for education.

Development budgets deal largely with infrastructural projects that are contracted to local firms. These include substantial works for resurfacing roads, as well as additions and improvements to water and sewer systems. A number of new projects, however, have been introduced in the 1981 budget, including a 330-bed woman's hospital, a marine communications station, and construction of a new power station at Ras Laffan. In addition to these projects, the Industrial Development Technical Center plans to establish joint ventures to study various aspects of solar energy, environmental protection, and water desalination.

Hydrocarbons

Petroleum.—Qatar is a member of the Organization of Petroleum Exporting Countries (OPEC) and the Organization of Arab Petroleum Exporting Countries (OAPEC). Qatar's production and pricing policies are based largely on the decisions of these groups. As in neighboring Gulf countries, the petroleum industry is the mainstay of economic growth in Qatar. Total control over oil production and marketing was acquired by the Government in 1976 and early 1977, with the Qatar General Petroleum Corporation (QGPC) becoming an umbrella organization for government joint ventures throughout the economy. In addition, QGPC manages Qatar's participation in regional ventures, including the Arab Petroleum Investments Company and the Arab Petroleum Services Company. While fully owned by the Qatari Government, some of QGPC's senior management and supervisory personnel are of British and American origin.

The Qatar Ministry of Finance and Petroleum exports the bulk of Qatar's crude through QGPC's facilities. Most is sold in long-term sales agreements directly to foreign governments and to international oil companies. Crude oil production increased steadily until 1972 but, reflecting the Government's desire to conserve petroleum reserves, has fluctuated at a slightly lower level since then. Production rose in 1979 to 185 million barrels in comparison to 177 million barrels in 1978.

Qatar's only oil refinery, located at Umm Said, is operated by the National Oil Distribution Company (NODCO). The facility, with a current capacity of 11,500 barrels per day, produces gasoline, diesel, aviation fuel, and kerosene. Although the refinery was adequate for domestic needs when completed in 1974, refined products must now be imported. Expansion of and additions to the refinery are now in progress and a capacity of 50,000 barrels per day is expected in 1983.

Natural Gas.—There are large deposits of natural gas in Qatar, both in association with crude oil and in nonassociated form, and the use of gas has become an important element in the Government's plans for industrial expansion and diversification. At present, associated gas is used as feedstock for power stations, water desalination plants, a steel mill, and a fertilizer complex.

The country's first natural gas liquids (NGL) plant, which opened in 1975 and was destroyed by fire in 1977, has been replaced by two fully integrated units. NGL1, designed to utilize associated gases produced from the Dukhan onshore fields, has a production capacity of 740 tons of propane, 470 tons of butane, and 310 tons of condensate daily. NGL2—utilizing associated gas from the offshore fields of Idd Al-Shargi, Maydan Mahzam, and Bul Hanine—has a daily capacity of 220 tons of propane, 730 tons of butane, and 73 tons of condensate.

The importance of natural gas in Qatar's economic future stems from the discovery in the early 1970's of a major offshore field known as the Northwest Dome. With recoverable reserves now estimated at over 150 billion cubic feet, it is among the world's largest fields of nonassociated natural gas. After several years of discussion and study, talks are underway between the State oil company, Qatar/General Petroleum Corporation (QGPC), and several foreign firms on construction of a $4 billion liquefied natural gas (LNG) plant. The plant will be located on the northwestern coast about 45 miles north of Doha, at Ras Laffan. Other aspects of the project will include offshore distribution facilities, pipelines to the mainland, and associated industries. In addition, the LNG facility, which will be developed to produce about 2 billion cubic feet per day, will need a fleet of approximately nine LNG tankers for distribution, each costing about $150 million.

Development of the Northwest Dome, along with a new industrial zone near Ras Laffan, will provide a significant source of income for Qatar well beyond the termination of oil reserves.

Other Industries

Resulting from the Qatari Government's program of large investment expenditures, industrial activity has shown significant growth in recent years. All large industrial enterprises are wholly or partially government owned, either directly or through the Qatar General Petroleum Corporation.

Fertilizer.—The Qatar Fertilizer Company (QAFCO) was formed in 1969 to use associated onshore gas as feedstock to produce ammonia and urea. Present shareholders in this joint venture include QGPC (70 percent), a Norwegian company (25 percent), and a U.K. banking group (5 percent). Located at Umm Said, the plant has been in operation since 1973. The facility's original capacity has recently been doubled, with production now at 1,800 tons of ammonia and 2,000 tons of prilled urea. Almost all of QAFCO's output is exported, mainly to India, Pakistan, and countries in Southeast Asia.

Petrochemicals.—The Qatar Petrochemical Company (QAPCO) was established in 1974 as a joint venture between QGPC (84 percent) and Cd. F. Chemie of France (16 percent). The Company's two plants, now under construction in Umm Said, are scheduled to be completed in 1981. One will produce 280,000 tons yearly of ethylene and the other 140,000 tons annually of low-density polyethylene. Future plans also call for the construction of a high-density polyethylene plant at Umm Said. In 1979, a mutually owned Qatari-French petrochemical plant was opened in Dunkirk, France for the production of ethylene and polyethylene.

Steel.—The Qatar Steel Company, Ltd. (QASCO), also established in 1975, is a joint venture between QGPC (70 percent), Kobe Steel of Japan (20 percent), and Tokyo Boeki, Ltd. (10 percent). Its facility at Umm Said, which started operations in 1978, is a direct reduction plant using electric arc furnaces, a continuous castor, and a rolling mill to make steel reinforcing rods. Production capacity is 400,000 metric tons per year, most of which is exported.

Cement.—The Qatar National Cement Company was established in 1965 to exploit the country's rich deposits of limestone, plaster, and gypsum. The plant, located on the west coast at Umm Bad, started production of Portland and sulfur-resident cement in 1979. Although recent expansions have raised production capacity to 1,600 tons per day, actual production is much lower and imports of cements are increasing. To meet demand, plans were announced in February 1981 for the construction of a new plant, also in Umm Bad, with a capacity of 2,000 tons of cement daily.

Agriculture and Fishing

Agricultural production in Qatar is limited by the scarcity of water and arable land. Less than one-half of 1 percent of the territory (approximately 6,000 hectares) is now under cultivation. Also, there is little useable surface water, with rainfall insufficient and groundwater high in salinity. At present, food accounts for about 13 percent of the country's total imports.

In general, agricultural land in Qatar is privately owned. To encourage local production and to reach a goal of agricultural self-sufficiency by the end of the century, the Government administers a subsidy program that supplies seeds, insecticides, water pumps, and fertilizers free of charge to farmers. In addition, farmers may qualify for government grants and aid in the event of crop or land damage.

The Government now undertakes various agricultural feasibility studies and farming projects. Experimental vegetable farms have been undertaken in an attempt to extend seasonal production and reduce the country's dependence on imports. The main vegetable crops now under cultivation include tomatoes, carrots, lettuce, cabbage, and beans.

Operation of a government-owned poultry and

egg-producing project, located north of Doha, began in 1975. Known as the Qatar General Poultry Establishment and producing 1 million chicken and 10 million eggs annually, the facility covers 25 percent of local demand. With government encouragement, a private Qatari firm is setting up in 1981 a turnkey poultry project with initial capacity of 50 million eggs and 5 million chickens per year. Other government pilot programs in Qatar include sheep raising and dairy farming.

The Qatari Government is in the process of divesting itself of the State-owned Qatar National Fishing Company (QNFC), which has dominated the fishing industry. The QNFC trawlers will be sold to the private sector.

Social Infrastructure

Education.—The State provides free education to all children living in Qatar. In 1978, approximately 34,000 students were enrolled in the country's 12-year system of education, which was first begun in 1956. By 1982, the Government hopes to achieve universal enrollment of primary school children and two-thirds enrollment of secondary school children in 24 elementary and 12 secondary schools.

The new University of Qatar, which is scheduled to open with a fully equipped campus in October 1982, will accommodate 3,000 to 4,000 students. Government allocations toward construction of University facilities have exceeded $225 million. Higher education is also provided at the Doha Regional Training Center, which specializes in technical education.

Public Health.—All residents of Qatar enjoy free medical services, ranging from outpatient clinics to hospitalization. If facilities in the country are insufficient to treat a patient, the patient is sent abroad, accompanied by a member of his/her family and at the expense of the State. In addition, visiting medical and surgical consultants spend several weeks each year in Doha to advise on difficult cases and to help upgrade local medical services. National hospital needs were largely met in 1980 when the 678-bed Hamad General Hospital commenced operations. The Ministry of Health is also expanding general health services with the construction of 20 new clinics around the country and the creation of a Health Training Center in Doha.

Trade Regulations

Trade Policy

Dependent on imports for most of its foodstuffs, consumer goods, and capital goods, Qatar maintains a liberal trade policy. Tariff duties are minimal, and very few products are subject to administrative control. Restrictive measures have been implemented only to ensure that the profits on foreign trade accrue to Qatari nationals or Qatari firms.

Qatar is a party to the Arab League Trade and Payments Agreements, which accord preferential rates to specified products of Arab League member states. While not a contracting member to the General Agreement on Tariffs and Trade (GATT), GATT's code is applied on a de facto basis in Qatar. Also, preferential tariff treatment is accorded to countries of the British Commonwealth.

The Government of Qatar prohibits imports from South Africa and Israel. It participates in the Arab League boycott against Israel and in the secondary boycott against third-country firms found to have certain economic relationships with Israel. In general, normal trade dealings are unaffected by the boycott, and many U.S. firms trading with Qatar successfully sell to both Israel and Qatar.

It is the policy of the U.S. Government to oppose restrictive trade practices or boycotts fostered or imposed by foreign countries against other countries friendly to the United States. The Export Administration Act of 1979 (Public Law 96-72) and the U.S. Department of Commerce's implementing regulations (Export Administration Regulations, 15 C.F.R. Part 369) prohibit certain forms of compliance with foreign boycotts, including furnishing information or entering into or implementing agreements. Violators of the U.S. antiboycott law are subject to severe penalties, including fines, imprisonment, and revocation of export license privileges. U.S. exporters are required by law to report to the U.S. Department of Commerce any request for action in support of such restrictive trade practices or boycotts in accordance with Section 369.6 of the Export Administration Regulations. Reporting forms (ITA-621P or ITA-6051P) may be obtained from the Office of Antiboycott Compliance, U.S. Department of Commerce, Washington, D.C. 20230.

U.S. exporters should also familiarize themselves with antiboycott provisions of the Tax Reform Act of 1976, administered by the U.S. Treasury Department. Violation of Treasury antiboycott regulations risks tax penalties rather than criminal prosecution. These tax penalties can extend to business operations in nonboycotting countries.

The U.S. Department of Commerce seeks to minimize the adverse impact on U.S. trade of foreign boycotts and other restrictive trade practices by furnishing information and assistance to U.S. firms directly affected. In addition to reporting such requests, as noted, firms confronted with boycott problems may wish to discuss them with the Commerce Action Group for the Near East.

Import Regulations

Qatar does not permit the import of narcotics, artificial pearls, certain firearms, and pork products. Special permits are required for the import of alcoholic beverages and specified drugs, and the Public Security Department must issue a direct order before stipulated arms and ammunition may be imported. Only licensed Qatari firms or individuals are authorized to import goods.

Otherwise, there are no administrative restrictions or prohibitions on imports. For the most part, open general import licenses are issued to well-established importers who have been operating in a variety of import fields. Others who have confined their operations to a few commodities are granted licenses to import specific goods. Licenses are normally valid for a period of one year but are renewable.

Import Tariff System

Qatar imposes a flat 2.5 percent ad valorum duty on the c.i.f. value of most imported goods. The exceptions are tobacco and tobacco products, which are dutiable at 10 percent; phonographs and records, 15 percent; and alcoholic beverages, 50 percent. No duty is levied on goods transshipped through Qatar.

All international trade transactions that involve weights and measures must use only the metric system as a unit of standards.

Information regarding Qatar's duties applicable to specific products may be obtained free of charge from the Commerce Action Group for the Near East, Office of Country Marketing, International Trade Administration, U.S. Department of Commerce, Washington, D.C. 20230, or from any Department of Commerce District Office. Inquiries should contain a complete product description.

Shipping Documents

A commercial invoice, certificate of origin, bill of lading, steamship certificate, and insurance certificate must be included with each shipment. Packing lists are not officially required, but their inclusion will facilitate the clearance of cargo through Qatari customs.

The commercial invoice (required in quad-ruplicate) should contain a detailed description of the goods, any identification marks (including serial numbers), sizes, quantities, and prices. Both the factory price and the c.i.f. value should be included. Prices should be indicated in U.S. dollars and Qatari Riyals on the invoice. The country of origin should be noted on the invoice, and the invoice signed by the shipper. The certificate of origin (usually issued in quad-ruplicate) must contain the name of the vessel and date of sailing, as well as a statement that the products being shipped are of U.S. origin and that they are manufactured in the United States. If the products contain any foreign components, the country of origin and percentage must be indicated. The full name and address of the U.S. manufacturer must also be included. There are no special requirements for the bill of lading; however, Qatari authorities emphasize that it must state whether the freight is prepaid or collectable.

Samples and Advertising

Samples of no commercial value are admitted free of duty. Unless meant only for temporary use and subsequent reexporting; samples of value are subject to duty. Small quantities of advertising material may be imported duty free.

Marking and Labeling

There are no regulations on marking and labeling. In keeping with normal shipping practice, however, packages should bear the consignee's mark and should be numbered.

A high standard of export packaging is essential because of the long sea voyage, the high temperatures that are experienced for most of the year, and the likelihood of transshipment.

Distribution and Sales Channels

Major Marketing Areas, Distribution Centers

Doha, with over 80 percent of Qatar's total population, is the commercial and marketing center of the country. The government ministries, major trading houses, and the banking community are all located within walking distance of the old "suq" or bazaar on Doha's Corniche.

Agents/Distributors

Any American firm wishing to sell in Qatar must adhere to the Civil and Commercial Law (Law No. 16 of 1971) and sell through an agent or distributor. This representative must be a Qatari national or a company with at least 51-percent Qatari ownership. In addition, all goods brought into Qatar for sale must be imported by the holder of an import license, which are issued only to Qatari citizens.

Serious consideration should be given to the selection of a representative; whenever possible, it should be done on the basis of a personal visit to Qatar. A well-chosen agent in Qatar would have good contacts in government decisionmaking circles, enabling him to collect valuable information on upcoming tenders and, if possible, acquainting key government officials with the product or service provided by the foreign firm.

The practice of appointing exclusive representation is widely followed in Qatar. American firms should avoid assigning one regional agent to cover the entire Middle East and should deal directly through a local Qatari establishment. American firms should also take care to see that their agent is not handling competitive lines.

Personal contact is an essential prerequisite for a successful marketing effort in Qatar. Representatives of foreign firms should visit Doha prior to selection of an agent, following up with regular trips thereafter. Qataris like to see home office representatives of the firm with which they are dealing, and the display of interest symbolized by frequent visits can make the difference between making and losing major sales.

Agency agreements between Qatari firms and foreign companies must be registered with the Ministry of Commerce and Economy. The Ministry also has responsibility for arbitrating disputes between parties to an agency agreement. Since termination of agency or distributor relationships can be tedious and damaging to a company's reputation, a thorough investigation of a potential agent should be conducted before a final agreement is signed.

Government Tendering Procedures

All government contracts are let under provisions of bidding and tender regulations included in Law No. 8 of 1979. The bidding process and the awarding of contracts are handled by the Central Trading Committee (CTC) under the direction of the Ministry of Finance and Petroleum.

The Ministry of Public Works, the principal construction supervisor of the Qatari Government, has primary responsibility for evaluation of bids and selection of contractors for civil construction and highway projects. The Industrial Development Technical Center plays a similar role for contracts involving construction of industrial facilities, as does the Ministry of Electricity and Water for power and desalination projects.

As a general rule, the Qatari Government does not award turnkey contracts, preferring to have separate agreements for consultants. In consultation with the consultants, the executing government agency will generally invite a relatively small number of firms to submit bids for a contract. Contracts for small projects (under QR 300,000 or approximately $80,000) are awarded only to locally based contractors, importers and merchants whose names are entered with the Qatar Chamber of Commerce. On large projects, a Central Tenders Committee announces the tender, using local media and, in some cases, Qatar's overseas embassies. Though bidding is not limited to prequalified firms, the Government continues to announce the opportunity to prequalify and to invite bids only from those companies that have prequalified. In addition, Law No. 8 of 1976 provides for the classification of contractors, by a committee, based on the firms' financial strength and areas of experience.

Fixed price bids are required without exception in Qatar. Escalation clauses are not used under any circumstances, and there are no cost-plus-fee contracts. Also, while some provision is made for qualitative differences in bids, contracts must by law be awarded to the firm submitting the lowest bid that is in accordance with tender specifications.

Bid and performance bonds in the form of unconditional bank guarantees with the Qatar National Bank are required. The standard bid bond is 5 percent; it can be negotiated down on large contracts and is returned to all bidders after the contract is signed. The performance bond is set at 10 percent of the value of the contract. However, the amount actually required will depend on the Qatari agent or partner, and the extent of the agent's connections with the Government and the ruling family. Imported equipment can be used to offset the performance bond to some extent, depending again on the negotiating capability of the Qatari partner.

Firms bidding on projects in Qatar are not required to have an association with a Qatari firm at the time a bid is submitted. However, before a contract can be signed, the foreign firm must have already concluded either a joint venture or an agency agreement.

The State Purchases Office, under the authority of the Ministry of Finance and Petroleum, handles all direct purchase requests for equipment and supplies not involving construction. Invitations to tender, in this case, are sent to local firms only. Tender calls from the Office involve hundreds of millions of dollars annually, and their annual value is expected to increase substantially in the next few years. The period for preparation of quotations is generally quite short, and the bid deadline is seldom more than 45 days after the tender announcement. In most cases, the deadline is less than 30 days after the announcement. Under these conditions, local representation is crucial for successful bidding.

Though Qatar has no specific regulations governing arbitration, Government contracts normally contain an arbitration clause. The typical clause states that arbitration will take place in Qatar; no provision is made for international arbitration. Foreign contractors have had mixed experience with local arbitration bodies; typically, those who lose say the procedure is unfair, and those who win tend to praise Qatar's arbitration process.

Contractors generally receive an advance payment of 20 percent against an unconditional bank guarantee, and progress payments are made as the project moves along. There have been cases where the progress payments have been delayed. This is a problem that can be alleviated by the influence and contacts of the Qatari agent.

The official language in Qatar is Arabic, though English is widely used. Bids should be in both English and Arabic. However, all official documents must be authenticated in Arabic. The translator's signature must appear on the authenticated document. Specifications are usually written to British standards. Qatar uses the metric system of measurement.

Consulting Firms

There are no formal registration or legal requirements for consulting engineers or architects. Such firms wishing to work in Qatar should indicate their interest by writing to the following agencies, including evidence of professional experience and qualifications:

Architects . . . . Director of Engineering,
E.S.D.
Ministry of Public Works
P.O. Box 38
Doha, Qatar

Technical Advisor
Office of the Amir
P.O. Box 923
Doha, Qatar

Consulting Engineers . . . . Director of Engineering
(civil projects   E.S.D.
and highways)   Ministry of Public Works
P.O. Box 38
Doha, Qatar

Consulting Engineers . . . . Director
(heavy and light   Industrial Development
industry, archi-   Technical Center
tecture)   P.O. Box 36
Doha, Qatar

Consultants interested in working in other areas should contact the Ministry of Public Works and the appropriate client agency—e.g., the Ministry of Electricity and Water for power or desalination projects. Information on government ministries and other relevant agencies is provided in the appendix.

Pricing and Terms of Payment

As Qatar has a substantial balance-of-payments surplus, no exchange restrictions are imposed by the Government. Also, there are no controls over what merchants pay for imported products.

Firms bidding on a tender contract should quote the c.i.f. rate, make their bids valid for 3 months, and use both dollar and riyal values.

Payment is usually made by an irrevocable letter of credit, but at times, it is also made by cash. A sight draft is also accepted occasionally, but flexible credit terms are often requested by private buyers. If an exporter, after consulting his/her agent's banker, offers to accept payment 3 to 6 months after the arrival of the goods, he/she will stand a better chance of making a sale.

Licensing and Franchising

Qatar has no formal regulations governing either licensing or franchising arrangements, and there are no restrictions on the payment of fees or royalties. Firms seeking potential licensees or franchises should identify local entities through the same exhaustive manner of identifying an agent. The identical restrictions and precautions apply.

Advertising and Market Research

The business framework within which most U.S. firms are accustomed to dealing has only begun to develop in Qatar. Such "service" related specialties as advertising agencies, government and nongovernment statistical services, consumer credit companies, public relations firms, and promotional agencies are either not available or have just begun operations.

Most publications in Qatar have a small readership, come out weekly or monthly, are in Arabic, and are purchased by specialized audiences. These include *Al Ahad* (P.O. Box 2531, Doha), a weekly political review; *Al Arab* (P.O. Box 633, Doha), the only daily newspaper; *Al Doha* (P.O. Box 1836, Doha), a monthly magazine issued by the Ministry of Information; *Al-Jawhara* (P.O. Box 2531, Doha), a monthly journal published for women; *Al-Ouroba* (P.O. Box 633, Doha), a weekly review; and *Al-Saqr* (P.O. Box 4925, Doha), a sports magazine issued monthly by the Qatari Armed Forces. The two English publications in Qatar are the *Gulf Time* (published by Gulf Publishing and Printing House, P.O. Box 533, Doha), a weekly newspaper; and *This is Qatar* (published by Gulf Public Relations, P.O. Box 4015, Doha), a quarterly publication.

Radio and Television

Qatar Radio, which began transmission in June 1968, utilizes both medium wave and FM frequencies. Most broadcasts on the medium wave are in Arabic, while the FM stereo station, which transmits for 18 hours daily, is mainly used for broadcasts in English. Plans for the development of Qatar Radio include the construction of a 250-kilowatt transmission station to beam programs to the United States.

There is one television station operating in Qatar, which transmits over 54 hours of programming per week; a second station, which will broadcast largely in English, is scheduled to open in early 1982. Color television studios were installed in 1974, and much of the programming is purchased from Western countries. Further information on advertising, which has recently been introduced for television, can be obtained from the Commercials Section, Qatar Television, Ministry of Information, P.O. Box 1944, Doha.

Transportation, Utilities, and Communications

Shipping from the United States

Two American flag carriers provide regular cargo service to Qatar from the United States. The Waterman Steamship Corporation, 120 Wall Street, New York, N.Y. 10005, telephone: (212) 747-8550, provides lash barge service from the gulf and east coasts. The Sea-Land Service, Inc., P.O. Box 900, Edison, N.J. 08817, telephone (201) 494-2500, provides service from the east coast.

The sailing time from east coast ports to Qatar around the tip of Africa is normally 30 to 40 days. The time is reduced by at least 5 to 6 days when using the Suez Canal and possibly by even more time for vessels with fewer stops before Qatar.

For more information on American flag capacities worldwide, contact: Division of Commercial Cargo, Office of Marketing Development, Maritime Administration, U.S. Department of Commerce, Washington, D.C. 20230, telephone: (202) 377-4180.

Port Facilities

Qatar has two ports capable of handling cargo. General cargo normally enters through the nine-berth port at Doha, which has a maximum depth of 30 feet. Following a dredging operation to widen the port's main channel, the Government plans to add three additional berths along with a small, floating bunkering station for oil and water tankers. Bulk shipments are handled at Umm Said, 30 miles south of Doha, which has six berths and depths ranging from 20 to 35 feet. General cargo is occasionally unloaded at Umm Said and barged to Doha by the Qatar National Navigation and Transport Company. Umm Said will serve increasingly as the export facility for the Umm Said industrial area, and a $13 million project is underway to add additional pier space to the port.

The port congestion experienced earlier in the 1970's has been eased by increased storage space, expanded work force, and mechanized cargo-handling facilities. Port facilities are now adequate, and there are no port delays.

Road Transport

Qatar has an excellent highway system, which connects all parts of the peninsula. There are over 600 miles of road, 200 miles of which are hard surfaced. Qatar is now connected with Europe via the Trans-Arabian Highway and with the United Arab Emirates and Oman via a recently completed expressway. About 30 percent of the country's imports are now brought in overland by truck, with increasing amounts coming from container facilities at the ports of Dubai and Sharjah in the United Arab Emirates.

Air Transport

Gulf Air—jointly owned by Qatar, Bahrain, the United Arab Emirates, and Oman—is the national airline. The International Airport of Doha is served by 13 international passenger airlines, including Gulf Air, and is capable of handling any shipments of air freight that can be accommodated by modern, wide-bodied aircraft. To cope with increasing passenger and freight traffic, which increased by 8 percent in 1979, plans call for the construction of a second international airport near Doha. The new facility will be able to handle 16 aircraft simultaneously and over 900 passengers per hour.

Utilities

Demand for both power and water have grown dramatically in the past decade, reflecting expansion of Qatar's industrial and social sectors. With electric power consumption growing at an annual rate of 27 percent, the Government has expanded the country's main electric power and desalination plant at Res Abu Fontas, located 20 miles south of Doha. By 1980, the gas turbine power station, fueled by natural gas, had a full-load capacity of 820 megawatts.

Although power generating capacity is currently sufficient, plans call for the construction of a 1,200-megawatt power and desalination facility to avoid an energy crunch in the mid-1980's. Over $750 million has been allocated for the construction of this plant, which will be located at Ras Laffan. Production of desalinated water, which is currently adequate for national demands, averages 30 million gallons per day. Underground water, produced from approximately 400 wells, is used primarily for agriculture and is often added to desalinated water to improve its taste. A major project to extend water mains throughout the city of Doha began in 1978 and will be completed in the early 1980's.

Communications

Qatar's rapidly growing telecommunications system provides excellent external telephone, telex, and cable facilities. An earth satellite station was completed in 1976, and the installation of a second is now planned. Automatic telephone dialing is available to most parts of Europe, the Middle East, and the United States.

Credit

The Qatar Monetary Authority (QMA) was established in 1973 to serve as Qatar's central banking institution. The Agency's major responsibilities include issuance and redemption of currency, protection of the value of the riyal, and regulation of the commercial banking system. Due to lack of sufficient staff, however, QMA has been prevented from fully exercising its powers.

There are currently 13 commercial banks operating in Qatar. The three locally owned banks are the Qatar National Bank, which serves as the depository for most government accounts, the Commercial Bank of Qatar, which is managed by Chase Manhattan, and the Doha Bank. Foreign-owned banks include the Arab Bank, the Bank de Paris, the British Bank of the Middle East, and the Oman Bank. The only American bank in Doha is Citibank. The presence of the foreign banking community, large relative to the small size of the banking market in Qatar, would appear to preclude additional foreign banks from entering the market.

Qatar has no foreign exchange restrictions, and banking regulations permit all usual types of commercial banking operations. In September 1976, Qatar, Bahrain, and the United Arab Emirates signed a currency agreement that made the three countries' currencies legal tender in each other's territories. This agreement was suspended in early 1979, however, when Qatar unilaterally revalued its currency. Such revaluations are normally small and infrequent in Qatar.

There is no stock market in Qatar, but a few joint stock companies are publicly held and trade shares through local banks. Non-Qataris may not own shares in Qatari companies except in development projects specifically approved by the Government. Foreign companies participating in a joint venture with the Government may own stock but may not trade on the local market.

In the insurance field, there are nine companies operating in Qatar, five of which are foreign owned. The Qatari Insurance Company (P.O. Box 666, Suq Wakef, Doha) controls most of the market and manages the Government's insurance business.

Foreign exchange rates are determined by the Qatar Monetary Agency. In May 1981, the exchange rate of the Qatar Riyal (QR) against the U.S. dollar was $1 to QR 3.64 or QR 1 to $0.2747.

Investment in Qatar

The Government of Qatar actively encourages foreign investment. While the country's oil wealth has eliminated the need for foreign capital, foreign investment is seen as necessary to ensure technology transfers and quality products. Incentives specifically designed to attract the foreign investor include exemption from customs duties on equipment and material imported for use in new industries, renewable 5-year tax holidays, government assistance through capital participation and provision of interest-free loans, and the provision of free land.

Foreign investors are also encouraged by the allowance for unrestricted repatriation of capital, net profits, royalties, and all other fees.

Law No. 20 of 1963, as amended by Decree 22 of 967, establishes guidelines for foreign participation in commerce and industry. It is legally required that all local companies have at least 51-percent Qatari ownership, although exemptions may be granted by special decree. Foreign companies wishing to establish a wholly owned branch or a company with less than majority Qatari ownership must apply to the Ministry of Economy and Commerce for a special exemption. Such requests are evaluated on a case-by-case basis.

Investment procedures are to be thoroughly defined in the proposed Investment Code for Qatar, now being developed by the country's Industrial Development Technical Center (IOTC).

Qatar has no bilateral investment agreements.

Industrial Property Protection*

Qatar is not a member of any international convention to which the United States belongs on the subject of patents, trademarks, or copyrights. There are no patent laws in effect in Qatar. Some protection, however, is afforded by advertising a Cautionary Notice in daily Qatari newspapers.

Labor

Qatar is heavily dependent on foreign labor and will continue to be so for the foreseeable future. Over three-quarters of Qatar's total population of about 250,000 are non-Qataris, with foreigners comprising well over 80 percent of the labor force.

There is no unemployment in Qatar; rather, the country's major development constraint is the shortage of skilled and unskilled labor. Therefore, foreign contractors on most projects are required to recruit much of their labor from overseas. The contractors must arrange for housing and other facilities for these employees.

A number of training centers, including the Technical Center for Industrial Development and the Institute for Management, have been set up to broaden educational and vocational training opportunities for Qataris. Efforts to increase the number of Qatari technicians have also included sending missions abroad for

*Prepared by Foreign Business Practices Division, Office of International Finance and Investment, International Trade Administration, U.S. Department of Commerce.

training and encouraging private enterprise—particularly the oil firms—to provide more training. A Regional Training Center, located in Doha, is operated with assistance from the International Labor Organization. This center provides vocational training for Qataris and nationals of other Gulf States.

Wages and Benefits

The need for imported labor and the expansion of economic activity have increased wage levels by an estimated 30 to 50 percent per year since 1973. Monthly salaries for Qataris and non-Westerners in 1980 were as follows: High level executives, $2,500; middle management, $1,700; technicians, $1,250; secretaries, $1,300; skilled workers, $1,200; and unskilled workers, $250 to $800. Salaries are usually paid in cash on a monthly or semimonthly basis.

Fringe benefits normally given to skilled workers can amount to more than 100 percent of the basic pay. These may include transportation to and from the work site, health services, and education and housing allowances. Many employers augment the salaries of unskilled workers with a food allowance as well as a housing allowance or company housing.

Regulations mandate a maximum 8-hour day, and a 48-hour work week most of the year. During the Moslem fasting month of Ramadan, the working day may not exceed 6 hours and the work week 36 hours. Overtime is paid at varying rates depending on circumstances.

Labor Legislation

Labor Law No. 3 of 1962, as amended, regulates labor conditions in Qatar. There are various categories of workers to whose employment the law does not apply, including domestic servants, workers in firms with less than 10 employees, and managerial and executive staff. The law sets conditions for work and compensation, outlaws strikes and labor unions, and gives Qataris preference in hiring.

The Ministry of Labor and Social Affairs, as directed by the Labor Law, appoints officials to monitor labor conditions and informally mediate disputes within the country. Ministry officials are also responsible for inspecting all labor sites and camps. There are no labor unions.

The Labor Law requires all expatriate workers to have valid documentation including a passport, a good conduct certificate, and a resident permit. The Ministry of Labor and Social Affairs issues authorizations to local employers to sponsor the import of expatriate workers. In late 1978, a four-person committee was established to oversee the status of sponsors and ensure that authorizations are not being abused.

Taxation

There are no personal income taxes or municipal taxes levied in Qatar. This applies alike to citizens and aliens residing in the country.

Companies are required to pay tax on their annual profits after deducting all necessary business expenses. These taxes are fixed on a sliding scale rising from 5 percent to a maximum of 55 percent on taxable profits above QR 5 million ($1.3 million).

If a project is considered beneficial to development, net annual profits by Qatari share companies may be exempted from taxes for 5 years. Foreign branches and individuals are not eligible for this tax holiday.

Guidance for Business Visitors Abroad

Entry Requirements

Business representatives wishing to visit Qatar must have a valid passport and possess a visa. The latter can be obtained from the Qatar Embassy in Washington or the Qatar Mission to the United Nations in New York. All business applicants must submit two visa applications and photographs together with a letter from the sponsoring Qatari firm that explains the purpose of the travel, states who the visitors will see, and guarantees that all expenses will be covered. The local sponsor must submit a letter to the immigration office in Qatar prior to the traveler's arrival or prior to the issuance of the visa.

A transit visa, valid for a maximum of 72 hours, can be obtained at the Doha airport if the business traveler is met by a representative of a bona fide Qatari business firm who brings an authorized letter of sponsorship. The U.S. Embassy cannot sponsor the visit of private Americans to Qatar.

A visitor must also have proof of health inoculations. Certificates of vaccination against cholera are required and travelers arriving from infected areas must have a certificate of vaccination against yellow fever.

Business Customs

Commercial language.—Arabic is the official language, but English is widely spoken and is generally acceptable in business and gov-

ernment circles. Catalogs and promotional material in English are acceptable. However, use of Arabic by foreign firms in corresponding with Qataris is greatly valued as a mark of consideration, and consequently could be of competitive value to the foreign firm.

Business Hours.—Qatari Government hours are Saturday through Thursday, 8 a.m. to 12:30 p.m. Commercial and banking hours are Saturday through Thursday, 8 a.m. to 12:30 p.m. Some firms reopen in the afternoon from 3:30 p.m. to 6:30 p.m. U.S. Embassy hours are Saturday through Wednesday, 7:30 a.m. to 3:30 p.m. All businesses and other offices are closed on Friday, the Muslim holy day.

Holidays.—Qatar uses a Heijira calendar, which is based on a lunar year about 11 days shorter than the Gregorian, or solar year. Religious holidays vary from year to year, therefore, on the Gregorian calendar. The holidays are Eid Al-Fitr (approximately August 1-3 in 1981), which celebrates the end of Ramadan, and Eid Al-Adha (approximately October 8-11 in 1981), which concludes the celebration of the pilgramage to Mecca. The only fixed holidays in Qatar are New Year's Day, the anniversary of the accession of the Emir on February 22, and Independence Day on September 3.

October through May or June generally is considered the best period for foreign business visits to Qatar. The summer months are very hot and many local businesspeople are absent from the country during that period.

Hotels.—Business travelers are advised to make hotel reservations in advance of their visit. The major hotels, all in Doha, are the Gulf (P.O. Box 1911, telex: 4214), Doha Palace (P.O. Box 710, telex: 4265), and the Ramada (P.O. Box 1768, telex: 4664). Daily rates range from $85 single/$110 double at the Gulf to $70 single/$85 double at the Ramada. Extra hotel charges include a 10-percent service charge and a 5-percent government tax. A Sheraton hotel/convention center is scheduled to open toward the end of 1981.

Transportation.—The major airlines serving Qatar are Gulf Air, British Airways, Royal Jordanian Airlines, Middle East Airlines, Air France, Sabena, Air India, Pakistan International, and Saudi Arabian Airlines.

Taxis (cars with yellow plates) are available at a cost of $5 to $10 per trip within Doha; out-of-town and all-day rates must be negotiated. Medium-sized cars can be rented for $50 per day; a driver can be hired for $30 to $35 per day. U.S. and international drivers' licenses are not accepted.

Sources of Economic and Commercial Information

Government Representation

Embassy of the United States
Fariq Bin Omran
P.O. Box 2399
Doha, Qatar
Telephone: 870701/2/3

Embassy of Qatar
600 New Hampshire Avenue, N.W.
Suite 1180
Washington, D.C. 20037
Telephone: (202) 338-0111

Qatari Mission to the United Nations
747 Third Avenue
New York, N.Y. 10017
Telephone: (212) 486-9335

Commerce Action Group for the Near East
Office of Country Marketing
U.S. Department of Commerce
Washington, D.C. 20230
Telephone: (202) 377-5545

U.S. Government Publications

Area Handbook for the Persian Gulf States, U.S. Government Printing Office, 1977
Foreign Economic Trends and Their Implications for the United States—Qatar, October 1980, prepared by the American Embassy, annual
Background Notes: Qatar, December 1976, U.S. Department of State, Washington, D.C., Publication No. 7905
An Introduction to Contract Procedures in the Near East and North Africa, October 1980, prepared by Commerce Action Group for the Near East

Qatari Government Publications

Qatar Year Book 1978-79, Press and Publications Department, Ministry of Information, Doha
Yearly Bulletin of Imports and Exports, Customs Department, Doha
Third Annual Report, Qatar Monetary Agency, 1978, Doha
Qatari Facts and Figures, Ministry of Information, 1980, Doha
Diaruna Wal Alam (monthly), Ministry of Finance and Petroleum, Doha

Other Sources

Mideast Markets (biweekly), published by Financial Times, London. Available in U.S. from F.T. Publications, 75 Rockefeller Plaza, New York, N.Y. 10019
Middle East Economic Survey (weekly), the Middle East Research and Publishing Center, P.O. Box 1224, Beirut, Lebanon
"Qatar," *The Financial Times*, February 22, 1980, London
A Survey of Selected Projects in the Gulf States, Projects Research, Inc., P.O. Box 2285, Falls Church, Va. 22042
Middle East Executive Reports (monthly), published by Middle East Executive Reports, Ltd., 1115 Massachusetts Avenue, N.W. #6, Washington, D.C. 20005
Middle East Economic Digest (weekly), published by MEED, 84-86 Chancery Lane, London WC 2A 1DL, United Kingdom

APPENDIX
Qatari Government Agencies
(P.O. Boxes are in Doha)

Ministries

Ministryof Agriculture and Industry
P.O. Box 1966
H.E. Sheikh Faisal Bin Thani al Thani,
Minister
Mr. Ahmad Al-Mana,
Deputy Minister
Mr. Sultan Kawari
Director of Agriculture
Mr. Michel Farah
Head of Interim Section in the Ministry

Ministry of Communications and Transport
P.O. Box 3416
H.E. Abdullah Bin Nasser al Suwaidi
Minister
Mr. Ahmad Muarafieh
Deputy Minister
Department of Civil Aviation
P.O. Box 4000
Mr. Ali al-Malki
Acting Director of Civil Aviation
Department of Ports
P.O. Box 313
Mr. Abdulrahman Jaber Al-Muftah
Director
Department of Posts
P.O. Box 3416
Mr. Mohammad Saif Mo'dadi
Director
Department of Telecommunications
P.O. Box 313
Mr. Ahmad Abu Huddoud
director

Ministry of Defense
P.O. Box 37
H.H. Sheikh Hamad bin Khalifa al Thani
Minister, Commander-in-Chief, and
Crown Prince
(Aide: Major Abdullah Said Abu Saleh)
Brigadier Mohammad al Attiyah
Deputy Commander-in-Chief
(Aide: Major Mohammed Khalil)

Ministry of Economy and Commerce
P.O. Box 1968
H.E. Sheikh Nasser bin Khalid Al-Thani
Minister
Mr. Ismail Sidke
Director of Economic and Commercial Affairs

Mr. Ali Hasan Khalaf
Director of Economic Administration
Mr. Hasan Mobsin
Director of Registration Section

Ministry of Education
P.O. Box 80
H.E. Sheikh Mohammed Bin Hamad al Thani
Minister
Mr. Abdul Aziz bin Turki
Deputy Minister

Ministry of Electricity and Water
P.O. Box 41
H.E. Sheikh Jasim bin Mohammed Al Thani
Minister
Department of Electricity
P.O. Box 41
Mr. Mohammad Yousif al Ali
Director
Mr. Owen Phillips
Senior Advisor
Department of Water
P.O. Box 162
Mr. Ahmad Jittal
Director
Mr. William Lee
Deputy Director

Ministry of Finance and Petroleum
P.O. Box 83
H.E. Sheikh Abdul Aziz bin Khalifa al Thani
Minister
Dr. Taher Hadidi
Advisor to the Minister
Mr. Abdullah Al-Attiyah
Director of Public Relations
Department of Petroleum Affairs
P.O. Box 3322
Mr. Abdullah Sallatt
Director
Mr. Nasir Mubarak Al Ali
Deputy Director
Department of Financial Affairs
P.O. Box 83
Mr. Abd Al Qadr al Qadi
Director
Mr. Hassain Habboub
Deputy Director
State Purchasing Department
P.O. Box 1908

QATAR

Mr. Mohammad al-Khulaifi
Director
Customs Department
P.O. Box 218
Mr. Ahmad Al-Uthman
director
Supply Department
P.O. Box 925
Mr. Ahmad Sowaidi
Director

Ministry of Foreign Affairs
P.O. Box 250

H.E. Sheikh Suhaym bin Hamad Al Thani
Minister
H.E. Sheikh Ahmad bin Saif Al Thani
Minister of State for Foreign Affairs

Ministry of Information
P.O. Box 1836

H.E. Issa Ghanim Al Kawari
Minister
Mr. Mohammad Abdul Rahman Al Khulaifi
Deputy Minister
(Vacant)
Director of Information

Ministry of Justice
P.O. Box 917

(Vacant)
Minister
Mr. Mohammad Abdullah Al-Malki
Director of Minister's Office

Ministry of Labor and Social Affairs
P.O. Box 201

H.A. Ali bin Ahmad al Ansari
Minister
Mr. Mohammad Mahmoud
Director of Ministry

Ministry of Interior
P.O. Box 2433

H.E. Sheikh Khalid bin Hamad al Thani
Minister
Mr. Saied Al-Sulaiti
Director of Passports and Immigration

Ministry of Municipal Affairs
P.O. Box 820

H.E. Sheikh Mohammad bin Jabor Al Thani
Minister
Mr. Ali Mohammad al Khater
Director of Doha Municipality

Ministry of Public Health
P.O. Box 42

H.E. Khalid al Mana
Minister
Dr. Abdullah al Baker
director of Health
Dr. Omar Hashisho
Director of Hospitals
Dr. John Busser
Advisor on Equipment Purchases
P.O. Box 3646

Ministry of Public Works
P.O. Box 38

H.E. Khalid al Attiyah
Minister
Mr. Khalid al Khater
Director of Engineering Services Department
Mr. Sidke Khader
Deputy Director of Engineering Services
    Department
Mr. Ian Jones
Engineer

Other Agencies

Office of the Technical Advisor to the Amir
P.O. Box 923

Mr. Hisham Qaddumi
Technical Advisor

Industrial Development Technical Center
P.O. Box 2599

Mr. Said Mishal
Director
(Vacant)
financial Advisor
Mr. Samir Ghali
Heavy Industry
Dr. Abu Baker Murad Ghalib
Medium and Light Industries

Chamber of Commerce
P.O.Box 402

Mr. Ahmad Sowaidi
President
Mr. Kamal Saleh
Director General

University of Qatar
P.O. Box 80

Mr. Mohammad Kazem
President

Gulf Organization for Industrial Consulting
P.O. Box 5114

Dr. Ali Khalaf
Secretary General

Market Profile—QATAR

Foreign Trade

Imports.—$1.5 billion in 1980; $1.4 billion in 1979. Major 1979 suppliers: Japan, $264 million; United Kingdom, $237 million; France, $175 million; United States, $152 million. Major imports: machinery, transport equipment, oilfield supplies, steel, cement, foodstuffs, tobacco, textiles, clothing.

Exports.—$6.2 billion in 1980; $4.2 billion in 1979. Major customers 1979: Japan, $879 million; Netherlands, $604 million; France, $473 million; United States, $265 million; Thailand, $247 million. Crude petroleum is principal export. Other exports include fertilizer (urea), hydrous liquid, shrimp, steel bars.

Trade Policy.—Liberal. Most imports are charged 2.5 percent ad valorem duty. Importation limited to Qatari nationals and firms. No exchange controls on imports.

Foreign Investment

Government anxious to diversify economy and welcomes foreign investment, particularly when output is intended for export. Foreign equity limited to 49 percent of total participation in most cases. Customs duty relaxation and free land often granted. No restriction on remittance of profits, nor are there any foreign exchange restrictions. No personal taxes and a 5-year exemption of corporate taxes is often granted. U.S. investment is primarily in the petroleum sector and banking. The Government is interested in developing petrochemical, food processing, and plastics industries.

Currency.—Qatar Riyal (QR) divided into 100 dirhams and equals US$.275 (US$1 = QR 3.64) in May 1981. Money supply in February 1980 was $736 million; currency in circulation, $200 million. Foreign exchange reserves in July 1979 were $281 million.

Domestic Credit and Investment.—Thirteen commercial banks—including one U.S. bank—and the Qatar National Bank, which is 50 percent owned by the Qatar Government and is the depository for government accounts. The Qatar Monetary Agency serves as the central bank.

State Budget.—The 1980 development budget calls for expenditures of $2.3 billion, 20 percent above 1979-80 expenditures.

Economy

GNP is derived largely from oil production and related industries; oil revenues were approximately $5.8 billion in 1980 and may exceed $6.5 billion in 1981. Per capita income at $26,000 in 1980. The estimated inflation rate for 1980 was 15 percent. Qatar has no development plan.

Agriculture.—Production limited by scarcity of arable land and water. Country has achieved self-sufficiency in production of a few vegetables; government-operating poultry project will supply greater part of demand for poultry and eggs. Long-range development programs in sheep-raising and dairy farming.

Minerals.—At present level of production, oil reserves are expected to last 20 years. Oil production averaged just over 500,000 barrels per day in 1980. Has natural gas deposits that can be produced well into the next century with one field, the

Northwest Dome, believed to be one of the world's biggest. Associated gas production in 1979 was 235.5 cubic feet, an increase of 29 percent from 1978.

Industry.—Most major industrial projects are based on petroleum and natural gas to produce fertilizers, gasoline, diesel, aviation fuel, and kerosene. The Qatar Steel Company has a direct reduction plant, an electric arc furnace, a continuous caster, and a rolling mill to make steel reinforcing rods. Smaller ventures—including an aluminum extrusion plant, flour mill, truck assembly plant, and concrete plants—are in operation or being constructed. The cement plant at Umm Bab has a rated capacity of 1,600 tons per day. Ethylene plants also are under construction. The NGL plant destroyed by fire in 1977 has been rebuilt and a second NGL facility is under construction.

Basic Economic Facilities

Transportation.—No railroads, but an excellent highway system reaches all settled parts of the peninsula. Doha International Airport accommodates jumbo jets and is served by a number of international airlines. Qatar owns 25 percent of Gulf Air, which provides regular service to the Middle East, Europe, and Hong Kong. A manmade port at Doha has nine berths. Umm Said, 40 kilometers south of Doha, has 13 berths and an oil loading terminal. In 1979, 1.7 million tons of freight were unloaded.

Communications.—Excellent telephone, telex, and cable facilities include an automatic telex and direct dialing to some Gulf States. An earth satellite station beams on the Indian Ocean satellite. Radio and TV available; expansion planned.

Power.—Generating capacity, 2,000 MW in 1980. Power production and peak demand have risen 30 and 35 percent annually in recent years. Surplus of desalinated water production was 7,000 million gallons in 1980.

Natural Resources

Land.—Peninsula about 100 miles long; total area 4,400 square miles. Flat desert except for hills on western coast; sand dunes and salt flats predominate in south.

Climate.—Extremely hot May through September. Pleasant remainder of year, although more humid; light rainfall.

Fishing.—Qatar National Fishing Company exported shrimp valued at $2 million in 1980.

Population

Size.—Estimated 250,000; only some 50,000 native Qataris, with major expatriates primarily Pakistanis, Indians, Iranians, and Europeans; 85 percent of population lives around Doha.

Language.—Arabic. English spoken in business circles.

Education.—Literacy rate is low, but improving. Educational systems free. Begun construction of university and plans increase number schools. Over 38,000 students enrolled in 1980.

Labor.—Labor force estimated at 50,000 to 70,000, of which 80 percent are expatriates.

2007

Trading and Investing In Romania

Contents

Report Revised September 1978

Introduction

Economic and commercial relations between the United States and Romania have shown marked improvement in recent years. Supported by initiatives from both governments and the signing of a number of bilateral agreements, these improved relations have resulted in a healthy surge in trade. Two-way trade reached an all-time high of $492.7 million in 1977, a six-fold increase since 1970. Both nations hope to surpass the $1 billion level by 1980. U.S.-Romanian trade has risen more sharply than Romanian trade with the West as a whole, and the United States is now Romania's second most active trading partner among free world industrialized countries. In 1977 U.S.-Romanian trade comprised about 4 percent of Romania's total trade.

The list of bilateral agreements in the economic sector reached in recent years has been impressive. They concern maritime affairs, aviation, taxation, agricultural trade and cooperation, fisheries, and long-term economic, industrial, and technical cooperation. Most important is the 1975 U.S.-Romanian Trade Agreement by which each country extends and receives most-favored-nation (MFN) tariff treatment. This agreement has gone far toward normalizing economic relations between the two countries.

Through its participation in the General Agreement on Tariffs and Trade (GATT), the International Monetary Fund (IMF), and the World Bank, Romania has increased its efforts to integrate its economy into the world economic system and to diversify its trade. In 1977 approximately 60 percent of Romania's trade was with non-communist nations, compared to about 45 percent in 1970. Romania also has passed legislation which facilitates cooperation with foreign firms, allows foreign equity ownership in joint companies with Romanian partners, and permits U.S. and other Western firms to open representative offices in Romania.

A continuous series of visits since 1969 by high-level government officials, working-level commercial delegations, and U.S. Congressional leaders has contributed to a continuing dialogue between the two countries on economic and commercial matters. Among the more significant of these visits have been trips to the United States by Romanian President Ceausescu in 1970, 1973, 1975, and 1978, and visits to Romania by President Nixon in 1969 and President Ford in 1974.

The Romanian Economy

Romania, once a predominantly agrarian country, has experienced extremely high industrial growth since the 1950's. Since 1970, according to Romanian statistics, industrial production has risen at an average annual rate of more than 12 percent despite extensive flooding in 1970 and 1975 and a major earthquake in 1977. Industry accounted for 60 percent of the country's national income in 1976. Growth has been greatest in the electronics, machine building, chemical, and metallurgical sectors and has been achieved at the expense of agricultural development and the Romanian consumer. The U.S. Government estimates that the Romanian Gross National Product (GNP) reached $52.5 billion in 1977. Romanian per capita GNP was approximately $2,442, roughly four-fifths that of most of the other East European countries.

About two-thirds of Romania's total investment goes to industry. Over 60 percent of industrial investment has gone to the electric power, metallurgy, machine building, and chemical sectors. In recent years energy and light industry also have been important.

Romania's rich natural resource base of oil deposits, natural gas, timber, and coal is impressive, but the country's oil reserves are rapidly depleting, and iron ore and coal shortages threaten impressive economic development. Romania's rapid industrial growth in recent years has made energy an increasingly important factor. In 1976 Romania became a net importer of crude oil, although it continues to export refined oil products. This situation created a strong interest in alternative sources of energy, especially nuclear and hydroelectric power, and offshore oil and gas exploration in the Black Sea.

Planning

Planning in Romania centers on a 5-year plan with specific annual and ancillary plans derived from it. These plans acquire legal status and establish compulsory priorities and targets for growth and development in industrial and agricultural production, raw materials use, investment, labor productivity, economic efficiency, scientific research and other areas. Over the years these targets have generally been met and sometimes exceeded. The 5-year plan and other plans are not available to foreigners, but the general guidelines of the plan, or "Directives," are published and provide the basic directions the Romanian economy will take. Copies of the "directives" can be obtained through the Romanian Embassy or the Romania Desk at the U.S. Department of Commerce.

The agency responsible for preparing, implementing, and monitoring Romania's plans is the State Planning Committee under the Council of Ministers. With the assistance of other government economic organizations, the Committee prepares the 5-year plans and annual economic plans and coordinates all planning activity.

The State Planning Committee submits its draft plan to the Council of Ministers, which in turn passes it on to the Supreme Council. After approval by the Supreme Council, the plan is enacted into law by the Grand National Assembly, Romania's chief legislative body. Once it has become law, the plan is distributed to the various ministries which translate the directives into specific assignments, targets and quotas for implementation by the ministries themselves and by subordinate units.

Within the 5-year plan and the annual plans, a specific foreign trade plan is developed by the State Planning Committee in collaboration with the Ministry of Foreign Trade and International Economic Cooperation and other ministries and agencies concerned with foreign trade, such as the Romanian Bank for Foreign Trade.

Recent Reforms

The Romanian Government has recognized the need for reform in the economy to make the transition from extensive to intensive economic development. Among the East European Communist States, Romania has the least experience with economic decentralization. This is, in part, because Romania's overall slower economic development required much longer to reach the

"bottleneck" crises that other communist states have encountered. The present economic mechanisms had been quite successful in achieving high rates of growth. The economy, nevertheless, is inefficient in its use of manpower, raw materials, and capital, and faces the threat of stagnation if changes are not adopted.

In 1978, President Ceausescu has announced a number of proposals to improve the economy's

---

HOW TO OBTAIN BACKGROUND INFORMATION ABOUT THESE COUNTRIES

Keeping this book within reasonable size limits has made it necessary to focus on material *directly* concerned with marketing and commerce, and set aside materials only indirectly related. The editors relize, however, that *general* data about a country are also vital to a company's preparations to enter a foreign market, and make a very definite recommendation as to how such expanded information needs can be served.

For those who wish *general* data about a country—data which goes beyond marketing and commerce—the editors recommend *Countries of the World and Their Leaders*, published as an annually updated yearbook by Gale Research Company, Detroit, Michigan 48226. Containing 4- to 20-page entries on 168 countries, the volume also provides several hundred pages of supplementary world data. Each country entry is prepared by the U.S. Department of State to provide a general briefing on the geography, people, culture, and political situation of the particular country. Each report provides some historical insight as well as a look at contemporary trends of lifestyle in the country. Reports also discuss a country's educational system, its press, ethnic groupings and religious practices.

Countries of the World and Their Leaders provides a fresh listing of cabinet ministers of each nation. In addition it lists health conditions the traveling businessman will wish to prepare for and includes information on passport procedures, customs and duties, and world climate conditions.

performance. These include the addition of qualitative measurements to gross output when assessing the performance of the economic enterprise. Salaries would be based on marketable output and not gross production.

Enterprises would be required to develop a plan and budget for both inputs and outputs. If output goals were surpassed, the enterprise could establish a fund for plant expansion and worker benefits such as added housing construction and possibly foreign travel. Presumably these monies would be controlled, at least to some extent, by the local enterprise.

Only the switch away from the gross output measure is scheduled to be implemented in 1978. The other proposals will undergo further discussion before adoption.

Current Five-Year Plan

The 1976-80 Five-Year Plan maintains the heavy emphasis of recent plans on rapid industrial development and also commits more money to investment in agriculture. It sets an annual target of 11.5 percent for expansion of gross industrial production and of 6.9 to 9 percent for agricultural growth. The plan emphasizes investments in export manufacturing facilities and sets approximately two-thirds of planned investments or about $126 billion for industrial production. Of this figure, 70 percent is allocated into four priority areas: Chemical/petrochemical, machine building, metallurgy, and mining and power engineering.

Under the plan, chemical/petrochemical output is expected to increase 160 to 180 percent. Within this sector, the development and expansion of synthetic yarn and fiber production, chemical fertilizers, synthetic rubber and plastics, and pharmaceuticals have priority. In addition, Romania is concentrating on improving the efficiency of its petroleum industry.

Over the 5-year period, growth in the machine building industry is scheduled to average from 11.5 to 12.5 percent annually; this sector is to produce 34 percent of the total Romanian industrial output by 1980. Priority areas within this sector include: electronics, fine optics, electrical engineering, machine tools, cars, trucks, tractors, and the aircraft industry.

In metallurgy, Romania will develop a new iron and steel manufacturing facility and will expand existing capacity in both ferrous and non-ferrous metallurgical industries, particularly aluminum. There is also an interest in establishing co-production arrangements with Western firms for processing copper, lead, and zinc concentrates.

In mining and power engineering, heavy emphasis is given to geological exploration for new energy resources, such as coal and lignite. Deep drilling for crude oil and gas, including Black Sea offshore operations, will expand. The plan calls for improved fuel efficiency by existing thermopower stations, increased use of bituminous shales as fuel, and construction and/or expansion of hydropower and thermopower stations. Romania is beginning a nuclear power program.

Agriculture has not fared nearly as well as industry. Investment in this area has remained rather modest, and Romanian agriculture has been severely affected by a number of natural disasters in this decade.

Agricultural growth between 1973 and 1975 averaged around 1.6 percent per year, although 1976, a very good year for Romanian agriculture, saw a better than 15 percent jump. In 1977, agricultural production slumped once again. The Romanian Government has taken steps to remedy structural weaknesses that led to low productivity and shortages of skilled labor in the agricultural sector. In the current Five-Year Plan, attention is focused on modernization of agricultural facilities, equipment and processes, increased mechanization, and more rational use of land. Extensive irrigation, drainage, and anti-soil erosion projects are of particular importance.

Foreign Trade

General Policy

Romanian foreign trade has grown rapidly in this decade from $3.8 billion in 1970 to $14 billion in 1977. This growth rate is expected to continue until at least 1980. While Romania's total external trade is balanced, there is an imbalance in hard currency trade. In 1977 Romania imported $2.4 billion and exported $1.9 billion. The current Five-Year Plan seeks to put this hard currency trade in balance by 1980.

The percentage of Romania's trade with the communist countries, the industrialized west, and the developing countries has been basically static since 1976. Prior to 1976, the percentage of Romanian trade with the communist countries, as a percentage of total Romanian trade, declined substantially since 1965. Table 1 demonstrates this redistribution. Romania remains a member of the Council for Mutual Economic Assistance (CEMA, also called COMECON)[1], a Soviet-organized multilateral organization founded in 1949 to further cooperation among member states; however, the Romanian Government has clearly embarked on a policy designed to avoid dependence on any particular trading partner or bloc. Romania maintains important trade relations with both the People's Republic of China and Yugoslavia.

Table 1.—Romanian External Trade

(percentages)

	1965	1970	1975
Exports			
Socialist Countries	68.9	58.4	47.8
OECD	25.4	32.9	36.9
Less Developed	5.7	8.7	15.3
Imports			
Socialist Countries	61.5	54.8	45.1
OECD	34.0	40.5	44.2
Less Developed	4.5	4.7	10.7

Source: Romanian Statistics

While trade with the communist countries has slipped, the Soviet Union remains Romania's most important trading partner. Major Romanian imports from the USSR include heavy industrial equipment, machine tools, installations for the chemical industry, mining equipment, coking coal, iron ore, nonferrous metal ores, and steel products. Unlike other CEMA countries Romania does not depend upon the Soviet Union for oil. Chief Romanian exports to the Soviet Union include electrical engineering equipment, drilling rigs, motor vehicles, railway cars, chemicals, chemical equipment, raw materials and agricultural products.

Romania's other major CEMA trading partners are the German Democratic Republic ($855 million total trade in 1976), Poland ($549 million) and Czechoslovakia ($540 million). CEMA has assigned Romania certain product specialization areas for intra-CEMA trade, including thermoelectric plants and gas-powered generators, deep-drilling rigs and oil-refinery equipment, petrochemicals, diesel locomotives, tractors, trucks, knitwear, and furniture. While Romania does export these products to CEMA countries, Romanian policy for the past 20 years has been to resist full CEMA integration and

[1] CEMA members include Bulgaria, Cuba, Czechoslovakia, German Democratic Republic, Mongolia, Hungary, Poland, Romania and the USSR. Vietnam and Yugoslavia have "observer" status.

conformity, and to proceed with its own rapid industrialization.

Romanian trade with the West and Japan grew significantly between 1965 and 1975, but the consistent trade deficits led to an alarming hard currency debt by 1974. Cutbacks on imports from the West did reduce this debt in 1975, and in 1976 Romania's trade position with OECD countries was almost in balance. In 1977 Romania may have run a sizeable deficit due in part to the March earthquake.

Romania generally confines its purchases from the West to the technology, installations, equipment, products, and raw materials necessary to carry out the directives of the Five-Year Plan and which absolutely cannot be produced

Table 2.—U.S.-Romanian Trade, 1974–77

(in millions of dollars)

Leading U.S. Exports to Romania

	1974	1975	1976	1977
Coal	5.5	17.5	10.7	53.6
Soybeans	0	3.5	45.3	38.6
Cattle hides	24.1	9.7	26.6	26.7
Wheat	0	11.8	48.5	16.0
Corn	63.0	58.6	7.5	15.8
Phosphate rock	9.7	6.2	6.8	14.9
Woodpulp	3.0	5.8	9.4	11.2
Soybean oilcake	25.5	1.9	17.7	9.4
Measurement and control instruments	1.3	5.2	3.6	6.7
Cotton	38.8	12.2	0	6.5
Steel plate, tinned	7.1	1.8	12.8	6.1
Grain sorghums	0	3.3	18.1	5.1
Machine tools	0.4	1.9	1.6	4.8
Computer equipment	1.0	3.4	2.9	4.1
Motor vehicle parts	0.1	.1	.5	2.8
Special purpose trucks	0.9	1.2	.7	2.5
Herbicides & other organic chemicals	2.9	2.7	.4	2.4
Rolling mill equipment	0.2	0	0	1.7
Internal combustion engines	0.1	.2	.2	1.5
Aircraft parts	3.3	1.2	.8	1.5
Subtotal	177.9	148.6	214.1	231.9

Leading U.S. Imports from Romania

Fuel oil	22.1	53.0	79.3	53.0
Footwear	11.4	8.2	17.8	20.4
Gasoline	40.1	18.8	2.6	19.2
Men's boys' outerwear	1.3	1.6	13.0	17.3
Canned ham & pork	9.9	8.3	13.0	14.8
Tractors	7.5	8.1	9.8	10.1
Women's, girls' outerwear	1.4	1.3	4.9	9.7
Furniture	1.7	1.9	4.1	6.9
Seamless steel pipe	0.9	.5	.2	6.8
Knit outerwear	0.3	.1	3.9	6.5
Knit underwear	1.6	.9	3.9	6.1
Misc. glassware	1.7	1.9	4.4	5.2
Steel plate and sheet	0.6	1.9	1.2	4.5
Ball bearings	0.0	.2	.7	4.2
Carpets	0.1	.4	1.9	4.2
Machine tools	0.6	1.4	3.1	3.3
Organic Chemicals	1.7	1.6	4.0	3.2
Synthetic fabric	0	0	.2	2.5
Semi-refined petroleum	6.0	8.2	0	2.3
Men's, boys' underwear	0.8	.2	1.1	2.3
Subtotal	109.7	118.5	169.1	202.6
Total U.S. Exports	277.1	189.3	249.0	259.4
Total U.S. Imports	130.5	133.0	198.8	233.3
Trade Turnover	407.6	322.3	447.8	492.7
U.S. Trade Balance	+146.6	+56.3	+50.2	+26.1

Table 3.—Leading Romanian Imports from
Industrial West and Japan, 1974–76

(in thousands of dollars)

SITC	IMPORT ITEM	1976	% U.S. share	1975	1974
0410	Unmilled wheat and meslin	119,514	40.5	60,280	1,608
7151	Machine tools for metal work	73,700	2.2	72,599	51,083
3218	Coke semi-coke of coal	62,372	—	49,860	28,514
6782	Iron/steel seamless pipes	48,689	3.6	81,621	45,747
2214	Soya beans	45,282	100.0	3,506	0
7198	Machinery and mach. appl.	31,246	9.3	37,837	54,708
67323	Alloy steel bars and rods	30,874	—	52,319	25,097
73289	Road motor vehicle parts	30,422	1.5	27,577	22,195
6747	Iron/steel tinned plates, sh	29,070	44.0	26,030	32,810
2111	Bovine hides (excl. calf)	28,508	93.2	11,114	27,009
67433	Ingots of alloy steel	25,794	—	13,812	38,791
6715	Ferro-alloys, excl. pig iron	23,949	—	19,718	8,847
53101	Synthetic organic dyestuffs	23,919	—	18,356	29,500
07321	Iron/steel rods—non-alloy	23,876	—	6,738	3,713
59999	Other chemical prods. and preps)	21,735	0.8	16,881	16,151
67581	Iron/steel strip, non-alloy	21,478	—	18,330	31,549
73492	Aircraft/airship parts	21,194	3.9	21,736	9,027
67413	Alloy steel heavy plates	19,276	4.8	22,750	26,688
5812	Plastic polymerization prod.	18,368	0.3	22,395	32,759
0459	Unmilled cereals	18,076	100.0	3,310	0

Source: OECD

or found at home. Romanian export efforts in the West have been directed toward machinery and equipment, fuels and lubricants, chemicals, textiles, vegetable and meat products, wood products and lumber, clothing, and footwear. Romania's major OECD trading partners in 1976 were: the Federal Republic of Germany ($997 million), United States ($448 million), France ($444 million), Italy ($427 million), Netherlands ($223 million), and Japan ($180 million). Romanian trade with the United States and Japan has grown faster in recent years than with other OECD countries. Japanese firms have done well in selling complete plants and equipment for the chemical/petrochemical, machine building and metallurgy industries and have purchased Romanian textiles and food products.

Romania's expanding industry has created a heavy demand for imported raw materials, and the Romanian Goverment is looking increasingly to the developing countries to fill these requirements. In these countries, Romania can sell or barter manufactured products for much needed raw materials such as crude oil, iron ore and rubber. Romania's major trading partner in the developing world is Iran ($490 million in 1976) followed by Libya ($256 million) and Iraq ($204 million), reflecting Romania's growing oil needs.

In recent years, Romania has emphasized the establishment of long-term cooperation projects in these and other developing countries, often involving joint cooperation with Western firms. This emphasis continues under the current five-year plan. Romania has established 34 joint production companies in the developing world.

Trade Regulations

Exchange Controls.—Romanian trading entities must apply to the Foreign Trade Bank to obtain the convertible currency necessary to pay for imports. The terms of payment are established in the sales contract concluded with foreign firms. Payment can be made by documentary letters or credit, payment on receipt of the documents, simple transfer or any other method used in banking practice. In putting letters of credit into effect, Romania customarily applies the rules of the "Uniform Customs and Practice for Documentary Credits" of the International Chamber of Commerce. Romania, however, does not adhere to the "uniform customs."

Tariffs and Taxes.—Goods imported by Romanian foreign trade organizations are now liable to customs duties. Customs clearance consists only of checking the goods to ascertain that they correspond to the shipping documents.

Transit goods, temporary imports and exports, samples, models, and articles for personal use belonging to tourist, business, and diplomatic visitors are entered duty free. Articles exceeding visitors' personal requirements which are taken into or out of the country are subject to duty. Articles which leave or enter the country by parcel post are also subject to customs duty.

Items imported to support a representative office or a joint venture are subject to duty. Therefore, unless specifically waived by the Romanian Government, a substantial duty will be levied on office equipment, some household articles, automobiles, supplies, raw materials, subassemblies, or other materials. Joint ventures are sometimes successful in negotiating free entry of needed products.

The Romanian sale price of imported goods, irrespective of origin, is generally set at the price level of similar or substitute domestic goods, with differences in quality taken into account. The domestic tax system is applied in a uniform way to imported and domestically-produced goods and, therefore, should not affect imports.

Documentation.—As a general rule, exporters should follow the instructions of their Romanian importers and of their contracts. The foreign trade organizations as government entities, know Romania's document requirements for their particular imports and any other regulations currently in force. These often vary from product to product.

The documents usually required for shipments to Romania are five copies of the commercial invoice and a bill of lading or airway bill. One of the copies must be the signed original. Certificates of origin and quality control verification are necessary if requested by the Romanian importer.

Government Structure

The Romanian economy is highly centralized and, like the other East European nations, is based on a system of planning including 5-year plans, annual plans, and foreign trade plans. While the planning process is diversified and involves a wide range of government institutions and economic organizations, economic decisions are reached at the highest levels of the government—by President Ceausescu, his advisors and the nine-member Permanent Bureau of the Political Executive Committee, chaired by President Ceausescu and representing the inner circle of the Romanian Government.

Romania's top economic body is the Supreme Council of Socio-Economic Development headed by President Ceausescu, composed of both party and government officials, and controlled by the Council of State. The Supreme Council has an overall policy-making role in concert with the subordinate Central Economic Research Institute, which coordinates all Romania's economic research activities. The Central Committee of the RCP also has its own economic departments divided by economic or industrial sector. The Party maintains control at all levels of the economy. Party bodies, for instance, establish guidelines for the Council of Ministers, which acts as the principal executive body for all questions relating to the economy.

Below these organizations, the economy is separated into economic/industrial ministries or "technical-production" ministries (See "Key Romanian Economic Units" for a listing). These ministries have broad responsibilities for their respective sectors. Below the ministry level are the industrial centrals, which combine several enterprises and/or suppliers having similar products, functions, or structures. Below the centrals are the actual producing units, such as factories and enterprises.

Ministry of Foreign Trade (MFT)

MFT formulates the annual foreign trade plan in coordination with the technical-production ministries, which are responsible for overall planning in their respective sectors. MFT then monitors and guides implementation of the Plan. It also issues import and export licenses to other government agencies and staffs foreign trade offices. In its role as promoter of Romanian exports, MFT is involved in trade fairs and foreign exhibits.

In a 1973 reorganization, a directorate for cooperation was established within the MFT, and increased cooperation activities with Western firms have become a primary goal of the Ministry. (See "Commercial Transactions" for a discussion of cooperation.)

Technical-Production Ministries

When looking at the industrial structure of Romania, it is best to look at the system as if each technical-production ministry were a western-style conglomerate. In this context, the senior officials of a ministry are equivalent to senior operating officers of the various industrial centrals, research and design institutes, and foreign trade organizations whose activities are subordinated to this ministry.

The various ministers of technical-production ministries are, in effect, the board chairmen of the companies under them. Generally speaking, the most important subunits of such a ministry are the industrial centrals. Research and design institutes are second in importance, while foreign trade organizations, the equivalent of an import-export department in a western firm, play a relatively minor role.

Industrial Centrals

Industrial Centrals (IC's) are groups of enterprises or producing units having related products, functions, or structures and under a single management. The IC's were established in the late 1960's as an attempt at economic decentralization. IC's have not become the semiautonomous industrial organizations they were intended to be, but rather serve basically as large-scale production entities with somewhat limited authority and responsibility. They are subordinate to the technical-production ministries.

In foreign trade, IC's provide data and information to the ministry to which they are responsible for purposes of developing the foreign trade plan. In some instances, IC's also are authorized to negotiate and sign contracts for trade transactions, as well as cooperation arrangements such as joint ventures. A list of IC's is included in "Key Romanian Economic Units."

Research and Design Institutes

Research and design is centrally planned and controlled through the Central Economic Research Institute. Actual research and design is carried out by R&D institutes which are subordinate to the technical-production ministries. The number of such institutes has been expanding. It is believed they play an important role in foreign trade planning and decision making.

Foreign Trade Organizations

Foreign trade organizations (FTO) are independent economic units which receive a percentage of their funds from shares of transactions they conclude. Each FTO deals with specific products, equipment, or areas even though these sometimes may cut across ministerial lines. FTO's have wide latitude in choosing their foreign partners subject to review by the MFT and the applicable ministry whenever the contract is large. They are authorized to sign contracts and other trade documents as principals, and may negotiate and conclude long-term contracts, re-export transactions, cooperation arrangements, compensation deals and the establishment of equity joint ventures. An annotated list of FTO's is found in "Key Romanian Economic Units."

Enterprises and End Users

Producing enterprises and factories cannot act as principals in foreign trade transactions and may not be open to direct contract with foreign firms. These enterprises, however, frequently provide information and advice to the appropriate FTO or industrial central. End-user representatives often participate in the negotiation phases of a contract. Enterprises which are not part of an industrial central are subordinated directly to the technical-production ministries.

Bank for Foreign Trade

The Romanian Bank for Foreign Trade is discussed in the Finance Section.

Chamber of Commerce and Industry

The Chamber of Commerce and Industry is a state organization made up of more than 700 member organizations. It includes all of Romania's foreign trade entities and related economic and industrial organizations. The Chamber provides information about Romania's economy, foreign trade system, and foreign trade laws and regulations. In addition it promotes Romanian products abroad, arranges contacts between foreign producers and Romanian foreign trade entities, and offers a wide range of services and facilities designed to assist the foreign businessman. Some activities are handled directly by the Chamber. For example, its Foreign Relations Department handles inquiries from abroad; its Arbitration Commission assists in resolving disputes arising from foreign trade transactions.

A.D.A.S.

ADAS is the State Insurance Administration which insures export and import shipments. ADAS also insures the motor vehicles of foreign tourists in Romania and acts as an agent for foreign insurance companies.

ONT—Carpati

ONT-CARPATI, the National Travel Office, organizes tourist activities and services in Romania and abroad and plans the promotion and development of tourism in Romania. ONT also handles the rental of office space and living accommodations for foreign businessmen.

National Council for Science and Technology

The National Council is charged with fulfilling RCP policy in science and technology, including the coordination of all research and technological development. Imports of high technology products and licenses are subject to National Council approval.

Development of U.S.-Romanian Trade Relations

The United States has taken a number of actions in this decade to support increased U.S.-Romanian commercial activity, including extension of Commodity Credit Corporation (CCC), U.S. Export-Import Bank, and Overseas Private Investment Corporation (OPIC) facilities. These programs are discussed in the section on Finance.

The Romanian Government has taken a number of steps to integrate itself into the world economic system. For example, it has joined the General Agreement on Tariffs and Trade (GATT) and is the only Warsaw Pact country to join both the International Monetary Fund (IMF) and the International Bank for Reconstruction and Development (World Bank). In addition, Romania has enacted legislation allowing foreign firms to open representational offices and permitting foreign equity ownership (up to 49 percent) in companies with Romanian partners. A number of U.S. firms have representation in Bucharest and one American company is engaged in a joint venture.

In 1973, the Governments of both countries created the Joint American-Romanian Economic Commission to review the progress of bilateral economic and commercial problems and to discuss and resolve trade problems. The Commission meets annually. It is headed by the American Secretary of Commerce and the Romanian Minister of Foreign Trade and International Economic Cooperation. In 1977, the Commission session focused on possibilities for increased cooperation activities between the two countries, exchange of economic data, availability of financing, and business facilitation measures. In connection with the Commission activities, trade officials from both countries meet often at the working level, and numerous expert and working group meetings have been held.

The U.S.-Romanian Economic Council was founded in December 1973 by the Presidents of the Romanian and U.S. Chambers of Commerce to expand contacts between private U.S. firms and Romanian economic organizations. The annual Council meeting is held alternately in the United States and Romania.

U.S.-Romanian Trade Agreement

The 1975 Trade Agreement provides the framework for economic and commercial relations between the two countries. Its most important section extends most-favored-nation (MFN) tariff treatment to the products of both countries. In addition, U.S. recognition of Romania as a developing country led to the granting of preferential tariff status under the Generalized System of Preferences (GSP). For example, chemicals, manufactured wood, rubber and plastic products may enter the United States duty-free under this program.

The Agreement allows the countries' firms to open representational offices. It also allows these firms to deal directly with buyers and end-users. Other portions of the business facilitation section of the Agreement provide for market information exchange and improvement of services and facilities available to businessmen. Both countries reaffirmed their obligations under the Paris Convention for the Protection of Industrial Property and under the Universal Copyright Convention. Should either party determine that actual or prospective imports of certain products are "causing or threaten to cause" market disruption to a domestic industry, the Agreement calls for prompt consultations, and permits either country to impose restrictions to remedy the disruption.

The Trade Agreement runs for 3 years, but is automatically renewed for successive 3-year periods unless 30 days prior to expiration either party notifies the other of its intention to terminate. The Trade Agreement was renewed in 1978. The President must annually submit to Congress a waiver of the 1974 Trade Act's emigration provisions to allow MFN to continue.

U.S.-Romanian Long-Term Agreement on Economic, Industrial, and Technical Cooperation

To supplement the Trade Agreement, the United States and Romania signed a 10-year agreement in November 1976. It protects U.S. investors against expropriation or impairment of their contractual rights by government action, and contains measures for improving business facilities and the availability of commercial information. It includes an annex designed to facilitate the establishment of joint ventures and other forms of business cooperation on terms familiar to U.S. businessmen.

Other Bilateral Agreements

U.S.-Romanian Income Tax Treaty.—This treaty, which entered into force in February 1976, is designed to avoid double taxation of business income, personal service income, and investment income. American citizens may credit most taxes paid in Romania against their U.S. income tax. Tax rates on interest and royalty income are reduced. In addition, the treaty assures nondiscriminatory treatment by providing that citizens and businesses of one country will not be taxed more in the other country than are the host country's own citizens and businesses.

Agricultural Protocols.—In September 1975 Romania and the United States signed two protocols; the first on cooperation in agriculture and the other on development of argicultural trade. The agreements increased contracts between government organizations, universities, research organizations, firms, and individuals. In addition, they call for the exchange of agricultural information on a regular basis. To review and implement the Protocols' provisions, the countries established a permanent working group that met in Bucharest in 1977 and in Washington in 1978.

Maritime Transport Agreement.—This Agreement, in force since September 1976, institutionalizes procedures for handling shipping issues which previously had been handled on an *ad hoc* basis. Among other things, it allows maritime enterprises to establish representational offices and it expedites traffic.

Fisheries Agreement.—In effect since November 1976, this Agreement governs fishing by Romanian vessels within the 200 mile U.S. fishery conservation zone. The amount of fishing allowed within this zone is determined annually by the U.S. Government.

Airworthiness Agreement.—In December 1976, the United States and Romania concluded this document to insure that Romanian-made gliders exported to the United States would meet this country's aviation safety standards.

Effects of 1977 Earthquake

On March 4, 1977, a severe earthquake, centered 100 miles north of Bucharest, killed more than 1,500, injured more than 11,000 and caused $2 billion in damages. Particularly hard hit were apartment buildings, schools, and hospitals. In addition, more than 700 industrial facilities, including some petrochemical complexes, were damaged. Chemical fertilizer production,

which was directly affected by the quake, rose by 6 percent over 1976 levels but fell 31.8 percent short of the 1977 goal. To date, however, the new goals of the current Five-Year Plan (1976–80) have not been revised.

Immediately following the earthquake, the United States responded with emergency relief and recovery assistance. On March 7, 1977, military airlifts delivered $626,000 worth of medical equipment, medicine, and food. In April 1977, Congress authorized an additional $20 million in humanitarian assistance. Most of this aid is being used to reconstruct damaged housing, schools, and medical facilities. In addition, Romania received approximately $500,000 from private U.S. sources.

Prospects for Expansion of U.S.-Romanian Trade

The 1977 trade turnover of $492.7 million is a record high for U.S.-Romanian trade. Large Romanian imports of U.S. agricultural products and easier access to the U.S. market afforded Romania by GSP and MFN, contributed to this sharp rise. It should be noted that the United States traditionally runs a trade surplus with Romania of $50 million or more. However, Romanian officials are seeking to balance the trade.

Romania, like other East European countries, is stressing the use of industrial cooperation agreements in its foreign trade. Agreements that involve countertrade are preferred to direct sales because they permit Romania to obtain needed technology while minimizing the outlay of hard currency.

For the past few years, seven U.S. agricultural commodities have accounted for about half of total U.S. exports to Romania, while fuel oil and gasoline have accounted for about one-third of all Romanian exports to the United States. To reach the desired goal of $1 billion in two-way trade by 1980, trade must become more diversified. Foreign trade organizations are especially interested in numerically controlled machine tools, mini-calculators, welding machinery, heavy plate equipment, stainless steel extrusion processes, scarfing machines, sulphur production equipment, ferroalloys, tinned sheet, special casting pipe, refractory material, hydraulic equipment and automatic processing equipment for the steel industry.

Commercial Transactions

Initiating Contact

Contacts between U.S. firms and Romanian foreign trade organizations or industrial centrals may be initiated by either side. U.S. companies can take the initiative by:

Contacting the Romanian Embassy in Washington, the Romanian Trade Office in New York or its satellite offices in Chicago and Los Angeles. While these groups do not take part in commercial negotiations or sign contracts, they are important sources of information and can be useful in initiating contact between Romanian foreign trade entities and American firms.

Writing or telexing directly the appropriate Romanian foreign trade organization or industrial central.

Sending company representatives to Romania to meet with appropriate FTO and IC authorities.

Participating in Romanian trade fairs and other trade promotion events in Romania (see "Trade Promotion").

Conveying commercial information to the FTO or IC through the Department of Commerce and the U.S. Embassy Commercial Section.

Arranging to meet with Romanian foreign trade officials who visit the United States. Information about such visits can be obtained from the Romanian Embassy or its New York Trade Office.

Romanian FTO's and IC's may take the initiative by:

Writing or telexing the U.S. firm.

Contacting a West European subsidiary or affiliate of a U.S. firm.

Contacting the U.S. firm through the Romanian Embassy or Trade Office.

Seeking help from the U.S. Embassy in Bucharest and/or Washington-based U.S. Government agencies, such as the Department of Commerce.

The American firm's initial correspondence or personal presentation should include a complete description of the company's background, capabilities, and products, as well as any specific proposals which it wishes to make. Correspondence can be conducted in English.

The Negotiating Process

Certain factors should be kept in mind in early negotiations, especially by firms new to the market. The process leading to a signed contract is essentially the same whether an American company is negotiating a major or small project in Romania. Normally several bids are required for each transaction. Only written contracts are valid in Romania; therefore, Romanian negotiators place heavy emphasis on extensive, often exhaustive, discussions of contract details.

As a result, negotiating sessions are usually time-consuming and costly. Numerous persons may be brought into the discussions at various points. Representatives of the FTO, the Foreign Trade Bank, the end-user plant, research and design institutes, and concerned ministries must be satisfied before a contract is signed. The vice president of the FTO or the head of the pertinent FTO department usually conducts the negotiations, which usually take place in Romania, but also may occur in the United States.

Unless the FTO is under pressure to complete the deal within a specified time period, talks are usually protracted, and several visits to Romania may be required. This is especially true when the trading partners are dealing with each other for the first time or have had minimal prior contact. The Romanians are cautious about accepting new methods and suppliers. After confidence is established, negotiations on subsequent projects are likely to be less protracted. U.S. companies have often had to overcome Romanian preferences for contracts with European sources with whom they have developed working relationships.

A U.S. company's chances of concluding a contract are better if its negotiators are of a sufficiently high rank and have authority to sign for the company. A personal working relationship developed with the Romanians can facilitate negotiations. For this reason, firms have often found it useful to have the same company representatives participate in each negotiating session.

Negotiations with each of the most promising bidders that have submitted preliminary proposals to the FTO are divided into two distinct phases—the technical and the commercial. During the former, project specifications are reviewed extensively and revised often to determine what best fulfills Romanian requirements.

At this stage, American firms have frequently had to provide substantially more information (in the form of drawings, blueprints, descriptions, samples and visual aids) than is normally the case in Western transactions. If the U.S. product is new in Romania or higher priced than that of competing bidders, the U.S. firm will have to demonstrate its product's advantage. Therefore, it is sometimes useful to arrange for Romanian technicians and negotiators to visit one of the U.S. firm's plants, either in the United States or Western Europe.

Because of the exhaustive format of the technical negotiations, a U.S. firm's negotiating team should include qualified specialists who do not need to refer technical questions to the home office. The Romanian side generally consists of well-informed technical personnel, including plant managers, product engineers and research institute staff.

After technical agreement is reached, Romanian officials hold discussions with the bidders and appraise their bids. Commercial talks, which lead to final selection of one bidder, may be conducted with several firms at the same time to obtain the best terms available. These sessions focus on the project's financial aspects, including price, financing, penalty payments and a myriad of other subjects such as delivery schedules, arbitration and training of personnel. Additional Romanian officials, usually from the Romanian Bank of Foreign Trade and central planning offices, may be brought into the talks.

Pricing

A company's pricing strategy when negotiating with Romanians can range from very simple to very complex depending upon the business proposal under consideration. The simplest case is selling an off-the-shelf item that has a standard price. The most complicated cases occur when product, technology, licenses, and technical assistance are all being included in one contract.

In the more complicated cases the Romanian buyer will try to get the seller to quote a firm price early in the negotiations. The seller should delay quoting a final price as long as possible and preferably only after all other terms and conditions have been set. Since this is not always possible, the seller, when quoting a price, should explicitly define what is included and what is not. This will preclude unforeseen costs

such as living expenses for Romanian technicians sent to the United States for preshipment inpections, additional expenses for the seller's technicians during technical assistance periods, and many other items.

During the price negotiations the Romanian side will seek to obtain the maximum price reduction possible. If a firm price is agreed to early in the negotiations, the seller may find the buyer trying to add additional items or services into this price, thus achieving what amounts to a price reduction. The seller should have sufficient flexibility built into the price to allow for some reductions during negotiations. Nevertheless, repeated discounts of substantial amounts will cause a loss of credibility for the original offer. If possible, the seller should try to receive a concession from the buyer for this price reduction. The buyer will have a reasonable idea of what a fair price should be and may, in fact, be negotiating with other firms at the same time. It also is important for the seller to specify the time period for which the price remains valid.

The pricing of technology and/or manufacturing licenses presents special problems. Romania and other East European countries prefer not to pay royalties on production but would rather pay a specific sum, sometimes over a period of years. In this case the seller must assure a fair return.

Other factors to be considered in quoting a price are inflation forecasts for the contract period, interest rate differentials that may occur as the result of using certain financing methods, and the increased costs of marketing in Romania. This last factor is especially important because a marketing campaign is more expensive in Eastern Europe than in Western Europe.

In no case should a company agree to a price that will not provide the minimum return on investment that the company requires. A company should not count on recovering initial losses in future contracts. Each contract should be considered separately.

During the negotiations, some firms have found it advisable to provide their own interpreters who are familiar with technical details. Often interpreters supplied by the Romanians are not fully qualified to translate necessary technical terminology. The Romanian negotiators should be informed immediately of an interpreter's presence. Some U.S. companies have not needed interpreters, as their counterparts spoke English.

A flexible approach with well-considered alternatives in case of impasse is invaluable during the arduous negotiating sessions. U.S. firms have sometimes found that difficult points, left temporarily unresolved, can be taken up successfully in later negotiations. It is also advisable to note in writing and initial those items that have been agreed to each day to preclude attempts to reopen the same questions at subsequent sessions, although this may be unavoidable as representatives of different Romanian agencies join the talks.

Standard Contract Provisions

As mentioned above, contract negotiations in Romania are divided into two phases, the technical and the commercial. During the technical discussions, there may be little attention devoted to commercial issues. Contract terms, other than price, are often not discussed until the technical phase has been successfully concluded. At that point commercial negotiations with the actual Romanian contractual party, the FTO, begin in earnest, although the FTO may attend the technical discussions.

When commercial negotiations with a U.S. firm begin, the Romanian FTO will usually offer one of its form contracts and urge its adoption. Most FTO's have several form contracts, each suitable for a different type of transaction. Those forms used for transactions involving technology transfers, such as licensing agreements and turnkey contracts, tend to be more complex and detailed than those designed for simple equipment purchases. The main body of a form contract outlines the basic commercial terms of the transaction. Often there are extensive appendices covering matters such as the technical specifications for the equipment and technology being purchased, the installation of the equipment, and the training of Romanian personnel.

Form contracts vary among the FTO's. However, the forms share many common elements because they are based on the COMECON General Conditions. (The COMECON General Conditions are a codification of commercial law for trade among the members of CEMA).

Romanian FTO's are often adamant about incorporating form contract provisions, and while changes and concessions are possible, the final product will generally resemble the form contract at least in its basic structure. The following discussion treats some of the provisions in form contracts that typically cause problems during commercial negotiations.

Financing, Price, and Terms of Payment.— Largely because of Romania's hard currency shortages, U.S.-Romanian trade financing continues to present problems. Given the shortage of convertible currency and increasing Romanian indebtedness, only a limited number of transactions can be handled on a cash or short-term credit basis. In these cases, traditional payment methods such as irrevocable letters of credit and cash against documents are normally used. Some U.S. companies have even agreed to extend unsecured short-term credits. However, currently this type of credit is extremely rare. In many instances, however, the Romanian trading partner will insist upon medium- or long-term financing or some form of countertrade.

Penalties for Late Delivery—The communist countries are "performance-oriented" in their approach to contracts, in contrast to Westerners who are more often considered "breach-oriented." Virtually all contracts in which the Romanians purchase equipment or technology include penalty clauses for late or incomplete delivery of goods and technical documentation, as well as rigorous performance or output guarantees. Given the nature of the planning system in centrally-run economies, it is not surprising that penalties rather than damages are the standard remedy for late delivery. In these countries each component of the economic plan, including foreign trade, is designed as part of an organically complete system. A breakdown or bottleneck at any single point has repercussions for many sectors of the economy. Thus, the stiff penalty clause in the contract is primarily meant to assure prompt delivery rather than to provide an accurate measure of damages.

A typical clause found in Romanian form contracts provides that delays in delivery of equipment, spare parts, and technical documentation are to be penalized at the rate of 0.5 percent of the value of the equipment overdue for every week up to a maximum stated percentage of the value of the delayed goods. Generally, there is a provision that if the delay exceeds a certain time period, usually somewhere between four and six months, the buyer may cancel the contract without compensation to the seller.

2021

Guarantees.—U.S.-Romanian contracts generally include a detailed and comprehensive clause spelling out all of the seller's guarantee obligations. These usually include boilerplate provisions such as guarantees that the equipment being delivered has been manufactured using high quality materials and workmanship and that it conforms to the terms and conditions of the contract.

The seller is uniformly obliged to guarantee normal operation of the equipment for a specified period of time—typically 12 months from the date the equipment is put into operation, but not more than 18 months from the date of delivery. The latter limitation is of utmost importance to a U.S. seller since Romanian buyers often fall far behind schedule in putting new equipment into operation. If the guarantee period were to run only from the date the equipment is put into operation, the seller's guarantee obligations might not begin to run until 2 or 3 years after delivery. Even worse, the seller would not be entitled to the 5 or 10 percent of the contract price that is often retained by the buyer during the guarantee period as a type of performance bond.

Romanian purchasers often require stricter performance and output guarantees in licensing agreements and turnkey contracts than in other types of contracts. The seller is typically requested to guarantee that the equipment and/or technology being supplied will enable the purchaser to manufacture a specified quantity of goods of an agreed quality. Such a guarantee is risky for a U.S. seller since it may have little control over the installation and operation of the equipment and technology it supplies. Thus the seller should attempt to substitute alternative language which may serve to limit the scope of its obligations.

Romanian purchasers of both equipment and technology usually require the seller to guarantee that he possesses the rights to all relevant patents and inventions for the materials supplied; that the purchaser may employ such equipment and technology in the manner called for in the contract without violating the rights of third parties; and that the seller will indemnify the purchaser against patent infringement claims. The typical provision calls for the seller or licensor to defend against any suit or settle any claims by a third party whose rights have been infringed by the purchaser's use of the equipment purchased. Specific contract provisions are generally included to permit factory equipment or technology furnished under the contract. Often the seller's maximum liability under such an indemnification clause is limited to a specific dollar amount.

Quality Control and Inspection.—Technical specifications and provisions for technical documentation are characteristically an important part of a supply contract, often filling dozens of pages of small type. The Romanian party will expect such contractual provisions to be followed to the letter, and will be certain to raise the issue if it believes that technical specifications or quality guarantees are not being met.

To assure compliance with specifications and guarantees, the Romanian FTO will generally insist on inspection before shipment of any equipment purchased. Specific contract provisions are generally included to permit factory inspection at the seller's or its subcontractor's plant, and to deal with issues such as who will pay the buyer's inspection costs. Similar provisions are necessary when the buyer's personnel are to be trained by the seller in the use of the equipment, either at the seller's plant or at the installation site. Final inspection and approval by the buyer usually take place after the goods have arrived at their destination, or in the case of equipment, when it has been installed and put into operation.

Shipping Terms and Insurance.—The majority of contracts for sales of U.S. equipment to Romania call for f.a.s. or f.o.b. port-of-shipment terms, under which the buyer assumes the risk of loss at the time the goods are brought alongside or loaded on board the ship. Sales to the United States are usually made on a c.i.f. basis. These arrangements allow the Romanian FTO's to arrange the insurance coverage.

Force Majeure.—A *force majeure* clause is an integral part of every U.S.-Romanian contract. The effect of such a clause is to release a party from responsibility for non-fulfillment of its contractual obligations if its failure to perform is caused by certain circumstances. A U.S. seller would want to include among such circumstances natural disasters, wars, strikes, unavailability of raw materials, and other unforeseen and unavoidable circumstances. The contract normally provides for notification of the event by the affected party within a specified time period.

Arbitration.—Almost universally, the communist countries prefer arbitration to court litigation of commercial disputes. For many years, FTO's insisted upon arbitration before the Arbitration Commission of the Romanian Chamber of Commerce. However, in the U.S.-Romanian Trade Agreement, the parties agreed to "encourage" arbitration in a third country. U.S. companies have recently found FTO's quite willing to agree to arbitration in countries such as Switzerland and France. As a form of pre-arbitration, firms may wish to use the conciliation procedures established by the Romanian-U.S. Economic Council. For further information firms should contact the International Division, Chamber of Commerce of the United States, 1615 II Street, N.W., Washington, D.C. 20062.

Economic and Industrial Cooperation

Cooperation activities have come to play an increasingly important role in Romania's foreign trade due to a chronic shortage of hard currency. As a more complex form of commercial activity than simple purchase/sale transactions, economic and industrial cooperation arrangements are generally characterized by their long-term duration and the frequent requirement for counter-deliveries of Romanian goods as part of the contractual terms. U.S. firms considering doing business with Romania should expect to discuss cooperation during commercial negotiations with their Romanian counterparts. Cooperation proposals may be for licensing or technical service arrangements, contract manufacturing and subcontracting, turnkey plants, co-production and specialization arrangements, or research and development. Currently, Romania has 180 cooperation agreements with Western firms.

Since the signing of the U.S.-Romanian Long Term Cooperation Agreement, Romania looks to U.S. firms in cooperation projects, particularly joint ventures, as a source of managerial and technical expertise, high-grade technology, marketing skills, and capital. The Romanian Government states that machine building, chemical and petrochemical, and energy development industries are priority areas for cooperation activities.

Joint Ventures

Since 1971 Romania has permitted the establishment of equity joint ventures between Romanian and foreign companies. The ventures are recognized as corporate bodies under Romanian law. Romania was the first CEMA country to allow foreign private investment.

Under Romanian law a foreign firm may own up to 49 percent equity of a joint company. The foreign party's investment and the repatriation of convertible currency profits are guaranteed by the Romanian Government.

Joint companies may be established in a broad range of economic sectors including industry, agriculture, construction, tourism, transportation, and scientific and technological research. At present seven Western companies —Control Data Corporation of the United States, Renk Zahnraederfabrik of West Germany, Romalfa of Italy, Dainippon of Japan, Citroen of France, Kohmaier of Austria, and General Maritime Co. of Libya—are operating joint ventures in Romania.

Information on the establishment and operation of joint ventures in Romania is contained in the Department of Commerce publication "Joint Ventures in Romania: Background for Implementation." This booklet may be obtained from the Romania Desk, Room 4324, U.S. Department of Commerce, Washington, D.C. 20230.

Licensing

Throughout the 1970's Romania has actively sought Western licenses. Licensing agreements are common throughout the economy, particularly in the machine building, and chemical/petrochemical sectors. In recent years, however, the Romanian Government has attempted to curtail its industries' expensive appetite for foreign licenses in favor of using Romanian research and design facilities.

Romania does not have a central licensing agency but rather negotiates license transactions through specialized staff in certain FTO's. The major FTO's involved in licensing are:

Uzinexportimport—(machine building)
Electroexportimport—(electrical machinery)
Electronum—(electronics)
Industrialexport—(oil and gas extraction and processing)
Tehnoimportexport–(medical and transportation equipment; instrumentation)
Romchim—(chemical and petrochemical)
Metarom—(metallurgy)
Romenergo—(electric power)
Romconsult—(consulting, export of Romanian licenses)

Where possible, Romania prefers to tie the purchase of a license to a cooperation arrangement whereby part, if not all, of the purchase is paid for in the resulting product. However, it has often purchased licenses with no counter-trade demands.

Industrial Property Protection

Inventions and Patents

Romania is a party to the "Paris Union" International Convention for the Protection of Industrial Property and has subscribed to all its amendments. Thus, non-Romanian inventors, as well as their assignees, such as corporations and other business associations, are entitled to the same treatment as Romanian citizens under Romanian patent law. Foreign nationals have one year from filing the original application in their home country to preserve their patent priority by filing a corresponding application in Romania.

The current patent law in Romania is Law No. 62 of October 30, 1974, on Inventions and Innovations. It provides full protection for foreign technical processes applied in Romania and offers important incentives to Romanian inventors. It also stipulates tight controls and selective standards for purchasing inventions.

Romanian patent applications are filed with and awarded by the State Office for Inventions and Trademarks (OSIM) which is an autonomous operation of the National Council for Science and Technology. OSIM is headed by a Director whose job is not unlike that of the U.S. Commissioner of Patents and Trademarks. OSIM staff is divided into sections of technology and science, which recommend the allowance, or rejection, of patent applications. Rejected applications may be resubmitted to an OSIM Commission and the Commission's decisions may be appealed to the courts. To file a patent application with OSIM, however, the foreign applicant must go through ROMINVENT, the Bureau of Foreign Patents and Inventions of the Chamber of Commerce and Industry. ROMINVENT acts as patent agent and attorney for all foreign nationals and legal entities wishing to obtain patent protection in Romania. Foreign applicants must provide ROMINVENT with a power of attorney in order to be represented before OSIM. ROMINVENT will provide a fee schedule to any foreign agent or attorney on request.

Once granted, a patent is valid for 15 years from the date of registration with OSIM.

Also, once issued a patent must be worked within 3 years from issue date or 4 years from filing date, whichever is later. If not worked, the patent is subject to compulsory state license.

Inventions are protected only by patents, which give the patentee exclusive rights to use the invention in Romania. A patent does not, however, confer on one patentee the right to organize the production of the patented product in Romania or to import into the country. In Romania the means of production belong to the State, and the State maintains a monopoly over all foreign trade.

Romanian law, in effect, prohibits Western companies from obtaining patents on certain types of inventions. Specifically, patents are granted only to socialist state organizations for the following: Substances obtained by nuclear fission or chemical means; pharmaceuticals; means of diagnosis and medicinal cores; methods for prophylaxis; food products and flavorings; strains of plants, bacteria, and fungi; and new animal and silkworm breeds. Patents are obtainable on new and progressive technical solutions which can be used in the economy, science, national defense, or other parts of economic and social life.

Trademarks and Copyrights

Romania has joined the Madrid Arrangement relating to the International Registration of Trademarks and has subscribed to all amendments of that arrangement. The current trademark law is Law No. 28 of December 29, 1976, on Trade and Service Marks and Brands.

As with patents, trademark applications are filed with OSIM through its intermediary ROMINVENT. Unlike patents, trademarks do not require prior registration in the owner's country. Trademark applications are examined by OSIM for their novelty and will be rejected if the mark is copied, imitated, deceptive, not of a generic character, or not sufficiently distinguishable from other marks for the same goods.

Accepted trademarks are published, and any opposition must be filed within 6 months of publication. Trademarks are valid for 10 years from date of application and may be renewed for the same period. There are 34 classes of goods and eight classes of services for registration purposes.

A registered trademark vests exclusive rights in the owner and is enforceable by him against its unauthorized use. Transfer or premature extinction of trademarks is handled through ROMINVENT.

Romania is a member of the Berne Convention on Copyrights and the Universal Copyright Convention. The copyright law is Decree 321 of 1956 on Copyrights. The United States has a bilateral reciprocal copyright agreement with Romania.

Opening An Office in Bucharest

A decree permitting the establishment of representational offices by foreign firms was issued in 1971, and today more than 150 firms, including 19 from the United States and from European subsidiaries of U.S. firms, are represented in Bucharest. Despite the cumbersome approval process requiring a minimum of several months, and the high cost of establishing and operating a representational office, many foreign firms engaged in long-term projects believe their presence in Bucharest improves chances for obtaining rapid, affirmative responses.

To obtain a license to open a representational office, the following documents must be filed with the Ministry of Foreign Trade and International Economic Cooperation:

An application, filed on a special form, in which the applicant describes the objective of the firm and enumerates the Romanian FTO's with which it conducts business;

A receipt showing payment of $300 for a 2-year stamp tax payment to the Romanian Foreign Trade Bank (Account No. 63.02. 00 of the Financial Administration of the People's Council of the Municipality of Bucharest);

A certificate issued by the Chamber of Commerce in the country of origin, testifying to the object of activity and the capital of the applicant firm;

A certificate of reliability issued by the firm's bank;

The deed of partnership or any other deed in the original and in authorized translation, testifying to the legal existence of the respective foreign trading firm or economic organization in the country where it is established;

A power of attorney enabling the firm's representative to act on its behalf and delineating the representative's competence.

Concurrently, the applicant firm must write a letter to ARGUS, Office for Representation and Commission of the Chamber of Commerce and Industry, applying for a recommendation to the Ministry of Foreign Trade enabling it to obtain a license for opening an office. This letter can be written in English and must specify the object of activity of the respective foreign firm in the Romanian market and the Romanian foreign trade organizations with which it is maintaining trade relations.

Once established, a representational office may conduct the following transactions with Romanian economic organizations:

Commercial operations, e.g., issuing and receiving orders and offers, and negotiating and signing contracts;

Commercial information and advertising;

Technical assistance and service on machinery and equipment;

Provide, in conjunction with Romanian agencies, international land, air, and sea transportation;

General services;

Other economic and commercial activities intended to promote trade with Romania.

Operating a representational office in Bucharest involves a number of costly taxes and fees —all payable in hard currency. An operating license costs $1,500 for a 2-year period. Customs duties must be paid on all imported equipment and effects. An annual tax ranging from $3,200 (for enterprises with one to two employees) to $18,170 (for enterprises with five to seven employees, non-Romanians included) is levied. Romanian personnel must be contracted through ARGUS. Salaries for Romanians presently run from $1,300 a month for a director to $810 a month for an engineer with 10 years experience to $430 a month for a typist. The National Travel Office arranges office space and housing for representational offices and their U.S. or foreign personnel. Rents are equivalent to West European rates, and suitable office space and housing are limited.

Because of the above issues and problems, some U.S. firms, including a number involved in technology transfer and licensing, have chosen to do business with Romania either through their West European subsidiaries or directly from the home office. Others have sought to join together with several companies in one representational office or to join with U.S. firms already located there and split costs, fees, and other expenses. Still others use the services of Western trading companies operating in Romania. Such firms are hired on a commission basis and are often quite effective in directing export opportunities to their clients.

U.S. Regulations

Export Controls

Export controls are imposed unilaterally by the United States and multilaterally through COCOM, a group of 15 nations corresponding to the NATO countries less Iceland and plus Japan. These controls are designed to prevent the export of goods or technology which could make a significant contribution to the military potential of any nation when this would prove detrimental to the national security of the United States or COCOM members. Judgments are made on a transaction-by-transaction basis, and the United States regards these controls as a non-negotiable matter of national security. Romania and Poland receive more liberal treatment from the United States in the application of these controls than other communist countries.

U.S. export control regulations and procedures are subject to continuous review, resulting in periodic narrowing of the number of items subject to security trade controls. A succession of reviews over the years has reduced the control list, and most of the products requiring a validated license have military applications or can contribute to the military potential of a country.

For detailed information on licensing requirements, U.S. exporters should consult the "Export Administration Regulations" and supplementary "Export Administration Bulletins," published by the Commerce Department's Office of Export Administration. Included in the Regulations is the Commodity Control List (CCL); this is the key to determining whether a specific shipment may be exported under an established general license authorization, or whether a validated license is required.

Once it has been determined that a validated export license is required for a specific export, an application should be submitted to the Office of Export Administration, U.S. Department of Commerce, Washington, D.C. 20230. These forms can be obtained free of charge from any U.S. Department of Commerce district office.

U.S. firms are encouraged to contact the Office of Export Administration for information on export licensing, including the status of pending transactions. Telephone inquiries may be directed to the Exporter Services Branch, (202) 377-4811. While no official determination on licensing can be made before formal application is filed, the Office of Export Administration can often informally indicate the prospects for a license.

Textiles

U.S. imports of Romanian textiles and apparel are subject to bilateral restraint agreements. The agreements set ceilings for Romanian exports of cotton, wool, and man-made fiber fabric, apparel, made-up textile products, such as household furnishings and cotton yarn. For further information, inquirers should contact the Office of Textiles, U.S. Department of Commerce (202/377-2184).

Finance

Romania's banking system, as in the other East European communist countries, is a state monopoly that exercises centralized control over both the domestic economy and foreign trade. The National Bank of Romania exercises the functions of a central bank and, together with the Ministery of Finance, sets the foreign exchange rate, establishes foreign exchange budgets, and decides on the distribution of exchange balances among various currencies and depositories.

Subordinate to the National Bank is the Romanian Bank of Foreign Trade (RBFT). Although the two banks interchange personnel, the Bank of Foreign Trade is primarily responsible for all payments related to international trade and service transactions. The services available include confirmation of letters of credit, endorsement of bills of exchange, payment against shipping documents, discount of commercial paper, credit guarantees, purchases and sale of foreign currency, and other similar commercial activities. The RBFT may also conclude agreements with foreign banks concerning financial transactions and accounting practices. The RBFT maintains correspondent relationships with hundreds of banks worldwide and has a good credit rating in world financial circles. The RBFT also provides foreign exchange facilities for tourists, diplomats, and visiting businessmen.

As a CEMA member, Romania also is a member of the International Bank for Economic Cooperation (IBEC) and the International Investment Bank (IIB), independent international legal and economic entities located in Moscow. Although these banks can provide short-, medium-, and long-term financing to member countries, their activities in Romania have been minimal.

Commercial Banks

The large commercial banks, located in the United States, Japan, and Europe, are the most important institutions in financing trade with Romania. In the United States, commercial banks provide most of the short-term (up to 1 year) and medium-term (1 to 5 years) financing of East-West trade. This includes both supplier's and buyer's credits. Generally, U.S. banks do not extend long-term financing, though such financing may be available through a European bank to a European subsidiary of a U.S. firm.

Long-term financing for Romania is available from the Export-Import Bank of the United States (Eximbank) with the participation of commercial banks. A U S commercial bank, on behalf of a client, might also arrange long term export financing through a syndication with various European banks or financial entities. A U.S. businessman seeking financing should start with his local bank, which in many instances can refer him to one of its large correspondent banks active in East West trade.

Romania is the only communist country which permits a foreign bank branch to operate within its territory. Manufacturers Hanover Trust Company of New York established a branch in Bucharest in 1974. All foreign exchange activities of the Manufacturers Hanover branch are conducted under the supervision of the Romanian Foreign Trade Bank. The branch performs many of the services customarily available at banks in the West.

U.S. Government Financing Sources

Since 1971, with the exception of a brief period in 1975, Romania has been eligible for Eximbank finanicng, guarantees and Foreign Credit Insurance Association (FCIA) insurance. Eximbank is an independent corporate agency of the U.S. Government founded to assist in financing the export trade of the United States. It extends and guarantees credits to overseas buyers of American goods and services, and guarantees and insures private export credits when required by commercial banks.

Eximbank provides "preliminary commitments" outlining the amount, terms, and conditions of the financial assistance it will extend to purchasers of U.S. goods and services. There is no charge or obligation to the applicant for a "preliminary commitment."

In recent months Eximbank has made wider use of Letters of Interest, in lieu of the Preliminary Commitment to see suppliers through the lengthy stage of Romanian technical negotiations. Letters of Interest express Eximbank's willingness to consider financing a requested amount for a named project but do not present specific financing terms. Letters of Interest representing exports of an additional $30 million were issued to U.S. suppliers for projects scheduled begin in late 1978.

Since September 1972 when Eximbank authorized its first direct loan to Romania, it has supported among other things the sale of three Boeing 707 jet aircraft, equipment for a heavy steel plate mill, and equipment for a gas processing plant. Total Export-Import Bank participation as of March 31, 1978, amounted to $91.5 million.

Eximbank is able to support a greater volume of exports to Romania over the near term. Romania maintains a good credit reputation and low portfolio with Western commercial banks, who have to date participated in Eximbank packages for Romania without the support of Eximbank's financial guarantee. For further information contact the European Division, Export-Import Bank of the United States, 811 Vermont Avenue, N.W., Washington, D.C., 20571.

Romania is also eligible for programs run by the Commodity Credit Corporation (CCC) in the U.S. Department of Agriculture, which finances commercial export sales of U.S. agricultural commodities. The commodities eligible under the program vary according to changes in available export supplies of private stocks. Therefore, exporters seeking CCC credit financing for agricultural sales to Romania should obtain a listing of currently eligible products from the Director, Export Programs Division, Commodity Credit Corporation, Foreign Agricultural Service, U.S. Department of Agriculture, Washington, D.C., 20250.

Although Romania received no CCC credits in fiscal 1977, a total of $158.2 million has been granted since 1970. The principal commodities purchased with these credits were cotton, feedgrains, soybeans, soybean meal, and wheat.

The Overseas Private Investment Corporation (OPIC) insures U.S. private investments against certain political risks in less developed countries, including Romania, and finances the investment or development of eligible projects involving U.S. investors in those countries. While the OPIC programs have not yet been used in Romania, their existence offers an important support to the U.S. business community. Further details are available from the Information Officer, Overseas Private Investment Corporation, 1129 20th Street, N.W., Washington, D.C., 20527.

Countertrade

Romania demands some of the highest countertrade (CT) percentages per transaction of any CMEA country (100 percent counterdelivery commitment may be initially requested for many Western imports). Whether such demands are met is determined during the negotiation process, where the nature and priority of the imports together with hard bargaining often can reduce the demand to lower percentages.

Specific guidelines may be provided by the various Romanian industrial ministries to the FTO's setting forth desirable CT goals in accordance with established annual export targets. Exceptions to CT obligations can be made, however, for important deals.

Most Romanian products offered for CT suffer from inflated prices, poor quality and lack of aftersale service. They range from forestry products to consumer goods, machinery, light industry goods, and chemicals. Romanian authorities will seek to restrict counterdelivery commitments to the original importing FTO or the industrial ministry to which the FTO is responsible.

Romanian FTO's are now giving serious consideration to tying future imports to firm CT

contractual obligations requiring the Western exporter to purchase a specified volume and value of a particular Romanian product within a year. Current practice is to require a frame contract which allows for a range of CT commodities "mutually agreed upon" by the parties expressed as a percentage of the Western export contract.

Since present emphasis is on increasing exports, Romanian FTO's might show flexibility in enforcing the terms of a CT contract if the Western party runs into difficulty securing or disposing of the CT goods within the allotted time frame. The FTO's, however, will insist on fulfillment of the CT obligations and are interested in securing the non-fulfillment penalties only as a last resort.

When confronted with countertrade demands and provided they agree to CT terms, the U.S. executives should first concentrate on a selection of goods that could be absorbed within their own company or by their clients. The American should be aware that the list of Romanian exports offered for counterpurchases may be years old and that many of the goods listed may be unavailable because of prior commitments or limited production. They may wish to use the services of an experienced trading house to dispose of the CT goods offered. Today, several hundred trading houses exist in the commercial centers of West Europe, Japan, and the United States.

Commerce's Industry and Trade Administration can provide more detailed information on CT practices in East-West trade and has published a monograph entitled "East-West Countertrade Practices: An Introductory Guide for Business."

Trade Promotion

One of the best ways to improve business contacts and promote sales in Romania is participation in specialized exhibitions, trade fairs, and trade seminars. The events are attended by FTO and ministry officials, representatives of research and design institutes, and endusers. Although these meetings are excellent opportunities for broad exposure to the Romanian market, sales seldom result solely from participation in fairs, seminars and exhibitions. Usually, Romanian purchases are the culmination of months of hard negotiations.

Romanian-Sponsored Events.—The most important event is the biannual Bucharest International Fair, usually held in October of even numbered years. The Department of Commerce traditionally sponsors an American Pavilion at this fair.

In addition, Romania sponsors numerous industrial exhibitions each year. Firms interested in more information or in participating in one of these shows should contact Publicom, 22 N. Balcescu Blvd., Bucharest; telex 11374. Firms or groups that would like to arrange a private display of their products should also contact Publicom, an organization under the Chamber of Commerce which arranges for advertising in Romania by foreign firms.

U.S. Trade Promotion Activities.—The U.S. Department of Commerce regularly sponsors trade promotion events in Romania. In 1974 and 1976 the Department organized specialized exhibits featuring industrial instrumentation, food processing, and agricultural machinery manufacturers at the Bucharest International Fair. Off-the-floor sales for the 35 exhibitors who participated in these two Fairs exceeded $500,000, and their projected sales over the 12-month periods following exhibits exceeded $14 million.

In addition to these biannual exhibits the Department sponsors several technical sales seminars (TSS) each year. These events are designed to introduce American exporters to the Romanian market and to assist them in establishing contact with potential buyers and end-users. Recent sales seminars focused on offshore oilfield equipment and chemical processing instruments and technology.

Companies wishing to participate in Department of Commerce promotional events should contact the Trade Promotion Division, Industry and Trade Administration, Room 4821, U.S. Department of Commerce, Washington, D.C. 20230. Announcements of trade promotion events in Romania are made regularly in *Commerce America* magazine and to firms listed in the *American International Traders' Register*.

Business Hints

Visiting Romania

Although correspondence can go far toward introducing products and technology, and perhaps eliciting inquiries, it is not a very effective sales method in Romania. Initial correspondence and catalogs should be followed up by direct visits. These visits, however, must be organized in advance for maximum effectiveness. An unplanned 2- or 3-day visit could well be spent waiting in a hotel lobby.

Romania offers American business good opportunities for sales, licensing, and joint ventures, primarily in high technology areas related to industrial products and processes. Key selling points in discussions with foreign trade organizations are the state of technical development of a product, product reliability and durability, availability of servicing, and required training.

Hurdles quite unlike anything in the West must be surmounted if opportunities are to be maximized. The American must accept a lengthy negotiation process, sometimes running 2 or more years and often requiring repeated trips to Romania. Access to end-users can also be problem. While the relevant foreign trade organization will negotiate and sign the contract, it is usually desirable to discuss a product's technical qualities with the eventual end user. Identifying and contacting end-users, however, is often complicated. The lack of reliable information presents a final hurdle. Data fundamental to making a business decision in the United States simply is not available in Romania.

Visa Requirements

Visas are required for entry into Romania. Multiple entry business visas can be obtained, normally without difficulty, from the Romanian Embassy in Washington and from Romanian embassies abroad. A single-entry visa can be obtained at the Bucharest International Airport.

Business and Hotel Facilities

All foreign trade organizations have their own interpreters available when needed for discussions with foreign business visitors. Alternatively, translating and interpreting services can be hired at major hotels through the National Tourist Office. Telex facilities are available at most major hotels. The following deluxe category hotels are located in Bucharest. Intercontinental, Blvd. Balcescu 4, phone 137040, telex 541, 542; Athenee Place, str. Episcopiei 1-3, phone 140899, telex 162; Hotel Bulevard, Blvd. Gheorghe Gheorghiu—Dej No.

1, phone 13108, telex 10886; Lido, Blvd. Magheru 5, phone 144930, telex 161; and the Hotel Continental, Calea Victoriei No. 56, phone 145349, telex 10380.

Exchange Rates

Romania's national currency is the leu (plural lei). The official rate is 4.47 lei to the dollar, while the non-commercial or tourist rate is 12 lei to the dollar. The tourist rate is normally used in business transactions. Foreign visitors entering Romania may bring with them any amount of foreign currency. Romanian currency can also be brought in, but only if it has been delivered to the tourist by the banks of East European countries which have received the corresponding amount in lei from the National Bank of Romania. Exports of lei in cash are prohibited.

While in Romania, foreign visitors may exchange currency only at the Foreign Trade Bank or other authorized bodies. Foreigners changing currency must ask for an exchange voucher which will enable them to prove, on leaving the country, that all transactions have been done legally. This voucher entitles them to reconvert the unspent lei.

Working Hours and Holidays

The normal hours of business for foreign trade companies and other Government offices are from 7 a.m. to 4 p.m. Monday through Friday and from 7 a.m. to 12:30 p.m. on Saturday. In Bucharest some office hours are scheduled half an hour later. Most staff members take a short lunch break around 11:30 a.m. or noon. Commercial holidays observed in Romania are January 1 (New Year's), May 1 (International Workers Day) and August 23 (National Liberation Day). The day following each of these holidays also is a public holiday. Sometimes depending on the incidence of weekends, this additional day may be taken the day before.

U.S. Embassy Services

The personnel of the U.S. Embassy Economic/Commercial Section are active in promoting trade and counseling American businessmen. Embassy assistance can be very useful in making contacts, obtaining market or negotiating advice, and resolving specific problems that may arise. The U.S. Embassy is located at Strada Tudor Arghezi 7–9 in Bucharest (telephone: 12–40–40; telex 11416 AMEMB R).

Bibliography

Romanian Business and Economic Publications

Romanian Foreign Trade, (quarterly), in English, French, German, Russian and Spanish.

Romanian Journal of Chemistry, (quarterly), in English, French, German, and Russian.

Romanian Engineering, (quarterly), in English, French, German and Spanish.

Forestra, (quarterly), in English.

Romanian Industrial Centrals and Research-Design Institutes, 1978.

Your Commercial Partners in Romania, 1978 (a list of foreign trade organizations).

Romanian Economic Data, (annually), in English.

Economic and Commercial Guide to Romania, (annually), in English.

Romanian Foreign Trade Law, (annually), in English, French, German and Spanish.

Doing Business with Romania: Opportunities for U.S. Businessmen, 1977, Romanian Chamber of Commerce.

Romania's Economic Development During the 1976–1980 Five-Year Plan.

Romania's Presence in the World Economic Flow, particularly emphasizes cooperation activities with capitalist countries.

Anuarul Statistic al Republicii Socialiste Romania, statistical yearbook published annually in Romanian.

Twenty Years of Progress in Socialist Romania's Chemical Industry, by Mihail Florescu, 1973.

U.S. Government Publications

Foreign Economic Trends and Their Implications for the United States—Romania, annually by the U.S. Foreign Service, U.S. Department of State and released by the U.S. Department of Commerce.

Background Notes—Romania, U.S. Department of State, March 1978.

East-West Trade Update: A Commercial Fact Sheet for U.S. Business, semiannually by the U.S. Department of Commerce.

Area Handbook for Romania, 1972, Foreign Area Studies, American University.

Trade of the United States with Communist Countries in Eastern Europe and Asia, 1975–

77, OBR 78–32, U.S. Department of Commerce, June 1977.

U.S. Trade Status with Communist Countries, monthly by the U.S. Department of Commerce.

East-West Trade Financing, An Introductory Guide, U.S. Department of Commerce, September 1976.

East-West Countertrade Practices: An Introductory Guide for Business, U.S. Department of Commerce, 1978.

Selected Trade and Economic Data of the Centrally Planned Economies, U.S. Department of Commerce, December 1977.

Commerce America, biweekly by the U.S. Department of Commerce. Of special note: semi-annual World Trade Outlook issues.

Eastern European Economies: Post-Helsinki, a compendium of papers submitted to the Joint Economic Committee of Congress, Government Printing Office, September 1977. In particular see: "Romania's Foreign Trade: An Overview," by John Michael Montias; "Industrialization, Trade and Mobilization in Romania's Drive for Economic Independence," by Marvin R. Jackson and "An Analysis of the United States-Romanian Long-Term Agreement on Economic, Industrial, and Technical Cooperation," by Jay A. Burgess.

Joint Venture Agreements in Romania: Background for Implementation, U.S. Department of Commerce, June 1977.

Other Publications

United States/Eastern Europe Technology and Patents: Sale and/or Licensing, edited by Edward P. White, Licensing Executives Society, Inc., 1977.

Economic Development in Communist Romania, by John Michael Montias, The M.I.T. Press, 1967.

Appendix—Key Romanian Economic Units

Central Institutions, Including Ministries

THE COUNCIL OF MINISTERS OF THE SOCIALIST REPUBLIC OF ROMANIA
2, Onesti St., Bucharest

STATE PLANNING COMMITTEE
152, Calea Victoriei, Bucharest

FOREIGN AFFAIRS MINISTRY
8, Ilie Pintilie Blvd, Bucharest

MINISTRY OF FOREIGN TRADE AND INTERNATIONAL ECONOMIC COOPERATION
14, Republicii Blvd., Bucharest

MACHINE BUILDING INDUSTRY MINISTRY
133, Calea Victoriei, Bucharest

INDUSTRIAL CONSTRUCTIONS MINISTRY
202 A, Splaiul Independentei, Bucharest

ELECTRIC POWER MINISTRY
33, Magheru Blvd., Bucharest

METALLURGY MINISTRY
21–25 Mendeleev St.

CHEMICAL INDUSTRY MINISTRY
202 A, Splaiul Independentei, Bucharest

MINING, PETROLEUM AND GEOLOGY MINISTRY
36–38, Mendeleev St., Bucharest

FOREST ECONOMY AND BUILDING MATERIALS MINISTRY
13, Republicii Blvd., Bucharest

LIGHT INDUSTRY MINISTRY
13, Ion Ghica St., Bucharest

MINISTRY OF AGRICULTURE AND FOOD INDUSTRY
24, Republicii Blvd., Bucharest

DOMESTIC TRADE MINISTRY
12, Doamnei St., Bucharest

MINISTRY OF TECHNICO-MATERIALS SUPPLY, CONTROL OF FIXED ASSETS ADMINISTRATION
152, Calea Victoriei, Bucharest

TRANSPORT AND TELECOMMUNICATIONS MINISTRY
38, Dinicu Golescu Blvd., Bucharest

FINANCE MINISTRY
8, Doamnei St., Bucharest

EDUCATION AND INSTRUCTION MINISTRY
12, Spiru Haret St., Bucharest

HEALTH MINISTRY
6, Ilfov St., Bucharest

TOURISM MINISTRY
7, Magheru Blvd., Bucharest

NATIONAL COUNCIL FOR SCIENCE AND TECHNOLOGY
32–34, Roma St., Bucharest

NATIONAL BANK OF THE SOCIALIST REPUBLIC OF ROMANIA
25 Lipscani St., Bucharest

ROMANIAN FOREIGN TRADE BANK
22 Calea Victoriei, Bucharest

CHAMBER OF COMMERCE AND INDUSTRY OF THE SOCIALIST REPUBLIC OF ROMANIA
22, N. Balcescu Blvd., Bucharest

UNCAP—NATIONAL UNION OF AGRICULTURAL PRODUCTION COOPERATIVES
25, Gheorghe Gheorghiu-Dej Blvd., Bucharest

UCECOM—CENTRAL UNION OF HANDICRAFT COOPERATIVES
46, Calea, Plevnei, Bucharest

BROADCASTING AND TELECASTING COMMITTEE
6C, Nuferilor St., Bucharest

Romanian Trade Offices in the United States

Office of the Economic Counselor
573–577 Third Ave.
New York, N. Y. 10016
Telephone: 212–682–9120 and 9121

Romanian Foreign Trade Promotion Office
100 West Monroe St.
Suite 2010
Chicago, Ill., 60603
Telephone: 312–782–4463

Romanian Foreign Trade Promotion Office
350 South Figuero St.
Suite 447
Los Angeles, Calif. 90071
Telephone: 213–614–1104

Embassy of the Socialist Republic of Romania
1607 23rd St., N.W.
Washington, D.C. 20008
Telephone: 202–232–4747

Industrial Centrals

Grouped by industrial ministry or sector and including major imports and exports, as described in the Romanian publication *Romanian Industrial Centrals and Research-Design Institutes.*

METALLURGY MINISTRY

CENTRALA INDUSTRIALA SIDERURGICA GALATI
(IRON AND STEEL
INDUSTRIAL CENTRAL, GALATI)

Galati—Romania
Galtati County
Sos. Galati-Smîrdan
Telephone: 930/31900; Telex: 51253, 51257

Ferrous metallurgy products: foundry coke, cast-iron, steel, thick and thin plates, zinc-coated sheet iron included; casting equipment, wire products, spare parts, bent sections and metallic structures.

CENTRALA INDUSTRIALA SIDERURGICA, HUNEDOARA
(IRON AND STEEL
INDUSTRIAL CENTRAL, HUNEDOARA)

Hunedoara—Romania
Hunedoara County
8, Dr. Petru Groza St.
Telephone: 957/12533; Telex: 32411, 32412

Ferrous metallurgy products: foundry coke, cast iron, steel, finished rolled steel, casting equipment, cast iron pipes, iron and steel castings.

CENTRALA INDUSTRIALA SIDERURGICA RESITA
(IRON AND STEEL
INDUSTRIAL CENTRAL, RESITA)

Resita—Romania
Caras Severin County
1, Podul Inalt St.
Telephone: 964/17211; Telex: 44214

Ferrous metallurgy products: foundry coke, cast iron, steel, finished rolled steel, thick and thin plates, railway rails, tyres and thrust plates, track material, drawn bars, metallurgical equipment, wire products and spare parts.

CENTRALA INDUSTRIALA DE PRELUCRARI METALURGICE, BUCURESTI
(INDUSTRIAL CENTRAL
FOR METAL PROCESSING, BUCHAREST)

Bucharest—Romania
256 Muncii Blvd.
Sector 3
Telephone: 27 59 45; Telex: 10862

Rolled and welded tubes, finished rolled steel, steel and copper wire, welding electrodes, drawn bars, wire products, bent sections, spare parts and metallurgical equipment.

CENTRALA INDUSTRIALA PENTRU METALE NEFEROASE SI RARE SLATINA
(INDUSTRIAL CENTRAL
FOR NONFERROUS AND RARE METALS, SLATINA)

Slatina—Romania
Olt County
116, Pitestilor St.
Telephone: 944/11900; Telex: 47218

Aluminum oxide production; aluminum smelting; processing of nonferrous metals and alloys; recovery of nonferrous metals from waste; manufacture of graphite anodes and electrodes.

CENTRALA INDUSTRIALA PENTRU PRODUSE REFRACTARE, BRASOV
(INDUSTRIAL CENTRAL FOR REFRACTORY PRODUCTS, BRASOV)

Brasov—Romania
Brasov County
127, Carierei St.
Telephone: 921/23966; Telex: 12307

Production of refractory bricks and products, chamotte, antishrinkage powders, carbon products, abrasive disks, various abrasive materials.

CENTRALA DE PRELUCRARE SI COLECTARE A DESEURILOR METALICE, BUCURESTI
(SCRAP METAL COLLECTING AND PROCESSING CENTRAL, BUCHAREST)

Bucharest—Romania
4, Theodor Aman St.
Sector 7
Telephone: 14 75 90; Telex: 10937

Processing of scrap metal; collecting of metal and refractory products scraps.

MACHINE BUILDING INDUSTRY MINISTRY

CENTRALA INDUSTRIALA DE AUTOCAMIOANE SI TURISME, BRASOV
(INDUSTRIAL CENTRAL FOR LORRIES AND MOTOR CARS, BRASOV)

Brasov—Romania
Brasov County
5 Poenelor St.
Telephone: 921/37222
Telex: 12204

Manufacture of motor vehicles.

CENTRALA INDUSTRIALA DE TRACTOARE SI MASINI AGRICOLE, BRASOV
(INDUSTRIAL CENTRAL FOR TRACTORS AND FARMING MACHINERY, BRASOV)

Brasov—Romania
Brasov County
5 Turnului St.
Telephone: 921/10422; 10423
Telex: 12311

Manufacture of tractors, and farming machinery.

CENTRALA INDUSTRIALA DE UTILAJ TEHNOLOGIC, CHIMIC, SI RAFINARIL, BUCURESTI
(INDUSTRIAL CENTRAL FOR TECHNOLOGICAL, CHEMICAL, EQUIPMENT AND REFINERIES, BUCHAREST)

Bucharest—Romania
355—357, Calea Grivitei
Sector 8
Telephone: 65 50 90; Telex; 11250

Manufacture of technological chemical equipment.

CENTRALA INDUSTRIALA DE UTILAJ ENERGETIC, METALURGIC SI MASINI DE RIDICAT, BUCURESTI
(INDUSTRIAL CENTRAL FOR POWER AND METALWORKING EQUIPMENT AND HOISTING MACHINES, BUCHAREST)

Bucharest—Romania
104, Sos. Berceni
Sector 5
Telephone: 84 20 20; Telex: 10243

Manufacture of power and metal working equipment and hoisting machines.

CENTRALA INDUSTRIALA DE MASINI SI UTILAJE PENTRU INDUSTRIA USOARA, BUCURESTI
(INDUSTRIAL CENTRAL FOR LIGHT INDUSTRY MACHINERY AND EQUIPMENT, BUCHAREST)

Bucharest—Romania
170, Sos. Bucurestii Noi
Sector 8
Telephone: 67 40 30; Telex: 10873

Manufacture of light industry machinery and equipment.

CENTRALA INDUSTRIALA DE UTILAJ TEHNOLOGIC SI MATERIAL RULANT, BUCURESTI
(INDUSTRIAL CENTRAL FOR TECHNOLOGICAL EQUIPMENT AND ROLLING STOCK, BUCHAREST)

Bucharest—Romania
256, Muncii Blvd.
Sector 3
Telephone: 27 70 40; Telex: 10344

Manufacture of technological equipment, rolling stock and building equipment.

CENTRALA INDUSTRIALA DE RULMENTI SI ORGANE DE ASAMBLARE, BRASOV (INDUSTRIAL CENTRAL FOR BALL BEARINGS AND ASSEMBLING PARTS, BRASOV)

Brasov—Romania
Brasov County
96, 13 Decembrie St.
Telephone: 921/20641; Telex: 12245

Manufacture of ball bearings, bearings, and assembling parts.

CENTRALA INDUSTRIALA NAVALA, GALATI (NAVAL INDUSTRIAL CENTRAL, GALATI)

Galati—Romania
132, Pacii St.
Telephone: 930/10800; Telex: 51293

Naval construction.

CENTRALA INDUSTRIALA DE MASINI UNELTE, MECANICA FINA SI SCULE, BUCURESTI (INDUSTRIAL CENTRAL FOR MACHINE-TOOLS, FINE MECHANICS AND TOOLS, BUCHAREST)

Bucharest—Romania
250, Muncii Blvd.
Sector 3
Telephone: 27 60 30; Telex: 11464

Manufacture of machine tools, fine mechanics and tools.

CENTRALA INDUSTRIALA DE MASINI SI APARATE ELECTRICE, CRAIOVA (INDUSTRIAL CENTRAL FOR ELECTRIC MACHINES AND APPARATUS, CRAIOVA)

Craiova—Romania
Dolj County
144, Calea Bucurestiului

Telephone: 941/40061; Telex: 41234

Manufacture of electric machines and apparatus.

CENTRALA INDUSTRIALA DE MOTOARE SI MATERIALE ELECTROTEHNICE, BUCURESTI (INDUSTRIAL CENTRAL FOR ELECTRICAL ENGINEERING, MOTORS AND MATERIALS, BUCHAREST)

Bucharest—Romania
4, Sos. Garii Catelu
Sector 3
Telephone: 27 20 90; Telex: 10781

Manufacture of electrical engineering motors and materials.

CENTRALA INDUSTRIALA DE ELECTRONICA SI TEHNICA DE CALCUL, BUCURESTI (INDUSTRIAL CENTRAL FOR ELECTRONICS AND COMPUTING TECHNIQUE, BUCHAREST)

Bucharest—Romania
7—9, Sos. Fabrica de Glucoza
Sector 2
Telephone: 33 71 70; Telex: 10895

Manufacture of electronic equipment and computing equipment.

CENTRALA INDUSTRIALA DE ECHIPAMENTE DE TELECOMUNICATII SI AUTOMATIZARI, BUCURESTI (INDUSTRIAL CENTRAL FOR TELECOMMUNICATIONS AND AUTOMATION EQUIPMENT, BUCHAREST)

Bucharest—Romania
18, Kalinin Blvd.
Sector 2
Telephone: 33 00 90; Telex: 11462

Manufacture of telecommunication and automation equipment.

CENTRALA INDUSTRIALA DE UTILAJ PETROLIER SI MINIER, PLOIESTI (INDUSTRIAL CENTRAL FOR OILFIELD AND MINING EQUIPMENT, PLOIESTI)

Ploiesti—Romania
Prahova County
121, Democratiei St.
Telephone: 971/42051; Telex: 19278

Manufacture of oilfield and mining equipment.

CHEMICAL INDUSTRY MINISTRY

CENTRALA INDUSTRIALA DE RAFINARII SI PEROCHIMIE, PLOIESTI
(INDUSTRIAL CENTRAL FOR REFINERIES AND PETROCHEMISTRY, PLOIESTI)

Brazi—Romania
Prahova County
Telephone: 2 04 00; Telex: 19343

Processing of crude oil and derivatives; production of petrochemicals, chemicals, and plastics.

CENTRALA INDUSTRIALA DE INGRASAMINTE CHIMICE, CRAIOVA
(INDUSTRIAL CENTRAL FOR CHEMICAL FERTILIZERS, CRAIOVA)

Isalnita—Romania
Dolj County
Telephone: 13405; 13327; Telex: 41239

Production of fertilizers and other chemicals, lacquers and paints.

CENTRALA INDUSTRIALA DE MEDICAMENTE, COSMETICE, COLORANTI SI LACURI, BUCURESTI
(INDUSTRIAL CENTRAL FOR MEDICAL DRUGS, COSMETICS, DYESTUFFS AND LACQUERS, BUCHAREST)

Bucharest—Romania
246, Ion Sulca Blvd.
Telephone: 43 35 50; Telex: 11849

Production of medical drugs, dyestuffs, cosmetics, lacquers, paints, inks, soap, detergents and other chemicals, rubber and plastic articles, metallic structures, PVC consumer goods, tire retreading, packing glassware.

CENTRALA INDUSTRIALA DE FIRE SI FIBRE CHIMICE, SAVINESTI
(INDUSTRIAL CENTRAL FOR CHEMICAL YARNS AND FIBRES, SAVINESTI)

Savinesti—Romania
Neamt County
Telephone: 13000; Telex: 25246

Production of chemical yarns and fibres and other chemicals, rubber technical articles and consumer goods.

CENTRALA INDUSTRIALA DE PRODUSE ANORGANICE, RIMNICU VILCEA
(INORGANIC PRODUCTS INDUSTRIAL CENTRAL, RIMNICU VILCEA)

Rimnicu Vilcea—Romania
Vilcea County
1, Uzinei St.
Telephone: 16100; Telex: 48271

Production of chlorosodium products, carbide and other chemicals, rubber and plastic articles, paints, domestic soap, and candles.

CENTRALA INDUSTRIALA DE PRELUCRARE CAUCIUC SI MASE PLASTICE, BUCURESTI
(INDUSTRIAL CENTRAL FOR RUBBER AND PLASTIC PROCESSING BUCHAREST)

Bucharest—Romania
Popesti-Leordeni
Telephone: 83 41 40; Telex 10276

Manufacture of tires, tubes and auxiliary products for the tire industry; manufacture of technical rubber goods and plastic goods manufacturing equipment, the required molds included; chemicals, metallic structures, castiron parts, glass craftware, mirrors, hand-made tufted carpets, textile ready mades.

CENTRALA DE UTILAJE, PIESE DE SCHIMB PENTRU INDUSTRIA CHIMICA, BUCURESTI
(CENTRAL FOR CHEMICAL INDUSTRY EQUIPMENT AND SPARE PARTS, BUCHAREST)

Bucharest—Romania
112, Sos. Vitan
Telephone: 44 11 94; Telex: 11613

Manufacture of chemical equipment, spare parts, armature, prototypes, measuring and control apparatus, anticorrosion protection installations and devices, equipment for pilot stations, various chemicals; co-ordination of nationwide production of oxygen and argon; determination of working conditions in chemical units and prevention of occupational diseases; acceptance of chemical industry equipment, rubber and plastic articles, wood products, textile ready-mades, rubber vulcarization.

TRUSTUL CONSTRUCTII MONTAJE SI REPARATII IN INDUSTRIA CHIMICA, BUCURESTI
(CHEMICAL INDUSTRY CONSTRUCTION-ERECTION AND REPAIR TRUST, BUCHAREST)

Bucharest—Romania
112, Sos. Vitan
Telephone: 49 11 94; Telex: 11613

Erection-assembling and repair and other specific jobs in the field of the chemical industry; secondary industrial production linked with these works.

CENTRALA DE DESFACERE A PRODUSELOR PETROLIERE "PECO"
(CENTRAL FOR THE SALE OF "PECO" PETROLEUM PRODUCTS)

Bucharest—Romania
11 bis, Gl Budisteanu St.
Telephone: 13 38 10; Telex: 10739

Sale and transport of petroleum products by pipeline, tank wagons, and tankers.

ELECTRIC POWER MINISTRY

CENTRALA INDUSTRIALA DE PRODUCERE A ENERGIEI ELECTRICE SI TERMICE, BUCURESTI
(INDUSTRIAL CENTRAL FOR ELECTRIC AND THERMAL POWER PRODUCTION, BUCHAREST)

Bucharest—Romania
16—18, Hristo Botev Blvd.
Sector 3
Telephone: 13 26 20; Telex: 10156

Production, transmission and distribution of electric and thermal power in Romania.

TRUSTUL "ENERGOCONSTRUCTIA," BUCURESTI
("ENERGOCONSTRUCTIA" TRUST, BUCHAREST)

Bucharest—Romania
103—105, Calea Dorobantilor
Sector 1
Telephone: 79 60 20; Telex: 10179

Construction of thermopower stations, smoke stacks and flues, cooling towers, etc.

TRUSTUL DE CONSTRUCTII HIDROENERGETICE, BUCURESTI
(HYDROPOWER CONSTRUCTION TRUST, BUCHAREST)

Bucharest—Romania
23—25, Dimitrie Onciul St.
Sector 3
Telephone: 35 54 70; Telex: 10244

Construction of hydropower stations and complex hydropower systems, dams, tunnels, sluices, river harnessing.

TRUSTUL "ENERGOMONTAJ," BUCURESTI
("ENERGOMONTAJ" TRUST, BUCHAREST)

Bucharest—Romania
103—105, Calea Dorobantilor
Telephone: 79 70 20; Telex: 11335

Assembling work for hydro- and thermopower stations.

TRUSTUL "ELECTRAMONTAJ," BUCURESTI
("ELECTROMONTAJ" TRUST, BUCHAREST)

Bucharest—Romania
158, Calea Mosilor
Sector 3
Telephone: 16 63 30; Telex: 10271

Erection of electric power transmission lines and transformer substations.

MINING, PETROLEUM AND GEOLOGY MINISTRY

DIRECTIA GENERALA AUTONOMA A PETROLULUI SI GAZELOR, BUCURESTI
(AUTONOMOUS DIRECTORATE OF PETROLEUM AND NATURAL GAS, BUCHAREST)

Bucharest—Romania
109, Calea Victoriei
Sector 1
Telephone: 14 71 90; Telex: 11720

Discharges the functions assigned to industrial centrals and departments, providing leadership for all petroleum and gas extraction units.

CENTRALA GAZULUI METAN, MEDIAS
(METHANE GAS CENTRAL, MEDIAS)

Medias—Romania
4, Unirii St.
Sibiu Conty
Telephone: 12262; Telex: 49718

Natural gas prospecting, well drilling, production and transport of natural gas, constructions, installations, laying of pipelines, research, design, service regarding these activities; natural gas burning and control equipment installation and equipment repair for the methane gas industry.

COMBINATUL MINIER, VALEA JIULUI
(MINING COMBINE, VALEA JIULUI)

Petrosani—Romania
Hunedoara County
2, 23 August St.
Telephone: 957/41460

Coal output and processing; geological, mining and industrial construction; production of mechanization equipment and installations for the coal industry, spare parts, metallic structures for the coal industry, repair and workover jobs (mining equipment), research, design, and manufacture of mining equipment.

CENTRALA MINEREURILOR, DEVA
(ORES CENTRAL, DEVA)

Deva—Romania
Deva County
4, Piata Unirii
Telephone: 956/13640; Telex: 32223

Output of ferrous, non-ferrous and gold-bearing ores and ore concentrates; geological surveys and investigations; mining and industrial constructions, research and design, related services.

CENTRALA MINEREURILOR
SI METALURGIEI NEFEROASE, BAIA MARE
(NONFERROUS ORES AND METALLURGY CENTRAL, BAIA MARE)

Baia Mare—Romania
Maramures County
Piata Gh. Gheorghiu Dej
Telephone: 994/11504; Telex: 33223

Output of non-ferrous ores and non-ferrous ore concentrates; output of heavy non-ferrous metals and associated metals from concentrates; geological surveys and investigations; mining and industrial constructions; research and design; production and repair of mining equipment.

CENTRALA SARII SI NEMETALIFERELOR, BUCURESTI
(SALT AND NON-METALLIC ORES CENTRAL, BUCHAREST)

Bucharest—Romania
220, Calea Victoriei
Sector 1
Telephone: 50 40 78; Telex: 10647

Output of salt from non-metallic ores and concentrates; geological surveys; mining and industrial construction; research and design; related services.

COMBINATUL MINIER, PLOIESTI
(MINING COMBINE, PLOIESTI)

Ploeisti—Romania
Prohova County
2 Bobilna St.
Telephone: 971/23610

Output and cleaning of lignite and brown coal, mine and pit opening; research and manufacture of lignite mining equipment, spare parts and subassemblies, repair of mining and transportation equipment.

COMBINATUL MINIER, OLTENIA
(MINING COMBINE, OLTENIA)

Farcascsti—Romania
Gorj County
Telephone: 929/13495

Output and dressing of lignite, research, design and execution of geological, hydrogeological and draining works, mine and pit opening.

INDUSTRIAL CONSTRUCTIONS MINISTRY

CENTRALA DE MECANIZARE PENTRU CONSTRUCTII INDUSTRIALE, BUCURESTI—C.M.C.I.B.
(INDUSTRIAL CONSTRUCTIONS MECHANIZATION CENTRAL, BUCHAREST)

Bucharest—Romania
164, Sos Giurgiului
Sector 5
Telephone: 85 34 90; Telex: 11605

Repair of building machinery and equipment; production of building machinery, equipment, devices and tools;

FOREST ECONOMY AND BUILDING MATERIALS MINISTRY

CENTRALA DE PRELUCRARE A LEMNULUI, BUCURESTI (WOODWORKING CENTRAL, BUCHAREST)

Bucharest—Romania
46—48, Sos. Pipera
Sector 2
Telephone: 33 55 40; Telex: 11380

Coordinates woodworking complexes and enterprises, timber factories, plywood and veneer factories, particle board factories, furniture and carpentry factories, parquetry and wood container factories.

CENTRALA DE EXPLOATARE A LEMNULUI, BUCURESTI (LUMBERING CENTRAL, BUCHAREST)

Bucharest—Romania
8, Calomfirescu St.
Sector 4
Telephone: 14 52 62; Telex: 11221

Coordinates log output and transport enterprises.

CENTRALA MATERIALELOR DE CONSTRUCTII, BUCURESTI (BUILDING MATERIALS CENTRAL, BUCHAREST)

Bucharest—Romania
136, Calea Grivitei
Sector 8
Telephone: 17 53 00; Telex: 10569

Coordinates enterprises producing building materials, bricks, tiles, sandstone and marble plates, sanitary items, prefab concrete panels for constructions, asbestos-cement and cast iron drain pipes, insulation materials for construction, etc.

CENTRALA CIMENTULUI, BUCURESTI (CEMENT CENTRAL, BUCHAREST)

Bucharest—Romania
8, Calomfirescu St.
Sector 4
Telephone: 150936; Telex: 10249

Coordinates cement, plaster and lime producing enterprises.

CENTRALA DE UTILAJE SI PIESE DE SCHIMB, BUCURESTI (EQUIPMENT AND SPARE PARTS CENTRAL, BUCHAREST)

Bucharest—Romania
12, Preciziei Blvd.
Sector 7
Telephone: 60 74 30; Telex: 10587

Coordinates enterprises producing equipment and spare parts for units subordinated to the Forest Economy and Building Materials Ministry.

CENTRALA DE CELULOZA, HIRTIE SI FIBRE ARTIFICIALE, BRAILA (PULP, PAPER AND ARTIFICIAL FIBRE CENTRAL, BRAILA)

Braila—Romania
Sos. Braila-Viziru, Km 10
Telephone: 938/31239; Telex: 55219

Coordinates combines and enterprises producing pulp, paper goods and artificial fibres.

DEPARTMENTUL SILVICULTURII (FORESTRY DEPARTMENT)

Bucharest—Romania
21 Calea Grivitei
Sector 4
Telephone: 150680

Coordinates national scale forestry activity: preservation and development of the growing stock: afforestation, improvement of species, phyto-sanitary campaigns, and marketing of forest by-products (fruit, mushrooms, resin, seeds, fodder, honey, etc.). Protection, industrial-scale development and management of game and salmonidae (trout); environment protection achieved by zoning and management of forests and hydrographic basins, correction etc.

CENTRALA DE EXPLOATARE INDUSTRIALA A AGREGATELOR MINERALE PENTRU CONSTRUCTII, TIRGOVISTE (CENTRAL FOR INDUSTRIAL EXPLOITATION OF BUILDING MINERAL AGGLOMERATES, TIRGOVISTE)

Tirgoviste—Romania
Dimbovita County
Castanilor Blvd.
Telephone: 926/12058

Coordinates the work of the building mineral agglomerates.

AGRICULTURE AND FOOD INDUSTRY MINISTRY

CENTRALA INDUSTRIALIZARII CARNII, BUCURESTI
(MEAT INDUSTRIALIZATION CENTRAL, BUCHAREST)

Bucharest—Romania
3, Piata Valter Maracineanu
Telephone: 15 91 04 Telex: 10392

Meat and meat products.

CENTRALA INDUSTRIALIZARII LAPTELUI, BUCURESTI
(MILK INDUSTRIALIZATION CENTRAL, BUCHAREST)

Bucharest—Romania
3, Piata Valter Maracineanu
Telephone 14 43 95 Telex: 11193

Dairy products.

CENTRALA PRODUCTIEI SI INDUSTRIALIZARII PESTELUI, BUCURESTI
(FISH BREEDING AND FISH INDUSTRIALIZATION CENTRAL, BUCHAREST)

Bucharest—Romania
3, Piata Valter Maracineanu
Telephone: 14 84 52

Fish and fishery products.

CENTRALA PRODUCTIEI SI INDUSTRIALIZARII SFECLEI DE ZAHAR, BUCURESTI
(SUGAR BEET PRODUCTION AND INDUSTRIALIZATION CENTRAL, BUCHAREST)

Bucharest—Romania
3, Piata Valter Maracineanu
Telephone 13 92 03; Telex 10056

Sugar.

CENTRALA BERII, SPIRTULUI SI AMIDONULUI, BUCURESTI

(BEER, ALCOHOL AND STARCH CENTRAL, BUCHAREST)

Bucharest—Romania
157 Calea Rahovei
Sector 6
Telephone: 23 81 10; Telex 10462

Various types of beer, alcohol and starch.

CENTRALA PRODUCTIEI SI INDUSTRIALIZARII TUTUNULUI, BUCURESTI
(TOBACCO PRODUCTION AND INDUSTRIALIZATION CENTRAL, BUCHAREST)

Bucharest—Romania
2, Regiei Blvd.
Sector 7
Telephone 49 71 45; Telex: 10696

Tobacco and cigarettes.

CENTRALA ULEIULUI, BUCURESTI
(OIL CENTRAL, BUCHAREST)

Bucharest—Romania
2, Spataru Preda St.
Sector 6
Telephone 23 70 70; Telex: 10860

Vegetable oil and derivatives.

CENTRALA VALORIFICARII A CEREALELOR SI PRODUCEREA NUTRETURILOR COMBINATE, BUCURESTI
(CENTRAL FOR MARKETING GRAIN AND PRODUCTION OF COMPOUND FODDER, BUCHAREST)

Bucharest—Romania
17 Republicii Blvd.
Telephone: 14 22 10; Telex: 11611 ABCD

Contracting, purchase, preservation and marketing of grain. Industrial production of compound fodder.

CENTRALA PENTRU LEGUME SI FRUCTE, BUCURESTI
(FRUIT AND VEGETABLES CENTRAL, BUCHAREST)

Bucharest—Romania
2, Dr. Marcovic St.
Telphone: 16 28 04; Telex 10530

Fresh, half-preserved and tinned vegetables and fruit, and potatoes.

CENTRALA VIEI SI VINULUI, BUCURESTI
(VINEYARD AND WINE CENTRAL, BUCHAREST)

Bucharest—Romania
2 Dr. Marcovic St.
Telephone: 15 39 96; Telex: 11649

Wines and alcoholic drinks.

CENTRALA DE MECANIZAREA AGRICULTURII SI PRODUCEREA DE UTILAJE PENTRU AGRICULTURA SI INDUSTRIA ALIMENTARA, BUCURESTI
(CENTRAL FOR AGRICULTURE MECHANIZATION AND PRODUCTION OF FARMING AND FOOD INDUSTRY EQUIPMENT, BUCHAREST)

Bucharest—Romania
24, Republicii Blvd.
Sector 4
Telephone 14 40 20; Telex 10737

Undertakes the mechanization of agriculture.

TRUSTUL INULUI, CINEPII SI BUMBACULUI
(FLAX, HEMP AND COTTON TRUST)

Bucharest—Romania
2, Dr. Marcovici St.
Telephone: 13 68 80; Telex: 10664

Organization of production, contracting and purchase of flax and hemp straws and cotton. Processing and marketing of flax and hemp straws.

TRUSTUL PLANTELOR MEDICALE "PLAFAR"
("PLAFAR" MEDICINAL HERBS TRUST)

Bucharest—Romania
50, Emil Bodnaras St.
Telephone: 60 56 55; Telex: 10436

Production, purchase, processing and marketing of medicinal herbs and aromatic plants.

CENTRALA INDUSTRIALA DE MORARIT, DECORTICAT, PANIFICATIE SI PRODUSE FAINOASE
(INDUSTRIAL CENTRAL FOR MILLING, DECORTICATION, BAKERY AND FLOUR PRODUCTS)

Bucharest—Romania
3, Piata Valter Maracineanu
Telephone: 14 24 13; Telex: 10468

Production of flour, maize flour, bread, flour paste ware and biscuits, rice decortication.

CENTRALA DELTA DUNARII
(DELTA DUNARII CENTRAL)

Tulcea—Romania
Tulcea County
1, Piata Republicii
Telephone: 14660; Telex: 52237

Capitalization of the resources of the Danube Delta (fishing, fish breeding, reed cultivation).

LIGHT INDUSTRY MINISTRY

CENTRALA INDUSTRIEI BUMBACULUI, BUCURESTI
(COTTON INDUSTRY CENTRAL, BUCHAREST)

Bucharest—Romania
2, Sos. Morarilor
Sector 3
Telephone: 27 60 80; Telex: 11265

Coordinates the production of: cotton and cotton type yarns and fabrics (bleached or dyed fabrics for bed sheeting, 100 p.c. cotton or mixed cotton and rayon and polyester; fabrics designed for clothing, piece-dyed, yarn-dyed or printed, or cotton or mixed cotton and rayon or polyester; shirtings, piece-dyed, yarn-dyed or printed, of mixed cotton and rayon and polyester; 100 p.c. rayon sateen lustre creaseless printed fabrics for dresses; printed fabrics for dresses of mixed cotton and polyester or rayon; checkered fabrics and flannels for sport shirts; suitings of cotton and mixed cotton and polyester; yarn-dyed cotton pajama fabrics; cotton and mixed cotton and polyester sewing thread; cotton and rayon yarns; technical fabrics).

Cotton and mixed yarns bedding (sheets, pillowcases, bed sets). Various textile raw materials (cotton and mixed yarns).

CENTRALA INDUSTRIEI MATASII, INULUI SI CINEPII, BUCURESTI
(SILK, FLAX AND HEMP INDUSTRY CENTRAL, BUCHAREST)

Bucharest—Romania
134, Ghencea Blvd.
Sector 6
Telephone: 31 64 00; Telex: 1183758

Pure silk, artificial silk and synthetic fibre fabrics (printed artificial fibre fabrics—acetate, triacetate or mixed type; plain or printed pure silk fabrics; printed nylon and polyester fabrics; printed pure silk, polyester, acetate or triacetate neckties; pure silk and polyester jacquard neckties; pure silk and artificial silk kerchiefs and scarves). Decorative fabrics (jacquard or schaft pattern upholstery fabrics; decorative artificial silk and mixed jacquard pattern fabrics; cotton or mixed fibre plush for furniture and home decoration; various fabrics blankets; fringes, elastic and non-elastic ribbons and other trimmings; hats, cloche hats, berets and fezes). Linen and hemp fabrics (for garments and bedding; linen and hemp—in admixture with other fibres—fabrics for table cloths and napkins; indoor decoration fabrics, camping articles; tarpaulins). Various textile raw materials (silk waste, flax and hemp bundle; non-rubberized fire hoses—100 percent polyester; silk and polyester yarns; mixed flax and polyester yarns.

CENTRALA INDUSTRIEI LINII, BUCURESTI
(WOOL INDUSTRY CENTRAL, BUCHAREST)

Bucharest—Romania
300, Sos. Pantelimon
Sector 3
Telephone: 27 44 80; Telex: 11510

Woolen carpets, blankets and cloth (machine-made carpets—100 percent wool or in admixture with synthetic and artificial fibres; tufting carpets—woolen or in admixture with synthetic or artificial fibres; suitings—100 percent wool or in admixture with synthetic or artificial fibres; blankets—100 percent wool or in admixture with synthetic fibres or 100 percent synthetic fibres; cotton and vicuna blankets). Various textile raw materials (technical felt for hydroinsulating support and upholstery requisites); flaw wool for carpets.

CENTRALA INDUSTRIEI TRICOTAJELOR, BUCURESTI
(KNITWEAR INDUSTRY CENTRAL, BUCHAREST)

Bucharest—Romania
220 Calea Serban Voda
Sector 5
Telephone: 23 68 90; Telex: 11664

Knitwear (cotton knitted underwear—men's undershirts, pants, trunks, pajamas, flannel or plush underwear; cotton knitted outerwear—T-shirts, terrycloth sweatsuits, polo and tennis shirts, sweat shirts, etc.; polyamide yarn garments—ladies' slips, nighties and panties, ny-

lon, helanca—in admixture with cotton—track suits, etc.; acryl knitwear—pullovers, jackets, slacks, dresses, overcoats, wintercoats, sets of pullovers, sets of jackets and trousers, gloves, caps, berets); cotton, acryl, helanca or polyamide fibres, socks and stockings for men, women and children; synthetic and artificial yarn tights.

CENTRALA INDUSTRIEI CONFECTIILOR, BUCURESTI
(GARMENTS INDUSTRY CENTRAL, BUCHAREST)

Bucharest—Romania
7, Armata Poporului Blvd.
Sector 7
Telephone: 31 00 70; Telex 11195

Ready-mades for men, women, teenagers and children (indoor and outdoor garments, sport and travel wear, underwear, protection clothes, school uniforms, workmen's special clothes).

CENTRALA INDUSTRIEI PIELARIEI, CAUCIUCULUI SI INCALTAMINTEI, BUCURESTI
(LEATHERWARE, RUBBER AND FOOTWEAR INDUSTRY CENTRAL, BUCHAREST)

Bucharest—Romania
96, Splaiul Unirii
Sector 5
Telephone: 20 60 20; Telex: 11523; 10154

Leather and artificial leather footwear for men, women and children; leather and leather substitute gloves; protection gloves; morocco goods; fur and leather garments; rubber footwear and sport articles; plastic-made toys and other articles, pvc foils; artificial leather and plastic foils.

CENTRALA INDUSTRIEI STICLARIEI SI CERAMICII FINE, BUCURESTI
(GLASS AND FINE CERAMICS INDUSTRY CENTRAL, BUCHAREST)

Bucharest—Romania
171, Muncii Blvd.
Sector 3
Telephone: 27 30 40; Telex: 11869

Household glassware; lighting glassware; earthenware and chinaware; technical and laboratory glassware; drawn glass and other glass products; bottles and jars.

CENTRALA INDUSTRIEI ARTICOLELOR CASNICE, BUCURESTI
(HOUSEHOLD REQUISITES INDUSTRY CENTRAL, BUCHAREST)

Bucharest—Romania
38, Fintinica St.
Sector 3
Telephone: 35 00 50; Telex: 10481

Cooking and heating lamps and accessories; carpet brushes; folding tables; enamelled metal, inox, cast iron and aluminum kitchen requisites; wrought iron flower and bottle stands; cutlery, pocket knives and other household items; scissors, sewing and knitting requisites; earthenware and chinaware; technical and lab-gardening tools; hurricane lanterns; accessories; screw drivers and tool kits; sport, camping, angling, shooting implements; perambulators, tricycles, scooters, rocking chairs. Metallic, plastic, rubber, textile, mechanical and plain tools; footwear and morroco goods accessories; plastic flowers, office requisites; alarm clocks and wall clocks.

CENTRALA DE PREINDUSTRIALIZARE SI ACHIZITII, BUCURESTI
(PRE-INDUSTRIALIZATION AND PURCHASE CENTRAL, BUCHAREST)

Bucharest—Romania
60, Calea Dorobanti
Sector 1
Telephone: 11 19 30; Telex: 11545

Goat's hair; jute sack waste; cotton and rayon waste.

*MINISTRY OF TRANSPORT
AND TELECOMMUNICATIONS*

CENTRALA MECANICA DE MATERIAL RULANT, BUCURESTI
(ROLLING STOCK MECHANICAL CENTRAL, BUCHAREST)

Bucharest—Romania
359, Calea Grivitei
Sector 8
Telephone: 65 54 75; Telex: 10639

Rolling stock, spare parts, special equipment, repair of rolling stock and railway equipment.

CENTRALA INDUSTRIALA DE REPARATII AUTO, BUCURESTI
(AUTO REPAIR INDUSTRIAL CENTRAL, BUCHAREST)

Bucharest—Romania

68, Clabucet St.
Telephone: 65 30 45; Telex: 11533

Motor vehicle overhaul.

CENTRALA DE TRANSPORTURI AUTO, BUCURESTI
(AUTO TRANSPORTATION CENTRAL, BUCHAREST)

Bucharest—Romania
38, Dinicu Golescu Blvd.
Sector 7
Telephone: 18 06 67; Telex: 10430

Inland and international transport of goods by motor vehicles; inland and international passengers' road service; technical assistance; training of professional and amateur motor vehicle drivers.

CENTRALA DE CONSTRUCTII CAI FERATE, BUCURESTI
(RAILWAY BUILDING CENTRAL, BUCHAREST)

Bucharest—Romania
38, D. Golescu Blvd.
Sector 7
Telephone: 18 01 28; Telex: 11657

Building and assembling of railway and hydro-technical installations.

REGIONALA DE CAI FERATE, BRASOV
(BRASOV RAILWAY BRANCH)

Brasov—Romania
Brasov County
1, Politehnicii St.
Telephone: 921/42009; Telex: 12265

Passenger and freight traffic on Romanian railways.

REGIONALA DE CAI FERATE BUCURESTI
(BUCHAREST RAILWAY BRANCH)

Bucharest—Romania
Piata Garü de Nord
Sector 7
Telephone: 18 16 96; Telex: 11401

Passenger and freight traffic on Romanian railways.

REGIONALA DE CAI FERATE CRAIOVA
(CRAIOVA RAILWAY BRANCH)

Craiova—Romania
Dolj County
5, Arges St.
Telephone: 23163

Passenger and freight traffic on Romanian railways.

REGIONALA DE CAI FERATE CLUJ
(CLUJ RAILWAY BRANCH)

Cluj-Napoca—Romania
Cluj County
17, Piata Victoriei
Telephone: 951/11390; Telex: 31361

Passenger and freight traffic on Romanian railways.

REGIONALA DE CAI FERATE IASI
(JASSY RAILWAY BRANCH)

Jassy—Romania
Jassy County
1, Garii St.
Telephone: 980/14829; Telex: 22280

Passenger and freight traffic on Romanian railways.

REGIONALA DE CAI FERATE GALATI
(GALATI RAILWAY BRANCH)

Galati—Romania
Galati County
51, Republicii Blvd.
Telephone: 930/14202; Telex: 51247

Passenger and freight traffic on Romanian railways.

REGIONALA DE CAI FERATE TIMISOARA
(TIMISOARA RAILWAY BRANCH)

Timisoara—Romania
Timis County
2, 6 Martie Blvd.
Telephone: 961/13744

Passenger and freight traffic on Romanian railways.

REGISTRUL NAVAL ROMAN, BUCURESTI
(ROMANIAN REGISTER OF SHIPPING, BUCHAREST)

Bucharest—Romania
38 Dinico Goleseu Blvd.
Sector 7
Telephone: 17 05 50; Telex: 10256

Technical supervision of ship building and equipment, ship classification.

Foreign Trade Organizations

The listing of the major exports and imports of the Foreign Trade Organizations has been extracted from the Romanian publication *Your Commercial Partners in Romania.*

AGROEXPORT

Bucharest—Romania
2, Ion Ghica St.
Telephone: 13 71 72
Telex: 11141

Exports.—Grain; oleaginous seeds, leguminous and technical plants; flour; grain and fodder exchange.

Imports.—Grain, oleaginous seeds; leguminous and technical plants; flour; grain and fodder exchange.

ARCOM

(Romanian construction and erection company)

Bucharest—Romania
91—93, Calea Victoriei
Telephone: 14 98 33
Telex: 11490

Exports.—Enginereing services, licenses, technology, designs and surveys in the field of construction.

Construction of industrial projects, socio-cultural centers, administrative buildings, hospitals, hotels and housing, as a general contractor or civil engineer, singly or in association with local partners or third parties.

Technical assistance in designing and constructing projects.

Services in the field of construction.

Imports.—Purchasing of machinery, installations, devices, transport equipment and materials required on its sites.

ARPIMEX

Bucharest—Romania
1, Al. Postolache St.
Telephone: 31 32 60
Telex: 11472; POB: 5650

Exports.—Footwear with leather and leather substitute uppers for men, women and children; leather gloves for men and women; protection gloves; leatherware (handbags, folios, attaché cases, beauty cases, bags, saddlery etc.); fur and leather garments; pvc foils; vinyl on textile support; pvc carpets; household items; rubber and sport items; rubber footwear; lohn operations.

Imports.—Raw sheepskins, goatskins and cowhides; leather; tanning materials; organic dyes and pigments; chemical auxiliaries for the leather industries; other raw materials, auxiliary materials for leather and footwear industry, inclusively for rubber footwear, plastic articles and artificial leather.

AUTO-DACIA

Bucharest—Romania
19, Lipscani St.
Telehone: 15 86 20
Telex: 11396

Exports.—Motor cars; four-wheel-drive cars; buses; utility vans; special purposes vehicles derived from motor cars; special purpose vehicles derived from utility vans; CKD and SKD; related spare parts and mounting lines; service.

Imports.—Components, subassemblies, CKD and SKD for the manufacture of specific products; spare parts for the specific products; motor cars; four-wheel-drive cars; buses; utility vans; special purpose vehicles derived from motor cars; special purpose vehicles derived from utility vans.

AUTOEXPORTIMPORT

2200—Brasov—Romania
45, Republicii St.
Telephone: 921—40 133
Telex: 12268, 12269

Exports.—Trucks of 3-30 tons with 2, 4 and 6 drive wheels, tractors, dump trucks, special purpose vehicles, trailers; assembly lines.

Imports.—Trucks, dump trucks, special purpose vehicles, tractors, and electric, hydraulic and pneumatic equipment for motor vehicle production.

CHIMIMPORTEXPORT

Bucharest—Romania
10, Republicii Blvd.
Telephone: 16 06 36
Telex: 11184; 11185
POB: 525

Export.—Inorganic substances; intermediaries and organic solvents; alkylamines; organic acids; synthetic and plastic resins; synthetic rubber of the butadiene-styrene type —CAROM ® trademark; carbon black; pestfighters; organo-phosphoric insecticides; pharmaceutical raw materials; original pharmaceutical preparations; conditioned medical drugs; organic pigments and dyestuffs; inter-

mediaries for dyestuffs production; inks and lacquers; thinners; inorganic pigments; plasticizers; soaps and detergent granules; perfumery products and cosmetics; chemical reagents.

Imports.—Natural and synthetic rubber, polyethylene, polypropylene, colophony, sulfur, chromium ore, ammonium chloride, fatty alcohols, chlorine hydride, polystyrene, cellophane, reagents, adhesives, catalysts and other chemicals which are not included in the export lists of other foreign trade companies; medical drugs (veterinary drugs excluded), raw materials for cosmetics, dyestuffs (those used in the light industry are excluded), intermediaries, pharmaceuticals, boron ore, naphthalene, organic solvents, styrene, titanium dioxide, zinc oxide, glycerine, plasticizers, bone and hide glue, suet, vegetable oils (tung oil, linseed oil and coconut oil) lacquers and dyes, melamine, organic and inorganic pigments, stearine soaps, etc.

COMTURIST

Bucharest—Romania
40-44, 30 Decembrie St
Telephone: 15 05 97; 13 59 89
Telex: 1117
POB: 833

Company selling goods at home with payment in freely convertible currency.

Comturist shops are to be found in Bucharest, Brasov and in the Black Sea coast resorts.

Goods can be bought either directly from the usual shops with payment in cash or from Special Order Shops where payment is made in checks, payment orders, letters of credit.

Comturist Agency offers:

—Romanian automobiles.

—long-term technical goods (refrigerators, heating stoves, washing machines, etc.)

—carpets, furniture.

—various other goods (handicrafts, fur and leather coats, cosmetics, cigaretes, drinks, etc.)

—automotive spare parts.

CONFEX

Bucharest—Romania
7, Armata Poporului Blvd.
Telephone: 31 37 51
Telex: 11195 c conf-r

Exports.—All types of ladies' wear, men's wear, teenagers' wear and children's wear; everyday dress; sports dress; traveling dress; formal dress; house dress; knitwear dress.

CONTRANSIMEX

Bucharest—Romania
38, Dinicu Golescu Blvd.
Telephone: 18 00 42
Telex: CTRIX 11606, A, B; POB: 2006

Exports.—Studies, projects, documentation, licenses, technical assistance, services, expert's accounts and carrying out of erection-mounting jobs and installations in the fields of transports and telecommunications abroad (highways, motorways, railways, level crossings, tunnels, channels, bridges, ports, airports, telecommunication jobs); box-pallets and containers and other products produced by transport and telecommunication units.

Imports.—Complex installations and technological completion equipment for the projects of the Transport and Telecommunications Ministry, licenses, technical documentation and assistance included; machinery, installations and working devices for building and repair jobs in the fields of rail, road and water transport, traffic signaling and security; electrification of railway jobs (which are not carried out by other foreign trade companies); ship repairs; garage equipment; mail and telecommunications machines and equipment which are not imported by other foreign trade companies; portal and semi-portal, floating and railway cranes; spare parts for maintenance and repair jobs in the field of rail, road and water transport, mail and telecommunications (spare parts for Dacia motor cars excepted); pit coal creosote; fishing tools for industrial fishing jobs; equipment and materials for assembling jobs carried out abroad.

DANUBIANA

Bucharest—Romania
202 A, Splaiul Independentei
Telephone: 49 50 10; 49 50 60
Telex: 11 489 danaz r; 11748 danzar r;
11842 danzar r
POB: 2350

Exports.—Chemical fertilizers: urea, ammonium nitrate, calcium ammonium nitrate, complex fertilizers, diammonium phosphate, superphosphate; radial and conventional tires as well as inner tubes for passenger cars, trucks, tractors, industrial and agricultural vehicles; technical rubber items; reclaimed rubber, V-belts, conveyor belts, high and low pressure tubes and hoses, accumulator hard rubber cases, profiled and pressed rubber gaskets, rubber car carpets; processed plastic items; PVC granules, foils, sheetings, floorings, pipes, tubes, profiles, simple and corrugated plates; polyethylene blown films, sacks and bags, injection molded articles for industry or consumer goods (barrels, cans, baskets etc.) thermoformed polystyrene products; chemical fibres and yarns; polyacryl, polyamide, polypropylene, polyester; adipic acid, cellulosic film; other chemical items; sodium nitrate, sodium nitrate, ammonium bicarbonate, butanol, methyl acetate, butyl acetate, etc.

Imports.—Phosphates; sulfuric acid; phosphoric acid; ion exchangers; catalysts; arsenic anhydride; monoethanolamine: diethanolamine; divinylbenzene; synthetic camphor; sodium sulphite; sodium sulfate; morpholine; photo gelatine; tyres; anti-oxidant; antiozone; accelerators for vulcanization (Vulcacite); cord net; rubber and plastic technical and insulation products (all assortments); chemical pulp; chemicals for the chemical fibres and yarns production.

DELTA

Bucharest—Romania
2, Intrarea Bibliotecii
Telephone: 15 00 71
Telex: 10570 Delta R
POB: 796
Cables: DELTA—Bucharest

Exports.—Chemical and petrochemical products, wood, wooden products, metal products, building materials, household articles, barter operations, triangular operations, etc.

Imports.—Various goods.

ELECTROEXPORTIMPORT

Bucharest—Romania
133, Calea Victoriei
Telephone: 50 28 70
Telex: 11388
POB: 17

Exports.—Electric motors; electric generators; welding converters powered by electric motors or heat engines; power capacitors; electrical insulation materials; galvanic cells and batteries; electric cables and conductors; lifts; household electric consumer goods (refrigerators, vacuum cleaners, washing machines); indoor and outdoor lighting fixtures, power and distribution transformers, high voltage equipment (switches, separators, lightning arresters, current and voltage transformers); electrical handtools, accumulators; diesel electric and electric locomotives, elevators.

Imports.—Rotary electric machines; electric motors; high voltage transformers and apparatus and electrical engineering equipment; carbon brushes for electric machines, equipment for the electric cable and conductor industry, winding benches; electric handtools; household electric consumer goods (refrigerators, sewing machines, washing machines); electrical insulation materials, insulators, accumulators; electric welding equipment; electric cables and conductors, accessories; electric locomotives and streetcars; electric furnaces (excepting those designed for steel and iron alloy production); licenses, invention patents, surveys, designs, know-how, engineering, technical assistance in the field of the electric engineering industry.

ELECTRONUM

Bucharest—Romania
8, Dimitrie Pompei Blvd.
Telephone: 33 71 70
Telex: 11547; 11584
POB: 105

Exports.—COMPUTING TECHNIQUE: medium and small capacity electronic computing systems; minicomputers, microcomputers; industrial process monitoring computing systems; off-line equipment for computing systems; integrated circuits invoicing and accounting machines; desk-top electronic computers (with display or printer); pocket electronic computers; electro-mechanical computing machines (two or three operations).

BLACK AND WHITE TV SETS: fixed tv sets with 47,51,59,61,65 cm kinescope hybrid or with printed circuits (modular system); portable television sets of 31 cm. kinescope, fully transistorized or with printed circuits (modular system).

RADIO RECEIVERS: MA-MF stationary radio receivers; MA-MF portable radio receivers; 3 band MA radio receivers for motor cars; TV-OIRT, RETMA, CCIR-VHF selectors; television and radio parts and components.

PASSIVE ELECTRONIC COMPONENTS: ceramic capacitors: semi-variable capacitors-trimmers; by-pass capacitors; resistors; varistors; thermistors; passive networks, resistors, capacitors.

KINESCOPES of 44,47,51,59,61 and 65 cm.

ELECTRONIC GUNS, TE 1 and TE 2.

ACTIVE ELECTRONIC COMPONENTS: integrated circuits-linear and logical; silicon transistors; germanium transistors; silicon diodes; germanium diodes; thyristors; power rectifying diodes; radiators; rectifying bridges.

FERRITES: complete set of ferrite cores for the television deflection system; anisotrope magnets for loudspeakers; magnetic tape for refrigerators; aerials for radio receivers; magnetic segments for electric motors; transmission paths; E-type transformer cores; plasto-ferrite rectification and focusing magnets; sets of radio-shielding plugs for motor cars.

CONNECTORS: linear connectors for double-plated printed circuits; linear plug-in connectors for automated telephone exchanges and carrier currents; rotary plug-in connectors with seven contacts (6+ mass); RACK plug-in connectors with 9,15,25,37,50 contacts; switches for television sets and radio receivers; parts and accessories for the electronic industry (line straight boxes, jacks, sockets, etc.).

ELECTRIC MEASURING INSTRUMENTS: measuring bridges with one and six channels; switching-balancing devices; electronic counters; universal and laboratory oscilloscopes; digital and electronic multimeters; versatesters; oscilloscopes-miniscopes; stabilized and continuous voltage source.

RADIOTELEPHONES: portable, stationary and mobile radiotelephones.

ELECTRIC MEASURING INSTRUMENTS: double tariff and CAM-63 single-phase counters; CA-43 S, CA-32 S three-phase and double tariff counters; MI, AI indicating milliampere-meters; LI indicating logometers; wattmeters; varimeters; electromagnetic and magnetoelectric apparatus.

ELECTRIC INSTALLATION EQUIPMENT: current breakers; switches; plugs; sockets; high breaking capacity and standard fuses; industrial sockets and plug-ins.

LOW VOLTAGE EQUIPMENT: automatic circuit breakers, standard and explosion-proof design; contactors; thermal relays; micro circuit breakers, standard and explosion-proof design; push buttons; signaling lamps; cam controllers.

TELEPHONE EXCHANGES: local, long-distance, tandem, rural, office and hotel telephone exchanges; line concentrators.

TELEPHONE SETS: calling-dial telephone sets; secretary telephone exchanges; flame-proof design mining telephone sets.

ELECTRICAL ENGINEERING AUTOMATION EQUIPMENT: single and three-phase thyristor-equipped static converters; thyristor-equipped speed variators; battery chargers with automatic voltage stabilization for buffer system; rectifiers for electrolytic installations; high voltage electric equipment batteries of condensers for the improvement of the power factor; static excitation equipment for synchronous generators.

LOW VOLTAGE TRANSFORMERS AND AUTOTRANSFORMERS OF POWERS UP TO 100 KVA: autotransformers; bell transformers; single-phase and three-phase transformers.

AUTOMATION ELEMENTS: electronic automation instruments: transducers for pressure, temperature, output, water quality, conductivity, pH; indicators; recorders; continuous and discrete regulators; signal converters; analog computing elements; panel secondary elements—auxiliary apparatus; static commutation equipment; fire detecting equipment; photoelectric relays for the automated control of public lighting; electronic time relays. Pneumatic automation instruments (panel mounted or process mounted): pen and selector recorders; indicating regulators; indicators; integrators; computing elements; function generators; programmers; deviation indicating controllers; local indicating regulators with measuring elements.

AUTOMATION EQUIPMENT AND INSTALLATIONS: distribution and control switchboard; monitoring switchboard; distribution and control panels; distribution and control cabinets; control desks; control boxes; automation relays for use in the industrial, transport and power field.

RESEARCH AND DESIGN IN THE FIELD OF INDUSTRIAL PROCESS AUTOMATION: research and production of automation equipment and elements; designing of automation systems and installations for all industrial branches; designing of computer-assisted automated process lines and elaboration of basic software; technical assistance and consulting in the commissioning of automation equipment for various industrial processes.

LIGHTING SOURCES: standard and special electric bulbs of 25–100 W; fluorescent tubes; mercury vapor lamps with magnesium germanate and with yttrium vanadite; sodium vapor lamps; ballasts, cast-in and cast-off design, for fluorescent tubes; ballasts, cast-in and cast-off design, for mercury vapor lamps; ballasts for sodium vapor lamps; igniters for sodium vapor lamps.

Imports.—Complex installations for the electronic and electrical engineering industry, licenses, patents, studies, know-how, engineering, technical assistance; computing technique machinery and equipment; typewriters; passive electronic components (resistors, potentiometers, thermistors, fixed and variable capacitors); materials for radio and television set production; active electronic components (semiconductors, diodes, transistors, thyristors, etc.; electronic valves: reception, emission, picture, special); lighting sources, TV mobile units, various studio electro-acoustic equipment, telecommunication elements; designing of automation systems and installations for all industrial branches; designing of computer-assisted automated process lines and elaboration of basic software; technical assistance and consulting in the commissioning of the automation equipment for various projects.

EXIMCOOP

(Foreign Trade Department of the Consumer Cooperatives)

Bucharest—Romania
31, Brezoianu St.
Telephone: 13 64 33
Telex: 11591 a-b

Exports.—Edible egg paste, egg powder, industrial egg powder, feathers, human hair, snails, frogs, frogs' legs, pigeons, rabbits, bees' honey and wax, beans and pumpkin seeds.

Imports.—Products designed to meet the needs of cooperatives (CENTROCOOP) which are not covered by other foreign trade companies.

FOREXIM

Bucharest—Romania
6, Edgar Quinet St.
Telephone: 16 11 33
Telex: 11120

Exports.—Licenses, surveys, technical documentation and projects worked out by own staff of the ministry institutes, engineering technical assistance, spare parts and cooperation ventures regarding installations for silviculture, the wood-processing industry, the pulp and paper industry, the building materials industry; equipment and spare parts turned out by the forest economy and building material units.

Imports.—Factories, complex installations, technological installations, subassemblies, documentation, projects, technical assistance and spare parts for the wood processing industry, the pulp and paper industry, the building materials industry (cement factories excluded); tools, cutters and devices for wood processing, pulp, paper and building materials processing, phosphorous bronze sieves; licenses, surveys, technical documentation, projects, know-how, technical assistance for factories, complex installations, technological completion installations and spare parts for the wood processing industry, the pulp and paper, and building materials (cement factories excluded) industries.

FRUCTEXPORT

Bucharest—Romania
43, Brezoianu St.
Telephone: 13 65 63
Telex: 10963
Cables: Fructexport—Bucharest

Exports.—Fresh orchard and hothouse fruit for household use; fresh orchard and forest fruit for industrial use; fresh hothouse and field vegetables for household use; grown and wild mushrooms: fresh, dried and in brine; semi-industrialized products: pulps, purées, juices, concentrated apple juice; dehydrated fruit and vegetables; walnuts in shell; walnut kernels; canned fruit: in water, in light and heavy syrup, jams, purées, nectars, syrups; canned vegetables in water, in vinegar, in oil or in tomato sauce; tomato paste and juice; frozen fruit and vegetables for household and industrial use; flowers and ornamental plants; medicinal plants, seeds and essential oils.

GEOMIN

(Company for Mining and Geological Cooperation)

Bucharest—Romania
109, Calea Victoriei
Telephone: 14 55 01
Telex: 11242

Carries out geological investigations, preliminary evaluations, laboratory analyses, technological research, feasibility studies, surveys, designs, construction-erection jobs, mining and geological engineering jobs; complete installation plants for mining projects, turnkey deliveries or ore processing plants; participation in joint mining ventures abroad.

Imports.—Installations and equipment for mining ore processing projects under construction abroad.

ICECOOP

Bucharest—Romania
12, Marin Serghiescu St.
Telephone: 12 10 69
Telex: 10 479

Exports.—Furniture, wooden articles (toys for little children, household items, handicrafts), wrought iron and copper. Oriental-type hand-knotted carpets. Kelim-type hand-woven carpets, textile handicrafts (fabrics, folk embroideries, folk garments, blouses and dolls), ready-mades and knitware, black and colored ceramics, basket-work, handicraft glassware, silverware, Christmas tree decorations, leatherware (footwear, morocco goods, furrier's goods), metallic articles and chemicals, painted wood and glass icons, etc.: **operations:** mainly in the field of ready-mades, footwear and precious metals; **services;** including selling of products against payment in foreign currency in the trading network of the handicraft cooperatives; **goods exchange:** with similar foreign enterprises, organizations and companies; **cooperation:** cooperation in the field of goods production and sale in foreign markets.

ILEXIM

Bucharest—Romania
3, 13 Decembrie St.
Telephone: 15 76 72
Telex: 11226

Exports.—Wooden and metal household articles; inner decoration articles from wood, metal, glass, alabaster, ceramics; white and decorative candles; handtools and gardening implements; vrious osier, reed, maize leaves and hazel twigs basket-work; occasional furniture with pleated seats; rubber and plastic articles; metallic structures; pig-iron cast articles; various quarry and building materials; certain textile ready-mades; sport and camping outfits; travel and beach articles; school and office requisites; wind and percussion instruments; certain agricultural produce and foodstuffs; table and medicinal mineral water; books, newspapers, magazines, periodicals, postage stamps and accessories; records.

Imports.—Books, newspapers, magazines, periodicals. postage stamps and accessories; records.

IMPEXMIN

Bucharest—Romania
109, Calea Victoriei
Telephone: 50 31 90
Telex: 10588
POB: 4664

Exports.—Raw materials: emulsifying-reduction agents, anionic surface active substances, ground asbestos, bentonite, organic colloids, kaolin clays, chalk, organofilic clay, dacite, diatomite, dolomite, bleaching earths, emulsifying agents for drilling fluids, feldspar, kaolin, quartz, quartz mass, filter agents, rock salt, quartz sand for foundries, mineral specimens, talc, witherite. Processed products: tools and apparatus used in oil and gas drilling (fishing tool magnets, dynamographs, weight indicators, multiple shot survey instruments for recording the direction and inclination of bore holes, torque assembly, pressure recorders etc.); devices for pipes (safety devices, natural gas pressure adjusting installations, industrial pressure regulators, gas filters for regulating stations, tronsons rotary devices, burners with radiant flame type TRICEM, burners in group); mining equipment and products for dressing (fixed trucks, hydrocyclones, electric sludge pumps, mechanical agitators, sample takers); diverse goods (rubber pistons, various rubber gaskets, rubber protectors, drillpipe wipers, miners' helmets).

Imports.—Products, equipment and installations for mining, oil and gas industries: kaolin, kieselguhr, perlite, atapulgite, mica, chalk, steatite, manganese dioxide, hard grinding materials, flotation reagents, ground silica, copper, lead and zinc concentrates, steam coal,

preparation plants for non-metal-bearing ores, complete technological lines, mechanized systems for coal face cutters, winches and extraction machines, loading machines for bags, drill carriages (JUMBO), perforating heads, geologic drilling installations, pumps for the mining industry, compressors, ventilators, pit lamps, apparatus for mine rescue, transformer substations of fire-proof design, fireproof electric apparatus, equipment, apparatus and materials for offshore platforms, spare parts for mining and oil equipment, pumps and valves etc. Gas processing plants, equipment for cryogenic plants, etc.

INDUSTRIALEXPORT

Bucharest—Romania
1-3, Scaune St.
Telephone: 13 10 09
Telex: 10052
POB: 768

Exports.—Complete oil refineries and complex chemical and petrochemical installations, parts of installations and technological lines in the field of chemical and petrochemical industries and of crude processing; drilling rigs and equipment, production equipment for crude and gas wells, geological investigation and water well drilling equipment, mining equipment, pumps and industrial fittings; studies, designs, technical assistance in construction jobs, training of operating personnel and other engineering jobs and services in the field of oil equipment, oil refineries, chemical and petrochemical units.

Imports.—Completion outfits for complex chemical and oil processing installations and equipment specific to oil and gas extraction industry; industrial fittings; pumps.

Cooperates with specialist firms in other countries in building industrial units, development of technologies in the chemical industry and crude processing, as well as in the manufacture of oil exploration and mining equipment.

MASINEXPORTIMPORT

Bucharest—Romania
1–3, Scaune St.
Telephone: 13 75 96; 33 27 20
Telex: 11206; 11216
Cables: MEXIM-Bucharest

Exports.—Metal cutting machine tools; engine lathes in the range of 400 to 800 mm swing and 750 to 5000 mm length; single spindle automatic lathes 16–25–42–60 mm; turret lathes 32–40–63–80 mm; vertical boring mills with maximum processing diameters of 1400–1650–2200–2700–3300 and 4300 mm; horizontal boring mills, 85–100–130 and 150 mm spindle diameter; plane milling machines, 660–1000 and 1600 mm table width; knee type milling machines (universal and vertical); spur gear hobbing machines; toolroom milling machines; broaching machines; cylindrical grinding machines; surface grinding machines; centerless grinding machines; tool and cutter grinding machines; bench and column drilling machines; vertical inner tapping machines; shaping machines, 425–700 and 800 mm stroke; metal cutting circular and hack saws; ball flashing and lapping machines; ball bearing race lapping machines; hydraulic press brakes; inclinable automatic presses; roll plate bending machines; flanging machines; structural steel shears; profile and section shears; guillotine shears; forging hammers; double-end grinders.

Woodworking machines. Textile industry machines. Measuring instruments (mass, length, pressure). Tools.

Imports.—MASINEXPORTIMPORT is sole importer of machine tools in Romania.

MECANOEXPORTIMPORT

Bucharest—Romania
10, Mihai Eminescu St.
Telephone: 12 46 00
Telex: 10269
POB: 130

Exports.—Freight cars and passenger railway cars, tank cars, spare parts, assembly lines for the above mentioned items, relevant components and subassemblies; building equipment, roadbuilding equipment, crushing and screening equipment; mechanical handling equipment, electric lift trucks and side loaders, metallic construction, cast and forged parts; Diesel hydraulic, Diesel electric locomotives and mining locomotives, 4HP-30HP and 120 HP Diesel engines; stationary gasoline engines, compressors; technological equipment for secondary thermal treatment, foundry furnaces and installations included; cast iron and brass sanitary fittings.

Imports.—Mechanical handling equipment (portal and semiportal cranes, floating cranes and railway cranes excluded), motor and electric lift trucks, motor and electric sideloaders; freight cars and passenger railway cars, tank cars; excavators building equipment (excepting road building and railway building equipment); furnaces and technological equipment for foundries, gas-heated secondary thermal treatment furnaces; pressure casting machines (for ferrous and nonferrous metals); asbestos sheets, railway car connections, industrial filters and filtering equipment; compressors, blowers and fans for commercial refrigeration installations and the food industry (excepting methane gas turbo-compressors, technological process turbo-compressors in the chemical industry and technological turbocompressors and turbo-blowers for furnace and coke gas); fire-fighting equipment, burners and hot air generators, (air conditioning installations for computing centers included), crushing and screening equipment; welding and oxyacetylene output stations; food industry equipment, bottling and packing equipment; stationary internal combustion engines and 300–6000 HP Diesel engines (excepting engines imported as spare parts for vehicles); general purpose equipment.

MERCUR

Bucharest—Romania
118, Calea Victoriei
Telephone: 15 66 00
Telex: 11366

Exchange of consumer goods with similar foreign organizations and firms, exchange of goods of the cooperative units with similar foreign organizations; exchange of commercial equipment and furniture, imports of goods on consignment to supply the domestic market stores; imports of foods; imports of cosmetics, metal haberdashery, buttons, costume jewelry, enameled dishes, household glassware, chinaware, pottery, crystals, cutlery, watches, petromax lamps and brackets, ironmongery, hunting arms, sport arms, precious stones, ropes of beads, statuettes, Christmas tree decorations, record players and spare parts, sports and beach articles, toys, smokers' outfits, school and office stationery, musical articles, razor blades; organization of sales of motor car spare parts, motor cars and oether long-use goods, homebuilt, imported or imported on consignment and paid for in foreign currency; shipping abroad of goods purchased by tourists; export of foodstuffs, craftware, guides and propaganda materials marketable in Romanian restaurants opened abroad, at congresses, gastronomic gatherings, exhibition, stands, etc.; import of amusement equipment, spare parts and similar products marketable in restaurants.

METALIMPORTEXPORT

Bucharest—Romania
21—25, Mendeleev St.
Telephone: 62 06 21
Telex: 11515 a, b, c
Cables: Metalimportexport

Exports-Imports.—Steel semifabs, commercial quality and alloy steel bars and profiles, flat products, tubes, drawn wire, pull ropes, nails, welding electrodes, aluminum ingots and aluminum products, other non-ferrous metals ingots and rolled goods.

METAROM

Bucharest—Romania
21—25, Mendeleev St.
Telephone: 15 05 43
Telex: 11705

Exports.—Technologies, licenses, projects, technical assistance in the field of metalworking.

Imports.—Complex installations and completion equipment; machinery, equipment for the ironworking and metalworking industries and for the coke-chemical, refractory products, abrasive and carbon materials industries which are not included in the import lists of other foreign trade specialist companies; turbo-blowers, electric blowers, turbo-compressors and electric compressors for top gas and coke gas (oxygen installations included); electric furnaces for steel and iron alloys smelting, spectro chemical analysis apparatus for assessment of hydrogen, nitrogen, oxygen and other elements in steel; steel and iron alloys smelting, spectrochemical licenses surveys, designs, technology, engineering, know-how, technical assistance for the iron and metalworking industry, for the coke-chemical, the refractory, abrasive and carbon materials industries.

MINERALIMPORTEXPORT

Bucharest—Romania
16, Republicii Blvd.
Telephone: 13 91 67
Telex: 11873 a, b, c

Exports.—Coal tar, Söderberg paste.

Imports.—Iron ore, manganese ore, pyrite, calcined alumina, bauxite, potassium chloride, potassium fertilizers, graphite electrodes, magnesite and chromemagnesite bricks, silica-alumina bricks, silica bricks, silimanite bricks, Corhart bricks and other refractory materials for the glass industry, magnesite and chrome magnesite mortar, furnace coke, foundry coke, coke breeze, aluminum oxide, abrasives, anthracite, coking coal, sinter and caustic magnesite, rutile, calcium fluoride, zirconium, refractory clay, aluminum fluoride, synthetic cryolite, pitch tar, carbon and cathode blocks, other materials (putties, refractories, foundry fluxes).

NAVLOMAR

Bucharest—Romania
26, Corneliei St.
Telephone: 23 96 00; 31 79 72
Telex: 11781; 11783 a, b, c, d;
POB: 1302

Chartering, shipping agency, ship chandler services; sale of goods and services payable in currency for foreign ships in Romanian ports.

PETROLEXPORT

Bucharest—Romania
139, Calea Plevnei
Telephone: 49 23 32
Telex: 11519 petex r

Exports.—Gasolines; various lube oils; gas oil; fuel oil; paraffins; petroleum asphalt; petroleum coke.

Imports.—Crude oil; special mineral oils; silicon oils; special greases; additives.

PRODEXPORT

Bucharest—Romania
5—9, Gabriel Péri St.
Telephone: 16 16 60
Telex: 11527

Exports.—Live animals (cattle, sheep, porcines), meat, tinned meat and meat products, Sibiu salami, animal organs and byproducts, frozen poultry, eggs, sugar, sunflower oil, sturgeon, zander fillet, ocean fish, canned fish, caviar, crayfish tails—frozen and in brine, crayfish soup, frogs' legs, live and shot game, bees honey and apiarian products, dairy products, tobacco, cigarettes, etc.

Imports.—Cocoa beans, hop, malt, tobacco, auxiliaries for the foodstuffs industry, etc.

ROMAGRIMEX

Bucharest—Romania
16 Alexandru Sahia St.
Telephone: 14 10 88; 13 48 29
Telex: 11522; 11693
Cables: ROMEX–R

Exports.—Surveys, projects, licenses, technical documentation, know-how, technical assistance in the field of land management and marketing of arable areas, land reclamation, dams and river improvement projects; general supplier of complete installations; equipment and installations included in the manufacturing program of the units subordinated to the Agriculture and Food Industry Ministry, immersion evaporators, cold accumulators and open basins; smooth pipe cooling elements; air coolers of large capacity (between 110–550 sq.m apiece); heat exchangers; CEF 180 and CEF 250 forced evaporation condensers; forced ventilation water cooling towers (between 50,000 and 600,000 kcal/h for industrial areas—85 CZ); valves and auxiliary parts for pipes; safety and control fittings; expanded polystyrene shells; equipment for ice factories after the conventional method, excepting compressors, electric pumps, tanks and ice molds; water well drilling, seeds and saplings, breeding and pedigree animals and fowl, in-breeding strains; veterinary medical drugs and products, cooperative ventures, joint production companies sited in Romania or abroad and other forms of cooperation.

Imports.—Protein meal, biostimulators, inseminated eggs; breeding and pedigree animals and fowl, and inbreeding strains, seeds and saplings; biological material for production of sera and vaccines for breeding and zoological purposes; veterinary medical drugs and substances; land reclamation installations and equipment which are not included in the import lists of other importing companies; equipment, installations spare parts and accessories for pre-industrialization of hemp, flax and cotton.

ROMANIA FILM

Bucharest—Romania
25, Iulius Fucik St.
Telephone: 11 13 08;
Telex 11144

Exports.—Films and tapes for cinematography and television.

Imports.—Films and tapes for cinematography.

ROMANIAN RADIO AND TELEVISION

(Export and Import Board)

Bucharest—Romania
191, Calea Dorobanti
Telephone: 31 15 77
Telex: 11251; 11252; 11746
POB: 111

Exports.—TV films and tapes.

Imports.—TV films and tapes; exchange of TV films.

ROMANOEXPORT

Bucharest—Romania
17—19, Doamnei St.
Telephone: 13 36 99; 16 23 10
Telex: 11186; 11400 REXPT R
POB: 594
Cables: Romanoexport

Exports.—Bleached or dyed bedsheeting, 100 p.c. cotton, cotton mixed with 33 p.c. rayon, various colors; body linen fabrics, piece-dyed, yarn-dyed or printed, of cotton, cotton with 33 p.c. rayon, polyester mixed with cotton or rayon in various designs and colors; shirtings and blouse fabrics, piece-dyed, yarn-dyed or printed, or cotton mixed with 33 p.c. rayon, polyester mixed with cotton, polyester and rayon blends in up-to-date designs and colors; printed fabrics for ladies' dresses of 100 p.c. rayon, sateen lustre, low creasing, in a wide range or designs and colors; printed fabrics for dresses, of polyester mixed with cotton, polyester with rayon, in up-to-date designs and colors; fabrics for sport shirts, checks, checkered flannels, in various designs and colors; suitings of cotton or mixed polyester and cotton, in various weaving effects; cotton pajama fabrics, yarn-dyed, in various designs and colors; various types of sewing thread of cotton or polyester mixed with cotton, in various colors; cotton and rayon yarns; technical cloths; machine-made carpets of 100 p.c. wool and wool mixed with synthetic and artificial fibres; tufted carpets made of wool mixed with artificial and synthetic fibres; piece goods for men's suiting, 100 p.c. wool, wool mixed with synthetic and artificial fibres; blankets, 100 p.c. wool, wool mixed with synthetic fibres, or 100 p.c. synthetic fibres; blankets of cotton and waste cotton; printed fabrics of artificial fibres (acetate, triacetate and mixed fibres); natural silk fabrics, plain, and printed; nylon and polyester printed fabrics; printed neckties of natural silk, polyester, acetate and triacetate for men and women; jacquard neckties of natural silk and polyester; scarves and kerchiefs of natural or artificial silk; upholstery fabrics, shaft and jacquard designs, various assortments; decorative jacquard fabrics of artificial silk and mixed fibres; velvets of cotton or cotton mixed with other fibres for upholstery and inner decorations; bed spreads of various fabrics; fringes, elastic ribbons, non-elastic ribbons and other haberdashery; hats and hat bodies; berets and fezzes; linen and hemp fabrics for garments and bedsheetings; linen and hemp and mixed fibres fabrics for table cloths, tables sets and kitchen napkins; linen and hemp fabrics for inner decorations and camping articles; tarpaulins; waste silk; felts and technical cloths; unwoven textiles for hydroinsulation support, upholstery wadding; hemp, bundle, hemp and flax tow, flax and hemp waste; fire hose, 100 p.c. polyester, nonrubberized; natural silk and PNA yarns; goat hair; scoured carding carpet wool; yarns: 100 p.c. cotton and blends; flax yarns blended with polyester; jute scrap bagging rags; mixed new cotton and staple fibre hosiery cuttings; old textile waste; cotton knitted underwear (men's undershirts, men's singlets, trunks, pajamas, plain, dyed and printed, flannels, and terry trousers, interlock and plush); cotton knitted garments (tee-shirts, terry cloth sweatpants and shorts, track suits, polo shirts, sweat shirts); polyamide knitted underwear (ladies' underdresses, nighties, nylon panties, polyester shirts); polyamide knitted garments (track suits of nylon, helanca and cotton); acrylic knitted garments (pullovers, jackets, trousers, dresses, overcoats, sets of pullovers, jackets and trousers, gloves, knitted gloves, caps, mufflers); ladies', children's and men's socks of cotton and acrylic fibres, of helanca and polyamide yarns of cotton and rayon and nylon stockings; tights.

Imports.—Raw cotton; carded cotton yarns; woolen waste; jute tow; sisal yarns and fibres; uncoated elastic yarns; ramie; fabrics from plain and teflon-coated glass yarns; glass fibre felting; coated elastic yarns; technical felt, technical cloth for the paper and asbestos cement industries; jute yarns and fabrics; jute and synthetic bags; technical screen for textile printing, for milling and for screen printing; raffia; animal hair; window glass and mirror polishing wheels; textile conveyor belts; spun rayon fibres; wool-type, cotton-type, polynosic fibres; acetate, triacetate, viscose and cotton waste yarns; synthetic, polyamide, poly-

ester yarns; metallic and metallized (metalloplastic) yarns; filter fabrics; synthetic, acrylic fibres for artificial furs; chemical fibres for artificial leather; cotton, wool, silk and blended fabrics; towels; machine-made woolen carpets; polyester jersey; various haberdashery; dyestuffs; adhesive for interlinings; auxiliaries for the textile and leather industries; pigments for the glassware, pottery and porcelain industries, and bright gold; various chemicals.

ROMCHIM

Bucharest—Romania
13, Dacia Blvd.
Telephone: 11 07 30/108; 114; 186
Telex: 10930

Imports.—Complex installations and technological projects, licenses, technological processes, documentation, reproduction rights, technical assistance, services for the chemical and crude processing industries; complex installations and completion equipment for the chemical yarn and fibre industry; industrial fixtures and assembling materials (fittings, flanges) for corrosive chemical media; compressors, blowers and fans for chemical industry technological processes (air, methane gas, commercial refrigeration plants and food industry excepted); pumps for corrosive chemical media; plastic processing equipment; oxygen, nitrogen etc., factories and plants, stocking and distribution stations.

ROMCONSULT

(Romanian Consulting Institute)

Bucharest—Romania
35, Armeneasca St.
Telephone: 12 89 40
Telex: 11650
POB: 757

Carries out a wide range of consulting services; preliminary and feasibility studies; general and execution designs; technical assistance; working out of specifications and organization of tenders; analysis of designs and of other documentation; works supervision; training of personnel; market survey and research; exports of patents, licenses, know-how; management. The relevant services are carried out in the following spheres: civil engineering, architecture, town planning; energetics; industry; transports; water supplies; farming; irrigation; education; hydrology, meteorology; tourism; sport.

ROMENERGO

Bucharest—Romania
1, Lacul Tei Blvd.
Telephone: 12 13 26; 12 05 51
Telex: 11525, ROMENG-R
POB: 736

Exports.—High, medium, and low voltage lines, transformer substations and posts, poles and fittings for high, medium and low voltage lines; studies, designs, erection and assembling of projects carried out abroad in the electric power field, dams, hydrotechnical constructions, export and transport of electric power; licenses, studies, designs, engineering, technical assistance, expert's accounts in the power field.

Imports.—Complex power installations for the electric and nuclear power field, equipment, apparatus and materials for the erection-assembling jobs carried out abroad.

ROMPETROL

(Company for Oil and Gas Cooperation)

Bucharest—Romania
109, Calea Victoriei
Telephone: 14 17 16
Telex: 10155

Carries out abroad: geological investigations, design, surveys, engineering, and technical assistance in the field of petroleum and gas extraction; oil well drilling jobs, construction of oilfields, petroleum pipelines, oil and natural gas bulk plants and distribution facilities as well as other construction-erection works in the oil and gas industry; participation in joint ventures for hydrocarbon development and production activities; leasing operations.

ROMSIT

Bucharest—Romania
13, Ion Ghica St.
Telephone: 13 89 77; 14 05 32;
Telex: 11836; 11855

Exports.—Engineering, consulting complete plants, machinery and aggregates for the light industry sectors household items of metal glass, porcelain, faience and plastic; silver and silver-plated decorative articles, metallic lighting fixtures; office requisites and artificial flowers; haberdashery; kitchen and pocket knives; hurricane lamps; plush and metal toys, dolls and sport articles; accessories for footwear and leatherware; alarm and wall clocks; gardening implements; lighting glassware; window glass, mirrors, technical and laboratory glassware.

Imports.—Technological installations and equipment for the light industry sectors (readymades, knit-wear, weaving mills, spinning mills, leatherware, glassware, chinaware, faience etc.); accessories for the equipment of the light industry sectors; licenses, patents, studies, designs, engineering, know-how, technical assistance for the light industry sectors.

ROMTRANS

Bucharest—Romania
196, Calea Rahovei
Telephone: 23 89 20
Telex: 11346
POB: 1311

Secures the best conditions for the forwarding of foreign trade goods from and to all important places in Europe, the Near and Middle East; transit of foreign goods through Romania, for international fairs and exhibitions included, warehousing; transport of collective goods and containers.

TEHNOFORESTEXPORT

Bucharest—Romania
4, Piata Rosetti
Telephone: 16 04 00; 14 30 02
Telex: 11382; 11763; 11362

Exports.—Finished wooden products (furniture, chairs, boats, sports articles, musical instruments, wood containers, windows, doors, prefab cottages); softwood, beech and oak timber, particle- and fiberboards—standard and enriched, plywood, panels, veneer, parquetry, pulp timber, charcoal, round beams, paper, pulp, paper and pulp products.

Imports.—Logs, veneer, seagrass, ironmongery and other accessories for furniture; musical instruments and sports articles; specific materials for the wood processing industry (lacquers, dyestuffs, adhesives, paints, polishing paste) which are not included in the import lists of other foreign trade companies; paper pulp, pulp for the footwear industry, paper, cardboard, tegofilm, tegotex, special technical paper (electrical engineering paper and cardboard excluded); special chemicals for the paper and pulp industry which are not included in the import lists of other foreign trade companies.

TEHNOIMPORTEXPORT

Bucharest—Romania
5, Doamnei St.
Telephone: 16 45 70
Telex: 11254; POB: 110

Exports.—Apparatus and installations manufactured by the Nuclear Physics Institute; apparatus (single piece series) produced by the research and design institutes; laboratory and metrology equipment, medical apparatus, atomic physics apparatus; oxyacetylene welding equipment; airplanes, helicopters, gliders, aviation equipment and materials, spare parts; bicycles, motorcycles, components and spare parts; assembling parts and elements, ball bearings, and rollers, bushings; microscopes, teaching aid apparatus and materials; film production equipment and materials; films and recorded tapes not designed for cinematography, TV and radio.

Imports.—Laboratory equipment, medical apparatus and equipment, atomic physics apparatus; airplanes, helicopters, gliders, aviation equipment, bicycles, motorcycles, components and spare parts; pressure-measuring apparatus and instruments; geophysical apparatus; ball bearings and rollers; optical, technical and laboratory glass; fault detectors and gas analysis devices; cameras and materials for film production, radio and TV; duplication equipment; technical clocks; medical and industrial Roentgen apparatus (accessories and components used in the manufacture of Roentgen apparatus included); industrial and laboratory apparatus and equipment used in physical-mechanical tests; optical-mechanical and photogrammetrical apparatus; laboratory furnaces; laboratory pumps; printing materials and equipment; records and recording tapes; films and recorded tapes not designed for cinematography and radio-TV; all types of measurement and gauging apparatus (non-unified system apparatus included); apparatus for measurement of methane gas concentration in mines, spectral analysis apparatus and apparatus for determination of hydrogen, nitrogen, oxygen, and other elements in steel excluded; products, equipment, apparatus and materials for scientific research units including hiring of aforesaid; manufacture lines, assembling parts and elements; cooperation ventures in the field of aeronautics and imports of equipment for aforesaid (if not included in the operations of other specialist foreign trade companies); airport equipment and air navigation protection and control installations; noxious gas and dust protection equipment, diving equipment; machines and equipment for production of lenses, vibration recording and compensating machines and apparatus.

TERRA

Bucharest—Romania
16, Republicii Blvd.
Telephone: 15 30 43; 15 84 83
Telex: 11571; 11341 Terra
Cables: TERRA BUCHAREST 4
POB: 86

Imports and exports of any kind of commodities, commercial and financial compensation operations, switch, foreign trade operations; carrying out of orders placed by public organizations; joint companies, conclusion of contracts with physical persons, services provided with payment in foreign currency; sale of customs clearance tickets.

UNIVERSAL TRACTOR

Bucharest—Romania
19, Lipscani St.
Telephone: 15 86 20;
Telex: 11889; POB: 454
Cables: UNIVERSAL TRACTOR-
Bucharest

Subsidiary in Brasov:
5, Turnului St.
Telephone: 10422
Telex: 12335

Exports.—Tire-mounted farming tractors, 35 HP class: U–350; 45 HP class; U–445, V–445, L–445, 445 HCP, 445 HCV, 445 DT, 445 DTE; 55 HP class: U–550 Super, V–550 Super, L–550 Super, 550 DT Super, 550 DTE Super; 65 HP class: U–650 M, 651 M, U–650 Super, 650 DT Super; 80 HP class: U–800, 800 DT; 180 HP class: A–1800 A. Tire-mounted industrial tractors, 45 HP class: 445 SD, 445 DT-SD, TIH–445; 55 HP class; 550 SD Super, 550 DT-SD Super; 360 HP class: A–3600 IF, A–3600 L. Caterpillar farming tractors, 45 HP class: S–445, SV–445, SM–445. Caterpillar industrial tractors, 65 HP class: S–651 LS; 150 HP class: S–1500 LS; 180 HP class: S–1800 IF, S–1800 LS.

Farming machinery and equipment: soil tilling machines and equipment; sowing, planting and fertilizer spraying machines, pest control installations; harvesting and threshing machines; vegetable cleaning, screening and drying equipment; animal husbandry equipment.

Trailers: 4-ton farming trailers; 3-5 ton motor vehicle trailers; 1800 and 3600 I fuel and lubricant trailed tankers; 4000 I fluid chemical fertilizer trailed tankers; high capacity fodder trailers.

Imports.—Wheel and track-type tractors; bulldozers; farming equipment: soil tilling; sowing and planting; culture maintenance; harvesting; farming machine engines; hothouse equipment; garden and park equipment.

UZINEXPORTIMPORT

Bucharest—Romania
133, Calea Victoriei
Telephone: 50 25 35;
POB: 2993
Telex: 11214

Exports.—Plants and complex installations for the production of equipment and installations in the field of mechanical engineering, electrical engineering and electronics, licenses, invention patents and manufacturing technologies, the relevant CKD; ships, boats, naval equipment, ship repair; thermoelectric power plants, thermal power stations, district heating plants, hydroelectric power plants, hydromechanical equipment, diesel electric stations, spare parts; metallurgical and iron and steel installations, the related individual equipment and the outfits, relevant spare parts; food industry installations: refrigerating warehouses, ice factories, milling installations, silos, meat, milk and fruit preparing lines, bread manufacturing factories, the relevant spare parts; cement lines, various individual equipment and outfits, spare parts; studies, designs, know-how, engineering, production lines, technologies for the above-mentioned factories, erection, technical assistance, training.

Imports.—Plants and complete installations for the mechanical engineering industry; equipment for boilers and turbines; equipment for metal surface protection; complex installations for the food industry, for the scientific institutes and the local industry units; ships, boats, naval equipment and outfits, completion outfits for naval industry included; parts of installations and equipment for cement factories; designs, licenses, technical assistance, training for the imported installations.

VINEXPORT

Bucharest—Romania
41, Brezoianu St.
Telephone: 14 31 94
Telex: 11132
POB: 34

Exports.—Natural bottled and bulk wines; wine brandy; vermouth, sparkling wines; fruit brandies; wine distillates; liqueurs; beer; starch, glucose; concentrated must; grapes.

VITROCIM

Bucharest—Romania
18, Blanari St.
Telephone: 13 16 38
Telex: 11330 vicim r

Exports.—BINDERS: BSS 12/58 Portland cement, anti-sulphatic cements, white cement, building plaster, hydrated plaster, burnt limestone; ASBESTOS CEMENT: asbestos cement corrugated boards, asbestos cement tubes; HYDROINSULATING MATERIALS: bituminized cardboard, bituminized felting, bituminized cloth; MINERAL WADDING THERMAL AND SOUND INSULATING MATERIALS: cushions, boards, felts, shells, cord, dialit bricks; MARBLE AND MARBLE PRODUCTS: blocks, plates, marmoroc, marble granules, mosaic slabs; CERAMIC MATERIALS: glazed ceramic slabs, glazed and nonglared sandstone slabs, faience tiles, ceramic sandstone tubes, tiles, bricks, granulite; WALLPAPERS: PVC wallpaper on paper support; FLOORINGS: PVC flooring on textile support; Polirom type thermal and sound-insulating carpet, synthetic moquette; SANITARY AND HEATING INSTALLATION MATERIALS: both tubs, radiators, brass sanitary fixtures, cast iron draining pipes, porcelain and enamelled cast iron sanitary articles.

Imports.—ASBESTOS AND ASBESTOS PRODUCTS: threads, yarns, boards, fabrics, belts, asbestos protection materials, gaskets, cord; CORK AND CORK PRODUCTS: boards, waste, rounds, granules, gaskets, corks; DYES: for the ceramic industry.

Market Profile—RWANDA

Foreign Trade

Imports.—$205 million in 1981; $206 million in 1982. Principal imports: electrical machinery, transport equipment, consumer goods, foodstuffs. Imports from United States: $6.2 million in 1981, $5.8 million in 1982. Principal suppliers: Japan (15.9 percent), Belgium (12.7 percent), PRC (11.2 percent); Kenya (10.4 percent) and United States (3.7 percent).

Exports.—$100 million in 1981; $82 million in 1982. Principal exports: coffee, tea, cassiterite, wolfram, and pyrethrum. Exports to the United States: $40.5 million in 1981 and $35 million in 1982. Principal customers: Tanzania (32.5 percent), United States (26.6 percent); Netherlands (8.5 percent), and West Germany (7.8 percent).

Trade Policy.—Associate member of the European Economic Community and member with Zaire and Burundi of the Economic Community of the Great Lakes. No trade preferences granted.

Trade Prospects.—Food processing machinery, road transport vehicles, chemicals, foodstuffs, consumer goods.

Foreign Investment

Liberal investment code, permitting 100 percent foreign-owned enterprises and full repatriation of profits. U.S. investment at present limited to tea factory.

Investment Prospects.—Tourism, mineral extraction, export agriculture.

Finance

Currency.—Rwandan francs (92.84 RwF=US$1, in Oct. 1983). Money supply was $175 million at end of 1982.

Domestic Credit and Investment.—National bank, three commercial banks, a development bank, and a government savings bank offer a wide spectrum of credit. Domestic credit totaled $89 million in May 1982.

National Budget.—Budget for 1982 shows expenditures of $191 million and revenues of $174 million.

Foreign Aid.—Official development assistance totaled $96 million in 1982.

Balance of Payments.—Reserves, including gold, were $128 million in 1982.

Economy

Largely dependent upon coffee exports; some tea and minerals production.

GDP.—$140 million in 1982.

Agriculture.—Generates about 60 percent of GDP. Coffee accounts for 80 percent of export earnings, with production 25,000 metric tons in 1982. Tea, pyrethrum, and chinchona becoming more important. Marketing and diversification of agricultural products managed by Rwandan Office of Industrial Crops.

Industry.—Little activity as yet. Beer, soft drinks, furniture, plastic tubing and utensils, and soap products are produced locally, while shoes and cigarettes receive final processing in-country.

Commerce.—Credit policies encourage small national traders. Considerable government participation. Consumer Price Index 98.9 in 1982 (average second quarter 1982=100).

Tourism.—Spectacular scenery and outstanding game parks offer major development potential.

Basic Economic Facilities

Transportation.—Network of about 1,300 miles of main roads and 2,400 miles of secondary roads. About 10,000 motor vehicles in late 1977, with new registrations about 2,000 vehicles a year.

Communications.—Government operated postal, telegraphic, telex, and international telephone service available. Local telephone system being improved, nationwide FM radio system completed in 1978. No television. Intelsat under consruction.

Power.—Consumption was 35 million kWh in 1978, much of it imported from Zaire.

Natural Resources

Land.—10,169 square miles, about the size of Vermont, landlocked between Zaire and Tanzania. Very mountainous terrain, with altitudes of up to 13,500 feet.

Climate.—Temperate because of high altitudes although the country is close to the Equator. Average annual rainfall of 50 inches occurs mainly February to May, November and December.

Minerals.—Cassiterite (tin oxide) production about 1,800 tons a year. Wolfram (tungsten ore) output 613 metric tons in 1982. Mining Code of 1974 and reforms aim to attract capital for mineral exploitation.

Population

Size.—Estimated 5.4 million 1982; Kigali, the capital, has about 90,000 people.

Language.—Kinyawanda, is the national language. French used for commerce.

Education.—25 percent literacy rate; about 10 percent of population is illiterate. Education received 22 percent of national budget in 1979, an increase of 35 percent from 1978.

Labor.—Over 80 percent engaged in agriculture or small handicrafts.

RWANDA

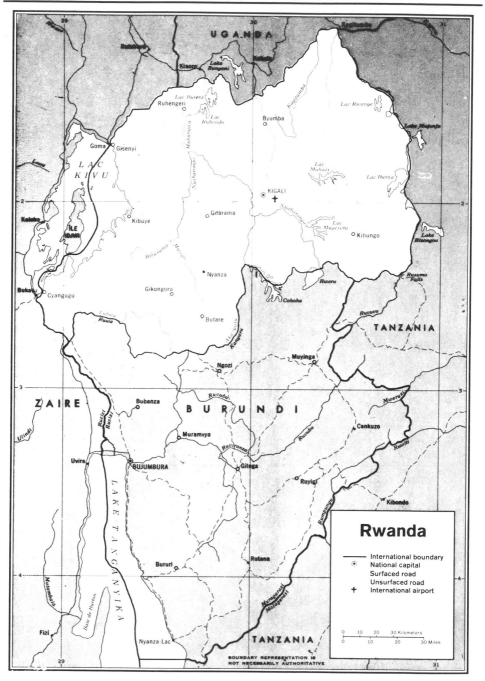

Rwanda

— International boundary
⊙ National capital
   Surfaced road
   Unsurfaced road
✈ International airport

| 0 | 10 | 20 | 30 Kilometers |
| 0 | 10 | 20 | 30 Miles |

BOUNDARY REPRESENTATION IS
NOT NECESSARILY AUTHORITATIVE

2058

Market Profile— SAO TOME AND PRINCIPE

Foreign Trade

Import.—$15.5 million in 1979; $10.1 million in 1978. Primarily foodstuffs and manufacturers. Mostly from Portugal.

Exports.—$26.6 million in 1979; $14.5 million in 1978. Principally cocoa (90 percent), coffee, palm oil, and copra. Mostly to Portugal. Trade virtually nil with United States.

Trade Policy.—Acceded to Lome Convention in 1977, ending reverse preferences to Portugal.

Foreign Investment

Investment Prospects.—Very limited. New Investment Code adopted 1981.

Finance

Currency.—Dobra (US$1=39 dobras in Oct. 1983).

National Budget.—1981 revenues, about $10 million and expenditures of about $13.6 million.

Balance of Payments.—Deficit of about $3.5 million in 1981.

Foreign Aid.—Official development assistance for 1980 is $4.4 million in 1980. The United States has supplied $300,000 for agricultural development. Arab Bank for Economic Development and African Development Bank made sizable loans in 1978.

Domestic Credit and Investment.—Central Bank and a government Savings and Loan Institute.

Economy

Dependent upon cocoa production and prices.

GDP.—About $35 million in 1980.

Agriculture.—Principal source of income and employment; largely plantation based. Cocoa principal crop; production has fallen from 10,000 tons a year before independence to about 8,000 tons in 1980. Government plans to rehabilitate 45,000 acres of cocoa estates.

Industry.—A few small-scale industries; fish and cocoa processing have greatest potential.

Commerce.—Socialist regime; Portuguese have departed. Limited free enterprise.

Tourism.—Spectacular mountain scenery. Virtually nonexistent at present but has great potential.

Basic Economic Facilities

Transportation.—International airport at Sao Tome, serviced by TAG and Air Gabon. Airport expansion to wait external financing. 288 km of roads. No railroad.

Communications.—Minimal system. Three wireless stations; 900 telephones; 1 AM and 1 FM, radio station and no TV stations.

Power.—3,000 km capacity (1980); 10 million kWh produced (1980), 120 kWh per capita.

Natural Resources

Land.—374 square miles; principally volcanic.

Climate.—Tropical; heavy rainfall, September to May.

Fisheries.—Catch, 1500 metric tons (1979 est.).

Population

Size.—85,000 (1981).

Language.—Portuguese, Crioulo.

Education.—Forty-six primary schools (10,015 students), four secondary schools (2,394 students). Literacy 5-10 percent.

Labor.—Majority of population engaged in subsistence agriculture and fishing. Skilled labor shortage.

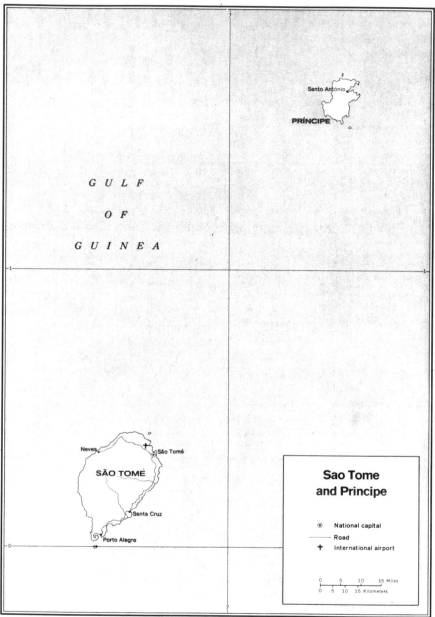

Santo António

PRÍNCIPE

G U L F

O F

G U I N E A

Neves

São Tomé

SÃO TOMÉ

Santa Cruz

Porto Alegre

Sao Tome and Principe

⊙   National capital

——   Road

✛   International airport

0	5	10	15 Miles
0	5	10	15 Kilometers

518148 8-76

Marketing in Saudi Arabia

Contents

Report revised December 1979

NOTE: Dashed lines between Israel and neighboring countries represent armistice lines. Borders are not necessarily authoritative.

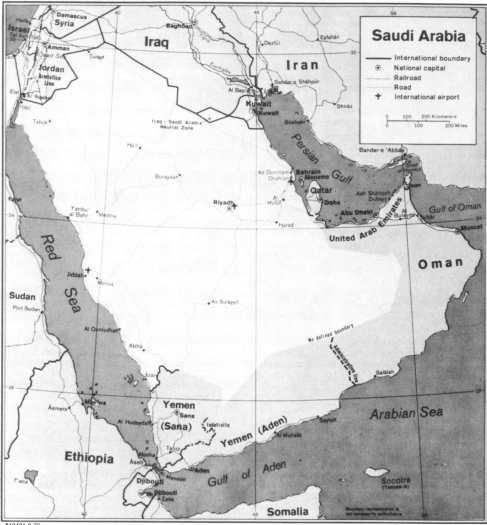

519421 9-79

Note: "Jiddah" is the Board of Geographic Names' approved spelling of Jidda. Makkah is the Board of Geographic Names' approved Arabic spelling of "Mecca."

Foreign Trade Outlook[1]

The Kingdom of Saudi Arabia was the United States' seventh largest foreign market in 1977-78 and will remain a key market for goods and services in the years ahead. Crude oil exports have provided the means by which the Saudi Government is pursuing its goals of modernizing the country's physical infrastructure, improving social services, diversifying and expanding the Kingdom's industrial sector, and encouraging private sector commercial and industrial initiatives in all fields of activity.

Trade statistics on Saudi Arabia are incomplete and vary according to source. It is believed that total Saudi imports reached $27 billion in calendar 1979, compared to $22 billion in 1978 and $17.2 billion in 1977. Imports have increased at about a 30 percent annual rate in recent years, and are expected to grow substantially in the next five years. Past restraints on economic growth, such as port congestion and inadequate infrastructure, are being eased as newly opened facilities increase absorptive capacity.

The Saudi economy is one of the strongest in the world although, as explained in succeeding sections, it remains inextricably linked to the oil sector. The sellers' market which prevailed in Saudi Arabia during 1976-77 has, however, changed to the point that Saudi and foreign observers alike note that the feeling of an unrelenting "boom period" is over. In the past 2 years the Saudi Government has taken actions to control the ill effects of the mid-1970s "boom," primarily inflation, and to channel economic growth in a more deliberate fashion.

This sophistication has changed the way business is conducted in Saudi Arabia. Saudi buyers, both governmental and private, are showing an ability to discriminate between fair and unfair bid packages. Local business and government officials demand detailed proposals and award contracts to the most cost-effective bidder. Saudis are acutely sensitive to what they consider to be overpriced bids.

They feel that foreign firms have often taken advantage of them in the past, and they will effectively shut out a company from the local market if its bids are considered unnecessarily

[1] This section was prepared by Philip Rimmler, Commerce Action group for the Near East.

Table 1. —U.S. Exports to Saudi Arabia, 1975–78
(in millions of dollars)

	1979	1976	1977	1978
Total by Trade Category	1,488.9	2,734.3	3,542.4	4,295.5
Food and Live animals	106.1	153.3	160.2	301.1
Beverages and Tobacco	18.2	21.8	68.0	93.7
Crude materials, inedibles	6.2	13.3	14.0	33.3
Mineral fuels, lubricants	13.0	18.8	20.6	37.4
Oils and fats	9.6	10.0	9.9	10.5
Chemicals	33.1	44.8	61.5	109.6
Manufactured goods	122.1	303.9	433.0	552.4
Machinery and transport equipment	927.6	1,880.9	2,101.2	2,532.5
Misc. Manufactured articles	69.8	134.1	173.1	969.4
Items not classified by kind	25.9	23.7	23.2	50.5

Major Product Exports

Rice—milled	37.0	48.8	39.7	150.1
Wheat flour	43.7	52.6	50.1	36.8
Beverages—nonalcoholic	0.3	1.1	33.9	51.8
Cigarettes	17.7	20.3	33.6	40.8
Lubricating oils and greases	9.7	16.3	17.1	35.0
Medical and pharmaceutical (prep., compounds, mixtures, etc.)	7.1	11.1	10.3	13.9
Cosmetics, toiletries exc. soaps	3.2	2.2	3.6	21.6
Chemical products, nec, incl. reagents etc.	4.6	8.9	10.11	N/A
Rubber tires	5.3	7.4	11.3	10.1
Builders woodwork and prefab. bldg.	6.9	26.3	61.4	37.0
Articles of paper pulp, paper and paperboard	2.7	4.4	5.1	5.4
Carpets and rugs	1.8	5.2	7.5	N/A
Iron and steel tube and pipe fittings	7.2	11.2	16.3	29.5
Finished struc. parts and structures, iron and steel	25.7	75.0	89.8	95.2
Engines, internal combustion, parts	13.5	28.8	47.5	60.4
Const. and mining machinery and parts	64.3	154.0	114.9	128.7
Heating and cooling machinery and equipment	58.8	117.4	178.1	200.1
Electric power machinery and parts	43.3	162.6	300.4	N/A
Telecommunications equipment	30.0	37.6	138.2	N/A
Electric household equipment, appliances and parts	14.6	30.7	37.5	58.2
Passenger cars and trucks	227.8	453.8	326.3	389.0
Motor vehicle and tractor parts, accessories	22.2	30.3	54.4	59.8
Aircraft: heavier than air	118.0	116.7	199.3	101.5
Furniture	15.4	39.5	37.9	55.2

Source: U.S. Bureau of Census, FT 450 (annual).

Table 2. —Saudi trade by major trading partners
(percentage)

Saudi Imports

	1974	1975	1976	1977
United States	21.9	23.0	18.7	22.6
West Germany	7.5	8.6	8.2	10.8
France	3.1	3.1	2.6	3.9
Japan	17.7	20.0	12.1	14.9
United Kingdom	7.3	6.7	5.9	6.4
Italy	3.0	4.9	4.8	6.8
Netherlands	3.4	2.0	3.7	.9

Saudi Exports

	1974	1975	1976	1977
United States	6.1	9.2	4.7	15.4
West Germany	6.8	5.2	3.1	4.2
France	10.1	9.6	11.5	9.5
Japan	17.5	19.7	20.0	18.9
United Kingdom	9.2	6.1	4.8	4.2
Italy	10.1	7.5	6.3	6.4
Netherlands	1.3	3.5	5.1	4.0

Source: International Monetary Fund, "Direction of Trade".

ing, plastics, rubber and chemical equipment, food processing and packaging machinery, water resources equipment including purification, distribution and recovery systems, and production process control equipment. There will be a continued need for building supplies and equipment and basic infrastructural products such as electric power generating and transmission equipment, communications equipment, and construction equipment.

Maintenance and other service industries are increasingly in demand.

Firms contemplating entering the Saudi market should familiarize themselves with local social and business customs, tax laws, agency and import regulations. A good personal relationship with a Saudi representative is a prerequisite for

costly. The mid-1970s maxim that the Saudis want and will pay for the best has been mellowed by time and experience. Saudi buyers now look not only at quality, but at the justification for high quality if somewhat lesser quality goods or services will do the job adequately at competitive prices.

Joint ventures, especially those involving the construction of a local manufacturing plant, are increasingly cost-effective methods of penetrating the Saudi market. As the Kingdom industrializes there will be increasing need for such specialized industrial equipment as metal work-

---

NEW TO EXPORT?

Many basic questions about export and overseas marketing are answered by material which appears at the end of the country-by-country market studies. Three of the information packages appearing there for the benefit of the new exporter are:

- **Basic guide to export marketing.**
- **East-west trade financing**
- **Metric laws and practices in international trade.**

Check the table of contents for page numbers of these and other special reports.

Table 3. —Saudi Arabia Trade
(in millions of dollars)
Major Markets (f.o.b. basis)

	1971	1972	1973	1974	1975	1976	1977[1]	1978[2]
U.S.	108	224	376	1,085	1,126	1,734	6,375[1]	3,791[2]
Canada	26	37	36	378	359	356	672[1]	42
Japan	509	684	1,141	4,944	5,443	7,243	7.790	5,637
West Germany	106	146	225	1,360	972	1,133	1,749[1]	992
Italy	323	506	767	3,204	2,098	2,295	2,644	1,405
France	304	419	707	3,578	3,000	4,165	3,923	2,450
U.K.	276	366	613	2,886	1,667	1,769	1,731	1,087
World	3,163	4,516	7,693	30,991	27,737	36,124	40,932	N/A

Major Suppliers (c.i.f. Basis)

	1971	1972	1973	1974	1975	1976	1977x	1978
U.S.	137	221	380	489	722	1,627	3,933	3,465
Canada	3	2	7	5	10	10	114	143
Japan	92	163	306	455	645	1,057	2,600	2,723
West Germany	64	71	124	173	289	719	1,884	1,638
Italy	36	46	53	79	164	426	1,183	1,079
France	18	26	42	51	95	233	680	682
U.K.	73	83	142	138	326	514	1,111	1,192
World	817	1,136	1,961	2,858	4,214	8,694	16,836	N/A

[1]Preliminary data.
[2]1st 3 quarters only.
Source: IMF, *"Direction of Trade"*.
x = preliminary
*1978 = first 3 quarters only

business success in Saudi Arabia, because Saudi custom stresses the binding ties of kinship, friendship and business partnership, and because government regulations maximize the business benefits to foreigners who have Saudi agents or partners.

Best Prospects

The Saudi economy's shift from a focus primarily on infrastructure to industry offers new prospects for sales of U.S. products, particularly consumer goods, business equipment, medical equipment, furniture, and semi-arid agriculture technology. Capital-intensive products such as data-processing equipment have a solid, long-term market because of the Kingdom's chronic manpower shortage.

U.S. exports to Saudi Arabia have paralleled the Kingdom's economic growth. The value of U.S. exports increased from $443 million in 1973 to $4.4 billion in 1978. While the majority of U.S. exports have been heavy machinery, construction equipment and structural materials, the pattern of U.S. exports is beginning to change along with the shift in emphasis within the Saudi economy. The growth of infrastructure-related goods is leveling-off, whereas the value of U.S. consumer goods, beverages, vehicles, furniture and chemicals shipped to the Kingdom is growing at an increasing rate. Table 1 provides U.S. export data to Saudi Arabia.

Major competitors in selling products or services to Saudi Arabia include the traditonally strong exporting countries of Japan, the United Kingdom, West Germany, France and Italy, and relative newcomers such as Brazil, Taiwan, Philippines and South Korea. The latter has been particularly successful in the construction sector in recent years.

Tables 2 and 3 indicate market shares and trade values held by leading trading partners of Saudi Arabia.

Industry Trends

GDP Movement

Since the discovery of oil in Saudi Arabia in the 1930s it has dominated the Saudi economy in terms of exports, government revenue and con-

Trade and economic statistics concerning Saudi Arabia are difficult to obtain, often dated or incomplete, and sometimes contradictory. Some Saudi Government agencies publish data by the Gregorian calendar year, others by the Muslim Hijra calendar year (which advances 11 days each year vis-a-vis the Gregorian calendar), and others by the Saudi Government fiscal year. This begins on the first day of Rajab, the seventh of the 12 Hijra months. Dates used in this report are Gregorian unless otherwise specified.

Table 4.—Saudi Arabian GDP by Economic Activity
(in millions of riyals, at current prices)*

Fiscal Years	1973		1974		1975		1976		1977	
Agriculture	1,139	2.8	1,242	1.2	1,392	1.0	1,586	1.0	1,810	0.9
Mining and quarrying										
Petroleum and natural gas	26,284	64.8	78,345	78.9	104,696	78.0	109,560	69.4	128,466	64.0
Other	90	0.2	146	0.1	248	0.2	677	0.4	1,260	0.6
Manufacturing										
Petroleum refining	1,811	4.5	4,347	4.4	5,766	4.3	5,962	3.8	6,221	3.1
Other	617	1.5	730	0.7	931	0.7	1,191	0.8	1,494	0.7
Electricity, gas and water	319	0.8	328	0.3	318	0.2	391	0.2	550	0.3
Construction	1,809	4.5	2,720	2.7	4,949	3.7	13,525	8.6	25,207	12.6
Trade, restaurants, hotels	1,544	3.8	2,355	2.4	3,045	2.3	4,940	3.1	7,952	4.0
Transport, storage and communications	2,121	5.2	2,718	2.7	3,946	2.9	5,854	3.7	8,662	4.3
Finance, insurance real estate, business services										
Ownership of dwellings	1,000	2.5	1,333	1.3	2,000	1.5	3,000	1.9	4,500	2.2
Other	523	1.3	746	0.8	1,107	0.8	1,655	1.0	2,508	1.2
Community social and personal services	339	0.8	403	0.4	523	0.4	712	0.5	918	0.5
Imputed bank service charges	−51	−0.1	−64	−0.1	−77	−0.1	−96	−0.1	−125	−0.1
Subtotal	37,555	92.6	95,349	96.0	128,844	96.0	148,956	94.4	189,423	94.4
Government services	2,533	6.3	3,490	3.5	4,990	3.7	8,271	5.2	10,613	5.3
Total GDP in producer's values	40,088		98,839		133,834		157,227		200,036	
Import duties	463	1.1	475	0.5	376	0.3	634	0.4	716	0.4
Total GDP in purchaser's values	40,551	100.0	99,315	100.0	134,211	100.0	157,861	100.0	200,752	100.0
(Equivalent in $ billion:)	(10.2)		(27.8)		(37.9)		(44.5)		(56.7)	

*In Italics, relative share of each activity in total GDP.
Source: Saudi Arabian Monetary Agency, 1978 Annual Report.

tribution to the gross domestic product (GDP). Oil has made the Saudi economy one of the world's strongest and most rapidly growing, with GDP totaling 222 billion riyals ($65.3 billion) in fiscal year (FY) 1978 (ending June 6, 1978). This represents a 25 percent increase in current prices and a 17 percent increase in real terms over the previous year.

The oil sector, including refining, contributes two-thirds of Saudi GDP. After sharp increases (peaking at 83 percent in FY 1974, following a period of oil price increases), the oil sector has returned to the reduced, but still significant, share it held earlier in this decade. It is anticipated that oil's role in the economy will not greatly expand in the years ahead because of the government's policy of restraining growth of the oil sector and promoting more dynamic activity in other areas, particularly construction and, to a lesser extent, non-oil industries. The importance of such industries is not yet reflected in Saudi Government statistics because the private Saudi/foreign joint venture factories are only now beginning to be built or enter into production.

As reflected in table 4, construction nearly quadrupled its GDP share in the three years ending FY 1977, when it accounted for nearly 13 percent of GDP. Agriculture and government services have both declined in relative importance to GDP over recent years; both were affected by heightened business activities in the

private trade and industrial areas. Real non-oil GDP increased rapidly in the mid- and late 1970s, propelled by sharp increases in government spending (averaging 23 percent annually during 1973–77) and by the private sector (up 16.2 percent annually during the same period). In Fy 1978 non-oil GDP showed a real growth rate of 17 percent (18 percent public sector, 17 percent private sector), while the oil sector actually declined by 2 percent in real terms.

Table 5 provides growth rates for various economic indicators discussed in this report. Further details are available from the Commerce Action Group for the Near East, U.S. Department of Commerce, Washington, D.C. 20230

Table 5.—Saudi Arabian Economic Indicators
(annual growth rates, in percent)

	FY 1975	FY 1976	FY 1977	FY 1978 est.
Private sector liquidity (M3)[1]	61	74	53	45
Private sector real supplies[2]	20	39	31	31
Non-oil real GDP	17	19	22	17
Private sector real imports	26	83	45	47
Non-oil GDP deflator[3]	25	52	30	18
Official cost-of-living index	35	32	11	4

[1] M3 includes currency in circulation, demand deposits, time and savings deposits, and quasi-monetary deposits.
[2] Consists of non-oil GDP plus real private sector imports.
[3] A factor used to translate current non-oil output of the economy into constant terms for year-to-year comparisons, determined by dividing non-oil GDP at current prices by non-oil GDP at FY 1970 constant prices.
Source: Saudi Arabian Monetary Agency, 1978 Annual Report.

Inflation Measures

Two Saudi Government indices measure domestic inflation rates, but neither of them is complete or fully reliable: (a) the consumer cost of living index, based on a hypothetical urban household earning SR 600–899 per month, and (b) the non-oil GDP deflator, which translates current non-oil output of the economy into constant terms for year-to-year comparisons. The latter is derived by dividing non-oil GDP at current prices by non-oil GDP at FY 1970 constant prices.

Both measures have noted strong declines in the domestic inflation rate since FY 1976 and have justified the government's efforts over the past 2 years to control costs at all levels. The cost of living index, see Table 6, registered a 4 percent increase in FY 1978 compared to 11 percent in FY 1977 and 32 percent in FY 1976. The non-oil GDP deflator also dropped considerably from 152 percent in FY 1976 to 30 percent in FY 1977 and 18 percent in FY 1978.

To such data must be added comments by Saudi officials and others who address inflation rates in specific areas. According to the Ministry of Planning, for example, construction costs in FY 1978 were up 5 to 6 percent, compared to 39 percent in FY 1977.

The Ministry of Commerce reports that in calendar year 1978 the cost of living declined by about 2 percent. Wage inflation rates apparently rose considerably last year as supply tightened after the government's crackdown on unregistered expatriate laborers and expulsion of illegal residents. Accurate data, however, are not available.

Government Budgets

Government spending under the current 1975-80 Plan has exceeded what was originally

Table 6.—Cost of Living Index

(for urban households in the income group SR 600- SR 899 per month)

Base Year 1970

Year (Weights)	Food (52.19)	Housing (24.88)	Clothing (6.58)	Misc. (16.35)	General (100.00)
1971	102.74	111.46	107.05	100.68	104.85
1972	104.44	121.55	117.55	102.89	109.32
1973	121.06	136.18	134.96	128.78	127.00
1974	142.72	189.22	152.73	138.08	154.19
1975	170.94	332.81	155.10	154.84	207.55
1976	210.28	479.80	192.51	191.03	273.02
1977	254.83	490.67	210.94	215.38	304.17
1978 3rd Q. ...	249.21	447.92	242.62	245.69	294.64
1979 est.	....	....	....	....	325.00

Sources: SAMA Annual Report 1977; Central Department of Statistics, 3rd Quarter 1978; "Saudi Business".

envisaged in 1975. Both budget allocations and actual expenditures have exceeded the planned $142 billion for the 5 year period. For the first three fiscal years, FY 1976 to FY 1978, budget allocations held steady at 111 billion riyals each year. Actual spending improved rapidly, from only 74 percent of allocations in FY 1976 to near equilibrium in FY 1978. FY 1979 saw a deficit budget, with expenditures exceeding allocations by 13 percent. Government revenues greatly exceeded spending in FY 1976 through FY 1978, but draws from reserves were necessary in FY 1979. Tables 7 and 8 provide recent budgetary data.

Of the FY 1980 budget of 160 billion riyals ($47 billion), defense spending accounts for 30 percent, transport and communications for 14 percent, other infrastructure for 11 percent, human resource development 11 percent, economic resource development 8 percent, and health 6 percent.

Development Planning

The current development plan, covering July 1975 to May 1980, is Saudi Arabia's Second Five-Year Plan. The Saudi Arabian Monetary Agency (SAMA) estimates that government expenditures during the 1975-80 period will approximate $180 billion, compared to $142 billion originally estimated when the Plan began. Fifty to 60 percent of expenditures represent project money.

The 1975–80 Plan was based on maintenance of the religious and moral values of Islam; assurance of the defense and internal security of the Kingdom; maintenance of a high rate of economic growth; reducing dependence on crude oil exports; developing human resources through education, training and health improvements; increasing the well-being of all groups within a stable society; and developing the physical infrastructure.

The Second Plan targeted a real GDP growth rate of 10 percent annually, with the non-oil pri-

Table 7.—Saudi Government Budgets, Annual Totals

(million riyals)

| | Expenditures | | Revenue | |
	Allocations	Actual	Anticipated	Actual
FY 1980	160,000	....	....	....
FY 1979	130,000	147,400	130,000	123,000
FY 1978	114,400	111,400	146,493	141,593
FY 1977	110,935	106,867	110,935	135,899
FY 1976	110,935	81,783	95,847	101,178

Note: one riyal = approx. $0.30 in 1979

Source: SAMA 1978 Annual Report; "Middle East Economic Digest;" "Saudi Business"

Table 8.—Saudi Government Budget Estimates [1]

(in millions of riyals) [2]

Fiscal Year	1976–77	1977–78	1978–79
Revenue			
Total revenue	110,935	146,493	130,000
Oil royalties	23,020	31,817	27,042
Income tax on businesses	76,854	99,337	89,492
Customs duties	500	1,000	1,400
Other	10,579	14,399	12,066
From general reserve			
Expenditure			
Total expenditure	110,935	146,493	130,000
Recurring expenditure	36,502	36,534	46,952
Project expenditure	74,433	74,866	83,048
Council of Ministers and related	4,757	4,925	4,399
Municipal & rural affairs	14,758	11,681	7,967
Public works & housing	9,061	7,857	5,649
Information	960	1,064	724
Civil aviation	4,470	4,370	3,913
Interior	3,079	3,293	3,331
Labor & social affairs	2,041	2,237	1,452
Health	1,737	1,758	1,855
Education	6,368	7,955	5,123
Communications	15,381	7,823	7,377
Finance & national economy	3,985	3,754	3,310
Industry, electricity, commerce	1,081	488	377
Agriculture & water	1,721	1,511	1,854
Public investment fund	N/A	N/A	4,000
Other	25,396	39,003	50,433
Less: expected shortfall	−20,361	−22,854	−18,676

[1] Note: According to Ministry of Finance information released in May 1979, actual revenue in FY 1979 was 132.9 billion riyals and actual expenditure was 147.4 billion riyals. The deficit was covered by withdrawals from reserves. Figures may not add because of rounding.

[2] In May 1979, US$1 = 3.38 riyals.

Source: Saudi Arabian Monetary Agency 1978 Annual Report, and news reports.

vate sector growing at a 13 percent real rate. As noted earlier, actual performance of the economy has exceeded these planned rates. Notable successes during the plan period include construction of roads, seaports and airports, initiation of a major automated telephone project, construction of schools at all levels and construction of numerous power, water desalination, and sewage plants.

Administration reforms since 1975 have allowed for creation of several autonomous government agencies to oversee key projects, such as the Royal Commission for Jubail and Yanbu. It is responsible for planning and building new cities at two new industrial complexes. Another agency, the Saudi Basic Industries Corporation (SABIC), is responsible for creating the heavy industrial facilities at Jubail and Yanbu in partnership with foreign firms. (See Appendix for list of Saudi Government agencies).

Numerous regulations have been issued, ranging from new Foreign Capital Investment Regulations, to product and testing standards issued by the Saudi Arabian Standards Organization, to new regulations for government tenders, appointment of agents bidding on government tenders, and the "Buy Saudi" program which promotes domestic industry.

The main constraint on Saudi development efforts has not been financing, but the shortage of trained, skilled manpower and managerial capability. This problem has been addressed both by a major expansion of the Saudi educational system and by increasing the numbers of Saudis in schools at all levels, and by relying to a great extent on the import of expatriate labor, skilled and unskilled.

A new 5-year plan for mid-1980 to mid-1985 is being negotiated within the Saudi Government. Although details were sketchy at this writing, broad outlines announced by Saudi officials suggested continued major expenditures probably exceeding $250 billion for the 5-year period. The plan will emphasize financing "productive" industrial and agricultural projects instead of infrastructure, which has received most funds to date.

Domestic assembly or manufacturing ventures will be encouraged, particularly for import-substituting products, and the Saudi Government intends to pursue its goal of creating major export-oriented petrochemical industries at Jubail and Yanbu. Social services are also expected to receive greater attention in the next 5 years, particularly skill training, designed to replace expatriate labor and managers with Saudis.

Industry

The industrial sector is still relatively small in Saudi Arabia. But is is growing rapidly with Government financial and administrative encouragement, such as interest-free loans for up to 50 percent of the cost of establishing manufacturing facilities and the "Buy Saudi" program under which Government procurement preference is given to Saudi-made products.

While the operative Saudi philosophy is free enterprise, the Government has taken the initiative in capital-intensive, long-term projects in which the Saudi private sector has been unable or unwilling to invest.

Two agencies are responsible for Government industrial projects: Petromin, which develops oil, gas, and minerals, and the Saudi Basic Industries Corporation (SABIC), which is responsible for all other basic heavy industries (petrochemicals, iron, steel, and fertilizer).

By 1978, according to the Ministry of Industry, some 800 private factories capitalized at $2 billion had been licensed and 1,300 factories are anticipated by 1980. Foreign capital licensed through 1977 included Saudi riyals (SR) 730 million in industry and SR 421 million in other fields. The Government is sensitive to concerns about creating "white elephant" industries relying on artificial protections and subsidies, and insists through its licensing mechanism that privately planned industrial ventures be not only profitable but practical and necessary to the economy.

Keystones of the Saudi industrialization program are two new industrial complexes being developed at Jubail on the Gulf 60 km. north of Dhahran, and at Yanbu on the Red Sea 350 km. north of Jidda. These sites are being developed by the Royal Commission for Jubail and Yanbu, an independent government agency set up in 1975. Two U.S. firms, Bechtel Corp. and Ralph M. Parsons, created the master plans and have management services contracts, respectively, for Jubail and for Yanbu. In 1979 SABIC announced that the value of its heavy industry projects in Jubail and Yanbu would exceed $9 billion. Jubail is planned to have a population of 175,000 by 1987; Yanbu will contain 75,000 inhabitants by 1984 and 150,000 by 2000.

Major facilities planned for Jubail and Yanbu include:

SABIC/Shell Pecten: 656,000 tons/year ethylene-based complex

SABIC-Dow: 400,000 tons/year ethylene-based complex;

SABIC-Exxon: 240,000 tons/year low-density polyethylene;

SABIC-Saudi Petrochemical Development Co. (consortium of 54 Japanese firms): 300,000 tons ethylene-based complex;

SABIC-Japanese Consortium (Mitsubishi, C. Itoh, W.R. Grace and others): 2,000 tons/day chemical grade methanol;

SABIC-Celanese/Texas Eastern: 2,000 tons/day chemical grade methanol;

SABIC-Korf Stahl (Germany): direct-reduced iron which with local scrap, will produce 850,000 tons/year of steel reinforcing bars;

SABIC-Taiwan Fertilizer: 1,000 tons/day ammonia and 1,600 tons/day urea;

PETROMIN-Royal Dutch Shell refinery: 250,000 barrels per day (b/d) with possible expansion to 500,000 b/d;

Petromin-Texaco-Chevron refinery: 120,000 b/d of lube base oil;

Petromin-Caltex blending plant: 500,000 barrels per year;

SABIC-Mobil: 450,000 tons/year ethylene-based complex;

Petromin-Mobil refinery: 250,000 b/d;

Petromin refinery: 170,000 b/d (under construction; scheduled for completion 1981).

Manufacturing

The largest manufacturing operations consist of hydrocarbon and cement plants, including the Aramco oil refinery at Ras Tanura (415,000 b/d capacity of crude throughout and 180,000 b/d of natural gas liquids) and Petromin refineries at Jidda (100,000 b/d) and Riyadh (20,000 b/d). The Riyadh plant is being expanded by an additional 120,000 b/d, but plans to expand Jidda's facility by 170,000 b/d were shelved in 1978 in favor of a planned new refinery at Yanbu. The Jidda petroleum complex includes a lube oil blending plant completed in 1968, producing 150,000 barrels per year, and a lube oil refinery completed in 1978, producing 1 million barrels per year of base stocks. The Arabian Oil Co. also operates a 30,000 b/d refinery at Ras al Khafji in the Saudi-Kuwait partitioned zone.

Cement plants at Jidda, Riyadh and Hofuf produced some 2 million tons in 1978. Another plant opened at Yanbu in 1978. New facilities are under construction at Jizan, Buraidah, Abqaiq and in the Saudi-Kuwait partitioned zone. Total cement consumption in 1978 is estimated at 10 million tons.

Other major manufacturing plants include: Saudi Arabian Fertilizer Co. (SAFCO) in Damman, producing urea, sulfur and sulfuric acid; Petromin's steel plant in Jidda, producing 11,000 tons of steel reinforcing bars annually (but expanding to 150,000 tons/year); Saudi Cables Co., Jidda, producing 6,000 tons annually of copper wire and cable (owned by Xenel Industries, of Saudi Arabia, Standard Oil of California and Anaconda Corp.); Saudi Automotive Industries, an assembler of Mercedes trucks, owned by Juffali and Daimler-Benz; and a joint venture between Ward Industries of Arkansas and the Saudi Research and Development Corp. (REDEC) to assemble buses near Jidda.

Under construction are a new sulfuric acid plant (100,000 tons per year capacity) for SAFCO, to start up in 1980; a 500,000-ton-per-year urea plant at Jubail by the Saudi Basic Industries Corporation (SABIC) and Taiwan Fertilizer; and a steel mill at Jubail, a joint venture between SABIC and Korf Stahl of West Germany, to produce 850,000 tons per year of reinforcing bars.

The Grain Silos and Flour Mills Organization has completed storage silos in Riyadh, Dammam and Jidda sufficient to stockpile a six-month supply of grain (80,000 tons each site) plus flour and animal feed mills with respective capacities of 540 tons and 100 tons per day at each location. A grain silo complex has also been built in Qasim.

The private manufacturing sector, in addition to the cement and vehicle assembly plants, consists of light manufacturing and processing of:

Foodstuffs: milk, fruit juice, soft drinks, pasta, biscuits, mineral water, poultry and cattle feed;

Textiles: cotton and silk textiles, towels, head scarfs, and prayer rugs;

Wood and paper: wooden doors and windows, wooden furniture, paper including Kraft bags and cardboard, paper tissues, baby diapers and feminine napkins, telex and office machine paper;

Chemicals: including oxygen, acetylene, caustic soda, hydrochloric acid, insecticides, soap, bleach, paint, adhesives, basic pharmaceuticals, tire recapping, plastic household products, containers, plastic sheets and pipes, PVC products, polyethylene products, foam rubber and fiberglass products; building materials: red bricks and tiles, cement blocks and pipes, hollow-core prestressed concrete panels, marble, prefab and precast concrete structures, gypsum;

Metal products: ironmongery, guard rails, fencing, aluminum and copper housewares, steel wool, metal office and house furniture, aluminum doors and windows, tanks for water/fuel storage, nails, tin-plate cans, barrels;

Finished products such as: desert coolers and air conditioning units, pumps, electric distribution panels, water heaters, car batteries, light poles, lamps, switchboxes, fiberglass boats, car radiators, dump truck bodies, eyeglass lenses, jewelry, traffic and road signs.

A wide range of other products has been licensed, but plants are either still under construction or in the planning stage.

Most of existing Saudi industry is located on industrial estates near Jidda, Riyadh, Dammam, Mecca and Hofuf. Other estates are planned at Jubail, Yanbu, Medina, Al Kharj and Khamis Mushait. Land and utilities are provided at nominal cost by the Saudi Government to firms in these estates.

Electricity

The electric power sector is predominantly privately-owned, although since 1976 the Government has made an effort to plan and control power development through creation of regional electrical companies and a central General Electricity Organization in Riyadh. Government loans through the Saudi Industrial Development Fund (SIDF) and the Public Investment Fund have encouraged creation of new private power companies in smaller towns as well as consolidated regional power companies in the eastern, central and northern regions. In 1978, a U.S. firm, Charles T. Main, through the aegis of the U.S.–Saudi Arabia Joint Economic Commission, completed a study of the Kingdom's electric power needs over the next 25 years which called for an eventual power capacity of 29,000 megawatts (MW) at a cost of $24 billion in 1977 values.

Current generating capacity in Saudi Arabia is about 2,400 MW; by 1982 capacity will reach 5,000 MW in the Eastern Province alone. Major desalination/power complexes under construction or planned will add nearly 4,000 MW to the Saudi power system by the early 1980s.

Relatively little attention has been paid to date to other sources of energy, especially nuclear and solar. The former is under study by the Ministry of Petroleum and the Institute for Public Administration, and the latter by the Saudi National Center for Science and Technology.

Petroleum Sector

Saudi Arabia is the world's largest oil exporter, the third largest oil producer (after the Soviet Union and the United States). It possesses the world's largest crude oil reserves. With proven reserves in 1977 estimated by the Saudi Government to be 153 billion barrels (cf. 1978 Aramco estimates of 113 billion barrels proved and 178 billion barrels probable reserves), Saudi Arabia has about 25 percent of the world's proven reserves. In 1977, Saudi Arabia accounted for about 15 percent of total world oil output and about 30 percent of output from the Organization of Petroleum Exporting Countries (OPEC).

Saudi oil production rose steadily each year until 1978 (see tables 9 and 10), when the Government imposed a maximum daily production lid on Aramco of 8.5 million barrels and limited the proportion of the more popular light (vs. heavy) crude production to 65 percent of the total. Saudi officials have indicated that the light/heavy production ratio will move from the present 65/35 ratio to a 50/50 ratio sometime in the late 1980s. During late 1978 Saudi oil production increased to occasional peaks of about 10.5 million b/d, mainly to offset declines in Iranian production. For 1979, the production varied between 8.5 and 9.5 b/d, although the official permanent ceiling remains 8.5 million b/d.

The Arabian American Oil Company (Aramco) produces about 97 percent of the Kingdom's oil. At this writing, the Saudi Government owns 60 percent of Aramco's producing assets, the remainder are held by Aramco's four original American owners: Standard Oil of California, Texaco, Exxon, and Mobil. Saudi Government takeover of 100 percent of Aramco's producing assets has been agreed in principel, although final details have not been worked out. The original Aramco partners are expected to retain a management role in its activities after the full takeover.

Two other foreign concessionnaires produce the remaining 3 percent of Saudi oil production: Getty Oil Company, which operates in the Saudi-Kuwait partitioned zone, and the Arabian Oil Company (Japanese) offshore in the Gulf.

Aramco is slowly expanding its productive capacity by 1 million b/d to reach about 12 million b/d in the mid-1980s.

Most Saudi oil production is exported, but domestic oil consumption is on the increase, estimated at 400,000 b/d in 1977 and 700,000 b/d by 1983.

Table 9.—Saudi Oil Production

(expressed as percentage share of following areas)

Year	Middle East[1]	OPEC[2]	World Excluding Sino-Soviet area	Total World
1960	24.8	15.1	7.5	6.3
1965	26.3	15.4	8.9	7.3
1970	27.3	16.2	10.0	8.3
1975	35.8	26.0	16.2	12.8
1977	40.7	29.5	18.9	14.8
1978	NA	NA	17.0	NA

[1]including Egypt but excluding other North African Countries.
[2]including present 13 members of Organization of Petroleum Exporting Countries.
Source: International Monetary Fund and Aramco.

Table 10.—Saudi Oil Production

(in million barrels)

	Total	Average daily Production
1960	481.3	1.32
1965	804.9	2.21
1970	1,386.7	3.80
1975	2,582.5	7.08
1976	3,139.2	8.58
1977	3,357.8	9.20
1978	3,000.0 (est.)	8.30 (est.)

Sources: Ministry of Petroleum and Mineral Resources; various.

Gas Program

Aramco's Natural Gas Liquids (NGL) production from gas associated with crude oil production averaged 216,100 barrels per day in 1977, for a total of 78.9 million barrels. About four-fifths of Saudi gas, produced in association with crude oil, is currently wasted by flaring.

In 1975 the Saudi Government asked Aramco to plan, design, construct and operate a program to gather and process associated gas from Aramco's concession area as the backbone of the Kingdom's long-range industrial development program. The first phase will come onstream in mid-1980, and the entire system is scheduled for completion in 1985. It will provide fuel gas for local industry, feedstocks for petrochemical plants, and propane, butane and natural gasoline (naphtha) for export. The program also includes construction (underway by the Argentine firm, Techint) of a transpeninsular 1,200 kilometer (km.) gas pipeline which will deliver propane, butane, natural gasoline and ethane to Yanbu, where it will be further processed and/or exported.

Although the program has been scaled down, total expenditures for the gas collection program may exceed $18 billion, to harness about 3.29 billion cubic feet of gas per day (worth $1.4 billion per year at 1978 prices). This is reduced from an original plan of 6 billion cubic feet/day production. The NGL center at Berri, near Jubail, came onstream in October 1977, processing 1 billion cubic feet per day. Other NGL centers are under construction at Shedgum and Uthmaniya. An NGL export terminal and gas fractionation plant is under construction at Juaymah and another is to be built at Yanbu. There are other NGL facilities at Ras Tanura and Abqaiq.

Gas reserves at the end of 1976 were estimated by Aramco to include proven reserves of 63,759 billion cubic feet and probable reserves of 113,646 billion cubic feet. About 500 million cubic feet of gas is associated with each million barrels of crude oil produced.

Agriculture

Cultivated land in Saudi Arabia totals about 525,000 hectares (ha.), or 12 percent of arable land estimates at 4.5 million ha. Approximately one-fourth of cultivated land is irrigated. The major impediment to increasing the amount of land under cultivation is scarcity of water. The country averages 10 millimeters of rainfall annually.

The Government has undertaken a program of building and rehabilitating water shortage dams, wells and drainage facilities to reduce salinity, agricultural settlement plans to encourage Bedouin settlement, and limited research, training, and agricultural extension. Cultivable land is being extended through distribution of fallow land by the Ministry of Agriculture and Water, with some 57,000 ha. distributed through 1976.

The Saudi Agricultural Bank administers a subsidy program which pays half of the cost of imported fertilizers and animal feed and 45 percent of the cost of imported farm machinery, and provides interest-free loans to Saudi farmers. Output subsidies encourage production of wheat, sorghum, rice and breeding of sheep and camels. The cost of importing dairy cattle to the farm site by air is financed by the government. Annual subsidies for imported foodstuffs and agricultural equipment exceed SR 5 billion.

Major crops include cereals such as wheat, sorghum and millet, alfalfa, tomatoes, onions, watermelons and cabbages. Cereals occupy two-thirds of cropland. Traditional date groves cover 27,000 ha. but this sector's relative importance is declining as vegetable production increases.

Production of poultry has increased sharply in recent years with 20 million chickens and 270 million eggs produced in 1976. Some 330 poultry projects have been financed by the Saudi Agricultural Bank in recent years, providing for 60 percent of poultry and 80 percent egg requirements of the Kingdom.

Imports account for 63 percent of Saudi food consumption.

Construction

Value added in the construction sector (construction of infrastruture housing, commercial and government structures) has grown 30 percent annually at constant prices during the four years ending FY 1977. More than 100,000 housing units were built by the private sector during 1976 and 1977 through Real Estate Development Fund loans. The Saudi Government was responsible for 90 percent of an estimated $18 billion in construction contracts let in 1978.

Large government expenditures have been devoted to road, airport and seaport construction, desalination/power complexes and telecommunications. Major Saudi projects currently underway include: new Jidda airport ($4 and $5 billion); new Riyadh airport (over $3 billion); new universities at Riyadh, Jidda, Mecca, Dammam and Hofuf; King Khalid Military City at Al-Batin, to house 70,000 people by 1985; a causeway to Bahrain, to cost $1 billion; a new diplomatic quarter in Riyadh for embassies and diplomatic housing, to be ready for occupancy about 1983; sports complexes in many large towns; and municipal improvements including sewers, water and drainage systems and street beautification.

Health

Several Saudi Government agencies operate or are building health facilities either for the general public or for the groups the agencies serve, including: the Ministries of Health, Education, Higher Education, Labor and Social Affairs, Defense and Aviation, Interior, Pilgrimage and Religious Trusts (Haj and Waqf), and the National Guard, the General Organization for Social Insurance, the Red Crescent Society and the Royal Diwan (Court).

Five large public hospitals built by Philip Holtzman of West Germany will become operational in 1979 at Jidda, Al Khobar, Medina, Jizan and Hofuf. Fifty clinics are under construction by Feal of Italy. By the end of 1980 the Ministry of Health is expected to contract for additional hospitals and clinics containing 6,000 beds. By 1985 all hospitals or clinics in the Kingdom are to be either new or renovated. The Ministry of Health provides interest-free loans for construction of private hospitals.

Most medical staffers in Saudi Arabia are expatriates. Only 8 percent of the 4,600 doctors are Saudi. Additional Saudi doctors and nurses are being trained, however, in three medical schools which have some 500 students.

Education

Great strides have been made in education in the past decade, with 11 percent of the Government budget ($4.5 billion) spent on education in FY 1978. In that year there were 1.2 million Saudis in 7,500 elementary and secondary schools containing 47,000 classrooms, with 58,200 teachers, and in major universities which include: University of Petroleum and Minerals, Dhahran; King Faisal University, Dammam and Hofuf; University of Riyadh and Iman Mohamed Ibn Saud University, both in Riyadh; King Abdulaziz University in Jidda and its Mecca branch (being developed as a separate institution); Islamic University, Medina; and the Government's Institute of Public Administration, Riyadh. About half of all teachers in Saudi schools are Saudi nationals; about one-third of the students are female.

In 1978 there were 3,600 adult night literacy schools enrolling 102,000 students. Ministry of Higher Education students on government scholarships abroad totaled 11,700 in the 1979 school year. Additional Saudis study abroad at their own expense or through scholarships from other Government agencies. About 11,000 Saudi students were in the United States in 1979. By 1980 the ministry expects to have produced 2,800 engineering graduates from Saudi universities, plus another 400 Saudi engineers matriculated from foreign schools. Only 15 percent are expected to practice their profession, however, because of other job opportunities.

Social Affairs

In addition to upgrading facilities at 10 vocational training schools, the Government has 15 new schools under design in a project associated with the U.S.-Saudi Joint Economic Commission. These schools train Saudi students in machine shop trades, automotive repair, welding, diesel engine repair, air conditioning and refrigeration, electricity, and plumbing.

Other agencies involved with social outreach include the Presidency for Youth Welfare, which sponsors sports teams and is constructing large sports complexes in most towns, including Olympic-sized facilities in Riyadh, Jidda and Dammam. This organization, with the municipality of Jidda, is planning major seaside recreation facilities on the Red Sea. Institutional care is provided through the Ministry of Labor and Social Affairs and other agencies for orphans, delinquents and the handicapped. Almost 100 cooperatives exist throughout the Kingdom, covering consumer, agricultural and general interests of their members.

Housing

The Government's first large public housing developments in Dammam and Jidda were to be ready for occupancy in late 1979. They consist of 32 eighteen-story buildings in Dammam and 24 buildings in Jidda. These were originally intended to house low and middle-income Saudis. However, there has been some discussion that such high rises are incompatible with Saudi traditions because of lack of privacy and private grounds. Additional public housing developments in these and other cities are being constructed as low-rise buildings.

According to the Ministry of Municipal and Rural Affairs, 114,000 building permits were issued in 1976 and 1977. It is believed that about 70 percent of private housing benefits from

financing from the Real Estate Development Fund, and the average house is 242 square meters in size. The average area of all new buildings, two-thirds of which are houses, was 400 square meters. However, data available from Dammam municipality shows that 9 percent of its building permits were for buildings averaging 4,400 square meters.

Building construction costs in 1978, according to the calculations of the Saudi Industrial Development Fund, averaged 2,548 riyals per square meter for housing and 2,112 riyals per square meter for other buildings.

According to data from all the above-mentioned sources, in recent years small towns have joined bigger cities in the building boom and increased their share of activity to 36 percent of all building construction in 1978.

Selling in Saudi Arabia

Distribution and Sales Channels

Commerce in Saudi Arabia has a long history of free enterprise. Trading was the principal economic activity before the development of the petroleum industry. Growth of the construction and manufacturing industries, which followed the income from oil revenues, was undertaken first by the traditional trading families. As the level of education and mobility has increased with the expansion, the ranks of commerce have swelled with new businesspeople and companies.

Marketing practices are becoming increasingly sophisticated in the Kingdom, both because of the influence of expatriate company managers and because of changing local tastes, perceptions and expectations. Company advertising, for example, has grown in the past few years, partly as a reflection of personal pride in one's products or services and also because it is increasingly effective. Most Saudis are general traders at heart, but some business specialization is beginning to appear.

An informal discussion of different kinds of Saudi firms follows. Many firms are a blend of these characteristics.

Commission agent, is similar to an indent agent in the Western world. They solicit orders for merchandise from Saudi merchants and arrange for their importation at a commission, usually of 5 percent. On rare occasions they stock the imported goods before selling them to retailers. They often act as exclusive agents or representatives for foreign firms in selling merchandise or services to retailers, or contractors, or directly to the Government on contract. Most commission agents work only for themselves. Some of the most successful are members of large Saudi business firms which carry on a commission agent business as an additional function of the firm.

Importer Wholesaler—One who acts as an exclusive distributor for foreign suppliers. Most wholesalers operate simultaneously as retailers. Other retailers with whom the wholesaler does business normally claim the status of "agent" or "dealer". Sometimes, they also act as subdistributors.

Travel or shipping agencies— Operate as agents of foreign transport firms, offering their services as airline booking or ticket agents and as shipping agents. They often act simultaneously as insurance agents. A number of firms included in the next category incorporate these functions within their business.

The "typical Arab trading firm."—This type of organization combines the functions of importer, wholesaler, exclusive distributor, retailer, et al. The larger trading firms often have interests in other activities such as construction, manufacturing, and shipping. They function largely as family-owned conglomerates.

Retailing is still conducted in traditional bazaars (suqs). However, the growth of new residential communities in the suburbs of Riyadh, Jidda, Al Khobar and other towns has generated modern supermarkets, shopping centers and showrooms with Western merchandising techniques.

Jidda remains the main financial, commercial, and distribution center in Saudi Arabia. However, the development of petroleum-related industries in the Eastern Province makes the Dammam-Al Khobar-Dhahran triangle perhaps the most industrialized and certainly the most American-oriented area. Most of the well-established trading firms of Jidda have opened branches in the Eastern Province. The number of new firms there is increasing. The capital of the Kingdom, Riyadh, has also become an important business center for large-scale government procurement of goods and services. Some Jidda firms have moved their headquarters to Riyadh.

Aramco

Doing business with Aramco is almost like doing business with a large American company (even though Aramco is 60 percent Saudi

Government-owned and eventually will be completely owned by the Government). As a buyer of $2.6 billion in goods and services in 1977, Aramco constitutes to some extent a separate market within Saudi Arabia for U.S. suppliers.

Aramco's procurement policy gives preference first to locally manufactured products, then to goods imported by Saudi agents/distributors of foreign suppliers, then to direct purchasing from overseas. Firms performing services for Aramco must in most cases be registered in the Kingdom by a relevant agency, generally the Ministry of Commerce.

A foreign service firm registering in the Kingdom usually finds it advantageous for tax and other reasons to do so as a joint venture with a Saudi partner. Exceptions to this Aramco requirement are few and limited to certain firms which provide services peculiar to Aramco operations and for which there is no other market in the Kingdom.

Goods procurement is the responsibility of Aramco's Materials Supply Organization. Technical experts who determine specifications of Aramco's materials are located in Dhahran. The central coordinators for Aramco purchasing are the Vice President, Materials Supply, and the Manager of Purchasing (both in Dhahran).

U.S. firms which wish to establish their capabilities and product specifications with Aramco should contact Aramco Services Co. (ASC), 1100 Milam, Houston, Texas 77002, Phone 717-651-5800, (or similar offices in The Hague and Tokyo). ASC's Purchasing Department determines that U.S. products meet normal Aramco specifications. In the case of major and specialized equipment, ASC's Project Liaison Coordinator can advise whether the products are relevant to Aramco's current needs and which Aramco projects might be able to use the product. For technical and quality determination, manufacturers of major and specialized equipment should contact the Administrator, Equipment Specialists, in the Engineering Department of ASCO. Manufacturers of unusual or technologically advanced products may find it useful, after initial contact with ASC, to discuss their products directly with engineers and end-users in Dhahran. Suppliers are encouraged to organize technical seminars in Dhahran to acquaint engineers and end-users with the firm's products or services.

Aramco's Contracting Department in Dhahran has overall responsibility for award-of-service contracts for work to be performed in Saudi Arabia. Purely out-of-Kingdom services, such as design engineering work, are procured by ASC Houston.

Competitive bidding is preferred on most contracts, although selective bids or negotiated bids directly with a single firm are also possible. Aramco contracts may be either lump sum (fixed price), unit price, or cost reimbursable.

Individual consultants may be engaged by Aramco to perform specified services of a limited duration in Saudi Arabia. Such consultants need not have a Saudi license or commercial registry.

Service firms may register with Aramco in the following steps: 1) make preliminary contact for technical quality with ASC, Houston; 2) contact ASC's Project Liaison Coordinator for applicability of the firm's services to Aramco's needs and to learn of active and proposed Aramco projects; 3) after the above steps have been taken, contact may be made with Aramco offices in Dhahran. A first point of contact is Aramco's Local Industrial Development Department (LIDD) for information on Aramco's requirements, finding a local partner, registration procedures, and aspects of doing business in Saudi Arabia; 4) if a firm decides that a market for its services exists within Aramco, it should next proceed with Saudi Government registration procedures; 5) after registration, the firm should send a letter to the Manager, LIDD, Aramco, providing information on the company and its services, including normal pre-qualification type information. Attached to the letter should be a certificate from the Saudi Government's Department of Income Tax stating that the firm's fiscal obligations have been paid; a copy of the company's commercial registration certificate; a list of names of persons authorized to sign for the company; and a copy of the company's membership papers in the Chamber of Commerce and Industry in Dammam.

Private Sector

Effective local representation is virtually essential for sales success in Saudi Arabia's private, non-oil sector. To be effective, a sales representative must be able to conduct business in the traditional, friendly, face-to-face manner which characterizes this highly personalized marketplace. This means representation not just by a Saudi, but by agents in each of the three main commercial centers of the country: Jidda, Riyadh, and Dammam/Al-Khobar. Unless distributors have active branches in all three they cannot adequately cover the market. For this reason, and because of the distances between cities, foreign firms sometimes divide their sales territories, appointing two or three distributors for the Kingdom. This is sometimes difficult, however, since most Saudi firms prefer an exclusive arrangement.

It is unwise to appoint a Saudi sales representative as a subagent to a Lebanese, Kuwaiti, or other non-Saudi commercial firm. Representatives in the Kingdom should have full agency powers with the authority to quote prices and the ability to deliver, because Saudi buyers no longer travel to Beirut or elsewhere to make purchases, as they can usually obtain their requirements from within the Kingdom. Moreover, most Saudis will reject appointment as subagents. Not only will it affront their considerable national pride, but it will also reduce price competitiveness and/or service because of the resultant commission splitting.

The capability to provide after-sales service and to maintain a stock of parts should be an important consideration in selecting an agent. The foreign firm must also support its agent for a complete marketing effort. This includes not only adequate product literature and training materials, but also frequent regular visits by the principal.

The agent or distributor should be chosen carefully. Any arbitrary effort to switch agents will be difficult once an agreement is signed, or even before a signed agreement if serious conversations may have led the Saudi to think or argue that a moral commitment to him was made. An agency agreement should specify the procedure for dissolving a relationship if it becomes necessary, including provision for compensating the old agent. It is best to sign an agency agreement for a fixed term. The Saudi business community remains close-knit through family and friendship ties, and many Saudis will not talk to a foreign firm contemplating switching agents, to avoid offending their colleagues.

While there is no requirement in Saudi law for compensating a terminated agent, Saudi courts may award compensation to terminated agents who can prove that they incurred extraordinary expenses while executing their obligations under the agreement. Since Saudi courts base decisions on the wording of the agency agreement, it may be difficult to change agents if there is no provision in the original agency agreement for doing so.

In the event of disappointment with the performance of one's Saudi agent or distributor, it frequently proves more beneficial to find ways to improve perceived weaknesses than try to terminate the relationship. Improvements may include sending technicians or marketing people to work with the Saudi firm for brief or extended periods, or bringing employees of the Saudi firm to the United States for training.

The best way to terminate an agency agreement in Saudi Arabia is through consensus, i.e., concurrence by the local agent that the two parties have no future together.

The U.S. Department of Commerce and the American Embassy in Saudi Arabia can assist in identifying potential agents or distributors through Commerce's Agent/Distributor Service. Local chambers of commerce (see list at end of this report) and commercial banks also can help.

Most foreign firms wishing to deal with the Saudi Government, whether manufacturers of goods or suppliers of services, find it essential to choose a good Saudi representative. The Saudi Bids and Tenders Law, which applies to most Government contracts, requires that bidders either reside in the Kingdom or have an agent or partner there. A 1978 decree requires foreign contractors and firms having a "consultancy" character (e.g. architects, engineers, consultants) to have either a Saudi agent or partner in order to bid on Government tenders. An October 1978 Ministry of Commerce regulation requires foreign suppliers and sub-contractors to be registered and open an office in the Kingdom when working for the Government, unless they have a Saudi agent.

A foreign company can expect a wide variety of services from its local agent. On a very basic but important level the representative will arrange for entrance visas, airline reservations, local transportation and appointments with officials during visits to Saudi Arabia by company officials. While it is possible to operate in Saudi Arabia without these services, a great deal of time and effort is usually required to accomplish relatively simple tasks.

On a higher level, a good local representative maintains close contacts with the various ministries to obtain timely information on upcoming contracts. Aggressive agents can convince officials that their principals' products or services are unique. When this is done, contract specifications can be written for a product. On the other hand, an alert agent can often spot this occurring on behalf of a competitor early enough to head it off. Basically, a good agent combines elements of public relations with information gathering. Both are essential for success in Saudi Arabia.

U.S. Corps of Engineers

The U.S. Army Corps of Engineers acts as a consultant to the Saudi Government, mainly the Ministry of Defense and Aviation, in contracting design and construction work for military installations. Annual contract awards range from $1 to $2 billion in value. On behalf of the Saudi Government the Corps contracts with architectural and engineering firms, usually American, to draw up and design specifications for these projects. After approval by the Saudi Government, the Corps issues tenders for international bid for the construction work.

The Corps has been responsible for Ministry of Defense and Aviation military cantonments at Tabuk and Khamis Mushayt and a third cantonment, King Khalid Military City, at Al Batin; the Saudi Naval Expansion Program (SNEP) facilities at Jidda and Jubail; the King Abdulaziz Military Academy near Riyadh; headquarters facilities in Riyadh; a new Saudi Arabian National Guard base to be built in the Qasim area; and other projects.

American firms must prequalify with the Corps at this address:

U.S. Army Engineer Division
Middle East (Rear)
P.O. Box 2250
Winchester, Virginia 22601
Phone: 703-667-2295, telex 89584

Construction firms must submit Form 3627 "Prequalification Statement for Prime Construction Contractors" to the above address, attn: MERPS-C, telephone extension 2179. Architect-engineering firms must submit Standard Forms 254 and 255 to the above Winchester, Va., address, attn: MEDED-MC, telephone extension 2206. Suppliers of other equipment and services must file Form SF 129 "Bidder's Mailing List Application" to the above address, attn: MERPS, telephone extension 2155. It also is recommended that suppliers obtain current lists of architect-engineers and contractors undertaking Corps-sponsored prjects, and supply them with information on products of interest.

Lists of Corps construction contract and design awards, prequalified construction contractors, and semiannual lists of future Corps projects in Saudi Arabia can be obtained from the above address, attn: MERPS-C.

Solicitations for architect-engineering services, certain supplies and other services are advertised only in "Commerce Business Daily," which may be ordered from the Superintendent of Documents, U.S. Government Printing Office,

Washington, D.C. 20402 ($105 per annual subscription). Construction and major supply and service projects are advertised in "Commerce Business Daily;" "International Construction Week," published by Engineering News-Record, McGraw-Hill Publications Co., P.O. Box 950, New York, N.Y. 10020; "Middle East Economic Digest," available from MABCO Inc., 61 Broadway, Suite 1400, New York, N.Y. 10006; and "Middle East Trade Letter," available from Airport Office Center, P.O. Box 3444, Charlotte, N.C. 28203.

Some relatively small projects also are awarded by the Corps' office in Saudi Arabia to local contractors. U.S. firms interested in smaller contracts and which are affiliated with Saudi companies should contact the Corps of Engineers Division Office, P.O. Box 2959, Riyadh, Saudi Arabia, phone 22346, 67017, for prequalification information.

U.S. firms bidding on Corps' projects are subject to Saudi regulations, including those providing preference to foreign firms if they have a Saudi agent or partner. The Corps accepts surety bonds in lieu of bank guarantees to cover bid and performance bonds on Saudi projects.

U.S.-Saudi Arabian Joint Commission for Economic Cooperation

The Joint Commission was established in 1974 to promote bilateral cooperation in industrialization, trade, manpower training, agriculture, and science and technology. A government-to-government program, the Joint Commission has signed several important supply, consulting, design and installation contracts with private U.S. and Saudi firms and constitutes another potential institutional market for U.S. goods and services.

Programs under the Joint Commission include agriculture, water resources and land management, development of the Asir National Park, vocational training and construction of training centers, statistics and data processing, electricity, desalination, consumer protection services, highway transportation, solar energy research, customs administration and training, and cooperating with the Saudi Arabian National Center for Science and Technology. Other programs under consideration may cover municipal water systems, meteorology and environment protection, health manpower development, and technical assistance to Saudi universities and other governmental institutions.

Further information on the Joint Commission for Economic Cooperation is available from the Office of Saudi Arabian Affairs, Room 1446, U.S. Department of Treasury, Washington, D.C. 20220, phone 202-566-8371.

Pricing and Terms of Payment

There are no price controls on imports into Saudi Arabia, apart from those on basic foodstuffs and certain building materials mentioned below in the Trade Regulations section. Saudi businesses generally prefer c.i.f. quotations, or c. and f. when the importers arrange insurance on their own.

Payment is typically by letter of credit, or even by cash in advance. Increasingly, however, some suppliers have begun to sell by draft and occasionally by open account. This is obviously risky unless the customer is well known to the seller and has proven reliability. There have been extreme instances where buyers have obtained documents from the local bank, and title to goods on the dock, before making payment to the bank.

Japanese sellers, and some European firms, are well known for their willingness to offer attractive time draft terms, extending for as much as two or three years. U.S. firms generally have been unable to offer more than 180-day terms.

The Export-Import Bank of the United States, 811 Vermont Ave., N.W., Washington, D.C. 20571, telex 89-461, phone 202-382-8400, and the Foreign Credit Insurance Association, (FCIA), One World Trade Center, 9th Floor, New York, N.Y. 10048, phone 212-432-6311, can help U.S. exporters cover the risk involved in lengthening their credit terms. A similar private organization is the Private Export Funding Corporation (PEFCO), 280 Park Ave., New York, NY 10017.

Import Subsidies

The Saudi Government directly subsidizes certain imports to mitigate the effects of imported inflation on consumers. Subsidized products include certain basic foodstuffs, pharmaceuticals, and some building materials such as cement and reinforcing bars.

The subsidies are paid directly to importers and operated in conjunction with wholesale and retail price controls on affected commodities. The system operates as follows: First, ceilings are set by the Government on retail prices. The subsidy then is determined and paid to the importer by calculating the difference between landed costs and the fixed price ceiling, with an allowance for profit of generally 10 percent. Costs are considered to be c.i.f. plus unloading, port charges and letter of credit costs. For some items, costs of warehousing and inland freight can also be included. The permitted profit margin on some products is higher, for example for cement it is 25 percent.

Other subsidy programs exist such as those of the Saudi Agricultural Bank, which pays directly to farmers and fishermen 45 or 50 percent of the landed costs of imported farm machinery, fertilizers, animal feeds, and fishing equipment. It also covers full air freight costs for imported dairy cattle, and provides subsidies per kilogram of grains or per head of sheep and camels to encourage domestic production.

Licensing, Leasing and Franchising

No specific regulations govern licensing, leasing or franchising agreements in Saudi Arabia. Payments of fees and royalties can be freely transferred abroad (see Section on Industrial Property Protection for information on patents and trademarks). Potential licensees and franchisees can be identified through the same methods described above for agents. In addition, periodic lists of Saudi entrepreneurs and industrialists who are contemplating new industrial ventures for which licensed technology may be desired are available from the Directorate General for Industry, Ministry of Industry and Electricity, Riyadh, or as loan copies from the Commerce Action Group for the Near East, U.S. Department of Commerce, Washington, D.C. 20230.

The terms of agreements between U.S. and Saudi parties for licensing, leasing or franchising can be set privately, but they should be complete and in writing. In the event of legal redress, the written agreement between the two parties forms the primary basis on which Saudi courts will judge the issue. There is no requirement that leases of personal property be registered. Under Saudi Arabia's religious-based (Shariah) law, the lessor would retain title to leased property during the lease period. Rental income from leased property is subject to Saudi income tax. Leased equipment may be imported into Saudi Arabia duty-free on a temporary basis. Customs duties must be paid upon entry but will be reimbursed if the leased property is reexported within six months (extendable for another six months). If the equipment is held in Saudi Arabia longer than 12 months, customs duties will be refundable only if the property is being used by a government agency and prior arrangement on this subject has been made.

Government Regulations

A 1962 royal decree restricts the operation of commercial agencies to Saudi nationals and wholly Saudi-owned companies. Non-Saudis may not import goods into the Kingdom for resale. In addition, the Bids and Tenders Law requires that bidders who win government contracts either reside in the Kingdom or have an agent there.

All agents, as well as all business enterprises, both Saudi and foreign-owned, must be registered in the Commercial Register of the city in which they are located within 1 month of establishment. These registers are maintained by the local Commercial Register Offices of the Ministry of Commerce and Industry in Jidda, Riyadh, Dhahran, Dammam, Al-Khobar, Medina, Mecca, Taif, and Jizan. The registers contain information on the range of the company's activities, managerial staff and capital holdings, as well as judgments filed against a company, such as bankruptcies. The fee schedule includes a 100 SR annual charge per registration.

Certain documents (e.g. articles of incorporation or by-laws) required for registration may have to be authenticated by a foreign company's home government. U.S. firms seeking to establish themselves in Saudi Arabia must have these documents notarized, certified by the county clerk and stamped with the state seal by that state's secretary of state. Documents so stamped should be sent to the Authentications Office, Room 2813, U.S. Department of State, Washington, D.C. 20520, phone 202-632-0406. The state seal will then be authenticated by the U.S. Department of State at a cost of $3 per document.

Government Procurement Practices

The Government's system for bidding and contracting is set out in numerous regulations and decrees, supplemented by interpretations or rulings on individual cases issued by the Ministry of Finance and National Economy. Key regulations include: Royal Decree M/6 (Tenders Regulations) published 8/3/1386 on the Muslim Hejira calendar, or 1966 in the Gregorian calendar; Royal Decree M/14 dated 7/4/1397 (1977) and the related Ministry of Finance Resolution No. 3131/97 dated 5/5/1397 (1977), entitled Rules for Implementation of Tenders Regulations. Decree M/14 supercedes M/6 in the event of any contradictions. The essence of these regulations is summarized below.

There is no central procurement office. Each ministry or autonomous agency can contract directly with suppliers, within the framework of the general tender regulations. (See Appendix for list of ministries and major agencies).

Direct, negotiated purchases are permitted in the following instances according to M/14, if the total value is less than one million riyals: machinery and equipment of various kinds, foodstuffs, construction works, operation and maintenance works, well drilling, consulting, spare parts of all kinds, and armaments.

For all contracts exceeding one million riyals in value, government agencies must solicit bids from at least three firms (five bids are required for construction work).

Bids are opened in public and a committee of three or more persons from the Ministry of Finance or from the government agency concerned with the project reviews the bids and awards the contract by majority vote. The award will normally go to the company with the lowest bid which meets the specifications. Negotiations take place only if all the bid prices are significantly higher than what the Saudis determine to be the market price of the project or if the conditions put forth by the lowest bidder are unacceptable.

Until now, firms wishing to submit proposals for projects in Saudi Arabia have been required to make themselves known to each ministry undertaking the work on which they wish to bid. Construction firms have been required in addition to register with the Ministry of Public Works and Housing (MPWH).

The Saudi Government recently began compiling a central list of foreign construction firms, including joint ventures, in which Saudi participation is less than 50 percent. All Government agencies can use the list to choose companies to bid on projects. The first list was published in October 1977 and will be periodically updated. Firms wishing to register must present a completed questionnaire (in Arabic and English), a copy of their latest annual report, two references, two copies of a list of completed projects, and a copy of two recently signed contracts to: Contractor's Classification Committee, Non-Saudi Contractors Division, Ministry of Public Works and Housing, Riyadh, Saudi Arabia, Attention: Director Abdullah Khanhal. Firms are classified as specializing in any or all of several categories.

In normal practice, a ministry undertaking a project will have a consultant draw up tender documents with the specifications against which the invited firms must bid. On small projects, turnkey proposals may be requested which will require an offer for the complete facility, including the training of personnel to operate it. On the large industrial and infrastructure projects, the contracts for the master plan, detailed engineering and management of construction may be awarded to separate firms. Often the companies which have performed the consulting and design phases of the project are not allowed to participate in its construction. The construction manager is usually required to provide for operational management and personnel training following construction.

The Saudi Government is required by law to give preference in awarding contracts to Saudi companies or joint-ventures with more than 50 percent Saudi participation. Foreign firms are awarded contracts only when a qualified Saudi company cannot be found. All bidders are required to have local addresses to which notices can be sent. This requirement can be met by establishing an office in Saudi Arabia or by using the address of a local agent or representative.

Local representation is required of all foreign companies, except consultants bidding on Government projects. In practice, a Saudi representative or joint venture partner is highly desirable and even essential to maintaining the contact with Government officials necessary to receive advance notice of upcoming projects and to ensure that the firm is placed on the bidders' lists. A competent local representative can also explain the highly technical goods or services a firm might be offering that are unfamiliar to the Saudi client, as well as ascertain and communicate to the firm how it might prepare a proposal to fit Saudi requirements, Since the bid specifications can be very general, too many U.S. companies have submitted proposals using state-of-the-art technology only to find themselves underbid by third-country firms offering less complex and less expensive facilities better suited to Saudi requirements.

In short, the Saudis do not want the best that money can buy if it is inordinately costly.

Performance Requirements.—The Saudi Government requires bid and performance bonds from most foreign firms of 1 percent and 5 percent, respectively, of the value of the contract. The bonds must be cash, a certified check drawn on a local bank, or a bank guarantee payable on demand. About 45 foreign banks, including some U.S. banks, are authorized to act as direct guarantors, though each guarantee must be approved by a bank in Saudi Arabia acting as the agent of the foreign bank. Unconditional surety bonds will be accepted as guarantees if they are payable on demand, issued by an approved U.S. surety company, and cover at least 25 percent of the value of the contract. The Saudi Government has published a list of acceptable insurance firms, and the limits which each insurance company may underwrite.

The performance bond is not required for consulting work, for the supply of spare parts, nor for contracts which the Government awards by direct purchase contracts of less than SR 1 million in value and do not have to be tendered. The performance bond is reduced on operation and maintenance contracts as work progresses on the project. However, it cannot go below 5 percent of the value of the uncompleted work.

The bid bond is always required. It is returned automatically to the bidders when the period specified in the tender announcement for the bids to remain open expires. The performance bond is generally due from the winning bidder within 10 days after notification of the award. It is returned to the contractor on completion of the project, though the contractor remains liable for the collapse of a structure and other defects for 10 years (unless the structure was not meant to last 10 years).

The Saudi client may make an advance payment of 20 percent of the cost of the project at the signing of construction contracts, although this is subject to negotiation. The advance must be backed by the contractor with a bank guarantee of an equal amount. Though this is sometimes referred to as a suicide bond, most contractors accept the payment and earn interest on it during the time between the contract signing and the start-up of work. The Government will also pay up to 75 percent of the value of construction materials when they are imported, if they are stored in a way that will avoid damage and deterioration. The Government will make progress payments of up to 90 percent of the work completed. The remaining 10 percent is held pending final delivery of the project or may be paid against bank guarantees as work progresses. However, Saudi companies and joint ventures in which the Saudi partner holds at least 60 percent of the capital will be paid in full for work completed without the requirement of submitting a bank guarantee.

The Saudi Tender Regulations allow for delays or default in completion of work due to *force majeure*, and clauses can be put in the contract to specify *force, majeure*. Labor strikes are not considered *force majeure* nor are delays due to port congestion, if these can be anticipated. A Saudi lawyer versed in the Shariah law (canonial law of Islam) should be employed to negotiate a *force majeure* clause.

Arbitration.—Contracts always include a provision for settling disputes. Most Governments agencies are prohibited by the tenders regulations from agreeing to international arbitration. Both public and private organizations strongly prefer to resolve commercial disputes through personal contacts and negotiations or through the Saudi arbitration system. Grievance boards have been established for settling commercial disputes with Government agencies. The decision of the boards can be appealed to the Shariah court. The Saudi Council of Ministers has been known to get involved in major disputes. Settlement out of court, careful drafting of contracts including provision of clauses which define procedures for dispute resolution, and use of private arbitration are recommended instead of going to court.

Arabic is the official language in Saudi Arabia, but English is widely spoken and understood. The Tender Regulations say that bids may be in any language, and in practice the tender announcement for each project generally specifies the language of the bid. English is used in most of the major contracts. However, any documents concerning the formation of a joint venture and representation or agency agreements must be in Arabic to be legally binding.

Price.—The Saudi Government has required fixed price, lump sum bids for almost all contracts, even those for services extending over a period of many years. New regulations allow cost-plus-fee contracts only for project management. Escalation clauses are known to have been negotiated in at least two contracts, both for the construction of large facilities. In one case, an escalation clause allows a price increase of 25 percent over 4½ years. In the other, changes in the price of specified items will be reflected in changes in the total value of the contract. The Tender Regulations allow price increases for changes in transportation charges, insurance rates, or in raw material prices. However there must be a limit to the increase and it must be approved by the Council of Ministers. The regulations also allow contractors to claim compensation for factors beyond their control, including costs incurred due to the Government's alleged failure to make decisions on time. Getting the supplementary payments can be a difficult process.

Foreign companies have sought to insure themselves against losses by making worst-case bids which in turn push up bid prices uncompetitively. In an effort to stop this practice, several ministries have cancelled bids when the prices have greatly exceeded the cost estimated by Government consultants. The Government is expected to continue to insist that the bid prices come reasonably close to its own estimates.

Equipment and Materials.—Most contracts provide for the importation of supplies, machinery and equipment duty free. However, the Government may recommend that equipment and material be purchased from Saudi dealers where possible. In these instances, the Government will not reimburse the dealer for duties already paid on stocked goods.

Used machinery does not have to be re-exported and re-exportation of trucks and other vehicles in working order is forbidden. There is heavy demand in Saudi Arabia for all types of construction machinery and equipment. It has a high attrition rate, however, due to the climate and the inexperience of operators. Most contractors, therefore, write off the costs of the equipment imported for construction projects.

"Standard Boycott Language in Contracts."—On January 21, 1979 the Ministry of Finance and National Economy issued Circular Note No. 17/11901 dated 12/7/98 A.H. to all Saudi Government ministries and agencies. It provides a standardized English-language text concerning the Kingdom's economic boycott against Israel. This text must be included in all contracts signed by Saudi Government agencies with foreign, particularly American, firms

The effect of this Circular Note is to permit American firms to sign Saudi Government contracts with language acceptable both to U.S. export administration regulations and Saudi regulations. However, receipt by U.S. firms of this text is reportable under the U.S. Export Administration Regulations.

The text of the Circular Note follows:

"1) In connection with the performance of this contract, the second party (contractor/supplier) specifically acknowledges that the import and customs laws and regulations of the Kingdom of Saudi Arabia shall apply to the furnishing and shipment of any products or components thereof to Saudi Arabia. The second party (contractor/supplier) specifically acknowledges that the aforementioned import and customs laws and regulations of the Kingdom of Saudi Arabia prohibit, among other things, the importation into Saudi Arabia of products or components thereof: (1) originating in Israel; (2) manufactured, pro-

duced or furnished by companies organized under the laws of Israel; and (3) manufactured, produced or furnished by nationals or residents of Israel.

"2) The first party (the Saudi Government agency concerned) in its exclusive power, reserves its rights to make the final unilateral and specific selection of any proposed carriers, insurers, suppliers of services to be performed within the Kingdom of Saudi Arabia or of specific goods to be furnished in accordance with the terms and conditions of this contract."

"Buy Saudi" Program.—Several regulations require foreign contractors to "buy Saudi" when local manufactures serve a similar purpose, even if they are of a higher price or lower quality than similar imports (the price/quality differential is stated to be 10 percent in the Tenders Regulations). Council of Ministers Resolution No. 1977 dated 17/11/1396 (1976) states: "Technical departments in ministries as well as consultants working for the government are hereby obligated to give priority to the products of Saudi industry in their specifications as long as the said products are satisfactory."

A related Council of Ministers 24851 dated 5/10/1397 (1977) states: "All contracts and agreements concluded between the government and companies executing governmental projects must contain a clause prohibiting (contractors) from establishing any manufacturing units of any size without a prior license from the Ministry of Industry and Electricity.

Furthermore, to protect the public interest, such companies are required to make maximum use of locally manufactured goods." Council of Ministers Resolution 377 dated 18/4/1398 (1978) states: "The Ministry of Industry and Electricity shall prepare every 6 months lists of locally manufactured goods suitable for government projects, having first ascertained the availability, quality and fair price of such goods . . . . All governmental contracts shall contain a clause obligating contractors to purchase the locally manufactured goods in the lists . . . . These contractors are prohibited from importing goods similar to those in the lists."

In August 1978, the Ministry of Commerce notified foreign companies operating in the Kingdom that they should obtain their supplies of consumer and food products for their own employees' consumption from the local market through Saudi agents rather than import such products directly. The Ministry of Commerce reportedly instructed Saudi customs officials to prohibit the entry of any consumer or food products that may be imported by foreign firms for their own use.

Advertising and Market Research

In the past 2 years printed advertising as a sales promotion tool has become quite popular in Saudi Arabia, a distinct contrast with years past when the primary form of advertising was oral—through personal contacts and the "grapevine." Key newspaper and business weeklies which accept advertising are listed below. All have Kingdom-wide coverage, except as otherwise indicated. Both Arabic and English ads should be considered; the former to appeal to most Saudis and the latter to attract attention of foreign managers of Saudi companies.

Direct mail is another useful advertising medium. One U.S. firm in 1977 discovered a little-used Saudi postal regulation which allows for special, low-cost bulk mailouts. After much negotiation on the spot, this firm was able to get permission to stuff every mailbox in major city post offices, without addressing the envelopes. In most cases, however, the use of post office box numbers is necessary.

English Language Media

Arab News (daily)
P.O. Box 4556,
Jidda
Telex: 401570 ARANEWS SJ

(Maintains U.S. offices at 2100 West Loop South, South Suite 1650, Houston, TX 77027 Phone: 713-961-0245)

Saudi Business (weekly) published by Arab News

Saudi Gazette (daily)
P.O. Box 5941
Jidda
Phone: 32166, 46283, Telex: 401360

Saudi Economic Survey (weekly)
P.O. Box 1989
Jidda

Saudi Review (daily)
P.O. Box 2043
Jidda

Arabic Language Media

Al-Jazirah (daily)
P.O. Box 354
Jidda

Ar-Riyadh (daily)
P.O. Box 851
Jidda

(Both the above newpapers reach government officials and have national distribution)

Okaz (daily)
P.O. Box 1508
Jidda

Al-Madina (daily)
P.O. Box 807
Jidda

An-Nadwa (daily)
% Mecca Establishment for Printing
Jidda

Al-Bilad (daily)
c/0 Al-Bilad Establishment for Press
Jidda

Al-Yawm (weekly)
P.O. Box 565
Dammam

Saudi Trade Post (monthly)
Mecca

Umm al-Qura (official gazette)
Mecca

(This is the official government gazette which publishes government regulations, details of newly registered companies and tenders)

The only other method of advertising in Saudi Arabia is the placement of signs along streets and roads, or attached to streetlight posts.

There are no public theatres and advertising is not permitted on public radio and television.

There is one permanent exhibition hall in Jidda which can be considered for displays of equipment by U.S. firms. Contact: A. Harithy Establishment, P.O. Box 6249, Jidda, phone 58149, telex 401103 SJ. Short-term production promotions and demonstrations at the U.S. Commercial Center in Jidda can be arranged by contacting the American Embassy's Commercial Section.

There are several Saudi market research companies. These include Saudi Research and Marketing Co., which publishes *Arab News* (see address above); Tihama for Advertising, Public Relations and Marketing Studies, P.O. Box 5455, Jidda, phone 22132, telex: 401205 TIHAMA SJ; Al Harithy; Saudi Advertising International, P.O. Box 6557, Jidda, phone 50830, telex: 401008 GAC SJ; and a Cypriot/Saudi joint venture, Riyadh P.O. Box 5978, Magherbi Bldg., Jidda, phone 38626.

Advertising firms include Saudi Research and Marketing Co., Tihama, Saudi Advertising International (addresses noted above) and the following: Raed Marketing & Advertising, P.O. Box 1076, Jidda, phone 59782; Marwah Company for Public Relations, Advertisement, and Distribution, P.O. Box 3029, Jidda, phone 57908, 676100; Bronze Establishment for Advertising and Publicity, P.O. Box 1518, Jidda, phone 42428, 48936; Al Madina Press Establishment, P.O. Box 807, Jidda, phone 72208, 71009; Farougui Agency for Trade and Publicity (signboards), P.O. Box 592, Jidda, phone 48401; Commercial Intermediary, P.O. Box 235, Jidda, phone 29277, 29288; National Information Advertising Agency, P.O. Box 2021, Jidda, phone 24810; Neon Abu Hassan (neon and other signs and calligraphy), P.O. Box 1057, Jidda, phone 42503, 44915; Transworld Publicity, P.O. Box 1482, Riyadh, phone 36898, 38465, telex: 201654 TRANS SJ; Arabian Public Relations Agency, P.O. Box 1249, Riyadh, phone 62588, 25831; Dar Al Manar for Information Services, P.O. Box 2325, Riyadh, phone 24739; National Press Agency, P.O. Box 3182, Riyadh, phone 28103; National Advertising Agency, P.O. Box 3434, Riyadh, phone 31275; and Tayer Agency, P.O. Box 2899, Riyadh, phone 27964.

According to a 1977 survey conducted in the Gulf countries, the most widely read regional business magazines circulating to key business and government readers include: Alam Attijarat (26 percent of respondents read it), Al Iktissad Al Arabi (14 percent), Business Week and Alaam Al Idarah (12 percent), the Economist (11 percent), Middle East Economic Digest and the Middle East (9 percent each). Others include International Management, Financial Times, Middle East Trade, Al Idari, Middle East Construction, Construction Today-Middle East, Modern Government, and Near East Business.

Credit

Banking is regulated by the central bank, the Saudi Arabian Monetary Authority (SAMA). There are 12 private commercial banks with 110 branches in the Kingdom. Some are still completely foreign-owned although the policy of Saudization of foreign banks is expected to be extended to them all in the near future. Major local banks include: National Commercial Bank, Riyadh Bank, Bank al-Jazira (with Pakistani interests), Al-Bank Al-Saudi al-Hollandi (partly owned by Algement Bank Nederland), Al-Bank Al-Saudi Al-Fransi (partly owned by Banque de l'Indochine et de Suez), and Al-Bank Al-Saudi Al-Britani (partly owned by British Bank of the Middle East). Banque du Caire and Citibank, the only U.S. commercial bank with offices in Jidda and Riyadh, are expected to complete Saudization soon. First National Boston Bank has a management contract with National Commercial Bank and Credit Lyonnais with Riyadh Bank.

Other foreign banks include Arab Bank, Banque du Liban et d'Outre Mer, Bank Melli Iran and the United Bank of Pakistan.

There are also private or mixed investment banks which finance new agriculture or industry projects. One such institution, partially owned by Chase Manhattan, is Saudi Investment Banking Corporation, P.O. Box 3533, Riyadh, phone 60532, telex: 201170 SIBCORP SJ, with a branch at P.O. Box 5557, Jidda, phone 56741, telex: 401413 SIBJED SJ. Others include First Arabian Corporation, P.O. Box 1313, Jidda, phone 34561, telex: 401235 su, and Saudi Arabian Investment Co., P.O. Box 2096, Jidda, phone 33689, telex: 401211 SAICO SJ.

Private money-changers are also important sources of day-to-day banking and foreign exchange transfers on the part of Middle Eastern residents of Saudi Arabia. Largest of these is Al-Rahiji Company for Currency Exchange and Commerce, which has paid-up capital of SR 600 million.

Commercial bank loans are given mainly for international trade financing, although increased emphasis is being placed on the needs of domestic businesses. Citibank, for example, offers business loans for up to 10 years. Because the lack of exchange controls permits free entry and exit of capital, the local cost of money is in large measure influenced by international rates.

Insurance Programs

The Export-Import Bank of the United States (Eximbank), 811 Vermont Ave. N.W., Washington, D.C. 20571, phone 202-566-8096, and the Foreign Credit Insurance Association, One World Trade Center, 9th Floor, New York, N.Y. 10048, phone 212-432-6300, offer a wide range of credit insurance and guarantees for exports to Saudi Arabia. Eximbank also offers a U.S. Contractors Guarantee Program which insures U.S. contractors against the risks of inconvertibility, confiscation, war and failure by the client to honor an arbitration award or comply with an agreed dispute-settling mechanism.

The U.S. Overseas Private Investment Corporation (OPIC), 1129 20th St., N.W. Washington, D.C. 20527, phone 202-632-9646, also provides political risk insurance for bid and performance bonds and advance guarantees which may be required by Saudi Government clients.

Other Sources of Capital

There is no stock exchange or capital market in the Kingdom. However, several government financial institutions offer credit facilities for a variety of domestic and foreign undertakings. U.S. firms, as partners with or suppliers to Saudi firms, can take advantage of some of these additional resources.

Saudi Industrial Development Fund, P.O. Box 4143, Yamama St., Riyadh, phone 33755., 33710, 33703, 33745, telex: 201065 SIDFUND SJ., Established 1974, has a capital of SR 3 billion for industrial projects and another SR 19 billion for electricity projects. Provides medium or long-term loans for up to 15 years at 2 percent to new, expanding industries for up to 50 percent of the capital requirement. Saudi/foreign joint ventures qualify for consideration if Saudi equity in the project is at least 25 percent of the total.

Saudi Arabian Agricultural Bank, Omar bin Al-Khattab Street, Riyadh, phone 39303, 23934, 23911. Established 1963, capital of SR 1.4 billion, provides loans or grants for agricultural or fishing projects including equipment, fertilizers, seeds, and livestock. Implements government subsidies to farmers. Since establishment, the bank has issued 113,000 loans to Saudi farmers. Its FY 1979 budget is SR 1.2 billion.

Real Estate Development Fund, Airport Street, Riyadh, phone 33500, 33523, 33927, 33737. Established 1974 to finance private sector housing and hotel/apartment construction: capital SR 33 billion. Provides interest-free loans to Saudi citizens of up to 70 percent of the cost of housing (maximum varies between SR 100,000 and SR 300,000 depending upon location) or up to 50 percent of construction costs (maximum SR 10 million) to Saudi firms.

Credit Fund for Contractors, Riyadh. Established 1974, capital SR 450 million, assists Saudi contractors (which may include Saudi/foreign joint ventures if Saudi equity is at least 60 percent of the total) by providing interest-free loans for purchase of equipment and building materials.

Public Investment Fund, Riyadh, phone 401–2666, established 1971, capital SR 11 billion. Finances commercial and industrial projects of government corporations such as Petromin, Saudia, or the electricity or desalination companies, and takes equity in mixed government/

private industrial companies such as Saudi Arabian Fertilizer Company, Maritime Company for Petroleum Transport or the Arab Shipyard Co.

Saudi Credit Bank, Riyadh, phone 29128, 29625, established 1973, capital SR 110 million, loans funds to low-income Saudi citizens for home repairs, medical treatment, weddings, and opening workshops or small businesses.

General Organization for Social Insurance, Riyadh. Established 1969. As the Government's social security fund, GOSI invests its funds in public companies and is a source of industrial finance.

Saudi Fund for Development, P.O. Box 5711, Al Washem Street, Riyadh, phone 36600, 38268, 69200, established 1975 as the Government's agency for lending to developing countries. Infrastructure, agriculture, health and education projects receive priority treatment. By the end of 1978, SFD had committed more than $3 billion in 130 loans to 50 countries in Asia and Africa.

Two other international financial institutions headquartered in Saudi Arabia are sources of finance in other countries:

Islamic Development Bank, P.O. Box 5925, Jidda, phone 33994, 33995, telex: 401137 BISLAMI SJ. Established 1975. Consists of 33 Muslim countries with an authorized capital of $2.4 billion. Provides loans, guarantees, foreign trade financing, leasing, and equity investment to the most needy in its member countries.

Arab Petroleum Investment Corporation, P.O. Box 448, Dhahran Airport, phone 43883, 43411, 44663, telex: 671009 PETMARK SJ ATTN APIC. Established 1976 with authorized capital of SR 3.6 billion, provides finance for the petroleum and related industries with an emphasis on joint ventures in Arab countries.

Another financial institution which assists foreign firms trading with or investing in the Middle East is the *Saudi International Bank*, London, established 1975 with capital of 25 million Pounds Sterling. The Saudi Arabian Monetary Agency is principal shareholder with the remainder held by several private banks including National Commercial Bank, Riyadh Bank, Morgan Guaranty Trust Co., and others.

Transportation and Utilities

Ports and Shipping

Saudi Arabia's two major general cargo ports, which together account for 90 percent of all cargo entering the Kingdom by sea, are Jidda on the Red Sea and Dammam on the Gulf. Both government-run facilities include container terminals and bulk cement terminals. Both are in the midst of major expansion programs. At the end of 1978 Jidda had 31 berths and Dammam 28, due to be expanded to 45 and 40, respectively, by 1981. Other ports which will assume greater relative importance include Jubail commercial port on the Gulf (10 berths in 1978, expanding to 16), Jubail industrial port, whose first two berths were planned to open in late 1978, with 15 berths plus a separate container terminal; and Jizan (Gizan) on the Red Sea in the southwest near Yemen, which had four berths in 1978. Total functioning Saudi sea berths were 82 at the end of 1978, with a throughout capacity of over 20 million tons. Additional ports are open at Ras al-Mishab and Rad Al-Ghar on the Gulf and Qadima north of Jidda.

Many U.S. shipping lines offer direct and transit service to Jidda and Dammam, including Waterman Steamship Corp., Central Gulf Lines, Seatrain, Sea-Land, Barber, Costa/Saudi National Lines, and others. Some 100 shipping lines call at Saudi ports.

Transit time from the U.S. to Jidda is about 15 days.

Shipping costs average $4,400 per 40 foot container from the United States to Saudi Arabia: breakbulk cargo costs between $60 and $75 per measurement ton.

Airports, Airlines, Air Couriers

There are three international airports: Jidda, Dhahran, and Riyadh, but only the national carrier, Saudia, calls at Riyadh. All three airports are undergoing major expansions. Jidda's new $6 billion airport (to be opened in phases between 1979–82) will be the biggest in the world when completed. Ralph M. Parsons/Daniel Joint Venture of the United States is supervising construction; Hochtief of West Germany is prime contractor. Bechtel is planning the new Riyadh airport which will exceed Jidda's in eventual size. A new Eastern Province airport designed by a U.S. firm will be located between the present Dhahran facility and Jubail.

Pan American Airways and Saudia presently operate a joint service between New York and Dhahran. Foreign carriers which serve Jidda or Dhahran include Alitalia, Air France, British Airways, Lufthansa, Middle East Airlines, Iran Air and many others. Saudia, which has a modern fleet of Boeing and Lockheed aircraft, flies to major European, North African, Arab and South Asian cities. TWA provides technical assistance to Saudia.

Air courier service between the United States and Saudi Arabia is an increasingly common way private U.S. firms send important packages with tight delivery dates. U.S. firms which operate to Saudi Arabia include DHL, Calico Air Courier Service and Air Courier International.

Domestic Transportation

Modern paved highways link nearly all settled towns at present. The amount of paved roads in 1978 totaled 19,000 km.; another 3,700 km. are under construction and 10,600 km. under design. Italian, Taiwanese and Saudi firms have landed most road projects. It is possible to drive on paved roads from Jordan either southeast along the Tapline to Dhahran, thence to Riyadh, or south to Jidda and Abha on paved roads. The Jidda-Riyadh road is also paved. Inland transport costs average as follows: Dammam-Riyadh, 461 km., $16 per measurement ton (MT); Jidda-Riyadh, 1,075 km. $37/MT; Jidda-Abha, 720 km., $50/MT.

Almost 300,000 commercial and passenger vehicles have been imported into Saudi Arabia each year from 1976–78, producing a total of more than 1 million registered vehicles. More than half of recent imports are Datsun or Toyotas. In 1978 a Mercedes truck assembly plant and a bus assembly plant opened in the Jidda area.

A semi-public Saudi National Transport Co. is in the process of establishing an inter—and intra-city bus service throughout the Kingdom. It is managed by an American consortium, ATE/DMJM.

The Saudi Government Railroad Organization operates a 380-mile standard-gauge track between Dammam and Riyadh, passing through Hofuf and Al Kharj. This line is being upgraded and may be rerouted. There are also several major rail projects in various stages of study, including reconstruction of the old Hejaz railroad from Damascus through Jordan to Medina, Yanbu and possibly Jidda; and the extension of the Dammam-Riyadh line to either Medina/Yanbu and/or Mecca and Jidda.

Power and Water

Electric power is generated by about 60 private electric power companies, whose numbers and investments have greatly expanded in the past 3 years along with demand and favorable government financing. The General Electricity Organization, a Government corporation under the Ministry of Industry and Electricity, was set up in 1976 to oversee national electrical planning and to consolidate the mostly small private power companies into regional grids, such as SCECO in the Eastern Province and new consolidated companies established in 1979 in the south (linking Abha, Jizan and Baha) and center (linking Riyadh and Qasim).

The largest existing private power companies include Saudi National Electric Co., Riyadh; Saudi National Co. for Electric Power, Jidda; and Saudi Electric Co., Jidda (covers Mecca and Taif). Power is available at fixed rates of SR .07 per Kwh for household and SR 0.5 per Kwh for industrial users. The Government makes up the difference and guarantees the power companies a 15 percent annual return on investment.

All the above thermal power units, whose total capacity was 2,400 MW in 1978, will be supplemented by the power facilities associated with large water desalination plants planned and under construction by the government's Saline Water Conversion Corporation, Riyadh.

Thus far, power capacity from desalination plants totals 330 MW in Jidda and 10 MW in Al Khobar. Plants under construction will add 500 MW in Jidda, 250 MW in Medina/Yanbu, 500 MW in Al-Khobar and 1,350 MW at Jubail by the early 1980s.

Although each municipality maintains its own electric current characteristics, the various systems are being integrated and standardized on 60 cycles, 127/220 volts. Major towns not yet on this standard include Hofuf, Buraidah, Mecca and Taif (they are on 50 cycles). Plugs are of the continental round 2-pin type although many electrical outlets also accept standard-type flat-pronged plugs.

By 1985, according to the Saudi Government, Western Province towns will require 194 million gallons per day (mgd) of potable water, of which half will be desalinated; Riyadh and the Central Province will consume 239 mgd, two-thirds from desalination, and the Eastern Province, 110 mgd, three-fourths from desalination.

Water rates for domestic and industrial consumption are subsidized by the government. The official charge is SR 0.25 per cubic meter from city water sources. However, sometimes municipal sources are curtailed because of insufficient supplies, and private suppliers are permitted to charge whatever the market will bear.

Trade Regulations

Trade Policy

The trade policy of Saudi Arabia is liberal and free-enterprise oriented. There are no exchange restrictions and few limits are imposed on trade. This situation has resulted from the coincidence of an ample supply of foreign exchange, a stable currency, and an economy still largely dependent on imports for development.

Nevertheless, certain imports are prohibited, including alcoholic beverages and pork products. Saudi Arabia prohibits trade with South Africa. It also participates in the Arab League economic boycott against Israel. Not only does Saudi Arabia prohibit direct trade with Israel, but it also subscribes to the secondary boycott against third-country firms found to have certain economic relationships with Israel. In general, normal trade dealings are unaffected by the boycott, and many U.S. firms successfully sell to both Israel and Saudi Arabia.

It is the policy of the U.S. Government to oppose restrictive trade practices or boycotts fostered or imposed by foreign counties against other countries friendly to the United States. The Export Administration Amendments of 1977 (Public Law 95–52) and the U.S. Department of Commerce's implementing regulations (Export Administration Regulations, 15 C.F.R. Part 369) prohibit certain forms of compliance with foreign boycotts including furnishing information or entering into or implementing agreements. Violators of the U.S. anti-boycott law are subject to severe penalties including fines, imprisonment, and revocation of export license privileges. U.S. exporters are required by law to report to the U.S. Department of Commerce any request for action in support of such restrictive trade practices or boycotts in accordance with Section 369.6 of the Export Administration Regulations. Reporting forms (ITA–621P or ITA–6051P) may be obtained from the Office of Export Administration, U.S. Department of Commerce, Washington, D.C. 20230.

U.S. exporters should also familiarize themselves with anti-boycott provisions of the Tax Reform Act of 1976, administered by the U.S. Treasury Department. Violation of Treasury anti-boycott regulations risks tax penalties rather than criminal prosecution. These tax penalties can extend to business operations in non-boycotting countries.

The U.S. Department of Commerce seeks to minimize the adverse impact on U.S. trade of foreign boycotts and other restrictive trade practices by furnishing information and assistance to U.S. firms directly affected. In addition to reporting such requests, as noted, firms confronted with boycott problems may wish to discuss them with the Commerce Action Group for the Near East.

Import Tariff System

Saudi Arabia's latest (June 1977) tariff book classifies goods according to the unified nomenclature of the Arab League, which is essentially the international Customs Cooperation Council Nomenclature (CCCN), formerly Brussels Tariff Nomenclature (BTN), system.

More than half of all items are exempted from customs duties entirely, including most equipment needed for development projects. Nearly all the remaining items are dutible at 3 percent *ad valorem*.

Some locally produced products have a protective duty. Following is a list of these products with protective duties of 20 percent unless otherwise specified.

Candy, sweets, and chocolate
Tahini
Ice cream
Biscuits (10 percent)
Mineral water
Macaroni
Marble, decorative stones, dolomite and quartz
Gypsum (SR 150 per ton)
Gasoline and kerosene (SR 0.16 per liter)
Oxygen and acetylene
Soap powder
Plastic foam
Plastic bags
Plastic bottles and other products
Paper towels and handerchiefs
Paper bags and boxes
Prayer carpets
Red ghotras (men's head covering)
Cotton towels
Tents (10 percent)
Tiles (floor and gypsum titles)
Glass bottles
Metal tanks and barrels, less than 300 liters capacity,
Extruded aluminum bars, rods, angles, shapes, and sections
Wheelbarrows
Metal shelves
Aluminum utensils
Water heaters
Furniture, of any material
Plastic pipes and sheets
Bleach and dry-powdered soap
Desert coolers
Plaited ropes (10 percent)
Paints (10 percent)

Imports of machinery, spare parts, and raw materials by approved industrial enterprises (both foreign and domestic) may be exempted from customs duties.

Preferential duty treatment is given to member states of the Arab League who are signatories to the Agreement to Facilitate Trade and Exchange and to Organize Transit between the Arab League States.* The agreement provides for duty-free entry of certain nonindustrial goods and a 25 percent reduction in the duty on some industrial products produced in signatory states. In addition, further duty reductions are accorded to imports from Arab States with which Saudi Arabia has concluded bilateral trade agreements. Tariff rates on individual commodities may be obtained from the Commerce Action Group for the Near East, U.S. Department of Commerce, Washington, D.C. 20230.

Duties are assessed on the cost, insurance, and freight (c.i.f.) value or, in the case of specific rates, on the metric weight of the product. The unit of currency is the Saudi riyal (SR3.36=US$1)

Special Customs Provisions

Entry and Reexport

All imported goods are deposited at Saudi Government customs warehouses or at other places within the port area. There are no private warehouse facilities. Goods deposited remain the sole responsibility of the shipping companies until received by the customs agent. After clearing customs, the goods become the responsibility of the importer. At no time will the customs authorities assume responsibility for the goods. Goods not claimed within 15 days are subject to public auction.

Port stevedoring is the responsibility of the Port Authority, and unloading fees, which vary according to the type of cargo, are fixed by the Government. The Government monopoly in this field has been successful in reducing the anarchy which prevailed until 1977 in Saudi ports, and has helped clear previously congested ports.

Goods in transit are not subject to customs duties. However, the shipping company must notify customs of all goods to be transshipped

---

*Iraq, Jordan, Lebanon, Syria, Egypt, Yemen Arab Republic and Saudi Arabia.

and the word "Transit" must be marked on each package and on the bill of lading and invoice accompanying the goods. A regular customs declaration must be completed when transshipment is delayed. Storage fees are collected after 10 days for warehoused goods and after 2 days for goods in transit, and porterage fees are charged.

Reexport of goods is possible but officially discouraged. The consignee must prove that the goods do not conform in quality to those ordered or that there is no market demand for the goods. Reimbursement of duties is difficult. Because of problems encountered in the past, many banks will not finance reexports.

Foreign-made items may be sent abroad for repair and reimported duty-free provided that they are registered with customs beforehand.

Commercial samples not suitable for sale are exempt from duties. Other samples are dutiable; however, duties of less than 50 Halala (about 15¢) are not collected. The duties collected on commercial samples imported for display for periods of up to 6 months (renewable for additional 6-month periods) are returned when the samples are reexported. Jewelry and watch samples are subject to a non-refundable 3 percent duty.

Factory advertising materials, excluding printed and illustrated calendars, imported for display only are exempt from duties of less than SR50. Duties exceeding this amount must be paid. All catalogs and brochures for which no charge is made are duty free.

Advance Rulings

No facilities are available for advance rulings on customs classification.

Fines and Penalties

Consignees not satisfied with the assessed valuation or penalties imposed may appeal to the Director General of Customs.

No special judicial process is followed for the recovery of confiscated goods. Anyone disagreeing with the customs may appeal to the Ministry of Finance and National Economy, Directorate General of Customs.

Shipping Documents

Documents required on all commercial shipments to Saudi Arabia are: commercial invoice, certificate of origin, bill of lading or air waybill, packing list, and, if shipment is insured by the exporter, an insurance certificate. In the case of letter of credit payment terms, the Saudi Government also requires a special shipping certificate (see Saudi Letter of Credit Requirements).

Commercial Invoice

Four notarized copies of this document are required: one for retention by the certifying chamber of commerce and three to be presented to the Saudi Consulate; two copies are returned to the shipper. Prices stated on the invoice must be certified by a relevant chamber of commerce then presented to a Saudi Consulate in the United States for "legalization." Sometimes, but not always, the Saudi consular official requests that the U.S. Department of State authenticate these documents before the Saudi Consulate will legalize them. Generally this is required only for documents such as power of attorney, affidavit, free sale certificate, price list, and company registration documents. One should be guided by the dictates of the Saudi Consulate.

If the Saudi Consulate requires U.S. Department of State authentication, the documents should be presented to the Authentications Office, Room 2813, U.S. Department of State, Washington, D.C. 20520, phone 202-632-0406.

All commercial invoices must be prepared on the letterhead of the company preparing the invoice. Merchandise should be described specifically and in full and, on shipments by sea, should indicate the name of the vessel and date of sailing. The invoice also must contain the following information (although sometimes the Saudi Consulate will accept certain of the data from the packing list instead): full, specific description of the goods, trademarks, quantity and price of each type of goods, number, volume and weight of goods, contents of each container, and itemized list of expenses, discounts, names and addresses of consignee and consignor. The commercial invoice, like the certificate of origin, should preferably indicate that the products being shipped are of U.S. origin and they have been manufactured in the United States. The copy of the commercial invoice to be retained by the chamber of commerce must contain the following affidavit:

I, (name, title, name of company), hereby swear that the prices stated in this invoice are the current export market prices and that the origin of the goods described herein is the United States of America, and I assume full responsibility for any inaccuracies or errors therein.

Certificate or Origin

A certificate of origin is to be issued by the supplier or exporting company and authenticated by the exporting country, attesting that the goods exported to Saudi Arabia are of indigenous origin, and stating the name of the factory or the manufacturing company. To the extent that the goods as described in the certificate of origin are not exclusively products of their country of origin indicated thereon, a declaration must be appended to the certificate of origin giving the name of the supplier/manufacturer and declaring:

"The undersigned, _____, does hereby declare on behalf of the above-named supplier/manufacturer, that certain parts or components of the goods described in the attached certificate of origin are the products of such country or countries, other than the country named therein as specifically indicated hereunder:

"Country of origin and percentages of value of parts or components relative to total shipment: _____." (notarized)

It is the U.S. Department of Commerce's position that furnishing a positive certificate of origin, such as the one stated here, falls within the exception contained in Section 369.3 (b) of the U.S. Export Administration Regulations for compliance with the import and shipping document requirements of Saudi Arabia.

Four notarized copies of this document also are required: one for the chamber of commerce and three for the Saudi Consulate, which retains one and legalizes and returns two to the shipper. The certificate of origin should also include the name of the ship and the date of sailing if goods are being shipped by sea.

Exporters from New York must have the commercial invoice and certificate of origin certified by the U.S.-Arab Chamber of Commerce, Inc., One World Trade Center, Suite 4657, New York, NY 10048, phone 212-432-0655; exporters from Illinois must use the Mid-American-Arab Chamber of Commerce, 135 South La Salle St., Suite 2050, Chicago, IL 60603, phone 312-782-4654; exporters from Texas must use the American Arab Chamber of Commerce, 319 World Trade Building, Houston, TX 77002, phone 713-222-6152; exporters from California must use the U.S.-Arab Chamber of Commerce, 230 California St., Suite 201, San Francisco, CA 94111, phone 415-397-5663. Exporters from other States can use any of these listed or any other recognized chamber of commerce.

Packing List

This is required for customs clearance at the port of entry in Saudi Arabia. It should describe accurately and in detail the contents of each case or container, giving the net and gross weight and the c.i.f. value.

Arrangement of Documents

Shipping documents must be presented to the Saudi Consulate in this manner: set one: shippers documents must be stapled and marked "return to shipper"; set two: Consulate's copies must be stapled together and marked "Consulate's Set."

Consular Fees

The Consulate fee for legalizing documents is $2 for the first page and 40 cents for each additional page per document. The fee for "legal documents" is $1.60. Legal documents include power of attorney, trademarks and the like. Before the latter documents will be legalized by the Sauid Consulate they must first be authenticated by the U.S. Department of State's Authentications Office.

The State Department requires these steps before it will authenticate documents: (a) documents must be notarized, (b) a clerk of court must certify the notary seal, (c) the Secretary of State of the exporter's State must certify the legitimacy of the clerk of court seal. Cost of State Department authentication: $3 per document.

Saudi Letter of Credit Requirements

In February 1978 the Ministry of Commerce issued a memorandum which established standard requirements for certificates of origin, insurance and ship certificates in all letters of credit issued by Saudi banks. A copy of the text of the Ministry's memorandum is available from the Commerce Action Group for the Near East, U.S. Department of Commerce, Washington, D.C. 20230.

Bill of Lading or Air Waybill

This should agree with the invoice and show gross weight, volume, measurement, marks and name/address of consignee and telephone number of consignee (all in Arabic if possible). Marks and numbers should agree with those on the invoice and containers.

Insurance Certificate

A certificate must be appended to the insurance policy stating: (1) name of insurance company; (2) address of its principal office; and (3) country of its incorporation, and declaring:

"The undersigned, _____, does hereby certify on behalf of the above-named insurance company that the said company has a duly qualified and appointed agent or representative in Saudi Arabia whose name and address appear below: _____."
(Notarized)

It is the U.S. Department of Commerce's position that the insurer itself may certify that it has a duly qualified and appointed agent or representative in Saudi Arabia, and may furnish the name and address of the agent or representative. Furnishing such a statement pertaining to one's own status offends no prohibition under the U.S. Export Administration Regulations.

Shipping Certificate

A certificate must be appended to the bill of lading stating: name of vessel, its nationality of registry and owner, and declaring:

(A) "The undersigned does hereby declare on behalf of the owner, master, or agent of the above-named vessel that said vessel is not registered in Israel or owned by nationals or residents of Israel and will not call at or pass through any Israeli port enroute to Saudi Arabia.

(B) "The undersigned further declares that said vessel is otherwise eligible to enter into the ports of Saudi Arabia in conformity with its laws and regulations." (Notarized)

It is the U.S. Department of Commerce's position that furnishing a certificate such as the one set in paragraph (A) above, falls within the exception contained in Section 369.3 (b) of the U.S. Export Administration Regulations for compliance with the import and shipping document requirements of Saudi Arabia. With regard to paragraph B, it is the U.S. Department of Commerce's position that the owner, charterer, or master of a vessel may certify that it is "eligible" or "otherwise eligible" to enter the ports of Saudi Arabia in conformity with its laws and regulations. Furnishing such a statement pertaining to one's own eligibility offends no prohibition under the U.S. Export Administration Regulations.

However, it is the U.S. Department of Commerce's position that furnishing such a certifica-tion (which does not reflect customary international commercial practice) by anyone other than the owner, charterer, or master of a vessel would fall within the prohibition set forth in Section 369.2 (d) of the U.S. Export Administration Regulations unless it is clear from all the facts and circumstances that the certification is not required for a boycott reason.

Special Requirements

Plants and plant material must be accompanied by U.S. Government Federal Phytosanitary Certificates or the goods will be refused entry. All shipments of plants will be inspected upon arrival in Saudi Arabia, with costs to be borne by the importer. Soil, sand and specified plant pests are prohibited. Plant propagative materials such as cuttings, seedlings, and bulbs, must be shipped in peat moss certified to have been sterilized by the country of origin. Firms which wish to ship plants in artificial materials other than peat moss should verify in advance from the Director, Plant Protection Branch, Ministry of Agriculture, Riyadh, that the artificial material will be acceptable.

Fresh or frozen meat or poultry must be accompanied by a certificate stating that it has been slaughtered in accordance with Muslim Law.

The Ministry of Health requires that imported pharamaceutical and medicinal products be accompanied by a certificate of "free sale" accepted and stamped by the Consulate General. The certificate may be obtained from the Commerce and Industry Association of New York. Commercial quantities of used clothing not accompanied by a disinfection certificate must pass through the local quarantine station.

Parcel-post packages, including air parcels, sent to Saudi Arabia may not weigh more than 22 pounds and may not exceed 42 inches in length or 6 feet in length and girth combined. These must be accompanied by two U.S. Customs declaration tags (Form 2966), an international parcel post sticker (Form 2922), and a dispatch note (Form 2972). Air parcels require, in addition, two air mail labels (one for the parcel itself and one for the dispatch note). Parcel post packages may not be registered or insured. Sealing is optional.

"Small-packet" mail may not exceed 2 pounds, 3 ounces and must be accompanied by a label (Form 29760) indicating that the packet is to be submitted for customs inspection. A customs declaration (Form 2876-A) may be enclosed if the mailer prefers not to list the contents on the label.

Merchandise cannot be sent by letter mail. The export or import by mail of bank notes and coins inside personal letters or packages also is prohibited. Printed matter, including catalogs up to a weight of 6 pounds and 9 ounces and books in packages up to 11 pounds may be sent by mail. Letters, "small-packet" mail, and printed matter can be registered but not insured.

Dogs are prohibited entry.

Persons wishing to bring animals into Saudi Arabia should check the latest regulations. If permitted, animals must be accompanied by a veterinary certificate showing vaccination against rabies and distemper.

Marking and Labeling

The containers of imported products should be marked with the gross weight and with either the initials or the name of the consignee. If the consignment includes two or more containers, they should be consecutively numbered. Imported flour must have the packing date clearly stamped on the container.

The price of imported pharmaceutical products must appear in Arabic on each article.

Food labeling regulations since 1976 require that certain items have Arabic labeling of product name, common or usual product name, list of ingredients, net contents (in metric units), name and address of the manufacturer, packer or importer, date of production or its code number, country of origin. The expiration date should be included on spoilable items.

The original list included: edible oils and fats, all milk, cream, juices, tomato paste, tea and coffee extracts.

Fifteen additional product categories were added in September 1978: noodle products, honey, jam and marmalade, tomato products, hummus (garbanzo beans) in cans, halava or tahini, tuna, mackeral, processed cheese, broad beans, green beans, bottled water, salt, green peas, all processed meats, and soups. Separate stick-on labels are acceptable. It is anticipated that other products will gradually be added to this list.

All goods consigned to Saudi Arabia should be packed to withstand rough handling, extreme heat and high humidity, and to afford protection against pilferage. The precautions are necessary because many shipments from the United States to Saudi Arabia are transshipped en route.

Boxes should be waterproofed inside and out and double strapped with metal bands. Simple crating of merchandise does not give sufficient protection from weather and possible careless stevedoring.

Positive color tones to Saudis: bold red, blue, black, black offset by white, and soft brown and green. Colors such as pink, violet and yellow have negative impact in Saudi Arabia. Human figures shown on packages, if any, should be in good taste.

There should be no Koranic or Islamic sayings written on packages, other than straight translations where needed of product contents, and photos or illustrations of pigs or wrappings simulating pigskin should be avoided.

Saudis like pictorial, pastoral scenes on packages such as mountain scenes, streams, or farms. Reusable bottles or tins have appeal.

Senate Concurrent Resolution 4, adopted July 30, 1953, invites U.S. exporters to inscribe, insofar as practicable, on their external shipping containers in indelible print of a suitable size: "United States of America."

Nontariff Import Controls

Import Licensing

Saudi Arabia imposes no quantitative restrictions and few licensing controls on commercial imports. Cigarettes, tobacco, tombac, jurak, cigarette paper, drugs and medical supplies may be imported only by persons licensed to deal in these products. Imported hunting arms require prior licensing. Other arms, ammunition and war material may be imported only by the Saudi Government.

Export Controls

Export licenses are not required; no control is exercised over export proceeds. All exports to Israel, and South Africa and the reexport of certain imported items benefiting from Government subsidy are prohibited.

The export or reexport of certain goods in short supply was prohibited effective June 1976.

These include: camels, cattle, sheep and poultry (live or slaughtered); all kinds of subsidized foodstuffs (rice, flour, sugar, milk powder, vegetable oils, ghee for cooking, locally produced grains, eggs, tea, coffee and cardamon); chemical fertilizers except for locally manufactured fertilizer, (after permission of the Ministry of Agriculture and Water and after refund of any subsidy already received); feeds and fodder; date palm saplings, except with permission of the Ministry of Agriculture and Water; subsidized medicines; cement; detergent and Clorox; spare parts of motor vehicles, agricultural and construction machinery and equipment, and Toyota motor vehicles; gasoline and by-products, diesel oil and motor oils and lubricants; antiques and works of art, except with permission of the Antiquities Department of the Ministry of Education.

Investing in Saudi Arabia

Investment Climate

The Government of Saudi Arabia encourages private direct investment from the United States and other countries, particularly in capital-intensive and high-technology fields. While the Saudis have ample funds to finance their development programs themselves, they see foreign capital participation in both private and semi-public ventures as a way to ensure that projects are soundly designed and managed. Although there is no minimum foreign equity required for Saudi joint ventures, the Government encourages a more-than-normal investment as evidence of the foreign partner's commitment to developing the country.

The Saudi Government has articulated a free-enterprise investment policy favoring diversification away from the still predominantly oil-based economy, increasing the national productive capacity at competitive costs, widening and deepening the Kingdom's access to modern technology, and skill-training of Saudi citizens to reduce its dependence upon expatriate labor.

A 1974 industrial policy statement issued by the Council of Ministers notes:

"Businessmen who are prepared to take their risks of success and failure, motivated by prospects of profits, will enjoy the full support of the government during all stages of preparation, establishment and operation of industrial projects which are beneficial for the Kingdom. The Government is also ready to supplement the efforts of businessmen in the private sector by establishing, financing and participating in the management of large industrial projects requiring wide technical experience and which the private sector cannot undertake alone. The govern-

ment considers that competition serving the interests of local consumers is the best means of influencing the business community in the industrial field toward beneficial manufacturing projects which suit market requirements, for encouraging low cost production and for fixing fair prices for both consumer and producer. However, the government will not permit harmful foreign competition, such as dumping."

The Foreign Capital Investment Regulations issued in January 1979 (revising similar 1964 regulations) accord foreign investors the same protections given to Saudi investors under the 1962 Regulations for the Protection and Encouragement of National Industries. The latter supports private investors with tax incentives, tariff protection and financial and technical assistance The Foreign Capital Investment Regulations guarantee foreign investors the freedom of capital flows and equal treatment with Saudi businessmen. Foreign capital is defined to include money, bonds, machinery, spare parts, raw materials, means of transport, patents, trademarks, and other values owned by an individual or corporate entity of non-Saudi nationality.

Ministry of Industry and Electricity Resolution 323, dated May 7, 1979, provide rules for implementation of the 1979 Foreign Capital Investment Regulations.

Government incentives offered to potential investors include: (1) inexpensive land (SR 0.08 per square meter annual rent) and utilities (power costs SR 0.05 per Kwh and water SR 0.25 per cubic meter) at industrial estates outside major cities; (2) financing from the Saudi Industrial Development Fund (up to 50 percent of the venture's capital requirements at a 2 percent annual administrative fee); (3) a tax holiday of 10 years for approved industrial or agricultural ventures and 5 years for other approved ventures; (4) the possibility (but not assurance) of special tariff protection (up to 20 percent duties imposed on competing imports); (5) customs exemptions for raw materials and capital goods used in manufacturing; (6) a 10 percent price and quality preference in government procurement.

Petroleum and mineral projects are not covered by the above regulations and operate, instead, on the basis of separate concession contracts.

In February 1975 the Ministry of Agriculture and Water published a statement on the government's agricultural policy which extends the same guarantees and concessions to foreign investors in agricultural and agribusiness projects which are available to industrial investors. In addition, the statement outlines the services and infrastructure the ministry will provide to investors, such as water for irrigation, land, research, and subsidies.

Certain sectors of the economy are reserved for local ownership. Foreigners cannot own land except as follows: A Saudi-registered company including foreign equity can buy land needed for the business and residences of personnel; certain arable land may be distributed to non-Saudis by the Ministry of Agriculture and Water, with concurrence by the Ministry of Interior, subject to the "Regulations for Distribution of Uncultivated Land". Also, Arabs from other Gulf states can own land on a reciprocal basis. Other exceptions to the policy on land ownership may be authorized by the King. Retail and wholesale trade is restricted to wholly Saudi-owned firms. The Saudi Government has required that private banks be owned 60 percent by Saudi citizens, and the Government (as noted earlier in this report) is negotiating an amicable settlement with the four U.S. Aramco partners to take full control of Aramco's producing assets.

The Saudi Government participates in industrial ventures either as sole partner with foreign investors, as is the case with petrochemical and hydrocarbon projects involving Petromin or SABIC, or as one among many investors in joint stock comapnies such as the Saudi Arabia Fertilizer Co. or the several cement or electricity companies.

Several government institutions have been established to assist in industrial development. The newly-created Saudi Consulting House, which replaces the Industrial Studies and Development Center, is charged with performing feasibility and other consultative studies for the Saudi Government and private sector. It is unclear whether the new organization will retain all the functions of its predecessor agency. The U.S. firms, Arthur D. Little and Leo Daly, won technical contracts to work with the Saudi Consulting House.

The Public Investment Fund and the Saudi Industrial Development Fund provide financing for investment projects in the Kingdom (see section on Credit).

Investment Application Procedures

Investment application forms for all ventures other than petroleum and minerals can be obtained from the Foreign Capital Investment Office, Ministry of Industry and Electricity, Riyadh. Required information must be submitted to this office, which then forwards it for approval by the Foreign Capital Investment Committee. This committee is composed of the Deputy Minister of Industry and representatives from the Ministries of Finance and National Economy, Agriculture and Water, Commerce, Planning, and Petroleum and Minerals. The committee's decision on each investment application is determined by majority vote which must be approved by the Ministry of Industry and Electricity. The process of seeking investment approval takes 6 to 12 months.

For manufacturing projects these documents must be submitted to the Foreign Capital Investment Office:

a) Application to the Foreign Capital Investment Office;

b) A statement describing how the project is to be financed and the total capital;

c) The project's estimated annual production capacity;

d) A feasibility study covering the technical, financial and economic aspects of the project (with Arabic translation);

e) Proposed plan for technical and managerial training of Saudi personnel;

f) If foreign patents are to be used, a certificate authorizing their use;

g) The contract between the Saudi and foreign partners;

h) Contracts for the purchase of machinery and equipment for the project, or correspondence concerning the acquisition of such machinery along with details as to whether the contract includes its installation and startup;

i) In the case of projects to produce medicines, the approval of the Saudi Ministry of Health;

j) Power of attorney authorizing the person submitting the application to submit it and pursue it on behalf of the partners;

k) Authenticated documents showing the activities and experience of the foreign partner (annual reports are acceptable) and important projects executed by the foreign partner in and outside the Kingdom;

l) The resolution of the board of directors of the foreign partner authorizing participation in the investment project in Saudi Arabia;

m) An authenticated certificate of incorporation of the foreign company in its country of origin (with Arabic translation);

n) A document specifying the facilities and support which the foreign company would render to the Saudi venture;

o) Address of the foreign partner;

p) In addition to these, the Saudi partner must supply documents establishing his identify and address and his commercial registration number.

For projects involving construction, maintenance work, technical services, specialized services, marine and land transportation services, hotels, catering, and hospitals, these following documents are required:

a) The agreement between the Saudi and foreign partner;

b) Application form containing information on the venture's purpose, capitalization, including the proportion contributed in kind and the distribution, including the proportion contributed in kind and the distribution of the share capital among the partners (in Arabic translation), 10 copies;

c) Power of attorney authorizing the person submitting the application to present it on behalf of the partners (with Arabic translations);

d) Authenticated documents showing the activities and experience of the foreign partner (annual reports can be accepted) and the most important projects executed by the foreign partner in and outside the kingdom;

e) Resolution of the board of directors of the foreign partner authorizing participation in the project in Saudi Arabia;

f) An authenticated certificate of incorporation of the foreign company in its country of origin (with Arabic translation);

g) Annual reports and audited budgets of the foreign company for the past 3 years;

h) A document specifying the facilities and support which the foreign company will render to the Saudi project;

i) Catalogs and brochures concerning the machinery and equipment to be used in the project;

j) If the project is for maintenance services, a full description of the equipment, machinery and other facilities to be used to establish a fully equipped maintenance facility in the Kingdom, along with a statement as to the value of the equipment;

k) Address of the foreign company in its country of origin;

l) In addition to the above, the Saudi partner must supply documents establishing his identity and address and his commercial registration number. In the case of construction contracting, he must also supply his Saudi Government classification certificate, if any.

After receipt of the license from the Foreign Capital Investment Committee, and the approval from the Minister of Industry and Electricity, the foreign investor must register his company with the Ministry of Commerce. The required procedure is:

a) A copy of the Minister of Industry and Electricity's approval and four copies of the contract between the partners (generally called Articles of Association) should be submitted to the Company Registration Department in the Ministry of Commerce to permit the Ministry to verify that the contract is in accord with the Companies Law.

b) When the articles of association are approved by the Ministry of Commerce, these should be notarized. The articles are copied in a register kept by the notary public. All the partners should sign the register in the presence of the notary public who then certifies the copies of the articles by stating on them that the notarization procedure has been completed. The copies of the Articles of Association, so certified, should then be returned to the Ministry of Commerce.

c) A Copy of the certified articles should then be sent to the official gazette ("Umm al Qura") in Mecca, for publication.

d) After that publication, one applies for registration of the company in the Commerce Register and the Companies Register. This requires submission of these documents:
(1) A Written application to the Ministry of Commerce requesting registration of the firm in the Commercial Register;

(2) A similar but separate application for registration in the Companies Register;

(3) The names of the members of the board of directors of the company to be registered, the name of the managing director and a photocopy of his passport or identity card;

(4) Four copies of the official gazette in which the Articles of Association were published;

(5) Four copies of the Articles of Association of the foreign company duly legalized by the Saudi Embassy in the country of origin of the foreign (note: the Saudi Embassy, Washington, requires prior authentications by the U.S. State Department's Authentications Office before it will legalize the documents);

(6) The certificate of incorporation of the foreign company in its country of origin;

(7) A certificate showing that the capital of the company to be registered has been deposited with a designated bank in Saudi Arabia;

(8) A copy of the lease of contract for the head office of the company;

(9) A letter from the company identifying the person authorized to sign the Commerce Register on its behalf.

All approved investments are subject to the country's labor regulations and to all inspection and control regulations applicable to domestic industry.

Mining and Petroleum

The Saudi Arabian Mining Code of 1972 applies to all mineral investments except petroleum, natural gas, pearls and similar substances. The Directorate General of Mineral Resources within the Ministry of Petroleum and Mineral Resources is responsible for administering the code.

Under the mineral categories, qualified applicants can obtain either individually or jointly reconnaissance permits, exploration licenses, mining, quarry, treatment plant and transportation leases. A firm with an exploration license has first claim on mining leases.

There is no formal petroleum code. The terms under which petroleum concessions are granted can be obtained from the Ministry of Petroleum and Mineral Resources, Riyadh.

Forms of Business Organization

There are numerous permissible forms of business organization. The most common is the limited liability partnership, which is often preferred by Saudi partners because it requires no public exposure of business secrets. The minimum capital normally required is one million riyals, but the amount varies according to the nature of the business.

The basic legislation governing the organization and operation of companies is the Regulations for Companies which became effective in 1965. Business entities defined by these regulations include—in addition to the Limited Liability Partnership—General Partnership, Partnership Limited by Share, Variable Capital Partnership, "Joint Venture", and Joint Stock Company.

The various types of partnerships differ as to number of partners, paid-in capital, and liability. In a joint stock company, capital is divided into negotiable shares of equal value. The minimum number of limited liability shareholders is five. Minimum capital is one million riyals for companies offering shares publicly; for other companies, the minimum is SR 200,000. The paid-up capital upon incorporation shall be not less than one half of the authorized capital, and the minimum par value shall be SR 50. Approval for incorporation is granted by the Ministry of Commerce and Industry and the Council of Ministers.

Although foreign/Saudi mixed companies are commonly called "joint ventures," legally they are not. A "joint venture" under Saudi law is a specific form of business organization whose existence remains unknown to third parties. Although sometimes used for licensing arrangements, foreign investors rarely choose this form of organization.

Temporary License.—Foreign firms which obtain Saudi Government contracts directly or foreign sub-contractors who must establish an in-country presence, must obtain a simplified "temporary license" from the Ministry of Commerce or register as a branch of a foreign firm. "Temporary licenses" authorize only such activity as is required by the company's government contract and they expire upon completion of the contract. Firms operating under "temporary licenses" are liable for Saudi income tax unless their contract provides for tax exemption or reimbursement.

Branch Office.—Although the Companies Law permits foreign firms to establish branches, offices or foreign agencies in the Kingdom, subject to approval by the Minister of Industry and Electricity, in practice Saudi authorities generally do not permit them.

Ministry of Commerce Resolution 680 of October 10, 1978, however, appears not only to permit but to require foreign sub-contractors or firms which win supply contracts to the Saudi Government to open branches or offices in the Kingdom. Firms are exempted from this requirement if they already have a Saudi agent or partner. While it is clear that such firms must register with the Ministry of Commerce before undertaking their project, the form that this registration must take (i.e. whether "branch" or "temporary license") is unclear.

Sponsorship.—A simple method for foreign firms to have a presence in the Kingdom is through sponsorship by a Saudi firm. The Saudi sponsor must register with the Ministry of Commerce as agent of the foreign firm, but the foreign firm has no legal registry requirements.

In effect, the foreign firm's staff working in the Kingdom under the sponsorship arrangement would be viewed by the Saudi Government as employees of the sponsoring Saudi firm. Under this arrangement, the foreign firm must use the business name of its Saudi sponsor rather than its own name. This sponsorship arrangement is completely informal in terms of Saudi Government regulations and offers the foreign firm no government benefits or protections. It nonetheless is relatively quick and easy to arrange and serves the interests of some Saudi and foreign firms better than other legal arrangements. The only protection available to the foreign firm under the sponsorship arrangement is the mutually-agreed language of the memorandum of understanding betweeen the Saudi sponsor and the sponsored foreign firm.

Investment Insurance

The U.S. Overseas Private Investment Corporation (OPIC), a U.S. government agency located at 1129 20th St., N.W. Washington, D.C. 20527, phone 202–632–9646, insures certain U.S. investors in Saudi Arabia against the risks of currency incovertibility, expropriation, and damage from war, revolution and insurrection. This insurance is generally available only to U.S. industrial firms with annual sales of less than $110 million or to non-industrial (e.g. construction) firms which have stockholders' equity of less than $36 million. Investment insurance may also be available from the U.S. private sector. Firms should consult their brokers to determine private insurance rates and terms.

Extent of Foreign Investment

The largest foreign investment in Saudi Arabia is still Aramco, although it is in the proc-

ess of completing transfer of full ownership to the Saudi Government. The value of American investment in Aramco is not published, but Aramco's net book value at the end of 1977 has been estimated at $5.9 billion.

In early 1977, the Foreign Investment Committee of the Ministry of Industry and Electricity stated that the value of all investment—foreign and Saudi, but excluding Aramco—licensed through that date by the ministry totaled 2.9 billion riyals (about $830 million). Some 40 percent of this total was foreign investment (i.e., about $330 million). Two-thirds of foreign investments, other than Aramco, included the Arabian Oil Co. (Japanese), Getty Oil Co., a German/Saudi Mercedes truck assembly plant, a U.S.-Saudi cable plant, and shipping (U.S., Kuwaiti, Greek, Japanese, and Saudi).

According to the Saudi Ministry of Finance, the value of U.S. investments in Saudi Arabia licensed under the Foreign Capital Investment Regulations totaled $148 million through August 1978, of which two-thirds was invested in industries.

Labor

Labor Force

Of an estimated population of 6 to 7 million, including expatriate residents, the total labor force was estimated at 2.1 million in early 1979, of which 900,000 were foreigners, according to a Saudi news report. Other sources have estimated expatriate workers to exceed 1.5 million.

A 1976 survey of business establishments in 61 urban areas counted a total urban workforce of 348,000 persons, both Saudi and foreign. Because of polling techniques, this figure excludes laborers, owner-operated vehicle drivers, servants and itinerant peddlers.

Government workers, excluding military, totaled 175,000 in 1976.

Distribution of non-government employment is: trade, 28 percent; construction, 23 percent; social and personal services, 15 percent; finance, real estate, business services, 4 percent; others; 14 percent.

Employment registered with the Ministry of Labor in major cities is: Riyadh, 95,000; Jidda, 63,000; Dammam, Al Khobar and Dhahran 60,000 combined; and Mecca, 23,000.

There is a serious shortage of skilled labor, including construction workers, electricians, carpenters, plumbers. This shortage has resulted in the hiring of large numbers of foreign workers from nearby Arab states, South Asia and Africa.

Manpower Training

The Ministries of Education and Labor and Social Affairs have developed extensive vocational and technical training programs for young Saudis in such trades as machine shop, automotive repair, welding, diesel engine repair, air conditioning and refrigeration, electricity and plumbing. On-the-job training is also encouraged.

Ministry funds are available to both Saudi and foreign firms operating in the Kingdom to train Saudis in technical fields.

The U.S.-Saudi Joint Economic Commission has a program to develop Ministry of Labor and Social Affairs training programs and to design and supervise construction of an instructor training institute, nine new vocational centers, and the expansion of 15 existing centers. A construction management contract has been awarded to CRS Design Associates and the master plan and design contract to Frank L. Hope/VTN joint venture of the United States.

Training is available to Government employees through the Institute of Public Administration, Riyadh, with branches in Jidda and Dammam. There are four secondary industrial training schools in Riyadh, Jidda, Medina, and Hofuf, and secondary commercial schools in large towns. Through 1975, vocational training schools had graduated 4,400 students.

The labor law includes mandatory provisions for on-the-job training.

Wages and Benefits

Because of inflation and increasing demand for scarce skills, wage rates in Saudi Arabia are among the highest in the world. In early 1979 unskilled laborers on the open market (mainly Yemenis) commanded about SR 100 ($30) daily, Other typical annual wage rates in 1979 include":

High-level executive: $40,000 to $70,000
Middle management: $24,000 to $40,000
Technicians: $15,000 to $25,000
Secretaries, male, English-speaking: $12,000 to $16,000 annually
Skilled workers: $15,000 to $25,000
Houseboy: $200 to $400 (monthly)
Cook: $300 to $400 (monthly)
Driver: $400 to $500 monthly)
Gardner: $100 to $150 (monthly part-time)
Fringe benefits offered to expatriate North Americans by U.S. and other foreign firms in Saudi Arabia are about double an individual's base salary. In a survey of 31 U.S. firms conducted in mid-1978 it was found that about half of them provided a foreign post allowance ranging from 15 to 50 percent and cost-of-living allowances ranging from 8 to 27 percent

Expatriates are provided with housing and most are given use of a car.

About half of the surveyed firms pay for expatriate children's school expenses (more than $6,000 annually per child at American schools in Jidda, Ryadh or Dhahran). Annual leave varies from 14 to 60 days, with most firms giving 45 days off annually, divided into combinations of home leave and rest and recreation (R & R). All firms grant home leave with transportation, usually every 12 months. One-half of the firms give R&R leave, with transportation paid, at 4 or 6-month intervals with Athens and London the most common destinations. Some 10 percent of the firms provide per diem for home leave or R&R.

Additional information is available on Saudi Arabian business costs in Commerce's Overseas Business Report 79–19, July 1979.

Labor Regulations

The 1969 Labor Code is the applicable law covering apprentices and all male and female employment in private or public enterprises. Companies should be thoroughly familiar with this law because it is applied by government labor inspectors and enforced by the Saudi labor court. Provisions of any labor contract, including that of foreigners, which contradict Saudi labor law, will be judged invalid if an employee chooses to bring the contradiction to the attention of Saudi labor officials.

Two provisions frequently overlooked include Article 80 which says, "except within the limits dictated by the need to attract foreign workmen, an employer who employes foreign workmen may not pay them wages and renumerations in excess of what he pays Saudi workmen of equal competence, technical proficiency and academic qualifications," and Article 9 which requires every establishment employing 20 or more people to display at a conspicuous place a set of rules duly approved by the Ministry of Labor containing classification of workmen by occupational categories, work periods, hours, holidays, work shifts, attendance, vacations, and disciplinary rules approved by the Ministry of Labor.

The specifications outlined are: minimum

working age, 14 years; maximum workday, 8 hours (6 hours during Ramadan); workweek, 6 days with Friday a non-workday; paid vacations, 15 to 21 days per year depending on seniority; paid holidays, up to 10 days; annual paid sick leave, up to 30 days at full pay and 60 days at three-fourths pay; and overtime pay of time-and-a-half. Paid leave is allowed for marriage, births, and deaths in the family.

The code also governs severance pay, disability compensation, fringe benefits, safety requirements, disciplinary procedurees, and dismissals.

There is no minimum wage proviso. This is usually subject to negotiation between the foreign company and the Ministry of Commerce.

The code includes instruction to employers for maintaining personnel records, health and safety reports, and requires mandatory training programs for the labor force. If more than 500 workmen are employed, the employer also may be obliged to supply these employee services at his own expense: shopping facilities for basic commodities; recreation and medical facilities; children's schools; and employee training programs in reading and writing.

Worker Benefits.—Social insurance regulations issued in 1969 provide for a formal social security system. The social security program basically applies to all workers regardless of nationality, with the exception of foreigners who work in the Kingdom less than 1 year. Exempted are Government workers, who have their own retirement plan, foreign diplomatic employees, servants, artisans, seamen, and agricultural workers. The General Organization for Social Insurance administers the system.

The contribution for occupational disability benefits, all paid by the employer, amounts to 2 percent of gross wages. The contribution for old age and survivors insurance is 13 percent, of which 8 percent is paid by the employer and 5 percent is deducted from the employee's gross wage. Company retirement plans are not mandatory but some companies have established retirement systems. The normal practice, however, is to give a lump sum payment upon retirement.

Labor Relations

A 1958 Royal Decree, reinforced by provisions and penalties in the labor code, forbids the formation of labor unions as well as other bodies organized to express labor demands. As a result, strikes and work stoppages are rare.

Responsibility for protecting employee rights is assumed by the Government. The labor code, for example, provides for a network of Government employment offices. In addition to functioning as employment centers coordinating labor supply and job openings, these offices have the responsibility of initiating actions to safeguard employee privileges contained in labor management contracts.

Labor commissions, attached to the local labor offices, have been established to arbitrate employer-employee disputes according to the Shariah (Islamic religious law). These offices have a history of fair treatment of foreigners and Saudis alike, whether their complaints are against Saudi or foreign employers.

Employment of Aliens

A work permit from the Ministry of Labor and Social Affairs is required for foreigners. U.S. firms should notify the ministry of their intention to employ foreigners and secure its approval in advance of their employee's individual applications.

The general policy on the issuance of a permit is that the foreign national must offer a job skill which the country requires and which Saudi nationals either do not have or do not have in sufficient quantities. Under the 1969 labor legislation, a firm's workforce must be at least 75 percent Saudi and its total payroll 51 percent Saudi. The Minister of Labor can reduce these percentages in cases where there are insufficient skilled Saudis available, which is true in most cases.

The 1969 regulations also require that an employer provide vocational training for his Saudi labor force to eventually replace his non-Saudi employees. Employers must maintain a register recording the names of Saudi workmen who have replaced non-Saudis.

The Ministry of Interior's Committee for the Admission of Foreigners will instruct the Ministry of Foreign Affairs to authorize the Saudi Embassy in the country of the prospective foreign worker to issue a work visa. This process takes anywhere from one week to two months, depending upon the amount of follow-up done by the employer in Saudi Arabia.

Applicants for work visas must prove to the Saudi Embassy that they are the person(s) described in the authorization, and present a letter of contract from their employer in Saudi Arabia notarized by a Saudi Chamber of Commerce. It is also helpful to carry either a copy of the Foriegn Ministry cable sent to the Saudi Embassy, or its date and number. Saudi embassies also usually ask for proof of the applicant's ability to do the work intended.

Bloc work visas also are possible. Such visas require an authoriziation by the Ministry of Labor and Social Affairs, through the Ministry of Foreign Affairs, to the relevent Saudi Embassy stating that a certain number of (unnamed) persons with certain skills can be given work visas in order to work for a certain firm in Saudi Arabia. Applicants for bloc work visas must present the same documentation to the Saudi Embassy as for an individual work visa. The bloc visa procedure helps employers reduce the time and paperwork necessary to hire large numbers of expatriates.

All persons arriving in the Kingdom on work visas must register within 3 days at the local passport office.

Workers cannot freely transfer jobs in Saudi Arabia. To do so legally, employees must obtain a "release" from their current sponsors (employers) which allows a new employer to become the sponsor.

On July 14, 1975 the Council of Ministers established regulations regarding the transfer of foreign laborers. These provide for the repatriation of workers who go to work for any new employer without the consent of a previous employer with whom a contract has expired.

In the summer of 1977, the Ministry of Interior supplemented this decree with regulations prohibiting expatriates working in Saudi Arabia on contract to transfer from one employer to another without advance approval of the first employer and transfer of its contractual sponsorship to the new employer.

In late 1977 the Council of Ministers issued another decree (date and number unavailable) requiring that all foreign workers not previously subject to labor recruitment regulations (mainly unskilled Yemenis) must obtain work permits from the Ministry of Labor and Social Affairs. This decree requires workers to have a work contract signed by their employers if the work takes more than one week to complete. It further specifies that employers must retain the passports of employees, except when employees need them for travel.

The late 1977 Council of Ministers decree supplements an earlier March 14, 1977, regulation which requires that all companies having contracts with ministries, government departments and public institutions for industrial, housing and other projects worth more than SR 50 million (approx. $14.5 million) must recruit all their skilled and unskilled workers and staff abroad without violating the priority for Saudi nationals and must provide them with necessary accommodations without exerting pressure on the local market. The late 1977 decree requires Saudi Government agencies to include the above clause in all contracts. It also states that all subcontractors carrying out work for the original signatory of contract are bound by the same regulation as the main contractor.

The decree also applies to Saudi Government agencies which carry out their own work if it involves 200 or more workers. Further, the decree amends Council of Ministers' Resolution Number 448 of March 14, 1977, as follows: in bids presented to the various government departments, those relying on automation and fewer workers shall be favored and the government departments concerned must rely on machinery to the utmost in bid specifications.

Another regulation of the General Bureau of the Civil Service dated October 31, 1977, prohibits individual expatriates who leave Saudi Government service from opening private business offices in the Kingdom upon termination of their government job. Exceptions may be granted only after a lapse of three years between termination of an expatriate's contract with the government and the beginning of their private business in the Kingdom. However, expatriates who complete their contracts can request a "release" of sponsorship in order to work in the Kingdom for someone else.

Taxation

Saudi citizens and companies are exempt from taxation on personal and corporate income. However, Saudi proprietorships, partnerships, corporations, and such legal entities as trusts and endowments, are obliged to pay a religious tithe called Zakat, amounting to 2½ percent of liquid assets. The Zakat is collected by the state and is obligated for the relief of the poor by the Ministry of Labor and Social Affairs. It is assessed on total capital resources, including capital, retained earnings, reserves not created for specific liabilities, and net profits, but excluding amounts invested in fixed assets. Only one-half of the Zakat is actually collected by the Government; it is expected that the remainder will be given to charity by Saudi firms as part of their religious tithe.

Income Taxes on Foreign Businesses and Individuals

The graduated income tax in Saudi Arabia

applies only to non-Saudi firms and to foreign partners in business enterprise. A Royal Decree issued on May 15, 1975, suspends the income tax on wages and salaries earned by foreigners in Saudi Arabia.

Non-Saudi companies operating in the Kingdom must pay taxes on income derived from operations within Saudi Arabia. Taxable income includes profits of foreign companies, dividends of Saudi companies paid to non-Saudis, and the full share of non-Saudi silent partners in the net profits of partnerships. Income, for tax purposes, is defined as gross revenue less expenses.

Expenses are defined as:

1. All normal and essential expenses required by the trade or business which are paid during the year, including a reasonable amount for employees' salaries and any awards that may be given for personal service.

2. Expenses related to trade or business.

3. Rental of properties in connection with trade or business.

4. Any losses that may be suffered by the trade or business that have not been recovered in any way.

5. A reasonable amount against depreciation of properties employed in business. (See adjacent box item for officially permitted rates).

For oil and mining companies, the conditions of taxation are included in the body of the negotiated agreement. Otherwise the applicable rates on business income are shown below.

Income (Saudi riyals)	Marginal Rate (Percent)
0–100,000	25
100,001–500,000	35
500,001–1,000,000	40
1,000,000 plus	45

Companies subject to the tax must declare their income and pay the corresponding tax on or before the 15th day of the month of the year following that year covered by the statement. In cases of delay, a fine of 10 percent of the amount due will be imposed for the first 15 days overdue. After 15 days the fine is 25 percent of the amount due.

Official Fixed Asset Depreciation Rates

	Percent per year		Percent per year
Electricity and Natural Gas		Ships	5
Above-ground network	5	Trailers	15
Generators (diesel)	5	Trucks	25
Generators (gas turbine)	5	Specialized Industries	
Natural gas bottling machinery	7½	Beverage-manufacturing machinery	10
Underground network	5	Carpentry machinery	12½
Warehouses (gas)	5	Cement industry machinery	7½
Offices and Showroom		Chemical industry machinery	10
Air coolers (desert)	20	Cloth-weaving and spinning machinery	12½
Air conditioners (compressor)	25	Flour-milling machinery	7½
Cold storage units	7½	Dairy machinery	10
Computers	12½	Furniture-making and wood-cutting equipment	12½
Electrical appliances (refrigerators,		Glass-producing machinery	7½
radios, etc.)	10	Ice cream-manufacturing equipment	10
Furniture and accessories	10	Metal-forming and metal-pressing equipment	10
Office Equipment	15	Plastic-producing machinery	10
Safes	2½	Rubber manufacturing machinery	7½
Roads, Ports, and Buildings		Soap manufacturing equipment	10
Brick- and stone-making machinery	7½	Steel furniture manufacturing equipment	10
Buildings	3	Tanning equipment	10
Compressors	20	Vegetable oil presses	7½
Earthmoving equipment (heavy)	12½	Miscellaneous	
Port construction equipment	10	Boilers	10
Road and building construction equipment	7½	Car-washing and greasing equipment	10
Ship repair equipment	10	Furnaces (electric)	12½
Surveying equipment	10	Gas station pumps	10
Tents	20	Generators (small, electric)	20
Transport Equipment		Handtools	20
Airplanes	15	Machinery (fixed)	7½
Bicycles	25	Machinery (movable)	10
Cars (passenger)	25	Ovens (electric)	12½
Launches (motor)	20	Pumps	20
Motorcycles	25	Welding equipment	7½

Tax returns may be based on the company's records, provided they are certified by an approved auditor. Alternatively, the tax can be based on an assessment of the company's profits as arbitrarily determined by the Ministry of Finance. The current minimum calculated rate of profit is 15 percent of invested capital.

There is no tax on dividends from a limited liability partnership or branch remittances. Royalties, interest, and management fees are taxed at the normal corporate rates and in the case of payments to persons or companies not present in Saudi Arabia, the payer is obligated to pay the tax.

Import Service Taxation

Saudi tax is applied to any income or profits having a source within the Kingdom. Tax Department Circular No. 2 of 1969 provides that suppliers of goods manufactured outside Saudi Arabia to a buyer in Saudi Arabia are not obliged to pay tax on the income derived from the sale *per se*. However, the foreign supplier will become subject to Saudi tax for any additional service such as delivery of the goods from the port to the buyer, or installation of the equipment. For this reason, sales contracts should be written either on an f.o.b. or c.i.f./c.&f. Saudi port basis. Suppliers who agree to any additional work for the buyer should sign separate contracts:

One for the sale *per se* and another for the follow-up services to be performed. If only one contract is possible, a separate clause should specify the value of services performed within Saudi Arabia so that the tax liability will be clear to tax authorities.

Double Taxation

Under U.S. law, credit against U.S. taxes is allowable for taxes paid to foreign countries by U.S. companies operating in those countries. However, there is no Saudi Arabia-United States "double taxation" treaty defining all deductible taxes.

Industrial Property Protection*

Saudi Arabia is not party to any bilateral or multilateral convention with the United States with respect to patent, trademark, or copyright protection.

* Prepared by Foreign Business Practices Division, Office of International Finance and Investment, Bureau of International Economic Policy and Research.

Saudi Arabia has no patent law. However, U.S. companies can publish a cautionary Notice of Foreign Patent Ownership in either the "Official Gazette" or a local newspaper for such ownership recognition as this may establish in seeking court action against possible infringement. An invention, however, cannot be fully protected by such a notice.

Trademark protection is afforded by Royal Decree 33/1/4 of 1939, as amended by Decree No. 8 of 1973 and No. M/24 of 1974. U.S. companies should address trademark applications, through their legal representative in Saudi Arabia, to the Ministry of Commerce in Riyadh.

Initial trademark registrations are valid for 10 years from application date and are renewable for similar periods, provided application is filed within 3 months prior to the expiration of the original trademark. The applicant for an initial trademark is entitled to registration in the Trademark Register and to the exclusive use of the mark. After examination and acceptance by the authorities, applications are published in "Umm al Qura," the official gazette, for 6-months of public scrutiny or opposition.

The registrant of a mark is deemed to be its exclusive owner. However, anyone proving that they used the mark for one year before its registration by another can also own and use the mark.

The trademark's validity can be contested during the ensuing 5 years from the date of registration. If no valid charge has been made in this period, the trademark becomes incontestable as to ownership.

Customs authorities can confiscate imported goods bearing marks that infringe upon those registered in Saudi Arabia. If a trademark is assigned, this transferral must be recorded in the Trademark Register. Use of a registered mark is not compulsory.

Trademark disputes are considered by the Court for Settlement of Commercial Disputes.

Although there is no formal system for copyright protection, one expatriate artist was able to preempt unauthorized copying of her work by obtaining a letter from the local governor of her city of residence in the Kingdom. It stated that her work might not be copied without the artist's permission. The protection afforded by this letter was based on the implied power of governing officials to mediate or prevent local business disputes.

Guidance for Business Travelers

Entrance Requirements

Business visas for entry for one to three months (depending upon the policy of the individual Saudi Consulate), and valid for use for one month from issuance date, can be obtained from these addresses in the United States:

Royal Embassy of Saudi Arabia
Visa Section
1580 18th St., N.W.
Washington, D.C. 20036
phone: 202-483-2100
telex: 440-132 NADJIAH

Royal Consulate of Saudi Arabia
866 United Nations Plaza, Suite 480
New York, NY 10017
phone: 212-752-2740
telex: 420-617 NAJDIAH

Royal Consulate of Saudi Arabia
5433 Westheimer, Suite 825
Houston, Texas 77056
phone: 713-961-3351
telex: 77-4389 NAJDIAH

Tourist visas are not issued by the Saudi Government.

Other kinds of visas include: transit visas (rarely given, which permit 3 days in country if required to stay overnight in Kingdom), visit visas (for close relatives of persons residing in the Kingdom), work visas and exit visas (required only for persons residing in the Kingdom). Foreign visitors to the Kingdom on a business visa routinely obtain an exist visa stamp at the airport before departure. Do not let visas expire; stiff penalities may result.

The Saudi Embassy or Consulates require the following for a business visa:

1. The sponsor must telex the Saudi Embassy or Consulate directly, inviting a named individual of a named firm to visit Saudi Arabia. Sometimes the Saudi consul will accept a copy of a telex or letter which has been sent to the visa applicant by the Saudi sponsor, but it is better to have the sponsor send this directly to the Embassy or Consulate. Sometimes the Saudi consular officer accepts none of these and, instead, requires that an official invitation be sent directly to him by the Saudi sponsor through the Ministry of Foreign Affairs.

2. Valid passport.

3. Letter from U.S. firm stating that it assumes financial responsibility for the traveler.

4. International Health Certificate showing valid smallpox and cholera immunizations.

5. Two photos.

6. Application form available from Saudi Embassy or Consulate.

7. A check or money order payable to the Saudi Embassy or Consulate, currently $6 per application.

There is no easy way to identify a Saudi sponsor or to circumvent these procedures in trying to enter Saudi Arabia. The American Embassy does not sponsor business visitors to the Kingdom.

While traveling within the Kingdom, travelers should carry their passports with them at all times. Extensions to business visas are possible, if arranged before its expiration. Extensions applied for after visas expire may result in penalties.

For Americans working and residing in the Kingdom, it should be noted that a Saudi Government regulation (Council of Ministers' Resolution No. 1235 of 9/25/77) requires employers to hold their employees' passports except when the employee needs to travel. Foreign residents must carry special identification cards issued by the Passport Office.

There are no currency restrictions upon entry or departure from Saudi Arabia. Currency may be exchanged at any bank, hotel or with money changers. Customs regulations strictly prohibit the importation of alcohol, pork products and printed matter that would be considered lewd or otherwise offensive to Islam.

Business Customs

Holidays.—The Islamic calendar followed in the Kingdom is the Hijra year of 12 lunar months, totaling 354 days. Therefore the two national holidays advance each year, vis-a-vis the Western or Gregorian calendar, by about 11 days. The holidays are Id al Fitr (approx. August 22–26 in 1979), which celebrates the end of Ramadan, and Id al Adha (approx. Oct. 26–Nov. 6 in 1979), which concludes the celebration of the pilgrimage to Mecca.

During the fasting month of Ramadan, Muslims refrain from eating, drinking, and smoking from sunrise to sunset. Non-Muslims also are cautioned to observe the fast while in public. During Ramadan, restaurants are closed during the day. Business meetings can be arranged successfully during this month, however, if the American traveler observes the Saudi custom of working during Ramadan evenings. Midnight business appointments are not unusual during Ramadan.

During the Pilgrimage (Haj) season, which brings 1½ million pilgrims to the Jidda/Mecca area, hotel rooms are extremely difficult to obtain and flights within Saudi Arabia are generally overbooked.

The weekend in Saudi Arabia is Thursday and Friday.

Business Hours.—Saudi Government hours are Saturday through Wednesday, approximately 8 a.m. to 2 p.m. During Ramadan the schedule is shortened to approximately 9 a.m. to noon. Senior Government officials are unlikely to be in their offices at the stated opening times, but, except during Ramadan, they frequently remain in their offices after official closing times.

Business establishments are normally open from 8 a.m. to 2 p.m. and from about 4:30 p.m. to 7:30 p.m. Saturday through Wednesday and until noon on Thursday. Banks are open during both business periods, but observe slightly shortened hours. During Ramadan daytime hours are greatly reduced; instead businesses open at night, 9 p.m. until around midnight.

U.S. Embassy and Consulate General hours are 8 a.m. to 5 p.m. Saturday through Wednesday. The U.S. Commercial Center in Jidda is also open Thursday from 8 a.m. to 2 p.m.

All businesses and other offices are closed on Friday, the Muslim holy day.

Correspondence.—The official language of Saudi Arabia is Arabic. However, English is widely spoken in both the Government and private business community. Letters, cables and telexes can be addressed to Saudi recipients in English. Post office boxes in most cases must be used rather than street addresses.

Telex.—This is the preferred medium of communication by Saudi businessmen when dealing with overseas suppliers. U.S. business visitors have access to telex facilities operated by the post office or the better hotels.

Clothing.—Lightweight, wash-and-wear clothing is essential for the hot (100–130°F, humid climate in Jidda and the Eastern Province. In Riyadh during January-February, heavier clothing including sweaters may be necessary. A tie is customary Western dress for the office, or for American business visitors. Women dress modestly; low necklines and sleeveless dresses should be avoided for religious reasons.

Tipping.—Fifteen percent service is added to hotel and restaurant bills. Allow SR 1 per bag for porters; tips to taxi drivers are unnecessary.

Health.—Drinking bottled water or other beverages is advised. With normal immunizations required for the visa, foreign visitors to Saudi Arabia can stay healthy.

Local time 3 hours ahead of Greenwich Mean Time; 8 hours ahead of Eastern Standard Time.

Hotels.—*Riyadh:* Intercontinental, Khurais Marriott, Khozama, Atallah House, Yamama, Ash-Sharq; *Jidda:* Meridien, Kandara Palace, Jeddah Kaki, Al-Attas Oasis, Airport, Sands, Golden, Sheraton, Al-Hamra; *Taif:* Intercontinental, Sheraton; *Dhahran Area:* Dhahran International, Ramad (Dhahran Palace), Al-Gosaibi, Carlton Al-Moabed, Dammam-Oberoi.

In early 1979, there were an estimated 4,400 hotel rooms in Saudi Arabia in 44 major hotels. Another 14,500 hotel rooms were under construction.

Social Etiquette

Personal contact is the key to successful marketing in Saudi Arabia. While written (letter or telex) communication offers a useful introduction of American firms to Saudis, it should not be expected that Saudis will reply to unsolicited mail. This may frustrate a U.S. firm trying to stir up some expression of interest prior to a visit to the Kingdom.

Private Saudi businessmen will readily make appointments with Americans representing any U.S. firm, but generally appointments are not confirmed until the visitor has arrived in the Kingdom. Representatives of U.S. firms should be senior-level individuals, empowered to commit their firms and they should come well prepared with price and technical information on their products. Frequently visitors will deal with expatriate (American, European, Arab or Asian) managers of Saudi companies as well as with the Saudi owners.

Appointments with Saudi Government officials may be more difficult to arrange but can be made with adequate advance preparation if one's product or service is of interest to the Saudi agency. It is suggested that before leaving the United States, Americans write or telex the Saudi official describing one's proposal and telling the official that they will contact him for an appointment when they arrive in Saudi Arabia.

For maximum effectiveness, correspondence with Saudi officials should include an Arabic translation. Arabic translations are a legal requirement for foreigners resident in the Kingdom who correspond with the Government.

While Saudi custom does not stress promptness, U.S. visitors should not be late for appointments. Business visitors should be prepared to spend considerable time waiting for a confirmed appointment, then waiting in outer offices where many others are ahead of them.

Business discussions are often prefaced by long conversations on unrelated topics, which in effect constitutes a warming-up period in which the Saudi decides whether or not the visitor is worth dealing with seriously. Often at the end of such conversations no business will have been discussed at all; the Saudi may simply invite the visitor to call again the next day to discuss the matter at hand.

All meetings include generous servings of juice, soft drinks, or the traditional sweet tea or bitter cardamon coffee. Following the warm-up session, Saudis appreciate a straight-foward presentation without a "hard sell." Seldom will any commitments be made as the result of one visit. Foreign business representatives should be careful to follow-up meetings with correspondence providing any added information requested and arranging for future discussions to reach a definitive agreement.

Hands are shaken in greeting and it is customary to look a man straight in the eye when talking to him.

Among Saudis it is offensive to allow the soles of one's shoes to be seen by others; if you cross your legs while sitting, keep the feet pointed toward the floor.

As devout Muslims, Saudis pray five times a day. The first prayer during business hours is at about 12:45 p.m. You should therefore be sensitive to Saudis who may wish to break off further discussion at this point, leaving visitors while they retire to a prayer room. In Government offices, particularly, visitors should avoid walking near the staff at prayer time, when they congregate in the halls. When at prayer, Saudis expect privacy and quiet.

During the holy month of Ramadan, foreign visitors should not eat or smoke in public during daylight hours.

Sources of Economic and Commercial Information

Government of Saudi Arabia

Office of the Commercial Attache
Embassy of Saudi Arabia
1155 15th St. N.W., Suite 428
Washington, D.C. 20005
Phone: 202-331-0422
Telex: 89-610 TIJARAH

Saudi Arabian Information Office
Suite 1022
1156 15th St. N.W.
Washington, D.C. 20005
Phone: 202-452-0525

U.S. Government

Commerce Action Group for the Near East
Room 3203
U.S. Department of Commerce
Washington, D.C. 20230
Phone 202-377-5341

Office of Saudi Arabian Affairs, Room 1446
U.S. Department of Treasury,
Washington, D.C. 20220
Phone 202-566-8371

U.S. Army Corps of Engineers
Middle East Division (Rear)
P.O. Box 2250
Winchester, Va. 22601
Phone: 703-667-2295, ext. 2179
Telex: 89-584

American Embassy
P.O. Box 149, Palestine Road
Jidda
(Mailing address from U.S.: APO New York
09697)
Phone: 67-0080
Telex: 401459 AMEMB SJ

U.S. Commercial Center
P.O. Box 149 (Palestine Road, opposite
American Embassy)
Jidda
(Mailing address from U.S.: APO New York
09697)
Phone: 67-0047
Telex: 401459 AMEMB SJ
Telex: 301459 AMEMB SJ

U.S. Embassy Liaison Office
P.O. Box 7442 (across Khourais Road from
Ministry of Petroleum)
Riyadh
(Mailing address from U.S.: APO New York
09038)

Phone: 477-2466, 477-2551, 477-2528, 477-2534

Telex: 201363 USRIAD SJ

American Consulate General
P.O. Box 81
Dhahran
(Mailing address from U.S.: APO New York 09616)
Phone: 864-3200, 864-3613, 864-3452

Regional Trade Development Office (for Near East)
% American Embassy
91 Vasilissis Sophias Blvd.
Athens, Greece
Phone: 712951, 718401
Telex: 21-5548

These U.S. Government agencies have programs in Saudi Arabia under the U.S.-Saudi Joint Commission for Economic Cooperation: Agriculture, Interior, Labor, Bureau of the Census, Treasury, Federal Highway Administration, Energy, National Science Foundation, Customs Service, Food and Drug Administration, General Services Administration.

Saudi Chambers of Commerce

Eastern Province Chamber of Commerce and Industry
P.O. Box 719
Dammam, Saudi Arabia
Phone: 21134 Cable: ALGHURFA
Telex: 601086 GHABR SJ

Jidda Chamber of Commerce and Industry
P.O. Box 1264
Jidda, Saudi Arabia
Phone: 31059, Cable ALGHURFA
Telex: 401069 GHURFA SJ

Riyadh Chamber of Commerce and Industry
P.O. Box 596
Riyadh, Saudi Arabia
Phone: 22600 Cable: TAJARIAH
Telex: 201054 TJARYH SJ

Mecca Chamber of Commerce and Industry
P.O. Box 866
Mecca, Saudi Arabia
Phone: 25775 Cable: ALGHURFA
Telex: 440011 CHAMEC SJ

Medina Chamber of Commerce and Industry
P.O. Box 442
Medina, Saudi Arabia
Phone: 1037
Telex: 470009 ICCMED SJ

Qasim Chamber of Commerce and Industry
P.O. Box 444
Buraidah, Saudi Arabia

U.S. Chambers of Commerce

American-Arab Association for Commerce and Industry, Inc.
342 Madison Ave.
New York, N.Y. 10017
Phone: 212-986-7229

U.S.-Arab Chamber of Commerce, Inc.
One World Trade Center, Suite 4657
New York, N.Y. 10048
Phone: 212-432-0655

American-Arab Chamber of Commerce, Inc.
World Trade Building
Suite 319
Houston, Texas 77002
Phone: 713-222-6152

U.S.-Arab Chamber of Commerce (Pacific), Inc.
230 California St., Suite 201
San Francisco, Calif. 94111
Phone: 415-397-5663

Mid-American-Arab Chamber of Commerce, Inc.
135 South LaSalle St., Suite 2050
Chicago, Ill. 60603
Phone: 312-782-4654

Publications

U.S. Government

(Available from the Superintendent of Documents, Government Printing Office, Washington, D.C. 20402)

Area Handbook for Saudi Arabia, Government Printing Office, Washington, D.C., 1977.

Foreign Economic Trends and Their Implications for the United States–Saudi Arabia (semi-annual).

Background Notes Saudi Arabia, January 1978.

Saudi Arabian Five Year Development Plan (1975–80-National Technical Information Service, 5285 Port Royal Rd., Springfield, Va. 22161. $19.

Other

Arabian American Oil Compnay (ARAMCO). *Handbook-Oil and Middle East*. Dhahran, Saudi Arabia: 1968.

Business International S.A. *Business Prospects in Arab Middle East*. Geneva, Switzerland: 1975.

Citibank: Investment Guide: Saudi Arabia, 1977

Doing Business in Saudi Arabia, N.A. Shilling, 1975

Doing Business in Saudi Arabia February 1979 Price, Waterhouse and Co., New York

A Hundred Million Dollars a Day: Inside the World of Middle East Money, Michael Field, London: Sedgweck & Jackson, 1975.

Guide to Industrial Investments in Saudi Arabia: Industrial Studies and Development Center, Riyadh, 1977.

Jeddah, 68/69, University Press of Arabia, Nairobi, Kenya, 1968.

Khoja, Ibrahim F. *A Short Guide to Doing Business in Saudi Arabia*. Washington, D.C.: World Wide Enterprises, Ltd. 1975.

Percival, John. *Oil Wealth-Middle East Spending and Investment Patterns*. New York: Financial Times Publications, Ltd., 1975

Mideast Markets (bi-weekly), published by Financial Times, London. Available in U.S. from F.T. Publications, 75 Rockefeller Plaza, New York, NY 10019

Middle East Economic Digest (weekly). London. Available in U.S. from MABCO Inc., 61 Broadway Suite 1400, New York NY 10006

Middle East Economic Survey (weekly), The Middle East Research and Publishing Center, P.O. Box 1224, Beirut, Lebanon

Quarterly Economic Review of Saudi Arabia, published by The Economist Intelligence Unit, London (quarterly)

Saudi Arabia, Samir Ahmed, New York: Chase World Information Service, 1976

Saudi Arabia: A Case Study in Development, Dr. Fouad al-Farsy, London, Stacey Int'l 1978.

Saudi Arabia Today, Peter Hobaday, New York: St. Martin's Press 1978

Saudi Business (weekly) published by Arab News, P.O. Box 4556, Jidda, Saudi Arabia

Saudi Economic Survey (weekly), Ashoor Public Relations, P.O. Box 1989, Jidda, Saudi Arabia.

Saudi Introspect (monthly) P.O. Box 659, Southington, CT 06489

Statistical Summary (annual), Saudi Arabian Monetary Agency, Research and Statistic Department, Riyadh, Saudi Arabia.

Winning Business in Saudi Arabia, Nicolas Fallon, London, Graham 1976.

Who's Who in Saudi Arabia, 2nd Edition, 1978 Tihama, Jidda, Saudi Arabia.

U.S. Foreign Service Officers in Economic/Commercial Sections are available to assist American business visitors to Saudi Arabia. A booklet, *Key to Officers of Foreign Service Posts*, is published quarterly by the U.S. Department of State. Copies can be purchased from the Government Printing Office. Washington, D.C. 20402

APPENDIX

Saudi Government Agencies*

MINISTRIES	FUNCTIONAL RESPONSIBILITIES
Ministry of Agriculture and Water, Riyadh phones: 401-2777, 401-1699 telex: 201108 AGRWAP SJ	Agriculture, irrigation, desalination, fisheries, animal resources, locust control
Ministry of Commerce, Riyadh phones: 401-2229, 40-4708 telex: 201057 TIJARA SJ	Foodstuff quality control, consumer protection, companies' registration, labeling regulations, standards
Ministry of Communications, Riyadh phones: 404-3000, 404-3440 telex: 201020 GENTEL SJ	Roads, railroads, bus systems
Ministry of Defense and Aviation, Riyadh phone: 404-0524 telex: 201071 MILFAC SJ	Construction of military bases, civilian airports, meteorology

*All Saudi telephones are being changed to seven digits.

MINISTRIES	*FUNCTIONAL RESPONSIBILITIES*
Ministry of Education, Riyadh phone: 404-2888, 404-2952	Primary, intermediate and secondary education, school lunch programs, Royal Technical Institute, programs for handicapped, antiquities and museums
Ministry of Finance and National Economy Riyadh phones: 404-2666, 404-2892 telex: 201021 FINACE SJ	Finance, customs, Central Department of Statistics, National Computer Center, U.S.-Saudi Joint Commission for Economic Cooperation
Ministry of Foreign Affairs Jidda phones: 58877, 58078 telex: 401104 KHARGIA SJ	Office of Saudi Projects in Yemen
Ministry of Health Riyadh phone: 401-2220	Hospitals
Ministry of Higher Education Riyadh phone: 36744	Most universities
Ministry of Industry and Electricity P.O. Box 5927 Riyadh phones: 689, 68764, 68558 telex: 201154m INDEL SJ	Industry and power projects, SABIC, ELECTRICO
Ministry of Information P.O. Box 843, Riyadh phones: 25500, 25555 telex: 201040 RINFORM SJ	Press, television
Ministry of Interior P.O. Box 3743 Riyadh phones: 30800, 30944, 30955 telex: 201090 INPORUH SJ 201063 DOMA SJ	Public security
Ministry of Justice, Riyadh phone: 51155	Court system
Ministry of Labor and Social Affairs P.O. Box 1182, Riyadh phone: 401-2225 telex: 201043	Vocational and on-job training, programs for handicapped, labor offices, Presidency for Youth Welfare, Government Organization for Social Insurance, Saudi Red Crescent Society
Ministry of Municipalities and Rural Affairs Riyadh phones: 21500, 21999	Town planning, water and sewage systems
Ministry of Petroleum and Mineral Resources Riyadh phones: 61133, 61661	Oil and gas, Petromin, oil refineries, Directorate General for Mineral Resources (other minerals)
Ministry of Pilgrimage and Endowments Riyadh phone: 22200	Concerned with annual pilgrimage to Mecca with land controlled by religious trusts

MINISTRIES	*FUNCTIONAL RESPONSIBILITIES*
Ministry of Planning P.O. Box 358, Riyadh phones: 23800, 23812 telex: 201075	National planning, Royal Commission for Jubail and Yanbu
Ministry of Posts, Telephone and Telegraph Riyadh phones: 440-0288, 404-0692 telex: 2012200 TELCOM SJ	Post offices, telecommunications
Ministry of Public Works and Housing Riyadh phones: 22723	Public works, construction, public housing projects
Major Autonomous Agencies	*Functional Responsibilities*
Agriculture Research Center P.O. Box 2579, Jidda Phone: 27840, 27777	Fisheries and fishing boats, locust control
Central Department of Statistics Riyadh Phone: 23355	Collects and publishes miscellaneous statistics
Customs Department, Riyadh Phones: 21655, 23655	Customs duties
Directorate General for Mineral Resources P.O. Box 345, Jidda Phone: 33133	Mineral exploration and concessions
Directorate General of Zakat and Income Tax Riyadh Phone: 22712	Tax collection
General Organization for Social Insurance (GOSI) Riyadh Phone: 478-5721	Social insurance agency
General Seaports Organization P.O. Box 5162, Riyadh Phones: 60531, 60600 Telex: 401158 PORTS SJ	Port development, port stevedoring
Jidda Seaport Jidda Phone: 32222 Telex: 401175 PORTS SJ	
Dammam Seaport, Dammam Telexes: 601130 DAMPA SJ 601139 DAMPA SJ 601005 DAMPORT SJ	

MINISTRIES	*FUNCTIONAL RESPONSIBILITIES*
General Secretariat for Arab Red Crescent and Red Cross, Riyadh Phones: 54080, 52081 Telex: 201192 ASHI SJ	Emergency health care
Government Electricity Organization (ELECTRICO), Riyadh Phones: 60923, 60921, 65733, 60917 Telex: 201052 SJ	Electricity planning, consolidated power companies
Grain Silos and Flour Mills Organization, P.O. Box 3402, Riyadh Phone: 33048 Telex: 401515 SAWAMI SJ	Silos, flour mills, wheat importing
International Airport Projects Office, P.O. Box 6326, Jidda Phone: 692700 Telex: 501521 IAPJED SJ	Approves work on new international airports
Meteorology and Environmental Protection Agency, P.O. Box 1358, Jidda Phones: 77233, 54188, 54189 Telex: 401236 ALSAAD SJ	Meteorology
Petromin P.O. Box 757 Riyadh Phones: 61145, 61133 Telex: 201048 PETROMIN SJ	Oil marketing, oil refineries, oil concessions to foreign firms
Presidency of Civil Aviation, Jidda Phone: 673644, 673624, 673700 Telex: 201093 CIVAIR SJ	Overflight
Royal Commission for Jubail and Yanbu, Headquarters office: Riyadh Phones: 39580, 39364, 24709 Telex: 201075 PLAN SJ	Construction of infrastructure at industrial complexes at Jubail and Tanbu towns
Directorate General for Yanbu, P.O. Box 6312, Jidda Phones: 59229, 59230, 59415 Telex: 401491 RCYANBU SJ	
Directorate General for Jubail, Jubail Industrial Complex, Jubail Phone: 20000 Telex: 631280 JABEEEN SJ 631281 JABEEN SJ	

MINISTRIES	*FUNCTIONAL RESPONSIBILITIES*
Saline Water Conversion Corporation (SWCC), P.O. Box 6086, Riyadh Phone 478-0872 Telex: 401473 TAHLIA SJ	Desalination/power complex
Saudi Arabian Agricultural Bank, Omar bin Al-Khattab St., Riyadh Phones: 39202, 23934, 23911	Purchases agricultural equipment, seeds, animals; provides loans to Saudi farmers
Saudi Arabian Airlines (Saudia), Airport Road, Jidda Phone: 25222	National airline
Saudi Arabian Monetary Agency (SAMA), P.O. Box 2922, Riyadh Phone: 478-7400 Telex: 201734 SJ	Central bank
Saudi Arabian National Center for Science and Technology (SANCST) Riyadh Phone: 29534	Research and development, solar energy projects
Saudi Arabian Standards Organization (SASO), P.O. Box 3437, Riyadh Phone: 401-3644	Development and publishing of standards
Saudi Basic Industries Corporation (SABIC) P.O. Box 5101, Riyadh Phones: 69700, 69728	Joint ventures with foreign firms for heavy industries at Jubail and Yanbu
Saudi Consulting House, P.O. Box 1267, Riyadh Phone: 20900 Telex: 201152 DEVIND SJ	Conducts market research and industrial feasibility studies, prepares and publishes data on industrial development
Saudi Fund for Development, P.O. Box 5711, Riyadh Phones: 38268, 36600, 69200 Telex: 201145, SUNDOQ SJ	Project loans to foreign countries

Saudi Government Railroad Organization,
Omar bin al-Khattab St.,
Riyadh
Phones: 24660, 24661
Also: P.O. Box 90
    Dammam
    Phone: 22042
    Telex: 601050 SAGRAIL SJ
	Runs Dammam-Riyadh railroad

MINISTRIES	*FUNCTIONAL RESPONSIBILITIES*
Saudi Industrial Development Fund (SIDF), P.O. Box 4134, Yamama St. Riyadh Phones: 33755, 33710, 33703, 33745 Telex: 201065 SIDFUND SJ	Loans to Saudi or Saudi/foreign joint industrial ventures
Youth Welfare Organization Riyadh Phones: 29598, 29599	sports complexes
Sama Building, South Tower Airport Road P.O. Box 4143 Riyadh Phone: 477-4002 Telex: 201065 SJ 202583 SJ	

Market Profile—SAUDI ARABIA

Foreign Trade

Imports.—(CIF) $26 billion, 1979 estimate; $20 billion, 1978. Principal suppliers: United States, 19.3 percent; Japan, 15.1 percent; West Germany, 9.6 percent. Principal imports: building materials, construction equipment, household furnishings and appliances, industrial machinery, aircraft and avionics, foodstuffs, and transportation equipment.

Exports.—(FOB) $59 billion, 1979 estimate; $38 billion, 1978. Petroleum constitutes 99 percent of total exports. Major markets in 1979: Japan, 18.4 percent; United States, 15.1 percent; Italy, 7.3 percent; Netherlands, 4.5 percent.

Trade Policy.—Liberal, no import licensing or other controls. Tariffs are zero or 3 percent ad valorem except for certain protected industries such as furniture and locally produced building materials.

U.S.-Saudi Trade.—Total U.S. exports to the Kingdom (including reexports) in 1979 were $4.9 billion and $4.4 billion in 1978. Saudi Government encourages small and medium size and minority firms to become active in the Kingdom. Principal imports from the United States: cars and trucks, aircraft and avionics, cereals and preparations, electric power equipment, construction and mining equipment, heating and cooling equipment.

Trade Prospects.—Best prospects: Building and construction materials and equipment; prefabricated building systems; materials handling equipment; office furnishings and machines; small computers and software; electrical power generation and distribution equipment; water resources equipment including purification, distribution, and recovery systems; hospital equipment and services; foodstuffs.

Foreign Investment

Foreign investment is strongly encouraged; 100 percent foreign ownership is permitted, however Saudi tax concessions and financing favor joint venture with Saudi firms. Minimum 25 percent Saudi equity participation required in joint venture to qualify for the 5–10 year tax holiday and investment credits. There is an Investment Guarantee Agreement with the United States.

Finance

Currency.—(SR 1=US$.30), (US$1=SR 3.32); Saudi Riyal issued by the Saudi Arabian Monetary Agency; money supply in 1979 $14.5 billion. There are 13 private commercial banks. Specialized government institutions include Saudi Industrial Development Fund, Saudi Fund for Development, Real Estate Development Fund, and Saudi Agricultural Bank. Inflation rate estimated at 8 percent in 1980, down from 9.2 percent in 1979.

National Budget.—Budget expenditures for FY 1981 (ending May, 1981) projected at $81 billion, up from $48 billion in FY 1980. Major budget items: defense and internal security, infrastructure (ports, roads, housing, airports, communications), education and training, health, agriculture and water, heavy industry.

Balance of Payments.—1979 current account surplus estimated at $14 billion. Official foreign exchange reserves and other foreign assets estimated at $59.5 billion at the end of 1979.

Economy

GDP.—1979 GDP estimated at $75.6 billion, more than 40 percent by the non-oil sector. In real terms, non-oil sector has grown nearly 14 percent annually during fiscal years 1978 and 1979. Per capita income estimated at $13,750 in FY 1980 (ending May, 1980).

Development Plan.—Expenditures during the Third Five-Year Plan are projected to exceed $285 billion, with emphasis on industry, agriculture, and mining, in addition to improved social services, education, and training.

Agriculture.—Only 2 percent of the land is cultivated, 25 percent of which is irrigated. Major products: Grains, vegetables, dairy products, and meat. Agriculture and fishing employ almost 30 percent of the Saudi work force.

Petroleum.—Saudi Arabia is the largest oil producer in the Near East and in OPEC. In 1978, output averaged 8.3 million barrels per day (MBD), production increased to 9.5 MBD in 1979. Completion of the master gas gathering project in 1983 will make available to the market 8.8 million tons/year NGL.

Industry.—Oil refining is the major industry. Other large industries planned to utilize natural gas and petroleum include petrochemical and steel plants. Local industries also include fertilizer, cement, furniture, food, and beverages. Heavy industry located at planned cities of Yanbu on the Red Sea and Jubail on the Gulf.

Commerce.—Centered in Jidda, Riyadh, and Damman/Al-Khobar. Strong commitment to private enterprise. Wholesale, retail, and commercial agencies can be handled only by Saudi citizens. Government is dominant purchaser of goods and services, but the private sector is developing rapidly. Large projects have been broken down to encourage a more active participation by the private sector (and small foreign firms).

Basic Economic Facilities

Transportation.—357 miles of single track railway connect Dammam and Riyadh, with plans to expand the rail network. There are 19,000 km of paved roads, with another 3,700 km under construction. International airports at Riyadh, Jidda, and Dhahran, with plans to expand those and construct smaller airports in cities and towns Kingdom-wide. Major ports at Jidda and Dammam. New ports have opened at Jubail, Yanbu, Ras Al-Mishab, Ras Al-Ghar, and Qadima.

Communications.—Telephone service in major cities with good inter-city service. Direct international dialing is possible. Multi-billion dollar communication system improvement underway, including plans to expand telex system.

Power.—Electricity is available in most cities. In 1978, Saudi Arabia produced 2,879 MW of power and projects to add 7,200 MW were under construction or in planning stages. Additional plans to increase generating capacity are underway.

Natural Resources

Land.—Estimated between 600,000 to 850,000 square miles.

Climate.—Hot and dry with average annual rainfall 10 millimeters; very humid on both coasts.

Minerals.—Huge petroleum and natural gas reserves; proven gas reserves in 1976 were estimated at 6.4 trillion cubic feet. Small-scale production of salt, gypsum, and limestone, with plans to mine gold and silver in addition to excavation of other minerals.

Fisheries.—Extensive plans to develop this sector, including expansion of fishing ports and increasing annual catch, presently estimated at 32,000 tons annually.

Population

Estimated at 5 million, with an additional 900,000 to 1.5 million expatriate workers. Total labor force estimated at 2.1 million, of which half are foreigners. Arabic is the official and principal spoken language. English is frequently used in commerce.

Market Profile—SENEGAL

Foreign Trade

Imports.—$1.069.5 million in 1981; $1.107.8 million in 1982. Major suppliers. 1981: France. Nigeria, Netherlands, Thailand. United States. Principal imports: foodstuffs, machinery and petroleum products. From United States 1982 ($30.5 million) rice. 24.8 percent; milled corn, 6.4 percent; wheel-type tractors, 6.2 percent; mechanical shovels, 4.7 percent; edible preparations, nspf. 3.2 percent.

Exports.— $425.6 million in 1981; $482.4 million in 1982. Major markets 1981: France, Ivory Coast, Mauritania, Mali, and the United States in 31st place. Principal exports: fish, peanuts, and phosphates. To United States 1982 ($1.1 million): live birds. 26.7 percent; shellfish (excl. clams), 4.1 percent; fresh beans (excl. lima).

Trade Policy.—Signatory of Lome Convention. Member of ECOWAS and West African Economic Community (CEAO).

Trade Prospects.—Greatest sales potential is for building and construction equipment, energy systems, communication equipment, fishing equipment, irrigation and pump equipment. Principal African market (1982): Ivory Coast; principal African supplier (1981): Nigeria.

Foreign Investment

Investment Code has been liberalized; the Dakar Industrial Free Zone for manufacturers of export-oriented goods is being revitalized, offers preferential access to CEAO countries; prices are being regulated; government participation in business is being minimized; and a special investors' facilitation center is being established. U.S. investment in Senegal amounts to approximately $24 million. Bilateral investment treaty and OPIC guarantees with the United States.

Investment Prospects.—Fishing, mining, agribusiness, tourism, textiles.

Finance

Currency.—CFA francs (399 CFA francs=US$1 in Oct. 1983), issued by the Central Bank of West African states which serves six member nations of the West African Monetary Union. France guarantees unlimited convertibility of CFA francs into French francs at 50 CFA francs to the French franc.

Domestic Credit and Investment. Five commercial banks plus three French and one U.S. bank offer full credit facilities.

National Budget.—1982/83 budget balances at $648.5 million; capital investment expenditures. $67.6 million.

Foreign Aid.—Major sources of development assistance are the World Bank, Saudi Arabia, Iraq, France, and the United States. U.S. Economic Assistance FY 1982, $29.3 million; development assistance, $16.2 million (55.2 percent); PL 480, $12.8 million (43.7 percent); IMET, $323,000 (1.1 percent).

Balance of Payments.—$281.5 million deficit in 1981.

Economy

A restructuring of the economy (reinforcement of the agricultural sector, more productive investment in industrial projects, and emphasis on private enterprise) is taking place.

GDP.—$2.2 billion (est.) in 1981; $381 per capita.

Agriculture.—Bad weather and poor prices helped diversification from peanuts into fruit, vegetables, cotton, fish, and livestock for export.

Industry.—Probably 90 percent controlled by foreign and semipublic enterprises. Over 200 firms, primarily engaged in processing raw materials into finished products for export and consumption.

Commerce.—French influence predominates. Foreign private sector centered in Dakar. Government pushing Senegalization; industrial estate under construction in Dakar.

Tourism.—Most promising sector of economy; total number of tourist class hotel rooms in Dakar is 2,000. Another major hotel planned for Dakar and a 2,500-bed resort will be located 60 miles south of Dakar.

Development Plan.—The Sixth Development Plan (July 1981-June 1985 calls for an investment of $1,623.8 million.

Basic Economic Facilities

Transportation.—8,636 miles of roads (2,150 paved); 642 miles of meter gauge railroad; an international airport and a port at Dakar.

Communications.—40,200 telephones (0.8 per 100 people). Eight AM radio stations; one TV station, three submarine cables, one Atlantic Ocean satellite station.

Power.—Thermal. 315,000 kW capacity in 1982; 1.106 billion kWh produced in 1982, 180 kWh per capita.

Natural Resources

Land.—76,124 square miles. Mostly high plains; semidesert; laced with four rivers.

Climate.—Four climate zones. Rainy season in July to October averages 60 inches.

Minerals.—Phosphates, limestone, titanium, and salt significant.

Forestry.—Covers about 13 percent of total land.

Fisheries.—Resources include tuna and shrimp. Industrial fishing sector composed of about 70 modern boats. Total catch in 1981 about 229,317 metric tons; export $119.6 million (1981).

Population

Size.—6.3 million (1983); 3.2 percent growth rate.

Language.—French.

Education.—Literacy rate 10 percent. School attendance: 53 percent primary, 11 percent secondary.

Labor.—Labor force of 1.7 million; about 170,000 salaried, private sector 40 percent, government and parapublic 60 percent.

SENEGAL

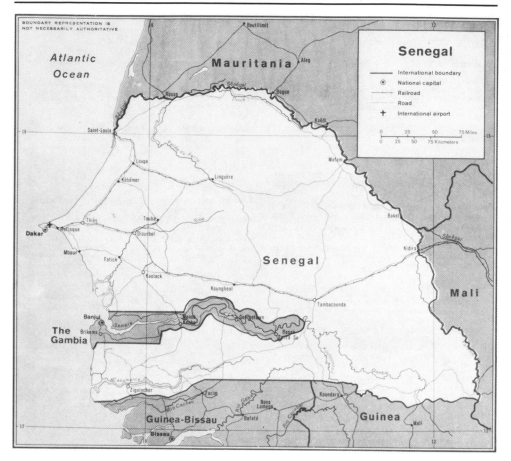

Market Profile—SEYCHELLES

Foreign Trade

Imports.—$92.4 million in 1981; $60.2 million in 1982. Major suppliers in 1981: Bahrain, $18.8 million: United Kingdom, $16.6 million. Japan, $5.2 million. Imports from United States: machinery and transportation equipment and industrial machinery; $15.4 million in 1982.

Exports.—$14 million in 1981; $33.7 million in 1982. Major markets in 1981: Pakistan, $2.7 million. United Kingdom, $0.6 million. Exports to United States: gemstones, metal coins; $212,000 in 1982.

Trade Policy.—Signatory to Lome Convention. No exchange controls or restrictions on foreign trade. 30 percent of c.i.f. value is generally permitted markup on imported goods. Payment for imports normally is by irrevocable letter of credit drawn on supplier's bank.

Foreign Investment

Since 1971, the United Kingdom has invested approximately $50 million in major projects.

Domestic Credit and Investment.—National Investment Corporation was organized in 1979 to establish and manage government-owned fishing industry. State farms. Seychelles Airlines, bus company, as well as government equity in tourism ventures.

Development bank is 56 percent government owned. French Caisse Central de Cooperation Economique and European Investment Bank each has 20 percent of equity. Barclays Bank International and Standard Bank Ltd., which are the largest commercial banks, each has 2 percent of equity.

Finance

Currency.—Rate fluctuates (6.82 Seychelles rupees=US$1, as of Oct. 1983). Foreign Exchange Reserves (1980): $15.7 million in November, up 3.9 percent from April. Money supply: $3 million in September 1980.

National Budget.—1978 current expenditures. $27 million; development expenditures. $15.3 million. Fiscal year is same as calendar year.

Balance of Payments.—Trade deficit has been offset by aid. private investment, and tourism earnings in most years.

Foreign Aid.—Mostly from United Kingdom: some PL-480 and AID self-help funds provided by the United States. All assistance to date has been on soft terms and debt repayment has not imposed burden on economy.

Economy

Agriculture.—Cash economy based largely on production of copra and cinnamon for export. Other major crops are vanilla

and patchouli (used in perfume). Bulk of food requirements are imported.

GDP.—GDP in real terms has grown at over 5 percent a year; per capita GDP estimated at $664 in 1978.

Industry.—Major areas: tourism, processing of copra and vanilla pods for export, essential oils, coconut processing, small cement plants, brewery, soft drinks plant, and cigarette factory.

Tourism.—Most promising source of future income: contributes about 16 percent of GDP annually.

Commerce.—Consumer Price Index (1975 = 100): 274.9 in September 1980, up 13.4 percent from April 1980.

Development Plan.—Main objectives of 1983-86 Plan is diversification, particularly in agriculture and fisheries.

Basic Economic Facilities

Transportation.—Interisland travel is accomplished by ferry among the major islands (Mahe, Praslin, and La Digue) and by auxiliary schooners to the outlying islands. International airport is served by British Caledonia and British Airways. 134 miles of highways, of which 90 have bituminous and 44 crushed stone or earth surfaces; seven usable airfields, no railroads. Victoria is a small port.

Communications.—Direct radiocommunications with adjacent island and African coastal countries: 3,900 telephones (6.4 per 100 population): two AM radio stations; no FM radio station: no TV station: one Indian Ocean satellite station.

Power.—In 1977: 11,000 kW capacity: 25 million kWh produced; 410 kWh per capita.

Natural Resources

Land.—About 92 islands comprise the 171 square miles of total land area.

Climate.—Equable and healthy, although quite humid.

Water.—200 nautical miles are limits of territorial waters claimed.

Population

Size.—(1979 est.) 65,000; annual growth rate, 2.6 percent. Victoria, Mahe Island (population 15,000) is capital city.

Language.—English and French (both official) and Creole.

Education.—Limited. 90 percent of schoolage population attends school. Seychelles College is secondary school. Literacy rate. 60 percent.

Labor.—Public sector is largest single employer. Private sector provides employment for 72 percent of wage earners.

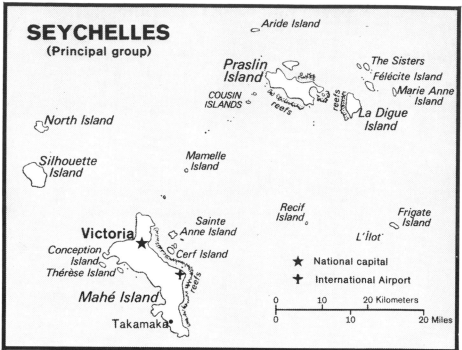

SEYCHELLES
(Principal group)

Aride Island

Praslin Island

The Sisters

Félécite Island

COUSIN ISLANDS

Marie Anne Island

reefs

reefs

La Digue Island

North Island

Silhouette Island

Mamelle Island

Recif Island

Frigate Island

L'Îlot

Victoria

Sainte Anne Island

Conception Island

Cerf Island

★ National capital

✈ International Airport

Thérèse Island

reefs

Mahé Island

0   10   20 Kilometers

0   10   20 Miles

Takamaka

519892 12–80

Market Profile—SIERRA LEONE

Foreign Trade

Imports.—$237 million in 1981; $199 million in 1982. Major suppliers 1981: United Kingdom, United States, France, Germany, Japan. Principal imports: machinery and transportation equipment, foodstuffs, and petroleum products. From United States 1982 ($15 million): rice, 19.8 percent; ships (small commercial), 15.8 percent; wheat, 7.5 percent; used clothing, 7.1 percent; dried milk and cream, 4.6 percent.

Exports.—$280 million in 1981; $169 million in 1982. Major markets, 1981: United Kingdom, United States, Germany. Principal exports: diamonds, coffee and bauxite. To United States 1982 ($34.7 million): coffee, 44.1 percent; titanium ore (rutile), 38 percent; shellfish (excl. clams), 13.1 percent; natural precious and semiprecious stones, 1.7 percent; diamonds, 0.8 percent.

Trade Policy.—An open door policy; nonpreferential tariff. Increased use of import licensing to protect infant industry. Import controls introduced in 1976. Mano River Customs Union with Guinea and Liberia. Signatory of Lome Convention. Member of ECOWAS.

Trade Prospects.—Agro-industries and mining equipment. Major African market (1982): Liberia. Major African supplier (1982): Liberia.

Foreign Investment

Government very interested in attracting foreign investment. No investment code in effect. U.S. investment in rutile (titanium ore) and diamond mining, an oil refinery, a fishing complex, and a flour mill and indirect participation in one bank. Investment guaranty agreement with United States in effect since 1961.

Investment Prospects.—Mining, fishing, tourism, and agro-industries.

Finance

Currency.—Exchange rate: 2.5 LER=US$1. OCT. 1983.

Domestic Credit and Investment.—Central bank, two foreign owned commercial banks (British), one government-owned commercial bank, National Development Bank, and the Post Office Savings Bank.

National Budget.—Expenditures, $354 million, revenues and grants, $211 million (1980/81). Budget deficit $143 million.

Foreign Aid.—Provided by IDA, EEC, ADB, US. economic assistance FY 1982, $7.5 million: development assistance, $3.1 million (41.2 percent); PL 480, $4.4 million (5.8 percent); IMET, $22.000 (0.3 percent).

Balance of Payments.—Deficit of $159 million in 1980/81. Severe shortage of foreign exchange, pipeline is 20 months.

Economy

Stagnating 1976-82. Austerity programs adopted 1976 and likely for some time.

GDP.—$999 million in 1980.

Agriculture

Agriculture.—Contributes 31 percent of GDP. Rice and cassava for consumption; expansion of palm kernel, coffee, and cocoa production for export. Ginger and piassava of some importance. Sugar development seen as a possibility by current Plan, in which $97 million in allocated for agriculture.

Industry.—Contributes 6 percent of GDP, basically unchanged for 10 years. Small-scale, foreign-owned and managed, mainly basic import substitution and fabricating.

Commerce.—Transportation sector and trade controlled by State monopolies. Large expatriate firms dominate commercial sector. Wholesale Price Index (1975=100) increased to 170.7 in 1979. Lebanese merchants very significant.

Basic Economic Facilities

Transportation.—Highways 4,637 miles, paved 761 miles. Railroads: 52 miles narrow gauge privately owned mineral line operated by the Sierra Leone Development company. Freetown, major port; smaller ports include Bonthe and Pepel. Modernized international airport at Lungi serves Freetown; 15 smaller airfields.

Communications.—International cable and telephone service. Two AM radio stations; one FM station; two TV stations; 16,000 telephones (0.5 per 100 people) INTELSAT Atlantic Ocean satellite-to-ground station.

Power.—Installed capacity estimated at 95,000 kW in 1982; 210 million kWh produced (1982), 60 kWh per capita. All diesel. Hydro facilities planned for the 1980's.

Natural Resources

Land.—27,925 square miles, about the size of South Carolina; mountains, plains, and plateaus situated on the western bulge of Africa.

Climate.—Tropical climate, high temperatures and humidity, rainfall heavy June to September.

Minerals.—Chiefly diamonds, iron ore, bauxite, large reserves of rutile (a titanium ore). Government policy of 51 percent interest in extractive operations is negotiable. Falling diamond production and world prices have had adverse impact. Iron mining resumed in 1982. Gold prospect growing.

Fisheries.—Local demand exceeds supply, necessitating imports. Catch: 57,600 metric tons (1979); imports: $2.7 million (1974).

Population

Size.—3.7 million in 1983; growing 2.6 percent a year; 17 percent urban. Freetown, the capital, estimated population 250,000; and Bo, 40,000.

Language.—English, Krio, Mende, Temne, and 10 other native languages.

Education.—Literacy rate is about 15 percent.

Labor.—Eighty percent agricultural. Labor force estimated at 1.5 million, of which about 65,000 are wage earners. Agriculture, 75 percent; industry and services, 15 percent.

SIERRA LEONE

- International boundary
- ✳ National capital
- Railroad
- Road
- ✝ International airport

0 10 20 30 40 50 Miles
0 10 20 30 40 50 Kilometers

BOUNDARY REPRESENTATION IS
NOT NECESSARILY AUTHORITATIVE

518120 7-76

Note: Sierra Leone is approximately 7,700 kilometers (4,800 mi.) from Washington, D.C.

2118

Marketing in Singapore

Contents

Report Revised June 1981

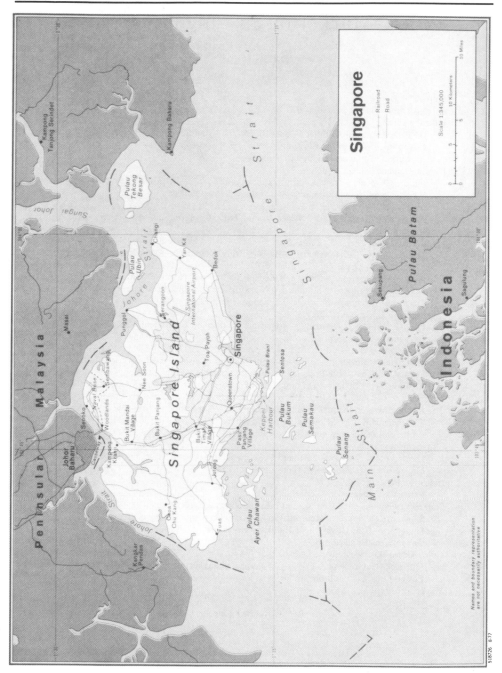

Note: Singapore is over 16,000 kilometers (10,000 mi.) from Washington, D.C.

Foreign Trade Outlook

Singapore—in its unquestionable role as a major regional trading, sales, servicing, and warehousing center—is one of the most lucrative markets for U.S. exports today. Supported by a booming economy and exceptionally favorable trade statistics, Singapore clearly favors a free trade policy in a competitive environment.

The U.S. share of Singapore's import market increased from $1,328 million (12.9 percent) in 1977 to $1,530 million (14.3 percent) in 1979. Figures for the first half of 1980 show a 42-percent increase over the first half of 1979 in imports from the United States. After being Singapore's leading trading partner in 1975, the United States has since slipped to second place behind Japan, a position that is now being taken over by Malaysia.

U.S. imports from Singapore increased 21.1 percent between 1978 and 1979. However, the U.S. share of Singapore's total exports decreased from 16 percent in 1978 to 13.8 percent in 1979, due in part to the overall increased export efforts of Singapore.

Singapore's other major trading partners include the United Kingdom, the Federal Republic of Germany, Thailand, Iraq, Saudi Arabia, and Indonesia. Singapore's trade with Indonesia is believed to be substantial; however, these figures are excluded from Singapore trade statistics out of concern that they would clash with those released by Indonesia.

To promote trade with China, Singapore and China have negotiated a trade agreement. However, trade statistics do not yet suggest that China is about to replace the United States, Japan, or Malaysia as one of Singapore's main trading partners. Bilateral trade between Singapore and China in 1979 was $582 million, with a $242 million balance in China's favor.

Singapore's balance-of-payments position is strong, due to foreign investments and income from services, which more than compensate for a large trade deficit. Singapore's balance of payments showed a $524 million surplus for 1979, and total official reserves of $5,789 million.

Table 1 lists Singapore's principal imports from the United States and provides the U.S. market share in these commodities.

Table 2 lists Singapore's major imports in descending order of value for 1979.

Table 3 lists the value of selected exports from Singapore to the United States and the world.

Table 1.—Singapore's Principal Imports from the United States and U.S. Market Share, 1979
(in millions of U.S. dollars)

Commodity	Imports from U.S.	U.S. Share (%)
Fruits and Nuts, fresh, dried	24.0	22.9
Plastic Materials	46.3	18.1
Chemical Products, n.e.s.*	35.8	36.9
Hand Tools	23.2	30.7
Piston Engines	61.7	33.7
Engines and Motors, nonelectric	37.5	94.3
Electric Plant and Parts, n.e.s.	33.7	44.3
Civil Engineering Equipment Parts	141.3	40.5
Specialized Machinery, n.e.s.	34.2	23.2
Machine Tools, metalworking	23.5	21.9
Heating and Cooling Equipment	25.0	25.7
Pumps for Liquids	25.2	42.8
Pumps, n.e.s.	26.1	34.1
Mechanical Handling Equipment	40.2	33.3
Nonelectric Machinery Parts, n.e.s.	77.6	30.0
Data Processing Machines	18.3	49.7
Parts for Office Machines/Data Processing Equipment	44.1	77.4
Telecommunications Equipment	41.9	15.0
Electrical Circuit Apparatus	32.9	17.0
Electronic Components	455.3	45.6
Electrical Machinery, n.e.s.	42.0	21.6
Aircraft	441.2	97.3
Ships and Boats	20.1	6.4
Measuring Instruments	54.6	40.7

*Not elsewhere specified.

Source: Singapore Half-Yearly Trade Statistics—Imports and Exports—Department of Statistics, Singapore.

Table 2.—Singapore Imports by Major Commodity Categories, 1979

(in millions of U.S. dollars)

Commodity	From World
Petroleum and Products	4,394.5
Electrical Machinery, n.e.s.*	1,609.3
Crude Rubber	917.2
Transport Equipment	771.8
Textile Manufactures	757.3
Iron and Steel	664.1
General Industrial Machinery	646.5
Industrial Machinery	584.9
Road Vehicles	440.0
Metal Manufactures	363.9

*Not elsewhere specified.

Source: Singapore Half-Yearly Trade Statistics—Imports and Exports—Department of Statistics, Singapore.

Table 3.—Singapore Total Exports (Includes Reexports and Domestic Exports) by Major Commodity Categories, 1979

(in millons of U.S. dollars)

Commodity	To U.S.	Total
Electrical Machinery, n.e.s.*	611.9	1,472.7
Telecommunications Apparatus	261.2	820.8
Crude Rubber	222.9	1,395.6
Petroleum and Products	125.6	3,335.1
Articles of Apparel and Clothing Accessories	124.1	368.6
Transport Equipment	68.8	399.7
General Industrial Machinery	29.0	300.1
Nonferrous Metals	96.4	189.1
Power-generating Machinery and Equipment	56.1	172.5

*Not elsewhere specified.

Source: Singapore Half-Yearly Trade Statistics—Imports and Exports—Department of Statistics, Singapore.

Principal Growth Sectors

The services sector is still the major contributor to the economy, accounting for over 70 percent of Singapore's GDP. During 1979, however, the goods sector experienced a growth rate of 12.6 percent as compared to 8.8 percent for the services sector, indicating a move towards more sophisticated and higher value-added operations within manufacturing, construction, and other goods industries.

Table 4 shows the contribution to GDP by the major industries and their annual rate of growth in recent years and over selected periods.

Industry Trends

GNP Development

Singapore's economy has experienced tremendous growth in comparison to setbacks during 1974-76 that were due to escalating oil prices and subsequent recessions in the industrial world. GDP achieved a 17.6-percent growth from 1977-78 and a 16.5 percent from 1978-79. Economic planning in 1979 centered around the launching of Singapore's "second industrial revolution," by which Singapore hopes

to increase the capital and skill-intensity of production in all sectors. No formal name has been given to this program, which emphasizes higher technologies and reduced labor intensity in response to the tight labor market that Singapore is now facing. Singapore also holds the distinction of having the second highest per capita GNP—$3,800—in Asia, trailing only behind Japan.

The outlook for the economy throughout the 1980's is bright, though the Government realizes that the high growth and low inflation performance of 1979 will not be matched. Singapore, however, is able to weather recession in the industrialized countries better than might be expected. By seeking out new markets and expanding market shares in existing ones, attracting foreign investment, and altering fiscal policy through government projects, Singapore retains buoyancy during economic downturns abroad.

Principal Growth Sector

Three major shifts occurred within Singapore's economy during 1979 that account for the rising growth of the goods sector. Manufacturing replaced transportation and communications as the economy's prime motivator with a 14-percent growth acceleration and the largest share contributed to overall GDP growth. The performance of the manufacturing sector reflected the shift in the industrial sector away from low valued-added activities to higher value-added industries, keeping in line with the aims of Singapore's second industrial revolution. Transportation and communications slowed to a 14-percent growth after 3 years of rapid advances. It was, however, the second largest

Table 4.—Gross Domestic Product by Industry, 1960 and 1978-79

(at 1968 factor cost)

Industry	1978	1979p	1960-1979	1969-1979	1978	1979
	Million Dollars		Annual Growth Rate (%)			
Agriculture and Fishing	151.1	155.3	3.1	2.2	-0.8	2.8
Quarrying	35.6	40.4	9.3	9.0	-13.4	13.5
Manufacturing	2,262.9	2,587.8	12.4	12.1	11.3	14.4
Utilities	303.0	332.1	10.1	10.1	14.0	9.6
Construction	514.9	553.7	10.8	7.0	-7.7	7.5
Trade	2,734.4	2,924.5	7.7	7.6	6.9	7.0
Transport and Communication	1,772.9	2,026.1	10.6	14.7	15.6	14.3
Financial and Business Services	1,525.4	1,648.0	10.5	10.2	10.0	8.0
Other Services	1,197.7	1,264.0	6.4	6.7	7.8	5.5
Less: Imputed Bank Service Charge	409.3	504.7	na	na	na	na

p=preliminary figures.

na=not available.

Source: Department of Statistics, Singapore.

source of growth and continues to be stimulated by expansions in air, telecommunications, and port services.

The second major movement took place in the construction sector. With a growth rate of 8 percent in 1979, it contrasted sharply to the declines experienced in 1977-78. The decline in public housing construction, which depressed past output, was offset by growing private sector construction in office and shopping complexes, hotels, and other industries. There are an estimated 1,000 projects to be completed in this decade. Included in these are the $1 billion petrochemical complex; the $400 million Raffles City project; and a new city center to be completed by 1984 on the east coast sea front, which will incorporate the $300 million marina center. There also is a mass rapid transit proposal under consideration. Consequently, business for domestic building suppliers is booming to the point where shortages and escalating costs are occurring. Many projects have had to be delayed until supply and demand conditions become better balanced.

The third motivator in 1979 was Singapore's shipbuilding and repairing industry, reviving after a 2-year decline. Growth was stimulated by increased oil exploration and mounting worldwide recognition of Singapore as one of the leading international shiprepairing centers. As Singapore's competitive posture increases, repair yards are continuing their efforts to improve productivity through more intensive skills improvement. Emphasis is also being placed on increasing mechanization to reduce overall turnaround time. According to industry sources, revenues increased by 29 percent to roughly $650 million. The oil-rig construction sector more than doubled its 1978 revenues, while ship repairing increased roughly 34 percent, the highest increase yet achieved. Shipbuilding improved only slightly but nonetheless reversed the 29-percent drop experienced in 1978.

Manufacturing

The industries that have attracted the newest manufacturing, investment commitments are petroleum, metal products and engineering, advanced electronics, transport equipment, and chemicals. Because of the shift in the industrial structure from low valued-added industries to those adding higher value, new industries and investment will from now on be capital intensive. By value added, the largest manufacturing sector is machinery and appliances, which includes the large electronics industry. The

fastest growing manufacturing subsector in 1979 was metal engineering and precision equipment, which grew by 32 percent. Sixty-five percent of the sector's output was exported.

The largest manufacturing subsector measured by value of production is petroleum refining (37 percent in 1979), which reflects the high price of crude oil more than the importance of this sector to the economy. Singapore, however, is the world's third largest petroleum refining center. To maintain high capacity utilization in the face of tight supplies, refiners have had to diversify their sources of crude oil to include more from the region than has been the case historically, but Singapore still relies heavily on Mid-East petroleum imports.

Some of the subsectors that in the past played a larger role in Singapore's economy than they do now (such as textiles, apparel, and a variety of raw materials processing activities), posted gains in growth of output that were lower than the manufacturing sector's average. Due to labor shortages, which are not expected to dissipate, decreased emphasis has been placed on the above-cited labor-intensive industries.

Table 5 exhibits quarterly performances of selected industries for 1978-1980.

Services

Singapore's booming tourist industry grew by 9.8 percent in 1979, as measured by arrivals (over 2.2 million). Malaysian tourists were the largest in number followed by Indonesians and Japanese. The Singapore Tourist Promotion Board (STPB) is expecting more than 3 million tourists by 1982 and 3.5 million visitors by 1985. An increased budget of 29 percent for late 1980 will encourage even more pronounced overseas promotions, advertising, convention, activities, and domestic operations.

The financial sector expanded rapidly in 1978. While its contribution to GDP only grew by 8 percent in real terms, notable developments in the sector centered around the increased sophistication of the capital market. The most interesting developments were in the Euromarket, where both the number of offshore banks and lending instruments and the size of the market grew rapidly. As a result, Singapore is now the largest Eurocurrency market in Asia.

Government Role in the Economy

The Government of Singapore has budgeted some $2,700 million for expenditure during the fiscal year April 1979 to March 1980. As in the

Table 5.—Quarterly Index of Industrial Production
(1974=100)

Selected Industries (Weights)	1975 (Quarter) 1	1979 (Quarter) 1	2	3	4	1980 (Quarter) 1
Food (42)	119.8	121.0	139.9	130.1	136.9	137.6
Textiles and Textile Manufactures (24)	103.3	87.9	93.5	91.6	114.1	104.8
Sawntimber and Wood Products Except Furniture (28)	115.0	93.6	97.9	98.2	97.7	90.2
Printing and Publishing (34)	146.2	124.6	132.6	149.0	156.3	126.0
Petroleum Products (245)	115.0	105.7	105.6	107.5	112.9	106.9
Iron and Steel (28)	178.9	145.2	168.4	181.8	195.1	180.1
Fabricated Metal Products (41)	104.3	101.3	107.6	109.4	115.9	98.1
Calculators, Refrigerators, Air-conditioners and Industrial Machinery (76)	207.8	222.6	231.5	201.6	208.7	238.5
Electrical and Electronic Equipment and Appliances (142)	232.1	219.4	249.6	294.5	300.6	294.3
Transport Equipment and Oil Rigs (152)	123.1	119.2	159.7	154.7	172.3	167.5
Other Manufacturing Industries Including Precision Equipment	160.7	139.3	164.8	173.3	159.7	130.6
Total Manufacturing Excluding Rubber Processing (1000)	148.7	141.2	154.7	158.0	165.6	161.2

Note: The quarterly indices have been revised to take into account the contributions of new firms since 1975.
Source: Department of Statistics, Singapore.

past, most of the money will be expended on capital equipment and infrastructural development projects. Although government expenditure has been increasing rapidly in recent years, it made up only about 22 percent of GDP in 1979.

Expenditure or servicing the public dept was increased by 25.7 percent in 1979. This marked increase is attributed to the large amount of government debt incurred in recent years and to new loans floated in FY 1979. The Government's growing emphasis on education is reflected in the substantial rise in the allocation of expenditure on this sector. While expenditure on transport and communications continues to rise, the allocation for housing declined for the first time since the Housing Development Board (HDB) began its aggressive housing program some 15 years ago. The HDB has recently caught up with the substantial backlog of demand for public housing. It now faces the opportunity, under its fifth 5-year building program, to emphasize design quality and individuality, rather than standardization and functionality.

In addition to numerous statutory boards, the Government of Singapore has interests in some 160 enterprises, ranging from food manufacturing to shipbuilding, banking, and various business services. Government investment in manufacturing is weighted toward heavy industry and capital- and skill-intensive industries. This trend is expected to continue in view of the increasing importance of sophisticated capital-intensive industries. Dr. Goh Keng Swee, the Deputy Prime Minister, defended the Government's role in business, saying that State enterprises are meant to "promote economic growth and not, except in special cases, to replace private businessmen."

Singapore has a number of government industrial and commercial enterprises besides government agencies and statutory public service authorities such as the Public Utilities Board. Some of these government enterprises are wholly owned by the Government, and others are partly owned by local or foreign companies. Among these State enterprises are the following: Development Bank of Singapore Ltd.—industrial and commercial development, Singapore International Airline—national airlines, Air Charter Enterprise Ltd.—air charter services, Neptune Orient Lines Ltd.—national shipping line, Jurong Shipbuilders (Pte.) Ltd.—shipbuilding and repairs, Keppel Shipyard (Pte.) Ltd.—ship repairs, Sembawang Shipyard Private Ltd.—ship repairs, NTUC Comfort Cooperative—transport cooperative, Chartered Industries of Singapore Ltd.—minting of coins and manufacture of munitions, and Jurong Bird Park (Pte.) Ltd.—tourist development.

Best U.S. Exports

The following product areas have been identified as holding the best prospects for U.S. exporters to Singapore. Many of these products will be featured at exhibitions and other trade promotion events at the U.S. International Marketing Center in Singapore. (See section entitled "U.S. Government Representation in Singapore.")

Metalworking Equipment.—The overall market for metalworking and finishing equipment is excellent. Total demand (local production, plus imports, minus exports), is expected to equal $184 million in 1980, a 10-percent increase over the 1979 level of $165.4 million, Imports are expected to account for $152 million of the total market in 1980, representing an 11.5 percent increase over 1979. By 1985, this market is expected to total $233.6 million, with imports accounting for $186 million.

The metal engineering industry has grown in recent years to become a major manufacturing industry in Singapore. The Government has encouraged an increased use of automation and mechanization in the metal engineering sector in an effort to reduce the labor input to production.

American manufacturers supplied $38.9 million worth of machine tools and metalworking equipment to Singapore in 1979, accounting for 28.5 percent of the import market. U.S.-made products are known for their high quality and efficiency. The increasing emphasis placed upon sophisticated, fully automated, and numerically controlled machines by the Singapore Government should help to increase the U.S. market share.

The major end-users of metalworking and machine tools in Singapore are the photographic and optical goods industry, the electronics industry, transportation equipment and oil rig manufacturers, and the air-conditioning and refrigeration machinery industry.

Business and Banking Equipment.—In recent years, Singapore's revitalized economy has fostered the development of a strong market for business and banking equipment. Demand will also stem from the accelerating automation of business and banking operations, spurred by the increasing importance of Singapore as a major trade and financial center servicing a vast and developing geographic area.

Singapore depends largely on imports to satisfy its growing demand for banking and business equipment since local production is, for the most part, limited to typewriters and calculators manufactured for export. Imports from the United States are expected to hold a roughly constant share of an import market, which is projected to reach $91 million in 1982.

The technical superiority of U.S. products and brandname recognition appear to be the main factors that provide U.S. suppliers with a favorable competitive edge over third-country manufacturers. Products offering high sales potential to U.S. manufacturers include minicomputers, microfilm equipment, plain paper copiers and duplicators, handheld calculators (five or more functions), bank teller terminals, coin sorting machines, bank proofing and encoding machines, and dictation transcribing machines.

Industrial Process Controls.—The current expansion of Singapore's industrial base is opening up new opportunities for sales of process control instrumentation, predicted to reach $20 million in 1982. No local producers cu;rrently exist.

Substantial sales should result from government spending in the electric, gas, and sanitary sectors.

Interested in broadening the scope and sophistication of their production processes, Singapore end-users have continued to seek the advanced technology of U.S.-made process control devices. The widespread use of U.S.-designed process control instrumentation in Singapore plants is only partially reflected by the 36 percent market share of U.S. manufacturers since significant amounts of equipment are shipped from foreign subsidiaries of American firms located elsewhere. Sales of U.S. devices are projected to increase at the rate of 15 percent annually by 1982, surpassing $7 million.

The trend in Singapore toward greater emphasis on applications of electronic/electric instruments is anticipated to total 40 percent of the market or $8 million by 1982. Not far behind, the market for nonelectric/nonelectronic controls in 1982 is expected to advance by 12 percent annually to $6 million.

Hospital and Medical Equipment.—All medical equipment in Singapore is imported except for disposables, which is a relatively new market entry. Total imports of medical equipment increased from $13.1 million in 1978 to $17.5 million in 1979. By 1984, imports of this category are expected to reach $21 million. Cardiological equipment is emerging as the fastest growing sector. Strong demand is also shown for operating room equipment, general hospital equipment, laboratory/scientific equipment, and orthotic and prosthetic equipment.

The major reason for the tremendous growth of this market is the Government's policy to promote Singapore as the region's medical center. The increased participation of private enterprise in health care industries and the numerous planned public and private hospital developments and expansions have aided in giving hospital and medical equipment needs a healthy boost. The growing standard of living in Singapore and in the neighboring ASEAN (Association of Southeast Asian Nations) countries has prompted people to seek more sophisticated and expensive methods of medical treatment. Although medical equipment manufacturing is identified as 1 of 11 industries earmarked for priority development, it is still in its infant stages, confined to disposables and low-technology items.

The United States held a 32.5-percent share of Singapore's total medical equipment import market in 1979. With U.S.-origin equipment being known for its sophisticated technological features and with strong marketing efforts and price competitiveness, the U.S. share of the future market will likely increase.

Computers and Peripheral Equipment.— Rising interest in computer technology, general economic expansion, and a growing need for replacements should combine to push the Singapore market for computers and peripheral equipment to $23 million in 1982. The market is estimated to average a 14-percent annual growth rate through 1982. Manufacturers in the United States have supplied 55 percent of Singapore's computers and peripheral equipment and are expected to maintain and strengthen that share through 1982. Approximately 82 percent of all computers installed in Singapore carry American brand names.

Among the best sales opportunities for the next 5 years are small mainframes valued at less than $350,000; minicomputers equipped with business software; medical computers; high-density diskette units; and standardized software for banking, accounting, inventory, and insurance. Sales of minicomputers look most promising, with forecasts of a 19-percent average annual growth rate and expenditures exceeding $4 million in 1982.

U.S. vendors have succeeded in Singapore because American products are held in high regard by Asian businesspersons. They consider U.S. industry to be the pioneer in the computer field. Approximately 30 percent by value of installed computers were owned or leased by the Government as of 1977, while the manufacturing sector emerged as the second largest customer with 16 percent by value of all installed computers.

Construction Equipment, Tools, and Building Materials.— Substantial opportunities exist for U.S. sales within the next 5 to 10 years. In 1979, imports of these product categories reached $791 million as compared with $712 million in 1978. Through 1990, over 1,000 projects will have to be developed. The total import market is expected to reach $1.5 billion by 1984 due to the various current and forthcoming multimillion dollar projects.

The United States held a 29.8-percent share of the total import market for construction equipment, tools, and building materials in 1979. Demand is expected to increase as Singapore is finding a greater need for higher technology and more sophisticated products. The level of U.S. technology and quality recognized by users offsets the 10 to 15 percent higher costs, as does the imperative need for laborsaving devices and equipment that the United States can supply.

The U.S. share of imports will continue to increase over the next 5 years, particularly for pumps, valves, and compressors; earthmoving equipment; lifting and loading equipment; and building materials such as air-conditioners, and quality polyvinyl chloride (PVC) pipes for sewage systems. Other related products with good potential include tractors for construction, concrete and building products, production equipment, power tools, and foundation and electrical equipment.

A related market category is building supplies and accessories. U.S. products that have good sales potential are floor coverings (carpets, vinyl tiles), ceiling boards, laminated boards, locksets, tinted glass, plastic molded doors, light fixtures, electric switchgears, and plastic sanitary fittings. Industry sources indicate the "open plan partition system" widely used in the United States is one product that may prove to be a winner in this market.

Telecommunication Systems.— Singapore has established itself as an important regional and global center for telecommunications and has the third highest telephone concentration in Asia, after Japan and Hong Kong. The Telecommunications Authority of Singapore (TAS); will continue its dynamic expansion and improvement programs, stimulating market potential for sophisticated U.S. communications equipment. TAS has earmarked approximately $455 million for investment in new capital equipment and network for the next 4 years and is the single major buyer of communications equipment. Other large end-users include the Ministry of Defense, the Broadcasting Division, and the Port of Singapore Authority.

Local production is confined to cables, wires, UHF radios, private branch exchange equipment, central office switching equipment, and telephone handsets. Therefore, U.S. suppliers of advanced technological equipment have a potentially lucrative market. American firms exported $48.4 million worth of telecommunications equipment in 1979.

Graphic Industries Equipment.— Purchases of new equipment by the expanding graphic industries in Singapore jumped to $17.3 million in 1978, and a robust 12-percent average annual growth to $30 million in 1983 is foreseen. With such an optimistic outlook, most companies have been enlarging production capacities and upgrading their equipment. The acute labor shortage in the country, together with the pressures of rising costs, has made purchases of automated equipment more desirable. The greatest demand will be for small- and medium-sized equipment with automated features.

Singapore printers rely exclusively on foreign sources for their graphic industries equipment. As demand for printed material continues to grow rapidly in Singapore, some printing companies are expected to grow large enough to require the high volume equipment in which American suppliers seem to specialize. U.S. suppliers are expected to raise their sales from $4.9 million in 1979 to $10 million in 1983, accounting for 26 percent of all imports. Prospects for American sellers seem optimistic, and printers operating U.S. machinery rate it as good as or better than other well-known competing foreign brands.

U.S. exporters will want to look into the legislation (PL 92-178) which permits U.S. firms to set up Domestic International Sales Corporations (DISCs). DISCs are entitled to defer Federal tax on up to 50 percent of export income. For information, write to the Foreign Business Practices Division, Office of Finance Investment and Services, International Trade Association, U.S. Department of Commerce, Washington, D.C. 20230.

Transportation, Communications, and Utilities

Transportation.—Singapore has a well-developed transportation network which continues to be improved and expanded. Its modern international airport at Paya Lebr is able to efficiently handle any civil aircraft now in operation. A new airport is being developed at Changi, and construction should be completed in 1982. Singapore is served by 33 international airlines, with frequent flights within the region as well as to all major global cities. American flag carriers are Pan American for both passenger and cargo flights and Flying Tigers for cargo only. ,

As the third largest port in the world in terms of cargo tonnage handled, Singapore has extensive facilities for passenger and cargo ships. Additional docks and wharfage are being prepared in both the Singapore City harbor area and the Jurong satellite area to handle more containerized cargo. Over 150 shipping lines representing some 84 countries and transporting freight and passengers, now serve Singapore. Singapore also has its own government-sponsored shipping line, Neptune Orient Lines Ltd.

American shipping lines serving both East and West Coasts are American President Lines; Sea-Land Service, Inc.; and United States Lines. Transit time is from 24 to 27 days from the West Coast and 33 to 36 days from the East Coast. Pacific Far East Lines serves the West Coast exclusively. Central Gulf Lines, Inc., provides LASH service from East Coast and Gulf ports. Lykes Bros. Steamship Co., Inc., sails from Gulf ports.

Singapore is linked to Malaysia and Thailand by highway and by the Malayan Railway System owned by the Government of Malaysia. Singapore possesses a network of approximately 1,200 miles of well-paved roads within its land area of 225 square miles, of which 800 miles are bituminous or concrete surfaced. The ratio of registered cars to people stands at approximately 1 car to every 16 persons, despite high import tariffs and local disincentives limiting automobile purchases. Authorities wish to reduce substantially the number of automobiles; however, continued growth in the standard of living is weakening the impact of current disincentives. Excellent bus and taxi service is available.

Communications.—Singapore, because of its geographic and commercial position, is one of the major regional and world centers of telecommunications. International telephone calls can be made to almost anywhere, with connections now available to 197 countries. A satellite station for cable and telephone communications came into operation in late 1971. Local telephone service provides a fully automated dial system with more than 167,000 instruments in operation. An instrument normally can be installed within a week of application. International telegraph service is readily available to all parts of the world via a worldwide system of integrated cable and radio networks. Telex channels are available to some 193 countries. Telegrams can be sent from Singapore at any time of day to almost all destinations, including ships at sea; and a photo-telegram service by which pictures may be transmitted is also in operation.

Airmail and surface mail services are available on a worldwide basis. Local mail is generally delivered on the same day as posted. The Post Office continues to provide three deliveries per day during weekdays in the central city area. Airmail deliveries between Singapore and the United States take only 4 to 7 days; to Europe, 3 to 5 days.

Utilities.—The Public Utilities Board (PUB) provides a reliable and continuous supply of electricity, water, and gas to meet rising utility demands from industrial, commercial, and domestic customers. Electricity is generated by the Board's four steam power stations (Pasir Panjang A&B, Jurong, and Senoko Power Stations) and two gas turbine stations (St. James and Senoko Power Stations), which have a total generating capacity of 1,610 megawatts. Total production in 1979 amounted to 6,448 million kilowatt hours and consumption amounted to 5,744 million kilowatt hours. Work is in progress on the construction of a second power station at Senoko on Singapore's north shore.

Electrical current availability is a.c., 50-cycle, single phase for 230 volts and three phase for 400 volts. The PUB is authorized to control water, gas, and electricity installations, and to establish rates for these utilities. Tariff schedules give preferential rates for large industrial power consumers. Electricity is available to almost every part of the country.

Singapore's water supply is considered the purest in Southeast Asia. Water consumption in the Republic averages around 146 million gallons per day, of which 44 percent is for domestic use. The water comes from waterworks in South Johore (across the causeway in Malaysia) after treatment. In addition to the Malaysian source, Singapore maintains three catchment areas and three reservoirs on the island itself. Further development is in process to increase water production and reservoir storage capacity.

Distribution and Sales Channels

Import Channels

The import of American goods is usually done through established trading firms that have branches in Singapore and throughout Singapore's marketing area. These firms handle sales and aftersales servicing as well as offering technical and engineering assistance. For a U.S. exporter, the aftersales support is of prime importance in gaining the confidence of a purchaser who may feel apprehensive about buying the equipment from a manufacturer thousands of miles away. To assure oneself of this product support, care should be taken in selecting an agent. It is frequently accomplished by the assignment of a company representative on the premises of the Singapore trading firm. This company representative is responsible for before- and after-sales supervision of distributors. This is a valuable function, since a large trading company may handle the product lines of several hundred foreign suppliers involving several thousand items. The smaller firms may be just as diversified or specialized by product or industry. Singapore trading companies offer every possible service. They will maintain spare parts inventories, provide main-

tenance services, sell or process indent orders, and market to both wholesalers and retailers. It is left to the U.S. firm to locate an agent who can best fulfill its marketing needs and then support and supervise that agent to assure the use of aggressive selling techniques.

As an alternative, if volume is substantial, U.S. exporters may find it advantageous to open a branch in Singapore, staff it with locals and/or Americans, and retain management authority over their sales efforts.

Sales to government agencies are still being done in response to international tendering. The importance of this practice is decreasing as foreign suppliers find it easier and more lucrative to deal through local agents or branches.

Ports and Warehousing

Port activities and accommodations are regarded as efficient and adequate as any in the world. Extensive port facilities are under the supervision of the well-administered Port of Singapore Authority. Public docking, cargo loading and unloading, and warehousing operations are maintained with the use of modern mechanical material-handling equipment in the Singapore City harbor area and at the facilities in the Jurong satellite area. All berths for oceangoing and coastal vessels are fully supported by transit sheds, warehouses, access roads, and direct rail connections with the Malayan Railway System. The Authority operates on a three-shift basis to assure minimum turnaround time of vessels, which averages about 2 days.

Public warehousing provided by the Port of Singapore Authority in the City area consists of transit sheds at wharfside and warehouses. The Jurong wharves include an open storage area and a covered storage warehouse. There are more than 860,000 square meters of covered warehouse space.

Goods delivered within 3 days of completion of discharge of vessel are not subject to storage charges in public warehouses. After 3 days, the charges are based on a sliding scale of rates, which changes weekly. Free storage is allowed up to 4 weeks for transshipment cargo; after that, a sliding scale of rates is levied.

Private trading companies own and maintain extensive warehouse facilities in connection with their trading activities in the local market and the reexport trade. Many of these are conveniently located on the banks of the Singapore River, which threads its way into a substantial part of the commercial district.

These facilities are easily reached by lighters servicing the ships in the roadstead and by trucks servicing the entire Singapore area. Reacting more quickly to increased demands for warehouse space, the trading companies are constantly expanding these facilities.

Pilferage from Singapore warehouses is considered negligible, reflecting the high security standards in effect.

Distribution Practices

With a population of over 2 million people within a 225 square mile area, Singapore is as much a city as it is a country. The trading companies discussed under "Import Channels" normally provide complete local and area distribution. A large trading company can blanket Singapore and the surrounding marketing area through innumerable outlets where this type of distribution is appropriate or, in the case of industrial equipment, through offices strategically located near target markets. One distributor will generally suffice for the Singapore market itself.

Wholesale and Retail Channels

Current figures for the wholesale and retail trades are incomplete. In 1978 some 50,000 employees were engaged in the wholesale trade, 109,000 in retailing, and 64,000 in the hotel-restaurant industry. Over 109,000 persons were engaged in transportation and storage activities. Facilities range from the most modern warehouses and department stores to small, owner-operated shops. Modern, western-style retail outlets are increasing in popularity as are U.S. merchandising methods.

Because Singapore comprises such a small area, there are very few large wholesalers. There are, however, a number of small wholesalers who will usually supply on credit the retailers who agree to stock their products. Generally, the trading companies handle the wholesaling and, to some degree, the retailing functions in Singapore. These companies maintain large warehouse complexes in connection with their trading activities, and it is from these facilities that the retail market is supplied. Payment is usually made by the retailer on a deferred basis. But just as an exporter, when selling to Singapore, may be in fact selling to the entire Far East, so the trading company may be wholesaling or retailing to a far wider market than just Singapore itself.

The U.S. Department of Commerce provides a variety of services to businesses that can assist in locating agents, distributors, and end-users and in obtaining background information on foreign companies. For information, contact a U.S. Department of Commerce District Office in one of the 47 cities where they are located or write: Office of Export Marketing Assistance, International Trade Administration, U.S. Department of Commerce, Room 1033, Washington, D.C. 20230.

Government Procurement

Almost all government purchasing is done by tenders. Invitations to bid on government projects are published in the Singapore Government Gazette (available from the Government Publications Bureau, Fullerton Building, Singapore). Invitations may be restricted to contractors registered with the department initiating the request or may be open to general bidding. The Department of Commerce publishes foreign tenders in various publications and contacts appropriate trade associations and other industry groups when bids are open to international competition.

Complete instructions are issued at the time invitations are published, indicating the sources of tender documents, drawings and specifications, and filing procedures.

The Government facilitates some of its overseas purchasing through Intraco, Ltd. Although it is a government/private industry joint venture, Intraco is in a competitive position in relation to other privately sponsored agents. Its address in Singapore is 2 Shenton Way, Singapore 0106.

Advertising and Research

Advertising Media

Advertising is widely used as a sales tool in Singapore. There are several advertising and public relations firms that will assist the U.S. export company or its agent in media presentations.

Product identification can be developed to associate the merchandise with either the U.S. manufacturer or the local distributor, depending upon the preferences of the exporter. Several of the large trading companies do their own advertising. This practice results in the product or service being associated with the distributor rather than the foreign supplier. Foreign suppliers, on the other hand, may purchase space in local newspapers. When the U.S. export company buys local advertising space, it often uses a format developed by a local advertising firm and, in this way, assures itself that its marketing campaign will conform to local customs and preferences.

The most effective media advertising is done in the daily newspapers. With a circulation of over 500,000, these publications circulate to readers in the three major local languages—English, Chinese, and Malay. Most of the Singapore business community can be reached in the English language press.

Radio and, more recently, television are being used increasingly by distributors to advertise consumer goods. Rising family incomes make these media a very popular method of advertising. Over 70 percent of the population listen daily to Radio Singapore broadcasts. Television Singapore operates 104 hours weekly on two channels, partly in color, offering a full range of programming. Both radio and television offer commercial "spots." Advertising in American publications also reaches the Singapore market. U.S. consumer and trade journals have a wide circulation, often reaching a worldwide readership, particularly among the more affluent business and professional customers, many of whom are headquartered in Singapore.

In addition, all types of advertising familiar to the exporter are available in Singapore. The type of promotion will, of course, depend upon the product and the target market. Flyers, billboards, store displays, radio, newspapers, etc. are all used as successful marketing techniques.

Market Research and Trade Organizations

Market research is recognized as an essential and effective marketing tool. It is being utilized with increasing frequency in Singapore with very satisfactory results. Several firms have been established to supply this service and have developed an acceptable competence in professional market research. These firms are constantly expanding their activities to meet the growing demand for their expertise.

Although professional market investigation services are available, many local trading firms conduct market inquiries on a rule-of-thumb basis. While the results are often good, they vary according to the competence of the firms and their staffs responsible for market planning and development. Foreign suppliers having agency contacts with local firms are able, in many cases, to obtain most useful market assessments and market development guidance from their agents.

For an indepth assessment of a product's market potential, an American supplier may also engage a U.S. or third-country market research firm, or the supplier may send his or her own

market specialist to Singapore to conduct the necessary research.

Business organizations, both government and private, may also be helpful as sources of market information. There are several chambers of commerce organized on an ethnic basis. They have good membership support and are loosely tied into a single united chamber in an effort to achieve a consolidated approach when representing the viewpoint of private enterprise in its relations with the Government. The largest of the chambers has been organized by business-people of Chinese origin. Membership includes a large number of importers and exporters. There is also the Singapore International Chamber of Commerce, which publishes a monthly *Economic Bulletin.* This periodical advertises trade inquiries and presents trade statistics and general business information helpful to the world trader. Their offices are located in the Denmark House, Raffles Quay, Singapore 0104.

Facilities of the Government to promote commerce and industry have limited application to the promotion of foreign export opportunities in the local markets; principal emphasis is on promotion and assistance to local industrial expansion and exports. In Singapore, the Economic Development Board (EDB) has the responsibility for industry and trade promotion. EDB publishes a monthly journal, *Singapore Trade and Industry,* in which a small number of foreign export opportunities sought by foreign suppliers in the Singapore market are published.

Credit and Banking

Singapore is the major financial center for Southeast Asia. Its financial activities have become an important adjunct to its export-oriented industries and its development as a manufacturing center. As of March 31, 1979, there were 81 commercial banks (68 of them foreign), 29 merchant banks, 44 representative offices of foreign banks, and multiple offices for over 34 major finance companies in Singapore.

On June 1, 1978, Singapore completely liberalized exchange control, thereby facilitating a freer flow of funds between Singapore and the rest of the world. As a result of exchange control liberalization, offshore banks are allowed to deal freely in foreign exchange and to provide credit facilities to Singapore residents without the need to extend a qualifying term loan. The current exchange is about US$1=S$2.10.

One unusual advantage of Singapore as a financial center is its position in world time zones. Seven and a half hours ahead of Greenwich

Mean Time, the Republic has a working day overlapping both European and Asian financial centers. Money dealers in Singapore can contact their counterparts in both London and Tokyo during normal working hours.

Prior to July 15, 1975, the Monetary Authority of Singapore set domestic interest rates in consultation with the Association of Banks. Since that date, all banks have been free to quote their own interest rates, resulting in lower rates for borrowers. The prime lending rate at yearend 1980 was 13 percent.

Local and foreign-owned commercial banks supply short-term credit through overdraft facilities that act as revolving accounts extending credit up to 5 years. American banks providing these services include Bank of America, Chase Manhattan, Citibank, First National Bank of Chicago, and American Express International Banking Corp.

The Development Bank of Singapore (DBS), which is owned by the Government and a number of financial institutions, is the major source of medium- and long-term loans; however, commercial banks are increasingly providing medium- and long-term loans to manufacturing firms. DBS extends credit for 5 to 10 years at competitive interest rates covering up to 50 percent of plant and machinery costs and up to 65 percent of the value of factory buildings. Higher percentages are available for especially desirable projects and for expansion loans.

Several merchant banks have recently been formed to assist in the financing of Singapore's rapid industrial growth. Activities of these banks cover areas not serviced by commercial banks and include capital equipment leasing, medium-term currency loans, direct investment in selected industries, and consultant services from their staffs of lawyers, brokers, and accountants.

Finance companies are present in Singapore and not only provide basic loans to firms but also finance commercial and trade purchases.

Quotations should be c.i.f. Singapore, whenever possible. The prices given may be either in U.S. or Singapore dollars. Exporters making quotations in Singapore dollars should consult their bank for the prevailing exchange rate.

Shipments to Singapore are made under letters of credit and drafts depending on the exporter's preference and the extent of past dealing with the purchaser. For payment by letters of credit, the normal periods are 60, 120, and 180 days. The foreign departments of most major banks are well equipped to give service and advice in matters of foreign trading and, particularly, terms of credit.

Commercial information on Singapore firms is available through *World Traders Data Reports*. These reports are compiled by the Foreign Service and are available from the U.S. Department of Commerce. Such information is also available from private agencies. Principal U.S. credit reporting agencies include Foreign Interchange Bureau, National Association of Credit Management, 475 Park Avenue, South, New York, New York 10022; American Foreign Credit Underwriters Corporation, 99 Church Street, New York, New York 10007; and Dun and Bradstreet, Inc., 299 Park Avenue, New York, New York 10017.

U.S. Bank Branches in Singapore

American Express International Banking
  Corporation
14th Floor, Shing Kwan House
4 Shenton Way, Singapore 0106

Bank of America NT & SA
Clifford Center
24 Raffles Place
Singapore 0104

The Bank of New York
2202-4 Ocean Building
Collyer Quay
Singapore 0104

Bankers Trust Company
Suite 506-8, Ocean Building
Collyer Quay
Singapore 0104

The Chase Manhattan Bank NA*
Shing Kwan House
4 Shenton Way
Singapore 0106

Chemical Bank
DBS Building Tower 3801
6 Shenton Way
Singapore 0106

Citibank NA*
UIC Building
6 Shenton Way
Singapore, 0106

Continental Illinois National Bank
  & Trust Company of Chicago
2101 OCBC Centre
Singapore 0104

First National Bank of Boston
10th Floor, Ocean Building
Collyer Quay
Singapore 0104

*Also have merchant banks incorporated in Singapore.

The First National Bank of Chicago*
150 Cecil Street
Singapore 0106

First National Bank in Dallas
10th Floor, UIC Building
Shenton Way
Singapore 0106

Harris Trust and Savings Bank
2505 OCBC Centre
Singapore 0104

Irving Trust Company
25th Floor, Ocean Building
Collyer Quay
Singapore 0104

Manufacturers Hanover Trust Company
21st Floor, UIC Building
5 Shenton Way
Singapore 0106

Marine Midland Bank
15th Floor, Shin Kwan House
4 Shenton Way
Singapore 0106

Morgan Guaranty Pacific Limited
3001 DBS Tower
6 Shenton Way
Singapore 0106

Republic National Bank of Dallas
1309 Shenton House
Shenton Way
Singapore 0106

United California Bank
22nd Floor, UIC Building
5 Shenton Way
Singapore 0106

Rainier National Bank (U.S.A.)
2003 CPF Building
79 Robinson Road
Singapore 0106

Wells Fargo
2 Shenton Way
Singapore 0106

Banks with Representative Offices

American National Bank & Trust Co. of
  Chicago
DBS Building, Tower 1602
6 Shenton Way
Singapore 0106

The Citizens and Southern National Bank
10th Floor

Bank of East Asia Building
137-K Market Street
Singapore 0104

First Pennsylvania Bank NA
Room 331, 3rd Floor
ICB Building
2 Shenton Way
Singapore 0106

First National Bank in St. Louis
3904 OCBC Centre
Singapore 0104

First National Bank of Houston
Suite 2307
Ocean Building
Collyer Quay
Singapore 0104

First National Bank of Oregon
22nd Floor, UIC Building
5 Shenton Way
Singapore 0106

Girard Bank
1203 Bangkok Building
180 Cecil Street
Singapore 0106

Marine Midland Bank
15th Floor, UIC Building
4 Shenton Way
Singapore 0106

Pacific National Bank of Washington
22nd Floor, UIC Building
5 Shenton Way
Singapore 0106

Pittsburgh National Bank
Suite 1108, Ocean Building
Collyer Quay
Singapore 0104

Security Pacific National Bank
5th Floor, Denmark House
Singapore 0104

State Street Bank & Trust Co.
Suite 909, Ocean Building
Collyer Quay
Singapore 0104

Trade Regulations

Trade Policy

Singapore has long been a regional distribution and sales center (entrepôt) for the trade of Southeast Asia, functioning basically as a free port with a few duties levied for revenue only. Before 1965, import levies were applied on a very small number of products, mainly alcoholic beverages, tobacco, and petroleum products. Later, embarking on more rapid industrialization, Singapore introduced protective duties and, in some cases, quota restrictions to protect new local industries. The emphasis on protective duties has declined in recent years as Singapore has concentrated on developing export industries. Moreover, import quotas have been eliminated. Government policy clearly favors free trade, and local industry is expected to be competitive on the world market.

Despite ensuing changes, Singapore's economy continues to be based heavily on its position as entrepôt for the surrounding region. In recent years, however, Singapore's neighbors have adopted more direct marketing of their raw materials, and they are also exporting them in more finished forms. Singapore's entrepôt role has changed to encompass greater quantities of capital goods (e.g., industrial raw materials and machinery).

Free trade zones were established in Singapore's port areas in September 1969, with special warehouses catering to the particular requirements.

Singapore is a subscriber to the obligations of the International Monetary Fund (November 9, 1968) and a contracting party to the General Agreement on Tariffs and Trade—GATT (August 20, 1973).

Tariff Structure

Effective January 1, 1979, the Singapore Trade Classification and Customs Duties are based on the Customs Cooperation Council Nomenclature (CCCN). Import duties, however, are no longer considered an important means of industrial protection since the emphasis on export-oriented industries has been established. Revenue from duties has declined quite considerably in the percentage that it supplies to total government revenues. While in the past protective tariffs were applied for some infant industries, these were lowered as the industries matured. Major dutiable items now include alcoholic beverages, tobacco, petroleum products, sugar, confectionery, perfumes, assembled televisions, motor vehicles, certain household appliances, clothing, and certain furniture items.

Approximately 50 percent of the duties are levied on a specific basis (certain amount of Singapore dollars per unit of measure); (43 percent are levied on an ad valorem basis (certain

percentage rate of the total invoice value of a shipment of goods); and 7 percent of the duties are either specific or ad valorem, whichever is higher, or a combination of the two. Ad valorem rates range from 10 to 45 percent and average about 20 percent.

Copies of the *Singapore Trade Classification and Customs Duties* are available from the Publications Bureau, Fullerton Building, Ground Floor, Singapore 0104, price S$10.

Basis of Duty Assessment

Ad valorem duties are based on the Singapore customs open-market value—i.e., at the c.i.f. value, plus cost (1 percent of c.i.f., covering handling and other incidental expenses), in the case of direct importation of goods from suppliers or manufacturers, or the c.i.f. value, plus cost and agent commission, in case of importation through an agent. Duties are payable in Singapore dollars at the time dutiable goods are cleared through customs.

Information regarding Singapore's import duties applicable to specific products may be obtained free of charge from the Office of Country Marketing, International Trade Administration, U.S. Department of Commerce, Washington, D.C. 20230; or from any Department of Commerce District Office. Inquiries should contain a complete product description, including BTN, SITC, or U.S. Schedule B Export Commodity numbers, if known.

Multilateral Trade Negotiations

The United States and Singapore reached a bilateral agreement in the Multilateral Trade Negotiations (MTN), completed in April of 1979. In the context of that agreement, Singapore agreed to bind import duties at zero—meaning that duties will not be allowed to rise above the bound rate—on a number of items of trade interest to the United States. These include vegetable protein concentrates, peptones, and similar products; insecticides, fungicides, and herbicides; filling station dispensing pumps for fuels; water coolers; telephone, telegraph, and radio wire and cables; and fats and oils processing machinery.

In the spring of 1980, Singapore became a signatory to the Standards Code negotiated during the MTN and at yearend indicated acceptance of the Government Procurement Code. The Standards Code aims to ensure that adoption of technical regulations or standards by governments or other bodies do not create unnecessary obstacles to trade. The Government Procurement Code is designed to make laws, regulations, and practices regarding government procurement more clear and to ensure there is no protection of domestic products or suppliers or discrimination against foreign products and suppliers.

ASEAN

Regional cooperation is progressing at an increasing rate between the five member countries (Indonesia, Malaysia, the Philippines, Singapore, and Thailand) of the Association of Southeast Asian Nations (ASEAN). In October 1980, a meeting of ASEAN economic ministers was held in Bangkok, with the continued purpose of strengthening trade and investment ties. Among the most favorable concessions decided upon was an increase in the preferential intra-ASEAN tariff reduction rate from 20 percent off on items now listed to 25 percent off. In addition, 1,500 new products were added to the Preferential Trade Arrangements (PTA), for a total of 5,825 items. The initial agreement on the ASEAN Preferential Trade Arrangements was signed February 1977 and effective January 1, 1978. 71 products were incorporated under this first agreement.

Generalized System of Preference

Many goods producted in Singapore (as in most developing countries) qualify for preferential access to markets in the United States, The European Economic Community, Japan, Australia, and the Scandanavian countries. Statistics for 1979 show eligible ASEAN nations shipping $490 million worth of Generalized System of Preferences (GSP), duty-free goods to the United States, as compared with $304 million in 1978. Singapore ranks seventh among all U.S. GSP beneficiaries and is by far the largest beneficiary of the member countries of ASEAN. In 1979, the United States imported $232 million worth of GSP, duty-free products from Singapore, as compared with $153 million in 1978.

The United States requires that 35 percent of the product's value be added in the eligible country. Also, goods from GSP-eligible nations retain their preferential access to the U.S. market if transshipped through Singapore.

The UNCTAD (United Nations Conference on Trade and Development), Form A, required to qualify for GSP status, is issued only by the Singapore Department of Trade. It is not available from the chambers of commerce.

Metrication

Singapore is in the process of shifting from imperial units to the International System of Units (SI), the updated version of the metric system. In the public sector, the changeover is substantially complete in the telephone and postal systems, land surveying, public utilities, public housing, sewerage, road work, and the Marine Department. Metric speed limits and distance markings on roads have been set and car speedometers are required to show kilometers per hour.

Progress by the private sector in converting from popular use of a diverse mix of British, Malay, and Chinese measures, all in common use, is slow. Having originally planned to require sole use of metric units in the retail sector by January 1976, the Government currently only requires that retailers be prepared to sell in metric units upon customer demand.

There are no metric packaging or labeling requirements applicable to prepackaged goods imported into Singapore, although customs and other trade documents must include declarations in SI units. Imports of weighing and measuring devices are subject to government approval, which usually requires calibration solely in SI units. Dually calibrated units are not acceptable. Instruments specifically subject to approval by the Singapore Department of Trade include barometers, calipers, flow meters, micrometers, odometers, pressure gages, rulers, speed indicators (including magnetic speed indicators), surveying instruments, thermometers, pyrometers, weighing machines, weighbridges, and weights of all kinds.

Certain domestic products are now subject to metric packaging guidelines that affect packaging materials going into Singapore. It is likely that these guidelines will be applied to imports in the near future.

More detailed information on worldwide metriation is contained in *Metric Laws and Practices in International Trade—a Handbook for U.S. Exporters* prepared by the U.S. Department of Commerce in 1976 and available through the U.S. Government Printing Office (Stock number: 210-801/422 1-3).

Information on metric requirements and usage in Singapore may be obtained from:

Singapore Metrication Board
Ministry of Science and Technology
1 Anson Road
Singapore 0207

U.S. exporters are advised to ascertain from their importers current practices and preferences concerning metric usage.

Antipollution Regulations

Most industrial and commercial enterprises are covered by antipollution legislation. The major laws include the "Clean Air Antipollution Regulations of 1971," "Clean Air Regulations, 1972," "Water Pollution and Drainage Act, 1975," and the "Trade Effluent Regulations, 1976." In March 1972, Singapore began instituting regulatory measures against motor vehicles, which covered, among others, air pollution measures.

Entry and Reexport

Entry.—Upon the arrival of goods in Singapore (by either surface or air), the importing company must present to the carrier's agent an appropriate import declaration certified by the Registrar of Imports and Exports in exchange for a delivery order that entitles the agent to take delivery of the company's shipment. Landing permits for dutiable goods must be obtained from customs officials, and goods must be landed at a quay, wharf, customs airport, or other designated place. Goods that are loaded, transshipped, or removed contrary to this procedure are liable to seizure. If goods are not accounted for within a prescribed period, fines are levied. Penalties are also imposed for goods not accounted for in event of short shipment, short lading, or overlading.

Transit, Transshipment, and Reexport.—Singapore's traditional function as a transit zone and transshipment point for the trade of nearby Southeast Asian countries continues practically unaffected by the country's minimal trade controls. Most of its trade continues to move without the imposition of customs duties or other restrictions, so that activities relating to trade may be undertaken throughout the island. For the storage of dutiable goods, government and private bonded warehouses are available both inside and outside port areas.

Much of Singapore's transit trade is handled within the free zone area immediately adjacent to the harbor under the jurisdiction of the Port of Singapore Authority. Within its confines, goods may be loaded, unloaded, stored, sorted, repacked, and transshipped with minimum customs involvement. Goods do not pass through Singapore customs unless they are removed from this area.

Sampling of cargoes held on Port Authority premises is subject to approval upon written application. While other forms of processing are generally not permitted, in some cases (again subject to written application and approval), assembly may be undertaken. Manufacturing is not permitted in Port Authority public warehouses but may be performed (with a license from the Customs Department) in the free trade zones and in other buildings specifically leased for such purposes within the port area or in other areas approved by the Government.

The entry, departure, or transfer of goods to or from transit sheds and storage warehouses within the general port area by shippers, agents, or consignees is subject to certain documentary requirements. Prior to the exportation, reexportation, or transshipment of goods from Singapore, export permits issued by the Registrar of Imports and Exports must be obtained. The Customs Unit of the Import and Export Office issues Customs Removal Permits in respect of dutiable goods for transshipments on through bills of lading. Shipping agents are also allowed to ship cargo overland on transshipment declaration permits.

Dutiable goods on which duties have not been paid may be reexported without payment of duty only if they are moved under Customs control and checked out at the port of boundary station. All or part of the customs duty paid may be refunded on goods, as prescribed by the Minister of Finance, if imported and reexported within a prescribed period. This applies also to goods imported, manufactured, and then reexported.

Samples and Advertising Matter.—Samples of no commercial value are admitted duty free into Singapore; other samples are subject to prevailing duties. Dutiable samples may be brought in by commercial travelers under bond or under deposit of duty. The bond is canceled or the deposit refunded if the samples are exported within 6 months or within such further time as the authorities may grant.

Commercial travelers' samples and samples imported by parcel post may enter duty free except for limited items, including liquor and tobacco. No restrictions are imposed on the reexportation of duty-free goods. No refund of duty is granted on liquor and tobacco samples. Only advertising material relating to a limited number of items, including tobacco and liquor, are subject to customs duties.

Advance Rulings on Classification.—When an importer is in doubt as to the classification of goods, a sample and description of the goods may be sent to appropriate Customs officers. Any ruling the Customs officer may make is purely advisory and not binding. The Customs officer may elect to send a sample of the goods to the Comptroller of Customs for a ruling on the classification of the article. Such a ruling is considered binding.

Fines and Penalties.—With the exception of a

Customs officer pursuing his/her duties, no person may have in his/her possession of control in a Customs or licensed warehouse any dutiable goods or denatured spirits imported contrary to the provisions of the Customs regulations. All goods dealt with in contravention of these regulations are liable to seizure, and any person found guilty of possessing such dutiable goods is liable to a fine.

Any person who makes false or fraudulent alterations on any document required by the Import and Export Control or Customs authorities is subject to punishment with imprisonment or fine.

Penalties are provided for the importation of prohibited goods, removal of goods before examination by a Customs officer, the illegal removal of goods from a warehouse or other place of security, the deliberate concealing of prohibited or undeclared goods or goods that have been removed illegally, or the fraudulent evasion or attempt at evasion of Customs duty.

The Singapore Customs (Dumping and Subsidies) Ordinance of 1962 provides for the imposition of antidumping and countervailing duties—in addition to normal import duties—on dumped and subsidized goods, if their import is likely to endanger an established industry or retard the establishment of an industry.

Internal Taxes

Excise taxes, equal to import duties, are levied on locally manufactured petroleum products. There is an excise tax imposed on certain locally manufactured alcoholic beverages. There is also a censorship fee on films and a levy on admission tickets.

On first registration of a new vehicle (including those locally assembled) in Singapore, a fee of 125 percent (plus a 45 percent duty for imports) of the open market value (to be determined by the Registrar) of all passenger cars is levied. There is also an annual registration fee (road tax) determined on the basis of the cubic capacity of the engine, which ranges from S$.175 to S$.40 per cubic centimeter. An additional tax, which is six times the road tax levied on gasoline powered vehicles, is imposed on motor vehicles fitted with engines using heavy oil. These rates went into effect on January 1, 1976, and represent the Government's attempt to alleviate the strain placed on Singapore's transport system by the large increase in the number of cars on the road.

Shipping Documents

Documents required by Import and Export Control and Customs authorities for air and surface shipments entering Singapore include the commercial invoice; the bill of lading for surface shipments; and air waybill for air freight, import declaration, packing lists, and insurance documents. Special documents are also required for the importation of certain plant materials, birds, and animals. Consumer documents are not required.

Commercial Invoice.—Special commercial invoice forms are not required. Invoices may be printed on an exporter's letterhead, but must be signed by a responsible person of the firm and must show the proper description, quantity or weight, c.i.f. value, country of origin of the goods, and name or number of the vessel or aircraft in which such goods are shipped. Two copies are forwarded under separate cover to the consignee in Singapore; the original copy must be submitted to the Customs authorities.

Bill of Lading.—The bill of lading should show the name of the shipper, consignee, and steamer; the exporter's mark and number of packages; and a description of the goods.

Certificate of Origin.—A certificate of origin is required only for banking purposes when dollar exchange is supplied by the local control authorities and for goods for which a preferential tariff rate is to be claimed. There is no special form for the certificate, which may be certified by a chamber of commerce, a recognized bank, or by a firm of international repute.

Import Declaration.—Importers are required to present an import declaration for all imports.

Singapore Standards

The Singapore Institute of Standards and Industrial Research (SISIR) seal is the official government certification mark guaranteeing the quality of Singapore-made products. A manufacturer is authorized by SISIR to use the seal only after the Institute has subjected his products to stringent quality tests and is satisfied with its quality and reliability.

Marking and Labeling Requirements

Labels are required on imports of food, drugs, liquors, paints, and solvents, and they must specify the country of origin. Prepacked foods must be labeled to show in English the appropriate designation of the food content, printed in capital letters at least 1/16 inch high; whether foods are compounded, mixed, or blended; the minimum quantity stated in metric net weight or measure (intoxicating liquors, soft drinks, and condensed or dried milk are exempt from this provision if prepacked in a container for retail sale); the name and address of the manufacturer or seller; and the country of origin. Sugar confectionery, chocolate, and chocolate confectionery are exempted from all the general labeling requirements for prepacked foods.

A description of the contents of the package may be added to the face of the label provided the additional language is not contrary to, or a modification of, any statement (in English) on the label. Pictorial illustrations must not be misleading as to the true nature or origin of the food.

Foods having defined standards must be labeled to conform to these standards and be free from added foreign substances. Packages of food described as "enriched," "fortified," "vitaminized," or in any other way which implies that the article contains added vitamins or minerals, must show the quantities of vitamins or minerals added per metric unit.

> *Senate Concurrent Resolution 40, adopted July 30, 1953, invites U.S. exporters to inscribe, insofar as practicable, on the external shipping containers in indelible print of a suitable size: "United States of America."*

Special labels are required for certain foods, medicinals, and goods such as edible and nonedible animal fats, as well as paints and solvents. Processed foods and pharmaceuticals must be inspected and passed by the Ministry of Health. Electrical goods must be checked by the Public Utilities Board (PUB) engineers before they can be installed in government establishments, while paints and solvents are the responsibility of the Chief Inspector of Factories, Ministry of Labor.

U.S. exporters are advised to ascertain from their importers current marking and labeling requirements.

Import Licensing

Most goods are freely importable into Singapore under general license, without recourse to a specific validated license for each transaction. There are, however, a few commodities subject to specific import licensing that are specified in the "Control of Imports (Licensing) Order, 1976." Amendments to the list appear from time to time, printed in the *Singapore Government Gazette* and announced in "Notices to Importers." Certain products on the list are further restricted by quotas, published quarterly in "Notices to Importers." If no quota is specified, special import licenses are issued, upon application, for reasonable quantities.

All imports originating in South Africa or in any territory administered by that country are prohibited. In addition, the open general license does not apply to goods originating in, wholly or mainly manufactured in, or consigned from, Albania, People's Republic of China, Cuba, Czechoslovakia, East Germany, Laos, Mongolia, or Vietnam. License applications for such goods must be submitted through the intermediary of Intraco, Ltd., which levies a surcharge of 0.5 percent on the c.i.f. value of imports from these countries, except for the People's Republic of China. Intraco, a State-sponsored trading company, conducts much of the importing business with State trading countries.

Import controls are administered by the Ministry of Trade and Industry. Some control functions of a statistical, implementive, and investigative nature have been delegated to the Controller of Customs. Information on goods currently listed in these notifications, and quotas where in effect, is available on request from the ASEAN/Southeast Asia Branch, Office of Country Marketing, International Trade Administration, U.S. Department of Commerce, Washington, D.C. 20230.

Exchange Controls

Exchange controls, first introduced in Singapore in 1939, were completely removed on June 1, 1978. This final step in exchange control liberalization made it possible for all Singapore residents, including corporations, to make freely payments in all currencies and to invest in any country. There are no restrictions placed on the movement of capital to and from Singapore, including the repatriation of profits derived from foreign investment there.

The Singapore currency, the Singapore dollar, was introduced on June 12, 1967, to replace the "Straits dollar" which was previously utilized in Malaysia, Singapore, and Brunei. Since 1973, the Singapore dollar has been floating freely against other world currencies. The exchange rate, as of December 1980, hovered around $S2.10-US$1.

Singapore's Export Control

All exports from Singapore are technically subject to control and must be declared. However, restrictions are imposed on only a few categories of exports. Export control functions are carried on by the Ministry of Trade and Industry.

Exports of certain textiles to Norway, Sweden, the United Kingdom, and the United States are subject to restrictive licensing, and all exports of metal scraps of iron and steel, and untreated bird feathers are restricted. Since August 1979, exports of footwear to the United States are under restrictive licensing. Other commodities do not require an export license.

Investment in Singapore

Foreign and U.S. Investment

Total American investment in Singapore at the end of 1978 was $1.6 billion and reached $1.7 billion by mid-1979. The entry of high-technology manufacturing industries and significant capital expansion by existing firms contributed to this substantial increase over previous years.

Petroleum refining and storage remained the leading sector, representing 31 percent of total U.S. investment, with investment in electronics manufacturing accounting for 22 percent.

For more than 10 years, the United States has been Singapore's top investor in the manufacturing sector. At the end of 1977, Japan overtook the United Kingdom and the Netherlands to reach second place, according to Singapore's Economic Development Board (EDB). Japan will soon replace the United States as the largest investor, particularly when the $910 million Sumitomo petrochemical complex is completed.

Total foreign investment in Singapore's manufacturing sectors by region (North America, Europe, and Asia) totaled $2.3 billion in 1978, and, by mid-1979, it had reached $2.6 billion. As of 1978, the Government of Singapore stopped publishing investment data by country; therefore, only regional totals are available. Europe, as a result, holds the highest investment figures for manufacturing, totaling $883 million in 1978 and $993 million by mid-1979.

Government Policy on Investment

Singapore welcomes private foreign investment and explicitly encourages multinationals. There are no restrictions on foreign ownership of companies in Singapore. In general, local equity participation is not required, but, in some industries, the Government may encourage it. Companies whose sole activity is to trade goods made elsewhere, none of which are reexported from Singapore, may be required to obtain local equity in certain cases. There are no ceilings on remittance of profits and no obstacles to capital repatriation.

The Government is particularly interested in petrochemicals, machine tools, precision engineering and equipment, sophisticated electronics, and heavy machinery. Although the Government's emphasis is on these industries, nearly all types of investment are welcome, including regional administrative and sales offices.

The sphere of development for foreign private investment is not limited by legislation. Consequently, foreign investment in Singapore has been marked by its diversification, covering a full range of light industry and many heavy industries (petroleum refining and related activities, chemicals, metal products, transport equipment and facilities, and electronic and electrical products), including those bunkering and entrepôt services that Singapore provides as the world's third largest port.

In principle, no distinction is made by the Government between local and foreign capital. Legislation offering incentives for private industrial development is open to both sources equally. However, there is a tendency, not reflected in written legislation, for the specific encouragement of joint ventures emphasizing foreign know-how and the joint participation of foreign and local capital. Maximum participation of Singapore personnel, eventually including the executive level, should be planned by foreign private investors contemplating investing in Singapore, even though not specifically required by legislation.

Singapore's Economic Development Board (EDB) encourages skill-intensive and technology-oriented manufacturing industries that add a high value per worker. Support for the Board's strategy is provided through domestic and overseas vocational and technical training schemes. For approved precision industries, the Government is prepared to subsidize in-plant training for up to S$9,200 per trainee. All technical education is conducted in English.

Certain categories of foreign investors are offered varying combinations of tax holidays, tax reductions, favorable loan terms, duty-free import in capital goods and raw materials, government equity participation, and industrial estate facilities. The main types of investment eligible for incentives are the following: (1) establishment of pioneer industries that "are not being carried on in Singapore on a scale adequate to the economic needs of Singapore"; (2) expansion of established enterprises by capital expenditure of at least S$10 million; and (3) export enterprises.

The procedure for seeking pioneer status involves applying in writing to the EDB. Then, with publication of the application, objections are invited. If after official consideration no objections have been made or no grounds for objection remain, the pioneer certificate is issued. The EDB plays an additional role of aiding investors during any necessary negotiations with other government agencies or ministries. Approvals for pioneer industries generally take less than 3 weeks. Currently over 400 pioneer enterprises hold investments that total over S\$3 billion. Most skill-intensive and high-technology industries that have applied have received pioneer status.

Details regarding incentives are available from the Singapore Economic Development Board, Ninth Floor, World Trade Center, Telok Blangah Road, Singapore 0409, or its offices in the United States (see the final section of this report for addresses).

Singapore Stock Exchange

Since May 1973, Singapore's stock exchange (SES) has been separate from Malaysia's. The SES is assuming an important role in the financing of both stocks and bonds. At the end of October 1979, 265 enterprises were listed. Of these, 96 were Singaporean companies. Several Asian dollar bond issues have been floated during the last few years.

Firms that can handle stock exchange issues include DBS (Daiwa Securities) and Singapore Nomura Merchant Banking.

Legislation Governing Investment

Entry and Repatriation of Capital.—The transfer of funds between Singapore and other countries is unrestricted. Importation of currency notes of all countries is permitted without restriction, and there are no restrictions on the repatriation of foreign currency.

Foreign industrialists may bring in any amount of capital, and both the remittance of profits and the repatriation of capital (including depreciation and capital appreciation) in the currency of the original investments are permitted without restriction. Transfer of profits and dividends in the currency of the original investment is permitted without restriction.

Foreign Ownership of Business Entities.—There are no restrictions against foreign ownership of business entities in Singapore, and completely foreign-owned businesses may operate. However, foreign investment that is associated with local capital and enterprise is particularly welcomed by the Government.

Foreign Ownership of Real Property.—Except for residential properties there are no restrictions on the foreign ownership of land in Singapore and privately owned land may be leased for a term of years up to 99 years. The Torrens System of land restriction prevails here, and is known as "The Land Titles Act." The foreign investor who contemplates purchasing land in Singapore should consult the Economic Development Board for appropriate assistance.

Investors may either purchase privately held land for plant construction or lease government land on the industrial estates, such as Jurong, for 30 to 60 years.

The 1976 Residential Property Act permits only Singapore citizens to buy and sell residential properties without restrictions. However, foreign individuals who make an economic contribution to Singapore are, under certain conditions, allowed to purchase residential properties.

Investment Agreements

The Government has signed investment guarantee treaties with France, the United Kingdom, Germany, Canada, the Netherlands, Switzerland, and the United States. Investments made by nationals of both parties in each other's territory will be protected against war and expropriation risks.

Investors may also obtain assistance through guaranties against loss from commercial as well as political risks; direct loans in dollars of local foreign currencies; and preinvestment information, counseling, and cost-sharing. Information on this program may be obtained from the Overseas Private Investment Corporation (OPIC), 1129 20th Street, N.W., Washington, D.C. 20036.

Business Organization

Types of Organization

There are three ways in which a business enterprise can be organized to operate in Singapore: as a single proprietorship, as a partnership, and as a corporation.

Single Proprietorship or Partnership.—Persons carrying on business under their own name, as well as persons who carry on business under names that are not the complete true names of the individuals or partners, are required to register under the Business Registration Act of 1973. Societies duly registered or exempted under the Societies Act and businesses consisting solely of the exercise of a profession that is regulated by law do not fall under this requirement. Partnerships have the option of registering under The Companies (Amendment) Act of 1970.

Corporation.—Corporations are governed by The Companies Act of 1970. Under this Act, any two or more persons may form an incorporated company. It becomes mandatory to register as a company once an organization, association, or partnership whose object is to realize profits or gains has more than 20 members.

A company may be: (a) limited by shares, (b) limited by guarantee, (c) limited by both shares and guarantee, or (d) unlimited. A company limited by shares is one where the liability of its members is limited to the amount of shares subscribed by them; in a company limited by guarantee, the liability of the members is limited to the amount that they undertake to contribute to the company's assets in event of its liquidation. An unlimited company is one in which no limit is placed on the liability of its members.

A company may be registered as a private company if it does not have more than 50 shareholders, restricts the right to transfer shares, and prohibits any invitation to the public to subscribe to its shares and debentures or to deposit money with it. Otherwise, the company becomes a public company.

A limited company must have the word "Limited" or "Berhad" at the end of its name. Nonprofit companies may be exempted from this requirement. A private company must have the word "Private" or "Sendirian" at the end of its name if it is unlimited, or immediately before the word "Limited" or "Berhad" if it is a limited company.

Steps for Approval and Registration

Except in the case of certain professions and occupations, potential investors should first write to the Foreign Branches/Immigration Section of the Trade Division, Ministry of Trade and Industry, Second Floor, World Trade Center, 1 Maritime Square, Singapore 0409.

Completed application forms must then be returned to the respective government departments/ministries for processing, which takes 2 to 3 weeks to complete. When approval is obtained from the respective government agencies, the next step is registration.

For registration under the Business Registration Act, the address is Registrar, Registry of Businesses, Room 406-416, Colombo Court, Singapore 0617. For registration under the Companies Act, the forms should be sent to the Registry of Companies at the same address.

It is advisable for foreigners to file company registration forms through a local lawyer since they can also handle all the statutory declaration requirements for registration.

Incorporation of a Local Company

Registration requirements for limited companies registered under the Companies Act are:

a. The name of corporation must be approved by the Registrar of Companies.
b. There must be a minimum of two individual persons each subscribing to at least one share in the corporation.
c. There must be a minimum of two directors, one of whom must have principal or only residence in Singapore. (A director must be a natural person and not a corporation.)
d. The following documents must be lodged with the Registrar of Companies:
   1. memorandum and articles of the proposed company,
   2. consent to act as director (on prescribed forms),
   3. notice of location of registered office and of office hours and particulars of changes (on prescribed forms),
   4. certificate of identity (on prescribed forms), and
   5. statutory declaration of compliance (on prescribed forms).
e. The company must have one or more secretaries, each of whom must be a natural person who has principal or only residence in Singapore.
f. The company must have authorized and paidup capital (no minimum amount).
g. Registration fees payable depend on the amount of authorized capital.

Incorporation as a local company is generally favored by the Singapore Government over establishment of a branch for foreign enterprises engaging in activities in the country. A domestic corporation must:

(a) have an authorized capital and a paid-up capital (while there is no minimum amount specified, there must be at least two subscriber shares);

(b) pay registration fees on the basis of the authorized capital of the company; and

(c) file annual audited statements with the Registrar of Companies unless it is an exempted private company (i.e., one with not more than 20 stockholders, all of whom are individuals rather than corporations).

A company can be dissolved only by liquidation procedures prescribed in the Companies Act of 1970. The powers of the board of directors of a company are governed by its articles of association.

The Government is eager to have local participation and is willing to assist foreign investors in finding partners.

Sole Proprietorship or Partnership

Registration requirements for a sole proprietorship or partnership registered under the Business Registration Act are:
a. the company must state the business name, the general nature of the business, and the principal place of business;
b. particulars of the proprietor (for sole proprietorship) and each partner (for partnership), whether individuals or corporations; and
c. registration fee of S$50 (S$25 for annual renewal).

Branch Office

Foreign banks and financial institutions must apply to the Monetary Authority of Singapore before setting up a branch office in Singapore. Similarly, insurance companies must apply to the Ministry of Finance.

Generally, foreign corporations engaged in other activities can establish a branch in Singapore without obtaining clearance from any government bodies. However, it is advisable for foreign corporations to consult the Trade Division on any legislation or acts that may be relevant to the various trades.

Within 1 month of establishing a place of business or commencing operations in Singapore, a branch must register with the Registrar of Companies and lodge with the Registrar the following documents:
a. certificate of incorporation in the foreign country,
b. charter and/or memorandum and articles of association,
c. list of its foreign directors and particulars of the directors,
d. list of directors resident in Singapore with a memorandum stating their powers,
e. memorandum of appointment of power of attorney stating names and addresses of two or more residents of Singapore authorized to accept legal notices on behalf of the company,
f. statutory declaration to be made by the agent of the foreign company on prescribed forms, and
g. notice of the location of its registered office in Singapore.

No authorized or paid-up capital is required for a branch office since the capital of the head office in effect acts for the branch.

Registration fees payable are half of those for incorporating a local company, but they are based on the authorized capital of the parent company.

Branch offices of foreign corporations engaged in trading and shipping activities must notify the Foreign Branches/Immigration Section of the Trade Division within 1 month of commencing business.

A branch can be dissolved after giving due notice to the Registrar of Companies. The powers of the agents or the local board of directors are contained in the memorandum of appointment or power of attorney. There are no restrictions as to citizenship for branches.

Representative Office

Other than for banks, financial institutions, and insurance companies, representative offices need ot apply for clearance nor register with the Registrar of Companies. However, trading and shipping companies must inform the Department of Trade after establishing a representative office in Singapore.

Representative offices are not allowed to engage in any trading activities; they serve purely as promotional or liaison offices. The Foreign Branches/Immigration Section of the Trade Division must be consulted if there is any question of whether a particular office can be considered a representative office.

Pros and Cons of Incorporation vs. Branch Operations

There appear to be no significant advantages from an operational standpoint to establishing a branch office versus setting up a local company. There are no restrictions on the operations of branch offices other than those laid down in legislation and regulations pertaining to the various trades. However, it is advisable to consult a local lawyer before making the decision on what type of operation best suits a firm's particular needs, especially with regard to the effects on a company's tax liability.

Locally incorporated companies are taxed on their taxable income at a flat rate of 40 percent. In the case of a branch office, only profits derived from or remitted to Singapore are taxed at 40 percent (i.e., income from sales outside Singapore and dividends and interest received in Singapore are taxable if remitted to Singapore; royalty income would normally follow the same rule, but, in some cases, it depends on where the contract was signed).

Since representative offices do not engage in any trading activities, they do not pay company taxes. However, the personnel in the representative office who are resident in Singapore will have to pay personal income tax. In the case of an area representative of a foreign firm who normally travels extensively on business but is based in Singapore, the representative is liable for income tax on the greater of:

a. the proportion of earnings earned while in Singapore, or

b. the amount of income received in or remitted to Singapore.

The representative is allowed the normal tax exemptions regardless of the period of residence.

Taxation

The basic legislation that imposes personal and corporate income taxes, defines deduction, establishes appellate procedures, and sets forth the tax forgiveness features of industries accorded pioneer status is the Income Tax (Amendment) Act of 1967, which amended the Income Tax Act (Chapter 166 of the Revised Edition), as of November 24, 1967. Copies of this legislation may be purchased from the Government Printer, Singapore. A few of the principal features of this ordinance are summarized here, but reference should be made to the original legislation. For more detailed information and official rulings on specific questions, inquiries should be directed to the Inland Revenue Department, Income Tax Division, Fourth Floor, Fullerton Building, Singapore 0104, telephone: 914-244.

Income Tax

Income is defined to include gains or profits from any trade, business, profession, or vocation; earnings from employment, direct or in the form of food, clothing, or housing provided by the employer, including wages, salary, leave pay, fees, commission, gratuities, and allowances, but excluding bona fide subsistence, travel, or entertainment allowances; net annual value of land and improvements used by the owner on a **rent-free basis; dividends, interest, and discounts; pensions and annuities; and rents, royalties, and earnings from property. There is no capital gains tax.**

In determining taxable income for individuals, it is necessary to calculate assessable and chargeable income. Assessable income is statutory income less deductions for losses incurred in any trade, profession, or vocation; losses incurred during the 6 years preceding the year of assessment that have not been allowed against the statutory income of the prior year; and gifts to public charitable institutions. The chargeable income is the assessable income after further deductions consisting of personal allowances. Under Singapore law, a flat S$2,000

is deductible from the assessable income of resident individual taxpayers, with additional deductions permitted for dependents in the case of married taxpayers. Life insurance premiums and certain contributions to pension and retirement funds are also deductible as personal allowances.

Since the personal allowances apply only to individuals, the chargeable income is identical with the assessable income in the case of companies, partnerships, and associations.

Singapore residents are taxed according to the following progressive rate schedule on their chargeable income:

		Percent
First S$	2,500	5
Next	2,500	8
"	2,500	10
"	2,500	12
"	5,000	15
"	5,000	20
"	5,000	25
"	10,000	30
"	15,000	35
"	50,000	40
"	100,000	45
"	200,000	50
"	200,000 and above	55

Individual Income Tax Liability

Temporary Residents.—Income from sources outside Singapore received by temporary residents of Singapore is exempt from Singapore income tax under certain conditions. The individual must not have any intent to establish residence there and must not have resided in Singapore for a period or periods equaling 6 months in a calendar year. Directors of companies are liable for a flat income tax rate of 40 percent irrespective of the length of their stay in Singapore.

Short-term Visiting Employees.—Income derived from employment in Singapore by nonresident employees who stay in Singapore for not more than 60 days in a calendar year is exempt from Singapore income tax.

Nonresidents.—Persons residing in Singapore for more than 60 days but less than 183 days in a calendar year are normally considered to be nonresidents. The income of such persons (whether paid in Singapore or not) derived from the exercise of employment in Singapore is taxable at a flat rate of 15 percent, provided such tax is not less than that which would be payable by a Singapore resident in the same circumstances. Income from most other sources is taxable at a flat rate of 40 percent. Whether a person is a nonresident is a question of interpretation, and some persons who may have been in Singapore for less than 183 days may be treated as residents. The criterion used to determine residence is similar to that applicable in the United States—each case being considered on its merits.

Residents.—An individual who has resided in Singapore for 183 days or more in a calendar year is considered a resident and is liable for tax on income derived from or received in Singapore on the same basis as Singapore citizens. As indicated above, the tax rates are progressive from 5 to 55 percent of chargeable income, after certain exemptions and deductions have been applied.

Special Note for Resident Individuals: A resident individual who is located in Singapore whose salary is partly paid in Singapore and the rest deposited in his/her bank in his/her home country is liable for payment of personal income tax in Singapore on his/her total salary. Section 12(4) of the Republic of Singapore Income Tax Act (Chapter 141) states that gains on profits from any employment exercised in Singapore shall be deemed to be derived from Singapore whether the gains or profits from such employment are received in Singapore or not.

Corporations Tax

In the case of companies and corporations, tax is levied at a flat rate of 40 percent on the adjusted net profits for income tax purposes, less any capital or depreciation allowances. Companies that are resident in Singapore are entitled to deduct tax at the rate of 40 percent from any dividends paid to shareholders. Resident shareholders who receive dividends must include the dividends together with other personal income in preparing income tax statements. However, resident shareholders can in turn set off the corporation taxes paid by the firm on the dividend against the income tax payable in Singapore on their total income. This provision affords tax relief to resident shareholders.

In the case of nonresident and other taxpayers whose rate of tax is also 40 percent, no further tax is payable on the dividend, since the tax is already accounted for by deduction.

Deductions are allowed for all direct and overhead expenses incurred in generating income. The list of allowable deductions includes, but is not limited to, the following items: interest on loans; dividends declared; rent; expenses incurred for repair of premises, plant, machinery, or fixtures; bad debts; contributions to approved pensions or to the Central Provident fund; and depreciation on buildings, machinery, and equipment.

Payroll Tax

Payroll tax is levied at the rate of 2 percent on the payroll of an employer for each month where the payroll exceeds S$500, provided that total payroll tax payable does not exceed the difference between the payroll and S$500. This tax is applicable to the whole of the remuneration comprising salaries, wages, commissions, bonuses, leave pay, etc., paid in cash to the employees. Contributions by the employer to an approved provident or pension fund are deducted from the total payroll for tax purposes. This tax is not applicable to persons who are self-employed.

Tax Incentives

The Government has granted tax incentives to businesspeople and firms investing in Singapore since 1967. In a period characterized by lagging economic growth and much unemployment, the Singapore Parliament passed the Economic Expansion Incentives (Relief from Income Tax) Act of 1967. These incentives included tax relief for a period up to 15 years. However, the Act as originally passed was considered no longer appropriate to Singapore's present economic situation of booming growth and adequate employment opportunities. Therefore, the Singapore Parliament passed the Economic Expansion Incentives (Relief from Income Tax) Amendment Act of 1970. The main changes made in Singapore's tax incentive structure were to decrease the length of time for which tax exemption could be granted and to tighten up the criteria for granting pioneer status. The tax incentives listed below incorporate the changes that have been made in the law by the Amendment Act of 1970 and further changes made in August 1975, March 1978, and April 1979.

Pioneer Industries.—Full exemption from tax on profits of pioneer companies is granted for a period of up to 10 years. (There is no longer a minimum capital expenditure requirement for small but especially high-quality product industries that provide supporting services.) The company should also be relatively new in its field in Singapore and should be sufficiently skill intensive.

Expanding Enterprises.—A special exemption from corporate tax for the additional income resulting from the expansion of an approved enterprise is granted for a period not exceeding 5 years, but the firm must incur a cost of not less than S$10 million on additional equipment to realize either increased production or profitability of an approved product.

Export Enterprise.—A company having

export sales not less than S$100,000 and not less than 20 percent of total sales may enjoy export status for:

a. a period of 5 years if not a pioneer enterprise; or

b. if also a pioneer enterprise, a period of 3 years after the expiration of the pioneer relief period.

During the period of its export status, the enterprise is entitled to a tax concession by paying 4 percent instead of 40 percent tax on profits from export sales (profits from domestic sales being still taxed at 40 percent). However, where an export enterprise has incurred or intends to incur a fixed capital expenditure of:

a. not less than S$1,000 million, or

b. not less than S$150 million but less than S$1,000 million, and with the two additional conditions that:

1. not more than 50 percent of the paidup capital of the export enterprise be held by permanent residents in Singapore,

2. the Minister for Finance believes the export enterprise will promote or enhance the economic or technological development of Singapore;

then, its export status period may be extended to:

a. 15 years if not a pioneer enterprise, or

b. 10 years after the expiration of its pioneer relief period if it is a pioneer enterprise.

Investment Allowance.—Under this incentive, companies planning to start up or increase the manufacture of any product can claim investment allowances up to 50 percent of fixed capital expenditure on specified items. Companies that specialize in engineering and technical services will also qualify for the benefits. A company can utilize the investment allowance granted by virtue of the new projects to claim tax exemption on profits from the current business. There is no statutory minimum requirement in terms of fixed investment or turnover for a project to be considered under this incentive. There is a time period within which a company cannot sell, lease, or dispose of any assets upon which an investment allowance has been given.

Warehousing and Servicing Incentive.—Companies engaged in regional warehousing and servicing operations for engineering products are entitled to a concessional 20 to 40 percent corporate tax rate for a period of 5 years. Companies that invest at least S$2 million in buildings and productive equipment are eligible.

International Consultancy Incentive.—This incentive is extended to companies engaged in technical advisory services, design and engineering fabrication of equipment,

management and supervision of installation or construction, and data processing. These services must be for overseas projects, and only companies earning more than S$1 million per year from such services are eligible. The incentive is a concessionary 20-percent corporate tax rate for a period of 5 years.

International Trade Incentive.—Companies that are exporting Singapore-made products or trading in nontraditional commodities (excluding tin, natural rubber, palm oil, coconut oil, logs, sawn timber, petroleum, and spices) are entitled to a concessionary 20 percent corporate tax rate for 5 years. To qualify for this incentive, companies must either export an annual minimum of S$10 million of the qualifying products or S$20 million of the nontraditional commodities.

Accelerated Depreciation Allowances.—Certain industrial enterprises may claim an accelerated allowance of 33.33 percent per annum for a period of 3 years on capital expenditures incurred on plant and machinery. The provision is also applicable to equipment and devices installed for the prevention of air and water pollution.

Double Deduction for Permanent Trading Office Abroad.—Companies setting up permanent trading offices overseas can claim twice the amount of operational expenses incurred in the first 2 years.

Allowances for Overseas Promotion.—Expenses for not more than two employees incurred by a firm for maintaining or participating in an approved overseas trade fair exhibition or trade mission for the purpose of export promotion of locally manufactured goods will be allowed double deductions.

Research and Development (R&D) Concessions.—A new concession announced by the Minister for Trade and Industry in March 1980 allows various incentives to aid in the development of new products and processes. Included will be the double deduction of R&D expenditures (other than on building and equipment); accelerated depreciation over 3 years for all plant and machinery relating to R&D; and an investment allowance of up to 50 percent of the capital investment in R&D, including building costs.

Allowances for Conventions.—Convention organizers can qualify for tax exemption on hosting expenses if such conventions are held by recognized bodies and the function is approved by the Government. Profits made from holding the convention will not be taxed if more than half of the income comes from the organization's members.

Tax Exemption for Nonresident.—
Exemption from tax is given to nonresidents on income derived from interest on:

a. moneys held on deposit in an approved bank in Singapore,

b. Asian dollar bonds issued in Singapore, and

c. credit facilities not less than S$200,000 for the purchase of productive equipment for approved development projects.

Exemption from Singapore estate duty is also given to nonresidents on:

a. deposits with Asian currency units and approved Asian dollar bonds, and

b. Singapore Government tax-free bonds.

Tax reductions in Special Cases.—

a. The withholding tax rate is reduced to 20 percent (full exemption in special cases) on certain approved royalties, technical assistance fees, or contributions to research and development costs paid by a Singapore firm to a nonresident person or company. Where such royalties, fees, or contributions are converted into equity in the local industrial company, they then become exempted from tax in Singapore, provided the tax liability of the nonresident is not increased in his/her country of physical domicile as a result of the exemption.

b. Offshore income of banks or other institutions in Singapore derived from loans to overseas borrowers from their Asian currency units will be charged the income tax rate of 10 percent or other special rate.

Shiping Enterprises.—Any shipping enterprise that registers a large seagoing ship in Singapore irrespective of whether it calls at Singapore or not will be exempted from income tax on its income derived from the operation of such a ship.

Changes in Pioneer Status Criteria. Incentives for Technology.—The Government announced on July 10, 1970, that some industries and products that had previously obtained pioneer status would no longer be eligible. The domestic requirements for many items in the early list of pioneer industries have been adequately met. Among some of the products removed from the lists are preserved foods, chewing gum, printing inks, industrial paper bags, toilet soap, household textile goods, and playing cards. All companies that have been granted pioneer status for products now removed from the pioneer list will continue to enjoy pioneer tax incentives until the scheduled expiry date of the previously granted tax incentives.

Under the new policy, pioneer status will not be granted to companies producing exclusively for the local market. The new policy is designed to encourage the establishment of export-oriented industries in Singapore.

As part of Singapore's policy of encouraging industries with a higher degree of technology, a new list of industries eligible for pioneer status has been published. Among the new industries and products declared eligible for pioneer status are aircraft components and accessories, compressors, transformers, diesel and petrol engines, electrical testing and measuring instruments, electric portable tools, telephone exchange equipment, microwave equipment, magnets and magnetic materials, typewriters, cameras, watches and clocks, miniature lamps, and a range of plastic raw materials such as polyethylene, polystyrene, polyvinylidene chloride, and other resins.

Additional industries and products will be added to this list as and when the Ministers for Finance considers it appropriate and in the economic interests of the Republic to do so.

Special Situations

Branch Office of a Foreign Firm.—For a branch office of a foreign firm established in Singapore but serving a wider geographic area, most of the income of which is derived from sales to other countries of the region, the tax liability depends on whether the business income is derived from the branch activities. If the sales are made from Singapore to persons in other countries, then the profits are derived from the activities of the branch business in Singapore, and profits of the branch office are taxed at the 40 percent rate.

Examples of revenue derived from operations of a branch that would be taxable are:

a. negotiations of sales originated in Singapore; and

b. commissions received from services performed in Singapore for instance, the branch acting as guarantors for overdraft facilities or as brokers for business transactions.

Operations of a branch that are not of a trading nature would not be taxable, such as service fees received from the head office for administrative work done by the branch on behalf of its head office.

Nonresident Firm.—A nonresident company that carries on a trade or business of which only part of the operations is carried on in Singapore is not liable to pay corporate tax on profits of the business if th eprofits are directly attributable to operations carried on outside Singapore. Only gains or profits derived from operations in Singapore are taxable.

Note: "Resident in Singapore," with respect to a company or body of persons, means a company or body of persons the control and management of whose business is exercised in Singapore. "Company" means any company incorporated or registered under any law in force in Singapore or elsewhere.

Singapore's Double Taxation Treaties

Provisions to eliminate or minimize double taxation have been incorporated into treaties with Malaysia, Japan, the United Kingdom, Australia, Belgium, West Germany, France, Thailand, Canada, Switzerland, Denmark, Sweden, Norway, Israel, the Netherlands, New Zealand, the Philippines, and Italy. The United States does not have a convention for avoidance of double taxation with Singapore.

Persons with questions about their liability for U.S. income tax should write directly to:

Internal Revenue Service
Unit 2
541 Liat Towers
Singapore 0923
or
Office of International Operations
Internal Revenue Service
1325 K Street, N.W.
Washington, D.C. 20225

Property Tax

Owners, rather than occupants of land, buildings, and houses, are liable to the payment of property tax. The Property Tax Act provides for a basic tax rate of 35 percent to be assessed against the annual value of the property (i.e., the gross annual rent that the property can reasonably be expected to earn). Over a period of time, however, a series of concessions has resulted in a schedule of different rates ranging from 12 to 33 percent and, in some exceptional cases, a complete waiver. A surcharge of 10 percent of the annual value of a property is levied from January 1, 1974 on all residential properties not allowed by Singapore citizens, by permanent residents, or by companies registered and carrying on business in Singapore. However, effective January 1, 1975, owners of flats or apartments in buildings of not less than six stories are exempted from the surcharge.

The rate of tax to be assessed depends greatly on the type of locality in which the property is situated. Usually, the rate of tax in developed areas, including urban, is 33 percent. The tax in certain rural areas may be at lower rates, dependent somewhat on whether the rural land is developed or vacant. In Jurong Industrial Estate, special rates apply: 18 percent on properties on which there are buildings, 12 percent on vacant lands.

Stamp and Documentary Tax

A stamp tax is imposed upon a wide variety of legal documents, including contracts, affidavits, conveyances, bills of exchange, sight drafts, checks, bills of lading, bills of sale, receipts, and securities. The rate of tax varies according to the type of document and the amount involved. Firms transacting business in Singapore should ascertain which, if any, of their business forms are subject to the stamp tax.

Employment

Labor Force

A major reason for Singapore's success in attracting new industry has been its energetic and conscientious labor force, which in 1979 totaled some 1 million. Most industrial workers speak English and are readily trainable in advanced industrial production techniques. Productivity per worker is recognized as being exceptionally high.

However, Singapore is experiencing a tight labor market, due in part to low birth rates and the Government's reluctance to allow permanent and large inflows of unskilled foreign workers. Also, previously unrealistic wage restraints spurred foreign and domestic investors to take advantage of abundant labor resources and establish operations. The high economic growth rates of the 1970's took their toll on Singapore's labor force.

Because of this labor scarcity, the National Wages Council (NWC) set the 1979 wage increase guideline so as to increase employer's wage bills by an average of 20 percent and wages by an average of 14 percent. This high wage policy was one of the forerunners for the "second industrial revolution" and is a key measure in restructuring Singapore's economy by reducing the labor intensity of production and conversely increasing labor productivity. As a result, Singaporean wage rates are higher than those prevailing in most other Southeast Asian nations. However, increased emphasis on already substantial worker training, impressive worker discipline, and increased productivity should still make Singapore's labor force very attractive to a large majority of investors. Labor disputes are rare, with no work stoppages having occurred in 2½ years.

The professional and technical work force is being enlarged by the Government through increased enrollment in local universities, colleges, and technical and vocational schools; through comprehensive apprenticeship and other labor-training programs; and by selective immigration. The Vocational and Industrial Training Board coordinates a number of industrial training programs.

The principal occupations in Singapore continue to be connected with commerce and finance, industry, public administration, and transport and communications.

Singapore's active program of increased industialization and diversification has kept unemployment low for several years. At the end of 1980, unemployment stood at 3.6 percent.

Wages, Related Benefits

Singapore's Employment Act and the Industrial Relations Act provide the legislative basis for the regulation of the principal terms and conditions of employment, such as hours of work, paid holidays, rest days, sick leave, and other fringe benefits.

In general, employees work a 44-hour week with a weekly rest day and have 11 paid holidays a year and 7 to 14 days of annual leave, depending on length of service.

The Workmen's Compensation Act provides for the payment of compensation of workers injured in the course of employment. The Central Provident Fund, established in 1955, makes provision for employees in their old age. It is essentially a compulsory savings fund to which both employers and employees contribute. Since July 1979, the employer's rate of contribution is 20.5 percent of the employee's basic wage, while the employee's contribution ranges from nil (for employees paid less than S$200) to 16.5 percent. The combined maximum contribution is S$1,110, plus 37 percent of any additional wages (overtime, allowances, etc.) beyond the basic wage.

Wages and salaries in Singapore vary from one employer to another. However, some guidelines on salaries may be drawn from the following averages for specific categories as of July 1978:

Production Workers:
  Skilled (fitters, turners, machinists, toolmakers, electricians, plumbers, welders, trimmers, linotype operators) . . . . S$2.70/hr.
  Semiskilled (assemblers, machine operators) . . . . S$1.55/hr.
  Unskilled (gardeners, cleaners, drivers, sweepers, storemen, oilers, materials handlers, laborers) . . . . S$1.30/hr.

Supervisory and Technical Employees:
  Graduate engineers . . . . S$1,610/mo.
  Foremen . . . . S$680/mo.
  Sales representatives (excluding commission) . . . . S$270/mo.
  Shop assistant . . . . S$270/mo.
Office Staff:
  Clerks, typists . . . . S$360-380/mo.
  Secretaries . . . . S$765/mo.
  Stenographers . . . . S$580/mo.

Fringe benefits, such as vacation pay, sick leave, holidays, retirement benefits, and contributions to the Central Provident Fund, would add approximately 30 to 45 percent to the above direct costs. The new wage policy increases of 1979 must also be taken into consideration. Actual pay scales would be determined by an employee's experience. The higher rates in the above ranges would be paid only to employees with substantial on-the-job experience.

Labor Organization and Labor-Management Relations

The labor situaiton in Singapore has generally been quite stable over recent years. This has been due largely to a sophisticated trade union movement, 3-year collective agreements, efficient officials of the Ministry of Labor who enjoy mutual trust of workers and employers, and an impartial Industrial Arbitration Court to which problems can be referred. Singapore enjoys oen of the lowest ratios of days lost per industrial worker in the world.

Most workers in big industrial plants and offices are unionized. The National Trade Union Congress (NTUC) has about 40 affiliates, organized mostly on an industry basis and represents about 23 percent of the total work force.

Employment and labor relations are regulated by the Employment Act, the Industrial Relations Act, the Central Provident Act, the Factories Act, the National Servicemen (Employment) Act, the Trade Disputes Act, the Workmen's Compensation Act, and other laws.

The Industrial Relations Act of 1960, as amended by the Industrial Relations (Amendment) Act of 1968, governs industrial relations in Singapore. The Act provides machinery for the prevention and settlement of trade disputes by collective bargaining conciliation and arbitration. The Ministry of Labor has an Industrial Relations Section whose officers assist employers and trade unions to settle their disputes through conciliation.

The Industrial Arbitration Court, established in 1960, has the status of a "High Court." A trade dispute may be referred to the Court either at the joint request of the parties to the dispute or by the Minister of Labor or, in special circumstances, by the President of the Republic.

Employers and trade unions may also enter into collective agreements on industrial matters that must be forwarded to the Court for registration and certification. On certification, a collective agreement is deemed to be an award of the Court and becomes binding upon the parties.

Worker/Employer Councils

Although works councils or productivity councils are officially encouraged by the Government, employer organizations, and the NTUC, few have been established. The councils that have been set up have played a purely consultative role for both parties. Management decisionmaking powers have remained intact. Under the model constitution, all issues covered by normal collective bargaining do not fall under the purview of the works councils.

Employment of Aliens

The Regulation of Employment Act of 1965 requires all noncitizens employed or seeking employment at a basic salary of S$750 per month or less to have a work permit. Such foreigners must apply to the Controller of Immigration for a Professional Visit Pass or an Employment Pass. Due to the current shortages of various types of workers, the Controller has discretion to waive various pertinent requirements. Long-term visas for necessary foreign managerial and technical personnel of manufacturing enterprises are readily granted.

Industrial Property Protection*

Singapore is not a member of any international convention on patents and trademarks to which the United States belongs. All inquiries, applications, or other correspondence on industrial property rights should be addressed to the Registrar of Trade Marks and Patents, 305, Tanglin Road, Singapore 1024.

Patents

Singapore uses the United Kingdom Patents Acts for the registration of patents. It only registers and protects patents that have been registered in the United Kingdom under the British legislation. When the patent has been

*Prepared by the Foreign Business Practices Division, Office of International Finance Investment and Services, U.S. Department of Commerce.

registered and sealed in the United Kingdom, one can apply to the Singapore Registry of Trade Marks and Patents for registration within 3 years from the date of sealing. Applications are not examined for novelty. There are no opposition proceedings.

Anyone may apply for a compulsory license of a confirmation patent, within 3 years of the issue of the basic British patent, on subject matter relating to metal products, glass, minerals, wool, textile and paper, and fixed construction, on grounds: that (1) the invention is not being fully worked, (2) demand for the product is not being adequately met, (3) the work is being hindered by imports, and (4) the patentee refuses to grant a license on reasonable terms. If the compulsory license is not issued after 2 years of the Government's order for such action, any interested person may apply to the Registrar for revocation of the patent.

The Registrar may grant compulsory licenses at any time on patents relating to foods, medicines, and surgical devices.

Trademarks

The governing law is the Trademarks Act, effective February 1, 1939; later Trademark Rules, effective May 1, 1968.

The first user or intended user of a mark is entitled to its registration. Any person claiming to be the proprietor of a mark may apply for its registration. Anyone who has applied for a registration in the United Kingdom or other country with which Singapore has reciprocal trademark relations may apply for the mark in Singapore within 6 months of the foreign registration and receive thereon the same filing date as the earlier foreign registration.

The Register of Trademarks is divided into Part A (distinctive marks) and Part B (marks used in Singapore for at least 2 years to indicate ownership of the proprietor's goods, even though not qualifying as distinctive under Part A). Marks registered in Part B of the United Kingdom Act from 1905 to 1937 qualify if used for 6 months preceding the filing date. Singapore uses the new British Classification System consisting of 34 classes of marks.

Applications are examined and, if acceptable, published for opposition for 2 months. If there is no opposition, or the opposition is successfully overcome, the mark is registered for 7 years from application filing date, renewable for 14 year periods. A mark must be used on a continuous basis for 5 years; otherwise, it may be canceled. The mark may also be canceled upon proof that it was obtained fraudulently or is similar to any well-known words used for the goods. The law contains "Registered User" provisions governing licensing of trademarks.

A mark is considered incontestable on prior user or ownership grounds after expiration of 7 years from its registration date.

Copyrights

The United Kingdom Copyright Act of 1911 continues in force in Singapore. The Government has enacted special legislation to prevent phonograph record piracy and infringement of musical works; however, the results of enforcement have been mixed.

Sources of Economic and Commercial Information

Singapore Government Representation

Investment information services of the Singapore Government are available from the Economic Development Board (EDB), located in the World Trade Center, Singapore. In the United States, the EDB has regional investment offices at 745 Fifth Avenue, New York, New York 10022; 223 N. Michigan Avenue, Chicago, Illinois 60601; 3 Greenway Plaza East, Houston, Texas 77046, and 333 S. Hope Street, Los Angeles, California 90071. The Singapore Embassy is at 1824 R Street, N.W., Washington, D.C. 20009

Singapore Government Representation

MINISTRY OF FINANCE
29th-40th Floor
CPF Building
79 robinson Road
Singapore 0106
Tel. 222-9666

MINISTRY OF TRADE AND INDUSTRY
Department of Trade
Suite 201, Second Floor
World Trade Center
Telok Blangah Road
Singapore 0409
Tel: 271-9388

ECONOMIC DEVELOPMENT BOARD
Ninth Floor
World Trade Center
Telok Blangah Road
Singapore 0409
Tel: 271-0844

SINGAPORE INSTITUTE OF STANDARDS AND INDUSTRIAL RESEARCH (SISIR)
179 River Valley Road
Singapore 0617
Tel: 360-933

NATIONAL PRODUCTIVITY BOARD
Sixth Floor
Jurong Flatted Factory (off Corporation Road)
Jurong Town
Singapore 2260
Tel: 652-555

INDUSTRIAL TRAINING BOARD
Annex Building
Ministry of Education Building
Kay Siang Road
Singapore 1024
Tel: 623-344

MINISTRY OF LAW
Second Floor, City Hall
St. Andrew's Road
Singapore 0617
Tel: 361-477

MINISTRY OF NATIONAL DEVELOPMENT
National Development Building
Maxwell Road
Singapore 0106
Tel: 222-1211

SENTOSA DEVELOPMENT CORPORATION
Block 10, Carlton Hill Road
Singapore 0208
Tel: 634-388

REGISTRY OF COMPANIES AND REGISTRY OF BUSINESSES
Third Floor
Colombo Court
Singapore 0617
Tel: ROC 361-203, ROB 361-282

THE MONETARY AUTHORITY OF SINGAPORE
SIA Building
77 Robinson Road
Singapore 0106
Tel: 222-5511

MINISTRY OF SCIENCE AND TECHNOLOGY
Kay Siang Road
Singapore 1024
Tel: 649-367

METRICATION BOARD
One Anson Road
Singapore 0207
Tel: 222-7755

STATISTICS DEPARTMENT
Fullerton Building
Singapore 0104
Tel: 436-121

MARINE DEPARTMENT
Fullerton Building
Singapore 0104
Tel: 910-511

PORT OF SINGAPORE AUTHORITY
PSA Towers, Maritime Square
Telok Blangah Road
Singapore 0409
Tel: 271-2211

JURONG TOWN CORPORATION
Jurong Town Hall
Singapore 2260
Tel: 650-133

MINISTRY OF CULTURE
Third Floor, City Hall
St. Andrew's Road
Singapore 0617

PRIME MINISTER'S OFFICE
Istana Annex
Singapore 0922
Tel: 375-133

MINISTRY OF THE ENVIRONMENT
Princess House
Alexandra Road
Singapore 0315
Tel: 635-111

THE TIMBER INDUSTRY BOARD
Fourth Floor, Realty Centre
15-16 Enggor Street
Singapore 0207
Tel: 220-5011

SINGAPORE TOURIST PROMOTION
  BOARD
131-133 Tanglin Road
Singapore 1024
Tel: 235-6611

MINISTRY OF LABOUR
Havelock Road
Singapore 0316
Tel: 436-141

SINGAPORE NATIONAL PRINTERS
  (PTE) LTD.
303 Upper Serangoon Road
Singapore 1334
Tel: 282-0611

CUSTOMS AND EXCISE DEPARTMENT
Customs House
Mexwell Road
Singapore 0106
Tel: 222-3511

INLAND REVENUE DEPARTMENT
Income Tax Division
Fullerton Building
Singapore 0104
Tel: 914-244

Chambers and Associations

THE SINGAPORE MANUFACTURER'S
  ASSOCIATION
Unit 118, First Floor
World Trade Center
Telok Blangah Road
Singapore 0409
Tel: 275-1211

SINGAPORE INTERNATIONAL
  CHAMBER OF COMMERCE
Denmark House
Collyer Quay
Singapore 0104
Tel: 981-255

SINGAPORE CHINESE CHAMBER OF
  COMMERCE AND INDUSTRY
47 Hill Street
Singapore 0617
Tel: 328-381

SINGAPORE INDIAN CHAMBER OF
  COMMERCE
55A Robinson Road
Singapore 0106
Tel: 222-2855

SINGAPORE MALAY CHAMBER OF
  COMMERCE
1901 International Plaza
Singapore 0207
Tel: 221-1066

SINGAPORE EMPLOYERS FEDERATION
23A Amber Mansion
Singapore 0923
Tel: 361-211

SINGAPORE ASSOCIATION OF SHIP-
BUILDERS AND REPAIRERS
850 World Trade Center
Telok Blangah Road
Singapore 0409

U.S. Government Representation in Singapore

The U.S. Embassy is located at 30 Hill Street, Singapore 0617, and the telephone number is 30251. U.S. Foreign Service Officers in the Economic/Commercial Section are available to assist American businesspeople visiting Singapore.
The U.S. Government maintains an International Marketing Center in Singapore available for the promotion and exhibition of U.S. products. The Center provides a variety of services for U.S. businesses interested in selling in Singapore. The International Marketing Center is located on the First Floor, Malayan Credit House, 96 Somerset Road, Singapore 0923. The telephone number is 737-3100.
Under the American Embassy, the U.S. Agricultural Trade Office carries out market development and trade servicing activities to promote markets for U.S. food products in Singapore and Southeast Asia. Its address is U.S. Agricultural Trade Office, 1500 Liat Towers, 541 Orchard Road, Singapore 0923, tel: 737-1233.
Alternatively, all official U.S. Government offices may receive mail through American Embassy, Singapore, FPO San Francisco 96699.

U.S. Government Publications

Foreign Economic Trends. Prepared on a semiannual basis by the U.S. Embassy, Singapore, and distributed by the U.S. Department of Commerce.

Trade USA. A bimonthly magazine, published by and on behalf of the U.S. commercial officers in the region to promote trade between Southeast Asia and the United States.

Commercial Newsletter. Published periodically by the U.S. Embassy in Singapore.

Other Publications

Singapore International Chamber of Commerce Economic Bulletin. Published monthly by the Singapore International Chamber of Commerce.

Singapore International Chamber of Commerce Report. Annual.

Singapore International Chamber of Commerce Investor's Guide. Annual.

Singapore. Published annually by the Singapore Ministry of Culture.

The Straits Times Directory of Singapore. Published yearly by Times Periodicals Pte. Ltd., Singapore.

Far Eastern Economic Review. Weekly magazine published in Hong Kong.

Asian Research Bulletin. A monthly economic report with political supplement, published by Asia Research Pte. Ltd., Singapore.

Singapore Business. Monthly magazine published by Times Periodicals Pte. Ltd., Singapore.

Asia Yearbook. Published annually by the Far Eastern Economic Review Ltd., Hong Kong.

South East Asia Oil Directory. Published annually by J. S. Metes & Co. (Pte.) Ltd., Singapore.

Singapore Manufacturer's Association Directory. Published by the Singapore Manufacturers' Association.

Shipbuilding & Repairing in Singapore Directory. Published by Singapore Association of Shipbuilders and Repairers.

Insight. Asia's monthly business magazine published by Pacific Magazines Ltd., Hong Kong.

Petroleum News. A monthly journal published by Petroleum News Southeast Asia Ltd., Hong Kong.

Companies Handbook of the Stock Exchange of Singapore Limited. Annual.

Singapore Banking and Finance. Published by the Institute of Banking and Finance.

The Singapore Manufacturer. A bimonthly newsletter, published by the Singapore Manufacturers' Association

Asia Business & Industry. A monthly magazine, published by Far East Trade Press Ltd., Hong Kong.

The Singapore Stock Exchange Journal. Monthly magazine published by the Stock Exchange of Singapore Limited, Singapore.

Economic Bulletin. Monthly newsletter published by the Indian Chamber of Commerce, Singapore.

Modern Asia. Monthly magazine, published by Business Publication Audit of Circulation Inc., Hong Kong.

Foreign Investment In Singapore. A report compiled by the Bank of America.

Doing Business in Singapore. Prepared by SGV-Goh Tan Pte. Ltd., Singapore.

Economic Profile. Prepared annually by SGV-Goh Tan Pte. Ltd., Singapore.

Singapore Banking, Finance, and Insurance. Published by Times Directories (Pte.) Ltd. on an annual basis.

Singapore Government Publications

Singapore Yearbook. Government Printing Office, Singapore.

Monthly Digest of Statistics. Department of Statistics,* Singapore.

Singapore Trade Statistics—Imports And Exports. A monthly publication published by the Department of Statistics.

Singapore Half-Yearly Trade Statistics. Department of Statistics, Singapore.

Singapore Investment News. Published monthly by the Singapore Economic Development board.

Commercial Bulletin. Monthly newsletter published by the Department of Trade, Singapore.

The Statutes of the Republic of Singapore, Volume 1-8. Revised Edition of Acts 1970 and Supplements.

Report on the Census of Industrial Production. Annual publication by the Department of Statistics, Singapore.

Guidance for Business Travelers

Entrance Requirements

Passports are required for all visitors. No visa is required for a business or pleasure visit of up to 14 days durations. Extensions can usually be obtained from the Controller of Immigration for up to 3 months. A National Registration Card must be obtained within 30 days of arrival if a stay of over 1 year is anticipated. Vaccinations or inoculations against smallpox, cholera, and

*Department of Statistics materials may be ordered from: Singapore National Printers Pte. Ltd., Publications Sales Division, Ground Floor, Fullerton Building, Singapore 0104.

yellow fever are not ordinarily required, unless the visitor has come from or, in the immediate past, has been in transit through a country where one or more of the diseases is present.

In general, household and personal effects may be brought into Singapore duty free. There is no limitation placed upon the amount of U.S. currency or travelers checks and letters of credit brought in by a visitor. Visitors are allowed to depart with all of the currency they brought with them, provided this amount was declared and noted on their passport by the Customs authorities at the time of arrival.

Foreign Exchange

The local currency is the Singapore dollar. Its value in relation to the U.S. dollar is now "floating," and a traveler should check with a local bank for the current exchange rate. The December 1980 exchange rate was US$1=S$2.10. The Singapore dollar has been appreciating against the U.S. dollar since mid-1973, when the "float" began.

Samples of no commercial value are admitted duty free. Other samples are subject to prevailing duties. Dutiable samples may be brought in by commercial travelers under bond or under deposit of duty. The bond is canceled or the deposit refunded if the samples are exported within 6 months, or within such further time as the authorities may grant, except in the case of liquor and tobacco, on which no refund is granted. Commercial travelers' samples and samples imported by parcel post may enter duty free except for a limited number of items including liquor and tobacco. No restrictions are imposed on the reexportation of duty-free goods. Advertising material is not subject to import duties unless it is related to tobacco, liquor, and a few other items.

Languages

English, Malay, Mandarin, and Tamil are all considered official languages in Singapore. Local traders usually have knowledge of at least two of the official languages and various dialects of Chinese, and, to some extent, Malay are used by the local businesspeople when dealing with each other and their customers. Japanese, Thai, and Indian are also used locally. Because of the international character of Singapore, almost every language is in evidence, but most people in business speak and understand English.

Workweek

Businesses operate on a 5½-day week, Monday through Saturday. Office hours are generally from 8:30 or 9 a.m. to 1 p.m., and from 2:30 to 4:40 or 5 p.m. Most offices are open for a half day on Saturday closing at 1 p.m. However, several foreign firms work 44 hours during a 5-day week. The hours observed by the government offices are 9 a.m. to 4:30 p.m. during the week and 9 a.m. to 1 p.m. on Saturday.

Holidays

Offices are closed on holidays. The following are the public holidays observed in Singapore: New Year's Day, Chinese New Year, Good Friday, Singapore Labor Day (May 1), National Day (Aug. 9), Vesak Day, Hari Raya Puasa, Deepavali, Hari Raya Haji, and Christmas Day. The Chinese, Hindu and Muslim holidays are based on the lunar calendar.

Power

Electrical current is 230 V, single phase, 50 cycle, a.c., and it is reliable. Any 110 V electrical equipment shipped to Singapore will need transformers or, more properly, should be converted to the local power requirements before shipment. Most motor driven appliances such as electric shavers, blenders, mixers, hair dryers, etc. will operate but will run hot unless they have a universal 50/60 cycle motor.

Living Conditions

Seasons in Singapore are nonexistent. The mean high is 87°F and the mean low is 75°F. While the humidity is high, averaging 70 percent, and the annual rainfall heavy, the weather is relatively pleasant due to the cooling sea breezes.

First-class hotels are numerous and expensive. Moderately priced hotels are also numerous. Restaurants are varied, and taxi service is inexpensive. Conference rooms and secretarial service are available at most hotels.

The Singapore International Chamber of Commerce has produced a pamphlet entitled "Expatriate Living Costs in Singapore," which Americans planning to live in Singapore should find informative. Copies can be obtained for S$3 from the Chamber's Secretariat, address: Fourth Floor, Denmark House, Singapore 0104.

Dental and medical facilities are adequate. There are American doctors at the Seventh Day Adventist Youngberg Memorial Hospital.

Market Profile— SINGAPORE

Economic Overview

Singapore has been able to maintain a relatively high level of growth during the present world recession despite its dependence on foreign trade. The Government encourages foreign trade and investment in capital-intensive equipment, manufacturing, and consumer goods. As the center of Southeast Asian commerce and trade, Singapore has stayed active although there has been an overall slowdown in growth. To deal with the worldwide economic pause in activity, the Singaporean Government is concentrating on maintaining domestic demand and investment to compensate for external sectors weakness and on continuing to retrain the work force in order to restructure the economy to lay the foundation for future growth. Singapore's real growth rate for 1982 was 6.3 percent. The country experienced a trade deficit of $6.6 billion and an inflation rate of 4 percent.

Major Developments

Major projects include the beginning of construction of a mass rapid transit system major expansion in the production of public housing units, continued construction of three major office-hotel-shopping developments, and plans to construct two large electrical generating plants.

Foreign Trade

Best U.S. Sales Prospects. — Computers and related components and systems; industrial electronics; precision engineering; robotics and computer-operated numerical controlled (CNC) metalworking equipment; aviation components and servicing; medical equipment; industrial and office products which can be used to increase labor productivity such as computers, word processors and process control equipment; consumer goods, such as fashionable clothing and processed foods.

Major Suppliers (January-June 1982). — Japan ($2.5 billion), Malaysia ($1.9 billion), United States ($1.8 billon), and EEC (1.5 billion).

Principal Exports. — Petroleum products, electrical machinery, telecommunications apparatus, rubber, tin, textiles and garmets and ships.

Major Markets (January-June 1982). — Malaysia ($1.8 billion), United States ($1.3 billion), Japan ($1.1 billion), EEC ($1 billion).

Finance

Currency.—Although its value dropped somewhat against the U.S. dollar, the Singapore dollar remained stronger than other major currencies during 1982. $2.10=US$1.

Domestic Credit. — The prime rate was about 11 percent. External debt reached an estimated $425 million in mid-July 1982.

National Budget (1982). — $5.9 billion; deficit: approximately $1.4 billion.

Balance of Payments. — International reserves totaled $7.7 billion (July 1982). A healthy balance-of-payments surplus of $917 million was recorded for 1981.

Foreign Investment

The Singaporean Government strongly encourages foreign investment, particularly in capital-intensive equipment. Not only does the Government provide financial and capital infrastructure assistance, but it also will provide financial and institutional support for worker training.

Import-Export Trade*
(millions of U.S. Dollars)

	1980	1981	1982**
Total Imports (c.i.f.)	23979	27566	14377
U.S. share	14.1	12.6	12.29
Total Exports, (f.o.b.)	19359	20961	10681
Domestic exports	12052	13938	7151
U.S. share	12.7	13.2	11.9

*Singapore data.
**First two quarters.

Principal Imports from the U.S. in 1981*
(millions of U.S. dollars)

	Value	Percent of Total
Food and live animals	165.0	5.6
Minerals fuels, lubricants	146.5	4.9
Chemicals and related products	252.0	8.5
Machinery and transport equipment	1,844.6	62.1
Manufactured goods	371.7	12.5

*U.S. Data.

Basic Economic Facilities

Transportation. — Singapore serves as a center for transportation in Southeast Asia. It is served by major international airlines and a modern airport. The transportation system links Singapore by road and rail to Malaysia and Thailand.

Communications. — Singapore is also the center for communication in Southeast Asia. Telecommunications and telephone facilities are modern and comprehensive. Radio and television stations are government owned and operated. There are also daily newspapers published in English, Chinese, and Malay.

Power. — Singapore's public utilities are reliable and efficient. The electrical system operates on a 230-volt, single-phase, 50 cycle alternating current. All 110-volt electrical equipment requires transformers. Unless electrical motors are specifically wired for 50/60 cycles, they are subject to failure.

Natural Resources

Terrain. — Land 224.3 square miles; one large island and 55 islets. Climate's tropical; average maximum temperature 87F; average rainfall 96 inches.

Resources. — Because of Singapore's size, agriculture and natural resources have no major impact on the economy. Rice and other staples are imported; fruits and vegetables are produced for domestic consumption and other resources, such as tropical fish, and exported in limited quantities.

Population

Size.— (1980) 2.4 million. Annual growth rate—1.3 percent. The people of Singapore are mostly Chinese (77 percent, but there are also Malays and Indians.

Labor Force. — 1,083,000. Agriculture 2 percent, industry and commerce 70 percent, and services: 21 percent.

Education. — Literacy rate—84 percent for those under 30 years old, literacy rate exceeds 90 percent. There is no compulsory education although the Government aims at providing 10 years of education for every child.

Language. — The National language is Malay. Chinese, English, and Tamil are also official languages. English is widely used and is the language of administration.

Market Profile—SOLOMON ISLANDS

Foreign Trade

Exports.—Total exports for 1979 were $69.2 million consisting primarily of fish, wood, and copra.

Imports.—Total imports for 1979 were $58.1 million, consisting primarily of petroleum and petroleum products, machinery, and transportation equipment.

Trade Policy.—Duties are applicable to most goods. The Brussels Tariff Nomenclature number is used for classification. The Government uses a single-line tariff scale. Manufacturing machinery and equipment, raw materials, chemicals, and building materials and equipment are admitted duty free or at low rates. Duty free import items include dairy products, staples, medical supplies, and fuel.

Best Trade Prospects.—Manufacturing and building machinery, building materials, and transportation equipment.

Trading Associations.—BSIP Chamber of Commerce; Honiara Junior Chamber of Commerce; Primary Producers and Trade Association of the Western Solomons; B.S. Trading Co., Ltd., and Breckwoldt Company.

Finance

Currency.—Australian currency used. There are plans to introduce a Solomon Islands currency.

Banks.—The major banks are located in Honiara: Commonwealth Banking Corp. of Australia; Australia and New Zealand Bank, Ltd.; and Hong Kong and Shanghai Banking Corp.

Foreign Aid.—The Asian Development Bank loaned $13.63 million to the Solomon Islands for the following development plans: $3.6 million for fishery development, $2.03 million for the Honiara Port development, and $8 million for the Lungga Hydropower construction. An additional $45,000 was given as technical assistance in the Honiara Port development project.

Foreign Investment.—Foreign investors are welcome, but the Government requires that it retain full control of natural resources. Projects approved by the Government receive assistance with site negotiations, tax relief, and import duty concessions. The islanders are ensured a reasonable share of the profits.

Economy

GDP.—The final figures for 1978 totaled $93.9 million. GDP from 1973-79 grew at an annual rate of 8 percent.

Agriculture.—The supply of fish is abundant, which enhances its strong export trade potential. The Asian Development Bank Loan will provide the capital to modernize the industry.

Development Plans.—Besides the emphasis on fishery development, there is major emphasis on public facilities. Hydroelectric plant development and port improvement projects are in progress.

Basic Economic Facilities

Transportation.—Overseas air service is provided by Air Niugini from Papua New Guinea, Air Pacific from Fiji and Australia, and Air Nauru connecting Nauru, Australia, and the northern Pacific. Internal services are operated by Solomon Islands Airways, Ltd. The Bank Line serves Solomons ports from Europe via Panama. Daiwa Line and Kyowa Shipping Lines operate out of Hong Kong, Japan, and other Far East ports. The New Guinea Australia Line connects from Sydney and Brisbane. SOFRANA—Unilines serves from New Zealand. Services and facilities are provided at Honiara, the main port of entry. There is a well-developed interisland shipline freight service. There is construction of new roads and upgrading the present road system is taking place.

Communications.—There are three radio-telephone circuits providing connections to almost anywhere in the world. A telephone exchange system serves Honiara.

Power.—Electricity is limited to areas of activity: Honiara, Auki, Gizo, Kua Kira, and Tulazi. The voltage supplied is 240/415 volts, 50 cycles.

Natural Resources

Location.—The Solomon Islands are located 1,300 miles west of Nadi, Fiji.

Climate.—Tropical, with a heavy annual rainfall that hurts the agricultural growing season.

Minerals.—A recent study concluded that there are sufficient bauxite reserves to merit the development of a bauxite-mining operation, and more in-depth studies are under consideration by the Government. In Panguage, North Solomons province, copper mining accounts for 20 percent of budget revenues.

Fisheries.—Abundant, commercial fishing well developed.

Population

Size.—As of 1982, 245,000 inhabitants.

Language.—English used as the business language. Many dialects of Papuan spoken.

Education.—Education is becoming a growing concern. Large amounts of money are being allocated to upgrade the entire system.

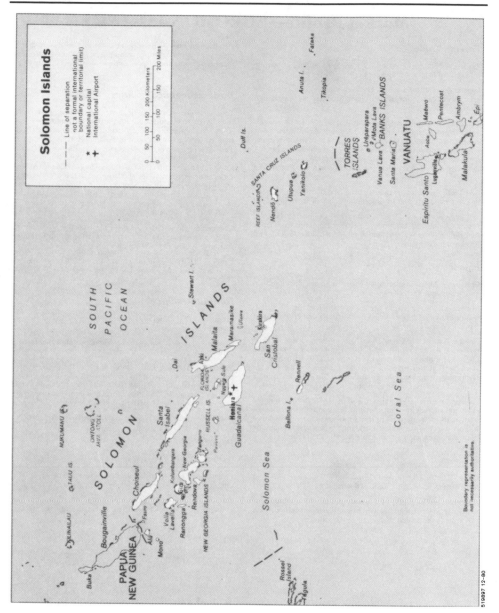

Solomon Islands

- - - - Line of separation
not a formal international
boundary or territorial limit)
★ National capital
✛ International Airport

0 50 100 150 200 Kilometers
0   50   100   150 200 Miles

519897 12-80

Market Profile—SOMALIA

Foreign Trade

Imports.—$427 million in 1981; $469 million in 1982. Major suppliers in 1981 (percent of total): Italy, 23; United States, 15.2; and West Germany, 7.5. From United States in 1982: $47 million; U.S. product value by percentage: soybean oil, 19; rice, 14; wheat, 8; dried milk and cream, 6. Imports from United States in 1982 valued at $46.6 million.

Exports.—$139 million in 1981; $143 million in 1982. Major markets, 1981 (percentage of product value): Saudi Arabia, 75.6; Yemen, 11.2; Italy, 6.7. Major exports: live animals (82.8 percent of total value), bananas, and hides and skins. Exports to United States valued at $0.9 million 1982.

Trade Prospects.—American goods are in demand when price competitive. Best prospects are in agricultural equipment, building materials, trucks, aircraft, machinery parts, pharmaceuticals, and fishing equipment.

Foreign Investment

Government encourages foreign investment. Bilateral investment guarantee with United States signed January 8, 1964.

Finance

Currency.—15.6 Somali shillings=US$1, as of Oct. 1983. Money and near-money supply: $305.9 million in September 1982.

Domestic Credit and Investment.—Modern banking system. Separate central, commercial, and development banks are government owned.

National Budget.—1981 expenditure $381 million.

Foreign Budget.—Infrastructure projects funded by U.S. agencies, EEC, and IDA (Mogadishu deepwater port); Peoples Republic of China (600-mile all weather road); and U.S.S.R. (major irrigation/hydroelectric project at Fanole). $142 million refugee relief in 1980.

Balance of Payments.—Deficit of 4.7 million in 1981. Foreign exchange reserves of $5.3 million (Sept. 1982).

Economy

Over 60 percent of people are nomadic herders. GNP (at current prices), $1,884 million; per capita GNP, $365 in 1981. Public sector includes most financial institutions, utilities and manufacturing. Government agricultural cooperatives and state farms expanding. International private enterprise important in oil exploration.

Agriculture.—Traditionally strong in livestock, bananas, sugar, corn, and sorghum. Diversification into wheat, rice,

tobacco, and cotton planned. Only 8 percent of arable land is used.

Industry.—Processing of agricultural products emphasized. Light industry includes tomato and fruit juice cannery; sugar; cigarette, match, shoe, paint, cardboard and textile factories; and a dairy. Small iron foundry planned for Mogadishu. Meat and fish processing plants were closed in 1978 for lack of spare parts and skilled labor. The textile industry was the only one to register an increase in production (6.8 percent in 1979).

Commerce.—Most wholesale commodity trading by public sector. State trading outlets for wide variety of retail goods. Consumer Price Index (1975=100): 244.1 in April 1980, up 23 percent from November 1979.

Basic Economic Facilities

Transportation.—Mogadishu and Hargeisa are chief air terminals. Commercial ports are Mogadishu, Berbera, Merca, and Chisimaio. 1,181 miles of paved roads, 478 miles of improved road and 6,775 miles of other. 13,000 vehicles in 1980.

Communications.—Domestic and international telephone service available. Two 5-kW AM radio stations; one TV station. 6,000 telephones. 2 newspapers.

Power.—1980 estimated production 100 million kWh; 90,000 kW installed capacity; 20 kWh per capita.

Natural Resources

Land.—Area of 246,000 square miles. Northern region is hilly; southern area flat.

Climate.—Ranges from tropical to subtropical.

Minerals.—Deposits of uranium are being explored. Commercial production confined to salt, charcoal, limestone, and meerschaum. Oil exploration has not yet produced results.

Fisheries.—The fishing industry was brought to a virtual stand-still in late 1977 with the end of the Somali-Soviet fishing agreement and the closing of the major fish processing plant because of mechanical problems.

Population

Size.—4 million (1979); annual growth rate of 2.6 percent. Principal cities: Mogadishu, the capital, 400,000; and Hargeisa, 500,000.

Language.—Somali (written form instituted by Government in 1972) government and business. Arabic, Italian, and English also used.

Labor.—Livestock production employs 70 percent of the total labor force; agriculture 20 percent; and industry, commerce, and transportation 5 percent.

SOMALIA

Somalia

— International boundary
— — Region boundary
★ National capital
⊛ Region capital
‥‥‥ Railroad
— Road
✛ International airport

0   50   100   150 Kilometers
0   50   100   150 Miles

Boundary representation is
not necessarily authoritative.

519738 8-80

2158

Marketing in South Africa

Contents

Report Revised March 1981

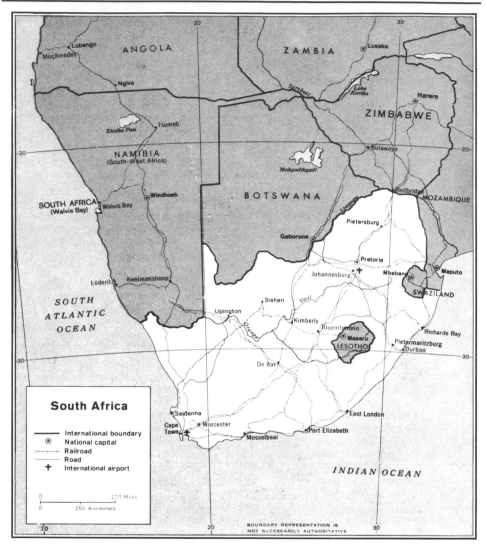

South Africa

— International boundary
⊛ National capital
┼┼┼ Railroad
— Road
✛ International airport

0   250 Miles
0   250 Kilometers

BOUNDARY REPRESENTATION IS
NOT NECESSARILY AUTHORITATIVE

2160

U.S. Government Policy

The United States and South Africa maintain normal diplomatic relations. Throughout the past two decades the U.S. Government has repeatedly expressed its disapproval of the South African Government's internal policy of separate racial development (apartheid) and the resulting institutionalized racial discrimination.

It is the U.S. Government view that South Africa should move toward a political system which provides for the full participation of all its people. In the June 1980 Security Council session, the U.S. Ambassador to the United Nations said: "Now is the time for South Africa to move toward fundamental social and political change.... At this moment, the Government of South Africa with its strong economy and formidable defenses should have the confidence and strength to commit itself to make necessary reforms. Those of us who are not citizens of South Africa cannot dictate the form that a final resolution of this dilemma will take . . . all of us stand ready to extend whatever assistance the South African Government and people need or desire if the goal of a full participatory government can be agreed upon."

The economic and commercial elements of the overall U.S. policy are designed to avoid giving the impression of closeness to the South African Government. While the United States maintains normal commercial relations with South Africa and seeks to maintain its share of the South African market, there are several major U.S. export controls on trade with South Africa. Since 1963, the United States has embargoed the sale of arms and ammunition and equipment for their manufacture and maintenance to South Africa. Enforcement of the arms embargo is the responsibility of the U.S. Department of State's Office of Munitions Control. The prior approval of the U.S. Department of Commerce's Office of Export Administration (OEA) is required for the export of goods of a dual-use nature.

Exports of crime control equipment, computers, and general aviation aircraft are subject to OEA review to prevent their use in the enforcement of apartheid. Since South Africa is not yet a signatory to the Nuclear Non-Proliferation Treaty, all exports of equipment to be used in that country's nuclear enrichment facility are prohibited.

In February 1978, the United States forbade all sales of U.S. origin goods and technical data to the South African military and police.

Specific questions regarding the implementation of U.S. Export Control Regulations should be addressed to the Office of Export Administration, U.S. Department of Commerce, Washington, D.C. 20230. U.S. firms and business representatives trading with South Africa in other non-strategic goods and services are placed under no restrictions peculiar to that country.

HOW TO OBTAIN BACKGROUND INFORMATION ABOUT THESE COUNTRIES

For those who wish *general* data about a country—data which goes beyond marketing and commerce—the editors recommend *Countries of the World and Their Leaders*, published as an annually updated yearbook by Gale Research Company, Detroit, Michigan 48226. Containing 4- to 20-page entries on 168 countries, the volume also provides several hundred pages of supplementary world data. Each country entry is prepared by the U.S. Department of State to provide a general briefing on the geography, people, culture, and political situation of the particular country. Each report provides some historical insight as well as a look at contemporary trends of lifestyle in the country. Reports also discuss a country's educational system, its press, ethnic groupings and religious practices.

Countries of the World and Their Leaders provides a fresh listing of cabinet ministers of each nation. In addition it lists health conditions the traveling businessman will wish to prepare for and includes information on passport procedures, customs and duties, and world climate conditions.

The latter are free to participate in South Africa's industrial exhibitions equally with any other international participant, to mount a private business visit, or to engage in any other promotional event they think appropriate to that market place.

The United States neither encourages or discourages investment in South Africa.

The U.S. Departments of Commerce and State, and the U.S. Embassy and Consulates in South Africa will, upon request, provide a complete briefing on the problems and prospects of doing business in South Africa. The final decision is up to the company. However, the U.S. Government encourages all American firms operating in South Africa to establish employment conditions in their South African plants consistent with standards in their U.S. plants. Racially discriminatory policies should be avoided. If South African law renders impossible the implementation of American standards in their entirety, compensatory programs, such as increased training opportunities or general education grants, should be considered. U.S. firms with or contemplating investments in South Africa are urged to become signators of the Sullivan Principles of Fair Employment Practices. (See Labor section for further information).

The U.S. Government discourages U.S. nationals from investing in South West Africa (Namibia). Prospective investors should be aware that U.S. nationals who invest there on the basis of rights acquired from the South African Government after October 27, 1966, will not receive U.S. Government assistance to protect such investments against the claims of a future lawful government of that territory.

U.S. firms seeking more detailed information on the commercial elements of U.S. policy towards South Africa are urged to call ITA's South Africa desk on 202-377-5148.

Trade Outlook

Foreign trade is a major sector of the South African economy. The $11.5 billion import bill in 1979 equalled 21 percent of the country's GNP while exports of $10.5 billion equalled another 19 percent (32 percent if gold is included). Major imports in 1979 included petroleum, machinery, transport equipment, chemicals (up 23 percent), metal products (up 24 percent), and textiles.

Two-way trade between the United States and South Africa during 1979 rose to $4,029 million, an increase of 17 percent from the 1978 level of $3,330 million. While South African exports to the United States increased 14 percent ($2,616 million) in 1979 after a 79 percent increase in 1978 due largely to gold coin, U.S. exports showed an important increase of 30% ($1,406 million) in 1979 after only a 2 percent increase in 1978.

Just over 27% of South Africa's non-gold exports in 1979 came to the United States, which represents South Africa's largest overseas market. The United States in 1979 supplied 17.6 percent of South Africa's non-military and non-oil imports.

Strong U.S. performers include capital and transportation equipment, but select consumer items also perform well. Nearly 12 percent of all U.S. exports are in the transportation sector— air, rail, and road. Construction, agriculture, engineering, mechanical handling, and machine and power tools account for over 20 percent. Chemicals and related products total 15 percent of U.S. exports, while articles of iron or steel and automatic data processing (ADP) equipment are still major markets for American manufacturers.

The Federal Republic of Germany continued to be South Africa's principal supplier in 1979. The United Kingdom is the second ranking supplier with the United States third, followed by Japan, France, and Italy. South African businesspeople are sophisticated, highly experienced foreign traders. American technology and product quality are respected. Foreign suppliers successful in the keenly competitive South African market pay attention to market developments and are aware of the importance of efficient delivery. These businesspeople keep in mind that competent servicing with readily available spare parts is vital to the penetration of the South African market.

The South African Economy

After the most severe economic downturn of the postwar period in the midseventies, South Africa experienced a modest recovery in 1978 which slowly gained momentum in the first half of 1979 and led to strong growth patterns by late 1979. The real growth rate for GDP was 3.7 percent for 1979, a significant improvement over the 2.3 percent growth in 1978 and zero growth in 1977. It represented the highest level of growth since 1974. Real GNP increased by 5 percent in 1979, surpassing growth in GDP due to the improved terms of trade. Due to record gold prices, public sector initiatives and renewed private sector confidence, South Africa is on its way toward a period of further economic growth.

Almost all sectors showed increased real growth in 1979. Non-gold mining was up 9 percent; manufacturing up 6.5 percent; utilities up 5 percent; construction up 1.5 percent after several years of decline; services up 5 percent; and agriculture up 1 percent. Although there was no growth in gold mining, record gold prices ($260 an ounce in early 1979, $600 by year end) contributed to the value of exports. Price increases in non-gold exports such as uranium, platinum, ferrochrome, copper, and diamonds also contributed to export values. There was a record current account surplus of $3.7 billion in 1979 compared to the $1.5 billion surplus of 1978. The strong economic surge was reflected in the private sector where expenditure was up 2.7 percent and domestic investment increased by 2 percent.

Despite the 13.8 percent inflation rate in 1979, real consumer spending began to increase with 1980 predictions for a 4.3 percent growth rate. Recent data indicate consumers have already increased their purchases of durables, such as autos and household supplies, with many buying on credit.

The South African budget for 1980/81 announced in March 1980 reflects the government's commitment to plow back a good portion of the record revenue into the economy. The government hopes to reduce its role in the economy and increase real growth by directing revenue into consumers' hands. Included in the budget were the following measures: Reduction of individual income tax by $720 million, elimination of the required loan levy on individuals and corporations, elimination of the 7.5 percent surcharge on imports, an increase for black education to $288 million, and pay raises of $576 million for civil servants and teachers.

With these expansionary measures, economic growth was expected to be 5 percent in 1980 and into 1981. Government spending was estimated to increase 14 percent, which would roughly keep pace with the 1979 inflation rate. By making use of tax cuts rather than increased real government spending, the impact on the inflation rate should be minimized, since South Africa currently suffers from cost-push (particularly oil prices) rather than demand-pull inflation.

As the South African economy strengthens, growth will bring pressure for social and political change by the majority non-white population. In addition, there is an immediate need for increased job training due to an acute

Table 1.—South African Imports

	Leading Imports in millions of U.S. dollars				Percentage Supplied by U.S.			
	1979	1978	1977	1976	1979	1978	1977	1976
Rice	49.3	39.2	35.5	30.8	87.2	99.7	91.6	91.0
Misc. chemical products	306.6	178.2	128.2	122.9	16.8	27.0	31.4	33.9
Artificial resins	295.4	192.1	161.6	197.5	15.2	6.8	22.3	17.5
Paper and Paperboard	153.0	126.7	115.0	126.9	20.5	26.1	30.3	28.2
Synthetic yarn and fibers	89.7	196.1	172.0	218.9	3.4	23.0	13.4	11.2
Precious and semiprecious stones and metals	42.5	33.6	57.5	64.5	NA	NA	2.4	2.7
Sheets and plates of iron or steel	9.8	8.7	5.3	8.4	9.1	11.2	37.0	11.0
Articles of iron or steel (other than sheets and plates)	80.2	210.7	168.2	236.5	11.4	2.5	10.2	11.9
Internal Combustion piston engines	132.0	116.2	72.5	101.4	30.7	40.4	45.2	32.3
Pumps, valves and compressors	118.6	53.2	50.1	53.2	21.4	25.7	24.8	23.8
Machinery for treatment of materials using heat	201.8	405.2	113.2	63.5	9.3	0.4	6.8	9.4
Lifting, handling and loading equipment	48.1	39.9	58.8	70.2	70.2	60.5	29.3	22.8
Excavating, level, boring, extracting equip.	162.0	191.7	140.0	162.3	57.9	55.4	57.4	51.1
Harvesting and threshing machines	17.1	23.8	27.4	28.4	21.6	15.0	14.7	18.2
Metalworking machine tools	116.6	79.5	46.3	66.5	14.0	11.6	9.7	12.6
ADP equipment	173.8	117.8	86.4	75.5	41.1	33.7	47.9	44.4
Misc. machines and machinery	98.1	98.1	67.9	84.9	NA	NA	16.4	17.1
Taps, corks and valves	74.5	57.2	49.4	47.0	19.1	31.0	22.8	27.9
Bearings: ball, roller, needle roller	54.3	44.9	33.5	34.6	15.5	13.0	22.3	26.2
Trans. shafts, cranks and casings	89.6	110.2	82.9	63.5	2.1	NA	34.9	35.3
Generators, motors, converters	110.8	118.5	137.3	139.3	9.1	8.5	15.8	12.3
Radio, TV, telegraph, telephone equipment	64.0	48.3	49.4	99.9	40.1	25.7	21.6	11.3
Switchgears	164.4	144.4	135.0	154.1	8.3	6.2	11.4	10.4
Railroad and tramway locomotive parts	63.9	32.3	28.4	61.7	41.1	65.5	53.0	78.2
Motor vehicles, chassis, parts	741.6	998.0	656.4	809.8	7.2	6.2	8.0	10.3
Tractors	160.8	167.7	153.9	172.3	16.5	21.9	20.8	32.2
Aircraft and parts	71.8	63.6	153.5	333.4	67.2	33.1	61.6	81.7
TOTAL IMPORTS[3]	8,345.1	7,212.1	5,893.1	6,738.3	17.6	15.7	18.9	21.5

[1]*South African Foreign Trade Statistics*, Vol. 1, Calendar Year 1979; Vol. 2, Calendar Years 1978 and 1976; Vol. 3, Calendar Years 1977 and 1976, Government of the Republic of South Africa, Pretoria.

[2]FT 410, Dec. 1978, U.S. Department of Commerce, U.S. converted at 1 R=$1.15.

[3]Total figures exclude arms and oil imports.

shortage of skilled labor. Prospects for sustained growth will depend on how South African Government officials respond to these pressures and, in turn, how South Africans and the international business community perceive that response.

Table 2.—U.S. Exports to South Africa
(in millions of dollars)

	1978	1979
Rice mill/semimill	30.4	41.6
Woodpulp-sulphate	22.3	19.7
Chemicals-cyclic and acyclic organic	18.8	39.3
Synthetic resins	13.3	26.6
Antiknock and fuel additives	18.9	27.8
Paper and paperboard	15.0	35.4
Textile fabrics and yarn	21.9	29.5
Aluminum and aluminum alloys	5.6	4.9
Piston internal combustion engines and parts	26.6	20.1
Aircraft engines and parts	17.3	9.7
Electric motors and generators and parts	9.6	10.0
Tractors, tracklaying type	17.1	13.8
Tractors, wheel	19.3	12.9
Construction and mining machinery	28.7	36.5
Construction and mining machinery parts	40.5	57.3
Metal working tools, parts	9.9	9.2
Lifting, loading and conveying machines	20.6	26.4
Taps, cocks, and valves	18.4	14.2
ADP equipment and parts	53.1	71.8
Parts of road vehicles and tractors	45.1	53.8
Railway cranes, workshops	21.7	26.3
Measuring, controlling instruments	37.3	52.9
Total	1,072.9	1.406.9

Source: EM 450/455, Tables 3 and 4 1978 and 1979, U.S. Department of Commerce

Agriculture

Although South Africa's 1979 crop yield was down due to drought conditions, agriculture is traditionally a strong sector in South Africa's economy and an important source for export trade. During the last 30 years the volume of production in agriculture has increased 300 percent. Despite these advances, however, the sector's overall contribution to the GDP has fallen from 16 percent in 1946 to 7.5 percent in 1978. Primary agricultural imports include coffee, tea, rice, natural rubber, and some meat (mostly live cattle and beef). Major sources of foreign exchange are corn, sugar, wool, fruits, and lobster. The total value of agricultural exports in 1979 was estimated at $1,665 million, a drop of 10 percent from 1978 when agricultural products represented 21 percent of the total value of exports. In 1978 a sharp rise in corn exports offset a major loss in sugar exports. Sugar exports fell from $263 million in 1977 to about $115 million in 1978 as South Africa reduced its exports in compliance with the International Sugar Agreement. There are hopes to export more sugar by-products such as high-test molasses and feedstock, which are new commercial ventures for South Africa.

Table 3.—Gross Domestic Product 1970, 1973-1979
(in millions of dollars)

	GDP at market prices	GDP at constant prices (1970)	Per capita real GDP (in dollars)
1972	20,871	19,356	560
1973	28,621	20,239	580
1974	35,932	21,911	606
1975	37,181	22,549	607
1976	35,692	22,625	865
1977	40,361	22,845	847
1978	45,864	23,377	840
1979	57,785	20,838	742

Source: South African Reserve Bank Quarterly Bulletin, March 1979, SARB, Pretoria.

South Africa's sheep population of 32 million ranks eighth in the world. The country is the fourth largest wool exporter after Australia, Argentina and New Zealand. Sales of wool, mohair, hides, and skins are doing well following a slump in the mid-1970's.

Meanwhile, cotton imports have fallen from 42 million kilograms in 1976 to an estimated 8 million kilograms for 1979 as domestic production expanded. Low-quality cotton will still be imported from Paraguay and the United States for the manufacture of jeans.

A serious drought during the 1979/80 growing season led to reduced crop yields and fewer lambs for future wool production. However, the fall in exports is expected to be cushioned by surplus carry-over from the excellent 1978/79 growing season.

Agriculture also may be called upon to supply corn, sugar, or cassava for the production of ethanol, an energy alternative which may be used to extend short supplies of diesel fuel. The Government has recently guaranteed water to growers putting sugar into the production of ethanol. The Corporation for Economic Development has already decided to build an ethanol plant in KwaZulu and draw upon plantings of cassava.

The major problem area for South African agriculture is the continuing rise in production costs. The price index of farm requisites increased 15 percent in 1978/79 which followed a 13 percent increase the previous year. Price increases were across the board from machinery to fuel to fertilizer to labor. A commission study on price increases found that gross farm income between 1973 and 1978 had increased by 129 percent while total farm expenses had increased 200 percent. The combination of inflation and the need to double production by the year 2000 in order to keep pace with population growth is driving South Africa to mechanize production and seek specialized expertise and more advanced technology. Several areas of

Table 4—South Africa's Economy: GDP by Sectors
1946-1979, Selected Years
(Millions of dollars)

	1979[1]	1978[2]	1977[2]	1976[2]	1975[2]	1970[3]	1962[4]
Agriculture, forestry, fishing	3,700	3,198	3,013	2,656	2,899	1,362	954
Mining and quarrying	9,680	6,374	4,591	3,778	4,148	1,689	1,038
Manufacturing	12,066	9,447	8,595	8,136	7,715	3,914	1,566
Utilities	2,008	1,708	1,284	913	843	429	201
Construction	2,164	1,844	1,737	1,710	1,697	709	219
Transport, communications	4,718	4,137	3,777	3,152	3,288	1,615	775
Finance	5,841	4,478	4,077	3,701	3,964	2,063	827
General government service	4,844	4,034	3,660	3,237	3,340	1,584	676
	(Percent share of total)						
Agriculture, forestry, fishing	8	8	8	8	8	8	10
Mining and quarrying	21	15	12	12	12	10	13
Manufacturing	27	22	22	23	22	23	21
Utilities	4	4	3	3	2	3	3
Construction	5	5	4	5	5	4	3
Transport, communications	10	10	11	10	10	10	10
Finance	13	10	11	11	11	12	11
General government service	11	10	10	10	10	10	9

[1]South African Reserve Bank Quarterly Bulletin, March 1980, SARB, Pretoria.
[2]South African Reserve Bank Quarterly Bulletin, Dec. 1979, SARB, Pretoria.
[3]South Africa Reserve Bank Quarterly Bulletin, Dec. 1978, SARB, Pretoria.
[4]South African Statistics, 1972, Government of The Republic of South Africa, Pretoria.

opportunities for U.S. companies are in irrigation, bigger tractors, food processing equipment, grain landing, storage equipment, and fertilizer blenders and spreaders.

Soil fertility and railfall limit crop production to 15 percent of the country's area. Rainfall averages 475 millimeters per year compared to a world average of 860 millimeters. Agriculture already uses over 85 percent of the available water and, therefore, any increase in production under irrigation will have to be based on a more efficient use of existing water.

South Africa is sparsely wooded in comparison with most other countries. The 1.3 million hectare forest area, of which 234,000 hectares is of indigenous species, represents about 1 percent of the Republic's total area. Compensation for this rather small area of commercial forest land is a climate conducive to a rapid growth rate. South Africa is entirely self-sufficient at present in timber for its mining industry, and provides 70 percent of its demand for paper and paper products, and about 90 percent of its softwood building timber requirements. South Africa's largest paper producer, Sappi. Ltd., is the largest on the continent and is expanding its facilities.

South Africa's (and Namibia's) fishing industry is among the top 10 in the world. The Namibian fishing industry is entirely controlled by South African conglomerates. There are four main sectors: Inshore fishing (also referred to as pelagic or shoal fishing), lobster fishing, deep sea trawling, and whaling.

The South African Continental Shelf is one of the most lucrative pelagic and demersal fishing grounds in the world. Overfishing, however, had drastically reduced catches and presented the distinct threat of commercial extinction of the principal pelagic specie, the pilchard. In November 1977 South Africa moved to save the industry by extending its exclusive fishing zone to 200 miles offshore. This limit now applies to the waters off the Namibian coast. Quotas were

Table 5.—Agricultural Production 1976-1979
(in 1,000 metric tons)

	1976[1]	1977[1]	1978[1]	1979[2]
Wheat	2,239	1,860	1,715	2,250
Rye	2	1	1	6
Corn	7,314	9,727	10,054	7,200
Barley	71	85	141
Oats	66	40	36	84
Sorghum	280	394	625	362
Beans, dry	62	76	80	46
Dry peas	9	7	8	8
Cowpeas	8	8	8	7
Potatoes	684	756	701	696
Sweet potatoes	41	44	44	47
Tobacco	32	41	47	45
Cotton	18	35	50	55
Cottonseed	36	70	102	110
Soybeans	28	31	37	25
Peanuts, in shell	143	234	298	125
Sunflower seed	255	478	446	321
Chicory	18	16	15	15
Tomatoes	330	335	270	293
Oranges	580	526	679	564
Apples	386	292	365	353
Pears	122	143	131	124
Peaches	177	175	170	164
Bananas	98	88	90	103
Pineapples	182	159	163	202
Grapes, for wine	816	655	953	963
Sugar, raw	2,042	2,084	2,050	2,100
Raisins	9	11	16	19
Meats	744	784	844	903
Milk	2,540	2,503	2,251	2,270
Wool, greasy basis	107	111	113	98
Mohair, greasy basis	4	4	5	5
Eggs	165	169	166	179

[1]U.S. Department of Agriculture, Statistical Bulletin No. 623.
[2]U.S. Department of Agriculture, Statistical Bulletin No. 637.

set for certain fish and only a few foreign fleets were licensed to fish in South African waters. These measures seem to have helped some species though catches of pilchard remain low. The 1978 catch of demersal fish (mainly hake, maasbanker and snoek) came to almost 200,000 tons. The pelagic catch (mainly the anchovy and pilchard) amounted to 800,000 tons. If properly managed, Namibia's fishing grounds have the potential to contribute more than 30 percent to the Namibian GDP, compared to the current 13 percent and less of recent years.

The main fish processing centers are at Walvis Bay, Port Nolloth, Lambert's Bay, Helena Bay, Saldanha Bay, Cape Town, Hout Bay, Gansbaai, and Luderitz Bay in Namibia. Capital investments in the fishing industry are estimated to be around R400 million.

Mining

Few countries are as richly endowed as South Africa in metals and minerals. With the notable exceptions of petroleum or bauxite, nearly every useful mineral resource exists, many in enormous proportions. South Africa consequently enjoys a highly developed metals and minerals industry. This industry supports a healthy and growing manufacturing sector and serves as the principal source of foreign exchange. Total sales in 1979 amounted to $11.6 billion (1978: $7.9 billion; 1974: $3.7 billion), with roughly about 90 percent of this from export sales. Mining thus plays a unique role in the South African economy, contributing 14.8 percent to the GDP in 1978—exceptionally high

by world standards. Gold was the largest money earner with $6.9 billion in 1979 compared to $4.6 billion in 1978.

The recent surge in export values is not accounted for solely by higher prices. The South African Government has embarked on ambitious and determined programs to effect eventual self-sufficiency in energy production and to develop a sophisticated industrial sector that is import independent. Discoveries of massive new ore reserves and the development of huge new ore port facilities at the Saldanha and Richards Bay harbors will make it easier for the mining industry to meet these goals.

World demand for South African metals and minerals is likely to remain firm as it is an important free-world supplier of platinum, chromite, manganese, vanadium, diamonds, gold, and, in the long run, of uranium and fluorspar.

Gold is by far South Africa's most important metal, earning $4,442 million in foreign exchange for 1978, 56 percent of the export value of all metals and minerals. Production at 704 tons was below the 1970 high of 1,000 tons but soaring gold prices led to record earnings. Gold exports at current prices were expected to yield at least $1,840 million more in 1979.

The higher gold prices have reversed a downward trend in production as marginal reefs and new mines become economically attractive. South Africa supplies 51 percent of the world's gold needs, 73 percent for the free world alone. Its sales are twice that of the U.S.S.R. One quarter of its gold shares are in the form of the South

Table 6.—Leading Mineral Production 1975-1979

	Unit	1975[1]	1976[1]	1977[1]	1978[1]	1979[2]
Antimony	1,000 metric tons	26	18	20	16	20
Asbestos	1,000 metric tons	355	370	383	257	249
Chrome	1,000 metric tons	2,075	2,409	3,319	3,145	3,296
Coal	1,000 metric tons	69,440	76,453	85,411	90,358	103,459
Copper	1,000 metric tons	179	197	205	206	227
Diamonds	1,000 carats	7,295	7,023	7,643	7,793	8,384
Flint clay	1,000 metric tons	255	191	193	167	180
Flourspar	1,000 metric tons	203	291	351	393	451
Gold	kilograms	713,447	713,390	699,887	704,576	703,001
Gypsum	1,000 metric tons	539	482	440	389	377
Iron Ore	1,000 metric tons	12,298	15,663	26,481	24,206	31,565
Iron Pyrites	1,000 metric tons	651	735	830	765	—
Lime and Limestone	1,000 metric tons	17,892	18,543	17,274	19,634	19,126
Magnesite	1,000 metric tons	61	63	49	37	65
Manganese	1,000 metric tons	5,881	5,503	5,290	4,413	5,182
Phosphates	1,000 metric tons	11,626	12,362	14,583	18,810	—
Salt	1,000 metric tons	264	224	242	490	538
Silica	1,000 metric tons	1,156	1,225	1,017	1,013	1,375
Sillimanite	1,000 metric tons	17	26	15	10	19
Silver	kilograms	95,923	87,736	97,364	96,544	100,664
Tin	1,000 metric tons	6	6	6	6	2
Vermiculite	1,000 metric tons	208	222	165	209	191

[1]Minerals, A Report for the Republic of South Africa, Oct.-Dec. 1977, 1978, Government of the Republic of South Africa, Pretoria.
[2]Republic of South Africa Minerals Production Statistics Questionnaire March 1980 American Consulate Johannesburg.

African Krugerrand, a 1-ounce gold coin. The Krugerrand dominates the international gold coin market with over 6 million sold in 1978. Gold reserves are immense. Known underground reserves amount to 35,000 tons and above ground stocks to 42,000 tons.

Uranium.—Uranium is a frequent by-product of gold production. In 1978, production rose 16 percent to 4,672 tons of uranium oxide. At the same time favorable prices brought an increase in earnings of 238 percent to R500 million. South Africa will be supplying an estimated 14,000 tons a year within a decade, compared to the 1979 annual production rate of just under 9,500 tons.

South Africa and Namibia combined have one-seventh of the world's uranium reserves, yet South Africa has produced about one-sixth of world supplies for more than 25 years. South Africa is the third largest producer after the United States and Canada; Namibia is the fourth largest. Reserves are estimated to be 350,000 tons. Production will continue to increase as existing mines are expanded, advanced extraction techniques implemented and new mines and recovery operations begun. The Rossing mine in Namibia, alone, expects to produce at a rate of 5,000 tons annually by the end of 1979 (up from 776 tons in 1976). The Rossing mine is currently larger than the biggest mines in Canada (2,163 tons/year) or Australia (420 tons/year). Two new mines have recently been announced by Beisa Mines Limited owned by Union Corporation and Harmony Gold Mining Company, the first ones to mine uranium as the primary product with gold as the by-product.

Most of this uranium is ultimately exported. However, domestic demand for enriched uranium will rise with the start of South Africa's nuclear power plant, Koeburg, at the end of 1982. South Africa plans to make its own fuel through locally developed uranium enrichment technology and to be able to fully supply Koeburg by around 1985, though fuel elements will still be imported.

Coal.—Since World War II, South Africa's coal industry has enjoyed a phenomenal growth rate. Production in 1978 totaled 90.3 million tons, up considerably from 69.4 million tons in 1975 and 44.6 million tons in 1961. Of this, 18 percent (15 million tons) was exported, earning $373 million in foreign exchange. Production for 1979 is expected to come to 97 million tons and exports may reach 20 million tons.

Coal reserves have been listed at more than 85 billion tons. This figure could range much higher, depending on various assumptions, new discoveries and improved extraction techniques.

Peak production projections have been pushed from the early to the latter part of the next century. The reserves are nearly all of the bituminous variety with barely 1 percent in anthracite. The quality of South African coal does not compare with the best European coals but geologic conditions enable it to be mined at exceptionally low costs. South Africa must import some of its coking coal for use in the iron and steel industry. However, a rich deposit of a 100 million tons of coking grade coal has recently been discovered in Venda. The Kemplust mine, 43 kilometers southwest of Paulpietersburg, became operational in January 1979 and is currently producing 30,000 tons of coking coal per month. The mine is conveniently situated along the Richards Bay rail line.

South Africa has 8 percent of the world coal market but hopes to become a major competitor with the United States and Australia for lucrative supply contracts. Starting in 1972 South Africa entered the export market and now exports significant quantities of coal to Europe and Japan. Industry goals are to export between 40 and 45 million tons annually by 1985. Coal is exported mainly through port facilities at The Richards Bay harbor, which can handle up to 20 million tons of coal per year. Plans are under consideration for extensions to double the capacity to 52 million tons in the mid 1980's. Train service linking the coal fields to the harbor has been improved and mining techniques refined. New mines are also being developed. The Reitspruit mine, 75 miles east of Johannesburg, produced 5 million tons in 1978 and anticipates 20 million tons in 1979, 25 percent of South African steam coal exports for 1979. The Reitspruit mine has reserves to last 22 years. The Kleinkopje strip mining operation near Witbank, Transvaal, will ultimately produce 100 million tons of coal. By 1983 it will produce 2 million tons annually for export and 1.5 million tons for domestic use.

Export goals may be difficult to obtain, however, as domestic needs grow. Coal already meets 75 percent of South Africa's energy needs—90 percent of electricity is coal-based—and short oil supplies make coal all the more attractive. South Africa's oil-from-coal plants (SASOL I, II, III) will soon be demanding a total of about 33 million tons annually. If South Africa decides to produce methanol as a fuel substitute it would likely be derived from coal. In addition, outside of the Koeburg reactors, further increases in generating capacity will likely come from coal-fired plants rather than nuclear reactors as the latter take more time and capital to construct. Finally, variable world demand may also dampen export growth. Exports for 1978 did.not rise as fast as in 1977 as world buyers withheld large orders following a slump in their country's iron and steel industries.

Iron—After several years of significant gains, iron ore production finally leveled off in response to depressed world demand. Output for 1978 fell to 24.2 million tons from 26.5 million tons in 1977, still far above 12.3 million tons in 1975. Total sales value for 1978 amounted to R219.7 million. Export volume remained a near constant 11.0 million tons, earning a significant R165.0 million in foreign exchange. Saldanha Bay harbor, northwest of Cape Town, is a major, ultra-modern port facility specifically designed to handle these exports.

Reserves are estimated to be 9.5 billion tons, the seventh largest in the world. Nearly 80 percent is in hematite, the remainder in magnetite. Extensive deposits of hematite occur in the Postmasburg-Sishen district of Cape Province and in the Thabazimbi district of northern Transvaal. Deposits of both are found in Pretoria-Series near Pretoria. Deposits of magnetites may be found in the Bushveld Complex in northeastern Transvaal.

Diamonds.—South Africa ranks as the leading world supplier of gem-quality stones, although other countries lead in the output of industrial diamonds. The largest diamond producer, DeBeers, through the Central Selling Organization (CSO) Controls 80 percent of the international diamonds sales. Since 1976 the volume of diamond sales has been falling while the sales value has continued to increase dramatically. The 1978 value of sales of $512.7 million represented an increase of 73 percent over 1977 while the volume sold, at 7,390,099 carats, fell by 1 percent.

Numerous other metals and minerals may be found in South Africa. The Republic's recoverable copper reserves are listed at 728.6 million tons. However, world oversupply conditions promise mixed returns on copper production through 1985. The country also has massive reserves of platinum, 200 million tons, or 75 percent of the world total. It currently produces 35 percent of the world output but by the year 2000 may be the only Western producer of any significance.

South Africa is the single largest producer of vanadium ore, providing 68 percent of the world output, or 88 percent of the free world's needs. Its reserves are the largest in the world: 49 percent of the world total, or 850-950 million tons of ore, enough to produce 7.8 million tons of vanadium. Vanadium is used in the making of high-strength specialty steels.

At 18 billion tons, South Africa has more than 80 percent of the world's chromite reserves. Measured on an output basis, South Africa produces some 33.8 percent of total world production. Four basic grades of ferrochrome are produced: Charge chrome, ferrochrome silicon, and high- and low-carbon ferrochromium. The bulk of South Africa's exports are of charge chrome. Since 1970, the South African contribution to world supply jumped from only 10 percent to about 50 percent (80 percent for the United States alone). A surge in demand is expected to bring almost $345 million in foreign exchange for 1979, far above the $51.7 million earned in 1970. Little of South Africa's total production is of high grade chrome ore; thus, most of the ore is too low in quality to smelt into the metallurgical grade ferrochrome used in stainless and other specialty steels.

Reserves of phosphates are enough to last 1,000 years. South Africa also has the world's largest reserves of fluorspar, more than 35 percent of the world total supply or about 116 million tons, and may become the major world supplier after 1985. Fluorspar is used in the manufacture of aluminum, steel and certain chemicals.

Titanium has been discovered in Zululand, enough to produce an annual yield in excess of current world use. Titanium is a very tough metal with great potential in the production of specialty steels.

South Africa is the world's second largest producer of manganese ores (after the U.S.S.R.), the free world's most important exporter, and the possessor of nearly 93 percent of the free world's reserves. Chief ores include draunite, bixbyite, pyrolusite, and psilomelan—the qualities of which meet all existing world standard specifications required for the manufacture of iron, steel, and ferroalloy products and in the chemical industry. The major portion of South Africa's manganese ore deposits is located in the Kuruman-Postmasburg area of the northwest Cape. Manganese reserves are a hefty 12.1 billion tons, enough to last at least 250 years. Total output for the various grades of ore for 1978 was 4.4 million tons, of which 2.95 million tons were exported.

South Africa's important asbestos areas are in the Transvaal and Cape Province (and to a lesser degree in Natal Province). Principal varieties mined include amosite, chrysotile, crocidolite (Cape and Transvaal Blue) and anthophyllite/tremolite. Of these, Cape blue crocidolite is South Africa's most important variety, accounting for over half of the total value of asbestos production. South Africa is the world's principal producer of blue asbestos crocidolite.

South Africa holds large quantities of cobalt sulphate. Production at the Rustenburg plantinum plant was expected to make South Africa self-sufficient in this mineral in 1979 and to allow for exports in 1980.

South Africa also has significant reserves of lead, silver, zirconium and silicon.

South Africa has several new and interesting mining projects underway. The Richards Bay heavy minerals projects began operation in 1979 and was scheduled to come to full production in 1980. It will mine sand dunes on the north coast of the bay for rutile, zircon, ilmenite (for titania slag) and low manganese pig iron. At peak production it will make 399,000 tons of slag annually, 217,000 tons of pig iron, 115,000 tons of zircon and 56,000 tons of rutile. As 90 percent of this will be exported it is expected to earn $3.5 billion in foreign exchange over a 30-year period, supplying 12 percent of the world's zircon, 33 percent of its low manganese pig iron, and 15 percent of its titania slag.

A second operation, the Black Mountain mining project, was due to start in 1980. It will mine lead, copper, silver and zinc, exporting lead and copper through the Saldanha Bay harbor at a rate of 165,000 tons per year.

South Africa also has a slimes recovery project on the East Rand, designed to reprocess effluent discarded from earlier mining operations when extraction techniques were less efficient. Recovery of gold and uranium will be so profitable that the project would break even at gold prices as low as $30 to $40 per troy ounce. The project is expected to last 22 years.

In December 1979 Auglo American Coal Corporation (Amcoal) announced plans for two new coal mines to supply two Escom power stations. The New Denmark mine near Bethal will supply 5 million tons of coal a year for the Tutuka power station while the Cornelia mine near Vereerniging will supply 6.5 million tons of coal. In addition Union Corporation announced in late 1979 that pregrouting would begin on a potential gold mine (Beatrix—southeast of its Beisa mine). A full feasibility study should be completed in 6 months. The Beisa gold mine is expected to reach full production of 100,000 tons a month by 1982.

South Africa imports a number of metals and minerals but few are of significant proportion. The single most important is crude oil which South Africa must purchase on the spot oil market or through third parties as the OPEC producing nations officially boycott the Republic (including Iran which used to supply 90 percent of South Africa's needs). Estimates put oil imports at a rate equal to 305,000 barrels per day (some 65,000 are re-exported) at a total cost of around $1.8 billion in 1978. Oil supplies some 25 percent of South Africa's energy needs. The price tag may yet approach $4.6 billion for 1979 despite a reduction in oil imports. The country is engaged in offshore oil explorations after abandoning the search on land.

South Africa must also import bauxite ore for use in the production of aluminum. Small reserves of bauxite have been discovered but are being held as an emergency reserve. Little of South Africa's metal and mineral imports originate in the United States. Our main exports to South Africa have included steel products, aluminum metal, and coking coal. With increasing self-sufficiency and depressed demand, metal and mineral imports have shown some decline.

U.S. business opportunities are best in the areas of advanced mining equipment and technology as well as capital investment. South Africa advertises a liberal foreign/investment policy which treats its foreign and domestic investors alike. The United States is currently the second largest foreign investor after the United Kingdom. In mining, U.S. businessmen are the preferred operating partners.

Manufacturing

The manufacturing sector is the leading branch of business activity in the Republic. The importance of this sector is reflected in the increasing percentage of GDP it represents (table 4).

The movement from mining and agriculture to industrial production indicates South Africa's growing economic maturity. Despite this trend, South Africa still depends importantly on foreign sources for its capital goods requirements.

South Africa's iron and steel industry is dominated by the large, mainly government-owned, South African Iron and Steel Industrial Corporation (ISCOR), established by parliament in 1928. Private sector firms engaged in the iron and steel industry include: Highweld Steel Industries, Southern Cross Steel Company and Cape Town Iron and Steel. No monopoly right over iron and steel production was conferred upon ISCOR, but the firm has developed into a vertically-integrated enterprise producing more than two-thirds of the Republic's steel requirements. ISCOR owns three complete steel works, at Pretoria, at Vanderbijlpark in the southern Transvaal, and at Newcastle in Natal. In 1978 ISCOR suffered its fifth consecutive and largest loss despite an increase in sales of 30 percent over 1977. Losses stem from world excess capacity and ISCOR's heavy interest burden from earlier, debt-financed expansions.

South African production of steel ingots, castings, and stainless steels in 1978 came to 7.9 million tons. Total steel production is to reach 10 million tons by 1980, 80 percent of this for export. Total iron production remained essentially constant at 6.3 million tons. Ferroalloys are performing the best with rising producer prices and production up 19 percent to a total of 1.1 million tons. Total 1978 exports increased in volume to 2 million tons, up 28 percent from 1977.

The iron and steel industry is of interest to U.S. business as a potential market for high-quality coking coal, speciality steels such as stainless steel bars, rods, and alloy tool steel or final products and equipment. South Africa is also a potential source of iron and semi-finished steel.

South Africa's clothing industry began 25 years ago with the manufacture of underwear. It has since grown with a 1977 sales turnover of more than $839 million and a 1978 record export value of $25 million. Both the textile and clothing industries were hard hit by the recent recession. Sales bottomed out in 1977 and the government imposed high import duties, forcing the local clothing industry to purchase textiles locally. Total textile sales in 1977 were $1,219 million, a 14 percent drop from 1976. At the same time, employment fell from its usual 127,000 down to 108,000. South Africa is becoming more independent of cotton imports as growers increase plantings and introduce higher quality strains. Although U.S. export prospects for cotton, textiles and clothing look poor, opportunities are present in textile machinery, parts and accessories, textile chemicals, dyestuffs and similar products, especially synthetics.

The automotive industry has advanced in the past 20 years from the assembly of cars from imported parts and components to the production of vehicles with a South African content of at least 66 percent by weight. The South African Government currently requires 66 percent local content for passenger cars by weight. Effective January 1, 1980, light commercial vehicles (approximately 2,800 lbs.) are also included in the local content regulation program. Manufacturers of light commercial vehicles had to achieve 50 percent local content by year-end 1980 and will have to achieve 66 percent by the end of 1981. There is a schedule of rebates of the excise tax on cars for a local content above 66 percent and light commercial vehicles with local content above 50 percent. There is currently no local content requirement for heavy commercial vehicles, but they must be assembled locally. South Africa's automotive industry has no monopolies, price rings, or cartels, though the number of manufacturers dropped from 12 to 10 following recent merger activity. There has been a trend toward nationalization in the industry though it is more likely due to the recent recession rather than to the reduction in automakers. Sales for 1979 of 209,000 units compared to a high of 229,000 in 1975 and a low of 165,000 in 1977. A shift toward smaller cars, noticeable since the late 1973 oil crisis, has been reinforced by soaring fuel prices. Small cars now account for over one-half of current sales. Predictably, sales of motorcycles are also doing very well. Registered new motor vehicles totalled 278,602 for Jan.-Oct. 1979 (260,778 in 1978) while registered used vehicles totalled 663,588 for Jan.-Oct. 1979 (718,453 in 1978).

Chemicals are of strategic importance, and South Africa is striving towards self-sufficiency. This involves the chemical industry in projects that could total $4.8 billion between 1977-87 (at current prices). A feature of the industry is the wide variety of products, ranging from fertilizers to explosives, from pesticides to plastics, and from mineral salts to synthetic fibers and rubber. Of overwhelming importance to the chemical industry is the fact that nearly 60 percent of its basic products are of petrochemical origin, and of this at least 75 percent is produced from South Africa's coal reserves.

Table 7.—*Manufacturing Production Index 1968, 1970, 1974-1979*

(Base 1970=100)

	1968	1970	1974	1975	1976	1977	1978	1979
Food	100.5	100.0	116.9	121.0	125.9	124.1	117.8	124.0
Textiles	86.9	100.0	111.8	105.5	115.0	106.5	108.8	113.5
Chemicals and chemical products	86.3	100.0	133.2	142.1	141.3	146.9	151.8	160.3
Non-metalic mineral products	83.4	100.0	121.1	120.8	114.4	96.1	98.2	100.5
Basic metals and metal products	83.8	100.0	118.9	125.5	121.8	116.9	135.5	153.1
Machinery incl. electrical machinery	93.8	100.0	109.5	113.0	108.4	89.7	88.5	91.4
Transport equipment	80.5	100.0	128.3	120.1	110.1	95.3	111.3	106.6
Other	80.4	100.0	126.0	129.1	129.9	117.7	123.0	132.2
TOTAL	86.4	100.0	121.2	123.7	123.6	115.8	121.7	129.9

Source: South African Reserve Bank Quarterly Bulletin, Sept. 1980, SARB, Pretoria.

Table 8.—Value of Manufacturing Sales 1975-1979

(in thousands of dollars)

	1975	1976	1977	1978	1979
Food and beverages	4,542	4,212	4,824	5,125	6,337
Tobacco	422	420	464	492	594
Textiles	1,184	1,250	1,206	1,375	1,640
Clothing, footwear	987	926	888	991	1,155
Paper and printing	1,243	1,219	1,286	1,483	1,779
Chemical and chemical products	3,738	3,901	4,443	5,130	6,570
Non-metallic mineral products	809	779	700	834	990
Basic metals	2,452	2,454	2,709	3,299	4,624
Fab. metal products	2,038	1,969	1,666	1,865	2,320
Machinery	1,553	1,411	1,519	1,509	1,704
Electrical machinery	1,226	1,271	1,181	1,190	1,569
Transport equipment	550	473	485	455	498
TOTAL	24,543	23,603	24,831	28,184	35,005

Source: South African Statistic, Sept. 1980. Bulletin of Statistics Government of the Republic of South Africa, Pretoria.

The new SASOL plants will be able to expand nitrogen output and produce enough ammonia and raw material for synthetic rubber to make South Africa import independent in these areas.

South Africa's chemical industry began with the need for blasting materials for diamond and gold mining in the late 1980's. Today, South Africa's R100 million a year explosives industry is the largest in the world.

South Africa's limited arable land has made it necessary to use fertilizers to increase yields on fixed acreage. Chemical fertilizers play a major role. About 60 percent of the fertilizer output is purchased by maize growers. Sugar, wheat, and citrus producers are also reliant on fertilizers. South Africa is expected to become a major world supplier of fertilizer and phosphoric acid in the 1980's. Exports in 1978 amounted to $102 million. Imports of fertilizers are limited to small amounts of ash, sulfur and, until about 1982, nitrogen.

As mentioned above, a number of new chemical projects are planned or underway. The single biggest undertaking is Coalplex, located in Sasolburg, at a cost of R230 million. Coalplex can convert coal to several chemicals, notably caustic soda, chlorine, and up to 100,000 tons of polyvinylchloride (PVC) plastic powder, needed for the plastic conversion industry and to make South Africa an exporter of PVC. The joint owners, African Explosive and Chemical Industry (AECI) and Sentrachem, have plans for a second plant at a later stage.

Other projects include an R125 million synthetic rubber plant sponsored by Sentrachem, which will draw materials from SASOL. AECI plans to produce polyether, now imported from the United States and Europe. This will save South Africa R5 million a year in foreign exchange. South Africa also is building the second largest lime factory in the world. It was scheduled to start production by late 1980.

In addition, several expansion plans are to begin in 1980. Sentrachem announced in early 1980 a $48 million investment project to expand the Germiston and Isipingo subsidiary sites of its National Chemical Products. Fedmis Ltd. announced a $120 million expansion for its phosphoric acid plants to increase production by 100,000 tons per annum.

Plans have also called for a hydrocarbon and aromatic solvents plant, a herbicide plant in Transvaal, and a seaweed processing plant in the Transkei. Opportunities are present for U.S. companies interested in any aspect of South Africa's continuing chemical projects, from supplying equipment and systems to providing technology.

South African demand for computers has grown with the increasing sophistication of business and industry. Annual income from the computer industry topped $310 million in 1977, far above the $209 million in 1975. Concern over U.S. sanctions temporarily dampened demand for U.S.-made computers as buyers feared parts and service could be cut off at a later date. Some of this apprehension has worn off, particularly among the larger, more well-informed buyers. Competition is strong but growth is assured with investments in computers increasing around 20 percent each year. Much is also needed in the way of training as South Africa has a serious shortage of computer analysts and programmers.

Other manufacturing prospects for U.S. exports in electronics may be found in the area of word-processing equipment. A 560-bed hospital is being built in Pietmaritzburg and is likely to be interested in U.S.-made equipment to outfit the hospital at a later stage, particularly for sophisticated items such as operating room and diagnostic equipment. In the area of printing and graphic arts, demand is expected to increase for technologically advanced, labor-saving equipment. The United States is seen as a leader in this area in both quality and service. The sound equipment market is $132 million a year and fast growing, particularly in car-sound, car-fi equipment. Further development is expected after electricity is brought to Soweto.

The production of energy has absorbed much attention and capital in South Africa. The main focus is on the oil-from-coal plants, SASOL I, II, and III. SASOL I, in Sasolburg, Orange Free State (OFS), already produces 50 million gallons of gases, fuels, and chemicals each year, earning an annual after-tax profit of $108 million. SASOL II and III are being built adjacent to each other in the eastern Transvaal, each 10 times as large as SASOL I. Construction of SASOL II and III will cost $6.7 billion, making it the most expensive industrial project now underway in the world. SASOL II began initial crude production in March 1980 with refined products to be produced within 3 months—all within the budget of $2.9 billion. It is hoped that both SASOL II and III will be in full production by end of 1982. Their combined estimated output will be at a rate of 120,000 bpd of gases, liquid fuels, and chemicals, enough to provide between 35-50 percent of South Africa's oil needs at current consumption. SASOL is a government-financed project, though the public (for the first time) is now able to purchase private shares.

In terms of U.S. participation, no further civil engineering contracts are expected and for the most part South African contractors and materials are preferred, although the U.S. company Fluor has a managing construction contract.

In other areas SASOL is to build a $30 million plant to produce transport fuels from coal tars in Secunda. The plant is to be constructed by Flour by mid-1982 and will produce diesel and naphtha streams.

Two large South African companies, General Mining and Sentrachem, are conducting a feasibility study for a oil from coal plant in the northern Transvaal which would use the process of direct liquefaction rather than the SASOL process which changes coal to gas and then to liquid.

Licensing Procedures

A South African firm that wishes to conclude a license agreement with a foreign firm must apply for permission to the South African Department of Industries. The Department of Industries will in turn advise the Exchange Control Authorities of the South African Reserve Bank whether the agreement should be accepted. The Reserve Bank then authorizes the use of foreign exchange to pay the royalties.

Certain conditions are considered null and void if included in a licensing agreement. The conditions are those which have the effect of prohibiting or restricting the purchaser or licensee from purchasing or using any article or class of articles, whether patented or not, supplied or owned by any person other than the seller or licensor or his nominee; prohibiting or restricting the licensee from using any article or process not protected by the patent; requiring the purchaser or licensee to acquire from the seller, licensor, or his nominee any article or class of articles not protected by the patent; requiring or

inducing the purchaser to observe a specified resale price in respect to any article or class of articles protected by the patent; and/or prohibiting or restricting the making, using, exercising or vending of the invention concerned in any country in which the invention is not patented.

The South African Government considers South Africa to be self-sufficient to a large extent in the manufacture of consumer goods, and is therefore not in favor of the payment of high rates of royalties on these items. In the field of intermediate goods or capital equipment, the Government will consider higher rates, ranging from 4 to 7.5 percent of manufacturing costs.

A tax of 12.5 percent is levied on the overseas payment of royalties. This tax is creditable under the U.S.-South African Taxation Treaty towards U.S. tax liabilities.

Distribution and Sales Channels

Distribution Centers

In a 1978 demographic study conducted by the University of South Africa, the population of the Republic numbered 27.4 million. The total population data is distributed into four racial population groups as follows: 19.6 million Blacks; 4.4 million Whites; 2.5 million Coloreds; and 778,000 Asians. Among the economically and politically dominant whites, 40 percent use English as their language, the remaining 60 percent speak Afrikaans, a basically Dutch language with German and French influences.

The descriptive terms for the various ethnic groups are neither standard nor necessarily acceptable to all shades of opinion. White South Africans are, for example, referred to as Europeans or whites. The Asians have been referred to as Asians, Asiatics, or Indians. Black South Africans have been called Black, African, African natives (or simply natives), Bantu, or Azanians. Coloured is most generally used to describe those persons of mixed racial origin. The terms used hereinafter are Black or African for the Black South African, white for the white South African, Asian for those South Africans of Asian descent; and coloured for those South Africans of racially mixed descent. These terms have been chosen arbitrarily for consistency, and their use does not imply any recognition or approval.

The 472,359 square mile area of South Africa is divided into four provinces, the 1970 population and area of which were respectively: Cape of

Good Hope[1]: 6.7 million and 278,465 square miles; Transvaal: 8.7 million, and 109,621 square miles: Orange Free State: 1.7 million and 49,866 square miles: Natal: 4.2 million, and 33,587 square miles. As of 1970, 48 percent of the population was urban.

Approximately 80 percent of the metropolitan population is found in the areas surrounding the cities of Johannesburg (Transvaal), Cape Town (Cape Province), Durban (Natal) and Port Elizabeth (Cape Province).

Johannesburg, the commercial hub of South Africa, is located in the heart of the Southern Transvaal, an area known as the Witwatersrand which also includes the administrative capital of South Africa, Pretoria. Nearly 50 percent of South Africa's white population lives in the Witwatersrand which provides 25 percent of all job opportunities country-wide. In the Johannesburg area approximately 600,000 are employed in industry, particularly in the steel works and petro-chemical installations. Manufacturing is also important, providing 52 percent of all domestic goods. Johannesburg is 456 miles from its major port, Durban, and 954 miles from Cape Town.

Durban with a population of 843,000 is the largest port of South Africa and one of the busiest in Africa. The triangle of Durban-Pietermaritz-burg-Pinetown is the manufacturing core of Natal. Natal's major industries are textiles, footwear, clothing, refined petroleum, chemicals, sugar, and processed food. Many of the export-oriented industries are located in the Durban area.

Cape Town (population 1.1 million) is South Africa's second busiest port and the site of the Republic's legislative assembly. The Department of Planning and the Environment projects that the area between Cape Town and Saldanha has an important developmental future. Saldanha Bay will be South Africa's ore-exporting port and also has processing industries for iron ore.

Port Elizabeth, population 469,000, is South Africa's third largest port. It is located 768 miles south of Johannesburg and 490 miles east of Cape Town. Port Elizabeth has a large concentration of motor vehicle assembly plants in addition to tire plants, clothing and textile mills and chemical and pharmaceutical industries. It is the main manufacturing center for South African footwear.

Two other important cities in South Africa are Bloemfontein and East London. Bloemfontein is the capital of the Orange Free State and the Republic's judicial capital. The city has 350 established factories which produce furniture.

A factor of increasing importance to business people concerned with marketing their products in South Africa is the role of African, Asians, and Coloreds in the country's personal consumption picture. A continuing white labor shortage has increased job and salary opportunities for non-whites, thereby raising income level. According to market research, the division of purchasing power among the different groups in 1975 was still highest among the whites (64.9 percent), followed by Africans (25.3 percent), Coloreds (7.2 percent), and Asians (2.6 percent). As a result of higher levels of education and training achieved by the non-whites sector, it was projected that the spread in incomes in 1980 would show a relative decline for the White group to 60.1 percent and an increase to 28.9 percent for the Africans, 8.2 percent for Coloreds, and 2.8 percent for Asians.

Distribution Channels

South Africa offers foreign suppliers a wide variety of methods of distributing and selling their products. The principal methods consist of employing the services of an agent or distributor; selling through established wholesalers or dealers; selling directly to department stores or other retailers; or establishing a branch or subsidiary with its own sales force in the Republic.—

Selling through an agent or distributor.— Agents are often used for the distribution of a wide range of both durable and non-durable consumer goods, and for some industrial raw materials. This form may be ideal when products are highly competitive and lack a large market. Agents are located in most of the large cities and may be able to cover the whole market through their branch offices. While some U.S. exporters have appointed an agent in each of the major population centers, a single agent capable of providing national coverage is generally preferable. As a rule, the agents most likely to have national coverage are located in Johannesburg. South African agents often represent several different product lines, and an exporter should be careful not to appoint one who is handling competitive lines.

Capital goods and equipment are often best handled by stocklist-distributors who buy on their own account and carry a wide range of spares. Distributors frequently also handle other commodities, such as chemicals, pharmaceuticals, and brand-new products, on an exclusive basis. Leading distributors often have branches throughout the Republic and sell to both wholesalers and retailers. In appointing an exclusive representative in South Africa, the

---

[1]While "Cape of Good Hope" is the formal designation of the province, it is frequently referred to by the shortened title of Cape Province.

U.S. exporter is legally entitled to certain exemptions from U.S. antitrust laws. The Webb-Pomerence Act allows a limited exemption from U.S. antitrust laws for direct exports by allowing exporters to agree on prices, sales terms, territorial divisions, and other activities in export trade which would be forbidden in U.S. domestic trade. More information on the Webb-Pomerence Act is available from the Foreign Business Practices Division, Office of Finance, Investment, and Services, U.S. Department of Commerce, Washington, D.C. 20230.

U.S. Exporters seeking an agent or distributor in South Africa should plan to visit the country, since firsthand knowledge of the market and the society is highly useful. Moreover, such a visit provides an opportunity for a personal appraisal of the relative merits of the prospective agents or distributors. For those products requiring service, exporters should ensure that qualified personnel and the necessary parts and components are close at hand, as more than one firm has lost valued customers by failing to provide prompt and efficient servicing.

Selling through established wholesalers.—Consumer goods requiring maintenance of stocks and industrial raw material are often exported to South Africa through established wholesalers.

Selling through retailers/wholesalers.—Many American exporters of consumer goods sell directly to South African retail organizations, such as consumer cooperatives, department stores, chain stores, and cooperative groups of independent retailers, to undertake the functions of wholesale buying, selling, and warehousing. Similarly, many manufacturers have established wholesale and retail outlets, and wholesalers have taken over some elements of retailing and manufacturing. Consequently, according to recent estimates, slightly less than 50 percent of total merchandise sales passes through both a wholesaler and a retailer before reaching the final consumer; 40 percent is sold from the manufacturer to the retailer, bypassing the wholesaler completely; 5 percent is sold by the wholesaler directly to the consumer, without passing through the retailer, and the remainder bypasses both the wholesaler and the retailer, reaching the consumer directly from the producer or the importer.

Wholesalers.—Although the wholesalers have diminished in their importance over the past two decades, they remain an important element in the distribution chain. In fact, in absolute terms wholesale turnover has actually grown as a result of the expansion of the South African economy. According to the 1971 census of wholesalers, there were over 7,000 such establishments in the country.

According to the type of merchandise handled, the wholesalers were organized as follows: mining, agricultural and industrial equipment and machinery, 1,664 establishments; clothing and textiles, 716; construction and building materials, 812; food and beverage suppliers, 722; books, stationery and office equipment 525; pharmaceuticals and toiletries, 248; agricultural and pastoral products, 517; furniture and household furnishings, 341; jewelry and precious stones, 177; industrial and heavy chemicals, 63; and general and miscellaneous dealers, 1,064. Even though most wholesalers are organized as limited liability companies, the majority are small- to medium-sized firms; some 55 percent have annual sales ranging between $15,000 and $120,000; the average turnover of all the establishments in the 1967 census was over 493,000 Rand. Wholesale sales in 1978 reached 19.5 billion rand in current prices.

Retailers.—Retailing is one of South Africa's most dynamic sectors, with total retail sales in 1978 of 11.6 billion rand in current prices. According to the 1971 census, over 52,000 retail firms were engaged, with over one-third located in the Transvaal and another third in the Cape. According to type of merchandise offered for sale, 19,891 carried food; 7,551 textiles and clothing; 3,023 furniture, household appliances and furnishings; 2,114, pharmaceuticals; 748, jewelry; 690 building materials and hardware; 406, cycles; 762, books and stationery; and 647, sporting and entertainment equipment.

In 1978, 50 percent of all retail sales occurred in the Transvaal. As a rule, South African retailers tend to be smaller than their U.S. counterparts with the majority of firms having annual sales of less than $7,500. Nonetheless, there are numerous large department stores, with branches in the main population centers, which are important outlets for U.S. products. The largest of these often have their own buying offices abroad, and import and frequently warehouse directly from foreign manufacturers. In the 1967 census the strength of the department stores was clearly indicated by the fact that while the 433 department stores represented less than 1 percent of the total number of retailing establishments, they transacted just slightly less than 14 percent of the Republic's retail sales. Self-service was introduced into South Africa in 1947, and is now widespread. A considerable variety of goods is marketed through self-service stores: groceries, foodstuffs, and clothing. Other articles will no doubt be added. Developments of the past decade have seen the advent of the American-type discount stores on the retailing scene. The stores sell only for cash, with a minimum amount of customer service, and at a price beneath "normal" retail. The discount operations did not meet with immediate success among the Republic's buying public who had accustomed themselves to the many services of the department store, including credit or installment purchasing.

The Black Consumer

As Black wages rise, so does the importance of the Black consumer in the South African economy. Black wage increases have been outpacing those of Whites and the rate of inflation, though a large absolute gap between White and Black earnings remains. Blacks' disposable income was estimated to be R9 billion per year in 1979 against R4.5 billion in 1977. Their share of total purchasing power was expected to be 28.9 percent in 1980 (up from 26 percent in 1977) and may rise to 50 percent in the next 12 years.

Despite these percentages, only 15 percent of market research and 9 percent of all advertising has focused on the Black consumer. Most of this attention is on the urban Black who comprises only 30 percent of the total Black population but who enjoys a higher average income. The Black consumer is very important in some markets such as food, drink, toiletries, medicine, clothing, footwear and furniture. Blacks make one-half of the purchases in skirts, trousers, and bedroom furniture, 60 percent of all record playing equipment and 70 percent of kitchen furniture. Further, as White markets reach their saturation point, many industries will depend upon the Black consumer for future growth. Manufacturers of durables such as electric refrigerators and stoves are hoping for increased sales as electricity is made available to Black townships.

A cautious note must be sounded, however, as the projections of Black earning power are based on possibly overly-optimistic estimates of high economic growth and low unemployment.

Historically, Blacks have been excluded from the business mainstream because of restrictive government policy, lack of education and training, no access to long-term credit, and confinement to Black areas. Out of the country's roughly 20 million Blacks, only 35,000 are entrepreneurs, largely in the petty trade and service establishments. However, recent changes in the law, the skills shortage, and subsequent pressure to upgrade Black education and training may substantially improve the lot of the Black businessperson. Among other advancements, Black companies may now be formed, capital may be raised among Blacks anywhere in the country, restrictions on shop size have been lifted and buildings may be erected privately in Black urban areas. As of this writing further liberalization of the law appears likely. Contact the South African Desk at the U.S. Department of Commerce for the most recent developments.

Commercial Practices

Quotations and Terms of Payment.— American and other foreign firms generally quote on an f.o.b. port of export basis. As a general rule, such quotations should also include a statement of the actual charges for freight and insurance plus any additional charges to the port of delivery. Quotations are usually in terms of the currency of the country of origin. The terms of payment for imported goods vary according to the type of buyer and the buyer's access to capital. Large organizations such as the Government or mining companies tend to transact business on a sight draft basis, while small companies tend to operate on documents against acceptable terms. Payment between 90 and 120 days after acceptance is most common, but terms may vary between 30 and 180 days. For large orders of capital equipment, longer terms are often required.

Consumer Financing.— Consumer credit is widely used in South Africa. Large retailers, along with many of the smaller ones (excluding the discount operations) extend credit to customers on a regular basis. The ratio of credit to cash sales has been steadily rising. By retail sector, the highest credit/cash ratios occur in household furnishings and clothing, 60 percent. The South African Hire Purchase Act enacted in 1942 and most recently amended in 1972 governs both installment purchasing and hire with purchase option contracts of most categories of goods whose value does not exceed $6,000. Down payment and length of credit terms range from 10 percent down and 24 months to pay for household furniture and domestic appliances, to 25 percent and 30 months for passenger cars.

Business Hours.— Provincial legislation in South Africa rigidly prescribes shopping hours. In most areas shopping starts between 7 and 8:30 a.m. and most close by 6 p.m. from Monday to Fridays, and by 1 p.m. on Saturdays. Exceptions are arranged for certain classes of merchandise, in particular perishable goods, and some grocers stay open until 10 p.m. even on Saturdays and Sundays. Banking hours vary slightly from area to area, but are generally 9 a.m. to 3:30 p.m. Monday, Tuesday, Thursday, and Friday, and 9 a.m. to 1 p.m. on Wednesday; Saturday banking hours run from 8:30 a.m. to 11 a.m. Lunch is generally from 1 to 2 p.m. and many businesses may be closed during this period.

Government Procurement

Government purchasing is an important factor in the South African economy. Virtually all such purchasing is done through competitive bidding on invitations for tenders, which are published periodically in official gazettes and newspapers. Even though both national and provincial procedures favor purchases from domestic firms, an overseas firm is not precluded from bidding if the firm has an agent in the Republic to act in its behalf. As a general practice, payment is made directly to the overseas firm, with the agent's fee deducted. Bids for government tenders must be on a c.i.f. basis, and normally must include rail charges inside the Republic to the point of delivery.

National Government Procurement.— South Africa's buying procedures are highly centralized. The Office for State Purchasers in Pretoria has responsibility for procuring for some 40 departments, and purchases goods worth roughly $350 million annually. The procedures for procurement of commodities and services at the national level are spelled out in Government Gazette No. R 99 of January 19, 1968. The Offices Director and Deputy Director call for tenders and arrange contracts on behalf of the Government. Tender notices are published only in the Republic, unless the supplies or services cannot be obtained domestically or if the price of purchasing domestically would be excessive; in this case, the board may approve the publishing of tender notices abroad. The due date for a bid is required to be at least 21 days from the date of first publication of the notice for supplies to be manufactured in the Republic; in other cases the due date must be not less than 30 days from date of announcement. As a general practice, a lead time of 30 to 45 days is allowed. Firms may subscribe to the State Tenders Bulletin at a cost of $30 per year. Bids on tenders should be addressed to the Director, Private Bag 49, Pretoria 0001 under sealed cover with the tender number, due date, and name and address of the tender or endorsed on the outside. As part of the Government's policy to encourage local industry, the Office of State Purchases grants several types of preferences to industries established in the Republic, with the major preference based on the percentage of local content. In comparing tenders for supplies produced, manufactured, or assembled within South Africa from imported and local materials, the Office of State Purchases deducts a certain percentage of the bid price, depending on the percentage of the local content, as follows:

Percent of local content	Percent deducted
5 or less	1
5-10	2
10-20	3
20-30	4
30-40	5
40-50	6
50-60	7
60-70	8
70-80	9
more than 80	10

To permit the Office of State Purchases to determine the level preference to be deducted, tenders must enclose with their bid a certificate showing classification of the supplies offered in terms of local content. In addition to local content preferences, an additional preference, not to exceed 15 percent, including customs duty, may be added. Thus, an item on which there is a 3 percent customs duty and with a local content of 85 percent could receive a total preference of 22 percent (10 percent for local content, plus the additional preference of 15 percent less the customs duty of 3 percent).

An additional preference of 2.5 percent may also be granted if the supplies bear the mark of the South African Bureau of Standards. Finally, an optional preference can be added if the Board of Trade and Industries so recommends. In considering the price of foreign bids, the office considers the customs duty ordinarily payable (even though not actually payable, since the commodity is for Government use). This has the effect of granting a slight preference to Commonwealth countries in some instances over goods coming from "most favored-nation" countries, such as the United States. The South African Railways and Harbors Administration maintains purchasing offices in the United States. The address is: Railways and Airways Purchasing Office, 1975 Linden Blvd., Elmont, New York 11003, 212-656-7266, 516-285-7150. The Administration's tender board regulations are patterned after those for the Office of State Purchases, and include similar preferences for local content and for using the Bureau of Standards mark.

Provincial Government Procurement.— Local government purchases have become increasingly significant, and in some cases are open to overseas bidding. The tender regulations of the four provinces—Cape Province, Natal, the Orange Free State, and the Transvaal—provide preferences for articles manufactured within the province, "all things being equal".

Tenders for the Transvaal Province are published weekly in the Province of Transvaal Official Gazette obtainable from the Provincial Secretary, Private Bag X64, Pretoria, at an annual rate of $7.50 plus postage. Orange Free State (OFS) tenders are published in the OFS Official Gazette which can be obtained from the Officer-in-Charge, Official Gazette, P.O. Box 517, Bloemfontein, O.F.S., at the cost of $4.50 per year. Tenders for the Cape Province are published in the Official Gazette of the Cape Province available from the Enquiry Office, Provincial Building, Cape Town at 15 cents per copy, or by subscription, $9 per annum in South Africa and $11.25 overseas. For Natal, tenders are published in the Official Gazette of the Province of Natal, available through the Natal Witness (Pty.) Ltd.; P.O. Box 362 Peitermaritzburg, Natal, at the subscription cost of $7.75 per annum. In terms of South Africa, the Republic's Limitation and Disclosure of Finance Charges Act #73 of 1968 as amended by Act #62 of 1974 provides much the same credit protection to the consumer and small borrower as does the U.S. Truth in Lending Act of 1968. Allowable interest rates are set periodically by the South African Government.

The Shops and Offices Act of 1964 established a 46-hour work week for full-time employees and an 8½-hour workday for part-time help. Provisions of the 1964 Act also regulate overtime, sick and annual leave, resignation and the maintenance of essential employer records.

Minimum wages for the distributive trades are governed by Wage Determination 356 as amended in July 1974. The Determination lists jobs and assigns a minimum wage to each according to seven pay scales corresponding to differing magisterial districts.

Transportation and Utilities

Rail, Road, Air, and Sea

South Africa has excellent sea and air passenger and freight connections with the United States and Western Europe. South African Airlines operates four flights a week from the United States directly to South Africa and daily flights to the United Kingdom/Europe. Other connections may be made through London with daily flights to South Africa on British Airways. In addition approximately two flights a day on other carriers leave New York for Johannesburg via connections. Airlines flying into Johannesburg include Iberian, Lufthansa,

Swissair and Sabena, Portuguese and Varig. South Africa's major airline, South African Airways (SAA) which is government-owned and operated offers a comprehensive network of services throughout the Republic as well as regional services to Lesotho, Swaziland, Botswana, Mauritius, Zimbabwe, and Mozambique. There are two SAA flights a week between Johannesburg and Sydney, Australia, and one flight a week to Hong Kong.

During the period 1977-78, SAA carried over 3 million passengers and 54,726 metric tons of cargo. Jan Smuts airport handles 3 million passengers annually and is ranked as one of the top five international airports in the world.

Nationally-owned airports are located in Johannesburg, Durban, Cape Town, Bloemfontien, and East London. Municipally-owned airports operate in numerous other cities including Kimberley, Port Elizabeth, and Beaufort West. In addition, there are private and public airfields scattered throughout the Republic. South Africa is continually expanding and updating airports and airport facilities. South African Airlines announced in late 1979 that it would purchase 12 737 aircraft for delivery in 1982 from Boeing in the U.S. to replace a fleet of nine 727's. Operations are expected to begin by 1982 at the La Mercy International Airport located 20 miles outside Durban. La Mercy is expected to handle 3.5 million domestic and 250,000 international passengers annually. A potential area for marketing is in South Africa's expanding regional air service operated by 10 commercial air companies. This service provides daily flights to 36 towns not serviced by South Africa Airlines. This sector offers a market for updated equipment, aircraft, and eventually short-range jet transports. It is estimated that the capital investment of these carriers in aircraft, spare parts and related equipment could reach $20 million.

Two American flag carriers maintain scheduled sea connections with South Africa: Farrell from U.S. Atlantic ports and Lykes Brothers Steamship from the U.S. Gulf ports. The Republic's principal harbors are Durban, Richard Bay, Cape Town, Saldanha Bay, Port Elizabeth and East London. The South Africa government owns all of the harbors which are constructed and directed by the Railways and Harbours Administration. Total international cargo handled by the six ports totaled 83.1 million tons in 1978. Durban handled 34.1 million of that amount; Richards Bay 15.4 million, Cape Town 9.7 million, Saldanha Bay 12.6 million, Port Elizabeth 7.5 million; and East London 3.8 million.

The Republic's two newest ports, Richards Bay on the east coast and Saldanha Bay northwest of Cape Town (both opened in 1976), have quickly grown in importance. With greater demands being placed on South African rail and shipping facilities these ports are considered to be of real strategic importance.

Richards Bay is a specialized port with coal exports comprising nearly 93 percent of tonnage. The coal handling facility is being upgraded to handle 24 million tons per year by mid-1980 and plans are under consideration to increase this to 52 million tons in the mid-1980's. Richards Bay and the surrounding area will continue to offer investment and product opportunities. In an effort to provide an alternative to the port of Maputo in Mozambique, the South African government is constructing a multi-purpose bulk handling facility at Richards Bay to permit the export of most free-flowing commodities. In addition, exports of Swaziland such as wood pulp, coal and timber could be switched to Richards Bay. Other construction plans being considered are a petrochemical complex and refinery designed to handle a wide range of petrochemical imports. Export facilities to handle wattle bark and sugar are contemplated.

Saldanha Bay represents a massive transportation system to receive iron ore from the Sishen mine. The ore is transported directly to the modern port facility by a 535-mile railway line. Almost all tonnage handled in Saldanha is comprised of ores and minerals. In 1979 a new dock for bulk loading of nickel and iron ore was completed. Plans are underway to construct a $1.4 billion steel plant and to build a multi-million dollar drydock.

The South African Government, through the South African Railways and Harbor Administration, owns and operates the country's 21,778 mile rail network. Of the total, some 6,351 miles of track are electrified. As a result of the increasing electrification, the need for greater mechanization and efficiency in track laying has become of prime importance. Most southern African territories use the 3-foot, 6-inch gauge. In the year ending March 31, 1978, South African Railways hauled 147 million tons of traffic and carried 610 million passengers. The South African Railways rate structure is classified according to 15 separate listings, each with its own freight rate. Rates vary widely depending on the class of grade and the distance travelled.

The Republic's road network comprises nearly 6,000 miles of national roads, 15,700 miles of major provincial roads, 38,000 miles of primary, and 33,000 miles of secondary provincial roads. The transport of commercial goods over this network is restricted under the Motor Carrier Transportation Act of 1930 to limit competition with the railroads. Firms themselves are allowed to deliver specified goods in their own vehicles within a 150 mile radius, and for an even shorter list of goods, within a 300 mile radius. For shipments beyond the allowed areas, a petition must be submitted to the respective local Road Transportation Board. Boards are located in Bloemfontein, Cape Town, Durban, East London, Johannesburg, Kimberly, Pietermaritzburg, Port Elizabeth, Potchefsroom, Pretoria, and Umtata. Appeals of rulings made by the local Boards are directed to the National Transport Commission. In the public transport service, Johannesburg's bus depot, the most modern in the world, has set an example that South Africa would like to continue. Other depots are planned, providing possible opportunities for U.S. firms interested in supplying equipment and/or services.

Port Capacities

South Africa's major ports have floating and mobile cranes for vessels to work cargo. Durban has two floating cranes with lifting capacities of 25 tons and 40 tons, respectively; Cape Town, 60 tons. Port Elizabeth and East London both have tow mobile cranes. Cargo is granted 48 hours free time by each of the ports, except East London, which only grants 24 hours. There are ample general cargo storage facilities at each of the ports.

The port facilities of South Africa are handling an unprecedented volume of cargo flowing in and out of the country. In Durban and East London, refrigerated cargo must be offloaded and transferred to refrigerated rail cars for shipment inland. Cape Town and Port Elizabeth possess refrigerated storage facilities. Container facilities were opened in July 1977 at Cape Town, Port Elizabeth, and Durban. The facilities are designed to handle up to 600,000 containers per year or 70 percent of South Africa's total break-bulk trade. Containerization is designed to reduce the time a vessel remains at a wharf to transfer cargo from a week or more to less than 24 hours. From March 1977-March 1978 containers conveyed totaled 371,992. Eventually, Durban will have five deep-sea berths, Cape Town, three, and Port Elizabeth two or three. The containerization system is designed to solve the frequent harbor congestion problems in South Africa with the expansion of containerization and the network of inland transport. The wharfage rate for imported goods is 61 cents per ton and $1.83 per $120 ad valorem pro rata (Note: the value of ad valorem for wharfage purposes is the free on-board price of the goods at the port of shipment excluding local excise or sales duty, if any, in respect to goods shipped from another harbor in the Republic or South West Africa. If there is no such value, the value as accepted for customs purposes shall apply).

Theft and pilferage are fairly well controlled in South African ports; however, handling is frequently rough and causes considerable damage to merchandise. Shippers are advised to use wooden boxes or cases instead of fiberboard cartons wherever possible. Protection against water damage is also desirable.

There are no free port facilities in South Africa.

Telecommunications

Annual telephone traffic is approaching 4.4 billion calls. There are more than 2 million telephones in use, with more than 120,000 new installations a year. The Ministry of Posts and Telecommunications, through the telecommunications activities of the South African Post Office, is the sole legal provider of public telecommunications services in South Africa and Namibia. Facilities for calls between South Africa and other countries via the undersea cable between Cape Town and Portugal or by radio-telephone are available to over 160 countries. Additional routes are provided by the satellite earth station at Hartebeeshoek opened in December 1975. It provides direct telephone and live television circuits with North and South America, Europe, and Africa via the Intelsat satellites above the Atlantic. A second earth station will provide direct circuits to the East, including Japan, Australia and New Zealand, via the Indian Ocean satellite.

National dialing is possible between all large centers and is gradually being extended to other towns. International dialing from South Africa to Lesotho, Western Germany, and Mbabane and Manzini in Swaziland is available. From the Witwatersrand, direct dialing is also available to Zimbabwe and Gaborone in Botswana. Subscribers on the Witwatersrand, in the Vaal Triangle, and in Pretoria are also able to dial subscribers in the United Kingdom direct.

Fully automated telex service is available to 47 countries from South Africa. As of March 1975, there were 10,772 telex subscribers utilizing nine inland telex exchanges and two international telex exchanges, one of which is manned. Facsimile transmission is still in very small demand; but data transmission is growing strongly with 2,448 modems in March 1974, up 60 percent from the previous year, and 3,373 data modems in March 1975.

The 736 post offices in South Africa, South West Africa, Botswana, Lesotho and Swaziland are able to dial each other directly, thus enabling them to transmit public telegrams. The automatic inland exchanges used for telex traffic are the same used for transmitting telegrams.

Electricity Rates

South Africa covers 4 percent of the total area of Africa, has less than 6 percent of the population and yet generates more than 50 percent of the total electricity generated on the continent. The Electricity Supply Commission (ESCOM) supplies 90 percent of the electricity used in South Africa. At present ESCOM operates 18 coal-fired power stations, 2 hydro-electric stations and 2 gas turbines. During the next 20 years demand for electricity is estimated to grow 20 percent. ESCOM is building two additional coal-fired power stations expected to increase generating capacity by more than 10,000 MW. ESCOM's newest power station, located at Kriel in the Eastern Transvaal, is capable of generating 3,000 MW. When in full production, Kriel will consume 1,500 tons of coal an hour. South Africa's abundant coal supplies have enabled ESCOM to sell power at the rate of $.043 per kWh. The power is generally of 220 volt, 50 cycle, three or four phase.

Hydroelectric Energy

Although coal provides nearly 98 percent of the fuel requirements for energy, it is predicted that coal production will not be able to keep up with demand by the year 2000. Thus South Africa is exploiting every possible source of power. The Tugela Vaal hydro project is in the final phases of construction. This project is designed to increase the Transvaal's future fresh water supply while simultaneously adding as much as 1,000 megawatts of power to the national electricity grid. This scheme uses the "pumped-storage" concept, whereby water pumped to a high level dam during periods of low electricity demand flows back to generate electricity in peak demand periods. In 1978 the Minister of Water Affairs in Natal disclosed that his department was considering a second hydro-electric scheme in the Drakensberg mountains between Natal and the Orange Free State. Provisional feasibility studies have been completed for two additional hydroelectric projects on the Tugela River in Natal. These projects could yield a total of 4,000 megavolts of power. U.S. suppliers should keep track of these future hydroelectric projects.

Atomic Energy

In order to benefit from South Africa's large reserves of low-cost uranium, the South African Atomic Energy Board is pursuing an active program for nuclear power. South Africa's first nuclear power station (Koeberg-25 miles north of Cape Town) is scheduled to start generating electricity in December 1982 with a second reactor operational a year later. The two reactors, which are located on an island strengthened to withstand floods and earthquakes, will generate 1.8 million kilowatts. In an effort to decrease dependence on foreign supplies of enriched uranium required by nuclear plants such as Koeberg, the Atomic Energy Board has plans to build a small commercial scale enrichment plant.

Marketing Aids

Advertising is a highly sophisticated profession in South Africa. In 1979 approximately $296 million was spent on advertising in the Republic. All major media are available to advertising. TV advertising which began in 1978 accounts for 16 percent of overall spending. The most popular medium is the English language daily press with advertising sales of $63.8 million. English language consumer magazines have a 12 percent share of press income with $24 million. Trade magazines have an 8 percent share with $18.9 million while black publications are showing an increasing share amounting to nearly 5 percent with $13 million. Radio advertising expenditures represent 14 percent with $43 million while cinema and outdoor advertising was approximately $20 million.

There are approximately 100 advertising agents throughout South Africa. Their branches in major retail outlets provide a full range of advertising, including market research and full media coverage. Customarily, advertising agencies are not paid by their clients in South Africa, but rather the newspapers, magazines, and radio corporations reduce their charges for space and time when the purchaser is a recognized advertising agency. The agency then bills the client at the full rate and retains the difference as a commission. The agency's profit is, in turn, limited by law to one-sixth of normal costs of the advertisement.

With this arrangement, the company seeking to bring its products to the public must pay the same charge if the company places the advertisement directly or through an advertising agent. Names and addresses of major advertising agents, newspapers, magazines, market research companies, public relations consultants, and outdoor advertising firms are published together with current rates and other data in the Advertising and Press Annual of Africa. Foreign subscriptions which include the annual and monthly updates are $45 per year and are available from the National Publishing Company (Pty) Ltd., 501 Capitol House, Commissioner St., P.O. Box 2735, Johannesburg.

Newspaper Advertising

Twenty-two daily newspapers are published in South Africa, 15 in English and 7 in Afrikaans. The newspaper industry is led by a few large organizations which publish regional newspapers throughout South Africa. There are seven Sunday newspapers which give national coverage, four English and three Afrikaans. In addition to these publications, there are numerous publications centered in smaller rural towns. These are published once, twice, or three times per week. They have a limited circulation, however, and are of interest only to residents of the particular regions or towns in which they are published.

Although television advertising was initiated in January 1978, there has not been a sharp decline in newspaper advertising. In the major urban areas where there is a large number of competing dailies and weeklies relative to circulation figures, competition for advertising is strong. As the South African economy continues to grow, the volume of advertising is anticipated to increase. It is also likely that there will be a continued emphasis on regional retail and classified advertising which is more efficiently served by newspapers rather than the limited volume national image advertising of television.

As the table below shows, circulation figures rose in 1978 after the recession years of 1976 and 1977. In addition a new morning daily began in 1976 with rapid growth in black readership. Circulation figures of afternoon dailies and weeklies, however, are still down from 1975.

Readership
(Percent change over previous year)[1]

Year	dailies/weeklies		dailies/weeklies		dailies/weeklies	
1976	+10.8	+5.8	+2.7	−18.7	+29.0	+25.9
1977	−15.3	−13.8	−10.5	−11.5	−25.7	−19.5
1978	+26.2	+3.2	+25.5	+4.3	+52.2	+8.5

[1]Standard Bank Review March 1979 p. 5.

Advertising tariffs vary according to size and

type of advertisement, circulation and other factors. Based on advertising volumes and values, however, the cost per single column inch has risen from $3.70 in 1975 to $5.90 in 1978.[2]

Advertising rates vary considerably depending on the media involved: $9-40 for weekend papers, and $5-15 for dailies. Color advertising rates are considerably higher.

Circulation figures vary from newspaper to newspaper and from area to area. The following July-December 1976 figures give an indication of the circulation of the more widely read papers: Rapport (weekend, Afrikaans: 458,540); Sunday Express (weekend, English: 119,582); Sunday Times (weekend, English: 492,187); Daily News (Durban: 133,081); Pretoria News (daily, Pretoria: 37,811); Rand Daily Mail (Johannesburg: 151,916); Star (daily, Johannesburg: 183,794).

Radio Advertising

Radio broadcasting in South Africa is monopolized by the South African Broadcasting Corporation (SABC), a semi-government body. There are seven commercial channels broadcast, including the three regional channels: Radio Port Natal (Natal), Radio Good Hope (Cape) and Radio Highveld (Transvaal and Orange Free State).

Radio SR began broadcasts in 1977 to cater to the urban black areas of Transvaal and Natal with programs and commercials in English—the language common to most Black ethnic groups.

Statistics indicate about one-quarter of the Republic's population listens to one or more of the channels. It is estimated that about 94 percent of white South Africans have access to a radio, while roughly 3 million Black adults have access.

Listenership statistics for the various channels are as follows: Radio 5—2.5 million each week of which 84 percent falls in the 16 to 34 age group; Radio Bantu—4.4 million Blacks; regional channels of Radio Highveld, 561,000; Radio Port Natal—144,000, and Radio Good Hope—436,000.

Approximately $43 million was spent on radio advertising in the period June 1978-June 1979. For the period January-December 1975-76, $32.6 million was spent on radio advertising. Of that total Springbok Radio had 14 million. Radio Bantu attracted advertising worth $8.9 million while Radio Haveld ($4.4 mil.) and Radio Good Hope ($2.6 mil.) were the next most popular. Radio Port Natal and Radio 5 achieved advertising sales of approximately $1 million each.

Advertising costs vary from channel to channel and from broadcast time to broadcast time.

²Standard Bank Review March 1979 p. 5.

SABC officials advise that there are also different rates for long- and short-term advertising campaigns. It is therefore difficult to give a general indication of charges on radio other than to say that costs range from $15 for a 7-second spot at low listenership periods to $290 per 30-second slot during peak hours on Springbok Radio. A short-term Monday through Saturday campaign consisting of 24 30-second spots will cost $2,700 on Springbok Radio. Costs on other channels are lower and range from $6.90 (quarter-minute low listenership period) to $100 for a full minute during peak listenership. Special rates apply where campaigns are concerned.

Radio Bantu operates seven separate services in seven different languages: Zulu, Xhosa, Southern Sotho, Northern Sotho, Tswana, Venda, and Tsonga. Quarter-minute and half-minute spot announcements are broadcast on all services and sold as packaged deals. All spot announcements must be broadcast in the language of the service in which they appear. Further information can be obtained from SABC, Radio Bantu, P.O. Box 4559, Johannesburg 2000. Information concerning advertising on channels other than Radio Bantu is available from the SABC at P.O. Box 1166, Johannesburg 2000.

Television Advertising

Television broadcasts began in January 1976 with nightly 5-hour broadcasts by the South African Broadcasting Corporation (SABC). Total average viewership is estimated at 1,690,000. Audience growth has been greater than expected and a SABC survey showed that 75 percent of white South Africans watch television at least once a week with peak viewing times attracting 38 percent of white adults. Television advertising began in January 1978 with commercials costing the sponsors between (R8,000) and (R15,000) to produce. The SABC policies prohibit the use of sex as a theme and ads for cigarettes or liquor are also prohibited. No ad is allowed to be screened more than three times a week. Bilingual ads are prohibited although half of the ads must be in English and half in Afrikaans. Based on an estimated audience of 900,000 adults for each quarter-hour of viewing, a 30-second peak-time ad in English costs R4,590 and a peak-time ad in Afrikaans costs R2,720.

Magazine Advertising

About 30 general interest magazines are published in South Africa on a weekly or fortnightly basis, while about the same number are published monthly or quarterly. In addition to this, there is a highly organized industrial, professional, technical, and commercial press which publishes numerous magazines of interest to particular organizations and groups. Despite tight advertising budgets, trade and technical magazines have increased their share of advertising expenditures consistently, and in 1976 this share amounted to R11.45 million. A listing of these magazines with current rates and data is available in the *South African Rates and Data Guide.*

Motion Picture Advertising

Motion picture companies now face strong competition from commercial television for advertising revenue. As movie attendance drops, advertisers are naturally turning to the growing audience share that television commands. Theater chains are battling to compete, and among measures aimed at making cinema viewing more attractive to audiences has been a move to shorten advertising programs featured before main attractions.

Cinemark (Pty) Limited is the major motion picture advertising company. Further information concerning their rates is available from the firm at P.O. Box 7884, Johannesburg 2000. Rates were about $700 per 30-second film commercial in 1977 through the entire circuit controlled by Cinemark. The rate for selected cycles or areas is calculated by taking the average weekly attendance of the cycles chosen, and multiplying this figure by the cost ($700) per thousand for the entire circuit, and adding a premium of 25 percent.

Other popular forms of advertising are outdoor advertising in the forms of posters, billboards and the like, and direct mail advertising. There are numerous companies specializing in outdoor advertising. These companies are organized on a regional basis as costs vary from area to area depending on the media used. An advantage of this type of organization is that they have direct access to local authorities who control public recreation, transport, and other utilities where outdoor advertising can be used.

Direct mail is also a popular form of advertising, generating over $20 million in advertising placements. Costs here are generally high when one takes printing and postage costs into account. Although the obvious advantage of select target audiences can be achieved, the effectiveness of this type of advertising is in question as many householders discard this type of mail without even perusing it. Names and addresses of companies involved in direct mail

advertising, as well as outdoor advertising, are contained in *The Advertising and Press Annual.*

Units other than correct metric units are prohibited in all types of advertising (including verbal communications and quotations) except in connection with non-metric fasteners, spanners, and thread cutting equipment.

Advertising Restrictions

Details about the regulation on the advertising of drugs (as stated in South Africa's Drug Control Act 101, 1965 amended to Act 95, 1971) can be obtained from the Drugs Control Council (c/o Secretary for Health, Private Bag 88, Pretoria). When advertising foodstuffs, cosmetics, and disinfectants, false or misleading descriptions are prohibited. A geographical name which is generally accepted as a generic name for a particular type or variety of foodstuff is allowed. Specific regulations on advertising these products can be found in the Foodstuffs, Cosmetics and Disinfectants Act 54, 1972.

Market Research and Trade Organizations

Numerous South African advertising agencies conduct market research activities, including market analysis, opinion research and pools, and specialized trade and industry studies for their clients.

In addition, several firms specialize in the preparation of market research studies. Some of these companies are Consumer Research Services (Pty) Ltd., 1001 Trust Bank Centre, 475 Smith St., P.O. Box 670, Durban; Market Research Africa (Pty) Ltd., Research House, 178 Fox St., P.O. Box 10483, Johannesburg; Marketing Information Organization (Pty), Ltd., P.O. Box 56213, Pinegorwie, Johannesburg; Intercontinental Marketing Services Africa, 1st Floor, Highpoint, Kotz St., Hillbrow, P.O. Box 11260, Johannesburg; Nielsen Company (Pty) Ltd., A.C. Longsbank Bldg., 187 Bree St., P.O. Box 5637, Johannesburg; Howard-Purdon Associates, 22nd Floor, Bosman Bldg., cor Eloff & Bree St., P.O. Box 7981, Johannesburg.

South African public banks also will provide assistance on market research in South Africa and frequently these services are available in the United States through correspondent arrangements. The Netherlands Bank of South Africa has established a subsidiary, Stats-Inform, to conduct both public and private market research studies. Many local Chambers of Commerce, which are members of the Association of Chambers of Commerce of South Africa (Allied Building, P.O. Box 694; Johannesburg), publish weekly newsletters containing information of interest to the trading community, as well as a listing of trade opportunities. The Association itself issues a monthly publication, *Commerce Opinion*, which is reported to have the largest circulation of any trade paper in South Africa. Manufacturing firms in South Africa may be represented in one of the eight regional Chambers of Industry; the regional Chambers in turn, along with 18 national Associations, are represented on the Federated Chamber of Industries (622 Sanlam Building; 63 Commissioner Street; Johannesburg). The Federated Chamber of Industries also issues its own monthly publication, FCI Viewpoint. The Afrikaanse Handelsinstituut, an organization of Afrikaans-speaking businessmen, is located in Pretoria and publishes the monthly journal *Volkshandel*.

Two organizations that specialize in the promotion of trade fairs, generally held in Johannesburg or Cape Town, are Specialized Exhibitions (Pty) Ltd., P.O. Box 2900, Johannesburg 2000 and Exhibition Promotions of South Africa (Pty) Ltd., P.O. Box 6110; Johannesburg.

Credit

The South African Reserve Bank (SARB) fulfills the functions of a Central Bank. It maintains both Government accounts and reserve accounts of South Africa's commercial banks. As of October 1979 total assets of SARB amounted to 4.9 billion rand.

The commercial banking system in South Africa is comparable to that of the British branch system. The major banks of South Africa include the following: Barclays, Standard, Nedbank, Citibank, French Bank of Southern Africa, the Bank of Lisbon and South Africa, South African Bank of Athens Ltd., The Trust Bank of Africa Ltd., and Volkskas Ltd.

Of 9.3 billion rand in assets in 1978, almost two-thirds were held by the two largest banks, Barclay's and Standard. As of September 1979 total deposits in commercial banks amounted to 10.4 billion rand. Total liabilities of the commercial banks were 11.2 billion rand in September 1979. Advances and discounts for the same period totaled 5.5 billion rand.

The monetary unit of the Republic of South Africa is the rand with an exchange value in 1980 of $1.31. The rand is decimally divided into 100 rand cents. South Africa is part of the sterling area. South Africa, Lesotho, and Swaziland form the monetary area for which the South African Reserve Bank acts as a central bank. Lesotho, Swaziland, and Botswana all have their own national currency although exchange rates follow the value of the rand. Thus the rand is legal tender but not necessarily the only legal tender. Citibank, Chase Manhatten, and First National Bank of New York are U.S. banks represented in South Africa.

South Africa's first Black-owned bank, the African Bank of South Africa (Afribank) has branches in DiepKloof, Soweto (established March 1977), Umtata, Transkei, and the Gra-Rankuwa branch in Pretoria. Afribank was founded to provide an almost entirely black banking institution to meet the needs of black business people and individuals with the participation by established banking institutions such as Standard and Barclays.

Under the International Banking Act of 1978, there is a requirement that once a foreign-owned bank reaches $24 million in share capital, it must open its shareholding to local participation with a goal of reaching 50 percent South African ownership within the next 10 years. However the Minister of Finance has flexibility in negotiating the implementation schedule. The U.S.-owned bank, Citibank has less than the $24 million in share capital so that the local shareholding requirement does not yet apply.

The National Finance Corporation, which was incorporated in 1949 by an Act of Parliament, supplements existing facilities for the investment of short-term funds. The creation of this facility led to the establishment of several acceptance and discount houses. A number of supplementary banking institutions have developed as the country's financial system grew in size. These include the Industrial Finance Corporation, insurance companies, building societies, and unit trusts, all of which are subject to regulations.

South African business people have traditionally used commercial banks for short-term credit facilities. For the small- to medium-size firm, banks are also the major source of permanent credit. Therefore, during periods of rapid expansion the banking facilities are over-taxed, causing a threat of inflation as during 1963-65. Ceilings on bank lending to help curb inflation were first instituted in 1965 by the Banks Act.

According to South African Reserve Bank regulation of August 1979, every banking institution must ensure that the total amount of its discounts, loans, and advances does not exceed 134 percent of its assets and that at the end of each month this amount plus an additional .5 percent does not exceed the total amount of assets as of December 1975.

The SARB, by the Currency and Exchange

Act, regulates allowable interest and discount rates. As of May 1980, the discount rate stood at 7 percent, the prime overdraft rate at 9.5 percent, and the home mortgage rate ranged from 9.5-11.5 percent.

The Johannesburg Stock Exchange (JSE) grew up around the mineral houses in South Africa. As of December 1979 membership on the JSE was 546 firms with 65 brokerage firms operating out of nine centers in South Africa. On an average day a total of 3.3 million shares, valued at $15.5 million dollars, were traded on the Stock Exchange. The Stock Exchange showed strong growth in 1979. The number of shares increased from 7.3 million in 1978 to 14.7 million in 1979. Based on a composite yield of 15.9 percent the sectors of textile and clothing, tobacco and motors showed growth while the earnings of building and engineering dropped off.

By the mid-1950's shares of manufacturing, industrial, and commercial companies began to challenge the domination of mining on the Exchange. As a result, a substantial number of institutional investors have appeared in the equity market bringing with them new ideas and attitudes which transformed the JSE. Modern financial techniques have been introduced and a period of rapid growth, particularly in the late 1960's has resulted.

Import and Tariff Regimes

Botswana, Lesotho, Swaziland, and South Africa form the Southern African Customs Union. It originated in 1910 and was renegotiated in 1969. The Customs Union provides for the general free entry and exit of goods within the four-country area, a common external tariff and a sharing of customs revenues.

The Customs Union utilizes the Brussels Tariff Nomenclature. The tariff itself is two column: MFN (United States and most other GATT members); and General (remaining trading partners). As far back as 1925, the South African Government embarked on a policy of active encouragement of secondary industries by means of the customs tariff. Protection is selective.

The tariff is not designed to encourage uneconomic or unsound development or to burden the basic industries unduly, particularly gold mining on which the country still depends for much of its foreign exchange. On the other hand, deserving secondary industries can rely on adequate protective duties for survival against strong competition from abroad. The Government does not hesitate to act effectively and quickly against dumping and other forms of disruptive competition.

Under the import control policy of South Africa, imported goods fall into one of three categories which determines the type of license required. The categories are: Group One—a wide range of items with no license required; Group Two—certain raw materials, capital plant, equipment, and consumer goods which can be imported with a license to meet full, reasonable requirements of bona fide merchants; Group Three—specified items which can be imported only with a license that specifically describes the goods. Included in this group are alcoholic beverages and clothing. Under certain circumstances, the Minister of Finance may grant duty rebates on certain classes of materials imported for manufacturing purposes. In many cases, machinery, apparatus and appliances for factory installations may be imported free of customs duty. For a preliminary ruling on customs duties, shippers may contact the Customs and Excise Board.

For articles subject to duty on a value basis, the dutiable value is the domestic value or f.o.b. (free-on-board) price of the goods in the country of origin, whichever is greater. Domestic value is considered to be the wholesale market price in the exporting country plus all costs, charges, and expenses incidental to the sale and to placing the goods on board, less excise taxes or sales taxes imposed by the country of origin, and less drawbacks, refunds, rebates, or remissions of customs duty granted by the exporting country.

Dutiable weight for the assessment of specific duties is the legal weight of the merchandise plus the weight of the immediate container in which it is sold, unless specified otherwise in the tariff. Import duties are payable by the importer in South African rand. For purposes of such payment, foreign values are converted to the exchange rate current on the date of purchase (date of supplier's confirmation of order) or the rate prevailing at the time of exportation to South Africa.

Sales Tax

In July 1978 a general sales tax of 4 percent was placed on all goods and services at final sale. The value for sales tax on imported commodities is the f.o.b. value plus 15 percent of that value, plus any non-rebated customs duty payable on such commodities. If part or all of the customs duty is to be rebated, that portion of the customs duty is not included in the value for sales tax.

Excise Tax

An excise tax is levied on a number of imported and locally produced goods such as tobacco, vinegar, alcohol, and petroleum products. The excise tax is computed on the f.o.b. value or the domestic value, whichever is higher, and is added to the customs duty. However, generally for goods with an excise tax, the sales tax does not apply.

Documentation

A shipper's commercial invoice which shows the actual price charged to the importer in addition to the cost of placing goods on board ship for export and the goods commission is required for all shipments to South Africa. At least three copies of the invoice should go forward under separate cover to the consignee, preferably by airmail to ensure their receipt prior to arrival of the goods. A Declaration of Origin (Form DA 59) is used for goods where a lower rate of duty is claimed and for goods that may fall in the category for anti-dumping or countervailing duty.

For detailed information concerning the proper preparation of an invoice form, including special invoicing requirements applied to a number of goods such as alcoholic beverages, medicaments, and textiles, U.S. business people should consult the Exporters Encyclopedia published by Dun and Bradstreet. Reference copies of this publication are available in all U.S. Department of Commerce District Offices and in major commercial and public libraries.

Information regarding customs duties applicable to specific products entering the Customs Union may be obtained from the Africa Division, Office of Country Marketing, U.S. Department of Commerce, Washington, D.C. 20230; or from any Department of Commerce District Office. Inquiries should give a complete product description, including BTN, SITC, or U.S. Schedule E Export Commodity number, if known.

Warehousing

South African regulations require that all goods must be landed and entered within 7 days after arrival of the importing ship unless the Secretary of Customs provides an exemption. If goods are not so entered, the Customs Officials may transfer them to a state customs warehouse where charges are assessed and after 3 months sold at public auction.

Goods may be stored in bond without payment of customs duties, except dumping or special duties, in any bonded warehouse licensed by the Commissioner of Customs. Alternatively, goods may be stored in an unbonded warehouse if the Commissioner approves and if the importer furnishes security. When such goods are later withdrawn from bond and shipped elsewhere in the Republic, the applicable duties must then be paid.

Non-Tariff Control

All firms conducting import operations in South Africa must register with the Director of Imports and Exports by category of goods handled and submit periodic reports of volume and nature of import transactions. From such data, the South African Government annually allocates the amount of foreign exchange it will make available for the purchase of all imports by broad categories. The current control categories are: Exempted, Restricted, and Prohibited.

Weights and Measures

South Africa officially shifted in 1974 to the metric system of weights and measures, known as the Scientific International (S.I.) system. All commercial and manufacturing enterprises must produce and package all of their grades in metric terms. The S.I. metric system is similar but not identical to the metric system used by the European Economic Community. For example S.I. markings are in centiliters rather than milliliters.

Labeling

The Trade Metrology Act of 1973 describes how metric units are to be used in the packaging of consumer and industrial commodities. All goods shipped to South Africa must conform with the S.I. system. Although packages can show U.S. denominations with metric equivalents, the metric figure must come first and be conspicious on the containers. While not mandatory under either U.S. or South African law, marks of origin are desirable on goods shipped from the United States, not only because of the invitation extended in Senate Concurrent Resolution 40, of July 30, 1953, but also because U.S. goods are held in high esteem by South Africa's buying public.

Pricing

Pricing in South Africa in the retail field was characterized by the resale price maintenance (RPM) system whereby manufacturers set a minimum retail price for their products. The RPM system came under attack as a result of a price war in the fall of 1967 in which domestic appliance retailers abandoned the system. Following the recommendations of a 1969 Board of Trade and Industries investigation, the Monopolistic Conditions Act of 1954/58 was amended in 1969 to declare unlawful any practice which has or is calculated to have the effect of compelling or inducing a reseller to observe a specified price, through such activities as withholding supplies, denial of distributioin rights, sales discrimination, or in any other manner. Manufacturers are,however, permitted to recommend suggested prices as guides for resellers. Maximum prices of certain commodities in South Africa are controlled under the 1967 Price Control Act. The Republic Price Controller is empowered to fix maximum wholesale and retail prices and service charges. In general, controlled prices apply to goods of primary interest to the agricultural sector, goods produced under near monopolistic conditioins, and goods in short supply. The current list includes such items as sugar, selected dairy products, bread, fertilizer, agricultural machinery, fish meal, building materials, coal, jewelery, cameras, radios, television receivers, and items manufactured from iron and steel. Other provisions of the 1967 Act include provisions to ensure that price controls are not evaded through auction sales and prohibition of the conditional selling of goods specified by the Price Controller. The same Price Control Act requires that persons offering goods or services for resale keep and retain records for possible recall, indicating purchase and manufacturing costs and selling prices. Details on South Africa's Price Control regulations may be obtained from the Price Controller, Department of Commerce, Pretoria, Transvaal, Republic of South Africa.

Samples and Advertising Matters

South Africa has acceded to the Customs Convention of ATA ("Admissions Temporaire-Temporary Admission") carnets for the temporary importation (and export) of goods. The ATA carnet may be used in the Republic of South Africa, Botswana, Lesotho, Swaziland and in other countries which are parties to the Customs Convention. A carnet simplifies customs procedures for certain classes of temporary imports (and exports) by replacing normal customs documentation and the provision of security (e.g., by deposit) in the country of temporary importation. Carnets may be used for: (1) goods for display or use at exhibitions, fairs, meetings and similar events, (2) professional equipment such as equipment for the press, cinematographic equipment, engineering, topographical, surgical, electrical, archeological, and ewntertainment equipment, and (3) commercial samples imported for the purpose of being shown or demonstrated in the Republic of South Africa for soliciting orders for goods to be supplied subsequently from abroad. It is the obligation of the holder of the carnet to ensure that the customs authorities of South Africa will accept an ATA carnet for the import in question. Inquiries should be addressed to Foreign Trade Manager, ASSCOM (Association of Chambers of Commerce of South Africa), P.O. Box 694, Johannesburg, Republic of South Africa.

Samples of no commercial value are received free of charge. Advertising samples issued gratis or intended for distribution gratis as advertising matter sent from the United States to South Africa are subject to a duty of 20 percent ad valorum or $.13 per kilo, whichever is greater. A similar duty is imposed on catalogs and price lists of South African firms and firms holding stocks of merchandise in Customs Union member countries. Catalogs, price lists, and trade publications of forms or persons having no established place of business in the Customs Union or no representative holding stocks in the Republic are admitted free. Publications and advertising matter relating to fairs, exhibitions, and travel in countries outside South Africa are likewise admitted free of duty.

Investment

The U.S. Department of Commerce estimated U.S. investment in South Africa to be $2.01 billion at year-end 1979. In 1978 the South African Reserve Bank put total foreign direct investments at $11.04 billion, of which $10.6 billion was on private account. The EEC countries accounted for 62 percent of the investments. South Africa maintains an open door policy for foreign capital which plays an active role in the country's economic development. While the Government has assumed an increasing role in strategic areas, private enterprise is seen as responsible for economic growth, rather than a large influx of government spending. In recent years the South African Government has lowered its emphasis on encouraging industries to locate in the Black homelands in an effort to promote separate development. Private business is encouraged to channel new development to the Black homelands but, in the words of Prime Minister Botha, "this does not mean that there should be a large-scale transfer of production assets to the Black State." Nonetheless concessions are offered to offset the added costs of locating in the more remote "homelands" and "harden areas". The incentives include: (1) financial assistance, specifically loans at favorable interest rates; (2) in the Black homelands, the Corporation for Economic Development Limited (CED) will provide land and buildings on a rental basis, (3) buildings and up to 45 percent of cost of machinery and working capital level housing will be provided by the Government through the Industrial Development Corporation; (4) Depending on the area, favorable interest rates on loans and lease rentals are granted for 10 years; (5) low-cost housing for white personnel is provided; and (6) other incentives such as significant rail transport rebates on goods manufactured in these homeland areas and cash grants towards the approved costs of moving from certain other areas to these designated areas. Additional information on this program can be obtained from The Decentralisation Board, Department of Industries, Private Bag x342, Pretoria, 0001 or the Corporation for Economic Development Limited, P.O. Box 213, Pretoria, 2001.

The 1946 United States-South Africa income tax convention applies to U.S. federal income taxes and excess profit taxes and to South African normal, super, undistributed profits, and non-resident shareholders taxes; excess profits duties, and trade profits special levies. South Africa may not tax U.S.-sourced income; the United States may tax the South African income of U.S. citizens, but allows credit for taxes paid to South Africa. A company's income must be allocated between the two countries if the firm maintains a permanent establishment in each.

1973 Companies Act (Amended 1974)

The Companies Act regulates the formation, conduct of affairs and liquidation of all companies whether locally owned or foreign owned.

A private, locally incorporated, limited liability company is a common organization to carry on operations as a subsidiary of another company. It may have 2 to 50 members, who may but are not required to possess non-public shares, and is identified by the words "Proprietary Limited" in its title. Its formation is effected by lodging with the Registrar of Companies (1) the original and two certified copies of the Memorandum and Articles of Association as specified in the October 19, 1973, Companies Administrative Regulations, (2) the registered address, (3) a share capital duty receipt, and (4) a power of attorney by the subscribers to the

Memorandum in favor of the person lodging the documents upon which the firm may commence operations. The company's directors need not be South African nationals or residents of South Africa. Private companies are required to render annual returns to the Registrar of Companies but not their balance sheet of profit and loss accounts.

A public, limited liability company is formed in all cases in which shares are to be held by a number (at least seven) of persons not bound by family or business ties. In addition to the documents required for a private company, a group seeking to organize a public company, must submit (1) a list of persons consenting to serve as directors, of which there must be at least two, neither of whom need be a South African national or resident; (2) written consent of the directors and auditors to serve in those capacities; (3) a statement of the sufficiency of the company's capital; and (4) an affidavit that the directors have paid for a minimum number contracted shares. Every public company must hold a statutory general meeting between 1 and 3 months after date of certification; the meeting must be announced at least 14 days in advance and each member must be furnished a copy of the statutory report. Thereafter annual meetings must be no later than 6 months after the end of the company's financial year, and at intervals no greater than 15 months. Within 30 days of these meetings; the following must be filed with the Registrar of Companies: (1) annual list of shareholders not fully paid up; (2) annual summary relating to the share capital, directors, etc. of the company, and (3) certified balance sheets of the company, its profit and loss account, and the directors' and auditors' reports. The principal differences between private and public companies include the following: (1) a private director need not lodge with the Registrar a written consent; (2) a minimum subscription is not required of a private company; (3) the public company may not commence operations until receipt of the Registrar's certification; (4) the private company need have only one director; (5) the private company is not subject to the statutory meeting and reports requirements; (6) private companies may not offer their shares for public subscriptions; and (7) a private company's shares are restricted in their freedom of transfer. An external company is open to any company registered in a country other than South Africa and is the usual form for locally incorporated subsidiaries of foreign firms. Under Section 322; external companies shall submit to the Registrar within 21 days of the establishment of a place of business in the Republic: (1) a certified copy of the memorandum of the company (notice of changes in the memorandum must be submitted within 3 months of their occurrence); (2) notice of registered office and postal address of the company; (3) consent and name and address of the company's South African auditor; (4) notice of the company's financial year; (5) consent and list of particulars on each of the company's directors and local manager; (6) proof of payment of the annual duty (see below). Section 329 requires the maintenance of accounting records and the submission of the register of an annual financial report as well as the annual finance report required by the laws of the incorporating foreign jurisdiction. Section 331 prescribes that every external company shall (1) conspicuously exhibit outside of the company and that of the foreign country within which it is incorporated; (2) present the same information on all company forms, correspondence and advertisements; and (3) include on all trade literature/letterhead the names and nationalities of the company's directors as well as the names of the local manager and secretary.

Annual Duties.—Both locally incorporated and external companies must pay a minimum duty of 50 Rand ($60). A second duty is payable on the basis of R2.50 per each R10,000 or part thereof either share capital, capital account (of a non-share issuing firm) on the combined total if a firm possesses both. The duty on an external firm is assessed on the total subscribed capital of the company's overseas parent. A local company must also pay (1) a capital duty of 25 rand cents per each R100 or part thereof of authorized capital, with a minimum payment of R10; (2) a stamp duty of 5 rand cents per R20 or part thereof of the par value of the number of share covered by the original issue of share certificates.

Protection of Businesses Act, 1978

This Act forbids South African firms from complying with foreign orders to provide information about their operations. In addition no judgment, order, arbitration award or letters of request delivered, given or issued outside the Republic can be enforced in South Africa except with the permission of the Minister of Industry, Commerce and Consumer Affairs. The official explanation is that the intent of the Act is to prevent foreign civil judgments from being enforced by South African courts without government control. In practice most requests for information on firms with more than 50 percent U.S. ownership have been complied with. In terms of replying to the Sullivan Principles Summary Report, South African firms may furnish the information without prior approval according to South African Economics Minister Heunis in 1978 in a statement to the U.S. Chamber of Commerce in South Africa.

Industrial Property Protection

South Africa is a member of the Paris Union International Convention for the Protection of Industrial Property (patents, trademarks, commercial names and industrial designs) to which the United States and about 80 other countries adhere. American business people and investors are thus entitled to receive national treatment in South Africa (i.e., treatment equal to that accorded local citizens) under that country's law regarding the protection of patents and trademarks. American nationals are also entitled to certain other benefits such as the protection of their patents against arbitrary forfeiture for nonworking and a 1-year "right of priority" for filing their patent applications (i.e., 1 year after first filing a patent application in the United States in which to file a corresponding application in South Africa and receive for the latter the benefit of the first U.S. application filing date).

Under the Patents Act of 1978, patents are granted for any invention which involves an inventive step capable of being used or applied in trade, industry, or agriculture. Applications and specifications for patents are made through South African patent agents who will process applications through the Registrar of Patents in Pretoria. The Registrar examines the application and if found in compliance grants the patent and publishes the acceptance. For the duration of the patent the patentee has the right to exclude other persons from making, using, exercising or disposing of the invention. Patents are granted for a period of 20 years from the filing date of the application. If a patentee does not work his patent within 3 years from date of grant (or 4 years from application date, whichever is later) a compulsory license may be ordered.

Trade registrations are valid for 10 years from the date of registration, renewable for similar periods. South Africa has adopted the Nice International Classification System for registration purposes (34 product and 8 service classes). Registrations on applications filed before Jan. 1, 1964, are valid 14 years, renewable for 10-year periods. First applicant, as user or intended user, is entitled to registration. Under certain conditions, a mark being used by more than one person can be registered to several parties for concurrent use. Marks are registrable as Part A (distinctive) and B (capable of becoming distinctive). Part A registration, if valid 7 years, becomes incontestable on prior use grounds. Applications are examined and published for 2 months. Also, under informal procedures, the Registrar can decide conflicting opposition cases with the consent of both parties. The Mark is cancellable if not used within 5 years. Official national or foreign emblems, or other markings contrary to public order or good morals are not registerable as trademarks.

Under the Copyright Act of 1978 the following are eligible for copyright in South Africa: Literary works, musical works, artistic works, cinematograph films, sound recordings, broadcasts, program carrying signals. Copyright protection for literary, musical and artistic works extends for the life of the author plus 50 years. For films and photographs and sound recordings, protection extends for 50 years from the year the work is publicly released. Protection for Broadcasts and program-carrying signals extends 50 years from when first transmission is made. The Republic is a member of the Berne Union Copyright Convention. Although the United States is not a member of the Convention, U.S. authors may obtain protection in Berne Union Countries by publishing a work in a Union member country at the time it is first published and copyrighted in the United States.

Application or inquiries should be addressed to the Registrar of Patents, Design, Trade Marks and Copyright, Zania Building, 116 Proes Street, Pretoria.

Land Ownership and Leasing

Land may be held either under freehold tenure whereby occupiers are the registered owners of their properties, or under leasehold tenure, encountered in mining areas and in certain areas of the larger municipalities, where the length of the tenure ranges from 30 to 99 years. Under the 99-year leasehold Act of 1978 Blacks with the backing of their employers can obtain mortgages from private lending companies to purchase, build, and improve homes. Rights to minerals under the surface may be separate from rights to ownership of the land (Sections 71 and 72, Act 47 of 1937). Most municipalities control the use of land within their jurisdiction through zoning provisions for residential and industrial development. There are restrictions on the areas in which members of a race can own real property.

Entry and Registration of Capital

South African Exchange Control (SAEC) seeks to maintain a favorable foreign investment climate in South Africa, and actively oversees capital flows to protect the equally important South African objectives of strategic sectors, local participation, and reserves levels. SAEC controls include: (1) the local borrowing of non-resident owned/or controlled South African companies, and (2) the overseas borrowings of South African companies. Its regulations contain no permissive or concessionary clauses. Foreign investment is categorized as portfolio investment or direct investment. A portfolio investment can occur either on foreign stock exchanges or locally by the remittance of funds to South Africa or by the use of Financial Rand. There is no need to refer such inward transfers to Exchange Control.

An important incentive for foreign investment in South Africa is the freely floating, financial rand exchange rate system introduced in 1979 which replaces the blocked rand procedure. In 1961, in order to slow the outflow of capital, an exchange control regulation known as the blocked rand was introduced. Shares sold locally by non-residents of South Africa could no longer be transferred abroad and in addition could be transferred between non-residents.

Blocked rand could only be used to invest in securities and government and municipal stocks with a maturity rate of 5 years. By 1976 blocked rands had evolved into security rands which could be transferred between non-residents and could be exchanged in the Johannesburg Stock Exchange (JSE).

In 1979 the DeKock Commission recommended the formulation of the financial rand which allowed investment in a wide range of assets including securities on the JSE, government, municipal and public utility stocks or savings certificates. The potential supply of the financial rand is the total amount of overseas investment in South Africa. Financial rand offers a considerable discount since the price during 1979 was 20-30 percent lower than the commercial rand. The financial rand is influenced by the difference between the cost of shares purchased abroad which is usually higher and the cost of the same shares purchased with foreign exchange in South Africa.

Due to the financial rand and the generally favorable economic climate, there was increased foreign investor interest in South Africa during 1979. The South African Reserve Bank stated that $610 million was invested through the financial rand and nearly two-thirds of this amount went into manufacturing investments. The United Kingdom direct investment grew at an estimated rate of 6 percent in 1978.

Other influxes of capital into new or existing

ventures in South Africa are termed direct investments. Exchange Control approval is not required for the inward transfer to South Africa of fixed capital. Loan capital transferred to a South African firm from abroad does, however, require SAEC approval. Approval is customarily only granted if the recipient firm can show that the loan is not required for acquiring fixed assets but only for providing necessary temporary finance of a working capital nature. South African companies, in which non residents own or control 25 percent or more of the voting securities, capital, or earnings, are subject to local borrowing restrictions enforced by Exchange Control. Normally, approval to borrow locally is not withheld, provided it can be shown that the funds are required for the purpose of financing current assets requirements and that the total local borrowing facilities do not, in the aggregate, exceed 25 percent of the total foreign investment in the local subsidiary. Understandably, the Exchange Control allows South African enterprises which are not wholly or largely owned from abroad, a priority right to financial resources. Thus, if a subsidiary of an overseas concern is South African owned, the policy would normally be to permit such concerns to borrow locally an "additional" percentage of the share holders fund, based primarily on the ratio of the resident to non-resident interest. There is no restriction on the transfer of dividends or profits of foreign owned local branches based on current profits, provided such transfers can be made from available cash funds without recourse to excessive local borrowing. Those firms whose local borrowing is subject to SAEC approval must obtain approval to remit dividends or profits. Wholly foreign-owned subsidiaries must supply SAEC with data attesting the profits to be remitted were indeed generated by the South African operation. Interest earned at reasonable rates may be freely remitted; salary transfers do, however, require SAEC approval. Royalty and licensing arrangements, technical service and management fee arrangements are all subject to prior SAEC approval.

Taxation

An understanding of "gross income," "income," and "taxable income" is essential to comprehension of the South African Income Tax Act of 1962. "Gross income" is the total amount received during the tax year less (1) all capital receipt and (2) receipt from non-South African sources. Although South African tax law is based on the "source" of income, the following examples have been determined as taxable by South Africa: (1) sale proceeds of a contract concluded in South Africa and (2) interest earned on loans to and deposits with South African banks. "Income" is the amount remaining after allowable exemptions are subtracted and "taxable income" is the amount remaining after deduction of expenditures incurred in the production of income. Such expenditures if not of a capital nature must have been incurred wholly and exclusively for the non-personal purpose of earning income.

Companies formed in South Africa must register with the local Receiver of Revenue, responsible for administering the tax laws under the Secretary of Inland Revenue. The taxable "year of assessment" coincides with a company's financial year for accounting purposes. The official tax year ends on the last day of February and any company wishing to end its financial year on any other date must obtain the tax authorities permission.

Taxation of Companies.—Companies are taxed at a flat rate of 40 percent of their taxable income plus a surcharge of 5 percent of basic tax plus a loan levy of 15 percent of basic tax except for companies in the fields of diamonds (45 percent plus 5 percent surcharge and 10 percent loan levy), petroleum (40 rand cents on each Rand of taxable income plus 5 percent surcharge and 15 percent loan levy), natural gas, and gold.

Although wear and tear allowances are settled individually, deductions generally allowed are furniture and fittings (10 percent) machinery and equipment (10-25 percent), automobiles (20 percent), and trucks (25 percent), and are based on the diminishing balance method. A scrapping allowance may be claimed when the amount realized from the disposition of a depreciable 25 percent initial allowance is also deductible for the cost of new or used plant and machinery while 15 percent is deductible for hotel equipment. There is a 30 percent investment allowance for new machinery brought into use after March 27, 1975. Twenty-five percent of capital expenditure for scientific research is likewise deductible. Should allowable deductions in a given tax year exceed that year's income, the "assessed loss" may be carried forward or set off against future income.

The undistributed profits tax (UPT) is assessed at the rate of 33-1/3 percent on the amount by which the distributable income of a firm, registered and conducting business in South Africa, exceeds the distributed dividends. The distributable income is the firm's net profit (taxable income plus interest on normal tax-exempt government stock, non-capital receipt income earned non-South Africa, and dividend income) less taxes paid, a 55 percent allowance of non-dividends net profits, plant and machinery costs, and, for public companies, a 35 percent allowance of dividend net profit. In effect, only financial companies are subject to UPT. Companies exempt from the UPT include companies with at least 50 percent of equity held by foreign shareholders, external companies serving not more than 50 percent of their total net profit from South African resources, and banks and building societies and mining companies.

Tax incentives

An exporter's allowance is made to taxpayers involved in the exportation of goods produced, manufactured or processed in South Africa. The allowance entitles a firm to claim as a deduction a percentage of the expenses incurred in developing overseas markets, ranging from 75 percent to 100 percent of the costs. To promote decentralization of its industry, South Africa has proclaimed certain regions as economic development areas. At the discretion of the Minister of Finance the following provisions apply to firms manufacturing or conducting business therein: (1) allowance of up to 10 percent of the cost of electric power; water and transport; (2) allowances for additional or abnormal administrative or manufacturing costs incurred in moving a factory from another area to an economic development area; (3) allowance of 35 percent of the cost of employee housing during the year of completion and 10 percent during the nine succeeding years; (4) new machinery investment allowance of 30-65 percent; (5) buildings investment allowance of 25-45 percent, (6) a 20-40 percent allowance in wages paid to Bantu or, in some cases, colored employees in each of the first 7 full financial years after establishment; and (7) 25-40 percent of cost of transferring manufacturing equipment at the end of the first financial year.

Other Taxation

Stamps must be affixed to many legal and other documents. Trading and other licenses are required of all firms engaging in business in South Africa. Some are required throughout the Republic, while others are only municipal or provincial requirements. A donations tax is imposed on all gifts made by South African resident and private companies; the tax is assessed on the cumulative value of the property involved and the rate varies from 3 percent on donations up to $9,600 to 25 percent on those over $108,000.

The South African government imposed a 4 percent sales tax in July 1978 on all transactions which includes the sale of new goods, leased property, hotel lodging and imported goods. A transfer duty for individuals is levied on the sale or transfer of ownership of immovable property at the rate of 3 percent for buildings valued above $24,000. For companies, the duty is 5 percent of the total price. Municipalities levy and assess their own taxes on residential and industrial properties within their jurisdiction.

Non-resident individuals carrying on business in South Africa are subject to ordinary income tax on these South African dividend receipts but are not required to pay a non-resident shareholders' tax. However, non-residents are liable for a non-resident withholding tax of 10 percent on interest received from South African services to be paid to tax authorities within 14 days of the date on which interest accrues.

The basis of determining an individual's taxable income is identical to that applied in arriving at a company's taxable income. Taxable income is the amount remaining after deducting exempt income and allowable deductions from gross income from a South African source.

Employment

Labor Force

Out of an estimated population of 28 million in March 1980, approximately 10.9 million were said to be "economically active" including employees, self-employed, unpaid family assistants, part-time and temporary workers.

Since the discovery of diamonds near Kimberley in 1870 followed by the discovery of gold in the Transvaal in 1886, the labor market in South Africa has been characterized by a shortage of skilled and technically qualified employees and a surplus of unskilled workers. The dean of the University of Witswatersrand's Graduate School of Business has projected that by 1990 South Africa will have a shortage of skilled and semi-skilled workers of 750,000. The fact that employers encounter today the same labor recruitment problems their predecessors encountered 110 years ago is due to a succession of governments which have imposed a racially restrictive system of education, training, and employment. The governments' failure to provide adequate education and training opportunities for the majority of South Africa's population has forced employers to accept much lower standards of education and talent for their South African employees than they would insist upon elsewhere. According to a presentation by the National Productivity Institute, over half of South Africa's black labor force has no education at all. Most of the rest have less than 5 years schooling. Progressive employers faced with the inefficiencies of attempting to operate productively with a badly educated workforce and faced with a shortage of skilled workers have been severe critics of government policies.

The shortage has been so severe that in the middle of the 1977 recession (the worst since 1930) 41 percent of the employers surveyed reported bottlenecks due to a skilled labor shortage.

Growth in employment traditionally lags behind the overall economic growth rate, but there was evidence of an acceleration of employment levels in the second half of 1979. While employment in non-agricultural sectors rose by only 1.8 percent in the first three quarters of 1979, certain key sectors for which full-year figures were available showed significantly larger increases. Employment in manufacturing, mining, construction, railways and electricity increased 6 percent between December 1978 and December 1979 with the increase for black workers being 5 percent. The employment figures have tended to confirm that the greatest demand is for skilled workers.

The black workforce is growing by around 200,000 persons a year; an estimated 5-6 percent rate of real growth is required to provide jobs for this number. For the first time in 4 years, the South African economy is generating enough new jobs to accommodate new job market entrants but not enough to make a dent in existing unemployment. Coexisting for over a century with the shortage of skilled workers has been massive unemployment of South Africa's black population. Official statistics place unemployment among Africans at 492,000 as of March 1980, but these statistics define as employed, casual laborers who succeed in finding a day's work one day out of three. Other, more reliable, estimates place the number of unemployed and underemployed Africans at 2 million.

In contrast to this high unemployment, South Africa has over the past 20 years actively recruited skilled whites from foreign sources with a target of attracting 30-40,000 immigrants annually. In the past few years, however, South Africa has failed to register a net gain in White foreign immigrants.

Average real wages for all workers showed a marginal decline of .9 percent in the first 9 months of 1979 compared to a slight increase of .2 percent in 1978. Real wages of whites declined by 1 percent in the first three quarters of 1979 while those of non-whites were virtually stagnant (+0.3 percent).

Labor Regulations

The Industrial Conciliation Act, No. 28 of 1978 and the Black Labors Relations Regulation Act, No. 48 of 1953 regulate the negotiation of conditions of employment and settlement of disputes. The Industrial Conciliation Act provides the machinery for collective bargaining and agreement between employers and employees on an industry-wide basis. It provides for the formation and registration of trade unions and employers associations, and for the establishment of industrial councils in which terms and conditions of employment are negotiated. Agreements reached by the councils are published in the Government Gazette and are binding on all employers and employees in the industry.

The general nature of the agreements is to establish minimum wages for various job categories. Generally a distinction is made between minimum wages for male and female employees, but no distinction is made on the basis of race or color. Many employers pay premium wages from those prescribed in the industry-wide agreements. An important function of the Act is the prevention of strikes. Disputes between employers and employees must be submitted to the Industrial Council, or, in the absence of an industrial council, to the Minister of Labour who then establishes an ad hoc conciliation board. If these approaches are not successful, the dispute may be referred to an arbitor. Arbitration is compulsory in industries providing essential services. During the period while these techniques are being employed, strikes or lockouts are absolutely prohibited. Between the period 1924-1979 there has been only one strike by a white union, the Mine Workers Union strike in March 1979. The MWU strike resulted in a major setback for the striking workers due to strong government opposition. Only registered trade unions can participate in the collective bargaining and dispute settlement procedures established by the Act.

The Black Labors Relations Regulation Act applies to Black employees and their employers in industries other than farming, domestic service, government service, or educational institutions and provides for employment negotiation and settlement of disputes through a committee system. As of the early months of 1980, the South African government has accepted in principle the Wiehahn Commission recommendations that the industrial councils of the Conciliation Act and the committee system of the Black Labors Relations Act be integrated into one system.

The Wage Act of 1957 provides for hiring wages and working conditions of workers not covered by collective agreements. The Factories, Machinery, and Building Work Act, 1941, as amended, provides for the registration of factories and establishes minimum hours of work and minimum conditions of employment for all factory workers. Legal authority to reserve jobs in a particular trade in certain areas by race existed from 1956 to 1979. Although only 2.5 percent of South Africa's industrial workforce was affected by this legislation, a far more pervasive system of reservation by race exists due to closed shop union contracts. A government White Paper, in response to a commission of inquiry report in 1979, stated that the government accepted the principle that no new closed shop agreements would be permitted, but no legislation to this effect has been introduced. The White Paper also accepted a recommendation that apprenticeships be opened to all races in all areas, but no legislation has been introduced. Under present practices, apprenticeships are controlled by apprenticeship committees made up of an equal number of employer and trade union representatives. White-only trade unions have the power, therefore, to effectively prevent the recruitment of apprentices from other race groups.

Recent Labor Developments

South Africa's industrial relations system is at the present time in the process of being restructured under the review of two Government appointed commissions, Wiehahn and Riekert. The Wiehahn Commission was empowered to investigate existing labor legislation and recommend changes to adjust the system to meet labor needs, provide dispute settlement methods, and eliminate labor bottlenecks. The Wiehahn Commission found that it had become "abundantly clear" that "Black trade unions have become part of the fabric of South Africa's industrial life and that their strength and position of influence can no longer be ignored."

Recommendations included in the Wiehahn Commission report are: The maintenance and development of individual economic freedom and competition by the removal of indefensible discrimination, the principle of freedom of association as the basis of trade union membership, the autonomy of trade unions in respect of membership and officials, the commercial use of

existing facilities for industrial training and geographic mobility for workers of all population groups. Although the South African government has in theory accepted the recommendations, the government has stated that only Black workers with fixed employment and permanent residence rights would automatically qualify for full trade union rights. This provision threatens the impact of Black trade unions whose membership consists largely of migrants and commuters. The Government subsequently agreed to allow independent homeland "foreign" workers to join, but not foreign workers from neighboring countries. All such blacks are now encompassed as "employees" under South African labor laws. In addition although the Commission recommended that any trade union regardless of race or sex should be eligible for registration under the amended Industrial Conciliation Act, unions with members "of more than one population group" are forbidden registration except by ministerial exemption. Legislation requires that trade unions be limited to members of a particular population group unless the Minister of Labor determines that the number of employees of a particular population group is too small to enable them to form an effective separate union or "that by reason of the ratio between the numbers of employees of the different population groups concerned it would be expedient to form a union in respect of more than one such population group." Although the rationale for the first exemption seems clear, no one seems to know what is meant, if anything, by the exemption "by reason of the ratio." By mid-1979, 21 of the 28 applications to the Minister to allow unions to enroll members of various population groups have been approved, while the remainder are "under consideration." As of August 1, 1980, no application for permission to form multiracial trade unions has been denied.

The second part of the Wiehahn Commission report tabled in Parliament in June 1980 emphasized training. The report recommended repeal of the Building Workers Act of 1951 which was found discriminatory as it prohibited skilled work by Blacks in White urban areas and permitted such work by White in Black residential areas in a supervisory capacity only. A second proposal recommended that Black apprentices as well as apprentices from other population groups should be trained at public centers established through legislation.

The Riekert Commission made a number of recommendations to streamline the contract labor and influx control systems. Under the Provisions of the Black Consolidation Act of 1945, no Black person may remain in a "prescribed area" for more than 72 hours unless he has lived continuously in the area since birth or, has worked for one employer for 10 years, or has been in continuous employment in the area for 15 years. Any other Blacks wishing to work in these areas are on a contract basis as migrant workers and are not allowed to bring their families into the area.

Among the Riekert Commission recommendations are: Workers in one urban area can move to another for a job provided they have "suitable accommodation;" workers do not have to report to a labor bureau if they change jobs; once a Black worker is employed, it is no longer necessary for him or his employer to appear at a labor bureau to register; there are no limitations on the amount of money an employer can lend to a Black worker; and registered workers can be employed in another job while off duty without being registered, provided their employer agrees. In addition, the Riekert Commission recommended that facilities should be provided for the "temporary sojourn of dependents who wish to visit the head of the family while he is working in the White area." Multi-racial trade centers would be created and employers would be allowed to register homes under their own name which they buy for their employees living in Black townships. Differences exist, however, between the Commission's proposals, Government action and the impact felt by the Black population. The Government thus far has decided to keep the highly controversial influx control pass system, including the 72-hour time limit.

Employment Codes

The United States Government neither encourages nor discourages private investment in South Africa. The U.S. Government, however, actively encourages all American firms with, or contemplating, operations in South Africa to establish employment conditions in their South African plants conforming as closely as possible to their U.S. labor practices. A decent standard of living, training and opportunities should be provided all personnel.

The U.S. government supports the Statement of Principles initiated by Rev. Leon Sullivan in regard to U.S. firms labor practices in South Africa. Each of the U.S. firms endorsing the Sullivan principles supports the following: 1. non-segregation of the races in all eating, comfort and work facilities; 2. equal and fair employment practices for all employees; 3. equal pay for all employees doing equal or comparable work for the same period of time; 4. initiation and development of training programs that will prepare in substantial numbers, Blacks and other non-White for supervisory, administrative, clerical and technical jobs; 5. increasing the number of Blacks and other non-Whites in management and supervisory positions; 6. improving the quality of employees lives outside the work environment in such areas as housing, transportation, schooling, recreation and health facilities. Additional information on the Sullivan principles and implementation guidelines in addition to reports monitoring the progress of signatory companies can be obtained from the International Council for Equality of Opportunity Principles, Inc., 1501 N. Broad Street, Philadelphia, Pa. 19122.

Notes for Business Travelers

Entrance Requirements

Individuals entering South Africa must have a valid passport and visa. Visas may be obtained free of charge from either the South African Embassy in Washington, D.C., or from one of the South African Consulates in the United States: 425 Park Avenue, New York, New York 10022; P.O. Box 2310 New Orleans, Louisiana 70176; and Suite 1600, 120 Montgomery St., San Francisco, California 94104. The visitor's visa is generally valid for entry into the Republic for a period of up to 12 months from the issuing date, and is valid for multiple entries. Normally the length of time a visitor may remain in the Republic is limited to a period not exceeding 6 months; under certain conditions, this may be extended upon application to the Commissioner of Immigration in Pretoria.

A valid International Health Certificate indicating vaccination against smallpox must be produced by all persons travelling to South Africa via other African countries which require a vaccination. In addition, all persons arriving in South Africa must have a certificate of inoculation or immunity against yellow fever. Passengers travelling directly from the United States are exempted from this latter requirement.

Visitors must satisfy the Passport Control Officer that they have sufficient means to maintain themselves for the period of their proposed stay and that they are in possession of a fully paid forward or return ticket. A visitor who does not so satisfy the Passport Control Officer may be required to pay a deposit generally equivalent to his fare home which is refunded upon departure from the Republic.

No American entering on a visitor's visa may

take up remunerative employment in South Africa without special permission from the Department of Interior in Pretoria, or from one of the Department's regional representatives.

There are no restrictions on the amount of dollar currency that may be taken into South Africa, but the traveler must declare the amount at the time of entry. Dollars cannot be used in South Africa and must be converted to rand by authorized foreign exchange dealers, hotels, commercial banks, and certain travel agencies. It is illegal to convey foreign currency to anyone else, and dollars may not be used in commercial or other private transactions. On leaving South Africa, visitors must declare the amount of foreign currency they are taking with them, which is restricted by the amount brought in and how much they spent in South Africa. A permit must be obtained from a bank if currency in excess of this amount is to be taken out. Travelers may take out South African currency to 50 Rand.

Passengers entering the Republic must declare all goods in their possession with the exception of personal clothing, essential toilet articles, and used sporting equipment. In order to be free of declaration, these goods must be for the passenger's personal use, and not to be intended as gifts to be sold, exchanged, or traded. All articles, used or unused, carried by the visitor as presents or parcels for other persons, must be declared.

Under cover of a valid triptyque-carnet, a visitor may take his automobile into the Republic for a period not exceeding 12 months with payment of duty. If the visitor wishes to dispose of his vehicle either during his stay or upon departure, he must first obtain an import permit and pay the relevant duty.

Business Etiquette

Business customs in South Africa are generally similar to those in the United States and Western Europe. South African business people tend to dress conservatively, and sport jackets and slacks are rarely seen at work. South African men tend to favor medium or heavy woolen suits, frequently with vests, for year-round wear. During the warmer months of November through March, darker light-weight fabrics such as tropical worsteds are most appropriate, although men's seersucker or cotton-cord suits are also worn. Men seldom wear hats in South Africa.

Business cards should be simple, including only the basics such as name, address, and business title. Punctuality is important to the South African business person, who generally makes every effort to be on time for appointments. As a general rule, appointments should be made in advance of a business call.

Living Conditions and Costs

There are more than 1,500 licensed hotels in the Republic, ranging from small country hotels to larger city hotels of high standards. Rates are very moderate, compared to most countries. However, reservations should be made in advance, particularly in resort areas during the South African summer months (December-January) as adequate accommodations are scarce in some areas.

Suitable longterm housing accommodations are often difficult to obtain promptly, and Americans planning lengthy stays should allow 4 to 8 weeks in a hotel until more permanent quarters can be located. Eating customs and types of food available in South Africa are similar to those in the United States, and Americans should find no difficulty in adjusting to South African cuisine. Drinking water is both ample and safe. Tipping is lower than in Europe or the United States and, as a rough guide, should not exceed 10 percent. It is customary to tip porters, taxi drivers, waiters, stewards, and hotel porters.

Local telephone service is available at reasonable rates, although delays of from one to several hours are often experienced on long distance calls within the Republic. A delay of several months may be encountered in procuring either a business or a home telephone. Long distance calls to the United States can be made for $9.30 for a 3-minute call and $3 per each additional minute, and by booking the call a day in advance, can ordinarily be placed at a specified time.

Telegraph service provided by the Department of Posts and Telegraphs is adequate and prices are reasonable. U.S.-South Africa cablegrams presently cost $0.28 per word, with a seven-word minimum, and arrive in 4-5 hours; night letters cost $0.14 per word with a 22-word minimum and arrive the following day. Air mail from the United States to South Africa generally takes 5 to 6 days, while surface mail takes from 3 to 6 weeks.

South Africa's medical facilities are excellent. Almost all pharmaceutical products are available, and general hospitals in the leading cities are equipped to handle almost all potential cases.

Commercial Language

Although English and Afrikaans are South

Africa's two official languages, English is most frequently used commercially. A considerable proportion of the white population speak both languages; the Coloureds speak Afrikaans. Most of the Africans and Asians speak English or Afrikaans and many speak both. In addition, the Africans generally speak at least one tribal language, while the Asians speak either Tamil, Hindi, Gujerati, or Telegu at home. Most firms in South Africa are able to correspond in either English or Afrikaans. However, there is some language sensitivity in South Africa, particularly among the Afrikaner population. Consequently, many firms print much of their literature, including annual statements, in both languages. While such a practice entails extra expense, it can pay large dividends in good will.

Holidays

There are 10 statutory public holidays in South Africa: New Year's Day, Good Friday, Easter Monday, Ascension Day, Republic Day (May 31), Settlers Day (first Monday in September), Kruger Day (October 10), Day of the Covenant (December 16), Christmas Day and Boxing Day (December 26). If a public holiday falls on a Sunday, the following Monday becomes a holiday. In addition, January 2, or if the 2nd falls on a Sunday, January 3, and Easter Saturday are holidays in Cape Prince and the Province of Natal. The manufacturing and construction industries generally close down for an "artisans' holiday" over the period December 16 to just after the New Year. The length of the closure varies. Vital industries do not follow this practice.

Bibliography

U.S. Department of Commerce

Market Profiles for Africa, OBR 78-20, March 1980.
Foreign Economic Trends for South Africa, FET 80-065, July 1980

South African Government

Bulletin of Statistics, Pretoria; Department of Statistics, September 1979
Monthly Abstract of Trade Statistics; Pretoria, Department of Customs and Excise, December 1978, December 1979
South African Statistics 1976; Pretoria: Bureau of Statistics
Annual Report: 1978-1979; Pretoria; South African Railways and Harbors
Economic Development Programme for the Republic of South Africa, Pretoria 1979-1981: Office of the Economic Advisor to the Prime Minister
South African Reserve Bank Quarterly Bulletin, Pretoria: South African Reserve Bank, December 1979, March 1980, June 1980.
A Report for the Republic of South Africa: Minerals, October-December 1977-1978, Pretoria: Government of the Republic of South Africa.

Other:

U.S. Department of Agriculture, Statistical Bulletin #623, 1978, Statistical Bulletin #637, 1979
South Africa Minerals Production Statistics—Questionnaire, March 1980
Advertising and Press Annual of Africa, 1977, Cape Town: National Publishing Company (Pty) Ltd.
Business Blue Book of South Africa, 1980, Cape Town: The Communications Group
Taxation in South Africa: Touche Ross International, October 1979
Doing Business in South Africa, Johannesburg: Barclays National Bank Limited, 1980
Ports of South Africa, 1979, Johannesburg: Industrial Publishing Corp. (Pty) Ltd.
Standard Bank Review, Standard Bank of South Africa, March 1979
South African Rates and Data (SARAD), January 1980

Market Profiles—REPUBLIC OF SOUTH AFRICA

Foreign Trade

Imports.—$21 billion in 1981, $18.5 billion in 1982. Principal 1982 suppliers by percentage: United States, 14.5; West Germany, 14.7; United Kingdom, 11.9; Japan, 10. Major imports: wide variety of industrial machinery and equipment, vehicle components; steel; textiles; office machinery and data processing equipment; transportation equipment. From United States: chemicals, resins, engineering and construction equipment, ADP equipment, measuring instruments, vehicle parts.

Exports.—$21 billion in 1981, $17.7 billion in 1982. Major customers by percentage 1982: United States (6.8 percent); Japan, 8.6 percent; United Kingdom, 7.3. Principal exports by percentage: precious stones and metals, 28; base metals, 17; gold coins, mineral products, 11.

Trade Policy.—The Customs Union Agreement with Botswana, Lesotho, and Swaziland provides for common external tariffs; preferences granted in selected items for most favored nations. Licensing and exchange control system tends to fluctuate in response to internal economic conditions and level of foreign exchange holdings. Signator of Tokyo Round of the MTN.

Trade Prospects.—With a real GDP growth rate of -1 percent in 1982, South Africa's economy is in recession. Gold price rise in second half of 1982 and a decline in imports lowered current account deficit. The strengthened dollar coupled with the lowered value of the rand will cause U.S. goods to be increasingly expensive to South African purchasers. U.S. exports during Jan.-June 1983 were down 22 percent from the same period 1982. Prospects over the next 6-12 months are good in the short term for electric power and coal technology equipment.

Finance

Currency.—South African rand (R1=US$0.89 in Oct. 1983). Money supply was $13.1 billion in 1982.

Domestic Credit and Investment.—Sophisticated financial institutions provide ample credit facilities; substantial installment buying. Short-term and long-term money market facilities available. Prime interest rate: 14 percent, 1982.

National Budget.—Revenues of $17.4 billion and expenditures of $19.3 billion in 1983. Budget in 1983-84 projects government spending will increase 10.3 percent.

Economy

Declining rate of economic growth since third quarter 1981. Principal causes: constraint on almost fully used production capacity, a shortage of skilled labor, and declining export demand.

GDP.—$66.9 billion total in 1982 represented a real decline in GDP of .9 percent. Manufacturing is the largest sector, contributing 23 percent of GDP; mining, 14 percent; and business services, 13 percent.

Agriculture.—Although diminishing in importance—falling from 8 percent of GDP in 1975 to 6 percent in 1979—improved world prices encourage production of a range of crops. Major products include corn, dairy products, sugar, wheat, cotton, corn. Self-sufficient in foodstuffs.

Industry.—Major foreign exchange earner with increasing emphasis placed on self-sufficiency and critical industries.

Major industries: mining, textiles, iron and steel, chemicals, fertilizer, automobiles, metalworking, electrical and nonelectrical machinery and equipment, construction, and mining machinery. Physical volume of manufacturing declined 2 percent during 1981.

Commerce.—Modern methods of marketing and advertising. Trend toward larger scale operations including shopping centers, supermarkets, department stores, retail chains, and discount outlets. Marketing is becoming increasingly price competitive. Consumer Price Index running at 15 percent annual rate.

Basic Economic Facilities

Transportation.—Well-developed rail system of 35,434 km (including Namibia); comprehensive air transport system with over 300 airports, international flights at Jan Smuts Airport, Johannesburg; about 299,090 km of road, 35 percent paved; 3.5 million motor vehicles registered in 1980. Half million new vehicles registered in 1981. Principal harbors at Durban, East London, Port Elizabeth, Cape Town, Saldanha Bay, Richards Bay.

Communications.—Best developed in Africa. Adequate facilities for both domestic and international needs. National television switched to commercial programming in 1977. TV broadcasts 5 hours a day.

Power.—Production of 119.8 GW per hour in 1982; 90.7 percent produced by the Electricity Supply Commission. Six coal fired stations under construction to increase capacity during 1980's.

Natural Resources

Land.—472,359 square miles, mostly high plateau.

Climate.—Generally temperate, annual mean temperature about 60°F. Rainfall unevenly distributed.

Minerals.—Extensive deposits of gold, platinum, coal, diamonds, antimony, iron ore, copper, uranium, manganese, chrome, asbestos, vanadium.

Fisheries.—177.8 tons of trawler catch; 379,176 tons of pelagic fish and 1.3 million kg of rock lobster landed in 1981; catch declining due to overfishing of the South Atlantic fishery.

Forestry.—9.8 million acres or 3 percent of total land area.

Population

Size.—30 million (July 1982); 70 percent Black, 10.6 percent colored, 16 percent white, 3 percent Asian. Principal cities (1976): Johannesburg, 1,748,000; Cape Town, 843,000; Durban, 855,000; Pretoria, 634,000.

Language.—English, Afrikaans, local dialects.

Education.—Almost 100 percent literacy, for whites; Government estimates 50 percent of Africans literate; primary education for nonwhites becoming compulsory. Black education funding being significantly increased.

Labor.—Employment 1982: agriculture, 30.2 percent; manufacturing, 30 percent; mining, 14 percent. Average monthly wage: White $1,005; Asian $475; Colored $336; Black $249 (1982).

Marketing in Spain

Contents

Report Revised July 1981

519428 4-80

2199

Foreign Trade Outlook

Spain has long been a major market for U.S. goods and services as well as U.S. direct investment. Like most developed countries, Spain has experienced a marked economic slowdown since the mid-1970's, largely due to worldwide economic changes and uncertainties surrounding its domestic political transition. Nevertheless, the United States continues as the single largest supplier and investor in Spain.

The economic downturn is in sharp contrast to the rapid growth and industrialization of the 1960's and early 1970's. The average annual increase in gross domestic product (GDP) was nearly 6 percent in real terms between 1970 and 1975, compared with about 2.1 percent between 1975 and 1980. This slow growth has been accompanied by falling investment, rising unemployment, high inflation, and a deteriorating balance-of-payments situation.

During the 1960's and early 1970's, the Government actively encouraged the development and restructuring of industry through National Development Plans and "concerted action programs" whereby firms in a given section were granted financial incentives in return for cooperating in meeting goals, output, and export promotion.

A favorable labor situation also facilitated industrial expansion as rural emigrants provided a continuing source of new and easily trained workers.

Spain already conducts a substantial portion of its foreign trade with the members of the European Communities (EC),[1] with which it already has an industrial preferential trade agreement. Full membership negotiations with the EC opened in February 1979 and are expected to be completed for Spanish accession by 1984 or 1985.

Trade with the World

The bulk of Spain's foreign trade involves the members of the European Communities and the European Free Trade Association (EFTA).[2] Since 1975, there have been substantial shifts in the volume, product composition, and geographic distribution of Spanish trade. Spain's trade policy also is influenced by its membership in the Organization for Economic Cooperation and Development (OECD), the General Agreement on Tariffs and Trade (GATT), and the International Monetary Fund (IMF). Historically, Spain has imported more than it has exported. Nevertheless, statistics for the latest 5-year period show exports growing faster than imports: Spanish exports grew from $8.7 billion in 1976 to $20.8 billion in 1980 or by 139 percent; Spanish imports grew by only 97 percent over the same period, from $17.4 billion in 1976 to $34.3 billion in 1980. Realignment of exchange rates and inflationary conditions account for much of this expansion.

The geographic distribution of trade as shown by table 1 indicates that the two European economic blocks, the EEC and EFTA, continue to dominate Spanish trade patterns. Spain's principal suppliers in 1979 were the United States, France, West Germany, and Saudi Arabia. Major customers for Spanish products were France, West Germany, the United States, and the United Kingdom.

Major product categories imported and exported by Spain in 1978 and 1979 are shown in table 2.

Trade with the United States

Spanish trade with the United States has expanded significantly over the past 10 years. Spanish imports from the United States totaled $4.5 billion in 1980, compared with $3.1 billion in 1979, an increase of 42 percent. At the same time, Spanish exports to the United States reached $1.1 billion in 1980, down from $1.3 billion in 1979. The United States has traditionally had a surplus in its trade with Spain: it reached $3.4 billion in 1980. As of 1980, the United States was Spain's major supplier (13 percent of total imports) and third best customer (5 percent of total exports).

Traditionally, almost one-third of U.S. exports to Spain have consisted of agricultural products, particularly corn, soybeans, and other cereals. U.S. industrial exports include iron or steel scrap, aircraft, nuclear reactors and parts, coal, automated data processing machines, tobacco manufactures, and control instruments. Major U.S. imports from Spain include footwear, prepared vegetables, rubber tires, iron and steel products, zinc alloys, metalworking tools, wines, and motor vehicle parts. The product composition of U.S.-Spanish trade in 1978 and 1979 is shown in table 3.

Best Export Prospects

The demand for imported goods and services in the Spanish market is wide and changing, but the following categories deserve special note.

---

[1] Members of the EC are Belgium, Denmark, France, Ireland, Italy, Luxembourg, the Netherlands, the United Kingdom, and West Germany. Greece joined the EC on January 1, 1981

[2] Members of EFTA are: Austria, Iceland, Norway, Portugal, Sweden, Switzerland, and Finland (associate member).

Electronic Components.—The Spanish electronic components market is strong and growing. Imports have risen significantly during the past few years and account for about 60 percent of overall consumption. Imports from the United States are expected to increase because end-users are seeking more sophisticated circuits where U.S.-made items are more competitive. The Spanish electronic components industry developed quite rapidly in the early 1970's and is now in a position to supply a portion of domestic requirements. However, there is still a substantial need for imports since local industry lacks the capacity to produce the more sophisticated types of components. National production predominantly includes transistors, diodes, and small thyristors. The most promising products are electron tubes, semiconductors, passive components, and printed circuits.

Computers and Peripheral Equipment.—Rapid modernization of Spanish business has led to high growth rates in the market for computers and peripherals. A continually increasing demand—mostly by industry, banking institutions, and the Government—is expected. Small businesses are numerous in Spain, and despite the present economic recession, prospects for mini-computers and small systems will continue to be good. While Spanish production of computers and peripheral equipment has reflected a sharp increase in the recent past, it is quite limited in quantity and scope. Imports, $402 million in 1979, predominate in the domestic market, with the United States as the major supplier. The most promising products are magnetic disk devices, semiconductor memory devices, magnetic tape units, automatic file mass storage systems, disc log entry devices, plotters, impact printers, CRT displays, and intelligence terminals.

Electrical Power Generation and Distribution Equipment.—This is a sector of prime interest to U.S. exporters since Spain is a very rapidly expanding market for electrical equipment. In order to reduce the heavy flow of foreign exchange resulting from crude oil imports, Spain is making considerable efforts to augment the capacity and the efficiency of coal-fired electrical energy production and expand nuclear power capacity. Domestic output of switchgear and ancillaries, transformers, controls, boilers, and generators is significant. But even in these product lines, Spanish buyers import if the quality and technology are superior. The most promising products are boilers, reactors, generator sets, and a wide range of transmission equipment.

Telecommunications Equipment.—Spain imports about 20 percent of its requirements for telecommunications equipment. The Spanish National Telephone Company (CTNE) is the principal purchaser of this equipment; its plans call for ever-increasing investments in order to meet the growing demand. Sophisticated American equipment and systems enjoy great preference. For example, satellite tracking equipment is practically all of U.S. origin. Local production of telecommunications equipment ranks high in the electronic sector although domestic manufacturers are for the most part subsidiaries of multinational companies, which import and export sizable quantities of such equipment. Since many of these imports are actually intracompany transfers, trade statistics tend to be somewhat distorted. The most promising products are advanced test equipment and test systems, marine radio sets, satellite tracking equipment, and facsimile transmission equipment.

Industrial Controls.—It is anticipated that the development plans over the next few years in

Table 1.—Distribution of Spain's Trade by Geographic Areas in 1979

(in millions of U.S. dollars with percent of total)

	Imports		Exports	
Total	25,386	100%	18,197	100%
Total OECD	14,595	57%	11,998	66%
United States	3,159	12%	1,305	7%
Japan	595	2%	366	2%
Europe	10,472	41%	10,079	55%
EEC	9,120	36%	8,730	48%
France	2,454	10%	2,936	16%
West Germany	2,431	10%	1,877	10%
Italy	1,432	6%	1,173	6%
United Kingdom	1,308	5%	1,304	7%
Netherlands	772	3%	774	4%
Belgium-Luxembourg	469	2%	475	3%
EFTA	1,271	5%	1,107	6%
Switzerland	465	2%	300	2%
Sweden	338	1%	167	1%
Portugal	114	—	417	2%
Other OECD Europe	80	—	242	1%
Africa	2,073	8%	1,932	11%
Libya	797	3%	174	1%
South Africa	199	1%	70	—
Algeria	195	1%	431	2%
Morocco	179	1%	394	2%
Ivory Coast	123	—	49	—
Middle East	5,016	20%	1,039	6%
Saudi Arabia	2,199	9%	373	2%
Iraq	916	4%	144	1%
United Arab Emirates	663	3%	44	—
Eastern Europe and U.S.S.R.	664	3%	748	4%
U.S.S.R.	217	1%	266	2%
Poland	139	1%	74	—
Latin America	2,175	9%	2,000	11%
Argentina	555	2%	410	2%
Mexico	415	2%	250	1%
Brazil	360	1%	178	1%
Venezuela	272	1%	408	2%
Far East	795	3%	381	2%

Source: OECD *Foreign Trade Statistics.*

Table 2.—Spanish Trade with the World, 1978 and 1979
(in millions of U.S. dollars)

Categories	Imports	
	1978	1979
Animal products	554.6	890.8
Vegetable products	1,899.9	2,033.6
Animal and vegetable oils	157.4	155.6
Prepared foodstuffs	783.5	821.5
Mineral products	6,351.3	8,488.1
Chemical products	1,743.2	2,233.5
Plastic materials and manufactures of	523.9	719.7
Skins and leather	327.8	424.8
Wood and cork and manufactures of	354.4	434.9
Paper and related products	358.7	476.3
Textiles, clothing, and raw cotton	570.4	753.7
Foodwear, etc.	27.6	48.8
Glass and pottery	217.7	283.6
Pearls, precious stones, and precious metals	338.6	392.7
Metals and manufactures of	1,196.8	1,711.1
Machinery and electrical machinery	3,002.9	3,512.6
Transportation equipment	747.6	1,180.8
Optical instruments and measuring instruments	730.6	847.6
Arms and munitions	10.6	13.3
Products not elsewhere classified	114.5	167.2
Art works and antiques	33.2	22.1
Total	**20,045.3**	**25,612.8**
	Exports	
Animal products	260.7	369.5
Vegetable products	1,274.0	1,826.1
Animal and vegetable oils	312.1	409.9
Prepared foodstuffs	995.4	1,129.0
Mineral products	818.1	926.9
Chemical products	807.2	1,142.2
Plastics materials and manufactures of	546.4	730.7
Skins and leather	268.8	368.4
Wood and cork and manufactures of	194.3	252.6
Paper and related products	496.3	688.4
Textiles, clothing, and raw cotton	823.7	960.0
Footwear, etc.	655.1	729.8
Glass and pottery	291.0	373.3
Pearls, precious stones, and precious metals	99.4	131.6
Metals and manufactures of	2,217.6	2,926.2
Machinery and electrical machinery	1,666.5	2,316.9
Transportation equipment	1,893.3	2,501.2
Optical instruments and measuring instruments	94.9	135.2
Arms and munitions	46.2	53.6
Products not elsewhere classified	259.2	292.4
Art works and antiques	6.3	9.6
Total	**14,026.9**	**18,359.2**

Source: Direccion General de Aduanas; valued for 1978 at 71.39 pesetas and for 1979 at 66.53 pesetas per $1.

the electric power, chemical processing, and primary metals sectors will lead to a heavier demand for industrial controls in Spain. Control valves and regulators will be furnished for the most part by domestic suppliers. However, there are important possibilities for American producers of electric and electronic industrial controls to increase their sales and share in this market. Except for control valves and regulators, local firms offer little competition, and the U.S. competitive position is good among foreign suppliers. Most promising products are electronic and nuclear controls. Also included are all process instruments required to operate under unusual conditions.

Medical Instruments and Equipment.— Spain has traditionally been an excellent market for medical instruments and equipment since its needs are largely filled by imports. Domestic production consists mainly of basic X-ray equipment or other product lines such as sterilizers, intensive care materials, and surgical instruments. The Social Security Administration controls about 72 percent of all Spanish purchases of medical instruments and equipment. It operates or controls virtually all of the well-equipped hospitals in the country. The most promising products are patient monitoring

Table 3.—Spanish Trade with the United States by Value of Principal Categories, 1978-79
(in millions of U.S. dollars)

Categories	Spanish Imports	
	1978	1979
Food and live animals	516.0	543.7
Corn	357.3	391.5
Animal feedstuffs	73.6	61.1
Beverages and tobacco	108.0	87.4
Tobacco and tobacco manufactures	56.2	26.1
Crude materials, inedible, except fuel	665.0	941.9
Oilseeds, oil nuts	441.8	524.9
Textile fibers	55.0	63.3
Iron and steel scrap	52.3	170.4
Mineral fuels	79.0	136.0
Coal	47.6	83.3
Oils and fats, animal and vegetable	22.0	27.6
Chemicals	263.0	335.7
Organic chemicals	75.0	121.3
Medicines	38.7	46.6
Synthetic resins and plastic materials	20.0	30.1
Manufactured goods, by chief value	117.0	148.3
Paper and paperboard	16.5	18.8
Textile yarn and fabrics	4.8	11.3
Iron and steel	16.0	16.6
Metal manufactures, n.e.s.	20.0	22.5
Machinery and transport equipment	549.0	744.2
Power generating machinery	118.0	130.5
Office machines	102.0	128.0
Construction and mining machinery	30.1	35.5
Machinery and appliances, n.e.s.	63.0	72.7
Transport equipment	53.0	170.9
Miscellaneous manufactured articles, n.e.c.	155.0	168.2
Total	**2,474.0**	**3,133.5**
	Spanish Exports	
Food and live animals	147.0	140.8
fish and fish preparations	18.0	13.5
Canned fruits and vegetables	109.0	104.4
Beverages and tobacco	43.0	41.9
Alcoholic beverages	36.5	35.6
Crude materials, inedible, except fuel	20.0	17.2
Mineral fuels and lubricants	24.0	23.3
Oils and fats, animal and vegetable	15.0	16.3
Vegetable oils and fats	15.0	16.3
Chemicals	41.0	46.4
Manufactured goods, by chief value	428.0	444.6
Rubber tires and tubes	70.0	80.5
Iron and steel	181.0	150.9
Nonferrous metals	44.0	51.1
Manufactures of metals, n.e.s.	65.0	78.3
Machinery and transport equipment	99.0	148.8
Metalworking machinery	16.0	26.1
Textile and leather machinery	7.9	8.8
Motor vehicle parts	18.6	29.7
Miscellaneous manufactured articles, n.e.c.	393.0	383.9
Clothing	17.0	10.5
Footwear	286.3	277.8
Furniture	16.3	16.1
Printed matter	16.4	17.1
Toys, games and sporting goods	10.2	9.1
Total	**1,214.0**	**1,268.5**

Source: *OECD Foreign Trade Statistics*, Series B, 1978 and 1979.

equipment, ultrasound equipment, blood analyzers, pacemakers, surgical tables, sterilizing equipment, heart/lung surgery units, and artificial kidneys.

Food Processing and Packaging Equipment.—This market has witnessed a remarkable increase in recent years due to the fact that in an effort to offset the sharp increase in labor costs the various subsectors attempted to reach the maximum possible degree of automation. Spanish manufacturers mainly focus on basic items for small-scale food processing. However, a number of foreign manufacturers, including some of the leading U.S. makers, are successfully established in the Spanish market where they manufacture more sophisticated equipment under license. The most promising products at the present time are meat, poultry, and egg processing equipment; beverage manufacturing machinery; and equipment for bakeries—primarily very sophisticated machinery. With Spain's accession to the Common Market, the most promising areas could be fruit and vegetable canning, meat processing, beverages, and ready-to-cook or convenience foods.

Electronics Industry Production and Test Equipment.—There is a drive on in Spain to modernize consumer electronics output and expand the range of electronic equipment manufactured to meet the demand for newer, more advanced equipment. The Spanish electronics industry is characterized by a forward-looking attitude; it is generally receptive to change and the use of innovative techniques, particularly in the consumer products field. Spain's electronics industry offers good prospects for future growth, and since domestic output of test and production materials does not suffice to meet requirements, many types of the more sophisticated items will have to be imported. The most promising products are circuit testing equipment, materials for the manufacture of semiconductors, panel meters, equipment for measuring radio interference, waveform measuring and analyzing equipment, coil-winding equipment, and ultrasonic cleaning systems.

Analytical and Scientific Instruments.—Future demand for this sector is clearly promising. Labor costs are at present a major cause for concern, and decisive action aimed at automating analysis and research procedures is required. The domestic sector is composed of some 14 firms, and, as a rule, these also act as representatives for foreign concerns. Local production is quite limited and offers practically no competition to imports, of which the United States enjoys a strong market share. The most promising products include practically the entire range of laboratory, engineering, and research instruments; materials testing and quality control items; and laboratory fixtures and equipment.

Other product categories offering strong sales potential for U.S. exports include industrial controls, air and water purification and pollution control equipment, and security and safety equipment.

Government's Role in Industry

The Spanish Government is an active participant in many economic sectors. It owns and operates the postal and telecommunications systems—including radio and television networks, the railroad, and the national airline. An autonomous public institution, the National Institute of Industry (INI), has widespread holdings, both direct and indirect, in the industrial and service sectors.

At the end of 1980, INI held direct, and in some cases majority, participation in 73 different firms and indirect holdings in 230 additional firms. Holdings are particularly significant in shipbuilding, coal mining, defense industry, and steel. (INI has control over two of the three integrated steel companies.) Other major holdings are in power generation, motor vehicles industry, chemicals, refining, and oil exploration. INI also has large holdings in service activities such as air transport, tourism, regional development, banks, foreign trade, and the development of new technology. More than 10 percent of gross industrial product in 1979 was attributable to INI firms.

Distribution and Sales Channels

The Approach to Selling

The key to successful selling in Spain is the appointment of a competent agent or distributor or the establishment of an effective sales subsidiary.

Spanish customers generally are reluctant to buy directly from foreign firms that do not have representatives in Spain because they want a local organization to be responsible for such matters as installation, training of technicians, and maintenance and repair. The more complex the product offered the more pronounced this reluctance becomes.

Moreover, Spanish Government agencies, which are important buyers of many types of products and services, are not permitted to buy directly from foreign firms, but only through representatives established in Spain.

Spanish commercial practices are somewhat different from those in the United States. For example, large volume purchasing by chains with numerous outlets, while growing, is a minor factor in Spain where retail trade is conducted largely by small specialty shops. Business relations are also more formal than in the United States.

In general, Spain conducts its foreign trade through regular commercial channels. This applies both to privately owned and publicly owned or operated enterprises. When selling in Spain, U.S. exporters should treat a government-owned or -operated enterprise like any other Spanish firm, for these nationalized enterprises do their purchasing on an individual basis.

American exporters should thoroughly acquaint themselves with the Spanish market, sell more aggressively with the help of advertising, and make every effort to meet prices, credit terms, servicing, and other facilities that may be offered by competitors, chiefly from Western Europe.

General import agencies, most of which are located in Madrid or Barcelona, provide the most effective access to the Spanish market. Dealers in provincial capitals usually obtain their supplies from such agencies rather than by importing them directly.

Regional Markets

There remain definite regional characteristics that affect business and commercial attitudes as well as purchasing habits, particularly in the Bilbao and Barcelona regions. These areas as well as other sections of Spain have been granted substantial tax and judicial powers formerly relegated to the Central Government.

Madrid and Barcelona are the two leading market centers. The capital Madrid serves the central and western parts of the country. To the northeast is Zaragoza (Aragon), one of the development centers; to the northwest, Valladolid and Badajoz (Extremadura) serve as secondary centers. Barcelona is the major industrial city, leading port, and center of activity in the northeast region of Cataluna.

The central Mediterranean coastal area is served from Valencia, a port and the center of the citrus industry. The southern provinces, which constitute Andalusia, are centered in Sevilla, the fourth largest city. It is also a shipping center via the Guadalquivir River. Other important trade centers in Andalusia are Cordoba, Granada, Malaga, Cadiz, and Huelva, also a development center.

Bilbao is the center of heavy industry on the northern coast. Burgos, Oviedo (Asturias), and Pamplona (Navarra) are secondary distribution centers in the northern provinces.

Agent/Distributors

Most manufacturers sell their products through agents (agents comerciales) or their own sales force. Agents usually are employed to handle a specific territory, and subagents report in turn to them. Some agents may represent more than one firm and work under a distribution agreement.

Some U.S. firms have found sales representatives difficult to find since many educated Spaniards prefer office jobs. Some firms have remedied the situation by training Spanish personnel at the company's home offices in the United States or at affiliates in Western Europe.

Agents may hold stock in warehouses in Spain since major lines such as chemicals and industrial apparatus are sold directly to end-users.

Industrial sales personnel are located in such primary trade and industrial centers as Madrid, Barcelona, Bilbao, La Coruna, Zaragoza, and Sevilla. Large companies may have sales branches, warehouses, or both, in some or all of these centers.

The principal-agent relationship is governed by the Civil and Commercial Codes, but there is no special legislation. Local commercial customs supplement the legal provisions and the will of the parties. The parties are free to agree on the terms of their agency agreement, including provisioins for cancellation. In the absence of such provisions, the Commercial Code provides that the principal may cancel the agency at any time on giving notice to the agent. The principal, however, remains liable for the value of the agent's efforts until such time as agreement is reached to terminate the dealership.

Quotations and Terms of Payment

Since a good portion of foreign merchandise in Spain is sold by importers stocking merchandise, the quotations are usually made f.o.b. warehouse, Spain. Quotations made from foreign suppliers in the absence of a representative are usually made f.o.b. foreign port. However, Spanish importers, in most casts, prefer quotations c.i.f. Spanish port.

Terms of payment vary, but the following are the usual arrangements: (1) by irrevocable letter of credit payable upon presentation of documents, (2) by irrevocable letter of credit payable 90 to 180 days after the presentation of documents, (3) by sight draft, (4) by 90-day draft, (5) by check or bank transfer after the presentation of documents, and (6) by check or bank transfer after the sale of the merchandise (this latter only when goods are on consignment).

U.S. firms do not generally extend credits to buyers in Spain for periods of longer than 90 days unless they are backed up by bank credit.

Wholesale and Retail Channels

Firms desiring to sell successfully in Spain need a network of merchandising-minded wholesalers responsible for an area market and its effective promotion.

Wholesalers are of two types: Mayoristas, large national or regional wholesalers selling to retailers; or menoristas, small retail wholesalers in the provinces. Some firms have found that specialized wholesalers can do a more effective selling job if they can develop sales personnel capable of furnishing technical service. Department stores, including the chain type, exist in all of Spain's urban centers and sell a wide range of merchandise similar to that found in U.S. stores. Major department store chains include El Cortes Ingles, Galerias Preciados, and Sears Roebuck de Espana. There is still, however, an abundance of family-type enterprises, especially in the food sector. The number of U.S.-type supermarkets is increasing. They are located principally in the larger urban centers.

Consumer Financing.—Installment selling is becoming widely accepted and there is a growing demand for consumer credit. The lending capacity and the conditions offered by finance institutions are strictly controlled by the Government. A number of manufacturing companies have established their own finance houses.

Franchises. Franchising operations currently exist in the quick food service area. The Ministry of Economy and Commerce authorizes the remittance of royalties and technical assistance fees. New operations are approved on an *ad hoc* basis, depending upon the Government's assessment of each project's utility to the Spanish economy. Prospective franchisors are encouraged to visit Spain before setting up their operations.

Mail-Order Selling.—Mail-order and door-to-door selling are growing but are still relatively insignificant retail sales techniques. In the past, the problem has been to convince the Spanish buyer of reasonable quality and overcoming the fear of nondelivery. Generally, those items selling well in the United States through the mail or from door-to-door should also be successful in Spain.

Licensing Agreements

Technical assistance and technological transfer contracts are governed by Decree 2343 of September 21, 1973. This decree covers such services as the use of patents and trademarks, transmission of unpatented knowledge, engineering services, technical studies, and consultant and study services. Registration of the contract and approval of the transferability of related payments are assigned to the Ministries of Industry and Energy and of Economy and Commerce. Once the contract has been approved by both ministries, it carries the right to transfer abroad the payments involved. The contract must be recorded in the Transfer of Technology Contracts Register of the Directorate General of Industrial and Technological Development in the Ministry of Industry and Energy.

Payments are freely transferable, provided the contract has been approved by the Directorate General for External Transactions in the Ministry of Economy and Commerce together with the documentary justifications and subject to the deduction of applicable taxes (See Taxation section). The Directorate General gives permission for such payments as soon as it has checked that the payments correspond with the terms of the contract.

Government Procurement

Government procurement in Spain is basically regulated by the Act on State Contracts, approved by Decree 923 of 1976 and the General Regulations on State Contracting, approved by Decree 3410 of 1975. There are no government purchasing agencies in Spain as such. Each government ministry, agency, or government-owned company does its own purchasing independently, normally from Spanish firms or from companies having local distributors or agents.

The various types of tenders used in government procurement are the auction (subasta), where the contract is awarded to the lowest bidder; the selective tender (concurso-subasta), where the contract is awarded to the lowest bidder from among a group of firms previously selected as meeting certain preestablished requirements; tender (concurso), where the contract is awarded to the bidder submitting the most advantageous proposal even though it may not be the cheapest; and the private tender, where the contract is awarded to whoever the administration wishes.

The tender is announced in the Official State Bulletin at least 20 working days before the date fixed for the submission of the tenders and documents validating the conditions that may be required. In the case of international tenders, the minimum notice is 40 days.

Under Article 24 of the General Regulations on State Contracting, foreign firms wishing to contract work with the Spanish Government must meet the following requirements: (1) have full capacity to contract and obligate themselves according to the laws of their respective country; (2) prove with documents submitted through the Spanish Embassy in the country of origin that Spanish firms can contract with their respective governments in a similar manner; and (3) have a branch office legally established in Spain that acts as its representative and for which the required foreign investment authorizations will have been obtained. The foreign firm and its representative must be registered in the Spanish Mercantile Registry and the Ministry of Industry's Industrial Registry.

In its tender, the firm must agree to abide by the jurisdiction of Spanish courts. To establish its juridical personality, a foreign firm must submit its documents of incorporation, translated into Spanish by the Ministry of Foreign Affairs and accompanied by a statement from the Spanish Embassy in the respective country to the effect that the firm has legal capacity to contract and to obligate itself. The proposal must state the participation in the work of the corresponding foreign firm or firms.

Provincial and local government agencies follow the same general procedures regarding foreign purchases as the National Government.

Contracts will be drawn up according to the laws of the territories where they are entered into and only with companies having the legal capacity to contract under the laws of their country. Construction work will be supervised by the government agency directly affected by the contract; supply and service contracts are approved by the Ministry having jurisdiction. In addition, approval of the Ministry of Economy and Commerce is required for contracts resulting in payments in foreign currencies.

Trade Fair Schedule

Spain hosts a number of national and international trade fairs. Occasionally, the U.S. Department of Commerce participates in Spanish fairs or sponsors promotional events;

e.g., trade missions, seminar missions, or industrial catalog shows. Additional information concerning these events may be obtained from the nearest Commerce Department District Office or the Office of Country Marketing, International Trade Administration, U.S. Department of Commerce, Washington, D.C. 20230. The trade fair schedule for Spain is shown below by city and month:

Barcelona
January .... International Nautical and Sports Salon (annual)
March .... ALIMENTARIA—Food Products and Equipment (biennial)
GRAPHISPACK—Printing and Packaging Equipment (quadrennial)
April .... CONSTRUMAT—Building Materials (biennial)
May .... International Automobile Salon (biennial)
June .... International General Trade Fair (annual)
September .... SONIMAG—Electronics (annual)
October .... HOGARTEL—Food & Hotel Equipment (annual)
EXPOQUIMIA—Chemicals (triennial)
EXPOAVICOLA—Poultry and Cattle (biennial)

Bilbao
March .... ELA—Electrical and Electronic Equipment (biennial)
April .... EXMA—Elevation and Transportation Equipment
May .... AMBIENTE—Heating and Refrigeration Equipment
SINAVAL—Naval and Maritime Equipment
October .... International Steel Industry Fair (biennial)

Elda
May/Nov. ..... Shoe Related Industries Fair (semiannual)
March/Sept.... FICIA—International Footwear (semiannual)

Madrid
March .... SICUR—Security Equipment
October .... INSTRUMENTALIA-EXPOMEDICA—Laboratory Instruments/Medical Equipment
November ..... SIMO—Office Equipment and Data Processing (annual)

Sevilla
April .... Ibero-American General Trade Fair (annual)

Valencia
January .... TEXTILHOGAR—Home and Decorative Textiles (annual)
February ..... International Toy Fair (annual)
April .... International Art in Metal (annual)
EXPOCARNE—Meat Industries (biennial)
May .... International General Trade Fair (annual)
September .... FIMODA—International Wearing Apparel Fair (annual)
November ..... International Woodworking Machinery Fair (annual)

Zaragoza
March .... FIMA—International Technical Agricultural Machinery (annual)

Trade Regulations

Trade Policy

Since 1959, the Spanish Government has had a program to gradually free its system of trade and payments restrictions. As membership negotiations with the European Communities progress, this liberalization should increase. Most items have been liberalized although quantitative restrictions still remain for a few products. All imports into Spain require either an import license or an "import declaration" issued by the Directorate General of Tariff Policy and Imports in the Ministry of Economy and Commerce.

Spain acceded to the General Agreement on Tariffs and Trade (GATT) in 1963 and participated in the Multilateral Trade Negotiations (MTN). In 1979, Spain signed the General Protocol to the GATT, which contains Spain's MTN offer. The Spanish offer affects some 1,700 tariff positions and includes bindings of the present rates of 1,300 products and tariff reductions on the remaining 400. The reductions will be phased in over an 8-year period, which began July 1, 1980.

Spain also has signed the MTN codes on customs valuation, technical barriers to trade, and dumping (implementation of Article VI of the GATT).

In early 1979, Spain started formal membership negotiations with the European Economic Community (EEC). Entry is expected sometime in 1984 or 1985. Spain already has a preferential trade agreement with the EEC, which was signed in 1970. Under its terms, Spain grants tariff reductions on a wide variety of products from the EEC. The reductions amount to 25 or 60 percent, depending on the product. In addition, special quotas were opened for the EEC for items under Spanish quantitative restrictions. For its part, the EEC has reduced its duty rates on most Spanish products by 60 percent.

Spain also signed in June 1980 a free trade agreement with the seven EFTA countries. As a first step, Spain reduced its duties on some industrial products imported from the EFTA countries by 60 percent and on a large number of industrial products by 25 percent. The EFTA countries, apart from Portugal, will reduce their import duties on almost all industrial products by 60 percent in one step. Elimination of the remaining tariffs will come at a later date.

Import Tariff System

The Spanish tariff schedule is based on the Customs Cooperation Council Nomenclature (CCCN), also referred to as the Brussels Tariff Nomenclature (BTN). Duty rates are separated into four columns: (1) the "normal rate," applicable to imports from the United States and all other countries except those that receive preferential treatment; (2) the "GATT rate," applicable to certain imports from GATT member countries when lower than the "normal rate"; (3) the "EEC rate," which gives the preferential rate, if any, extended to imports from the European Economic Community (EEC); and (4) the "EFTA rate," which gives the preferential rate, if any, extended to imports from the European Free Trade Association (EFTA).

Spain is a relatively high tariff country. Most imports are dutiable at rates ranging from 10 to 35 percent. Imports of raw materials are usually subject to lower rates. The tariff provides for temporarily reduced rates relating to certain capital goods not available from domestic production.

Spanish import duties are levied almost entirely on an *ad valorem* basis. The basis for valuation is the normal price of the merchandise, plus the cost of transportation and all other expenses connected with sale and delivery to the Spanish customs territory. The normal price is the price that could be obtained for the goods in a sale negotiated in the open market between a buyer and a seller independent of each other at the time of entry. The normal price is not the price actually paid in cases where the goods are sold with allowances or discounts exceeding those normally granted for similar transactions or when such discounts are not granted to all buyers under the same conditions. When there is proof of the existence of unusual discounts or of "special relationships" between buyer and seller, the customs administration is authorized to increase the declared value of imported goods for duty-levying purposes.

A few duty rates are levied on a specific basis and are indicated in the tariff. Such duties are based on net or gross weight, length, volume, or on the number of units imported. The metric system of weights and measures is used in customs transactions.

Duties are payable in Spanish pesetas, and the conversion rates used are those announced by the customs office for the day of clearance.

Spain has no customs surcharges, but nearly all imports are subject to a Compensatory Import Tax and a few products to Luxury Taxes. These taxes are explained more fully in the section on internal taxes.

Information regarding Spanish duties applicable to specific products may be obtained free of charge from the Office of Country

Marketing/International Trade Administration, U.S. Department of Commerce, Washington, D.C. 20230, telephone 202-377-4508; or from any Department of Commerce District Office. Inquiries should contain a complete description, including BTN, SITC, or U.S. Schedule B Export Commodity numbers, if known.

Nontariff Import Controls

Spain maintains four principal licensing arrangements: liberalized imports, global quotas, bilateral trade, and State trading.

Most imports, including raw materials, semi-manufactures, machinery, and chemicals, are classified as liberalized goods and may be imported into Spain from the United States and other countries on the import free list without quantitative restrictions. The import free list does not apply to Afghanistan, Albania, Andorra, Bhutan, People's Republic of China, North Korea, Laos, Mongolia, Nepal, Vietnam, San Marino, Tibet, and the U.S.S.R. or to the payments agreements countries (see below). Only specified imports from Iran and Japan are accorded free list treatment. No import license is necessary for liberalized goods, although import declarations are required for statistical and foreign exchange purposes. While these declarations are normally approved freely, the Directorate General of Tariff Policy has the power to suspend the issuance of declarations for commodities for which prices are suspected of being abnormal, pending a full investigation into the prices of the commodities in question.

Commodities for which global quotas are set may be imported from countries to which the free list applies. Global quotas establish the maximum amounts, in pesetas, of import licenses that the Spanish authorities will grant annually for items that fall within the globalized system. These quotas while indicative, are not binding, because in actual practice, importation may exceed or fall short of the announced figure. In recent years, the Ministry of Economy and Commerce has maintained a policy of increasing the individual items within the globalized list by a flat 10 percent. Only 26 items were subject to import quotas in 1981.

Spain admits certain products under a licensing system controlled by bilateral trading agreements between Spain and certain countries. Licenses for imports of these products from countries not enjoying bilateral status are granted on a case-by-case basis. The issue of these licenses is guided by various criteria, including the protection of domestic industries and commitments under the bilateral agreements.

State traded goods include certain agricultural products (generally basic foodstuffs), some raw materials, and goods over which the State has a monopoly (e.g., petroleum products and tobacco). Importation is restricted to State trading agencies or monopolies. Some agricultural products are subject to variable import levies.

Applications for licenses must be submitted to the Directorate General for Tariff Policy and Imports in the Ministry of Commerce, or to a regional office of that ministry. The foreign exporter must furnish the Spanish importer with a *pro forma* invoice, in sextuplicate, to be attached to the import license application or to the import declaration. Indication of the foreign port price (f.o.b. value), freight and insurance charges, as well as Spanish port price (c.i.f. value), should be included on the invoice. The American exporter should assure himself/herself that the importer has a valid license or import declaration. Import licenses are normally valid for 6 months: an extension is possible if justified.

The Spanish Monetary Area—defined as the Peninsular Territories of the Spanish State, the Canary Islands, the Balearic Islands, Ceuta and Melilla—constitutes a single exchange control area.

Payment for imports may be made in U.S. and Canadian dollars or any of the externally convertible European currencies, but in practice, payment is usually made in the current of the country of origin or destination. Countries with which Spain has bilateral payments agreements settle their accounts in U.S. dollars. These include Colombia, Cuba, Czechoslovakia, and Equatorial Guinea. Payments for authorized imports in the appropriate currencies are permitted freely.

Shipping Documents

The documents required by Spain from the exporter on all shipments include a commercial invoice, a bill of lading, a certificate of origin (in triplicate), and, in certain instances, special certificates. Pro forma invoices (six copies) are required by importers in order to support license applicaiton for applicable goods. Spanish consular offices sell certificate of origin blanks ($0.35 each). If the importer or bank requests consular legalization of the various shipping documents, the fees are as follows: the certificate of origin is $9.50 and the commercial invoice is $3.70.

A detailed commercial invoice is required and should contain an accurate and complete description of the merchandise as a basis for levying import duty. One copy is sufficient and may be written in English.

A bill of lading is required and must show gross weight in pounds and kilos.

A certificate of origin is required for all goods with the following exceptions: vehicles subject to registration in Spain whose origin that may be proven by appropriate markings or other signs appearing on the article, such as automobiles, airplanes, and tractors; commercial shipments with a value of less than 50,000 pesetas f.o.b.; and crude petroleum and radioactive isotopes imported by the Nuclear Energy Board. All parcel post packages require a certificate of origin although such a certificate is not usually demanded for packages valued at less than $10.

Commercial printers sell the general form of the certificate of origin that requires only certification before forwarding to the consignee. Certification may be obtained by U.S. chambers of commerce and by the New York Chamber of Commerce and Industry. If legalization has been requested, all three copies of the certificate of origin are presented to the Consulate after certification, with a copy of the commercial invoice for checking purposes. The Consulate will retain two copies of the certificate and return the original. The validity period of a certificate of origin is 6 months from the date of issuance with the possibility of extension by the Directorate General of Customs on a case-by-case basis.

For goods exported to Spain through a third country, a certificate of origin may be issued in the country by a Spanish chamber of commerce or Spanish Commercial Offices, or by career consular officers of Spain. In addition, the Director General of Customs may empower a foreign authority or agency to issue certificates of origin when none of the above-mentioned offices exist.

Importation of all living plant material including plants, plant products, and seeds into Spain is subject to provisions decreed by the Ministry of Agriculture. Sanitary certificates from the appropriate agencies in the United States are required. Health inspection requirements also govern the importation of animals and parts of animals (including meat products, skins, hides, and similar products), marine mammals, fish, crustaceans, or molluscs and parts.

The certifying agency in the United States, the Animal and Plant Health Inspection Service (APHIS) of the U.S. Department of Agriculture, is located in the Federal Building, Hyattsville, Maryland 20782. Inspections usually are carried out in local offices of APHIS, which are located in major U.S. ports and airports. Export agents or brokers may present products for inspection; likewise, inspection of air shipments may be handled by the airlines.

Information on documents required for the importation of agricultural products (including food items), plants, and animals is available from the Foreign Agricultural Service, U.S. Department of Agriculture, Washington, D.C. 20250. Owing to the complexity of sanitary and health regulations, U.S. exporters should also obtain information directly from the importer prior to shipment. Information can also be obtained from the Ministry of Agriculture, P. Infanta Isabel, 1, Madrid-7, Spain.

Internal Taxes

The most important tax affecting imports is the Compensatory Import Tax, known officially as the "Impuesto de Compensacion de Gravamenes Interiores" or ICGI. Spain is considering adoption of a value-added tax (VAT) to replace the Compensatory Import Tax. The current tax is intended to recover the sales, excise, stamp, and other taxes and fees that would have been paid had the imported item been manufactured in Spain. The tax is levied at the time of customs clearance on the total value of the import including freight, insurance, and duty. For most raw materials, the rate varies between 5 and 10 percent, and for finished goods the rate is generally between 10 and 15 percent although it may be higher in certain cases.

In addition to the Compensatory Import Tax, domestic Luxury Taxes also are assessed on certain imports. Items subject to the Luxury Tax include tobacco products, automobiles, cameras, jewelry, watches, antiques, musical instruments, art and decorative objects, rugs and tapestries, cosmetics, perfumes, alcoholic beverages, luggage, purses, and furs. The importer must pay the Luxury Tax based on the value of the goods, which is usually defined as the total of the c.i.f. price, plus the import duty, plus the Compensatory Import Tax.

Spain also uses a cascade-type Turnover Tax by which each stage in the production of a good is taxed. For imports, only the last two stages are applicable. Sales from the manufacturer to the wholesaler are taxed at 2 percent, and sales from the wholesaler to the retailer are taxed at 0.4 percent. Although not particularly large in themselves, for imports they are calculated on top of all the previously mentioned taxes and may therefore be far more cumbersome than for domestically produced goods.

Advance Rulings on Classifications

Advanced rulings on tariff classifications may be obtained by presenting an application directly to the Tariff Study Service, Direccion General de Politica Arancelaria e Importacion, Serrano, 37, Madrid. Applications should be accompanied by samples of the article in question, labeled and signed by the petitioners, with a petition declaring the commercial or industrial name of the product, the raw materials that entered into its composition, its applications and uses, value, the place from which it will be shipped to Spain, and the place of its manufacture or origin. In the case of machines, apparatus, and other articles for which it is not possible to present samples, a set of drawings, models, or photographs—accompanied by a detailed description of the quantity and kind of component parts and the purpose for which the machine or apparatus is intended—may be substituted for the actual sample.

Spain is a member of the Customs Cooperation Council (CCC) in Brussels, works in close conjunction with the Council, and abides by the Council's decisions on nomenclature classifications. The classification rulings of the service are binding unless publicly revoked. All rulings are published.

Fines and Penalties

Fines and penalties may be imposed for failure to present a customs declaration within the prescribed time and for variations between volume and value of goods declared and those actually presented for customs clearance. Variations due to damage or spoilage are not penalized. Deficiencies or excesses of less than 4 percent are not penalized.

For failure to pay the assessed duties within 3 working days, there is a fine of 5 percent of the duty. For all official examinations and verifications of declarations, a charge of 5 percent of the sum of all duties is levied.

For an attempt to circumvent customs regulations or to obtain a lower rate of duty by importing separately all of the parts of a whole mechanism, apparatus, or other object, the duty will be assessed at the rate levied on the assembled mechanism, apparatus, or object, and a fine will be charged based on the differences in the rates of duties concerned.

For failure to present the original commercial invoice and one copy thereof, the importer will be subject to a fine of 5 percent of the total amount of duties due.

Antidumping and Countervailing Duties

The Spanish Government introduced regulations for the establishment of antidumping and countervailing duties through Decree 3519. The primary purpose of the Decree was to adopt existing Spanish antidumping legislation to Article VI of the GATT and to comply fully with the requirements of the EEC-Spain Trade Agreement signed on June 29, 1970.

According to Article VI of the GATT, dumping and export subsidization are defined as importation of products into the commerce of another country at less than their normal value, which thereby causes or threatens to cause material injury to domestic industry or materially retard the establishment of a domestic industry.

Dumping is considered to take place when the export price of a product is less than its domestic price or less than the price charged for export to a third country. Dumping also is considered to take place when, in the absence of a domestic price, the export price is less than the production cost in the country of origin plus a reasonable addition for selling cost and profit. Due allowance will be made in each case for differences in conditions and terms of sale, for differences in taxation, and for other differences affecting price comparability. To offset or prevent dumping, an antidumping duty may be levied in an amount not greater than the difference between the dumped price and the comparable price of the product.

A countervailing duty is a special duty levied for the purpose of offsetting any bounty or subsidy bestowed, directly or indirectly, upon the manufacture, production, or export of any merchandise. No countervailing duty will be levied for more than an amount equal to the estimated bounty or subsidy determined to have been granted by a foreign country, directly or indirectly, on the manufacture, production, exportation, or transportation of the product.

A request for the imposition of antidumping or countervailing duties is filed with the Ministry of Economy and Commerce, Tariff and Import Policy Division by any agency or person representing the injured national production sector. Antidumping and countervailing duties are imposed for a 3-month period, extendible for a maximum of 3 months.

Special Customs Provisions

It is necessary to employ a customs agent or broker to clear goods through the Spanish customs.

For all imported goods an import declaration must be filed in duplicate within 72 hours of the time of unloading or a fine of 5 percent of the amount of the duties and charges will be levied. Declarations must contain the exact wording of the tariff items under which the goods are dutiable.

The presentation of the bill of lading is a prerequisite for obtaining possession of goods shipped to Spain. Should this document be lost, however, the goods may be procured by presenting a bank guarantee covering the full value of the goods involved. The shipper is therefore adequately protected insofar as documentary procedure is concerned.

If, at the time of customs clearance, the importing company or its agent does not have the origin invoice and its copy, the company must give a guarantee that he will present them within 3 months, beginning on the date of dispatch for shipments of non-European origin and within 2 months for shipments of European origin. The goods may then be cleared provisionally.

Goods may be declared for consumption, transit, reexport, or warehousing. Goods that have been declared for consumption may not be reexported unless subject to export controls.

When goods are unloaded at a customs house, they may be declared for transit, whether or not so declared in the manifest. Transit shipments include goods for foreign destinations passing through Spain, merchandise directed under customs surveillance to a warehouse or to a customs office in the interior of Spain for declaration, merchandise withdrawn from warehouses or declared and verified at a Spanish customs office and directed to a customs office on the frontier for reexport, and merchandise shipped by land from one warehouse to another. When goods of any kind intended for maritime transit are so declared on the ship's manifest, no further customs declaration is required since they do not have to be unloaded at a customs house.

Marking and Labeling Requirements

There are no general requirements that imports be marked as to the country of origin, nor are there any requirements concerning specific commodities. In addition, there are no requirements to post signs at the place of sale indicating country of origin or requiring that locally produced articles indicate the inclusion of foreign components or parts. The quality of imported goods must correspond to the description shown on import documents, declarations, licenses, and labels, or packages. Inspection for quality is conducted by the Spanish Customs Inspection Service of SOIVRE (Servicio Oficial de Inspeccion y Vigilancia del Comercio Exterior) and takes place before clearance through customs.

Imports of foodstuffs and beverages of all kinds are subject to the health provisions decreed by the Directorate General of Health. Foodstuffs, in particular, must have the following information indicated in Spanish by means of an engraved or lithographed legend or by means of a label securely attached to the container: the country of origin, common name or classification, form of preparation (e.g., in olive oil, tomato juice, brine, etc.), month and year of preparation, detailed ingredients, and instructions for preparation. Inscriptions must be written in the same way, with the same type, and in the same colors, as those that appear in the original language. Preparations containing saccharin must carry a label to that effect. Other specific regulations apply to the labeling of milk, butter, margarine, chocolate, and soaps. Wines and alcoholic beverages that do not conform to the characteristics stipulated by Spanish legislation on the subject are prohibited or restricted from importation into Spain.

Regulations have been issued with respect to the labeling and composition of textile products manufactured in or imported into Spain. The regulations define the different types of products included within such headings as yarn and thread, trimmings, readymade clothing, and the standard composition of these products. Such goods must bear the appropriate labels when they are put on sale to the public. Foreign words or expressions must be accompanied by their Spanish equivalent in letters of the same size or larger. The manufacturer may use a registered trademark or its fiscal identification number instead of the manufacturer's name and address as previously required.

Drugs, pharmaceutical products, and cosmetics (in a finished state) must first be registered with the Directorate General of Health in the Ministry of Interior and are subject to detailed marking and labeling requirements. Various types of fertilizers and additives for soil and crop preparation must carry special labeling information in Spanish. All manufactures of precious metals must be hallmarked with the Government's stamp at the Spanish Guaranty Bureau prior to import clearance. Firearms must have affixed the official stamp from the Spanish Government Proving Grounds. Imported tires and tubes, except solid tires mounted on metallic rims, must bear a serial number. Serial numbers must be wrought into the metal of motorcar engines and chassis.

In view of the complexity of this field, U.S.

exporters should request Spanish marking and labeling regulations from their importers prior to shipment. Imported goods that do not comply with the regulations are denied entry. Goods that are deemed to carry fraudulent labels or markings are confiscated by the Spanish customs. Customs authorities may also confiscate imported goods whose labels are deemed to contain false claims of credit and industrial reputation. Statements made on the labels that the products have been granted official recognition or that the products have won prizes in competition must be exact and specific.

Packages should bear the consignee's mark, including port mark, and should be numbered unless the contents of the packages can be readily identified without numbers.

Senate Concurrent Resolution 40, adopted July 30, 1953, invites U.S. exporters to inscribe, insofar as practicable, on the external shipping containers in indelible print of a suitable size: "United States of America." Although such marking is not compulsory under our laws, U.S. shippers are urged to cooperate in thus publicizing American-made goods.

Free Trade Zones

Spain maintains three free trade zones: in Barcelona, Cadiz, and Vigo. Merchandise of foreign origin not permanently prohibited from importation into Spain may be brought into the free trade zone without payment of Spanish customs duties or other national taxes and remain free of such duties and taxes while held in the zone or if subsequently transshipped or reexported. Duties become payable, however, if the merchandise is removed from the zone for consumption in Spain.

Operations authorized in the free trade zone include sorting, packaging, mixing, processing, exhibiting, sampling, marking, selling, auctioneering, dividing goods from bulk to commercial quantities, and manufacturing. The storage of goods not used in manufacturing is limited to a 6-year period. This period may be extended with permission of the customs authorities.

Any type of industry may be established except those that may be considered detrimental to the national economy. The establishment of an industry in the zone requires a permit issued by the Ministry of Finance. Applications for such permits must be submitted through the Ministry of Finance of the zone's administering authority.

Special Facilities

In addition to the free trade zones, Spain has established four types of special facilities: free ports, customs warehouses, free deposits, and commercial deposits. These facilities are comparable in many respects to those offered in other countries under bonded warehousing systems.

Free Ports.—Spanish free ports are located in the Canary Islands at Las Palmas and Santa Cruz de Tenerife and the cities of Ceuta and Melilla on the North African coast. In the free ports, the entry and exit of goods is controlled by license. Although Spanish customs duties are not levied in the ports or in their limited hinterlands, excise taxes may be payable. Foreign goods transferred from these areas into other parts of Spain become liable to payment of all applicable duties and taxes. Goods may remain "in transit" without being cleared through customs or placed in a customs warehouse for 1 year. The activities permitted in the free ports are similar to those permitted in the free deposits. Control of free port operations is vested in the Directors of Customs of the respective ports.

Customs Warehouses.—Goods may be stored in customs warehouses for 4 months. Storage fees are collected for each 10 days or fraction thereof. No manipulation is permitted in customs warehouses. Partial withdrawals may be made but only of complete packages. If goods are not withdrawn at the expiration of the storage period, they are considered abandoned.

Free Deposits.—These facilities are available in the cities of Algeciras, Alicante, Bilbao, Cartagena (Murcia), Gijon (Oviedo), La Coruna, Pasajes, Santander, and all major maritime ports on the Spanish mainland. A free deposit is a limited area in a major port containing the office of a martime customs authority and is operated by a concessionary company under the general supervision of the customs authorities. Goods may be held in free deposits without payment of customs duties or other taxes.

General operations permitted in free deposits include storing, repacking, dividing goods from bulk to commercial quantities, mixing, and all other operations that increase the value of the goods deposited without changing essentially the nature of the goods. In addition special operations such as shelling and roasting coffee and cocoa, washing wool, and extracting oil from oilseeds may be undertaken. Spanish merchandise licensed for export may also be stored in free deposits. Maximum storage time in the free deposits is limited to 4 years. The time limit does not apply to merchandise destined for use in the free deposit.

For detailed information concerning a free deposit, inquiry should be addressed to the

Deposito Franco in the particular city in question. The Director of Customs in each city may also be consulted.

Commercial Deposits.—Facilities are maintained in the ports of Huelva, Malaga, and Valencia on the Spanish mainland and in Las Palmas in the Canary Islands.

Commercial deposits are similar to free deposits but offer more limited privileges. They are operated by concessionary companies. With the approval of the customs authorities, merchandise may be stored, repacked, and removed in small quantities as samples. Goods may be freely sold in the commercial deposits; however, the customs authorities must be notified of the sale. Goods may be stored in the deposits for 4 years and may be removed for reexportation abroad, for transfer to another commercial deposit, for consumption in the same locality, or for shipment in coastal trade to another Spanish customs area.

Additional information about commercial deposits may be obtained from the Deposito de Comercio in the particular city of interest. In all cases, inquiries may also be addressed to the Director of Customs in each city.

Reexport

There are four systems that affect goods reexported from Spain. They are drawback, temporary admission, replacement, and temporary import.

Drawback.—"El Drawback" is a system in which duties and taxes are paid in the normal manner, but they are reimbursed when the imported goods are processed or incorporated into another product and reexported within 6 months (period extendible upon request). The importer must submit a detailed list of the goods at the time of customs clearing and must state that they are destined for reexport.

Temporary Admission.—"Admissiones Temporales" is a system in which a bond or bank guarantee is deposited for the amount of import duty and tax due; this deposit is released by the customs authorities upon reexportation. In addition, the temporary admission system allows for the tax to be paid upon entry (when bond is placed for duties), and a tax rebate will be rendered upon reexportation. It is usually more profitable to pay the tax based on the value of the imported product and to receive a rebate based on the value of the exported product. Application for temporary admission must be submitted to the Director General of Customs Policy of the Ministry of Economy and Commerce prior to importation, and any processing or

manufacturing to take place must involve an industrial change and enhance the value of the goods. Goods entering Spain under this system must be licensed and must be reexported before the expiration of the time limit approved by the Government.

Replacement.—Under this system ("sistema de reposicion con franquicia arancelaria"), Spanish companies that exported during the previous year may import free-of-duty primary materials and intermediate products of the same kind and having similar characteristics as those incorporated into the previous exports. The import tax may either be paid outright and a rebate received upon reexportation, or a deposit may be made for the amount of the tax that will be refunded upon reexportation. There is no obligation to reexport under the replacement system.

Temporary Import.—"Importationes temporales" applies to the importation of finished goods that do not undergo essential changes before reexport. Simple incorporation of finished parts or pieces is not considered a modification or transformation of the goods. This is similar to the temporary admissions system in that the goods are cleared on bond without payment of duties.

Refund of Duty

Goods imported for free replacement of identical goods that have been returned or destroyed under customs supervision because they were defective or did not comply for any other reason with the terms of a current sales contract are admitted duty free.

Samples, Advertising Matter, and Carnets

Spain is a member of the "International Convention to Facilitate the Importation of Commercial Samples and Advertising Matter."

Samples of negligible value are admitted duty free. Those samples having commercial value or not so mutilated as to render them unsalable are subject to the duties regularly applied commercial shipments of such commodities.

Samples having commercial value or otherwise failing to qualify under provisions for free entry may be imported temporarily into Spain by bona fide commercial travelers for a maximum period of 1 year upon deposit with the customs collector of a sum adequate to cover the full import duties. Such deposit will be refunded by the customs collector at the point of exit upon outward clearance of the goods originally entered and upon presentation of the deposit receipt, provided always that the goods are removed within 1 year from the date of entry.

To qualify as a bona fide commercial traveler, an individual must bear a letter from his/her principals certifying his/her status and visaed by the Spanish consular officer nearest the home office of such principals. This letter or certificate must also list and identify the samples carried by the traveler and indicate that they are not for sale.

As a result of various customs conventions, to which both Spain and the United States are parties, simplified procedures in the form of the "carnet" are available to U.S. business executives and professionals for the importation of commercial samples, advertising materials including film, and medical or other professional equipment into Spain for a limited time. The carnet eliminates extensive customs procedures for temporary imports; with the carnet such goods may be imported without the payment of duty and tax or the provision of additional security.

Professional equipment includes, but is not limited to, equipment for the press or for radio and television broadcasting; cinematographic equipment; and engineering, topographical, surgical, electrical, archeological, and entertainment equipment. Commercial samples generally refer to those imported solely for demonstration purposes in the solicitation of orders from abroad. Not included in the carnet system are items already sold or offered for sale and items such as paints, cleaning materials, food, leaflets, and other consumable items that are either given away, disposed of, or used abroad.

Carnets are issued for a fee in the United States by the U.S. Council of the International Chamber of Commerce, Inc., 1212 Avenue of the Americas, New York, New York 10036 (telephone (212) 354-4480). Applications for carnets are available from the U.S. Council or from U.S. Department of Commerce District Offices. Carnets are valid for 1 year from the date of issuance.

Advertising material, price lists, catalogs, and trade notices are admitted free of duty provided they do not exceed one document. If they exceed one document, they are admitted duty free if the total weight of such material does not exceed 1 kilogram.

System of Weights and Measures

The metric system is used in Spain and should be used, if at all possible, in every quotation where measurement or weight is involved.

Electric Current

AC 50-cycle, one- or three-phase, and nominal voltage is 127/220 and 220/380. Most outlets for ordinary current are European (tubular prong) type and require an adapter. Transformers also may be needed.

Spain's Export Controls

Exports from Spain are subject to export licenses or a customs export declaration. Export declarations are issued by the Directorate General of Exports of the Ministry of Economy and Commerce, and they are granted freely.

Transportation and Utilities

Spain's international transportation links are well developed, and a number of airlines and steamship companies provide scheduled service between Spain and the United States. Ocean transit time from the East Coast of the United States to Spanish ports ordinarily is about 3 weeks.

Spain's internal transportation system has been considerably improved, and upgrading of transport facilities continues to receive high priority. In recent years, there has been a marked shift of passenger traffic from railroads to highways and to air transport. The main growth in freight traffic has benefited trucking and coastal shipping.

The network of the Spanish National Railways (RENFE) is comprised of 16,700 kilometers of broad gage lines, including 1,920 kilometers with double tracks. In addition, there are a number of narrow gage lines, mostly operated by small private companies in connection with mining operations. Spain's highway system consists of 79,600 kilometers of national roads and 67,300 kilometers of provincial and local roads.

Both freight and passenger traffic have grown rapidly. Parts of the system suffer from congestion, but major efforts are being made to improve road conditions. As of 1979, the number of motor vehicles in circulation was nearly 7.1 million, or approximately 188 per 1,000 inhabitants; this compares with 60.7 per 1,000 in 1969. Spain is lacking in navigable rivers, and there is little inland water navigation.

Spain's coastlines, including those of the Balearic and Canary Islands, are dotted with many ports. Most tonnage is handled by the nine largest ports, led by Bilbao, Tarragona, and Barcelona.

Air transport has undergone rapid growth. Domestic passenger traffic has been stimulated by Spain's growing tourist industry. Most Spanish cities are now served by the expanding airport network. The most important airports are those at Palma, Madrid, Malaga, Barcelona, and the Canary Islands. Iberia, the Spanish national airline, provides service throughout Spain and flies to a number of foreign countries. TWA provides passenger service to Spain.

The State-owned Compania Telefonica Nacional de Espana (CTNE) operates telephone service in all parts of the country. As of 1979, there were some 11 million telephones in service. The national telegraph system is administered by the State in conjunction with the post office system.

Most radio and television broadcasting is also under State control. Some 33 television broadcasting stations are in operation, with coverage throughout the country; of these, 22 broadcast the "National Program" and 11, the "Second Program." Color broadcasts are available on both programs.

Electricity is produced and distributed by INI and a few large private companies together with a number of very small companies. In 1980, domestic electricity production totaled an estimated 110.1 billion kWh. Under the second National Energy Plan, total power generation is expected to reach 145 billion kWh by 1987 with a substantial and rapid increase in nuclear power. However, there are indications that there may be a hiatus in Spain's nuclear power program due to cost, fuel, and political considerations. New emphasis is being placed on the construction of coal-fired generation plants over the next few years.

Advertising and Market Research

Advertising has developed rapidly in Spain over the past 10 years, and many leading foreign companies, including U.S. firms, now have agencies there. Daily newspapers are the predominant outlet for advertising followed by magazines, television, radio, motion picture theaters, and outdoor display.

Newspapers are the strongest advertising medium. There are about 150 daily papers and 19 special Monday papers called Hojas del Lunes. Evening papers do not appear on Sunday, and morning papers do not appear on Monday. The majority of Spanish newspapers are privately owned and are either regional or local. The largest daily newspapers are the following: ABC (Madrid and Seville), La Vanguardia (Barcelona), El Pais (Madrid), Ya (Madrid), and El Pueblo (Madrid).

There are more than 5,700 weekly, biweekly, and quarterly publications in Spain; most of them have very limited circulation. Trade and technical publications are important although some care must be taken in their selection because quality and coverage are uneven. The use of these publications has increased commensurately with technological development.

Television is the second largest advertising medium. There are an estimated 7.3 million sets covering about 96 percent of Spanish households. The number of sets is increasing rapidly despite their high cost. All 33 stations are owned and operated by the Government and they carry advertising.

Radio advertising has grown considerably. There are 271 radio stations in Spain with more than 90 percent of Spanish households having at least one radio set. Two national radio chains are in operation: Nacional and Peninsulares.

Advertising agencies are of different types, and foreign advertisers should know the distinctions before making a selection. The principal types are full service, general distribution, exclusive, and technical study.

Commissions and rates are not uniform in Spain and are subject to negotiations in many instances. Agency commissions are generally 15 to 17.5 percent. Radio advertising may be booked directly or through brokers and advertising agencies. Cost varies greatly from one location to another.

In large cities, television spots are from 20 to 30 seconds. Due to the great cost of television advertising, a number of Spanish firms are turning back to radio and newspapers. Filmed commercials shown in movie theaters range from 15 to 30 seconds in length and vary in cost by category and number of meters of film.

Market research is carried out by a few specialized firms and a number of advertising agencies. A list of market research consultants can be obtained from the U.S. Department of Commerce.

Credit

Currency

The basic monetary unit of Spain is the peseta, written as "Ptas." There are 100 centimos to a peseta. As of July 21, 1981, its exchange rate in terms of the U.S. dollar was 1.02 cents (US$1=98.4 pesetas). Banknotes are issued in denominations of 5,000, 1,000, 500, and 100 pesetas; and coins in 50, 25, 5, and 1 pesetas and also 50, 10, and 5 centimos.

Sources of Credit

The following institutions largely form the structure of the Spanish financial system: the Bank of Spain, the Institute of Official Credit, private banks (commercial and industrial), nonprofit savings banks, nonbanking financial intermediaries, and the stock market.

Bank of Spain.—In addition to its responsibilities in the control of the money supply, the Bank of Spain or Banco de Espana has the usual regulato·y powers over credit institutions and establishι· maximum interest rates and reserve requirements. The Bank is the only institution entitled to manage the country's foreign exchange reserves and control the movement of foreign payments.

Institute of Official Credit.—The Institute is the permanent link between official credit entities and the Ministry of Finance. Separate specialized credit agencies function under supervision of the Institute. Each agency applies medium- and long-term funds at preferential interest rates to the private sector. The seven agencies are as follows: the Industrial Credit Bank, the Construction Credit Bank, the Agricultural Credit Bank, the Local Credit Bank, the Mortgage Bank, the Fishing Credit Bank, and the External Bank of Spain.

Private banks.—Since a banking reform act was passed in 1962, commercial and investment banking functions have been separated, with the latter being reserved to industrial banks. Industrial banks are responsible for promoting the creation of new industrial or agricultural companies and the extension or modernization of existing firms, along with their medium- and long-term financing.

Although industrial banks have undergone substantial growth, commercial banks are the main suppliers of credit to the private sector, principally in the form of short-term loans. Commercial banking operations are dominated by seven large banks: Banco Espanol de Credito, Banco Central, Banco Hispano Americano, Banco de Bilbao, Banco de Vizcaya, Banco de Santander, and Banco Popular Espanol.

From the end of Spain's Civil War until 1978, foreign banks were not allowed to establish branches in Spain although some banks that had branches before the Civil War were allowed to retain them.

Under a Royal Decree approved by the Council of Ministers in May 1978, foreign banks now have the option of opening, subject to the approval of the Bank of Spain, three types of banking activities: representative offices, branches, or wholly owned subsidiaries. Required capital is 750 million pesetas with wholly owned subsidiaries subject to 1.5 billion peseta capitalization. Profit and dividend repatriation rules will be the same as those applied to other foreign investors and local banks.

The following American banks are located in Madrid: Bank of America, Bankers Trust, Chemical Bank, Continental Illinois National Bank, Chase Manhattan Bank, First National Bank of Chicago, First National Bank of Boston, Citibank, Manufacturers Hanover Trust, Marine Midland Bank, Morgan Guaranty Trust, First Wisconsin National Bank, United California Bank, and Wells Fargo Bank. A system of 90 nonprofit savings banks is in operation under the general supervision of the Bank of Spain to provide credit to small borrowers. The savings banks and their 11,000 branches operate somewhat like ordinary banks and obtain most of their resources from savings deposits. They are required to allocate a portion of their deposits for loans to specified sectors on preferential terms.

Stock Exchanges

Stock exchanges are located in Madrid, Barcelona, and Bilbao. The Madrid exchange is the most important and handles about one-half of total trading. Although activity on the stock exchanges has expanded considerably in recent years, the Spanish security markets remain thin, both in terms of international standards and in relation to Spanish economic activity. All issues must be authorized by the Directorate General for Financial Policy in the Ministry of Finance.

Investment in Spain

U.S. Investment

The value of total U.S. direct investment in Spain amounted to nearly $2.5 billion at the end of 1979, largely in petroleum and manufacturing operations. U.S. investment comprises about 42 percent of all foreign investment in Spain in 1979; other major investors were France (about 11 percent), the Netherlands (9 percent), West Germany (8.5 percent), and Switzerland (5 percent). An estimated 350 U.S. firms have a substantial direct capital investment in Spain in the form of stock, as the sole owner or as a partner in an enterprise.

Foreign investment is welcomed in Spain, and the investment climate is considered excelent for U.S. firms. Since 1959, the Spanish Government has followed a liberal policy for foreign capital investments. In that year, a program of economic stabilization and reforms was enacted that was accompanied by a fundamental change in the Government's attitude toward foreign investment and trade. Investment in Spain by foreign firms is now in principal open in all fields except those relating to national defense, public information, and public services.

Treaty Relations with the United States

According to the Treaty of Friendship and General Relations of 1902, Americans have the right—as long as they conform to the laws of Spain—to enter, travel, and reside in all parts of the country, and to enjoy, for the protection of their persons and their property, the same treatment and the same rights as Spaniards. Furthermore, Americans may freely exercise their industry or their business without being subjected to any taxes (general or local), imposts, or conditions different than those that are imposed upon Spanish subjects or subjects of the most-favored nation.

Americans have the right to possess real estate in Spain, subject to the law of October 23, 1935, and other legislation placing restrictions on the acquisition and ownership of real estate by foreigners in so-called strategic zones. Americans also have full power to dispose of their personal property within the Spanish territory, by testament, donation, or otherwise. Their heirs, legatees, and donees—whether resident or nonresident—may succeed to their personal property, may take possession of it either by themselves or by others acting for them, and dispose of it at their pleasure, paying only such duties as Spanish subjects shall be liable to pay in like case.

American citizens have free access to Spanish courts, upon conforming to the laws regulating the matter. They may be represented by lawyers and enjoy the same rights and the same advantages that are granted to the citizens or subjects of the most-favored nation concerning arrest of persons or the seizure of property.

Foreign Investment Legislation

Spain has long encouraged foreign investment as a means of obtaining additional investment capital, advanced technology, creation of new jobs, and an offset to its balance-of-trade deficits. Decrees 3021 and 3022, both of October 31, 1974, and Royal Decree 3099 of November 1976 form the general legal framework for foreign investment.

Until 1977, the guiding principle of Spanish investment legislation was to grant foreign individuals and firms complete freedom to subscribe up to 50 percent of the capital of any Spanish company. For such an investment, approval is almost automatic, the only requirement being that an industrial permit be obtained and the investment must be registered with the Foreign Investment Registry of the Directorate General for External Transactions (Direccion General de Transacciones Exteriores, Castellano 162, Madrid-16) in the Ministry of Economy and Commerce. Such registration ensures rights to subsequent transfer of capital and earnings; although, in the case of the latter, it is not unusual for limitations to be imposed on the amount of dividends that may be declared. Foreign participation or holdings exceeding 50 percent of the Spanish company requires prior authorization from the Directorate General of External Transactions and the Council of Ministers.

Royal Decree 3099 of 1976, which was promulgated in January 1977, eased the requirements for foreign investors wishing to acquire more than 50 percent of a Spanish company, if certain balance-of-payments and employment conditions were met by making approval automatic in the absence of any objection by the Spanish Government within 90 days.

The requisite conditions of Royal Decree 3099 are that (1) the investment consists of foreign currency or convertible pesetas, imported equipment or foreign technical assistance, or patents or licenses; (2) the incremental investment be not less than 100 million pesetas, or that exports be at least 50 percent of production with a value not less than 100 million pesetas; (3) the Spanish company make no payments for the transfer of technology to the foreign investor except those agreed upon for previous services, and in no case can such payments be stated as a constant percentage or related to the volume of business activity; (4) the company must provide at least 100 new permanent jobs within the first year of operation; and (5) after 1 year its operations must have a positive annual balance in its foreign exchange account. If the company does not have a positive annual balance, it must provide at least 1,000 new permanent jobs.

Foreign participation is not normally permitted in activities that are directly connected with national defense or public information; there is a 25-percent foreign investment limit in companies operating public utilities.

Foreign investments in the following sectors are governed by special legislation: mining, motion pictures, hydrocarbon prospecting and processing, banking, insurance, gambling, shipping, and air transport.

Investment Incentives

Since 1963 when the law of "preferential interest" was established, domestic and foreign investors in specified industries have been offered special incentives for their investment. For now the following industries are affected: electronics, telecommunications, zinc, automobile accessories, chemicals production, and pharmaceuticals. In 1976, the Government expanded the incentives available to new industries and new investment, both domestic and foreign. Tax incentives were offered to companies that located their facilities in industrial or agricultural "preferential zones" where there is excessive dependence upon agriculture or relatively high unemployment. The legislation also covered activities or industries involving mining, steel, food processing, agriculture, shipbuilding, and fishing.

Under the 1976 Decree Law, a credit of 10 percent is deductible from the profits tax on the investment. The investment must have been established on a firm basis before March 31, 1977, and must be received or constructed before 1981. The incentives include assistance in plant location by means of expropriation of land; reduction of up to 95 percent of the transfer tax and other taxes related to setting up businesses; freedom of depreciation during the first 5 years, starting with the first year of operation; priority in obtaining official low-interest credits; and subsidies to be determined on a case-by-case basis. Earlier incentives, such as accelerated depreciation rates and reduction of import duties for plant equipment not available in Spain, continue to be granted.

Performance Requirements

Performance requirements are applied to both domestic and foreign investments on a case-by-case basis and comprise a broad range of measures, including quantitative employment quotas, export and import requirements, local content, capital flow, and access to local capital markets. The imposition of any of these requirements is generally open to negotiation.

Access to Domestic Credit

Medium- or long-term bank credit to Spanish firms with foreign participation exceeding 25 percent is subject to special provisions. Domestic bank credit for up to 18 months may be granted, irrespective of the degree of foreign participation, on the same conditions as to wholly Spanish-owned firms.

Profit and Dividend Repatriation

Once an investment has been made in full compliance with Spanish foreign investment legislation, legally distributed profits and dividends may, in theory, be repatriated freely. Proceeds from the disposal of investments, including the capital initially contributed, plus capital gains, may also be transferred freely. Nevertheless, the Spanish Government has on certain occasions placed dividend limits on all Spanish companies, whether foreign or locally owned. This has acted as a restriction on profit repatriation. The last dividend limitation was relaxed in January 1978.

Real Estate Investment

In general, both urban and rural property may be purchased freely by foreign individuals or legal entities with the following exceptions: The Ministry of Defense must authorize in advance purchases of rural property in the Balearic Islands, the province of Galicia, the Canary Islands, and the sovereign cities in North Africa. The purchaser applies for authorization in these areas through appropriate local military channels and must include a plan illustrating the layout and location of the property.

Approval by Spanish authorities is required for any purchase, exchange, private bidding, or donation of property that exceeds 4 hectares of irrigated land or 20 hectares of unirrigated land.

All property purchases must be recorded in the Registro de la Propriedad or Property Register. Registration is of paramount importance since land purchases are not effective in any respect until duly registered. Registration is prima facie evidence of title and therefore necessary to ensure that the purchaser is not later dispossessed of the property.

A distinction is made by Spanish authorities between real estate purchases classified as business-oriented (all purchases by foreign legal entities) and purchases by nonresident individuals of rural property, urban land for development of more than three dwelling units in the same building, or private oriented (villas or apartments for individual use). All purchases by foreign corporations require prior authorization by the Directorate General for External Transactions. This office also establishes the general conditions and rights of transfer abroad to be applied in each specific case.

Forms of Business Organization

Spanish law provides for four basic types of commercial organization other than the individual trader: partnerships, limited partnerships, limited liability companies, and corporations. Due to the advantage of limited liability of the shareholders, the corporation is probably the most common of these forms and is believed to be the most interesting one to U.S. firms considering investing in Spain.

Corporation (sociedad anonima).—The establishment, operation, and dissolution of corporations in Spain are governed by the law of July 17, 1951, on the Juridical Regime of Incorporated Companies (published in the Official Bulletin of August 6, 1951).

This basic law makes the corporate form mandatory for all firms that limit the responsibility of their members in any way and that have paid-in capital of more than 50 million pesetas. Simple limited partnerships are excepted from this provision. The capital must be divided into shares and must be composed of contributions from the members, whose responsibility is limited to the amount invested in the company. Foreigners may acquire shares through the investment of capital, capital goods, technical assistance, or patents. The words "Sociedad Anonima" must appear in the name, and the name may not duplicate that of any existing firm. The corporation must be domiciled in Spain.

A corporation must be established by public contract, which must be inscribed in the Mercantile Register. To be established, a corporation must have its capital fully subscribed and at least one-fourth paid in. A corporation may be formed by agreement among the founders—who retain all the shares and who must number at least three—or by public subscription. In the latter case, a prospectus must be published and various other formalities must be complied with.

Cash contributions to the capital of a corporation should be made in Spanish currency. If foreign currency is used, the Spanish currency equivalent thereof must be determined.

The law cited provides in great and specific detail for registration, shares, reports, balance sheets, voting rights, shareholders' meetings, and other requirements, generally following what may be considered common practice in corporation law.

A corporation with over 500 full-time employees, having at least three directors and having existed over 3 years, must have employee representatives on its board of directors. Firms with over 100 full-time employees must have a committee elected from among the employees. The committee is presided over by a representative of the company management. Foreign citizens may not serve on such committees.

Limited Liability Company (sociedad de responsabilidad limitada).—The law of July 17, 1953, on the Juridical Regime of Limited Liability Companies (published in the Official Bulletin of July 18, 1953), sets forth the regulations and limitations applicable to this type of commercial organization.

The limited liability company has a fixed capital that is divided into equal portions or participations, which are indivisible and non-negotiable. The capitalization may not exceed 50 million pesetas and must be fully paid in from the start. The number of participating members is limited to 50, and they are not personally responsible for the firm's debts. The firm must be domiciled in Spain.

A limited liability company is established by public contract, which must be inscribed in the Mercantile Register. Cash contributions to the capital should be in Spanish currency. If the contributions are in foreign currency, the Spanish currency equivalent must be determined. The 1953 law sets forth in some detail further regulations governing limited liability companies.

Partnership (compania colectiva).—The Spanish Commercial Code of 1885 contains the basic legal provisions concerning partnerships (Articles 125 to 144). This law sets forth the minimum requirements for the formation of a partnership, the form of the agreement, registration, operation, responsibilities, and other requirements. All partners are fully responsible for the acts and debts of the firm to the full extent of their common and personal property. The social contract or partnership agreement must be registered in the Mercantile Register.

Limited Partnership (sociedad en comandita).—As in the United States, this form of organization comprises one or more limited or silent partners who invest capital but do not participate in the management of the firm and one or more active partners who manages the business. Responsibility of the limited partners is restricted to the extent of their investment. This can take the form of shares (share-issuing limited partnership) or stock (simple limited partnership). Responsibility of the active or managing partners is not limited. The name of the firm must include the name of at least one of the general partners and the phrase "y Compania, Sociedad en Comandita" (and company, in limited partnership).

The social contract of a limited partnership must be registered in the Mercantile Register and must contain full details about the members and the firm.

Joint Ventures.—Joint ventures are increasingly encouraged as a means of gaining access to foreign technology and developing small and medium-sized firms. Also, foreign companies sometimes enter into joint ventures with Spanish firms for limited periods or objectives.

A joint venture with a separate legal identity (associacion de empresas) can be formed under the merger law of 1963. The partners may be corporations, companies, partnerships, or individuals. Except with special authorization from the Ministry of Finance, no member may hold more than one-third of the capital and none may hold more than a one-third interest. Although the joint venture is managed by one of the partners, liability for its debts is joint, several, and unlimited. Details of its objectives, administration, and financial structure, as well as copies of the last annual reports of the partners, must be submitted to the Instituto de Credito Oficial, on whose recommendation the Ministry of Finance will grant tax reliefs on the registration of the joint venture and on transactions between it and its constituent partners. The formation contract must be recorded in the Mercantile Registry.

A joint venture without a separate legal identity may be formed to promote the individual partners' businesses. The tax authorities must be told how income and expenditure will be shared and recorded in the returns of the individual partners. If a foreign entity is to be one of the partners, the Ministry of Economy and Commerce must give its approval.

Industrial Property Protection

Legislation in force governing the protection of industrial property rights (patents, trademarks, industrial designs, and commercial names) is contained in the Decree Law of July 26, 1929, as amended.

Spain and the United States are members of the "Paris Union" International Convention for the Protection of Industrial Property. Thus, U.S. business and investors are entitled to the same treatment in Spain (i.e., national treatment) for the protection of their industrial property rights as that country extends to its own nationals. U.S. nationals also are entitled to certain special advantages such as preservation of patent and trademark filing rights after first filings abroad and protection against arbitrary cancellation for nonworking.

Spain recognizes four main types of patents: patents of invention, patents of addition, utility models, and patents of importation.

Patents of invention cover apparatus, machines, instruments, and mechanical or chemical processes for obtaining an industrial result or product. These patents are granted for a nonrenewable period of 20 years from date of issue.

A patent of invention must be worked in Spain or a license for its operation must be tendered within 3 years from its date of issue, except upon proof of the existence of a "force majeure." An annual fee must be paid and evidence shown that the patent is being worked; otherwise, it may be subject to cancellation.

Patents of addition are granted only to the owner of a patent of invention who wishes to introduce a modification in the patent; no more than three patents of addition will be granted in connection with an invention. These are issued for the unexpired term of the main patent.

Patents on utility models or petty patents are granted for 20 years for instruments, tools, devices, and objects or accessoaries that afford an advantage or new effect.

A patent of importation (also known as a patent of introduction) is granted for no longer than 10 years concurrent with the basic patent and covers inventions known or patented in a foreign country but not patented or known in Spain. However, this patent is not protection against imported products.

Applications for patents are examined as to the patentability and form but not as to novelty or usefulness. There is no provision in the law for opposition. Cancellation of patents and utility models may be applied for before the courts during their first 15 years.

Trademark registrations are valid for 20 years from date of grant and are renewable indefinitely for similar periods. The first applicant is entitled to registration and exclusive use of the mark. Registrations are incontestable on prior-use grounds after 3 years. Applications are examined, and if approved, they are published in the *Official Bulletin* for opposition for 2 months. The trademark registration must be used for 5 consecutive years; otherwise, it can be canceled upon petition by any party to the courts. If the registrant can show that such non-use was due to "force majeure," the mark will not be canceled. Service marks are registrable.

Registration also can be canceled or subject to forfeiture upon termination and failure to renew its validity, failure to pay any of advance 5-year installment fees, and upon the proprietor's death or dissolution of the business in which the mark is used.

Protection also is granted to industrial designs containing a combination of fines or ornamentation of a product involving manual, mechanical, or chemical processes. Industrial models and designs are registered for 10 years and may be renewed.

Spain and the United States are also members of the Universal Copyright Convention. Under this Convention, U.S. authors are accorded virtual automatic copyright protection in member countries for their literary and artistic works first published and copyrighted in the United States. To acquire such protection, all they need show on their works is their name, date of the work's first publication and the symbol "c" in circle.

Under Spanish law, copyright protection for scientific, literary, or artistic works belongs to authors during their lives and to their heirs for 80 years after their death.

Applications for the registration of industrial property rights and copyrights should be addressed to: Registro de la Propriedad Industrial, Ministry of Industry and Energy, Av. Generalisimo 59, Madrid. Nonresidents requesting patent or trademark registrations must designate an official agent to act on their behalf in Spain.

Taxation

The power to impose taxes rests largely with the Central Government. Provincial and municipal authorities have the power to impose surcharges. Much of the Spanish revenue system has been recently revised.

The principal taxes applicable are summarized below to furnish a general picture of the structure of the Spanish tax system. Taxes of lesser importance or those of limited application are omitted. The Corporation Tax or Impuesta General Sobre la Renta de las Sociedades is assessed on the net income, whether realized in Spain or abroad, of Spanish resident firms (created under Spanish law or with headquarters in Spain). Firms resident abroad that carry on business operations in Spain through permanent establishments are taxed only on profits realized in Spain. This includes foreign firms that possess or operate through offices in Spain or if they employ representatives authorized to contract in the name of or for account of the firm. Also falling in this category are firms that construct, install or assembly projects for more than 12 months and firms that operate in Spain through a sales organization.

Under a corporate taxation law effective January 1, 1979, the basic tax rate for corporations is set at 33 percent. Taxable income is computed on the basis of gross revenues from all sources, including net capital gains, less necessary expenses. Included among allowable expenses are investment reserves of up to 50 percent of nondistributed profits, provided the company's declared earnings equal at least 6 percent of its paid-in capital and reserves. The maximum allowable depreciation rates are industrial buildings, 3 percent; office buildings, 2 percent; machinery, 8 percent; tools, 20 percent; office equipment, 10 percent; and motor vehicles, 10 to 14 percent.

Effective January 1, 1979, Spain also introduced a new Personal Income Tax (Law 44/78) which applies to (1) all individuals residing in Spain for more than 183 days during the calendar year (total income and the total wealth increases are taxable, independently of where they originated or the place of residence of the taxpayer), and (2) all individuals obtaining income or wealth increases originated on Spanish territory or paid by an individual or legal entity resident in Spain.

Residents of Spain will pay for their worldwide income and nonresidents for their income from a source within Spain.

Covered under taxable income are the following items: income deriving from work, from capital, and from businesses; the actual profits obtained from capital; other changes in wealth that are not taxable by the Inheritance Tax; profits earned by civil corporations, estates, and communities of property; and other legal entities. Nonresidents are required to designate an individual or corporation domiciled in Spain to act as their personal representative in dealings with tax authorities.

Taxable income is the gross income, minus deductible expenses to produce it.

The tax rates on peseta income are:

From	To	Rate (percent)
0	200,000	15.00
200,001	400,000	16.02
400,001	600,000	17.04
600,001	800,000	18.06
800,001	1,000,000	19.08
1,000,001	1,400,000	20.61
1,400,001	1,800,000	22.65
1,800,001	2,200,000	24.69
2,200,001	2,600,000	26.73
2,600,001	3,000,000	28.78
3,000,001	3,400,000	30.82
3,400,001	3,800,000	32.86
3,800,001	4,200,000	34.90
4,200,001	4,600,000	36.94
4,600,001	5,000,000	38.98
5,000,001	5,400,000	41.02
5,400,001	5,800,000	43.06
5,800,001	6,200,000	45.10
6,200,001	6,600,000	47.14
6,600,001	7,000,000	49.18

7,000,001	7,400,000	51.22
7,400,001	7,800,000	53.27
7,800,001	8,200,000	55.31
8,200,001	8,600,000	57.35
8,600,001	9,000,000	59.39
9,000,001	9,400,000	61.43
9,400,001	9,800,000	63.47
More than	9,800,001	65.51

Until Spain introduces a value-added tax, it will continue to apply a Sales Turnover Tax that is a cascade tax in which each stage of production of an item is taxed. The operations of all mercantile, industrial, and commercial firms are subject to the tax, as well as the operations of firms supplying services and performing functions under contract. Specific types of business activities subject to this tax include sales of products realized by manufacturers, importers, exporters, and wholesalers, and fees and income received for services rendered by hotels, restaurants, banks, insurance companies, transportation companies, advertising agencies, and theaters. Retail sales are exempt from the tax.

Tax rates are as follows: sales from manufacturers to wholesalers, 2 percent; sales from manufacturers to retailers, 2.4 percent; sales from wholesalers to retailers, 0.4 percent; for real estate sales, 3.5 percent.

A Consumption Tax is charged on certain nonessential or luxury items and services including the following major products: Tobacco, perfumes and cosmetics, jewelry, motorcars, beverages, and radio and television sets. Rates vary according to product or service.

An Inheritance Tax is levied on the entire estate of Spanish residents, and in the case of nonresidents, it is levied on property located in Spain. Rates vary according to the value of the property and the relationship of the beneficiaries to the decreased.

Double Taxation Treaty.—To protect taxpayers benefiting from certain tax reductions or exemptions within Spain, double taxation agreements, in general, give the taxpayer resident abroad the right to reduce the tax payable in the country of residence by the full amount of Spanish tax that would have been payable without the reduction of exemption. Spain has double taxation agreements with Austria, Belgium, Denmark, Finland, France, Ireland, Japan, the Netherlands, Norway, Portugal, West Germany, South Africa, Sweden, Switzerland, and the United Kingdom. There is none between the United States and Spain.

Labor Relations

The Spanish labor force contained approximately 13.2 million persons in 1980 or about 37 percent of the country's total population of 36 million. The ratio of the labor force to population, which in Spain is lower than the average for Western Europe due to relatively low employment of females and temporary emigration, has remained relatively stable. Movement of workers out of agriculture and into industry and services has been continuous since the 1960's. As of 1979, the bulk of the labor force was divided among services (42 percent), manufacturing (26 percent), agriculture (18 percent), and construction (10 percent).

Emigration of Spanish workers to other European countries was substantial until the mid-1960's but has declined markedly since then as the gap between income in Spain and abroad has narrowed and as the economic slump persists in Western Europe. Estimated net emigration was only 12,000 in 1979, compared with 103,000 in 1972. There are an estimated one million Spaniards employed in other European countries: chiefly France, West Germany, and Switzerland.

Minimum standards for wages, hours, social security, health and safety protection, holidays and vacations, personnel classification, and incentives are set forth by the Ministry of Labor after consultation with the labor unions involved. Noncompliance with these regulations may be penalized by the Ministry. The minimum standards may be improved either by collective bargaining or voluntary action of an employer.

Most Spanish labor legislation has undergone or is expected to undergo substantial revision over the next few years as Spain adjusts to free trade unionism and increased worker demands. Businesses with over 10 employees are now required to have elected labor representatives who are allowed to participate in the administration of the business. The number of labor representatives is proportionate to the firm's total labor force.

In general, Spain has relatively strict laws regarding worker dismissal. Workers may be dismissed for such reasons as insubordination, repeated absenteeism, and deliberate work slowdowns. Employees dismissed for reasons other than those listed before are entitled to indemnity. Workers may not be dismissed due to union membership, race, sex, religion, politics, or social origin.

To dismiss a worker, the local labor delegate must be given an application stating the reasons for the dismissal and anticipated severance pay.

Once this application has been agreed upon, it is sent to the provincial delegate or to the Ministry of Labor in Madrid. If accepted, notification will be given within 30 days.

Minimum rates of pay are set by the Ministry of Labor for each occupational category within an industry or region. The national general minimum daily wage was raised to 759 pesetas in June 1980, but most Spanish workers earn considerably more than the minimum. Rates for women are generally lower than for men in comparable classifications.

The national workweek averages 44 hours for most sectors. Ordinances and agreements set the actual duration of hourly, weekly, monthly, or annual work within this limit, but the number of hours worked in any 1 day may not exceed 9.

The law requires a paid annual vacation of at least 21 work days, but vacations average 1 month for most white-collar workers. In addition, workers are entitled to national holidays, which are paid unless they fall on Sunday.

Bonuses are paid twice yearly (in July and at Christmas) and range from a legal minimum of 21 days' to 1 month's pay. Many companies pay a one-third bonus in lieu of profit sharing or earmark a fixed amount for profit saving.

Spain's extensive social security system includes government-sponsored obligatory insurance covering old age, disability, survivor's health, maternity, unemployment, accident benefits, and family allowance. The entire system is under control of one government agency, the Instituto Nacional de Prevision.

Social security contributions are based on minimum wage rates for each job category. Although the nominal rates of contribution are very high, actual earnings are substantially higher than the minimum wages.

Since 1977, the "national syndicalist" structure (government-controlled labor-management associations) has been dismantled and replaced by a free trade union movement. Altogether there are more than 1,000 trade unions, although four major and four lesser trade unions are the major participants in the labor scene in Spain. Most of the Spanish labor force remains unaffiliated with any union. Due to the large number of unions, companies often are required to deal with more than one union. This can be done by a "mixed" committee representing any or all unions included in the specific enterprise along with representatives of management.

Guidance for Business Visitors

Entrance Requirements

U.S. citizens need valid U.S. passports, but neither visas nor health certificates are required. Business visitors need no additional documentation. Visitors to Spain bearing U.S. diplomatic and official passports are required to obtain Spanish visas.

In general, travelers are permitted to bring in, duty free, clothing and personal effects contained in their luggage and intended for their personal use.

Foreigners living in Spain are considered to be tourists for the first 6 consecutive months of their stay. After this period, foreigners are normally classified as residents unless approval is obtained for extension of their status as tourists. To remain in Spain as residents, foreigners must register with the police authorities in the district in which they will reside and obtain residence permits.

As a resident, a foreigner becomes subject to Spanish income tax laws.

Further information may be obtained from the nearest Consulate of Spain in the United States.

Employment of Aliens

The employment and work regulations pertaining to alien workers in Spain are governed by Decree 1870 of July 27, 1968. The Decree provides that in order to work in Spain, either as an employee or self-employed person, an alien must obtain a work permit in advance.

Work permits are not issued to aliens if Spanish workers signify their desire to obtain the positions applied for and establish their qualifications. Wages paid an alien worker may not in any case be less than those established for Spanish workers in the same job category. If a company employing both aliens and Spanish citizens is authorized to discharge workers, aliens must be discharged first within each occupational category. When a work permit is authorized on the basis of the specialized qualifications of the alien concerned, it may be stipulated that the employer hire a qualified Spaniard to assist the foreign national and train the native for the position in question.

The restriction against hiring aliens when qualified Spaniards are available may be waived for the spouses of Spanish citizens, in the case of foreign technicians who are temporarily in Spain to install or repair imported machinery, and in certain other specified instances.

As a general rule, American companies operating in Spain employ Spanish nationals to the maximum extent possible. These companies employ very few Americans in Spain. They are usually executives with long experience with their companies.

Applications for work permits must be submitted to the Ministry of Labor through the Provincial Labor Office (Delegacion Provincial de Trabajo). When the application is received, notice is publicized so that any Spaniard may have the opportunity to seek the same position for which the alien is applying. If no Spaniard applies within 15 days, it is assumed that no national applicants are available. If the application is approved, the work permit is issued upon payment of a tax that varies from 50 to 1,500 pesetas depending on the estimated amount of earnings. In addition to the work, a residence permit is required.

Foreigners who wish to practice one of the professions in Spain that require, under Spanish law, a university degree must submit their degrees to the Ministry of National Education for evaluation. Foreign degrees and transcripts of school records must be legalized by a Spanish Consul and translated into Spanish before they may be submitted to the Ministry of National Education.

Foreign engineers wishing to practice in Spain must be members of one of the Colleges of Engineers. Only persons having completed training in Spain or whose degree has been validated by the Spanish Government are eligible to become members. Otherwise, they could practice in an unofficial status only, and all work would have to be signed by an authorized engineer.

For specific, current information about work permits, the interested party should write to the Ministry of Labor, Seccion de Trabajo de Extranjeros, Agustin de Betancourt 4, Madrid-3.

Other Information

Foreign Exchange Regulations.—There are no restrictions on the amount of dollars that may be brought into Spain, but the law requires that all foreign exchange be declared at the frontier.

Visitors leaving Spain may depart with no more foreign currency than they declared on entry and no more than 3,000 pesetas in Spanish currency.

Business Etiquette.—Spain's traditional courtesy and hospitality apply to business relations. It is customary to entertain only intimate friends in the home. On the other hand, many public places of entertainment are located in the larger cities, and business visitors should be prepared to reciprocate the courtesies accorded to them.

Commercial Language.—Spanish is the commercial language, although Catalan is used extensively in the Barcelona region and Basque in the Bilbao region. The importance of having trade literature, catalogs, and instructions for the use and servicing of products printed in Spanish cannot be overemphasized. Business cards should be printed in both English and Spanish. Many large commercial houses, however, conduct correspondence in English or French in addition to Spanish.

Interpreters.—Interpreters are usually available for hire on an hourly or daily basis in Spain's larger cities. Names of reputable organizations can be obtained from the American Embassy and Consulates in Spain.

Communications.—Airmail to and from the United States usually takes between 3 and 4 days. Regular surface mail requires from 3 to 4 weeks.

The regular parcel post facilities existing between Spain and the Unites States are not entirely satisfactory. Considerable delays may occur after a package arrives at a Spanish post office for customs inspection and handling.

Local telephone and telegraph service within Spain is good and rates are reasonable. Long-distance telephone and cable services from Spain to the United States and elsewhere are also very good.

Business Hours.—The average work week is 44 hours. Business hours are generally from 9 a.m. to 7 p.m. with a 2-3 hour lunchbreak. Businesses are closed on Sunday. Spanish standard time is 1 hour ahead of Greenwich Mean Time, and 6 hours ahead of U.S. Eastern Standard Time.

Holidays.—Public holidays vary in number according to the locality. Local patron saints' days for each city have been omitted in this listing. Spanish national holidays are: January 1 (New Year's), January 6 (Epiphany), March 19 (St. Joseph's), Holy Thursday (date varies), Holy Friday (date varies), May 1 (Labor Day), Corpus Christi (date varies), July 25 (Santiago, Patron Saint of Spain), August 15 (Assumption), October 12 (Columbus Day), December 8 (Immaculate Conception), and December 25 (Christmas).

Regional and municipal holidays include the following: Easter Monday (date varies), Barcelona; Fair Day (date varies), Sevilla; June 24 (St. John the Baptist and King's Day), Central Government and Barcelona; July 31 (St. Ignatius), Bilbao; August 31 (Semana Grande), Bilbao; September 11 (Catalonia Day), Barcelona and Catalan provinces; September 24 (Our Lady of Mercy), Barcelona; October 9 (Valencia Day), Valencia; November 9 (Nuestra Senora),

Madrid; December 4 (Andalucia Day); December 26 (St. Stephen), Barcelona.

In addition to Spanish legal holidays, many businesses observe other local holidays and feast days.

Source of Economic and Commercial Information

Government Offices and Chambers of Commerce

U.S. Foreign Service Officers in Spain are located at the American Embassy, Serrano 75, Madrid; the American Consulate General, Via Layetana 33, Barcelona; the American Consulate General, Paseo de las Delicias 7, Seville; and the American Consulate, Avda. del Ejercito, 11, Deusto-Bilbao 12. U.S. Consular Agencies exist in Las Palmas, Palma de Mallorca, Valencia, Malaga, and La Coruna. U.S. Foreign Commercial Service Officers are available to brief and assist American firms and individuals visiting Spain.

In the United States, the Spanish Government maintains commercial offices at the following addresses: 2558 Massachusetts Avenue, N.W., Washington, D.C. 20008; Room 5410, 405 Lexington Avenue, New York, New York 10017; Suite 1028, 180 N. Michigan Avenue, Chicago, Illinois 60601; Room 850, 870 Market Street, Flood Building, San Francisco, California 94102; 350 South Figueroa Street, Los Angeles, California 90071; 1840 International Trade Mart, New Orleans, Louisiana 70130; and the World Trade Center, P.O. Box 75258, Dallas, Texas 75258.

The American Chamber of Commerce in Spain, which has more than 2,500 members, has its headquarters at Avda. Diagonal, 477, Barcelona-11; a branch office is located at the Eurobuilding, Padre Damian 23, Madrid-16.

The Spain-U.S. Chamber of Commerce also helps promote trade between the United States and Spain. It is located at 500 Fifth Avenue, New York, New York 10036, with branch offices at 180 North Michigan Avenue, Chicago, Illinois 60601; P.O. Box 452, San Juan, Puerto Rico 00902; and the Los Angeles Trade Center, 350 S. Figueroa Street, Los Angeles, California 90071.

Trade Associations

A list of the principal Spanish trade associations follows. These organizations are similar to trade associations and professional organizations in the United States and generally provide the same types of information and services.

Asociacion Nacional de Confeccion (Apparel)
Av. Jose Antonio, 32
Madrid-13

Asociacion Espanola de Tecnicos de Maquinaria para la Construccion de Obras Publicas (Public works machinery)
Cruz del Sur
Madrid-30

Asociacion Nacional de Quimicos de Espana (Chemicals)
Lagasca, 81
Madrid-1

Asociacion de Investigacion Tecnica de la Industria Papelera Espanola (Paper industry)
Plaza del Marques de Salamanca, 9
Madrid-6

ANIEL (Asociacion Nacional de Industrias Electronicas-Electronic)
General Mola, 74
Madrid-6

UNESID (Union de Empresas Siderurgicas-Iron and steel)
Castello, 128
Madrid-6

SERCOBE (Servicio Tecnico Comercial de Constructores de Bienes de Equipo-Capital goods)
General Mola, 9
Madrid

CONSTRUNAVES (Asociacion de Constructores Navales Espanoles-Shipbuilding)
Orense, 11
Madrid-20

Asociacion de Constructores de Maquinas Herramientas (Machine tools)
Avda. Zarauz
San Sebastian

Federacion Espanola de Armadores de Buques de Pesca (Fishing boats)
Montera, 48
Madrid-14

ASINEL-Asociacion de Investigacion Electrica (Electrical Industry)
Francisco Gervas, 3
Madrid-15

Instituto Espanol del Envase y Embalajes, S.A. (Packaging)
Breton de los Herreros, 57
Madrid-3

Asociacion Nacional de Contratistas de Obras Publicas (Public Works)
Cruz del Sur
Madrid-30

Asociacion Electronica Espanola (Electronics)
Nunez de Balboa
Madrid-1

Consejo Superior de las Camaras Officales de Comercio
(Chambers of Commerce)
Claudio Coello, 19-1
Madrid-1

Publications

The following publications and periodicals are useful sources of economic and commercial information (in English unless otherwise noted):

OECD Economic Surveys-Spain
OECD Publications Center
1700 Penna. Ave., N.W.
Washington, D.C. 20006

Spain-U.S. Trade Bulletin
Spain-U.S. Chamber of Commerce, Inc.
500 Fifth Avenue
New York, N.Y. 10036

Spanish Economic News Service-weekly
Informaciones Economicas, S.A.
Avda. de Jose Antonio, 70
Madrid-13, Spain

*A Guide to Business in Spain-*8 brochures
*Informacion Comercial Espanola-*weekly
(Span. language - Spanish Commercial News)
General Technical Secretariat
Ministry of Economy and Commerce
Madrid, Spain

The New Spain: Business Problems & Opportunities
Investing, Licensing & Trading Conditions Abroad: Spain
Business International
One Dag Hammarskjold Plaza
New York, N.Y. 10017

Report on Spain
Banco Urquijo
One Liberty Plaza
New York, N.Y. 10006

Legal Aspects of Foreign Investments in Spain
Ventura Graces
Banco Industrial de Cataluna
Madrid, Spain

Business Opportunities in Spain for the 1980's
Banco de Santander
375 Park Avenue
New York, N.Y. 10022

Doing Business in Spain
Price Waterhouse & Co.
New York, N.Y.
June 1980

Ernst & Whinney International Series: Spain (1980)
Ernst & Whinney
New York, N.Y.

Espana: Anuario Estadistico
(Sp. Language - Statistical annual)
National Statistical Institute
Madrid, Spain

Area Handbook for Spain
Superintendent of Documents
U.S. Government Printing Office
Washington, D.C. 20402

Quarterly Economic Review—Spain
Economist Intelligence Unit
London, United Kingdom

International Customs Journal—Spain
International Customs Tariff Bureau
Rue de l'Association, 38
B-1000 Brussels, Belgium

Background Notes: Spain
U.S. Department of State
Washington, D.C.
June 1980

Foreign Economic Trends: Spain
U.S. Department of Commerce
Washington, D.C.
June 1981

Business Operations in Spain
Tax Management, Inc.
The Bureau of National Affairs
Washington, D.C.

Directory of Spanish Industry
1980-81
PRODEI
Madrid, Spain

American Firms, Subsidiaries & Affiliates
Operating in Spain
World Trade Academy Press, Inc.
50 East 42nd St.
New York, N.Y. 10017

Market Profile—SPAIN

Foreign Trade

Imports.—Total $34,255 million in 1980; $23,008 million in 1979. Principal products: crude petroleum, organic chemicals, corn, oilseeds, minerals, machinery, and electrical equipment. U.S. is the leading supplier with 13 percent of total. Other major suppliers: West Germany; Saudi Arabia, France, and Iran. Imports from U.S.: $4,471 million in 1980, $3,152 million in 1979. Principal imports from U.S.: soybeans, corn, aircraft, iron and steel scrap, coal, machinery and appliances, and organic chemicals.

Exports.—Total $20,831 million in 1980, $18,191 million in 1979. Principal products: footwear, ships, citrus fruit, canned vegetables, motor vehicles, iron and steel products, chemicals. U.S. is a leading market with a 5-percent share. Other major markets: France, West Germany, United Kingdom, and Italy. To U.S.: $1,103 million in 1980; $1,266 million in 1979. Leading exports to U.S.: footwear, canned vegetables, rubber tires and tubes, iron and steel plates, leather goods, unwrought zinc, and wines.

Trade Policy.—Major share of imports liberalized but some products subject to quotas. Membership negotiations with EEC opened in 1977. Industrial tariff reductions under Tokyo Round. Member of GATT, OECD, and IMF.

Trade Prospects.—Specific product groups with good sales potential: electronic components, computers and peripherals, electrical power equipment, telecommunications equipment, industrial controls, metalworking equipment, medical instruments, analytical instruments, food processing and packaging equipment, and electronics industry production and test equipment.

Foreign Investment

Direct U.S. investment estimated at $2.4 billion end of 1979. Principal areas: petroleum, automobile industry, chemicals, foodstuffs, retail and wholesale trade, and electrical machinery. Liberal foreign investment code. No tax agreement with the United States.

Finance

Currency. —Peseta; floating, approximately 98 pesetas = $1 (July 21, 1981).

Domestic Credit and Investment.—Bank loans available for short and medium terms. Private bank credit has been expanding rapidly. Stock exchanges in Madrid, Barcelona, and Bilbao.

Balance of Payments. —In 1980, $5,960 million deficit; in 1979, $1,182 million surplus. Estimated foreign exchange reserves, $12.4 billion (November 1980).

Central Government Budget.—Expenditures and revenue in 1979 estimated at 1.7 trillion pesetas. Emphasis on unemployment, education, health, social security, and pensions.

Economy

Industry has excellent long-term records, but agriculture still important. GDP at current prices $227 billion in 1980 ($197 billion in 1979). Agriculture accounted for 8 percent of GDP, industry and construction 35 percent, and services 52 percent (1978 data). Real GDP averaged 6 percent growth between 1970-75, but has since significantly declined: 1980, 1.7 percent (est.); 1979, 0.6 percent. Per capita GDP in 1980, $5,600.

Agriculture.—Employs 20 percent of working population and furnishes 20 percent of exports. There is a great need for modern equipment and technology. Principal crops: cereals, fruits, vegetables, olives, and wine.

Industry.—Rapid development since 1959 with help of foreign capital. Principal industries: processed foods, textiles, footwear, petrochemicals, steel automobiles, consumer goods, and shipbuilding. Production Index (July 1980) 132; 1979, 130 (1972=100).

Commerce.—Inflation of major concern. Cost of living in 1980 rose 15 percent. Numerous small- and medium-size retail establishments. Department stores and supermarkets increasing in urban areas.

Tourism.—Of major importance to balance of payments. Tourist earnings from overseas visitors totaled $5.6 billion in 1979.

Natural Resources

Land.—196,607 square miles. Largely mountainous or flat plains.

Climate.—Extremely variable. Damp and cool in North, hot and dry in South.

Minerals.—Of growing importance. Coal, iron, zinc, copper, and potash are mined. Large imports of coal.

Forestry.—Limited resources. Large producer of cork. Extensive reforestation plans.

Fisheries.—Catch in 1978 1.3 million metric tons.

Population

Size.—37.8 million; annual growth, about 1.2 percent. Madrid, capital, 3.5 million; Barcelona, 2 million; Valencia, 700,000; Sevilla, 560,000.

Languages.—Spanish (official), Catalan, and Basque. English and French also used in business.

Education.—97 percent literate; compulsory school to age 14.

Labor.—More than 13.2 million workers; skilled labor increasingly available; unemployment about 12 percent (1980); wages rising rapidly in response to inflation. Wage increases limited.

Marketing in Sri Lanka

Contents

Report Revised November 1982

Sri Lanka

- ⊛ National capital
- Railroad
- Road
- ✝ International airport

40 Kilometers
40 Miles

India

Tondi
Palk Strait
Kankesanturai
Point Pedro
Jaffna
Delft Island
Palk Bay
Dhanushkodi
Mankulam
Mullaittivu
Mannar
Pulmoddai
Vavuniya
Bay of Bengal
Gulf of Mannar
Trincomalee
Anuradhapura
Kalpitiya
Polonnaruwa
Puttalam
Maho
Batticaloa
Kurunegala
Matale
Kandy
Ampara
Gal Oya
Negombo
Kegalla
Nuwara Eliya
Badulla
Colombo
Moneragala
Pottuvil
Moratuwa
Ratnapura
Opanake
Kalutara
Galle
Hambantota
Matara

Indian Ocean

2229

The Sri Lankan Market

Background

A rarity among developing countries, Sri Lanka enjoys a vibrant, functioning democracy with an educated, politically aware electorate. Formerly known as Ceylon, the island achieved independence from Great Britain in 1948, and since then has seen an unbroken string of democratically elected governments. Partly as a result of the need to respond to the wishes of the electorate, successive governments—regardless of party—until 1977 pursued consumption and welfare-oriented policies which contributed to an exceptionally high physical quality-of-life rating, with a life expectancy of close to 70 years, literacy rate above 80 percent, and extensive education and medical care facilities. These policies did not, however, produce much economic growth. Problems related to economic stagnation, including unemployment in the range of 24 percent, became increasingly evident in the early and middle 1970's.

The present United National Party (UNP) Government was swept into office in 1977 with a mandate to get the economy moving again. It immediately set about rechannelling resources from consumer subsidies and other welfare programs into growth-oriented capital expenditures, notably the accelerated Mahaweli hydroelectric/irrigation/resettlement project. Price controls and import barriers were lifted and greater incentives given to private entrepreneurs.

The results have been quite striking. Real gross national product (GNP) growth since 1977 has averaged over 6 percent, in contrast to the 3 percent average recorded during 1970–77. Unemployment, according to census figures, has been reduced from 24 to 15 percent. Foreign trade—imports and exports combined—expanded fivefold between 1976 and 1980. However, the picture has not been uniformly favorable. High-growth policies, combined with the release of pent-up demand from earlier years, higher oil prices, and other factors, have pushed the inflation rate up to the 20–40 percent range, have contributed to serious trade deficits, and have increased the economy's reliance on foreign assistance. The public perception of how the economy has fared on balance and whether Sri Lankans are better off under the present free-market, open economy were the key issues in the October 20, 1982 presidential election, which returned President J. R. Jayewardene to office. Following the presidential election, the Government of Sri Lanka announced that it would seek a referendum to continue the present parliament, rather than to schedule a general election. The referendum is scheduled for December 22, 1982.

The Economy

Sri Lanka's gross domestic product (GDP) grew to Rs. 78.5 billion (about $4 billion) in 1981 (see table 1). Assuming a population of 14.85 million (1981 census figures), this amounts to a per capita income in the $265 range.

Taking a closer look at the composition of Sri Lanka's GDP, the services sector predominates, with 44 percent of total GDP in 1981; in part this reflects the exceptionally dominant role played by the government budget. Next comes agriculture, with about 28 percent. Within the agricultural sector, the traditional plantation crops—tea, rubber, and coconuts—continue to play an important role, accounting for some 14 percent of GDP. Tea and rubber are Sri Lanka's major traditional export earners, though rubber has declined in relative importance recently due to poor world market conditions. Coconut plantations occupy more land than any other tree crop, but coconuts are mostly for domestic consumption. Rice output has expanded considerably in recent years. Sri Lanka is also a major producer and exporter of certain spices, most notably cinnamon.

Industry accounts for only 18 percent of GDP, reflecting the lack of development of that sector of the economy. With the exception of one steel mill and several cement plants, there is little heavy industry in the country. The size of the market and income levels have not permitted sufficiently large economies of scale. There is some variety in light industry, including soaps, paints, foodstuffs, drugs, pharmaceuticals, leather goods, and light engineering industries. Again, most are small scale by world standards.

The present Government's efforts to stimulate investment has borne some fruit. An Investment Promotion Zone (IPZ) set up near Colombo in 1978, already has employed some 22,000 workers in 50 factories. More than three-fourths of the

IPZ's workers are involved in garment manufacture, as foreign investors took advantage of investment and tax incentives to set up factories using the country's inexpensive, educable labor force. Average wages in the zone are about $1 per day.

In 1979, the Greater Colombo Economic Commission (GCEC), which administers the IPZ, signed agreements for 37 new projects with a total investment of $116 million. In 1980, 48 agreements worth $191 million were signed. As the emphasis on garment industries declined, the number of new projects signed in 1981 was only 17. Despite the leveling off of new entrants into the zone, annual exports from these plants were projected at $60 million, almost double the $32 million projected for projects signed the previous year.

Outside the IPZ, foreign investments are the responsibility of the Foreign Investment Advisory Committee (FIAC), an interagency group. In 1979, the FIAC approved 113 projects with an investment of $110 million; in 1980, it approved 137 projects worth $217 million; and in 1981, 151 projects worth $354 million.

Few of these investments are from American companies. There is only one 100-percent American-owned firm in the IPZ, although two electronics firms have signed agreements to build plants and one of these has now broken ground for plant construction. Of the 250 projects approved by the FIAC in 1979 and 1980, only 14 were American. The largest number came from the United Kingdom (33), Hong Kong (29), Singapore and India (21 each), and West Germany (20). Total American investment at the end of 1981 was an estimated $7 million, though that figure is expected to grow severalfold in the next few years.

A large portion of new investment has gone into the tourist industry. Exploiting Sri Lanka's climate, beach, and historical resources has been one of the present Government's major thrusts. In 1981, some 370,000 tourists visited Sri Lanka, a hefty increase over the previous year's 322,000 and 1979's 250,000. With an average stay of more than 10 days, the foreign exchange inflow is not insignificant, and the industry was reportedly the third largest foreign exchange earner in 1981.

In 1981, the construction industry accounted for 9 percent of GDP. The Government's two most important development projects account for a large proportion of this sector. The biggest is the Accelerated Mahaweli Project, a multibillion dollar irrigation and hydroelectric project consisting of several dams and associated

Table 1.—KEY ECONOMIC INDICATORS

(Money values in millions of rupees except where noted)

	1980	1981	% Change	(Proj.)[1] 1982
Production and Investment				
GDP at Current Prices	62,246	78,506	26.1	102,000
GNP at Current Prices	61,814	76,831	24.3	99,500
Resident Population (Thousands)	14,738	14,988	1.7	15,242
Per Capita GNP at Current Prices (Rs.)	4,194	5,126	22.2	6,528
GNP at Constant (1970) Prices	19,456	20,268	4.2	21,180
Real GNP Growth Rate (%)	5.6	4.2	-	4.5
Gross Fixed Capital Formation	20,845	24,528	17.7	30,660
Labor, Employment, and Wages				
Labor Force (Millions)	5.6	5.7	2.2	5.8
Unemployment (%)	15.6	15.3	-	15.0
Minimum Wage Rates (% Growth)				
Agriculture	24.7	-0.2	-	n.a.
Industry and Commerce	21.7	12.7	-	n.a.
Government	11.2	14.6	-	n.a.
Money and Prices				
M1 Growth Rate (%)	29	6	-	25
M2 Growth Rate (%)	32	23	-	30
Cost of Living Index (% Growth)	38	24	-	25
Wholesale Price Index (% Growth)	34	17	-	20
Commercial Loan Interest Rates (%)	10-30	11-32	-	n.a.
Government Accounts				
Expenditures	28,627	28,582	0	39,629
of which Mahaweli investment	(3,416)	(3,750)	(9.8)	(7,217)
Revenue	13,262	15,259	15	19,205
Budget Deficit	-15,365	-13,323	-13	-20,424
Balance of Payments ($ Million)				
Exports, f.o.b.	1,065	1,061	0	1,124
U.S. Share	(116)	(146)	26	(155)
Imports, c.i.f.	2,052	1,904	-7	2,261
U.S. Share	(90)	(129)	43	(153)
Trade Balance	-987	-843	15	-1,137
Current Account				
Balance	-660	-635	4	-866
Tourist Receipts	111	130	17	140
Private Remittances	152	229	51	280
Foreign Aid Commitments	639	794	24	668
Gross External Assets (Yearend)	376	449	19	400
External Debt (Yearend)	1,435	1,695	18	2,100
Debt Service Ratio [2]	12.4	13.4	-	18
Terms of Trade (1978 = 100)	58	46	-	43

Main Imports From U.S. (1981): Wheat and Meslin ($62.0 m.), Aircraft and Parts ($14.9 m.), Earthmoving Equipment ($3.7 m.).

[1] GSL and Embassy projections.
[2] Ratio of all public/commercial debt services payments, including IMF repurchases, to exports of goods and services.

Note: Exchange rates, SL rupees per U.S. dollar:

	1980	1981
Yearend	18.00	20.55
Annual average	16.53	19.25

Sources: Central Bank Annual Report, 1981; Public Investment, 1982–86.

irrigation canals and civil works. Designed to achieve in 6 years what the previous government said would take 30 years, the project has put a tremendous strain on the country's physical and financial resources. Although largely financed by aid from multilateral donors and Western countries, a large proportion of the Government's domestic resources are involved as well. For example, in 1982 the Mahaweli project will take close to one half of the Government's entire capital budget.

The second large project is the Government's housing program. When it took office the Government promised to build 100,000 houses, a feat unparalleled in the country's history. The target may yet be met by 1983, but only because the Government has switched from direct construction to "aided self-help," i.e., providing materials and some technical assistance to homeowners who are then supposed to supply the labor for their own houses.

While boosting the construction industry's share of GDP, both projects have strained resources and caused construction industry material and labor costs to grow faster than general inflation. The situation has been exacerbated by the outflow of skilled construction workers to greener pastures in the Middle East, where, even after inflation in Sri Lanka is taken into account, salaries are four to six times higher than domestic wage scales.

Infrastructure

Poor infrastructure is one of the major bottlenecks still inhibiting growth in Sri Lanka. Present power, communications, and transport systems are badly outdated, and the unforeseen growth generated by the present Government's new policies has severely strained what little is available.

Electric Power.—Electric power is the number one infrastructure problem. Since 1977, demand has grown by an average of 15 percent, far above projections. Two-thirds of the country's 501 megawatt installed capacity is hydroelectric, dependent on good rainfall. Poor rains in 1979 and 1980 meant nationwide power cuts during the dry season of from 4 to 8 hours a day.

New power from the Mahaweli project dams will bring relief, but the first of these units will not come on-stream until 1984. To provide interim relief, the Government has purchased six gas turbines with a combined capacity of 120 megawatts in addition to the 50 megawatts of thermal power already available. These units have helped, but they are expensive to run and can only supplement hydroelectric power production, not replace it. There will be no real relief until the Mahaweli dams start generating power.

Telecommunications.—The antiquated telecommunications system has also hampered development. Although the Government has improved international telecommunications in the past few years, with new electronic telex and direct dialing telephone exchanges using a satellite station, domestic communications remain difficult. Within the greater Colombo area, where business and government are concentrated, the antiquated system is overloaded and suffers frequent breakdowns. Outside of Colombo the situation is often worse. Most towns are not yet connected by direct dialing facilities. A significant portion of the Government's resources are being invested in improving the situation. World Bank and French and Japanese aid have also been enlisted, but growing demand seems to continue to outstrip improvements.

Transportation.—A similar situation exists in transportation. International facilities are generally good and improving. Many international airlines now serve Colombo, and the Port of Colombo, which handles more than 90 percent of the country's seaborne trade, has been reorganized and improved. A new container terminal and berth is also being built with Japanese aid. Turnaround time for container vessels is less than 24 hours, and the port may now be the most efficient in South Asia.

Shipping from U.S. Atlantic and Gulf ports to Sri Lanka (Colombo) takes about 40 days; from the Pacific Coast, about 34 days. Lines regularly serving U.S.-Sri Lanka routes include American President Lines, Hoegh Lines, Scindia Steam Navigation, Co., Ltd., and Waterman-Isthmian Line. In addition, The Hellenic Line and the Shipping Corporation of India (S.C.I.) offer service "on inducement," i.e., if the cargo to be shipped is sufficiently large.

Domestic travel, however, is difficult. Although most major roads are paved, the paving has not held up well, and the roads are not wide. Public road and rail transportation equipment is not in good repair. In 1980, the Government allowed private buses to operate after a lapse of more than 20 years, helping to meet the growing demand that was straining public resources.

Population and Labor Force

According to the 1981 census, Sri Lanka's population was 14.85 million people. The growth rate for the previous decade averaged 1.7 percent per year, relatively low for a developing nation. High literacy is one factor in reducing birth rates, and in 1981 literacy reached an estimated 86.5 percent, an increase from 1971's 78.5 percent.

The decline in the birth rate is reflected in the decline in the proportion of the population in the 0–14 age group from 39 percent in 1971 to 35 percent in 1981. However, previous higher birth rates have meant an increase in the 15–64 age group from 57 percent of the population to 60 percent.

This has meant increasing numbers of new entrants to the labor market and increasing problems in generating new jobs. The present Government has made employment creation a key goal and claims to have reduced the unemployment rate from 24 percent in 1977 to less than 15 percent by 1981. However, labor statistics are not considered to be very accurate.

One way the Government has reduced the unemployment problem has been the export of labor. The 1978 constitution made travel a right, and by 1981 an estimated 70,000 Sri Lankans were working in the Middle East alone, remitting more than $200 million in foreign exchange. To help ease the unemployment situation even further, President Jayewardene announced in early 1982 that he hoped to find 100,000 more jobs for Sri Lankans in the Middle East by the end of the year. Although many of those emigrating are unskilled, a significant number are managers and technicians, particularly in the building trades and accounting and engineering professions. Their departure has created shortages, sometimes severe, in the domestic economy. However, the Government has as yet made no move to restrict the outflow, publicly stating that travel is a citizen's right and that the country needs the foreign exchange.

Economic Assistance

Most of the Sri Lankan Government's capital budget (i.e., public investment) is financed by foreign aid, and much of the country's growth under the present government can be attributed to the success it has had attracting foreign assistance. New aid commitments amounted to $566 million in 1979, $642 million in 1980, and $865 million in 1981. The Government projects about the same level in 1982 as in 1981. Almost all aid comes from either the multilateral development banks or Western countries, as well as Japan.

The United States has been one of the largest donors. Assistance in (fiscal year) 1980 totaled $63 million; in 1981, $95.3 million; and 1982 assistance is expected to reach $97 million. Most U.S. aid is project assistance, including a part of the Mahaweli project. More than 20 percent consists of concessional food sales under the PL 480 program, and another 25 percent is in the form of housing investment guarantees.

Other U.S. aid-related agencies are also active in Sri Lanka. By the end of 1981, U.S. Export-Import Bank (Eximbank) exposure totaled $60 million, including financing guarantees for two new aircraft and direct financing for a new luxury hotel. Investments in Sri Lanka are eligible for insurance coverage for expropriation and inconvertibility through the Overseas Private Investment Corporation (OPIC), which already insures several million dollars worth of investments in the country. The U.S. Agency for International Development has established a small project to study ways in which foreign investment in Sri Lanka might be facilitated as a means of promoting the development process.

Trade

Imports.—As part of its policy of opening up the economy, the present Government lifted most import restrictions when it took office in 1977. At the same time, however, it "rationalized" the previous government's two-tier exchange rate and set the dollar equal to 16 Sri Lanka rupees, in effect devaluing from an average Rs. 12 rate under the two-tier system.

Nevertheless, loosening restraints brought a massive surge of imports. In 1977, imports were valued at Rs. 6.1 billion.* In 1978, the first full year under the new devalued exchange rate, imports increased to Rs. 14.7 billion.* As table 2 shows, they increased to Rs. 22.5 billion in 1979 and Rs. 33.9 billion in 1980. However, an austerity budget in 1981 limited import growth in rupee terms to Rs. 35.3 billion. With depreciation of the rupee from an average rate of 16.65 in 1980 to 19.35 in 1981 the net effect was a decline in imports in dollar terms.

As table 2 indicates, Saudi Arabia is the leading supplier, reflecting Sri Lanka's dependence on Saudi oil since the beginning of the Iran-Iraq war. Second in importance is Japan. The United

---

*Average 1977 and 1978 exchange rates were as follows.
1977—Jan. 1-Nov. 15: Rs. 7.89 = US$1. Nov. 16-Dec. 31: Rs. 15.76 = US$1. (There was a big devaluation in 1977. Average for year as a whole was Rs. 9.15 = US$1.)
1978—Rs. 15.61 = US$1.

States was the third largest supplier, and Iran, despite the war, was fourth in 1981.

Despite the wide variety of consumer items now available on Sri Lankan retail shelves, most imports have either been primary or intermediate goods or basic foodstuffs (table 3). Oil and oil products lead the list, not surprisingly since no oil has yet been discovered in the country. Sec-

Table 2.—FOREIGN TRADE BY COUNTRY

(Rupees Million)

	1979	1980	1981
Exports (f.o.b.) to:			
United States	1,585	1,925	2,806
United Kingdom	1,244	1,278	1,291
Pakistan	686	568	1,074
Japan	1,037	552	686
Saudi Arabia	449	607	632
Egypt	432	567	623
Iraq	465	613	588
India	194	568	564
Communist Countries	1,631	1,582	1,636
Other	7,518	9,034	10,685
Total Exports	15,241	17,294	20,585
Imports (c.i.f.) from:			
Saudi Arabia	1,570	3,527	5,247
Japan	3,005	4,302	4,970
United States	1,211	1,493	2,489
Iran	740	1,814	2,350
United Kingdom	2,015	3,206	2,139
Singapore	1,359	1,520	1,905
India	2,334	1,594	1,460
France	482	1,310	770
Iraq	704	2,082	6
Communist Countries	1,716	1,300	1,010
Other	7,405	11,794	12,905
Total Imports	22,541	33,942	35,251

Note: Average Monthly Exchange Rate: 1979, $1 = 15.57 SL rupees; 1980, $1 = 16.65 SL rupees; 1981, $1 = 19.35 SL rupees.
Source: External Trade Statistics, Sri Lanka Customs.

Table 3.—FOREIGN TRADE BY COMMODITY

(Rupees Million)

	1979	1980	1981
Exports (f.o.b.)			
Tea	5,722	6,170	6,444
Petroleum Products	1,926	2,999	3,375
Textiles & Garments	1,108	1,814	3,000
Rubber	2,491	2,590	2,826
Coconut	1,699	1,234	1,438
Minor Agricultural Products	825	840	1,301
Gems	490	458	634
Other	980	1,189	1,498
Total Exports	15,241	17,294	20,585
Imports (c.i.f.)			
Petroleum	3,912	8,090	8,627
Machinery & Equipment	2,900	4,212	3,876
Sugar	936	2,026	2,826
Textiles & Garments	1,536	1,721	2,334
Transport Equipment	1,615	2,421	2,229
Fertilizer	664	1,339	1,202
Rice	891	882	992
Other	10,087	13,251	13,165
Total Imports	22,541	33,942	35,251

Note: Average Monthly Exchange Rate: 1979, $1 = 15.57 SL rupees; 1980, $1 = 16.65 SL rupees; 1981, $1 = 19.35 rupees.
Source: External Trade Statistics, Sri Lanka Customs

ond is machinery and equipment and third is sugar. Sri Lanka produces less than 20 percent of its sugar needs. Other imports include wheat grain; in 1981, Sri Lanka imported 530,000 metric tons of wheat, almost all from the United States and Australia.

Exports.—The large jump in imports to satisfy demand pent up under the previous government's restrictions has not been matched by a concomitant increase in exports, and a large balance-of-trade deficit has opened up in the past few years. In 1977, a particularly good year for tea prices, exports valued at Rs. 6.6 billion exceeded imports by Rs. 500 million. However, in the 3 succeeding years there were trade deficits of Rs. 1.5 billion, Rs. 7.3 billion, and Rs. 16.6 billion respectively. In 1980, exports amounted to slightly over 50 percent of imports (table 3).

The jump in imports was partially fueled by heavy government deficit spending, which leveled off considerably in the austerity budget of 1981. Exports increased 19 percent to Rs. 20.6 billion in rupee terms (unchanged in dollar terms), but imports grew less than 4 percent in rupee terms and actually declined 7 percent in dollar terms. Exports reached 58 percent of imports in 1981.

As table 3 shows, tea remains by far the largest single source of export earnings. Petroleum products, largely aviation and bunker fuels and naphtha, rank second and rubber ranks third. However, textiles and garments were fourth in 1981 and, given the growth in this sector, may well soon replace rubber as the number three export earner.

Invisibles, not shown in the table, have become important factors in the economy as well. In terms of foreign exchange earnings, private remittances from abroad at Rs. 4.4 billion were ahead of everything except tea, and earnings from tourism ranked fifth behind textiles and garments.

Trade with the United States.—The United States is the only one of Sri Lanka's major trading partners with which it runs a trade surplus. As table 4 indicates, although the surplus has been of varying sizes in 1979–81, the balance of trade has been consistently in Sri Lanka's favor.

Although Sri Lanka normally ranks among the top two or three suppliers of tea to the U.S. market, tea is no longer its major export to the United States. Garments are by far the largest item, dating from the Government's opening the

Table 4.—TRADE WITH THE UNITED STATES

(Rupees Million)

Product	1979	1980	1981
Exports to U.S.			
Garments	590	968	1,550
Tea	330	396	453
Rubber	119	277	150
Minor Agricultural Products	48	41	48
Gems	40	56	37
Other	458	187	568
Total Exports to U.S.	1,585	1,925	2,806
Imports from U.S.			
Wheat and Meslin	95	452	1,194
Aircraft and Parts	13	75	286
Earthmoving Equipment	23	120	72
Cereal Flour	374	72	21
Fertilizer	117	92	5
Other	589	682	911
Total Imports from U.S.	1,211	1,493	2,489

Note: Average Monthly Exchange Rate: 1979, $1=15.57 SL rupees; 1980, $1=16.65 SL rupees; 1981, $1=19.35 SL rupees.

Source: External Trade Statistics, Sri Lanka Customs

economy to foreign investment. Despite the existence of U.S. import quotas, garments are likely to remain Sri Lanka's most important export to the United States as the local industry expands into other categories and quota limits grow as provided for in the quota agreement.

Tea is likely to remain second, as U.S. demand generally remains steady. Despite a depressed world market and a U.S. automobile industry in decline, rubber should remain third for the foreseeable future.

In recent years, the most important U.S. export to Sri Lanka has been wheat and wheat flour. In 1980, a new flour mill was opened with capacity sufficient to handle all of the country's needs. This means that flour will no longer be imported, only wheat grain. Although a large proportion of U.S. sales is under the government-to-government PL 480 aid program, most U.S. wheat sales are made on commercial terms, in competition with Australia.

Aircraft and related parts are becoming increasingly important imports. The new government-owned flag carrier, Air Lanka, operates an entirely American fleet of Lockheed Tristars and a Boeing 737. Several small American private aircraft have also been imported in the past 2 years.

Construction equipment was a major import from the United States in 1980, a boom year for the construction industry. The boom ended with the austerity budget of 1981.

U.S. exports of fertilizer have been significant in the past few years, but they declined precipitously in 1981 in the face of severe competition.

For information on U.S. export opportunities, see the "Best Export Prospects for U.S. Firms" section.

Foreign Trade Outlook.—Despite the huge balance-of-trade deficits of recent years, the Government shows no signs of changing its policy of open trade. Instead, it has increased taxes on imports by levying the "Business Turnover Tax" (BTT), i.e., a sales tax, on almost all imports and allowing the rupee to depreciate from 16 to the U.S. dollar in 1977, to almost 21 to the dollar by the beginning of 1982.

A projection by the Sri Lankan Ministry of Finance shows imports and exports increasing by 72 percent and 73 percent respectively in the 5 years from 1981 to 1986. Table 5 shows the top six import and export items in 1981 and 1986, their value in each year and the percentage increase during the 5-year period.

Petroleum and petroleum products will remain the major import, but intermediate goods, including industrial processing inputs, will move up to second place. Concomitantly industrial goods are forecast to become the largest export item, surpassing tea and petroleum products. Imports of investment goods and most consumer goods, including wheat, will increase. Sugar imports are forecast to decrease as new domestic sugar projects come on-stream. Similarly, rice imports are expected to decline gradually to near zero by the mid-1980's as Sri Lanka approaches self-sufficiency in paddy production.

Tea, while remaining an important export, is expected to slip to second place. The largest jump in exports after industrial goods is projected to be in coconut, with "minor agricultural products," e.g., spices, a not-too-distant fifth. Only rubber exports are forecast to decline.

TABLE 5.—TRADE GROWTH 1981–86

(US $ Millions)

Product:	1981 Position/ Value	1986 Position/ Value	Per cent Change
Imports			
Petroleum	1/581	1/1091	+88
Other Intermediate goods	3/413	2/914	+121
Investment goods	2/425	3/670	+58
Other Consumer goods	4/160	4/280	+75
Wheat	6/100	5/188	+88
Sugar	5/120	6/111	–8
Exports			
Industrial goods	2/183	1/490	+268
Tea	1/361	2/396	+10
Petroleum Products	2/183	3/323	+77
Coconut	6/65	4/278	+427
Minor Agricultural Prods.	5/96	5/211	+220
Rubber	4/159	6/140	–12

Source: Ministry of Finance and Planning.

The presidential election of October 20, 1982, returned President J. R. Jayewardene, the UNP candidate, to office for 6 years. As noted above, the Government of Sri Lanka announced shortly thereafter that it would seek a referendum to continue the present parliament rather than to schedule a general election; the referendum is scheduled for December 22, 1982. It is reasonable to expect that the United National Party would continue its open trade policy. The policies of the leading opposition party, the Sri Lanka Freedom Party, in its past terms of office (most recently from 1971–77), have been more protectionist—oriented toward import substitution, import licensing, and foreign exchange controls.

Best Export Prospects for U.S. Firms

Based on economic trends and estimates of U.S. competitiveness, there are several areas where near-term prospects for U.S. exports should be good, even if American penetration to date has been poor. Success will require aggressive marketing and appropriate local agents or distributors.

Chemicals.—Chemicals, especially fertilizer, are the most promising area in terms of size. Fertilizer imports alone have grown from $16 million in 1978 to $63 million in 1981, despite elimination of most government subsidies. A urea factory, commissioned in 1981, uses naphtha as a feedstock, making its output more expensive than imported urea made with natural gas. Although Sri Lanka has phosphate deposits, they are not yet developed, and phosphate fertilizers and blends will continue to be imported for some time. Most fertilizer is bought by the Government's Ceylon Fertilizer Corporation through public tenders. American performance to date has not been particularly good, but aggressive marketing could help.

Other chemicals, especially artificial resins and plastics, are good prospects as well. The plastics and packaging industries in Sri Lanka are still in their infancies, and market size does not encourage producing raw materials locally. Imports therefore will continue to increase. In 1981, imports were $16 million, almost double 1978 levels. Some U.S. penetration has already been made in polyethylene and polyvinylchloride. Pharmaceutical imports continue to grow. While not expanding rapidly, the market for other chemicals, especially inorganic products, remains substantial. In 1981, imports were $29 million, compared to $25 million in 1978.

Power Generation and Transmission Equipment.—This equipment is the second best prospect for U.S. exporters. Rapid economic growth has strained existing hydroelectric capacity, forcing the Government, which owns the monopoly public utility, the Ceylon Electricity Board, to import gas turbines and impose occasional power cuts. New hydroelectric capacity is being built, but it will not come on-stream until 1984 and beyond. At present growth rates, even this new capacity will need to be supplemented by large-scale thermal units going into operation by 1990. In addition, the Government is continuing a major rural electrification project. In the private sector, there is a growing market for standby power units. This is the only product line where U.S. goods have to date done well, supplying 20 percent of imports in 1981. In 1981, imports of $40 million were almost triple 1979's $14 million.

Construction Equipment.—The third best prospect is construction equipment. With imports severely restricted and the construction industry stagnant under the previous government, the last few years have seen the release of pent-up demand and large increases in construction equipment imports. The United States has made some headway, especially in bulldozers, where it ranks second to Japan. Although imports declined in 1981, the outlook for the next few years should be good. A government projection under Ministry of Finance and Planning predicts that the construction industry will be the fastest growing sector of the economy between 1981 and 1986, increasing at an 11 percent annual real rate. In 1979, imports were valued at $18 million; 1980, at $35 million; and 1981, at $25 million.

Telecommunications.—Along with electricity, telecommunications remains a major bottleneck to increased growth and development, and telecommunications equipment should be a good export prospect for many years to come. Public telecommunications are a government monopoly, although in recent years the Government has allowed private service bureaus and mobile telephone services to be established. The existing national system is antiquated, unwieldy and in poor condition, and will require extensive expenditures in the near and long term. Although Japanese suppliers dominate the market, American products could be competitive in quality and prices. Since imports fluctuate as projects are completed, 1979 imports were $16 million, but 1981 imports were only $10 million.

Hotel and Restaurant Equipment.—Tourism is one of the Government's prime areas for exploitation, and tourist arrivals have more than doubled since the present Government took office, reaching 370,000 in 1981. The Government's target is 500,000 visitors annually. Not only are more hotels being built, but the Government has issued foreign investment permits for 37 new restaurants, primarily in the Colombo area. All this means that the market for hotel and restaurant equipment, although relatively small (less than $16 million in 1981), is growing and will continue to do so. American products have not yet made much impact, but local interest is increasing.

Automated Data Processing and Business Equipment.—Automated data processing and business equipment, the smallest best prospect category, may be the fastest growing. Although there are numbers of educated unemployed in the country, there is a critical shortage of clerical staff, especially stenographers and secretaries, fluent in English. This has boosted interest in word processing equipment as well as computers, and the United States is the top supplier in this field. In 1981, imports were less than $7 million, but this was one-third more than in 1979. U.S. products are already establishing a good reputation, and the market is only beginning. Imports, valued at $6 million in 1979, reached $8 million in 1981.

Trade Policy and Trade Regulations

General Information

Although Sri Lanka is a member of the British Commonwealth, it is a republic, and Commonwealth member nations receive no special preferences in terms of imports or customs duties. Sri Lanka is not a member of any other trade or customs grouping. In 1981, Sri Lanka applied for membership in the Association of South East Asian Nations (ASEAN), but ASEAN has yet to take action on Sri Lanka's application.

Since 1977, as part of the Government's decision to open up the economy, import policies and procedures have been greatly liberalized, and importing made significantly easier (see "Import Procedures" section).

U.S. trade with Sri Lanka is affected by certain policy measures of the U.S. Government. The U.S. Generalized System of Preferences (GSP) and the U.S. bilateral textile agreement with Sri Lanka (covered on pages 9 and 10) are those of most interest to U.S. traders.

Duties and Taxes on Imports

The Sri Lanka Customs Tariff is based on the Brussels Tariff Nomenclature (BTN) system, also known as CCCN (Customs Cooperative Council Nomenclature). Standard rates of duty are basically ad valorem and are calculated on the c.i.f. value.

Tariff rates range from 0 percent (duty free), e.g. on pharmaceuticals, to 300 percent, e.g., on cigarettes. Most duties are in the 5 to 100 percent range. Duties on investment and other capital goods, intermediate goods, and raw materials are generally 25 percent or less, while most consumer and luxury goods, e.g. color televisions and air conditioners, are assessed at between 50 to 100 percent.

The Government offers a duty rebate for imported raw materials which have been used in the manufacture of commodities exported from Sri Lanka. The rate of rebate, calculated on an f.o.b. basis, ranges from 2 to 105 percent.

In October 1981, the Government revised import duties on a number of goods listed under the Revenue Protection Ordinance in order to encourage local production. Certain items, such as black and white television receiving sets, which were subject to 12½ percent duty can now be imported into the country free of duty if these sets are imported in completely knocked down condition.

As of November 1981, a Business Turnover Tax (BTT) is collected in addition to import duties. Under the 1982 budget, the BTT has a three-tier basic rate structure (2, 5, and 10 percent) and is levied on most imports as well as domestic products, with a few stated exceptions. In the case of imports, the tax is calculated on the basis of c.i.f. value. The 2 percent tax is applicable to (a) agricultural inputs, (b) building materials, (c) food items, (d) fishing boats and nets, (e) petroleum and petroleum products, and (f) pharmaceuticals. The 5 percent rate applies to almost all other items. Some items are taxed above the 10 percent rate, e.g. cigarettes and tobacco, which are taxed at 35 percent. The excise duty on liquor was increased appreciably after the 1981 budget.

Information regarding Sri Lankan duties applicable to specific products may be obtained free of charge from the Office of International Economic Policy, U.S. Department of Commerce, Washington, D.C. 20230; or from any Department of Commerce District Office. Inquiries should contain a complete product description, including BTN (CCCN), SITC, or U.S. Schedule E Export Commodity numbers.

Import Procedures

The Special Import License (S.I.L.) system introduced in 1977 promoted the importation of consumer and certain capital goods. Changes and amendments during each fiscal year are announced in the *Government Gazette*. Under the S.I.L. system, items can be imported without specific permission from the Controller of Imports and Exports, provided the goods fall within the 144 products in the S.I.L. list, which covers most imports. Certain items—e.g. pharmaceuticals, textiles and automobiles—can only be imported under specific licenses obtained from the Controller of Imports and Exports. Licenses are normally issued on a c.i.f. basis. Any variation in the value or quantity of imports is not usually permitted except for goods being imported under the S.I.L. system. No letters of credit can be established nor can any other form of remittance be made without a valid import license for items that require a license.

S.I.L. No. 1 of 1977 came into effect in November 1977 and clearly stated that all imports should be through letters of credit valid for shipment for a period not exceeding 180 days, except with the authority of the Controller of Exchange. The importer must furnish the Controller of Imports and Exports a copy of the application made to the bank for opening the letter of credit (L/C) not later than 2 working days after the date of opening the L/C. The importer must also furnish the Business Turnover Tax reference number assigned to him by the Commissioner of Inland Revenue when application is made for the L/C.

Goods imported in consignments valued at more than Rs.700,000 (US$35,000) c.i.f. require prior approval from the Foreign Investment Advisory Committee.

Imports into Sri Lanka normally should be under Letter of Credit D.P. (documents against payments) terms. D.A. (documents against acceptance) terms are allowed where imports are mainly for projects that are export oriented, i.e. an exporter can import raw materials or components needed for the final product, which is to be exported, on D.A. terms. On D.A. terms, the supplier is normally expected to give credit for a maximum of 90 days. Other priority areas for D.A. terms include agriculture, fisheries, and development oriented projects at the discretion of the Government.

Labeling and Marking Requirements

All labeling of packages should be in large bold lettering in indelible ink or paint. For containerized cargo, the weight, center of gravity, and sling or grab points may be marked as aids for careful handling. Goods shipped to Sri Lanka should be well packed in order to withstand heat, moisture, rough handling, and pilferage. Even small packages and cartons should carry proper labeling. Shipping marks should show consignee order number as specified and port of entry.

Goods arriving at the port of Colombo which are not cleared within a reasonable time period are sold at public auction by the Port Authority unless the consignee specifically requests an exemption. Shipments by air cargo require the same documentation as those arriving by ocean freight. Copies of the air waybill, along with the other documents, are needed for Customs clearance.

> **Senate Concurrent Resolution 40, adopted July 30, 1953, invites U.S. exporters to inscribe, insofar as practicable, on the external shipping containers in indelible print of a suitable size: "United States of America."**

Standards and Measures

Although Sri Lanka is converting to the metric system, some English measurements are still used. Weights are calculated in pounds and ounces; distances in miles. Gasoline is measured in liters; car oil in pints. The Sri Lanka Bureau of Standards (53 Dharmapala Mawatha, Colombo 3) has authority to set voluntary standards for most items. Exceptions include pharmaceuticals. Electricity is 230 volts, 50 cycles, alternating current.

U.S. Generalized System of Preferences (GSP)

Title V of the Trade Act of 1975 authorized the President of the United States to grant generalized tariff preferences to imports from developing nations for a period of 10 years. Other major industrialized countries had previously adopted this program of assistance to developing countries, which aims to decrease their need for outside financial help by building up their export opportunties. The scheme permits voluntary, general and nonreciprocal tariff preferences for imports of certain products from the developing countries. In 1981, Sri Lankan products entering the United States duty free under GSP amounted to $3.2 million, an increase of about 90 percent over 1980's $1.7 million of duty-free imports under GSP. Imports from Sri Lanka receiving duty-free treatment under GSP in 1981 included electromechanical appliances; seamless gloves of rubber or plastic; wooden furniture parts; game, sport, and playground equipment; electric heating equipment; precious and semi-precious stones; chars and carbons; and earthenware or stoneware.

U.S. Bilateral Textile Agreement with Sri Lanka

The current bilateral U.S. textile agreement with Sri Lanka covers all textiles and apparel of cotton, wool, and man-made fibers. It was signed on July 7, 1980, and its term is the 3-year period of May 1, 1980 through April 30, 1983. Annual imports from Sri Lanka in 14 apparel categories are currently limited by provisions of this agreement. Talks on renegotiation of this agreement are scheduled to begin in early 1983.

Selling in Sri Lanka

Distribution Channels

Imports and wholesale trade are centered in the capital, Colombo. The city itself has a population of some 650,000, and with its suburbs, the metropolitan area numbers about one million. There are no other cities of similar size, the next largest being Jaffna with a population of 120,000. More than 75 percent of the total population is in rural or semirural areas.

Over 90 percent of the country's imports enter through the port of Colombo. Accordingly, almost all importing and wholesaling of imported goods are concentrated in the Colombo area. Few if any business people outside of Colombo import directly for wholesaling or retailing in their home areas.

Under the previous government much major trade was channelled through various state trading corporations. Since the present government liberalized imports, literally hundreds of firms have become involved in importing, competing with the government trading corporations. However, imports are dominated by 10 to 20 relatively large groups of companies, most of which are descendants of British trading houses started in the last century and which still maintain extensive British contacts. Many are also involved in manufacturing, and as a group they represent several hundred different product lines, from machinery to chemicals to consumer goods. Major companies include the Brown's

Group, Walker Sons and Co. Ltd., The Maharaja Organization, and Hayley's Limited. Among state-owned trading companies are the State Trading (General) Corporation, The Cooperative Wholesale Establishment, and the Building Materials Corporation.

Few of the private sector importers have branches elsewhere in the country, although several of the public sector importers do. Instead they wholesale to independent regional distributors or direct to retailers. There are many small importers concentrated in the Pettah area of Colombo, near the port, and they do business from there.

Transport to areas outside of Colombo is mainly by truck, since such service is more frequent and flexible than the government railroad, and almost any area of the country can be reached by truck in 1 day. There are almost no large fleets of trucks, most being owned by individuals with no more than three or four vehicles.

There are also large numbers of individuals and small firms acting as indenting agents for products sold on a one-time or irregular basis. Many operate from their residences and use telex service bureaus to communicate with suppliers. They depend on their individual contacts in industry and government, and frequently are retired from the industry or government agency to which they cater.

Selecting Representation

The specific type of representation for a new-to-market firm will depend on the product and the market. Firms producing machinery or other goods requiring servicing and spare parts inventories will require one of the larger local trading companies, because only they have access to the resources necessary to get into the business. However, local interest rates are over 20 percent, and even good sized companies find it difficult to finance large inventories. Skilled maintenance personnel frequently migrate to other countries with higher salary levels, often as soon as their apprenticeships are completed. Perhaps more importantly, many of these large-size firms are not used to competing in an open economy. Their experience has been with limited imports and short-term profits. Reorienting their thinking to the long term in order to get them to make the necessary investments is often not easy.

Also, unless the particular product involved forms a significantly large part of the company's business, the product line can easily "get lost in the shuffle" among the hundreds of other products the company imports or represents. Smaller firms, even without large capitalizations, may make better representatives, if they are sufficiently knowledgeable and aggressive. They may be even better choices if the product is sold on a one-time or irregular basis or requires no servicing or spare parts.

An ongoing contract between an American company and a Sri Lankan agent can be dishonored or terminated by the American company on grounds of inefficiency, misappropriation, death or incapacity of the agent to fulfill terms of the contract. If the agency agreement is for a fixed period of time, the principal must pay compensation to the agent for premature revocation or termination of the agency for causes not justified. Whatever the case may be, the principal must inform the agent, with due notice or prior warning, of his intention to terminate the agreement in order to avoid legal implications.

Government Purchasing

Considering that the government budget equals about 40 percent of gross national product, government imports are an important part of overall trade. Large aid inflows in recent years have also generated large-scale imports. Although most bilateral aid is "tied" at least to some degree, the multilateral development banks, especially the World Bank and the Asian Development Bank, are major donors, and procurement for projects they finance are open to bidders from all countries that are members of those banks. The United States belongs to both banks.

Although there is a Department of Government Supplies which can make purchases for any government agency, all ministries and departments have the option of purchasing directly, and almost all do. There is therefore no central registry of tenders and purchases.

Most major government purchases are made by public tenders, which are published in local newspapers. The American Embassy cables these to the Department of Commerce in Washington and to the American Embassy in Singapore and the American Consulate General in Hong Kong, where many American companies have regional offices responsible for the Sri Lankan sales territory. All tenders valued at over $150,000 must be approved by the Cabinet and follow a complicated tender procedure.

However, almost all tenders close relatively soon after they are announced. This usually means that bids must be submitted 4 to 6 weeks after the tenders are announced, and on the forms prescribed in the tender. This makes it difficult for American firms to compete by mail, since 10–15 days must be allowed each way for international air mail. It is therefore almost imperative that American firms interested in bidding on government tenders be represented in Sri Lanka by either a dealer or an authorized agent.

Although Sri Lanka was a British colony from 1815 until 1947, there does not appear to be any bias towards British products in government purchasing. In recent years, other European countries and Japan have won the bulk of government tenders. U.S. performance to date has not been good, either because American firms were not competitive, did not have local agents, or did not market aggressively.

Payment of commission to agents is generally permitted, but must be specified in the bid. Almost all government purchases are paid for by irrevocable letter of credit, although because of tight budget restrictions, tenders frequently include supplier or other financing requirements or alternatives. Government purchases are normally made on price only, with quality and reputation secondary considerations, assuming all bids meet specifications.

Banking and Credit

Sri Lanka is not a member of any international monetary grouping such as the Sterling Area. Exchange and banking are controlled by the Government's Central Bank of Ceylon, the equivalent of the Federal Reserve Board. The unit of currency is the rupee, consisting of 100 cents. The exchange rate for different currencies varies and is set daily by a managed float by the Central Bank. In mid-1982, the exchange rate was approximately Rs. 20.70 to US $1, a 30 percent depreciation compared with the Rs. 16 to US $1 rate the UNP Government established in 1977 when it took office. The rupee is not freely convertible; most exchange transactions must be approved by the Central Bank's Controller of Exchange.

There are 4 domestic and 20 foreign commercial banks in the country. The two largest, each with several hundred branches nationwide, are the People's Bank and the Bank of Ceylon, both owned by the Government. Together they control 85 percent of all commercial bank deposits. There are two private commercial banks, Hatton National Bank and the Commercial Bank of Ceylon. Both have fewer than 25 branches each, considerably smaller than the government-owned banks. All four maintain correspondent relationships with major American banks. Seven of the 20 foreign banks have been in Colombo for many years, and they are mostly Indian and British. However, as part of its policy of opening the economy, the present Government allowed other foreign banks to open branches in Colombo. By 1982, there were 13 new banks operating, including three American banks. Citibank, American Express International Banking Corporation, and the Bank of America. A fourth bank, Girard Bank of Philadelphia, has been given permission to open a representative office, Sri Lanka's first. A complete list of commercial banks is provided in the "Guidance for Business Travelers" section.

All commercial banks in Sri Lanka are permitted to operate "Foreign Currency Banking Units" (FCBU's). This program was introduced in May 1979. FCBU's are permitted to deal only in foreign currency and only with non-residents, approved residents, and enterprises approved by the Greater Colombo Economic Commission (GCEC).

FCBU's accept time and fixed deposits (but not savings or current accounts) and also borrow funds from, extend loans to, and make advances to their customers. They also are permitted to establish, open, or advise letters of credit; issue guarantees; issue indemnities; and discount bills and acceptances in permitted foreign currencies. The Central Bank's eventual aim is to set up a full-fledged offshore banking center in Sri Lanka.

Depositors of foreign currency in FCBU's are exempt from income tax on their interest income. FCBU's themselves are totally exempt from tax on their profits from all offshore and specified onshore operations.

There are also several other government banking institutions, including the National Development Bank and Development Finance Corporation of Ceylon. These two specialize in medium- and long-term lending, an area where resources are chronically short of demand.

Stimulated by government financial requirements and demand from importers as trade restrictions were lifted, interest rates have generally been high for the past few years, with prime rates about 24 percent. There are special incentive programs for exporters, using Central Bank refinancing, which offer rates as low as 13 percent. However, there are no such programs for importers, and American firms new to market

whose product requires the dealer to spend significant initial amounts for inventory and equipment should be prepared to consider offering supplier credit.

Although Sri Lanka is eligible for Eximbank credits, borrowing through this channel in recent years has been heavy, especially for new aircraft for the Government's flag carrier, Air Lanka. As a result, Eximbank examines additional credits to Sri Lanka on a case-by-case basis.

Most imports are paid for by irrevocable letters of credit. There have been very few defaults in recent years by private companies and almost none in the public sector.

Market Research

There are no specialized marketing research firms in Sri Lanka. Banks are a good source of information, as is the Ceylon Chamber of Commerce—127, Lower Chatham Street, Fort, Colombo 1 (Telex 21193). There is also a new public library in Colombo with reference facilities, as well as a library at the American Center and a small reference library in the American Embassy Commercial Section.

The best statistical information is found in the *Monthly Bulletin* of the Central Bank and its *Annual Report* and *Review of the Economy*. The former is normally published by June of the following year and the latter by October. Customs statistics are available for reference in the office of the Principal Collector of Customs, who usually publishes a bound volume of annual statistics within 4 months after the end of the year. The Brussels Tariff Nomenclature (BTN) system is used.

An excellent reference source is *Ferguson's Ceylon Directory*, published every other year by Associated Newspapers Ltd., D. R. Wijewardene Mawatha, Colombo 2. In its more than 2,000 pages, the Directory covers most government, financial, and business institutions—including officials, board members, and product lines represented for most major companies in the country. The latest edition, published in 1981, is priced at Rs.225 ($11) plus postage.

Marketing Aids

Advertising is available in all media, including newspapers, magazines, radio, television, billboards, direct mail, posters, films in movie theaters, and local exhibitions and displays. Among

Sri Lanka's highly literate population, newspapers are very widely read. There are four English dailies alone, plus a number of dailies and weeklies in the two major languages, Sinhala and Tamil. The Government owns most but not all of the newspapers.

International newspapers, including the *Asian Wall Street Journal* and the *International Herald Tribune* are available in Colombo, but circulation is small. More popular are the international and regional weeklies, including *Time* and *Newsweek* (both Asian editions) and the *Far Eastern Economic Review* and *Asia Week*.

Radio and television are controlled by the Government, the former through the Sri Lanka Broadcasting Corporation (SLBC) and the latter through the Independent Television Network (ITN) and Rupavahini. INT, which began broadcasting in 1978, covers only the Colombo area, but Rupavahini, which began service in 1982, is nationwide. The SLBC broadcasts in English and local languages and offers advertising time in both its domestic and international (shortwave) services. Both television channels also sell commercial time. There is radio coverage 18 hours a day and television service in the evenings.

There are more than 40 advertising agencies in the country, including affiliates of Grant, Kenyon and Eckhardt, and J. Walter Thompson. Most are concentrated in the Colombo area. Print and radio materials are prepared locally, but television and movie theater films are usually produced elsewhere, e.g. Singapore and Malaysia.

Investing in Sri Lanka

The Investment Climate and Government Policy

There is no good estimate of total foreign investment in Sri Lanka. The largest proportion of investment is British, stemming from the country's colonial heritage. It is certain that the American share, estimated to be about $7 million, as of the end of 1981, is relatively small. Several major American multinationals do have plants in Sri Lanka, including Pfizer, Warner-Lambert, Singer, and Union Carbide, but their output is limited and only for domestic consumption. However, two major electronics firms, Motorola and Harris, have signed agreements for 100 percent export-oriented plants in the Investment Promotion Zone. Their combined value would quadruple existing American investment levels. There are several other major projects either under discussion or in negotiation in which American firms are participants.

One of the keystones of the present Government's economic policy is attracting foreign investment. Although inexpensive, trainable labor is perhaps the country's main attraction for foreign investors, the Government is attempting to attract resource-based projects as well, e.g., rubber, phosphates, graphite, and rare earths.

To encourage investors, the Government offers a wide variety of tax concessions, depending mainly on whether the project is 100 percent for export or whether some or all production is intended for the domestic market.

Projects designed entirely for the export market are usually licensed through the Greater Colombo Economic Commission (GCEC). Established in 1978, the Commission was given charge of an area north of Colombo, and set up its first Investment Promotion Zone, commonly referred to as the Free Trade Zone or FTZ, 20 miles north of the city, across from the international airport. In November 1980, the GCEC was given the authority to license 100 percent export projects anywhere in the country, not just the FTZ.

GCEC tax incentives are quite liberal, including complete tax exemption for up to 10 years. Incentives are negotiable, depending on the number of jobs to be created, the net value added in terms of foreign exchange earnings, and the level of new technology being brought into the country through the project. Foreign investors are allowed to own 100 percent of the equity in GCEC-licensed companies.

Incentives for projects aimed entirely or partially at the domestic market are not so generous. Foreign equity participation is generally limited to 49 percent and tax holidays to 5 years, although in industries where the Government is anxious to attract investment, such as tourism, the percentage may be as high as 70 and the tax holidays as long as 10 years. Conversely, for a project creating few jobs or introducing no new technology, foreign equity participation can be limited to even less than 49 percent. As with GCEC projects, incentives are negotiable. Applications for projects for the domestic market must be approved by the interagency Foreign Investment Advisory Committee (FIAC), whose chairman is, *ex officio*, Mr. C. Chanmugam, the Deputy Secretary of the Ministry of Finance and Planning.

The appendix summarizes and compares the different incentives offered for GCEC and FIAC projects.

Interested American firms should contact either the Investment Promotion Division, Greater Colombo Economic Commission, 14, Sir Baron Jayatileke Mawatha, Colombo 1, telex 21332 or the International Economic Cooperation Division, Ministry of Finance and Planning, Third Floor, Room 361 B, Galle Face Secretariat, Colombo 1, telex 21409 (for FIAC projects).

International Agreements

Sri Lanka is a signatory of the Convention on the Settlement of Investment Disputes between States and Nationals of other States, which has also been ratified by the United States. Sri Lanka and the United States concluded an Investment Guarantee Agreement in 1966, which makes available the investment insurance services of the U.S. Overseas Private Investment Corporation to U.S. investors with Sri Lankan Government approval (see "OPIC" section). Article 157 of the 1978 Sri Lanka Constitution gives constitutional protection to this and similar agreements with other countries.

Overseas Private Investment Corporation

The Overseas Private Investment Corporation (OPIC), a U.S. Government entity, provides insurance against loss of investment due to currency inconvertibility, expropriation, and war, revolution, or insurrection. OPIC also insures against loss due to the arbitrary drawing by host governments on letters of credit posted by U.S. exporters and contractors. It also underwrites special risks relating to energy and minerals exploration. OPIC insurance is available to eligible U.S. investors doing business in Sri Lanka as well as in over 90 other developing countries.

The types of investment OPIC insures include equity, loans, loan guarantees, fees and royalties, and physical assets. As OPIC insures only new investments or expansions of existing investments, investors must notify OPIC before an irrevocable commitment to invest has been made.

To assist in the financing of joint ventures, OPIC also provides direct loans, all-risk guarantees, and feasibility study funding for projects involving U.S. companies with a successful record in the business concerned.

For more information on OPIC programs, potential investors should write to either the Insurance or Finance Officer, Asia Division, Overseas Private Investment Corporation, 1129 20th Street, N.W., Washington, D.C. 20527, or phone (202) 653-2920.

U.S. A.I.D.'s Private Enterprise Promotion Program

U.S. investors will be interested to note that Sri Lanka is one of a handful of developing countries, worldwide, singled out for special emphasis in the new "Private Enterprise Promotion" program under the U.S. Agency for International Development (A.I.D.). A small project has already been set up, under A.I.D. auspices, to study ways in which foreign investment in Sri Lanka might be facilitated as a means of promoting the development process.

Intellectual and Industrial Property Protection

Sri Lanka is a member of the World Intellectual Property Organization. The code of Intellectual Property Act, No. 52 of 1979, came into effect on January 3, 1980, and a separate office was set up on January 1, 1982, separate from the Registrar of Companies, which previously had responsibility.

Sri Lanka is not a member of the Universal Copyright Convention of September 1952, to which the United States belongs. It is a party to the Berne Copyright Convention, of which the United States is not a member. U.S. authors may receive atuomatic copyright protection in Sri Lanka for a work if it is published in one of the 60 other countries adhering to the Berne Convention at the same time it is published in the United States.

Sri Lanka is a member of the International Union for the Protection of Industrial Property (Paris Union), London 1934 revision. U.S. nationals are entitled to national equal treatment in maintaining their patent and trademark rights in Sri Lanka.

Business Organization

Foreign investors may incorporate either as resident or nonresident companies, although taxation rates for each differ (see section entitled "Taxation"). Businesses can also be organized as partnerships or sole proprietorships.

Information relating to procedures for setting up a business should be obtained from legal counsel.

Taxation

Resident companies are taxed on income at the rate of 50 percent. A lower rate of 40 percent is levied on "people's" companies, i.e., those with widely held shares. Public companies whose shares are quoted and that make available a minimum percentage of shares to be purchased by the general public will also be liable to tax at the lower 40 percent rate.

Dividends paid by resident companies are taxable, and a company paying a dividend is required to withhold tax at 20 percent on such dividends. Quoted public companies, i.e., those whose shares are publicly traded, are not required to deduct tax at source on dividends declared by them.

In addition to the 50 percent basic income tax rate, nonresident companies pay an additional 5% in lieu of estate duties. They must also pay a nonrefundable 33⅓ percent tax on remittance of profits.

Dividends, interest, and royalties generated in Sri Lanka and received by a nonresident are liable to Sri Lanka income tax at whatever rates are applicable to nonresident individuals and companies. Reduced rates have been extended to residents of countries with which Sri Lanka has signed double taxation treaties. Such a treaty is now being negotiated by Sri Lanka and the United States. Until it is signed, under U.S. law American companies operating in Sri Lanka may claim a credit against U.S. taxes for such taxes paid to Sri Lanka.

Other Taxes.—The most important tax after income tax is the Business Turnover Tax or BTT (see "Trade Regulations" section). In 1982, BTT was extended to cover imports and is levied in addition to customs duties.

There are numerous license taxes on motor vehicles, radios, televisions, etc. In addition, municipalities levy property taxes, which vary from city to city. In Colombo, the tax is 30 percent of assessed value.

There is a 100 percent tax on the transfer of company shares to a nonresident, and a 500 percent tax on the sale of land to a nonresident.

Personal Income Tax.—Personal income taxes are levied on a graduated scale from 5 to 50 percent of income. Civil servant and public corporation salaries are exempt from income tax. Most expatriates involved in foreign investments are eligible for a flat 25 percent tax rate for their first 3 years in Sri Lanka. Thereafter, their income is taxed at normal rates.

Labor Laws and Regulations

Sri Lanka has a well-developed body of labor legislation and case law. There are more than 1,500 trade unions and an estimated 25 percent of the entire labor force are union members. Public sector workers do not have the right to bargain collectively, although they do have the right to strike, unless the Government bans strikes through the Essential Public Services Act or a state of emergency. Private sector workers have the right to bargain collectively and to strike, but private employers also have the right to "lock out."

Employers must contribute 12 percent of workers' salaries to the Employees Provident Fund, a form of social security. Workers contribute 9 percent. In addition, employers must also contribute an additional 3 percent of salaries to the Employees Trust Fund, which then invests the proceeds on behalf of the workers in new and existing companies.

The Employers' Federation of Ceylon, 30 Sulaiman Avenue, Colombo 5, can provide more information on labor laws and legislation. More than 180 private sector companies are members of the Federation, and the Federation bargains collectively on behalf of many of them with several joint trade union councils.

There are 33 wage boards for most trades. The boards—which include government, employer and worker representatives—set minimum wages and benefits for the trades for which they are responsible.

Guidance for Business Travelers

Passport and Visa Requirements for U.S. Business Travelers

A valid U.S. passport and a Sri Lankan visa are required for U.S. nationals proceeding to Sri Lanka for specific purposes such as business, lectures, tours, academic research, etc., if the stay is more than 30 days. Visitors coming without a visa are issued a 30-day entry permit, which may be extended or converted to a temporary residence visa, if necessary.

Applicants for visas for business purposes are required to file application forms which can be obtained from the Embassy of Sri Lanka in Washington, D.C., the Permanent Mission of Sri Lanka to the United Nations in New York, and the honorary consulates for Sri Lanka in Chicago, Los Angeles, and New Orleans. All pages of the form should be carefully completed, and the applicant should sign in the spaces indicated on page two of the form. No stamps should be affixed to the form. The completed application form should be sent, together with one passport-size photograph, the passport of the applicant, and a money order or check for the fee (see below) to the Embassy of Sri Lanka, 2148 Wyoming Avenue, N.W., Washington, D.C. 20008.

Applicants for visas to Sri Lanka for business purposes should also annex a letter from their organization sponsoring the application, together with a copy of a letter of invitation from an individual or organization setting out the business purpose of the visit. The Embassy of Sri Lanka in Washington, D.C., is the only consular authority in the United States empowered to issue visas. The Embassy of Sri Lanka does not, as a general policy, issue visas for a stay in Sri Lanka exceeding 3 months.

The visa fee for U.S. nationals is $0.42. A remittance of $2 per passport must be paid to cover the cost of returning the passport by certified mail. Please contact the Embassy of Sri Lanka, 2148 Wyoming Avenue, N.W., Washington, D.C. 20008, phone (202) 483-4025, to ascertain the visa fees for other nationals.

Immunizations and Health Precautions

Every visitor to Sri Lanka is required to have (1) a valid vaccination certificate against smallpox if the visitor has been in an infected area 14 days prior to arrival in Sri Lanka, (2) a valid inoculation certificate against cholera if coming from infected areas, (3) a valid inoculation certificate against yellow fever if the visitor has been in an infected area 6 days prior to arrival in Sri Lanka. Typhoid and tetanus shots are recommended. Malaria prophylaxis (for those going outside the Colombo area) and hepatitis prophylaxis should be started before leaving home.

The following simple health precautions should be followed:

- Drink only boiled, filtered water. Bottled water, soft drinks and beer available.

- Wash all salads, vegetables, and fruit before eating.

- Get plenty of rest.

- Get daily physical exercise to maintain body muscle tone. However, it is advisable to stay out of the sun during mid-day, because of Sri Lanka's proximity to the equator.

Exchange Regulations

When entering Sri Lanka, visitors must make a currency declaration. This will enable the visitor not only to exchange currency brought in, but to take the unspent foreign currency out of Sri Lanka on departure.

Foreign currency brought into Sri Lanka and declared to Customs may be exchanged through any authorized foreign currency dealer or through the commercial banks, which will endorse the amount exchanged on the currency declaration form. Exchange facilities are also available at the International Airport as well as most major hotels. However, exchange rates at hotels are generally lower than those at banks. Many shops are also authorized to accept foreign exchange. The rates for currency notes are up to 10 percent lower than for traveler's checks. Most major hotels and some shops also honor major travel and bank credit cards.

General Information

Languages. — While Sinhala is the official language, almost all transactions in private and certain public sector offices are done in English. There are only three languages used in Sri Lanka—Sinhala, Tamil, and English—and all companies doing business overseas almost without exception use English in correspondence and communications.

Business Hours and Local Time. — Working hours for most Sri Lankan Government offices are 8:00 a.m. to 12 noon and 1 p.m. to 4:15 p.m. Monday through Friday. Typical private sector organizations function from 8:30 a.m. to 12:30 p.m. and 1 p.m. to 4:30 p.m. Most business executives prefer business appointments late in the morning. The U.S. Embassy in Sri Lanka is open Monday through Friday from 8 a.m. to 12:45 p.m. and 1:45 p.m. to 5 p.m.

Sri Lanka is G.m.t. plus 5½ hours. No daylight savings time is observed. The local time is 9½ or 10½ hours ahead of New York, depending on whether New York is on e.d.t. or e.s.t.

Holidays. — Most Sri Lankan official holidays are connected with the country's four religions—Buddhism, Hinduism, Islam, and Christianity; therefore, they fluctuate and do not have fixed dates. In an average year there are some 25 official holidays, including all full moon days, Buddhist and Tamil New Year (April) and several Muslim holidays. Fixed date holidays include Independence Day (February 4), National Heroes' Day (May 22), Christmas, and New Year's Day. In addition June 30 and December 31 are bank holidays. Holidays which fall on weekends are observed either on the preceding Friday or following Monday, except for full moon days.

Climate and Dress. —Most areas of Sri Lanka are generally hot and humid year round, with daytime temperatures around 90 degrees Fahrenheit. The monsoon (rainy season) on the eastern side of the country lasts from December to February, and in the rest of the country, including Colombo, from May to September. April and May are generally the hottest months.

Clothing of the weight worn in Washington, D.C., during the hottest summer months is suitable year round in Colombo. The carrying of rainwear is recommended. Business dress is usually washable, lightweight suits. Heavier clothing is necessary for evenings in the mountains ("upcountry"), at an elevation of 4,000 to 6,000 feet.

Business Courtesy. —Business cards are a necessity for any serious business traveler. Courtesy is highly valued in Sri Lanka; displays of temper and impatience are usually counterproductive; and personal friendliness probably plays a greater role than in U.S. business. Appointments and other commitments are scrupulously observed, although the sense of time in Sri Lanka is probably not so finely honed as in the United States.

Tipping. —Tipping is not a particularly strong institution in Sri Lanka. All taxis are metered, and customers are expected to pay the amount on the meter, although some pay to the next highest rupee. In international class hotels, service charges are almost always added to the bill; if not, a nominal tip is in order for personal services rendered. It is normal to give about 5 rupees to a hotel porter carrying bags to the room, and about 50–100 rupees to the driver of a hired car after 3–4 days' service.

Domestic Transportation. —There are regularly scheduled domestic flights from Colombo's domestic airport at suburban Ratmalana to Jaffna, Trincomalee and Batticaloa. There are also day and night express trains to most major cities. However, no place is more than a day's drive from Colombo.

Both self-drive and chauffeur-driven rental cars are available. Because of local road and traffic conditions and the minimal extra cost, hiring a car with driver is generally preferable. Rates for medium-size sedans, e.g., Peugeot 504's, with driver, average $0.35 per mile with air conditioning and $0.30 per mile without. Gas is included.

Cars with drivers can be rented from:

Hertz	— Quickshaws Limited Kalinga Place Colombo 5
	Telephone: 83133-4-5
Avis	— Mack Transport Limited York Street Colombo 1
	Telephone: 29288, 33043, 20760
Toyota	— Ebert Silva Touring Company Limited P.O. Box 11 Dehiwela
	Telephone: 71-3356, 71-7854, 71-2994
Inter-Rent American	— Mercantile Tours (Ceylon) Limited 23, York Arcade Colombo 1
	Telephone: 28706
Mackinnons Travel Services (Ceylon) Limited	— 7 York Street Colombo 1 Telephone: 22641

In Colombo metered taxis and "autorickshaws" are also available. Rates for the former average $0.50 per mile and for the latter $0.25 per mile.

Telex/Cable Service. —International telegraph, telex, and telephone services are available 24 hours a day at the Central Telegraph Office, Duke Street, Colombo 1 (Telephone: 27176).

Direct telephone services via satellite are available 24 hours daily to the United States, United Kingdom, Australia, Singapore, Malaysia, Hong Kong, Italy, People's Republic of China, Japan, and India and through connections to almost all parts of the world.

There are several private international telephone and telex bureaus providing 24-hour service. Major hotels in Colombo can also send telexes.

International Airmail.—Ten to 15 days each way should be allowed for airmail between Sri Lanka and the United States.

Hotels.—All the following hotels are air-conditioned:

HOTEL CEYLON INTERCONTI-
NENTAL
(250 rooms)
48, Janadhipathi Mawatha
Colombo 1
Telephone: 21221/2/3/4
Telex: CMB 21188

Category: Single with bath	$68
Twin with bath	$74
Suite	$150 to $240

Fully air-conditioned, coffee/shop, roof top restaurant, seafood restaurant, two bars, massage, health club, swimming pool, tennis, squash. Located in the heart of the city overlooking the Indian Ocean. Thirty minutes from International airport. Hotel taxi service.

HOTEL LANKA OBEROI
(376 rooms)
77–83 Steuart Place
Galle Road
Colombo 3
Telephone: 21171, 20001
Telex: CMB 21201

Category: Single with bath	$70
Twin with bath	$80
Suite	$150

Fully air-conditioned, two restaurants, bar service in lounge, massage, health club, swimming pool, tennis, shops. Five minutes from city center, 45 minutes from International airport. Hotel taxi service.

GALLE FACE HOTEL
(180 rooms, presently
only 83 in operation)
Galle Face Center Road
Colombo 3
Telephone: 28211, 26369
Telex: 21281 GFH CE

| Category: Single with bath | $63.25 |
| Twin with bath | $67.50 |

Two restaurants, bars, salt water swimming pool, overlooking the Indian Ocean. Forty minutes from International airport.

HOLIDAY INN
(100 rooms)
30, Sir Macan Markar Mawatha
P.O. Box 1200
Colombo 3
Telephone: 22001—10 lines
Telex: 21200 HOLINN CE

Category: Single with bath	$62
Twin with bath	$70
Suite	$130

Fully air-conditioned, coffee shop, specialty restaurant, seafood restaurant, two bars, massage, golf and tennis arranged on request, shopping arcade, swimming pool. Five minutes from city, 45 minutes from International airport.

Dry Cleaning and Laundry Service.—Dry cleaning is available in the Hotel Ceylon Intercontinental and Hotel Lanka Oberoi. Service is available for anyone, not just hotel guests. Laundry service is available in all hotels.

Electric Current.—Current is 230 volts, 50 cycles, alternating, but transformers can be used with 110–volt appliances.

Sri Lankan Banks
Bank of Ceylon
Central Office
York Street
Colombo 1
Telephone: 28521, 25742, 26260
Telex: 21126 FORBANK CE
21331 LANKABK CE.

Central Bank of Ceylon
34–36, Janadhipathi Mawatha
Colombo 1
Telephone: 21191, 20863, 29938, 22738/9, 27325, 22819, 22094, 22918
Telex: 21176 and 21290 CENTRABANK CBO

Commercial Bank of Ceylon
57 Sir Baron Jayatileke Mawatha
P.O. Box 148
Colombo 1
Telephone: 28193-5
Telex: 21274
COMBANK CE, 21520 COMEX CE.

Hatton National Bank
16 Janadhipathi Mawatha
P.O. Box 98
Colombo 1
Telephone: 21885-7, 21460, 21466-9
Telex: 21259 HATNABK CE.

National Savings Bank
Savings House
Galle Road
Colombo 3
Telephone: 20101.

People's Bank, 75 Sir Chittampalam Gardiner
Mawatha
Colombo 2
Telephone: 27841
Telex: 21143 PLBNK CE and 21364 PLBKINT
CE

Foreign Banks

Algemene Bank of Netherlands N.V. (ABN),
30 Sir Baron Jayatileke Mawatha
Colombo 1
Teephone: 20205/6/7/8.
Telex: 21590 ABNA CE.

American Express International Banking Corpo-
ration Limited
45, Janadhipathi Mawatha
Colombo 1
Telephone: 31288-9
Telex: 21469 AMBANK CE

Amsterdam-Rotterdam Bank (AMRO)
90, Chatham Street
Colombo 1
Telephone: 23023, 548107, 548108
Telex: 21818 AMRO CE

Bank of America
324, Galle Road
Colombo 3
Telephone: 547372-5
Telex: 21481 BOFACOL CE

Bank of Credit and Commerce International
(Overseas) Ltd.
52, Mudalige Mawatha
Colombo 1
Telephone: 21597, 23303-6
Telex: 21411 BCCICE

Chartered Bank
17 Janadhipathi Mawatha
P.O. Box 27
Colombo 1

Telephone: 26671-4
Telex: 21117 BANCHAR CE

Citibank
49/16, Iceland Building
Galle Face
Colombo 3
Telephone: 547316
Telex: 21445 CTBK CE.

Dubai Bank Ltd.
48, Mudalige Mawatha
Colombo 1
Telephone: 33719, 37868
Telex: 21724 DUBANK CE

European Asian Bank
90, Union Place
Colombo 2
Telephone: 37062-7
Telex: 21508 and 21589 EURAS CE

Habib Bank Ltd.
163 Keyzer Street
Colombo 11
Telephone: 26565, 28713, 24528, 29412
Telex: 21258 CEY HABIB

Hongkong & Shanghai Banking Corporation
24 Sir Baron Jayatileke Mawatha
Colombo 1
Telephone: 25435
Telex: 21152 HSBC CE

Grindlays Bank Limited
142, Dam Street
Colombo 12
Telephone: 20376
Telex: 21130 GRNDLAY CE

Banque de L'Indochine Et de Suez (Indoseuz)
Ceylinco House
69, Janadhipathi Mawatha
Colombo 1
Telephonc: 36181-5
Telex: 21402 INDOSU CE, 21554 INSUEZ CE,
21733 INDOFX CE

Indian Overseas Bank
139, Main Street
P.O. Box 671
Colombo 11
Telephone: 20515
Telex: 21456 OFFIOB CE

Overseas Trust Bank
39, Bristol Street
Colombo 1

Telephone: 547655-9
Telex: 21489 OTBSL CE

State Bank of India
16 Sir Baron Jayatileke Mawatha
Colombo 1
Telephone: 26133
Telex: 21286 THISTLE CE

Union Bank of the Middle East Ltd.
69 Chatham Street
Colombo 1
Telephone: 23467, 35483
Telex: 21769 UBME CE

Roman Catholic Churches

All Saints Church
Campbell Place
Colombo 8
Telephone: 93051
(6:00 a.m., 7:00 a.m., & 6:00 p.m.)

Holy Rosary Church
De Soysa Circus
Colombo 2
Telephone: 20158
(8:15 a.m.)

St. Lucia's Cathedral
Kotahena
Colombo 13
Telephone: 32080
(6:00 a.m., 7:00 a.m. & 6:00 p.m.)

St. Mary's Church
Lauries Road
Colombo 4
Telephone: 588745
(7:00 a.m. & 6:30 p.m.)

St. Philip Neri's Church
Norris Canal Road
Colombo 11
Telephone: 21367
(6:45 a.m., 5:15 p.m., & 6:30 p.m.)

St. Theresa's Church
364 Thimbirigasyaya Road
Colombo 5
Telephone: 83425
(7:00 a.m. & 6:30 p.m.)

Anglican (Episcopalian)

Christ Church
Galle Face

Colombo 3
Telephone: 25166
(6:45 a.m. & 6:00 p.m.)

St. Michael's & All Angels
St. Michael's Road
Colombo 3
Telephone: 23660
(7:30 a.m. & 5:30 p.m.)

St. Paul's Church
Kynsey Road
Colombo 8
Telephone: 93037
(6:00 a.m., 7:00 a.m. & 5:00 p.m.)

St. Luke's Church
Borella
Colombo 8
Telephone: 91543
(6:30 a.m., 8:30 a.m. & 5:30 p.m.)

Presbyterian Church

St. Andrew's Church
Galle Road
Colombo 3
Telephone: 23765
(6:30 p.m.)

Methodist Church

Methodist Church
Galle Road
Colombo 3
Telephone: 23033
(5:30 p.m.)

Hospitals

General Hospital
Regent Street
Colombo 8
Telephone: 91111
(24 hours emergency service)

Joseph Frazer Memorial Nursing Home
Joseph Frazer Road
Colombo 5
Telephone: 588385

Laboratories and X-Ray Clinics

Electro Medics Limited (X-rays only)
16, Galle Face Court
Colombo 3
Telephone: 27468

Glass House
48 Edinburgh Crescent
Colombo 7
Telephone: 95528 & 91322

Medi-Clinic
77 Galle Road
Bambalapitiya
Colombo 4
Telephone: 85551.

Medi-Lab
155 Dharmapala Mawatha
Colombo 3
Telephone: 34702
(Open 24 hours)

Medical Doctors (Generalists)

The following are Foreign Service post
medical advisers:
    Dr. Theva Buell
        Telephone: 92417
    Dr. D.W. Walpola
        Telephone: 91772

Foreign Embassies with Offices in Sri Lanka

Australia
P.O. Box 742
Colombo 7
Telephone: 598767, 598768, 598769

Bangladesh
207/1 Dharmapala Mawatha
Colombo 7
Telephone: 595963

Belgium
31A, Horton Place
Colombo 7
Telephone: 595554, 594596

Bulgaria
29/9 Jayasingha Road
Colombo 6
Telephone: 553173

Burma
23, Havelock Road
Colombo 5
Telephone: 587607, 587608

Canada
P.O. Box 1006
Colombo 7
Telephone: 595841, 595842, 595843

China
191 Dharmapala Mawatha
Colombo 7
Telephone: 96459, 96418, 95700, 93277

Cuba
34 Ward Place
Colombo 7
Telephone: 595450

Czechoslovakia
P.O. Box 238
Colombo 7
Telephone: 91596

Egypt
39,. Dickman's Road
Colombo 5
Telephone: 83621

Finland
35/2 Guildford Crescent
Colombo 7
Telephone: 598819, 598820

France
P.O. Box 880
Colombo 7
Telephone: 93615, 93018

Germany (East)
101 Rosmead Place
Colombo 7
Telephone: 93753

Germany (West)
P.O. Box 658
Colombo 7
Telephone: 595814, 595816/7

Holy See
Apostolic Nunciature,
1 Gower Street
Colombo 5
Telephone: 82554

Hungary
79/2 Horton Place
Colombo 7
Telephone: 91966

India
Third Floor
State Bank of India Building
18–3/1, Sir Baron Jayatileke Mawatha
Colombo 1
Telephone: 21604, 22788, 22789

Indonesia
1, Police Park Terrace
Colombo 5
Telephone: 580113

Iran
6, Sir Ernest De Silva Mawatha
Colombo 7
Telephone: 29071

Iraq
P.O. Box 79
Colombo 3
Telephone: 25827

Italy
586 Galle Road
Colombo 3
Telephone: 588622, 588388

Japan
20, Gregory's Road
Colombo 7
Telephone: 93831

Korea (South)
98, Dharmapala Mawatha
Colombo 7
Telephone: 91325

Libya
P.O. Box 155
Colombo 7
Telephone: 94874

Malaysia
63A, Ward Place
Colombo 7
Telephone: 94837

Maldives
25 Melbourne Avenue
Colombo 4
Telephone: 86762

Netherlands
25 Torrington Avenue
Colombo 7
Telephone: 589626, 589627, 589628

Pakistan
17, Sir Ernest de Silva Mawatha
Colombo 7
Telephone: 596301, 596302

Philippines
5 Torrington Place

Colombo 7
Telephone: 596861, 596862, 596863

Poland
120, Park Road
Colombo 5
Telephone: 81903

Romania
15, Clifford Avenue
Colombo 3
Telephone: 34217

Sweden
P.O. Box 1072
Colombo 2
Telephone: 20201

Switzerland
7 1/1 Upper Chatham Street
Colombo 1
Telephone: 547157, 547663

Thailand
10, Sir Ernest de Silva Mawatha
Colombo 7
Telephone: 27280

Union of Soviet Socialist Republics
62, Sir Ernest de Silva Mawatha
Colombo 7
Telephone: 27885

United Kingdom
190, Galle Road
Colombo 3.
Telephone: 27611, 27615

Vietnam
2, Dudley Senanayake Mawatha,
Colombo 8.
Telephone: 595188

Yugoslavia
32, Cambridge Place,
Colombo 7
Telephone: 592624

International Organizations

United Nations
202/204, Bauddhaloka Mawatha
Colombo 7
Telephone: 85287/8, 83804, 588954, 82792/3

United Nations Development Program
202/204, Bauddhaloka Mawatha
Colombo 7
Telephone: 81111

Food & Agricultural Organization
202/204, Bauddhaloka Mawatha
Colombo 7
Telephone: 588537

United Nations Children's Fund (UNICEF)
5, Queens Avenue
Colombo 3
Telephone: 86136

World Health Organization (WHO)
228, Havelock Road
Colombo 5
Telephone 84636

United Nations Fund for Population Activities
(UNFPA)
202/204, Bauddhaloka Mawatha
Colombo 7
Telephone: 86674

World Tourism Organization (WTO)
10,. Albert Crescent
Colombo 7
Telephone: 595091

Government Offices

Presidency
Republic Building
Colombo 1
Telephone: 25306

Ministry of Posts & Telecommunications
Old C.T.O. Building
Colombo 1
Telephone: 29567

Ministry of Foreign Affairs
Republic Building
Colombo 1
Telephone: 24109

Ministry of Finance & Planning
Galle Face Secretariat
Colombo 1
Telephone: 23365

Ministry of Plan Implementation
7th & 8th North Towers
Central Bank of Ceylon Building
Colombo 1
Telephone: 27741

Ministry of Industries & Scientific Affairs
48, Sri Jinaratana Mawatha
Colombo 2
Telephone: 27599

Ministry of Trade & Shipping
7th Floor
Insurance Corporation Building
21, Vauxhall Stret
Colombo 2
Telephone: 26539

Ministry of Defense
Republic Building
Colombo 1
Telephone: 29983

Chamber of Commerce

Ceylon Chamber of Commerce
127, Lower Chatham Street
Fort
Colombo 1
(P.O.B. 274)
Telex: 21193

Airlines Serving Colombo

Air Lanka
Telephone: 21161, 21291

Aeroflot
Telephone: 25580, 33062

British Airways
Telephone: 20231, 20236-9

Garuda Indonesian Airlines
Telephone: 25984, 21819

Gulf Air Company
Telephone: 35903, 29881, 26633, 32594

Indian Airlines
Telephone: 23136

K.L.M. Royal Dutch Airlines
Telephone: 26359, 25984/5/6

Korean Airlines
Telephone: 22921, 26144

Kuwait Airways
Telephone: 547828

Pakistan International Airlines
Telephone: 29215

Royal Nepal Airlines
Telephone: 24045, 28945

Singapore Airlines
Telephone: 22711-0

Swissair
Telephone: 35403

Thai International Airways
Telephone: 36201–5

U.T.A. French Airlines
Telephone: 27605/6

American Airline Representation

Pan American World Airways
Telephone: 23177, 20671

Transworld Airlines (TWA)
Telephone: 27506, 36724/5, 27911

Northwest Orient Airlines
Telephone: 20456, 29881, 29563, 22641

Diplomatic Representation

Embassy of the Democratic Socialist
Republic of Sri Lanka
2148 Wyoming Avenue, N.W.
Washington, D.C. 20008
Telephone: (202) 483-4025

Mission of the Democratic Socialist Republic
of Sri Lanka to the United Nations
630 3rd Avenue,
New York, NY 10017
Telephone: (212) 986-7040

American Embassy
44 Galle Road
P.O. Box 106
Colombo 3, Sri Lanka
Telephone: 21271, 21520, 21532
Telex: 21305 AMFMB CE

Foreign Service Officers in the Economic/Commercial Section of the Embassy are available and willing to brief and assist American business persons and representatives of American companies visiting Sri Lanka.

Published Sources of Economic and Commercial Information

U.S. Government Publications

More detailed information on current economic developments in Sri Lanka and an analysis of their implication for American business interests may be obtained by requesting the most recent Foreign Economic Trends Report from the U.S. Department of Commerce in Washington, D.C. or from the nearest District Office. Political and other background information on Sri Lanka is available in the Background Notes series of reports prepared by the U.S. Department of State, Washington, D.C. 20520. Annual subscriptions for all of the reports appearing in the Foreign Economic Trends and Background Notes series may be purchased by writing to the Superintendent of Documents, Government Printing Office, Washington, D.C. 20402.

Sri Lankan Government Publications
Review of the Economy (annual), Central Bank of Ceylon, Colombo.

Bulletin (monthly), Central Bank of Ceylon, Colombo.

Annual Report of the Monetary Board to the Hon. Minister of Finance and Planning, Central Bank of Ceylon, Colombo.

External Trade Statistics–Sri Lanka, Sri Lanka Customs, Colombo.

Sri Lanka–Register of Investors, International Economic Cooperation Division, Ministry of Finance and Planning, Colombo.

Other Publications

Economic Review (monthly), published by the People's Bank, Research Department. Head Office: Sir Chittampalam A. Gardinar Mawatha, Colombo 2, Sri Lanka.

Ferguson's Ceylon Directory, published by Associated Newspapers Ltd., Wijewardene Mawatha, Colombo 2.

Appendix

Incentives for Foreign Investment

I. VISIBLE INCENTIVES FOR FOREIGN INVESTMENT IN SRI LANKA (MANUFACTURING INDUSTRIES)

Greater Colombo Economic Commission—GCEC—Incentives (100-percent Export-Oriented Industries)	Foreign Investment Advisory Committee—FIAC (Domestic Sales Permitted)

A. Concessions during life of the project

1. No limits on equity holdings of foreign investors.	1. Maximum foreign equity is 49 percent.
2. Free transfer of shares within or outside Sri Lanka.	2. Free transfer to foreigners not permitted. 100 percent tax.
3. No tax or exchange control on such transfers.	3. Subject to exchange control and tax.
4. Dividends of nonresident shareholders exempt from any taxes, and remittances of such dividends exempt from exchange control	4. Dividends of nonresident shareholders free of tax in holiday period. Dividends exempt from exchange control.
5. No import duty on machinery, equipment, construction materials and raw materials.	5. 12½ percent duty on import on machinery equipment, construction materials, rebate on customs duty on imported raw materials at the point of export of finished products.
6. Such imports and exports exempt from normal import control and exchange control procedures.	6. Subject to exchange control and import control regulations.
7. Transfer of capital and proceeds of liquidation exempt from exchange control.	7. Subject to exchange control.

B. During Tax Holiday Period

1. Tax holiday of minimum 2 to maximum 10 years based on: a. employment, b. net foreign exchange earnings, c. introduction of new technology, and d. substantial exports to new markets.	1. Export-oriented industries/import substitution industries are entitled to a 5-year tax holiday.
2. No income tax on remuneration of foreign personnel employed.	2. Taxable.
3. No tax on royalties.	3. 10 percent tax on royalties.
4. No tax on dividends of resident and nonresident shareholders.	4. No taxes.

C. After Tax Holiday

1. A further concessionary tax period of up to 15 years. Thereafter, Inland Revenue laws in force will apply.	1. Inland Revenue laws in force will apply.

II. Invisible Incentives (GCEC Projects)

1. Speedy processing of applications and service. GCEC entrusted with wide ranging powers; it is the only agency with which foreign investors need to deal.

2. Investments protected under Section 157 of the Sri Lanka Constitution. (Only for investors from countries with bilateral investment protection agreements with Sri Lanka. (The United States has such an agreement for OPIC-insured projects.)

3. Developed factory sites and all infrastructure requirements in zones at a nominal charge. These facilities, to an extent, cut down the time required for setting up factories.

4. Speedy customs clearance at port or airport or factory site.

5. Foreign Currency Banking Units and offshore banking facilities.

6. GCEC makes available to investors a register of qualified graduates in different fields and facilities of a "Job Bank" where unskilled people living within a radius of 10 miles of the zone have registered.

Market Profile—SRI LANKA

Foreign Trade

Imports.—$1.79 billion in 1981; $2.02 billion in 1980. Major suppliers in 1981: Saudi Arabia 15 percent, Japan 14 percent, U.S. 7 percent, Iran 7 percent, U.K. 6 percent. Principal imports: oil and petroleum products, machinery and equipment, sugar, vehicles; from U.S.; wheat, aircraft and parts, earthmoving equipment, organic chemicals. Total 1981 imports from U.S.: $129 million.

Exports.—$1.03 billion in 1981, $1.04 billion in 1980. Major customers in 1981: U.S. 14 percent, U.K. 6 percent, Pakistan 5 percent, Japan 4 percent, Saudi Arabia 3 percent. Principal exports: tea, refined petroleum products, rubber, textiles and garments, coconut products; to U.S.: garments, tea, rubber. Total 1981 exports to U.S.: $146 million.

Trade Policy.—Not a member of any regional trade or customs grouping, although has applied for Association of South East Asian Nations (ASEAN) membership. Liberal import policy; few items require licenses, exchange control approvals generally routine.

Trade Prospects.—Chemicals, including fertilizer, power generation and transmission equipment, construction equipment, telecommunications equipment, hotel and restaurant equipment, automated data processing and business machines.

Foreign Investment

Diversified, but largest thought to be British. U.S. investment small, estimated $7 million. Free Trade Zone, established in 1978, has 22,000 employees and 50 factories (1982).

Investment Prospects.—Labor-intensive manufacturing, agribusiness, tourism, fisheries, rubber and coconut-based industries.

Finance

Currency. Sri Lanka rupee (Rs. 20.875 – US$1 as of October 1982) issued by Central Bank of Ceylon. Not member of any currency area, not freely convertible.

Domestic Credit.—Two government and two private local commercial banks; 20 branches of foreign banks, including 3 U.S. Medium- and long-term credit from government National Development Bank and government-affiliated Development Finance Corporation of Ceylon.

National Budget.—$1.9 billion in 1982, up 10 percent (U.S. dollar terms) from 1981. Budget growth likely to be in same range for next several years.

Foreign Aid.—$865 million in commitments in 1981. Major donors World Bank, U.S., Japan, West Germany, U.K.

Balance of Payments.—Overall deficits in 1980 and 1981. Gross external assets at end 1981: $449 million.

Economy

GDP.—$4 billion in 1981, $265 per capita.

Agriculture.—33 percent of total land area is under cultivation, producing 24 percent of GNP. Major export crops: tea, rubber, coconut, spices. Main crop and diet staple is paddy: output approaching self-sufficiency.

Industry.—30 percent of GNP. Major products: petroleum products and chemicals, plantation crop processing, textiles and garments.

Commerce.—60 percent of all productive capacity owned by government. Both public and private sector involved in retail and foreign trade. End 1981 wholesale price index 289.7 (1974 = 100).

Development Plan.—Rolling public investment plan changes yearly and is mainly descriptive. Major projects, i.e., Mahaweli Irrigation/Power and Housing take two-thirds of all government capital resources.

Basic Economic Facilities

Transportation.—16,000 miles of roads; 8,000 motorable. 900 miles of rail track. 16,000 new motor vehicles (excluding motorcycles) registered in 1981. Main deepwater port Colombo. Others at Trincomalee and Galle. International airport at Colombo; four domestic operating airports. $19 million spent on highways in 1981.

Communication.—Radio, TV, international cable, direct dial telephone, telex. Automatic domestic inter-city dialing by 1983.

Power.—Total 1981 production 1,482 million kWh; 45 percent consumed by industry. Installed capacity 501 MW, two-thirds hydroelectric. Mahaweli project to provide 300–400 MW hydroelectric capacity by 1987.

Natural Resources

Land.—25,322 square miles. Low plain in the north, hills and mountains in the south.

Climate.—Tropical with two monsoon seasons; May–September on western side and December–February on eastern side.

Minerals.—Gemstones, rare earths, graphite, industrial clays, limestone. No petroleum, but offshore prospecting underway. Large phosphate deposits recently discovered.

Forestry.—Forests and forests reserves cover 36 percent of land area. Wood used for fuel as well as manufacturing.

Population

Size.—14.85 million (1981 census); 75 percent rural. Principal cities: Colombo, capital (about 1 million in metropolitan area), Jaffna (120,000), Kandy (100,000).

Languages.—Sinhala, Tamil, English. English widely used in business.

Education.—Free through university, almost all schools government-controlled, 86.5 percent literacy (1981) census).

Labor.—Labor force estimated at 6.3 million with 15 percent unemployment. 25 percent of work force belongs to unions. Legal minimum wages for most workers.

Marketing in Sudan

Contents

Report Revised November 1981

The Sudanese Economy

The Sudan, with an area of 967,491 square miles, is the largest country in Africa. It has a population of about 18 million and a per capita income of about $320. Much of the country is unoccupied or sparsely populated. In contrast to many developing countries there is little population pressure on presently developed land. The manufacturing sector is relatively small and—apart from the processing of such agricultural commodities as cotton, oil seeds, and sugar—is limited to the production of consumer goods and building materials.

While the basic physical and human potential of Sudan is considerable, its economic performance has been disappointing. During the 1960's and early 1970's, the economy grew by little more than the rate of growth of the population. In 1973, the Government formulated an Interim Action Program that marked the beginning of an accelerated development effort. Since then, the Government's development expenditure has increased rapidly and gross domestic product (GDP) has grown at an annual average rate of about 4.5 percent. Increasing external and internal strains on the economy have come with growth.

The Sudan relies on its agricultural sector to generate the majority of its export earnings. Cotton, as the Sudan's major cash crop, dominates the economy. Varying levels of cotton production over the past several years has had a significant effect on the Sudan's balance of payments and its GDP. Other export crops that have a high potential for expanding output include peanuts and sesame. New economic measures have been designed to encourage increased production and export of these crops. Livestock is another sector receiving increased attention for development, particularly those projects which emphasize exports. Petroleum offers future potential for increasing the Sudan's export earnings. Chevron of the United States, which has oil concessions in the Sudan, recently found oil in Darfur and Southern Khordofan.

The most immediate problem facing the Sudan is the crisis in the balance of payments. From 1973 to 1975, the deficit on current account increased from $65 million to $640 million and, since then, has changed little. In spite of high levels of external aid commitments, disbursements actually declined between 1976 and 1978. Debt service obligations mounted, and external payments had accumulated to a level of about $1.2 billion by September 1979. In response to the increasingly difficult financial situation, the Government, in consultation with the International Monetary Fund (IMF), took a number of measures, which include incentives to encourage exports and an economic stabilization program based on limiting the growth of nondevelopment expenditures and increasing tax revenues. It is hoped that with these and other policies, financial imbalances can be corrected within the 1980's, and that during the recovery period a moderate real increase in the GDP will be possible.

Trade Outlook

The United States ranked fifth among the non-petroleum suppliers to the $1.6 billion Sudanese market in 1980, with exports of $142.5 million, as compared with $6 million in 1972. The market for U.S. goods and services has become much more broadly based. In addition to opportunities for exports of heavy construction equipment and agro-industrial machinery, sales potential has increased for trucks and irrigation and oil drilling equipment.

An expansion of the U.S. market share from its 1980 level of 5 percent is possible if financing becomes available. U.S. Export-Import Bank financing is not currently available. The World Bank, U.S. Agency for International Development, and several Arab donors are funding improvements in official agricultural projects. Several million dollars worth of equipment is being financed annually from these sources. The market will be supplied largely through government tenders and will be receptive to U.S. companies that have products that meet their specifications.

Best Export Prospects

Most opportunities for U.S. suppliers are for agricultural machinery, storage facilities, and chemicals. About 1,200 tractors are now being imported per year, most in the 70 to 80 horse-power range and most from the United Kingdom. The market could, if financing were available, easily absorb at least 2,500 units a year as a base. Comparable needs exist for disc plows, ridgers, disc harrows, seeders, planters, multipurpose blades, ditchers, diggers, shakers, etc. Wheat, peanut, and sorghum mechanical harvesters are being sold at a rate of some 120 units per year, while another 120 or more might easily be sold. Cotton pickers are being introduced into the country and should provide a good market in the future as mechanization proceeds. Similarly, the country is short of most types of pumps and other irrigation equipment, as well as grain handling equipment and storage facilities. In chemicals, some 10,000 metric tons of insecticides are imported annually, mainly from France, the United States, Italy, and the United Kingdom.

There is a substantial market in both the public and private industrial sectors for modern oil seed handling and crushing machinery, as well as some interest in new equipment for spinning and weaving, cement manufacture, and clay brick and cement block manufacturing equipment. Large over-the-road trucks will continue to find a good market. In both public and private sectors, however, financing for both new equipment and spares is very scarce, with payment delays running at about 16 months. The Sudanese Government will continue to focus on equipment and spare parts for the Sudanese Railway Corporation financed by the World Bank and Arab donors, on power generation spares (much of the major power equipment is financed under tied loans and grants from non-U.S. donors), and on agricultural and industrial equipment and spares.

Road construction projects offer opportunities for U.S. consultants, engineers, and construction firms. While some of these projects will be limited to firms from the country providing financing, Arab- and World Bank-financed projects are open to all qualified bidders.

In the transportation sector the best prospects for commercial sales lie in the vehicle market. Truck purchases by both the Government and private sector are expected to continue at a high level in support of the country's numerous development projects and expanding road network. Most government purchases will continue to be effected through tenders financed by foreign donors. Private sector purchases should begin constituting a larger share of total demand as the larger transport companies expand their fleets. Japanese and West European firms have a predominant share of the market for heavy trucks, but U.S. firms recently have been successful in some government tenders. American pickup trucks command a good share of the market in areas such as western Sudan. The Japanese have made substantial inroads in this market, and U.S. suppliers will have to market aggressively in order to maintain sales.

There will be substantial demand for modern truck maintenance and service centers and facilities in the years ahead, both in urban areas and along newly constructed highways. Sales opportunities will be limited by the foreign exchange shortage. Joint ventures with Sudanese firms offer a promising alternative for the interested U.S. firm.

Development Planning.—The Sudan Government has reordered national priorities within the framework of the 1979-83 Six-Year Plan (with planning to be done on a rolling 3-year basis) through the Three-Year Public Investment Programs. The main objective of these programs is to concentrate on completion of ongoing projects and on investments that will quickly contribute to the growth of exports and domestic revenues. New projects are to be limited to those that rehabilitate existing projects and help alleviate infrastructural bottlenecks.

As part of its strategy, the Government has embarked upon an Export Action Program (EAP) designed to achieve an annual increase of 7 percent in the volume of cotton production in the Sudan during the period 1979-91. This program is a package of short- and medium-term investments designed to develop an appropriate price-cost-income policy for the irrigated subsector and the parastatals.

Identifiable commitments of assistance total $950 million. This amount includes IMF credits and compensatory financing totaling $472 million, the major share of which will be disbursed in 1981-82 in conjunction with the implementation of the IMF/Sudanese Government stabilization program. Emphasis is being placed on agricultural rehabilitation, energy development, highway construction, railway rehabilitation, port improvement, and telecommunications expansion. Major efforts include the development of more dependable and efficient transportation links between Port Sudan on the Red Sea and the productive areas in the east central and western regions and between the southern region and potential markets in Kenya and Uganda.

World Bank Group commitments to Sudan through May 1980 totaled US$715.1 million. About 45 percent of the total Bank lending has gone into agricultural development; for irrigation projects, including the New Halfa Irrigation Rehabilitation Project; three rain-fed mechanized farming projects; three smallholder development projects—two in the southern region and one in the west; a livestock marketing project; an agricultural research project; and the Agricultural Rehabilitation Program (ARP).

Agriculture

General.—The agriculture sector in the Sudan contributes about 40 percent of the country's gross domestic project, is the source of virtually all exports, provides employment for over two-thirds of the labor force, and supplies inputs for a large proportion of industrial activity. Cotton is the major cash and export crop, accounting for some 56 percent of all exports in recent years; peanuts, sesame, and gum arabic follow at 10,

7.5, and 7 percent, respectively. Recent crop diversification has concentrated on import substitution, with expansion in wheat and sugar output, in part at the expense of cotton. Incomes are relatively low in the agricultural sector. Of the Sudan's total population of about 18 million, an estimated 85 percent live in rural areas. To augment their incomes, many subsistence farmers also work on mechanized or irrigated tenancies to harvest cotton, peanuts, sesame, and cereals. They form a highly mobile labor force of about 1 million people. Labor shortages have occurred in recent years for operations such as cotton picking.

The Sudan's agricultural development has for many years largely depended on the irrigation subsector, which produces over 50 percent by value of the nation's exports. Over the last decade, the area of irrigated land increased on average by 3.5 percent a year. At the same time, the area devoted to cotton, the Sudan's most remunerative export crop, fell by nearly 20 percent. Average cotton yields declined from 4.3 to 2 kantars[1] of seed cotton per feddan[2], and the total volume of cotton exports fell by 35 percent from 1971 to 1977.

The performance of existing irrigation schemes has suffered from the overall economic downturn in the Sudan and higher priority given to development of new schemes. The Sudan's economy should be realizing considerable benefits from its previous irrigation investment, but the Gezira, Blue Nile, White Nile, and New Halfa schemes currently are performing below expectations and have required additional funds to cover budget deficits. This has been due largely to static or declining yields. Technical, financial, and institutional constraints have been the major contributing factors. These have included poor timing of orders for spare parts and other inputs and the neglect of maintenance, as well as a profit-sharing system that stifles farmer incentives. The government recognizes these problems and as part of the new Export Action Program and current Three-Year Public Investment Program has embarked on a new strategy of rehabilitating/modernizing existing irrigation schemes and reforming marketing and incentive policies.

Private investments include the Seleit agro-industrial project, which is expected to have an annual production of 4,500 tons of beef and 3,200 tons of lamb, mainly for export. The Damazin scheme in the south, another private enterprise project, is expected to produce up to 100,000 tons

of crops, but it will not be completed for several years.

Semi-public Arab investment institutions, such as the Arab Authority for Agriculture Investment and Development (AAAID), are expected to make substantial, essentially private investments over the next several years.

The result could be a gradual diminution of public sector dominance in agriculture, although the balance is unlikely to shift for many years. While cotton will certainly remain a government near-monopoly for some time to come, as will most cane, irrigated rice, and perhaps wheat, other products should increasingly come from individual holdings. Much of the country's sorghum (dura) and peanut and sesame production is private. Upland rice will be grown in the South, as will tea, coffee, and tobacco.

Livestock.—Animal husbandry is largely outside the modern sector. Although probably half of all Sudanese agriculturists have at least some animals, most are held under traditional nomadic patterns. Camels, sheep, goats, and cattle are bought and sold, but these animals are held by many nomads for subsistence and prestige more than for commercial purposes. Distances often are great and nomadic herders are less likely than subsistence farmers to receive credit from the few banks. The Government is aware of the problems and has established the Livestock and Meat Marketing Board and the Animal Production Public Corporation to encourage the production and, especially, the marketing of livestock. A number of local, Arab, European, and American firms have become interested in the obvious opportunities in Sudanese poultry, ranching, and meat marketing, and some investments have taken place.

Forestry.—Forestry land covers more than one-fifth of the Sudan's total area. Most of the country's natural and planted forests are located in the southern region. The principal commercial forest product is gum arabic, of which the Sudan provides over 80 percent of the world's supply. Gum arabic production in some years has exceeded 45,000 metric tons. Production varies significantly from year to year depending on weather conditions and availability of labor.

Fishing.—Sudan's total annual catch has been estimated at 16,000 metric tons, but exact data are not available. Each year 300 to 500 tons of fish from the White Nile are dried and exported to Zaire. Commercial fishing in the rivers and along the Red Sea coast has been expanding. The Sudanese Government through its Fisheries Corporation (subsidiary of the Animal Production Corporation) has drawn up a $12.3

---

[1] kantar usually weighs 99 pounds.
[2] feddan equals 1.03 acres.

million program to finance a range of projects aimed at boosting production to 57,000 tons per year by 1985. This would include the production of shrimp (Red Sea) and other fish (Nuba Lake and Malakal).

Manufacturing

Manufacturing contributes about 10 percent of the Sudan's GDP. Much of the Sudan's industrial development is related to the processing of agricultural products. Textile development has been by far the largest, but edible oil pressing, sugar processing, grain milling, tanning, and sack production (from kenaf) are being expanded. Agriculture is likely to continue to be the base upon which industrial expansion will depend.

The bulk of private sector investment has gone into the textile, soap, edible oil pressing, footwear, soft drinks, printing, packaging, and milling industries.

Most large enterprises manufacturing import substitutes were started in the 1960's. In 1962, the Government formed the Industrial Development Corporation (IDC) to manage several public sector factories. The IDC and certain public agencies, such as the government printing press and the mint, have continued to manage a number of industries. In addition to four sugar factories and a tannery, the Government operates five food processing plants, a cannery and date factory at Kareima, a second cannery at Wau, an onion dehydrating plant at Kassala, and a powdered milk factory at Babanousa. The supply of agricultural raw materials often does not match the productive capacity of the factories. Emphasis on the textile and sugar production increased greatly during the 1970's. The Sennar Sugar Factory was completed in 1976 and the Hagar Asalaya plant in 1980. The Kenana Sugar Factory, the world's largest sugar complex, near Kosti began production in February 1980.

Five of the planned seven textile plants and the first phase of a sixth factory, the Friendship Weaving and Textile Factory built by the Chinese, have been completed. With the completion of all seven plants, the Sudan expects to be able to satisfy local demand and to export yarn by the end of 1982.

Telecommunications

In recent years, the Sudan's international telecommunications links have become the most advanced in Africa. Because of the country's size, domestic telecommunication services are still poor. Internal central telephone, telex, and television facilities will be greatly improved with the installation of 14 microwave stations during the 1980's. Several other projects under the ongoing telecommunications program will provide submarine cable links with Jidda, Saudi Arabia; a domestic subscriber truck dialing system; a 500-line automatic telex exchange; and up to 45,000 telephone lines in the capital.

Most telecommunications projects have been financed by loans from the Arab Fund, Saudi Arabia, the African Development Bank, and loans and credit facilities from Japan, American banks, and many European countries.

Transportation

General.—The country's transportation system consists of one railroad with a feeder line, the deep water port of Port Sudan, river steamers, Sudan Airways (the flag carrier), and about 1,640 kilometers of paved roads. The high cost of hauling agricultural exports and essential imports over great distances is a major impediment to economic development.

Independent public corporations manage the railway, ports, and the airlines. By far the largest in the Sudan Railways Corporation (SRC). Others are the Seaports Corporation, the River Transport Corporation, and the Civil Aviation Department.

Southern Sudan has two methods of moving lower value freight—the railway branch to Wau and river transport to Malakal and Juba, the capital of the southern region.

Railway.—The railway is the dominant means of transportation in the Sudan. The State-owned Sudan Railways handles 75 percent of the total intercity freight traffic. The railway system is mainly a single track on the Port Sudan-Khartoum line. This line serves the heart of the agricultural region, carrying about 50 percent of the freight on the rail network. Major emphasis is being directed toward improving the railway's services, efficiency, and reliability. Improvement of the railway track system, workshops, and signaling and communications is underway. The railway projects are financed by loans and technical assistance programs from the World Bank, the African Development Bank, Kuwait, and credits from several other sources, including loans from Germany and other European countries.

Civil Aviation.—The Civil Aviation Department, under the control of the Ministry of Defense since 1970, is responsible for the adinistration of all civil airports in Sudan. The Department is responsible for licensing all private airports to ensure compliance with minimum operational standards. Although 71 well-distributed airports throughout the country are used regularly in transporting passengers and freight within Sudan, only 18 are used in scheduled operations. The remainder are used mainly by light aircraft in aerial work operations, charter, or private aircraft operations.

The Sudan's Civil Aviation Development Plan calls for several important projects for improving and upgrading existing airports and constructing new airports. With limited availability of local funds, the projects are relying heavily on substantial international assistance. The International Bank for Reconstruction and Development (IBRD), International Development Association (IDA), the European Development Fund, and the Saudi Development Fund are supporting the construction of regional airports at Port Sudan, Wau, Juba, and Malakal, but about 50 percent of the financing still needs to be secured before the projects can get underway.

The physical capabilities of Khartoum International Airport are connected closely with the utilization of all airports as all domestic flights originate and terminate in Khartoum. The Khartoum airport was designed to handle 100,000 passengers per year, but the number of passengers embarking and disembarking had exceeded 450,000 by 1978. This has resulted in serious congestion and a slowdown in passenger handling and customs clearance. Although originally scheduled for completion in 1986, the construction of the new Khartoum International Airport at Haj Yousif, 20 kilometers north of Khartoum, is being delayed until financing can be arranged. The Abu Dhabi Fund has pledged $100 million toward construction costs, but sources of the remaining funds have not been identified.

Substantial potential exists for increased U.S. sales of aircraft and equipment for development of the Sudan's aviation sector. In July 1980, Sudan Airways signed a $60 million contract with Boeing for the purchase of three 737's to be delivered in 1982. Opportunities for the sale of additional passenger and cargo aircraft must await the availability of financing.

The Civil Aviation Department will be in the market for essential equipment and services, but such procurement in the short term is severely limited by the country's weak financial situation and lack of financing. Lighting systems will be crucial for increasing aircraft utilization and improving scheduling on domestic routes. Opportunities also exist for the sale of cargo handling equipment as operations are expanding in this area. Sudan Airways is currently interested in the computerization of various airline activities to improve billing and ticketing, reservation services, and financial analysis. Sudan's National Aviation Plan also includes renewal of telecommunications equipment and radio navigation aids.

There is scope for increasing managerial and technical assistance to Sudan Airways. Sudan Airways also will be in the market for a longer term management contract once money is available.

Roads.—Phase One of road construction under the Six-Year Plan was completed in 1980. It increased the length of the Sudanese paved highway system from 782 kilometers (km) in July 1977 to about 1,640 km in October 1980. In addition, there are about 3,600 km of laterite roads, mostly in southern Sudan, and 15,000 to 18,000 km of rough tracks, mainly in northern and western Sudan. The latter can be used only during the dry season. Since 1974, the Sudan Government has given greater priority to the expansion of the country's road network than to other modes of transportation. Funds for construction increased rapidly due in part to several foreign loans and grants in the 1970's. The decision to increase expenditures for road construction reflected a recognition of the railroad's inability to support the country's development effort. Between 1975 and 1980, the paved road network tripled in size. The five-stage highway linking Port Sudan and Khartoum was completed in 1980. Several roads in central Sudan, the country's main agricultural section, are nearing completion.

The Khartoum-Port Sudan highway is the most important road in the country, as virtually all the country's exports and imports are made through Port Sudan. The road also crosses eastern Sudan, the largest mechanized farming region of the country. Many foreign contractors participated in the construction of the 1,200 km road,ᐟ which is of excellent quality. The easternmost section of the road, from Port Sudan through the Red Sea Hills to Haiya, was financed by Abu Dhabi and constructed by Strabag Bau of West Germany.

Road development outside central Sudan and the Khartoum-Port Sudan corridor is planned for 1982 and later, when existing projects are complete.

Ambitious plans developed by the Organization of African Unity for the Pan-African highway system directly involve the Sudan. Both the Cairo-Gaborone and Massawa-Ndjamena roads will pass through the Sudan. The former will include 1,452 km in the Sudan from Wadi Halfa on the border with Egypt to Gallabat on the Ethiopian border. Of this road, the northern portion from Aswan to Khartoum is part of the Egyptian-Sudanese transportation integration program.

Ports.—Port Sudan in the Red Sea is the only deepwater port in the country. It is managed by the Sea Ports Corporation. While Port Sudan can handle current traffic, development projects underway and planned elsewhere in the economy are creating a need for additional port capacity. A World Bank project is financing expansion and improvements at Port Sudan, and the Government is actively seeking funds for the development of a second port at Suakin, 40 km further south.

Mining

There has been considerable interest in the exploration of the Sudan's mineral resources. These include gypsum, chromite, asbestos, and iron. Large deposits of iron ore have been found in the northern Red Sea areas and in western Sudan. A new public corporation for mining has been established to consolidate the various exploratory activities and to facilitate foreign participation in the further exploitation of commercial deposits.

Energy

Electric Power.—At present, hydroelectric power is the only indigenous source of commercial energy available in the Sudan. Existing hydro stations supply about 50 percent of the country's electric energy requirements. The country's noncommercial sources of energy are forests and vegetable wastes (charcoal, sugar cane bagasse, and stalks from cotton fields). Bagasse is used in the sugar factories and charcoal in the households (especially in rural areas) as a source of heat.

Electricity supply is very limited in urban centers, which are distant from the developed area of the Blue Nile Grid (BNG). At present, about 50 such centers, each with more than 5,000 inhabitants, and with a total population of 470,000, are without public electricity. According to the 1978 development program, the Government of Sudan has defined a development strategy for electrification of such centers in which priority will be given to schemes with potential for outstanding economic benefits.

The Public Electricity and Water Corporation (PEWC), the main producer and sole distributor of electricity in the Sudan, generates about 90 percent of the total electricity produced in the country. Self-generating industrial undertak-

ings account for the balance. PEWC's operational areas are Khartoum, Blue Nile, Damazin, Kordofan, Darfur, Southern Region, Red Sea, and the Northern and Eastern Regions. Most of these areas contain small, diesel plants operating at individual population centers. Only the BNG and Eastern areas include two or more interconnected power plants feeding the major load centers in their respective areas. At present, each of these two areas operates independently. A transmission line linking the two systems is planned to be constructed in the near future.

PEWC's installed power capacity is about 234 megawatts (MW), of which 118 MW are hydroelectric and the balance is thermal. The principal generating and transmission facilities are located in the BNG along the Blue Nile, with an installed capacity of 177 MW, of which 105 MW are hydro. The BNG system produces about 90 percent of PEWC's total energy and supplies the city of Khartoum and surrounding areas, as well as Sennar, Damazin, Wad Medani, Hassa Heissa, Es Suki, Singa, and other population centers. It also supplies various irrigation schemes at N.W. Sennar, Wad El Hadad, Guneid, Rahad, and Gezira.

Petroleum.—One factor that could considerably improve the Sudan's long-term economic prospects is the commercial value of recent oil finds. Five of the 23 oil wells dug by Standard Oil of California (Chevron) in Unity Field and other Chevron wells have a total reserve in excess of 80 million barrels, which is estimated to be sufficient to meet local consumption needs for 15 years. The Government is seeking co financing for the planned $700-$900 million Rahak refinery. The refinery would have an initial capacity of 25,000 barrels per day (bbl/d) and a minimum production level of 15,000 bbl/d. Its crushing unit would produce a full range of petroleum products.

At the present time, petroleum imports are processed at the Port Sudan refinery. About 35 percent of the gasoline and 44 percent of the kerosene consumed are imported, mainly from Kuwait.

The recently completed pipeline from Port Sudan to Khartoum has facilitated deliveries at least to the Greater Khartoum area. Several major road projects being implemented will further improve marketing and distribution.

Currency and Credit

Currency

The Sudanese pound is the basic unit of currency. It is divided into 100 piasters (PT) or

1,000 milliemes (M/Ms). Bank of Sudan notes in denominations of LS20, LS10, LS5, LS1, PT50, and PT25 are legal tender up to any amount. Coins are legal tender for any payment up to PT200 in value.

In September 1979, the Sudan instituted a new two-tier system of currency exchange with an official and a parallel rate. The official rate of US$2=LS1 (one Sudanese pound) applies to "essential" imports and exports, while all other transactions are subject to a fluctuating parallel rate of about US$1=LS1.25.

Commodities subject to the new parallel rate include medical, pharmaceutical, and laboratory equipment; seeds; spare parts; nonagricultural chemicals; tires; various types of electrical equipment; cement; glass; wood; rope; trucks; and buses. Also included are many types of consumer goods, such as tape recorders, rugs, stationery, canned food, fresh fruit, plastic and rubber products, and lighting and heating equipment.

Applications to import these commodities will be considered in light of available parallel market resources. The currency reforms are expected to stimulate foreign investment and to increase bank deposits from remittances by expatriate Sudanese workers, thereby freeing more foreign exchange in the Sudan.

Banking Institutions

The structure of the Sudanese banking system was altered in May 1970 when all commercial banks were nationalized. Under the Banks Nationalization Act of 1970, the entire Sudanese banking system came under public sector control. Under a concurrent amendment to the Bank of Sudan Act, the board of directors of the Bank of Sudan has effective control of the nationalized commercial banks.

The Sudan has a well-organized, commercial banking establishment with five State-owned commercial banks operating in open competition with one another. In addition the Sudan Industrial Bank, the Agricultural Bank, the Estates Bank, and the Sudan Investment Bank provide assistance to private sector enterprises. There is capital in reasonable amounts in private banks outside the banking system, and an attractive project may draw sufficient attention to meet local currency needs through such sources. A stock exchange being organized by the Bank of Sudan also may become a source of local capital in the future (see Appendix A for listing of banking institutions).

The Sudan Development Corporation (SDC) is a financial and investment corporation of the Government. SDC mobilizes both local and foreign capital for projects and enterprises in the following fields: Agriculture, irrigation, animal production, infrastructure, foreign trade, industry, and mining. SDC provides financing through loans, guarantees, and equity participation and assists in coordinating project financing.

Other possible sources of foreign exchange capital include the Arab Investment Company, the Sudanese-Kuwaiti Investment Company, TRIAD Natural Resources (Sudan) Ltd., the International Finance Corporation, and large Western commercial banks.

Specialized Banks

All three specialized banking institutions (the Agricultural Bank, the Industrial Bank, and the Estates Bank) are fully owned by the Bank of Sudan and their financial resources consist mainly of funds provided by the Bank of Sudan and budgetary contributions.

The Agricultural Bank received LS2 million from the Bank of Sudan during 1975-76 in the form of increased capitalization. It has expanded its operations considerably.

The Industrial Bank intends short- and medium-term loans as well as technical support to private sector industrial enterprises. Ordinarily, the Industrial Bank extends loans for 2 to 15 years. Interest rates charged are 8.5 percent on 2- to 5-year loans and 9.5 percent on loans of 6 to 15 years. There also is a commitment charge of 0.5 percent per annum on the unused balance of the loan. The Industrial Bank may lend up to two-thirds of the total capital of an enterprise. In general, the Bank encourages firms to rely on suppliers' credits (which it is empowered to guarantee) to the maximum extent possible. In some cases, the Bank participates in the share capital of companies. The Industrial Bank extends services, mainly for enterprises such as flour mills, vegetable oil factories, and textile plants which will use domestically produced agricultural inputs.

The Sudanese Estates Bank extends financing for low-cost housing. Low-income borrowers pay 4.5 percent interest and middle- and high-income borrowers 6 percent for 20-year loans.

Banking Act

The Banks Nationalization Act of 1970, as amended in october 1975, requires each commercial bank to register as a private company under the Companies Act of 1925, with the majority of shares to be owned by the Bank of Sudan. The remainder of the shares are to be owned by the Government, as represented by the Ministry of Finance, Planning and National Economy.

In February 1976, the Bank of Sudan issued conditions under which foreign banks may operate in the Sudan. They are allowed to open branches according to the following conditions: (1) The foreign bank is required to strictly adhere to and comply with all laws, circulars, and instructions relating to banking business in the Sudan whether issued or to be issued in the future, (2) The foreign bank also is required to transfer to the Sudan a minimum capital of LS3 million within 6 months from the date of opening the first branch in the Sudan.

Exchange Control

Exchange control is administered by the Bank of Sudan, with most of the details being carried by authorized State banks. Foreign commerce payments are channeled through the following banks which have been designated by the Ministry of Finance, Planning and National Economy as approved foreign exchange dealers: Khartoum Bank, Unity Bank, the Sudan Commercial Bank, People's Cooperative Bank, and El Nilein Bank. These banks may approve applications for the release of the foreign exchange in the designated currencies by one of the following methods, provided that the application is accompanied by a valid import license and in some cases a contract of purchase.

Advance Payments.—With respect to goods imported against advance payment, authorized Sudanese dealers are restricted to supplying $250 or 25 percent of the value of the goods, whichever is less. Payments in excess of this amount must be arranged through the Exchange Control Section of the Bank of Sudan.

On Consignment or On Credit.—Goods may be imported on consignment. A Customs Certificate of Value evidencing actual entry of goods must be produced before foreign exchange is released. In all cases, the amount shown on the Customs Certificate of Value has to be the same as that remitted abroad in settlement for the goods.

Administration of Controls

There is close coordination between the Exchange Control Authorities (Bank of Sudan) and the Ministry of Finance, Planning and National Economy. Import licenses and registration forms approved by the Ministry are valid only when certified by the Bank of Sudan.

In practice, the granting of foreign exchange is automatic once an import license has been issued

cash against documents (c.a.d.) or documents against acceptance of a bill. When payment for imports is made against the release of documents, an Exchange Control form is required to be completed at the time of payment. If documents are to be released against acceptance of a bill, the forms are completed when payment is actually effected (i.e., on maturity of the bill). In both cases, the authorized dealer is required to cancel the Customs Certificate of Value presented by the importer as evidence the goods were imported.

Letter of Credit.—A letter of credit can be opened and used in connection with imports provided that: (1) the duration of its validity does not exceed 6 months beyond the expiration date of the import license/registration form, and (2) the terms of the credit require evidence that the goods were shipped to the Sudan. (An on-board bill of lading or similar certificate will satisfy this requirement.)

Foreign goods often are purchased on the basis of cash against documents. In view of possible delays in obtaining onward transportation after the goods have arrived at Port Sudan, letters of credit can tie up local capital for as long as 6 months. For this reason letters of credit generally are not required by European and Japanese suppliers selling to established firms in the Sudan. The U.S. supplier's insistence on a letter of credit could influence the Sudanese merchant to buy elsewhere, even if the American price were more attractive.

Price Controls

Wholesale prices in the manufacturing sector are controlled by the Government. They are generally fixed well above production costs to allow companies to have a reasonable profit margin, but delays in the adjustment of prices to reflect inflation and higher input costs frequently reduce or eliminate this margin entirely. When more than one factory is involved, sales prices are fixed as a percentage of the weighted average production per unit. This procedure allows the better managed factory to achieve profits above the average of other factories.

Consumer price indices cover only greater Khartoum; i.e., Khartoum, Omdurman, and Khartoum North.

commodities subject to price control are gasoline and the main consumer items. Recently, the control system has been made more flexible through the frequent revision of official prices to reflect supply and demand conditions.

Repatriation of Capital and Profits

All profits accruing from the investment of foreign capital may be remitted abroad in the same currency in which they entered the Sudan after payment of all taxes, dues, and other liabilities. Bona fide savings of foreign employees of approved industries can be transferred abroad.

In case of liquidation of any enterprise, the Government permits remittance of the net value of that enterprise on the date of liquidation.

Trade Regulations

Trade Policy

The Sudan maintains a liberal trade policy, although some imports considered competitive with local production are subject to quantitative restrictions. The customs tariff, primarily revenue producing rather than protective, is applicable to goods from all countries except Egypt and Jordan, which are granted preferences.

All imports from Israel are prohibited in accordance with the Arab League boycott policy. Imports from the Republic of South Africa also are excluded.

Imports into the Sudan must be made directly from the country of origin except in the case of certain items, such as spare parts and accessories, which may be imported from a third country.

Multilateral Trade Agreements

Among the recently agreed-upon tariff cuts resulting from the Multilateral Trade Negotiations (MTN), the one of greatest interest to the Sudan was long staple cotton. Tariff cuts from 4.9 percent to 2.8 percent were agreed to as part of the Tokyo Round.

Under the Trade Agreements Act of 1979, the Sudan became eligible, on January 1, 1980, to receive the benefit of full U.S. MTN tariff cuts on approximately 2,500 products.

Import System.—Imports have been recategorized into four sections, comprising goods which can be imported under open general license, goods imported on an annual quota basis, goods imported after authorization from the relevant ministry, and banned goods. The move is an attempt to simplify the complex import regulations.

Duties and Taxes on Imports

Tariff Structure.—The customs tariff schedule, organized along the Brussels Tariff Nomenclature (BTN), is three-column. Column I is the list of commodities. Column II is a general rate listing applicable to imports from all countries other than Egypt and Jordan. Column III is a preferential rate for goods of Egyptian and Jordanian origin.

Duties.—The Sudanese tariff makes use of both specific and ad valorem rates. Specific rates are applied almost exclusively to alcoholic beverages and tobacco. Ad valorem duties range from "free" to 1,100 percent. Commodities not specifically mentioned in the Sudanese Customs Tariff Schedule are dutiable at a 40 percent ad valorem rate. Most duties imposed ad valorem are based on the c.i.f. value of the goods. Duties are payable in Sudanese currency. When the invoice cost is expressed in a foreign currency, it is converted at a rate determined by the Sudanese Director of Customs.

The highest duty rates apply to beer and wine, both of which are produced locally, and to items classified as luxuries or nonessential. The rate of duty on capital goods and raw materials varies from "free" to 60 percent.

Technical Standards

The Sudan uses both the metric and the British weights and measures systems. The metric system is used in international trade. Weights and measures still in use in the provinces are based on the old Egyptian systems with the dirhem of 3.12 grams as the fundamental unit of weight and the keila of 16.5 liters as the basic unit of liquid measure. A feddan equals 1.038 acres or 4,200 square meters. Cotton is often measured by the kantar. A kantar of ginned cotton usually weighs 99 pounds. In different regions the kantar's weight varies from 99 pounds to 312 pounds. A bale of Sudanese unginned cotton averages 420 pounds, but, depending on the region of origin, a bale can weigh from 300 to 450 pounds. The Sudan Almanac has a complete conversion table for Sudanese weights, which should be consulted if further details are required.

Internal Taxes

Quay Dues.—Quay dues are assessed at Port Sudan on all goods discharged from any ship or transferred from one ship to another at the rate of 2.5 percent ad valorem on the c.i.f. value of the goods.

Royalties.—A royalty is levied on a limited group of items, whether imported or exported. The group includes ivory, gum, hides, cattle, peanuts, and manganese ore.

Consumption Taxes.—Consumption taxes are collected at the time of import of certain products into the Sudan. These taxes are primarily specific and apply to a variety of goods, including alcohol and preparations containing alcohol, shoes, tobacco, soaps, and various other goods.

Defense Tax.—A 10 percent tax is levied on a number of products.

Nontariff Import Controls

Import Licensing.—All imports into the Sudan are subject to import licensing. Imports are placed under one of two classifications: (1) specifically licensed goods that are likely to compete with locally produced commodities or are considered luxuries, and (2) goods considered essential, either for consumption or for economic development (generally, these are under open general license). Import licenses or registration forms for imports under open general licenses are usually valid for 3 months but subject to extension provided application for extension is made at least 3 weeks before the expiration date and reasons supporting the extension are given.

The following goods may be imported without a license: (1) goods imported by the Government; (2) goods imported by parcel post and air freight with a value not exceeding LS2, or bona fide gifts, declared as such, not exceeding LS5; (3) trade samples of no commercial value; and (4) vehicles traveling across the customs boundary for the purpose of carrying passengers, goods, or accessories.

There are no special restrictions against importations from the dollar area.

There is no separate foreign exchange license requirement. The allocation of foreign exchange for import purposes is determined solely by the Ministry of Finance, Planning and National Economy, which partly bases its allocations on advice received from the Ministry of Commerce and Supply. This Ministry is responsible for forecasting the needs of the country's different import sectors, relying to some degree on the estimates of the State Trading Corporation (STC) for its planned purchases over a 2-year period. Imports made by government agencies are not subject to licensing procedures. These are relaxed somewhat for goods considered essential for the country's economic development, which are purchased abroad by private companies. These include most raw materials. The latter category of products are usually imported under "Open General License." This license is granted by a special committee of the Council of Ministers after they have screened the application using the same criteria applied to goods likely to compete with locally produced commodities or that fall into the luxury category.

In screening license applications, this committee generally looks for the best quality products at the most favorable prices from suppliers offering the most advantageous payment terms. During periods of limited foreign exchange, the committee either may delay approval of certain license applications, or return them without approval.

The importer may wait from 2 weeks to 2 months before his license application is approved. An import license generally is valid for 3 months, as are registrations for imports made under "Open General License." This period may be extended, provided the application for extension is made at least 3 weeks before the original license expires.

Certain categories of imports.—Imports such as household furnishings and office equipment require special licenses granted on an ad hoc basis, subject to the availability of foreign exchange.

Special Requirements

No live plants may be imported into the Sudan without a permit from the Ministry of Agriculture, Food and Natural Resources. Fresh vegetables and fresh fruits may be imported without a permit provided they are presented to the proper customs officer and are certified as to examination by a plant quarantine officer.

Importation of animals, plants, and seeds is subject to quarantine regulations. Every imported animal must be accompanied by a certificate from a veterinary authority indicating that it was free from disease at the time of exportation.

Imported articles of gold must bear a recognizable hallmark.

Applications to import cotton seed must be made to the Director of Agriculture, Khartoum, and must indicate all details regarding quantity, variety, and place of origin. Cotton seed will be subject to fumigation before delivery to the addressee. A specific import license is required for all textile/apparel products except knit apparel, carpets, impregnated and rubberized fabrics, jute sacks, and textile/apparel products, including wool and blended wool blankets.

The Ministry of Industry and Mining does not consider most applications for importation, unless insurance has been taken out with a Sudanese company. Exceptions are made when the national Sudanese interest requires that insurance be taken out with countries outside the

Sudan. Such cases should be submitted to the Ministry of Finance, Planning and National Economy for approval.

Advance Rulings on Customs Classification

Requests for advance ruling on customs classification of merchandise may be submitted in writing to the Director Customs, Department of Customs, Box 323, Khartoum, Sudan.

Fines and Penalties

At present even minor violations of customs regulations are taken to court. Penalties usually include fines and/or imprisonment. All penalties shall be in addition to any forfeiture of the goods.

Abandoned Goods

Goods are considered as abandoned after 3 months in storage, after 6 months in bonded warehouses, and after 12 hours if the goods are subject to rapid deterioration or decay. The customs authority will destroy such goods or dispose of them at the owner's expense. The proceeds for such goods, after deduction of all charges, are retained by the customs for the account of the shipper or importer for 3 years from the date of sale.

Export Duties

In October 1973 the basis of the export duty was changed from a specific to an ad valorem assessment and at the same time its coverage was widened to include additional exports. The rates imposed vary from 15% of f.o.b. value for hides and skins, 10% for long-staple cotton, to 20% for livestock and meat.

Shipping Documents

Documents required from U.S. exporters on ocean, air or mail shipments from the United States to the Sudan are the commercial invoice, the bill of lading (air waybill for air cargo) and, in certain cases, sanitary or quarantine certificates. Consular invoices or special certificates of origin are not required. A packaging list is not necessary if the commercial invoice contains all the required information. A specific import declaration form is required by the Sudanese customs authorities for clearance of imported goods.

Insurance

Insurance on all imports into the Sudan by both the public and the private sectors has to be obtained from Sudanese insurance companies. The Ministry of Industry does not consider most applications for importation unless insurance has been taken out with a Sudanese company. Exceptions are made when the national Sudanese interest requires that insurance be taken out with countries outside the Sudan. Such cases should be submitted to the Ministry of Finance and National Economy for approval.

Marking, Labeling, and Packing Requirements

Marking and Labeling.—Other than for cotton piece goods, the Sudan has few specific marking and labeling requirements. To facilitate accurate identification of items listed on accompanying forms, goods and containers should be labeled and marked clearly.

All cotton piece goods, other than handwoven head and body wraps not exceeding 5 yards in length and 54 inches in width, are required to be folded in uniform yard and meter lengths. Each piece should be visibly marked on the exterior to indicate the exact number of meters or yards contained in the piece. Where the width is specified, it is to be correctly marked in inches or centimeters. Sudanese law requires that these markings be stapled into the material or be shown on labels affixed to the piece. Cotton velvets may be folded in laps of one-half yard or meter, if markings conform to regulations in other respects. Cotton goods rolled and not folded are required to comply with marking regulations. Hanks, skeins, balls, spools, and cards of cotton thread, including sewing, darning, embroidery, and knitting cotton for retail trade, should be labeled to indicate the length of width weight in one of the units prescribed by Sudanese law (i.e., in kilos or meters).

Marks-of-origin are not mandatory for goods imported into the Sudan. It is considered good practice to label products "Made in U.S.A."

Packing.—Secure packing is recommended to protect merchandise from rough handling and pilferage. Whenever possible, goods should be baled or fastened with hoop iron or packed in strong wooden boxes. Fiberboard and other cartons should not be used as they may be inadequate to protect the shipment.

Specialized Customs Provisions

Samples and Advertising Matter.—Bona fide trade samples of no commercial value may be admitted duty free but may not include tobacco or alcoholic liquids.

When dutiable samples accompany a traveler,

a refund of any customs duty paid will be allowed if the samples are reexported from the Sudan within 6 months from date of imports.

Imports of advertising matter can benefit by a reduction in duty of 30 percent if not for sale, if not of a size used in commercial practice, and if clearly marked with the name or trademark of the advertised firm or commodity.

Magazines, Books, and Printed Matter.— Imports of magazines, books and other printed matter do not require registration or licensing; however, remittances for such imports are subject to exchange control approval.

Investment in the Sudan

Investment Climate

Throughout most of the Sudanese economy, private investment, local and foreign, is welcome. Government companies are not given special advantages, such as priority for import permits. While businesspeople would be hard put to complain about the Sudan's investment policies, they do face significant problems, such as an underdeveloped transportation system and a shortage of foreign exchange. Headway is being made against transportation and communications problems through well-planned projects.

On balance, the Sudan offers local entrepreneurship, a relatively well-trained work force, and an open, friendly attitude toward foreigners in general and Americans in particular. Private activity declined from 1965 through 1972 due to an unstable political environment and the uncertainty generated by the nationalization/confiscation measures of 1970 and 1971. The Government returned some confiscated property to private ownership and settled compensation claims. It also enacted legislation that provides incentives and guarantees for private enterprises, both domestic and foreign. The thrust of the legislation has been to make clear that the Sudan Government desires to carry out flexible and attractive investment policies.

Legislation Governing Investment

A unified investment law has been promulgated by the People's Assembly. The most important features of the draft law concern streamlining investment applications, easing exchange controls, and protecting investors against confiscation. The major existing investment incentives are described in the following laws.

The Encouragement of Investment Act 1980.—This act is generally a progressive piece of legislation which emphasized incentives rather than restrictions. Examples of such incentives include tax reductions for up to 15 years, facilitated land acquisition, protective tariffs, customs exemptions, favorable electrical and freight rates and full remittance of profits and capital. To qualify for these concessions, a firm should propose to do at least one of the following: manufacture products that increase national income; remove bottlenecks in development; provide necessary services for consolidating economic and social development; utilize local raw materials; assisting in achieving self sufficiency, and consolidating the balance of payment; provide direct or indirect local labor opportunities; or undertake operations having defense or strategic importance or contributing to the objectives of economic cooperation or integration with Arab and African countries.

The most important element of this Act is the creation of a single body, called the "Secretariat General for Investment", headed by a Secretary General who is the Minister of State for Finance and National Economy. He is overseen by a Ministerial Committee whose function is to decide general policy and investment priorities, without becoming involved in day-to-day decisions. A consultative committee chaired by the Secretary General is charged with making specific recommendations on applications for investment licenses, the extent of privileges granted under those licenses and any changes which later might become necessary. A working Staff called the "Technical Secretariat", evaluates feasibility studies and investment license requests, coordinates among the various interested ministries and follows up on licensing procedures to ensure reasonably expeditious handling.

Petroleum Resources Act (1972).—This law provides for a 13-member Board of Petroleum Affairs (BPA) chaired by the Minister of Industry and Mining. BPA submits recommendations to the Council of Ministers, which makes the final decisions on applications for exploration licenses and production leases. While such licenses are theoretically granted only to companies registered in the Sudan in accordance with the Companies Ordinance of 1925, in practice U.S. firms have been able to negotiate terms which protect their interests under U.S. tax laws.

Each exploration license covers an area not to exceed 800 square kilometers (with a minimum width of 15 kilometers) and has a validity period of 2 years, extendable up to 8 years. Each production lease normally covers an area not to exceed 250 square kilometers and has a validity period of no more than 60 years. There is no limit to the number of licenses and leases a company can obtain. If it elects to do so, the Government, directly or through one of its corporations, may take an interest in the capital of the producing company of up to 25 percent. The Minister is empowered to grant exemptions for import and reexport duties during the exploration stage. Exploration licenses cost LS500 ($625) a piece to obtain. Thereafter, there is an exploration fee of LS10 ($12.50) per 100 square kilometers annually during the first 4 years and LS200 ($400) for each additional year of the validity period. Royalties (12.5 percent ad valorem at well head), fees (LS60 or $120 per square kilometer), and taxes on oil production are not to total less than 50 percent of net profits (with royalties defined as a production expense), unless the Government becomes a partner in which case no minimum tax is prescribed. The Act authorizes the prospecting company that discovers oil to establish a refinery in the Sudan in accordance with conditions laid down by the Council of Ministers.

The text of the Act and related documents are obtainable at a nominal charge from the Director, Geological Survey Department, Ministry of Industry and Mining, P.O. Box 410, Khartoum, Sudan.

Mines and Quarries Act (1972).—This Act affirms the Government's control of all mineral resources and establishes a Mines and Quarries Board to issue prospecting licenses and mining leases. The Minister of Industry and Mining retains ultimate control, however, including the right to decide appeals against board decisions. As few specifics are offered in the Act, the Minister of the Board is legally able to agree to practically any proposal, including ones which seek concessions such as those granted in the Industrial Investment Act. Further information may be obtained from the Director, Geological Survey Department, Ministry of Industry and Mining, P.O. Box 410, Khartoum, Sudan.

A joint Sudanese-Saudi Arabian authority has been formed to determine how the Sudan's offshore mineral resources are to be prospected and mined. No details are available on the size of the resources, which Sudanese sources have described as enormous.

Organization and Promotion of Investment in Economic Services Act (1972).—Economic services covered by this Act include tourism, transportation, warehousing, and fertilizer and insecticide spraying, as well as any other services provided by the Ministry of Finance, Planning and National Economy. The act provides for con-

cessions similar to those in the Industrial Investment Act, including a tax holiday for periods of up to 6 years, land at low cost, and guarantees for repatriation of foreign capital and profits. Moreover, it states that guarantees contained in the Industrial Investment Act pertaining to noncommercial risks will be applicable to investments in the services sector as well.

Agricultural Investment Act.—This Act, issued in late 1975, provides incentives similar to those contained in the Industrial Investment Act, including the allocation of land and other facilities at favorable rates. Tax incentives, however, are offered over a more extended time frame in recognition of the longer startup periods of such ventures.

Foreign Ownership of Business

The legislation and procedures described above apply equally to all investors, both Sudanese and foreign. Foreign companies may be established in the Sudan for industrial and other legitimate purposes with the only rigid restriction being that enterprises dealing solely in wholesale/retail activities are reserved for Sudanese citizens. The government and the law are flexible in regard to equity participation. There is no requirement that Sudanese capital—even a token percentage—be associated with a foreign undertaking, nor are there laws or regulations in force that create any distinction between foreign-owned and domestically owned firms. In practice, some local equity is expected by the Sudanese. Foreign investors with reputable and knowledgeable local partners probably will find such joint ventures advantageous.

Land transactions generally are subject to government control. Foreigners usually are not allowed to purchase land from Sudanese citizens. They may buy land already owned by foreigners. In practice, the Government owns most of the land, inasmuch as all land not officially registered to an individual is government property. The Government is prepared to lease land to foreigners for long periods of time at low rates. There is a surplus of land for leasing both for agriculture and for industrial sites. Land is available within easy reach of the major urban center of Khartoum. In terms of property other than land, there is no law making ownership more difficult for foreigners than for Sudanese.

Registration

Registration is done under the provisions of the Companies Ordinance Act, 1927, as amended, and at the discretion of the Ministry of Industry and Mining. A certified company charter, statutes, articles of association, or a similar instrument should contain the names of company directors and authorized Sudanese representatives. The registration fee is LS25 ($31.25).

Investment Guarantees

In addition to the provisions in Sudanese investment laws, U.S. investors in the Sudan can be protected under the "Guarantee of Private Investments" signed on March 17, 1959, by the United States and the Sudan. Under this agreement, prospective American investors can obtain guarantees against currency inconvertibility, expropriations, and war losses through the Overseas Private Investment Corporation (OPIC). Information on this insurance can be obtained from the Insurance Division, Overseas Private Investment Corporation, 1129 20th Street, N.W., Washington, D.C. 20527. Telephone: (202) 653-2920.

The Sudan is a signatory of the Settlement of Investment Disputes Between States and Nationals of Other States, which also has been ratified by the United States.

Extent of Foreign Investment

Accurate data on foreign investment are not available. At the end of 1980, total foreign investment was estimated at $500 million. Investment by U.S. companies presently totals about $400 million, most in the area of oil and exploration. The principal U.S. investors are Mobil Oil Company (distribution services), Sterling Drug International (pharmaceutical manufacture), Union Carbide (battery plant), and Chevron International (oil exploration).

Business Organization

Business organization in the Sudan closely follows British practice. In general, the three types of business organizations are:

Limited Company.—A limited company is organized in much the same as an American corporation. The business is owned in shares, and a shareholder's liability is limited to his actual investment. An American investor establishing a business in the Sudan in most cases would organize his/her business as a limited company.

Partnership.—Each partner is liable to the full extent of his/her assets for the liabilities of the firm, unless the partnership is limited.

Sole Proprietorship.—The owner has unlimited liability.

No laws or regulations are in effect that require that Sudanese capital be associated with an investment, but there is an unwritten preference for Sudanese participation. Obtaining permission to engage in business and to register the company are the two main legal steps to be accomplished. Approval for the first step is granted jointly by the Ministry of Finance, Planning and National Economy and the Ministry of Industry and Mining. Their approval is extended under the Traders License and Taxation of Business Profits Tax Ordinance, 1930, as amended. Without this approval, a business cannot be carried on legally.

Franchising and Licensing

Sudanese law does not contain specific provisions for franchising or licensing. The primary consideration in either type of arrangement is the formalization of a remittance procedure for any fees and royalties to the franchisor or licensor.

Trademarks and Patents

Trademarks may be registered in the Sudan after payment of nominal fees and the deposit of certain forms. The Sudan's Trade Marks Ordinance closely follows British law and contains essentially the same provisions as the U.S. law for protection of trademarks. The Sudan is not a member of any international trademark protection organization. When a convention of investment is negotiated, trademark protection clauses should be included in the contract.

No patent law is in effect. Original inventions and discoveries, together with exact descriptions in words and drawings, can be notarized before qualified commissioners of oaths. If inventions thereafter are infringed or pirated, legal proceedings for appropriate relief can be instituted.

Employment of Aliens.—The employment of foreigners in the Sudan and Sudanese abroad is regulated by the Manpower Act of 1973. By law, a labor permit will not be granted to an alien if a qualified Sudanese is available to fill the job. Priority is to be given to residents rather than incoming aliens and to nationals of Arab and African countries. In practice, when applying for approval of an investment, a company can request permission to employ foreign personnel. Although documentation such as labor permits, residence permits, and subsequent reentry permits are still required, approval of the investment constitutes general permission to employ such expatriate personnel.

An alien is not allowed to change his work specialization or to transfer to another firm without authorization of the Ministry of Public Service and Administration Reform (which has jurisdiction over all labor questions). The employer of an alien is required to assign a qualified Sudanese counterpart to be trained by that alien. Government authorities have proven to be flexible on the duration of such training, particularly for top management positions in new enterprises. Appeals against decisions regarding employment of foreigners are to be directed to the Minister of Public Service and Administration Reform whose decision is final.

Taxation

For any enterprise established in accordance with the investment laws, the Minister of Finance and National Economy may exempt or reduce business profit taxes, municipal dues, etc., for 5 to 15 years. Without such concessions, the investor is required to pay taxes as outlined in Appendix C of this report. Customs duties averaging 40 percent ad valorem of the c.i.f. value plus a 5 to 10 percent development tax in addition to quay and port dues are levied on all machinery and equipment. Municipal land rents and dues vary in accordance with the location of the enterprise (e.g., in Khartoum North, the main industrial area, the cost of land plus service fees amounts to LS0.18 or $23 per square meter per annum.

The rate of tax on business profits is progressive, with the maximum rate of 60 percent being imposed on annual profits exceeding LS40,000 for public companies and LS20,000 for private companies. Personal income tax progresses from 15 percent of the second LS1000 of taxable income to 70 percent of income in excess of LS14,000.

Selling in the Sudan

Distribution Channels

The commercial distribution system in the Sudan is a mixture of State and private enterprises. There are numerous examples of complementary, overlapping, and competitive operations between the public and private sectors. Wholesaling and distribution functions are about equally divided between the public sector and private interests. Retailing is largely a function of the private sector which is dominated by family enterprises.

Distribution Centers

The Sudan's estimated population of 17 million is distributed unevenly. More than 2 million people reside in a 64,000-square-mile area at the juncture of the White and Blue Niles. The principal marketing area is the Three Towns, which is comprised of Khartoum, Khartoum North (the leading industrial center), and Omdurman (largely residential). Known also as the "triangular capital," these three towns form a single metropolitan area, which is the focus of commerce and industry. Demand for higher priced and more sopisticated products is generally greatest in the Three Towns. Port Sudan (100,000) is the country's only major port. Smaller towns having about 13 percent of the total urban population include Kassala with 86,000 people, Wad Medani (67,000), Qedaref (61,000), Atbara (55,000) and Al Fashir (50,000). An estimated 45 percent of the population is in the 0-14 years age bracket and 7 percent is 50 years or older.

Government Procurement

Sales to the Government may be made through private agents, State trading companies, government ministries and agencies, State-owned agricultural entities and irrigation schemes, and government-controlled industries. Local agents acting for foreign manufacturers are required to be registered with the Government to qualify as bidders on government contracts. The Government purchases about 10 percent of its requirements through the Sudanese Government Purchasing Agent, 3-4 Cleveland Road, St. James, London, England. The remaining 90 percent is purchased through government procurement agencies in Khartoum, Atbara, and Barakat.

Announcements of tender requests are carried in the government-owned Arabic newspapers. It is important to do as much preparatory work as possible on a project before the publication of the tender announcement. Bid deadlines are often short and contracts rarely are awarded to firms that begin to compete only after the tender documents are in hand. Some tenders are not announced. In some cases, firms negotiate directly for contracts on projects they propose to the Government.

State Trading

The State Trading Corporation (Telex No. 311, P.O. Box 211, Khartoum) includes the following branches:

The Trade and Service Corporation (Telex No. 335, P.O. Box, Khartoum) is the country's biggest importer of general merchandise (textiles, building materials, chemicals, pharmaceuticals, and foodstuffs). It distributes consumable goods and acts as an agent for international companies for general merchandise and general insurance.

The Engineering Equipment Corporation (Telex No. 331, P.O. Box 97, Khartoum) is an importer and distributor of agricultural, engineering, accounting, electronic, and household equipment.

The Automobile Corporation (Telex No. 311, P.O. Box 221, Khartoum) is a leading Sudanese importer of diesel trucks, vehicles, tires, spare parts, and related assembly plants.

The Silos and Storage Corporation (P.O. Box 62, Khartoum) owns warehouses and silos throughout the Sudan. It handles storage and distribution of all types of agricultural products.

Selling Under AID Programs

The U.S. Agency for International Development (AID) program in the Sudan was reestablished in 1978 after several years absence. Since that time, AID's program has focused on two major components: development assistance (funds allocated for specific projects such as upgrading the traditional agricultural sector and rural health services) and P.L. 480 or Food for Peace (loan financing of surplus U.S. agricultural commodities and direct grants of food aid to private voluntary agencies).

For U.S. fiscal year 1982, AID has requested economic support funding for a Commodity Import Program (C.I.P.). This grant would be used to help alleviate balance-of-payments problems. The fund, governed by Security Supporting Assistance legislation, has a greater degree of built-in flexibility then many other AID programs, including Development Assistance. The C.I.P. is designed to support three major sectors: Agriculture, transportation, and industry. In general, use of those monies should meet the following criteria: funds should go to enterprises that use existing idle capacity and that encourage export promotion or import substitution. The Sudanese Government has stated its intention to allocate 25 percent of Commodity Import Program funds to the private sector.

Marketing Aids

Advertising Media.—Advertising is available in newspapers, magazines, billboards, neon signs, slides and short films in movie theaters, radio and television, local exhibitions and displays, and direct mail. The advice of local specialists should be sought before embarking on a publicity campaign. The major advertising agencies are located in Khartoum and include the following: Al Ayam Printing and Publishing House, P.O. Box 363; Al Sahafa Printing and Publishing House, P.O. Box 1228; the Com-

mercial Office, Ministry of Information and Culture, P.O. Box 291; Al Gorashy Publishing House, P.O. Box 536; and FAL Advertising and Printing, P.O. Box 2158.

Market Research

There are no specialized market research firms. Local support for market research projects can be obtained from the Sudanese Chamber of Commerce, P.O. Box 663, Khartoum. American and Sudanese researchers and visitors are encouraged to use the commercial services of the American Embassy, Khartoum. In the public sector, the Industrial Research and Consultancy Corporation, the Industrial Bank of Sudan, and the Sudan Development Corporation offer information services to potential participants in business ventures.

The National Council for Research administers all activities of the various local research institutes, most of which are attached to the University of Khartoum. The Arid Zone Research Unit conducts scientific investigations into the problems of soils in the arid regions of the Sudan. The Hydrobiological Research Unit explores problems of the Nile River with special interest in inland fisheries. The National Building Research Station studies problems related to building design and construction. The Ministry of Health maintains the Wellcome Chemical Laboratory.

The Gezira Research Library and Research Division Library are operated by the Ministry of Agriculture. Both are in Wad Medani and specialize in agriculture. The Geographical Survey Library in Khartoum publishes annual reports and other bulletins, which also are part of its small specialized collection. The University of Khartoum library is a depository for publications of international agencies, including the Food and Agriculture Organization (FAO), the World Health Organization (WHO), the International Labor Organization (ILO), and the United Nations Economic and Social Council (UNESCO).

Guidance for U.S. Business Travelers

General

To facilitate contracts for foreigners interested in investment opportunities in the Sudan, an Economic Corporation Committee has been set up to prepare for visits, arrange meetings, and conduct negotiations with potential foreign investors. The committee headed by the Under

Secretary of the National Planning Commission, includes representatives from the Ministries of Industry and Mining, Agriculture, Foreign Affairs, and Finance. Other interested government organizations include the Sudan Development Corporation, the Industrial Research and Consultancy Institute (a unit of the Ministry of Industry and Mining), the Regional Development Corporation (for Southern Region projects), and the Sudan Industrial Bank (which makes loans to private businesspeople for small-scale projects). There also is an advisor for Arab Investment in the Secretariat General of the Presidency of the Republic who is prepared to see Americans interested in "trilateral" investment opportunities. In the private or quasi-private sector, investors might call on the Sudanese-Kuwaiti Investment Company, the Arab Investment Company, the Sudan Chamber of Commerce, and the representative office of Chase Manhattan Bank. Addresses of some possible business contacts are given in Appendix B.

Entrance Requirements

A valid U.S. passport and a visa are required for American citizens traveling to the Sudan. Application for a visa may be made by mail or in person to the Embassy of the Sudan in Washington, D.C., or to the Sudanese Mission to the United Nations in New York. The visa application should be submitted in triplicate with a passport-size photograph attached to each form. An international health certificate showing vaccination against smallpox should accompany the application. If the applicant is traveling on business, a letter from his firm is required.

A visa to the Sudan will be invalidated by an Israeli visa or stamp in the passport and entry to the Sudan will be denied. To avoid such problems the U.S. Department of State Passport Office will issue a second passport to the U.S. citizen. (That passport will be limited in its validity to Israel.) The fee is $25.63 for a business (8 days to 3 months) and $15.60 for a transit (1-7 days) visa.

Travel in the Sudan

Most business travel in the Sudan is by air. Sudan Airways provides domestic service to many urban centers. The road network is very limited, and poor roads cause damage even to four-wheel-drive vehicles. Distance between towns is often vast. Many rural roads can only be used in the dry months. The country's extensive railway system permits access to the more isolated towns such as Nyala in the west and Wau in the south. Journey by train, however, tends to be long and is not popular.

Climate

Khartoum has one of the hottest climates in the world. The lowest average maximum temperatures for any month is 69 degrees in February. The hottest months are May and June with average maximum temperatures of 118 degrees. Temperatures on individual days often run 130 degrees in the midday sun. Average mean temperatures of 100 degrees or more prevail from March through October, and 90 to 98 degrees from November through February. Humidity is low during the hot months but is high (56-58 percent) during the short rainy season. The average rainfall in Khartoum is 8 inches, all of which falls in occasional showers between June and early summer. Lightweight washable clothing can be worn year-round. A topcoat may be needed during the evening hours from November to February.

Correspondence and Cables

Arabic and English are both commercial languages of the Sudan. Arabic is official. However, most local businesspeople and officials speak and correspond in English. Business correspondence normally is conducted by air mail, which arrives from the United States twice a week. Transit time varies from 7 to 14 days. International airmail letters from the United States to Khartoum cost $0.40 for a letter weighing one-half ounce; airform letters cost $0.30.

Cables frequently are used to supplement airmail communications. In estimating the time of arrival of a radio or cable message in Khartoum, 7 hours should be added to the time of dispatch (Eastern Standard Time). For telegrams, the full rate per word from all places in the United States is $0.34 subject to a seven word minimum.

Telephone and Telex Service

Khartoum has excellent international telephone and telex connections since the Sudan's first satellite ground station completed in November 1974. A microwave relay network under construction will provide equally good connections to several provincial capitals. Telephone service between Khartoum and the United States costs about $16.00 for 3 minutes.

Commercial Practices

An important feature of Sudanese business practice is the Sudanese preference for a personalized buyer-seller and principal-agent relationship. It is taken for granted that the prospective U.S. supplier will come in person to the Sudan, hold discussions with officials in ministries and state organizations as appropriate, with potential agents in the public and private sectors, with a local financial institution, and with the U.S. Embassy. An accepted practice for new-to-market U.S. businessmen is to have an introductory letter from a senior company official. Company brochures should be enclosed, preferably with both English and Arabic texts. If a visit is planned, the letter should propose a date on which the businessman could call on the Sudanese official or businessman.

The appointment of Sudanese agents and representatives who are in positions to have regular meetings with key procurement officials is recommended.

In appointing an exclusive representative in the Sudan, the U.S. exporter is legally entitled to certain exemptions from U.S. antitrust laws. The Webb-Pomerene Act allows a limited exemption from U.S. antitrust legislation for direct exports by allowing exporters to agree on prices, sales terms, territorial division, and other activities in export trade which could be prohibited in U.S. domestic commerce. Further information concerning the Webb-Pomerene Act is available from Foreign Business Practices Division, Office of International Finance and Investment, U.S. Department of Commerce, Washington, D.C. 20230.

Business Hours.—Most business firms and government offices are open 6 days a week. Office hours are 8:30 a.m. to 2 p.m. in the summer, and winter hours are 7:30 a.m. to 2:30 p.m. All government offices and many businesses are closed Fridays. Banking hours are 8:30 a.m. to 12 noon, Saturday through Thursday. Office hours at the American Embassy are 7:30 a.m. to 2:30 p.m. Monday through Friday and 7:30 a.m. to 12 noon on Saturday.

Holidays.—Fixed official holidays observed in the Sudan include January 1 (Independence Day and New Year's Day), March 3 (Unity Celebration), May 1 (Labor Day), May 25 (Anniversary of the May Revolution), October 12 (Republican Day), October 21 (Sudan Revolution Day), and December 25 (Christmas). The following religious holidays vary according to the Muslim calendar: Muslim New Year, Sham al-Nasim, Kurban Bairam (5 days), Ramadan Bairam (4 days), and the Prophet's Birthday.

Diplomatic Representation

Embassy of the Democratic Republic of the

Sudan
2210 Mass. Ave., NW
Washington, D.C. 20008
Tel: (202) 338-8565

Mission of the Sudan to the United Nations and Consulate
General of the Sudan
210 East 49th Street
New York, New York 10017
Tel: (212) 421-2680

American Embassy
P.O. Box 699
Khartoum
Democratic Republic of the Sudan

Sources of Economic and Commercial Information

Government of the Sudan

Foreign Trade Statistics, Ministry of Planning, Department of Statistics, Khartoum, annual.

Sudan Almanac, Central Office of Information, Khartoum, 1971.

Sudanow, Ministry of Culture and Information, P.O. Box 2651, Khartoum. Annual subscription $62 (airmail) and $46 (surface mail).

Government of the United States

(Available from the Superintendent of Documents, U.S. Government Printing Office, Washington, D.C. 20402.)

Background Notes—Sudan, biannual.

Foreign Economic Trends and Their Implications for the United States—Sudan. FET 80-76.

Area Handbook for the Democratic Republic of the Sudan, 1973.

The following publications may be obtained from the Country Specialist for the Sudan, Office of Country Marketing, International Trade Administration, U.S. Department of Commerce, Washington, D.C. 20230.

Agriculture in the Sudan, 1979

Air Transportation in the Sudan, 1980

Banking and Credit in the Sudan, 1980

Guide to Mineral Investment in the Sudan, 1980

Port Sudan, 1980

Provisional Order Encouragement of Investment Act, 1980

Rural Financial Markets in the Sudan, 1980

Sudan's Sugar Industry

The Sudanese Cement Industry, 1980

The Sudanese Hides, Skins, and Leather Industry, 1980

The Sudanese Railway System, 1980

Textile Industry in the Sudan, 1980

Other Publications

AED African Economic Digest, Weekly Business News and Forecast, MEED Publications Ltd., 21 John Street, London WC1N 2BP, England.

Africa Report, African American Institute, 833 United Nations Plaza, New York, N.Y. 10017 (bimonthly).

Export Shipping Manual and U.S. Export Weekly International Trade Reporter, Bureau of National Affairs, Washington, D.C. 20036.

Exporters Encyclopedia, Dun and Bradstreet, New York, N.Y. 10007 (annual)

International Financial Statistics, International Monetary Fund, Bureau of Statistics, Washington, D.C. 20431 (monthly).

Appendix A
Banking Institutions and Insurance Companies

Bank of Sudan
P.O. Box 313, Khartoum
Banker and financial advisor of Government
of the Sudan.

El Nilein Bank
P.O. Box 466, Khartoum

Omdurman-Juba National Bank
P.O. Box 1186, Khartoum

People's Bank
P.O. Box 922, Khartoum

Red Sea Commercial Bank
P.O. Box 1838, Khartoum

State Bank for Foreign Trade
P.O. Box 1028, Khartoum

Sudan Commercial Bank
P.O. Box 1116, Khartoum

Agricultural Bank
P.O. Box 1363, Khartoum

Estates Bank
P.O. Box 2193, Khartoum

Industrial Bank of Sudan
P.O. Box 1722, Khartoum

Unity Bank
P.O. Box 408, Khartoum

Bank of Credit and Commerce International SA
P.O. Box 5, Khartoum

Chase Manhattan Bank
P.O. Box 2679, Khartoum

Citibank
P.O. Box 2743, Khartoum

Faisal Islamic Bank
P.O. Box 2415, Khartoum

National Bank of Abu Dhabi
P.O. Box 2465, Khartoum

Arab-Africa Bank
P.O. Box 2721, Khartoum

Arab Bank for Economic Development in Africa
P.O. Box 2640, Khartoum

Sudanese Estates Bank
P.O. Box 309, Khartoum

Blue Nile Insurance Co. (Sudan) Ltd.
P.O. Box 2215, Khartoum

General Insurance Co. (Sudan) Ltd.
P.O. Box 1555, Khartoum

Sudanese Insurance and Re-insurance Co. Ltd.
P.O. Box 2332, Khartoum

Khartoum Insurance Co. Ltd.
P.O. Box 737, Khartoum

United Insurance Co. (Sudan) Ltd.
P.O. Box 318, Khartoum

Appendix B

Selected Sudanese Sources of
Business Assistance

Advisor for Arab Investment
Secretariat-General of the Presidency of the
  Republic
P.O. Box 781
Khartoum, Sudan

Ministry of Agriculture, Food and Natural Re-
  sources
Attention: Under Secretary
P.O. Box 285
Khartoum, Sudan

Arab Investment Company
Attention: Manager for the Sudan
O.O. Box 2242
Khartoum, Sudan

National Planning Commission
Attention: Director General
P.O. Box 2092
Khartoum, Sudan

Regional Development Corporation
Attention: Managing Director
P.O. Box 29
Juba, Sudan

Sudan Chamber of Commerce
Attention: Secretary/General
P.O. Box 81
Khartoum, Sudan

Sudan Development Corporation
Attention: Managing Director
P.O. Box 427
Khartoum, Sudan

Sudan Industrial Bank
Attention: Managing Director
P.O. Box 172
Khartoum, Sudan

Sudan Investment Bank
Attention: Managing Director
P.O. Box 81
Khartoum, Sudan

Sudanese Kuwaiti Investment Co.
Attention: Managing Director
P.O. Box 1745
Khartoum, Sudan

TRIAD Natural Resources (Sudan) Ltd.
Attention: Managing Director
P.O. Box 1069
Khartoum, Sudan

Ministry of National Planning Economy
Attention: Under Secretary
P.O. Box 2092
Khartoum, Sudan

Ministryof Industry and Mining
Attention: Under Secretary
P.O. Box 2184
Khartoum, Sudan

Industrial Research and Consultancy Institute
Attention: Director
P.O. Box 26
Khartoum, Sudan

Mechanized Farming Corporation
P.O. Box 2182
Khartoum, Sudan

The National Chemical Company
P.O. BAG
Khartoum, Sudan

Ministry of Irrigation and Hydroelectric
  Power
P.O. Box 878
Khartoum, Sudan

Arab Authority for Agricultural and
  Industrial Development (AAAID)
c/o Ministry of Finance, Planning and
  National Economy

Sudan-U.S. Business Council
Attention: Ar-Rahman al-Beshir, Chairman
c/o Shereif Group of Companies
P.O. Box 1828
Khartoum, Sudan

National Water Administration
P.O. Box 381
Khartoum, Sudan

Gezira Board
Barakat, Sudan

Storage and Silos Corporation
P.O. Box 1183
Khartoum, Sudan

Public Corporation for Agricultural
   Production
P.O. Box 518
Khartoum, Sudan

Appendix C

The Sudan's Income Tax Rates

A. Taxes are payable on business profits and

Limited public companies

On the first	LS1,000	25 percent
On the next	LS9,000	40 percent
On the next	LS10,000	45 percent
On the next	LS20,000	50 percent
On the balance		60 percent

Private limited companies, trustees,
executors, and administrators

On the first	LS1,000	25 percent
On the next	LS9,000	40 percent
On the next	LS10,000	50 percent
On the balance		60 percent

B. Taxes are payable on personal income at the following rates:

Resident individuals

On the first LS1000	Nil
On the next LS1000	15 percent
On the next LS1000	20 percent
On the next LS2,000	30 percent
On the next LS2,000	40 percent
On the next LS3,000	50 percent
On the next LS4,000	60 percent
Over LS14,000	70 percent

Nonresident individuals

On the first LS1,000	10 percent
On the next LS1,000	20 percent
On the next LS1,000	30 percent
On the next LS1,000	40 percent
On the next LS3,000	60 percent
Over LS7,000	80 percent

Appendix D

Shipping Lines Serving the Sudan From the United States

U.S. Flag Ships

American Export Lines, Inc. (monthly from
   Atlantic and Gulf ports)
17 Battery Place
New York, N.Y. 10004
   Local Agent:
   Red Sea Shipping
   P.O. Box 184
   Port Sudan
      and
   P.O. Box 116
   Khartoum, Sudan
   Tel. 71266

American President Lines
601 California Street
San Francisco, Calif. 94108

Isbrandtsen Co. Inc.
26 Broadway
New York, N.Y.
   Local Agent:
   Red Sea Shipping
   P.O. Box 116
   Khartoum, Sudan
   Tel. 71266

Overseas Tankship Corporation
380 Madison Avenue
New York, N.Y.
   Local Agent:
   Contomichalos & Sons Co.
   P.O. Box 326
   Khartoum, Sudan
   Tel. 74040

United States Lines
1 Broadway
New York, N.Y.
   Local Agent:
   May Trading & Services Co.
   P.O. Box 17
   Port Sudan
     and
   P.O. Box 215
   Khartoum, Sudan
   Tel. 70203

Waterman Steamship Corporation
   (fortnightly)
120 Wall Street
New York, N.Y. 10005
   Local Agent:
   May Trading and Services Co.
   P.O. Box 17
   Port Sudan
     and
   P.O. Box 215
   Khartoum, Sudan
   Tel. 70203

Central Gulf Lines, Inc.
Houston First Savings Bldg.
Houston, Tex.
   Local Agent:
   Sudan Shipping Line, Ltd.
   P.O. Box 426
   Port Sudan

**Foreign Flag Ships (all monthly from
Atlantic and Gulf Ports)**

Barber Steamship Lines
17 Battery Place
New York, N.Y. 10004
   Local Agent:
   Red Sea Shipping Co.
   P.O. Box 116
   Khartoum, Sudan
   Tel. 71266

Hellenic Lines Ltd.
39 Broadway
New York, N.Y.
   Local Agent:
   Commercial and Shipping Co.
   P.O. Box 308
   Khartoum, Sudan
   Tel. 74220

The Shipping Corporation of India, Ltd.
U.S. Agent: Norton, Lilly & Co., Inc.
          90 West Street
          New York, N.Y. 10006
   Local Agent:
   Commercial and Shipping Co.
   P.O. Box 308
   Khartoum, Sudan
   Tel. 74220

Triton International Carriers, Ltd.
U.S. Agent: Mercury Shipping (Touston) Inc.
          Suite 610
          Houston Center Two
          Houston, Tex.
   Local Agent:
   Contomichalos & Sons. Co.
   P.O. Box 326
   Khartoum, Sudan
   Tel. 74040

Market Profile—SUDAN

Foreign Trade

Imports.—$1.6 billion in 1981; $1.9 billion in 1982. Major suppliers. 1981: Saudi Arabia. 15.9 percent; United Kingdom, 13.3 percent; United States. 11.8 percent; and West Germany, 6.1 percent. Imports from the United States: $270.1 million in 1982.

Exports.—$658 million in 1981; $583 million in 1982. Principal markets: Saudi Arabia. 20.5 percent; People's Republic of China. 17.5 percent; Italy. 8.2 percent; and United States, 6.9 percent. Major exports: cotton, sesame, peanuts, sugar, durra, hides and skins. and live animals. Exports to United States: gum arabic, cotton, and hides and skins; $15.7 million 1982.

Trade Policy.—Open general license policy applies to raw materials for local industry, spare parts, agricultural equipment, medicines, and certain capital and consumer goods. Import quotas applied to goods supplementing locally produced commodities, luxury goods, and certain capital and consumer goods. Importers required to file a special "Application for Import License." Exports regulated to ensure local supply.

Trade Prospects.—Machinery and equipment for agriculture, food processing, textiles, transport, and construction.

Foreign Investment

New investment law pending, promulgation expected to provide tax holidays and other important concessions to authorized industries. Friendly attitude toward foreigners, especially Americans. At yearend 1979, direct foreign investment estimated at $175 million, of which the U.S. portion was $21 million.

Finance

Currency.—Official rate (1983) US$1=1.30 Sudanese pounds. Money supply: $2.405.2 million at the end of July 1982. up 14 percent from year earlier.

Domestic Credit and Investment.—Bank credit tight, at least as far as long-term loans are concerned. Limited capital in private hands outside the banking system available for well-conceived enterprises.

National Budget.—FY (July-June) 1982/83 current expenditures $2.5 billion; development expenditures, $652.6 million; deficit, $737.1 million.

Balance of Payments. Deficit $906 million in 1980. For eign exchange reserves totaled $18.8 million in November 1982. IMF standby and official debt rescheduling agreed upon in 1983.

Foreign Aid.—World Bank Group is leading donor. U.S. aid exceeded $100 million in 1982.

Economy

Predominately agricultural. In December 1981, GDP at current prices was $5,850 million; $370 per capita at yearend 1982.

Agriculture.

Agriculture.—Main crops: cotton, oilseeds, gum arabic, and peanuts. Fifteen million acres cultivated (3 million irrigated). Additional 6 million acres for irrigation, plus 70 million of rainfed acres and 200 million acres for grazing may have potential.

Commerce.—Cost of Living Index of greater Khartoum in year ending December 1982 rose 4.7 percent.

Development Plan.—$7 billion Six Year-Development Plan (1977-83) emphasizes agricultural, transportation, telecommunications.

Industry.—Cotton ginning, edible oil processing, breweries, and tanneries.

Basic Economic Facilities

Transportation.—Direct sea freight service between U.S. ports and Port Sudan (on Red Sea) good. Inland transport extension is development aim. The 2,895-mile Sudan Railway is mostly single track. 7,800 miles of roads in 1973, 294 paved.

Telecommunications.—Khartoum has international telex and telephone connections via satellite. Long-term contracts underway to improve telex, telephone, and radio links. 13 daily newspapers; 56,000 telephones in 1978; two AM radio stations; two television stations.

Power.—231,800 kW; 672 million kWh produced; 40 kWh per capita in 1977.

Natural Resources

Land.—Largest country in Africa; immense plateau of 967,500 square miles, with sand and arid hills in north; swampland and tropical savana in south.

Water.—5,310 km of inland waterways. 12 nautical miles (nm), plus 6 nm "supervision zone," are limits of territorial waters claimed.

Climate.—North of latitude 19° N, there is movement of dry wind southward in summer. May and June are hottest months.

Minerals.—Some production of chrome, gold, iron ore, manganese, gypsum and oil. Also deposits of lead, asbestos, copper, talc, silver and zinc. Small-scale production of iron ore, chromite, manganese, ore, slate, gold, and gypsum. Exploitation of deposits of petroleum and asbestos underway.

Fisheries.—Annual catch of about 16,000-18,000 tons.

Population

Size.—18.5 million (1980 est.); annual rate of increase 3.2 percent. Principal cities: Khartoum, the capital, 300,000; Omdurman, 195,000; and North Khartoum, 105,000. 71 percent rural; 19 percent urban; 7 percent semiurban; and 1 percent nomadic.

Language.—Arabic is official.

Health.—145 hospitals.

Labor.—8.6 million wage earners. 85 percent of population occupied in agriculture-related activities.

Marketing in Sweden

Contents

Report Revised November 1980

Sweden

International boundary
National capital
Railroad
Road
International airport

Foreign Trade Outlook

Introduction

The Swedish market, containing over 8 million persons, is in most respects a microcosm of the U.S. market. Industrial production covers a broad spectrum of products, including petrochemicals, forest products, automobiles, and mining equipment. The lighter industries include electronics, business machines, furniture, food processing, textiles, footwear, sporting goods, and home appliances. Because of Sweden's relatively small population base, industry must look to foreign markets to assume optimal production runs. This fact, in turn, demands a high standard of production technology for Swedish industry to maintain an internationally competitive position. Because of its highly developed economy and continuing need to upgrade its production apparatus, Sweden offers an excellent market for current, state-of-the-art capital equipment. Machinery, transport equipment and instrumentation account for over 50 percent of U.S. sales to the Swedish market. The Swedish consumer enjoys one of the highest standards of living in the world. Lengthy vacations together with substantial disposable income support a lively, leisure time market. Rapid growth of suburban communities and growing onwership of weekend cottages have expanded demand for virtually all products familiar to the American consumer.

Swedish imports in 1979 were $28.5 billion, an increase of 3.8 percent over the 20.6 billion recorded in 1978. Imports from the United States amounted to $2.1 billion in 1979 as compared to $1.5 billion in 1978. The U.S. share of the Swedish market in 1979 was 7.3 percent.

Best Export Prospects

Several of the most promising prospects for export to Sweden are described below. This list is not exhaustive. Swedish market potential covers a broad range of industrial, consumer and agricultural products.

Electronic Data Processing.—The value of the computer market in Sweden (including data services), is expected to rise to $1,697 million in 1980. Sales of computer equipment, which amounted to $532 million in 1976, are expected to grow 16 percent a year (at constant prices) to $977 million in 1980 and will continue to rise by at least 15 percent a year through 1982. Swedish imports of computer-related equipment, worth $394 million in 1978, should rise at a rate of 18 percent a year (constant prices) to a value of $783 million in 1982. The United States has a dominant position among foreign suppliers, accounting for 54 percent of Swedish imports of computer-related equipment in 1977. This share is expected to widen to 58 percent by 1982. Exports achieved by the U.S. computer and peripherals industry exceed, by far, those of any other industry sectors, but, as Swedish and third country competitors gain more experience and technical sophistication, American manufactur-

---

HOW TO OBTAIN
BACKGROUND INFORMATION

Keeping this book within reasonable size limits has made it necessary to focus on material *directly* concerned with marketing and commerce, and set aside materials only indirectly related. The editors relize, however, that *general* data about a country are also vital to a company's preparations to enter a foreign market, and make a very definite recommendation as to how such expanded information needs can be served.

For those who wish *general* data about a country—data which goes beyond marketing and commerce—the editors recommend *Countries of the World and Their Leaders*, published as an annually updated yearbook by Gale Research Company, Detroit, Michigan 48226. Containing 4- to 20-page entries on 168 countries, the volume also provides several hundred pages of supplementary world data. Each country entry is prepared by the U.S. Department of State to provide a general briefing on the geography, people, culture, and political situation of the particular country. Each report provides some historical insight as well as a look at contemporary trends of lifestyle in the country. Reports also discuss a country's educational system, its press, ethnic groupings and religious practices.

Countries of the World and Their Leaders provides a fresh listing of cabinet ministers of each nation. In addition it lists health conditions the traveling businessman will wish to prepare for and includes information on passport procedures, customs and duties, and world climate conditions.

ers will not be able to slacken the pace of their promotional efforts if they wish to maintain their dominant position.

The following products have good sales potential for U.S. exporters: Programmable controllers for automated industrial production systems; computer-aided design and manufacturing systems; computer systems for medical analysis and for the printing and graphic arts industry; data-base management systems; and minicomputers for small business operations.

Health Care Equipment.—Sweden is one of the most advanced medical equipment markets in the world in its appreciation of new ideas and techniques. Sweden's medical equipment market is expected to grow at an average annual rate of 4.6% from 1978 to 1983 (at constant prices). American manufacturers are second only to West German firms in supplying medical equipment in Sweden, and U.S. exports in this category should increase 15 percent a year (in current prices) over the next three years. The sophistication of American equipment, together with very competitive pricing, should lead to an increase in the U.S. share of the Swedish market if American firms continue to gear their marketing prices to local conditions.

Recent trends indicate excellent prospects for U.S. equipment, especially in computer-based systems for EEG and ECG, telemetry systems, tomographic X-ray scanners, and ultrasonic diagnostic apparatus. Market research highlights the following equipment for export promotion by U.S. firms: Cardiological (especially patient monitoring and intensive care systems) equipment; pulmonary function (IPPB) equipment; neurological (especially EEG) equipment; pediatric (especially infant intensive care) equipment; and operating room (especially diathermy and heart-lung machinery) equipment and clinical laboratory equipment. Swedish trade statistics show increasing exports of U.S. equipment that have a significant share of the Swedish market in the following categories: Medical; surgical and dental instruments; orthopedic articles and artificial prostheses; electromedical instruments; and physiotherapy and respiratory apparatus.

Metalworking Machinery.—Metalworking is Sweden's largest industry, accounting for about 40 percent of all industrial production. Approximtaely 4,500 establishments produce metal products. U.S. metalworking machinery with high sales potential in Sweden includes: Adaptive control systems; direct numerical control systems; drilling machines (N/C); electrochemical machining; lathes (automatic, N/C); punching

machines, transfer lines and automatic feed devices; thread forming screws; and electrolytic grinding machines. As this partial list indicates, Swedish manufacturers are in the market for highly sophisticated equipment. Swedish industry is attempting to attain greater output in the face of frequent shortages of skilled labor, rising energy and raw materials costs, and labor costs that rank among the highest in the world. Swedish manufacturers expect to increase their investment in machine tools to $345 million in 1982.

Pulp and Papermaking Equipment.— Sweden's second most important industry, forest products provides a solid market for U.S. equipment. This sector appears to have pulled itself out of the doldrums in the late 70's and is now moving ahead with several plant expansion and improvement plans in both pulpmaking and papermaking, with the emphasis on major grades of paper, notably newsprint. In the paper sector, present plans provide for an overall capacity expansion of 1.3 million metric tons to 8.3 million tons by 1983. This is equivalent to an average annual increase of 3.5 percent. In the field of paperboard, capacity additions totaling some 340,000 tons are planned, most of which will be for kraft liner and bleached folding boxboard. Projects planned and under way should offer U.S. equipment suppliers excellent sales prospects in Sweden for pollution prevention systems and equipment. The industry's environmental protection program for 1979–84 calls for investment of about $262 million for pollution control measures. Measures to reduce water pollution will focus on improving the recovery of chemicals through higher pulp-washing efficiency; shifting to oxygen bleaching; expanded biological and chemical purification facilities; and improving sludge separation, sludge handling and internal fiber recovery. Discharges into the atmosphere are to be reduced primarily by more efficient dust separation from flue gases, and by controls on sulphur dioxide emissions. There will also be a need for a wide range of other sophisticated plant equipment and know how.

Process Control Instrumentation. — Sweden's accelerated industrialization during the postwar years has made it a sizeable market for process controls. Swedish industry is expected to spend $107 million for instrumentation in 1982, up an average 5.5 percent annually from $86 million in 1978. Investments in control devices are expected to show an increase as buyers initiate modernization and cost reduction projects. Equipment to aid in energy and raw materials conservation and pollution reduction will be of special importance. Pulp and paper manufacturers account for about 45 percent of sales of control and chemicals and primary metals together accounted for some 28 percent.

The Swedish process industries are also trying to compensate for high labor and raw material costs by developing a more competitive international marketing position. With wage rates in Sweden at such a high level, greater industrial automation is being encouraged. Because U.S. suppliers are leaders in innovative technology and new process control instrument designs, Swedish end-users look for them for sophisticated electronic instruments and process control computers and peripherals. New firms can expect the best reception for equipment that provides unique capabilities and applications.

Food Processing and Packaging Equipment.—The market for food processing and packaging equipment is growing about 4 percent a year. By 1983, it is expected to reach $164 million annually. While local production is substantial, particularly in the dairy equipment, there is a sizeable import market. In 1978, Swedish imports of food-processing equipment totaled $44.3 million. The well-developed domestic industry produced an estimated $186 million with almost 52 percent going for exports.

The principal foreign supplier is West Germany, which in 1978 accounted for 35 percent of all food processing and 40 percent of all food packaging equipment needs. Other leading supplier countries were Denmark, which accounted for 20 percent of all food processing equipment needs. The Netherlands with 12 percent is another leading supplier to the market.

U.S. exporters now have a good chance to offer serious competition to their European rivals as U.S. equipment has become more price competitive in recent years. U.S. suppliers could enhance their market share substantially from the present 9.5 percent of total imports. The outlook for U.S. equipment is favorable in advanced meat-processing machinery, continuous process and quality control equipment as well as packaging machinery.

New-to-the-market firms will find the market very well covered, and should therefore be prepared to offer equipment with unique capabilities and applications. In addition, they should be prepared to offer prompt after-sale service.

Electronics Industry Production and Test Equipment.—U.S. producers of electronics production and test equipment are expected to find prime marketing opportunities in Sweden's growing electronics industry. Demand is expected to be particularly strong for test equipment, semiconductor production equipment, wiring assemblies and other interface equipment. In 1976, the Swedish market for this amounted to $30.6 million, of which the U.S. supplied roughly one-third. In 1980, the total is expected to reach $60 million. Among semiconductor and integrated circuit production equipment the following specific products were found to have high sales potential: Dicing machines; conveyor dryers; ultrasonic bonders; soldering systems and equipment; leak detectors. In the printed circuit field, excellent sales potential is forecast for: Automatic etching and precision drilling machines; fusing machines; plating machines; component inserting and sequencing machines. Point-to-point wiring equipment, automatic strippers and cutters are among high potential items in the wiring assembly operations while micromaterials handling equipment and positioning equipment, and metal forming machines are among the other types of production equipment expected to sell well in Sweden.

Electronic Components.—The Swedish market for electronic components is growing on an average annual rate of about six percent. In 1980, the total market is expected to be $477 million. Sweden imports almost 50 percent of its electronic component needs. Imports of electronic components from the United States are rising, from $60.5 million in 1976 to almost $65 million in 1980.

The country's communications industry occupies first place as a consumer of electronic components. Sweden's multinational communications equipment company L.M. Ericsson is the most important and is the largest buyer. Its move into computer controlled telephone exchanges has had a stimulating effect on the entire Swedish electronics market. U.S. suppliers are expected to find a good marketing opportunity for power transistors, thyristors, microwave diodes, optoelectronics, multilayer printer circuits, readout devices, relays and solid state switches.

Communications Equipment

Swedish telecommunications manufacturers are in the forefront of technology and provide a good market for complementary U.S. equipment and components. Swedish imports of telecommunications equipment totaled $435 million in 1978. Of that figure, $28 million came from the U.S.

L.M. Ericsson sells communication systems throughout the world. A sizeable portion of the equipment that it exports contains U.S. components and parts.

The best prospects for U.S. telecommunications equipment are those for data communications devices and for alarm and signal systems. In the next few years, the most rapid growth in the Swedish market is expected to be in data communications devices of the sophisticated kind that American firms make best.

Swedish firms that deal in this kind of equipment do not wait for the seller, but aggressively seek out new developments. U.S. companies interested in this market should be ready to respond rapidly to enquiries.

Textiles and Apparel

Sweden currently imports more than 75 percent of its clothing and textile needs. In 1978, Swedish imports of apparel totaled $862 million; imports of textiles were $729 million.

A rapid decline in the domestic textile and apparel manufacturing industry is taking place as a result of the high volume of imports. Despite government action to keep the industry at its present size, it seems likely that import penetration will increase with surviving manufacturers concentrating on the production of high-quality, high-priced merchandise for export as well as for the home market. Swedish consumers are showing considerable interest in distinctive U.S. apparel, particularly leisure and sports wear. Among younger persons there is a great desire for American style jeans, sweatshirts, tee-shirts, football shirts, jogging clothes and other sports/fashion wear. Opportunities exist, although limited, for increasing U.S. apparel sales; where the styles, novelty, and quality of U.S. merchandise are an advantage, and where consumers would be willing to pay a premium for the products. However, in order to realize long-term demand, U.S. manufacturers must be prepared to commit time, effort, and money to marketing.

Other Products With Sales Potential.—In addition to those industries and products already mentioned, the Swedish market appears to offer good prospects for expanded U.S. exports in a number of other product categories. Among these are laboratory, scientific and engineering instruments, aircraft and parts, security and safety equipment, and pollution control equipment.

Industry Trends

GDP Developments

The Swedish standard of domestic living measured in terms of per capita gross product (GDP) is comparable to the United States. In 1978, Sweden's per capita GDP reached approximately $10,452 in current prices. Other economic measurements, such as per capita housing, automobile ownership, and health services place Sweden among the world's most economically advantaged countries.

The Swedish economy, through the decades of the 1950's and 1960's may be characterized as one of moderate balanced growth. During 1965–70, real GDP increased by approximately 4 percent annually. The sharp international recession of 1974–75, together with the slow pace of recovery and lackluster developments in international demands, resulted in a down turn for Sweden in 1976–78. In 1977, GDP declined 2.4 percent in constant prices from 1976.

Growth rates began to go up in 1978, as moderate increases in total labor costs enabled Swedish exporters to take advantage of recovery abroad and earlier devaluations of the Swedish krona. However, as the rate of recovery accelerated in 1979, other sectors of the economy began to claim their share. Private consumption will probably grow by more than 3 percent in volume after two years of negative growth. The public sector, despite boom conditions, is continuing to stimulate the economy to the tune of 3 percent of GDP. Inventory accumulation will be up strongly and private investment will not be far behind. Meanwhile, the 1978 trade surplus has evaporated in the face of oil price increases and a strong resumption of demand for imports. Inflation rates are already on the way up, even though to date, the excess above 5 percent is largely attributable to import prices.

In 1980, a case of excessive demand could develop. If the current collective bargaining round results in total labor cost increases in excess of 10 percent in 1980, a sizeable cost-push element would be added to inflationary pressure. Unit labor costs have declined steadily vis à vis Sweden's major competitors in 1977, 78 and 79, and a reversal of that trend would seriously delay the nation's effort to return to external balance in the mid-80's. Bottlenecks, especially skilled labor supply may also pose a serious problem.

Economic policy makers must also wrestle with the fact that tax increases, as a tool to limit domestic demand, can have a pernicious effect by way of causing increased wage demands. There continues to be optimism about Sweden's ability to cope with its problems. Decision-makers in labor, business and government are remarkably adept at assessing the realities facing the economy. The oil price increases prove paradoxically beneficial in the sense that they have strongly brought home the external realities facing any small, open industrialized economy today. The best guess is that consumer prices can be held to a rate of increase under 10 percent in 1980, the current account deficit can be kept under Skr 10 billion and GDP can still go up by well over 3 percent. These results can be attained without a devaluation of the krona, and without threatening Sweden's still fairly substantial foreign exchange reserves, although more external borrowing will clearly be in store.

Swedish manufacturing facilities, among the most up-to-date in the world, are constantly being modernized. Gross investment totaled $3.8 billion in 1978. While this was a decline of 4.2 percent from the previous year, projections for 1979 indicate a growth of 7.0 percent.

The three most important natural resources in Sweden are iron ore, timber, and hydroelectric power. Sweden's rapid growth during this century as an industrial economy has been based primarily on these resources.

Sweden's metal-based industries (primary metals, metalworking) are the most important in terms of employment and output. The strong primary metals sector produces specialty steels and nonferrous metals. The metalworking ("engineering") sector produces industrial machinery, motor vehicles, aircraft, ships, electrical equipment, and other metal products. Stimulated by heavy domestic investment, the metal-based industries expanded rapidly since World War II. A relatively high rate of investment is expected to continue.

Sweden's forest product industries (paper, pulp, lumber, wood products) rank second in importance in the Swedish economy. Historically, these industries have undergone a change of emphasis from semimanufactures (e.g. sawn timber) to processed goods such as paper, paperboard, etc. Increased attention is now given to research and development.

Among other Swedish industries, the chemicals and petrochemicals have experienced rapid growth. The petrochemical industry is concentrated on the west coast of Sweden. Ethyl alcohol, a byproduct of the chemical pulp industry, has been replaced by petrochemical ethylene as the most important base for organic chemical

production. Along with the petrochemical industry, petroleum refining has also been growing. Investment in the chemical industry during the past few years has averaged about $200 million a year. Chemical industry production exceeded $2.6 billion in 1977. The fastest growing sectors in the chemical industry are pharmaceuticals and plastics.

Government Role in the Economy

More than 93 percent of Sweden's manufacturing industry is privately-owned. In general, government ownership developed not out of any policy of nationalization, but rather in response to specific situations (e.g., the need to prevent unemployment when a plant in a rural area threatened to close). In fact, most instances of state ownership date from the period before 1932.

While government ownership of productive facilities remains small, the Government during the past few years has taken several steps to increase the influence of the State on industrial development. The increase in governmental activity is designed to assist in the maintenance of full employment, particularly in such areas as northern Sweden where pronounced unemployment exists, to influence restructuring and modernization of Swedish industry; and to provide resources for projects which are unattractive to private industry because of the risks involved. Among the chief state institutions formed to stimulate industrial development are the Swedish Investment Bank (Sveriges Investeringsbank—AB); and the National Industrial Establishment Company (SVETAB).

Most Swedish state-owned business enterprises have been brought together under a holding company, Statsforetag AB, which is administered by the Ministry of Industry. The largest government-owned business firm is LKAB, which exploits the iron-ore deposits in northern Sweden. Other large state-owned firms are found in the steel and forest product industries. The value of production by all government-owned business is approximately 6 percent of GDP.

Sweden combines a free enterprise economy with extensive government social welfare activities. The State, in cooperation with local authorities, plays a vital role in providing medical, family, old age, disability, unemployment and other social services.

The economic philosophy currently prevailing in Sweden includes the theory that monetary and fiscal policies can and should be actively utilized for achieving full employment, restraining inflation, maintaining a favorable balance of payments, and moderating business cycles.

Transportation and Utilities

Shipping from United States.—Ocean shipping to Sweden via U.S. flag carriers from the eastern United States is rapid and convenient. Voyage time from New York to Goteborg for general cargo on scheduled carriers is normally about 10 days if shipment is direct. The voyage time is longer, of course, if the cargo is routed via other European ports.

Four U.S. shipping lines offer services to Sweden, three of which have weekly sailings from Atlantic Coast ports and the fourth offering service from the major Gulf ports to Sweden. The Atlantic Coast carriers are Farrell Lines, Inc.; Sea-Land Service, Inc.; and United States Lines, Inc. Lykes Bros. Steamship Co., Inc. provides Gulf Coast services.

Farrell Lines provides container service to Sweden via Bremerhaven from New York, Norfolk, and Baltimore with feeder service from Savannah, Philadelphia and Boston. Transit time from Boston to Sweden is 10 days. For additional information call (212) 440-4291 or write Farrell Lines, Inc., One Whitehall St., New York, New York 10004.

Sea-Land Service, Inc. has weekly container ship sailings from New York, Boston, Baltimore, Charleston, Portsmouth, Savannah, and Wilmington, N.C. Cargo for Sweden is transshipped at Bremerhaven. Transit time from New York to Sweden is 14 days. For further information, call (202) 494-7400 or write Sea-Land Service, Inc., P.O. Box 800 Edison, New Jersey 08817.

United States Lines, Inc. provides weekly containerized service sailing from New York, Boston, Philadelphia, Baltimore, Norfolk, Charleston, Jacksonville, and Savannah. Cargo is transshipped to Sweden via Bremerhaven or Felixstowe. United States Lines also offers refrigerated, and open-top equipment on request. Transit time to Sweden is 15 days. For further information, call (201) 272-9600 or write to United States Lines, Inc., 27 Commerce Drive, Cranford, N.J. 07016.

Lykes Bros. provides Sea Bee barge ships through the major Gulf ports of New Orleans, Houston, Mobile and also inland river ports. See Bee barge and break cargo is transshipped to Sweden through Bremerhaven. Call (504) 523-6611 for additional information, or write Lykes

Bros. Steamship Co., Inc., Lykes Center, 300 Poydras Street, New Orleans, Louisiana 70130.

The most important ports serving international shipping are Goteborg, Stockholm, Helsingborg and Malmo. Goteborg, on the west coast, is the principal port for overseas trade; Stockholm is the chief Baltic port and Helsingborg is the principal port for traffic with the Continent. These ports are accessible to large vessels, having depth at quayside of 10, 10, and 9.2-meters, respectively. Other large ports are Trelleborg, connected by rail ferry with Germany, Lulea and Gavle, which handle iron-ore exports; Sundsvall, which exports large quantities of forest products; and Norrkoping, Kalmar, Landskrona, Soderhamn, and Ornskoldsvik. All have modern quays, cranes, railway connections, and warehouses.

Shipping and dock facilities in the principal Swedish harbors for both general and specialized cargoes such as oil and grain are good. Shipping to Sweden by air freight or air express is facilitated by frequent regularly scheduled air passenger and freight service. International aircraft arriving at Stockholm use Arlanda Airport, situated 27 miles north of Stockholm. Other major Swedish airports are situated in Goteborg adn Malmo. From the U.S., Sweden is served by Northwest and SAS.

Once cargo has arrived in Sweden from the United States, it can be forwarded to any point in the country within 24 hours. Domestic rail, truck, and air services are well equipped for efficient movement of goods in the Swedish market. Rail service is available to the Arctic north and the sparsely settled north central area, as well as to the more densely populated sections of the country. Truck services are well developed throughout the country.

Utilities.—Electricity, generated mainly by hydroelectric plants, is abundant and relatively inexpensive. Swedish production of electric energy was 90,200 million kilowatt hours in 1978. Of that total 63 percent was hydroelectric, 25 percent nuclear and 12 percent conventional thermal. Three fourths of electric power is generated in the north and conveyed to the populous south by high voltage transmission lines. Electricity rates in Sweden are reasonable.

Currently, Sweden has six nuclear power generation plants in operation. An additional two reactors have been fueled. The active development programs for nuclear power, which were underway, are now in a state of flux due to the demand that the industry develop satisfactory nuclear waste disposal and safety programs prior to placing future plants in operation.

All forms of electronic communication are supervised and controlled by the Telecommunications Administration, a Swedish Government agency.

The Swedish telephone system is completely automated. Per capita ownership of telephones (744 per 1000 persons) is second to the United States. Telex is also well-developed.

Distribution and Sales Channels

Major Marketing Areas

Sweden is the third largest country in Europe, with a land area of 173,423 square miles (roughly the size of California). Marketing in Sweden is simplified by the existence of several distinct marketing regions, containing sizeable population concentrations, which may be serviced through sales and distribution organizations located in principal cities in each region. The population of Sweden was 8.3 million in 1977. Over 90 percent of the population is located in the central and southern portions of the country.

Rapid industrialization has transformed Sweden from a predominantly rural to an urban economy during the century. Since World War II, the population movement from farm to city has accelerated. While nearly 40 percent of the population lived on farms and in villages with fewer than 200 inhabitants in 1945, less than 25 percent are found in such areas today. More than 30 percent of the Swedish population now resides in the three major population areas, Stockholm, Goteborg, and Malmo. The remainder of the population is divided almost equally between towns of 200–10,000 inhabitants and cities of 10,000–90,000 inhabitatns. Rapid urbanization has created new markets, new demands, and vast changes in distribution systems. These trends have frequently paralleled developments in the United States.

The capital and business center of Sweden is Stockholm. The city proper has a population of approximately 700,000, while the Stockholm metropolitan area numbers about 1.4 million. Many of the suburbs are noteworthy for their modern shopping facilities and excellent transportation links with the central city. Industrial development is advanced and diversified. Average personal income in the Stockholm area is estimated to be about 30 percent higher than the national Swedish average.

Several of Sweden's most important industrial cities lie within 125 miles of Stockholm. The nation's sixth most populous city, Vasteras (118,000 population), is located about 50 miles west of the capital. Heavy industry is located in that city, including the ASEA Corporation, third largest corporation in Sweden in terms of sales and a leading world producer of electrical equipment. Other major centers within 125 miles of Stockholm include Uppsala (141,000), Norrköping (121,000) Örebro (117,000), Köping, (111,000), Gävele (87,000), and Eskilstuna (92,000).

Most of the head offices for Swedish industrial and commercial associations, as well as the head offices for many of Sweden's largest corporations, are located in Stockholm and its environs. Most of the large purchasing organizations, such as the Cooperative Union, (which is the central purchasing agent for most Swedish consumer cooperatives), the major retail buying organizations and chains, and many of the largest wholesalers, are based in the capital. Stockholm or its environs, is an excellent all-around location for sales offices and sales subsidiaries.

Sweden's second-largest city, Goteborg, also provides the focal point for a large and important marketing area. The southwestern quadrant of the country is the most rapidly growing part of Sweden in terms of population and is a burgeoning industrial region. Many of Sweden's most modern industrial plants are situated in or near Goteborg. The city is also Sweden's foremost port for international shipping.

The city of Goteborg has a population of 440,000 with a total of almost 700,000 in the metropolitan area. Average personal income is estimated to be about 15 percent higher than the national average. A significant feature of Goteborg, from the marketing standpoint, is its proximity to Denmark and Norway and its accessibility to Atlantic shipping routes. As a major world port, Goteborg has long been the site of several large shipyards. The industrial complex centered in Goteborg produces a wide range of industrial machinery and petrochemicals.

At the southern tip of Sweden, only a few miles from neighboring Denmark, is Malmo, the third largest city. Greater Malmo has a population of approximately 450,000, of which almost 40 percent live in the suburbs. Malmo is an important center for Swedish shipping to Continental Europe. Like Goteborg, Malmo benefits from its location in the rapidly developing southwestern part of Sweden. Its personal average income is above the national average. An outstanding current development is the growth of very close commercial ties between Malmo and the Danish capital, Copenhagen, only a few miles to the west across the Oresund, a narrow body of water separating Denmark and Sweden. Other cities in the southwestern quadrant of Sweden include Helsingborg (101,000), Boras (104,000), Jonkoping (109,000), Karlstad (73,000), Lund (77,000) and Halmstad (75,000). Major industrial facilities are scattered throughout the area.

Although the northern half of Sweden contains less than 10 percent of the population, it is the site of many large industrial plants, especially in the forest products field. It includes Sweden's largest mines (chiefly iron ore) and hydroelectric facilities. The northern part of Sweden therefore has significant market potential for certain types of products, and should not be overlooked in any assessment of the Swedish market. Major population centers include Sundsvall (94,000), Skelleftea (73,000), Lulea (66,000), and Umea (77,000).

Importers, Agents, Distributors

Sweden offers the American exporter a wide range of methods for distributing and selling a product. This section will briefly consider the most generally used of these methods.

Selling Through an Agent or Distributor— Exporters of capital goods, industrial raw materials, and related commodities usually employ Swedish commission agents. Normally, one exclusive agent or representative is appointed to cover the country. Swedish agents often represent several different foreign firms and carry a number of different product lines. In selecting an agent, the exporter should avoid commissioning one who handles directly competing products. Swedish commercial agents are organized in the Federation of Swedish Commercial Agents (Svenska Handelsagenters Forening), which is based in Stockholm and has about 500 members.

Specific Swedish legislation sets out the rights and obligations of each party to an agency/principal contract or arrangement. The basic law covering such agreements is found in the Swedish Code (SFS) 1974:219 published May 21, 1974 with effect as of July 1, 1974. A summary of the more important sections of this law may be obtained from the Foreign Business Practices Division, Office of International Economic Policy and Research, U.S. Department of Commerce, Washington, D.C. 20230.

Manufacturers seeking an agent in Sweden should also plan to visit the country. It is the best way of making a first-hand appraisal of the relative merits of prospective agents. Besides acquainting the exporter directly with the market, it also gives him an opportunity to discuss policy and sales campaigns with the agent.

Close contact between the American principal and the Swedish distributor is very desirable and should be developed early. Certain products and equipment entail servicing to maintain them during their useful life. The exporter should make provision for such servicing by qualified personnel in Sweden or a neighboring country.

Selling Through Established Wholesalers— Approximately two-thirds of all Swedish imports are purchased through wholesalers-importers. Consumer goods (which require maintenance of stocks) and industrial raw materials are very often imported through these channels.

Selling Directly to Retailing Organizations— American exporters of consumer goods may find it advantageous to sell directly to department stores, consumer cooperatives, voluntary chains, and other retail outlets. Some of the larger Swedish retailers have purchasing agents in the United States.

Establishing a Sale Subsidiary in Sweden— This method of reaching the Swedish market has become increasingly significant in recent years. Many U.S. firms operate their own sales offices.

Commercial Practices

Sales quotations are usually given either c.i.f. port of destination, or f.a.s. or f.o.b. port of shipment. The former method is generally preferred by Swedish importers. Large firms and department stores, however, sometimes buy on f.a.s. or f.o.b. terms since they may prefer to arrange for shipping and insuring the goods themselves. Quotations and invoicing are usually in terms of the currency and country of origin.

There is no uniformity in the method of payment for imports to Sweden. All of the normal methods for payment are used. In recent years there has been a trend toward more liberal financing, as opposed to payment by letters of credit or cash. Letters of credit are customarily used mainly for handling certain staple commodities and transit shipments. Knowledge of the market competition, and of the customer, are generally the prime considerations in deciding whether to use sight drafts, time drafts or open accounts. General terms of sale are payment within 30 to 90 days after delivery varying with the commodity and the credit standing of the purchaser.

Wholesale and Retail Channels

Because of rising labor costs and continued concentration of the Swedish population in urban centers, there is a strong trend in both wholesale as well as retail trade toward offering directly from local manufacturers and foreign suppliers, these include: Purchasing organizations, voluntary groups, various types of chains, cooperatives, and department stores.

Wholesaling—The Federation of Swedish Wholesale Merchants and Importers (Sveriges Grossistforbund), is the principal organization for the private wholesale and import trade in Sweden. Its membership includes about 55 branch associations, whose member firms are importers, wholesalers, distributors, agents, and general agents of all types of goods. The number of firms belonging to the Federation approximates 1,030. Total sales of member enterprises in 1977 was $22.3 billion. Almost half of the members' turnover consists of capital equipment, and fuels. Members of the Federation are responsible for an estimated two-thirds of all Swedish imports.

An important wholesale organization in Sweden is ICA (Inkopscentralernas Aktiebolag). This is a voluntary association of retailers owned by approximately 4400 retailers, whose total turnover in 1977 was about $3.4 billion. ICA includes, in addition to its associated retail members, several other distributive companies. ICA was originally only a purchasing organization, but now performs other functions for its members, e.g. financing marketing, and consulting services. Other important wholesalers are DAGAB and KF (the Cooperative Union and Wholesale Society). DAGAB is associated with the NK/Ahlens department store chain. A.S.K.-Bolagens Ekonomiska Forening (A.S.K.) is also an association of wholesalers. It is one of Sweden's largest companies, including voluntary retail chains in addition to its wholesaling activities.

Retailing—Retail methods and organization are undergoing rapid changes not unlike those in the United States. The past decade has seen a strong trend toward fewer and larger retail outlets. Shopping centers featuring supermarkets have multiplied around Stockholm and other cities. The centralizing trend is especially evident in the food retail business. At the same time, some high quality specialty shops have strengthened their position. Increasing prosperity has generated demand for household equipment, sporting goods, toys and other specialties.

Three large concerns dominate the retail scene. The largest, Kooperative Forbundet (KF), is discussed in a separate section since it is active in both wholesaling and retailing. The other major concern is NK-Ahlens AB, formed by a merger of two formerly independently owned companies, Nordiska Kompaniet (NK) and Ahlen & Holm AB. The combined concern dominates department store retailing in Sweden. Its total sales were $1.7 billion in 1977. The NK/Ahlens group has 165 department and variety stores.

Perhaps the most important new development in retailing in Sweden is the growth of voluntary single-line chains. These chains usually start with a few shops featuring a single line. Other shops wishing to join the group pay an initial subscription, agree to pay an annual subscription, and enter into contractual arrangements calling for: (1) sales cooperation, (2) coordination of design, (3) joint staff and management training, and (4) joint contract purchase of large quantities. The voluntary chains now extend to most product lines, including readymade clothing, home furnishings, textiles, children's wear, glass and china ware, furniture, radio and television. One of the largest single-line voluntary chains (Jarnia), specializes in hardware and includes dealers throughout Scandinavia.

An outstanding development on the Swedish retail scene is the growth of planned shopping centers which emphasize convenience, good transportation links with the city center, and excellent architectural design. In 1977, there were about 36 large shopping centers, with total sales of $710 million. Most of these are suburban complexes, which include a wide range of housing, as well as schools, churches, and shops of all kinds. One of the first of the new planned suburban communities was Vallingby, started in 1953, and situated near Stockholm. Other major centers near Stockholm include Farsta, Taby and Hogdalen.

Self-service has become widespread in Sweden. Some 95 percent of sales of convenience goods are handled by self-service stores. The development of self-service has created demand for modern packaging and merchandising techniques. Of Sweden's 47,100 retail outlets more than 8,000 are self-service, most of them are concentrated in the food sector.

Supermarkets are also increasing rapidly. In Sweden, these are defined as self-service stores offering a complete food line (and frequently other consumer articles) and having a minimum annual turnover of at least SKr. 4 million. In 1977, there were some 1,450 supermarkets with a total turnover of $4.6 billion; almost one quarter of total retail trade supermarkets, accounting for more than 45 percent of total retail sales. Over 300 of the larger department and variety stores maintain connected supermarkets, or a section within the main store for that purpose.

Consumer Cooperative Societies—These play a vital role in Swedish wholesaling and retailing. In the consumer goods field, the cooperatives may be viewed as the largest single importer (they import through a central importing organization). Local consumer cooperative societies are the backbone of the system. In keeping with the general trend toward concentration in Sweden, the actual number of societies and outlets has been reduced during the past ten years, but sales have continued to increase rapidly. Owned by their members, the cooperatives are not in any sense state-owned or operated; they are part of the private sector. The local societies belong to a central organization, Kooperativa Forbundet (KF) or Cooperative Union, owned by them. KF is the wholesale arm of the cooperative movement, and is the central buying organization. It is also heavily engaged in manufacturing.

In 1977, there were approximately 2200 cooperative outlets, of which 180 are department, variety or discount stores, and 1,919 are food markets. The organization estimates that it has a total retail trade of 48 percent of department and variety store trade, 31 percent of supermarket trade and 13 percent of furniture and home furnishings trade. Cooperative department stores use the trade name "Domus" stores, while the recently inaugurated discount stores are called "OBS." As Sweden's largest concern, KF (including its constituent societies) had total sales of $4.3 billion in 1977.

Independent Retailing

While large chain stores and cooperatives have become important in retail trade in Sweden, nearly two thirds of all retail trade sales are made through private firms. The majority of them are still small in size and run by the owner. The widespread closing of businesses has meant that small businesses, in regard to turnover, have declined in importance. However, by establishing new businesses and by setting up branches, many retailing firms have been able to grow. A large number of private firms have joined together in voluntary chains to meet competition from the cooperatives and the department store enterprises.

Wholesale and Retail Sales

There are some 16,000 wholesale establishments in Sweden. Most of these are independent firms, although consumer cooperatives and some large retailing businesses also are engaged in wholesaling and importing. Members of the Federation of Swedish Wholesalers and Importers represent the overwhelming proportion of wholesale turnover. Of the total sales of $22.3 billion in 1977, producer goods represented 31.2 percent of total wholesale turnover in 1977 while consumer goods made up 25.6 percent, fuel 18.0 percent and other goods 25.2 percent.

Sweden's retail establishments in 1978 had an estimated total turnover of 125.9 billion SEK (about $27.9 billion), excluding value added tax.

In terms of commodities, retail trade in 1978 was distributed as follows: Food, 27 percent; automobiles, 15 percent; home furnishings, 10 percent; wearing apparel, 8 percent; gasoline and lubricants, 7 percent; wine and liquor, 6 percent; jewelry, watches, and recreational items, 4 percent; tobacco and books, 4 percent; pharmaceuticals, 2 percent. Highest retail turnover per capita was in the Stockholm area. Of total retail turnover, roughly 20 percent is transacted in the Stockholm area, 10 percent in Goteborg, and 6 percent in the greater Malmo area. Total retail sales increased in value by 8.1 percent in 1978. Of the major retail categories, sales of wine and liquors made the greatest percentage (up 14.7 percent), followed by gasoline and lubricant sales (13.4 percent), pharmaceuticals (12.8 percent), jewelry, watches, and recreation (12 percent, tobacco and books (10.6 percent), wearing apparel (10 percent), automobiles (3.4 percent), and food (9.3 percent).

Retail trade margins—Pricing within the retail trade is free in principle, although some items, mainly foods, are subject to government regulation. Average gross profits on turnover in various retail establishments in 1977 were as follows: Food, tobacco and newspaper establishments, 20 percent; fruit and confectionery establishments and newsstands, 20–25 percent; furniture, hardware, radio-TV, books, photographic articles, and leisure time equipment establishments, 25–30 percent; apparel, china and glass, paints, shoes, flowers, lighting equipment, and yarn establishments, 30–40 percent; watches, optical goods and gold articles, gloves and handbags, 40–50 percent.

Principal Buying and Merchandising Offices

In view of the large number of buying and merchandising firms, the following list includes only a few of the largest firms.

ICA (Inköpscentralernas Aktiebolag)
Odengatan 69
Box 6187
102 33 Stockholm 6
(Central purchasing organization and wholesaler for associated retailers

A.S.K.—Bolagens Ekonomiska Forening
Fack
104 01 Stockholm 60
(Association of wholesalers; also operates voluntary retail chains)

Kooperativa Förbundet
Fack
104 65 Stockholm 15
(Central purchasing organization for consumer cooperatives)

NK—Ahlens AB
Box 16343
S–103 26 Stockholm
(Largest department store chain)

Järnia AB
Brunskogsgatan 5
Box 112
S–523 01 Ulricehamn
(Purchase and sale of hardware)

The above-listed firms are briefly described in the section of this report "Wholesale and Retail Channels."

Licensing and Franchising

Licensing—Licensing agreements for production in Sweden of U.S. originated goods are common both for consumer products and capital equipment. Royalty and license fee payments may be freely transferred out of Sweden. Information on licensing abroad is available from the Office of International Finance and Investment, Bureau of International Economic Policy and Research, U.S. Department of Commerce, Washington, D.C. 20230

Franchising—While franchising is not yet a widespread practice in Sweden, the outlook is excellent for future development. A study indicated that the following areas offer favorable opportunities for franchising in Sweden: Convenience foods; laundry and dry cleaning, business aids and services (e.g. reproduction services, office equipment rentals, etc.); speciality clothing stores; do-it-yourself stores; fast food restaurants; motels; automotive services. Franchising is not, as such, subject to any body of law in Sweden. Certain laws are applicable on parts of the franchise arrangement. It is strongly recommended that any U.S. company considering franchising in Sweden conduct a qualified legal study to ensure full validity and enforcement of its franchise agreements. To use an American form of franchising agreement without adjustments to Swedish laws and practices could be detrimental to the franchisor's business.

Government Procurement

National Government Procurement—The procedures for procurement of goods, services and construction at the national level is established by legislative enactment. (The Royal Purchasing Proclamation, dated 29th of June 1973). These regulations superseded the Royal Decree No. 496 dated June 6, 1952, and became effective on January 1, 1974. Government-owned companies are not subject to the government purchasing proclamation but are completely free to establish their own procurement and purchasing policies, which are generally based on purely commercial considerations.

Under the new purchasing proclamation, two main forms of procurement procedures are provided for in addition to private contracts. These are "strict tender" and "negotiated tender." Both forms may be either public or selective tenders. Whatever procedure is used, however, all bids, including bids from non-invited bidders, must be examined and evaluated. The procuring entity is free to choose the tender procedure considered economically most advantageous for the entity. In the "strict tender" procedure, bids are assessed and awarded without negotiations with bidders. In the "negotiated tender" procedure, negotiations with bidders may take place after the initial bids have been received. For private contracts, which are intended only for purchases of minor value and for supplies needed at once because of fire, flood, explosion or other disasters, no formal procedure for inviting bids has to be followed.

Suppliers may be invited through public announcement or letters of invitation in the case of both strict and negotiated tenders. If the negotiated tender procedure is used, other ways to invite bids may, however, be used. When public announcement is not used, a sufficient number of suppliers are to be invited to bid so as to ensure effective competition. In practice, public announcement has been the most prevalent form of soliciting bids for public works contracts, while mostly selective tenders and private contracts are used in the procurement of goods. Procurement for the armed forces is normally effected through selective tenders. When public announcement is used, the tender is published in a special appendix to the official Gazette (Tidning for leveranser till staten) or both in this Gazette and in one or more other newspapers. Procuring entities are required to give bidders sufficient time to prepare and submit bids, the time depending on the circumstances in each case.

The National Swedish Audit Bureau (Riksrevisionsverket Fack) S-100 26 Stockholm is the material agency generally responsible for the application of the new Purchasing Proclamation by procuring entities and for the coordination of government procurement procedures. Other useful addresses are:

> Forenade Fabriksverken, (the Swedish National Industries Corporation) S631 87 Eskilstuna.
>
> Forsvarets Materielverk (the Materiel Administration of the Swedish Armed Forces) Fack S-104 50 Stockholm
>
> Postverket (The Swedish Post Office Administration) S-101 10, Stockholm
>
> Statens Jarnvagar (the Swedish State Railways) S-105 50 Stockholm
>
> Statens Vattenfallsverk (the Swedish State Power Board) S-162 87 Vallingby.
>
> Statens Vagvewerk Fack (The National Swedish Road Administration) S-78187 Borlange
>
> Televerkets central-forvaltning (the National Swedish Telecommunications Administration) S-123 86 Farsta.

Local Government Procurement — Local government purchases have become increasingly significant, and may in some cases offer American companies excellent trading opportunities. Local governments are not subject to the national procurement procedures outlined above but are free to adopt their own procurement rules. The Swedish Association of Local Authorities and the Federation of Swedish County Councils have, however, adopted a recommendation aiming at rules for local government procurement which follow closely the rules of the national purchasing regulations.

As is also the case with procurement on the national government level, purely business considerations determine the methods and sources of procurement by local governments and similar bodies, and no distinction is made between domestic and foreign suppliers or contractors. The normal procedure in inviting bids is through circular letters addressed directly to firms known to be reputable and reliable. Such firms could be Swedish or foreign, the latter often being the local subsidiary or sales representative of a foreign company. With respect to small orders or supplementary deliveries, contact with suppliers is often made by oral communication, usually by telephone. Local government procurement agencies do not require publication of bids for contracts or purchases exceeding certain limits; this is left to the discretion of the local procurement organization and is inconsistent with practices among state purchasing organizations.

Local governments and their procurement procedures and practices are reputed to be liberal and completely non-discriminatory in character. Foreign firms, including many American companies, are often awarded contracts if the quality of other procurement terms and conditions are advantageous from a purely economic and business viewpoint.

The period allowed for tendering, i.e., the time elapsing between the first day from which the documents detailing the special conditions of the contract can effectively be consulted, and the day on which the tenders are open — varies from contract to contract and is dependent on the time required to adequately prepare for such bids.

Hospital Procurement — The organization of the medical care sector in Sweden makes centralized equipment purchases through the County Councils rather easy to arrange. The twenty-five County Councils, however, are autonomous units, and the degree of centralization varies.

The normal purchasing procedure is for the County Medical Care Authority, together with end-users of the equipment, to survey the equipment needs for new or expanded hospitals and forward them to the purchasing departments. In the case of replacements, the purchase request originates in the hospital department involved. Tenders are requested by the purchasing departments and are evaluated by the Equipment Sections together with the end-users. Upon their recommendation, the decision to purchase is made by the Delegation for Economy.

The LIC (Landstingens Inkopscentral) located at Svetsarvägen 20, S-17183 Solna, is a supply and distribution organization of the County Councils Association.

There is a high degree of uniformity in the Swedish hospital organiation. Once a piece of equipment has been tested and approved in one hospital, the chances are good that it will be installed in a number of other hospitals.

Advertising and Research

Advertising Media—With the important exception of television and radio, all major types of media are available in Sweden. Advertising plays a major role in Sweden's commercial life.

Daily newspapers and other publications are by far the most important media for advertising in Sweden. These account for almost half of all expenditures. Direct mail advertising is second, accounting for about 16 percent of the total. Other forms, useful for certain types of products, are point-of-sale advertising, motion picture advertising, outdoor posters and billboards, and transit cards.

Television and radio in Sweden do not carry any commercial advertising. Programs are financed through payment of annual license fees by television owners.

Advertising agencies in Sweden are rather tightly organized. In order to place advertisements in newspapers, magazines, and trade journals, an agency must be authorized to do so by the Swedish Publishers Association (Svenska Tidningsutgivareforeningen). Acceptance requires that the agency have experience in advertising, and that its books be open for audit by the association. Owing to the restrictions of the Publishers Association, it is difficult for foreign agencies to maintain Swedish branches; however, several Swedish agencies have representative arrangements with U.S. firms.

Publications—Sweden has one of the world's highest rates of newspaper readership. There are 138 newspapers with a total circulation of about 4.7 million, or more than 571 copies per 1000 inhabitants.

Detailed statistical information about the income distribution, age distribution, etc., of newspaper readers is available. The Swedish information service Tidningsstatistik (TS) acts as the nation's audit bureau of circulation. On the basis of statistics revised, usually at five year intervals, Sweden is divided into "TS areas," of which there are currently approximately 90. A TS area is formed within a radius where the newspapers published in one town have a higher circulation than papers from any nearby town. Certain exceptions to this definition are made for the large metropolitan dailies.

A distinction is drawn between the major metropolitan papers in Stockholm, Goteborg and Malmo, which have wide geographical circulation, and local daily newspapers in other Swedish cities and town. The four large Stockholm dailies enjoy nationwide circulation. They are Dagens Nyheter (morning), Svenska Dagbladet (morning), Aftonbladet (afternoon) and Expressen (afternoon). In spite of their wide circulation, however, these papers do not provide complete coverage of households outside the capital area. The large dailies in Goteborg and Malmo are important media for advertising exposure in western and southern Sweden. Advertisers wishing to obtain more thorough national coverage also may make use of the numerous local dailies. In addition to the 138 newspapers, there are more than two thousand other periodical publications. Most noted among these are the weekly and monthly magazines. There are some 45 of these publications with a combined circulation of almost seven million. It is estimated that 90 percent of the Swedish population reads one or more of these periodicals.

The largest popular weeklies are: Aret Runt, circulation of 387,150 and Hemmets Veckotidning 341,360. Two specialized weekly consumer magazines should be mentioned: ICA-Kuriren (668,850 copies), sponsored by the retail grocery trade and devoted to home and family matters, and Vi (301,036) with serious reporting on social and economic issues, published by the Cooperative Union and Wholesale Society.

Another important group of periodicals consists of some 500 trade and professional journals of varying size. The largest of these are published by trade unions and organized agricultural interests.

Direct Mail Advertising—Bulk addressed mailing is simplified through the ready availability of mailing lists. These may be purchased from the Swedish Post Office, which compiles lists for about fifty professions and 200 industries and institutions. These are available from Postverkets Address-register, Box 1, S-10120 Stockholm 1. In addition, a number of private firms compile mailing lists for use by direct mail advertisers.

Market Research—In preparing a preliminary survey of the Swedish market for any product, the exporter may wish to make use of the excellent Swedish statistical publications (see "Sources of Economic and Commercial Information" for a listing of the most important of these). Detailed trade data giving Swedish imports and exports of commodities by country are issued on a current basis. Production data, also very complete, usually lags by about two years. These data may be obtained through the Department of Commerce or any of its District Offices.

Market research is well developed in Sweden, and the techniques used in the United States are available. Market research firms are prepared to conduct interviews to determine customer attitudes. They also run regular opinion surveys directed at special groups. Many Swedish advertising agencies have market research divisions which will undertake limited market studies in connection with advertising compaigns. In addition to market research bureaus, there are firms composed of marketing consultants. A retail audit service showing customer purchases, on a trade section basis is available. Audits are usually supplied on a bi-monthly basis. A list of Swedish firms is contained in the Trade List — *Market Research Organizations Worldwide — 1979* available from the Office of Export Marketing Assistance U.S. Department of Commerce, Washington, D.C. 20230.

Several research institutes follow market trends and issue regular reports. These are connected with the Swedish industrial or trade associations. Leading institutes of this type include:

(1) The Swedish Retail Research Institute (Detaljhandelns Utredningsinstitut) — issues reports on retailing trends such as the expansion of voluntary chains and department stores.

(2) The Swedish Wholesalers' Research Institute (Grosshandelns Utredningsinstitut) — traces wholesaling developments.

(3) The Industrial Research Institute (Industriens Utredningsinstitut) — is concerned with general industrial trends and developments and issues numerous reports of its findings.

The reports issued by these organizations are normally in Swedish.

Credit

Availability of Capital

The Swedish credit market is well developed, and capital can usually be obtained to finance ventures which appear sound. The Central Bank of Sweden (Riksbanken) controls the money supply through its discount rate, through liquidity ratios and through open-market operations. The Central Bank also establishes credit policy guidelines after consultation with the commercial banks. Currently, liquidity in Sweden is high. Total private lending in the first six months of 1979 was 25 percent above the first half of 1978. The Riksbanken has recently been tightening the screws to prevent capital outflows and stimulate private borrowing abroad. It will also help reduce domestic demand. Fairly substantial increases in interest rates paid on savings accounts offers savers the possibility of a positive real rate of return. This should help increase the savings rate and restrain the growth of consumption.

Sources of Financing

Commercial banks. — The well-developed commercial banking system is the most important source of credit. According to Swedish law, commercial bank loans cannot exceed 1 year, but may be renewed under certain circumstances. The banks also buy and sell bonds and stock shares. However, they are not allowed to purchase securities for themselves. Approximately 82 percent of the total assets of Sweden's commercial banks are held by the four largest banks. Their total assets at year end 1978 were Post- och Kreditbanken (PKbanken); $13.1 billion; Skandinaviska Enskilda Banken; $11.5 billion; Svenska Handelsbanken; $10.8 billion and Götabanken $3.1 billion. The first three of these are based in Stockholm and maintain hundreds of branches throughout southern and central Sweden, Of the 14 commercial banks in Sweden, all but one are privately owned. The state-owned bank. Post- och Kredibanken (also called PKbanken) was created in 1974 through the merger of two state-owned banking institutions.

Head offices of the four largest Swedish banks are as follows:
Skandinaviska Enskilda Banken
Box 16067
S-103 22 Stockholm

Svenska Handelsbanken
Box 12128
S-103 28 Stockholm

PK Banken
S-103 71 Stockholm
Götabanken

S-405 09 Goteborg

There are currently no branches of foreign banks in Sweden. A few foreign banks have representative offices in Stockholm. While not engaged in actual banking operations, the representative offices maintain and develop contracts, respond to inquiries, and cooperate with Swedish banks in banking transactions. U.S. banks with representative offices are First National Bank of Chicago, Citibank, and Chase Manhattan Overseas Corp.

Specialized credit institutions—Long-term loans for specific purposes can be obtained from several specialized credit institutions. They include housing, agriculture, shipbuilding, and small industry. Two of the specialized credit institutions provide capital to small businesses for development and modernization, they are AB Industrikredit and AB Företagskredit. Both organizations are jointly owned by the Government and the commercial banks. Also jointly owned by the Government and the banks is AB Svensk Exportkredit, which provides credit to finance exports of ships and heavy machinery.

Bonds and Stocks—The use of bonds to obtain funds for investment is well established. Approximately 51 percent of total outstanding bonds are issued by mortgage institutions and credit companies. The national government accounts for 37 percent of bonds outstanding, municipalities 2 percent, and other borrowers 11 percent.

The Swedish stock market has grown rapidly in recent years. Share ownership has broadened to include new categories of investors and the market has become increasingly important as a source of capital. At the end of 1978, 134 corporations were listed on the Stockholm Stock Exchange or on the stockbroker's list. There are 23 security dealers in Sweden with permission to trade in securities and to charge commissions. About 40 percent of the total trade in shares takes place on the Stock Exchange. In 1978, total trade volume was nearly $1.1 billion. Capital raised through new issues was in the past comparatively small, but in recent years has grown considerably due to favorable market conditions.

Insurance Companies—These are a significant source of capital. Approximately 320 insurance firms are covered by special legislation. Of these, about 50 operate nationally. Insurance companies are restricted in the uses to which they may put their funds; most funds may only be invested in prime bonds, bank deposits, or promissory notes secured by first mortgages on real estate.

Savings banks—Sweden has a strong savings bank system. Loans are generally for housing construction, agriculture, and local industry. They are, therefore, not a significant source of capital for foreign investors in Sweden.

The Swedish Investment Bank—Established in 1967, the Swedish Investment Bank (Sveriges Investeringsbank AB Box 16051, S-103 22 Stockholm) is a State-owned institution formed to provide capital for large industrial projects, especially those for restructuring and modernizing Swedish industry. The bank is also authorized to provide export credits. Though generally charging commercial interest rates, the Bank can pursue a more liberal lending policy than the commercial banks. It may draw on the huge National Pension Fund to finance its capital needs. Its lending capacity is over $2 billion. The Investment Bank finances major industrial enterprises and risk projects which cannot raise funds through normal capital market channels. By the end of 1978, the bank had granted credits totaling $1.5 billion.

The Fund for Northern Sweden—In 1961, the Swedish parliament established a regional/industrial development fund for the northern half of Sweden, called Norrlandsfonden. The basic purposes of the fund are: To stimulate the development and diversification of business enterprises in the north of Sweden; to upgrade existing natural resources and establish local manufacturing enterprises; to promote production and service industries in northern Sweden and coordinate their activities towards certain regional and industrial targets. The fund provides financing to companies within its territory, either in the form of working capital loans, or financing in connection with a new corporate establishment, or loans for product development. In the latter case, the loan repayments are frequently conditional upon the product development being commercially successful. The lending capacity of the Fund varies slightly from year to year, depending on the repayment of and return on outstanding loans. In 1979, the Fund had approximately $16 million available for financing various corporate activities. Information about the Fund is available from Norrlandfonden Smedjegation 17 S-951 32 Sweden.

Consumer Financing

Installment and other means of credit purchases have become increasingly important to the Swedish economy. During the past decade, there has been a steady expansion in the use of consumer credit facilities. Installment credit is used extensively in the purchase of automobiles and household articles. Regulations concerning the length of credit vary according to the type of commodity. In general, installment credit practices are similar to those in the United States, and installment purchase contracts normally run from 12-24 months. Part-payment arrangements are also used. Partial payment is made on delivery of the article, with the balance payable in 30-90 days. There is no interest charge under this procedure.

Account credit is well developed in Sweden; charge account and credit account systems are similar to those in the United States. Most of the larger department stores have offered such payment facilities for many years. In 1960, smaller retailers joined together to form Köpkort, which offers credit card facilities to small retailers. The use of various credit cards has expanded rapidly during the past few years. The number of credit cards in use in 1978 increased by more than 30 percent and outstanding debt on credit cards rose to about $400 million. Credit cards can be used to purchase almost any product except alcoholic beverages.

Two types of consumer loans are widely used. Savings loans are offered to depositors of commercial banks and savings banks who have maintained regular deposits for a stipulated period. Cooperative loan purchases are offered by local cooperative societies to their members. Credit is granted in conjunction with purchases at a moderate annual interest rate. The amount of such loans is limited by the annual salary of the borrower.

Trade Regulations

Sweden traditionally has maintained a policy favoring the liberalization and expansion of international trade, and presently has one of the lowest tariff levels in the world. Import licenses are required for only a few commodities. Sweden has taken an active part in international organizations engaged in promoting the freer movement of trade. It participates in the General Agreement on Tariffs and Trade (GATT), the Organization for Economic Cooperation and Development (OECD), the European Free Trade Association (EFTA), The International Monetary Fund, the International Bank for Reconstruction and Development (World Bank), and the United Nations Economic Commission for Europe (ECE).

Sweden, like some other EFTA members that did not apply for European Economic Community (EEC) membership, signed a trade agreement with the EEC on July 22, 1972.

Tariff Structure

Sweden's tariff is a single-column tariff using the Brussels nomenclature. Import duties apply to all countries receiving most-favored-nation (MFN) treatment, including the United States. At the present time, Sweden grants MFN treatment to all countries. Sweden maintains one of the lowest tariff levels in the world on industrial goods. Some representative rates are as follows: 5 percent on most semimanufactures and finished products; 10 percent on automobiles; 3 to 13 percent on textiles; and 13 to 17 percent on clothing. Most raw materials, basic chemicals, pharmaceuticals, wood pulp, newsprint, pig iron and some finished goods, including most ships and aircraft are admitted duty free. Certain items, mainly machinery, of a type not produced in Sweden or produced in small quantities only, may be admitted duty free.

Certain agricultural products are subject to import fees, which are imposed in connection with a Swedish Government program designed to support agriculture. These import fees are generally flexible in character and are raised and lowered depending upon world market prices. Among the products subject to these fees are cattle, hogs, meat, poultry, butter, cheese, eggs, cereals, flour and certain fats and oils.

As a member of European Free Trade Association (EFTA), Sweden began a gradual elimination of its duties on practically all products originating in other EFTA nations on July 1, 1960. The final reduction to duty free entry was made on December 31, 1966. In addition to Sweden, EFTA members are Austria, Finland, Iceland, Norway, Portugal, and Switzerland.

Sweden, as well as other EFTA countries not joining the EEC, has entered into separate preferential trade agreements with the EEC. The Swedish agreement provided that in the trade between Sweden, and the members of the EEC (Belgium, France, Germany, Italy, Luxembourg, the United Kingdom, Denmark, the Netherlands and Ireland), duties will be eliminated on most industrial goods in stages over a five-year period. The first step, a 20 percent cut, was taken on April 1, 1973, followed by cuts of the same magnitude on January 1, 1974, 1975 and 1976. The final 20 percent reduction took place on July 1, 1977, so that now there is virtually free trade in industrial goods between Sweden, the other members of EFTA, and the nine member nations in the EEC. For a few sensitive items (e.g., paper products and metals), duties are being phased out over a longer period. On January 1, 1972, Sweden put into effect a generalized system of tariff preferences in favor of developing nations. Almost all industrial products considered to be of origin in these developing nations may enter free of duty. A few nonindustrial products (e.g., crustaceans and preserved fish, fresh quinces, peaches and melons, some canned fruits, juices, and certain spirituous beverages) may also enter duty free.

Basis of Duty Assessment—Virtually all Swedish import duties are on an ad valorem basis. The basis for valuation is the normal price of the merchandise plus costs of transportation and all other expenses, such as insurance and freight, connected with the sale and delivery of the merchandise up to the point of its introduction into Swedish customs territory. This normal price is defined as the price which could be obtained for the merchandise at the time and place of its introduction into Swedish customs territory in the course of a sale in the open market effected between a buyer and seller independent of each other. Under these conditions, the normal price can be determined on the basis of the invoice price.

Information regarding Swedish duties applicable to specific products may be obtained free from any U.S. Department of Commerce District office or from the Swedish Country Specialist, Office of Country Marketing, International Trade Administration,. U.S. Department of Commerce, Washington, D.C. 20230. The Country Specialist also can provide information about Swedish duty rate concessions resulting from the GATT negotiations.

Customs Surcharges and Taxes—Sweden levies no customs surcharges as such, but nearly all imports are subject to a value added tax and some products to special taxes. These are explained more fully in the section on Taxation.

Shipping Documents

The documents required by Sweden from the exporter include a commercial invoice, a bill of lading, and such special certificates as may be necessary. Consular invoices and regular certificates of origin are not required. There are no stipulations as to the form of commercial invoices, bills of lading or other shipping documents.

Commercial Invoice—Swedish customs regulations specify that the invoice (in triplicate) must contain the seller's name, signature, and address; the buyer's name and address; date the

invoice was prepared; date the purchase contract was concluded; number of cases, parcels, or containers; type and gross weight plus marking and number; product's commercial name; quantity of the merchandise, price of each type of product; eventual discounts (and the nature of the discount); and also conditions of delivery and payment. Goods liable to an ad valorem duty shipped on consignment should be accompanied by an invoice as though they had been sold.

All shipping documents may be made out in the English language. The use of the metric system of weights and measures, though preferable, is not compulsory.

Bill of Lading—The usual ocean bill of lading (or air waybill on air shipments) suffices for shipments to Sweden. The bill of lading must be compiled in accordance with the invoice. "To order" bills of lading are accepted.

Sanitary Certificates—Sanitary certificates which must show the country or origin are required for goods which may be suspected of bringing contagious animal or vegetable diseases into the country or for goods for which special stipulations as to quality are prescribed. Goods subject to these sanitary certificates of origin include: Live animals, certain aminal products (including meat and meat products), used dairy hollow wares, used sacks, feedstuff, potatoes, live plants, seed, margarine, cheese, and fatty emulsions, syrup and molasses, preparations containing spirits, concentrated alcohol, and shaving brushes. The sanitary certificate of origin must be legalized by a Swedish consul or an official authority in the country of production or export.

Documents on Air Cargo—The documentary requirements for air express or air freight shipment are the same as for other shipments to Sweden except that the air waybill replaces the bill of lading.

Marketing and Labeling Requirements

There is no general requirement in Sweden that imports be marked as to the country of origin. However, goods carrying incorrect designations or origin are prohibited, and a product which has been made to appear as though it has been produced or manufactured in Sweden may not be imported unless its foreign origin is clearly, conspicuously; and durably marked thereon. It would suffice if the marking in this case consisted only of the word "imported." There are, however, special marking regulations on a few products, e.g., shoes, pharmaceuticals, poisons, seeds and certain foods.

If not already marked before arrival, goods must be properly marked under customs supervision, within 30 days after arrival. Goods not properly marked may be reexported by the owner, under customs supervision, within the 30-day period after arrival. If neither properly marked nor reexported, the goods become the property of the state.

Importers of food products must present to Swedish customs officials a certificate showing that the imported food products contain only additives authorized by the Swedish Board of Trade. Information about food import regulations, food additives, and labeling of prepackaged foods is available from the Staten Livsmedelsverk (Swedish National Food Administration,) Box 622, S-751 26 Uppsala, Sweden.

Most imported articles of precious metals must be sent to the Swedish assay office for hallmarking before clearance through the customs. There are no special regulations for marking outside cases or packages except that packages upon arrival must be marked to correspond with the bill of lading and the invoice, and gross weight must be marked on single packages exceeding 1 metric ton in weight (2,204 lbs.).

Senate Concurrent Resolution 40, adopted July 30, 1953, invites U.S. exporters to inscribe, insofar as practicable, on the external shipping containers in indelible print of a suitable size: "United States of America." Although such marking is not compulsory under our laws, U.S. shippers are urged to cooperate in thus publicizing American-made goods.

Free Zones and Ports

There are free port facilities at Stockholm, Goteborg and Malmö where goods may enter without customs declarations or inspection. The facilities are municipal enterprises operated under the supervision of the Royal Board of Customs. The Board has authority over all goods and traffic passing through the ports in order to insure that Swedish laws and regulations are observed.

Goods may be stored, sorted, repacked, sold, exported, or returned to the country of origin without payment of customs duties or other import charges. They may also be cleared through customs for domestic consumption. In order to carry on industrial operations in freeport areas, special authorization must be obtained. Retail trade is prohibited, except as may be authorized to provision and service ships and aircraft.

Technical Standards and Requirements

Since Sweden uses the metric system, equipment for sale in Sweden should be adapted to it whenever possible.

Electric current is 50 hertz, 220/380 volts A.C., single and three phase. Electrical equipment sold in Sweden must be approved by the Swedish Institute for Testing and Approval of Electrical Equipment (SEMKO), unless it is to be used solely by qualified technical personnel. SEMKO's address is Box 30049, S-104 25 Stockholm, Sweden.

Information about Swedish industrial standards may be obtained free from the Standards Information Service of the National Bureau of Standards, (301) 921-2587. This reference service can determine if there is a standard for a specific product, provide a reference number and the name of a private U.S. organization from which to obtain the standard.

Since the diversity of foreign standards, regulations, inspection procedures, and certification requirements constitute a considerable barrier to increasing U.S. exports, U.S. firms may want to take advantage of the Technical Help to Exporters program provided by the National Technical Information Service of the U.S. Department of Commerce. This service can provide foreign standards and regulations that a product must meet in a specific or regional market overseas. Customized work projects may also be undertaken to meet your needs in the standards area on a cost reimbursable basis. For additional information contact the National Technical Information Service, Technical Help to Exporters, U.S. Department of Commerce, Springfield, Va. 22161, (703) 557-4732. Information about industrial standards may also be obtained from the American National Standards Institute, Inc., 1430 Broadway, New York, N.Y. 10018, Telephone (212) 354-3300.

Samples, Carnets

Sweden is a member of the International Convention to facilitate the Importation of Commercial Samples and Advertising Matter." Samples may be imported into Sweden free of customs charges if they are of little or no commercial value, or if they have been made unfit for use. If they do not meet these requirements, the samples are subject to customs duty. Small quantities of advertising matter are admitted duty and tax free. Other samples and advertising films not exceeding 16 mm. may be imported free of duties and taxes for a 6-month period, provided the amount of customs charges is deposited with the customs authorities or a bond posted upon entry of the goods into Sweden. When the merchandise is reexported, the cash deposit is refunded or the bond canceled.

Samples may also be imported temporarily by using the ATA Carnet. The ATA Carnet is a simplified customs document by which commercial samples or professional equipment may be sent or taken into Sweden and any of the other 34 foreign countries participating in this arrangement. The ATA Carnet is a guarantee to the Customs authorities that duties and taxes will be paid if the goods are not taken out of the country. The carnet permits making customs arrangements in advance in the United States and is especially useful when visiting several countries, since the same document may be used and remains valid for a 12-month period.

In the United States, ATA Carnets are issued for a fee by the U.S. Council of the International Chamber of Commerce, 1212 Avenue of the Americas, New York, N.Y. 10036, (212) 354-4480. Application forms may be obtained from your local U.S. Department of Commerce district Office.

Investment in Sweden

U.S. Investment in Sweden

U.S. direct investment in Sweden at year's end 1979 totaled $1399 million. Of that total, $369 million was in machinery manufacturing, $39 million in primary and fabricated metals, $137 million in trade, $14 million in finance, and the remainder divided among other activities including petroleum, chemicals, and food and transportation equipment.

At the present time, there are about 170 subsidiaries and affiliates of U.S. companies operating in Sweden. Over one half of these are sales and distribution firms, just under one fifth operate assembly or manufacturing plants. In addition to several of the leading American oil companies, other large U.S. companies active in Sweden include, AMF, Burroughs, Dow, Du Pont, Ford, General Motors, General Foods, Hercules, Honeywell, IBM, ITT, 3M Corp., NCR, Sperry Rand, and Texas Instruments. A few American firms are active in the service trades such as: Advertising, management consulting, news and travel services and consulting engineers. A listing of *American Firms, Subsidiaries and Affiliates Operating in Sweden* is published by World Trade Academy Press Inc., 50 East 42nd St., New York, New York 10017.

Swedish Policy and Investment

Sweden is receptive to foreign direct investment. With few exceptions, Sweden accords foreign investors the same treatment as Swedish nationals. However, Sweden does not offer special tax or other inducements to attract foreign capital.

With few exceptions, Swedish law accords the same treatment of foreign-owned subsidiaries and branches as to Swedish companies. The few fields in which foreign ownership is not permitted include air transport facilities within Sweden, ownership of Swedish vessels, and the manufacture of war materials. Potential takeover of existing Swedish firms by foreign transnational companies is a subject of sensitive public concern. To meet these concerns and to exercise surveillance, the Government now has authority to reject the foreign take-over of a Swedish-owned firm if it is considered "detrimental to the national interest."

There are certain limitations on foreigners with regard to the formation of a corporation, membership on the board of directors, and the managing directorship of a corporation. None of these special regulations is a serious barrier to the establishment and operation of a subsidiary in Sweden, however. Sweden generally maintains a highly restrictive policy toward foreign portfolio investment in Swedish shares. Likewise, portfolio investment aborad by Swedish residents is generally restricted.

Forms of Business Organizations

Foreigners are, in principal, permitted to carry on in Sweden any of the legally recognized forms of business enterprise, subject to the exceptions noted in the following paragraphs. The types of organizations are:

Joint stock company (limited liability corporation) Aktiebolag (AB)
Branch of a foreign corporation (Filial)
Individual business activity
Partnership
Limited Partnership
Cooperative

The nontrading office—The two forms of particular interest to foreign investors in Sweden are the joint stock company and the branch of a foreign corporation. Of possible interest are the individual business activity and the nontrading office. These forms of organization are described in the following paragraphs.

Joint stock company (corporation)—The great majority of American-owned firms in Sweden are joint-stock companies. A Swedish corporation may be entirely foreign-owned. This is the only Swedish form of business based on share ownership. It is an independent legal entity. Shareholders are not individually responsible for liabilities and obligations.

The basic Swedish legislation governing the formation of a joint stock company is the Swedish Companies Act (1975:1385) as implemented and amended by Act (1975:1386) on the Implementation of the Companies Act. These acts became effective on January 1, 1977. Under this legislation, a company may be formed by one or several founders. The minimum subscribed share capital is established at 50,000 Swedish kronor. The founder(s) must be a resident Swedish citizen or Swedish legal entity. The Government, however, may permit founders other than mentioned above, in certain cases.

The corporation's board of directors must consist of at least three members in all cases, in which the share capital of the company is one million Swedish kronor or more. Companies capitalized at less than one million kronor may have only one or two directors provided that at least one deputy director is appointed. There are special provisions concerning membership of non-Swedish nationals on a Swedish corporation's board of directors. Not more than one-third of the board members may ordinarily be non-Swedish. Non-Swedish nationals elected to the board must have specific permission from the Board of Commerce. Likewise, specific permission is required for a non-Swedish national to serve as managing director of a corporation (such permission normally is forthcoming). The board of directors has final responsibility for the management of the firm. The Swedish Companies Act has been translated into English and published by the Federation of Swedish Industries. (Sveriges Industriforbund), Box 5501, S-11485 Stockholm, Sweden.

Branch of a Foreign Company—Since 1955, foreign companies have been permitted to establish branch operations in Sweden. The parent company must be properly registered and carrying on business in its home country. The branch is required to have a managing director resident in Sweden (though he need not be a Swedish citizen). He is fully responsible for operations in Sweden and has power-of-attorney from the parent company to act on behalf of the company.

In many respects, a branch in Sweden is treated as if it were a Swedish corporate entity. The branch pays the Swedish corporate income

tax on its revenues in Sweden (see section on Taxation). In respect to exchange transactions, the branch is treated as if it were a Swedish subsidiary. The Swedish branch establishment law also contains detailed provisions for auditing of the branches' books. The Swedish branch must have the same name as the parent company, with the addition of the word "filial" (branch) and a clear indication of the parent company's country of domicile.

Individual business activity—A foreign businessman may carry on a business as a single individual. If his business requires the keeping of books of account, he must register with the administration of the county in which he is doing business. In certain instances, a foreign businessman carrying on his own business must also obtain a "license to trade." The Swedish Board of Trade (Kommerskollegium) is the agency granting licenses to trade, but application must be made through the county administration. Such professions as teaching and medical practice do not require a license to trade but are subject to other special regulations. A license to trade is not needed for such occasional business activities by foreigners as obtaining a sales agreement with a Swedish firm or installing a specific lot of equipment. The license is needed only if a foreigner carries on a regular business in Sweden over a period of time. Licenses to trade are liberally granted, as a rule.

Partnerships—There are two types of partnerships in Sweden, trading partnerships and limited partnership. The principal difference between them is that in a limited partnership one or more, but not all of the partners may limit his liability to the amount of his investment. To join a Swedish partnership, a foreign national must secure a permit from the Board of Commerce and receive approval from the Riksbanken.

The nontrading office—A foreign firm may establish an office in Sweden which does not actually conclude contracts or make sales. Such office may make preliminary market studies in behalf of the foreign firm. It may also solicit orders (without actually making sales). Under these conditions, the office is not considered a business or trading establishment. There are no special registration or other requirements.

Entry and Repatriation of Capital

Permission must be obtained from the Swedish Central Bank (Riksbanken) to import capital into Sweden either to finance the establishment of a business or to buy a share of an existing Swedish firm. The Riksbanken normally grants permission for this type of capital import. However, the Bank is not likely to approve import of capital for purely portfolio investment.

The Riksbanken has a liberal policy on repatriation of earnings and capital. In general, yields on invested funds may be freely transferred. This includes dividends on shares, interest on bonds, or other receipts from invested capital and from real estate in Sweden.

Riksbanken permission is normally granted to repatriate proceeds accruing from the liquidation of a foreign subsidiary or branch in Sweden.

Royalties and license fees—Royalty and license fee payments may be freely transferred out of Sweden, and no special license is required from the Riksbanken. Similarly, a subsidiary or branch in Sweden may transfer fees without special license to the parent company for management services, research expenditures, and the like.

Foreign Ownership of Real Property

A special concession is required from the Swedish Government for a foreigner to purchase real estate. Normally it is not difficult to obtain permission to buy property for use as a plant site, or to purchase factory buildings, business office buildings, warehouses, or other real property for use in the course of operating the business. A foreign subsidiary or branch may rent office or industrial space without statutory restriction; no special permission is required.

Certain forms of real property, however, are restricted as to ownership by foreign persons or entities. The Government's policy is highly restrictive toward foreign ownership or mineral rights and mines. The authorities also are not likely to grant permission for ownership of agricultural and forest land.

Incentive Legislation

Regional development incentives—The Swedish Government, to achieve a more balanced distribution of resources, and reduce unemployment offers significant incentives to firms locating in development areas, particularly the more sparsely settled parts of the country (mainly the northern two thirds). A firm's application for special assistance is evaluated in terms of the planned location and its prospects for profitable operation. Incentives are in the form of grants and loans for financing new buildings and equipment, training of personnel, moving machinery and employees from other locations, and extra costs that may be incurred for trans-

portation and communication. Also, payroll taxes are reduced for investments in the development areas. The incentives are available to companies engaged in industrial or similar activities, and those serving industry (including machine repair and testing laboratories, but not marketing). To a limited extent, incentives are also available for tourism ventures. Companies that operate in the development or "support" areas receive a reduction on the payroll tax—2 percent instead of the usual 4 percent.

Industrial Property Protection

Sweden is a member of the "Paris Union," International Convention for the Protection of Industrial Property (patents, trade marks, commercial names, and industrial designs) to which the United States and about 80 other countries adhere. American businessmen and inventors are thus entitled to receive national treatment in Sweden (treatment equal to that accorded Swedish citizens), under laws regarding the protection of patents and trademarks. American nationals are also entitled to certain other benefits, such as the protection of patents against arbitrary forfeiture for nonworking and a 1 year "right of priority" for filing patent applications (one year after first filing a patent application in the United States in which to file a corresponding application in Sweden, and receive in the latter the benefit of the first U.S. application filing date). The right-of-priority period for trade marks is 6 months. Applications or inquiries pertaining to industrial property rights should be addressed to: Director General, Patent & Registeringsverket (Royal Patents and Registration Office), Box 5055, S-102 42 Stockholm.

Sweden is also a member of the Universal Copyright Convention to which the United States and about 60 other countries adhere. Works of American authors first copyrighted in the United States are entitled to automatic protection in Sweden. The author need only show on such works, his name, year of first publication, and the symbol "C" in a circle to obtain copyright protection.

Sweden is also a member of the "Berne Union" Copyright Convention. Although the United States is not a member of this Convention, U.S. authors may obtain protection in Berne Union countries by publishing work in a Union country at the same time it is first published in the United States (simultaneous publication).

Patents—The Patents Act of 1978 became effective June 1, 1978. Patents are granted for 20 years from the effective date of filing the application — three years longer than the preceding Patent Act of 1967. The new law also provides that patents less than 12 years old on June 1, 1978 can be extended to 20 years by paying the prescribed annual fees. Applications are examined for novelty and, if accepted, published for opposition for 3 months. If no opposition is filed or it is successfully overcome, the application is allowed and a patent granted. If a patentee does not work his patent within 3 years from date of grant or 4 years from the application date, a compulsory license may be ordered.

Trademarks—Trademarks are protected under the Trade Mark Act of 1960, effective January 1, 1961. Sweden has adopted the Nice International Classification System for registration purposes (34 product and 8 service classes). Trademark registrations are valid for 10 years from the date of registration and are renewable for like periods. The first applicant for a mark is entitled to receive a registration and exclusive ownership. If another party, however, can prove he was the first user, he may have the mark canceled and reregistered to himself. After 5 years, a registration becomes incontestable on grounds of prior use. Applications are examined and, if acceptable, published for opposition for 2 months. Swedish or foreign official emblems or words, or markings contrary to public order or good morals, cannot be registered as trademarks. A trademark registration may be canceled if not used within 5 years, unless the registrant shows an acceptable reason for non-use.

Copyrights—Protection of copyrights in Sweden is governed by Law No. 729 (of 1960) as amended. The term of copyright protection of a work is for the author's life plus 50 years after his death. It includes all literary, dramatic, musical, and artistic works. Copyright includes the sole right to produce and reproduce the work or a translation of it; to publish such a work or translation; to perform it in public; and to authorize others to do so.

Further information on the general features of Sweden's laws on patent, trademark, and copyright protection may be obtained from the Foreign Business Practices Division, Office of International Finance and Investment, Bureau of International Economic Policy and Research. That Division, however, cannot provide detailed information on fees or other step-by-step procedures in seeking protection under the laws. Competent legal counsel should be consulted.

Taxation

Corporate Taxes—Corporations are subject to both national and local income taxes. They pay a 40 percent corporate income tax to the national government, to as well as a local income tax which averages about 25 percent. The latter tax rate varies somewhat in different localities. The amount paid for local income tax is fully deductible before payment of the national income tax, however. Thus, the effective rate of corporate income tax (national and local combined) is about 55 percent.

Swedish tax law is generally liberal with regard to allowable deductions which can be made to compute "net taxable income." Ordinary deductions include: Rent paid by the corporation to a third party for premises; wages and salaries including most fringe benefit costs; interest paid on borrowed capital; expenditures for repair or maintenance of machinery and buildings; indirect taxes paid in the course of business; royalties paid for the right to use a patent or copyright; and other expenses incurred in operating the business.

Depreciation allowances—The Swedish corporate income tax includes liberal rules for depreciation of machinery and equipment. The taxpayer may choose either the 20-percent, straight-line method or the 30-percent, declining-balance method of computing depreciation. The cost of assets with a service life of less than 3 years may be written off at once. The depreciation on factories and office buildings is on a straight-line basis. Factories are generally depreciated at 4 percent a year and office buildings are depreciated at 2 percent.

Investment reserve system—Firms may build up investment reserves for purposes of economic stabilization. Any Swedish company is allowed to allocate up to 40 percent of its profits before taxes in any one year to an investment reserve fund. Such amounts are deductible from taxable income. Of this allocation, 50 percent must be deposited with the Central Bank of Sweden (Riksbanken) in a blocked account on which no interest is paid. The remainder can be held by the firm as working capital. The reserve fund is then completely tax-free if it is used under conditions specified by the Government.

Personal Income Taxes—Swedish residents are subject to personal income taxes at both the national and local levels. The tax burden on middle and upper income brackets is heavy because of the steeply progressive character of the national personal income tax.

Value added tax—By far the most important indirect tax is the value added tax (VAT). It is levied at a rate of 23.46 percent. The VAT was introduced on January 1, 1969. It applies at the same 23.46 percent rate to both domestic transactions and imported goods and services. Exports from Sweden are not subject to the VAT. The value added tax is levied at each sale transaction along the production and distribution chain. But, as the name of the tax implies, it is only the value added at each phase of production or distribution that is taxed. In effect, each taxpayer pays the difference between the tax calculated on his own sales and the tax included on his purchases from other producers or distributors. On imported goods, the value added tax is payable to Swedish Customs Authorities at the time of entry in much the same way as customs duties. The VAT is levied on the c.i.f., duty-paid value of the imported product.

The Swedish VAT applies to almost all goods and services. A few items are exempt from the VAT, however, including medical and dental services; prescription medicines; certain ships and aircraft used in business; electrical energy and certain other fuels used for heating or production of energy; ordinary newspapers; certain types of periodicals (religious, political); and works of art. Generally, foreign advertisers are not required to pay value added taxes on their advertising. In addition, a lower effective VAT rate applies to building contractor and restaurant services, prefabricated houses, and a few other services.

Of great importance to U.S. exporters of machinery and equipment is the fact that all capital equipment enjoys practical exemption from the VAT. When the equipment is entered, the importer must pay the 23.46 percent VAT. However, VAT paid at time of purchase of capital equipment can be deducted from the buyer's VAT remittances to the Government on his sales. Thus, in effect, the VAT does not apply to capital equipment. This provision of VAT provides a significant stimulus to capital equipment outlays by companies in Sweden.

Other taxes—The Swedish Government levies excise taxes on several items, among which are motor vehicles, liquor and wines, sugar, malt, carbonated beverages, tobacco, fuels, and electrical energy. There are luxury taxes on jewelry, cosmetics and other luxury items. There are also other types of taxes, such as capital distribution, net wealth real estate transfer, inheritance and gifts taxes.

Tax Treaty With the United States—A Convention for the Avoidance of Double Taxation between the United States and Sweden came into force in 1939, and was modified by a Supplementary Convention in 1963. It applies to national income taxes in the United States and Sweden and the local income tax in Sweden. Its benefits apply both to individual citizens and to corporations in the two countries. The key, for Swedish taxation purposes, is whether an American enterprise operates in Sweden through a "permanent establishment" (Article II). If so, then all "industrial and commercial profits" allocable to the permanent establishment in Sweden are taxable by the Swedish Government (and exempt from taxation by the United States). The identical rule applies, of course, to Swedish-operated permanent establishments in the United States.

Tax treatment of royalties is spelled out in Article VI of the Convention, as follows: "Royalties from real property or in respect to the operation of mines, quarries, or other natural resources shall be taxable only in the contracting States in which such property, mines, quarries, or other natural resources are located. Other royalties and amounts derived from within one of the contracting States by a resident or by a corporation or other entity of the other contracting State as consideration for the right to use copyrights, patents, secret processes and formulas, trademarks and other analogous rights, shall be exempt from taxation in the former State."

Tax treatment of interest on bonds, etc., is dealt with in Article VIII of the Convention, as modified in 1963, as follows: "Interest on bonds, debentures, other securities and notes, or on any other form of indebtedness received from sources within one of the contracting States by a resident or corporation or other entity of the State not having a permanent establishment in the former State shall be exempt from tax by such former State."

The Convention spells out detailed rules for the taxation of dividends (Article VII as modified by the Supplementary Convention). In general, it limits the extent to which dividends may be taxed at their source prior to remittance abroad. Copies fo the tax treaty and supplementary convention are available from the Superintendent of Documents, U.S. Government Printing Office Washington, D.C. 20402 in the following publications: *Double Taxation Convention and Protocol Between the United States and Sweden* (Treaty Series No. 958) and *Supplementary Convention Between the United States and Sweden* (Treaty series No. 5656).

Labor Force

Sweden's labor force totals 4.2 million. The working population by sector is as follows: Public service, 27.1 percent; mining and manufacturing, 24.9 percent wholesale and retail trade, 12.3 percent; transportation and communications, 6.7 percent; construction, 8.0 percent; agriculture, 4.8 percent; and forestry, 1.5 percent.

Payments and Benefits

Labor costs in Sweden are among the highest in Europe. The average hourly wage for all workers in manufacturing during the second quarter was 30.3 SEK. To this figure must be added remuneration for time not worked (vacation, public holidays, payments in kind and so on) equivalent to about 5.0 SEK. Social benefit costs which average 37.9 percent (in 1980) of cash wages before taxes must also be added. These social benefit costs include pension contributions, health insurance, unemployment insurance. Social benefit costs for salaried employees are even greater, averaging 44 percent (1980) of cash salaries before taxes.

Guidance for Business Travelers

Entrance Requirements

Every traveler must be in possession of a valid passport. Sweden has no vaccination requirements. Certain vaccinations, however, are recommended or required by the United States for Americans traveling abroad. Since the regulations governing these requirements may change with prevailing conditions, anyone contemplating a trip abroad should obtain the latest information from the Division of Foreign Quarantine, U.S. Public Health Service, Department of Health, Education, and Welfare, Washington, D.C. 20201, or from any local facility of the Service.

Entrance and Residence—Foreigners entering Sweden must have a passport or other valid document of identification. The general rule is that this document must be visaed by a Swedish Embassy or Consulate only if the visit to Sweden is to be longer than 3 months. A residence longer than 3 months requires a special residence permit (uppehallstillstand), which is granted by the National Immigration and Naturalization Administration. (Statens Invandrarverk). American citizens may enter Sweden without a Swedish visa and do not require a residence permit during the first 3 months after their entry. (Certain exemptions from the requirements are granted citizens of Denmark, Finland and Norway).

Work Permit.—An alien who wishes to accept employment must first obtain a work permit. This rule applies to American citizens. However, Swedish-born American citizens, their wives, and unmarried children under 21 years of age, (provided they accompany the husband or parent) may be exempt from the work-permit requirement.

Foreign Exchange Regulations

Foreign exchange restrictions is Sweden have been continuously reduced, and remaining requirements are applied liberally. In general, commercial transactions are not subject to any restrictions. Payments for imported and exported goods as well as commissions, royalties, wages, licenses, other fees, etc., may thus be remitted freely to other countries and received from them.

A non-resident's account with a Swedish bank is, in principle, convertible. The only condition for free disposal is that the funds on the account either represent such Swedish payment as could have been made by direct transfer to other countries (e.g. normal commercial payments) or transfer from another convertible account in Sweden or a sale of freely convertible currencies. Such a non-resident's account may be used for payments in Sweden, transfers to other countries or purchase of foreign exchange. A foreign national with employment in Sweden may transfer abroad, in any currency, what he has been able to save out of his income derived from work in Sweden.

For capital transactions and transfers a Riksbanken (the Central Bank of Sweden) license is required and is normally granted. Direct investments thus licensed, require no special license for dividend or interest payments to the foreign investor. Repatriation of the principal sum invested and of undistributed profits, however, does require a special license, but this license also is ordinarily granted.

Language, Business Hours, Holidays

Commercial Language—Many Swedish businessmen, particularly those dealing in export and import, are fluent in English, the preferred commercial language. The business visitor will discover, however, that as he travels from the main centers such as Stockholm, Goteborg and Malmo, he will find fewer English-speaking businessmen. A knowledge of German often is useful, particularly with older, non-English-speaking Swedes. Swedish business executives travel extensively in the United States and in Europe. Moreover, they generally read English-language trade and technical magazines and books. The American businessman will quickly note that they are often very well acquainted with the trade and business practices in the United States.

Business Hours—Offices generally open at 8:30 or 9 a.m. and close at 5 p.m. on weekdays (sometimes at 3 p.m. or 4 p.m. in summer). Most business offices are closed on Saturdays. Banks are open weekdays usually from 9:30 a.m. to 3 p.m. Banks are closed Saturdays throughout the year. On Monday to Friday, many banks, especially in large towns, are open one or more evenings, e.g. 4:30 p.m. to 6 p.m.

Holidays—Sweden has 11 national holidays: New Years Day; Good Friday; Easter Sunday; Easter Monday; Labor Day (May 1); Ascension Day (sixth Thursday after Easter); Whitmonday; Mid-Summer Day (the Saturday between June 19 and 26); All Saints Day (first Saturday in November); Christmas (December 25 and 26). Most organizations also close on Mid-Summer Eve, Christmas Eve and New Year's Eve. Government, banks, commercial institutions and offices generally close at 1 p.m. on the day before major holidays such as Labor Day, Ascension Day and All Saints Day.

July is a traditional vacation month in Sweden. Many offices and factories are closed or work with very reduced staffs during the entire month. The business slowdown begins the last week of June and lasts through mid-August. Business visitors are advised to avoid traveling to Sweden during this period as they could find Swedish executives unavailable, unless they have made prior arragements. Business appointments are also difficult to make between December 22 and January 6.

Sources of Economic and Commercial Information

General information concerning the Swedish market (economic trends, commercial development, trade regulations and duties, production, trade, etc.) may be obtained from the German/Nordic Section, Office of Country Marketing, Export Development, U.S. Department of Commerce, Washington, D.C. 20230, or from any of the Department's District Offices.

Government Representation

Sweden has an Embassy in the United States at 600 New Hampshire Ave., N.W., Washington, D.C. 20008. Telephone: (202) 298-3500.

Sweden maintains Consulates General at 333 N. Michigan Ave., Chicago, Il. 60601; 17 Briar Hollow Lane, Houston, Texas 77006; 730 Second Ave. South, Minneapolis, Minn. 55402; 825 Third Ave., New York, N.Y. 10022; and 1960 Jackson St., San Francisco, Calif. 94109.

Consulates are located in Anchorage, Atlanta, Baltimore, Boston, Cleveland, Dallas, Detroit, Buffalo, Cincinnati, Denver, Duluth, Jacksonville, Kansas City, Mobile, Phoenix, Portland Me, Portland Ore., San Diego, San Juan, St. Louis, Honolulu, Los Angeles, Miami, Milwaukee, New Orleans, Norfolk, Omaha, Philadelphia, and Seattle.

In addition to its Embassy and Consulates, the Swedish Government maintains Trade Commissioners in New York, Chicago, Houston, Los Angeles, and Detroit. These officials, oriented toward business and trade, can supply information on Swedish exports to the United States. The New York Trade Commissioner, which has national coordinating responsibility, is located at 1 Dag Hammarskjold Plaza, New York 10017 (telephone 212-593-0045).

The United States maintains an Embassy in Stockholm at Strandvagen 101 S-115 27 (telephone 63 05 20). It also maintains the American Cultural Center at Sveavagen 118, Stockholm.

Swedish Investment Information

The Swedish Industrial Development Corporation may prove very helpful to the U.S. firm contemplating investment in Sweden. It is located at 600 Steamboat Road, Greenwich, Conn., telephone 203-661-2500. Its parent company is a corporation wholly owned by the Swedish Government. Its aim is to stimulate the exchange of technology between U.S. and Swedish firms and to facilitate joint ventures, licensing agreements, and other forms of cooperation. Detailed Information about the Swedish Industrial Development Corporation and its services may be obtained by writing or calling its Greenwich office.

Swedish Trade Organizations

Specific industries, trades, and professions are almost invariably grouped into associations. In turn, these associations are often represented in larger trade federations which have more general purposes. The most important, from the standpoint of export and import trade as well as domestic business activity, are listed below:

1. The Federation of Swedish Industries (Sveriges Industriforbund), located at Storgatan 19, Stockholm. Its membership consists of all the major trade associations as well as individual Swedish industries. The Federation plays an active role in the formulation of Swedish industrial, business and trade legislation. Its staff of professional economists charts Swedish business trends, studies the impact of international commerce on Swedish industry, examines problems of technological development.

2. Federation of Swedish Wholesale Merchants and Importers (Sveriges Grossistforbund), located at Storgatan 19, S114 85 Stockholm. It is the principal organization for the private wholesale and import trade in Sweden. It is based upon about 55 branch associations (e.g., textiles, chemicals, machine tools) whose member firms act as importers, wholesalers, distributors, agents, and general agents for all kinds of goods. The Federation's foreign trade department can supply registers of importers of different articles in Sweden. It supplies information about customs and license regulations, Swedish trade fairs, terms of payment, etc. It publishes a monthly review called Svensk Handel (trans. Swedish Trade).

3. The Swedish Export Council, also located at Storgatan 19, S 114 85 Stockholm, is jointly funded and operated by Swedish industries and the Government. It gathers and disseminates information on foreign markets, manages Sweden's export promotion program, provides technical data, etc.

4. The Stockholm Chamber of Commerce, because of its location in the capital, includes in its membership many of Sweden's prominent business enterprises. Its address is Box 16050 S-103 22 Stockholm. All major Swedish cities have local chambers of commerce, many of them engaged in promoting foreign trade.

5. The Swedish-American Chambers of Commerce are devoted to increasing trade and improving commercial relations between Sweden and the United States. Their membership includes both Swedish and American companies.

The Swedish-American Chamber of Commerce Inc. is located at One Dag Hammarskjold Plaza, New York, New York 10017. Telephone 212-838-5530.

The Swedish-American Chamber of Commerce of the Western U.S. covers the 13 Western states. It is located in the World Trade Center, San Francisco, California 94111. Telephone 415-781-4188.

6. Federation of Commercial Agent of Sweden (Sveriges handel sagenters Forbund) Hantverkargatan 46, S-112 21 Stockholm, comprising over 500 commission agents operating in all product areas will include announcements for foreign firms seeking Swedish representation.

Publications

Swedish Government

Allman Manads Statistik (Monthly Bulletin of General Statistics). Stockholm: Central Bureau of Statistics.

Fact Sheets on Sweden. A series of informative profiles, in English, of various aspects of the Swedish economy, political system, educational system, social structure, etc. Available without charge from: Swedish Information Service, 825 Third Avenue, New York, N.Y. 10022.

Industri. Stockholm: Central Bureau of Statistics. Detailed annual production statistics. Includes number of establishments and employees and other industrial information.

Manadsstatistik over Utrikeshandeln (Monthly Trade Statistics). Stockholm: Central Bureau of Statistics.

Utrikeshandel (Annual Trade Statistics). Stockholm: Central Bureau of Statistics.

Statistik Arsbok (Yearbook of Swedish Statistics). Stockholm: Central Bureau of Statistics.

The Swedish Budget, A summary. Stockholm: Ministry of Economic Affairs and Ministry of the Budget. Includes excellent summary of Swedish tax system, industrial policy, social security, etc. Annual, available in English.

The Swedish Economy. Stockholm: Ministry of Finance. A quarterly series with authoritative discussion of economic trends, available in English.

The Swedish Economy 1971-1975 and the General Outlook up to 1990-The 1970 Long-term Survey. Stockholm: Ministry of Finance. Detailed study with projections of trends in population, labor, industrial investment, productivity, etc. In English.

Other

The Swedish Companies Act 1975. Stockholm: Federation of Swedish Industries. A translation of relevant Swedish legislation regulating the founding and workings operation of joint stock companies in Sweden.

Factu: Mediahandbok Annonstaxa. Stockholm: The Swedish Association of Business Press. Describes many Swedish magazines and advertising rates. Brief Summary in English.

Nordisk Handels Kalender. Copenhagen: Scan-Report A/C. Comprehensive directory by industry of firms in Sweden and other Nordic countries.

Quarterly Review. Stockholm: Skandinaviska Enskilda Banken. Review of economic trends and developments in Sweden.

Some Data About Sweden. Stockholm: Skandinaviska Enskilda Banken. Excellent, detailed presentation of Swedish economy, revised biennially. In English.

Sweden (Annual Economic Survey). Paris: Organization for Economic Cooperation and Development. May be obtained from OECD Publications Center, Suite 1207, 1750 Pennsylvania Avenue N.W., Washington, D.C. 20006 for $3.50

Sweden Now. Stockholm. Industria-Press, Naringslivets Forslags A.B. Box 27315 S-102 54 Stockholm. Monthly magazine about Swedish economic, political, cultural affairs, in English.

Swedish Export Directory. Stockholm. Swedish Export Council. Lists main Swedish exporting manufacturers by type of product, with information about share capital, address, products manufactured, annual turnover, subsidiaries and provides much additional useful information. Most of these firms are also importers. In English, published annually.

Svensk Industri Kalender. Stockholm: Federation of Swedish Industries. Comprehensive directory of Swedish firms, giving information as to location, type of business, share capital number of employees, annual turnover, subsidiaries, chief executives, etc. Issued annually.

Veckans Affarer. Stockholm: Veckans Affarer, Box 3263, S-103 65 Stockholm. An important business weekly focusing on current industrial and commercial developments in the Nordic area.

Dagens Industri. Stockholm: Box 3177 S-103 63 Stockholm. An influential Swedish business periodical, published twice a week.

Business practice in Sweden. Published by Coopers and Lybrand AB, Sturegatan 1, S-114 35 Stockholm, Sweden.

Starting a business in Sweden, The Nordic Market 1979. Current Business in Sweden (quarterly business and economic survey), and *Sweden's Economy in Figures* (annual) are four reports published by Svenska Handelsbanken and available from their subsidiary, the Nordic American Banking Corp., 600 Fifth Ave., New York, N.Y. 10020.

Tax and Trade Guide—Sweden. Published by Arthur Andersen and Co. (Swedish Office: Box 16310, S-103 26 Stockholm).

Doing business in Sweden. Published by Price Waterhouse and Co. Box 1612 S-111 86 Stockholm, Sweden.

Sweden-Your Market, Your Guide to Investment in Sweden. Outlook on the Swedish Economy (quarterly), and *Highlights on the Swedish economy* (monthly survey)—published by PK Banken and available from their representative office, Pk Banken, 375 Park Ave., Suite 1705, New York, N.Y. 10022).

Establishing a business in Sweden. Published by Skandinaviska Enskilda Banken and available from their affiliate: Scandinavian Securities Corp., 125 Broad St., New York, N.Y. 10004.

Business with Sweden. Published annually by Svenska Dagbladet, S-105 17 Stockholm (one of the two largest daily newspapers in Sweden with nation-wide circulation).

Investment and Taxation—Sweden. Published by touche Ross Int'l (Swedish Office: Touche Ross and Co. AB, Box 1356, S-111 83 Stockholm.

Product Directory–Swedish State Company Limited. Statsforetag AB Fack S-103 80 Stockholm. In English.

Yearbook of Nordic Statistics. Presentation of statistical information in English on the five Nordic countries. Nordic Council Box 19506 S-104 32 Stockholm Sweden.

The Swedish Credit Market. In English, published by the Swedish Bankers Association Box 161 43 S-103 23 Stockholm.

Technical Capability and Industrial Competence. A comparative study, in English, on Sweden's future competitiveness. Royal

Swedish Academy of Engineering Science. Meddelande 224 Stockholm Sweden.

Research Activities of the National Swedish Industrial Board. Contains short description of investigations being conducted on various sectors of Swedish industry. In English. Published by the National Swedish Industrial Board Box 16315 S-103 26 Stockholm.

Newsletter from Sweden. Abstracts in English from the Swedish press convering current affairs, trade, industry, science and technology. Issued by the Swedish International Press Bureau Skeppargatan 37 S-114 52 Stockholm.

Kompass—Sverige Register of Swedish Industry and Commerce. Issued by Kompass Box 3303 S-103 66 Stockholm.

Swedish Industry Today. Published by the International Council of Swedish Industry Box 5501 S-11485 Stockholm. The Council, sponsored jointly by the Swedish Employers Conferation and the Federation of Swedish Industries, serves to strengthen Swedish industry's international relations.

Nordic Economic Outlook. An English language semiannual analysis of the Nordic economies issued jointly by the federations of industries in the Nordic countries. Published by Swedish Industrial Publications Box 5501 S-11485 Stockholm, Sweden.

Swedish Economy at the Crossroads. In English. Federation of Swedish Industries Box 5501 S-11485 Stockholm, Sweden.

Market Profile—SWEDEN

Foreign Trade

Imports.—$20,600 million in 1978; $20,122 million in 1977. From U.S. $1,511 million in 1978, $1,432 in 1977. U.S. share (1978) 7.3 percent. Other major suppliers (1978): Federal Republic of Germany, 18.4 percent, U.K., 11.1 percent; Denmark, 7.1 percent; Finland 6.2 percent; Norway 5.4 percent; Japan 3.8 percent. Major imports: Petroleum and products, nonelectric machinery, transport equipment, chemicals, foodstuffs, iron and steel. From U.S.: Nonelectric machinery, telecommunications equipment, chemicals, pharmaceuticals, plastic materials, electrical machinery, transport equipment (mainly aircraft), foodstuffs, and tobacco, instruments and optical goods.

Exports.—$21,800 million in 1978; $19,091 million in 1977. To U.S. $1,383 million in 1978; $1,022 million in 1977. U.S. share 1978, 6.3 percent. Other major customers (1978): Norway, 10.3 percent, U.K., 10.9 percent; Germany 11 percent, Denmark, 9.1 percent; Finland 5.7 percent Japan 1.4 percent. Major exports: nonelectric machinery, transport equipment, paper and paper products, steel, wood pulp, lumber. To U.S.: Automobiles, nonelectric machinery, steel, electrical machinery, chemicals, instruments.

Trade Policy.—Tariffs generally low. No import license requirement on nonagricultural goods. Industrial free trade agreement with EEC, has removed tariffs on most nonagricultural trade with EEC. Sweden retains its own tariff schedule. Member EFTA, GATT, OECD, and IMF. Sweden was a participant in the Tokyo Round of the GATT multilateral trade negotiations concluded in 1979, and agreed to make substantial duty concessions. The reductions will be staged over an eight-year period beginning January 1, 1980.

Trade Prospects.—Most promising U.S. export categories include: EDP equipment; instruments; health care equipment; metal working equipment; consumer goods, especially sporting and leisure time equipment; construction equipment and building supplies; communications equipment, and systems; and occupational safety equipment.

Foreign Investment

U.S. Direct Investment.—U.S. direct investment end 1978 totaled $1,195 million, including $311 million in machinery manufacturing, $29 million in food products, $96 million in trade, $13 in finance, and the remainded divided among other activities including petroleum, metals and chemicals.

Investment Policy.—Sweden is generally receptive to foreign investment.

U.S. Direct Investment.—U.S. direct investment end 1978 totaled $1,195 million, including $311 million in machinery manufacturing, $29 million in food products, $96 million in trade, $13 in finance, and the remainded divided among other activities including petroleum, metals and chemicals.

Investment Policy.—Sweden is generally receptive to foreign investment.

Finance

Currency.—Swedish Krona (pural kronor) or crown. The value of the krona is determined in relation to a weighted average of the 15 most important currencies in Swedish foreign trade. The rate of exchange fluctuates. On November 7, 1979 the krona traded at US$1.00=4.24.

Domestic Credit and Investment.—Commercial banking highly developed and centralized, moderately active stock market. Bond market oriented to mortgage institutions and government borrowing.

Balance of Payments.—Improved export performance reduced the 1978 current account deficit to $900 million. Foreign exchange reserves, at year end 1978 $4.1 billion.

National Budget.—The proposed budget for FY 1979/80 calls for expenditure of kr 171.9 billion (about $40.9 billion) and income of 126.8 billion (about $30.2 billion)

Economy

GDP.—$87.5 billion in 1978, a real increase of 2.8 percent over 1977. Per capita GDP $10,452. GDP by kind of economic activitry, 1977: manufacturing, 26.6 percent; agriculture, forestry, and fishing 4.2 percent; mining 0.7 percent; electricity, gas and water 2.3 percent; wholesale and retail trade, 10 percent; transportation and communication, 4.6 percent; finance insurance and real estate 11.8 percent, government and public services 19.9 percent.

Industry.—Based primarily of forest and mineral resources plus hydroelectric power. Chief manufacturing sectors are: machinery and equipment, automobiles, paper and pulp, steel, electronics and electrical equipment, chemicals, ships, wood products.

Consumer Prices.—Index rose by 10.1 percent, in 1978; forecast to increase 10.5 percent in 1979.

Commerce.—Rapid growth of self service, supermarkets, department stores, shopping centers. Total number of retail outlets declining. Retail establishments 54,000.

Basic Economic Facilities

Transportation.—Excellent highway, railroad, and air transport, 7,500 miles of rail track. Three major seaports; Gothenburg, Stockholm, Malmo. Number of motor vehicles 2.9 million (year end 1978) of which 180,000 were trucks.

Communications.—Highly developed, government operated. 352 TV sets per 1000 population. 794 telephones per 1,000 population.

Power.—Hydroelectric power a major natural resource. Total 1978 production 90.2 billion kWh, of which 63 percent hydroelectric, 25 percent nuclear, and 12 percent conventional thermal.

Natural Resources

Land.—173,423 square miles—978 miles along and 310 miles at widest—about size and shape of California. 8.6 percent area inland waters, 10 percent cultivated or grazing land, 50 percent forests.

Minerals.—High grade iron ore primary mineral. Small supplies gold, silver, lead, copper, zinc, pyrites, tungsten, manganese, granite, quartz, marble.

Population

Size.—8.3 million. Metropolitan areas in 1977: Stockholm, 1,357,000; Goteborg, 693,000; Malmo, 454,000.

Labor—Labor force 4.2 million. Working population by sector in 1977: Public services 27.1 percent; mining and manufacutring 24.9 percent; wholesale and retail trade 12.3 percent; transportation, and communications 6.7 percent; construction, 8 percent; agriculture 4.8 percent, forestry 1.5 percent.

Marketing in Switzerland

Contents

Report Revised April 1981

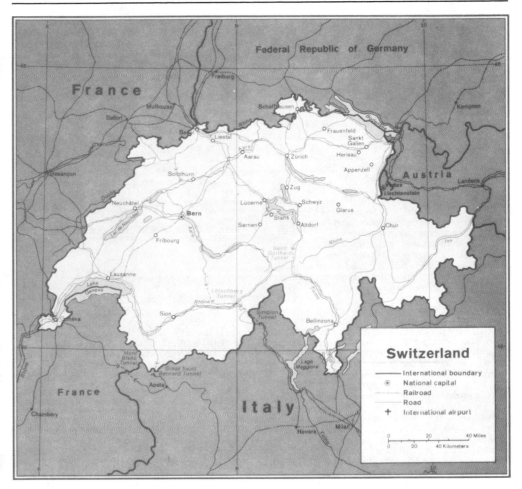

Foreign Trade Outlook

Principal Imports from the World and from the United States

The Swiss Confederation, commonly called Switzerland, is a fiercely independent, economically powerful nation in South Central Europe. The Swiss have been free of foreign intervention, with few interruptions, since 1515. The mainstay of this independence has been Swiss neutrality and the Swiss economy. Switzerland is devoid of natural resources except for hydroelectric power, thus its economy must be supported by a vigorous foreign trade. In 1979, imports accounted for 28 percent of Switzerland's gross national product (GNP). The current account surplus in 1979 was estimated at $1.2 billion in 1979; however, this figure is expected to decline as Switzerland faces higher energy costs and labor shortages.

Within the export sector, Switzerland's most successfully marketed items are precision, specialty, and chemical goods. Items such as watches, textiles, chocolate, home furnishings, and energy generators are among the strongest products for export.

Over 50 percent of all Swiss imports are in raw materials and energy related items. (See table 1.) With 1979 per capita GNP at $15,939, the Swiss appetite for imports is among the most voracious in the world. This is reflected in the value of Swiss imports of consumer goods, a figure twice that of imported capital goods.

Regionally, Switzerland gets about two-thirds of its imports from the European Economic Community (EEC), and depends on the Common Market to buy nearly one-half of its exports. Developing countries are also increasing their share of Swiss trade. During 1979, the developing countries are estimated to have provided the Swiss with over 10 percent of their imports and received over 25 percent of their exports.

The United States is usually Switzerland's fourth largest supplier and customer, preceded by West Germany, France, and Italy. (See table 2.) In 1979, the U.S. share in Switzerland's overall trade constituted 6.9 percent of exports and 7 percent of imports. The U.S. trade balance with Switzerland usually shows a slight surplus that is offset by a larger deficit in "invisible" transactions, particularly foreign travel.

The Swiss have developed a taste for quality and progress. While constantly automating their industry, they will excel at products requiring individual care and craftsmanship. The Swiss reputation for consumer goods makes their exports in this area slightly more competitive

Table 1.—Switzerland: Foreign Trade by Commodity Groups, 1977-79

	$ millions			% of total		
	1977	1978	1979	1977	1978	1979
Exports						
Metals and machines	6,762.2	9,169.8	8,407.0	34.4	34.2	29.7
Chemicals and pharmaceuticals	3,438.5	4,711.8	5,332.9	17.5	17.6	18.7
Watchmaking	3,638.2	4,703.5	5,418.1	18.5	17.5	19.1
Textiles	1,296.4	1,665.2	1,943.8	6.6	6.2	6.9
Other	4,529.4	6,600.5	7,244.7	23.0	24.5	25.6
TOTAL	19,664.7	26,850.8	28,346.5	100	100	100
Imports						
Raw materials and semi-finished products	7,484.7	9,448.0	11,858.0	41.8	40.0	40.2
Fuels and lubricants	1,644.8	1,845.0	3,359.0	9.2	7.8	11.4
Capital goods	2,775.6	4,258.3	4,811.6	15.5	18.1	16.3
Consumer goods	5,994.0	8,052.1	9,502.0	33.5	34.1	32.1
TOTAL	17,899.1	23,603.4	29,530.6	100	100	100

Source: Statistique Annuelle du Commerce Extérieur de la Suisse

than those of the United States. This is seen by the fact that 30 percent of Swiss exports to the United States are in consumer goods, while the United States provides Switzerland with less than that figure. (See table 4.) An estimated 30 percent of Switzerland's imports from the United States are capital goods; the value of U.S. imports of capital goods from Switzerland is much lower.

Best Export Prospects

The appreciation of the Swiss franc against the U.S. dollar has helped U.S. exports to Switzerland. However, some of this advantage is lost to the Common Market countries. The EEC is geographically closer to the Swiss market and enjoys duty-free treatment for most industrial products. Still, there remain a number of U.S. industries with high export potential to Switzerland.

Computers and Peripheral Equipment.— Computers are America's most marketable product in Switzerland. Within the last 4 years, the United States has had an average 44 percent share of the Swiss market. In 1978, the United States sold over $100 million worth of computers to Switzerland, the second largest per capita user of computers in the world. The domestic computer industry in Switzerland is practically nonexistent. These two facts, combined with aggressive marketing techniques, should be

Table 2.—Switzerland: Trade by Geographic Area
(in millions of U.S. dollars)

	1978	1979
Imports		
TOTAL	23,657.6	29,307.5
Total OECD	20,712.9	25,567.8
United States	1,776.1	1,323.6
Europe	18,089.3	22,741.3
EEC	16,053.1	20,240.5
West Germany	6,842.0	8,387.8
France	2,956.2	3,772.9
Italy	2,319.7	3,040.1
United Kingdom	1,889.0	2,258.3
Belgium-Luxembourg	911.5	1,204.7
Netherlands	864.0	1,256.5
EFTA	1,706.9	1,771.7
Austria	922.4	1,100.6
Sweden	489.6	626.2
Finland	128.9	164.8
Centrally Planned Economies	890.9	1,206.6
U.S.S.R.	513.1	780.0
Africa	413.6	562.6
Nigeria	66.0	82.3
Latin America	564.7	578.9
Panama	149.6	129.8
Brazil	80.5	126.5
Far East	528.1	631.6
Hong Kong	180.9	227.9
India	87.8	83.6
Middle East	399.9	563.2
Middle East	399.9	563.2
Bahrain	156.7	225.2
Israel	98.0	118.3
Exports		
TOTAL	23,366.6	26,477.3
Total OECD	16,642.4	19,375.4
United States	1,678.4	1,817.2
Europe	13,893.4	16,331.9
EEC	11,038.6	13,139.8
West Germany	4,215.4	5,197.8
United Kingdom	2,020.4	2,312.6
Italy	1,473.0	1,880.8
Netherlands	676.8	746.3
Belgium-Luxembourg	663.2	755.0
EFTA	2,153.0	2,404.0
Austria	1,084.3	1,209.4
Sweden	497.4	561.2
Centrally Planned Economies	1,174.8	1,203.4
U.S.S.R.	266.0	265.3
Poland	186.9	192.7
Africa	992.4	837.8
Nigeria	235.7	158.3
Latin America	1,068.1	1,231.1
Brazil	249.8	291.0
Venezuela	135.6	120.5
Far East	1,009.1	1,275.5
Hong Kong	428.4	481.6
India	109.4	129.2
Middle East	1,933.9	1,918.8
Israel	538.8	585.1
Saudi Arabia	519.4	572.3
Iran	383.8	221.3

Source: OECD Foreign Trade Statistics, Series A; Statistique Annuelle du Commerce Exterieur de la Suisse.

sufficient to secure U.S. manufacturers a commanding position in the Swiss computer market.

Although EEC competitors are favored by duty-free rates, such factors as cost effectiveness and technological advance favor U.S. sellers of computers. Further, foreign competitors are known to experience software problems. The strong U.S. position will continue to rest on its ability to supply complete systems with strong support services.

With the introduction of more powerful systems to deal with Switzerland's enormous service sector (banks, insurance companies, tourism, transportation, etc.), large computers are still in demand. Microcomputer and advanced semiconductor technology spur sales in distributed computing, real-time systems, networks, transaction and dialog systems, intelligent terminals, clusters, and related peripherals. According to trade sources, consumption of computers is expected to grow at an annual rate of at least 40 percent until 1982.

Process Control Instruments and Systems.—The export-oriented Swiss industry is continuing to invest in advanced process control equipment to cut production costs that are among the highest in the world. Although the United States has lost some of its market share in a growing market for process-control related

Table 3.—Selected Items of Swiss Trade with the United States
(in million of U.S. dollars)

	1978[1]	1979[2]
Imports		
Wheat	27.1	16.3
Corn	30.4	33.0
Oil cake	47.9	37.9
Tobacco manufactured	96.6	131.1
Organic chemicals	38.7	38.0
Photo and cinematographic goods	38.4	45.8
Jewelry	106.9	161.2
Nonelectric machinery	288.4	314.3
Electrical machinery	106.6	130.3
Vehicles	77.3	114.7
Aircraft	414.1	216.0
Optical and precision instruments	88.8	130.0
Works of art	21.9	42.2
Other	385.8	437.2
TOTAL	1,768.9	1,848.0
Exports		
Cheese	21.1	22.2
Organic chemicals	136.4	184.7
Synthetic organic dyes	47.1	42.1
Odoriferous substances	14.3	10.7
Jewelry	129.4	181.6
Nonelectric machinery	475.1	314.3
Electric machinery	119.3	173.1
Optical and precision instruments	98.2	109.5
Watches	19.6	19.6
Works of art	36.9	49.5
Other	319.1	704.3
TOTAL	1,416.5	1,814.0

Source: Statistique Annuelle du Commerce Exterieur de la Suisse
[1] US$1=SF1.79
[2] US$1=SF1.65

Table 4.—Economic Indicators: Percentage
Change from Previous Year

	1977	1978	1979
Increase of GNP			
in constant prices	6.4	3.4	5.1
in real prices	4.3	2.7	0.2
Industrial production	5.5	0	2.0
Average wage for skilled			
worker	0.1	-0.2	-1.2
Industrial wages	1.0	2.8	3.0
Consumer prices	1.3	1.1	4.0
Retail sales	3.3	0.5	0.5
Inflation (percent			
each yr.)	1.3	1.0	3.6

Source: Embassy of Switzerland; U.S. Federal Reserve; *La Vie Economique,*
April 1980.

items, it is still considered a major source of supply. Despite the unwillingness of U.S. suppliers to adapt to local requirements, American products are still generally preferred because of their technological innovation and originality. To increase competitiveness, U.S. firms will need to pay stricter attention to Swiss standards. West Germany, for example, has health and safety codes similar to those of Switzerland, which gives German products an advantage over American products.

The Swiss economic situation still favors imports that are cheaper than locally made items. The need for automation in industry continues at all levels. The following products have proven to be the most marketable in Switzerland: programmable controls and systems, data acquisition units, electronic displays, digital counters, panel meters, multiplexers, minicomputers, ultra-sound and doppler effect systems, instruments for radio-active measurements, and flow and liquid meters.

Microprocessors.—The market for solid-state devices in Switzerland is highly developed and sophisticated. American firms control at least 90 percent of the market. Microprocessors, solid-state memories, and related devices undoubtedly offer the highest sales potential in electronic componentry, with annual growth rates of up to 150 percent. Switzerland's machinery and precision instrument industry represents the largest sector for U.S. sales of solid-state devices and semiconductor memories, followed by communications, watches, and consumer electronics. American firms will have to maintain their high-quality production to maintain their position. The quality-conscious Swiss may shortly begin production of microprocessors domestically and spark strong

competition in this traditionally U.S.-dominated sector.

Industrial and Commercial Security Systems.—The growing security consciousness in Switzerland is expected to be reflected in increased sales. Banks, insurance firms, post offices, and private concerns will devote more money to security to help stop the growing rate of burglaries and theft of government property.

Swiss security firms, known for their reliability, export many security items containing U.S. components. This permits Swiss manufacturers to adhere to their local regulations without requiring American adaptation.

The market for security equipment in Switzerland will reach maturity by 1985 when most large government and industrial programs will have been completed. The United States is viewed as the major source of innovation. Especially well received are American advances in sensing and detecting technology using radar, IR, or seismic systems. American manufacturers should find attractive market possibilities in these areas: lasers, shoplifting detection equipment, narrow beam motion and other microwave systems, body armour and personal protection devices, easy-to-install residential burglar alarms, and arms and bomb detectors for post offices or airports.

Consumer Goods.—Switzerland ranks among the richest consumer markets in the world. In 1979, for example, the country had an import bill of $26.4 billion of which $9 billion, or 34 percent, was consumer goods. This figure is twice that of capital goods and nearly equal to the figure for raw materials. Marketing possibilities in consumer goods are ranked as good overall.

Apparel: To the fashionable Swiss, Geoffrey Bean, Calvin Klein, Bill Blass, and John Weitz are all household names. New opportunities for U.S. clothing manufacturers have emerged in sportswear. Skiing garments and jogging and tennis outfits should do well. However, there will be stiff competition from experienced European firms.

Sporting Goods: A good-to-high sales potential exists for the following items of sporting goods: table tennis sets, water skis, wind surfing equipment, small sailboats, marine accessories, swim wear, bicycle carriers, and sporting goods carrier bags.

Other: Based on marketing research, reports by major Swiss department stores, and inquiries by Swiss trade circles, a number of miscellaneous items also have a high potential for incremental export sales to Switzerland. These include housewares and hardware, cosmetics and

toiletries, home furnishings and home entertainment articles.

Biomedical Equipment.—The Swiss are
planning a major renovation of their hospital/
health care system. Within the last 4 years, the
United States has supplied over 20 percent of the
biomedical equipment market. The EEC,
European Free Trade Association (EFTA),
Japan, and Israel are the major competitors.
These countries have a good command of X-ray,
intensive care systems, imaging systems, and
medical electronics. Switzerland itself is an
exporter of certain biomedical instruments and
health care items. Despite a strong domestic
instruments sector, U.S. suppliers can
consolidate their position by emphasizing cost
effectiveness, technological advance, and
adaptation, and by following a vigorous, well-
planned marketing strategy.

Industry Trends

GNP Movement

The Swiss economy, long a dynamo of Europe,
was one of the last countries to feel the recession
of 1974-75. (See table 4.) In constant prices,
Switzerland's 1979 real GNP crept up a scant 0.7
percent over 1978, but it is still far from the 1975
low of a 7.7 percent decline in real GNP. Real
GNP growth in 1980 is expected to rise above 1
percent.

In part, recovery from this slump will depend
upon traditional Swiss fiscal/monetary con-
servatism and industriousness. Apropos to that,
the Swiss National Bank has reestablished the
primacy of inflation control in fiscal/monetary
policy with the full agreement of the Federal
Government.

Not all indices are gloomy. Per capita GNP in
current prices, still among the world's highest,
rose 2.9 percent in 1979 to $15,939. Unemploy-
ment is very low, amounting to only 0.3 percent in
1979. The Swiss economy, sensitive to exchange
rate fluctuations and foreign demand (35 percent
of GNP is exported), enjoyed increases in sales in
its export dependent industries. Heavy
machinery, chemical/pharmaceutical, and
textile industries increased sales from 1 to 5
percent in 1979. This helped stave off a current
account deficit but could not stop the erosion of
the current account surplus to only SF 4 billion—
a 50 percent decrease over 1978.

Agriculture and forestry have contributed a
steady 7 percent to the country's GNP. The
service and industry sectors continue to slowly
change to reflect modern, Western European
trends. The Swiss have reached the stage where

the contribution of the service sector to GNP
ranks as important as that of the industry sector.
The slightly higher growth rate of the service
sector follows the shift within the labor force. In
1979, an estimated 40 percent of the labor force
worked in industry while 53 percent worked in
the service sector.

Growth Sectors

The Swiss economy, dedicated to stability and
a strong currency, sometimes suffers for its
strength. The repeated revaluations of the Swiss
franc make Swiss exports much more expensive
and thus less competitive. In general, Swiss
industry has been able to withstand the adverse
effect of the appreciation of the Swiss franc.
Manufacturers, in the mid-1970's, began to
experience diminishing profit margins. To
counter this trend, the Swiss reorganized their
managerial structure. They grouped numbers of
similar companies under a few umbrella holding
companies geared to strengthen the firms'
competitive capacity. This was achieved by
coordinating research, production, and
marketing techniques.

To overcome the drawback of a too-strong
currency in an export-oriented economy, the
Swiss have taken a further step. Following the
lead of German and Japanese manufacturers
facing similar situations, the Swiss transferred
production facilities to other countries. In this
way, the Swiss overcame not only the drawbacks
of their appreciated currency but also high
foreign tariffs and high domestic labor costs.

Switzerland takes its commercial sector
seriously. Modernization of industry, and strict
inflation control are two examples of the Swiss
concern for their continued economic success.
Another important aspect of a strong business
sector is research and development. Swiss R&D
expenditures, as a percentage of gross domestic
product, are the highest in the world—3.2
percent. The chemical and machinery industries
sharply outspend all other sectors in R&D
research. Government and other nonprivate
R&D account for only 24 percent of the total
amount; private industry supplies the rest.

The effects of appreciation of the Swiss franc
on the economy have not been uniform. The
construction industry, one of the most important
indicators of domestic prosperity, is expected to
grow by 8 percent in 1980. The tourist industry,
generally hurt by an overvalued franc, may have
edged out of its slump. Stagnating revenues gave
way in 1979-80 to one of the best winter seasons in
years.

The machinery and metals industry has also

seen an upturn. Aluminum production rose by 4 percent in 1979, and the expectations for 1980 are guardedly optimistic. According to surveys by the Swiss Machinery Manufacturers Association, total orders for machinery from abroad rose 5.3 percent and domestic orders rose 9.1 percent.

Swiss watches, traditionally well marketed, are suffering a falloff in foreign sales. Since 97 percent of Swiss watch production is exported, this may be an ominous trend for Switzerland. Despite drastic restructing of the industry to make it more competitive with electric and digital design, exports declined by 5 percent in 1979.

Chemicals and pharmaceuticals, another export-intensive industry, fared better. With 80 percent of domestic production exported, the volume of chemical exports increased by 5 percent. This was due partially to the Swiss ability to minimize costs and pass on the savings to consumers in the form of a 1.5 percent average reduction in chemical prices.

Government Controls

A strong work ethic and an active business sector make Switzerland one of the most prosperous nations. The Swiss attachment to free enterprise and a free market economy is historical. Developments abroad such as inflation, recession, regional integration, and the appreciation of the Swiss franc have brought greater powers of regulation to the Federal Government.

The Federal Government as an entrepreneur is limited to the railroad (SBB/CFF) and to the post, telegraph, and telephone (PTT). Government-operated facilities manufacture armaments and assemble military aircraft. A government energy agency operates experimental atomic reactors for peaceful uses. Further, the Government owns 24 percent of Swissair, the national airline. Cantonal and municipal governments participate in public utilities and in low-cost housing developments.

Switzerland relies, to a large extent, on voluntary arrangements to achieve policy objectives. Those Federal decrees that have no constitutional basis must be sanctioned by the majority of the voters and by the cantons. For example, in 1973 the Federal Government requested a constitutional amendment that would give the Government more power to control cyclical fluctuations in the Swiss economy. In 1975, the business cycle proposal was defeated by a narrow margin. The article was finally passed in February 1978.

Government policy in monetary affairs is carried out through the Swiss National Bank.

The majority of the bank's board of directors are appointed by the Federal Government. Due to the country's high dependence on foreign trade, its economic situation is greatly influenced by external developments. To ward off unwanted capital inflow that increases domestic liquidity and exerts pressure on the Swiss currency, the Swiss National Bank has occasionally imposed restrictions on capital inflows at the expense of the country's reputation as an international financial center.

The Swiss Export Risk Guarantee Program (ERG) was initiated in 1933. In 1970, a new commission for the protection of investments was added as well. Both are administered by Federal commissions in Zurich. The ERG covers credits extended by Swiss exporters to foreign customers or by the commercial banks to exporters. The coverage of Swiss goods and certain services abroad extends to political and commercial risks, now up to 95 percent of the invoice value, and since 1973 to risks resulting from the appreciation of the Swiss franc. In 1976, about 18 percent of total Swiss exports were covered by this program.

Investment guarantees are granted against political risks up to 70 percent of the amount invested in developing countries. The ceiling for possible losses to be paid is set at SF 500,000.

The Swiss Science Council is entrusted with the preparation and execution of government policy on research and development. Its members are appointed by the Government. Most government subsidies on research and development are assigned to the Federal Technical Institutes in Zurich and Lausanne, cantonal universities, and to the Swiss National Fund for Scientific Research.

Distribution and Sales Channels

Importers and Agents

Most importers are engaged in wholesale trade. Import wholesalers usually specialize in one commodity or group of commodities and rarely handle a wide range of unrelated products. Cooperatives and retail purchasing associations are also involved in importing.

Agency agreements are covered by a 1949 law contained in the Swiss Code of Obligations. The agent may be a single person or a company and represent one or several foreign firms or products. An agent must be registered with the Commercial Register. The Swiss Association of Commercial Travelers and Agents has drafted a standard agency agreement. Under Swiss law a principal is not allowed to inspect the books of the Swiss agent.

Wholesale and Retail Channels

The number of outlets decreased slightly in wholesale trade from 12,243 in 1965 to 11,763 in 1975, and in retail trade from 50,608 to 49,902. The trend in the reduction of retail outlets reflects, in part, the growing role of the large department stores, e.g. Jelmoli and Globus. In addition, the impetus toward mergers, so apparent in the United States and Western Europe, also accounts for a part of the relative decline in the number of independent retail outlets. This is most marked in the reaction of independent Swiss retailers to the success of consumer co-ops and chain stores. Retailers have begun to counter the co-op and chain store encroachment upon their traditional markets by forming associations for purchase and other services.

Despite lower profit margins and a more competitive market, independent retailers still accounted for 52 percent of retail sales in 1976. The share of the large cooperatives, Migros and Coop., increased to 22 percent, that of department stores to 11 percent, chain stores to 9 percent, discount stores to 4 percent, and mail order houses to 2 percent.

Licensing, Leasing and Franchising

The Swiss have relatively few import restrictions. Special import permits are required for a few products such as defense materials, foodstuffs, many textiles, and items subject to health regulations. Licensing is always subject to the Swiss Code of Obligations, the equivalent of a commercial code. There are no limitations on the transfer of royalties or fees.

Leasing was introduced in 1964 through the establishment of Industrie Leasing A.G., in Zurich, a subsidiary of the Swiss Banking Corporation. Subsequently, other large banks also entered the leasing business by establishing companies. In 1977, more than 20 companies and banks were engaged in leasing operations.

Franchising is not widely used in Switzerland. It is practiced in car maintenance and repair, temporary help services, dry cleaning, retail food, and restaurants.

Principal Professional and Purchasing Organizations

Swiss firms engaged in foreign trade are members of the following organization:

Union of Swiss Firms for World and Transit Trade
(Syndicat des maisons suisses du commerce mondial et du commerce de transit)

Aeschenvorstadt 4
4000 Basel

Most Swiss importers and wholesalers belong to the following organization:

Swiss Federation of Importers and Wholesalers and Traders
(Federation suisse des importateurs et du commerce de gros)
Centralbahnstrasse 9
4010 Basel

Consumer buying cooperatives have the following central organizations:

Federation of MIGROS Cooperatives
Limmatstrasse 152
8005 Zurich

Coop Schweiz
Thiersteinerallee 14
4002 Basel

Department stores, of which Jelmoli and Globus are the largest, have the following central buying organizations:

Grannds Magasins Jelmoli SA
8112 Otelfingen.

Manor Ac,
Untergasse 6
4005 Basel

Magazine zum Globus Ag
Eichstrasse 27
8045 Zurich

Independent retailers have established several purchasing cooperatives to compete with large cooperatives, department stores, and chain stores in the wholesale and import trade. The most important of them in the food sector is:

USEGO—AG
Solothurnerstrasse 231
4600 Olten

Hotels and caterers have their own purchasing cooperative:

HOWEG
Leimenstrasse 91
2540 Granges

Procurement Practices

Government procurement is limited because the Federal Government usually is involved only in projects dealing with transportation, communication, utilities, defense, and construction. Many public projects are carried out by cantonal and communal authorities.

In general, the Federal Government exercises a great deal of discretion in inviting bids. Selective discretionary tenders are more common than public discretionary tenders and private contracts. Contrary to cantonal and communal authorities, Federal authorities are not required to inform the bidders of the tender that has been accepted or of the reasons for the choice. However, technical superiority is frequently more important than price in accepting the bid. Cantonal and communal authorities usually prefer suppliers located in their own area. Foreign firms are sometimes required to have a Swiss bank guarantee.

Trade Shows

Basel

March.—DIDACTA. Educational Materials.
April.—International Watch, Clock, and Jewelry Fair. Annual.
June.—SWISSPACK. Packaging. Every 2-3 years.
June.—Pro-Aqua Pro-Vita. Environmental Protection. Triennial.
September.—INTERFEREX. Hardware, Tools, Housewares. Biennial.
September.—ILMAC. Laboratory Instruments. Every 3 years.
October.—INELTEC. Electronics. Biennial.
October.—NUCLEX. Nuclear Power. Triennial.

Bern

September.—SAMA. Automation. Annual.
October.—BESPO. Summer Sporting Equipment and Apparel. Annual.

Geneva

March.—International Motor Show
June.—MMM. Microprocessors, Minicomputers, and Microcomputers. Annual.
September.—TELECOM. Telecommunications. Triennial.

Lausanne

April.—COMPUTER. Data Processing Equipment. Biennial.
September.—COMPTOIR SUISSE. Swiss National Fair. Annual.

Zurich

March.—SWISSPO. Winter Sporting Goods.
March.—SEMICON EUROPA. Semiconductors. Biennial.
May.—SICHERHEIT. Security. Biennial.
October.—IFAS. Medical Supplies. Biennial.
September.—BUFA. Office Equipment.
April/October.—MODEXPO. Women's Apparel. Semiannual.

Transportation and Utilities

Domestic Transportation System

Switzerland's geographic position makes it the crossroads of Europe. The country's efficient and comprehensive transportation system is constantly being improved. The Swiss are aware of the benefits of their central position and have undertaken a number of ambitious transportation projects. One of these, presently half completed, will link West Germany's autobahns with Italy's autostradas. The nerve centers of Swiss transportation are Zurich, Basel, and Geneva. From these cities span the major rail, highway, and air links to the rest of Switzerland and to a number of other countries. The principal river port on the Rhine is Basel.

Government-owned railroads connect all major cities, while railroads owned by cantons and municipalities reach remote mountain areas. So important is this service that the frugally minded Swiss continue to run the railroads, with no service reductions, despite the fact that in 1979 the railroads ran at a $414 million deficit.

Trans-European rail traffic passing through Switzerland uses the tunnels at Simplon, Lotschberg, and St. Gothard. Nearly all Swiss rails are electrified and 80 percent of the regular track belongs to the Swiss Federal Railway (SBB/CFF).

In 1978, SBB/CFF carried some 203 million passengers, and moved about 39 million tons of freight. In 1978, Swiss imports moved as follows: rail, 25 percent; highway, 32 percent; water, 24 percent; and pipeline, 18 percent. Exports were: rail, 45 percent; highway, 51 percent; water, 4 percent; and air, 1 percent.

Basel, on the Rhine, has connections to Strasbourg, Rotterdam, and Antwerp. At the beginning of 1979, the Swiss merchant fleet on the Rhine consisted of 462 vessels with total cargo capacity of more than 582,201 tons.

Goods destined for Switzerland are channeled through Antwerp and Rotterdam to Basel or shipped through Italian, French, or German ports. Frequent sailings occur from all ports of the United States to Antwerp and Rotterdam. A Swiss oceangoing merchant fleet was established during World War II. At the beginning of 1979, this fleet consisted of 29 vessels with a capacity of about 422,800 deadweight tons.

Swissair is the government-owned national airline. It has related investments in hotels, restaurants, and travel agencies in Switzerland and other countries. In 1979, Swissair carried 6.9 million people and over $408 million worth of merchandise. There are two charter airline companies—Balair in Basel, owned 60 percent by Swissair, and CTA (Corporation de Transport Aerien) in Geneva—and a Swiss helicopter operator, Heliswiss in Bern.

Telecommunications

The Government controls the post, telephone, telegraph and telex services through PTT, the Swiss communications corporation. The postal service provides 1-day service and its postal check system is used frequently. The telephone system is totally automated and the ratio of telephones to people is among the highest in the world. Switzerland has the densest telex network in the world. Satellite communications are handled by an Intelsat Station at Levuk for the Atlantic region and through cooperative arrangement with West Germany for the use of an Indian Ocean Satellite.

Radio and television broadcasts are operated by the Swiss Radio and Television Corporation (SRG/SSR). Each of the three television networks broadcasts in one of three languages: German, French, or Italian.

Utilities: Sources and Costs of Fuel

The breakdown of fuel consumption by type in Switzerland in 1978 was as follows: liquid fuel, 75 percent; electricity, 17 percent; gas, 5 percent, and coal and wood, 3 percent.

Crude oil is imported from various Middle Eastern countries and is processed in the country's two refineries, operated by Exxon and Shell. Most heating oil and gasoline is imported from neighboring EEC countries.

In the near future, Swiss energy needs can be met either by increased reliance on oil or development of nuclear energy since the country's hydropower potential has been exhausted. In 1979, about 70 percent of the electric energy production came from hydroelectric plants, 22 percent from nuclear power plants, and 5 percent from thermal (mostly oil-generated) plants. By 1985, an estimated 50 percent of Swiss electricity needs will be powered by nuclear energy, 46 percent by hydroelectric plants (4 percent by thermal plants). Currently, four nuclear power plants are in operation and a fifth is under construction. Construction of further plants has been halted due to growing financial, environmental, and political considerations.

Advertising and Research

Advertising Media

Advertising is widely used in Switzerland. Advertisements, commercials, and other types of publicity are of high quality and are very expensive. The division of the country into three language zones, the high standard of living, a liberal import policy, and keen competition contributed to advertising expenditures of $300 million in 1979, some 2 percent of Swiss GNP.

Switzerland has the highest number of newspapers per capita in the world. With few exceptions, these newspapers appeal to local interests. The press is the most important media for advertising even though only a handful of the more than 400 newspapers have more than 50,000 subscribers. There are also some 6,480 periodicals with circulations ranging from several hundred to several hundred thousand.

The growing trend towards consolidation in the publications industry has continued. Technical magazines and smaller regional newspapers are merging with others in their respective areas.

Television is also a popular medium, but its advertising rates are among the highest in the world. Switzerland has no commercial radio, but significant audiences hear radio advertisements from surrounding countries. Posters and billboards are frequently used with Swiss poster design and printing of a high standard. Outdoor advertising is carefully controlled and is largely restricted to urban sites. Other advertising media include direct mail campaigns and movie theaters.

Retail advertising is geared to capture the public's attention with such devices as displays, posters, novel containers, or samples. In addition, full-scale promotion campaigns such as games and contests are used.

Direct mail advertising is handled by specialized firms such as the Adressen and Werbezentrale (Centrale suisse d'adresse et de publicite directe) with offices throughout the country. These firms provide lists of addresses and distribute unaddressed folders and leaflets.

The Swiss have divided advertising into space sellers (announce-expedition, agence de publicite), which plan specific campaigns and have consultants who specialize in market research and the planning of advertising and public relations campaigns. Government controls and self-policing by industry have led to high advertising standards and to limitations on the promotion of certain products. Both the ethical rules and the nature of the market make it advisable for foreign exporters to deal with one of the many Swiss or international consultants available. For example, it is often difficult or impossible to obtain production or sales data because of the Swiss tradition of commercial secrecy. Also advertising for the German market will not suit German-speaking Switzerland because of differences in accent and phraseology.

Market Research Services

The Swiss are very cautious and wish to maintain their commercial superiority. As a result, Swiss commercial secrecy laws hamper the collection of pertinent data for market research purposes. Production and sales figures, as well as information on plant and equipment expenditures, are lacking.

Information on some manufacturing and service sectors can be obtained from the semiofficial Swiss Office for the Development of Trade, which has offices in Lausanne and Zurich, and from the Swiss Federation of Commerce and Industry, also known as Vorort, in Zurich. The latter has chambers of commerce and trade associations as members. Many Swiss firms conduct market research for third parties.

Credit

International Financial Position

Switzerland's political and economic stability, the relative abundance of capital and freedom of capital movements, and the high standards of Swiss banks are some of the reasons that Switzerland is one of the world's financial centers. Switzerland has long attracted long-term capital borrowers from all over the world. Its influence has increased with the formation of the Euro-dollar market as Swiss banks have at times been able to place almost half of the Eurobond issues with their customers. In addition, about three-fourths of the world's gold transactions are conducted through intermediaries at the gold market in Zurich which is maintained by the three largest Swiss banks.

Organization of the Banking System

The Swiss banking system is characterized by its strong links with financial institutions abroad and close cooperation between the central bank and other banks in carrying out the Government's monetary policy. The banking network is the densest in the world.

The banking system is headed by the Swiss National Bank (Schweizerische Nationalbank/ Banque National Suisse). About 58 percent of its capital stock is held by cantons, cantonal banks, and public agencies. More than half of its board of directors, as well as the president and vice president, are appointed by the Federal Government. In 1978 a new National Bank Law gave the Bank more authority for policy operations.

At present, there are 71 banks obliged to submit monthly statements to the National Bank. They consist primarily of the "Big Five" of Switzerland: Union Bank of Switzerland, Swiss Bank Corporation, Swiss Credit Bank, Swiss Popular Bank, and Leu & Company. Together, these banks control one-third of the financial assets of Switzerland. Enjoying wide international connections, these banks also perform a major role in managing large investment trusts and mutual funds. In addition to the Big Five, there are 28 cantonal banks and 38 municipal banks that submit monthly reports to the central bank. There are also nearly 400 other banks and finance companies in Switzerland. There are 84 foreign banks established in Switzerland of which 14 are branches of American banks.

Each canton has its own bank. Cantonal and local banks finance local business and carry out mortgage lending, financed out of their savings deposits and subscription to savings bonds. The Cantonal Bank in Zurich is the fourth largest in Switzerland as measured by balance sheet totals.

Banking Procedures

A salient feature of the Swiss banking system is its tradition of secrecy. The principle of secrecy applies to all accounts, numbered or not. Secrecy, however, does not mean that bankers can refuse to divulge information when they are required to do so by law. Since 1934, bank secrecy has been protected by law, but can be invoked in criminal cases. The names of all depositors, when identified by numbers, are known to the bank.

Foreign Exchange and Credit Regulations

Based on the special powers that have been granted to the Federal Government, the inflow of foreign capital since 1972 has been discouraged to a smaller or larger extent to stem the appreciation of the Swiss currency. This upward revaluation has adversely affected the tourist industry and some exports. As a result, the Swiss Government has been given wide-ranging powers that it may invoke to alleviate high capital inflows to Switzerland. Such powers include: limiting the amount of Swiss bonds foreigners can purchase, banning the purchase of Swiss securities by nonresident foreigners, interest rate restrictions, and limiting the amount of Swiss bank notes that foreigners can bring into the country.

Several measures are carried out through a gentlemen's agreement with the National Bank of Switzerland. Thus banks and multinational corporations based in Switzerland since 1975 have renewed yearly agreements to report foreign exchange transactions over SF 5 million to the National Bank. In addition, since 1976 all large Swiss enterprises with activities abroad have agreed to notify the National Bank every month of the capital movements they plan to carry out in the following month.

Purchases of real estate by foreigners living abroad or in Switzerland for less than 5 consecutive years, unless they have a residence permit, are subject to approval by the canton where the property is located.

Sources and Availability of Capital

The money market is characterized by excessive liquidity and a downward trend of interest rates. Short-term and medium-term finance is widely available in all usual forms, subject to any government credit restrictions. Swiss borrowers usually take an overdraft rather than a fixed loan. Medium-term finance is normally provided by a fixed loan secured on real estate.

Consumer credit plays a minor role in Switzerland and is far below the European average on a per capita basis. Consumer credit is used mainly for the financing of purchases of durable consumer goods. Consumer credit is provided by banks and special financing agencies. Competition between these institutions has depressed costs to the consumer but credit charges can still amount to 18 percent because of expenses involved.

Long-term loans are handled on the bond, stock, and mortgage loan markets. Utilities, banks, the Federal Government, and cantons have been the main borrowers on the bond market. Most bonds are purchased by private investors such as pension funds and by insurance companies.

There are three main stock exchanges located in Zurich, Basel, and Geneva. Stock exchanges are regulated by their respective cantons. The larger part of the newly issued shares is placed directly with private investors outside the stock exchange. The Swiss stock exchange is not used by foreign companies to obtain long-term capital. Many U.S. companies, however, are listed on the Zurich stock exchange.

Mortgage loans are used not only for dwellings, but to a lesser extent for industrial and commercial construction. Switzerland has the highest mortgage indebtedness per capita. Only a little more than one-half of the mortgages granted are amortized. However, the lender, on

short notice, has the right to call the mortgage at any time, usually for changing the interest rate. The largest part of the mortgages is financed by the cantonal and local banks, followed by pension funds, insurance companies and by other private and public entities.

Trade Regulations

Switzerland's dependence on foreign markets causes it to follow a policy of trade liberalization where it can without compromising its neutrality. Thus Switzerland would not become a member of the ECC because of the Common Market's concerted economic, social, and political policies. By its membership in EFTA, Switzerland retains full autonomy in matters of labor mobility, economic policies, commercial laws, and political involvement. Switzerland is also a member of the Organization for Economic Cooperation and Development (OECD) and the General Agreement on Tariffs and Trade (GATT).

Customs Duties

Switzerland's customs tariff uses the Customs Cooperation Council Nomenclature (CCCN), which was formerly the Brussels Tariff Nomenclature (BTN), and consists of a single column. Assessments are made on gross weight, mostly in Swiss francs per 100 kilograms (about 220 lbs.) or in some cases by the unit.

In line with Switzerland's liberal approach to trade, normal duties are charged at 5 percent or less on more than half of all imports. Notable exceptions to this are agricultural products that are generally assessed at rates of 12 to 15 percent. These percentages are rough equivalents of actual duties.

Additional Taxes

All imported items are subject to a statistical tax of 3 percent of the customs duty. Most imports are also charged with a sales tax, mainly at 8.4 percent on the wholesale value c.i.f. at the Swiss border or 5.6 percent on the delivered price if the merchandise is not for resale. Switzerland does not levy export duties. Excise taxes are levied on a few products such as cigarettes and alcohol.

Free Zones

Goods not cleared through customs can be stored in free zones, Federal bonded warehouses, or private bonded warehouses. There are 16 free zones and 6 cold storage free zones in Switzerland. They are, in effect, bonded warehouses in which goods can be stored without time limit.

Goods in the nine Federal bonded warehouses are subject to customs control and may not remain in storage for more than 5 years. Similar rules apply to private bonded warehouses where only certain types of products can be stored.

Samples, Advertising Matter, and Carnets

Switzerland is a member of the International Convention to Facilitate the Importation of Commercial Samples and Advertising Matter and adheres to the conventions that introduced carnets to facilitate temporary duty-free importation of commercial samples. Carnets, designed to eliminate customs procedure for temporary imports, can be purchased from the U.S. Council of the International Chamber of Commerce, Inc., 1212 Avenue of the Americas, New York, N.Y. 10036, telephone (212) 354-4480. Applications for carnets are available from the U.S. Council or from the U.S. Department of Commerce District Offices. Carnets are valid 1 year from date of issuance, and eliminate duty on samples whose value is less than SF 10 or weigh less than 100 grams. Other samples are liable to duty, although duties may be recovered if the samples are reexported within a year.

Documentation and Registration

In addition to the usual description and markings, every invoice is required to show the ex-factory price of the merchandise, all additional costs including insurance to the Swiss border, net and gross weights, and the name of the country of origin. All documents must be presented to the customs authorities promptly or the consignee may be fined.

Like all business entities, importers must be inscribed in the Commercial Register in the canton of their residence. This requirement also extends to individual proprietorships if their sales exceed SF 10,000.

Customs Classification

The Swiss Customs Administration will furnish information about the classification of goods not specifically mentioned in the tariff schedule and not included under any category in the Swiss tariff.

Applications for such information should be accompanied by samples and should be made on the official forms furnished by the Swiss customs authorities for this purpose.

Rulings are furnished in writing. An appeal of any action taken by Swiss Customs may be made by a person directly concerned. Appeals must be drawn up in writing and addressed to the Swiss customhouse initiating the action leading to the appeal.

Nontariff Barriers

While Switzerland's customs tariffs are quite low, imports of nearly all agricultural products are subject to regulations to protect farmers from low-priced imports. This is also to maintain a certain degree of self-sufficiency in food production.

Quotas exist mostly for meat, animals for slaughter, grains and feed-grains, potatoes, and bulk wine. Licenses are granted within the quota limits. Other agricultural products are subject to supplementary import charges. The charges are revised in response to world market prices and the situation of Swiss agriculture.

Import permits are required for specific products that are not quantitatively restricted but fall under health and security regulations.

Imports of foodstuffs and beverages must meet Federal requirements that are enforced by the Federal Office for Public Health (Eidenassiche Gesundheitsamt/Service Federal de l'hygiene publique) and the Veterinary Office (Veterinaramt/Office veterinaire), both in Bern.

Marking and Labeling

The rules are generally liberal but prohibit any deception. Labels should include the name of the product, indicate measures and weights in the metric system, and list ingredients in either German or French, preferably in both languages. Food products should show whether additives have been used for preserving, coloring, or flavoring purposes.

Imported gold and silver jewelry must bear the imprint of an identification mark of the manufacturer who must be registered with the Swiss Custom Administration in Bern.

There is no general requirement that all imports should be marked as to the country of origin. However, indication of origin is required for certain food products.

Multilateral Trade Negotiations

The most recent series of Multilateral Trade Negotiations (MTN) held under the General Agreement on Tariffs and Trade (GATT)—the Tokyo round—was concluded in 1979. These comprehensive and far-reaching negotiations, in which the United States and its trading partners played major roles, have resulted in agreements that should liberalize world trade over the next decade.

Of particular interest to U.S. exporters to Switzerland are the six agreements that establish new rules, or "codes," on government procurement, product standards, import licensing procedures, subsidies, trade in civil aircraft and customs valuation, and the protocol that lowers tariffs on industrial and other products in general. Switzerland has signed all of the codes.

The codes will increase the opportunities for foreign suppliers to sell to government entities, discourage the manipulation of product standards that discriminate against imported products, simplify and harmonize import licensing procedures, provide recourse when facing subsidized competition in foreign markets, reduce government influence on civil aircraft purchase decisions, and eliminate tariffs on civil aircraft and their principal components, and replace a number of different systems of customs valuation with a uniform system. The tariff protocol will reduce the Swiss average tariff level on industrial product imports from the United States by approximately 23.5 percent.

The agreements on product standards, subsidies and countervailing measures, import licensing procedures, trade in civil aircraft, and tariffs came into force on January 1, 1980. The codes on government procurement and customs valuation became effective on January 1, 1981.

Tariffs on civil aircraft and their principal components were completely eliminated by Switzerland on January 1, 1980. On the other hand, Swiss tariff reductions on other industrial products will, with a few exceptions, be spread in equal installments over a period of 8 years. The first cut was made on January 1, 1980; the seven additional cuts are scheduled for each January 1 from 1981 to 1987 (for certain chemicals and plastics the first cut was made on July 1, 1980). For textiles and steel, six equal cuts are scheduled for each January 1 from 1982 to 1987.

Investment in Switzerland

Value of U.S. Investment

U.S. direct investment in Switzerland amounted to $7.4 billion at the end of 1978 of which 48 percent was in retailing, 29 percent in finance, 15 percent in manufacturing, and 8 percent in other areas.

The majority of the 550 U.S. firms with financial interests in Switzerland maintain sales and regional administrative offices. Profits from U.S. investments in Switzerland have been reinvested by U.S. holding companies in third-country subsidiaries. In this context, Switzerland may be the largest center for U.S. holding companies in manufacturing, metal processing, chemical, watch, and textile industries outside the United States.

Pertinent Treaties

The 1850 Treaty of Frendship between the United States and Switzerland forms the basis for bilateral commercial relations. It provides for reciprocal freedom in establishing business entities.

The convention between the two countries for the avoidance of double taxation on income has been in effect since 1951. The convention covers U.S. Federal income and excess profits taxes and Swiss Federal, cantonal, and municipal taxes on income.

A Swiss Federal decree was designed in 1962 to limit abuses resulting from the application of double taxation treaties.

The Judicial Assistance Treaty, which went into effect in 1977, will also help U.S. authorities track down criminal activities in cooperation with Swiss authorities.

Government Policy

The Swiss Federal Government has no specific policy on foreign direct investment. The complete freedom of transfer of investment income and repatriation of capital is a strong inducement to foreign investment in Switzerland.

According to regulations issued in February 1978, the establishment of a foreign-owned corporation must be approved by the National Bank.

Special tax, utility, and land concessions in predominantly agricultural cantons also can be considered as inducements for foreign investment. The Swiss Government insists on reciprocity when it permits foreign banks to open branch offices in Switzerland.

Information about government policy towards investors is available from the Federal Office for Industry, Trade, and Labor, a division of the Federal Department of Public Economy, Bundeshaus, 3000-Bern, or the Swiss Office of the Development of Trade, rue Bellefontaine 18, 1003-Lausanne.

Switzerland is a signatory to the Convention on the Settlement of Investment Disputes. Under this treaty, a department was set up to resolve differences over investment projects where one party is a government agency and the other a foreign national.

Problems Facing Investors

Short-term government controls are introduced periodically by federal authorities in order to manage the economy. Prospective investors should therefore always ascertain the current regulations when a new project is contemplated.

The biggest problem likely to face a new enterprise is the chronic shortage of labor. Foreign investors who wish to bring managers or technicians from their home countries will find difficulty in obtaining the necessary permits.

Forms of Business Organization

All business forms that are authorized and regulated by the Swiss Federal Code of Obligations, adopted in 1911, can be used by foreign firms. Business organizations fall into two categories—those whose members are personally liable and those whose liability is limited to the shareholder's investment.

Among the first category, the sole proprietorship is the most prevalent form, followed by general, and limited partnerships (Killektivgesellschaft, Societe en nom collectif and Kommanditgesellschaft, Societe en commandite). Unless the sole proprietorship's annual turnover is more than SF 100,000, it need not be registered in the Commercial Register. Both partnership forms are in most respects similar to those in the United States. They are formed by registering the necessary information with the Commercial Register. There is no citizenship requirement for partners.

In the second category, the most common type is the corporation (Aktiengesellschaft A.G., Societe Anonyme S.A.), which resembles in form and operation the U.S. corporation. The limited liability company (Gesellschaft mit beschrankter Haftung, G.m.b.H., Societe a responsibilite limitee, S.A.R.L.) has not become as popular in Switzerland as in other European countries. This form of organization has features of a corporation and a partnership. Like a partnership, it does not have freely negotiable shares, although its capital is divided into shares, but like a corporation the equity is limited to shareholders' investment. The limited liability partnership (Kommanditaktiengesellschaft, Societe en commandite par actions) is rarely used. It differs from the limited partnership in that its capital is divided into shares. Despite the unlimited responsibility of general partners, taxes are levied on the company, not on the individual partners.

Foreigners who intend to set up a corporation need the services of a Swiss notary. There must be at least three founders who declare their intention to form a corporation through a public notification, setting forth the corporate articles and naming the officers. The public act is followed by registration with the Commercial Register in the canton of the company's domicile after which the corporation comes into existence and becomes a juridical entity.

The legal minimum for subscribed capital is SF 50,000; of this amount, 20 percent, but not less than SF 20,000 must be paid in. Capital is divided into shares with a registered par value of not less than SF 100 that are either as to bearer or to a person.

The majority of the board of directors must be Swiss citizens residing in Switzerland. However, this requirement may be waived if the largest part of the holding company's investment is in companies outside of Switzerland.

Each year financial statements of corporations must be examined by independent auditors. The auditing firm is elected at the shareholders' meeting and does not need to be a Swiss firm.

The branch also must be registered in the Commercial Register. At least one of the branch managers must be a Swiss resident.

Under the Swiss law the parent company is liable for the obligations of the branch.

Intellectual Property Protection

The Federal Office for the Protection of Intellectual Property (Eidgenossiche Amt fur Geistiges Eigentum/Bureau de la propriete intellectuelle), Eschmannstrasse 2, 3000-Bern, is in charge of trademarks, patents, and copyrights.

Trademarks other than company names are regulated under the Federal Trademark Law of 1980 and subsequent amendments. Switzerland is a member of the Madrid Arrangement of 1891, which provides uniform trademark registration in all signatory countries.

Registration of a trademark lasts for 20 years and may be renewed for similar periods. Application for renewal must be made no later than 6 months after the expiration of registration.

Applications for trademarks requested in Switzerland for international protection have to be directed to the World Organization for Intellectual Property in Geneva.

Switzerland has signed the European Patent Convention, which became effective in 1977.

Taxation

Fiscal authority is divided between the Federal Government and the 26 cantons which, in addition, have conferred the right to levy taxes upon the more than 3,000 municipalities. Taxes such as customs duties, stamp taxes, and some excise taxes are the exclusive prerogative of the Federal Government. Others, such as the Federal direct tax and the sales tax, are assigned to the Federal Government on a temporary basis. In general, the Federal Government relies heavily on indirect taxes while the local authorities derive the bulk of their revenue from direct taxes.

Incorporated businesses as well as individuals are subject to all levels of taxation in Switzerland. The Federal direct tax (also called the Federal or national defense tax) is levied on the income and capital of business entities and on the income of individuals. The tax is collected by cantonal authorities. The Federal direct tax is assessed on the average net income of the preceding 2 years. The tax for corporations varies from 3.63 to 9.8 percent, depending on the ratio of net profits to net worth. The Federal tax on net worth is levied annually at a uniform ratio of 0.0825 percent. The maximum rate of Federal tax on personal income is 11.5 percent.

Dividend income is subject to a 35 percent Federal withholding tax. Since the recipient corporation or individual is required to include in the taxable income the gross amount of the dividend, the tax is refunded or credited against the recipient's Federal and cantonal tax liabilities.

Cantonal taxes on corporate and personal income and net worth vary in terms of the tax base. Most municipal taxes are fixed as a percentage of similar cantonal taxes. The combined cantonal rate and municipal tax rates on corporate and individual income does not exceed 30 percent.

Sales stamp taxes are the principal indirect taxes, the proceeds of which revert back to the Federal Government. The sales tax is an ad valorem tax on the sale of goods in Switzerland. Sales of real property, intangible property, and securities are exempt from the sales tax. Sales of certain essential items, i.e., water, gas, electricity, fuel, food, and medicine, also are exempt. Exports are also exempt from sales tax. The tax is a single-phase tax levied on the last sale, i.e., by a wholesaler or manufacturer to a retailer and by a retailer to a consumer. Since 1975, the tax has been assessed at 8.4 percent at the wholesale level and at 5.6 percent at the retail level. Imports are taxed at the wholesale rate.

However, if the importer is a registered wholesaler, he or she does not pay the sales tax since it is already collected in the usual manner when the product is subsequently sold to the consumer.

The enactment of a value added tax to replace the turnover tax was rejected by the Swiss electorate in 1977.

Federal stamp taxes are levied on securities transactions. The term itself is a misnomer since no stamps are in fact used. For all transactions through banks and other dealers, the stamp tax for Swiss securities involving the sale or exchange of securities is 0.1 percent and for those of foreign origin is 0.2 percent.

Employers have to pay one-half of the 10 percent contribution that is applied to wages and salaries to support the Federal Pension Plan. This plan includes such benefits as old age and survivors insurance, disability insurance, and reimbursement of individuals for lost salary during compulsory military service. The other 5 percent to support these programs is withheld from employee's wages.

Switzerland only taxes a foreign corporation's profits when those profits are attributable to the activities of its permanent establishment in Switzerland. Switzerland reserves the right to modify the industrial or commercial profits shown on the books of the permanent establishment in order to bring its profit picture in line with that of a resident enterprise engaged in similar work.

An agreement has recently been signed that clears up previous difficulties between the United States and Switzerland on social security taxes. The treaty permits U.S. citizens to pay social security taxes only to the country in which they are permanently employed. Other points also lessen undue personnel costs incurred in the past by a lack of common U.S./Swiss social security requirements.

Double Taxation

Switzerland has concluded a number of treaties for the avoidance of double taxation. While taxes on wealth are not covered by the treaties, foreign corporations established in Switzerland may generally expect a reduced rate of withholding taxes on dividends and interest.

The terms in the treaties vary, but common to all are the following principles: (1) All Swiss Federal, cantonal, and communal taxes on income, and where applicable, on net assets, are covered; (2) with minor and always reciprocal exceptions, the treaties are applicable to all corporations domiciled and individuals resident in the countries of the two parties; (3) recovery of foreign withholding taxes is not available to branches or permanent establishments of foreign entities in Switzerland. In these cases, the existing treaties between the country of source of the income and that of the registration or principal establishment of the recipient are applicable.

A fixed place of business (branch office, workshop, warehouse, etc.) that an enterprise domiciled or incorporated in one country maintains in the other country constitutes a permanent establishment. This does not apply to an agent who only solicits business, or to offices that only purchase goods, or to a warehouse not for display but for convenience of delivery. Investments in subsidiary companies are not considered permanent establishments.

Income or profit, as well as assets or reserves attributable to the permanent establishment, are subject to tax in the country in which the establishment is situated. Any tax relief must be given in the country where the enterprise is domiciled or incorporated. There are no fixed rules as to the manner in which the income or profit and net assets must be apportioned. Each case is judged on its merits.

Switzerland has general double taxation agreements with a number of countries, including the United States, Canada, France, West Germany, Japan, the Netherlands, Portugal, South Africa, Spain, Sweden, and the United Kingdom.

Labor Relations

Labor Force

Despite some relief in recent recessions, Switzerland is likely to continue to suffer from a chronic shortage of labor, particularly in the professional and skilled areas. The labor force in Switzerland consists of some 3 million workers, of which 1 million are women and approximately 650,000 are foreign workers. Foreigners are generally found in less skilled jobs. The breakdown by sector is as follows:

	Swiss	Foreign	Total
Agriculture	221,000	10,000	231,000
Mining, construc- tion and manufac- turing	1,007,000	438,000	1,445,000
Services.............	1,110,000	210,000	1,320,000
Total...............	2,338,000	658,000	2,996,000

Source: Touche Ross International

Working Conditions

A standard work week of 46 hours, prescribed by Federal law, applies to most industrial, office, and retail employees. In many instances, actual working time has been reduced by collective agreements to 40 hours. A 5-day work week is now normal. There are eight legal holidays, but some cantons give extra days. Annual paid vacations vary, but may not be less than 2 weeks.

There continues to be a wide disparity between average wages for men and women. In 1979, the average yearly wage for men was SF 34,600 and for women SF 24,600.

Labor Organizations

Swiss labor unions are organized nationally, not by canton. There is complete freedom to join labor unions or abstain. One-quarter of the workforce belongs to unions. All collective bargaining is done on the workers' side by unions; contracts are negotiated for 2-3 years. Swiss unions are grouped into four main associations. Traditionally, Switzerland has enjoyed labor peace.

Like unions, employers' associations are usually parties to collective agreements. Aside from cantonal and municipal chambers of commerce, there is a national employers' association called the Zentraverband Schweizerischer Arbeitgeberorganisationen/Union des Associations Patronales Suisses. There is also the Vorort, an organization of 17 chambers of commerce and over 100 other employers' associations that aids new enterprises and issues numerous business publications.

In 1976, the Swiss voters rejected a referendum to introduce the principle of workers' participation in industrial management. Swiss managers deal with workers through workers' councils whose members are elected by all employees.

Work Permits

Several attempts have been made to reduce the number of foreign workers, but all have been defeated in popular referendums, the last of which was in 1977. The Federal Government has tried to stabilize the number of foreign workers by tightening existing regulations. The annual quota as of 1979 was 6,000 for cantons and 2,500 for the Federal Government. At present it is nearly impossible to get a work permit except for managerial positions or highly skilled/technicians on intercompany transfer. Depending on the nationality of the foreign worker, and the canton involved, an annual permit holder may apply for permanent status after living in Switzerland for 5 to 10 years.

U.S. business residents representing their firms have long been included in the restricted category and must apply for work permits at the cantonal or Federal level.

Guidance for Business Travelers

Entrance Requirements

Every traveler entering Switzerland must have a valid passport. No visa is required for tourists, commercial travelers, or students. A visitor may remain in Switzerland for an uninterrupted period of not more than 3 months. After 3 months, the visitor may apply to the municipal authorities to stay another 3 months. U.S. citizens who remain in Switzerland for more than a week for business reasons are required to notify the Police Section for aliens and inform it of any changes in address. Permission to take up residence must be obtained from cantonal authorities. If a work permit has been authorized, the resident permit is automatically granted.

There are no inoculation requirements for visitors entering Switzerland.

Foreign Exchange Regulations

Foreign exchange is controlled only in transactions with the few countries with which Switzerland maintains bilateral payments agreements. Foreign bank notes can be purchased and sold freely in Switzerland at rates determined by supply and demand.

Languages

According to the latest census, German was spoken by 65 percent of the population, French by 18 percent, and Italian by 12 percent. German is spoken in Bern, Basel, and Zurich; French in Geneva and Lausanne; and Italian in Lugano. For Swiss companies, the general practice is to prepare the financial statements in the language used in their headquarters. English is widely understood and spoken in business transactions.

Holidays

Businesses are closed on the following Federal holidays: January 1 (New Years' Day), January 2 (Baerzelisday), God Friday, Ascension Day, Whitmonday, August 1 (Swiss National Day), December 24 afternoon (Christmas Eve),

December 25 (Christmas Day) and December 26 (St. Stephan's Day).

In addition, the afternoon of May 1 is observed in all major cities as Labor Day. Other holidays are celebrated locally. In Zurich, the second-to-last Monday in April (Sechsrlauten) and the second Monday in September (Knabenschiessen) are celebrated. Businesses are closed in Basel on carnival days during the first week in Lent, in Geneva on the second Thursday in November (Thanksgiving), and December 31 (Reformation Day).

Business Hours

Daily business hours are from 8 a.m. to 5 p.m. with a 1-2 hour lunch break Monday through Friday. Banks normally open one-half hour later and close one-half hour earlier, and are closed on Saturdays. Stores are usually closed Monday mornings.

Time in Switzerland is 6 hours ahead of Eastern Standard time, and 6 hours ahead of Eastern Daylight Savings Time.

Weights and Measures

The metric system is used for all weights and measures. Temperatures are measured in centigrade. Domestic electric supply is usually 220 volts, and plugs have two or three round pin lamp fittings and are of the screw type. Adaptors maybe necessary for appliances such as electric razors.

Sources of Economic and Commercial Information

Swiss Commercial Representation in the United States

Swiss commercial representatives are located in the Swiss Embassy in Washington, D.C. Consulates General are located in Chicago, Los Angeles, New Orleans, New York, and San Francisco. Consulates are located in other major cities in the United States.

U.S. Representation in Switzerland

American Embassy
Jubilaeumstrasse 93
3005 Bern
Tel. (031) 43-70-11

American Consulate General
Zollikerstrasse 141
8008 Zurich
Tel. (01) 55-25-66

American Embassy (Branch for Consular Services Only)
Route de Pregny 11
P.O. Box 1292
Chambesy-Geneva
Tel. (022) 34-60-31

U.S. Foreign Commercial Officers are available to brief and assist American firms and individuals visiting Switzerland.

Business Associations

In addition to market research organizations, the Swiss Chamber of Commerce in various cantons and principal cities can provide information to businesspeople.

The Swiss-American Chamber of Commerce in Zurich, Talacker 41, represents the interests of its more than 1,200 members and provides information in matters affecting Swiss-American economic relations.

The semiofficial Swiss Office for the Development of Trade, in Zurich, Stampfenbachstrasse 85, and in Lausanne, Rue de Bellefontaine 18, works in close cooperation with Swiss foreign service posts and chambers of commerce abroad in providing information to Swiss and foreign business visitors.

Publications

General:
Business Study Switzerland/Liechtenstein. Touche Ross International.
Focus of Switzerland. Four volumes prepared by the Coordinating Committee for the Presence of Switzerland Abroad. Published by the Swiss Office for the Development of Trade, Lausanne. 1975.
Background Notes: Switzerland. U.S. Department of State, Washington, D.C.

Economy:
Economic Survey of Switzerland. Union Bank of Switzerland, Zurich. Annual.
OECD Economic Surveys. Switzerland, Paris. Annual.
Foreign Economic Trends and their Implications for the U.S. American Embassy, Bern. Semiannual.

Newsletters
Swiss Economic News. Swiss Office for the Development of Trade, Lausanne.

Market Profile—SWITZERLAND

Foreign Trade

Imports.—$29.3 billion in 1979; $23.6 billion in 1978. In real terms imports increased 13 percent in 1979 and 9.6 percent in 1978. Main suppliers in 1979: West Germany, 28.2 percent; France, 12.2 percent; Italy, 9.7 percent; United Kingdom, 7.3 percent; and United States, 6.7 percent. Main imports in 1979: Machinery, agricultural goods, chemical products, textiles, and metals. From the United States: Nonelectric machinery, aircraft, jewelry, tobacco, optical and precision goods, and electrical equipment.

Exports.—$26.5 billion in 1979; $23.3 billion in 1978. In real terms exports increased 5.1 percent in 1979 and 4.7 percent in 1978. Main customers were: West Germany, 16.5 percent; France, 8.7 percent; Italy, 8.1 percent; United States, 6.6 percent, United Kingdom, 5.7 percent. Main exports in 1979 were: Machinery, watches, chemicals, metals, and textiles. Main exports to the United States were: nonelectric machinery, organic chemicals, jewelry, electrical machinery, works of art, and watches.

Foreign Investment

Swiss direct investments abroad exceeded $19 billion at the end of 1977; the book value of U.S. direct investments in Switzerland amounted to $7.4 billion while Swiss direct investments in the United States were estimated at $2.8 billion.

Finance

Currency.—Floating since 1973. The National Bank has tried to stem the appreciation of the Swiss franc by restraining the inflow of foreign capital and by intervening from time to time on the foreign exchange market. The Swiss franc has appreciated from SF 1.79 per dollar in 1978 to SF 1.66 per dollar in 1979. On July 8, 1980, the exchange rate stood at 1SF=$.62.

Domestic Credit and Investment

The demand for credit has seen a slight increase since 1978, which the National Bank has met by carefully regulating the discount rate. It has gone from 1 percent in 1978 to 3 percent in 1980. On the capital market, domestic bond issues are usually over-subscribed due to the abundance of capital and limited investment opportunities.

Budget

Taxes are levied at the Federal, cantonal, and municipal levels. The plan to replace the turnover tax with a value-added tax in order to reduce budgetary deficits of the Federal Government was rejected by the electorate.

Balance of Payments

Trade deficit is covered by invisible transactions, mostly by investment income and receipts from tourism, which produce a surplus in the current account. In 1978, the current account surplus amounted to $7.8 billion, and in 1979 it was estimated at $2.4 billion.

Economy

GNP.—Swiss GNP in 1978 was $95.1 billion, in 1979, $98 billion, and for 1980 is projected at $100 billion. GNP per capita in current prices was $13,925 in 1978, $15,546 in 1979, and an estimated $15,889 in 1980.

Agriculture.—Meets about one-half the need for food. Domestic producers are subsidized and protected from foreign competition. In 1979, agriculture accounted for less than 5 percent of GNP.

Industry.—Contributes about one-half of GNP. The watch-making industry exports 95 percent of its production, the chemical industry about 85 percent, and the machine-building industry 65 percent.

Domestic Commerce.—Retail sales increased in 1979 by 3.6 percent and in 1980 by an estimated 3.7 percent.

Tourism.—In 1977, 6.5 million tourists visited Switzerland and brought in $2.3 billion. In terms of visitors, the United States ranked second in Switzerland.

Basic Economic Facilities

Transportation.—Excellent highway and railroad networks. The main inland port is at Basel on the Rhine. International airports are at Zurich, Geneva, and Basel. Swissair provides worldwide air service.

Communications.—Highly developed post, telegraph, and telephone system and a broad television audience. The major part of Swiss overseas communications is handled by an Intelsat Satellite.

Power.—Petroleum accounts for 75 percent of all energy needs; electricity accounts for 17 percent and gas 4 percent. Water resources for the generation of additional electric energy are virtually exhausted. An increase in the production of electric energy is being achieved through nuclear power plants. Four nuclear power plants are in operation, one is under construction.

Natural Resources

Land.—15,956 square miles of which 26 percent is non-productive.

Minerals.—Negligible with the exception of salt.

Population

Size.—6.3 million, of which 16 percent is foreign. Major cities: Zurich: 708,200; Basel: 368,900; Geneva: 323,100; and Bern: 293,300.

Language.—German, 65 percent; French, 18 percent; and Italian, 12 percent.

Labor Force.—2.7 million. 7.7 percent in agriculture, 44.2 percent in industry, 47.5 percent in services; unemployment 0.6 percent. Approximately 25 percent of the labor force is foreign.

Market Profile—SYRIAN ARAB REPUBLIC

Foreign Trade

Imports.—Estimate $3 billion in 1979; $2.3 billion in 1978. Major suppliers: Italy, 12.1 percent; Iraq, 10.4 percent; West Germany, 9.4 percent; France, 7.3 percent; United States, 5.1 percent; United Kingdom, 3.6 percent. Principal imports: machinery, petroleum products, vehicles, iron and steel, foodstuffs.

Exports.—Estimated $1.5 billion for 1979; $990 million in 1978. Major customers: Italy, 28.7 percent; France, 17.1 percent; United States, 10.7 percent. Principal exports: petroleum, raw cotton, phosphates, food products, wool, textiles.

Trade Policy.—Most foreign trade undertaken by public agencies.

Foreign Investment

Most old foreign investment nationalized, but new investment strongly encouraged and treated liberally. Almost no American investment; some investment from Arab oil producing countries. Investment Guarantee Agreement signed with United States in 1976.

Finance

Currency.—Foreign exchange controls liberalized. Syrian Pound (SL) divided into 100 piastres. Official rate, 1 SL equals US$.256; US$1 equals SL 3.90. Unofficial rate has been as high as US$1 equals SL 4.62. Inflation rate in 12–15 percent range.

Domestic Credit and Investment.—All banks government owned. Institutions include the Commercial Bank (for foreign trade and large domestic transactions), the Agricultural Cooperative Bank, the Industrial Bank, the Real Estate Bank, and the Popular Credit Bank for smaller domestic loans.

Balance of Payments.—There were large balance of payments deficits estimated at near $500 million for 1976 and $400 million in 1977. Problem was caused by military intervention in Lebanon and greatly reduced Arab aid during that period. Situation improved in 1978 due to restoration of aid and reduction of expenditures by Syrian Government. The deficit for 1978 was estimated at $150 million or less and 1979 may have seen a slight surplus. A slight deficit again projected for 1980. The trend has been one of rising deficits financed by foreign aid.

Foreign Aid.—Heavily dependent on foreign assistance. Major donors: Arab oil producers, some Socialist countries, and the United States. Proposed U.S. assistance in fiscal 1980 about $60 million.

Economy

Agricultural, with increasing industrialization. Major industries and commercial enterprises are government owned. Active private sector in services and non-government controlled sectors. Growth rate at the end of the 1970s estimated at 3–5 percent.

GDP.—$7.3 billion in 1978. Approximate sector contributions: industry, 26 percent; agriculture, 18 percent; trade, 17 percent; government, 16 percent; and other services, 20 percent. Smuggling may account for about 20 percent of the GDP.

Agriculture

Agriculture.—Employs about half of work force, but country is still a net importer of food. Production, particularly cereals, fluctuates with rainfall. Primary products: Wheat, barley, sugar beets, cotton, olives, lentils. Undertaking large program of irrigation and land development in Euphrates Basin. 5.5 million hectares of cultivated land, 32 percent of which is fallow.

Industry.—Mostly small-scale, geared to the domestic market. Major industries: textiles, food processing, oil refining, tobacco, cement. Light industries: glass, refrigerators, batteries, TVs and washing machines. All large industries owned by the government. Public sector industry operating at about 40 percent capacity.

Development Program.—Fourth Five Year Plan (1976–80) originally set total investment at $13.7 billion; a drop in foreign aid receipts reduced the investment level to an estimated $9.9 billion. Priority given to completion of ongoing projects, including land reclamation, oil refining, cement, sugar refining, and phosphates. Fifth Five Year Plan, to begin 1981, will emphasize port development, mining, transportation, and public works.

Tourism.—Becoming foreign exchange earner with heavy investment in tourist infrastructure.

Basic Economic Facilities

Transportation.—Railway: About 7,720 miles in two different gauge systems; integrated network to total 14,966 miles planned. Roads: 6,820 miles of paved roads; 1,054 miles of gravel roads, and 1,488 miles of earth roads; system being expanded. International airport at Damascus. Other airports at Aleppo, Dier-Al Zawr, and Al-Qamishli. Main ports at Latakia and Tartous; Banias used mostly for oil exports.

Communications.—Government-owned. Good international and domestic communications services. Radio and television.

Power.—Electric generating capacity has increased with the completion of the Euphrates Dam, which will eventually supply most of the country's output. In 1977 production was 1389 MW. In short run, Syria will be an energy exporter. Expects to spend $1.25 billion on electrical power generation and distribution 1981–85.

Natural Resources

Land.—71,722 square miles. Coastal plain bounded by mountains, central plateau, desert in southeast.

Climate.—Mediterranean along coast; semi-arid on plateau; hot and dry in desert.

Minerals.—Petroleum reserves estimated at 7 billion barrels. Record of more than 10 million barrels produced in 1976; since then production has been in 9.1–9.9 million range. Phosphate reserves estimated at 500 million tons, with 1976 production of 500,000 tons.

Population

Size.—Estimated at 8.1 million in 1978; annual growth rate 3.4 percent. More than 50 percent urban. Principal cities: Damascus (capital), Aleppo, Homs.

Language.—Arabic. Some French and English also used.

Education.—Free compulsory elementary education. Four universities. In 1976, 67 percent of males and 52 percent of females over age 10 were literate.

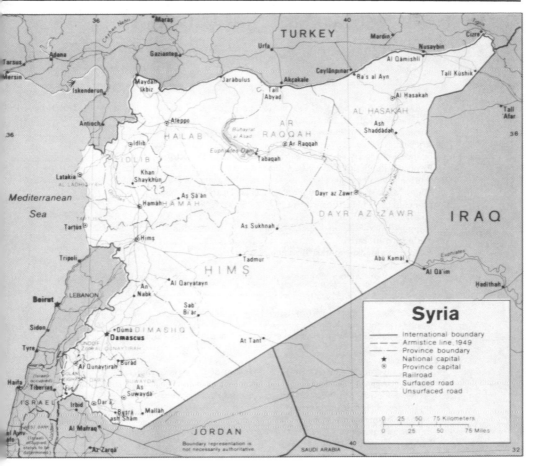

Marketing in Taiwan

Contents

Report Revised October 1981

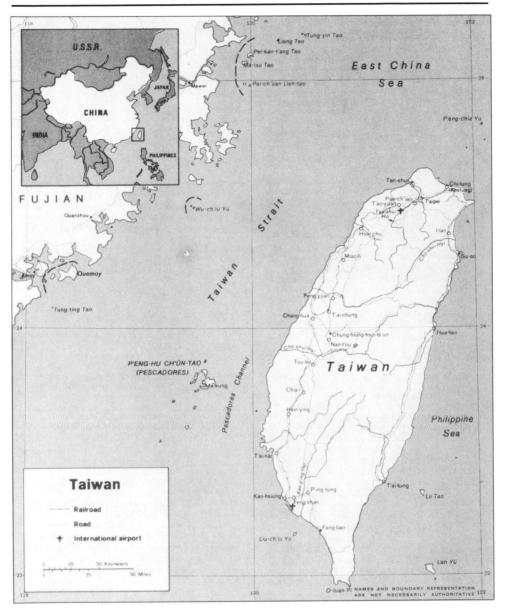

U.S.-Taiwan Relations

U.S. Public Law 96-8 (Taiwan Relations Act) was passed and became effective April 10, 1979, following the decision to establish diplomatic relations with the Peoples' Republic of China on January 1, 1979. The Act authorizes the continuation of commercial, cultural, and other relations between the people of the United States and the people on Taiwan. One prime objective was to assure that existing business relations with Taiwan would not be jeopardized. The Act stipulates that the U.S. Government will continue to encourage trade and investment between the United States and Taiwan.

Programs, transactions, and other relations with Taiwan are conducted by or through the American Institute in Taiwan (AIT), a nonprofit corporation incorporated under the laws of the District of Columbia. The Institute has its main office in Arlington, Virginia, and subsidiary offices in Taipei and Kaohsiung, Taiwan. The Institute also maintains the American Trade Center as part of its Taipei offices.

The Coordination Council for North American Affairs (CCNAA) is Taiwan's counterpart organization to AIT in the United States. Addresses for both AIT and CCNAA may be found under the heading, "Sources of Economic and Commercial Information," page 2359.

Foreign Trade Outlook

Introduction

During the past three decades, Taiwan has developed from an agricultural to an industrial economy. With the exception of 1974 when the economy stagnated briefly as a result of worldwide recession, economic growth has been rapid and sustained. The secret of success has been, and will continue to be, the emphasis given to international trade and to domestic and foreign investment.

Taiwan is the United States' ninth largest trading partner worldwide, and consistently registers a trade surplus with the United States. On the other hand, as Taiwan's largest supplier, Japan enjoys a consistent surplus in bilateral trade. These imbalances have been a matter of serious concern and, as a result, Taiwan authorities have attempted since 1972 to increase imports of American products and to decrease dependency on Japanese goods. Taiwan has favored procurement from the United States in the application screening process by restricting certain classes of goods from Asian nations and, since 1978, has sent special buying missions to the United States. To date, these missions have purchased approximately $5.5 billion worth of U.S. products. Reversing the long-running imbalance on the merchandise trade account cannot be done overnight, but progress is being made. With the continuing efforts of Taiwan, and most importantly, with the efforts of American businesses, the rate of improvement should accelerate.

Although growth in U.S. exports to Taiwan is expected to continue, serious competition for the U.S. share of the market is emerging. In order to be less vulnerable to economic slumps in the United States and Japan, its two major trading partners, Taiwan has implemented a program to diversify trade. Measures have been taken to improve trade ties in other regions of the world, particularly with Western Europe, and they are proving successful. American suppliers should therefore intensify promotion efforts in order to sell the advanced-technology capital goods that Taiwan requires.

Table 1 shows the value of principal imports from the world; table 2 shows value of selected U.S. exports to Taiwan, by major commodities.

Best Export Prospects

Prospects are very good for the sale of sophisticated industrial, manufacturing, and research equipment, and design and engineering services. While price is extremely important in selling to Taiwan, financing, delivery, and after-sales service also are highly important. American firms that pay attention to these considerations and pursue opportunities aggres-

---

BACKGROUND INFORMATION ABOUT THESE COUNTRIES

For those who wish *general* data about a country—data which goes beyond marketing and commerce—the editors recommend *Countries of the World and Their Leaders*, published as an annually updated yearbook by Gale Research Company, Detroit, Michigan 48226. Containing 4- to 20-page entries on 168 countries, the volume also provides several hundred pages of supplementary world data. Each report provides some historical insight as well as a look at contemporary trends of lifestyle in the country. Reports also discuss a country's educational system, its press, ethnic groupings and religious practices.

Table 1.—Value of Principal Imports from the World
(Millions of dollars)

Commodity	1977	1978	1979
Agriculture, Forestry, and Fishery Products	1.179	1.466	2.083
Minerals	1.414	1.809	2.552
Chemical and Pharmaceutical Products	1.025	1.305	1.817
Basic Metal	841	1.104	1.479
Machinery	893	1.212	1.587
Electrical Machinery and Appratus	869	1.337	1.630
Transportation Equipment	602	831	1.176
Total	8.511	11.027	14.774

Source: Taiwan Statistical Data Book, 1980.

Table 2.—Selected U.S. Exports to Taiwan by Major Commodities
(Millions of dollars)

Commodity	1978	1979	1980
Nonagricultural Products			
Machinery	637.8	962.3	1.621.2
Office Machines, Computers and Equipment	37.5	44.5	81.0
Electronic Components and Parts	80.1	84.2	124.7
Telecommunications and Sound Re-producing Equipment	107.7	110.0	163.7
Aircraft and Parts	147.2	163.9	260.9
Railroad and Road Vehicles and Parts.	66.4	79.6	90.0
Scientific and Control Instru-mentation	48.9	71.8	99.9
Photo Equipment, Optical Goods and Timing Apparatus	40.6	22.5	35.9
Chemicals	226.4	448.1	501.6
Iron and Steel	40.3	59.8	74.2
Coal, Coke and Briquets	13.6	17.9	32.0
Agricultural Products			
Corn	195.7	274.7	271.5
Wheat	77.6	115.8	103.7
Soybeans	254.6	308.9	261.7
Cotton	141.5	135.7	203.5
Tobacco	55.1	92.5	37.0
Total	2.341.9	3.271.3	4.336.6

Source: U.S. Department of Commerce, Bureau of the Census.

sively will secure growing sales in the Taiwan market and assist the United States in balancing its unfavorable bilateral trade account.

The following is a brief review of the 10 product categories that are considered to have the highest sales potential for U.S. suppliers to Taiwan over the next few years.

INDUSTRIAL PROCESS CONTROLS.—Over the next few years, Taiwan plans to step up development of technology-intensive industries such as petrochemical, chemical, basic metals, cement, and portions of the food processing industry. These developments will increase demand for sophisticated process control instruments such as instruments for level measurement, flow measurement, pressure measurement, temperature control, power control, chemical analysis, and physical analysis.

LABORATORY, SCIENTIFIC, AND ENGINEERING INSTRUMENTS.—The development of high-technology industry is crucial to Taiwan's development plans for the 1980's. Under a program of special incentives, many private firms and some academic institutions are increasing their budgets for research and development. The market should grow at a rate of 10 to 20 percent annually with the following products considered to be in demand: Microscopes (optical and electron), oscilloscopes, X-ray apparatus for laboratories, spectrophotometers, atomic absorption, micrometers, water meters, hydrometers, gas meters, mechanical appliances for testing physical properties and industrial materials, centrifuges, laser instruments, and compressibility testing machines.

COMPUTERS AND PERIPHERAL EQUIPMENT.—The demand for sophisticated computers and peripheral equipment is continuing to grow significantly in Taiwan. In order to improve production efficiency and reduce production costs, many large companies are adopting computerized operations. A fast growing wage rate in the manufacturing sector is likely to accelerate the pace of computerization in industry. Best sales prospects include microprocessor computers, graphic computer systems, personal computer systems, Chinese/English line printers, flexible discs, data terminals, CRT terminals, Chinese data processing systems, keypunch units, disc products, small business computer systems, and programmable data terminals.

FOOD PROCESSING EQUIPMENT.—Food manufacture on Taiwan has been expanding since 1961. The major food processing industries are sugar refining, food canning, rice milling, wheat flour milling, and vegetable oil extraction with sugar and canned food industries being the most important. Canned foods are mostly exported. The majority of the food processing plants are traditional, family-type businesses, which face serious competition from the rapidly growing modernized large-scale plants. Although these smaller firms are eager to upgrade production patterns to meet the competition, the six to eight large plants will continue to be the main end-users of advanced food processing equipment. Best sales prospects include grading machines; vacuum evaporation equipment; fitting machines; food freezing equipment (with the use of liquid nitrogen or liquid freon); rapid freezing systems; high-temperature, short-time aseptic canning facilities; sophisticated, food-product packaging equipment; and related printing equipment and technology.

TELECOMMUNICATIONS EQUIPMENT.—The Taiwan market for telecommunications systems has been expanding significantly in recent years. The high growth of income and rapid expansion of foreign trade are major contributors to a booming market. Some of the major expansion projects in this area are increasing local telephone facilities on a large scale, expanding international and domestic toll communications facilities, promoting new services such as push-button telephones, intensifying research, and development in the field of telecommunications science and technology. Also, modernization of the military sector provides trade opportunities for special telecommunications equipment. Best sales prospects include microwave radios; communications test systems; transmission test systems; telephone sets; electronic telephone sets; system noise monitors; automatic cable tester systems; computerized branch exchanges; precision, automatic noise figure indicators; wire wrapping and unwrapping tools; integrated circuit inserters and extractors; and digital, key telephone systems.

DRUGS AND PHARMACEUTICALS.—More than 90 percent of Taiwan's domestic market for Western-type drugs and pharmaceuticals depends on imports, although Taiwan does have a thriving Chinese medicine industry. These two forms of medicine coexist easily since Taiwan's population uses both. Annual growth of imported drugs and pharmaceuticals over the past few years has averaged more than 19 percent and this growth rate seems likely to continue.

CONSTRUCTION MACHINERY AND BUILDING PRODUCTS.—In recent years construction has attained the highest growth rate of the entire Taiwan business spectrum. For the most part, Taiwan has been self-sufficient in most categories of building materials and in some building equipment. In the next few years, it is expected there will be an increased demand for high-quality building supplies and sophisticated equipment such as air-conditioning machines, fans and blowers, hand tools, elevators, circuit breakers, switchgear assemblies and switchboards, panelboards and distribution boards, electricity meters and standard meters insulating fittings, structures and structural parts of iron and steel, cast-iron pipe fittings, building wire and cable, and asbestos products.

ELECTRONIC COMPONENTS.—The electronics industry has achieved the highest growth rate of all major industries in Taiwan. It is export oriented and the second largest foreign exchange earner. Electronic components make up 84 percent of total electronic imports. Products with best sales prospects include integrated circuits digitalic, linear, monolithic, and hybrid; tuners for TV receivers; semiconductors other than integrated circuit—silicon transistors, selenium transistors, other transistors, diodes, silicon rectifiers, display including LED, LCD, and digital tubes, crystal valves; reactors; printed circuit boards; ferrite cores; coils; fixed and variable capacitors; ceramic, polyester film,

electrolytic; and tubes electronic microwave, cathode ray for color TV, and electronic tubes for industrial use.

POLLUTION CONTROL EQUIPMENT.—Industrial pollution is a serious problem in Taiwan. The ratio of existing equipment investment for pollution control and the paid in capital of individual firms is less than 1 percent. Growing pressure on factories to control pollution should speed up growth in this market. Best sales prospects include professional engineering services in industrial/municipal water and wastewater treatment, air pollution abatement equipment, environmental planning studies, filtration systems, sludge concentrating systems, chlorine analyzers, turbidimeters, conductivity meters, spectrophotometers, BOD apparatus, water quality test kits, hydragard automatic liquid samplets, filters, screens and strainers, flow recording and sampling equipment, wastewater treatment systems, pressure reducing and check valves, in-line separators, pulsed flourescent ambient SO_2 analyzers, and chemicluminescent NO/NO_2 ambient air analyzers.

MEDICAL INSTRUMENTS AND EQUIPMENT.—Taiwan's strong economy has resulted in a higher standard of living for Taiwan's citizens, who continue to demand more and better services from both public and private medical institutions. A proposed national health insurance program may go into effect in 1981, and several large hospitals are undertaking major expansions that will generate substantial purchases of medical apparatus (almost all from abroad) during the next few years. Best sales prospects are spectrophotometers, clinical analyzers, double-beam spectrophotometers, vision testers, tonometers, aspirators, phacoemulsifiers, respiratory intensive care systems, flowmeters, ocutomes, fragmatomes, fetal monitors, neonatal monitors, Ph meters, automatic computing densitometers, sterile procine skin dressings, X-Y recorders, transducers, and patient monitors.

Industry Trends

Economic Progress

Taiwan officials have implemented a successful economic development program over the past two decades. The result has been the emergence of one of the fastest growing economies in the world. In the years since the launching of the first Four-Year Economic Development Plan in 1953, real gross national product (GNP) has increased at an average annual rate of almost 10 percent and manufacturing by about 15 percent a year.

There have been two distinct phases of growth to date. The first, extending from 1953 to 1962, stressed stability and the establishment of a solid economic base. During this period, Taiwan generally followed a four-pronged policy approach, which consisted of a strengthening of the agricultural base, development of a physical and social infrastructure, achievement of price stability, and emphasis on import-substitution industries. The result was a system of power, transportation, and communications facilities, second only to Japan in Asia and a secure base for an industrial economy supported by a productive agricultural sector. With increased per capita income and purchasing power, these improved conditions enhanced the climate for industrial activity and enabled local producers to rely more confidently on the development of domestic markets. By the early 1960's, Taiwan was able to pursue a pattern of self-sustaining growth, which launched the island into its second phase of rapid industrial development.

The Four-Year Economic Development Plans covering 1961 to 1972 called for intense industrialization. Primary consideration was assigned to the improvement of the investment climate and the promotion of exports. Midway through the third Economic Development Plan, the economic indicators began to grow. In 1963, real GNP increased over 9.4 percent largely due to the increased contribution of industry (see table 3). For the first time in the history of Taiwan, industry represented a greater share of net domestic products than agriculture. Industry was concerned with import substitution. Priority was assigned to such industries as cotton, textiles, clothing, shoes, and leather products. This was designed to alleviate the pressure caused by scarce foreign exchange. During this period, food processing was the only major export industry. As the orientation of industry shifted to the promotion of exports, the profile of growth industries changed. The island's inexpensive labor force, coupled with exchange reforms and export promotion, resulted in the acceleration of such light, basic industries as textiles, apparel, and wood and paper products. As the composition of industry with export capabilities shifted away from agricultural products, foreign markets began to open up, and industry moved into the production of more sophisticated products such as electronics and plastics.

By 1977, GNP had reached $21.4 billion and per capita GNP, $1,282. Industry's contribution to net domestic product had increased from 17.7 percent in 1953 to 43.7 percent in 1977. At the same time, the share held by agriculture dropped from 38.3 percent to 12.5 percent. Taiwan's 1978 economic performance was its best ever. The rate of real growth in GNP was 13.9 percent, and its value was $26 billion. Industrial production grew

Table 3.—Growth of Real Gross National Product in Taiwan, 1952-80

(NT$ Million, 1976 Prices[1])

Year	GNP	% Increase
1952	89,864	12.05
1953	98,239	9.32
1954	107,641	9.57
1955	116,349	8.09
1956	122,748	5.50
1957	131,684	7.28
1958	140,323	6.56
1959	151,197	7.75
1960	160,978	6.47
1961	171,970	6.83
1962	185,467	7.85
1963	202,852	9.37
1964	227,816	12.31
1965	252,909	11.01
1966	275,691	9.01
1967	304,799	10.56
1968	332,439	9.07
1969	362,370	9.00
1970	403,210	11.27
1971	455,226	12.90
1972	515,825	13.31
1973	581,928	12.82
1974	588,459	1.12
1975	613,414	4.24
1976	696,101	13.48
1977	764,706	9.86
1978	870,621	13.85
1979	940,973	8.08
1980	1,003,599	6.66

[1]Exchange Rate: NT$36 ~ US$1.

Source: Directorate-General of Budget, Accounting and Statistics.

by 25 percent, and agriculture production as a percentage of total output showed further decline. In 1979, GNP dropped to 8.1 percent, caused principally by escalating crude oil prices, but the growth rate still outpaced other non-oil exporting countries.

The increased emphasis being given to the heavy, basic industries (such as iron and steel, aluminum, shipbuilding, and machinery) and to the more capital intensive, higher technology industries (such as electronics and petrochemicals) are resulting in greatly increased opportunities for overseas suppliers and foreign investors. Likewise, Taiwan's infrastructure development program presents many additional opportunities.

Economic Priorities and Growth Sectors

The basic elements of the authorities' plan to further industrialize Taiwan were set forth in the first Six-Year Economic Development Plan (1976-81). The Plan called for strengthening the economic structure through deemphasis on labor-intensive, light industry and the promotion of technologically oriented, capital-intensive, sophisticated industrial operations. Specifically, the Plan aimed for completion of the 10 major infrastructure projects followed by an additional 12 projects discussed below. The basic objective is to raise Taiwan to developed-nation status by the end of the 1980's.

In order to ensure a continuous economic development that takes future needs and contingencies into consideration, the new Ten-Year Economic Development Plan covering the period 1980 to 1989 has been implemented. Whereas the availability of cheap energy, an ample supply of low-cost labor, and rapid expansion of foreign trade has contributed to Taiwan's economic growth, these conditions could not be expected to continue into the 1980's. The Ten-Year Plan focuses on changes in these factors of production.

To combat the problem of escalating costs of imported oil and increasing energy consumption by the industrial sector, the Plan calls for diversifying energy sources by shifting to coal and nuclear power, making major industries more energy efficient through technological improvements and the use of energy-saving machinery, as well as improving the industrial structure by expanding the share of total industrial output produced by less energy-intensive industries.

As Taiwan's industrial structure continues to be upgraded, the need for a labor force that is better educated and more highly skilled is crucial. To that end, the authorities have drafted a "Science and Technology Development Program" to intensify scientific and technological education, recruit overseas Chinese experts to serve the economy, and to strengthen on-the-job vocational training of mid-level technical personnel.

In view of the importance of foreign trade to Taiwan's economy as well as growing export competition worldwide, major emphasis has been placed on export promotion measures. This includes upgrading and controlling the quality of commercial and industrial products to meet the competition, diversifying export markets and expanding the share of existing markets, and reducing tariff rates. Tariff reduction would not only make goods imported from Taiwan's trading partners more competitive but could also help combat inflation by decreasing the retail cost of imports. This decrease in the cost of imports would also help Taiwan's industries, which depend so heavily on imported capital goods and raw materials.

The Ten-Year Plan calls for an annual growth rate of 7.9 percent, which might elsewhere in the world appear optimistic in light of economic slowdown worldwide. However, it is not too ambitious when compared with the past performance of Taiwan's economy which registered an average annual growth rate of 9.2 percent from 1953 to 1979. All previous economic development plans have proceeded on target; it is

anticipated that the present Plan will also be successful.

Twelve Major Projects

Of major significance to Taiwan's economic development has been the completion of the "10 major projects" in the 1970's. These have been a major step in the transition to an industrialized economy. Between 1964 and 1973, economic growth was very rapid, averaging about 10 percent annually, and had largely outgrown the island's infrastructure—growth had outstripped power supplies; trade and travel had outgrown ports, rail facilities, roads, and airports; and industry had to rely on imports of steel and petrochemicals to keep producing. To solve the problem, the authorities initiated 10 projects to bring the infrastructure in line with long-range growth needs. These included the North-South Freeway, Taichung Harbor, Taoyuan International Airport, Kaohsiung Shipyard, nuclear power plants, an integrated steel mill, and a petrochemical development program.

With the completion of these 10 projects, 12 new major endeavors are in various stages of development.

Round-the-Island Railway Networks.—The network, as planned, includes three projects: the north link line, east line track widening, and the south link line. The north link line was completed in December 1979. The track for the east line (Taitung-Hualien) will be widened to be of the same standard as that for the west line. This project will cost about $80 million and will be completed in 1982. The south link line will connect Taitung and Pingtung, a distance of 84 kilometers. Total construction expense is estimated at $135 million. Completion date for the project is June 1986.

THREE NEW CROSS-ISLAND HIGHWAYS.— These highways, totaling 265.6 kilometers, will connect Chiayi and Yushan, Shuili and Yushan, and Yushan and Yungli. This project was started in July 1978 and is to be completed in June 1985. The budget is $102 million.

KAOPING REGION TRAFFIC IMPROVEMENT. —Broadening of highways to meet the needs of growing traffic volume in this highly industrialized region.

CHINA STEEL MILL-FIRST STAGE, SECOND PHASE.—With a total construction fund of $1.4 billion, the China Steel Corporation is slated to install additional equipment with a capacity of producing 710,000 metric tons of hot rolled plate, strip and steel, 690,000 metric tons of cold rolled strip, sheet and base plate per year, and bring total mill production to 3.25 million metric tons.

The United States Steel Corporation was contracted to do the design work. The project is scheduled for completion by June 1982.

NUCLEAR PLANTS #2 AND #3.—Units 1 and 2, with 985-megawatt capacity each, will be installed in Nuclear Power Station #2 in 1981 and 1982 respectively at a total cost of $1.5 billion. Installation of Units 1 and 2, each with 951 megawatts in Nuclear Station #3 will be completed in 1984 and 1985 respectively at a cost of $1.8 billion.

TAICHUNG HARBOR PHASE 2 AND 3.—Phase 2 involves a total construction fund of $192 million to achieve a total cargo handling volume of 4.5 million metric tons annually. This project includes the completion of an outer dike at the southern and northern sides of the harbor together with five deep-water wharves and scheduled for completion in 1980. Some $273 million is slated for phase 3 of the project, which will bring the annual cargo handling volume to 11 million metric tons, and a fishing port. These are scheduled for completion in October 1982.

NEW COMMUNITY AND HOUSING PROJECTS.
—New communities in Linkou, Nanken, Taichung Harbor, Tapingting, and Cheng-Ching Lake are planned to accommodate a population of approximately 314,000. The housing projects call for 88,100 units to be built and 62,516 to be repaired.

IMPROVEMENT OF FARM DRAINAGE SYSTEMS.—This long-term project involves the improvement of the island-wide farm irrigation and drainage systems covering an area of 199,969 hectares. It is expected to be completed this year. The estimated cost is $38 million.

WEST COAST AND RIVER DIKES RECONSTRUCTION.—A long-term program is underway to reconstruct dikes on the west coast and rivers throughout the island.

FOUR-LANE HIGHWAY BETWEEN PINGTUNG AND OLUANPI.—The highway sector between Pingtung and Oluanpi, 110 kilometers, will be rebuilt by 1982 into a higher standard four-lane highway at a cost of approximately $55 million.

FARM MECHANIZATION.—A fund of $110 million has been appropriated to promote farm mechanization between 1978 and 1982.

COUNTY AND CITY CULTURAL CENTERS.—Sizable aquariums. science museums, libraries, and music halls will be built in counties and cities on the island between 1979 and 1983.

Public Role in the Economy

Taiwan has a free market economy based on private ownership as the means of production and distribution. The authorities espouse an effective laissez faire philosophy about Taiwan's private sector, although there is public ownership in certain industries and considerable centralized planning for the economy. The authorities also formulate separate long-range plans for transportation, electric power, and labor force development.

While the authorities have played a very active role in the planning of industrial development, its share of ownership and operation of industries has declined. The private sector now dominates almost all industries except those considered to be of strategic importance (power, petroleum refining, aluminum, steel, and certain chemical facilities). The public corporations include the following: Chinese Petroleum Corporation, Taiwan Metal Mining Corporation, Taiwan Fertilizer Company, Taiwan Power Company, Taiwan Sugar Corporation, Taiwan Aluminum Corporation, China Steel Corporation, Taiwan Machinery Manufacturing Corporation, China Shipbuilding Corporation, BES Engineering Corporation, Taiwan Alkali Company, China Petrochemical Development Corporation, Chung-Tai Industries Corporation, and China Phosphate Industries Corporation.

In addition to overall economic development planning, the authorities have traditionally exercised some degree of control over the economy through specific industry expansion plans, price controls, and other special economic measures taken to achieve stabilization and growth.

Distribution and Sales Channels

Major Marketing Areas

Taiwan's population of almost 18 million is involved in a continuing process of urbanization. More than 27 percent of the island's inhabitants live in the five major urban centers along the west coast: Keelung, Taipei, Taichung, Tainan, and Kaohsiung.

Taiwan's 59,500 manufacturing concerns are concentrated near the capital of Taipei, along the west coast highway and rail lines, and near the industrial districts and export processing zones. Taipei is not only the administrative seat, but it is also the principal cultural and economic center and the hub of transportation. Kaohsiung is the largest port, second largest city, and main industrial complex. It is also the site of the largest of the island's three export processing zones.

While much business can be conducted in Taipei, it is now essential for U.S. suppliers wishing to meet strong Japanese and growing European competition to visit plants and firms outside of Taipei, especially in the Taichung and Kaohsiung areas. Factory managers play important roles in procurement decisions. The possibility of doing business with smaller but growing companies that do not have offices in the capital is enhanced by personal contact.

Importers, Agents, Distributors

There are three basic channels of distribution in Taiwan: private traders (importer-wholesalers who buy and sell for their own account), end-users (manufacturers, public utilities, hospitals, schools, etc.), and publicly owned trading agencies (Central Trust of China and Taiwan Supply Bureau). Any of these may import directly or through local Taiwan commission agents appointed by the supplier.

Imported machinery and equipment are generally sold directly to the end-user or through an agent or importer. Industrial users enjoy certain benefits such as special import credits and utilization of deferred payment instruments. The agent, however, plays an important role in sales promotion and in providing aftersales service. Where official procurement is involved, almost all purchases are accomplished by open bidding. U.S. suppliers interested in opening this market must have capable representatives in Taiwan who can identify requirements for their types of equipment at the planning stage of a project. At U.S. exhibitions in Taipei, however, some purchases are made on the floor during the event.

Local representation in Taiwan is becoming increasingly necessary for successful marketing. U.S. suppliers have a number of alternatives: set up a branch sales office, establish a regional office in another Asian city to service the Taiwan market, appoint one of the American trading firms in Taiwan as representative, or select a local trading firm to act as agent. (See section on authorized importers under Trade Regulations.)

U.S. suppliers seeking representation in the Taiwan market can obtain assistance through the Agent Distributor Service (ADS) offered for a nominal fee by the U.S. Department of Commerce District Offices. The American Trade Center, which opened in 1974, offers "REP-FIND" services for those firms planning to visit Taipei. These services include bonded entry of demonstration equipment and samples, identification and contacting of prospects, and hiring for the account of the U.S. firm a qualified interpreter/secretary. In effect, the visitor will have ready on arrival a temporary office and staff. He/she can devote his/her full time to interviewing agency prospects and potential customers.

Selling Factors

PERSONAL CONTACT.—In selling to manufacturers, personal contact is important not only because of the value Asians place on personal discussions but also because such discussions serve to bring the end-user in touch with new processes and equipment. Taiwan businesspeople are open to new ideas and technology, but their knowledge of what is available may be limited. Frequently, Taiwan firms in the market for equipment to expand and modernize their plants are not aware of what U.S. suppliers can offer, and by default the contract may be given to a Japanese firm. Such occurrences reflect the underrepresentation of U.S. suppliers in Taiwan and the weak dissemination of catalogs and similar information by U.S. manufacturers.

With the competition offered by Japanese suppliers who often visit potential and existing customers throughout Taiwan, American suppliers should consider (1) making visits to Taiwan to augment the efforts of the local representative; (2) holding more demonstrations, seminars, and exhibitions of their products utilizing such facilities as the American Trade Center; (3) increasing distribution of technical data and descriptive brochures to possible buyers, teachers and industry associations (the Commercial Library at the Trade Center displays catalogs of American firms); and (4) improving followup on initial sales leads.

Discussions with potential Taiwan buyers should exhibit knowledge of developments and technology in the customer's industry and underline how the purchase of a U.S. product will specifically benefit the customer's operations, particularly with respect to cost reduction and quality improvement. To sell, it is essential that the supplier be able to talk in terms of solving the problems faced by the industrialist. To make a sales presentation couched in these terms, plant visits are necessary. This gives the supplier the opportunity to talk to plant engineers and other plant managers and thereby help pave the way for a favorable procurement decision. Typically, after consulting plant engineers, purchase decisions are made by the headquarters staff of the company whose offices are often in the downtown area rather than at the plant location.

DELIVERY.—The ability to supply goods in a prompt and timely manner is a positive factor when competing in any market. Delivery schedules take on an added significance in the Taiwan importer's purchasing decisions because prevailing high interest rates become costly if delivery is delayed. Under these conditions, fast turnover and prompt delivery become crucial considerations to the buyer.

Japan, of course, has a very favorable advantage in respect to delivery time. Goods shipped to Taiwan from the United States take considerably longer. While little can be done to reduce transit time direct from the United States, the possibility of maintaining stocks of rapid-turnover goods needs to be given more serious consideration in the future. In addition, American suppliers should make every effort to handle foreign orders on a priority basis to speed delivery as much as possible. Production schedules should be more flexible, promised delivery dates more accurate, and the importer should be made aware that the U.S. supplier is doing everything possible to effect delivery in a timely manner.

SERVICING.—When foreign exchange was scarce in Taiwan and imports were at a minimum, owners of machinery learned to rely on their own resources or those of the many small machine shops to repair machinery. Equipment parts were often replaced by locally tooled spares. This tradition is still prevalent. But with heavy competition among foreign suppliers, servicing has become a more important factor in selling.

Japan's proximity to Taiwan allows Japanese manufacturers to send teams of specialists at low cost to offer skilled advice in installation, maintenance, and repair. Some agents for U.S. firms have qualified maintenance personnel. Emphasis has been given recently to training such personnel in formal programs in the United States. American firms should give consideration to establishing regional servicing facilities that can effectively support equipment sold in Taiwan.

PRICING.—U.S. goods have a reputation in Taiwan for quality and performance; yet the people on Taiwan tend to be very price conscious and often regard the U.S. label as too expensive. Two important factors help to explain this. First, a tight money policy has resulted in very high local interest rates that favor the smallest possible outlay of capital. Second, in an export-oriented economy where finished products must be able to meet keen competition, many local manufacturers feel it essential to buy raw materials and equipment from the least expensive source. Under these conditions, goods from Japan and other countries are frequently considered to be a better buy, even though it is widely recognized that their quality and durability often do not compare with products made in the United States.

The currency realignments of recent years have made U.S. goods more price competitive vis-a-vis the Japanese, but in the face of rising raw material costs U.S. suppliers must continue to take all possible steps to maintain this advantage. U.S. exporters might consider (1) adapting their products for the Taiwan market by stripping them down to the basic production unit; (2) taking into account in their price quotations, as their competitors do, the repeat business generated by the demand for spare parts and components and auxiliary equipment; (3) emphasizing and selling the idea that the superior quality of U.S. products ultimately results in lower production costs; and (4) investigating possible warehousing arrangements that would allow larger shipments and cheaper freight rates for the trans-Pacific voyage.

Franchising

Opportunities for foreign franchising in Taiwan are limited due to a reluctance by the authorities to approve any foreign operation in a field that a local entrepreneur is capable of exploiting. Most types of foreign investment are generally encouraged, but franchising operations are subject to vigorous scrutiny and must fulfill stringent requirements. Only when the technology is unavailable in Taiwan and the authorities feel the proposed venture is needed to improve the standard of living is a favorable decision made; e.g., hotel management and leasing of sophisticated equipment.

There are no laws specifically relating to franchising. Such operations fall under the Statute for Technical Cooperation. Any foreign investment application that does not fall under the Statute for the Encouragement of Investment or the Patent and Trademark Laws is subject to the Statute for Technical Cooperation.

Public Procurement

The Central Trust of China, through its procurement and services mission in New York, imports various products for administrative and military organizations and for public and private enterprises. The Taiwan Supply Bureau handles imports of similar kind for the Taiwan Provincial Government and others. Public enterprises may import for themselves but usually do not.

At the beginning of each fiscal year, every official organization must file a detailed estimate of its import needs for that year. If approved, the necessary foreign exchange is set aside for allocation at the appropriate time. Approval is granted on two conditions: (1) if the proposed import is not available locally in adequate quantity or quality, and (2) if available locally, the domestic price is 15 percent higher than the landed cost (c.i.f. cost, plus import duty and surtaxes).

Once approved, the procurement must be

handled by one of the two public trading agencies, the Central Trust of China or the Taiwan Supply Bureau. In some cases, the end-user may request a "restricted tender" and designate a specific foreign supplier; in cases where suppliers are limited, negotiation may be undertaken. However, a requirement that "approved equals" must be considered tends to inhibit the gearing of specifications to certain suppliers. Thus, in practice, most procurement is open to competitive worldwide bidding.

In the case of bidding, the Central Trust or the Supply Bureau announces scheduled procurement in newspapers and bulletin boards, with invigations to bid made available at advertised localities. Sometimes, notices also are issued abroad throughout the Central Trust's branch offices when open bids call for supplies from a specific country. Otherwise official invitations to bid are obtainable only from the Procurement Division, Central Trust of China, Taipei, Taiwan. Bids may be tendered direct by the foreign supplier or through his/her local Taiwan agent with a power of attorney. Each bidder must pay a bid bond of 1 percent of the bidding price which is returned if the bid is unsuccessful. The successful bidder must deposit a performance bond equivalent to 5 percent of the contract value within 14 days after the notice of award. Cargo delivery must conform to the terms of the contract. Normally, payments are made by letters of credit without the extension of foreign credit to save interest payments in foreign exchange.

In addition to handling all procurement for official end-users, Central Trust and the Supply Bureau also are authorized to buy certain items for their own account. These are usually essential foods or raw materials that, if bought in bulk when the world market price is lowest, would save foreign exchange as well as permit regulation of the supply to be allocated domestically. Included are crude oil and petroleum products, fertilizers, tallow, rubber, leather, timber, glass, cement, motor vehicles, chemicals, metals, foods, and textile materials.

Transportation and Utilities

Taiwan's transportation and communications facilities are among the best in Asia. Situated on the edge of Asia's continental shelf, 750 miles south of Japan, and 200 miles north of the Philippines, Taiwan is at a crossroads of one of the busiest air and sea routes in East Asia. Transportation between Taiwan and the rest of the world is well developed, and major East Asian cities can be reached in a few hours by air. Most of the communications facilities are publicly owned

and operated. They are modern and provide excellent service to the public.

Shipping from the United States

OCEAN FREIGHT.—Taiwan is serviced by scheduled American, Japanese, and other foreign flag lines. Depending on the vessel and the number of stops en route, shipping time from San Francisco to Taiwan ranges from 13 to 15 days. From New York, the time varies from 25 to 30 days. Most imports enter Taiwan via the two ports of Keelung and Kaohsiung. These ports can accommodate oceangoing cargo ships at alongside berths. In the past, the rapid growth in Taiwan's foreign trade placed an increasing burden on existing harbor facilities. During the peak of the shipping season both Kaohsiung and Keelung were so busy that ships had to be diverted to Hualien, where inland transportation facilities were not as well developed. To ease congestion, a new ocean port was constructed in central Taiwan, near Taichung. The first phase of construction was completed in 1976 and the harbor was opened to traffic. When finished in 1982, the harbor will be able to handle an annual volume of 12 million metric tons and accommodate vessels up to 200,000 dead weight tons (DWT).

Keelung can handle vessels of 25,000 DWT, Kaohsiung vessels up to 100,000 DWT, and Taichung can handle vessels to 50,000 DWT. Both Kaohsiung and Keelung have piers for handling containerized cargo, which has been increasing rapidly.

AIR FREIGHT.—Taiwan has two major airports: Chiang Kai-shek International and Kaohsiung. The Chiang Kai-shek Airport, one of the most modern in Asia, is located about 25 miles south of Taipei. It was completed in 1978. In addition to China Air Lines (CAL), the flag carrier, a number of other internaitonal airlines, including Northwest and Flying Tigers, maintain scheduled passenger and aircargo service between Taipei and other major cities in the Far East and the United States, while one all-cargo carrier provides scheduled air freight service to European countries.

Domestic Transportation System

RAILROADS.—Taiwan's railroads are operated by the Taiwan Railway Administration. The rail system consists of two separate lines. The west coast trunk line double track links the main ports of Keelung in the north and Kaohsiung in the south and serves most of the industrial centers and key cities of Taiwan. There are 416 kilometers of branch lines connected to the trunk. The east coast line connects Hualien in the north with Taitung in the south and provides the eastern part of Taiwan with passenger and freight services.

Recent improvements in the railway system include the electrification of signals, the mechanization of freight handling, and modernization of rolling stock.

Additions to the eastern trunk line have produced a uniform gauge round-the-island network. Electrification of the west coast line has substantially increased the system's capacity and reduced the travel time between Keelung and Kaohsiung to 4 hours from 6 hours.

HIGHWAYS.—Taiwan's highway network system, consisting of the freeway, the around-island, the cross-island, the inland, the coastal, and the connecting highways, has a total length of about 17,447 kilometers of roads. Most of these are in the western part of the island. Some 12,137 kilometers (67 percent) are paved, 4,065 graveled, and the remaining 1,244 dirt surfaced. Some are single-lane roads, with traffic passing only in one direction at specified hours during the day.

The volume of highway freight traffic in 1980 was 7.7 billion ton-kilometers, up 7.8 percent over 1979. The number of motor vehicles in Taiwan in 1980 stood at well over 4 million. As a result there was increasing congestion on roads connecting major industrial centers on the west coast. This led to construction of a 230-mile superhighway between Keelung in the north and Fengshan, just south of Kaohsiung, at a cost of $1.2 billion. Completed in 1978, the six-lane highway has reduced the travel time between Keelung and Kaoshiung to less than 6 hours (from 8 to 10 hours). Motor freight is handled by private trucking companies.

PORTS.—Taiwan relies heavily on its ports in both international and interisland trade. There are four international harbors: Keelung, Kaohsiung, Hualien, and Taichung. In addition, a new port is being constructed at Suao in the northeast and is expected to be completed in 1981.

AIRPORTS.—Taiwan's airports are situated at Taipei, Hualien, Taichung, Tainan, Taitung, Taoyuan, Kaoshiung, and Makung (in the Pescadores Islands). Of these, Chiang Kai-shek at Taoyuan (near Taipei) and Kaohsiung are international airports. International traffic at Taiwan's airports has increased greatly, with freight up 10.8 percent in 1980 to 210,000 metric tons. Passenger traffic increased by 3.9 percent to 3.8 million in 1980. There are six local airline companies, two of which, China Air Lines (CAL) and Far Eastern Air Transportation Corporation (FAT), provide scheduled flights to Taiwan's major cities. The other four operate charter flights, lease aircraft, and provide maintenance services.

Utilities

FUEL.—Oil, natural gas, and coal are the major fuels in Taiwan. A number of natural gas wells in northern and central Taiwan are operated by the publicly owned Chinese Petroleum Corporation (CPC). Natural gas pipes have been installed in the major cities in the northern and central areas. In Taipei, natural gas is furnished by the Greater Taipei Gas Corporation. Almost all of Taiwan's petroleum requirements are filled by imports. Petroleum production and sales, including the import of crude oil, are controlled by the CPC.

ELECTRICITY.—Electricity is available in all industrial areas and towns and to about 98 percent of the population. Almost all electric power is supplied by the publicly owned Taiwan Power Company. Production facilities are comprised of thermal (67.8 percent in 1979), hydroelectric (16.8 percent), and nuclear (15.4 percent). The first of six planned nuclear power plants was operating fully in 1979. Although the total installed generating capacity has increased dramatically in less than a decade (from 3.5 million kilowatts in 1972 to 9 million kilowatts in 1980), the growth of industrial production also grew rapidly, with the demand for power increasing. To meet these demands, great effort has been made in the last few years to increase generating capacity, expand transmission facilities, and to use energy more efficiently. Despite the rapid increase in installed capacity, the supply of power is beginning to meet the demands of Taiwan's expanding industries. Power can be curtailed at times during dry seasons. There is also limited reserve to provide for equipment failure. Taiwan Power Company added emergency facilities with a capacity of 500,000 kilowatts to satisfy requirements until the first nuclear power unit came on-stream in early 1979. When the second unit is installed, the nuclear facility will have a capacity of 1.3 million kilowatts. Two other nuclear power plants, with a capacity of 1.9 million kilowatts each, are planned for completion in 1982 and 1985. By 1992, Taiwan expects to triple its 1980 capacity to 27 million kilowatts. Coal-fired thermal plants at Hsinta, Taichung, and Suao are expected to add 6.5 million kilowatts of capacity by 1992.

Taiwan's electricity is alternating current (a.c.) 60 cycles, single and three phase, 110/220 volts.

WATER.—Taiwan's waterworks supply water to about 50 percent of the population. The other half depends on wells or rivers. Only about 10 percent of Taiwan's treated water supply is used for industrial purposes, as many factories develop their own water resources to meet requirements. Rates charged to industrial users vary with each locality. These rates may be adjusted under certain circumstances for larger users of industrial water. Although the island's rainfall is heavy, most of the water runs quickly out to sea. As a result, during the summer months, Taiwan often experiences water shortages that necessitates water rationing. To alleviate the problem, a program to build sufficient new reservoirs over the next 15 years has been activated. All water has a high calcium carbonate content.

COMMUNICATIONS.—A modern communications network spans Taiwan. Its post office is known for its efficient management and prompt delivery of mail twice daily. To keep pace with increasing volume resulting from social progress and economic advance, the postal system has been largely mechanized and a zip code system adopted. Surface mail letters can reach any part of the island the day after mailing, while special delivery letters reach their destinations in 6 to 8 hours.

A well maintained telephone system has more than 2,322,800 million subscribers. More than 97.5 percent enjoy automatic dialing service. The major cities on the west coast are joined by cable and microwave links with direct distance dialing capability. The international telephone network consists of microwave systems connecting Taiwan with Hong Kong and the Philippines and communications via satellite with the United States, Japan, Europe, and Africa. Overseas telegraph service is readily available, and rates compare favorably with those of other Asian countries.

Advertising and Research

Advertising Media

In Taiwan, advertising plays a significant role in promoting and maintaining sales of most products. The print media, radio, television, and the cinema are used for advertising purposes. Space is available in these media at reasonable rates. The biggest share of the advertising dollar goes to the newspapers; television is second. Radio, outdoor advertising, direct mail, magazines, and movies follow in order of usage.

NEWSPAPERS.—Newspapers are the oldest of the mass media and still the most popular mode of advertising. There are 31 daily papers with a combined circulation of approximately 2-1/3 million copies. Most of these are published in Taipei, including two English language newspapers—China Post and China News. The three major papers—the Central Daily News, the China Times, and the United Daily News—are distributed for morning reading. Ads tend to be institutional and heavy with reading matter. Many papers use color for advertising. Retail price advertising is a new practice.

MAGAZINES.—Although there are some 1,485 magazines in Taiwan, these are less sophisticated than the newspapers and less popular as a medium of advertising than newspapers and television. Periodicals of general interest are uncommon. Specialized magazines are prevalent. Women's magazines are popular, and the Chinese edition of *Reader's Digest* has a large circulation.

RADIO.—The availability of inexpensive, mass-produced transistorized radios and the proliferation of radio stations throughout the island make radio a popular medium of advertising in Taiwan. There are 134 radio stations, giving Taiwan the distinction of having the world's largest number of stations per capita and per square mile. Taiwan does not have a newspaper in every small town. The local radio station takes its place.

TELEVISION.—It is the second most popular advertising medium in Taiwan. About 35 percent of the population lives in rural areas, but almost every farmhouse has a television set. There are three island-wide commercial television networks. All programs are produced in color.

MOVIES.—Theater-screen advertising is popular in Taiwan. The people on Taiwan are ardent movie fans. All motion picture houses project advertising strips or stills prior to the feature film. Cinema advertising is especially popular for promoting products to the under-25 age group.

Market Research Services

Local firms set up to provide market research are a comparatively recent development in Taiwan. There are four or five companies in Taipei. Several with foreign affiliates offer a range of services from product and consumer research to trade surveys, advertising and media research, and credit information. Two American firms are International Research Associates (Asia) Ltd. and Needham Standard Advertising (Taiwan) Ltd.

The American Institute in Taiwan supplies the U.S. Department of Commerce with information on the Taiwan economy as well as commercial developments and market information.

ADVERTISING AGENCIES.—Taiwan has a number of advertising agencies to assist in preparing and placing advertisements in the mass communications media. Generally speaking, these agencies sometimes run advertising copy taken from their client—a parent company—rather than create their own. The *1980 Taiwan Buyers' Guide* lists nine agencies and an additional four American agencies are Needham (listed above), Brantingham and Associates, Cambridge Advertising Company, Ltd., and Trade Winds, Inc.

Credit

Availability of Capital

To achieve price stability and orderly economic growth, Taiwan authorities acting through the Central Bank have traditionally sought to encourage savings and restrict credit. The rate of saving has increased steadily.

All local banks, mutual loan and savings companies, credit cooperative associations and credit departments of farmers' associations are authorized to accept demand, savings, and time deposits. Foreign banks are permitted to accept only demand deposits (checking accounts), passbook ordinary deposits, and notice deposits. All appointed foreign exchange banks are authorized to accept Hong Kong and U.S. dollar demand deposits and time deposits for redeposit with the Central Bank. Deposits in other currencies can be accepted only after conversion to Hong Kong or U.S. dollars. Only foreign currency deposits made by bank draft or inward remittance may be transferred abroad (i.e., cash deposits and traveler's check deposits cannot be remitted out).

Taiwan companies rely primarily on banks to supply operating capital and financing for expansion. New Taiwan (NT) dollar loans are available at virtually all financial institutions, but foreign currency financing (including financing of imports) can be transacted only by appointed foreign exchange banks. The cost of NT dollar funds is high. The Central Bank's rediscount rate is 12 percent, and the interest rates that are charged by other banks range from 11 percent per year for export credit to 14.75-16.80 percent per year for short-term unsecured NT dollar loans.

Since exchange controls dictate that every outward remittance (including loan repayments) must be approved, foreign currency loans are subject to a number of restrictions. Under regulations, all long-term (i.e., with a maturity in excess of 1 year) foreign currency financing must be specifically approved by the Central Bank of China and must be denominated in one of the seven authorized currencies. Thus virtually all offshore term obligations incurred by foreign-invested enterprises are for projects outlined in the Foreign Investment Application (FIA), which must specify both the sources of the financing and its purpose.

For normal short-term financing needs, offshore borrowing is restricted to export promotion loans, for which repayment must come from the proceeds of exports. To control the money supply, the Central Bank has established a ceiling for export loans against foreign exchange settlement for each individual foreign bank.

Sources of Financing

BANKING SYSTEM.—The banking system in Taiwan is composed of commercial banks, development banks, investment and trust companies, savings and loan associations, and credit cooperatives. The official and the private sectors are involved in banking. By the end of 1980, loans and investments of the private sector totaled $22.8 billion, up 22.9 percent over 1979.

Taiwan's banking system is supervised by the Central Bank of China. The Central Bank is responsible for regulation of money and credit, management of foreign exchange, bank examination, and economic research. It also acts as the fiscal agent for the central-level administration. Only the appointed foreign exchange banks can process transactions involving foreign exchange; in this capacity they act only as agents for the Central Bank of China.

The Bank of Taiwan is the island's largest bank. Aside from its commercial banking activities, it acts as the fiscal agent for the provisional-level administration, and issues New Taiwan (NT) dollar notes as agent of the Central Bank. The City Bank of Taipei is the fiscal agent for Taipei municipality.

Foreign banks are not permitted to establish more than one branch on Taiwan. Since 1958, 21 foreign banks have opened branches in Taipei. In 1980, for the first time, five European banks opened branches in Taiwan and more are expected in 1981. A list of American banking and financial services institutions can be found in the appendix.

There also are 278 credit departments of farmers' associations, which receive deposits and extend loans to members of the association. They also serve as agents of the Land Bank and the

Cooperative Bank, both of which specialize in the extension of farm credit. Seventy-five credit cooperatives engage in commercial banking for their members while eight medium business banks and savings and loan associations accept deposits from members, and extend loans (usually up to 70 percent) against these deposits.

There are three finance companies in Taiwan. Because standards for the opening of checking accounts are rigid, most of the general public uses cash to settle commercial transactions.

There are two development banks in Taiwan. The China Development Corporation specializes in medium- and long-term lending to private industry, and supplements its capital with credits from international and foreign financial institutions. The Taiwan Land Development and Trust Corporation is owned by the administration, Taiwan Sugar Corporation, and several banks, and finances tidal land reclamation, construction of industrial estates, and other development projects. The Bank of Communications has recently been reorganized as a development bank.

The Export-Import Bank of Taiwan, patterned after the Export-Import Bank of the United States (Eximbank), was established in 1979. The Bank's refinance program offers loans repayable in 2 to 7 years at an annual interest rate of 8.5 percent.

INVESTMENT AND TRUST COMPANIES.— Despite the rapid growth in savings, Taiwan has experienced a shortage of long- and medium-term capital from domestic sources to finance the development of the infrastructure and heavy industry. In addition, many companies have found it necessary to turn to such sources as family connections or the unorganized money market (where interest rates average 16 to 34 percent per annum) to obtain financing. According to some estimates, borrowing from such sources accounts for as much as one-fifth of the domestic capital supply. For this reason, among others, the authorities in early 1971 provided for the establishment of trust and investment companies in Taiwan. Now eight in number, these combine the features of a trust company, an investment bank, a development bank, and an industrial finance company. As such, they are equipped to provide financing in the form of term loans, equipment leasing, and securities underwriting, in addition to other forms of lending. Funds are obtained through the sale of trust certificates, which usually guarantee a minimum rate of return and pay dividends according to the issuing company's profitability.

TAIWAN STOCK EXCHANGE.—The Taiwan stock market, located in Taipei, is still in the developmental stages with only about 102 com-

panies listed. Activity on the exchange varies widely.

The Taiwan Stock Exchange was established in February 1962 with an original capital investment of $250,000. This represented the investment of 43 public and private banks and enterprises. It is the only exchange in Taiwan and operates under the supervision of the Securities and Exchange Commission (SEC). There are 25 member brokers and 9 traders on the floor of the exchange. (Brokers are defined as those who trade in securities on behalf of their clients, whereas traders conduct business for their accounts.) Securities traded include stocks, corporate bonds, and public bonds. The market price for an individual security is determined by bids and offers made by various dealers on the trading floor. To prevent violent price fluctuations in individual securities, the SEC sets a daily limit for the maximum rise or fall of a security's market price.

The stock exchange had not been a significant source of new funds until October 1976. To stimulate investments in the market and to stop a decline in share prices, the SEC announced that income tax on securities transactions would be excluded from annual personal income taxation for 2 years. (This exclusion was extended through 1979.)

PUBLIC FINANCE.—Modest surpluses in budgets last 17 consecutive years produced monetary and price stability. Therefore, Taiwan has not needed to rely on the issuance of bonds to meet deficits. Instead, it has used surpluses to direct funds in low interest loans to various sectors of the economy.

A shift in development toward heavy industry will require increased expenditure in the form of outlays for infrastructure projects. Since nearly half of public expenditures are for general administration and defense, external credits have been sought in the past to finance long-term development projects. In recent years, price stability, together with increases in per-capita income and a highly successful national savings program have made more long-term capital available from domestic sources, so that the authorities have reportedly decided to issue new bonds to help finance important development projects.

FOREIGN FINANCING.—The U.S. foreign aid program played a significant role in the early development of Taiwan's economy. It was terminated in 1963. After that, Taiwan's external capital sources have been mainly the World Bank and Asian Development Bank until 1971 as well as other foreign financial institutions and private foreign investment. Taiwan is becoming increasingly dependent on commercial loans and credits such as those extended by export-import banks. Eximbank has played an important role in financing U.S. exports to Taiwan in recent years. Loans, commitments, and guarantees of the Eximbank aggregated to more than $2.24 billion as of September 30, 1980, the second highest Eximbank exposure in the world, behind Korea.

Importance of Credit in Selling to Taiwan

The ability of U.S. exporters to extend credit to buyers in the Taiwan market is an important factor in the exporter's competitive position vis-a-vis suppliers from other countries. The low level of equity capital in many Taiwan firms, the resultant high debt-equity ratio, and the high interest rates on routine commercial banks all contribute to making credit a very important factor in selling in Taiwan. The general unwillingness of American suppliers to sell on credit, to accept commercial risks unless guaranteed by a bank in Taiwan, are in contrast to the selling practices of Japanese and other foreign suppliers.

For some equipment, it is common for suppliers to extend credit of 60 to 180 days after a satisfactory working relationship has been established. In other cases, longer terms are extended. The financing package is a critical factor in selling major equipment to end-users on the island. Taiwan has been a major recipient of Eximbank credits, and the demand for these outstripped the supply. U.S. suppliers of industrial machinery and other big-ticket items should be prepared to discuss alternative long-term financing arrangements with propsective Taiwan purchasers.

Trade Regulations

Trade Policy

The foreign trade policy aims to diversify markets and sources of supply, broaden Taiwan's export base, and protect local industry. Although endorsing freer trade as an ultimate objective, Taiwan trade policy long has been characterized by protectionism and strict licensing controls on imports. This policy was regarded as necessary to stimulate industrial development and to balance international payments.

Through import licensing and, to a lesser extent, import duties and commodity taxes, the authorities have controlled the volume and composition of imports. Since Taiwan has few natural resources and produces little heavy machinery and equipment, imports of most industrial raw materials and capital goods have always been encouraged. However, Taiwan still discourages imports of nonessentials, such as consumer durables and articles of adornment and recreation. To protect developing industry, the authorities also discourage the importation of goods that can be produced locally.

From time to time, import restrictions are lifted and duty rates lowered as the supply of foreign exchange increases and as local industries become competitive.

Import Tariff System

TARIFF STRUCTURE.—Although Taiwan is not a party to the General Agreement on Tariffs and Trade (GATT), the tariff system is designed in accordance with the rules of the GATT.

A single-column import tariff schedule was maintained until September 1980 at which time a two-tier tariff system was implemented. Under the new system, the second column carries 1,719 items receiving preferential treatment with the average level of tariff reduced from 39.28 percent to 29.4 percent. The reduced rate applies to goods imported from 113 countries and regions that have reciprocal treatment with Taiwan, which includes the United States.

Tariff rates range from free to 100 percent ad valorem. Generally, the duties under 20 percent apply to books, essential raw materials, machinery, and fuels; those between 20 percent and 35 percent to products essential to education and health; those between 35 percent and 80 percent to most manufactured articles; and those above 80 percent to luxury goods.

A few imports are admitted duty free, such as scientific instruments for teaching or research, relief articles, and petty gift parcels.

Under the Statute for Encouragement of Investment, approved industries may obtain exemption of duty on machinery and equipment at the time of establishment or expansion, provided similar domestically manufactured items are unavailable.

Capital equipment, as well as raw materials, can be imported freely into approved bonded factories and into Taiwan's three export processing zones (Kaohsiung, Taichung, and Nantze), as long as these remain there or are reexported.

Information regarding Taiwan import duties applicable to specific products may be obtained free from the East Asia Marketing Group, Office of Country Marketing, International Trade Administration, U.S. Department of Commerce, Washington, D.C. 20230, or from any Department of Commerce District Office. Inquiries should contain a complete product description, including CCCN commodity number.

PAYMENT OF DUTY.—Duties are payable within 14 days from the date of issuance of the duty statement. Under the Statute for Encouragement of Investment, an approved enterprise may, with the prior permission of the Ministry of Finance, import machinery and equipment under an arrangement whereby the customs duties are paid in installments after the machinery and equipment are put into operation.

The dutiable value is defined as the c.i.f. price plus 15-percent customs uplift tax. If customs officials consider the invoiced value to be too low, they may elect to estimate the dutiable value on the basis of the wholesale market value of the goods in local currency at the port of importation. If neither the wholesale market value nor the c.i.f. price is available, the dutiable value may be determined by the customs officials on the basis of the c.i.f. price of the most recent import of the commodity or a similar commodity.

Regulations stipulate that prices must be quoted c.i.f. or c.f. to the ports of Keelung, Kaohsiung, Taichung, or Hualien.

CUSTOMS SURCHARGES.—In addition to the duty, importers must also pay harbor dues, which are 4 percent of the dutiable value of the import. Shipments by air freight and parcel post are exempt from harbor dues.

CUSTOMS CLASSIFICATION.—Taiwan's tariff classification is based on the Customs Cooperation Council Nomenclature (CCCN). Rulings on customs classification of items not shown in the tariff schedule or the dutiable status of goods in doubt, may be obtained in advance of shipment upon written application to the Inspector General of Customs in Taipei. It is desirable to submit samples but not always necessary. However, in the event samples are not possible, photographs, specifications, and descriptive literature may be required.

Internal Taxes

In addition to the import duty and customs surcharges, an importer may also be required to pay a commodity tax.

The commodity tax, which ranges from 3 to 120 percent ad valorem, is levied on 19 types of commodities sold for consumption on Taiwan. The tax rates are the same for imported and locally produced goods, but the bases or taxable values differ. For imported goods, the taxable value is c.i.f. plus 15-percent customs uplift tax plus tariff. The commodity tax on imports is due at the time of payment of the import duty.

The commodity tax need not be paid if the goods are exported or used as raw materials in the manufacture of other taxable commodities (except for leaf tobacco). A refund of the commodity tax paid may be obtained if the goods are exported or are used in the manufacture of export items.

Reexport

Goods may be entered into bonded warehouses on arrival, provided the consignee has made prior application to customs for such entry. Within prescribed time limits, the goods may be reexported free of import duty.

Industries in the export processing zones are exempt from all duties and taxes on imports of machinery, equipment, and materials used in production for export.

Manufacturers in Taiwan using imported raw materials in making goods for reexport are eligible for a rebate of the import duty and commodity tax paid on such imports. Duties levied on goods imported for reexport may be satisfied by having a bonding agency guarantee payment. Rebates range from 70 to 100 percent of the total duty and taxes paid. The time period allowed for reexportation is normally 1 year from importation, but it may be extended in special circumstances up to an additional year. One hundred percent of the duty is rebated on goods reexported within the authorized time limit. When reexported within 6 months after expiration of the time limit, 80 percent is refunded if the duty was actually paid, and 70 percent is written if the d;uty was recorded against a bond. If exportation takes place more than 6 months after expiration of the time limit, the recorded duty may still be written off, but a delinquency fee is levied at the rate of 0.04 percent per day of the recorded amount of the duty, calculated from the day following that on which the duty was recorded.

Nontariff Import Controls

IMPORT LICENSING.—Most goods brought into Taiwan must be covered by an import permit. Under this comprehensive licensing system, merchandise is divided into three categories: permissible, controlled, and prohibited imports. In demand items such as capital equipment, raw materials and essential consumer goods are classified as permissible and import licenses are freely granted, subject to the availability of foreign exchange. Goods on the permissible list include about 97 percent of product classification categories.

Products that tend to compete with locally produced goods are controlled. These can only be imported directly by end-users, who apply to the

Board of Foreign Trade for approval on a case-by-case basis. Items still on the controlled list include certain luxury goods, alcohol, goods subject to regulation and allocation, and goods that the authorities believe should be produced locally in sufficient quantity and quality to meet domestic needs and whose ex-factory prices are not more than 10 percent higher than the c.i.f. prices of comparable imported goods.

Prohibited items are those regarded as dangerous or unessential to the economy. The prohibited list includes only caviar, cloisonne, narcotics, and firearms.

Licenses to import goods on the permissible list are granted liberally. In general, the import permit is issued automatically for permissible goods whether the applicant is a registered trader, end-user, or public trading agency. However, in the case of many items, import permits are granted only to end-users or to public agencies. Items on the controlled list are licensed restrictively. Under Board of Foreign Trade rules, imports of controlled goods generally are handled by public trading agencies. However, for the import of raw materials, machinery, and equipment for their own use, factories and other end-users may import controlled items if they follow certain procedures. (The bulk of all machinery imports are items on the permissible list that traders may import.) Goods on the prohibited list may not be authorized for entry into Taiwan.

The Board of Foreign Trade announced that 2,110 items of commodities were exempt from import licensing in July 1981. The license-exempted items account for about 7 percent of the total importable goods. The list will be made public in the near future.

AUTHORIZED IMPORTERS.—Goods may be brought into Taiwan by any one of three major groups of importers: end-users, public trading agencies, and private traders. End-users include enterprises, both domestic and foreign engaged in manufacturing, mining, fishing, and other fields, as well as hospitals, cultural organizations, and tourist hotels. The main public trading agencies are the Central Trust of China and the Taiwan Supply Bureau.

Registration with the Board of Foreign Trade is required of all traders, who must have minimum paid-in capital of NT$2 million ($56,000) and first export over $200,000 worth of goods in a single year. This restriction limits the number of companies able to import and market foreign goods in Taiwan and encourages the establishment of large, stable import/export operations. A registered trader may import and sell on his or her own account or operate on a commission basis as the local agent of a foreign supplier.

Until November 1977, Taiwan companies acting as agents of foreign firms had to register under the Control of Agents Regulations, in addition to the regular registration with the Board of Foreign Trade. With the abolition of those regulations, foreign suppliers are free to deal directly with end-users; i.e., exclusive local agents are no longer necessary in presenting bids and quotations to buyers. However, designated agents often offer advantages to the American firms seeking to sell in Taiwan. For example, agents can keep abreast of portending and newly issued public invitations to bid, maintain inventories, and provide aftersales service. Consequently, most successful U.S. companies still employ agents.

ENTRY REQUIREMENTS.—Regulations require that all imports be carried by ship except commodities of high value in relation to weight or are urgently needed. Such goods may be shipped by air. Most imports enter at the principal seaports of Keelung, Kaohsiung and Taichung. Goods bound for the east coast may enter at the secondary international seaport of Hualien. Air freight enters through the international airports at Taoyuan and Kaohsiung.

In general, imports must be sent to Taiwan directly from the producing country. With the prior approval of the Board of Foreign Trade, certain goods may be shipped from a free port or entrepot outside the producing country.

Shipping Documents

Documents required for shipments to Taiwan include the commercial invoice, bill of lading or air waybill, packing list, and certificate of origin. Shipments of agricultural products, plants, and animals may require certificates of inspection or quarantine issued in the country of origin and are subject to inspection and quarantine upon importation into Taiwan.

The commercial invoice must show the import license number and must be itemized as to f.o.b. value, insurance, freight, and other charges. There is no requirement as to form. The commodity description and value shown on the commercial invoice must agree with those on the import license.

There is no requirement as to the form of a bill of lading. However, all marks and case numbers appearing on packages must be shown. Customs does not permit the grouping of marks of numbers on a shipment of mixed commodities.

A general discharge permit, secured by the shipping agent prior to the arrival of the cargo, is the authority for the discharge of cargo from the vessel.

The importer may request a survey at the port of export and a certificate stating that the goods meet the specifications of the order.

Remittances for imports are made only against the shipping documents forwarded to designated exchange banks.

Marking and Labeling Requirements

There are no specific regulations governing the labeling of goods imported into Taiwan. It is recommended, however, that labels on containers of prepared foods and pharmaceuticals show a quantitative analysis of the contents.

Rules governing the marking and numbering of foreign import cargo are as follows:

All import cargo must bear a mark of distinctive design, a set of three or more letters or a combination of design and letters indelibly painted, stenciled, stamped, or burned on the packing or on the cargo itself.

For cargo packed in cases, boxes, crates, casks, drums, or cylinders, each container should bear a separate number, which is not repeated for 2 years. Bags or bales also must bear a nonrecurring number, date, or set of three or more letters.

In addition, each package of a consignment must be numbered consecutively. However, numbering is not essential for large lots of cargo except when packed in cases, boxes, or crates, provided that each package of the consignment contains cargo of identical weight.

There are no special packing requirements for goods destined for Taiwan, but precautions against rough handling, pilferage, water seepage, and high heat and humidity are recommended.

Senate Concurrent Resolution 40, adopted July 30, 1953, invites U.S. exporters to inscribe, insofar as practicable, on the external shipping containers in indelible print of a suitable size: "United States of America."

Free Zones and Warehousing

FREE ZONES.—Three zones have been designated for the bonded processing of imported materials into finished goods for export. The free zones are specially established industrial areas. Industries in the three zones are exempt from all duties and taxes on imports of machinery, equipment, and materials used in production for export. Generous tax incentives and necessary facilities are provided to encourage foreign firms to locate in these zones. The Kaohsiung Export Processing Zone is located on a peninsula in the harbor at Kaohsiung. The Nantze Zone is less than 15 miles away, while the Taichung Export Processing Zone is on the west coast in central Taiwan, near the Taichung Port facility.

There are 303 factories in the three zones, including 128 at Kaohsiung, 130 at Nantze, and 45 at Taichung. Employment at the end of 1980 was 80,000 with combined sales of more than $1.2 billion. Because the three zones are operating at capacity, a new export processing zone is planned for a still-to-be-determined location.

Information on these zones is available from the Export Processing Zone Administration. Nantze, Kaohsiung, Taiwan.

Although investors may choose to locate in one of the export processing zones to avoid paying duty on imported capital equipment and raw materials, they may also obtain similar duty-free status for a factory located elsewhere by establishing a bonded enterprise. Customs bonded factories may be established for enterprises that are "exclusively engaged in the manufacture of export goods not for domestic sales and have a paid-up capital of more than NT$5 million" (approximately $140,000).

SCIENCE-BASED INDUSTRIAL PARK.—The Hsinchu Industrial Park was formally opened in late 1980 for the purpose of developing science and technology so as to bring the economy into a higher plateau of sophistication. Located 45 miles south of Taipei and accessible to a number of leading universities and research institutes, the park will be active in project development and engineering as well as being a manufacturing zone. It will operate as a bonded, duty-free area with a computerized inventory control system. So far, 17 firms (foreign and domestic) have been approved to set up plants and factories, and when the park is eventually completed, it will be able to accommodate 200.

WAREHOUSING.—Adequate bonded storage facilities are available in Taiwan and are limited almost entirely to those under the direct supervision of the Inspector General of Customs. Goods may be entered into bonded warehouses on arrival in Taiwan, provided the consignee has made prior application to Customs for such entry. Within prescribed time limits, the goods may be reexported free of import duty.

Samples and Advertising Matter

Samples and other advertising materials are subject to Customs examination. Those of no commercial value are admitted duty free; those having commercial value, such as pens and calendars, are dutiable under the appropriate tariff classifications. Advertising materials should be sent early since customs classification and clearance of such articles often take time.

Technical Standards and Requirements

Three measurement systems are used in Taiwan: Chinese, English, and metric. The metric system has been adopted, but the English system is used locally in some instances.

The Central Bureau of Standards is the highest agency responsible for establishing industrial standards. The Bureau usually adopts or follows the standards of those developed countries which first export or register a product in Taiwan. This has been especially true for instruments and electronic equipment.

Investment in Taiwan

Foreign Investment

Foreign investment in Taiwan from 1952 through 1980 totaled $2.7 billion. This huge amount of foreign and overseas investment can be attributed to the excellent investment climate. Of the total, $1.8 billion was invested by non-Chinese foreigners and the remaining approximately $965 million by "Overseas Chinese." (The Taiwan authorities record investments by non-Chinese foreign residents by country of origin, but investments by foreign residents of Chinese ancestry are recorded as "Overseas Chinese" investments, regardless of country of residence.) Investments in the electrical and electronic industries have absorbed well over $852 million, another $388 million has gone to the chemical industry and machinery and apparatus manufacturing took approximately $164 million. The United States led the list of foreign investors with a total of $776.3 million, and Japan ranked second with $457.7 million.

More than half of the U.S. investment in Taiwan concentrated in the electronics industry, where such firms as RCA, Motorola, and Zenith carry on assembly operations and manufacturers such as IBM, Corning Glass, and General Instrument produce components. Other significant areas of U.S. investment include chemicals, plastics machinery and metal products, banking, insurance, and other services.

Investment Policy

Officials place a high priority on attracting new foreign investment to Taiwan. Recognizing the importance of foreign investment to its development plans, Taiwan has sought to maintain a climate conducive to attracting foreign

business. Foreign investors are needed to provide much of the technology and know-how required to develop sophisticated industries. They are also needed in certain manufacturing industries to help secure overseas markets that may be precluded to local manufacturers.

The investment policy in the past has drawn labor-intensive industries but has now been modified in an effort to shift to more capital-intensive and high-technology industries (including petrochemicals, steel, and shipbuilding). Taiwan offers U.S. firms an attractive investment climate: rapid development of the economy and the increasingly equitable distribution of income; political stability; a comparatively low rate of inflation; established adequate infrastructure and viable supporting industries; an educated, easily trained work force at competitive wages; absence of labor strife; and a positive, consistent attitude of the authorities toward foreign investment in most sectors.

The attitude toward foreign investors is best illustrated by the tax incentives offered, the wide range of services available to investors, and efforts to prepare comprehensive economic plans as a guide for both the public and private sectors. The Statute for Encouragement of Investment provides liberal tax and other incentives to attract foreign capital.

Generally, the authorities welcome foreign investment if it falls in one of the following four categories: (1) those productive and manufacturing endeavors needed in Taiwan; (2) those enterprises with export markets; (3) those which will improve and develop Taiwan's industry, mining, and communications; and (4) those that promote economic and social development.

Taiwan is capable of absorbing considerable new investment. The 12 major industrial and infrastructure development projects offer many opportunities for the sale of U.S. goods and services and, with much of the required capital expected to come from foreign sources, new opportunities for U.S. investment as well. Once the 12 major projects are completed, more funds will be required for development of other aspects of the economy.

Initial contact should normally be made with the Industrial Development and Investment Center (IDIC), a service organization established to assist potential investors in their initial investigations and throughout the investment process. Inquiries may be addressed to the Director, Industrial Development and Investment Center, Ministry of Economic Affairs, 5th floor, 7 Roosevelt Road, Section 1, Taipei, Taiwan. Prospective American investors can contact the following investment service organization in New York that works closely with IDIC: CCNAA Investment and Trade Office, 515 Madison Avenue, New York, New York 10022. Also, representatives at the Coordination Council and its branch offices in the United States offer assistance. (See the section on Sources of Economic and Commercial Information.)

Forms of Business Organization

In Taiwan, the Civil Code stipulates that a business may be organized as a proprietorship, a partnership, or as a company. Any person, whether an alien or a citizen, may engage in business as a sole proprietor, a partner, or as a stockholder. The various forms of doing business are roughly similar to those in the United States and Europe. As far as proprietorships and partnerships are concerned, the only difference is that for tax purposes they are considered entities separate from the individuals constituting them. In other words, the proprietorship or partnership is required to file tax returns, declaring income from all sources including the profits or share in the profits, after tax, of the firm owned or in partnership.

Under the Chinese Company Law, a company is defined as an entity organized and incorporated to make a profit. Companies are divided into five types, differentiated by the number of shareholders and the extent to which they are liable for the obligations incurred by the organization. Almost every important enterprise in Taiwan, commercial and industrial, is organized as a "Company Limited by Shares," which most nearly corresponds to a corporation in the United States. Under this type of business organization, seven or more shareholders are required, each of whom is liable only to the extent of his/her capital contribution.

Foreign companies may set up operations in Taiwan in any of the following forms: As a company organized under the Chinese Company Law and the Statute for Investment by Foreign Nationals, as an ordinary domestic company, as a branch, or by appointing an agent.

FOREIGN INVESTED FIRMS.—Most foreign investors establish their operations in Taiwan as a company organized under the Chinese Company Law and the Statute for Investment by Foreign Nationals. A foreign investor who comes in under the Statute may supply cash, machinery and equipment, raw materials, technical know-how, or a combination thereof to either a new or an existing company. The basic criterion for eligibility under the Statute is that the foreign company engage in general manufacturing, production of exportable products or any other business conducive to the development or improvement of any important industrial, mining, or communication sector of the economy or to the general economic and social development of the country. The investment may be used to set up a new firm or to expand existing facilities through increased capitalization or buying into an existing business. Although joint ventures are frequent, local participation is not required by law or policy.

Both the foreign investor and the enterprise he/she invests in enjoy privileges under the Statute. The original capital and any subsequent approved additions may be repatriated at the rate of 20 percent per year commencing 2 years after the completion of the approved investment plan. A higher percentage rate would require special approval. Dividends may be repatriated at any time, so long as the dividends declared do not exceed the profit or accumulated profit per the tax return. Companies formed under the Statute are exempt from the residence requirement normally applicable to shareholders and officers.

An export enterprise also may avail itself of exchange settlement benefits and exemption from import taxes by applying to locate in an Export Processing Zone.

DOMESTIC COMPANY.—Investors who cannot, or do not wish to, qualify for investment under the Statute for Investment by Foreign Nationals may join in organizing an ordinary domestic company under the Company Law. The foreign shareholders of such a company are not entitled to the incentives and privileges enjoyed by foreign investors under the Statute for Investment by Foreign Nationals—such as repatriation of capital—but otherwise are entitled to all the privileges and are subject to all the responsibilities of local businesses.

BRANCH.—A foreign company may operate in Taiwan by setting up a branch. No foreign company is allowed to do business or to establish a branch office in Taiwan unless it has been recognized by appropriate authorities. Thus, the first step in establishing a foreign branch is to apply for official recognition of the foreign company.

AGENT.—A foreign company may appoint a registered, profit-seeking enterprise in Taiwan as its agent to conduct business on its behalf. A recognized branch office of a foreign company may act as agent for another foreign company.

Licensing Agreements

In addition to equity and loan investment, foreign companies can furnish technical know-how or patent rights to existing enterprises as capital investment or for fixed royalty. Licensing and technical assistance agreements may be concluded between foreign companies and Taiwan firms covering a wide range of industrial and consumer products. Such an agreement whereby the foreign company agrees to furnish the Taiwan firm with technical skill or patent rights, not as capital stock but for fixed royalty, falls under the Statute for Technical Cooperation. Japan has been the leader in the field of licensing and technical agreements in Taiwan.

Incentive Legislation

The incentive laws, procedures, and guidelines for foreign investors are set forth in the Statute for Investment by Foreign Nationals and the Statute for the Encouragement of Investment. Incentives are provided for foreign investment in a wide range of industries with special attention being given to certain high-priority industries: electrical machinery, automotive equipment, precision machine tools, minicomputers, computer terminals and peripherals.

In addition to tax incentives (discussed below), Taiwan offers foreign investors the same incentives that are afforded domestic investors. They are allowed the following: 100-percent ownership of the invested enterprise; remittance of all net profits and interest; annual repatriation of 20 percent of the invested capital permitted commencing 2 years after the completion of the approved investment plan; and to employ foreign nationals in supervisory, technical, or advisory positions.

Investment Procedures

The simplification of investment procedures is one of the most important measures adopted in Taiwan to improve the investment climate. Generally, a decision on approval will be made with 3 to 4 weeks following the formal submission of the application, provided all the necessary supporting documents, certificates, and credentials are attached.

Prospective investors should perform the following tasks:
- Apply to Investment Commission of the Ministrty of Economic Affairs, 73 Kuling Street, 7th Floor, Taipei, Taiwan. In case the projected enterprise is to be established in an export processing zone, apply directly to the Export Processing Zone Administration, MOEA (Nantze, Kaohsiung Hsien, Taiwan)
- Remit capital into Taiwan after the investment application is approved (notify the Commission after remittance is made)
- Apply to Investment Commission for company registration
- Apply to the local administration for registration as a profit-seeking enterprise
- Purchase or lease land for plant site. Investors may apply for assistance from the Industrial Development Bureau of the Ministry of Economic Affairs
- Apply to the local administration for registration of the establishment of and for a license for construction of factories
- Apply to the regional office of the Taiwan Power Company for supply of electricity
- Apply to the local municipal or county government for factory registration.

A wide range of investment services is offered free of charge by the IDIC to investors and potential investors. Such services include, but are not limited to the supply of data and information for pre-investment studies; arrangement for potential investors to visit related factories and agencies in charge of matters relating to investment; assistance in the selection and purchase of industrial land; assistance in applying for enjoyment of various benefits and incentives provided by law; and after an investment is made, assistance in solving problems the invested enterprise may encounter.

An investor in Taiwan can always be assured of local support for his/her productive activities. Experienced contractors can undertake almost all types of construction. Financing facilities are available from a number of foreign banking institutions. There are also law offices and accounting firms in addition to advisory agencies such as data processing centers and management and engineering consultants capable of performing extensive services to meet operational requirements.

Industrial Property Rights*

Taiwan is not a party to any of the international conventions on patents, trademarks, and copyrights. The bilateral Treaty of Friendship, Commerce, and Navigation of November 4, 1946 remains in effect and entitles U.S. citizens to the same treatment for patent and trademark rights in Taiwan as Taiwan extends to its own people The protection provided U.S. firms under the Treaty is less extensive than that available under the international conventions.

Patent, trademark, and copyright registrations may be obtained by filing applications with Taiwan authorities pursuant to the Patent Act of 1949, as amended in 1979; the Trademark Law, effective 1972; and the Revised Copyright Law of 1964, as appropriate. Inquiries regarding patent and trademark matters should be addressed to the National Bureau of Standards, 61-1

*Prepared by Foreign Business Practices Division, Office of International Services, International Trade Administration, U.S. Department of Commerce.

Sungchiang Rd., Taipei, Taiwan. Inquiries on copyrights should be addressed to the Copyright Screening Committee, Ministry of Interior, 107 Roosevelt Road, Section 4, Taipei, Taiwan.

PATENTS AND TRADEMARKS.—Foreign persons may file for patents through an authorized agent of Chinese nationality on any new invention of productive utilization value. The term of patent protection for an invention is 15 years from publication date. Applications are examined for novelty. Prior publication or public use of the invention destroys its patentibility. Applications are published for a 3-month opposition period. If a patent is not adequately worked, its compulsory licensing or revocation is possible. A patent confers upon the holder exclusive rights to manufacture, sell, or use the patented item.

Trademark protection can be obtained for specially distinctive words, devices, marks, or combinations thereof which meet the approval of the authorities. The granting of a trademark confers upon the registered owner the exclusive right of its use for 10 years from the date of registration, renewable for 10 years at a time. The first applicant is entitled to registration. Applications are examined and published for a 3-month opposition period. Trademark registrations must be used within 1 year of registration and such use not discontinued for 2 years. A foreigner having no residence or place of business in Taiwan cannot register a trademark unless he/she appoints an agent having a residence or place of business in Taiwan.

COPYRIGHTS.—Taiwan is not a member of any international copyright convention, and reproduction of foreign works not copyrighted in Taiwan is prevalent. A specific copyright registration in Taiwan may be necessary on a work to prevent unauthorized reproductions.

Taxation

Although there are 19 taxes levied, Taiwan offers foreign investors a number of tax exemptions and benefits under the Statute for Encouragement of Investment.

Major taxes relating to foreign investment are discussed below.

INCOME TAX.—A Business Income Tax is levied on the net profit of a productive enterprise after deduction of all costs, expenses, losses and other taxes. Rates range from 15 to 25 percent.

A consolidated Income Tax is levied on an individual's gross consolidated income. Rates range from 6 to 60 percent. For a person having no domicile or residence within Taiwan, 15 to 35 percent of the dividends received from invested enterprises is withheld.

CUSTOMS DUTY.—This is levied on the basis of the duty paying value (c.i.f. value plus 15 percent) of imported goods.

Tariff rates on imported machinery and equipment are about 15 percent, and on raw materials, 11 percent.

BUSINESS TAX.—This is levied on a profit-seeking enterprise's gross business revenue each month. Rates vary with different types of businesses: manufacturing industries, 0.6 percent; transportation services, 1.2 percent; hotels, 1.5 percent; and banking institutions, 4 percent.

LAND TAX.—Levied on the assessed land value each year. The rate is 1.5 percent for factory operations.

HOUSE TAX.—Levied on the assessed value of buildings. Rates vary with types of buildings: business buildings, 3 percent; residential buildings, 1.38 percent; and buildings for manufacturing operations, 1.5 percent.

HARBOR DUES.—These are levied together with customs duty on imported goods that pass through any harbor of Taiwan. The present rate is 4 percent of duty-paying value of imported goods. On those imported raw materials for processing and export, harbor dues are only 1 percent.

Incentives

The Statute for Encouragement of Investment also provides a broad range of incentives for a variety of industries. These include the following:

- Business income tax exemption for 5 years or accelerated depreciation of fixed assets for newly established encouraged productive enterprises
- Business income tax exemption for 4 years or accelerated depreciation of fixed assets for encouraged productive enterprises at the time of increasing capital and expanding machinery and equipment
- Business income tax limited to 22 to 25 percent of total annual income
- Export sales exempted from business tax
- Special encouraged industries are exempted from import duty on imported machinery and equipment
- Productive enterprises may apply for installment payment of import duty on imported machinery and equipment
- Import duties paid or payable on imported raw materials used in export products may be refunded or bonded.

As of July 1977 new tax laws have been passed to further encourage investment. Several laws worth noting are explained below.

Besides the 4- and 5-year business income tax exemption laws, the new law allows important eligible enterprises to defer the beginning of the tax-free period for up to 4 years after the utilization of the new equipment. Eligible industries are classified as capital intensive or high-technology industries. This term along with "important" are defined in the Categories and Criteria of the Productive Enterprises Eligible for Encouragement.

Another beneficial regulation provides that research and development expenditures are allowed to be listed as legitimate business expenses.

Subject to their meeting certain general and special criteria, the following manufacturing industries are eligible for tax incentives:

- Food processing
- Pulp and paper
- Rubber processing
- Chemicals/petrochemicals
- Nonmetallic mineral processing
- Basic metals
- Machinery
- Electrical equipment
- Electronic equipment
- Transportation equipment
- Ceramics
- Textiles
- Construction materials
- Clinical and surgical instruments
- Photographic and optical instruments
- Watches, clocks, and parts thereof
- Precision instruments

Potential investments that do not fall into these categories but meet criteria similar to those used in establishing the foregoing list also may qualify for incentives, including the following:

- Handicrafts
- Mining
- Forestry
- Fishery
- Agriculture
- Transportation
- Warehousing
- Public utilities
- Housing
- Tourist hotel operations
- Heavy construction.

Labor Force

Taiwan, known for its plentiful supply of inexpensive labor, has recently entered a new phase. A shortage of both skilled and unskilled workers has emerged and can be expected to continue. The problem is a result of the rapidly expanding economy and is exacerbated by the large num-bers of workers required to complete the major infrastructure and overseas projects. As these projects are completed over the next few years, many of these workers will become available to industry.

At the same time, however, there are always new major projects on the horizon necessary to accommodate future industrial development. If the economy continues to expand rapidly, then the labor shortage will become chronic. In 1980, the unemployment rate was only 1.9 percent; since 1968, it has risen over 2 percent in only 1 year when the economy was recovering from the 1974 oil crisis. In some industries, electronics in particular, the labor shortage is already serious. Although authorities estimate that the additional potential labor force is 3 million above the current 6.5 million workers, industries hard hit by the labor shortage have not been able to attract significant numbers of workers from the potential to the actual labor force. To obtain workers, companies have been forced to compete with each other, thereby raising the wage rates. Supervisory and management personnel also are in short supply.

Nevertheless the labor force is one of Taiwan's major resources. Virtually all potential workers coming into the job market have a minimum of a ninth grade education with emphasis on technical and vocational training. Trained personnel will have as much as 6 years of additional formal education. Workers are diligent and adept at learning new skills.

PAYMENTS AND BENEFITS.—While wages have been rising over the past few years, both skilled and unskilled labor of manufacturing is available at a rate, which is 20 percent of comparable U.S. rates, even after adjustment for productivity. Supervisors and executives are paid accordingly. An increase of at least 25 percent per year is forecast for the foreseeable future. This is in line with other Asian wage trends.

Fringe benefits for workers in Taiwan are 20 to 25 percent of the base wage rate. Benefits include an annual bonus of about 1 to 3 month's salary, uniforms, and insurance (80 percent paid by the company). Many employers provide their workers with free accommodations or a meal allowance.

WORKING HOURS.—The standard work week in factories is six 8-to-10 hour days. While two-shift operation is not common as yet in Taiwan, this is becoming a reality as industries become more capital-intensive. While productivity is still somewhat lower than that of equivalent U.S. workers, it is improving rapidly primarily because of improvements in manufacturing techniques and management.

MANPOWER DEVELOPMENT PROGRAMS.—
In an effort to keep manpower supply in balance
with demand in the face of Taiwan's high rate of
economic growth, a highly organized manpower
development planning process has been adopted.
Projections of industrial labor demand and
supply, by industry and by occupation, are made,
which are available for annual periods. To meet
projected needs, the authorities have developed a
variety of vocational education and training programs aimed at keeping the output of trained
manpower closely aligned with emerging requirements. Highest priority is being given to the
training of workers in the metalworking crafts—
e.g., tool makers, machinists, plumbers, welders,
skilled workers in precision instrument manufacture, electricians, and related electrical and
electronics workers. In addition to publicly
operated schools, cooperative training programs
and special courses are being given increasing
attention.

Most larger firms established in Taiwan
operate a variety of in-plant training programs
as a matter of self-interest. The smaller and
medium-sized firms, however, have generally
neglected such activity, offering training to new
workers strictly on an on-the-job basis. Accordingly, to encourage such firms to strengthen their
activities, a law passed in April 1973 requires all
firms employing 40 or more persons to contribute
1.5 percent of their payroll to the National Vocational Training Fund Board, which finances
training activities for contributing companies.
Although this statute is still in effect, contributions to the Fund have been suspended since
December 1974.

Labor Relations

Taiwan does not have an active labor movement and the authorities do not interject themselves into wage negotiations. Strikes are
virtually unheard of. The average employment
period for production work is 3 years.

Both industrial and craft unions operate in
Taiwan under the Trade Unions Act of 1949, but
unionism is not prevalent in Taiwan. For certain
industries and all levels of public employment,
unions may not be formed.

The unions' primary function is in the settlement of disputes, usually arising out of the dismissal of workers. The procedure for settlement
begins with a factory council composed of labor
and management representatives. If the dispute
cannot be resolved satisfactorily at this level, it is
submitted first to an ad hoc conciliation board
and ultimately, though rarely, to an ad hoc
arbitration board whose decision is binding.

Strikes and lockouts are permitted by law in
nongovernmental enterprises other than public
utilities, transportation, and communications,
except in times of national emergency or during
conciliation and arbitration proceedings. In
practice, however, since Taiwan continues to be
technically and legally in a state of emergency,
strikes are prohibited.

Investment in Industrial Districts

To encourage investment and assist investors
in the acquisition of plant sites, more than 50
tracts of land with good accessibility and power
and water supplies have been designated as
industrial land. As such their use is not restricted
to agriculture, but they may be purchased for
factory sites or other commercial purposes. The
assessed value serves as a guide to the purchase
price, which is determined by negotiation
between buyer and seller. Land experts of the
IDIC help investors locate plant sites and
negotiate purchases in case private land is
involved. If an agreement cannot be reached, the
buyer can apply for land requisition at an
arbitrated price, but this is usually a lengthy
process. All arrangements for roads, sewage
systems, drainage systems, and public utilities
must be made by the buyer.

Because of the difficulties involved in negotiating a purchase price and arranging for utilities,
most investors have chosen to locate their plant
facilities in one of the island's 15 industrial
districts, or in one of the 3 export processing
zones. The districts, each administered by the
agency that developed it, are complete with
roads, drainage and sewage systems, water
supply (either from city mains or from district
waterworks), electric power, telecommunications, road lights, sewage treatment plants, and a
service center. In addition, there are also
standard factory buildings available for lease to
investors. Prices of land within the industrial
districts are generally quite reasonable, as they
are set just high enough to cover the cost of development. Arrangement of public utilities
building permits, and the like is eased by dealing
through the district administration.

Guidance for Business Travelers

Entrance Requirements

Visitors to Taiwan must have a valid passport
and a visa. Visas may be obtained gratis from
Taiwan's representative offices overseas. Transit
visas are valid for 3 months from the date of issue
and are good for a 2-week stay; they may not be

extended. Tourist visas are valid for 6 months from the date of issue and are available in two types. Type A is good for a 1-month stay and may be extended for one additional month. Type B is valid for 2 months and may be extended twice for 6 months. Business people who wish to stay for more than 6 months must apply to the Ministry of Foreign Affairs in Taipei for an entry visa.

Quarantine regulations require the traveler to produce a current (not more than 3 years old) smallpox vaccination certificate upon arrival. However, it is advisable for the traveler to have an international immunization record and to keep it up to date. Travelers to Taiwan who are from, or have passed through, cholera-infected areas require inoculations more than 7 days but less than 6 months prior to arrival.

Pertinent Treaties

A Treaty of Friendship, Commerce, and Navigation reciprocally grants rights of residence and trade in Taiwan and the United States and confers unconditional, most-favored-nation treatment in commercial matters.

Foreign Exchange Controls

Taiwan's strict exchange control system is administered by the Foreign Exchange Department of the Central Bank of China. The Central Bank regulates all foreign exchange transactions and designates authorized foreign exchange banks. Unlimited conversion from authorized currencies into New Taiwan (NT) dollars is permitted but this function and foreign currency financing of imports and exports is limited to appointed foreign exchange banks. Generally, all transactions involving foreign currencies require a license or prior permission.

The basic unit of exchange is the NT dollar. The NT dollar has traditionally been pegged to the U.S. dollar, most recently at the rate of NT$38=US$1. The exchange rate is allowed to float within a limited range since the establishment of a foreign exchange market early in 1979.

No more than NT$8,000 in cash may be brought in or taken out of Taiwan. Traveler's checks and bank drafts need not be declared. Unlimited foreign currency may be brought in and, if declared on arrival, may be taken out. Without a declaration, not more than $1,000 in cash or the equivalent in any other foreign currency may be taken out.

Foreign currencies may be exchanged at designated banks, hotels, and shops. To convert NT dollars back to foreign exchange just prior to departure from Taiwan, appropriate exchange conversion receipts proving prior conversion of foreign currency to NT dollars must be in the foreigner's possession.

Language, Business Hours, Holidays

COMMERCIAL LANGUAGE.—While Mandarin Chinese is the official language, a southern Fukien dialect known as Taiwanese is spoken by the majority of the people. Mandarin Chinese is the language of business; however, many businesspeople speak and understand English to some extent, and many business firms correspond in English. Japanese is also widely used. Catalogs, promotional literature, and instructions are acceptable in English.

BUSINESS HOURS.—Most offices, public and private, are open from 8:30 a.m. to 5:30 p.m. on weekdays with 1 hour for lunch, but close at 1 p.m. on Saturday. Banks close at 3 p.m. daily and are open until 1 p.m. on Saturday. Department stores, shops, restaurants, hospitals, barber shops, or other service establishments remain open as late as 10 p.m. and are open over weekends and even on public holidays, except for Chinese New Year.

HOLIDAYS.—Public and business offices close on the following statutory holidays: January 1 and 2, New Year Celebration; Chinese New Year's Eve (afternoon), Chinese New Year Holiday, and following day (moveable dates); March 29, Youth Day; April 5, Tomb Sweeping Day; Dragon Boat Festival (afternoon) (moveable date); Moon Festival (moveable date); September 28, Confucius' Birthday; October 10, National Day; October 25, Taiwan Retrocession Day; October 31, Chiang Kai-shek's Birthday; November 12, Dr. Sun Yat Sen's Birthday; and December 25, Constitution Day.

Sources of Economic and Commercial Information

General information on the Taiwan market (i.e., economic trends, commercial developments, production, and trade) may be obtained from the East Asia Marketing Group, Office of Country Marketing, International Trade Administration, U.S. Department of Commerce, Washington, D.C. 20230.

The American Institute in Taiwan (AIT), an unofficial organization incorporated under the laws of the District of Columbia, represents U.S. interests in Taiwan. Economic/Commercial Officers are available to brief and assist American business people visiting Taiwan, and they may be contacted at the American Trade Center.

The American Trade Center in Taipei is located at 261 Nanking East Rd., Section 3. The telephone number is 781-2171; TELEX number is 23890 USTRADE.

Representation in the United States

The Coordination Council for North American Affairs (CCNAA), the unofficial counterpart to AIT, represents Taiwan's interests in the United States. CCNAA is headquartered at 5161 River Road, Washington, D.C. 20016. The Economic Division is located at 4301 Connecticut Avenue, N.W., Washington, D.C. 20008. The telephone number is (202) 686-6400. Branch offices of the CCNAA are in the following cities:

Atlanta, Georgia 30303: Peachtree Center, Suite 1602 Cain Tower, 229 Peachtree Street, N.E. Telephone (404) 522-0182/0183

Chicago, Illinois 60606: 222 N. Dearborn Street, 9th Floor,
Telephone: (312) 372-1213/1214

Honolulu, Hawaii 96817: 2746 Pali Highway, Telephone: (808) 595-6347/6348

Houston, Texas 77002: 810 World Trade Building, 1520 Texas Avenue,
Telephone: (713) 228-0059

Los Angeles, California 90010: 3660 Wilshire Boulevard, Suite 1050,
Telephone: (213) 389-1215

New York, New York 10017: 801 Second Avenue, Telephone: (212) 697-1250

San Francisco, California 94104: 300 Montgomery Street, Suite 535,
Telephone: (415) 362-7680

Seattle, Washington 98104: 413 Lyon Building, 607 Third Avenue,
Telephone: (206) 682-4586.

In addition, the CCNAA Investment and Trade Office is at 515 Madison Avenue, New York, New York 10022. The telephone number is (212) 752-2340. The China External Trade Development Council—with offices in New York, Chicago, Dallas, Los Angeles, and San Francisco—has information on Taiwan manufacturers and suppliers.

Publications

The following is a list of publications available from public and private sources to provide the trader and investor with detailed economic and commercial information on Taiwan.

PUBLIC.—
Board of Foreign Trade, *Foreign Trade Handbook.*

Central Bank of China, Economic Research Department, *Taiwan Financial Statistics Monthly.*

China Productivity Center, *Taiwan Buyers-Guide.*

Directorate-General of Budget, Accounting and Statistics, *Commodity-Price Statistics Monthly, Taiwan District. Monthly Bulletin of Labor Statistics. Monthly Statistics, National Income: National Accounts in Taiwan* (annual). *Statistical Abstract.*

Economic Planning Council, *Industry of Free China* (monthly). *Long-Range Economic Development Plan, 1971-80. Taiwan Statistical Data Book* (annual).

Export Processing Zone Administration, *Export Processing Zones: Development, Production and Sales.*

Industrial Development and Investment Center. *A Brief Introduction to the Investment Climate. Customs Law. Economic Progress and Investment Climate. Foreign-Invested Enterprises in Taiwan. Regulations Governing Customs Bonded Factories. Statute of Encouragement of Investment. Enforcement Rules of the Statute for Encouragement of Investment. Statute for Investment by Foreign Nationals. Statute for Technical Cooperation. Taxes in Taiwan.*

Inspectorate-General of Customs, Statistical Department, *The Trade of China (Taiwan),* annual. *Monthly Statistics of Trade.*

PRIVATE.—
China Publishing Company, *China Yearbook.*

Chung Hwa Information Service, *Free China Weekly.*

Citibank, *Investment Guide to Taiwan.*

Deloitte Haskins and Sells, *Taxation in Taiwan.*

Far Eastern Economic Review, *Yearbook, Review of Taiwan.*

Importers and Exporters Association of Taipei, *Taiwan International Trade* (monthly).

Pan-Orient Corporation, *Business and Industry Taiwan* (weekly).

Price Waterhouse, *Doing Business in Taiwan.*

SGV-Soong and Company, *Doing Business in Taiwan* (annual).

The Research Institute of America, *The Business Guide to Taiwan.*

TSU, E.T., *Business Directory of Taiwan.*

APPENDIX
List of U.S. Banking and Financial
Services Institutions in Taiwan

American Express International Banking Corporation
Taipei Branch
137 Nanking East Rd.
Section 2, Taipei
Telephone: 563-3182

Bank of America N.T. & S.A.
Taipei Branch
205 Tun Hua North Rd.
Taipei
Telephone: 731-4111

Bank of California
8 Hsiang Yang Rd.
Taipei
Telephone: 311-0551

Bankers Trust Company
8/F, 46 Kuan Chien Rd.
Taipei
Telephone: 361-7228

The Chase Manhattan Bank, N.A.
Taipei Branch
72 Nanking East Rd.
Section 2
Taipei
Telephone: 521-3262

Chemical Bank
Taipei Branch
261 Nanking East Rd.
Section 3
Taipei
Telephone: 741-1181

Citibank, N.A.
Taipei Branch
742 Min Sheng East Rd.
Taipei
Telephone: 731-5931

Continental Illinois National Bank & Trust Company
  of Chicago
62 Nanking East Rd.
Section 2
Taipei
Telephone: 521-0242

The First National Bank of Boston
Taipei Branch
5/F, 137 Nanking East Rd.
Section 2
Taipei
Telephone: 563-3443

Irving Trust Company
Taipei Branch
10 Chung King South Rd.
Section 1
Taipei
Telephone: 311-4682

Kaplan, Russin, Vecchi & Parker
5F, Citicorp Center
742 Min Sheng East Rd.
Taipei
Telephone: 752-8756

Manufacturers Hanover Trust Company
4/F, 261 Nanking East Rd.
Section 3
Taipei
Telephone: 772-2562

Morgan Guaranty Trust Company
  of New York and Taipei, Taiwan
Bank Tower, 10th Floor
205 Tun Hua North Rd.
Taipei
Telephone: 772-2333

Ranier National Bank
Taipei Branch
125 Sung Chiang Rd.
Taipei
Telephone: 536-3244

Seattle-First National Bank
Taipei Branch
333 Nanking East Rd.
Taipei
Telephone: 773-3433

Security Pacific National Bank
261 Nanking East Rd.
Section 3
Taipei
Telephone: 752-4237

Taiwan First Investment & Trust Co., Ltd.
4/F, 742 Ming Shen East Rd.
Taipei
Telephone: 752-5353

United California Bank
Taipei Branch
221 Nanking East Rd.
Section 3
Taipei
Telephone: 752-5353

Market Profile—TAIWAN

Economic Overview

Taiwan's economic growth has recently been lagging compared with its 9 percent per year average of the last 30 years. GNP growth in 1981 was 5.4 percent; the forecast for 1982 is 3.6 percent. Investment growth was positive at 2.8 percent, but much lower than 1980's growth of 15.5 percent. Inflation has been reduced substantially to about 5 percent. Unemployment in 1981 remained very low, averaging 1.35 percent, but underemployment is on the rise, especially in the agricultural sector.

Major Developments

A new Joint Industrial Investment Service Center has been established to assist prospective and already resident foreign investors. In addition, the authorities are considering the establishment of a free trade zone in Taiwan, which would offer incentives for high technology, nonpolluting industry and provide bonded warehousing and other services.

Foreign Trade

Best U.S. Sales Prospects. — Electronics industry production and test equipment, energy conservation equipment, laboratory testing equipment, computers, and precision instrumentation.

Major Suppliers (1981). — Japan (28 percent) United States (22.5 percent).

Principal Exports. — Textile products, electronic/electrical goods, machinery, footwear, plywood and furniture, and processed foods.

Major Markets (1981). — United States (36.1 percent) and Japan (10.9 percent).

Finance

Currency. — New Taiwan dollar; NT $39=$1.

Domestic Credit. — Secured loan rate 18 percent in 1981 and expected to be 15.25 percent in 1982.

National Budget. — Proposed FY 1983 (ending June 30, 1983) expenditures $8.9 billion, mainly for defense, economic development, and social services. Deficit, $1.25 billion

Balance of Payments. — Balance of payments showed a positive $1,336 million at end of 1981, up substantially from 1980 balance of $241 million.

Foreign Investment

Private foreign investment approved 1953-81, $3,114 million; from the United States, $979 million, mainly in electronics/electrical products and chemicals.

Investment Prospects. — Investment climate favorable with liberal tax incentives in approved manufacturing sectors. Emphasis on technology and capital-intensive projects,

Basic Economic Facilities

Transportation. — Railroad system of 5,100 kilometers and highway system of 17,488 kilometers (as of 1980). Port facilities: Kaohsiung, Keelung, Taichung, and Huallen.

Import—Export Trade*
(millions of U.S. dollars)

	1979	1980	1981
Total Imports (c.i.f.)	14,774	19,733	21,200
Imports from the U.S.	3,381	4,673	4,766
Manufactured goods	4,577	5,765	6,738
Agricultural and industrial raw materials	10,197	13,968	14,461
Total Exports (c.i.f.)	16,103	19,811	22,611
Exports to the U.S.	5,652	6,760	8,163
Manufactured goods	14,581	17,990	20,859
Agricultural goods	1,523	1,821	1,743

*Taiwan data.

Principal Imports from the U.S. — 1981*
(millions of U.S. dollars)

	Value	Percent of Total
Machinery and tools	1,459	30.6
Electrical machinery and equipment	624	13.1
Chemicals	536	11.2
Soybeans	383	8.0
Corn	293	6.1
Transportation equipment	154	3.2
Wheat	133	2.8
Cotton	117	2.5

*Taiwan data.

Communications. — Good international cable, telex, and telephone facilities. Three television networks, 134 radio stations, and satellite links.

Power. — Power generation was 40.1 billion kilowatt hours in 1981. Capacity was 10,077 megawatts in 1981 and will need capacity of 15,836 megawatts by 1985.

Natural Resources

Land. — 13,895 square miles; about 25 percent cultivated; many mountain peaks over 10,000 feet.

Minerals. — More important minerals: coal, natural gas, marble, limestone, glass sand, copper, and salt (sea).

Forestry. — A major resource, but inaccessibility in steep mountain areas has held back exploitation.

Population

Size. — 18.1 million end 1981; annual growth rate of 1.92 percent.

Labor Force. — About 6.9 million end 1981; unemployment rate, 1.35 percent; some underemployment.

Education. — Free and compulsory to ninth grade; 101 colleges/universities. Nearly universal literacy.

Language. — Mandarin Chinese (official). Principal local dialects; Taiwanese and Hakka.

Market Profile— TANZANIA

Foreign Trade

Imports.—$1.197 million in 1981; $1,046 million in 1982. Major suppliers in 1981 by percentage: United Kingdom, 19.6; Japan, 9; West Germany, 8.3; and Netherlands, 3.7. Principal imports: machinery, transportation equipment, metals, fuel, textiles, wearing apparel, food, beverages, and tobacco. Imports from United States: cereals, grain, seeds, agricultural tractors, agricultural chemicals. Total $41.2 million in 1982.

Exports.—$578 million in 1981; $480 million in 1982. Principal markets in 1981 by percentage: West Germany, 14.6; Indonesia, 10.5; United Kingdom, 8.7; and Italy 4.9. Major exports: coffee, spices, sisal cordage, and edible nuts. Exports to United States: $29 million in 1982.

Trade Policy.—State-owned Board of Internal Trade imports and distributes most products other than textiles, stationery, toys, books, and office equipment. Stringency on import controls reflects stern financial picture.

Trade Prospects—Earthmoving, leveling, construction, telecommunications, mining and dairy equipment, agricultural tractors, trucks, grain storage facilities, machinery for cement, textile, and paper plants seem to have the best prospects.

Foreign Investment

U.S. investment guaranty agreement in effect with mainland Tanzania. Foreign investment restricted to certain sectors; some areas reserved for public and semipublic enterprises. Fiscal incentives; import duty relief. Direct U.S. investment, $15 million in 1978. State tourism, spare parts and highly technical intermediate industries are good prospects. No foreign holdings are permitted on Zanzibar.

Finance

Currency.—Tanzanian shilling (TSh 12.15=US$ in Oct. 1983). Money supply: $2.250 million at yearend 1981.

Domestic Credit and Investment.—State-owned National Bank of Commerce is the only commercial bank. National Investment Bank, Tanganyika Development Fund, and parastatal entities mobilize invesment funds.

National Budget.—FY (July-June) 1980 receipts: $5,340 million.

Foreign Aid.—Substantial (usually $500 million per year), 50 percent in grant form. Major donors: World Bank, UNDP, China, Sweden, Netherlands, Canada, United States, Norway, and Japan.

Balance of Payments.—Trade deficit $580.4 million; foreign exchange reserves, $6.7 million (November 1982).

Economy

GDP.—$4,4708 million (current prices) 1981; $240.4 real per capita income. Agriculture accounted for 50.9 percent, commerce 12.2 percent, manufacturing, 9.3 percent.

Agriculture.—Village is basic production-marketing channel. Coffee, cotton, tea, and sisal are principal exports; other cash crops include oilseeds, nuts, tobacco, and sugar. Zanzibar is principal world clove producer.

Industry.—Textile, cement, sugar refining, galvanized and aluminum rolling plants; oil refinery.

Commerce.—Dar es Salaam 1981 general Cost of Living Index (1970 = 100) 389 (up 6.9 percent from 1980).

Tourism.—Tanzania Tourist Corporation is developing the tourism sector.

Development Plan.—Fourth Five-Year Plan (1981-86) emphasizes expansion of and development in manufacturing, water and power, construction, transport, communications and mining.

Basic Economic Facilities

Transportation.—Two railways: 2,800-mile Tanzania Railway and 1,200-mile Tanzania-Zambia (TAZARA) railway. There is a total of 26,000 miles of roads on mainland including TANZAM highway: 1,635 paved; 84,305 motor vehicles. Three main Indian Ocean ports (Dar es Salaam, Tanga, and Mtwara). Inland ports on Lakes Victoria and Tanganyika. 60 percent of domestic cargo moves by truck.

Communications.—1979: 75,000 telephones; five AM radio stations; color television on Zanzibar but not TV on mainland. Four submarine cables. Microwave network is major endeavor.

Electric Current.—377 MW capacity with preparation for two large hydro schemes.

Natural Resources

Land.—363,450 square miles; 50 percent agricultural. Low, flat coastal strip; central plateau with Lakes Victoria and Tanganyika. Kilimanjaro is highest African peak.

Climate.—Tropical near coast; subtropical and temperate inland; semiannual monsoons.

Minerals.—Diamonds exported. Production of salt, mica sheets, gem stones, tin concentrates is increasing. Songwe/Kiwira and Ketewaka/Mchuchuma major coal and iron ore deposits. 30 billion cubic liters of natural gas have been found on Songo Songo island.

Population

Size.—18.6 million, 1981; 2.8 percent growth rate. Principal cities: Dar es Salaam (capital), 630,000 (42 percent of urban population); Arusha, 94,000; Tanga, 90,000; Tabora, 69,000. About 75 percent of the rural population is settled in "kaya," village cooperatives of 250-400 families. "Ujaama" (collective villages) are a long-term goal.

Language.—Swahili is official. English widely used in commerce and government.

Labor.—572,000 employed in monetary sector. Over 90 percent engaged in related occupations. Minimum wage $58 per month.

Education.—66 percent literacy rate.

Note: Dar es Salaam is more than 10,000 kilometers (6,500 miles) from Washington, D.C.

Marketing in Thailand

Contents

Report Revised June 1984

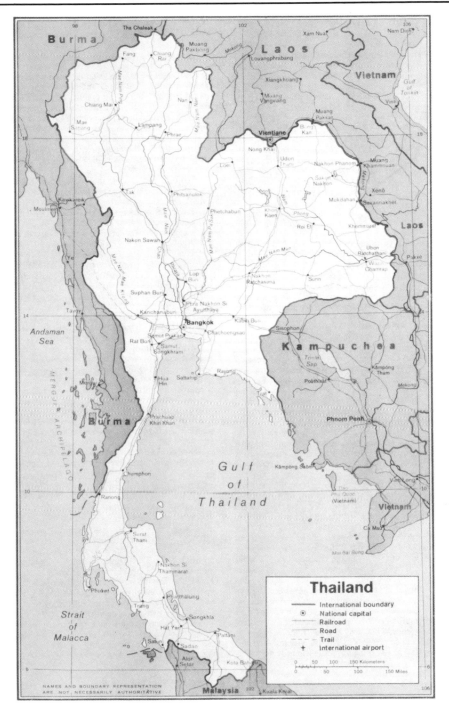

2367

THAILAND

Foreign Trade Outlook

Despite a slowdown from the more rapid growth of 1981, the Thai economy performed well in 1982, chalking up a real growth rate of 4.2 percent and outperforming all of Thailand's ASEAN economic partners except Singapore. Considerable progress was made in reducing the rate of inflation, which fell below 5 percent, and in dealing with the country's chronic balance of trade problems. The current account deficit, at $1.1 billion, was less than half its 1981 level, due primarily to a 13-percent drop in imports.

The most rapid growth in the economy occurred in the banking, insurance and real estate sector, which expanded 11.5 percent in real terms. Due to poor commodity prices and insufficient rains early in the planting season, the 1982 agricultural sector shrank from $8.5 billion to $7.7 billion. Agriculture's share of GDP dropped to 20.6 percent, while on the other hand, the manufacturing sector grew from $7.2 billion to $7.7 billion in 1982.

U.S. exports to Thailand in 1982 totaled $862 million, which was 15 percent lower than in 1981. U.S. imports from Thailand totaled $884 million, 6.5 percent lower than in the 1981. U.S. exports continued to decrease in 1983 and in the first eight months totaled $575 million, as opposed to $607 million in 1982. Table 1 shows Thailand's imports by economic classification for 1980-81.

The year 1983 promises a pickup in the rate of economic activity. Real GDP growth is forecast at 6.0 percent, in contrast to 4.2 percent in 1982. Inflation should be about 4 percent. This year's revival of domestic economic activity should result in increased imports from all sources, including the United States. Foreign borrowing has been restrained: external debt exceeded $10 billion in 1982, but debt servicing, at 20 percent of export earnings, is still considered manageable.

Thailand remains primarily an agricultural country with a strongly agro-based industrial sector. Its largest farm export earners are rice, sugar, tapioca, and jute. Agricultural production should increase only moderately over the 1982-83 harvest due to lower crop prices and production controls.

A major economic development has been the bringing onstream of Thailand's offshore natural gas reserves. Despite a sharp reduction in estimated reserves between 1981 and 1983, the Thai government is proceeding with plans for a large-scale petrochemical complex and other projects along the Eastern Seaboard, to the southeast of Bangkok. Overall plans call for investments of over $4.9 billion, most of which would be undertaken during 1983-1991. The government expects to be responsible for infrastructure development and will take equity positions in essential enterprises only where necessary to attract private capital. Other major industrial projects planned for the area include a gas separation plant, and production facilities for chemical fertilizers, vinyl chloride monomer, soda ash, and methanol.

Additional major projects in Thailand include nationwide upgrading of the telecommunications system, the Mae Moh power transmission project, and expansion of port facilities on the Eastern Seaboard and in the south.

Best Export Prospects

Thailand's Fifth National Economic and Social Development Plan (1982-86) stresses the expansion of rural income and employment, expanding agro-based and export-oriented industries utilizing local resources to create employment, and reduction of the disparity between urban and rural incomes.

Consequently, some of the best investment opportunities for U.S. companies in Thailand are in agroindustry. Sales prospects look particularly attractive for exporters of agricultural and food processing machinery and equipment, as well as for a wide variety of products and services needed for the planned development of the rural economy.

According to the Plan, the government is expected to allocate considerable sums for irrigation projects, expansion of power generation and transmission facilities, rural electrification, and international and regional telecommunications expansion.

Another important objective of the Plan is development of Thailand's sizable natural resources. While oil and natural gas have been discovered in the Gulf of Thailand, only the gas deposits are considered large enough to make exploitation feasible, but exploration for additional gas and oil deposits continues. Thailand has commercial deposits of antimony, lignite, limestone, phosphate, tin, tungsten, wolfram, and zinc.

Development of these natural resources offers excellent sales opportunities for a wide range of products and services including engineering consulting services, mining equipment, and mineral processing and materials handling equipment. There will be additional opportunities for roadbuilding and construction equipment since new roads will be needed to connect mining areas with the coast, and new port facilities to handle agricultural and mineral exports as well as finished imports.

Other equipment categories that offer excellent prospects for American exporters are described below.

Food Processing and Packaging Equipment

Thailand is a major food producer and is one of the few developing countries capable of exporting food products on a large scale. Major food export items include rice, tapioca, corn, sugar, pineapple, beans, grapes, and other fruits, and vegetables. Because of the sector's obvious potential, the Thai Government has been placing major emphasis on agriculture and food-related industries. The Fifth Development plan sets a clear target of improving the structure of agriculture productivity, stressing an increase in production efficiency to achieve a 4.5 percent growth rate per year.

The Thai market for food processing and packaging equipment totaled $46 million in 1982, of which 65 percent was for food processing equipment and the remainder for food packaging equipment.

Table 1—Thailand's 1980-81 Imports by Economic Classification
(In millions of U.S. dollars)

Commodity	1980	1981	% Change 80–81
Consumer Goods	598	615	3
Nondurables	302	290	−1
Food & Beverages	148	168	14
Clothing and Footwear	99	109	10
Medical and Pharmaceutical Products	44	47	7
Other Nondurables	343	435	27
Durables	111	120	8
Household Goods	141	170	21
Electrical Appliances	92	144	57
Other Durables	1878	2098	12
Total, Consumer Goods			
Intermediate Products and Raw Materials	1376	1548	13
Chiefly for Consumer Goods	193	237	23
Textile Fiber, Yarn, and Thread	731	833	14
Chemicals	452	477	6
Other	836	903	8
Chiefly for Capital Goods	505	546	8
Iron and Steel	332	357	8
Other	4425	4901	11
Total, Intermediate			
Capital Goods	206	238	16
Fertilizers and Pesticides	153	239	56
Metal Manufactures	996	1181	19
Nonelectrical Machinery and Parts	547	501	92
Electrical Machinery and Parts	112	136	21
Scientific and Optical Instruments	31	146	471
Aircraft and Ships	204	156	−24
Other	2249	2599	15
Total, Capital			
Other Imports	338	433	28
Land Vehicles and Parts	1919	2165	13
Crude Oil	949	819	−14
Other Fuel and Lubricants	604	409	−32
Miscellaneous	3810	3826	0.4
Total, Other	12362	13422	9
Grand Total			

Source: Thai Department of Customs

There is no known local producer of food processing equipment in Thailand. All food processing equipment is imported. In 1982, the major sources of supply were Japan (21.7 percent), W. Germany (19.9 percent) and the United States (9.5 percent).

There are five domestic manufacturers of filling, wrapping and sealing machines in Thailand, with an annual output of about $6 to $7 million (including non-food packaging machinery).

Imported equipment is preferred by Thai food processors and packers due to its high quality, dependability and durability. Imported food processing and packaging equipment is usually distributed through local agents/distributors, who provide installation and after-sales services. Major food processors occasionally order their equipment directly from overseas suppliers.

Medical Equipment

Thailand's total market for medical, surgical, and hospital equipment and supplies was estimated to be $48 million in 1982. Most of the market is satisfied by imports, which totaled $42 million in 1982. Domestic production is limited to hospital furniture, fixtures, and a few supplies like cotton wool, bandages, and gauze.

American medical products are well known in Thailand for their high quality, design practicality, and reliability. A large proportion of Thai doctors were trained in the United States and are both familiar with and anxious to recommend the purchase of U.S. equipment.

The Ministry of Public Health is the single largest consumer of medical supplies, with an annual budget of about $10 million. Of the more than 600 hospitals in Thailand, some 85 percent are operated by the Ministry. The Ministry also runs about 5,700 clinics, compared to 4,400 by the private sector. Government facilities must purchase equipment through government-issued tenders.

In additon, the Royal Thai Air Force is constructing a new hospital building, to be completed by the end of 1984. It is expected to be the most modern facility in the

2369

region and will require some $10 million worth of medical equipment. The project consultant is an American professor of medicine, and the facilities and equipment are therefore expected to be of U.S. standards.

During the 1982-86 period, the Ministry of Public Health plans to spend about $1.6 billion for various projects included in the Fifth Development Plan.

Products with the best sales prospects include electro-medical apparatus, medical instruments, breathing appliances, artificial limbs, and X-ray equipment.

Computers and Business Equipment

Thailand is entirely dependent on imports for computers, peripherals, and other business machines and computer-related equipment. The total apparent market for these products in 1982 was approximately $70 million.

In Thailand the computerization trend is toward smaller and less expensive computers that render higher efficiency. The need for computerization has persistently increased as the advantages become more apparent, especially for expanding enterprises. For that reason and in spite of conservative spending patterns, many large businesses, not only in Bangkok but also in the provinces, have been computerized.

About 50-60 new computer systems are sold each year. Principal customers are banks, finance companies, large business firms, manufacturing companies, and government agencies.

Historically U.S. computers and business machines have dominated the Thai market, but in recent years the U.S. market share has been diminishing. Japanese suppliers have recently made concerted efforts to promote the sale of their equipment and their initiatives appear to be successful. While U.S. firms still dominate the computer market, their percentage share of the business machine market is declining.

The number of computers and advanced business machines users is low considering the increasing sophistication of industry and commerce in Thailand, leaving room for impressive growth and market opportunities for aggressive U.S. suppliers.

A large untapped market lies with smaller companies that can use (and afford) a computer priced at $50,000 or less. Microcomputers appear to have a bright future and positive market potential. Automatic typewriters, typewriters with memory, word processors, automatic banking equipment, personal computers, blueprint machines, and paper shredders also have a receptive and growing market in Thailand.

Pumps, Valves, and Compressors

The demand for pumps, valves, and compressors is projected to increase steadily due to the high pace of development in the agricultural and manufacturing sectors. As the economy picks up in 1983 and succeeding years, local demand for pumps, valves, and compressors will grow.

The Thai market is divided into two sectors: agricultural and industrial. In 1982, Thailand's apparent market for pumps, valves, and compressors was $92 million.

Thailand's 1982 imports of these products were $86 million, representing approximately 50 percent of the total demand. Japan was the main supplier.

About 80 percent of the imported pumps are used in industry. The pumps imported for agricultural use are usually low quality, low cost.

Valves made of cast iron for use in low pressure water works are produced locally primarily for domestic consumption. Special valves, requiring high technology, are imported.

The major end-user sectors for pumps, valves, and compressors are plants and organizations involved in the following industries: electrical appliances, utility services, food and kindred products, petroleum refining, petroleum exploration, mining, electricity generation, hotels, and high rise buildings. It is estimated that these consumers account for about 65 percent of Thailand's total requirements for pumps, valves, and compressors.

Electric Power Generation Equipment

In Thailand there are three state-enterprises—the Electricity Generating Authority of Thailand (EGAT), the Metropolitan Electricity Authority (MEA), and the Provincial Electricity Authority (PEA)—involved in power generation, transmission, and distribution. EGAT, which supplies over 95 percent of the overall power supply, generates and sells electricity to MEA, PEA, and other major industries such as cement production, petroleum refining, and iron and steel reforming. MEA provides distribution facilities and purchases electricity from EGAT for resale to customers in Bangkok and nearby provinces. PEA's activities are similar to MEA's but cover provincial areas. PEA also operates diesel generating plants in the areas not yet covered by PEA's power distribution system.

Most industrial firms in Thailand rely on power supplied by EGAT, MEA, or PEA, but standby diesel generators are widely used for non-stop production lines and services. Hospitals usually install standby diesel generators. There are no records of the generating capacity of these standby and self-sufficient generating systems. However, the Ministry of Public Health is trying to install standby generators in all of its hospitals in the provincial areas. The Ministry of Public Health allocates a budget of about $250,000 per year for the purchase of about 15 generators ranging in capacity from 60-100 MW. Health units in various districts, which are also under the Ministry of Public Health, are to have smaller standby generators of under 25 MW installed. The Telephone Organization of Thailand (TOT) will spend nearly $7 million for standby diesel generators which will be installed at its store-program-computerized telephone exchanges.

During 1982-86, to increase its generating capacity, EGAT plans to construct the following power plants:

(1) Sirindhorn Dam: hydro-electric power, third unit of 12 MW capacity.

(2) Bang Pakong Thermal Unit 2: oil/gas-fired power plant of 550 MW capacity.

(3) Lang Suan Dam: hydro-electric power, 3 units with

Table 2—Gross Domestic Product at 1972 Prices

(In Millions of Baht)

Sector	1977	1978	1979[1]	1980[1]	1981[2]
Agriculture	65,537	72,513	71,408	72,784	78,200
	(27.6)	(27.8)	(25.8)	(24.9)	(24.8)
Mining and quarrying	3,526	4,104	4,531	4,780	4,600
	(1.5)	(1.6)	(1.6)	(1.6)	(1.5)
Manufacturing	48,071	52,521	57,841	60,597	66,700
	(20.3)	(20.1)	(20.9)	(20.7)	(21.1)
Construction	11,996	13,583	14,547	16,576	17,600
	(5.1)	(5.2)	(5.3)	(5.7)	(5.6)
Electricity and water supply	4,144	4,500	5,178	5,560	6,000
	(1.7)	(1.7)	(1.8)	(1.9)	(1.9)
Transportation and communications	14,474	16,205	17,663	18,811	20,400
	(6.1)	(6.2)	(6.4)	(6.4)	(6.5)
Wholesale and retail trade	41,213	43,658	45,497	48,227	51,700
	(17.4)	(16.7)	(16.4)	(16.5)	(16.4)
Banking, insurance and real estate	11,574	13,443	15,582	17,419	18,800
	(4.9)	(5.1)	(5.6)	(6.0)	(5.9)
Ownership of dwellings	3,823	4,052	4,289	4,502	4,800
	(1.6)	(1.6)	(1.6)	(1.5)	(1.5)
Public administration and defense	9,555	10,166	11,594	12,423	13,100
	(4.0)	(3.9)	(4.2)	(4.2)	(4.1)
Services	23,260	26,352	28,777	31,173	33,800
	(9.8)	(10.1)	(10.4)	(10.6)	(10.7)
Gross Domestic Product (GDP)	237,173	261,097	276,907	292,852	315,700
	(100.0)	(100.0)	(100.0)	(100.0)	(100.0)

Source: Office of the National Economic and Social Development Board, as given in Bank of Thailand Annual Economic Report, 1981.
[1] Revised.
[2] Bank of Thailand figures.
Note: Figures in parentheses denote percentage of the GDP.

a generating capacity of 45 MW each.

(4) Srinagarind Dam Stage 2: hydro-electric power, fourth and fifth units with a generating capacity of 180 MW each.

(5) Chiew Larn Dam: hydro-electric power, 3 units with a generating capacity of 80 MW each.

(6) Mae Moh Project: lignite-fired power plant, sixth and seventh units with generating capacities of 300 MW each.

The transmission line system in Thailand is now 230 and 115 KV type while the distribution system is 69 KV and under. The power system for domestic consumption is 220V, 50 HZ.

1982 imports into Thailand of electric power equipment totalled $106 million, about 20 percent over 1981's figure. Imports of U.S. electric power equipment into Thailand in 1982 were $15 million.

Industry Trends

GDP Movement

Recovering from a decade-low growth rate of 4.2 percent in 1982—a disappointing year for Thailand but good by world and regional standards—real GDP growth was expected to reach 6 percent in 1983. Fairly strong growth should continue, ranging from 6.2-6.8 percent during the 1984-85 period. The composition of the Thai economy is reflected in Table 2.

Major Sectors

Agriculture—Thailand is a major producer and exporter of agricultural commodities. Of Thailand's estimated population of 50 million, about 74 percent is employed in the agricultural sector. The agricultural sector has been expanding in absolute terms and continues to be the mainstay of the Thai economy, but it will progressively account for a diminishing share of GDP. In 1975 the agricultural sector accounted for 31 percent of GDP, but by 1982 its contribution had fallen to 21 percent.

Thailand's major crops include, rice, maize, rubber, sugar cane, kenaf, and tapioca. Adverse weather conditions have often affected crop yields and the nation's foreign exchange earnings; however, to remedy this situation, the government is actively promoting programs supporting crop diversification, irrigation, and value-added food processing industries. These programs offer opportunities to U.S. exporters in areas ranging from hybrid seed to canning machinery.

Mining—Mineral production for export began decreasing in 1981 and accelerated its decrease in 1982 in response to lower world demand and, in the case of tin, export controls imposed by the International Tin Council. Even in cases such as lead and acid-grade fluorite, where exported quantities increased, export earnings declined. Two minor minerals—barite and gypsum—were the only mineral exports to increase in quantity and earnings.

Production of minerals for domestic consumption, responding to a still expanding Thai economy, continued to increase with lignite, limestone, shale, and gypsum leading the growth.

After a 25.7 percent decline in mineral export earnings between 1980 and 1981, exports suffered an additional 22 percent decline in 1982, or a reduction of $119.7 million. Tin remained the leading mineral export, although volume dropped by 18.7 percent and value fell 21.5 percent.

Recent declines in estimated natural gas reserves in Union Oil's Erawan field have forced the Thai government to postpone some minerals and related projects while others, because of a question of economic viability, have been shelved.

Industry—The manufacturing sector has become increasingly important and in 1982 accounted for 21 percent of GDP. This sector, concentrated heavily in labor-intensive industries, including food processing and textiles, employs approximately 10 percent of the Thai labor force. Performance of the textile industry in 1983 is improving following a two-year downturn, and overall food processing performance continues to be strong. Electronics assembly is another important industry in this sector. The construction industry should show impressive gains in 1984. Declining interest rates and Thai government initiatives in support of Eastern Seaboard Development projects (ports, petrochemicals, and fertilizer plants) are expected to increase activity in the construction industry.

Business Climate

The Thai government has a history of changing hands peacefully with relative frequency, but the basic orientation towards a free enterprise system is embedded in the Thai philosophy and does not change with the leaders. Thailand is committed to trade and welcomes foreign private investment. Thailand's pro-business stance, conservative fiscal and monetary policies, abundant natural resources, skilled labor, and impressive infrastructure all help to create a generally good investment climate.

There is still some ambiguity in the application of some of Thailand's laws. Customs problems related to classification, valuation, advance duty deposits, and retroactive reassessments continue. Revised interpretations of certain laws and their strict enforcement have resulted in retroactive punitive measures against a few foreign businesses.

In order to encourage investment in priority sectors, the Thai Board of Investment (BOI) offers certain "promotion privileges" to investors. Any firm may invest in Thailand without BOI approval if it complies with local laws, but BOI approval is necessary to qualify for promotional privileges.

Privileges granted to firms may include tax holidays, guarantees against competition, waiver of import duties on machinery, components and raw materials, and assistance with residency permits. Preconditions for receipt of promotional privileges vary from industry to industry, but may include export performance requirements, local content requirements, local ownership requirements, and minimum capital investment requirements.

The BOI has been hampered in the past because it could not issue permits itself. In order to achieve greater efficiency, the cabinet, in 1982, established two Investment Service Centers (ISC). The centers aid investors by helping them make appropriate applications. The centers may also issue permits or arrange for other government agencies to issue them. Permits must be processed and completed within 90 days. In the past, the procedure could take up to 15 months. The ISCs, however, have two drawbacks. First, because the ISCs will not completely control the issuance of permits, investors may still have to intercede with the issuing ministry in order to get a response on their applications. Second, the new system is limited since it can issue industrial permits in only seven areas.

U.S. firms, except in certain fields, are accorded national treatment under the 1966 Treaty of Amity and Economic Relations between Thailand and the United States. Foreign firms are allowed to repatriate profits. Thai labor practices present few impediments in the management of work forces. Relatively few restrictions, good benefits, and a strong economy contribute to Thailand's generally good investment climate.

Government Role

Public Industries—The Thai government owns or controls a substantial sector of the country's economy. It owns and operates the postal services, telephone, telegraph, radio, and television communications, the railroads, ports, and an airline. Government monopolies exist in the tobacco, opium, and alcoholic beverage industries and in the manufacture of playing cards, cigarettes, arms and ammunition, and explosives. Manufacturing industries in which the Government participates or has interests include cement, paper, matches, textile piece goods, canned fish products, alum, rubber footwear, automobile batteries, glass, textiles, and petroleum refining and marketing. Teak extraction has been nationalized and extraction of other forest products is under government control. Other fields controlled by the Government through direct participation or special arrangements (including concessions to private operators) include the exploitation of minerals and mining, the exploration and production of petroleum, electricity, water supply, passenger transport (other than the wholly government-owned railway), and banking and insurance, including life insurance.

Development Planning—Thailand's Fifth National Economic and Social Development Plan (1982-86) was discussed on page 3. Total foreign loan requirements are $5.89 billion.

Distribution and Sales Channels

Import Marketing

Methods for marketing imports in Thailand have tended to be simple and akin to merchant trading but, as competition grows, businesses are realizing that there are benefits to modern promotional methods.

There are four main categories of importers or agents. Each offers advantages and disadvantages depending upon the product to be covered. First there are long-established expatriate firms with strong resources and large turnover. However, in such diverse operations, the value of business from a medium-sized principal is often small in the firm's overall activities, and the product may be neglected. On the other hand, a particular product may be central to the firm's operations.

The second category comprises smaller importers who generally specialize in one line of business in which they have valuable contacts. They may specialize in selling to one or more government departments or have special contacts within only one industry.

The third category, which offers good prospects for many medium-sized U.S. exporters, comprises the relatively new companies that are trying to grow into major marketing organizations. They frequently have technical backing and modern marketing techniques.

The fourth category comprises private firms heavily involved in the import/export business, known as International Trading Companies (ITCs). The advantage of using an ITC is that ITCs are granted certain privileges by the BOI. ITCs are exempted from import and business taxes on imported raw materials for domestic production of export goods, while suppliers of raw materials and other items to ITCs are exempted from business tax.

The importance of careful agency selection is underlined. In almost all cases a local representation arrangement is the best way, at least initially, by which an American exporter can obtain worthwhile business. An agent is also useful for foreign companies bidding on Government tenders, although this is not usually required. The experience and knowledge of the Foreign Commercial Service officers at the U.S. Embassy in Bangkok can be drawn upon to try to match product with representation. Lists of major importers are also available from the Thailand Country Specialist at the Department of Commerce.

Direct Selling—The Alien Business Act (ABA) of 1979 places some limitations on direct selling. (See following section entitled "Regulation of Marketing Firms.") Consequently, patterns and procedures for direct selling to consumers are undergoing some changes.

At the time that the above decree was issued, direct selling was largely limited to petroleum sales by three major international oil companies. Their sales organizations and terminal facilities were located primarily in Bangkok, while service stations were dispersed throughout the country. Otherwise, direct selling is used mainly to market soaps (mostly detergents), cosmetics, paper products, proprietary drugs, and low-priced consumer products for the home.

Any company considering direct selling in Thailand should concentrate first upon Bangkok, where per capita income is three or four times the national average of $748 (1982 dollars).

Regulation of Import Marketers—Foreign firms wishing to establish a marketing subsidiary in Thailand must conform to provisions of the ABA. Most marketing subsidiaries would fall within Category C of the ABA—namely, wholesale trade except in native agricultural products and real estate. Class "C" businesses also include retail trade in machinery, engines, and tools, and sales of foods and beverages to promote tourism.

Any alien wishing to operate a business in Thailand pertaining to the above outlined activities must file an application for a license with the Director of Commercial Registration.

Domestic Trade Channels

Agriculture, forestry, hunting, and fishing provide work and the means of living for a high proportion of the population. Many essential commodities are grown and consumed by the producer or distributed only locally. An increasing production surplus is being used for the purchase of other articles, most of which are imported and enjoy a reasonable measure of countrywide distribution. Both distribution and collection of commodities that enter trade are centered in Bangkok; exceptions are a few export commodities such as rubber, tin, and glutinous rice, which are exported from points near production. Domestic trade is carried on mostly by private enterprise. Some establishments employ 100 persons or more.

Trade is carried on by a wide variety of commercial organizations: some are devoted exclusively to wholesale trade; others exclusively to retail trade; and still others engaged in both wholesale and retail trade. Wholesale and retail enterprises also are combined with office organizations. In some instances, retail outlets are connected with production centers.

Wholesale firms located in Bangkok and Thonburi areas are agents for the sale of imported goods and, in some instances, exporting firms themselves serve as wholesalers.

Retail goods are distributed by outlets that vary from highly sophisticated and modernized urban establishments to small general stores, itinerant peddlers, and door-to-door traders selling food. Rural needs are usually met by small general stores or by traveling salespeople.

Almost every kind of retail outlet, ranging from modern supermarkets to the traditional floating market, is represented in Bangkok. In addition to the ubiquitous small general store, over 40 department stores served Bangkok and suburban areas in 1982. Consumer needs also were filled by almost every kind of specialty shop, including dress shops, florists, jewelers, shoe dealers, furniture shops, electric equipment shops, and many others. Several supermarkets are open in the area and shops are increasing in suburban centers. Personal, technological, and professional services also are available in the metropolitan area.

THAILAND

Among the leading retailers in Bangkok are Central Trading Company Ltd., Central Building, Silom Road; Nightingale-Olympic Co. Ltd., 1145/1 Lardya Road, Thonburi; Robinson Department Store; Metro Department Store; The Mall Department Store; and Thai Daimaru Co. Ltd., 6 Rajaprasong.

Government Procurement—The Government is Thailand's largest buyer. It usually purchases by means of tenders issued by the various end-user agencies and departments. Among the most active buyers of foreign goods for the public account are Foreign Purchasing Section, Supply and Procurement Department, Electricity Generating Authority of Thailand, Nonthaburi, Bangkok; Purchase and Stores Department, Metropolitan Electricity Authority, 121 Chakpetch Street, Bangkok; Provincial Electricity Authority, 200 Ngarm Wong Waan Road, Bangkhen, Bangkok; Telephone Organization of Thailand, Ploenchit Road, Bangkok; Thailand Tobacco Monopoly, Rama IV Road, Bangkok; Royal Irrigation Department, Samsen Road, Bangkok; and Department of Highways, Ministry of Communications, Rama VI Road and Sri Ayudhaya Road, Bangkok. Other government agencies are listed on pages 2387-2388.

Available information on such tenders is published in the biweekly *Business America* and *Commerce Business Daily,* both prepared by the U.S. Department of Commerce. These publications may be ordered through District Offices of the Department of Commerce or from the Superintendent of Documents, U.S. Government Printing Office, Washington, D.C. 20402.

Invitations to bid on Government tenders usually require that a deposit of up to 5 percent accompany the bid. The deposit is refunded to unsuccessful bidders and the successful bidder's deposit is retained as a performance bond and returned after the bidder has satisfactorily completed the work. In some cases, successful bidders are required to furnish a performance bond in addition to their original deposit.

Price is only one of several considerations for a government award: quality, delivery, credit terms, maintenance and service facilities are also weighed. On the other hand, price bidding does have the advantage of minimizing the danger of collusion, since it maximizes objectivity in awarding contracts.

Major Private-Sector Purchasers—These include rubber estates, mines, and industrial enterprises that do not generally cover their requirements directly. Usually their needs are supplied by the larger import companies with which they have standing orders for recurring deliveries and which go into the market for them to contract for nonrecurring (one-time) purchases.

In dealing with these large customers, the import companies sometimes trade on their own account but more frequently act as indent agents. Where maintenance and servicing of equipment are involved, the foreign supplier is likely to appear as a party in the sales contract. However, even in the maintenance and servicing fields, the large import houses are quite active, often undertaking to service equipment they sell on their own account.

Market Characteristics and Preferences

Thailand is located in Southeast Asia, covers almost 200,000 square miles of the Indochinese peninsula, and is roughly four-fifths the size of Texas. It has four main geographic regions, each with somewhat different natural resources and economic development. Its highly fertile central plain is one of the richest sources of food in Asia. Vast quantities of rice are grown throughout the region. Consequently, Thailand is a leading exporter of rice.

About 85 percent of the people are Thai ethnic origin and another 12 percent are of Chinese descent. The remaining 3 percent consist of Malays concentrated in southern Thailand near the Malaysian border, hill people along the borders with Burma and Laos, and a sizeable group of Vietnamese refugees in the northeast along the Mekong River.

Most Thai are Buddhists, generally religious in their own lives and tolerant of foreigners of other faiths; no important religious taboos affect their trade. The national diet consists chiefly of rice and fish, supplemented by fruits and vegetables available locally.

The country and its people are a mixture of old and new, conservative and progressive. The market for new housing, modern housing conveniences, and up-to-date production and marketing facilities is gradually spreading. Several general tastes and preferences regarding marketing are discernible.

Price—Price is probably of paramount importance, particularly in the purchase of general consumer goods, small machinery, and appliances. Although Thai businesspersons and consumers are aware of the general benefits of higher-priced, more durable goods, they are often in the position of being able to finance only less expensive merchandise. Experienced American exporters appreciate the pricing advantage in the Thai market. They eliminate from their product and price any components that are related entirely to distribution within the United States. This effort can be the deciding factor in achieving a competitive position for specific American products.

Package Labels—Most Thai prefer to have labels, instructions, and descriptions that accompany imported products printed in the Thai language. Although there is local support for "buying Thai," most Thai still generally prefer foreign products if higher price is not a significant obstacle.

Quality—Thai buyers are quality conscious, although this factor is often outweighed by considerations of price and credit. Buyers are aware that products manufactured outside the United States by subsidiaries or affiliates of American firms often differ in quality from those manufactured in the United States. Sometimes they prefer the American-made product, as in the case of toiletries and cigarettes. In other instances, preference is for the product manufactured outside the United States.

Service—Servicing of sales is necessary, particularly in selling machinery and equipment. Parts inventories, trained repair personnel, and expeditious servicing are provided as a standard function by many foreign suppliers, and the Thai buyer is demanding greater service back-up from all sources.

Specifications—Product specifications and the initiative of the supplier in altering products to meet local demand can often be the determining factor in making sales. The ability of the American manufacturer to supply up-to-date equipment for medium or small-scale production can determine the success of the marketing effort. Product flexibility is particularly important in meeting the Government's procurement requirements.

Merchandising—Foreign suppliers now cultivating the Thai market are beginning to apply more up-to-date merchandising techniques. The use of imaginative advertising, proper attention to the effective display of products, care in selection and appropriate supervision of distributors, and the introduction of other modern selling methods are helping foreign suppliers win sales from their competitors.

Regarding brand preferences, a survey by one advertising firm in Bangkok revealed that 50 percent of the customers of 10 supermarkets and grocery stores in Bangkok bought the products because of their brand name. Somewhat conflicting guidance comes from a Thai brewery official who claims that the criteria in buying a brand would appear to depend on the kind of premium offered at that particular time. He notes that Thai women have a greater tendency than Thai men to try new products.

Purchaser's Power

Thailand's population is 50.7 million and is increasing at 2 percent annually. The largest concentration of population is in the Bangkok-Thonburi metropolitan area, which had an estimated 6 million persons at the end of 1981. As in all developing countries, Bangkok's population is being swelled by unemployed and displaced farmers and their families. Bangkok is the commercial hub of the country. Only two cities, Chiang Mai in the north and Nakhon Ratchasima on the Korat Plateau, have populations exceeding 100,000.

In Bangkok, the average household size is 5.2 persons. The average annual household income is $3,800. Major employment categories are: 28.2 percent private business; 25 percent clerical, sales and service workers; 16.8 percent production workers; and 8.1 percent professional, administrative and technical workers.

Transportation and Utilities

Water Transport

Most maritime trade enters and clears Thailand via the principal port of Bangkok with the balance being handled primarily through the ports of Songkhla, Phuket, and Pattani, three ports in the southern provinces. An international deep-sea port is planned as a long term project at Laem Chabang, about 126 km. southeast of Bangkok. A portion of the Sattahip naval base, 184 km. southeast of Bangkok, is being converted for commercial use, including a container terminal.

Bangkok lies approximately 45 km. inland on the Chao Phraya River. Constant dredging of the river is required, and navigation is limited to smaller vessels because of draft and length limitations. Larger vessels discharge into lighters at an open roadstead in the Gulf of Thailand near the mouth of the river. The East Quay, part of the Port of Bangkok, is the principal container facility for Thailand. Most container traffic to Thailand is by feeder line service from other ports such as Singapore and Hong Kong.

The transit times from the United States to Thailand range from 36-40 days from the Eastern United States, about 30 days from the U.S. Gulf area, and from 20-30 days from the U.S. Pacific Coast, depending upon vessel itinerary and port of transshipment in the Far East.

American President Lines offers weekly service to Bangkok from the West Coast with transshipment at Singapore. For further information call (415) 271-8000 or write: American President Lines, 1950 Franklin Street, Oakland, California 94612.

Lykes Bros. Steamship Co., Inc. offers service to Bangkok via Taiwan at 17/18 day intervals from the West Coast and on an inducement basis from the U.S. Gulf. For further information call (504) 523-6611 or write: Lykes Bros. Steamship Co., Inc. 300 Poydras Street, New Orleans, LA 70130.

Sea-Land Service, Inc. offers a weekly service to Bangkok from the U.S. East, West, and Gulf Coasts with transshipment at Hong Kong. For further information call (201) 632-2000 or write: Sea Land Service, Inc., P.O. Box 800, Iselin, New Jersey 08830.

Information and assistance regarding ocean transportation is also available from regional and area offices of the Maritime Administration, U.S. Department of Transportation, or at any local office of the carriers named above.

Air Transport

Don Muang International Airport, some 20 miles from the center of Bangkok, is an important port of call for regional air carriers and for international airplanes operating around-the-world schedules. Passenger movements have been steadily increasing and were up 7 percent in 1981. The Thai government has decided to expand Don Muang and may also build a new international airport for Bangkok. Expansion of the present site will cost $650-$700 million and will expand the life of Don Muang 10-15 years. The new airport would cost slightly more and would take 8-10 years to build.

Expansion is underway on the airports at Phuket and Surat Thani.

Thai International, the national airline, flies to Europe, the Middle East, and the West Coast of the United States. Thai International plans to buy two Airbus 300s and one Boeing 747 by 1986.

Some 30 scheduled airlines provide international services at Don Muang. Thai Airways Company, parent company of Thai International, provides domestic air services and operates and maintains a number of Thai airports. Thai Airways plans to buy its fifth Boeing 737-200 by 1984.

Rail Transport

The Thai Railway (State Railway of Thailand), government-owned and operated, has a network of approximately 3,897 kilometers of single meter gauge, mainly single track. Lines radiate south, east, and north from Bangkok to connect with important administrative and commercial centers. The southern line extends along the entire east coast of peninsular Thailand and joins the Malaysian railroad system at the border. The eastern line connects with the Cambodian railroad. The northern line terminates at Chiang Mai and a fourth line branches to the east from the Bangkok-Chiang Mai line about 50 miles from Bangkok and at Nakhon Ratchasima forks northeast to the Laos boarder and east to Muang Ubon.

There are four freight terminals in the Bangkok area equipped with minimal but adequate mechanical handling equipment (primarily forklift trucks). Terminal facilities elsewhere are quite limited. Most of the freight-handling operations are performed either at the Bangkok or the Paholyothin freight terminals. The railway has six yards, with the main marshalling yard located at Bangsue. All major locomotive and rolling stock repair work is carried out at the Makasan workshop in Bangkok.

Two container services are offered: one is Bangkok-Chiang Mai and the other is Bangkok-Kuala Lumpur. A new line is under construction from Chachoengsao to Sattahip to serve the new port. Plans call for a new line to serve the northeast extension of the northern line to Chiang Mai. The current Five-Year Plan of the SRT calls for $99 million to be spend for expansion and improvement.

Road Transport

By far the most important mode of transport in Thailand is the highway system. It consists of about 34,950 kilometers of highways, 21,597 of which are paved or improved. The major arteries of the network radiate from Bangkok, north to Chiang Mai, northeast toward Vientiane in Laos, and south to Songhkla and the Malaysian border. During 1981, nearly 81,000 new vehicles were sold in Thailand; 20,000 private cars, 45,000 LCV, and 16,000 six-to-ten wheelers.

Truck and passenger transport is carried out primarily by large private companies or by small independent owner-operators owning one or two vehicles. However, the interprovincial trucking business is shared by private operators and the government-sponsored Express Transport Organization (ETO). ETO provides an integrated long-distance trucking service with depots nationwide. It operates an inland waterway service at Swasdi port, three bus routes, and exclusive trucking services at Klong Toey port. It has a trucking monopoly in the area of railway stations in certain provinces.

Most of the vehicles in Thailand operate in the Bangkok metropolitan area, causing severe traffic congestion, which is compounded by an inadequate city highway network and no rapid transit system. Three elevated highways linking provincial trunk routes into Bangkok are under various stages of design, but construction will not be completed for a few years. An elevated rapid transit system is under consideration. In the meantime, the city administration is building overpasses and eliminating traffic circles in the worst areas.

The Highway Department is inviting contractors to submit prequalification bids for improvement of 1,300 kilometers of provincial roads and strengthening and rehabilitation of another 1,300 kilometers of roads in other areas.

Electricity

The Electricity Generating Authority of Thailand (EGAT) is responsible for electricity generation in Thailand. Present capacity is 3,910 megawatts. Sources are thermal (50.2 percent), hydropower (34.3 percent), gas turbine (14.7 percent), and diesel (0.8 percent). The Fifth Five-Year Plan identifies 37 projects estimated to cost $4,447 million for power generation, distribution, and transmission.

The Metropolitan Electricity Authority (MEA) is responsible for distribution of electricity in the Bangkok metropolitan area. Power is supplied by EGAT at six terminal stations.

Distribution of electricity in the provinces is handled by the Provincial Electricity Authority (PEA). PEA will invest $846 million under the Fifth Five-Year Plan to supply electricity to 92 percent of Thailand's rural areas.

Indigenous fuel resources for Thailand's thermal power plants consist primarily of lignite coal deposits at Mae Moh and Krabi and oil deposits at Fang. Mae Moh deposits amount to 678 million tons of proven reserves of 6,000 Btu per pound of lignite. Besides the nearby existing fertilizer plant, three 75 MW thermal generating facilities are utilizing the lignite at Mae Moh. Krabi lignite reserves of 5 to 8 million tons of 6,000 Btu per pound are used to power a nearby mine. The production of the Fang Oil Field is 1,000 barrels a day and dedicated to military use.

Imported petroleum cost Thailand $3.2 billion in 1981. Imported crude is refined at three locations. The Petroleum Authority of Thailand operates a 65,000 barrel-per-day refinery at Bangchak, a suburb of Bangkok. ESSO Standard Thailand Ltd. operates a refinery in Si Racha District, Chonburi Province; its daily capacity has been 35,000 barrels, but in 1983 the government approved ESSO's proposal to increase its capacity to 65,000 barrels per day. Thai Oil Refinery Company (TORC) Ltd., operates a facility with a production capacity of 130,000 barrels per day.

Advertising and Research

Advertising Agencies

There are about two full pages of listings of advertising agencies in the Greater Bangkok Metropolitan Area Telephone Directory for January 1983. These listings cover "Agencies and Counselors" (130), "Direct Mail" (4), "Directory and Guide" (1), "Indoor" (1), "Motion Picture" (10), "Newspaper" (3), "Outdoor" (25), "Radio" (8),

"Specialties" (1), "Television" (6), and "Transportation" (1).

Leading agencies include Adplan Ltd., Dentsu Advertising Ltd., Kenyon & Eckhardt (Thailand) Ltd., Leo Burnett Ltd., McCann-Erickson (Thailand) Ltd., Media Direction Enterprises, Ogilvy & Mather (Thailand) Ltd., Ted Bates Ltd. (Thailand), Temple Publicity Services, Letter-Ads Direct Mail Co., Ltd., Pan Advertising Co., Ltd., SSC & B-Lintas Thailand Ltd., and Diethelm Advertising.

The above classification of agencies pertains to firms engaged in a much wider range of activities than in most other countries. Some Thai advertising agencies may deal solely in space brokerage, or sign-making or any other allied business. A more precise description for a number of the agencies may be "advertising subagencies."

Agency earnings are roughly 18 percent of advertisers' net expenditures. This yields relatively low returns in that the bulk of an advertising agency's income is derived from commissions received from media, which have relatively low rates.

The U.S. exporter buying local advertising space is well advised to use a format developed by persons thoroughly familiar with Thai cultural characteristics. Many advertisers and agency employees believe that although the English-language media reach only a small audience, they do reach the most affluent and influential segment of the Thai population. Thus advertising of industrial equipment and materials as well as some consumer goods in the English-language media in Thailand is probably well advised.

Media

The $600 million turnover in the advertising industry is distributed as follows: radio, 30 percent; television, 30 percent; daily newspapers, 22 percent; movie theaters, 5 percent; magazines, 6 percent; and other media, 7 percent.

Television—Thailand has nine television stations. They are licensed by the government. The Thai television stations located in Bangkok telecast an average of more than 100 hours per week. They are considered excellent media for advertising, although more expensive than newspapers. They have modern studio facilities and broadcast about 60 percent live and 40 percent filmed material. U.S. television programs are popular in Thailand, and there is a good market there for "canned" programs. The five provincial stations, located in the cities of Khon Kaen (northeast); Haadyai, Surat Thani and Phuket (south); and Lampang (north), serve the people in these areas on a much more limited basis.

Advertising provides nearly all revenue for operation of television stations. The number of television receivers is roughly 1.5 million. Television and motion pictures are very effective media in that Thai consumers tend to be more responsive to graphic display than written text.

Radio—Thailand has 196 broadcasting stations scattered throughout the country. Three FM stations and more than 50 AM transmitting terminals serve metropolitan Bangkok. Two Bangkok stations operate with FM stereo multiplex systems. All areas of the country can be reached by radio advertising, although not all stations carry commercials.

Motion Pictures—Thai people are avid moviegoers. Seventy percent of the people in Bangkok and more than 50 percent of those in the provinces reportedly attend at least once a week. Bangkok has a number of large ultramodern, air-conditioned movie houses. The motion picture theaters in the provinces are usually among the most modern buildings in town. Screen advertising is considered an effective means of promoting the sale of goods and services.

Magazines—There are several Thai magazines. English language magazines include "Business in Thailand," "Business Review," "The ASEAN Investor," and "T-AB" (Thai-American Business—the bimonthly publication of the American Chamber of Commerce in Thailand).

Newspapers—Newspapers may be the most preferred media. Most advertising occurs during December and January for visual promotion of consumer gift products. Among the most prominent Thai newspapers are *Thai Rath, Siam Rath, Ban Muang, Mati Chon,* and *Daily News.* There are three English-language newspapers published in Bangkok, *Bangkok Post, The Nation,* and *Bangkok World.*

Market Research

Business research agencies in Bangkok offer two main types of service and supplement these with several other functions. The first general service is market research, offering a description and analysis of market conditions at a given time. The second type of service is the feasibility study to determine whether or not to set up a new factory or plant or to launch a new product.

Among the 18 firms listed under "Marketing Research & Analysis," "Research Organizations & Companies," and "Public Relations Service" in the Bangkok January 1983 Telephone Directory, the most active independent firms include: Research Ltd., Orient Research Ltd., Deemar, Presko Public Relations Co., Ltd., International Research Associates and Impress Public Relations.

Besides the research conducted by independent agencies, major companies in Thailand maintain their own market research units. One example is the subsidiary of one important international marketer of toilet soaps, shampoos, detergents, and instant foods. It maintains a regular staff of 35 and a field force of 27. It completes about 100 studies per year for the parent company on a budget in seven figures (baht). About 30 percent of the company's effort revolves around a consumer market index conducted monthly in Bangkok, bimonthly in "upcountry" towns, and quadrennially in rural areas. Other research carried out on an *ad hoc* basis includes product tests, retail shop audits, various promotional tests, and regular media surveys.

In general comments upon market research, one source indicates that interviewing is the most widely used method to obtain opinions from Bangkok consumers. Telephone surveys and questionnaires by mail

2377

are not highly regarded as a source of candid responses form a public that is wary of dealing with strangers. One Thai with 15 years experience believes that the tendency of Thai not to offend the interviewer by critical responses is declining.

About 50 firms in Bangkok regularly use market research to promote their products, according to the director of one research agency. He further estimates that 100-150 firms may commission a research project once in 5 years. The biggest customers for market research may be local branches of international companies.

U.S. exporters may be wise to keep in mind that good cross-culture research requires a questionnaire designed by individuals having an extensive knowledge of Thai cultural characteristics. Thus, a questionnaire in the Thai language, understood in purpose by the person being interviewed, can elicit valuable information that might otherwise be lost in the tendency to give the answer that will please. On the other hand, politeness leads to extension of discussion, openings to add desired points, and opportunities to inquire further into one or many aspects of the questionnaire.

Further information regarding Thai tastes and preferences that may be weighed in advertisement planning is located in the foregoing section entitled "Market Characteristics and Preferences."

Credit

Capital Availability

As an anti-inflationary tactic, the money market tightened in 1982, though later there was evidence of an easing of controls. The following interest rates prevailed at commercial banks in Bangkok:

Deposits	% per year
Savings	9
Time Certificate of Deposit	
3 months	9
1 year	11
Nonresident US$	
3 months	6
1 year	7.5
Loans	
Overdrafts & other baht loans	17
U.S. $ import/export financing	10.5
(loan rates subject to negotiation)	

With Thailand paying more for what it buys abroad and receiving less for what it sells, with the current account expected to continue in deficit, and private foreign investment still at a very low level, money is expected to be tight for the next year at least. However, the Thai Government is welcoming new investment, especially in promoted industries such as integrated steel, fertilizer, petrochemicals, oil, and mining. In export-oriented manufacturing and those businesses related to development, there will of course be little difficulty in getting credit and doing business in Thailand.

Regulation of Supply

Money supply regulation is accomplished by the government's central bank, The Bank of Thailand (BOT). It has the authority to control credit by rediscounting short-term commercial paper and engaging in open market operations, although the latter authority has not been exercised extensively or effectively. It has the authority under the Commercial Banking Act of 1979 to establish reserve requirements for commerical banks. In January 1974, the ratio of cash reserves to total deposits that commercial banks are required to maintain at BOT was increased to 8 percent from 7 percent.

Under the Commercial Banking Act B. E. 2522 (1979), the BOT, with the approval of the Ministry of Finance, is empowered to regulate maximum deposit rates, maximum interest rates and discounts, maximum rates for services rendered by commercial banks, maximum deposits for letters of credit, and maximum deposits for security demanded as surety on transactions. Maximum rates of interest vary from 0.01 percent per year on demand deposits and time deposits of less than 3 months, to 7 percent per year on time deposits of 12 months or more. Interest on foreign currency deposits is limited to 12 percent. Maximum rates of interest on loans can vary by as much as five percentage points; secured loans to industry may not exceed 12 percent.

Financing Sources

The private capital market structure in Thailand consists of five kinds of institutions, of which commercial banks are the most familiar. They numbered 30 (16 Thai banks and 14 foreign banks) at the end of 1982 and accounted for roughly four-fifths of total assets of private financial institutions in Thailand.

Bank of America and Chase Manhattan have full operations (branches) in Thailand. Many other American banks have representative offices in Bangkok.

Thai finance companies borrow from the public at comparatively higher rates of interest. They then buy short-term commerical paper and work for a very rapid turnover of funds. Their impact is felt most in the money market. However, their stock in trade is consumer credit. The number of finance companies has expanded considerably in recent years to approximately 70 at the end of 1982.

Insurance companies in Thailand totaled 20 in 1982. They are generally conservative in their dealings and distribute funds received in the market for long-term debt instruments and government securities and in such entities as the State Railway of Thailand and the Electricity Generating Authority of Thailand.

Among the finance companies and investment banks, American banks have interests in Asian and Euro-American Capital Corporation (Bank of America), Multi-Credit Corporation of Thailand Ltd. (Philadelphia National), Wang Lee Bank (First National City Bank), Thai Investment and Securities Co. (Bankers Trust), and Bangkok First Investement and Trust (Citicorp).

The Stock Exchange and the government-sponsored Securities Exchange of Thailand are now active in generating significant new capital.

Other Thai financial institutions include the Industrial Finance Corporation of Thailand (IFCT), which was established in October 1959 under government sponsorship. Its purpose is to provide long-term credits to private small or medium-size industries primarily engaged in manufacturing consumer goods with local raw materials.

The chief institution for rural savings deposits is the Government Savings Bank, which makes medium- and long-term loans. However, the Bank for Agriculture and Agricultural Cooperatives accounts for roughly 85 percent of all institutional credit for the rural sector. Institutional credit meets only 15 percent of total agricultural credit requirements; the rest is provided by money lenders at rates of interest of 30-40 percent per year.

Trade Regulations

Documentation and Procedures

Shipping Documents—Normally required for shipments are a commercial invoice, a bill of lading, sanitary certificate if appropriate, and any other documents prescribed in the instrument of payment. Packing lists are recommended as a service to the customer.

Import Licensing—A license must be obtained from the Ministry of Commerce for a few import items including some foods, materials, and industrial products. In general, the items under import licensing and control may be classified into three categories: goods whose import is normally prohibited in order to protect local industries; goods whose import is subject to a requirement for concurrent purchase of similar goods produced domestically; and goods whose import is controlled for health, security or other reasons. The category of goods whose import is normally prohibited for protective reasons is the largest. Domestic production of practically all these items is considered sufficient for home consumption. Examples of goods for which a license is required are steel bars and rods, vinyl chloride monomer, diesel engines, compressors, soy beans, soy bean oil, and palm oil.

In addition to the licensing by the Ministry of Commerce, importers should be aware of the laws administered by various other agencies that regulate trade in certain goods. Goods covered by these laws include arms, ammunition, and explosives; opium and dangerous drugs; playing cards; television, radio and wireless sets; tobacco; certain plants; and weighing and measuring instruments. A sanitary certificate is required for seeds, fruits, and live animals.

Entry—Most goods exported from the United States to Thailand, whether by sea or air, enter at Bangkok. Provincial ports such as Phuket and Songkhla play small roles.

All merchandise entering Thailand except for transshipment or transit is subject to customs examination. Customs entry forms must be prepared and submitted, together with original or duplicate shipping documents, to the Chief of the Import and Export Division, Department of Customs, Bangkok, or to the designated official at any other entry point.

Transit and Transshipment—Goods may be cleared through customs upon application submitted on special forms by the intermediate consignee. Physical examination of the goods is usually waived.

Reexport—Under section 17 of the Customs Code of Thailand, drawback of nine-tenths (but not exceeding one thousand baht) of the duty paid is allowed when goods are reexported within one year, provided that the reexported goods have not been used or processed in Thailand. Refund of the duty paid can be requested, on a case-by-case basis, from the Department of Customs when goods have been imported for processing in Thailand and reexported within one year from the date of import. Import duties are exempted only when a prior request for a bonded warehouse has been approved by the Department of Customs or if written approval has been issued by the BOI. However, the goods must be processed locally and reexported within one year from the date of import.

Samples and Advertising Matter—Samples of commercial value are dutiable under the applicable tariff category while those of no commercial value are admitted duty free. Commercial travelers bringing in dutiable samples may either post bond or pay the duty. If the samples are then reexported within 6 months, the bond is canceled or the deposit refunded.

Advertising matter, whether for sale or free distribution, is subject to duty; for printed advertising matter it is 30 percent *ad valorem* or 3.00 baht per kilogram, whichever is higher.

Abandoned Goods—Goods held in customs custody become subject to Government disposal if not claimed within 4 months of entry or if in arrears in rent or warehouse charges. The agent of the importing vessel is given a 14-day option of either clearing the goods through customs or reexporting them.

Fines and Penalties—The Legal Division of the Customs Department is responsible for levying and enforcing any fines or penalties with regard to cases of fraud. Very seldom do these cases involve fraudulent intent but instead result from carelessness, confusion, or general misunderstanding.

Thailand adopted antidumping legislation in 1964. The Antidumping Act, B.E. 2507, applies to the importation and sale of merchandise at less than its normal price which might cause damage to domestic industry.

Taxation of Imports

Tariff Structure—Since 1960, the Thai customs tariff has been based on the Brussels tariff nomenclature (BTN). Most duties are *ad valorem*; some are specific. When the tariff lists both specific and *ad valorem* rates for an item, the rate yielding the higher revenue applies. The *ad valorem* duties range from zero to a high of 60 percent.

Basis of Duty Assessment—*Ad valorem* duties are assessed on the "wholesale cash price (exclusive of import duty) for which goods of like kind and quality are capable of being sold without loss at the time and place of importation, without deduction or abatement." Specific duties are calculated on the unit, volume, or weight. Duties based on weight refer to the net weight exclusive of packing materials, except where expressly stated otherwise.

All duties are payable in baht, the Thai currency, at the time goods are cleared through customs (US$1=23 baht.) The metric system is used for expressing weights and measures. There are no customs surcharges.

Tariff Classification—Importers may request an advance ruling from the Tariff Classification Section of the Customs Department. The request may be accompanied by samples, illustrations, a description of the goods, and a narrative justifying a certain classification. If the Classification Section seeks advice from outside technical experts, the cost of obtaining this advice is charged to the applicant.

Internal Taxes—The business tax is the most important internal tax as far as exporters to Thailand are concerned. As a sales tax, business tax is levied on almost all imports. The business tax is assessed on the "normal" selling price. The "normal" selling price is determined as follows:

C.I.F. value + import duty = X
X times standard rate of profit for item = Y
X + Y = "normal" selling price
(X + Y) times rate of business tax = amount of business tax

The standard rate of profit is an estimate of the retail markup, assigned by the Ministry of Finance to each category of goods.

Business tax is payable only on the first sale (i.e., sale by manufacturer to distributor), unless the imported product is materially altered. All tax is paid at the time of importation. With certain exceptions, the tax rate is the same for both imported and locally produced goods of the same type, varying from 1.5 percent on educational matter to 30 percent on alcoholic beverages.

In addition, there are excise taxes levied on certain articles such as tobacco, alcoholic beverages, and playing cards. All business transactions, including imports that involve the issuance of receipts and similar instruments, are subject to a small stamp tax. A municipal surtax of 10 percent is levied on the amount payable under the business tax.

Marking and Labeling Requirements

Whenever weights and measures shown on containers or merchandise offered for sale are in foreign systems, the equivalent in the metric system, carried out to one decimal place, must also be given. The Thai language also must be used. Certain products must meet special labeling requirements. For example, canned milk must be labeled to show the kind, trademark of the milk, name of the manufacturer, and location of the factory. In the case of skimmed milk, the label must state in Thai script of not less than 7 millimeters: "Skimmed milk. Not to be used for nursing babies."

Most food products must now be labeled in the Thai language to show the name of the food and its registration number, the name and address of the manufacturer, date of manufacture, net weight of contents and all additives used.

The United States Senate Concurrent Resolution 40, adopted July 30, 1953, invites U.S. exporters to inscribe, insofar as practicable, on external shipping containers in indelible print of a suitable size: United States of America.

Investment in Thailand

U.S. Investment

U.S. direct investment in Thailand totaled $594 million at the end of 1982. The figure does not necessarily represent the current value of the U.S. investments, of which a substantial portion was made before the last decade.

A recent announcement of the Thai Board of Investment indicated that registered U.S. capital of firms granted promotion certificates from 1960 to September 1982 amounted to $34 million. It should be noted that many firms have invested in Thailand without the benefit of "promoted industry" status, and they, therefore, would not be represented in the above figure.

U.S.-Thailand Commercial Agreements

On June 8, 1966, a new Treaty of Friendship, Commerce, and Navigation between the United States and Thailand came into force. In the treaty each of the two parties (1) formally endorsed high standards regarding protection of persons, their property and interests; (2) recognized the need for special attention to the stimulation of international movement of investment capital for economic development; (3) affirmed its adherence to the principles of nondiscriminatory treatment in trade and shipping; and (4) agreed to accord within its territories to citizens and corporations of the other, treatment no less favorable than it accords its own citizens and corporations (i.e., "national treatment") in respect to establishing and carrying on commercial and industrial activities. However, each country reserves the right to prohibit or limit the interest of aliens in enterprises in domestic trade in indigenous agricultural products; communications; transport or fiduciary functions; banking involving depository functions; or the exploitation of land or other natural resources; provided that it accords to nationals and companies of the other party treatment no less favorable than that given nations and companies of any third country. Each party may reserve for its own nationals the practices of professions or callings. This Treaty, also called the Thai-American Treaty of Amity and Economic Relations (AER), may be terminated by either party with 1 year's advance notice at any time thereafter.

The U.S. Investment Guaranty Program established in 1954 is operative in Thailand. Under the program, now administered by the Overseas Private Investment Corporation (OPIC), U.S. investors may be insured against (1) confiscation, nationalization or expropriation of their enterprises; (2) inconvertibility and non-transferability of the invested capital and profits; and (3) war damages inflicted upon the physical assets of the enterprises.

The Foreign Assistance Act of 1961 extended the protection to cover the following additional risks: (1) Risks incurred by wholly owned subsidiaries of U.S. companies; (2) *defacto* expropriation due to a foreign government's breach of contract; and (3) damages inflicted upon the physical assets of the enterprises through revolution or insurrection.

In addition, since December 1965, American investors may be provided with "extended risk" coverage under the Investment Guaranty Program.

Forms of Business Organization

With the exception of those restrictions noted in the section entitled "Foreign Investment Policy and Regulations" below, foreign companies in Thailand generally operate under the same laws, rules and regulations as do Thai companies. Foreign businesses must, however, obtain a license from the Alien Business Registration Section, Department of Commercial Registration, Ministry of Commerce, before commencing business. U.S. firms which claim an exemption from the provisions of the Alien Business Law under the provisions of the Treaty of Amity and Economic Relations must obtain a written confirmation from the Director-General of the Department of Commercial Registration. This procedure is quite straightforward. Assistance is available through the Commercial Section of the U.S. Embassy in Bangkok.

The principal forms of business organization under Thai law are sole proprietorships, partnerships, limited companies and public limited companies. In addition, branches of foreign corporations are recognized, and may be required to be registered to do business in many sectors. A "representative" or "liaison" office of a foreign company is not recognized as a distinct legal entity, and may be treated as a branch office for tax and other purposes.

Sole Proprietorship—An individual may, subject to various formalities and authorizations that apply to specific types of activities, establish a business without incorporating. The owner has the sole responsibility for its operation. In settlement of debts, not only business assets but also personal goods and property may be attached. If the proprietorship is commercial, the proprietor must register with the government.

Partnership—Two types of partnerships are recognized: (1) "Ordinary" partnerships, both registered and unregistered, and (2) "limited" partnerships. Although the liabilities attaching to these different partnerships vary, the general rules governing partnerships are similar. Thai and western partnership laws have many similarities. In Thailand a partnership is defined as a contract whereby two or more persons agree to unite to form a common undertaking with a view to sharing profits that may be derived therefrom.

One of the two types of partnership is the "ordinary" type, in which all the partners are jointly liable for all obligations of the partnership. If the ordinary partnership is registered, the entry must contain the following particulars: (1) name of the partnership firm; (2) its purpose; (3) address of the principal business office and all branch offices; (4) name, address, and occupation of every partner; (5) names of the managing partners, in case not all of the partners have been appointed as such; (6) restrictions, if any, imposed upon the powers of managing partners, and (7) the seal, or seals, that are binding on the partnership. The application for registration must be signed by every partner and sealed with the common seal. A certificate of registration will then be delivered to the partnership.

The second type of partnership is called "limited" in that there are (1) one or more partners whose liability is limited to such amount as they may respectively undertake to contribute to the partnership, and (2) one or more partners who are jointly and unlimitedly liable for all the obligations of the partnership. A limited partnership must be registered. The entry in the register must contain the following particulars in addition to the items required for registration of the ordinary partnership: (1) statement that the firm is a limited partnership; (2) amount of the limited-liability partners' contribution; (3) the names of the unlimited partners; and (4) the restrictions, if any, on the power of the managing partners to bind the partnership.

Limited Liability Company—A limited company in Thailand has basic legal characteristics similar to a western corporation. A limited company is formed with a Memorandum of Association (Articles of Incorporation) and Articles of Association (By-laws). The Memorandum of Association should be filed with the Department of Commercial Registration, Ministry of Commerce, on the form provided. The memorandum must contain the following particulars: (1) name of the proposed company, which must always end with the word "limited", (2) the geographic location of the corporation; (3) the purpose of the corporation; (4) a declaration that the liability of the shareholders shall be limited; (5) the amount of registered share capital and its division into shares of fixed amount; and (6) the names, addresses, occupations, and signature of the promoters and the number of shares subscribed by each of them.

Shareholders enjoy limited liability. Subject to the Alien Business Law and other applicable laws and regulations, all shareholders may be aliens.

A limited company is managed by a Board of Directors in accordance with the laws and the Articles of Association and subject to the control of the shareholders. Subject to the Alien Business Law and other restrictive laws and regulations, all directors may be aliens. However, it may be necessary to register that one of the directors authorized to bind the company be either an alien holding a non-immigrant visa or a Thai national.

For a private limited company, a minimum of seven shareholders is required at all times.

Recognition of the public limited company represents a new development in Thai corporate law. The relevant law is the Public Companies Act B.E. 2522 (1979). As in the case of private limited companies, liability of shareholders is limited to no more than the par value of the shares remaining unpaid.

The procedure for incorporating a public limited company is similar to that for a private limited company under the Civil and Commercial Code; there are, however, several important differences, as indicated below:

(1) In a private limited company, there must be at least seven natural persons as promoters; for a public limited company this number is increased to 15.

(2) In a private limited company, there must be at least seven shareholders; in a public limited company, there must be at least 100 shareholders.

(3) Unlike a private limited company, a public limited company is entitled to issue debentures.

(4) A private limited company may not offer its shares for sale to the public nor issue a prospectus. A public limited company may offer both shares and debentures for sale to the public if a prospectus has been registered.

(5) A public limited company may have greater flexibility in issuing securities of various kinds.

It is a prerequisite for most applicants for BOI "promoted investor" status, discussed in the following section entitled "Foreign Investment Policy and Regulations," that they set up a limited liability company equivalent to the Western type of corporation. Such a company can be wholly owned by aliens.

Foreign Corporation Branch—There is no general requirement for foreign companies to register to do business in Thailand. However, most businesses fall within the scope of one or more laws or regulations which require registration, either prior to or within 30 days after starting an eligible business.

In the case of a branch office of a foreign company, the following documents are required for registration:

(1) **Affidavit of Company Officer.** This affidavit must set forth the following information: name of corporation, registration number, date of registration, jurisdiction in which registered, address of registered office, authorized capital and share structure, amount of paid up capital, information about each director (name, address, age, race, nationality and number of shares owned), and information about shareholders (nationalities and number of shares owned, except for large public corporations).

(2) **Power of Attorney.** This power of attorney must authorize the branch manager to establish a branch office in Thailand, to act as branch manager thereof, and to effect registration of the branch office with Thai government authorities, in addition to giving him normal powers.

(3) **Memorandum of Association.** In addition to listing the company's objectives, this document should include the power to establish a branch office abroad. The proposed activities in Thailand must be consistent with these objectives.

(4) **Articles of Association.**

(5) **Resolution.** A copy of a Board of Directors' resolution must be provided, containing the decision to establish a branch office in Thailand and the appoint-

ment of the branch manager named in the power of attorney.

(6) **Other Documents.** Documentation must be submitted for any other procedure specifically required by the Articles of the company or otherwise as a prerequisite to establish a branch office in Thailand.

Each of the above documents must be notarized by the Thai Consulate or Embassy in the country of domicile of the foreign company. The proper procedure in each case will depend upon such Thai Consulate or Embassy, and upon current requirements of the Department of Commercial Registration in Bangkok, which should be investigated.

The branch office is required to comply with the laws of the land, to keep proper accounts and records, and to file tax and other returns as required by the authorities, but the documents refer only to the activities of the branch or branches in Thailand; those relating to the head office and branches in other countries are not required. It is imperative that the manager of a branch of a foreign corporation have resident status, but if this cannot be immediately arranged, a qualified stand-in, usually a lawyer or accountant, is appointed through a Deed of Substitution to act temporarily on behalf of the manager.

Charges for registering a firm or company are moderate. Registration fees, revenue stamps and forms should not cost more than 400 baht for a limited company with a capital of 100,000 baht or less. Legal fees are more costly, especially if considerable translation into Thai is required. They range from a possible minimum of 1,000 baht for establishing a sole proprietorship to a possible 8,000 baht for establishing a limited company.

Joint Ventures—A joint venture is not recognized by the civil and commercial code, but it is recognized under the Petroleum Act and the Revenue Code. A joint venture, as a legal entity, can be incorporated as a limited company but the Commercial Registration Department has no authority to register the names of shareholders and the numbers of their shares. Under Thai law, foreigners cannot own more than 49 percent of the equity.

Foreign Investment Policy and Regulations

Investor Incentives—The Government has long officially recognized that foreign investment is an important development tool. Its BOI provides many incentives and guarantees to "promoted investors" (with joint ventures and export-oriented industries given priority) including tax holidays, tariff waivers, assurance against nationalization, and government protection from competition.

At present, BOI's emphasis is upon nine types of industries: agricultural, metal mining, ceramic, chemical, mechanical, electronics, construction materials, textiles, and services, including tourism. Especially desired are new industries that would use local agricultural products.

Ownership Limitations—Late in 1972, the Government enacted the Alien Business Decree (ABD) designed to promote the development of domestic enterprise and to reserve some fields of business to Thai nationals. The ABD sets forth three groups of businesses, Categories A, B, and C, in which all foreign firms must apply for licenses to operate.

Those in Category A—including accounting, law, brokerage, and advertising—must reduce foreign ownership to 49 percent or less within 2 years. Firms in the other categories may grow at a rate of 30 percent a year (not compounded) based on 1972 sales or production unless exceptions are granted by the Commerce Ministry, which has stated that exceptions will be given where a strong case is made. In almost all cases, the Ministry has been granting exceptions to the 30 percent limitation, but usually on only a year-to-year basis.

Most American-owned firms affected have registered under the ABD, even though they are exempted from doing so under the terms of the Thai-American Treaty of Amity and Economic Relations. As a matter of co-operation, some American firms have even reorganized and merged in Category A to bring themselves into compliance with the 49 percent requirement.

Clause four of the ABD gives the Director General of the Commercial Registration Department authority not to apply the ABD to Category C firms, if they hold "promoted investor" certificates issued by the Board of Investment. Among the businesses in Category C are (1) export trade, (2) most wholesale trade, (3) retail trade in machinery, engines, and tools, (4) sale of food and beverages to promote tourism, (5) production of animal feed, vegetable oils, textile and knotted products, containers made from glass, cups, bowls and dishes, production of writing paper and printing papers, (6) rock salt farming, (7) mining, (8) miscellaneous businesses not included in Category A or B.

Effective December 8, 1973, the Thai Government officially protects alien companies classified under Category B of the ABD from its restrictions if the companies have an investment promotion certificate from the Board of Investment and a letter of guarantee from the Director General of the Commercial Registration Department. In the case of any such company whose promotion certificate is revoked, the firm must forfeit the right to operate the business within 180 days. Among businesses in Category B are (1) agricultural, processing, manufacturing, and retail and other trade businesses not mentionaed above as included in Categories A or C (2) land, water, and air transport businesses, and (3) service businesses such as tourist guide, hotels, entertainment, photography, laundry and tailoring.

The Director General may impose conditions upon such alien firms in accordance with regulations issued as they pertain to: (1) the ratio between capital and loans to be used in the operation of the licensed business, (2) money that the licensee shall bring in from foreign countries for financing the operation of the licensed business, (3) the ratio between capital of Thai nationals and that of aliens in operation of the licensed business, and (4) the ratio between the number of Thai workers and that of aliens, or those who are responsible for the operation of the licensed business—they being necessarily local residents.

Under various Thai laws, there are limitations on foreign ownership of land, natural resources such as minerals and forest reserves, real property and most businesses not mentioned above. Further information about these limitations is provided elsewhere in this publication.

Entry and Repatriation of Capital—Thailand has a comprehensive Exchange Control Act, B.E. 2485 (1942), which is administered by the Foreign Exchange Control Division in the Bank of Thailand on behalf of the Ministry of Finance. In practice, restrictions are minimal on payments and transfers for current international transactions provided that requisite formalities are complied with.

In the fields that have not been specifically closed to foreigners, entry of capital for investment purposes is unrestricted. However, foreign exchange created as the result of investment in Thailand must be sold to an authorized agent within 7 days.

The Bank of Thailand maintains a Special Register in which all amounts of foreign exchange remitted or brought to Thailand by investors, either as capital or as a loan for use in the establishment or expansion of industrial enterprises, are recorded. When an investor wishes to remit any dividends, profits, interest, or principal recorded in the Special Register, the Exchange Control Office is prepared to approve (1) transfers of profits or dividends after deduction of income and other taxes and after appropriation of reserves, (2) tranfers of 50 percent of the estimated net profit earned up to 6 months before the end of the fiscal year of each enterprise, (3) transfers of funds in payment of interest or principal in accordance with a contract, and (4) transfers of capital invested upon liquidation of the enterprise in which the capital had been invested or upon submission of proof that such enterprise no longer requires the use of the amount of capital to be repatriated.

Taxation—Most of Thailand's revenue is obtained from indirect taxes such as customs duties on imports and exports. However, there are several other types of tax that are of increasing importance.

Import duties are levied on nearly all goods. The rate can be as high as 60 percent for luxury goods or goods which are produced by local industries and have been placed under government protection. However, it is normal for statutory rates to be markedly lower on agricultural and industrial equipment and supplies for industries that have received promoted industry status from the Board of Investment.

Export duties are imposed on a limited number of products including rice, scrap iron and steel, hides, skins, leather, and rubber.

All companies and partnerships registered under Thai law, or incorporated under foreign laws and conducting business in Thailand (e.g., branches), are subject to company income tax. The tax rate is 30 percent for companies listed on the stock exchange and 40 percent for others.

The Personal Income Tax applies to residents who spend more than 180 days of any tax year in Thailand. The graduated rates are 10 percent on 10,000 baht to 50 percent on income of 400,000 baht or more.

The sales or business tax is based upon monthly gross receipts. Rates vary considerably. For instance, the tax is 20 percent on passenger cars, 25 percent on alcoholic beverages, 12 percent on refrigerators and television sets. However, it may be only 1.5 percent for some kinds of service.

The transfer of profits to a head office overseas is taxed at an effective rate of 16.66 percent of the sum transferred. Other forms of income such as dividends or interest transmitted to juristic persons overseas are taxed at 25 percent of the sums transmitted. In the case of remittances of interest and fees by Thai companies to foreign corporate shareholders, the amounts are tax-deductible. This is not the case for similar remittances by a branch to its head office.

Labor Relations

The Labor Relations Act of 1975 regulates the establishment of employee unions and employer associations. In general, the same procedures apply to both. They must be licensed and registered with the Central Employees' Union and Employers' Association Registration Office of the Department of Labor in order to operate.

Many large industries are owned or controlled by the Royal Thai Government. As previously noted, most small industries are family-owned and operated. Thus, independent employers still are a small minority in Thai industry, and employer or management associations are not widely established.

The Labor Relations Act of 1975 establishes procedures for settling labor disputes by a conciliation officer, arbitrator, and labor relations committee and establishes rules governing the conduct of strikes and lockouts. Over the past year, however, disputes have generally been resolved on an *ad hoc* basis, often with intervention by the Labor Department, the Ministry of Interior and/or the Office of the Prime Minister.

Licensing and Franchising

Under Section 70 of the Revenue Code of Thailand (1930) on submission of returns by companies abroad, royalties from licensing and franchising are subject to revenue tax. Levels of taxation differ and need to be considered and assessed by the Department of Revenue on a case-by-case basis. Franchising is open to all industries, commodities, and services if not restricted by other laws, such as the Alien Business and Occupation Laws.

Intellectual Property Rights

Patents are protected under the Patent Act B.E. 2522 (1979). Under the law, patents on inventions are valid for 15 years. Foreign nationals are permitted to apply for patents if Thai nationals are able to receive reciprocal treatment in the applicant's country. As of March 1983, only 50 patents had been issued, the majority of which are owned by foreigners.

Trademarks are protected under the Trademarks Act B.E. 2474 (1931) and B.E. 2504 (1961). According to Thai law, a trademark includes "a device, brand, heading, label, ticket, name, signature, word, letter, numeral, or any combination thereof used or proposed to be used, or in connection with goods of the proprietor of such trademark by virtue of manufacture, selection, certification, dealing with, or offering for sale." Trademarks not fulfilling specified criteria may be registered after long and extensive use. Three years is generally the required time for registration in this manner. There is some trademark piracy, particularly in the areas of pharmaceuticals and some consumer products.

Under the terms of the Treaty of Amity and Economic Relations, U.S. and Thai entities enjoy bilateral copyright relations, subject to compliance with certain formalities. The principal formalities under the Thai Copyright Act are that the author be a Thai national, or that the work first be published in Thailand. The effect of these two formalities on the level of protection for U.S. nationals is unclear. However, under the Thai law the requirement of nationality is satisfied when the author is a corporate or juristic person.

The Copyright Act of B.E. 2521 (1978) does extend copyright protection to nationals of countries which are parties to the Berne Convention, but the United States is not a member.

Guidance for Business Travelers Abroad

Entrance Requirements

All aliens entering Thailand must carry valid passports. Normally, some sort of visa also is required. The visa requirement may be waived in the case of certain aliens who enter by air or sea, who are transiting Thailand and who possess confirmed onward reservations. American citizens may be granted a "stay without visa" for up to 15 days as may nationals of certain other countries. The majority of aliens, however, are given "transit without visa stays" of only 7 days. Listed below are the requirements for a Thai visa:

(1) A valid passport must be submitted with the applications

(2) Two visa application forms (applicant must sign the forms)

(3) Three passport-size photographs

(4) Visa fees:

    Transit Visa—$5.00 for one entry

    Tourist Visa—$10.00 for one entry

    Non-Immigrant Visa—$15.00 for one entry

Fees are payable in cash, U.S. Postal Money Order, or company check. Personal checks are not accepted. Applications submitted *in person* and not requiring approval of the Immigration Division in Thailand are usually processed within 48 hours. Those submitted by mail are requested to enclose a self-addressed stamped envelope by certified mail. The visa must be utilized within 90 days from the date of issuance.

For transit visas, the maximum stay is 30 days; for tourist visas, 60 days. The maximum stay for non-immigrant visas is 90 days, but an alien who wishes to stay longer must obtain prior approval through the Immigration Division in Bangkok. Such a visa can be obtained in one of two ways:

(1) The applicant may submit the applications through the Thai Embassy or Consulate abroad.

(2) The firm in Thailand where the alien wishes to work may represent the alien by applying directly to the Immigration Division in Bangkok.

For a non-quota immigrant visa (indefinite stay), applicants must submit applications together with certificate of residence directly to the Immigration Division in Bangkok.

There are no health requirements unless entering Thailand from an infected area.

Thai transit and tourist visas are obtainable without delay from Thai Embassies and Consulates throughout the world, provided the applicant is a *bona fide* transient or tourist. Thai non-immigrant visas are also available throughout the world, although aliens applying in a country of which they are not nationals must anticipate a waiting period of approximately 3 to 4 weeks. Thai Embassies and Consulates must refer non-immigrant visa applications to the Ministry of Foreign Affairs in Bangkok for approval prior to issuance of non-immigrants who are not nationals of the country in which their applications are being processed. Thus, in the United States, the Thai Embassy and Thai Consulates can issue non-immigrant visas to American citizens without prior referral to their headquarters in Bangkok. All applications for immigrant visas, regardless of where they are made, must be referred to the Ministry of Foreign Affairs in Bangkok for approval.

American businesspeople who intend to work in Thailand for an indefinite period, as opposed to business trips of less than 30 to 60 days, should obtain non-immigrant or immigrant visas prior to entry. In certain circumstances, the non-immigrant visa-holder may be allowed to stay beyond the normal 30 to 90 days.

Visitors are allowed to bring in duty-free 200 cigarettes or 250 grams of tobacco; one liter of wine and one liter of spirits; one cinema and one still camera with three and five rolls of film respectively; a reasonable amount of clothing for personal use, toilet articles, and professional instruments; and a reasonable amount of household effects if taking up resident status. Imports of narcotics are prohibited, and a license has to be obtained for imports of firearms, ammunition, and certain kinds of plants and fruits. Pets can enter duty-free at the airport, providing a veterinarian's vaccination certificate can be produced.

Pertinent Treaties and Regulations

The Amity and Economic Relations Treaty between the United States and Thailand governs the activities of visiting U.S. businesspeople. It provides that each party may reserve for its own nationals the practice of any profession or calling. Related is the Thai Law of Occupations of Aliens, Decree No. 322, which came into force March 13, 1973. The Law concerns largely three categories of foreigners: (1) those legally resident before the above date, (2) those with investment promotion privileges, and (3) almost everybody else. The first two categories are automatically allowed to choose their pro-

fessions; the third category is subject to the Decree. Besides most skilled and unskilled trade occupations, aliens are prohibited from occupations such as accounting, law, architecture, advertising, brokerage, and civil engineering. They are also prohibited from major industries including farming, fruit growing, fisheries, rice milling, sugar production, hotel operation, pharmaceuticals production, and retailing.

Foreigners entering Thailand and desiring to work for more than 15 days must obtain a work permit as well as the non-immigrant or immigrant visa mentioned above. In theory, foreigners intending to work in Thailand must have their prospective employer file a request for a work permit with the Labor Department. If the Ministry of Labor approves the employment, the foreigner will be granted an appropriate visa and, once in Thailand, shall apply in person for the permit. Questions and initiation of actions to obtain the work permit may be directed to the nearest Thai Embassy or Consulate.

Foreign Exchange

Visitors to Thailand may bring in or take out a maximum of 500 baht each or 1,000 baht in the case of a family traveling under one passport. However, there is no restriction on the amount of foreign currencies that may be brought into the country.

When converting foreign currencies into baht, visitors may obtain favorable rates of exchange at commercial banks or money changers. The Bank of Thailand encourages nonresidents to place foreign currency deposits with commercial banks in Thailand. No restrictions are maintained on opening a foreign currency account as long as the fund originates from abroad. The balance on such account may be transferred without formality or restriction. In addition, a commercial bank may pay an interest rate of up to 12 percent per year on such deposits.

Upon leaving Thailand, the following noncurrency articles may be taken out by a foreigner without authorization from a commercial bank or the Bank of Thailand: (1) precious stones and gold or platinum jewelry with no limit in value; and (2) any effects other than those in (1) above which are valued at less than 10,000 baht. When the tourist wishes to take out articles over the limits as described in (2), he must acquire a Certificate of Exportation from the Bank of Thailand through a commercial bank.

Thailand's exchange controls are considered relatively liberal, and the baht is regarded as a comparatively "hard" currency.

The exchange rate of the baht with the dollar is 23 to 1. Further details are found in the foregoing section entitled "Foreign Investment Policy and Regulations."

Language

English is an accepted language for business and is widely spoken in Bangkok commercial and government circles. English alone may be sufficient for dealings with large private firms and high-level government officials. However, in dealings pertaining to consumer goods (which must be retailed by Thai nationals in accordance with the Alien Occupations Law), a local agent or representative will be necessary to reach the non-English reading and speaking population.

Holidays

Thai national holidays and their respective dates in chronological order for 1984 are: Jan. 1 (New Year's Day), Feb. 16 (Maka Bucha Day), Apr. 6 (Chakri Day), Apr. 13 (Songkran Day), May 5 (Coronation Day), May 14 (Visaka Bucha Day), July 13 (Buddhist Lent), Aug. 12 (Queen's Birthday), Oct. 23 (Chulalongkorn Day), Dec. 5 (King's Birthday), Dec. 10 (Constitution Day).

Information Sources

Government Representation

Thailand's commercial interests in the United States are represented by the Office of the Economic Counselor (Board of Investment), Five World Trade Center, Suite 3443, New York, N.Y. 10048 (tel. 212-466-1745); by the Commercial Counselor of the Royal Thai Embassy, 1990 M St., N.W., Suite 380, Washington, D.C., 20036 (tel. 202-467-6790); and by consular offices and missions at the following locations throughout the United States: (1) 3211 Lebron Avenue, Montgomery, Ala. 36106, (2) 3460 Wilshire Blvd., Suite 814, Los Angeles, Ca. 90010, (3) 1401 Brickell Ave., 9th Floor, Miami, Fla. 33131, (4) 841 Bishop St., Honolulu, Ha. 96813, (5) 111 E. Wacker Dr., Chicago, Ill. 60601, (6) 280 Moross Road, Grosse Pointe Farms, Mi. 48236, (7) Three Dunford Circle, Kansas City, Mo. 64112, (8) 7836 Montgomery Ave., Elkins Park, Pa. 19117, (9) 1900 Wyoming Ave., El Paso, Tx. 79987, (10) Eight Roslyn Rd., Richmond, Va. 23226, (11) 101 Tremont St., Boston, Mass. 02108.

Government of Thailand Publications

Annual Economic Reports, Bank of Thailand, Bangkok.
Monthly Report, Bank of Thailand, Bangkok.
The Fifth National Economic and Social Development Plan. (1982-1986) International Translation, Bangkok.
Thailand Official Yearbook, Office of the Prime Minister, Bangkok.
Thailand Business-Legal Handbook, Prepared by Charles Kirkwood and Associates for the Board of Investment, Bangkok.
The Investor (Monthly), produced on behalf of the Board of Investment by Siam Publications Ltd., Bangkok.
Investing in the Dynamic Growth of Thailand, Private Enterprise Investment Opporinties in Thailand, Board of Investment, Bangkok.
Exchange Control in Thailand, A Guide for the General Reader, Bank of Thailand.

Investment Guide to Thailand, Bangkok First Investment and Trust Limited, Bangkok.
Business in Thailand, (Monthly), Business Information and Research Co., Ltd., Bangkok.
Annual Report, Bangkok Bank Ltd., Bangkok.
Monthly Review, Bangkok Bank Ltd., Bangkok.

United States Government Publications

Economic Trends—Thailand, September 1983, Department of Commerce, Washington, D.C.
Background Notes—Thailand, U.S. Department of State, Washington, D.C.

Other

The Bangkok Post (Daily), Allied Newspapers Ltd., Bangkok.
Businessman's Visa for Thailand, Siam Cement Group, Bangkok.

Key Thai Government and Quasi-Government Agencies

The Bank of Thailand
273 Samsen Rd.
Bangkok 10200, Thailand
Tel. 281-3311

Office of the Prime Minister
Government House
Nakhon Pathom Rd.
Bangkok 10300, Thailand
Tel. 281-2500

Office of the National Economic and Social Development Board
962 Krung Kasem Rd.
Bangkok 10100, Thailand
Tel. 282-1151; 282-3861

Office of the Board of Investment
68 Mansion Rd.
Rajdamnern Ave.
Bangkok 10200, Thailand
Tel. 233-3939/50

Ministry of Defense
Sanamchai Rd.
Bangkok 10200, Thailand
Tel. 222-3121/2

Ministry of Finance
Na Pralan Rd.
Bangkok 10200, Thailand
Tel. 221-4161

The Customs Department
Art Narong Rd.
Klong Toey
Bangkok 10110, Thailand
Tel. 286-1010/9

The Treasury Department
Charkrapong Rd.
Bangkok 10200, Thailand

Ministry of Foreign Affairs
Saranrom Palace
Bangkok 10200, Thailand
Tel. 221-9171/8

Ministry of Agriculture and Cooperatives
Thanon Rajdamnern Nok
Bangkok 10200, Thailand
Tel. 281-5955

The Royal Irrigation Department
Samsen Rd.
Bangkok 10300, Thailand
Tel. 241-0740/9

Department of Livestock Development
Phyathai Rd.
Bangkok 10400, Thailand
Tel. 251-5136

Department of Fisheries
Thanon Rajdamnern Nok
Bangkok 10200, Thailand
Tel. 281-8600

Department of Agriculture
Kaset-Klang, Bangkhan
Phaholyothin Rd.
Bangkok 10900, Thailand
Tel. 579-0151/8

Ministry of Communications
Thanon Rajdamnern Nok
Bangkok 10100, Thailand
Tel. 281-3422

Department of Land Transport
Phaholyothin Rd.
Bangkok 10900, Thailand
Tel. 278-1055/7

Department of Aviation
Tong Mahmek, Yannaua
Bangkok 10120, Thailand
Tel. 286-0921/5

Harbor Department
Yotha Rd.
Bangkok 10100, Thailand
Tel. 233-1311/8

Department of Highways
Sri Ayudhaya Rd.
Bangkok 10400, Thailand
Tel. 281-7421; 281-7404

Ministry of Commerce
Sanamchai Rd.
Bangkok 10200, Thailand
Tel. 222-0855

Department of Foreign Trade
Sanamchai Rd.
Bangkok 10200, Thailand
Tel. 223-1481/5

Ministry of Interior
Asdang Rd.
Bangkok 10200, Thailand
Tel. 222-1141/51

Department of Public Works
Pan Fah Bridge
Larn Luang Rd.
Bangkok 10100, Thailand
Tel. 231-3647

Ministry of Public Health
Devaves Palace
Samsen Rd.
Bangkok 10200, Thailand
Tel. 281-9433

Ministry of Science, Technology and Energy
Department of Science Service, 6th Fl.
Yothi Rd., Phayathai
Bangkok 10400, Thailand
Tel. 281-4767

Market Profile—THAILAND

Foreign Trade

Imports—(c.i.f.) $8,548 million in 1982 and estimated $9,435 million in 1983. Thai imports from the U.S. in 1982 were $1,173 million and estimated to be $1,321 million in 1983. Main imports from the U.S.: electrical machinery; machinery, mechanical appliances and parts, chemicals and chemical products; tobacco; cotton; plastic; and fertilizer.

Exports—(f.o.b.) $6,949 million in 1982 and estimated $6,896 million in 1983. Thai exports to the U.S. in 1982 were $888 million and estimated to be $903 million in 1983. Chief Thai exports: Rice, corn, rubber, sugar, tapioca, tin, artifacts, and pineapple.

Trade Policy—Moderate to heavy tariffs except authorized items for preferred industries. Licensing controls limited mainly to selected locally produced, health, and security items. GATT signatory, as of 1982. Most-favored nation agreement with the United States.

Trade Prospects—There is a wide range of potential markets, but the ten sectors thought to be offering the best sales prospects for U.S. exporters are: food processing and packaging equipment; medical equipment; computers and peripherals; pumps, valves, and compressors; electric power generation equipment; avionic and ground support equipment; marine ports and ship building equipment; material handling machinery and equipment; and telecommunications equipment.

Foreign Investment

U.S. direct investment in Thailand totaled $594 million at the end of 1982. The Japanese account for 25 percent of all registered foreign capital of Board of Investment promoted companies, while the United States and Taiwan each account for about 10 percent. American investors can take advantage of the investment guarantee and insurance program offered by the Overseas Private Investment Corporation (OPIC) to cover their investments in Thailand.

Investment Prospects—Investment climate good except for some problems with commercial counterfeiting. U.S. firms receive national treatment in most cases through the 1966 Treaty of Amity and Economic Relations. Promotional privileges available from Board of Investment.

Finance

Currency—The baht: valued against a basket of currencies. Currently 23 baht equals US$1.

Domestic Credit and Investment—Commercial bank prime rate was 17.2 percent at mid-year 1982 and moved down to 16.0 percent at the end of 1982.

National Budget—FY 1984 (ending Sept. 30, 1984) budget expenditures are authorized at $8.3 billion, mainly for social services and defense. This is an 8.5 percent increase over FY 1983. Revenues are projected to be $6.9 billion.

Foreign Aid—U.S. aid grants and loans in 1982 totaled $36.4 million. The World Bank is the largest supplier of soft loans with $252 million committed in FY 1981. The Asian Development Bank is second with $55 million.

Balance of Payments—International reserves were $2.4 billion at the end of 1982. Balance of payments showed a surplus of $144 million in 1982, up from $116 million in 1981.

Economy

Mainly agricultural (about 78 percent of labor force). Growing industrial and mining sector, favorable growth rate.

GNP—Estimated at $14.3 billion in 1983, compared to $13.5 billion in 1982. Per capita GNP in 1983 prices about $805.

Basic Economic Facilities

Transportation.—Railroad system of 3,897 kilometers and highway system of 34,950 kilometers.

Communications.—Limited but improving. About 314,000 telephone lines in Bangkok in 1980. Microwave system for interregional communications nearing completion. Thailand has 196 radio broadcasting stations, 9 television stations, and roughly 1.5 million television receivers.

Power.—Capacity was 3,910 megawatts in 1982; country will need capacity of 7,000 megawatts by 1990. Household current is 220 volts/50 cycles.

Natural Resources

Land.—200,000 square miles. Over 27 million acres cultivated.

Minerals.—Sizable natural gas, tin, tungsten, and lignite reserves. Tin is a major export. Unexploited deposits of manganese, molybdenum, antimony, and others.

Forestry.—Teak a major export.

Population

Size.—50.7 million at mid-1983. About 85 percent Thai, 12 percent Chinese.

Labor Force.—22 million at mid-1983, expanding by 500,000 annually. Over 50 percent of total are unpaid family workers in agricultural sector.

Education.—Literacy rapidly increasing; over 85 percent for those 10 years and older.

Language.—Thai; English usable in business.

Import—Export Trade*
(millions of dollars)

	1980	1981	1982
Total Imports, (c.i.f.)	9,216	9,933	8,548
Imports from the U.S.	1,328	1,170	1,173
Manufactured goods	5,106	5,502	4,919
Agricultural goods	427	356	340
Other	3,683	4,075	3,289
Total Exports, (f.o.b)	6,506	7,013	6,949
Exports to the U.S.	822	946	888
Manufactured goods	2,225	2,066	2,154
Agricultural goods	2,976	3,566	3,881
Other	1,305	1,381	914

*Thailand data.

Principal Imports from the U.S. in 1982*
(millions of U.S. dollars)

	Value	Percent of Total
Electronic components	168.9	18.6
Tobacco	67.4	7.4
Cotton	54.5	6.0
Synthetic resins, plastics	34.2	3.8
Telecommunications equipment	25.2	2.8
Refined petroleum products	24.7	2.7
Aircraft	23.6	2.6
Organic chemicals	23.2	2.6
Civil engineering and contractors' equipment	21.7	2.4
Measuring, checking instruments	21.6	2.4

*U.S. data.

Market Profile—TOGO

Foreign Trade

Imports.—$433.1 million in 1981; $526 million in 1982. Major suppliers, 1981: France. Nigeria. United Kingdom, Netherlands, Japan. and United States. Major imports: machinery, and heavy equipment, transportation equipment, textiles, and foodstuffs. From United States 1982 ($25 million): wheat, 17.6 percent; used clothing, 17.2 percent; rags and scrap of cordage, 10.8 percent; turkeys, 8.4 percent; and rice, 5 percent.

Exports.—$207 million in 1981; $213 million in 1982. Major markets: France. Yugoslavia, Netherlands, Nigeria, Germany, the United States, in 10th place. Major exports: phosphates, coffee, cocoa, peanuts, cotton, and palm oil. To United States, 1982 ($10.1 million): coffee, 96.9 percent; ethnographic objects, 1.1 percent; gold bullion ore, 0.5 percent. From Ghana: animals (excl. birds). 0.5 percent; live birds, 0.5 percent.

Trade Policy.—Nondiscriminatory policy. One of five members of Conseil de l'Entente. Signed International Coffee Agreement. Member of Economic Community of West African States. Signed Lome Convention between EEC and 58 other developing nations.

Trade Prospects.—Food processing equipment, consumer products, agricultural chemicals and equipment, and electical machinery offer best sales potential. Important transit trade with Niger. Mali, and Upper Volta which have warehouses in Togo's port zone. Major African market (1982): Ghana; Major African supplier (1982): Ivory Coast.

Foreign Investment

Predominantly French. U.S. investment in petroleum exploration and distribution and two banks. Investment guaranty agreement and treaty of amity and economic relations in effect with United States. Liberal investment code.

Finance

Currency.—CFA franc. 399 CFA francs=US$1 in Oct. 1983.

Foreign Aid.—France and West Germany are the major contributors, with United States, Canada, EEC, World Bank, and the UNDP of increasing significance. U.S. economic assistance FY 1982. $5.3 million: development assistance, $3.4 million (63.7 percent); PL 480, $1.9 million (35.6 percent); IMET, $36,000 (0.7 percent).

Balance of Payments.—Deficit of $141.2 million estimated for 1980.

Economy

Primarily agricultural with industry, phosphate mining, transport services, and commerce sectors expanding. Has an extensive private sector. Government monopoly on certain products.

GDP.—$812.5 million in 1982; 316.6 per capita 4.8 percent growth rate. Commerce and services make greatest contribution to GDP.

Agriculture.—Predominantly subsistence. Food crops: manioc, yams, maize, millet, sorghum, beans, and rice. Main cash crops: coffee and cocoa.

Industry.—40 medium-sized manufacturing plants producing such products as phosphates, petroleum products, cement, steel, glass, textiles, palm oil, sugar, and milk.

Development Plan.—Preparation of Five-Year Development Plan 1981-85 (367 billion CFA Francs). Will emphasize transforming industries, agricultural development, grain storage facilities, and solar energy development.

Basic Economic Facilities

Transportation.—About 4,350 miles of road (820 miles paved). Total 275 miles of railroad. Modernized deep water port at Lome moves imports and exports. Jet airport at Lome.

Communications.—System based on skeletal network of open-wire lines supplemented by a rapid relay route and radio communication stations. 7,800 telephone system is state-operated (0.3 per 100 people). Two AM radio stations, three TV stations; one Atlantic Ocean satellite station.

Power.—Domestic capacity (all thermal) over 95,000 kW capacity (1982); produced 150 million kWh in 1982, 20 kWh per capita. Imports 250 million kWh from Ghana.

Natural Resources

Land.—21,853 square miles, about the size of West Virginia. Six distinct zones; littoral, plateau, mountains, hills, savanna, and valley.

Climate.—Equatorial, hot and humid in the central mountains. April to October, rainy season.

Minerals.—High-grade phosphate production, 2.2 million metric tons in 1981. Total production capacity 3.2 million metric tons.

Population

Size.—2.8 million 1983; 3.1 percent average annual growth rate; 15 percent urban. Lome, largest city and capital, has a population of 130,000 (1980 estimate).

Language.—French.

Education.—Literacy rate 18 percent. Approximately 55 percent of school-age (7-14) children attend schools.

Labor.—About 1 million labor force. Agriculture 80 percent; industry and private sectors 88,600 wage earners evenly divided between public and private sectors.

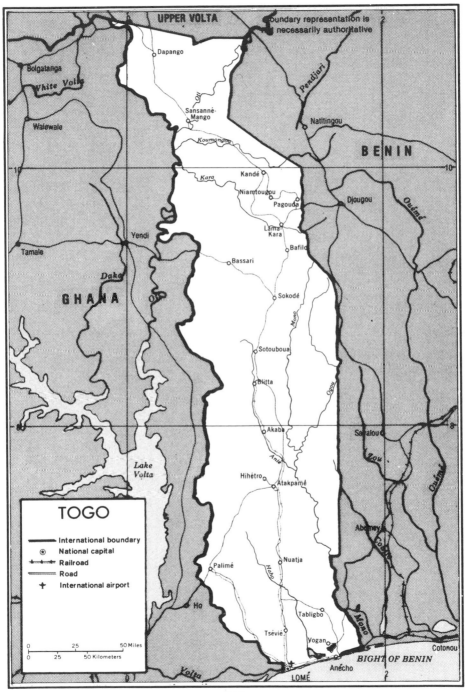

UPPER VOLTA

...oundary representation is
...necessarily authoritative

Bolgatanga

White Volta

Dapango

Pendjari

BENIN

Waiewaie

Sansanné-
Mango

Natitingou

Koumongou

10

Kandé

Kara

Niamtougou

Pagouda

Djougou

Ouémé

Lama-
Kara

Yendi

Bafilo

Tamale

Bassari

Daka

Oti

GHANA

Sokodé

Mono

Sotouboua

Blitta

Oyou

Akaba

Saralou

Zou

Anié

Lake
Volta

Hihétro

Atakpamé

Ossini

Abomey

TOGO

——— International boundary
⊛ National capital
╬ Railroad
═══ Road
✛ International airport

Palimé

Nuatja

Haho

Ho

Tabligbo

Mono

Tsévié

Vogan

Cotonou

| 0 | 25 | 50 Miles |
| 0 | 25 | 50 Kilometers |

LOMÉ

Anécho

BIGHT OF BENIN

Volta

2391

Market Profile—TONGA

Foreign Trade

Exports.—In 1978, $5.6 million, primarily fruit and fruit products, nuts and copra.

Imports.—In 1978, $12.4 million consisting mostly of meat and meat products, machinery and transport systems, wood products, and petroleum products. New Zealand is the major trading partner.

Trade Policy.—Tonga has two tariff rates; the Commonwealth Preference rate from 15 to 25 percent, and the General Tariff of 20 to 45 percent. Books and periodicals, corn, eggs, meat, music, photographs, pictures, seeds and samples are admitted duty free. There are no excise taxes; however, bananas, coconuts, corn, gold, silver and copra are subject to export duties.

Trading Agencies.—Burns Philp Co., Ltd., and Morris Hedstran, Ltd.

Best Trade Prospects.—Agricultural equipment, canning facilities, fishing equipment, manufacturing machinery.

Finance

Currency.—US $1 = $0.91 Tongan.

Bank.—The Treasury fills the role of a trading bank; the formation of a commercial bank and an industrial development fund is under consideration.

Foreign Aid.—As of September 1977, the Asian Development Bank had loaned $2.9 million for road improvement and construction projects. Another Asian Development Bank Loan of $370,000 was made for further development and expansion of light industries.

Economy

GDP.—GDP for 1979 totaled $31 million; per capita income was $355.

Development Plans.—The coconut and timber industries need further development. However, improvements in Tonga's ports and other modes of transportation are required for economic growth.

Basic Economic Facilities

Air Transportation.—The international airport on Tongatapu provides service through Air Pacific, South Pacific Island Airways, and Polynesian Airlines. Air Pacific handles traffic between Fiji and Auckland, New Zealand, via Tonga as well as regular service to Apia, Pago Pago, Suva, and Niva.

Road Transportation.—Thre are approximately 588 miles of road, mostly earth or coral; 54 miles are paved. Priority is given to road construction and maintenance connecting villages and population centers.

Communications.—Radio is the basic mode of communication for the Tonga Islands, although there is limited telephone service in Nukualofa.

Power.—Nukualofa, the center of trade activity, is well supplied with electricity of 240 volts AC.

Natural Resources

Location.—The Tonga Islands, commonly called the Friendly Islands, are located approximately 450 miles southwest of Pago Pago, American Samoa.

Climate.—Tropical with a rainy season extending from December to April.

Forestry.—Good quality timber has the potential of becoming a major export commodity. Presently it is not commercially exploited.

Fisheries.—The fishing industry is relatively underdeveloped. It is a potentially important export industry.

Population

Size.—As of 1982, 102,000 inhabitants.

Language.—English is the language of business. Tongan is spoken in many dialects.

Education.—Compulsory schooling for children ages 6 to 14.

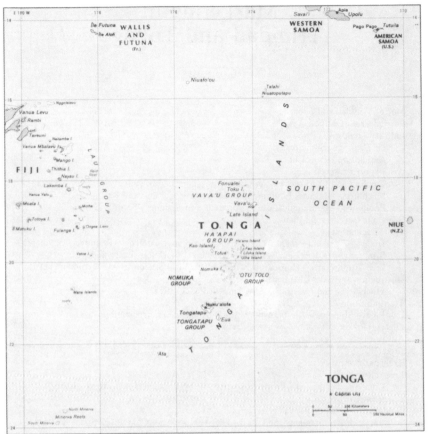

519517 10-79

2393

Marketing in
Trinidad and Tobago

Contents

Report Revised September 1980

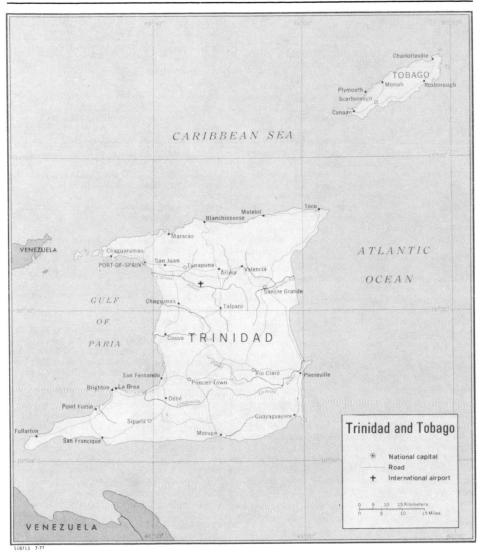

CARIBBEAN SEA

TOBAGO
Charlotteville
Plymouth
Scarborough
Moriah
Roxborough
Canaan

VENEZUELA

ATLANTIC

OCEAN

Toco
Matelot
Blanchisseuse
Maracas
Chaguaramas
San Juan
PORT-OF-SPAIN
Tunapuna
Arima
Valencia
Sangre Grande
GULF
Chaguanas
Talparo
OF
Couva
TRINIDAD
PARIA
San Fernando
Rio Claro
Pierreville
Brighton
La Brea
Princes Town
Point Fortin
Débé
Siparia
Guayaguayare
Fullarton
Moruga
San Francique

Trinidad and Tobago

⊛ National capital
Road
✚ International airport

| 0 | 5 | 10 | 15 Kilometers |
| 0 | 5 | 10 | 15 Miles |

VENEZUELA

518713 7-77

Foreign Trade Outlook

Prospects for U.S. trade with Trinidad and Tobago look very good for the next several years as that country's industrialization program, based on the petroleum and natural gas industries, is moving ahead in high gear. While total imports rose 8.7 percent in 1978, non-petroleum imports increased 21.5 percent with the United States supplying about 34 percent of that category. U.S. market share is declining however, since non-traditional suppliers have been attracted by the industrial development program and the government is making a concerted effort to diversify its economic relationships from dependence on traditional partners such as the United States, the United Kingdom, and Canada. Trinidad and Tobago's total import figures are not yet available for 1979. Total U.S. exports in 1979 were $462 million. In the first 4 months of 1979, U.S. exports rose to $208.6 million, a 28 percent increase over the same period of 1978.

Several factors have restricted imports. These include port congestion resulting in a surcharge on ocean freight. This has diverted some freight to air cargo that is more expensive and is straining the airlines' freight capacity. A temporary port has been established at Point Lisas, site of a growing industrial complex, to handle equipment and materials for the major projects under construction. A permanent, industrial port is under construction there, but completion is still some time off.

Trinidad still has a strong balance of payments surplus in spite of slight declines in exports, largely petroleum products (90 percent of the total), in 1977 and 1978, as well as growing imports. The surplus stood at $391 million at the end of 1979, while foreign exchange reserves were just over $2 billion, an increase of 23 percent over 1978, which also showed a 23 percent increase over 1977.

Besides goods and services for the development program, there will be strong demand for food products, construction equipment and materials, equipment for metalworking, plastic, woodworking, oilfield use, communications, and security plus a broad range of consumer goods. Competition is getting tighter, however. Major trading partners' market shares for non-oil imports in 1978 were United Kingdom, 21 percent, Canada, 6 percent, and the European Community, 12 percent, with Japan's share growing although not specified.

Industry Trends

Trinidad and Tobago has embarked upon a massive $3-5 billion industrialization program aimed at employing its oil revenue and natural resources to create employment, to convert raw materials into export products with high value

---

HOW TO OBTAIN BACKGROUND INFORMATION ABOUT THESE COUNTRIES

Keeping this book within reasonable size limits has made it necessary to focus on material *directly* concerned with marketing and commerce, and set aside materials only indirectly related. The editors relize, however, that *general* data about a country are also vital to a company's preparations to enter a foreign market, and make a very definite recommendation as to how such expanded information needs can be served.

For those who wish *general* data about a country—data which goes beyond marketing and commerce—the editors recommend *Countries of the World and Their Leaders*, published as an annually updated yearbook by Gale Research Company, Detroit, Michigan 48226. Containing 4- to 20-page entries on 168 countries, the volume also provides several hundred pages of supplementary world data. Each country entry is prepared by the U.S. Department of State to provide a general briefing on the geography, people, culture, and political situation of the particular country. Each report provides some historical insight as well as a look at contemporary trends of lifestyle in the country. Reports also discuss a country's educational system, its press, ethnic groupings and religious practices.

Countries of the World and Their Leaders provides a fresh listing of cabinet ministers of each nation. In addition it lists health conditions the traveling businessman will wish to prepare for and includes information on passport procedures, customs and duties, and world climate conditions.

---

added content and to reduce the country's dependence upon the petroleum sector. A fertilizer plant was completed in 1979. Other major government projects at various stages of implementation or planning include an iron and steel mill, a second fertilizer plant, a petrochemical plant, a methanol plant, an aluminum smelter, an LNG (liquid natural gas) plant and expansion of a state-owned petroleum refinery. Other top priority projects include a new cement plant, refractories, and a pulp and paper project. Implementation of these projects will mean vast additional expenditure on electric power generation, port and harbor construction, water resources development, and infrastructural changes. These projects should be complete and in operation by the mid 1980's.

U.S. firms should be in a good position to provide engineering, design, training, and consulting services for these high technology projects, particularly in joint ventures. The government also is actively promoting investment in light manufacturing industries, especially those, such as metalworking industries, that will complement the major projects.

Current Economic Situation

High technology industrial projects are the basis of the government's development strategy and are based on use of the country's oil and gas reserves. These and other major construction projects have sustained strong economic growth, even though petroleum production and refining began declining in 1978. Real growth was 11.7 percent in 1977 and 7.7 percent in 1978. Per capita income is presently estimated at $3,750.

Unemployment has fallen from 15.2 percent in 1975 to 11.9 percent in 1979, although employment in agriculture has declined. There are, nevertheless, shortages of skilled workers and managerial personnel, aggravated by the construction boom, that has also caused substantial wage increases and shortages of building materials.

To meet these problems the Government has made agreements with friendly governments under which the latter will oversee the implementation of specific projects in Trinidad. It is hoped these "government to government" arrangements will assure timely completion of key projects.

Inflation has been another concern which is caused partly by the huge petroleum revenues of the past 6 years, but also by the inflation in

pricipal supplier countries—a situation over which the Government has little control. The retail price index climbed 9.6 percent in 1978 and 14.7 percent in 1979, and it is now thought to be close to 20 percent.

Manufacturing sector output has also been expanding, although exports to CARICOM (Caribbean Community and Common Market, comprising the English-speaking Caribbean lands) members have declined somewhat. The high level of oil revenues and the capital intensive nature of the petroleum industry and the major plants in the development program have contributed high levels of capital formation throughout the 1970's. Capital expenditure was 24.3 percent of total expenditure in 1977 and 29.4 percent in 1978.

Construction has been dynamic in both the government and private sectors during recent years. It has been growing substantially in industrial plants, infrastructure, offices, and housing and will continue to grow as new major projects are implemented. The government is also aiming at a 6,500 unit per year housing program.

Agriculture

The agriculture sector declined in relative importance throughout the 1970's. In 1978, the sector accounted for 3 percent of Growth Domestic Product (GDP), as compared to 6 percent of GDP at the beginning of the decade. Almost all sectors shared in the production decline in 1978. On the whole, Trinidad and Tobago continues to rely heavily on imports to meet its food requirements.

The sugar industry output in 1978 was only 144.7 thousand tons, the lowest since 1952. It declined further in 1979. The marked drop in production was due to adverse price and weather conditions, high production costs, numerous incidence of fires, and reduction in the crop area. Cocoa production also declined significantly due to labor shortages and adverse weather conditions. Coffee production has remained stable in recent years.

Domestic agricultural production also declined in most key areas. Copra production declined in 1978, despite government initiatives and assistance. After a sharp decline in 1977, citrus production rebounded in 1978 in response to favorable weather conditions. After 2 years of steady gain, production of meat dropped in 1978, mostly due to a fall in pork output. The only upward trend in livestock production was that of the poultry and egg industry. Milk production declined due to the reduction in dairy cattle population that resulted from drought and disease.

Petroleum

Growth has been sluggish in the petroleum sector. Its contribution to GDP dropped from 22 percent in 1970 to 16 percent in 1978.

Crude oil production, mostly from two large offshore refineries, remains high. However, the steady increase from 1972 leveled off in 1978 with crude output of 230,000 barrels a day, and then declined to 215,000 barrels in 1979. Low refinery throughout is largely responsible for the sector's sluggish growth. This is because crude imports also declined, bringing utilization down to 53 percent of capacity in 1978. Considerable exploration of offshore resources indicates potential for future growth.

A bright spot in the petroleum sector is the increase in petrochemical and asphalt production. After major setbacks in 1977, petrochemical production grew by 84.7 percent in 1978, largely on account of the contributions from the ammonia plant that began operation in October 1977.

An independent study of the natural gas reserves was recently commissioned by the government. As a result of this study, the government is operating on an assumption of 12 trillion cubic feet proven or presumed provable reserves, and a total reserve of 21 trillion cubic feet considered not unrealistic. These reserves are considered sufficient for a project to convert natural gas into industrial uses.

Best Export Prospects

Best export prospects are in capital goods because consumer items are strongly affected by the "Negative List". This is a protective device to encourage local processing, packaging, light manufacturing, and assembly industries.

The U.S. Embassy in Port of Spain has identified industry sectors that show especially strong growth potential over the next several years. These sectors should result in excellent opportunities for U.S. exporters.

Building and Construction Supplies, Equipment, and Machinery

Trinidad and Tobago is experiencing fundamental changes in the construction industry, in size of projects, and in construction technology. Along with the major industrial projects, the government has given major impetus to housing construction. They have set a goal of 6,500 housing units per year for the 10-year period which began in 1978. Substantial outlays also have been made for construction of hospitals, schools, and public buildings.

These construction programs are placing severe strain on available local resources. Imports include cement, clay, limestone, sand, gravel, plaster, and wood products. The cement shortage will be alleviated with the completion of a new cement plant this year. Steel and steel pipes are imported in large quantities, although increased local production of some steel products has caused imports in this category to drop. A new iron and steel mill is to begin production in late 1980.

Metalworking Machinery

As a result of the industrial development program launched by the government, a sharp increase in demand for metalworking machinery is expected, especially welding equipment. According to local importers and metalworking firms, the expected market growth is estimated at 50 percent and could possibly double, when all planned major projects are actually carried out. The U.S. market is growing and stands at about

Table 1.—Trinidad and Tobago Exports to the World 1977 and January–August 1978
(in thousands of U.S. dollars)

Commodity group	1977	1978
Animals and animal products	3,462	2,869
Vegetable products	8,003	7,993
Animal and vegetable oils, fats, and waxes	1,544	970
Prepared foodstuffs beverages and tobacco	62,807	53,549
Mineral products	2,026,483	1,850,313
Chemical products	35,607	61,610
Rubber and plastic and articles thereof	1,512	1,225
Hides, skins, leather and articles thereof	4	110
Wood, charcoal, cork, straw, and basket ware	129	111
Paper and paperboard and articles thereof	5,951	5,142
Textiles and products	10,191	9,497
Artificial flowers, human hair, footwear, headgear, etc.	995	886
Stone, cement, and asbestos	1,209	1,533
Jewelry	1,154	1,055
Base metals and products	4,871	5,269
Machinery, electrical equipment and parts	7,666	10,801
Transport equipment	3,300	20,411
Optical, measuring and scientific instruments	2,544	3,292
Arms and ammunition	0.4	.05
Manufactured, articles NES	743	649
Works of Art, antiques	1	11
Special Transactions	1,546	2,340
Grand Total	2,179,996	2,039,636

Source: Overseas Trade Bi-Monthly Report. Central Statistical Office of the Republic of Trinidad and Tobago, December, 1977 and December 1978.

Table 2.—United States: 1977-79 Exports to Trinidad and Tobago by Principal Commodity Groups

(in thousands of U.S. dollars)

	1977	1978	1979
Food and live animals	35,009	45,610	61,500
Wheat, unmilled	1,455	6,458	8,513
Corn, unmilled	7,916	8,438	10,155
Oilseed cake, meal and residues	4,668	2,176	2,539
Potatoes, except sweet potatoes, fresh	935	—	892
Crude materials, inedible, except fuel	5,963	6,934	13,993
Wood, rough, roughly shaped or simply worked	2,397	1,666	7,228
Mineral fuels, lubricants and related materials	2,466	2,386	2,498
Lubricating oils and greases	1,883	—	1,906
Oils and fats, animals and vegetable	3,939	5,001	8,210
Fixed vegetable oils	2,125	3,133	4,833
Chemicals	25,822	27,058	38,089
Ammonia, anhydrous, or aqueous solution, fertilizer grade	1,486	237	—
Synthetic resins and plastic materials	4,472	6,250	8,820
Additives for lubricating and fuel oils	1,883	1,681	1,906
Machinery and transport equipment	154,805	145,573	206,361
Machinery, non-electric	93,476	86,106	127,099
Internal combustion engines, except aircraft and parts	2,878	3,770	6,583
Gas turbines and parts for mechanical drives	3,065	942	649
Tractors, except road and industrial	4,454	2,961	2,226
Metalworking machinery, except machine tools and parts	1,358	3,155	3,601
Construction and mining machinery and parts	34,378	33,068	26,740
Heating and cooling machinery and equipment, and aprts	6,349	8,631	17,122
Pumps for liquids and gases, blowers, compressors, centrifuges (other than cream separators and filtering and purifying machinery and parts	7,547	12,184	20,809
Mechanical and handling machinery and equipments and parts	8,967	7,395	15,643
Electrical Machinery, apparatus and appliances	17,187	11,867	16,457
Electric power machinery and parts	1,996	1,139	2,024
Electric apparatus for making and breaking or for protecting electrical circuits and parts	1,301	2,180	2,690
Telecommunications apparatus, and parts	6,054	12,728	9,399
Electric household equipment and appliances, and parts	3,590	4,692	6,388
Transport equipment	44,142	18,359	28,899
Passenger cars, trucks, buses, special purpose vehicles, chassis with engines mounted, new or used, all fuels	7,242	7,497	7,339
Motor vehicle parts and accessories	3,549	4,705	5,913
Aircraft and parts	3,217	13,237	14,553
Ships and boats, excluding military, including special purpose	1,462	4,993	235
Other manufactured goods	144	62,135	84,339
Iron and steel	12,911	18,655	19,770
Iron or steel bars, rods, angles, shapes, sections and sheet piling	1,163	1,015	4,903
Iron or steel tubes, pipes and fittings	11,300	15,916	12,512
Finished structural parts and structures, iron and steel, aluminum and Zinc	1,868	5,453	12,629
Tools for use in hand or machine use	1,565	2,043	3,023
Clothing and accessories except fur; elastic or rubber knit fabric, knit house furnishings and articles	2,083	2,503	2,140
Measuring, controlling and scientific instruments	2,641	5,170	7,959
Misc commodities and transactions NEC	5,939	829	1,064
Total domestic exports	301,824	326,304	455,696
Reexports	3,847	4,077	6,172
Total exports, including reexports	305,671	330,381	461,868
Total exports, including special category	305,695	330,412	462,037

NOTE: Certain commodities are designated as special category commodities for which regulations prevent the release of detailed commodity information. Source: U.S. Department of Commerce, Bureau of the Census, U.S. Exports, World Areas by Schedule B Commodity Groupings, Report FT 455, Annual 1977 and unpublished 1978 and 1979.

45 percent, compared to 21 percent from the United Kingdom.

With construction of an iron and steel mill now under way, and an aluminum smelter planned, the Government has given high priority to investment in metal working industries to maximize employment opportunities. At the same time, the development program itself will involve a significant increase in demand for a wide variety of metal products. These factors will mean a high demand for imports of metalworking machinery over the next few years. The Government also is actively seeking licensing and joint venture proposals from foreign firms for these industries.

Most local manufactures of domestic metal products, such as shop fronts, furniture, and louvres, import their metalworking machinery directly, since this is a highly specialized field and it would be difficult for any agent to represent such a variety of lines. However, there is a reasonably large number of established local firms importing welding equipment and machine tools, either for distribution or leasing, or for their own manufacturing purposes.

Business Equipment and Systems

Many local business establishments in various sectors of the market are expanding and modernizing their present range of operations, resulting among other things, in an increased demand for office machines. From interviews with local importers and distributors it appears that an increase in imports of 40–50 percent a year can be expected.

IBM, 3M and Xerox have their own affiliate/subsidiary marketing and distribution operations in Trinidad. IBM, apart from supplying computers and computer services, has at present the largest market share for electric typewriters, many of which are manufactured in Canada. In the line of duplicating machines, the estimated market share of 3M is 20–25 percent and 70 percent for Xerox.

Although the business equipment market has not grown significantly in the past few years, the economic development program will required a substantial increase in clerical services, and a corresponding growth in demand for related hardware. Computer softwear also is expected to be in demand.

Cooling and Refrigeration Equipment

While the United States presently dominates the market or air conditioning and cooling equipment, growing opportunities and competition will occur as industrial development broadens and diversifies the use of this equipment. Major industrial plants requiring large scale cooling installations will provide the largest sales opportunities. This equipment will usually form an integral part of the original installation and suppliers should be prepared to work closely with potential foreign contractors and investors in planning the overall plant construction.

Light industry in a tropical climate also requires cooling systems for both the comfort of employees and efficient operation of machinery. The use of local agents as a source of information on new opportunities in this area and for adequate servicing of new units is highly desirable. While some business and residential air conditioners are assembled locally, there is a large import market for commercial and specialized cooling and air conditioning systems. With standards of living improving markedly since the oil boom, a substantial increase is foreseen in the use of homes and office air conditioning systems.

Communications Equipment and Systems

Trinidad has made considerable progress on updating the obsolete and inadequate telephone system. There is an increasing demand for communications systems in both the private and public sectors as the economy becomes more industrialized and sophisticated. Imports in this category can be increased significantly. The United States has enjoyed about 70 percent of the market in recent years.

The Trinidad and Tobago Telephone Co., Ltd. (TELCO), which is wholly-owned by the government, provides automatic telephone services throughout Trinidad and Tobago, and a semi-automatic international service. New lines are being installed at the rate of 20–25,000 every 3 years. As most equipment is purchased directly by the company, exporters should contact the General Manager, Trinidad and Tobago Telephone Co., Ltd., 54 Frederick Street, Port of Spain, Trinidad, W.I.

The Trinidad and Tobago External Telecommunications Co., Ltd. (TEXTEL), a joint enterprise between the government (51 percent) and the British firm, Cable and Wireless Ltd. (49 percent), operates international transmission facilities via earth satellite station. Prior to acquisition of majority ownership by the Government of Trinidad and Tobago in 1973, most equipment had been imported from the United Kingdom and Europe. During recent years the United States has become a major supplier of communications systems, due to lower prices and faster deliveries.

TEXTEL's expansion plans will necessitate additional radio equipment (both small and large), new technology for the satellite station and new record services equipment. U.S. manufactures interested in exporting such equipment should send their specifications to: The Chief Engineer, Trinidad and Tobago External Telecommunications Col, Ltd., 1 Edward Street, Port of Spain, Trinidad.

Because of difficulties in transport and communications between Port of Spain and Point Lisas, companies working on the development projects there are considering installation of internal communications systems. There is only a very small number of agents in Trinidad handling radio and telecommunications equipment, due to the difficulty in finding skilled technicians in this field. The market growth for communications systems was expected to be 25 percent per annum through 1980, both for the government sector and for the private sector.

Security Systems

The security systems market, a new dimension of communication equipment, is evolving rapidly as economic affluence brings with it a greater number of criminal incidents. Sales opportunities include radios, alarms, closed circuit television systems, and similar items.

Economic Development Plan

The government's development strategy centers around plans for a number of high technology industrial projects which will benefit from Trinidad and Tobago's oil and gas reserves. In some cases, these plants will use petroleum products directly, and in others as a relatively cheap source of energy. Implementation is now proceeding. Construction of the iron and steel mill is well advanced, and the plant should begin production by the middle of 1980. Engineering of the third ammonia plant has been completed and construction begun. Foreign partners have been selected for the aluminum smelter, and design and engineering work on the upgrading of the TRINTOC refinery has been started. Studies on the proposed LNG liquefaction plant are also continuing. Urea and methanol plants also are under active consideration. Infrastructure construction and other complementary work appear to be moving ahead in tandem with the industrial plants. Total investment is expected to reach about $6 billion when the major plants are completed. The site of the major portion of this program is the Point Lisas Industrial Port, a 2,000 acre site about 23 miles south of Port of Spain formerly devoted to raising sugarcane.

Considerable attention is also being given to meeting social needs. Health centers, schools, housing, public transport, utilities, government office space and other public services are being developed, although results may not be immediately visible.

The Government's industrial development program envisages a major role for foreign private investors, normally as minority partners with local investors. For major projects in which the Government is itself the majority partner, this split is normally 51 to 49 percent. For smaller private projects, the Government is moving to bring existing foreign investments into line with these criteria, and localization of the financial sector is well under way. To date, localization has been arrived at through negotiation, and expropriation has not been an issue.

In October 1979, the National Energy Corporation set up the National Energy Commission (NEC) to serve as a holding company for the energy-based industrial development projects. The NEC will evaluate the energy-based projects as they progress and will report directly to the Cabinet. The Industrial Development Corporation (IDC) will continue to be the overall focal point for attracting and guiding foreign investors in Trinidad and Tobago, and will coordinate with the NEC on the larger industrial projects. The addresses are as follow:

National Energy Corporation
28 Sackville Street
Port of Spain, Trinidad, West Indies

Industrial Development Corporation
10-12 Independence Square
Port of Spain, Trinidad, West Indies

The energy-based projects the Government is pursuing are in various stages of planning or development. The following summaries of each give completion date targets and brief comments on developments to date:

Fertilizers of Trinidad and Tobago Ltd. (FERTRIN).—Design of all facilities was to be completed by the end of 1979 by Pullman-Kellog, the prime contractor, while actual construction of the two ammonia plants by Kellog Pan American Corporation got well underway. The first ammonia plant and marine facilities are scheduled for completion March 1, 1981, with the second plant to be ready by May 31, 1981. Production should commence July 30, 1981, with the first shipment being made in September. Thus far, $130 million in financing has been arranged and some $89 million was to be expended in 1979. This overall joint venture between the Government and Amoco will also utilize urea through a marketing arrangement with Agrico Chemicals to increase the value added of a large part of the ammonia production.

Aluminium Smelter Project.—Construction should begin in 1980 with the project to be completed in 1983. Trinidad agreed in October 1979 to accept two U.S companies, National Steel and South Wire Aluminium, as joint venture partners for this smelter. Preparatory work on project economics, a definitive cost estimate, and finalization of the marketing agreements should be completed in time for mid-1980 start-up. Close to $2 million was spent on preliminaries in 1979. Total investment could reach over $300 million. Full production will be 180,000 metric tons per year.

Methanol Project.—Work continues on the methanol plant although it remains in the planning stage. Design and finance arrangements were to be completed in 1979, with detailed engineering and field construction contracts awarded by the end of December. Mechanical completion of facilities is slated for December 1981, with the plant to be ready March 1982.

Cement Expansion.—This expansion project is being carried out under a government-to-government agreement between Trinidad and Austria, or more specifically between Trinidad Cement Limited and Voest-Alpine, which is responsible for engineering and construction. The total cost is nearly $20 million, and Voest-Alpine secured financing for 85 percent of the contract price through the Austrian Export Bank. Design was to be completed in 1979 with civil engineering and construction started during the year. All equipment should be in place by February, 1981 and the project fully completed in April, 1981.

Liquid Natural Gas (LNG) Project. — A trans-island natural gas pipeline was completed in 1977 bringing gas from the offshore fields in the southeast to the Point Lisas industrial area on the west coast. Further pipelines are now planned from the offshore fields to the north, although construction of these will probably not begin until 1983.

In 1978, it was decided to study the advantages of a liquefication plant, so that gas not needed for Trinidad's own industrial program might be shipped as LNG to the U.S. market. The Government has decided to go ahead with the project and is proceeding with a complete engineering analysis and cost estimate for pipelines, production facilities, infrastructure, liquefication plant, and marine handling equipment. Detailed design should be completed in 1980 and the actual engineering/construction contract is to be awarded by January 1981. Completion of construction is targeted for the end of 1985 with LNG production starting in early 1986. Total investment could exceed $1 billion.

Closely associated with the LNG plant which will provide feedstock will be the establishment of an ethylene-based (olefins/aromatics) petrochemical complex. This project is still under study.

Port and Harbor Project. — A deepwater port is being constructed at Point Lisas, in the Gulf of Paria, to service the heavy industries to be located there. The port will be able to handle importation of iron ore and alumina, and bulk exportation of steel, aluminum, liquid ammonia, fertilizer, and cement. Facilities will include a 40 foot deep channel, 500 feet wide; a 2,000 foot turning basin; a 1,100 foot marginal wharf with two berths and expansion potential to 6,000 feet; and loading eqqipment for handling up to 200 ton units (vital for the power station planned for the area).

The Point Lisas Industrial Port Development Corporation (PLIPDECO) was founded several years ago as a joint private sector-government industrial development endeavor, but all of its shares were acquired by the Government. PLIPDECO's master plan calls for the development of 1,600 acres of land for heavy industry, with an additional 400 acres devoted to roads, drains, and utilities. A new highway was constructed to link the industrial area with Trinidad's major north-south highway located 5 miles away.

Dredging of the channel and turning basin for the port was largely completed by the end of 1979 and construction of the dock facilities was completed in mid-year, although dredging continues. The water supply and drainage systems also were largely finished in 1979. Work is well underway on factory shell construction for light industry, a commercial center, and housing. The port and industrial area should be nearly completed by the end of 1980.

Trade Regulations

The Government of Trinidad and Tobago adopted, effective January 1, 1971, a new customs tariff, an amended version of which was issued on January 1, 1979. The new Common External Tariff (so called because it was adopted within the framework of the Caribbean Community, CARICOM), is a one-column tariff based on the Brussels Tariff Nomenclature (BTN), but provision is also made for the statistical classification in accordance with revision 2 of the Standard International Trade Classification (SITC) system.

No preferential treatment is accorded, other than for goods produced in member states of CARICOM which are generally duty-free.

Duties

Most duties are levied on the value, ad valorem, although certain vegetable products, spiritous liquors, and petroleum products, are assessed specific duties according to weight or volume. Duties are levied as a percentage of the c.i.f. value; i.e., the value of the item delivered to the custom house of entry, to include the cost of containers and preparation of goods for shipment. Buying commissions paid to purchasing agents must be included in the value of the goods unless the supplier of the goods produces a statutory declaration stating that he is the bonafide buying agent of the importer, that he is not the manufacturer, and specifying the rate of commission and basis for establishment of that rate. The maximum excludable commission is 5 percent.

Suppliers outside the Commonwealth just attest to such declaration before a Trinidadian or in the absence of such, a British consul in the country of supply. On shipments by air cargo, freight charges for duty purposes are to be taken as either one-fourth of the actual charges paid or the minimum charges of an ocean bill of lading, whichever is greater.

Duties average 20–35 percent ad valorem, with a few items bearing duties over 50 percent. A number of essential products are duty-free or are dutiable at low rates of up to 15 percent ad valorem. Certain items used in basic industries, such as the oil field industry, construction, and "pioneer" industries which have been adjudged eligible for fiscal incentives are admitted free of duty when specified conditions have been met.

Information regarding Trinidad and Tobago duties applicable to specific products may be obtained from the International Trade Administration, Office of Country Marketing, U.S. Department of Commerce, Washington, D.C. 20230, or through any Department of Commerce District Office. Inquiries should contain a complete product description, including BTN, SITC or U.S. schedule B Export Commodity numbers, if known. Responsibility for determining the correct tariff classification for any specific item of course rest with the Trinidad and Tobago Customs and Excise Division.

Fines and Penalties

For custom purposes the invoice must contain a careful description of all goods and all details necessary to arrive at the c.i.f. value. Errors or omissions will render the shipment subject to penalty.

Import and Exchange Controls

In local terminology, imports are subject to either specific license or open general license. In practice, all items are on open general license (for which no license is actually required) unless subject to specific license. The latter are detailed on the so-called "Negative List" which comprises over 400 tariff items. Licenses for these items must be obtained prior to placing a firm order for shipment, and are valid for 6 months when issued. While information on items included on the negative list is available through the Department of Commerce, exporters of these items are advised to seek current advice from importers in Trinidad and Tobago as to the likelihood that licenses will be issued for their particular products, as practice depends considerably on the adequacy of local-produced substitutes. Licenses will not be granted if applications are received after goods have been shipped. The goods should arrive in Trinidad before the expiration of the license.

Trade advertising material, commercial catalogs and the like are dutiable at the rate of 45 percent of value, other than for occasional copies mailed for informational purposes. Audiovisual materials and equipment may be brought in for demonstration purposes, but the Customs may require a bond to be posted on arrival.

Payments for all imports into Trinidad and Tobago require foreign exchange approval of the Central Bank. Payments for goods from the United States may be made in dollars or sterling credited to an external account, or in any foreign currency in the manner prescribed by the exchange control authorities.

The exchange control system provides for compulsory surrender of foreign currency and for control over both current and capital transactions.

Imports of goods produced or originating in South Africa and Rhodesia are prohibited by law.

Required Documents

Commercial Invoice. — No special form of invoice is required but the documents should be prepared at least in duplicate, with one copy for customs purposes and one for import licensing. (The Jamaica invoice and declaration of value, Form C-23 is commonly used in the English-speaking Caribbean and it can be purchased from commercial stationers.)

For customs purposes the invoice must contain a careful and detailed description of the goods, and all details necessary to arrive at the c.i.f. value. Where the c.i.f. value is not given, the invoice should indicate that all charges which would be included in reaching a c.i.f. value have been stated. All discounts listed on the invoice must be explained.

In the case of imports under general license, a signed declaration of origin must be included as follows. "We hereby declare that the within goods were manufactured (or produced or grown) in (name of country)." The invoice must be signed by the declarer and one witness. Facsimile signatures are not accepted. Chamber of Commerce certification and consular legalization are not required.

Bill of Lading. — There are no regulations specifying the form, or number of bills of lading required for any particular shipment. A bill of lading customarily shows the name of shipper, name and address of consignee, port of destination, description of goods, listing of freight and other charges, number of bills of lading in the full set, and date and signature of the carrier official acknowledging receipt onboard of the goods for shipment. The information should correspond with that shown on the invoices and the packages. "To order" bills are permitted. Goods are obtainable by the cosignee without representation of the bill if a bond is deposited. Consolidated bills of lading are generally not accepted, especially where the marks and numbers on the packages are similar. Trinidad banks will not accept responsibility for delivery orders on consolidated bills of lading. The air waybill replaces the bill of lading on air cargo shipments.

The minimum bill of lading U.S. steamship companies will accept from Atlantic and Pacific ports is $100.

U.S. Shipper's Export Declaration. — This document is a U.S. Government requirement for shipments valued over $500 or when a validated U.S. export license is needed. The $500 exemption applies to goods under each Schedule B number in a single shipment from one exporter to one exporter.

Special Requirements. — Shipments of dried peas, beans, lentils, and other pulses, and of shelled and unshelled peanuts must be accompanied by certificates, in duplicate, signed by a state or federal authority stating that the products are of a type, quality and grade that could be legally sold for human food under federal law in the country of origin and that the products are substantially free from mold, insect damage or live insects.

Cotton products may be imported only with permission from the Trinidad and Tobago Ministry of Agriculture, Lands and Fisheries.

Canned meats are to be heated in their metal cans at 165 degrees F.

Fresh and frozen meat products exported from the United States must be accompanied by a certificate, prepared on forms available through the Trinidad and Tobago Embassy in Washington, that they meet United States Department of Agriculture quality and health standards. Temporary import restrictions may be imposed from time to time if animal health problems arise in the country of origin of the animals.

Samples and Advertising Material

Trinidad and Tobago is a signatory to the International Convention to facilitate the importation of commercial samples and advertising material. Samples of no commercial value and other articles imported temporarily may be entered after a deposit in the amount of the duty is made or after a bond is posted, except for items in finished form which appear on the negative list; a license must be obtained prior to importation of such samples. The full amount of any deposit will be returned or the bond cancelled upon exportation within 3 months. Detailed lists of samples or patterns must be prepared for submission to Customs officers. Printed advertising material is dutiable.

Labeling

Goods from the United States should be labeled "Made in USA" to avoid confusion as to the place of origin of the goods. Containers of imported foods, beverages, and drugs must be labeled to comply with Food and Drug Regulations, 1965, as amended.

Labels for foodstuffs, including beverages and ingredients for manufacturing food, should state on the main panel the brand name, or trade name, if applicable, of the food; common name of the food; and net contents of the package in terms of weight, measure, or number, according to usual practice.

The following information must be given in one place, either on the main panel or on any panel other than the bottom: declaration by name of any Class II, Class III or Class IV preservative used; declaration of any food color additives; any artificial or imitation flavorings added; and other declarations as may be required by the regulations as to be obtained from the importer. Labels must also include name and address of the preparer (in Trinidad and Tobago) if not the manufacturer; and name of country of preparation ("Made in Trinidad") if other than country of manufacture.

Labels for drug products (excluding most antibiotics and narcotics) must include the following information on the main panel of both the outer and inner labels: Proper name and standard under which the drug was manufactured, including the standard or abbreviation if mentioned in the regulations; common name if no proper name; name of manufacturer or distributor, required on outer label only when contents are less than 5 milliliters; lot number or batch number so indicated for drugs intended for internal or parenteral use, except for patent or proprietary medicines; directions for use, in English; and proper name (or common name) of all medicinal ingredients except on official drugs, patent or proprietary medicines, shipping cases, and wrapping material.

The outer labels must show net contents in terms of weight, measure, or number and name and proportion of any preservatives for parenteral drugs. Any medicine containing a narcotic or controlled drug must show the name and proportion of that drug on the label. All labeling must be clearly and prominently displayed.

Compulsory standards on labeling of most clothing items have been instituted. Labels must show percentage of fiber content by mass in descending order of magnitude where the fiber constitutes more than 5 percent of the total fiber content of the garment; name and address of the manufacturer or brand name registered with the Trinidad and Tobago Bureau of Standards; country of origin; and appropriate garment size. Full information on these requirements can be obtained from the Trinidad and Tobago Bureau of Standards, Salvatori Building, Port of Spain.

Marking

There are no stipulations regarding how shipments must be marked, and any common shipping practice may be followed. In general, all identifying marks, including the consignee's mark with port marks, should be plainly inscribed on the packages to facilitate arrival of the shipment. Packages should be numbered unless the contents are such that they can be readily identified without numbers.

Senate Concurrent Resolution 40, adopted July 30, 1953, invites U.S. exporters to inscribe, insofar as practicable, on the external shipping containers in indelible print of a suitable size: "United States of America." Although such marking is not compulsory under our laws, U.S. shippers are urged to cooperate in thus publicizing American-made goods.

Entry and Reexport

With specified exceptions, 4 days is allowed between the date of unloading and that of customs entry and clearance before storage fees are levied. Exceptions from this rule include transshipment goods (4 days are allowed), cargo destined for San Fernando (a town in Trinidad and Tobago), and in cases of documents held up by customs.

If goods are not entered within 10 days of arrival, they will be removed to the Government warehouse to await entry and in that case storage charges will be applied. Goods not entered within 3 months will be considered abandoned and will be offered for sale at public auction.

Goods imported for repairs, processing and the like and subsequent reexport, upon submission of satisfactory proof thereof to the Comptroller of Customs and Excise, may be exempted from payment of duty. Duty exemption also may be granted to temporary imports upon their return to the country of origin within 3 months.

Free Trade Zones

There are no free trade zones in Trinidad and Tobago.

Household Effects

Household effects which have been used by the passenger for at least 1 year and brought in for personal use and not for sale or exchange may be admitted duty free.

Technical Standards and Requirements

Electrical current: A.C. 60 cycles, 115/220 volts.

Weights and measures: All imports are required to conform to the metric system.

For most industries, compliance with United States or British technical standards is acceptable. Local standards are being developed, but at present affect only a few locally-produced items. Questions as to acceptability of standards should be addressed to the Trinidad and Tobago Bureau of Standards, Salvatori Building, Port of Spain.

Distribution and Sales Channels

Companies which intend to maintain ongoing sales to Trinidad and Tobago are advised to appoint a local agent or distributor. Trinidad is a small community where personal relationships are important. Furthermore, government policy encourages the development of local enterprise, and having a local agent can be an asset in obtaining government supply contracts.

There is a relatively active group of a number of importers and distributors, and U.S. firms appear to have little difficulty in locating suitable representation. Agreements with agents are voluntary. It is customary to include provision for 3 to 6 months notice by either party before terminating a business relationship of this nature.

Many retail outlets in Trinidad and Tobago import merchandise directly for their own account. Travel between Trinidad and Tobago and the United States is frequent, and many wholesalers and retailers enjoy buying trips to the United States.

Trinidad has several department stores, and chain supermarkets are popular. However, much of the retailing is done through small shops. There are also a number of "duty free" shops catering to tourist trade, which specialize in cameras, watches, and gifts.

Because the market in Trinidad and Tobago is relatively small and there is a large imported component in retail sales of consumer products, firms dealing solely in wholesaling are rare. On one hand, there is a group of large firms which handle a variety of activities: Importers, exporters, distributors, wholesalers, manufacturers representatives, commission agents, etc., are frequently housed under one roof. On the other hand, a number of small companies has been successfully formed in recent years to supply a limited variety of products, competing aggressively with the established firms in their chosen lines. Branching out is frequent, and most responsible businessmen can be approached to handle imported goods in their own or similar product lines, even if they have not previously been engaged in importing activities.

Franchising and Licensing

Franchises have become popular in recent years, particularly in the fast food line. Hotels in Port of Spain currently have excess capacity, so this field is not promising. There may be scope for hotel franchises on the island of Tobago, which is being developed as a tourist center, although the lack of direct transportation from the United States and Europe at present poses a constraint on the growth of tourism, a problem to which the Government is directing some attention.

Licensing for manufacture has also been popular. U.S. brands are known here, as Trinidad has long depended on imports of consumer goods from aboard and there is a tendency to manufacture under the brand name already familiar. The technical assistance normally provided by such agreements is welcome. This trend is enforced by liberal government policies toward transfer of licensing fees abroad.

Government Procurement

Government procurement is conducted under competitive bidding, with tenders well advertised in the local press. Prospective bidders are normally required to establish their qualifications, to show proof of purchase of the tender documents, and to post a performance bond. While contracts are awarded under the supervision of the Central Tenders Board, tender documents, specifications, and information concerning the bids are frequently made available through the purchasing ministry or agency or through the contracting engineers supervising the project.

On some key development projects, the Government has turned to friendly foreign governments to assist in identifying appropriate firms and assist in the screening of bids, particularly for construction and consultancy contracts.

Transportation

Ports

All merchandise imports into Trinidad and Tobago are entered through the Port of Spain harbor, with the exception of some bulk cargoes (such as cement and lumber) which are entered through the old naval facilities at Chaguaramas, and some specialized materials and equipment which may be offloaded from shallow draft vessels at the Point Lisas Industrial Port.

The Port of Spain harbor has 5,500 feet of wharfage, 10 transit sheds, and approximately 450,000 square feet of storage space. Lift capacity is 60 tons. There is a cold storage plant and a conveyor belt facility to handle wheat or grain in bulk direct from the ship. New container facilities have recently been installed, and additional facilities are planned. The Port Authority encourages palletization. The port and cargo handling operations are administered by the Port Authority of Trinidad and Tobago, P.O. Box 549, Port of Spain.

Goods intended for Tobago are transshipped through Port of Spain. Scarborough Harbor has facilities and accommodations for tourists and inter-island transport, but does not have the capacity to handle oceangoing cargo vessels. The 350 foot wharf was completed at the end of 1973.

Shipping

From Atlantic Ports:

Atlantic Lines LTD. (from New York, Newport News and Miami to Port of Spain).

L. Figuerado S.A. (from New York and Baltimore to Port of Spain).

Nobal lines (from Miami and New York to Port of Spain).

Royal Netherlands Steamship Co. (Antilles) (from New York, Baltimore, Philadelphia, and Miami to Port of Spain).

Sea-Land Service, Inc., Caribbean Division (from New York to Port Elizabeth) (Baltimore, Charleston, Jacksonville, Miami and Portsmouth to Port of Spain).

Tropical Shipping Co. Ltd. (West Palm Beach to Port of Spain).

From Great Lakes Ports:

Great Lakes Transcaribbean Lines (from Great Lakes port, during period of navigation, to Port of Spain).

From Gulf Ports:

Royal Netherlands Steamship to the Netherlands Antilles (from Gulf Ports to Port of Spain).

Sea-Land Service, Inc., Caribbean Division (from New Orleans to Port of Spain).

Air Transportation

Passenger and cargo aviation services between Trinidad and Tobago and the United States are well developed. Pan American Airways provides services between New York and Piarco International Airport in Trinidad, and between Miami and Piarco. Eastern Airlines flies between San Juan and St. Croix and Piarco. The Trinidad and Tobago national air carrier, TTIA (Formerly BWIA) provides service from Miami and New York to Trinidad, and has direct flights from Miami to Tobago's Crown Point Airport.

Domestic Transportation

Internal transportation is almost exclusively by road. The network connecting major cities and industrial sites is generally good, although only a few well traveled routes are capable of carrying very large transport vehicles.

Transportation between the islands of Trinidad and Tobago is provided by air, with heavy cargo and some passengers carried by ship.

Fuel and Power

Presently Trinidad's local petroleum and natural gas production are more than sufficient to satisfy the domestic and industrial needs of the country. Trinidad and Tobago currently exports much of its crude, either directly or as product, and also imports crude from other producing countries for refining and reexport. Gas is presently converted to power through the electrical system, and is used as feedstock for petrochemicals. Demands for both uses are likely to increase substantially with the installation of a number of major industrial projects now at various stages of development. Nevertheless, it is believed that sufficient gas resources exist to permit the installation of an LNG facility for export; this matter is now under study.

Electrical generating capacity is being substantially increased to accommodate the major industrial plants under construction. Present generation is running at a rate of about 1.8 million kilowatt hours per annum, but this will increase markedly when the iron and steel mill begins operation later this year. Current is A.C., 60 cycles. High and low voltages are available and special industrial rates can be arranged with the Electricity Commission.

Advertising and Research

The principal advertising media in Trinidad and Tobago are the press, radio and television. Locally-edited magazines are becoming increasingly important. There are four daily newspapers—the Trinidad Guardian and its afternoon edition, the Evening News, and the Express, which also publishes the afternoon tabloid, the Sun.

There are two AM and two FM radio stations with advertising facilities available. A color television station also provides a major source of advertisement.

Advertising agencies include:
All Media Projects Ltd. (AMPLE)
Beston/Benton & Bowles Ltd.
Corbin-Compton (Trinidad) LTD
Creative Advertising
Kenyon & Eckhardt/Caribbean Advertising Ltd.
McCann Erickson (Trinidad) Ltd.
Trinity Advertising Ltd.
Key Caribbean Publications Ltd.
Radio 610
Trinidad and Tobago Television Ltd.
Trinidad Broadcasting Ltd.

Market research facilities are available from the following companies (in Port of Spain unless otherwise stated):

A.M. Provan & Associates
Caribbean Industrial Relations Ltd.
Consumer Relations & Market Research Consultants Ltd.
Del Caribe Management Consultants Ltd.
Inpro Associates
Management Services Ltd.
Peat, Marwick, Mitchell & Co.
Scicon Associates
Trinidad Industrial Relations Consultants Ltd. (San Fernando)

Credit

The major commercial banks in the country are: Barclay's Bank; the Bank of Commerce; Chase Manhattan; Citibank; National Commercial Bank, Scotiabank, and Royal Bank.

In the absence of merchant banks, the only institutions that provide medium- and long-term financing are the development banks. Commercial banks, however, offer extensive overdraft facilities as well as some long-term capital.

The Trinidad and Tobago Dvelopment Finance Company and the Agricultural Development Bank are two development banks in Trinidad and Tobago. Both banks offer medium- and long-term loans. The Development Finance Company offers services mainly for industrial purposes and tourism and the Agricultural Development Bank confines itself to commercially oriented agriculture and forestry. The Loan Fund of the industrial Development Corporation makes loans to private industry.

The U.S. Export-Import Bank (Eximbank) assists exporters through U.S. commercial banks and through the Foreign Credit Insurance Association (FCIA). In other cases, Eximbank deals directly with exporters or with borrowers abroad.

For short-term financing up to 180 days, FCIA credit insurance is available under a "whole turnover" basis where the exporter agrees to insure all his short-term export sales over a period of time. For medium-term export ranging from 180 days to 5 years, credit is available, as follows:

Contract Price	Payment Terms
up to $50,000	up to 2 years
over $50,000 to $100,000	up to 3 years
over $100,000 to $200,000	up to 4 years
over $200,000	up to 5 years

Coverage under short and medium terms usually begins from the date of shipment. However, suppliers may elect to insure from the date of the sales contract.

Long-term capital loans are available for sizable purchases of U.S. industrial equipment, materials and services, usually associated with a specific undertaking abroad.

Other agencies that help to finance foreign trade are the Overseas Private Investment Corporation (OPEC), the World Bank, the Inter-American Development Bank, and the Private Export Funding Corporation.

Exchange Controls

Authority is vested in the Central Bank through the Exchange Control Act of 1970 to exercise control over all gold and currency transactions between Trinidad and Tobago and nonresident foreign nationals or entities.

The repatriation of capital, profit, dividends, or interest by foreign corporations is permissible but the conditions under which this is done are regulated by the Bank with the approval of the Ministry of Finance and in accordance with the investment status assigned the particular corporation. The Exchange Control Act also provides for repatriation of funds in respect to licensing arrangements and royalty payments.

Approval for foreign exchange for import payments is contingent on compliance with all relevant customs and licensing requirements.

Investment

United States investment in Trinidad and Tobago in 1978 was estimated at about $850 million, most of it in petroleum and related industries.

The Government welcomes new private foreign investment consistent with its development and economic policy objectives. Every proposed investment is reviewed on its merits. In general, however, it seeks ventures which will provide new technology, access to foreign markets, and/or increased employment opportunities. It is expected that foreign investment will enter on a joint venture basis with local firms or in some cases, with the Government, with the local partners owning a majority share of the company.

Foreign staff transferred to Trinidad and Tobago are required to obtain a work permit. These are normally issued only for technical and administrative skills that cannot be supplied from the local workforce. Applications are considered for a named individual on the basis of his or her qualifications, and should be submitted by the employee's local employer.

Purchase or lease of property used in connection with foreign investments must be approved by the Aliens Landholding Committee.

Certain sectors of the economy such as distribution, news media, public utilities, commercial banking, insurance, the furniture industry, and boat building, are reserved for local investors and no new foreign investments will be permitted in these industries except where the Government determines that this would be in the interest of the nation. Existing investors in these sectors are being urged to transfer a controlling share of their ownership to local investors.

Investment in certain key industries including the petroleum sector and energy-based heavy industries are reserved for the government, possibly with minority participation by foreign investors.

Potential investors should be aware that there is a well-organized and active labor movement, that the Government enforces a restrictive policy toward the issuance of work permits for foreigners, that a tax is withheld from all remittances of profits, dividends, and private interest paymemts, and that foreign exchange transactions are controlled by the Central Bank. The Overseas Private Investment Corporation in Washington is available to consider guarantees for American investors. There is a double taxation treaty in effect between the United States and Trinidad and Tobago.

The harmonization of Fiscal Incentives to Industry under a Caribbean Common Market Agreement (CARICOM) provides for:

1. A tax holiday and rebate on customs duty up to 10 years.

2. Tax exemption of dividends for equivalent period but with no time limit on distributions.

3. Twenty percent initial allowances on capital expenditure after tax holiday period.

4. Export allowances.

5. Carry forward of aggregate net losses for 5 years after end of tax holiday period.

To qualify for a benefit an enterprise must:

1. Be incorporated in the country from which it seeks the benefit.

2. Be engaged in industry.

3. Obtain approved status for itself and for its product.

4. Not be in an "established industry"—a condition which does not apply to enclave and highly capital intensive industries.

In Trinidad and Tobago, specific incentives to be extended from among those authorized under CARICOM rules are negotiated on a case by case basis, and depend on the extent of local value added as well as a determination of the economic requirements of the project.

Import substitution manufacturing industries may also benefit through the addition of the imported product to the negative list, which has the effect of requiring an import license and providing protection for the locally manufactured product.

The authority designated to negotiate with potential investors on specific investment incentives to be granted is the Industrial Development Corporation, 10-12 Independence Square, Port of Spain, Trinidad, W.I.

Prospective investors who have determined that their project is economically viable and acceptable to the Government are urged to retain legal counsel to advise them on the procedures for registration, tax obligations, and other matters related to the establishment of their business.

While the discussion below will describe these requirements in general terms, relevant legislation such as the Companies' Law, the petroleum tax law, and income and withholding tax rates are subject to revision.

Company Formation

The private company is the most common form of enterprise established by foreign companies operating in Trinidad and Tobago and may be formed by a minimum of two persons. A private company is one which by its articles:

1. Restricts the right of transfer of its shares;

2. Limits the number of members to 50, exclusive of employees or former employees.

3. Prohibits any invitation to the public to subscribe for shares or debentures of the company.

Although private companies have the same rights and obligations as public companies, they differ from public companies in that they are exempted from the obligation to file or register with the Registrar of Companies a statement in lieu of prospectus and copies of their annual profit and loss account and balance sheet. Neither do they need to hold a statutory meeting nor file a statutory report.

Authorized Capital	Fee to Register
Up to $50,000	$50
From $50,000 to $150,000	$50 plus 50¢ for every $1,000 in excess of $50,000
Over $150,000	$100 plus 25¢ for every $1,000 in excess of $150,000

In addition, there will be legal costs which will normally vary from $1,000 to $5,000 depending on the size and complexity of the company. Other incidental costs such as printing the memorandum and articles of association will be incurred.

Registration of Branches of Foreign Corporations.—All companies incorporated outside of, but which establish a business within Trinidad and Tobago are required to register certain information with the Registrar. The information required to be registered includes:

1. A certified copy of the charter, statutes or memorandum and articles of the company defining the constitution of the company.

2. A list of the directors with general biographic data.

3. The names and addresses of one or more persons residing in Trinidad and Tobago authorized to accept, on behalf of the company, services of legal processes or notices to be served on the company.

4. A copy of the annual balance sheet and profit and loss account of the company.

Each such company must exhibit its name and the country of incorporation at its place of business and on all letterheads. The statement must indicate that the liability of the members is limited, if this is the case.

Property Ownership by Foreigners

Generally speaking, foreigners (companies or individuals) may not own property in Trinidad and Tobago. This covers anyone who is not a citizen of Trinidad and Tobago either by naturalization, registration or birth. Exceptions must be authorized by the Ministry of Finance. Property can be obtained, however, on long-term leases.

Companies who wish to come into Trinidad must see to it that not more than one third of the nominal license of the outstanding debentures of the company are held by unlicensed aliens. A property extent of, say around 10,000 feet, would be regarded as normal, whether one is buying freehold or leasehold. In this way, the Government is able to regulate the extent of foreign investment by putting limits on the amounts of acreage to be acquired.

Taxation

Taxation on Resident Corporations.—The principal taxes to which a company incorporated in Trinidad and Tobago is liable are: A corporation tax of 45 percent (50 percent in the case of petroleum companies) on its net annual income; an unemployment levy of 5 percent on the full amount of its annual chargeable profits; and a withholding tax at a statutory rate of 25 percent which is leviable on the gross remittances of distribution and payments to non-residents.

There are reduced rates of withholding tax for countries with which there is a double taxation agreement.

Taxes on Nonresident Individuals and Corporation.—Withholding taxes are payable in respect of investment income arising from any "distribution" or any "payments" made to non-resident individuals or companies that are not engaged in trade or business in Trinidad and Tobago. "Payments" include interest, discounts, annuities, rentals, royalties, management charges and premiums.

The rates of withholding tax are:

1. Any distribution to a parent company — 15 percent
2. Any other distribution — 25 percent
3. Any payment to a company — 30 percent
4. Any payment to an individual — 20 percent

There are tax incentives in some industries, e.g. construction, tourism, and export.

Labor Relations

Trinidad and Tobago has an adaptable labor force of 452,000 persons, of which 312,400 are male and 139,600 are female. The levels of education are relatively high; overall illiteracy is less than 5 percent. Unemployment is about 12 percent, but the rate of unemployment has been declining in recent years and there are shortages of some skills.

Wage levels vary considerably, but earnings have been ranging between TT$100 to TT$500 per week in the manufacturing sector. In general, wage increases have exceeded the rise in the cost of living in recent years. The highest paid workers are in the petroleum and petrochemical sector, followed closely by the construction sector.

Labor relations in Trinidad and Tobago are governed by the Industrial Relations Act of 1972, as amended. There are about 21 active unions, 15 of which represent some 24.6 percent of the labor force.

Strikes and lockouts are theoretically prohibited for persons in certain public services and in what are designated as "essential services."

Guidance for Business Travelers

Entrance Requirements for U.S. Citizens

A passport is absolutely required for entry into Trinidad. U.S. citizens, for stays of less than 6 months, do not need a visa unless seeking employment. Travelers must have a return or through ticket or deposit sufficient funds for purchase of a ticket with immigration authorities upon arrival.

Further details on entry requirements can be obtained from the Trinidad and Tobago Consulates.

Holidays

The following is a list of Trinidad and Tobago national holidays:

New Year's Day
Good Friday
Easter Monday
Whit Monday
Corpus Christi
June 19 (Labor Day)
August 4 (Discovery Day)
August 31 (Independence Day)
September 24 (Republic Day)
December 25, 26

Communications

Calls to the United States and elsewhere can be made from the principal hotels or from the Textel offices. The minimum rates for calls to the United States range from $7.00 to $14.00 for the first three minutes or fraction, depending on the point of destination of the call.

Telegrams are charged at the rate of about 22 cents per word; a night letter is $2.40 for 22 words or less, plus 11 cents for each additional word.

The rate for telex service is $8.40 for the first three minutes plus $2.80 for each additional minute.

Postage Rates

Air mail letters to the United States are currently charged at the equivalent of 15 cents for each half ounce up to and including 2 ounces. As this is written, it is expected that postage rates will be amended shortly. Rates should be confirmed after arrival in Trinidad.

Foreign Exchange

U.S. dollars can be changed at any bank, at the rate of U.S. $1.00=TT $2.397 (slightly less for cash). Rates given by hotel cashiers are sometimes less favorable. An exchange permit from the Central Bank is required to purchase foreign currencies, although the banks have been authorized to make certain limited transactions directly. Further information and application forms (Form E) can be obtained from a commercial bank.

Time Differential

Add one hour to Eastern Standard Time. Trinidad and Tobago does not use Daylight Saving Time.

Sources of Economic and Commercial Information

Business Information Offices

Trinidad and Tobago Chamber of Industry and Commerce
P.O. Box 499
Port Spain

Trinidad Manufacturers Association
P.O. Box 971
Port of Spain

Government Information Offices

Ministry of Industry and Commerce
Salvatori Building
Port of Spain

Trinidad and Tobago Industrial Development Corporation
10–12 Independence Square
Port of Spain

Comptroller of Customs
Customs House Queen's Wharf
Port of Spain

U.S. Foreign Service Posts in Trinidad and Tobago

The United States is represented in Trinidad and Tobago by an Embassy at 15 Queen's Park West, Port of Spain. A U.S. Foreign Service Officer in the Economic/Commercial Section is available to assist U.S. business people visiting Trinidad and Tobago. A booklet *Key Officers at Foreign Service Posts*, is published quarterly by the U.S. Department of State.

Copies may be purchased for $1.50 each or $4.50 per year on a subscription basis from the Superintendent of Documents, Government Printing Office, Washington, D.C. 20402.

Trinidad and Tobago Representation in the United States

Embassy of Trinidad and Tobago
1708 Massachusetts Avenue, N.W.
Washington, D.C. 20008

Trinidad and Tobago Consulate
331-3 Graybar Building
420 Lexington Avenue
New York, New York 10017

Permanent Delegation of Trinidad and Tobago
to the United Nations
801 Second Avenue
New York, New York 10017

Trinidad and Tobago Industrial Development
Corporation and Tourist Board
Suite 712-14
400 Madison Avenue
New York, New York 10017

Publications

Trinidad and Tobago: Background Notes, September 1977, U.S. Department of State

Economic Trends, October 1978*

Businessman's Guide to Trinidad and Tobago, 1977, (available from Price Waterhouse and Co., 1251 Avenue of the Americas, New York, New York 10020. Attention: International Tax Dept.)

Foreign Investment Climate and Statistics, Port of Spain 1959, August 6, 1975.*

Trinidad and Tobago Directory of Commerce, Industry and Tourism, annual, (available from International Publications, LTD, 17 Queen's Park West, Port-of-Spain, Trinidad and Tobago.)

Businessman's Guide to Trinidad and Tobago, (available from Trinidad and Tobago Businessman's Association; c/o Carib Publications, Port-of-Spain, Trinidad and Tobago.

Trinidad and Tobago, Building, Construction Engineering and Services, annual (available from Trinidad Chamber of Commerce, Inc., 31 Frederick Street, P.O. Box 499, Port-of-Spain).

Trinidad and Tobago Directory of Industries (available from Trinidad and Tobago Industrial of Industries Corporation, Port-of-Spain).

Area Handbook for Trinidad and Tobago, 1976, Superintendent of Documents, U.S. Government Printing Office, Washington, D.C. 20402.

*Available from Room 4320, U.S. Department of Commerce, Washington, D.C. 20230. (Telephone Number (202) 377-2521.

Market Profile—TRINIDAD and TOBAGO

Foreign Trade

Exports.—$1,963 million (1978). Principal exports: petroleum and products, sugar, fertilizer. Destinations: United States ($1,347), CARICOM, Canada, United Kingdom.

Imports.—$1,970 (1978). Principal imports: Crude oil, transport equipment, machinery, foodstuffs, chemicals, metals. Suppliers: United States ($404 million), OPEC, United Kingdom, other EC, Japan, Canada, CARICOM.

Trade Policy.—Members of CARICOM are exempt from customs duties and import restrictions. Local and CARICOM producers protected by the use of a "negative list" of items for which a specific import license must be obtained. Some sanitary requirements exist for animal and vegetable products.

Trade Prospects.—Trinidad's robust economy with large oil revenues and its ambitious industrialization program all offer unusually good opportunities for U.S. exports. Trade prospects for wheat, corn and soybean, industrial plants, engineering design and construction services and construction equipment and machinery are especially bright.

Foreign Investments

Trinidad and Tobago expects majority local participation in all new investments, and encourages existing foreign organizations to bring in local partners. U.S. foreign investments in Trinidad and Tobago in 1979 are estimated about $850 million, most of it in the petroleum and petrochemical sector.

Finance

Currency.— Trinidad and Tobago dollar (TT12.40 = US $1.00).

Domestic Credit.—Bank loans are available from seven commercial banks, although loans to foreign firms are restricted. New domestic credit, currently totaling somewhat over $1 million, consists largely of loans and advances to the private sector as the government, with substantial petroleum tax revenues, is not a significant borrower.

National Budget.—Total government revenues for 1979 amounted to $1.5 billion, roughly two-thirds of it originating in the petroleum sector.

Foreign Aid.—Loans from international institutions were estimated at about $6 million in 1979. U.S. bilateral assistance was phased out in the late 1960's.

Balance of Payments.—Surplus in balance on current account of $16 million in 1978, with an overall surplus of $309 million.

Economy

Estimated GDP $3.7 billion (1978 current prices), or $3,200 per capita, annual real growth about 6 percent.

Agriculture.—Chief export crop is sugar. Over a quarter of Trinidad and nearly half of Tobago under cultivation.

Products.—Petroleum, petrochemicals, processed food, cement.

Natural Resources.—Petroleum, natural gas.

Basic Economic Facilities

Transportation.—4,000 miles of all-weather roads. Domestic and foreign airlines with good connections to North America, South America, Europe, and other islands of the Caribbean. Several shipping lines connect various Atlantic and Gulf ports with Port of Spain.

Communications.—Inland: Phone services, 5 per 100 of population. Telex services (new lines not now available). External: Telex, telegraph, telephone, ship to shore. Radio broadcasting through two local AM and two FM stations. There is one color television station.

Power.—Total electric power is generated by three plants in Trinidad and a standby in Tobago. Present generation 1.8 million kilowatt hours per annum.

Geography

Area 1,980 square miles (1 ½ times the size of Rhode Island).

Capital.—Port of Spain (pop. 250,000 metropolitan). Other cities: San Fernando (50,000). Scarborough, Tobago (40,000).

Climate.—West season from June to December; dry season from January to May. Annual mean temperature 78°F; it varies from 92°F. in the day to 64° at night.

Population

Size.—Population 1,155,000 (1979 estimate). Annual growth rate estimated at 1.5 percent. Desity 583 per square mile.

Ethnic Groups.—Negro, East Indian, Chinese, Caucasian

Religion.—Roman Catholic, Hindu, Church of England, Muslim, Protestant.

Language.—English

Literacy.—94 percent

Life Expectancy.—Males 64 years; females 68 years.

Government

Type.—Parliamentary Republic

Independence.—August 31, 1962. Date of Republican Constitution August 31, 1976.

Head of State.—President

Head of Government.—Prime Minister with Cabinet, responsible to Parliament.

Legislative. Bicameral Parliament; House of Representatives Elected, Senate Appointed by President with advice of Prime Minister and the Leader of the Oppositiion.

Judiciary.—Independent court system, headed by Supreme Court. Final appeal to Privy Council in London.

Political Parties.—People's National Movement (majority), United Labor Front, Democratic Action Congress currently represented in Parliament.

Suffrage.—Universal over 18.

Political Subdivisions.—Nine Counties.

Membership in International Organizations.—UN and most of its specialized Agencies; Organization of American States; Caribbean Community (CARICOM), Commonwealth Nations (British); Lome Convention (EC); Inter-American Development Bank; Caribbean Development Bank.